P9-AEW-174

Minor English Poets
1660-1780

A selection from the twenty-one volume *"The Works of the English Poets,"* edited by Alexander Chalmers, first published London 1810.

Compiled, with a new Introduction by David P. French

Minor English Poets

1660-1780

A Selection from Alexander Chalmers'
The English Poets [1810]

Compiled, with an Introduction by
David P. French

Vol. 9

Benjamin Blom
Publishers

First issued London 1810 as
The Works of the English Poets
in 21 volumes, selected and edited by Alexander Chalmers

New edition compiled and edited with
a new Introduction by David P. French
First published in 10 volumes 1967 by Benjamin Blom, Inc., New York 10452

Library of Congress Catalog Card No. 66-29423

Printed in U.S.A. by
NOBLE OFFSET PRINTERS, INC.
NEW YORK 3, N. Y.

CONTENTS.

VOL. IX.

ROWE'S TRANSLATION OF LUCAN'S PHARSALIA.

GRAINGER'S TRANSLATIONS.

FAWKES'S TRANSLATIONS.

THE IDYLLIUMS OF THEOCRITUS.

THE EPIGRAMS OF THEOCRITUS.

ARGONAUTICS OF APOLLONIUS RHODIUS.

THE RAPE OF HELEN:

THE ODES OF ANACREON.

THE EPIGRAMS OF ANACREON.

THE WORKS OF SAPPHO.

FRAGMENTS.

TRANSLATIONS FROM BION AND MOSCHUS.

THE IDYLLIUMS OF BION.

FRAGMENTS.

THE IDYLLIUMS OF MOSCHUS.

OVID'S METAMORPHOSES,

IN FIFTEEN BOOKS,

TRANSLATED BY DRYDEN, ADDISON, GARTH, MAINWARING, CONGREVE, ROWE, POPE, GAY, EUSDEN, CROXALL, AND OTHER EMINENT HANDS.

THE THEBAIS OF STATIUS,

TRANSLATED BY LEWIS.

THE WORKS AND DAYS OF HESIOD,

TRANSLATED BY COOKE.

LUCAN'S PHARSALIA.

TRANSLATED BY ROWE.

——— Ne tanta animis assuescite bella :
Neu patriæ validas in viscera vertite vires.—Virg.

TO THE KING.

SIR,

WHILE my deceased husband was engaged in the following long and laborious work, he was not a little supported in it, by the honour which he proposed to himself of dedicating it to your sacred majesty. This design, which had given him so much pleasure for some years, out-lasted his abilities to put it in execution: for, when his life was despaired of, and this part of the book remained unfinished, he expressed to me his desire, that this translation should be laid at your majesty's feet, as a mark of that zeal and veneration which he had always entertained for your majesty's royal person and virtues. Had he lived to have made his own address to your majesty upon this occasion, he would have been able, in some measure, to have done justice to that exalted character, which it becomes such as I am to admire in silence: being incapable of representing my dear husband in any thing, but in that profound humility and respect with which I am,

may it please your majesty,

your majesty's most dutiful and most obedient servant,

ANNE ROWE.

PREFACE,

GIVING SOME ACCOUNT OF LUCAN AND HIS WORKS.

BY JAMES WELWOOD, M.D.

FELLOW OF THE ROYAL COLLEGE OF PHYSICIANS, LONDON.

I COULD not resist Mr. Rowe's request in his last sickness, nor the importunities of his friends since, to introduce into the world this his posthumous translation of Lucan, with something by way of preface. I am very sensible how much it is out of my sphere, and that I want both leisure and materials, to do justice to the author, or to the memory of the translator. The works of both will best plead for them; the one having already out-lived seventeen ages, and both one and the other like to endure as long as there is any taste for liberty or polite learning left in the world. Hard has been the fate of many a great genius, that while they have conferred immortality on others, they have wanted themselves some friend to embalm their names to posterity. This has been the fate of Lucan, and perhaps may be that of Mr. Rowe.

All the accounts we have handed down to us of the first are but very lame, and scattered in fragments of ancient authors. I am of opinion, that one reason why his life is not to be found at any length in the writings of his contemporaries, is the fear they were in of Nero's resentment, who could not bear to have the life of a man set in a true light, whom, together with his uncle Seneca, he had sacrificed to his revenge. Notwithstanding this, we have some hints in writers who lived near this time, that leave us not altogether in the dark, about the life and works of this extraordinary young man.

Marcus Annæus Lucan was of an equestrian family of Rome, born at Corduba in Spain, about the year of our Saviour 39, in the reign of Caligula. His family had been transplanted from Italy to Spain a considerable time before, and were invested with several dignities and employments in that remote province of the Roman empire. His father was Marcus Annæus Mela, or Mella, a man of a distinguished merit and interest in his country, and not the less in esteem for being the brother of the great philosopher Seneca. His mother was Acilia the daughter of Acilius Lucanus, one of the most eminent orators of his time: and it was from his grandfather that he took the name of Lucan. The story that is told of Hesiod and Homer, of a swarm of bees hovering about them in their cradle, is likewise told of Lucan, and probably with equal truth: but whether true or not, it is a proof of the high esteem paid to him by the ancients, as a poet.

He was hardly eight months old when he was brought from his native country to Rome that he might take the first impression of the Latin tongue in the city where it was spoke in the greatest purity. I wonder then to find some critics detract from his language, as if it took a tincture from the place of his birth; nor can I be brought to think otherwise, than that the language he writes in, is as pure Roman as any that was writ in Nero's time. As he grew up, his parents educated him with a care that became a promising genius, and the rank of his family. His masters were Rhemmius Polæmon, the grammarian; then Flavius Virginius, the rhetorician; and lastly, Cornutus, the Stoic philosopher; to which sect he ever after addicted himself.

It was in the course of these studies he contracted an intimate friendship with Aulus Persius, the satirist. It is no wonder that two men, whose geniuses were so much alike, should unite and become agreeable to one another; for if we consider Lucan critically, we shall find in him a strong bent towards satire. His manner, it is true, is more declamatory and diffuse than Persius: but satire is still in his view, and the whole Pharsalia appears to me a continued invective against ambition and unbounded power.

The progress he made in all parts of learning must needs have been very great, considering the pregnancy of his genius, and the nice care that was taken in cultivating it by a suitable education: nor is it to be questioned, but besides the masters I have named, he had likewise the example and instructions of his uncle Seneca, the most conspicuous man then of Rome for learning, wit, and morals. Thus he sat out in the world with the greatest advantages possible, a noble birth, an opulent fortune, great relations, and withal, the friendship and protection of an uncle, who, besides his other preferments in the empire, was favourite, as well as tutor, to the emperor. But rhetoric seems to have been the art he excelled most in, and valued himself most upon; for all writers agree, he declaimed in public when but fourteen years old, both in Greek and Latin, with universal applause. To this purpose it is observable, that he has interspersed a great many orations in the Pharsalia, and these are acknowledged by all to be very shining parts of the poem. Whence it is that Quintilian, the best judge in these matters, reckons him among the rhetoricians, rather than the poets, though he was certainly master of both these arts in a high degree.

His uncle Seneca being then in great favour with Nero, and having the care of that prince's education committed to him, it is probable he introduced his nephew to the court and acquaintance of the emperor: and it appears from an old fragment of his life, that he sent for him from Athens, where he was at his studies, to Rome for that purpose. Every one knows that Nero, for the five first years of his reign, either really was, or pretended to be, endowed with all the amiable qualities that became an emperor and a philosopher. It must have been in this stage of Nero's life, that Lucan has offered up to him that *poetical incense* we find in the first book of the Pharsalia; for it is not to be imagined, that a man of Lucan's temper would flatter Nero in so gross a manner, if he had then thrown off the mask of virtue, and appeared in such bloody colours as he afterwards did. No! Lucan's soul seems to have been cast in another mould: and he that durst, throughout the whole Pharsalia, espouse the party of Pompey, and the cause of Rome against Cæsar, could never have stooped so vilely low, as to celebrate a tyrant and a monster in such an open manner. I know some commentators have judged that compliment to Nero to be meant ironically; but it seems to me plain to be in the greatest earnest: and it is more than probable, that if Nero had been as wicked at that time as he became afterwards, Lucan's life had paid for his irony. Now it is agreed on by all writers, that he continued for some time in the highest favour and friendship with Nero; and it was to that favour, as well as his merit, that he owed his being made quæstor, and admitted into the college of Augurs, before he attained the age required for these offices: in the first of which posts he exhibited to the people of Rome a show of gladiators at a vast expense. It was in this sunshine of life Lucan married Polla Argentaria, the daughter of Pollius Argentarius, a Roman senator; a lady of noble birth, great fortune, and famed beauty; who, to add to her other excellencies, was accomplished in all parts of learning; insomuch, that the three first books of the Pharsalia are said to have been revised and corrected by her in his life-time.

How he came to decline in Nero's favour, we have no account that I know of in history; and it is agreed by all that he lost it gradually, till he became his utter aversion. No doubt, Lucan's virtue, and his principles of liberty, must make him hated by a man of Nero's temper. But there appears to have been a great deal of envy in the case, blended with his other prejudices against him, upon the account of his poetry.

Though the spirit and height of the Roman poetry was somewhat declined from what it had been in the time of Augustus, yet it was still an art beloved and cultivated. Nero himself was not only fond of it to the highest degree, but, as most bad poets are, was vain and conceited of his performances in that kind. He valued himself more upon his skill in that art, and in music, than on the purple he wore; and bore it better to be thought a bad emperor, than a bad poet or musician. Now Lucan, though then in favour, was too honest and too open to applaud the bombast stuff that Nero was every day repeating in public. Lucan appears to have been much of the temper of Philoxenus, the philosopher; who, for not approving the verses of Dionysius the tyrant of Syracuse, was by his order condemned to the mines. Upon the promise of amendment, the philosopher was set at liberty; but Dionysius repeating to him some of his wretched performances in full expectation of having them approved, "Enough," cries out Philoxenus, "carry me back to the mines." But Lucan carried this point further, and had the imprudence to dispute the prize of eloquence with Nero in a solemn public assembly. The judges in that trial were so just and bold as to adjudge the reward to Lucan, which was fame and a wreath of laurel; but in return he lost for ever the favour of his competitor. He soon felt the effects of the emperor's resentment, for the next day he had an order sent him, never more to plead at the bar, nor repeat any of his performances in public, as all the eminent orators and poets were used to do. It is no wonder that a young man, an admirable poet, and one conscious enough of a superior genius, should be stung to the quick by this barbarous treatment. In revenge, he omitted no occasion to treat Nero's verses with the utmost contempt, and expose them and their author to ridicule.

In this behaviour towards Nero, he was seconded by his friend Persius; and no doubt, they diverted themselves often alone at the emperor's expense. Persius went so far, that he dared to attack openly some of Nero's verses in his first satire, where he brings in his friend and himself repeating them. I believe a sample of them may not be unacceptable to the reader, as translated thus by Mr. Dryden:

FRIEND. But to raw numbers and unfinish'd verse,
Sweet sound is added now, to make it terse.
'T is tagg'd with rhyme like Berecynthian Atys,
The mid part chimes with art that never flat is.
"The dolphin brave,
That cut the liquid wave,
Or he who in his line,
Can chime the long-rib Apennine."

PERSIUS. All this is doggrel stuff.

FRIEND. What if I bring
A nobler verse? "Arms and the man I sing."

PERSIUS. Why name you Virgil with such fops as these?
He's truly great, and must for ever please;
Not fierce, but awful in his manly page,
Bold in his strength, but sober in his rage.

FRIEND. What poems think you soft? and to be read
With languishing regards, and bending head?

PERSIUS. "Their crooked horns the Mimallonian crew
With blasts inspir'd: and Bassaris, who slew
The scornful calf, with sword advanc'd on high,
Made from his neck his haughty head to fly.
And Mænas, when with ivy bridles bound,
She led the spotted lynx, then Evion rung around,
Evion from woods and floods repairing echoes sound."

The verses marked with commas are Nero's, and it is no wonder that men of so delicate a taste as Lucan and Persius could not digest them, though made by an emperor.

About this time the world was grown weary of Nero, for a thousand monstrous cruelties of his life, and the continued abuse of the imperial power. Rome had groaned long under the weight of them, till at length several of the first rank, headed by Piso, formed a conspiracy to rid the world of that abandoned wretch. Lucan hated him upon a double score; as his country's enemy and his own, and went heartily into the design. When it was just ripe for execution, it came to be discovered by some of the accomplices, and Lucan was found among the first of the conspirators. They were condemned to die, and Lucan had the choice of the manner of his death. Upon this occasion some authors have taxed him with an action, which, if true, had been an eternal stain upon his name, that, to save his life, he informed against his mother. This story seems to me to be a mere calumny, and invented only to detract from his fame. It is certainly the most unlikely thing in the world, considering the whole conduct of his life, and that noble scheme of philosophy and morals he had imbibed from his infancy, and which shines in every page of his Pharsalia. It is probable Nero himself, or some of his flatterers, might invent the story, to blacken his rival to posterity; and some unwary authors have afterwards taken it up on trust, without examining into the truth of it. We have several fragments of his life, where this particular is not to be found; and which makes it still the more improbable to me, the writers that mention it have tacked to it another calumny yet more improbable, that he accused her unjustly. As this accusation contradicts the whole tenour of his life, so it does the manner of his death. It is universally agreed, that having chose to have the arteries of his arms and legs opened in a hot bath, he supped cheerfully with his friends, and then, taking leave of them with the greatest tranquillity of mind and the highest contempt of death, went into the bath, and submitted to the operation. When he found the extremities of his body growing cold, and death's last alarm in every part, he called to mind a passage of his own in the IXth book of the Pharsalia, which he repeated to the standers-by, with the same grace and accent, with which he used to declaim in public, and immediately expired, in the 27th year of his age, and tenth of Nero. The passage was that where he describes a soldier of Cato's dying, much after the same manner, being bit by a serpent, and is thus translated by Mr. Rowe:

So the warm blood at once from every part
Ran purple poison down, and drain'd the fainting heart.
Blood falls for tears, and o'er his mournful face
The ruddy drops their tainted passage trace.
Where'er the liquid juices find a way,
There streams of blood, there crimson rivers stray.
His mouth and gushing nostrils pour a flood,
And e'en the pores ouse out the trickling blood;
In the red deluge all the parts lie drown'd,
And the whole body seems one bleeding wound.

He was buried in his garden at Rome; and there was lately to be seen, in the church of Santo Paulo, an ancient marble with the following inscription:

MARCO ANNAEO LVCANO CORDVBENSI POETAE, BENEFICIO NERONIS, FAMA SERVATA.

This inscription, if done by Nero's order, shows that, even in spite of himself, he paid a secret homage to Lucan's genius and virtue, and would have atoned in some measure for the injuries and the death he gave him. But he needed no marble or inscription to perpetuate his memory; his Pharsalia will out-live all these.

Lucan wrote several books, that have perished by the injury of time, and of which nothing remains but the titles. The first we are told he wrote, was a poem on the combat between Achilles and Hector, and Priam's redeeming his son's body, which, it is said, he wrote before he had attained eleven years of age. The rest were, the descent of Orpheus into Hell; the burning of Rome, in which he is said not to have spared Nero that set it on fire; and a poem in praise of his wife Polla Argentaria. He wrote likewise several books of Saturnalia; ten books of Silvæ; an imperfect tragedy of Medea; a poem upon the burning of Troy, and the fate of Priam; to which some have added the panegyric to Calphurnius Piso, yet extant, which I can hardly believe is his, but of a later age. But the book he staked his fame on was his Pharsalia; the only one that now remains, and which Nero's cruelty has left us imperfect in respect of what it would have been, if he had lived to finish it.

Statius in his Sylvæ gives us the catalogue of Lucan's works in an elegant manner, introducing the Muse Calliope accosting him to this purpose: "When thou art scarce past the age of childhood (says Calliope to Lucan) thou shalt play with the valour of Achilles, and Hector's skill in driving of a chariot. Thou shalt draw Priam at the feet of his unrelenting conqueror, begging the dead body of his darling son. Thou shalt set open the gates of Hell for Eurydice, and thy Orpheus shall have the preference in a full theatre, in spite of Nero's envy;" alluding to the dispute for the prize between him and Nero, where the piece exhibited by Lucan was Orpheus's descent into Hell. "Thou shalt relate (continues Calliope) that flame which the execrable tyrant kindled, to lay in ashes the mistress of the world; nor shalt thou be silent in the praises that are justly due to thy beloved wife; and when thou hast attained to riper years, thou shalt sing, in a lofty strain, the fatal fields of Philippi, white with Roman bones, the dreadful battle of Pharsalia, and the thundering wars of that great captain, who, by the renown of his arms, merited to be enrolled among the gods. In that work (continues Calliope) thou shalt paint, in never-fading colours, the austere virtues of Cato, who scorned to out-live the liberties of his country; and the fate of Pompey, once the darling of Rome. Thou shalt, ike a true Roman, weep over the crime of the young tyrant Ptolemy; and shalt raise to Pompey, by the power of thy eloquence, a higher monument than the Egyptian pyramids. The poetry of Ennius (adds Calliope) and the learned fire of Lucretius, the one that conducted the Argonauts through such vast seas to the conquest of the golden fleece, the other that could strike an infinite number of forms from the first atoms of matter, both of them shall give place to thee without the least envy, and even the divine Æneid shall pay thee a just respect."

Thus far Statius concerning Lucan's works; and even Lucan in two places of the Pharsalia has promised himself immortality to his poem. The first is in the seventh book, which I beg leave to give in prose, though Mr. Rowe has done it a thousand times better in verse. "One day (says he) when these wars shall be spoken of in ages yet to come, and among nations far remote from this clime, whether from the voice of fame alone, or the real value I have given them by this my history, those that read it shall alternately hope and fear for the great events therein contained. In vain (continues he) shall they offer up their vows for the righteous cause, and stand thunder-struck at so many various turns of fortune; nor shall they read them as things that are already past, but with that concern as if they were yet to come, and shall range themselves, O Pompey, on thy side."

The other passage, which is in the ninth book, may be translated thus: "Oh! Cæsar, profane thou not through envy the funeral monuments of these great patriots, that fell here sacrifices to thy ambition. If there may be any renown allowed to a Roman Muse, while Homer's verses shall be thought worthy of praise, they that shall live after us, shall read his and mine together: my Pharsalia shall live, and no time nor age shall consign it to oblivion."

This is all that I can trace from the ancients, or himself, concerning Lucan's life and writings; and indeed there is scarce any one author, either ancient or modern, that mentions him but with the greatest respect and the highest encomiums, of which it would be tedious to give more instances.

I design not to enter into any criticism on the Pharsalia, though I had ever so much leisure or ability for it. I hate to oblige a certain set of men, that read the ancients only to find fault with them, and seem to live only on the excrements of authors. I beg leave to tell these gentlemen, that Lucan is not to be tried by those rules of an epic poem, which they have drawn from the Iliad or Æneid; for if they allow him not the honour to be on the same foot with Homer or Virgil, they must do him the justice at least, as not to try him by laws founded on their model. The Pharsalia is properly an historical heroic poem, because the subject is a known true story. Now with our late critics, truth is an unnecessary trifle for an epic poem, and ought to be thrown aside as a curb to invention. To have every part a mere web of their own brain, is with them a distinguishing mark of a mighty genius in the epic way. Hence it is, these critics observe, that the favourite poems of that kind do always produce in the mind of the reader the highest wonder and surprise; and the more improbable the story is, still the more wonderful and surprising. Much good may this notion of theirs do them; but, to my taste, a fact very extraordinary in its kind, that is attended with surprising circumstances, big with the highest events, and conducted with all the arts of the most consummate wisdom, does not strike the less strong, but leaves a more lasting impression on my mind, for being true.

If Lucan therefore wants these ornaments, he might have borrowed from Helicon, or his own invention; he has made us more than ample amends, by the great and true events that fall within the compass of his story. I am of opinion, that, in his first design of writing this poem of the civil wars, he resolved to treat the subject fairly and plainly, and that fable and invention were to have had no share in the work: but the force of custom, and the design he had to induce the generality of readers to fall in love with liberty, and abhor slavery, the principal design of the poem, induced him to embellish it with some fables, that without them his books would not be so universally read: so much was fable the delight of the Roman people.

If any shall object to his privilege of being examined and tried as an historian, that he has given in to the poetical province of invention and fiction, in the sixth book, where Sixtus inquires of the Thessalian witch Erictho the event of the civil war, and the fate of Rome; it may be answered, that perhaps the story was true, or at least it was commonly believed to be so in his time, which is a sufficient excuse for Lucan to have inserted it. It is true, no other author mentions it. But it is usual to find some one passage in one historian, that is not mentioned in any other, though they treat of the same subject. Nor though I am fully persuaded that all these oracles and responses, so famous in the pagan world, were the mere cheats of priests; yet the belief of them, and of magic and witchcraft, was universally received at that time. Therefore Lucan may very well be excused for falling in with a popular errour, whether he himself believed it or no, especially when it served to enliven and embellish his story. If it be an errour, it is an errour all the ancients have fallen into, both Greek and Roman: and Livy, the prince of the Latin historians, abounds in such relations. That it is not below the dignity and veracity of an historian to mention such things, we have a late instance in a noble author of our time, who has likewise wrote the civil wars of his country, and intermixt in it the story of the ghost of the duke of Buckingham's father.

In general, all the actions that Lucan relates in the course of his history are true; nor is it any impeachment of his veracity, that sometimes he differs in place, manner, or circumstances of actions, from other writers, any more than it is an imputation on them, that they differ from him. We ourselves have seen, in the course of the late two famous wars, how differently almost every battle and siege has been represented, and sometimes by those of the same side, when at the same time there be a thousand living witnesses, ready to contradict any falsehood, that partiality should impose upon the world. This I may affirm, the most important events, and the whole thread of action in Lucan, are agreeable to the universal consent of all authors, that have treated of the civil wars of Rome. If now and then he differs from them in lesser incidents or circumstances, let the critics in history decide the question: for my part, I am willing to take them for anecdotes first discovered and published by Lucan, which may at least conciliate to him the favour of our late admirers of secret history.

After all I have said on this head, I cannot but in some measure call in question some parts of Cæsar's character as drawn by Lucan; which seem to me not altogether agreeable to truth, nor to the universal consent of history. I wish I could vindicate him in some of his personal representations of men, and Cæsar in particular, as I can do in the narration of the principal events and series of his story. He is not content only to deliver him down to posterity, as the subverter of the laws and liberties of his country, which he truly was, and than which, no greater infamy can possibly be cast upon any name: but he describes him as pursuing that abominable end, by the most execrable methods, and some that were not in Cæsar's nature to be guilty of. Cæsar was certainly a man far from revenge, or delight in blood; and he made appear, in the exercise of the supreme power, a noble and generous inclination to clemency on all occasions: even Lucan, though never so much his enemy, has not omitted his generous usage of Domitius at Corfinium, or of Afranius and Petreius, when they were his prisoners in Spain. What can be then said for Lucan, when he represents him riding in triumph over the field of Pharsalia, the day after the battle, taking delight in that horrid landscape of slaughter and blood, and forbidding the bodies of so many brave Romans to be either buried or burnt? Not any one passage of Cæsar's life gives countenance to a story like this: and how commendable soever the zeal of a writer may be, against the oppressor of his country, it ought not to have transported him to such a degree of malevolence, as to paint the most merciful conqueror that ever was, in colours proper only for the most savage natures. But the effects of prejudice and partiality are unaccountable; and there is not a day of life, in which even the best of men are not guilty of them in some degree or other. How many instances have we in history of the best princes treated as the worst of men, by the pens of authors that were highly prejudiced against them!

Shall we wonder then, that the Roman people, smarting under the lashes of Nero's tyranny, should exclaim in the bitterest terms against the memory of Julius Cæsar, since it was from him that Nero derived that power to use mankind as he did? Those that lived in Lucan's time did not consider so much what Cæsar was in his own person, or temper, as what he was the occasion of to them. It is very probable, there were a great many dreadful stories of him handed about by tradition among the multitude; and even men of sense might give credit to them so far as to forget his clemency, and remember his ambition, to which they imputed all the cruelties and devastations committed by his successors. Resentments of this kind in the soul of a man, fond of the ancient constitution of the commonwealth, such as Lucan was, might betray him to believe, upon too slight grounds, whatever was to the disadvantage of one he looked upon as the subverter of that constitution. It was in that quality, and for that crime alone, that Brutus afterwards stabbed him; for personal prejudice against him he had none, and had been highly obliged by him: and it was upon that account alone, that Cato scorned to owe his life to him, though he well knew, Cæsar would have esteemed it one of the greatest felicities of his, to have had it in his power to pardon him. I would not be thought to make an apology for Lucan's thus traducing the memory of Cæsar; but would only beg the same indulgence to his partiality, that we are willing to allow to most other authors; for I cannot help believing all historians are more or less guilty of it.

I beg leave to observe one thing further on this head, that it is odd, Lucan should thus mistake this part of Cæsar's character, and yet do him so much justice in the rest. His greatness of mind, his intrepid courage, his indefatigable activity, his magnanimity, his generosity, his consummate knowledge in the art of war, and the power and grace of his eloquence, are all set forth in the best light upon every proper occasion. He never makes him speak, but it is with all the strength of argument and all the flowers of rhetoric. It were tedious to enumerate every instance of this; and I shall only mention the speech to his army before the battle of Pharsalia, which in my opinion surpasses all I ever read, for the easy nobleness of expression, the proper topics to animate his soldiers, and the force of an inimitable eloquence.

Among Lucan's few mistakes in matters of fact, may be added those of geography and astronomy; but finding Mr. Rowe has taken some notice of them in his notes, I shall say nothing of them. Lucan had neither time nor opportunity to visit the scenes where the actions he describes were done, as some other historians both Greek and Roman had, and therefore it was no wonder he might commit some minute errours in these matters. As to astronomy, the schemes of that noble science were but very conjectural in his time, and not reduced to that mathematical certainty they have been since.

The method and disposition of a work of this kind must be much the same with those observed by other historians, with one difference only, which I submit to better judgments: an historian who like Lucan has chosen to write in verse, though he is obliged to have strict regard to truth in every thing he relates, yet perhaps he is not obliged to mention all facts, as other historians are. He is not tied down to relate every minute passage, or circumstance, if they be not absolutely necessary to the main story; especially if they are such as would appear heavy and flat, and consequently encumber his genius, or his verse. All these trifling parts of action would take off from the pleasure and entertainment, which is the main scope of that manner of writing. Thus the particulars of an army's march, the journal of a siege, or the situation of a camp, where they are not subservient to the relation of some great and important event, had better be spared than inserted in a work of that kind. In a prose writer, these perhaps ought, or at least may be properly and agreeably enough mentioned; of which we have innumerable instances in most ancient historians, and particularly in Thucydides and Livy.

There is a fault in Lucan against this rule, and that is his long and unnecessary enumeration of the several parts of Gaul, where Cæsar's army was drawn together, in the first book. It is enlivened, it is true, with some beautiful verses he throws in, about the ancient Bards and Druids; but still in the main it is dry, and but of little consequence to the story itself. The many different people and cities there mentioned were not Cæsar's confederates, as those in the third book were Pompey's; and these last are particularly named, to express how many nations espoused the side of Pompey. Those reckoned up in Gaul were only the places where Cæsar's troops had been quartered, and Lucan might with as great propriety have mentioned the different routes by which they marched, as the garrisons from which they were drawn. This therefore, in my opinion, had been better left out; and I cannot but likewise think, that the digression of Thessaly, and an account of its first inhabitants, is too prolix, and not of any great consequence to his purpose. I am sure, it signifies but little to the civil war in general, or the battle of Pharsalia in particular, to know how many rivers there are in Thessaly, or which of its mountains lies east or west.

But if these be faults in Lucan, they are such as will be found in the most admired poets, nay, and thought excellencies in them; and besides, he has made us most ample amends in the many extraordinary beauties of his poem. The story itself is noble and great; for what can there be in history more worthy of our knowledge and attention, than a war of the highest importance to mankind, carried on between the two greatest leaders that ever were, and by a people the most renowned for arts and arms, and who were at that time masters of the world? What a poor subject is that of the Æneid, when compared with this of the Pharsalia? And what a despicable figure does Agamemnon, Homer's king of kings, make, when compared with chiefs, who, by saying only, "be thou a king," made far greater kings than him! The scene of the Iliad contained but Greece, some islands in the Ægean and Ionian seas, with a very little part of the Lesser Asia: this of the civil war of Rome drew after it almost all the nations of the then known world. Troy was but a little town, of the little kingdom of Phrygia; whereas Rome was then mistress of an empire, that reached from the Straits of Hercules, and the Atlantic Ocean, to the Euphrates, and from the bottom of the Euxine and the Caspian seas, to Æthiopia and Mount Atlas. The inimitable Virgil is yet more straitened in his subject. Æneas, a poor fugitive from Troy, with a handful of followers, settles at last in Italy; and all the empire that immortal pen could give him, is but a few miles upon the banks of the Tiber. So vast a disproportion there is between the importance of the subject of the Æneid and that of the Pharsalia, that we find one single Roman, Crassus, master of more slaves on his estate, than Virgil's hero had subjects. In fine, it may be said, nothing can excuse him for his choice, but that he designed his hero for the ancestor of Rome, and the Julian race.

I cannot leave this parallel, without taking notice, to what a height of power the Roman empire was then arrived, in an instance of Cæsar himself, when but proconsul of Gaul, and before it is thought he ever dreamed of what he afterwards attained to: it is in one of Cicero's letters to him, wherein he repeats the words of Cæsar's letters to him some time before. The words are these: "As to what concerns Marcus Furius, whom you recommended to me, I will, if you please, make him king of Gaul; but, if you would have me advance any other friend of yours, send him to me." It was no new thing for citizens of Rome, such as Cæsar was, to dispose of kingdoms as they pleased: and Cæsar himself had taken away Deiotarus's kingdom from him, and given it to a private gentleman of Pergamum. But there is one surprising instance more, of the prodigious greatness of the Roman power, in the affair of king Antiochus, and that long before the height it arrived to, at the breaking forth of the civil war. That prince was master of all Egypt; and, marching to the conquest of Phœnicia, Cyprus, and the other appendixes of that empire, Popilius overtakes him in his full march, with letters from the senate, and refuses to give him his hand till he had read them. Antiochus, startled at the command that was contained in them, to stop the progress of his victories, asked a short time to consider of it. Popilius makes a circle about him with a stick he had in his hand. "Return me an answer," said he, "before thou stirrest out of this circle, or the Roman people are no more thy friends." Antiochus, after a short pause, told him with the lowest submission, he would obey the senate's commands. Upon which, Popilius gives him his hand, and salutes him a friend of Rome. After Antiochus had given up so great a monarchy, and such a torrent of success, upon receiving only a few words in writing, he had indeed reason to send word to the senate, as he did by his ambassadors, that he had obeyed their commands with the same submission, as if they had been sent him from the immortal gods.

To leave this digression. It were the height of arrogance to detract ever so little from Homer or Virgil, who have kept possession of the first places, among the poets of Greece and Rome, for so many ages: yet I hope I may be forgiven, if I say there are several passages in both, that appear to me trivial, and below the dignity that shines almost in every page of Lucan. It were to take both the Iliad and Æneid in pieces, to prove this: but I shall only take notice of one instance, and that is, the different colouring of Virgil's hero, and Lucan's Cæsar, in a storm. Æneas is drawn weeping, and in the greatest confusion and despair, though he had assurance from the gods that he should one day settle and raise a new empire in Italy. Cæsar, on the contrary, is represented perfectly sedate, and free from fear. His courage and magnanimity brighten up as much upon this occasion, as afterwards they did at the battles of Pharsalia and Munda. Courage would have cost Virgil nothing, to have bestowed it on his hero; and he might as easily have thrown him upon the coast of Carthage in a calm temper of mind, as in a panic fear.

St. Evremont is very severe upon Virgil on this account, and has criticized upon his character of Æneas in this manner. When Virgil tells us,

Extemplo Æneæ solvuntur frigore membra,
Ingemit, et duplices tendens ad sidera palmas, &c.

"Seized as he is," says St. Evremont, "with this chillness through all his limbs, the first sign of life we find in him, is his groaning; then he lifts up his hands to Heaven, and, in all appearance, would implore its succour, if the condition wherein the good hero finds himself would afford him strength enough to raise his mind to the gods, and pray with attention. His soul, which could not apply itself to any thing else, abandons itself to lamentations; and like those desolate widows, who upon the first trouble they meet with, wish they were in the grave with their dear husbands, the poor Æneas bewails his not having perished before Troy with Hector, and esteems them very happy who left their bones in the bosom of so sweet and dear a country. Some people," adds he, "may perhaps believe he says so, because he envies their happiness; but I am persuaded," says St. Evremont, "it is for fear of the danger that threatens him." The same author, after he has exposed his want of courage, adds, "The good Æneas hardly ever concerns himself in any important or glorious design: it is enough for him that he discharges his conscience in the office of a pious, tender, and compassionate man. He carries his father on his shoulders, he conjugally laments his dear Creüsa, he causes his nurse to be interred, and makes a funeral pile for his trusty pilot Palinurus, for whom he sheds a thousand tears. Here is (says he) a sorry hero in paganism, who would have made an admirable saint among some Christians." In short, it is St. Evremont's opinion, "he was fitter to make a founder of an order than a state."

Thus far, and perhaps too far, St. Evremont: I beg leave to take notice, that the storm in Lucan is drawn in stronger colours, and strikes the mind with greater horrour than that of Virgil; notwithstanding the first has no supernatural cause assigned for it, and the latter is raised by a god, at the instigation of a goddess, that was both wife and sister of Jupiter.

In the Pharsalia, most of the transactions and events, that compose the relation, are wonderful and surprising, though true, as well as instructive and entertaining. To enumerate them all, were to transcribe the work itself, and therefore I shall only hint at some of the most remarkable. With what dignity, and justness of character, are the two great rivals, Pompey and Cæsar, introduced in the first book; and how beautifully, and with what a masterly art, are they opposed to one another? Add to this, the justest similitudes by which their different characters are illustrated in the second and ninth book. Who can but admire the figure that Cato's virtue makes, in more places than one? And I persuade myself, if Lucan had lived to finish his design, the death of that illustrious Roman had made one of the most moving, as well as one of the most sublime episodes of his poem. In the third book Pompey's dream, Cæsar's breaking open the temple of Saturn, the siege of Marseilles, the sea-fight, and the sacred grove, have each of them their particular excellence, that in my opinion come very little short of any thing we find in Homer or Virgil.

In the fourth book, there are a great many charming incidents, and among the rest, that of the soldiers running out of their camp to meet and embrace one another, and the deplorable story of Vulteius. The fifth book affords us a fine account of the oracle of Delphi, its origin, the manner of its delivering answers, and the reason of its then silence. Then, upon the occasion of a mutiny in Cæsar's camp near Placentia, in his manner of passing the Adriatic in a small boat, amidst the storm I hinted at, he has given us the noblest and best image of that great man. But what affects me above all, is the parting of Pompey and Cornelia, in the end of the book. It has something in it as moving and tender, as ever was felt, or perhaps imagined.

In the description of the witch Erictho, in the sixth book, we have a beautiful picture of horrour; for even works of that kind have their beauties in poetry, as well as in painting. The seventh book is most taken up with what relates to the famous battle of Pharsalia, which decided the fate of Rome. It is so related, that the reader may rather think himself a spectator of, or even engaged in, the battle, than so remote from the age it was fought. There is, towards the end of this book, a noble majestic description of the general conflagration, and of that last catastrophe, which must put an end to this frame of Heaven and Earth. To this is added, in the most elevated style, his sentiments of the "immortality of the soul," and of rewards and punishments after this life. All these are touched with the nicest delicacy of expression and thought, especially that about the universal conflagration; and agrees with what we find of it in holy writ. In so much that I am willing to believe Lucan might have conversed with St. Peter at Rome, if it be true he was ever there; or he might have seen that epistle of his, wherein he gives us the very same idea of it.

In the eighth book, our passions are again touched with the misfortunes of Cornelia and Pompey; but especially with the death, and unworthy funeral, of the latter. In this book is likewise drawn, with the greatest art, the character of young Ptolemy and his ministers; particularly that of the villain Photinus is exquisitely exposed in his own speech in council.

In the ninth book, after the apotheosis of Pompey, Cato is introduced as the fittest man after him to head the cause of liberty and Rome. This book is the longest, and, in my opinion, the most entertaining in the whole poem. The march of Cato through the deserts of Lybia, affords a noble and agreeable variety of matter; and the virtue of his hero, amidst these distresses through which he leads him, seems every where to deserve those raptures of praise he bestows upon him. Add to this, the artful descriptions of the various poisons with which these deserts abounded, and their different effects upon human bodies, than which nothing can be more moving or poetical.

But Cato's answer to Labienus in this book, upon his desiring him to consult the oracle of Jupiter Hammon about the event of the civil war, and the fortune of Rome, is a master-piece not to be equalled. All the attributes of God, such as his omnipotence, his prescience, his justice, his goodness, and his unsearchable decrees, are painted in the most awful and the strongest colours, and such as may make Christians themselves blush, for not coming up to them in most of their writings upon that subject. I know not but St. Evremont has carried the matter too far, when, in mentioning this passage, he concludes, "If all the ancient poets had spoke as worthily of the oracles of their gods, he should make no scruple to prefer them to the divines and philosophers of our time. We may see," says he, "in the concourse of so many people, that came to consult the oracle of Hammon, what effect a public opinion can produce, where zeal and superstition mingle together. We may see in Labienus, a pious sensible man, who to his respect for the gods, joins the consideration and esteem we ought to preserve for virtue in good men. Cato is a religious severe philosopher, weaned from all vulgar opinions, who entertains those lofty thoughts of the gods, which pure undebauched reason and a true elevated knowledge can give us of them; every thing here," says St. Evremont, "is poetical, every thing is consonant to truth and reason. It is not poetical upon the score of any ridiculous fiction, or for some extravagant hyperbole, but for the daring greatness and majesty of the language, and for the noble elevation of the discourse. It is thus," adds he, "that poetry is the language of the gods, and that poets are wise; and it is so much the greater wonder to find it in Lucan," says he, "because it is neither to be met with in Homer nor Virgil." I remember Montaigne, who is allowed by all to have been an admirable judge in these matters, prefers Lucan's character of Cato to Virgil, or any other of the ancient poets. He thinks all of them flat and languishing, but Lucan's much more strong, though overthrown by the extravagancy of his own force.

The tenth book, imperfect as it is, gives us, among other things, a view of the Ægyptian magnificence, with a curious account of the then received opinions of the increase and decrease of the Nile. From the variety of the story, and many other particulars I need not mention in this short account, it may easily appear, that a true history may be a romance or fiction, when the author makes choice of a subject that affords so many and so surprising incidents.

Among the faults that have been laid to Lucan's charge, the most justly imputed are those of his style; and indeed how could it be otherwise? Let us but remember the imperfect state, in which his sudden and immature death left the Pharsalia; the design itself being probably but half finished, and what was writ of it, but slightly, if at all, revised. We are told, it is true, he either corrected the three first books himself, or his wife did it for him, in his own life-time. Be it so: but what are the corrections of a lady, or a young man of six-and-twenty, to those he might have made at forty, or a more advanced age? Virgil, the most correct and judicious poet that ever was, continued correcting his Æneid for near as long a series of years together as Lucan lived, and yet died with a strong opinion that it was imperfect still. If Lucan had lived to his age, the Pharsalia without doubt would have made another kind of figure than it now does, notwithstanding the difference to be found in the Roman language, between the times of Nero and Augustus.

It must be owned he is in many places obscure and hard, and therefore not so agreeable, and comes short of the purity, sweetness, and delicate propriety of Virgil. Yet it is still universally agreed among both ancients and moderns, that his genius was wonderfully great, but at the same time too haughty and headstrong to be governed by art; and that his style was like his genius, learned, bold, and lively, but withal too tragical and blustering.

I am by no means willing to compare the Pharsalia to the Æneid; but I must say with St. Evremont, that for what purely regards the elevation of thought, Pompey, Cæsar, Cato, and Labienus, shine much more in Lucan, than Jupiter, Mercury, Juno, or Venus, do in Virgil. The ideas which Lucan has given us of these great men are truly greater, and affect us more sensibly, than those which Virgil has given us of his deities: the latter has clothed his gods with human infirmities, to adapt them to the capacity of men: the other has raised his heroes so, as to bring them into competition with the gods themselves. In a word, the gods are not so valuable in Virgil, as the heroes: in Lucan, the heroes equal the gods. After all, it must be allowed, that most things throughout the whole Pharsalia are greatly and justly said, with regard even to the language and expression; but the sentiments are every where so beautiful and elevated, that they appear, as he describes Cæsar in Amyclus's cottage in the fifth book, noble and magnificent in any dress. It is in this elevation of thought that Lucan justly excels: this is his forte, and what raises him up to an equality with the greatest of the ancient poets.

I cannot omit here the delicate character of Lucan's genius, as mentioned by Strada, in the emblematic way. It is commonly known that Pope Leo the Tenth was not only learned himself, but a great patron of learning, and used to be present at the conversations and performances of all the polite writers of his time. The wits of Rome entertained him one day, at his villa on the banks of the Tiber, with an interlude in the nature of a poetical masquerade. They had their Parnassus, their Pegasus, their Helicon, and every one of the ancient poets in their several characters, where each acted the part that was suitable to his manner of writing, and among the rest one acted Lucan. "There was none," says he, "that was placed in a higher station, or had a greater prospect under him, than Lucan. He vaulted upon Pegasus with all the heat and intrepidity of youth, and seemed desirous of mounting into the clouds upon the back of him. But as the hinder feet of the horse stuck to the mountain, while the body reared up in the air, the poet with great difficulty kept himself from sliding off, insomuch that the spectators often gave him for gone, and cried out now and then, he was tumbling." Thus Strada.

I shall sum up all I have time to say of Lucan, with another character, as it is given by one of the most polite men of the age he lived in, and who, under the protection of the same Pope Leo X, was one of the first restorers of learning in the latter end of the fifteenth and the beginning of the sixteenth century; I mean, Johannes Sulpitius Verulanus, who, with the assistance of Beroaldus, Badius, and some others of the first form in the republic of letters, published Lucan with notes at Rome in the year 1514, being the first impression, if I mistake not, that ever was made of him. Poetry and painting, with the knowledge of the Greek and Latin tongues, rose about that time to a prodigious height in a small compass of years; and whatever we may think to the contrary, they have declined ever since. Verulanus, in his dedication to Cardinal Palavicini, prefixed to that edition, has not only given us a delicate sententious criticism on his Pharsalia, but a beautiful judicious comparison between him and Virgil, and that in a style which in my opinion comes but little short of Sallust, or the writers of the Augustan age. It is to the following purpose:

"I come now to the author I have commented upon," says Sulpitius Verulanus, "and shall endeavour to describe him, as well as observe in what he differs from that great poet Virgil. Lucan, in the opinion of Fabius, is no less a pattern for orators than for poets; and always adhering strictly to truth, he seems to have as fair a pretence to the character of an historian; for he equally performs each of these offices. His expression is bold and lively; his sentiments are clear, his fictions within compass of probability, and his digressions proper: his orations artful, correct, manly, and full of matter. In the other parts of his work, he is grave, fluent, copious, and elegant; abounding with great variety, and wonderful erudition. And in unriddling the intricacy of contrivances, designs, and actions, his style is so masterly, that you rather seem to see, than read of those transactions. But as for enterprises and battles, you imagine them not related, but acted: towns alarmed, armies engaged, the eagerness and terrour of the several soldiers, seem present to your view. As our author is frequent and fertile in descriptions; and none more skilful in discovering the secret springs of action, and their rise in human passions: as he is an acute searcher into the manners of men, and most dextrous in applying all sorts of learning to his subject: what other cosmographer, astrologer, philosopher, or mathematician, do we stand in need of, while we read him? Who has more judiciously handled, or treated with more delicacy, whatever topics his fancy has led him to, or have casually fallen in his way? Maro is, without doubt, a great poet; so is Lucan. In so apparent an equality, it is hard to decide which excels: for both have justly obtained the highest commendations. Maro is rich and magnificent; Lucan sumptuous and splendid: the first is discreet, inventive, and sublime; the latter free, harmonious, and full of spirit. Virgil seems to move with the devout solemnity of a reverend prelate: Lucan to march with the noble haughtiness of a victorious general. One owes most to labour and application; the other to nature and practice: one lulls the soul with the sweetness and music of his verse, the other raises it by his fire and rapture. Virgil is sedate, happy in his conceptions, free from faults; Lucan quick, various, and florid: *he* seems to fight with stronger weapons, *this* with more. The first surpasses all in solid strength; the latter excels in vigour and poignancy. You would think that the one sounds rather a larger and deeper toned trumpet; the other a less indeed, but clearer. In short, so great is the affinity, and the struggle for precedence between them, that though nobody be allowed to come up to that divinity in Maro; yet had *he* not been possessed of the chief seat on Parnassus, our author's claim to it had been indisputable.

February 26, 1718-19.

LUCAN'S PHARSALIA.

TRANSLATED BY ROWE.

LUCAN'S PHARSALIA.

IN TEN BOOKS.

BOOK I.

THE ARGUMENT.

In the first book, after a proposition of his subject, a short view of the ruins occasioned by the civil wars in Italy, and a compliment to Nero, Lucan gives the principal causes of the civil war, together with the characters of Cæsar and Pompey: after that, the story properly begins with Cæsar's passing the Rubicon, which was the bound of his province towards Rome, and his march to Ariminium. Thither the tribunes and curio, who had been driven out of the city by the opposite party, come to him, and demand his protection. Then follows his speech to his army, and a particular mention of the several parts of Gaul from which his troops were drawn together to his assistance. From Cæsar, the poet turns to describe the general consternation at Rome, and the flight of great part of the senate and people at the news of his march. From hence he takes occasion to relate the foregoing prodigies, which were partly on occasion of those panic terrours, and likewise the ceremonies that were used by the priests for purifying the city, and averting the anger of the gods; and then ends this book with the inspiration and prophecy of a Roman matron, in which she enumerates the principal events which were to happen in the course of the civil war.

EMATHIAN plains with slaughter cover'd o'er,
And rage unknown to civil wars before,
Establish'd violence, and lawless might,
Avow'd and hallow'd by the name of right;
A race renown'd, the world's victorious lords,
Turn'd on themselves with their own hostile swords;
Piles against piles oppos'd in impious fight,
And eagles against eagles bending flight;
Of blood by friends, by kindred, parents, spilt,
One common horrour and promiscuous guilt;
A shatter'd world in wild disorder tost,
Leagues, laws, and empire, in confusion lost;
Of all the woes which civil discords bring,
And Rome o'ercome by Roman arms, I sing.
What blind, detested madness could afford
Such horrid license to the murdering sword?
Say, Romans, whence so dire a fury rose,
To glut with Latian blood your barbarous foes?
Could you in wars like these provoke your fate?
Wars, where no triumphs on the victor wait!
While Babylon's proud spires yet rise so high,
And rich in Roman spoils invade the sky;
While yet no vengeance is to Crassus paid,
But unatton'd repines the wandering shade!
What tracts of land, what realms unknown before,
What seas wide-stretching to the distant shore,
What crowns, what empires, might that blood have gain'd,
With which Emathia's fatal fields were stain'd!
Where Seres in their silken woods reside,
Where swift Araxes rolls his rapid tide:
Where'er (if such a nation can be found)
Nile's secret fountain springing cleaves the ground;
Where southern suns with double ardour rise,
Flame o'er the land, and scorch the mid-day skies;
Where winter's hand the Scythian seas constrains,
And binds the frozen floods in crystal chains:
Where'er the shady night and day-spring come,
All had submitted to the yoke of Rome.
O Rome! if slaughter be thy only care,
If such thy fond desire of impious war;
Turn from thyself, at least, the destin'd wound,
Till thou art mistress of the world around,
And none to conquer but thyself be found.
Thy foes as yet a juster war afford,
And barbarous blood remains to glut thy sword.
But see! her hands on her own vitals seize,
And no destruction but her own can please.
Behold her fields unknowing of the plough!
Behold her palaces and towers laid low!
See where o'erthrown the massy column lies,
While weeds obscene above the cornice rise.
Here gaping wide, half-ruin'd walls remain,
There mouldering pillars nodding roots sustain.

The landscape, once in various beauty spread,
With yellow harvests and the flowery mead,
Displays a wild uncultivated face,
Which bushy brakes and brambles vile disgrace:
No human footstep prints th' untrodden green,
No cheerful maid nor villager is seen.
E'en in her cities famous once and great,
Where thousands crowded in the noisy street,
No sound is heard of human voices now,
But whistling winds through empty dwellings blow;
While passing strangers wonder, if they spy
One single melancholy face go by.
Nor Pyrrhus' sword, nor Cannæ's fatal field,
Such universal desolation yield:
Her impious sons have her worst foes surpass'd,
And Roman hands have laid Hesperia waste.
But if our fates severely have decreed
No way but this for Nero to succeed;
If only thus our heroes can be gods,
And Earth must pay for their divine abodes;
If Heaven could not the thunderer obtain,
Till giants wars made room for Jove to reign,
'T is just, ye gods, nor ought we to complain:
Opprest with death though dire Pharsalia groan,
Though Latian blood the Punic ghosts atone;
Though Pompey's hapless sons renew the war,
And Munda view the slaughter'd heaps from far;
Though meagre famine in Perusia reign,
Though Mutina with battles fill the plain;
Though Leuca's isle, and wide Ambracia's bay,
Record the rage of Actium's fatal day;
Though servile hands are arm'd to man the fleet,
And on Sicilian seas the navies meet;
All crimes, all horrours, we with joy regard,
Since thou, O Cæsar, art the great reward.
Vast are the thanks thy grateful Rome should [pay
To wars, which usher in thy sacred sway.
When, the great business of the world achiev'd,
Late by the willing stars thou art receiv'd,
Through all the blissful seats the news shall roll,
And Heaven resound with joy from pole to pole.
Whether great Jove resign supreme command,
And trust his sceptre to thy abler hand;
Or if thou choose the empire of the day,
And make the Sun's unwilling steeds obey;
Auspicious if thou drive the flaming team,
While Earth rejoices in thy gentler beam;
Where'er thou reign, with one consenting voice,
The Gods and Nature shall approve thy choice.
But, oh! whatever be thy godhead great,
Fix not in regions too remote thy seat;
Nor deign thou near the frozen Bear to shine,
Nor where the sultry southern stars decline;
Less kindly thence thy influence shall come,
And thy blest rays obliquely visit Rome.
Press not too much on any part the sphere:
Hard were the task thy weight divine to bear;
Soon would the axis feel th' unusual load,
And groaning bend beneath th' incumbent god:
O'er the mid orb more equal shalt thou rise,
And with a juster balance fix the skies.
Serene for ever be that azure space,
No blackening clouds the purer Heaven disgrace,
Nor hide from Rome her Cæsar's radiant face.
Then shall mankind consent in sweet accord,
And warring nations sheath the wrathful sword;
Peace shall the world in friendly leagues compose,
And Janus' dreadful gates for ever close.
To me thy present godhead stands confest,
Oh let thy sacred fury fire my breast!
So thou vouchsafe to hear, let Phœbus dwell
Still uninvok'd in Cyrrha's mystic cell;
By me uncall'd, let sprightly Bacchus reign,
And lead the dance on Indian Nysa's plain.
To thee, O Cæsar, all my vows belong;
Do thou alone inspire the Roman song.
And now the mighty task demands our care,
The fatal source of discord to declare;
What cause accurst produc'd the dire event,
Why rage so dire the madding nations rent,
And peace was driven away by one consent.
But thus the malice of our fate commands,
And nothing great to long duration stands;
Aspiring Rome had risen too much in height,
And sunk beneath her own unweildy weight.
So shall one hour at last this globe control,
Break up the vast machine, dissolve the whole,
And time no more through measur'd ages roll.
Then Chaos hoar shall seize his former right,
And reign with Anarchy and eldest Night;
The starry lamps shall combat in the sky,
And lost and blended in each other die;
Quench'd in the deep the heavenly fires shall fall,
And ocean cast abroad o'erspread the ball:
The Moon no more her well-known course shall run,
But rise from western waves, and meet the Sun;
Ungovern'd shall she quit her ancient way,
Herself ambitious to supply the day:
Confusion wild shall all around be hurl'd,
And discord and disorder tear the world.
Thus power and greatness to destruction haste,
Thus bounds to human happiness are plac'd,
And Jove forbids prosperity to last.
Yet Fortune, when she meant to wreak her hate,
From foreign foes preserv'd the Roman state,
Nor suffer'd barbarous hands to give the blow,
That laid the queen of earth and ocean low;
To Rome herself for enemies she sought,
And Rome herself her own destruction wrought;
Rome, that ne'er knew three lordly heads before,
First fell by fatal partnership of power.
What blind ambition bids your force combine?
What means this frantic league in which you join?
Mistaken men! who hope to share the spoil,
And hold the world within one common toil!
While Earth the seas shall in her bosom bear,
While Earth herself shall hang in ambient air,
While Phœbus shall his constant task renew;
While through the zodiac night shall day pursue;
No faith, no trust, no friendship, shall be known
Among the jealous partners of a throne;
But he who reigns, shall strive to reign alone.
Nor seek for foreign tales to make this good,
Were not our walls first built in brother's blood?
Nor did the feud for wide dominion rise,
Nor was the world their impious fury's prize;
Divided power contention still affords,
And for a village strove the petty lords.
The fierce triumvirate, combin'd in peace,
Preserv'd the bond but for a little space,
Still with an awkward disagreeing grace.
'T was not a league by inclination made,
But bare agreement, such as friends persuade.
Desire of war in either chief was seen,
Though interposing Crassus stood between.
Such in the midst the parting isthmus lies,
While swelling seas on either side arise;
The solid boundaries of earth restrain
The fierce Ionian and Ægean main;

But, if the mound gives way, straight roaring loud
In at the breach the rushing torrents crowd;
Raging they meet, the dashing waves run high,
And work their foamy waters to the sky.
So when unhappy Crassus, sadly slain,
Dy'd with his blood Assyrian Carre's plain;
Sudden the seeming friends in arms engage,
The Parthian sword let loose the Latian rage.
Ye fierce Arsacidæ! ye foes of Rome,
Now triumph, you have more than overcome:
The vanquish'd felt your victory from far,
And from that field receiv'd their civil war.
The sword is now the umpire to decide,
And part what friendship knew not to divide.
'T was hard, an empire of so vast a size
Could not for two ambitious minds suffice;
The peopled earth, and wide-extended main,
Could furnish room for only one to reign.
When dying Julia first forsook the light,
And Hymen's tapers sunk in endless night,
The tender ties of kindred-love were torn,
Forgotten all, and bury'd in her urn.
Oh! if her death had haply been delay'd,
How might the daughter and the wife persuade!
Like the fam'd Sabine dames she had been seen
To stay the meeting war, and stand between:
On either hand had woo'd them to accord,
Sooth'd her fierce father, and her furious lord,
To join in peace, and sheath the ruthless sword.
But this the fatal sisters doom deny'd;
The friends were sever'd, when the matron dy'd.
The rival leaders mortal war proclaim,
Rage fires their souls with jealousy of fame,
And emulation fans the rising flame.
Thee, Pompey, thy past deeds by turns infest,
And jealous glory burns within thy breast;
Thy fam'd piratic laurel seems to fade,
Beneath successful Cæsar's rising shade;
His Gallic wreaths thou view'st with anxious eyes
Above thy naval crowns triumphant rise.
Thee, Cæsar, thy long labours past incite,
Thy use of war, and custom of the fight;
While bold ambition prompts thee in the race,
And bids thy courage scorn a second place.
Superior power, fierce faction's dearest care,
One could not brook, and one disdain'd to share.
Justly to name the better cause were hard,
While greatest names for either side declar'd:
Victorious Cæsar by the gods was crown'd,
The vanquish'd party was by Cato own'd.
Nor came the rivals equal to the field;
One to increasing years began to yield,
Old age came creeping in the peaceful gown,
And civil functions weigh'd the soldier down;
Disus'd to arms, he turn'd him to the laws,
And pleas'd himself with popular applause;
With gifts and liberal bounty sought for fame,
And lov'd to hear the vulgar shout his name;
In his own theatre rejoic'd to sit,
Amidst the noisy praises of the pit.
Careless of future ills that might betide,
No aid he sought to prop his failing side,
But on his former fortune much rely'd.
Still seem'd he to possess, and fill his place;
But stood the shadow of what once he was.
So, in the field with Ceres' bounty spread,
Uprears some ancient oak his reverend head;
Chaplets and sacred gifts his boughs adorn,
And spoils of war by mighty heroes worn.
But, the first vigour of his root now gone,
He stands dependent on his weight alone;
All bare his naked branches are display'd,
And with his leafless trunk he forms a shade:
Yet, though the winds his ruin daily threat,
As every blast would heave him from his seat;
Though thousand fairer trees the field supplies,
That rich in youthful verdure round him rise;
Fix'd in his ancient state he yields to none,
And wears the honours of the grove alone.
But Cæsar's greatness, and his strength, was more
Than past renown and antiquated power;
'T was not the fame of what he once had been,
Or tales in old records and annals seen;
But 't was a valour, restless, unconfin'd,
Which no success could sate, nor limits bind;
'T was shame, a soldier's shame untaught to yield,
That blush'd for nothing but an ill-fought field;
Fierce in his hopes he was, nor knew to stay,
Where vengeance or ambition led the way;
Still prodigal of war whene'er withstood,
Nor spar'd to stain the guilty sword with blood;
Urging advantage, he improv'd all odds,
And made the most of fortune and the gods;
Pleas'd to o'erturn whate'er withheld his prize,
And saw the ruin with rejoicing eyes.
Such, while Earth trembles, and Heaven thunders loud,
Darts the swift lightning from the rending cloud;
Fierce through the day it breaks, and in its flight
The dreadful blast confounds the gazer's sight;
Resistless in its course delights to rove,
And cleaves the temples of its master, Jove:
Alike where'er it passes or returns,
With equal rage the fell destroyer burns;
Then with a whirl full in its strength retires,
And recollects the force of all its scatter'd fires.
Motives like these the leading chiefs inspir'd;
But other thoughts the meaner vulgar fir'd.
Those fatal seeds luxurious vices sow,
Which ever lay a mighty people low.
To Rome the vanquish'd Earth her tribute paid,
And deadly treasures to her view display'd:
Then Truth and simple Manners left the place,
While Riot rear'd her lewd dishonest face;
Virtue to full prosperity gave way,
And fled from rapine, and the lust of prey.
On every side proud palaces arise,
And lavish gold each common use supplies.
Their fathers' frugal tables stand abhorr'd,
And Asia now and Afric are explor'd
For high-pric'd dainties, and the citron board.
In silken robes the minion men appear,
Which maids and youthful brides should blush to wear.
That age by honest poverty adorn'd,
Which brought the manly Romans forth, is scorn'd;
Wherever aught pernicious does abound,
For luxury all lands are ransack'd round,
And dear-bought deaths the sinking state confound
The Curii's and Camilli's little field,
To vast extended territories yield;
And foreign tenants reap the harvest now,
Where once the great dictator held the plough.
Rome, ever fond of war, was tir'd with ease;
E'en liberty had lost the power to please:
Hence rage and wrath their ready minds invade,
And want could every wickedness persuade:
Hence impious power was first esteem'd a good,
Worth being sought with arms, and bought with blood:

With glory, tyrants did their country awe,
And violence prescrib'd the rule to law.
Hence pliant servile voices were constrain'd,
And force in popular assemblies reign'd;
Consuls and tribunes, with opposing might,
Join'd to confound and overturn the right:
Hence shameful magistrates were made for gold,
And a base people by themselves were sold:
Hence slaughter in the venal field returns,
And Rome her yearly competitions mourns:
Hence death unthrifty, careless to repay,
And usury still watching for its day:
Hence perjuries in every wrangling court;
And war, the needy bankrupt's last resort.
Now Cæsar, marching swift with winged haste,
The summits of the frozen Alps had past;
With vast events and enterprizes fraught,
And future wars revolving in his thought.
Now near the banks of Rubicon he stood;
When lo! as he survey'd the narrow flood,
Amidst the dusky horrours of the night,
A wondrous vision stood confest to sight.
Her awful head Rome's reverend image rear'd,
Trembling and sad the matron form appear'd;
A towery crown her hoary temples bound,
And her torn tresses rudely hung around:
Her naked arms uplifted ere she spoke,
Then groaning thus the mournful silence broke.
"Presumptuous men! oh, whither do you run?
Oh, whither bear you these my ensigns on?
If friends to right, if citizens of Rome,
Here to your utmost barrier are you come."
She said; and sunk within the closing shade:
Astonishment and dread the chief invade;
Stiff rose his starting hair, he stood dismay'd,
And on the bank his slackening steps were stay'd.
"O thou" (at length he cry'd) "whose hand controls
The forky fire, and rattling thunder rolls;
Who from thy capitol's exalted height,
Dost o'er the wide-spread city cast thy sight!
Ye Phrygian gods, who guard the Julian line!
Ye mysteries of Romulus divine!
Thou, Jove! to whom from young Ascanius came
Thy Alban temple and thy Latian name:
And thou, immortal sacred Vestal flame!
But chief, oh! chiefly, thou, majestic Rome!
My first, my great divinity, to whom
Thy still successful Cæsar am I come;
Nor do thou fear the sword's destructive rage,
With thee my arms no impious war shall wage.
On him thy hate, on him thy curse bestow,
Who would persuade thee Cæsar is thy foe;
And since to thee I consecrate my toil,
Oh favour thou my cause, and on thy soldier smile."
He said; and straight, impatient of delay,
Across the swelling flood pursu'd his way.
So when on sultry Libya's desert sand
The lion spies the hunter hard at hand,
Couch'd on the earth the doubtful salvage lies,
And waits awhile till all his fury rise;
His lashing tail provokes his swelling sides,
And high upon his neck his mane with horrour rides:
Then, if at length the flying dart infest,
Or the broad spear invade his ample breast,
Scorning the wound, he yawns a dreadful roar,
And flies like lightning on the hostile Moor.
While with hot skies the fervent summer glows,
The Rubicon an humble river flows;
Through lowly vales he cuts his winding way,
And rolls his ruddy waters to the sea.
His bank on either side a limit stands,
Between the Gallic and Ausonian lands.
But stronger now the wintery torrent grows,
The wetting winds had thaw'd the Alpine snows,
And Cynthia rising with a blunted beam
In the third circle, drove her watery team,
A signal sure to raise the swelling stream.
For this, to stem the rapid water's course,
First plung'd amidst the flood the bolder horse;
With strength oppos'd against the stream they lead,
While to the smoother ford, the foot with ease succeed.
The leader now had pass'd the torrent o'er,
And reach'd fair Italy's forbidden shore:
Then rearing on the hostile bank his head,
"Here, farewell peace and injur'd laws!" (he said.)
"Since faith is broke, and leagues are set aside,
Henceforth thou, goddess Fortune, art my guide;
Let fate and war the great event decide."
He spoke; and, on the dreadful task intent,
Speedy to near Ariminum he bent;
To him the Balearic sling is slow,
And the shaft loiters from the Parthian bow.
With eager marches swift he reach'd the town,
As the shades fled, the sinking stars were gone,
And Lucifer the last was left alone.
At length the morn, the dreadful morn arose,
Whose beams the first tumultuous rage disclose:
Whether the stormy south prolong'd the night,
Or the good gods abhorr'd the impious sight,
The clouds awhile withheld the mournful light.
To the mid forum on the soldier pass'd,
There halted, and his victor ensigns plac'd:
With dire alarms from band to band around,
The fife, hoarse horn, and rattling trumpets sound.
The starting citizens uprear their heads;
The lustier youth at once forsake their beds;
Hasty they snatch the weapons, which among
Their houshold-gods in peace had rested long;
Old bucklers of the covering hides bereft,
The mouldering frames disjoin'd and barely left;
Swords with foul rust indented deep they take,
And useless spears with points inverted shake.
Soon as their crests the Roman eagles rear'd,
And Cæsar high above the rest appear'd;
Each trembling heart with secret horrour shook,
And silent thus within themselves they spoke:
"Oh, hapless city! oh, ill-fated walls!
Rear'd for a curse so near the neighbouring Gauls!
By us destruction ever takes its way,
We first become each bold invader's prey;
Oh, that by fate we rather had been plac'd
Upon the confines of the utmost east!
The frozen north much better might we know,
Mountains of ice, and everlasting snow.
Better with wandering Scythians choose to roam,
Than fix in fruitful Italy our home,
And guard these dreadful passages to Rome.
Through these the Cimbrians laid Hesperia waste;
Through these the swarthy Carthaginian pass'd;
Whenever Fortune threats the Latian states,
War, death, and ruin, enter at these gates."
In secret murmurs thus they sought relief,
While no bold voice proclaim'd aloud their grief,
O'er all one deep, one horrid silence reigns;
As when the rigour of the winter's chains
All Nature, Heaven, and Earth at once constrains;
The tuneful feather'd kind forget their lays,
And shivering tremble on the naked sprays;

E'en the rude seas compos'd forget to roar,
And freezing billows stiffen on the shore.
The colder shades of night forsook the sky,
When, lo! Bellona lifts her torch on high:
And if the chief, by doubt or shame detain'd,
Awhile from battle and from blood abstain'd;
Fortune and fate, impatient of delay,
Force every soft relenting thought away.
A lucky chance a fair pretence supplies,
And justice in his favour seems to rise.
New accidents new stings to rage suggest,
And fiercer fires inflame the warrior's breast.
The senate threatening high, and haughty grown,
Had driven the wrangling tribunes from the town;
In scorn of law, had chas'd them through the gate,
And urg'd them with the factious Gracchi's fate.
With these, as for redress their course they sped
To Cæsar's camp, the busy Curio fled;
Curio, a speaker turbulent and bold,
Of venal eloquence, that serv'd for gold,
And principles that might be bought and sold.
A tribune once himself, in loud debate,
He strove for public freedom and the state:
Essay'd to make the warring nobles bow,
And bring the potent party-leaders low.
To Cæsar thus, while thousand cares infest,
Revolving round, the warrior's anxious breast,
His speech the ready orator addrest:
"While yet my voice was useful to my friend;
While 't was allow'd me, Cæsar to defend,
While yet the pleading bar was left me free,
While I could draw uncertain Rome to thee;
In vain their force the moody fathers join'd,
In vain to rob thee of thy power combin'd;
I lengthen'd out the date of thy command,
And fix'd thy conquering sword within thy hand.
But since the vanquish'd laws in war are dumb,
To thee, behold, an exil'd band we come;
For thee, with joy our banishment we take,
For thee our houshold hearths and gods forsake;
Nor hope to see our native city more,
Till victory and thou the loss restore.
Th' unready faction, yet confus'd with fear,
Defenceless, weak, and unresolv'd, appear;
Haste then thy towering eagles on their way:
When fair occasion calls, 't is fatal to delay.
If twice five years the stubborn Gaul withheld,
And set thee hard in many a well-fought field;
A nobler labour now before thee lies,
The hazard less, yet greater far the prize:
A province that, and portion of the whole;
This the vast head that does mankind control.
Success shall sure attend thee, boldly go
And win the world at one successful blow.
No triumph now attends thee at the gate;
No temples for thy sacred laurel wait:
But blasting envy hangs upon thy name,
Denies thee right, and robs thee of thy fame;
Imputes as crimes, the nations overcome,
And makes it treason to have fought for Rome:
E'en he who took thy Julia's plighted hand,
Waits to deprive thee of thy just command.
Since Pompey then, and those upon his side,
Forbid thee, the world's empire to divide;
Assume that sway which best mankind may bear,
And rule alone what they disdain to share."
He said; his words the listening chief engage,
And fire his breast, already prone to rage.
Not peals of loud applause with greater force,
At Grecian Elis, rouse the fiery horse;
When eager for the course each nerve he strains,
Hangs on the bit, and tugs the stubborn reins,
At every shout erects his quivering ears,
And his broad breast upon the barrier bears.
Sudden he bids the troops draw out, and straight
The thronging legions round their ensigns wait:
Then thus, the crowd composing with a look,
And, with his hand commanding silence, spoke:
"Fellows in arms, who chose with me to bear
The toils and dangers of a tedious war,
And conquer to this tenth revolving year;
See what reward the grateful senate yield,
For the lost blood which stains yon northern field;
For wounds, for winter camps, for Alpine snow,
And all the deaths the brave can undergo.
See! the tumultuous city is alarm'd,
As if another Hannibal were arm'd:
The lusty youth are cull'd to fill the bands,
And each tall grove falls by the shipwright's hands;
Fleets are equipp'd, the field with armies spread,
And all demand devoted Cæsar's head.
If thus, while Fortune yields us her applause,
While the gods call us on and own our cause,
If thus returning conquerors they treat,
How had they us'd us flying from defeat;
If fickle chance of war had prov'd unkind,
And the fierce Gauls pursued us from behind!
But let their boasted hero leave his home,
Let him, dissolv'd with lazy leisure, come,
With every noisy talking tongue in Rome:
Let loud Marcellus troops of gown-men head,
And their great Cato peaceful burghers lead.
Shall his base followers, a venal train,
For ages, bid their idol Pompey reign?
Shall his ambition still be thought no crime,
His breach of laws, and triumph ere the time?
Still shall he gather honours and command,
And grasp all rule in his rapacious hand?
What need I name the violated laws,
And famine made the servant of his cause?
Who knows not, how the trembling judge beheld
The peaceful court with armed legions fill'd;
When the bold soldier, justice to defy,
In the mid forum rear'd his ensigns high;
When glittering swords the pale assembly scar'd,
When all for death and slaughter stood prepar'd,
And Pompey's arms were guilty Milo's guard?
And now, disdaining peace and needful ease,
Nothing but rule and government can please.
Aspiring still, as ever, to be great,
He robs his age of rest, to vex the state:
On war intent, to that he bends his cares,
And for the field of battle now prepares.
He copies from his master Sylla well,
And would the dire example far excel.
Hyrcanian tigers fierceness thus retain,
Whom in the woods their horrid mothers train,
To chase the herds, and surfeit on the slain.
Such, Pompey, still has been thy greedy thirst,
In early love of impious slaughter nurst;
Since first thy infant cruelty essay'd
To lick the curst dictator's reeking blade.
None ever give the salvage nature o'er,
Whose jaws have once been drench'd in floods of gore.
"But whither would a power so wide extend?
Where will thy long ambition find an end?
Remember him who taught thee to be great;
Let him who chose to quit the sovereign seat,
Let thy own Sylla warn thee to retreat.

Perhaps, for that too boldly I withstand,
Nor yield my conquering eagles on command;
Since the Cilician pirate strikes his sail,
Since o'er the Pontic king thy arms prevail;
Since the poor prince, a weary life o'erpast,
By thee and poison is subdued at last;
Perhaps, one latest province yet remains,
And vanquish'd Cæsar must receive thy chains.
But though my labours lose their just reward,
Yet let the senate these my friends regard;
Whate'er my lot, my brave victorious bands
Deserve to triumph, whosoe'er commands.
Where shall my weary veteran rest? Oh where
Shall virtue worn with years and arms repair?
What town is for his late repose assign'd?
Where are the promis'd lands he hop'd to find,
Fields for his plough, a country village seat,
Some little comfortable safe retreat;
Where failing age at length from toil may cease,
And waste the poor remains of life with peace?
But march! your long-victorious ensigns rear,
Let valour in its own just cause appear.
When for redress entreating armies call,
They who deny just things, permit them all.
The righteous gods shall surely own the cause,
Which seeks not spoil, nor empire, but the laws.
Proud lords and tyrants to depose we come,
And save from slavery submissive Rome."
He said; a doubtful sullen murmuring sound
Ran through the unresolving vulgar round;
The seeds of piety their rage restrain'd,
And somewhat of their country's love remain'd;
These the rude passions of their soul withstood,
Elate to conquest, and inur'd to blood:
But soon the momentary virtue fail'd,
And war and dread of Cæsar's frown prevail'd.
Straight Lelius from amidst the rest stood forth,
An old centurion of distinguish'd worth;
The oaken wreath his hardy temples wore,
Mark of a citizen preserv'd he bore.
"If against thee" (he cry'd) "I may exclaim,
Thou greatest leader of the Roman name;
If truth for injur'd honour may be bold,
What lingering patience does thy arms withhold?
Canst thou distrust our faith so often try'd,
In thy long wars not shrinking from thy side?
While in my veins this vital torrent flows,
This heaving breath within my bosom blows;
While yet these arms sufficient vigour yield
To dart the javelin, and to lift the shield;
While these remain, my general, wilt thou own
The vile dominion of the lazy gown?
Wilt thou the lordly senate choose to bear,
Rather than conquer in a civil war?
With thee the Scythian wilds we'll wander o'er,
With thee the burning Libyan sands explore,
And tread the Syrt's inhospitable shore.
Behold! this hand, to nobler labours train'd,
For thee the servile oar has not disdain'd,
For thee the swelling seas were taught to plough,
Through the Rhine's whirling stream to force thy prow,
That all the vanquish'd world to thee might bow.
Each faculty, each power, thy will obey,
And inclination ever leads the way.
No friend, no fellow-citizen I know,
Whom Cæsar's trumpet once proclaims a foe.
By the long labours of thy sword, I swear,
By all thy fame acquir'd in ten years' war,
By thy past triumphs, and by those to come,
(No matter where the vanquish'd be, nor whom)
Bid me to strike my dearest brother dead,
To bring my aged father's hoary head,
Or stab the pregnant partner of my bed;
Though Nature plead, and stop my trembling hand,
I swear to execute thy dread command.
Dost thou delight to spoil the wealthy gods,
And scatter flames through all their proud abodes?
See through thy camp our ready torches burn,
Moneta soon her sinking fane shall mourn.
Wilt thou yon haughty factious senate brave,
And awe the Tuscan river's yellow wave?
On Tiber's bank thy ensigns shall be plac'd,
And thy bold soldier lay Hesperia waste.
Dost thou devote some hostile city's walls?
Beneath our thundering rams the ruin falls;
She falls, e'en though thy wrathful sentence doom
The world's imperial mistress, mighty Rome."
He said; the ready legions vow to join
Their chief belov'd, in every bold design;
All lift their well-approving hands on high,
And rend with peals of loud applause the sky.
Such is the sound when Thracian Boreas spreads
His weighty wing o'er Ossa's piney heads:
At once the noisy groves are all inclin'd,
And, bending, roar beneath the sweeping wind;
At once their rattling branches all they rear,
And drive the leafy clamour through the air.
Cæsar with joy the ready bands beheld,
Urg'd on by fate, and eager for the field;
Swift orders straight the scatter'd warriors call,
From every part of wide-extended Gaul;
And, lest his fortune languish by delay,
To Rome the moving ensigns speed their way.
Some, at the bidding of the chief, forsake
Their fix'd encampment near the Leman lake:
Some from Vogesus' lofty rocks withdraw,
Plac'd on those heights the Lingones to awe;
The Lingones still frequent in alarms,
And rich in many-colour'd painted arms.
Others from Isara's low torrent came,
Who winding keeps through many a mead his name;
But seeks the sea with waters not his own,
Lost and confounded in the nobler Rhone.
Their garrison the Ruthen city send,
Whose youths long locks in yellow rings depend.
No more the Varus and the Atax feel
The lordly burthen of the Latian keel.
Alcides' fane the troops commanded leave,
Where winding rocks the peaceful flood receive;
Nor Corus there, nor Zephyrus resort,
Nor roll rude surges in the sacred port;
Circius' loud blast alone is heard to roar,
And vex the safety of Monœchus' shore.
The legions move from Gallia's farthest side,
Wash'd by the restless ocean's various tide;
Now o'er the land flows in the pouring main,
Now rears the land its rising head again,
And seas and earth alternate rule maintain.
If driven by winds from the far distant pole,
This way and that, the floods revolving roll;
Or if, compell'd by Cynthia's silver beam,
Obedient Tethys heaves the swelling stream;
Or if, by heat attracted to the sky,
Old ocean lifts his heavy waves on high,
And briny deeps the wasting Sun supply;
What cause so'er the wondrous motion guide,
And press the ebb, or raise the flowing tide;

Be that your task, ye sages, to explore,
Who search the secret springs of Nature's power:
To me, for so the wiser gods ordain,
Untrac'd the mystery shall still remain.
From fair Nemossus moves a warlike band,
From Atur's banks, and the Tarbellian strand,
Where, winding round, the coast pursues its way,
And folds the sea within a gentle bay.
The Santones are now with joy releas'd
From hostile inmates, and their Roman guest;
Now the Bituriges forget their fears,
And Suessons nimble with unwieldy spears:
Exult the Leuci, and the Remi now,
Expert in javelins, and the bending bow.
The Belgæ taught on cover'd wains to ride,
The Sequani the wheeling horse to guide;
The bold Averni who from Ilium come,
And boast an ancient brotherhood with Rome;
The Nervi, oft rebelling, oft subdued,
Whose hands in Gotta's slaughter were imbrued;
Vangiones, like loose Sarmatians drest,
Who with rough hides their brawny thighs invest:
Batavians fierce, whom brazen trumps delight,
And with hoarse rattlings animate to fight;
The nations where the Cinga's waters flow,
And Pyrenæan mountains stand in snow;
Those where slow Arar meets the rapid Rhone,
And with his stronger stream is hurried down;
Those o'er the mountain's lofty summit spread,
Where high Gebenna lifts her hoary head;
With these the Trevir, and Ligurian shorn,
Whose brow no more long falling locks adorn;
Though chief amongst the Gauls he wont to deck,
With ringlets comely spread, his graceful neck:
And you, where Hesus' horrid altar stands,
Where dire Teutates human blood demands;
Where Taranis by wretches is obey'd,
And vies in slaughter with the Scythian maid:
All see with joy the war's departing rage,
Seek distant lands, and other foes engage.
You too, ye bards! whom sacred raptures fire,
To chant your heroes to your country's lyre;
Who consecrate, in your immortal strain,
Brave patriot souls in righteous battle slain;
Securely now the tuneful task renew,
And noblest themes in deathless songs pursue.
The Druids now, while arms are heard no more,
Old mysteries and barbarous rites restore:
A tribe who singular religion love,
And haunt the lonely coverts of the grove.
To these, and these of all mankind alone,
The gods are sure reveal'd, or sure unknown.
If dying mortals doom they sing aright,
No ghosts descend to dwell in dreadful night:
No parting souls to grisly Pluto go,
Nor seek the dreary silent shades below:
But forth they fly immortal in their kind,
And other bodies in new worlds they find.
Thus life for ever runs its endless race,
And like a line, death but divides the space,
A stop which can but for a moment last,
A point between the future and the past.
Thrice happy they beneath their northern skies,
Who that worst fear, the fear of death, despise;
Hence they no cares for this frail being feel,
But rush undaunted on the pointed steel;
Provoke approaching fate, and bravely scorn
To spare that life which must so soon return.
You too tow'rds Rome advance, ye warlike band,
That wont the shaggy Cauci to withstand;
Whom once a better order did assign,
To guard the passes of the German Rhine;
Now from the fenceless banks you march away,
And leave the world the fierce barbarian's prey.
While thus the numerous troops, from every part,
Assembling, raise their daring leader's heart;
O'er Italy he takes his warlike way,
The neighbouring towns his summons straight [obey,
And on their walls his ensigns high display.
Meanwhile the busy messenger of ill,
Officious Fame, supplies new terrour still:
A thousand slaughters, and ten thousand fears,
She whispers in the trembling vulgar's ears.
Now comes a frighted messenger, to tell
Of ruins which the country round befell;
The foe to fair Mevania's walls is past,
And lays Clitumnus' fruitful pastures waste;
Where Nar's white waves with Tiber mingling fall,
Range the rough German and the rapid Gaul.
But when himself, when Cæsar they would paint,
The stronger image makes description faint;
No tongue can speak with what amazing dread
Wild thought presents him at his army's head;
Unlike the man familiar to their eyes,
Horrid he seems, and of gigantic size:
Unnumber'd eagles rise amidst his train,
And millions seem to hide the crowded plain.
Around him all the various nations join,
Between the snowy Alps and distant Rhine.
He draws the fierce barbarians from their home,
With rage surpassing theirs he seems to come,
And urge them on to spoil devoted Rome.
Thus fear does half the work of lying fame,
And cowards thus their own misfortunes frame;
By their own feigning fancies are betray'd,
And groan beneath those ills themselves have made.
Nor these alarms the crowd alone infest,
But ran alike through every beating breast;
With equal dread the grave Patricians shook,
Their seats abandon'd, and the court forsook.
The scattering fathers quit the public care,
And bid the consuls for the war prepare.
Resolv'd on flight, yet still unknowing where
To fly from danger, or for aid repair,
Hasty and headlong differing paths they tread,
As blind impulse and wild distraction lead;
The crowd, a hurrying, artless train, succeed.
Who that the lamentable sight beheld,
The wretched fugitives that hid the field,
Would not have thought the flames, with rapid [haste
Destroying wide, had laid their city waste;
Or groaning Earth had shook beneath their feet,
While threatening fabrics nodded o'er the street.
By such unthinking rashness were they led;
Such was the madness which their fears had bred,
As if, of every other hope bereft,
To fly from Rome were all the safety left.
So when the stormy South is heard to roar,
And rolls huge billows from the Libyan shore;
When rending sails flit with the driving blast,
And with a crash down comes the lofty mast;
Some coward master leaps from off the deck,
And, hasty to despair, prevents the wreck;
And though the bark unbroken hold her way,
His trembling crew all plunge into the sea.
From doubtful thus they run to certain harms,
And flying from the city rush to arms.
Then sons forsook their sires unnerv'd and old,
Nor weeping wives their husbands could withhold;

Each left his guardian Lares unador'd,
Nor with one parting prayer their aid implor'd:
None stopp'd, or sighing turn'd for one last view,
Or bid the city of his birth adieu.
The headlong crowd regardless urge their way,
Though e'en their gods and country ask their stay,
And pleading nature beg them to delay.
What means, ye gods! this changing in your doom?
Freely you grant, but quickly you resume.
Vain is the short-liv'd sovereignty you lend;
The pile you raise you deign not to defend.
See where, forsaken by her native bands,
All desolate the once great city stands!
She whom her swarming citizens made proud,
Where once the vanquish'd nations wont to crowd,
Within the circuit of whose ample space
Mankind might meet at once, and find a place;
A wide defenceless desert now she lies,
And yields herself the victor's easy prize.
The camp intrench'd securest slumbers yields,
Though hostile arms beset the neighbouring fields;
Rude banks of earth the hasty soldier rears,
And in the turfy wall forgets his fears:
While, Rome, thy sons all tremble from afar,
And scatter at the very name of war;
Nor on thy towers depend, nor rampart's height,
Nor trust their safety with thee for a night.
Yet one excuse absolv'd the panic dread;
The vulgar justly fear'd when Pompey fled.
And, lest sweet hope might mitigate their woes,
And expectation better times disclose,
On every breast presaging terrour sate,
And threaten'd plain some yet more dismal fate.
The gods declare their menaces around,
Earth, air, and seas, in prodigies abound;
Then stars, unknown before, appear'd to burn,
And foreign flames about the pole to turn;
Unusual fires by night were seen to fly,
And dart obliquely through the gloomy sky.
Then horrid comets shook their fatal hair,
And bade proud royalty for change prepare:
Now dart swift lightnings through the azure clear,
And meteors now in various forms appear:
Some like the javelin shoot extended long,
While some like spreading lamps in Heaven are hung.
And though no gathering clouds the day control,
Through skies serene portentous thunders roll;
Fierce blasting bolts from northern regions come,
And aim their vengeance at imperial Rome.
The stars, that twinkled in the lonely night,
Now lift their bolder head in day's broad light.
The Moon, in all her brother's beams array'd,
Was blotted by the Earth's approaching shade:
The Sun himself, in his meridian race,
In sable darkness veil'd his brighter face;
The trembling world beheld his fading ray,
And mourn'd despairing for the loss of day.
Such was he seen, when backward to the east
He fled, abhorring dire Thyestes' feast.
Sicilian Ætna then was heard to roar,
While Mulciber let loose his fiery store;
Nor rose the flames, but with a downward tide
Tow'rds Italy their burning torrent guide;
Charybdis' dogs howl doleful o'er the flood,
And all her whirling waves run red with blood;
The vestal fire upon the altar dy'd,
And o'er the sacrifice the flames divide;
The parting points with double streams ascend,
To show the Latian festivals must end:
Such from the Theban brethren's pile arose,
Signal of impious and immortal foes.
With openings fast the gaping earth gave way,
And in her inmost womb receiv'd the day.
The swelling seas o'er lofty mountains flow,
And nodding Alps shook off their ancient snow.
Then wept the demigods of mortal birth,
And sweating Lares trembled on the hearth.
In temples then, recording stories tell,
Untouch'd the sacred gifts and garlands fell.
Then birds obscene, with inauspicious flight,
And screamings dire, prophan'd the hallow'd light.
The salvage kind forsook the desert wood,
And in the streets disclos'd their horrid brood.
Then speaking beasts with human sounds were heard,
And monstrous births the teeming mothers scar'd.
Among the crowd, religious fears disperse
The saws of Sybils, and foreboding verse.
Bellona's priests, a barbarous frantic train,
Whose mangled arms a thousand wounds distain,
Toss their wild locks, and, with a dismal yell,
The wrathful gods and coming woes foretel.
Lamenting ghosts amidst their ashes mourn,
And groanings echo from the marble urn.
The rattling clank of arms is heard around,
And voices loud in lonely woods resound.
Grim spectres every where affright the eye,
Approaching glare, and pass with horrour by.
A fury fierce about the city walks,
Hell-born, and horrible of size, she stalks:
A flaming pine she brandishes in air,
And hissing loud up-rise her snaky hair:
Where'er her round accurst the monster takes,
The pale inhabitant his house forsakes.
Such to Lycurgus was the phantom seen,
Such the dire visions of the Theban queen;
Such, at his cruel stepmother's command,
Before Alcides, did Megæra stand:
With dread, till then unknown, the hero shook,
Though he had dar'd on Hell's grim king to look.
Amidst the deepest silence of the night,
Shrill-sounding clarions animate the fight;
The shouts of meeting armies seem to rise,
And the loud battle shakes the gloomy skies.
Dead Sylla in the Martian field ascends,
And mischiefs mighty as his own portends.
Near Anio's stream old Marius rears his head;
The hinds beheld his grisly form, and fled.
The state thus threaten'd, by old custom taught,
For counsel to the Tuscan prophets sought:
Of these the chief for learning fam'd, and age,
Aruns by name, a venerable sage,
At Luna liv'd; none better could descry
What bodes the lightning's journey through the sky;
Presaging veins and fibres well he knew,
And omens read aright, from every wing that flew.
First he commands to burn the monstrous breed,
Sprung from mix'd species, and discordant seed;
Forbidden and accursed births, which come
Where Nature's laws design'd a barren womb.
Next, the remaining trembling tribes he calls,
To pass with solemn rites about their walls,
In holy march to visit all around,
And with lustrations purge the utmost bound.
The sovereign priests the long procession lead,
Inferior orders in the train succeed,
Array'd all duly in the Gabine weed.
There the chaste head of Vesta's choir appears,
A sacred fillet binds her reverend hairs;

To her, in sole pre-eminence, is due,
Phrygian Minerva's awful shrine to view.
Next the fifteen in order pass along,
Who guard the fatal Sybils' secret song:
To Almon's stream Cybele's form they bear,
And wash the goddess each returning year.
The Titian brotherhood, the Augurs' band,
Observing flights on the left lucky hand;
The seven ordain'd Jove's holy feast to deck;
The Salii blithe, with bucklers on the neck;
All marching in their order just appear:
And last the generous Flamens close the rear.
While these through ways uncouth, and tiresome ground,
Patient perform their long laborious round,
Aruns collects the marks of Heaven's dread flame;
In earth he hides them with religious hand,
Murmurs a prayer, then gives the place a name,
And bids the fix'd bidental hallow'd stand.
Next from the herd a chosen male is sought,
And soon before the ready altar brought.
And now the seer the sacrifice began,
The pouring wine upon the victim ran;
The mingled meal upon his brow was plac'd;
The crooked knife the destin'd line had trac'd;
When with reluctant rage th' impatient beast
The rites unpleasing to the god confest.
At length compell'd his stubborn head to bow,
Vanquish'd he yields him to the fatal blow;
The gushing veins no cheerful crimson pour,
But stain with poisonous black the sacred floor.
The paler prophet stood with horrour struck;
Then with a hasty hand the entrails took,
And sought the angry gods again; but there
Prognostics worse, and sadder signs, appear;
The pallid guts with spots were marbled o'er,
With thin cold serum stain'd, and livid gore;
The liver wet with putrid streams he spy'd,
And veins that threaten'd on the hostile side:
Part of the heaving lungs is no where found,
And thinner films the sever'd entrails bound;
No usual motion stirs the panting heart;
The chinky vessels ouze on every part;
The caul, where wrapt the close intestines lie,
Betrays its dark recesses to the eye.
One prodigy superior threaten'd still,
The never-failing harbinger of ill:
Lo! by the fibrous liver's rising head,
A second rival prominence is spread;
All sunk and poor the friendly part appears,
And a pale, sickly, withering visage wears;
While high and full the adverse vessels ride,
And drive, impetuous, on their purple tide.
Amaz'd, the sage foresaw th' impending fate;
"Ye gods!" (he cry'd) "forbid me to relate
What woes on this devoted people wait.
Nor dost thou, Jove, in these our rites partake,
Nor smile propitious on the prayer we make;
The dreadful Stygian gods this victim claim,
And to our sacrifice the Furies came.
The ills we fear command us to be dumb;
Yet somewhat worse than what we fear shall come.
But may the gods be gracious from on high,
Some better prosperous event supply,
Fibres may err, and augury may lie;
Arts may be false, by which our sires divin'd,
And Tages taught them, to abuse mankind."
Thus darkly he the prophecy exprest,
And riddling sung the double-dealing priest.

But Figulus exclaims (to science bred,
And in the gods mysterious secrets read;
Whom nor Ægyptian Memphis' sons excell'd,
Nor with more skill the rolling orbs beheld:
Well could he judge the labours of the sphere,
And calculate the just revolving year).
"The stars" (he cries) "are in confusion hurl'd,
And wandering errour quite misguides the world;
Or, if the laws of Nature yet remain,
Some swift destruction now the Fates ordain.
Shall earth's wide-opening jaws for ruin call,
And sinking cities to the centre fall?
Shall raging drought infest the sultry sky?
Shall faithless earth the promis'd crop deny?
Shall poisonous vapours o'er the waters brood,
And taint the limpid spring and silver flood?
Ye gods! what ruin does your wrath prepare!
Comes it from Heaven, from earth, from seas, or air?
The lives of many to a period haste,
And thousands shall together breathe their last.
If Saturn's sullen beams were lifted high,
And baneful reign'd ascendant o'er the sky,
Then moist Aquarius deluges might rain,
And earth once more lie sunk beneath the main:
Or did thy glowing beams, O Phœbus, shine
Malignant in the Lion's scorching sign,
Wide o'er the world consuming fires might roll,
And Heaven be seen to flame from pole to pole:
Through peaceful orbits these unangry glide,
But, God of Battles! what dost thou provide?
Who in the threatening Scorpion dost preside?
With potent wrath around thy influence streams,
And the whole monster kindles at thy beams:
While Jupiter's more gentle rays decline,
And Mercury with Venus faintly shine;
The wandering lights are darken'd all and gone,
And Mars now lords it o'er the Heavens alone.
Orion's starry falchion blazing wide,
Refulgent glitters by his dreadful side.
War comes, and salvage slaughter must abound,
The sword of violence shall right confound;
The blackest crime fair virtue's name shall wear,
And impious fury rage for many a year.
Yet ask not thou an end of arms, O Rome,
Thy peace must with a lordly master come.
Protract destruction, and defer thy chain,
The sword alone prevents the tyrant's reign,
And civil wars thy liberty maintain."

The heartless vulgar to the sage give heed,
New rising fears his words foreboding breed.
When, lo! more dreadful wonders strike their eyes,
Forth through the streets a Roman matron flies,
Mad as the Thracian dames that bound along,
And chant Lyæus in their frantic song:
Enthusiastic heavings swell'd her breast,
And thus her voice the Delphic god confest:
"Where dost thou snatch me, Pæan! wherefore bear
Through cloudy heights and tracts of pathless air?
I see Pangean mountains white with snow,
Æmus and wide Philippi's fields below.
Say, Phœbus, wherefore does this fury rise?
What mean these spears and shields before my eyes?
I see the Roman battles crowd the plain!
I see the war, but seek the foe in vain.
Again I fly, I seek the rising day,
Where Nile's Ægyptian waters take their way:
I see, I know upon the guilty shore,
The hero's headless trunk besmear'd with gore.

The Syrts and Libyan sands beneath me lie,
Thither Emathia's scatter'd relics fly.
Now o'er the cloudy Alps I stretch my flight,
And soar above Pyrene's airy height:
To Rome, my native Rome, I turn again,
And see the senate reeking with the slain.
Again the moving chiefs their arms prepare;
Again I follow through the world the war.
Oh, give me, Phœbus! give me to explore,
Some region new, some undiscover'd shore;
I saw Philippi's fatal fields before."
She said: the weary rage began to cease,
And left the fainting prophetess in peace.

BOOK II.

THE ARGUMENT.

Amidst the general consternation that foreran the civil war, the poet introduces an old man giving an account of the miseries that attended on that of Marius and Sylla; and comparing their present circumstances to those in which the commonwealth was when that former war broke out. Brutus consults with Cato, whether it were the duty of a private man to concern himself in the public troubles; to which Cato replies in the affirmative: then follows his receiving Marcia again from the tomb of Hortensius. While Pompey goes to Capua, Cæsar makes himself master of the greatest part of Italy, and among the rest of Corfinium, where Domitius, the governor for Pompey, is seized by his garrison, and delivered to Cæsar, who pardons and dismisses him.

Pompey, in an oration to his army, makes a trial of their disposition to a general battle; but not finding it to answer his expectation, he sends his son to solicit the assistance of his friends and allies; then marches himself to Brundusium, where he is like to be shut up by Cæsar, and escapes at length with much difficulty.

Now manifest the wrath divine appear'd,
And Nature thro' the world the war declar'd;
Teeming with monsters, sacred law she broke,
And dire events in all her works bespoke.
Thou Jove, who dost in Heaven supremely reign,
Why does thy providence these signs ordain,
And give us prescience to increase our pain?
Doubly we bear thy dread-inflicting doom,
And feel our miseries before they come.
Whether the great creating parent Soul,
When first from chaos rude he form'd the whole,
Dispos'd futurity with certain band,
And bade the necessary causes stand;
Made one decree for ever to remain,
And bound himself in Fate's eternal chain;
Or whether fickle Fortune leads the dance,
Nothing is fix'd, but all things come by chance;
Whate'er thou shalt ordain, thou ruling power,
Unknown and sudden be the dreadful hour:
Let mortals to their future fate be blind,
And hope relieve the miserable mind.
While thus the wretched citizens behold
What certain ills the faithful gods foretold;
Justice suspends her course in mournful Rome,
And all the noisy courts at once are dumb;
No honours shine in the distinguish'd weed,
Nor rods the purple magistrate precede;
A dismal silent sorrow spreads around,
No groan is heard, nor one complaining sound.
So when some generous youth resigns his breath,
And parting sinks in the last pangs of death;
With ghastly eyes, and many a lift-up hand,
Around his bed the still attendants stand;
No tongue as yet presumes his fate to tell,
Nor speaks aloud the solemn last farewell;
As yet the mother by her darling lies,
Nor breaks lamenting into frantic cries;
And though he stiffens in her fond embrace,
His eyes are set, and livid pale his face;
Horrour awhile prevents the swelling tear,
Nor is her passion grief, as yet, but fear;
In one fix'd posture motionless she keeps,
And wonders at her woe before she weeps.
The matrons sad, their rich attire lay by,
And to the temples madly crowding fly:
Some on the shrines their gushing sorrows pour,
Some dash their breasts against the marble floor,
Some on the sacred thresholds rend their hair,
And howling seek the gods with horrid prayer.
Nor Jove receiv'd the wailing suppliants all,
In various fanes on various powers they call,
No altar then, no god was left alone,
Unvex'd by some impatient parent's moan.
Of these, one wretch her grief, above the rest,
With visage torn, and mangled arms confest.
"Ye mothers! beat" (she cry'd) "your bosoms now,
Now tear the curling honours from your brow;
The present hour e'en all your tears demands,
While doubtful fortune yet suspended stands.
When one shall conquer, then for joy prepare,
The victor chief, at least, shall end the war."
Thus, from renew'd complaints they seek relief,
And only find fresh causes out for grief.
The men too, as to different camps they go,
Join their sad voices to the public woe;
Impatient to the gods they raise their cry,
And thus expostulate with those on high:
"Oh hapless times! oh that we had been born,
When Carthage made our vanquish'd country mourn!
Well had we then been number'd with the slain
On Trebia's banks, or Cannæ's fatal plain.
Nor ask we peace, ye powers, nor soft repose;
Give us new wars, and multitudes of foes;
Let every potent city arm for fight,
And all the neighbour nations round unite;
From Median Susa let the Parthians come,
And Massagetes beyond their Ister roam:
Let Elbe and Rhine's unconquer'd springs send forth
The yellow Suevi from the farthest north:
Let the conspiring world in arms engage,
And save us only from domestic rage.
Here let the hostile Dacian inroads make,
And there his way the Gete invader take.
Let Cæsar in Iberia tame the foe;
Let Pompey break the deadly eastern bow,
And Rome no hand unarm'd for battle know.
But if Hesperia stand condemn'd by fate,
And ruin on our name and nation wait;
Now dart thy thunder, dread Almighty Sire,
Let all thy flaming heavens descend in fire;
On chiefs and parties hurl thy bolts alike,
And, ere their crimes have made them guilty, strike.
Is it a cause so worthy of our care,
That power may fall to this, or that man's share?
Do we for this the gods and conscience brave,
That one may rule, and make the rest a slave?

When thus e'en liberty we scarce should buy,
But think a civil war a price too high."
Thus groan they at approaching dire events,
And thus expiring piety laments.
Meanwhile the hoary sire his years deplores,
And age that former miseries restores:
He hates his weary life prolong'd for woe,
Worse days to see, more impious rage to know.
Then fetching old examples from afar,
"'T was thus" (he cries) "fate usher'd in the war:
When Cimbrians fierce, and Libya's swarthy lord,
Had fall'n before triumphant Marius' sword;
Yet to Minturnæ's marsh the victor fled,
And hid in oozy flags his exil'd head.
The faithless soil the hunted chief reliev'd,
And sedgy waters fortune's pledge receiv'd.
Deep in a dungeon plung'd at length he lay,
Where gyves and rankling fetters eat their way,
And noisome vapours on his vitals prey.
Ordain'd at ease to dine in wretched Rome,
He suffer'd then, for wickedness to come.
In vain his foes had arm'd the Cimbrian's hand,
Death will not always wait upon command;
About to strike, the slave with horrour shook,
The useless steel his loosening gripe forsook;
Thick flashing flames a light unusual gave,
And sudden shone around the gloomy cave;
Dreadful the gods of guilt before him stood,
And Marius terrible in future blood;
When thus a voice began: 'Rash man forbear,
Nor touch that head which fate resolves to spare;
Thousands are doom'd beneath his arm to bleed,
And countless deaths before his own decreed;
Thy wrath and purpose to destroy is vain:
Would'st thou avenge thee for thy nation slain?
Preserve this man; and in some coming day
The Cimbrian slaughter well he shall repay.'
No pitying god, no power to mortals good,
Could save a salvage wretch who joy'd in blood:
But fate reserv'd him to perform its doom,
And be the minister of wrath to Rome.
By swelling seas too favourably tost,
Safely he reach'd Numidia's hostile coast;
There, driven from man, to wilds he took his way;
And on the earth, where once he conquer'd, lay;
There in the lone unpeopled desert field,
Proud Carthage in her ruins he beheld;
Amidst her ashes pleas'd he sat him down,
And joy'd in the destruction of the town.
The genius of the place, with mutual hate,
Rear'd its sad head, and smil'd at Marius' fate;
Each with delight survey'd their fallen foe,
And each forgave the gods that laid the other low.
There with new fury was his soul possest,
And Libyan rage collected in his breast.
Soon as returning fortune own'd his cause,
Troops of revolting bond-men forth he draws;
Cut-throats and slaves resort to his command,
And arms were given to every baser hand.
None worthily the leader's standard bore,
Unstain'd with blood or blackest crimes before:
Villains of fame, to fill his bands, were sought,
And to his camp increase of crimes they brought.
Who can relate the horrours of that day,
When first these walls became the victor's prey!
With what a stride devouring Slaughter past,
And swept promiscuous orders in her haste!
O'er noble and plebeian rang'd the sword;
Nor pity or remorse one pause afford.
The sliding streets with blood were clotted o'er,
And sacred temples stood in pools of gore.
The ruthless steel, impatient of delay,
Forbad the sire to linger out his day:
It struck the bending father to the earth,
And cropt the wailing infant at his birth.
(Can innocents the rage of parties know,
And they who ne'er offended find a foe?)
Age is no plea, and childhood no defence,
To kill is all the murderer's pretence.
Rage stays not to inquire who ought to die,
Numbers must fall, no matter which, or why;
Each in his hand a grisly visage bears,
And as the trophy of his virtue wears.
Who wants a prize, straight rushes thro' the streets,
And undistinguish'd mows the first he meets;
The trembling crowd with fear officious strive,
And those who kiss the tyrant's hand survive.
Oh could you fall so low, degenerate race!
And purchase safety at a price so base?
What though the sword was master of your doom,
Though Marius could have given you years to come.
Can Romans live by infamy so mean?
But soon your changing fortune shifts the scene;
Short is your date; you only live to mourn
Your hopes deceiv'd, and Sylla's swift return.
The vulgar falls, and none laments his fate,
Sorrow has hardly leisure for the great.
What tears could Bæbius' hasty death deplore!
A thousand hands his mangled carcass tore;
His scatter'd entrails round the streets were tost,
And in a moment all the man was lost.
Who wept, Antonius' murder to behold,
Whose moving tongue the mischief oft foretold?
Spite of his age and eloquence he bled;
The barbarous soldier snatch'd his hoary head;
Dropping he bore it to his joyful lord,
And while he feasted plac'd it on the board.
The Crassi both by Fimbria's hand were slain,
And bleeding magistrates the pulpit stain.
Then did the doom of that neglecting hand,
Thy fate, O holy Scævola, command;
In vain for succour to the gods he flies,
The priest before the vestal altar dies:
A feeble stream pour'd forth the exhausted sire,
And spar'd to quench the everliving fire.
The seventh returning fasces now appear,
And bring stern Marius' latest destin'd year:
Thus the long toils of changing life o'erpast,
Hoary and full of days he breath'd his last,
While Fortune frown'd, her fiercest wrath he bore,
And while she smil'd enjoy'd her amplest power:
All various turns of good and bad he knew,
And prov'd the most that chance or fate could do.
"What heaps of slain the Colline gate did yield!
What bodies strew'd the Sacriportan field,
When empire was ordain'd to change her seat,
To leave her Rome, and make Præneste great!
When the proud Samnites' troops the state defy'd,
In terms beyond their Caudine treaty's pride.
Nor Sylla with less cruelty returns,
With equal rage the fierce avenger burns:
What blood the feeble city yet retain'd,
With too severe a healing hand he drain'd:
Too deeply was the searching steel employ'd,
What maladies had hurt, the leach destroy'd.
The guilty only were of life bereft:
Alas! the guilty only then were left.
Dissembledhate and rancour rang'd at will
All as they pleas'd took liberty to kill;

And while revenge no longer fear'd the laws,
Each private murder was the public cause.
The leader bade destroy: and at the word,
The master fell beneath the servant's sword.
Brothers on brothers were for gifts bestow'd,
And sons contended for their father's blood.
Nor refuge some to caves and forests fled;
Some to the lonely mansions of the dead;
Some, to prevent the cruel victor, die;
These strangled hang from fatal beams on high;
While those, from tops of lofty turrets thrown,
Came headlong on the dashing pavement down.
Some for their funerals the wood prepare,
And build the sacred pile with hasty care:
Then bleeding to the kindling flames they press,
And Roman rites, while yet they may, possess.
Pale heads of Marian chiefs are borne on high,
And heap'd together in the Forum lie;
There join the meeting slaughters of the town,
There each performing villain's deeds are known.
No sight like this the Thracian stables knew,
Antæus' Libyan spoils to these were few:
Nor Greece beheld so many suitors fall,
To grace the Pisan tyrant's horrid hall.
At length, when putrid gore, with foul disgrace,
Hid the distinguish'd features of the face,
By night the miserable parents came,
And bore their sons to some forbidden flame.
Well I remember, in that woeful reign,
How I my brother sought amongst the slain;
Hopeful by stealth his poor remains to burn,
And close his ashes in a peaceful urn;
His visage in my trembling hand I bore,
And turn'd pacific Sylla's trophies o'er;
Full many a mangled trunk I try'd, to see
Which carcass with the head would best agree.
Why should my grief to Catullus return,
And tell the victim offer'd at his urn;
When, struck with horrour, the relenting shade
Beheld his wrongs too cruelly repay'd?
I saw where Marius' hapless brother stood,
With limbs all torn, and cover'd o'er with blood;
A thousand gaping wounds increas'd his pain,
While weary life a passage sought in vain;
That mercy still his ruthless foes deny,
And, whom they mean to kill, forbid to die.
This from the wrist the suppliant hands divides,
That hews his arms from off his naked sides;
One crops his breathing nostrils, one his ears,
While from the roots his tongue another tears;
Panting awhile upon the earth it lies,
And with mute motion trembles ere it dies:
Last, from the sacred caverns where they lay,
The bleeding orbs of sight are rent away.
Can late posterity believe, whene'er
This tale of Marius and his foes they hear,
They could inflict so much, or he could bear?
Such is the broken carcass seen to lie,
Crush'd by some tumbling turret from on high;
Such to the shore the shipwreck'd corse is borne,
By rending rocks and greedy monsters torn.
Mistaken rage! thus mangling to disgrace,
And blot the lines of Marius' hated face!
What joy can Sylla take, unless he know
And mark the features of his dying foe?
Fortune beheld, from her Prænestine fane,
Her helpless worshippers around her slain;
One hour of fate was common to them all,
And like one man she saw a people fall.
Then dy'd the lusty youth in manly bloom,
Hesperia's flower, and hope for times to come;
Their blood, Rome's only strength, distains the fold,
Ordain'd th' assembling centuries to hold.
Numbers have oft been known, on sea and land,
To sink of old by death's destructive hand;
Battles with multitudes have strown the plain,
And many perish on the stormy main:
Earthquakes destroy, malignant vapours blast,
And plagues and famines lay whole nations waste:
But justice, sure, was never seen, till now,
To massacre her thousands at a blow.
Satiety of death the victors prove,
And slowly through th' encumbering ruin move:
So many fall, there scarce is room for more,
The dying nod on those who fell before;
Crowding in heaps their murderers they aid,
And, by the dead, the living are o'erlaid.
Meanwhile the stern dictator, from on high,
Beholds the slaughter with a fearless eye;
Nor sighs, to think his dread commands ordain
So many thousand wretches to be slain.
Amidst the Tiber's waves the load is thrown,
The torrent rolls the guilty burthen down;
Till rising mounds obstruct his watery way,
And carcasses the gliding vessels stay.
But soon another stream to aid him rose,
Swift o'er the fields a crimson deluge flows:
The Tuscan river swells above his shores,
And floating bodies to the land restores:
Struggling at length he drives his rushing flood,
And dyes the Tyrrhene ocean round with blood.
Could deeds like these the glorious style demand
Of prosperous, and saviour of the land?
Could this renown, could these achievements build
A tomb for Sylla in the Martian field?
Again, behold the circling woes return,
Again the curse of civil wars we mourn;
Battles and blood, and vengeance, shall succeed,
And Rome once more by Roman hands shall bleed.
Or if, for hourly thus our fears presage,
With wrath more fierce the present chiefs shall rage,
Mankind shall some unheard-of plagues deplore,
And groan for miseries unknown before.
Marius an end of exile only sought;
Sylla to crush a hated faction fought;
A larger recompense these leaders claim,
And higher is their vast ambition's aim:
Could these be satisfy'd with Sylla's power;
Nor, all he had possessing, ask for more;
Neither had force and impious arms employ'd,
Or fought for that which guiltless each enjoy'd."

Thus wept lamenting age o'er hapless Rome,
Remembering evils past, and dreading those to come.

But Brutus' temper fail'd not with the rest,
Nor with the common weakness was opprest;
Safe and in peace he kept his manly breast.
'Twas when the solemn dead of night came on,
When bright Calisto with her shining son
Now half their circle round the pole had run;
When Brutus, on the busy times intent,
To virtuous Cato's humble dwelling went:
Waking he found him, careful for the state,
Grieving and fearing for his country's fate;
For Rome, and wretched Rome, alone he fear'd;
Secure within himself, and for the worst prepar'd.

To him thus Brutus spoke: "O thou, to whom
Forsaken virtue flies, as to her home,

Driv'n out, and by an impious age oppress,
She finds no room on earth but Cato's breast:
There, in her one good man, she reigns secure,
Fearless of vice, or fortune's hostile power.
Then teach my soul, to doubt and errour prone,
Teach me a resolution like thy own.
Let partial favour, hopes, or interest guide,
By various motives, all the world beside,
To Pompey's, or ambitious Cæsar's side;
Thou, Cato, art my leader. Whether peace
And calm repose amidst these storms shall please:
Or whether war thy ardour shall engage,
To gratify the madness of this age, [rage.
Herd with the factious chiefs, and urge the people's
The ruffian, bankrupt, loose adulterer,
All who the power of laws and justice fear,
From guilt learn specious reasons for the war.
By starving want and wickedness prepar'd,
Wisely they arm for safety and reward.
But, oh! what cause, what reason, canst thou find?
Art thou to arms for love of arms inclin'd?
Hast thou the manners of this age withstood,
And for so many years been singly good,
To be repaid with civil wars and blood?
Let those to vice inur'd for arms prepare,
In thee 't will be impiety to dare;
Preserve at least, ye gods, these hands from war.
Nor do thou meanly with the rabble join,
Nor grace their cause with such an arm as thine.
To thee, the fortune of the fatal field
Inclining, unauspicious fame shall yield;
Each to thy sword should press, and wish to be
Imputed as thy crime, and charg'd on thee.
Happy thou wert, if with retirement blest,
Which noise and faction never should molest,
Nor break the sacred quiet of thy breast;
Where harmony and order ne'er should cease,
But every day should take its turn in peace.
So, in eternal steady motion, roll
The radiant spheres around the starry pole:
Fierce lightnings, meteors, and the winter's storm,
Earth and the face of lower Heaven deform,
Whilst all by Nature's laws is calm above;
No tempest rages in the court of Jove.
Light particles and idle atoms fly,
Toss'd by the winds, and scatter'd round the sky;
While the more solid parts the force resist,
And fix'd and stable on the centre rest.
Cæsar shall hear with joy, that thou art join'd
With fighting factions, to disturb mankind:
Though sworn his foe, he shall applaud thy choice,
And think his wicked war approv'd by Cato's
voice.
See! how to swell their mighty leader's state
The consuls and the servile senate wait:
E'en Cato's self to Pompey's yoke must bow,
And all mankind are slaves but Cæsar now.
If war, however, be at last our doom,
If we must arm for liberty and Rome:
While undecided yet their fate depends,
Cæsar and Pompey are alike my friends;
Which party I shall choose, is yet to know,
That let the war decide; who conquers is my foe."
Thus spoke the youth. When Cato thus exprest
The sacred counsels of his inmost breast:
"Brutus! with thee, I own the crime is great;
With thee, this impious civil war I hate;
But virtue blindly follows, led by fate.
Answer yourselves, ye gods, and set me free;
If I am guilty, 't is by your decree.
If yon fair lamps above should lose their light,
And leave the wretched world in endless night;
If chaos should in Heaven and Earth prevail,
And universal Nature's frame should fail:
What stoic would not the misfortune share,
And think that desolation worth his care?
Princes and nations whom wide seas divide,
Where other stars far distant Heavens do guide,
Have brought their ensigns to the Roman side.
Forbid it, gods! when barbarous Scythians come
From their cold north, to prop declining Rome,
That I should see her fall, and sit secure at home.
As some unhappy sire by death undone,
Robb'd of his age's joy, his only son,
Attends the funeral with pious care,
To pay his last paternal office there;
Takes a sad pleasure in the crowd to go,
And be himself part of the pompous woe;
Then waits till, every ceremony past,
His own fond hand may light the pile at last.
So fix'd, so faithful to thy cause, O Rome,
With such a constancy and love I come,
Resolv'd for thee and liberty to mourn,
And never! never from your sides be torn;
Resolv'd to follow still your common fate,
And on your very names, and last remains to wait.
Thus let it be, since thus the gods ordain;
Since hecatombs of Romans must be slain,
Assist the sacrifice with every hand,
And give them all the slaughter they demand.
Oh! were the gods contented with my fall,
If Cato's life could answer for you all,
Like the devoted Decius would I go,
To force from either side the mortal blow,
And for my country's sake, wish to be thought
her foe.
To me, ye Romans, all your rage confine,
To me, ye nations from the barbarous Rhine,
Let all the wounds this war shall make be mine.
Open my vital streams, and let them run,
Oh, let the purple sacrifice atone
For all the ills offending Rome has done.
If slavery be all the faction's end,
If chains the prize for which the fools contend,
To me convert the war, let me be slain;
Me, only me, who fondly strive, in vain,
Their useless laws and freedom to maintain:
So may the tyrant safely mount his throne,
And rule his slaves in peace, when I am gone.
Howe'er, since free as yet from his command,
For Pompey and the commonwealth we stand.
Nor he, if fortune should attend his arms,
Is proof against ambition's fatal charms;
But, urg'd with greatness, and desire of sway,
May dare to make the vanquish'd world his prey.
Then, lest the hopes of empire swell his pride,
Let him remember I was on his side;
Nor think he conquer'd for himself alone,
To make the harvest of the war his own,
Where half the toil was ours." So spoke the sage.
His words the listening eager youth engage
Too much to love of arms, and heat of civil rage.
Now 'gan the Sun to lift his dawning light,
Before him fled the colder shades of night;
When lo! the sounding doors are heard to turn,
Chaste Martia comes from dead Hortensius' urn.
Once to a better husband's happier bed,
With bridal rites, a virgin was she led:
When, every debt of love and duty paid,
And thrice a parent by Lucina made,

The teeming matron, at her lord's command,
To glad Hortensius gave her plighted hand;
With a fair stock his barren house to grace;
And mingle by the mother's side the race.
At length this husband in his ashes laid,
And every rite of due religion paid,
Forth from his monument the mournful dame,
With beaten breasts, and locks dishevell'd, came;
Then with a pale dejected rueful look,
Thus pleasing, to her former lord she spoke:
"While nature yet with vigour fed my veins,
And made me equal to a mother's pains,
To thee obedient, I thy house forsook,
And to my arms another husband took:
My powers at length with genial labours worn,
Weary to thee, and wasted, I return.
At length a barren wedlock let me prove,
Give me the name, without the joys of love;
No more to be abandon'd, let me come,
That Cato's wife may live upon my tomb.
So shall my truth to latest times be read,
And none shall ask if guiltily I fled,
Or thy command estrang'd me from thy bed.
Nor ask I now thy happiness to share,
I seek thy days of toil, thy nights of care:
Give me, with thee, to meet my country's foe,
Thy weary marches and thy camps to know;
Nor let posterity with shame record,
Cornelia follow'd, Martia left her lord."
She said: the hero's manly heart was mov'd,
And the chaste matron's virtuous suit approv'd.
And though the times far differing thoughts demand,
Though war dissents from Hymen's holy band;
In plain unsolemn wise his faith he plights,
And calls the gods to view the lonely rites.
No garlands gay the cheerful portal crown'd,
Nor woolly fillets wove the posts around;
No genial bed with rich embroidery grac'd,
On ivory steps in lofty state was plac'd;
No hymeneal torch preceding shone,
No matron put the towering frontlet on,
Nor bade her feet the sacred threshold shun.
No yellow veil was loosely thrown, to hide
The rising blushes of the trembling bride;
No glittering zone her flowing garments bound,
Nor sparkling gems her neck encompass'd round;
No silken scarf, nor decent winding lawn,
Was o'er her naked arms and shoulders drawn:
But, as she was, in funeral attire,
With all the sadness sorrow could inspire,
With eyes dejected, with a joyless face,
She met her husband's, like a son's embrace.
No Sabine mirth provokes the bridegroom's ears,
Nor sprightly wit the glad assembly cheers.
No friends, not e'en their children, grace the feast,
Brutus attends, their only nuptial guest:
He stands a witness of the silent rite,
And sees the melancholy pair unite.
Nor he, the chief, his sacred visage cheer'd,
Nor smooth'd his matted locks, or horrid beard;
Nor deigns his heart one thought of joy to know,
But met his Martia with the same stern brow.
(For when he saw the fatal factions arm,
The coming war, and Rome's impending harm;
Regardless quite of every other care,
Unshorn he left his loose neglected hair;
Rude hung the hoary honours of his head,
And a foul growth his mournful cheeks o'erspread.
No stings of private hate his peace infest,
Nor partial favour grew upon his breast;
But, safe from prejudice, he kept his mind
Free, and at leisure to lament mankind.)
Nor could his former love's returning fire,
The warmth of one connubial wish inspire,
But strongly he withstood the just desire.
These were the stricter manners of the man,
And this the stubborn course in which they ran;
The golden mean unchanging to pursue,
Constant to keep the purpos'd end in view;
Religiously to follow Nature's laws,
And die with pleasure in his country's cause,
To think he was not for himself design'd,
But born to be of use to all mankind.
To him 't was feasting, hunger to repress;
And home-spun garments were his costly dress:
No marble pillars rear'd his roof on high,
'T was warm, and kept him from the winter sky:
He sought no end of marriage, but increase,
Nor wish'd a pleasure, but his country's peace:
That took up all the tenderest parts of life,
His country was his children and his wife.
From justice' righteous lore he never swerv'd,
But rigidly his honesty preserv'd.
On universal good his thoughts were bent,
Nor knew what gain, or self-affection meant;
And while his benefits the public share,
Cato was always last in Cato's care.
Meantime, the trembling troops, by Pompey led,
Hasty to Phrygian Capua were fled.
Resolving here to fix the moving war,
He calls his scatter'd legions from afar;
Here he decrees the daring foe to wait,
And prove at once the great event of fate;
Where Apennine's delightful shades arise,
And lift Hesperia lofty to the skies.
Between the higher and inferior sea,
The long-extended mountain takes his way;
Pisa and Ancon bound his sloping sides,
Wash'd by the Tyrrhene and Dalmatic tides;
Rich in the treasure of his watery stores,
A thousand living springs and streams he pours,
And seeks the different seas by different shores.
From his left falls Crustumium's rapid flood,
And swift Metaurus red with Punic blood;
There gentle Sapis with Isaurus joins,
And Sena there the Senones confines;
Rough Aufidus the meeting ocean braves,
And lashes on the lazy Adria's waves;
Hence vast Eridanus with matchless force,
Prince of the streams, directs his regal course;
Proud with the spoils of fields and woods he flows,
And drains Hesperia's rivers as he goes.
His sacred banks, in ancient tales renown'd,
First by the spreading poplar's shade were crown'd;
When the Sun's fiery steeds forsook their way,
And downward drew to Earth the burning day:
When every flood and ample lake was dry,
The Po alone his channel could supply.
Hither rash Phaeton was headlong driven,
And in these waters quench'd the flames of Heaven.
Nor wealthy Nile a fuller stream contains,
Though wide he spreads o'er Ægypt's flatter plains;
Nor Ister rolls a larger torrent down,
Sought he the sea with waters all his own;
But meeting floods to him their homage pay,
And heave the blended river on his way.
These from the left; while from the right there come
The Rutuba and Tiber dear to Rome;

Thence slides Vulturnus' swift-descending flood,
And Sarnus hid beneath his misty cloud;
Thence Lyris, whom the Vestin fountains aid,
Winds to the sea through close Marica's shade;
Thence Siler through Salernian pastures falls,
And shallow Macra creeps by Luna's walls.
Bordering on Gaul the loftiest ridges rise,
And the low Alps from cloudy heights despise;
Thence his long back the fruitful mountain bows,
Beneath the Umbrian and the Sabine plows;
The race primeval, natives all of old,
His woody rocks within their circuit hold;
Far as Hesperia's utmost limits pass,
The hilly father runs his mighty mass;
Where Juno rears her high Lucinian fane,
And Scylla's raging dogs molest the main.
Once, farther yet ('t is said) his way he took,
Till through his side the seas conspiring broke;
And still we see on fair Sicilia's sands,
Where, part of Apennine, Pelorus stands.
But Cæsar for destruction eager burns,
Free passages and bloodless ways he scorns;
In fierce conflicting fields his arms delight,
He joys to be oppos'd, to prove his might,
Resistless through the widening breach to go,
To burst the gate, to lay the bulwark low,
To burn the villages, to waste the plains,
And massacre the poor laborious swains.
Abhorring law, he chooses to offend,
And blushes to be thought his country's friend.
The Latian cities now, with busy care,
As various they inclin'd, for arms prepare.
Though doom'd before the war's first rage to yield,
Trenches they dig, and ruin'd walls rebuild;
Huge stone and darts their lofty towers supply,
And guarded bulwarks menace from on high.
To Pompey's part the proner people lean,
Though Cæsar's stronger terrours stand between.
So when the blasts of sounding Auster blow,
The waves obedient to his empire flow;
And though the stormy god fierce Eurus frees,
And sends him rushing cross the swelling seas;
Spite of his force, the billows yet retain
Their former course, and that way roll the main;
The lighter clouds with Eurus driving sweep,
While Auster still commands the watery deep.
Still fear too sure o'er vulgar minds prevails,
And faith before successful fortune fails.
Etruria vainly trusts in Libo's aid,
And Umbria by Thermus is betray'd;
Sylla, unmindful of his father's fame,
Fled at the dreadful sound of Cæsar's name,
Soon as the horse near Auximon appear,
Retreating Varus owns his abject fear,
And with a coward's haste neglects his rear;
On flight alone intent, without delay,
Through rocks and devious woods he wings his way.
Th' Esculean fortress Lentulus forsakes,
A swift pursuit the speedy victor makes;
All arts of threats and promises apply'd,
He wins the faithless cohorts to his side.
The leader with his ensigns fled alone,
To Cæsar fell the soldier, and the town.
Thou, Scipio, too, dost for retreat prepare;
Thou leav'st Luceria, trusted to thy care;
Though troops well try'd attend on thy command,
(The Roman power can boast no braver band)
By wily arts of old from Cæsar rent,
Against the hardy Parthians were they sent;
But their first chief the legion now obeys,
And Pompey thus the Gallic loss repays;
Aid to his foe too freely he affords,
And lends his hostile father Roman swords.
But in Corfinium bold Domitius lies,
And from his walls th' advancing power defies;
Secure of heart, for all events prepar'd,
He heads the troops once bloody Milo's guard.
Soon as he sees the cloudy dust arise,
And glittering arms reflect the sunny skies:
"Away, companions of my arms!" he cry'd,
"And haste to guard the river's sedgy side:
Break down the bridge. And thou that dwell'st below,
Thou watery god, let all thy fountains go,
And rushing bid thy foamy torrent flow;
Swell to the utmost brink thy rapid stream,
Bear down the planks, and every floating beam;
Upon thy banks the ling'ring war delay,
Here let the headlong chief be taught to stay;
'T is victory to stop the victor's way."
He ceas'd; and, shooting swiftly 'cross the plain,
Drew down the soldier to the flood in vain.
For Cæsar early from the neighbouring field,
The purpose to obstruct his march beheld:
Kindling to wrath, "Oh basest fear!" (he cries)
"To whom nor towers, nor sheltering walls suffice.
Are these your coward stratagems of war?
Hope you with brooks my conquering arms to bar?
Though Nile and Ister should my way control,
Though swelling Ganges should to guard you roll,
What streams, what floods soe'er athwart me fall,
Who pass'd the Rubicon shall pass them all.
Haste to the passage then, my friends." He said;
Swift as a storm the nimble horse obey'd;
Across the stream their deadly darts they throw,
And from their station drive the yielding foe:
The victors at their ease the ford explore,
And pass the undefended river o'er.
The vanquish'd to Corfinium's strength retreat,
Where warlike engines round the ramparts threat.
Close to the wall the creeping vinea lies,
And mighty towers in dread approaches rise.
But see the stain of war! the soldier's shame!
And vile dishonour of the Latian name!
The faithless garrison betray the town,
And captive drag their valiant leader down.
The noble Roman, fearless, though in bands,
Before his haughty fellow-subject stands,
With looks erect, and with a daring brow,
Death he provokes, and courts the fatal blow:
But Cæsar's arts his inmost thoughts descry,
His fear of pardon, and desire to die.
"From me thy forfeit life" (he said) "receive,
And, though repining, by my bounty live;
That all, by thy example taught, may know,
How Cæsar's mercy treats a vanquish'd foe:
Still arm against me, keep thy hatred still,
And if thou conquer'st, use thy conquest, kill.
Returns of love, or favour, seek I none;
Nor give thy life to bargain for my own."
So saying, on the instant he commands
To loose the galling fetters from his hands.
Oh fortune! better were it, he had dy'd,
And spar'd the Roman shame, and Cæsar's pride.
What greater grief can on a Roman seize,
Than to be forc'd to live on terms like these!
To be forgiven, fighting for the laws,
And need a pardon in his country's cause!

Struggling with rage, undaunted he represt
The swelling passions in his labouring breast;
Thus murmuring to himself: "Wilt thou to Rome,
Base as thou art, and seek thy lazy home?
To war, to battle, to destruction fly,
And haste, as it becomes thee well, to die;
Provoke the worst effects of deadly strife,
And rid thee of this Cæsar's gift, this life."
Meanwhile, unknowing of the captiv'd chief,
Pompey prepares to march to his relief.
He means the scattering forces to unite,
And with increase of strength expect the fight.
Resolving with the following sun to move,
First he decrees the soldier's heart to prove:
Then into words like these, rever'd, he broke,
The silent legions listening while he spoke:
"Ye brave avengers of your country's wrong,
You who to Rome and liberty belong;
Whose breasts our fathers virtue truly warms,
Whose hands the senate's sacred order arms;
With cheerful ardour meet the coming fight,
And pray the gods to smile upon the right.
Behold the mournful view Hesperia yields,
Her flaming villages and wasted fields!
See where the Gauls a dreadful deluge flow,
And scorn the boundaries of Alpine snow.
Already Cæsar's sword is stain'd in blood,
Be that, ye gods, to us an omen good;
That glory still be his peculiar care,
Let him begin, while we sustain the war.
Yet call it not a war to which we go;
We seek a malefactor, not a foe;
Rome's awful injur'd majesty demands
The punishment of traitors at our hands.
If this be war, then war was wag'd of old
By curst Cethegus, Catiline the bold,
By every villain's hand who durst conspire
In murder, robbery, or midnight fire.
Oh wretched rage! thee, Cæsar, fate design'd
To rank amongst the patrons of mankind;
With brave Camillus to enrol thy fame,
And mix thee with the great Metelli's name:
While to the Cinna's thy fierce soul inclines,
And with the slaughter-loving Marii joins.
Since then thy crimes, like theirs, for justice call,
Beneath our axe's vengeance shalt thou fall:
Thee rebel Carbo's sentence, thee the fate
Of Lepidus and bold Sertorius wait.
Believe me yet (if yet I am believ'd),
My heart is at the task unpleasing griev'd:
I mourn to think that Pompey's hand was chose,
His Julia's hostile father to oppose,
And mark thee down amongst the Roman foes.
Oh that, return'd in safety from the east,
This province victor Crassus had possest;
New honours to his name thou might'st afford,
And die like Spartacus beneath his sword:
Like him have fall'n a victim to the laws,
The same th' avenger, and the same the cause.
But since the gods do otherwise decree,
And give thee, as my latest palm, to me;
Again my veins confess the fervent juice,
Nor has my hand forgot the javelin's use.
And thou shalt learn, that those who humbly know
To peace and just authority to bow,
Can, when their country's cause demands their care,
Resume their ardour, and return to war.
But let him think my former vigour fled;
Distrust not, you, your general's hoary head;
The marks of age and long-declining years,
Which I your leader, his whole army wears:
Age still is fit to counsel, or command,
But falters in an unperforming hand.
Whate'er superior power a people free
Could to their fellow-citizens decree,
All lawful glories have my fortunes known,
And reach'd all heights of greatness but a crown;
Who to be more, than Pompey was, desires,
To kingly rule, and tyranny aspires.
Amidst my ranks, a venerable band,
The conscript fathers and the consuls stand.
And shall the senate and the vanquish'd state
Upon victorious Cæsar's triumph wait?
Forbid it, gods, in honour of mankind!
Fortune is not so shameless, nor so blind.
What fame achiev'd, what unexampled praise,
To these high hopes the daring hero raise?
Is it his age of war, for trophies calls
His two whole years spent on the rebel Gauls?
Is it the hostile Rhine forsook with haste?
Is it the shoaly channel which he past,
That ocean huge he talks of? Does he boast
His flight on Britain's new-discover'd coast?
Perhaps abandon'd Rome new pride supplies,
He views the naked town with joyful eyes,
While from his rage an armed people flies.
But know, vain man, no Roman fled from thee;
They left their walls, 't is true; but 't was to follow me,
Me, who ere twice the Moon her orb renew'd,
The pirates formidable fleet subdu'd:
Soon as the sea my shining ensigns bore,
Vanquish'd they fled, and sought the safer shore;
Humbly content their forfeit lives to save,
And take the narrow lot my bounty gave.
By me the mighty Mithridates chas'd
Through all the windings of his Pontus pass'd,
He who the fate of Rome delay'd so long,
While in suspense uncertain empire hung;
He who to Sylla's fortune scorn'd to yield,
To my prevailing arms resign'd the field:
Driv'n out at length, and press'd where'er he fled,
He sought a grave to hide his vanquish'd head.
O'er the wide world my various trophies rise,
Beneath the vast extent of distant skies;
Me the cold Bear, the northern climates know,
And Phasis' waters through my conquests flow;
My deeds in Egypt and Syene live,
Where high meridian suns no shadow give.
Hesperian Bætis my commands obeys,
Who rolls remote to seek the western seas.
By me the captive Arabs hands were bound,
And Colchians for their ravish'd fleece renown'd;
O'er Asia wide my conquering ensigns spread,
Armenia me, and lofty Taurus dread;
To me submit Cilicia's warlike powers,
And proud Sophene veils her wealthy towers:
The Jews I tam'd, who with religion bow
To some mysterious name, which none beside them know.
Is there a land, to sum up all at last,
Through which my arms with conquest have not past?
The world, by me, the world is overcome,
And Cæsar finds no enemy but Rome."
He said: the crowd in dull suspension hung,
Nor with applauding acclamations rung;
No cheerful ardour waves the lifted hand,
Nor military cries the fight demand.
The chief perceiv'd the soldiers' fire to fail,
And Cæsar's fame forerunning to prevail;

His eagles he withdraws with timely care,
Nor trusts Rome's fates to such uncertain war.
As when, with fury stung and jealous rage,
Two mighty bulls for sovereignty engage;
The vanquish'd far to banishment removes,
To lonely fields and unfrequented groves;
There, for a while, with conscious shame he burns,
And tries on every tree his angry horns:
But when his former vigour stands confest,
And larger muscles shake his ample breast,
With better chance he seeks the fight again,
And drives his rival bellowing o'er the plain;
Then uncontroll'd the subject herd he leads,
And reigns the master of the fruitful meads.
Unequal thus to Cæsar, Pompey yields
The fair dominion of Hesperia's fields:
Swift through Apulia march his flying powers,
And seek the safety of Brundusium's towers.
This city a Dictæan people hold,
Here plac'd by tall Athenian barks of old;
When with false omens from the Cretan shore,
Their sable sails victorious Theseus bore.
Here Italy a narrow length extends,
And in a scanty slip projected ends.
A crooked mole around the waves she winds,
And in her folds the Adriatic binds.
Nor yet the bending shores could form a bay,
Did not a barrier isle the winds delay,
And break the seas tempestuous in their way.
Huge mounds of rocks are plac'd by Nature's hand,
To guard around the hospitable strand:
To turn the storm, repulse the rushing tide,
And bid the anchoring bark securely ride.
Hence Nereus wide the liquid main displays,
And spreads to various ports his watery ways;
Whether the pilot from Corcyra stand,
Or for Illyrian Epidamnus' strand.
Hither when all the Adriatic roars,
And thundering billows vex the double shores;
When sable clouds around the welkin spread,
And frowning storms involve Ceraunia's head;
When white with froth Calabrian Sason lies,
Hither the tempest-beaten vessel flies.
Now Pompey, on Hesperia's utmost coast
Sadly survey'd how all behind was lost;
Nor to Iberia could he force his way;
Long interposing Alps his passage stay.
At length amongst the pledges of his bed,
He chose his eldest-born; and thus he said:
"Haste thee, my son! to every distant land,
And bid the nations rouse at my command:
Where fam'd Euphrates flows, or where the Nile
With muddy waves improves the fattening soil;
Where'er diffus'd by victory and fame,
Thy father's arms have borne the Roman name.
Bid the Cilician quit the shore again,
And stretch the swelling canvass on the main:
Bid Ptolemy with my Tigranes come,
And bold Pharnaces lend his aid to Rome,
Through each Armenia spread the loud alarm,
And bid the cold Riphean mountains arm.
Pontus and Scythia's wandering tribes explore,
The Euxine and Mæotis' icy shore;
Where heavy-loaded wains slow journeys take,
And print with groaning wheels the frozen lake.
But wherefore should my words delay thy haste?
Scatter my wars around through all the east.
Summon the vanquish'd world to share my fate,
And let my triumphs on my ensigns wait.
But you whose names the Roman annals bear,
You who distinguish the revolving year;
Ye consuls! to Epirus strait repair,
With the first northern winds that wing the air;
From thence the powers of Greece united raise,
While yet the wintery year the war delays."
So spoke the chief; his bidding all obey;
Their ships forsake the port without delay,
And speed their passage o'er the yielding way.
But Cæsar, never patient long in peace,
Nor trusting in his fortune's present face;
Closely pursues his flying son behind,
While yet his fate continued to be kind.
Such towns, such fortresses, such hostile force,
Swept in the torrent of one rapid course;
Such trains of long success attending still,
And Rome herself abandon'd to his will;
Rome, the contending parties' noblest prize,
To every wish but Cæsar's might suffice.
But he with empire fir'd and vast desires,
To all, and nothing less than all, aspires;
He reckons not the past, while aught remain'd
Great to be done, or mighty to be gain'd.
Though Italy obey his wide command,
Though Pompey linger on the farthest strand,
He grieves to think they tread one common land;
His heart disdains to brook a rival power,
E'en on the utmost margin of the shore;
Nor would he leave, or earth, or ocean free;
The foe he drives from lands, he bars from sea.
With moles the opening flood he would restrain,
Would block the port, and intercept the main;
But deep devouring seas his toil deride,
The plunging quarries sink beneath the tide,
And yielding sands the rocky fragments hide.
Thus, if huge Gaurus headlong should be thrown,
In fathomless Avernus' deep to drown;
Or if from fair Sicilia's distant strand,
Eryx uprooted by some giant hand,
If, ponderous with his rocks, the mountain vast,
Amidst the wide Ægean should be cast;
The rolling waves o'er either mass would flow,
And each be lost within the depths below.
When no firm basis for his work he found,
But still it fail'd in ocean's faithless ground,
Huge trees and barks in massy chains he bound.
For planks and beams he ravages the wood,
And the tough boom extends across the flood.
Such was the road by haughty Xèrxes made,
When o'er the Hellespont his bridge he laid.
Vast was the task, and daring the design,
Europe and Asia's distant shores to join,
And make the world's divided parts combine.
Proudly he pass'd the flood tumultuous o'er,
Fearless of waves that beat, and winds that roar:
Then spread his sails, and bid the land obey,
And through mid Athos find his fleet a way.
Like him bold Cæsar yok'd the swelling tide,
Like him the boisterous elements defy'd;
This floating bank the straitening entrance bound,
And rising turrets trembled on the mound.
But anxious cares revolve in Pompey's breast,
The new surrounding shores his thoughts molest;
Secret he meditates the means, to free
And spread the war wide-ranging o'er the sea.
Oft driving on the work with well-fill'd sails,
The cordage stretching with the freshening gales,
Ships with a thundering shock the mole divide,
And through the watery breach securely glide.

Huge engines oft by night their vengeance pour,
And dreadful shoot from far a fiery shower;
Through the black shade the darting flame descends,
And kindling o'er the wooden wall extends.
At length arriv'd with the revolving night,
The chosen hour appointed for his flight;
He bids his friends prevent the seamens roar,
And still the deafening clamours on the shore;
No trumpets may the watch by hours renew,
Nor sounding signals call aboard the crew.
The heavenly Maid her course had almost run,
And Libra waited on the rising Sun;
When hush'd in silence deep they leave the land:
No loud-mouth'd voices call with hoarse command,
To heave the flooky anchors from the sand.
Lowly the careful master's orders past,
To brace the yards, and rear the lofty mast;
Silent they spread the sails, and cables haul,
Nor to their mates for aid tumultuous call.
The chief himself to Fortune breath'd a prayer,
At length to take him to her kinder care;
That swiftly he might pass the liquid deep,
And lose the land which she forbad to keep.
Hardly the boon his niggard fate allow'd,
Unwillingly the murmuring seas were plow'd;
The foamy furrows roar'd beneath his prow,
And sounding to the shore alarm'd the foe.
Straight through the town their swift pursuit they sped,
(For wide her gates the faithless city spread)
Along the winding port they took their way,
But griev'd to find the fleet had gain'd the sea.
Cæsar with rage the lessening sails descries,
And thinks the conquest mean, though Pompey flies.
A narrow pass the horned mole divides,
Narrow as that where Euripus' strong tides
Beat on Eubœan Chalcis' rocky sides:
Here two tall ships become the victor's prey:
Just in the strait they stuck; the foes belay;
The crooked grappling's steely hold they cast,
Then drag them to the hostile shore with haste.
Here civil slaughter first the sea profanes,
And purple Nereus blush'd in guilty stains.
The rest pursue their course before the wind,
These of the rear-most only left behind.
So when the Pegasæan Argo bore
The Grecian heroes to the Colchian shore;
Earth her Cyanean islands floating sent,
The bold adventurers' passage to prevent;
But the fam'd bark a fragment only lost,
While swiftly o'er the dangerous gulf she crost:
Thundering the mountains met, and shook the main,
But move no more, since that attempt was vain.
Now through night's shade the early dawning broke,
And changing skies the coming Sun bespoke;
As yet the Morn was drest in dusky white,
Nor purpled o'er the east with ruddy light;
At length the Pleïades' fading beams gave way,
And dull Boötes languish'd into day;
Each larger star withdrew his fainting head,
And Lucifer from stronger Phœbus fled;
When Pompey, from Hesperia's hostile shore
Escaping, for the azure offing bore.
O hero, happy once, once styl'd the great!
What turns prevail in thy uncertain fate!
How art thou chang'd since sovereign of the main,
Thy navies cover'd o'er the liquid plain!
When the fierce pirates fled before thy prow,
Wherever waves could waft, or winds could blow!
But Fortune is grown weary of thee now.
With thee, thy sons, and tender wife, prepare
The toils of war and banishment to bear;
And holy houshold-gods thy sorrows share.
And yet a mighty exile shalt thou go,
While nations follow to partake thy woe.
Far lies the land in which thou art decreed,
Unjustly, by a villain's hand to bleed.
Nor think the gods a death so distant doom,
To rob thy ashes of an urn in Rome;
But Fortune favourably remov'd the crime,
And forc'd the guilt on Egypt's cursed clime;
The pitying powers to Italy were good,
And sav'd her from the stain of Pompey's blood.

BOOK III.

THE ARGUMENT.

The third book begins with the relation of Pompey's dream in his voyage from Italy. Cæsar, who had driven him from thence, after sending Curio to provide corn in Sicily, returns to Rome: there, disdaining the single opposition of L. Metellus, then tribune of the people, he breaks open the temple of Saturn, and seizes on the public treasure. Then follows an account of the several different nations that took part with Pompey. From Rome Cæsar passes into Gaul, where the Massilians, who were inclinable to Pompey, send an embassy to propose a neutrality; this Cæsar refuses, and besieges the town. But meeting with more difficulties than he expected, he leaves C. Trebonius his lieutenant before Massilia, and marches himself into Spain, appointing at the same time D. Brutus, admiral of a navy which he had built and fitted out with great expedition. The Massilians likewise send out their fleet, but are engaged and beaten at sea by Brutus.

THROUGH the mid ocean now the navy sails,
Their yielding canvass stretch'd by southern gales.
Each to the vast Ionian turns his eye,
Where seas and skies the prospect wide supply:
But Pompey backward ever bent his look,
Nor to the last his native coast forsook.
His watery eyes the lessening objects mourn,
And parting shores that never shall return;
Still the lov'd land attentive they pursue,
Till the tall hills are veil'd in cloudy blue,
Till all is lost in air, and vanish'd from his view.
At length the weary chieftain sunk to rest,
And creeping slumbers sooth'd his anxious breast:
When, lo! in that short moment of repose,
His Julia's shade a dreadful vision rose;
Through gaping earth her ghastly head she rear'd,
And by the light of livid flames appear'd.
" Thy impious arms," she cry'd, "my peace infest,
And drive me from the mansions of the blest:
No more Elysium's happy fields I know,
Dragg'd to the guilty Stygian shades below:
I saw the fury's horrid hands prepare
New rage, new flames to kindle up thy war.
The sire no longer trusts his single boat,
But navies on the joyless river float.
Capacious Hell complains for want of room,
And seeks new plagues for multitudes to come.

Her nimble hands each fatal sister plies,
The sisters scarcely to the task suffice.
When thou wert mine, what laurels crown'd thy head!
Now thou hast chang'd thy fortune with thy bed.
In an ill hour thy second choice was made,
To slaughter thou, like Crassus, art betray'd.
Death is the dower Cornelia's love affords,
Ruin still waits upon her potent lords:
While yet my ashes glow'd, she took my place,
And came a harlot to thy loose embrace.
But let her partner of thy warfare go,
Let her by land and sea thy labours know;
In all thy broken sleeps I will be near,
In all thy dreams sad Julia shall appear.
Your loves shall find no moment for delight,
The day shall all be Cæsar's, mine the night.
Not the dull stream, where long oblivions roll,
Shall blot thee out, my husband, from my soul.
The powers beneath my constancy approve,
And bid me follow wheresoe'er you rove.
Amidst the joining battles will I stand,
And still remind thee of thy plighted hand.
Nor think, those sacred ties no more remain;
The sword of war divides the knot in vain,
That very war shall make thee mine again."

The phantom spoke, and, gliding from the place,
Deluded her astonish'd lord's embrace.
But he, though gods forewarn him of his fate,
And furies with destruction threatening wait,
With new resolves his constant bosom warms,
And sure of ruin rushes on to arms.
"What mean these terrours of the night?" he cries;
"Why dance these visions vain before our eyes?
Or endless apathy succeeds to death,
And sense is lost with our expiring breath;
Or, if the soul some future life shall know,
To better worlds immortal shall she go:
Whate'er event the doubtful question clears,
Death must be still unworthy of our fears."

Now headlong to the west the Sun was fled,
And half in seas obscur'd his beamy head;
Such seems the Moon, while, growing yet, she shines,
Or waning from her fuller orb declines:
When hospitable shores appear at hand,
Where fair Dyrrachium spreads her friendly strand.
The seamen furl the canvass, strike the mast,
Then dip their nimble oars, and landward haste.

Thus, while they fled, and lessening by degrees
The navy seem'd to hide beneath the seas;
Cæsar, though left the master of the field,
With eyes unpleas'd the foe's escape beheld:
With fierce impatience victory he scorns,
And, viewing Pompey's flight, his safety mourns.
To vanquish seems unworthy of his care,
Unless the blow decides the lingering war.
No bounds his headlong vast ambition knows,
Nor joys in aught, though fortune all bestows.
At length his thoughts from arms and vengeance cease,
And for awhile revolve the arts of peace;
Careful to purchase popular applause,
And gain the lazy vulgar to his cause,
He knew the constant practice of the great,
That those who court the vulgar bid them eat.
When pinch'd with want, all reverence they withdraw;
For hungry multitudes obey no law:
Thus therefore factions make their parties good,
And buy authority and power with food.
The murmurs of the many to prevent,
Curio to fruitful Sicily is sent.
Of old the swelling sea's impetuous tide
Tore the fair island from Hesperia's side:
Still foamy wars the jealous waves maintain,
For fear the neighbouring lands should join again.
Sardinia too, renown'd for yellow fields,
With Sicily her bounteous tribute yields;
No lands a glebe of richer tillage boast,
Nor waft more plenty to the Roman coast:
Not Libya more abounds in wealthy grain,
Nor with a fuller harvest spreads the plain;
Though northern winds their cloudy treasures bear,
To temper well the soil and sultry air,
And fattening rains increase the prosperous year.

This done, to Rome his way the leader took:
His train the rougher shows of war forsook;
No force, no fears their hands unarmed bear,
But looks of peace and gentleness they wear.
Oh! had he now his country's friend return'd,
Had none but barbarous foes his conquest mourn'd;
What swarming crowds had issued at the gate,
On the glad triumph's lengthening train to wait!
How might his wars in various glories shine,
The ocean vanquish'd, and in bonds the Rhine!
How would his lofty chariot roll along,
Through loud applauses of the joyful throng!
How might he view from high his captive thralls,
The beauteous Britons, and the noble Gauls;
But, oh! what fatal honours has he won!
How is his fame by victory undone!
No cheerful citizens the victor meet,
But hush'd with awful dread his passage greet.
He too the horrours of the crowd approv'd,
Joy'd in their fears, and wish'd not to be lov'd.

Now steepy Anxur past, and the moist way,
Which o'er the faithless Pontine marshes lay;
Through Scythian Dian's Aricinian grove,
Cæsar approach'd the fane of Alban Jove.
Thither with yearly rites the consuls come,
And thence the chief survey'd his native Rome:
Wondering awhile he view'd her from afar,
Long from his eyes withheld by distant war.
"Fled they from thee, thou seat of gods!" he cry'd
"Ere yet the fortune of the fight was try'd?
If thou art left, what prize can Earth afford,
Worth the contention of the warriour's sword?
Well for thy safety now the gods provide,
Since Parthian inroads spare thy naked side;
Since yet no Scythians and Pannonians join,
Nor warlike Daci with the Getes combine;
No foreign armies are against thee led,
While thou art curst with such a coward head.
A gentler fate the heavenly powers bestow,
A civil war, and Cæsar for thy foe."

He said; and strait the frighted city sought:
The city with confusion wild was fraught,
And labouring shook with every dreadful thought.
They think he comes to ravage, sack, and burn;
Religion, gods, and temples to o'erturn.
Their fears suggest him willing to pursue
Whatever ills unbounded power can do.
Their hearts by one low passion only move,
Nor dare show hate, nor can dissemble love.
The lurking fathers, a dishearten'd band,
Drawn from their houses forth, by proud command,
In Palatine Apollo's temple meet,
And sadly view the consul's empty seat;
No rods, no chairs curule, adorn the place,
Nor purple magistrates th' assembly grace.
Cæsar is all things in himself alone,
The silent court is but a looker-on;

With humble votes obedient they agree,
To what their mighty subject shall decree:
Whether as king, or god, he will be fear'd,
If royal thrones, or altars, shall be rear'd.
Ready for death, or banishment, they stand,
And wait their doom from his disposing hand:
But he, by secret shame's reproaches staid,
Blush'd to command, what Rome would have obey'd.
Yet liberty, thus slighted and betray'd,
One last effort with indignation made;
One man she chose to try th' unequal fight,
And prove the power of justice against might.
While with rude uproar armed hands essay
To make old Saturn's treasuring fane their prey;
The bold Metellus, careless of his fate,
Rush'd through, and stood to guard the holy gate.
So daring is the sordid love of gold!
So fearless death and dangers can behold!
Without a blow defenceless fell the laws;
While wealth, the basest, most inglorious cause,
Against oppressing tyranny makes head,
Finds hands to fight, and eloquence to plead.
The bustling tribune, struggling in the crowd,
Thus warns the victor of the wrong aloud:
"Through me, thou robber! force thy horrid way,
My sacred blood shall stain thy impious prey.
But there are gods, to urge thy guilty fate;
Sure vengeance on thy sacrilege shall wait.
Remember, by the tribunes' curse pursued,
Crassus, too late, the violation rued.
Pierce then my breast, nor shall the crime displease,
This crowd is us'd to spectacles like these.
In a forsaken city are we left,
Of virtue, with her noblest sons bereft.
Why seek'st thou ours? Is there not foreign gold?
Towns to be sack'd, and people to be sold?
With those reward the ruffian soldier's toil;
Nor pay him with thy ruin'd country's spoil.
Hast thou not war? Let war thy wants provide."
He spoke: the victor, high in wrath, reply'd:
"Sooth not thy soul with hopes of death so vain,
No blood of thine my conqu'ring sword shall stain.
Thy titles and thy popular command,
Can never make thee worthy Cæsar's hand.
Art thou thy country's sole defender! thou!
Can liberty and Rome be fall'n so low!
Nor time, nor chance breed such confusions yet,
Nor are the mean so rais'd, nor sunk the great;
But laws themselves would rather choose to be
Suppress'd by Cæsar, than preserv'd by thee."
He said: the stubborn tribune kept his place,
While anger redden'd on the warrior's face;
His wrathful hand descending grasp'd his blade,
And half forgot the peaceful part he play'd.
When Cotta, to prevent the kindling fire,
Thus sooth'd the rash Metellus to retire:
"Where kings prevail, all liberty is lost,
And none but he who reigns can freedom boast;
Some shadow of the bliss thou shalt retain,
Choosing to do what sovereign powers ordain:
Vanquish'd and long accustom'd to submit,
With patience underneath our loads we sit;
Our chains alone our slavish fears excuse,
While we bear ill, we know not to refuse.
Far hence the fatal treasures let him bear,
The seeds of mischief, and the cause of war.
Free states might well a loss like this deplore;
In servitude none miss the public store,
And 't is the curse of kings for subjects to be poor."
The tribune with unwilling steps withdrew,
While impious hands the rude assault renew:
The brazen gates with thundering strokes resound,
And the Tarpeian mountain rings around.
At length the sacred store-house, open laid,
The hoarded wealth of ages past display'd;
There might be seen the sums proud Carthage sent,
Her long impending ruin to prevent.
There heap'd the Macedonian treasures shone,
What great Flaminius and Æmilius won
From vanquish'd Philip, and his hapless son.
There lay, what flying Pyrrhus lost, the gold
Scorn'd by the patriot's honesty of old:
Whate'er our parsimonious sires could save,
What tributary gifts rich Syria gave;
The hundred Cretan cities' ample spoil;
What Cato gather'd from the Cyprian isle,
Riches of captive kings by Pompey borne,
In happier days his triumph to adorn,
From utmost India and the rising morn;
Wealth infinite, in one rapacious day,
Became the needy soldiers' lawless prey:
And wretched Rome, by robbery laid low,
Was poorer than the bankrupt Cæsar now.
Meanwhile the world, by Pompey's fate alarm'd,
Nations ordain'd to share his fall had arm'd.
Greece first with troops the neighbouring war supply'd,
And sent the youth of Phocis to his side;
From Cyrrha and Amphisa's towers they mov'd,
And high Parnassus by the Muse belov'd;
Cephissus' sacred flood assistance lends,
And Dirce's spring his Theban leaders sends.
Alphæus too affords his Pisa's aid:
By Pisa's wall the stream is first convey'd,
Then seeks through seas the lov'd Sicilian maid.
From Mænalus Arcadian shepherds swarm,
And warriors in Herculean Trachyn arm;
The Dryopes Chaonia's hills forsook,
And Sellæ left Dodona's silent oak.
Though Athens now had drain'd her naval store,
And the Phœbean arsenal was poor,
Three ships of Salamis to Pompey came,
To vindicate their isle's contested name,
And justify the ancient Attic claim.
Jove's Cretan people hastening to the war,
The Gnossian quiver and the shaft prepare;
The bending bow they draw with deadly art,
And rival e'en the flying Parthian's dart.
With Athamans who in the woods delight,
With Dardan Oriconians unite;
With these th' Encheliæ who the name partake,
Since Theban Cadmus first became a snake:
The Colchians planted on Illyrian shores,
Where rushing down Absyrtos foamy roars;
With those where Peneus runs, and hardy swains,
Whose ploughs divide Iolcos' fruitful plains.
From thence, ere yet the seaman's art was taught,
Rude Argo through the deep a passage sought:
She first explor'd the distant foreign land,
And show'd her strangers to the wondering strand:
Then nations nations knew, in leagues were join'd,
And universal commerce mix'd mankind.
By her made bold, the daring race defy'd
The winds tempestuous, and the swelling tide:
Much she enlarg'd destruction's ample power,
And open'd ways to death unknown before.
Then Pholoe's heights, that fabled Centaurs boast,
And Thracian Hæmus then his warriors lost.

Then Strymon was forsook, whose wintery flood
Commits to warmer Nile his feather'd brood;
Then bands from Cone and from Peuce came,
Where Ister loses his divided stream;
From Idalis where cold Caïcus flows,
And where Arisbe, thin, her sandy surface strows;
From Pytane, and sad Celenæ's walls, [falls:
Where now in streams the vanquish'd Marsyas
Still his lamenting progeny deplore
Minerva's tuneful gift, and Phœbus' power;
While through steep banks his torrent swift he
leads,
And with Mæander winds among the meads.
Proud Lydia's plains send forth her wealthy sons,
Pactolus there, and golden Hermus runs: [vey,
From Earth's dark womb hid treasures they con-
And rich in yellow waters rise to-day.
From Ilium too ill-omen'd ensigns move,
Again ordain'd their former fate to prove;
Their arms they rang'd on Pompey's hapless side,
Nor sought a chief to Dardan kings ally'd:
Though tales of Troy proud Cæsar's lineage grace,
With great Æneas and the Julian race.
The Syrians swift Orontes' banks forsake,
And from Idume's plains their journey take;
Damascus obvious to the driving wind,
With Ninos' and with Gaza's force is join'd.
Unstable Tyre now knit to firmer ground,
With Sidon for her purple shells renown'd,
Safe in the Cynosure, their glittering guide,
With well-directed navies stem the tide.
Phœnicians first, if ancient fame be true,
The sacred mystery of letters knew;
They first, by sound in various lines design'd,
Exprest the meaning of the thinking mind;
The power of words by figures rude convey'd,
And useful science everlasting made.
Then Memphis, ere the reedy leaf was known,
Engrav'd her precepts and her arts in stone;
While animals in various order plac'd,
The learned hieroglyphic column grac'd.
Then left they lofty Taurus' spreading grove,
And Tarsos, built by Perseus, born of Jove;
Then Mallian, and Corycian towers they leave,
Where mouldering rocks disclose a gaping cave.
The bold Cilicians, pirates now no more,
Unfurl a juster sail, and ply the oar;
To Egæ's port they gather all around,
The shores with shouting mariners resound.
Far in the east war spreads the loud alarm,
Where worshippers of distant Ganges arm;
Right to the breaking day his waters run,
The only stream that braves the rising Sun.
By this strong flood, and by the ocean bound,
Proud Alexander's arms a limit found;
Vain in his hopes the youth had grasp'd at all,
And his vast thought took in the vanquish'd ball;
But own'd, when forc'd from Ganges to retreat,
The world too mighty, and the task too great.
Then on the banks of Indus nations rose,
Where unperceiv'd the mix'd Hydaspes flows:
In numbers vast they coast the rapid flood,
Strange in their habit, manners, and their food.
With saffron dyes their dangling locks they stain,
With glittering gems their flowing robes constrain,
And quaff rich juices from the luscious cane.
On their own funerals and death they smile,
And living leap amidst the burning pile;
Heroic minds! that can e'en fate command,
And bid it wait upon a mortal hand;
Who full of life forsake it as a feast,
Take what they like, and give the gods the rest.
Descending then fierce Cappadocian swains,
From rude Amanus' mountains sought the plains.
Armenians from Niphates' rolling stream,
And from their lofty woods Coastrians came.
Then wondering Arabs from the sultry line
For ever northward saw the shade incline.
Then did the madness of the Roman rage
Carmanian and Olostrian chiefs engage:
Beneath far distant southern heavens they lie,
Where half the setting Bear forsakes the sky,
And swift our slow Boötes seems to fly.
These furies to the sun-burn'd Æthiops spread,
And reach the great Euphrates' rising head.
One spring the Tigris and Euphrates know,
And join'd awhile the kindred rivers flow;
Scarce could we judge between the doubtful claim,
If Tigris, or Euphrates, give the name:
But soon Euphrates' parting waves divide,
Covering like fruitful Nile the country wide;
While Tigris, sinking from the sight of day,
Through subterranean channels cuts his way;
Then from a second fountain springs again,
Shoots swiftly on, and rushing seeks the main.
The Parthian powers, to neither chief a friend,
The doubtful issue in suspense attend;
With neutral ease they view the strife from far,
And only lend occasion to the war.
Not so the Scythians where cold Bactros flows,
Or where Hircania's wilder forest grows,
Their baneful shafts they dip, and string their
deadly bows.
Th' Heniochi of Sparta's valiant breed,
Skilful to press, and rein the fiery steed;
Sarmatians with their fiercer Moschi join'd,
And Colchians rich where Phasis' waters wind,
To Pompey's side their aid assembling bring,
With Halys, fatal to the Lydian king;
With Tanais, falling from Riphean snows,
Who forms the world's division as he goes:
With noblest names his rising banks are crown'd,
This stands for Europe's, that for Asia's bound;
While, as they wind, his waves with full command,
Diminish, or enlarge th' adjacent land.
Then arm'd the nations on Cimmerian shores,
Where through the Bosphorus Mæotis roars,
And her full lake amidst the Euxine pours.
This strait, like that of Hercules, supplies
The midland seas, and bids th' Ægean rise.
Sithonians fierce, and Arimaspians bold,
Who bind their plaited hair in shining gold.
The Gelon nimble, and Areian strong,
March with the hardy Massagete along:
The Massagete, who at his salvage feast
Feeds on the generous steed which once he prest.
Not Cyrus when he spread his eastern reign,
And hid with multitudes the Lydian plain;
Not haughty Xerxes, when, his power to boast,
By shafts he counted all his mighty host;
Not he who drew the Grecian chiefs along,
Bent to revenge his injur'd brother's wrong;
Or with such navies plough'd the foamy main,
Or led so many kings, amongst their warlike train.
Sure in one cause such numbers never yet,
Various in countries, speech, and manners, met;
But Fortune gather'd o'er the spacious ball, [fall.
These spoils, to grace her once-lov'd favourite's
Nor then the Lybian Moor withheld his aid,
Where sacred Ammon lifts his horned head:

All Afric, from the western ocean's bound,
To eastern Nile, the cause of Pompey own'd.
Mankind assembled for Pharsalia's day,
To make the world at once the victor's prey.
Now trembling Rome forsook, with swiftest haste,
Cæsar the cloudy Alpine hills had past.
But while the nations, with subjection tame,
Yield to the terrours of his mighty name;
With faith uncommon to the changing Greeks,
What duty bids, Massilia bravely seeks:
And, true to oaths, their liberty and laws,
To stronger fate prefer the juster cause,
But first to move his haughty soul they try,
Entreaties and persuasion oft apply;
Their brows Minerva's peaceful branches wear,
And thus in gentlest terms they greet his ear:
"When foreign wars molest the Roman state,
With ready arms our glad Massilians wait,
To share your dangers, and partake your fate.
This our unshaken friendship vouches well,
And your recording annals best can tell.
E'en now we yield our still devoted hands,
On foreign foes to wreak your dread commands;
Would you to worlds unknown your triumphs spread?
Behold! we follow wheresoe'er you lead.
But if you rouse at discord's baleful call,
If Romans fatally on Romans fall;
All we can offer is a pitying tear,
And constant refuge for the wretched here.
Sacred to us you are: oh, may no stain
Of Lucian blood our innocence profane!
Should Heaven itself be rent with civil rage,
Should giants once more with the gods engage;
Officious piety would hardly dare
To proffer Jove assistance in the war.
Man unconcern'd and humble should remain,
Nor seek to know whose arms the conquest gain,
Jove's thunder will convince them of his reign.
Nor can your horrid discords want our swords,
The wicked world its multitudes affords;
Too many nations at the call will come,
And gladly join to urge the fate of Rome.
Oh, had the rest like us their aid deny'd,
Yourselves must then the guilty strife decide;
Then, who but should withhold his lifted hand,
When for his foe he saw his father stand?
Brothers their rage had mutually represt,
Nor driven their javelins on a brother's breast.
Your war had ended soon; had you not chose
Hands for the work, which Nature meant for foes:
Who, strangers to your blood, in arms delight,
And rush remorseless to the cruel fight.
Briefly, the sum of all that we request
Is, to receive thee as our honour'd guest;
Let those thy dreadful ensigns shine afar,
Let Cæsar come, but come without the war.
Let this one place from impious rage be free;
That, if the gods the peace of Rome decree,
If your relenting angers yield to treat,
Pompey and thou, in safety, here may meet.
Then, wherefore dost thou quit thy purpos'd way?
Why, thus, Iberia's nobler wars delay?
Mean, and of little consequence we are,
A conquest much unworthy of thy care.
When Phocis' towers were laid in ashes low,
Hither we fled for refuge from the foe;
Here, for our plain integrity renown'd,
A little town in narrow walls we bound:
No name in arms nor victories we boast,
But live poor exiles on a foreign coast.
If thou art bent on violence at last,
To burst our gates, and lay our bulwarks waste,
Know we are equally resolv'd, whate'er
The victor's fury can inflict, to bear.
Shall death destroy, shall flames the town o'erturn?
Why—let our people bleed, our buildings burn.
Wilt thou forbid the living stream to flow?
We 'll dig, and search the watery stores below.
Hunger and thirst with patience will we meet,
And, what offended nature nauseates, eat.
Like brave Saguntum daring to be free,
Whate'er they suffer'd, we 'll expect from thee.
Babes, ravish'd from the fainting mother's breast,
Shall headlong in the burning pile be cast.
Matrons shall bare their bosoms to their lords,
And beg destruction from their pitying swords;
The brother's hand the brother's heart shall wound,
And universal slaughter rage around.
If civil wars must waste this hapless town,
No hands shall bring that ruin but our own."
Thus said the Grecian messengers. When lo!
A gathering cloud involv'd the Roman's brow;
Much grief, much wrath, his troubled visage spoke;
Then into these disdainful words he broke:
"This trusting in our speedy march to Spain,
These hopes, this Grecian confidence is vain;
Whate'er we purpose, leisure will be found
To lay Massilia level with the ground:
This bears, my valiant friends, a sound of joy;
Our useless arms, at length, shall find employ.
Winds lose their force, that unresisted fly,
And flames, unfed by fuel, sink and die.
Our courage thus would soften in repose,
But fortune and rebellion yield us foes.
Yet mark! what love their friendly speech exprest!
Unarm'd and single, Cæsar is their guest.
Thus, first they dare to stop me on my way,
Then seek with fawning treason to betray.
Anon, they pray that civil rage may cease:
But war shall scourge them for those hopes of peace;
And make them know the present times afford,
At least while Cæsar lives, no safety like the sword."
He said; and to the city bent his way:
The city, fearless all, before him lay,
With armed hands her battlements were crown'd,
And lusty youth the bulwarks mann'd around.
Near to the walls, a rising mountain's head
Flat with a little level plain is spread:
Upon this height the wary chief designs
His camp to strengthen with surrounding lines.
Lofty alike, and with a warlike mien,
Massilia's neighbouring citadel is seen;
An humble valley fills the space between.
Straight he decrees the middle vale to fill,
And run a mole athwart from hill to hill,
But first a lengthening work extends its way,
Where open to the land this city lay,
And from the camp projecting joins the sea.
Low sinks the ditch, the turfy breast-works rise,
And cut the captive town from all supplies:
While, gazing from their towers, the Greeks bemoan
The meads, the fields, and fountains once their own.
Well have they thus acquir'd the noblest name,
And consecrated these their walls to fame.
Fearless of Cæsar and his arms they stood,
Nor drove before the headlong rushing flood:

And while he swept whole nations in a day,
Massilia bade th' impatient victor stay,
And clogg'd his rapid conquest with delay.
Fortune a master for the world prepar'd,
And these th' approaching slavery retard.
Ye times to come, record the warrior's praise,
Who lengthen'd out expiring freedom's days.
Now while with toil unweary'd rose the mound,
The sounding ax invades the groves around;
Light earth and shrubs the middle banks supply'd,
But firmer beams must fortify the side;
Lest when the towers advance their ponderous height,
The mouldering mass should yield beneath the weight.
Not far away for ages past had stood
An old inviolated sacred wood;
Whose gloomy boughs, thick interwoven, made
A chilly cheerless everlasting shade:
There, nor the rustic gods, nor satyrs sport,
Nor fauns and sylvans with the nymphs resort:
But barbarous priests some dreadful pow'r adore,
And lustrate every tree with human gore.
If mysteries in times of old receiv'd,
And pious ancientry be yet believ'd,
There not the feather'd songster builds her nest,
Nor lonely dens conceal the salvage beast:
There no tempestuous winds presume to fly,
Even lightnings glance aloof, and shoot obliquely by.
No wanton breezes toss the dancing leaves,
But shivering horrour in the branches heaves.
Black springs with pitchy streams divide the ground,
And bubbling tumble with a sullen sound.
Old images of forms misshapen stand,
Rude and unknowing of the artists hand;
With hoary filth begrim'd, each ghastly head
Strikes the astonish'd gazer's soul with dread.
No gods, who long in common shapes appear'd,
Were e'er with such religious awe rever'd:
But zealous crowds in ignorance adore,
And still the less they know, they fear the more.
Oft (as Fame tells) the earth in sounds of woe
Is heard to groan from hollow depths below;
The baleful yew, though dead, has oft been seen
To rise from earth, and spring with dusky green;
With sparkling flames the trees unburning shine,
And round their boles prodigious serpents twine.
The pious worshippers approach not near,
But shun their gods, and kneel with distant fear:
The priest himself, when, or the day, or night,
Rolling have reach'd their full meridian height,
Refrains the gloomy paths with wary feet,
Dreading the demon of the grove to meet;
Who, terrible to sight, at that fix'd hour,
Still treads the round about his dreary bower.
This wood near neighb'ring to th' encompass'd town
Untouch'd by former wars remain'd alone;
And since the country round it naked stands,
From hence the Latian chief supplies demands.
But lo! the bolder hands, that should have struck.
With some unusual horrour trembling shook:
With silent dread and reverence they survey'd
The gloom majestic of the sacred shade:
None dares with impious steel the bark to rend,
Lest on himself the destin'd stroke descend.
Cæsar perceiv'd the spreading fear to grow,
Then, eager, caught an axe, and aim'd a blow.
Deep sunk within a violated oak
The wounding edge, and thus the warrior spoke:
"Now let no doubting hand the task decline;
Cut you the wood, and let the guilt be mine."
The trembling bands unwillingly obey'd;
Two various ills were in the balance laid,
And Cæsar's wrath against the gods was weigh'd.
Then Jove's Dodonian tree was forc'd to bow;
The lofty ash and knotty holm lay low;
The floating alder by the current born,
The cypress by the noble mourner worn,
Veil their aërial summits, and display
Their dark recesses to the golden day;
Crowding they fail, each o'er the other lies,
And heap'd on high the leafy piles arise.
With grief, and fear, the groaning Gauls beheld
Their holy grove by impious soldiers fell'd;
While the Massilians, from th' encompass'd wall,
Rejoic'd to see the sylvan honours fall.
They hope such power can never prosper long,
Nor think the patient gods will bear the wrong.
But, ah! too oft success to guilt is given,
And wretches only stand the mark of Heaven.
With timber largely from the wood supply'd,
For wains the legions search the country wide;
Then from the crooked plough unyoke the steer,
And leave the swain to mourn the fruitless year.
Meanwhile, impatient of the lingering war,
The chieftain to Iberia bends afar,
And gives the leaguer to Trebonius' care.
With diligence the destin'd task he plies;
Huge works of earth with strengthening beams arise:
High tottering towers, by no fix'd basis bound,
Roll nodding on along the stable mound.
The Greeks with wonder on the movement look,
And fancy Earth's foundations deep are shook;
Fierce winds they think the beldame's entrails tear,
And anxious for their walls and city fear:
The Roman from the lofty top looks down,
And rains a winged war upon the town.
Nor with less active rage the Grecians burn,
But larger ruin on their foes return;
Nor hands alone the missile deaths supply,
From nervous cross-bows whistling arrows fly;
The steely corslet and the bone they break,
Through multitudes their fatal journeys take;
Nor wait the lingering Parcæ's slow delay,
But wound, and to new slaughter wing their way.
Now by some vast machine a ponderous stone,
Pernicious, from the hostile wall is thrown;
At once, on many, swift the shock descends,
And the crush'd carcasses confounding blends.
So rolls some falling rock, by age long worn,
Loose from its root by raging whirlwinds torn,
And thundering down the precipice is borne,
O'er crashing woods the mass is seen to ride,
To grind its way, and plane the mountain's side.
Gall'd with the shot from far, the legions join,
Their bucklers in the warlike shell combine;
Compact and close the brazen roof they bear,
And in just order to the town draw near:
Safe they advance, while with unweary'd pain
The wrathful engines waste their stores in vain;
High o'er their heads the destin'd deaths are tost,
And far behind in vacant earth are lost;
Nor sudden could they change their erring aim.
Slow and unwieldy moves the cumbrous frame.
This seen, the Greeks their brawny arms employ,
And hurl a stony tempest from on high:
The clattering shower the sounding fence assails;

But vain, as when the stormy winter hails,
Nor on the solid marble roof prevails:
Till tir'd at length the warriors fall their shields;
And, spent with toil, the broken phalanx yields.
Now other stratagems the war supplies,
Beneath the vinea close th' assailant lies. [spread,
The strong machine, with planks and turf be-
Moves to the walls its well-defended head;
Within the covert safe the miners lurk,
And to the deep foundation urge their work.
Now justly pois'd the thundering ram they sling,
And drive him forceful with a lanching spring;
Haply to loose some yielding part at length,
And shake the firm cemented bulwark's strength.
But from the town the Grecian youth prepare
With hardy vigour to repel the war:
Crowding they gather on the rampart's height,
And with tough staves and spears maintain the
fight; [throw,
Darts, fragments of the rock, and flames they
And tear the planky shelter fix'd below;
Around by all the warring tempest beat,
The baffled Romans sullenly retreat.
Now by success the brave Massilians fir'd,
To fame of higher enterprise aspir'd;
Nor longer with their walls defence content,
In daring sallies they the foe prevent. [go,
Nor arm'd with swords, nor pointed spears they
Nor aim the shaft, nor bend the deadly bow:
Fierce Mulciber supplies the bold design,
And for their weapons kindling torches shine,
Silent they issue through the gloomy night,
And with broad shields restrain the beamy light:
Sudden the blaze on every side began,
And o'er the Latian works resistless ran;
Catching, and driving with the wind it grows,
Fierce through the shade the burning deluge glows;
Nor earth, nor greener planks its force delay,
Swift o'er the hissing beams it rolls away:
Embrown'd with smoke the wavy flames ascend,
Shiver'd with heat the crackling quarries rend;
Till with a roar at last, the mighty mound,
Towers, engines, all, come thundering to the
Wide-spread the discontinuous ruins lie, [ground:
And vast confusion fills the gazer's eye.
Vanquish'd by land, the Romans seek the main,
And prove the fortune of the watery plain:
Their navy, rudely built, and rigg'd in haste,
Down through the rapid Rhone descending past.
No golden gods protect the shining prow,
Nor silken streamers lightly dancing flow;
But rough in stable floorings lies the wood,
As in the native forest once it stood.
Rearing above the rest her towery head,
Brutus' tall ship the floating squadron led.
To sea soon wafted by the hasty tide,
Right to the Stœchades their course they guide.
Resolv'd to urge their fate, with equal cares,
Massilia for the naval war prepares;
All hands the city for the task requires,
And arms her striplings young, and hoary sires.
Vessels of every sort and size she fits,
And speedy to the briny deep commits
The crazy hulk, that, worn with winds and tides,
Safe in the dock, and long neglected, rides,
She planks anew, and calks her leaky sides.
Now rose the morning, and the golden Sun
With beams refracted on the ocean shone;
Clear was the sky, the waves from murmur cease,
And every ruder wind was hush'd in peace:
Smooth lay the glassy surface of the main,
And offer'd to the war its ample plain:
When to the destin'd stations all repair;
Here Cæsar's powers, the youth of Phocis there.
Their brawny arms are bar'd, their oars they dip,
Swift o'er the water glides the nimble ship;
Feels the strong blow the well-compacted oak,
And trembling springs at each repeated stroke.
Crooked in front the Latian navy stood,
And wound a bending crescent o'er the flood.
With four full banks of oars advancing high,
On either wing the larger vessels ply,
While in the centre safe the lesser galliots lie.
Brutus the first, with eminent command,
In the tall admiral is seen to stand;
Six rows of lengthening pines the billows sweep,
And heave the burthen o'er the groaning deep.
Now prow to prow advance each hostile fleet,
And want but one concurring stroke to meet,
When peals of shouts and mingling clamours roar,
And drown the brazen trump and plunging oar.
The brushing pine the frothy surface plies,
While on their banks the lusty rowers rise:
Each brings the stroke back on his ample chest,
Then firm upon his seat he lights represt.
With clashing beaks the lanching vessels meet,
And from the mutual shock alike retreat.
Thick clouds of flying shafts the welkin hide,
Then fall, and floating strow the ocean wide.
At length the stretching wings their order leave,
And in the line the mingling foe receive:
Then might be seen, how, dash'd from side to side,
Before the stemming vessel drove the tide;
Still as each keel her foamy furrow plows,
Now back, now forth, the surge obedient flows.
Thus warring winds alternate rule maintain,
And this, and that way, roll the yielding main.
Massila's navy, nimble, clean, and light,
With best advantage seek or shun the fight;
With ready ease all answer to command,
Obey the helm, and feel the pilot's hand.
Not so the Romans; cumbrous hulks they lay,
And slow and heavy hung upon the sea;
Yet strong, and for the closer combat good,
They yield firm footing on th' unstable flood.
Thus Brutus saw, and to the master cries
(The master in the lofty poop he spies,
Where streaming the prætorian ensign flies),
"Still wilt thou bear away, still shift thy place,
And turn the battle to a wanton chase?
Is this a time to play so mean a part,
To tack, to veer, and boast thy trifling art?
Bring to. The war shall hand to hand be try'd;
Oppose thou to the foe our ample side,
And let us meet like men." The chieftain said;
The ready master the command obey'd,
And side-long to the foe the ship was laid.
Upon his waste fierce fall the thundering Greeks,
Fast in his timber stick their brazen beaks;
Some lie by chains and grapplings strong com-
pell'd,
While others by the tangling oars are held:
The seas are hid beneath the closing war,
Nor need they cast the javelin now from far;
With hardy strokes the combatants engage,
And with keen falchions deal their deadly rage:
Man against man, and board by board they lie,
And on those decks their arms defended die.
The rolling surge is stain'd around with blood,
And foamy purple swells the rising flood;

The floating carcasses the ships delay,
Hang on each keel, and intercept her way;
Helpless beneath the deep the dying sink,
And gore, with briny ocean mingling, drink.
Some, while amidst the tumbling waves they strive,
And struggling with destruction float alive,
Or by some ponderous beam are beaten down,
Or sink transfix'd by darts at random thrown.
That fatal day no javelin flies in vain,
Missing their mark they wound upon the main.
It chanc'd, a warrior ship on Cæsar's side,
By two Massilan foes was warmly ply'd;
But with divided force she meets th' attack,
And bravely drives the bold assailants back:
When from the lofty poop, where fierce he fought,
Tagus to seize the Grecian ancient sought.
But double death his daring hand repress'd,
One spear transfix'd his back, and one his breast,
And deadly met within his heaving chest.
Doubtful awhile the flood was seen to stay,
At length the steely shafts at once gave way;
The fleeting life a twofold passage found,
And ran divided from each streaming wound.
Hither his fate unhappy Telon led,
To naval arts from early childhood bred;
No hand the helm more skilfully could guide,
Or stem the fury of the boisterous tide;
He knew what winds should on the morrow blow,
And how the sails for safety to bestow;
Celestial signals well he could descry,
Could judge the radiant lights that shine on high,
And read the coming tempest of the sky.
Full on a Latian bark his beak he drives,
The brazen beak the shivering elder rives;
When from some hostile hand, a Roman dart,
Deep piercing, trembled in his panting heart:
Yet still his careful hand its task supplies,
And turns the guiding rudder as he dies,
To fill his place bold Gyareus essay'd,
But passing from a neighbouring ship was stay'd:
Swift through his loins a flying javelin struck,
And nail'd him to the vessel he forsook.
Friendlike, and side by side, two brethren fought,
Whom, at a birth, their fruitful mother brought:
So like the lines of each resembling face,
The same the features, and the same the grace,
That fondly erring oft their parents look,
And each, for each, alternately mistook:
But death, too soon, a dire distinction makes.
While one, untimely snatch'd, the light forsakes,
His brother's form the sad survivor wears,
And still renews his hapless parents tears:
Too sure they see their single hope remain,
And while they bless the living, mourn the slain.
He, the bold youth, as board and board they stand,
Fix'd on a Roman ship his daring hand;
Full on his arm a mighty blow descends,
And the torn limb from off the shoulder rends;
The rigid nerves are cramp'd with stiff'ning cold,
Convulsive grasp, and still retain their hold.
Nor sunk his valour by the pain deprest,
But nobler rage inflam'd his mangled breast:
His left remaining hand the combat tries,
And fiercely forth to catch the right he flies;
The same hard destiny the left demands,
And now a naked helpless trunk he stands.
Nor deigns he, though defenceless to the foe,
To seek the safety of the hold below;
For every coming javelin's point prepar'd,
He steps between, and stands his brother's guard,
Till fix'd, and horrid with a wood of spears,
A thousand deaths, at others aim'd he wears.
Resolv'd at length his utmost force t' exert,
His spirits gather'd to his fainting heart,
And the last vigour rous'd in every part;
Then nimble from the Grecian deck he rose,
And with a leap sprung fierce amidst his foes:
And when his hands no more could wreak his hate,
His sword no more could minister to fate,
Dying he prest them with his hostile weight.
O'ercharg'd the ship with carcasses and blood,
Drunk fast at many a leak the briny flood;
Yielding at length the waters wide give way,
And fold her in the bosom of the sea;
Then o'er her head returning rolls the tide,
And covering waves the sinking hatches hide.
That fatal day was slaughter seen to reign,
In wonders various, on the liquid plain.
On Lycidas a steely grappling struck;
Struggling he drags with the tenacious hook,
And deep had drown'd beneath the greedy wave,
But that his fellows strove their mate to save;
Clung to his legs, they clasp him all they can,
The grappling tugs, asunder flies the man.
No single wound the gaping rupture seems,
Where trickling crimson wells in slender streams;
But from an opening horrible and wide,
A thousand vessels pour the bursting tide:
At once the winding channel's course was broke,
Where wandering life her mazy journey took:
At once the currents all forgot their way,
And lost their purple in the azure sea.
Soon from the lower parts the spirits fled,
And motionless th' exhausted limbs lay dead:
Not so the nobler regions, where the heart
And heaving lungs their vital powers exert;
There lingering late, and long conflicting, life
Rose against fate, and still maintain'd the strife;
Driven out at length, unwillingly and slow,
She left her mortal house, and sought the shades below.
While, eager for the fight, an hardy crew
To one sole side their force united drew,
The bark, unapt th' unequal poise to bear,
Turn'd o'er, and rear'd her lowest keel in air;
In vain his active arms the swimmer tries,
No aid the swimmer's useles art supplies;
The covering vast o'erwhelming shuts them down,
And helpless in the hollow hold they drown.
One slaughter terrible above the rest,
The fatal horrour of the fight exprest.
As o'er the crowded surface of the flood
A youthful swimmer swift his way pursued;
Two meeting ships, by equal fury prest,
With hostile prows transfix'd his ample breast;
Suspended by the dreadful shock he hung,
The brazen beaks within his bosom rung;
Blood, bones, and entrails, mashing with the blow,
From his pale lips a hideous mixture flow.
At length the backing oars the fight restrain,
The lifeless body drops amidst the main;
Soon enter at the breach the rushing waves,
And the salt stream the mangled carcass laves.
Around the watery champaign wide dispread,
The living shipwrecks float amidst the dead;
With active arms the liquid deep they ply,
And panting to their mates for succour cry:
Now to some social vessel press they near,
Their fellows pale the crowding numbers fear;

With ruthless hearts their well-known friends withstand,
And with keen falchions lop each grasping hand;
The dying fingers cling and clench the wood,
The heavy trunk sinks helpless in the flood.
Now spent was all the warriors steely store,
New darts they seek, and other arms explore,
This wields a flag-staff, that a ponderous oar.
Wrath's ready hands are never at a loss:
The fragments of the shatter'd ship they toss.
The useless rower from his seat is cast,
Then fly the benches and the broken mast.
Some seizing, as it sinks, the breathless corse,
From the cold grasp the blood-stain'd weapon force.
Some from their own fresh bleeding bosoms take,
And at the foe the dropping javelin shake:
The left-hand stays the blood, and soothes the pain,
The right sends back the reeking spear again.
Now gods of various elements conspire;
To Nereus, Vulcan joins his hostile fire;
With oils, and living sulphur, darts they frame,
Prepar'd to spread afar the kindling flame;
Around the catching mischiefs swift succeed,
The floating hulks their own destruction feed;
The smeary wax the brightening blaze supplies,
And wavy fires from pitchy planks arise:
Amidst the flood the ruddy torrent strays,
And fierce upon the scattering shipwrecks preys.
Here one with haste a flaming vessel leaves:
Another, spent and beaten by the waves,
As eager to the burning ruin cleaves.
Amidst the various ways of death to kill,
Whether by seas, by fires, or wounding steel,
The dreadfullest is that, whose present force we feel.
Nor valour less her fatal rage maintains
In daring breasts that swim the liquid plains:
Some gather up the darts that floating lie,
And to the combatants new deaths supply.
Some struggling in the deep the war provoke,
Rise o'er the surge, and aim a languid stroke.
Some with strong grasp the foe conflicting join,
Mix limbs with limbs, and hostile wreathings twine,
Till plunging, pressing to the bottom down,
Vanquish'd, and vanquishers' alike they drown.
One, chief above the rest, is mark'd by fame,
For watery fight, and Phoceus was his name:
The heaving breath of life he knew to keep,
While long he dwelt within the lowest deep;
Full many a fathom down he had explor'd,
For treasures lost, old Ocean's oozy hoard;
Oft when the flooky anchor stuck below,
He sunk, and bade the captive vessel go.
A foe he seiz'd close cleaving to his breast,
And underneath the tumbling billows prest.
But when the skilful victor would repair
To upper seas, and sought the freer air;
Hapless beneath the crowding keels he rose,
The crowding keels his wonted way oppose;
Back beaten, and astonish'd with the blow,
He sinks, to bide for ever now below.
Some hang upon the oars with weighty force,
To intercept the hostile vessel's course;
Some to the last the cause they love defend,
And valiant lives by useful deaths would end;
With breasts oppos'd the thundering beaks they brave,
And what they fought for living, dying save.
As Tyrrhen, from a Roman poop on high,
Ran o'er the various combat with his eye;
Sure aiming, from his Balearic thong,
Bold Ligdamus a ponderous bullet slung;
Through liquid air the ball shrill whistling flies,
And cuts its way through hapless Tyrrhen's eyes.
Th' astonish'd youth stands struck with sudden night,
While bursting start the bleeding orbs of sight.
At first he took the darkness to be death,
And thought himself amidst the shades beneath;
But soon recovering from the stunning sound,
He liv'd, unhappily he liv'd, he found.
Vigour at length, and wonted force returns,
And with new rage his valiant bosom burns:
"To me, my friends," he cry'd, "your aid supply,
Nor useless let your fellow-soldier die;
Give me, oppos'd against the foe to stand,
While like some engine you direct my hand.
And thou, my poor remaining life, prepare
To meet each hazard of the various war;
At least, my mangled carcass shall pretend
To interpose, and shield some valiant friend:
Plac'd like a mark their darts I may sustain,
And, to preserve some better man, be slain."
Thus said, unaiming he a javelin threw,
The javelin wing'd with sure destruction flew;
In Argus the descending steel takes place,
Argus, a Grecian of illustrious race.
Deep sinks the piercing point, where to the loins
Above the naval high the belly joins:
The staggering youth falls forward on his fate,
And helps the goring weapon with his weight.
It chanc'd, to ruthless destiny design'd,
To the same ship his aged sire was join'd:
While young, for high achievements was he known,
The first in fair Massilia for renown;
Now an example merely, and a name,
Willing to rouse the younger sort he came,
And fire their souls to emulate his fame.
When from the prow, where distant far he stood,
He saw his son lie weltering in his blood;
Soon to the poop, oft stumbling in his haste,
With faltering steps the feeble father past.
No falling tears his wrinkled cheeks bedew,
But stiffening cold and motionless he grew:
Deep night and deadly shades of darkness rise,
And hide his much-lov'd Argus from his eyes.
As to the dizzy youth the sire appears,
His dying, weak, unwieldy head he rears;
With lifted eyes he cast a mournful look,
His pale lips mov'd, and fain he would have spoke;
But unexpress'd th' imperfect accent hung,
Lost in his falling jaws and murmuring tongue:
Yet in his speechless visage seems exprest,
What, had he words, would be his last request,
That aged hand to seal his closing eye,
And in his father's fond embrace to die:
But he, when grief with keenest sense revives,
With nature's strongest pangs conflicting strives;
"Let me not lose this hour of death," he cries,
"Which my indulgent destiny supplies;
And thou forgive, forgive me, oh my son,
If thy dear lips and last embrace I shun.
Warm from thy wound the purple current flows,
And vital breath yet heaving comes and goes:
Yet my sad eyes behold thee yet alive,
And thou shalt, yet, thy wretched sire survive."
He said; and fierce, by frantic sorrow prest,
Plung'd his sharp sword amidst his aged breast:

And though life's gushing streams the weapon stain,
Headlong he leaps amidst the greedy main;
While this last wish ran ever in his mind,
To die and leave his darling son behind;
Eager to part, his soul disdain'd to wait,
And trust uncertain to a single fate.
And now Massilia's vanquish'd force gives way,
And Cæsar's fortune claims the doubtful day.
The Grecian fleet is all dispers'd around,
Some in the bottom of the deep lie drown'd;
Some, captives made, their haughty victors bore,
While some, but those a few, fled timely to the shore.
But, oh! what verse, what numbers, can express
The mournful city, and her sore distress!
Upon the beach lamenting matrons stand,
And wailings echo o'er the lengthening strand;
Their eyes are fix'd upon the waters wide,
And watch the bodies driving with the tide.
Here a fond wife, with pious errour, prest
Some hostile Roman to her throbbing breast;
There to a mangled trunk two mothers run,
Each grasps, and each would claim it for her son;
Each, what her boding heart persuades, believes,
And for the last sad office fondly strives.
But Brutus, now victorious on the main,
To Cæsar vindicates the watery plain;
First to his brow he binds the naval crown,
And bids the spacious deep the mighty master own.

BOOK IV.

THE ARGUMENT.

Cæsar having joined Fabius, whom he had sent before him to Spain, encamps upon a rising ground near Ilerda, and not far from the river Sicoris: there, the waters being swollen by great rains, endanger his camp; but the weather turning fair, and the floods abating, Pompey's lieutenants, Afranius and Petreius, who lay over-against him, decamp suddenly. Cæsar follows, and encamps so as to cut off their passage, or any use of the river Iberus. As both armies lay now very near to each other, the soldiers on both sides knew, and saluted one another; and forgetting the opposite interests and factions they were engaged in, ran out from their several camps, and embraced one another with great tenderness. Many of Cæsar's soldiers were invited into the enemy's camp, and feasted by their friends and relations. But Petreius apprehending this familiarity might be of ill consequence to his party, commanded them all (though against the rules of humanity and hospitality) to be killed. After this, he attempts in vain to march back towards Ilerda; but is prevented, and enclosed by Cæsar; to whom, both himself and Afranius, after their army had suffered extremely for want of water and other necessaries, are compelled to surrender, without asking any other conditions than that they might not be compelled to take on in his army; this Cæsar, with great generosity, grants, and dismisses them. In the mean while, C. Antonius, who commanded for Cæsar near Salonæ, on the coast of Dalmatia, being shut up by Octavius, Pompey's admiral, and destitute of provisions, had attempted, by help of some vessels, or floating machines of a new invention, to pass through Pompey's fleet: two of them by advantage of the tide found means to escape, but the third, which carried a thousand Opitergians commanded by Vulteius, was intercepted by a boom laid under the water. Those when they found it impossible to get off, at the persuasion, and by the example of their leader, ran upon one another's swords and died. In Africa the poet introduces Curio inquiring after the story of Hercules and Antæus, which is recounted to him by one of the natives, and afterwards relates the particulars of his being circumvented, defeated, and killed by Juba.

But Cæsar in Iberian fields afar,
E'en to the western ocean spreads the war;
And though no hills of slaughter heap the plain,
No purple deluge leaves a guilty stain,
Vast is the prize, and great the victor's gain.
For Pompey with alternative command,
The brave Petreius and Afranius stand:
The chiefs in friendship's just conditions join,
And, cordial to the common cause combine;
By turns they quit, by turns resume the sway,
The camp to guard, or battle to array;
To these their aid the nimble Vectons yield,
With those who till Asturia's hilly field;
Nor wanted then the Celtiberians bold,
Who draw their long descent from Celtic Gauls of old.
Where rising grounds the fruitful champaign end,
And unperceiv'd by soft degrees ascend;
An ancient race their city chose to found,
And with Ilerda's walls the summit crown'd.
The Sicoris, of no ignoble name,
Fast by the mountain pours his gentle stream.
A stable bridge runs cross from side to side,
Whose spacious arch transmits the passing tide,
And jutting piers the wintery floods abide.
Two neighbouring hills their heads distinguish'd raise;
The first great Pompey's ensigns high displays;
Proud Cæsar's camp upon the next is seen;
The river interposing glides between.
Wide spread beyond, an ample plain extends,
Far as the piercing eye its prospect sends;
Upon the spacious level's utmost bound,
The Cinga rolls his rapid waves around.
But soon in full Iberus' channel lost,
His blended waters seek Iberia's coast;
He yields to the superior torrent's fame,
And with the country takes his nobler name.
Now 'gan the lamp of Heaven the plains to gild,
When moving legions hide th' embattled field;
When front to front oppos'd in just array,
The chieftains each their hostile powers display:
But whether conscious shame their wrath represt,
And soft reluctance rose in every breast;
Or virtue did a short-liv'd rule resume,
And gain'd one day for liberty and Rome;
Suspended rage yet linger'd for a space,
And to the west declin'd the Sun in peace.
Night rose, and black'ning shades involv'd the sky,
When Cæsar, bent war's wily arts to try,
Through his extended battle gives command,
The foremost lines in order fix'd shall stand;
Mean-while the last, low lurking from the foe,
With secret labour sink a trench below:
Successful they the destin'd task pursue,
While closing files prevent the hostile view.

Soon as the morn renew'd the dawning gray,
He bids the soldier urge his speedy way,
To seize a vacant height that near Ilerda lay.
This saw the foe, and wing'd with fear and shame,
Through secret paths with swift prevention came.
Now various motives various hopes afford,
To these the place, to those the conquering sword:
Oppress'd beneath their armour's cumbrous weight,
Th' assailants labouring tempt the steepy height;
Half bending back they mount with panting pain,
The following crowd their foremost mates sustain;
Against the shelving precipice they toil,
And prop their hands upon the steely pile: [stay,
On cliffs and shrubs, their steps, some climbing
With cutting swords some clear the woody way;
Nor death, nor wounds, their enemies annoy,
While other uses now their arms employ.
Their chief the danger from afar survey'd,
And bade the horse fly timely to their aid.
In order just the ready squadrons ride,
Then wheeling to the right and left divide,
To flank the foot, and guard each naked side.
Safe in the middle space retire the foot,
Make good the rear, and scorn the foe's pursuit;
Each side retreat, though each disdain to yield,
And claim the glory of the doubtful field.

Thus far the cause of Rome by arms was try'd,
And human rage alone the war supply'd;
But now the elements new wrath prepare,
And gathering tempests vex the troubled air.
Long had the earth by wintery frosts been bound,
And the dry north had numb'd the lazy ground.
No furrow'd fields were drench'd with drisly rain,
Snow hid the hills, and hoary ice the plain.
All desolate the western climes were seen,
Keen were the blasts, and sharp the blue serene,
To parch the fading herb, and dip the springing green.
At length the genial heat began to shine,
With stronger beams in Aries' vernal sign;
Again the golden day resum'd its right,
And rul'd in just equation with the night:
The Moon her monthly course had now begun,
And with increasing horns forsook the Sun;
When Boreas, by night's silver empress driven,
To softer airs resign'd the western Heaven.
Then with warm breezes gentler Eurus came,
Glowing with India's and Arabia's flame.
The sweeping wind the gathering vapours prest,
From every region of the farthest east;
Nor hang they heavy in the midway sky,
But speedy to Hesperia driving fly;
To Calpe's hills the sluicy rains repair,
From north, and south, the clouds assemble there,
And darkening storms lower in the sluggish air.
Where western skies the utmost ocean bound,
The watery treasures heap the welkin round;
Thither they crowd, and, scanted in the space,
Scarce between Heaven and Earth can find a place.
Condens'd at length the spouting torrents pour,
Earth smokes, and rattles with the gushing shower;
Jove's forky fires are rarely seen to fly,
Extinguish'd in the deluge soon they die;
Nor e'er before did dewy Iris show
Such fady colours, or so maim'd a bow;
Unvary'd by the light's refracting beam,
She stoop'd to drink from ocean's briny stream;
Then to the dropping sky restor'd the rain:
Again the falling waters sought the main.
Then first the covering snows began to flow
From off the Pyrenean's hoary brow;
Huge hills of frost, a thousand ages old,
O'er which the summer suns had vainly roll'd,
Now melting, rush from every side amain,
Swell every brook, and deluge all the plain.
And now o'er Cæsar's camp the torrents sweep,
Bear down the works, and fill the trenches deep.
Here men and arms in mix'd confusion swim,
And hollow tents drive with th' impetuous stream;
Lost in the spreading floods the land-marks lie,
Nor can the forager his way descry.
No beasts for food the floating pastures yield,
Nor herbage rises in the watery field.
And now, to fill the measure of their fears,
Her baleful visage meagre famine rears;
Seldom alone, she troops among the fiends,
And still on war and pestilence attends.
Unpress'd, unstraiten'd by besieging foes,
All miseries of want the soldier knows.
Gladly he gives his little wealth, to eat,
And buys a morsel with his whole estate.
Curs'd merchandise! where life itself is sold,
And avarice consents to starve for gold!
No rock, no rising mountain, rears his head,
No single river winds along the mead,
But one vast lake o'er all the land is spread.
No lofty grove, no forest haunt is found,
But in his den deep lies the savage drown'd:
With headlong rage resistless in its course,
The rapid torrent whirls the snorting horse;
High o'er the sea the foamy freshes ride,
While backward Tethys turns her yielding tide.
Mean-time continued darkness veils the skies,
And suns with unavailing ardour rise;
Nature no more her various face can boast,
But form is huddled up in night and lost.
Such are the climes beneath the frozen-zone,
Where cheerless winter plants her dreary throne;
No golden stars their gloomy Heavens adorn,
Nor genial seasons to their Earth return:
But everlasting ice and snows appear, [year.
Bind up the summer signs, and curse the barren

Almighty Sire! who dost supremely reign,
And thou great ruler of the raging main!
Ye gracious gods! in mercy give command,
This desolation may for ever stand.
Thou Jove! for ever cloud thy stormy sky;
Thou Neptune! bid thy angry waves run high:
Heave thy huge trident for a mighty blow,
Strike the strong earth, and bid her fountains flow;
Bid every river-god exhaust his urn,
Nor let thy own alternate tides return;
Wide let their blended waters waste around,
These regions, Rhine, and those of Rhone confound.
Melt ye hoar mountains of Riphæan snow;
Brooks, streams, and lakes, let all your sources go:
Your spreading floods the guilt of Rome shall spare,
And save the wretched world from civil war.

But Fortune stay'd her short displeasure here,
Nor urg'd her minion with too long a fear;
With large increase her favours full return'd,
As if the gods themselves his anger mourn'd;
As if his name were terrible to Heaven,
And Providence could sue to be forgiven.

Now 'gan the welkin clear to shine serene,
And Phœbus potent in his rays was seen.
The scattering clouds disclos'd the piercing light,
And hung the firmament with fleecy white;
The troublous storm had spent his wrathful store,
And clattering rains were heard to rush no more.
Again the woods their leafy honours raise,
And herds upon the rising mountains graze.

Day's genial heat upon the damps prevails,
And ripens into earth the slimy vales.
Bright glittering stars adorn night's spangled air,
And ruddy evening skies foretel the morning fair.
Soon as the falling Sicoris begun
A peaceful stream within his banks to run,
The bending willow into barks they twine,
Then line the work with spoils of slaughter'd kine:
Such are the floats Venetian fishers know,
Where in dull marshes stands the settling Po;
On such to neighbouring Gaul, allur'd by gain,
The bolder Britons cross the swelling main;
Like these, when fruitful Egypt lies afloat,
The Memphian artist builds his reedy boat.
On these embarking bold with eager haste,
Across the stream his legions Cæsar past:
Straight the tall woods with sounding strokes are fell'd,
And with strong piles a beamy bridge they build;
Then mindful of the flood so lately spread,
They stretch the lengthening arches o'er the mead.
And, lest his bolder waters rise again,
With numerous dikes they canton out the plain,
And by a thousand streams the suffering river drain.
Petreius now a fate superior saw,
While elements obey proud Cæsar's law;
Then straight Ilerda's lofty walls forsook,
And to the farthest west his arms betook;
The nearer regions faithless all around,
And basely to the victor bent, he found.
When with just rage and indignation fir'd,
He to the Celtiberians fierce retir'd;
There sought, amidst the world's extremest parts,
Still daring hands, and still unconquer'd hearts.
Soon as he view'd the neighbouring mountain's head
No longer by the hostile camp o'erspread,
Cæsar commands to arm. Without delay
The soldier to the river bends his way;
None then with cautious care the bridge explor'd,
Or sought the shallows of the safer ford;
Arm'd at all points, they plunge amidst the flood,
And with strong sinews make the passage good:
Dangers they scorn that might the bold affright,
And stop e'en panting cowards in their flight.
At length the farther bank attaining safe,
Chill'd by the stream, their dropping limbs they chafe:
Then with fresh vigour urge the foes' pursuit,
And in the sprightly chase the powers of life recruit.
Thus they; till half the course of life was run,
And lessening shadows own'd the noon-day Sun;
The fliers now a doubtful fight maintain,
While the fleet horse in squadrons scour the plain;
The stragglers scattering round they force to yield,
And gather up the gleanings of the field.
'Midst a wide plain two lofty rocks arise
Between the cliffs an humble valley lies;
Long rows of ridgy mountains run behind,
Where ways obscure and secret passes wind.
But Cæsar, deep within his thought, foresees
The foes attempt the covert strong to seize:
So may their troops at leisure range afar,
And to the Celtiberians lead the war.
"Be quick" he cries "nor minding just array,
Swift, to the combat, wing your speedy way.
See! where yon cowards to the fastness haste,
But let your terrours in their way be plac'd;
Pierce not the fearful backs of those that fly,
But on your meeting javelins let them die."
He said. The ready legions took the word,
And hastily obey their eager lord;
With diligence the coming foe prevent,
And stay their marches, to the mountains bent.
Near neighbouring now the camps intrench'd are seen,
With scarce a narrow interval between.
Soon as their eyes o'ershoot the middle space,
From either host, sires, sons, and brothers trace
The well-known features of some kindred face.
Then first their hearts with tenderness were struck,
First with remorse for civil rage they shook;
Stiffening with horrour cold, and dire amaze,
Awhile in silent interviews they gaze:
Anon with speechless signs their swords salute,
While thoughts conflicting keep their masters mute.
At length, disdaining still to be represt,
Prevailing passion rose in every breast,
And the vain rules of guilty war transgress'd.
As at a signal, both their trenches quit,
And spreading arms in close embraces knit:
Now friendship runs o'er all her ancient claims,
Guest and companion are their only names;
Old neighbourhood they fondly call to mind,
And how their boyish years in leagues were join'd.
With grief each other mutually they know,
And find a friend in every Roman foe.
Their falling tears their steely arms bedew,
While interrupting sighs each kiss pursue;
And though their hands are yet unstain'd by guilt,
They tremble for the blood they might have spilt.
But speak, unhappy Roman! speak thy pain,
Say for what woes thy streaming eyes complain?
Why dost thou groan? why beat thy sounding breast?
Why is this wild fantastic grief exprest;
Is it that yet thy country claims thy care?
Dost thou the crimes of war unwilling share?
Ah! whither art thou by thy fears betray'd?
How canst thou dread that power thyself hast made?
Do Cæsar's trumpets call thee? scorn the sound.
Does he bid, march? dare thou to keep thy ground.
So rage and slaughter shall to justice yield,
And fierce Erinnys quit the fatal field:
Cæsar in peace a private state shall know,
And Pompey be no longer call'd his foe.
Appear, thou heavenly Concord! blest appear!
And shed thy better influences here.
Thou who the warring elements dost bind,
Life of the world, and safety of mankind,
Infuse thy sovereign balm, and heal the wrathful mind.
But if the same dire fury rages yet,
Too well they know what foes their swords shall meet;
No blind pretence of ignorance remains,
The blood they shed must flow from Roman veins.
Oh; fatal truce! the brand of guilty Rome!
From thee worse wars and redder slaughters come.
See! with what free and unsuspected love,
From camp to camp the jocund warriors rove;
Each to his turfy table bids his guest,
And Bacchus crowns the hospitable feast.
The grassy fires refulgent lend their light,
While conversation sleepless wastes the night:
Of early feats of arms by turns they tell,
Of fortunes that in various fields befell,
With well-becoming pride their deeds relate,
And now agree, and friendly now debate:
At length their unauspicious hands are join'd,
And sacred leagues with faith renew'd they bind.

But oh! what worse could cruel fate afford!
The furies smil'd upon the curst accord,
And dy'd with deeper stains the Roman sword.
By busy fame Petreius soon is told,
His camp, himself, to Cæsar all are sold;
When straight the chief indignant calls to arm,
And bids the trumpet spread the loud alarm.
With war encompass'd round he takes his way,
And breaks the short-liv'd truce with fierce affray;
He drives th' unarm'd and unsuspecting guest,
Amaz'd, and wounded, from th' unfinish'd feast;
With horrid steel he cuts each fond embrace,
And violates with blood the new-made peace.
And lest the fainting flames of wrath expire,
With words like these he fans the deadly fire:
"Ye herd! unknowing of the Roman worth,
And lost to the great cause which led you forth;
Though victory and captive Cæsar were
Honours too glorious for your swords to share;
Yet something, abject as you are, from you,
Something to virtue and the laws is due:
A second praise ev'n yet you may partake!
Fight, and be vanquish'd for your country's sake.
Can you, while fate as yet suspends our doom,
While you have blood and lives to lose for Rome,
Can you with tame submission seek a lord;
And own a cause by men and gods abhorr'd;
Will you in lowly wise his mercy crave?
Can soldiers beg to wear the name of slave?
Would you for us your suit to Cæsar move?
Know we disdain his pardoning power to prove:
No private bargain shall redeem this head:
For Rome, and not for us, the war was made.
Though peace a specious poor pretence afford,
Baseness and bondage lurk beneath the word.
In vain the workmen search the steely mine
To arm the field, and bid the battle shine;
In vain the fortress lifts her towery height;
In vain the warlike steed provokes the fight;
In vain our oars the foamy ocean sweep;
In vain our floating castles hide the deep;
In vain by land, in vain by sea we fought,
If peace shall e'er with liberty be bought.
See! with what constancy, what gallant pride,
Our steadfast foes defend an impious side!
Bound by their oaths, though enemies to good,
They scorn to change from what they once have vow'd.
While each vain breath your slackening faith withdraws,
Yours! who pretend to arm for Rome and laws,
Who find no fault, but justice in your cause.
And yet, methinks, I would not give you o'er,
A brave repentance still is in your power;
While Pompey calls the utmost east from far,
And leads the Indian monarchs on to war,
Shall we (oh shame!) prevent his great success,
And bind his hands by our inglorious peace?"
He spoke; and civil rage at once returns,
Each breast the fonder thought of pity scorns,
And ruthless with redoubled fury burns.
So when the tiger, or the spotted pard,
Long from the woods and savage haunts debarr'd,
From their first fierceness for a while are won,
And seem to put a gentler nature on;
Patient their prison, and mankind they bear,
Fawn on their lords, and looks less horrid wear:
But let the taste of slaughter be renew'd,
And their fell jaws again with gore imbru'd;
Then dreadfully their wakening furies rise,
And glaring fires rekindle in their eyes;
With wrathful roar their echoing dens they tear,
And hardly ev'n the well-known keeper spare;
The shuddering keeper shakes and stands aloof for fear.
From friendship freed, and conscious nature's tie,
To undistinguish'd slaughters loose they fly;
With guilt avow'd their daring crimes advance,
And scorn th' excuse of ignorance and chance.
Those whom so late their fond embraces prest,
The bosom's partner, and the welcome guest;
Now at the board unhospitable bleed,
While streams of blood the flowing bowl succeed.
With groans at first each draws the glittering brand,
And lingering death stops in th' unwilling hand:
Till urg'd at length returning force they feel,
And catch new courage from the murdering steel:
Vengeance and hatred rise with every blow,
And blood paints every visage like a foe.
Uproar and horrour through the camp abound,
While impious sons their mangled fathers wound,
And, lest the merit of the crime be lost,
With dreadful joy the parricide they boast;
Proud to their chiefs the cold pale heads they bear,
The gore yet dropping from the silver hair.
But thou, O Cæsar! to the gods be dear!
Thy pious mercy well becomes their care;
And though thy soldier falls by treacherous peace,
Be proud, and reckon this thy great success.
Not all thou ow'st to bounteous Fortune's smile,
Not proud Massilia, nor the Pharian Nile;
Not the full conquest of Pharsalia's field,
Could greater fame, or nobler trophies yield;
Thine and the cause of justice now are one,
Since guilty slaughter brands thy foes alone.
Nor dare the conscious leaders longer wait,
Or trust to such unhallow'd hands their fate:
Astonish'd and dismay'd they shun the fight,
And to Ilerda turn their hasty flight.
But, ere their march achieves its destin'd course,
Preventing Cæsar sends the winged horse:
The speedy squadrons seize th' appointed ground,
And hold their foes on hills encompass'd round.
Pent up in barren heights, they strive in vain
Refreshing springs and flowing streams to gain;
Strong hostile works their camp's extension stay,
And deep-sunk trenches intercept their way.
Now deaths in unexpected forms arise,
Thirst and pale famine stalk before their eyes.
Shut up and close besieg'd, no more they need
The strength or swiftness of the warlike steed;
But doom the generous coursers all to bleed.
Hopeless at length, and barr'd around from flight,
Headlong they rush to arms, and urge the fight:
But Cæsar, who with wary eyes beheld,
With what determin'd rage they sought the field,
Restrain'd his eager troops. "Forbear," he cry'd,
"Nor let your sword in madmens blood be dy'd.
But, since they come devoted by despair,
Since life is grown unworthy of their care,
Since 't is their time to die, 't is our's to spare.
Those naked bosoms that provoke the foe,
With greedy hopes of deadly vengeance glow;
With pleasure shall they meet the pointed steel,
Nor smarting wounds, nor dying anguish feel,
If, while they bleed, your Cæsar shares the pain,
And mourns his gallant friends among the slain.
But wait awhile, this rage shall soon be past,
This blaze of courage is too fierce to last;

This ardour for the fight shall faint away,
And all this fond desire of death decay."
He spoke; and at the word the war was stay'd
Till Phœbus fled from night's ascending shade.
Ev'n all the day, embattled on the plain,
The rash Petreians urge to arms in vain:
At length the weary fire began to cease,
And wasting fury languish'd into peace;
Th' impatient arrogance of wrath declin'd,
And slackening passions cool'd upon the mind.
So when, the battle roaring loud around,
Some warrior warm receives a fatal wound;
While yet the griding sword has newly past,
And the first pungent pains and anguish last;
While full with life the turgid vessels rise,
And the warm juice the sprightly nerve supplies;
Each sinewy limb with fiercer force is prest,
And rage redoubles in the burning breast:
But if, as conscious of th' advantage gain'd,
The cooler victor stays his wrathful hand;
Then sinks his thrall with ebbing spirits low
The black blood stiffens and forgets to flow:
Cold damps and numbness close the deadly stound,
And stretch him pale and fainting on the ground.
For water now on every side they try,
Alike the sword and delving spade employ;
Earth's bosom dark, laborious they explore,
And search the sources of her liquid store;
Deep in the hollow hill the well descends,
Till level with the moister plain it ends.
Not lower down from cheerful day decline
The pale Assyrians, in the golden mine.
In vain they toil, no secret streams are found
To roll their murmuring tides beneath the ground;
No bursting springs repay the workman's stroke,
Nor glittering gush from out the wounded rock;
No sweating caves in dewy droppings stand,
Nor smallest rills run gurgling o'er the sand.
Spent and exhausted with the fruitless pain,
The fainting youth ascend to light again.
And now less patient of the draught they grow,
Than in those cooler depths of earth below;
No savory viands crown the cheerful board,
Ev'n food for want of water stands abhorr'd:
To hunger's meagre refuge they retreat,
And, since they cannot drink, refuse to eat.
Where yielding clods a moister clay confess,
With griping hands the clammy glebe they press;
Where-e'er the standing puddle loathsome lies,
Thither in crowds the thirsty soldier flies;
Horrid to sight, the miry filth they quaff,
And drain with dying jaws the deadly draff.
Some seek the bestial mothers for supply,
And draw the herds extended udders dry;
Till thirst, unsated with the milky store,
With labouring lips drinks-in the putrid gore.
Some strip the leaves, and suck the morning dews;
Some grind the bark, the woody branches bruise,
And squeeze the sapling's unconcocted juice.
Oh happy those, to whom the barbarous kings
Left their envenom'd floods, and tainted springs;
Cæsar be kind, and every bane prepare,
Which Cretan rocks, or Libyan serpents bear:
The Romans to thy poisonous streams shall fly,
And conscious of the danger, drink, and die.
With secret flames their withering entrails burn,
And fiery breathings from their lungs return:
The shrinking veins contract their purple flood,
And urge laborious on the beating blood;
The heaving sighs through straiter passes blow,
And scorch the painful palate as they go: [draws,
The parch'd rough tongue night's humid vapours
And restless rolls within the clammy jaws;
With gaping mouths they wait the falling rain,
And want those floods that lately spread the plain.
Vainly to Heaven they turn their longing eyes,
And fix them on the dry relentless skies.
Nor here by sandy Afric are they curst,
Nor Cancer's sultry line inflames their thirst;
But to enhance their pain, they view below,
Where lakes stand full, and plenteous rivers flow;
Between two streams expires the panting host.
And in a land of water are they lost.
Now prest by pinching want's unequal weight,
The vanquish'd leaders yield to adverse fate:
Rejecting arms, Afranius seeks relief,
And sues submissive to the hostile chief.
Foremost himself, to Cæsar's camp he leads
His famish'd troops, a fainting band succeeds.
At length in presence of the victor plac'd,
A fitting dignity his gesture grac'd,
That spoke his present fortunes, and his past.
With decent mixture in his manly mein,
The captive and the general were seen:
Then, with a free, secure, undaunted breast,
For mercy thus his pious suit he prest.
"Had fate and my ill fortune laid me low,
Beneath the power of some ungenerous foe;
My sword hung ready to protect my fame,
And this right-hand had sav'd my soul from shame:
But now with joy I bend my suppliant knee,
Life is worth asking, since 't is given by thee.
No party-zeal our factious arms inclines,
No hate of thee, or of thy bold designs.
War with its own occasions came unsought,
And found us on the side for which we fought:
True to our cause as best becomes the brave,
Long as we could, we kept that faith we gave.
Nor shall our arms thy stronger fate delay,
Behold! our yielding paves thy conquering way:
The western nations all at once we give,
Securely these behind thee shalt thou leave;
Here while thy full dominion stands confest,
Receive it as an earnest of the east.
Nor this thy easy victory disdain,
Bought with no seas of blood, nor hills of slain;
Forgive the foes that spare thy sword a pain.
Nor is the boon for which we sue too great,
The weary soldier begs a last retreat;
In some poor village, peaceful at the plough,
Let them enjoy the life thou dost bestow.
Think, in some field, among the slain we lie,
And lost to thy remembrance cast us by.
Mix not our arms in thy successful war,
Nor let thy captives in thy triumph share.
These unprevailing bands their fate have try'd,
And prov'd that fortune fights not on their side.
Guiltless to cease from slaughter we implore,
Let us not conquer with thee, and we ask no more."
He said. The victor, with a gentler grace,
And mercy softening his severer face,
Bad his attending foes their fears dismiss,
Go free from punishment, and live in peace.
The truce on equal terms at length agreed,
The waters from the watchful guard are freed:
Eager to drink, down rush the thirsty crowd,
Hang o'er the banks and trouble all the flood.
Some, while too fierce the fatal draughts they drain,
Forget the gasping lungs that heave in vain;

No breathing airs the choking channels fill,
But every spring of life at once stands still.
Some drink, nor yet the fervent pest assuage,
With wonted fires their bloated entrails rage;
With bursting sides each bulk enormous heaves,
While still for drink th' insatiate fever craves.
At length returning health dispers'd the pain,
And lusty vigour strung the nerves again.
Behold! ye sons of luxury, behold!
Who scatter in excess your lavish gold;
You who the wealth of frugal ages waste,
T' indulge a wanton supercilious taste:
For whom all earth, all ocean are explor'd,
To spread the various proud voluptuous board:
Behold! how little thrifty nature craves,
And what a cheap relief the lives of thousands saves!
No costly wines these fainting legions know,
Mark'd by old consuls many a year ago;
No waiting slaves the precious juices pour,
From myrrhine goblets, or the golden ore:
But with pure draughts they cool the boiling blood,
And seek their succour from the crystal flood.
Who, but a wretch, would think it worth his care,
The toils and wickedness of war to share,
When all we want thus easily we find?
The field and river can supply mankind.
Dismiss'd, and safe from danger and alarms,
The vanquish'd to the victor quits his arms;
Guiltless from camps, to cities he repairs,
And in his native land forgets his cares.
There in his mind he runs repenting o'er
The tedious toils and perils once he bore;
His spear and sword of battle stands accurst,
He hates the weary march, and parching thirst;
And wonders much, that e'er with pious pain
He pray'd so oft for victory in vain:
For victory! the curse of those that win,
The fatal end where still new woes begin.
Let the proud masters of the horrid field
Count all the gains their dire successes yield;
Then let them think what wounds they yet must feel,
Ere they can fix revolving Fortune's wheel:
As yet th' imperfect task by halves is done,
Blood, blood remains, more battles must be won,
And many a heavy labour undergone:
Still conquering, to new guilt they shall succeed,
Where-ever restless fate and Cæsar lead.
How happier lives the man to peace assign'd,
Amidst this general storm that wrecks mankind!
In his own quiet house ordain'd to die,
He knows the place in which his bones shall lie.
No trumpet warns him 'put his harness on,
Though faint, and all with weariness fore-done:
But when night falls, he lies securely down,
And calls the creeping slumber all his own;
His kinder fates the warrior's hopes prevent,
And ere the time, the wish'd dismission sent;
A lowly cottage, and a tender wife,
Receive him in his early days of life;
His boys, a rustic tribe, around him play,
And homely pleasures wear the vacant day.
No factious parties here the mind engage,
Nor work th' imbitter'd passions up to rage;
With equal eyes the hostile chiefs they view,
To this their faith, to that their lives are due:
To both oblig'd alike, no part they take,
Nor vows for conquest, nor against it, make.
Mankind's misfortunes they behold from far,
Pleas'd to stand neuter, while the world's at war.

But Fortune, bent to check the victor's pride,
In other lands forsook her Cæsar's side;
With changing cheer the fickle goddess frown'd,
And for a while her favourite cause disown'd.
Where Adria's swelling surge Salonæ laves,
And warm Iader rolls his gentle waves,
Bold in the brave Curictan's warlike band,
Antonius camps upon the utmost strand:
Begirt around by Pompey's floating power,
He braves the navy from his well-fenc'd shore.
But while the distant war no more he fears,
Famine, a worse, resistless foe, appears:
No more the meads their grassy pasture yield,
Nor waving harvests crown the yellow field.
On every verdant leaf the hungry feed,
And snatch the forage from the fainting steed;
Then ravenous on their camp's defence they fall,
And grind with greedy jaws the turfy wall.
Near on the neighbouring coast at length they spy,
Where Basilus with social sails draws nigh;
While, led by Dolabella's bold command,
Their Cæsar's legions spread th' Illyrian strand:
Straight with new hopes their hearts recovering beat,
Aim to elude the foe, and meditate retreat.
Of wond'rous form a vast machine they build,
New, and unknown upon the floating field.
Here, nor the keel its crooked length extends,
Nor o'er the waves the rising deck ascends;
By beams and grappling chains compacted strong,
Light skiffs, and casks, two equal rows prolong:
O'er these, of solid oak securely made,
Stable and tight a flooring firm is laid;
Sublime, from hence, two planky towers run high,
And nodding battlements the foe defy.
Securely plac'd, each rising range between,
The lusty rower plies his task unseen.
Mean-while nor oars upon the sides appear,
Nor swelling sails receive the driving air;
But living seems the mighty mass to sweep,
And glide self-mov'd athwart the yielding deep.
Three wond'rous floats, of this enormous size,
Soon by the skilful builder's craft arise;
The ready warriors all aboard them ride,
And wait the turn of the revolving tide,
Backward at length revolving Tethys flows,
And ebbing waves the naked sands disclose:
Straight by the stream the lanching piles are borne,
Shields, spears, and helms, their nodding towers adorn;
Threatening they move in terrible array,
And to the deeper ocean bend their way.
Octavius now, whose naval powers command
Adria's rude seas, and wide Illyria's strand,
Full in their course his fleet advancing stays,
And each impatient combatant delays:
To the blue offing wide he seems to bear,
Hopeful to draw th' unwary vessels near;
Aloof he rounds them, eager on his prey,
And tempts them with an open roomy sea.
Thus, when the wily huntsman spreads his nets
And with his ambient toil the woods besets;
While yet his busy hands, with skilful care,
The meshy hayes and forky props prepare;
Ere yet the deer the painted plumage spy;
Snuff the strong odour from afar, and fly;
His mates, the Cretan hound and Spartan bind,
And muzzle all the loud Molossian kind;
The quester only to the wood they loose,
Who silently the tainted track pursues:
Mute signs alone the conscious haunt betray,
While fix'd he points, and trembles to the prey.

'Twas at the season when the fainting light,
Just in the evening's close, brought on the night:
When the tall towery floats their isle forsook,
And to the sea their course adventurous took.
But now the fam'd Sicilian pirates, skill'd
In arts and warfare of the liquid field,
Their wonted wiles and stratagems provide,
To aid their great acknowledg'd victor's side.
Beneath the glassy surface of the main,
From rock to rock they stretch a ponderous chain;
Loosely the slacker links suspended flow,
T' enwrap the driving fabrics as they go.
Urg'd from within, and wafted by the tide,
Smooth o'er the boom the first and second glide;
The third the guileful latent chain infolds,
And in his steely grasp entwining holds:
From the tall rocks the shouting victors roar,
And drag the resty captive to the shore.
For ages past an ancient cliff there stood,
Whose bending brow hung threatning o'er the flood;
A verdant grove was on the summit plac'd,
And o'er the waves a gloomy shadow cast;
While near the base wild hollows sink below,
There roll huge seas, and bellowing tempests blow:
Thither whate'er the greedy waters drown,
The shipwreck, and the driving corpse, are thrown:
Anon the gaping gulph the spoil restores,
And from his lowest depths loud-spouting pours.
Not rude Charybdis roars in sounds like these,
When thundering, with a burst, she spews the foamy seas.
Hither, with warlike Opitergians fraught,
The third ill-fated prisoner float was brought;
The foe, as at a signal, speed their way,
And haste to compass in the destin'd prey;
The crowding sails from every station press,
While armed bands the rocks and shores possess.
Too late the chief, Vulteius, found the snare,
And strove to burst the toil with fruitless care;
Driv'n by despair at length, nor thinking yet
Which way to fight, or whither to retreat,
He turns upon the foe; and though distrest,
By wiles intangled, and by crowds opprest,
With scarce a single cohort to his aid,
Against the gathering host a stand he made.
Fierce was the combat fought, with slaughter [great,
Though thus an odds unequally they meet,
One with a thousand match'd, a ship against a [fleet.
But soon on dusky wings arose the night,
And with her friendly shade restrains the fight;
The combatants from war consenting cease,
And pass the hours of darkness o'er in peace.

When to the soldiers, anxious for his fate,
And doubtful what success the dawn might wait,
The brave Vulteius thus his speech addrest,
And thus compos'd the cares of every beating breast.

"My gallant friends! whom our hard fates de- [cree,
This night, this short night only, to be free;
Think what remains to do, but think with haste,
Ere the brief hour of liberty be past.
Perhaps, reduc'd to this so hard extreme,
Too short, to some, the date of life may seem;
Yet know, brave youths, that none untimely fall,
Whom death obeys, and comes but when they call.
'T is true, the neighbouring danger waits us nigh;
We meet but that from which we cannot fly;
Yet think not but with equal praise we die.
Dark and uncertain is man's future doom,
If years, or only moments, are to come:
All is but dying; he who gives an hour,
Or he who gives an age, gives all that's in his power.
Sooner, or late, all mortals know the grave,
But to choose death distinguishes the brave.
Behold, where waiting round, yon hostile band,
Our fellow-citizens, our lives demand.
Prevent we then their cruel hands, and bleed;
'Tis but to do what is too sure decreed,
And where our fate would drag us on, to lead.
A great conspicuous slaughter shall we yield,
Nor lie the carnage of a common field:
Where one ignoble heap confounds the slain,
And men, and beasts, promiscuous strew the plain.
Plac'd on this float by some diviner hand,
As on a stage, for public view we stand.
Illyria's neighbouring shores, her isles around,
And every cliff, with gazers shall be crown'd;
The seas and earth our virtue shall proclaim,
And stand eternal vouchers for our fame;
Alike the foes and fellows of our cause,
Shall mark the deed, and join in vast applause.
Blest be thou, Fortune, that has mark'd us forth,
A monument of unexampled worth;
To latest times our story shall be told,
Ev'n rais'd beyond the noblest names of old.
Distinguish'd praise shall crown our daring youth,
Our pious honour, and unshaken truth.
Mean is our offering, Cæsar, we confess:
For such a chief, what soldier can do less?
Yet oh! this faithful pledge of love receive!
Take it, 'tis all that captives have to give.
Oh! that, to make the victim yet more dear,
Our aged sires, our children had been here:
Then with full horrour should the slaughter rise,
And blast our paler foes' astonish'd eyes;
Till, aw'd beneath that scorn of death we wear,
They bless the time our fellows 'scap'd their snare:
Till with mean tears our fate the cowards mourn,
And tremble at the rage with which we burn.
Perhaps they mean our constant souls to try,
Whether for life or peace we may comply.
Oh grant, ye gods! their offers may be great,
That we may gloriously disdain to treat,
That this last proof of virtue we may give,
And show we die not now because we could not live.
That valour to no common heights must rise,
Which he, our god-like chief himself, shall prize
Immortal shall our truth for ever stand,
If Cæsar thinks this little faithful band
A loss, amidst the host of his command.
For me, my friends, my fix'd resolve is ta'en,
And fate, or chance, may proffer life in vain;
I scorn whatever safety they provide,
And cast the worthless trifling thought aside.
The sacred rage of death devours me whole,
Reigns in my heart, and triumphs in my soul:
I see, I reach the period of my woe,
And taste those joys the dying only know.
Wisely the gods conceal the wondrous good,
Lest man no longer should endure his load;
Lest every wretch like me from life should fly,
Seize his own happiness himself, and die."

He spoke. The band his potent tongue confest,
And generous ardour burn'd in every breast.
No longer now they view, with watery eyes,
The swift revolving circle of the skies;
No longer think the setting stars in haste,
Nor wonder slow Böotes moves so fast;

But with high hearts exulting all, and gay,
They wish for light, and call the tardy day.
Yet, nor the heavenly axis long delays,
To roll the radiant signs beneath the seas;
In Leda's Twins now rose the warmer Sun,
And near the lofty Crab exalted shone;
Swiftly night's shorter shades began to move,
And to the west Thessalian Chiron drove.
At length the morning's purple beams disclose
The wide horizon cover'd round with foes;
Each rock and shore the crowding Istrians keep,
While Greeks and fierce Liburnians spread the [deep:
When yet, ere fury lets the battle loose,
Octavius wooes them with the terms of truce;
If haply Pompey's chains they choose to wear,
And captive life to instant death prefer.
But the brave youth regardless of his might,
Fierce in the scorn of life, and hating light,
Fearless, and careless of whate'er may come,
Resolv'd and self-determin'd to their doom;
Alike disdain the threatning of the war,
And all the flattering wiles their foes prepare.
Calmly the numerous legions round they view,
At once by land and sea the fight renew;
Relief, or friends, or aid, expect they none,
But fix one certain truth in death alone.
In opposition firm awhile they stood,
But soon were satisfy'd with hostile blood.
Then turning from the foe with gallant pride,
"Is there a generous youth," Vulteius cry'd,
"Whose worthy sword may pierce your leader's [side?"
He said; and at the word, from every part,
A hundred pointed weapons reach'd his heart;
Dying he prais'd them all, but him the chief,
Whose eager duty brought the first relief:
Deep in his breast he plung'd his deadly blade,
And with a grateful stroke the friendly gift repaid.
At once all rush, at once to death they fly,
And on each other's sword alternate die,
Greedy to make the mischief all their own,
And arrogate the guilt of war alone.
A fate like this did Cadmus' harvest prove,
When mortally the earth-born brethren strove;
When by each other's hands of life bereft,
An omen dire to future Thebes they left.
Such was the rage inspir'd the Colchian foes,
When from the dragon's wondrous teeth they rose;
When urg'd by charms, and magic's mystic power,
They dy'd their native field with streaming gore,
Till e'en the fell enchantress stood dismay'd,
And wonder'd at the mischiefs which she made.
Furies more fierce the dying Romans feel,
And with brave breasts provoke the lingering steel;
With fond embraces catch the deadly darts,
And press them plunging to their panting hearts.
No wound imperfect for a second calls;
With certain aim the sure destruction falls.
This last best gift, this one unerring blow,
Sires, sons, and brothers, mutually bestow;
Nor piety, nor fond remorse prevail,
And if they fear, they only fear to fail.
Here with red streams the blushing waves they [stain,
Here dash their mangled entrails in the main.
Here with a last disdain they view the skies,
Shut out Heaven's hated light with scornful eyes,
And, with insulting joy, the victor foe despise.
At length the heapy slaughter rose on high,
The hostile chiefs the purple pile descry;
And while the last accustom'd rites they give,
Scarcely the unexampled deed believe:
Much they admire a faith by death approv'd,
And wonder lawless power could e'er be thus be-lov'd.
Wide through mankind eternal fame displays
This happy crew, this single vessel's praise.
But, oh! the story of the godlike rage
Is lost, upon a vile, degenerate age;
The base, the slavish world will not be taught
With how much ease their freedom may be bought.
Still arbitrary power on thrones commands,
Still liberty is gall'd by tyrants bands,
And swords in vain are trusted to our hands.
O Death! thou pleasing end of human woe,
Thou cure for life, thou greatest good below;
Still may'st thou fly the coward and the slave,
And thy soft slumbers only bless the brave.
Nor war's pernicious god less havoc yields,
Where swarthy Libya spreads her sun-burnt fields.
For Curio now the stretching canvass spread,
And from Sicilian shores his navy led;
To Afric's coast he cuts the foamy way,
Where low the once victorious Carthage lay.
There landing, to the well-known camp he hies,
Where from afar the distant seas he spies;
Where Bagrada's dull waves the sands divide,
And slowly downward roll their sluggish tide.
From thence he seeks the heights renown'd by fame,
And hallow'd by the great Cornelian name:
The rocks and hills which long, traditions say,
Were held by huge Antæus' horrid sway.
Here, as by chance, he lights upon the place,
Curious he tries the reverend tale to trace.
When thus, in short, the ruder Libyans tell,
What from their sires they heard, and how the case befel:
"The teeming Earth, for ever fresh and young,
Yet, after many a giant son, was strong;
When labouring, here, with the prodigious birth,
She brought her youngest-born Antæus forth.
Of all the dreadful brood which erst she bore,
In none the fruitful beldame glory'd more:
Happy for those above, she brought him not
Till after Phlegra's doubtful field was fought.
That this, her darling, might in force excel,
A gift she gave: whene'er to earth he fell,
Recruited strength he from his parent drew,
And every slackening nerve was strung anew.
Yon cave his den he made; where oft for food,
He snatch'd the mother lion's horrid brood.
Nor leaves, nor shaggy hides, his couch prepar'd;
Torn from the tiger, or the spotted pard;
But stretch'd along the naked earth he lies:
New vigour still the native earth supplies:
Whate'er he meets his ruthless hands invade,
Strong in himself, without his mother's aid.
The strangers that unknowing seek the shore,
Soon a worse shipwreck on the land deplore.
Dreadful to all, with matchless might he reigns,
Robs, spoils, and massacres the simple swains,
And all unpeopled lie the Libyan plains.
At length, around the trembling nations spread,
Fame of the tyrant to Alcides fled.
The godlike hero, born by Jove's decree,
To set the seas and earth from monsters free;
Hither in generous pity bent his course,
And set himself to prove the giant's force.
"Now met, the combatants for fight provide,
And either doffs the lion's yellow hide,

Bright in Olympic oil Alcides shone,
Antæus with his mother's dust is strown,
And seeks her friendly force to aid his own.
Now seizing fierce their grasping hands they mix,
And labour on the swelling throat to fix;
Their sinewy arms are writh'd in many a fold,
And, front to front, they threaten stern and bold.
Unmatch d before, each bends a sullen frown,
To find a force thus equal to his own.
At length the godlike victor-Greek prevail'd,
Nor yet the foe with all his force assail'd.
Faint dropping sweats bedew the monster's brows,
And panting thick with heaving sides he blows;
His trembling head the slackening nerves confess'd,
And from the hero shrunk his yielding breast.
The conqueror pursues, his arms entwine,
Infolding gripe, and strain his crashing chine,
While his broad knee bears forceful on his groin.
At once his faltering feet from earth he rends,
And on the sands his mighty length extends.
The parent Earth her vanquish'd son deplores,
And with a touch his vigour lost restores:
From his faint limbs the clammy dew she drains,
And with fresh streams recruits his ebbing veins;
The muscles swell, the hardening sinews rise,
And bursting from th' Herculean grasp he flies.
Astonish'd at the sight Alcides stood:
Nor more he wonder'd, when in Lerna's flood
The dreadful snake her falling heads renew'd.
Of all his various labours, none was seen
With equal joy by Heav'n's unrighteous queen;
Pleas'd she beheld, what toils, what pains he prov'd,
He who had borne the weight of Heaven unmov'd.
Sudden again upon the foe he flew,
The falling foe to earth for aid withdrew;
The Earth again her fainting son supplies,
And with redoubled forces bids him rise:
Her vital powers to succour him she sends,
And Earth herself with Hercules contends.
Conscious at length of such unequal fight,
And that the parent touch renew'd his might,
'No longer shalt thou fall,' Alcides cry'd,
'Henceforth the combat standing shall be try'd;
If thou wilt lean, to me alone incline,
And rest upon no other breast but mine.'
He said; and as he saw the monster stoop,
With mighty arms aloft he rears him up:
No more the distant Earth her son supplies,
Lock'd in the hero's strong embrace he lies;
Nor thence dismiss'd, nor trusted to the ground,
Till death in every frozen limb was found."
Thus, fond of tales, our ancestors of old
The story to their children's children told;
From thence a title to the land they gave,
And call'd this hollow rock Antæus' cave.
But greater deeds this rising mountain grace,
And Scipio's name ennobles much the place;
While, fixing here his famous camp, he calls
Fierce Hannibal from Rome's devoted walls.
As yet the mouldering works remain in view,
Where dreadful once the Latian eagles flew.
Fond of the prosperous victorious name,
And trusting fortune would be still the same,
Hither his hapless ensigns Curio leads,
And here his inauspicious camp he spreads.
A fierce superior foe his arms provoke,
And rob the hills of all their ancient luck.
O'er all the Roman powers in Libya's land,
Then Atius Varus bore supreme command;
Nor trusting in the Latian strength alone,
With foreign force he fortify'd his own;
Summon'd the swarthy monarchs all from far,
And call'd remotest Juba forth to war.
O'er many a country runs his wide command;
To Atlas huge, and G[illegible]des' western strand;
From thence to horned Ammon's fane renown'd,
And the waste Syrts' inhospitable bound:
Southward as far he reigns, and rules alone
The sultry regions of the burning zone.
With him, unnumber'd nations march along,
Th' Autololes with wild Numidians throng;
The rough Getulian, with his ruder steed;
The Moor, resembling India's swarthy breed;
Poor Nasamons, and Garamantines join'd,
With swift Marmaridans that match'd the wind;
The Mazax, bred the trembling dart to throw,
Sure as the shaft that leaves the Parthian bow;
With these Massilia's nimble horsemen ride,
They, not the bit, nor curbing rein provide,
But with light rods the well-taught courser guide.
From lonely cots the Libyan hunters came,
Who still unarm'd invade the savage game,
And with spread mantles tawny lions tame.
But not Rome's fate, nor civil rage alone,
Incite the monarch Pompey's cause to own;
Stung by resenting wrath, the war he sought,
And deep displeasures past by Curio wrought.
He, when the tribune's sacred power he gain'd,
When justice, laws, and gods were all prophan'd,
At Juba's ancient sceptre aim'd his hate,
And strove to rob him of his royal seat:
From a just prince would tear his native right,
While Rome was made a slave to lawless might.
The king, revolving causes from afar,
Looks on himself as party to the war.
That grudge, too well remembering, Curio knew;
To this he joins, his troops to Cæsar new,
None of those old experienc'd faithful bands,
Nurs'd in his fear, and bred to his commands;
But a loose, neutral, light, uncertain train,
Late with Corfinium's captive fortress ta'en,
That wavering pause, and doubt for whom to strike,
Sworn to both sides, and true to both alike.
The careful chief beheld, with anxious heart,
The faithless centinels each night desert:
Then thus, resolving, to himself he cry'd,
"By daring shows our greatest fears we hide:
Then let me haste to bid the battle join,
And lead my army, while it yet is mine;
Leisure and thinking still to change incline.
Let war, and action, busy thought control,
And find a full employment for the soul.
When with drawn swords determin'd soldiers stand,
When shame is lost, and fury prompts the hand,
What reason then can find a time to pause,
To weigh the differing chiefs, and juster cause?
That cause seems only just for which they fight,
Each likes his own, and all are in the right.
On terms like these, within th' appointed space,
Bold gladiators gladiators face:
Unknowing why, like fiercest foes they greet,
And only hate, and kill, because they meet."
He said; and rang'd his troops upon the plain,
While Fortune met him with a semblance vain,
Covering her malice keen, and all his future pain.
Before him Varus' vanquish'd legions yield,
And with dishonest flight forsake the field,

Expos'd to shameful wounds their backs he views,
And to their camp the fearful rout pursues.
Juba with joy the mournful news receives,
And haughty in his own success believes.
Careful his foes in errour to maintain,
And still preserve them confident, and vain;
Silent he marches on in secret sort,
And keeps his numbers close from loud report.
Sabbura, great in the Numidian race,
And second to their swarthy king in place,
First with a chosen slender band precedes,
And seemingly the force of Juba leads:
While hidden he, the prince himself, remains,
And in a secret vale his host constrains.
Thus oft th' ichneumon, on the banks of Nile,
Invades the deadly aspic by a wile;
While artfully his slender tail is play'd,
The serpent darts upon the dancing shade;
Then turning on the foe with swift surprise,
Full at his throat the nimble seizer flies:
The gasping snake expires beneath the wound,
His gushing jaws with poisonous floods abound,
And shed the fruitless mischief on the ground.
Nor Fortune fail'd to favour his intent,
But crown'd the fraud with prosperous event.
Curio, unknowing of the hostile power,
Commands his horse the doubtful plain to scour,
And e'en by night the regions round explore.
Himself, though oft forewarn'd by friendly care,
Of Punic frauds, and danger to beware,
Soon as the dawn of early day was broke,
His camp, with all the moving foot, forsook.
It seem'd, necessity inspir'd the deed,
And fate requir'd the daring youth should bleed.
War, that curst war which he himself begun,
To death and ruin drove him headlong on.
O'er devious rocks, long time, his way he takes,
Through rugged paths, and rude encumbering brakes;
Till, from afar, at length the hills disclose,
Assembling on their heights, his distant foes.
Oft hasty flight with swift retreat they feign,
To draw th' unwary leader to the plain.
He, rash and ignorant of Libyan wiles,
Wide o'er the naked champaign spreads his files;
When, sudden, all the circling mountains round
With numberless Numidians thick are crown'd;
At once the rising ambush stands confess'd,
And dread strikes cold on every Roman breast.
Helpless they view th' impending danger nigh,
Nor can the valiant fight, nor coward fly.
The weary horse neglects the trumpet's sound,
Nor with impatient ardour paws the ground;
No more he champs the bit, nor tugs the rein,
Nor pricks his ears, nor shakes his flowing mane:
With foamy sweat his smoking limbs are spread,
And all o'er-labour'd hangs his heavy head;
Hoarse, and with pantings thick, his breath he draws,
While ropy filth begrimes his clammy jaws;
Careless the rider's heartening voice he hears,
And motionless the wounding spur he bears.
At length, by swords and goading darts compell'd,
Dronish he drags his load across the field;
Nor once attempts to charge, but drooping goes,
To bear his dying lord amidst his foes.
Not so the Libyans fierce their onset make;
With thundering hoofs the sandy soil they shake;
Thick o'er the battle wavy clouds arise,
As when through Thrace Bistonian Boreas flies,
Involves the day in dust, and darkens all the skies.
And now the Latian foot encompass'd round,
Are massacred, and trodden to the ground;
None in resistance vainly prove their might,
But death is all the business of the fight.
Thicker than hail the steely showers descend;
Beneath the weight the falling Romans bend.
On every side the shrinking front grows less,
And to the centre madly all they press:
Fear, uproar, and dismay, increase the cry,
Crushing, and crush'd, an armed crowd they die;
E'en thronging on their fellows' swords they run,
And the foe's business by themselves is done.
But the fierce Moors disdain a crowd should share
The praise of conquest, or the task of war:
Rivers of blood they wish, and hills of slain,
With mangled carcasses to strow the plain.
Genius of Carthage! rear thy drooping head,
And view thy fields with Roman slaughter spread.
Behold, O Hannibal, thou hostile shade!
A large amends by Fortune's hand is made,
And the lost Punic blood is well repaid.
Thus do the gods the cause of Pompey bless?
Thus! is it thus, they give our arms success?
Take, Afric, rather take the horrid good,
And make thy own advantage of our blood.
The dust, at length, in crimson floods was laid,
And Curio now the dreadful field survey'd.
He saw 't was lost, and knew in vain to strive,
Yet bravely scorn'd to fly, or to survive;
And though thus driven to death, he met it well,
And in a crowd of dying Romans fell.
Now what avail thy popular arts and fame,
Thy restless mind that shook thy country's frame;
Thy moving tongue that knew so well to charm,
And urge the madding multitude to arm?
What boots it, to have sold the senate's right,
And driven the furious leaders on to fight?
Thou the first victim of thy war art slain,
Nor shalt thou see Pharsalia's fatal plain.
Behold! ye potent troublers of the state,
What wretched ends on curst ambition wait!
See! where a prey, unbury'd Curio lies,
To every fowl that wings the Libyan skies.
Oh! were the gods as gracious as severe,
Were liberty, like vengeance, still their care;
Then, Rome! what days, what people might'st thou see,
If Providence would equally decree,
To punish tyrants, and preserve thee free.
Nor yet, O generous Curio! shall my verse
Forget, thy praise, thy virtues, to rehearse:
Thy virtues, which with envious time shall strive,
And to succeeding ages long survive.
In all our pregnant mother's tribes, before,
A son of nobler hope she never bore:
A soul more bright, more great, she never knew,
While to thy country's interest thou wert true.
But thy bad fate o'er-rul'd thy native worth,
And in an age abandon'd brought thee forth;
When vice in triumph through the city pass'd,
And dreadful wealth and power laid all things waste.
The sweeping stream thy better purpose cross'd,
And in the headlong torrent wert thou lost.
Much to the ruin of the state was done,
When Curio by the Gallic spoils was won;
Curio, the hope of Rome, and her most worthy son.
Tyrants of old, whom former times record,
Who rul'd, and ravag'd with the murdering sword;
Sylla, whom such unbounded power made proud;
Marius, and Cinna, red with Roman blood;

E'en Cæsar's mighty race who lord it now,
Before whose throne the subject nations bow,
All bought that power which lavish Curio sold,
Curio, who barter'd liberty for gold.

BOOK V.

THE ARGUMENT.

In Epirus the consuls assemble the senate, who unanimously appoint Pompey general of the war against Cæsar, and decree public thanks to the several princes and states who assisted the commonwealth. Appius, at that time prætor of Achaia, consults the oracle of Delphos concerning the event of the civil war. And, upon this occasion, the poet goes into a digression concerning the origin, the manner of the delivery, and the present silence of that oracle. From Spain, Cæsar returns into Italy, where he quells a mutiny in his army, and punishes the offenders. From Placentia, where this disorder happened, he orders them to march to Brundusium; where, after a short turn to Rome, and assuming the consulship, or rather the supreme power, he joins them himself. From Brundusium, though it was then the middle of winter, he transports part of his army by sea to Epirus, and lands at Palæste. Pompey, who then lay about Candavia, hearing of Cæsar's arrival, and being in pain for Dyrrachium, marched that way: on the banks of the river Apsus they met and encamped close together. Cæsar was not yet joined by that part of his troops which he had left behind him at Brundusium, under the command of Mark Anthony; and being uneasy at his delays, leaves his camp by night, and ventures over a tempestuous sea in a small bark to hasten the transport. Upon Cæsar joining his forces together, Pompey perceived that the war would now probably be soon decided by a battle; and upon that consideration, resolved to send his wife to expect the event at Lesbos. Their parting, which is extremely moving, concludes this book.

Thus equal, Fortune holds awhile the scale,
And bids the leading chiefs by turns prevail;
In doubt the goddess, yet, their fate detains,
And keeps them for Emathia's fatal plains.
And now the setting Pleiades grew low,
The hills stood hoary in December's snow;
The solemn season was approaching near,
When other names renew'd the Fasti wear,
And double Janus leads the coming year.
The consuls, while their rods they yet retain'd,
While, yet, some show of liberty remain'd,
With missives round the scatter'd fathers greet,
And in Epirus bid the senate meet.
There the great rulers of the Roman state,
In foreign seats, consulting, meanly sate.
No face of war the grave assembly wears,
But civil power in peaceful pomp appears:
The purple order to their place resort,
While waiting lictors guard the crowded court.
No faction these, nor party, seem to be,
But a full senate, legal, just, and free.
Great, as he is, here Pompey stands confest
A private man, and one among the rest.
Their mutual groans, at length, and murmurs cease,
And every mournful sound is hush'd in peace;
When from the consular distinguish'd throne,
Sublimely rais'd, thus Lentulus begun.
"If yet our Roman virtue is the same,
Yet worthy of the race from which we came,
And emulates our great forefathers name,
Let not our thoughts, by sad remembrance led,
Bewail those captive walls from whence we fled.
This time demands, that to ourselves we turn,
Nor, fathers, have we leisure now to mourn;
But let each early care, each honest heart,
Our senate's sacred dignity assert.
To all around proclaim it, wide, and near,
That power which kings obey, and nations fear,
That only legal power of Rome, is here.
For whether to the northern Bear we go,
Where pale she glitters o'er eternal snow;
Or whether in those sultry climes we burn,
Where night and day with equal hours return;
The world shall still acknowledge us its head,
And empire follow whereso'er we lead.
When Gallic flames the burning city felt,
At Veiæ Rome with her Camillus dwelt.
Beneath forsaken roofs proud Cæsar reigns,
Our vacant courts, and silent laws constrains;
While slaves obedient to his tyrant will,
Outlaws, and profligates, his senate fill;
With him a banish'd guilty crowd appear,
All that are just and innocent are here.
Dispers'd by war, though guiltless of its crimes,
Our order yielded to these impious times;
At length returning each from his retreat,
In happy hour the scatter'd members meet.
The gods and Fortune greet us on the way,
And with the world lost Italy repay.
Upon Illyria's favourable coast,
Vulteius with his furious band are lost;
While in bold Curio, on the Libyan plain,
One half of Cæsar's senators lie slain.
March then, ye warriors! second fate's design,
And to the leading gods your ardour join,
With equal constancy to battle come,
As when you shunn'd the foe, and left your native Rome.
The period of the consuls power is near,
Who yield our fasces with the ending year:
But you, ye fathers, whom we still obey,
Who rule mankind with undetermin'd sway,
Attend the public weal, with faithful care,
And bid our greatest Pompey lead the war."
In loud applause the pleas'd assembly join,
And to the glorious task the chief assign:
His country's fate they trust to him alone,
And bid him fight Rome's battles, and his own.
Next, to their friends their thanks are dealt around,
And some with gifts, and some with praise are crown'd:
Of these the chief are Rhodes, by Phœbus lov'd,
And Sparta rough, in virtue's lore approv'd.
Of Athens much they speak; Massilia's aid
Is with her parent Phocis' freedom paid.
Deiotarus his truth they much commend,
Their still unshaken faithful Asian friend.
Brave Cotys and his valiant son they grace,
With bold Rhasipolis from stormy Thrace.
While gallant Juba justly is decreed
To his paternal sceptre to succeed.
And thou too, Ptolemy, (unrighteous fate!)
Wert rais'd unworthy to the regal state;

The crown upon thy perjur'd temples shone
That once was borne by Philip's godlike son.
O'er Egypt shakes the boy his cruel sword:
(Oh! that he had been only Egypt's lord!)
But the dire gift more dreadful mischiefs wait,
While Lago's sceptre gives him Pompey's fate:
Preventing Cæsar's, and his sister's hand,
He seiz'd his parricide, and her command.
  Th' assembly rose, and all on war intent
Bustle to arms, and blindly wait th' event.
Appius alone, impatient to be taught
With what the threatening future times were fraught,
With busy curiosity explores
The dreadful purpose of the heavenly powers.
To Delphos straight he flies, where long the god
In silence had possess'd his close abode;
His oracles had long been known to cease,
And the prophetic virgin liv'd in peace.
  Between the ruddy west and eastern skies,
In the mid-earth Parnassus' tops arise:
To Phœbus, and the cheerful god of wine,
Sacred in common stands the hill divine.
Still as the third revolving year comes round,
The Mænades, with leafy chaplets crown'd,
The double deity in solemn songs resound.
When, o'er the world, the deluge wide was spread,
This only mountain rear'd his lofty head;
One rising rock, preserv'd, a bound was given,
Between the vasty deep, and ambient Heaven.
Here, to revenge long-vex'd Latona's pain,
Python by infant Pæan's darts was slain,
While yet the realm was held by Themis' righteous reign.
But when the god perceiv'd, how from below
The conscious caves diviner breathings blow,
How vapours could unfold th' inquirer's doom,
And talking winds could speak of things to come;
Deep in the hollows plunging he retir'd,
There, with foretelling fury first inspir'd,
From hence the prophet's art and honours he acquir'd.
  So runs the tale. And oh! what god indeed
Within this gloomy cavern's depth is hid?
What power divine forsakes the Heaven's fair light,
To dwell with Earth, and everlasting night?
What is this spirit, potent, wise, and great,
Who deigns to make a mortal frame his seat;
Who the long chain of secret causes knows,
Whose oracles the years to come disclose;
Who through eternity at once foresees,
And tells that fate which he himself decrees?
Part of that soul, perhaps, which moves in all,
Whose energy informs the pendent ball,
Through this dark passage seeks the realms above,
And strives to re-unite itself to Jove.
Whate'er the demon, when he stands confest
Within his raging priestess' panting breast,
Dreadful his godhead from the virgin breaks,
And thundering from her foamy mouth he speaks.
Such is the burst of bellowing Ætna's sound,
When fair Sicilia's pastures shake around;
Such from Inarimè Typhœus roars,
While rattling rocks bestrew Campania's shores.
  The listening god, still ready with replies,
To none his aid, or oracle, denies;
Yet, wise and righteous ever, scorns to hear
The fool's fond wishes, or the guilty's prayer;
Though vainly in repeated vows they trust,
None e'er find grace before him, but the just.
Oft to a banish'd, wandering, houseless race,
The sacred dictates have assign'd a place.
Oft from the strong he saves the weak in war:
This truth, ye Salaminian seas, declare!
And heals the barren land, and pestilential air.
Of all the wants with which this age is curst,
The Delphic silence surely is the worst.
But tyrants, justly fearful of their doom,
Forbid the gods to tell us what's to come.
Meanwhile, the prophetess may well rejoice,
And bless the ceasing of the sacred voice:
Since death too oft her holy task attends,
And immature her dreadful labour ends.
Torn by the fierce distracting rage she springs,
And dies beneath the god for whom she sings.
  These silent caves, these tripods long unmov'd,
Anxious for Rome, inquiring Appius prov'd:
He bids the guardian of the dread abode
Send in the trembling priestess to the god.
The reverend sire the Latian chief obey'd,
And sudden seiz'd the unsuspecting maid,
Where careless in the peaceful grove she stray'd.
Dismay'd, aghast, and pale, he drags her on;
She stops, and strives the fatal task to shun:
Subdu'd by force, to fraud and art she flies,
And thus to turn the Roman's purpose tries:
"What curious hopes thy wandering fancy move,
The silent Delphic oracle to prove?
In vain, Ausonian Appius, art thou come:
Long has our Phœbus and his cave been dumb.
Whether, disdaining us, the sacred voice
Has made some other distant land its choice;
Or whether, when the fierce barbarians' fires
Low in the dust had laid our lofty spires,
In heaps the mouldering ashes heavy rod,
And chok'd the channels of the breathing god:
Or whether Heaven no longer gives replies,
But bids the Sibyls mystic verse suffice;
Or, if he deigns not this bad age to bear,
And holds the world unworthy of his care;
Whate'er the cause, our god has long been mute,
And answers not to any suppliant's suit."
  But, ah! too well her artifice is known,
Her fears confess the god, whom they disown.
Howe'er each rite she seemingly prepares;
A fillet gathers up her foremost hairs;
While the white wreath and bays her temples bind,
And knit the looser locks which flow behind.
Sudden, the stronger priest, though yet she strives,
The lingering maid within the temple drives:
But still she fears, still shuns the dreadful shrine,
Lags in the outer space, and feigns the rage divine.
But far unlike the god, her calmer breast
No strong enthusiastic throes confest;
No terrours in her starting hairs were seen
To cast from off her brow the wreathing green;
No broken accents half obstructed hung,
Nor swelling murmurs roll her labouring tongue.
From her fierce jaws no sounding horrours come,
No thunders bellow through the working foam,
To rend the spacious cave, and shake the vaulted dome.
Too plain, the peaceful groves and fane betray'd
The wily, fearful, god-dissembling maid.
The furious Roman soon the fraud espy'd,
And, "Hope not thou to 'scape my rage," he cry'd;
"Sore shalt thou rue thy fond deceit, profane,
(The gods and Appius are not mock'd in vain)
Unless thou cease thy mortal sounds to tell,
Unless thou plunge thee in the mystic cell,

Unless the gods themselves reveal the doom,
Which shall befall the warring world and Rome."
He spoke, and, aw'd by the superior dread,
The trembling priestess to the tripod fled:
Close to the holy breathing vent she cleaves,
And largely the unwonted god receives.
Nor age the potent spirit had decay'd,
But with full force he fills the heaving maid;
Nor e'er so strong inspiring Pæan came,
Nor stretch'd, as now, her agonizing frame:
The mortal mind driv'n out forsook her breast,
And the sole godhead every part possest.
Now swell her veins, her turgid sinews rise,
And bounding frantic through the cave she flies;
Her bristling locks the wreathy fillet scorn,
And her fierce feet the tumbling tripods spurn.
Now wild she dances o'er the vacant fane,
And whirls her giddy head, and bellows with the [pain.
Nor yet the less th' avenging wrathful god
Pours in his fires, and shakes his sounding rod:
He lashes now, and goads her on amain;
And now he checks her stubborn to the rein,
Curbs in her tongue, just labouring to disclose,
And speak that fate which in her bosom glows.
Ages on ages throng, a painful load,
Myriads of images, and myriads crowd;
Men, times, and things, or present, or to come,
Work labouring up and down, and urge for room.
Whatever is, shall be, or e'er has been,
Rolls in her thought, and to her sight is seen.
The ocean's utmost bounds her eyes explore,
And number every sand on every shore;
Nature, and all her works, at once they see,
Know when she first begun, and when her end shall be.
And as the Sibyl once in Cumæ's cell,
When vulgar fates she proudly ceas'd to tell,
The Roman destiny distinguish'd took,
And kept it careful in her sacred book;
So now, Phemonoë, in crowds of thought,
The single doom of Latian Appius sought.
Nor in that mass, where multitudes abound,
A private fortune can with ease be found.
At length her foamy mouth begins to flow,
Groans more distinct, and plainer murmurs go:
A doleful howl the roomy cavern shook,
And thus the calmer maid in fainting accents spoke:
"While guilty rage the world tumultuous rends,
In peace for thee, Eubœa's vale attends;
Thither, as to thy refuge shalt thou fly,
There find repose, and unmolested lie."
She said; the god her labouring tongue suppress,
And in eternal darkness veil'd the rest.
Ye sacred tripods, on whose doom we wait!
Ye guardians of the future laws of fate!
And thou, O Phœbus! whose prophetic skill
Reads the dark counsels of the heavenly will;
Why did your wary oracles refrain,
To tell what kings, what heroes must be slain,
And how much blood the blushing earth should stain?
Was it that, yet, the guilt was undecree'd?
That yet our Pompey was not doom'd to bleed?
Or chose you wisely, rather, to afford
A just occasion to the patriot's sword?
As if you fear'd t' avert the tyrant's doom,
And hinder Brutus from avenging Rome?
Through the wide gates at length by force dis-[play'd,
Impetuous sallies the prophetic maid;
Nor yet the holy rage was all suppress'd,
Part of the god still heaving in her breast:
Urg'd by the demon, yet she rolls her eyes,
And wildly wanders o'er the spacious skies.
Now horrid purple flushes in her face,
And now a livid pale supplies the place;
A double madness paints her cheeks by turns,
With fear she freezes, and with fury burns:
Sad breathing sighs with heavy accent go,
And doleful from her fainting bosom blow.
So when no more the storm sonorous sings,
But noisy Boreas hangs his weary wings;
In hollow groans the falling winds complain,
And murmur o'er the hoarse-resounding main.
Now by degrees the fire ethereal fail'd,
And the dull human sense again prevail'd;
While Phœbus sudden, in a murky shade,
Hid the past vision from the mortal maid.
Thick clouds of dark oblivion rise between,
And snatch away at once the wondrous scene;
Stretch'd on the ground the fainting priestess lies,
While to the tripod, back, th' informing spirit flies.
Meanwhile, fond Appius, erring in his fate,
Dream'd of long safety, and a neutral state;
And, ere the great event of war was known,
Fix'd on Eubœan Chalcis for his own.
Fool! to believe that power could ward the blow,
Or snatch thee from amidst the general woe!
In times like these, what god but death can save?
The world can yield no refuge, but the grave.
Where struggling seas Charystos rude constrains,
And, dreadful to the proud, Rhamnusia reigns;
Where by the whirling current barks are tost
From Chalcis to unlucky Aulis' coast;
There shall thou meet the gods' appointed doom,
A private death, and long remember'd tomb.
To other wars the victor now succeeds,
And his proud eagles from Iberia leads:
When the chang'd gods his ruin seem'd to threat,
And cross the long successful course of fate.
Amidst his camp, and fearless of his foes,
Sudden he saw where inborn dangers rose,
He saw those troops that long had faithful stood,
Friends to his cause, and enemies to good,
Grown weary of their chief, and satiated with blood.
Whether the trumpet's sound too long had ceas'd,
And slaughter slept in unaccustomed rest:
Or whether, arrogant by mischief made,
The soldier held his guilt but half repaid:
Whilst avarice and hope of bribes prevail,
Turn against Cæsar, and his cause, the scale,
And set the mercenary sword to sale.
Nor, e'er before, so truly could he read
What dangers strow those paths the mighty tread,
Then, first he found, on what a faithless base
Their nodding towers ambition's builders place:
He who so late, a potent faction's head,
Drew in the nations, and the legions led;
Now stript of all, beheld in every hand
The warriors' weapons at their own command;
Nor service now, nor safety they afford,
But leave him single to his guardian sword.
Nor is this rage the grumbling of a crowd,
That shun to tell their discontents aloud;
Where all with gloomy looks suspicious go,
And dread of an informer chokes their woe:
But, bold in numbers, proudly they appear,
And scorn the bashful mean restraints of fear.

For laws, in great rebellions, lose their end,
And all go free, when multitudes offend.
Among the rest, one thus: "At length 't is time
To quit thy cause, O Cæsar! and our crime:
The world around for foes thou hast explor'd,
And lavishly expos'd us to the sword;
To make thee great, a worthless crowd we fall,
Scatter'd o'er Spain, o'er Italy, and Gaul;
In every clime beneath the spacious sky,
Our leader conquers, and his soldiers die.
What boots our march beneath the frozen zone,
Or that lost blood which stains the Rhine and Rhone?
When scarr'd with wounds, and worn with labours hard,
We come with hopes of recompense prepar'd,
Thou giv'st us war, more war, for our reward.
Though purple rivers in thy cause we spilt,
And stain'd our horrid hands in every guilt;
With unavailing wickedness we toil'd,
In vain the gods, in vain the senate spoil'd;
Of virtue, and reward, alike bereft,
Our pious poverty is all we 've left.
Say to what height thy daring arms would rise?
If Rome's too little, what can e'er suffice?
Oh, see at length! with pity, Cæsar, see
These withering arms, these hairs grown white for thee.
In painful wars our joyless days have past,
Let weary age lie down in peace at last:
Give us, on beds, our dying limbs to lay,
And sigh, at home, our parting souls away.
Nor think it much we make the bold demand,
And ask this wondrous favour at thy hand:
Let our poor babes and weeping wives be by,
To close our drooping eyelids when we die.
Be merciful, and let disease afford
Some other way to die, beside the sword;
Let us no more a common carnage burn,
But each be laid in his own decent urn.
Still wilt thou urge us, ignorant and blind,
To some more monstrous mischief yet behind?
Are we the only fools, forbid to know
How much we may deserve by one sure blow?
Thy head, thy head is ours, whene'er we please;
Well has thy war inspir'd such thoughts as these:
What laws, what oaths, can urge their feeble bands,
To hinder these determin'd daring hands?
That Cæsar, who was once ordain'd our head,
When to the Rhine our lawful arms he led,
Is now no more our chieftain, but our mate;
Guilt equal, gives equality of state.
Nor shall his foul ingratitude prevail,
Nor weigh our merits in his partial scale;
He views our labours with a scornful glance,
And calls our victories the works of chance:
But his proud heart, henceforth, shall learn to own
His power, his fate, depends on us alone.
Yes, Cæsar, spite of all those rods that wait,
With mean obsequious service, on thy state;
Spite of thy gods, and thee, the war shall cease,
And we thy soldiers will command a peace."
He spoke, and fierce tumultuous rage inspir'd,
The kindling legions round the camp were fir'd,
And with loud cries their absent chief requir'd.
Permit it thus, ye righteous gods, to be;
Let wicked hands fulfil your great decree;
And, since lost faith and virtue are no more,
Let Cæsar's bands the public peace restore.
What leader had not now been chill'd with fear,
And heard this tumult with the last despair?
But Cæsar, form'd for perils hard and great,
Headlong to drive, and brave opposing fate,
While yet with fiercest fires their furies flame,
Secure, and scornful of the danger, came.
Nor was he wroth to see the madness rise,
And mark the vengeance threatening in their eyes;
With pleasure could he crown their curst designs,
With rapes of matrons and the spoils of shrines;
Had they but ask'd it, well he could approve
The waste and plunder of Tarpeian Jove:
No mischief he, no sacrilege, denies,
But would himself bestow the horrid prize.
With joy he sees their souls by rage possest,
Sooths and indulges every frantic breast,
And only fears what reason may suggest.
Still, Cæsar, wilt thou tread the paths of blood?
Wilt thou, thou singly, hate thy country's good?
Shall the rude soldier first of war complain,
And teach thee to be pitiful in vain?
Give o'er at length, and let thy labours cease,
Nor vex the world, but learn to suffer peace.
Why shouldst thou force each, now, unwilling hand,
And drive them on to guilt, by thy command?
When e'en relenting rage itself gives place,
And fierce Enyo seems to shun thy face."
High on a turfy bank the chief was rear'd,
Fearless, and therefore worthy to be fear'd;
Around the crowd he cast an angry look,
And, dreadful, thus with indignation spoke:
"Ye noisy herd! who in so fierce a strain
Against your absent leader dare complain;
Behold! where naked and unarm'd he stands,
And braves the malice of your threatening hands.
Here find your end of war, your long-sought rest,
And leave your useless swords in Cæsar's breast.
But wherefore urge I the bold deed to you?
To rail, is all your feeble rage can do.
In grumbling factions are you bold and loud,
Can sow sedition, and increase a crowd;
You! who can loath the glories of the great,
And poorly meditate a base retreat.
But, hence! be gone from victory and me,
Leave me to what my better fates decree:
New friends, new troops, my fortune shall afford,
And find a hand for every vacant sword.
Behold, what crowds on flying Pompey wait,
What multitudes attend his abject state!
And shall success, and Cæsar, droop the while?
Shall I want numbers to divide the spoil,
And reap the fruits of your forgotten toil?
Legions shall come to end the bloodless war,
And shouting follow my triumphal car.
While you, a vulgar, mean, abandon'd race,
Shall view our honours with a downward face,
And curse yourselves in secret as we pass.
Can your vain aid, can your departing force,
Withhold my conquest, or delay my course?
So trickling brooks their waters may deny,
And hope to leave the mighty ocean dry;
The deep shall still be full, and scorn the poor supply.
Nor think such vulgar souls as yours were given,
To be the task of fate, and care of Heaven:
Few are the lordly, the distinguish'd great,
On whom the watchful gods, like guardians, wait:
The rest for common use were all design'd,
An unregarded rabble of mankind.

By my auspicious name, and fortune, led,
Wide o'er the world your conquering arms were spread,
But say, what had you done, with Pompey at your head?
Vast was the fame by Labienus won,
When, rank'd amidst my warlike friends, he shone:
Now mark what follows on his faithful change,
And see him with his chief new-chosen range;
By land, and sea, where'er my arms he spies,
An ignominious runagate he flies.
Such shall you prove. Nor is it worth my care,
Whether to Pompey's aid your arms you bear:
Who quits his leader, wheresoe'er he go,
Flies like a traitor, and becomes my foe.
Yes, ye great gods! your kinder care I own,
You made the faith of these false legions known:
You warn me well to change these coward bands,
Nor trust my fate to such betraying hands.
And thou too, Fortune, point'st me out the way,
A mighty debt, thus, cheaply to repay;
Henceforth my care regards myself alone,
War's glorious gain shall now be all my own.
For you, ye vulgar herd, in peace return,
My ensigns shall by manly hands be borne.
Some few of you my sentence here shall wait,
And warn succeeding factions by your fate.
Down! groveling down to earth, ye traitors, bend,
And with your prostrate necks, my doom attend.
And you, ye younger striplings of the war,
You, whom I mean to make my future care;
Strike home! to blood, to death, inure your hands,
And learn to execute my dread commands."

He spoke; and, at the impious sound dismay'd,
The trembling unresisting crowd obey'd:
No more their late equality they boast,
But bend beneath his frown a suppliant host.
Singly secure, he stands confess'd their lord,
And rules, in spite of him, the soldier's sword.
Doubtful, at first, their patience he surveys,
And wonders why each haughty heart obeys;
Beyond his hopes he sees the stubborn bow,
And bare their breasts obedient to the blow;
Till e'en his cooler thoughts the deed disclaim,
And would not find their fiercer souls so tame.
A few, at length, selected from the rest,
Bled for example; and the tumult ceas'd;
While the consenting host the victims view'd,
And, in that blood, their broken faith renew'd.

Now to Brundusium's walls he bids them tend,
Where ten long days their weary marches end;
There he commands assembling barks to meet,
And furnish from the neighbouring shores his fleet.
Thither the crooked keels from Leuca glide,
From Taras old, and Hydrus' winding tide;
Thither with swelling sails their way they take,
From lowly Sipus, and Salapia's lake;
From where Apulia's fruitful mountains rise,
Where high along the coast Garganus lies,
And beating seas and fighting winds defies.

Meanwhile the chief to Rome directs his way,
Now fearful, aw'd, and fashion'd to his sway.
There, with mock prayers, the suppliant vulgar wait,
And urge on him the great dictator's state.
Obedient he, since thus their wills ordain,
A gracious tyrant condescends to reign.
His mighty name the joyful Fasti wear,
Worthy to usher in the curst Pharsalian year.
Then was the time, when sycophants began
To heap all titles on one lordly man;
Then learn'd our sires that fawning lying strain,
Which we, their slavish sons, so well retain:
Then, first, were seen to join, an ill-match'd pair,
The axe of justice, with the sword of war;
Fasces, and eagles, mingling, march along,
And in proud Cæsar's train promiscuous throng.
And while all powers in him alone unite,
He mocks the people with the shows of right.
The Martian field th' assembling tribes receives,
And each his unregarded suffrage gives;
Still with the same solemnity of face,
The reverend augur seems to fill his place:
Though now he hears not when the thunders roll,
Nor sees the flight of the ill-boding owl.
Then sunk the state and dignity of Rome,
Thence monthly consuls nominally come:
Just as the sovereign bids, their names appear,
To head the calendar, and mark the year.
Then too, to finish out the pageant show,
With formal rites to Alban Jove they go;
By night the festival was huddled o'er,
Nor could the god, unworthy, ask for more;
He who look'd on, and saw such foul disgrace,
Such slavery befall his Trojan race.

Now Cæsar, like the flame that cuts the skies,
And swifter than the vengeful tigress, flies
Where waste and overgrown Apulia lies;
O'erpassing soon the rude abandon'd plains,
Brundusium's crooked shores, and Cretan walls he gains.
Loud Boreas there his navy close confines,
While wary seamen dread the wintery signs.
But he, th' impatient chief, disdains to spare
Those hours that better may be spent in war:
He grieves to see his ready fleet withheld,
While others boldly plow the watery field.
Eager to rouse their sloth, "Behold," he cries,
"The constant wind that rules the wintery skies,
With what a settled certainty it flies!
Unlike the wanton fickle gales, that bring
The cloudy changes of the faithless spring.
Nor need we now to shift, to tack, and veer:
Steady the friendly north commands to steer.
Oh! that the fury of the driving blast
May swell the sail, and bend the lofty mast!
So, shall our navy soon be wafted o'er,
Ere yon Phæacian galleys dip the oar,
And intercept the wish'd-for Grecian shore.
Cut every cable then, and haste away;
The waiting winds and seas upbraid our long delay.

Low in the west the setting Sun was laid,
Up rose the night in glittering stars array'd,
And silver Cynthia cast a lengthening shade;
When loosing from the shore the moving fleet,
All hands at once unfurl the spreading sheet;
The slacker tacklings let the canvass flow,
To gather all the breath the winds can blow.
Swift, for a while, they scud before the wind,
And leave Hesperia's lessening shores behind;
When, lo! the dying breeze begins to fail,
And flutters on the mast the flagging sail:
The duller waves with slower heavings creep,
And a dead calm benumbs the lazy deep.
As when the winter's potent breath constrains
The Scythian Euxine in her icy chains;
No more the Bosphori their streams maintain,
Nor rushing Ister heaves the languid main;
Each keel enclos'd, at once forgets its course,
While o'er the new-made champaign bounds the horse:

Bold on the crystal plains the Thracians ride,
And print with sounding keels the stable tide.
So still a form th' Ionian waters take,
Dull as the muddy marsh and standing lake:
No breezes o'er the curling surface pass,
Nor sun-beams tremble in the liquid glass;
No usual turns revolving Tethys knows,
Nor with alternate rollings ebbs and flows:
But sluggish ocean sleeps in stupid peace,
And weary nature's motions seem to cease.
With differing eyes the hostile fleets beheld
The falling winds, and useless watery field.
There Pompey's daring powers attempt in vain
To plough their passage through th' unyielding main;
While, pinch'd by want, proud Cæsar's legions here
The dire distress of meagre famine fear.
With vows unknown before they reach the skies,
That waves may dash, and mounting billows rise;
That storms may with returning fury reign,
And the rude ocean be itself again.
At length the still, the sluggish darkness fled,
And cloudy morning rear'd its low'ring head.
The rolling flood the gliding navy bore,
And hills appear'd to pass upon the shore.
Attending breezes waft them to the land,
And Cæsar's anchors bite Palæste's strand.
 In neighbouring camps the hostile chiefs sit down,
Where Genusus the swift, and Apsus run;
Among th' ignobler crowd of rivers, these
Soon lose their waters in the mingling seas:
No mighty streams nor distant springs they know,
But rise from muddy lakes, and melting snow.
Here meet the rivals who the world divide,
Once by the tenderest bands of kindred ty'd.
The world with joy their interview beheld,
Now only parted by a single field.
Fond of the hopes of peace, mankind believe,
Whene'er they come thus near, they must forgive.
Vain hopes! for soon they part to meet no more,
Till both shall reach the curst Ægyptian shore;
Till the proud father shall in arms succeed,
And see his vanquish'd son untimely bleed;
Till he beholds his ashes on the strand,
Views his pale head within a villain's hand;
Till Pompey's fate shall Cæsar's tears demand.
 The latter yet his eager rage restrains,
While Antony the lingering troops detains.
Repining much, and griev'd at war's delay,
Impatient Cæsar often chides his stay,
Oft he is heard to threat, and humbly oft to pray.
 "Still shall the world," he cries, "thus anxious wait?
Still wilt thou stop the gods, and hinder fate?
What could be done before, was done by me:
Now ready fortune only stays for thee.
What holds thee then? Do rocks thy course withstand,
Or Libyan Syrts oppose their faithless strand?
Or dost thou fear new dangers to explore?
I call thee not, but where I pass'd before.
For all those hours thou losest, I complain,
And sue to Heaven for prosperous winds in vain.
My soldiers (often has their faith been try'd),
If not withheld, had hasten'd to my side.
What toil, what hazards will they not partake?
What seas and shipwrecks scorn, for Cæsar's sake?
Nor will I think the gods so partial are,
To give thee fair Ausonia for thy share;
While Cæsar, and the senate, are forgot,
And in Epirus bound their barren lot."
 In words like these, he calls him oft in vain,
And thus the hasty missives oft complain.
At length the lucky chief, who oft had found
What vast success his rasher darings crown'd;
Who saw how much the favouring gods had done,
Nor would be wanting, when they urg'd him on;
Fierce, and impatient of the tedious stay,
Resolves by night to prove the doubtful way:
Bold, in a single skiff, he means to go,
And tempt those seas that navies dare not plough.
 'Twas now the time when cares and labour cease,
And e'en the rage of arms was hush'd to peace:
Snatch'd from their guilt and toil, the wretched lay,
And slept the sounder for the painful day.
Through the still camp the night's third hour resounds,
And warns the second watches to their rounds;
When through the horrours of the murky shade,
Secret the careful warrior's footsteps tread.
His train, unknowing, slept within his tent,
And Fortune only follow'd where he went.
With silent anger he perceiv'd, around,
The sleepy centinels bestrew the ground:
Yet, unreproving, now, he pass'd them o'er,
And sought with eager haste the winding shore.
There through the gloom his searching eyes explor'd,
Where to the mouldering rock a bark was moor'd.
The mighty master of this little boat
Securely slept within a neighbouring cot:
No massy beams support his humble hall,
But reeds and marshy rushes wove the wall;
Old shatter'd planking for a roof was spread,
And cover'd in from rain the needy shed.
Thrice on the feeble door the warrior struck,
Beneath the blow the trembling dwelling shook.
"What wretch forlorn," the poor Amyclas cries,
"Driven by the raging seas, and stormy skies,
To my poor lowly roof for shelter flies?"
He spoke; and hasty left his homely bed,
With oozy flags and withering sea-weed spread.
Then from the hearth his smoking match he takes,
And in the tow the drowsy fire awakes;
Dry leaves, and chips, for fuel, he supplies,
Till kindling sparks and glittering flames arise.
O happy poverty! thou greatest good,
Bestow'd by Heaven, but seldom understood!
Here nor the cruel spoiler seeks his prey,
Nor ruthless armies take their dreadful way:
Security thy narrow limits keeps,
Safe are thy cottages, and sound thy sleeps.
Behold! ye dangerous dwellings of the great,
Where gods and godlike princes choose their seat;
See in what peace the poor Amyclas lies,
Nor starts, though Cæsar's call commands to rise.
What terrours had you felt, that call to hear!
How had your towers and ramparts shook with fear,
And trembled as the mighty man drew near!
The door unbarr'd: "Expect," the leader said,
"Beyond thy hopes, or wishes, to be paid;
If in this instant hour thou waft me o'er,
With speedy haste, to yon Hesperian shore.
No more shall want thy weary hand constrain,
To work thy bark upon the boisterous main;
Henceforth good days and plenty shall betide;
The gods and I will for thy age provide.

A glorious change attends thy low estate,
Sudden and mighty riches round thee wait;
Be wise, and use the lucky hour of fate." [dress'd,
Thus he; and though in humble vestments
Spite of himself, his words his power express'd,
And Cæsar in his bounty stood confess'd.
To him the wary pilot thus replies:
" A thousand omens threaten from the skies;
A thousand boding signs my soul affright,
And warn me not to tempt the seas by night.
In clouds the setting Sun obscur'd his head,
Nor painted o'er the ruddy west with red:
Now north, now south, he shot his parted beams,
And tipp'd the sullen black with golden gleams:
Pale shone his middle orb with faintish rays,
And suffer'd mortal eyes at ease to gaze.
Nor rose the silver queen of night serene,
Supine and dull her blunted horns were seen,
With foggy stains and cloudy blots between.
Dreadful awhile she shone all fiery red,
Then sicken'd into pale, and hid her drooping head.
Nor less I fear from that hoarse hollow roar,
In leafy groves, and on the sounding shore.
In various turns the doubtful dolphins play,
And thwart, and run across, and mix their way.
The cormorants the watery deep forsake,
And soaring herns avoid the plashy lake;
While, waddling on the margin of the main,
The crow bewets her, and prevents the rain.
Howe'er, if some great enterprize demand,
Behold, I proffer thee my willing hand:
My venturous bark the troubled deep shall try,
To thy wish'd port her plunging prow shall ply,
Unless the seas resolve to beat us by."
He spoke; and spread his canvass to the wind,
Unmoor'd his boat, and left the shore behind.
Swift flew the nimble keel; and as they past,
Long trails of light the shooting meteors cast;
E'en the fix'd fires above in motion seem,
Shake through the blast, and dart a quivering beam;
Black horrours on the gloomy ocean brood,
And in long ridges rolls the threatening flood;
While loud and louder murmuring winds arise,
And growl from every quarter of the skies.
When thus the trembling master, pale with fear,
" Behold what wrath the dreadful gods prepare;
My art is at a loss; the various tide
Beats my unstable bark on every side:
From the north-west the setting current swells,
While southern storms the driving rack foretells.
Howe'er it be, our purpos'd way is lost,
Nor can one relic of our wreck be tost
By winds, like these, on fair Hesperia's coast.
Our only means of safety is to yield,
And measure back with haste the foamy field;
To give our unsuccessful labour o'er, [shore."
And reach, while yet we may, the neighbouring
But Cæsar, still superior to distress,
Fearless, and confident of sure success,
Thus to the pilot loud—" The seas despise,
And the vain threatening of the noisy skies.
Though gods deny thee yon Ausonian strand;
Yet, go, I charge thee, go at my command.
Thy ignorance alone can cause thy fears,
Thou know'st not what a freight thy vessel bears;
Thou know'st not I am he, to whom 't is given
Never to want the care of watchful Heaven.
Obedient Fortune waits my humble thrall,
And always ready comes before I call.
Let winds, and seas, loud wars at freedom wage,
And waste upon themselves their empty rage;
A stronger, mightier demon is thy friend,
Thou, and thy bark, on Cæsar's fate depend.
Thou stand'st amaz'd to view this dreadful scene;
And wonder'st what the gods and Fortune mean!
But artfully their bounties thus they raise,
And from my dangers arrogate new praise;
Amidst the fears of death they bid me live,
And still enhance what they are sure to give.
Then leave yon shore behind with all thy haste,
Nor shall this idle fury longer last.
Thy keel auspicious shall the storm appease,
Shall glide triumphant o'er the calmer seas,
And reach Brundusium's safer port with ease.
Nor can the gods ordain another now,
'T is what I want, and what they must bestow."
Thus while in vaunting words the leader spoke;
Full on his bark the thundering tempest struck;
Off rips the rending canvass from the mast,
And whirling flits before the driving blast;
In every joint the groaning alder sounds,
And gapes wide-opening with a thousand wounds.
Now, rising all at once, and unconfin'd,
From every quarter roars the rushing wind:
First from the wide Atlantic ocean's bed,
Tempestuous Corus rears his dreadful head;
Th' obedient deep his potent breath controls,
And, mountain-high, the foamy flood he rolls.
Him the north-east encountering fierce defy'd,
And back rebuffeted the yielding tide.
The curling surges loud conflicting meet,
Dash their proud heads, and bellow as they beat;
While piercing Boreas, from the Scythian strand,
Ploughs up the waves, and scoops the lowest sand.
Nor Eurus then, I ween, was left to dwell,
Nor showery Notus in th' Æolian cell;
But each from every side, his power to boast,
Rang'd his proud forces, to defend his coast.
Equal in might, alike they strive in vain,
While in the midst the seas unmov'd remain:
In lesser wars they yield to stormy Heaven,
And captive waves to other deeps are driven;
The Tyrrhene billows dash Ægean shores,
And Adria in the mix'd Ionian roars.
How then must Earth the swelling ocean dread,
When floods ran higher than each mountain's head!
Subject and low the trembling beldame lay,
And gave herself for lost, the conquering water's prey.
What other worlds, what seas unknown before,
Then drove their billows on our beaten shore!
What distant deeps, their prodigies to boast,
Heav'd their huge monsters on th' Ausonian coast!
So when avenging Jove long time had hurl'd,
And tir'd his thunders on a harden'd world:
New wrath, the god, new punishment display'd,
And call'd his watery brother to his aid:
Offending Earth to Neptune's lot he join'd,
And bade his floods no longer stand confin'd;
At once the surges o'er the nations rise,
And seas are only bounded by the skies.
Such now the spreading deluge had been seen,
Had not th' Almighty Ruler stood between;
Proud waves the cloud-compelling sire obey'd,
Confess'd his hand suppressing, and were stay'd.
Nor was that gloom the common shade of night,
The friendly darkness that relieves the light;
But fearful, black, and horrible to tell,
A murky vapour breath'd from yawning Hell:

So thick the mingling seas and clouds were hung,
Scarce could the struggling lightning gleam along.
Through Nature's frame the dire convulsion struck,
Heaven groan'd, the labouring pole and axis shook:
Uproar, and chaos old, prevail'd again,
And broke the sacred elemental chain:
Black fiends, unhallow'd, sought the blest abodes,
Profan'd the day, and mingled with the gods.
One only hope, when every other fail'd,
With Cæsar, and with nature's self, prevail'd;
The storm that sought their ruin, prov'd them strong,
Nor could they fall, who stood that shock so long.
High as Leucadia's lessening cliffs arise,
On the tall billow's top the vessel flies;
While the pale master, from the surge's brow,
With giddy eyes surveys the depth below.
When straight the gaping main at once divides,
On naked sands the rushing bark subsides,
And the low liquid vale the topmast hides.
The trembling shipman, all distraught with fear,
Forgets his course, and knows not how to steer;
No more the useless rudder guides the prow,
To meet the rolling swell, or shun the blow.
But, lo! the storm itself assistance lends,
While one assaults, another wave defends:
This lays the sidelong alder on the main,
And that restores the leaning bark again.
Obedient to the mighty winds she plies,
Now seeks the depths, and now invades the skies;
There borne aloft, she apprehends no more,
Or shoaly Sason, or Thessalia's shore;
High hills she dreads, and promontories now,
And fears to touch Ceraunia's airy brow.
At length the universal wreck appear'd,
To Cæsar's self, e'en worthy to be fear'd.
"Why all these pains, this toil of fate," he cries,
"This labour of the seas, and earth, and skies?
All nature and the gods, at once alarm'd,
Against my little boat and me are arm'd.
If, O ye powers divine! your will decrees
The glory of my death to these rude seas;
If warm, and in the fighting field to die,
If that, my first of wishes, you deny;
My soul no longer at her lot repines,
But yields to what your providence assigns.
Though immature I end my glorious days,
Cut short my conquest, and prevent new praise;
My life, already, stands the noblest theme,
To fill long annals of recording fame.
Far northern nations own me for their lord,
And envious factions crouch beneath my sword;
Inferior Pompey yields to me at home,
And only fills a second place in Rome.
My country has my high behests obey'd,
And at my feet her laws obedient laid;
All sovereignty, all honours are my own,
Consul, dictator, I am all alone.
But thou, my only goddess, and my friend,
Thou, on whom all my secret prayers attend,
Conceal, O Fortune! this inglorious end.
Let none on Earth, let none beside thee, know
I sunk thus poorly to the shades below.
Dispose, ye gods! my carcass as you please,
Deep let it drown beneath these raging seas;
I ask no urn my ashes to infold,
Nor marble monuments, nor shrines of gold;
Let but the world, unknowing of my doom,
Expect me still, and think I am to come;
So shall my name with terrour still be heard,
And my return in every nation fear'd."
He spoke, and sudden, wond'rous to behold,
High on a tenth huge wave his bark was roll'd;
Nor sunk again, alternate, as before,
But rushing, lodg'd, and fix'd upon the shore.
Rome and his fortune were at once restor'd,
And Earth again receiv'd him for her lord.
Now, through the camp his late arrival told,
The warriors crowd, their leader to behold;
In tears, around, the murmuring legions stand,
And welcome him, with fond complaints, to land.
"What means too-daring Cæsar," thus they cry,
"To tempt the ruthless seas, and stormy sky!
What a vile helpless herd had we been left,
Of every hope at once in thee bereft?
While on thy life so many thousands wait,
While nations live dependent on thy fate,
While the whole world on thee, their head, rely,
'T is cruel in thee to consent to die.
And could'st thou not one faithful soldier find,
One equal to his mighty master's mind,
One that deserv'd not to be left behind?
While tumbling billows tost thee on the main,
We slept at ease, unknowing of thy pain.
Were we the cause, oh shame! unworthy we,
That urg'd thee on to brave the raging sea?
Is there a slave whose head thou hold'st so light,
To give him up to this tempestuous night?
While Cæsar, whom the subject Earth obeys,
To seasons such as these, his sacred self betrays.
Still wilt thou weary out indulgent Heaven,
And scatter all the lavish gods have given?
Dost thou the care of Providence employ,
Only to save thee when the seas run high?
Auspicious Jove thy wishes would promote;
Thou ask'st the safety of a leaky boat:
He proffers thee the world's supreme command;
Thy hopes aspire no farther than to land,
And cast thy shipwreck on th' Hesperian strand."
In kind reproaches thus they waste the night,
Till the gray east disclos'd the breaking light:
Serene the Sun his beamy face display'd,
While the tir'd storm and weary waves were laid.
Speedy the Latian chiefs unfurl their sails,
And catch the gently-rising northern gales:
In fair appearance the tall vessels glide,
The pilots, and the wind, conspire to guide,
And waft them fitly o'er the smoother tide:
Decent they move, like some well-order'd band,
In rang'd battalions marching o'er the land.
Night fell at length, the winds the sails forsook,
And a dead calm the beauteous order broke.
So when, from Strymon's wintery banks, the cranes,
In feather'd legions, cut th' ethereal plains;
To warmer Nile they bend their airy way,
Form'd in long lines, and rank'd in just array:
But if some rushing storm the journey cross,
The wingy leaders all are at a loss:
Now close, now loose, the breaking squadrons fly,
And scatter in confusion o'er the sky.
The day return'd, with Phœbus Auster rose,
And hard upon the straining canvass blows.
Scudding afore him swift the fleet he bore,
O'er-passing Lyssus, to Nymphæum's shore;
There safe from northern winds, within the port they moor.
While thus united Cæsar's arms appear,
And fortune draws the great decision near;

Sad Pompey's soul uneasy thoughts infest,
And his Cornelia pains his anxious breast.
To distant Lesbos fain he would remove,
Far from the war, the partner of his love.
Oh, who can speak, what numbers can reveal,
The tenderness which pious lovers feel?
Who can their secret pangs and sorrows tell,
With all the crowd of cares that in their bosoms dwell?
See what new passions now the hero knows,
Now first he doubts success, and fears his foes;
Rome and the world he hazards in the strife,
And gives up all to fortune, but his wife.
Oft he prepares to speak, but knows not how,
Knows they must part, but cannot bid her go;
Defers the killing news with fond delay,
And, lingering, puts off fate from day to day.
The fleeting shades began to leave the sky,
And slumber soft forsook the drooping eye:
When, with fond arms, the fair Cornelia prest
Her lord, reluctant, to her snowy breast:
Wondering, she found he shunn'd her just embrace,
And felt warm tears upon his manly face.
Heart-wounded with the sudden woe, she griev'd,
And scarce the weeping warrior yet believ'd.
When, with a groan, thus he: "My truest wife,
To say how much I love thee more than life,
Poorly expresses what my heart would show,
Since life, alas! is grown my burthen now;
That long, too long delay'd, that dreadful doom,
That cruel parting hour at length is come.
Fierce, haughty, and collected in his might,
Advancing Cæsar calls me to the fight.
Haste then, my gentle love, from war retreat;
The Lesbian isle attends thy peaceful seat:
Nor seek, oh! seek not to increase my cares,
Seek not to change my purpose with thy prayers;
Myself, in vain, the fruitless suit have try'd,
And my own pleading heart has been deny'd.
Think not, thy distance will increase thy fear:
Ruin, if ruin comes, will soon be near,
Too soon the fatal news shall reach thy ear.
Nor burns thy heart with just and equal fires,
Nor dost thou love as virtue's law requires;
If those soft eyes can e'en thy husband bear,
Red with the stains of blood, and guilty war.
When horrid trumpets sound their dire alarms,
Shall I indulge my sorrows with thy charms,
And rise to battle from these tender arms?
Thus mournful, from thee, rather let me go,
And join thy absence to the public woe.
But thou be hid, be safe from every fear,
While kings and nations in destruction share:
Shun thou the crush of my impending fate,
Nor let it fall on thee with all its weight.
Then if the gods my overthrow ordain,
And the fierce victor chase me o'er the plain,
Thou shalt be left me still, my better part,
To soothe my cares, and heal my broken heart;
Thy open arms I shall be sure to meet,
And fly with pleasure to the dear retreat."
Stunn'd and astonish'd at the deadly stroke,
All sense, at first, the matron sad forsook.
Motion, and life, and speech, at length returns,
And thus in words of heaviest woe she mourns:
"No, Pompey! 't is not that my lord is dead,
'T is not the hand of fate has robb'd my bed;
But like some base plebeian I am curs'd,
And by my cruel husband stand divorc'd.
But Cæsar bids us part! thy father comes!
And we must yield to what that tyrant dooms!
Is thy Cornelia's faith so poorly known,
That thou should'st think her safer whilst alone?
Are not our loves, our lives, our fortunes one?
Canst thou, inhuman, drive me from thy side,
And bid my single head the coming storm abide?
Do I not read thy purpose in thy eye?
Dost thou not hope, and wish, e'en now to die?
And can I then be safe? Yet death is free,
That last relief is not deny'd to me?
Though banish'd by thy harsh command I go,
Yet I will join thee in the realms below.
Thou bidst me with the pangs of absence strive,
And, till I hear thy certain loss, survive.
My vow'd obedience, what it can, shall bear;
But, oh! my heart's a woman, and I fear.
If the good gods, indulgent to my prayer,
Should make the laws of Rome, and thee, their care;
In distant climes I may prolong my woe,
And be the last thy victory to know.
On some bleak rock that frowns upon the deep,
A constant watch thy weeping wife shall keep!
There from each sail misfortune shall I guess,
And dread the bark that brings me thy success.
Nor shall those happier tidings end my fear,
The vanquish'd foe may bring new danger near!
Defenceless I may still be made a prize,
And Cæsar snatch me with him, as he flies:
With ease my known retreat he shall explore,
While thy great name distinguishes the shore:
Soon shall the Lesbian exile stand reveal'd,
The wife of Pompey cannot live conceal'd.
But if th' o'er-ruling powers thy cause forsake,
Grant me this only last request I make;
When thou shalt be of troops and friends bereft,
And wretched flight is all thy safety left;
Oh! follow not the dictates of thy heart,
But choose a refuge in some distant part.
Where'er thy inauspicious bark shall steer,
Thy sad Cornelia's fatal shore forbear,
Since Cæsar will be sure to seek thee there.'
So saying, with a groan the matron fled,
And, wild with sorrow, left her holy bed:
She sees all lingering, all delays are vain,
And rushes headlong to possess the pain;
Nor will the hurry of her griefs afford
One last embrace from her forsaken lord.
Uncommon cruel was the fate, for two,
Whose lives had lasted long, and been so true,
To lose the pleasure of one last adieu.
In all the woeful days that cross'd their bliss,
Sure never hour was known so sad as this;
By what they suffer'd now, inur'd to pain,
They met all after-sorrows with disdain,
And Fortune shot her envious shafts in vain.
Low on the ground the fainting dame is laid;
Her train officious hasten to her aid:
Then gently rearing, with a careful hand,
Support her, slow-descending, o'er the strand.
There, while with eager arms she grasp'd the shore,
Scarcely the mourner to the bark they bore.
Not half this grief of heart, these pangs, she knew,
When from her native Italy she flew:
Lonely, and comfortless, she takes her flight,
Sad seems the day, and long the sleepless night.
In vain her maids the downy couch provide,
She wants the tender partner of her side.

When weary oft in heaviness she lies,
And dozy slumbers steals upon her eyes; [prest,
Fain, with fond arms, her lord she would have
But weeps to find the pillow at her breast.
Though raging in her veins a fever burns,
Painful she lies, and restless oft she turns.
She shuns his sacred side with awful fear,
And would not be convinc'd he is not there.
But, oh! too soon the want shall be supply'd,
The gods too cruelly for that provide:
Again, the circling hours bring back her lord,
And Pompey shall be fatally restor'd.

BOOK VI.

THE ARGUMENT.

Cæsar and Pompey lying now near Dyrrachium, after several marches and counter-marches, the former with incredible diligence runs a vast line, or work, round the camp of the latter. This, Pompey, after suffering for want of provisions, and a very gallant resistance of Scæva, a centurion of Cæsar s, at length breaks through. After this, Cæsar makes another unsuccessful attempt upon a part of Pompey's army, and then marches away into Thessaly: and Pompey, against the persuasion and counsel of his friends, follows him. After a description of the ancient inhabitants, the boundaries, the mountains, and rivers of Thessaly; the poet takes occasion, from this country being famous for witchcraft, to introduce Sextus Pompeius, inquiring the event of the civil war from the sorceress Erictho.

Now, near encamp'd, each on a neighbouring height,
The Latian chiefs prepare for sudden fight.
The rival pair seem hither brought by fate,
As if the gods would end the dire debate,
And here determine of the Roman state.
Cæsar, intent upon his hostile son,
Demands a conquest here, and here alone;
Neglects what laurels captive towns must yield,
And scorns the harvest of the Grecian field.
Impatient he provokes the fatal day,
Ordain'd to give Rome's liberties away,
And leave the world the greedy victor's prey.
Eager, that last great chance of war he waits,
Where either's fall determines both their fates.
Thrice, on the hills, all drawn in dread array,
His threatening eagles wide their wings display;
Thrice, but in vain, his hostile arms he show'd,
His ready rage, and thirst of Latian blood.
But when he saw, how cautious Pompey's care,
Safe in his camp, declin'd the proffer'd war;
Through woody paths he bent his secret way,
And meant to make Dyrrachium's towers his prey.
This Pompey saw; and swiftly shot before,
With speedy marches on the sandy shore:
Till on Taulantian Petra's top he stay'd,
Sheltering the city with his timely aid. [boast,
This place, nor walls, nor trenches deep can
The works of labour, and expensive cost.
Vain prodigality! and labour vain! [pain!
Lost is the lavish wealth, and lost the fruitless
What walls, what towers soe'er they rear sublime,
Must yield to wars, or more destructive time;
While fences like Dyrrachium's fortress made,
Where Nature's hand the sure foundation laid,
And with her strength the naked town array'd,
Shall stand secure against the warrior's rage,
Nor fear the ruinous decays of age.
Guarded, around, by steepy rocks it lies,
And all access from land, but one, denies.
No venturous vessel there in safety rides,
But foaming surges break, and swelling tides
Roll roaring on, and wash the craggy sides:
Or when contentious winds more rudely blow,
Then mounting o'er the topmost cliff they flow,
Burst on the lofty domes, and dash the town below.
Here Cæsar's daring heart vast hopes conceives,
And high with war's vindictive pleasures heaves;
Much he revolves within his thoughtful mind,
How, in this camp, the foe may be confin'd,
With ample lines from hill to hill design'd.
Secret and swift he means the task to try,
And runs each distance over with his eye.
Vast heaps of sod and verdant turf are brought,
And stones in deep laborious quarries wrought;
Each Grecian dwelling round the work supplies,
And sudden ramparts from their ruins rise.
With wond'rous strength the stable mound they [rear,
Such as th' impetuous ram can never fear,
Nor hostile might o'erturn, nor forceful engine tear.
Through hills, resistless, Cæsar planes his way,
And makes the rough unequal rocks obey.
Here deep, beneath, the gaping trenches lie,
There forts advance their airy turrets high.
Around vast tracts of land the labours wind,
Wide fields and forests in the circle bind,
And hold as in a toil the savage kind.
Nor e'en the foe too strictly pent remains,
At large he forages upon the plains;
The vast enclosure gives free leave around,
Oft to decamp, and shift the various ground.
Here, from far mountains, streams their channels trace,
And, while they wander through the tedious space,
Run many a mile their long extended race:
While some, quite worn and weary of the way,
Sink, and are lost before they reach the sea:
E'en Cæsar's self, when through the works he goes,
Tires in the midst, and stops to take repose.
Let fame no more record the walls of Troy,
Which gods alone could build, and gods destroy;
Nor let the Parthian wonder, to have seen
The labours of the Babylonian queen:
Behold this large, this spacious tract of ground!
Like that, which Tigris or Orontes bound;
Behold this land! that majesty might bring,
And form a kingdom for an eastern king;
Behold a Latian chief this land enclose,
Amidst the tumult of impending foes:
He bad the walls arise, and as he bad they rose.
But ah! vain pride of power! ah! fruitless boast!
E'en these, these mighty labours are all lost!
A force like this what barriers could withstand?
Seas must have fled, and yielded to the land;
The lovers shores united might have stood,
Spite of the Hellespont's opposing flood;
While the Ægean and Ionian tide,
Might meeting o'er the vanquish'd isthmus ride,
And Argive realms from Corinth's walls divide;
This power might change unwilling nature's face,
Unfix each order, and remove each place.
Here, as if clos'd within a list, the war
Does all its valiant combatants prepare;

Here ardent glows the blood, which fate ordains
To dye the Libyan and Emathian plains;
Here the whole rage of civil discord join'd,
Struggles for room, and scorns to be confin'd.
Nor yet, while Cæsar his first labours try'd,
The warlike toil by Pompey was descry'd.
So, in mid Sicily's delightful plain,
Safe from the horrid sound, the happy swain
Dreads not loud Scylla barking o'er the main.
So, northern Britons never hear the roar
Of seas, that break on the far Cantian shore.
Soon as the rising ramparts' hostile height,
And towers advancing, struck his anxious sight,
Sudden from Petra's safer camp he led,
And wide his legions on the hills dispread;
So, Cæsar, forc'd his numbers to extend,
More feebly might each various strength defend.
His camp far o'er the large enclosure reach'd,
And guarded lines along the front were stretch'd;
Far as Rome's distance from Aricia's groves,
(Aricia which the chaste Diana loves)
Far as from Rome old Tiber seeks the sea,
Did he not wander in his winding way.
While yet no signals for the fight prepare,
Unbidden, some the javelin dart from far,
And, skirmishing, provoke the lingering war.
But deeper cares the thoughtful chiefs distress,
And move, the soldiers ardour to repress.
Pompey, with secret anxious thought, beheld,
How trampling hoofs the rising grass repell'd;
Waste lie the russet fields, the generous steed
Seeks on the naked soil, in vain, to feed:
Loathing from racks of husky straw he turns,
And, pining, for the verdant pasture mourns.
No more his limbs their dying load sustain,
Aiming a stride, he falters in the strain,
And sinks a ruin on the withering plain:
Dire maladies upon his vitals prey,
Dissolve his frame, and melt the mass away.
Thence deadly plagues invade the lazy air,
Reek to the clouds, and hang malignant there.
From Nesis such, the Stygian vapours rise,
And with contagion taint the purer skies;
Such do Typhœus' steamy caves convey,
And breathe blue poisons on the golden day.
Thence liquid streams the mingling plague receive,
And deadly potions to the thirsty give:
To man the mischief spreads, the fell disease
In fatal draughts does on his entrails seize.
A rugged scurf, all loathsome to be seen,
Spreads, like a bark, upon his silken skin;
Malignant flames his swelling eye-balls dart,
And seem with anguish from their seats to start;
Fires o'er his glowing cheeks and visage stray,
And mark, in crimson streaks, their burning way;
Low droops his head, declining from its height,
And nods, and totters with the fatal weight.
With winged haste the swift destruction flies,
And scarce the soldier sickens ere he dies;
Now falling crowds at once resign their breath,
And doubly taint the noxious air with death.
Careless their putrid carcasses are spread;
And on the earth, their dank unwholesome bed,
The living rest in common with the dead.
Here none the last funereal rites receive;
To be cast forth the camp is all their friends can give.
At length kind Heaven their sorrows bad to cease,
And staid the pestilential foe's increase;
Fresh breezes from the sea begin to rise,
While Boreas through the lazy vapour flies,
And sweeps, with healthy wings, the rank polluted skies.
Arriving vessels now their freight unload,
And furnish plenteous harvests from abroad:
Now sprightly strength, now cheerful health, returns,
And life's fair lamp, rekindled, brightly burns.
But Cæsar, unconfin'd, and camp'd on high,
Feels not the mischief of the sluggish sky:
On hills sublime he breathes the purer air,
And drinks no damps, nor poisonous vapours, there.
Yet hunger keen an equal plague is found;
Famine and meagre want besiege him round:
The fields, as yet, no hopes of harvest wear,
Nor yellow stems disclose the bearded ear.
The scatter'd vulgar search around the fields,
And pluck whate'er the doubtful herbage yields;
Some strip the trees in every neighbouring wood,
And with the cattle share their grassy food.
Whate'er the softening flame can pliant make,
Whate'er the teeth, or labouring jaws, can break;
What flesh, what roots, what herbs so'er they get,
Though new, and strange to human taste as yet,
At once the greedy soldiers seize and eat.
What want, what pain soe'er they undergo,
Still they persist in arms, and close beset the foe.
At length, impatient longer to be held
Within the bounds of one appointed field,
O'er every bar which might his passage stay,
Pompey resolves to force his warlike way;
Wide o'er the world the ranging war to lead,
And give his loosen'd legions room to spread.
Nor takes he mean advantage from the night,
Nor steals a passage, nor declines the fight;
But bravely dares, disdainful of the foe,
Through the proud towers and ramparts breach to go.
Where shining spears, and crested helms are seen,
Embattled thick to guard the walls within;
Where all things death, where ruin all afford,
There Pompey marks a passage for his sword.
Near to the camp a woody thicket lay,
Close was the shade, nor did the greensward way
With smoky clouds of dust, the march betray.
Hence, sudden they appear in dread array,
Sudden their wide-extended ranks display;
At once the foe beholds with wondering eyes
Where on broad wings Pompeian eagles rise;
At once the warriors' shouts and trumpet-sounds surprise.
Scarce was the sword's destruction needful here,
So swiftly ran before preventing fear;
Some fled amaz'd, while vainly valiant some
Stood, but to meet in arms a nobler doom.
Where'er they stood, now scatter'd lie the slain,
Scarce yet a few for coming deaths remain,
And clouds of flying javelins fall in vain.
Here swift consuming flames the victors throw,
And here the ram impetuous aims a blow;
Aloft the nodding turrets feel the stroke,
And the vast rampart groans beneath the shock.
And now propitious Fortune seem'd to doom
Freedom and peace, to Pompey, and to Rome;
High o'er the vanquish'd works his eagles tower,
And vindicate the world from Cæsar's power.
But (what nor Cæsar, nor his fortune cou'd)
What not ten thousand warlike hands withstood,
Scæva resists alone; repels the force,
And stops the rapid victor in his course.

Scæva! a name erewhile to fame unknown,
And first distinguish'd on the Gallic Rhone;
There seen in hardy deeds of arms to shine,
He reach'd the honours of the Latian vine.
Daring and bold, and ever prone to ill,
Inur'd to blood, and active to fulfil
The dictates of a lawless tyrant's will;
Nor virtue's love, nor reason's laws he knew,
But, careless of the right, for hire his sword he drew.
Thus courage by an impious cause is curst,
And he that is the bravest, is the worst.
Soon as he saw his fellows shun the fight,
And seek their safety in ignoble flight,
"Whence does," he said, "this coward's terrour grow,
This shame, unknown to Cæsar's arms till now?
Can you, ye slavish herd, thus tamely yield?
Thus fly, unwounded, from the bloody field?
Behold, where pil'd in slaughter'd heaps on high,
Firm to the last, your brave companions lie;
Then blush to think what wretched lives you save,
From what renown you fly, from what a glorious grave.
Though sacred fame, though virtue yield to fear,
Let rage, let indignation keep you here.
We! we the weakest, from the rest are chose,
To yield a passage to our scornful foes!
Yet, Pompey, yet, thou shalt be yet withstood,
And stain thy victor's laurel deep in blood.
With pride 't is true, with joy I should have dy'd,
If haply I had fall'n by Cæsar's side;
But Fortune has the noble death deny'd.
Then Pompey, thou, thou on my fame shall wait,
Do thou be witness, and applaud my fate.
Now push we on, disdain we now to fear,
A thousand wounds let every bosom bear,
Till the keen sword be blunt, be broke the pointed spear.
And see the clouds of dusty battle rise!
Hark how the shout runs rattling through the skies!
The distant legions catch the sounds from far,
And Cæsar listens to the thundering war.
He comes, he comes, yet ere his soldier dies,
Like lightning swift the winged warrior flies:
Haste then to death, to conquest haste away;
Well do we fall, for Cæsar wins the day."
He spoke, and straight, as at the trumpet's sound,
Rekindled warmth in every breast was found;
Recall'd from flight, the youth admiring wait,
To mark their daring fellow-soldier's fate,
To see if haply virtue might prevail,
And, e'en beyond their hopes, do more than greatly fail.
High on the tottering wall he rears his head,
With slaughter'd carcasses around him spread;
With nervous arms uplifting these he throws,
These rolls oppressive, on ascending foes.
Each where materials for his fury lie,
And all the ready ruins arms supply:
Even his fierce self he seems to aim below,
Headlong to shoot, and dying dart a blow.
Now his tough staff repels the fierce attack,
And tumbling, drives the bold assailants back:
Now heads, now hands he lops, the carcass falls,
Whilst the clench'd fingers gripe the topmost walls:
Here stones he heaves; the mass descending full,
Crushes the brain, and shivers the frail scull.
Here burning pitchy brands he whirls around;
Infix'd, the flames hiss in the liquid wound,
Deep drench'd in death, in flowing crimson drown'd.
And now the swelling heaps of slaughter'd foes,
Sublime and equal to the fortress rose;
Whence, forward with a leap, at once he sprung,
And shot himself amidst the hostile throng.
So daring, fierce with rage, so void of fear,
Bounds forth the spotted pard, and scorns the hunter's spear.
The closing ranks the warrior straight infold,
And, compass'd in their steely circle, hold.
Undaunted still, around the ring he roams,
Fights here and there, and every where o'ercomes;
Till, clogg'd with blood, his sword obeys but ill
The dictates of its vengeful master's will;
Edgeless it falls, and though it pierce no more,
Still breaks the batter'd bones, and bruises sore.
Mean time, on him the crowding war is bent,
And darts from every hand, to him are sent:
It look'd as Fortune did in odds delight,
And had in cruel sport ordain'd the fight;
A wond'rous match of war she seem'd to make,
Her thousands here, and there her one to stake;
As if on nightly terms in lists they ran,
And armies were but equal to the man.
A thousand darts upon his buckler ring,
A thousand javelins round his temples sing;
Hard bearing on his head, with many a blow,
His steely helm is inward taught to bow.
The missive arms, fix'd all around, he wears,
And e'en his safety in his wounds he bears,
Fenc'd with a fatal wood, a deadly grove of spears.
Cease, ye Pompeian warriors! cease the strife,
Nor, vainly, thus attempt this single life;
Your darts, your idle javelins cast aside,
And other arms for Scæva's death provide:
The forceful rams' resistless horns prepare,
With all the ponderous vast machines of war;
Let dreadful flames, let massy rocks be thrown,
With engines thunder on, and break him down,
And win this Cæsar's soldier, like a town.
At length, his fate disdaining to delay,
He hurls his shield's neglected aid away,
Resolves no part whate'er from death to hide,
But stands unguarded now on every side.
Encumber'd sore with many a painful wound,
Tardy and stiff he treads the hostile round;
Gloomy and fierce his eyes the crowd survey,
Mark where to fix, and single out the prey.
Such, by Getulian hunters compass'd in,
The vast unweildy elephant is seen:
All cover'd with a steely shower from far,
Rousing he shakes, and sheds the scatter'd war;
In vain the distant troops the fight renew,
And with fresh rage the stubborn foe pursue;
Unconquer'd still the mighty savage stands,
And scorns the malice of a thousand hands.
Not all the wounds a thousand darts can make,
Though all find place, a single life can take.
When lo! addrest with some successful vow,
A shaft, sure flying from a Cretan bow,
Beneath the warrior's brow was seen to light,
And sunk, deep piercing the left orb of sight.
But he (so rage inspir'd, and mad disdain)
Remorseless fell, and senseless of the pain,
Tore forth the bearded arrow from the wound,
With stringy nerves besmear'd and wrapp'd around,
And stamp'd the gory jelly on the ground.
So in Pannonian woods the growling bear,
Transfix'd, grows fiercer for the hunter's spear,

Turns on her wound, runs madding round with
And catches at the flying shaft in vain. [pain,
Down from his eyeless hollow ran the blood,
And hideous o'er his mangled visage flow'd;
Deform'd each awful, each severer grace,
And veil'd the manly terrours of his face.
The victors raise their joyful voices high,
And with loud triumph strike the vaulted sky:
Not Cæsar thus a general joy had spread,
Though Cæsar's self like Scæva thus had bled.
Anxious, the wounded soldier, in his breast,
The rising indignation deep represt, [drest:
And thus, in humble vein, his haughty foes ad-
"Here let your rage, ye Romans, cease," he said,
"And lend your fellow-citizen your aid;
No more your darts nor useless javelins try,
These, which I bear, will deaths enow supply,
Draw forth your weapons, and behold I die.
Or rather bear me hence, and let me meet
My doom beneath the mighty Pompey's feet:
'T were great, 't were brave, to fall in arms, 't is
But I renounce that glorious fate for you. [true,
Fain would I yet prolong this vital breath,
And quit e'en Cæsar, so I fly from death."
The wretched Aulus listen'd to the wile,
Intent and greedy of the future spoil;
Advancing fondly on, with heedless ease,
He thought the captive and his arms to seize,
When, ere he was aware, his thundering sword
Deep in his throat the ready Scæva gor'd.
Warm'd with the slaughter, with fresh rage he
burns,
And vigour with the new success returns.
"So may they fall," he said, "by just deceit,
Such be their fate, such as this fool has met,
Who dare believe that I am vanquish'd yet!
If you would stop the vengeance of my sword,
From Cæsar's mercy be your peace implor'd,
There let your leader kneel, and humbly own his
Me! could you meanly dare to fancy me [lord.
Base, like yourselves, and fond of life to be!
But know, not all the names which grace your
cause,
Your reverend senate, and your boasted laws,
Not Pompey's self, not all for which you fear,
Were e'er to you, like death to Scæva, dear."
Thus while he spoke, a rising dust betray'd
Cæsarian legions marching to his aid.
Now Pompey's troops with prudence seem to yield,
And to increasing numbers quit the field;
Dissembling shame, they hide their foul defeat,
Nor vanquish'd by a single arm retreat.
Then fell the warrior, for till then he stood;
His manly mind supply'd the want of blood.
It seem'd as rage had kindled life anew,
And courage to oppose, from opposition grew.
But now, when none were left him to repel,
Fainting for want of foes, the victor fell.
Straight with officious haste his friends draw near,
And, raising, joy the noble load to bear:
To reverence and religious awe inclin'd,
Admiring, they adore his mighty mind,
That god within his mangled breast enshrin'd.
The wounding weapons, stain'd with Scæva's
blood,
Like sacred relics to the gods are vow'd:
Forth are they drawn from every part with care,
And kept to dress the naked god of war.
Oh! happy soldier, had thy worth been try'd,
In pious daring, on thy country's side!
Oh! had thy sword Iberian battles known,
Or purple with Cantabrian slaughter grown;
How had thy name in deathless annals shone!
But now no Roman pæan shalt thou sing,
Nor peaceful triumphs to thy country bring,
Nor loudly blest in solemn pomp shalt move,
Through crowding streets to Capitolian Jove,
The laws defender, and the people's love:
Oh, hapless victor thou! oh, vainly brave!
How hast thou fought, to make thyself a slave!
Nor Pompey, thus repuls'd, the fight declines,
Nor rests encompass'd round by Cæsar's lines;
Once more he means to force his warlike way,
And yet retrieve the fortune of the day.
So when fierce winds with angry ocean strive,
Full on the beach the beating billows drive;
Stable awhile the lofty mounds abide,
Check the proud surge, and stay the swelling tide:
Yet restless still the waves unweary'd roll,
Work underneath at length, and sap the sinking
mole.
With force renew'd the baffled warrior bends,
Where to the shore the jutting wall extends:
There proves, by land and sea, his various might,
And wins his passage by the double fight.
Wide o'er the plains diffus'd his legions range,
And their close camp for freer fields exchange.
So, rais'd by melting streams of Alpine snow,
Beyond his utmost margin swells the Po,
And loosely lets the spreading deluge flow:
Where'er the weaker banks opprest retreat,
And sink beneath the heapy waters' weight,
Forth gushing at the breach, they burst their way,
And wasteful o'er the drowned country stray:
Far distant fields and meads they wander o'er,
And visit lands they never knew before;
Here, from its seat the mouldering earth is torn,
And by the flood to other masters borne;
While gathering, there, it heaps the growing soil,
And loads the peasant with his neighbour's spoil.
Soon as, ascending high, a rising flame,
To Cæsar's sight, the combat's signal came,
Swift to the place approaching near, he found
The ruins scatter'd by the victor round,
And his proud labours humbled to the ground.
Thence to the hostile camp his eyes he turns,
Where for their peace, and sleep secure, he
mourns, [burns.
With rancorous despite, and envious anguish,
At length resolv'd, (so rage inspir'd his breast)
He means to break the happy victor's rest;
Once more to kindle up the fatal strife,
And dash their joys with hazard of his life.
Straight to Torquatus fierce he bends his way,
(Torquatus near a neighbouring castle lay)
But he, by prudent caution taught to yield,
Trusts to his walls, and quits the open field;
There, safe within himself, he stands his ground,
And lines the guarded ramparts strongly round.
So when the seamen from afar descry
The clouds grow black upon the low'ring sky,
Hear the winds roar, and mark the seas run high,
They furl the fluttering sheet with timely care,
And wisely for the coming storm prepare.
But now the victor, with resistless haste,
Proud o'er the ramparts of the fort had past;
When swift descending from the rising grounds,
Pompey with lengthening files the foe surrounds.
As when in Ætna's hollow caves below,
Round the vast furnace kindling whirlwinds blow;

Rous'd in his baleful bower the giant roars,
And with a burst the burning deluge pours;
Then pale with horrour shrieks the shuddering swain,
To see the fiery ruin spread the plain.
Nor with less horrour Cæsar's bands behold
Huge hostile dusty clouds their rear infold;
Unknowing whom to meet, or whom to shun,
Blind with their fear, full on their fates they run.
Well, on that day, the world repose had gain'd,
And bold rebellion's blood had all been drain'd,
Had not the pious chief the rage of war restrain'd.
Oh, Rome, how free, how happy hadst thou been!
Thy own great mistress, and the nations' queen!
Had Sylla, then, thy great avenger stood,
And dy'd his thirsty sword in traitors' blood.
But, oh! for ever shalt thou now bemoan
The two extremes, by which thou wert undone,
The ruthless father, and too tender son.
With fatal pity, Pompey, hast thou spar'd,
And given the blackest crime the best reward:
How had that one, one happy day, withheld
The blood of Utica, and Munda's field!
The Pharian Nile had known no crime more great
Than some vile Ptolemy's untimely fate!
Nor Afric, then, nor Juba, had bemoan'd,
Nor Scipio's blood the Punic ghosts aton'd;
Cato had, for his country's good, surviv'd,
And long in peace a hoary patriot liv'd;
Rome had not worn a tyrant's hated chain,
And fate had undecreed Pharsalia's plain.
But Cæsar, weary of th' unlucky land,
Swift to Æmathia leads his shatter'd band;
While Pompey's wary friends, with caution wise,
To quit the baffled foe's pursuit advise.
To Italy they point his open way,
And bid him make the willing land his prey.
"Oh! never," he replies, "shall Pompey come,
Like Cæsar arm'd, and terrible to Rome;
Nor need I from those sacred walls have fled,
Could I have borne our streets with slaughter red,
And seen the forum pil'd with heaps of dead.
Much rather let me pine in Scythia's frost;
Or burn on swarthy Libya's sultry coast;
No clime, no distant region, is too far,
Where I can banish, with me, fatal war.
I fled, to bid my country's sorrows cease;
And shall my victories invade her peace?
Let her but safe and free from arms remain,
And Cæsar still shall think she wears his chain."
He spoke, and eastward sought the forest wide,
That rising clothes Candavia's shady side;
Thence to Æmathia took his destin'd way,
Reserv'd by fate for the deciding day.
Where Eurus blows, and wintry suns arise,
Thessalia's boundary, proud Ossa lies;
But when the god protracts the longer day,
Pelion's broad back receives the dawning ray.
Where through the Lion's fiery sign he flies,
Othrys his leafy groves for shades supplies.
On Pindus strikes the fady western light,
When glittering Vesper leads the starry night.
Northward, Olympus hides the lamps, that roll
Their paler fires around the frozen pole.
The middle space, a valley low depress'd,
Once a wide, lazy, standing lake possess'd;
While growing still the heapy waters stood,
Nor down through Tempe ran the rushing flood:
But when Alcides to the task apply'd,
And cleft a passage through the mountains wide;
Gushing at once the thundering torrent flow'd,
While Nereus groan'd beneath th' increasing load.
Then rose (oh, that it still a lake had lain!)
Above the waves Pharsalia's fatal plain,
Once subject to the great Achilles' reign.
Then Phylace was built, whose warriors boast
Their chief first landed on the Trojan coast;
Then Pteleos ran her circling wall around,
And Dorion, for the Muses' wrath renown'd:
Then Trachin high, and Melibœa stood,
Where Hercules his fatal shafts bestow'd;
Larissa strong arose, and Argos, now
A plain, submitted to the labouring plough.
Here stood the town, if there be truth in fame,
That from Bœotian Thebes receiv'd its name.
Here sad Agave's wandering sense return'd,
Here for her murder'd son the mother mourn'd;
With streaming tears she wash'd his ghastly head,
And on the funeral pile the precious relic laid.
The gushing waters various soon divide,
And every river rules a separate tide;
The narrow Æas runs a limpid flood,
Evenos blushes with the Centaur's blood;
That gently mingles with th' Ionian sea,
While this, through Calydonia, cuts his way.
Slowly fair Io's aged father falls,
And in hoarse murmurs his lost daughter calls.
Thick Acheloüs rolls his troubled waves,
And heavily the neighbour isles he laves;
While pure Amphrysus winds along the mead,
Where Phœbus once was wont his flocks to feed:
Oft on the banks he sat a shepherd swain,
And watch'd his charge upon the grassy plain.
Swift to the main his course Sperchios bends,
And, sounding, to the Malian gulf descends.
No breezy air near calm Anauros flies,
No dewy mists, nor fleecy clouds arise.
Here Phœnix, Melas, and Asopus run,
And strong Apidanus drives slow Enipeus on.
A thousand little brooks, unknown to fame,
Are mix'd, and lost in Peneus' nobler name:
Bold Titaresus scorns his rule, alone,
And, join'd to Peneus, still himself is known:
As o'er the land his haughty waters glide,
And roll, unmingling, a superior tide.
'T is said, through secret channels winding forth,
Deep as from Styx he takes his hallow'd birth:
Thence, proud to be rever'd by gods on high,
He scorns to mingle with a mean ally.
When rising grounds uprear'd at length their heads,
And rivers shrunk within their oozy beds;
Bebrycians first are said, with early care,
In furrows deep to sink the shining share.
The Lelegians next, with equal toil,
And Dolopes, invade the mellow soil.
To these the bold Æolidæ succeed,
Magnetes, taught to rein the fiery steed,
And Minyæ, to explore the deep, decreed.
Here pregnant by Ixion's bold embrace,
The mother Cloud disclos'd the Centaurs' race:
In Pelethronian caves she brought them forth,
And fill'd the land with many a monstrous birth.
Here dreadful Monychus first saw the light,
And prov'd on Pholoe's rending rocks his might;
Here tallest trees uprooting Rhœcus bore,
Which baffled storms had try'd in vain before.
Here Pholus, of a gentler human breast,
Receiv'd the great Alcides for his guest.

Here, with brute-fury, lustful Nessus try'd
To violate the hero's beauteous bride,
'T is justly by the fatal shaft he dy'd.
This parent land the pious leach confest,
Chiron, of all the double race the best:
'Midst golden stars he stands refulgent now,
And threats the Scorpion with his bended bow.
Here love of arms and battle reign'd of old,
And form'd the first Thessalians fierce and bold:
Here, from rude rocks, at Neptune's potent stroke,
Omen of war, the neighing courser broke;
Here, taught by skilful riders to submit,
He champ'd indignant on the foamy bit.
From fair Thessalia's Pegasæan shore,
The first bold pine the daring warriors bore,
And taught the sons of Earth wide oceans to explore.
Here, when Itonus held the regal seat,
The stubborn steel he first subdu'd with heat,
And the tough bars on sounding anvils beat:
In furnaces he ran the liquid brass,
And cast in curious works the molten mass,
He taught the ruder artist to refine,
Explor'd the silver and the golden mine,
And stamp'd the costly metal into coin.
From that old era avarice was known,
Then all the deadly seeds of war was sown;
Wide o'er the world, by tale, the mischief ran,
And those curst pieces were the bane of man.
Huge Python, here, in many a scaly fold,
To Cyrrha's cave a length enormous roll'd:
Hence, Pythian games the hardy Greeks renown,
And laurel wreaths the joyful victor crown.
Here proud Alæus durst the gods defy,
And taught his impious brood to scale the sky:
While mountains pil'd on mountains interfere
With Heaven's bright orbs, and stop the circling sphere.
To this curst land, by fate's appointed doom,
With one consent the warring leaders come;
Their camps are fix'd, and now the vulgar fear,
To see the terrible event so near.
A few, and but a few, with souls serene,
Wait the disclosing of the dubious scene.
But Sextus, mix'd among the vulgar herd,
Like them was anxious, and unmanly fear'd:
A youth unworthy of the hero's race,
And born to be his nobler sire's disgrace.
A day shall come, when this inglorious son
Shall stain the trophies all by Pompey won:
A thief, and spoiler, shall he live confess'd,
And act those wrongs his father's arm redress'd.
Vex'd with a coward's fond impatience now,
He pries into that fate he fears to know;
Nor seeks he, with religious vow, to move
The Delphic tripod, or Dodonian Jove;
No priestly augur's arts employ his cares,
Nor Babylonian seers, who read the stars;
He nor by fibres, birds, or lightning's fires,
Nor any just, though secret, rights inquires;
But horrid altars, and infernal powers,
Dire mysteries of magic, he explores,
Such as high Heaven and gracious Jove abhors.
He thinks, 't is little those above can know,
And seeks accurst assistance from below.
The place itself the impious means supplies,
While near Hæmonian hags incamp'd he lies:
All dreadful deeds, all monstrous forms of old,
By fear invented, and by falshood told,
Whate'er transcends belief, and reason's view,
Their art can furnish, and their power makes true

The pregnant fields a horrid crop produce,
Noxious, and fit for witchcraft's deadly use:
With baleful weeds each mountain's brow is hung,
And listening rocks attend the charmer's song.
There, potent and mysterious plants arise,
Plants that compel the gods, and awe the skies;
There, leaves unfolded to Medea's view,
Such as her native Colchos never knew.
Soon as the dread Hæmonian voice ascends,
Through the whole vast expanse, each power attends;
E'en all those sullen deities, who know
No care of Heaven above, or Earth below,
Hear and obey. Th' Assyrian then, in vain,
And Memphian priests, their local gods detain;
From every altar loose at once they fly,
And with the stronger foreign call comply.
The coldest hearts Thessalian numbers warm,
And ruthless bosoms own the potent charm;
With monstrous power they rouse perverse desire,
And kindle into lust the wint'ry fire:
Where noxious cups, and poisonous philtres fail,
More potent spells and mystic verse prevail.
No draughts so strong the knots of love prepare,
Cropt from her younglings by the parent mare.
Oft, sullen bridegrooms, who unkindly fled
From blooming beauty, and the genial bed,
Melt, as the thread runs on, and sighing, feel
The giddy whirling of the magic wheel.
Whene'er the proud enchantress gives command,
Eternal motion stops her active hand;
No more Heaven's rapid circles journey on,
But universal nature stands foredone:
The lazy god of day forgets to rise,
And everlasting night pollutes the skies.
Jove wonders, to behold her shake the pole,
And, unconsenting, hears his thunders roll.
Now, with a word, she hides the Sun's bright face,
And blots the wide ethereal azure space;
Loosely, anon, she shakes her flowing hair,
And straight the stormy lowering Heavens are fair:
At once, she calls the golden light again,
The clouds fly swift away, and stops the drizly rain.
In stillest calms, she bids the waves run high,
And smooths the deep, though Boreas shakes the sky;
When winds are hush'd, her potent breath prevails,
Wafts on the bark, and fills the flagging sails.
Streams have run back at murmurs of her tongue,
And torrents from the rock suspended hung.
No more the Nile his wonted seasons knows,
And in a line the strait Mæander flows.
Arar has rush'd with headlong waters down,
And driven unwillingly the sluggish Rhone.
Huge mountains have been levell'd with the plain,
And far from Heaven has tall Olympus lain.
Riphæan crystal has been known to melt,
And Scythian snows a sudden summer felt.
No longer prest by Cynthia's moister beam,
Alternate Tethys heaves her swelling stream;
By charms forbid, her tides revolve no more,
But shun the margin of the guarded shore.
The ponderous earth, by magic numbers struck,
Down to her inmost centre deep has shook;
Then rending with a yawn, at once made way,
To join the upper, and the nether day;
While wondering eyes the dreadful cleft between,
Another starry firmament have seen.
Each deadly kind, by nature form'd to kill,
Fear the dire hags, and execute their will.

Lions, to them, their nobler rage submit,
And fawning tigers couch beneath their feet;
For them, the snake foregoes her wint'ry hold,
And on the hoary frost untwines her fold:
The poisonous race they strike with stronger death,
And blasted vipers die by human breath.
What law the heavenly natures thus constrains,
And binds e'en godheads in resistless chains?
What wond'rous power do charms and herbs imply,
And force them thus to follow, and to fly?
What is it can command them to obey?
Does choice incline, or awful terrour sway?
Do secret rites their deities atone,
Or mystic piety to man unknown?
Do strong enchantments all immortals brave?
Or is there one determin'd god their slave?
One, whose command obedient nature awes,
Who, subject still himself to magic laws,
Acts only as a servile second cause?
Magic the starry lamps from Heaven can tear,
And shoot them gleaming through the dusky air;
Can blot fair Cynthia's countenance serene,
And poison with foul spells the silver queen:
Now pale the ghastly goddess shrinks with dread,
And now black smoky fires involve her head;
As when Earth's envious interposing shade
Cuts off her beamy brother from her aid;
Held by the charming song, she strives in vain,
And labours with the long pursuing pain;
Till down, and downward still, compell'd to come,
On hallow'd herbs she sheds her fatal foam.
But these, as arts too gentle, and too good,
Nor yet with death, or guilt enough embru'd,
With haughty scorn the fierce Erictho view'd.
New mischief she, new monsters durst explore,
And dealt in horrours never known before.
From towns and hospitable roofs she flies,
And every dwelling of mankind defies;
Through unfrequented deserts lonely roams,
Drives out the dead, and dwells within their tombs.
Spite of all laws, which Heaven or nature know,
The rule of gods above, and man below;
Grateful to Hell the living hag descends,
And sits in black assemblies of the fiends.
Dark matted elf-locks dangling on her brow,
Filthy, and foul, a loathsome burthen grow;
Ghastly, and frightful-pale her face is seen,
Unknown to cheerful day, and skies serene:
But when the stars are veil'd, when storms arise,
And the blue forky flame at midnight flies,
Then, forth from graves, she takes her wicked way,
And thwarts the glancing lightnings as they play.
Where'er she breathes, blue poisons round her spread,
The withering grass avows her fatal tread,
And drooping Ceres hangs her blasted head.
Nor holy rites, nor suppliant prayer she knows,
Nor seeks the gods with sacrifice, or vows:
Whate'er she offers is the spoil of urns,
And funeral fire upon her altars burns;
Nor needs she send a second voice on high,
Scar'd at the first, the trembling gods comply.
Oft in the grave the living has she laid,
And bid reviving bodies leave the dead:
Oft at the funeral pile she seeks her prey,
And bears the smoking ashes warm away;
Snatches some burning bone, or flaming brand,
And tears the torch from the sad father's hand;
Seizes the shroud's loose fragments as they fly,
And picks the coal where clammy juices fry.
But when the dead in marble tombs are plac'd,
Where the moist carcass by degrees shall waste,
There, greedily on every part she flies,
Strips the dry nails, and digs the gory eyes.
Her teeth from gibbets gnaw the strangling noose,
And from the cross dead murderers unloose:
Her charms the use of sun-dry'd marrow find,
And husky entrails wither'd in the wind;
Oft drops the ropy gore upon her tongue,
With cordy sinews oft her jaws are strung,
And thus suspended oft the filthy hag has hung.
Where'er the battle bleeds, and slaughter lies,
Thither, preventing birds and beasts, she hies;
Nor then content to seize the ready prey,
From their fell jaws she tears their food away:
She marks the hungry wolf's pernicious tooth,
And joys to rend the morsel from his mouth.
Nor ever yet remorse could stop her hand,
When human gore her cursed rites demand.
Whether some tender infant, yet unborn,
From the lamenting mother's side is torn;
Whether her purpose asks some bolder shade,
And by her knife, the ghost she wants, is made;
Or whether, curious in the choice of blood,
She catches the first gushing of the flood;
All mischief is of use, and every murder good.
When blooming youths in early manhood die,
She stands a terrible attendant by;
The downy growth from off their cheeks she tears,
Or cuts left-handed some selected hairs.
Oft when in death her gasping kindred lay,
Some pious office would she feign to pay;
And while close hovering o'er the bed she hung,
Bit the pale lips, and cropt the quivering tongue;
Then, in hoarse murmurs, ere the ghost could go,
Mutter'd some message to the shades below.
A fame like this around the region spread,
To prove her power, the younger Pompey led.
Now half her sable course the night had run,
And low beneath us roll'd the beamy Sun;
When the vile youth in silence cross'd the plain,
Attended by his wonted worthless train.
Through ruins waste and old, long wandering round,
Lonely upon a rock, the hag they found.
There, as it chanc'd, in sullen mood she sate,
Pondering upon the war's approaching fate:
At that same hour, she ran new numbers o'er,
And spells unheard by Hell itself before;
Fearful, lest wavering destiny might change,
And bid the war in distant regions range.
She charm'd Pharsalia's field with early care,
To keep the warriors and the slaughter there.
So may her impious arts in triumph reign,
And riot in the plenty of the slain:
So, many a royal ghost she may command,
Mangle dead heroes with a ruthless hand,
And rob of many an urn Hesperia's mourning land.
Already she enjoys the dreadful field,
And thinks what spoils the rival chiefs shall yield;
With what fell rage each corse she shall invade,
And fly rapacious on the prostrate dead.
To her, a lowly suppliant, thus begun
The noble Pompey's much unworthy son:
"Hail! mighty mistress of Hæmonian arts,
To whom stern Fate her dark decrees imparts;
At thy approving, bids her purpose stand,
Or alters it at thy rever'd command.

From thee my humbler awful hopes presume
To learn my father's, and my country's doom:
Nor think this grace to one unworthy done,
When thou shalt know me for great Pompey's son;
With him all fortunes am I bound to share,
His ruin's partner, or his empire's heir.
Let not blind Chance for ever wavering stand,
And awe us with her unresolving hand:
I own my mind unequal to the weight,
Nor can I bear the pangs of doubtful fate:
Let it be certain what we have to fear,
And then—no matter—let the time draw near.
Oh let thy charms this truth from Heaven compel,
Or force the dreadful Stygian gods to tell.
Call death, all pale and meagre, from below,
And from herself her fatal purpose know;
Constrain'd by thee, the phantom shall declare
Whom she decrees to strike, and whom to spare.
Nor ever can thy skill divine foresee,
Through the blind maze of long futurity,
Events more worthy of thy arts, and thee."
Pleas'd that her magic fame diffusely flies,
Thus, with a horrid smile, the hag replies.
"Hadst thou, O noble youth, my aid implor'd,
For any less decision of the sword;
The gods, unwilling, should my power confess,
And crown thy wishes with a full success.
Hadst thou desir'd some single friend to save,
Long had my charms withheld him from the grave:
Or would thy hate some foe this instant doom,
He dies, though Heaven decrees him years to come.
But when effects are to their causes chain'd,
From everlasting, mightily, ordain'd;
When all things labour for one certain end,
And on one action centre and depend:
Then far behind we own our arts are cast,
And magic is by fortune's power surpass'd.
Howe'er, if yet thy soul can be content,
Only to know that undisclos'd event;
My potent charms o'er nature shall prevail,
And from a thousand mouths extort the tale:
This truth the fields, the floods, the rocks, shall tell,
The thunder of high Heaven, or groans of Hell:
Though, still, more kindly oracles remain,
Among the recent deaths of yonder plain.
Of these a corse our mystic rites shall raise,
As yet unshrunk by Titan's parching blaze;
So shall no maim the vocal pipes confound,
But the sad shade shall breathe, distinct in human sound."
While yet she spoke, a double darkness spread,
Black clouds and murky fogs involve her head,
While o'er th' unbury'd heaps her footsteps tread.
Wolves howl'd, and fled where'er she took her way,
And hungry vultures left the mangled prey:
The savage race, abash'd, before her yield,
And while she culls her prophet, quit the field.
To various carcasses by turns she flies,
And, griping with her gory fingers, tries;
Till one of perfect organs can be found,
And fibrous lungs uninjur'd by a wound.
Of all the flitting shadows of the slain,
Fate doubts which ghosts shall turn to life again.
At her strong bidding (such is her command)
Armies at once had left the Stygian strand;
Hell's multitudes had waited on her charms,
And legions of the dead had ris'n to arms.
Among the dreadful carnage strow'd around,
One, for her purpose fit, at length she found;
In his pale jaws a rusty hook she hung,
And dragg'd the wretched lifeless load along:
Anon, beneath a craggy cliff she staid,
And in a dreary delve her burthen laid;
There evermore the wicked witch delights,
To do her deeds accurs'd, and practise Hellish rites.
Low as the realms where Stygian Jove is crown'd,
Subsides the gloomy vale within the ground;
A downward grove, that never knew to rise,
Or shoot its leafy honours to the skies,
From hanging rocks declines its drooping head,
And covers in the cave with dreadful shade;
Within dismay, and fear, and darkness dwell,
And filth obscene besmears the baleful cell.
There, lasting night no beamy dawning knows,
No light but such as magic flames disclose;
Heavy, as in Tænarian caverns, there
In dull stagnation sleeps the lazy air.
There meet the boundaries of life and death,
The borders of our world, and that beneath;
Thither the rulers of th' infernal court
Permit their airy vassals to resort;
Thence with like ease the sorceress could tell,
As if descending down, the deeds of Hell.
And now she for the solemn task prepares,
A mantle patch'd with various threads she wears,
And binds with twining snakes her wilder hairs.
All pale, for dread, the dastard youth she spy'd,
Heartless his mates stood quivering by his side.
"Be bold," she cries, "dismiss this abject fear;
Living and human shall the form appear,
And breathe no sounds but what e'en you may hear.
How had your vile, your coward souls been quell'd,
Had you the livid Stygian lakes beheld;
Heard the loud floods of rolling sulphur roar,
And burst in thunder on the burning shore?
Had you survey'd yon prison-house of woe,
And giants bound in adamant below?
Seen the vast dog with curling vipers swell,
Heard screaming Furies, at my coming, yell,
Double their rage, and add new pains to Hell?"
This said, she runs the mangled carcass o'er,
And wipes from every wound the crusty gore;
Now with hot blood the frozen breast she warms,
And with strong lunar dews confirms her charms.
Anon she mingles every monstrous birth,
Which nature, wayward and perverse, brings forth.
Nor entrails of the spotted lynx she lacks,
Nor bony joints from fell hyænas' backs;
Nor deer's hot marrow, rich with snaky food;
Nor foam of raging dogs that fly the flood.
Her store the tardy remora supplies,
With stones from eagles warm, and dragons' eyes;
Snakes that on pinions cut their airy way,
And nimbly o'er Arabian deserts prey;
The viper bred in Erythræan streams,
To guard in costly shells the growing gems;
The slough by Libya's horned serpent cast,
With ashes by the dying phœnix plac'd
On odorous altars in the fragrant east.
To these she joins dire drugs without a name,
A thousand poisons never known to fame:
Herbs o'er whose leaves the hag her spells had sung,
And wet with cursed spittle as they sprung;
With every other mischief most abhorr'd,
Which Hell, or worse Erictho, could afford.
At length, in murmurs hoarse her voice was heard,
Her voice, beyond all plants, all magic fear'd,
And by the lowest Stygian gods rever'd.

Her gabbling tongue a muttering tone confounds,
Discordant, and unlike to human sounds:
It seem'd, of dogs the bark, of wolves the howl,
The doleful screeching of the midnight owl;
The hiss of snakes, the hungry lion's roar,
The bound of billows beating on the shore;
The groan of winds amongst the leafy wood,
And burst of thunder from the rending cloud:
'Twas these, all these in one. At length she breaks
Thus into magic verse, and thus the gods bespeaks
"Ye Furies, and thou black accursed Hell!
Ye woes! in which the damn'd for ever dwell;
Chaos, the world, and form's eternal foe!
And thou sole arbiter of all below,
Pluto! whom ruthless fates a god ordain,
And doom to immortality of pain;
Ye fair Elysian mansions of the blest,
Where no Thessalian charmer hopes to rest;
Styx! and Persephone, compell'd to fly
Thy fruitful mother, and the cheerful sky!
Third Hecate! by whom my whispers breathe
My secret purpose to the shades beneath;
Thou greedy dog, who at th' infernal gate,
In everlasting hunger, still dost wait!
And thou old Charon, horrible and hoar!
For ever labouring back from shore to shore:
Who murmuring dost in weariness complain,
That I so oft demand thy dead again;
Hear, all ye powers! If e'er your Hell rejoice
In the lov'd horrours of this impious voice;
If still with human flesh I have been fed,
If pregnant mothers have, to please you, bled;
If from the womb these ruthless hands have torn
Infants, mature, and struggling to be born;
Hear and obey! nor do I ask a ghost,
Long since receiv'd upon your Stygian coast;
But one that, new to death, for entrance waits,
And loiters yet before your gloomy gates.
Let the pale shade these herbs, these numbers hear,
And in his well-known warlike form appear.
Here let him stand, before his leader's son,
And say what dire events are drawing on:
If blood be your delight, let this be done."
Foaming she spoke: then rear'd her hateful head,
And hard at hand beheld th' attending shade.
Too well the trembling sprite the carcass knew,
And fear'd to enter into life anew;
Fain from those mangled limbs it would have run,
And, loathing, strove that house of pain to shun.
Ah! wretch! to whom the cruel fates deny
That privilege of human kind, to die!
Wrath was the hag at lingering death's delay,
And wonder'd Hell could dare to disobey;
With curling snakes the senseless trunk she beats,
And curses dire, at every lash, repeats;
With magic numbers cleaves the groaning ground,
And, thus, barks downwards to th' abyss profound:
"Ye fiends hell-born, ye sisters of despair!
Thus? is it thus my will becomes your care?
Still sleep those whips within your idle hands,
Nor drive the loitering ghost this voice demands?
But mark me well! my charms, in fate's despite,
Shall drag ye forth, ye Stygian dogs, to light;
Through vaults and tombs, where now secure you roam,
My vengeance shall pursue, and chase you home.
And thou, O Hecate! that dar'st to rise,
Various and alter'd to immortal eyes,
No more shalt veil thy horrours in disguise;
Still in thy form accursed shalt thou dwell,
Nor change the face that Nature made for Hell.
Each mystery beneath I will display,
And Stygian loves shall stand confess'd to day.
Thee, Proserpine! thy fatal feast I'll show,
What leagues detain thee in the realms below,
And why thy once-fond mother loaths thee now.
At my command, earth's barrier shall remove,
And piercing Titan vex infernal Jove;
Full on his throne the blazing beams shall beat,
And light abhorr'd afflict the gloomy seat.
Yet, am I yet, ye sullen fiends, obey'd?
Or must I call your master to my aid?
At whose dread name the trembling Furies quake,
Hell stands abash'd, and Earth's foundations shake?
Who views the Gorgons with intrepid eyes,
And your inviolable flood defies?"
She said; and, at the word, the frozen blood
Slowly began to roll its creeping flood;
Through the known channels stole the purple tide,
And warmth and motion through the members glide;
The nerves are stretch'd, the turgid muscles swell,
And the heart moves within its secret cell;
The haggard eyes their stupid lights disclose,
And heavy by degrees the corpse arose.
Doubtful and faint th' uncertain life appears,
And death, all-o'er, the livid visage wears.
Pale, stiff, and mute, the ghastly figure stands,
Nor knows to speak, but at her dread commands.
When thus the hag: "Speak what I wish to know,
And endless rest attends thy shade below;
Reveal the truth, and, to reward thy pain,
No charms shall drag thee back to life again;
Such hallow'd wood shall feed thy funeral fire,
Such numbers to thy last repose conspire,
No sister of our art thy ghost shall wrong,
Or force thee listen to her potent song.
Since the dark gods in mystic tripods dwell,
Since doubtful truths ambiguous prophets tell;
While each event aright and plain is read,
To every bold inquirer of the dead:
Do thou unfold what end these wars shall wait,
Persons, and things, and time, and place relate,
And be the just interpreter of fate."
She spoke, and, as she spoke, a spell she made,
That gave new prescience to th' unknowing shade.
When thus the spectre, weeping all for woe:
"Seek not from me the Parcæ's will to know.
I saw not what their dreadful looms ordain,
Too soon recall'd to hated life again;
Recall'd, ere yet my waiting ghost had pass'd
The silent stream, that wafts us all to rest.
All I could learn, was from the loose report
Of wandering shades, that to the banks resort.
Uproar, and discord, never known till now,
Distract the peaceful realms of death below;
From blissful plains of sweet Elysium some,
Others from doleful dens, and torments, come;
While in the face of every various shade,
The woes of Rome too plainly might be read.
In tears lamenting, ghosts of patriots stood,
And mourn'd their country in a falling flood;
Sad were the Decii, and the Curii seen,
And heavy was the great Camillus' mien:
On Fortune loud indignant Sylla rail'd,
And Scipio his unhappy race bewail'd;
The censor sad foresaw his Cato's doom,
Resolv'd to die for liberty, and Rome.

Of all the shades that haunt the happy field,
Thee only, Brutus! smiling I beheld;
Thee, thou first consul, haughty Tarquin's dread,
From whose just wrath the conscious tyrant fled,
When freedom first uprear'd her infant head.
Meanwhile the damn'd exult amidst their pains,
And Catiline audacious breaks his chains.
There the Cethegan naked race I view'd,
The Marii fierce, with human gore imbru'd,
The Gracchi, fond of mischief-making laws,
And Drusi, popular in faction's cause;
All clapp'd their hands in horrible applause.
The crash of brazen fetters rung around,
And Hell's wide caverns trembled with the sound.
No more the bounds of fate their guilt constrain,
But proudly they demand th' Elysian plain.
Thus they, while dreadful Dis, with busy cares,
New torments for the conquerors prepares;
New chains of adamant he forms below,
And opens all his deep reserves of woe:
Sharp are the pains for tyrants kept in store,
And flames yet ten times hotter than before.
But thou, O noble youth! in peace depart,
And sooth, with better hopes, thy doubtful heart;
Sweet is the rest, and blissful is the place,
That wait thy sire, and his illustrious race.
Nor fondly seek to lengthen out thy date,
Nor envy the surviving victor's fate;
The hour draws near when all alike must yield,
And death shall mix the fame of every field.
Haste then, with glory, to your destin'd end,
And proudly from your humbler urns descend;
Bold in superior virtue shall you come,
And trample on the demigods of Rome.
Ah! what shall it import the mighty dead,
Or by the Nile or Tiber to be laid?
'T is only for a grave your wars are made.
Seek not to know what for thyself remains,
That shall be told in fair Sicilia's plains;
Prophetic there, thy father's shade shall rise,
In awful vision to thy wondering eyes:
He shall thy fate reveal; though doubting yet,
Where he may best advise thee to retreat.
In vain to various climates shall you run,
In vain pursuing fortune strive to shun,
In Europe, Afric, Asia, still undone.
Wide as your triumphs shall your ruins lie,
And all in distant regions shall you die.
Ah, wretched race! to whom the world can yield
No safer refuge, than Emathia's field."
He said, and with a silent, mournful look,
A last dismission from the hag bespoke.
Nor can the sprite, discharg'd by death's cold hand,
Again be subject to the same command;
But charms and magic herbs must lend their aid,
And render back to rest the troubled shade.
A pile of hallow'd wood Erictho builds,
The soul with joy its mangled carcass yields;
She bids the kindling flames ascend on high,
And leaves the weary wretch at length to die.
Then, while the secret dark their footsteps hides,
Homeward the youth, all pale for fear, she guides;
And, for the light began to streak the east,
With potent spells the dawning she repress'd;
Commanded night's obedient queen to stay,
And, till they reach'd the camp, withheld the rising day.

BOOK VII.

THE ARGUMENT.

In the seventh book is told, first, Pompey's dream the night before the battle of Pharsalia; after that, the impatient desire of his army to engage, which is reinforced by Tully. Pompey, though against his own opinion and inclination, agrees to a battle. Then follows the speech of each general to his army, and the battle itself; the flight of Pompey; Cæsar's behaviour after his victory; and an invective against him, and the very country of Thessaly, for being the scene (according to this and other authors) of so many misfortunes to the people of Rome.

LATE, and unwilling, from his watery bed,
Uprear'd the mournful Sun his cloudy head;
He sicken'd to behold Emathia's plain,
And would have sought the backward east again:
Full oft he turn'd him from the destin'd race,
And wish'd some dark eclipse might veil his radiant face.
Pompey, meanwhile, in pleasing visions past
The night, of all his happy nights the last.
It seem'd, as if, in all his former state,
In his own theatre secure he sate:
About his side unnumber'd Romans crowd,
And, joyful, shout his much-lov'd name aloud:
The echoing benches seem to ring around,
And his charm'd ears devour the pleasing sound.
Such both himself, and such the people seem,
In the false prospect of the feigning dream;
As when in early manhood's beardless bloom,
He stood the darling hope and joy of Rome.
When fierce Sertorius by his arms suprest,
And Spain subdued, the conqueror confest:
When rais'd with honours never known before,
The consul's purple, yet a youth, he wore:
When the pleas'd senate sat with new delight,
To view the triumph of a Roman knight.
Perhaps, when our good days no longer last,
The mind runs backward, and enjoys the past:
Perhaps, the riddling visions of the night
With contrarieties delude our sight;
And when fair scenes of pleasure they disclose,
Pain they foretel, and sure ensuing woes.
Or was it not, that, since the Fates ordain
Pompey should never see his Rome again,
One last good office yet they meant to do,
And gave him in a dream this parting view?
Oh, may no trumpet bid the leader wake!
Long, let him long the blissful slumber take!
Too soon the morrow's sleepless night will come,
Full fraught with slaughter, misery, and Rome;
With horrour, and dismay, those shades shall rise,
And the lost battle live before his eyes.
How blest his fellow-citizens had been,
Though but in dreams, their Pompey to have seen!
Oh! that the gods, in pity, would allow,
Such long-try'd friends their destiny to know;
So each to each might their sad thoughts convey,
And make the most of their last mournful day.
But now, unconscious of the ruin nigh,
Within his native land he thinks to die:
While her fond hopes with confidence presume,
Nothing so terrible from fate can come,
As to be robb'd of her lov'd Pompey's tomb.
Had the sad city fate's decree foreknown,
What floods, fast falling, should her loss bemoan!

Then should the lusty youth, and fathers hoar,
With mingling tears, their chief renown'd deplore;
Maids, matrons, wives, and babes, a helpless train,
As once for godlike Brutus, should complain;
Their tresses should they tear, their bosoms beat,
And cry loud-wailing in the doleful street.
Nor sha't thou, Rome, thy gushing sorrows keep,
Though aw'd by Cæsar, and forbid to weep;
Though, while he tells thee of thy Pompey dead,
He shakes his threatening falchion o'er thy head.
Lamenting crowds the conqueror shall meet,
And with a peal of groans his triumph greet;
In sad procession, sighing shall they go,
And stain his laurels with the streams of woe.
But now, the fainting stars at length gave way,
And hid their vanquish'd fires in beamy day;
When round the leader's tent the legions crowd,
And, urg'd by fate, demand the fight aloud.
Wretches! that long their little life to waste,
And hurry on those hours that fly too fast!
Too soon, for thousands, shall the day be done,
Whose eyes no more shall see the setting Sun.
Tumultuous speech th' impulsive rage confest,
And Rome's bad genius rose in every breast.
With vile disgrace they blot their leader's name,
Pronounce e'en Pompey fearful, slow, and tame,
And cry, "He sinks beneath his father's fame."
Some charge him with ambition's guilty views,
And think 't is power, and empire, he pursues,
That, fearing peace, he practises delay,
And would, for ever, make the world obey.
While eastern kings of lingering wars complain,
And wish to view their native realms again.
Thus when the gods are pleas'd to plague mankind,
Our own rash hands are to the task assign'd;
By them ordain'd the tools of fate to be,
We blindly act the mischiefs they decree;
We call the battle, we the sword prepare,
And Rome's destruction is the Roman prayer.
The general voice, united, Tully takes,
And for the rest the sweet persuader speaks;
Tully, for happy eloquence renown'd,
With every Roman grace of language crown'd;
Beneath whose rule and government rever'd,
Fierce Catiline the peaceful axes fear'd:
But now, detain'd amidst an armed throng,
Where lost his arts, and useless was his tongue,
The orator had borne the camp too long,
He to the vulgar side his pleading draws,
And thus enforces much their feeble cause:
"For all that Fortune for thy arms has done,
For all thy fame acquir'd, thy battles won;
This only boon her suppliant vows implore,
That thou would'st deign to use her aid once more:
In this, O Pompey! kings and chiefs unite,
And, to chastise proud Cæsar, ask the fight.
Shall he, one man against the world combin'd,
Protract destruction, and embroil mankind?
What will the vanquish'd nations murmuring say,
Where once thy conquests cut their winged way;
When they behold thy virtue lazy now,
And see thee move thus languishing and slow?
Where are those fires that warm'd thee to be great?
That stable soul, and confidence in fate?
Canst thou the gods ungratefully mistrust?
Or think the senate's sacred cause unjust?
Scarce are th' impatient ensigns yet withheld:
Why art thou, thus, to victory compell'd?
Dost thou Rome's chief, and in her cause, appear?
'T is hers to choose the field, and she appoints it here.
Why is this ardour of the world withstood,
The injur'd world, that thirsts for Cæsar's blood?
See! where the troops with indignation stand,
Each javelin trembling in an eager hand,
And wait, unwillingly, the last command.
Resolve the senate then, and let them know,
Are they thy servants, or their servant thou?"
Sore sigh'd the listening chief, who well could read
Some dire delusion by the gods decreed;
He saw the Fates malignantly inclin'd,
To thwart his purpose and perplex his mind.
"Since thus," he cry'd, "it is by all decreed,
Since my impatient friends and country need
My hand to fight, and not my head to lead;
Pompey no longer shall your fate delay,
But let pernicious Fortune take her way,
And waste the world on one devoted day.
But, oh! be witness thou, my native Rome,
With what a sad foreboding heart I come;
To thy hard fate unwillingly I yield,
While thy rash sons compel me to the field.
How easily had Cæsar been subdu'd,
And the blest victory been free from blood!
But the fond Romans cheap renown disdain,
They wish for deaths to purple o'er the plain,
And reeking gore their guilty swords to stain.
Driv'n by my fleets, behold, the flying foe
At once the empire of the deep forego;
Here by necessity they seem to stand,
Coop'd up within a corner of the land.
By famine to the last extremes compell'd,
They snatch green harvests from th' unripen'd field;
And wish we may this only grace afford,
To let them die like soldiers, by the sword.
'T is true, it seems an earnest of success,
That thus our bolder youth for action press:
But let them try their inmost hearts with care,
And judge betwixt true valour and rash fear;
Let them be sure this eagerness is right,
And certain fortitude demands the fight.
In war, in dangers, oft it has been known,
That fear has driven the headlong coward on.
Give me the man, whose cooler soul can wait,
With patience, for the proper hour of fate.
See what a prosperous face our fortunes bear!
Why should we trust them to the chance of war?
Why must we risk the world's uncertain doom,
And rather choose to fight, than overcome?
Thou goddess Chance! who to my careful hand
Hast given this wearisome supreme command;
If I have, to the task of empire just,
Enlarg'd the bounds committed to my trust;
Be kind, and to thyself the rule resume,
And, in the fight, defend the cause of Rome:
To thy own crowns, the wreath of conquest join;
Nor let the glory, nor the crime, be mine.
But see! thy hopes, unhappy Pompey! fail:
We fight; and Cæsar's stronger vows prevail.
Oh, what a scene of guilt this day shall show!
What crowds shall fall, what nations be laid low!
Red shall Enipeus run with Roman blood,
And to the margin swell his foamy flood.
Oh! if our cause my aid no longer need,
Oh! may my bosom be the first to bleed:
Me let the thrilling javelin foremost strike,
Since death and victory are now alike.
To day, with ruin shall my name be join'd,
Or stand the common curse of all mankind;

By every woe the vanquish'd shall be known,
And every infamy the victor crown."
He spoke; and, yielding to th' impetuous crowd,
The battle to his frantic bands allow'd.
So, when long vex'd by stormy Corus' blast,
The weary pilot quits the helm at last;
He leaves his vessel to the winds to guide,
And drive unsteady with the tumbling tide.
Loud through the camp the rising murmurs sound,
And one tumultuous hurry runs around;
Sudden their busy hearts began to beat,
And each pale visage wore the marks of fate.
Anxious, they see the dreadful day is come,
That must decide the destiny of Rome.
This single vast concern employs the host,
And private fears are in the public lost.
Should Earth be rent, should darkness quench the Sun,
Should swelling seas above the mountains run,
Should universal nature's end draw near,
Who could have leisure for himself to fear?
With such consent his safety each forgot,
And Rome and Pompey took up every thought.
And now the warriors all, with busy care,
Whet the dull sword, and point the blunted spear;
With tougher nerves they string the bended bow,
And in full quivers steely shafts bestow;
The horseman sees his furniture made fit,
Sharpens the spur, and burnishes the bit;
Fixes the rein, to check or urge his speed,
And animates to fight the snorting steed.
Such once the busy gods' employments were,
If mortal men to gods' we may compare,
When Earth's bold sons began their impious war.
The Lemnian power, with many a stroke, restor'd
Blue Neptune's trident, and stern Mars's sword;
In terrible array, the blue-ey'd maid
The horrours of her Gorgon shield display'd;
Phœbus his once victorious shafts renew'd,
Disus'd, and rusty with the Python's blood;
While, with unweary'd toil, the Cyclops strove
To forge new thunders for imperial Jove.
Nor wanted then dire omens, to declare
What curst events Thessalia's plains prepare;
Black storms oppos'd against the warriors lay,
And lightnings thwarted their forbidden way;
Full in their eyes the dazzling flashes broke,
And with amaze their troubled senses struck:
Tall fiery columns in the skies were seen,
With watery typhons interwove between.
Glancing along the bands swift meteors shoot,
And from the helm the plumy honours cut;
Sudden the flame dissolves the javelin's head,
And liquid runs the shining steely blade.
Strange to behold! their weapons disappear,
While sulphurous odour taints the smoking air.
The standard, as unwilling to be borne,
With pain from the tenacious earth is torn:
Anon, black swarms hang clustering on its height,
And press the bearer with unwonted weight.
Big drops of grief each sweating marble wears,
And Parian gods and heroes stand in tears.
No more th' auspicious victim tamely dies,
But furious from the hallow'd fane he flies;
Breaks off the rites with prodigies prophane,
And bellowing seeks Emathia's fatal plain:
But who, O Cæsar! who were then thy gods?
Whom didst thou summon from their dark abodes?
The Furies listen'd to thy grateful vows,
And dreadful to the day the powers of Hell arose.
Did then the monsters, fame records, appear?
Or were they only phantoms form'd by fear?
Some saw the moving mountains meet like foes,
And rending earth new gaping caves disclose.
Others beheld a sanguine torrent take
Its purple course through fair Bœbeis' lake;
Heard each returning night, portentous, yield
Loud shouts of battle on Pharsalia's field.
While others thought they saw the light decay,
And sudden shades oppress the fainting day;
Fancied wild horrours in each other's face,
And saw the ghosts of all their bury'd race;
Beheld them rise and glare with pale affright,
And stalk around them, in the new-made night.
Whate'er the cause, the crowd, by fate decreed,
To make their brothers, sons, and fathers bleed,
Consenting, to the prodigies agreed;
And, while they thirst impatient for that blood,
Bless these nefarious omens all as good.
But wherefore should we wonder, to behold
That death's approach by madness was foretold?
Wild are the wandering thoughts which last survive;
And these had not another day to live.
These shook for what they saw; while distant climes,
Unknowing, trembled for Emathia's crimes.
Where Tyrian Gades sees the setting Sun,
And where Araxes' rapid waters run,
From the bright orient to the glowing west,
In every nation, every Roman breast
The terrours of that dreadful day confest.
Where Aponus first springs in smoky steam;
And full Timavus rolls his nobler stream;
Upon a hill that day, if fame be true,
A learned augur sat the skies to view:
"'T is come, the great event is come," he cry'd,
"Our impious chiefs their wicked war decide."
Whether the seer observ'd Jove's forky flame,
And mark'd the firmament's discordant frame;
Or whether, in that gloom of sudden night,
The struggling Sun declar'd the dreadful fight:
From the first birth of morning in the skies,
Sure never day like this was known to rise;
In the blue vault, as in a volume spread,
Plain might the Latian destiny be read.
Oh Rome! oh people, by the gods assign'd
To be the worthy masters of mankind!
On thee the Heavens with all their signals wait,
And suffering nature labours with thy fate.
When thy great name 's to latest times convey'd,
By fame, or by my verse immortal made,
In free-born nations justly shall prevail,
And rouse their passions with this noblest tale;
How shall they fear for thy approaching doom,
As if each past event were yet to come!
How shall their bosoms swell with vast concern,
And long the doubtful chance of war to learn!
E'en then the favouring world with thee shall join,
And every honest heart to Pompey's cause incline.
Descending, now, the bands in just array,
From burnish'd arms reflect the beamy day;
In an ill hour they spread the fatal field,
And with portentous blaze the neighbouring mountains gild.
On the left wing, bold Lentulus, their head,
The first and fourth selected legions led:
Luckless Domitius, vainly brave in war,
Drew forth the right with inauspicious care.
In the mid battle daring Scipio fought,
With eight full legions from Cilicia brought.

Submissive here to Pompey's high command,
The warrior undistinguished took his stand,
Reserv'd to be the chief on Libya's burning sand.
Near the low marshes and Enipeus' flood,
The Pontic horse and Cappadocian stood,
While kings and tetrarchs proud, a purple train,
Liegemen and vassals to the Latian reign,
Possess'd the rising grounds and drier plain.
Here troops of black Numidians scour the field,
And bold Iberians narrow bucklers wield;
Here twang the Syrian and the Cretan bow,
And the fierce Gauls provoke their well-known foe.
Go, Pompey, lead to death th' unnumber'd host,
Let the whole human race at once be lost.
Let nations, upon nations, heap the plain,
And tyranny want subjects for its reign.
Cæsar, as chance ordain'd, that morn decreed
The spoiling bands of foragers to lead;
When, with a sudden, but a glad surprise,
The foe descending struck his wondering eyes.
Eager, and burning for unbounded sway,
Long had he borne the tedious war's delay;
Long had he struggled with protracting time,
That sav'd his country, and deferr'd his crime:
At length he sees the wish'd-for day is come:
To end the strife for liberty and Rome;
Fate's dark mysterious threat'nings to explain,
And ease th' impatience of ambition's pain.
But, when he saw the vast event so nigh,
Unusual horrour damp'd his impious joy;
For one cold moment sunk his heart suppress'd,
And doubt hung heavy on his anxious breast.
Though his past fortunes promise now success,
Yet Pompey, from his own, expects no less.
His changing thoughts revolve with various cheer,
While these forbid to hope, and those to fear.
At length his wonted confidence returns,
With his first fires his daring bosom burns;
As if secure of victory, he stands,
And fearless thus bespeaks the listening bands:
"Ye warriors! who have made your Cæsar great,
On whom the world, on whom my fortunes wait,
To day, the gods, whate'er you wish, afford,
And fate attends on the deciding sword.
By your firm aid alone your leader stands,
And trusts his all to your long-faithful hands.
This day shall make our promis'd glories good,
The hopes of Rubicon's distinguish'd flood.
For this blest morn we trusted long to fate,
Deferr'd our fame, and bad the triumph wait,
This day, my gallant friends, this happy day,
Shall the long labours of your arms repay;
Shall give you back to every joy of life,
To the lov'd offspring and the tender wife;
Shall find my veteran out a safe retreat,
And lodge his age within a peaceful seat.
The long dispute of guilt shall now be clear'd,
And conquest shall the juster cause reward.
Have you, for me, with sword and fire laid waste
Your country's bleeding bosom, as you past?
Let the same swords as boldly strike to day,
And the last wounds shall wipe the first away.
Whatever faction's partial notions are,
No hand is wholly innocent in war.
Yours is the cause to which my vows are join'd,
I seek to make you free, and masters of mankind.
I have no hopes, no wishes of my own,
But well could hide me in a private gown:
At my expense of fame, exalt your powers,
Let me be nothing, so the world be yours.
Nor think the task too bloody shall be found,
With easy glory shall our arms be crown'd:
Yon host come learn'd in academic rules,
A band of disputants from Grecian schools.
To these, luxurious eastern crowds are join'd,
Of many a tongue, and many a different kind:
Their own first shouts shall fill each soul with fears,
And their own trumpets shock their tender ears.
Unjustly this, a civil war, we call,
Where none but foes of Rome, barbarians, fall.
On then, my friends! and end it at a blow;
Lay these soft, lazy, worthless nations low.
Show Pompey, that subdu'd them, with what ease
Your valour gains such victories as these:
Show him, if justice still the palm confers,
One triumph was too much for all his wars.
From distant Tigris shall Armenians come,
To judge between the citizens of Rome?
Will fierce barbarian aliens waste their blood,
To make the cause of Latian Pompey good?
Believe me, no. To them we 're all the same,
They hate alike the whole Ausonian name;
But most those haughty masters whom they know,
Who taught their servile vanquish'd necks to bow.
Meanwhile, as round my joyful eyes are roll'd,
None but my try'd companions I behold;
For years in Gaul we made our hard abode,
And many a march in partnership have trod.
Is there a soldier to your chief unknown?
A sword, to whom I trust not, like my own?
Could I not mark each javelin in the sky,
And say from whom the fatal weapons fly?
E'en now I view auspicious furies rise,
And rage redoubled flashes in your eyes.
With joy those omens of success I read,
And see the certain victory decreed;
I see the purple deluge float the plain,
Huge piles of carnage, nations of the slain:
Dead chiefs, with mangled monarchs, I survey,
And the pale senate crowns the glorious day.
But, oh! forgive my tedious lavish tongue,
Your eager virtue I withhold too long;
My soul exults with hopes too fierce to bear,
I feel good fortune and the gods draw near.
All we can ask, with full consent they yield,
And nothing bars us but this narrow field.
The battle o'er, what boon can I deny?
The treasures of the world before you lie.
Oh, Thessaly! what stars, what powers divine,
To thy distinguish'd land this great event assign?
Between extremes, to day our fortune lies,
The vilest punishment, and noblest prize.
Consider well the captive's lost estate,
Chains, racks, and crosses, for the vanquish'd wait,
My limbs are each allotted to its place,
And my pale head the rostrum's height shall grace;
But that 's a thought unworthy Cæsar's care,
More for my friends than for myself I fear.
On my good sword securely I rely,
And, if I conquer not, am sure to die.
But, oh! for you my anxious soul foresees,
Pompey shall copy Sylla's curst decrees;
The Martian field shall blush with gore again,
And massacres once more the peaceful Septa stain.
Hear, O ye gods, who in Rome's strugglings share,
Who leave your Heaven, to make our Earth your care;
Hear, and let him the happy victor live,
Who shall with mercy use the power you give;

Whose rage for slaughter with the war shall cease,
And spare his vanquish'd enemies in peace.
Nor is Dyrrhachium's fatal field forgot,
Nor what was then our brave companions lot;
When, by advantage of the straiter ground,
Successful Pompey compass'd us around;
When quite disarm'd your useless valour stood,
Till his fell sword was satiated with blood.
But gentler hands, but nobler hearts you bear,
And, oh! remember 't is your leader's prayer,
Whatever Roman flies before you, spare.
But, while oppos'd and menacing they stand,
Let no regard withhold the lifted hand:
Let friendship, kindred, all remorse, give place,
And mangling wounds deform the reverend face:
Still let resistance be repaid with blood,
And hostile force by hostile force subdu'd;
Stranger, or friend, whatever be the name,
Your merit still, to Cæsar, is the same.
Fill then the trenches, break the ramparts round,
And let our works lie level with the ground;
So shall no obstacles our march delay,
Nor stop one moment our victorious way.
Nor spare your camp; this night we mean to lie
In that from whence the vanquish'd foe shall fly."
 Scarce had he spoke, when, sudden at the word,
They seize the lance, and draw the shining sword:
At once the turfy fences all lie waste,
And through the breach the crowding legions haste;
Regardless all of order and array
They stand, and trust to fate alone the day.
Each had propos'd an empire to be won,
Had each once known a Pompey for his son;
Had Cæsar's soul inform'd each private breast,
A fiercer fury could not be express'd.
 With sad presages, Pompey, now, beheld
His foes advancing o'er the neighbouring field:
He saw the gods had fix'd the day of fate,
And felt his heart hang heavy with new weight.
Dire is the omen when the valiant fear,
Which yet he strove to hide, with well-dissembled cheer.
High on his warrior steed, the chief o'er-ran
The wide array, and thus at length began:
 "The time to ease your groaning country's pain,
Which long your eager valour sought in vain;
The great deciding hour at length is come,
To end the strivings of distracted Rome:
For this one last effort exert your power,
Strike home to day, and all your toils are o'er.
If the dear pledges of connubial love,
Your houshold-gods, and Rome, your souls can move,
Hither by fate they seem together brought,
And for that prize, to day, the battle shall be fought.
Let none the favouring gods' assistance fear;
They always make the juster cause their care.
The flying dart to Cæsar shall they guide,
And point the sword at his devoted side:
Our injur'd laws shall be on him made good,
And liberty establish'd in his blood.
Could Heaven, in violence of wrath, ordain
The world to groan beneath a tyrant's reign,
It had not spar'd your Pompey's head so long,
Nor lengthen'd out my age to see the wrong.
All we can wish for, to secure success,
With large advantage here our arms possess:
See, in the ranks of every common band,
Where Rome's illustrious names for soldiers stand.
Could the great dead re-visit life again,
For us, once more, the Decii would be slain;
The Curii, and Camilli, might we boast,
Proud to be mingled in this noblest host.
If men, if multitudes, can make us strong,
Behold what tribes unnumber'd march along!
Where'er the zodiac turns its radiant round,
Wherever earth, or people, can be found;
To us the nations issue forth in swarms,
And in Rome's cause all human nature arms.
What then remains, but that our wings enclose,
Within their ample folds, our shrinking foes?
Thousands, and thousands, useless may we spare;
Yon handful will not half employ our war.
Think, from the summit of the Roman wall,
You hear our loud lamenting matrons call;
Think with what tears, what lifted hands, they sue,
And place their last, their only hopes in you.
Imagine kneeling age before you spread,
Each hoary reverend majestic head;
Imagine, Rome herself your aid implor'd,
To save her from a proud imperious lord.
Think how the present age, how that to come,
What multitudes from you expect their doom:
On your success dependant all rely;
These to be born in freedom, those to die.
Think (if there be a thought can move you more,
A pledge more dear than those I nam'd before)
Think you behold (were such a posture meet)
E'en me, your Pompey, prostrate at your feet.
Myself, my wife, my sons, a suppliant band,
From you our lives and liberties demand;
Or conquer you, or I, to exile born,
My last dishonourable years shall mourn,
Your long reproach, and my proud father's scorn.
From bonds, from infamy, your general save,
Nor let his hoary head descend to earth a slave."
 Thus while he spoke, the faithful legions round,
With indignation caught the mournful sound;
Falsely, they think, his fears those dangers view,
But vow to die, ere Cæsar proves them true.
What differing thoughts the various hosts incite,
And urge their deadly ardour for the fight!
Those bold ambition kindles into rage,
And these their fears for liberty engage.
How shall this day the peopled Earth deface,
Prevent mankind, and rob the growing race!
Though all the years to come should roll in peace,
And future ages bring their whole increase;
Though Nature all her genial powers employ,
All shall not yield what these curst hands destroy.
Soon shall the greatness of the Roman name,
To unbelieving ears, be told by fame;
Low shall the mighty Latian towers be laid,
And ruins crown our Alban mountain's head;
While yearly magistrates, in turns compell'd
To lodge by night upon th' uncover'd field,
Shall at old doting Numa's laws repine,
Who could to such bleak wilds his Latine rites assign.
E'en now behold! where waste Hesperia lies,
Where empty cities shock our mournful eyes;
Untouch'd by time, our infamy they stand,
The marks of civil discord's murderous hand.
How is the stock of human-kind brought low!
Walls want inhabitants, and hands the plough.
Our fathers' fertile fields by slaves are till'd,
And Rome with dregs of foreign lands is fill'd:
Such were the heaps, the millions of the slain,
As 't were the purpose of Emathia's plain,
That none for future mischiefs should remain.
Well may our annals less misfortunes yield,
Mark Allia's flood, and Cannæ's fatal field;

But let Pharsalia's day be still forgot,
Be ras'd at once from every Roman thought.
'T was there, that Fortune, in her pride, display'd
The greatness her own mighty hands had made;
Forth in array the powers of Rome she drew,
And set her subject nations all to view;
As if she meant to show the haughty queen,
E'en by her ruins, what her height had been.
Oh countless loss! that well might have supply'd
The desolation of all deaths beside.
Though famine with blue pestilence conspire,
And dreadful earthquakes with destroying fire;
Pharsalia's blood the gaping wounds had join'd,
And built again the ruins of mankind.
Immortal gods! with what resistless force,
Our growing empire ran its rapid course!
Still every year with new success was crown'd,
And conquering chiefs enlarge the Latian bound;
Till Rome stood mistress of the world confess'd,
From the gray orient, to the ruddy west;
From pole to pole, her wide dominions run,
Where'er the stars, or brighter Phœbus shone;
As Heaven and Earth were made for her alone.
But now, behold, how Fortune tears away
The gift of ages in one fatal day!
One day shakes off the vanquish'd Indians' chain,
And turns the wandering Däæ loose again:
No longer shall the victor consul now
Trace our Sarmatian cities with the plough:
Exulting Parthia shall her slaughters boast,
Nor feel the vengeance due to Crassus' ghost.
While liberty, long wearied by our crimes,
Forsakes us for some better barbarous climes;
Beyond the Rhine and Tanaïs she flies,
To snowy mountains, and to frozen skies;
While Rome, who long pursu'd that chiefest good,
O'er fields of slaughter, and through seas of blood,
In slavery, her abject state shall mourn,
Nor dare to hope the goddess will return.
Why were we ever free? Oh why has Heaven
A short-liv'd transitory blessing given?
Of thee, first Brutus, justly we complain!
Why didst thou break thy groaning country's chain,
And end the proud lascivious tyrant's reign?
Why did thy patriot hand on Rome bestow
Laws, and her consuls' righteous rule to know?
In servitude more happy had we been,
Since Romulus first wall'd his refuge in,
E'en since the twice six vultures bad him build,
To this curst period of Pharsalia's field.
Medes and Arabians of the slavish east
Beneath eternal bondage may be blest;
While, of a differing mold and nature, we,
From sire to son accustom'd to be free,
Feel indignation rising in our blood,
And blush to wear the chains that make them proud.
Can there be gods, who rule yon azure sky?
Can they behold Emathia from on high,
And yet forbear to bid their lightnings fly?
Is it the business of a thundering Jove,
To rive the rocks, and blast the guiltless grove?
While Cassius holds the balance in his stead,
And wreaks due vengeance on the tyrant's head.
The Sun ran back from Atreus' monstrous feast,
And his fair beams in murky clouds suppress'd;
Why shines he now? why lends his golden light
To these worse parricides, this more accursed sight?
But chance guides all; the gods their task forego,
And Providence no longer reigns below.
Yet are they just, and some revenge afford
While their own Heavens are humbled by the sword,
And the proud victors, like themselves, ador'd:
With rays adorn'd, with thunders arm'd they stand,
And incense, prayers, and sacrifice demand;
While trembling, slavish, superstitious Rome,
Swears by a mortal wretch, that moulders in a tomb.

Now either host the middle plain had pass'd,
And front to front in threatening ranks were plac'd;
Then every well-known feature stood to view,
Brothers their brothers, sons their fathers knew.
Then first they feel the curse of civil hate,
Mark where their mischiefs are assign'd by fate,
And see from whom themselves destruction wait.
Stupid a while, and at a gaze, they stood,
While creeping horrour froze the lazy blood:
Some small remains of piety withstand,
And stop the javelin in the lifted hand;
Remorse for one short moment stepp'd between,
And motionless, as statues, all were seen.
And oh! what savage fury could engage,
While lingering Cæsar yet suspends his rage?
For him, ye gods! for Crastinus, whose spear
With impious eagerness began the war,
Some more than common punishment prepare;
Beyond the grave long lasting plagues ordain,
Surviving sense and never ceasing pain.
Straight, at the fatal signal, all around
A thousand fifes, a thousand clarions, sound;
Beyond where clouds, or glancing lightnings fly,
The piercing clangors strike the vaulted sky.
The joining battles shout, and the loud peal
Bounds from the hill, and thunders down the vale;
Old Pelion's caves the doubling roar return,
And Oeta's rocks and groaning Pindus mourn;
From pole to pole the tumult spreads afar;
And the world trembles at the distant war.

Now flit the thrilling darts through liquid air,
And various vows from various masters bear:
Some seek the noblest Roman heart to wound,
And some to err upon the guiltless ground;
While chance decrees the blood that shall be spilt,
And blindly scatters innocence and guilt.
But random shafts too scanty death afford,
A civil war is business for the sword:
Where face to face the paricides may meet,
Know whom they kill, and make the crime complete.

Firm in the front, with joining bucklers clos'd,
Stood the Pompeian infantry dispos'd;
So crowded was the space, it scarce affords
The power to toss their piles, or wield their swords.
Forward, thus thick embattled though they stand,
With headlong wrath rush furious Cæsars band;
In vain the lifted shield their rage retards,
Or plaited mail devoted bosoms guards;
Through shields, through mail, the wounding weapons go,
And to the heart drive home each deadly blow;
Oh rage ill match'd! oh much unequal war,
Which those wage proudly, and these tamely bear!
These, by cold, stupid piety disarm'd;
Those, by hot blood, and smoking slaughter warm'd.

Nor in suspense uncertain fortune hung,
But yields, o'ermaster'd by a power too strong,
And borne by fate's impetuous stream along.
From Pompey's ample wings, at length the horse
Wide o'er the plain extending take their course;
Wheeling around the hostile line they wind,
While lightly arm'd the shot succeed behind.
In various ways the various bands engage,
And hurl upon the foe the missile rage:
There fiery darts and rocky fragments fly,
And heating bullets whistle through the sky:
Of feather'd shafts, a cloud thick shading goes,
From Arab, Mede, and Ituræan bows:
But driven by random aim they seldom wound;
At first they hide the Heaven, then strow the ground;
While Roman hands unerring mischief send,
And certain deaths on every pile attend.
But Cæsar, timely careful to support
His wavering front against the first effort,
Had plac'd his bodies of reserve behind,
And the strong rear with chosen cohorts lin'd.
There, as the careless foe the fight pursue,
A sudden band and stable forth he drew;
When soon, oh shame! the loose barbarians yield,
Scattering their broken squadrons o'er the field,
And show, too late, that slaves attempt in vain
The sacred cause of freedom to maintain.
The fiery steeds, impatient of a wound,
Hurl their neglected riders to the ground;
Or on their friends with rage ungovern'd turn,
And trampling o'er the helpless foot are borne.
Hence foul confusion and dismay succeed,
The victors murder, and the vanquish'd bleed:
Their weary hands the tir'd destroyers ply,
Scarce can these kill, so fast as those can die.
Oh, that Emathia's ruthless guilty plain
Had been contended with this only stain;
With these rude bones had strown her verdure o'er,
And dy'd her springs with none but Asian gore!
But if so keen her thirst for Roman blood,
Let none but Romans make the slaughter good;
Let not a Mede nor Cappadocian fall,
No bold Iberian, or rebellious Gaul:
Let these alone survive for times to come,
And be the future citizens of Rome.
But fear on all alike her powers employ'd,
Did Cæsar's business, and like fate destroy'd.
Prevailing still the victors held their course,
Till Pompey's main reserve oppos'd their force;
There, in his strength, the chief unshaken stood,
Repell'd the foe, and made the combat good;
There in suspense th' uncertain battle hung,
And Cæsar's favouring goddess doubted long;
There no proud monarchs led their vassals on,
Nor eastern bands in gorgeous purple shone;
There the last force of laws and freedom lay,
And Roman patriots struggled for the day.
What parricides the guilty scene affords!
Sires, sons, and brothers, rush on mutual swords!
There every sacred bond of nature bleeds;
There met the war's worst rage, and Cæsar's blackest deeds.
But, oh! my Muse, the mournful theme forbear,
And stay thy lamentable numbers here;
Let not my verse to future times convey
What Rome committed on this dreadful day;
In shades and silence hide her crimes from fame,
And spare thy miserable country's shame.
But Cæsar's rage shall with oblivion strive,
And for eternal infamy survive.
From rank to rank, unweary'd, still he flies,
And with new fires their fainting wrath supplies.
His greedy eyes each sign of guilt explore,
And mark whose sword is deepest dy'd in gore;
Observe where pity and remorse prevail,
What arm strikes faintly, and what cheek turns pale.
Or, while he rides the slaughter'd heaps around,
And views some foe expiring on the ground,
His cruel hands the gushing blood restrain,
And strive to keep the parting soul in pain:
As when Bellona drives the world to war,
Or Mars comes thundering in his Thracian car;
Rage horrible darts from his Gorgon shield,
And gloomy terrour broods upon the field;
Hate, fell and fierce, the dreadful gods impart,
And urge the vengeful warrior's heaving heart;
The many shout, arms clash, the wounded cry,
And one promiscuous peal groans upwards to the sky.
Nor furious Cæsar, on Emathia's plains,
Less terribly the mortal strife sustains:
Each hand unarm'd he fills with means of death,
And cooling wrath rekindles at his breath:
Now with his voice, his gesture now, he strives,
Now with his lance the lagging soldier drives:
The weak he strengthens, and confirms the strong,
And hurries war's impetuous stream along.
"Strike home," he cries, "and let your swords erase
Each well-known feature of the kindred face:
Nor waste your fury on the vulgar band;
See! where the hoary doting senate stand;
There laws and right at once you may confound,
And liberty shall bleed at every wound."
The curs'd destroyer spoke; and, at the word,
The purple nobles sunk beneath the sword:
The dying patriots groan upon the ground,
Illustrious names, for love of laws renown'd.
The great Metelli and Torquati bleed,
Chiefs worthy, if the state had so decreed,
And Pompey were not there, mankind to lead.
Say thou! thy sinking country's only prop,
Glory of Rome, and liberty's last hope;
What helm, O Brutus! could, amidst the crowd,
Thy sacred undistinguish'd visage shroud?
Where fought thy arm that day! But, ah! forbear!
Nor rush unwary on the pointed spear;
Seek not to hasten on untimely fate,
But patient for thy own Emathia wait:
Nor hunt fierce Cæsar on this bloody plain,
To day thy steel pursues his life in vain.
Somewhat is wanting to the tyrant yet,
To make the measure of his crimes complete;
As yet he has not every law defy'd,
Nor reach'd the utmost heights of daring pride.
Ere long thou shalt behold him Rome's proud lord,
And ripen'd by ambition for thy sword;
Then, thy griev'd country vengeance shall demand,
And ask the victim at thy righteous hand.
Among huge heaps of the patricians slain,
And Latian chiefs, who strow'd that purple plain,
Recording story has distinguish'd well,
How brave, unfortunate Domitius fell.
In every loss of Pompey still he shar'd,
And dy'd in liberty, the best reward;
Though vanquish'd oft by Cæsar, ne'er enslav'd,
E'en to the last, the tyrant's power he brav'd:
Mark'd o'er with many a glorious streaming wound,
In pleasure sunk the warrior to the ground;

No longer forc'd on vilest terms to live,
For chance to doom, and Cæsar to forgive.
Him, as he pass'd insulting o'er the field,
Roll'd in his blood, the victor proud beheld:
" And can," he cry'd, " the fierce Domitius fall,
Forsake his Pompey, and expecting Gaul?
Must the war lose that still successful sword,
And my neglected province want a lord?"
He spoke; when lifting slow his closing eyes,
Fearless the dying Roman thus replies:
" Since wickedness stands unrewarded yet,
Nor Cæsar's arms their wish'd success have met;
Free and rejoicing to the shades I go,
And leave my chief still equal to his foe;
And if my hopes divine thy doom aright,
Yet shalt thou bow thy vanquish'd head ere night.
Dire punishments the righteous gods decree,
For injur'd Rome, for Pompey, and for me;
In Hell's dark realms thy tortures I shall know,
And hear thy ghost lamenting loud below."
He said; and soon the leaden sleep prevail'd,
And everlasting night his eyelids seal'd.
But, oh! what grief the ruin can deplore!
What verse can run the various slaughter o'er!
For lesser woes our sorrows may we keep;
No tears suffice, a dying world to weep.
In differing groups ten thousand deaths arise,
And horrours manifold the soul surprise.
Here the whole man is open'd at a wound,
And gushing bowels pour upon the ground;
Another through the gaping jaws is gor'd,
And in his utmost throat receives the sword:
At once, a single blow a third extends;
The fourth a living trunk dismember'd stands.
Some in their breasts erect the javelin bear,
Some cling to earth with the transfixing spear.
Here, like a fountain, springs a purple flood,
Spouts on the foe, and stains his arms with blood.
There horrid brethren on their brethren prey;
One starts, and hurls a well-known head away.
While some detested son, with impious ire,
Lops by the shoulders close his hoary sire:
E'en his rude fellows damn the cursed deed,
And bastard-born the murderer aread.
No private house its loss lamented then,
But count the slain by nations, not by men.
Here Grecian streams and Asiatic run,
And Roman torrents drive the deluge on.
More than the world at once was given away,
And late posterity was lost that day:
A race of future slaves receiv'd their doom,
And children yet unborn were overcome.
How shall our miserable sons complain,
That they are born beneath a tyrant's reign?
" Did our base hands," with justice shall they say,
" The sacred cause of liberty betray?
Why have our fathers given us a prey?
Their age, to ours, the curse of bondage leaves;
Themselves were cowards, and begot us slaves."
'Tis just; and Fortune, that impos'd a lord,
One struggle for their freedom might afford;
Might leave their hands their proper cause to fight,
And let them keep, or lose themselves, their right.
But Pompey, now, the fate of Rome descry'd,
And saw the changing gods forsake her side.
Hard to believe, though from a rising ground
He view'd the universal ruin round,
In crimson streams he saw destruction run,
And in the fall of thousands felt his own.
Nor wish'd he, like most wretches in despair,
The world one common misery might share:
But with a generous, great, exalted mind,
Besought the gods to pity poor mankind,
To let him die, and leave the rest behind:
This hope came smiling to his anxious breast,
For this his earnest vows were thus address'd:
" Spare man, ye gods! oh let the nations live!
Let me be wretched, but let Rome survive.
Or if this head suffices not alone,
My wife, my sons, your anger shall atone:
If blood the yet unsated war demand,
Behold my pledges left in Fortune's hand!
Ye cruel powers, who urge me with your hate,
At length behold me crush'd beneath the weight:
Give then your long-pursuing vengeance o'er,
And spare the world, since I can lose no more."
So saying, the tumultuous field he cross'd,
And warn'd from battle his despairing host.
Gladly the pains of death he had explor'd,
And fall'n undaunted on his pointed sword;
Had he not fear'd th' example might succeed,
And faithful nations by his side would bleed.
Or did his swelling soul disdain to die,
While his insulting father stood so nigh?
Fly where he will, the gods shall still pursue,
Nor his pale head shall 'scape the victor's view.
Or else, perhaps, and fate the thought approv'd,
For her dear sake he fled, whom best he lov'd:
Malicious Fortune to his wish agreed,
And gave him in Cornelia's sight to bleed.
Borne by his winged steed at length away,
He quits the purple plain and yields the day.
Fearless of danger, still secure and great,
His daring soul supports his lost estate;
Nor groans his breast, nor swell his eyes with tears,
But still the same majestic form he wears.
An awful grief sat decent in his face,
Such as became his loss, and Rome's disgrace:
His mind, unbroken, keeps her constant frame,
In greatness and misfortune still the same;
While Fortune, who his triumphs once beheld,
Unchanging sees him leave Pharsalia's field.
Now disentangled from unwieldy power,
O Pompey! run thy former honours o'er:
At leisure now review the glorious scene,
And call to mind how mighty thou hast been.
From anxious toils of empire turn thy care,
And from thy thoughts exclude the murderous war;
Let the just gods bear witness on thy side,
Thy cause no more shall by the sword be try'd.
Whether sad Afric shall her loss bemoan,
Or Munda's plains beneath their burthen groan,
The guilty bloodshed shall be all their own.
No more the much-lov'd Pompey's name shall charm
The peaceful world, with one consent, to arm;
Nor for thy sake, nor aw'd by thy command,
But for themselves, the fighting senate stand:
The war but one distinction shall afford,
And liberty, or Cæsar, be the word.
Nor, oh! do thou thy vanquish'd lot deplore,
But fly with pleasure from those seas of gore:
Look back upon the horrour, guiltless thou,
And pity Cæsar, for whose sake they flow.
With what a heart, what triumph shall he come,
A victor, red with Roman blood, to Rome?
Though misery thy banishment attends,
Though thou shalt die, by thy false Pharian friends;

Yet trust securely to the choice of Heaven,
And know thy loss was for a blessing giv'n:
Though flight may seem the warrior's shame and curse;
To conquer, in a cause like this, is worse.
And, oh! let every mark of grief be spar'd,
May no tear fall, no groan, no sigh be heard;
Still let mankind their Pompey's fate adore,
And reverence thy fall, e'en as thy height of power.
Meanwhile survey th' attending world around,
Cities by thee possess'd, and monarchs crown'd:
On Afric, or on Asia, cast thy eye,
And mark the land where thou shalt choose to die.
Larissa first the constant chief beheld,
Still great, though flying from the fatal field:
With loud acclaim her crowds his coming greet,
And sighing, pour their presents at his feet.
She crowns her altars, and proclaims a feast;
Would put on joy to cheer her noble guest;
But weeps, and begs to share his woes at least.
So was he lov'd e'en in his lost estate,
Such faith, such friendship, on his ruins wait;
With ease Pharsalia's loss might be supply'd,
While eager nations hasten to his side;
As if misfortune meant to bless him more,
Than all his long prosperity before.
" In vain," he cries, " you bring the vanquish'd aid;
Henceforth to Cæsar be your homage paid,
Cæsar, who triumphs o'er yon heaps of dead."
With that, his courser urging on to flight,
He vanish'd from the mournful city's sight.
With cries, and loud laments, they fill the air,
And curse the cruel gods, in fierceness of despair.
Now in huge lakes Hesperian crimson stood,
And Cæsar's self grew satiated with blood.
The great patricians fall'n, his pity spar'd
The worthless, unresisting, vulgar herd.
Then, while his glowing fortune yet was warm,
And scattering terrour spread the wild alarm,
Straight to the hostile camp his way he bent,
Careful to seize the hasty flyer's tent,
The leisure of a night, and thinking to prevent.
Nor reck'd he much the weary soldiers toil,
But led them prone, and greedy to the spoil.
" Behold," he cries, " our victory complete,
The glorious recompense attends you yet:
Much have you done to day, for Cæsar's sake;
'Tis mine to show the prey, 'tis yours to take.
'Tis yours, whate'er the vanquish'd foe has left;
'Tis what your valour gain'd, and not my gift.
Treasures immense yon wealthy tents infold,
The gems of Asia, and Hesperian gold;
For you the once-great Pompey's store attends,
With regal spoils of his barbarian friends:
Haste then, prevent the foe, and seize that good,
For which you paid so well with Roman blood."
He said; and with the rage of rapine stung,
The multitude tumultuous rush along.
On swords, and spears, on sires and sons they tread,
And all remorseless spurn the gory dead.
What trench can intercept, what fort withstand
The brutal soldier's rude rapacious hand;
When eager to his crime's reward he flies,
And, bath'd in blood, demands the horrid prize?
There, wealth collected from the world around,
The destin'd recompense of war they found.
But, oh! not golden Arimaspus' store,
Nor all the Tagus or rich Iber pour,
Can fill the greedy victors griping hands:
Rome, and the Capitol, their pride demands;
All other spoils they scorn, as worthless prey,
And count their wicked labours robb'd of pay.
Here in patrician tents, plebeians rest,
And regal couches are by ruffians press'd:
There impious parricides the bed invade,
And sleep where late their slaughter'd sires were laid.
Meanwhile the battle stands in dreams renew'd,
And Stygian horrours o'er their slumbers brood.
Astonishment and dread their souls infest,
And guilt sits painful on each heaving breast.
Arms, blood, and death, work in the labouring brain,
They sigh, they start, they strive, and fight it o'er again.
Ascending fiends infect the air around,
And Hell breathes baleful through the groaning ground:
Hence dire affright distracts the warriors' souls,
Vengeance divine their daring hearts controls,
Snakes hiss, and livid flame tormenting rolls.
Each, as his hands in guilt have been imbru'd,
By some pale spectre flies all night pursu'd.
In various forms the ghosts unnumber'd groan,
The brother, friend, the father, and the son:
To every wretch his proper phantom fell,
While Cæsar sleeps the general care of Hell.
Such were his pangs as mad Orestes felt,
Ere yet the Scythian altar purg'd his guilt.
Such horrours Pentheus, such Agave knew;
He when his rage first came, and she when hers withdrew.
Present and future swords his bosom bears,
And feels the blow that Brutus now defers.
Vengeance, in all her pomp of pain, attends;
To wheels she binds him, and with vultures rends,
With racks of conscience, and with whips of fiends.
But soon the visionary horrours pass,
And his first rage with day resumes its place:
Again his eyes rejoice to view the slain,
And run unweary'd o'er the dreadful plain.
He bids his train prepare his impious board,
And feasts amidst the heaps of death abhorr'd.
There each pale face at leisure he may know,
And still behold the purple current flow.
He views the woeful wide horizon round,
Then joys that earth is no where to be found,
And owns, those gods he serves, his utmost wish have crown'd;
Still greedy to possess the curs'd delight,
To glut his soul, and gratify his sight,
The last funereal honours he denies,
And poisons with the stench Emathia's skies.
Not thus the sworn inveterate foe of Rome,
Refus'd the vanquish'd consul's bones a tomb:
His piety the country round beheld,
And bright with fires shone Cannæ's fatal field,
But Cæsar's rage from fiercer motives rose;
These were his countrymen, his worst of foes.
But, oh! relent, forget thy hatred past,
And give the wandering shades to rest at last.
Nor seek we single honours for the dead,
At once let nations on the pile be laid:
To feed the flame, let heapy forests rise,
Far be it seen to fret the ruddy skies,
And grieve despairing Pompey where he flies.
Know too, proud conqueror, thy wrath in vain
Strows with unbury'd carcasses the plain.
What is it to thy malice, if they burn,
Rot in the field, or moulder in the urn?
The forms of matter all dissolving die,
And lost in nature's blending bosom lie.
Though now thy cruelty denies a grave,
These and the world one common lot shall have;

One last appointed flame, by fate's decree, [sea;
Shall waste yon azure heavens, this earth, and
Shall knead the dead up in one mingled mass,
Where stars and they shall undistinguish'd pass.
And though thou scorn their fellowship, yet know,
High as thy own can soar these souls shall go;
Or find, perhaps, a better place below.
Death is beyond thy goddess Fortune's power,
And parent Earth receives whate'er she bore.
Nor will we mourn those Romans' fate, who lie
Beneath the glorious covering of the sky;
That starry arch for ever round them turns,
A nobler shelter far than tombs or urns.
But wherefore parts the loathing victor hence?
Does slaughter strike too strongly on thy sense?
Yet stay, yet breathe the thick infectious stream,
Yet quaff with joy the blood-polluted steam.
But see, they fly! the daring warriors yield!
And the dead heaps drive Cæsar from the field!
Now to the prey, gaunt wolves, a howling train,
Speed hungry from the fair Bistonian plain;
From Pholoe the tawny lion comes,
And growling bears forsake their darksome homes:
With these, lean dogs in herds obscene repair,
And every kind that snuffs the tainted air.
For food the cranes their wonted flight delay,
That erst to warmer Nile had wing'd their way:
With them the feather'd race convene from far,
Who gather to the prey, and wait on war.
Ne'er were such flocks of vultures seen to fly,
And hide with spreading plumes the crowded sky:
Gorging on limbs in every tree they sat,
And dropp'd raw morsels down and gory fat:
Oft their tir'd talons, loosening as they fled,
Rain'd horrid offals on the victor's head.
But while the slain supply'd too full a feast,
The plenty bred satiety at last;
The ravenous feeders riot at their ease,
And single out what dainties best may please.
Part borne away, the rest neglected lie,
For noon-day suns, and parching winds, to dry;
Till length of time shall wear them quite away,
And mix them with Emathia's common clay.
Oh fatal Thessaly! oh land abhorr'd!
How have thy fields the hate of Heav'n incurr'd;
That thus the gods to thee destruction doom,
And load thee with the curse of falling Rome!
Still to new crimes, new horrours, dost thou haste,
When yet thy former mischiefs scarce were past.
What rolling years, what ages, can repay
The multitudes thy wars have swept away!
Though tombs and urns their numerous store should spread,
And long antiquity yield all her dead;
Thy guilty plains more slaughter'd Romans hold,
Than all those tombs, and all those urns, infold.
Hence bloody spots shall stain thy grassy green,
And crimson drops on bladed corn be seen:
Each ploughshare some dead patriot shall molest,
Disturb his bones, and rob his ghost of rest.
Oh! had the guilt of war been all thy own,
Were civil rage confin'd to thee alone;
No mariner his labouring bark should moor,
In hopes of safety, on thy dreadful shore;
No swain thy spectre-haunted plain should know,
Nor turn thy blood-stain'd fallow with his plough:
No shepherd e'er should drive his flock to feed,
Where Romans slain enrich the verdant mead:
All desolate should lie thy land and waste,
As in some scorch'd or frozen region plac'd.
But the great gods forbid our partial hate
On Thessaly's distinguish'd land to wait;
New blood, and other slaughters, they decree,
And others shall be guilty too, like thee.
Munda and Mutina shall boast their slain,
Pachynus' waters share the purple stain,
And Actium justify Pharsalia's plain.

BOOK VIII.

THE ARGUMENT.

From Pharsalia Pompey flies, first to Larissa, and after to the sea-shore; where he embarks upon a small vessel for Lesbos. There, after a melancholy meeting with Cornelia, and his refusal of the Mitylenians' invitations, he embarks with his wife for the coast of Asia. In the way thither he is joined by his son Sextus, and several persons of distinction, who had fled likewise from the late battle; and among the rest by Deiotarus, king of Gallo-Græcia. To him he recommends the soliciting of supplies from the king of Parthia, and the rest of his allies in Asia. After coasting Cilicia for some time, he comes at length to a little town called Syedra or Syedræ, where great part of the senate meet him. With these, he deliberates upon the present circumstances of the commonwealth, and proposes either Mauritania, Ægypt, or Parthia, as the proper places where he may hope to be received, and from whose kings he may expect assistance. In his own opinion he inclines to the Parthians; but this Lentulus, in a long oration, opposes very warmly; and, in consideration of young Ptolemy's personal obligations to Pompey, prefers Ægypt. This advice is generally approved and followed, and Pompey sets sail accordingly for Ægypt. Upon his arrival on that coast, the king calls a council, where, at the instigation of Pothinus, a villanous minister, it is resolved to take his life; and the execution of this order is committed to the care of Achillas, formerly the king's governor, and then general of the army. He, with Septimius, a renegado Roman soldier, who had formerly served under Pompey, upon some frivolous pretences, persuades him to quit his ship, and come into their boat; where, as they make towards the shore, he treacherously murders him, in the sight of his wife, his son, and the rest of his fleet. His head is cut off, and his body thrown into the sea. The head is fixed upon a spear, and carried to Ptolemy; who, after he had seen it, commands it to be embalmed. In the succeeding night, one Cordus, who had been a follower of Pompey, finds the trunk floating near the shore, brings it to land with some difficulty; and, with a few planks that remained from a shipwrecked vessel, burns it. The melancholy description of this mean funeral, with the poet's invective against the gods, and fortune, for their unworthy treatment of so great a man, concludes this book.

Now through the vale, by great Alcides made,
And the sweet maze of Tempe's pleasing shade,
Cheerless, the flying chief renew'd his speed,
And urg'd, with gory spurs, his fainting steed.
Fall'n from the former greatness of his mind,
He turns where doubtful paths obscurely wind.

The fellows of his flight increase his dread,
While hard behind the trampling horsemen tread:
He starts at every rustling of the trees,
And fears the whispers of each murmuring breeze.
He feels not yet, alas! his lost estate;
And, though he flies, believes himself still great;
Imagines millions for his life are bid,
And rates his own, as he would Cæsar's head.
Where'er his fear explores untrodden ways,
His well-known visage still his flight betrays.
Many he meets unknowing of his chance,
Whose gathering forces to his aid advance.
With gaze astonish'd, these their chief behold,
And scarce believe what by himself is told.
In vain, to covert, from the world he flies,
Fortune still grieves him with pursuing eyes:
Still aggravates, still urges his disgrace,
And galls him with the thoughts of what he was.
His youthful triumph sadly now returns,
His Pontic and piratic wars he mourns, [burns.
While stung with secret shame and anxious care he
Thus age to sorrows oft the great betrays,
When loss of empire comes with length of days.
Life and enjoyment still one end shall have,
Lest early misery prevent the grave.
The good, that lasts not, was in vain bestow'd,
And ease once past becomes the present load:
Then let the wise, in Fortune's kindest hour,
Still keep one safe retreat within his power;
Let death be near, to guard him from surprise,
And free him, when the fickle goddess flies.
Now to those shores the hapless Pompey came,
Where hoary Peneus rolls his ancient stream:
Red with Emathian slaughter ran his flood,
And dy'd the ocean deep in Roman blood.
There a poor bark, whose keel perhaps might glide
Safe down some river's smooth descending tide,
Receiv'd the mighty master of the main,
Whose spreading navies hide the liquid plain.
In this he braves the winds and stormy sea,
And to the Lesbian isle directs his way.
There the kind partner of his every care,
His faithful, lov'd Cornelia, languish'd there:
At that sad distance more unhappy far,
Than in the midst of danger, death, and war.
There on her heart, e'en all the live-long day,
Foreboding thought a weary burthen lay:
Sad visions haunt her slumbers with affright,
And Thessaly returns with every night.
Soon as the ruddy morning paints the skies,
Swift to the shore the pensive mourner flies;
There, lonely sitting on the cliff's bleak brow,
Her sight she fixes on the seas below;
Attentive marks the wide horizon's bound,
And kens each sail that rises in the round:
Thick beats her heart, as every prow draws near,
And dreads the fortunes of her lord to hear.
At length, behold! the fatal bark is come!
See! the swoln canvass labouring with her doom.
Preventing fame, misfortune lends him wings,
And Pompey's self his own sad story brings.
Now bid thy eyes, thou lost Cornelia, flow,
And change thy fears to certain sorrows, now.
Swift glides the woeful vessel on to land;
Forth flies the headlong matron to the strand.
There soon she found what worst the gods could do,
There soon her dear much-alter'd lord she knew;
Though fearful all and ghastly was his hue.
Rude, o'er his face, his hoary locks were grown,
And dust was cast upon his Roman gown.
She saw, and, fainting, sunk in sudden night;
Grief stopp'd her breath, and shut out loathsome light;
The loosening nerves no more their force exert,
And motion ceas'd within the freezing heart;
Death kindly seem'd her wishes to obey,
And, stretch'd upon the beach, a corse she lay.
But now the mariners the vessel moor,
And Pompey, landing, views the lonely shore.
The faithful maids their loud lamentings ceas'd,
And reverendly their ruder grief suppress'd
Straight, while with duteous care they kneel around,
And raise their wretched mistress from the ground,
Her lord infolds her with a strict embrace,
And joins his cheek close to her lifeless face:
At the known touch her failing sense returns,
And vital warmth in kindling blushes burns.
At length, from virtue thus he seeks relief,
And kindly chides her violence of grief:
"Canst thou then sink, thou daughter of the great,
Sprung from the noblest guardians of our state;
Canst thou thus yield to the first shock of fate?
Whatever deathless monuments of praise
Thy sex can merit, 't is in thee to raise.
On man alone life's ruder trials wait,
The fields of battle, and the cares of state;
While the wife's virtue then is only try'd,
When faithless Fortune quits her husband's side.
Arm then thy soul, the glorious task to prove,
And learn, thy miserable lord to love.
Behold me of my power and pomp bereft,
By all my kings, and by Rome's fathers left:
Oh make that loss thy glory; and be thou
The only follower of Pompey now.
This grief becomes thee not, while I survive;
War wounds not thee, since I am still alive:
These tears a dying husband should deplore,
And only fall when Pompey is no more.
'T is true, my former greatness all is lost;
Who weep for that, no love for me can boast,
But mourn the loss of what they valued most."
Mov'd at her lord's reproof, the matron rose;
Yet, still complaining, thus avow'd her woes:
"Ah! wherefore was I not much rather led,
A fatal bride, to Cæsar's hated bed?
To thee unlucky, and a curse, I came,
Unblest by yellow Hymen's holy flame:
My bleeding Crassus, and his sire, stood by,
And fell Erynnis shook her torch on high.
My fate on thee the Parthian vengeance draws,
And urges Heaven to hate the juster cause.
Ah! my once greatest lord! ah! cruel hour!
Is thy victorious head in Fortune's power?
Since miseries my baneful love pursue,
Why did I wed thee, only to undo?
But see, to death my willing neck I bow;
Atone the angry gods by one kind blow.
Long since, for thee, my life I would have given;
Yet, let me, yet prevent the wrath of Heaven.
Kill me, and scatter me upon the sea,
So shall propitious tides thy fleets convey,
Thy kings be faithful, and the world obey.
And thou, where'er thy sullen phantom flies,
Oh! Julia! let thy rival's blood suffice;
Let me the rage of jealous vengeance bear,
But him, thy lord, thy once-lov'd Pompey spare."
She said, and sunk within his arms again;
In streams of sorrow melt the mournful train:

E'en his, the warrior's eyes, were forc'd to yield,
That saw, without a tear, Pharsalia's field.
 Now to the strand the Mitylenians press'd,
And humbly thus bespoke their noble guest:
 "If to succeeding times, our isle shall boast
The pledge of Pompey left upon her coast,
Disdain not, if thy presence now we claim,
And fain would consecrate our walls to fame.
Make thou this place in future story great,
Where pious Romans may direct their feet,
To view with adoration thy retreat.
This may we plead, in favour of the town;
That, while mankind the prosperous victor own,
Already, Cæsar's foes avow'd, are we,
Nor add new guilt, by duty paid to thee.
Some safety too our ambient seas secure:
Cæsar wants ships, and we defy his power.
Here may Rome's scatter'd fathers well unite,
And arm against a second happier fight.
Our Lesbian youth with ready courage stands,
To man thy navies, or recruit thy bands.
For gold, whate'er to sacred use is lent,
Take it, and the rapacious foe prevent.
This only mark of friendship we entreat,
Seek not to shun us in thy low estate;
But let our Lesbos, in thy ruin, prove,
As in thy greatness, worthy of thy love."
 Much was the leader mov'd, and joy'd to find
Faith had not quite abandon'd human kind.
"To me," he cry'd, "for ever were you dear;
Witness the pledge committed to your care:
Here in security I plac'd my home,
My houshold-gods, my heart, my wife, my Rome.
I know what ransom might your pardon buy,
And yet I trust you, yet to you I fly.
But, oh! too long my woes you singly bear;
I leave you, not for lands which I prefer,
But that the world the common load may share.
Lesbos! for ever sacred be thy name;
May late posterity thy truth proclaim!
Whether thy fair example spread around,
Or whether, singly, faithful thou art found:
For 't is resolv'd, 't is fix'd within my mind,
To try the doubtful world, and prove mankind.
Oh! grant, good Heaven! if there be one alone,
One gracious power so lost a cause to own,
Grant, like the Lesbians, I my friends may find;
Such who, though Cæsar threaten, dare be kind:
Who, with the same just hospitable heart,
May leave me free to enter, or depart."
 He ceas'd; and to the ship his partner bore,
While loud complainings fill the sounding shore.
It seem'd as if the nation with her pass'd,
And banishment had laid their island waste.
Their second sorrows they to Pompey give,
For her, as for their citizen, they grieve.
E'en though glad victory had call'd her thence,
And her lord's bidding been the just pretence;
The Lesbian matrons had in tears been drown'd,
And brought her weeping to the watery bound.
So was she lov'd, so winning was her grace,
Such lowly sweetness dwelt upon her face;
In such humility her life she led,
E'en while her lord was Rome's commanding head,
As if his fortune were already fled.
 Half hid in seas descending Phœbus lay,
And upwards half, half downwards shot the day;
When wakeful cares revolve in Pompey's soul,
And run the wide world o'er, from pole to pole.
Each realm, each city, in his mind are weigh'd
Where he may fly, from whence depend on aid.
Weary'd at length beneath the load of woes,
And those sad scenes his future views disclose,
In conversation for relief he sought,
And exercis'd on various themes his thought.
Now sits he by the careful pilot's side,
And asks what rules their watery journey guide;
What lights of Heaven his art attends to most,
Bound by the Libyan or the Syrian coast.
 To him, intent upon the rolling skies,
The Heaven-instructed shipman thus replies:
"Of all yon multitude of golden stars,
Which the wide rounding sphere incessant bears,
The cautious mariner relies on none,
But keeps him to the constant pole alone.
When o'er the yard the lesser Bear aspires,
And from the topmast gleam its paly fires,
Then Bosphorus near-neighbouring we explore,
And hear loud billows beat the Scythian shore:
But when Calisto's shining son descends,
And the low Cynosure tow'rds ocean bends,
For Syria straight we know the vessel bears,
Where first Canopo's southern sign appears.
If still upon the left those stars thou keep,
And, passing Pharos, plough the foamy deep,
Then right a-head thy luckless bark shall reach
The Libyan shoals, and Syrts' unfaithful beach.
But say, for lo! on thee attends my hand,
What course dost thou assign? what seas, what land?
Speak, and the helm shall turn at thy command."
 To him the chief, by doubts uncertain tost;
"Oh, fly the Latian and Thessalian coast:
Those only lands avoid. For all beside,
Yield to the driving winds, and rolling tide;
Let Fortune, where she please, a port provide.
Till Lesbos did my dearest pledge restore,
That thought determin'd me to seek that shore:
All ports, all regions, but those fatal two,
Are equal to unhappy Pompey now."
 Scarce had he spoke, when straight the master veer'd,
And right for Chios, and for Asia steer'd.
The working waves the course inverted feel,
And dash and foam beneath the winding keel.
With art like this, on rapid chariots borne,
Around the column skilful racers turn:
The nether wheels bear nicely on the goal,
The farther, wide in distant circles roll.
 Now day's bright beams the various earth disclose,
And o'er the fading stars the Sun arose;
When Pompey gathering to his side beheld
The scatter'd relics of Pharsalia's field.
First from the Lesbian isle his son drew near,
And soon a troop of faithful chiefs appear.
Nor purple princes, yet, disdain to wait
On vanquish'd Pompey's humbler low estate.
Proud monarchs, who in eastern kingdoms reign,
Mix in the great illustrious exile's train.
From these, apart, Deiotarus he draws,
The long-approv'd companion of his cause:
"Thou best," he cries, "of all my royal friends!
Since with our loss Rome's power and empire ends;
What yet remains, but that we call from far
The eastern nations to support the war;
Euphrates has not own'd proud Cæsar's side,
And Tigris rolls a yet unconquer'd tide.
Let it not grieve thee, then, to seek for aid
From the wild Scythian, and remotest Mede.
To Parthia's monarch my distress declare,
And at his throne speak this my humble prayer.

'If faith in ancient leagues is to be found,
Leagues by our altars and your magi bound,
Now string the Getic and Armenian bow,
And in full quivers feather'd shafts bestow.
If when o'er Caspian hills my troops I led,
'Gainst Allans, in eternal warfare bred,
I sought not once to make your Parthians yield,
But left them free to range the Persian field.
Beyond th' Assyrian bounds my eagles flew,
And conquer'd realms that Cyrus never knew;
E'en to the utmost east I urg'd my way,
And ere the Persian, saw the rising day:
Yet while beneath my yoke the nations bend,
I sought the Parthian only as my friend.
Yet more; when Carræ blush'd with Crassus' blood,
And Latium her severest vengeance vow'd;
When war with Parthia was the common cry,
Who stopp'd the fury of that rage, but I?
If this be true, through Zeugma take your way,
Nor let Euphrates' stream the march delay;
In gratitude to my assistance come;
Fight Pompey's cause, and conquer willing Rome.'"
He said; the monarch cheerfully obey'd,
And straight aside his royal robes he laid;
Then bid his slaves their humbler vestments bring:
And in that servile veil conceals the king.
Thus majesty gives its proud trappings o'er,
And humbly seeks for safety from the poor:
The poor, who no disguises need, nor wear;
Unblest with greatness, aud unvex'd with fear.
His princely friend now safe convey'd to land,
The chief o'erpass'd the fam'd Ephesian strand,
Icaria's rocks, with Colophon's smooth deep,
And foamy cliffs which rugged Samos keep.
From Coan shores soft breathes the western wind,
And Rhodes and Gnidos soon are left behind.
Then crossing o'er Telmessos' ample bay,
Right to Pamphilia's coast he cuts his way.
Suspicious of the land, he keeps the main,
Till poor Phaselis, first, receives his wandering train.
There, free from fears, with ease he may command
Her citizens, scarce equal to his band.
Nor lingering there, his swelling sails are spread,
Till he discerns proud Taurus' rising head:
A mighty mass it stands, while down his side
Descending Dipsas rolls his headlong tide.
In a slight bark he runs securely o'er
The pirates' once-infested dreadful shore.
Ah! when he set the watery empire free,
And swept the fierce Cilician from the sea,
Could the successful warrior have forethought
'T was for his future safety, then, he fought!
At length the gathering fathers of the state,
In full assembly on their leader wait:
Within Syedra's walls their senate meets,
Whom, sighing, thus th' illustrious exile greets.
"My friends! who, with me fought, who with me [fled,
And now are to me in my country's stead;
Though quite defenceless and unarm'd we stand,
On this Cilician, naked, foreign strand;
Though every mark of Fortune's wrath we bear,
And seem to seek for council in despair;
Preserve your souls undaunted, free, and great,
And know I am not fall'n entirely, yet,
Spite of the ruins of Emathia's plain,
Yet can I rear my drooping head again.
From Afric's dust abandon'd Marius rose,
To seize the fasces, and insult his foes.
My loss is lighter, less is my disgrace;
Shall I despair to reach my former place?
Still on the Grecian seas my navies ride,
And many a valiant leader owns my side.
All that Pharsalia's luckless field could do,
Was to disperse my forces, not subdue.
Still safe beneath my former fame I stand,
Dear to the world, and lov'd in every land.
'T is yours to counsel and determine, whom
We shall apply to, in the cause of Rome;
What faithful friend may best assistance bring;
The Libyan, Parthian, or Ægyptian king.
For me, what course my thoughts incline to take,
Here freely, and at large I mean to speak.
What most dislike me in the Pharian prince,
Are his raw years, and yet unpractis'd sense:
Virtue, in youth, no stable footing finds,
And constancy is built on manly minds.
Nor, with less danger, may our trust explore
The faith uncertain of the crafty Moor:
From Carthaginian blood he draws his race,
Still mindful of the vanquish'd town's disgrace;
From thence Numidian mischiefs he derives;
And Hannibal in his false heart survives:
With pride he saw submissive Varus bow,
And joys to hear the Roman power lies low.
To warlike Parthia therefore let us turn,
Where stars unknown in distant azure burn;
Where Caspian hills to part the world arise,
And night and day succeed in other skies;
Where rich Assyrian plains Euphrates laves,
And seas discolour'd roll their ruddy waves.
Ambition, there, delights in arms to reign,
There rushing squadrons thunder o'er the plain;
There young and old the bow promiscuous bend,
And fatal shafts with aim unerring send.
They first the Macedonian phalanx broke,
And hand to hand repell'd the Grecian stroke;
They drove the Mede and Bactrian from the field,
And taught aspiring Babylon to yield;
Fearless against the Roman pile they stood,
And triumph'd in our vanquish'd Crassus' blood.
Nor trust they to the points of piercing darts,
But furnish death with new improving arts,
In mortal juices dipt their arrows fly,
And if they taste the blood, the wounded die.
Too well their powers and favouring gods we know,
And wish our fate much rather would allow
Some other aid against the common foe.
With inauspicious succour shall they come,
Nurs'd in the hate and rivalship of Rome.
With these the neighbouring nations round shall [arm,
And the whole east rouze at the dire alarm.
Should the barbarian race their aid deny,
Yet would I choose in that strange land to die:
There let our shipwreck'd poor remains be thrown,
Our loss forgotten, and our names unknown:
Securely there ill-fortune would I brave,
Nor meanly sue to kings, whose crowns I gave:
From Cæsar free, enjoy my latest hour,
And scorn his anger's and his mercy's pow'r.
Still, when my thoughts my former days restore,
With joy, methinks, I run those regions o'er;
There, much the better parts of life I prov'd,
Rever'd by all, applauded, and belov'd;
Wide o'er Mæotis spread my happy name,
And Tanaïs ran conscious of my fame;
My vanquish'd enemies my conquests mourn'd,
And cover'd still with laurels, I return'd.
Approve then, Rome, my present cares for thee;
Thine is the gain, whate'er th' event shall be.

What greater boon canst thou from Heaven demand,
Than in thy cause to arm the Parthian's hand?
Barbarians thus shall wage thy civil war,
And those that hate thee in thy ruin share.
When Cæsar and Phraates battle join,
They must revenge, or Crassus' wrongs, or mine."
The leader ceas'd; and straight a murmuring sound
Ran through the disapproving fathers round.
With these, in high pre-eminence, there sat
Distinguish'd Lentulus, the consul late:
None with more generous indignation stung,
Or nobler grief, beheld his country's wrong.
Sudden he rose, rever'd, and thus began,
In words that well became the subject and the man:
"Can then Pharsalia's ruins thus control
The former greatness of thy Roman soul?
Must the whole world, our laws and country, yield
To one unlucky day, one ill-fought field!
Hast thou no hopes of succour, no retreat,
But mean prostration at the Parthian's feet?
Art thou grown weary of our earth and sky,
That thus thou seek'st a fugitive to fly;
New stars to view, new regions to explore,
To learn new manners, and new gods adore?
Wilt thou before Chaldean altars bend,
Worship their fires, and on their kings depend?
Why didst thou draw the world to arms around?
Why cheat mankind with liberty's sweet sound?
Why on Emathia's plain fierce Cæsar brave,
When thou canst yield thyself a tyrant's slave?
Shall Parthia, who with terrour shook from far,
To hear thee nam'd, to head the Roman war,
Who saw thee lead proud monarchs in thy chain,
From wild Hyrcania and the Indian main;
Shall she, that very Parthia, see thee now,
A poor, dejected, humble suppliant bow?
Then haughtily with Rome her greatness mate,
And scorn thy country, for thy groveling fate?
Thy tongue, in eastern languages untaught,
Shall want the words that should explain thy thought:
Tears, then, unmanly, must thy suit declare;
And suppliant hands, uplifted, speak thy prayer.
Shall Parthia (shall it to our shame be known)
Revenge Rome's wrongs, ere Rome revenge her own?
Our war no interfering kings demands,
Nor shall be trusted to barbarian hands:
Among ourselves our bonds we will deplore,
And Rome shall serve the rebel son she bore.
Why would'st thou bid our foes transgress their bound,
And teach their feet to tread Hesperian ground?
With ensigns, torn from Crassus, shall they come,
And, with his ravish'd honours, threaten Rome;
His fate those blood-stain'd eagles shall recall,
And hover dreadful o'er their native wall.
Canst thou believe the monarch, who withheld
His only forces from Emathia's field,
Will bring his succours to thy waining state,
And brave y now defy the victor's hate?
No eastern courage forms a thought so great.
In cold laborious climes the wint'ry north
Brings her undaunted hardy warriors forth,
In body and in mind untaught to yield,
Stubborn of soul, and steady in the field;
While Asia's softer climate, form'd to please,
Dissolves her sons in indolence and ease.
Here silken robes invest unmanly limbs,
And in long trains the flowing purple streams.
Where no rude hills Salmatia's wilds restrain,
Or rushing Tigris cuts the level plain,
Swifter than winds along the champaign borne,
At liberty they fly, or fight, or turn,
And, distant still, the vain pursuer scorn.
Nor with like ease they force their warlike way,
Where rough unequal grounds their speed delay.
Whene'er the thicker shades of night arise,
Unaim'd the shaft, and unavailing, flies.
Nor are they form'd with constancy to meet
Those toils that make the panting soldier sweat:
To climb the heights, to stem the rapid flood,
To make the dusty noon-day battle good,
Horrid with wounds, and crusted o'er in blood.
Nor war's machines they know, nor have the skill
To shake the rampire, or the trench to fill:
Each fence that can their winged shafts endure,
Stands, like a fort impregnable, secure.
Light are their skirmishes, their war is flight,
And still to wheel their wavering troops delight.
To taint their coward darts, is all their care,
And then to trust them to the flitting air.
Whene'er their bows have spent their feather'd store,
The mighty business of the war is o'er:
No manly strokes they try, nor hand to hand
With cleaving swords in sturdy combat stand.
With swords the valiant still their foes invade;
These call in drugs and poison to their aid.
Are these the powers to whom thou bidst us fly?
Is this the land in which thy bones would lie?
Shall these barbarian hands for thee provide
The grave, to thy unhappy friend deny'd?
But be it so! that death shall bring thee peace,
That here thy sorrows and thy toils shall cease.
Death is what man should wish. But, oh! what fate
Shall on thy wife, thy sad survivor, wait!
For her, where lust with lawless empire reigns,
Somewhat more terrible than death remains.
Have we not heard, with what abhorr'd desires
The Parthian Venus feeds her guilty fires?
How their wild monarch, like the bestial race,
Spreads the pollution of his lewd embrace?
Unaw'd by reverence of connubial rites,
In multitudes, luxurious, he delights:
When gorg'd with feasting, and inflam'd with wine,
No joys can sate him, and no laws confine;
Forbidding nature, then, commands in vain,
From sisters and from mothers to abstain.
The Greek and Roman with a trembling ear,
Th' unwilling crime of Oedipus may hear;
While Parthian kings like deeds, with glory, own,
And boast incestuous titles to the throne.
If crimes like these they can securely brave,
What laws, what power shall thy Cornelia save?
Think, how the helpless matron may be led,
The thousandth harlot to the royal bed.
Though when the tyrant clasps his noble slave,
And hears to whom her plighted hand she gave,
Her beauties oft in scorn he shall prefer,
And choose t' insult the Roman name in her.
These are the powers to whom thou wouldst submit,
And Rome's revenge and Crassus' quite forget.
Thy cause, preferr'd to his, becomes thy shame,
And blots, in common, thine and Cæsar's name.
With how much greater glory might you join,
To drive the Daci, or to free the Rhine!
How well your conquering legions might you lead,
'Gainst the fierce Bactrian and the haughty Mede!

Level proud Babylon's aspiring domes,
And with their spoils enrich our slaughter'd leaders' tombs?
No longer, Fortune! let our friendship last,
Our peace, ill-omen'd, with the barbarous east;
If civil strife with Cæsar's conquest end,
To Asia let his prosperous arms extend;
Eternal wars there let the victor wage,
And on proud Parthia pour the Roman rage.
There I, there all, his victories may bless,
And Rome herself make vows for his success.
Whene'er thou pass the cold Araxes o'er,
An aged shade shall greet thee on the shore,
Transfix'd with arrows, mournful, pale, and hoar.
'And art thou,' shall he cry, complaining, 'come
In peace and friendship, to these foes of Rome?
Thou! from whose hand we hop'd revenge in vain,
Poor naked ghosts, a thin unbury'd train,
That flit, lamenting, o'er this dreary plain?'
On every side new objects shall disclose
Some mournful monument of Roman woes;
On every wall fresh marks thou shalt descry,
Where pale Hesperian heads were fix'd on high:
Each river, as he rolls his purple tide,
Shall own his waves in Latian slaughter dy'd.
If sights like these thou canst with patience bear,
What are the horrours, which thy soul would fear?
E'en Cæsar's self with joy may be beheld,
Enthron'd on slaughter in Emathia's field.
Say then, we grant, thy cautions were not vain,
Of Punic frauds and Juba's faithless reign;
Abounding Egypt shall receive thee yet,
And yield, unquestion'd, a secure retreat.
By nature strengthen'd with a dangerous strand,
Her Syrts and untry'd channels guard the land.
Rich in the fatness of her plenteous soil,
She plants her only confidence in Nile.
Her monarch, bred beneath thy guardian cares,
His crown, the largess of thy bounty, wears.
Nor let unjust suspicions brand his truth;
Candour and innocence still dwell with youth.
Trust not a power accustom'd to be great,
And vers'd in wicked policies of state.
Old kings, long harden'd in the regal trade,
By interest and by craft alone are sway'd,
And violate with ease the leagues they made:
While new ones still make conscience of the trust,
True to their friends, and to their subjects just."
He spoke; the listening fathers all were mov'd,
And with concurring votes the thought approv'd.
So much e'en dying liberty prevail'd,
When Pompey's suffrage, and his counsel fail'd.
And now Cilicia's coast the fleet forsake,
And o'er the watery plain for Cyprus make.
Cyprus to love's ambrosial goddess dear,
For ever grateful smoke the altars there:
Indulgent still she hears the Paphian vows,
And loves the favourite seas from whence she rose.
So Fame reports, if we may credit Fame,
When her fond tales the birth of gods proclaim,
Unborn, and from eternity the same.
The craggy cliffs of Cyprus quickly past,
The chief runs southward o'er the ocean vast.
Nor views he, through the murky veil of night,
The Casian mountains' far distinguish'd height,
The high-hung lantern, or the beamy light.
Haply at length the labouring canvass bore
Full on the farthest bounds of Ægypt's shore,
Where near Pelusium parting Nile descends,
And in her utmost eastern channel ends.
'T was now the time, when equal Jove on high
Had hung the golden balance of the sky:
But, ah! not long such just proportions last,
The righteous season soon was chang'd and pass'd;
And spring's encroachment, on the shortening shade,
Was fully to the wintery nights repaid:
When to the chief from shore they made report,
That, near high Casium, lay the Pharian court.
This known, he thither turns his ready sail,
The light yet lasting with the favouring gale.
The fleet arriv'd, the news flies swiftly round,
And their new guests the troubled court confound.
The time was short; howe'er the council met,
Vile ministers, a monstrous motley set.
Of these, the chief in honour, and the best,
Was old Achorëus the Memphian priest:
In Isis and Osiris he believ'd,
And reverend tales, from sire to son receiv'd;
Could mark the swell of Nile's increasing tide,
And many an Apis in his time had dy'd;
Yet was his age with gentlest manners fraught,
Humbly he spoke, and modestly he taught.
With good intent the pious seer arose,
And told how much their state to Pompey owes:
What large amends their monarch ought to make,
Both for his own, and for his father's sake.
But fate had plac'd a subtler speaker there,
A tongue more fitted for a tyrant's ear,
Pothinus, deep in arts of mischief read,
Who thus, with false persuasion, blindly led
The easy king, to doom his guardian dead:
"To strictest justice many ills belong,
And honesty is often in the wrong:
Chiefly when stubborn rules her zealots push,
To favour those whom Fortune means to crush.
But thou, O royal Ptolemy, be wise;
Change with the gods, and fly whom Fortune flies.
Not Earth, from yon high Heavens which we admire,
Not from the watery element the fire,
Are sever'd by distinction half so wide,
As interest and integrity divide.
The mighty power of kings no more prevails,
When justice comes with her deciding scales.
Freedom for all things, and a lawless sword,
Alone support an arbitrary lord.
He that is cruel must be bold in ills,
And find his safety from the blood he spills.
For piety and virtue's starving rules,
To mean retirements let them lead their fools:
There may they still ingloriously be good;
None can be safe in courts, who blush at blood.
Nor let this fugitive despise thy years,
Or think a name, like his, can cause thy fears:
Exert thyself, and let him feel thy power,
And know, that we dare drive him from our shore.
But if thou wish to lay thy greatness down,
To some more just succession yield thy crown;
Thy rival sister willingly shall reign,
And save our Ægypt from a foreign chain.
As now, at first, in neutral peace we lay,
Nor would be Pompey's friends, nor Cæsar's prey.
Vanquish'd where'er his fortune has been try'd,
And driv'n, with scorn, from all the world beside,
By Cæsar chas'd, and left by his allies,
To us a baffled vagabond he flies,
The poor remaining senate loath his sight,
And ruin'd monarchs curse his fatal flight:
While thousand phantoms from th' unbury'd slain,
Who feed the vultures of Emathia's plain,

Disastrous still pursue him in the rear,
And urge his soul with horrour and despair.
To us for refuge now he seeks to run,
And would once more with Ægypt be undone.
Rouse then, O Ptolemy, repress the wrong;
He thinks we have enjoy'd our peace too long:
And therefore kindly comes, that we may share
The crimes of slaughter, and the woes of war.
His friendship shown to thee suspicions draws,
And makes us seem too guilty of his cause:
Thy crown bestow'd, the victor may impute;
The senate gave it, but at Pompey's suit.
Nor, Pompey! thou thyself shall think it hard,
If from thy aid, by fate, we are debarr'd.
We follow where the gods, constraining, lead;
We strike at thine, but wish 't were Cæsar's head.
Our weakness this, this fate's compulsion call;
We only yield to him who conquers all.
Then doubt not if thy blood we mean to spill;
Power awes us; if we can, we must, and will.
What hopes thy fond mistaken soul betray'd,
To put thy trust in Egypt's feeble aid?
Our slothful nation, long disus'd to toil,
With pain suffice to till their slimy soil;
Our idle force due modesty should teach,
Nor dare to aim beyond its humble reach.
Shall we resist where Rome was forc'd to yield,
And make us parties to Pharsalia's field?
We mix'd not in the fatal strife before:
And shall we, when the world has given it o'er?
Now! when we know th' avenging victor's power?
Nor do we turn, unpitying, from distress;
We fly not Pompey's woes, but seek success.
The prudent on the prosperous still attends,
And none but fools choose wretches for their friends."
He said; the vile assembly all assent,
And the boy-king his glad concurrence lent,
Fond of the royalty his slaves bestow'd,
And by new power of wickedness made proud.
Where Casium high o'erlooks the shoaly strand,
A bark with armed ruffians straight is mann'd,
And the task trusted to Achillas' hand.
Can then Ægyptian souls thus proudly dare!
Is Rome, ye gods! thus fall'n by civil war?
Can you to Nile transfer the Roman guilt,
And let such blood by cowards' hands be spilt?
Some kindred murderer at least afford,
And let him fall by Cæsar's worthy sword.
And thou, inglorious, feeble, beardless boy!
Dar'st thou thy hand in such a deed employ?
Does not thy trembling heart, with horrour, dread
Jove's thunder, grumbling o'er thy guilty head?
Had not his arms with triumphs oft been crown'd;
And e'en the vanquish'd world his conquest own'd;
Had not the reverend senate called him head,
And Cæsar given fair Julia to his bed,
He was a Roman still: a name should be
For ever sacred to a king, like thee.
Ah, fool! thus blindly by thyself undone,
Thou seek'st his ruin, who upheld thy throne:
He only could thy feeble power maintain,
Who gave thee first o'er Ægypt's realm to reign.
The seamen, now, advancing near to shore,
Strike the wide sail, and ply the plunging oar;
When the false miscreants the navy meet,
And with dissembled cheer the Roman greet.
They feign their hospitable land address'd,
With ready friendship, to receive her guest;
Excusing much an inconvenient shore,
Where shoals lie thick, and meeting currents roar:
From his tall ship, unequal to the place,
They beg him to their lighter bark to pass.
Had not the gods, unchangeably, decreed
Devoted Pompey in that hour to bleed,
A thousand signs the danger near foretel,
Seen by his sad presaging friends too well.
Had their low fawning justly been design'd,
If truth could lodge in an Ægyptian mind,
Their king himself with all his fleet had come,
To lead, in pomp, his benefactor home.
But thus Fate will'd; and Pompey chose to bear
A certain death before uncertain fear.
While, now, aboard the hostile boat he goes,
To follow him the frantic matron vows,
And claims her partnership in all his woes.
"But, oh! forbear," he cries, "my love, forbear;
Thou and my son remain in safety here.
Let this old head the danger first explore,
And prove the faith of yon suspected shore."
He spoke; but she, unmov'd at his commands,
Thus loud exclaiming, stretch'd her eager hands:
"Whither, inhuman! whither art thou gone?
Still must I weep our common griefs alone?
Joy still, with thee, forsakes my boding heart;
And fatal is the hour whene'er we part.
Why did thy vessel to my Lesbos turn?
Why was I from the faithful island borne?
Must I all lands, all shores, alike, forbear,
And only on the seas thy sorrows share?"
Thus, to the winds, loud plain'd her fruitless tongue,
While eager from the deck on high she hung;
Trembling with wild astonishment and fear,
She dares not, while her parting lord they bear,
Turn her eyes from him once, or fix them there.
On him his anxious navy all are bent,
And wait, solicitous, the dire event.
No danger aim'd against his life they doubt;
Care for his glory only, fills their thought:
They wish he may not stain his name renown'd,
By mean submission to the boy he crown'd.
Just as he enter'd o'er the vessel's side,
"Hail, general!" the curs'd Septimius cry'd,
A Roman once in generous warfare bred,
And oft in arms by mighty Pompey led;
But now (what vile dishonour must it bring)
The ruffian slave of an Egyptian king.
Fierce was he, horrible, inur'd to blood,
And ruthless as the savage of the wood.
Oh, Fortune! who but would have call'd thee kind,
And thought thee mercifully now inclin'd,
When thy o'er-ruling providence withheld
This hand of mischief from Pharsalia's field?
But, thus, thou scatter'st thy destroying swords,
And every land thy victims thus affords.
Shall Pompey at a tyrant's bidding bleed!
Can Roman hands be to the task decreed!
E'en Cæsar, and his gods, abhor the deed.
Say you! who with the stain of murder brand
Immortal Brutus's avenging hand,
What monstrous title, yet to speech unknown,
To latest times shall mark Septimius down!
Now in the boat defenceless Pompey sate,
Surrounded and abandon'd to his fate.
Nor long they hold him in their power, aboard,
Ere every villain drew his ruthless sword:
The chief perceiv'd their purpose soon, and spread
His Roman gown, with patience, o'er his head:
And when the curs'd Achillas pierc'd his breast,
His rising indignation close repress'd.

No sighs, no groans, his dignity profan'd,
No tears his still unsully'd glory stain'd:
Unmov'd and firm he fix'd him on his seat,
And dy'd, as when he liv'd and conquer'd, great.
Meanwhile, within his equal parting soul,
These latest pleasing thoughts revolving roll.
"In this my strongest trial, and my last,
As in some theatre I here am plac'd:
The faith of Ægypt, and my fate, shall be
A theme for present times, and late posterity.
Much of my former life was crown'd with praise,
And honours waited on my early days:
Then, fearless, let me this dread period meet,
And force the world to own the scene complete.
Nor grieve, my heart! by such base hands to bleed;
Whoever strikes the blow, 't is Cæsar's deed.
What, though this mangled carcass shall be torn,
These limbs be tost about for public scorn;
My long prosperity has found its end,
And death comes opportunely, like a friend:
It comes, to set me free from Fortune's power,
And gives, what she can rob me of no more.
My wife and son behold me now, 't is true;
Oh! may no tears, no groans, my fate pursue!
My virtue rather let their praise approve,
Let them admire my death, and my remembrance love."
Such constancy in that dread hour remain'd,
And, to the last, the struggling soul sustain'd.
Not so the matron's feebler powers repress'd
The wild impatience of her frantic breast:
With every stab her bleeding heart was torn,
With wounds much harder to be seen than borne.
"'T is I, 't is I have murder'd him!" she cries,
"My love the sword and ruthless hand supplies.
'T was I allur'd him to my fatal isle,
That cruel Cæsar first might reach the Nile;
For Cæsar sure is there; no hand but his
Has right to such a parricide as this.
But whether Cæsar, or whoe'er thou art,
Thou hast mistook the way to Pompey's heart:
That sacred pledge in my sad bosom lies,
There plunge thy dagger, and he more than dies.
Me too, most worthy of thy fury know,
The partner of his arms, and sworn your foe.
Of all our Roman wives, I singly bore
The camp's fatigue, the sea's tempestuous roar:
No dangers, not the victor's wrath, I fear'd;
What mighty monarchs durst not do, I dar'd.
These guilty arms did their glad refuge yield,
And clasp'd him, flying from Pharsalia's field.
Ah, Pompey! dost thou thus my faith reward?
Shalt thou be doom'd to die, and I be spar'd?
But fate shall many means of death afford,
Nor want th' assistance of a tyrant's sword.
And you, my friends, in pity, let me leap
Hence headlong, down amidst the tumbling deep:
Or to my neck the strangling cordage tie;
If there be any friend of Pompey nigh,
Transfix me, stab me, do but let me die.
My lord, my husband! Yet thou art not dead;
And see! Cornelia is a captive led:
From thee their cruel hands thy wife detain,
Reserv'd to wear th' insulting victor's chain."
She spoke; and stiffening sunk in cold despair;
Her weeping maids the lifeless burthen bear;
While the pale mariners the bark unmoor,
Spread every sail, and fly the faithless shore.
Nor agonies, nor livid death, disgrace
The sacred features of the hero's face;
In the cold visage, mournfully serene,
The same indignant majesty was seen;
There virtue still unchangeable abode,
And scorn'd the spite of every partial god.
The bloody business now complete and done,
New furies urge the fierce Septimius on.
He rends the robe that veil'd the hero's head,
And to full view expos'd the recent dead;
Hard in his horrid gripe the face he press'd,
While yet the quivering muscles life confess'd;
He drew the dragging body down with haste,
Then cross a rower's seat the neck he plac'd;
There, awkward, haggling, he divides the bone
(The headsman's art was then but rudely known.)
Straight on the spoil his Pharian partner flies,
And robs the heartless villain of his prize.
The head, his trophy, proud Achillas bears;
Septimius an inferior drudge appears,
And in the meaner mischief poorly shares.
Caught by the venerable locks, which grow
In hoary ringlets, on his generous brow,
To Ægypt's impious king that head they bear,
That laurels us'd to bind, and monarchs fear.
Those sacred lips and that commanding tongue,
On which the listening forum oft has hung;
That tongue which could the world with ease restrain,
And ne'er commanded war or peace in vain;
That face, in which success came smiling home,
And doubled every joy it brought to Rome:
Now pale, and wan, is fix'd upon a spear,
And borne, for public view, aloft in air.
The tyrant, pleas'd, beheld it; and decreed
To keep this pledge of his detested deed.
His slaves straight drain the serous parts away,
And arm the wasting flesh against decay;
Then drugs and gums through the void vessels pass,
And for duration fix the stiffening mass.
Inglorious boy! degenerate and base!
Thou last and worst of the Lagæan race!
Whose feeble throne, ere long, shall be compell'd
To thy lascivious sister's reign to yield:
Canst thou, with altars, and with rites divine,
The rash vain youth of Macedon inshrine;
Can Ægypt such stupendous fabrics build;
Can her wide plains with pyramids be fill'd;
Canst thou, beneath such monumental pride,
The worthless Ptolemæan fathers hide;
While the great Pompey's headless trunk is toss'd
In scorn, unbury'd, on thy barbarous coast?
Was it so much? Could not thy care suffice,
To keep him whole, and glut his father's eyes?
In this, his fortune ever held the same,
Still wholly kind, or wholly cross, she came.
Patient, his long prosperity she bore,
But kept his death, and this sad day in store.
No meddling god did e'er his power employ,
To ease his sorrows, or to damp his joy;
Unmingled came the bitter and the sweet,
And all his good and evil was complete.
No sooner was he struck by Fortune's hand,
But, see! he lies unbury'd on the sand;
Rocks tear him, billows toss him up and down,
And Pompey by a headless trunk is known.
Yet ere proud Cæsar touch'd the Pharian Nile,
Chance found his mangled foe a funeral pile;
In pity half, and half in scorn, she gave
A wretched, to prevent a nobler grave.
Cordus, a follower long of Pompey's fate,
(His quæstor in Idalian Cyprus late)

From a close cave, in covert where he lay,
Swift to the neighbouring shore betook his way:
Safe in the shelter of the gloomy shade,
And by strong ties of pious duty sway'd,
The fearless youth the watery strand survey'd.
'Twas now the thickest darkness of the night,
And waining Phœbe lent a feeble light;
Yet soon the glimmering goddess plainly show'd
The paler corse, amidst the dusky flood.
The plunging Roman flies to its relief,
And with strong arms infolds the floating chief.
Long strove his labour with the tumbling main,
And dragg'd the sacred burthen on with pain.
Nigh weary now, the waves instruct him well,
To seize th' advantage of th' alternate swell:
Borne on the mounting surge, to shore he flies,
And on the beach in safety lands his prize.
There o'er the dead he hangs with tender care,
And drops in every gaping wound a tear:
Then, lifting to the gloomy skies his head,
Thus to the stars, and cruel gods, he pray'd:
"See, Fortune! where thy Pompey lies! and oh!
In pity, one, last little boon bestow.
He asks no heaps of frankincense to rise,
No eastern odours to perfume the skies;
No Roman necks his patriot corse to bear,
No reverend train of statues to appear;
No pageant shows his glories to record,
And tell the triumphs of his conquering sword;
No instruments in plaintive notes to sound,
No legions sad to march in solemn round;
A bier, no better than the vulgar need,
A little wood the kindling flame to feed,
With some poor hand to tend the homely fire,
Is all, these wretched relics now require.
Your wrath, ye powers! Cornelia's hand denies;
Let that, for every other loss, suffice;
She takes not her last leave, she weeps not here,
And yet she is, ye gods! she is too near."
Thus while he spoke, he saw where through the shade
A slender flame its gleaming light display'd;
There, as it chanc'd, abandon'd and unmourn'd,
A poor neglected body lonely burn'd.
He seiz'd the kindled brands; and "Oh!" he said,
"Whoe'er thou art, forgive me, friendless shade;
And though unpity'd and forlorn thou lie,
Thyself a better office shalt supply.
If there be sense in souls departed, thine
To my great leader shall her rites resign:
With humble joy shall quit her meaner claim,
And blush to burn, when Pompey wants the flame."
He said; and, gathering in his garment, bore
The glowing fragments to the neighbouring shore.
There soon arriv'd, the noble trunk he found,
Half wash'd into the flood, half resting on the ground
With diligence his hands a trench prepare,
Fit it around, and place the body there.
No cloven oaks in lofty order lie,
To lift the great patrician to the sky:
By chance a few poor planks were hard at hand,
By some late shipwreck cast upon the strand;
These pious Cordus gathers where they lay,
And plants about the chief, as best he may.
Now while the blaze began to rise around,
The youth sat mournful by upon the ground:
And, " Ah!" he cry'd, " if this unworthy flame
Disgrace thy great, majestic, Roman name;
If the rude outrage of the stormy seas
Seem better to thy ghost, than rites like these;
Yet let thy injur'd shade the wrong forget,
Which duty and officious zeal commit
Fate seems itself, in my excuse to plead,
And thy hard fortune justifies my deed.
I only wish'd, nor is that wish in vain,
To save thee from the monsters of the main;
From vultures' claws, from lions that devour,
From mortal malice, and from Cæsar's power.
No longer, then, this humbler flame withstand;
'T is lighted to thee by a Roman hand.
If e'er the gods permit unhappy me,
Once more, thy lov'd Hesperian land to see,
With me thy exil'd ashes shall return,
And chaste Cornelia give thee to thy urn.
Meanwhile, a signal shall thy care provide,
Some future Roman votary to guide;
When with due rites thy fate he would deplore,
And thy pale head to these thy limbs restore:
Then shall he mark the witness of my stone,
And, taught by me, thy sacred ghost atone."
He spoke; and straight, with busy, pious hands,
Heap'd on the smoking corse the scatter'd bands:
Slow sunk amidst the fire the wasting dead,
And the faint flame with dropping marrow fed.
Now 'gan the glittering stars to fade away,
Before the rosy promise of the day,
When the pale youth th' unfinish'd rites forsook,
And to the covert of his cave betook.
Ah! why thus rashly would thy fears disclaim
That only deed, which must record thy name?
E'en Cæsar's self shall just applause bestow,
And praise the Roman that inters his foe.
Securely tell him where is son is laid,
And he shall give thee back his mangled head.
But soon behold! the bolder youth returns,
While, half consum'd, the smouldering carcass burns;
Ere yet the cleansing fire had melted down
The fleshy muscles, from the firmer bone.
He quench'd the relics in the briny wave,
And hid them, hasty, in a narrow grave:
Then with a stone the sacred dust he binds,
To guard it from the breath of scattering winds:
And lest some heedless mariner should come,
And violate the warrior's humble tomb;
Thus with a line the monument he keeps,
" Beneath this stone the once great Pompey sleeps."
Oh Fortune! can thy malice swell so high?
Canst thou with Cæsar's every wish comply?
Must he, thy Pompey once, thus meanly lie?
But oh! forbear, mistaken man, forbear!
Nor dare to fix the mighty Pompey there:
Where there are seas, or air, or earth, or skies,
Where'er Rome's empire stretches, Pompey lies:
Far be the vile memorial then convey'd!
Nor let this stone the partial gods upbraid.
Shall Hercules all Oeta's heights demand,
And Nysa's hill, for Bacchus only, stand;
While one poor pebble is the warrior's doom,
That fought the cause of liberty and Rome?
If fate decrees he must in Ægypt lie,
Let the whole fertile realm his grave supply:
Yield the wide country to his awful shade,
Nor let us bear on any part to tread,
Fearful to violate the mighty dead.
But if one stone must bear the sacred name,
Let it be fill'd with long records of fame.

There let the passenger, with wonder, read,
The pirates vanquish'd, and the ocean freed;
Sertorius taught to yield; the Alpine war;
And the young Roman knight's triumphal car.
With these, the mighty Pontic king be plac'd,
And every nation of the vanquish'd east:
Tell with what loud applause of Rome, he drove
Thrice his glad wheels to Capitolian Jove:
Tell too, the patriot's greatest, best renown,
Tell, how the victor laid his empire down,
And chang'd his armour for the peaceful gown.
But ah! what marbles to the task suffice!
Instead of these, turn Roman, turn thy eyes;
Seek the known name our Fasti us'd to wear,
The noble mark of many a glorious year;
The name that wont the trophy'd arch to grace,
And e'en the temples of the gods found place:
Decline thee lowly, bending to the ground,
And there that name, that Pompey may be found.
Oh fatal land! what curse can I bestow,
Equal to those, we to thy mischiefs owe?
Well did the wise Cumæan maid of yore
Warn our Hesperian chiefs to shun thy shore.
Forbid, just Heavens! your dews to bless the soil,
And thou withhold thy waters, fruitful Nile!
Like Ægypt, like the land of Ethiops, burn,
And her fat earth to sandy deserts turn.
Have we, with honours, dead Osiris crown'd,
And mourn'd him to the tinkling timbrel's sound;
Receiv'd her Isis to divine abodes,
And rank'd her dogs deform'd with Roman gods;
While in despite of Pompey's injur'd shade,
Low in her dust his sacred bones are laid!
And thou, O Rome! by whose forgetful hand
Altars and temples, rear'd to tyrants, stand,
Canst thou neglect to call thy hero home,
And leave his ghost in banishment to roam?
What though the victor's frown, and thy base fear,
Bad thee, at first, the pious task forbear;
Yet now, at least, oh let him now return,
And rest with honour in a Roman urn.
Nor let mistaken superstition dread,
On such occasions, to disturb the dead;
Oh! would commanding Rome my hand employ,
The impious task should be perform'd with joy:
How would I fly to tear him from the tomb,
And bear his ashes in my bosom home!
Perhaps, when flames their dreadful ravage make,
Or groaning earth shall from the centre shake;
When blasting dews the rising harvest seize,
Or nations sicken with some dire disease:
The gods in mercy to us, shall command
To fetch our Pompey from th' accursed land.
Then, when his venerable bones draw near,
In long processions shall the priests appear,
And their great chief the sacred relics bear.
Or if thou still possess the Pharian shore,
What traveller but shall thy grave explore;
Whether he tread Syene's burning soil,
Or visit sultry Thebes, or fruitful Nile:
Or if the merchants, drawn by hopes of gain,
Seek rich Arabia, and the ruddy main;
With holy rites thy shade shall he atone,
And bow before thy venerable stone.
For who but shall prefer thy tomb above
The meaner fane of an Ægyptian Jove?
Nor envy thou, if abject Romans raise
Statues and temples, to their tyrant's praise;
Though his proud name on altars may preside,
And thine be wash'd by every rolling tide;
Thy grave shall the vain pageantry despise,
Thy grave, where that great god, thy fortune, lies.
E'en those who kneel not to the gods above,
Nor offer sacrifice or prayer to Jove,
To the Bidental bend their humble eyes,
And worship where the bury'd thunder lies.
Perhaps fate wills, in honour to thy fame,
No marble shall record thy mighty name.
So may thy dust, ere long, be worn away,
And all remembrance of thy wrongs decay:
Perhaps a better age shall come, when none
Shall think thee ever laid beneath this stone;
When Ægypt's boast of Pompey's tomb shall prove
As unbeliev'd a tale, as Crete relates of Jove.

BOOK IX.

THE ARGUMENT.

The poet having ended the foregoing book with the death of Pompey, begins this with his apotheosis; from thence, after a short account of Cato's gathering up the relics of the battle of Pharsalia, and transporting them to Cyrene in Africa, he goes on to describe Cornelia's passion upon the death of her husband. Amongst other things, she informs his son Sextus of his father's last commands, to continue the war in defence of the commonwealth. Sextus sets sail for Cato's camp, where he meets his elder brother Cn. Pompeius, and acquaints him with the fate of their father. Upon this occasion the poet describes the rage of the elder Pompey, and the disorders that happened in the camp, both which Cato appeases. To prevent any future inconvenience of this kind, he resolves to put them upon action, and in order to that to join with Juba. After a description of the Syrts, and their dangerous passage by them, follows Cato's speech to encourage the soldiers to march through the deserts of Libya; then an account of Libya, the deserts, and their march. In the middle of which is a beautiful digression concerning the temple of Jupiter-Ammon, with Labienus's persuasion to Cato to inquire of the oracle concerning the fate of the war, and Cato's famous answer. From thence, after a warm eulogy upon Cato, the author goes on to the account of the original of serpents in Africa; and this, with the description of the various kinds, and the several deaths of the soldiers by them, is perhaps the most poetical part of this whole work. At Leptis he leaves Cato, and returns to Cæsar, whom he brings into Egypt, after having shown him the ruins of Troy, and from thence taken an occasion to speak well of poetry in general, and himself in particular. Cæsar, upon his arrival on the coast of Ægypt, is met by an ambassador from Ptolemy with Pompey's head. He receives the present (according to Lucan) with a feigned abhorrence, and concludes the book with tears, and a seeming grief for the misfortunes of so great a man.

NOR in the dying embers of its pile
Slept the great soul upon the banks of Nile.
Nor longer by the earthy parts restrain'd,
Amidst its wretched relics was detain'd;
But, active and impatient of delay,
Shot from the mouldering heap, and upwards urg'd its way.

Far in those azure regions of the air
Which border on the rolling starry sphere,
Beyond our orb, and nearer to that height,
Where Cynthia drives around her silver light;
Their happy seats the demigods possess,
Refin'd by virtue, and prepar'd for bliss;
Of life unblam'd, a pure and pious race,
Worthy that lower Heaven and stars to grace,
Divine, and equal to the glorious place.
There Pompey's soul, adorn'd with heavenly light,
Soon shone among the rest, and as the rest was
New to the blest abode, with wonder fill'd, [bright.
The stars and moving planets he beheld;
Then looking down on the Sun's feeble ray,
Survey'd our dusky, faint, imperfect day,
And under what a cloud of night we lay.
But when he saw, how on the shore forlorn
His headless trunk was cast for public scorn;
When he beheld, how envious fortune, still,
Took pains to use a senseless carcass ill,
He smil'd at the vain malice of his foe,
And pity'd impotent mankind below.
Then lightly passing o'er Emathia's plain,
His flying navy scatter'd on the main,
And cruel Cæsar's tents; he fix'd at last,
His residence in Brutus' sacred breast:
There brooding o'er his country's wrongs he sate,
The state's avenger, and the tyrant's fate;
There mournful Rome might still her Pompey find,
There, and in Cato's free unconquer'd mind.
  He, while in deep suspense the world yet lay,
Anxious and doubtful whom it should obey,
Hatred avow'd to Pompey's self did bear,
Though his companion in the common war.
Though, by the senate's just command they stood
Engag'd together for the public good;
But dread Pharsalia did all doubts decide,
And firmly fix'd him to the vanquish'd side.
His helpless country, like an orphan left,
Friendless and poor, of all support bereft,
He took and cherish'd with a father's care,
He comforted, he bad her not to fear; [of war.
And taught her feeble hands once more the trade
Nor lust of mpire did his courage sway,
Nor hate, nor proud repugnance to obey:
Passions and private interest he forgot;
Not for himself but liberty he fought.
Straight to Corcyra's port his way he bent,
The swift advancing victor to prevent;
Who marching sudden on to new success,
The scatter'd legions might with ease oppress.
There, with the ruins of Æmathia's field,
The flying host, a thousand ships he fill'd.
Who that from land, with wonder, had descry'd
The passing fleet, in all its naval pride,
Stretch'd wide, and o'er the distant ocean spread,
Could have believ'd those mighty numbers fled?
Malea o'erpast, and the Tænarian shore,
With swelling sails he for Cythera bore:
Then Crete he saw, and with a northern wind
Soon left the fam'd Dictæan isle behind.
Urg'd by the old Phycuntines' churlish pride,
(Their shores, their haven, to his fleet deny'd)
The chief reveng'd the wrong, and as he pass'd,
Laid their inhospitable city waste.
Thence wafted forward, to the coast he came
Which took of old from Palinure its name.
(Not Italy this monument alone
Can boast, since Libya's Palinure has shown
Her peaceful shores were to the Trojan known.)

From hence they soon descry with doubtful pain
Another navy on the distant main.
Anxious they stand, and now expect the foe,
Now their companions in the public woe:
The victor's haste inclines them most to fear:
Each vessel seems a hostile face to wear,
And every sail they spy, they fancy Cæsar there.
But oh, those ships a different burthen bore,
A mournful freight they wafted to the shore:
Sorrows that might tears, e'en from Cato, gain,
And teach the rigid stoic to complain.
  When long the sad Cornelia's prayers, in vain,
Had try'd the flying navy to detain,
With Sextus long had strove, and long implor'd
To wait the relics of her murder'd lord;
The waves, perchance, might the dear pledge restore,
And waft him bleeding from the faithless shore:
Still grief and love their various hopes inspire,
Till she beholds her Pompey's funeral fire,
Till on the land she sees th' ignoble flame
Ascend, unequal to the hero's name;
Then into just complaints at length she broke,
And thus with pious indignation spoke:
  Oh Fortune! dost thou then disdain t' afford
My love's last office to my dearest lord?
Am I one chaste, one last embrace deny'd?
Shall I not lay me by his clay-cold side,
Nor tears to bathe his gaping wounds provide?
Am I unworthy the sad torch to bear,
To light the flame, and burn my flowing hair?
To gather from the shore the noble spoil,
And place it decent on the fatal pile?
Shall not his bones and sacred dust be borne,
In this sad bosom to their peaceful urn?
Whate'er the last consuming flame shall leave,
Shall not this widow'd hand by right receive,
And to the gods the precious relics give?
Perhaps, this last respect, which I should show,
Some vile Ægyptian hand does now bestow,
Injurious to the Roman shade below.
Happy, my Crassus, were thy bones, which lay
Expos'd to Parthian birds and beasts of prey!
Here the last rites the cruel gods allow,
And for a curse my Pompey's pile bestow.
For ever will the same sad fate return?
Still an unbury'd husband must I mourn,
And weep my sorrows o'er an empty urn?
But why should tombs be built, or urns be made?
Does grief like mine require their feeble aid?
Is he not lodg'd, thou wretch! within thy heart,
And fix'd in every dearest vital part?
O'er monuments surviving wives may grieve,
She ne'er will need them, who disdains to live.
But oh! behold where yon malignant flames
Cast feebly forth their mean inglorious beams:
From my lov'd lord, his dear remains, they rise,
And bring my Pompey to my weeping eyes;
And now they sink, the languid lights decay,
The cloudy smoke all eastward rolls away,
And wafts my hero to the rising day.
Me too the winds demand, with freshening gales;
Envious they call, and stretch the swelling sails.
No land on Earth seems dear as Ægypt now,
No land that crowns and triumphs did bestow,
And with new laurels bound my Pompey's brow.
That happy Pompey to my thoughts is lost,
He that is left, lies dead on yonder coast;
He, only he, is all I now demand,
For him I linger near this cursed land;

Endear'd by crimes, for horrours lov'd the more,
I cannot, will not, leave the Pharian shore.
Thou Sextus, thou shalt prove the chance of war,
And through the world thy father's ensigns bear,
Then hear his last command, intrusted to my care.
'Whene'er my last, my fatal hour shall come,
Arm you, my sons, for liberty and Rome;
While one shall of our free-born race remain,
Let him prevent the tyrant Cæsar's reign.
From each free city round, from every land,
Their warlike aid in Pompey's name demand.
These are the parties, these the friends he leaves,
This legacy your dying father gives.
If for the sea's wide rule your arms you bear,
A Pompey ne'er can want a navy there,
Heirs of my fame, my sons, shall wage my war.
Only be bold, unconquer'd in the fight,
And, like your father, still defend the right.
To Cato, if for liberty he stand,
Submit, and yield you to his ruling hand,
Brave, just, and only worthy to command.'
At length to thee, my Pompey, I am just,
I have surviv'd, and well discharg'd my trust;
Through chaos now, and the dark realms below,
To follow thee, a willing shade I go:
If longer with a lingering fate I strive,
'T is but to prove the pain of being alive,
'T is to be curst for daring to survive.
She, who could bear to see thy wounds, and live,
New proofs of love, and fatal grief, shall give.
Nor need she fly for succour to the sword,
The steepy precipice, and deadly cord;
She from herself shall find her own relief,
And scorn to die of any death but grief."
  So said the matron; and about her head
Her veil she draws, her mournful eyes to shade.
Resolv'd to shroud in thickest shades her woe,
She seeks the ship's deep darksome hold below:
There lonely left, at leisure to complain,
She hugs her sorrows and enjoys her pain:
Still with fresh tears the living grief would feed,
And fondly loves it, in her husband's stead.
In vain the beating surges rage aloud,
And swelling Eurus grumbles in the shroud;
Her, nor the waves beneath, nor winds above,
Nor all the noisy cries of fear can move;
In sullen peace compos'd for death she lies;
And, waiting, longs to hear the tempest rise;
Then hopes the seamen's vows shall all be crost,
Prays for the storm, and wishes to be lost.
  Soon from the Pharian coast the navy bore,
And sought through foamy seas the Cyprian shore;
Soft eastern gales prevailing thence alone,
To Cato's camp and Libya waft them on.
With mournful looks from land (as oft, we know,
A sad prophetic spirit waits on woe),
Pompey his brother and the fleet beheld,
Now near advancing o'er the watery field:
Straight to the beach with headlong haste he flies:
"Where is our father, Sextus, where?" he cries:
"Do we yet live? Stands yet the sovereign state?
Or does the world, with Pompey, yield to fate?
Sink we at length before the conquering foe?
And is the mighty head of Rome laid low?"
He said; the mournful brother thus reply'd;
"O happy thou! whom lands and seas divide
From woes, which did to these sad eyes betide:
These eyes! which of their horrour still complain,
Since they beheld our godlike father slain.
Nor did his fate an equal death afford,
Nor suffer'd him to fall by Cæsar's sword.
Trusting in vain to hospitable gods,
He dy'd, oppress'd by vile Ægyptian odds:
By the curs'd monarch of Nile's slimy wave
He fell, a victim to the crown he gave.
Yes, I beheld the dire, the bloody deed;
These eyes beheld our valiant father bleed:
Amaz'd I look'd, and scarce believ'd my fear,
Nor thought th' Ægyptian could so greatly dare;
But still I look'd, and fancy'd Cæsar there.
But, oh! not all his wounds so much did move,
Pierc'd my sad soul, and struck my filial love,
As that his venerable head they bear,
Their wanton trophy, fix'd upon a spear;
Through every town 't is shown the vulgar's sport,
And the lewd laughter of the tyrant's court.
'T is said that Ptolemy preserves this prize,
Proof of the deed, to glut the victor's eyes.
The body, whether rent, or borne away,
By foul Ægyptian dogs, and birds of prey:
Whether within their greedy maws entomb'd,
Or by those wretched flames, we saw, consum'd;
Its fate as yet we know not, but forgive:
That crime unpunish'd, to the gods we leave,
'T is for the part preserv'd alone we grieve."
  Scarce had he ended thus, when Pompey, warm
With noble fury, calls aloud to arm;
Nor seeks in sighs and helpless tears relief,
But thus in pious rage express'd his grief:
  "Hence all aboard, and haste to put to sea,
Urge on against the winds our adverse way;
With me let every Roman leader go,
Since civil wars were ne'er so just as now.
Pompey's unbury'd relics ask your aid,
Call for due rites and honours to be paid.
Let Ægypt's tyrant pour a purple flood,
And sooth the ghost with his inglorious blood.
Not Alexander shall his priests defend,
Forc'd from his golden shrine he shall descend:
In Mareotis deep I'll plunge him down,
Deep in the sluggish waves the royal carcass drown.
From his proud pyramid Amasis torn,
With his long dynasties my rage shall mourn,
And floating down their muddy Nile be borne.
Each stately tomb and monumental stone,
For thee, unburied Pompey, shall atone.
Isis no more shall draw the cheated crowd,
Nor god Osiris in his linen shroud;
Stript of their shrines, with scorn they shall be cast,
To be by ignominious hands defac'd;
Their holy Apis, of diviner breed,
To Pompey's dust a sacrifice shall bleed,
While burning deities the flame shall feed.
Waste shall the land be laid, and never know
The tiller's care, not feel the crooked plough:
None shall be left for whom the Nile may flow:
Till, the gods banish'd, and the people gone,
Ægypt to Pompey shall be left alone."
  He said; then hasty to revenge he flew,
And seaward out the ready navy drew;
But cooler Cato did the youth asswage,
And praising much, comprest his filial rage.
  Meantime the shores, the seas, and skies around,
With mournful cries for Pompey's death resound.
A rare example have their sorrows shown,
Yet in no age beside, nor people known,
How falling power did with compassion meet,
And crowds deplor'd the ruins of the great.

But when the sad Cornelia first appear'd,
When on the deck her mournful head she rear'd,
Her locks hang rudely o'er the matron's face,
With all the pomp of grief's disorder'd grace;
When they beheld her, wasted quite with woe,
And spent with tears that never ceas'd to flow,
Again they feel their loss, again complain,
And Heaven and Earth ring with their cries again.
Soon as she landed on the friendly strand,
Her lord's last rites employ her pious hand;
To his dear shade she builds a funeral pile,
And decks it proud with many a noble spoil.
There shone his arms with antic gold inlaid,
There the rich robes which she herself had made,
Robes to imperial Jove in triumph erst display'd:
The relics of his past victorious days,
Now this his latest trophy serve to raise,
And in one common flame together blaze.
Such was the weeping matron's pious care:
The soldiers, taught by her, their fires prepare:
To every valiant friend a pile they build,
That fell for Rome in curst Pharsalia's field:
Stretch'd wide along the shores, the flames extend,
And, grateful to the wandering shades, ascend.
So when Apulian hinds, with art, renew
The wintery pastures to their verdant hue,
That flowers may rise, and springing grass return,
With spreading flames the wither'd fields they [burn,
Garganus then and lofty Vultur blaze,
And draw the distant wandering swains to gaze;
Far are the glittering fires descry'd by night,
And gild the dusky skies around with light.
  But, oh! not all the sorrows of the crowd
That spoke their free impatient thoughts aloud,
That tax'd the gods, as authors of their woe,
And charg'd them with neglect of things below;
Not all the marks of the wild people's love,
The hero's soul, like Cato's praise, could move;
Few were his words, but from an honest heart,
Where faction and where favour had no part,
But truth made up for passion and for art.
  "We 've lost a Roman citizen," he said:
"One of the noblest of that name is dead;
Who, though not equal to our fathers found,
Nor by their strictest rules of justice bound,
Yet from his faults this benefit we draw,
He, for his country's good, transgress'd her law,
To keep a bold licentious age in awe.
Rome held her freedom still, though he was great;
He sway'd the senate, but they rul'd the state.
When crowds were willing to have worn his chain,
He chose his private station to retain,
That all might free, and equal all remain.
War's boundless power he never sought to use,
Nor ask'd, but what the people might refuse:
Much he possess'd and wealthy was his store,
Yet still he gather'd but to give the more,
And Rome, while he was rich, could ne'er be poor.
He drew the sword, but knew its rage to charm,
And lov'd peace best, when he was forc'd to arm;
Unmov'd with all the glittering pomp of power,
He took with joy, but laid it down with more:
His chaster houshold and his frugal board,
Nor lewdness did, nor luxury afford,
E'en in the highest fortunes of their lord.
His noble name, his country's honour grown,
Was venerably round the nations known,
And as Rome's fairest light and brightest glory shone.
When betwixt Marius and fierce Sylla tost,
The commonwealth her ancient freedom lost,
Some shadow yet was left, some show of power;
Now e'en the name with Pompey is no more:
Senate and people all at once are gone,
Nor need the tyrant blush to mount the throne.
Oh, happy Pompey! happy in thy fate,
Happy by falling with the falling state,
Thy death a benefit the gods did grant,
Thou might'st have liv'd those Pharian swords to [want.
Freedom, at least, thou dost by dying gain,
Nor liv'st to see thy Julia's father reign;
Free death is man's first bliss, the next is to be [slain.
Such mercy only I from Juba crave,
(If Fortune should ordain me Juba's slave)
To Cæsar let him show, but show me dead,
And keep my carcass, so he takes my head."
  He said, and pleas'd the noble shade below,
More than a thousand orators could do;
Though Tully too had lent his charming tongue,
And Rome's full forum with his praise had rung.
  But discord now infects the sullen crowd,
And now they tell their discontents aloud:
When Tarchon first his flying ensigns bore;
Call'd out to march, and hastened to the shore;
Him Cato thus, pursuing as he mov'd,
Sternly bespoke, and justly thus reprov'd:
  "Oh, restless author of the roving war,
Dost thou again piratic arms prepare?
Pompey, thy terrour and thy scourge is gone,
And now thou hop'st to rule the seas alone."
  He said, and bent his frown upon the rest,
Of whom one bolder thus the chief address'd,
And thus their weariness of war confess'd:
  "For Pompey's sake, nor thou disdain to hear,
The civil war we wage, these arms we bear;
Him we preferr'd to peace: but, Cato, now,
That cause, that master of our arms lies low.
Let us no more our absent country mourn,
But to our homes and houshold gods return;
To the chaste arms from whose embrace we fled,
And the dear pledges of the nuptial bed.
For oh! what period can the war attend,
Which nor Pharsalia's field nor Pompey's death can end?
The better times of flying life are past,
Let death come gently on in peace at last.
Let age at length with providential care
The necessary pile and urn prepare,
All rites the cruel civil war denies,
Part ev'n of Pompey yet unbury'd lies.
Though vanquish'd yet by no barbarian hand,
We fear not exile in a foreign land,
Nor are our necks by fortune now bespoke,
To bear the Scythian or Armenian yoke;
The victor still a citizen we own,
And yield obedience to the Roman gown.
While Pompey liv'd, he bore the sovereign sway;
Cæsar was next, and him we now obey;
With reverence be the sacred shade ador'd,
But war has given us now another lord:
To Cæsar and superior chance we yield:
All was determin'd in Amathia's field.
Nor shall our arms on other leaders wait,
Nor for uncertain hopes molest the state,
We follow'd Pompey once, but now we follow fate.
What terms, what safety, can we hope for now,
But what the victor's mercy shall allow?
Once Pompey's presence justify'd the cause,
Then fought we for our liberties and laws;

With him the honours of that cause lie dead,
And all the sanctity of war is fled.
If, Cato, thou for Rome these arms dost bear,
If still thy country only be thy care,
Seek we the legions where Rome's ensigns fly,
Where her proud eagles wave their wings on high:
No matter who to Pompey's power succeeds,
We follow where a Roman consul leads."
  This said, he leap'd aboard; the youthful sort
Join in his flight, and haste to leave the port;
The senseless crowd their liberty disdain,
And long to wear victorious Cæsar's chain.
Tyrannic power now sudden seem'd to threat
The ancient glories of Rome's free-born state,
Till Cato spoke, and thus deferr'd her fate:
  "Did then your vows and servile prayers conspire
Nought but a hasty master to desire?
Did you, when eager for the battle, come
The slaves of Pompey, not the friends of Rome?
Now, weary of the toil, from war you fly,
And idly lay your useless armour by;
Your hands neglect to wield the shining sword,
Nor can you fight but for a king and lord.
Some mighty chief you want, for whom to sweat;
Yourselves you know not, or at least forget,
And fondly bleed, that others may be great:
Meanly you toil, to give yourselves away;
And die, to leave the world a tyrant's prey.
The gods and Fortune do at length afford
A cause most worthy of a Roman sword.
At length 't is safe to conquer. Pompey now
Cannot, by your success, too potent grow;
Yet now, ignobly, you withhold your hands,
When nearer liberty your aid demands.
Of three who durst the sovereign power invade,
Two by your fortune's kinder doom lie dead;
And shall the Pharian sword and Parthian bow
Do more for liberty and Rome than you?
Base as you are, in vile subjection go,
And scorn what Ptolemy did ill bestow.
Ignobly innocent, and meanly good,
You durst not stain your hardy hands in blood;
Feebly awhile you fought, but soon did yield,
Aud fled the first from dire Pharsalia's field;
Go then secure, for Cæsar will be good,
Will pardon those who are with ease subdu'd;
The pitying victor will in mercy spare
The wretch, who never durst provoke his war.
Go, sordid slaves! one lordly master gone,
Like heir-looms go from father to the son.
Still to enhance your servile merit more,
Bear sad Cornelia weeping from the shore;
Meanly for hire expose the matron's life,
Metellus' daughter sell, and Pompey's wife;
Take too his sons: let Cæsar find in you
Wretches that may e'en Ptolemy out-do.
But let not my devoted life be spar'd.
The tyrant greatly shall that deed reward;
Such is the price of Cato's hated head,
That all your former wars shall well be paid;
Kill me, and in my blood do Cæsar right,
'Tis mean to have no other guilt but flight."
  He said, and stopp'd the flying naval power;
Back they return'd, repenting, to the shore.
As when the bees their waxen town forsake,
Careless in air their wandering way they take;
No more in clustering swarms condens'd they fly,
But fleet uncertain through the various sky;
No more from flowers they suck the liquid sweet,
But all their care and industry forget:
Then if at length the tinkling brass they hear,
With swift amaze their flight they soon forbear;
Sudden their flowery labours they renew,
Hang on the thyme, and sip the balmy dew.
Meantime secure on Hybla's fragrant plain,
With joy exults the happy shepherd swain;
Proud that his art had thus preserv'd his sto e,
He scorns to think his homely cottage poor.
With such prevailing force did Cato's care
The fierce impatient soldiers' minds pre.are,
To learn obedience, and endure the war.
  And now their minds, unknowing of repose,
With busy toil to exercise he chose;
Still with successive labours are they ply'd,
And oft in long and weary marches try'd.
Before Cyrene's walls they now sit down;
And here the victor's mercy well was shown,
He takes no vengeance of the captive town;
Patient he spares, and bids the vanquish'd live,
Since Cato, who could conquer, could forgive.
Hence, Libyan Juba's realms they meant t' explore,
Juba, who borders on the swarthy Moor;
But Nature's boundaries the journey stay,
The Syrts are fix'd athwart the middle way;
Yet led by daring virtue on they press,
Scorn opposition, and still hope success.
  When Nature's hand the first formation try'd,
When seas from lands she did at first divide,
The Syrts, not quite of sea nor land bereft,
A mingled mass uncertain still she left;
For nor the land with seas is quite o'er-spread,
Nor sink the waters deep their oozy bed,
Nor earth defends its shore, nor lifts aloft its head.
The site with neither, and with each complies,
Doubtful and inaccessible it lies;
Or 't is a sea with shallows bank'd around,
Or 't is a broken land with waters drown'd;
Here shores advanc'd o'er Neptune's rule we find,
And there an inland ocean lags behind.
Thus Nature's purpose by herself destroy'd,
Is useless to herself and unemploy'd,
And part of her creation still is void.
Perhaps, when first the world and time began,
Her swelling tides and plenteous waters ran;
But long confining on the burning zone,
The sinking seas have felt the neighbouring Sun:
Still by degrees we see how they decay,
And scarce resist the thirsty god of day.
Perhaps, in distant ages, 'twill be found,
When future suns have run the burning round,
These Syrts shall all be dry and solid ground;
Small are the depths their scanty waves retain,
And earth grows daily on the yielding main.
  And now the loaden fleet with active oars
Divide the liquid plain, and leave the shores,
When cloudy skies a gathering storm presage,
And Auster from the south began to rage.
Full from the land the sounding tempest roars,
Repels the swelling surge, and sweeps the shores;
The wind pursues, drives on the rolling sand,
And gives new limits to the growing land.
'Spite of the seaman's toil, the storm prevails;
In vain with skilful strength he hands the sails,
In vain the cordy cables bind them fast,
At once it rips and rends them from the mast;
At once the winds the fluttering canvass tear,
Then whirl and whisk it through the sportive air.
Some, timely for the rising rage prepar'd,
Furl the loose sheet, and lash it to the yard:

In vain their care; sudden the furious blast
Snaps by the board, and bears away the mast;
Of tackling, sails, and masts, at once bereft,
The ship a naked helpless hull is left.
Forc'd round and round, she quits her purpos'd way,
And bounds uncertain o'er the swelling sea.
But happier some a steady course maintain,
Who stand far out, and keep the deeper main.
Their masts they cut, and driving with the tide,
Safe o'er the surge beneath the tempest ride:
In vain did, from the southern coast, their foe,
All black with clouds, old stormy Auster blow;
Lowly secure amidst the waves they lay,
Old Ocean heav'd his back, and roll'd them on their way.
Some on the shallows strike, and doubtful stand,
Part beat by waves, part fix'd upon the sand.
Now pent amidst the shoals the billows roar,
Dash on the banks, and scorn the new-made shore:
Now by the wind driven on in heads they swell,
The stedfast banks both winds and waves repel:
Still with united force they rage in vain,
The sandy piles their stations fix'd maintain,
And lift their heads secure amidst the watery plain.
There 'scap'd from seas, upon the faithless strand,
With weeping eyes the shipwreck'd seamen stand,
And, cast ashore, look vainly out for land.
Thus some were lost; but far the greater part,
Preserv'd from danger by the pilot's art,
Keep on their course, a happier fate partake,
And reach in safety the Tritonian lake.
These waters to the tuneful god are dear,
Whose vocal shell the sea-green Nereids hear;
These Pallas loves, so tells reporting fame,
Here first from Heaven to Earth the goddess came,
(Heaven's neighbourhood the warmer clime betrays,
And speaks the nearer Sun's immediate rays)
Here her first footsteps on the brink she staid,
Here in the watery glass her form survey'd,
And call'd herself from hence the chaste Tritonian maid.
Here Lethe's streams, from secret springs below,
Rise to the light; here heavily, and slow,
The silent dull forgetful waters flow.
Here by the wakeful dragon kept of old,
Hesperian plants grew rich with living gold;
Long since, the fruit was from the branches torn,
And now the gardens their lost honours mourn.
Such was in ancient times the tale receiv'd,
Such by our good forefathers was believ'd;
Nor let inquirers the tradition wrong,
Or dare to question, now, the poet's sacred song.
Then take it for a truth, the wealthy wood
Here under golden boughs low bending stood;
On some large tree his folds the serpent wound,
The fair Hesperian virgins watch'd around,
And join'd to guard the rich forbidden ground.
But great Alcides came to end their care,
Stript the gay grove, and left the branches bare;
Then back returning sought the Argive shore,
And the bright spoil to proud Eurystheus bore.

These famous regions and the Syrts o'erpast,
They reach'd the Garamantian coast at last;
Here, under Pompey's care the navy lies,
Beneath the gentlest clime of Libya's skies.
But Cato's soul, by dangers unrestrain'd,
Ease and a dull inactive life disdain'd.
His daring virtue urges to go on,
Through desert lands, and nations yet unknown;
To march, and prove th' inhospitable ground,
To shun the Syrts, and lead the soldier round.
Since now tempestuous seasons vex the sea,
And the declining year forbids the watery way;
He sees the cloudy drizzling winter near,
And hopes kind rains may cool the sultry air:
So haply may they journey on secure,
Nor burning heats, nor killing frosts endure;
But while cool winds the winter's breath supplies,
With gentle warmth the Libyan sun may rise,
And both may join and temper well the skies.

But ere the toilsome march he undertook,
The hero thus the list'ning host bespoke:
"Fellows in arms! whose bliss, whose chiefest good,
Is Rome's defence, and freedom bought with blood;
You, who, to die with liberty, from far
Have follow'd Cato in this fatal war,
Be now for virtue's noblest task prepar'd,
For labours, many, perilous, and hard.
Think through what burning climes, what wilds we go:
No leafy shades the naked deserts know,
Nor silver streams through flowery meadows flow,
But horrours there, and various deaths abound,
And serpents guard th' inhospitable ground.
Hard is the way; but thus our fate demands;
Rome and her laws we seek amidst these sands.
Let those who, glowing with their country's love,
Resolve with me these dreadful plains to prove,
Nor of return nor safety once debate,
But only dare to go, and leave the rest to fate.
Think not I mean the dangers to disguise,
Or hide them from the cheated vulgar's eyes.
Those, only those, shall in my fate partake,
Who love the daring for the danger's sake;
Those who can suffer all the worst can come,
And think it what they owe themselves and Rome.
If any yet shall doubt, or yet shall fear,
If life be, more than liberty, his care;
Here, ere we journey farther, let him stay,
Inglorious let him, like a slave, obey,
And seek a master in some safer way.
Foremost, behold, I lead you to the toil,
My feet shall foremost print the dusty soil:
Strike me the first, thou flaming god of day,
First let me feel thy fierce, thy scorching ray;
Ye living poisons all, ye snaky train,
Meet me the first upon the fatal plain.
In every pain, which you, my warriors, fear,
Let me be first, and teach you how to bear.
Who sees me pant for drought, or fainting first,
Let him upbraid me, and complain of thirst.
If e'er for shelter to the shades I fly,
Me let him curse, me, for the sultry sky.
If while the weary soldier marches on,
Your leader by distinguish'd ease be known,
Forsake my cause, and leave me there alone.
The sands, the serpents, thirst, and burning heat,
Are dear to patience, and to virtue sweet;
Virtue, that scorns on cowards' terms to please,
Or cheaply to be bought, or won with ease;
But then she joys, then smiles upon her state,
Then fairest to herself, then most complete,
When glorious danger makes her truly great.
So Libya's plains alone shall wipe away
The foul dishonours of Pharsalia's day;
So shall your courage now transcend that fear:
You fled with glory there, to conquer here."

He said; and hardy love of toil inspir'd;
And every breast with godlike ardour fir'd.
Straight, careless of return, without delay,
Through the wide waste he took his pathless way.

Libya, ordain'd to be his last retreat,
Receives the hero, fearless of his fate;
Here the good gods his last of labours doom,
Here shall his bones and sacred dust find room,
And his great head be hid, within an humble tomb.
If this large globe be portion'd right by fame,
Then one third part shall sandy Libya claim:
But if we count, as suns descend and rise,
If we divide by east and west the skies,
Then, with fair Europe, Libya shall combine,
And both to make the western half shall join.
Whilst wide-extended Asia fills the rest,
Of all from Tanais to Nile possest,
And reigns sole empress of the dawning east.
Of all the Libyan soil, the kindliest found
Far to the western seas extends its bound;
Where cooling gales, where gentle zephyrs fly,
And setting suns adorn the gaudy sky:
And yet e'en here no liquid fountain's vein
Wells through the soil, and gurgles o'er the plain;
But from our northern clime, our gentler Heaven,
Refreshing dews and fruitful rains are driven;
All bleak, the god, cold Boreas, spreads his wing,
And with our winter gives the Libyan spring.
No wicked wealth infects the simple soil,
Nor golden ores disclose their shining spoil:
Pure is the glebe, 'tis earth, and earth alone,
To guilty pride and avarice unknown:
There citron groves, the native riches, grow,
There cool retreats and fragrant shades bestow,
And hospitably screen their guests below.
Safe by their leafy office long they stood
A sacred, old, unviolated wood,
Till Roman luxury to Afric past,
And foreign axes laid their honours waste.
Thus utmost lands are ransack'd, to afford
The far-fetch'd dainties, and the costly board.
But rude and wasteful all those regions lie
That border on the Syrts, and feel too nigh
Their sultry summer sun, and parching sky.
No harvest, there, the scatter'd grain repays,
But withering dies, and ere it shoots decays:
There never loves to spring the mantling vine,
Nor wanton ringlets round her elm to twine:
The thirsty dust prevents the swelling fruit,
Drinks up the generous juice, and kills the root:
Through secret veins no tempering moistures pass,
To bind with viscous force the mouldering mass;
But genial Jove, averse, disdains to smile,
Forgets, and curses the neglected soil.
Thence lazy Nature droops her idle head,
As every vegetable sense were dead;
Thence the wide dreary plains one visage wear,
Alike in summer, winter, spring appear,
Nor feel the turns of the revolving year.
Thin herbage here (for some e'en here is found)
The Nasamonian hinds collect around;
A naked race, and barbarous of mind,
That live upon the losses of mankind:
The Syrts supply their wants and barren soil,
And strow th' inhospitable shores with spoil.
Trade they have none, but ready still they stand,
Rapacious, to invade the wealthy strand,
And hold a commerce, thus, with every distant [land.
Through this dire country Cato's journey lay,
Here he pursu'd, while virtue led the way.
Here the bold youth, led by his high command,
Fearless of storms and raging winds, by land
Repeat the dangers of the swelling main,
And strive with storms and raging winds again.

Here all at large, where nought restrains his force,
Impetuous Auster runs his rapid course;
Nor mountains here, nor stedfast rocks resist,
But free he sweeps along the spacious list.
No stable groves of ancient oaks arise,
To tire his rage, and catch him as he flies;
But wide, around, the naked plains appear,
Here fierce he drives unbounded through the air,
Roars and exerts his dreadful empire here.
The whirling dust, like waves in eddies wrought,
Rising aloft, to the mid Heaven is caught;
There hangs a sullen cloud; nor falls again,
Nor breaks, like gentle vapours, into rain.
Gazing, the poor inhabitant descries,
Where high above his land and cottage flies;
Bereft, he sees his lost possessions there,
From Earth transported, and now fix'd in air.
Not rising flames attempt a bolder flight;
Like smoke by rising flames uplifted, light
The sands ascend, and stain the Heavens with night.
But now, his utmost power and rage to boast,
The stormy god invades the Roman host;
The soldier yields, unequal to the shock,
And staggers at the wind's stupendous stroke.
Amaz'd he sees that earth, which lowly lay,
Forc'd from beneath his feet, and torn away.
Oh Libya! were thy pliant surface bound,
And form'd a solid, close-compacted ground;
Or hadst thou rocks, whose hollow deeps below
Would draw those raging winds that loosely blow;
Their fury, by thy firmer mass oppos'd,
Or in those dark infernal caves enclos'd,
Thy certain ruin would at once complete,
Shake thy foundations, and unfix thy seat:
But well thy flitting plains have learn'd to yield;
Thus, not contending, thou thy place hast held,
Unfix'd art fix'd, and flying keep'st the field.
Helms, spears, and shields, snatch'd from the warlike host,
Through Heaven's wide regions far away were tost;
While distant nations, with religious fear,
Beheld them, as some prodigy in air,
And thought the gods by them denounc'd a war.
Such haply was the chance, which first did raise
The pious tale, in priestly Numa's days;
Such were those shields, and thus they came from Heaven,
A sacred charge to young patricians given;
Perhaps, long since, to lawless winds a prey,
From far barbarians were they forc'd away;
Thence through long airy journeys safe did come,
To cheat the crowd with miracles at Rome.
Thus, wide o'er Libya, rag'd the stormy south,
Thus every way assail'd the Latian youth:
Each several method for defence they try,
Now wrap their garments tight, now close they lie:
Now sinking to the earth, with weight they press,
Now clasp it to them with a strong embrace,
Scarce in that posture safe; the driving blast
Bears hard, and almost heaves them off at last.
Meantime a sandy flood comes rolling on,
And swelling heaps the prostrate legions drown;
New to the sudden danger, and dismay'd,
The frighted soldier hasty calls for aid,
Heaves at the hill, and struggling rears his head.
Soon shoots the growing pile, and, rear'd on high,
Lifts up its lofty summit to the sky:
High sandy walls, like forts, their passage stay,
And rising mountains intercept their way:

The certain bounds which should their journey
The moving earth and dusty deluge hide: [guide,
So landmarks sink beneath the flowing tide.
As through mid-seas uncertainly they move,
Led only by Jove's sacred lights above:
Part e'en of them the Libyan clime denies,
Forbids their native northern stars to rise,
And shades the well-known lustre from their eyes.
Now near approaching to the burning zone,
To warmer, calmer skies they journey'd on. [fess,
The slackening storms the neighbouring Sun con-
The heat strikes fiercer, and the winds grow less,
Whilst parching thirst and fainting sweats in-
As forward on the weary way they went, [crease.
Panting with drought, and all with labour spent,
Amidst the desert, desolate and dry,
One chanc'd a little trickling spring to spy:
Proud of the prize, he drain'd the scanty store,
And in his helmet to the chieftain bore.
Around, in crowds, the thirsty legions stood,
Their throats and clammy jaws with dust be-
strew'd, [view'd.
And all with wishful eyes the liquid treasure
Around the leader cast his careful look,
Sternly the tempting envy'd gift he took,
Held it, and thus the giver fierce bespoke:
"And think'st thou then that I want virtue most!
Am I the meanest of this Roman host!
Am I the first soft coward that complains!
That shrinks, unequal to these glorious pains!
Am I in ease and infamy the first!
Rather be thou, base as thou art, accurs'd,
Thou that dar'st drink, when all beside thee thirst."
He said; and wrathful stretching forth his hand,
Pour'd out the precious draught upon the sand.
Well did the water thus for all provide,
Envy'd by none, while thus to all deny'd,
A little thus the general want supply'd.
Now to the sacred temple they draw near,
Whose only altars Libyan lands revere;
There, but unlike the Jove by Rome ador'd,
A form uncouth, stands Heaven's almighty lord.
No regal ensigns grace his potent hand,
Nor shakes he there the lightning's flaming brand:
But, ruder to behold, a horned ram
Belies the god, and Ammon is his name.
There though he reigns unrivall'd and alone,
O'er the rich neighbours of the torrid zone;
Though swarthy Æthiops are to him confin'd,
With Araby the blest, and wealthy Inde;
Yet no proud domes are rais'd, no gems are seen,
To blaze upon his shrines with costly sheen;
But plain and poor, and unprophan'd he stood,
Such as, to whom our great forefathers bow'd:
A god of pious times, and days of old,
That keeps his temples safe from Roman gold.
Here and here only, through wide Libya's space,
Tall trees, the land, and verdant herbage grace;
Here the loose sands by plenteous springs are
Knit to a mass, and moulded into ground: [bound,
Here smiling Nature wears a fertile dress,
And all things here the present god confess.
Yet here the Sun to neither pole declines,
But from his zenith vertically shines:
Hence, e'en the trees no friendly shelter yield,
Scarce their own trunks the leafy branches shield;
The rays descend direct, all round embrace,
And to a central point the shadow chase.
Here equally the middle line is found,
To cut the radiant Zodiac in its round:
Here unoblique the Bull and Scorpion rise,
Nor mount too swift, nor leave too soon the skies;
Nor Libra does too long the Ram attend,
Nor bids the Maid the *fishy* sign descend.
The Boys and Centaur justly time divide,
And equally their several seasons guide:
Alike the Crab and wintery Goat return,
Alike the Lion and the flowing Urn.
If any farther nations yet are known,
Beyond the Libyan fires, and scorching zone;
Northward from them the Sun's bright course is
made,
And to the southward strikes the leaning shade:
There slow Boötes, with his lazy wain
Descending, seems to reach the watery main.
Of all the lights which high above they see,
No star whate'er from Neptune's waves is free,
The whirling axle drives them round, and plunges
in the sea.
Before the temple's entrance, at the gate,
Attending crowds of eastern pilgrims wait:
These from the horned god expect relief:
But all give way before the Latian chief.
His host, (as crowds are superstitious still)
Curious of fate, of future good and ill,
And fond to prove prophetic Ammon's skill,
Entreat their leader to the god would go,
And from his oracle Rome's fortunes know:
But Labienus chief the thought approv'd,
And thus the common suit to Cato mov'd:
"Chance, and the fortune of the way," he said,
"Have brought Jove's sacred counsels to our aid:
This greatest of the gods, this mighty chief,
In each distress shall be a sure relief;
Shall point the distant dangers from afar,
And teach the future fortunes of the war.
To thee, O Cato! pious! wise! and just!
Their dark decrees the cautious gods shall trust!
To thee their fore-determin'd will shall tell:
Their will has been thy law, and thou hast kept it
well.
Fate bids thee now the noble thought improve;
Fate brings thee here, to meet and talk with Jove.
Inquire betimes, what various chance shall come
To impious Cæsar, and thy native Rome;
Try to avert, at least, thy country's doom.
Ask if these arms our freedom shall restore:
Or else, if laws and right shall be no more.
Be thy great breast with sacred knowledge fraught,
To lead us in the wandering maze of thought:
Thou, that to virtue ever wert inclin'd,
Learn what it is, how certainly defin'd,
And leave some perfect rule to guide mankind."
Full of the god that dwelt within his breast,
The hero thus his secret mind express'd,
And in-born truths reveal'd; truths which might
well
Become e'en oracles themselves to tell.
"Where would thy fond, thy vain inquiry go?
What mystic fate, what secret would'st thou know?
Is it a doubt if death should be my doom,
Rather than live till kings and bondage come,
Rather than see a tyrant crown'd in Rome?
Or would'st thou know if, what we value here,
Life, be a trifle hardly worth our care?
What by old age and length of days we gain,
More than to lengthen out the sense of pain?
Or if this world, with all its forces join'd,
The universal malice of mankind,
Can shake or hurt the brave and honest mind?

If stable virtue can her ground maintain,
Whilst fortune feebly threats and frowns in vain?
If truth and justice with uprightness dwell,
And honesty consist in meaning well?
If right be independent of success,
And conquest cannot make it more nor less?
Are these, my friend, the secrets thou would'st know,
Those doubts for which to oracles we go?
'T is known, 't is plain, 't is all already told,
And horned Ammon can no more unfold.
From God deriv'd, to God by nature join'd,
We act the dictates of his mighty mind:
And though our priests are mute, and temples still,
God never wants a voice to speak his will.
When first we from the teeming womb were brought,
With in-born precepts then our souls were fraught,
And then the Maker his new creatures taught.
Then when he form'd, and gave us to be men,
He gave us all our useful knowledge then.
Canst thou believe, the vast Eternal Mind
Was e'er to Syrts and Libyan sands confin'd?
That he would choose this waste, this barren [ground,
To teach the thin inhabitants around,
And leave his truth in wilds and deserts drown'd?
Is there a place that God would choose to love
Beyond this earth, the seas, yon Heaven above,
And virtuous minds, the noblest throne for Jove?
Why seek we farther then? Behold around,
How all thou seest does with the God abound,
Jove is alike in all, and always to be found.
Let those weak minds, who live in doubt and fear,
To juggling priests for oracles repair;
One certain hour of death to each decreed,
My fix'd, my certain soul from doubt has freed.
The coward and the brave are doom'd to fall;
And when Jove told this truth, he told us all."
So spoke the hero; and, to keep his word,
Nor Ammon, nor his oracle explor'd;
But left the crowd at freedom to believe,
And take such answers as the priest should give.
  Foremost on foot he treads the burning sand,
Bearing his arms in his own patient hand;
Scorning another's weary neck to press,
Or in a lazy chariot loll at ease:
The panting soldier at his toil succeeds,
Where no command, but great example leads.
Sparing of sleep, still for the rest he wakes,
And at the fountain, last, his thirst he slakes;
Whene'er by chance some living stream is found,
He stands, and sees the cooling draughts go round,
Stays till the last and meanest drudge be past,
And, till his slaves have drunk, disdains to taste.
If true good men deserve immortal fame,
If virtue, though distress'd, be still the same;
Whate'er our fathers greatly dar'd to do,
Whate'er they bravely bore, and wisely knew,
Their virtues all are his, and all their praise his due.
Whoe'er, with battles fortunately fought,
Whoe'er, with Roman blood, such honours bought?
This triumph, this, on Libya's utmost bound,
With death and desolation compass'd round,
To all thy glories, Pompey, I prefer,
Thy trophies, and thy third triumphal car, [war.
To Marius' mighty name, and great Jugurthine
His country's father here, O Rome, behold,
Worthy thy temples, priests, and shrines of gold!
If e'er thou break'st thy lordly master's chain,
If liberty be e'er restor'd again,
Him shalt thou place in thy divine abodes, [gods.
Swear by his holy name, and rank him with thy
  Now to those sultry regions were they past,
Which Jove to stop inquiring mortals plac'd,
And as their utmost, southern, limits cast.
Thirsty, for springs they search the desert round,
And only one, amidst the sands, they found.
Well stor'd it was, but all access was barr'd:
The stream ten thousand noxious serpents guard:
Dry aspics on the fatal margin stood,
And dipsas thirsted in the middle flood.
Back from the stream the frighted soldier flies,
Though parch'd, and languishing for drink, he dies:
The chief beheld, and said, "You fear in vain,
Vainly from safe and healthy draughts abstain,
My soldier, drink, and dread not death or pain.
When urg'd to rage, their teeth the serpents fix,
And venom with our vital juices mix;
The pest infus'd through every vein runs round,
Infects the mass, and death is in the wound.
Harmless and safe, no poison here they shed:"
He said; and first the doubtful draught essay'd;
He, who through all their march, their toil, their thirst,
Demanded, here alone, to drink the first.
  Why plagues, like these, infect the Libyan air,
Why deaths unknown in various shapes appear;
Why, fruitful to destroy, the cursed land
Is temper'd thus, by Nature's secret hand;
Dark and obscure the hidden cause remains,
And still deludes the vain inquirer's pains;
Unless a tale for truth may be believ'd,
And the good-natur'd world be willingly deceiv'd.
  Where western waves on farthest Libya beat,
Warm'd with the setting Sun's descending heat,
Dreadful Medusa fix'd her horrid seat.
No leafy shade, with kind protection, shields
The rough, the squalid, unfrequented fields:
No mark of shepherds, or the ploughman's toil,
To tend the flocks, or turn the mellow soil:
But, rude with rocks, the region all around
Its mistress, and her potent visage, own'd.
'T was from this monster, to afflict mankind,
That nature first produc'd the snaky kind:
On her, at first their forky tongues appear'd;
From her, their dreadful hissings first were heard.
Some wreath'd in folds upon her temples hung;
Some backwards to her waist depended long;
Some with their rising crests her forehead deck;
Some wanton play, and lash her swelling neck:
And while her hands the curling vipers comb,
Poisons distil around, and drops of livid foam.
  None, who beheld the fury, could complain;
So swift their fate, preventing death and pain:
Ere they had time to fear, the change came on,
And motion, sense, and life, were lost in stone.
The soul itself, from sudden flight debarr'd,
Congealing, in the body's fortune shar'd.
The dire Eumenides could rage inspire,
But could no more; the tuneful Thracian lyre
Infernal Cerberus did soon assuage,
Lull'd him to rest, and sooth'd his triple rage;
Hydra's seven heads the bold Alcides view'd,
Safely he saw, and what he saw, subdu'd:
Of these in various terrours each excell'd;
But all to this superior fury yield.
Phorcus and Ceto, next to Neptune be,
Immortal both, and rulers of the sea,
This monster's parents did their offspring dread;
And from her sight her sister Gorgons fled.

Old ocean's waters and the liquid air,
The universal world her power might fear:
All nature's beauteous works she could invade,
Through every part a lazy numbness shed,
And over all a stony surface spread. [grown,
Birds in their flight were stopt, and ponderous
Forgot their pinions, and fell senseless down.
Beasts to the rocks were fix'd, and all around
Were tribes of stone and marble nations found.
No living eyes so fell a sight could bear;
Her snakes themselves, all deadly tho' they were,
Shot backward from her face, and shrunk away
By her, a rock Titanian Atlas grew, [for fear.
And Heaven by her the giants did subdue:
Hard was the fight, and Jove was half dismay'd,
Till Pallas brought the Gorgon to his aid:
The heavenly nation laid aside their fear,
For soon she finish'd the prodigious war;
To mountains turn'd, the monster race remains,
The trophies of her power on the Phlegræan plains.
   To seek this monster, and her fate to prove,
The son of Danaë and golden Jove
Attempts a flight through airy ways above.
The youth Cyllenian Hermes' aid implor'd;
The god assisted with his wings the sword,
His sword which late made watchful Argus bleed,
And Iö from her cruel keeper freed.
Unwedded Pallas lent a sister's aid;
But ask'd, for recompense, Medusa's head.
Eastward she warns her brother bend his flight,
And from the Gorgon realms avert his sight;
Then arms his left with her refulgent shield,
And shows how there the foe might be beheld.
Deep slumbers had the drowsy fiend possest,
Such as drew on, and well might seem, her last:
And yet she slept not whole; one half her snakes
Watchful, to guard their horrid mistress, wakes;
The rest dishevell'd, loosely, round her head,
And o'er her drowsy lids and face were spread.
Backward the youth draws near, nor dares to look,
But blindly, at a venture, aims a stroke:
His faltering hand the virgin goddess guides,
And from the monster's neck her snaky head
      divides.
But oh! what art, what numbers can express
The terrours of the dying Gorgon's face!
What clouds of poison from her lips arise,
What death, what vast destruction, threaten'd in
      her eyes!
'T was somewhat that immortal gods might fear,
More than the warlike maid herself could bear.
The victor Perseus still had been subdu'd,
Though, wary still, with eyes averse he stood:
Had not his heavenly sister's timely care
Veil'd the dread visage with the hissing hair.
Seis'd of his prey, heavenwards, uplifted light,
On Hermes' nimble wings, he took his flight.
Now thoughtful of his course, he hung in air,
And meant through Europe's happy clime to steer;
Till pitying Pallas warn'd him not to blast
Her fruitful fields, nor lay her cities waste.
For who would not have upwards cast their sight,
Curious to gaze at such a wond'rous flight?
Therefore, by gales of gentle Zephyrs borne,
To Libya's coast the hero minds to turn.
Beneath the sultry line, expos'd it lies
To deadly planets, and malignant skies.
Still, with his fiery steeds, the god of day
Drives through that Heaven, and makes his burn-
      ing way.
No land more high erects its lofty head,
The silver Moon in dim eclipse to shade;
If through the summer signs direct she run,
Nor bends obliquely, north or south, to shun
The envious Earth, that hides her from the Sun.
Yet could this soil accurst, this barren field,
Increase of deaths, and poisonous harvests yield.
Where'er sublime in air the victor flew,
The monster's head distill'd a deadly dew;
The Earth receiv'd the seed, and pregnant grew.
Still as the putrid gore dropt on the sand,
'T was temper'd up by Nature's forming hand;
The glowing climate makes the work complete,
And broods upon the mass, and lends it genial
      heat.
   First of those plagues the drowsy asp appear'd,
Then first her crest and swelling neck she rear'd;
A larger drop of black congealing blood
Distinguish'd her amidst the deadly brood.
Of all the serpent race are none so fell, [swell;
None with so many deaths, such plenteous venom
Chill in themselves, our colder climes they shun,
And choose to bask in Afric's warmer sun;
But Nile no more confines them now: What bound
Can for insatiate avarice be found!
Freighted with Libyan deaths our merchants come,
And poisonous asps are things of price at Rome.
   Her scaly folds th' hæmorrhoïs unbends,
And her vast length along the sand extends;
Where'er she wounds, from every part the blood
Gushes resistless in a crimson flood.
   Amphibious some do in the Syrts abound,
And now on land, in waters now are found.
   Slimy chelyders the parch'd earth distain,
And trace a reeking furrow on the plain.
   The spotted cenchris, rich in various dyes,
Shoots in a line, and forth directly flies:
Not Theban marbles are so gaily dress'd,
Nor with such party-colour'd beauties grac'd.
   Safe in his earthly hue and dusky skin,
Th' ammodites lurks in the sands unseen:
The swimmer there the crystal stream pollutes;
And swift, through air, the flying javelin shoots.
The scytale, ere yet the spring returns,
There casts her coat; and there the dipsas burns;
The amphisbæna doubly arm'd appears,
At either end a threatening head she rears.
Rais'd on his active tail the pareas stands,
And, as he passes, furrows up the sands.
The prester by his foaming jaws is known;
The seps invades the flesh and firmer bone,
Dissolves the mass of man, and melts his fabric
      down.
The basilisk, with dreadful hissings heard,
And from afar by every serpent fear'd,
To distance drives the vulgar, and remains
The lonely monarch of the desert plains.
   And you, ye dragons of the scaly race,
Whom glittering gold and shining armours grace,
In other nations harmless are you found,
This, guardian genii and protectors own'd;
In Afric only are you fatal; there,
On wide-expanded wings, sublime you rear
Your dreadful forms, and drive the yielding air.
The lowing kine in droves you chase, and cull
Some master of the herd, some mighty bull:
Around his stubborn sides your tails you twist,
By force compress, and burst his brawny chest.
Not elephants are by their larger size
Secure, but, with the rest, become your prize.

Resistless in your might, you all invade,
And for destruction need not poison's aid. [spread,
Thus, though a thousand plagues around them
A weary march the hardy soldiers tread,
Thro' thirst, thro' toil and death, by Cato led.
Their chief, with pious grief and deep regret,
Each moment mourns his friends untimely fate;
Wond'ring, he sees some small, some trivial wound
Extend a valiant Roman on the ground.
Aulus, a noble youth of Tyrrhene blood,
Who bore the standard, on a dipsas trod;
Backward the wrathful serpent bent her head,
And, fell with rage, th' unheeded wrong repaid.
Scarce did some little mark of hurt remain,
And scarce he found some little sense of pain;
Nor could he yet the danger doubt, nor fear
That death, with all its terrours, threaten'd there.
When lo; unseen, the secret venom spreads,
And every nobler part at once invades;
Swift flames consume the marrow and the brain,
And the scorch'd entrails rage with burning pain;
Upon his heart the thirsty poisons prey,
And drain the sacred juice of life away.
No kindly floods of moisture bathe his tongue,
But cleaving to the parched roof it hung;
No trickling drops distil, no dewy sweat,
To ease his weary limbs, and cool the raging heat.
Nor could he weep; e'en grief could not supply
Streams for the mournful office of his eye,
The never-failing source of tears was dry.
Frantic he flies, and with a careless hand
Hurls the neglected eagle on the sand;
Nor hears, nor minds, his pitying chief's command.
For springs he seeks, he digs, he probes the ground,
For springs, in vain, explores the desert round,
For cooling draughts, which might their aid impart,
And quench the burning venom in his heart.
Plung'd in the Tanaïs, the Rhone, or Po,
Or Nile, whose wandering streams o'er Ægypt flow,
Still would he rage, still with the fever glow.
The scorching climate to his fate conspires,
And Libya's sun assists the dipsa's fires.
Now every where for drink in vain he pries,
Now to the Syrts and briny seas he flies;
The briny seas delight, but seem not to suffice.
Nor yet he knows what secret plague he nurs'd,
Nor found the poison, but believ'd it thirst.
Of thirst, and thirst alone, he still complains,
Raving for thirst, he tears his swelling veins;
From every vessel drains a crimson flood,
And quaffs in greedy draughts his vital blood.
This Cato saw, and straight, without delay,
Commands his legions on to urge their way;
Nor give th' inquiring soldier time to know
What deadly deeds a fatal thirst could do.
But soon a fate more sad, with new surprise,
From the first object turns their wond'ring eyes.
Wretched Sabellus by a seps was stung;
Fix'd to his leg, with deadly teeth, it hung:
Sudden the soldier shook it from the wound,
Transfix'd and nail'd it to the barren ground.
Of all the dire destructive serpent race,
None have so much of death, though none are less.
For straight, around the part, the skin withdrew,
The flesh and sinking sinews backward flew,
And left the naked bones expos'd to view.
The spreading poisons all the parts confound,
And the whole body sinks within the wound.
The brawny thighs no more their muscles boast,
But, melting, all in liquid filth are lost;
The well-knit groin above, and ham below,
Mixt in one putrid stream, together flow;
The firm peritonæum, rent in twain,
No more the pressing entrails could sustain,
It yields, and forth they fall, at once they gush amain.
Small relics of the mouldering mass were left,
At once of substance, as of form bereft;
Dissolv'd, the whole in liquid poison ran,
And to a nauseous puddle shrunk the man.
Then burst the rigid nerves, the manly breast,
And all the texture of the heaving chest;
Resistless way the conquering venom made,
And secret nature was at once display'd;
Her sacred privacies all open lie
To each prophane, inquiring, vulgar eye.
Then the broad shoulders did the pest invade,
Then o'er the valiant arms and neck it spread;
Last sunk, the mind's imperial seat, the head.
So snows dissolv'd by southern breezes run,
So melts the wax before the noon-day Sun.
Nor ends the wonder here; though flames are known
To waste the flesh, yet still they spare the bone:
Here none were left, no least remains were seen;
No marks to show that once the man had been.
Of all the plagues which curse the Libyan land,
(If death and mischief may a crown demand)
Serpent, the palm is thine. Though others may
Boast of their power to force the soul away,
Yet soul and body both become thy prey.
A fate of different kind Nasidius found,
A burning prester gave the deadly wound;
And straight a sudden flame began to spread,
And paint his visage with a glowing red.
With swift expansion swells the bloated skin,
Nought but an undistinguish'd mass is seen,
While the fair human form lies lost within.
The puffy poison spreads, and heaves around,
Till all the man is in the monster drown'd.
No more the steely plate his breast can stay,
But yields, and gives the bursting poison way.
Not waters so, when fire the rage supplies,
Bubbling on heaps, in boiling cauldrons rise:
Nor swells the stretching canvass half so fast,
When the sails gather all the driving blast,
Strain the tough yards, and bow the lofty mast.
The various parts no longer now are known,
One headless formless heap remains alone;
The feather'd kind avoid the fatàl feast,
And leave it deadly to some hungry beast;
With horrour seiz'd, his sad companions too,
In haste from the unbury'd carcass flew; [grew.
Look'd back, but fled again, for still the monster
But fertile Libya still new plagues supplies,
And to more horrid monsters turns their eyes.
Deeply the fierce hæmorrhoïs imprest
Her fatal teeth on Tullus' valiant breast:
The noble youth, with virtue's love inspir'd,
Her, in her Cato, follow'd and admir'd;
Mov'd by his great example, vow'd to share,
With him, each chance of that disastrous war.
And as when mighty Rome's spectators meet
In the full theatre's capacious seat,
At once, by secret pipes and channels fed,
Rich tinctures gush from every antique head;
At once ten thousand saffron currents flow,
And rain their odours on the crowd below:
So the warm blood at once from every part
Ran purple poison down, and drain'd the fainting heart.

Blood falls for tears, and o'er his mournful face
The ruddy drops their tainted passage trace:
Where'er the liquid juices find a way,
There streams of blood, there crimson rivers stray:
His mouth and gushing nostrils pour a flood,
And e'en the pores ooze out the trickling blood;
In the red deluge all the parts lie drown'd,
And the whole body seems one bleeding wound.
Lævus, a colder aspic bit, and straight
His blood forgot to flow, his heart to beat;
Thick shades upon his eye-lids seem'd to creep,
And lock him fast in everlasting sleep:
No sense of pain, no torment, did he know,
But sunk in slumbers to the shades below.
Not swifter death attends the noxious juice,
Which dire Sabæan aconites produce.
Well may their crafty priests divine, and well
The fate which they themselves can cause, foretell.
Fierce from afar a darting javelin shot,
(For such, the serpent's name has Afric taught)
And through unhappy Paulus' temples flew;
Nor poison, but a wound, the soldier slew.
No flight so swift, so rapid none we know,
Stones from the sounding sling, compar'd, are slow,
And the shaft loiters from the Scythian bow.
A basilisk bold Murrus kill'd in vain,
And nail'd it dying to the sandy plain;
Along the spear the sliding venom ran,
And sudden, from the weapon, seiz'd the man:
His hand first touch'd, ere it his arm invade,
Soon he divides it with his shining blade:
The serpent's force by sad example taught,
With his lost hand his ransom'd life he bought.
Who that the scorpion's insect form surveys,
Would think that ready death his call obeys?
Threatening, he rears his knotty tail on high;
The vast Orion thus he doom'd to die,
And fix'd him, his proud trophy, in the sky.
Or could we the salpuga's anger dread,
Or fear upon her little cell to tread?
Yet she the fatal threads of life commands,
And quickens oft the Stygian sisters hands.
Pursu'd by dangers, thus they pass'd away
The restless night, and thus the cheerless day;
E'en earth itself they fear'd, the common bed,
Where each lay down to rest his weary head:
There no kind trees their leafy couches strow,
The sands no turf nor mossy beds bestow;
But tir'd, and fainting with the tedious toil,
Expos'd they sleep upon the fatal soil.
With vital heat they brood upon the ground,
And breathe a kind attractive vapour round.
While chill, with colder night's ungentle air,
To man's warm breast his snaky foes repair,
And find, ungrateful guests, a shelter there.
Thence fresh supplies of poisonous rage return,
And fiercely with recruited deaths they burn.
"Restore," thus sadly oft the soldier said,
"Restore Emathia's plains, from whence we fled;
This grace, at least, ye cruel gods afford,
That we may fall beneath the hostile sword.
The dipsas here in Cæsar's triumph share,
And fell cerastæ wage his civil war.
Or let us haste away, press farther on,
Urge our bold passage to the burning zone,
And die by those ethereal flames alone.
Afric, thy deserts we accuse no more,
Nor blame, O Nature! thy creating power.
From man thou wisely didst these wilds divide,
And for thy monsters here alone provide;
A region waste and void of all beside.
Thy prudent care forbad the barren field
The yellow harvest's ripe increase to yield;
Man and his labours well thou didst deny,
And bad'st him from the land of poisons fly.
We, impious we, the bold irruption made;
We, this the serpents world, did first invade;
Take then our lives a forfeit for the crime,
Whoe'er thou art, that rul'st this cursed clime:
What god soe'er, that only lov'st to reign,
And dost the commerce of mankind disdain;
Who, to secure thy horrid empire's bound,
Hast fix'd the Syrts, and torrid realms around;
Here the wild waves, there the flame's scorching breath,
And fill'd the dreadful middle space with death.
Behold, to thy retreats our arms we bear,
And with Rome's civil rage prophane thee here;
E'en to thy inmost seats we strive to go,
And seek the limits of the world to know.
Perhaps more dire events attend us yet;
New deaths, new monsters, still we go to meet.
Perhaps to those far seas our journey bends,
Where to the waves the burning Sun descends;
Where, rushing headlong down Heaven's azure steep,
All red he plunges in the hissing deep.
Low sinks the pole, declining from its height,
And seems to yield beneath the rapid weight.
"Nor farther lands from Fame herself are known,
But Mauritanian Juba's realms alone.
Perhaps, while, rashly daring, on we pass,
Fate may discover some more dreadful place;
Till, late repenting, we may wish in vain
To see these serpents, and these sands again.
One joy at least do these sad regions give,
E'en here we know 't is possible to live:
That, by the native plagues, we may perceive.
Nor ask we now for Asia's gentler day,
Nor now for European suns we pray;
Thee, Afric, now, thy absence we deplore,
And sadly think we ne'er shall see thee more.
Say, in what part, what climate, art thou lost?
Where have we left Cyrene's happy frost?
Cold skies we felt, and frosty winter there,
While more than summer suns are raging here,
And break the laws of the well-order'd year.
Southward, beyond earth's limits, are we pass'd,
And Rome, at length, beneath our feet is plac'd.
Grant us, ye gods, one pleasure ere we die,
Add to our harder fate this only joy,
That Cæsar may pursue, and follow where we fly."
Impatient, thus the soldier oft complains,
And seems, by telling, to relieve his pains.
But most the virtues of their matchless chief
Inspire new strength, to bear with every grief;
All night, with careful thoughts and watchful eyes,
On the bare sands expos'd the hero lies;
In every place alike, in every hour,
Dares his ill fortune, and defies her power.
Unweary'd still, his common care attends
On every fate, and cheers his dying friends:
With ready haste at each sad call he flies,
And more than health, or life itself, supplies;
With virtue's noblest precepts arms their souls,
And e'en their sorrows, like his own, controls.
Where'er he comes, no signs of grief are shown;
Grief, an unmanly weakness, they disown,
And scorn to sigh, or breathe one parting groan.

Still urging on his pious cares, he strove
The sense of outward evils to remove;
And, by his presence, taught them to disdain
The feeble rage and impotence of pain.
But now, so many toils and dangers past,
Fortune grew kind, and brought relief at last.
Of all who scorching Afric's sun endure,
None like the swarthy Psyllians are secure.
Skill'd in the lore of powerful herbs and charms,
Them, nor the serpent's tooth, nor poison harms;
Nor do they thus in arts alone excel,
But nature too their blood has temper'd well,
And taught with vital force the venom to repel.
With healing gifts, and privileges grac'd,
Well in the land of serpents were they plac'd;
Truce with the dreadful tyrant, Death, they have,
And border safely on his realm, the grave.
Such is their confidence in true-born blood,
That oft with asps they prove their doubtful brood;
When wanton wives their jealous rage inflame,
The new-born infant clears or damns the dame;
If subject to the wrathful serpent's wound,
The mother's shame is by the danger found;
But if unhurt the fearless infant laugh,
The wife is honest, and the husband safe.
So when Jove's bird, on some tall cedar's head,
Has a new race of generous eaglets bred,
While yet unplum'd, within the nest they lie,
Wary she turns them to the eastern sky;
Then if, unequal to the god of day,
Abash'd they shrink, and shun the potent ray,
She spurns them forth, and casts them quite away:
But if with daring eyes unmov'd they gaze,
Withstand the light, and bear the golden blaze;
Tender she broods them with a parent's love,
The future servants of her master Jove.
Nor safe themselves, alone, the Psyllians are,
But to their guests extend their friendly care.
First, where the Roman camp is mark'd, around
Circling they pass, then chanting, charm the ground,
And chase the serpents with the mystic sound.
Beyond the farthest tents rich fires they build,
That healthy medicinal odours yield;
There foreign galbanum dissolving fries,
And crackling flames from humble wall-wort rise;
There tamarisk, which no green leaf adorns,
And there the spicy Syrian costus burns.
There centaury supplies the wholesome flame,
That from Thessalian Chiron takes its name;
The gummy larch-tree, and the thapsos there,
Wound-wort and maiden-weed perfume the air.
There the large branches of the long-liv'd hart,
With southern-wood, their odours strong impart.
The monsters of the land, the serpents fell,
Fly far away, and shun the hostile smell.
Securely thus they pass the nights away;
And if they chance to meet a wound by day,
The Psyllian artists straight their skill display.
Then strives the leach the power of charms to show,
And bravely combats with the deadly foe:
With spittle first, he marks the part around,
And keeps the poison prisoner in the wound;
Then sudden he begins the magic song,
And rolls the numbers hasty o'er his tongue;
Swift he runs on; nor pauses once for breath,
To stop the progress of approaching death:
He fears the cure might suffer by delay,
And life be lost but for a moments stay.
Thus oft, though deep within the veins it lies,
By magic numbers chas'd the mischief flies:
But if it hear too slow, if still it stay,
And scorn the potent charmer to obey;
With forceful lips he fastens on the wound,
Drains out, and spits the venom to the ground.
Thus, by long use and oft experience taught,
He knows from whence his hurt the patient got;
He proves the part through which the poison past,
And knows each various serpent by the taste.
The warriors thus reliev'd, amidst their pains,
Held on their passage through the desert plains:
And now the silver empress of the night
Had lost, and twice regain'd, her borrow'd light,
While Cato, wandering o'er the wasteful field,
Patient in all his labours, she beheld.
At length condens'd in clods the sands appear,
And show a better soil and country near:
Now from afar thin tufts of trees arise,
And scattering cottages delight their eyes.
But when the soldier once beheld again
The raging lion shake his horrid mane,
What hopes of better lands his soul possest!
What joys he felt, to view the dreadful beast!
Leptis at last they reach'd, that nearest lay,
There free from storms, and the Sun's parching ray,
At ease they pass'd the wintery year away.
When sated with the joys which slaughters yield,
Retiring Cæsar left Emathia's field;
His other cares laid by, he sought alone
To trace the footsteps of his flying son.
Led by the guidance of reporting fame,
First to the Thracian Hellespont he came.
Here young Leander perish'd in the flood,
And here the tower of mournful Hero stood:
Here, with a narrow stream, the flowing tide,
Europe from wealthy Asia does divide.
From hence the curious victor passing o'er,
Admiring sought the fam'd Sigæan shore,
There might he tombs of Grecian chiefs behold,
Renown'd in sacred verse by bards of old.
There the long ruins of the walls appear'd,
Once by great Neptune, and Apollo, rear'd:
There stood old Troy, a venerable name;
For ever consecrate to deathless fame.
Now blasted mossy trunks with branches sear,
Brambles and weeds, a loathsome forest rear;
Where once, in palaces of regal state,
Old Priam, and the Trojan princes, sat.
Where temples once, on lofty columns borne,
Majestic did the wealthy town adorn,
All rude, all waste and desolate is laid,
And even the ruin'd ruins are decay'd.
Here Cæsar did each storied place survey,
Here saw the rock, where, Neptune to obey,
Hesione was bound the monster's prey.
Here, in the covert of a secret grove,
The blest Anchises clasp'd the queen of love:
Here fair Oenone play'd, here stood the cave
Where Paris once the fatal judgment gave;
Here lovely Ganymede to Heaven was borne,
Each rock, and every tree, recording tales adorn.
Here all that does of Xanthus' stream remain,
Creeps a small brook along the dusty plain.
Whilst careless and securely on they pass,
The Phrygian guide forbids to press the grass;
This place, he said, for ever sacred keep,
For here the sacred bones of Hector sleep.
Then warns him to observe, where, rudely cast
Disjointed stones lay broken and defac'd:
Here his last fate, he cries, did Priam prove;
Here, on this altar of Hercæan Jove.

O poesy divine! O sacred song!
To thee, bright fame and length of days belong;
Thou, goddess! thou eternity canst give,
And bid secure the mortal hero live.
Nor, Cæsar, thou disdain, that I rehearse
Thee, and thy wars, in no ignoble verse;
Since, if in aught the Latian Muse excel,
My name, and thine, immortal I foretell;
Eternity our labours shall reward,
And Lucan flourish, like the Grecian bard;
My numbers shall to latest times convey
The tyrant Cæsar, and Pharsalia's day.
When long the chief his wond'ring eyes had cast
On ancient monuments of ages past;
Of living turf an altar straight he made,
Then on the fire rich gums and incense laid,
And thus, successful in his vows, he pray'd.
"Ye shades divine! who keep this sacred place,
And thou, Æneas! author of my race,
Ye powers, whoe'er from burning Troy did come,
Domestic gods of Alba, and of Rome,
Who still preserve your ruin'd country's name,
And on your altars guard the Phrygian flame:
And thou, bright maid, who art to men deny'd;
Pallas, who dost thy sacred privilege confide
To Rome, and in her inmost temple hide;
Hear, and auspicious to my vows incline,
To me, the greatest of the Julian line:
Prosper my future ways; and lo! I vow
Your ancient state and honours to bestow;
Ausonian hands shall Phrygian walls restore,
And Rome repay, what Troy conferr'd before."
He said; and hasted to his fleet away,
Swift to repair the loss of this delay.
Up sprung the wind, and with a freshening gale,
The kind north-west fill'd every swelling sail;
Light o'er the foamy waves the navy flew,
Till Asia's shores and Rhodes no more they view.
Six times the night her sable round had made,
The seventh now passing on, the chief survey'd
High Pharos shining through the gloomy shade;
The coast descry'd, he waits the rising day,
Then safely to the port directs his way.
There wide with crowds o'erspread he sees the shore,
And echoing hears the loud tumultuous roar.
Distrustful of his fate, he gives command
To stand aloof, nor trust the doubted land;
When lo! a messenger appears, to bring
A fatal pledge of peace from Ægypt's king:
Hid in a veil, and closely cover'd o'er,
Pompey's pale visage in his hand he bore.
An impious orator the tyrant sends,
Who thus, with fitting words, the monstrous gift commends.
"Hail! first and greatest of the Roman name;
In power most mighty, most renown'd in fame:
Hail! rightly now, the world's unrivall'd lord!
That benefit thy Pharian friends afford.
My king bestows the prize thy arms have sought,
For which Pharsalia's field in vain was fought.
No task remains for future labours now;
The civil wars are finish'd at a blow.
To heal Thessalia's ruins, Pompey fled
To us for succour, and by us lies dead.
Thee, Cæsar, with this costly pledge we buy,
Thee to our friendship, with this victim, tie.
Ægypt's proud sceptre freely then receive,
Whate'er the fertile flowing Nile can give:
Accept the treasures which this deed has spar'd;
Accept the benefit, without reward.
Deign, Cæsar! deign to think my royal lord
Worthy the aid of thy victorious sword:
In the first rank of greatness shall he stand;
He, who could Pompey's destiny command.
Nor frown disdainful on the proffer'd spoil,
Because not dearly bought with blood and toil:
But think, oh think, what sacred ties were broke,
How friendship pleaded, and how nature spoke:
That Pompey, who restor'd Auletes' crown,
The father's ancient guest was murder'd by the son.
Then judge thyself, or ask the world and fame,
If services like these deserve a name.
If gods and men the daring deed abhor,
Think, for that reason, Cæsar owes the more;
This blood *for thee*, though not *by thee*, was spilt;
Thou hast the benefit, and we the guilt."
He said, and straight the horrid gift unveil'd,
And stedfast to the gazing victor held.
Chang'd was the face, deform'd with death all o'er,
Pale, ghastly, wan, and stain'd with clotted gore,
Unlike the Pompey Cæsar knew before.
He, nor at first disdain'd the fatal boon,
Nor started from the dreadful sight too soon.
Awhile his eyes the murderous scene endure,
Doubting they view; but shun it, when secure.
At length he stood convinc'd, the deed was done;
He saw 't was safe to mourn his lifeless son:
And straight the ready tears, that staid till now,
Swift at command with pious semblance flow:
As if detesting, from the sight he turns,
And groaning, with a heart triumphant mourns.
He fears his impious thought should be descried,
And seeks in tears the swelling joy to hide.
Thus the curst Pharian tyrant's hopes were crost,
Thus all the merit of his gift was lost;
Thus for the murder Cæsar's thanks were spar'd;
He chose to mourn it, rather than reward.
He who, relentless, through Pharsalia rode,
And on the senate's mangled fathers trod;
He who, without one pitying sigh, beheld
The blood and slaughter of that woeful field;
Thee, murder'd Pompey, could not ruthless see,
But paid the tribute of his grief to thee.
Oh mystery of fortune, and of fate!
Oh ill-consorted piety and hate!
And canst thou, Cæsar, then thy tears afford
To the dire object of thy vengeful sword?
Didst thou, for this, devote his hostile head,
Pursue him living, to bewail him dead?
Could not the gentle ties of kindred move?
Wert thou not touch'd with thy sad Julia's love?
And weep'st thou now? Dost thou these tears provide
To win the friends of Pompey to thy side?
Perhaps, with secret rage thou dost repine,
That he should die by any hand but thine:
Thence fall thy tears, that Ptolemy has done
A murder due to Cæsar's hand alone.
What secret springs soe'er these currents know,
They ne'er, by piety, were taught to flow.
Or didst thou kindly, like a careful friend,
Pursue him flying, only to defend?
Well was his fate deny'd to thy command!
Well was he snatch'd by fortune from thy hand!
Fortune withheld this glory from thy name,
Forbad thy power to save, and spar'd the Roman shame.
Still he goes on to vent his griefs aloud,
And artful, thus, deceives the easy crowd.
"Hence from my sight, nor let me see thee more;
Haste, to thy king his fatal gift restore.

At Cæsar have you aim'd the deadly blow,
And wounded Cæsar worse than Pompey now;
The cruel hands by which this deed was done,
Have torn away the wreaths my sword had won,
That noblest prize this civil war could give,
The victor's right to bid the vanquish'd live.
Then tell your king, his gift shall be repaid;
I would have sent him Cleopatra's head;
But that he wishes to behold her dead.
How has he dar'd, this Ægypt's petty lord,
To join his murders to the Roman sword?
Did I, for this, in heat of war, distain
With noblest blood Emathia's purple plain,
To license Ptolemy's pernicious reign?
Did I with Pompey scorn the world to share?
And can I an Ægyptian partner bear?
In vain the warlike trumpet's dreadful sound
Has rous'd the universe to arms around;
Vain was the shock of nations, if they own,
Now, any power on Earth but mine alone.
If hither to your impious shores I came,
'Twas to assert at once my power and fame;
Lest the pale fury, Envy, should have said,
Your crimes I damn'd not, or your arms I fled.
Nor think to fawn before me and deceive;
I know the welcome you prepare to give.
Thessalia's field preserves me from your hate,
And guards the victor's head from Pompey's fate.
What ruin, gods! attended on my arms,
What dangers unforeseen! what waiting harms!
Pompey, and Rome, and exile, were my fear;
See yet a fourth, see Ptolemy appear!
The boy-king's vengeance loiters in the rear.
But we forgive his youth, and bid him know
Pardon and life 's the most we can bestow.
For you, the meaner herd, with rites divine,
And pious cares, the warrior's head enshrine:
Atone with penitence the injur'd shade,
And let his ashes in their urn be laid;
Pleas'd, let his ghost lamenting Cæsar know,
And feel my presence here, e'en in the realms [below.
Oh, what a day of joy was lost to Rome,
When hapless Pompey did to Ægypt come!
When, to a father and a friend unjust
He rather chose the Pharian boy to trust.
The wretched world that loss of peace shall rue,
Of peace which from our friendship might ensue:
But thus the gods their hard decrees have made;
In vain, for peace, and for repose, I pray'd;
In vain implor'd, that wars and rage might end,
That, suppliant like, I might to Pompey bend,
Beg him to live, and once more be my friend.
There had my labours met their just reward,
And, Pompey, thou in all my glories shar'd,
Then, jars and enmities all past and gone,
In pleasure had the peaceful years roll'd on;
All should forgive, to make the joy complete;
Thou shouldst thy harder fate, and Rome my wars forget."

Fast falling still the tears, thus spoke the chief,
But found no partner in the specious grief.
Oh glorious liberty! when all shall dare
A face, unlike their mighty lord, to wear!
Each in his breast the rising sorrow kept,
And thought it safe to laugh, though Cæsar wept.

BOOK X.

THE ARGUMENT.

Cæsar, upon his arrival in Ægypt, finds Ptolemy engaged in a quarrel with his sister Cleopatra; whom, at the instigation of Photinus, and his other evil counsellors, he had deprived of her share in the kingdom, and imprisoned: she finds means to escape, comes privately to Cæsar, and puts herself under his protection. Cæsar interposes in the quarrel, and reconciles them. They in return entertain him with great magnificence and luxury at the royal palace in Alexandria. At this feast Cæsar, who at his first arrival had visited the tomb of Alexander the Great, and whatever else was curious in that city, inquires of the chief priest Achoreus, and is by him informed of the course of the Nile, its stated increase and decrease, with the several causes that had been till that time assigned for it. In the mean time Photinus writes privately to Achillas, to draw the army to Alexandria, and surprise Cæsar; this he immediately performs, and besieges the palace. But Cæsar, having set the city and many of the Ægyptian ships on fire, escapes to the island and tower of Pharos, carrying the young king and Photinus, whom he still kept in his power, with him; there, having discovered the treachery of Photinus, he puts him to death. At the same time Arsinoë, Ptolemy's younger sister, having by the advice of her tutor, the eunuch Ganymedes, assumed the regal authority, orders Achillas to be killed likewise, and renews the war against Cæsar. Upon the mole between Pharos and Alexandria he is encompassed by the enemy, and very near being slain, but at length breaks through, leaps into the sea, and with his usual courage and good fortune swims in safety to his own fleet.

Soon as the victor reach'd the guilty shore,
Yet red with stains of murder'd Pompey's gore,
New toils his still prevailing fortune met,
By impious Ægypt's genius hard beset.
The strife was now, if this detested land
Should own imperial Rome's supreme command,
Or Cæsar bleed beneath some Pharian hand.
But thou, O Pompey! thy diviner shade,
Came timely to this cruel father's aid;
Thy influence the deadly sword withstood, [blood.
Nor suffer'd Nile, again, to blush with Roman
Safe in the pledge of Pompey, slain so late,
Proud Cæsar enters Alexandria's gate:
Ensigns on high the long procession lead;
The warrior and his armed train succeed.
Meanwhile, loud-murmuring, the moody throng,
Behold his fasces borne in state along;
Of innovations fiercely they complain,
And scornfully reject the Roman reign.
Soon saw the chief th' untoward bent they take,
And found that Pompey fell not for his sake.
Wisely, howe'er, he hid his secret fear,
And held his way with well-dissembled cheer.
Careless, he runs their gods and temples o'er,
The monuments of Macedonian power;
But neither god, nor shrine, nor mystic rite,
Their city, nor her walls, his soul delight:
Their caves beneath his fancy chiefly led,
To search the gloomy mansions of the dead:
Thither with secret pleasure he descends,
And to the guide's recording tale attends. [prize,
There the vain youth who made the world his
That prosperous robber, Alexander, lies. [kind,
When pitying death, at length, had freed man-
To sacred rest his bones were here consign'd;

His bones, that better had been toss'd and hurl'd,
With just contempt, around the injur'd world.
But Fortune spar'd the dead; and partial Fate,
For ages, fix'd his Pharian empire's date.
If e'er our long-lost liberty return,
That carcass is reserv'd for public scorn:
Now, it remains a monument confest,
How one proud man could lord it o'er the rest.
To Macedon, a corner of the Earth,
The vast ambitious spoiler ow'd his birth:
There, soon, he scorn'd his father's humbler reign,
And view'd his vanquish'd Athens with disdain.
Driv'n headlong on, by fate's resistless force,
Through Asia's realms he took his dreadful course:
His ruthless sword laid human nature waste,
And desolation follow'd where he pass'd.
Red Ganges blush'd, and fam'd Euphrates' flood,
With Persian this, and that with Indian blood.
Such is the bolt which angry Jove employs,
When, undistinguishing, his wrath destroys:
Such to mankind, portentous meteors rise,
Trouble the gazing Earth, and blast the skies.
Nor flame, nor flood, his restless rage withstand,
Nor Syrts unfaithful, nor the Libyan sand:
O'er waves unknown he meditates his way,
And seeks the boundless empire of the sea;
E'en to the utmost west he would have gone,
Where Tethys' lap receives the setting Sun;
Around each pole his circuit would have made,
And drunk from secret Nile's remotest head,
When Nature's hand his wild ambition stay'd.
With him, that power his pride had lov'd so well,
His monstrous universal empire, fell:
No heir, no just successor left behind,
Eternal wars he to his friends assign'd,
To tear the world, and scramble for mankind.
Yet still he died the master of his fame,
And Parthia to the last rever'd his name:
The haughty east from Greece receiv'd her doom,
With lower homage than she pays to Rome.
Though from the frozen pole our empire run,
Far as the journies of the southern Sun;
In triumph though our conquering eagles fly,
Where'er soft zephyrs fan the western sky;
Still to the haughty Parthian must we yield,
And mourn the loss of Cannæ's dreadful field:
Still shall the race untam'd their pride avow,
And lift those heads aloft which Pella taught to bow.
  From Casium now the beardless monarch came,
To quench the kindling Alexandrians' flame.
Th' unwarlike rabble soon the tumult cease,
And he, their king, remains the pledge of peace;
When, veil'd in secrecy, and dark disguise,
To mighty Cæsar Cleopatra flies.
Won by persuasive gold, and rich reward,
Her keeper's hand her prison-gates unbarr'd,
And a light galley for her flight prepar'd.
O fatal form! thy native Ægypt's shame!
Thou lewd perdition of the Latian name!
How wert thou doom'd our furies to increase,
And be what Helen was to Troy and Greece!
When with an host, from vile Canopus led,
Thy vengeance aim'd at great Augustus' head;
When thy shrill timbrel's sound was heard from far,
And Rome herself shook at the coming war;
When doubtful fortune, near Leucadia's strand,
Suspended long the world's supreme command.
And almost gave it to a woman's hand.
Such daring courage swells her wanton heart,
While Roman lovers Roman fires impart:
Glowing alike with greatness and delight,
She rose still bolder from each guilty night.
Then blame me, hapless Anthony, no more,
Lost and undone by fatal beauty's power;
If Cæsar, long inur'd to rage and arms,
Submits his stubborn heart to those soft charms;
If, reeking from Emathia's dreadful plain,
And horrid with the blood of thousands slain,
He sinks lascivious in a lewd embrace,
While Pompey's ghastly spectre haunts the place:
If Julia's chastest name he can forget,
And raise her brethren of a bastard set;
If indolently he permits, from far,
Bold Cato to revive the fainting war;
If he can give away the fruits of blood,
And fight to make a strumpet's title good.
  To him disdaining, or to feign a tear,
Or spread her artfully-dishevell'd hair,
In comely sorrow's decent garb array'd,
And trusting to her beauty's certain aid,
In words like these began the Pharian maid:
  "If royal birth and the Lagæan name,
Thy favouring pity, greatest Cæsar, claim,
Redress my wrongs, thus humbly I implore,
And to her state an injur'd queen restore.
Here shed thy juster influence, and rise
A star auspicious to Ægyptian skies.
Nor is it strange for Pharos to behold
A woman's temples bound with regal gold:
No laws our softer sex's powers restrain,
But undistinguish'd equally we reign.
Vouchsafe my royal father's will to read,
And learn what dying Ptolemy decreed:
My just pretensions stand recorded there,
My brother's empire and his bed to share.
Nor would the gentle boy his love refuse,
Did curs'd Photinus leave him free to choose;
But now in vassalage he holds his crown,
And acts by power and passions not his own.
Nor is my soul on empire fondly set,
But could with ease my royal rights forget;
So thou the throne from vile dishonour save,
Restore the master, and depose the slave.
What scorn, what pride, his haughty bosom swell,
Since, at his bidding, Roman Pompey fell!
(E'en now, which O ye righteous gods avert!
His sword is levell'd at thy noble heart)
Thou and mankind are wrong'd, when he shall dare,
Or in thy prize, or in thy crime to share."
  In vain her words the warrior's ears assail'd,
Had not her face beyond her tongue prevail'd;
From thence resistless eloquence she draws,
And with the sweet persuasion gains her cause.
His stubborn heart dissolves in loose delight,
And grants her suit for one lascivious night.
Ægypt and Cæsar, now, in peace agreed,
Riot and feasting to the war succeed:
The wanton queen displays her wealthy store,
Excess unknown to frugal Rome before.
Rich, as some fane by slavish zealots rear'd,
For the proud banquet, stood the hall prepar'd:
Thick golden plates the latent beams infold,
And the high roof was fretted o'er with gold:
Of solid marble all the walls were made,
And onyx e'en the meaner floor inlay'd;
While porphyry and agat, round the court,
In massy columns, rose a proud support.
Of solid ebony each post was wrought,
From swarthy Meroë profusely brought:

With ivory was the entrance crusted o'er,
And polish'd tortoise hid each shining door;
While on the cloudy spots enchas'd was seen
The lively emerald's never-fading green.
Within, the royal beds and couches shone,
Beamy and bright with many a costly stone.
In glowing purple rich the coverings lie;
Twice had they drunk the noblest Tyrian dye;
Others, as Pharian artists have the skill
To mix the party-colour'd web at will,
With winding trails of various silks were made,
Where branching gold set off the rich brocade.
Around, of every age, and choicer form,
Huge crowds, whole nations of attendants swarm:
Some wait in yellow rings of golden hair,
The vanquish'd Rhine show'd Cæsar none so fair:
Others were seen with swarthy woolly heads,
Black as eternal night's unchanging shades.
Here squealing eunuchs, a dismember'd train,
Lament the loss of genial joys in vain:
There Nature's noblest work, a youthful band,
In the full pride of blooming manhood stand.
All duteous on the Pharian princes wait,
The princes round the board recline in state,
With mighty Cæsar, more than princes great.
On ivory feet the citron board was wrought,
Richer than those with captive Juba brought.
With every wile ambitious beauty tries
To fix the daring Roman's heart her prize.
Her brother's meaner bed and crown she scorns,
And with fierce hopes for nobler empire burns;
Collects the mischiefs of her wanton eyes,
And her faint cheeks with deeper roses dyes;
Amidst the braidings of her flowing hair,
The spoils of orient rocks and shells appear;
Like midnight stars, ten thousand diamonds deck
The comely rising of her graceful neck:
Of wond'rous work, a thin transparent lawn
O'er each soft breast in decency was drawn;
Where still by turns the parting threads withdrew,
And all the panting bosom rose to view.
Her robe, her every part, her air, confess
The power of female skill exhausted in her dress.
Fantastic madness of unthinking pride,
To boast that wealth, which prudence strives to [hide!
In civil wars such treasures to display,
And tempt a soldier with the hopes of prey!
Had Cæsar not been Cæsar, impious, bold,
And ready to lay waste the world for gold,
But just as all our frugal names of old;
This wealth could Curius or Fabricius know,
Or ruder Cincinnatus from the plough,
As Cæsar, they had seiz'd the mighty spoil,
And to enrich their Tiber robb'd the Nile.
Now, by a train of slaves, the various feast
In massy gold magnificent was plac'd:
Whatever earth, or air, or seas afford,
In vast profusion crowns the labouring board.
For dainties, Ægypt every land explores,
Nor spares those very gods her zeal adores.
The Nile's sweet wave capacious crystals pour,
And gems of price the grapes delicious store;
No growth of Mareotis' marshy fields,
But such as Meroë maturer yields;
Where the warm Sun the racy juice refines,
And mellows into age the infant wines.
With wreaths of nard the guests their temples bind,
And blooming roses of immortal kind;
Their dropping locks with oily odours flow,
Recent from near Arabia, where they grow:
The vigorous spices breathe their strong perfume,
And the rich vapour fills the spacious room.
 Here Cæsar Pompey's poverty disdain'd,
And learn'd to waste that world his arms had gain'd.
He saw th' Ægyptian wealth with greedy eyes,
And wish'd some fair pretence to seize the prize.
Sated at length with the prodigious feast,
Their weary appetites from riot ceas'd;
When Cæsar, curious of some new delight,
In conversation sought to wear the night:
Then gently thus addrest the good old priest,
Reclining decent in his linen vest:
" O wise Achoreus! venerable seer!
Whose age bespeaks thee Heaven's peculiar care,
Say from what origin thy nation sprung,
What boundaries to Ægypt's land belong?
What are thy people's customs, and their modes,
What rites they teach, what forms they give their [gods?
Each ancient sacred mystery explain,
Which monumental sculptures yet retain.
Divinity disdains to be confin'd,
Fain would be known, and reverenc'd by mankind.
'Tis said, thy holy predecessors thought
Cecropian Plato worthy to be taught:
And sure the sages of your schools have known
No soul more form'd for science than my own.
Fame of my potent rival's flight, 'tis true,
To this your Pharian shore my journey drew;
Yet know the love of learning led me too.
In all the hurries of tumultuous war,
The stars, the gods, and heavens, were still my [care.
Nor shall my skill to fix the rolling year
Inferior to Eudoxus' art appear.
Long has my curious soul, from early youth,
Toil'd in the noble search of sacred truth:
Yet still no views have urg'd my ardour more,
Than Nile's remotest fountain to explore.
Then say what source the famous stream supplies,
And bids it at revolving periods rise;
Show me that head from whence, since time begun,
The long succession of his waves has run;
This let me know, and all my toils shall cease,
The sword be sheath'd, and Earth be blest with peace."
 The warrior spoke; and thus the seer replied:
" Nor shalt thou, mighty Cæsar, be denied.
Our sires forbad all, but themselves, to know,
And kept with care profaner laymen low:
My soul, I own, more generously inclin'd,
Would let in daylight to inform the blind.
Nor would I truth in mysteries restrain,
But make the gods, their power and precepts, plain;
Would teach their miracles, would spread their praise,
And well-taught minds to just devotion raise.
Know then, to all those stars, by Nature driven
In opposition to revolving Heaven,
Some one peculiar influence was given.
The Sun the seasons of the year supplies,
And bids the evening and the morning rise;
Commands the planets with superior force,
And keeps each wandering light to his appointed [course.
The silver Moon o'er briny seas presides,
And heaves huge ocean with alternate tides.
Saturn's cold rays in icy climes prevail;
Mars rules the winds, the storm, and rattling hail;
Where Jove ascends the skies are still serene;
And fruitful Venus is the genial queen:
While every limpid spring, and falling stream,
Submits to radiant Hermes' reigning beam.

When in the Crab the humid ruler shines,
And to the sultry Lion near inclines,
There fix'd immediate o'er Nile's latent source,
He strikes the watery stores with ponderous force;
Nor can the flood bright Maïa's son withstand,
But heaves, like ocean, at the Moon's command;
His waves ascend, obedient as the seas,
And reach their destin'd height by just degrees.
Nor to its bank returns th' enormous tide,
Till Libra's equal scales the days and nights divide.
Antiquity, unknowing and deceiv'd,
In dreams of Ethiopian snows believ'd:
From hills they taught, how melting currents ran,
When the first swelling of the flood began.
But, ah how vain the thought! no Boreas there
In icy bonds constrains the wintery year,
But sultry southern winds eternal reign,
And scorching suns the swarthy natives stain.
Yet more, whatever flood the frost congeals,
Melts as the genial spring's return he feels;
While Nile's redundant waters never rise,
Till the hot Dog inflames the summer skies;
Nor to his banks his shrinking stream confines,
Till high in Heaven th' autumnal Balance shines.
Unlike his watery brethren he presides,
And by new laws his liquid empire guides.
From dropping seasons no increase he knows,
Nor feels the fleecy showers of melting snows.
His river swells not idly, ere the land
The timely office of his waves demand;
But knows his lot, by Providence assign'd,
To cool the season, and refresh mankind.
Whene'er the Lion sheds his fires around,
And Cancer burns Syene's parching ground;
Then, at the prayer of nations, comes the Nile,
And kindly tempers up the mouldering soil.
Nor from the plains the covering god retreats,
Till the rude fervour of the skies abates;
Till Phœbus into milder autumn fades,
And Meroä projects her lengthening shades.
Nor let inquiring sceptics ask the cause,
'T is Jove's command, and these are Nature's laws.
"Others of old, as vainly too, have thought
By western winds the spreading deluge brought;
While at fix'd times, for many a day, they last,
Possess the skies, and drive a constant blast;
Collected clouds united Zephyrs bring,
And shed huge rains from many a dropping wing,
To heave the flood, and swell th' abounding spring.
Or when the airy brethrens stedfast force
Resists the rushing current's downward course,
Backward he rolls indignant to his head:
While o'er the plains his heapy waves are spread.
"Some have believ'd, that spacious channels go
Through the dark entrails of the Earth below;
Through these, by turns, revolving rivers pass,
And secretly pervade the mighty mass;
Through these the Sun, when from the north he flies,
And cuts the glowing Ethiopic skies,
From distant streams attracts their liquid stores,
And through Nile's spring th' assembled waters pours:
Till Nile, o'er-burden'd, disembogues the load,
And spews the foamy deluge all abroad.
"Sages there have been too, who long maintain'd,
That ocean's waves through porous earth are drain'd;
'T is thence their saltness they no longer keep,
By slow degrees still freshening as they creep:
Till at a period, Nile receives them all,
And pours them loosely spreading as they fall.
"The stars, and Sun himself, as some have said,
By exhalations from the deep are fed;
And when the golden ruler of the day
Through Cancer's fiery sign pursues his way,
His beams attract too largely from the sea;
The refuse of his draughts the nights return,
And more than fill the Nile's capacious urn.
"Were I the dictates of my soul to tell,
And speak the reasons of the watery swell,
To Providence the task I should assign,
And find the cause in workmanship divine.
Less streams we trace, unerring, to their birth,
And know the parent Earth which brought them forth:
While this, as early as the world begun,
Ran thus, and must continue thus to run;
And still, unfathom'd by our search, shall own
No cause, but Jove's commanding will alone.
"Nor, Cæsar, is thy search of knowledge strange;
Well may thy boundless soul desire to range,
Well may she strive Nile's fountain to explore;
Since mighty kings have sought the same before;
Each for the first discoverer would be known,
And hand, to future times, the secret down;
But still their powers were exercis'd in vain,
While latent nature mock'd their fruitless pain.
Philip's great son, whom Memphis still records,
The chief of her illustrious scepter'd lords,
Sent of his own, a chosen number forth,
To trace the wond'rous stream's mysterious birth.
Through Æthiopia's plains they journied on,
Till the hot Sun oppos'd the burning zone:
There, by the god's resistless beams repell'd,
An unbeginning stream they still beheld.
Fierce came Sesostris from the eastern dawn;
On his proud car by captive monarchs drawn;
His lawless will, impatient of a bound,
Commanded Nile's hid fountain to be found:
But sooner much the tyrant might have known
Thy fam'd Hesperian Po, or Gallic Rhone.
Cambyses too his daring Persians led,
Where hoary age makes white the Ethiop's head;
Till sore distress'd and destitute of food,
He stain'd his hungry jaws with human blood;
Till half his host the other half devour'd,
And left the Nile behind them unexplor'd.
"Of thy forbidden head, thou sacred stream!
Nor fiction dares to speak, nor poets dream.
Through various nations roll thy waters down,
By many seen, though still by all unknown;
No land presumes to claim thee for her own.
For me, my humble tale no more shall tell,
Than what our just records demonstrate well;
Than God, who bade thee thus mysterious flow,
Permits the narrow mind of man to know.
"Far in the south the daring waters rise,
As in disdain of Cancer's burning skies;
Thence, with a downward course, they seek the main,
Direct against the lazy northern wain;
Unless when, partially, thy winding tide
Turns to the Libyan or Arabian side.
The distant Seres first behold thee flow;
Nor yet thy spring the distant Seres know.
'Midst sooty Ethiops, next, thy current roams;
The sooty Ethiops wonder whence it comes;
Nature conceals thy infant stream with care,
Not lets thee, but in majesty, appear.

Upon thy banks astonish'd nations stand,
Nor dare assign thy rise to one peculiar land.
Exempt from vulgar laws thy waters run,
Nor take their various seasons from the Sun:
Though high in Heaven the fiery solstice stand,
Obedient winter comes at thy command.
From pole to pole thy boundless waves extend;
One never knows thy rise, nor one thy end.
By Meroë thy stream divided roves,
And winds encircling round her ebon groves;
Of sable hue the costly timbers stand,
Dark as the swarthy natives of the land:
Yet, though tall woods in wide abundance spread,
Their leafy tops afford no friendly shade;
So vertically shine the solar rays,
And from the Lion dart the downward blaze.
From thence, thro' deserts dry, thou journiest on,
Nor shrink'st, diminish'd by the torrid zone,
Strong in thyself, collected, full, and one.
Anon thy streams are parcell'd o'er the plain,
Anon the scatter'd currents meet again;
Jointly they flow, where Philæ's gates divide
Our fertile Ægypt from Arabia's side;
Thence, with a peaceful, soft descent, they creep,
And seek, insensibly, the distant deep;
Till through seven mouths, the famous flood is lost,
On the last limits of our Pharian coast;
Where Gaza's isthmus rises, to restrain
The Erythræan from the midland main.
Who that beholds thee, Nile! thus gently flow,
With scarce a wrinkle on thy glassy brow,
Can guess thy rage, when rocks resist thy force,
And hurl thee headlong in thy downward course;
When spouting cataracts thy torrent pour,
And nations tremble at the deafening roar;
When thy proud waves with indignation rise,
And dash their foamy fury to the skies?
These wonders reedy Abatos can tell,
And the tall cliffs that first declare thy swell;
The cliffs with ignorance of old believ'd
Thy parent veins, and for thy spring receiv'd.
From thence huge mountains Nature's hand provides
To bank thy too luxurious river's sides;
As in a vale thy current she restrains,
Nor suffers thee to spread the Libyan plains:
At Memphis, first, free liberty she yields,
And lets thee loose to float the thirsty fields."
  In unsuspected peace securely laid,
Thus waste they silent night's declining shade.
  Meanwhile accustom'd furies still infest,
With usual rage, Photinus' horrid breast;
Nor can the ruffian's hand from slaughter rest.
Well may the wretch, distain'd with Pompey's blood,
Think every other dreadful action good.
Within him still the snaky sisters dwell,
And urge his soul with all the powers of Hell.
Can Fortune to such hands such mischief doom,
And let a slave revenge the wrongs of Rome!
Prevent th' example, pre-ordain'd to stand
The great renown of Brutus' righteous hand!
Forbid it, gods! that Cæsar's hallow'd blood,
To liberty by fate a victim vow'd,
Should on a less occasion e'er be spilt,
And prove a vile Ægyptian eunuch's guilt.
Harden'd by crimes, the bolder villain, now,
Avows his purpose with a daring brow;
Scorns the mean aids of falsehood and surprise,
And openly the victor chief defies.
Vain in his hopes, nor doubting to succeed,
He trusts that Cæsar must, like Pompey, bleed.
  The feeble boy to curs'd Achillas' hand
Had, with his army, given his crown's command;
To him, by wicked sympathy of mind,
By leagues and brotherhood of murder join'd,
To him, the first and fittest of his friends,
Thus, by a trusty slave, Photinus sends:
  "While stretch'd at ease the great Achillas lies,
And sleep sits heavy on his slothful eyes,
The bargain for our native land is made,
And the dishonest price already paid.
The former rule no longer now we own,
Usurping Cleopatra wears the crown.
Dost thou alone withdraw thee from her state,
Nor on the bridals of thy mistress wait?
Tonight at large she lavishes her charms,
And riots in luxurious Cæsar's arms.
Ere long her brother may the wanton wed,
And reap the refuse of the Roman's bed;
Doubly a bride, then doubly shall she reign,
While Rome and Ægypt wear, by turns, her chain.
Nor trust thou to thy credit with the boy,
When arts and eyes, like hers, their powers employ.
Mark with what ease her fatal charms can mould
The heart of Cæsar, ruthless, hard, and old:
Were the soft king his thoughtless head to rest,
But for a night, on her incestuous breast,
His crown and friends he'd barter for the bliss,
And give thy head and mine for one lewd kiss;
On crosses, or in flames, we should deplore
Her beauty's terrible resistless power.
On both, her sentence is already pass'd,
She dooms us dead, because we kept her chaste.
What potent hand shall then assistance bring?
Cæsar's her lover, and her husband king.
Haste, I adjure thee by our common guilt,
By that great blood which we in vain have spilt,
Haste, and let war, let death, with thee return,
And the funereal torch for Hymen's burn.
Whate'er embrace the hostile charmer hold,
Find, and transfix her in the luscious fold.
Nor let the fortune of this Latian lord
Abash thy courage, or restrain thy sword;
In the same glorious guilty paths we tread,
That rais'd him up, the world's imperious head,
Like him, we seek dominion for our prize,
And hope, like him, by Pompey's fall to rise.
Witness the stains of yonder blushing wave,
Yon bloody shore, and yon inglorious grave.
Why fear we then to bring our wish to pass?
This Cæsar is not more than Pompey was.
What though we boast nor birth, nor noble name,
Nor kindred with some purple monarch claim?
Conscious of fate's decree, such aid we scorn,
And know we were for mighty mischief born.
See, how kind Fortune, by this offer'd prey,
Finds means to purge all past offence away:
With grateful thanks Rome shall the deed approve,
And this last merit the first crime remove.
Stripp'd of his titles, and the pomp of power,
Cæsar's a single soldier and no more.
Think then how easily the task were done,
How soon we may an injur'd world atone;
Finish all wars, appease each Roman shade,
By sacrificing one devoted head.
Fearless, ye dread united legions, go;
Rush, all undaunted, on your common foe:
This right, ye Romans! to your country do;
Ye Pharians! this your king expects from you.

But chief, Achillas! may the praise be thine;
Haste thou, and find him on his bed supine,
Weary with toiling lust, and gorg'd with wine.
Then strike, and what their Cato's prayers demand,
The gods shall give to thy more favour'd hand."
Nor fail'd the message, fitted to persuade;
But, prone to blood, the willing chief obey'd.
No noisy trumpets sound the loud alarm,
But silently the moving legions arm:
All unperceiv'd for battle they prepare,
And bustle through the night with busy care.
The mingled bands who form'd this mongrel host,
To the disgrace of Rome were Romans most;
A herd, who had they not been lost to shame,
And long forgetful of their country's name,
Had blush'd to own e'en Ptolemy their head;
Yet now were by his meaner vassal led.
O mercenary War! thou slave of gold!
How is thy faithless courage bought and sold!
For base reward thy hireling hands obey;
Unknowing right or wrong, they fight for pay,
And give their country's great revenge away.
Ah, wretched Rome! for whom thy fate prepares,
In every nation, new domestic wars;
The fury, that from pale Thessalia fled,
Rears on the banks of Nile her baleful head.
What could protecting Ægypt more have done,
Had she receiv'd the haughty victor's son?
But thus the gods our sinking state confound,
Thus tear our mangled empire all around;
In every land fit instruments employ,
And suffer ruthless slaughter to destroy.
Thus ev'n Ægyptian parricides presume
To meddle in the sacred cause of Rome;
Thus, had not fate those hands of murder ty'd,
Success had crown'd the vile Achillas' side.
Nor wanted fit occasion for the deed;
Timely the traitors to the place succeed,
While in security the careless guest,
Lingering as yet, his couch supinely prest:
No gates, no guards, forbad their open way,
But all dissolv'd in sleep and surfeits lay;
With ease the victor at the board had bled,
And lost in riot his defenceless head;
But pious caution now their rage withstands,
And care for Ptolemy withholds their hands:
With reverence and remorse, unknown before,
They dread to spill their royal master's gore;
Lest, in the tumult of the murderous night,
Some erring mischief on his youth may light.
Sway'd by this thought, nor doubting to succeed,
They hold it fitting to defer the deed.
Gods! that such wretches should so proudly dare!
Can such a life be theirs to take, or spare;
Till dawn of day the warrior stood repriev'd,
And Cæsar at Achillas' bidding liv'd.
Now o'er aspiring Casium's eastern head
The rosy light by Lucifer was led;
Swift thro' the land the piercing beams were borne,
And glowing Ægypt felt the kindling morn:
When from proud Alexandria's walls afar,
The citizens behold the coming war.
The dreadful legions shine in just array,
And firm, as to the battle, hold their way.
Conscious, meanwhile, of his unequal force,
Straight to the palace Cæsar bends his course:
Nor in the lofty bulwarks dares confide,
Their ample circuit stretching far too wide:
To one fix'd part his little band retreats,
There mans the walls and towers, and bars the gates.
There fear, there wrath, by turns, his bosom tears;
He fears, but still with indignation fears.
His daring soul, restrain'd, more fiercely burns,
And proudly the ignoble refuge scorns.
The captive lion thus, with generous rage,
Reluctant foams, and roars, and bites his cage.
Thus, if some power could Mulciber enslave,
And bind him down in Ætna's smoky cave,
With fires more fierce th' imprison'd god would glow,
And bellow in the dreadful deeps below.
He who so lately, with undaunted pride,
The power of mighty Pompey's arms defy'd,
With justice and the senate on his side;
Who, with a cause which gods and men must hate,
Stood up, and struggled for success with fate;
Now abject foes and slaves insulting fears,
And shrinks beneath a shower of Pharian spears.
The warrior who disdain'd to be confin'd
By Tyrian Gades, or the eastern Ind,
Now in a narrow house conceals that head
From which the fiercest Scythians once had fled,
And horrid Moors beheld with awful dread.
From room to room irresolute he flies,
And on some guardian bar or door relies.
So boys and helpless maids, when towns are won,
To secret corners for protection run.
Still by his side the beardless king he bears,
Ordain'd to share in every ill he fears:
If he must die, he dooms the boy to go,
Alike devoted to the shades below;
Resolves his head a victim first shall fall,
Hurl'd at his slaves from off the lofty wall.
So from Æetes fierce Medea fled,
Her sword still aim'd at young Absyrtos' head;
Whene'er she sees her vengeful sire draw nigh,
Ruthless she dooms the wretched boy should die.
Yet ere these cruel last extremes he proves,
By gentler steps of peace the Roman moves;
He sends an envoy, in the royal name,
To chide their fury, and the war disclaim.
But impious they nor gods nor kings regard,
Nor universal laws by all rever'd;
No right of sacred characters they know,
But tear the olive from the hallow'd brow;
To death the messenger of peace pursue,
And in his blood their horrid hands imbrue.
Such are the palms which curs'd Ægyptians claim,
Such prodigies exalt their nation's name.
Nor purple Thessaly's destructive shore,
Nor dire Pharnaces, nor the Libyan Moor,
Nor every barbarous land, in every age,
Equal a soft Ægyptian eunuch's rage.
Incessant still the roar of war prevails,
While the wild host the royal pile assails.
Void of device, no thundering rams they bring,
Nor kindling flames with spreading mischief fling:
Bellowing around they run with fruitless pain,
Heave at the doors, and thrust and strive in vain:
More than a wall, great Cæsar's fortune stands,
And mocks the madness of their feeble hands.
On one proud side the lofty fabric stood
Projected bold into th' adjoining flood
There, fill'd with armed bands, their barks draw near;
But find the same defending Cæsar there:
To every part the ready warrior flies,
And with new rage the fainting fight supplies:
Headlong he drives them with his deadly blade,
Nor seems to be invaded, but t' invade.

Against the ships Phalaric darts he aims;
Each dart with pitch and livid sulphur flames.
The spreading fire o'er-runs their unctuous sides,
And, nimbly mounting, on the top-mast rides:
Planks, yards, and cordage, feed the dreadful blaze;
The drowning vessel hisses in the seas;
While floating arms and men, promiscuous strow'd,
Hide the whole surface of the azure flood.
Nor dwells destruction on their fleet alone,
But, driv'n by winds, invades the neighb'ring town;
On rapid wings the sheety flames they bear,
In wavy lengths, along the redd'ning air.
Not much unlike, the shooting meteors fly,
In gleamy trails, athwart the midnight sky.
Soon as the crowd behold their city burn,
Thither, all headlong, from the siege they turn.
But Cæsar, prone to vigilance and haste,
To snatch the just occasion ere it pass'd,
Hid in the friendly night's involving shade,
A safe retreat to Pharos timely made.
In elder times of holy Proteus' reign,
An isle it stood, encompass'd by the main:
Now by a mighty mole the town it joins,
And from wide seas the safer port confines.
Of high importance to the chief it lies,
To him brings aid, and to the foe denies:
In close restraint the captive town is held,
While free behind he views the wat'ry field.
There safe, with curs'd Photinus in his power,
Cæsar defers the villain's doom no more.
Yet, ah! by means too gentle he expires;
No gashing knives he feels, no scorching fires;
Nor were his limbs by grinning tigers torn,
Nor pendent on the horrid cross are borne:
Beneath the sword the wretch resigns his breath,
And dies too gloriously by Pompey's death.
Meanwhile, by wily Ganymede convey'd,
Arsinoë, the younger royal maid,
Fled to the camp; and with a daring hand
Assumes the sceptre of supreme command:
And, for her feeble brother was not there,
She calls herself the sole Lagæan heir.
Then, since he dares dispute her right to reign,
She dooms the fierce Achillas to be slain.
With just remorse, repenting Fortune paid
This second victim to her Pompey's shade.
But oh! nor this, nor Ptolemy, nor all
The race of Lagos doom'd at once to fall,
Not hecatombs of tyrants shall suffice,
Till Brutus strikes, and haughty Cæsar dies.
Nor yet the rage of war was hush'd in peace,
Nor would that storm, with him who rais'd it, cease.
A second eunuch to the task succeeds,
And Ganymede the power of Ægypt leads:
He cheers the drooping Pharians with success,
And urg'd the Roman chief with new distress.
Such dangers did one dreadful day afford,
As annals might to latest times record,
And consecrate to Fame the warrior's sword.
While to their barks his faithful band descends,
Cæsar the mole's contracted space defends.
Part from the crowded quay aboard were pass'd,
The careful chief remain'd among the last;
When sudden Ægypt's furious powers unite,
And fix on him alone th' unequal fight.
By land the numerous foot, by sea the fleet,
At once surround him, and prevent retreat.
No means for safety or escape remain,
To fight, or fly, were equally in vain.
A vulgar period on his wars attends,
And his ambitious life obscurely ends.
No seas of gore, no mountains of the slain,
Renown the fight on some distinguish'd plain:
But meanly in a tumult must he die,
And, overborne by crowds, inglorious lie:
No room was left to fall as Cæsar should,
So little were the hopes his foes and fate allow'd.
At once the place and danger he surveys,
The rising mound, and the near neighbouring seas:
Some fainting struggling doubts as yet remain:
Can he, perhaps, his navy still regain?
Or shall he die, and end th' uncertain pain?
At length, while madly thus perplex'd he burns,
His own brave Scæva to his thought returns;
Scæva, who in the breach undaunted stood,
And singly made the dreadful battle good;
Whose arm advancing Pompey's host repell'd,
And, coop'd within a wall the captive leader held.
Strong in his soul the glorious image rose,
And taught him, sudden, to disdain his foes;
The force oppos'd in equal scales to weigh,
Himself was Cæsar, and Ægyptians they;
To trust that fortune, and those gods, once more,
That never fail'd his daring hopes before.
Threat'ning, aloft his flaming blade he shook,
And through the throng his course resistless took:
Hands, arms, and helmed heads before him fly,
While mingling screams and groans ascend the sky.
So winds, imprison'd, force their furious way,
Tear up the earth, and drive the foamy sea.
Just on the margin of the mount he staid,
And for a moment, thence, the flood survey'd:
"Fortune divine! be present now," he cry'd;
And plung'd, undaunted, in the foamy tide.
Th' obedient deep, at Fortune's high command,
Receiv'd the mighty master of the land;
Her servile waves officious Tethys spread,
To raise with proud support his awful head.
And, for he scorn'd th' inglorious race of Nile
Should pride themselves in aught of Cæsar's spoil,
In his left hand, above the water's power,
Papers and scrolls of high import he bore;
Where his own labours faithfully record
The battles of ambition's ruthless sword:
Safe in his right the deadly steel he held,
And plough'd, with many a stroke, the liquid field;
While his fix'd teeth tenaciously retain
His ample Tyrian robe's imperial train;
Th' encumber'd folds the curling surface sweep,
Come slow behind, and drag along the deep.
From the high mole, from every Pharian prow,
A thousand hands a thousand javelins throw;
The thrilling points dip bloodless in the waves,
While he their idle wrath securely braves.
So when some mighty serpent of the main
Rolls his huge length athwart the liquid plain,
Whether he range voracious for the prey,
Or to the sunny shore directs his way,
Him if by chance the fishers view from far,
With flying darts they wage a distant war:
But the fell monster, unappall'd with dread,
Above the seas exerts his poisonous head;
He rears his livid crest and kindling eyes,
And, terrible, the feeble foe defies;
His swelling breast a foamy path divides,
And, careless, o'er the murmuring flood he glides.
Some looser Muse, perhaps, who lightly treads
The devious paths where wanton fancy leads,

In Heaven's high court, would feign the queen of love,
Kneeling in tears before the throne of Jove,
Imploring, sad, th' Almighty Father's grace,
For the dear offspring of her Julian race.
While to the just recording Romans' eyes,
Far other forms, and other gods arise;
The guardian furies round him rear their heads,
And Nemesis the shield of safety spreads;
Justice and fate the floating chief convey,
And Rome's glad genius wafts him on his way;
Freedom and laws the Pharian darts withstand,
And save him for avenging Brutus' hand.
His friends, unknowing what the gods decree,
With joy receive him from the swelling sea;
In peals on peals their shouts triumphant rise,
Roll o'er the distant flood, and thunder to the skies.

THE

ELEGIES OF TIBULLUS;

AND THE

POEMS OF SULPICIA.

TRANSLATED BY GRAINGER.

Μοισας Ερως καλεοι, Μοισαι τον Ερωτα φεροιεν,
Μολπαν ται Μοισαι μοι αει ποθεοντι διδοιεν
Ταν γλυκεραν μολπαν, τας φαρμακον ἁδιον ουδεν.

BION.

TO

JOHN BOURRYAU, ESQ.

SIR,

WHEN I first thought of prefixing your name to this translation of Tibullus, I found myself considerably embarrassed; as I would choose to avoid the strain of adulation, so common in addresses of this kind, on the one hand, without suppressing the just sense I have of your rising merit, on the other. I shall not however, I flatter myself, incur the imputation of the first, by declaring, even in this public manner, my satisfaction at the progress you have made in every branch of useful and polite literature; and this too, at a time of life, when young men of fashion are generally engrossed by the idle amusements of an age abounding in all the means of dissipation.

If your maturer years answer, as I am convinced they will, so favourable a dawn, I need not a moment hesitate to foretel the happiness of your friends, in an agreeable companion, and polite scholar; and of your country, in a principled and unshaken patriot.

It is with particular pleasure, sir, that I dwell, though but in idea, on this part of your future character. The time is not far off, when you will have finished the plan of your education, by a survey of foreign countries: and as it will then, of course, be expected from one of your opulent and independent fortune, you will, I hope, devote the fruits of your industry to the service of the public:

> Hunc precor, hunc utinam nobis Aurora nitentem
> Luciferem roseis candida portet equis. TIBULLUS.

When you become a member of the most august assembly of the nation, every well-wisher to the community will exult to see you unawed by power, undazzled by riches, and unbiassed by faction: an impartial assertor of the just prerogatives of the crown, and the liberties of the people: equally a foe to corruption, and a friend to virtue.

Such, sir, are the hopes which all your friends at present conceive of you: and as your talents, both natural and acquired, seem strongly to confirm these hopes, the more inexcusable you will prove, should they hereafter be disappointed.

In regard to the translation, with which I here take the liberty to present you; I will not pretend to say, I set no value upon it: my offering it to you is a proof of the contrary. Indeed, the chief merit it has with me, is, that it formerly pleased you. It served also to make many of my hours pass agreeably, which otherwise would have been extremely irksome, amid the din of arms, and hurry of a camp-life.

But while you peruse Tibullus as a poet, let not his integrity, as a member of the commonwealth, be forgotten. In this light he merits your highest regard: for though he justly obtained a distinguished rank among the great writers of the Augustan age; yet ought it more especially to be remembered to his honour, that neither the frowns of a court, nor the distresses of fortune, could ever induce him to praise those powerful but wicked men, who had subverted the liberties of his country; and this, at a time, when the practice of the poets his cotemporaries might have countenanced in him the most extravagant adulation.

I am, sir,

your most obedient humble servant,

JAMES GRAINGER.

ADVERTISEMENT.

THE following version of Tibullus was begun and completed several years ago, when the author was in the army. A military man, even in the most active campaign, has many hours of leisure; and as these cannot be spent more rationally than in some literary pursuit, he employed that part of his time, which was not devoted to his profession, in perusing the classics.

Time and place influence us more in our opinions of, and relish for, particular writers, than is commonly imagined. Amid the horrours of war, the translator could most readily sympathize with, and best account for, his poet's aversion to a military life: and while exposed to all the hurry and tumult of a camp, could not but taste with a peculiar relish all descriptions of the unruffled and tranquil scenes of the country: beside these, every motive conspiring to make him regard the fair sex as the chief ornaments of society, was it surprising that Tibullus, who abounds in sentiments of this kind, should soon become a favourite; and that what delighted him, he should at last be tempted to translate?

A pleasing employment is seldom neglected. Those elegies which particularly touched him, were first rendered into English; and as these make the greater part of Tibullus's poems, he was contented afterwards to complete the work, by finishing as a task, what he began as an amusement.

A favourite author, on whom some labour has been employed, is not easily forgotten; the version, therefore, was retouched as often as opportunity served. All this while, indeed, the translator had no intention of making the public acquainted with his poetical amusements: he knew his poet too well, and admired him too much, to think he had done him justice: yet when Mr. Dart's translation of Tibullus was sent him, he was resolved to publish his own; that those who did not understand the original might not form an idea of the most exact, elegant, and harmonious of the Roman elegiac poets from the most inaccurate, harsh, and inelegant version of the present century.

The translator hopes, he will be acquitted of vanity, in preferring his own performance to Mr. Dart's: indeed that gentleman often missed the meaning of his author, while his poetry always escaped him. Neither does he appear to have been a competent judge of his own language; and from the little tenderness transfused into his verses, it may be concluded, that he was an utter stranger to that passion which gave rise to most of the elegies of Tibullus.

What advantages the present translator may have over his predecessor in these respects, does not become him to determine: yet he is well apprised, that no translator, however qualified, can give Tibullus the genuine air of an Englishman.

It is true, that amorous elegy is less local than many other of the minor kinds of poetry, the passion of love operating pretty nearly the same upon the human mind in all ages. Yet as the modes of expressing that passion differ much in different countries, so these modes must not be confounded: a Grecian ought to make love like a Grecian, and a Roman like a Roman.

Besides this, Tibullus abounds in images of rural theology. He has even preserved some superstitious usages, which are to be met with in no other poet: but as these are also characteristical, and must be preserved in the version, who can hope to give a translation of Tibullus the easy air of a modern original?

Verbal translations are always inelegant, because always destitute of beauty of idiom and language; for by their fidelity to an author's words, they become treacherous to his reputation: on the other hand, a too wanton departure from the letter often varies the sense, and always alters the manner.

The translator chose the middle way, and meant neither to tread on the heels of Tibullus, nor yet to lose sight of him. He had not the vanity to think, he could improve on his poet: and though he has sometimes endeavoured to give a more modern polish to his sentiments, he has seldom attempted to change them. To preserve the sense of his original was his first care; his next was, to clothe it in as elegant and becoming a dress as possible. Yet he must confess, that he has now and then taken the liberty to transpose, and sometimes paraphrastically to enlarge the thoughts. Where a sentiment was too much contracted by the closeness of the Latin idiom to be unfolded in a corespondent expression in English, or from its peculiarity might, in a modern language, seem flat, he has endeavoured to inspirit it by collateral thoughts from other poets; and where its colours were languid, to heighten them—with what success, the reader must determine.

The hexameter and pentameter is said to be peculiarly suited to plaintive subjects. The English have no stanza correspondent to that, but the alternate, which is supposed to possess a solemnity and kind of melancholy flow in its numbers. This Mr. Hammond chose for his imitation of Tibullus; and it must be confessed, that he has happily succeeded. Yet, as in this stanza the sense naturally ends at the fourth line, the translator thought he could not in general have adopted it, without violence to the original: he therefore preferred the heroic measure, which is not better suited to the lofty sound of the epic muse, than to the complaining tone of elegy. The reader, however, will find one or two elegies rendered in the alternate stanza, which is by no means so difficult as the heroic.

As Tibullus wrote love poems like a Roman, any translation of them without notes, would have been extremely obscure to an English reader: most of his commentators are mere philologers, or at best they have only displayed their erudition in the history of a heathen god, or the topography of a river. From this censure, however, Broekhusius, his Dutch editor, and Vulpius, his Italian commentator, may in part be exempted; they have, indeed, sometimes entered into the propriety of our poet's thoughts. Yet even their chief excellence consists in arranging the text; in selecting the most approved readings; and in giving those passages, which they suppose Tibullus either borrowed from his predecessors, or the moderns copied from him. The design of the translator is very different; he has commented on his author as a Roman poet, and as a Roman lover: and although he owns himself enamoured of his beauties, (as who can draw a pleasing resemblance of a face which disgusts him?) he hopes he has not been blind to his imperfections. These, indeed, he has touched upon with the tenderness of a friend, not the acrimony of a critic.

Yet as most of the commentators were consulted, the translator has taken from each of them such notes, as he imagined would be most serviceable to an English reader, always ascribing them however to the author who furnished them. Thus, beside Broekhusius and Vulpius, the name of Mr. Dart will sometimes be found at the bottom of an observation. Nor must it be forgotten, that the translator has been obliged to that gentleman for ten or twelve lines in his version.

It has been judged necessary to print the Latin text[1] along with the version: this the translator would willingly have declined, as his work can hope to find favour with those only who understand not the original. Yet, when he considered, that the English press had afforded no one accurate edition of Tibullus; and that even the best of those printed abroad were not

[1] This is omitted in the present edition.—*C.*

exempted from material errours; he surmounted his scruples, and has endeavoured to give a less exceptionable text of his poet than any hitherto published.

Before he concludes, the translator must return his sincere thanks to a worthy friend, for his elegant version of the first elegy, and of Ovid's poem on the death of Tibullus. By what accident his own translation of the first elegy was lost, is of no consequence; especially too, as the reader, from a perusal of Mr. P———'s specimen, will probably be induced to wish, that more of those now published had undergone a like fate, provided the same gentleman had likewise translated them.

Nor is that the only good office which challenges his gratitude: the translator is particularly obliged to his friend, for having procured him the valuable acquaintance of another learned gentleman; who not only took the trouble to compare his version of the three last books with the original; but who also favoured him with some notes, which constitute the chief ornament of the second volume. Thus, like the Britons of old, the translator has called in auxiliaries to conquer him.

THE

LIFE OF TIBULLUS.

WE are not only unacquainted with the prænomen of Tibullus, but with the year of his birth. The biographers, from a line [1] in the fifth elegy of his third book, indeed inform us, that Ovid and he were born the day that Hirtius and Pansa were killed, viz. on the tenth of the calends of April, A. U. C. 710. This was the opinion of the learned for many centuries; nor was it controverted, till Joseph Scaliger first entertained some doubts of it; and Janus Douza the younger, about a hundred and seventy years ago, was induced, by comparing what our poet had said of himself, with what Horace and Ovid have wrote concerning him, to reject that line as spurious, and to assert that Tibullus must have been born almost twenty years sooner. Although we think some considerable objections may be raised against Douza's opinion [2], yet as the old account is liable to still greater, we shall venture with that critic to inform the reader, that Albius Tibullus, the prince of elegiac poets, was born at Rome, A. U. C. 690, six years after the birth of Virgil, and one after that of Horace.

Tibullus might say with his great admirer, Ovid,

——— usque a proavis vetus ordinis hæres,
Non modo militiæ turbine factus eques [3],

being descended from an equestrian branch of the Albian family: and though some of the old biographers [4] assert, that his ancestors made a figure in the forum and in the field, yet as history makes no mention of them, posterity would have been unacquainted with this branch of that illustrious house, had it not been for our poet.

As the ancient writers of Tibullus's life have favoured us with no particulars of his infancy, it is probable it was distinguished by nothing remarkable. The human mind does not always blossom at the same period; and it by no means follows that his childhood must have flourished, whose mature age has produced fair fruits of science. Perhaps too, details of early excellence are less useful than is commonly imagined, as they often dispirit those who would otherwise in due time have expanded into an extensive reputation.

But if such accounts are less useful, it would have been no unprofitable gratification of curiosity to have known by what plan his studies were conducted, and who were his preceptors. Antiquity, however, having left us in the dark with regard to these matters, we can only suppose that as his father's condition was considerable, so nothing was omitted to render our poet an useful and elegant member of society.

[1] Natalem nostri primum videre parentes
Quum cecidit fato consul uterque pari.

[2] See the arguments on both sides of the question in the notes to the fifth elegy of the third book.

[3] Amor. lib. iii. el. 14.

[4] Crinitus, &c.

The Romans possessed a real advantage over the moderns in point of education; for as the same citizen might plead causes, command armies, and arrive at the first dignities of the priesthood, so their literary institutions were made to comprehend these several objects. It is easy to see of what vast utility so general a plan must have been to a state; and perhaps it is not paying letters too high a compliment, to say, that the successes of the Romans were in a great measure owing to this advantage.

In the year of Rome 705, the civil war broke out between Cæsar and Pompey. The army and corrupt part of the legislature followed Cæsar; while the majority of the senate and of the knights, with all those who dreaded a perpetual dictator, sided with Pompey, as the person from whom the republic had less danger to apprehend. Of this number was the father of Tibullus; and there is reason to suspect, that he either fell in the field, or was butchered by proscription, for we know that a considerable part of his estate was left a prey to the rapacious soldiery[5]. These events probably determined our author's public attachments; but without these motives to revenge, it is not unlikely that Tibullus had, before this time, adopted the political opinions of his father[6].

At what actions in the civil war our young knight was present, as it was not prudent in him to mention in his poems, so historians do not inform us: but as principle and revenge equally conspired to rouse his courage (and courage he certainly possessed[7]), may we not safely infer, that Tibullus did not run away, like his friend Horace, from Philippi[8], at which battle he was present with his patron the illustrious Messala Corvinus?

But the fortune of Octavius prevailing over the better cause of Brutus and Cassius, Messala too (who was next in command to these patriot citizens) going over with his forces to the conqueror, Tibullus, although he paid the greatest regard to the sentiments of that excellent soldier and orator, yet determined to leave the army; for as he would not fight against the party which his friends had now espoused, so neither could he appear in arms against those whom his principles taught him to regard as the assertors of liberty. Besides, the bad success of the patriot-party, and his own experience, had now inspired him with an abhorrence of the war; he therefore retired, A. U. C. 712, to his country-seat at Pedum, there, by an honest industry, to raise his impaired fortune to its ancient splendour, while his hours of leisure were either devoted to philosophy or the Muses[9].

But we are not to imagine that rural objects and study solely engaged our poet's attention; for being formed with a natural tenderness of disposition, he began to enlarge the sphere of his pleasures by conversing with the fair sex. The first object of his affection was probably Glycera; and we have Horace[10] on our side, when we add, that she at first gave him hopes of success: but though his person was elegant[11], his fortune not contemptible, and his life was then in the prime, Glycera deserted him for a younger lover[12]. As he entertained a real affection for that lady, her infidelity gave him much uneasinesss; he therefore endeavoured, by exerting his elegiac genius, to reclaim her. But his poems producing in Glycera no change to his advantage, his friend and old fellow-soldier, Horace, advised him to abate of his sorrow for her loss, and send her no more elegies.

None of these elegies having come down to our times, Lilio Giraldi[13] supposes that Nemesis and Glycera were the same; but the poems which are inscribed to Nemesis[14] do not favour this

5 Vide Panegyr. ad Messalam, lin. 191. Jan. Douz. Sched. Succid.

6 See Francis's notes on the thirty-third ode of the first book of Horace.

7 Tibull. lib. i. el. 8.

8 Vell. Patercul. lib. ii. cap. 71.

9 Panegyr. Tibull. ad Messalam, lin. 184.

10 Lib. i. ode 33.

11 Horat. lib. i. ep. 4.

12 Horat. lib. i. ode 33. Albi ne doleas plus nimio, &c.

No more in elegiac strain
Of cruel Glycera complain.

13 Dialog. de Poet.

14 Lib. ii.

supposition: and indeed, it seems more likely, that Tibullus was so piqued at the ill success of his first amour, that he destroyed all those elegies which it gave rise to.

Some time after this (A. U. C. 718), the fierce inhabitants of Pannonia rebelling, and Messala being one of the generals appointed by Augustus to reduce them, that nobleman invited Tibullus to attend him in the expedition. As this service was not against the Pompeian party [15], and as he hoped in the hurry of a military life to find a remedy for his melancholy, he complied with his noble friend's request, and in every action behaved with his usual bravery. In proof of this the commentators quote our poet's description of the old soldier of Arupinum:

> Testis Arupinas, & pauper natus in armis,
> Quem si quis videat, vetus ut non fregerit ætas,
> Terna minus Pyliæ miretur sæcula famæ,
> Namque senex longæ peragit dum sæcula vitæ,
> Centum fecundos Titan renovaverit annos:
> Ipse tamen velox celerem super edere corpus
> Audet equum, validisque sedet moderator habenis [16].

Besides these verses, some others may be brought from the panegyric, and in particular the three following, to strengthen their assertion:

> Nam bellis experta cano, testis mihi victæ
> Fortis Japidiæ miles, testis quoque fallax
> Pannonius, gelidas passim disjectus in Alpes [17].

In this manner did our poet subdue his passion for Glycera: but being by nature addicted to the love of the fair sex, at his return from the army he fixed his affections on Delia.

Cyllenius, in his commentary on Tibullus [18], conjectures that she obtained the name of Delia from the Greek word δηλεῖν, on account of her surpassing in beauty the Roman ladies. But we have the more respectable authority of Apuleius [19], for asserting that Delia was an appellation given her by our poet, her real name being Plania.

Some critics [20] contend, that Delia was a woman of the town: but many passages in the elegies, addressed to her [21], contradict this assertion. Which of these poems were first written, cannot now be determined; but it is certain, they were not composed in the order they are now printed.

It would seem, that some time after his attachment to Delia, Messala invited our poet to accompany him in some military expedition: but he was then too deeply enamoured of Delia, to attend the call of honour. Tibullus therefore composed his first elegy, in which, as he prefers a country retirement with Delia and a moderate income, to all the triumphs of war and allurements of fortune, so Corvinus could not well urge, with propriety, our poet's departure.

Messala having soon after obtained the consulship, Tibullus composed his panegyric. This poem is in heroic numbers, and though not destitute of poetical beauties, is inferior to his elegies: it seems rather an effusion of friendship, than an effort of genius: it has therefore not been translated.

In the year of Rome 725 [22], Messala being entrusted by Augustus Cæsar with an extraordinary command over Syria, insisted on Tibullus's accompanying him thither, to which our poet consented. This sacrifice to friendship was not however obtained without much reluctance; for

15 An amnesty was granted by the triumvirate to all Pompey's party, A. U. C. 715.

16 Panegyr. ad Messalam, lin. 110.

17 Ibid. lin. 107.

18 This commentary was published at Venice, A. D. 1487.

19 In apologia accusent—& Tibullum, quod ei sit Plania in animo, Delia in versu. Casaubon and Colvius think, it should be read either *Flavia* or *Planca*. In one of Fulvius Ursinus's MS. copies of the Apology, it was written *Plantia*. "*Plania*, however," says Broekhusius, "is found in Roman inscriptions, and therefore the name need not be altered."

20 Erat libertinæ conditionis muliercula.—Broekh.

21 Vide lib. i. passim.

22 Noris Cenotaph. Pisan. Diss. ii. cap. 16. § 7.

Delia, it would seem, opposed his departure. But as Messala, in this expedition, was to visit Greece, Asia, &c. and as Tibullus, in his panegyric, had said,

Pro te vel rapidas ausim maris ire per undas,
Adversis hyberna licet tumeant freta ventis.
Pro te vel solus densis subsistere turmis:
Vel pavidum Ætneæ corpus committere flammæ
Sum quodcunque tuum est[23], &c.

he embarked with his patron. He, however, had not been long at sea, before he was taken so ill, that Messala was obliged to put him ashore, and leave him in Phæacia[24]. In this island, so famous for the gardens of Alcinous, our poet composed the third elegy of the first book; which shows, that whatever effect this sickness had upon his constitution, it did not in the least impair his poetical talents.

From the sentiments of tenderness expressed in that beautiful poem, it would not have been surprising had Tibullus on his recovery returned to Italy: but he had too sincere a regard for his friend, to desert him; he therefore, as soon as he was able to renew his voyage, hastened after Messala, and with that nobleman[25] travelled through Cilicia, Syria, Ægypt, and Greece, being then probably initiated into the Eleusinian Mysteries at Athens[26].

What were the political consequences of this expedition, historians do not mention: but the consequences to Tibullus were highly disagreeable; for if any stress, in this point, is to be laid on his elegies, there is reason to suspect, that Delia married before his return.

This, doubtless, occasioned much uneasiness to, and rendered our poet the less unwilling to embrace another offer made him, soon after, by Messala, of going to Aquitaine; which province having revolted (A. U. C. 726.), Augustus had entrusted that excellent officer with the important business of its reduction[27].

"The Romans," says an elegant writer, "fought with other nations for glory, but with the Gauls for liberty." This observation was at least verified at this time; for it was not till after many sharp actions, in which both the general and his soldiers distinguished themselves, that Messala completed the service he was sent upon. In all these battles, our poet signalized his courage in so remarkable a manner, that the success of the expedition was, in no small degree, owing to him.

Non sine me est tibi partus honos: Tarbella Pyrene
    Testis, & oceani littora Santonici:
Testis Arar, Rhodanusque celer, magnusque Garumna,
    Carnuti & Flavi cœrula lympha Liger[28].

For which reason he had military honour conferred on him; militaribus donis ornatus est, as the old writer of his life informs us[29].

The reduction of Aquitaine was so acceptable to the emperor, that Messala had a triumph decreed him the year after[30]: and as our poet had borne so distinguished a share in the war, it is not to be supposed but he was present at that superb solemnity; which, as an ancient inscription[31] acquaints us, was celebrated on the seventh of the calends of October.

But his Gallic expedition not having banished Delia from his breast, he again paid his addresses to her: and, from some passages in the second and seventh elegies of the first book, it would seem that they were but too successful.

23 Panegyr. ad Messalam, lin. 193.
24 Now Corfu.
25 Lib. i. el. 8. also Broekhusius's notes on the third elegy of the first book.
26 Non ego tentavi nulli temeranda virorum
    Audax laudandæ sacra docere deæ. Lib. iii. el. 5.
27 Steph. Vinand Pighii Annal. & Norris Cenotaph. Pisan. Diss. ii. cap. 16. § 7.
28 Lib. i. el. 8.
29 In the life prefixed to that edition of Tibullus which was published at Venice, A. D. 1475.
30 Cenotaph. Pisan. Diss. ii. cap. 16. § 7.
31 Pighii Annales.

When a woman has once so far forgot herself, as to bestow improper favours on a lover, nothing is more natural than for that lover to suspect he is not the only favourite. Our poet is an instance of the truth of this observation; for to such a height did his ungenerous suspicions of Delia arise (notwithstanding all her protestations of innocence), that he made her husband acquainted with his intrigue[32]. Whether Delia was innocent or not, she could never forgive this discovery. Or had she been willing to forget the past, we cannot suppose that her husband would ever admit Tibullus again into his house.

Such then was the extraordinary conclusion of our poet's intimacy with Delia; and therefore, the poem which furnished these particulars is justly made the last of the poems inscribed to that beauty.

Although the elegies of Tibullus warrant, in some sort, these surmises; yet, it ought to be considered, that poets write from imagination more frequently than from reality, because ideal subjects afford greater scope to their faculties than occurrences in common life: and indeed, if what Ovid tells us may be depended on, Delia was again enamoured with our poet, at the time of his decease, when probably her husband was dead.

Some time elapsed, before Tibullus entered into any new engagements: in this interval, he composed his famous elegy on Messala's birth-day, the ninth and the following elegies of the first book, with the first and second of the second book; endeavouring to forget his disasters, by dividing his time between his country-seat and Rome, but chiefly by conversing, more than ever, with the learned and polite: of these, the most eminent among his acquaintance were Messala, Valgius, Macer, and Horace.

Messala was now in the height of his reputation: in eloquence and military knowledge he was excelled by none of his cotemporaries; and yet the goodness of his heart surpassed his abilities. His house was the rendezvous of the learned; and his patronage, as an admirable poet[33] expresses it, was

The surest passport to the gates of fame.

Happy in the approbation of all parties, his siding with Augustus, after the defeat at Philippi, did not lose him the esteem of his old friends; and his interesting himself in their behalf, to the honour of that emperor, made him not the less beloved by Augustus[34].

J. Valgius Rufus was eminent, not only for heroic poetry, but also for his elegies, especially those on the death of his son Mystes[35]. He also wrote some excellent epigrams. But all his poems are now lost. As Tibullus thought him the best poet next to Homer, posterity has suffered much in their loss[36].

Of Macer, all that is known is mentioned in the notes to the sixth elegy of the second book.

But although Tibullus himself informs us of his acquaintance with these eminent scholars, yet should we not have known of the friendship which Horace and he entertained for one another, had it not been for Horace, who probably about this time sent our poet an epistle, which is thus translated by Mr. Francis:

[32] Lib. i. el. 7.

[33] Dr. Young.

[34] Messala had a brother, who was also a polite scholar, as Horace informs us. According to St. Jerome, this illustrious Roman married Terentia, Cicero's widow, and by her had two sons, Marcus and Lucius, who both attained to the consulship, and were an ornament to their families, by their military and civil capacities. Messala himself was so old before he died, as to forget his own name. Pliny the elder tells us, that he would not permit a person of his family to have his statue placed among those of his ancestors, because he was a disgrace to them.

[35] We learn this circumstance from Horace, who wrote Valgius a beautiful consolatory ode on the occasion.

Non semper imbres nubibus hispidos
Manant in agros, &c. Lib. ii. ode 9.

[36] The critics have been able, from all antiquity, to glean only seven lines of Rufus's poetry, which the reader, if curious of such literary scraps, will find collected by Broekhusius, in his notes on Tibullus's panegyric to Messala.

Albius! in whom my satires find
A candid critic and a kind,
Do you, while at your country-seat,
Some rhyming labours meditate,
That shall in volum'd bulk arise,
And e'en from Crassus bear the prize;
Or, sauntering thro' the silent wood,
Think what befits the wise and good.
Thou art not form'd of lifeless mould,
With breast inanimate and cold;
To thee the gods a form complete,
To thee the gods a large estate,
In bounty give, with skill to know
How to enjoy what they bestow.
Can a fond nurse one blessing more
E'en for her favourite boy implore,
With sense and clear expression blest,
Of friendship, honour, wealth possest;
A table elegantly plain,
And a poetic easy vein?
By hope inspir'd, deprest by fear,
By passion warm'd perplex'd with care
Believe that every morning's ray
Hath lighted up thy latest day;
Then, if to morrow's sun be thine,
With double lustre shall it shine.
Such are the maxims I embrace,
And here in sleek and joyous case,
You'll find for laughter fitly bred,
A hog by Epicurus fed [37].

FRANCIS.

Mons. Dacier[38] observes, that this epistle is all ironical; for Tibullus, according to him, having exhausted his fortune by extravagance, had now retired to the country, to recruit his finances, and avoid the importunity of his creditors.

To find out these things from the epistle before quoted, required a strange obliquity of understanding; as to support them demanded some learning: however it must be confessed, that the French editor of Horace is not the first author who maintained this extraordinary opinion. An old grammarian[39], whose comment on Horace Caspar Barthius owns he perused, but to whom Dacier was willing to sink his obligations, though he also must have seen him, has out-done the French critic in what he writes of Tibullus. Fuit hic Albius, says this uncommon genius, eques Romanus, qui primus in amatorio carmine habetur: eum per ironiam irridet Horatius, quasi rem bene gesserit, cum in juventa omnia prodegerit, et postea versibus victum quæsiverit. Ergo ubi eum laudat, se innuit Horatius; ubi vituperat se, & Epicurum nominat, Albium intelligit, quem ridendum ait quod prodegerit omnia, jam nihil habens, quo, ut solebat, cutem curare posset: quod vero ait

Di tibi divitias dederint, &c.

manifesta ironia est, nam Epicuri non credentes deos habere curam rerum humanarum, omnia prodigunt; quod postquam factum est omnibus sunt ridiculi.

Whence this semi-priscus grammaticus (for so Broekhusius calls him) drew these particulars relating to our poet, is not known: but that Dacier should adopt them, is matter of wonder; as, in

37 Lib. i. ep. 4.

38 Voyez ses notes sur l' Horace, lib. i. ep. 4.

39 Casp. Barth. Adversar. lib. xxxvii. cap. 19.

all probability, the Frenchman had read Tibullus's panegyric[40], which plainly shows that the diminution of his fortune was not owing to his own intemperance. And if the grammarian had perused his elegies[41] with ever so little attention, he would have seen, that Tibullus was rather religious than otherwise, and by no means an Epicurean, at least in belief.

"But," say some critics, who have too thoughtlessly embraced this opinion, "does not Horace confirm it, where he tells us, that his father warned him, when a young man, from pursuing extravagant courses, by setting before his eyes the infamy and miserable life of Albius,

Nonne vides Albi ut male vivat filius?"

To make this objection decisive, the critics must first prove, that there were no other Albiusses in Rome than the father of Tibullus; which, by the way, is false: and then they must show, that this infamous and indigent son of Albius's was our poet; which cannot be done, especially as we know that he died a knight, and of course was worth upwards of three thousand pounds sterling. There are also innumerable passsages in his elegies[42], which prove, that he was by no means in distressed circumstances, though less wealthy than his ancestors. Again, is it to be imagined, that the rich and generous Messala would have suffered so fine a genius, and one whom he regarded so much, to have been distressed by his creditors? And, to crown all, as Tibullus was confessedly some years younger than Horace, with what propriety could Horace's father propose Tibullus as an example not to be followed by his son?

When such were the friends of Tibullus, and his poetical abilities had long since obtained him universal applause, he could have found no difficulty in getting admission to the learned court of Augustus.: "How then," ask the commentators, "has it come to pass, that he never once mentions either that emperor, or Mæcenas, both whom his brother poets celebrated with such a lavishness of praise?" "And yet," add they, "there are many parts of his writings, where those patrons of genius might have been introduced with uncommon propriety?"

True to the principles of the republic, and a real friend to the liberties of the people, Tibullus never could prevail upon himself to flatter those, whatever affection they expressed for the Muses, whom his principles taught him to detest as the enslavers of his country.

This, as Pope emphatically expresses it, "kept him sacred from the great," who doubtless perceived with secret displeasure (for Augustus and Mæcenas well knew the importance of having the poets on their side) that no loss of fortune, and no allurement of ambition, could induce Tibullus to join in the general chorus of their praise. Although both the emperor and his favourite must in their hearts have applauded our poet's integrity, yet that mental applause, in all probability, would not have secured Tibullus from the effects of their displeasure, had it not been for the interest which he had with Messala.

Besides Messala, Valgius, and Macer, Tibullus mentions Cornutus, Marathus, Titius, and Messalinus: the conjectures of the critics concerning these Romans are inserted in the notes to the elegies, where their names occur.

Soon after this, Tibullus fell in love with Neæra. It is true, that the elegies he wrote to Neæra, in every edition of our poet, follow those in which he celebrates Nemesis: yet as Ovid (who could not well be mistaken in what related to one whom he regarded so much as Tibullus) says, that Nemesis was his last mistress; and, as it is probable, that the fifth elegy of the second book (our poet being then certainly very fond of Nemesis) was written between the years 732 and 734, when Augustus wintered in Samos, that is, a short time before our poet's death, we suppose, although the learned gentleman who favoured the author with the notes marked B, is of a different opinion, that Neæra was the third object of his affections.

[40] ———————— quamvis
Fortuna, ut mos est illi, me adversa fatiget.

And some lines lower,

————————non cura novatur,
Quum memor anteactos semper dolor admovet annos.
Sed licet asperiora cadant, spolierque relictis. Lin. 190.

[41] Book i. el. 1, 3, 8, 11.

[42] See the notes on the first elegy of the first book, and on the first and third elegy of the second.

Fabricius conjectures, from her name, that she was a woman of the town; Neæra, in the declension of the Roman empire, being a synonimous term for a courtezan[43]: but Fabricius should have considered that Tibullus wrote in the Augustan age. Besides, it appears from Homer[44], from Valerius Flaccus[45], and from an old marble statue preserved by Pignonius[46], that women of the first rank and most unsuspected modesty were called by that name. Without, however, these authorities, Tibullus himself screens this favourite from the imputation of libertinism, by bestowing on her the epithet *casta*[47]: he also characterizes her parents, as people of virtue and fortune.

It appears from the second and third elegy of the first book, that Neæra, after a long courtship, having consented to marry Tibullus, was somehow or other forced away from him. This gave our poet an uncommon concern; which was redoubled, when he discovered, that she herself had not only been accessary to her being carried off, but meant also to marry his rival.

Mr. Dart, in his life of Tibullus[48], is of opinion, that Neæra was the same with Glycera: but why then does our poet not call her by that name? Besides, if any one will attentively peruse Horace's consolatory ode to our author on the infidelity of Glycera, and compare it with many passages in the third book of Tibullus, he will easily see, that Mr. Dart must be mistaken.

Tibullus, who had hitherto been unsuccessful in his addresses to the fair, was not more fortunate in his last mistress; for, if Nemesis (for so was she called) possessed beauties of mind and person equal to those of Delia, and Neæra, her extreme avarice obscured them all: and though Martial[49] founds Tibullus's chief claim to poetical reputation on the elegies he addressed to that lady,

Fama est arguti Nemesis formosa Tibulli,

we have our poet's authority for asserting, that they produced no effect upon her.

Whether Nemesis ever abated of her rigour to Tibullus, his elegies do not inform us: it is indeed probable she did, especially since Ovid represents her as sincerely grieved at Tibullus's death, which, according to Marsus, a cotemporary poet, happened soon after that of Virgil:

Te quoque, Virgilio comitem, non æqua, Tibulle,
Mors juvenem campos misit ad Elysios:
Ne foret, aut elegis molles qui fleret amores;
Aut caneret forti regia bella pede.

Thee! young Tibullus, to th' Elysian plain
Death bid accompany great Maro's shade;
Determin'd that no poet should remain
Or to sing wars, or weep the cruel maid.

For Tibullus died either A. U. C. 735, the year of Virgil's death, or the year after, in the forty-fourth or forty-fifth year of his age.

Nor was Marsus the only poet who celebrated this melancholy event: Ovid[50], who had no less friendship than admiration for Tibullus, has immortalized both himself and his friend, in the following beautiful elegy, which containing some further particulars relating to our poet, will make a proper conclusion to this life, which, from the scantiness as well as the little authority of many of the materials, the author is sorry he cannot render more complete.

If Thetis, if the blushing queen of morn,
If mighty goddesses could taste of woe
For mortal sons; come, Elegy forlorn!
Come, weeping dame! and bid thy tresses flow:

43 Thus Iso, the old glossarist of Prudentius, interprets Neæra by *pellex* and *concubina*.
44 Odys. lib. xii. ver. 133.
45 Argonaut. lib. ii. ver. 141.
46 Epist. Symbolic. vid. Reines, ep. 28.
47 Lib. iii. el. 4.
48 P. 20.
49 Lib. viii. ep. 73.
50 Lib. iii. el. 8.

Thou bear'st, soft mistress of the tearful eye,
    From grief thy name, now name alas too just!
For see thy favourite bard, thy glory lie,
    Stretch'd on yon funeral pile, ah! lifeless dust!

See Venus' son, his torch extinguish'd brings,
    His quiver all revers'd, and broke his bow;
See pensive how he droops with flagging wings,
    And strikes his bared bosom many a blow:

Loose and neglected, scatter'd o'er his neck,
    His golden locks drink many a falling tear:
What piteous sobs, as if his heart would break,
    Shake his swoln cheek! Ah! sorrow too severe!

Thus, fair Iülus! for thy godlike sire,
    'T is said, he weeping from thy roof withdrew:
Nor deeper mourn'd the queen of soft desire,
    When the grim boar her lov'd Adonis slew.

And yet we bards are fondly call'd divine,
    Are sacred held, the gods' peculiar care:
There are, that deem us of th' ethereal line,
    That something of the deity we share.

But what can Death's abhorred stroke withstand?
    Say what so sacred he will not profane?
On all the monster lays his dusky hand,
    And poets are immortal deem'd in vain.

Thee, Orpheus, what avail'd thy heavenly sire?
    Thy mother-muse, and beast-enchanting song?
The god for Linus swept his mournful lyre,
    And with a father's woes the forests rung.

Great Homer see, from whose eternal spring
    Pierian draughts the poet-train derive,
Not he could 'scape the fell remorseless king,
    His lays alone the greedy flames survive.

Still live, the work of ages, Ilion's fame,
    And the slow web by nightly craft unwove:
So Nemesis' shall live, and Delia's name;
    This his first passion, that his recent love.

Now what avails, ye fair! each holy rite,
    Each painful service for your lover paid?
Recluse and lonely that you pass'd the night?
    Or sought th' Egyptian cymbal's fruitless aid?

When partial fate thus tears the good away,
    (Forgive, ye just! th' involuntary thought)
I'm led to doubt of Jove's eternal sway,
    And fear that gods and heaven are words of nought.

Live pious, you must die: religion prize,
    Death to the tomb will drag you from the fane:
Confide in verse; lo! where Tibullus lies!
    His all a little urn will now contain!

Thee, sacred bard! could then funereal fires
Snatch from us? on thy bosom durst they feed?
Not fanes were safe, nor Jove's refulgent spires,
From flames that ventur'd on this impious deed.

The beauteous queen that reigns in Eryx's towers,
From the sad sight averts her mournful face;
There are, that tell of soft and pearly showers
Which down her lovely cheeks their courses trace.

Yet better thus, than on Phæacia's strand,
Unknown, unpitied, and unseen to die:
His closing eyes here felt a mother's hand,
Her tender hands each honour'd rite supply.

His parting shade here found a sister's care,
Who sad attends, with tresses loose and torn:
The fair he lov'd his dying kisses share,
Nor quit the Pyre, afflicted and forlorn.

"Farewel, dear youth!" thus Delia parting cry'd,
"How blest the time, when I inspir'd the lay!
You liv'd, were happy; every care defy'd,
While I possess'd your heart, untaught to stray."

To whom thus Nemesis, in scornful mood,
"Mine was the loss, then why art thou distress'd?
Me, only me, with parting life he view'd;
My hand alone with dying ardour press'd."

And yet, if aught beyond this mouldering clay
But empty name and shadowy form remain,
Thou liv'st, dear youth! for ever young and gay,
For ever blest, shalt range th' Elysian plain.

And thou, Catullus! learned gallant mind,
(Fast by thy side thy Calvus will attend)
With ivy wreaths thy youthful temples twin'd,
Shalt spring to hail th' arrival of thy friend.

And Gallus, too profuse of life and blood,
If no sad breach of friendship's law deprive,
This band immortal of the blest and good,
Thy shade shall join, if shades at all survive.

Thou, polish'd bard! thy loss tho' here we mourn,
Hast swell'd the sacred number of the blest;
Safe rest thy gentle bones within their urn!
Nor heavy press the earth upon thy breast!

THE

ELEGIES OF TIBULLUS.

TRANSLATED BY GRAINGER.

TIBULLUS.

BOOK THE FIRST. ELEGY THE FIRST.

THE glitt'ring ore let others vainly heap,
O'er fertile vales extend th' enclosing mound;
With dread of neighb'ring foes forsake their sleep,
And start aghast at ev'ry trumpet's sound.

Me humbler scenes delight, and calmer days;
A tranquil life fair poverty secure!
Then boast, my hearth, a small but cheerful blaze,
And riches grasp who will, let me be poor.

Nor yet be Hope a stranger to my door,
But o'er my roof, bright goddess, still preside!
With many a bounteous autumn heap my floor,
And swell my vats with must, a purple tide.

My tender vines I'll plant with early care,
And choicest apples, with a skilful hand;
Nor blush, a rustic, oft to guide the share,
Or goad the tardy ox along the land.

Let me, a simple swain, with honest pride,
If chance a lambkin from its dam should roam,
Or sportful kid, the little wanderer chide,
And in my bosom bear exulting home.

Here Pales I bedew with milky show'rs,
Lustrations yearly for my shepherd pay,
Revere each antique stone bedeck'd with flow'rs
That bounds the field, or points the doubtful way.

My grateful fruits, the earliest of the year,
Before the rural god shall duly wait:
From Ceres' gifts I'll cull each browner ear,
And hang a wheaten wreath before her gate.

The ruddy god shall save my fruit from stealth,
And far away each little plund'rer scare:
And you, the guardians once of ampler wealth,
My household gods, shall still my off'rings share.

My num'rous herds, that wanton'd o'er the mead,
The choicest fatling then could richly yield;
Now scarce I spare a little lamb to bleed
A mighty victim for my scanty field.

And yet a lamb shall bleed, while, rang'd around,
The village youths shall stand in order meet,
With rustic hymns, ye gods, your praise resound,
And future crops and future wines entreat.

Then come, ye pow'rs, nor scorn my frugal board,
Nor yet the gifts clean earthen bowls convey;
With these the first of men the gods ador'd,
And form'd their simple shape of ductile clay.

My little flock, ye wolves, ye robbers, spare,
Too mean a plunder to deserve your toil;
For wealthier herds the nightly theft prepare;
There seek a nobler prey, and richer spoil.

For treasur'd wealth, nor stores of golden wheat,
The hoard of frugal sires, I vainly call;
A little farm be mine, a cottage neat,
And wonted couch where balmy sleep may fall.

"What joy to hear the tempest howl in vain,
And clasp a fearful mistress to my breast:
Or lull'd to slumber by the beating rain,
Secure and happy sink at last to rest [1]."

These joys be mine! O grant me only these,
And give to others bags of shining gold,
Whose steely heart can brave the boist'rous seas,
The storm wide-wasting, or the stiff'ning cold.

Content with little, I would rather stay
Than spend long months amid the wat'ry waste:
In cooling shades elude the scorching ray,
Beside some fountain's gliding waters plac'd.

O perish rather all that's rich and rare,
The diamond quarry, and the golden vein,
Than that my absence cost one precious tear,
Or give some gentle maid a moment's pain.

[1] Hammond's translation.

With glitt'ring spoils, Messala, gild thy dome,
Be thine the noble task to lead the brave:
A lovely foe me captive holds at home,
Chain'd to her scornful gate, a watchful slave.

Inglorious post! and yet I heed not fame:
Th' applause of crowds for Delia I'd resign:
To live with thee I'd bear the coward's name,
Nor 'midst the scorn of nations once repine.

With thee to live I'd mock the ploughman's toil,
Or on some lonely mountain tend my sheep;
At night I'd lay me on the flinty soil,
And happy 'midst thy dear émbraces sleep.

What drooping lover heeds the Tyrian bed,
While the long night is pass'd with many a sigh:
Nor softest down with richest carpets spread,
Nor whisp'ring rills, can close the weeping eye.

Of threefold iron were his rugged frame,
Who when he might thy yielding heart obtain,
Could yet attend the calls of empty fame,
Or follow arms in quest of sordid gain.

Unenvy'd let him drive the vanquish'd host,
Thro' captive lands his conquering armies lead;
Unenvy'd wear the robe with gold emboss'd,
And guide with solemn state his foaming steed.

O may I view thee with life's parting ray,
And thy dear hand with dying ardour press:
Sure thou wilt weep—and on thy lover's clay,
With breaking heart, print many a tender kiss!

Sure thou wilt weep—and woes unutter'd feel,
When on the pile thou seest thy lover laid!
For well I know, nor flint, nor ruthless steel,
Can arm the breast of such a gentle maid.

From the sad pomp, what youth, what pitying fair,
Returning slow can tender tears refrain?
O Delia, spare thy cheeks, thy tresses spare,
Nor give my ling'ring shade a world of pain.

But now while smiling hours the Fates bestow,
Let love, dear maid, our gentle hearts unite!
Soon Death will come and strike the fatal blow;
Unseen his head, and veil'd in shades of night.

Soon creeping age will bow the lover's frame,
And tear the myrtle chaplet from his brow:
With hoary locks ill suits the youthful flame,
The soft persuasion, or the ardent vow.

Now the fair queen of gay desire is ours,
And lends our follies an indulgent smile:
'T is lavish youth's t' enjoy the frolic hours,
The wanton revel, and the midnight broil.

Your chief, my friends, and fellow-soldier, I
To these light wars will lead you boldly on:
Far hence ye trumpets sound and banners fly:
To those who covet wounds and fame begone.

And bear them fame and wounds; and riches bear;
There are that fame and wounds and riches prize:
For me, while I possess one plenteous year,
I'll wealth and meagre want alike despise.

THE SECOND ELEGY.

With wine, more wine, my recent pains deceive,
Till creeping slumber send a soft reprieve:
Asleep, take heed no whisper stirs the air,
For wak'd, my boy, I wake to heart-felt care.
Now is my Delia watch'd by ruthless spies,
And the gate, bolted, all access denies.
Relentless gate! may storms of wind and rain,
With mingled violence avenge my pain!
May forky thunders, hurl'd by Jove's red hand,
Burst every bolt, and shatter every band!
Ah no! rage turns my brain; the curse recall;
On me, devoted, let the thunder fall!
Then recollect my many wreaths of yore,
How oft you 've seen me weep, insensate door!
No longer then our interview delay,
And as you open let no noise betray.
In vain I plead!—Dare then my Delia rise!
Love aids the dauntless, and will blind your spies!
Those who the godhead's soft behests obey,
Steal from their pillows unobserv'd away;
On tiptoe traverse unobserv'd the floor;
The key turn noiseless, and unfold the door:
In vain the jealous each precaution take,
Their speaking fingers assignations make.
Nor will the god impart to all his aid:
Love hates the fearful, hates the lazy maid;
But through sly windings, and unpractis'd ways,
His bold night-errants to their wish conveys:
For those whom he with expectation fires,
No ambush frightens, and no labour tires;
Sacred the dangers of the dark they dare,
No robbers stop them, and no bravoes scare.
Tho' wintery tempests howl, by love secure,
The howling tempest I with ease endure:
No watching hurts me, if my Delia smile,
Soft turn the gate, and beckon me the while.
She 's mine. Be blind, ye ramblers of the night,
Lest angry Venus snatch your guilty sight:
The goddess bids her votaries' joys to be
From every casual interruption free:
With prying steps alarm us not, retire,
Nor glare your torches, nor our names inquire:
Or if ye know, deny, by Heaven above,
Nor dare divulge the privacies of love.
From blood and seas vindictive Venus sprung,
And sure destruction waits the blabbing tongue!
Nay, should they prate, you, Delia, need not fear;
Your lord (a sorceress swore) should give no ear!
By potent spells she cleaves the sacred ground,
And shuddering spectres wildly roam around!
I 've seen her tear the planets from the sky!
Seen lightning backward at her bidding fly!
She calls! from blazing pyres the corse descends,
And, re-enliven'd, clasps his wondering friends!
The fiends she gathers with a magic yell,
Then with aspersions frights them back to Hell!
She wills,—glad summer gilds the frozen pole!
She wills,—in summer wintery tempests roll!
She knows, 't is true, Medea's awful spell!
She knows to vanquish the fierce guards of Hell!
To me she gave a charm for lovers meet,
("Spit thrice, my fair, and thrice the charm repeat.")
Us, in soft dalliance, should your lord surprise;
By this impos'd on, he'd renounce his eyes!
But bless no rival, or th' affair is known;
This incantation me befriends alone.
Nor stopp'd she here; but swore, if I 'd agree,
By charms or herbs to set thy lover free.

With dire lustrations she began the rite!
(Serenely shone the planet of the night)
The magic gods she call'd with hellish sound,
A sable sacrifice distain'd the ground—
I stopp'd the spell: I must not, cannot part:
I begg'd her aid to gain a mutual heart.

THE THIRD ELEGY.

WHILE you, Messala, plough th' Ægean sea,
O sometimes kindly deign to think of me.
Me, hapless me, Phæacian shores detain,
Unknown, unpitied, and oppress'd with pain.
Yet spare me, Death, ah spare me and retire:
No weeping mother's here to light my pyre:
Here is no sister, with a sister's woe,
Rich Syrian odours on the pile to throw:
But chief, my soul's soft partner is not here,
Her locks to loose, and sorrow o'er my bier.
What tho' fair Delia my return implor'd,
Each fane frequented, and each god ador'd:
What tho' they bad me every peril brave;
And Fortune thrice auspicious omens gave;
All could not dry my tender Delia's tears,
Suppress her sighs, or calm her anxious fears;
E'en as I strove to minister relief,
Unconscious tears proclaim'd my heart-felt grief:
Urg'd still to go, a thousand shifts I made,
Birds now, now festivals my voyage staid:
Or, if I struck my foot against the door,
Straight I return'd, and wisdom was no more.
Forbid by Cupid, let no swain depart,
Cupid is vengeful, and will wring his heart.
What do your offerings now, my fair, avail?
Your Isis heeds not, and your cymbals fail!
What, though array'd in sacred robes you stood,
Fled man's embrace, and sought the purest flood?
While this I write, I sensibly decay,—
"Assist me, Isis, drive my pains away:
That you can every mortal ill remove,
The numerous tablets in your temple prove:
So shall my Delia, veil'd in votive white,
Before your threshold sit for many a night;
And twice a day, her tresses all unbound,
Amid your votaries fam'd, your praises sound:
Safe to my household gods may I return,
And incense monthly on their altars burn."
How blest man liv'd in Saturn's golden days,
Ere distant climes were join'd by lengthen'd ways.
Secure the pine upon the mountain grew,
Nor yet o'er billows in the ocean flew;
Then every clime a wild abundance bore,
And man liv'd happy on his natal shore:
For then no steed to feel the bit was broke,
Then had no steer submitted to the yoke;
No house had gates, (blest times!) and, in the grounds
No scanty landmarks parcell'd out the bounds:
From every oak redundant honey ran,
And ewes spontaneous bore their milk to man:
No deathful arms were forg'd, no war was wag'd,
No rapine plunder'd, no ambition rag'd.
How chang'd, alas! Now cruel Jove commands;
Gold fires the soul, and falchions arm our hands:
Each day, the main unnumber'd lives destroys;
And slaughter, daily, o'er her myriads joys.
Yet spare me, Jove, I ne'er disown'd thy sway,
I ne'er was perjur'd; spare me, Jove, I pray.
But, if the Sisters have pronounc'd my doom,
Inscrib'd be these upon my humble tomb.
"Lo! here inurn'd a youthful poet lies,
Far from his Delia, and his native skies!
Far from the lov'd Messala, whom to please
Tibullus follow'd over land and seas!"
Then Love my ghost (for Love I still obey'd)
Will grateful usher to th' Elysian shade:
There joy and ceaseless revelry prevail;
There soothing music floats on every gale;
There painted warblers hop from spray to spray,
And, wildly-pleasing, swell the general lay:
There every hedge, untaught, with cassia blooms
And scents the ambient air with rich perfumes:
There every mead a various plenty yields;
There lavish Flora paints the purple fields:
With ceaseless light a brighter Phœbus glows,
No sickness tortures, and no ocean flows;
But youths associate with the gentle fair,
And stung with pleasure to the shade repair:
With them Love wanders wheresoe'er they stray,
Provokes to rapture, and inflames the play:
But chief, the constant few, by death betray'd,
Reign, crown'd with myrtle, monarchs of the shade.
Not so the wicked; far they drag their chains,
By black lakes sever'd from the blissful plains;
Those should they pass, impassable the gate
Where Cerb'rus howls, grim sentinel of fate.
There snake-hair'd fiends with whips patrole around,
Rack'd anguish bellows, and the deeps resound:
There he, who dar'd to tempt the queen of Heaven,
Upon an ever-turning wheel is driven:
The Danaids there still strive huge casks to fill,
But strive in vain, the casks elude their skill:
There Pelop's sire, to quench his thirsty fires,
Still tries the flood, and still the flood retires:
There vultures tear the bow'ls, and drink the gore,
Of Tityus, stretch'd enormous on the shore.
Dread love, as vast as endless be their pain
Who tempt my fair, or wish a long campaign.
O let no rival your affections share,
Long as this bosom beats, my lovely fair!
Still on you let your prudent nurse attend;
She'll guard your honour, she's our common friend.
Her tales of love your sorrowings will allay,
And, in my absence, make my Delia gay:
Let her o'er all your virgin train preside,
She'll praise th' industrious, and the lazy chide.
But see! on all enfeebling languors creep;
Their distaffs drop, they yawn, they nod, they sleep.
Then, if the destinies propitious prove,
Then will I rush, all passion, on my love:
My wish'd return no messenger shall tell,
I'll seem, my fair, as if from Heaven I fell.
A soft confusion flushes all your charms,
Your graceful dishabille my bosom warms,
You, Delia, fly and clasp me in your arms.
For this surprise, ye powers of love, I pray,
Post on Aurora, bring the rosy day.

THE FOURTH ELEGY.

POET.

So round, my god, may shady coverings bend,
No sun-beams scorch thy face, no snows offend!
Whence are the fair so proud to win thy heart,
Yet rude thy beard, and guiltless thou of art?
Naked thou stand'st, expos'd to wintery snows!
Naked thou stand'st, when burning Sirius glows!

Thus I—and thus the garden-power reply'd,
A crooked sickle glittering by his side.

PRIAPUS.

Take no repulse—at first what tho' they fly!
O'ercome at last, reluctance will comply.
The vine in time full ripen'd clusters bears,
And circling time brings back the rolling spheres:
In time soft rains thro' marble sap their way,
And time taught men to tame fierce beasts of prey.
Nor aw'd by conscience meanly dread to swear;
Love-oaths, unratify'd, wild tempests bear!
Banish then scruples, if you'd gain a heart;
Swear, swear by Pallas' locks, Diana's dart;
By all that's most rever'd—if they require:
Oaths bind not eager love, thank Heaven's good sire!
Nor be too slow; your slowness you'll deplore;
Time posts; and, oh! youth's raptures soon are o'er:
Now forests bloom, and purple earth looks gay;
Bleak winter blows, and all her charms decay:
How soon the steed to age's stiffness yields,
So late a victor in th' Olympic fields?
I've seen the aged oft lament their fate,
That senseless they had learnt to live too late.
Ye partial gods, and can the snake renew,
His youthful vigour, and his burnish'd hue?
But youth and beauty past; is art in vain
To bring the coy deserters back again?

POET.

Jove gives alone the pow'rs of wit and wine,
In youth immortal, spite of years, to shine.

PRIAPUS.

Yield prompt compliance to the maid's desires;
A prompt compliance fans the lover's fires:
Go pleas'd where'er she goes, tho' long the way,
Tho' the fierce Dog-star dart his sultry ray;
Tho' painted Iris gird the bluish sky,
And sure portends, that rattling storms are nigh:
Or, if the fair-one pant for sylvan fame,
Gay drag the meshes, and provoke the game:
Nay, should she choose to risk the driving gale;
Or steer, or row, or agile hand the sail:
No toil, tho' weak, tho' fearful, thou forbear;
No toils should tire you, and no dangers scare:
Occasion smiles, then snatch an ardent kiss;
The coy may struggle, but will grant the bliss:
The bliss obtain'd, the fictious struggle past,
Unbid, they'll clasp you in their arms at last.

POET.

Alas! in such degenerate days as these,
No more love's gentle wiles the beauteous please!
If poor, all gentle stratagems are vain!
The fair-ones languish now alone for gain!
O may dishonour be the wretch's share,
Who first with hateful gold seduc'd the fair!

PRIAPUS.

Ye charming dames, prefer the tuneful quire,
Nor meanly barter heavenly charms for hire.
What cannot song? The purple locks that glow'd
On Nisus' head, harmonious song bestow'd!
What cannot strains? By tuneful strains alone
Fair iv'ry, Pelops, on thy shoulder shone!
While stars with nightly radiance gild the pole,
Earth boasts her oaks, or mighty waters roll,
The fair, whose beauty poets deign to praise,
Shall bloom uninjur'd in poetic lays:
While she who hears not when the Muses call,
But flies their fav'rites, gold's inglorious thrall!
Shall prove, believe the bard, or soon, or late,
A dread example of avenging fate!
Soft, flattering songs, the Cyprian queen approves;
And aids the suppliant swain with all her loves.

POET.

The god, no novice in th' intriguing trade,
This answer, Titius, to my question made:
But caution bids you fly th' insidious fair,
And paints the perils of their eyes and air;
Nor these alone, devoted man subdue,
Devoted man their slightest actions woo.
Be cautious those who list—but ye who know
Desire's hot fever, and contempt's chill woe;
Me grateful praise—contempt shall pain no more;
But wish meet wish, instructed by my lore:
By various means, while others seek for fame,
Scorn'd love to counsel be my noblest aim.
Wide stands my gate for all—I rapt foresee
The time, when I love's oracle shall be!
When round my seat shall press th' enamour'd throng,
Attend my motions, and applaud my song.
Alas! my hopes are fled, my wiles are vain;
The fair, I doat on, treats me with disdain:
Yet spare me, charmer, your disdain betrays
To witty laughter my too boastful lays.

THE FIFTH ELEGY.

Of late I boasted I could happy be,
Resume the man, and not my Delia see!
And boasts of manhood, boasts of bliss are vain;
Back to my bondage I return again!
And like a top am whirl'd, which boys, for sport,
Lash on the pavement of a level court!
What can atone, my fair, for crimes like these?
I'll bear with patience, use me as you please!
Yet, by Love's shafts, and by your braided hair,
By all the joys we stole, your suppliant spare.
When sickness dimm'd, of late, your radiant eyes;
My restless, fond petitions won the skies.
Thrice I with sulphur purified you round,
And thrice the rite, with songs, th' enchantress bound:
The cake, by me thrice sprinkled, put to flight
The death-denouncing phantoms of the night:
And I nine times, in linen garbs array'd,
In silent night, nine times to Trivia pray'd.
What did I not? Yet what reward have I?
You love another, your preserver fly!
He tastes the sweet effects of all my cares,
My fond lustrations, and my solemn prayers.
Are these the joys my madding fancy drew,
If young-ey'd Health restor'd your rosy hue?
I fondly thought, sweet maid, oh thought in vain!
With you to live a blithesome village-swain.
When yellow Ceres asks the reaper's hand,
"Delia" (said I) "will guard the reaper's band;
Delia will keep, when hinds unload the vine,
The choicest grapes for me, the richest wine:
My flocks she'll count, and oft will sweetly deign
To clasp some prattler of my menial train:

With pious care will load each rural shrine,
For ripen'd crops a golden sheaf assign,
Cates for my fold, rich clusters for my vine:
No, no domestic care shall touch my soul;
You, Delia, reign despotic o'er the whole!
And will Messala fly from pomp of state,
And deign to enter at my lowly gate?
The choicest fruitage, that my trees afford,
Delia will cull herself, to deck the board;
And wondering, such transcendant worth to see,
The fruit present, thy blushing hand-maid she."
Such were the fond chimeras of my brain,
Which now the winds have wafted o'er the main.
O power of love, whom still my soul obey'd,
What has my tongue against my mother said?
Guiltless of ill, unmark'd with incest's stain,
I stole no garland from her holy fane:
For crimes, like these, I'd abject crawl the ground,
Kiss her dread threshold, and my forehead wound.
But ye who, falsely wise, deride my pains,
Beware; your hour approaches—Love has chains.
I've known the young, who ridicul'd his rage,
Love's humblest vassals, when oppress'd with age:
Each art I've known them try to win the fair,
Smooth their hoarse voice, and dress their scanty hair;
I've known them in the street, her maid detain;
And weeping, beg her to assist their pain.
At such preposterous love, each school-boy sneers:
Shuns, as an omen; or pursues with fleers.
Why do you crush your slave, fair queen of joy?
Destroying me, your harvest you destroy!

The sons of opulence are folly's care,
But want's rough child is sense, and honour's heir.
In vain we sing—the gate still bolted stands;
Come, Vengeance, let us burst its sullen bands.
Learn, happy rival, by my wrongs to know
Your fate; since Fortune governs all below.

THE SIXTH ELEGY.

WITH wine, I strove to sooth my love-sick soul,
But vengeful Cupid dash'd with tears the bowl:
All mad with rage, to kinder nymphs I flew;
But vigour fled me, when I thought on you.
Balk'd of the rapture, from my arms they run,
Swear I'm devoted, and my converse shun!
By what dire witchcraft am I thus betray'd?
Your face and hair unnerve me, matchless maid:
Not more celestial look'd the sea-born fair,
Receiv'd by Peleus from her pearly chair.
A rich admirer his addresses paid;
And brib'd my mistress by a beldam's aid.
From you my ruin, curst procuress, rose;
What imprecations shall avenge my woes?
May Heaven, in pity to my sufferings, shed
Its keenest mischief on your plotting head!
The ghosts of those, you robb'd of love's delight,
In horrid visions haunt your irksome night!
And, on the chimney, may the boding owl
Your rest disturb, and terrify your soul!
By famine stung, to church-yards may you run;
There, feast on offals, hungry wolves would shun!
Or, howling frantic, in a tatter'd gown,
Fierce mastiffs bait you thro' each crowded town!
T'is done! a lover's curse the gods approve;
But keenest vengeance fires the queen of love.
Leave then, my fair, the crafty venal jade;
What passion yields not, when such foes invade?
Your hearts, ye fair, does modest merit claim?
Tho' small his fortunes, feed his gentle flame;
For, genuine love's soft raptures would ye know?
These raptures merit can alone bestow:

THE SEVENTH ELEGY.

LOVE still invites me with a smiling eye!
Beneath his smiles, what pains and anguish lie?
Yet since the gods, dread power, must yield to thee!
What laurels canst thou gain from conquering me?
Me Delia lov'd; but by thy subtle wiles,
The fair, in secret, on another smiles:
That my suspicion's false, 'tis true, she swears;
And backs her imprecations with her tears!
False fair, your oaths, and syren tears refrain;
Your syren tears and oaths no credit gain;
For when your lord suspected me of yore,
As much you wept, as many oaths you swore.
Yet wherefore blame I Love? the blame is mine;
I, wretched I, first taught her to design!
I first instructed her, her spies to foil!
Back on myself my wanton arts recoil:
Herbs of rare energy my skill supplied,
All marks of too-fond gallantry to hide!
More artful now, alone the wanton lies;
And new pretexts her cozening brains devise.
Uncautious lord of a too cunning spouse!
Admittance grant me, she shall keep her vows!
Be warn'd, my friend, observe her when her tongue
Commends in wanton phrase the gay-dress'd young;
O let her not her heaving bosom bare,
Expos'd to every fop's immodest stare.
When leaning on the board, with flowing wine,
She seems to draw some inconsiderate line;
Take heed, take heed, (I know the warning true)
These random lines assign an interview.
Nor let your wife to fanes so frequent roam,
A modest wife's best temple is at home:
But if your prohibitions all are vain,
Give me the hint, I'll dodge her to the fane;
What tho' the goddess snatch my curious sight,
I'll bring her wanton privacies to light.
Some gem she wore, I'd oft pretend to view,
But squeez'd her fingers unperceiv'd of you:
Oft with full racy bowls I seal'd your eyes,
Water my bev'ridge, and obtain'd the prize.
Yet since I tell, forgive the pranks I play'd,
Love prompted all, and love must be obey'd!
Nay, 'twas at me (be now the truth avow'd)
Your watchful mastiff us'd to bark so loud;
But now some other, with insidious wait,
Intent observes each creaking of your gate,
At which, whoever of the house appears,
Passing, the mien of quick despatch he wears;
But comes again, the minute they remove,
And coughs, sure signal of impatient love!
What boots, tho' marriage gave a wife so fair,
If careless you, or she eludes your care?
While men are artful, and your wife can feign,
Vain are your brazen bolts, your mastiffs vain.
Cold to the raptures of the genial bed,
She lays the fault upon an aching head:
'Tis false; the wanton for some other sighs;
From this, her coolness, this, her aches arise.

Then, then be warn'd, entrust her to my care;
Whips, chains I laugh at, if you grant my prayer.
"Hence from my ward, ye sparkish essenc'd beaus;
Illegal love oft springs from essenc'd clothes."
Where'er she walks, not distant I'll attend;
And guard your honour from the casual friend!
"Off, gallants, off; for so the gods ordain,
So, the dread priestess, in unerring strain!"
(When holy fury fires the frantic dame,
She mocks all torture, and exults in flame;
Her snow-white arms and heaving breast she tears;
And with the gushing gore Bellona smears;
Deep in her side she plants the glittering sword;
And the dread goddess prompts each fateful word.)
"Ye youths beware, nor touch whom Cupid guards,
Unpunish'd none attempt his gentle wards:
As my blood flows, and as these ashes fly;
Their wealth shall perish, and their manhood die."
She menac'd then the fair, with dreadful pain;
E'en were you guilty, may her threats be vain:
Not on your own account; your mother's age,
Your worthy mother, deprecates my rage:
When Love and Fortune smil'd, her gentle aid
Oft me conducted to the blooming maid;
My footsteps, wakeful, from afar she knew,
Unbarr'd the gate, nor fear'd the nightly dew:
Half of my life's long thread I'd pleas'd resign,
My sweet conductress, could I lengthen thine!
Still, still, tho' much abus'd, I Delia prize;
She's still thy daughter, and enchants my eyes.
Yet tho' no coy cimarr invest the fair;
Nor vestal fillet bind her auburn hair;
Teach her what decent modesty requires;
To crown my fire, alone, with equal fires.
Me too confine; and if, in wanton praise
Of other maids, my tongue luxuriant strays;
Let thy suspicion then no limits know,
Insult me, spurn me, as thy greatest foe!
But if your jealousies are built in air,
And patient love your usage cannot bear;
What wrath may perpetrate, my soul alarms;
For wrath, I warn you, heeds not female charms.
Nor yet be chaste, from mean unamorous fear;
Be still most modest, when I am not near.
For those, whom neither wit, nor worth secure,
Grow old, unpitied; palsied, worthless, poor;
Yet with each servile drudgery they strive,
To keep their being's wretchedness alive!
The gay regard their woe with laughing eyes;
Swear they deserve it, and absolve the skies!
Nor Venus less exults! "May such a fate,"
(From Heaven she prays) "upon th' inconstant wait."
The same my wish! but O may we two prove,
In age, a pattern of unalter'd love!

THE EIGHTH ELEGY.

"THIS day," (the Fates foretold in sacred song,
And singing drew the vital twine along,)
"He comes, nor shall the gods the doom recal,
He comes, whose sword shall quell the rebel Gaul.
With all her laurels, him shall conquest crown,
And nations shudder at his awful frown;
Smooth Atur, now that flows through peaceful lands,
Shall fly affrighted at his hostile bands."
'Tis done! this prophecy Rome joys to see,
Far-fam'd Messala, now fulfill'd in thee:
Long triumphs ravish the spectators eyes,
And fetter'd chieftans of enormous size:
An ivory-car, with steeds as white as snow,
Sustains thy grandeur through the pompous show.
Some little share, in those exploits I bore;
Witness Tarbella; and the Santoigne shore;
Witness the land, where steals the silent Soane;
Where rush the Garonne; and th' impetuous Rhone;
Where Loire, enamour'd of Carnutian bounds,
Leads his blue water through the yellow grounds.
Or shall his other acts adorn my theme;—
Fair Cydnus, winding with a silver stream?
Taurus, that in the clouds his forehead hides,
And rich Cilicia from the world divides;
Taurus, from which unnumber'd rivers spring,
The savage seat of tempests, shall I sing?
Why should I tell, how sacred through the skies
Of Syrian cities the white pigeon flies?
Why sing of Tyrian towers, which Neptune laves;
Whence the first vessel, venturous, stemm'd the waves?
How shall the bard the secret source explore,
Whence, father Nile, thou draw'st thy watery store?
Thy fields ne'er importune for rain the sky;
Thou dost benignly all their wants supply:
As Egypt, Apis mourns in mystic lays,
She joins thy praises to Osiris' praise.
Osiris first contriv'd the crooked plough,
And pull'd ripe apples from the novice bough;
He taught the swains, the savage-mould to wound,
And scatter'd seed-corn in th' unpractis'd ground.
He first with poles sustain'd the reptile vine,
And show'd its infant tendrils how to twine;
Its wanton shoots instructed men to shear,
Subdue their wildness, and mature the year:
Then too, the ripen'd cluster first was trod;
Then in gay streams its cordial soul bestow'd;
This as swains quaff'd, spontaneous numbers came,
They prais'd the festal cask, and hymn'd thy name;
All ecstacy! to certain time they bound,
And beat in measur'd awkwardness the ground.
Gay bowls serene the wrinkled front of care;
Gay bowls the toil-oppressed swain repair!
And let the slave the laughing goblet drain;
He blithesome sings, though manacles enchain.
Thee sorrow flies, Osiris, god of wine!
But songs, enchanting Love, and dance are thine;
But flowers and ivy thy fair head surround,
And a loose saffron-mantle sweeps the ground.
With purple-robes invested, now you glow;
The shrine is shown, and flutes melodious blow:
Come then, my god, but come bedew'd with wine!
Attend the rites, and in the dance combine;
The rites and dances are to genius due!
Benign Osiris, stand confess'd to view!
Rich unguents drop already from his hair,
His head and neck soft flowery garlands share!
O come, so shall my grateful incense rise,
And cates of honey meet thy laughing eyes!
On thee, Messala, ('tis my fervent prayer,)
May Heaven bestow a wise, a warlike heir:
In whom, increas'd, paternal worth may shine,
Whose acts may add a lustre to thy line,
And transports give thee in thy life's decline.
But should the gods my fervent pray'r deny,
Thy fame, my glorious friend, shall never die.
Long as (thy bounteous work) the well-made way
Shall its broad pavement to the Sun display.

The bards of Alba shall in lofty rhyme
Transmit thy glory down the tide of time:
They sing from gratitude: nor less the clown
Whom love or business have detain'd in town
Till late, as home he safely plods along,
Thee chants, Messala, in his village-song.
Blest morn, which still my grateful Muse shall sing,
Oft rise, and with you greater blessings bring.

THE NINTH ELEGY.

In vain would lovers hide their infant-smart,
From me a master in the amorous art;
I read their passion in their mien and eyes,
O'erhear their whispers, and explain their sighs.
This skill no Delphian oracles bestow'd,
No augurs taught me, and no victims show'd;
But Love my wrists with magic fillets bound,
Lash'd me, and lashing, mutter'd many a sound.
No more then, Marathus, indifference feign,
Else vengeful Venus will inhance your pain!
What now, sweet youth, avails your anxious care,
So oft to essence, oft to change your hair?
What tho' cosmetics all their aid supply?
And every artifice of dress you try?
She's not oblig'd to bredes, to gems, to clothes,
Her charms to Nature Pholoe only owes.
What spells devote you? say, what philtres bind?
What midnight sorceress fascinates your mind?
Spells can seduce the corn from neighbouring plains!
The headlong serpent halts at magic strains!
And did not cymbals stop thy prone career,
A spell thee Luna from thy orb would tear!
Why do I magic for your passion blame,
Magic is useless to a perfect frame!
You squeez'd her hands, your arms around her threw,
Join'd lip to lip, and hence your passion grew.
Cease then, fair maid, to give your lover pain;
Love hates the haughty, will avenge the swain.
See youth vermillions o'er his modest face!
Can riches equal such a boy's embrace?
Then ask no bribe—when age affects the gay,
Your every smile let hoary dotage pay;
But you your arms around the stripling throw,
And scorn the treasure monarchs can bestow.
But she who gives to age her charms for pay,
May her wealth perish, and her bloom decay.
Then when impatience thrills in every vein,
May manhood shun her, and the young disdain.
Alas! when age has silver'd o'er the head,
And youth that feeds the lamp of love is fled,
In vain the toilette charms; 'tis vain to try,
Grey scanty locks with yellow nuts to die;
You strip the tell-tales vainly from their place;
And vainly strive to mend an aged face.
Then in thine eyes while youth triumphant glows,
And with his flowers thy cheeks my fair-one sows,
Incline thine heart to love, and gentle play;
Youth, youth has rapid wings and flies away!
The fond old lover vilify, disdain;
What praise can crown you from a stripling's pain?
Spare then the lovely boy; his beauties die;
By no dire sickness sent him from the sky:
The gods are just; you, Pholoe, are to blame;
His sallow colour from your coyness came.
Oh, wretched youth! how oft, when absent you,
Groans rend his breast, and tears his cheeks bedew? [cries,
"Why dost thou rack me with contempt?" he
"The willing ever can elude their spies.
Had you, O had you felt what now I feel,
Venus would teach you from your spies to steal.
I can breathe low; can snatch the melting kiss,
And noiseless ravish love's enchanting bliss;
At midnight I securely grope my way;
The floor tread noiseless, noiseless turn the key.
Poor fruitless skill! my skill if she despise,
And cruel from the bed of rapture flies.
Or if a promise haply I obtain,
That she will recompense at night my pain;
How am I dup'd? I wakeful listen round,
And think I hear her in each casual sound.
Perish the wiles of Love and arts of dress!
In russet weeds I'll shrowd my wretchedness.
The wiles of love, and arts of dress are vain,
My fair to soften, and admittance gain."
Youth, weep no more; your eyes are swoln with tears;
No more complain; for O! she stops her ears.
The gods, I warn you, hate the haughty fair,
Reject their incense, and deny their prayer.
This youth, this Marathus, who wears your chains,
Late laugh'd at love, and ridicul'd its pains!
Th' impatient lover in the street would stay!
Nor dreamt that vengeance would his crimes repay.
Now, now he moans his past misdeeds with tears,
A prey to love, and all its frantic fears:
Now he exclaims at female-scorn and hate;
And from his soul abhors a bolted gate!
Like vengeance waits you; trust th' unerring Muse,
If still you're coy, and still access refuse!
Then how you'll wish, when old, contemn'd of all,
But vainly wish, these moments to recal!

THE TENTH ELEGY.

Why did you swear by all the powers above?
Yet never meant to crown my longing love.
Wretch, tho' at first the perjur'd deed you hide,
Wrath comes with certain, tho' with tardy stride;
Yet, yet, offended gods, my charmer spare!
Yet pardon the first fault of one so fair!
For gold the careful farmer ploughs the plain,
And joins his oxen to the cumbrous wane;
For gold, thro' seas that stormy winds obey,
By stars, the sailor steers his watery way.
Yet, gracious gods, this gold from man remove,
That wicked metal brib'd the fair I love.
Soon shall you suffer greatly for your crime,
A weary wanderer in a foreign clime;
Your hair shall change, and boasted bloom decay,
By wintry tempests, and the solar ray.
"Beware of gold, how oft did I advise?
From tempting gold what mighty mischiefs rise?
Love's generous power," I said, "with ten-fold pain
The wretch will rack, who sells her charms for gain.
Let torture all her cruelties exert,
Torture is pastime to a venal heart.
"Nor idly dream your gallantries to hide,
The gods are ever on the sufferer's side.

With sleep or wine o'ercome, so fate ordains,
You'll blab the secret of your impious gains."
Thus oft I warn'd you; this augments my shame;
My sighs, tears, homage, henceforth I disclaim.
"No wealth shall bribe my constancy," you swore,
"Be mine the bard," you sigh'd, "I crave no more:
Not all Campania shall my heart entice,
For thee Campania's autumns I despise.
Let Bacchus in Falernian vineyards stray,
Not Bacchus' vineyards shall my faith betray."
Such strong professions, in so soft a strain,
Might well deceive a captivated swain;
Such strong professions might aversion charm,
Slow doubt determine, and indifference warm.
Nay more, you wept, unpractis'd to betray,
I kiss'd your cheeks, and wip'd the tears away.
But if I tempting gold unjustly blame,
And you have left me for another flame;
May he, like you, seem kind, like you deceive,
And O may you, like cheated me, believe.
Oft I by night the torch myself would bear,
That none our tender converse might o'erhear;
When least expected, oft some youth I led,
A youth all beauty, to the genial bed,
And tutor'd him your conquest to complete,
By soft enticements, and a fond deceit.
By these, I foolish hop'd to gain your love!
Who than Tibullus could more cautious prove?
Fir'd with uncommon powers I swept the lyre,
And sent you melting strains of soft desire:
The thought o'erspreads my face with conscious shame,
Doom, doom them victims to the seas or flame.
No verse be theirs, who love's soft fires profane,
And sell inestimable joys for gain.
But you who first the lovely maid decoy'd,
By each adulterer be your wife enjoy'd.
And when each youth has rifled all her charms,
May bed-gowns guard her from your loathed arms!
May she, O may she like your sister prove,
As fam'd for drinking, far more fam'd for love!
'Tis true, the bottle is her chief delight,
She knows no better way to pass the night;
Your wife more knowing, can the night improve,
To joys of Bacchus joins the joys of love.
Think'st thou for thee, the toilette is her care?
For thee, that fillets bind her well-dress'd hair?
For thee, that Tyrian robes her charms enfold?
For thee, her arms are deck'd with burnish'd gold?
By these, some youth the wanton would entice,
For him she dresses, and for him she sighs;
To him she prostitutes, unaw'd by shame,
Your house, your pocket, and your injur'd fame:
Nor blame her conduct, say, ye young, what charms
Can beauty taste in gout and age's arms?
Less nice my fair-one, she for money can
Caress a gouty impotent old man;
O thou, by generous love too justly blam'd!
All, all that love could give, my passion claim'd.
Yet since thou could'st so mercenary prove,
The more deserving shall engross my love;
Then thou wilt weep when these ador'd you see;
Weep on, thy tears will transport give to me.
To Venus I'll suspend a golden shield,
With this inscription grav'd upon the field.
"Tibullus, freed at last from amorous woes,
This offering, queen of bliss, on thee bestows:
And humbly begs, that henceforth thou wilt guard,
From such a passion, thy devoted bard."

THE ELEVENTH ELEGY.

WHO was the first that forg'd the deadly blade?
Of rugged steel his savage soul was made;
By him, his bloody flag Ambition wav'd,
And grisly Carnage thro' the battle rav'd:
Yet wherefore blame him? we're ourselves to blame;
Arms first were forg'd to kill the savage game:
Death-dealing battles were unknown of old;
Death-dealing battles took their rise from gold;
When beachen bowls on oaken tables stood,
When temperate acorns were our father's food;
The swain slept peaceful, with his flocks around,
No trench was open'd, and no fortress frown'd.
O had I liv'd in gentle days like these,
To love devoted, and to home-felt ease;
Compell'd I had not been those arms to wear,
Nor had the trumpet forc'd me from the fair:
But now I'm dragg'd to war, perhaps my foe
E'en now prepares th' inevitable blow!
Come then, paternal gods, whose help I've known
From birth to manhood, still protect your own,
Nor blush, my gods, tho' carv'd of ancient wood,
So carv'd in our fore-fathers times you stood;
And though in no proud temples you were prais'd,
Nor foreign incense on your altar blaz'd;
Yet white-rob'd Faith conducted every swain;
Yet meek ey'd Piety seren'd the plain;
While clustering grapes, or wheat-wreaths round your hair,
Appeas'd your anger, and engag'd your care:
Or dulcet cakes himself the farmer paid,
When crown'd his wishes by your powerful aid;
While his fair daughter, brought with her from home,
The luscious offering of a honey-comb:
If now you'll aid me in the hour of need,
Your care I'll recompense—a boar shall bleed.
In white array'd I'll myrtle baskets bear,
And myrtle foliage round my temples wear:
In arms redoutable let others shine,
By Mars protected mow the hostile line;
You let me please, my head with roses crown,
And every care in flowing goblets drown;
Then when I'm joyous let the soldier tell,
What foes were captiv'd, and what leaders fell;
Or on the board describe with flowing wine,
The furious onset, and the flying line.
For Reason whispers, "Why will short-liv'd man
By war contract his too contracted span?"
Yet when he leaves the chearful realms of light,
No laughing bowls, no harvests cheer the sight,
But howl the damn'd, the triple monster roars,
And Charon grumbles on the Stygian shores:
By fiery lakes, the blasted phantoms yell,
Or shrowd their anguish in the depths of Hell.
In a thatch'd cottage happier he by far,
Who never hears of arms, of gold, or war,
His chaste embrace a numerous offspring crown,
He courts not Fortune's smile, nor dreads her frown;
While lenient baths at home his wife prepares,
He, and his sons, attend their fleecy cares,
As old, as poor, as peaceful may I be,
So guard my flocks, and such an offspring see.
Mean-time, soft Peace, descend, O! bless our plains!
Soft Peace to plough with oxen taught the swains.

Peace plants the orchard, and matures the vine,
And first gay-laughing prest the ruddy wine;
The father quaffs, deep quaff his joyous friends,
Yet to his son a well-stor'd vault descends. [joy!
Bright shine the plough-share, our support and
But rust, deep rust, the veteran's arms destroy!
The villager (his sacred offerings paid
In the dark grove, and consecrated shade,)
His wife and sons, now darkness parts the throng,
Drives home, and whistles, as he reels along.
Then triumphs Venus; then love-feuds prevail;
The youth all jealous then the fair assail;
Doors, windows fly, no deference they pay,
The chastest suffer in th' ungentle fray:
These beat their breasts, and melt in moving tears;
The lover weeps, and blames his rage and fears;
Love sits between, unmov'd with tears and sighs,
And with incentives sly the feud supplies.
Ye youths, though stung with taunts, of blows beware;
They, they are impious, who can beat the fair:
If much provok'd, or rend their silken zone,
Or on their tresses, be your anger shown:
But if nor this your passion can appease,
Until the charmer weep, the charmer tease!
Blest anger, if the fair dissolves in tears!
Blest youth, her fondness undisguis'd appears!
But crush the wretch, O War, with all thy woes,
Who to rough usage adds the crime of blows.
Bland Peace descend, with plenty on our plains,
And bless with ease and laughing sport the swains.

BOOK II.

ADVERTISEMENT.

This book, though shorter than the former, is not inferior to it in point of poetical fancy and amorous tenderness; the numbers flow with the same easy correctness, and perhaps the sentiments are more delicate; for, being wholly dedicated to rural devotion, friendship, and love, the reader will meet with nothing in it offensive to the strictest chastity.

ELEGY THE FIRST.

Attend! and favour! as our sires ordain;
The fields we lustrate, and the rising grain:
Come, Bacchus, and thy horns with grapes surround;
Come, Ceres, with thy wheaten garland crown'd;
This hallow'd day suspend each swain his toil,
Rest let the plough, and rest th' uncultur'd soil:
Unyoke the steer, his racks heap high with hay,
And deck with wreaths his honest front to day.
Be all your thoughts to this grand work apply'd!
And lay, ye thrifty fair, your wool aside!
Hence I command you mortals from the rite,
Who spent in amorous blandishment the night,
The vernal powers in chastity delight.
But come, ye pure, in spotless garb array'd!
For you the solemn festival is made!
Come! follow thrice the victim round the lands!
In running water purify your hands!
See! to the flames the willing victim come!
Ye swains with olive crown'd, be dumb! be dumb!
"From ills, O sylvan gods, our limits shield,
To day we purge the farmer and the field;
O let no weeds destroy the rising grain;
By no fell prowler be the lambkin slain;
So shall the hind dread penury no more;
But gaily smiling o'er his plenteous store,
With liberal hand shall larger billets bring,
Heap the broad hearth, and hail the genial spring.
His numerous bond-slaves all in goodly rows,
With wicker huts your altars shall enclose. [play,
That done, they'll cheerly laugh and dance, and
And praise your goodness in their uncouth lay."
The gods assent! see! see! those entrails show,
That Heaven approves of what is done below!
Now quaff Falernian, let my Chian wine,
Pour'd from the cask in massy goblets shine!
Drink deep, my friends; all, all, be madly gay,
'Twere irreligion not to reel to day!
Health to Messala, every peasant toast,
And not a letter of his name be lost! [grace,
O come, my friend, whom Gallic triumphs
Thou noblest splendour of an ancient race;
Thou whom the arts all emulously crown,
Sword of the state, and honour of the gown;
My theme is gratitude, inspire my lays!
O be my genius! while I strive to praise
The rural deities, the rural plain,
The use of foodful corn they taught the swain.
They taught man first the social hut to raise,
And thatch it o'er with turf, or leafy sprays:
They first to tame the furious bull essay'd,
And on rude wheels the rolling carriage laid.
Man left his savage ways; the garden glow'd,
Fruits not their own admiring trees bestow'd,
While thro' the thirsty ground meandring runnel flow'd.
There bees of sweets despoil the breathing spring,
And to their cells the dulcet plunder bring.
The ploughman first to sooth the toilsome day,
Chanted in measur'd feet his sylvan lay:
And, seed-time o'er, he first in blithesome vein,
Pip'd to his household gods the hymning strain.
Then first the press with purple wine o'er-ran,
And cooling water made it fit for man.
The village-lad first made a wreath of flowers
To deck in spring the tutelary powers:
Blest be the country, yearly there the plain
Yields, when the Dog-star burns, the golden grain:
Thence too thy chorus, Bacchus, first began,
The painted clown first laid the tragic plan.
A goat, the leader of the shaggy throng,
The village sent it, recompens'd the song.
There too the sheep his woolly treasure wears;
There too the swain his woolly treasure shears;
This to the thrifty dame long work supplies;
The distaff hence, and basket took their rise.
Hence too the various labours of the loom,
Thy praise, Minerva, and Arachne's doom!
'Mid mountain herds Love first drew vital air,
Unknown to man, and man had nought to fear;
'Gainst herds, his bow th' unskilful archer drew;
Ah my pierc'd heart, an archer now too true!
Now herds may roam untouch'd, 'tis Cupid's joy,
The brave to vanquish, and to fix the coy.
The youth whose heart the soft emotion feels,
Nor sighs for wealth, nor waits at grandeur's heels:
Age fir'd by love is touch'd by shame no more,
But blabs its follies at the fair one's door!
Led by soft love, the tender trembling fair
Steals to her swain, and cheats suspicion's care,
With out-stretch'd arms she wins her darkling
And tip-toe listens that no noise betray! [way,

Ah wretched those, on whom dread Cupid frowns!
How happy they, whose mutual choice he crowns!
Will Love partake the banquet of the day?
O come—but throw thy burning shafts away.
Ye swains, begin to mighty Love the song,
Your songs, ye swains, to mighty Love belong!
Breathe out aloud your wishes for my fold,
Your own soft vows in whispers may be told.
But hark! loud mirth and music fire the crowd—
Ye now may venture to request aloud!
Pursue your sports; night mounts her curtain'd wane;
The dancing stars compose her filial train
Black muffled sleep steals on with silent pace,
And dreams flit last, imagination's race!

THE SECOND ELEGY.

Rise, happy morn, without a cloud arise!
This morn, Cornutus blest his mother's eyes!
Hence each unholy wish, each adverse sound,
As we his altar's hallowed verge surround!
Let rich Arabian odours scent the skies,
And sacred incense from his altar rise;
Implor'd, thou tutelary god, descend!
And deck'd with flowery wreaths the rites attend!
Then as his brows with precious unguents flow,
Sweet sacred cakes and liberal wine bestow.
O Genius, grant whate'er my friend desires:
The cake is scatter'd, and the flame aspires!
Ask then, my noble friend, whate'er you want:
What silent still? your prayer the god will grant:
Uncovetous of rural wide domains,
You beg no woody hills, no cultur'd plains:
Not venal, you request no eastern stores,
Where ruddy waters lave the gemmy shores:
Your wish I guess; you wish a beauteous spouse,
Joy of your joy, and faithful to your vows.
'Tis done! my friend! see nuptial Love appears!
See! in his hand a yellow zone he bears!
A yellow zone, that spite of years shall last,
And heighten fondness, e'en when beauty's past.
With happy signs, great power, confirm our prayer,
With endless concord bless the married pair.
O grant, dread Genius, that a numerous race
Of beauteous infants crown their fond embrace;
Their beauteous infants round thy feet shall play,
And keep with custom'd rites this happy day.

THE THIRD ELEGY.

My fair, Cornutus, to the country's flown,
Oh how insipid is the city grown!
No taste have they for elegance refin'd;
No tender bosoms, who remain behind:
Now Cytherea glads the laughing plain,
And smiles and sports compose her sylvan train.
Now Cupid joins to learn the ploughman's phrase,
And clad a peasant o'er the fallows strays.
O how the weighty prong I'll busy wield!
Should the fair wander to the labour'd field;
A farmer then the crooked plough-share hold,
Whilst the dull ox prepares the vigorous mould:
I'd not complain tho' Phœbus burnt the lands,
And painful blisters swell'd my tender hands.
Admetus' herds the fair Apollo drove,
In spite of med'cines power, a prey to love;
Nor aught avail'd to sooth his amorous care,
His lyre of silver sound, or waving hair.
To quench their thirst, the kine to streams he led,
And drove them from their pasture to the shed:
The milk to curdle, then, the fair he taught,
And from the cheese to strain the dulcet draught.
Oft, oft his virgin-sister blush'd for shame,
As bearing lambkins o'er the field he came!
Oft would he sing the list'ning vales among,
Till lowing oxen broke the plaintive song.
To Delphi, trembling anxious chiefs repair,
But got no answer, Phœbus was not there.
Thy curling locks that charm'd a step-dame's eye,
A jealous step-dame, now neglected fly!
To see thee, Phœbus, thus disfigur'd stray!
Who could discover the fair god of day?
Constrain'd by Cupid in a cot to pine,
Where was thy Delos, where thy Pythian shrine?
Thrice happy days, when Love almighty sway'd!
And openly the gods his will obey'd.
Now Love's soft power 's become a common jest—
Yet those, who feel his influence in their breast,
The prude's contempt, the wiseman's sneer despise,
Nor would his chains forego, to rule the skies.
Curst farm! that forc'd my Nemesis from town,
Blasts taint thy vines, and rains thy harvests drown.
Though hymns implore your aid, great god of wine,
Assist the lover, and neglect the vine;
To shades, unpunish'd, ne'er let beauty stray;
Not all your vintage can its absence pay!
Rather than harvest should the fair detain,
May rills and acorns feed th' inactive swain!
The swains of old no golden Ceres knew,
And yet how fervent was their love and true?
Their melting vows the Paphian queen approv'd,
And every valley witness'd how they lov'd.
Then lurk'd no spies to catch the willing maid;
Doorless each house; in vain no shepherd pray'd.
Once more ye simple usages obtain!
No—lead me, drive me to the cultur'd plain!
Enchain me, whip me, if the fair command;
Whipp'd, and enchain'd, I'll plough the stubborn land!

THE FOURTH ELEGY.

Chains, and a haughty fair I fearless view!
Hopes of paternal freedom all adieu.
Ah when will Love compassionate my woes?
In one sad ténour my existence flows:
Whether I kiss or bite the galling chain,
Alike my pleasure, and alike my pain.
I burn, I burn! oh banish my despair!
Oh ease my torture, too too cruel fair:
Rather than feel such vast, such matchless woe,
I'd rise some rock o'erspread with endless snow!
Or frown a cliff on some disastrous shore,
Where ships are wreck'd, and tempests ever roar!
In pensive gloominess I pass the night,
Nor feel contentment at the dawn of light.
What tho' the god of verse my woes indite,
What tho' I soothing elegies can write,
No strains of elegy her pride control;
Gold is the passport to her venal soul.
I ask not of the Nine the epic lay;
Ye Nine! or aid my passion, or away.
I ask not to describe in lofty strain,
The Sun's eclipses, or the lunar wane;
To win admission to the haughty maid,
Alone I crave your elegiac aid;

But if she still contemns the tearful lay,
Ye, and your elegies, away, away!
In vain I ask, but gold ne'er asks in vain;
Then will I desolate the world for gain!
For gold, I'll impious plunder every shrine;
But chief, O Venus, will I plunder thine!
By thee compell'd I love a venal maid,
And quit for bloody fields my peaceful shade:
By thee compell'd, I rob the hallowed shrine,
Then chiefly, Venus, will I plunder thine!
Perish the man! whose curst industrious toil
Or finds the gem, or dyes the woolly spoil;
Hence, hence the sex's avarice arose,
And art with nature not enough bestows:
Hence, the fierce dog was posted for a guard,
The fair grew venal, and their gates were barr'd.
But weighty presents vigilance o'ercome,
The gate bursts open, and the dog is dumb.
From venal charms, ye gods! what mischiefs flow?
The joy, how much o'er-balanc'd by the woe!
Hence, hence so few, sweet Love, frequent thy fane,
Hence impious slander loads thy guiltless reign.
But ye! who sell your heavenly charms for hire,
Your ill-got riches be consum'd with fire!
May not one lover strive to quench the blaze,
But smile malicious, as o'er all it preys!
And, when ye die, no gentle friend be near
To catch your breath, or shed a genuine tear!
Behind the corpse, to march in solemn show,
Or Syrian odours on the pile bestow.
Far other fates attend the generous maid;
Tho' age and sickness bid her beauties fade,
Still she's rever'd; and when death's easy call
Has freed her spirit from life's anxious thrall,
The pitying neighbours all her loss deplore,
And many a weeping friend besets the door;
While some old lover touch'd with grateful woe,
Shall yearly garlands on her tomb bestow;
And home returning, thus the fair address,
"Light may the turf thy gentle bosom press."
'Tis truth; but what has truth with love to do?
Imperious Cupid, I submit to you!
To sell my father's seat should you command;
Adieu my father's gods, my father's land!
From madding mares, whate'er of poison flows,
Or on the forehead of their offspring grows,
Whate'er Medea brew'd of baleful juice,
What noxious herbs Æmathian hills produce;
Of all, let Nemesis a draught compose,
Or mingle poisons, feller still than those;
If she but smile, the deadly cup I'll drain,
Forget her av'rice, and exult in pain!

THE FIFTH ELEGY.

To hear our solemn vows, O Phœbus deign!
A novel pontiff treads thy sacred fane:
Nor distant hear, dread power! 'tis Rome's request,
That with thy golden lyre thou stand'st confest:
Deign mighty bard! to strike the vocal string,
And praise thy pontiff; we, his praises sing:
Around thy brows, triumphant laurels twine,
Thine altar visit, and thy rites divine:
New flush thy charms, new curl thy waving hair;
O come the god in vestment, and in air!
When Saturn was dethron'd, so crown'd with bays,
So rob'd, thou sung'st th' almighty victor's praise.
What fate, from gods and man, has wrapt in night,
Prophetic flashes on thy mental sight:
From thee, diviners learn their prescient lore,
On reeking bowels, as they thoughtful pore:
The seer thou teachest the success of things,
As flies the bird, or feeds, or screams, or sings:
The Sibyl-leaves if Rome ne'er sought in vain;
Thou gav'st a meaning to the mystic strain:
Thy sacred influence may this pontiff know,
And as he reads them, with the prophet glow.
When great Æneas snatch'd his aged sire,
And burning Lares, from the Grecian fire,
She [1], she foretold this empire fix'd by fate,
And all the triumphs of the Roman state;
Yet when he saw his Ilion wrapp'd in flame,
He scarce could credit the mysterious dame.
(Quirinus had not plann'd eternal Rome,
Nor had his brother met his early doom,
Where now Jove's temple swells, low hamlets stood,
And domes ascend, where heifers cropp'd their food.
Sprinkled with milk, Pan grac'd an oak's dun shade,
And scythe-arm'd Pales watch'd the mossy glade;
For help from Pan, to Pan on ev'ry bough
Pipes hung, the grateful shepherd's vocal vow,
Of reeds, still lessening, was the gift compos'd,
And friendly wax th' unequal junctures clos'd.
So where Velabrian streets like cities seem,
One little wherry plied the lazy stream,
O'er which the wealthy shepherd's favourite maid
Was to her swain, on holidays, convey'd;
The swain, his truth of passion to declare,
Or lamb, or cheese, presented to the fair.)

The Cumæan Sibyl speaks.

"Fierce brother of the power of soft desire,
Who fly'st, with Trojan gods, the Grecian fire!
Now Jove assigns thee Laurentine abodes,
Those friendly plains invite thy banish'd gods!
There shall a nobler Troy herself applaud,
Admire her wanderings, and the Grecian fraud!
There, thou from yonder sacred stream shalt rise
A god thyself, and mingle with the skies!
No more thy Phrygians for their country sigh,
See conquest o'er your shatter'd navy fly!
See the Rutulian tents, a mighty blaze!
Thou, Turnus! soon shalt end thy hateful days!
The camp I see, Lavinium greets my view!
And Alba! brave Ascanius! built by you:
I see thee, Ilia! leave the vestal fire;
And, clasp'd by Mars, in amorous bliss expire!
On Tyber's bank, thy sacred robes I see,
And arms abandon'd, eager god! by thee.
Your hills crop fast, ye herds! while fate allows;
Eternal Rome shall rise, where now ye brouse:
Rome, that shall stretch her irresistless reign,
Wherever Ceres views her golden grain;
Far as the east extends his purple ray,
And where the west shuts up the gates of day.
The truth I sing; so may the laurels prove
Safe food, and I be screen'd from guilty love."
Thus sung the Sibyl, and address'd her prayer,
Phœbus! to thee, and madding, loos'd her hair.
Nor, Phœbus! give him only these to know,
A farther knowledge on thy priest bestow:
Let him interpret what thy fav'rite maid,
What Amalthea, what Mermessia said:
Let him interpret what Albuna bore
Thro' Tyber's waves, unwet, to Tyber's farthest shore.

[1] The Sybil.

When stony tempests fell, when comets glar'd,
Intestine wars their oracles declar'd:
The sacred groves (our ancestors relate)
Foretold the changes of the Roman state:
To charge the clarion sounded in the sky,
Arms clash'd, blood ran, and warriors seem'd to die:
With monstrous prodigies the year began:
An annual darkness the whole globe o'er-ran;
Apollo, shorn of every beamy ray,
Oft strove, but strove in vain, to light the day:
The statues of the gods wept tepid tears;
And speaking oxen fill'd mankind with fears!
These were of old: No more, Apollo! frown,
But in the waves each adverse omen drown.
O! let thy bays in crackling flames ascend;
So shall the year with joy begin and end!
The bays give prosp'rous signs; rejoice ye swains!
Propitious Ceres shall reward your pains.
With must the jolly rustic purpled o'er,
Shall squeeze rich clusters, which their tribute pour,
Till vats are wanting to contain their store.
Far hence, ye wolves! the mellow shepherds bring
Their gifts to Pales, and her praises sing.
Now, fir'd with wine, they solemn bonfires raise,
And leap, untimorous, thro' the strawy blaze!
From every cot, unnumber'd children throng,
Frequent the dance, and louder raise the song:
And while in mirth the hours they thus employ,
At home the grandsire tends his little boy;
And in each feature pleas'd himself to trace,
Foretels his prattler will adorn the race.
The sylvan youth, their grateful homage paid,
Where plays some streamlet, seek th' embowering shade;
Or stretch'd on soft enamel'd meadows lie,
Where thickest umbrage cools the summer-sky:
With roses, see! the sacred cup is crown'd,
Hark! music breathes her animating sound:
The couch of turf, and festal tables stand
Of turf, erected by each shepherd-hand;
And all well-pleas'd, the votive feast prepare,
Each one his goblet, and each one his share.
Now drunk, they blame their stars and curse the maid;
But sober, deprecate whate'er they said.
Perish thy shafts, Apollo! and thy bow,
If Love unarmed in our forests go.
Yet since he learn'd to wing th' unerring dart,
Much cause has man to curse his fatal art:
But most have I; the Sun has wheel'd his round
Since first I felt the deadly festering wound;
Yet yet I fondly, madly, wish to burn,
Abjure indifference, and at comfort spurn;
And tho' from Nemesis my genius flows;
Her scarce I sing, so weighty are my woes!
O cruel Love! how joyous should I be,
Your arrows broke, and torch extinct to see!
From you, my want of reverence to the skies!
From you, my woes and imprecations rise!
Yet I advise you, too relentless fair!
(As Heaven protects the bards) a bard to spare!
E'en now, the pontiff claims my loftiest lay,
In triumph, soon he'll mount the sacred way.
Then pictur'd towns shall show successful war,
And spoils and chiefs attend his ivory car:
Myself will bear the laurel in my hand;
And pleas'd, amid the pleas'd spectators stand:
While war-worn veterans, with laurels crown'd,
With Io-triumphs shake the streets around.
His father hails him, as he rides along,
And entertains with pompous shows the throng.
O Phœbus! kindly deign to grant my prayer;
So may'st thou ever wave thy curled hair;
So ever may thy virgin-sister's name
Preserve the lustre of a spotless fame.

THE SIXTH ELEGY.

MACER campaigns; who now will thee obey
O Love! if Macer dare forego thy sway?
Put on the crest, and grasp the burnish'd shield,
Pursue the base deserter to the field:
Or if to winds he gives the loosen'd sail,
Mount thou the deck, and risk the stormy gale:
To dare desert thy sweetly-pleasing pains!
For stormy seas, or sanguinary plains!
'Tis Cupid! thine, the wanderer to reclaim,
Regain thy honour, and avenge thy name!
If such thou spar'st, a soldier I will be,
The meanest soldier, and abandon thee.
Adieu, ye trifling loves! farewel, ye fair!
The trumpet charms me, I to camps repair;
The martial look, the martial garb assume,
And see the laurel on my forehead bloom!
My vaunts how vain! debarr'd the cruel maid,
The warrior softens, and my laurels fade.
Piqu'd to the soul, how frequent have I swore,
Her gate so servile to approach no more?
Unconscious what I did, I still return'd,
Was still deny'd access, and yet I burn'd!
Ye youths, whom Love commands with angry sway,
Attend his wars, like me, and pleas'd obey.
This iron age approves his sway no more:
All fly to camps for gold, and gold adore:
Yet God clothes kindred states in hostile arms!
Hence blood and death, confusion and alarms!
Mankind, for lust of gold, at once defy
The naval combat, and the stormy sky!
The soldier hopes, by martial spoils, to gain
Flocks without number, and a rich domain:
His hopes obtain'd by every horrid crime,
He seeks for marble in each foreign clime:
A thousand yoke sustain'd the pillar'd freight,
And Rome, surpris'd, beholds th' enormous weight.
Let such with moles the furious deep enclose,
Where fish may swim unhurt, tho' winter blows:
Let flocks and villas call the spoiler lord!
And be the spoiler by the fair ador'd!
Let one we know, a whipp'd barbarian slave,
Live like a king, with kingly pride behave!
Be ours the joys of economic ease,
From bloody fields remote, and stormy seas!
In gold, alas! the venal fair delight!
Since beauty sighs for spoil, for spoil I'll fight!
In all my plunder Nemesis shall shine,
Yours be the profit, be the peril mine:
To deck your heavenly charms the silk-worm dies,
Embroidery labours, and the shuttle flies!
For you be rifled ocean's pearly store!
To you Pactolus send his golden ore!
Ye Indians! blacken'd by the nearer sun,
Before her steps in splendid liveries run;
For you shall wealthy Tyre and Afric vie,
To yield the purple, and the scarlet dye.

THE SEVENTH ELEGY.

THOUSANDS in death would seek an end of woe,
But Hope, deceitful Hope! prevents the blow!

Hope plants the forest, and she sows the plain;
And feeds, with future granaries, the swain;
Hope snares the winged vagrants of the sky,
Hope cheats in reedy brooks the scaly fry;
By Hope, the fetter'd slave, the drudge of fate,
Sings, shakes his irons, and forgets his state;
Hope promis'd you, you haughty still deny;
Yield to the goddess, O my fair! comply.
Hope whisper'd me, " Give sorrow to the wind!
" The haughty fair-one shall at last be kind."
Yet, yet you treat me with the same disdain:
O let not Hope's soft whispers prove in vain!
Untimely fate your sister snatch'd away;
Spare me, O spare me, by her shade I pray!
So shall my garlands deck her virgin-tomb;
So shall I weep, no hypocrite, her doom!
" So may her grave with rising flowers be drest,
" And the green turf lie lightly on her breast[1].
Ah me! will nought avail? the world I'll fly,
And, prostrate at her tomb, a suppliant sigh!
To her attentive ghost, of you complain;
Tell my long sorrowing, tell of your disdain:
Oft, when alive, in my behalf she spoke:
Your endless coyness must her shade provoke:
With ugly dreams she'll haunt your hour of rest,
And weep before you an unwelcome guest!
Ghastly and pale, as when besmear'd with blood,
Oh fatal fall! she pass'd the Stygian flood.
No more, my strains! your eyes with tears o'erflow,
This moving object renovates your woe:
You, you are guiltless! I your maid accuse;
You generous are! she, she has selfish views.
Nay, were you guilty, I'll no more complain;
One tear from you o'erpays a life of pain!
She, Phryne, promis'd to promote my vows:
She took, but never gave my billet-doux.
You're gone abroad, she confidently swears,
Oft when your sweet-ton'd voice salutes mine ears:
Or, when you promise to reward my pains,
That you're afraid, or indispos'd, she feigns:
Then madding jealousy inflames my breast;
Then fancy represents a rival blest;
I wish thee, Phryne! then, a thousand woes;
And if the gods with half my wishes close,
Phryne! a wretch of wretches thou shalt be,
And vainly beg of death to set thee free.

INTRODUCTION

TO THE THIRD BOOK.

Some words in the elegies of this book are of that sort, which are frequently used by the best writers catachrestically, sometimes denoting more lax, sometimes more intimate relations. The difficulty of ascertaining the sense in which Tibullus has used them, has thrown a seeming obscurity on a poet, who will ever have the first place amongst the wits of Greece and Rome, for elegant simplicity; and has caused such illustrious annotators as Scaliger, Lipsius, and Muretus, to stumble. The great difficulty is contained in the following lines; and if this can be cleared up, all the rest will be easy and intelligible. El. I. lin. 23.

Hæc tibi vir quondam, nunc frater, casta Neæra,
Mittit, & accipias munera parva, rogat.
Teque suis jurat caram magis esse medullis,
Sive sibi conjunx sive futura soror.
Sed potius conjunx hujus spem nominis illi
Auferet extincto pallida ditis aqua.

Where it is first inquired, what is meant by *frater* and *soror?* It is readily seen, that they cannot be understood in their primitive sense, because a marriage betwixt brother and sister would never have been tolerated at Rome: the very thoughts of it would have been regarded with abhorrence. These words sometimes mean cousin-germans, and in this sense Muretus here understands them; but this is too cold and unanimated to be admitted into poetry, or to flow from the pen of Tibullus, when he is expressing the tender feelings of a fond doating lover. It is much more probable, that he designed to represent by them one of those delicate connections, which have their foundation in the will and the affections; that by *frater* he would have us to understand a fond admirer; and by *soror*, a beloved mistress, who had entertained a reciprocal kindness and esteem for her lover. This sense of the words is familiar to most languages. Nothing can be more full to this purpose than what we meet with in the canticles of Solomon,—"Thou hast ravished my heart, my sister, my spouse,"—ch. iv. ver. 9. and in several other places.

Ovid also has used the words in this sense:

Alloquor Hermione nuper fratremque virumque,
Nunc fratrem, nomen conjugis alter habet.

And the Greeks had so accustomed themselves to this use of them, that we find their Venus has a title given her by Lycophron, which his scholiast explains by " την αδελφοποιον, the author of brotherly associations." And assigns this pretty whimsical reason for it: " For a commerce in love matters makes those who were strangers, brothers; and those who would carry on an amorous commerce secretly, say of one they favour he is my brother, he is my relation."

Having solved, we hope, this difficulty, we shall next consider what is the import of *vir* and *conjunx*. They certainly were designed to express some nearer connection, some closer tie, than mere friendship, or whatever else is comprehended in *frater* and *soror*. The epithet *casta*, given to Neæra, will not permit us to understand them of any loose amour; that title never could belong to a jilt, who had granted favours to one lover, and, upon some caprice, had thrown herself into the arms of another: but divorces were common enough at Rome, so that even a wife might dismiss her husband upon some displeasure taken, at least before actual matrimony, without hurting her reputation by it: so that I think husband and wife are the true meaning of *vir* and *conjunx*.

This interpretation however is not without difficulties: the silence of antiquity, and several other circumstances, make the marriage of Tibullus appear improbable; it has therefore been supposed by Lipsius, that *quondam* was intended to express future, and not past time. It cannot be denied, that it is sometimes thus used; but it more commonly signifies the time past, or formerly; and to understand it otherwise here, would

[1] Pope's verses To the Memory of an unfortunate Lady. *C.*

make the construction harsh and ungrammatical. In further confirmation of this, it appears that the following elegies of this book relate to the same persons and the same distress: they were probably the new-year's gift which Lygdamus, by the advice of the Muses, proposes to send to Neæra: now these furnish us with passages which can be understood of nothing else but a marriage-contract, and a subsequent separation: thus, in El. II. we find,

> Sed veniat caræ matris comitata dolore,
> Mæreat hæc genero, mæreat illa viro.

And again,

> Lygdamus hic situs est, dolor huic & cura Neæræ
> Conjugis ereptæ causa perire fuit.

In the third Elegy,

> Oh niveam quæ te poterit mihi reddere lucem,

And again,

> Aut, si fata negant reditum tristesque sorores.

In El. iv.

> Nec gaudet casta nupta Neæra domo.

One must torture these passages extremely, to make them consistent with any thing else but a previous marriage, or at least a very solemn contract. Was Tibullus then married? or did he intend at all to marry Neæra? I am not inclined to think so, as none of the ancient writers have given us the least hint of it. But the poet is not tied down to actual life:

> Pictoribus atque poetis
> Quid libet audendi semper fuit æqua potestas.

The sacrifice of Iphigenia at Aulis, is probably a mere fable; and yet what noble, what affecting, what interesting scenes of distress have both the tragedian and painter formed upon it? And might not Tibullus, to indulge his plaintive humour, and to display the soft feelings of his soul, chuse to represent himself in a situation that forms one of the most melting and agonizing distresses, to be found amongst those beds of thorns and roses which Love prepares for his capricious votaries? A beloved wife, grown dearer by more intimate acquaintance, charming without the help of artifice, and rooted in the soul by a thousand repeated endearments, torn from the arms of an enraptured husband, whilst he still doats upon her, and ready to be sacrificed to another;—what feeling heart but shudders at the thought?—especially when the delicate affecting colours are laid on by the pencil of Tibullus? The names certainly are fictitious; Neæra was as trite a name for a mistress in Rome, as Phyllis or Cloe with our modern sonnetteers. And what confirms me in the opinion, that the distress painted in these elegies is also fictitious, so far as Tibullus is concerned in it, is, that Ovid, in his poem on Tibullus's death, takes notice of no other mistress but Delia and Nemesis; to one of whom he assigns the last, to the other the first interest in him, without any intermediate favourite.

> Sic Nemesis longum, sic Delia nomen habebit:
> Altera cura recens, altera primus amor.

Ovid seems to have carefully searched out every curious particular of Tibullus's life, and therefore could not have overlooked so striking a circumstance as the distresses celebrated in these Elegies, if they had really happened to Tibullus. He and his cotemporaries of the Augustan age, were probably well informed of the true reason of Tibullus's composing the following book. Some such distress might have happened, and been much talked of in Rome; and Tibullus might seize upon it as a favourable opportunity for displaying his elegiac genius in its full lustre. Propertius has made the same use of the misfortunes of a noble family, in the twelfth Elegy of Book iv. It is a common artifice with delicate writers, to sigh and tell a piteous tale, while their hearts are not at all affected.

BOOK III.

ELEGY THE FIRST.

POET.

THY calends, Mars! are come, from whence of old,
The year's beginning our forefathers told:
Now various gifts thro' every house impart,
The pleasing tokens of the friendly heart.
To my Neæra, tuneful virgins! say,
What shall I give, what honour shall I pay?
Dear, e'en if fickle; dearer, if my friend!
To the lov'd fair, what present shall I send?

MUSES.

Gold wins the venal, verse the lovely maid:
In your smooth numbers be her charms display'd.
On polish'd ivory let the sheets be roll'd,
Your name in signature, the edges gold.
No pumice spare to smooth each parchment scroll,
In a gay wrapper then secure the whole.
Thus to adorn your poems be your care;
And thus adorn'd, transmit them to the fair.

POET.

Fair maids of Pindus! I your counsel praise:
As you advise me, I'll adorn my lays:
But by your streams, and by your shades, I pray,
Yourselves the volume to the fair convey.
O let it lowly at her feet be laid,
Ere the gilt wrapper, or the edges fade;
Then let her tell me, if her flames decline,
If quite extinguish'd, or if still she's mine.
But first your graceful salutations paid,
In terms submissive thus address the maid:
"Chaste fair! the bard, who doats upon your charms,
And once could clasp them in his nuptial arms,
This volume sends; and humbly hopes, that you,
With kind indulgence, will the present view.
You, you! he prizes more, he vows, than life;
Still a lov'd sister, or again his wife.
But oh! may Hymen bless his virtuous fire,
And once more grant you to his fond desire!
Fix'd in this hope, he'll reach the dreary shore,
Where sense shall fail, and memory be no more.',

THE SECOND ELEGY.

HARD was the first, who ventur'd to divide
The youthful bridegroom, and the tender bride:

More hard the bridegroom, who can bear the day,
When force has torn his tender bride away.
Here too my patience, here my manhood fails;
The brave grow dastards, when fierce grief assails:
Die, die I must! the truth I freely own;
My life too burthensome a load is grown.
Then, when I flit a thin and empty shade,
When on the mournful pile my corse is laid,
With melting grief, with tresses loose and torn,
Wilt thou, Neæra! for thy husband mourn?
A parent's anguish will thy mother shew,
For the lost youth, who liv'd, who dy'd for you?
  But see the flames o'er all my body stray!
And now my shade ye call, and now ye pray
In black array'd; the flame forgets to soar,
And now pure water on your hands ye pour;
My lov'd remains next gather'd in a heap,
With wine ye sprinkle, and in milk ye steep.
The moisture dry'd, within the urn ye lay
My bones, and to the monument convey.
Panchaian odours thither ye will bring,
And all the produce of an eastern spring:
But what than eastern springs I hold more dear,
O wet my ashes with a genuine tear!
  Thus, by you both lamented, let me die,
Be thus perform'd my mournful obsequy!
Then shall these lines, by some throng'd way [relate
The dear occasion of my dismal fate:
"Here lies poor Lygdamus; a lovely wife,
Torn from his arms, cut short his thread of life."

THE THIRD ELEGY.

WHY did I supplicate the powers divine?
Why votive incense burn at every shrine?
Not that I marble palaces might own,
To draw spectators, and to make me known;
Not that my teams might plough new purchas'd plains,
And bounteous autumn glad my countless swains:
I begg'd with you my youthful days to share,
I begg'd in age to clasp the lovely fair;
And when my stated race of life was o'er,
I begg'd to pass alone the Stygian shore.
  Can treasur'd gold the tortur'd breast compose?
Or plains, wide-cultur'd, sooth the lover's woes?
Can marble-pillar'd domes, the pride of art,
Secure from sorrow the possessor's heart?
Not circling woods, resembling sacred groves,
Not Parian pavements, nor gay-gilt alcoves,
Not all the gems that load an eastern shore,
Nor what e'er else the greedy great adore,
Possess'd, can shield the owner's breast from woe,
Since fickle Fortune governs all below:
Such toys, in little minds may envy raise;
Still little minds improper objects praise.
Poor let me be; for poverty can please
With you; without you, crowns could give no ease.
  Shine forth, bright morn! and every bliss impart,
Restore Neæra to my doating heart!
For if her glad return the gods deny,
If I solicit still in vain the sky,
Nor power, nor all the wealth this globe contains,
Can ever mitigate my heartfelt pains;
Let others these enjoy; be peace my lot,
Be mine Neæra, mine a humble cot!
Saturnia, grant thy suppliant's timid prayer!
And aid me, Venus! from thy pearly chair!
  Yet, if the sisters, who o'er fate preside,
My vows contemning, still detain my bride,
Cease, breast, to heave! cease anxious blood to flow!
Come, Death! transport me to thy realms below.

THE FOURTH ELEGY.

LAST night's ill-boding dreams, ye gods, avert!
Nor plague, with portents, a poor lover's heart!
But why? From prejudice our terrours rise;
Vain visions have no commerce with the skies:
Th' event of things the gods alone foresee,
And Tuscan priests foretell what they decree.
Dreams flit at midnight round the lover's head,
And timorous man alarm with idle dread:
And hence oblations to divert the woe,
Weak superstitious minds on Heaven bestow.
But since whate'er the gods foretel is true,
And man's oft warn'd, mysterious dreams! by you
Dread Juno! make my nightly visions vain,
Vain make my boding fears, and calm my pain!
The blessed gods, you know, I ne'er revil'd,
And nought iniquitous e'er my heart defil'd.
  Now night had lav'd her coursers in the main,
And left to dewy dawn a doubtful reign;
Bland sleep, that from the couch of sorrow flies,
(The wretch's solace) had not clos'd my eyes;
At last, when morn unbarr'd the gates of light,
A downy slumber shut my labouring sight:
A youth appear'd, with virgin-laurel crown'd,
H emov'd majestic, and I heard the sound.
Such charms, such manly charms, were never seen,
As fir'd his eyes, and harmoniz'd his mien:
His hair, in ringlets of an auburn hue,
Shed Syrian sweets, and o'er his shoulders flew;
As white as thine, fair Luna! was his skin,
So vein'd with azure, and as smoothly thin;
So soft a blush vermilion'd o'er his face,
As when a maid first melts in man's embrace;
Or when the fair with curious art unite
The purple amaranth and lily white.
A bloom like his, when ting'd by autumn's pride,
Reddens the apple on the sunny side;
A Tyrian tunic to his ancles flow'd, [show'd.
Which thro' its sirfled plaits his godlike beauties
A lyre, the present Mulciber bestow'd,
On his left arm with easy grandeur glow'd:
The peerless work of virgin gold was made,
With ivory, gems, and tortoise interlaid;
O'er all the vocal strings his fingers stray,
The vocal strings his fingers glad obey,
And, harmoniz'd, a sprightly prelude play:
But when he join'd the music of his tongue,
These soft, sad elegiac lays he sung:
  "All hail, thou care of Heaven! (a virtuous bard
The god of wine, the Muses, I regard;)
But neither Bacchus nor the Thespian Nine,
The sacred will of destiny divine:
The secret book of destiny to see,
Heaven's awful sire has given alone to me:
And I, unerring god, to you explain
(Attend and credit) what the Fates ordain.
  "She who is still your ever constant care,
Dearer to you than sons to mothers are,
Whose beauties bloom in every soften'd line,
Her sex's envy, and the love of thine:
Not with more warmth is female fondness mov'd,
Not with more warmth are tenderest brides belov'd.
For whom you hourly importune the sky,
For whom you wish to live nor fear to die,

Whose form when night has wrapp'd in black the
Cheats in soft vision your enamour'd soul; [pole,
Neæra! whose bright charms your verse displays,
Seeks a new lover, and inconstant strays!
For thee no more with mutual warmth she burns,
But thy chaste house, and chaste embrace, she
spurns.
"O cruel, perjur'd, false, intriguing sex!
O born with woes poor wretched man to vex!
Whoe'er has learn'd her lover to betray,
Her beauty perish, and her name decay!
"Yet, as the sex will change, avoid despair;
A patient homage may subdue the fair.
Fierce love taught man to suffer, laugh at pain;
Fierce love taught man, with joy to drag the
Fierce love, nor vainly fabulous the tale, [chain;
Forc'd me, yes forc'd me, to the lonely dale:
There I Admetus' snowy heifers drove,
Nor tun'd my lyre, nor sung, absorb'd in love.
The favourite son of Heaven's almighty sire,
Prefer'd a straw-pipe to his golden lyre.
"Tho' false the fair, tho' Love is wild, obey:
Or, youth, you know not Love's tyrannic sway.
In plaintive strains address the haughty fair;
The haughty soften at the voice of prayer.
If ever true my Delphian answers prove,
Bear this my message to the maid you love.
"Pride of your sex, and passion of the age!
No more let other men your love engage;
A bard on you the Delian god bestows,
This match alone can warrant your repose."
He sung. When Morpheus from my pillow flew,
And plung'd me in substantial griefs anew.
Ah! who could think that thou had'st broke thy
vows,
That thou, Neæra! sought'st another spouse?
Such horrid crimes, as all mankind detest,
Could they, how could they, harbour in thy breast.
The ruthless deep, I know was not thy sire;
Nor fierce Chimæra, belching floods of fire;
Nor didst thou from the triple monster spring,
Round whom a coil of kindred serpents cling;
Thou art not of the Lybian lion's seed,
Of barking Scylla's, nor Charybdis' breed;
Nor Afric's sands, nor Scythia gave thee birth;
But a compassionate, benignant earth.
No; thou, my fair! deriv'st thy noble race
From parents deck'd with every human grace.
Ye gods! avert the woes that haunt my mind,
And give the cruel phantoms to the wind.

THE FIFTH ELEGY.

WHILE you at Tuscan baths for pleasure stay,
(Too hot when Sirius darts his sultry ray,
Tho' now that purple spring adorns the trees,
Not Baia's more medicinal than these,)
Me harder fates attend, my youth decays;
Yet spare, Persephone! my blameless days:
With secret wickedness unstung my soul;
I never mix'd, nor gave the baneful bowl;
I ne'er the holy mysteries proclaim'd;
I fir'd no temple, and no god defam'd;
Age has not snow'd my jetty locks with white,
Nor bent my body, nor decay'd my sight;
(When both the consuls fell, ah fatal morn!
Fatal to Roman freedom! I was born.)
Apples unripe, what folly 'tis to pull,
Or crush the cluster ere the grapes are full!
Ye gloomy gods! whom Acheron obeys,
Dispel my sickness, and prolong my days!
Ere to the shades my dreary steps I take,
Or ferry o'er th' irremeable lake,
Let me (with age when wrinkled all my face)
Tell ancient stories to my listening race;
Thrice five long days and nights consum'd with
(O sooth its rage!) I gradually expire; [fire,
While you the Naiad of your fountain praise,
Or lave, or spend in gentle sport your days:
Yet, O my friends! whate'er the Fates decree,
Joy guide your steps, and still remember me!
Mean time, to deprecate the fierce disease,
And hasten glad returns of vigorous ease,
Milk mix'd with wine, O promise to bestow,
And sable victims, on the gods below.

THE SIXTH ELEGY.

LOVER.

COME, Bacchus, come! so may the mystic vine
And verdant ivy round thy temples twine!
My pains, the anguish I endure, remove;
Oft hast thou vanquish'd the fierce pangs of love.
Haste, boy, with old Falernian crown the bowl,
In the gay cordial let me drench my soul.
Hence, gloomy care! I give you to the wind;
The god of fancy frolics in my mind!
My dear companions, favour my design,
Let's drown our senses all in rosy wine!

COMPANION.

Those may the fair with practis'd guile abuse,
Who, sourly wise, the gay dispute refuse:
The jolly god can cheerfulness impart,
Enlarge the soul, and pour out all the heart.

LOVER.

But love the monsters of the wood can tame,
The wildest tigers own the powerful flame:
He bends the stubborn to his awful sway,
And melts insensibility away:
So wide the reign of love!

COMPANION.

Wine, wine, dear boy!
Can any here in empty goblets joy?
No, no! the god can never disapprove,
That those who praise him, should a bumper love.
What terrours arm his brow? the goblet drain:
To be too sober is to be profane!
Her son, who mock'd his rites, Agave tore,
And furious scatter'd round the yelling shore!
Such fears be far from us, dread god of wine!
Thy rites we honour, we are wholly thine!
But let the sober wretch thy vengeance prove:

LOVER.

Or her, whom all my sufferings cannot move!
—What pray'd I rashly for? my madding prayer,
Ye winds! disperse, unratified, in air:
For though, my love! I'm blotted from your soul,
Serenely rise your days, serenely roll!

COMPANION.

The love-sick struggle past, again be gay:
Come, crown'd with roses, let's drink down the
day!

LOVER.

Ah me! loud-laughing mirth how hard to feign!
When doom'd a victim to love's dreadful pain:

How forc'd the drunken catch, the smiling jest,
When black solicitude annoys the breast!

COMPANION.

Complaints, away! the blythsome god of wine
Abhors to hear his genuine votaries whine.

* * * * * *

LOVER.

You, Ariadne! on a coast unknown,
The perjur'd Theseus wept, and wept alone;
But learn'd Catullus, in immortal strains,
Has sung his baseness, and has wept your pains.

* * * * * *
* * * * *

COMPANION.

Thrice happy they, who hear experience call,
And shun the precipice where others fall.
When the fair clasps you to her breast, beware,
Nor trust her, by her eyes altho' she swear;
Not tho', to drive suspicion from your breast,
Or love's soft queen, or Juno she attest;
No truth the women know; their looks are lies.

LOVER.

Yet Jove connives at amorous perjuries.
Hence, serious thoughts! then why do I complain?
The fair are licenc'd by the gods to feign.
Yet would the guardian powers of gentle love,
This once indulgent to my wishes prove,
Each day we then should laugh, and talk, and toy,
And pass each night in hymeneal joy.
O let my passion fix thy faithless heart!
For still I love thee, faithless as thou art!
Bacchus the Naiad loves; then haste, my boy!
My wine to temper cooler streams employ.
What though the smiling board Neæra flies,
And in a rival's arms perfidious lies,
The live-long night, all sleepless, must I whine?
Not I—

COMPANION.

Quick, servants! bring us stronger wine.

LOVER.

Now Syrian odours scent the festal room,
Let rosy garlands on our foreheads bloom.

THE SEVENTH ELEGY.

To you my tongue eternal fealty swore,
My lips the deed with conscious rapture own;
A fickle libertine I rove no more,
You only please, and lovely seem alone.

The numerous beauties that gay Rome can boast,
With you compar'd, a e ugliness at best;
On me their bloom and practis'd smiles are lost,
Drive then, my fair! suspicion from your breast.

Ah no! suspicion is the test of love:
I dread two rivals, I'm suspicious grown;
Your charms the most insensate heart must move;
Would you were beauteous in my eyes alone!

I want not man to envy my sweet fate,
I little care that others think me blest;
Of happy conquests let the coxcomb prate;
Vain-glorious vaunts the silent wise detest.

Supremely pleas'd with you, my heavenly fair!
In any trackless desert I could dwell;
From our recess your smiles would banish care,
Your eyes give lustre to the midnight cell.

For various converse I should long no more,
The blythe, the moral, witty, and severe;
Its various arts are her's, whom I adore;
She can depress, exalt, instruct, and cheer.

Should mighty Jove send down from Heaven a maid,
With Venus' cestus zon'd, my faith to try,
(So, as I truth declare me Juno aid!)
For you I'd scorn the charmer of the sky.

But hold! you're mad to vow, unthinking fool!
Her boundless sway, you're mad to let her know:
Safe from alarms, she'll treat you as a tool—
Ah, babbling tongue! from thee what mischiefs flow!

Yet let her use me with neglect, disdain;
In all, subservient to her will I'll prove;
Whate'er I feel, her slave I'll still remain,
Who shrinks from sorrow, cannot be in love!

Imperial queen of bliss! with fetters bound,
I'll sit me down before your holy fane;
You kindly heal the constant lover's wound,
Th' inconstant torture with increase of pain.

THE POEMS OF SULPICIA.

ADVERTISEMENT.

Some of the best modern commentators contend, that the little poems which compose this fourth book are not the work of Tibullus. Their chief arguments are derived from the language and sentiment; in both which, it is said, and with more justice than is common on such occasions, that they bear no resemblance to our poet's productions.

But if the following little pieces are not the composition of Tibullus, to whom shall we impute them? Shall we, with Caspar Barthius, and Broekhusius, ascribe them to Sulpicia, the wife of Calenus, who flourished in the reign of Domitian? This opinion is by no means improbable, for we know from Martial and Sidonius Apolinaris, that Sulpicia was eminent in those days for her poetry.

Omnes Sulpiciam legant puellæ,
Uni quæ cupiunt viro placere.
Omnes Sulpiciam legant mariti,
Uni qui cupiunt placere nuptæ.
Non hæc Colchidos asserit furorem,
Diri prandia nec refert Thyestæ;
Scyllam, Byblida, nec fuisse credit:
Sed castos docet & pios amores,
Lusus, delicias, facetiasque,
Cujus carmina qui bene æstimarit,
Nullam dixerit esse nequiorem,
Nullam dixerit esse sanctiorem.
Tales egregiæ jocos fuisse
Udo crediderim Numæ sub antro.
Hac condiscipula, vel hac magistra
Esses doctior & pudica, Sappho:
Sed tecum pariter simulque visam
Durus Sulpiciam Phaon amaret.
Frustra: namque ea nec Tonantis uxor,
Nec Bacchi, nec Apollinis puella,
Erepto sibi viveret Caleno.

MART. l. x. ep. 35.

But to this proof, it is objected by Vulpius, that as the following pieces are of a strain different from those celebrated by Martial, so they could not be written by the wife of Calenus, but are Tibullus's; and that the Sulpicia they praise was the daughter of Servius Sulpicius, the famous lawyer, some of whose epistles to Cicero are still extant: for she, who is called Sulpicia in this book, adds he, certainly lived in the reign of Augustus, as Horace himself mentions Cerinthus, and Messala is named in the eighth poem. To this it may be answered, that it cannot be proved that Sulpicia had never been in love before she married Calenus; or had never composed any other poems, besides those of the conjugal kind, so much extolled by Martial? Nay, have we not her own testimony, that she wrote some thousands of pieces?

Cetera quin etiam, quot denique millia lusi!

And we know from some of Sulpicia's lines, preserved by the old scholiast on Juvenal, that she sometimes wrote in a manner the very reverse of that which the epigrammatist celebrates; and of course she may still be the author of these poems. Nor does it follow from Horace's having made mention of one Cerinthus, (lib. i. sat. 2. line 81.) who was fond of a rich mistress, that therefore this mistress was Sulpicia; unless it could be proved that Cerinthus never loved any but Sulpicia; and that there never was a person of the name of Cerinthus but in the age of Augustus. Again, though Messala is mentioned in the eighth poem of this book, it cannot thence be inferred that this was our poet's patron; unless it could be proved that the name Messala (which is not true) expired with that illustrious Roman. Therefore the following poems may still be the offspring of Martial's Sulpicia.

But against this opinion it is further urged by Vulpius, that Quintilian (lib i. cap. 11.) plainly alludes to,

Illam quidquid agit, quoquo vestigia movet
Componit, furtim subsequiturque decor,

in the following sentence: Neque enim gestum oratoris componi ad similitudinem saltationis volvo, sed subesse aliquid ex hac exercitatione puerili, unde nos non id agentes, furtim decor ille descentibus traditus prosequatur. But that eloquent rhetorician, says Vulpius, would have been ashamed to use the words of a woman, who was then alive; and therefore it is more probable, that he borrowed his illustration from Tibullus, a poet of an established reputation.

We cannot see any reason, however, why Quintilian should be more ashamed to borrow from a cotemporary poetess, if her words suited his purpose, than from a dead poet, let his character be ever so great. Nay, the great rhetorician, we apprehend, would rather have chosen to have expressed himself in the words of a woman, who was honoured with the epithet of learned, which was Sulpicia's case, than to have used the language of Tibullus, or any other person, when treating of a subject (viz. decency of gesture) wherein the fair sex must be allowed to be the most competent judges. But why might not Quintilian stumble upon *componit* and *furtim decor*, without ever having read this poem? Can any reason be assigned to the contrary? Or rather, did not his subject naturally lead him to express his sentiments of oratorial gesture in these very words?

Some critics, however, whom the translator has consulted, and who acknowledge the futility of Vulpius's arguments, are yet of opinion, that the first, third, and fifth poems of this book cannot be of Sulpicia's writing, but must be the work of Cerinthus, or some poet; as Sulpicia, they say, could not, with any grace, write the encomium on her own person; nor can the poem on her birth-day be, with any more propriety, ascribed to her; and it is evident, they think, that the fifth poem is the composition of a common friend.

Nor, granting this, every difficulty is not yet surmounted: the twelfth poem, according to some others, cannot be Sulpicia's, for from the following lines,

Nunc licet, e cœlo, mittatur amica Tibullo;
Mittetur frustra, deficietque Venus.

it is, they assert, plainly the composition of Tibullus. Tibulli carmen arbitror, says Broekhusius, ipsa dictione ita persuadente & numeris ad Albianum charactere martificiose conformatis: adding, that it has certainly slipt out of its place, and must belong to the third book, as the old critics inform us that Tibullus wrote no more than three books of elegies.

Although we have so far admitted this opinion, as to place that poem at the end of the third book, yet that our poet certainly wrote more elegies than we have of his at present is obvious, both from his works themselves, and from Horace: nor can the translator help being of opinion, that, however similar the metrical composition in the twelfth poem may be to that of Tibullus, yet the mode of thinking is very different from his; and therefore, if Tibullus is the author, he either in this piece imitated Ovid, or the piece itself was written by somebody else, perhaps in the age of Domitian, who was so fond of Tibullus, as to be willing to usher his own productions into the world under the sanction of his name.

But if the fourth book was composed by Sulpicia, how comes it, objects Vulpius, to be found in all the ancient MSS. of Tibullus? To this it may be answered, that the old librarians used commonly, in order to enhance the price of their MSS. to join to an author, who had not left many works behind him, any writer who composed in what they thought a similar taste. By this means, a satire, which our Sulpicia certainly wrote, was long ascribed by some to Juvenal, and by others to Ausonius, from having been found in the MS. works of those two poets; till some critics of more understanding[1] proved to the learned, neither Juvenal, nor Ausonius, but Martial's Sulpicia wrote it.

Such are the arguments by which the commentators support their different opinions. The reader must determine for himself. But if the translator might be permitted to pronounce on the subject, he would say, that if any weight might be laid on difference of style, and especially of thought, the following poems cannot be the work of Tibullus:—but whether Martial's Sulpicia, or who else wrote them, is not in his power to determine. But as Sulpicia is the only person to whom the critics attribute them, the translator, not knowing any one else, who can show a preferable claim, has retained her name in the title page.

Notwithstanding, however, it cannot be absolutely ascertained (and how can controversies of this sort be absolutely ascertained?) who was the person to whose happy talent we owe the following poems; every reader of taste will allow that they abound with striking beauties; and that upon the whole those critics do no great injury to Tibullus, who still ascribe them to that poet.

As Sulpicia and Cerinthus perfectly understood one another, we must not expect in their poems those sallies and transitions of passion, that frantic and despondent air, so observable in Tibullus: for these are the natural emanations of a heated fancy and a distracted heart. But the poems before us abound in what the moderns denominate gallant flattery. Most of them show the poet and happy lover. They give us little anecdotes of their passion, and make us regret we have not more.

POEM THE FIRST.

GREAT god of war! Sulpicia, lovely maid,
To grace your calends, is in pomp array'd.
If beauty warms you, quit th' ethereal height,
E'en Cytherea will indulge the sight:
But while you gaze o'er all her matchless charms,
Beware your hands should meanly drop your arms!
When Cupid would the gods with love surprise,
He lights his torches at her radiant eyes.
A secret grace her every act improves,
And pleasing follows wheresoe'er she moves:
If loose her hair upon her bosom plays,
Unnumber'd charms that negligence betrays:
Or if 'tis plaited with a labour'd care,
Alike the labour'd plaits become the fair,
Whether rich Tyrian robes her charms invest,
Or all in snowy white the nymph is drest,
All, all she graces, still supremely fair,
Still charm spectators with a fond despair.
A thousand dresses thus Vertumnus wears,
And beauteous equally in each appears.
The richest tints and deepest Tyrian hue,
To thee, O wonderous maid! are solely due:
To thee th' Arabian husbandman should bring
The spicy produce of his eastern spring:
Whatever gems the swarthy Indians boast,
Their shelly treasures, and their golden coast,
Alone thou merit'st! Come, ye tuneful choir!
And come, bright Phœbus! with thy plausive lyre!
This solemn festival harmonious praise,
No theme so much deserves harmonious lays.

THE SECOND POEM.

WHETHER, fierce churning boars! in meads ye stray,
Or haunt the shady mountain's devious way;
Whet not your tusks, my lov'd Cerinthus spare!
Know, Cupid! I consign him to your care.
What madness 'tis, shagg'd trackless wilds to beat,
And wound, with pointed thorns, your tender feet:
O! why to savage beasts your charms oppose?
With toils and blood-hounds why their haunts enclose?
The lust of game decoys you far away;
Ye blood-hounds perish, and ye toils decay!
Yet, yet could I with lov'd Cerinthus rove
Thro' dreary deserts, and the thorny grove:
The cumbrous meshes on my shoulders bear,
And face the monsters with my barbed spear:
Could track the bounding stags through tainted grounds,
Beat up their cover, and unchain the hounds:
But most to spread our artful toils I'd joy,
For while we watch'd them, I could clasp the boy!
Then, as entranc'd in amorous bliss we lay,
Mix'd soul with soul, and melted all away!
Snar'd in our nets, the boar might safe retire,
And owe his safety to our mutual fire.
O! without me ne'er taste the joys of love,
But a chaste hunter in my absence prove.
And O! may boars the wanton fair destroy,
Who would Cerinthus to their arms decoy!
Yet, yet I dread!—Be sports your father's care;
But you, all passion! to my arms repair!

THE THIRD POEM.

COME, Phœbus! with your loosely floating hair,
O sooth her torture, and restore the fair!
Come, quickly, come! we supplicant implore,
Such charms your happy skill ne'er sav'd before!
Let not her frame consumptive pine away,
Her eyes grow languid, and her bloom decay;
Propitious come! and with you bring along
Each pain-subduing herb, and soothing song;
Or real ills, or whate'er ills we fear,
To ocean's farthest verge let torrents bear.
O! rack no more, with harsh, unkind delays,
The youth, who ceaseless for her safety prays;

[1] Scaliger, &c.

'Twixt love and rage his tortur'd soul is torn;
And now he prays, now treats the gods with scorn.
Take heart, fond youth! you have not vainly pray'd,
Still persevere to love th' enchanting maid:
Sulpicia is your own! for you she sighs,
And slights all other conquests with your eyes:
Dry then your tears; your tears would fitly flow
Did she on others her esteem bestow.
O come! what honour will be yours to save
At once two lovers from the doleful grave?
Then both will emulous exalt your skill;
With grateful tablets, both your temples fill;
Both heap with spicy gums your sacred fire;
Both sing your praises to th' harmonious lyre:
Your brother-gods will prize your healing powers,
Lament their attributes, and envy yours.

THE FOURTH POEM.

On my account, to grief a ceaseless prey,
Dost thou a sympathetic anguish prove?
I would not wish to live another day,
If my recovery did not charm my love:
For what were life, and health, and bloom to me,
Were they displeasing, beauteous youth! to thee.

THE FITFH POEM.

With feasts I'll ever grace the sacred morn,
When my Cerinthus, lovely youth! was born.
At birth, to you th' unerring Sisters sung
Unbounded empire o'er the gay and young:
But I, chief I! (if you my love repay,)
With rapture own your ever-pleasing sway.
This I conjure you, by your charming eyes,
Where love's soft god in wanton ambush lies!
This by your genius, and the joys we stole,
Whose sweet remembrance still enchants my soul!
Great natal genius! grant my heart's desire,
So shall I heap with costly gums your fire!
Whenever fancy paints me to the boy,
Let his breast pant with an impatient joy:
But if the libertine for others sigh
(Which Love forbid!) O Love! your aid deny.
Nor, Love! be parital, let us both confess
The pleasing pain, or make my passion less.
But O! much rather 'tis my soul's desire,
That both may feel an equal, endless fire.
In secret my Cerinthus begs the same,
But the youth blushes to confess his flame:
Assent, thou god! to whom his heart is known,
Whether he public ask, or secret own.

THE SIXTH POEM.

Accept, O natal queen! with placent air,
The incense offer'd by the learned fair.
She's rob'd in cheerful pomp, O power divine!
She's rob'd to decorate your matron-shrine;
Such her pretence; but well her lover knows
Whence her gay look, and whence her finery flows.
Thou, who dost o'er the nuptial bed preside,
O! let not envious night their joys divide,
But make the bridegroom amorous as the bride!
So shall they tally, matchless lovely pair!
A youth all transport, and a melting fair!
Then let no spies their secret haunts explore;
Teach them thy wiles, O Love! and guard the door.
Assent, chaste queen! in purple pomp appear;
Thrice wine is pour'd, and cakes await you, here.
Her mother tells her for what boon to pray;
Her heart denies it, tho' her lips obey.
She burns, that altar as the flames devour;
She burns, and slights the safety in her power.
So may the boy, whose chains you proudly wear,
Thro' youth the soft indulgent anguish bear;
And when old age has chill'd his every vein,
The dear remembrance may he still retain!

THE SEVENTH POEM.

At last the natal odious morn draws nigh,
When to your cold, cold villa I must go;
There, far, too far from my Cerinthus sigh:
Oh why, Messala! will you plague me so?

Let studious mortals prize the sylvan scene,
And ancient maidens hide them in the shade;
Green trees perpetually give me the spleen;
For crowds, for joy, for Rome, Sulpicia's made!

Your too officious kindness gives me pain.
How fall the hail-stones! hark! how howls the wind!
Then know, to grace your birth-day should I deign,
My soul, my all, I leave at Rome behind.

THE EIGHTH POEM.

At last the fair's determin'd not to go:
My lord! you know the whimsies of the sex.
Then let us gay carouse, let odours flow;
Your mind no longer with her absence vex:
For oh! consider, time incessant flies;
But every day's a birth-day to the wise!

THE NINTH POEM.

That I, descended of patrician race,
With charms of fortune, and with charms of face,
Am so indifferent grown to you of late,
So little car'd for, now excites no hate.
Rare taste, and worthy of a poet's brain,
To prey on garbage, and a slave adore!
In such to find out charms, a bard must feign
Beyond what fiction ever feign'd of yore.
Her friends may think Sulpicia is disgrac'd;
No! no! she honours your transcendent taste.

THE TENTH POEM.

If from the bottom of my love-sick heart,
Of last night's coyness I do not repent,
May I no more your tender anguish hear,
No longer see you shed th' impassion'd tear.
You grasp'd my knees, and yet to let you part—
O night more happy with Cerinthus spent!
My flame with coyness to conceal I thought,
But this concealment was too dearly bought.

THE ELEVENTH POEM.

FAME says, my mistress loves another swain;
Would I were deaf, when fame repeats the wrong!
All crimes to her imputed, give me pain,
Not change my love: Fame, stop your saucy tongue!

THE TWELFTH POEM.

LET other maids, whose eyes less prosperous prove,
Publish my weakness, and condemn my love.
Exult, my heart! at last the queen of joy,
Won by the music of her votary's strain,
Leads to the couch of bliss herself the boy;
And bids enjoyment thrill in every vein:
Last night entranc'd in ecstacy we lay,
And chid the quick, too quick return of day!
But stop, my hand! beware what loose you scrawl,
Lest into curious hands the billet fall.
No—the remembrance charms—begone, grimace!
Matron! be yours formality of face.
Know, with a youth of worth, the night I spent,
And cannot, cannot for my soul repent!

THE

IDYLLIUMS OF THEOCRITUS.

TRANSLATED BY FAWKES.

Τοις Βουκολικοις, πλην ολιγων των εξωθεν, ο Θεοκριτος επιτυχεστατος,

LONGINUS.

TO THE HONOURABLE

CHARLES YORKE.

SIR,

THE complaint which Theocritus makes in one of his Idylliums, of the neglect shown to his Muse, naturally reminded me of my own necessity. The utmost ambition of my wishes could not have aspired after a more illustrious patron than Mr. Yorke; I was not kept long in suspense, having, through a worthy friend, received permission to inscribe to you the subsequent sheets; and the favour was granted in a manner so peculiarly polite, that I esteemed the obligation more than doubled.

It was customary among the ancient Romans for the plebeians to choose out of the body of the patricians protectors or patrons, whose care it was to assist their clients with their interest, and defend them from the oppression of the great; to advise them in points of law, to manage their suits, and secure their peace and happiness: what a powerful advocate in this respect you would prove, let the pleadings at the bar, the decisions in Westminster-hall, and the debates in the senate determine. But the friend I seek at present must be eminent for his enlivened genius, the delicacy of his taste in literature, his classical learning, and his generous protection of the Muses: and where can I find these shining abilities and these benevolent virtues so happily combined, as in that eminent patron who does me the honour to countenance the following work? you, sir, are not only Musis amicus, but

—Musarumq; comes cui, carmina semper
Et citharæ cordi.

You have long since sacrificed to the Muses with success, and had not the tenour of your studies, warmed by the example, and improved by the knowledge and experience of your admirable father, formed you to shine with so much lustre in a more active and exalted sphere, you had been ranked with the most celebrated authors in polite learning. But I cease to wonder that you should have attained qualifications like these, in the early culture of your talents, when I consider your zeal to vindicate the privilege of your predecessors; for the great lawgivers of antiquity were generally poets: Themis and the Muses are nearly joined in affinity; both derived from Heaven, they both distribute concord, harmony, and good-will among the inhabitants of the Earth.

To whom then can I present these Arcadian scenes with so much propriety as to the friend of ancient eloquence and ancient poetry; one whom I know to have been an intelligent reader and admirer of Theocritus? let me congratulate myself on my good fortune, in having, by this performance, found more distinguished favour from Mr. Yorke, than Theocritus experienced at the court of Hiero.

That the honours and reputation you have so deservedly acquired may increase more and more; that you may live long and happily, for the encouragement of the liberal sciences, and the service of your country, is the earnest wish of,

sir,

your most obliged,

and obedient servant,

FRANCIS FAWKES.

Orpington,
Jan. 10, 1767.

PREFACE.

WHEN I had formed a resolution of publishing a translation of this inimitable Greek poet, I intended to have availed myself of every elegant and faithful version of any particular Idyllium that fell in my way; and then have endeavoured, to the best of my ability, to make up the deficiency. With this view, I carefully examined Mr. Dryden, who has left translations of four Idylliums, the 3d, the 18th, the 23d, and the 27th. There are many beautiful lines in the third, but take it altogether and it is a tedious paraphrase; for the original contains only 54 verses, which he has multiplied into no fewer than 127; particularly there are three lines, beginning at the 18th,

> Ω το καλον τοθορωσα· το παν λιθος· ω κυανοφρυ
> Νυμφα. κ. τ. λ.
>
> Sweet black-ey'd maid, &c.

which he has expanded into twelve. Now though English heroic verse consists of no more than ten syllables, and the Greek hexameter sometimes rises to seventeen, but if upon an average we say fifteen, then two Greek verses is equal in point of syllables to three of English: but if a translator is so extravagantly licentious, he must lose sight of his original, and by introducing new thoughts of his own, disguise his author so that nobody can know him again. But Mr. Dryden has a far greater foible than this, which effectually prevents me from inserting any of his translations in this volume, which is, that whenever he meets with any sentiment in an author which has the least tendency to indecency, he always renders it worse; nay, even in these Idylliums where the original has given him no handle at all, he has warpt the simple meaning of Theocritus into obscenity. Sed vitiis nemo sine nascitur; no man had more excellencies as a poet than Mr. Dryden, therefore the hand of candour should draw a veil over constitutional blemishes.

In Dryden's Miscellany Poems there are seven or eight translations of other Idylliums, viz. the 2d, 10th, 14th, and 20th by W. Bowles; the 11th by Duke, and the 1st and some others by different hands; but none of these, I found, would suit my purpose: there are so many wild deviations from the original, such gross mistakes, and so many incorrect and empty lines, that they will sound very harshly in the polished ears of the present age. Fully satisfied with this inquisition, I then determined to undertake the whole work myself; considering that every translation from an ancient author, as well as every original work, is generally most agreeable to the reader which is finished by the same hand: because in this case there is kept up a certain uniformity of style, an idiomatical propriety of diction, which is infinitely more pleasing than if some different, though more able hand, had here and there interlarded it with a shining version, than if

> Purpureus, late qui splendeat, unus et alter
> Assuitur pannus.

I have been informed by some venerable critics, that Creech's translation of Theocritus was well done, and a book of reputation; that he thoroughly understood the classics, and had a peculiar facility in unfolding their beauties, and that if there was published a new edition of his translation, there would be no necessity for its being superseded by another. I beg leave to dissent entirely from these gentlemen, who probably having read Creech when they were young, and having no ear for poetical numbers, are better pleased with the rough music of the last age than the refined harmony of this; and will not easily be persuaded, that modern improvements can produce any thing superior. However Creech may have approved himself in Lucretius or Manilius, I shall venture to pronounce his translation of Theocritus very bald and hard, and more rustic than any of the rustics in the Sicilian bard: he himself modestly entitles his book, The Idylliums of Theocritus done into English: and they are done as well as can be expected from Creech, who had neither an ear for numbers, nor the least delicacy of expression.

It will be incumbent upon me to make good this bold assertion, which I can easily do by producing a few examples. In the first Idyllium, he calls that noble pastoral cup, a fine two handled pot; and the ελιξ, the tendrils or claspers with which scandent plants use to sustain themselves in climbing, he transforms into kids;——"where kids do seem to brouze." In the description of the fisherman, ver. 43. he has these lines,

> The nerves in's neck are swoln, look firm and strong,
> Altho' he's *old*, and fit for one that's *young*.

Ver. 112. He makes Daphnis say to Venus,

> Go now stout Diomed, go soon pursue,
> Go nose him now, and boast, my arts o'erthrew:
> Young Daphnis, fight, for I'm a match for you.

Ελικας ριον and *σᾶμα Λυκαονίδαο*, he renders, Helick's cliff, and Licon's tomb.—A little further on, and likewise in the 5th Idyllium, he turns nightingales into thrushes.

Idyllium III. Where Olpis is looking out for tunnies, he makes him stand, To snare his *trouts.*—The girl Erithacis he calls Tawney Bess—and Alphesibœa's mother, Alphish's mother.

Idyllium V. ver. 11. He translates Crocylus into Dick, and Idyllium XIV. Argivus, Apis and Cleunicus, into Tom, Will and Dick. Near the end of the 5th, Lacon says;

> I love Eumedes much, I gave my *pipe*,
> How sweet a kiss he gave; ah charming *lip*!

Then come successively the following delicate rhymes: strains, swans; shame, lamb; piece, fees; joy, sky: afterwards he makes Comates say;

> I'll *toot* at Lacon, I have won the lamb,
> Go foolish shepherd, pine, and die for shame.

Idyllium VII. ver. 120. He renders *απιος* parsley, thinking it the same as apium, whereas it signifies a pear.

Idyllium XI. He makes Polyphemus say of himself;

> Sure I am somewhat, they my worth can see,
> And I myself will now grow proud of me.

He says of Cynisca, Idyl. XIV. 23.

> That you might light a candle at her nose.

Idyllium XV. One of the gossips says to a stranger,

> —————You are a sawcy friend,
> I'm ne'er beholding t'ye, and there's an end.

And so there's an end of my animadversions upon Mr. Creech; were I to quote all his dull insipid lines, I should quote above half his book: this much was proper for me to say in my own vindication; and to add more might to some people seem invidious.

It has been hinted to me by more ingenious judges, that if Theocritus was translated in the language of Spenser, he would appear to great advantage, as such an antique style would be a proper succedaneum to the Doric idiom. There appeared to me at first something plausible in this scheme; but happening to find part of Moschus's first Idyllium, which is a Hue and Cry after Cupid, paraphrastically translated by Spenser himself, I had reason to alter my opinion. I shall transcribe the passage, that the reader may judge whether such a version would be more agreeable than one in modern language.

> It fortun'd fair Venus having lost
> Her little son, the winged god of love,
> Who for some slight displeasure which him crost,
> Was from her fled, as flit as any dove,
> And left her blissful bower of joy above;
> (So from her often he had fled away,
> When she for aught him sharply did reprove,
> And wander'd in the world in strange array,
> Disguis'd in thousand shapes, that none might him bewray:)
>
> Him for to seek, she left her heavenly house,
> And searched every way, thro' which his wings
> Had borne him, or his tract she mote detect:
> She promis'd kisses sweet, and sweeter things,
> Unto the man that of him tidings to her brings.

Fairy Queen, b. 3. ch. 6.

From this specimen I could not be persuaded to think that a translation of Theocritus, even in the purest language of Spenser, would afford any pleasure to an English reader: and therefore I have given him the dress which I apprehend would best become him. How I have executed this work, I leave to the decision of the candid and impartial, desiring they will allow me all the indulgence which the translator of so various and difficult an author can reasonably require; an author on whom there are but few Greek scholia published, only to the 17th Idyllium inclusive, and these often extremely puerile; an author on whom fewer notes have been written than upon any other equally excellent. Scaliger, Casaubon, Heinsius and Meursius frequently leave the most difficult passages untouched; their observations are sometimes trifling and unsatisfactory, often repugnant to each other, and now and then learnedly obscure: amidst these disadvantages I have endeavoured to conduct myself with the utmost caution; and if I may be allowed to speak of the following sheets, I will briefly explain what I have attempted to accomplish. First then as to the translation; I have neither followed my author too closely nor abandoned him too wantonly, but have endeavoured to keep the original in view, without too essentially deviating from the sense: no literal translation can be just; as to this point, Horace gives us an excellent caution;

> Nec verbum verbo curabis reddere fidus
> Interpres.

> Nor word for word too faithfully translate.

A too faithful interpretation, Mr. Dryden says, must be a pedantic one: an admirable precept to this purpose is contained in the compliment sir John Denham pays sir Richard Fanshaw on his version of the Pastor Fido;

> That servile path thou nobly dost decline,
> Of tracing word by word, and line by line;
> A new and nobler way thou dost pursue,
> To make translations, and translators too;
> They but preserve the ashes, thou the flame,
> True to his sense, but truer to his fame.

And as I have not endeavoured to give a verbal translation, so neither have I indulged myself in a rash paraphrase, which always loses the spirit of an ancient by degenerating into the modern manners of expression; and to the best of my recollection, I have taken no liberties but those which are necessary for exhibiting the graces of my author, transfusing the spirit of the original, and supporting the poetical style of the translation. This is the plan, and these are the rules by which every translator should conduct himself: how I have acquitted myself in these points must be left to the determination of superior judges. As to the notes, which I found the most laborious part of my task, they are intended either to illustrate the most difficult, and exemplify the beautiful passages; or else to exhibit the various imitations of authors, which I look upon as an agreeable comment, for they not only show the manner in which the ancients copied each other's excellencies, but likewise often help to elucidate the passages that are quoted. Upon a review of my notes, I have instanced too many passages from Virgil as imitations of Theocritus: what I have to say in my defence is, they appeared to me at the time to be similar, if they do not appear in the same light to the reader, they are easily overlooked: if I have in this respect committed a fault, this acknowledgment will plead in mitigation of it.

Besides these errours and mistakes, I am conscious of many more, though I hope not very material ones; those the learned and judicious, who are sensible of the difficulty of this undertaking, will readily excuse. This work has already met with the approbation of the best critics of the age, therefore what the worst may think or say of it, will give me no concern. I must acknowledge a fault or two *quas incuria fudit:* there are, I believe, two or three proper names falsely accented: I have also mistaken the sense of my author in the first Idyllium, ver. 31,

> This goat with twins I'll give, &c.

It should have been translated, " I will give you three milkings of this goat; ες τρις αμελξαι, that you may milk her three times;" not the goat herself and twins, which would have been a most extravagant present from a poor goat-herd, in return for a song. The reader therefore may correct the passage thus,

> Thrice shall you milk this goat; she never fails
> Two kids to suckle, though she fill two pails;
> To this I'll add, &c.

This mistake was imparted to me by the ingenious and learned Dr. Jortin, together with the following emendation; see note on ver. 57, " for χρυσεια you read with Pierson, Κροισοιο; which, as to the sense, seems to be right. But, as the Ionic dialect is not often used in a Doric song, I should prefer the adjective Κροισεια, which is also a smaller alteration. As from χρυσος comes χρυσειος, so from Κροισος, Κροισειος." I am much obliged to the same gentleman for the following short but full account of the bucolic measure.

" Whosoever shall carefully examine in Theocritus the composition of his verses, may perceive that, in his opinion, the nature of bucolic or pastoral metre requires that the fourth foot of the verse be a dactyl, and that the last syllable of this dactyl be the end of a word, which must not run into the next foot. The first foot also should rather be a dactyl than a spondee, and the *cæsura* is here likewise to be shunned. If after the fourth foot there be a pause, of a comma at least, the verse will be still more elegant; as,

Αρχετε | βωκολικας, Μωσαι φιλαι, | αρχετ' αοιδας.

Thus the verses will abound with dactyls, which, together with the broad Doric dialect, gives a certain rustic vivacity and lightness to the poesy. But yet the above-mentioned rules, if they were constantly observed, would displease by a tiresome uniformity, and confine the poet too much; and therefore a variety is better, as in the line,

Αμφωες, νεοτυχες, ετι γλυφα | -νοιο ποτοσδον,

And it is sufficient if the other structure predominate. These rules Virgil hath quite neglected; except in those verses of his eighth Eclogue, which are called, *versus intercalares:*

Incipe Mænalios mecum, mea | tibia, versus,

And

Ducite ab urbe domum, mea carmina, | ducite Daphnim.

For a further account of this matter, the curious reader is referred to the Memoires de L'Acad. tom. vi. p. 238."

AN ACCOUNT OF SOME MSS. AND CURIOUS EDITIONS OF THEOCRITUS.

It may be asked, why I have not acted the part of a verbal critic in this performance? My reason was, that far more able men had considered Theocritus in that light. The late Mr. D'Orville, the author of the Critica Vannus, and Sicula, during his travels in Italy and Sicily, collated upwards of forty MSS. of Theocritus: his collation is now at Amsterdam. Mr. St. Amand, a few years ago, left to the university of Oxford a large collection of collations, which Mr. Thomas Warton, who has prepared a noble edition of this author, has the use of. Mr. Taylor, late Greek professor of Cambridge, left likewise a Theocritus almost ready for the press. In the public library at Cambridge, there are some notes on Theocritus by Isaac Casaubon, written in the margin of Henry Stephens' Poetæ Græci; likewise manuscript notes in the edition of Commelin printed in quarto; and also some notes by Thomas Stanley, the author of the Lives of the Philosophers: all these, and likewise a MS. Theocritus, are in the public library at Cambridge. There is also a MS. of the first eight Idylliums in Emanuel college library. Mr. Hoblyn, late member for the city of Bristol, left behind him many notes and observations for an edition of Theocritus. Besides these, there are great materials for illustrating this author in private libraries.

As to the editions of Theocritus, which are very numerous, I think proper to say something; as we have but an imperfect account of them in Fabricius and Maittaire. Reiske, in the preface to his late edition of this Greek poet, has given us an account of the various editions, but this account is far from being satisfactory. The first edition of Theocritus was printed at Milan in the year 1493, the letter is the same with the Isocrates of the same place and date: see the catalogue of the Leyden library, page 251. The second edition was printed by Aldus Manutius at Venice in the year 1495; this is the only edition Aldus ever printed; there are some leaves cancelled in it, which is the reason why Reiske and others have imagined that Aldus printed two editions: Mr. Maittaire, in the first volumes of his Annales Typographici, page 244, has given us an account of these differences. In the year 1515, we have an edition by Philip Junta at Florence; and another in 1516, by Zachary Caliergus at Rome.

These are all the editions that came out before the year 1520. Besides these, and those mentioned by Reiske, which I have seen, there are some curious editions, viz. that of Florence by Benedict Junta, printed in the year 1540; the Basil edition of 1558, and the Paris edition of 1627, printed by John Libert. I have purposely omitted mentioning the others, as they are already taken notice of, either by Fabricius, Maittaire, or Reiske.

I cannot conclude this preface without paying my acknowledgments to those gentlemen who have kindly assisted me in this undertaking. Dr. Pearce, the present lord bishop of Rochester, many years eminent for his critical disquisitions, has in the friendliness of conversation furnished me with several useful rules for conducting my translation. Dr. Jortin has favoured me with a concise but full account of the old bucolic measure; and a few valuable notes. The celebrated Mr. Samuel Johnson has corrected part of this work, and furnished me with some judicious remarks. In a short conversation with the ingenious Mr. Joseph Warton, I gathered several observations, particularly in regard to the superiority of Theocritus to Virgil in pastoral, which are interspersed amongst the notes. The learned Dr. Plumptre, archdeacon of Ely, has, with great candour and accuracy, done me the honour to peruse and amend every sheet as it came from the press. Dr. Askew, so eminently distinguished in his profession, as well as for a large and most curious collection of the classics, and an intimate knowledge of them, with the sincerity of an old acquaintance and a friend, gave me many various readings, showed me every valuable edition of Theocritus that is extant, and furnished me with the account of some MSS. and scarce editions of my author, which were never taken notice of by former editors. Swithin Adee, M. D. and the rev. Mr. John Duncombe of Canterbury, have at my own request sent me several notes and strictures upon my performance, which are candid, and valuable. Mr. Burnaby Greene, author of Juvenal paraphrastically imitated, very obligingly supplied the Essay on Pastoral, and some ingenious observations: and Dr. William Watson lent me his friendly assistance in the botanical part. I could mention other eminent names of gentlemen who have corrected and improved this work;

————————Each finding, like a friend,
Something to blame, and something to commend.

The list I have given, I am apprehensive, will appear ostentatious—however, I had rather be convicted of the foible of vanity, than thought guilty of the sin of ingratitude.

SOME ACCOUNT OF THE LIFE AND WRITINGS OF THEOCRITUS.

AS the life of Theocritus has been several times written in English, I flattered myself that I might single out the account I liked best, and save myself the trouble of compiling it afresh: I depended a good deal upon Kennet, but when I came to peruse his account of Theocritus, I found it unsatisfactory, and no ways answerable to my purpose: he seems more solicitous, in an affected quaintness of style, to exhibit a display of his own learning, than studious, by the investigation of truth, to give information to his readers: his thoughts lie loose and unconnected, and therefore are generally tedious and perplexing.

The account of our author in the Biographical Dictionary, published in twelve volumes octavo, is nothing but a servile epitome of Kennet, and, where the conciseness of it will allow, expressed in his very words. Thus dissatisfied with the moderns, I had recourse to the ancients: in the life generally prefixed to his works by Suidas, we are told, "that Theocritus was a Chian, a rhetorician: but that there was another Theocritus, the son of Praxagoras and Philina, though some say of Simichidas, a Syracusian;" others say, "he was born at Cos, but lived at Syracuse;" now this was the case of Epicharmus, and might easily occasion the mistake. See the note on Epigram XVII.

In another Greek account in the front of his works, we are told, "that Theocritus the Bucolic poet was born at Syracuse, and that his father's name was Simichidas." Gyraldus says, "some have thought him of Cos, some of Chios." From such a confused jumble of relations, what can with certainty be made out?

> Then take him to develop, if you can,
> And hew the block off, and get out the man.

There are but few memorials left of this poet; those that I produce, I shall endeavour to establish on good authority, and whenever an opportunity offers, which is but very reasonable, will let him speak for himself.

Theocritus was a Sicilian, as is evident from many testimonies: Virgil invokes the Sicilian Muses because Theocritus, whom he professedly imitates, was of that country; Sicilides Musæ, paulo majora canamas. Ecl. 4. 1. and, Extremum hunc, Arethusa, mihi concede laborem. Ecl. 10. 1. He is called a Sicilian poet by the emperor Julian in one of his epistles; and by Terentianus Maurus, in his book de Metris, ver. 407, Siculæ telluris alumnus: by Manilius, B. 2. ver. 40, he is said to be Siculâ tellure creatus, which fixes his birth on that island: and that he was born at Syracuse, Virgil seems to intimate when he says, Prima Syracosio dignata est ludere versu. Ecl. 6. 1. But in one of his own Epigrams, which generally stands in the front of his works, probably according to his own original intention, he assures us he was born at Syracuse, and gives us the names of his parents:

> Αλλος ο Χῖος· εγω δε Θεοκριτος ος ταδε γραψα,
> Εις απο τῶν πολλῶν ειμι Συρακοσιων
> Υιος Πραξαγοραο περικλειτῆς τε Φιλινης·
> Μῶσαν δ' οθνειην ϐποτ' εφελκυσαμην.

> A Syracusian born, no right I claim
> To Chios, and Theocritus my name:
> Praxagoras' and fam'd Philina's son;
> My laurels from unborrow'd verse are won.

After this plain declaration, it is amazing that the old grammarians will not rest satisfied, but endeavour to rob him both of his parents and his country. The chief view which the poet had in writing this epigram, though perhaps it may not appear at first sight, seems to be this; he had a namesake of Chios, a rhetorician, and pretender to poetry, who, according to Plutarch, suffered an ignominious death, for some crime committed against king Antigonus; and therefore Theocritus the poet, by this epigram, took all possible precaution to be distinguished from his namesake the rhetorician. "The other Theocritus," says he, "is of Chios; I that am the author of these poems am a Syracusian, the son of Praxagoras and the celebrated Philina: I never borrowed other people's numbers." The last sentence is an honest declaration, that the poet had not been a plagiary, like many of his predecessors and contemporaries.

Theocritus is said to have been the scholar of Philetas, and Asclepiades, or Sicelidas: Philetas was an elegiac poet of the island of Cos, had the honour to be preceptor to Ptolemy Philadelphus, and is celebrated by Ovid and Propertius: Sicelidas was a Samian, a writer of epigrams: he mentions both these with honour in his seventh Idyllium, see ver. 53.

As to the age in which he flourished, it seems indisputably to be ascertained by two Idylliums that remain, one is addressed to Hiero king of Syracuse, and the other to Ptolemy Philadelphus, the Egyptian monarch. Hiero began his reign, as Casaubon asserts in his observations on Polybius, in the second year of the 126th Olympiad, or about 275 years before Christ; and Ptolemy in the fourth year of the 123d Olympiad. Though the exploits of Hiero are recorded greatly to his advantage by Polybius, in the first book of his history; though he had many virtues, had frequently signalized his courage and conduct, and distinguished himself by several achievements in war; yet he seems, at least in the early part of his reign, to have expressed no great affection for learning or men of letters: and this is supposed to have given occasion to the 16th Idyllium, inscribed with the name of Hiero; where the poet asserts the dignity of his profession, complains that it met with neither favour nor protection, and in a very artful manner touches upon some of the virtues of this prince, and insinuates what an illustrious figure he would have made in poetry, had he been as noble a patron, as he was an argument for the Muses.

His not meeting with the encouragement he expected in his own country, was in all probability the reason that induced Theocritus to leave Syracuse for the more friendly climate of Alexandria, where Ptolemy Philadelphus then reigned in unrivalled splendour, the great encourager of arts and sciences, and the patron of learned men. In his voyage to Egypt he touched at Cos, an island in the Archipelago not far from Rhodes, where he was honourably entertained by Phrasidamus and Antigenes, who invited him into the country to celebrate the festival of Ceres, as appears by the seventh Idyllium.

We have all the reason in the world to imagine that he met with a more favourable reception at Alexandria, than he had experienced at Syracuse, from his encomium on Ptolemy, contained in the 17th Idyllium; where he rises above his pastoral style, and shows that he could upon occasion (as Virgil did afterwards) exalt his Sicilian Muse to a sublimer strain, *paulo majora:* he derives the race of Ptolemy from Hercules, he enumerates his many cities, he describes his great power and immense riches, but above all he commemorates his royal munificence to the sons of the Muses. Towards the conclusion of the 14th Idyllium, there is a short, but very noble panegyric on Ptolemy: in the 15th Idyllium he celebrates Berenice, the mother, and Arsinoe, the wife of Ptolemy.

I do not recollect any more memorials of this poet's life, which can be gathered from his works, except his friendship with Aratus, the famous author of the Phænomena; to whom he addresses his sixth Idyllium, and whose amours he describes in the seventh.

There is one circumstance more in regard to Theocritus, which is so improbable, that I should not have thought it worth while to have troubled the reader with it, if it had not been mentioned by all his biographers; viz. that he lies under the suspicion of having suffered an ignominious death; this takes its rise from a distich of Ovid in his Ibis,

> Utque Syracosio præstrictâ fauce poetæ,
> Sic animæ laqueo sit via clausa tuæ.

But it does not appear, that by the Syracusian poet Ovid means Theocritus; more probably, as some commentators on the passage have supposed, Empedocles, who was a poet and philosopher of Sicily, is the person pointed at: others think that Ovid by a small mistake or slip of his memory might confound Theocritus the rhetorician of Chios, who was executed by order of king Antigonus, with Theocritus the poet of Syracuse; and the epigram quoted above very strongly indicates how apprehensive our poet was of being confounded with that person: it seems indeed, as I hinted before, composed on purpose to manifest the distinction.

After this short account of our author, it will be proper to say something of his works; for to write the life of a poet without speaking of his compositions, would be as absurd as to pretend to publish the memoirs of a hero, and omit the relation of his most material exploits.

All the writings of Theocritus that now remain are his Idylliums and Epigrams; in regard to the word idylliums, D. Heinsius tells us, that the grammarians termed all those smaller compositions Ειδη, (a species of poetry) which could not be defined from their subjects, which were various: thus the Sylvæ of Statius, had they been written in Greek, would have been called Ειδη and Ειδυλλια; even the Roman poets make use of this term; thus Ausonius styles one of his books of poems on various subjects Edyllia: this ancient title then may serve to express the smallness and variety of their natures; they would now perhaps be called Poems on Several Occasions. Though in deference to so great an authority, I shall take the liberty to make a conjecture: Heinsius tells us, that originally there were different titles or inscriptions prefixed to the poems of Theocritus; first of all his Bucolics were separated and distinguished by the title of Επη Βουκολικα, and were called by the grammarians Ειδυλλια Βουκολικα; but might it not at first have been written Επυλλια, which signifies poems or verses, and by an easy mistake of the transcriber altered into Ειδυλλια? This reading delivers us at once from the embarrassment attending the derivation of the word idyllium, and the same as versiculi, very naturally flows from the word Επη, the plural of Επος, carmen; thus we have Επη χρυσεια: it is to be observed that Aristophanes uses the word three times, see his Ranæ, ver. 973, Acharnenses, ver. 397; and in his Pax, ver. 531, he has επυλλιων Ευριπιδυ, *versiculorum Euripidis:* this however is only conjecture. Under the second title, every poem that was ascribed to Theocritus, though the character and argument were very different, was inserted. Under the third were contained a collection of bucolic poems, whether written by Theocritus, Moschus, Bion, or others, and the name of Theocritus prefixed to the whole; on which occasion there is an epigram in the Anthologia, ascribed to Artemidorus;

Βουκολικαι Μῦσαι σποραδην ποκα, νῦν δ' αμα πᾶσαι
Εντι μιᾶς μανδρας, εντι μιᾶς αγελας.

Wild rov'd the pastoral Muses o'er the plains,
But now one fold the single flock contains.

Besides the Idylliums that we now have, Theocritus is said by Suidas to have written Προιτιδας, Ελπιδας, Υμνους, Ηρωινας Επικηδεια μελη, Ελεγειας, και Ιαμβους; that is, Prœtides, Hopes, Hymns, Heroines, Dirges, Elegies, and Iambics; the Prœtides were the daughters of Prœtus, king of the Argives, who preferring themselves to Juno, went mad, and imagined themselves turned into cows, but were cured by Melampus; the Idyllium in praise of Castor and Pollux is supposed to be one of the Hymns, and there are five verses remaining of a poem, in praise of Berenice, which may be classed among the Heroines.

It is to be observed that Theocritus generally wrote in the modern Doric, sometimes indeed he used the Ionic; the Doric dialect was of two sorts, the old and the new; the old sounded harsh and rough, but the new was much softer and smoother; this, as Mr. Pope justly observes, in the time of Theocritus had its beauty and propriety, was used in part of Greece, and frequent in the mouths of many of the greatest persons. It has been thought by some that the Dorian phrase in which he wrote has a great share in his honours; but exclusive of this advantage, he can produce other ample claims to secure his rural crown from the boldest competitor. A proof of this, I think, will appear from this circumstance; that Virgil, who is the great rival of the Sicilian, has few images in his Eclogues but what are borrowed from Theocritus; nay, he not only continually imitates, but frequently translates several lines together, and often in these very passages falls short of his master, as will appear in the notes.

Though Theocritus is generally esteemed only a pastoral poet, yet he is manifestly robbed of a great part of his fame, if his other pieces have not their proper laurels. At the same time his pastorals are, without doubt, to be considered as the foundation of his credit; upon this claim he will be admitted for the happy finisher, as well as the inventor of his art; and will be acknowledged to have excelled all his imitators, as much as originals usually do their copies. He has the same advantage in bucolic, as Homer had in epic poetry, which is to make the critics turn his practice into eternal rules, and to measure Nature herself by his accomplished model: therefore, as to enumerate the glories of heroic poetry, is the same thing as to sum up the praises of Homer, so to exhibit the beauties of pastoral verse is only an indirect way of making panegyrics on Theocritus. Indeed the Sicilian has in this respect been somewhat more fortunate than Homer, as Virgil's Eclogues are reckoned more unequal mitations of his Idylliums, than the Æneis of the Iliad.

I think I cannot conclude this account of Theocritus with more propriety than by collecting the sentiments not only of the ancients, but likewise of the moderns, in regard to the character of our author. Longinus says, (see the motto) "Theocritus has shown the happiest vein imaginable for pastorals, excepting those in which he has deviated from the country;" or perhaps it may more properly be rendered, as Fabricius understands it, "excepting in those few pieces that are of another argument." Quintilian says, Admirabilis in suo genere Theocritus sed Musa illa rustica & pastoralis non forum modo verum etiam urbem reformidat:——, "Theocritus is admirable in his way, but his rustic and pastoral Muse is not only afraid of appearing in the forum, but even in the city:" by which he means, that the language and thoughts of Theocritus' shepherds ought not to be imitated in public speaking, nor in any polite composition; yet for all this, "he was admirable in his way." Manilius in the second book of his Astronomicon gives a just character of our poet [1];

Quinetiam pecorum ritus, & Pana sonantem
In calamos, Siculâ memorat tellure creatus:
Nec sylvis sylvestre canit: perque horrida motus
Rura serit dulces: Musamque inducit in auras.

The sweet Theocritus, with softest strains,
Makes piping Pan delight Sicilian swains;
Through his smooth reed no rustic numbers move,
But all is tenderness, and all is love;
As if the Muses sat in every vale,
Inspir'd the song, and told the melting tale.

CREECH.

One would imagine these authorities were sufficient to establish, or at least to fix the reputation of Theocritus on a very respectable footing: and yet Dr. John Martyn, who has translated Virgil's Eclogues and Georgics into prose, with many learned notes, seems to be of a different persuasion. In the latter end of his preface to the Eclogues, after observing that Virgil, in almost every Eclogue, entertains the reader with a rural scene, a sort of fine landscape, and enumerating these scenes, he says, "and having now seen this excellence in Virgil, we may venture to affirm, that there is something more required in a good pastoral, than the affectation of using coarse, rude, or obsolete expressions; or a mere nothingness, without either thought or design, under a false notion of rural simplicity." That he here means Theocritus, or else he means nothing, is plain from his mention of him immediately after: in regard to the charge of his "affectedly using coarse, rude, and obsolete expressions," I imagine he alludes to the fifth Idyllium, which indeed must be allowed to be too rustic and abusive: but we must remember that Theocritus intended this poem as a specimen of the original old bucolic idyllium which was very rude, and often obscene; as the learned Heinsius has more than once observed; his words are, Multum a reliquis differunt quæ αἰπολικα sunt, in quibus major est incivilitas; ut in quinto apparet, quod Idyllium singulare est, & in suo genere exemplem, antiquæ nimirum βȣκολιας; ubi nunquam fere sine obsceno sensu rixatur caprarius. And in another place; veræ βȣκολιας exemplum in quinto Theocriti, in Virgilii tertio habemus. Therefore instead of condemning Theocritus, we ought to think ourselves much obliged to him for leaving us one example of the ancient, rustic bucolic; Virgil certainly thought so, otherwise he would not have imitated that very piece. As to the scenery with which the Eclogues are embellished, all the Idylliums, or at least the greatest part of them, are ornamented in the same manner, which will appear so evident to every reader, that it would be impertinent to point it out. As to the other part of the doctor's observation, "a mere nothingness, without thought or design," it is such a despicable falsity that it is not worth notice.

Throughout his whole preface and life of Virgil, the doctor is very singular in giving Virgil the preference to Theocritus upon every occasion: particularly he declaims against the cup in the

[1] Instead of *pecorum ritus*, Dr Bentley reads, *ritus pastorum.*

first Idyllium, says the description of it is long and tedious, and far exceeded by Virgil in the third Eclogue; notwithstanding the doctor's assertion, some gentlemen whose critical disquisitions have deservedly announced them the best judges of polite literature, think that the images in Theocritus' cup, viz. "the beautiful woman and two lovers, the striking figure of the fisherman labouring to throw his net, the rock, the vineyard, the foxes, and the boy sitting carelessly and framing traps for grasshoppers," are charming embellishments, and far more pastoral and natural than Virgil s Orpheaque in medio posuit, sylvasque sequentes, "Orpheus in the middle, and the woods following him." In regard to the length of the description, it is observed that the cup of Theocritus was very large and capacious; he calls it βαθυ κισσυβιον, a deep pastoral cup; and Casaubon says it was Amplissimi vasis pastoritii genus; capacitatem ejus licet colligere ex cœlaturæ multiplici argumento: and I am informed, that when Mr. Thomas Warton's long-expected edition of Theocritus appears, it will be evidently proved, perhaps from some old scholia not yet printed, that this κισσυβιον was of an extraordinary size, very deep and wide, and therefore capable of being adorned with such a variety of figures in the sculpture; it was not intended for the use of drinking out of, or mixing any pastoral beverage, but chiefly for ornament; and therefore the vessel being so capacious and remarkable, the poet will be cleared from the charge of being thought tedious in the description of it.

In the preface above mentioned the doctor says, "It is not a little surprising, that many of our modern poets and critics should be of opinion, that the rusticity of Theocritus is to be imitated rather than the rural delicacy of Virgil." How can it be thought surprising that Theocritus should be imitated rather than Virgil? the reason is manifest, because the generality of poets and critics prefer the Sicilian far before the Roman, as a pastoral writer. I should not have troubled myself about Dr. Martyn's opinion; but, only as it is prefixed to Virgil, I thought perhaps it might possibly mislead the unwary young scholar into a wrong judgment, and induce him to prefer Virgil without first considering the more original beauties of Theocritus. As a contrast to the doctor's strange and singular decision, who acknowledges himself to be *no poet*, and therefore cannot be deemed a competent judge of poetical writings, I shall conclude this account with the sentiments of several of the finest writers, both as critics and poets, of the last and present age, in regard to the matter in question; two of them are translators of Virgil, and therefore cannot be supposed to be partial to Theocritus.

I shall begin with Mr. Dryden; "That which distinguishes Theocritus," says he, "from all other poets, both Greek and Latin, and which raises him even above Virgil in his Eclogues, is the inimitable tenderness of his passions, and the natural expression of them in words, so becoming of a pastoral. A simplicity shines throughout all he writes. He shows his art and learning by disguising both. His shepherds never rise above their country education in their complaints of love. There is the same difference between him and Virgil, as there is between Tasso's Aminta, and the Pastor Fido of Guarini. Virgil's shepherds are too well read in the philosophy of Epicurus and Plato; and Guarini's seem to have been bred in courts. But Theocritus and Tasso have taken theirs from cottages and plains. It was said of Tasso, in relation to his similitudes, that "he never departed from the woods," that is, all his comparisons were taken from the country: the same may be said of Theocritus. He is softer than Ovid; he touches the passions more delicately, and performs all this out of his own fund, without diving into the arts and sciences for a supply. Even his Doric dialect has an incomparable sweetness in its clownishness, like a fair shepherdess, in her country russet, talking in a Yorkshire tone. This was impossible for Virgil to imitate, because the severity of the Roman language denied him that advantage. Spenser has endeavoured it in his Shepherd's Calendar, but it can never succeed in English." Thus far Mr. Dryden in the preface to his Translations; in another place he says, "Theocritus may justly be preferred as the original, without injury to Virgil, who modestly contents himself with the second place, and glories only in being the first who transplanted pastoral into his own country."

Dr. Felton observes, "The Idylliums of Theocritus have something so inimitably sweet in the verse and thoughts, such a native simplicity, and are so genuine, so natural a result of the rural life, that I must, in my judgment, allow him the honour of the pastoral."

Mr. Blackwall upon the Classics, says, "Theocritus is another bright instance of the happy abilities and various accomplishments of the ancients. He has writ in several sorts of poetry, and ucceeded in them all. It seems unnecessary to praise the native simplicity, and easy freedom of his astorals, when Virgil himself sometimes invokes the Muse of Syracuse; when he imitates him through all his own poems of that kind, and in several passages translates him. In many of his other poems he shows such strength of reason and politeness, as would qualify him to plead among the orators, and make him acceptable in the courts of princes. In his smaller poems of Cupid stung, Adonis killed by the Boar, and others, you have the vigour and delicacy of Anacreon; in his Hylas, and Combat of Pollux and Amycus, he is much more pathetical, clear and pleasant, than Apollonius on the same, or any other subject. In his conversation of Alcmena and Tiresias, of Hercules and the old servant of Augeas, in Cynisca and Thyonichus, and the women going to the ceremonies of Adonis, there is all the easiness and engaging familiarity of humour and dialogue which reign in the Odyssey; and in Hercules destroying the Lion of Nemea, the spirit and majesty of the Iliad. The Panegyric upon king Ptolemy is justly esteemed an original and model of perfection in that way of writing. Both in that excellent poem, and the noble Hymn upon Castor and Pollux, he has praised his gods and his hero with that delicacy and dexterity of address, with those sublime and graceful expressions of devotion and respect, that in politeness, smoothness of turn, and refined art of praising without offence, or appearance of flattery, he has equalled Callimachus; and in loftiness and flight of thought, scarce yields to Pindar or Homer."

The author of the Guardian, No. 28, observes, "The softness of the Doric dialect, which Theocritus is said to have improved beyond any who came before him, is what the ancient Roman writers owned their language could not approach. But, besides this beauty, he seems to me to have had a soul more softly and tenderly inclined to this way of writing than Virgil, whose genius led him naturally to sublimity."

Mr. Pope briefly remarks, that "Theocritus excels all others in nature and simplicity: that the subjects of his Idylliums are purely pastoral: that other pastoral writers have learnt their excellencies from him, and that his dialect alone has a secret charm in it, which no other could ever attain."

Lord Lyttelton beautifully says,

From Love, Theocritus, on Enna's plains,
Learnt the wild sweetness of his Doric strains. Ecl. 2.

Mr. Warton, the worthy master of Winchester-school, gives us his sentiments on this subject in his prefatory dedication of Virgil to lord Lyttelton; "There are few images and sentiments in the Eclogues of Virgil, but what are drawn from the Idylliums of Theocritus: in whom there is a rural, romantic wildness of thought, heightened by the Doric dialect; with such lively pictures of the passions, and of simple unadorned nature, as are infinitely pleasing to such lovers and judges of true poetry as yourself. Theocritus is indeed the great store-house of pastoral description; and every succeeding painter of rural beauty (except Thomson in his Seasons) hath copied his images from him, without ever looking abroad upon the face of nature themselves." To the same purpose, in his dissertation on pastoral poetry, he says, "If I might venture to speak of the merits of the several pastoral writers, I would say, that in Theocritus we are charmed with a certain sweetness, a romantic rusticity and wildness, heightened by the Doric dialect, that are almost inimitable. Several of his pieces indicate a genius of a higher class, far superior to pastoral, and equal to the sublimest species of poetry: such are particularly his Panegyric on Ptolemy, the fight between Amycus and Pollux, the Epithalamium of Helen, the young Hercules, the grief of Hercules for Hylas, the death of Pentheus, and the killing of the Nemean Lion."

AN ESSAY ON PASTORAL POETRY.

BY EDWARD BURNABY GREENE, ESQ.

Gaudentes rure Camænæ.

HORACE.

THE precise time when the pastoral Muse made her appearance in the world, history seems to have left uncertain. Conjectures have been hazarded, and presumptions[1] multiplied, yet her origin is still unravelled; and the less inquisitive genius sits down contented with ascertaining her first perfection in the writings of Theocritus.

Indeed researches of this nature are rather curious than interesting; for though we may perhaps meet with some plausible accounts, we can trace none that carry conviction. The very few writers[2], handed down to us from Greece and Rome in that species of composition, are but insufficient guides to the rise of the art itself.

As it is more entertaining, it is likewise more to the honour of pastoral to observe, that it must necessarily have existed in the earlier ages of the world; existed, not indeed in the set form and elegance of numbers, but in the genuine sentiments of the heart, which nature alone inspired.

For the mind being on all sides surrounded with rural objects, those objects would not fail to make an impression; and whether the patriarchs of old with our parents in Milton piously broke out into the praise of their Creator, or reflected in silent admiration on the beauties of the earth, their hymns, or their meditations, must have been purely pastoral.

It has been remarked by a laborious commentator on the Eclogues of Virgil, that the lives of our earliest forefathers were spent in husbandry, and the feeding of cattle. And indeed it could not have been otherwise. At a period, when the numbers of mankind were comparatively insignificant, and their thoughts engaged in procuring subsistence, while luxury and ambition were yet unknown, it is inconsistent to suppose, but that the sons of earth were all in a manner the sons of agriculture.

When the world however increased, and its inhabitants dispersed into various regions, when societies were formed, and laws established, and when (the natural consequence of such expansion) the plagues of war and contention arose, different orders, and conditions were settled for the regulation of kingdoms; rustic awkwardness received the polish of civil life, and the plough-share was converted into instruments of destruction. Thus by degrees from an honourable situation husbandry became the employment of those alone, who had the least ambition, and the greatest probity.

But in those climates, whither emigrations being less fashionable, the people retained their primitive simplicity, it is no wonder, if in process of time considerable advance was made, and regularity introduced into pastoral reflections; that the dictates of unrefined nature were improved by the harmony of numbers.

We may accordingly observe, that in the countries which suffered the least variation from their original form, pastoral was most esteemed; there the thoughts were still allured, and the imagination feasted with rural scenes unimproved, or more properly uncorrupted; for the cottage had not felt the infection of the court.

[1] See what may be called the Prolegomena to the Θεοκριτου ευρισκομενα cum Græcis Scholiis, printed at London 1743, περι του που και πως ευρηθη τα βουκολικα, where the reputed invention of pastoral poetry has neither the air of probability nor ingenuity.

[2] Moschus, and Bion, with Theocritus, among the Greeks, and Virgil among the Romans, are the only standard writers of pastoral, mentioned by Warton in the dissertation prefixed to his edition of Virgil; that editor, with the critic * Rapin, seeming to explode all other ancient authors in that branch of poetry.

* Rapin's Critical Works, vol. 2. remarks on pastoral poetry.

Arcadia, so usually painted the flowery kingdom of romance, is more ingeniously accounted the land of pastoral. Its inland situation, and the plenty of its pasture[3], with the well-known characters of its inhabitants conspire to favour the title. That the ancient poets described this place as the seat of pastoral, is evident; a shepherd[4] peculiarly skilled in singing, being familiarly termed an Arcadian. There appears, however, in many traditions of the country such a strong mixture of the fabulous, that we may well suspect them to be the product rather of fancy than of truth.

Nor less fantastic are the descriptions of the golden age, the ideal manners of which are esteemed, by the more refined critic, the genuine source of pastoral.

To a taste so delicate, the least appearance of the rustic is disgusting. A becoming, indeed an elegant simplicity, and the purest innocence, must compose the character of the shepherd. No passions but of the softest and most engaging kind are to be introduced: in short, the swain is to be what no swain ever was.

In these elevated notions of humble pastoral, reality is sacrificed to the phantoms of the imagination; the more characteristic strokes in the picture of rural life being utterly erased; the bright colours of unspotted integrity are indeed more pleasing to the eye, but in a piece where nature should predominate, are more properly blended with the shade of frailty. For if mankind are to be represented entirely free from faults, we cannot look for their existence later than the fall.

On this fastidious principle it is esteemed necessary, that rural happiness should be described perfect and uninterrupted. The life of the shepherd is to be one perpetual spring, without a cloud to disturb its calmness. The vicissitudes indeed of love, which gives birth to more than half our modern pastorals, are admitted into the piece: for it seems to be with some as essential for a shepherd to be in love, as to have been born.

Yet even here the representation is confined; the swain after whining and crying (as Achilles did to his good mother Thetis) calls on the trees and bushes, and every thing in nature, to be witnesses of his unhappiness; but after all, the performance, like our novels and romances, those standards of propriety, must have a fortunate conclusion[5].

But whatever fond and amusing prospects the country naturally opens to the mind, experience teaches us, that even there vexations will arise: the seasons of quiet and uneasiness succeed as familiarly as summer and winter: groves and lawns, and purling streams, sound very prettily in description, chiefly when flowing through the numbers of some under-aged amorato; but reason cannot set her seal to the luxuriancy of this Mahometan paradise.

From sentiments so extravagantly refined, let us turn to those of a more sordid complexion. As the former satiate the judicious reader with beds of roses, the latter disgust him with the filthiness of a dunghill. With critics of this cast, the manners of the mere peasant are the sole foundation of pastoral; even less rustic and homely appellations are banished from the characters, and the Melibœus, or Neæra of Virgil are so much too courtly, that in their place are to be substituted the Αιπολος, and Βουκολισκος of Theocritus, and the Colin-clout or Hobbinol of Spenser.

The Doric dialect, which transfuses such a natural gracefulness over the Idylliums of the Grecian, has been a stumbling-block to these lovers of inelegance. There is a rustic propriety in the language of this dialect, which was familiar to the cottager in the age of Theocritus; but it must be remembered, that his pastorals contain likewise a delicacy of sentiment which may well be presumed to have attracted the attention of Ptolemy[6], whose polished court was the asylum of genius.

But though it should be allowed, that pastoral ought strictly to be limited to the actions of the peasant, it is not solely intended for his perusal. The critic, as he cannot on the one hand permit nature to be excluded, cannot relish on the other her being exposed in disgraceful colours.

There are in almost every situation some circumstances, over which we should draw the veil, for all is not to be painted with a close exactness. Coarseness of sentiment and indelicacy of expression are an offence to decorum, and give modesty the blush. Writings of such illiberal tendency counteract the best and principal end of composition; they hold up the mirror to vice and immorality[7], and sacrifice virtue to contempt.

To those, who live in our meridian of more refined simplicity, pastoral appears most properly in the dress of rural elegance. Something is indulged to the character of the shepherd, and something to the genius of the writer. They, who should place the former on the toilette, would betray an ab-

[3] Dr. Martyn in his preface to the Eclogues of Virgil calls Arcadia "mountainous and almost inaccessible;" another reason in support of the pastoral disposition of its people.

[4] Virgil in his 7th Eclogue says of two shepherds, that they were Arcades ambo, upon which Servius remarks, that they were not Arcadians, but so skilful in singing, that they might be esteemed Arcadians.

[5] It has indeed a tendency altogether immoral to represent with Theocritus a disappointed lover hanging himself. The present mode of indifference in these concerns is more eligible, and on the whole may be thought more natural. Love-sorrows are very rarely fatal.

[6] Ptolemy Philadelphus, king of Egypt, to make amends for many atrocious crimes, was remarkable for his singular regard to the welfare of his subjects, and was a distinguished encourager of learned men.—See Anc. Univ. Hist. vol. 9, p. 386, note T.

[7] On this principle, it were to be wished, that the subject of Virgil's second eclogue were not greatly liable to exception: though the morals of the poet should not be personally impeached, we must lament, that he has varnished in his Alexis the depravity of his times. Several representations in Theocritus are glaringly obscene.

surdity which would no less extend to the latter, whose thoughts flowed in the rude channel of uninformed rusticity.

The country is the scene in which pastoral is naturally laid; but various may be the subjects of this little drama. The spirit of the poet would be wretchedly cramped, if never permitted to step aside. An insipid sameness runs through the pieces [8], founded on the impropriety of this indulgence, and most of our later pastorals are in this respect but unmeaning paraphrases of earlier authors.

Were we to attempt an historical epitome of pastoral composition, we might place Theocritus in its dawn; in that earlier age when rural simplicity was cultivated and revered. Though we are sometimes struck with the rays of his genius, breaking out into more exalted descriptions, pastoral appears to be his favourite province [9].

Considering him as a writer, who drew his sentiments from the principles of nature, we may rather admire, that his Idylliums are so engaging, than cavil at his blemishes; we may reflect upon Theocritus, as the hive, whence the most established writers of eclogues have derived their sweets, or as a diamond, whose intrinsic worth has received a lustre from the refinement of succeeding times.

There is a very considerable gap in the history of pastoral, between the age of Theocritus and Virgil, who was reserved for the noon of its perfection. It would scarcely at first sight appear, that the period when civil war desolated the provinces, and spread all its horrours over the neighbourhood of Rome, should tend to the improvement of the pastoral Muse, whose spirit it was likely to have totally destroyed. Yet to this seemingly unfavourable situation we owe the most pleasing and interesting bucolics of Virgil, who has made the history of his country subservient to the efforts of his genius [10].

In those several pieces, to which the distresses of his times, or other political considerations gave rise, he seems more elaborately to have exercised the faculty of invention. But where genuine nature was to be represented, he borrowed largely from Theocritus [11]; many of his similies, sentiments and descriptions, being literal translations from his Grecian master.

Even in this less original task the merits of the Roman are conspicuous; he has separated the ore from the dross, and transplanted those flowers alone, which could add a fragrance to his work.

On the whole, the pastorals of Virgil are most agreeably conducted; they are not set forth in jewels or arrayed in silks, nor sordidly dressed in rags. In the "paulo majora," of his Muse, the poet rarely loses sight of the shepherd, and we may style him the refined Theocritus of an Augustan age.

From this elegant era, when the language of the country and court was purity itself, let us pass over to the days of our excellent Spenser, when the conversation of the latter had just emerged from rusticity.

The genius of Spenser was formed for poetry. The rich luxuriance of fancy which shines through the Fairy Queen surpasses the sublime of antiquity. Such bold conceptions little speak a writer qualified for pastoral. The fire of imagination, which strikes us in more elevated compositions, must in this be suspended; for nature is most advantageously shown, when she seems to borrow the least from art.

Our author was too great to rise by imitation. Though he had both Theocritus and Virgil for his models, his Shepherd's Calendar is altogether original. The dialect of his times is as happily adapted to rustic life, as the Doric of the former, and the easy flow of his descriptions, with the natural variety of his landscapes, rivals the poetic excellence of the latter.

Proverbial sayings, not too closely crowded, add to the simplicity of pastoral; Spenser is fortunate in such applications; but I own myself most peculiarly attracted with his short lessons of morality; they add a pleasing innocence to the character of the shepherd, and reflect a lustre on the poet.

Yet amidst this superior merit it must be observed, that a masterly writer of our own days has censured the dialogue of Spenser as affectedly barbarous, and the reflections of his peasants as too exalted.

It is necessary however to premise, that the criticism of this author is confined to the September of the Shepherd's Calendar; an eclogue which is indeed conveyed in a dialect singularly rustic; and the subject being the depravity of ecclesiastical manners in popish countries, the sordid language, under which the satire is couched, gives the greater offence to the critic; who concludes with this exclamation: "Surely at the same time that a shepherd learns theology, he may gain some acquaintance with his native language!"

The more ancient dialect seems here to have been selected, as a disguise to the real purport or

[8] Modern eclogues from this reason abound with repetitions of amorous scenes, or of swains piping for a reward. Not to mention other subjects of a like interesting nature, which from constant use are worn to tatters.

[9] The praises of Ptolemy, the Hylas, and the Hiero, are by no means pastoral; but, if Theocritus is entitled to a greater share of praise for any particular parts of those performances, it is where he deviates into pastoral representations.

[10] The first and ninth eclogues deserve attention on this account. To these we may also join the fourth and fifth.

[11] See the third, seventh, and eighth eclogues, where imitations from Theocritus abound.

characters of the piece. The reign of Mary, when England was under the bondage of an arbitrary religion, and oppressed by foreign counsels, may be esteemed the period of the pastoral. The violence, which had been so barbarously exerted throughout the country, at that baleful season, was too recent to have been forgotten; and the shepherd [12] is very naturally described as having fled from a persecution, the censure of which was a compliment to the principles of Elizabeth.

A rural metaphor is manifestly sustained through the performance, as if to obviate the inconsistency, which is alleged. So far from discussing knotty points of theological learning, the province of the peasant is closely preserved; unless it should be insisted that nothing relative to religion ought to concern a shepherd.

To descend from the writings of Spenser to the succeeding age, would be to point out the decline of the pastoral Muse. Indeed she has scarcely existed, but in the productions of Philips [13] and of Pope. Philips is so often on the whine, that we are apt to overlook his less exceptionable descriptions; he has injudiciously blended the polish of Virgil's language with the simplicity of Spenser's; and so great is his want of original matter, that he is at best to be regarded as a graceful copyist [14].

Pope has been so assiduous to refine his periods, that his spirit is greatly evaporated; and his pastorals, excepting the Messiah, only merit our attention as the marks of early genius. Sweetness of versification, and purity of expression, may constitute the character of a poet; but courtliness is not the whole that is expected in a writer of eclogues.

That love of the country, which is inherent in the bosom of reflection, has occasionally produced many later attempts on pastoral, but the most successful ones are fainter traces of rural life; the Muse has at last varied her form, and united the charms of elegance and nature in the ballads of Shenstone.

[12] The late Romish brutality was at that time so interesting a topic, and so flattering to the crown, that Spenser has employed three eclogues on the subject.

[13] The pastorals of Gay seem to have been designed as burlesque representations of scenes altogether rustic, and particularly as a ridicule of preceding authors, of whom many, it must be confessed, deserved such a treatment. I have on this account omitted his name as a pastoral writer, though his genius sufficiently qualified him for the task of eclogue.

[14] The fifth pastoral, which relates the contest of the Swain and Nightingale, is prettily turned on the whole; but the thought, like Philips's other more agreeable ones, is borrowed. The same may be remarked of the pastorals of Pope.

THE

IDYLLIUMS OF THEOCRITUS.

TRANSLATED BY FAWKES.

IDYLLIUM I.

THYRSIS, OR THE HYMERÆAN ODE.

THE ARGUMENT.

This Idyllium contains a dialogue between the shepherd Thyrsis and a goatherd. Thyrsis, at the request of his friend, sings the fate of Daphnis who died for love; for which he is rewarded with a milch goat, and a noble pastoral cup of most excellent sculpture. This piece is with great propriety prefixed to all the other Idylliums, and may be considered as the pattern and standard of the old bucolic poems. The scene changes from a rising ground to a lower situation near a fountain, where there is a shepherd's bower facing the statues of Priapus and the Nymphs, and not far distant a grove of oaks.

THYRSIS.

SWEET are the whispers of yon vocal pine,
Whose boughs projecting o'er the springs, recline;
Sweet is thy warbled reed's melodious lay;
Thou, next to Pan, shalt bear the prize away:
If to the god a horn'd he-goat belong,
The gentler female shall reward thy song;
If he the female claim, a kid 's thy share,
And, till you milk them, kids are dainty fare.

GOATHERD.

Sweeter thy song, O shepherd, than the rill,
That rolls its music down the rocky hill:

1. Sweet are the whispers, &c.] Poets frequently speak of the whispering or murmuring of trees: the word ψιθυρισμα, which Theocritus uses, is very expressive of the thing he describes, and properly signifies to whisper softly in the ear. Thus our author says the two lovers, Idyl. 27. αλληλεις ψιθυριζον, and Idyl. 2. ver. 141. εψιθυρισδομες αδυ. Virgil has, argutum nemus, pinosque loquentes, Ecl. 8. 22.; and, Sæpe levi somnum suadebit inire susurro, Ecl. 1. 56. Mr. Pope seems to have had this passage in view, and even improved it, in his Eloisa to Abelard.

> The darksome pines that o'er yon rocks reclin'd,
> Wave high, and murmur to the hollow wind.

He has also finely imitated this passage, and the beginning of the goatherd's speech, "Sweeter thy song," &c.

> Thyrsis, the music of that murmuring spring
> Is not so mournful as the strains you sing:
> Nor rivers winding thro' the vales below,
> So sweetly warble, or so smoothly flow.
> Past. 4.

4. Next to Pan.] Virgil comparing a shepherd with Pan says,

> Tu nunc eris alter ab illo. Ecl. 5. 49.

9. Than the rill, &c.] The Greek is—η το καταχες Την απο τας πετρας καταλειβεται υψοθεν υδωρ.

These ten words flow with most melodious sweetness; every one of them contributes to heighten the image they are to represent.

Homer has the same image in nearly the same words,

> ——Κατα δε ψυχρον ρεεν υδωρ
> Υψοθεν εκ πετρης, &c. Odyss. b. 17.

If one white ewe content the tuneful Nine,
A stall-fed lamb, meet recompense, is thine;
And if the Muses claim the lamb their due,
My gentle Thyrsis shall obtain the ewe.

THYRSIS.

Wilt thou on this declivity repose,
Where the rough tamarisk luxuriant grows,
And gratify the nymphs with sprightly strain?
I'll feed thy goats, and tend the browsing train.

GOATHERD.

I dare not, dare not, shepherd, grant your boon,
Pan's rage I fear, who always rests at noon,
When tir'd with hunting, stretch'd in sleep along,
His bitter rage will burst upon my song:
But well you know love's pains, which Daphnis rues,
You the great master of the rural Muse;
Let us beneath yon shady elm retreat,
Where Nature forms a lovely pastoral seat,
Where sculptur'd Naiads and Priapus stand,
And groves of oaks extending o'er the land;
There if you sing as sweetly as of yore,
When you the prize from Lybian Chromis bore,
This goat with twins I'll give, that never fails
Two kids to suckle, and to fill two pails:
To these I'll add, with scented wax o'er-laid,
Of curious workmanship, and newly made,
A deep two-handled cup, whose brim is crown'd
With ivy join'd with helichryse around;

Where, from the rock with liquid lapse distils
A limpid fount, &c. Pope.

Virgil has imitated this passage,

Tale tuum carmen nobis, divine Poeta,
Quale sopor fessis in gramine; quale per æstem
Dulcis aquæ saliente sitim restinguere rivo.
Ecl. 5. 45.

And again,

Nam neque me tantùm venientis sibilus austri,
Nec percussa juvant fluctu tam litora, nec quæ
Saxosas inter decurrunt flumina valles.
Ecl. 5. 82.

15. On this declivity repose, Where the rough tamarisk, &c.] The Greek is, Ως το καταντες τȣτο γεωλοφον, ατε μυρικαι. The same verse occurs, Idyl. 5. ver. 101. in the Greek; in the translation, 110.

18. Pascentes servabit Tityrus hœdos——
Ecl. 5. 12.

20. Pan's rage I fear,] Goats and their keepers were under the protection of Pan; it is with good reason therefore that the goatherd is afraid of offending that deity.

Who always rests at noon,] Horace, describing the middle of a hot day, says, caretque Ripa vagis taciturna ventis. Ode 29. b. 3. On which Dacier observes, "The ancients believed that at mid-day every thing was calm and serene, because at that season the sylvan deities reposed themselves," and quotes this passage of Theocritus in confirmation of it.

22. His bitter rage will burst upon my song:] Horace describes Faunus as a very choleric god, ode 18. b. 3. and begs he would pass through his grounds in good temper. The Greek is remarkable, Και οι αει δριμεια χολα ποτι ρινι καθηται—"And bitter choler always remains on his nostrils." Casaubon observes, that all violent passions cause a sensation in the nostrils, arising from the ebullition of the spirits, which mount towards the brain, and endeavouring to free themselves from restraint, find a vent by the nostril, and crowding through it, dilate it in their passage. This is evident from animals, and the nobler kinds of them, as the bull, the horse, the lion, whose nostrils always dilate when moved to anger. Homer has a similar expression in his Odyssey, b. 24.—ανα ρινας δε οι ηδη δριμυ μενος προυτυψε—"A sharp sensation struck his nostrils:" though this is to express another passion, viz. that of sorrow arising from filial tenderness; and is a description of Ulysses and his interview with Laertes. Persius in the same manner says—Ira cadat naso, rugosaque sanna. Sat. 5. 91.

23. Si quos aut Phyllidis ignes,
Aut Alconis habes laudes, aut jurgia Codri.
Ecl. 5. 10.

24. Montibus in nostris solus tibi certet Amyntas. Ecl. 5. 8.

25. ——Si quid cessare potes, requiesce sub umbrâ.—Ecl. 7. 10.

32. Bis venit ad mulctram, binos alit ubere fœtus. Ecl. 3. 30.

33. With scented wax, &c.] Heinsius observes, that we have here a description of that art which the ancients called Κηρογραφια, or inlaying with wax, which in the days of Theocritus was very much practised by the Egyptians and Sicilians. In beautifying the prows of their ships, the ancients made use of several colours, which were not barely varnished over with them, but very often annealed by wax melted in the fire, so as neither the Sun, winds, nor water were able to deface them: the art of doing this was called from the wax Κηρογραφια. See Potter's Ant. and Vitruvius, l. 7. cap. 9.

35. A deep two-handled cup, &c.] This is a very striking description of those large pastoral cups which the ancient shepherds occasionally filled with wine, milk, &c. We may guess at the capaciousness of this cup from the multiplicity of subjects which are carved upon it. Virgil imitates this passage.

—————— pocula ponam
Fagina, cælatum divini opus Alcimedontis;
Lenta quibus torno facili superaddita vitis
Diffusos hederâ vestit pallente corymbos.
Ecl. 3. 36.

And I this bowl, where wanton ivy twines,
And swelling clusters bend the curling vines.
Pope. Past. 1.

36. Here are three sorts of ivy mentioned, κισσος ελιχρυσος, and ελιξ. Pliny and Theophrastus say, that κισσος is a kind of ivy that grows alone without a support; ελιχρυσος is probably the poetical ivy which Virgil mentions, Ecl. 8. 12: Hanc sine tempora circum Inter victrices hederam tibi serpere lauros: it has golden or saffron-coloured berries, and is styled Hedera baccis aureis, and chrysocarpum; the ελιξ bears no fruit at all, but has white twigs, and small, angular, reddish leaves, which are more neat than the other sorts. Martyn.

Small tendrils with close-clasping arms uphold
The fruit rich speckled with the seeds of gold.
Within a woman's well-wrought image shines,
A vest her limbs, her locks a caul confines;
And near, two neat-curl'd youths in amorous strains
With fruitless strife communicate their pains:
Smiling, by turns, she views the rival pair;
Grief swells their eyes, their heavy hearts despair.
Hard by, a fisherman advanc'd in years,
On the rough margin of a rock appears;
Intent he stands t' enclose the fish below,
Lifts a large net, and labours at the throw:
Such strong expression rises on the sight,
You'd swear the man exerted all his might;
For his round neck with turgid veins appears—
"In years he seems, yet not impair'd by years."
A vineyard next, with intersected lines,
And red ripe clusters load the bending vines:
To guard the fruit, a boy sits idly by,
In ambush near, two skulking foxes lie;
This plots the branches of ripe grapes to strip,
But that, more daring, meditates the scrip;
Resolv'd ere long to seize the savoury prey,
And send the youngster dinnerless away:
Meanwhile on rushes all his art he plies,
In framing traps for grasshoppers and flies;
And earnest only on his own designs,
Forgets his satchel, and neglects his vines:
All round the soft acanthus spreads its train—
This cup, admir'd by each Æolian swain,
From far a Calydonian sailor brought,
For a she-goat and new-made cheese I bought;
No lip has touch'd it, still unus'd it stood;
To you I give this masterpiece of wood,
If you those Himeræan strains rehearse
Of Daphnis' woes—I envy not your verse—
Dread fate, alas! may soon demand your breath,
And close your music in oblivious death.

THYRSIS.

Begin, ye Nine, that sweetly wont to play,
Begin, ye Muses, the bucolic lay.

Nonnus in his Dionysiacs, b. 19. has elegantly imitated this and many other passages of Theocritus.

37. Small tendrils, &c.] Creech has thus translated this passage,

With crocus mix'd, where seem the *kids* to brouze,
The berries crop, and wanton in the boughs—

On which Dr. Martyn observes, "It is hardly possible for a translation to be more erroneous: καρπω κροκοεντι signifies a fruit of a yellow or saffron colour, which Creech has rendered crocus: but crocus or saffron is a flower, not a fruit. I was a long time puzzled to discover where he found the *kids:* but suppose it must be from mistaking the sense of the word ελιξ; it signifies those *tendrils* which sustain the vine in climbing: the Romans call it *capreolus*, hence the translator finding ελιξ to be *capreolus* in Latin, which also signifies a *kid*, took it in the latter sense: but he ought to have known, that though *capreolus* is used both for a *kid* and a *tendril*, yet ελιξ signifies only the latter." There is a translation of this Idyllium in the second volume of Whaley's Poems, which retains the same absurdity,

Around its lips the circling ivy strays,
And a young *kid* in wanton gambols plays.

39. Orpheaque in medio posuit, sylvasque sequentes. Ecl. 3. 46.

50. Fert ingens toto connixus corpore saxum. Æn. 10. 127.

51. ——Plenis tumuerunt guttura venis— Ovid. Met. 3. 73.

53. This is similar to an image in Homer's Iliad, b. 18. thus translated by Mr. Pope,

Next, ripe in yellow gold, a vineyard shines,
Bent with the ponderous harvests of its vines.

56. Foxes are observed by many authors to be fond of grapes, and to make great havoc in vineyards; Aristophanes in his Equites compares soldiers to foxes, who spoil whole countries, as the other do vineyards: Galen in his book of Aliments, tells us, that hunters did not scruple to eat the flesh of foxes in autumn, when they were grown fat with feeding on grapes. In the Song of Solomon, chap. ii. ver. 15, we read, "Take us the foxes, the little foxes that spoil the vines," &c. And agreeably to this, Nicander in Alexiph. v. 185. assures us that foxes will spoil the vines, Πιοτερην κ. τ. λ.

Cum pingui nocuit vulpes versuta racemo.

62. —— gracili fiscellam texit hibisco. Vir. ecl. 10. 71.

65. —— molli circùm est ansas amplexus acantho. Ecl. 3. 45.

67. Though Homer, in his catalogue of the ships, reckons Calydon among the Ætolian cities, yet it is certain that formerly it not only belonged to the Æolians, but was likewise called Æolis: Thucydides says in his third history αναχωρησαν ες την Αιολιδα την νυν καλουμενην Καλυδωνα.—Casaubon.

69. Necdum illis labra admovi, sed condita servo. Ecl. 3. 47.

Homer mentions the not having been used as a commendation of a cup in the 16th Iliad.

From thence he took a bowl of antique frame,
Which never man had stain'd with ruddy wine—
Pope.

71. —Those Himeræan strains] The Greek is τον εφιμερον υμνον, and is generally rendered amabile carmen: thus Horace, Epist. 3. b. 1. ver. 24. Seu condis amabile carmen: but the correction which Heinsius makes is undoubtedly genuine; he reads τον εφ' Ιμερα υμνον, the Hymn of Himera, a river in Sicily, the banks of which were the scene of the loves of Daphnis, as is evident from a passage in the 7th Idyllium ver. in the Greek 73. &c.—Besides, we have the indisputable authority of Ælian, who speaking of Daphnis and this hymn, says it is that which the goatherd calls, τον εφ' Ιμερα υμνον, and that Stesichorus the Himeræan bard first sung this celebrated hymn.

72. I envy not] Non equidem invideo. Ecl. 1. 11.

75. Incipe Mænalios mecum, mea tibia, versus. Ecl. 8. 21.

Thyrsis my name, to Ætna I belong,
Sicilian swain, and this is Thyrsis' song:
  Where were ye, Nymphs, in what sequester'd grove?
Where were ye, Nymphs, when Daphnis pin'd with love?
Did ye on Pindus' steepy top reside?
Or where through Tempe Peneus rolls his tide?
For where the waters of Anapus flow,
Fam'd streams! ye play'd not, nor on Ætna's brow;
Nor where chaste Acis laves Sicilian plains—
  Begin, ye Muses, sweet bucolic strains.
Him savage panthers in wild woods bemoan'd,
For him fierce wolves in hideous howlings groan'd;
His fate fell lions mourn'd the live-long day—
  Begin, ye Nine, the sweet bucolic lay.
Meek heifers, patient cows, and gentle steers,
Moan'd at his feet, and melted into tears;
Ev'n bulls loud bellowing wail'd the shepherd-swain—
  Begin, ye Nine, the sweet bucolic strain.
First from the mountain winged Hermes came;
"Ah! whence," he cried, "proceeds this fatal flame?

77. Thyrsis, &c.] Θυρσις οδ' ωξ Αιτνας, και Θυρσιδος αδεα φωνα, Thyrsis Ætnæus hic est, & hæc est Thyrsidis cantilena; Heinsius observes, this is the title or prelude to the hymn, very agreeable to the manner of the ancients: thus Herodotus —Herodoti Halicarnassensis hæc est Historia; he mentions his name, his country, and writings, exactly in the same manner as Thyrsis.

79. Virgil, Milton, Mr. Pope, and lord Lyttelton have imitated this passage—

> Quæ nemora, aut qui vos saltus habuere, puellæ
> Naïdes, indigno cùm Gallus amore periret?
> Nam neque Parnassi vobis juga, nam neque Pindi
> Ulla moram fecere, neque Aoniæ Aganippes.
> Ecl. 10. 9.

> Where were ye, Nymphs, when the remorseless deep
> Clos'd o'er the head of your lov'd Lycidas?
> For neither were ye playing on the steep,
> Where your old bards, the famous Druids, lie,
> Nor on the shaggy top of Mona high,
> Nor yet where Deva spreads her wizard stream.
> Lycidas.

> Where stray ye, Muses, in what lawn or grove,
> While your Alexis pines in hopeless love?
> In those fair fields where sacred Isis glides,
> Or else where Cam his winding vales divides?
> Pope.

Where were ye, Muses, &c. See Lord Lyttelton's beautiful Monody.

The 10th Eclogue of Virgil is indeed only a sort of parody on this first Idyllium of Theocritus.

87. Daphni, tuum Pœnos etiam ingemuisse leones
Interitum, montesque feri sylvæque loquuntur. Ecl. 5. 27.

91. Stant & oves circùm. Ecl. 10. 16.

95. Pan, deus Arcadiæ venit. Ecl. 10. 26.

96. ——————— dicat Opuntiæ
Frater Megillæ, quo beatus
Vulnere, quâ pereat sagittâ.
Hor. l. 1. Od. 27.

What nymph, O Daphnis, steals thine heart away?"
  Begin, ye Nine, the sweet bucolic lay.
Goatherds and hinds approach'd; the youth they hail'd,
And shepherds kindly ask'd him what he ail'd.
Priapus came, soft pity in his eye,
"And why this grief," he said, "ah! Daphnis, why?"
Meanwhile the nymph disconsolately roves,
With naked feet thro' fountains, woods, and groves,
And thus of faithless Daphnis she complains;
  (Begin, ye Muses, sweet bucolic strains)
"Ah youth! defective both in head and heart,
A cowherd styl'd, a goatherd sure thou art,
Who when askance with leering eye he notes
The amorous gambols of his frisking goats,
He longs to emulate their wanton play:"
  Begin, ye Nine, the sweet bucolic lay.
"So when you see the virgin train advance
With nimble feet, light-bounding in the dance;
Or when they softly speak, or sweetly smile,
You pine with grief, and envy all the while."
Unmov'd he sat, and no reply return'd,
But still with unavailing passion burn'd;
To death he nourish'd love's consuming pain—
  Begin, ye Nine, the sweet bucolic strain.
Venus insulting came, the youth addrest,
Forc'd a faint smile, with torture at her breast;
"Daphnis, you boasted you could Love subdue,
But, tell me, has not Love defeated you?
Alas! you sink beneath his mighty sway."
  Begin, ye Nine, the sweet bucolic lay.
"Ah, cruel Venus!" Daphnis thus began,
"Abhorr'd and curs'd by all the race of man,
My day's decline, my setting sun I know,
I pass a victim to the shades below,

99. Venit & upilio; tardi venere bubulci:
Omnes, unde amor iste, rogant tibi.—
Ecl. 10. 19.

102. Galle, quid insanis? inquit; tua cura, Lycoris,
Perque nives alium, perque horrida castra secuta est.
Ecl. 10. 22.

107. Ah youth! &c.] The Greek scholiast supposes this verse, and as far as to the 116th verse inclusive, to be the speech of Priapus comforting Daphnis; whereas it is undoubtedly that of the nymph Echenais, the mistress of Daphnis, upbraiding him for his incontinent passion; for he had been guilty of a breach of promise to her, and had offended her by following other women; taken in this light, the whole passage is beautiful, simple, and easy; "Daphnis," says she, "you was used to be styled a cowherd, a man of continency; but behold! you have adopted the manners of a goatherd, who when he observes the lasciviousness of his flock, wishes himself a goat:" Heinsius.—Virgil alludes to this place, Novimus & qui te transversa tuentibus hircis. Ecl. 3.

Τακεται οφθαλμως is a very strong expression, and emphatically denotes the effect which is produced in the eyes of any person who vehemently longs after an object which he can never attain; Horce has a similar expression,

> Cum semel fixæ cibo
> Intabuissent populæ. Epode 5. 39.

122. —— premit altum corde dolorem.
Vir. Æn. b. 4.

129. My setting sun I know] That is, he fore-

Where riots Love with insolent disdain"—
  Begin, ye Nine, the sweet bucolic strain.
" To Ida, Venus, fly, expose your charms,
Rush to Anchises', your old cowherd's arms;
There bowering oaks will compass you around,
Here low cyperus scarcely shades the ground,
Here bees with hollow hums disturb the day."
  Begin, ye Nine, the sweet bucolic lay.
" Adonis feeds his flocks, tho' passing fair,
With his keen darts he wounds the flying hare,
And hunts the beasts of prey along the plain."
  Begin, ye Nine, the sweet bucolic strain.
" Say, if again arm'd Diomed you see,
I conquer'd Daphnis, and will challenge thee;
Dar'st thou, bold chief, with me renew the fray?"
  Begin, ye Nine, the sweet bucolic lay.
" Farewel, ye wolves, and bears and lynxes dire;
My steps no more the tedious chase shall tire:
The herdsman, Daphnis, now no longer roves,
Through flowery shrubs, thick woods, or shady groves.
Fair Arethusa, and ye streams that swell
In gentle tides near Thymbrian towers, farewel,
Your cooling waves slow-winding o'er the plains."
  Begin, ye Muses, sweet bucolic strains.
" I Daphnis here my lowing oxen fed,
And here my heifers to their watering led,
With bulls and steers no longer now I stray."
  Begin, ye Nine, the sweet bucolic lay.
" Pan, whether now on Mænalus you rove,
Or loiter careless in Lycæus' grove,
Leave yon aerial promontory's height,
Of Helicè, projecting to the sight,
Where fam'd Lycaon's stately tomb is rear'd,
Lost in the skies, and by the gods rever'd;
Haste, and revisit fair Sicilia's plains."
  Cease, Muses, cease the sweet bucolic strains.
" Pan, take this pipe, to me for ever mute,
Sweet-ton'd, and bent your rosy lip to suit,
Compacted close with wax, and join'd with art,
For Love, alas! commands me to depart;
Dread Love and Death have summon'd me away."—
  Cease, Muses, cease the sweet bucolic lay.
" Let violets deck the bramble-bush and thorn,
And fair Narcissus junipers adorn.
Let all things Nature's contradiction wear,
And lofty pines produce the luscious pear:
Since Daphnis dies, let all things change around,
Let timorous deer pursue the flying hound;
Let screech-owls soft as nightingales complain"—
  Cease, cease, ye Nine, the sweet bucolic strain.
He died—and Venus strove to raise his head,
But Fate had cut the last remaining thread—
The lake he past, the whelming wave he prov'd,
Friend to the Muses, by the Nymphs belov'd.
  Cease, sacred Nine, that sweetly wont to play,
  Cease, cease, ye Muses, the bucolic lay.
Now, friend, the cup and goat are fairly mine,
Her milk's a sweet libation to the Nine:
Ye Muses, hail! all praise to you belongs,
And future days shall furnish better songs.

GOATHERD.

O, be thy mouth with figs Ægilean fill'd,
And drops of honey on thy lips distill'd!
Thine is the cup (for sweeter far thy voice
Than when in spring the grasshoppers rejoice)

saw his death; that he should no more behold the light of the Sun: an expression usual to the ancient poets; thus in Homer's Odyssey, b. 20. when the prophet Theoclymenus foresaw the death of the suitors, he says, ηελιος δε Ουρανυ εξαπολωλε, The Sun has perished from Heaven. Mr. Pope renders it,

  Nor gives the Sun his golden orb to roll,
  But universal night usurps the pole.

135. Hic virides tenerâ prætexit arundine ripas
  Mincius, éque sacrâ resonant examina quercu. Ecl. 7. 12.

137. Here bees, &c.] The Greek verse is very expressive of the sense: we hear the humming and buzzing of bees.

Ωδε καλον βομβευντι ποτι σμανεσσι μελισσαι.

139. Et formosus oves ad flumina pavit Adonis. Ecl. 10. 18.

Adonis was the son of Cynaras, king of Cyprus, by his own daughter Myrrha—he was the great favourite of Venus, and has been abundantly celebrated by the Greek poets. Martyn.

140. Auritosque sequi lepores, tum figere damas. Geor. 1. 308.

143. Say, if again arm'd Diomed] See Homer's Iliad, b. 5.

147. Farewell, &c.] Thus Virgil says, Vivite sylvæ, i. e. valete. Ecl. 8. 58.

155. Daphnis ego in sylvis, hinc usque ad sidera notus,
  Formosi pecoris custos. Ecl. 5. 43.

Here Virgil exceeds Theocritus, who only mentions the rural employments of Daphnis, whereas Virgil represents his Daphnis as a person whose fame had reached up to Heaven. Martyn.

159. Ipse nemus linquens patrium, saltusque Lycæi,
  Pan ovium custos, tua si tibi Mænala curæ,
  Adsis, O Tegææ favens——— Geor. 1. 1. v. 16.

167. Hos tibi dant calamos (en accipe) Musæ,
  Ascræo quos antè seni. Ecl 6. 69.

169. Pan primus calamos cerâ conjungere plures
  Instituit——————— Ecl. 2. 32.

The shepherd's pipe was composed of seven reeds, unequal in length, and of different tones, joined together with wax. Indeed in the 8th Idyllium there are two pipes described, composed of nine reeds each, but seven was the usual number.

171. ——————— sed me
  Imperiosa trahit Proserpina— Hor. l. 2. sat. 5.

172. Desine, Mænalios jam desine, tibia, versus. Virg. Ecl. 8. 61.

173. Virgil and Pope have imitated this passage:

  Nunc & oves ultro fugiat lupus; aurea duræ
  Mala ferant quercus; narcisso floreat alnus. Ecl. 8. 52.

  Let opening roses knotted oaks adorn,
  And liquid amber drop from every thorn. Pope. Past. 3.

178. Cum canibus timidi venient ad pocula damæ. Ecl. 8. 28.

179. Certent & cycnis ululæ— Ecl. 8. 55.

182. ————Extremaque Lauso
  Parcæ fila legunt. Æn. l. 10. 814.

190. Carmina tum meliùs, cum venerit ipse, canemus. Ecl. 9. 67.

Sweet is the smell, and scented as the bowers
Wash'd by the fountains of the blissful Hours
Come, Ciss! let Thyrsis milk thee—Kids, forbear
Your gambols, lo! the wanton goat is near.

IDYLLIUM II.

PHARMACEUTRIA.

ARGUMENT.

Simæthea is here introduced complaining of Delphis, who had debauched and forsaken her: she makes use of several incantations in order to regain his affection; and discovers all the variety of passions that are incident to a neglected lover.

WHERE are my laurels? and my philtres where?
Quick bring them, Thestylis—the charm prepare;
This purple fillet round the cauldron strain,
That I with spells may prove my perjur'd swain:
For since he rapt my door twelve days are fled,
Nor knows he whether I'm alive or dead:
Perhaps to some new face his heart's inclin'd,
For Love has wings, and he a changeful mind.
To the Palæstra with the morn I'll go,
And see and ask him, why he shuns me so?
Meanwhile my charms shall work: O queen of night!
Pale Moon, assist me with refulgent light;

197. Come, Ciss!] Κισσαιθα, the name of the goat, from κισσος, ivy, and αιθων, bright or shining.

1. This whole Idyllium, as Heinsius observes, seems to have been pronounced with great gesticulation, as is evident from the exordium, Πα μοι ται Δαφναι; τα δε τα φιλτρα; which is a direct imitation of the beginning of an ancient song, that used to be frequently rehearsed in the streets, and was called ανθεμα, Πȣ μοι τα ροδα; πȣ μοι τα ια; Where are my roses? where are my violets?

3. The cauldron] It is uncertain what sort of vessel the Κελεβη was; Nicander uses the word in his Theriacis, and there it signifies a mortar in which any thing is pounded. Casaubon thinks it may be taken in the same sense here. It is worth observation, that though Virgil has studiously imitated this whole Idyllium, he chose not to mention any sort of vessel, but says, molli cinge hæc altaria vitâ. Ecl. 8. 64.

4. Conjugis ut magicis sanos avertere sacris
Experiar sensus——— Ecl. 8. 66.

9. The Palæstra] The place for wrestling, and other exercises.

11. O queen of night!] Sorcerers addressed their prayers to the Moon and to Night, the witnesses of their abominations. Thus Medea in Ovid, Met. b. vii.

Nox, ait, arcanis fidissima—
Tuque triceps Hecate quæ cœptis conscia nostris
Adjutrixque venis.

Canidia addresses the same powers—O rebus meis
Non infideles arbitræ,
Nox, & Diana quæ silentium regis
Arcana cum fiunt sacra;
Nunc, nunc adeste. Hor. Epode 5. 49.

My imprecations I address to thee,
Great goddess, and infernal Hecatè
Stain'd with black gore, whom ev'n gaunt mastiffs [dread,
Whene'er she haunts the mansions of the dead;
Hail, horrid Hecatè, and aid me still
With Circe's power, or Perimeda's skill,
Or mad Medea's art—Restore, my charms,
My lingering Delphis to my longing arms.
The cake's consum'd—burn, Thestylis, the rest
In flames; what frenzy has your mind possest?
Am I your scorn, that thus you disobey,
Base maid, my strict commands?—Strew salt, and say,
"Thus Delphis' bones I strew"——Restore, my [charms,
The perjur'd Delphis to my longing arms.
Delphis inflames my bosom with desire;
For him I burn this laurel in the fire:
And as it fumes and crackles in the blaze,
And without ashes instantly decays,
So may the flesh of Delphis burn—My charms,
Restore the perjur'd Delphis to my arms.
As melts this waxen form, by fire defac'd,
So in Love's flames may Myndian Delphis waste:
And as this brazen wheel, tho' quick roll'd round,
Returns, and in its orbit still is found,
So may his love return—Restore, my charms,
The lingering Delphis to my longing arms.
I'll strew the bran: Diana's power can bow
Rough Rhadamanth, and all that's stern below.

19. My charms,] The Greek is Ιυγξ, a bird which magicians made use of in their incantations, supposed to be the wryneck. Virgil has, Ducite ab urbe domum, mea Carmina, ducite Daphnim. Ecl. 8. 68.

22. What frenzy] Ah, Corydon, Corydon, quæ te dementia cepit? Ecl. 2. 69.

28. Fragiles incende bitumine lauros.
Daphnis me malus urit, ego hanc in Daphnide laurum. Ecl. 8. 82.

The laurel was burnt in order to consume the flesh of the person, on whose account the magical rites were performed; it was thought, according to Pliny, b. 16. chap. the last, by its crackling noise, to express a detestation of fire. Mr. Gay has finely imitated this passage in his fourth Pastoral.

Two hazel-nuts I threw into the flame,
And to each nut I gave a sweetheart's name:
This with the loudest bounce me sore amaz'd,
That in a flame of brightest colour blaz'd:
As blaz'd the nut, so may thy passion grow,
For 'twas thy nut that did so brightly glow.

33. It was customary to melt wax, thereby to mollify the heart of the person beloved: the sorceress in Virgil, Ecl. 8. makes use of two images, one of mud, and the other of wax.

Limus ut hic durescit, & hæc ut cera liquescit
Uno eodemque igni: sic nostro Daphnis amore.

35. It was also usual to imitate all the actions they wished the loved person to perform; thus Simætha rolls a brazen wheel, believing that the motion of this magic machine had the virtue to inspire her lover with those passions which she wished. Canidia makes use of this wheel. See Hor. Epode 17. 6, 7.

Canidia, parce vocibus tandem sacris,
Citumque retro solve, solve turbinem.

Hark! hark! the village-dogs! the goddess soon
Will come—the dogs terrific bay the Moon—
Strike, strike the sounding brass—Restore, my charms,
Restore false Delphis to my longing arms.
Calm is the ocean, silent is the wind,
But grief's black tempest rages in my mind.
I burn for him whose perfidy betray'd
My innocence; and me, ah, thoughtless maid!
Robb'd of my richest gem—Restore, my charms,
False Delphis to my long-deluded arms.
I pour libations thrice, and thrice I pray;
O, shine, great goddess, with auspicious ray!
Whoe'er she be, blest nymph! that now detains
My fugitive in Love's delightful chains;
Be she for ever in oblivion lost,
Like Ariadne, 'lorn on Dia's coast,
Abandon'd by false Theseus—O, my charms,
Restore the lovely Delphis to my arms.
Hippomanes, a plant Arcadia bears,
Makes the colts mad, and stimulates the mares,
O'er hills, thro' streams they rage: O, could I see
Young Delphis thus run madding after me,
And quit the fam'd Palæstra!—O, my charms,
Restore false Delphis to my longing arms.

41. ——Hylax in limine latrat—
Virg. Ecl. 8. 107.
———visæque canes ululare per umbram,
Adventante Deâ— Æn. 6. 257.

The reason why Hecate was placed in the public ways, was because she presided over piacular pollutions: every new moon there was a public supper provided at the charge of the richer sort in a place where three ways met, hence she was called Trivia, which was no sooner brought, but the poor people carried it all off, giving out that the Hecate had devoured it; these suppers were expiatory offerings to move this goddess to avert any evils, which might impend by reason of piacular crimes committed in the highways. Potter's Ant.

43. Tinnitusque cie, et matris quate cymbala circum. Virg. Geor. 4. 64.

45. Et nunc omne tibi stratum silet æquor, et omnes
(Aspice) ventosi ceciderunt murmuris auræ.
Ecl. 9. 57.

51. The number three was held sacred by the ancients, being thought the most perfect of all numbers, as having regard to the beginning, middle, and end. We shall see a further propriety in it, if we consider that Hecate, who presided over magical rites, had three faces.

Terna tibi hæc primum triplici diversa colore
Licia circundo, terque hæc altaria circum
Effigiem dúco: numero Deus impare gaudet.
Ecl. 8. 73.

59. Hippomanes here undoubtedly signifies a plant, which is described as having the fruit of the wild cucumber, and the leaves of the prickly poppy; perhaps a kind of mullein; though in Virgil, Geor. 3. 280, it means a poison.
See Martyn.

60. Cum tibi flagrans amor et libido,
Quæ solet matres furiare equorum, &c.
Hor. b. 1. od. 25.

This garment's fringe, which Delphis wont to wear,
To burn in flames I into tatters tear.
Ah, cruel Love! that my best life-blood drains
From my pale limbs, and empties all my veins,
As leeches suck young steeds—Restore, my charms,
My lingering Delphis to my longing arms.
A lizard bruis'd shall make a potent bowl,
And charm, to morrow, his obdurate soul;
Meanwhile this potion on his threshold spill,
Where, though despis'd, my soul inhabits still;
No kindness he nor pity will repay;
Spit on the threshold, Thestylis, and say,
"Thus Delphis' bones I strew"—Restore, my charms,
The dear, deluding Delphis to my arms.
She's gone, and now, alas! I'm left alone!
But how shall I my sorrow's cause bemoan?
My ill-requited passion, how bewail?
And where begin the melancholy tale?
When fair Anaxa at Diana's fane
Her offering paid, and left the virgin train,
Me warmly she requested, breathing love,
At Dian's feast to meet her in the grove:
Where savage beasts, in howling deserts bred,
(And with them a gaunt lioness) were led
To grace the solemn honours of the day—
Whence rose my passion, sacred Phœbe, say—
Theucarila's kind nurse, who lately died,
Begg'd I would go, and she would be my guide;
Alas! their importunity prevail'd,
And my kind stars, and better genius fail'd;
I went adorn'd in Clearista's clothes—
Say, sacred Phœbe, whence my flame arose—
Soon as where Lyco's mansion stands I came,
Delphis the lovely author of my flame

65. Simætha burns the border of Delphis's garment, that the owner may be tortured with the like flame: Virgil's enchantress deposites her lover's pledges in the ground, under her threshold, in order to retain his love, and secure his affections from wandering.

Has olim exuvias mihi perfidus ille reliquit
Pignora cara sui; quæ nunc ego limine in ipso,
Terra, tibi mando—— Ecl. 8. 91.

71. Has herbas, atque hæc Ponto mihi lecta venena. Ecl. 8. 95.

Horace has—

Majus parabo, majus infundam tibi
Fastidienti poculum—— Epod. 5. 77.

Mr. Gay had this passage in view.

These golden lines into his mug I'll throw,
And soon the swain with fervent love shall glow. Past. 4.

83. The Athenian virgins were presented to Diana before it was lawful for them to marry, on which occasion they offered baskets full of little curiosities to that goddess, to gain leave to depart out of her train, and change their state of life.
Potter.

95. This is a stroke on the pride of those women who trick themselves in hired clothes; and

I saw with Eudamippus, from the crowd
Distinguish'd, for like helichrysus glow'd
The gold down on their chins, their bosoms far
Outshone the Moon, and every splendid star;
For lately had they left the field of fame—
Say, sacred Phœbe, whence arose my flame—
O, how I gaz'd! what ecstasies begun
To fire my soul? I sigh'd, and was undone:
The pompous show no longer could surprise,
No longer beauty sparkled in my eyes:
Home I return'd, but knew not how I came;
My head disorder'd, and my heart on flame:
Ten tedious days and nights sore sick I lay—
Whence rose my passion, sacred Phœbe, say—
Soon from my cheeks the crimson colour fled,
And my fair tresses perish'd on my head:
Forlorn I liv'd, of body quite bereft,
For bones and skin were all that I had left:
All charms I tried, to each enchantress round
I sought; alas! no remedy I found:
Time wing'd his way, but not to sooth my woes—
Say, sacred Phœbe, whence my flame arose—
Till to my maid, opprest with fear and shame,
I told the secret of my growing flame;
" Dear Thestylis, thy healing aid impart—
The love of Delphis has engross'd my heart.
He in the school of exercise delights,
Athletic labours, and heroic fights;
And oft he enters on the lists of fame"—
Say, sacred Phœbe, whence arose my flame—
" Haste thither, and the hint in private give,
Say that I sent you—tell him where I live."
She heard, she flew, she found the youth I sought,
And all in secret to my arms she brought.
Soon at my gate his nimble foot I heard,
Soon to my eyes his lovely form appear'd;
Ye gods! how blest my Delphis to survey!
Whence rose my passion, sacred Phœbe, say—
Cold as the snow my freezing limbs were chill'd,
Like southern vapours from my brow distill'd
The dewy damps; faint tremors seiz'd my tongue,
And on my lips the faultering accents hung;
As when from babes imperfect accents fall,
When murmuring in their dreams they on their mothers call.
Senseless I stood, nor could my mind disclose—
Say, sacred Phœbe, whence my flame arose—
My strange surprise he saw, then prest the bed,
Fix'd on the ground his eyes, and thus he said;
" Me, dear Simætha, you have much surpast,
As when I ran with young Philinus last
I far out-stript him, though he bravely strove;
But you have all prevented me with love;
Welcome as day your kind appointment came"—
Say, sacred Phœbe, whence arose my flame—
" Yes, I had come, by all the powers above,
Or, rather let me swear by mighty love,
Unsent for I had come, to Venus true,
This night attended by a chosen few,
With apples to present you, and my brows
Adorn'd like Hercules, with poplar boughs,
Wove in a wreathe with purple ribands gay"—
Whence rose my passion, sacred Phœbe, say—
" Had you receiv'd me, all had then been well,
For I in swiftness and in form excel;
And should have deem'd it no ignoble bliss
The roses of your balmy lips to kiss:
Had you refus'd me, and your doors been barr'd,
With axe and torch I should have come prepar'd,
Resolv'd with force resistance to oppose"—
Say, sacred Phœbe, whence my flame arose—
" And first to beauty's queen my thanks are due,
Next, dear Simætha, I'm in debt to you,
Who by your maid, love's gentle herald, prove
My fair deliverer from the fires of love:

is entirely similar to a passage in Juvenal, Sat. 6. 351.

Ut spectet ludos conducit Ogulnia vestem.
Ogulnia borrows clothes to see the show.

105. The Greek is Χως ιδον, ως εμανην κ. τ. λ. There is a similar line in the 3d Idyl. ver. 42. Ως ιδεν, ως εμανη, ως εις βαθυν αλλετ' ερωτα. Virgil has—

Ut vidi, ut perii, ut me malus abstulit error.
Ecl. 8. 41.

which is confessedly inferior to the Greek.

113. The literal translation of this passage is, And my colour was like thapsus:—θαψος is a Scythian wood of a boxen or golden colour; some take it to be the Indian guaiacum. The women that chose to look pale tinged their cheeks with it.
Heinsius's Notes.

116. Our poet uses the same proverb, Idyl. 4. ver. 16, and Virgil has——vix ossibus hærent.
Ecl. 3. 102.

119. Sed fugit interea, fugit irreparabile tempus.
Geor. b. 3. 284.

121. Cùm sic unanimem alloquitur malè sana sororem. Æn. B. 4. 8.

124. Solus hic inflexit sensus, animumque labantem
Impulit———— Ver. 22.

137. Diriguit visu in medio: calor ossa reliquit. Æn. b. 3. 308. If the learned reader will compare this passage with Sappho's celebrated ode Εις την ερωμενην, he will find great similarity both in the thoughts and expressions.

153. Heinsius observes there was a custom at Athens, that whenever a young man was smitten with the beauty of any lady, especially that of a courtezan, he wrote her name in a place appointed for the purpose, with some encomium upon her, and having acknowledged his passion, the day following he appointed for a festival, προς την αναδησιν, that is, to crown her head with a wreath of flowers and ribbands. Thus in Plato, Alcibiades, at a festival, resorts to Agatho, with a crown and ribands to adorn his head.

158. With poplar] The poplar was sacred to Hercules. Virgil has,

Populeis adsunt evincti tempora ramis.
Æn. 8. 286.

166. With axe and torch, &c.] If after rapping at the door, the lover was refused admittance, προς την αναδησιν, to place the flowery crown on the head of his mistress, he then threatened axes and torches, to break or burn the door—Thus Horace

Hic hic ponite lucida
Funalia, et vectes, et arcus
Oppositis foribus minaces— B. 3. od. 26.

"More raging fires than Ætna's waste my frame"—
Say, sacred Phœbe, whence arose my flame—
"Love from their beds enraptur'd virgins charms,
And wives new-married from their husbands' arms."
He said, (alas, what frenzy seiz'd my mind!)
Soft press'd my hand, and on the couch reclin'd:
Love kindled warmth as close embrac'd we lay,
And sweetly whisper'd precious hours away.
At length, O Moon, with mutual raptures fir'd,
We both accomplish'd—what we both desir'd.
E'er since no pause of love or bliss we knew,
But wing'd with joy the feather'd minutes flew;
Till yester morning, as the radiant Sun
His steeds had harness'd, and his course begun,
Restoring fair Aurora from the main,
I heard, alas! the cause of all my pain;
Philista's mother told me, "she knew well
That Delphis lov'd, but whom she could not tell:
The marks are plain, he drinks his favourite toast,
Then hies him to the maid he values most:
Besides with garlands gay his house is crown'd:"
All this she told me, which too true I found.
He oft would see me twice or thrice a day,
Then left some token that he would not stay
Long from my arms; and now twelve days are past
Since my fond eyes beheld the wanderer last—
It must be so—'tis my unhappy lot
Thus to be scorn'd, neglected, and forgot.
He wooes, no doubt, he wooes some happier maid—
Meanwhile I'll call enchantment to my aid:
And should he scorn me still, a charm I know
Shall soon dispatch him to the shades below;
So strong the bowl, so deadly is the draught;
To me the secret an Assyrian taught.

175. Love from their bowers] The Greek is παρθενον εκ θαλαμοιο, the thalami signified the inner chambers where the virgins were kept closely confined, and not permitted to converse with men. In Homer, Iliad, b. 6. the rooms where Priam's daughters lived are called τεγεοι θαλαμοι, as being placed at the top of the house; for the women's lodgings were usually in the uppermost rooms, as Eustathius remarks upon the passage; which was another means to keep them from company.

180. And sweetly whisper'd] Εψιθυριζδομες αδυ. See Idyl. 1. ver. 1.

193. That it was usual for lovers to adorn their houses with flowers and garlands in honour of their mistresses, is evident from a passage in Catullus, de Aty, ver. 66.

> Mihi floridis corollis redimita domus erat,
> Linquendum ubi esset orto mihi sole cubiculum.

> Fair flowery wreaths around my house are spread,
> When with the rising Sun I leave my bed.

202. His ego Daphnim aggrediar.
Ecl. 8. 102.

203. A charm I know] Majus parabo, majus infundam tibi
Fastidienti poculum. Hor. Epod. 5. 77.

206. Has herbas, atque hæc Ponto mihi lecta venena
Ipse dedit Mœris. Ecl. 8. 95.

The Assyrians were greatly addicted to magic.

Now, Cynthia, drive your coursers to the main;
Those ills I can't redress I must sustain.
Farewell, dread Moon, for I have ceas'd my spell,
And all ye stars, that rule by night, farewell.

IDYLLIUM III*.

AMARYLLIS.

ARGUMENT.

A goatherd declares his passion for his mistress Amaryllis, laments her cruelty, commends her charms, solicits her favours, and distracted at the thoughts of not obtaining them, threatens to drown himself, tries experiments to know if she loves him, sings love-songs, and seems resolved to die, and be devoured by wolves.

To Amaryllis, lovely nymph, I speed,
Meanwhile my goats along the mountain feed:
O Tityrus, tend them with assiduous care,
In freshest pasture, and in purest air;
At evening see them to the watering led,
And ware the Libyan ram with butting head.
Sweet Amaryllis! once how blest my lot
When here you met me in the conscious grot?
I, whom you call'd your dear, your love, so late,
Say, am I now the object of your hate?

* This Idyllium affords us a specimen of ancient gallantry, namely, of the παρακλαυσιθυρον, or mournful song, which excluded lovers used to sing at the doors of their mistresses: they had two methods of performing this, one was to sing it as they lay on the ground, thus Horace, ode 10. b. 3, was sung while the lover was porrectus ante fores; but this was performed standing, and with great gesticulation of body, and motion of the feet: it is called Comastes, which signifies, according to Hesychius, a shepherd that dances and sings at the same time. The turns in this song are very abrupt, sudden, and striking, and give us a lively picture of a distracted lover.

2. Pascuntur vero sylvas et summa Lycæi.
Geor. 3. 314.

3. O Tityrus, &c.] Virgil has translated these three lines;

> Tityre, dum redeo, brevis est via, pasce capellas:
> Et potum pastas age, Tityre: et inter agendum
> Occursare capro, cornu ferit ille, caveto.
> Ecl. 9. 23.

This passage of Virgil, Dr. Martyn thinks, seems to intimate, that he was engaged in translating the Idylliums of our poet.

6. The ram] The Greek is ενορχαν, which in this place undoubtedly signifies a ram. Thus Homer has Πεντεκοντα δ' ενορχα κ. τ. λ. Full fifty rams to bleed in sacrifice.
Pope's Iliad, b. 23

Creech and Dryden have rendered it ridgil: Dryden and Warton also have rendered the word capro in Virgil by the same term.

10. Dumque tibi est odio mea fistula, dumque capellæ,
Hirsutumque supercilium, prolixaque barba.
Ecl. 8. 33.

Does my flat nose or beard your eyes offend?—
This love will surely bring me to my end—
Lo! ten fair apples, tempting to the view,
Pluck'd from your favourite tree, where late they grew;
Accept this boon, 'tis all my present store—
To morrow shall produce as many more;
Meanwhile these heart-consuming pains remove,
And give me gentle pity for my love—
Oh! were I made, by some transforming power,
A bee to buzz in your sequester'd bower!
To pierce your ivy shade with murmuring sound,
And the fern leaves which compass you around—
I know thee, Love, and to my sorrow find
A god thou art, but of the savage kind;
A lioness sure suckled the fell child,
Fed with her whelps, and nurs'd him in the wild:
On me his scorching flames incessant prey,
Glow in my veins, and melt my soul away—
Sweet, black-ey'd maid! what charms those eyes impart!
Soft are your looks, but flinty is your heart;
With kisses kind this rage of love appease,
For me the joys of empty kisses please.
Your scorn distracts me, and will make me tear
The flowery crown I wove for you to wear,

12 This love, &c.] Mori me denique coges.
Ecl. 2. 7.

13. Quod potui, puero sylvestri ex arbore lecta
Aurea mala decem misi: cras altera mittam.
Ecl. 3. 70.

20. A bee to buzz] The Greek is, A βομβευσα μελισσα, and is very expressive of the sense. See Idyl. 1. 137.

22. And the fern leaves, &c.] The ancient shepherds often made themselves beds of fern, because they imagined that the smell of it would drive away serpents.

23. I know thee, Love, &c.] Virgil has,

> Nunc scio quid sit Amor: duris in cotibus illum
> Ismarus, aut Rhodope, aut extremi Garamantes,
> Nec nostri generis puerum nec sanguinis edunt.
> Ecl. 8. 43.

These ideas, not owing their original to rural objects, are not pastoral, and therefore improper: sentiments like these, as they have no ground in nature, are indeed of little value in any poem, but in pastoral they are particularly liable to censure, because they are more proper for tragic or heroic writings.

Rambler, No. 37.

Pope, endeavouring to copy Virgil, was carried to still greater impropriety;

> I know thee Love! on foreign mountains bred,
> Wolves gave thee suck, and savage tigers fed.
> Thou wert from Ætna's burning entrails torn,
> Got by fierce whirlwinds, and in thunder born.

32. For me, &c.] Εστι και εν κενεοισι φιλαμασιν αδεια τερψις;

Exactly the same verse occurs, Idyl. 27. l. 4. Moschus calls it, γυμνον το φιλαμα, a naked kiss.

Where rose-buds mingled with the ivy-wreath,
And fragrant parsley sweetest odours breathe—
Ah me! what pangs I feel? and yet the fair
Nor sees my sorrows, nor will hear my prayer—
I'll doff my goat-skin, since I needs must die,
And thence, where Olpis views the scaly fry
Inquisitive, a dire impending steep,
Headlong I'll plunge into the foamy deep;
And though perchance I buoyant rise again,
You'll laugh to see me flouncing in the main—
By one prophetic orpine-leaf I found
Your chang'd affection, for it gave no sound,
Though on my hand struck hollow as it lay,
But quickly wither'd, like your love, away—
An old witch brought sad tidings to my ears,
She who tells fortunes with the sieve and sheers;
For, leasing barley in my fields of late,
She told me, "I should love, and you should hate"—
For you my care a milk-white goat supplied,
Two wanton kids skip gamesome at her side,
Which Mermnon's girl, Erithacis the brown,
Has oft petitioned me to call her own;
And since you thus my ardent passion slight,
Hers they shall be before to morrow night—
My right eye itches; may it lucky prove!
Perchance I soon shall see the nymph I love;
Beneath yon pine I'll sing distinct and clear—
Perchance the fair my tender notes may hear;

35. Floribus, atque apio crines ornatus amaro.
Ecl. 6. 68.

The ancients thought that ivy and parsley had the virtue of dissipating the vapours of wine.

42. Headlong I'll plunge, &c.] Virgil has,

> Præceps aërii speculâ de montis in undas
> Deferar. Ecl. 8. 59.

45. Orpine] Τηλεφιλον is probably orpine, a low plant whose branches trail on the ground; the leaves are small, roundish, and of a glaucous colour, the flowers small and of a whitish green.

> Cool violets, and orpine growing still,
> Embathed balm, and cheerful galingale.
> Spenser.

49. An old witch.] The Greek is Αγροιω, and generally taken for a proper name; but Heinsius, with good reason, thinks it should be wrote α γραια, an old woman. We have a similar passage in the 6th Idyl. ver. 40. Ταυτα γαρ α γραια με Κοτυτταρις εξεδιδαξεν.

For this the old woman Cottytaris taught me.

50. Sieve and sheers] This was another sort of divination.

53. For you my care, &c.] Virgil has entirely copied this;

> Præterea duo nec tutâ mihi valle reperti
> Capreoli sparsis etiam nunc pellibus albo,
> Bina die siccant ovis ubera; quos tibi servo.
> Jampridem a me illos abducere Thestylis orat;
> Et faciet; quoniam sordent tibi munera nostra.
> Ecl. 2. 40.

59. My right eye itches] The palpitation of the right eye was reckoned a lucky omen.

Potter

Perchance may pity my melodious moan—
She is not metamorphos'd into stone—
Hippomanes, provok'd by noble strife,
To win a mistress, or to lose his life,
Threw golden fruit in Atalanta's way,
The bright temptation caus'd the maid to stay;
She look'd, she languish'd, all her soul took fire,
She plung'd into the gulph of deep desire.
From Othrys' top the bard Melampus came,
He drove the herd to Pyle, and won the dame:
Alphesibœa's mother, fam'd for charms
Of beauty, blest heroic Bias' arms.
Adonis fed his flocks upon the plain,
Yet heavenly Venus lov'd the shepherd-swain;
She mourn'd him wounded in the fatal chase,
Nor dead dismiss'd him from her warm embrace.
Though young Endymion was by Cynthia blest,
I envy nothing but his lasting rest.
Iäsion too was happy to obtain
The pleasures too divine for ears profane.
My head grows giddy—love affects me sore;
Yet you regard not, so I'll sing no more—

Stretch'd near your grotto, when I've breath'd my last,
My flesh will give the wolves a rich repast,
This will be sweet as honey to your taste.

IDYLLIUM IV.

THE SHEPHERDS.

ARGUMENT.

We have here a dialogue between Battus a shepherd, and Corydon a neatherd. The beauty of this Idyllium consists in that natural representation of sorrow which the poet makes the herds affected with in the absence of their master: Battus laments the death of Amaryllis. The latter part of this piece is very natural, but too much inclining to rusticity.

BATTUS.

Are these Philonda's cows that graze the mead?

CORYDON.

No; Ægon's—Ægon gave them me to feed.

BATTUS.

Don't you play false, and milk them by the by?

CORYDON.

My shrewd old master keeps too strict an eye;
The calves he suckles, and prevents the fraud.

BATTUS.

But where is Ægon? is he gone abroad?

CORYDON.

What, han't you heard it from the mouth of Fame?
Milo entic'd him to th' Olympic game.

BATTUS.

Will he engage in that athletic toil,
Who never yet beheld Olympic oil?

CORYDON.

Fame says, his strength with Hercules may vie;

65. Hippomanes, &c.] See the story in Ovid's Met. b. 10. v. 664.

69. She look'd, she languish'd, &c.] The Greek is,

Ως ιδεν, ως εμανη, ως ες βαθυν αλλετ' ερωτα!

There is a similar ver. Idyl. 2. 82.

Χως ιδον, ως εμανην, ως μευ περι θυμος ιαφθη—

Virgil has, Ut vidi, ut perii, ut me malus abstulit error! Ecl. 8. 41. Which is far inferior to the Greek; abstulit error is much more languid.

71. Othrys'] This was a mountain in Thessaly; which country was famous for such an extraordinary breed of oxen, that Neleus king of Pylus refused to give his daughter in marriage to Melampus king of Tyrius, except he procured him some of them, which he soon after accomplished by the help of his brother Bias.

Univer. Hist. vol. vi. p. 215. 8vo.

Turpia perpessus vates est vincla Melampus.
Prop. b. 2. ecl. 3.

78. Nor dead dismiss'd him, &c.] Bion, in his epitaph on Adonis, has a beautiful thought in allusion to this, ver. 45.

Εγρεο τυτθον Αδωνι, το δ' αυ πυματον με φιλασον. κ. τ. λ.

Raise, lov'd Adonis, raise thy drooping head,
And kiss me ere thy parting breath be fled;
The last fond token of affection give,
O kiss thy Venus, while the kisses live;
Till in my breast I draw thy lingering breath,
And with my lips imbibe thy love in death.
F. F.

81. Iâsion] The son of Jupiter and Electra; he lay with Ceres, and was by Jupiter struck with thunder;

Scarce could Iäsion taste her heavenly charms,
But Jove's swift lightning scorch'd him in her arms.
Pope's Od. b. 5.

82. Ears profane] Procul, ô, procul este profani.
Æn. b. 6. 258.

84. You regard not] Amor non talia curat.
Ecl. 10. 28.

87. Hoc juvat, et melli est.
Hor. b. 2. sat. 6. ver. 32.

Virgil begins his third Eclogue with almost the same words.

1. Dic mihi, Damœta, cujum pecus? an Melibœi?
D. Non, verum Ægonis: nuper mihi tradidit Ægon.
3. Hic alienus oves custos bis mulget in horâ.
Ecl. 3. 5.

There was a peculiar kind of theft which the mercenary herdsmen among the ancients were guilty of, which was to milk the cattle they tended clandestinely in the absence of their masters: these delinquents were called *αμολγοι*.

10. Olympic oil?] It was customary for the wrestlers, and other combatants at the Olympic games, to anoint themselves with oil, not only to render their limbs more supple, but likewise that their antagonists might have no advantage over them.

BATTUS.

And that stout Pollux is worse man than I.

CORYDON.

He with his spade is gone, at honour's call,
And twenty sheep to keep himself withal.

BATTUS.

To Milo surely high regard is had;
The wolves at his persuasion will run mad.

CORYDON.

These heifers want him, moaning o'er the mead.

BATTUS.

Alas! they've got a wretched groom indeed.

CORYDON.

Poor beasts, I pity them! they ev'n refrain
To pick the scanty herbage of the plain.

BATTUS.

Yon heifer's bones are all that strike the view:
Say, does she live, like grasshoppers, on dew?

CORYDON.

No, troth! by Æsar's banks she loves to stray,
And there I bring her many a lock of hay;
And oft she wantons in Latymnus' shades,
And crops fresh pasture in the opening glades.

13. His spade and sheep] Casaubon observes, that those who intended to be competitors at the Olympic games, came thirty days at least before they began, to be trained up and exercised by those who presided over the games, which lasted five days; so that the combatants remained at Elis near forty, at least five and thirty days: the twenty sheep therefore which Ægon carried with him were for his provision during his stay at Elis, and perhaps for sacrifice, and to entertain his friends. A spade, ςκαπανη, was the emblem or badge of a wrestler, and therefore painters and sculptors, as Festus Pompeius observes, represented wrestlers with this instrument in their hands; his words are, Rutrum tenentis juvenis est effigies in capitolio, ephebi, more Græcorum, arenam ruentis exercitationis gratiâ; in the capitol there is the effigy of a youth holding a spade, and, after the Grecian manner, turning the sand for the sake of exercise.

16. The wolves] The Greek scholiast observes, that madness is a distemper to which dogs of all animals are most liable: thus Virgil, Geor. 3. 496. Hinc canibus blandis rabies, Hence gentle dogs run mad; at least much more so than wolves; therefore, says Battus, if Milo can prevail on the rustic Ægon to go to the Olympic games, he might persuade even wolves to run mad.

17. These heifers, &c.] Moschus, idyl. 3. ver. 23. has a passage extremely similar to this,

Ωρεα δ'εςιν αφωνα, και αι βοες αι ποτι ταυροις
Πλαζομεναι γοαοντι, και ουκ εθελοντι νεμεσθαι.

And now each straggling heifer strays alone,
And to the silent mountains makes her moan;
The bulls loud-bellowing o'er the forests rove,
Forsake their pasture, and forget their love.
F. F.

21. ——— vix ossibus hærent. Ecl. 3. 102.

22. Dumque thymo pascentur apes, dum rore cicadæ. Ecl. 5. 77.

BATTUS.

That red bull 's quite reduc'd to skin and bone,
May the Lampriadæ, when they atone
The wrath of Juno, sacrifice his mate!
A wretched offering suits a wretched state.

CORYDON.

And yet on Physcus, or the marsh he feeds,
Or where Neæthus laves the verdant meads;
Where bright-ey'd flowers diffuse their odours round,
Buckwheat and fleabane bloom, and honey-bells abound.

BATTUS.

Alas! these herds will perish on the plain,
While Ægon courts fair Victory in vain;
His pipe, which sweetest music could produce,
His pipe too will be spoil'd for want of use.

CORYDON.

No fear of that, for when he went away,
He left it me, and I can sing and play:
I warble Pyrrhus' songs, and Glauca's lays,
Zacynthus fair, and healthful Croton praise;
And proud Lacinium, rising to the east,
Where Ægon swallow'd fourscore cakes at least:
There too a bull he boldly dar'd pursue,
Seiz'd by the hoof, and down the mountain drew;
Then gave it Amaryllis; with glad shout
The maids approv'd the deed, loud laugh'd the lubber lout.

BATTUS.

Sweet Amaryllis! though entomb'd you lie,
With me your memory shall never die:

27. Eheu, quam pingui macer est mihi taurus in arvo; Ecl. 3.
How lean my bull on yonder clover'd plain.
Warton.

28. Lampriadæ] Heinsius takes the Lampriadæ to have been the inhabitants of Lacinium, a promontory not far from Croton, where there was a celebrated temple erected to Juno—Attollit se diva Lacinia contra. Æn. 3. 552. They formerly were opulent, but afterwards reduced to extreme penury and wretchedness.

31. Saltibus in vacuis pascant, & plena secundum
Flumina; muscus ubi & viridissima gramine ripa. Geor. 3.

34. The Greek is, Αιγιπυρος, και κνυζα, και ευωδης μελιτεια.

The virgins that attended at the feast held in honour of Ceres, called Θεσμοφορια, strewed on their beds such herbs as were thought effectual to destroy all appetite for venereal pleasures, as κνυζα, fleabane, agnus castus, &c. See Potter.

40. I can sing] —— & me fecere poetam
Pierides; sunt & mihi carmina.
Ecl. 9. 32.

41. Glauca was a lutanist of Chios, Pyrrhus a Lesbian poet.

44. Horace says of a glutton——Porcius infra,
Ridiculus totas simul absorbere placentas.
B. 2. Sat. 8.

49. Sweet Amaryllis] This short elogy on the deceased Amaryllis, late the mistress of Battus,

I lov'd you dearer than my flocks of late,
And now, alas! I mourn your cruel fate.

CORYDON.

Yet, courage, friend; to morrow Fortune's ray
May shine with comfort, though it lours to day:
Hopes to the living, not the dead, remain
And the soft season brightens after rain.

BATTUS.

Firm is my trust—but see! these hungry cows
(White-face, away!) my tender olives browze!

CORYDON.

Away, Cymætha, to the bank! by Jove,
If I come near you, faith! I'll make you move—
See! she returns—Oh, that I had my pike!
I'd give the beast a blow she would not like.

BATTUS.

Pray, Corydon, see here! thy aid I beg;
A long sharp-pointed prick has pierc'd my leg:
How high these thorns, and spindling brambles grow!
Do'st see't?—'twas long of her; plague take the cow!

CORYDON.

Here comes the thorn! your throbbing pain I've found.

BATTUS.

How great the anguish! yet how small the wound!

CORYDON.

These thorny, furzy hills should ne'er be trod
With legs unguarded, and by feet unshod.

BATTUS.

Does your old master still persist to prize
His quondam mistress with the jet-black eyes?

CORYDON.

The same, for lately in the wattled ground
In the soft scene of love the carle I found.

BATTUS.

O, nobly done! lascivious old man!
Meet match for Satyrs, or salacious Pan.

---

is beautifully introduced on Corydon's mentioning her name.

53. Yet courage] ———sed credula vitam
Spes fovet, & melius cras fore semper ait.
Tibul. b. 2. el. 6.

And Horace,
———informes hyemes reducit Jupiter: idem
Summovet:
Non, si male nunc & olim Sic erit.
B. 2. od. 10.

Jove spreads the Heavens with dusky clouds;
The clouds he chides away;
To morrow's Sun shall shine serene,
Though Fortune lours to day.
Duncombe.

61. Oh that I had my pike] Unde mihi lapidem? unde sagittas? Hor. b. 2. Sat. 7.

IDYLLIUM V.

THE TRAVELLERS.

ARGUMENT.

This Idyllium is of the dramatic kind: Comates a goatherd, and Lacon a shepherd, after exchanging some very coarse railleries, a true image of vulgar freedom, contend in singing. The beauty of this piece consists in that air of simplicity in which the shepherds are painted; full of themselves, boastful of favours received, and making sudden transitions agreeable to the desultory genius of uncivilized nature.

COMATES.

My goats, of Lacon, Sybarite base, take heed;
He stole my goatskin—at a distance feed.

LACON.

Fly, fly, my lambs, these springs—nor longer stay,
Comates comes who stole my flute away.

COMATES.

What flute, thou servile, Sybaritic brute!
Pray when wast thou e'er master of a flute?
'Twas all thy pride, with Corydon, to draw
The rustic route with scrannel pipes of straw.

LACON.

The flute which Lycon gave me frank and free:
But pray, what goatskin did I steal from thee?
What goatskin e'er hadst thou, thou lubber lout?
It is well known thy master sleeps without.

COMATES.

What Crocylus bestow'd, of special note,
When to the nymphs he sacrific'd a goat;
Thou envied'st me the present, and by theft
Hast basely of the speckled pelt bereft.

---

1. Sybarite] Sybaris was once a powerful city of Calabria near Croton, in the bay of Tarentum; the inhabitants were so much addicted to pleasure and effeminacy, that their luxury became a proverb.

5. What flute] —aut unquam tibi fistula cerâ
Juncta fuit? non tu in triviis, indocte, solebas
Stridenti miserum stipulâ disperdere carmen?
Virg. ecl. 3. 25.

8. The Greek is καλαμας αυλον ποππυσδεν εχοντι. The word ποππυσδεν seems very expressive of the mean idea Comates had of the shepherd's piping. —Milton had both Theocritus and Virgil in view.

———Their lean and flashy songs
Grate on their scrannel pipes of wretched straw.
Lycidas.

9. ——Damœtas dono mihi quam dedit olim.
Ecl. 2. 37.

12. Thy master sleeps] The ancients used to sleep on various sorts of skins; thus in Homer, Iliad 10, speaking of Diomed,

Ευδ', υπο δ' ἔςρωτο ρινον βοος αγραυλοιο.

A bull's black hide compos'd the hero's bed;
A splendid carpet roll'd beneath his head.
Pope.

LACON.

I stole it not, I swear by mighty Pan;
Comates, thou'rt mistaken in thy man;
Or may I, seiz'd with instant frenzy, leap
Headlong from this high rock into the deep.

COMATES.

Thy flute I stole not; by the nymphs I swear,
The fountain-nymphs, to me for ever dear.

LACON.

If I believe thee, goatherd, may I prove
The desperate pains of Daphnis, pin'd with love:
Nought now is sacred!—yet a kid stake down,
Thou'lt find my skill superior to thy own.

COMATES.

A sow Minerva brav'd: for singing's sake,
I'll lay a kid, if thou a lamb wilt stake.

LACON.

Ah, sly old fox! but how can this be fair?
For good sheep's wool who ever shear'd goat's
    hair?
What booby, blown to folly's utmost pitch,
E'er left an udder'd goat to milk a bitch?

COMATES.

He that's as sure, as thou art to excel,
Though wasps may sing with grasshoppers as well:
But, lest thou turn thy challenge to a flam,
I'll stake this full-grown goat against thy lamb.

LACON.

Soft, hasty goatherd! let us hence remove
To yon wild olive-shade beside the grove;
There sing thy best, while in pure streams below,
Grateful to swains, the cooling fountains flow;
There spring sweet herbs, soft couches wait thy
    choice,
And there the sprightly grasshoppers rejoice.

COMATES.

Hasty I'm not, but greatly vex'd at heart
That thou dar'st brave thy teacher at his art;
Requital base!——Breed hounds, or wolf-whelps
    breed,
Ungrateful, they'll devour you for the deed.

LACON.

Ye goatherds love beyond the truth to stretch;
When learnt I ought of thee, invidious wretch?
But, come, vain boaster, to the grove along,
No more thou'lt challenge shepherds at the song.

COMATES.

Here rest we; lo! cyperus decks the ground,
Oaks lend their shade, and sweet bees murmur
    round   [spring;
Their honied hives; here two cool fountains
Here merrily the birds on branches sing;
Here pines in clusters more umbrageous grow,
Wave high their heads, and scatter cones below.

LACON.

With me retreat, where skins of lambs I keep,
Whose wool's a pillow softer far than sleep:
Thy goat-skins ill with cleanliness agree,
So rank they smell, nay rather worse than thee.
There to the nymphs, I'll crown, delightful toil!
One bowl of milk, and one of sweetest oil.

COMATES.

Retire with me to more sequester'd bowers,
There thou shalt rest on fern, and fragrant flowers;
O'er these the skins of tender kids I'll spread,
A softer far than thine and sweeter bed:

20. Into the deep] The Greek is ες Κραθιν, into Crathis, the name of a river near Sybaris.

25. Nought now is sacred] This is a proverb that seems to have taken its rise from the following circumstance: Hercules, on his arrival at Dios, a city of Macedonia, saw several people coming out of a temple; and being himself desirous to enter and worship, he inquired to whom it belonged; and being informed it was dedicated to Adonis, he answered, ȣδεν ιερον, nothing is sacred; for Adonis being no deity, he did not think him deserving of any honour or worship; by which seems to be meant, things that make a show of something great and sacred, but in reality are nothing but sorry and ridiculous trifles. Potter.

27. A sow, &c.] Υς ποτ' Αθαναιαν εριν ηρισεν, an adage that is used, when ignorant people put themselves in competition with men of learning.

32. ——Τις κακαν κυνα δηλετ' αμελγειν; Virgil has,

——Idem jungat vulpes et mulgeat hircos.
Ecl. 3. 91.

40. Hic gelidi fontes, hic mollia prata, Lycori;
Hic nemus. Ecl. 10. 42.

42. ——Resonant arbusta cicadis. Ecl. 2. 13.

48. When learnt I, &c.] There was a necessity in this place to omit translating four lines in the original, which are infinitely too indelicate for modest ears.

50. Efficiam posthàc ne quenquam voce lacessas.
Ecl. 3. 51.

51. Lo! cyperus, &c.] The Greek is—Τȣτω δρυες, ωδε κυπειρος,
Ωδι καλον βομβευντι ποτι σμανεσσι μελισσαι.
Which occurs in the first Idyllium. See ver. 136.

52. Bees murmur, &c.] Eque sacrâ resonant examina quercu. Ecl. 7. 13.

56. Scatter cones] The Greek word is, κωνȣς; Virgil has,

Strata jacent passim sua quæque sub arbore poma. Ecl. 7. 54.

58. Softer than sleep] The Greek is, υπνω μαλακωτερα. We find the same expression in the fifteenth Idyl. ver. in the Greek, 125.

Πορφυρεοι δε ταπητες ανω, μαλακωτεροι υπνω,

Virgil has, somno mollior herba. Ecl. 7. 45.
Softer than sleep, seems full as proper a figure as downy sleep, which is frequently used by modern poets.

62. Pocula bina novo spumantia lacte quotannis,
Craterasque duos statuam tibi pinguis olivi.
Ecl. 5. 67.

64. Fern] See the note on ver. 22. Idyl. III.
Fragrant flowers] The Greek is, γλαχων, which an eminent botanist informs me is the horned poppy.

Eight bowls of milk to Pan, great god, shall foam,
And eight of honey, and the honey-comb.

LACON.

Agreed: the contest lest thou shouldst evade,
I'll wait thy summons at thy oaken shade.
Who shall decide the honours of the day?
Perhaps Lycopas is not far away.

COMATES.

No need of him for judge; for here's as good,
Morson the keeper of thy master's wood;
He's cleaving faggots.

LACON.

Call the woodman near.

COMATES.

Call him thyself, for thou canst make him hear.

LACON.

Friend, hither haste while we in song contest,
And judge impartial who performs the best.

COMATES.

Let merit only thy just judgment guide,
Lean not to mine, or favour Lacon's side.
Thurius commits to Lacon's care his sheep;
Eumara's goats of Sybaris I keep.

LACON.

Who ask'd thee, goatherd, of thy tongue too free,
Whether the flock belong'd to him or me?

COMATES.

By Jove, I vow the simple truth I've told;
But thou grow'st vain, and scurrilously bold.

LACON.

Sing on, proud swain, nor thus consume thy breath;
But not, like Sirens, sing thy judge to death.

COMATES.

Me more than Daphnis the chaste Muses love;
Two kids I offer'd in their laurel grove.

LACON.

Me Phœbus loves, for him a ram I feed,
Which at the next Carnean feast shall bleed.

COMATES.

Twin-bearing goats I milk; "Ah, hapless swain!"
Alcippe cries, "dost thou their udders drain?"

LACON.

Full twenty presses I with cheese can fill,
And have a love-intrigue whene'er I will.

COMATES.

Gay Clearista, when perchance we meet,
Pelts me with apples, and says something sweet.

LACON.

Young Cratidus inspires my heart to glow,
For down his comely neck the lovely tresses flow.

COMATES.

Can dog-briar, or anemonies that bloom
In hedges, match with roses in perfume?

LACON.

Can acorns crude, whose coat is rough and dry,
With the soft fruitage of the chesnut vie?

COMATES.

In yonder juniper there broods a dove,
The young, when fledg'd, I'll carry to my love.

LACON.

Soft wool to weave a garment, if I live
To shear my sheep, to Cratidas I'll give.

COMATES.

Leave those wild olives, kids, and feed below,
Where the rough tamarisks luxuriant grow.

LACON.

Conarus, Cymy, leave those oak-crown'd meads,
And pasture eastward, where the white ram feeds.

COMATES.

A cypress pail is mine, and sculptur'd bowl,
I'll keep them for the charmer of my soul.

LACON.

This wolf-dog, to his flock and master true,
I'll give my boy, the wild beasts to pursue.

COMATES.

Ye prowling locusts, that devour my fruits,
Touch not my vines, for tender are the shoots.

LACON.

Ye grasshoppers, how I this goatherd vex!
Thus you the reapers of the field perplex.

69. Nunquam hodiè effugies; veniam quocunque vocaris. Ecl. 3.

77. Friend, hither haste] ———Ocyus, inquit, Huc ades, ô Melibœe. Ecl. 7. 8.

87. Sing on, &c.] Quin age si quid habes, &c. Ecl. 3. 52.

89. Theocritus, as well as Virgil, lays it down as an indispensable rule to himself, in these Amœbæan verses, to make the respondent shepherd answer his opponent in exactly the same number of lines: which must be allowed to be extremely difficult in a translation: how I have succeeded must be left to the determination of the candid reader, who, it is hoped, will make proper allowances for such a constraint.

91. Me Phœbus loves] Et me Phœbus amat. Ecl. 3. 62.

92. Carnean feast] This was a festival observed in most of the cities of Greece, in honour of Apollo, surnamed Carneus, from one Carnus an Acarnanian, who was instructed by this god in the art of divination, but afterwards murdered by the Dorians; this fact Apollo revenged upon them by a dreadful plague, to avert which they instituted this festival. See Potter's Ant.

97. Malo me Galatea petit, lasciva puella. Ecl. 3. 64.

99. At mihi sese offert ultro meus ignis Amyntas. Ecl. 3. 66.

100. Long hair was peculiar to the Lacedæmonians; they looked on it as the emblem of liberty, and those who wore it as uncapable of committing any illiberal action.

105. Parta meæ Veneri sunt munera; namque notavi
Ipse locum, aëriæ quo congressere palumbes. Ecl. 3. 68.

110. Where the rough tamarisks, &c.] See Idyl. I. ver. 16.

COMATES.

I hate the brush-tail foxes, that by night
Steal Myco's grapes, and then escape by flight.

LACON.

I hate dull beetles, that devour for prey
Philonda's figs, then buzzing wheel away.

COMATES.

Have you forgot, when once beneath my stroke,
You writh'd with pain, and ran to yonder oak?

LACON.

Yes, faith! but when Eumara lash'd thee well,
And bound with thongs, I readily can tell.

COMATES.

Morson, who's angry now?—Go, frantic swain,
Go, gather squills to calm your ruffled brain.

LACON.

Morson, I've nettled somebody full sore—
Go, gather sowbread, and be mad no more.

COMATES.

May Himera with milk, and Crathis flow
With wine, and fruits on plants aquatic grow.

LACON.

May Sybaris with honey-streams distil,
And maids each morn their urns with honey fill.

COMATES.

My goats on cytisus and wild oats browse,
And rest on arbatus and lentisck boughs.

LACON.

With fragrant balm my sheep are daily fed,
And ivy mixt with roses is their bed.

COMATES.

Alcippe charms not, though I sent a dove,
She neither prest my ears, nor kiss'd me for my [love.

LACON.

I love with warmest ardour young Eumede,
Who gave me kisses for a pastoral reed.

COMATES.

Can pies contend with nightingales? the owl
With swans? but you love discord at your soul.

MORSON.

Cease, Lacon, cease thy song; for I decree,
The lamb, Comates, as thy due, to thee:
Go, to the nymphs the welcome offering make,
And let thy Morson of the feast partake.

COMATES.

By mighty Pan, thou shalt, auspicious boy;
See how my goats leap wantonly for joy!
I too will leap, victorious as I am,
And laugh at Lacon, since I've gain'd the lamb.
Rejoice, my kids for in the cooling wave
Of Sybaris to morrow ye shall lave.
Yon butting, wanton goat I must forbid,
Till I have sacrific'd, to touch a kid—
What ruttish still!—your courage I'll abate,
Or may I suffer poor Melanthius' fate.

122. Steal Myco's grapes] See note of Idyl. I. ver. 56.

133. Ovid has a similar passage, Met. b. 1. ver. 111.

Flumina jam lactis, jam flumina nectaris ibant.

134. Plants aquatic] The Greek is, σια, which my botanic friend takes to be water-parsnips.

135. Mella fluant illi, ferat & rubus asper amomum. Ecl. 3.

137. Florentum cytisum sequitur lasciva capella. Ecl. 2. 64.

138. Lentisck] The Greek is, σχινος, the tree that produces mastich.

142. Prest my ears,] There was a particular sort of kiss which is called by Suidas χυτρον, the pot, when they took the person, like a pot, by both his ears: it is mentioned by Tibullus,

——————Natusque parenti
Oscula comprensis auribus eripiet.
B. 2. eleg. 5.

145. Can pies, &c.] Certent et cycnis ululæ. Ecl. 8. 55.

155. In the cooling wave, &c.] Ipse, ubi tempus erit, omnes in fonte lavabo. Ecl. 3. 97.

160. Melanthius' fate.] The fate of Melanthius, one of the suitors of Penelope, is thus described by Homer. See his Odyssey, b. 22, as translated by Mr. Pope.

Then forth they led Melanthius, and began
Their bloody work: they lopp'd away the man,
Morsel for dogs! then trimm'd with brazen sheers
The wretch, and shorten'd of his nose and ears;
His hands and feet next felt the cruel steel:
He roar'd, and torments gave his soul to Hell.

IDYLLIUM VI.

THE HERDSMEN.

ARGUMENT.

Damœtas and Daphnis drive their herds together into one place, and sing alternately the passion of Polyphemus for Galatea. Daphnis begins first, and addresses himself to Damœtas, as to the Cyclops; Damœtas answers him, as in the person of Polyphemus. Galatea's love is described from her wanton actions, and Polyphemus's obduracy from his neglect of the sea-nymph. This Idyllium is inscribed to Aratus, who was the friend of Theocritus, and supposed to be the author of an astronomical poem, called Arati Phœnomena.

DAMŒTUS and young Daphnis, tuneful wains,
Late fed their herds, Aratus, on the plains;
The first was ruddy, with a golden beard;
On Daphnis' cheek scarce doubtful down appear'd.
Fast by the margin of a murmuring spring,
'Midst noon-tide heat, they thus essay'd to sing.
And, while their cattle sought the cooling wave,
First Daphnis sung, for he the challenge gave.

1. Compulerantque greges Corydon et Thyrsis in unum. Vir. ecl. 7. 2.

DAPHNIS.

O Polyphemus, while your flocks you keep,
With apples Galatea pelts your sheep,
And calls you goatherd, and ungrateful swain;
Meanwhile you pipe in sweetly warbled strain,
Nor see the wild nymph, senseless as a log;
And, lo! again she pelts your faithful dog:
List! list! he barks, and in a strange amaze
His dancing shadow in the sea surveys:
Ah! call him back, lest on the maid he leap,
And tear her limbs emerging from the deep.
Lo! where she wantons, frolic, light, and fair,
As down of bearsfoot in soft summer air;
And, still impell'd by strange, capricious fate,
Flies those that love, and follows those that hate.
In vain the blandishments of love she plies,
For faults are beauties in a lover's eyes.
Thus Daphnis sung, Damœtas thus reply'd:

DAMŒTAS.

By mighty Pan, the wily nymph I spy'd
Pelting my flock, I saw with this one eye—
May Heaven preserve its lustre till I die:
Though Telemus presages ills to come;
Let him reserve them for his sons at home.
To tease, I seem regardless of her game,
And drop some items of another flame:
Soon to her ears the spreading rumour flies,
For envy then and jealousy she dies;
And furious, rising from her azure waves,
She searches all my folds, and all my caves:
And then my dog, obedient to command,
Barks as she walks, and bays her off the strand:
For when I lov'd, he wagg'd his tail with glee,
Fawn'd, whin'd, and loll'd his head upon her knee.
This practice shortly will successful prove,
She'll surely send me tidings of her love.
But I'll exclude this sea-jilt, till she swears
To press with me the bed herself prepares.
Nor am I so deform'd, for late I stood,
And view'd my face in ocean's tranquil flood;
My beard seem'd fair, and comely to the sight;
My eye, though single, sparkling, full, and bright:
My teeth array'd in beauteous order shone,
Well-match'd, and whiter than the Parian stone.
And lest enchantment should my limbs infest,
I three times dropt my spittle on my breast;
This charm I learnt from an old sorceress' tongue,
Who harvest-home at Hipocoön's sung.
Damœtas ended, and with eager joy
Daphnis embrac'd, and kiss'd the blooming boy;
Then gave, as best his sprightly taste might suit,
A pipe melodious, and receiv'd a flute.
Damœtas deftly on the flute could play,
And Daphnis sweetly pip'd, and caroll'd to his lay:
Their heifers gambol'd on the grass-green fields;
In singing neither conquers, neither yields.

10. With apples, &c.] See Idyl. V. ver. 97.

12. Meanwhile you pipe, &c.] ——Tu, Tityre, lentus in umbrâ
Formosam resonare doces Amaryllida sylvas. Ecl. 1. 4.

20. Bearsfoot] Ακανθα; see Martyn's note on Geor. b. 4. 123.

22. Flies those that love, &c.] Horace has a passage similar to this,

——Meus est amor huic similis, nam
Transvolat in medio posita, et fugientia captat.
B. 1. sat. 2.

29. Though Telemus, &c.] Polyphemus, in the 9th book of Homer's Odyssey, gives an account of Telemus, which I beg leave to lay before the reader in Mr. Pope's translation, ver. 593.

Th' astonish'd savage with a roar replies:
Oh Heav'ns! oh faith of ancient prophecies!
This Telemus Eurymedes foretold,
(The mighty seer who on these hills grew old;
Skill'd the dark fate of mortals to declare,
And learn'd in all wing'd omens of the air)
Long since he menac'd, such was Fate's command;
And nam'd Ulysses as the destin'd hand.

Dii capiti ipsius generique reservent.
Æn. b. 8. 484.

39. He wagg'd his tail with glee, &c.] Horace, speaking of Cerberus fawning upon Bacchus, expresses himself almost in the same words,

——————Leniter atterens
Caudam, & recedentis trilingui
Ore pedes, tetigitque crura. B. 2. od. 19.

45. Nor am I so deform'd, &c.] Nothing can be better fancied than to make this enormous son of Neptune use the sea for his looking-glass; but is Virgil so happy when his little landman says,

Non sum adeo informis: nuper me in littore vidi,
Cum placidum ventis staret mare? Ecl. 2. 25.

His wonderful judgment for once deserted him, or he might have retained the sentiment with a slight change in the application.

Hurd's Letter on the Marks of Imitation.

Ovid also imitates this passage in his Metam. b. 13. ver. 840.

Certè ego me novi, liquidæque in imagine vidi
Nuper aquæ: placuitque mihi mea forma videnti.

50. Whiter than the Parian stone] Horace has,

——————Glyceræ nitor
Splendentis Pario marmore purius.
B. 1. od. 19.

52. The ancients imagined that spitting in their bosoms three times (which was a sacred number, see note on Idyl. II. ver. 51.) would prevent fascination.

53. An old sorceress] The Greek is α γραια κοτυτταρις, which all the interpreters have taken for a proper name, whereas it undoubtedly signifies an enchantress or sorceress; for Horace calls the magical arts, which Canidia makes use of, Cotyttia; See Canidia's answer.

Inultus ut tu riseris Cotyttia
Vulgata, sacrum liberi Cupidinis?

Safely shalt thou Cotytto's rites
Divulge, and lawless Love's delights?
Duncombe.

Cotys, as Dacier observes, was the goddess that presided over enchantments and all the abominations that were practised in Greece and Thrace. See Juvenal, Sat. 2. ver. 91.

54. Who harvest-home, &c.] This verse occurs Idyl. X. ver. 16.

59. Tu calamos inflare leves, ego dicere versus.
Ecl. 5. 2.

61. Their heifers gambol'd, &c.] Horace has the same thought,

IDYLLIUM VII*.

THALYSIA, OR, THE VERNAL VOYAGE.

ARGUMENT.

This is a narration of a journey which Theocritus, along with two friends, took to Alexandria; as they are travelling, they happen to meet with the goatherd Lycidas, with whom they join company, and entertain each other with singing. Our poet had contracted a friendship, in the isle of Cos, with Phrasidamus and Antigenes, who invited him into the country to celebrate the feast of Ceres. The Thalysia was a sacrifice offered by husbandmen, after harvest, in gratitude to the gods, by whose blessing they enjoyed the fruits of the earth.

WHEN Eucritus and I, with one consent,
Join'd by Amyntas, from the city went,
And in our progress, meditating slow,
March'd where the waters of Halenta flow:
Antigenes and Phrasidamus, names
Renown'd afar, for each bright honour claims,
The sons of Lycopéus, at the shrine
Of fruitful Ceres offer'd rites divine:
In their rich veins the blood divinely roll'd
Of Clytia virtuous, and of Chalcon bold;
Chalcon, supreme of Cos, at whose command
The Burine fountain flow'd, and fertiliz'd the land;
Near it tall elms their amorous arms inwove
With poplars pale, and form'd a shady grove.
Scarce had we measur'd half our destin'd way,
Nor could the tomb of Brasilas survey;
When, travelling on the road, we chanc'd to meet
The tuneful goatherd, Lycidas, of Crete;
His very looks confest his trade; you'd swear
The man a goatherd by his gait and air:
His shoulders broad a goatskin white array'd,
Shaggy and rough, which smelt as newly flay'd;
A thread-bare mantle wrapt his breast around,
Which with a wide-wove surcingle he bound:
In his right hand, of rough wild-olive made,
A rustic crook his steps securely stay'd;
A smile serenely cheer'd his gentle look,
And thus, with pleasure in his eye, he spoke:
"Whither, Simichidas, so fast away,
Now when meridian beams inflame the day?
Now when green lizards in the hedges lie,
And crested larks forsake the fervid sky.
Say, does the proffer'd feast your haste excite,
Or to the wine-press some old friend invite?
For such your speed, the pebbles on the ground,
Dash'd by your clogs, at every step resound!"

Ludit herboso pecus omne campo, &c.
B. 3. od. 18.

In pastures all the cattle sport,
Soon as returns thy hallow'd day;
To meads the vacant hinds resort,
And, round th' unharness'd oxen, play.
Duncombe.

* This Idyllium is called ΘΑΛΥΣΙΑ, η ΕΑΡΙΝΗ ΟΔΟΙΠΟΡΙΑ, which has always been translated THALYSIA, or, THE VERNAL JOURNEY, but certainly very absurdly, as it implies a contradiction, the Thalysia being celebrated in autumn. Heinsius has proved, that οδοιπορια signifies ο πλυς, a navigation or voyage; this poem, therefore, may be styled the Vernal Voyage of Ageanax. It is well known that the ancients undertook no voyages but in the spring or autumn; the vernal navigation was called εαρινη, and the other θερινη; Lycidas therefore, the preceding spring, had composed a poem on the vernal voyage of his friend, which, as they are travelling on the road, he repeats. It contains the most ardent wishes and vows for his safety, and seems to have given Horace the hint for his third ode of the first book, on Virgil's voyage.

10. Of Clytia, &c.] The scholiast says, that Clytia was the daughter of Merops, and married to Eurypilus, king of the Coans, who was contemporary with Hercules; she was the mother of Chalcon. Homer mentions Eurypilus as king of Cos;

Cos, where Eurypilus possest the sway
Till great Alcides made the realms obey.
Pope's Il. b. 1.

13. ————Hic candida populus antro
Imminet, et lentæ texunt umbracula vites.
Ecl. 9. 41.

Here, o'er the grotto, the pale poplar weaves
With blushing vines, a canopy of leaves. Warton.

15. Scarce had we measur'd half our destin'd way, &c.]

Hinc adeo media est nobis via: namque sepulchrum
Incipit apparere Bianoris. Ecl. 9. 59.

Ancient tombs were usually placed by the road side; hence the expression, *siste viator*, which is absurdly introduced into modern epitaphs not placed in such situations.

29. Quo te, Mœri, pedes? an, quo via ducit, in urbem? Ecl. 9. 1.

Simichidas.] The grammarians have puzzled themselves to find out who this Simichidas was; it is strange they did not recollect a passage of Theocritus, in his poem called the Syrinx, where he claims this appellation to himself:

Ω, τοδε τυφλοφορων ερατον
Παμα Παρις θετο Σιμιχιδας

Ψυχαν. Cui (Pani) hunc peras-portantium amabilem thesaurum Paris posuit Simichidas animo; where, in a mystical manner, he confesses Simichidas and Theocritus to be the same person: Paris and Theocritus are the same: for Paris, when he was made judge of the beauty of the three goddesses, was Theocritus, that is, Θεων Κριτης: Thus Paris metaleptically is taken for Theocritus.
Heinsius.

31. Now when green lizards, &c.] The green lizard is very common in Italy; it is larger than our common eft, or swift: this circumstance strongly marks the time of the day.—Virgil imitates the passage,

Nunc virides etiam occultant spineta lacertos.
Ecl. 2. 8.

36. Dash'd by your clogs, &c.] The Greek is αρβυλιδεσσιν: αρβυλη was a kind of wooden shoe armed with iron nails, peculiar to the Bœotians, with which they used to tread the grapes in the wine-press.

Then I; "Dear Lycidas, so sweet your strains,
You shame the reapers and the shepherd-swains;
Your pipe's fam'd numbers, though they please me well,
Hope spurs me on to rival, or excel:
We go great Ceres' festival to share;
Our honour'd friends the sacred rites prepare:
To her they bring the first fruit of their store,
For with abundance she has blest their floor.
But since, my friend, we steer one common way,
And share the common blessings of the day,
Let us, as thus we gently pace along,
Divert the journey with bucolic song.
Me the fond swains have honour'd from my youth,
And call the Muses' most melodious mouth;
They strive my ears incredulous to catch
With praise, in vain; for I, who ne'er can match
Sicelidas, or sweet Philetas' song,
Croak like a frog the grasshoppers among."
Thus with alluring words I sooth'd the man,
And thus the goatherd, with a smile, began:
"Accept this crook, small token of my love,
For sure you draw your origin from Jove!
I scorn the builder, who, to show his skill,
Rears walls to match Oromedon's proud hill;

44. For with abundance, &c.] ——Neque illum
Flava Ceres alto nequicquam spectat Olympo.
Georg. b. 1. 95.

47. Cantantes licet usque, minus via lædet, eamus.
Ecl. 9. 64.

49. Me the fond swains, &c.] ——Et me fecere poetam [dicunt
Pierides: sunt et mihi carmina: me quoque
Vatem pastores, sed non ego credulus illis.
Ecl. 9. 32.

52. I, who ne'er can match, &c.] Virgil follows very close;

Nam neque adhuc Varo videor, nec dicere Cinnâ
Digna, sed argutos inter strepere anser olores.
Ecl. 9. 35.

53. Sicelidas.] That is, Asclepiades, the son of Sicelidas; the father's name is put for the son's: he was a Samian poet, a writer of epigrams. Philetas was of Cos. Both these are mentioned in that beautiful idyllium which Moschus wrote on the death of Bion; indeed this mention is in the six verses which were wanting in the ancient editions of that poet, and which are supposed to have been supplied by Marcus Musurus of Crete; though Scaliger affirms that they were written by Moschus:

Sicelidas, the Samian shepherd sweet,
And Lycidas, the blithest bard of Crete, [elate,
Whose sprightly looks erst spoke their hearts
Now sorrowing mourn thy sad untimely fate;
Mourns too Philetas' elegiac muse. F. F.

57. Accept this crook, &c.] At tu sume pedum.
Ecl. 5. 88.

60. Oromedon] This was the name of a mountain in the island of Cos, which seems to have taken its appellation from a giant who was slain and buried there. Propertius mentions Oromedon as one of the giants who waged war against the gods;

——Canam cœloque minantem
Cœum, & Phlegræis Oromedonta jugis.
B. 2. el. 8.

Nor do those poets merit more regard
Who dare to emulate the Chian bard.
Since songs are grateful to the shepherd-swain,
Let each rehearse some sweet bucolic strain;
I'll sing those lays (and may the numbers please)
Which late last spring I labour'd at my ease."
"Oh, may Ageanax, with prosperous gale,
To Mitylene, the pride of Lesbos, sail!
Tho' now the south winds the vext ocean sweep,
And stern Orion walks upon the deep;
So will he sooth those love-consuming pains
That burn my breast and glow within my veins.
May halcyons smooth the waves, and calm the seas,
And the rough south-east sink into a breeze;

Oromedon on Phlegra's heights I'll sing,
And Cœus threatening Heaven's eternal king.

61. Nor do those poets, &c.] The literal sense of the original is, as Heinsius observes; "And those birds, or cocks of the Muses, (poets) that pretend to rival the Chian cock, or bard, (Homer) strive to no purpose:" for the word ορνις and αοιδος means the same thing: Theocritus calls Homer the Chian bard or cock, in the same manner as Horace styles Varius the cock of the Mæonian song, or the prince of epic poetry:

Scriberis Vario fortis, & hostium
Victor Mæonii carminis alite. B. 1. ode 6.

This passage of Theocritus might, perhaps, be thus translated:

Nor do those muse-cocks merit more regard,
Who crow defiance to the Chian bard.

65. Imo hæc, in viridi nuper quæ cortice fagi
Carmina descripsi, et modulans alterna notavi,
Experiar. [tavi,
Ecl. 5. 13.

66. Last spring] The Greek is εν ορει, in a mountain; instead of which, Heinsius rightly reads εν ωρα, in the spring; for ωρα sometimes signifies το εαρ the spring.

70. And stern Orion, &c.] ——Quam magnus Orion,
Cum pedes incedit medii per maxima Nerei
Stagna, viam scindens, humero supereminet undas. Æn. 10. 763.

So thro' mid ocean when Orion strides,
His bulk enormous tow'rs above the tides.
Pitt.

Mr. Warton observes, that Virgil has not borrowed this thought from Homer. But does he not seem to have taken it from Theocritus?

73. May halcyons] The fable of Ceyx and his wife Halcyone being turned into birds, is beautifully related in the eleventh book of Ovid's Metamorph. The mutual love of these persons subsisted after their change; in honour of which the gods are said to have ordained, that while they sit on their nest, which floats on the sea, there should be no storm;

————Alcyone comprest,
Seven days sits brooding on her floating nest,
A wintery queen: her sire at length is kind,
Calms every storm, and hushes every wind;
Prepares his empire for his daughter's ease,
And for his hatching nephews smooths the seas.
Dryden.

Halcyons, of all the birds that haunt the main,
Most lov'd and honour'd by the Neraid train.
May all things smile propitious while he sails!
To the wish'd port convey him safe, ye gales!
Then shall my brows with violets be crown'd,
Or dill sweet-smelling, or with roses bound:
Before the hearth I'll quaff the Ptelean bowl;
Parch'd beans shall stimulate my thirsty soul:
High as my arms the flowery couch shall swell
Of fleabane, parsley, and sweet asphodell.
Mindful of dear Ageanax, I'll drink,
Till to the lees the rosy bowl I sink.
Two shepherds sweetly on the pipe shall play,
And Tityrus exalt the vocal lay;
Shall sing how Daphnis the coy damsel lov'd,
And, her pursuing, o'er the mountains rov'd;
How the rough oaks bewail'd his fate, that grow
Where Himera's meandring waters flow;
While he still urg'd o'er Rhodope his flight,
O'er Hæmus, Caucasus, or Atho's height,

81. Ante focum, si frigus erit; si messis, in umbrâ;
Vina novum fundam calathis arvisia nectar.
Ecl. 5. 70.

In winter shall the genial feast be made
Before the fire; by summer in the shade.
Dryden.

The ancients held three things requisite towards indulging their genius, namely, a good fire, wine, and music: Lycidas promises himself these three blessings, if Ageanax is favoured with a prosperous voyage. Heinsius.

84. Fleabane] See note on Idyl. 4. 34. Asphodell, or the day-lily: asphodells were by the ancients planted near burying-places, in order to supply the manes of the dead with nourishment.
Johnson's Dict.

By those happy souls who dwell
In yellow meads of asphodell.
Pope's St. Cecilia.

86. Till to the lees, &c.] At entertainments, when they drank healths, it was usual to drain the vessel they drank out of as far as the sediment: thus Horace, b. 3. ode 15, addressing himself to an ancient lady, says, it did not become her to empty the vessel of wine to the lees; nec poti vetulam fæce tenus cadi.

87. Cantabunt mihi Damœtas, et Lyctius Ægon.
Ecl. 5. 72.

89. The coy damsel] The Greek is, Ξενεας, and commonly understood as a proper name, but Heinsius observes, that it is here only appellative, and signifies a certain damsel: as ξενος Αθηναιος is Atheniensis quidam, a certain Athenian: the mistress of Daphnis was named Echenais. See note on Idyl. 1. 107.

91. Illum etiam lauri, illum etiam flevere myricæ. Ecl. 10. 13.

92. Where Himera's] See note on Idyl. 1. 71.

93. Rhodope, Atho, &c.] Virgil imitates this passage twice:

Aut Tmarus, aut Rhodope, aut extremi Garamantes. Ecl. 8. 44.
Aut Atho, aut Rhodopen, aut alta Ceraunia.
Geor. 1. 332.

The disjunctive particle aut, in each verse, is thrice repeated agreeable to Theocritus,

Η Αθω, η Ροδοπαν, η Καυκασον.

And, like the snow that on their tops appears,
Dissolv'd in love, as that dissolves in tears.
Next he shall sing the much-enduring hind
By his harsh lord in cedar chest confin'd;
And how the honey bees, from roseat bowers,
Sustain'd him with the quintessence of flowers;
For on his lips the Muse her balm distill'd,
And his sweet mouth with sweetest nectar fill'd.
O blest Comatas! nobly hast thou sped,
Confin'd all spring, to be with honey fed!
O had'st thou liv'd in these auspicious days!
I'd drive thy goats on breezy hills to graze,
Whilst thou should'st under oaken shades recline,
Or sweetly chant beneath the verdant pine."
He sung—and thus I answer'd: "Friendly swain,
Far other numbers me the wood-nymph train
Taught, when my herds along the hills I drove,
Whose fame, perchance, has reach'd the throne of Jove.
Yet, for thy sake, the choicest will I choose;
Then lend an ear, thou darling of the Muse!
"On me bland Cupids sneez'd, who Myrto love
Dearly, as kids the spring-embellish'd grove:
Aratus too, whose friendship is my joy,
Aratus fondly loves the beauteous boy:
And well Aristis, to the Muses dear,
Whose lyre Apollo would vouchsafe to hear,
And well Aristis knows, renown'd for truth,
How fond Aratus loves the blooming youth.
O Pan! whom Omole's fair mountain charms,
Place him, uncall'd, in dear Aratus' arms!
Whether Philinus, or some softer name:
Then may Arcadian youths no longer maim,
With scaly squills, thy shoulders or thy side,
When in the chase no venison is supply'd.

105. Atque utinam ex vobis unus, vestrique fuissem
Aut custos gregis, &c. Ecl. 10. 35.

115. Cupids sneez'd] Some sneezes were reckoned profitable, others prejudicial: Casaubon observes, that sneezing was a disease, or at least a symptom of some infirmity; and therefore, when any one sneezed, it was usual to say, Ζηθι, May you live; or Ζευ σωσον, God bless you. See Potter's Antiq. ch. 17.

117. Aratus] Supposed to be the author of the Phænomena.

123. Omole] A mountain of Thessaly, near Othrys, the seat of the Centaurs. See Virg. Æn. b. 7. 674.

126. It was usual for the ancient heathens to treat the images of their gods well or ill, just as they fancied they had been used by them: in like manner the modern Indians chastise their idols with scourges whenever any calamity befals them. There is a passage in Anacreon, ode 10, where a rustic thus addresses a little waxen image of Cupid;

This instant, Love, my breast inspire,
There kindle all thy gentle fire;
But, if thou fail'st to favour me,
I swear I'll make a fire of thee. F. F.

Pan had a festival in Arcadia, the country he chiefly delighted in, at which the Arcadians, if they missed of their prey in hunting, in anger at the god whom they reputed the president of that sport, used to beat his statue with squills, or sea onions. Potter's Ant. ch. 20.

But may'st thou, if thou dar'st my boon deny,
Torn by fell claws, on beds of nettles lie,
All the cold winter freeze beneath the pole
Where Hebrus' waves down Edon's mountains roll;
In summer, glow in Æthiopia's fires,
Where under Blemyan rocks scorch'd Nile retires.
Leave, O ye Loves, whose cheeks out-blush the rose!
The meads where Hyetis and Byblis flows:
To fair Dione's sacred hill remove,
And bid the coy Philinus glow with love.
Though as a pear he's ripe, the women say,
Thy bloom, alas! Philinus, fades away!
No more, Aratus, let us watch so late,
Nor nightly serenade before his gate:
But in this school let some unmeaning sot
Toil when the first cock crows, and hanging be his lot.
Rest be our portion! and, with potent charm,
May some enchantress keep us free from harm!"
I sung: he view'd me with a smiling look;
And for my song presented me his crook:
Then to the left he turn'd, through flowery meads,
The winding path-way that to Pyxa leads;
While with my friends I took the right-hand road
Where Phrasidamus makes his sweet abode;
Who courteous bad us on soft beds recline
Of lentisck, and young branches of the vine;
Poplars and elms above, their foliage spread,
Lent a cool shade, and wav'd the breezy head;
Below, a stream, from the Nymphs' sacred cave,
In free meanders led its murmuring wave:
In the warm sun-beams, verdant shrubs among,
Shrill grasshoppers renew'd their plaintive song:
At distance far, conceal'd in shades, alone,
Sweet Philomela pour'd her tuneful moan:
The lark, the goldfinch warbled lays of love,
And sweetly pensive coo'd the turtle dove:
While honey-bees, for ever on the wing,
Humm'd round the flowers, or sipt the silver spring.
The rich, ripe season gratified the sense
With summer's sweets, and autumn's redolence.
Apples and pears lay strew'd in heaps around,
And the plum's loaded branches kiss'd the ground.
Wine flow'd abundant from capacious tuns,
Matur'd divinely by four summers suns.
Say, Nymphs of Castaly! for ye can tell,
Who on the summit of Parnassus dwell,
Did Chiron e'er to Hercules produce
In Pholus' cave such bowls of generous juice?
Did Polypheme, who from the mountain's steep
Hurl'd rocks at vessels sailing on the deep,
E'er drain the goblet with such nectar crown'd,
Nectar that nimbly made the Cyclops bound,
As then, ye Nymphs! at Ceres' holy shrine
Ye mix'd the milk, the honey, and the wine.
O may I prove once more that happy man
In her large heaps to fix the purging fan!
And may the goddess smile serene and bland,
While ears of corn and poppies grace her hand.

131. Nec si frigoribus mediis Hebrumque bibamus,
Sithoniasque nives hiemis subeamus aquosæ:
Nec si, cum moriens altâ liber aret in ulmo,
Æthiopum versemus oves sub sidere Cancri.
Ecl. 10. 65.

Thus also Horace, b. 1. ode 22. Pone me pigris, &c.

Place me where no soft summer gale
Among the quivering branches sighs,
Where clouds, condens'd, for ever veil
With horrid gloom the frowning skies:
Place me beneath the burning zone,
A clime deny'd to human race;
My flame for Lalagé I'll own;
Her voice and smiles my song shall grace.
Duncombe.

132. Hebrus and Edon.] A river and mountain of Thrace.

140. Thy bloom, alas! &c.] Thus Anacreon, ode 11th, Λεγουσιν αι γυναικες.

Oft, with wanton smiles and jeers,
Women tell me I'm in years.

150. Pyxa] This is supposed to be a city in the island of Cos.

154. Lentisck] See Idyl. V. 138.

160. Shrill grasshoppers] I am aware that the Greek word, τεττιξ, and the Latin cicada, means a different insect from our grasshopper; for it has a rounder and shorter body, is of a dark green colour, sits upon trees, and makes a noise five times louder than our grasshopper; it begins its song as soon as the Sun grows hot, and continues singing till it sets: its wings are beautiful, being streaked with silver, and marked with brown spots; the outer wings are twice as long as the inner, and more variegated; yet, after the example of Mr. Pope, (see Iliad 3. ver. 200) I retain the usual term.

164. Nec gemere aëriâ cessabit turtur ab ulmo.
Ecl. 1. 59.

167. ————— Tuis hic omnia plena
Muneribus; tibi pampineo gravidus autumno
Floret ager; spumat plenis vindemia labris.
Geor. 2. 5.

Here all the riches of thy reign abound;
Each field replete with blushing autumn glows,
And in deep tides for thee the foaming vintage flows.
Warton.

172. By four summers] Horace has, quadrimum merum. B. 1. ode 9.

175. Chiron and Pholus] Two Centaurs: Chiron is said to have taught Æsculapius physic, Apollo music, and Hercules astronomy, and was tutor to Achilles.

178. Hurl'd rocks] A larger rock then heaving from the plain,
He whirl'd it round; it sung across the main;
It fell and brush'd the stern; the billows roar,
Shake at the weight, and refluent beat the shore.
Pope's Odys. b. 9.

180. Made the Cyclops bound,] Horace seems to allude to this,

Pastorem saltaret uti Cyclopa, rogabat.
B. 1. Sat. 5.

182. Cui tu lacte favos, et miti dilue Baccho.
Geor. b. 1. 344.

Mix honey sweet, with milk and mellow wine.
Warton.

IDYLLIUM VIII.

THE BUCOLIC SINGERS.

ARGUMENT.

A contest in singing, between the shepherd Menalcas and the neatherd Daphnis, is related; a goatherd is chosen judge; they stake down their pastoral pipes as the reward of victory; the prize is decreed to Daphnis. In this Idyllium, as in the fifth, the second speaker seems to follow the turn of thought used by the first. Dr. Spence observes, there are persons in Italy, and particularly in Tuscany, named Improvisatori, who are like the shepherds in Theocritus, surprisingly ready at their answers, respondere parati, and go on speech for speech alternately, alternis dicetis, amant alterna camenæ. This Idyllium is addressed to his friend Diophantus.

DAPHNIS, MENALCAS, GOATHERD.

DEAR Diophantus, some few days ago,
Menalcas, on the mountain's breezy brow,
By chance met Daphnis, bonny, blithe, and fair;
This fed his herds, and that his fleecy care.
Both grac'd with golden tresses, both were young,
Both sweetly pip'd, and both melodious sung:
Then first Menalcas, with complacent look,
Survey'd the master of the herd, and spoke:

MENALCAS.

Daphnis, thou keeper of the bellowing kine!
Wilt thou to me the palm of song resign?
Or try thy skill, and then thy master own?
Thus Daphnis answer'd:

DAPHNIS.

Thou sheep-tending clown,
Poor-piping shepherd! sing'st thou e'er so well,
Thou canst not Daphnis at the song excel.

MENALCAS.

Stake then some wager; let us trial make:

DAPHNIS.

I'll make the trial, and the wager stake.

MENALCAS.

What shall we lay, to equal our renown?

DAPHNIS.

I'll lay a calf, and thou a lamb full-grown.

MENALCAS.

A lamb I dare not; for my parents keep
Strict watch, and every evening count my sheep.

DAPHNIS.

What wilt thou stake? and what the victor's gains?

MENALCAS.

A pipe I form'd, of nine unequal strains,
Sweet-ton'd, with whitest wax compacted tight;
This, this I'll stake—but not my parent's right.

DAPHNIS.

And I have one of nine unequal strains, [pains,
Sweet-ton'd, and wax'd throughout with nicest
Which late I made; ev'n now my finger bleeds,
Sore wounded by a splinter of the reeds.
Who shall decide the honours of the day?

MENALCAS.

Yon goatherd, let him judge the vocal lay;
Our dog barks at him—call—the man is near:
The shepherds call'd, the goatherd came to hear:
The last decided, while the former sung.
Menalcas first essay'd his tuneful tongue:
Thus in alternate strains the contest ran,
Daphnis reply'd—Menalcas first began;

1. Dear Diophantus] The Greek is, Μαλα νεμων (ως φαντι) κατ' ωρεα μακρα Μεναλκας· the expression ως φαντι, as they say, seems very flat, and not correspondent with the native elegance of Theocritus: and therefore the learned and ingenious John Pierson (see his Verisimilia, p. 46.) proposes to read, Μαλα νεμων, Διοφαντε, κατ' ωρεα κ. τ. λ. observing that Theocritus inscribes several Idylliums to his intimate friends; for instance, he addresses the 6th to Aratus; the 11th and the 13th to Nicias the physician; and to this same Diophantus the 21st. This very plausible emendation I have followed in my translation. That the librarians often obliterated proper names will appear in the note on ver. 55 of this Idyllium. Virgil imitates this passage:

> Compulerantque greges Corydon et Thyrsis in unum;
> Thyrsis oves, Corydon distentas lacte capellas:
> Ambo florentes ætatibus, Arcades ambo:
> Et cantare pares, et respondere parati.
> Ecl. 7. 2.

6. Tu calamos inflare leves, ego dicere versus. Ecl 5. 2.

15. Vis ergo inter nos, quid possit uterque, vicissim Experiamur? Ecl. 3. 28.

18. ——— Ego hanc vitulam, ne forte recuses, Depono. Ecl. 3. 28.

19. De grege non ausim quicquam deponere tecum:
Est mihi namque domi pater, est injusta noverva:
Bisque die numerant ambo pecus, alter et hœdos. Ecl. 3. 32.

22. Nine equal strains,] Though nine strains, or reeds, are here mentioned, yet the shepherd's pipe was generally composed of seven reeds, unequal in length, and of different tones, joined together with wax. See note on Idyl. I. 169; and Virgil,

> Est mihi disparibus septem compacta cicutis
> Fistula. Ecl. 2. 36.

It is difficult to conceive how the ancient shepherds could pipe and sing at the same time: certainly that was impracticable. The most probable opinion is, that they first play'd over the tune, and then sung a verse or stanza of the song answering thereto, and so play'd and sung alternately: which manner of playing and singing is very common with the pipers and fiddlers at our country wakes, who, perhaps, originally borrowed the custom from the Romans, during their residence in Britain. We find the old English minstrels used to warble on their harps, and then sing.—See Percy's essay on the subject.

29 Who shall decide, &c.] The same verse occurs Idyl. V. 71.

35. Alternis igitur contendere versibus ambo Cœpêre:
Hos Corydon, illos referebat in ordine Thyrsis. Ecl. 7. 18.

MENALCAS.

Ye vales, ye streams, from source celestial sprung,
If e'er Menalcas sweetly pip'd or sung,
Feed well my lambs, and if my Daphnis need
Your flowery herbage, let his heifers feed.

DAPHNIS.

Fountains and herbs, rich pasturage, if e'er
Sung Daphnis meet for nightingales to hear,
Fatten my herds; if to these meadows fair
Menalcas drives, O feed his fleecy care.

MENALCAS.

When here my fair one comes, Spring smiles around,
Meads flourish, and the teats with milk abound,
My lambs grow fat; if she no longer stay,
Parch'd are the meads, the shepherd pines away.

DAPHNIS.

Where Milo walks, the flower-enamour'd bees
Work food nectareous, taller are the trees,
The goats bear twins; if he no longer stay,
The herdsman withers, and the herds decay.

MENALCAS.

O goat, the husband of the white-hair'd flock!
Drink at the shady fount by yonder rock,
'Tis there he lives; and let young Milo know,
Proteus fed sea-calves in the deep below.

DAPHNIS.

Not Pelops' lands, not Crœsus' wealth excite
My wish, nor speed to match the winds in flight;
But in yon cave to carol with my friend,
And view the ocean while our flocks we tend.

MENALCAS.

To teats the drought, to birds the snare, the wind
To trees, and toils are fatal to the hind!
To man the virgin's scorn. O, father Jove!
Thou too hast languish'd with the pains of love.
Thus in alternate strains the contest ran,
And thus Menalcas his last lay began:
"Wolf, spare my kids, my young and tender sheep;
Though low my lot, a numerous flock I keep.
Rouse, Lightfoot, rouse from indolence profound;
Ill fits a shepherd's dog to sleep so sound.
Fear not, my sheep, to crop the verdant plain;
The pastur'd herbage soon will grow again:
Feed well, and fill your udders in the vale,
And when my lambs have suckled, fill the pail."
He sung, and Daphnis sweetly thus reply'd:
"Me, from her grot, a lovely nymph espy'd,
As late I drove my cattle cross the plain;
A long, long look she cast, and call'd me handsome swain.
I answer'd not, but, as in thought profound,
Pursued my road with eyes upon the ground.
The heifer sweetly breathes, and sweetly lows,
Sweet is the bullock's voice, and sweet the cow's:
'Tis passing sweet to lie by murmuring streams,
And waste long summer-days in gentle dreams.

45. Phyllidis adventu nostræ nemus omne virebit. Ecl. 7. 59.

48. Aret ager; vitio moriens sitit aeris herba. ib. 57.

Pope has finely imitated both Theocritus and Virgil;

Str. All Nature mourns, the skies relent in showers,
Hush'd are the birds, and clos'd the drooping flowers;
If Delia smile, the flowers begin to spring,
The skies to brighten, and the birds to sing.

Daph. All Nature laughs, the groves are fresh and fair,
The Sun's mild lustre warms the vital air,
If Sylvia smiles, new glories gild the shore,
And vanquish'd Nature seems to charm no more.

51. If he no longer stay] ——At si formosus Alexis
Montibus his abeat, videas & flumina sicca. Ecl. 7. 55.

56. Proteus turpes pascit sub gurgite phocas. Geor. 4. 395.

57. Not Pelops' lands, not Cræsus' wealth, &c. The Greek is, Μη μοι γαν Πελοπος, μη μοι χρυσεια ταλαντα Ειη εχειν! May the territories of Pelops, and golden talents never fail to my share! χρυσεια ταλαντα is very frigid; one expects something better than this from the Sicilian Muse, and therefore the ingenious Pierson (see his Verisimilia) observing that the librarians frequently obliterated proper names, instead of χρυσεια reads Κροισοιο ταλαντα; then a new beauty arises in the opposition between the extensive territories of Pelops, and the talents, or treasures of Crœsus; and what adds to the probability that this is the true reading, Theocritus mentions the riches of Crœsus in the 10th Idyl. ver. 39. and likewise Anacreon, ode 26. ver. 3. Δοκων δ' εχειν τα Κροισȣ, Rich I seem as Lydia's king: indeed every school-boy knows that the riches of Crœsus became a proverb.

58. Nor speed, &c.] ——Cursuque pedum prævertere ventos. Æn. 7. 807.

61. To teats, &c.] The present reading in the original is, υδασι δ' αυχμος, the draught is fatal to waters; but a friend of mine reads ȣθασιν αυχμος, draught is fatal to the teats, which is far more natural, and agreeable to the idea of a shepherd.

Triste lupus stabulis, maturis frugibus imbres,
Arboribus venti; nobis Amaryllidis iræ. Ecl. 3. 80.

70. Ill fits, &c.] This seems to be an imitation of a verse in Homer: Ου χρη παννυχιον ευδειν βȣληφορον ανδρα. Il. b. 2. 24.

Ill fits a chief, who mighty nations guides,
To waste long nights in indolent repose.
Pope.

72. Thus Virgil,——Gregibus non gramina desunt, &c. Geor. b. 2. 200.

There for thy flocks fresh fountains never fail,
Undying verdure clothes the grassy vale;
And what is cropt by day, the night renews.
Warton.

78. Et longum, formose, vale, vale, inquit, Iola! Ecl. 3. 79.

81. This verse occurs, Idyl. 9. ver. 7. in the Greek.

83. Fortunate senex, hic inter flumina nota,
Et fontes sacros, frigus captabis opacum.
Ecl. 1. 52.

On oaks smooth acorns ornamental grow,
And golden apples on the pippin glow;
Calves grace the cows, light-skipping on the plain,
And lusty cows commend the careful swain."
They sung; the goatherd thus:

GOATHERD.

Thy verse appears
So sweet, O Daphnis! to my ravish'd ears,
More pleasing far thy charming voice to me
Than to my taste the nectar of the bee.
Receive these pipes, the victor's rightful meed:
And wouldst thou teach me, while my kids I feed,
This goat rewards thy pains, that never fails
Each morn to fill the largest of my pails.
As skips the fawn her mother doe around,
So Daphnis leap'd for joy, and dancing beat the ground:
As grieve new-married maids their sires to leave
So, deeply sighing, did Menalcas grieve.
Since that time, Daphnis, chief of shepherd-swains,
Daphnis supreme without a rival reigns:
And, to complete his happiness, he led
The blooming Naïs to his nuptial bed.

IDYLLIUM IX.

DAPHNIS AND MENALCAS.

ARGUMENT.

The herdsman Daphnis and the shepherd Menalcas are urged by a neighbouring shepherd to contend in singing; the song is in alternate strains, and each receives a prize; Daphnis a finely-finished club, and Menalcas a conch. The beauty of this Idyllium consists in the true character of low life, full of self-commendation, and boastful of its own fortune.

DAPHNIS, begin! for merrily you play,
Daphnis, begin the sweet bucolic lay;
Menalcas next shall sing; while pasturing near
Calves mix with cows, the heifer with the steer;
The bulls together with the herd may browze,
Rove round the copse, and crop the tender boughs;
Daphnis, begin the sweet bucolic strain;
Menalcas next shall charm the shepherd-swain.

DAPHNIS.

Sweet low the herds along the pastur'd ground,
Sweet is the vocal reed's melodious sound;
Sweet pipes the jocund herdsman, sweet I sing,
And lodge securely by yon cooling spring,
Where the soft skins of milk-white heifers, spread
In order fair, compose my decent bed:
Ah luckless! browsing on the mountain's side
The south-wind dash'd them headlong, and they died.
There I regard no more bright summer's fires
Than youthful lovers their upbraiding sires.
Thus Daphnis chanted his bucolic strain;
And thus Menalcas charm'd the shepherd-swain.

MENALCAS.

Ætna's my parent; there I love to dwell,
Where the rock-mountains form an ample cell:
And there, with affluence blest, as great I live,
As swains can wish, or golden slumbers give;
By me large flocks of goats and sheep are fed,
Their wool my pillow, and their skins my bed:
In caldrons boil'd their flesh sustains me well;
Dry beechen faggots wintry frosts expel.
Thus I regard no more the cold severe
Than toothless men hard nuts when pulse is near.

Here ceas'd the youths; I prais'd their pastoral strains,
And gave to each a present for his pains:
A well-form'd club became young Daphnis' due,
Which in my own paternal woodlands grew,

85. Vitis ut arboribus decori est, ut vitibus uvæ,
Ut gregibus tauri, segetes ut pinguibus arvis.
Ecl. 5. 32.

As vines the trees, as grapes the vines adorn,
As bulls the herds, and fields the yellow corn.
Dryden.

91. Tale tuum carmen nobis, divine poeta, &c.
Ecl. 5. 45.

Mr. Gay has imitated this passage, in his fifth pastoral;

Albeit thy songs are sweeter to mine ear,
Than to the thirsty cattle rivers clear;
Or winter porridge to the labouring youth,
Or buns and sugar to the damsel's tooth.

93. Hos tibi dant calamos, en accipe, Musæ
Ecl. 6. 69.

101. Ex illo Corydon, Corydon est tempore nobis.
Ecl. 7. 70.

1. Daphnis, begin, &c.] The first eight lines in the translation of this Idyllium are supposed to be spoken by the shepherd, who endeavours to engage Daphnis and Menalcas to sing:

Incipe, Mopse, prior. Ecl. 4. 10.

2. Incipe, Damœta; tu deinde sequêre, Menalca. Ecl. 3. 58.

9. This verse occurs Idyllium 8th, 77, in the original;

Dulce satis humor, depulsis arbutus hœdis,
Lenta salix fœto pecori, mihi solus Amyntas.
Ecl. 3. 82.

19. Hos Corydon, illos referebat in ordine Thyrsis. Ecl. 7. 20.

22. Ovid has a similar description of Polyphemus's cave:

Sunt mihi pars montis vivo pendentia saxo
Antra. Metamorph. b. 13. 810.

23. Hic focus, & tædæ pingues; hîc plurimus ignis
Semper, & assiduâ postes fuligine nigri.
Hîc tantum Boreæ curamus frigora, quantum
Aut numerum lupus, aut torrentia flumina ripas. Ecl. 7. 49.

Here ever-glowing hearths embrown the posts,
Here blazing pines expel the pinching frosts,
Here cold and Boreas' blasts we dread no more
Than wolves the sheep, or torrent streams the shore.
Warton.

30. Pulse] The Greek is αμυλοιο, which I apprehend signifies wheat boiled, without having been first ground in the mill, something in the nature of frumenty.

31. Here the shepherd resumes his account of the contest between Daphnis and Menalcas, and describes the presents he made them.

So exquisitely shap'd from end to end,
An artist might admire, but could not mend.
A pearly conch, wreath'd beautifully round,
Late on th' Icarian rocky beach I found,
The shell I gave Menalcas for his share;
Large was the conch, its flesh was rich and rare,
(This in five equal portions I divide)
And to five friends a plenteous meal supply'd.
Pleas'd he receiv'd, and lik'd his present well,
And thus he sweetly blew the shining shell:
Hail, rural Muses! teach your bard those strains
Which once I sung, and charm'd the listening swains:
Then would my tongue repeat the pleasing lore,
And painful blisters never gall it more.
To grasshoppers the grasshoppers are friends,
And ant on ant for mutual aid depends;
The ravenous kite projects his brother kite;
But me the Muse and gentle song delight.
O, may my cave with frequent song be blest!
For neither roseat spring, nor downy rest
So sweet the labourer sooth; nor to the bee
Are flowers so grateful, as the Muse to me:
For Circe's strongest magic ne'er can harm
Those whom the Muses with soft rapture charm.

IDYLLIUM X*.
THE REAPERS.

ARGUMENT.

Milo and Battus, two reapers, have a conference as they are at work; Battus not reaping so fast as usual, Milo asks him the reason of it; he frankly confesses it was owing to love; and, at the request of Milo, sings a song in praise of his mistress: Milo afterwards repeats the poetical maxims of Lytierses.

MILO and BATTUS.

MILO.

BATTUS, some evil sure afflicts you sore;
You cannot reap as you have reap'd before;
No longer you your sheaves with vigour bind,
But, like a wounded sheep, lag heavily behind,
If thus you fail with early morning's light,
How can you work till noon or slow-pac'd night?

BATTUS.

Milo, thou moiling drudge, as hard as stone,
An absent mistress didst thou ne'er bemoan?

MILO.

Not I—I never learnt fair maids to woo;
Pray what with love have labouring men to do?

BATTUS.

Did love then never interrupt thy sleep?

MILO.

No, Battus: dogs should never run at sheep.

BATTUS.

But I have lov'd these ten long days and more.

MILO.

Yes, you're a wealthy man, and I a poor.

BATTUS.

Hence all things round me in confusion lie.

MILO.

But tell me who's this charmer of your eye?

BATTUS.

Old Polybuta's niece, the gay, the young,
Who harvest-home at Hypocoön's sung.

45. Nymphæ, noster amor, Libethrides, aut mihi carmen,
Quale meo Codro, concedite. Ecl. 7. 21.

Give me the lays, Nymphs of th' inspiring springs,
Which Codrus, rival of Apollo sings.
Warton.

48. And painful blisters, &c.] The ancients believed that a lie was always followed by some punishment, as a blister on the tip of the tongue, a pimple on the nose, &c. See Idyl. 12, verse 32. See also Hor. b. 2. ode 8.

49. Juvenal has a similar passage, Sat. 15. 163.

Indica tigris agit rabidâ cum tygride pacem
Perpetuam: sævis inter se convenit ursis.

Tiger with tiger, bear with bear you'll find
In leagues offensive and defensive join'd.
Tate.

52. Me verò primùm dulces ante omnia Musæ,
Quarum sacra fero, ingenti perculsus amore,
Accipiant. Geor. 2. 475.

Ye sacred Muses, with whose beauty fir'd,
My soul is ravish'd, and my brain inspir'd,
Whose priest I am, give me, &c. Dryden.

Tale tuum carmen nobis, divine poeta,
Quale sopor fessis in gramine, quale per æstum
Dulcis aquæ saliente sitim restinguere rivo.
Ecl. 5. 46.

Mr. Pope has something very similar:
Not bubbling fountains to the thirsty swain,
Not balmy sleep to labourers faint with pain,
Not showers to larks, or sunshine to the bee,
Are half so charming as thy sight to me.
Past. 3.

* This Idyllium, as Dr. Martyn observes, being a dialogue between two reapers, is generally excluded by the critics from the number of the pastorals: and yet, perhaps, if we consider that a herdsman may very naturally describe a conversation between two of his country neighbours, who entertain each other with a rural song, we may soften a little the severity of our critical temper, and allow even this to be called a pastoral.

4. Like a wounded sheep, &c.] Virgil, speaking of a sickening sheep, says, you will see it.

Extremamque sequi, aut medio procumbere campo
Pascentem. Geor. b. 3. 466.

12. Ut canis a corio nunquam absterrebitur uncto. Hor. b. 2. sat. 8.

14. The original is, Εκ πιθω αντλευς δηλον· εγω δ' εχω ϑδ' αλις οξος. instead of δηλον, Hoelzinus (see his notes on Apollonius, b. 3. ver. 902.) reads πηλον, and then the interpretation will be, you drink red wine out of a hogshead; but I have scarcely vinegar enough.

18. Who harvest-home, &c.] This line occurs Idyllium 6. 54.

MILO.

Then for your sins you will be finely sped;
Each night a grizzle grasshopper in bed.

BATTUS.

Yet spare your insults, cruel and unkind!
Plutus, you know, as well as Love, is blind.

MILO.

No harm I mean—but, Battus, as you play
On the sweet pipe, and sing an amorous lay,
With music's charms our pleasing toils prolong;
Your mistress be the subject of your song.

BATTUS.

Ye Muses, sweetly let the numbers flow!
For you new beauty on all themes bestow.
Charming Bombyce, though some call you thin,
And blame the tawny colour of your skin;
Yet I the lustre of your beauty own,
And deem you like Hyblæan honey brown.
The letter'd hyacinth's of darksome hue,
And the sweet violet a sable blue;
Yet these in crowns ambrosial odours shed,
And grace fair garlands that adorn the head.
Kids flowery thyme, gaunt wolves the kid pursue,
The crane the plough-share, and I follow you.
Were I as rich as Crœsus was of old,
Our statues soon should rise of purest gold,
In Cytherea's sacred shrine to stand,
You with an apple, rose, and lute in hand;
I like a dancer would attract the sight,
In gaudy sandals gay, and habit light.

20. A grizzle grasshopper, &c.] Heinsius observes, that a grasshopper, here called μαντις, is the same that was called γραυς: σεριφος γραυς was a proverbial expression, and equal to anus quæ in virginitate consenuit: metaphora sumpta est a sylvestri locustâ, quam vocant γραυν σεριφην ϗ μαντιν. Suid. Milo therefore humorously laughs at Battus for falling in love with an old virgin.

33. The Greek is, Και το ιον μελαν εντι, και α γραπτα υακινθος, which Virgil has literally translated;

———Quid tum si fuscus Amyntas?
Et nigræ violæ sunt, & vaccinia nigra.
Ecl. 10. 38.

What if the boy's smooth skin be brown to view,
Dark is the hyacinth and violet's hue.
Warton.

Virgil likewise has, Inscripti nomina regum flores.
Ecl. 3. 106.

37. Torva leæna lupum sequitur, lupus ipse capellam;
Florentem cytisum sequitur lasciva capella:
Te Corydon ô, Alexi. Ecl. 2. 63.

39. Crœsus] A king of Lydia, whose riches became a proverb.

40. Nunc te marmoreum pro tempore fecimus: at tu,
Si fœtura gregem suppleverit, aureus esto.
Ecl. 7. 36.

But if the falling lambs increase my fold,
Thy marble statue shall be turn'd to gold.
Dryden.

Charming Bombyce, you my numbers greet;
How lovely, fair, and beautiful your feet!
Soft is your voice—but I no words can find
To represent the moral of your mind.

MILO.

How sweetly, swain, your carols you rehearse?
How aptly scan the measures of your verse?
A wit so barren with a beard so long!—
Attend to tuneful Lytierses' song.

46. How lovely, fair, and beautiful your feet!] Thus in Solomon's Song, ch. 7. 1. we read, How beautiful are thy feet with shoes! On which Mr. Percy observes, "Or more exactly within thy sandals." The Hebrew women were remarkably nice in adorning their sandals, and in having them fit neatly, so as to display the fine shape of the foot: Vid. Clerici Comment. Judith's sandals are mentioned along with the bracelets and other ornaments of jewels, with which she set off her beauty when she went to captivate the heart of Holofernes, chap. 10. 4. And it is expressly said, that her sandals ravished his eyes, chap. 16. 9.

51. A beard so long!] A long beard was looked on as a mark of wisdom; see Hor. sat. 3. b. 2. ver 35. Sapientem pascere barbam.

52. Lytierses] Lytierses was a bastard son of Midas, king of Phrygia; the poets tell us, that in a trial of skill in music between Apollo and Pan, Midas gave sentence in favour of the latter, whereupon Apollo clapt a pair of asses ears on his head. On the other hand, Conon, in his first narration (apud Phot. biblioth.) tells us, that Midas had a great many spies dispersed up and down the country, by whose information he knew whatever his subjects did or said; thus he reigned in peace and tranquillity to a great age, none daring to conspire against him. His knowing by this means whatever his subjects spoke of him, occasioned the saying, that Midas had long ears; and as asses are said to be endowed with the sense of hearing to a degree of perfection above other animals, he was also said to have asses ears; thus what was at first spoken in a metaphorical sense, afterwards ran current in the world for truth. As to Lytierses, he reigned, after Midas, at Celænæ, the chief city of Phrygia, and is described as a rustic, unsociable, and inhuman tyrant; of an insatiable appetite, devouring, in one day, three large baskets of bread, and drinking ten gallons of wine. He took great pleasure in agriculture; but, as acts of cruelty were his chief delight, he used to oblige such as happened to pass by while he was reaping, to join with him in the work; and then, cutting off their heads, he bound up their bodies in the sheaves. For these, and such like cruelties, he was put to death by Hercules, and his body thrown into the Mæander: however, his memory was cherished by the reapers of Phrygia, and an hymn, from him, called Lytierses, sung in harvest-time, in honour of their fellow labourer. See Univ. Hist. vol. 4. 8vo. page 459.

This anecdote is taken from one of the tragedies of Sosibius, an ancient Syracusian poet, who, according to Vossius, flourished in the 166th Olympiad. As this passage is scarce, I shall take the liberty to lay it before the learned reader, exactly as the illustrious Casaubon has corrected and amended it, together with a translation: the

O fruitful Ceres, bless with corn the field;
May the full ears a plenteous harvest yield!
Bind, reapers, bind your sheaves, lest strangers say,
"Ah, lazy drones! their hire is thrown away."
To the fresh north-wind, or the zephyrs rear
Your shocks; those breezes fill the swelling ear.

two verses between commas, are supposed to be spoken by a different person of the drama, and therefore omitted in the translation.

Αιθ' οι Κελαιναι πατρις, αρχαια πολις
Μιδȣ γεροντος, οςις ωτ' εχων ονȣ,
Ηνασσε· 'και νυν φανος ευειδης' αγαν,'
Ουτος δ' εκεινȣ παις παραπλαςος νοθος.
" Μητρος δ' οποιας η τεκȣς' επιςαται."
Εσθει μεν αρτων τρεις ονȣς κανθηλιȣς.
Τρις της βραχειας ημερας πινειθ' αμα,
Καλων μετρητην τον δεκαμφορον πιθον·
Εργαζεται δ' ελαφρα προς τα σιτια.
Ογμον θεριζει τη μια δ' εν ημερα
Δεκάγυον ομπνην συντιθησιν εις τελος·
Χ' ωταν τις ελθη ξεινος, η παρεξιη,
Φαγειν τ' εδωκεν ευ, ϗ ευ πεχορτασεν.
Και τȣ ποτȣ πρȣτεινεν ως αν εν θερει
Πλεον· φθονειν γαρ ωκνει τοις θανȣμενοις·
Επει δ' αγων εδειξε Μαιανδρȣ ροαις
Καρπευμα των αρδευτα δαψιλει ποτω
Τον ανδρομηκη πυρον ηκονημενη
Αρπη θεριζει. τον ξενον δε δραγματι
Αυτω κυλισας, κρατος ορφανον φερει.
Γελων θεριςην ως ανȣν ηριςισεν.

LYTIERSES.

Celænæ, city fam'd in former years,
Where Midas reign'd, renown'd for asses ears:
Whose bastard son, that like a monster fed,
Daily devour'd three* asses loads of bread;
A large wine-cask, which once a day he drain'd,
He call'd two gallons, though it ten contain'd.
Daily he labour'd in the corn-clad ground,
Reap'd ten whole acres, and in bundles bound.
If chance a stranger in his fields he spy'd,
Abundant wine and viands he supply'd,
Largely to drink, and sumptuously to feed,
Nor envied he the wretch he doom'd to bleed.
He points to meadows, arrogant and vain,
Of richest pasture, fields of golden grain,
Where through irriguous vales Mæander winds;
Then lops his head, and in the sheaves he binds
The trembling carcase, and with horrid jest
Laughs at the rashness of his murder'd guest.

Menander mentions this song in his Carchedonium; Αδοντα Λιτυερσην απ' αριςȣ τεως, Singing Lytierses soon after dinner.

Heinsius very justly observes, that this Lytierses is only a set of formulary maxims, or old sayings, and as such I have distinguished them in distichs, as they are in the Greek.

* A close translation would be, three asses of bread, that is, the burthen which three asses carry; agreeable to that passage in Samuel, ch. xvi. ver. 20. Jesse took an ass laden with bread; the Hebrew is, he took an ass of bread.
See Pool's Synopsis.

Ye threshers, never sleep at noon of day;
For then the light chaff quickly blows away.
Reapers should rise with larks, to earn their hire,
Rest in the heat, and when they roost, retire.
How happy is the fortune of a frog!
He wants no moisture in his watery bog.
Steward, boil all the pulse; such pinching's mean;
You'll wound your hand by splitting of a bean.
These songs the reapers of the field improve;
But your sad lay, your starveling tale of love,
Which soon will bring you to a crust of bread,
Keep for your mother, as she yawns in bed.

IDYLLIUM XI.

CYCLOPS.

ARGUMENT.

This is the last of those Idylliums that are generally allowed to be true pastorals, and is very beautiful. The poet addresses himself to Nicias, a physician of Miletus, and observes, there is no cure for love but the Muses: he then gives an account of Polyphemus's passion for Galatea, a sea-nymph, the daughter of Nereus and Doris: he describes him sitting upon a rock that overlooked the ocean, and soothing his passion with the charms of poetry.

No remedy the power of love subdues;
No medicine, dearest Nicias, but the Muse:
This plain prescription gratifies the mind
With sweet complacence—but how hard to find!
This well you know, who first in physic shine,
And are the lov'd familiar of the Nine.
Thus the fam'd Cyclops, Polypheme, when young,
Calm'd his fond passion with the power of song;
When blooming years imbib'd the soft desire,
And Galatea kindled amorous fire;

59. Virgil has something similar;

At rubicunda Ceres medio succiditur æstu,
Et medio tostas æstu terit area fruges.
Geor. b. 1. 297.

But cut the golden corn at mid-day's heat,
And the parch'd grain at noon's high ardor beat.
Warton.

The ancients did not thresh or winnow their corn: in the heat of the day, as soon as it was reaped, they laid it on a floor, made on purpose, in the middle of the field, and then they drove horses and mules round about it, till they trod all the grain out.
Benson.

66. Splitting of a bean] A sordid miser used formerly to be called κυμινοπριςης, that is, a bean-splitter.

1. No remedy, &c.] Ovid makes Apollo express the same sentiment as he is pursuing Daphne;

Hei mihi, quod nullis Amor est medicabilis herbis!
Nec prosunt domino, quæ prosunt omnibus, artes!
Metam. b. 1. 523.

To cure the pains of love no plant avails;
And his own physic the physician fails.
Dryden.

He gave no wreaths of roses to the fair,
Nor apples, nor sweet parsley for her hair:
Love did the tenour of his mind control,
And took the whole possession of his soul.
His flocks untended oft refus'd to feed,
And, for the fold, forsook the grassy mead;
While on the sedgy shore he lay reclin'd,
And sooth'd with song the anguish of his mind.
From morn to night he pin'd; for Love's keen dart
Had pierc'd the deep recesses of his heart:
Yet, yet a cure he found—for on a steep,
Rough-pointed rock, that overlook'd the deep,
And with brown horrour high-impending hung,
The giant monster sat, and thus he sung:
" Fair nymph, why will you thus my passion slight!
Softer than lambs you seem, than curds more white,
Wanton as calves before the udder'd kine,
Harsh as the unripe fruitage of the vine.
You come when pleasing sleep has clos'd mine eye,
And, like a vision, with my slumbers fly,
Swift as before the wolf the lambkin bounds,
Panting and trembling, o'er the furrow'd grounds.
Then first I lov'd, and thence I date my flame,
When here to gather hyacinths you came:
My mother brought you—'twas a fatal day;
And I, alas! unwary led the way:
E'er since my tortur'd mind has known no rest;
Peace is become a stranger to my breast:
Yet you nor pity, nor relieve my pain—
Yes, yes I know the cause of your disdain;
For, stretcht from ear to ear with shagged grace,
My single brow adds horrour to my face;
My single eye enormous lids enclose,
And o'er my blubber'd lips projects my nose.
Yet, homely as I am, large flocks I keep,
And drain the udders of a thousand sheep;
My pails with milk, my shelves with cheese they fill,
In summer scorching, and in winter chill.
The vocal pipe I tune with pleasing glee,
No other Cyclops can compare with me:
Your charms I sing, sweet apple of delight!
Myself and you I sing the live-long night.
For you ten fawns, with collars deck'd, I feed,
And four young bears for your diversion breed:

11. He gave not wreaths of roses, &c.] The Greek is, Ηςατο δ' ϐτι ϱοδοις, ϐ μαλοις, ϐδε κικινοις; which Heinsius has very properly corrected, and reads ϐδε σελινοις, nor with parsley-wreaths; and observes, that our author is never more entertaining than when he alludes to some old proverb, as in this place he does: your common lovers, such as were not quite stark staring mad, and not extravagantly profuse in their presents to their mistresses, were said, ερων μηλοις, ϗ ϱοδοις, to love with apples and roses; or, as others affirm, μηλοις ϗ ςεφανοις, with apples and garlands, which were generally composed of roses and parsley. See Idyllium 3. ver. 35.

> Where rose-buds mingled with the ivy-wreath,
> And fragrant parsley, sweetest odours breath.

21. For on a steep, &c.] Bion imitates this passage, see his 7th Idyl. ver. 3.

> Such as the Cyclops, on a rock reclin'd,
> Sung to the sea-nymph, to compose his mind,
> And sent it in the whispers of the wind. F.F.

This fable of Polyphemus and Galatea has furnished matter for several poets, particularly Ovid, who, in the 13th book of the Metamorphoses, fable the 6th, has borrowed very freely from Theocritus. See Dryden's elegant translation of that fable.

25. Nerine Galatea, thymo mihi dulcior Hyblæ,
Candidior cycnis, hederâ formosior albâ.
Ecl. 7. 37.

> O Galatea! nymph than swans more bright,
> More sweet than thyme, more fair than ivy white. Warton.

Are not our author's images far more natural, and consequently more adapted to pastoral than Virgil's?

27. Ovid has, Splendidior vitro; tenero lascivior hœdo.

Brighter than glass seems but a puerile sentiment.

31 Quem tu, cervus uti vallis in alterâ
Visum parte lupum graminis immemor,
Sublimi fugies mollis anhelitu.
Hor. b. 1. ode 15.

> Whose rage thou fly'st, with trembling fear,
> As from the wolf the timorous deer. F.F.

——Quam tu fugis, ut pavet acres agna lupos.
Ibid. b. 5. ode 12.

34. When here to gather hyacinths, &c.]
Sepibus in nostris parvam te roscida mala,
(Dux ego vester eram) vidi cum matre legentem.
Ecl. 8. 37.

41. Stretcht from ear to ear with shagged grace,]
O digno conjuncta viro! dum despicis omnes,
Dumque tibi est odio mea fistula, dumque capellæ,
Hirsutumque supercilium, prolixaque barba.
Ecl. 8. 32.

Has not Virgil's wonderful judgment once more deserted him? Hirsutum supercilium, the shaggy eyebrow, being mentioned only as a single one, might suit a Cyclops with great propriety; it is indeed a translation of Theocritus's λασια οφϱυς; μια μαϰϱα; but can this horrid eye-brow, with any accuracy, come into the description of an Italian shepherd?

43. My single eye, &c.] Unum est in mediâ lumen mihi fronte. Ovid. Metam.

45. Mille meæ Siculis errant in montibus agnæ:
Lac mihi non æstate novum, non frigore desit.
Ecl. 2. 21.

47. Cheese] Martyn thinks this τυϱος, or, as in Virgil, pressi copia lactis, means curd, from which the milk has been squeezed out, in order to make cheese. We find in the third Georgic, ver. 400, that the shepherds used to carry the curd, as soon as it was pressed, into the towns; or else salt it, and so lay it by for cheese against winter, Quod surgente die, &c.

53. Ten fawns, with collars, &c.] The Greek is, ενδεκα νεβϱως Πασας αμνοφοϱως, eleven young hinds, and all of them pregnant; which certainly, as Casaubon observes, cannot be probable, viz. that young hinds should be pregnant: there is an old Roman edition of Theocritus, which elucidates this passage, for it reads πασας μαννοφοϱως, all bearing collars: and nothing is more manifest, than that the ancients, as well as moderns, were fond of ornamenting those animals which they brought up tame with such sort of appendages.

54. Four young bears, &c.] Ovid imitates

Come, live with me; all these you may command,
And change your azure ocean for the land:
More pleasing slumbers will my cave bestow,
There spiry cypress and green laurels grow;
There round my trees the sable ivy twines,
And grapes, as sweet as honey, load my vines:
From grove-crown'd Ætna, rob'd in purest snow,
Cool springs roll nectar to the swains below.
Say, who would quit such peaceful scenes as these
For blustering billows, and tempestuous seas?
Though my rough form's no object of desire,
My oaks supply me with abundant fire;
My hearth unceasing blazes—though I swear
By this one eye, to me for ever dear,
Well might that fire to warm my breast suffice,
That kindled at the lightning of your eyes.
Had I, like fish, with fins and gills been made,
Then might I in your element have play'd,
With ease have div'd beneath your azure tide,
And kiss'd your hand, though you your lips deny'd!
Brought lilies fair, or poppies red that grow
In summer's solstice, or in winter's snow;
These flowers I could not both together bear
That bloom in different seasons of the year.
Well, I 'm resolv'd, fair nymph, I 'll learn to dive,
If e'er a sailor at this port arrive,
Then shall I surely by experience know
What pleasures charm you in the deeps below.
Emerge, O Galatea! from the sea,
And here forget your native home like me.
O would you feed my flock, and milk my ewes,
And ere you press my cheese the runnet sharp infuse!

Theocritus,

Inveni geminos, qui tecum ludere possunt,
Villosæ catulos in summis montibus ursæ.
Met. 13. 831.

These bears are highly in character, and well-adapted presents from Polyphemus to his mistress.

55. Huc ades, O Galatea! quis est nam ludus in undis?
Hic ver purpureum, varios hic flumina circum
Fundit humus flores; hic candida populus antro
Imminet, & lentæ texunt umbracula vites.
Huc ades: insani feriant sine littora fluctus.
Ecl. 9. 39.

O lovely Galatea! hither haste!
For what delight affords the watery waste?
Here purple Spring her gifts profusely pours,
And paints the river-banks with balmy flowers;
Here, o'er the grotto, the pale poplar weaves
With blushing vines a canopy of leaves;
Then quit the seas! against the sounding shore
Let the vext ocean's billows idly roar.
Warton.

69. I here follow the interpretation of Heinsius.

75. Lilies and poppies.] Tibi lilia plenis
Ecce ferunt nymphæ calathis: tibi candida Naïs
Pallentes violas, & summa papavera carpens.
Ecl. 2. 45.

85. O tantum libeat mecum tibi sordida rura,
Atque humiles habitare casas, & figere cervos,

My mother is my only foe I fear;
She never whispers soft things in your ear,
Although she knows my grief, and every day
Sees how I languish, pine, and waste away.
I, to alarm her, will aloud complain,
And more disorders than I suffer feign,
Say my head aches, sharp pains my limbs oppress,
That she may feel, and pity my distress.
Ah, Cyclops, Cyclops, where's your reason fled!--
If with the leafy spray your limbs you fed,
Or, ev'n wove baskets, you would seem more wise;
Milk the first cow, pursue not her that flies:
You'll soon, since Galatea proves unkind,
A sweeter, fairer Galatea find.
Me gamesome girls to sport and toy invite,
And meet my kind compliance with delight:
Sure I may draw this fair conclusion hence,
Here I 'm a man of no small consequence.''
Thus Cyclops learn'd love's torments to endure,
And calm'd that passion which he could not cure.
More sweetly far with song he sooth'd his heart,
Than if his gold had brib'd the doctor's art.

IDYLLIUM XII.

AITES.

ARGUMENT.

This piece is in the Ionic dialect, and supposed not to have been written by Theocritus. The word Aites is variously interpreted, being taken for a person beloved, a companion, a man of probity, a cohabitant, and fellow-citizen: see the argument. The amoroso addresses his friend, and wishes an union of their souls, a perpetual friendship, and that, after death, posterity may celebrate the affection and harmony that subsisted between them. He then praises the Megarensians for the divine honours they paid to Diocles, who lost his life in the defence of his friend.

Hœdorumque gregem viridi compellere hibisco! Ecl. 2. 28.

O that you lov'd the fields and shady grots,
To dwell with me in bowers and lowly cots,
To drive the kids to fold! &c. Warton.

95. Ah, Corydon, Corydon, quæ te dementia cepit? Ecl. 2.

What phrensy, Corydon, invades thy breast?

98. Thus Ovid,—Melius sequerere volentem
Optantemque eadem, parilique cupidine captam. Met. b. 14. 28.

When maids are coy, have manlier arts in view;
Leave those that fly, but those that like pursue. Garth.

100. Invenies alium, si te hic fastidit, Alexim. Ecl. 2. 73.

Theocritus here greatly excels his imitator; for to wave the superiority he holds in his application to one of the fair sex, there seems to be great consolation implied in the assurance that he shall find ισως ἢ καλλιον αλλαν, perhaps a fairer mistress; in Virgil is implied desperation, si te hic fastidit.

SAY, are you come? but first three days are told;
Dear friend, true lovers in one day grow old.
As vernal gales exceed the wintry blast,
As plums by sweeter apples are surpast,
As in the woolly fleece the tender lambs
Produce not half the tribute of their dams;
As blooming maidens raise more pleasing flames
Than dull, indifferent, thrice-married dames;
As fawns outleap young calves; as Philomel
Does all her rivals in the grove excel;
So me your presence cheers; eager I run,
As swains seek umbrage from the burning Sun.
O may we still to nobler love aspire,
And every day improve the concord higher;
So shall we reap renown from loving well,
And future poets thus our story tell:
" Two youths late liv'd in friendship's chain combin'd,
One was benevolent, the other kind;
Such as once flourish'd in the days of old,
Saturnian days, and stampt the age with gold."
O grant this privilege, almighty Jove!
That we, exempt from age and woe, may rove
In the blest regions of eternal day;
And when six thousand years have roll'd away,
Some welcome shade may this glad message bear
(Ev'n in Elysium would such tidings cheer)
" Your friendship and your love by every tongue
Are prais'd and honour'd—chiefly by the young!"
But this I leave to Jove's all-ruling care;
If right he'll grant, if wrong reject my prayer.
Mean-time my song shall celebrate your praise,
Nor shall the honest truth a blister raise:
And though keen sarcasms your sharp words impart,
I find them not the language of your heart;
You give me pleasure double to my pain,
And thus my loss is recompens'd with gain.
 Ye Megarensians, fam'd for well-tim'd oars,
May bliss attend you still on Attic shores!
To strangers kind, your deeds themselves commend,
To Diocles the lover and the friend:
For at his tomb each spring the boys contest
In amorous battles who succeeds the best;
And he who master of the field is found,
Returns with honorary garlands crown'd.
Blest who decides the merits of the day!
Blest, next to him, who bears the prize away!
Sure he must make to Ganymede his vow,
That he sweet lips of magic would bestow,
With such resistless charms and virtues fraught,
As that fam'd stone from Lydia's confines brought,
By whose bare touch an artist can explore
The baser metal from the purer ore.

1. Are you come?] —Longo post tempore venit. Ecl. 1. 30.

3. Lenta salix quantum pallenti cedit olivæ,
Puniceis humilis quantum saliunca rosetis:
Judicio nostro tantum tibi cedit Amyntas.
Ecl. 5. 16.

4. As plums] Βϱάβυλος is a sort of large indifferent plum.

11. So me your presence cheers] Horace has something similar;

——— Vultus ubi tuus
Affulsit populo, gratior it dies,
Et soles melius nitent. B. 4. ode 5.

So, in thy presence, smoother run
The hours, and brighter shines the Sun.
Duncombe.

17. His amor unus erat. Æn. 9. 182.

20. With gold] The Greek is, χϱυσειοι ανδϱες, which Heinsius takes to mean something amiable and delightful; thus Horace,

Qui nunc te fruitur credulus aureâ:
Qui semper vacuam, semper amabilem
Sperat. B. 1. ode 5.

Auream and amabilem he looks upon as synonymous: The Greeks have χϱυση Αφϱοδιτη, and Virgil, Venus aurea,

Aureus hanc vitam in terris Saturnus agebat.
Geor. b. 2. 538.

22. Exempt from age] αγηϱω, thus in the Odyssey, b. 5. Calypso says of Ulysses,

She promis'd (vainly promis'd) to bestow
Immortal life, exempt from age and woe.
Pope.

24. Six thousand years] The Greek is, γενεαις διηκοσιησιν, two hundred ages: an age, according to the common computation, is thirty years; thus Mr. Pope understands the word γενεα in the first book of the Iliad, speaking of the age of Nestor,

Two generations now had pass'd away,
Wise by his rules, and happy by his sway.

32. A blister raise] See Idyl. 9. ver. 48, and the note.

40. To Diocles] At Megara, a city of Achaia, between Athens and the Isthmus of Corinth, was an annual festival held in the spring in memory of the Athenian hero Diocles, who died in the defence of a certain youth whom he loved: whence there was a contention at his tomb, wherein a garland was given to the youth who gave the sweetest kiss. Potter's Arch. ch. 20.

IDYLLIUM XIII*.

HYLAS.

ARGUMENT.

If the severity of critics will not allow this piece the title of a pastoral, yet as the actions of gods and heroes used to be sung by the ancient herdsmen, we may venture to affirm that our author intended it as such. It contains a relation of the rape of Hylas by the Nymphs, when he went to fetch water for Hercules, and the wandering of that hero, and his extreme grief for the loss of him.

LOVE, gentle Nicias, of celestial kind,
For us alone sure never was design'd;

* Theocritus addresses this Idyllium, as he did the eleventh, to his friend Nicias, a Milesian physician.

1. Love, &c.] Omne adeo genus in terris hominum, &c. Geor. 3. 242.

Thus man and beast, the tenants of the flood,
The herds that graze the plain, the feathery brood,

Nor do the charms of beauty only sway
Our mortal breasts, the beings of a day:
Amphitryon's son was taught his power to feel,
Though arm'd with iron breast, and heart of steel,
Who slew the lion fell, lov'd Hylas fair,
Young Hylas graceful with his curling hair.
And, as a son by some wise parent taught,
The love of virtue in his breast he wrought,
By precept and example was his guide,
A faithful friend, for ever at his side;
Whether the morn return'd from Jove's high hall
On snow-white steeds, or noontide mark'd the wall,
Or night the plaintive chickens warn'd to rest,
When careful mothers brood, and flutter o'er the nest:
That, fully form'd and finish'd to his plan,
Time soon might lead him to a perfect man.
But when bold Jason, with the sons of Greece,
Sail'd the salt seas to gain the golden fleece,
The valiant chiefs from every city came,
Renown'd for virtue, or heroic fame,
With these assembled, for the host's relief,
Alcmena's son, the toil-enduring chief.
Firm Argo bore him cross the yielding tide
With his lov'd friend, young Hylas, at his side;
Between Cyane's rocky isles she past,
Now safely fix'd on firm foundations fast,
Thence as an eagle swift, with prosperous gales
She flew, and in deep Phasis furl'd her sails.
When first the pleasing Pleïades appear,
And grass-green meads pronounc'd the summer near,
Of chiefs a valiant band, the flower of Greece,
Had plann'd the emprise of the golden fleece,
In Argo lodg'd they spread their swelling sails,
And soon past Hellespont with southern gales,
And smooth Propontis, where the land appears
Turn'd in straight furrows by Cyanean steers.
With eve they land; some on the greensward spread
Their hasty meal; some raise the spacious bed
With plants and shrubs that in the meadows grow,
Sweet flowering rushes, and cyperus low.
In brazen vase fair Hylas went to bring
Fresh fountain-water from the crystal spring
For Hercules, and Telamon his guest;
One board they spread, associates at the feast:
Fast by, in lowly dale, a well he found
Beset with plants, and various herbage round,

Rush into love, and feel the general flame,
"For Love is lord of all, and is in all the same."
Warton.

6. Iron breast] Thus Horace, Illi robur & æs triplex
Circa pectus erat. B. 1. od. 3.

And Moschus, in his poem entitled Megara, speaking of Hercules,

——— Πετρης ογ' εχων νοον, ηε σιδηρω
Καρτερον εν ςηθεσσι.

——— His heart, like iron or a rock,
Unmov'd, and still superior to the shock.

7. Hylas] Hylas was the son of Theodamas, whom Hercules slew because he denied him a supply of provision.

9. ——— Insuevit pater optimus hoc me, &c. Hor. b. 1. Sat. 4.

14. On snow-white steeds] The Greek is λευκιππος· Dr. Spence very justly observes, that the poets are very inconsistent in their descriptions of Aurora, particularly in the colour of her horses; here they are white, whereas Virgil represents them rose-colour'd, roseis Aurora quadrigis. Æn. 6. 535. and b. 7. 26. Aurora in roseis fulgebat lutea bigis. The best critics have ever thought, that consistency is required in the most unbounded fictions: if I mistake not, Homer is more regular in this, as in all other fictions.
Essay on the Odyssey.

18. Thus Bion,———Ην δ' ανερος ες μετρον ελθης. Idyl. 2.

As soon as time shall lead you up to man.
F. F.

21. Valiant chiefs] Alter erit tum Tiphys & altera quæ vehat Argo
Delectos heroas. Ec. 4. 34.

27. Cyane's rocky isles] The Cyanean isles, or Symplegades, are two small islands near the entrance of the Euxine, or Black Sea, in the mouth of the straits of Constantinople, over against one another; at so small a distance, that to a ship passing by they appear but one; whence the poets fancied, that they sometimes met, and came together, therefore called them concurrentia saxa Cyanes. Juvenal, sat. 15. 19. See also Idyl. 22. ver. 29.

29. As an eagle swift] ——— Illa noto citius, volucrique sagittâ
Ad terram fugit, & portu se condidit alto.
Æn. 5. 242.

30. Phasis] A large river of Colchis which dischargeth itself into the Euxine. Ovid, speaking of the Argonauts, says,

Multaque perpessi claro sub Jäsone, tandem
Contigerant rapidas limosi Phasidos undas.
Met. b. 7. 5.

31. Pleïades] The Pleïades rise with the Sun on the twenty-second of April, according to Columella.

33. A valiant band] The Argonauts were fifty-two in number: Pindar calls them the flower of sailors, Theocritus, the flower of heroes, and Virgil, chosen heroes, delectos heroas; see ver. 21.

42. Sweet flowering rushes] The Greek is Βετομον οξυ, which there is great reason to believe is the carex acuta of Virgil,

Frondibus hirsutis, & carice pastus acutâ.
Geor. b. 3. 231.

On prickly leaves, and pointed rushes fed.
Warton.

Ovid applies the same epithet to the juncus, acutâ cuspide junci. The word comes from Βες, an ox, and τεμνω to cut, so called because the leaves of this plant are so sharp, that the tongue and lips of oxen, who are great lovers of it, are wounded by it. See Butomus in Miller.

49. Cerulean celandine] The Greek is, Κυανεον χελιδονιον

— Bright maiden-hair] Χλωρον τ' αδιαντον, capillus Veneris.

Cerulean celandine, bright maiden-hair,
And parsley green, and bindweed flourish'd there.
Deep in the flood the dance fair Naiads led,
And kept strict vigils, to the rustic's dread,
Eunica, Malis form'd the festive ring,
And fair Nychéa, blooming as the spring:
When to the stream the hapless youth apply'd
His vase capacious to receive the tide,
The Naiads seiz'd his hand with frantic joy,
All were enamour'd of the Grecian boy;
He fell, he sunk; as from th' etherial plain
A flaming star falls headlong on the main;
The boatswain cries aloud, "Unfurl your sails,
And spread the canvas to the rising gales."
In vain the Naiads sooth'd the weeping boy,
And strove to lull him in their laps to joy.
But care and grief had mark'd Alcides' brow,
Fierce, as a Scythian chief, he grasp'd his bow,
And his rough club, which well he could command,
The pride and terrour of his red right hand:
On Hylas thrice he call'd with voice profound,
Thrice Hylas heard the unavailing sound;
From the deep well soft murmurs touch'd his ear,
The sound seem'd distant, though the voice was [near.
As when the hungry lion hears a fawn
Distressful bleat on some far-distant lawn,
Fierce from his covert bolts the savage beast,
And speeds to riot on the ready feast.
Thus, anxious for the boy, Alcides takes
His weary way through woods and pathless brakes;
Ah, wretched they that pine away for love!
O'er hills he rang'd and many a devious grove.
The bold adventurers blam'd the hero's stay,
While long equipt the ready vessel lay; [night,
With anxious hearts they spread their sails by
And wish'd his presence by the morning light:
But he with frantic speed regardless stray'd,
Love pierc'd his heart, and all the hero sway'd.
Thus Hylas, honour'd with Alcides' love,
Is number'd with the deities above,
While to Amphitryon's son the heroes give
This shameful term, "The Argo's fugitive:"
But soon on foot the chief to Colchos came,
With deeds heroic to redeem his fame.

50. Bindweed] The Greek is, Ειλιτενης αγρωςις; as it is difficult to determine what plant Theocritus here means, I have rendered it bindweed, or convolvulus, which seems an exact translation of ειλιτενης.

55. When to the stream] The Greek is, Ητοι ο κουρος επειχε ποτῳ πολυχανδεα κρωσσον; instead of ποτῳ, Pierson reads ροῳ, which is properly right, being the same word which Apollonius Rhodius makes use of, when treating of the same subject. See b. 1. ver. 1234.

Αυταρ ογ' ως ταπρωτα ροῳ ενι καλπιν ερεισε.

59. He fell] Hylas, falling into a well, was said to be snatched away by the nymphs. Ovid, speaking of Phaeton, has something very similar to this passage;

> Volvitur in præceps, longoque per aëra tractu
> Fertur; ut interdum de cœlo stella sereno,
> Etsi non cecidit, potuit cecidisse videri.
> Met. b. 2. 319.

> The breathless Phaeton, with flaming hair,
> Shot from the chariot, like a falling star
> That in a summer's evening from the top
> Of Heav'n drops down, or seems at least to drop. Addison.

60. A star falls headlong] These sort of meteors were reckoned prognostics of winds,

> Sæpe etiam stellas, vento impendente, videbis
> Precipites cœlo labi. Geor. b. 1. 365.

61. Unfurl your sails] Solvite vela citi. Æn. 4. 574.

65. But care and grief, &c.] Virgil says of Hercules,

> Hic vero Alcidæ furiis exarserat atro
> Felle dolor; rapit arma manu, nodisque gravatum
> Robur. Æn. b. 8. 219.

> Alcides seiz'd his arms, inflam'd with ire,
> Rage in his looks, and all his soul on fire;
> Fierce in his hands the ponderous club he shook. Pitt.

69. On Hylas] Ut littus, Hyla, Hyla, omne sonaret. Ec. 6. 44.

And Spenser,

> And every wood and every valley wide
> He fill'd with Hylas' name, the nymphs eke Hylas cride. Fairy Queen, b. 3. c. 12.

Antoninus has given us an explanation of the circumstance of Hylas's name being so often repeated, which is so particularly insisted on by the poets: "Hercules," says he, "having made the hills and forests tremble, by calling so mightily on the name Hylas; the nymphs who had snatched him away, fearing lest the enraged lover should at last discover Hylas in their fountain, transformed him into Echo, which answered Hylas to every call of Hercules."

Warton's Observations.

73. As when the hungry lion, &c.] This simile seems to have pleased Apollonius so well, that writing on the same subject, the Rape of Hylas, he has imitated it twice; see book 1. ver. 1243, &c. Ovid also had it in view;

> Tigris ut, auditis diversâ valle duorum
> Extimulata fame mugitibus armentorum, &c.
> Met. b. 5. 164.

79. Ah, virgo infelix, tu nunc in montibus erras! Ec. 6. 52.

87. Horace says,

> ——Sic Jovis interest
> Optatis epulis impiger Hercules.
> B. 4. ode 8.

This Κατακοιμησις, or fate of Hylas, as Heinsius observes, with which the poet concludes this charming poem, is extremely elegant and agreeable;

> Ουτω μεν καλλιςος Υλας μακαρων αριθμειται,
> Thus the beautiful Hylas is numbered among the blessed.

He would not say, Ουτως ο Υλας τεθνηκεν, thus Hylas died; but, thus he is numbered with the blessed. See his notes.

IDYLLIUM XIV.

CYNISCA'S LOVE.

ARGUMENT.

Æschines being in love with Cynisca is despised by her, she having placed her affections on Lycus. Æschines accidentally meets with his friend Thyonichus, whom he had not seen of a long time, and tells him his lamentable tale, and that he is determined to turn soldier. Thyonichus advises him to enter into the service of Ptolemy Philadelphus, on whom he bestows a short but very noble encomium.

ÆSCHINES *and* THYONICHUS.

ÆSCHINES.

ALL health to good Thyonichus, my friend.

THYONICHUS.

May the same blessing Æschines attend.

ÆSCHINES.

I see you seldom.—

THYONICHUS.

Well, what ails you now?

ÆSCHINES.

All is not well with me.

THYONICHUS.

You therefore grow
So much a sloven, so exceeding thin,
Your hair untrimm'd, your beard deforms your chin.
A poor Pythag'rist late I chanc'd to meet,
Pale-fac'd, like you, and naked were his feet;
He came from learned Athens, as he said,
And was in love too—with a loaf of bread.

ÆSCHINES.

You jest; but proud Cynisca makes me sad;
Nay, I'm within a hair-breadth raving mad.

THYONICHUS.

Such is your temper, so perverse you grow,
You hope all smooth: but what affects you now?

ÆSCHINES.

I and Cleunicus and the Greek agreed,
With Apis, skill'd Thessalian colts to breed,
In my green court, with wine to cheer our souls:
A sucking pig I dress'd, and brace of fowls:
And fragrant wine produc'd, four summers old,
Phœnicia's generous wine that makes us bold:
Onions and shell-fish last the table crown'd,
And gayly went the cheering cup around;
Then healths were drank, and each oblig'd to name
The lovely mistress that inspir'd his flame.
Cynisca (she was by) then charm'd my soul,
And to her health I drain'd the foaming bowl:
She pledg'd me not, nor deign'd a kind reply:
Think how my rage, inflam'd with wine, ran high.
" What, are you mute?" I said—a waggish guest,
" Perhaps she's seen a Wolf," rejoin'd in jest:
At this her cheeks to scarlet turn'd apace;
Sure you might light a candle at her face.
Now Wolf is Laba's son, whom most men call
A comely spark, is handsome, young and tall.
For him she sigh'd; and this by chance I heard;
Yet took no note, and vainly nurst my beard.
We four, now warm, and mellow with the wine,
Arch Apis, with a mischievous design,
Nam'd Wolf, and sung encomiums of the boy,
Which made Cynisca fairly weep for joy,
Like a fond girl, whom love maternal warms,
That longs to wanton in her mother's arms.
I swell'd with rage, and, in revengeful pique,
My hand discharg'd my passion on her cheek:
" Since thee, I cry'd, my love no more endears,
Go court some other with those tender tears."

1. Thus Terence,

Salvere Hegionem plurimûm Jubeo.
Adelph. act. 3. sc. 5.

6. ——— Vultus gravis, horrida siccæ
Sylva comæ. Juven. sat. 9. 12.

8. Pale-fac'd, &c.] He ridicules and distinguishes the Pythagorists by the same marks as Aristophanes does the disciples of Socrates,

Τȣς ωχριωντας, τȣς ανυποδητας λεγεις.
Plut. act 1. sc. 1.

You would say that they were pale-fac'd, and barefoot.

9. Learned Athens] — Mediis sed natus Athenis. Juv. sat. 3.

17. In my green court] The Greek is, Εν χωρω παρ εμιν, which Heinsius corrects Εν χορτω παρ εμιν, that is, in that part of the house where the ancients used to dine and sup; which being originally εν χορτω, on the grass, well-adapted to the ancient shepherds, still retained its name, though it was afterwards surrounded with various apartments; therefore it probably means the inner court.

20. Wine] The Greek is, βυβλινον οινον, which Athenæus, b. 1. chap. 28. allows to be Phœnician wine.

28. Quid mihi tunc animi credis, germane, fuisse? Ovid. Epist. Can. to Macar.

30. She's seen a Wolf] That is, Λυκον, Wolf, her sweetheart.

——— Lupi Mœrim videre priores.
Ec. 9. 54.

On which Dr. Martyn observes, that a notion obtained among the ancient Italians, that if a wolf saw any man first, it deprived him of his voice for the present; but, says he, Theocritus gives this story a contrary turn; as if the seeing a wolf, instead of being seen by him, made a person mute. The doctor, and likewise Mr. Warton, did not observe our author's double meaning, viz. that λυκος signified not only a wolf, but was likewise the name of Cynisca's lover.

36. And vainly nurst my beard] Ματαν εις ανδρα γενειων, quod de iis dicebatur, quorum conjuges impune cum aliis solebant; quique hanc contumeliam leni & pacato animo ferebant.

Heinsius.

She rose, and, gathering in a knot her vest,
Flew swiftly: as the swallow from her nest,
Beneath the tiling skims in quest of food,
To still the clamours of her craving brood.
Thus from her downy couch in eager haste,
Through the first door, and through the gate she past,
Where'er her feet, where'er her fancy led;
The proverb says, "The bull to wood is fled."
Now twenty days are past, ten, nine, and eight,
Two and eleven add—two months complete,
Since last we met, and like the boors of Thrace,
In all that time I never trimm'd my face.
Wolf now enjoys her, is her sole delight;
She, when he calls, unbars the door at night:
While I, alas! on no occasion priz'd,
Like the forlorn Megareans am despis'd.
Oh could I from these wild desires refrain,
And love her less, all would be well again!
Now like a mouse insnar'd on pitch I move;
Nor know I any remedy for love.
Yet in love's flames our neighbour Simus burn'd,
Sought ease by travel, and when cur'd return'd;
I'll sail, turn soldier, and though not the first
In fighting fields, I would not prove the worst.

47. Gathering, &c.]—Nodoque sinus collecta fluentes. Æn. 1. 324.

Close, in a knot, her flowing robes she drew.
Pitt.

48. As swallows, &c.] Virgil has plainly borrowed this simile from our author, though Mr. Warton says he is obliged to Apollonius for it: it is not improbable but that Virgil's may be the copy of the copier.

Nigra velut magnas domini cum divitis ædes
Pervolat, et pennis alta atria lustrat hirundo,
Pabula parva legens, nidisque loquacibus escas,
Et nunc porticibus vacuis, nunc humida circum
Stagna sonat. Æn. b. 12. 473.

As the black swallow, that in quest of prey,
Round the proud palace wings her wanton way,
When for her children she provides the feast,
To still the clamours of the craving nest;
Now wild excursions round the cloyster takes;
Now sportive winds, or skims along the lakes.
Pitt.

Virgil has spun this simile into more than four lines, whereas Theocritus comprehends it in two.

54. The bull to wood is fled] A proverb signifying that he will not return.

55. The literal interpretation is, And now twenty and eight, and nine,' and ten days are past, to day is the eleventh, add two more, and there will be two months. A similar but more perplexing method of numeration we meet with in the 17th Idyl. ver. 95.

62. The Megareans, entertaining a vain conceit that they were the most valiant of the Grecians, inquired of the oracle if any nation excelled them: the conclusion of the answer was,

Υμεις δ', Μεγαρεις, ουτε τριτοι, ουτε τεταρτοι,
Ουτε δυωδεκατοι, ουτ' εν λογῳ, ουτ' εν αριθμῳ.

Nor in the third, nor fourth, Megareans call,
Nor in the twelfth, nor any rank at all.

65. Now like a mouse] The Greek is, ως μυς γευμεθα πισσας, like a mouse I have tasted pitch.

THYONICHUS.

May all that's good, whate'er you wish, attend
On Æschines, my favourite and friend.
If you're resolv'd, and sailing is your plan,
Serve Ptolemy, he loves a worthy man.

ÆSCHINES.

What is his character?—

THYONICUS.

A royal spirit,
To point out genius, and encourage merit:
The poet's friend, humane, and good, and kind;
Of manners gentle, and of generous mind.
He marks his friend, but more he marks his foe;
His hand is ever ready to bestow:
Request with reason, and he'll grant the thing,
And what he gives, he gives it like a king.
Go then, and buckle to your manly breast
The brazen corslet, and the warrior vest;
Go brave and bold, to friendly Ægypt go,
Meet in the tented field the rushing foe.
Age soon will come, with envious hand to shed
The snow of winter on the hoary head,
Will sap the man, and all his vigour drain—
'Tis ours to act while youth and strength remain.

IDYLLIUM XV.

THE SYRACUSIAN GOSSIPS.

ARGUMENT.

Two Syracusian women, who had travelled to Alexandria, go to see the solemnity of Adonis's festival, which had been prepared by Arsinoe, the queen of Ptolemy Philadelphus: the

71. — Tibi Dî, quæcunque preceris, Commoda dent. Hor. b. 2. sat. 8.

82. To this noble encomium of Ptolemy by the Sicilian poet, I shall briefly show the favourable side of his character, as it is given by the historians. He was a prince of great learning, and a zealous promoter and encourager of it in others, an industrious collector of books, and a generous patron to all those who were eminent in any branch of literature. The fame of his generosity drew seven celebrated poets to his court, who from their number, were called the Pleïades: these were Aratus, Theocritus, Callimachus, Lycophron, Apollonius, Nicander and Philicus. To him we are indebted for the Greek translation of the scripture, called the Septuagint. Notwithstanding his peculiar taste for the sciences, yet he applied himself with indefatigable industry to business, studying all possible methods to render his subjects happy, and raise his dominions to a flourishing condition. Athenæus called him the richest of all the princes of his age; and Appian says, that as he was the most magnificent and generous of all kings in laying out his money, so he was of all the most skilful and industrious in raising it. He built an incredible number of cities, and left so many other public monuments of his magnificence, that all works of an extravagant taste and grandeur were proverbially called Philadelphian works. Univ. Hist.

90. While youth, &c.] Dumque virent genua. Hor. Epod. 13.

humours of these gossips are naturally described. Theocritus, to gratify the queen, introduces a Grecian singing-girl, who rehearses the magnificence of the pomp which Arsinoe had provided.

GORGO, EUNOE, PRAXINOE, OLD-WOMAN, *and* STRANGER.

GORGO.

PRAY, is Praxinoe at home?

EUNOE.

Dear Gorgo, yes—how late you come!

PRAXINOE.

Well! is it you? Maid, bring a chair
And cushion.

GORGO.

Thank you.

PRAXINOE.

Pray sit there.

GORGO.

Lord bless me! what a bustling throng!
I scarce could get alive along:
In chariots such a heap of folks!
And men in arms and men in cloaks—
Besides I live so distant hence,
The journey really is immense.

PRAXINOE.

My husband, Heav'n his senses mend!
Here will inhabit the world's end,
This horrid house, or rather den;
More fit for savages than men.
This scheme with envious aim he labours,
Only to separate good neighbours—
My plague eternal!

GORGO.

Softly, pray,
The child attends to all you say;
Name not your husband when he's by—
Observe how earnest is his eye!

PRAXINOE.

Sweet Zopy! there's a bonny lad,
Cheer up! I did not mean your dad.

GORGO.

'Tis a god dad.—I'll take an oath,
The urchin understands us both.

PRAXINOE.

(Let's talk as if some time ago,
And then we shall be safe, you know)
This person happen'd once to stop
To purchase nitre at a shop,
And what d' ye think? the silly creature
Bought salt, and took it for salt-petre.

GORGO.

My husband's such another honey,
And thus, as idly, spends his money;
Five fleeces for seven drachms he bought,
Coarse as dog's hair, not worth a groat.
But take your cloak, and garment grac'd
With clasps, that lightly binds your waste;
Adonis' festival invites,
And Ptolemy's gay court delights;
Besides our matchless queen, they say,
Exhibits some grand sight to day.

PRAXINOE.

No wonder—every body knows
Great folks can always make fine shows:
But tell me what you went to see,
And what you heard—'tis new to me.

GORGO.

The feast now calls us hence away,
And we shall oft keep holiday.

PRAXINOE.

Maid! water quickly—set it down—
Lord! how indelicate you're grown!
Disperse these cats that love their ease—
But first the water, if you please—
Quick! how she creeps; pour, hussy, pour;
You've spoil'd my gown—so, so—no more.
Well, now I'm wash'd—ye gods be blest!—
Here—bring the key of my lage chest.

GORGO.

This robe becomes you mighty well;
What might it cost you? can you tell?

PRAXINOE.

Three pounds, or more; I'd not have done it,
But that I'd set my heart upon it.

GORGO.

'Tis wonderous cheap.

PRAXINOE.

You think so?—maid,
Fetch my umbrella and my shade;
So, put it on—fye, Zopy, fye!
Stay within doors, and don't you cry:
The horse will kick you in the dirt—
Roar as you please, you shan't get hurt.
Pray, maid, divert him — come, 'tis late:
Call in the dog, and shut the gate.
Lord! here's a bustle and a throng—
How shall we ever get along!

1. Anne est intus Pamphilus?
Ter. And. act. 5. sc. 2.

17. Softly, pray, &c.] Nil dictu fœdum, visuque, &c. Juv. sat. 14. 44.

Suffer no lewdnesss, or indecent speech
Th' apartment of the tender youth to reach.
Dryden.

33. Drachms] A drachma is seven pence three farthings.

35. Garment grac'd with clasps] Hence we learn, says Casaubon, that the ladies formerly had an under garment, which was fastened to the breast by clasps: the ladies of fashion had clasps of gold;

Aurea purpuream subnectit fibula vestem.
Æn. b. 4. 139.

A golden clasp her purple garment binds.
Pitt.

51. Quick] —— Move vero ocyus te, nutrix.
Ter. Eun. act. 5.

67. Dî boni, quid turbæ est!
Ter. Heaut. act. 2.

Such numbers cover all the way,
Like emmets on a summer's day.
O Ptolemy, thy fame exceeds
Thy godlike sire's in noble deeds!
No robber now with Pharian wiles
The stranger of his purse beguiles;
No ruffians now infest the street,
And stab the passengers they meet.
What shall we do? lo here advance
The king's war-horses—how they prance!
Don't tread upon me, honest friend—
Lord, how that mad horse rears an end!
He'll throw his rider down, I fear—
I'm glad I left the child, my dear.

GORGO.

Don't be afraid; the danger's o'er;
The horses, see! are gone before.

PRAXINOE.

I'm better now, but always quake
When'er I see a horse or snake;
They rear, and look so fierce and wild—
I own, I've loath'd them from a child.
Walk quicker—what a crowd is this!

GORGO.

Pray, come you from the palace?

OLD-WOMAN.

Yes.

GORGO.

Can we get in, d'ye think?

OLD-WOMAN.

Make trial—
The steady never take denial;
The steady Greeks old Ilium won:
By trial, all things may be done.

GORGO.

Gone, like a riddle, in the dark;
These crones, if we their tales remark,
Know better far than I or you know
How Jupiter was join'd to Juno.
Lo! at the gate, what crowds are there!

PRAXINOE.

Immense, indeed! Your hand, my dear:
And let the maids join hands, and close us,
Lest in the bustle they should lose us.
Let's crowd together through the door—
Heav'ns bless me! how my gown is tore!
By Jove, but this is past a joke—
Pray, good sir, don't you rend my cloak.

MAN.

I can't avoid it; I'm so prest.

PRAXINOE.

Like pigs they justle, I protest.

MAN.

Cheer up, for now we're safe and sound.

PRAXINOE.

May you in happiness abound;
For you have serv'd us all you can—
Gorgo!—a mighty civil man—
See how the folks poor Eunoe justle!
Push through the crowd, girl!—bustle, bustle—
Now we're all in; as Dromo said,
When he had got his bride in bed.

GORGO.

Lo! what rich hangings grace the rooms—
Sure they were wove in heavenly looms.

PRAXINOE.

Gracious! how delicately fine
The work! how noble the design!
How true, how happy is the draught!
The figures seem inform'd with thought—
No artists sure the story wove;
They're real men—they live, they move,
From these amazing works we find,
How great, how wise the human mind.
Lo! stretch'd upon a silver bed,
(Scarce has the down his cheeks o'erspread)

70. Like emmets, &c.] Ac veluti ingentem formicæ, &c. Æn. 4. 401.

78. War-horses] Post bellator equus. Æn. 11. 89.

80. Rears an end] Tollit se arrectum quadrupes. Æn. 10. 892.

86. Snake] The Greek is Ψυχρον οφιν, a cold snake: thus Virgil,

> Frigidus, ô pueri, fugite hinc, latet anguis in herbâ. Ec. 3. 93.

And

> Frigidus in pratis cantando rumpitur anguis. Ec. 8. 71.

97. Plautus seems to have imitated this,

> Id quod in aurem rex reginæ dixerit
> Sciunt, quod Juno fabulata est cum Jove.

117. Thus Telemachus expresses his surprise to Pisistratus at the magnificent furniture of Menalaus's palace at Sparta;

> View'st thou unmov'd, O ever honour'd most!
> These prodigies of art, and wondrous cost!
> Above, beneath, around the palace shines
> The sumless treasure of exhausted mines:
> The spoils of elephants the roof inlay,
> And studded amber darts a golden ray:
> Such, and not nobler, in the realms above
> My wonder dictates is the dome of Jove.
> Pope's Odyss. b. 4.

124. They live, they move] ——— Velut si Re verâ pugnent, feriant, vitentque moventes Arma viri. Hor. b. 2. sat. 7.

127. Lo, stretch'd upon a silver bed, &c.] At the feast of Adonis they always placed his image on a magnificent bed; thus Bion,

> Ες᾽ αγαθα ςιβας κ. τ. λ. Idyl. 1. 69.
>
> ——— Behold the stately bed,
> On which Adonis, now depriv'd of breath,
> Seems sunk in slumbers, beauteous ev'n in death. F. F.

128. ——— Flaventem prima lanugine malas. Æn. b. 10. 324.

Adonis lies; O, charming show!
Lov'd by the sable pow'rs below.

STRANGER.

Hist! your Sicilian prate forbear;
Your mouths extend from ear to ear,
Like turtles that for ever moan;
You stun us with your rustic tone.

GORGO.

Sure! we may speak! what fellow's this?
And do you take it, sir, amiss?
Go, keep Ægyptian slaves in awe:
Think not to give Sicilians law:
Besides we're of Corinthian mould,
As was Bellerophon of old:
Our language is entirely Greek—
The Dorians may the Doric speak.

PRAXINOE.

O sweet Proserpina, sure none
Presumes to give us law but one!
To us there is no fear you shou'd
Do harm, who cannot do us good.

GORGO.

Hark! the Greek girl 's about to raise
Her voice in fair Adonis' praise;
She's a sweet pipe for funeral airs:
She's just beginning, she prepares:
She'll Sperchis, and the world excel,
That by her prelude you may tell.

THE GREEK GIRL SINGS.

"O chief of Golgos, and the Idalian grove,
And breezy Eryx, beauteous queen of love!
Once more the soft-foot Hours approaching slow,
Restore Adonis from the realms below;
Welcome to man they come with silent pace,
Diffusing benisons to human race.
O Venus, daughter of Dione fair,
You gave to Berenice's lot to share
Immortal joys in heavenly regions blest,
And with divine Ambrosia fill'd her breast.
And now in due return, O heavenly born!
Whose honour'd name a thousand fanes adorn,
Arsinoe pays the pompous rites divine,
Rival of Helen, at Adonis' shrine;
All fruits she offers that ripe autumn yields,
The produce of the gardens, and the fields;
All herbs and plants which silver baskets hold;
And Syrian unguents flow from shells of gold.
With finest meal sweet paste the women make,
Oil, flowers and honey, mingling in the cake:
Earth and the air afford a large supply
Of animals that creep, and birds that fly.
Green bow'rs are built with dill sweet-smelling crown'd,
And little Cupids hover all around;

134. You stun us, &c.] A citizen of Alexandria finds fault with the Syracusian gossips for opening their mouths so wide when they speak; the good women are affronted, and tell him, that as they are Dorians, they will make use of the Doric dialect: hence we may observe, that the pronunciation of the Dorians was very coarse and broad, and sounded harsh in the ears of the politer Grecians. Martyn's Pref. to Virgil.

145. Here I entirely follow the ingenious interpretation of Heinsius.

151. Sperchis] A celebrated singer.

153. Golgos] Golgos was a small but very ancient town in Cyprus, where Venus was worshipped. Catullus has translated this verse of Theocritus,

> Quæque regis Golgos, quæque Idalium frondosum. De Nup. Pel. & Thet.

154. Eryx] Eryx was a mountain in Sicily.

162. With divine Ambrosia, &c.] Ovid has imitated this passage; speaking of the deification of Æneas, he says,

> ——Ambrosiâ cum dulci nectare mistâ
> Contigit os; fecitque Deum.
> Met. b. 14. 606.

164. A thousand fanes, &c.] This is similar to the beginning of Sappho's first ode,

> Ποικιλοθρον' κ. τ. λ.
>
> Venus bright goddess of the skies,
> To whom unnumber'd temples rise. F. F.

169. All herbs and plants, &c.] The Greek is απαλοι καποι, soft gardens; Archbishop Potter observes, that at the feast of Adonis, there were carried shells filled with earth, in which grew several sorts of herbs, especially lettuces, in memory that Adonis was laid out by Venus on a bed of lettuces: these were called κηποὶ, gardens; whence Αδωνιδος κηποί are proverbially applied to things unfruitful, or fading, because those herbs were only sown so long before the festival, as to sprout forth, and be green at that time, and afterwards cast in the water. See Antiquit. vol. 1.

> Nam quotcunque ferunt campi, quos Thessala magnis
> Montibus ora creat. Catull. & de Pel. & Thet.

176. Thus Bion, Αμφι δε μιν κ. τ. λ. Epit. Adon.

> Surrounding Cupids heave their breasts with sighs.

And Moschus,

> The little Loves lamenting at his doom,
> Strike their fair breasts, and weep around his tomb. F. F.

But as Longipierre observes, images of Cupids were never omitted at this festival. Ovid seems to have had this in view when he wrote,

> Ecce puer Veneris fert eversamque pharetram,
> Et fractos arcus, et sine luce facem.
> Aspice demissis ut eat miserabilis alis,
> Pectoraque infestâ tundit aperta manu.
> Excipiunt lacrymas sparsi per colla capilli,
> Oraque singultu concutiente sonant.
> Amor. b. 3. el. 9.

> See Venus' son his torch extinguish'd brings,
> His quiver all revers'd, and broke his bow!
> See, pensive how he droops with flagging wings,
> And strikes his bared bosom many a blow!
> Loose and neglected, scatter'd o'er his neck,
> His golden locks drink many a falling tear:
> What piteous sobs, as if his heart would break,
> Shake his swol'n cheek? Ah, sorrow too severe!

And, as young nightingales their wings essay,
Skip here and there, and hop from spray to spray.
What heaps of golden vessels glittering bright!
What stores of ebon black, and ivory white!
In ivory carv'd large eagles seem to move,
And thro' the clouds bear Ganymede to Jove.
Lo! purple tapestry arrang'd on high
Charms the spectators with the Tyrian dye;
The Samian and Milesian swains, who keep
Large flocks, acknowledge 'tis more soft than sleep:
Of this Adonis claims a downy bed,
And lo! another for fair Venus spread!
Her bridegroom scarce attains to nineteen years,
Rosy his lips, and no rough beard appears.
Let raptur'd Venus now enjoy her mate,
While we, descending to the city gate,
Array'd in decent robes that sweep the ground,
With naked bosoms, and with hair unbound,
Bring forth Adonis, slain in youthful years,
Ere Phœbus drinks the morning's early tears.
And while to yonder flood we march along,
With tuneful voices raise the funeral song.
"Adonis, you alone of demigods,
Now visit Earth, and now Hell's dire abodes:
Not fam'd Atrides could this favour boast,
Nor furious Ajax, though himself an host;
Nor Hector, long his mother's grace and joy
Of twenty sons; not Pyrrhus safe from Troy;
Not brave Patroclus of immortal fame;
Nor the fierce Lapithæ, a deathless name;
Nor sons of Pelops, nor Deucalion's race,
Nor stout Pelasgians, Argos' honour'd grace.
"As now, divine Adonis, you appear
Kind to our prayers, O bless the future year!
As now propitious to our vows you prove,
Return with meek benevolence and love."

178. Skip here and there, &c.] Thus Bion, speaking likewise of Cupid,

Τᾳ καὶ τᾳ τον Ερωτα μεταλμενον,

How here and there he skipt, and hopt from tree to tree.

181. Large eagles, &c.] Virgil has an image of this sort,

Intextusque puer ———— quem præpes ab Idâ, &c. Æn. b. 5.

There royal Ganymede, inwrought with art,
O'er hills and forests hunts the bounding hart:
The beauteous youth, all wondrous to behold;
Pants in the moving threads, and lives in gold:
From towering Ida shoots the bird of Jove,
And bears him struggling thro' the clouds above;
With out-stretch'd hands his hoary guardians cry,
And the loud hounds spring furious at the sky.
Pitt.

I transcribed this fine passage from Mr. Pitt's translation of Virgil, that I might lay before the reader Mr. Warton's note upon it. "The description of this beautiful piece of tapestry is extremely picturesque: the circumstances of the boy's panting, the old men lifting up their hands, and above all, the dogs looking up and barking after him, are painted in the liveliest manner imaginable. There is a very fine painting by Michael Angelo on this subject, who has exactly copied Virgil's description, except that he has omitted the circumstance of the dogs, which Spenser has likewise, in describing this story, as part of the tapestry with which the house of Busyrane was adorned."

———— When as the Trojan boy so faire
He snatch'd from Ida hill, and with him bare,
Wondrous delight it was, there to behold
How the rude shepherds after him did stare,
Trembling thro' fear lest he down fallen should,
And often to him calling to take surer holde.
F. Q. b. 3. c. 11.

185. Milesian] Thus Virgil,

Quamvis Milesia magno
Vellera mutentur Tyrios incocta rubores.
Geor. b. 3. 306.

186. More soft than sleep] See Idyl. v. ver. 58, and the note.

210. O bless the future, &c.] Sis bonus ô felixque tuis. Ecl. 5. 65.

Sis felix, nostrumque leves quæcunque laborem. Æn. 1. 330.

Ver. 212. This superstitious mystery, of lamenting for Adonis, may be thus explained: Adonis was the Sun; the upper hemisphere of the Earth, or that which we think so, was anciently called Venus; the under, Proserpine; therefore, when the Sun was in the six inferior signs, they said, he was with Proserpine; when he was in the six superior, with Venus. By the Boar that slew Adonis, they understood winter; for they made the Boar, not unaptly, the emblem of that rigid season. Or, by Adonis, they meant the fruits of the earth, which are for one while buried, but at length appear flourishing to the sight; when therefore the seed was thrown into the ground, they said, Adonis was gone to Proserpine; but when it sprouted up, they said, he had revisited the light and Venus. Hence probably it was that they sowed corn, and made gardens for Adonis.

Univers. Hist. vol. ii.

Milton has some fine melodious lines, on this subject.

———— Thammuz came next behind,
Whose annual wound in Lebanon allur'd
The Syrian damsels to lament his fate
In amorous ditties all a summer's day,
While smooth Adonis, from his native rock,
Ran purple to the sea, suppos'd with blood
Of Thammuz yearly wounded.
Par. Lost. b. 1.

Give me leave here to insert the account given by the late Mr Maundrel of this ancient piece of worship, and probably the first occasion of such a superstition. "We had the fortune to see what may be supposed to be the occasion of that opinion which Lucian relates, viz. That this stream (the river Adonis) at certain seasons of the year, especially about the feast of Adonis, is of a bloody colour; which the heathens looked upon as proceeding from a kind of sympathy in the river for the death of Adonis, who was killed by a wild boar in the mountains, out of which this stream rises. Something like this we saw actually come to pass; for the water was stained to a surprising redness; and, as we observed in traveling, had discoloured the sea a great way into a reddish hue, occasioned doubtless by a sort of minium or red earth, washed into the river by the violence of the rain, and not

GORGO.

O, fam'd for knowledge in mysterious things!
How sweet, Praxinoë, the damsel sings!
Time calls me home to keep my husband kind,
He's prone to anger if he has not din'd.
Farewell, Adonis, lov'd and honour'd boy;
O come, propitious, and augment our joy.

IDYLLIUM XVI*.

THE GRACES, OR HIERO.

ARGUMENT.

This Idyllium is addressed to Hiero, the last tyrant of Sicily. Theocritus having before celebrated this prince, without being recompensed for his trouble, composed this poem, in which he complains of the ingratitude of princes to poets, who can alone render their actions immortal. He observes, that not only the Lycian and Trojan heroes, but even Ulysses himself, would have been buried in oblivion, if their fame had not been celebrated by Homer.

It fits the Muse's tongue, the poet's pen,
To praise th' immortal gods, and famous men:
The Nine are deities, and gods resound,
But bards are men, and sing of men renown'd.
Yet who that lives beneath Heaven's cope regards
The incense, or the sacrifice of bards?

by any stain from the blood of Adonis." The prophet Ezekiel saw the women at Jerusalem lamenting Tammuz, ch. 8. ver. 14. "He brought me to the door of the gate of the Lord's house, which was towards the north, and behold there sat women weeping for Tammuz."

216. ——— If he has not din'd.] Thus Horace,

Impransus non qui civem dignosceret hoste.
B. 1. Ep. 15.

——————— With hunger keen,
On friends and foes he vented his chagrin.
Duncombe.

* This little piece abounds with so many beauties and graces, that it is with great propriety styled Χαριτες, or THE GRACES. Hiero, the subject of this poem, was the son of Hierocles, one of the descendents of Gelon the first king of Syracuse. Hiero succeeded to the throne of Syracuse 265 years before Christ. He was remarkable for his constant attachment to, and generous friendship for the Romans.

2. To praise th' immortal gods and famous men] In like manner Horace says,

Quem virum, aut heroa, lyrâ, vel acri
Tibiâ sumes celebrare, Clio?
Quem Deum? B. 1. Ode 12.

What man, what hero shall inspire
My Clio's fife with sprightly lays?
Or will she choose to strike the lyre
Devoted to the gods in hymns of praise?

5. Quis tibi Mecænas? quis nunc erit aut Proculeius.
Aut Fabius? quis Cotta iterum? quis Lentulus alter? Juv Sat. 7. 94

All these great men were celebrated for their generosity and liberality to the Muses.

Who opens now the hospitable door,
And makes the Muses richer than before?
Barefoot, unpaid, indignant they return,
Reproach my zeal, and unavailing mourn:
To the dark chest their labours they consign,
And on cold knees the languid head recline;
For none, alas! the race of men among,
Receives the bard, or hears his lofty song;
Men thirst not now for glory, as of old,
But all their passions are confin'd to gold;
To their mean breasts their thrifty hands they join,
And scarce will give the canker of their coin.
Hint at a recompense, they thus begin;
"Close is my shirt, but closer is my skin:
My own I'll keep! and may the gods reward,
And crown with honours every living bard.
Homer's the prince of poets—sure 'tis sense,
To read the noblest works, at no expense."
What profit, wretched churls, can gold afford,
Which thus in coffers ye abundant hoard?
The wise a different use for riches know,
And love on men of genius to bestow;

7. Who opens, &c.] Nemo cibo, nemo hospitio, tectoque juvabit. Juv. Sat. 3. 211.

Through the wide world a wretched vagrant roam,
For where can starving merit find a home?
In vain your mournful narrative disclose,
While all neglect, and most insult your woes.
S. Johnson.

9. Barefoot, unpaid, &c.] The protection of princes is the greatest incentive to the diligence of poets, and often of more avail than the inspiration of Apollo, Et spes et ratio studiorum in Cæsare tantum. Juvenal says,

Tædia tunc subeunt animos, tunc seque, suamque
Terpsichoren odit facunda et nuda senectus.
Sat. 7.

Last, crush'd by age, in poverty ye pine,
And sighing curse the unavailing Nine.
Bur. Greene.

17. To their mean breasts, &c.] Illiberal persons were said to hold their hands in their bosoms.

20. Close is my shirt, &c.] The Greek is, απωτερω η γονυ κναμα, My leg is further off than my knee. I could not recollect an English proverb more correspondent to the original than what I have substituted; the Romans have one similar,

Tunica pallio proprior, Plaut.

My waistcoat is nearer than my cloak.

23. Homer's the prince of poets—]
Priores Mæonius tenet
Sedes Homerus. Hor. b. 4. O. 9.

25. What profit, &c.]
Nullus argento color est, avaris
Abditæ terris inimice lamnæ
Crispe Sallusti, nisi temperato
Splendeat usu. Hor. b. 2. O. 2.

My Sallust's generous thoughts disdain
The sordid miser's hoarded gain;
Since silver with no lustre glows,
But what a moderate use bestows.
Duncombe.

28. Love on men of genius to bestow] Horace has something similar; Cur eget indignus quisquam te divite? &c. B. 2. S. 2.

Part on themselves, to others part they spare,
And some their friends, and some their kinsmen share:
To every man their bounty shines display'd,
And yet the offerings of the gods are paid.
With prudent hospitality they spend,
And kindly greeting speed the parting friend.
But most the Muses' sons these honours claim,
Whose deathless lays immortalize their fame;
Then will they never rove, in glorious shades,
(Like those who living labour'd with their spades)
Along cold Acheron's infernal river,
And mourn hereditary want for ever.
Aleua and Antiochus, we're told,
Reign'd rich, and mighty potentates of old,
And to a thousand slaves, their menial train,
In lots distributed the monthly grain:
In Scopas' fields unnumber'd heifers fed,
And bulls that proudly toss'd the rough-horn'd head:
For good Creondas' use the shepherd-swains
Fed flocks in myriads on Cranonian plains:
These after death their sweet enjoyments lost,
When in Hell's spacious barge their ghosts had crost
Th' infernal river, and unhonour'd all,
To other heirs their vast possessions fall;
And these among the miserable train
Had long in darkness and oblivion lain,
Had not the Céan Muse extoll'd their name,
Awak'd his sounding lyre, and given them deathless fame.
Verse crowns the race-horse with fair honour's meed,
That in the field has signaliz'd his speed.
Who had the Lycian chiefs and Trojan known,
Or Cycnus, delicate with milk-white crown,
Had not THE BARD delighted to rehearse
Their bold achievements in heroic verse?
Ulysses ne'er had endless glory gain'd,
Though for ten tedious summers he sustain'd
Unnumber'd toils, while he observant stray'd
From clime to clime, and men and states survey'd;
Ev'n though he scap'd the Cyclops' gloomy cell,
And quick descended to the realms of Hell:
Philœtius and Eumæus with the dead
Had lain as nameless as the beasts they fed;
And brave Laertes with his parting breath
Had dy'd, but Homer snatch'd their names from death.
All human fame is by the Muses spread,
And heirs consume the riches of the dead.
Yet 'tis an easier task, when tempests roar,
To count the waves that ceaseless lash the shore,
'Tis easier far to bleach the Ethiop foul,
Than turn the tenour of the miser's soul.
Curse on the wretch, that thus augments his store!
And much possessing, may he wish for more!
I still prefer fair fame, with better sense,
And, more than riches, men's benevolence.
And yet, alas! what guardian shall I choose,
What princely chief to patronize my Muse?

Then, like the Sun, let bounty spread her ray,
And shine that superfluity away.
Oh, impudence of wealth! with all thy store,
How dar'st thou let one worthy man be poor.
Pope.

Vain was the chief's, the sage's pride;
They had no poet, and they dy'd.
In vain they schem'd, in vain they bled!
They had no poet, and are dead. Pope.

34. And kindly greeting, &c.] Here are some admirable precepts for social life; some of them seem to be borrowed from Homer's Odyssey, b. 15. which I shall give in Mr. Pope's version.

True friendship's laws are by this rule exprest,
Welcome the coming, speed the parting guest.

Which he has adopted in his imitation of the 2d Satire of the 2d book of Horace.

38. Like those, &c.] The sense of the original is, Like some ditcher, who by labouring hard with his spade, has rendered his hands callous.

40. Nunc et pauperiem et duros preferre labores. Æn. b. 6. 436.

41. Antiochus was king of Syria: the Aleuadæ and Scopadæ reigned in Thessaly and the neighbouring islands.

44. In lots, &c.] Anciently the masters of families used to distribute to their slaves, every month, such a measure of corn as would keep them the month, which they called demensum; thus Terence,

Quod ille unciatum vix de demenso suo,
Suum defraudens genium, comparsit miser.
Phor. act 1. sc. 1.

48. Cranonian] Cranon was a city of Thessaly.

50. Et ferrugineâ subvectat corpora cymbâ. Æn. 6. 304.

52. To other heirs, &c.]
Linquenda tellus, et domus, et placens
Uxor—— Hor. b. 2. O. 14.

53. And these, &c.] ——Omnes illachrymabiles
Urgentur, &c.
Hor. b. 4. O. 9.

55. Céan Muse] Simonides, a native of Céos, an island in the Ægéan sea. He was a moving and a passionate writer, and succeeded chiefly in elegies: he gained as much honour as he gave by his poems on the four celebrated battles at Marathon, Thermopylæ, Salamis, and Platæa.

59. Lycian chiefs] These were Sarpedon and Glaucus: Cycnus, the son of Neptune, was slain by Achilles, and turned into a swan: Hesiod, according to the scholiast, describes Cycnus with a white head.

65. Thus Horace,——Multorum providus urbes,
Et mores hominum inspexit, latumque per æquor,
Dum sibi, dum sociis reditum parat, aspera multa
Pertulit.—— B. 1. Ep. 2.

69 It is here worth observation, that after the enumeration of these great heroes, Theocritus does not forget his pastoral capacity, or omit to mention the swineherd Eumæus, and the neatherd Philœtius. See Homer's Odyssey.

73. All human fame, &c.] Dignum laude virum Musa vetat mori. Hor. b. 4. O. 8.

74. And heirs, &c.] —Extructis in altum
Divitiis potietur hæres. Hor. b. 2. O. 3.

75. 'Tis an easier task, &c.] Virgil seems to have imitated this passage. Quem qui scire velit, &c. Geor. b. 2. 105.

Or tell the billows, as they beat the shores,
When all th' Ionian sea with raging Boreas roars. Warton.

In perilous paths the race of poets rove,
Dubious their [illegible], without the aid of Jove.
But still the Sun rolls glorious in the skies;
And future victors in the race will rise:
The chief will rise, who shall my numbers claim
Equal to great Æacides in fame,
Equal to Ajax on the Phrygian plains,
Where Ilus' tomb near Simois' streams remains.
The bold Phœnicians, sons of Libya far,
Shrink at the rumour of approaching war:
For lo! their spears the Syracusians wield,
And bend the pliant sallow to a shield:
These Hiero leads, superior to the rest,
And on his helmet nods the horse-hair crest.
O Jupiter, and thou Minerva chaste,
And Proserpine, to our protection haste,
With Ceres thou delightest to partake
Those fair built walls by Lysimelia's lake;

88. And future victors, &c.] Thus Virgil;

Alter erit Tiphys, et altera quæ vehat Argo
Delectos heroas: erunt etiam altera bella,
Atque iterum ad Trojam magnus mittetur Achilles. Ecl. 4.

Another Tiphys shall new seas explore,
Another Argos land the chiefs on shore;
New wars the bleeding nations shall destroy,
And great Achilles find a second Troy.
Dryd. and War.

92. Where Ilus' tomb] Homer has,
—— Θεισ παρα σηματι Ιλȣ. Iliad, b. 11. 415.

From ancient Ilus' ruin'd monument. Pope.

96. And bend, &c.] Thus Virgil,
—— Flectuntque salignas
Umbonum crates. Æn. b. 7. 632.

And for the shield, the pliant sallow bend.
Pitt.

Pindar seems to make an allusion to this circumstance, in his first Pythian Ode, which I shall give in the excellent translation of the late Gilbert West, esq.

And do thou aid Sicilia's hoary lord,
To form and rule his son's obedient mind;
And still in golden days of sweet accord,
And mutual peace the friendly people bind,
Then grant, O son of Saturn, grant my pray'r!
The bold Phœnician on his shore detain, &c.

98. And on his helmet, &c.] —Cristâ hirsutus equinâ. Æn. 10. 869.

High on his head the crested helm he wore.
Pitt.

99. O Jupiter, &c.] Αι γαρ, Ζευ κυδιϛε πατερ κ. τ. λ.

This verse is an imitation of that of Homer;

Αι γαρ, Ζευ τε πατερ ϗ Αθηναιη ϗ Απολλον.
Sic pater ille deûm faciat, sic altus Apollo.
Virg. Æn. 10. 875.

So may great Jove, and he, the god of light.
Pitt.

100. Proserpine and Ceres] These deities were worshipped by the Syracusians.

102. Lysimelia.] A lake not far from Syracuse.

Oh, may the fates, in pity to our woes,
On the Sardonian main disperse our foes!
And let the few that reach their country tell
Their wives and children how their fathers fell!
And let the natives dwell in peace and rest
In all the cities which the foes possest!
May swains, along the pastures, fat and fair,
In flocks of thousands tend their bleating care!
And lowing herds, returning to the stall,
Wind o'er the plain, as slow as foot can fall!
May the crops flourish, and with feeble voice,
On leafy shrubs the grasshopper rejoice!
While spiders stretch their webs along the shore,
And war's dread name be never mention'd more!
May godlike poets, in undying strain,
Bear Hiero's praise beyond the Scythian main,
Beyond the walls, with black bitumen made,
Where proud Semiramis the sceptre sway'd!
I am but one; Jove's daughters fair regard
With sweetest favour many a living bard;
These shall Sicilian Arethusa sing,
The happy people, and the valiant king.
Ye Graces Eteoclean, who reside
Where Minyas, curst by Thebans, rolls his tide,
Unask'd I'll rest; yet not, if call'd, refuse
With you to bring my sweet associate Muse:
Without you, what to men can pleasures give?
Oh! may I ever with the Graces live!

104. Our foes] These were the Carthaginians, who used frequently to invade Sicily.

105. The few] The Greek is, αριθματως, numerabiles, easy to be told, which is elegantly used for a few: Horace has the same expression, Quo sane populus numerabilis, utpote parvus.
Art Poet. 206.

110. Flocks of thousands, &c.] Thus the Psalmist, That our flocks may bring forth thousands and ten thousands in our streets; that is, in their pastures or walks; or, may they increase so as not only to fill our pastures, but the streets of our villages.

114. Sole sub ardenti resonant arbusta cicadis.
Virg. Ec. 2.

115. In foribus laxos suspendit aranea casses.
Virg. Geor. 4. 247.

119. Beyond the walls, &c.] Thus Ovid;

————Ubi ducitur altam
Coctilibus muris cinxisse Semiramis urbem.
Met. 4. 57.

————Where proud Semiramis, for state,
Rais'd walls of brick magnificently great.
Eusden.

125. Ye Graces Eteoclean] By the Graces are meant the Muses: Eteocles was the elder son of Œdipus by Jocasta: he is said to have first sacrificed to the Muses at Orchomenos; whence they are called the Eteoclean deities, or Graces. Homer mentions the river Minyas. Iliad. b. 11.

Soft Minyas rolls his waters to the main.
Pope.

130. O may I ever with the Graces live] Milton seems to allude to this,

These delights if thou canst give,
Mirth, with thee I mean to live.

There is a beautiful passage in my friend Mr. William Whitehead's excellent poem called The

IDYLLIUM XVII*.

PTOLEMY.

ARGUMENT.

Theocritus rises above his pastoral style when he celebrates the praises of Ptolemy Philadelphus, the son of Ptolemy Lagus and Berenice: he derives his race from Hercules; enumerates his many cities; describes his immense treasures; and though he extols him for his military preparations, he commends his love of peace: but above all he commemorates his royal munificence to the sons of the Muses.

WITH Jove begin, ye Nine, and end with Jove,
Whene'er ye praise the greatest god above:
But if of noblest men the song ye cast,
Let Ptolemy be first, and midst, and last.

Danger of writing Verse, which I shall beg leave to transcribe, as the subject is the same with this Idyllium, and the last line refers to our next poem, The Encomium of Ptolemy: complaining that the great showed no regard to the Muses, he says,

> Yet let ev'n these be taught in mystic rhyme,
> 'Tis verse alone arrests the wings of Time.
> Fast to the thread of life, annex'd by fame,
> A sculptur'd medal bears each human name:
> O'er Lethe's streams the fatal threads depend,
> The glittering medal trembles as they bend;
> Close but the shears, when chance or nature calls,
> The birds of rumour catch it as it falls;
> A while from bill to bill the trifle's tost,
> The waves receive it, and 'tis ever lost.
> But should the meanest swan that cuts the stream,
> Consign'd to Phœbus, catch the favour'd name,
> Safe in her mouth she bears the sacred prize
> To where bright Fame's eternal altars rise:
> 'Tis there the Muse's friends true laurel wear,
> There Egypt's monarch † reigns, and great Augustus there.

† Ptolemy Philadelphus.

* The common title of this Idyllium is The Encomium of Ptolemy. Heinsius makes no doubt but that the inscription should be simply Ptolemy: for Theocritus had written two poems, one was called Ptolemy, the other Berenice; the first celebrated the virtues of that illustrious monarch, the second those of his royal mother, who at that time was enrolled among the gods. For Ptolemy's character, see Idyllium XIV. and the note on verse 82.

1. With Jove begin, &c.] The Greek is Εκ Διος αρχωμεσθα, which are the very words with which Aratus begins his poem called Phænomina: as Theocritus and Aratus were intimate friends, and flourished nearly at the same time, though the Sicilian bard was older, it is hard to say which borrowed from the other: Virgil has,

> A Jove principium, Musæ. Ecl. 3.
> A te principium, tibi desinet. Ecl. 8.
> With thee began my sons, with thee shall end.
> Warton.

4. Let Ptolemy be first, and midst, and last] Milton has,

Heroes of old, from demigods that sprung,
Chose lofty poets who their actions sung:
Well skill'd, I tune to Ptolemy my reed;
Hymns are of gods above the honour'd meed.
To Ida, when the woodman winds his way,
Where verdant pines their towering tops display,
Doubtful he stands, with undetermin'd look,
Where first to deal the meditated stroke:
And where shall I commence? new themes arise,
Deeds that exalt his glory to the skies.
If from his fathers we commence the plan,
Lagus, how great, how excellent a man!
Who to no earthly potentate would yield
For wisdom at the board, or valour in the field:
Him with the gods Jove equals, and has given
A golden palace in the realm of Heaven:
Near him sits Alexander, wise and great,
The fell destroyer of the Persian state.
Against them, thron'd in adamant, in view
Alcides, who the Cretan monster slew,
Reclines, and, as with Gods the feast he shares,
Glories to meet his own descendant heirs,
From age and pain's impediments repriev'd,
And in the rank of deities receiv'd.
For in his line are both these heroes class'd,
And both deriv'd from Hercules the last.

> On Earth join all ye creatures to extol
> Him first, him last, him midst, and without end.

Milton has greatly improved this by adding, "and without end;" as he is celebrating God, and Theocritus only a man.

8. Hymns, &c.] Carmine Dî superi placantur, carmine manes. Hor. b. 2. Ep. 1.
Verse can the gods of Heaven and Hell appease.

16. Lagus] Ptolemy Lagus was one of Alexander's captains, who upon that monarch's death, and the division of his empire, had Egypt, Libya, and that part of Arabia which borders upon Egypt, allotted to his share: but at the time of his death, he held several other countries, which are enumerated below, see ver. 97, &c.

21. Near him, &c.] Quos inter Augustus recumbens. Hor. b. 3. O. 3.

——— wise, &c.] I would choose to read, αιολομητας, varium consilium habens, and not αιολομιτρας with Casaubon.

24. Who slew, &c.] Tu Cressia mactas
Prodigia. Æn. 8. 294.

> You slew the bull, whose rage dispeopled Crete. Pitt.

25. The feast he shares] ——Sic Jovis interest
Optatis epulis impiger Hercules.
Hor. b. 4. O. 8.

26. His own descendant heirs] The Greek is, Αθανατοι δε καλευνται θεοι νεποδες γεγαωτες, which is rendered, immortales vero vocantur Dii, sine pedum usu facti; and being formed without feet they are called immortal gods. It is amazing how a clear and elegant passage should be corrupted into such nonsense: Heinsius undoubtedly reads right; οι νεποδες γεγαωτες, that is, αυτω υιωνοι οντες, those that were his nephews; he rejoices that his nephews are called (or are become) immortal.

30. Julius, a magno demissum nomen Julo.
Æn. 1. 288.

Thence, when the nectar'd bowl his love inspires,
And to the blooming Hebe he retires,
To this his bow and quiver he allots,
To that his iron club, distinct with knots;
Thus Jove's great son is by his offspring led
To silver-footed Hebe's rosy bed.
How Berenice shone! her parents pride;
Virtue her aim, and wisdom was her guide:
Sure Venus with light touch her bosom prest,
Infusing in her soft ambrosial breast
Pure, constant love: hence faithful records tell,
No monarch ever lov'd his queen so well;
No queen with such undying passion burn'd,
For more than equal fondness she return'd.
Whene'er to love the chief his mind unbends,
To his son's care the kingdom he commends.
Unfaithful wives, dissatisfied at home,
Let their wild thoughts on joys forbidden roam:
Their births are known, yet, of a numerous race,
None shows the features of the father's face.
Venus, than all the goddesses more fair,
The lovely Berenice was thy care;
To thee 'twas owing, gentle, kind, and good,
She past not Acheron's woe-working flood.
Thou caught'st her e'er she went where spectres dwell,
Or Charon, the grim ferryman of Hell;
And in thy temple plac'd the royal fair,
Thine own high honour's privilege to share.
Thence gentle love in mortals she inspires,
And soft solicitudes and sweet desires.
The fair Deïpyle to Tydeus bare
Stern Diomed, the thunderbolt of war:
And Thetis, goddess of the azure wave,
To Peleus brought Achilles, bold and brave:
But Berenice nobler praise hath won,
Who bore great Ptolemy as great a son:
And sea-girt Cos receiv'd thee soon as born,
When first thine eyes beheld the radiant morn.
For there thy mother to Lucina pray'd,
Who sends, to those that suffer child-bed, aid.
She came, and friendly to the genial bed,
A placid, sweet tranquillity she shed
O'er all her limbs; and thus serene and mild,
Like his lov'd sire, was born the lovely child.
Cos saw, and fondling in her arms the boy,
Thus spoke, transported, with the voice of joy;
"Quick rise to light, auspicious babe be born!
And me with equal dignity adorn
As Phœbus Delos:—on fam'd Triops' brow,
And on the neighbouring Dorian race bestow
Just honours, and as favourably smile,
As the god views with joy Rhenæa's fertile isle."
The island spoke; and thrice the bird of Jove
His pinions clang'd, resounding from above;
Jove's omen thunder'd from his eagle's wings;
Jove loves and honours venerable kings.
But whom in infancy his care befriends,
Him power, and wealth, and happiness attends:
He rules belov'd unbounded tracts of land,
And various oceans roll at his command.

31. The nectar'd bowl] Purpureo bibit ore nectar. Hor. b. 3. O. 3.

33. To this his bow, &c.] Thus Ovid. Met. b. 3. 165.

——— Nympharum tradidit uni
Armigeræ jaculum, pharetramque arcusque retentos.

45. To his son's care, &c.] Ptolemy made his son Philadelphus partner with him in the empire.

49. Their births are known] The Greek is, Ρηϊδιαι δε γοναι, which is wrong translated, faciles quidem partus sunt, their births are easy; whereas it should be rendered, as Casaubon rightly observes, their births are easily to be judged of, viz. that they are adulterous; the latter part of the verse explains the former, Ρηϊδιαι δε γοναι, τεκνα δ' ουποτ' εοικοτα πατρι, their births are easy to be judged, for the children do not resemble their father. The ancients imagined those children not to be legitimate who were unlike their parents; and therefore Hesiod reckons it among the felicities which attend good men, that

The wives bear sons resembling their own sires.
Τικτουσιν δε γυναικες εοικοτα τεκνα γονευσι.
Ver. 233.

56. Portitor has horrendus aquas et flumina servat
Terribili squalore Charon.
Æn. b. 6. 298.

72. A placid, &c.] Virgil has something similar,

At Venus Ascanio placidam per membra quietem
Irrigat, &c. Æn. b. 1. 695.

Mean time the goddess on Ascanius throws
A balmy slumber, and a sweet repose;
Lull'd in her lap to rest, &c. Pitt.

75. Cos saw, &c.] The personifying of this island is sublime and noble, and bears a great resemblance to that passage in Isaiah; "Break forth into singing, ye mountains! O forest, and every tree therein!" Virgil has,

Ipsi lætitiâ voces ad sidera jactant
Intonsi montes. Ecl. 5. 62

79. Delos] An island in the Ægean sea, where Latona was delivered of Apollo and Diana; it was once a floating island, but fixed by Apollo. Quam pius Arcitenens, &c. Virg. Æn. 3. 75.

Which Phœbus fix'd; for once she wander'd round
The shores, and floated on the vast profound;
But now, unmov'd, the peopled region braves
The roaring whirlwinds, and the furious waves.
Pitt.

79. Triops] The scholiast says Triops was a king of Cos, from whom the Promontory near Cnidus took its denomination.

82. Rhenæa] An island separated from Delos by a narrow strait about three times as big as Delos.

86. Jove loves, &c.] Thus Callimachus, Εκ δε Διος βασιληες, kings are from Jupiter; which Virgil has translated, Ab Jove sunt reges: but they all seem to have copied after Hesiod. Theog. ver. 96.

Εκ δε Διος βασιληες. Ο δ' ολβιος οντινα Μουσαι Φιλευνται.————
——————— Kings are deriv'd from Jove;
And blest the mortal whom the Muses love.

Unnumber'd nations view their happy plains,
Fresh fertiliz'd by Jove's prolific rains:
But none, like Egypt, can such plenty boast,
When genial Nile o'erflows the humid coast:
No realm for numerous cities thus renown'd,
Where arts and fam'd artificers abound:
Three times ten thousand towery towns obey
Illustrious Ptolemy's pacific sway.
He o'er Phœnicia, Syria, Lybia reigns,
Arabian deserts, Ethiopian plains,
Pamphylians, and Cilicians bold in war,
And Carians brave, and Lycians fam'd afar;
The distant Cyclades confess his reign,
Whose fleets assert the empire of the main;
So far his ships their conquering flags display,
Him seas, and lands, and sounding floods obey.
Horsemen and spearmen guard the monarch round,
Their arms resplendent send a brazen sound;
Such tributes daily aggrandize his store,
No king e'er own'd such boundless wealth before.
His peaceful subjects ply at ease their toil, 111
No foes invade the fertile banks of Nile,
Nor pitch their camps along the peaceful plains
With war to terrify the village swains:
No pirates haunt the shore in quest of prey,
Nor bear by stealth the lowing herds away;
For graceful Ptolemy, renown'd in arms,
Guards his extended plains from hostile harms.

94. Genial Nile] The Nile is the greatest wonder of Egypt: as it seldom rains there, this river, which waters the whole country by its regular inundations, supplies that defect, by bringing, as a yearly tribute, the rains of the other countries. To multiply so beneficent a river, Egypt was cut into numberless canals, of a length and breadth proportioned to the different situation and wants of the lands; the Nile brought fertility every where with its salutary streams; it united cities one with another, and the Mediterranean with the Red-sea, maintained trade at home and abroad, and fortified the kingdom against the enemy; so that it was at once the nourisher and protector of Egypt. There cannot be a more delightful prospect than the Nile affords at two seasons of the year; for if you ascend some mountain, or one of the great pyramids of Grand Cairo, about the months of July and August, you behold a vast sea, in which a prodigious number of towns, villages, turrets, and spires appear, like the isles in the Ægean sea, with causeys leading from place to place, intermixed with groves and fruit-trees, whose tops only are visible; this view is terminated by mountains and woods, which, at a distance, form the most agreeable perspective that can be imagined. But in the winter, that is, in the months of January and February, the whole country is like one continued scene of beautiful meadows, enamelled with all kinds of flowers: you see on every side herds and flocks scatter'd over the plain, with infinite numbers of husbandmen and gardeners: the air is then embalmed by the great quantity of blossoms on the orange, lemon, and other trees; and is so pure, that a wholesomer and more agreeable is not to be found in the world: so that nature, which is then as it were dead in so many other climates, seems to revive only for the sake of so delightful an abode.

Rollin's Anc. Hist.

97. Three times ten thousand] The original is extremely perplexing, literally translated it would run thus,

He has three hundred cities, — —	300
Add three thousand — — — — —	3000
To thirty thousand, — — — —	30000
Twice three, — — — — — —	6
And three times eleven, — — —	33
	33339

I have made it the round number of thirty thousand. We meet with an embarrassed method of numeration in the 14th Idyl. ver. 55.

104. Whose fleets, &c.] Waller has a passage resembling this,

Where'er thy navy spreads her canvass wings,
Homage to thee, and peace to all she brings.

Which Creech stuck in his translation. Ptolemy intended to engross the whole trade of the east and west to himself, and therefore fitted out two great fleets to protect his trading subjects; one of these he kept in the Red-sea, the other in the Mediterranean: the latter was very numerous, and had several ships of an extraordinary size; two of them in particular had thirty oars on a side, one of twenty, four of fourteen, two of twelve, fourteen of eleven, thirty of nine, thirty-seven of seven, five of six, seventeen of five, and besides these, an incredible number of vessels with four and three oars on a side. By this means, the whole trade being fixed at Alexandria, that place became the chief mart of all the traffic that was carried on between the east and the west, and continued to be the greatest emporium in the world above seventeen hundred years, till another passage was found out by the Cape of Good Hope: but as the road to the Red-sea lay cross the deserts, where no water could be had, nor any convenience of towns or houses for lodging passengers, Ptolemy, to remedy both these evils, opened a canal along the great road, into which he conveyed the water of the Nile, and built on it houses at proper distances; so that passengers found every night convenient lodgings, and necessary refreshments for themselves, and their beasts of burden.

Univ. Hist. vol. ix. 8vo. p. 383.

111. His peaceful, &c.] The amiable picture Theocritus here gives us of the happiness the Egyptians enjoyed under the mild administration of Ptolemy, very much resembles that which Paterculus gives us of the happiness of the Romans, in the reign of Augustus, b. 2. ch. 89. Finita vicesimo anno bella civilia, sepulta externa, revocata pax, sopitus ubique armorum furor; restituta vis legibus, judiciis auctoritas, senatui majestas, &c. prisca illa et antiqua reipublicæ forma revocata; rediit cultus agris, sacris honos, securitas hominibus, certa cuique rerum suarum possessio; leges emendatæ utiliter, latæ salubriter. "In his twentieth year all wars, both civil and foreign, were happily extinguished; peace returned; the rage of arms ceased; vigour was restored to the laws; authority to the tribunals; majesty to the senate, &c. the ancient and venerable form of the republic revived; the fields were again cultivated; religion honoured, and every one enjoyed his own possessions with the utmost security; the old laws were revised and improved, and excellent new ones added."

118. Guards, &c.] Thus Horace;

Like a wise king, the conquests of his sire
He knows to keep, and new ones to acquire.
And yet he hoards not up his useless store
Like ants, still labouring, still amassing more;
The holy shrines and temples are his care,
For they the first-fruits of his favour share:
To mighty kings his bounties he extends,
To states confederate, and illustrious friends.
No bard at Bacchus' festival appears,
Whose lyre has power to charm the ravish'd ears,
But he bright honours and rewards imparts,
Due to his merits, equal to his arts:
And poets hence, for deathless song renown'd,
The generous fame of Ptolemy resound.
At what more glorious can the wealthy aim,
Than thus to purchase fair and lasting fame?
The great Atridæ this alone enjoy,
While all the wealth and spoil of plunder'd Troy,
That scap'd the raging flame, or whelming wave,
Lies buried in oblivion's greedy grave.
Close trode great Ptolemy, at virtue's call,
His father's footsteps, but surpast them all.
He rear'd the fragrant temple, and the shrine,
And to his parents offer'd rites divine;
Whose forms in gold and ivory are design'd,
And worshipp'd as the guardians of mankind.
There oft as circling moons divide the year,
On the red altar bleeds the fatten'd steer;
His hands the thighs for holy flames divide,
Fair blooms the lov'd Arsinoë at his side;
Than whom no nobler queen of mortal race
A greater prince detains in fond embrace;
And, as kind nature the soft tye approves,
Dearly the brother and the husband loves.
Such are the nuptials in the blest abodes,
And such the union of immortal gods:
Iris, who still retains her virgin bloom,
Whose radiant fingers breathe divine perfume,
For Jove prepares the bed, where at his side
Fair Juno sleeps, his sister and his bride.
Hail, noble Ptolemy! illustrious king!
Thee peer to mighty demigods I'll sing;
And future ages shall the verse approve:
Hail! and fair virtue only ask of Jove.

Custode rerum Cæsare, non furor
Civilis, aut vis exiget otium.
B. 4. O. 15.

While Cæsar reigns, nor civil jars
Shall break our peace, nor foreign wars.
Duncombe.

122. Like ants, &c.]
Ore trahit quodcunque potest, atque addit acervo.
Hor. b. 1. S. 1.

123. The holy shrines, &c.] —— Tua largâ
Sæpe manu multisque oneravit limina donis.
Virg. Æn. b. 10. 619.

To thy great name due honours has he paid,
And rich oblations on thy altars laid.
Pitt.

131. And poets, &c.] The fame of Ptolemy's munificence drew several celebrated poets to his court. See the note to verse 82 of Idyl. xiv.

139. Close trode, &c.] The original is a little perplexed, but I follow Heinsius, and take the sense to be this; Ptolemy alone treading close in the footsteps of his forefathers, yet warm in the dust, defaced and rose over them. Theocritus alludes to a contest usual among the ancients, wherein the antagonist used to place his right foot in the left footstep of his competitor, who went before him, and his left foot in the right footstep, which if he could exceed, he would cry aloud, Επιβεβηκα σοι, Υπερανω ειμι, I have stept over you, I am beyond you. Homer, speaking of Ulysses contending with Ajax in the race, has something very similar. Iliad, b. 23. 763.

———— Αυταρ οπισθεν,
Ιχνια τυπτε ποδεσσι, παρος κονιν αμφιχυθηναι,

Graceful in motion thus, his foe he plies,
And treads each footstep ere the dust can rise.
Pope.

150. Virgil thus speaks of Venus embracing Vulcan;

——Niveis hinc atque hinc, &c.
Æn. b. 8. 387.

——Her arms, that match the winter snows,
Around her unresolving lord she throws.
Pitt.

158. His sister and his bride] Juno, speaking of herself, says,

Ast ego, quæ divûm incedo regina, Jovisque
Et soror & conjux. Æn. 1. 47.

But I, who move supreme in Heav'n's abodes,
Jove's sister-wife, and empress of the gods.
Pitt.

162. Fair virtue only ask of Jove] Theocritus having already celebrated Ptolemy's riches and power, which were so great, that he could not even wish an increase of them, nobly concludes his poem with this fine precept Αρεταν γε μεν εκ Διος αιτευ, Ask virtue of Jupiter: as if he could not have too large a share of virtue, though eminently renowned for it: by this the poet proves himself an excellent moralist, and plainly hints at that maxim of the Stoics, who maintained that virtue was entirely sufficient for a happy life.

IDYLLIUM XVIII.

THE EPITHALAMIUM OF HELEN.*

ARGUMENT.

Twelve Spartan virgins of the first rank are here introduced singing this song at the nuptials of Helen, before the bride-chamber: first they are jocular; then they congratulate Menelaus on his being preferred to so many rival princes, and made the son-in-law of Jupiter: they celebrate the beauty of Helen, and conclude with wishing the married couple prosperity.

When Sparta's monarch, Menelaus, led
The beauteous Helen to his bridal bed,

* There were two sorts of epithalamiums, or nuptial songs, among the ancients; the first was sung in the evening, after the bride was introduced into the bride-chamber, it was named Κοιμητικον, and intended to dispose the married couple to sleep; the second was sung in the morning, termed Εγερτικον, and designed to awaken them: see the

Twelve noble virgins, blooming, young, and fair,
With hyacinthine wreaths adorn'd their hair,
And, pleas'd the vocal benison to shower,
To the soft cithern danc'd before the bower:
As bounding light in circling steps they move,
Their feet beat time, and every heart beat love:
This was the nuptial song,—"Why, happy groom,
Steal you thus early to the genial room?
Has sleep or wine your manly limbs opprest,
That thus, thus soon you seek the bed of rest?
If drowsy slumbers lull you to a drone,
Go take refreshing sleep, but sleep alone;
Leave Helen with her maiden mates, to play
At harmless pastimes till the dawn of day:
This night we claim, then yield her yours for life,
From morn to night, from year to year, your wife.
Hail happy prince! whom Venus wafted o'er,
With prosperous omens, to the Spartan shore;
To bless her bed, from all the princely crowd,
Fair Helen chose you—Cupid sneez'd aloud.
Of all our dem'gods 'tis you aspire,
Alone, to call Saturnian Jove your sire:
Jove's daughter now your warm embraces meets,
The pride of Greece, between two lily sheets.
Sure will the offspring, from that soft caress,
The mother's charms in miniature express.
Thrice eighty virgins of the Spartan race,
Her equals we in years, but not in face,
Our limbs diffusing with ambrosial oil,
Were wont on smooth Eurota's banks to toil
In manly sports; and though each nymph was fair,
None could with her in beauty's charms compare:
When Winter thus in night no longer lours,
And Spring is usher'd by the blooming Hours,
The rising Morning, with her radiant eyes,
Salutes the world, and brightens all the skies.
So shines fair Helen, by the Graces drest,
In face, shape, size superior to the rest:
As corn the fields, as pines the garden grace,
As steeds of Thessaly the chariot-race;
So Helen's beauties bright encomiums claim,
And beam forth honour on the Spartan name.
What nymph can rival Helen at the loom,
And make fair art, like living nature bloom?
The blended tints, in sweet proportion join'd,
Express the soft ideas of her mind.
What nymph, like her, of all the tuneful quire,
Can raise the voice, or animate the lyre?
Whether of Pallas, great in arms, she sings,
Or Dian bathing in the silver springs.
A thousand little Loves in ambush lie,
And shoot their arrows from her beaming eye.
O lovely Helen, whom all hearts adore,
A matron now you rise, a maid no more!
Yet ere another Sun shall gild the morn,
We'll gather flowers, your temples to adorn,
Ambrosial flowers, as o'er the meads we stray,
And frequent sigh that Helen is away;
Mindful of Helen still, as unwean'd lambs
Rove round the pastures, bleating for their dams;
Fair flowers of lote we'll cull, that sweetly breathe,
And on yon spreading plane suspend the wreath.

conclusion of this Idyllium. As Theocritus lived at the polite court of Ptolemy Philadelphus, during the time that the seventy interpreters resided there, he would probably, by reading their translation of the Old Testament, borrow some beautiful images from the Scriptures, conceived in oriental magnificence; a few specimens of these will be found in the notes on this Idyllium.

6. Thus Horace,—Junctæque Nymphis Gratiæ decentes
Alterno terram quatiunt pede. B. 1. o. 4.

22. Cupid sneez'd, &c.] Sneezing was sometimes reckoned a lucky omen. See Potter's Archæologia, ch. 17, and Catullus de Acme et Septimio;
—Hoc ut dixit, Amor sinistram, ut ante
Dextram, sternuit approbationem.

See also the note on Idyllium 7, ver. 115.

That new-married persons were attended by singers and dancers, Homer acquaints us in his description of the shield of Achilles. Iliad, b. 18.

Here sacred pomp, and genial feast delight,
And solemn dance, and Hymenæal rite;
Along the street the new-made brides are led,
With torches flaming, to the nuptial bed:
The youthful dancers in a circle bound
To the soft flute and cithern's silver sound:
Thro' the fair streets, the matrons in a row,
Stand in their porches, and enjoy the show.
Pope.

31. Our limbs, &c.] Thus the handmaids of Nausicäa in Homer anoint themselves with oil. Odys. b. 6.

Then with a short repast relieve their toil,
And o'er their limbs diffuse ambrosial oil.
Pope.

35. Thus Solomon's Song, ch. ii. ver. 11. Lo, the winter is past, the rain is over and gone.

37. The rising Morning, &c.] Who is she that looketh forth as the Morning, Solomon's Song, ch. vi. ver. 10. and in the book of Job, ch. xli. ver. 18. speaking of the Leviathan we read, His eyes are like the eye-lids of the Morning.

Here the marks of imitation appear very strong.

41. Pines the garden grace] Virgil has,
Fraxinus in sylvis pulcherrima, pinus in hortis.
Ecl. 7. 65.

42. As steeds of Thessaly, &c.] Theocritus still seems to borrow from the royal author: I have compared thee, O my love, to a company of horses in Pharaoh's chariots, Solomon's Song, ch. i. ver. 9.—The original literally signifies, I have compared thee to my mare, &c. Nor ought we to think the comparison coarse or vulgar, if we consider what beautiful and delicate creatures the eastern horses are, and how highly they are valued. See Percy on Solomon's Song.

53. A thousand little Loves, &c.]
Thus Hero is described in Musæus,

Εις δε τις Ηρως Οφθαλμος γελοων. κ. τ. λ.
Ver. 64.

When Hero smiles, a thousand Graces rise,
Sport on her cheek, and revel in her eyes.
F. F.

63. Flowers of lote] Miller says the leaves of the lote-tree, or nettle-tree, are like those of the nettle; the flower consists of five leaves, expanded in form of a rose, containing many short stamina in the bosom; the fruit, which is a roundish berry, grows single in the bosom of its leaves. Dr. Martyn says, it is more probable, that the lotus of the Lotophagi is what we call zizyphus or the jujube-tree: the leaves of this are about an inch and

But first from silver shells shall unguents flow,
Bedew the spreading plane and all the flowers
below:
And on the rind we'll write, that all may see,
'Here pay your honours, I am Helen's tree.'
Joy to the bride, and to the bridegroom joy,
And may Latona bless you with a boy!
May Venus furnish both with equal love!
And lasting riches be the gift of Jove!
May these descend, and by possession grow,
From sire to son, augmenting as they flow!
"Now sweetly slumber, mutual love inspire,
And gratify the fullness of desire:
Rise with the blushing morning, nor forget
The due of Venus, and discharge the debt:
And, ere the day's loud herald has begun
To speak his early prologue to the Sun,
Again we'll greet your joys with cheerful voice,
O Hymen, Hymen, at this match rejoice!"

IDYLLIUM XIX *.

THE HONEY-STEALER.

ARGUMENT.

As Cupid is stealing honey from a bee-hive, he is stung by a bee; on which he runs and complains to his mother, that so small an animal should inflict so great a wound; she immediately answers, that he himself is but little like a bee, yet the wounds he gives are grievous.

As Cupid, the slyest young wanton alive,
Of its hoard of sweet honey was robbing a hive,
The sentinel bee buzz'd with anger and grief,
And darted his sting in the hand of the thief.
He sobb'd, blew his fingers, stamp'd hard on the
ground,
And leaping in anguish show'd Venus the wound;
Then began in a sorrowful tone to complain,
That an insect so little should cause so great pain.
Venus smiling, her son in such taking to see,
Said, "Cupid, you put me in mind of a bee;
You're just such a busy, diminutive thing,
Yet you make woeful wounds with a desperate
sting."

IDYLLIUM XX *.

EUNICA, OR THE NEATHERD.

ARGUMENT.

A rough neatherd complains of the pride and insolence of a city girl, who refused to let him kiss her, and rallied his awkward figure: he appeals to the neighbouring shepherds, and asks them if he is not handsome; if his voice is not sweet, and his songs enchanting; and relates examples of goddesses that have been enamoured of herdsmen. In this Idyllium the poet is thought to be severe on those who with arrogance despise the sweetness and simplicity of bucolic numbers. It is strange, that the commentators will not allow this piece to be styled a pastoral: surely it is bucolical enough.

---

half in length, and an inch in breadth, of a shining green colour, and serrated about the edges: the fruit is of the shape and size of olives, and the pulp of it has a sweet taste like honey; and therefore cannot be the nettle-tree, the fruit of which is far from that delicacy which is ascribed to the lotus of the ancients. See Martyn on the Geor. b. 2. 84. But the lotus here spoken of is most probably an herb, the same Homer describes in the Odyssey, b. 9, and which Eustathius takes to be an herb; he says, there is an Egyptian lotus which grows in great abundance along the Nile, in the time of its inundations. Prosper Alpinus, an author of good credit, who travelled into Egypt, assures us, that the Egyptian lotus does not at all differ from our great white water-lily.

67. The custom of writing on the bark of trees was very common among the ancients, thus Virgil;

Certum est in sylvis, inter spelæa ferarum
Malle pati, tenerisque meos incidere amores
Arboribus: crescent illæ, crescetis amores.
Ecl. 10.

See Ovid in Oenone, Propertius, b. 1. Eleg. 18, &c.

Nothing can be more beautifully pastoral than this inscription on the bark of the plane-tree, as also the simile at the 61st and 62d verses.

75. Mutual love inspire] Quæ spirabat amores. Hor. b. 4. O. 11.

81. Again we'll greet, &c.] The chorus of virgins here promise to return early in the morning, and sing the Carmen Εγερτικον.

82. O Hymen, &c.] Thus Catullus, Carm. Nup.

Hymen, O Hymenæe, Hymen ades, O Hymenæe

* In this small poem Theocritus has copied the 40th ode of Anacreon, in every thing but the measure of his verse: the original of this is in hexameter, and therefore I thought it improper to give it Anacreontic numbers. I shall take the liberty to insert a translation of the Teian bard's little poem, that the English reader may have the pleasure to see the manner in which the ancient poets copied their predecessors.

Once as Cupid, tir'd with play,
On a bed of roses lay,
A rude bee, that slept unseen,
The sweet breathing buds between,
Stung his finger, cruel chance!
With its little pointed lance.
Straight he fills the air with cries,
Weeps, and sobs, and runs, and flies;
Till the god to Venus came,
Lovely, laughter-loving dame:
Then he thus began to plain;
"Oh! undone—I die with pain—
Dear mamma, a serpent small,
Which a bee the ploughmen call,
Imp'd with wings, and arm'd with dart,
Oh!—has stung me to the heart."
Venus thus replied, and smil'd;
"Dry those tears, for shame! my child;
If a bee can wound so deep,
Causing Cupid thus to weep,
Think, O think, what cruel pains
He that's stung by thee sustains!" F. F.

* This Idyllium has by Daniel Heinsius, and other learned critics, been ascribed to Moschus, and for that reason I published a translation of it some time ago, along with a version of the other

WHEN lately I offer'd Eunica to kiss,
She fleer'd, and she flouted, and took it amiss;
"Begone, you great booby," she cry'd with a frown,
"Do you think that I long to be kiss'd by a clown?
The sparks of the city my kisses esteem;
You never shall kiss me, no, not in a dream.
How pleasing your look! and how gently you play!
How soft is your voice! and what fine things you say!
So neat is your beard, and so comely your hair!
Your hands are so white, and your lips, a sweet pair!
But on your dear person I never shall doat;
So pray keep your distance—you smell like a goat."
Thus spoke the pert hussy, and view'd me all round
With an eye of disdain, and thrice spit on the ground,
Look'd proud of her charms, with an insolent sneer,
And sent me away with a flea in my ear.
My blood quickly boil'd in a violent pique,
And, red as a rose, passion glow'd in my cheek;
For it vex'd me, that thus in derision she jeer'd
My looks, and my voice, and my hair, and my beard.
But, am I not handsome, ye shepherds, say true?
Or has any god alter'd my person anew?
For lately, on oaks like the ivy, with grace
My hair and my beard added charms to my face:
My eye-brows were sable, my forehead milk-white,
And my eyes, like Minerva's, were azure and bright;
My lips, sweet as cream, were with music replete,
For from them flow'd sounds as the honey-comb sweet:
My songs are enchanting; nor ought can exceed
The tunes of my pipe, or the notes of my reed.
The girls of the country, if they had their wills,
Would kiss me, and press me to stay on the hills;
For they say, that I'm fair: but this flirt of the town
Refus'd my sweet kisses, and call'd me a clown.
Alas! she forgot, or perhaps did not know,
That Bacchus fed herds in the valley below;
That Venus a swain lov'd with hearty good will,
And help'd him his cattle to tend on the hill;
Adonis, while living, in groves she ador'd,
And dead, in the groves and on mountains deplor'd.
If right my conjecture, Endymion, I ween,
Like me too once tended his steers on the green;
Yet the Moon in this neatherd took such a delight,
That she met him at Latmos, and kiss'd him all night.
Ev'n Cybele mourn'd for a herdsman; and Jove
Snatch'd a boy from his herd to be waiter above.
But Eunica disdains me, nor lists to my vow;
Is she better than Cynthia, or Cybele, trow?
Does she think that in bloom, and the beauty of face
She is equal to Venus? if that be the case;
May she never behold sweet Adonis again
On the hill, in the vale, in the city or plain;
And may the proud minx, for her crime to atone,
If she can, sleep contented—but always alone!

beautiful pieces of that, and of four other Greek poets, viz. Anacreon, Sappho, Bion, and Musæus; but as in all probability Theocritus is the real author, I here insert it with several alterations and corrections, as I shall entirely omit it in the second edition of my work above mentioned, which will shortly be published; the first having been very favourably received by the public.

5. The sparks of the city, &c.] The Greek is, μεμαθηκα αςυκα χειλεα θλιβειν, Didici urbana labra terere, which Virgil seems to have had an eye to, when he says, Calamo trivisse labellum; on which Mr. Warton observes, there is a fondness in mentioning this circumstance of wearing his lip. The constant effect of playing on the fistula, which is used to this day in the Grecian islands, is making the lips thick and callous. Mr. Dawkins assured me he saw several shepherds with such lips.

13. View'd me all round] Virgil has something similar,

> Talia dicentem jamdudum aversa tuetur,
> Huc illuc volvens oculos, totumque pererrat
> Luminibus tacitis. Æn. b. 4. 362.

14. Thrice spit on the ground] The Greek is, τρις εις εον επτυςε κολπον, and should be rendered, She thrice spit into her bosom. Archbishop Potter observes, see Archæol. ch. 17, it was customary for the ancient Grecians to spit three times into their bosoms at the sight of a madman, or one troubled with an epilepsy; this they did in defiance, as it were, of the omen; for spitting was a sign of the greatest contempt and detestation, whence πτυειν, to spit, is put for to contemn.

22. Has any god alter'd, &c.] The poet here seems to allude to a passage in Homer's Odys. b. 13, where Minerva changes Ulysses into the figure of an old beggar.

> She spake, and touch'd him with her powerful wand:
> The skin shrunk up, and wither'd at her hand:
> A swift old age o'er all his members spread;
> A sudden frost was sprinkled on his head;
> No longer in the heavy eye-ball shin'd
> The glance divine, forth beaming from the mind.
> Pope.

26. And my eyes, &c.] Theocritus seems to have Anacreon in view, ode 28.

> All thy art her eyes require,
> Make her eyes of living fire,
> Glowing with celestial sheen,
> Like Minerva's, bright and keen;
> On her lips, that sweetly swell,
> Let divine persuasion dwell. F.F.

27. My lips, &c.] This is entirely taken from Solomon's Song, ch. iv. 11. Thy lips, O my spouse, drop as the honeycomb; honey and milk are under thy tongue.

40. And dead, &c.] See Bion's beautiful Idyllium on the death of Adonis.

41. Endymion] Latmius Endymion non est tibi, Luna, rubori. Ovid Art. Aman. 3. 85.

54. Always alone] Sappho, with the most elegant simplicity, complains, that she is deserted and left alone.

> Δεδυκε μεν α σελανα, κ. τ. λ. See her Frag.
>
> The Pleiads now no more are seen,
> Nor shines the silver Moon serene,
> In dark and dismal clouds o'ercast;
> The love-appointed hour is past;
> Midnight usurps her sable throne,
> And yet, alas! I lie alone. F.F.

IDYLLIUM XXI.

THE FISHERMEN.

ARGUMENT.

This piece is a dialogue between two fishermen, which for its singular simplicity of sentiment, as well as character, is peculiarly beautiful and regular: one of them relates his dream, which was, that he had caught a large fish of solid gold, on which he resolves to follow his laborious occupation no longer, but live luxuriously: in the morning his fish and his hopes vanish, and necessity compels him to return to his accustomed labours. This Idyllium admonishes every one to rest content with his lot; and under the shadow of a golden dream, beautifully displays the vanity of all human hopes and desires.

Need, Diophantus, ready wit imparts,
Is Labour's mistress, and the nurse of arts:
Corroding cares the toiling wretch infest,
And spoil the peaceful tenour of his breast;
And if soft slumbers on his eye-lids creep,
Some cursed care steals in, and murders sleep.
Two ancient fishers in a straw-thatcht shed,
Leaves were their walls, and sea-weed was their bed,
Reclin'd their weary limbs; hard by were laid
Baskets, and all their implements of trade,
Rods, hooks, and lines compos'd of stout horse-hairs,
And nets of various sorts, and various snares,
The seine, the cast-net, and the wicker maze,
To waste the watery tribes a thousand ways:
A crazy boat was drawn upon a plank;
Matts were their pillow, wove of osiers dank,
Skins, caps, and rugged coats a covering made:
This was their wealth, their labour, and their trade.
No pot to boil, no watch-dog to defend;
Yet blest they liv'd, with Penury their friend.
None visited their shed, save, every tide,
The wanton waves that wash'd its tottering side.
When half her course the Moon's bright car had sped,
Joint labour rous'd the tenants of the shed.
The dews of slumber from their eyes they clear'd,
And thus their mind with pleasing parley cheer'd.

ASPHALION.

I hold, my friend, that trite opinion wrong,
That summer-nights are short, when days are long.
Yes—I have seen a thousand dreams to night,
And yet no morn appears, nor morning light:
Sure on my mind some strange illusions play,
And make short nights wear heavily away.

FRIEND.

Fair summer-seasons you unjustly blame,
Their bounds are equal, and their pace the same;
But cares, Asphalion, in a busy throng,
Break on your rest, and make the night seem long.

ASPHALION.

Say, hast thou genius to interpret right
My dream? I've had a jolly one to night.
Thou shalt go halves, and more thou canst not wish,
We'll share the vision, as we share our fish.
I know thee shrewd, expert of dreams to spell;
He's the best judge, who can conjecture well.
We've leisure time, which can't be better spent
By wretched carles in wave-wash'd cabin pent,
And lodg'd on leaves; yet why should we repine,
While living lights in Prytaneum shine?

1. Need, &c.] Thus Virgil,

> Tum variæ venêre artes: labor omnia vincit
> Improbus, & duris urgens in rebus egestas.
> Geor. 1. 145.

> Then all those arts that polish life succeed;
> What cannot ceaseless toil, and pressing need!
> Warton.

And Persius, Prol.

> Quis expedivit psittaco suum χαιρε,
> Picasque docuit verba nostra conari?
> Magister artis, ingenîque largitor Venter.

> Who taught the parrot human notes to try,
> Or with a voice endued the chattering pye?
> 'Twas witty Want, fierce hunger to appease:
> Want taught their masters, and their masters these.
> Dryd.

3. Corroding cares.]

> Nec plocidam membris dat cura quietem.
> Virg.

5. And if soft slumbers, &c.] Juvenal has,

> Nocte brevem si forte indulsit cura soporem.
> Sat. 13. 217.

6. Some cursed care] ——Sub noctem cura recursat. Virg. Æn. b. 1.

19. No watch-dog] The Greek is ȣ κυνα, and is an emendation of the learned Johannes Auratus; before it was read ȣχ ενα. Heinsius.

33. Fair summer-seasons, &c.] Here I entirely follow the emendation of Heinsius; the text stands thus:

> Ασφαλιων, μεμφῃ το καλον θερος, ȣ γαρ ο καιρος
> Αυτοματως παρεβα τον εον δρομον.

Asphalion, you accuse the fair summer; for that season never willingly passes its bounds: which is nonsense; but by transposing the first word of each verse, thus,

> Αυτοματως μεμφῃ το καλον θερος, ȣ γαρ ο καιρος,
> Ασφαλιων, ταρεβα τον εον δρομον.

In vain and without reason you accuse the fair summer, &c.

42. He's the best judge, &c.] This seems to be taken from that verse of Euripides, which we read in Plutarch,

> Μαντις δ' αριςος οςις εικαζει καλως,

Which Tully has thus translated,

> Qui bene conjecit, vatem perhibebo optumum.

46. Prytaneum] The Prytaneum was a common-hall in the cities of Greece, where those that had deserved well of their country were maintained at the public charge; where also the fire consecrated to Vulcan was kept, as that sacred to Vesta at Rome. Cicero de Orat. 1. 54, says, Ut ei victus quotidianus in Prytaneo, publice præberetur. If this be understood of the Prytaneum at Athens, Scaliger observes, that there is great impropriety in Sicilian fishermen mentioning places so far remote from the scene of their labours: but from what follows it appears, there was a place in the neighbourhood, very commodious for fishing, named Prytaneum, on which nocturnal lamps were

FRIEND.

To thy fast friend each circumstance recite,
And let me hear this vision of the night.

ASPHALION.

Last evening, weary with the toils of day,
Lull'd in the lap of rest secure I lay;
Full late we supp'd, and sparingly we eat;
No danger of a surfeit from our meat.
Methought I sat upon a shelfy steep,
And watch'd the fish that gambol'd in the deep:
Suspended by my rod, I gently shook
The bait fallacious, which a huge one took;
(Sleeping we image what awake we wish;
Dogs dream of bones, and fishermen of fish)
Bent was my rod, and from his gills the blood,
With crimson stream, distain'd the silver flood.
I stretch'd my arm out, lest the line should break;
The fish so vigorous, and my hook so weak!
Anxious I gaz'd, he struggled to be gone;
"You're wounded——I'll be with you friend, anon—
Still do you teise me?" for he plagu'd me sore;
At last, quite spent, I drew him safe on shore,
Then graspt him with my hand, for surer hold,
A noble prize, a fish of solid gold!
But fears suspicious in my bosom throng'd,
Lest to the god of ocean he belong'd;
Or, haply wandering in the azure main,
Some favourite fish of Amphitrite's train.
My prize I loos'd, and strictest caution took,
For fear some gold might stick about the hook;
Then safe secur'd him, and devoutly swore,
Never to venture on the ocean more;
But live on land as happy as a king:
At this I wak'd: what think you of the thing!
Speak free, for know, I am extremely loth,
And greatly fear, to violate my oath.

fixed, as was customary, for the convenience of fishing by night. Sannazarius was not ignorant of this custom, who in his second piscatory eclogue says,

> Dumque alii notosque sinus, piscosaque circum
> Æquora collustrant flammis.

> While others on the well-known bay,
> Or fishy seas their lights display.

55. Suspended by my rod, &c.] Ovid has something similar,

> Nunc in mole sedens moderabar arundine linum. Met. b. 13. 923.

57. Sleeping we image, &c.] There is something very beautiful in what Ovid makes Sappho say to Phaon,

> Tu mihi cura, Phaon; te somnia nostra reducunt;
> Somnia formoso candidiora die, &c.

Which Mr. Pope has greatly improved upon,

> Oh night more pleasing than the brightest day,
> When fancy gives what absence takes away,
> And, dress'd in all its visionary charms,
> Restores my fair deserter to my arms!

77. Happy as a king, &c.] The expression in the original is remarkable, τω χρυσω βασιλευειν, to reign in riches; speaking of the happiness of the old Corycian farmer, Virgil says,

> Regim æquabat opes animis. Geor. 4. 132.

FRIEND.

Fear not, old friend; you took no oath, for why?
You took no fish—your vision's all a lye.
Go search the shoals, not sleeping, but awake,
Hunger will soon discover your mistake;
Catch real fish; you need not, sure, be told,
Those fools must starve who only dream of gold.

IDYLLIUM XXII*.

CASTOR AND POLLUX.

ARGUMENT.

This is a hymn, after the manner of the ancient Arcadians, in praise of Castor and Pollux. The first part describes the combat between Pollux and Amycus, the son of Neptune and king of the Bebrycians, who, valuing himself on his superiority in strength and the art of boxing, used to compel every stranger, that touched upon his coast, to take up the cæstus, and make trial of his skill in the management of that rude instrument of death; for so it proved to many, till Pollux, who arrived there with the Argonauts, encountered him and conquered: Apollonius says, he slew him, but this is denied by other authors.

---

81. Fear not] Solve metus. Virg.

*Virgil, in his description of the contest between Dares and Entellus, has borrowed some circumstances from this encounter between Amycus and Pollux, which shall be specified in their course: Apollonius Rhodius, in his second book of the Argonautics, has likewise described this last mentioned contest, but is, in the opinion of Casaubon, far surpassed by Theocritus; speaking of the first part of this Idyllium, he says, Porro qui contulerit priorem partem, quæ Pollucis pugilatum cum Amyco describit, cum iis quæ habet Apollonius, reperiet profecto Theocritum tantum excellere Apollonium,

> Quantum lenta solent inter viburna cupressi.
> As lofty cypresses low shrubs exceed.
> Warton.

And yet Scaliger, in his dogmatical manner, gives the preference to Apollonius; Splendore et arte ab Apollonio Theocritus superatur. Poet. b. 5. c. 6, whose determination the ingenious translator of Virgil's Eclogues and Georgics has adopted; but I am inclined to think, that my friend Mr. Warton, who perhaps admires Apollonius more, and understands him better than any man in the kingdom, may be too partial to his favourite author: I shall not take upon me to decide in this point, but after the Epigrams of Theocritus, I propose to print a translation of the combat between Pollux and Amycus from Apollonius, which I hope will be acceptable to the curious reader, as it has never, that I know of, been translated into English; he will then have an opportunity of forming a comparison, and in some sort judging of the merits of the two originals: I profess, without any kind of partiality, I have endeavoured to do all the justice in my power to them both. It is to be observed, that Apollonius flourished in

THE sons of Leda, and of Jove I sing,
Immortal Jove, the ægis-bearing king,
Castor and Pollux, with the cæstus grac'd,
Which round his wrist thick thongs of bull-hide brac'd:
In strains repeated shall my Muse resound
The Spartan Twins, with manly virtues crown'd:
Safeguards of men distrest, and generous steeds,
When in the fields of death the battle bleeds;
Safeguards of sailors, who the Twins implore,
When on the deep the thundering tempests roar.
These in the hollow vessel from the side,
Or head or helm, pour the high-swelling tide;
Burst are the planks, the tackling torn, the mast
Snapt, the sails rent before the furious blast:
Suspended showers obscure the cheerful light,
Fades the pale day before approaching night,
Rise the rough winds, resounding storms prevail,
And the vext ocean roars beneath the scourging hail.
Still you the wreck can save, the storm dispel,
And snatch the sailors from the jaws of Hell.
The winds disperse, the roaring waves subside,
And smooth'd to stillness sleeps the lenient tide.

the reign of Ptolemy Euergetes, and therefore, as he wrote after Theocritus, he probably borrowed many things from him.

1. The sons of Leda, &c.] In the same manner Horace,

Dicam et Alcidem, puerosque Ledæ;
Hunc equis, illum superare pugnis
Nobilem. B. 1. O. 12.

3. Cæstus] "The cæstus," says Gilbert West, esq. "consisted of many thongs of leather, or raw hides of bulls, wound about the hand and arm up to the elbow: I must here observe, that none of the three Greek poets, Homer Il. b. 23, Apollonius, nor our author, who all have given us a description of the cæstus, make any mention of plates of lead or iron;" as Virgil has done,

————Tantorum ingentia septem
Terga boum plumbo insuto, ferroque rigebant.
Æn. b. 5.

Seven thick bull-hides, their volumes huge dispread,
Ponderous with iron and a weight of lead.
Pitt.

Amycus is said to have invented the combat of the cæstus.

19. Still you the wreck can save, &c.] Archbishop Potter observes, "When the two lambent flames, about the heads of Castor and Pollux, appeared together, they were esteemed an excellent omen, foreboding good weather:" thus Horace,

Clarum Tyndaridæ sidus, &c. B. 4. O. 8.

Thus the twin-stars, indulgent, save
The shatter'd vessel from the wave.
Duncombe.

And b. 1. O. 12. Quorum simul alba nautis stella refulsit, &c.

Soon as their happy stars appear,
Hush'd is the storm, the waves subside,
The clouds disperse, the skies are clear,
And without murmurs sleeps th' obedient tide. Dunc.

When shine the Bears, and 'twixt the Asses seen,
Though faint, their manger, ocean proves serene.
O, friends of human kind in utmost need,
Fam'd for the song, the lyre, the gauntlet, and the steed!
Whose praises first shall my rapt Muse rehearse?
Both claim my praise, but Pollux first my verse.
When Argo reach'd (Cyane's islands past)
Cold Pontus harass'd by the northern blast,
Soon to Bebrysia, with the sons of fame,
A freight of chiefs and demigods, she came.
Forth from her sides, the country to explore,
The crew descended to the breezy shore:
On the dry beach they raised the leafy bed,
The fires they kindled, and the tables spread.
Meanwhile the royal brothers devious stray'd
Far from the shore, and sought the cooling shade.
Hard by, a hill with waving forests crown'd
Their ey s attracted; in the dale they found
A spring perennial in a rocky cave,
Full to the margin flow'd the lucid wave:
Below small fountains gush'd, and, murmuring near,
Sparkled like silver, and as crystal clear:
Above tall pines and poplars quivering play'd,
And planes and cypress in dark green array'd:
Around balm-breathing flowers of every hue,
The bee's ambrosia, in the meadows grew.
There sat a chief tremendous to the eye,
His couch the rock, his canopy the sky;
The gauntlet's strokes, his cheeks and ears around,
Had mark'd his face with many a desperate wound.
Round as a globe and prominent his chest,
Broad was his back, but broader was his breast:
Firm was his flesh, with iron sinews fraught,
Like some Colossus on an anvil wrought.
As rocks, that in the rapid streams abound,
Are wash'd by rolling torrents smooth and round,

24. Their manger] According to Aratus, there is a little cloud in the shell of the crab, between the shoulders, on each side of which is a star, called the Asses, the intermediate cloud therefore is probably styled their Manger.

29. Cyane's islands] See Idyllium 31. v. 27, and note.

31. Bebrycia] A country near Bithynia in Asia, bounded on the north by the Euxine sea.

35. On the dry beach, &c.]
Tunc littore curvo Extruimus toros. Virg.

37. Meanwhile, &c.] We may look upon every circumstance relating to this remarkable combat to commence here, the preceding lines being chiefly a noble encomium on these illustrious twin-sons of Jupiter, and then it is observable, that this conflict in Theocritus takes up 103 verses, and the episode on the same subject in Apollonius 97.

45. Tall pines, &c.] Qua pinus ingens, albaque populus. Hor.

49. Tremendous to the eye] Virgil speaking of the Cyclops, says,

Nec visu facilis, nec dictu affabilis ulli.
Æn. 3. 621.

A savage fiend! tremendous to the sight.
Pitt.

57. As rocks, &c.] This is surely a new and

The ridges rise, in crystal streams beheld:
So on his brawny arms the rising muscles swell'd.
A lion's spoils around his loins he draws,
Beneath his chin suspended by the paws:
Victorious Pollux, with attentive look,
View'd, and complacent, thus the chief bespoke:

POLLUX.

Peace, gentle friend! to wandering strangers tell
What tribes, what nations in these regions dwell?

AMYCUS.

What peace to me, while on my native shore,
I see strange guests I never saw before?

POLLUX.

Fear not; no foes, nor mean of birth are here.

AMYCUS

Thou hast no cause to bid me not to fear.

POLLUX.

Rude are your words, and wrongfully apply'd,
Your manners fierce, your bosom swoln with pride.

AMYCUS.

Thou see'st me as I am: these lands are mine;
I never yet have troubled thee on thine.

POLLUX.

Whene'er you come, you will a welcome find,
And presents, as befits a liberal mind.

AMYCUS.

Nor I thy welcome, nor thy gifts partake;
I give no welcome, and no presents make.

POLLUX.

May I not taste the stream that murmurs by?

AMYCUS.

I'll solve that question when thy throat is dry.

POLLUX.

Will gold, or other bribe the purchase gain?

AMYCUS.

Nought but to prove thy prowess on the plain;
Stand forth; let man oppos'd to man provoke,
With gauntlet-guarded arm, th' impending stroke;
Eye meeting eye, exert thy utmost might,
By feint or force to triumph in the fight.

POLLUX.

Whom must I fight? mine adversary who?

AMYCUS.

Thou see'st thy match, no despicable foe.

POLLUX.

But what reward shall the stout victor have?

AMYCUS.

The conquer'd man shall be the conqueror's slave.

POLLUX.

This is cock's play, and such the terms severe
In fight of scarlet-crested chanticleer.

AMYCUS.

Or be it cock's, or be it lion's play,
These are the fix'd conditions of the fray.

This said, his hollow conch he instant blew,
Quick through the coast the sounds alarming flew;
The signal rous'd the stout Bebrycian train,
Who join'd their chief beneath the shady plane.
Illustrious Castor from the neighbouring strand,
Call'd to the conflict Argo's chosen band.
Meanwhile the combatants, of mind elate,
Drew on their hands the dreadful gloves of fate;
The leathern thongs, that brac'd their shoulders round,
Firm to their arms the ponderous gauntlets bound.
Amid the circle now the champions stood,
Breathing revenge, and vehement for blood.
Studious each strove the piercing light to shun:
And on his shoulders catch the gleaming sun:
You call'd, O Pollux, Prudence to your aid;
In Amycus his eyes the solar splendours play'd.
This did th' enormous chieftain's rage provoke
To strike at once some death-denouncing stroke;
But watchful Pollux dealt a weighty blow
Full on the cheek of his advancing foe:

noble thought, to compare the protuberant muscles of a giant to the rocky shelves under water, that are worn smooth and round by the transparent stream.

61. A lion's spoils, &c.] Diomed is thus arrayed. Il. b. 10.

> This said, the hero o'er his shoulders flung
> A lion's spoils, that to his ankles hung.
> Pope.

95. His hollow conch] Before trumpets were invented, conchs were used to sound the signal for battle. Virgil says of Misenus,

> Sed tum forte cavâ dum personat æquora conchâ. Æn. b. 6.

97. The signal rous'd, &c.] Thus in Virgil, the rustics are stirr'd up to war by Alecto,

> Tum vero ad vocem celeres, &c.
> Æn. 7. 519.

> Then the mad rustics caught the dire alarms,
> And at the horrid signal flew to arms.
> Nor less in succour of the princely boy,
> Pour forth to battle all the troops of Troy.
> Pitt.

101. Satus Anchisâ cæstus pater extulit æquos, &c. Æn. 5. 424.

> Then the great prince with equal gauntlets bound
> Their vigorous hands, and brac'd their arms around. Pitt.

105. Amid the circle, &c.] Theocritus has Homer frequently in view in describing the combat of the cæstus. See Il. 23. 685.

> Ες μεσσον αγῶνα.

> Amid the circle now each champion stands.
> Pope.

113. But watchful Pollux, &c.]

> Επι δ' ωρνυτο θειος Επειος,
> Κοψε δε παπτηναντα παρηϊον. Il. b. 23. 689.

> At length Epeus dealt a weighty blow,
> Full on the cheek of his unwary foe. Pope.

Incens'd more ardent to the fight he came,
And forward bent to take the surer aim.
Through the Bebrycian band loud clamours run;
Nor less the Greeks encourag'd Leda's son.
Yet rising fears their generous breasts appal,
Lest on their friend the bulk of Amycus should fall:
Vain fears! for with both hands brave Pollux ply'd
His furious blows, and storm'd on every side;
The quick repeated strokes his rival stun,
And curb the force of Neptune's lawless son.
Giddy with blows the tottering hero stood,
And from his mouth discharg'd the purple blood.
Loud shouted the Greek warriors when they saw
Bebrycia's champion's batter'd cheeks and jaw.
His eyes, within their sockets deep impell'd,
Seem'd lessen'd, and his bruised visage swell'd.
Still the prince ply'd his mighty rival hard,
And feintful soon surpris'd him off his guard;
And as he stagger'd, full upon his brow
With all his force he drove the furious blow,
And mash'd his front; the giant with the wound
Fell flat, and stretch'd his bulk unwieldy on the ground.
But soon his vigour and his strength return'd,
He rose, and then again the battle burn'd:
With iron hands their hollow sides they pound,
And deal vindictive many a desperate wound.
Fierce on his foe Bebrycia's monarch prest,
And made rude onsets on his neck and breast;
But Jove's unconquer'd son far better sped,
Who aim'd his thunder at his rival's head.
Fast down their limbs the sweat began to flow,
And quickly lay the lofty champion low;
Yet Pollux firmer stood, with nobler grace,
And fresher was the colour of his face.
How Amycus, before Jove's offspring fell,
Sing, heaven-descended Muse; for you can tell:
Your mandates I implicitly obey,
And gladly follow where you lead the way.
Resolv'd by one bold stroke to win renown,
He seiz'd on Pollux' left hand with his own;
Then bent oblique to guard against a blow,
And sped his right with vengeance on the foe;
In hopes to strike his royal rival dead,
Who scap'd the blow, declining back his head;
Then Pollux aim'd his weighty stroke so well,
Full on the crest of Amycus it fell,
And gor'd his temples with an iron wound;
The black blood issuing flow'd and trickled to the ground.
Still with his left he maul'd his faltering foe,
Whose mash'd teeth crackled with each boisterous blow;
With strokes redoubled he deform'd his face;
Bruis'd cheeks and jaws proclaim'd his foul disgrace.
All on the ground he measur'd out his length,
Stunn'd with hard thwacks, and destitute of strength,
And, hands uprais'd, with death presaging mind,
At once the fight and victory declin'd.
Brave son of Jove, though you the conquest gain'd,
With no base deed the glorious day you stain'd:
The vanquish'd by his father Neptune swore,
That he would never, never injure strangers more.

115. Incens'd, &c.] Tum pudor incendit vires. Æn. 5. 455.

117. Loud clamours, &c.] It clamor, cœlo, &c. 451.

At once the Trojans and Sicilians rise,
And with divided clamours rend the skies. Pitt.

121. With both hands, &c.] Thus Virgil,

Creber utrâque manu pulsat versatque Dareta. 460.

126. His mouth discharg'd, &c.] Thus Homer,

Αἷμα παχυ πτυοντα.

His mouth and nostrils pour the clotted gore. Pope.

And Virgil,

——— Crassumque cruorem ore rejectantem. 469.

137. But soon his vigour, &c.] Acrior ad pugnam, &c. 454.

Improv'd in spirit, to the fight he came. Pitt.

139. Multa viri nequicquam inter se vulnera jactant,
Multa cavo lateri ingeminant, & pectore vastos
Dant sonitus. 433.

145. Fast down their limbs, &c.]

——— Ερρει δ' ἱδρως
Παντοθεν εκ μελεων. Il. b. 23. 688.

And painful sweat from all their members flows. Pope.

150. Sing heav'n-descended Muse, &c.] These addresses to the Muses are frequent in the best poets,

Pandite nunc Helicona, Deæ, &c. Æn. 7. 641.

Et meministis enim, Divæ, & memorare potestis.

156. And sped his right, &c.] Virgil follows very close;

Ostendit dextram insurgens Entellus, & alte
Extulit: ille ictum venientem a vertice velox
Prævidit, celerique elapsus corpore cessit. Æn. b. 5. 443.

162. The Greek verse consists of seventeen syllables,

Εκ δε χυθη μελαν αιμα θοας κροταφοιο χανοντος,

and was certainly intended to image the trickling of the blood, which I have endeavoured to preserve in an Alexandrine.

163. He maul'd, &c.]

——— Erratque aures & tempora circum
Crebra manus: duro crepitant sub vulnere malæ. 435

With swift-repeated wounds their hands fly round
Their heads and cheeks; their crackling jaws resound. Pitt.

169. And, hands uprais'd, &c.] It was customary in the ancient combats for the vanquished person to stretch out his hands to the conqueror, signifying that he declined the battle, acknow-

IDYLLIUM XXII.

PART THE SECOND.

ARGUMENT.

Castor and Pollux had carried off Phœbe and Talaira, the daughters of Leucippus, brother of deceased Aphareus, who were betrothed to Lynceus and Idas, the sons of Aphareus; the husbands pursued the ravishers, and claimed their wives; on this a battle ensued, in which Castor kills Lynceus, and Idas is slain by lightning. Ovid relates the event of this combat very differently; see the note.

POLLUX, thy name has dignify'd my song:
To Castor now the lofty lays belong;
Fam'd for bright armour on th' embattled plain,
And forming steeds obedient to the rein.
The bold twin-sons of Jove by stealth had led
Leucippus' daughters to their lawless bed.

ledged he was conquered, and submitted to the discretion of the victor: thus Turnus in Virgil:

——— Vicisti, et victum tendere palmas
Ausonii videre.

Thine is the conquest; lo! the Latian bands
Behold their general stretch his suppliant hands. Pitt.

I shall finish my observations on this Idyllium, with a translation of a Greek epigram of Lucillius, showing that the consequences of these kind of battles were sometimes very terrible, though the combatants might escape with their lives and limbs.

On a conqueror in the cæstus, Anthol. b. 2.

This victor, glorious in his olive-wreath,
Had once eyes, eye-brows, nose and ears, and teeth;
But turning cæstus-champion, to his cost,
These and still worse! his heritage he lost;
For by his brother su'd, disown'd, at last
Confronted with his picture he was cast.

5. Ovid's account of this battle begins at verse 700 of the 5th book of his Fasti;

Abstulerant raptas Phœben, &c.

The sons of Tyndarus, with conquest crown'd,
For boxing one, and one for steeds renown'd,
Had stoln, injurious, as their lawful prey,
Leucippus' daughters from their mates away;
Lynceus and Idas claim superior right,
Long since affianc'd, and prepare for fight.
Love urges both to combat on the plain,
These to retake, the others to retain.
The brother-twins might well escape by speed,
But held it base by flying to succeed.
All on an open plain the champions stood,
Aphidna nam'd, fit place for scenes of blood.
Castor by Lynceus' sword receiv'd a wound
Deep in his side, and lifeless prest the ground;
Avengeful Pollux, quick advancing near,
Thro' Lynceus' shoulders drove the forceful spear:
On him prest Idas, but Jove's flaming brand
Dash'd the pois'd javelin from his lifted hand.
F. F.

Lynceus and Idas, much for strength renown'd,
Long since by promise to the damsels bound,
Aphareus' sons, the foul dishonour view'd,
And fir'd with wrath the ravishers pursued.
But when they reach'd deceas'd Aphareus' tomb,
Encompass'd round with venerable gloom,
Each hero leap'd impetuous from his car,
All arm'd, and well appointed for the war.
Lynceus aloud beneath his helmet spoke:
"Why will ye frantic thus the fight provoke?
Of others wives why make unjust demands?
Why gleam the naked falchions in your hands?
To us Leucippus has betroth'd them both
Long since, and seal'd the contract with an oath:
'Tis base to make of others wives your prey,
And bear their riches, mules, and lowing herds away,
To threat the sire with force, or bribe with wealth,
And seize on others' properties by stealth.
Oft, though ungrac'd with eloquence and art,
Thus have I spoke the language of my heart:
'Princes, my friends, should not on any score
Solicit maids that are espous'd before:
Sparta for virgins, Elis for swift steeds
Are fam'd, large flocks and herds Arcadia breeds;
Messene, Argos numerous natives boast,
And fair looks Corinth on the sea-beat coast:
There nymphs unnumber'd bloom, a lovely race,
Acknowledg'd beauties both of mind and face:
There ye may gain the dames your fancies chuse;
No parents will the rich and brave refuse.
For you the love of noble deeds inspires;
Ye are the sons of honourable sires.
Let us our nuptials undisturb'd pursue,
And we'll unite to find fit brides for you.'
My words ne'er mov'd your unrelenting minds,
The waves receiv'd them from the driving winds.
Yet now, ev'n now your deeds let justice guide;
We both are cousins by the father's side.
But if mad rage impels you not to yield,
And arms must fix the fortune of the field;
Let Idas and brave Pollux both refrain
From the fell combat on the listed plain:
And only I and Castor prove our might,
By birth the youngest, in decisive fight.

16. Why will ye, &c.] Quo, quo scelesti, ruitis? aut cur dexteris
Aptantur enses conditi? Hor. Epod. 7.

Say, ye vile race, what frenzy draws
Your daring falchions in sedition's cause?
Duncombe.

33. There nymphs unnumber'd bloom, &c.] Thus Æneas says,

Sunt aliæ innuptæ Latio & Laurentibus agris,
Nec genus indecores. Æn. b. 12. 24.

38. Ye are the sons, &c.]
Turnus avis atavisq; potens. Æn. 7. 56.

47. Let Idas, &c.] Teucrûm arma quiescant
Et Rutulûm; nostro dirimatur sanguine bellum. Æn. 12. 78.

The celebrated ballad called Chevy Chace has the same thought;

Let thou and I the battle try,
And set our men aside, &c.

Why should we give our parents cause to grieve,
And their fond arms of all their sons bereave?
Let some survive our drooping friends to cheer,
And mate the virgins whom they hold so dear.
The wise with prudence their dissensions state,
And lesser ills conclude the great debate."
 Thus he, nor thus in vain; for on the ground
Pollux and Idas plac'd their arms around.
Lynceus first march'd undaunted to the field,
And shook his spear beneath his ample shield.
Castor to war his brandish'd lance addrest;
And on each helmet wav'd the nodding crest.
First with their spears began the dreadful strife,
Each chief explor'd the avenues of life.
But thus unhurt the battle they maintain'd,
Broke in their shields the spears' sharp points remain'd:
Then from their sheaths their shining swords they drew,
And fierce to fight the raging heroes flew:
On Lynceus' buckler Castor boldly prest,
And his bright helmet with the triple crest;
Lynceus, sharp-sighted, kept his foe at bay,
And struck his helmet's purple plume away;
Who quick retreating all his art display'd,
And lopt the hand that held the glittering blade;
Down dropt the sword; to his sire's tomb he flew,
Where Idas sat the fatal fight to view;
Close follow'd Castor, all his force apply'd,
And furious drove the falchion in his side,
Out gush'd his bowels through the gaping wound,
And vanquish'd Lynceus prest the gory ground;
In dim, dark mists the shades of death arise,
And in eternal slumber seal his eyes.
Nor was brave Idas by his mother led,
Laocöossa, to the nuptial bed:
For he, vindictive of fall'n Lynceus' doom,
Tore up a column from Aphareus' tomb.
Aiming at Castor, dreadfully he stood,
The bold avenger of his brother's blood;
Jove interpos'd, and with the forked brand
Quick struck the polish'd marble from his hand;
He wreath'd convulsive, scorch'd on every side,
And in a peal of rattling thunder dy'd.
 Thus shall the brothers be with conquest crown'd,
Brave of themselves, and sprung from chiefs renown'd.
Hail, Leda's valiant sons! my Muse inspire,
And still preserve the honour of my lyre.
Ye, and fair Helen, to all bards are dear,
With joy the names of those bold chiefs they hear,
Who in the cause of Menelaus drew
Their conquering swords, proud Ilium to subdue.
Your praise, O kings, the Chian Muse recites,
Troy's famous city, and the Phrygian fights,

51. Why should we give, &c.] Thus Nisus addresses Euryalus in the same sense,

> Neu matri miseræ tanti sim causa doloris.
> Æn. 9. 216.

> Why should I cause thy mother's soul to know
> Such heart-felt pangs; unutterable woe!
> Pitt.

60. And shook his spear, &c.] Thus Mezentius in Virgil,

> At vero ingentem quatiens Mezentius hastam
> Ingreditur campo. Æn. 10. 762.

63. First with their spears, &c.] In almost all heroic duels, the combatants first threw their spears, and then made use of their swords: Thus Hector and Achilles, Iliad b. 20. 22. Menelaus and Paris, b. 3. and the rest of the heroes attack one another. Potter.

64. Each chief explor'd, &c.]

> Partes rimatur apertas,
> Quà vulnus lethale ferat.
> Virg. Æn. b. 11. 748.

67. Then from their sheaths, &c.]

> Vaginâque cavâ fulgentem diripit ensem.
> Æn. b. 10.

> And from the sheath the shining falchion drew.
> Pitt.

71. Lynceus, sharp-sighted] Horace says,

> Non possis oculo quantum contendere Lynceus. B. 1. Ep. 1.

Hence the proverb of Lyncean eyes: Pindar tells us, Lynceus could discover Castor and Pollux hid in the trunk of a tree from the top of mount Taygetus: nay, he had so piercing a sight, that if we believe the poets, he could see what was doing in Heaven and Hell: the ground of the fable was, that he understood the secret powers of nature. Though it may admit of a doubt, whether this is the sharp-sighted Lynceus that attended the Argonautic expedition; from the poet's words, Ακριβης ομμασι Λυγκευς, I think it manifest that he was.

72. And struck, &c.]

> Summasq; excussit vertice cristas.
> Æn. 12. 492.

> But the swift javelin strikes his plume away.
> Pitt.

74. And lopt the hand]

> Strymonio dextram fulgenti diripit ense.
> Æn. b. 10. 414.

> The falchion lops his hand.

81. In dim, dark mists, &c.]

> Olli dura quies oculos, et ferreus urget
> Somnus; in æternum clauduntur lumina noctem. Æn. 10. 745.

94. Brave of themselves, &c.] Fortes creantur fortibus. Hor. b. 4. O. 4.

99. Who in the cause, &c.]

> Quicunque Iliacos ferro violavimus agros.
> Æn. 11. 255.

101. Your praise, O kings, &c.] I do not remember that Homer any where mentions Castor and Pollux, except in the third book of the Iliad, where the commemoration of them by their sister Helen is finely introduced, and in the true spirit of poetry: I shall beg leave to transcribe the whole passage in the admirable translation of Mr. Pope, because I think it as beautiful and pathetic as almost any part of the whole work;

> " Yet two are wanting of the numerous train,
> Whom long my eyes have sought, but sought in vain;

He sings the Grecian fleet renown'd afar,
And great Achilles, bulwark of the war.
I bring the tribute of a feebler lyre,
Sweet warbling what the rapturous Nine inspire,
The best I may; verse to the gods belongs;
The gods delight in honorary songs.

IDYLLIUM XXIII*.

THE DESPAIRING LOVER.

ARGUMENT.

An unhappy lover, despairing to gain the affections of his mistress, by whom he is despised, makes

Castor and Pollux, first in martial force,
One bold on foot, and one renown'd for horse;
My brothers these; the same our native shore,
One house contain'd us, and one mother bore.
Perhaps the chiefs, from warlike toils at ease,
For distant Troy refus'd to sail the seas:
Perhaps their swords some nobler quarrel draws,
Asham'd to combat in their sister's cause"
So spoke the fair, nor knew her brothers' doom,
Wrapt in the cold embraces of the tomb;
Adorn'd with honours in their native shore,
Silent they slept, and heard of wars no more.

101. The Chian Muse] As Theocritus, both here and in the 7th Idyllium, styles Homer the Chian bard Χῖον Αοιδον, we have reason to conjecture, that Chios has the honour of being the place of his nativity: Simonides in his Epigram on Human Life, calls him the man of Chios; for quoting a verse of Homer he says,

Εν δε το καλλιςον Χιος εειπεν ανηρ.

The Chians pleaded these ancient authorities for Homer's being born among them: they mention a race they had, called the Homeridæ, whom they accounted his posterity; they cast medals of him; they show to this day an Homerium, or temple of Homer, near Bolissus; and close their arguments with a quotation from the hymn to Apollo, (which is acknowledged for Homer's by Thucydides) where he calls himself, "The blind man that inhabits Chios." One cannot avoid being surprised at the prodigious veneration for his character, which could engage mankind with such eagerness in a point so little essential; that kings should send to oracles for the inquiry of his birth-place; that cities should be in strife about it; that whole lives of learned men should be employed upon it; that some should write treatises, others call up spirits about it; that thus, in short, Heaven, Earth and Hell, should be sought to, for the decision of a question which terminates in curiosity only. Thus far Mr. Pope in his essay on Homer: Yet though this point is not essential, and only matter of curiosity, we may observe, that these inquiries, disputes, and contentions, plead strongly in favour of the Muses, and set the character of a poet in the most eminent and exalted station.

* The argument of this Idyllium is similar to the argument of Virgil's second eclogue, though this is more tragical; I have taken the liberty to make a general transformation, which renders it a thousand times more natural, decent, and gallant.

away with himself: the cruel fair is soon after killed by the image of Cupid that fell upon her as she was bathing.

An amorous shepherd lov'd a cruel fair;
The haughty beauty plung'd him in despair:
She loath'd the swain, nor aught her breast could move,
She scorn'd the lover, and the god of love;
Nor knew the puissance of his bow and darts,
To tame the stubbornness of human hearts.
With cold disdain she griev'd the shepherd sore,
The more he sigh'd, she scorn'd him still the more.
No solace she afforded, no soft look,
Nor e'er the words of sweet compassion spoke:
Her eye, her cheek ne'er glow'd, her flame to prove,
No kiss she gave the lenient balm of love:
But as a lion, on the desert plain,
With savage pleasure views the hunter train;
Thus in her scorn severe delight she took;
Her words, her eyes were fierce, and death was in her look.
She look'd her soul; her face was pal'd with ire;
Yet she was fair; her frowns but rais'd desire.
At length, he could no more, but sought relief
From tears, the dumb petitioners of grief;
Before her gate he wept, with haggard look,
And, kissing the bare threshold, thus he spoke:
"Ah, savage fair, whom no entreaties move!
Hard heart of stone, unworthy of my love!
Accept this cord, 'tis now in vain to live,
This friendly gift, the last that I shall give;
I go where doom'd; my love, my life are o'er,
No more I grieve, and you are teas'd no more;
I go the last kind remedy to prove,
And drink below oblivion to my love.

1. An amorous, &c.] Formosum pastor Corydon ardebat Alexim. Virg. Ec. 2.

Young Corydon with hopeless love ador'd
The fair Alexis, favourite of his lord.
Warton.

7. With cold disdain, &c.] Ovid says of Anaxareté,

Spernit et irridet; factisque immitibus addit
Verba superba ferox; et spe quoque fraudat amantem. Met. b. 14. 714.

16. Death was in her look] The Greek is, Ειχεν αναγκαν, or as Heinsius more plausibly reads, Ειδεν αναγκαν, she looked necessity, that is, death or fate; thus Horace has,

Semotique priûs tarda necessitas
Lethi corripuit gradum. B. 1. O. 3.

And,

Te semper anteit sæva necessitas.
B. 1. O. 35.

Which elegant use of the word necessitas, he has taken from the Grecians; Pindar has, εχθρα αναγκα; and Euripides, δεινη αναγκη, which is exactly the dira necessitas of Horace, b. 3. O. 24.

21. Before her gate, &c.] Thus Ovid speaking of Iphis,

Non tulit impatiens longi tormenta doloris
Iphis, et ante fores hæc verba novissima dixit.
Met. b. 14.

30. And drink oblivion] Virgil says of souls that endure transmigration,

Lethæi ad fluminis undam
Securos latices, et longa oblivia potant.
Æn. b. 6.

But ah! what draughts my fierce desires can
Or quench the raging fury of my flame? [tame,
Adieu, ye doors! eternally adieu!
I see the future, and I know it true.
Fragrant the rose, but soon it fades away;
The violet sweet, but quickly will decay;
The lily fair a transient beauty wears;
And the white snow soon weeps away in tears:
Such is the bloom of beauty, cropt by time,
Full soon it fades, and withers in its prime.
The days will come when your hard heart shall burn
In scorching flames, yet meet no kind return.
Yet grant this boon, the last that I implore:
When you shall see, suspended at your door,
This wretched corse, pass not unheeding by,
But let the tear of sorrow dim your eye:
Then loose the fatal cord, and from your breast
Lend the light robe, and skreen me with your vest:
Imprint one kiss when my sad soul is fled;
Ah, grudge not thus to gratify the dead!
Fear not—your kisses cannot life restore:
Though you relent, yet I shall wake no more.
And last, a decent monument prepare,
And bury with my love my body there;
And thrice repeat, 'Here rests my friend his head;'
Or rather add, 'My dearest lover's dead.'
With this inscription be the stone supplied;
'By Cupid's dart this hapless shepherd dy'd:
Ah! passenger, a little moment spare
To stop, and say, He lov'd a cruel fair.'"
This said, he tries against the wall to shove
A mighty stone, and to a beam above

To yon dark streams the gliding ghosts repair'
And quaff deep draughts of long oblivion there'
Pitt.

34. I see the future] Haud ignara futuri.
Virg. Æn. 4. 50.

36. The violet sweet, &c.] Thus Ovid in his Art of Love;

Nec violæ semper nec hiantia lilia florent,
Et riget amissâ spina relicta rosâ.
B. 2. 115.

39. Such is the bloom, &c.] Thus Horace,
Fugit retrò
Levis juventas et decor. B. 2. O. 11.

46. Let the tear of sorrow, &c.]
Debitâ sparges lacrymâ favillam
Vatis amici. Hor. b. 2. O. 6.

53. And last a decent monument, &c.] Thus Virgil,

Et tumulum facite, et tumulo superaddite carmen. Ec. 5.

With grateful hands his monument erect,
And be the stone with this inscription deck'd.
Warton.

55. And thrice repeat] Of the inclamation at the tomb, Æneas thus tells Deiphobus, Magnâ Manes ter voce vocavi. Æn. 6. 506.

61. This said, &c.] The fate of Iphis in Ovid is very similar,

Dixit, et ad postes, &c. Met. b. 14.
Then o'er the posts, once hung with wreaths, he throws
The ready cord, and fits the fatal noose;
For death prepares, and bounding from above,
At once the wretch concludes his life and love.
Garth.

Suspends the cord, impatient of delay,
Fits the dire noose, and spurns the stone away;
Quivering in air he hung, till welcome death
Securely clos'd the avenues of breath.
The fair one, when the pendent swain she saw,
Nor pity felt, nor reverential awe;
But as she pass'd, for not a tear she shed
Her garments were polluted by the dead,
Then to the circus, where the wrestlers fought,
Or the more pleasing bath of love she sought:
High on a marble pedestal above,
Frown'd the dread image of the god of love,
Aiming in wrath the meditated blow,
Then fell revengeful on the nymph below;
With the pure fountain mix'd her purple blood—
These words were heard emerging from the flood:
"Lovers, farewell, nor your admirers slight;
Resign'd I die, for Heav'n pronounces right."

IDYLLIUM XXIV.

THE YOUNG HERCULES.

ARGUMENT.

This Idyllium is entirely narrative: it first of all gives an account how Hercules, when only ten months old, slew two monstrous serpents which Juno had sent to devour him; then it relates the prophecy of Tiresias, and afterwards describes the education of Hercules, and enumerates his several preceptors. The conclusion of this poem is lost.

WASH'D with pure water, and with milk well fed,
To pleasing rest her sons Alcmena led,
Alcides, ten months old, yet arm'd with might,
And twin Iphiclus, younger by a night:
On a broad shield of fine brass metal made,
The careful queen her royal offspring laid;
(The shield from Pterilus Amphitryon won
In fight, a noble cradle for his son!)

79. Lovers, farewel, &c.] Moschus, Idyl. 6. has nearly the same thought. Ταυτα λεγω πασιν, κ. τ. λ.

Ye scornful nymphs and swains, I tell
This truth to you; pray mark it well:
"If to your lovers kind you prove,
You'll gain the hearts of those you love."
F. F.

The fate of this scornful beauty is similar to that of a youth who was killed by the statue of his step-mother falling upon him. See Callimachus, Epigram 11. thus translated by Mr. Duncombe.

A youth, who thought his father's wife
Had lost her malice with her life,
Officious with a chaplet grac'd
The statue on her tomb-stone plac'd;
When, falling sudden on his head,
With the dire blow it struck him dead:
Be warn'd from hence, each foster-son,
Your step-dame's sepulchre to shun.

7. The shield from Pterilus, &c.] Virgil says nearly the same thing of the coat of mail which was taken from Demoleus,

Loricam, quam Demoleo detraxerat ipse
Victor apud rapidum Simoenta sub Ilio alto.
Æn. b. 5. 260.

Fondly the babes she view'd, and on each head
She plac'd her tender hands, and thus she said;
" Sleep, gentle babes, and sweetly take your rest,
Sleep, dearest twins, with softest slumbers blest;
Securely pass the tedious night away,
And rise refresh'd with the fair-rising day."
She spoke, and gently rock'd the mighty shield;
Obsequious slumbers soon their eye-lids seal'd.
But when at midnight sunk the bright-ey'd Bear,
And broad Orion's shoulder 'gan appear;
Stern Juno, urg'd by unrelenting hate,
Sent two fell serpents to Amphitryon's gate,
Charg'd with severe commission to destroy
The young Alcides, Jove-begotten boy:
Horrid and huge, with many an azure fold,
Fierce through the portal's opening valves they roll'd;
Then on their bellies prone, high swoln with gore,
They glided smooth along the marble floor:
Their fiery eye-balls darted sanguine flame,
And from their jaws destructive poison came.
Alcmena's sons, when near the serpents prest
Darting their forked tongues, awoke from rest;
All o'er the chamber shone a sudden light,
For all is clear to Jove's discerning sight.
When on the shield his foes Iphiclus saw,
And their dire fangs that arm'd each horrid jaw,
Aghast he rais'd his voice with bitter cry,
Threw off the covering, and prepar'd to fly:
But Hercules stretch'd out his arms to clasp
The scaly monsters in his iron grasp;
Fast in each hand the venom'd jaws he prest
Of the curst serpents, which ev'n gods detest.
Their circling spires, in many a dreadful fold,
Around the slow-begotten babe they roll'd,
The babe unwean'd, yet ignorant of fear,
Who never utter'd cry, nor shed a tear.
At length their curls they loos'd, for rack'd with pain
They strove to 'scape the deathful gripe in vain.
Alcmena first o'er-heard the mournful cries,
And to her husband thus: " Amphitryon, rise;
Distressful fears my boding soul dismay;
This instant rise, nor for thy sandals stay:
Hark, how for help the young Iphiclus calls!
A sudden splendour, lo! illumes the walls!
Though yet the shades of night obscure the skies;
Some dire disaster threats; Amphitryon, rise."
She spoke; the prince obedient to her word,
Rose from the bed, and seiz'd his rich-wrought sword,
Which, on a glittering nail above his head,
Hung by the baldric to the cedar bed.
Then from the radiant sheath, of lotos made,
With ready hand he drew the shining blade;
Instant the light withdrew, and sudden gloom
Involv'd again the wide-extended room:
Amphitryon call'd his train that slumbering lay,
And slept secure the careless hours away.
" Rise, rise, my servants, from your couches straight,
Bring lights this instant, and unbar the gate."
He spoke; the train obedient to command,
Appear'd with each a flambeau in his hand;
Rapt with amaze, young Hercules they saw
Grasp two fell serpents close beneath the jaw:
The mighty infant show'd them to his sire,
And smil'd to see the wreathing snakes expire;
He leap'd for joy that thus his foes he slew,
And at his father's feet the scaly monsters threw.
With tender care Alcmena fondly prest,
Half-dead with fear, Iphiclus to her breast,

By observing the use this shield is put to, we have an agreeable picture presented to the mind: it is an emblem of the peace and tranquillity which always succeed the tumults of war; and likewise a prognostic of the future greatness of this mighty champion in embryo.

19. Stern Juno, &c.] Pindar in his first Nemean Ode tells this same story, which, as it may be a satisfaction to the curious to see how different writers manage the same subject, I shall take the liberty to give in Mr West's translation.

Then glowing with immortal rage,
The gold-enthroned empress of the gods,
Her eager thirst of vengeance to asswage,
Straight to her hated rival's curs'd abodes
Bad her vindictive serpents haste.
They through the opening valves with speed
On to the chamber's deep recesses past,
To perpetrate their murderous deed:
And now, in knotty mazes to enfold
Their destin'd prey, on curling spires they roll'd,
His dauntless brow when young Alcides rear'd,
And for their first attempt his infant arms prepar'd.
Fast by their azure necks he held,
And grip'd in either hand his scaly foes;
Till from their horrid carcasses expell'd,
At length the poisonous soul unwilling flows.

27. Their fiery eye-balls, &c.] The Greek is, απ' οφθαλμον δε κακον πυρ Ερχομενοις λαμπεσκε; a pernicious flame shot from their eyes as they approached: Pierson (see his Verisimilia) reads with much more elegance and propriety Δερκομενοις, looking very keenly, as the eyes of serpents are always represented: Hesiod, speaking of dragons, uses the same word twice, εκ κεφαλων πυρ καιετο δερκομενοιο. Theog. ver. 828, and in the shield of Hercules, ver. 145. λαμπομενοισι δεδορκως. He brings likewise the authorities of Homer, Æschylus, and Oppian, to support this reading. Virgil has,

Ardentesq; oculi suffecti sanguine et igni,
Sibila lambebant linguis vibrantibus ora.
Æn. b. 2. 210.

41. Their circling spires, &c.] Thus Virgil, speaking of the serpents that devoured Laocoon's sons,

—— Parva duorum Corpora natorum, &c.
Æn. b. 2. 213.

And first in curling fiery volumes bound
His two young sons, and wrapt them round and round.
Pitt.

64. And slept secure, &c.] The Greek is, υπνον βαρυν εκφυσωντας, similar to what Virgil says of Rhamnes, Æn. 9. 326.

——— In slumbers deep he lay,
And, labouring, slept the full debauch away.
Pitt.

75. With tender care, &c.] Thus Virgil,

Et trepidæ matres pressere ad pectora natos
Æn. b. 7. 518

While o'er his mighty son Amphitryon spread
The lamb's soft fleece, and sought again his bed.
When thrice the cock pronounc'd the morning near,
Alcmena call'd the truth-proclaiming seer,
Divine Tiresias; and to him she told
This strange event, and urg'd him to unfold
Whate'er the adverse deities ordain;
"Fear not," she cry'd, "but Fate's whole will explain;
For well thou know'st, O! venerable seer,
Those ills which Fate determines, man must bear."
She spoke; the holy augur thus reply'd;
"Hail, mighty queen, to Perseus near ally'd;
Parent of godlike chiefs: by these dear eyes,
Which never more shall view the morning rise,
Full many Grecian maids, for charms renown'd,
While merrily they twirl the spindle round,
Till day's decline thy praises shall proclaim,
And Grecian matrons celebrate thy fame.
So great, so noble, will thy offspring prove,
The most gigantic of the gods above.
Whose arm, endow'd with more than mortal sway,
Shall many men, and many monsters slay:
Twelve labours past, he shall to Heav'n aspire,
His mortal part first purified by fire,
And son-in-law be nam'd of that dread power
Who sent these deadly serpents to devour
The slumbering child: then wolves shall rove the lawns,
And strike no terrour in the pasturing fawns.
But, O great queen! be this thy instant care,
On the broad hearth dry faggots to prepare,
Aspalathus, or prickly brambles bind,
Or the tall thorn that trembles in the wind,
And at dark midnight burn (what time they came
To slay thy son) the serpents in the flame.
Next morn, collected by thy faithful maid,
Be all the ashes to the flood convey'd,
And blown on rough rocks by the favouring wind,
Thence let her fly, but cast no look behind.
Next with pure sulphur purge the house, and bring
The purest water from the freshest spring,
This, mix'd with salt, and with green olive crown'd,
Will cleanse the late contaminated ground.
Last let a boar on Jove's high altar bleed,
That ye in all achievements may succeed."
Thus spoke Tiresias, bending low with age,
And to his ivory car retir'd the reverend sage.
Alcides grew beneath his mother's care,
Like some young plant, luxuriant, fresh, and fair,

84. Fear not, &c.] Thus Achilles says to Calchas, Il. b. 1.

> From thy inmost soul
> Speak what thou know'st, and speak without control. Pope.

86. Those ills, &c.] Homer puts a sentiment similar to this in the mouth of Hector, b. 6. which is finely translated by Mr. Pope;

> Fix'd is the term to all the race of Earth,
> And such the hard condition of our birth:
> No force can then resist, no flight can save,
> All sink alike, the fearful and the brave.

96. The most gigantic, &c.] The words of Theocritus are *απο ϛερνων πλατυς ηρως*, the broad breasted hero; I am in doubt how it should be rendered; Creech has translated it, The noblest burthen of the bending sky. In Homer's Odyssey, b. 11. Hercules is thus represented among the shades below,

> Now I the strength of Hercules behold,
> A towering spectre of gigantic mould;
> A shadowy form! for high in Heaven's abodes
> Himself resides a god among the gods. Pope.

On which Mr. Pope observes, "The ancients imagined, that immediately after death, there was a partition of the human composition into three parts, the body, image, and mind: the body is buried in the earth; the image, or *ειδωλον*, descends into the regions of the departed; the mind, or *φρην*, the divine part is received into Heaven; thus the body of Hercules was consumed in the flames, his image is in Hell, and his soul in Heaven."

100. His mortal part first purified by fire] The Greek is, *θνητα δε παντα πυρα Τραχινιος εξει*, The Trachinian pyre will consume his mortal part; Trachin was a city of Thessaly built by Hercules, and the place to which he sent to Dejanira for the shirt which proved fatal to him, and was the occasion of throwing himself into the fire that consumed him; hence therefore, probably, Theocritus calls it the Trachinian pyre.

103. Then wolves, &c.] Virgil has,

> Nec lupus insidias pecori, &c.

Both authors seem to have borrowed from Isaiah, chap. ii, ver. 6. "The wolf shall dwell with the lamb, and the leopard shall lie down with the kid."

105. But, O great queen, &c.] Archbishop Potter observes, "sometimes the ominous thing was burnt with ligna infelicia, that is, such sort of wood as was in tutelâ inferûm deorum avertentiumque, sacred to the gods of Hell, and those which averted evil omens, being chiefly thorns, and such other trees, as were fit for no other use than to be burned. Sometimes the prodigy, when burnt, was cast into the water, and particularly into the sea, as Theocritus has described." Chap. 17.

107. A spalathus] A plant called the rose of Jerusalem, or our lady's thorn.

Johnson's Dict.

—— Prickly brambles] The Greek is, *παλιυρος*, paliurus; which Martyn says, is most probably the plant which is cultivated in our gardens under the name of Christ's thorn, and is supposed to be the thorn of which the crown was made, that was put upon our Saviour's head. Notes on Virgil, Ecl. 5.

108. Or the tall thorn, &c.] The Greek is, *η ανεμῳ δεδονημενον αυον αχερδον*, or the dry acherdus which is agitated by the wind; it is uncertain what plant will answer to the acherdus of the ancients; Homer in the Odyssey, b. 14. ver. 10. has fenced the sylvan lodge of Eumæus with acherdus, *Και εθριγκωσεν αχερδῳ*,

> The wall was stone, from neighb'ring quarries born,
> Encircled with a fence of native thorn.
> Pope.

111. Next morn, &c.] The most powerful of all incantations was to throw the ashes of the sacrifice backward into the water; thus Virgil,

> Fer cineres, Amarylli, foras; rivoq; fluenti
> Transque caput jace; ne respexeris. Ecl. 8.

124. Like some young plant, &c.] Theocritus has

That screen'd from storms defies the baleful blast,
And for Amphitryon's valiant son he past.
Linus, who claim'd Apollo for his sire,
With love of letters did his youth inspire,
And strove his great ideas to enlarge,
A friendly tutor, faithful to his charge.
From Eurytus his skill in shooting came,
To send the shaft unerring of its aim.
Eumolpus tun'd his manly voice to sing,
And call sweet music from the speaking string.
In listed fields to wrestle with his foe,
With iron arm to deal the deathful blow,
And each achievement where fair fame is sought,
Harpalycus, the son of Hermes, taught,
Whose look so grim and terrible in fight,
No man could bear the formidable sight.
But fond Amphitryon with a father's care,
To drive the chariot taught his godlike heir,
At the sharp turn with rapid wheels to roll,
Nor break the grazing axle on the goal;
On Argive plains, for generous steeds renown'd,
Oft was the chief with race-won honours crown'd;
And still unbroke his ancient chariot lay,
Though cankering time had eat the reins away.
To lanch the spear, to rush upon the foe,
Beneath the shield to shun the falchion's blow,
To marshal hosts, opposing force to force,
To lay close ambush, and lead on the horse,
These Castor taught him, of equestrian fame,
What time to Argos exil'd Tydeus came,
Where from Adrastus he high favour gain'd,
And o'er a kingdom, rich in vineyards, reign'd.
No chief like Castor, till consuming time
Unnerv'd his youth, and cropp'd the golden prime.
  Thus Hercules, his mother's joy and pride,
Was train'd up like a warrior: by the side
Of his great father's his rough couch was spread,
A lion's spoils compos'd his grateful bed.
Roast-meat he lov'd at supper to partake,
The bread he fancied was the Doric cake,
Enough to satisfy the labouring hind;
But still at noon full sparingly he din'd.
His dress, contriv'd for use, was neat and plain,
His skirts were scanty, for he wore no train.

The conclusion of this Idyllium is wanting in the original.

IDYLLIUM XXV*.

HERCULES THE LION-SLAYER.

ARGUMENT.

Hercules having occasion to wait upon Augéas king of Elis, meets with an old herdsman, by whom he is introduced to the king, who, with his

---

borrowed this from Homer, Il. b. 18. Thetis, speaking of her son, says,

> Τον μεν εγω θρεψασα, φυτον ως γουνω αλωης.
>
> Like some fair plant, beneath my careful hand,
> He grew, he flourish'd, and he grac'd the land.
> Pope.

140. No man could bear, &c.] Virgil says of Dares,

> —— Nec quisquam ex agmine tanto
> Audet adire virum, manibusq; inducere cæstus.
> Æn. b. 5.

144. Nor break, &c.] In the chariot-race, the greatest care was to be taken to avoid running against the goal; Nestor in the 23d book of the Iliad, very particularly cautions his son in regard to this point; and Horace says,

> —— Metaque fervidis Evitata rotis. Od. 1.

154. What time to Argos, &c.] The Greek is,

> Καςωρ ιππαλιδας εδαεν, φυγας Αργεος ελθων,
> Οπποκα κλαρον απαντα ϗ οινοπεδον μεγα Τυδευς
> Ναιε, παρ Αδραςοιο λαβων ιππηλατον Αργος.

These accomplishments Castor, skilled in horsemanship, taught him, when he came an exile from Argos, at the time that Tydeus ruled over the whole kingdom famed for vineyards, having received Argos from Adrastus. There is great inconsistency in this passage, which nobody, that I know of, has observed or tried to remedy: we have no account in history, that Castor came a fugitive to Argos, but that Tydeus did, we have indisputable authority. See Homer's Il. b. 14. ver. 119. Diomed says of his father, πατηρ δ' ενθος Αργει νασθη, κ. τ. λ.

> ———— My sire: from Calydon expell'd
> He past to Argos, and in exile dwell'd;
> The monarch's daughter there (so Jove ordain'd)
> He won and flourish'd where Adrastus reign'd:
> There rich in fortune's gifts his acres till'd,
> Beheld his vines their liquid harvest yield,
> And numerous flocks that whiten'd all the field.
> Pope.

On which Eustathius observes; "This is a very artful colour: Diomed calls the flight of his father, for killing one of his brothers, travelling and dwelling at Argos, without mentioning the cause or occasion of his retreat." Might I venture to offer an emendation, I would read, φυγας Αργει ελθων, and then the construction might be, Castor taught him these accomplishments, at the time that Tydeus reigned over the kingdom of Argos, whither he had fled in exile, having received the sovereignty from Adrastus. Thus the passage becomes correspondent with Homer, with good sense and history; for Tydeus fled from Calydonia to Argos for manslaughter, where he married Deipyle, the daughter of Adrastus, and, it should seem by this passage, afterwards succeeded him in the kingdom.

164. Doric cake] A coarse bread like those cakes which the Athenians called πελανοι.

* Though this noble Idyllium is by far the longest of any that Theocritus has left us, containing, exclusive of the beginning which is lost, no less than 281 verses, yet the commentators, Scaliger, Casaubon, and D. Heinsius, have not left us one single emendation or note upon it; and therefore I shall trouble the reader with but few observations: yet these grey old critics have been lavish of their remarks upon the 27th Idyllium, infinitely the most obscene of all the pieces that have been attributed to Theocritus. One remark is very obvious, that the first part of this Idyllium, as far as ver. 170 in the translation, is entirely pastoral and bucolic, containing beautiful descriptions of mea-

son Phyleus, had come into the country to take a view of his numerous herds: afterwards Hercules and Phyleus walk together to the city; in the way the prince admiring the monstrous lion's skin which Hercules wore, takes occasion to inquire where he had it; this introduces an account how Hercules slew the Nemean lion.

The beginning is wanting.

THE good old herdsman laid his work aside,
And thus complacent to the chief reply'd:
"Whate'er you ask, O stranger, I'll impart,
Whate'er you wish, and with a cheerful heart:
For much I venerate the son of May,
Who stands rever'd in every public way:
Those most he hates, of all the gods on high,
Who the lone traveller's request deny.
"The numerous flocks your eyes behold around,
With which the vales are stor'd, the hills are crown'd,
Augéas owns; o'er various walks they spread,
In different meads, in different pastures fed;
Some on the banks of Elisuntus stray,
Some where divine Alphëus winds his way,
Some in Buprasium, where rich wines abound,
And some in this well-cultivated ground.
And though exceeding many flocks are told,
Each separate flock enjoys a separate fold.
Here, though of oxen numerous herds are seen,
Yet springs the herbage ever fresh and green
In the moist marsh of Menius: every mead,
And vale irriguous, where the cattle feed,
Produce sweet herbs, embalm'd in dewy tears,
Whose fragrant virtue fattens well the steers.
Behold that stall beyond the winding flood,
Which to the right appears by yonder wood
Where the wild olive, and perennial plane
Grow, spread, and flourish, great Apollo's fane,
To which the hinds, to which the shepherds bow,
And deem him greatest deity below!
Next are the stalls of swains, whose labours bring
Abundant riches to the wealthy king;
Four times each year the fertile soil they plow,
And gather thrice the harvests which they sow;
The lab'ring hinds, whose hands the vineyards dress,
Whose feet the grapes in purple autumn press,
Know well the vast domain Augéas owns,
Rich fields whose lap the golden ear imbrowns,
Or shaded gardens, far as yonder hills,
Whose brows are water'd by resplendent rills;
This spacious tract we tend with daily care,
As fits those swains who rural labours share.
"But say, (and all my service you shall claim)
Say for what cause you here a stranger came:
Would you the king or his attendants see?
I can conduct you; only trust to me.
For such your form, and such your manly grace,
You seem deriv'd from no ignoble race:
Sure thus the gods, that boast celestial birth,
Appear majestic to the sons of Earth.
He spoke, and thus Jove's valiant son reply'd;
"My wandering steps let some kind shepherd guide
To king Augéas, whom these realms obey;
To see Augéas am I come this way.
But if fair justice the good monarch draws
To Elis, to administer the laws;

dows, pastures, hills, vales, rivers, shepherds, herdsmen, and their stalls and dogs, flocks and herds innumerable: the second part is an account of a famous exploit performed by Hercules, and therefore the whole must surely belong to the Arcadian poetry.

6. Who stands rever'd, &c.] The ancients erected statues to Mercury in the public roads, as guides to travellers, which they called Hermæ; they were of marble and four square, nothing but the head was finished: thus Juvenal, Sat. 8. 53.

———Truncoque simillimus Hermæ.
Nullo quippe alio vincis discrimine, quam quod
Illi marmoreum caput est, tua vivit imago.

13. Elisuntus] A river near Elis.

14. Alphëus] A famous river of Arcadia near Elis, which the ancients feigned to have sunk under ground, and so passed through the sea, without mixing its streams with the salt waters, till arriving at Sicily, it mingled its current with the fountain Arethusa near Syracuse. Thus Virgil, Æn. 3. 694, Alpheum fama est, &c.

Hither, 'tis said, Alphëus from his source
In Elis' realms, directs his watery course:
Beneath the main he takes his sacred way,
And mounts with Arethusa up to day. Pitt.

15. Buprasium] A city and country of Achaia near Elis, from Buprasius its founder.

Those where fair Elis and Buprasium join.
Pope's Il. b. 2.

20. Yet springs, &c.]

Non liquidi gregibus fontes, non gramina desunt. Geor. 2. 200.

There for thy flocks fresh fountains never fail,
Undying verdure clothes the grassy vale.
Warton.

27. Wild olive] This tree was sacred to Apollo, and substituted as a temple where presents were offered to him: Virgil speaking of an olive tree, Æn. 12. 766, says,

Servati ex undis ibi figere dona solebant
Laurenti divo.

The shipwreck'd sailors, on the hallow'd wood,
Hung their devoted vests in honour of the god.
Pitt.

33. Four times, &c.] Virgil says that the soil for vines, Quotannis
Terque quaterque solum scindendum.
Georg. b. 2.

Thrice and four times the soil, each rolling year,
The ponderous ploughs, and heavy drags must bear. Warton.

49. Sure thus the gods, &c.]

Credo equidem, nec vana fides, genus esse deorum. Virgil.

54. To see Augéas, &c.] Evandrum petimus.
Æn. b 8. 55.

55. But if fair justice, &c.] Thus Dido in Virgil,

Jura dabat legesq; viris, operumque laborem
Partibus æquabat justis. Æn. b. 1. 511.

Conduct me to some honourable swain,
Who here presides among his rural train,
That I to him my purpose may disclose,
And follow what his prudence shall propose:
For Heaven's eternal wisdom has decreed,
That man of man should ever stand in need."
 Thus he; the good old herdsman thus reply'd:
" Sure some immortal being is your guide:
For lo! your business is already done:
Last night the king, descendant of the Sun,
With royal Phyleus, from the town withdrew,
His flocks unnumber'd, and his herds to view.
Thus when great kings their own concerns explore,
By wise attention they augment their store.
But let me quick, for time is on the wing,
In yonder tent conduct you to the king."
 This said, he walk'd before his royal guest,
Much wondering, much revolving in his breast,
When at his back the lion's spoils he saw,
And in his hand the club infusing awe.
He wish'd to ask the hero, whence he sprung?
The rising query dy'd upon his tongue:
He fear'd the freedom might be deem'd a fault:
'Tis difficult to know another's thought.
 The watchful dogs, as near the stalls they went,
Perceiv'd their coming by their tread and scent,
With open mouths from every part they run,
And bay'd incessant great Amphitryon's son;
But round the swain they wagg'd their tails and play'd,
And gently whining secret joy betray'd.
Loose on the ground the stones that ready lay
Eager he snatch'd, and drove the dogs away;
With his rough voice he terrified them all,
Though pleas'd to find them guardians of his stall.
" Ye gods!" the good old herdsman thus began,
" What useful animals are dogs to man?
Had Heav'n but sent intelligence to know
On whom to rage, the friendly or the foe,
No creature then could challenge honour more,
But now too furious, and too fierce they roar."
 He spoke; the growling mastives ceas'd to bay,
And stole obsequious to their stalls away.
The Sun now westward drove his radiant steeds,
And evening mild the noontide heat succeeds;

64. Sure, &c.] Dîs equidem auspicibus reor, & Junone secundâ,
Huc cursum Iliacas vento tenuisse carinas.
Æn. 4.

81. The watchful dogs, &c.] Here Theocritus imitates Homer, see Odys. b. 14. 29.

Soon as Ulysses near th' enclosure drew,
With open mouths the furious mastives flew.
Pope.

On which Mr. Pope observes, " What Homer speakes of Ulysses, Theocritus applies to Hercules; a demonstration that he thought it to be a picture of nature, and therefore inserted it in that heroic Idyllium."

88. And drove the dogs away] Thus also Eumæus did,

With showers of stones he drives them far away,
The scattering dogs around at distance bay.
Pope.

100. And evening mild, &c.] Thus the herds in Virgil return home in the evening,

His orb declining from the pasture calls
Sheep to their folds, and oxen to their stalls.
Herd following herd, it joy'd the chief to see
Unnumber'd cattle winding o'er the lea.
Like watery clouds arising thick in Heaven,
By the rough South, or Thracian Boreas driven;
So fast the shadowy vapours mount on high,
They cover all the region of the sky;
Still more and more the gathering tempest brings,
And weightier burdens on its weary wings.
Thus thickening march the cattle o'er the plain,
More than the roads or meadows can contain;
The lusty herds incessant bellowing keep,
The stalls are fill'd with steers, the folds with sheep.
Though numerous slaves stand round of every kind,
All have their several offices assign'd.
Some tie the cow's hind legs, to make her stand
Still, and obedient to the milker's hand.
Some give to tender calves the swelling teat,
Their sides distend with milky beverage sweet.
Some form fat cheeses with the housewife's art,
Some drive the heifers from the bulls apart.
Augéas visited the stalls around,
To see what stores in herds and flocks abound;
With curious eye he mov'd majestic on,
Join'd by Alcides and his royal son.
Here Hercules, of great and steady soul,
Whom mean amazement never could control,
Admir'd such droves in myriads to behold,
Such spreading flocks, that never could be told,
Not one king's wealth he thought them, nor of ten,
Though greatest of the rulers over men:
The Sun his sire this privilege assign'd,
To be in flocks and herds more rich than all mankind:
These still increas'd; no plague e'er render'd vain
The gainful labour of the shepherd-swain;

Vesper ubi e pastu vitulos ad tecta reducit.
Geor. 4. 433.

When evening homewards drives the calves and sheep.
Warton.

105. Like watery clouds, &c.] This simile finely represents the unnumbered herds of Augéas, and is very like a passage in Homer's Il. b. 4. which I shall beg leave to transcribe;

In one firm orb the bands were rang'd around,
A cloud of heroes blacken'd all the ground.
Thus from a lofty promontory's brow,
A swain surveys the gathering storm below;
Slow from the main the heavy vapours rise,
Spread in dim streams, and sail along the skies,
Till black as night the swelling tempest shows,
The clouds condensing as the west-wind blows.
Pope.

122. Thus Virgil says in regard to the management of bulls;

Aut intus clausos satura ad præsepia servant.
Geor. 3. 214.

126. Join'd by Alcides, &c.] Thus Virgil,

——— Ibat rex obsitus ævo;
Et comitem Æneam juxta natumque tenebat.
B. 8.

133. The Sun his sire, &c.] We may here observe, that Theocritus makes the great increase of the herds of Augéas to arise from the gift and influence of the Sun, his father.

Year following year his industry was blest,
More calves were rear'd, and still the last were best.
No cows e'er cast their young, or e'er declin'd,
The calves were chiefly of the female kind.
With these three hundred bulls, a comely sight,
Whose horns were crooked, and whose legs were white;
And twice an hundred of bright glossy red,
By whom the business of increase was sped:
But twelve, the flower of all, exulting run
In the green pastures, sacred to the Sun;
The stately swan was not so silver white,
And in the meads they took ineffable delight:
These, when gaunt lions from the mountain's brow
Descend terrific on the herds below,
Rush to the war, the savage foe they gore,
Their eyes look death, and horribly they roar.
But most majestic these bold bulls among
Stalk'd Phaëton, the sturdy and the strong;
So radiant, so refulgent from afar,
The shepherd-swains compar'd him to a star.
When round the shoulders of the chief he spy'd,
Alarming sight! the lion's tawny hide,
Full at his flank he aim'd his iron head,
And proudly doom'd the matchless hero dead:
But watchful Hercules, devoid of fear,
Seiz'd his left horn, and stopp'd his mad career;
Prone to the earth his stubborn neck he prest,
Then writh'd him round, and bruis'd his ample chest,
At one bold push exerted all his strength,
And high in air upheld him at arm's length.
Through all the wondering train amazement ran,
Silent they gaz'd, and thought him more than man.
Phyleus and Hercules (the day far spent)
Left the rich pastures, and to Elis went;
The footpath first, which tow'rd the city lay,
Led from the stalls, but narrow was the way;
Through vineyards next it past, and gloomy glades,
Hard to distinguish in the greenwood shades.
The devious way as noble Phyleus led,
To his right shoulder he inclin'd his head
And slowly marching through the verdant grove,
Thus mild bespoke the progeny of Jove:
"By your last bold achievement it appears,
Great chief, your fame long since has reach'd my ears.
For here arriv'd a youthful Argive swain,
From Helicé that borders on the main,
Who for a truth among th' Epëans told,
That late he saw a Grecian, brave and bold,
Slay a fell lion, fell to husbandmen,
That in the Nemean forest made his den:
Whether the chief from sacred Argos came,
Or proud Mycené, or Tirynthé claim
His birth, I heard not; yet he trac'd his line,
If true my tale, from Perseus the divine.
No Greek but you could such a toil sustain:
I reason from that mighty monster slain,
A perilous encounter! whose rough hide
Protects your shoulders, and adorns your side.
Say then, if you are he, the Grecian bold,
Of whom the Argive's wondrous tale was told:
Say, what dread weapon drank the monster's blood,
And how he wander'd to the Nemean wood.
For not in Greece such savages are found,
No beasts thus huge infest Achaian ground;
She breeds the ravenous wolf, the bear, the boar,
Pernicious monsters: but she breeds no more.
Some wonder'd at accounts so strange and new,
Thought the Greek boastful, and his tale untrue."
Thus Phyleus spoke, and as the path grew wide,
He walk'd attentive by the hero's side,
To hear distinct the toil-sustaining man,
Who thus, obsequious, to the prince began:
"Son of Augéas, what of me you heard
Is strictly true, nor has the stranger err'd.
But since you wish'd to know, my tongue shall tell,
From whence the monster came, and how he fell:
Though many Greeks have mention'd this affair,
None can the truth with certainty declare.
'Tis thought some god, by vengeful anger sway'd,
Sent this sore plague for sacrifice unpaid,
To punish the Phoroneans; like a flood
He delug'd the Pisæan fields with blood:

140. The calves, &c.] This circumstance must occasion a prodigious propagation: thus exceedingly increased the cattle of Jacob. Genesis, xxx. 30—43. "Thy cattle is now increased to a multitude: and the man increased exceedingly, and had much cattle:" and chap. xxxi. 38. Jacob says, "This twenty years have I been with thee; thy ewes and thy she-goats have not cast their young."

149. Lions] The Greek word is θηρες, and in this place properly signifies lions, as it does also in the Iliad, b. 15. ver. 586; and the bull Phaëton's being alarmed at seeing the skin of the Nemean lion, ver. 158, seems in a very agreeable manner to determine this construction.

182. Helicé] Was once a city of Achaia, three quarters of a league from Corinth, but swallowed up by the sea.

186. That in the Nemean forest, &c.] Thus Virgil,

> Tu mactas vastum Nemeâ sub rupe leonem.
> Æn. 8. 294.
> Beneath thy arm the Nemean monster fell.
> Pitt.

188. Tirynthé] A city near Argos where Hercules was nursed, whence he is called Tirynthius.

190. Perseus] Was grandfather to Amphitryon, the husband of Alcmena.

200. No beasts thus huge] Thus Horace,

> Quale portentum neque militaris
> Daunia in latis alit esculetis, &c.
> B. 1. Od. 22.

202. She breeds no more] At rabidæ tigres absunt, et sæva leonum Semina.
Virg. Geor. 2. 151.

211. But since, &c.]

> At si tantus amor casus cognoscere nostros.
> Æn. b. 2. 10.

217. Phoroneans] Inhabitants of a city in Argos: Phoroneus, the son of Inachus, succeeded his father, enlarged his territories, and gathered the people who were before dispersed about the country into one city, which was called from him Phoronium. Universal Hist. b. 1. ch. 16.

—Like a flood] Virgil compares Pyrrhus to a flood. Æn. 2. 496.

> Not half so fierce the foamy deluge bounds,
> And bursts resistless o'er the levell'd mounds;
> Pours down the vale, and roaring o'er the plain,
> Sweeps herds and hinds, and houses to the main.
> Pitt.

The Bembinæans, miserable men,
Felt his chief rage, the neighbours to his den.
The hardy task, this hideous beast to kill,
Eurystheus first enjoin'd me to fulfil,
But hop'd me slain: on the bold conflict bent,
Arm'd to the field with bow and darts I went:
A solid club, of rude wild olive made,
Rough in its rugged rind my right hand sway'd:
On Helicon's fair hill the tree I found,
And with the roots I wrench'd it from the ground.
When the close covert I approach'd, where lay
The lordly lion, lurking for his prey,
I bent my bow, firm fix'd the string, and straight
Notch'd on the nerve the messenger of fate:
Then circumspect I pry'd with curious eye,
First, unobserv'd, the ravenous beast to spy.
Now mid-day reign'd; I neither could explore
His paw's broad print, nor hear his hideous roar;
Nor labouring rustic find, nor shepherd-swain,
Nor cowherd tending cattle on the plain,
To point the lion's lair: fear chill'd them all,
And kept the herds and herdsmen in the stall.
I search'd the groves and saw my foe at length;
Then was the moment to exert my strength.
Long ere dim evening clos'd, he sought his den,
Gorg'd with the flesh of cattle and of men:
With slaughter stain'd his squalid mane appear'd,
Stern was his face, his chest with blood besmear'd,
And with his pliant tongue he lick'd his gory beard.
Mid shady shrubs I hid myself with care,
Expecting he might issue from his lair.
Full at his flank I sent a shaft, in vain,
The harmless shaft rebounded on the plain.
Stunn'd at the shock, from earth the savage rais'd
His tawny head, and all around him gaz'd;
Wondering from whence the feather'd vengeance flew,
He gnash'd his horrid teeth, tremendous to the view.
Vex'd that the first had unavailing fled,
A second arrow from the nerve I sped:
In his broad chest, the mansion of his heart,
I lanch'd the shaft with ineffectual art;
His hair, his hide the feather'd death repel;
Before his feet it innocently fell.
Enrag'd, once more, I try'd my bow to draw,
Then first his foe the furious monster saw:
He lash'd his sturdy sides with stern delight,
And rising in his rage prepar'd for fight.
With instant ire his mane erected grew,
His hair look'd horrid, of a brindled hue;
Circling his back, he seem'd in act to bound,
And like a bow he bent his body round:
As when the fig-tree skilful wheelers take,
For rolling chariots rapid wheels to make;
The fellies first, in fires that gently glow,
Gradual they heat, and like a circle bow;
Awhile in curves the pliant timber stands,
Then springs at once elastic from their hands,
On me thus from afar, his foe to wound,
Sprung the fell lion with impetuous bound.
My left hand held my darts direct before,
Around my breast a thick strong garb I wore;
My right, club-guarded, dealt a deadly blow
Full on the temples of the rushing foe:
So hard his skull, that with the sturdy stroke,
My knotted club of rough wild-olive broke:
Yet e'er I clos'd, his savage fury fled,
With trembling legs he stood, and nodding head;
The forceful onset had contus'd his brain,
Dim mists obscur'd his eyes, and agonizing pain.
This I perceiv'd; and now, an easy prey,
I threw my arrows and my bow away,
And ere the beast recover'd of his wound,
Seiz'd his thick neck, and pinn'd him to the ground;
With all my might on his broad back I prest,
Lest his fell claws should tear my adverse breast;
Then mounting, close my legs in his I twin'd,
And with my feet secur'd his paws behind;
My thighs I guarded, and with all my strength
Heav'd him from earth, and held him at arm's length,

222. Eurystheus, &c.]—Ut duros mille labores
Rege sub Eurystheo, fatis Junonis iniquæ,
Pertulerit. Æn. b. 8. 291.

The thousand labours of the hero's hands,
Enjoin'd by proud Eurystheus' stern commands. Pitt.

224. Arm'd to the field, &c.] Virgil says of Hercules;

——Rapit arma manu, nodisque gravatum
Robur. Æn. b. 8. 220.

232. Notch'd on the nerve, &c.] Thus Pandarus in Homer, Il. 4.

————Couching low,
Fits the sharp arrow to the well-strung bow. Pope.

239. Fear chill'd them all, &c.] Ovid speaking of the Calydonian boar, says,

Diffugiunt populi; nec, se nisi mœnibus urbis,
Esse putant tutos. Met. b. 8. 298.

256. Vex'd that the first, &c.] Thus Hector is vexed, that his lance did not penetrate the armour of Ajax, Il. b. 14.

Then back the disappointed Trojan drew,
And curs'd the lance that unavailing flew. Pope.

264. He lash'd his sturdy sides, &c.] There is an image in Virgil very similar to this; b. 12. ver. 6. Tum demum, &c.

As, pierc'd at distance by the hunter's dart,
The Libyan lion rouses at the smart;
And loudly roaring traverses the plain;
Scourges his sides; and rears his horrid mane;
Tugs furious at the spear; the foe defies,
And grinds his teeth for rage, and to the combat flies. Pitt.

270. Fig-tree] The Greek is, ἐρινεος, caprificus, a wild fig-tree: the same word occurs in Homer, Il b. 21, 37, which Mr. Pope renders a sycamore;

As from a sycamore, his sounding steel
Lopp'd the green arms, to spoke a chariot wheel.

278. My left hand, &c.] Thus Cadmus encountering with the dragon;

Instantiaque ora retardat
Cuspide prætentâ. Ovid. Met. b. 3.

297. Heav'd him from earth, and held him at arm's length] The construction of this passage is perplexed, but I hope I have hit upon the right, as the circumstance of Hercules's heaving the lion from the ground, is exactly the same as happened to the bull Phaëton,

And high in air upheld him at arm's length.
Ver. 166.

Indeed the words in the original are very similar.

And strangled thus the fellest of the fell;
His mighty soul decending sunk to Hell.
The conquest gain'd, fresh doubts my mind divide,
How shall I strip the monster's shaggy hide?
Hard task! for the tough skin repell'd the dint
Of pointed wood, keen steel, or sharpest flint:
Some god inspir'd me, standing still in pause,
To flay the lion with the lion's claws.
This I accomplish'd, and the spoil now yields
A firm security in fighting fields:
Thus, Phyleus, was the Nemean monster slain,
The terrour of the forest and the plain,
That flocks and herds devour'd, and many a village swain."

IDYLLIUM XXVI.

BACCHÆ *.

ARGUMENT.

This Idyllium contains a short account of the death of Pentheus, king of Thebes; who refusing to own the divinity of Bacchus, and endeavouring to prohibit his orgies, is torn in pieces by his own mother Agavé, and by his aunts Ino and Autonoë.

Autonoe, and Agavé, whose rough cheeks
Resembled the ripe apple's ruddy streaks,
With frantic Ino had resolv'd to keep
Three holy revels on the mountain's steep:
Green ivy and sweet asphodel they took,
And leafy branches from the shagged oak,
With these the madding Bacchanalians made
Twelve verdant altars in an opening glade;
Three to fair Semele they rais'd, and nine
To youthful Bacchus, jolly god of wine.
From chests they take, and, joyful shouting, lay
Their offerings on the fresh erected spray;
Such rites they practis'd, and such offerings brought,
As pleas'd the god, and what himself had taught.
Lodg'd in a lentisck-tree, conceal'd from sight,
Astonish'd Pentheus saw the mystic rite;
Autonoë first the latent monarch spy'd,
With horrid yellings down the hill she hy'd,
The orgies of the frantic god o'erthrew,
Which no profane, unhallow'd eye must view.
Maddening she rag'd, the rest all rag'd; and dread
Supplied with pinions Pentheus as he fled;
He hop'd by flight their fury to elude;
With robes tuck'd up they eagerly pursued:
Then Pentheus thus; "What means this rage? forbear;"
Autonoë thus; "You'll feel before you hear."
His mother roar'd, and snatch'd his head away,
Loud as the female lion o'er her prey:
Ino her foot upon his breast display'd,
Wrench'd off his shoulder, and the shoulder-blade;
Autonoë steep'd her hands in royal gore;
And all the monarch limb from limb they tore:
Thus drench'd in blood the Theban towers they sought,
And grief, not Pentheus, from the mountain brought.

298. Fellest of the fell] Thomson, in his Seasons, joins this epithet to the hyena: The keen hyena, fellest of the fell.

306. Aventinus, the son of Hercules, is represented by Virgil in the same dress.

Ipse pedes tegmen torquens immane leonis, &c.
Æn. b. 7. 666.

He stalk'd before his host; and, wide dispread,
A lion's teeth grinn'd horrid o'er his head;
Then sought the palace in the strange attire,
And look'd as stern, and dreadful as his sire.
Pitt.

* Mr. Warton observes, "That Euripedes, in his Bacchantes, has given a very fine description of the Bacchanalian women tearing Pentheus in pieces, for secretly inspecting their mysteries, which is worked up with the greatest fire, and the truest poetical enthusiasm. Theocritus has likewise nobly described this event."

1. Autonoë, Agavé, Ino] These were all sisters, and the daughters of Cadmus and Hermonia.

5. Green ivy, &c.] Anacreon, Epig. 4. describes three Bacchæ, and ivy is one of their oblations to Bacchus:

First Heliconias with a thyrsus past,
Xanthippe next, and Glauca was the last:
Lo! dancing down the mountains they repair,
And grateful gifts to jolly Bacchus bear;
Wreaths of the rustling ivy for his head,
With grapes delicious, and a kid well fed.
F. F.

8. Twelve altars, &c.] Thus Virgil, Ec. 5.
En quatuor aras:
Ecce duas tibi, Daphni, duoque altaria Phœbo.

15. The story of Pentheus is told by Ovid in the Metam. b. 3. in a manner something different, which I shall give in Mr. Addison's translation.

Here the rash Pentheus, with unhallow'd eyes,
The howling dames and mystic orgies spies.
His mother sternly view'd him where he stood,
And kindled into madness as she view'd:
Her leafy javelin at her son she cast,
And cries, "The boar that lays our country waste!
The boar, my sisters! aim the fatal dart,
And strike the brindled monster to the heart."
Pentheus astonish'd heard the dismal sound,
And sees the yelling matrons gathering round.
He sees, and weeps at his approaching fate,
And begs for mercy, and repents too late.
"Help! help! my aunt Autonoë," he cry'd;
"Remember how your own Actæon dy'd:"
Deaf to his cries, the frantic matron crops
One stretch'd-out arm, the other Ino lops.
In vain does Pentheus to his mother sue,
And the raw bleeding stumps presents to view:
His mother howl'd, and heedless of his prayer,
Her trembling hand she twisted in his hair,
"And this," she cry'd, "shall be Agavé's share;"
When from the neck his struggling head she tore,
And in her hands the ghastly visage bore.
With pleasure all the hideous trunk survey;
Then pull'd and tore the mangled limbs away,
As starting in the pangs of death it lay.
Soon as the wood its leafy honours casts,
Blown off and scatter'd by autumnal blasts,
With such a sudden death lay Pentheus slain,
And in a thousand pieces strow'd the plain.

27. And snatch'd his head away]
Quid? caput abscissum demens cum portat Agavé
Nati infelicis, sibi tum furiosa videtur?
Hor. b. 2. Sat. 3.

34. And grief, not Pentheus, &c.] There is great beauty in the original, Εξ ορεος πενθημα, ϗ

Be warn'd; let none the jolly god offend,
Lest sorer penalties the wretch attend;
Let none behold his rites with eyes impure;
Age is not safe, nor blooming youth secure.
For me, the works of righteousness I love,
And may I grateful to the righteous prove!
For this is pleasing to almighty Jove.
The pious blessings on their sons derive;
But can the children of the impious thrive?
Hail Bacchus, whom the ruler of the sky,
Great Jove, enclos'd, and foster'd in his thigh!
Hail, with thy sisters, Semele renown'd!
Offsprings of Cadmus, with bright praises crown'd,
In hymns of heroines: let none defame
This act; from Bacchus the incentive came:
'Tis not for man the deeds of deities to blame.

IDYLLIUM XXVII.

Is by the commentators generally attributed to Moschus, and therefore I may well be excused from translating it as a work of Theocritus. Were that not the case, it is of such a nature that it cannot be admitted into this volume: Scaliger, Casaubon, and Dan. Heinsius, have left more notes upon it in proportion, than upon any of the other Idylliums. Creech has done it into English, but the spirit is evaporated, and nothing remains but a caput mortuum. Dryden generally improves and expatiates upon any subject that is ludicrous, and therefore the tenour of his translation will be found very different. The last five lines in Greek, he has expanded into fourteen.

IDYLLIUM XXVIII.

THE DISTAFF.

ARGUMENT.

Theocritus going to visit his friend Nicias, the Milesian physician, to whom he has addressed the 11th and 13th Idylliums, carries an ivory distaff as a present for Theugenis, his friend's wife, and accompanies it with these verses, in which he modestly commends the matron's industry and virtue.

O DISTAFF, friend to warp and woof,
Minerva's gift in man's behoof,
Whom careful housewives still retain,
And gather to their households gain;
With me repair, no vulgar prize,
Where the fam'd towers of Nileus rise,
Where Cytherea's swayful power
Is worshipp'd in the reedy bower.
Thither, would Jove kind breezes send,
I steer my course to meet my friend,
Nicias, the Graces, honour'd child,
Adorn'd with sweet persuasion mild;
That I his kindness may requite,
May be delighted, and delight.
Thee, ivory distaff, I provide,
A present for his blooming bride.
With her thou wilt sweet toil partake,
And aid her various vests to make.
For Theugenis, the shepherds shear
The sheep's soft fleeces twice a year.
So dearly industry she loves,
And all that wisdom points approves.
I ne'er design'd to bear thee hence
To the dull house of Indolence:
For in that city thou wert fram'd
Which Archias built, Corinthian fam'd,
Fair Syracuse, Sicilia's pride,
Where troops of famous men abide.
Dwell thou with him whose art can cure
Each dire disease that men endure;
Thee to Miletus now I give,
Where pleasure-crown'd Ionians live,
That Theugenis by thee may gain
Fair honour with the female train;
And thou renew within her breast
Remembrance of her muse-charm'd guest.
Admiring thee each maid will call
The favour great, the present small;
For love the smallest gift commends,
All things are valued by our friends.

IDYLLIUM XXIX.

THE MISTRESS.

ARGUMENT.

This is an expostulation with his mistress for her inconstancy in love. In the original it is called Παιδικα: I have taken the liberty to make a

Πενθηα, φερουσαι, which arising from the similarity of the words πενθημα and Πενθηα, cannot be kept up in the translation.

45. Jove, enclos'd, &c.] Ovid mentions the same thing, Met. b. 3. 310.

> Imperfectus adhuc infans genetricis ab alvo
> Eripitur, patrioque tener (si credere dignum)
> Insuitur femori, maternaque tempora complet.

46. Semele] She was the mother of Bacchus, and sister to Ino, Agavé, and Autonoë.

50. 'Tis not, &c.] There is a similar thought in Bion, Idyl. 6.

> Κρινειν ουκ επεοικε θεμιία εργα βροτοισι.
>
> It ill becomes frail mortals to define
> What's best and fittest of the works divine.
> F.F.

6. The towers of Nileus] That is, Miletus, a famous city of Ionia, lying south of the river Mæander on the sea-coast; it was founded, according to Strabo, by Nileus the son of Codrus, king of Athens, when he first settled in that part of Asia. See Universal History. The fine garments made of Milesian wool were in great esteem with the Roman ladies: Horace has, Mileti textam chlamydem, b. 1. ep. 17. and Virgil, Milesia vellera, Geor. 3.

25. In that city] Syracuse, once the metropolis of all Sicily, and a most flourishing commonwealth, was, according to Tully, the greatest and most wealthy of all the cities possessed by the Greeks. Thucydides equals it to Athens, when that city was at the height of its glory; and Strabo calls it one of the most famous cities of the world for its advantageous situation, the stateliness of its buildings, and the immense wealth of its inhabitants. It was built by Archias, one of the Heraclidæ, who came from Corinth into Sicily, in the second year of the eleventh Olympiad. Univ. Hist.

38. Inest sua gratia parvis.

change in the application of it, which renders it far more obvious and natural.

WINE, lovely maid, and truth agree;
I'm mellow—learn this truth from me;
And hear my secret thoughts; I find,
"You love me not with all your mind."
Your beauty life and vigour gives,
In you my half-existence lives,
The other half has sadly sped,
The other half, alas! is dead.
Whene'er you smile auspicious love,
I'm happy as the gods above;
Whene'er your frowns displeasure show,
I'm wretched as the fiends below.
Sure 'tis unmeet with cold disdain
To torture thus a love-sick swain:
But could my words your thoughts engage,
Experience is the boast of age,
Take counsel, and when crown'd with store
Of blessings, then you'll praise me more.
"Build in one tree a single nest,
Which no curst reptile can infest."
Fond and unfix'd you wander now
From tree to tree, from bough to bough.
If any youth your charms commends
You rank him with your faithful friends,
Your first true lovers set aside;
This looks like vanity and pride.
Would you live long and happy too,
Love some fond equal that loves you.
This will esteem and favour gain,
Such love will never give you pain;
This wins all hearts, and will control
The stubborn temper of my soul.
If with my counsel you agree,
Give me sweet kisses for my fee.

IDYLLIUM XXX *.

THE DEATH OF ADONIS.

ARGUMENT.

Venus orders the Cupids to bring the boar that had slain Adonis before her: she severely upbraids him with his crime, but being satisfied that it was accidentally done, she orders him to be released. The measure of the verse is Anacreontic.

WHEN Venus saw Adonis dead,
And from his cheeks the roses fled,
His lovely locks distain'd with gore:
She bad her Cupids bring the boar,
The boar that had her lover slain,
The cause of all her grief and pain.
Swift as the pinion'd birds they rove
Through every wood, through every grove;
And when the guilty boar they found,
With cords they bound him, doubly bound;
One with a chain secure and strong,
Haul'd him unwillingly along;
One pinch'd his tail to make him go,
Another beat him with his bow:
The more they urg'd, the more they dragg'd,
The more reluctantly he lagg'd.
Guilt in his conscious looks appear'd;
He much the angry goddess fear'd.
To Venus soon the boar they led—
"O cruel, cruel beast!" she said,
"Durst thou that thigh with blood distain?
Hast thou my dearest lover slain?"
Submissive he replies; "I swear
By thee, fair queen; by all that's dear;
By thy fond lover; by this chain;
And by this numerous hunter-train;
I ne'er design'd with impious tooth,
To wound so beautiful a youth:
No; but with love and frenzy warm,
(So far has beauty power to charm!)
I long'd, this crime I'll not deny,
To kiss that fair, that naked thigh.
These tusks then punish, if you please,
These are offenders, draw out these.
Of no more use they now can prove
To me, the votaries of love!
My guilty lips, if not content,
My lips shall share the punishment."
These words, so movingly exprest,
Infus'd soft pity in her breast;
The queen relented at his plea,
And bad her Cupids set him free:
But from that day he join'd her train,
Nor to the woods return'd again;
And all those teeth he burnt with fire,
Which glow'd before with keen desire.

---

1. Wine and truth] In vino veritas.
6. Half-existence] Thus Horace,

Et serves animæ dimidium meæ. B. 1. Od. 3.

10. I'm happy, &c.]

Deorum vitam adepti sumus.
Ter. Heaut. act. 4. sc. 3.

16. Experience, &c.]—Seris venit usus ab annis.
Consilium ne sperne meum. Ovid. Met. b. 6.

* This little poem is a fine imitation of Anacreon: Theocritus had before in his nineteenth Idyllium copied that delicate master in every thing but the measure of his verse. Bion has a most beautiful Idyllium on the same subject. Longepierre says of this ode of Theocritus, Cette petite piéce m' a toujours paru si jolie, que je croy qu'on me pardonnera aisément si j'en donne icy une traduction.

14. Another beat him with his bow:] Thus Ulysses drives the horses of Rhesus with his bow, I. b. 10.

Ulysses now the snowy steeds detains,
And leads them, fasten'd by the silver reins;
These, with his bow unbent, he lash'd along.
Pope.

23. I swear by thee, fair Venus, &c.] Thus Sinon in Virgil,

Vos, æterni ignes, &c.

You, the eternal splendours, he exclaims,
And you divine inviolable flames,
Ye fatal swords, and altars, which I fled,
Ye wreaths, which circled this devoted head;
All, all attest. Pitt.

45. And all those teeth, &c.] The Greek is, Εκαιε τως ερωτας, exussit amores, i. e. amatorios dentes.

*THE EPIGRAMS OF THEOCRITUS**.

I.

OFFERINGS TO THE MUSES AND APOLLO.

This wild thyme, and these roses, moist with [dews,
Are sacred to the Heliconian Muse;
The bay, Apollo, with dark leaves is thine;
Thus art thou honour'd at the Delphic shrine;
And there to thee this shagg'd he-goat I vow,
That loves to crop the pine-tree's pendent bough.

II.

AN OFFERING TO PAN.

Daphnis the fair, who with bucolic song,
And pastoral pipe could charm the listening throng,
To Pan presents these emblems of his art,
A fawn's soft skin, a crook, and pointed dart,
Three rural pipes, adapted to his lip,
And for his homely food a leathern scrip.

III.

TO DAPHNIS SLEEPING.

On earth's soft lap, with leafy honours spread,
You, Daphnis, lull to rest your weary head:
While on the hill your snares for birds are laid,
Pan hunts your footsteps in the secret shade,
And rude Priapus, on whose temples wave
Gold ivy's leaves, resolv'd to find your cave:
Ah! fly these revellers, at distance keep,
And instant burst the silken bands of sleep.

IV.

A VOW TO PRIAPUS.

If by those oaks with roving step you wind,
An image fresh of fig-tree form'd you'll find;
Though cloth'd with bark, three-legg'd and void of ears,
Prompt for the pranks of pleasure he appears.
Springs gush perennial from the rocky hill,
And round the grotto roll their sparkling rill:
Green myrtles, bays, and cypress sweet abound,
And vines diffuse their circling arms around.
The vernal ousels their shrill notes prolong,
And modulate the loudly-varied song;
Sweet nightingales in soft-opponent strain,
Perch'd on the spray melodiously complain.
Repose you there, and to Priapus pray,
That Daphne may no more my bosom sway:
Grant this, a goat shall at his altar bleed[8];
But if I gain the maid, three victims are decreed;
A stall-fed lamb, a goat, and heifer fair:
Thus may the god propitious hear my prayer.

V.

THE CONCERT.

Say wilt thou warble to thy double flute,
And make its melody thy music suit?
Then, by the Nymphs I swear, I'll snatch the quill,
And on the rural lyre essay my skill:
The herdsman, Daphnis, on his reed shall play,
Whose sprightly numbers make the shepherds gay:
Fast by yon rugged oak our stand we'll keep,
And rob th' Arcadian deity of sleep.

VI.

THYRSIS HAS LOST HIS KID.

What profit gain you, wretched Thyrsis, say,
Thus, thus to weep and languish life away?
Lost is your favourite kid; the wolf has tore
His tender limbs, and feasted on his gore:
Your very dogs exclaim, and cry, "What gain,
When neither bones, nor ashes now remain?"

VII.

ON THE STATUE OF ÆSCULAPIUS.

At fam'd Miletus, Pæon's son the wise
Arriv'd, with learned Nicias to advise,
Who to his shrine with daily offerings came,
And rais'd this cedar statue to his fame;

* These Epigrams were never translated into English before. The six that first present themselves, are a true model of the rustic sweetness, and delicate simplicity of the ancient Greek epigram.

I. 2. Are sacred, &c.] That the rose was consecrated to the Muses, appears from Anacreon, ode 53. χαρίεν φυτον τε Μυσεων.

> In fabled song, and tuneful lays,
> Their favourite rose the Muses praise.

And Sappho, frag. 2.

> For thy rude hand ne'er pluck'd the lovely rose,
> That on the mountain of Pieria blows. F. F.

I. 5. Virgil and Horace have something similar:

> ——— Illius aram
> Sæpe tener nostris ab ovilibus imbuet agnus.
> Ecl. 1.

> Voveram album Libero caprum. B. 3. O. 8.

II. 1. Daphnis] This Daphnis was probably the son of Mercury, the same whose story is sung in the first Idyllium: Diodorus Siculus supposes him to be the author of bucolic poetry; and agreeable to this, Theon, an old scholiast on Theocritus, in his note on the first Idyllium, ver. 141, mentioning Daphnis, says, Καθο πρωτος ευρατο Βυκολικην, Inasmuch as he was the inventor of bucolics; however that be, probably this Daphnis was the first subject of bucolic songs.

III. 6. Gold ivy's leaves, &c.] The Greek is, κροκοέντα κισσον: This is probably the pallens, or alba hedera of Virgil, on which Dr. Martyn observes, (see his notes on Ecl. 7. ver. 38.) it is most likely that sort of ivy with yellow berries, which was used in the garlands with which poets used to be crowned, and Ecl. 8. ver. 13. The poetical ivy is that sort with golden berries, or hedera baccis aureis.

IV. 2. Of fig-tree] The ancients often hewed the image of Priapus out of a fig-tree.

> Olim truncus eram ficulnus, &c.
> Hor. Sat. 8. b. 1.

14. That Daphne, &c.] I have taken the liberty to address this epigram to Daphne, instead of Daphnis, puellæ et non pastori.

15. Grant this, &c.] Here I follow the ingenious interpretation of Dan. Heinsius.

V. 8. And rob, &c.] In the first Idyllium the shepherds are afraid of disturbing the Arcadian god's repose. See ver. 20.

VII. 1. Pæon's son] Æsculapius, the son of Apollo, was called Pæon or Παιων, because of his art in asswaging and curing diseases.

The cedar statue by Eëtion wrought,
Illustrious artist! for large sums he bought;
The work is finish'd to the owner's will,
For here the sculptor lavish'd all his skill.

VIII.

ORTHON'S EPITAPH.

To every toping traveller that lives,
Orthon of Syracuse this warning gives;
With wine o'erheated, and depriv'd of light,
Forbear to travel on a winter's night;
This was my fate; and for my native land
I now lie buried on a foreign strand.

IX.

ON THE FATE OF CLEONICUS.

O STRANGER! spare thy life so short and frail,
Nor, but when times are seasonable, sail.
Poor Cleonícus, innocent of guile,
From Syria hasten'd to rich Thaso's isle;
The Pleiads sunk as he approach'd the shore;
With them he sunk, to rise, alas! no more.

X.

ON A MONUMENT ERECTED TO THE MUSES.

HERE Xenocles hath rais'd this marble shrine,
Skill'd in sweet music, to the tuneful Nine:
He from his art acquires immortal fame,
And grateful owns the fountain whence it came.

XI.

EPITAPH ON EUSTHENES THE PHYSIOGNOMIST.

To Eusthenes, the first in wisdom's list,
Philosopher and physiognomist,
This tomb is rais'd: he from the eye could scan
The cover'd thought, and read the very man.
By strangers was his decent bier adorn'd,
By strangers honour'd, and by poets mourn'd:
Whate'er the Sophist merited he gain'd,
And dead, a grave in foreign realms obtain'd.

XII.

ON A TRIPOD DEDICATED TO BACCHUS BY DEMOTELES.

DEMOTELES, who near this sacred shrine
This tripod plac'd, with thee, O god of wine!

VIII. 5. And for my native land, &c.] I here follow the ingenious emendation of Heinsius.

IX. In all the editions of Theocritus in the original, there is only the first distich of this epigram, but in Pierson's Verisimilia, I find two more added from a MS. in the Palatine library, which was collated by D. Ruhnkenius; as I have translated, I likewise take the liberty to transcribe, the whole.

Ανθρωπε, ζωης περιφειδεο, μηδε παρ ωρ'αν
Ναυτιλος ισθι, ως ȣ πολυς ανδρι βιος.
Δειλαιε Κλεονικε, συ δ' εις λιπαρην Θασον ελθειν
Ηπειγευ κοιλης εμπορος εκ Συρινς.
Εμπορος, α Κλεονικε, δυσιν δ' απο πλειαδος αυτην,
Ποντοπορων αυτηι πλειαδι συνκατεδυς.

4. Thasos] An island near Thrace, formerly famous for gold, marble, and wine.

XI. Heinsius has rendered this epigram intelligible, whose emendations I follow.

XII. 6. And fair the tenour, &c.] The Greek is,

Και το καλον, ϗ το προσηκον ορων.

Thus Horace,

Quid verum, atque decens, curo et rogo, et omnis in hoc sum. B. 1. Ep. 1. 11.

Whom blithest of the deities we call,
In all things prov'd, was temperate in all:
In manly dance the victory he gain'd,
And fair the tenour of his life maintain'd.

XIII.

ON THE IMAGE OF THE HEAVENLY VENUS.

HERE Venus, not the vulgar, you survey;
Style her celestial, and your offering pay:
This in the house of Amphicles was plac'd,
Fair present of Chrysogona the chaste:
With him a sweet and social life she led,
And many children bore, and many bred.
Favour'd by thee, O venerable fair,
Each year improv'd upon the happy pair;
For long as men the deities adore,
With large abundance Heav'n augments their [store.

XIV.

EPITAPH ON EURYMEDON.

DEAD in thy prime, this tomb contains,
Eurymedon, thy dear remains;
Thou, now with pious men inshrin'd,
Hast left an infant heir behind;
The state due care of him will take,
And love him for his father's sake.

XV.

ON THE SAME.

O TRAVELLER, I wish to know
If you an equal praise bestow
On men of honourable fame,
Or to poltroons you give the same:
Then "Fair befal this tomb," you'll cry,
As oft you pass attentive by,
"Eurymedon, alas! is dead;
Light lie the stone upon his head."

XVI.

ON ANACREON'S STATUE.

WITH curious eye, O traveller, survey
This statue's form, and home-returning say,
"At Teos late with infinite regard,
I saw the image of the sweetest bard,
Anacreon; who, if ancient poets claim
The meed of praise, deserves immortal fame;"
Add this; "He lov'd" (for this with truth you can)
"The fair, the gay, the young," you'll paint the very man.

XVII.

ON EPICHARMUS.

THE style is Doric; Epicharmus he,
The poet who invented comedy:
This statue, Bacchus, sacred stands to you;
Accept a brazen image for the true.
The finish'd form at Syracuse is plac'd,
And, as is meet, with lasting honours grac'd.
Far-fam'd for wisdom, the preceptive bard
Taught those who gave the merited reward:
Much praise he gains who form'd ingenuous youth,
And show'd the paths to virtue, and to truth.

XIII. 1. Venus, not the vulgar, &c.] Plato in Convivio says, there were two Venuses, one was the daughter of Cœlus, which we call ουρανιαν, or celestial; the other the daughter of Jupiter and Dione, which we call πανδημον, or popular.

XVII. 1. Epicharmus] Was brought to Sicily when an infant from the island of Cos, and is there-

XVIII.

EPITAPH ON CLITA, THE NURSE OF MEDEUS.

MEDEUS rais'd, inspir'd by grateful pride,
This tomb to Clita by the high-way side:
We still commend her for her fostering care;
And praise the matron when we praise the heir.

XIX.

ON ARCHILOCHUS.

ARCHILOCHUS, that ancient bard, behold!
Arm'd with his own iambics keen and bold;
Whose living fame with rapid course has run
Forth from the rising to the setting Sun.
The Muses much their daring son approv'd,
The Muses much, and much Apollo lov'd;
So terse his style, so regular his fire,
Composing verse to suit his sounding lyre.

XX.

ON THE STATUE OF PISANDER, WHO WROTE A POEM STYLED, THE LABOURS OF HERCULES.

THIS statue fam'd Pisander's worth rewards,
Born at Camirus, first of famous bards
Who sung of Hercules, the son of Jove,
How with the lion he victorious strove,
And all the labours of this hero bold
The faithful bard in lofty numbers told.
The state regardful of the poet's name,
Hath rais'd this brazen statue to his fame.

XXI.

EPITAPH ON THE POET HIPPONAX.

OLD Hipponax the satirist lies here;
If thou'rt a worthless wretch, approach not near:
But if well bred, and from all evil pure,
Repose with confidence, and sleep secure.

XXII.

THEOCRITUS ON HIS OWN WORKS.

A SYRACUSIAN born, no right I claim
To Chios, and Theocritus my name:
Praxagoras' and fam'd Philina's son;
All praise I scorn'd but what my numbers won.

fore called a Sicilian; he was the disciple of Pythagoras, and said to be the first inventor of comedy. Plautus imitated him, according to Horace,

Plautus ad exemplar Siculi properare Epicharmi. B. 2. Ep. 1. 58.

Even Plato himself borrowed many things from him. He presented fifty-five, or as some say, thirty-five plays, which are all lost. He lived, according to Lucian, 97 years. Laertius has preserved some verses which were inscribed on one of his statues, which, as they are a testimony of the high esteem antiquity had for his worth, I shall transcribe.

Ει τι παραλλασσει φαεθων μεγας αλιος αστρων,
Και ποντος πόταμων μειζον εχει δυναμιν
Φαμι τοσουτον εγω σοφια προεχειν Επιχαρμον,
Ον πατρις εστεφανωσ' αδε Συρακοσιων.

As the bright Sun outshines the starry train,
And streams confess the empire of the main;
We first in wisdom Epicharmus own,
On whom fam'd Syracuse bestow'd the crown.

9. Much praise, &c.] The Greek is,

Πολλα γαρ ποτταν ζωαν τοις παισιν ειπε χρησιμα.
Μεγαλα χαρις αυτω.

Mr. Upton, in his observations on Shakespeare, instead of παισὶν children, reads πασιν all mankind; which is plausible, for the philosophic comedian spoke what was useful for all mankind to know, and fitting for common life; and then the translation may run,

Much praise, much favour he will ever find,
Whose useful lessons mended all mankind.

XIX. 1. Archilochus] He was a Greek poet, born at Paros, in the third Olympiad. His invectives against Lycambes (who after having promised his daughter in marriage, gave her to another) were so keen and severe, that they made him hang himself. He is said to have been the inventor of iambic verse. Thus Horace,

Archilochum proprio rabies armavit iambo.

XX. Pisander was a native of Camirus, a city of Rhodes; he is mentioned by Strabo and Macrobius, as the author of a poem styled Heraclea, which comprehended in two books all the exploits of Hercules: he is said to have been the first that represented Hercules with a club.
Univ. Hist. b. 2. ch. 1.

XXI. Hipponax was a witty poet of Ephesus, but so deformed, that the painters drew hideous pictures of him; particularly Bupalus and Anthermus, two brothers, eminent statuaries, made his image so ridiculous, that in resentment he dipped his pen in gall, and wrote such bitter iambics against them, that, it is said, they dispatched themselves: at least they left Ephesus upon the occasion. Horace calls Hipponax, Acer hostis Bupalo, Epod. 6.

Alcæus on Hipponax. Anthol. b. 3. ch. 25.

No vines the tomb of this old bard adorn
With lovely clusters, but the pointed thorn,
And spiry brambles that unseen will tear
The eyes of passengers that walk too near:
Let travellers that safely pass request,
That still the bones of Hipponax may rest.

Leonidas on the same. Ibid.

Softly this tomb approach, a cautious guest,
Lest you should rouse the hornet in his nest:
Here sleeps at length old Hipponax's ire,
Who bark'd sarcastic at his harmless sire.
Beware; stay not on this unhallow'd ground;
His fiery satires ev'n in death will wound.

Another on the same. Ibid.

Fly, stranger, nor your weary limbs relax
Near the tempestuous tomb of Hipponax,
Whose very dust, deposited below,
Stings with iambics Bupalus his foe,
Rouse not the sleeping hornet in his cell;
He loads his limping lines with satires fell;
His anger is not pacified in hell.

THE

ARGONAUTICS OF

APOLLONIUS RHODIUS.

TRANSLATED BY FAWKES.

TO THE

MOST REVEREND FATHER IN GOD,

FREDERIC,

LORD ARCHBISHOP OF CANTERBURY,

PRIMATE OF ALL ENGLAND, AND METROPOLITAN,

THE FOLLOWING TRANSLATION OF

APOLLONIUS RHODIUS

IS, BY PERMISSION,

AND WITH ALL HUMILITY,

INSCRIBED,

BY HIS GRACE'S MOST DUTIFUL,

AND MOST OBLIGED SERVANT,

THE EDITOR.

PREFACE.

THE author of this poem was the son of Silleus and Illeus. He was born at Alexandria in Egypt, and educated under Callimachus. He received the name of Rhodius, or the Rhodian, either from his mother, whose name was Rhoda, or, more probably, from the city Rhodes. During his stay in this place he finished his Argonautic poem, and founded a school of rhetoric. Ptolemy Euergetes, in whose reign our poet flourished, two hundred and forty-four years before Christ, recalled him from his retirement at Rhodes, and appointed him successor to Eratosthenes in the care of the Alexandrian library. The favours which had been conferred on Callimachus in the court of Ptolemy Philadelphus, were continued to him by his successor Ptolemy Euergetes. So that Callimachus, no less than his scholar, was protected and patronised by his prince. This circumstance, among others, gave occasion to those jealousies and dissensions, which subsisted between these rival poets. Callimachus is supposed to have alluded, in the following lines, to that invidious spirit which prevailed in his scholar.

> Ὁ φθόνος Ἀπόλλωνος ἐπ᾽ οὔατα λάθριος εἶπεν,
> Οὐκ ἄγαμαι τὸν ἀοιδὸν, ὃς οὐδ᾽ ὅσα Πόντος ἀείδει.
>
> Call. Hymn. ad. Ap. v. 105.

For Apollonius, anxious to establish his own reputation, and jealous of his master's, had depreciated those more numerous, but lighter productions, in which the muse of Callimachus excelled; epigrams, hymns, and elegies.

It will be no improper introduction to the following poem to trace the subject of it to its source: nor can we expect to be guided through its intricacies by a safer clue, than that which the ancients have afforded us.

Ino was the wife of Athamas, king of Orchomenos; from whom he was soon after divorced, and married Nephele. But she incurring his displeasure, he restored the repudiated Ino to his bed. By her he had two children, Learchus and Melicerta; by Nephele he had Phrixus and Helle. Ino beheld the children of her rival with a jealous eye. For they, being the eldest, had a prior claim to their father's inheritance. Resolved on their destruction, she concerted the following plan, as most likely to effect it. A grievous famine laying waste the country, it was judged expedient to consult the oracle about the means of suppressing it. Ino having gained over the priests to her interest, prevailed on them to return this answer; that the ravages of famine could no otherwise be suppressed, than by the sacrifice of Nephele's children. Phrixus, who was made acquainted with the cruel purpose of Ino, freighted his vessel with his father's treasures, and embarked with his sister Helle for Colchis. The voyage proved fatal to her; and the sea, into which she fell, was named from her the Hellespont. But Phrixus arrived safe at Colchis; and was protected from the cruelties of his step-mother Ino, at the court of Æetes his kinsman, who bestowed on him his daughter Chalciope in marriage. Upon his arrival he consecrated his ship to Mars; on whose prow was represented the figure of a ram. This embellishment, it is supposed by some of the historians, gave rise to the fiction, of his having swam to Colchis on the back of that animal, of his having sacrificed it to Mars, and hung up its fleece in the temple of that god. It is this imaginary fleece which is celebrated by the poets for having given birth to the expedition of the Argonauts. A variety of whimsical conjectures have been formed concerning it. Some are of opinion, that it was a book of sheep-skins, containing the mysteries of the chymic art. Others have assured us, that it signified the riches of the country; with which their rivers, that abounded in gold, supplied its inhabitants, and that, from the sheep-skins made use of in collecting the golden dust, it was called the golden fleece.

For a further illustration of the subject of this poem, it will be necessary to insert the following history.

Tyro, the daughter of Salmoneus, had two sons by Neptune, Neleus and Pelias: by Cretheus she had Æson, Pheres and Amithaon. The city of Iolcos in Thessaly, which Cretheus built, was the capital of his dominions. He left his kingdom at his death to Æson his eldest son; but made no provision for Pelias. Pelias, however, growing every day more powerful, at length dethroned Æson. And hearing that his wife Alcimeda was delivered of a son, he was resolutely bent on his destruction. For he had been forewarned by the oracle, that he must be dethroned by a prince, descended from Æolus, and who should appear before him with one foot bare. Æson and Alcimeda being informed of the tyrant's intention, conveyed their son to mount Pelion, where he was educated by Chiron. Having attained to maturity, he consulted the oracle; who encouraged him to repair to the court of Iolcos. Pelias, hearing of the arrival of this stranger, and of the circumstance of his appearance with only one sandal, concluded that this must be the person, whom the oracle had foretold. Having made himself and his situation known to his uncle, Jason demanded of him the crown, which he had so unjustly usurped. Pelias was greatly alarmed at this requisition. But knowing that a thirst for glory is the darling passion of youth, he contrived to appease his nephew's resentment by disclosing to him the means of gratifying his ambition. He assured him, that Phrixus, when he sailed from Orchomenos, had carried with him a fleece of gold, the possession of which would at the same time enrich and immortalize him. The proposal had its desired effect. Jason signified his acceptance of it, and collected speedily the most illustrious princes of Greece, who were eager to embark in a cause, that was at once advantageous and honourable. Who these heroes were, the route they took, the dangers which they encountered, and the success they met with, are particulars recorded by Apollonius, and on which he has lavished all the graces of poetry.

Such is the history of the golden fleece, as delivered down to us by the ancient poets and historians. This celebrated expedition is generally supposed to be the first era of true history. Sir Isaac Newton places it about forty-three years after the death of Solomon, and nine hundred and thirty-seven years before the birth of Christ. He apprehends, that the Greeks, hearing of the distractions of Egypt, sent the most renowned heroes of their country in the ship Argo, to persuade the nations on the coast of the Euxine sea to throw off the Egyptian yoke, as the Libyans, Ethiopians, and Jews had before done. But Mr. Bryant has given us a far different account of this matter in his very learned system of mythology: whose sentiments on this head I have endeavoured to collect, and have ventured to give them a place in this preface. For the novelty of his hypothesis, and the learning and ingenuity with which it is supported, cannot fail to entertain and instruct us.

"The main plot," says the learned and ingenious mythologist, "as it is transmitted to us, is certainly a fable, and replete with inconsistencies and contradictions. Yet many writers, ancient and modern, have taken the account in gross; and without hesitation, or exception to any particular part, have presumed to fix the time of this transaction. And having satisfied themselves in this point, they have presumed to make use of it for a stated era. Mr. Bryant is of opinion, that this history, upon which sir Isaac Newton built so much, did certainly not relate to Greece; though adopted by the people of that country. He contends, that sir Isaac's calculation rested upon a weak foundation. That it is doubtful, whether such persons as Chiron or Musæus ever existed; and still more doubtful, whether they formed a sphere for the Argonauts. He produces many arguments to convince us, that the expedition itself was not a Grecian operation; and that this sphere at any rate was not a Grecian work: and if not from Greece, it must certainly be the produce of Egypt. For the astronomy of Greece confessedly came from that country: consequently the history to which it alludes must have been from the same quarter. Many of the constellations, says our author, are of Egyptian original. The zodiac, which sir Isaac Newton supposed to relate to the Argonautic expedition, was, he asserts, an assemblage of Egyptian hieroglyphics.

"After having enumerated all the particulars of their voyage, the different routes they are supposed to have taken, and the many inconsistencies with which the whole story abounds, Mr. Bryant proceeds to observe, that the mythology, as well as the rites of Greece, was borrowed from Egypt; and that it was founded upon ancient histories, which had been transmitted in hieroglyphical representations. These, by length of time, became obscure; and the sign was taken for the reality, and accordingly explained. Hence arose the fable about the bull of Europa, and the like. In all these is the same history under a different allegory and emblem. In the wanderings of Rhea, Isis, Astarte, Iona, and Damater, is figured out the separation of mankind by their families, and their journeying to their places of allotment. At the same time, the dispersion of one particular race of men, and their flight over the face of the earth, is principally described. Of this family were the persons, who preserved the chief memorials of the ark in the Gentile world. They represented it under different emblems, and call it Demater, Pyrrha, Selene, Meen, Argo, Argus, Archas, and Archaius, or Archite. The Grecians," proceeds the learned writer, "by taking this story of the Argo to themselves, have plunged into numberless difficulties. In the account of the Argo, we have undeniably the history of a sacred ship, the first that was ever constructed. This truth the best writers among the Grecians confess, though the merit of the performance they would fain take to themselves. Yet after all their prejudices they continually betrayed the truth, and show that the history was derived to them from Egypt. The cause of all the mistakes in this curious piece of mythology arose from hence. The Arkites, who came into Greece, settled in many parts, but especially in Argolis and Thessalia; where they introduced their rites and worship. In the former of these regions, they were commemorated under a notion of the arrival of Da-naus, or Danaus. It is supposed to have been a person who fled from his brother Ægyptus, and came over in a sacred ship given him by Minerva. This ship, like the Argo, is said to have been the first ship constructed; and he was assisted in the building of it by the same deity, Divine Wisdom. Both histories relate to the same event. Danaus, upon his arrival, built a temple, called Argus, to Iona, or Juno; of which he made his daughters priestesses. The people of the place had an obscure tradition of a deluge, in which most perished, some few only escaping. The principal of these was Deucalion, who took refuge in the acropolis, or temple. Those who settled in Thessaly carried with them the same memorials concerning Deucalion, and his deliverance; which they appropriated to their own country. They must have had traditions of this great event strongly impressed upon their minds; as every place, to which they gave name, had some reference to that history. In process of time, these impressions grew more and more faint, and their emblematical worship became more obscure and unintelligible. Hence they at last confined the history of this event to their own country; and the Argo was supposed to have been built, where it was originally enshrined. As it was reverenced under the symbol of the Moon, called Man or Mon, the people from this circumstance name their country Ai-mona, in after times rendered Aimonia."

This extract from the ingenious and learned mythologist will enable the reader to form some idea of his sentiments on this subject.

But whatever disgust the grave historian may have conceived at this unsightly mixture of the marvellous and the probable, the poet needs not be offended at it. Fiction is his province. He may be allowed to expatiate in the regions of fancy without control, and to introduce his fiery bulls and sleepless dragons without the dread of censure.

The Argonautic expedition has been the admired subject of the Greek and Roman poets from Orpheus, or rather from Onomacritus, who lived in the times of Pisistratus, to those of our author's imitators, who lived in the decline of the Roman empire. To weigh the merits of these ancient poets in the just scale of criticism, and to appropriate to each his due share of praise, is a task too arduous and assuming for an humble editor to engage in. Yet such is the partiality of translators and editors to their favourite poets, that they wish, either to find them seated above their rivals and contemporaries on the summit of Parnassus, or, if possible, to fix them there. But vain are these wishes, unless the testimonies of the first writers of antiquity concur to gratify them. The reputation of Apollonius can neither be impaired nor enhanced by the strictures of Scaliger and Rapin: the judgment of Quintilian and Longinus may, indeed, more materially affect it. They have delivered their opinions on our author in the following words:

Ἐπεῖτοι γε καὶ ἄπτωτος ὁ Ἀπολλώνιος, ὁ τῶν Ἀργοναυτικῶν ποιητής, ἆρ' οὖν Ὅμηρος ἂν μᾶλλον ἢ Ἀπολλώνιος ἐθέλοις γενέσθαι; Sect. xxxiii. Longin. de Sublim.

Non contemnendum edidit opus æquali quadam mediocritate. Quinctil. Inst. Orat. L. x. c. 1.

Unfortunately, as it should seem, for the Rhodian, these celebrated strictures wear the double face of approbation and censure. The praise that is conveyed under the term ἄπλωτος, that he no where sinks, is lost in the implication that he is no where elevated. The expression, non contemnendum opus, apparently a flattering meiosis, is limited to its lowest sense by the subsequent observation, æquali quadam mediocritate. But we must not desert our poet even in this extremity; for, if imitation implies esteem and admiration, Apollonius's noblest eulogy will be found in the writings of Virgil. Those applauded passages in this poet, which are confessedly imitated from our author, may serve as a counterpoise to the sentence of the critics. Apollonius was Virgil's favourite author. He has incorporated into his Æneid his similies and his episodes; and has shown the superiority of his judgment by his just application and arrangement of them.

But it is not the Mantuan poet only, who has fetched from this storehouse the most precious materials. Valerius Flaccus, who has made choice of the same subject with the Rhodian, has discovered through every part of his work a singular predilection for him. He is allowed to have imitated the style of Virgil with tolerable success; but he is indebted for the conduct of his poem chiefly to Apollonius. It is remarkable, that Quintilian, who has objected mediocrity to our author, has mentioned this his closest imitator in terms of the highest respect. Yet must it be confessed, that the genius of Flaccus seldom soars so high, as when it is invigorated and enlightened by the Muse of Apollonius.

But the admiration, in which this writer has been held by the Roman poets, did not expire with them. The rage of imitation, far from ceasing, has caught congenial spirits in every succeeding period; and the most approved passages in this elegant poem have been diffused through the works of the most admired moderns. It were needless to mention any others than Milton and Camoens. Milton's imitations of Apollonius are, many of them, specified in the notes inserted in bishop Newton's valuable edition of all that writer's poetical works. Camoens, who has hitherto been known to the English reader only through the obscure and crude version of Fanshaw, has appeared of late greatly to advantage, in the very animated translation of Mr. Mickle. That the refined taste of Camoens was formed on the model of the Greek and Roman poets, is evident throughout the Lusiad; which abounds in allusions to the pagan mythology, and is enriched with a profusion of graces derived from the ancient classics. In the number of these it can be no disparagement to his poem to reckon Apollonius Rhodius; to the merit of whose work Camoens, if I misjudge not, was no stranger. The subject of the Portuguese poem bears a striking resemblance to that which our author has chosen. For the heroes both of Portugal and Greece traversed unknown seas, in pursuit of the wealth with which an unknown country was expected to supply them. Camoens not only alludes to Argo and her demigods, but seems particularly fond of drawing a comparison betwixt the heroes of his country and those of Thessaly.

Here view thine Argonauts, in seas unknown, &c.
B. i. p. 9.

With such bold rage the youth of Mynia glow'd,
When the first keel the Euxine surges plow'd;
When bravely venturous for the golden fleece,
Orac'lous Argo sail'd from wondering Greece.
B. iv. p. 172.

And soon after;

While each presage that great as Argo's fame,
Our fleet should give some starry band a name.

"The solemnity of the night spent in devotion, the affecting grief of their friends and fellow-citizens, whom they were never more to behold; and the angry exclamations of the venerable old man, give a dignity and interesting pathos to the departure of the fleet of Gama, unborrowed from any of the classics." See the concluding note to B. iv.

Apollonius has admitted into his first book, on a similar occasion, most of the above-mentioned particulars, and many others equally interesting. The prayer of Jason, and the sacrifices previous to their embarkation, are circumstantially related. The lamentations of Alcimeda at the loss of her son, the silent grief of Æson his father, and the tears of his friends, contribute to make this parting scene the most pathetic imaginable. Through the whole of this affecting interview Camoens seems not to have lost sight of Apollonius. But, lest it should be said, that a similarity of situations naturally produces a similarity of sentiments; and that we ought not to interpret a resemblance like this, which might be casual only, to be the effect of studied imitation; another passage may be selected from the Lusiad, which is universally admired for its genuine sublimity, and is affirmed to be the happiest effort of unassisted genius. "The apparition, which in the night hovers athwart the Cape of Good Hope, is the grandest fiction in human composition; the invention his own!" See the dissertation prefixed to Mr. Mickle's translation of the Lusiad.

There is a passage in the third book of Apollonius, to which the description of the apparition at the Cape bears a striking resemblance; I mean, the appearance of the ghost of Sthenelus, standing on his tomb, and surveying the Argonauts as they sail beside him. The description of Camoens is indeed heightened by many additional circumstances, and enriched with a profusion of the boldest images. The colouring is his own; but the first design and outlines of the piece appear to be taken from our poet.

But it is time to quit the imitators of Apollonius, and to give some account of his translators.

Dr. Broome, well known in the literary world for the part he took in the translation of the Odyssey, and for his notes annexed to it, has given an elegant version of the loves of Jason and Medea, and of the story of Talus; which are published with his original poems. Mr. West, who has transfused into his version of the odes of Pindar much of the spirit of his sublime original, has presented us in an English dress with one or two detached pieces from our author. Mr. Ekins has translated the third book, and about two hundred lines of the fourth. Had this gentleman undertaken a version of the whole poem, Mr. Fawkes, I am confident, would have desisted from the attempt. The public has long been in possession of several translations by this latter writer. Those of Anacreon and Theocritus are acknowledged to have considerable merit. The work before us was undertaken at the request of Mr. Fawkes's particular friends: and the encreasing number of his subscribers encouraged him to persevere in his design; but the completion of it was prevented by the premature stroke of fate. What part the editor has taken in this work, is a matter of too small importance to need an explanation. But lest his motive should be mistaken, and vanity should be supposed to have instigated what friendship only suggested, he begs leave to add, as the best apology he can offer for engaging in this work; that with no other ambition than to assist his friend, did he comply with his solicitations to become his coadjutor; and with no other motive does he now appear as his editor, than to enable the widow to avail herself of those generous subscriptions, for which she takes occasion here to make her thankful acknowledgments.

March 27, 1780.

THE

ARGONAUTICS

OF

APOLLONIUS RHODIUS.

TRANSLATED BY FAWKES.

BOOK I.

THE ARGUMENT.

This book commences with the list and character of the Argonauts. Before they embark, two of the chiefs quarrel; but are pacified by the harmony of Orpheus. They set sail, and land at Lemnos, an island inhabited by female warriors; who, though they had slain their husbands and turned Amazons, are so charmed with these heroes, that they admit them to their beds. Thence they sail to the country of the Dolions, and are kindly received by their king Cyzicus. Loosing from thence in the night, and being driven back by contrary winds, they are mistaken for Pelasgians, with whom the Dolions were then at war. A battle ensues, in which Cyzicus and many of his men are slain. The morning discovers the unhappy mistake. Thence they sail to Mysia. Hercules breaks his oar; and while he is gone into a wood to make a new one, Hylas is stolen by a nymph, as he is stooping for water at a fountain. Hercules and Polyphemus go in search of him. Meanwhile the Argonauts leave them behind, and sail to Bithynia.

INSPIR'D by thee, O Phœbus, I resound
The glorious deeds of heroes long renown'd,
Whom Pelias urg'd the golden fleece to gain,
And well-built Argo wafted o'er the main,
Through the Cyanean rocks. The voice divine
Pronounc'd this sentence from the sacred shrine;
" Ere long, and dreadful woes, foredoom'd by fate,
Thro' that man's counsels shall on Pelias wait,
Whom he, before the altar of his god,
Shall view in public with one sandal shod."
And, lo! as by this oracle foretold,
What time adventurous Jason, brave and bold,
Anaurus past, high swoln with winter's flood,
He left one sandal rooted in the mud.
To Pelias, thus, the hasty prince repair'd,
And the rich banquet at his altar shar'd:
The stately altar, with oblations stor'd,
Was to his sire erected, ocean's lord,
And every power that in Olympus reigns,
Save Juno, regent of Thessalia's plains.
Pelias, whose looks his latent fears express'd,
Fir'd with a bold adventure Jason's breast;
That, sunk in ocean, or on some rude shore
Prostrate, he ne'er might view his country more.
Old bards affirm this warlike ship was made
By skilful Argus, with Minerva's aid.
'Tis mine to sing the chiefs, their names and race,
Their tedious wanderings on the main to trace,
And all their great achievements to rehearse:
Deign, ye propitious Nine, to aid my verse.
First in the list, to join the princely bands,
The tuneful bard, enchanting Orpheus, stands;
Whom fair Calliope, on Thracia's shore,
Near Pimpla's mount, to bold Œägrus bore.
Hard rocks he soften'd with persuasive song,
And sooth'd the rivers as they roll'd along.

Yon beeches tall, that bloom near Zona, still
Remain memorials of his vocal skill:
His lays Pieria's listening trees admire,
And move in measures to his melting lyre.
Thus Orpheus charm'd, who o'er the Bistons reign'd,
By Chiron's art to Jason's interest gain'd.
Asterion next; whose sire rejoic'd to till
Piresian valleys by Phylleion's hill,
Born near Apidanus, who sportive leads
His winding waters thro' the fertile meads;
There where, from far, Enipeus, stream divine,
And wide Apidanus their currents join.
The son of Elatus, of deathless fame,
From fair Larissa, Polyphemus came.
Long since, when in the vigour of his might,
He join'd the hardy Lapithæ in fight
Against the Centaurs; now his strength declin'd
Thro' age, yet young and martial was his mind.
Not long at Phylace Iphiclus staid,
Great Jason's uncle; pleas'd he join'd his aid,
And march'd to meet th' adventurous band from far,
Urg'd by affinity and love of war.
Nor long Admetus, who at Pheræ reign'd,
Near high Chalcodon's bleating fields remain'd.
Echion, Erytus, for wiles renown'd,
Left Alope, with golden harvests crown'd;
The gainful sons of Mercury: with these
Their brother came, the bold Æthalides;
Whom fair Eupolema, the Phthian, bore
Where smooth Amphrysos rolls his watery store:
Those, Menetus, from thy fair daughter sprung,
Antianira, beautiful and young.
Coronus came, from Gyrton's wealthy town,
Great as his sire in valour and renown,
Cæneus his sire; who, as old bards relate,
Receiv'd from Centaurs his untimely fate.
Alone, unaided, with transcendent might,
Boldly he fac'd, and put his foes to flight.
But they, reviving soon, regain'd their ground;
Yet fail'd to vanquish, and they could not wound.
Unbroke, unmov'd, the chief his breath resigns,
O'erwhelm'd beneath a monument of pines.
From Titaresus Mopsus bent his way,
Inspir'd an augur by the god of day.
Eurydamas, to share fair honour's crown,
Forsook near Xynias' lake his native town,
Nam'd Ctimena: Menœtius join'd the band,
Dismiss'd from Opuns by his sire's command.
Next came Eurytion, Irus' valiant son,
And Eribotes, seed of Teleon.
Oïleus join'd these heroes, fam'd afar
For stratagems and fortitude in war;
Well skill'd the hostile squadrons to subdue,
Bold in attack, and ardent to pursue.
Next, by Canethus, son of Abans, sent,
Ambitious Canthus from Eubœa went;
Doom'd ne'er again to reach his native shore,
Nor view the towers of proud Cerinthus more.
For thus decreed the destinies severe,
That he and Mopsus, venerable seer,
After long toils and various wanderings past,
On Afric's dreary coast should breathe their last.
How short the term assign'd to human woe,
Clos'd, as it is, by death's decisive blow!
On Afric's dreary coast their graves were made,
From Phasis distant far their bones were laid;
Far as the east and western limits run,
Far as the rising from the setting Sun.
Clytius and Iphitus unite their aid,
Who all the country round Œchalia sway'd;
These were the sons of Eurytus the proud,
On whom his bow the god of day bestow'd;
But he, devoid of gratitude, defy'd,
And challeng'd Phœbus with a rival's pride.
The sons of Æacus, intrepid race!
Separate advanc'd, and from a different place.
For when their brother unawares they slew,
From fair Ægina diverse they withdrew.
Fair Salamis king Tèlamon obey'd,
And valiant Peleus Phthia's sceptre sway'd.
Next Butes came from fam'd Cecropia far,
Brave Teleon's son, a chief renown'd in war.
To wield the deadly lance Phalerus boasts,
Who, by his sire commission'd, joins the hosts:
No son, save this, e'er bless'd the hoary sage,
And this Heaven gave him in declining age:
Yet him he sent, disdaining abject fears,
To shine conspicuous 'midst his gallant peers.
Theseus, far more than all his race renown'd,
Fast in the cave of Tænarus was bound
With adamantine fetters, (dire abode!)
E'er since he trod th' irremeable road
With his belov'd Pirithoüs: had they sail'd,
Much had their might, their courage much avail'd.
Bœotian Tiphys came, experienc'd well
Old ocean's foaming surges to foretell,
Experienc'd well the stormy winds to shun,
And steer his vessel by the stars, or Sun.
Minerva urg'd him by her high command,
A welcome mate to join the princely band.
For she the ship had form'd with heavenly skill,
Tho' Argus wrought the dictates of her will.
Thus plann'd, thus fashion'd, this fam'd ship excell'd
The noblest ships by oar or sail impell'd.
From Aræthyrea, that near Corinth lay,
Phlias, the son of Bacchus, bent his way:
Bless'd by his sire, his splendid mansion stood
Fast by the fountains of Asopus' flood.
From Argos next the sons of Bias came,
Areius, Talaus, candidates for fame,
With bold Leodocus, whom Pero bore,
Neleus' fair daughter, on the Argive shore;
For whom Melampus various woes sustain'd,
In a deep dungeon by Iphiclus chain'd.
Next Hercules, endued with dauntless mind,
At Jason's summons, stay'd not long behind.
For warn'd of this adventurous band, when last
The chief to Argos from Arcadia past,
(What time in chains he brought the living boar,
The dread, the bane of Erymanthia's moor,
And at the gate of proud Mycenæ's town,
From his broad shoulders hurl'd the monster down:)
Unask'd the stern Mycenian king's consent,
Instant to join the warlike host he went.
Young Hylas waited with obsequious care,
The hero's quiver and his bow to bear.
Next came, the list of demigods to grace,
He who from Danaüs deriv'd his race,
Nauplius; of whom fam'd Prætus was the son,
Of Prætus Lernus; thus the lineage run:
From Lernus Naubolus his being claim'd,
Whose valiant son was Clytoneüs nam'd.
In navigation's various arts confess'd
Shone Nauplius' skill, superior to the rest:
Him to the sea's dread lord, in days of yore,
Danaüs' fair daughter, Amymone bore.
Last of those chiefs who left the Grecian coast,
Prophetic Idmon join'd the gallant host;

(Full well he knew what cruel fate ordain'd;
But dreaded more than death his honour stain'd)
The son of Phœbus by some stolen embrace,
And number'd too with Æolus's race.
He learn'd his art prophetic from his sire,
Omens from birds, and prodigies from fire.
Illustrious Pollux, fam'd for martial force,
And Castor, skill'd to guide the rapid horse,
Ætolian Leda sent from Sparta's shore:
Both at one birth in Tyndarus' house she bore.
No boding fears her generous mind depress'd;
She thought like them whom Jove's embrace had bless'd.
Lynceus and Idas, from Arene's wall
Heard Fame's loud summons, and obey'd her call:
The sons of Aphareus, of matchless might,
But Lynceus stands renown'd for piercing sight:
So keen his beam, that ancient fables tell,
He saw, thro' Earth, the wondrous depths of Hell.
With these bold Periclymenus appears,
The son of Neleus, most advanc'd in years
Of all his race; his sire's unconquer'd pride:
Him with vast strength old ocean's lord supply'd,
And gave the power, when hard in battle press'd,
To take whatever form might suit him best.
From Tegea's towers, where bore Aphidas sway,
Amphidamas and Cepheus took their way,
The sons of Aleus both; and with them went
Ancæus, by his sire Lycurgus sent.
Of those the brother, and by birth the first,
Was good Lycurgus; tenderly he nurs'd
His sire at home; but bade his gallant son
With the bold chiefs the race of glory run.
On his broad back a bear's rough spoils he wore,
And in his hand a two-edg'd pole-axe bore,
Which, that the youth might in no danger share,
Were safe secreted by his grandsire's care.
Augeas too, lord of the Elean coast,
Sail'd, brave associate, with the warlike host.
Rich in possessions, of his riches proud,
Fame says his being to the Sun he ow'd.
Ardent he wish'd to see the Colchian shore,
And old Æeta who the sceptre bore.
Asterius and Amphion, urg'd by fame,
The valiant sons of Hyperasius, came
From fair Pellene, built in days of yore
By Pelle's grandsire on the lofty shore.
From Tænarus, that yawns with gulf profound,
Euphemus came, for rapid race renown'd.
By Neptune forc'd, Europa give him birth,
Daughter to Tityus, hugest son of Earth.
Whene'er he skimm'd along the watery plain,
With feet unbath'd he swept the surging main,
Scarce brush'd the surface of the briny dew,
And light along the liquid level flew.
Two other sons of Neptune join'd the host,
This from Miletus on th' Ionian coast,
Erginus nam'd, but that from Samos came,
Juno's lov'd isle, Ancæus was his name;
Illustrious chiefs, and both renown'd afar
For the joint arts of sailing and of war.
Young Meleager, Œneus' warlike son,
And sage Laocoon march'd from Calydon.
From the same father he and Œneus sprung;
But on the breasts of different mothers hung.
Him Œneus purpos'd with his son to send,
A wise companion, and a faithful friend.
Thus to the royal chiefs his name he gave,
And green in years was number'd with the brave.
Had he continu'd but one summer more
A martial pupil on th' Ætolian shore,
First on the lists of fame the youth had shone,
Or own'd superior Hercules alone.
His uncle too, well-skill'd the dart to throw,
And in th' embattled plain resist the foe,
Iphiclus, venerable Thestius' son,
Join'd the young chief, and boldly led him on.
The son of Lernus, Palæmonius, came,
Olenian Lernus; but the voice of Fame
Whispers, that Vulcan was the hero's sire,
And therefore limps he like the god of fire.
Of nobler port or valour none could boast;
He added grace to Jason's godlike host.
From Phocis Iphitus with ardour press'd
To join the chiefs; great Jason was his guest,
When to the Delphic Oracle he went,
Consulting fate, and anxious for th' event.
Zetes and Calaïs of royal race,
Whom Orithyïa bore in wintry Thrace
To blustering Boreas in his airy hall,
Heard Fame's loud summons, and obey'd the call.
Erectheus, who th' Athenian sceptre sway'd,
Was parent of the violated maid,
Whom dancing with her mates rude Boreas stole,
Where the fam'd waters of Ilissus roll;
And to his rock-fenc'd Sarpedonian cave
Convey'd her, where Erginus pours his wave:
There, circumfus'd in gloom and grateful shade,
The god of tempests woo'd the gentle maid.
They, when on tip-toe rais'd, in act to fly,
Like the light-pinion'd vagrants of the sky,
Wav'd their dark wings, and, wondrous to behold!
Display'd each plume distinct with drops of gold;
While down their backs, of bright cerulean hue,
Loose in the winds their wanton tresses flew.
Not long with Pelias young Acastus stay'd;
He left his sire to lend the Grecians aid.
Argus, whom Pallas with her gifts inspir'd,
Follow'd his friend, with equal glory fir'd.
  Such the compeers of Jason, highly fam'd;
And all these demigods were Minyans nam'd.
The most illustrious heroes of the host
Their lineage from the seed of Minyas boast:
For Mianys' daughter, Clymena the fair,
Alcimeda, great Jason's mother, bare.
  When all was furnish'd by the busy band
Which vessels destin'd for the main demand;
The heroes from Iölcos bent their way,
To the fam'd port, the Pagásæan bay
And deep-environ'd with thick-gathering crowds,
They shone like stars resplendent thro' the clouds.
Then thus among the rout, with wondering look,
Some swain survey'd the bright-arm'd chiefs and spoke:
"Say, what can Pelias, mighty Jove, intend,
Far, far from Greece so great a force to send!
Sure, should Æeta spurn the sons of Greece,
And to their claims refuse the golden fleece,
That self-same day shall see his palace, crown'd
With glittering turrets, levell'd to the ground.
But endless toils pursue them as they go,
And Fate hath mark'd their desperate steps with woe."
Thus, when he saw the delegated bands,
Spoke the rude swain with heaven-uplifted hands:
The gentler females thus the gods implore;
"Safe may they reach again their native shore:"
And thus some matron mild her mind express'd;
(Tears in her eye, and terrours at her breast)
"Unfortunate Alcimeda, thy fate
Now frowns malignant, tho' it frowns so late;

Nor wills the tenour of thy life to run
Serene and peaceful, as it first begun.
On Æson too attend unnumber'd woes;
Far, better far, a lingering life to close,
And bury all his sorrows in the tomb,
Unconscious of calamities to come.
Oh! had both Phrixus and the ram been drown'd,
When Helle perish'd in the gulf profound:
But the dire monster was with voice endu'd,
And human accents from his mouth ensu'd,
To sad Alcimeda denouncing strife,
And woes to cloud the evening of her life."
Thus spoke some matron as the heroes went;
Around their lords the menial train lament:
Alcimeda embrac'd her son with tears,
Each breast was chill'd with sad presaging fears.
Age-drooping Æson heard the general moan,
Wrapp'd in soft robes, and answer'd groan for groan.
But Jason sooths their fears, their bosom warms,
And bids his servants bring the burnish'd arms.
They, with a downcast look and lowly bow,
Obey their chief with silent steps and slow.
The pensive queen, while tears bedew her face,
Her son still circles with a fond embrace.
Thus to her nurse an infant orphan springs,
And weeps unceasing as she closely clings;
Experienc'd insults make her loath to stay
Beneath a step-dame's proud, oppressive sway.
Thus in her royal breast the sorrows pent
Forc'd sighs and tears, and struggled for a vent.
Still in her arms she held her favourite son,
And comfortless with faltering speech begun:
"Oh had I died on that detested day,
And with my sorrows sigh'd my soul away,
When Pelias publish'd his severe decree,
Severe and fatal to my son and me!
Thyself had then my aged eyelids clos'd,
And those dear hands my decent limbs compos'd;
This boon alone I wish'd thee to impart,
This wish alone lay dormant at my heart.
But now, alas! tho' first of Grecian names,
Admir'd and envy'd by Thessalian dames,
I, like an hand-maid, now am left behind,
Bereav'd of all tranquillity of mind.
By thee rever'd, in dignity I shone,
And first and last for thee unloos'd my zone,
For unrelenting hate Lucina bore,
Thee, one lov'd son, she gave, but gave no more.
Alas! not ev'n the visions of the night
Foretold such fatal woes from Phrixus' flight."
Thus mourn'd Alcimeda; her handmaids hear,
Sigh back her sighs, and answer tear with tear.
Then Jason these consoling words address'd,
To sooth the rising anguish of her breast:
"Cease, mother, cease excess of grief to show,
Oh! cease this wild extravagance of woe.
Tears cannot make one dire disaster less;
They cherish grief, and aggravate distress.
Wisely and justly have the gods assign'd;
Unthought-of miseries to all mankind.
The lot they give you, though perchance severe,
Confiding in Minerva, bravely bear.
Minerva first this bold adventure mov'd,
Apollo, and the Oracles approv'd.
These calls of Heaven our confidence command,
Join'd with the valour of this princely band.
Haste, royal mother, to your native tow'rs,
Pass with your handmaids there the peaceful hours.
Forebode not here calamities to come:
Your female train will re-conduct you home."
He spoke; and from the palace bent his way,
Graceful of port; so moves the god of day
At Delos, from his odour-breathing fanes,
Or Claros situate on Ionian plains,
Or Lycia's ample shores, where Xanthus leads
His winding waters thro' irriguous meads.
Thus Jason march'd majestic thro' the crowd;
And Fame auspicious rais'd her voice aloud:
When lo! the priestess of Diana came,
Their guardian goddess, Iphias was her name,
Bending with age, and kiss'd the chief's right hand;
In vain she wish'd to speak; the hasty band
With speedy footsteps from the dame withdrew,
And Jason mingled with his valiant crew.
Then from the tower-fenc'd town he bent his way,
And reach'd ere long the Pagasæan bay;
There join'd his comrades waiting on the coast,
And there saluted his confederate host.
When from Iölcos, lo, the wondering train
Observe Acastus hastening o'er the plain,
And with him Argus, his compeer and friend;
Unknown to Pelias, to the ship they tend.
Argus around his brawny shoulders flung
A bull's black spoils that to his ancles hung.
Acastus wore a mantle, rich and gay,
Wrought by his sister, lovely Pelopa.
Thus rob'd, the chiefs approach'd the crowded shore;
Illustrious Jason stay'd not to explore
What cause so long detain'd them, but commands
To council all the delegated bands.
On shrouds and sails that cover'd half the beach,
And the tall, tapering mast, in order each,
The heroes sat; then rising o'er the rest,
His bold associates Jason thus address'd:
"Since now the stores lie ready on the strand,
And since our chiefs and arms are all at hand,
No longer let us waste the golden day,
But the first summons of the breeze obey.
And, since we all with equal ardour burn
For Colchian spoils, and hope a safe return,
Impartial choose some hero fam'd afar
To guide the vessel, and conduct the war;
Let him, your sovereign chief, with foreign foes
The terms of treaty, and of fight propose."
He spoke; with earnest eyes the youthful band
Mark bold Alcides for supreme command;
On him with voice unanimous they call,
Own him their leader, and the lord of all.
In the mid circle sat the godlike man,
His broad right hand he wav'd, and thus began:
"Let none to me this arduous task assign,
For I the glory with the charge decline.
Jason alone shall lead this valiant band,
The chief who rais'd it, let that chief command."
Thus briefly spoke th' unconquerable man;
Loud approbation thro' the circle ran:
Then Jason rose, (complacence fill'd his breast)
And thus the pleas'd, attentive throng address'd:
"Friends and associates, since your wills decree
This great, this honourable trust to me,
No longer be our enterprise delay'd:
To Phœbus first be due oblations paid;
Let then a short repast our strength renew:
And, till my herdsmen to our gallant crew
With beeves return, the best my stalls contain,
Strive we to lanch our vessel in the main.

And when close stow'd our military stores,
Each take his post, and ply the nimble oars.
To Phœbus first, Embasian Phœbus, raise
The smoking altar; let the victims blaze.
He promis'd, if due rites to him I pay,
To point thro' ocean's paths our dubious way."
He said, and instant to the task he flew;
Example fir'd his emulative crew.
They heap'd their vestments on a rock, that stood
Far from the insults of the roaring flood,
But, in times past, when wintry storms prevail'd,
Th' encroaching waves its towering top assail'd.
As Argus counsel'd, with strong ropes they bound,
Compacting close, the vessel round and round;
Then with stout nails the sturdy planks they join'd,
To brave the fury of the waves or wind:
Next delv'd with spades a channel deep and wide,
Thro' which the ship might lanch into the tide.
Near to the water deeper was the way,
Where wooden cylinders transversely lay;
On these they heav'd the vessel from the plain,
To roll her, smoothly-gliding, to the main.
Then to the benches, tapering oars they fix'd;
A cubit's measure was the space betwixt:
This was the station for the labouring bands,
To tug with bending breasts, and out-stretch'd hands.
First Tiphys mounted on th' aerial prow
To issue orders to the train below,
That at his word, their strength uniting, all
Might join together, and together haul.
With eager look th' attentive heroes stand,
And wait impatient till he gave command;
Then all at once, with full exerted sway,
They move her from the station where she lay,
And pushing instant, as the pilot guides,
On smooth round rollers Pelian Argo glides;
Glibly she glides; loud shouts the jovial band;
They haul, they pull, they push her from the strand.
Beneath the huge hulk groan the rollers strong;
Black smoke arises as she moves along;
With swift descent she rushes to the main:
Coercive ropes her rapid race restrain.
Then, next, their sails they hoisted, fix'd their oars,
The mast erected, and embark'd the stores.
By lots on benches were the heroes plac'd,
And with two heroes every bench was grac'd.
On great Alcides, formidable name,
And on Ancæus, who from Tegea came,
With voice unanimous the martial host
Bestow'd the centre's honourable post.
To watchful Tiphys was the helm assign'd,
To stem the waves, and catch the favouring wind.
This done, with stones beside the shore which lay,
They rear'd an altar to the god of day,
Embasian Phœbus, and the surface round
With the dry branches of an olive crown'd.
Meanwhile the herdsman drove two beeves well fed
From Jason's stalls; youths to the altar led
The victims; some brought water from the lake;
Some the due offering of the salted cake.
Jason, while these the sacrifice prepare,
Thus to his parent god prefers his pray'r:
"Patron of Pagasæ, thine ear we claim,
Guard of the city grac'd with Æson's name:
When to consult thine oracle I went,
It promis'd to reveal this great event,
The final issue of our bold emprise:
On thee, chief author, all our hope relies.
Conduct my comrades to the far-fam'd fleece,
Then safe restore them to the realms of Greece.
And here I vow, whatever chiefs return,
So many bulls shall on thine altar burn;
A sacrifice at Delphos is decreed,
And in Ortygia shall the victims bleed.
But now these humble offerings which we pay,
Gracious accept, far-darting god of day.
Be thou, O father, our auspicious guide,
When hence we sail across the sounding tide.
Smooth the rough billows, and let breezes bland
Propitious waft us to the Colchian land."
Thus pray'd he suppliant, and prepar'd to make
The sacred offering of the salted cake.
Alcides, fam'd for manly strength and sway,
And bold Ancæus rose the beeves to slay.
Alcides' club impress'd a deadly wound
On the steer's front, and felled him to the ground.
Thy axe, Ancæus, at one sturdy stroke,
The steer's skull fractur'd, and the neck-bone broke,
Down fell the victim, floundering with the blow,
Prone on his horns, and plough'd the sand below.
The ready train, that round in order stood,
Stab the fallen beeves, and shed the life-warm blood;
Then from the body strip the smoking hide,
The beasts they quarter, and the joints divide;
The thighs devoted to the gods they part,
On these the fat, involv'd in cawls, with art
They spread, and as the lambent flame devours,
The Grecian chief the pure libation pours.
Joy fill'd the breast of Idmon to behold,
How from the thighs the flame relucent roll'd
In purple volumes, and propitious smoke;
And thus the seer, inspir'd by Phœbus, spoke:
"Tho' various perils your attempt oppose,
And toils unnumber'd bring unnumber'd woes;
Yet shall ye safe return, ye sons of Greece,
Adorn'd with conquest, and the golden fleece.
Me cruel Fate ordains on Asia's shore
To die, nor e'er behold my country more.
And tho' my destiny long fix'd I knew,
Yet, still resolv'd, I join'd the martial crew;
Inflam'd with glory to the host I came,
Of life regardless, emulous of fame."
Thus he; the host the fate of Idmon mourn,
But joy transports them for their wish'd return.
The Sun, remitting now his fiercer ray,
Pours from the west the faint remains of day:
Low as he sinks, the lofty rocks expand
Their lengthen'd shadows o'er the distant land.
On leafy couches now the warlike train
Repose along the beach that skirts the main.
Before the chiefs are savoury viands plac'd,
And generous wines, delicious to the taste.
The hours in mutual converse they employ,
In festive songs and undissembled joy.
Thus at the banquet sport the young and gay,
When Mirth breaks in, and Envy skulks away.
But not unmark'd was Jason's pensive look;
Idas beheld him, and licentious spoke:
"What doubts, what fears do Æson's son perplex?
What dangers fright him, and what sorrows vex?
Proclaim thy thoughts: or is thy dubious mind
Dismay'd with terrours of the dastard kind?
Now by this stout, unconquer'd lance, I swear,
On which in war victorious wreaths I bear,
(Scorning from Jove's assistance to receive
Those palms, which this resistless lance can give)

No foes shall brave, no wiles of war withstand,
Tho' Jove frown adverse, this impetuous hand.
Such Idas is, for prowess fam'd afar,
Arene's boast, the thunder-bolt of war."
This said, the boaster seiz'd a goblet, fill'd
With racy wine, and to the bottom swill'd.
O'er his black beard and cheeks the liquor flow'd:
Th' assembled host with indignation glow'd.
Then Idmon rose and boldly thus reply'd:
"Vain wretch! to brand our leader and our guide;
And more irreverent still, thus flush'd with wine,
To dare reproach superior powers divine.
Far different speech must cheer the social train;
Thy words are brutish, and thy boasts are vain.
Thus, Fame reports, the Aloïdæ strove
Long since to irritate the powers above
By vile aspersions, infamously free;
Yet they in valour far exceeded thee.
Slain by the shafts of Phœbus, down they fell,
Tho' high aspiring, to the depths of Hell."
He said; but Idas, with sarcastic sneer,
Laughing, provok'd the venerable seer:
"Declare, wise augur, if the gods decree,
The same perdition shall be hurl'd on me,
Which fam'd Aloëus' impious sons befel
When slain by Phœbus, and condemn'd to Hell.
Meantime escape, or manfully withstand,
Vain seer, the fury of this vengeful hand."
Thus Idas spoke, impatient of control,
And rising rage inflam'd his fiery soul;
Nor had they here ceas'd fiercely to contest,
But Jason and his friends their wrath repress'd.
'Twas then, the jarring heroes to compose,
Th' enchanting bard, Œagrian Orpheus rose,
And thus, attuning to the trembling strings
His soothing voice, of harmony he sings:
"How at the first, beneath chaotic sway,
Heaven, earth and sea, in wild disorder lay;
Till Nature parted the conflicting foes,
And beauteous order from confusion rose.
How in yon bright etherial fields above
The lucid stars in constant orbits move;
How the pale queen of night and golden Sun,
Thro' months and years their radiant journeys run:
Whence rose the mountains, clad with waving woods,
The crystal founts, and hoarse-resounding floods,
With all their nymphs; from what celestial seed
Springs the vast species of the serpent breed:
How o'er the new-created world below,
On high Olympus' summits crown'd with snow,
Ophion, and, from Oean sprung of old,
The fair Eurynome reign'd uncontroll'd:
How haughty Saturn, with superior sway,
Exil'd Ophion from the realms of day;
Eurynome before proud Rhea fled,
And how both sunk in ocean's billowy bed.
Long time they rul'd the blest Titanian gods,
While infant Jove possess'd the dark abodes
Of Dictè's cave; yet uninform'd his mind
With heavenly wisdom, and his hand confin'd.
Forg'd by Earth's giant sons, with livid rays
Flam'd not as yet the lightning's piercing blaze;
Nor roar'd the thunder thro' the realms above,
The strength and glory of almighty Jove."
Here the sweet bard his tuneful lyre unstrung,
And ceas'd the heavenly music of his tongue;
But, with the sound entranc'd, the listening ear
Still thought him singing, and still seem'd to hear:
In silent rapture every chief remains,
And feels within his heart the thrilling strains.
Forthwith the bowl they crown with rosy wine,
And pay due honours to the powers divine;
Then on the flaming tongues libations pour,
And wait salubrious sleep's composing hour.
Soon as the bright-ey'd morning's splendid ray
On Pelion's summit pour'd the welcome day,
Light skimm'd the breezes o'er the liquid plain,
And gently swell'd the fluctuating main;
Then Tiphys rose, and, summon'd by his care,
Embark the heroes, and their oars prepare.
Portentous now along the winding shores
Hoarse sounding Pagasæan Neptune roars:
From Pelian Argo's keel loud murmurs broke,
Urgent to sail; the keel of sacred oak,
Endu'd with voice, and marvellously wrought,
Itonian Pallas from Dodona brought.
Now on their destin'd posts, arrang'd along,
In seemly order sat the princely throng;
Fast by each chief his glittering armour flames:
The midmost station bold Ancæus claims,
With great Alcides, (whose enormous might
Arm'd with a massy club provokes the fight,)
Close plac'd beside him: in the yielding flood
The keel deep-sinking owns the demigod.
Their hausers now they loose, and on the brine
To Neptune pour the consecrated wine:
Then from his native shore sad Jason turns
His oft-reverted eye, and silent mourns.
As in Ortygia, or the Delphic fane,
Or where Ismenus laves Bœotia's plain,
Apollo's altar round, the youthful quire,
The dance according with the sounding lyre,
The hallow'd ground with equal cadence beat,
And move in measure their alternate feet;
Together so Thessalia's princes sweep
With well-tim'd oars the silver-curling deep:
While, raising high the Thracian harp, presides
Melodious Orpheus, and the movement guides.
Dash'd by their oars the foaming billows broke,
And loud remurmur'd to each mighty stroke.
Swift sail'd the ship, the Sun refulgent beam'd,
And bright as flame their glittering armour gleam'd.
While to their outstretch'd oars the heroes bow,
The parted ocean whitening foams below.
So shines the path, along some grassy plain,
Worn by the foosteps of the village-swain.
Th' immortal powers that Jove's proud palace crown,
All on that memorable day look'd down,
The godlike chiefs and Argo to survey,
As thro' the deep they urg'd their daring way.
Then too on Pelion's cloud-capt summit stood
The nymphs that wander in that sacred wood;
Wondering they view'd below the sailing pine,
(Itonian Pallas fram'd the work divine)
And bold Thessalia's labouring hero sweep
With stretching oars the navigable deep.
Lo! from the mountain's topmost cliff descends
The Centaur Chiron; to the shore he bends
His hasty footsteps: on the beach he stood,
And dipp'd his fetlocks in the hoary flood.
He hail'd the heroes with his big, broad hand,
And wish'd them safe to gain their native land.
With Chiron came Chariclo to the shore;
The young Achilles in her arms she bore.
Peleus, his sire, with secret pleasure smil'd,
As high in air she rais'd the royal child.
And now the winding bay's safe precincts past,
Thessalian Argo plough'd the watery waste;

On Tiphys' care the valiant chiefs rely'd,
To steer the vessel o'er the foaming tide,
The smooth well-modell'd rudder to command,
Obsequious to the movement of his hand.
And next inserting in the keel below
The mast tall-tapering, to the stern and prow,
With ropes that thro' the rolling pulleys glide,
They rear upright, and firm on every side.
Then high in air the swelling sails they raise,
While on their bosoms buxom Zephyr plays.
With favouring gales their steady course they keep
To where Tisæum frowns upon the deep.
Meanwhile sweet Orpheus, as they sail'd along,
Rais'd to Diana the melodious song,
Who sav'd them, where her guardian power presides,
From treacherous rocks that lurk beneath the tides.
The fish in shoals, attentive to his lay,
Pursu'd the poet o'er the watery way;
And oft emerging from their liquid sphere,
Strove more distinct his heavenly notes to hear.
As sheep in flocks thick-pasturing on the plain
Attend the footsteps of the shepherd-swain,
His well-known call they hear, and fully fed,
Pace slowly on, their leader at their head;
Who pipes melodious, as he moves along,
On sprightly reeds his modulated song:
Thus charm'd with tuneful sounds, the scaly train
Pursu'd the flying vessel o'er the main.
And now the winds with favouring breezes blew,
Corn-crown'd Thessalia lessen'd to the view,
The Grecian heroes pass by Pelion's steep,
Whose rocky summit nodded o'er the deep.
Now Sepias' cliffs beneath the waves subside,
And sea-girt Sciathos surmounts the tide.
Next, but far distant, was Piresiæ seen,
(Built on Magnesia's continent serene)
And Dolops' tomb, for this pacific shore,
Blest with mild evening's soften'd gales, they bore.
To him with victims was an altar crown'd,
While night prevail'd, and ocean roar'd around.
Two days they tarried, till propitious gales
Rose with the third, and bellied all their sails.
Assiduous then, the well-known shore they fill,
The shore call'd Aphetæ of Argo still.
Next Melibœa, on Thessalia's shore,
They pass, where winds and thundering tempests roar.
At early dawn, incumbent o'er the deep,
They view high Omole's aspiring steep.
Next by the streams of Amyrus they steer,
And where thy vales, Eurymena, appear,
And Ossa and Olympus' shady brow;
Loud from deep caverns gush the waves below.
By night beside Pallene's heights they sail,
And rough Canastra frowning o'er the vale.
But when the morn display'd her orient light,
Tall Athos rose conspicuous to the sight;
Which tho' from Lemnos far remov'd it lay,
As far as ships can sail till noon of day,
Yet the proud mountain's high-exalted head,
A gloom umbrageous o'er Myrina spread.
All day till eve the soft, indulgent gales
Their succour lent, and fill'd the swelling sails.
But when with eve the breezes ceas'd to blow,
The mariners to Sintian Lemnos row,
Ill-fated island! where the female train
Had all the males, the year preceding, slain.
For, deep-enamour'd with the nymphs of Thrace,
The men declin'd the conjugal embrace;
Their wives they slighted, and unwary led
War's pleasing spoils, fair captives, to their bed.
For angry Venus robb'd of love's delights
The Lemnian females, for neglected rites.
Ah miserable train! with envy curs'd
And jealousy, of passions far the worst!
One fatal night this unrelenting crew
Their mates, and all the lovely captives, slew,
And every male; lest in the course of time
Should rise some hero to revenge the crime.
Hypsipyla alone, illustrious maid,
Spar'd her sire Thoas, who the sceptre sway'd.
With pious care, in reverence to his age,
In a capacious ark she plac'd the sage,
Confiding in the mercy of the wave
The monarch from the massacre to save.
Some faithful fishers, to their mandate just,
Convey'd with care the delegated trust
Safe to a neighbouring, sea-surrounded shore,
Œnœa nam'd, so nam'd in days of yore,
Now Sicinum; from Sicinus it takes
Its title, whom a naiad of the lakes,
The nymph Œnœa, beautiful and fair,
Compress'd by Thoas, to the monarch bare.
The widow'd Lemnians, tho' by waves secur'd,
Oft shone in arms, to martial toils inur'd.
To feed their cattle was their daily care,
Or cleave the furrow with the crooked share:
Expert at these, Minerva's arts they scorn'd,
Which once employ'd them, and which once adorn'd.
Oft to the main, oppress'd with dire alarms,
They look'd; for much they fear'd the Thracian arms.
And when Thessalian Argo caught their view,
Quick from Myrina to the shore they flew.
All clad in glittering arms they press'd the strand,
Impetuous; (like the Bacchanalian band,
When with raw flesh their horrid feasts they close;)
They deem'd the vessel stor'd with Thracian foes.
Hypsipyla advanc'd among the rest,
In the bright armour of her father dress'd;
Anxious, astonish'd all the dames appear,
And by their silence testified their fear.
Meanwhile Æthalides the heroes send;
To him their peaceful mandates they commend.
Invested with the office of the god,
They grace their herald too with Hermes' rod,
Hermes his sire; who bless'd his favourite heir
With memory nor time, nor place impair.
In vain around him Acheron's waters roll;
They pour no dull oblivion o'er his soul.
To him the fates this privilege bestow,
By turns to wander with the shades below;
By turns with men to view the golden day,
And feel the Sun's invigorating ray.
But why expatiate on such themes as these?
Why tell the fame of great Æthalides?
The herald to Hypsipyla address'd,
With mild benevolence, this joint request;
That now, at evening-close, the friendly land
Might hospitably treat this gallant band,
Who fear'd at morn to hoist their swelling sails,
For Boreas blew with unpropitious gales.

The queen had summon'd to the council-hall
The Lemnian dames, the dames obey'd her call:
Who mildly, with persuasion in her look,
In order rang'd, the heroines bespoke:
"Let us, my mates, and ye my words attend,
Commodious presents to these strangers send;
Such as their friends to mariners consign,
Salubrious viands, and delicious wine;

So will they peaceful on our borders stay,
Nor need compel them to the town to stray.
Here will they learn the story of our guilt,
The vows we broke, the kindred blood we spilt;
And sure a tale, thus horrid, must appear
Cruel and impious to a foreign ear.
These are the counsels of your faithful friend,
Prompt to advise, and steady to defend.
She who can furnish counsel more discreet,
Now let her offer—for this cause we meet."
Thus spoke the queen, and press'd her father's throne,
A royal seat, compos'd of solid stone.
Then rose Polyxo, venerable dame,
Once the queen's nurse, oppress'd with age, and lame;
A staff sustain'd her (for her limbs were weak)
Tottering with age, yet vehement to speak.
Near her four damsels, blooming, fresh, and fair,
Sat crown'd with ringlets of the whitest hair.
Full in the midst she stood, then rais'd her head,
Her back was bent with years, and thus she said:
"The queen's advice I greatly must commend,
Commodious presents to our guests to send.
And what more saving counsel shall I give
To those my friends who shall hereafter live;
Whene'er the sons of Thrace, or hostile hosts
From other kingdoms shall infest our coasts;
Which well may happen, we must all allow,
As this invasion that alarms us now?
But should some god avert th' impending ill,
Yet greater evils may befall, and will.
For when the oldest die, as die they must,
And our wise matrons be transform'd to dust,
And you, now young, oppress'd at last with age,
Shall unprolific tread life's irksome stage:
What wretched mortals ye, who then survive!
Who to their labour, then, the steers shall drive?
Will oxen then their necks spontaneous bow
Beneath the yoke, and drag the ponderous plough?
Or will they reap the harvest on the plain,
And every autumn house the golden grain?
I, tho' preserv'd to this important day,
(For death from me abhorrent turns away,)
Yet, ere the Sun completes his annual round,
If right I judge, shall mingle with the ground,
Lodg'd in the lap of Earth, at Nature's call,
And 'scape the ruin that involves you all.
Hear then, young damsels, what my years advise;
Before you now the fair occasion lies:
Commit your city to these strangers' care,
Let them your mansions and possessions share."
She spoke, pleas'd murmurs fill'd the spacious hall;
Polyxo's counsel was approv'd by all.
From her sire's throne Hypsipyla arose,
Thus in few words the conference to close:
"My mates, since all this sage advice commend,
An instant message to the ship I send."
She said, and to Iphinoa gave command;
"Haste, find the leader of yon martial band,
Invite him (of our amity a proof)
To lodge beneath my hospitable roof;
There time will furnish leisure to relate
The genius and the manners of our state.
But let his comrades rove, as pleasure leads,
And pitch their tents along the fertile meads:
Or to the tower-defended town repair,
Assur'd of safety, and our royal care."
Th' assembly rose, as thus the princess spoke,
Then to the regal dome her way she took.
Iphinoa, mindful of the queen's command,
Approach'd the Minyans scatter'd o'er the strand,
Who throng'd around her, eager to explore
Wherefore she came, and what commands she bore.
Then thus she said; "Strangers, to you as friends
Hypsipyla, the seed of Thoas, sends
Her faithful herald, with this strict command
To find the leader of your martial band;
Him she invites (of amity a proof)
To lodge beneath her hospitable roof:
There time will furnish leisure to relate
The genius and the manners of our state.
But let his comrades rove, as pleasure leads,
And pitch their tents along the fertile meads:
Or to the tower-defended town repair,
Assur'd of safety, and the royal care."
These words were grateful to the warlike band;
From her they learn'd whose sceptre rul'd the land;
Instant they urg'd their chief's assent, and all
Prepar'd obsequious to accept the call.
A mantle doubly lin'd, of purple hue,
The son of Æson o'er his shoulders threw.
This Pallas gave him, when, with wondrous art,
She plann'd his ship, and measur'd every part.
'Twere safer to survey the radiant globe
Of rising Phœbus, than this splendid robe.
Full in the middle beam'd a crimson blaze,
The verge surrounding darted purple rays.
In every part historic scenes were wrought;
The moving figures seem'd inform'd with thought.
Here, on their work intent, the Cyclops strove
Eager to forge a thunder-bolt for Jove;
Half-rough, half-form'd, the glowing engine lay,
And only wanted the fire-darting ray;
And this they hammer'd out on anvils dire;
At each collision flash'd the fatal fire.
Not distant far, in lively colours plann'd,
Two brothers, Zethus and Amphion, stand,
Sons of Antiopa: no turrets crown'd
Thy city, Thebes, but walls were rising round.
A mountain's rocky summit Zethus bore
On his broad back, but seem'd to labour sore.
Behind, Amphion tun'd his golden shell,
Amphion deem'd in music to excel:
Rocks still pursu'd him as he mov'd along,
Charm'd by the music of his magic song.
Crown'd with soft tresses, in a fairer field,
Gay Venus toy'd with Mars's splendid shield.
Down from her shoulder her expanded vest
Display'd the swelling beauties of her breast.
She in the brazen buckler, glittering bright,
Beheld her lovely image with delight.
On a rich plain appear, not distant far,
The Taphians, and Electryon's sons at war;
Fat steers the prize for which the swains contend,
Those strive to plunder, these their herds defend;
The meads were moist with blood and rosy dew:
The powerful many triumph'd o'er the few.
Two chariots next roll'd lightly o'er the plains,
This Pelops drove, and shook the sounding reins;
Hippodamia at his side he view'd:
In the next chariot, Myrtilus pursu'd,
And with him Œnomas; approaching near,
At Pelops' back he aim'd the vengeful spear;

The faithless axle, as the wheels whirl'd round,
Snapp'd short, and left him stretch'd along the ground.
Here young Apollo stood, in act to throw
The whirring arrow from the twanging bow,
At mighty Tityus aim'd, who basely strove
To force his mother, erst belov'd by Jove:
He from fair Elara deriv'd his birth,
Tho' fed and nourish'd by prolific Earth.
There Phryxus stoop'd to listen to the ram,
On whose broad back the Hellespont he swam.
The beast look'd speaking; earnest could you gaze,
The lively piece would charmingly amaze.
Long might you feast your eye, and lend an ear,
With pleasing hope the conference to hear.
Such was the present of the blue-ey'd maid—
In his right hand a missile lance he sway'd,
Which Atalanta, to reward the brave,
Sure pledge of friendship, to the hero gave,
When on the breezy Mænalus she rov'd,
And wish'd the company of him she lov'd;
But he, of suitors' amorous strife afraid,
Repress'd the fond intention of the maid.
Thus rob'd, thus arm'd, he to the city went,
Bright as a star that gilds the firmament,
Which maids assembled view with eager eyes
High o'er their roof in orient beauty rise.
On the bright signal, as it darts its rays,
Attentive they with silent transport gaze.
Each, with this omen charm'd, expects, tho' late,
Return'd from distant climes her destin'd mate.
Thus shone the chief, for high achievements known,
Majestic as he mov'd to Lemnos' town.
The noble heroines his footsteps meet,
With courteous joy the Grecian guest to greet,
Whose downcast eye ne'er wander'd, till he came
To the proud palace of the royal dame;
Obsequious damsels at the portal wait,
And quick unbar the double-folding gate:
Then thro' the various courts extending wide,
And stately rooms, Iphinoa was his guide;
On a bright throne, with rich embroidery grac'd,
Fronting her sovereign she the hero plac'd.
Th' embarrass'd queen, her face with blushes spread,
In courteous terms address'd the prince, and said:
" Why, gentle stranger, should your warlike train
At distance far, without the walls remain?
The men who till'd these ample fields before,
Now turn rich furrows on the Thracian shore.
But hear, while I our matchless woes relate;
So shall you know the story of our fate.
When o'er this realm my father Thoas reign'd,
The Lemnian youth, to fraud and rapine train'd,
On Thracian borders seiz'd the trembling prey,
And brought whole flocks, and lovely maids away.
This Venus plann'd, with mischievous intent,
And fierce among them fatal discord sent.
Their wives they loath'd, and vainly impious led
War's spoils, fair captives, to the lawless bed.
Long we endur'd, forgiving insults past,
And hop'd the faithless would reform at last.
In vain; each day but doubled our disgrace,
Our children yielded to a spurious race.
The widow'd mother, the discarded maid,
Forlorn, neglected thro' the city stray'd.
No tender pity touch'd the parent's breast,
To see his darling child abus'd, oppress'd
Beneath a step-dame's proud, imperious sway:
No sons would then maternal duty pay,
Nor, as before, their mother's cause defend;
No sister then to sister prov'd a friend:
But the gay troops of Thracian captives fair
Inthrall'd the men, and challeng'd all their care;
At home, abroad, the first, at pleasure's call,
To share the banquet, and conduct the ball.
At length, but strange! some favouring power divine
In female mind inspir'd this bold design,
That, when return'd from Thracia's hateful shore,
Our roofs these traitors might protect no more;
That, thus constrain'd, they might forego their crimes,
Or with their captives flee to distant climes.
They sail, return, the few remaining males
Demand, then quit us with auspicious gales;
And now the frigid fields of Thrace they plough,
And countries whiten'd with Sithonian snow.
Haste then, conduct your comrades to the town:
Here fix your seat, and Lemnos is your own.
And if to high dominion you aspire,
Reign here, and wield the sceptre of my sire.
You must approve; for not so fair a coast,
Or isle so fertile can the Ægean boast.
Haste to your friends, and make my pleasure known,
Nor let them longer lodge without the town."
Artful she spoke, forbearing to relate
How in one night each woman slew her mate.
Then Jason thus: " Whate'er your bounty grants,
Stores for our voyage, or our present wants,
Pleas'd we accept: I to my valiant bands
Will speed to signify your kind commands,
Then soon conduct my comrades to the town:
But still, O queen, still wear your father's crown.
Not from disdain I shun imperial sway,
But great achievements call me hence away."
He spoke, and gently press'd her fair right hand,
Then sought his comrades scatter'd o'er the strand.
Unnumber'd damsels round the hero wait,
Gazing with joy, and follow to the gate;
Then grateful presents in swift cars convey
To the land's margin, where the warriors lay.
When Jason now to his adventurous bands
Had signified Hypsipyla's commands,
With eager joy the Minyans haste to share
Her friendly roofs, and hospitable fare.
The queen of love Thessalia's chiefs inspires,
For Vulcan's sake, with amorous desires;
That Lemnos, Vulcan's sacred isle, agen
May flourish, peopled with a race of men.
Great Jason hastens to the regal walls;
The rest proceed where chance or pleasure calls,
Save great Alcides; with a chosen train,
Ambitious he in Argo to remain.
Eager with joy the jolly crowds advance
To share the genial feast, or lead the dance;
To Venus' and to Vulcan's fane they throng,
And crown the day with victims and with song.
Sunk in soft ease th' enamour'd heroes lay,
(Their voyage still deferr'd from day to day)
And longer still, and longer had declin'd,
Full loath to leave the lovely place behind,
Had not Alcides, the fair dames apart,
Thus spoke incens'd the language of his heart:

"Mistaken comrades, does our kindred, say,
From our own country drive us far away?
Or are we fondly thus enamour'd grown
Of foreign damsels, and despise our own?
Here shall we stay to till the Lemnian fields?
Small fame to heroes this base commerce yields.
No god, propitious to the sons of Greece,
Without our toil, will grant the golden fleece.
Our course pursue we; for the breeze invites;
And let him revel in love's soft delights,
Who here but stays to propagate his kind,
And leave a memorable name behind."
Alcides thus: none dar'd to lift his eye,
To breathe a murmur, or to make reply;
But keenly stung with this sarcastic style,
They haste to leave the lov'd Vulcanian isle.
Soon as the damsels their fix'd purpose knew,
Around the chiefs in busy crowds they flew.
As bees from some deep cavern'd rock proceed,
Buzz o'er the lilies of the laughing mead,
The sweets of all ambrosial herbs devour,
And suck the soul of every fragrant flow'r;
Thus they in swarms the parting Greeks address,
With hands salute, with soothing words caress;
Then to the powers above with fervour pray,
Safe to their arms the heroes to convey.
Hypsipyla the hand of Jason press'd,
And thus with tears the parting chief address'd:
"Adieu!—and may you with the sons of Greece
Return triumphant with the golden fleece.
Here shall you then my father's sceptre sway,
And his domains your sovereign will obey.
The neighbouring states will furnish large supplies,
And a vast empire by your wisdom rise.
But if on nobler plans your thoughts are bent,
And vainly I presage the wish'd event;
Absent or present, to my memory kind,
Still let Hypsipyla possess your mind.
And if with offspring Heav'n should bless me, say,
How shall I then my Jason's will obey?"
The prince beheld the queen with rapturous look,
And thus with mild benevolence bespoke:
"May these events, foredoom'd by Heaven's decree,
Successful prove, Hypsipyla, to thee.
But still of Jason nobler thoughts retain:
Enough for me o'er my own realms to reign;
May but the powers of Heaven (I ask no more)
Safe reconvey me to my native shore.
If that's denied, and you, my source of joy,
Bear, the soft token of our loves, a boy;
Him, when mature, in kindness to your friend,
My parents' solace, to Iölcos send;
If then perchance the venerable pair
Survive their woes, and breathe this vital air.
There may he live, from Pelias far remov'd,
By Grecians honour'd, who his father lov'd."
He spoke his last farewell: then first ascends
The ship, and with him his illustrious friends.
In their due stations plac'd, each seiz'd an oar,
While Argus loos'd the cable from the shore.
With active strokes the vigorous heroes sweep
The sounding bosom of the billowy deep.
As Orpheus counsel'd, and mild evening near,
To Samothrace, Electra's isle, they steer;
That there initiated in rites divine,
Safe might they sail the navigable brine.
But, Muse, presume not of these rites to tell:
Farewell, dread isle! dire deities, farewell!
Let not my verse these mysteries explain;
To name is impious, to reveal profane.
Thence the black main they lash'd with all their might,
Thrace on their left, and Imbros on the right;
And safely, with the now-declining Sun,
To far-projecting Chersonesus run.
Then stemm'd they, aided by the southern gales,
The stormy Hellespont with swelling sails,
Left the high-surging sea with morning light,
And reach'd Sigæum with approaching night.
Dardania past, and high exalted Ide,
They saw Abydos on the stormy tide.
Thence sail'd they by Percote's pasture lands,
Pityëa's meadows, and Abarnis' sands:
And nightly, favour'd by the friendly blast,
The purple-foaming Hellespont they past.
An ancient island in Propontis lies,
That towering lifts its summit to the skies;
Near Phrygia's corn-abounding coast it stands,
And far-projecting all the main commands;
An island this, save where the isthmus' chain
Connects both lands, and curbs the boisterous main.
Round its rough sides the thundering tempests roar,
And a safe bay is form'd on either shore.
Æsepus' waters near this isthmus fall:
And bordering tribes the mountain Arcton call.
On this rough mountain, barbarous, fierce, and bold,
Dwell mighty giants, hideous to behold;
And, wonderful to tell! each monster stands
With six huge arms, and six rapacious hands;
Two pendent on their shaggy shoulders grow,
And four deform their horrid sides below.
The lowland isthmus, verging to the main,
The Dolions till'd, and all the fertile plain.
O'er these reign'd Cyzicus the brave, the young,
Who from the gallant warrior, Æneus, sprung.
The daughter of Eusorus, first in fame,
Bore Cyzicus, Æneta was her name.
Secure they liv'd, and free from war's alarms,
Tho' Earth's huge sons were terrible in arms.
Sprung from the monarch of the hoary tide,
On Neptune's aid the Dolian race rely'd.
To this fair port, with gentle-breathing gales,
This friendly shore, Thessalian Argo sails.
Here the rope-fasten'd stone they heave on shore,
Which serv'd as anchor to the ship before,
But now too light, so Typhis bids, they bring,
And leave it at the pure Artacian spring;
Then choose another on the rocky bay,
More ponderous far, the rolling ship to stay.
There the first stone unnumber'd years remain'd,
Till, as Apollo's oracle ordain'd,
Th' Ionians found, with rites mysterious grac'd,
And sacred to Jasonian Pallas plac'd.
Soon as the Dolians, near approaching, knew
Thessalian Argo, and the godlike crew,
Led on by Cyzicus they haste to meet
The princely band, and amicably greet;
Invite them down the winding bay to fall,
And fix their cable near the city-wall.
Thus friendly treated, the Pelasgic train
Strive with their oars th' interior port to gain.
Then first Ecbasian Phœbus they adore,
And rear an altar on the sounding shore.
To them the king dispatch'd, with heart benign,
Fat sheep, and strong, exhilarating wine.
For thus the sacred oracle foretold,
"When here arrives a band of heroes bold,

With kind complacence treat the godlike crew,
Meet not in arms, but pay them honours due!"
Scarce had the down the monarch's cheeks o'erspread;
No children yet had bless'd the nuptial bed.
Clita, his lovely queen, the young, the fair,
Renown'd for beauty, and her golden hair,
Sprung from Percosian Merops, still remains
A stranger to Lucina's cruel pains.
Late from her father's court the king convey'd,
With ample dower enrich'd, the blameless maid;
Yet he neglects the genial bed, and feasts,
All fears far banishing, with foreign guests.
Oft he inquires of Pelias' stern command,
And why the heroes left their native land.
As oft they ask'd what cities neighbouring lay,
And in Propontis which the safest bay.
But scanty knowledge could the king bestow,
Tho' it behov'd them much these truths to know.
When morning rose, the Dindymean steep
Some mount, to view the navigable deep,
And all its winding bays; the road they came
They honour'd with illustrious Jason's name.
The chiefs, who chose aboard the ship to stay,
Remov'd her from the moorings where she lay.
Mean while the sons of Earth, a numerous train,
From their bleak mountains rush into the plain,
Besiege the pervious bay, and strive to block
Its mouth with massy fragments from the rock;
Intending there Thessalia's pine to keep
Hemm'd up, like some huge monster of the deep.
But Hercules remain'd; his bow he drew,
And heaps of giants with his arrows slew.
The rest enrag'd, rough, rocky fragments tore,
Hurl'd high in air, and thunder'd from the shore.
(This labour still for Hercules remain'd,
By Juno, Jove's imperial queen, ordain'd)
And fiercely now the glowing battle burn'd,
When lo! the chiefs from Dindymus return'd,
Attack'd the desperate giants in the rear,
And dealt destruction with the dart and spear;
Till Earth's fierce sons, defil'd with wounds and gore,
Dropp'd dead; their bodies cover'd half the shore.
As near the sea's broad brink, with sturdy strokes,
Assiduous woodmen fell aspiring oaks;
Then draw them in due order from the flood,
And thus well drench'd they cleave with ease the wood:
Thus at the entrance of the hoary bay,
The frequent corse of many a giant lay;
Some, tumbled headlong, made the sea their grave,
While their legs rose above the briny wave;
Some o'er the sands their horrid visage show,
Their feet deep-rooted in the mud below.
Thus their huge trunks afford abundant fare
To Neptune's fishes, and the birds of air.
Soon as concluded was the bloody fray,
And favouring breezes call'd the chiefs away,
They loos'd; o'er swelling ocean southern gales
Breath'd all day long, and fill'd their bellying sails.
Night rose, the favouring gales no longer last,
The ship drives backward with the stormy blast.
Again they harbour on the friendly coast,
Where late the Dolians entertain'd the host;
And round the rock the steady cable bind,
The rock ev'n now to sacred fame consign'd.
Here thro' the gloom of night again they came,
And knew not that the country was the same.
Nor knew the Dolians, so dark night prevail'd,
That back to Cyzicum the Greeks had sail'd;
But deem'd the chiefs a band of Macrian foes:
To arms they call, and force to force oppose.
A gleamy lustre glanc'd along the field,
While spear met spear, and shield encounter'd shield.
In sun-scorch'd bushes thus the bickering blaze
Flames forth, and crackling on the branches preys.
Dire was the conflict; on the fatal plain
Their prince, alas! was number'd with the slain,
His queen and bridal bed beheld he ne'er again.
For Jason spy'd the prince advancing near,
And thro' his bosom plung'd the furious spear;
The ribs it broke, and circumscrib'd his date,
Wing'd with th' inevitable will of fate.
Fate, like a wall, devoted man surrounds,
And fast confines him in its circling bounds.
Himself he deem'd, in that disorder'd fight,
Vainly he deem'd! protected by the night:
The favouring night, alas! produc'd his bane,
And chiefs unnumber'd with their prince were slain.
For Hercules, with his all-conquering bow,
Dispatch'd Telecles to the shades below,
And Megabrontes: by Acastus' hand
Pale Sphodris lay extended on the strand.
Peleus to Pluto's dark dominions gave
Zelys the hardy, and Gephyrus brave.
Bold Telamon, well-skill'd the lance to wield,
Left Basileus expiring on the field.
Next Idas vanquish'd Promeus by his side;
By warlike Clytius Hyacinthus died.
Fair Leda's sons, in bloody combat skill'd,
Fierce Megalossacus and Phlogius kill'd.
And Meleager added two to these,
Itymoneus and valiant Artaces.
These all were chiefs in fighting fields approv'd,
Deplor'd as heroes, and as brothers lov'd.
The rest for safety on their flight rely;
(As trembling doves before the falcon fly)
Then to the city-gates tumultuous press,
And raise the piercing cry of deep distress;
The city mourn'd: they deem'd, return'd from far,
That hostile Macrians had renew'd the war.
But when the rosy morn began to wake,
All found their irretrievable mistake.
Heart-rending grief oppress'd the Grecian train,
To see the hospitable monarch slain,
A clay-cold corse, extended on the shore,
Deform'd with dust, and all besmear'd with gore.
The Greeks and Dolians, sunk in deep despair,
Mourn three long days, and rend their graceful hair.
A tomb they rear upon the rising ground,
And clad in brazen arms thrice march around;
Then for the monarch, on Limonia's plain,
Of rites observant, funeral-games ordain.
There stands the tomb, adorn'd with honours due,
Which distant ages will with sorrow view.
When the sad news at Clita's ear arriv'd,
Not long the queen the monarch's fate surviv'd;
But woe augmenting, round her neck she tied
The noose dishonest, and unseemly died.
Her mournful dirge the weeping Dryads sung,
While Dindymus with lamentations rung;

And all the tears that from their eye-lids fell,
The gods transform'd, in pity, to a well;
In crystal streams it murmurs still, and weeps,
And still the name of wretched Clita keeps.
A day so dismal, so replete with woes,
Till this sad day, to Dolians never rose.
Deep, deep immers'd in sorrow they remain'd,
And all from life-supporting food abstain'd;
Save such poor pittance as man's needs require,
Of corn unground, or unprepar'd by fire.
And annual, on this day, the Dolians still
Sift coarsest meal, and at the public mill.
Thenceforth twelve days and nights dire storms prevail,
Nor could the chiefs unfurl the swelling sail.
The following night, by sleep's soft power oppress'd,
Once more in Cyzicum the heroes rest;
Mopsus alone and brave Acastus keep
The watch nocturnal, while their comrades sleep;
When, lo! a halcyon, of cerulean hue,
O'er the fair head of slumbering Jason flew,
In airy circles, wond'rous to behold,
And screaming loud, the ceasing storm foretold.
The grateful sound attentive Mopsus heard,
And mark'd the meaning of the sea-bred bird;
(Which gently rising from the deck below,
Perch'd on the summit of th' aerial prow)
Then rous'd he Jason from his fleecy bed,
Of sheeps' soft skins compos'd, and thus he said;
" O son of Æson, hear! be this thy care,
Haste, to the fane of Dindymus repair;
There Cybele with sacrifice implore;
So will the winds tempestuous cease to roar.
For this proclaim'd the boding halcyon true,
As round thee, sunk in deep repose, she flew.
By Cybele's dread power the vast profound,
And all the winds in harmony are bound.
By her subsists prolific earth below,
And high Olympus, ever crown'd with snow.
Jove yields, when she ascends the courts of day,
And all the powers immortal own her sway."
To Jason thus the venerable seer;
And welcome came the tidings to his ear.
Instant the chief, exulting with a bound,
Sprung from the bed, and wak'd his comrades round.
Elate with joy his looks, his words unfold
The glad presage which Mopsus had foretold.
Then from the stalls the youth appointed drove
Selected oxen to the heights above.
Some from the rock unloos'd the corded stay,
And with fleet oars approach'd the Thracian bay.
From thence the top of Dindymus they gain'd;
Few were the heroes that aboard remain'd:
By those the Macrian rocks, and Thracian land
Directly opposite, appear'd at hand;
The Thracian Bosphorous here, involv'd in shade,
And Mysia's rising mountains were survey'd;
There, where his waters black Æsepus pours,
Nepea's plain, and Adrasteia's tow'rs.
A vine's vast trunk adorn'd with branches stood,
Though old, yet sound, and long had grac'd the wood:
This trunk they hew'd, and made, by Argus' skill,
An image of the goddess of the hill;
Which on the rocky eminence they plac'd,
With the thick boughs of circling beeches grac'd.
They rear an altar, then, on rising ground,
Of stones that readiest lay, and wide around
Dispose the branches of the sacred oak,
And Dindymus's deity invoke,
The guardian power of Phrygia's hills and woods;
The venerable mother of the gods.
On Tityas and Cyllenus too they call,
Of all her priests most lov'd, and honour'd most of all;
For skill prophetic they alone are fam'd;
Idean Dactyli these priests are nam'd;
Both whom Anchiala in Dicte's cave
Brought forth, where chill Oaxis rolls his wave.
While on the burning victims Jason pours
Libations due, the goddess he implores
To smile propitious on the Grecian train,
And still the tempests of the roaring main.
Then Orpheus call'd, and youthful chiefs advance,
All clad in arms, to lead the martial dance;
With clashing swords they clatter'd on their shields,
And fill'd with festive sounds th' aerial fields.
Lost in these sounds was every doleful strain,
And their loud wailings for their monarch slain.
The Phrygians still their goddess' favour win
By the revolving wheel and timbrel's din.
Of these pure rites the mighty mother show'd
Her mind approving, by these signs bestow'd;
Boughs bend with fruit, Earth from her bosom pours
Herbs ever green, and voluntary flow'rs.
Fierce forest-beasts forsake the lonely den,
Approach with gentleness, and fawn on men.
A pleasing omen, and more wondrous still
The goddess gave: the Dindymean hill,
That ne'er knew water on its airy brow,
Bursts into streams, and founts perennial flow.
This wonder still the Phrygian shepherds sing,
And give the name of Jason to the spring.
Then on the mount the chiefs the feast prolong,
And praise the venerable queen in song.
But when the morning rose, they plied their oars,
And, the wind ceasing, left the Phrygian shores.
Then fair contention fir'd the princely train,
Who best the toil of rowing could sustain.
For now the howling storm was lull'd to sleep;
Etherial mildness had compos'd the deep.
On the calm sea the labouring chiefs rely'd;
Fleet flew the ship along the yielding tide;
Not Neptune's steeds so swift, with loosen'd reins,
Skim the light level of the liquid plains.
But when with even-tide the blustering breeze
Brush'd the broad bosom of the swelling seas,
The wearied chiefs their toilsome course repress'd,
And all, save great Alcides, sunk to rest.
Swift thro' the waves his arm unaided drew
The ship, deep-laden with the drowsy crew.
Thro' all her planks the well-compacted pine
Shook, as his oar dispers'd the foamy brine.
But soon the heroes view'd the Mysian shore,
As by the mouth of Rhyndacus they bore.
On Phrygia's fields a wishful look they cast,
And huge Ægæon's promontory pass'd,
When great Alcides, at one luckless stroke,
His oar, hard straining, near the middle broke.
One part was swallow'd in the whelming main,
One, though he fell, his grasping hands retain;
Backward he fell, but soon his seat regain'd,
And, loathing rest, in mute amaze remain'd.
What time the weary labourer, wanting rest,
Hies to his cot with pining fast oppress'd;
Ev'n in the entrance of his rural door
His tottering knees he bends, and moves no more;
His dusty limbs he views, and callous hands,
And curses hunger's insolent demands:
Then, nor till then, the chiefs to Chius row,
Chius, whose streams around Arganthon flow.

The friendly Mysians on their peaceful coast
Receive with hospitality the host;
Abundant stores they send, with hearts benign,
Fat sheep, and strong exhilarating wine.
Some bring dry wood, and some in order spread
Soft leaves and herbage for a spacious bed;
Some from the flint elicit living fire;
Some mix the wines that generous deeds inspire:
The feast they crown, and rites to Phœbus pay,
Ecbasian Phœbus, at the close of day.
But Hercules the genial feast declin'd,
And sought the wood, a fitting oar to find.
Nor long he sought, before a fir he found;
Few leaves adorn'd it, and few branches crown'd;
Yet as the poplar's stem aspires on high,
This fir, so stout and tall, attracts his eye.
On the green grass his bow he laid aside,
His arrowy quiver, and the lion's hide.
First with his club the solid soil he shook,
Then in both arms, assur'd, the fir-tree took;
Firm on his feet he stood, with bended knee;
His big broad shoulder lean'd against the tree;
Then heav'd it up, deep-rooted in the ground,
Clogg'd with the soil's impediments around.
As when, beneath Orion's wintry reign,
The sudden tempest rushes from the main,
Some tall ship's mast it tears, and every stay,
And all the cordage, all the sails away:
Thus he the trunk; then took, in haste to go,
The hide, the club, his arrows and his bow.
  Meanwhile, preparing for his friend's return
A ready supper, with his brazen urn
Alone rov'd Hylas o'er the fields, to bring
The purest water from the sacred spring.
For to such tasks Alcides train'd his squire,
Whom first he took an infant from his sire
Theodamas; but him with sword severe
He slew, who churlish had refus'd a steer.
For when Theodamas, oppress'd with care,
Turn'd the fresh furrow with his shining share,
He disobey'd, ah wretch! the chief's command,
Who claim'd the labouring ox that till'd the land.
But know, Alcides sought for cause to bring
War on Dryopia's kingdom and the king,
For barbarous acts, and rights neglected long.
  But rove not, Muse, digressive from the song.
Soon faithful Hylas to the fountain came,
Which Mysian shepherds crystal Pegæ name;
It chanc'd the nymphs, in neighbouring streams that dwell,
Then kept a concert at the sacred well.
In Dian's praise they rais'd the nightly song,
All who to high, aerial hills belong;
All who in caverns hide, or devious rove
The mountain-forest, or the shady grove.
When from her spring, unsullied with a stain,
Rose Ephydatia, to attend the train,
The form of Hylas rush'd upon her sight,
In every grace of blushing beauty bright:
For the full Moon a beamy lustre shed,
And heighten'd all the honours of his head.
Fir'd with love's sudden flame, by Venus rais'd,
The frantic Naiad languish'd as she gaz'd:
And soon as, stooping to receive the tide,
He to the stream his brazen urn apply'd,
In gush'd the foaming waves; the nymph with joy
Sprung from the deep to kiss the charming boy.
Her left arm round his lovely neck she threw,
And with her right hand to the bottom drew.

First Polyphemus heard, as wandering nigh
This fatal fount, the youth's distressful cry,
(In search of Hercules he rov'd the wood)
And hied with hasty footsteps to the flood.
As when a lion from his cavern'd rock,
At distance hears the bleatings of the flock,
To seize his prey he springs, with hunger bold,
But faithful shepherds had secur'd the fold;
Defeated of his prize, he roars amain,
Rends his hoarse throat, and terrifies the swain:
Thus Polyphemus call'd with voice profound,
And vainly anxious rov'd the forest round.
At length retreating, he the path explor'd
Thro' which he came, and drew his trusty sword,
Lest savage beasts should seize him for their prey,
Or nightly robbers intercept his way.
And as he brandish'd the bright burnish'd blade,
He met Alcides in the gloomy shade,
Unknown at first, but as he nearer drew,
His friend returning to the ship he knew.
Though his breath faulters, and his spirits fail,
He thus reveals the melancholy tale:
" Hard is my lot, and much averse my will,
To be the first sad messenger of ill;
Young Hylas went to fetch fresh water late,
Not yet return'd; I tremble for his fate:
By robbers seiz'd or beasts, 'tis hard to guess;
I heard his cry, the signal of distress:"
Thus he: the sweat from great Alcides flow'd,
And the black blood thro' all his body glow'd:
Enrag'd, the fir-tree on the ground he threw,
And, where his feet or frenzy hurried, flew.
  As when a bull, whom galling gadflies wound,
Forsakes the meadows, and the marshy ground,
The flowery food, the herd and herdsmen shuns,
Now stands stock-still, and restless now he runs;
Stung by the breese, he maddens with the pain,
Tosses aloft his head, and roars amain:
Thus ran the raging chief with matchless force,
Then sudden stopp'd he, wearied with the course.
Anxious in vain, he rov'd the forest round,
The distant hills and vales his voice rebound.
Now o'er the lofty mountains rose in view
The morning star, and mildest breezes blew:
That instant Tiphys bade the heroes sail,
Ascend the vessel, and enjoy the gale.
The ready crew obey the pilot's word,
Their anchor weigh, and haul the cords aboard;
Then give the stretching canvas to the wind,
And leave the Posidean rocks behind.
When from the rosy orient, beaming bright,
Aurora tipp'd the foot-worn paths with light;
And o'er moist meads the glittering dew-drops shin'd,
They miss'd those friends their folly left behind.
Then rose contention keen, and pungent grief,
For thus abandoning their bravest chief.
In silence Jason sat, and long suppress'd,
Though griev'd, the labouring anguish of his breast.
Brave Telamon, with anger kindling, spoke:
  " Mute is thy tongue, and unconcern'd thy look:
To leave unconquer'd Hercules behind
Was a base project, and by thee design'd;
Lest, when to Greece we steer the sailing pine,
His brighter glories should out-dazzle thine.
But words avail not—I renounce the band,
Whose selfish wiles this stratagem have plann'd:"
  Thus spoke Æacides, inflam'd with ire,
His eye-balls sparkling like the burning fire;
On Tiphys then, by rage impell'd, he flew:
And once more Mysia had receiv'd the crew;

Again the heroes the same course had sail'd,
Though roaring winds and raging waves prevail'd,
Had not bold Boreas' sons the chief address'd,
And, nobly daring, his rough rage repress'd.
(Ill-fated youths! for that heroic deed,
Doom'd by the hands of Hercules to bleed.
For when returning home their course they sped,
From funeral games perform'd for Pelias dead,
In sea-girt Tenos he the brothers slew,
And o'er their graves in heapy hillocks threw
The crumbling mould; then with two columns crown'd,
Erected high the death-devoted ground;
And one still moves, how marvellous the tale!
With every motion of the northern gale—
But these are facts reserv'd for future years)
Lo! sudden, Glaucus to their sight appears,
Prophet of Nereus, rising from the main,
Most skill'd of all his fate-foretelling train.
High o'er the waves he rear'd his shaggy head,
With his strong hand the rudder seiz'd, and said:
"Why strive ye thus, tho' Jove's high will withstands,
To bear Alcides to the Colchian lands?
He must at Argos, so the fates ordain,
And so Eurystheus has decreed, sustain
Twelve mighty labours, thence be rais'd above,
To high Olympus, and the court of Jove.
Cease for Amphytrion's son, your murmurs cease,
And lull the sorrows of your souls to peace.
In Mysia, where meandering Chius strays,
Must Polyphemus a proud city raise:
Then, mid' the Calybes, a desperate clan,
Expires on Scythian plains the gallant man.
But strange is Hylas' fate: his youthful charms
Entic'd a nymph, who clasp'd him in her arms.
Now the blest pair the bands of Hymen bind;
In search of him the chiefs are left behind."
This said, he plung'd into the gulf profound,
The purple ocean foam'd in eddies round.
The god, descending with resistless sway,
Impell'd the hollow vessel on her way.
The chiefs rejoic'd this prodigy to view,
And instant Telamon to Jason flew
In friendly sort, and in his right he took
The prince's hand, and thus embracing spoke:
"Illustrious chief, let not thine anger rise
At aught I said impetuous and unwise.
Grief for my friend has made me indiscreet,
And utter words for Jason's ear unmeet;
Those to the winds wide-scattering let us give,
And, as before, in friendly concord live."
Then Jason thus; "Thy censures wound my mind,
Which say, I left the bravest Greek behind.
Yet though thy words reproachful guilt suggest,
Rage dwells not long in Jason's generous breast;
Since not for flocks or riches we contend,
But a bold hero, and a faithful friend.
And thou, I trust, if reason calls, wilt be
As firm and warm an advocate for me."
He spoke; and now, the hateful contest o'er,
The chiefs resum'd the seats they held before.
But for those heroes whom they left behind,
By Jove's decree are various cares design'd.
Nam'd from its stream, the boast of future days,
Must one on Mysian plains a city raise:
One (great Alcides) other toils must share,
And learn Euristheus' stern commands to bear.
Long time he threaten'd, for his Hylas lost,
Instant destruction to the Mysian coast,
Unless the Mysians to his arms restor'd,
Alive or dead, the partner of his board.
Of all their bands the choicest youths they chose,
And them as pledges of their faith propose;
Then swore they all, their search should never end,
Till haply they had found the hero's friend.
Still to this day the fond Cianians seek
(All who at Trachin dwell) the lovely Greek.
For beauteous youths, to Trachin's walls convey'd,
Were there as pledges to Alcides paid.
Meanwhile all day and night brisk breezes blew,
Fleet o'er the foaming flood the vessel flew;
But when the dawn gave promise of the day,
The winds expiring gently died away.
A land projecting o'er the bay below
The chiefs discover'd, and to this they row;
This peaceful port awhile the Minyans chose,
And, as they reach'd it, grateful morning rose.

BOOK II.

ARGUMENT.

This book contains the combat between Amycus and Pollux; the former of whom is slain. A battle ensues between the Argonauts and Bebrycians, in which the Argonauts come off conquerors. They sail to Salmydessus, a city of Thrace, where they consult Phineus, a soothsayer, on the success of their expedition. He promises, if they would deliver him from the harpies, to direct them safely to Colchos. His request is granted, and he gives them instructions. The story of Paræbius, Cyrene, and Aristæus. They sail through the Symplegades, and thence to the island Thynia, where they land. Apollo, who here appears to them, is rendered propitious by sacrifice. The course of the river Acheron is described. They land on the coast of the Mariandyni, and are hospitably entertained by Lycus, the king of that country. Here Idmon is killed by a wild boar, and here Tiphys dies. Ancæus is appointed pilot in his stead. They sail by the monument of Sthenelus, whose ghost is released by Proserpine, and gratified with the sight of the Argonauts. At the island of Mars they meet the sons of Phrixus, who had just before been shipwrecked. They are kindly received by the Argonauts, who take them on board. Sailing by Mount Caucasus they come in sight of the eagle that preys on the entrails of Prometheus. The end of their voyage.

TENTS o'er the beach Bebrycia's king had spread,
And stalls erected where fat oxen fed.
To genial Neptune a Bithynian dame
Bore the fierce tyrant, Amycus his name,
Proudest of me. ; who this hard law decreed,
That from his realm no stranger should recede,
Till first with him compell'd in fight to wield
The dreadful gauntlet in the listed field.
Unnumber'd guests his matchless prowess slew:
Stern he accosts swift Argo's valiant crew,
Curious the reason of their course to scan,
Who, whence they were; and scornful thus began:

"Learn what 'tis meet ye knew, ye vagrant host;
None that e'er touches on Bebrycia's coast,
Is thence by law permitted to depart,
Till match'd with me he prove the boxer's art.
Choose then a chief who can the gauntlet wield,
And let him try the fortune of the field:
Should ye contemptuous scorn my fix'd decree,
Know, your proud hearts shall yield to fate and me."
Thus spoke the chief with insolent disdain,
And rous'd resentment in the martial train;
But Pollux most his vaunting words provoke,
Who thus, a champion for his fellows, spoke:
"Threat not, whoe'er thou art, the bloody fray;
Lo, we obsequious thy decrees obey!
Unforc'd, this instant to the lists I go,
Thy rival I, thy voluntary foe."
Stung to the heart with this severe reply,
On him he turn'd his fury-flaming eye:
As the grim lion, pierc'd by some keen wound,
Whom hunters on the mountain-top surround;
Though close hemm'd in, his glaring eye-balls glance
On him alone who threw the pointed lance.
The Greek stript off his mantle richly wrought,
Late from the Lemnian territory brought,
Which some fair nymph, who had her flame avow'd,
The pledge of hospitable love bestow'd:
His double cloak, with clasps of sable hue,
Bebrycia's ruler on the greensward threw,
And his rough sheep-hook of wild olive made,
Which lately flourish'd in the woodland shade.
Then sought the heroes for a place at hand
Commodious for the fight, and on the strand
They plac'd their friends, who saw, with wondering eyes,
The chiefs how different, both in make and size;
For like Typhœus' race the tyrant stood
Enormous, or that miscreated brood
Of mighty monsters, which parturient Earth,
Incens'd at Jove, brought forth, a hideous birth.
But Pollux shone like that mild star on high,
Whose rising ray illumes fair evening's sky.
Down spread his cheek, ripe manhood's early sign,
And in his eye-balls beam'd the glance divine.
But like a lion, glorying in his might
Stood Jove's puissant son, prepar'd for fight.
His arms he pois'd, advancing in the ring,
To try if still they kept their pristine spring;
If pliant still, and vigorous as before,
Nor rigid grown with labouring at the oar.
Trial like this the haughty king disdain'd:
Aloof and silent Amycus remain'd.
Full on his foe his vengeful eyes he turn'd,
For blood he thirsted, and for conquest burn'd.
With that his squire Lycoreus, full in view,
Two pair of gauntlets in the circle threw,
Of barbarous fashion, harden'd, rough, and dry'd.
Then thus the king, with insolence and pride:
"Lo, two stout pair; the choice I leave to thee;
(No lot appoints them) choose, and blame not me.
Bind them secure, and after trial tell,
How greatly I in either art excel,
Whether to form the cestus firm and good,
Or stain the cheeks of mighty men with blood."
He spoke: brave Pollux nothing deign'd to say,
But smiling chose the pair which nearest lay.
To cheer their champion, Castor, honour'd name!
And Talaüs, the son of Bias, came;
Firm round his arms the gloves of death they bind,
And animate the vigour of his mind.
Aratus, and bold Ornytus his friend,
To Amycus their kind assistance lend:
Fools! for they knew not, this one conflict o'er,
Those gauntlets never should be buckled more.
Accoutred thus each ardent hero stands,
And raises high in air his iron hands;
With clashing gauntlets fiercely now they close,
And mutual meditate death-dealing blows.
First Amycus a furious onset gave,
Like the rude insult of the battering wave,
That, heap'd on high by driving wind and tide,
Bursts thundering on some gallant vessel's side;
The wary pilot, by superior skill,
Foresees the storm, and shuns the menac'd ill.
Thus threatening Amycus on Pollux press'd,
Nor suffer'd his antogonist to rest:
But Jove's brave son observes each coming blow,
Quick leaps aside, and disappoints the foe;
And where a weak unguarded part he spies,
There all the thunder of his arms he plies.
As busy shipwrights stoutly labouring strive
Through sturdy planks the piercing spikes to drive,
From head to stern repeated blows go round,
And ceaseless hammers send a various sound;
Thus from their batter'd cheeks loud echoes sprung,
Their dash'd teeth crackled, and their jaw-bones rung:
Nor ceas'd they from the strokes that threaten'd death,
Till tir'd with toil they faintly gasp'd for breath:
Awhile they then remit the bloody fray,
And panting wipe the copious sweat away.
But adverse soon they meet, with rage they glow,
Like bulls fierce fighting for some favourite cow.
Then Amycus, collecting all his might,
Rose to the stroke, resolv'd his foe to smite,
And by one blow the dubious war conclude:
The wary prince, his ruin to elude,
Bent back his head; defeated of its aim,
The blow impetuous on his shoulder came.
Then Pollux with firm steps approaching near,
Vindictive struck his adversary's ear;
Th' interior bones his ponderous gauntlet broke;
Flat fell the chief beneath his dreadful stroke:
The Grecians shouted, with wild rapture fir'd,
And, deeply groaning, Amycus expir'd.
 The griev'd Bebrycians saw their monarch slain,
And big with vengeance rush'd into the plain;
With season'd clubs and javelins arm'd they ran,
And aim'd their fury at the conquering man.
Their keen-edg'd swords the friends of Pollux drew,
And to the succour of their comrade flew.
First Castor slaughter'd, with victorious hand,
A hero of the bold Bebrycian band;
The griding sword at once his head divides,
And on his shoulders hang the parted sides.
Mimans, Itymoneus of giant-size,
Each by the arm of conquering Pollux dies.
On this his foot impress'd a deadly wound
Full on his side, and stretch'd him on the ground:
His right hand dash'd, with unresisted sway,
Mimans' left eye, and tore the ball away.
Orcides, Amycus's proud compeer,
Then lanch'd at Talaüs his brazen spear;
Just near his flank the point he lightly felt,
That ras'd the skin beneath his 'broider'd belt.
Aratus, with his club of harden'd oak,
Aim'd at brave Iphitus a deadly stroke:
Vain thought! too soon, alas! it is decreed,
The hero by his brother's sword must bleed.

Then rush'd, to succour the Thessalian band,
Ancæus, with his pole-axe in his hand:
O'er his broad back a bear's dark spoils he threw,
And boldly mingled with the hostile crew.
The sons of Æacus, renown'd for might,
And Jason join'd them in the fields of fight.
As when, what time both dogs and shepherds keep
Close in warm cots, neglectful of their sheep,
Wolves, pinch'd with hunger and bleak winter's cold,
Leap o'er the fence, and terrify the fold,
With ravening eyes the crowded sheep survey,
And doubt where first to rend the trembling prey:
Thus the bold Greeks, as near their foes they drew,
Intimidate the congregated crew.
As swains with smoke, of honey studious, strive
From some rock's cleft the swarming bees to drive;
Alarm'd and trembling, with a murmuring sound,
They crowd to all their waxen rooms around;
But if the fumes prevail, their wings they ply,
And rove uncertain thro' the various sky:
Dispersing thus, the wild Bebrycians fled,
And loud proclaim'd that Amycus was dead.
Ah, hapless race of men! they little knew,
That, soon, far greater evils must ensue:
Soon must they see, their monarch now no more,
Their lands a drear, depopulated shore;
Their vineyards spoil'd, and wasted all their coast
By Lycus, and the Mariandine host:
For 'twas their fate, with spear and steely brand,
Hard lot! to battle for an iron land.
The Greeks then seiz'd their herds, an easy prey,
And from the sheep-folds drove the flocks away;
The live provision to their ship they sent:
Then thus some sailor gave his boasting vent;
"What had these miscreants done, with fears dismay'd,
Had Heaven indulg'd us with Alcides' aid?
No fierce contention then, I judge had been,
No bloody boxing on the listed green:
The chief's stout club had tam'd the tyrant's pride,
And set his execrable laws aside.
But now, impell'd by swelling waves and wind,
We leave at land the matchless chief behind;
Whose loss distress to every Greek will prove."
He said;—but all things own the will of Jove.
All night the heroes on the coast remain,
To heal the bruises of the wounded train.
First to the gods they give the honours due,
And next, a banquet for the princely crew.
Nor can night's shades the chiefs to sleep incline,
Or o'er the sacrifice, or o'er the wine;
Mirthful they sit, their brows with laurel crown'd:
To a green laurel was the cable bound.
While Orpheus strikes the lyre, the hymn they raise,
And Jove's fam'd offspring, mighty Pollux, praise:
Soft breathes the breeze, the billows cease to roar,
And festive joy exhilarates the shore.
But when the Sun illum'd the hills and plains,
Dank with the dew, and rous'd the shepherd-swains,
They sent abundant flocks and herds aboard,
And from the laurel-stem unloos'd the cord;
And while the favourable winds prevail'd,
Thro' the rough-rolling Bosphorus they sail'd.
When, lo! a wave by gathering surges driv'n,
Swoln big for bursting, is up-heav'd to Heav'n,
Still rises higher, and still wider spreads,
And hangs a watery mountain o'er their heads;
Like a black cloud it frowns, prepar'd to fall,
And threatens quick destruction to them all.
Yet the train'd pilot, by superior skill,
Well knows to 'scape this last impending ill:
Safe through the storm the vessel Tiphys steer'd,
And sav'd the heroes from the fate they fear'd.
Fronting Bithynia's coast, next morn they reach
New land, and fix their halsers on the beach.
There on the margin of the beating flood
The mournful mansions of sad Phineus stood,
Agenor's son; whom Heaven ordain'd to bear
The grievous burden of unequall'd care.
For, taught by wise Apollo to descry
Unborn events of dark futurity,
Vain of his science, the presumptuous seer
Deign'd not Jove's awful secrets to revere;
But wantonly divulg'd to frail mankind
The sacred purpose of the omniscient mind:
Hence Jove indignant gave him length of days,
But dimm'd in endless night his visual rays.
Nor would the vengeful god indulge his taste
With the sweet blessings of a pure repast,
Tho' (for they learn'd his fate) the country round
Their prophet's board with every dainty crown'd.
For, lo! descending sudden from the sky,
Round the pil'd banquet shrieking harpies fly,
Whose beaks rapacious, and whose talons tear
Quick from his famish'd lips th' untasted fare.
Yet would some slender pittance oft remain
Life to support and to perpetuate pain.
Such odours still the nauseous scraps exhal'd,
That with the stench the loathing stomach fail'd.
Aloof the guests amaz'd and hungry stood,
While their sick hearts abhorr'd the putrid food.
But now the princely crew approaching near,
The welcome sound invades the prophet's ear;
Taught by almighty Jove, that now was come
The long-wish'd period of Heaven's vengeful doom;
When, by these heroes' destin'd aid restor'd,
Peace should hereafter bless his feastful board.
Then heaves he from the couch his haggard head,
(Like some pale, lifeless, visionary shade)
Propp'd on his staff his way explores, and crawls
With lingering step along the lonely walls:
Diseas'd, enfeebled, and by age unbrac'd,
Thro' every limb he trembled as he pass'd;
Shrunk was his form, with want adust and thin,
The pointed bones seem'd bursting thro' his skin:
But faint and breathless as he reach'd the gate,
Down on the threshold, tir'd with toil, he sat.
In dizzy fumes involv'd, his brain runs round,
And swims beneath his feet the solid ground;
No more their functions the frail senses keep,
But speechless sinks he in a death-like sleep.
This saw the chiefs amaz'd, and gather'd round;
When from his labouring lungs a hollow sound
(His breath and utterance scarce recover'd) broke,
And thus th' enlighten'd seer prophetic spoke:
"Princes of Greece, attend; if ye be they
Whom o'er the main Thessalia's pines convey,
And Jason leads to Colchos' magic land;
Such is your cruel tyrant's stern command.
Yes, ye are they; for yet my mental eye
Undimm'd, past, present, future, can descry:
Thanks to thy son, Latona, who bestows
This grace, this only solace of my woes.
By Jove, to whom the suppliant's cause belongs,
Who hates the cruel, and avenges wrongs;
By Phœbus, and by Juno, from on high
Who marks your progress with compassion's eye,
Aid me, and, oh! a sufferer's pangs asswage,
And bid corrosive famine cease to rage:

Leave me not thus, unpitied and unbless'd;
But ere you sail, ah! pity the distress'd.
For not these orbs alone, depriv'd of sight,
Vindictive Heaven hath veil'd in doleful night;
But to extreme old age his cruel law
Dooms me th' unwasting thread of life to draw.
Still weightier woes from sorrow's lengthen'd chain
Depend, and pain is ever link'd to pain.
From secret haunts, aërial, unexplor'd,
Flights of devouring harpies vex my board;
Swift, instantaneous, sudden they descend,
And from my mouth the tasteful morsel rend.
Meanwhile my troubled soul, with woe oppress'd,
No means of aid, no comfort can suggest.
For when the feast I purpose to prepare,
They see that purpose, and prevent my care:
But cloy'd and glutted with the luscious spoil,
With noisome ordure parting they defile
Whate'er remains, if ought perchance remain,
That none approaching may the stench sustain,
Tho' his strong heart were wrapp'd in plated mail,
The filthy fragments such dire steams exhale.
Yet me fell hunger's all-subduing pain
Compels reluctant, loathing to remain;
Compels the deadly odours to endure,
And gorge my craving maw with food impure.
From these invaders (so hath fate decreed)
By Boreas' offspring shall my board be freed.
Nor on a stranger to your house and blood,
O sons of Boreas, is your aid bestow'd.
Phineus behold, Agenor's hapless son,
Once for phrophetic skill and riches known;
Who, while I sway'd the Thracian sceptre, led
Your portion'd sister to my spousal bed."
Here Phineus ceas'd, and touch'd each pitying chief:
But Boreas' sons were pierc'd with double grief;
Compassion kind was kindled in their breast:
Their tears abating, friendly Zetes press'd
His trembling hand, and thus the seer address'd:
"O most disastrous of all human kind,
Whence spring these evils that o'erwhelm thy mind?
Hast thou, intrusted with the book of fate,
By folly merited celestial hate?
Hence falls this indignation on thy head?
Fain would the sons of Boreas grant thee aid;
Fain would they execute what Heaven ordains,
But awful dread their willing hands restrains.
To frighted mortals well thy sufferings prove
How fierce the vengeance of the gods above.
Swear, or we dare not, as we wish, essay
To drive these hateful harpies far away:
Swear that the succours, which our arms intend,
Shall no superior deity offend."
He spoke; and straight to Heaven disclosing wide
His sightless eye-balls, thus the seer reply'd:
"My son, th' injustice of thy tongue restrain,
Nor let such thoughts thy pious soul profane.
By Phœbus, heavenly augur, who inspires
My conscious bosom with prophetic fires;
By every woe fate destines me to bear,
And by these eyes, involv'd in night, I swear;
By the fell demons of the realms below,
(Whom ever unpropitious may I know,
From their resentment not in death secure,
If falsely their dread godheads I adjure;)
That, should a captive by your arms be freed,
No god vindictive will avenge the deed."
Then acquiescing in the solemn pray'r,
To aid the prophet Boreas' sons prepare.
The youthful train a banquet spread; the last
Which those fell harpies were decreed to taste.
Nigh stand the brothers, ardent to oppose
With glittering falchions their invading foes.
But scarce the first sweet morsel Phineus took,
When from the clouds with swift prevention broke,
(Swift as the lightning's glance, or stormy blast,
Whose rapid fury lays the forest waste)
Shrill-clamouring for their prey, the birds obscene;
The watchful heroes shouting rush'd between;
But they with speediest rage the cates devour'd,
And round intolerable odours pour'd;
Then o'er th' Ægean far away they flew;
The sons of Boreas arm'd with swords pursue;
Close they pursue; for Jove, that signal day,
Their strength proportion'd to the desperate fray;
The strength he gave had Jove, that day, deny'd,
In vain their pinions had the brothers plied.
For when to Phineus furious they repair,
Or quitting Phineus seek the fields of air,
The light-wing'd monsters, fleeter than the wind,
Leave the careering Zephyrs far behind.
As when swift hounds, experienc'd in the chase,
Through some wide forest, o'er the scented grass
The bounding hind, or horned goat pursue,
Near, and more near their panting prey they view;
And eager stretching, the short space to gain,
They snap, and grind their gnashing fangs in vain:
Thus ever near, the rapid chiefs pursu'd,
The harpies thus their grasping hands elude.
But now far off in the Sicilian main,
By the wing'd brothers, sons of Boreas, slain,
The harpy-race, tho' every god withstood,
Had stain'd the Plotian isles with sacred blood;
Their sore distress had Iris not survey'd,
And darting from the skies the heroes staid:
"O sons of Boreas, the dread laws above
Permit you not to wound the dogs of Jove:
And, lo! my oath I pledge, that never more
Shall these fell dogs approach the Thracian shore."
This said, adjuring the tremendous floods,
Most fear'd, most honour'd by immortal gods;
By the slow-dripping urn of Styx she swore;
The prophet's peaceful mansions on the shore
For ever from these spoilers should be free;
Such was the fatal sisters' fix'd decree.
The goddess swore, the brothers straight obey,
And back to Argo wing their airy way:
The Strophades from thence derive their name,
The Plotian islands styl'd by ancient fame.
Disparting then, to different regions flew
The maid celestial and the monster-crew.
Those to the grots retir'd, the dark retreat
Of Dicte's caverns in Minoian Crete;
While the gay goddess of the watery bow
Soar'd on fleet pinions to Olympus' brow.
Mean-while the princes, with unwearied pains,
Wash from their seer the harpies' filthy stains:
Next from the spoils, which on Bebrycia's shore
From vanquish'd Amycus brave Pollux bore,
The fleecy victims they select with care;
And sooth the gods with sacrifice and pray'r.
Then in the palace each heroic guest
Partakes the pleasures of the sumptuous feast:
With them sat Phineus, and refresh'd his soul
With savoury viands, and the cheering bowl:
While yet he feasts, insatiate still he seems,
And shares a bliss beyond the bliss of dreams.

Tho' now the rage of hunger was repress'd,
And generous wine had open'd every breast;
Yet still the chiefs prolong the banquet late,
And for the feather'd sons of Boreas wait.
Plac'd in the midst, before the cheerful fire,
Thus of their voyage spoke the sacred sire:
"Hear what the gods permit me to relate;
For 'tis profane to publish all your fate.
Unnumber'd woes I felt, and feel them still,
For erst divulging Jove's almighty will:
To man he gives fate's dark events to scan
In part, but always leaves dependant man.
When hence your destin'd voyage ye pursue,
Two rocks will rise, tremendous to the view,
Just in the entrance of the watery waste,
Which never mortal yet in safety past:
Not firmly fix'd; for oft with hideous shock
Adverse they meet, and rock encounters rock:
The boiling billows dash their airy brow,
Loud thundering round the ragged shore below.
Safe if ye hope to pass, my counsel hear,
Be rul'd by prudence, and the gods revere;
Nor on your unexperienc'd youth depend,
The want of caution brings you to your end.
First from your ship a nimble dove let fly,
And on the sure prognostic bird rely;
Safe thro' the rocks if she pursue her way,
No longer ye the destin'd course delay;
Steer for the strait, and let the rowers sweep
With stretching oars the close-contracted deep:
For not in prayers alone your safety stands;
But nervous vigour, and the strength of hands.
Ply then your oars, and strain at every stroke;
But first with prayer the deities invoke.
The dove's sad fate should you desponding view,
Crush'd by the closing fragments as she flew,
Steer back, lest you against those rocks be driv'n,
Steer back; 'tis safest to submit to Heav'n.
'Twere death thro' them to force the foaming keel,
Tho' heaven-built Argo were compos'd of steel.
O friends, be warn'd by me, nor rashly dare
To venture farther than my words declare;
Me though ye deem the righteous gods pursue
With direful vengeance, threefold more than due;
Tempt not without the dove this dangerous strait,
For man must suffer what's ordain'd by fate.
But if with active oars ye safely gain,
Through these tremendous rocks, the distant main;
Close to Bithynia let your vessel run,
And on the left the dangerous shallows shun;
Till Rhebas, rapid-rolling stream, ye reach,
The gloomy shore, and Thynia's sheltering beach.
Thence o'er the billows fronting Thynia's strand,
Soon will ye gain the Mariandine land.
Here lies the path to Pluto's dreary caves,
Here Acherusia frowns above the waves,
Whose skirts the gulfy Acheron divides,
And from deep whirlpools disembogues his tides.
Thence, not far distant, with the western gale,
Near Paphlagonia's towering heights ye sail,
The hardy sons of which inclement coast
Enetean Pelops for their founder boast.
"Full to the north a promontory fam'd
Lifts the high head in air, Carambis nam'd;
The northern winds below its summit sweep,
So loftily it rises o'er the deep.
This point once doubled, a new coast expands
Its ample plains, and on the limit stands
A cape far-jutting, from whose rocky shores
The rapid Halys in old ocean roars.
Near him clear Iris draws his humbler train,
In silver torrents foaming to the main.
Beyond projects an headland tall and steep,
And forms a peaceful harbour in the deep.
Here o'er extensive fields Thermodon pours,
Near Themiscyria's heights, his watery stores.
Next lie the spacious Dœan plains, and near
Three cities of the Amazons appear:
And next the Chalybes, inur'd to toil,
Work at the forge, and turn the stubborn soil.
Near these the wealthy Tiberenians till,
Sacred to Jove, the Genetæan hill.
The Mossynœcians, next, the country round
Possess, with mountains and with forests crown'd.
In towers they live of solid timber fram'd,
Mossynes call'd, and thence the nation nam'd.
When these are past, an island bleak and bare
Lies full in view, there guide your ship with care,
And thence with care those noxious birds expel,
Which on the desert shore unnumber'd dwell.
Here form'd of solid stone, and seen from far,
Stands the rough temple of the god of war.
Two Amazonian queens, renown'd for arms,
Had rais'd the fane, when stunn'd with war's alarms.
Steer to this island through the stormy main,
And, all that mariners can wish, ye gain.
But why should I each circumstance disclose,
And make again the powers of Heaven my foes?
Beyond that isle, but on the fronting shores,
The Philyreans feed their fleecy stores:
The brave Macronians till the neighbouring coast;
Next these the numerous Bechirian host:
Near them Sapirians and Byzerians dwell,
And next the Colchians, who in arms excel.
But ye, your steady course in Argo keep,
Shun the false shores, and plough secure the deep,
Till that rich coast ye reach, where Phasis leads
From Amarantine hills o'er Colchian meads
His liquid stores, and through fam'd Circe's plain;
Then rolls his widening current to the main.
To this fam'd stream pursue your watery way,
Soon will your eyes Æeta's towers survey,
And Mars's grove, where, wondrous to behold!
Hangs on a spreading oak the fleecy gold.
A hideous dragon of enormous size
Turns all around his circumspective eyes:
O'er the bright spoil the strictest watch he keeps;
He never slumbers, and he never sleeps."
He spoke, and terrour curdled all their blood;
Deep fix'd in silence long the warriors stood.
At length thus Jason, though possess'd with fear:
"Tell us, O tell us, venerable seer,
Th' event of all our toils; the sign explain
How safely we may pass into the main
Thro' those dire rocks: and, O! indulgent, say,
Shall we once more our native land survey?
Unskill'd am I, unskill'd our martial train;
How shall I act, how measure back the main?
For far as ever flying sails were furl'd
Lies Colchos, on the limits of the world."
Thus Jason spoke; and thus the prophet old:
"Those dangerous rocks once pass'd, my son, be bold.
Some god from Æa shall thro' seas untry'd,
Skirted by others' coasts, your vessel guide,
But you, to Æa sailing, on your crew confide.
But, friends, to Venus be due honours paid;
Still in remembrance keep her secret aid.
On all your toils she kindly will bestow
A glorious end——expect no more to know."

Scarce had he spoke, when speeding back repair
The sons of Boreas through the fields of air:
At the seer's door with nimble feet they light;
Up rose the chiefs rejoicing at the sight.
When Zetes trembling, and with toils oppress'd,
While thick short sobs incessant heav'd his chest,
Tells how they drove the harpies far away,
How Iris screen'd them, and forbad to slay,
And pledg'd her solemn oath: while they retreat
To the huge caves of mountain-cover'd Crete.
These joyful tidings cheer'd the hearts of all,
But most the prophet's, in the feastful hall;
Whom Jason thus: "Sure from his heavenly state
Some god look'd down, and wail'd thy woeful fate,
And fore-decreed from far our bands to send,
That Boreas' sons might their assistance lend.
Should the same god restore thy long-lost sight,
My gladden'd soul would feel as great delight,
As ev'n my native country could bestow."
Then thus sage Phineus with dejected brow:
"My eyes, alas! shall ne'er behold the day;
Shrunk are these balls, and quench'd the visual ray:
Heaven round me soon death's gloomy shade shall spread,
And every honour will await me dead."
With converse thus the fleeting hours they cheer'd,
When rosy morning beaming bright appear'd.
The neighbouring peasants round, with early day,
Flock to the seer, their due regards to pay;
This daily custom love and reverence taught,
And some provision for the sage they brought.
All came to learn by his prophetic lore:
He to the rich divin'd, and to the poor:
For numerous votaries he reliev'd from dread,
Who dearly lov'd him, and who daily fed.
With these his steady friend Paræbius came,
Who saw with joy these gallant sons of fame.
To him prophetic Phineus had foretold,
That a young band of Grecians, brave and bold,
Should in their voyage to the Colchian shore,
In Thynia's bay their well-built vessel moor,
And from these coasts, those ravenous birds of prey,
The harpies drive, though sent by Jove, away.
The seer well pleas'd dismiss'd his friendly train,
But bade Paræbius with the Greeks remain,
And fetch him instant from his numerous stock
A sheep, the best and fairest of the flock.
The willing swain obey'd the seer's request,
And Phineus thus the mariners address'd:
"We are not all unciviliz'd and rude,
My friends, nor guilty of ingratitude.
That shepherd to my mansion came of late,
To learn from me the colour of his fate;
For the more labours and fatigues he bore,
Pale, pining want oppress'd him still the more;
New woes succeeded to the woes that past,
And every day was darker than the last:
And yet no crime had poor Paræbius wrought,
Alas! he suffered for his father's fault:
Who, when alone, and on the mountain's brow,
With cruel axe he laid the forest low,
Deaf to a doleful Hamadryad's pray'r,
The nymph neglected, and refus'd to spare,
Though oft she urg'd this lamentable plea;
'Pity, ah! pity my coeval tree,
Where I so many blissful ages dwelt!'
But his hard heart no soft compassion felt:
The tree he fell'd; and for this foul disgrace
The nymph ordain'd him woes, and all his race.
To me Paræbius came oppress'd with fear,
The cause I found, and counsel'd him to rear
An altar to the goddess of the shore,
And pardon for his father's crimes implore.
Thus was the guilt aton'd; e'er since the man
Pays all regards that grateful mortal can;
For ever at my side he loves to stay,
And always goes unwillingly away."
Thus Phineus spoke, when from his fleecy stock
His friend brought two, the fairest of the flock:
Then Jason rose, and, urg'd by Phineus blind,
Rose the bold offspring of the northern wind;
Their sacred offerings on the flames they lay,
Invoking Phœbus at the dawn of day.
The choicest viands with assiduous care
The younger heroes for their friends prepare.
Thus feasted, some their vessel's cordage press'd,
Some in the prophet's mansion sunk to rest.
Etesian breezes with the morning blow,
Which, sent by Jove, o'er every region flow.
The nymph Cyrene, in old times, 'tis said,
Her flocks beside Thessalian Peneus fed,
Pleas'd with the honours of her virgin-name,
Till day's bright god seduc'd the rural dame.
Far from Hæmonia he convey'd the fair,
Brought to the nymphs, and trusted to their care,
The mountain-nymphs that in parch'd Libya keep
Their airy mansions on Myrtosia's steep.
Cyrene there, along the winding shore,
Thee, Aristæus, to Apollo bore;
To whom rich swains, who in Thessalia live,
The names of Agreus, and of Nomius give.
With length of days the god her love repaid,
And fix'd her huntress of the woodland shade;
But the young boy to Chiron's care he gave,
To reap instruction in his learned cave.
To him, when blooming in the prime of life,
The Muses gave Autonoë to wife;
And taught their favourite pupil to excel
In arts of healing, and divining well.
To him they gave their numerous flocks to feed,
Which Phthia's Athamantine pastures breed;
And those that stray on Othrys' lofty brow,
Or where Apidanus' fam'd waters flow.
But when fierce Syrius scorch'd the Cyclades,
The realms of Minos, in th' Ægean seas,
Nought could the burning malady allay;
The islanders implor'd the god of day,
Who sent young Aristæus to their aid,
By whom the fatal pestilence was staid.
At his sire's call he left fair Phthia's land,
Attended by a bold Arcadian band,
Who from Lycaon their extraction boast,
And sail'd to Ceos with his numerous host.
He there an altar rais'd to showery Jove,
And made oblation on the heights above
To the red star that desolates the land,
And to Heaven's king; at whose supreme command
Th' Etesian winds, while forty days they blow,
Refresh with balmy gales the soil below.
Ev'n now the Cean priests pay rites divine
Before the burning star begins to shine.
Thus fame reports; and by these winds detain'd,
With Phineus still the Argonauts remain'd.
The grateful Thynians daily, while they staid,
To their lov'd seer abundant stores convey'd.
Yet, ere they leave this hospitable land,
To the twelve gods erect they on the strand

An altar, and with sacrifice and pray'r
Appease the powers of Heaven, and to their ship repair,
Eager their long-neglected oars to prove;
Yet not unmindful of the timorous dove:
Which safely fasten'd by a slender band
Euphemus carry'd trembling in his hand.
Quick from the stay they lopp'd the doubled cord:
Minerva saw the heroes haste aboard:
On a thin cloud she lighted from above,
(The cloud upheld the mighty seed of Jove)
And sped her voyage to the Euxine main,
For much she lov'd the delegated train.
So when some shepherd quits his native home,
(As men adventurous much delight to roam)
No roads too distant, or too long appear,
In thought he sees, and thinks his mansion near;
O'er sea, o'er land, with keen inquiring eyes
He views all ways, and in idea flies:
Thus to the Thynian shore, from Heaven above,
Swift flew the daughter of imperial Jove.
When now the heroes through the vast profound
Reach the dire straits with rocks encompass'd round,
Though boiling gulphs the sailing pine detain'd,
Still on their way the labouring Grecians gain'd,
When the loud-justling rocks increas'd their fears:
The shores resounding thunder'd in their ears.
High on the prow Euphemus took his stand,
And held the dove that trembled in his hand.
The rest with Tiphys on their strength rely'd,
To shun the rocks and stem the roaring tide.
Soon, one sharp angle past, the joyful train
Saw the cleft crags wide opening to the main.
Euphemus loos'd the dove, the heroes stood
Erect to see her skim the foaming flood.
She through the rocks a ready passage found;
The dire rocks met, and gave a dreadful sound.
The salt-sea spray in clouds began to rise;
Old Ocean thunder'd; the cerulean skies
Rebellow'd loudly with the fearful din;
The caves below remurmur'd from within.
O'er wave-worn cliffs, the coast's high margin o'er
Boil'd the light foam, and whiten'd all the shore.
Round whirl'd the ship; the rocks with rapid sway
Lopp'd from the dove her steering tail away;
Yet still securely through the straits she flew:
Loud joy inspir'd the circumspective crew.
But Tiphys urg'd the chiefs their oars to ply,
For the rocks yawn'd, tremendous to the eye.
Then terrour seiz'd them, when with sudden shock
The refluent billows forc'd them on the rock;
With chilling fears was every nerve unstrung,
While o'er their heads impending ruin hung.
Before, behind, they saw the spacious deep,
When instant, lo! a billow, vast and steep,
Still rises higher, and still wider spreads,
And hangs a watery mountain o'er their heads.
The heroes stoop'd, expecting by its fall
That mighty billow would o'erwhelm them all;
But Tiphys' art reliev'd the labouring oars:
On Argo's keel th' impetuous torrent pours,
Which rais'd the ship above the rocks so high,
She seem'd sublimely sailing in the sky.
Euphemus hastening urg'd the valiant crew
Their course with all their vigour to pursue.
Shouting they plied their oars, but plied in vain;
For the rough billows beat them back again.
And as the heroes unremitting row,
Their labouring oars were bent into a bow.
Swift down the mountainous billows Argo glides,
Like a huge cylinder along the tides,
Entangled with thick, craggy rocks around,
Her seams all bursting, and her planks unbound.
In that nice moment the Tritonian maid
To sacred Argo lent the timely aid.
Her left hand heav'd her from the craggy steep,
Her right dismiss'd her gently to the deep:
Then like an arrow from th' elastic yew,
Swift o'er the foaming waves the vessel flew.
Yet had the clashing rocks with adverse sway
Torn the tall prow's embellishments away.
When thus the Greeks had safely reach'd the main,
To Heaven Minerva wing'd her flight again.
The parted rocks at once concurrent stood,
Fix'd on one firm foundation in the flood:
This had been long determin'd by the fates,
If mortal ever past those dangerous straits.
Now freed from fears, the Greeks with eager eyes
View the broad ocean and serener skies:
Their anxious doubts for Argo they dispel,
And deem her rescued from the jaws of Hell.
Then Tiphys thus: "Sure to this ship we owe
That fearless safety we experience now,
For tho' wise Argus with ingenious art
Form'd the fair ship compact in every part,
Vigour divine propitious Pallas gave,
And power assign'd her o'er the wind and wave.
All now is safe: fear not thy haughty lord,
But mark, illustrious chief, the prophet's word,
The rocks escap'd, no future fears remain,
Your toils are easy, and your voyage plain."
Thus he; and steering through the spacious sea,
Near fair Bithynia plough'd the liquid way.
Then Jason mild the pilot thus address'd:
"Why, Tiphys, this to me with grief oppress'd?
Yes, I have err'd—my faults afflict my soul:
When Pelias gave command without control,
'Twas mine to 've shunn'd this wild-projected plot,
Though instant death had been my certain lot.
Now fears and cares my tortur'd bosom rend;
I dread those ills that from the deep impend,
I dread the savage coast, and every place
Where dwells the bloody, or the barbarous race.
No peace by day, no sleep at night I take,
Since these brave chiefs assembled for my sake.
With cold indifference may'st thou look down,
For no man's safety anxious but thy own;
But I, the least solicitous for mine,
Feel for this friend's, that comrade's, and for thine.
Much shall I feel for all this martial band,
Unless they safe regain their native land."
Thus spoke the prince, his gallant host to try;
With animating sounds they rend the sky.
The loud acclaim was grateful to his ears,
And thus he boldly hails his brave compeers:
"Your valour, friends, encourages my soul:
And since no fears your gallant hearts control,
Boldly will I each coward thought repel,
Though doom'd to enter the abyss of Hell.
For these rocks past, no dangers can dismay,
If we the counsel of the seer obey."
The Greeks applauding what their leader spoke,
Ply their stout oars and bend to every stroke;
And first by Rhebas' rapid stream they fly,
And where Colona's rocks invade the sky,
And where the black-brow'd promontary low'rs,
And where lov'd Phillis his broad current pours.
There Dipsacus receiv'd, in days of yore,
Young Phryxus landing on his friendly shore,

When, exil'd from Orchomenos, he swam
On the broad shoulders of the gold-fleec'd ram.
For to that stream a nymph of rural race
Bore Dipsacus, who, fearful of disgrace,
Dwelt with his mother, and along the mead
Chose, near his father's stream, his fleecy flocks to feed.
The chiefs soon pass'd his celebrated fane,
The river Calpis, and th' extended plain;
And all the night, along the tranquil tide,
And all the day their oars incessant ply'd.
As when laborious steers, inur'd to toil,
With the bright plough-share turn the stubborn soil;
Sweat from their sides distils in foamy smoke;
Their eyes obliquely roll beneath the yoke;
Their scorching breath heaves quick with panting sound,
While all day long they tread the weary ground:
So toil'd the Greeks; nor yet the morning-light
Had pass'd the doubtful confines of the night,
But, faintly glimmering on this earthly ball,
Produc'd what mortals morning-twilight call.
To Thynia's neighbouring isle their course they bore,
And safely landed on the desert shore,
When bright Apollo show'd his radiant face,
From Lycia hastening to the Scythian race.
His golden locks, that flow'd with grace divine,
Hung clustering like the branches of the vine:
In his left hand, his bow unbent he bore,
His quiver pendent at his back he wore:
The conscious island trembled as he trod,
And the big rolling waves confess'd the god.
Nor dar'd the heroes, seiz'd with dire dismay,
The splendours of his countenance survey,
But on the ground their downward eyes they cast:
Meanwhile Apollo o'er the watery waste,
And through thin ether on his journey flew.
Then thus spoke Orpheus to the martial crew:
" Let us, my honour'd chiefs, with joint acclaim
This island sacred to bright Phœbus name,
Who early here to all this host appear'd;
Here let an altar on the shore be rear'd,
And paid the rites divine: and if he deign
That safe we reach our native land again,
Young horned goats shall on his altars bleed,
And the choice thighs to Phœbus be decreed.
Now, comrades, due libations let us pay:
Be gracious, O be gracious, god of day!"
  Thus he: and some the stony altar raise,
And some explore the forest's devious maze;
Haply within its lone retreats to find
A kid wild wandering, or a bounding hind:
Latona's son soon led them to the prey;
Then on the altar, blazing bright, they lay
The choicest parts involv'd in sacred smoke,
And fair Apollo, early god, invoke.
Around the flame in sprightly dance they spring,
And Iö Pæan, Iö Pæan sing.
Then on the Thracian harp Œager's son
In soothing strains his tuneful tale begun:
  How once beneath Parnassus' rocky brow
He lanch'd an arrow from his deadly bow,
And the fell serpent slew; though young and fair
And beardless yet, but grac'd with golden hair:
(O prove propitious, thou whose radiant head
Is deck'd with curls unclip'd, that never shed,
Worthy thyself! Latona only knows
With nicest art those ringlets to dispose)
Corycian nymphs their joys in rapture show'd,
And Iö, Iö Pæan call'd aloud:
Encomium grateful to the god of day.
Thus having prais'd him in the solemn lay,
They swear devoutly, due libations made,
To league for ever, and lend mutual aid;
Then touch the hallow'd alta with their hands
Concordant; and ev'n now a temple stands
Sacred to Concord, by the Grecians rais'd,
When here that mighty deity they prais'd.
  Now the third morn began on Earth to smile,
When with fresh gales they left the lofty isle.
The foaming Sangar at a distance seen,
The Mariandine meads for ever green,
And Lycus' winding waters they forsake
All on the right, and Anthemoisia's lake.
So fast before the wind the vessel went,
Crack'd was the cordage, and the canvas rent:
But the gale ceasing with the dawning day,
Joyful they reach the Acherusian bay,
Begirt with rocks so towering tall and steep,
They frown tremendous on Bithynia's deep;
And yet so firmly founded in the main,
The raging billows round them roar in vain:
Above, upon the promontory's brow,
Umbrageous planes in beauteous order grow.
Thence, downward, thro' a deep and dreary dell,
Descends the path-way to the cave of Hell,
With woods and shaggy rocks obscure; from whence
Exhaling vapours, chilly, damp and dense,
Scatter hoar frost along the whitening way,
Which melts before the Sun's meridian ray.
On these rough cliffs, which many a storm molests,
The pleasing power of silence never rests.
From hollow caverns through the leafy boughs,
Above, the whistling wind for ever blows;
And while mad billows lash the sounding shores,
Below, the raging main for ever roars.
There, bursting from the promontory's sides,
Sad Acheron along the valley glides;
Deep hollow'd beds his turbid streams convey,
As eastward to the main he winds his way.
This sable flood, in ancient story fam'd,
The Megarensians Soönautes nam'd
In after ages, when their course they bore
By ocean to the Mariandine shore:
For when the deep in deathful billows heav'd,
This peaceful port their shatter'd ships receiv'd.
To this the labouring Grecians bent their way,
Row'd round the cape, and anchor'd in the bay.
When Lycus and his Mariandine host,
Lycus, the mighty monarch of the coast,
Knew these brave Greeks who Amycus had slain,
They welcom'd Jason and his conquering-train:
But most on Pollux fix'd their wondering eyes,
And view'd him as a hero from the skies:
For long the fierce Bebrycians' rude alarms
Had rous'd the Mariandyni to arms.
That day, the Grecian band with one consent
To the king's hospitable palace went:
Cheerful they there on choicest dainties din'd,
And there with converse sweet regal'd the mind.
Then Jason to the king recounts the name,
And race of all these chosen sons of fame,
Who lent their aid at Pelias' dire command;
Their strange adventures on the Lemnian land;
What griefs, what woes at Cyzicus they bore;
And how they landed on the Mysian shore,
Where Hercules, distress'd his friend to find,
They left at land, unwillingly, behind;

What Glaucus spoke prophetic from the main,
How with his subjects Amycus was slain,
The prince relates: what Phineus poor and old,
Worn out with sufferings to the chiefs foretold;
How thro' Cyanean rocks they safely steer'd,
And in what isle the god of day appear'd.
The king rejoic'd his guests so well had sped,
But griev'd that Hercules was left, and said:
"Think how, my friends, this hero's aid deny'd,
Rashly ye tempt a length of seas untry'd.
Full well I knew that valiant son of fame,
When here on foot thro' Lydia's coast he came
(For here my hospitable father dwelt)
To fetch Hippolita's embroider'd belt.
The hero found me then a beardless swain,
Mourning my brother by the Mysians slain;
(The nation dearly lov'd the blooming chief,
And still lament in elegies of grief)
Then at the funeral games he prov'd his might,
And vanquish'd Titias in the gauntlet-fight;
Tho' young and stout, and eager for the fray,
From his bruis'd jaws he dash'd the teeth away.
The Mysian country, and the Phrygian plains
The conqueror added to my sire's domains;
And the rude nations that Bithynia till,
To foaming Rhebas and Colona's hill;
And Paphlagonia to its utmost bounds,
Which sable Billis with his waves surrounds.
But now proud Amycus, and all his host,
Since Hercules has left the neighbouring coast,
Have spoil'd my realms, and spread their hostile bands
Wide as where Hipias' streams enrich the lands.
At length their lawless insolence they rue,
And by your hands have suffer'd vengeance due.
And sure some god afforded his relief
When Pollux slew that proud Bebrycian chief.
I for this deed my due regard will show;
'Tis what the meanest to the mighty owe.
My son, your comrade, shall at my command
Attend o'er distant seas your gallant band:
O'er distant seas, with Dascylus your guide,
You still with faithful friends shall be supply'd,
Far as Thermodon rolls his foaming tide.
Meanwhile on yon bold cape that mates the skies
To Leda's sons a sacred fane shall rise,
Admir'd by all that cross the boundless main,
For all shall venerate the sacred fane:
To them will I, as to the powers divine,
Some fruitful acres near the town assign."
Conversing thus, the genial feast they share,
And to the ship at early day repair:
With his brave son the friendly Lycus went,
Who store of viands to the ship had sent.
'Twas here the cruel destinies decreed
That Idmon, fam'd for augury, should bleed:
The fate of others he had oft foreshown,
But fail'd, unhappy! to prevent his own.
Here, in a covert near the reedy flood,
A fell wild boar lay deep immers'd in mud.
With horrid tusks so dreadful he appear'd,
The fountain-nymphs the savage monster fear'd:
No living wight in miry marsh or moor
E'er saw so fierce, so horrible a boar.
On the lake's verge as luckless Idmon stood,
From his close covert, in the reedy mud,
Up sprung the furious beast with might and main,
Tore the chief's thigh, and snapp'd the bone in twain;
He groans, he falls, and on the bank he lies,
His griev'd companions answer to his cries;
When Peleus instantly approaching near,
Lanch'd at the boar his unavailing spear:
But Idas aim'd his pointed dart so well,
Low in the marsh the dying monster fell.
The chiefs with Idmon to the ship retir'd,
Who deeply groaning in their arms expir'd.
Immers'd in grief, they now neglect to sail;
For three whole days their comrade they bewail;
But on the fourth, with pensive sorrow, paid
The last sad honours due to Idmon's shade.
The king, the people join'd the mournful crew,
And, loud-lamenting, numerous victims slew:
They dug the grave, and on the greensward raise
A tomb on which posterity will gaze:
For near the tomb a tall wild olive grows,
Beneath the cape, and beautifully blows.
Me would the Nine commission to unfold
This truth, which Phœbus had long since foretold,
This, this is he, the tutelary lord,
Henceforth to be by mighty states ador'd:
For here Bœotians and Megarians join'd,
Near the wild olive wavering in the wind,
To build a city; though due honours they
To Agamestor, not to Idmon, pay.
Who fell beside? for, lo! the chiefs intend
Another tomb for some lamented friend.
Ev'n now two mournful monuments appear:
Tiphys, Fame says, was stretch'd upon the bier.
Him cruel fate ordain'd no more to roam;
He died far distant from his native home.
For while to Idmon funeral rites they pay,
Untimely sickness snatch'd the chief away.
Then heart-felt sadness seiz'd the pensive train;
Who, prostrate on the margin of the main,
Forgetful of their necessary food,
Mourn'd in sad silence to the roaring flood.
For they, now skilful Tiphys is no more,
Despair'd returning to their native shore;
And here had staid, with bitter grief oppress'd,
Had not Saturnia in Ancæus' breast
Breath'd courage: him Astypalæa bore,
Near winding Imbrasus on Samos' shore,
To ocean's god; a chief expert to guide
The flying vessel o'er the foaming tide.
Then thus to Peleus, Neptune's valiant son,
By Heaven inspir'd, in cheering terms begun:
"Ill suits the brave in foreign climes to stay,
And waste, O Peleus, precious time away.
I left not Samos less for sailing skill'd
Than fierce contention in the fighting field.
For Argo cherish not one abject fear,
Since many skill'd, besides myself, are here.
And he, to whom the steerage we ordain,
Will safely guide the vessel o'er the main.
'Tis thine to stimulate the fainting crew
With hardy oars their voyage to pursue."
He spoke, and transport touch'd the Phthian's breast;
Instant he rose, and thus the host address'd:
"Why are we here by fruitless grief detain'd?
Two friends are dead, and this the fates ordain'd;
Yet many pilots in this host remain,
To steer firm Argo o'er the watery plain.
To sorrows unavailing bid adieu!
Let us, bold peers, our destin'd course pursue."
He said, and Jason anxious thus reply'd;
"Where are those pilots, say, our course to guide?
For those whom late we boasted as the best
And ablest chiefs, are most with grief oppress'd.

I therefore deem a like sad fate attends
On us, as on our late departed friends,
If neither in Æeta's ports we moor,
Nor thro' those rocks regain our native shore,
But here inactive and inglorious stay,
Years following years, and linger life away."
He spoke; Ancæus seiz'd the steerage, driv'n
By power instinctive from the queen of Heav'n.
Erginus next the glorious charge desir'd;
Euphemus, Nauplius to the helm aspir'd.
But these the congregated chiefs declin'd,
And bold Ancæus to the post assign'd.
With the twelfth rising morn the heroes sail;
Favonius breath'd a favourable gale;
And soon they leave sad Acheron behind,
Then give the swelling canvas to the wind:
On the smooth sea the ship serenely rides,
And light along the liquid level glides.
Ere long with stretching sails the coast they gain,
Where broad Callichorus augments the main.
To Thebes returning from his Indian fights,
Here Bacchus solemniz'd mysterious rites,
The dance before the sacred cave ordain'd,
And here full many a doleful night remain'd.
This name the country to the river gave,
Callichorus; and Aulion to the cave.
Still as their course the daring Greeks pursue,
The monument of Sthenelus they view.
With honours grac'd, obtain'd in realms afar,
Returning from the Amazonian war,
On the bleak shore (Alcides at his side)
Pierc'd by a fatal dart the hero died.
Slow sail'd they on, for, eager to survey
His kindred warriors on the watery way,
At his request, from her infernal coast
Pluto's grim queen releas'd the pensive ghost.
The pensive ghost beheld with eager ken
From the tall monument the ship and men.
As arm'd for war the martial phantom seem'd;
Four crests high-towering on his helmet beam'd,
With purple rays intolerably bright;
Then soon it sunk beneath the shades of night.
In mute amazement stood the Grecian host;
But Mopsus counsel'd to appease the ghost
With offerings due; the chiefs approach the strand,
And round the tomb of Sthenelus they stand.
They pour libations, and the victims slay,
And on the fire the destin'd offerings lay.
Apart, to guardian Phœbus next they raise
An altar meet, and bid the victims blaze.
Here Orpheus plac'd his lyre for music fam'd;
Apollo's altar hence was Lyra nam'd.
And now, invited by the favouring gales,
They climb the ship and spread their swelling sails;
Swift o'er the deep the winged vessel flies,
Swift as the rapid hawk that cleaves the skies,
And lightly thro' the liquid ether springs,
Nor moves, self-poiz'd, his wide-expanded wings.
Thence by Parthenius sail'd the social train,
The gentlest stream that mingles with the main.
Fatigued with traversing the mazy grove,
Here, ere she re-ascends the courts of Jove,
The chaste Diana, huntress of the wood,
Bathes her fair limbs, and gambols in the flood.
Then during night by Sesamus they sail,
And Erythinus rising o'er the vale;
By Cromna and Crobrialus, and where
Thy groves, Cytorus, ever green appear.
Thence with the rising Sun they stoutly row
Near where Carambis lifts his rocky brow.
All day, all night with unremitted oar
They coast along Ægialus's shore.
Then to the Syrian clime the heroes sped,
Where Jove, by hasty promises misled,
Sinope plac'd, and, all she wish'd to claim,
Gave her the honours of a virgin's name.
For, know, the god, by love's strong power oppress'd,
Promis'd to grant whate'er she might request:
And this request th' insidious damsel made,
That her virginity might never fade.
Hence Phœbus foil'd could no one wish obtain;
Hence winding Alys wooed the maid in vain.
No mortal force such virtue could o'ercome,
Defeat Jove's promise, and impair her bloom.
Here dwelt Deïmachus's offspring fam'd,
Deileon, Autolycus and Phlogius nam'd,
What time they ceas'd with Hercules to roam,
And at Sinope found a settled home.
They, when they saw the bold Thessalian band,
Met them on shore and welcom'd them to land;
And, loathing longer in these climes to stay,
Join'd the brave crew, and with them sail'd away.
Bless'd with the zephyr's breeze that briskly blew,
Near Halys' stream and Isis' sail'd the crew;
Near Syria's coast, and, ere night's shades abound,
Near th' Amazonian cape, for many a bay renown'd.
Where Hercules surpris'd, in days of yore,
Bold Menalippe wandering on the shore:
A belt Hippolyta her sister paid,
And for this ransom he restor'd the maid.
Here in Thermodon's bay firm Argo moor'd;
For lash'd with tempests the vex'd ocean roar'd.
No river like the fam'd Thermodon leads
Such numerous currents o'er the fertile meads:
A hundred streams to him their waters owe;
Yet from one source, one only source they flow.
On Amazonian hills, that reach the skies,
The great Thermodon first begins to rise;
Hence soon emerging many a course he takes,
Sinks but to mount, and various channels makes.
The different streams from different founts distil,
In soft meanders wandering down the hill;
Some public notice and fair titles claim,
Some flow obscurely, and without a name;
But confluent soon, along the winding plain,
He rolls his waves, and foams o'er half the main.
Had the Greeks landed on this hostile coast,
War would have soon pursu'd the gallant host:
(For the fierce Amazons regard not right,
Strife is their sport, and battles their delight:
From Mars and Harmony these warlike maids
Sprung where Acmonius spreads its bowery shades)
But favour'd with the soft Favonian wind,
The heroes left the crooked shore behind,
Where the bold Amazons, perceiv'd from far,
Stood sheath'd in arms, prepar'd for speedy war.
Not in one city dwelt this martial band,
But in three parties scatter'd o'er the land:
The first tribe at Themiscyra remain'd,
O'er this Hippolyta, their empress, reign'd;
There dwelt the fair Lycastian dames apart,
Here the Chadesians, skill'd to lance the dart.
Th' ensuing day the delegated band
Approach'd with oars the rough Chalybian land;
Whose sons ne'er yoke their oxen to the plough,
Nor healing plants, nor fruits delicious know:
Nor aught delight they in th' irriguous mead,
Retir'd and still, their fleecy flocks to feed;

But they dig iron from the mountains side,
And by this ore are nature's wants supply'd.
Devoid of toil ne'er beam'd Aurora's ray,
And dust and smoke obscur'd the dismal day.
From thence they pass where Tibarenians till,
Sacred to Jove, the Genetæan hill.
Here, when the teeming wives are brought to bed,
Their groaning husbands hang the drooping head;
Equal attendance with their wives they claim;
The same their diet, and their baths the same.
Next by the sacred hill their oars impel
Firm Argo, where the Mossynœcians dwell.
In towers they live, of solid timber fram'd,
Mossynes call'd, and thence the nation nam'd:
Of manners strange; for they with care conceal
Those deeds which others openly reveal;
And actions, that in secret should be done,
Perform in public and before the Sun:
For, like the monsters of the bristly drove,
In public they perform the feats of love.
Exalted in his tower that mates the sky,
The monarch here dispenses law from high:
But if his judgment err, this rigid state
Condemns their chief, and starving is his fate.
These nations past, with unremitting oar
They reach, Aretias, thy sea-girt shore.
Then sunk the breezes with the closing day,
When down the sky descending they survey
A winged monster of enormous might,
Which toward the ship precipitates her flight.
Her wings she shook, and from her pinions flung
A dart-like quill, which on Oïleus hung;
Down his left shoulder swift it fell: no more,
Faint and enfeebled, could he hold his oar.
In silence long the Grecian heroes gaze,
And view the feathery javelin with amaze.
But Erybotes, soon approaching near,
Extracted from the chief the winged spear;
Then from his side his pendent belt unbound,
And wrapp'd that bandage o'er the gaping wound.
When, lo! a second bird appear'd in view,
But ready Clytius first had bent his yew;
By his keen shaft the feather'd monster slain
Fast by the ship fell headlong in the main.
Then thus Amphidamas: " My friends, ye know,
And these obscene voracious fiends foreshow
Aretias near: then list to what I say,
Fruitless are shafts to drive these pests away;
But, would you here a fit reception find,
Recall th' advice of Phineus to your mind.
For when Alcides to Arcadia went
Well arm'd with arrows, on his toils intent,
From the Stymphalian lake he fail'd to fright
These ravenous harpies (I beheld the sight);
But when he rung a cymbal with his spear;
The clanging cymbal fill'd the birds with fear:
In wild confusion far away they fly,
And with shrill clamours pierce the distant sky.
'Tis ours to practise this expulsive art;
But hear ye first the counsel I impart:
Let half our crew, in glittering armour dress'd,
Nod, as by turns they row, the high-plum'd crest;
The rest bright spears and swords and shields provide,
And meet dispose them round the vessel's side.
Then all at once your voices raise on high,
And with loud pealing shouts assail the sky;
The deafening clamours, the protended spears,
And nodding crests will fill the birds with fears.
And when Aretias' barren isle ye gain,
Ring your broad bucklers, and all shout amain."
He spoke, the chiefs approv'd the wise design;
High on their heads the brazen helmets shine,
Whose purple crests wav'd dreadful in the wind;
To these alternate were stout oars assign'd;
The rest with care their vessel's side conceal'd
With glittering spears, and many a shining shield.
As when industrious builders cover o'er
With tiles the walls their hands had rais'd before;
In chequer'd squares they decorate the roof,
And make it fair to view, and tempest-proof:
Thus they with shields, dispos'd in order due,
Shelter'd their vessel, and adorn'd it too.
As when embattled hosts their foes assail,
Tumultuous shouts, and martial sounds prevail;
So from the ship loud clamours pierc'd the sky;
No more the Greeks their feather'd foes descry:
Rattling their bucklers, near the land they drew,
And far away the winged furies flew.
So when great Jove on close-throng'd cities pours
From hyperborean clouds his haily show'rs;
Within, the dwellers sit in peace profound,
Nor heed the rattling storms that rage around;
In vain the hail descends, the tempests roar,
Their roofs from harm were well secur'd before:
Thus on their shields the furies shot their quills,
Then clamouring vanish'd to far distant hills.
Say, Muse, why Phineus counsel'd here to land,
On Mars's isle, this delegated band?
And what advantage could the Grecians gain
From all the toils and perils of the main?
To fam'd Orchomenos, with favouring gale,
From Æa's walls the sons of Phrixus sail,
Their grandsire's vast inheritance to share,
Who dying left this voyage to their care.
Near Mars's island on this signal day
The sons of Phrixus plough'd the liquid way.
But Jove ordain'd that Boreas' blast should blow,
While moist Arcturus soak'd the vales below.
First on the mountains, rising by degrees,
All day rough Boreas shook the trembling trees;
Then, night approaching, he with hideous sound
Roll'd the big wave, and heav'd the vast profound.
No stars appear translucent thro' the clouds,
But gloomy darkness every object shrouds.
The sons of Phrixus, tost by whelming waves,
With horrour shudder'd at the watery graves;
For the fierce blast, impell'd with might and main,
Tore all their canvas, split the ship in twain
And dash'd to pieces; but by Heaven's kind aid
On a large fragment of the wreck convey'd,
The winds and waves the trembling brothers bore
Aghast, and half expiring to the shore.
Instant in floods descended copious rain,
Drench'd the whole island, and increas'd the main;
(These shores, the neighbouring coast, and sacred hill
The rude, the barbarous Mossynœcians till)
Borne on a broken plank, the forceful blast
The sons of Phrixus on this island cast,
Who met the Grecians with the rising Sun;
Ceas'd was the rain, and Argus thus begun:
" Adjur'd by Jove, whose circumspective ken
Surveys the conduct and the cares of men,
Whate'er your name or race, our tale attend,
And to the wretched your assistance lend.
The raging storms that Neptune's empire sweep
Have wreck'd our luckless vessel in the deep;

To you we pray, if pity touch your heart,
Some scanty raiment for our wants impart;
The sons of misery for mercy call;
To one low level sorrow sinks us all.
They who to prostrate suppliants lend an ear,
The laws of hospitable Jove revere.
All-present he hath listen'd to our pray'r,
And sinking sav'd us with a parent's care."
  Then Æson's son (fulfilling Phineus' plan)
Thus question'd mild the miserable man;
"But first, of truth observant, frankly tell,
In what far region of the world ye dwell;
What business call'd you from your native coast,
What race ye sprung from, and what names ye boast."
  Then Argus thus: "Ye, sure, have heard the fame
Of Phrixus, who from Greece to Æa came.
To great Æeta's citadel he swam
Supported on the shoulders of the ram,
Whose fleece now high suspended ye behold
By Hermes metamorphos'd into gold.
On the tall oak's high top it hangs in view,
The ram to Jove, propitious, Phrixus slew.
The generous king receiv'd him as his guest,
And with undower'd Chalciope he bless'd.
From these we sprung; but Phrixus breathes no more,
His bones lie buried on the Colchian shore.
We now to fam'd Orchomenos repair,
The wide domains of Athamas to share;
Such were the last injunctions of our sire:
Our business this—if ye our names require,
This Cytisorus, that will Phrontis claim,
He surnam'd Melas, Argus is my name."
He spoke: the Argonauts with still amaze,
And secret transport on the strangers gaze.
Then Jason mark'd the much-enduring man,
And thus with mild benevolence began:
"Friends as ye are, and near relations too,
To us for succour not in vain ye sue.
Cretheus and Athamas their sire the same;
And Cretheus was my honour'd grandsire's name:
With these companions join'd, I sail from Greece
To Colchos, famous for the golden fleece—
Some distant day, at ease may we relate
These strange events, and all our various fate.
Now shall warm robes to clothe your limbs be giv'n,
We meet conducted by the hand of Heav'n."
  He said, and from the ship rich vestments sent;
Then to the sacred fane of Mars they went.
From fleecy flocks they drain'd the life-warm blood,
And all devoutly round the altar stood;
This, of small stones compos'd, was plac'd before
The lofty temple's double-folding door:
(Within the fane a stone of sable hue
Stood where the Amazons their victims slew;
Who held it lawless, when they sojourn'd here,
To slay the sheep, or sacrifice the steer;
Instead of these the full-fed, pamper'd steed
Was doom'd, a victim at this fane, to bleed.)
These rites dispatch'd, and hunger's rage repress'd,
Thus Æson's son the listening host address'd:
  "Impartial Jove the race of man regards;
The bad he punishes, the just rewards:
As from a bloody stepdame's rage of yore
He sav'd your sire, and blest with ample store,
So he preserv'd you from the whelming deep,
And in this vessel will securely keep;
Whether for Æa in our ship ye sail,
Or to fair Phthia court the favouring gale.
For this fam'd ship of Pelion's pines was made,
And form'd by Argus, with Minerva's aid;
But storms had lash'd her, ere, with hideous shock,
She reach'd those straits, where rock encounters rock.
Then lend your aid to gain the golden fleece,
And be our guides to bring it back to Greece.
Jove seems incens'd, and we this voyage take,
To sooth his anger, and for Phrixus' sake."
  Ardent he spoke; but they despair'd to find
Æeta of so tractable a mind,
To yield the fleece: then Argus thus replies,
Alarm'd and troubled at their bold emprise;
"Whate'er our powers can grant, or wishes gain,
The sons of Greece shall never ask in vain.
But proud Æeta, cruel and severe,
I loath the tyrant, and his power I fear;
The Sun his sire, so fame relates, he boasts;
Unnumber'd subjects guard his ample coasts;
For mighty strength he stands renown'd afar,
And voice terrific as the god of war.
The golden prize a monstrous dragon keeps;
Hard task to seize it, for he never sleeps.
Earth on rough Caucasus a being gave
To this fierce beast near Typhaonia's cave,
Where huge Typhœus, as old stories prove,
Was struck by lightning from almighty Jove,
When fierce in arms against Heaven's king he stood;
From his head issu'd warm corrupted blood;
To Nysa's hills, to Nysa's plains he flies,
And now beneath Serbonian marshes lies."
  He said; distress'd so sad a tale to hear,
On every countenance sat pallid fear;
When Peleus thus with confidence reply'd,
And gave that courage which their fears deny'd:
  "Despair not, friend; for we disdain to yield,
Nor dread to meet Æeta in the field.
We too are skill'd in war, and draw our line
From godlike chiefs, and origin divine.
Incens'd should he the fleecy gold detain,
He'll ask, I trust, the Colchians' aid in vain."
  Conversing thus the chiefs their thoughts express'd,
And sated with repast reclin'd to rest.
With rising morn the gently-breathing gales
Play'd round the pine, and fill'd the swelling sails;
The swelling sails expanded by the wind
Soon left Aretias' barren shore behind;
And swiftly skimming o'er the watery vast,
The Philyræan isle at eve they past;
Where Saturn first fair Philyra survey'd,
When on Olympus he the Titans sway'd,
(Nurs'd by the fierce Curetes, yet a child,
Young Jove was hid in Cretan caverns wild)
Unknown to Rhea he the maid compress'd;
But soon to Rhea was the crime confess'd;
Detected Saturn left his bed with speed,
And sprung all-vigorous as a mane-crown'd steed.
Swift fled fair Philyra, abash'd with shame,
And to the hills of Thessaly she came:
Fam'd Chiron sprung from this embrace so odd,
Ambiguous, half a horse, and half a god.
From thence they sail by long Macronian strands,
And where Bechira's ample coast expands;
Shores where Byzerians wander far and wide,
And fierce Sapirians, stigmatiz'd for pride;
And favour'd by the soft impelling wind,
Leave numerous coasts and lands unnam'd behind:
And, sailing swiftly o'er the waves, survey,
Far on the Pontic main, an opening bay;

Then, Caucasus, thy hills were seen on high,
That rear their rocky summits in the sky;
Fix'd to these rocks Prometheus still remains,
For ever bound in adamantine chains:
On the rude cliffs a rav'nous eagle breeds,
That on the wretch's entrails ever feeds.
The Grecians saw him, ere th' approach of night,
Soar high in air, loud hissing in his flight:
Around the ship he flew in airy rings,
The sails all shivering as he shook his wings:
Not as a light aerial bird he soars,
But moves his pinions like well-polish'd oars.
The ravenous bird now rushing from the skies,
Sudden, they heard Prometheus' piercing cries:
The Heavens re-echo'd to the doleful sound,
While the fell eagle gnaw'd the recent wound.
Till gorg'd with flesh the bird of Jove they spy'd
Again descending from the mountain's side.
  Night now approaching, near the land they drew,
And Argus well his native country knew;
For, Phasis, thy wide-spreading flood they gain,
And the last limits of the Pontic main.
At length arriv'd, so many dangers past,
They furl the mainsail, and they lower the mast:
Their bending oars the mighty stream divide;
The stream receives them on his foaming tide.
All on the left, in ancient rolls renown'd,
Rise Æa's walls with glittering turrets crown'd;
And on the right the field, not distant far,
And grove, both sacred to the god of war;
Where on an oak the fleece, suspended high,
A dragon guards with ever-watchful eye.
Then Jason hastes, impatient to consign
To the pure stream the unpolluted wine,
And from a golden vase fulfils the rite divine,
Sacred to earth, to gods that guard the coasts,
And ancient heroes' long-departed ghosts:
For their protection he preferr'd his pray'r,
To keep the ship with tutelary care.
Then thus Ancæus: " Numerous perils past,
Colchos and Phasis we behold at last;
Behoves you now your sage advice to lend,
Whether to treat Æeta as a friend,
With speech accordant, and compliance bland,
Or in rough terms the golden prize demand."
  Thus he; but Jason urg'd, at Argus' call,
High up the sedgy stream the ship to haul;
Which, undisturb'd, might there at anchor ride
In the calm bosom of the peaceful tide:
There sought the chiefs the blessings of repose,
And slept secure till grateful morning rose.

BOOK III.

ARGUMENT.

Juno and Pallas intercede with Venus. They request that she would persuade Cupid to inspire Medea with love for Jason. Venus consents; and the shafts of Cupid, at her suit, have their desired effect. Jason, Augeas and Telamon proceed to the court of Æetea, where they are hospitably entertained. But, having heard the occasion of their voyage, Æetea is incensed, and refuses to bestow the golden fleece on Jason, unless on such terms, as he presumed he durst not comply with. The passion of Medea for Jason is described with great simplicity and delicacy. Medea early in the morning repairs to the temple of Hecate: thither Jason, at the suggestion of Mopsus, follows her. The poet dwells particularly on their interview and conference. Medea instructs, him how to subdue the brazen bulls and armies of giants. With Jason's combat, and the success of it, the book concludes.

Come, heavenly maid, thy timely succour bring,
And teach thy poet, Erato, to sing,
How Jason, favour'd by the Colchian maid,
To Grecian realms the golden prize convey'd.
Thy songs the rites of Cyprian bliss proclaim,
And in young virgins raise the melting flame;
For the soft passion thy behests approve,
And Erato's the kindred name of love.
  Conceal'd in sedges as the heroes lie,
Juno and Pallas mark'd them from the sky;
Apart from all the gods their seats they took
In Heaven's high hall, and thus Saturnia spoke:
" Daughter of Jove, thy sage advice impart,
By what nice fraud, what well-dissembled art,
These venturous chiefs shall gain the golden fleece,
And safe convey it to the realms of Greece.
Say, shall they call entreaties to their aid?
Will soft address the wayward king persuade,
So fam'd for fierce barbarity and pride?
No art, no effort, must be left untry'd."
She said; and Pallas thus: " O queen, I find
The same ideas rising in my mind:
To lend assistance to the Grecian train
My heart is willing, but my counsel vain."
  This said, their minds on various projects ran,
On earth their eyes were fix'd, when Juno thus began:
  " To Venus instant let us speed our way,
(Her soft persuasions Cupid will obey)
Entreat her that the wily god inspire
Medea's soul with love's unconquer'd fire,
Love for great Æson's son; applauding Greece
Will by her aid regain the glorious fleece."
  She said; Minerva patronis'd the plan,
And thus with mild benevolence began:
  " I, who arose from Jove's immortal brain,
Stranger to love, his pleasure or his pain,
Thy sage proposal from my soul approve;
Do thou explain it to the queen of love."
  This said, with speed the two immortals came
To the grand mansion of the Cyprian dame,
Which crippled Vulcan rais'd, when first he led
The Paphian goddess to his nuptial bed.
The gate they pass, and to the dome retire
Where Venus oft regales the god of fire:
(He to his forge had gone at early day,
A floating isle contain'd it on the bay,
Here wondrous works by fire's fierce power he wrought,
And on his anvil to perfection brought.)
Fronting the door, all lovely and alone,
Sat Cytherea on a polish'd throne.
Adown the shoulders of the heavenly fair,
In easy ringlets flow'd her flaxen hair;
And with a golden comb, in matchless grace,
She taught each lock its most becoming place.
She saw the deities approach her dome,
And from her hand dismiss'd the golden comb;
Then rose respectful, all with beauty grac'd,
And on rich thrones the great immortals plac'd;

Resum'd her seat, and with a ready hand
Bound her loose ringlets, and thus question'd bland:
"What cause, ye visitants from Heaven, relate,
Has brought such guests to Cytherea's gate?
Ye who excel in high Olympus' sphere,
Such mighty deities, and strangers here?"
Then thus Saturnia: "Wantonly you jest,
When pressing grief sits heavy on our breast.
Now in the Phasis, with his warlike train,
Great Jason moors, the golden fleece to gain:
For that fam'd chief, and for his martial host,
Dire fears alarm us, but for Jason most:
This potent arm, whate'er our prowess can,
Shall snatch from misery the gallant man,
Tho' far as Hell he, rash adventurer! go,
To free Ixion, link'd in chains of woe;
Lest Pelias proudly Heaven's decrees deride,
Who on my altars sacrifice de ny'd.
Nay more, young Jason claims my love and grace,
Whom late I met returning from the chase,
Returning met, as o'er the world I stray'd,
And human kind, and human works survey'd;
Hard by Araurus I beheld the man,
Wide o'er its banks whose rapid currents ran;
(From snow-clad hills, in torrents loud and strong,
Roar'd the swoln streams the rugged rocks among.)
He on his back, though like a crone I stood,
Securely brought me o'er the foaming flood;
This won my love, a love for ever true,
Nor will the haughty-minded Pelias rue
His flagrant crimes, till you propitious deign
To speed my Jason to his Greece again."
She spoke, and Venus stood amaz'd to find
The queen of Heaven to humble prayer inclin'd;
Then thus familiar said: "O wife of Jove,
Basest of beings call the queen of love,
Unless her every word and work conspire
To give you all the succour you require:
All that my hand, my feeble hand can do,
Shall unrewarded be perform'd for you."
Then Juno thus: "Not difficult the task;
No mighty force, no strength of arm I ask.
Bid gentle Love the Colchian maid inspire,
And for my Jason fan the rising fire;
If kind she prove, he gains the golden fleece,
And by her subtle aid conducts it safe to Greece."
Love's queen replied: "Cupid, ye powers divine,
Will reverence your injunctions more than mine:
Your looks will awe him, tho', devoid of shame,
Of me the urchin makes eternal game;
Oft he provokes my spleen, and then I vow,
Enrag'd, I'll break his arrows and his bow:"
"Restrain your ire," exclaims the sneering elf,
"Lest you find reason to upbraid yourself."
  At this the powers with smiles each other view'd,
And Venus thus her woeful tale pursu'd:
"Others may ridicule the pains I feel,
Nor boots it all my sufferings to reveal.
But since ye jointly importune my aid,
Cupid shall yield, and Venus be obey'd."
She said; and Juno press'd her hand and smil'd,
Then answer'd thus, benevolent and mild:
"O grant this boon; do instant as you say;
Chide not the boy, and he will soon obey."
  This said, both hasten'd to the realms above,
And left the mansions of the queen of love:
The Cyprian goddess o'er Olympus flies,
To find her son in every dale she pries,
Through Heaven's gay meads the queen pursu'd her way,
And found him there with Ganymede at play.
Him Jove translated to the blest abodes,
And, fam'd for beauty, plac'd among the gods.
With golden dice, like boon compeers they play'd:
Love in his hollow hand some cubes convey'd,
Resolv'd to cheat young Ganymede with those,
While on his cheeks the conscious crimson rose.
The Phrygian boy was vanquish'd to his cost,
Two dice alone remain'd, and those he lost.
Silent he sat in dull dejected state,
Enrag'd that Cupid should deride his fate:
His loss increasing with protracted play,
He went a wretch with empty hands away,
Nor saw he Venus: she her Cupid took
Fast by the cheek, and thus upbraiding spoke:
  "And can you laugh, you sly, deceitful elf?
Such tricks will bring a scandal on yourself.
But haste, my Cupid, my commands obey,
And a nice plaything shall your toils repay,
What once to Jove dear Adrastæa gave,
When Jove was nourish'd in the Cretan cave,
A sweet round ball; oh! keep it for my sake,
A finer ball not Vulcan's hands can make.
Gold are the circles, beauteous to behold,
And all the finish'd seams are wrought in gold;
But all so close they scarcely can be found:
And the pale ivy winds its wreaths around.
If high in air you fling this ball afar,
It shines and glimmers like a radiant star.
This prize I'll give, if you propitious prove,
And lure Medea to the toils of love;
Fire all her soul for Jason: haste away;
The favour is diminish'd by delay."
She said, and Cupid listening long'd to hear,
For her sweet words are music to his ear.
He ceas'd his pastime, and with both his hands
Hangs on the goddess, and the ball demands.
She kiss'd her boy, and press'd him to her cheek,
And fondly smiling, thus she answer'd meek:
"By thee, my son, and by myself I swear,
By all that's sacred, and by all that's dear,
This ball I'll give thee, if thy fatal dart
Thou fix unerring in Medea's heart."
  This said; he gather'd all his dice with haste,
And in his mother's splendid lap he plac'd.
Then snatch'd his bow and quiver from the ground,
And to his back with golden girdle bound.
From Jove's all-fertile plains he swift withdrew,
And thro' Olympus' golden portals flew.
Thence the descent is easy from the sky,
Where the two poles erect their heads on high,
Where the tall mountains their rough tops display,
And where the Sun first gives the radiant day.
Hence you behold the fertile earth below,
The winding streams, the cliffs' aerial brow,
Cities extended on the distant plain,
And thro' the vast expanse the roaring main.
  On the broad Phasis, in a sedgy bay,
Stretch'd on the deck the Grecian heroes lay;
Till call'd to council rose each godlike man,
And Jason thus the conference began:
"To you, my comrades, be my counsel known,
'Tis yours that counsel with success to crown.
One common cause our great emprise is made;
The common cause demands the common aid.
He who unutter'd can his counsel keep,
Stays our resailing o'er the sounding deep.

I to Æeta's court will speed my way,
The rest well arm'd shall in the vessel stay;
With me shall go, the palace to explore,
Phrixus' brave sons, and two associates more.
First will I prove the power of soft address
To gain the fleece; complacence wins success.
If in his arms he sternly should confide,
And spurn our claims with insolence and pride,
Consult we whether, when such powers oppress,
By arms or arts to free us from distress.
Be force the last alternative we take,
For soothing speeches deep impressions make;
And oft, where force and martial prowess fail,
The milder powers of eloquence prevail.
Once king Æeta kind reception gave
To blameless Phrixus, when escap'd the wave
He fled from Ino's unrelenting hate,
And the dire altars that denounc'd his fate.
Savage or social, all alike approve
The sacred rites of hospitable Jove."
He said: the Greeks his sage advice rever'd;
No voice dissentient thro' the host was heard:
Augeas then, and Telamon attends,
And with them Phrixus' sons, his faithful friends;
Jason they follow: he thy peaceful wand,
All-sapient Hermes, brandish'd in his hand.
Soon from the ship they gain the rising ground,
Mount every steep, and o'er the marshes bound,
Till Circe's plain they reach; in many a row
Here humble shrubs and lonely willows grow;
On whose tall branches, wavering o'er the fen,
Suspended hang the carcases of men.
At Colchos still this barbarous rite prevails:
They never burn the bodies of the males,
Nor deep in earth their decent limbs compose,
And with sepulchral dust the dead enclose;
But in raw hides they hang them high in air:
And yet, that earth may equal portions share,
Departed females to the grave they doom,
(Such are their rites) and close them in the tomb.
The chiefs advance; but friendly Juno shrouds
Her favourite heroes in a veil of clouds,
That none, too curious, might their steps delay,
While to the regal dome they bent their way:
But when unseen they pass'd the vulgar crowd,
The same kind deity dissolv'd the cloud.
Full in the court they stand with fix'd amaze,
On the proud gates, strong walls and columns gaze,
Which, rear'd in rows, erect their heads on high,
And lift the brazen cornice to the sky.
The portal past, young branching vines appear,
And high in air their verdant honours rear:
Beneath whose boughs, by matchless Vulcan made,
Four copious fountains in four currents play'd;
The first with milk, with wine the second glow'd,
Ambrosial oil the third, the fourth with water flow'd;
This, as by turns the Pleiads set or rose,
Dissolv'd in summer, and in winter froze.
Such were the wonders which the chiefs admire,
All highly finished by the god of fire.
With these were brass-hoof'd bulls, of curious frame,
From brazen nostrils breathing living flame.
And, near, a plough of burnish'd steel was laid,
Which for the god of day great Vulcan made,
When Phœbus brought him in his friendly car,
Sore harass'd in the fierce Phlegræan war.
The midmost court they reach; on either side
Large folding doors the various rooms divide.
Two painted porticoes salute their eyes,
And high in air transverse two turrets rise;
In this, which far in stately height excels,
Æeta with his royal consort dwells:
Absyrtus that contains, his royal heir,
Descended from Asterode the fair,
A Scythian nymph, ere yet Æeta led
Idya, Ocean's daughter, to his bed.
Him Phaeton the youthful Colchians call,
For he in beauty far surpass'd them all.
The proud apartments that remain'd contain
Chalciope, Medea, and their train.
Ordain'd a priestess to the Stygian queen,
She at the palace now was seldom seen:
But artful Juno, on this signal day,
Within the regal court decreed her stay.
Here now, from room to room, the pensive maid,
To find Chalciope her sister, stray'd.
Soon as she spied them in the spacious hall,
Aloud she call'd, her sister heard her call,
And with her maidens sallied from the door;
Their growing webs were scatter'd on the floor.
Well pleas'd her sons she sees, and raptur'd stands,
While high to Heaven she rears her greeting hands;
With equal joy to her embrace they fly.
Then thus Chalciope with plaintive cry:
"Here tho' you left me, heedless of my cries,
See! fate hath frown'd upon your bold emprise;
Hath check'd your voyage o'er the distant main,
And soon restor'd you to these arms again.
Wretch that I was, when by your sire's command,
Ye sought in evil hour the Grecian land!
Sad was the task your dying sire enjoin'd,
Sad and distressful to a mother's mind.
Ah! whence the wish Orchomenos to see,
His city visit, and abandon me?
Yes, Athamas's fancied wealth to gain,
Ye left me sorrowing, and ye sought the main."
Rous'd by her cries, at length Æeta came,
And to the hall repair'd his royal dame.
With busy crowds the spacious hall is fill'd;
The steer is chosen, and the victim kill'd.
Some heat the baths, some cleave the knotty wood,
And all attentive round their monarch stood.
Cupid mean time, thro' liquid air serene,
Speeds to the Colchian court his flight unseen;
Like that large fly, which breese the shepherds call,
That hastes to sting the heifers in the stall.
The nimble god, unseen, the porch ascends,
And there his bow behind a pillar bends;
A fatal arrow from his quiver took,
And quick advancing with insidious look,
Behind great Æson's son, conceal'd from sight,
He fits the arrow, fatal in its flight;
Bends the tough bow with all his strength and art,
And deep he hides it in Medea's heart.
A sudden transport seiz'd the melting maid:
The god, exulting now, no longer staid.
The glowing shaft the virgin's heart inspires,
And in her bosom kindles amorous fires.
On Jason beam'd the splendour of her eyes;
Her swoln breast heav'd with unremitting sighs:
The frantic maid had all remembrance lost,
And the soft pain her sickening soul engross'd.
As some good housewife, who, to labour born,
Fresh to her loom must rise with early morn;
Studious to gain what human wants require,
In embers heap'd preserves the seeds of fire;
Renew'd by these the brand rekindling burns,
And all the glowing heap to ashes turns:

Thus, kindling slow, love's secret flames invade,
And torture, as they rise, the troubled maid;
Her changeful cheeks the heartfelt anguish show,
Now pale they turn, now like the ruby glow.
The rich repast by seneschals prepar'd,
Fresh from their baths return'd, the strangers shar'd;
And when the rage of hunger was suppress'd,
His grandsons thus the Colchian king address'd:
"Sons of my child, and Phrixus, honour'd most
Of all the guests that reach'd the Colchian coast,
Say, why so soon return'd? what loss constrains
This speedy visit to your native plains?
In vain, with terrours for your safety fraught,
I urg'd the distance of the climes ye sought;
Warn'd, since of old my sire's bright chariot bore
Me and fair Circe to Hesperia's shore,
Where now o'er Tuscan realms my sister reigns,
A long, long distance from the Colchian plains.
But what of this? come now, the cause declare
That brought you back, and who these heroes are."
Then Argus, anxious for the Grecian band,
By birthright eldest, rose, and answer'd bland:
"Our ship, O king, by nightly tempests tost,
On Mars's isle, a dreary coast, was lost;
We, on the wreck by furious surges driv'n,
Were sav'd at last by kind protecting Heav'n.
Nor did those birds then desolate the shore,
Dire harpies, that infested it before;
For these brave warriors, the preceding day,
Had driv'n the curst, infernal fiends away.
Sure to our prayer some god inclin'd his ear;
For when of Phrixus and your name they hear,
Food for our wants, and raiment they convey,
And to your city now they bend their way.
But would you know, I'll tell their purpos'd plan:
Lo! sprung from Æolus the godlike man,
Whom a fierce tyrant's stern decree constrains
To quit his country and his rich domains:
Nor can he scape Jove's rage, unless the fleece,
Base theft of Phrixus, be restor'd to Greece.
Their ship was fashion'd by Minerva's aid;
How different are the Colchian vessels made!
Ours, far the worst that ever rear'd a mast,
Split with the tempest's desolating blast;
Theirs, firm-compacted, and of fittest wood,
Defied each storm that heav'd the troubled flood:
With equal speed their nimble vessel sails,
Impell'd by oars alone, or favouring gales.
In this their chief, with chosen Greeks, explores
Unnumber'd seas, and towns, and wide-extended shores.
And now he sues the golden fleece to gain;
But that as best your princely will ordain—
Nor hostile comes he; as a friend he brings
Large gifts proportion'd to the state of kings.
Inform'd the fierce Sarmatians waste your lands,
He vows destruction to their barbarous bands.
"Their names and lineage should you wish to hear,
Lend to my narrative a listening ear.
He, in whose cause the Grecian chiefs conspire,
Is valiant Jason, Æson is his sire,
The son of Cretheus: thus are we ally'd
By blood, relations on the father's side:
The sons of Æolus were Cretheus fam'd,
And Athamas, whose heir was Phrixus nam'd.
'Mid yon brave chiefs, Augeas you survey,
Illustrious offspring of the god of day;
And Telamon, who high his birth can prove,
His sire is Æacus, his grandsire Jove:
The rest, that visit your august abodes,
Are all the sons or grandsons of the gods."
This said, the king with indignation swell'd,
But chief enrag'd his grandsons he beheld;
Thro' them he deem'd the Greeks to Colchos came:
His eye-balls redden'd with avenging flame,
While thus he spoke: "Hence from my sight away,
Nor longer, traitors, in my kingdom stay:
Back, back to Greece your speedy course pursue,
Nor idly hope the golden fleece to view.
Not for that fleece (vain pretext ye must own)
But for my sceptre came ye, and my crown.
Had ye not first my feast partook to day,
Your tongues and hands, torn out and lopp'd away,
Should for your bold atrocious crimes atone:
My just revenge had spar'd your feet alone,
To bear you hastily to Greece again,
Dreading to visit more my just domain,
And with your perjuries the gods profane."
He said: bold Telamon with fury burn'd,
And to the king stern answer had return'd,
But Jason check'd his warmth, and mild reply'd:
"Let not Æeta falsely thus decide.
Nor crowns, nor empires come we here to gain;
Who for such wealth would measure half the main?
But fate, and Pelias' more severe command,
Have forc'd the suppliant on your friendly land.
Aid us, and Greece your praises shall record,
And thank you, sovereign, with their conquering sword;
Whether the fierce Sarmatians to inthrall,
Or realms more barbarous for your vengeance call."
While Jason thus in gentlest terms reply'd,
The tyrant's breast distracting thoughts divide,
Whether with vengeance on the foe to fly,
Or in the field of Mars his courage try.
On this resolv'd, "What need," he thus begun,
"With tedious tales my harass'd ears to stun?
For whether from immortals ye descend,
Or match'd in might ye dare with me contend,
Soon will I prove; that proof must thou display;
Then, if victorious, bear the fleece away;
Nor shall my hand the golden prize withhold:
Like your proud lord, I envy not the bold.
This nervous arm shall now sustain the fight,
Which calls to speedy proof thy boasted might.
Two bulls in Mars's field your wonder claim,
Their hoofs of brass, their nostrils breathing flame.
These oft I seize, and to the yoke constrain
To plough four acres of the stubborn plain.
No seeds I sow, but scatter o'er the land
A dragon's teeth; when, lo! an armed band
Of chiefs spring up: but soon as they appear,
I slay th' embattled squadrons with my spear.
Each morn I yoke the bulls, at eve resign:
Perform this labour, and the fleece is thine.
These are the terms; on these the prize I quit:
The weaker to the stronger must submit."
He said; and Jason, sunk in thought profound,
Sat mute, his eyes fast fix'd upon the ground;
Long time he ponder'd o'er the vast design,
Nor dar'd with confidence the battle join.
So hard the task, he stood embarrass'd long,
At last these words dropp'd cautious from his tongue:
"Cruel thy terms, but just: my strength I'll try
In this dread conflict, though ordain'd to die.
For, say, what law so rigorous can there be,
As the hard law of fix'd necessity?

That law which forc'd me from my native home,
And bade me thus in search of dangers roam?"
  Perplex'd he spoke: then thus the king in rage,
"Rejoin thy comrades, since thou dar'st engage.
But if the bulls constrain thy heart to yield,
Or the dread dangers of the martial field,
Be mine the toil; that hence the coward-slave
May dread to combat with the bold and brave."
  Imperious thus the haughty king replies:
And from their seats incens'd the heroes rise.
To warn his brothers here, at home, to wait,
Argus stopt short awhile: then rush'd they thro' the gate.
  Far o'er the rest, in grace unmatch'd alone,
And charms superior youthful Jason shone.
Him thro' her veil the love-distracted maid
With melting eyes, and glance oblique survey'd:
Her mind, as in a dream, bewilder'd ran,
And trac'd the footsteps of the godlike man.
Sorrowing they went: to shun the monarch's ire,
With fond Chalciope her sons retire;
Medea follow'd, but with cares oppress'd;
Such cares as love had rais'd within her breast.
His graceful image in her mind she bore,
His gait, his manner, and the robe he wore,
His pointed words: thro' Earth's remotest bound
No prince she deem'd with such perfections crown'd.
His tuneful voice still, still she seems to hear,
Still the sweet accents charm her listening ear.
The bulls and wrathful king excite her dread:
She mourns his fate, as if already dead.
From her bright eyes the shower of anguish breaks,
And thus, o'erwhelm'd with woe, Medea speaks:
  "Why fall the tears of sorrow from my eyes,
Tho' he the first or last of heroes dies?
Perish the man!—no, safely let him sail;
And may my prayer, kind Hecate, prevail!
Safe sail he home! but, ah! if doom'd to bleed,
Teach him, that I rejoice not in the deed."
  Thus mourn'd the maid: meantime to join their train,
The chiefs pursue their course along the plain;
Then Argus thus: "Though, Jason, you may blame,
And spurn the counsel which I now proclaim;
Yet sure for us, with threat'ning dangers press'd,
To try some safe expedient must be best.
A maid there is whose wondrous art excels,
Long taught by Hecate, in magic spells:
If she propitious to our wishes yield,
Thou com'st victorious from the martial field:
But if Chalciope decline her aid,
Be mine with tenderest motives to persuade.
Instant I'll go, on her for succour call;
For, lo! one general ruin threatens all.'
Humane he spoke, and Jason thus rejoin'd;
"Much I admire the purpose of thy mind.
Go, friend, to thy Chalciope repair,
Sue her with soft entreaty and with pray'r:
But, ah! vain hopes our vacant minds must fill,
Who trust for conquest to a woman's skill."
  He said; and soon they join'd their social train,
Rejoic'd to meet their princely peers again.
Then Jason thus began his mournful tale:
"With proud Æeta soft entreaties fail;
Our purpos'd end unable to attain,
Vain are my words, and your inquiries vain.
Two monstrous bulls the tyrant bids me tame;
Their hoofs of brass, their nostrils breathing flame;
These must my prowess to the yoke constrain,
To plough four acres of the stubborn plain;
My seed a dragon's teeth, to sow the land;
When, lo! up springs a formidable band
Of bright-arm'd giants; soon as they appear,
Poiz'd by this arm, my well-directed spear
Must pierce the foe: intrepid I accede
To the hard terms, nor future dangers heed."
  He said: they deem'd it all a desperate deed:
Silent they stood, with sad dejected look
Each gaz'd on other, till bold Peleus spoke:
"Time calls for our resolves; our safety stands
No more in counsel, but in strength of hands.
If, Jason, eager of the honour, thou
Wilt yoke these fiery monsters to the plough,
Haste to the charge; but if thy soul relent,
Sunk in sad bodings of the dire event,
Nor dar'st thou go; then go not, nor look round,
If haply here some fitter man be found;
Myself will go, and risk my dearest breath;
No greater evil can befall than death."
  He spoke; and Telamon with rage inspir'd
Starts up, and Idas with like fury fir'd;
Next the twin-race of Tyndarus arise;
Last Oeneus' son, who with the bravest vies;
Tho' o'er his cheeks scarce spreads the callow down,
His heart beats high for honour and renown.
And while the rest in mute attention stand,
Argus bespeaks the emulative band:
"Tho' hard the task, O chiefs, I still portend
My parent will assist, and prove a friend.
Still in your ship awhile with patience wait;
For rashness will accelerate your fate.
Know, at Æeta's court a maiden dwells,
Deep skill'd by Hecate in magic spells:
All plants she knows that grow on mountains steep,
On vales, or meads, or in the boundless deep;
By these she quells the fire's relentless force,
Stops the mad torrent in its headlong course,
Retards the planets as they roll on high,
And draws the Moon reluctant from the sky.
As from the palace o'er the plain we came
We mention'd oft my mother's honour'd name;
If she perchance her sister could persuade,
And fix our interest in the magic maid.
Back, if you bid, my ready steps I bend;
Fortune may smile, and fair success attend."
He said; when, lo! this signal of their love
Was kindly given them by the powers above;
For, by the falcon chas'd, a trembling dove,
Far from his foe, to Jason's bosom flies;
Stunn'd on the deck the felon falcon lies.
Then Mopsus thus divin'd: "The powers of Heav'n,
They, they alone this gracious sign have giv'n.
Be then the maid in mildest terms address'd;
She'll listen friendly to our joint request,
I ween she will; if Phineus could foreknow
That we to Venus must our safety owe.
For, lo! her bird escapes: oh! may we prove
With safety crown'd, like her auspicious dove..
Entreat we now for Cytherea's aid,
And let th' advice of Argus be obey'd."
  Thus he; the chiefs approv'd, remembering well
What Phineus deign'd prophetic to foretell:
Idas alone with indignation burn'd,
And with loud voice thus insolent return'd:
"Gods! what a crew hath Argo wafted o'er!
Women, not heroes, throng the hostile shore.

Women, who still to Venus' altars fly,
Nor dare but only on her aid rely.
No warlike deeds your dastard souls inflame:
To you is Mars an unregarded name.
As doves or falcons but direct your flight,
You flinch at danger, and you dread the fight.
Go; and all manly, martial toils forbear,
Sue to weak women, and deceive the fair."
Furious he spoke; a general murmur ran
Thro' the whole train; yet none oppos'd the man:
Indignant then he sat. Of dauntless breast
Thus Æson's son the listening train address'd:
"This instant Argus to the town I send,
For thus the general suffrages intend:
Meanwhile approach we nearer to the land,
And fix, in sight, our halsers to the strand:
Ill suits us longer thus to lie conceal'd;
We neither shun, nor dread the fighting field."
He said, and Argus went without delay,
And to the city backward sped his way;
At Jason's call they ply the labouring oar,
And land their beds and couches on the shore.
Meantime the king a council call'd, and sat,
(So were they wont) without the palace-gate.
Assembled there, unceasing toils they plann'd,
And wiles destructive to the Grecian band.
Thus he ordain'd, that when the bulls had slain
And stretch'd this dauntless hero on the plain,
Himself would lay the lofty forest low,
And for the funeral-pile prepare the bough:
Their boasted ship should be consum'd with fire,
And every traitor in the flames expire.
No hospitable rites had Phrixus shar'd,
Though much he wish'd and merited regard,
Had not Jove hasten'd Hermes from above
To win his favour and bespeak his love.
Were these invaders of his native soil
To thrive unpunish'd by rapacious spoil,
Soon would they make his lowing herds a prey,
And drive the shepherds and their flocks away.
But Phrixus' sons, who join'd the lawless crew,
He vow'd with double vengeance to pursue:
Base plunderers! come to spoil him of his crown,
So had the Sun, his sapient sire, foreshown:
Who warn'd him to suspect his faithless race,
And dread from them destruction and disgrace.
Therefore dismiss'd he, by his sire's command,
The youths far distant, ev'n to Grecian land.
His daughters gave him no perplexing care,
Nor young Absyrtus, his adopted heir;
But from Chalciope's detested race
He look'd for injuries, and fear'd disgrace.
Thus stern denouncing, as with rage he swells,
Death on each daring subject that rebels,
His guards he charg'd, and threaten'd vengeance due,
If either 'scap'd, the vessel or the crew.
Swift to the palace Argus now repairs,
And to his pitying mother pours his pray'rs,
That she might importune Medea's aid;
Nor had the queen her son's request delay'd,
But boding fears her willing mind restrain,
Lest all her fond entreaties should be vain;
And should the project be disclos'd to view,
Her father's ire the magic maid must rue.
As on her couch reclin'd the virgin lay,
Soft slumbers chas'd her anxious cares away;
But frantic dreams, which love-sick minds infest,
Present false terrours, and disturb her rest.
Her hero seem'd the task to undertake,
But not for honour, or the fleece's sake;
For her alone he risk'd the glorious strife,
To gain her love, and win her for his wife.
She then in dreams her utmost succour lends,
And with the bulls herself in fight contends.
Her parents she, in fancied rage, aver'd
False and regardless of their promis'd word,
Who Jason doom'd the brazen bulls to foil,
But made not her a partner of the toil.
Then warm disputes and fierce contentions reign,
Between Æeta and the Grecian train:
On her decision both the parties wait,
And deem what she determines to be fate.
In spite of parents, the fond maid express'd
Her choice in favour of her godlike guest.
Rage wrung their souls, and grief, and dire dismay,
Till the loud clamour chas'd her sleep away.
Trembling she starts; pale fears confus'd her look;
Her soul reviv'd, and thus the virgin spoke:
"Alas! what frightful dreams alarm my breast
For these fam'd chiefs, but most the royal guest?
I fear, some mighty mischief will ensue
From this bold leader and his gallant crew.
Yes, let him wed far off some Grecian dame:
Be mine my parents' house, my virgin's fame.
If from my headstrong purpose I refrain,
My sister's counsel might relieve my pain:
Oh! for her sons would she my aid implore,
My griefs would cease, my sorrows be no more!"
She said, and rose, no longer deign'd to wait,
But pass'd the threshold of her sister's gate,
Barefoot, undrest; long time she there remain'd,
(For modest fears her passing step restrain'd;)
Then back retreats; new courage soon acquires;
Again advances, and again retires:
Passions so various sway'd the virgin's breast,
That when fierce love impell'd her, fear repress'd:
Thrice she essay'd, and thrice retreating fled;
Then on the pillow sunk her drooping head.
As some young damsel, whom her friends had join'd
In marriage to the darling of her mind,
Conceal'd in secret, mourns her blooming mate
Snatch'd from her arms by some untimely fate,
Ere yet kind Heaven indulg'd them to employ
The golden moments in connubial joy:
In silence she, tho' stung with torturing grief,
Seeks on the widow'd bed the wish'd relief;
Looks eager round, then sheds the trembling tear,
Screen'd from the female eye, and tongue severe.
Thus mourn'd Medea, not unseen; her pain
Was mark'd by one, the youngest of her train!
Who told Chalciope Medea's grief;
And the sad tale exceeded her belief!
Her sons consulting, she with them essay'd
To sooth the sorrows of the love-sick maid.
Instant she rose, and trembling with dismay
Came to the chamber where her sister lay;
Torn were her cheeks, the tears her grief confess'd;
And thus Chalciope the maid address'd:
"Say, why those tears that thus incessant fall?
What mighty ills your feeble mind appal?
Say, does some heaven-sent woe your grief inspire?
Or in your bosom dwells Æeta's ire,
My sons and I the cause? Oh! far from home,
On the world's utmost limits may I roam,
Nor see my parents, nor my native shore,
Nor hear the hated name of Colchos more!"

She said: Medea's cheeks the crimson stain'd;
She strove to speak, but shame her words restrain'd.
Now on her lips the ready accents hung,
Now stifled in her breast: her faltering tongue
Long time the purpose of her soul withheld,
Artful at length she spoke, by love impell'd:
"Dire fears, Chalciope, my soul dismay,
Lest with these guests my sire thy children slay,
My frightful dreams such horrid scenes present:
May some kind deity these woes prevent!
Lest for thy sons the tears eternal flow:"
Thus spoke the maid, inquisitive in woe,
If haply, for her children's fate afraid,
Chalciope might first solicit aid.
Mix'd grief and terrour all the mother shook,
At last, impassion'd, thus she trembling spoke:
"'Tis for their sakes I now before thee stand;
Lend me, O lend thy salutary hand!
But swear by Earth and Heaven what I unfold
Rests in thy bosom, never to be told:
By the great gods, and all that's dear I call,
Swear thou wilt never see my children fall,
Lest I too perish, and in fell despight
Rise a dread fury from the shades of night."
Earnest she spoke, and tears incessant shed,
Then on her sister's breast reclin'd her head,
And mix'd their mutual sighs; groan answer'd groan,
And the wide palace echo'd to their moan.
Medea thus in mournful terms replies:
"Alas! what succour can my thoughts devise,
Thus with thy cruel menaces oppress'd?
Oh, still uninjur'd may thine offspring rest!
By Heaven above I swear, and Earth below,
Earth, the great mother of the gods, I vow,
(If aught my power can do, or words persuade)
To give thee counsel, and to lend my aid."
Thus spoke the maid; and thus Chalciope;
"Perhaps, in favour of my sons and me,
Thy mind, to save the hero, might impart
Some secret counsel, some mysterious art.
From Jason Argus comes, imploring aid;
They rest their safety on the magic maid."
Thus she; with joy exults the virgin's heart,
And rising blushes rosy charms impart;
But soon o'ercast with grief she thus reply'd:
"To serve thee, sister, be no art untry'd.
Ne'er may I see with pleasurable eyes
In yon bright orient cheerful morning rise,
If aught on Earth be half so dear to me
As is the welfare of thy sons and thee.
As brethren they my fond regard engage,
By blood related, and the same our age.
My sister, most esteem'd, and ever dear,
Thee with a daughter's love, I still revere.
For with thy children, nurs'd by thee, I shar'd
(So fame reports) a mother's fond regard.
Go then, and from my prying parents hide
The means of succour which I now provide.
All-potent spells will I, at dawn of day,
To Hecate's mysterious shrine convey."
Pleas'd with the tale, Chalciope departs,
And with the proffer'd aid transports her children's hearts,
Fear mix'd with shame now seiz'd the lonely maid,
Who dare, her sire reluctant, lend her aid.
Now rising shades a solemn scene display
O'er the wide Earth, and o'er th' etherial way;
All night the sailor marks the northern team,
And golden circlet of Orion's beam:
A deep repose the weary watchman shares,
And the faint wanderer sleeps away his cares;
Ev'n the fond maid, while yet all breathless lies
Her child of love, in slumber seals her eyes:
No sound of village-dog, no noise invades
The death-like silence of the midnight shades;
Alone Medea wakes: to love a prey,
Restless she rolls, and groans the night away:
For lovely Jason cares on cares succeed,
Lest vanquish'd by the bulls her hero bleed;
In sad review dire scenes of horrours rise,
Quick beats her heart, from thought to thought she flies:
As from the stream-stor'd vase with dubious ray
The sun-beams dancing from the surface play;
Now here, now there the trembling radiance falls,
Alternate flashing round th' illumin'd walls:
Thus fluttering bounds the trembling virgin's blood,
And from her eyes descends a pearly flood.
Now raving with resistless flames she glows,
Now sick with love she melts with softer woes,
The tyrant god, of every thought possess'd,
Beats in each pulse, and stings and racks her breast:
Now she resolves the magic to betray—
To tame the bulls—now yield him up a prey.
Again the drugs disdaining to supply,
She loaths the light, and meditates to die:
Anon, repelling with a brave disdain
The coward thought, she nourishes the pain.
Then pausing thus: "Ah, wretched me!" she cries,
"Where'er I turn what varied sorrows rise!
Tost in a giddy whirl of strong desire,
I glow, I burn, yet bless the pleasing fire:
Oh! had this spirit from its prison fled,
By Dian sent to wander with the dead,
Ere the proud Grecians view'd the Colchian skies,
Ere Jason, lovely Jason, met these eyes!
Hell gave the shining mischief to our coast,
Medea saw him, and Medea's lost—
But why these sorrows? if the powers on high
His death decree, die, wretched Jason, die!
Shall I elude my sire? my art betray?
Ah, me! what words shall purge the guilt away!
But could I yield——O whither must I run
To find the chief—whom virtue bids me shun?
Shall I, all lost to shame, to Jason fly?
And yet I must——if Jason bleeds I die!
Honour farewell! adieu for ever shame!
Hail black disgrace! and branded be my fame!
Live, Jason, live! enjoy the vital air!
Live thro' my aid! and fly where winds can bear.
But when he flies, cords, poisons, lend your powers;
That day Medea treads th' infernal shores!
Yet what reproach will after death be cast?
The maids of Colchos will my honour blast—
I hear them cry—'the false Medea's dead,
Thro' guilty passion for a stranger's bed;
Medea, careless of her virgin fame,
Preferr'd a stranger to a father's name!'
O may I rather yield this vital breath,
Than bear that base dishonour worse than death!"
Thus wail'd the fair, and seiz'd, with horrid joy,
Drugs foes to life, and potent to destroy;
A magazine of death! again she pours
From her swoln eye-lids tears in shining show'rs:
With grief insatiate, comfortless she stands,
And opes the casket, but with trembling hands.

A sudden fear her labouring soul invades,
Struck with the horrours of th' infernal shades:
She stands deep-musing with a faded brow,
Absorb'd in thought, a monument of woe!
While all the comforts that on life attend,
The cheerful converse, and the faithful friend,
By thought deep imag'd in her bosom play,
Endearing life, and charm despair away.
Enliv'ning suns with sweeter light arise,
And every object brightens to her eyes.
Then from her hand the baneful drugs she throws,
Consents to live, recover'd from her woes;
Resolv'd the magic virtue to betray,
She waits the dawn, and calls the lazy day:
Time seems to stand, or backward drive his wheels;
The hours she chides, and eyes the eastern hills:
At length the morn displays her rosy light,
And the whole town stands pictur'd to her sight.
Back to the ship (his brothers left behind
To mark the motions of Medea's mind)
Argus return'd; meanwhile her golden hair,
That flow'd diffusive in the wanton air,
The virgin binds; then wipes the tears away,
And from her eyes bids living lightning play;
On every limb refreshing unguents pours,
Unguents, that breathe of Heaven, in copious show'rs.
Her robe she next assumes; bright clasps of gold
Close to the lessening waist the robe infold:
Down from her swelling loins the rest unbound
Floats in rich waves redundant o'er the ground:
Then takes her veil, and stately treads the room
With graceful ease, regardless of her doom.
 Thus forward moves the fairest of her kind,
Blind to the future, to the present blind.
Twelve maids, attendants on her virgin bow'r,
Alike unconscious of the bridal hour,
Join to the car her mules; dire rites to pay,
To Hecate's fair fane she bends her way.
A juice she bears, whose magic virtue tames
(Thro' fell Persephone) the rage of flames:
For one whole day it gives the hero might,
To stand secure of harms in mortal fight;
It mocks the sword; the sword without a wound
Leaps as from marble shiver'd to the ground.
This plant, which rough Caucasean mountains bore,
Sprung from the venom of Prometheus' gore.
(While on the wretch the savage eagle storm'd)
In colour like Corycian crocus form'd:
On two tall stems up-springs the flowery shoot,
A cubit high; like red raw flesh its root.
From this root's juice, as black as that distill'd
From mountain beeches, the fair maid had fill'd
A Caspian conch; but first, as best beseems,
Array'd in black seven times in living streams
She bath'd; and call'd seven times on Brimo's name,
At midnight hour, the ghost-compelling dame.
She pluck'd the root, Earth murmur'd from below,
And sad Prometheus groan'd with agonizing woe.
This root the Colchian maid selecting plac'd
In the rich zone that bound her slender waist:
Then issuing mounts the car, but not alone,
On either side two lovely damsels shone:
Her hand with skill th' embroider'd rein controls,
Back fly the streets as swift the chariot rolls.
Along the wheel-worn road they speed their way,
The domes retreat, the sinking towers decay:
Bare to the knee succinct a damsel-train
Close throng behind them, hastening to the plain.
 As when her limbs divine Diana laves
In fair Parthenius, or th' Amnesian waves,
Sublime in royal state the bounding roes
Whirl her bright car along the mountain brows:
Swift to some sacred feast the goddess moves,
The nymphs attend that haunt the shady groves;
Th' Amnesian fount or silver-streaming rills,
Nymphs of the vales, or Oreads of the hills:
The fawning beasts before the goddess play,
Or, trembling, savage adoration pay:
 Thus on her car sublime the nymph appears,
The crowd falls back, and, as she moves, reveres:
Swift to the fane aloft her course she bends,
The fane she reaches, and on earth descends;
Then to her train—"Ah, me! I fear we stray,
Misled by folly to this lonely way!
Alas! should Jason with his Greeks appear,
Where should we fly? I fear, alas, I fear!
No more the Colchian youths, and virgin train,
Haunt the cool shade, or tread in dance the plain.
But since alone—with sports beguile your hours,
Collect sweet herbs, and pluck the fairest flow'rs:
If due attention to my words ye pay,
With richest spoils ye shall return to day.
For Argus and Chalciope require,
(But sacred keep this secret from my sire)
That for large presents, for my succour paid,
To this rash stranger I should lend my aid.
I pass'd my word, and soon without his train
The Grecian will attend me at the fane:
In equal portions we the spoil will share—
For him a dose more fatal I prepare—
But when he comes, ye nymphs, retire apart."
She spoke; the nymphs approv'd the virgin's art.
 When Argus heard the maid with early day
To Hecate's fair fane would speed her way,
He beckon'd Jason from his bold compeers
Apart, and Mopsus most renown'd of seers;
For prescient Mopsus every omen knew
Of birds that parting or approaching flew.
No mortal ever of the first-born race
Display'd like Jason such superior grace,
Whether from demigods he trac'd his line,
Or Jove himself immortal and divine,
As grac'd by Juno, Jove's imperial queen,
With soft address, and dignity of mien.
His comrades gaz'd with wonder as he went;
Mopsus foresaw and hail'd the blest event.
Hard by the path, and near the temple, stands
A poplar tall that wide its arms expands;
Here frequent rooks their airy pastime take,
And on the boughs their spray-form'd mansions make:
One shook its pinions, (louder than the rest)
And croaking, thus Saturnia's mind express'd:
"Vain seer! whose divinations fail to tell
Those plain events which children know so well;
That maids will not, with comrades in the train,
Tell the soft love-tale to their favour'd swain.
False prophet, hence! for thee nor love inspires,
Nor Venus gratifies with soft desires."
Then Mopsus laugh'd, as scoffing thus she spoke,
To hear the bird her dark predictions croak;
And thus: "Hence, Jason, to the fane, and find
The maiden to thy warmest wishes kind;
Venus approves, and fortune will ensue,
If what prophetic Phineus said prove true.
Myself and Argus here will wait apart,
Go and unfold the secrets of thy heart;

Be every mode of soft persuasion try'd."
He counsel'd wisely, and the chief comply'd.
  Meanwhile the maid her secret thoughts enjoy'd,
And one dear object all her soul employ'd:
Her train's gay sports no pleasure can restore,
Vain was the dance, and music charm'd no more;
She hates each object, every face offends,
In every wish her soul to Jason sends;
With sharpen'd eyes the distant lawn explores,
To find the hero whom her soul adores;
At every whisper of the passing air,
She starts, she turns, and hopes her Jason there;
Again she fondly looks, nor looks in vain,
He comes, her Jason shines along the plain.
As when, emerging from the watery way,
Refulgent Sirius lifts his golden ray,
He shines terrific! for his burning breath
Taints the red air with fevers, plagues, and death;
Such to the nymph approaching Jason shows,
Bright author of unutterable woes;
Before her eyes a swimming darkness spread,
Her flush'd cheeks glow'd, her very heart was dead:
No more her knees their wonted office knew,
Fix'd, without motion, as to earth they grew.
Her train recedes—the meeting lovers gaze
In silent wonder, and in still amaze.
As two fair cedars on the mountain's brow,
Pride of the groves! with roots adjoining grow;
Erect and motionless the stately trees
Short time remain, while sleeps each fanning breeze,
Till from th' Æolian caves a blast unbound
Bends their proud tops, and bids their boughs resound:
Thus gazing they; till by the breath of love,
Strongly at last inspir'd, they speak, they move;
With smiles the love-sick virgin he survey'd,
And fondly thus address'd the blooming maid:
  "Dismiss, my fair, my love, thy virgin fear;
'Tis Jason speaks, no enemy is here!
Dread not in me a haughty heart to find,
In Greece I bore no proud inhuman mind.
Whom would'st thou fly? stay, lovely virgin, stay!
Speak every thought! far hence be fears away!
Speak! and be truth in every accent found!
Scorn to deceive! we tread on hallow'd ground.
By the stern power who guards this sacred place,
By the fam'd authors of thy royal race;
By Jove, to whom the stranger's cause belongs,
To whom the suppliant, and who feels their wrongs;
O guard me, save me, in the needful hour!
Without thy aid thy Jason is no more.
To thee a suppliant, in distress I bend,
To thee a stranger, one who wants a friend!
Then, when between us seas and mountains rise,
Medea's name shall sound in distant skies;
All Greece to thee shall owe her heroes' fates,
And bless Medea thro' her hundred states.
The mother and the wife, who now in vain
Roll their sad eyes fast-streaming o'er the main,
Shall stay their tears: the mother, and the wife,
Shall bless thee for a son's or husband's life!
Fair Ariadne, sprung from Minos' bed,
Sav'd valiant Theseus, and with Theseus fled,
Forsook her father, and her native plain,
And stem'd the tumults of the surging main;
Yet the stern sire relented, and forgave
The maid, whose only crime it was to save;
Ev'n the just gods forgave: and now on high
A star she shines, and beautifies the sky:
What blessings then shall righteous Heaven decree
For all our heroes sav'd, and sav'd by thee?
Heaven gave thee not to kill, so soft an air;
And cruelty sure never look'd so fair!"
  He ceas'd, but left so charming on her ear
His voice, that listening still she seem'd to hear;
Her eyes to earth she bends with modest grace,
And Heaven in smiles is open'd on her face.
A look she steals; but rosy blushes spread
O'er her fair cheek, and then she hangs her head.
A thousand words at once to speak she tries;
In vain—but speaks a thousand with her eyes;
Trembling the shining casket she expands,
Then gives the magic virtue to his hands;
And had the power been granted to convey
Her heart—had given her very heart away.
For Jason beam'd in beauty's charms so bright,
The maid admiring languish'd with delight.
Thus, when the rising Sun appears in view,
On the fair rose dissolves the radiant dew.
Now on the ground both cast their bashful eyes,
Both view each other now with wild surprise.
The rosy smiles now dimpling on their cheeks,
The fair at length in faltering accents speaks:
  "Observant thou to my advice attend,
And hear what succour I propose to lend.
Soon as my sire Æeta shall bestow
The dragon's teeth in Mars's field to sow,
The foll'wing night in equal shares divide;
Bathe well thy limbs in some perennial tide;
Then all retir'd, thyself in black array,
Dig the round foss, and there a victim slay,
A female lamb; the carcase place entire
Above the foss, then light the sacred pyre,
And Perseus' daughter, Hecate, appease
With honey, sweetest labour of the bees;
This done, retreat, nor, while the relics burn,
Let howling dogs provoke thee to return,
Nor human footsteps; lest thou render vain
The charm, and with dishonour join thy train.
Next morn, the whole enchantment to fulfil,
This magic unguent on thy limbs distil:
Then thou with ease wilt strong and graceful move,
Not like a mortal, but the gods above.
Forget not with this unguent to besmear
Thy sword, thy buckler, and tremendous spear:
No giant's falchions then can harm thy frame,
Nor the fell rage of bulls expiring flame.
One day, nor longer, wilt thou keep the field;
Nor thou to perils, nor to labour yield.
But mark my words; when thou, with ceaseless toil,
Hast yok'd the bulls and plough'd the stubborn soil;
And seest up-springing on the teeth-sown land
Of giant foes a formidable band,
Hurl slily 'midst their ranks a rough hard stone,
And they, like dogs contending for a bone,
Will slay each other: thou with speed renew
The glowing fight, and conquest will ensue.
Thus shalt thou bear from Æa's realms to Greece,
If such thy fix'd resolve, the golden fleece."
  This said, her eyes were fix'd upon the ground,
And her fair cheeks with streaming sorrows drown'd;
Desponding anguish seiz'd her gentle mind,
Lest he should leave her comfortless behind.
Imbolden'd thus, him by the hand she press'd,
And in the language of her soul address'd;
  "If safely hence thou sail'st, O, think of me!
As I for ever shall remember thee!

And freely tell me, to relieve my pain,
Where lies thy home beyond the boundless main?
Say, is Orchomenos thy native soil?
Or dwell'st thou nearer on th' Ææan isle?
Let me that far-fam'd virgin's name inquire,
Who boasts the same high lineage with my sire."
She said; her tears his soft compassion won,
And thus the chief, by love inspir'd, begun:
"While on my fancy bright ideas play,
Thy image never from my soul shall stray,
If safe I sail, preserv'd by thee, to Greece,
Nor heavier labours interrupt my peace.
But if the distant country where I dwell
Thy will demands, my ready tongue shall tell.
A land there is which lofty hills surround,
For fertile pastures and rich herds renown'd,
Where from Prometheus good Deucalion came,
His royal heir, Hæmonia is the name.
Deucalion here the first foundations laid
Of towns, built fanes, and men by empire sway'd;
There my Iolcos stands, and many more
Fair ample cities, that adorn the shore.
What time, as rumour'd by the voice of fame,
Æolian Minyas to that country came,
He built, close bordering on the Theban ground,
Orchomenos, a city far renown'd.
But why your wonder should I vainly raise?
My birth-place tell, and Ariadne's praise?
For this the virgin's name you now inquire,
A lovely maid, and Minos is her sire.
Oh! may, like hers, your sire propitious prove,
Who honour'd Theseus with his daughter's love!"
Complacent thus he sooth'd her sorrowing soul;
Yet anxious cares within her bosom roll.
"Perchance in Greece," the pensive maid rejoin'd,
"Oaths are rever'd, and solemn compacts bind.
But Minos greatly differs from my sire,
Nor I to Ariadne's charms aspire.
Then mention hospitality no more;
But, safe conducted to thy native shore,
Grant this, 'tis all I ask, Oh! think of me,
As I for ever shall remember thee,
In my great sire, the Colchian king's despite:
But if thy pride my ardent passion slight,
Fame, or some bird the hateful news will bring;
Then will I chase thee on the tempest's wing,
Brand thy false heart, thy curs'd familiar be,
And prove thou ow'st thy life, thy all to me."
Medea thus, and tears abundant shed;
And mildly thus the son of Æson said:
"In vain, dear nymph, thy missive bird shall soar
Thro' air sublime, in vain the tempest roar.
But if towards Greece thou deign'st thy course to bear,
Immortal honours shall attend thee there;
There husbands, brothers, sons, so long deplor'd,
Safe to their native land by thee restor'd,
Shall as a goddess reverence thy name,
And pay thee rites which only gods can claim.
But would'st thou grace my bed with bridal state,
Our love can only be dissolv'd by fate."
His words with raptures all her soul subdue;
Yet gloomy objects rise before her view,
Ordain'd, ere long, Thessalia's realms to see;
For such was Juno's absolute decree,
That soon to Greece the Colchian maid should go,
To Pelias, source of unremitting woe.
Meanwhile apart her anxious handmaids stay,
In silence waiting till the close of day:
Such pleasing transports in her bosom roll,
His form, his words so captivate her soul,
On feather'd feet the hours unheeded fled,
Which warn'd her home: "Hence" (cautious Jason said)
"Hence let us hasten unperceiv'd away,
And here enraptur'd pass some future day."
Thus the blest hours in converse sweet they spent,
And both unwilling from the temple went;
He to his comrades bordering on the main,
The fair Medea to her virgin train.
Her train approach'd, but stood unnotic'd by;
Her soul sublime expatiates in the sky.
Her rapid car she mounts; this hand sustains
The polish'd thong, and that the flowing reins.
Fleet o'er the plain the nimble mules convey'd
To Æa's walls the love-transported maid.
Meanwhile Chalciope astonish'd stands,
And instant tidings of her sons demands;
In vain: sad cares had clos'd Medea's ears,
No answers gives she, and no questions hears;
But on a footstool low, beside her bed,
All bath'd in tears she sits; her hand sustains her head.
There sits she pondering, in a pensive state,
What dire distresses on her counsels wait.
But Jason, eager to return, withdrew
With his two friends, and join'd his social crew,
Who throng'd impatient round, while he display'd
The secret counsels of the Colchian maid,
And show'd the potent herbs: Idas apart
Conceal'd the choler rankling in his heart.
Meanwhile the rest, when glimmering day-light clos'd,
Wrapp'd in the mantle of the night repos'd.
Next morn they sent Æthalides the son
Of Mercury, and valiant Telamon,
(For thus in council had the Greeks decreed)
Of fierce Æeta to demand the seed,
The serpent's teeth, whose ever-wakeful sight
Watch'd o'er the fountain of the god of fight.
This baneful monster was by Cadmus slain,
Seeking Europa o'er the Theban plain;
An heifer to his seat of regal sway,
So will'd prophetic Phœbus, led the way.
These teeth Minerva from the monster rent,
And part to Cadmus and Æeta sent:
Sow'd on Bœotia's ample plains, from those
A hardy race of earth-born giants rose.
To Jason these he gave, a precious spoil;
Nor, tho' his matchless arm the bulls might foil,
Deem'd he, that victory would crown his toil.
The Sun now sinking with a feeble ray
To distant Ethiopians slop'd his way;
Night yok'd her steeds: the Grecian heroes spread
Around the halsers and the sails their bed.
The northern Bear was sunk beneath the hills,
And all the air a solemn silence fills:
Jason to lonely haunts pursu'd his way;
(All rites adjusted the preceding day.)
'Twas Argus' care a lambkin to provide,
And milk, the rest the ready ship supply'd.
A sweet sequester'd spot the hero found,
Where silence reigns, and welling streams abound;
And here, observant of due rites, he laves,
His limbs immerging in the cleansing waves;
Then o'er his shoulders, pledge of favours past,
The gift of fair Hypsipyla, he cast,

A sable robe: a deep round foss he made,
And on the kindling wood the victim laid:
The mix'd libation pouring o'er the flame,
Loud he invok'd infernal Brimo's name;
Then back retires: his call her ears invades,
And up she rises from the land of shades:
Snakes, wreath'd in oaken boughs, curl'd round her hair,
And gleaming torches cast a dismal glare.
To guard their queen the hideous dogs of Hell
Rend the dark welkin with incessant yell;
The heaving ground beneath her footsteps shakes;
Loud shriek the Naiads of the neighbouring lakes,
And all the fountain-nymphs astonish'd stood
Where Amaranthine Phasis rolls his flood.
Fear seiz'd the chief, yet backward he withdrew,
Nor, till he join'd his comrades, turn'd his view.
  And now on Caucasus, with snow o'erspread,
The rising morn her silver radiance shed,
When proud Æeta, earlier than the rest,
The fencing corslet buckled to his breast,
The spoils of Mimas of gigantic race,
Whom Mars had vanquish'd on the plains of Thrace:
His golden helmet to his head he bound,
With four fair crests of glittering plumage crown'd,
Bright as the Sun new rising from the main;
His nervous arms a mighty spear sustain:
From his broad shoulder beams his sevenfold shield,
Which not a chief of all the Greeks could wield,
Since great Alcides, of his friend bereft,
Was (sad mischance!) on Mysia's borders left.
His son hard by with ready chariot stands;
The king ascends; the reins adorn his hands;
Fierce to the field he hastes in regal state,
And crowds of Colchians round their monarch wait.
  As ocean's god, when drawn by rapid steeds,
To Isthmian games, or Calaureia speeds,
To Tænarus, or rocky Petra roves,
Or where Geræstus boasts her oaken groves,
Onchestus' woods, or Lerna's limpid spring;
So to the combat drives the Colchian king.
  Meanwhile, instructed by the magic maid,
The chief his shield, his spear and trenchant blade
With unguents smear'd: the Greeks approaching nigh
In vain their efforts on his armour try;
But chief the spear such magic charms attend,
No force can break it, and no onset bend.
Idas enrag'd deals many a furious wound,
But, as hard hammers from an anvil bound,
So from the spear his sword recoiling sprung:
The distant vales with loud applauses rung.
Next, with the potent charm the chief anoints
His well-turn'd limbs, and supples all his joints.
And, lo! new powers invigorate his hands,
And arm'd with strength intrepidly he stands.
  As the proud steed, exulting in his might,
Erects his ears, impatient for the fight,
And pawing snuffs the battle from afar;
So pants the hero for the promis'd war.
Firmly he moves, incapable of fear;
One hand his shield sustains, and one the spear.
Thus, when black clouds obscure the darkening day,
And rains descend, the living lightnings play.
  And now the fight draws near; the Grecian train
Sail up the Phasis to the martial plain;
From which as far the towers of Æa stand,
As when the chieftains, who the games command
For some dead king, the bounding barriers place
For steeds or men contending in the race.
Æeta there they found, of mind elate;
On Phasis' banks his chariot rolls in state.
On the Caucasian summits, that command
The field of Mars, the crowded Colchians stand.
Now Argo moor'd, the prince invades the field,
Arm'd with his magic spear, and ample shield;
With serpents' teeth his brazen helm was stor'd,
And cross his shoulder gleam'd his glittering sword:
Like Mars the chief enormous power display'd,
Or Phœbus brandishing his golden blade.
O'er the rough tilth he cast his eyes around,
And soon the plough of adamant he found,
And yokes of brass: his helm (approaching near)
He plac'd on earth, and upright fix'd his spear.
To find the bulls he farther went afield,
And trac'd their steps, arm'd only with his shield.
In a dark cave which smoky mists surround,
Horrid and huge their safe retreat he found.
With rage impetuous forth the monsters came,
And from their nostrils issued streams of flame.
Fear seiz'd the Greeks, but he their fury braves,
Firm as a rock defies the roaring waves;
Screen'd by his shield, intrepidly he scorns
The bulls loud bellowing, and their butting horns;
Collected firm he wards each threatening blow.
As at the forge where melting metals glow,
While now the bellows heave, now sink by turns,
The flame subsides, or with fresh fury burns;
Stirr'd to the bottom roars the raging fire:
So roar the bulls, and living flame respire,
That fierce as lightning round the hero play'd,
In vain, now shelter'd by the magic maid.
One bull he seiz'd, that aim'd a deadly stroke,
Seiz'd by his horns, and dragg'd him to the yoke;
Then hurl'd the roaring monster on the ground:
An equal fate his fellow captive found.
Loos'd from his arm he flung his shield aside,
And the two monsters manfully he ply'd,
Dragg'd on their knees, his fiery foes o'ercame,
And shifting artfully escap'd the flame.
Æeta view'd him with astonish'd eyes;
When, lo! the sons of Tyndarus arise,
As erst it was decreed, and from the land
Heav'd the strong yokes and gave them to his hand:
These o'er the bulls' low-bended necks he flung;
The brazen beam by rings suspended hung.
The youths retreating from the burning field,
The chief resum'd his loaded helm, his shield
Behind him thrown; then grasp'd his massy spear,
(Thus arm'd the hinds of Thessaly appear,
With long sharp goads to prick their bullocks' sides)
And the firm plough of adamant he guides.
The restiff bulls with indignation fir'd,
From their broad nostrils living flames expir'd,
Loud as the blasts when wintry winds prevail,
And trembling sailors furl the folding sail.
Urg'd by his spear the bulls their task fulfil,
Prove their own prowess, and the ploughman's skill.
As the sharp coulter cleft the clodded ground,
The roughen'd ridges sent a rattling sound.
Firm o'er the field undaunted Jason treads,
And scattering wide the serpent's teeth he spreads;
Yet oft looks back, suspecting he should find
A legion rising up in arms behind:
Unwearied still the bulls their toil pursue;
Their brazen hoofs the stubborn soil subdue.
  When now three portions of the day were spent,
And weary hinds at evening homeward went,
The chief had till'd four acres of the soil;
He then releas'd the monsters from their toil.

Away they scamper'd wildly o'er the plain;
Himself rejoin'd his delegated train,
Till on the field his earth-born foes appear:
The Greeks their animated hero cheer.
He in his helm, replenish'd at the springs,
To slake his burning thirst fresh water brings.
His limbs renew'd with forceful vigour play,
His heart beats boldly and demands the fray.
Thus the fell boar disdains the hunter-bands,
Foams, whets his tusks, and in defiance stands.
Now rose th' embattled squadron in the field,
In glittering helms array'd, with spear and shield,
Bright o'er the martial plain the splendours rise,
And dart in streams of radiance to the skies.
Thus, when thick snow the face of nature shrouds,
And nightly winds dispel the wintry clouds,
The stars again their splendid beams display;
So shone the warriors in the face of day.
But Jason, mindful of the maid's command,
Seiz'd a vast rock, and rais'd it from the land:
Not four stout youths, for strength of limbs renown'd,
Could lift a weight so pond'rous from the ground:
This 'midst his foes, embattled on the field,
He hurl'd, and safe retir'd behind his shield.
The Colchians shout, as when the raging main
Roars round tremendous rocks, but roars in vain.
In silence fix'd, Æeta stands aghast
To see the fragment with such fury cast.
The host, like dogs contending o'er their prey,
With curs'd ferocity their comrades slay,
Then leave on earth their mangled trunks behind,
Like pines or oaks uprooted by the wind.
As shoots a star from Heaven's etherial brow,
Portending vengeance to the world below,
Who thro' dark clouds descry its radiant light:
Thus Jason rush'd, in glittering armour bright.
His brandish'd falchion fell'd the rising foes:
Succinct in arms, some half their lengths disclose,
Some scarce their shoulders; others feebly stand,
While others, treading firm, the fight demand.
As on the bounds which sep'rate hostile states,
Eternal source of battle and debates,
The cautious hind the cruel spoiler fears,
And reaps his wheat with yet unripen'd ears;
Ere yet the spikes their wonted growth attain,
Ere yet the sun-beams have matur'd the grain:
So Jason's arms the rising squadrons mow'd;
Their blood profusely in the furrows flow'd.
Some sidelong fall on earth, and some supine,
Some prone lie groveling and their lives resign,
Like whales incumbent on the buoyant main:
Some wounded perish ere they tread the plain;
As late in air they held their heads on high,
So lowly humbled in the dust they lie.
Thus tender plants, by copious torrents drown'd,
Strew their fresh leaves, uprooted from the ground;
The tiller views with heart-corroding pain
His fostering care, and all his labours vain.
Æeta thus with wild vexation burn'd,
And with his Colchians to the town return'd,
Some weightier task revolving in his mind:
Thus clos'd the combat, and the day declin'd.

BOOK IV.

ARGUMENT.

Jason obtains the golden fleece by the assistance of Medea. She embarks with the Argonauts for Greece. Æeta pursues them. Having crossed the Euxine sea, they sail up the Ister; and by an arm of that river enter the Adriatic. Absyrtus is treacherously murdered by Jason. They sail into the Sardinian sea by the way of the Eridanus and the Rhone. The murder of Absyrtus is expiated by Circe, at whose island they land. Thetis and her nymphs conduct the heroes through the straits of Scylla and Charybdis. They sail by the island infested with the Sirens, from whose enchantments Orpheus delivers them. At Corcyra, once called Drepane, they meet with the Colchians that pursued them through the Symplegades; who request Alcinous, king of the island, to deliver up Medea. He agrees to send her back to her father, if unmarried; but if married to Jason, he refuses to separate them. Upon this determination her nuptials are immediately celebrated. They again put to sea, and are driven upon the quicksands of Africa. The tutelary deities of the country extricate them from their distresses. They bear Argo on their shoulders as far as the lake Tritonis. The Hesperides, who were bewailing the death of the serpent, slain the preceding day by Hercules, give some account of that hero. The death of Canthus and Mopsus, two of their comrades, is related. Triton, whose figure is particularly described, gives them directions about their voyage. They sail near Crete. The story of Talus. At Hippuris they sacrifice to Phœbus, who, standing on the top of a hill, enlightens their way. The clod of earth, given by Triton to Euphemus, becomes an island, called Calliste. They anchor at Ægina; and loosing from thence, arrive without further interruption at Thessaly.

O GODDESS, daughter of th' eternal king,
Medea's various cares and counsels sing:
Far from my mind the sad suspense remove,
Whether to celebrate her lawless love,
Or whether her base flight from Colchis' bay,
Best claims the tribute of my tuneful lay.
In solemn council to his faithful chiefs
The vengeful king disclos'd his bosom-griefs:
Sore disconcerted at the recent fight,
He spent in long debate the doleful night;
Mistrusting still, these schemes, so deeply laid,
Were all conducted by his daughters' aid.
Meanwhile th' imperial queen of Heaven had shed
O'er the fair virgin's breast despondent dread.
She starts, she trembles, as, pursu'd by hounds,
The fawn light skipping o'er the meadow bounds.
She fears the secrets of her soul betray'd,
And her sire's vengeance for her proffer'd aid.
Her handmaids, conscious of her crimes, she fears;
Her eyes fierce flames emit, loud murmurs fill her ears.
Her death she meditates in wild despair,
And, sadly sighing, tears her golden hair.
Now fate imbibing from the poison'd bowl,
Soon had she freed her voluntary soul,
And Juno's projects all been render'd vain,
But, kindly pitying a lover's pain,
The goddess urg'd with Phrixus' sons her flight,
And eas'd her bosom of its sorrow's weight.
Forth from her casket every drug she pours,
And to her lap consigns the magic stores.

Then with a parting kiss her bed she press'd,
Clung round each door, and ev'n the walls caress'd.
A lock she tore of loosely-flowing hair,
And safe consign'd it to her mother's care,
The sacred relic of her virgin fame;
And wailing thus, invok'd Idya's name:
"This lock, O mother, at my hand receive,
Which I, far-distant roaming, with thee leave.
Farewell, Chalciope; far hence I roam!
And thou farewell, my first, my dearest home!
Oh! hadst thou, stranger, in deep ocean drown'd,
Perish'd, and never trod on Colchian ground!"
She spoke, and tears her heart-felt woe betray'd;
Then fled she instant. Thus the captive maid,
When from her friends and country banish'd far,
She shares the miserable fate of war,
Disus'd to toil beneath a tyrant's sway,
Flies from oppression's rod with speed away.
With speed like her's the weeping fair withdrew:
The doors spontaneous open'd as she flew,
Shook by her magic song; barefoot she strays
Thro' winding paths and unfrequented ways.
Before her face one hand her vesture holds,
And one confines its border's flowing folds.
Beyond the city-walls with trembling haste,
Unseen of all the centinels, she pass'd,
Then by accustom'd paths explor'd the fane,
Where spectres rise, and plants diffuse their bane;
(Thus practise magic maids their mystic art)
Fears ill portending flutter round her heart.
Her frenzy Cynthia, rising bright, survey'd,
And this soliloquy in triumph made:
"Yes, with Endymion's heavenly charms o'ercome,
I to the cave at Latmos once could roam,
Of love regardful, when your potent lay
Had from the starry spheres seduc'd my ray,
That you, protected by the gloom of night,
Might celebrate unseen the mystic rite,
Your lov'd employ: now Cupid's shafts subdue,
Not Cynthia only, but, fair sorceress, you.
For you his toils the wily god hath wove,
And all your heart inflam'd with Jason's love.
Come then, those pangs which love ordains endure,
And bear with courage what you cannot cure."
She said: impetuous hastening to the flood,
Soon on its lofty banks Medea stood.
A fire, which midnight's deadly gloom dispell'd,
Signal of conquest gain'd, she here beheld.
Involv'd in shade, the solitary dame
Rais'd her shrill voice, and call'd on Phrontis' name.
Known was her voice to Phrixus' sons, who bear
The grateful tidings to their leader's ear.
The truth discover'd, the confed'rate host
All silent stood, in wild amazement lost.
Loud call'd she thrice; and with responsive cries,
His friends requesting, Phrontis thrice replies.
Quick at her call they ply the bending oar;
Nor were their halsers fasten'd to the shore,
When Æson's son at one decisive bound
Leaps from the lofty deck upon the ground;
Phrontis and Argus hasten to her aid,
Whose knees embracing, thus Medea pray'd:
"Oh! save me, friends, from my offended sire,
Oh! save yourselves from dread Æeta's ire.
Known are our projects: sail we hence afar,
Ere Æa's monarch mounts his rapid car.
My magic charms shall close the dragon's eyes,
And soon reward you with the golden prize.
But thou, lov'd guest, continue faithful still,
And swear whate'er thou promis'd to fulfil:
Ah! leave me not to infamy a scorn,
By all my friends abandon'd and forlorn."
Plaintive she spoke: his arms around her waist
Rapt'rous he threw, then rais'd her and embrac'd,
And solac'd thus in terms of tend'rest love:
"By Heaven's high king I swear, Olympian Jove,
By Juno, goddess of the nuptial rite,
Soon as my native land transports my sight,
Thou, lovely virgin, shalt be duly led,
Adorn'd with honours, to my bridal bed."
This said, in her's he clos'd his plighted hand:
To Mars's grove Medea gave command,
Spite of her sire, the vessel to convey,
And bear by night the golden fleece away.
Swift at the word they sprung; the Colchian maid
Embark'd, and instant was their anchor weigh'd.
Their crashing oars resound: she oft to land
Reverts her eye, and waves her trembling hand:
But Æson's son his ready aid affords,
And sooths her sorrows with consoling words.
Wak'd by their hounds, what time the huntsmen rise,
And shake the balm of slumber from their eyes,
At twilight, ere Aurora's dreaded ray
Efface the tracks, and waft the scent away:
Jason, then landing with the fair, attains,
With flowers diversified, the verdant plains,
Where first the ram, with Phrixus' weight oppress'd,
His wearied knee inclin'd, and sunk to rest.
Hard by, an altar's stately structure stands,
To favouring Jove first rais'd by Phrixus' hands,
Where he the golden monster doom'd to bleed;
So his conductor Hermes had decreed.
Here, as by Argus taught, the chiefs withdrew,
While their lone course the regal pair pursue
Thro' the thick grove, impatient to behold
The spreading beech that bears the fleecy gold.
Suspended here, it darts a beamy blaze,
Like a cloud tipp'd with Phœbus orient rays.
With high-arch'd neck, in front the dragon lies,
And towards the strangers turns his sleepless eyes;
Aloud he hisses: the wide woods around,
And Phasis' banks return the doleful sound.
Colchians, far distant from Titanus' shore,
Heard ev'n to Lycus' streams the hideous roar;
Lycus, who, sever'd from Araxis' tides,
A boisterous flood, with gentle Phasis glides:
One common course their streams united keep,
And roll united to the Caspian deep.
The mother starting from her bed of rest,
Fears for her babe reclining on her breast,
And closely clasping to her fondling arms,
Protects her trembling infant from alarms.
As from some wood, involv'd in raging fires,
Clouds following clouds ascend in curling spires:
The smoky wreaths in long succession climb,
And from the bottom rise in air sublime;
The dragon thus his scaly volumes roll'd,
Wreath'd his huge length, and gather'd fold in fold.
Him winding slow, beheld the magic dame,
And Sleep invok'd the monster's rage to tame.
With potent song the drowsy god she sway'd
To summon all his succour to her aid;
And Hecate from Pluto's coasts she drew,
To lull the dauntless monster, and subdue.
Jason advanc'd with awe, with awe beheld
The dreaded dragon by her magic quell'd.

Lifeless he lay, each languid fold unbound,
And his vast spine extended on the ground.
Thus, when the boisterous wave forbears to roar,
It sinks recumbent on the peaceful shore.
Still strove the monster his huge head to heave,
And in his deadly jaws his foe receive.
A branch of juniper the maid applies,
Steep'd in a baneful potion, to his eyes:
Its odours strong the branch diffus'd around,
And sunk th' enormous beast in sleep profound.
Supine he sunk; his jaws forgot to move,
And his unnumber'd folds are spread o'er half the grove.
Then Jason to the beech his hand applies,
And grasps, at her command, the golden prize.
Still she persists to ply the potent spell,
And the last vigour of the monster quell,
Till he advis'd her to rejoin the crew;
Then from the grove of Mars the maid withdrew.
As some fair dame, when Cynthia rises bright,
Beholds the beamy splendours with delight,
Which from her vestment strong-reflected rise;
Thus gloried Jason in the glistering prize.
The flaming rays, that from its surface flow'd,
Beam'd on his cheeks, and on his forehead glow'd.
Large as the heifer's hide, or as the hind's,
Which in Achaia's plains the hunter finds,
Shone the thick, pond'rous fleece, whose golden rays
Far o'er the land diffus'd a beamy blaze.
He on his shoulders, now, the spoil suspends,
Low at his feet the flowing train descends;
Collecting, now, within its ponderous folds,
His grasping hand the costly capture holds.
Fearful he moves, with circumspect survey,
Lest men or gods should snatch the prize away.
Now as returning morn illumes the land,
The royal pair rejoin the gallant band.
The gallant band beheld with wondering eyes,
Fierce as Jove's fiery bolt, the radiant prize.
Their hands extending as they flock around,
All wish to heave the trophy from the ground.
But Jason interdicting singly threw
O'er the broad fleece a covering rich and new;
Then in the ship he plac'd the virgin-guest,
And thus the listening demigods address'd:
"No longer doubt ye, comrades, to regain
Far o'er a length of seas your lov'd domain.
For see, the end of all our glorious toil,
Won by Medea's aid, this precious spoil!
Her, not reluctant, I to Greece will bear,
And with connubial honours crown her there.
Guard your fair patroness, ye gallant crew,
Who sav'd your country when she succour'd you.
Soon will Æeta with his Colchian train
Preclude, I ween, our passage to the main.
Some with your oars resume your destin'd seat;
Some with your shields secure your wish'd retreat;
This rampire forming, we their darts defy,
Nor, home returning, unreveng'd will die.
Lo! on our prowess all we love depends,
Our children, parents, country, and our friends.
Greece, as we speed, thro' future times shall boast
Her empire fix'd, or wail her glory lost."
He said, and arm'd; the heroes shout applause:
Then from its pendent sheath his sword he draws,
Severs the halser, and, in arms array'd,
His station fixes near the magic maid,
And where Ancæus' hand the pilot's art display'd.
Keen emulation fir'd the labouring crew,
As down the stream of Phasis Argo flew.
Medea's flight now reach'd Æeta's ear,
And all her crimes in all their guilt appear.
To council call'd, in arms the Colchian train
Rush thick as billows on the roaring main,
Thick as the leaves that flutter from above,
When blasting autumn strips the faded grove;
So thick the shouting Colchians rush to war,
Led by Æeta in his splendid car,
Glorying in Phœbus' gifts, his rapid steeds,
Whose swiftness far the speed of winds exceeds.
His left a buckler's wide circumference rais'd;
In his extended right a flambeau blaz'd;
His girded belt a mighty spear sustains;
His son Absyrtus grasps the flowing reins.
Now by tough oars impell'd and prosp'rous tides,
The vessel glibly down the river glides.
Th' indignant king invok'd the powers above,
His parent Phœbus, and almighty Jove,
His wrongs to witness: and to sudden fate
Doom'd in his fury the devoted state.
Who dar'd delay the guilty maid to bring,
From land or ocean, to their injur'd king,
On their rebellious heads his wrath should fall,
And vengeance merited o'ertake them all.
Thus menac'd he; and, lo! the Colchian train
Lanch'd on that day their vessels in the main;
Swift, on that day, unfurl'd their bellying sails,
And all embarking caught the balmy gales.
Nor deem ye this a well-train'd naval host;
Like flocks of birds they scream around the coast.
Juno, propitious to her favourite crew,
Inspir'd the breezes that serenely blew,
That soon on Grecian land the fair might tread,
And pour destruction down on Pelias' head.
With the third morn, on Paphlagonia's shore,
Where Halys rolls his stream, the heroes moor.
Medea here ordain'd a solemn rite
To Hecate, the magic queen of night.
But what, or how she form'd the potent spell,
Let none inquire, nor shall my numbers tell:
Fear holds me silent. Here the pious band
Erect a sacred temple on the strand,
Sacred to Hecate, night's awful queen;
And still beside the beach the holy fane is seen.
And now the words of Phineus, old and blind,
Recurr'd to Jason, and each hero's mind.
From Æa he advis'd them to pursue
A different course, a course no pilot knew,
Which Argos thus delineates to the crew:
"When towards Orchomenos our course we bent,
We took that route th' instructive prophet meant.
For in times past a different road was known,
And this thy priests, Ægyptian Thebes, have shown.
Before the stars adorn'd the saphire-sphere,
Or Danaus' race had reach'd th' inquirer's ear;
In Greece the bold Arcadians reign'd alone,
And, ere bright Cynthia deck'd her silver throne,
On acorns liv'd, the food of savage man;
Before Deucalion's sons their reign began;
With harvests, then, was fertile Ægypt crown'd,
Mother of mighty chiefs, of old renown'd;
Then the broad Triton, beauteous to behold,
His streams prolific o'er the country roll'd.
For Jove descends not there in bounteous rains,
But inundations fertilise the plains.
Hence rose the matchless chief (if fame says true)
Who conquer'd Europe's realms and Asia's too;

His hardy troops embattled at his side,
He on his valour and those troops rely'd.
He built and peopled with superior skill
Unnumber'd cities, some remaining still.
Though many ages now have pass'd away,
Yet Æa stands, nor hastens to decay;
Peopled at first by his adventurous train,
Whose long-continued race ev'n now remain.
With care they still recording tablets keep
Of all the limits of the land and deep,
Wherever rivers flow, or storms prevail,
Wherever men can march, or ships can sail.
A river, stately-winding, deep and wide,
From far, far distant mountains rolls its tide;
Where ships of burthen sure protection claim:
Long is its course, and Ister is its name.
Far, o'er Riphæan hills, where Boreas reigns,
He undivided flows thro' various plains;
But when thro' Thrace and Scythian climes he glides,
In two broad streams his rapid flood divides:
This to th' Ionian sea its circuit sweeps,
That wider stretches to Trinacria's deeps,
Whose lofty shores your Grecian coast command,
If Achelöus flow through Grecian land."
He said: a favouring sign the goddess gave,
Which with new courage animates the brave.
Celestial fires emit a living ray,
And beams of glory point the certain way.
Here, leaving Lycus' valiant son behind,
They spread with joy their canvas to the wind.
Afar the Paphlagonian hills appear;
And from Carambis' cape remote they steer,
Led by the heavenly light and kindly gales,
Till in broad Ister's flood the vessel sails.
Where the Cyanean rocks o'erlook the main,
Part of the Colchians steer their course in vain;
While they, whose counsels sage Absyrtus guides,
Cut through the mouth call'd Calon Ister's tides.
Outsailing thus yon tardy ships, they sweep
With skilful oars the wide Ionian deep.
An isle, which Ister's branching streams comprise,
Peuce, triangular, before them lies:
Wide o'er the beach its ample base extends,
And in the flood its pointed angle ends.
The two broad streams, that round the island flow,
They by Arecos' name and Calon know.
Below this isle Absyrtus and his crew
Through the wide Calon their swift course pursue:
Above it sailing Jason's comrades stray,
And through Arecos wind their distant way.
Such naval force dismay'd the neighbouring swains;
They left their fleecy flocks and verdant plains:
The ships in view, with terrour struck they stood,
And deem'd them monsters rising from the flood:
Never beheld they from their native shore
Ships proudly sailing on the seas before.
For the fierce Scythians and Sigynnian race
Maintain'd no commerce with the sons of Thrace:
Nor Sindians e'er, who roam the desert plain,
Nor e'er Graucenians cross'd the seas for gain.
When Argo's crew the mount Angurus pass'd,
And reach'd the rock Cauliacus at last,
(Ister near which his stately stream divides
And mingles with the deep his sever'd tides;)
And distant left the wide Taurian plain,
Then had the Colchians plough'd the Chronian main.
Here, lest the vessel scape, they cautious stay,
And strive to intercept her in her way.
At length appears to their expecting view
On Ister's flood the enterprising crew.
Two lovely sea-girt isles their notice claim'd,
Dear to Diana, and the Brugi nam'd.
Superb in one a sacred temple rose,
And one secur'd them from their Colchian foes.
Her power revering whom these isles obey,
The foe had quitted them without delay.
Each isle beside was throng'd with Colchian hosts,
Who, guarding every pass, protect the coasts.
For troops of enemies embattled stood,
Far ev'n as Nestis and Salango's flood.
Their numbers few, the Mynian chiefs forbear
To wage with numerous foes unequal war.
Preventive of debate, this truce was seal'd;
That, since the king propos'd the fleece to yield,
Whether by open force, or arts unknown,
Conquest the daring combatant might crown,
He, though reluctant, must resign his right,
And the contested prize the victor's toil requite.
That, from the crowd with secrecy convey'd,
Diana's fane should guard the magic maid,
Till mid' the sceptred princes one arose
To fix their vague opinions, and propose,
Or to restore her to her sire's embrace,
Or in Orchomenos's city place,
Or freely grant her to embark in peace,
And with the Grecian heroes visit Greece.
When now, long pondering, the suspicious maid
Had learn'd, and all their secret counsels weigh'd,
Tormenting cares disturb'd her mind's repose,
And keen reflection added woes to woes.
Aside she then, from all th' assembled crew,
With cautious secrecy her Jason drew:
Him, thus withdrawn, th' impassion'd maid address'd,
And hold the secret sorrows of her breast:
"Say, what the cause that hostile hosts are join'd,
And leagues, destructive of my peace, combin'd?
Say, have these charms, with rapture once explor'd,
Lull'd to forgetfulness my faithless lord?
Hath time effac'd the promises he made,
When in the needful hour he ask'd mine aid?
Where now thine oaths, preferr'd to mighty Jove?
Where now thy tenders of unalter'd love?
Curs'd oaths! which bade me all I love disclaim,
Friends, parents, country, every honour'd name!
Forlorn and vex'd lest thou should'st toil in vain,
I with the plaintive halcyon sought the main.
I follow'd but to shield thee from alarms,
When bulls breath'd fire, and giants rose in arms.
Now is the fleece, for which ye sail'd, possess'd,
And by my foolish fondness thou art bless'd.
Bless'd thou; but me what secret sorrows vex,
Whose deeds reflect dishonour on my sex!
Me as thy daughter, sister, wife they brand,
Who dare attend thee to a distant land.
But stay, protect me, ease my weight of woe,
Nor to my royal sire without me go.
Oh! think on justice, and revere thine oath,
Which both consented to, which bound us both:
Or instant, should'st thou every tie evade,
In this frail bosom plunge the pointed blade.
Thus frantic love its due desert shall see,
And death come grateful to a wretch like me.
Think, should the king exert his sovereign sway,
And with my brother destine me to stay,

(That king with whom ye both with treacherous aim
Have form'd a league, subversive of my fame;)
Oh! how shall I behold my father's face?
With courage I! not shrinking at disgrace!
No; stung by conscience, I forestall my fate,
And feel the horrours which my crimes create.
Back o'er the seas, mid' raging tempests borne,
Long may'st thou wander joyless and forlorn.
Ne'er may thy boasted patroness and friend,
Juno, to thee her wonted aid extend.
Stern fate may still severer toils ordain,
And thou, false wretch, remember me in vain.
Oh! may the fleece deceive thy ravish'd sight,
And, like a vision, vanish into night.
Rise may my Furies, vengeance to demand,
And distant drive thee from thy native land.
From thee, their guilty source, my sorrows flow:
Share now thy part, and suffer woe for woe.
Thine oaths no more a slighted maid shall wrong,
Nor this perfidious truce protect thee long."
  Stung with despair, she utter'd thus her grief,
Thus to her angry spirit gave relief.
To burn the ship forth rush'd th' impetuous dame,
And wrap its heaven-built sides in sudden flame;
Resolv'd in thought, as now the vessel blaz'd,
To perish dauntless in the flame she rais'd:
But Jason thus, with boding fears impress'd,
Sooth'd the mad tumults of Medea's breast:
  "Cease, heavenly maid, nor wound a lover's ear
With words unwelcome, and unfit to hear.
The common safety bids us all unite
To gain a timely respite from the fight.
See, fair protectress, to restore thee lost,
What clouds of enemies surround the coast.
The country arms thy brother's cause to aid,
And bear thee to thy sire a captive maid.
Against such force should we our arms oppose,
Perish might all our host, o'erpower'd by foes:
Then, sad to think! if, every hero slain,
In long captivity must thou remain.
Our arts perfidious will this truce conceal,
Whose baneful influence must thy brother feel.
Bereav'd of him, the Colchians' cause to aid,
And to recover thee, a captive maid,
No more the neighbouring forces will unite:
Instant will I renew the desperate fight,
Secure my wish'd return, and vindicate my right."
  Thus spoke he mild: the mischief-brooding maid
Told her dark purpose, and, "O think," she said,
"Think, Jason, now: oppose we, as beseems,
To their destructive deeds destructive schemes.
Urg'd first by Love, in errour's maze I stray'd,
And through that god is every lust obey'd.
Decline the fight, till I the youth betray,
And to your hands consign an easy prey.
With presents be the heedless stripling lur'd:
Heralds, of faith approv'd, by me procur'd,
Ere long a seret audience shall obtain,
And to my purposes Absyrtus gain.
My plan (I reck not) if it please, pursue:
Go, slay my brother, and the fight renew."
  Such were the snares the treacherous lovers laid;
And by large presents was the prince betray'd.
The heralds with these specious presents bore
The veil Hypsipyle so lately wore.
Each Grace in Naxos' isle, with art divine,
Wrought the rich raiment for the god of wine;
He gave it Thoas, his illustrious heir,
And Thoas to Hypsipyle the fair;
She gave it Jason: wondering you behold,
And with new transport trace th' embroider'd gold.
What time with large nectareous draughts oppress'd,
On the soft vesture Bacchus sunk to rest,
Close by his side the Cretan maid reclin'd,
At Naxos' isle whom Theseus left behind;
From that bless'd hour the robe, with odours fill'd,
Ambrosial fragrance wide around distill'd.
  Her guileful purposes the magic maid
In order thus before the heralds laid:
That, soon as night her sable shade had spread,
And to the temple was Medea led,
Thither Absyrtus should repair, and hear
A project pleasing to a brother's ear:
How she, the golden fleece in triumph borne,
Would to Æeta speed her wish'd return;
How Phrixus' treacherous sons prolong'd her stay,
And her to cruel foes consign'd a prey.
Then far she flung her potent spells in air,
Which lur'd the distant savage from his lair.
Curse of mankind! from thee contentions flow,
Disastrous love! and every heart-felt woe:
Thy darts the children of thy foes infest,
As now they rankle in Medea's breast.
How, vanquish'd by her wiles, Absyrtus fell,
In seemly order now my Muse must tell.
  Medea now secur'd in Dian's fane,
The Colchians hasten to their ships again.
Jason meanwhile lies in close ambush, bent
Absyrtus and his friends to circumvent,
Him, yet unpractis'd in his sister's guile,
His ready ship had wafted to the isle:
Conceal'd in night they tugg'd their toilsome oars,
Till in the bay secure the vessel moors.
Alone, in confidence, the stripling came,
And at Diana's porch approach'd the dame,
(She like a torrent look'd, when swoln with rain,
Which foaming terrifies the village-swain;)
To learn what snare her wily art could lay,
To drive these bold adventurers away.
And all was plann'd; when from his ambuscade
Sprung Æson's son, and shook his lifted blade.
The conscious sister, stung with secret dread,
Lest her own eyes should view Absyrtus dead,
Turn'd from the murderous scene aside distress'd,
And veil'd her guilty face beneath her vest.
As falls an ox beneath the striker's blow,
So was Absyrtus laid by Jason low.
Near that bright fane the neighbouring Brugi built,
He eyes his victim, and completes his guilt.
Here sunk he low; and to his bleeding side,
Compressing both his hands, the hero died.
Medea's veil receiv'd the purple flood,
And her fair vesture blush'd with brother's blood.
Hell's blackest fury the dire scene survey'd,
And mark'd with sidelong eye the reeking blade.
The pious rite for blood in secret spilt,
Jason fulfils, and expiates his guilt.
The skin he rases from the body slain,
Thrice licks the blood, thrice spits it out again.
Then with collected earth the corse he press'd;
And still his bones with Absyrteans rest.
  When in full prospect the bright flambeau blaz'd,
Which to conduct the chiefs Medea rais'd,
Elate with hope the radiant guide they view,
And near the Colchian vessel Argo drew.

As lions fierce the timorous flocks dismay,
Leap o'er the folds, and drive them far away;
As trembling doves before the kite retreat,
So before Argo flies the Colchian fleet.
Furious as flame, on all the host they prey'd,
And low in death was each assailant laid.
Jason at length, to aid his valiant crew,
Who little need his aid, appear'd in view.
For not a fear their gallant hearts oppress'd,
Save what their Jason's safety might suggest.
The chiefs assembled with Medea sat,
And on their future voyage thus debate;
Peleus began: "Now, ere Aurora rise,
A speedy embarkation I advise:
A different course with caution let us choose,
From that far different which the foe pursues.
For (such my sanguine hope) when morning-light
Yon slaughter'd heaps discloses to their sight,
No words will win them to pursue us far,
No tongue entice them to renew the war.
Sedition soon, their prince Absyrtus dead,
Will, like a pest, o'er all their navy spread:
Secure and free shall we recross the main,
Their forces scatter'd, and their sovereign slain."
He said; the chiefs consented, and with haste
Re-enter'd Argo, and their oars embrac'd.
Hard by Electris, last of isles, they row,
Near which, Eridanus, thy waters flow.
Soon as their leader's fate the Colchians knew,
They vow'd destruction to the Grecian crew;
And, eager to o'ertake the Mynian train,
Had travers'd in their wrath the boundless main,
But Juno, as her thunder awful roll'd,
Presag'd her vengeance, and their pride control'd.
Dreading Æeta's ire, the vanquish'd host
Far distant voyag'd from the Colchian coast.
Unnumber'd ports the scatter'd fleet explor'd:
Some to those isles repair'd where Jason moor'd,
Nam'd from Absyrtus: some, where stately flows
The flood Illyricum, expect repose;
Beside whose bank a lofty tower they rear'd,
Where Cadmus' and Harmonia's tomb appear'd;
Here with the natives dwell they. Others roam
Till midst Ceraunian rocks they find a home;
Ceraunian nam'd, since Jove's red thunder tore
Their ships that anchor'd on the neighbouring shore.
But towards th' Hyllean port the heroes bear,
And, fortune smiling, fix their halsers there.
For many an isle projected o'er the tide,
Near which no vessel could with safety ride.
No hostile arts th' Hylleans now devise:
They teach the Mynians where their voyage lies;
And for their friendly intercourse obtain
The largest tripod from Apollo's fane.
For, doubtful of the fleece, when Jason came
To hear responses from the Pythian dame,
Enrich'd, and honour'd from the shrine he trod
With two bright tripods, given by Delphi's god.
'Twas doom'd no power should lay the country waste,
Within whose confines were these tripods plac'd.
Hid, for this cause, in earth the sumptuous prize
Hard by the fair Hyllean city lies;
Deep, deep it lies, with ponderous earth oppress'd,
That there unseen it might for ever rest.
King Hyllus, whom in fam'd Phæacia's shore
Fair Melite to great Alcides bore,
To mortal view was manifest no more.
Nausithoüs, to youthful Hyllus kind,
The heedless stripling in his courts confin'd;
(For, when to Macris' isle Alcides fled,
That far-fam'd isle, which infant Bacchus fed,
To expiate his guilt, and wash the stain
Of blood yet streaming from his children slain,
Here, as beside his favourite-beach he rov'd,
The Naiad Melite he saw and lov'd,
The daughter of Ægëus, fair and young,
From whose caresses hopeful Hyllus sprung.)
But he, to manhood ripening, wish'd to roam
Far from his sovereign's eye and regal home:
The native islanders augment his train,
And with their leader tempt the Chronian main.
Nausithoüs complied with each demand,
And Hyllus settled on the Illyric strand:
But, as he strove his scatter'd herd to shield,
A boor's rude weapon stretch'd him on the field.
How cross these seas, how round th' Ausonian shores,
And the Ligurian isles they plied their oars,
Ye Muses tell: what tokens still remain
Of Argo's voyage, what her feats, explain:
Say, to what end, by what impelling gales
She o'er remotest seas unfurl'd her sails.
All-seeing Jove their perfidy discern'd,
And for Absyrtus slain with anger burn'd.
By Circe's mystic rites Heaven's sire decreed
The guilt to expiate of so base a deed.
To sufferings dire, but what no mortal knew,
He, ere they safe return'd, foredoom'd the crew.
Beyond th' Hyllean land their course they steer'd:
Remote the vast Liburnian isles appear'd,
Late fill'd with Colchians; Pityëa fair,
And rocky Issa, are the names they bear.
These islands past, Cercyra's cliffs they greet,
Where dwelt (for here had Neptune chose her seat)
Cercyra: he, by tender passions sway'd,
From distant Philiuns fetch'd the black-ey'd maid;
Melaine her admiring sailors name,
As through dark groves they view the swarthy dame.
Fleet as the vessel sails before the wind,
Cerossus, Melite they leave behind.
Soon on Nymphæa, though remote, she gains,
Where Atlas' daughter, queen Calypso, reigns.
The crew conjectur'd, through far distant skies
They saw the tall Ceraunian mountains rise.
And now Jove's purposes and vengeful rage
Propitious Juno's anxious thoughts engage.
That every toil with glory might be crown'd,
And no disastrous rocks their ship surround,
She wak'd the brisker gales in Argo's aid,
Till in Electris' isle she rode embay'd.
Sudden, the vessel, as she sail'd along,
Spoke, wondrous portent! as with human tongue:
Her sturdy keel of Dodonean oak,
By Pallas vocal made, prophetic spoke.
This solemn voice shook every heart with fear:
They deem'd the thunderer's threaten'd vengeance near.
"Expect," says Argo, "storms and wintry seas,
'Till Circe's rites the wrath of Jove appease.
Ye guardian twins, who aid our great design,
By humble prayer the heavenly powers incline
To steer me safe to each Ausonian bay,
And to the haunts of Circe point my way."
Thus Argo spoke, as night her shades display'd:
The sons of Leda listen'd and obey'd.
Before th' immortal powers their hands they spread;
All, save these chiefs, were struck with silent dread.

The canvas wide-distended by the gales,
Swift down Eridanus the galley sails.
Here Jove's dread bolt transfix'd the stripling's side,
Who greatly dar'd the car of Phœbus guide.
This flood receiv'd him; and the flaming wound
Still steams, and spreads offensive vapours round.
The feathery race, as o'er the flood they fly,
Wrapp'd in sulphureous exhalations die.
The poplar's winding bark around them spread,
Apollo's daughters wail their brother dead.
Down their fair cheeks bright tears of amber run,
Sink in the sand, and harden by the Sun.
When boisterous winds the troubled waters urge,
And o'er its bank ascends the swelling surge,
These amber gems, swept by the tide away,
Their pearly tribute to the river pay.
But, down the stream, as Celtic legends tell,
The tears of Phœbus floated as they fell
In amber drops, what time from angry Jove
The god withdrew, and left the realms above:
To the far Hyperborean race he fled,
Griev'd for his favourite Æsculapius dead.
From fair Coronis sprung this godlike son,
Where Amyros' streams near Lacerea run.
  Strangers to mirth, the pensive Mynians muse
On their hard lot, and strengthening food refuse.
Loathing the stench these putrid streams emit,
Sickening and spiritless whole days they sit;
Whole nights they hear the sorrowing sisters tell,
How by the bolts of Jove their brother fell.
Their mingled tears, as o'er the stream they weep,
Like drops of oil float down the rapid deep.
The Rhone's broad channel Argo's keel divides,
Which mingles with Eridanus its tides:
There, where the confluent floods unite their force,
Boisterous they foam. The Rhone derives its source
From caverns deep, which, far from mortal sight,
Lead to the portals, and the realms of night.
One stream its tribute to th' Ionian pays,
One to the wide Sardinian ocean strays;
Thro' seven wide mouths it disembogues its tides,
Where foaming to the sea its stream divides.
This winding stream transmits th' adventurous train
To lakes that delug'd all the Celtic plain.
Disastrous fate had here their labour foil'd,
And of her boasted prowess Argo spoil'd,
(For through a creek to ocean's depths convey'd,
To sure destruction had the heroes stray'd;)
But Juno hasten'd from on high, and stood
On a tall rock, and shouted o'er the flood.
All heard, and all with sudden terrour shook;
For loud around them bursts of thunder broke.
Admonish'd thus, submissive they return,
And, steering back, their better course discern.
Mid' Celtæ and Ligurians long they stray'd,
But reach'd the sea-beat shore by Juno's aid:
O'er them each day her cloudy veil she drew,
And thus from human sight conceal'd the crew;
Whose ship had now the broad, mid channel pass'd,
And rode amidst the Stœchades at last:
For Jove's twin sons had pray'd, nor pray'd in vain.
Hence rear thy altars, and due rites ordain
To these kind powers, whose influential aid
Not only Argo's bold adventurers sway'd;
But later voyagers, by Jove's decree,
Have own'd their happy influence o'er the sea.
  The Stœchades now lessening from their view,
Swift to Æthalia's isle the vessel flew.
With chalks, that, as they cover'd, ting'd the shore,
The heroes rubb'd their wearied bodies o'er.
Here are their quoits and wondrous armour fram'd,
Here is their port display'd, Argoüs nam'd.
Hence sailing, they the Tyrrhene shores survey,
As through Ausonia's deeps they cleave their liquid way.
Æea's celebrated port they reach,
And fasten here their halsers to the beach.
Here saw they Circe, as in ocean's bed,
Dismay'd with nightly dreams, she plung'd her head.
For thus the sorceress dream'd; that blood and gore
Had smear'd her walls, and flow'd around her floor:
That all her treasur'd stores were wrapp'd in flame,
With which she lur'd each passenger that came:
That copious streams of blood her hand apply'd,
And her fears vanish'd as the flames subside.
For this the magic dame, as morning rose,
Wash'd in the cleansing wave her locks and clothes.
Monsters, unlike the savage, bestial race,
Unlike to humankind in gait or face,
Limbs not their own support whose hideous frame,
As sheep their shepherd follow, these their dame.
Such monsters once the pregnant earth disclos'd,
Of heterogeneous shapes and limbs compos'd:
No drying winds had then the soil condens'd,
No solar rays their genial warmth dispens'd;
But time perfection to each creature gave:
Monsters like these were seen in Circe's cave.
All, stedfast gazing on her form and face,
Pronounc'd the sorceress of Æeta's race.
Those terrours vanish'd, which her dream inspir'd,
Back to her gloomy cell the dame retir'd.
Close in her guileful hand she grasp'd each guest,
And bad them follow where her footsteps press'd.
The crowd aloof at Jason's mandate stay'd,
While he accompanied the Colchian maid.
Together thus they Circe's steps pursue,
Till her enchanting cave arose in view.
  Their visit's cause her troubled mind distress'd;
On downy seats she plac'd each princely guest.
They round her hearth sat motionless and mute:
(With plaintive suppliants such manners suit)
Her folded arms her blushing face conceal;
Deep in the ground he fix'd the murderous steel;
Nor dare they once, in equal sorrow drown'd,
Lift their dejected eyelids from the ground.
Circe beheld their guilt: she saw they fled
From vengeance hanging o'er the murderer's head.
The holy rites, approv'd of Jove, she pays:
(Jove, thus appeas'd, his hasty vengeance stays)
These rites from guilty stains the culprits clear,
Who lowly suppliant at her cell appear.
To expiate their crime in order due,
First to her shrine a sucking pig she drew,
Whose nipples from its birth distended stood:
Its neck she struck, and bath'd their hands in blood.
Next with libations meet and prayer she ply'd
Jove, who acquits the suppliant homicide.
Without her door a train of Naiads stand,
Administering whate'er her rites demand;
Within, the flames, that round the hearth arise,
Waste, as she prays, the kneaded sacrifice:
That thus the Furies' vengeful wrath might cease,
And Jove appeas'd dismiss them both in peace,
Whether they came to expiate the guilt
Of friends' or strangers' blood by treachery spilt.
  Circe arose, her mystic rites complete,
And plac'd the princes on a splendid seat.

Near them she sat, and urg'd them to explain
Their plan and progress o'er the dangerous main:
Whence rose the wish to visit Circe's isle,
And thus beneath the roof converse awhile.
For still on every thought the vision press'd,
And its remembrance still disturb'd her rest.
Soon as the sorceress saw Medea raise
From earth those eyes which shot a beamy blaze,
Anxious she wish'd to hear her native tongue,
Conjecturing from her features whence she sprung.
For all Sol's race are beauteous as their sire;
Their radiant eyes emit celestial fire.
The willing maid complied with each demand,
And in the language of her native land
Her story told; each strange event declar'd,
What countries they had seen, what dangers shar'd;
Her sister's counsels how they sway'd her breast,
How with the sons of Phrixus she transgress'd;
How from her father fled, his threats disdain'd:
But still untold her brother's fate remain'd.
His fate th' enchantress knew; no arts could hide
The murderous deed: she pitied and reply'd:
"Ah! wretch, dire mischiefs thy return await.
Hope not to shun thy father's vengeful hate;
Resolv'd on right, he to the realms of Greece
Will close pursue thee, nor his fury cease,
Till he avenge the murder of his son:
For deeds of blackest darkness hast thou done.
But go, at once my kin and suppliant, free,
Nor fear additional distress from me.
Thy lover hence, far hence thyself remove,
Who scorn'dst a father's for a vagrant's love.
Here supplicate no more: my heart disclaims
Thy guilty wanderings and sinister aims."
She spoke: the maid lamented; o'er her head
Her veil she cast, and many a tear she shed.
Her trembling hand the hero rais'd with speed,
And from the cave of Circe both recede.
By watchful Iris taught, Saturnia knew
What time from Circe's cave they both withdrew.
To mark their steps commission'd Iris staid,
On whom these fresh injunctions Juno laid:
"Haste, Iris, now; thy pinions wide expand,
And bear once more Saturnia's dread command.
Go, Thetis rouse from ocean's dark retreat;
Her potent aid my projects will complete.
Spread then towards Vulcan's shores thy speedy wing,
Where round his anvils ceaseless hammers ring.
Bid him no more his boisterous bellows ply,
Till heaven-built Argo sail securely by.
Then to the deity, whose sovereign sway
Controls the winds, whom raging storms obey,
Haste; and request that every rising gale
Be hush'd, and silence o'er the seas prevail:
That round the waves serenest zephyrs play,
'Till Argo anchors in Phæacia's bay."
She said: and Iris, poiz'd on airy wings,
From the bright summit of Olympus springs:
Descends impetuous down th' Ægean deeps,
Where in his watery caverns Nereus sleeps.
To Thetis first repairs the winged maid;
Solicits and obtains her potent aid.
Vulcan she next in humble prayer address'd;
The god of fire complied with her request:
His bellows heave their windy sides no more,
Nor his shrill anvils shake the distant shore.
Her wants to Æolus she next disclos'd:
And while her wearied limbs she here repos'd,
Thetis from all her Naiad train withdrew,
And from her Nereus to Olympus flew.
Juno with transport hail'd her sea-born guest,
Whom near her throne she seated and address'd:
"O, hear my tale, bright goddess of the main:
Thou know'st my care for Jason and his train;
Thou know'st how Juno's arm alone upheld,
And through the jutting rocks their ship impell'd:
Around whose sides fierce, fiery tempests rave,
And the huge crag is whiten'd by the wave.
Now must they sail near Scylla's awful height,
And where the rock Charybdis forms a streight.
Thee yet an infant in my arms I press'd,
And more than all thy sister-nymphs caress'd.
Revering me, the wife of sovereign Jove,
Thou scorn'dst the tenders of his lawless love.
(For him a mortal beauty now inflames,
And now he revels with celestial dames.)
And Jove, in vengeance for his slighted bed,
Swore, not a deity should Thetis wed.
Nor could the fervour of his love abate,
Till Themis thus disclos'd the will of fate;
That from thy womb in future times should spring,
Superior to his sire, an infant-king.
Dreading th' event, lest in some future day
This infant-king should claim celestial sway,
Thee Jove abandon'd to secure his throne,
And reign unrival'd ever and alone.
But, lo! I gave, thy bridal bed to grace,
A mortal husband worthy thy embrace;
I made thee mother of a happy line,
And to thy nuptials call'd the powers divine.
Myself, in honour to the godlike pair,
Deign'd on that day the bridal torch to bear.
Soon as thy son (believe the truths you hear)
Shall in Elysium's blissful plains appear,
Whom kindly now the fostering Naiads guard
In Chiron's mansion, of thy milk debarr'd,
In Hymen's silken chains the hero led,
Must share the honours of Medea's bed.
Oh! be a mother's tenderest care display'd,
Succour thy Peleus, aud thy daughter aid.
Hath he transgress'd? thy rising wrath subdue;
For Ate's dire effects th' immortals rue.
Vulcan, I ween, obsequious to my will,
His fires will stifle, and his bellows still;
His boisterous waves will Æolus restrain,
And zephyrs only fan the curling main,
Till Argo anchors in Phæacia's bay.
But shelves and stormy seas obstruct her way;
These, these I dread: but with thy train expert,
Be thine the care these mischiefs to avert.
Safe from Charybdis' gulf the vessel guide,
Safe from loud Scylla's all-absorbing tide;
Scylla, the terrour of Ausonia's shore,
Whom Phorcus to infernal Hecat bore,
Cratæis nam'd. Oh! summon all thy pow'r,
Lest her voracious jaws my chiefs devour.
Hope's cheerly dawn if haply thou discern,
Snatch from the watery grave the sinking stern."
"If 'tis resolv'd," replies th' assenting queen,
"Tempests to curb, and oceans to serene,
Fear not; but in my proffer'd aid confide:
This arm shall convoy Argo o'er the tide.
The surge subsiding shall confess my sway,
While harmless zephyrs round the canvas play.
Now must I traverse the wide fields of air,
And to my sisters' crystal grots repair;
Request their aid, and hasten to the shores,
Where anchor'd Argo unmolested moors:

That each brave comrade, at the dawn of day,
With heart elate may cleave the liquid way."
She spoke, and through th' aërial regions sped,
Then in the pools of ocean plung'd her head.
At Thetis' call the sister Nereids came,
And flock'd obedient round their oozy dame.
Juno's commands she bade the sisters heed,
And to th' Ausonian deep descend with speed.
Swifter than lightning, or than Phœbus' beams,
The goddess darted thro' the yielding streams;
Till, gliding smooth beside the Tyrrhene strand,
Her speedy footstep press'd th' Ææan land.
Along the winding beach the Mynians stray,
And while with quoits and darts their hours away.
Here Thetis singled from the gallant band
Peleus her spouse, and press'd the hero's hand:
Unseen by all the host, his hand she press'd;
By all, save Peleus, whom she thus address'd:
"Loiter not here; but with returning light
Unfurl your sails, nor Juno's counsels slight.
Safe thro' th' Erratic rocks your ship to guide,
Which frown tremendous o'er the tossing tide,
For this the sea-green sisters join their force,
And smooth through dangerous seas your destin'd course.
My form, what time we urge the foaming keel,
By you not unobserv'd, to none reveal;
Lest, as before, your folly I chastise,
And to more desperate heights my vengeance rise."
She said, and vanish'd to the deeps below.
The wondering chief was pierc'd with keenest woe.
For since the dame, with indignation fir'd,
Had from her Peleus' hated bed retir'd,
Unseen till now she lurk'd: the strife begun
From this unweeting cause, her infant-son.
For, soon as night diffus'd its darkest shade,
Her young Achilles o'er the flame she laid,
And, at return of day, with ceaseless toil
Applied to all his limbs ambrosial oil,
That youth might triumph o'er th' attacks of time,
Nor creeping age impair his vigorous prime.
The father saw, as from his bed he rose,
Fierce, ambient flames his infant's limbs enclose;
And, as he gaz'd, his rueful cries confess'd
The boding sorrows of a parent's breast.
Fool! for his queen, who heard her lord deplore,
Dash'd in a rage her infant on the floor.
Then fleet as air, or like a dream of night,
She vanish'd sudden from his odious sight;
Plung'd in her fury down the whelming main,
Nor e'er emerg'd she from the waves again.
For this he sorrow'd: but each sage command
Which Thetis gave, he told his gallant band.
They heard, and from their sports retir'd in haste;
Then shar'd, recumbent, in a short repast.
Sated, they catch the comforts of repose,
Till, every toil renewing, morn arose.
Soon as her radiant light illumin'd Heaven,
And to their wish were breezy zephyrs giv'n,
Quitting the land, they climb with nimble feet
The lofty decks, and reassume their seat.
Each to his toil returns alert and bold:
They tear the griping anchor from its hold;
They hoist the yard, their bracing ropes unbind,
And give the flapping canvas to the wind.
Swift sails the ship: soon to th' expecting crew
Anthemoessa's isle arose in view.
The Sirens here, from Achelous sprung,
Allure the loitering sailors with their tongue,
Who, fastening to the beach the corded stay,
Neglect their voyage, and attend the lay.
What time to Achelous' longing arms
The Muse Terpsichore resign'd her charms,
Their mutual love these wily songsters crown'd;
Who lur'd, in times remote, with tempting sound
Ceres' fair daughter, and fallacious shew
A virgin-face, while wing'd like fowls they flew.
On a bright eminence the charmers stand,
And watch the vessels as they tug to land.
Full many a mariner their songs betray,
Who lists and lingers till he pines away.
As Argo sail'd they rais'd their tuneful tongue;
And here their halsers had the heroes hung,
But Thracian Orpheus wak'd his wonted fire,
And sung responsive to his heavenly lyre;
That each resounding chord might pierce their ear,
And none the music of the Sirens hear.
Yet still they sung: still briskly with the breeze,
The vessel tilted o'er the curling seas.
Butes alone became an easy prey,
Who all enraptur'd listen'd to their lay.
Erect, above the towering chiefs, he stood,
And frantic sprung into the faithless flood.
His helpless hands he rais'd, the ship to gain,
And, but for Venus' aid, had rais'd in vain:
She, Eryx' honour'd queen, the wretch descry'd,
And snatch'd him floundering from the foaming tide,
His kind protectress, as her course she bends
Where Lilybœum's ample cape extends.
This dire mishap dishearten'd all the band,
Who row with vigour from the traitorous strand.
But other pests, more fatal to their freight,
Threaten their progress to that dangerous streight,
Where Scylla's rock projects its wave-worn side,
And where Charybdis' gulf absorbs the tide.
Dash'd by the driven waves the Planctæ roar'd,
From whose cleft summits flames sulphureous pour'd.
Thick, dusky clouds involve the darken'd skies,
And hid are Phœbus' splendours from their eyes.
Though Vulcan ceas'd from his assiduous toils,
The fires flash thick, and fervid ocean boils.
Here o'er the sailing pine the nymphs preside,
While Thetis' forceful hands the rudder guide.
As oft in shoals the sportive dolphins throng,
Circling the vessel as she sails along,
Whose playful gambols round the prow and stern
The much-delighted mariners discern;
Round Argo thus the toiling nymphs attend,
And, led by Thetis, their assistance lend.
O'erhanging black th' rocks' bleak brow they see,
And gird their azure vestures to their knee.
Now here, now there, as danger warns, they glide,
And stem mid' crushing crags the troubled tide.
Pendent on mountain-waves the vessel hung,
That pierc'd her solid planks, and foam'd the rocks among.
Above these rocks, here now the Nereids rise,
And float on billows hid amidst the skies;
Descending now to ocean's secret bed,
They in his gulfy deeps conceal their head.
As when along the beach, succinct for play,
To toss the flying ball the Nereids stray,
From hand to hand the sphere unerring flies,
Nor ever on the ground inglorious lies;
The sisters thus, with coadjutant force,
High o'er the surge impel the vessel's course:

From secret shelves her wave-dash'd sides they shove,
Tho' sturdy billows strong against them strove.
On a tall fragment that o'erlook'd the flood,
His shoulder resting on his hammer, stood
The sooty god: and from her starry skies
Juno beheld the scene with steadfast eyes.
Her hand around Minerva's neck she threw;
For much Saturnia trembled at the view.
  Long as the vernal suns protract the light,
So long in Argo's cause the nymphs unite.
Propitious to their labours sprung the breeze,
And the free vessel shot across the seas.
Trinacria's verdant meads they soon survey,
Where graze thy herds, illustrious god of day.
Juno's commands obey'd, the watery train,
Like diving mews, explore the deeps again.
Coasting along, the bleating flocks they hear,
And herds loud bellowing strike their listening ear.
Sol's youngest daughter, Phaëthusa, leads
The bleating flocks along the dewy meads;
Propp'd on her silver crook the maid reclin'd:
A shorter staff, with brazen ringlets join'd,
Lampetie takes; whose herds the heroes see
Slunk to the brook, or browsing on the lea.
Of sable hue no cattle you behold;
Milkwhite are all, and tipp'd their horns with gold.
They pass'd these meads by day; at day's decline
They brush'd with pliant oars the yielding brine.
At length Aurora's all-reviving ray
Redden'd the waves, and show their certain way.
  A fertile isle towers o'er th' Ionian tide,
Ceraunia nam'd; the land two bays divide.
Fame says, (forgive me, Muse, while I unveil,
Reluctant too, a legendary tale;)
A sickle lies conceal'd within this land,
With which rash Saturn's mutilating hand
His father castrated: for Ceres' aid
Others assert this rural sickle made.
For Ceres once, with love of Macris fir'd,
To this fam'd isle, her favourite seat, retir'd.
The Titans here she taught her arms to wield,
And crop the bearded harvest of the field.
This island hence, nurse of Phæacian swains,
Th' expressive name of Drepane obtains.
From mangled Uranus's blood they trace
The source inglorious of Phæacia's race.
  Trinacria left, and numerous perils past,
Here heaven-protected Argo moors at last.
The heroes disembark'd Alcinoüs hails,
And at their festive sacrifice regales.
Mirth unremitted through the city runs,
As though they welcom'd home their darling sons.
The godlike guests their social part sustain,
Joyous as though they press'd Hæmonia's plain:
But ere that distant plain delights their view,
The chiefs must buckle on their arms anew.
For, lo! those Colchians who adventurous stray'd
Through deeps unknown, and enter'd undismay'd
The dire Cyanean rocks, here throng the coast,
And wait th' arrival of the Grecian host.
The forfeit maid should Argo's crew refuse,
War in each sad, disastrous shape ensues.
Arm'd and resolv'd they threaten instant fight,
And future fleets t' assert their monarch's right.
But king Alcinoüs interpos'd his aid,
And, ere they rush'd to fight, their wrath allay'd.
Arete's knee the suppliant virgin press'd,
And thus th' associate band and queen address'd:
  "O queen," exclaim'd she, "lend thy timely aid
To save from Colchian hands a suffering maid.
With ruffian rage to bear me hence they come,
And to my wrathful sire conduct me home.
Thou know'st, if one, like me, of humankind,
How prone to err is man's unstable mind.
Deem me no slave to lust's usurping pow'r;
Prudence forsook me in the needful hour.
Be witness, Sun, and thou, whose every rite
Is wrapp'd, dire Hecate, in sable night,
How I reluctant left my native home,
And with rude foreigners abhor'd to roam.
Fear wing'd my flight; and, having once transgress'd,
To flee I judg'd my last resource and best.
Still have I liv'd, as with my father, chaste,
My spotless zone fast girded to my waist.
Oh! may my tale, fair princess, claim thy tears;
Oh! teach thy lord compassion as he hears.
On thee may all th' immortal gods bestow
Beauty and life, exempt from age and woe;
Cities, that need no bold invaders dread,
And a fair progeny to crown thy bed."
  In tears she spoke: then to each gallant chief
Told in these plaintive strains her tale of grief:
  "Low at your feet, ye warriors, suppliant view
A princess doom'd to wretchedness for you.
Yok'd were the bulls, and, desperate as they rose,
Crush'd by my aid were hosts of giant-foes.
Yes, soon Hæmonia the rich prize will see,
And boast of conquests which she owes to me.
My country I, my parents, palace left,
To pine through life, of all its joys bereft;
But gave to you, a base, ungrateful train,
To see your country and your friends again.
Spoil'd of my beauty's bloom by fate severe,
In endless exile must I languish here.
Revere your oaths; Erynnis' vengeance dread,
Who heaps her curses on the perjur'd head:
Dread Heaven's sure wrath, if, to my sire restor'd,
My shame or ruin wait his desperate word.
No sheltering shrine, no fortress near, I fly
To you alone, on your defence rely.
Yet why on you? who, merciless and mute,
Have heard my cries, nor seconded my suit;
Unmov'd have seen me lift my suppliant hand
To the kind princess of this foreign land.
Elate with hope the golden fleece to gain,
Colchos oppos'd you, and her king in vain:
But fearful now the battle to renew,
Ye dread detachments, nor will fight with few."
  She said; and all, who heard her suppliant moan,
Cheer'd her sad heart, and check'd the rising groan.
Each gallant man his brandish'd spear display'd,
And vow'd assistance to the suffering maid,
Shook his drawn sword, a prelude to the fight,
Resolv'd on vengeance, and resolv'd on right.
  Night now dispers'd the faint remains of day,
And all the slumbering world confess'd its sway:
Grateful its gloom to men with toils oppress'd;
Grateful to all but her, with sleep unbless'd.
She, hapless fair, her painful vigils kept;
Revolving still her griefs, she watch'd and wept.
  As at the distaff toils th' industrious dame,
Whose frequent tears her orphan children claim.
All night she toils, while clinging round they stand,
Wail their lost sire, and his return demand.
Swift down her cheek descends the silent tear:
So hard the lot fate destines her to bear!

Like hers Medea's copious tears descend,
Such agonizing griefs her tortur'd bosom rend.
The royal pair retir'd with wonted state
From the throng'd city to their palace-gate.
On their soft couch reclin'd, at evening's close,
Long conference held they on Medea's woes.
Thus to Alcinöus the queen express'd
The kind suggestions of her pitying breast:
"Oh! may the Minyans, prince, thy favours share:
Oh! shield from Colchian foes an injur'd fair.
Not distant far Hæmonia's plains extend,
And near our island Argos' frontiers end.
But far remote Æeta reigns; his name
Unknown to us, or faintly known by fame.
She, in whose sorrows now I bear a part,
Hath, to redress them, open'd all my heart.
Let no rude Colchian bear her hence away,
To her sire's vengeance a devoted prey.
Her errour this: the fiery bulls to quell,
Fond and officious she prepar'd the spell.
Augmenting then (as oft offenders will)
Her first with future errours, ill with ill,
Far from her native home, impress'd with dread,
Far from her angry sire the damsel fled.
But bound is Jason by strong ties, says fame,
To wed the wanderer, and retrieve from shame.
Urge him not then, with many an added threat,
His faith to violate, his oaths forget;
Nor stimulate Æeta's wrath to rise:
Their daughters parents rigorously chastise.
Thus Pycteus, with parental zeal o'ercome,
Compell'd his child Antiope to roam.
Thus Danaë, by her wrathful sire secur'd,
Toss'd in the troubled deep distress endur'd.
Nor long since Echetus, a wretch accurs'd,
With brazen pins his daughter's eye-balls pierc'd:
Pent in a dungeon's awful gloom she pin'd,
Doom'd by her savage sire obdurate brass to grind."
She said: soft pity touch'd the sovereign's breast,
Who thus his supplicating queen address'd:
"In me, O queen, these heroes should descry,
For the fair sufferer's sake, a firm ally;
Soon should my arms the Colchian foes remove,
But I revere the just decrees of Jove.
Unsafe I deem Æeta to deride,
Who sways the sceptre with a monarch's pride;
Able, though distant, if averse from peace,
To scatter discord through the realms of Greece.
Hear my proposal then; which you, I trust,
And all who hear it, will applaud as just:
If still a virgin's spotless name she bear,
Safe to her sire's domains conduct the fair:
But if one bed the wedded pair contain,
I will not sever Hymen's silken chain.
Forbid it, Heav'n! that I in wrath expose
Her sinless offspring to insulting foes."
He said, and sunk to rest: his sage resolves
Anxious and oft the wakeful queen revolves.
She rose: their princess' footstep heard, arise
Her femaletrain, and each her wants supplies.
"Go," to her page apart Arete said,
"Bid Æson's valiant son the virgin wed.
Bid him no more Alcinöus' ears assail
With long entreaties and a well-known tale.
Himself, unask'd, his advocate will go,
And tender these conditions to the foe:
If still the fair a spotless maid remain,
Soon shall she view her father's courts again;
But, if a matron's honour'd name she bear,
He will not separate the wedded pair."
She said: her herald, eager to convey
The royal message, sped without delay;
To Æson's son he told Arete's word,
And the kind counsels of her sovereign lord.
Hard by their ship, in glistering arms array'd,
Deep in the port of Hyllicus embay'd,
He spies the chiefs, his embassy repeats,
And every gallant heart with transport beats.
They crown the goblets to the powers divine,
And drag th' accustom'd victims to the shrine:
Then for the pensive fair officious spread
In a sequester'd grot the bridal bed.
Hither, in days of yore, fair Macris came,
Daughter of Aristæus, honour'd name!
He taught mankind the virtues and the use
Of the bee's labours, and the olive's juice.
For, know, when Hermes infant-Bacchus bore,
Snatch'd from the flames, to fair Eubœa's shore,
Macris embrac'd him with a mother's love,
And there, awhile, she nurs'd the seed of Jove,
And there with honey fed; till Juno's spite
Far from Eubœa's isle compell'd her flight.
At length, of this Phæacian grot possess'd,
She with vast opulence the natives bless'd.
To deck with honours due the bridal bed,
Around it wide the golden fleece was spread.
With sweetest flowers, that deck or dale or hill,
Th' assiduous nymphs their snowy bosoms fill.
The golden fleece emits so bright a ray,
They shone all radiant as the star of day,
Inspiring love: the prize though strong desire
Prompts them to touch, with reverence they retire.
These are the daughters of the Ægeän flood,
Those, Meletæum, haunt thy lofty wood.
From groves, from streams, at Juno's call they ran,
To grace the nuptials of this godlike man.
The sacred grot, recorded still by fame,
Bears to this day Medea's honour'd name.
For here the nymphs, their veils around them spread,
To nuptial joys the happy lovers led:
And every chief, to guard the blissful spot,
Clad in bright armour, stood before the grot,
Lest hostile troops, with rude tumultuous noise,
Should force an entrance, and distract their joys.
Thus station'd, they protect the hallow'd ground,
Their festive brows with leafy chaplets crown'd.
As Orpheus struck his tuneful lyre, they sung,
And Hymeneals round the grotto rung.
But in Alcinöus' court the fair to wed,
O'er Jason's anxious mind disquiet spread:
Full oft he wish'd Iolcos' coast to gain,
And wed the virgin in his sire's domain;
Such too Medea's wish: but fate severe
Forc'd him to celebrate his nuptials here.
For pleasure unalloy'd we look in vain;
Pleasure to suffering man is mix'd with pain.
Whether the Colchian foe had scorn'd or clos'd
With the just terms Phæacia's prince propos'd,
Of this they doubted: mid' the mirthful scene
Fears, which these doubts suggested, intervene.
Aurora now her orient beams display'd,
And pierc'd the sullen night's surrounding shade.
The circling shores and dew-bespangled ground
Reflect her rays: the streets with noise resound.
The citizens and Colchians, who possess'd
The distant coast, awake from balmy rest.

Impatient now his purpose to disclose,
To plead Medea's cause the monarch rose.
His hand sustain'd a sceptre's massy gold,
Which kings, deciding right, were wont to hold.
Around their prince, in glistering arms array'd,
Phœacia's peers a seemly pomp display'd.
Eager on each adventurous chief to gaze,
A female troop beyond the city strays.
In festive bands the distant swains unite:
(For Juno had divulg'd the nuptial rite)
One from his fold a ram selected brought,
A heifer one, to feel the yoke untaught;
Flagons of wine some for libation bear:
The smoke of victims blacken'd all the air.
As women wont, the female train select
Their costly veils, with gay embroidery deck'd:
Such golden toys, such trinkets they provide,
As on a nuptial day adorn the bride.
The comely chiefs their admiration won;
But more than all Æager's tuneful son,
As lightly to the lyre's melodious sound
Tripp'd the brisk dancer o'er the measur'd ground.
In concert full the virgin-choir prolong
The happy day with hymeneal song.
Here a fair band, collected in a ring,
Praises to thee, auspicious Juno, sing.
By thee inspir'd, disclose the royal dame
The friendly terms her prince was pleas'd to name.
Nor are the terms Alcinöus nam'd disown'd:
(For now their faithful loves hath Hymen crown'd)
True to his oath, he heard with fix'd disdain
And deem'd Æeta's vengeful fury vain.
Soon as the Colchians saw their purpose cross'd,
Defeated all their schemes, their labour lost;
That to the sovereign's terms they must accede,
Or quit his ports, and sail away with speed;
Dreading the monarch's wrath, submiss they try
To win his friendship, and commence ally.
Settling at last, long time the Colchian host
Dwelt with the natives on Phæacia's coast:
Till Bacchus' hated race from Corinth fled,
Exil'd these Colchians, and the isle o'erspread.
They sought the neighbouring shores: in times to come
Their sons emigrating explor'd a home,
Where far and wide extends th' Illyric coast,
And the Ceraunian hills in clouds are lost.
But these events, which now my Muse engage,
Were late fulfill'd in some succeeding age.
Yet still, in Phœbus' fane, uninjur'd stand
The altars rais'd by fair Medea's hand:
Some to the fates are pil'd with victims due,
Some to the nymphs their annual rites renew.
Towards the parting train the royal pair
Their generous love by costly gifts declare.
Twelve fair Phæacians, at the queen's command,
Conduct Medea to the sea-beat strand.
On the seventh morn with gently-breathing gales
Propitious Jove expanded Argo's sails;
Argo, decreed fresh dangers to sustain,
Ere Greece beholds her gallant sons again.
Ambracia's bay had open'd to their view,
Beside Curetes' land the galley flew,
The clustering isles, Echidanes, they pass'd,
And Pelops' distant realm beheld at last.
Nine tedious nights and days the vessel sweeps
The troubled surface of the Libyan deeps:
Till, driven by rapid tides and storms astray,
She near the Syrtes' quicksands plough'd her way:
Whirl'd in whose gulfy pools, their destin'd grave,
Nor sails nor oars the sinking galleys save.
Burst from its black abyss, the boiling flood
Up-heaves its shaggy weeds, involv'd in shelves of mud.
With the far-spreading spray the sands arise;
But nought discern they here that creeps or flies.
The tide (which now retreats into the main;
And now returns upon the beach again;)
Far o'er the shore, impell'd with fury, shew
All Argo's slimy keel expos'd to view.
They disembark, and gaze with aching eyes
On ridgy mountains lost amid the skies.
No grateful streams, no beaten paths appear,
No rural cot discern they, far or near;
A death-like silence reign'd around: dismay'd
His comrade each interrogating said:
"What country this? on what bleak clime at last
Have the rude tempests heaven-built Argo cast?
Oh! had we dar'd, devoid of vulgar fear,
Our course undaunted through those fragments steer,
Like heroes then (though Jove success deny'd)
We in the bold attempt had bravely died.
What can our skill devise? the least delay
Is fatal here; the winds forbid our stay.
How bleak and barren is the coast we tread!
And what a desert waste is wide around us spread!"
He said; and, joining in the loud lament,
Ancæus thus foreboded the event:
"What dire mishaps our gallant host befall!
Thus by stern fate's decree we perish all!
What woes await us, on this desert coast,
If from the land awakes the furious blast!
For slimy seas my sight far off commands,
And whitening billows bursting o'er the sands.
And dreadfully had Argo's yawning sides,
Remote from shore, receiv'd the gushing tides,
Had not the surge, which lifted her to Heav'n,
Full on the pebbly beach the vessel driv'n.
But now the tide retiring quits the strand,
And waves unfaithful skim the levell'd sand.
Our projects baffled, and hope's cheerly dawn
From our expecting sight thus soon withdrawn,
Let other hands the pilot's art display,
And they who fear not danger steer the way.
But our joint labours Jove decrees to foil,
Nor will our native home reward our toil."
He said; and all, renown'd for naval skill,
Close with his words, and wait th' impending ill.
From every heart the vital motion fled,
O'er every face a deadly paleness spread.
As when from street to street, in wild dismay,
Affrighted mortals, like pale spectres, stray;
Expecting wars, or plagues, or bursting rains,
That deluge all the harvest of the plains:
Or, as when statues drops of blood distil,
And fancied bellowings the temples fill;
The noon-day Sun eclips'd involves in night
Th' astonish'd world, and stars emit their light:
Thus on the beach they stalk'd, a heartless clan!
Like sweating statues, or like spectres wan.
His feeble arm each round his comrade cast,
Then sunk into the sand to breathe his last,
Resolv'd, as now the star of Hesper rose,
To share the solace of united woes.
Some here, some there select their clay-cold bed,
And round their shivering limbs their garments spread:

Resign'd to death, in midnight's sullen shade
And at mid-day, here languishing they laid.
Remote, Medea's fair attendants moan,
Cling round their queen, and groan return for groan.
  As when a nest, surcharg'd with callow young,
Falls from the lofty cliff to which it clung,
Th' unfeather'd brood by shrillest cries attest
Their far-flown mother, and their ruin'd nest:
As on the banks Pactolus' streams bedew,
Melodious swans their dying notes renew;
The rivers, gliding the rich vales among,
Bear on their silver streams the soothing song:
Thus they, their golden locks besmear'd with gore,
All night in plaintive elegies deplore.
Their toils yet incomplete, the godlike band
Had now ignobly perish'd on the sand,
But the bold heroines, who guard the coast,
Beheld with pitying eye the drooping host:
Those nymphs, who, when in glistering arms array'd,
Rush'd from the thunderer's brain the martial maid,
In needful hour their kind assistance gave,
And cleans'd her infant-limbs in Triton's wave.
  'Twas noon: o'er Libya's sands the god of day
Darted the splendours of his fiercest ray.
Full before Jason stood the nymphs confess'd,
And gently from his head withdrew the vest.
Sudden he starts, impress'd with silent dread,
And from his fair protectors turns his head.
They in compassion's mild address began
To free from terrours vain the hopeless man!
  " Why griev'st thou thus ? Oh! bid thy sorrows cease:
We know thy coming's cause, the golden fleece.
We know the various toils by land you bore;
How toss'd on ocean, how distress'd on shore.
Terrestrial powers, for acts of friendship known,
We make the shepherd's rural cares our own.
We, Libya's daughters and avengers, boast
Our sway extended o'er the Libyan coast.
Arise, nor sink beneath thy sorrow's weight;
But rouse thy fellows from their drooping state.
When Amphitrite with officious speed
Unreins from Neptune's car the fiery steed,
Thy mother then with duteous care repay,
Whose womb hath borne thee many a toilsome day.
Discharge this duty, and resail to Greece,
Safe and triumphant with the golden fleece."
  They spoke, and vanish'd: from his sandy bed
Jason arose, and looking round he said;
  " Ye godlike powers, the desert plains who rove,
Ye fair, who tend the flocks, propitious prove.
Those dark mysterious truths your tongues foretold,
I go, if haply can my friends unfold.
Conven'd, may they some prudent scheme devise,
For in th' advice of numbers safety lies."
  He said: and, wading thro' the driven sand,
Rous'd with loud voice the sad, desponding band.
Thus, while the lion his lost mate explores,
The forests ring, Earth trembles as he roars:
Herdsmen and herds o'erwhelm'd with equal fear,
All mute and trembling deem destruction near.
But grateful to the host was Jason's call;
No fears it cherish'd, but gave hope to all.
Yet with dejected looks the heroes meet.
Beside the female train to each his seat
He, near the shore, assign'd; in order due
His wondrous tale relates, and cheers the pensive crew:
  " Attend, my friends: three virgin-forms, who claim
From Heaven their race, to sooth my sorrows, came.
Their shoulders round were shaggy goat-skins cast,
Which, low descending, girt their slender waist.
High o'er my head they stood; with gentle hand
My vesture rais'd, and gave this dread command:
That I with speed my piteous bed forsake,
And, risen, haste my comrades to awake.
That mindful we our mother's cares repay,
Whose womb sustain'd us many a toilsome day,
When Amphitrite with officious speed
Unreins from Neptune's car the fiery steed.
Long have I sought this wonder to explain,
And, still revolving, I revolve in vain.
In the bold name of heroines they boast,
Daughters and guardians they of Libya's coast.
Known to these nymphs are all the toils we bore
On the rough ocean, and the faithless shore.
Nor staid they long; but, sudden, from my view
Their radiant forms an ambient cloud withdrew."
He said: on every face sat boding fears;
When, lo! a portent, greater far, appears.
Fierce from the foamy deep, of wondrous size,
Springs a huge horse; his mane expanded flies.
From his strong sides he shakes th' adherent spray,
Then towards the coast directs his rapid way.
Skill'd in whate'er this prodigy portends,
With pleasure Peleus thus consoles his friends:
  " Now by his consort's hand releas'd I see
The car of Neptune, and his horses free.
A mother's name (or I predict in vain)
Argo may boast; she feels a mother's pain.
Her pregnant womb a troop of heroes bears,
And endless perils for their safety shares.
Come, let us now our boasted strength display,
And on our shoulders bear our ship away.
Steer we through depths of sand our dangerous course,
Led by the steps of this portentous horse.
His steps reluctant press the dusty plain,
But rapid bear him to his kindred main;
Thither attend his flight." Thus spoke the seer:
His pleasing counsels gratified their ear.
  This wondrous tale the tuneful Nine recite,
And as the Muses dictate must I write.
This have I heard, and this as truth proclaim,
That you, O princely peers, of deathless fame,
By the joint efforts of united hands,
Twelve days and nights, through Libya's burning sands,
High on your shoulders rais'd the vessel's weight,
All that its womb contain'd, a mighty freight!
What woes o'ertook them, and what toils befell,
No verse can celebrate, no tongue can tell.
Such brave exploits proclaim'd their godlike line,
For, as their lineage, were their deeds, divine.
But when Tritonis' lake the chiefs attain,
They eas'd their shoulders, and embark'd again.
Doom'd to acuter griefs they now are curs'd
With all the miseries of burning thirst;
Like dogs they run its fury to assuage,
And at a fountain's head suppress its rage.
Nor wander'd they in vain; but soon explor'd
The sacred spot with golden apples stor'd,
In Atlas' realm: the serpent's wakeful eyes
Watch'd, till but yesterday, the golden prize.
The fair Hesperides with kind survey
Tended the serpent as they tun'd their lay.

But, lo ! the monster, by Alcides slain,
Beneath a branching pear-tree press'd the plain.
His tail still vibrates, though his ghastly head
And spine immense lie motionless and dead.
Flies in thick swarms his gory sides surround,
Drink his black blood, and dry the dripping wound,
Made by the darts, whose poison'd tips detain
The deadly venom of the hydra slain.
As Ladon's fate the pensive maids deplore,
Their hands they wrung, their golden locks they tore ;
But, sudden, as the heroes hasten'd near,
They to the dust descend and disappear.
Struck with the prodigy his eyes survey'd,
Thus to the nymphs observant Orpheus pray'd :
  " Ye goddesses, with blooming beauty bless'd,
Look with benevolence on men distress'd.
Whether ye grace the splendid courts of Jove,
Or on this humbler Earth auspicious move;
Whether to flowery pastures ye repair,
And the lov'd name of shepherdesses bear;
Illustrious nymphs, from ocean sprung, arise,
Bless with a recent view our longing eyes.
Bid from the thirsty soil a torrent burst,
Or open some hard rock to slake our thirst.
Should we again our tatter'd sails expand,
And greet at last the dear Achaian land,
Grateful we then these favours will repay,
And choicest offerings on your altars lay :
No goddess, who frequents the courts of Jove,
Shall greater honour share, or greater love."
  Thus Orpheus pray'd, with feeble voice and low:
The listening nymphs commiserate their woe.
First tender grass they bade the soil disclose:
Then high above it verdant branches rose.
Erect and strong, the spreading boughs display'd
Wide o'er the barren soil an ample shade.
A poplar's trunk fair Hespera receives,
And in a weeping willow Ægle grieves.
But Erytheïs in an elm remains:
Each in her tree her proper shape retains ;
Stupendous sight ! first Ægle silence broke,
And kindly thus the suppliant band bespoke :
  " Hither some lawless plunderer came of late,
Who will reverse the colour of your fate.
Yon beast he slew, for whom we sorrow now,
And tore the golden apples from their bough.
But yesterday the desperate giant came ;
From his black eye-brows flash'd the livid flame:
A lion's shaggy skin, besmear'd with gore,
Wide o'er his shoulders spread, the monster wore.
On his stout staff his fearless step rely'd,
And by his deadly dart the serpent died.
He, like a sturdy traveller, stalk'd along,
Seeking some fount to cool his fiery tongue.
With eager haste he trod the dusty plain,
And still for water look'd, but look'd in vain.
To this tall rock, hard by Tritonis' lake,
Some god conducted him, his thirst to slake.
Struck by his heel, its deep foundations shook,
And from the yawning clefts a torrent broke.
Prone on the ground the limpid streams he swills,
And, groveling like a beast, his belly fills."
  Elated with the tale, they speed their course,
To find, as Ægle told, the fountain's source.
  As when assembled ants with joint essay
Strive in some chink their lifted grain to lay :
Or as when flies some liquid sweet explore,
They hang in clusters round the honied store;
Like them the Mynians: such their numbers seem,
And such their haste to gather round the stream.
Conjecturing thus some grateful hero said,
As from the rill refresh'd he rais'd his head :
  " Ye gods! though absent, great Alcides gives
These limpid streams ; by him each hero lives.
Come, haste we now the country to explore,
And the lost wanderer to our host restore."
  Instant to council rose th' associate band,
Selecting heroes to explore the land.
For nightly winds dispersing o'er the plains
The light, loose sands, no step impress'd remains.
Boreas' fleet sons, who wing their airy flight,
Sagacious Lynceus bless'd with keenest sight,
Euphemus swift of foot, and Cantheus speed:
Him his brave spirit urg'd and Heaven decreed
To ask Alcides, on what fatal coast
He left his comrade, Polyphemus lost.
When this bold chief had rear'd on Mysian ground,
And fenc'd with circling walls a city round,
Wide o'er the country, Argo's fate to learn,
He roam'd, with Argo anxious to return.
Scarce had his feet Calybian frontiers press'd,
Ere fate consign'd him to eternal rest.
Along the beach, with stately poplars spread,
They rear'd a tomb in honour of the dead.
But Lynceus deems, that, o'er the distant lands
His sight the long-lost Hercules commands.
Thus sees the clown, or thinks he can descry
The new Moon breaking through a cloudy sky.
Back to his comrades hastes the joyous chief,
Precludes their further search, and gives their mind relief.
Euphemus soon, and Boreas' sons, his friends,
Whose search in empty expectation ends,
Rejoin'd the host: but thee, brave Canthus, slain,
Stern fate foredoom'd to press the Libyan plain.
To feast his comrades with the grateful prey,
He forc'd through scatter'd flocks his desperate way.
Sudden, his flock to guard, the shepherd flew,
And with a rock's huge fragment Canthus slew.
This sturdy villager, Caphaurus nam'd,
His lofty lineage from Apollo claim'd,
And Acacallis : conscious of his might,
He fear'd no rival, nor declin'd the fight.
Minos her sire, to Libya's coast remov'd
Fair Acacallis, by the god belov'd.
To Phœbus here a hopeful son she gave,
Amphithemis or Garamans the brave.
Thy love, Amphithemis, Tritonis crown'd,
And grac'd thy bed with Nasamon renown'd,
And bold Caphaurus ; whose decisive blow
Transmitted Canthus to the shades below.
The bloody deed divulg'd to all the host,
Not long his conquest could Caphaurus boast.
They to its sepulchre the corse convey,
Weeping ; and make the shepherd's flocks their prey.
  To Pluto's realms prophetic Mopsus fled,
And join'd, on that sad day, the mighty dead.
With fate's decrees must mortal man comply,
And the wise seer, in spite of prescience, die.
For, shelter'd from the fierce meridian ray,
Beneath a sandy bank, a serpent lay.
Innoxious till incens'd, he ne'er annoy'd,
But strove th' affrighted traveller to avoid.
But all, whome'er the foodful earth contains,
Who feel his darted venom in their veins,

Nor long, nor distant deem the dreary road,
That leads direct to Pluto's dark abode.
His fangs infix'd when once the wretches feel,
In vain would medicine's god attempt to heal.
For when brave Perseus (this her godlike son
His mother oftener nam'd Eurymedon)
O'er Libya flew, the Gorgon's head to bring,
Fresh-slain and dripping, to th' expecting king,
From every drop, that dyed the soil with blood,
A serpent sprung, and thus increas'd the brood.
The monster's spiry tail rash Mopsus press'd
With his unheeding foot: his tortur'd breast
Upward he turn'd, and writh'd his spires around,
Then with his venom'd fang infix'd a deadly wound.
Medea trembled and her female train:
Fearless he bathes the wound, nor heeds the pain.
But now, lost wretch! each sense is clos'd and dead,
And o'er his sinking eyes death's gloomy shade is spread.
Prone to the dust he falls: his cold remains
Press with unwieldy weight the desert plains.
His faithful friends, and Jason with the rest,
Weep o'er the corse, with heart-felt grief impress'd.
His flesh all putrid from the taint within,
And hanging round him loose his flabby skin,
The burning Sun unable long to bear,
His busy comrades, with officious care,
Deep in the soil conceal their delving spade,
And soon a decent sepulchre was made.
Men, matrons, all, as round the grave they flock,
Lamenting loud select the sacred lock:
His corse the bright-arm'd heroes thrice surround,
And raise in seemly form the hallow'd mound,
Then hasten to their ship: the southern breeze
Curl'd, as it blew, the surface of the seas.
In sad suspense, still wishing to forsake,
And cross with favouring gales Tritonis' lake,
They loiter long, and waste the useful day
In idle contest and in vain delay.
A serpent thus, long scorch'd with summer's heat,
Winds to some secret chink, his cool retreat.
Enrag'd he hisses, rears his crest on high,
And furious darts his fire-emitting eye,
Till haply he the wish'd-for chink pervade,
And in its cool recess secure a shade.
Uncertain thus, the ship explor'd in vain
The lake's wide mouth that open'd to the main.
With pious care, as Orpheus gives command,
They place Apollo's tripod on the strand;
That those auspicious powers the coast who guard,
Pleas'd with th' oblation, may their toils reward.
Clad like a youth, before them stood confess'd
The mighty Triton: in his hands he press'd
The gather'd soil; this amicable sign
He to the heroes held, and spoke benign:
"The hospitable pledge my hand extends,
The best I now can give, accept my friends.
Would you o'er ocean's paths your course discern,
And learn the tracks, which strangers wish to learn,
Hear: from my sire, the monarch of the main,
I boast my science: o'er these seas I reign.
Perchance ev'n you, though distant far you came,
May recognise Eurypylus's name,
In Libya born." He said: Euphemus took
The proffer'd soil, and thus responsive spoke:
"If such thy knowledge, friendly chief, explain
Where Atthis lies, where rolls the Cretan main.
Reluctant sail'd we towards the Libyan coast,
By angry Heaven and adverse tempests tost:
By land, with Argo o'er our shoulders cast,
We toil'd, and lanch'd her in this lake at last.
Nor can we yet our certain course devise,
Where full in prospect Pelops' realms will rise."
He said: his hand out-stretching, Triton shew
The lake's wide mouth, and sea expos'd to view.
"Where the lake blackens, and its waters sleep,
Expect," he cries, "a passage to the deep.
Observe the cliffs high towering on each side,
And through the streight they form your vessel guide.
There, above Crete, where, mingling with the skies,
Yon ocean spreads, the land of Pelops lies.
When to the right th' expanded lake ye leave,
And the safe seas your mighty freight receive,
Still cautious coast along the winding strand,
Till you the cape's projecting sides command:
Your course, that cape once doubled, safe pursue,
Your ship uninjur'd, and undaunted you.
Thus gladden'd go; nor let your vigorous arms
Droop with fatigue, and shake with vain alarms."
Heartening he spoke: the decks they re-ascend,
And, rowing brisk, to cross the lake contend.
The proffer'd tripod friendly Triton takes,
And hides his head beneath the dimpling lakes.
Thus with the costly prize the god withdrew,
Instant invisible to mortal view.
Inspir'd with joy, that some superior guest
Had comfort given them, and with counsel bless'd,
The choicest sheep they bade their leader slay,
And to the power benign due honours pay
He to the galley's poop with speed convey'd
The choicest sheep, and, as he offer'd, pray'd:
"Dread deity, who late conspicuous stood
On the clear margin of this rolling flood,
Whether great Triton's name delight thine ear,
Triton, whom all the watery gods revere;
Or Ocean's daughters, as they sound thy fame,
Thee mighty Nereus, or thee Phorcuns name,
Be bounteous still: bid all our labours cease,
And reinstate us in our native Greece."
Thus pray'd the chief, as on the poop he stood,
And sunk the slaughter'd victim in the flood.
His head above the billows Triton rear'd,
And in his proper shape the god appear'd.
As when, intent his fiery steed to train,
The horseman leads him to the dusty plain,
His floating mane firm twisted in his hand,
He runs, yet holds him subject to command:
Superb he paces, by his master led,
Curvetting still, and tossing high his head.
His bits, all white with gather'd foam around,
Craunch'd by his restless jaw, aloud resound:
Thus Triton's hands the vessel's head sustain,
And safely guide her to the seas again.
His every limb, down to his swelling loin,
Proclaims his likeness to the powers divine.
Below his loin his tapering tail extends;
Arch'd like a whale's on either side it bends.
Two pointed fins, projecting from his side,
Cleave, as he scuds along th' opposing tide.
Acute and tapering, these indented thorns
A semblance bear to Phœbe's budding horns.
His arm conducts her, till, from danger free,
She rides imbosom'd in the open sea.
This prodigy the shouting warriors saw,
Impress'd at once with gratitude and awe.

Here shatter'd ships Argous' port receives,
Here tokens of her voyage Argo leaves:
To Triton here, high towering o'er the strand,
And here to Neptune stately altars stand.
For here they linger'd out one useless day;
But with fresh breezes sail'd, at morn, away.
Far to the right they leave the desert land,
And the stretch'd canvas to the winds expand.
Gaining mid ocean with returning light,
The doubled cape diminish'd from their sight.
The zephyrs ceasing, rose the southern gale,
And cheer'd the shouting heroes as they sail.
* The evening star now lifts, as day-light fades,
* His golden circlet in the deepening shades;
* Stretch'd at his ease the weary labourer shares
* A sweet forgetfulness of human cares:
* At once in silence sleep the sinking gales,
* The mast they drop, and furl the flagging sails;
* All night, all day, they ply their bending oars
* Towards Carpathus, and reach the rocky shores;
* Thence Crete they view, emerging from the main,
* The queen of isles; but Crete they view in vain.
* There Tagus mountains hurls with all their woods;
* Whole seas roll back, and tossing swell in floods.
* Amaz'd the towering monster they survey,
* And trembling view the interdicted bay.
* His birth he drew from giants sprung from oak,
* Or the hard entrails of the stubborn rock:
* Fierce guard of Crete! who thrice each year explores
* The trembling isle, and strides from shores to shores,
* A form of living brass! one part beneath
* Alone he bears, a part to let in death,
* Where o'er the ankle swells the turgid vein,
* Soft to the stroke, and sensible of pain.
Pining with want, and sunk in deep dismay,
From Crete far distant had they sail'd away,
But the fair sorceress their speed repress'd,
And thus the crew disconsolate address'd:
"Attend. This monster, ribb'd with brass around,
My art, I ween, will level to the ground.
Whate'er his name, his strength however great,
Still, not immortal, must he yield to fate.
But from the far-thrown fragments safe retreat,
Till prostrate fall the giant at my feet."
She said: retiring at the sage command,
They wait the movement of her magic hand.
Wide o'er her face her purple veil she spread,
And climb'd the lofty decks, by Jason led.
* And now her magic arts Medea tries;
* Bids the red furies, dogs of Orcus, rise,
* That starting dreadful from the th' infernal shade,
* Ride Heaven in storms, and all that breathes invade.
* Thrice she applies the power of magic pray'r,
* Thrice, hellward bending, mutters charms in air;
* Then, turning towards the foe, bids mischief fly,
* And looks destruction, as she points her eye.
* Then spectres, rising from Tartarean bow'rs,
* Howl round in air, or grin along the shores.
Father supreme! what fears my breast annoy,
Since not disease alone can life destroy,
Or wounds inflicted fate's decrees fulfil,
But magic's secret arts have power to kill!
For, by Medea's incantations plied,
Enfeebled soon the brazen monster died.

☞ The lines thus marked * are Broome's, who has translated the story of Talus, not without several omissions, which are here supplied.

* While rending up the earth in wrath he throws
* Rock after rook against th' aerial foes,
* Lo! frantic as he strides, a sudden wound
* Bursts the life-vein, and blood o'erspreads the ground.
* As from a furnace, in a burning flood
* Pours melting lead, so pours in streams his blood:
* And now he staggers, as the spirit flies,
* He faints, he sinks, he tumbles, and he dies.
* As some huge cedar on a mountain's brow,
* Pierc'd by the steel, expects a final blow,
* Awhile it totters with alternate sway,
* Till freshening breezes through the branches play;
* Then tumbling downward with a thundering sound,
* Headlong it falls, and spreads a length of ground:
* So, as the giant falls, the ocean roars,
* Outstretch'd he lies, and covers half the shores.
Crete thus delivered from this baneful pest,
The Mynians unmolested sunk to rest.
Soon as Aurora's orient beams appear,
A temple they to Cretan Pallas rear.
With water stor'd, once more the busy train
Embark, and lash the foamy brine again.
Assiduous all with equal ardour glow
Distant to leave Salmonis' lofty brow.
As o'er the Cretan deep the galley flew,
Around them night her sable mantle threw;
Pernicious night, whose all-investing shade
Nor stars, nor Phœbe's brighter rays pervade.
Thick darkness, or from Heaven, or Hell profound,
Spread, as it rose, its rueful shades around.
Uncertain whether, on huge billows tost,
Sublime they sail, or sink to Pluto's coast,
Uncertain where the bursting wave may throw,
They to the sea commit their weal or woe.
Jason aloud, with lifted hands, address'd
The god of day to succour the distress'd.
The tears fast trickling down his sorrowing face,
He vow'd with gifts the Delphic shrine to grace,
He vow'd with choicest gifts, an ample store,
To load Amyclæ, and Ortygia's shore.
Attentive to his tears and meek request,
Phœbus from Heaven descends, and stands confess'd,
Where, frowning hideous o'er the deeps below,
The rocks of Melans lift their shaggy brow.
Awhile on one of these he takes his stand,
His golden bow high lifting in his hand;
Assisted by whose far-reflected light,
An isle of small extent attracts their sight,
Amid the Sporades; against it stood
Hippuris, circled by the rolling flood.
Their anchors here they drop. Aurora's ray
Glimmer'd, and sunk before the light of day.
A temple here o'er-arch'd with woods they raise,
And bid an altar to Apollo blaze,
On whom the name Æglete they bestow;
For here the god display'd his beamy bow.
Here, since on Argo's crew all bright he shone,
By the name Anaphe the isle is known.
The scanty produce of this barren isle
To Phœbus they on humble altars pile.
Each fair Phæacian in Medea's train,
Who oft had seen the fatted oxen slain
In king Alcinoüs' court, in laughter joins
At sight of water pour'd on burning pines.
With well-dissembled wrath the chiefs reprove
The laughing damsels, and the mirth they love.

A wordy altercation soon began,
And pleasant raillery through the circle ran.
Hence, to Æglete, on this festive day,
All who in Anaphe due honours pay,
Maidens and men, a mix'd assembly, join
In friendly contests and debates benign.
The halsers now were loosen'd from their hold,
And unrestrain'd in ocean Argo roll'd,
When thus the dream of night, yet uneffac'd,
Revering Maia's son, Euphemus trac'd.
How, with close grasp the sacred clod compress'd,
Stream'd with a milky current at his breast. [eyes
And from this clod, though small, his wondering
Beheld a lovely, female form arise.
Charm'd with the beauteous fair, he soon resign'd
To nuptial joys his love-devoted mind,
Lamenting still that he the maid should wed,
Whom at his fostering breast with milk he fed.
"Thy children's nurse am I," (the fair began,
Accosting mild the disconcerted man;)
"But not thy daughter: I from Triton came;
(Triton and Libya my parents' name)
He fix'd near Anaphe my watery cell,
And bade me here with Nereus' daughters dwell.
But now I hasten towards the Sun's bright ray,
And to thy race the choicest boon convey."
This dream recurring to his mind again,
He told the leader of the gallant train,
Who, long revolving, thus at length reveal'd
Those mystic truths the Pythic shrine conceal'd:
"Ye gods! what glory waits thy valorous deeds,
What fame, Euphemus, to thy toil succeeds!
For, when in ocean's bed this earth you fling,
Thence (so the gods ordain) an isle shall spring;
Here shall thy children's children late repose.
Triton this hospitable gift bestows:
He tore from Afric's coast the treasur'd soil;
To him, of all the gods, ascribe the isle."
Thus spoke he prescient, nor in vain divin'd:
Euphemus heard him with attentive mind;
Transported with the presage, forth he sprung,
And the mysterious clod in ocean flung.
Instant emerging from the refluent tides,
Calliste's isle display'd its wave-wash'd sides,
Nurse of Euphemus' race: in days of yore,
They dwelt on Sintian Lemnos' sooty shore.
Exil'd from Lemnos by Etrurian force,
To Sparta's friendly walls they bent their course:
Ejected thence, Theras, Autesion's heir,
Bade him to fam'd Calliste's isle repair;
His name it took: th' events we now display
Were unaccomplish'd in Euphemus' day.
Vast tracts of ocean pass'd, the joyous host
Steer'd towards, and anchor'd on Ægina's coast.
They here propose a trial of their skill;
What chief can first the weighty bucket fill,
And, ere his fellows intercept his way,
First to the ship the watery store convey.
For parching thirst, and winds that briskly blew,
To the fleet course inclin'd the gallant crew.
His bucket now, replenish'd at the springs,
Each stout Thessalian on his shoulder brings;
Intent the palm of conquest to obtain,
He scours with speedy foot across the plain.
Hail, happy race of heroes, and repay
With tributary praise my tuneful lay!,
With pleasure still may distant times rehearse,
And added years on years exalt my verse!
For here I fix the period of your woes,
And with your glorious toils my numbers close.
Your galley loosen'd from Ægina's shore,
Waves discompos'd, and winds detain'd no more.
Serene ye sail'd beside th' Achaian strand,
Where Cecrops' towers the subject main command,
Where opposite Eubœa Aulis lies,
And where the Locrian cities lofty rise,
Till Pagasæ her friendly port display'd,
Where rode triumphant Argo safe embay'd.

NOTES TO THE ARGONAUTICS.

BOOK I.

V. 1 Inspir'd by thee] Thus begins Homer's Batrachomyachia, the 17th Id. of Theocritus, and Aratus's poem.

See also on these words the Gr. Schol. and Hoelzlinus's note.

3. Whom Pelias] For Pelias, Æson, &c. See the preface.

Colchos, now called Mingrelia, is bounded on the north by part of Sarmatia, on the west by so much of the Euxine sea as extends from the river Corax to the mouth of the river Phasis, on the south by part of Cappadocia, and on the east by Iberia.

5. Thro' the Cyanean rocks]

——————— when Argo pass'd
Through Bosphorus betwixt the justling rocks.
Milton's Par. Lost. b. ii. 1017.

Two rocks at the entrance of the Euxine sea, called symplegades by the Grecians, by Juvenal concurrentia saxa; because they were so near, that, as a ship varied its course, they seemed to open and shut; or, as Milton expresses it, to justle one another. They were also called cyanean, from their dark colour.

13. Anaurus past] A river in Thessaly, according to Apollonius, Callimachus, and others. But some are of opinion, that Anaurus, as its etymology implies, is the general name of any torrent. Valerius Flaccus, relating the same story, mentions the river Enipeus.

33. Whom fair Calliope, on Thracia's shore] The Pæonians of Thrace lived upon the Hebrus; and all the people of that region were at one time great in science. The Grecians acknowledged they were greatly indebted to them; and the Muses were said to have come from those parts. The Pierians were as famed for poetry and music, as the Pæonians were for physic. Thamyras, Eumolpus, Linus, Thymætes, and Musæus, were supposed to have been of this country. Orpheus also is ascribed to Thrace; who is said to have soothed the savage rage, and to have animated the very rocks to harmony. Bryant's Myth.

35. Hard rocks, &c.] Mulcentem tigres et agentem carmine quercus.—Virg. Georg. iv. 510.

42. By Chiron's art to Jason's interest gain'd] Orpheus, in the Argonautic poem ascribed to him, gives the same account of himself.

Καὶ μ' ἔκιχεν κιθάρην πολυδαίδαλον ἐντύνοντα,
Ὄφρα κέ τοι μέλπων προχέω μελιγήρυν ἀοιδὴν,
Κηλήσω δέ τε θῆρας ἰδ' ἑρπετὰ καὶ πετεηνά.
Orph. Arg. 71.

71. Cœneus] It is fabled that this person was Thessalian virgin, the daughter of Elatus, one of

the Lapithæ; who, having been violated by Neptune, obtained of him, as the reward of her prostitution, that she might be transformed into a man, and rendered invulnerable. Thus changing her sex, she changed her name into Cœneus, being before called Cœnis. See Ovid's Met. and Virg. Æn. vi. 448.

79. From Titaresus] Mopsus was surnamed the Titaresian, from Titaresus, the name of a place and river in Thessaly. Thus Hesiod in Scut. Herc. l. 181.

Μόψοντ' Ἀμπυκίδην Τιταρήσιον——

125. Theseus] Theseus, by the help of his friend Pirithoüs, had stolen Helen from the temple of Diana, and carried her off: in return for this service, he assisted Pirithöus in the rape of Proserpine. In order to accomplish this design, they went down to the infernal regions together: but Pluto, having discovered their intentions, exposed Pirithöus to the dog Cerberus, who devoured him, and chained Theseus to the mountain Tænarus. Plutarch's life of Theseus.

138. Tho' Argus wrought] Apollonius calls him Ἄργος ἀρεστορίδης, the son of Arestor. But Banier remarks that we ought to read (as Meziriac has recommended) ἀλεκτορίδης, the son of Alector. For Argus, the son of Arestor, preceded the time of the Argonauts eight or nine generations: but most of the ancients agree, that the ship Argo was built by Argus, the son of Alector, who lived in the time of the Argonauts. Banier's Myth. vol. iv.

147. Pero] Iphiclus had seized upon the oxen of Tyro, the mother of Neleus. These Neleus demands, but is denied by Iphiclus. Pero, the daughter of Neleus, was promised in marriage to him who recovered these oxen from Iphiclus. Melampus undertakes the recovery; but being vanquished is thrown into prison. See Homer's Od. b. xi. 290.

174. Prophetic Idmon] He is mentioned in the same manner by Orpheus and Valerius Flaccus:

———— Ἄβαντος παῖς νόθος ἤλυθε κάρτερος Ἴδμων,
Τόν ῥ' ὑποκυσσαμένη τέκεν Ἀπόλλωνι ἄνακτι
Ἀμβρόσιον παρὰ χεῦμα φερητιὰς Ἀντιάνειρα,
Τῷ καὶ μαντοσύνην ἔπορε καὶ θέσφατον ὀμφὴν
Φοῖβος. Orph. Arg. 185.

———————— Phebeius Idmon,
Cui genitor tribuit monita prænoscere Divûm
Omnia, seu flammas, seu lubrica cominus exta,
Seu plenum certis interroget aera pennis.
Val. Flac. b. i. 228.

180. Omens from birds, and prodigies from fire] There were two grand divisions of the religious ceremonies of the ancients, viz. into ἔμπυρα and ἄπυρα, i. e. those where fire was heaped upon the altar, and those which were not accompanied with fire. The σήματα ἔμπυρα were observations made from the victims at the time they were burning; which was the province of the haruspices: the σήματα ἄπυρα referred to the flight of birds, and such observations as the augurs collected from them. Thus Euripides in Bacchæ, v. 257.

Σκοπεῖν πτερωτοὺς, κἀμπύρων μισθοὺς φέρειν·

197. And gave the power] Thus Ovid:

———————— cui posse figuras
Sumere quas vellet, rursusque reponere sumptas,
Neptunus dederat, Nelei sanguinis auctor.
Met. xii. 5.

And Seneca:

Sumere innumeras solitum figuras. Med. 635.

222. Euphemus] The text has Polyphemus; which is undoubtedly a false reading, as Valerius Flaccus and Pausanias seem to confirm. The annotator to Mr. Pope's Odyssey, not suspecting this, was led into a pleasant mistake. "If Polyphemus," says he, Od. ix. 569. "had really this quality of running upon the waves, he might have destroyed Ulysses without throwing this mountain: but Apollonius is undoubtedly guilty of an absurdity, and one might rather believe that he would sink the earth at every step, than run upon the waters with such lightness as not to wet his feet." As this description of the swiftness of Euphemus is originally taken from Homer's account of the mares of Ericthonius, so Virgil's description of Camilla's swiftness seems copied from these beautiful lines of Apollonius. See Pope's Il. b. xx. 270.

These lightly skimming, when they swept the plain,
Nor ply'd the grass, nor bent the tender grain:
And when along the level seas they flew,
Scarce on the surface curl'd the briny dew.

Illa vel intactæ segetis per summa volaret
Gramina, nec teneres cursu læsisset aristas:
Vel mare per medium, fluctu suspensa tumenti,
Ferret iter, celeres nec tingeret æquore plantas.

251. Palæmonius] Our poet in his account of this hero follows Orpheus very closely: Valerius Flaccus makes no mention of him.

273. They, when on tip-toe] Milton's description of Raphael is similar to this:

———— ———— like Maia's son he stood,
And shook his plumes, that heavenly fragrance fill'd
The circuit wide, &c. Par. L. b. v. 285.

Apollonius in this beautiful description has far exceeded his venerable master; who says only,

———————— ταρσοῖσιν ὑπαιτίοις πεπότηντο
Ζήτης καὶ Κάλαϊς, δέμας εἴκελοι ἀθανάτοισιν.
Orph. Arg. 219.

287. Minyas' daughter] The Argonauts were distinguished by the appellation of Minyæ: a title which they took as being descended from the daughters of Minyas, a Bœotian prince, the son of Orchomenus, who built a city of that name in Bœotia.

291. Iolchos] A city of Thessaly, and the birth-place of Jason. It was also called Larissa (as Pomponius Mela asserts); hence Larissæus Achilles. Virg.

292. The Pagasæan bay] Pagasæ is a town and promontory of Thessaly. Here Argo was built; and from that circumstance, ἀπὸ τῆς ναυπηγίας, the bay is supposed to have derived its name.

319. Phrixus] For an account of Phrixus see the preface.

327. Alcimeda embrac'd her son with tears] This affecting scene is extremely natural, and drawn by our poet in a manner the most masterly. He is no where happier than in the execution of these pathetic pieces. This parting interview, the episode of Hypsipyla, and the loves of Medea

and Jason have been admired and imitated by the poets of ancient and modern times.

379. Haste, royal mother] Thus Telemachus addresses his mother in Homer, and Turnus in Virgil.

Tears and apprehensions of danger were deemed bad presages, when the people were going to war.

> Ne, quæso, ne me lacrymis, neve omine tanto
> Prosequere, in duri certamina Martis euntem.
> Virg. Æn. xii. 72.

> ——— O royal mother, cease your fears,
> Nor send me to the fight with boding tears.
> Pitt.

384. So moves the god of day] Virgil has manifestly borrowed this comparison, and applied it to Æneas. B. iv. 143.

> As when from Lycia, bound in wintry frost,
> Where Xanthus' streams enrich the smiling coast,
> The beauteous Phœbus in high pomp retires,
> And hears in Delos, &c. Pitt.

447. With beeves return, the best] It was requisite to reserve the best of the flocks and herds for the altar: they must be sound and perfect in all their limbs, or they would be deemed a very unfit offering for the gods. Thus Achilles in Homer offers up to Apollo—ἀρνῶν κνίσσην αἰγῶντε τελέιων. τοῖς θέιοις ὥς τελείοις προσάγειν χρὴ τέλεια, says Eustathius on this passage. It is the precept of Virgil, that the cattle which are designed for the plough, for breeding and sacrifices, should be distinguished by particular marks, and separated from the rest.

> Continuoque notas, et nomina gentis inurunt.
> Georg. iii. 158.

456. Example fir'd] The poet through this whole description is agreeably circumstantial. He paints the busy scene before us in the liveliest colours. We are present to all the labours of his heroes. We see them constructing, lanching, and manning their ship, choosing their seats, erecting their altar, and offering sacrifice. We feel ourselves already interested, and cannot help joining with Jason in his prayer, that success may crown their enterprise.

503. Embasian Phœbus] Embasian and Ecbasian are epithets which they applied to their tutelar god at the instant of their embarkation, and when they were about to land.

551. Tho' various toils] This speech of Idmon is calculated to excite our admiration and pity. We cannot but admire the courage and calmness of the hero, when he discloses to his comrades the purpose of Apollo. He tells them, in a prophetic strain, that they would be exposed to dangers, but successful at last; that, as to himself, he knew his doom, which was, that he must die in a distant country long before their return. Homer represents his hero weeping at his fate, Ὡς ἄρ ἔφη δακρυχέων: our poet reserves the tears of sorrow for them, from whom they fall with a better grace;

> ——— the host the fate of Idmon mourn.

581. Now by this lance] This circumstance seems to be borrowed from that noble one of Achilles swearing by his sceptre in Homer; which passage both Virgil and Valerius Flaccus have closely imitated.

599. The Aloïdæ] Iphimedia, the daughter of Triopas and wife of Alöeus, fell in love with Neptune, by whom she had two sons, Ephialtes and Otus. Presuming on their gigantic strength, they attempted to dethrone Jupiter; but were slain (as Homer and Pindar relate, and after them Apollonius) by Apollo at Naxus, and thrown into Tartarus by Pluto.

617. 'Twas then] The following lines, to 720, are taken from Mr. West's translation of the song of Orpheus, and the setting out of the Argonauts; but many passages are much altered.

621. How at the first]

> Namque canebat, uti magnum per inane coacta
> Semina terrarumque animæque marisque fuissent, &c. Virg. Ec.

For a full illustration of the propriety and beauty of this song, which Scaliger condemns, I beg leave to subjoin Mr. Wharton's judicious criticism, in his Observations on Spenser's Fairy Queen. "Scaliger finds great fault with the subject of this song, and prefers to it the subject of Orpheus's song in Valerius Flaccus. By this piece of criticism he has betrayed his ignorance of the nature of ancient poesy, and of the character of Orpheus. But the propriety of the subject of this song is easily to be defended without considering the character of Orpheus. The occasion of it was a quarrel among the Argonauts, whom Orpheus endeavours to pacify with the united powers of music and verse. To this it may be added, that a song whose subject is religious, and which asserts the right of Jupiter to the possession of Olympus, was even expedient, as one of the chiefs had but just before spoken blasphemy against him. Nor were the auditors of so mean a rank as Scaliger would represent them: he terms them viri militares; but it should be considered, that they were princes and demi-gods. There is one circumstance belonging to the song of Orpheus in Apollonius, which gives it a manifest superiority to that of Orpheus in Valerius Flaccus, I mean the design of it, which was, to express the vehemence of the passions, at once so agreeable to the well-known character of Orpheus, and so expressive of the irresistible influence of music. In the Latin poet, Orpheus sings upon no occasion, and to no end, unless to make the night pass away more pleasantly."

636. Ophion] Milton has undoubtedly copied this passage. Par. L. b. x. 580.

> ——— how the serpent whom they call'd
> Ophion with Eurynome, the wide
> Encroaching Eve, perhaps, had first the rule
> Of high Olympus, &c.

Apollonius, as well as Milton, has hinted that Ophion was of the serpent race. ——— the vast species of the serpent breed.

The upper part of Eurynome was a perfect figure of a woman; the lower part, from the thighs downward, terminated in the tail of a fish. Lucian.

649. Here the sweet bard] The effect, which the harp and voice of Orpheus had upon the Argonauts, is here elegantly described. When the poet had ended his song, they, intent and bending

towards him, still listened, and imagined him still singing. Milton follows Apollonius very close:

> The angel ended, and in Adam's ear
> So charming left his voice, that he awhile
> Thought him still speaking, still stood fix'd to hear. Par. L. b. viii. 1.

657. Then on the flaming tongues] It was the custom of the ancients at their solemn festivals, before they went to rest, to sacrifice the tongues of the victims to Mercury, the god of eloquence, pouring on them a libation of wine. This was done, either with a design to make an expiation for any indecent language that had been spoken (as was the case about fifty lines above) or to signify, that what had been there spoken, ought not to be divulged or remembered afterward.

669. Endu'd with voice] The ancient writers, as well historians as poets, are full of these wonders. The speech of Achilles's horse to his master is well known. Among the many prodigies, which are said to have appeared at the death of Julius Cæsar, this, Virgil informs us, was one,—pecudesque locutæ. Appian expressly says, that an ox spoke with a human voice. Livy has given us the speech of one of these animals on a certain occasion:

> Quod maximè terrebat Consulem Cn. Domitium, bovem locutum, "Roma tibi cave." Lib. xxxv.

This ship was indeed built out of some sacred timber from the grove of Dodona, which was sacred to Jupiter Tomarias: and on this account it was said to have been oracular, and to have given verbal responses.

670. Itonian] Minerva was so called from Itonis, a city of Thessaly, where she was worshipped.

698. The parted ocean whitening] The poets are fond of expressing the activity of the rowers, and the velocity of the ship, by the effect which the stroke of their oars and the track of the keel produce on the waters.

> —— λεύκαινον ὕδωρ ξεστῆς ἐλάτῃσιν. Od. μ'. 172.

> Totaque remigio spumis incanuit unda. Catull.
> Et freta canescunt, sulcam ducente carinâ. Manil.

701. Th' immortal powers] Apollonius, anxious to impress on his readers a just idea of the importance of his subject, has, in the true spirit of Homer, represented all the gods looking down upon Argo, as if interested in the success of her voyage.

717. With Chiron came] Achilles was educated under Chiron. The circumstance of Chariclo's raising up young Achilles in her arms, to show him his father Peleus, is exceedingly beautiful and striking. From this action we may also fairly conjecture, that this famous expedition preceded the siege of Troy, probably, about thirty years, viz. from the infancy of Achilles to his arrival at perfect manhood.

752. Corn-crown'd Thessalia] On the epithet ἠερίη, which the poet here applies to Thessaly, and which seems to have perplexed the commentators, Mr. Bryant makes the following ingenious remark: "The Pelasgi settled very early in Thessaly, to which they gave the name Aëria. This was the ancient name of Egypt, from whence this people came. They likewise called the same country Ai Monah, Regio Lunaris; which the poets changed to Hæmonia."

759. And Dolops' tomb] The scholiast tells us, this Dolops was the son of Hermes, and slain at Magnesia; where they erected a monument, near the shore, to his memory.

766. Aphetæ] The place from which they set sail was named from that event Aphetæ. It is a town and port of Magnesia in Thessaly.

778. Tall Athos] Plutarch and Pliny assert, that this mountain is so high, as to project its shade, when the Sun is in the summer solstice, on the market-place of the city Myrina. Univ. Hist.

> ———— ingenti tellurem proximus umbrâ
> Vestit Athos, nemorumque obscurat imagine pontum. Stat. Theb.

793. For angry Venus] "The description of Venus, enraged against the men of Lemnos for neglecting her temple, represents her," says Mr. Spence in his Polymetis, "rather as the goddess of jealousy, than of love. There is no figure of her under this character, nor any description in any of the Roman poets before the third age." Had the learned author consulted Apollonius, he would have seen to whom Valerius was indebted for this description of Venus, as the goddess of jealousy. The passage is indisputably borrowed from our poet. So true is it, what Mr. Gray has observed of this writer, that had he consulted the Greek authors, they would have afforded him more instruction on the very heads he professes to treat, than all the other writers put together. See Gray's 5th letter to Mr. Walpole.

826. Like the bacchanalian band] The Lemnian women are here represented as savage as the Thyades, who delighted in bloody banquets. Upon this the scholiast observes, that the Mænades and Bacchæ used to devour the raw limbs of animals which they had cut or torn asunder. In the island of Chios it was a religious custom to tear a man limb from limb by way of sacrifice to Dionusus: the same in Tenedos. Hence we may learn one sad truth, that there is scarce any thing so impious and unnatural, as not at times to have prevailed. Bryant's Myth. vol. ii. p. 13.

852. For Boreas] There is a judicious note on this passage, inserted in an elegant edition of our poet, lately published at Oxford; which I shall venture to give the reader: "Licet ventus Boreas Argonautis ad cursum continuandum secundus esset, non tamen solverunt." Mihi perspectum est nihil veri his inesse. Non enim ventus Aquilo secundus est tendentibus in Pontum, sed adversum tenet. Hoc ergo Apollonius indicat. Minyas non solvisse illo mane, ex insulâ Lemno, quod Aquilo, qui ipsis in Pontum porrecturis adversus erat, flaret. Wesseling. Observ. p. 130.

This observation appears to be just. Yet is it no unusual thing with the poets to put one wind for another. The most judicious and accurate of the Roman poets is not exempt from errours of this kind. "The description of the departure of Æneas from Carthage is not only inconsistent with truth and probability, in this respect, but contradictory to itself. He sails in the morning with a west wind, which is very improperly called favourable; but before he is out of sight of Carthage, we find him pursuing his course with a north wind, which is still more contrary to his intended course." See an Essay on the original Genius and Writings of Homer.

913. — Hypsipyla arose] Dido is the Hypsipyla of Virgil. The latter, as Hoelzlinus speaks, is the archetype of the former.

949. A mantle] This mantle, which Pallas gave to Jason, and the simile of the star, to which he is compared, are beautiful specimens of our poet's talent for description. We shall find him, in the more descriptive parts of his poem, rising greatly above that equal mediocrity which some critics have ascribed to him.

971. Behind, Amphion] The fable of Thebes being built by the power of music is not in Homer, and therefore may be supposed to be of later invention. See Pope's Od. b. xi. 320.

982. The Taphians] The Teleboans, or Taphians (so called from the island Taphos which they inhabited) coming to Argos, stole the oxen of Electryon, the father of Alcmena: a battle ensued, in which himself and sons were slain.

988. This Pelops drove] Hippodamia was the daughter of Œnomaüs, king of Elis and Pisa. She was a princess of great beauty, and had many admirers. Œnomaüs having been informed by the oracle, that he should be slain by his son-in-law, endeavoured to deter the suitors from paying their addresses to his daughter, by proposing a chariot-race. The terms were; that he who conquered him in the race should obtain his daughter, but that he who proved unsuccessful should be put to death. Pelops, whom Hippodamia was most attached to, accepted the dangerous conditions, and contended with Œnomaüs. The plan which his daughter had concerted with Myrtilus, the charioteer, of loosening the pin of the wheel, succeeded to her wish. The pin flew out, the chariot was overthrown, and victorious Pelops claimed the lady as his prize.

997. At mighty Tityus aim'd] Elara being pregnant by Jupiter, he, to avoid the jealousy of Juno, concealed her in a cavern of the Earth, where Tityus was born: who, from his being immersed in worldly cares, and from his centering all his affections on the Earth, as if he had sprung from it, is fabled to be the son of the Earth.

1132. And let him revel] This is an oblique, but very severe sarcasm on Jason.

1161. And if with offspring] That there was offspring appears from Homer's Il. b. vii.

> And now the fleet, arriv'd from Lemnos' sands,
> With Bacchus' blessings cheer'd the generous bands.
> Of fragrant wines the rich Eunæus sent
> A thousand measures to the royal tent;
> Eunæus, whom Hypsipyle of yore
> To Jason, shepherd of his people, bore.

These verses, says Mr. Pope, afford us the knowledge of some points of history and antiquity: as that Jason had a son by Hypsipyle; who succeeded his mother in the kingdom of Lemnos: that Samos was anciently famous for its wines; and that coined money was not in use at the time of the Trojan war; but the trade of the countries carried on by exchange in brass, oxen, slaves, &c. as appears by two lines farther:

> Each, in exchange, proportion'd treasures gave,
> Some brass, or iron, some an ox, or slave.

1187. That there initiated] All that were initiated into the Cabiritic mysteries were thought effectually secured from storms at sea, and all other dangers: and the influence of the Cabirian priests was particularly implored by mariners for success in their voyages. Potter. Bryant.

1193. Thence the black main] So named from a bay which lies west of the Thracian Chersonesus; called Melas from a river of that name.

1207. An ancient island] Cyzicus, or Cyzicum according to Strabo, is an island in the Propontis, joined by two bridges to the continent. The strait, over which these bridges were thrown, being in a course of years filled up, an isthmus was formed, and the island became a peninsula: to this isthmus the poet alludes. Strabo. Hoelz.

1235. Here the rope-fasten'd stone] It is observable that the name of an anchor does no where occur in Homer. The ships of which he speaks had only a rudder and ballast. Neither was there any metal employed in the construction of them; the timbers were fastened together with pegs.

We must not therefore wonder at the rude expedient, to which the Argonauts had recourse, in these still earlier times.

1299. As near]

> Ac veluti magnâ juvenum cum densa securi
> Silva labat; cuneisque gemit grave robur adactis;
> Jamque abies, piceæque suunt: sic dura sub ictu
> Ossa virûm malæque sonant, sparsusque cerebro
> Albet ager. Val. Flac. l. iii. 163.

1380. There stands the tomb] The most ancient tombs were very simple: they were nothing more than hillocks of earth heaped up over the grave. This the Romans called tumulus. Sometimes we find an oar, or pillar erected over it in honour of the deceased. Thus we read in Homer;

> Τύμβον χεύαντες, καὶ ἐπὶ στήλην ἐρύσαντες,
> Πήξαμεν ἀκροτάτῳ τύμβῳ εὐῆρες ἐρετμόν.
> See Bp. Lowth's note on Isaiah liii. 9.

1384. — round her neck she tied] Some nicer critics may be offended that Clita should die in so vulgar a manner: but this objection is owing to a want of considering the notions and manners of different ages and countries. Amata, the mother of Turnus, in the 12th book of the Æneid, hangs herself. In the 11th book of the Odyssey Jocasta dies in like manner, and likewise in the Œdipus of Sophocles.

1399. Sift coarsest meal, and at the public mill] It was customary for families to grind their own corn. For this purpose they made use of hand-mills. Wind and water-mills were a later invention. They employed their slaves at this work: and sometimes it was inflicted on them as the heaviest punishment.

> Molendum in pistrino, vapulandum, habendæ compedes. Ter. Phorm.
> See Bp. Lowth's Isaiah, page 217.

Here we find, not a single family, but a whole people, annually, in token of mortification and sorrow, labouring together at one common mill, and partaking of the bread of affliction, which is of the coarser kind, and unbaked.

1406. A beauteous Halcyon] Ceyx, king of Thrace, married Alcyone, the daughter of Æolus,

On a voyage to consult the Delphic oracle, he was shipwrecked. His corpse was thrown ashore in sight of his wife, who, in the agonies of love and despair, threw herself into the sea. The gods, in pity to her fidelity, changed her and her husband into the birds which bear her name. The halcyons very seldom appear, but in the finest weather: whence they are fabled to build their nests on the waves. The female is no less remarkable than the turtle for her conjugal affection. When the halcyons are surprised by a tempest, they fly about as in the utmost terrours, and with the most lamentable cries.

1418. There Cybele] The worship of Cybele was famous in Phrygia. Her priests, sounding their tabrets and striking their bucklers with spears, danced and distorted their whole bodies. To these dances and distortions they add shrieks and howlings; whence they were called Corybantes. Thus it was that they deplored the loss of their goddess's favourite Atys; thus they drowned the cries of Jupiter, concealed among the Curetes in Crete; and thus they stifled the grief of these Dolians for their slaughtered monarch. See Banier's Myth.

1422. — by Cybele the vast profound] Orpheus, in his hymn to this goddess, has ascribed to her the same unlimited dominion:

> Μήτηρ μέντε θεῶν ἠδὲ θνητῶν ἀνθρώπων,
> Ἐκ σοῦ γὰρ καὶ γαῖα καὶ οὐρανὸς εὐρὺς ὕπερθεν,
> Καὶ πόντος, πνοιαίτε. Orph. Hymn. 13.

1448. This trunk they hew'd] It sometimes happens, that the roots and branches of aged trees bear a faint likeness to the human fabric. The ancients seem to have taken advantage of this fancied similitude, which they improved by a little art; and their first efforts towards imagery were from these rude and rotten materials. Bryant's Myth. vol. i.

1461. Idean Dactyli] The Dactyli were the priests of Cybele: they first inhabited mount Ida in Phrygia; hence they were styled Idæi. They were originally five in number, as their name, derived from the fingers of the hand, imports.

1463. — Oaxis rolls his wave] There is a river of this name, not only in Mesopotamia, but in Crete.

Thus Virg. Ecl. i.

> Et rapidum Cretæ veniemus Oaxem.

1469. — martial dance] Called also the Pyrrhic dance, from fire, with which it was accompanied. It was esteemed a martial exercise, and was performed by persons in armour, who gave it the name of Berarmus, from the temple of the deity, where it was probably first practised; or from the regularity of their movements in dancing. Schol. Bryant.

1478. Boughs bend with fruit] It was the general opinion of the ancients, that when they had appeased their deities by sacrifice and prayer, the tokens of reconciliation would appear by an uncommon fertility of the soil.

The poets have not failed to avail themselves of this popular opinion. It is customary with them to represent fruits and flowers of every kind, as springing up and coming to perfection in a manner that seemed to indicate the immediate agency of some propitious deity.

Besides; Cybele was taken for the earth; on which account she was called the mother of the gods; for the earth gives birth to all things. Hence her worship was blended with several circumstances which bore a relation to the earth. Its fertility therefore, at the instant of the celebration of her festival, is something more than a poetical embellishment.

1509. — Ryndacus] A river of Mysia, which empties itself into the Propontis. Near its banks, as some assert, stood the tomb of Ægæus or Briareus.

1525. — Arganthon] A mountain near Cios. Cios is the name of a river, and of a city in Mysia.

1530. Some bring dry wood] Thus Theocritus, speaking of the employments of the Argonauts, when they landed in the country of the Bebrycians, says,

> Εὐνάς τ' ἐστόρνυντο, κ. τ. λ. Id. 22.
>
> On the dry beach they rais'd the leafy bed,
> The fires they kindled, and the tables spread.

1556. Meanwhile, preparing] This story is told with great simplicity and elegance by our poet's rival and contemporary Theocritus; Id. 13. Nor has his faithful imitator, Valerius Flaccus, neglected to embellish his poem with the same story. The learned editor of Theocritus, published in 2 vol. at Oxford, portions out to each poet his share of merit in the following words: Egregiè quidèm Valerius Flaccus Herculis vehementem et repentinam perturbationem depingit: qui, vesperi reversus, Hylam ad sociorum mensas, in littore constructas, non deprehendit. Nihil nisi dictionem Virgilianam, castam, teretem, simplicem, pro turgidulâ illâ, et duriusculâ, desidero. Conferatur et Hercules Apollonii Rhodii: quem credibile est omnes intendisse nervos, ut in simili materiâ poetam coævum superaret. Pulchrum profectò illud Herculis, a manu abietem abjicientis. At fortassis, ad summum, simpliciora Theocriti et luculentiora fatebere, et minus frequentata circumstantiis et elaborata. Not. ad V. lv. Id. 13.

1568. But know, Alcides] Hercules, arriving at the country of the Dryopians, a people of Epirus, applied to their prince Theodamas for refreshment. Upon his refusal, he unyoked one of the oxen with which he was plowing, and sacrificed it. Theodamas, attempting to redress this grievance by force of arms, was killed, and his son Hylas was carried off by the conqueror. Some attribute this exploit to the rapacity of Hercules, others to his desire of civilizing an inhospitable people. Callimachus, speaking of the rapacity of Hercules, says,

> Οὐ γὰρ ὅγε Φρυγίῃ περ ὑπὸ δρυὶ γυῖα θεωθεὶς
> Παύσατ' ἀδηφαγίης· ἔτι οἱ πάρα νηδὺς ἐκείνη
> Τῇ ποτ' ἀροτριόωντι συνήντετο Θειοδάμαντι.
> In Dian. 159.

1576. In Dian's praise] Thus Callimachus, in his hymn to Diana, celebrates her as encircled with a choir of nymphs:

> —— αἱ νύμφαι σε χορῷ ἔνι κυκλώσονται
> Ἀγχόθι πηγάων. In Dian. 170.

1598. As when a lion] Virgil has closely imitated this simile in the following lines, where, speaking of the impetuosity of Turnus, he thus compares him:

Ac veluti pleno lupus insidiatus ovili,
Cum fremit ad caulas, ventos perpessus & imbres,
Nocte super mediâ; tuti sub matribus agni
Balatum exercent: ille asper & improbus irâ,
Sævit in absentes: collecta fatigat edendi
Ex longo rabies, et siccæ sanguine fauces.

Æn. b. ix. 59.

1626. As when a bull, whom galling gadflies wound] Apollonius, within the compass of a very few lines, makes use of two different words to express the same animal, μύωψ and οἶστρος. The former, he tells us, is the more general appellation: ὅν [οἶστρον] μύωπα βοῶν κλείουσι νομῆες. B. iii. 276.

The correspondent names in Latin are asilus and tabanus: asilus vulgò tabanus vocatur, says Servius.

——— ——— cui nomen asilo
Romanum est, æstron Græci vertere vocantes.
Arcebis gravido pecori.

Virg. Georg. iii.

Homer also speaks of this fly as being very pernicious to cattle:

Οἱ δ' ἐφέβοντο κατὰ μέγαρον, βόες ὥς ἀγελαῖοι,
Τὰς μέντ' αἰόλος οἶστρος ἐφορμηθεὶς ἐδόνησεν.

Od. xxii. 299.

Confus'd, distracted thro' the rooms they fling,
Like oxen madden'd by the breese's sting.

This simile is common to the poets: Virgil, Coluthus, and Tryphiodorus have made use of it.

1676. And one still moves] It was usual with the ancients to place one vast stone upon another for a religious memorial. The stones thus placed they poized so equally, that they were affected with the least external force: a breath of wind would sometimes make them vibrate. These were called rocking stones. Of such an one Apollonius is here speaking, as being moved by the wind, and the admiration of spectators. Bryant.

1746. A land projecting] The coast of Bebryeia; the ancient name of Bithynia, a country of Asia Minor, near Troas, bounded on the north by the Euxine sea.

Orpheus has given us, at the beginning of his poem, a catalogue of the heroes that accompanied Jason to Colchis. Apollonius has followed his example. And he has shown himself a judicious imitator of Homer, by diversifying and enlivening his narration with an account of the family, character, and birth-place of his Argonauts. He constantly inserts some little history or anecdote, which may serve to impress their names on our memory, and to interest us in their future fortunes. He has contrived to throw the utmost variety into the voyage, by describing particularly the situation of the coasts, and the customs and manners of the inhabitants. The lanching of Argo, the episode of Hypsipyla, the night-adventure of the Dolians, the story of Hylas, the sacrifices and similes, are severally possessed of such distinguished merit, as cannot fail to give the reader a favourable idea of our poet's taste and genius.

NOTES TO BOOK II.

16. Till match'd with me] This encounter between Amycus and Pollux is described likewise by Theocritus, who, in the opinion of Casaubon, far surpasses Apollonius; but Scaliger gives the preference to our author, who has certainly furnished Virgil with many circumstances in his description of the contest between Dares and Entellus. See Æn. b. v.

Neither Apollonius nor Theocritus have lost sight of Homer's description of the combat of the cæstus, Il. xxiii. 683.

Mr. Warton, in his valuable edition of Theocritus, delivers his opinion of the description of this combat, by the three poets, Apollonius, Theocritus, and Valerius, in the following words: Apollonio sane, auctore suo, Flaccum inferiorem censeo; quippe quod Flaccus minus simplex sit, et omnia, sublimitatis affectato studio, magnificentius efferat et inflatius. Utroque præstantior Theocritus, quod utroque simplicior. Tantum illi cedit Apollonius, quantum Flaccus Apollonio."

112. Like bulls] This simile is borrowed by Virgil, Æn. xii. 715.

With frowning front two mighty bulls engage,
A dreadful war the bellowing rivals wage, &c.

Pitt.

163. As swains with smoke] Virgil has also taken this simile from Apollonius; a poet, as Catrou observes, very rich in beautiful comparisons. See Pitt's Virg. Æn. xii. 832.

So when the swain invades with stifling smoke
The bees, close-cluster'd in a cavern'd rock,
They rise; &c.

It was the custom of the ancients to force bees out of their hives by fumigation. To this practice the poets frequently allude. Thus Ovid de rem. amor. l. i. 185.

Quid, cum suppositos fugiunt examina fumos,
Ut relevent dempti vimina curva fagi?

——— τῦφε πολλῷ τῷ καπνῷ.

Aristoph. in vesp.

178. — an iron land] The land of the Chalybes, which bordered upon that of the Mariandyni.

199. — their brows with laurel crown'd] Crowns and garlands were thought so necessary to recommend men to the gods, and were so anciently used, that some have derived the custom of putting them on at feasts, from the primitive entertainments, at which the gods were thought to be present. Potter.

221. Fronting Bithynia's coast] The storm drove them to Salmydessus, a city on the coast of Thrace opposite to Bithynia.

The scholiast speaks of more than one Bithynia. There is a country of that name, he tells us, both on the coast of Europe and of Asia. The storm drove the Argonauts to Salmydessus, which is opposite to the Asiatic Bithynia.

224. — sad Phineus] Phineus was a king of Thrace, or, as some say, of Arcadia. He ordered the eyes of his two sons to be torn out, to satisfy their mother-in-law. The gods punished his cruelty: they struck him with blindness, and sent the Harpies to him, who took the meat from his mouth; so that he would have perished with hunger, if Zetes and Calaïs had not delivered him from them, and pursued them to the Strophades, where they gave over the chace. These Harpies were called out of Hell, and seem to be of the

number of the furies. A permission was given them to dwell upon Earth to punish the wicked: by which the poets would represent to us the remorse of a bad conscience. Catrou.

237. For, lo! descending] Apollonius has furnished Virgil with many hints on this subject of the harpies. See Æn. b. iii. 225.

At subitæ horrifo lapsu de montibus adsunt
Harpyiæ; &c.

When from the mountains, terrible to view,
On sounding wings the monster-harpies flew.
Pitt.

The harpies were a kind of birds which had the faces of women, and foul, long claws. When the table was furnished for Phineus, they flew in, and either devoured or carried away the greater part of his repast, or polluted what they left. Raleigh.

256. Like some pale, lifeless, visionary shade] The person and distresses of this old man are represented to us in a manner the most striking and pathetic. Virgil had this description in view, when speaking of Achemenides, he says,

Cum subitò e silvis, macie confecta supremâ,
Ignoti nova forma viri, miserandaque cultu
Procedit, supplexque manus ad litora tendit,
Respicimus: dira illuvies, immissaque barba,
Consertum tegmen spinis —— Æn. iii. 590.

347, 347. By every woe—And by these eyes] Thus Telemachus swears, not only by Jupiter, but by the sorrows of his father.

By great Ulysses, and his woes I swear.
See Pope's Odyss. xx. 406.

Adjurations of this sort are frequently to be met with in the Greek tragedians.

377. As when swift hounds] Virgil has closely copied the conclusion of this comparison: the eager hound, says he,

Hæret hians, jam jamque tenet, similisque tenenti
Increpuit malis, morsuque elusus inani est.
Æn. xii. 754.

They snap, and grind their gnashing teeth in vain.

393. — the dogs of Jove] The ancient name of a priest was cahen, rendered mistakenly κυν, and canis. Hence the harpies, who were priests of Ur are styled by Apollonius the dogs of Jove. Iris accosting Calaïs and Zetes, tells them, it would be a profanation to offer any injury to those personages. The Sirens and harpies were of the same vocation. Bryant's Myth. vol. ii.

404. The Strophades] The word Strophades is derived from a Greek verb that signifies to turn. These islands therefore were named Strophades, because near them the sons of Boreas left off pursuing the harpies, and turned back to the house of Phineus.

437. Two rocks] This is very similar to a passage in the Odyssey, b. xii. v. 71.

High o'er the main two rocks exalt their brow,
The boiling billows thundering roll below;
Thro' the vast waves the dreadful wonders move,
Hence nam'd erratic by the gods above.——
Scarce the fam'd Argo pass'd these rapid floods,
The sacred Argo, fill'd with demigods!
Ev'n she had sunk, but Jove's imperial bride
Wing'd her fleet sail, and push'd her o'er the tide.
Pope.

It is observed in the note on this passage, "that Homer, to render his poetry more marvellous, joins what has been related of the Symplegades to the description of Scylla and Charybdis.--The story of the dove being reported of the Symplegades might give him the hint of applying the crushing of the doves to Scylla and Charybdis." But we must remember that Argo passed, in her return, through Scylla and Charybdis, and that Apollonius, as well as Homer, has mentioned these rocks by the name πλαγκταὶ, erratic, which is supposed to be more strictly applicable to the Symplegades. If the Cyanean rocks were called Symplegades from their justling together, and that appearance was occasioned by the different views in which they were seen, sometimes in a direct line, and sometimes obliquely, why might not Scylla and Charybdis, for the same reason, be said to justle together, and consequently without impropriety be called πλαγκταὶ or erratic? Minerva, according to Apollonius, guided Argo through the Symplegades; but her course through Scylla and Charybdis was directed by Thetis, at the intercession of Juno, agreeable to what Homer here mentions.

448. — a nimble dove let fly] The dove which returned to Noah with a leaf of olive, and brought the first tidings that the waters of the deep were assuaged, was held in many nations as particularly sacred: it was looked upon as a peculiar messenger of the Deity, an emblem of peace and good fortune. Among mariners it was thought to be particularly auspicious; who as they sailed used to let a dove fly from their ships, to judge of the success of their voyage. The most favourable season for setting sail was at the Heliacal rising of the seven stars, near the head of Taurus; and they are, in consequence of it, called Pleiades. It was at their appearance that the Argonauts sat out upon their expedition. Ἆμος δ' ἀντέλλοντι πελείαδες.—Theoc. Id. xiii. 25. When first the pleasing Pleiades appear. And this was thought a fortunate time for navigation in general. The Argonauts, in a time of difficulty and danger, made the experiment of letting a dove fly, and formed from it a fortunate presage. Bryant's Myth. vol. ii. 285.

It is indeed the opinion of many learned men, that the science of augury, or of predicting future events by the flight of birds, arose from the dismission of the raven and the dove from Noah's ark at the time of the deluge. This species of divination is undoubtedly very ancient: it is mentioned in many places of the Old Testament, and made a considerable part of the religion of the heathen world.

479. — Acherusia] Is a cave, through which, according to the fable, is a passage to the regions below. Hercules is said to have descended through it to bring up Cerberus. Tokens of which exploit they show, says Xenophon, even to this day. Near this spot stands the principal city of the Maryandyni, named from Hercules, Heraclea. Here, as our poet informs us, runs the river Acheron, so called from the abovementioned lake.

493. — Halys] This river, which rises in Cappadocia, and empties itself into the Euxine, took its name from the beds of salt through which it runs. Strabo. Tournefort says, this country is so full of fossil-salt, that it is to be found in the high roads and ploughed lands.

498. — Thermodon] This river, says Strabo, after having received many others, runs through Themiscyra, formerly inhabited by the Amazons, and then falls into the Euxine sea.

502. — the Chalybes] It is commonly believed, that the ancient Chalybes were the descendants of Tubal; for they are celebrated by the ancients for their extraordinary skill in working of iron, and making of steel-armour; whence they are said to have had their name. Univ. Hist.

Strabo is of opinion, that they are the same whom Homer mentions by the name of ἄλυβες. For he joins them with the Paphlegonians, and characterizes them thus, ὅθεν ἀργύρȣ ἐςὶ γενέθλη.

Chalybes nudi ferrum —— Virg. Georg.

505. — the Genetæan hill] A promontory, so named from Genetes, a neighbouring river, which ran through the country of the Chalybes. A temple was erected here to Jupiter the hospitable.

530. — Phasis] Pliny informs us, that the bird called the pheasant derives its name from this river, whose banks they frequented in great abundance; and that they were first brought over into Greece by the Argonauts.

Argivâ primum sunt transportata carinâ;
Ante mihi notum nil nisi nomen erat.

Mart.

535. A hideous dragon] Tarchon, which, according to the learned and ingenious Mr. Bryant, signifies a hill with a tower, or temple on it, was in later times rendered Trachon; from whence the region Trachonitis received its name. This word, it seems, was still further sophisticated by the Greeks, and expressed Δρακων, dragon: from whence in a great measure arose the notion of treasures being guarded by dragons. The gardens of the Hesperides, and the golden fleece at Colchis, were entrusted to a sleepless serpent. The dragons are represented as sleepless; because in towers there were commonly lamps burning, and a watch maintained. The eyes of the dragon were windows in the uppermost part of the building, through which the fire appeared. Bryant's Myth.

553. Lies Colchos] All the countries which lie on the north and north-east parts of the Euxine, the region of Colchos, and the country at the foot of Caucasus, were of old esteemed Scythia, and these the Greeks looked upon to be the boundaries, northward, of the habitable world.

556. — Æa] The region termed Αια, above Colchis, was a name peculiarly given by the Amonians to the places where they resided. Among the Greeks the word grew general; and Αια was made to signify any land. But among the Egyptians, as well as among those of Colchis Pontica, it was used for a proper name of their country.

It was owing to this, that the name given to the chief person of the country was Aiates. Bryant's Myth.

626. — coeval tree] It was the common opinion of the ancients, that the Hamadryads lived and died together with their trees, and therefore were extremely grateful to those, who at any time preserved them. The scholiast tells a remarkable story to this purpose: A person called Rhœcus, observing a beautiful oak ready to fall, ordered it to be set upright and supported. The nymph of the tree appeared to him, and bade him, in return, ask whatever he pleased. She being exceedingly handsome, Rhœcus desired he might be entertained as her lover: which she promised, and accordingly sent a bee to summon him. But the young man, happening to be playing at dice when the bee came, was so offended with its buzzing, that he drove it from him. The nymph, provoked at this uncivil treatment of her embassador, in revenge, deprived Rhœcus of the use of his limbs. He also speaks of another nymph, who was grateful to the man that preserved her oak.

—— τότε δρύες ἠνίκα νύμφαι.

Call. Hymn. in Del. v. 83.

662. The names of Agreus and of Nomius] Thus Callimachus:

Φοῖβον ϗ Νόμιον κικλήσκομεν, ἐξ ἔτι κείνȣ
'Εξότ' ἐπ' 'Αμφυρσῷ ζευγήτιδας ἔτρεφεν ἵππȣς,
'Ηϊθέȣ ὑπ' ἔρωτι κεκαυμένος 'Αδμήτοιο.

Hymn. ad Ap. 47.

'Αγρεὺς and Νόμιος were undoubtedly the names of Apollo; but they were also bestowed on his son Aristæus, on account of his fondness for a country life, and his many useful discoveries.

'Ανδράσι χάρμα φίλοις,
'Αγχιςον ὀπάονα μήλων,
'Αγρεα καὶ Νόμιον
Τοῖς δ' 'Αριςαῖον καλεῖν.

Pynd. Pyth. ix. 115.

671. To him they gave their numerous flocks to feed] Almost all the principal persons, whose names occur in the mythology of Greece and Italy, are represented as shepherds. It is reported of the Muses, that they were of shepherd extraction, and tended flocks, which they entrusted to their favourite Aristæus; the same whom Virgil styles Pastor Aristæus. Bryant.

685. — showery Jove] Jupiter is frequently represented under the character of pluvius, or the dispenser of rain, both by poets, painters, and statuaries. For it was his province, as chief ruler of the air, to direct not only the thunders and lightnings, but the rain. Virgil has given us a noble description of the Jupiter pluvius in the following description:

—— cum Jupiter, horridus austris,
Torquet aquosam hyemem, et cælo cava nubila rumpit.

Æn. ix. 670.——Spence's Polym.

693. — and by these winds detain'd] For these Etesian winds, the history of which the poet has just given us, blew north-east, and consequently in a direction the most unfavourable for them who were sailing up the Euxine.

735. Old ocean thunder'd] This storm seems to have been copied by Virgil, Æn. i. by Lucan, Ovid, and Valerius Flaccus.

813. With cold indifference] The great out-

lines of Jason's character are piety, humanity, and valour. The sentiment before us is replete with philanthropy, and prejudices us highly in favour of the hero of the poem.

861. His golden locks] Milton thus describes Adam's hair:

> —— ———————— hyacinthine locks
> Round from his parted forelock manly hung
> Clust'ring. B. iv. 303.

The circumstance of the hair hanging like bunches of grapes has been justly admired. But it is literally translated from the description of Apollo's hair in the Greek poet.

> ————————— χρύσεοι δὲ παρειάων ἑκάτερθε
> Πλοχμοὶ ΒΟΤΡΥΟ'ΕΝΤΕΣ ἐπεῤῥώοντο κιόντι.

The word βοτρυόεντες could hardly be rendered into English by any other word than by clustering. Warton's Observ.

867. Nor dar'd the heroes] Thus Hesiod in Scuto, speaking of Hercules,

> ——————————— οὐδέ τις αὐτοῦ
> Ἔτλη ἐς ἄντα ἰδὼν χεδὸν ἐλθεῖν.

There was probably, in the old pictures of Apollo, a certain brightness beaming from his eyes, and perhaps diffused all over his face; in the same manner, as the body of the principal figure is all luminous and resplendent in the famous nativity of Correggio, of the transfiguration by Raphael. What made me then suspect this, was the ancient poets speaking so often of the brightness of Apollo's face, and the beaming splendours of his eyes. Virgil does not only compare his Æneas (under whom is generally supposed to be meant Augustus) to Apollo for beauty; but, in another place, he seems to call Augustus himself (who was really very beautiful) by the name of this god. Spence's Polym.

771. Then like an arrow] Virgil has adopted this comparison, where he represents Cloanthus's ship as moved forward by Portunus:

> —— Et pater ipse manu Portunus euntem
> Impulit: illa noto citius volucrique sagittâ
> Ad terram fugit, et portu se condidit alto.
> Æn. v. 241.

900. —with curls unclipp'd] Nothing was deemed by the ancients more essential to the beauty of a young person (and Apollo was always represented a youth) than fine, long hair. Hence the epithets crinitus and intonsus are so often given to Apollo.

> ————— crinitus Apollo,
> Nube sedens Virg. Æn. ix. 638.
> ——— sic tibi sint intonsi, Phœbe, capilli.
> Tibull.

946. The Megarensians Soönautes nam'd] They are called by our poet in this place, and by Theocritus, Id. xii. 27. Νισαῖοι Μεγαρῆες; from Nisa, which, as the scholiast informs us, was the name of their dock. It was so named from Nisus, son of Pandion, and king of this people.

The Megarensians, going out to plant a colony in Heraclea, were driven by distress of weather into the river Acheron, which, from the protection it afforded them, they called Soönautes.

1028. But fail'd, unhappy!—]

> Sed non augurio potuit depellare pestem.
> Æn. ix. 328.

> The fate of others he had oft foreshown,
> But fail'd, unhappy! to prevent his own.
> Pitt.

1029. Here, in a covert] This description of a boar hid among the rushes, and the terrour of the neighbourhood, reminds us of the following beautiful lines of Ovid, who is describing the Caledonian boar:

> Concava vallis erat, quo se dimittere rivi
> Assuerant pluvialis aquæ: tenet ima lacunæ
> Lenta salix, alvæque leves, juncique palustres,
> Viminaque, et longæ parvâ sub arundine cannæ:
> Hinc aper excitus, medios violentus in hostes
> Fertur, ut excussis elisus nubibus ignis.
> Ov. Met. l. viii.

1167. Parthenius] This river rises in Paphlagonia, and derives its name from the cheerful meadows through which it flows. Strabo.

1176. Thy groves, Cytorus]

> Thy groves of box, Cytorus, ever green.
> Pope's Il. b. ii.

Hence things made of box were called Cytoriaca.

> Sæpe Cytoriaco deducit pectine crines.

1204. The Amazonian cape] The Greeks, who would fain deduce every thing from their own language, imagined, that by the term Amazon was signified a person without a breast. From this wrong etymology proceed all the absurdities with which the history of this extraordinary people abounds. They were in general Cuthite colonies from Egypt and Syria; and as they worshipped the Sun, they were called Azones, Amazones, Alazones; which are names of the same import. The most noted were those, who settled near the river Thermodon, in the region of Pontus.

> Quales Theïciæ, cum flumina Thermodontis
> Pulsant, et pectis bellantur Amazones armis.
> Æn. xi. 658.

1229. From Mars and Harmony] The Amazons worshipped the deity from whom they received their name; viz. Azon and Amazon, the same as Ares, the Sun. They worshipped also Harmon, the Moon; which the Grecians changed to a feminine, Harmonia. So that by γενεῇ Ἄρεος καὶ Ἁρμονίης is meant the children of the Sun and Moon. Bryant's Myth.

1251. —Tibarenians] It is remarked of this people, that they are uncommonly addicted to laughter and buffoonery. Some have accounted for the absurd custom, here alluded to, from this cause. But it is difficult to assign a reason for the many absurd customs which different nations have adopted. It has been recorded by grave historians, that the ancient Spaniards and the Americans follow the practice of the Tibareneans.

1260. Mossynes call'd,] Xenophon gives us the most authentic account of this people in the fifth book of his Anabasis. He tells us, that they do those things in private, which others do in public; that they talk to themselves, laugh by themselves, and dance alone, as if they were showing their skill in public. Savage and indecent as the custom, alluded to by our poet, may seem, Strabo ascribes the same barbarities to the Irish, and

Cæsar makes the same observations on the ancient Britons.

1269. But if his judgment err] Thus Pomponius Mela, l. i. c. 19. Reges suffragio deligunt, vinculisque et arctissimâ custodiâ tenent; atque ubi culpam pravè quid imperando meruere, inediâ totius diei afficiunt.

1301. But when he rung a cymbal] This cymbal, or crotalum, was made, the scholiast tells us, by Vulcan; Hercules received it from Pallas. The description of this instrument is differently given by different authors. Our poet tells us it was made of brass; others represent it as formed of a rod or reed cut in two; both parts of which, when struck together, emitted a sound after the manner of castanets. This latter description agrees with the opinion of Suidas, and the scholiast of Aristophanes.

1386. The laws of hospitable Jove revere] Thus Virgil, Æn. i. 784.

Jupiter (hospitibus nam te dare jura loquuntur)

Almighty Jove! who pleads the stranger's cause;
Great guardian God of hospitable laws. Pitt.

And Homer, in the words of Mr. Pope; Od. b. ix.

The poor and stranger are Jove's constant care;
To Jove their cause and their revenge belongs,
He wanders with them, and he feels their wrongs.

1430. Round the altar stood] The tombs, of which frequent mention is made by the ancient writers, were in reality high altars or pillars, and not, as has been supposed, monuments erected in honour of the dead. Such an one the Argonauts are said to have found in the temple of Mars, when they landed upon the coast of Pontus. This was the express object to which the Amazonians paid their adoration; as they lived in an age when statues were not known: Bryant's Myth.

1472. Typhaonia's cave] Apollonius mentions an ancient Typhonian petra in the hollows of the mountain. It was an ophite temple, where the deity was probably worshipped under the figure of a serpent. Hence the poet supposes the serpent, with which Jason engages, to have been produced in those parts. Bryant's Myth.

1497. Where Saturn first fair Philyra] Saturn, to avoid being discovered by his wife Ops, while he was engaged with Philyra his mistress, turned himself into a beautiful horse.

Chiron, the famous Centaur, was the son of this nymph Philyra.

1547. Where on an oak] The Greek here, and at v. 1399, is δρυὸς; but at v. 534 the word is φηγοῖο, a beech: both which trees bearing mast, they may perhaps be indiscriminately used.

NOTES TO BOOK III.

2. AND teach thy poet Erato,] Apollonius with great propriety invokes Erato, the Muse who presided over love affairs. For this book contains the loves of Medea and Jason, and abounds with the most beautiful sentiments descriptive of the tender passion. Virgil's invocation of Erato, Nunc age, qui reges, Erato, &c. is a transcript of Apollonius, Εἰ δ' ἄγε νῦν, Ἐρατώ, &c. Virgil seems to have copied our poet in this instance, at the expence of his judgment: for it is difficult to assign a reason for his invocation of this Muse, when he was about to sing, as he informs us, reges et tempora rerum.

The fourth book of Virgil, Servius tells us, is borrowed from this of Apollonius Rhodius. Virgil's Æneid, says Hoelzlinus, would not have been enriched with the episode of Dido, had not the amours of Hypsipyla and Medea been worked up ready to his hand by Apollonius.

10. Juno and Pallas] Having conducted his heroes to the banks of the Phasis, our poet shifts the scene, and takes occasion to introduce the two goddesses, Juno and Pallas, consulting for the safety of Jason. There is a necessity for such machinery, in order to preserve the dignity of epic poetry. And the propriety of its introduction in this place will be acknowledged, if we recollect, that on the successful application of these goddesses to Venus the future fortunes of Jason depend. There needs no greater proof of the beauty of this passage, than that it has been imitated by Virgil in that part of his first book, where Cupid is commissioned by his mother to kindle in Dido's breast a passion for Æneas.

46. A floating isle] The Greek is Νήσοις πλαγκτῆς. Homer has a similar expression, Πλωτῇ 'νὶ νήσῳ. Odyss. x. 3.

A floating isle! high-rais'd by toil divine.
Pope.

50. Sat Cytherea on a polish'd throne] This whole passage is imitated by Claudian, who, speaking of Venus, says,

Cæsariem tunc forte Venus subnixa corusco
Fingebat solis: dextrâ lævâque sorores
Stabant Idaliæ: largos hæc nectaris imbres
Irrigat; hæc morsu numerosi dentis eburno
Multifidum discrimen arat; sed tertia retro
Dat varios nexus, et justo dividit orbes
Ordine, neglectam partem studiosa relinquens.

74. To free Ixion] He, for making love to Juno, and boasting afterwards that he had dishonoured Jupiter, was hurled headlong by him into Tartarus, and bound to a wheel, which he was doomed to turn without intermission.

79. As o'er the world I stray'd] It was the opinion of the ancients, that the gods frequently assumed the human shape. Thus Homer, Odyss. xvii. 485.

They (curious oft of mortal actions) deign
In forms like these to round the earth and main,
Just and unjust recording in their mind,
And with sure eyes inspecting all mankind.
Pope.

——————— summo delabor Olympo,
Et Deus humanâ lustro sub imagine terras.
Ov. Met. l. 1.

1[illegible]1. With golden dice] The Greek is ἀστραγάλοισι. Homer has the same expression, Il. xxiii. 88. but it is omitted in Pope's translation.

141. — Adrastæa gave] She was nurse to Jove when an infant. Thus Callimachus;

——————— σὲ δὲ κοίμισεν Ἀδρήστεια
Λίκνῳ ἐνὶ χρυσέῳ. Hymn. ad Jov. v. 47.

149. A sweet round ball] It is partly from the wanton and playful character of these little Cupids, that they are almost always given us under the figures of children.

Thus Ovid;

Et puer es, nec te quicquam nisi ludere oportet:
Lude, decent annos mollia regna tuos.
Ov. Rem. Am.

In conformity to this puerile character, Venus promises to reward her favourite boy with play-things.

210. To blameless Phrixus.] See the preface.

227. At Colchos still this barbarous rite prevails] These extraordinary rites of the Colchians are mentioned by Ælian in his fourth book. The earth and air are said to be the principal objects of their worship. Hoelz. and Schol.

235. But friendly Juno shrouds] Thus Pallas spreads a veil of air around Ulysses, and renders him invisible:

Propitious Pallas to secure her care,
Around him threw a veil of thicken'd air.
Homer's Odyss. b. vii.

Thus Venus conceals Æneas and his companions:

At Venus obscuro gradientes aere sepsit.
Virg. Æn. l. i.

251. The Pleiads set or rose] The Pleiades are said to be the daughters of Atlas by the nymph Pleione. They were seven in number. Their name is derived, either from their mother, or their number, or, more probably, from the Greek word, which signifies to sail. They are called in Latin Vergiliæ, from the vernal season when they rise. They rise about the vernal equinox, and set in autumn. See a further account of them in the note on v. 448. b. ii.

260. Phlegræan war] The battle between the gods and giants is supposed to have been fought at Phlegra, near Pallene, in Thessaly.

299. Athamas's fancied wealth to gain] These sons of Phrixus and Chalciope had sailed from Colchis to Orchomenos, a city of Bœotia, to receive the inheritance of their grandfather Athamas.

327. As some good housewife] Virgil seems to have copied this simile from Apollonius. Æn. viii. v. 408.

What time the poor, laborious frugal dame,
Who plies her distaff, stirs the dying flame;
Employs her handmaids by the winking light,
And lengthens out their tasks with half the night;
Thus to her children she divides the bread.
And guards the honours of her homely bed.
Pitt.

356. On Mars's isle] One of those islands called the Strophades, in the Ionian sea.

387. The fierce Sarmatians] The Sarmatians, or Sauromatæ, were Scythians, who dwelt in the country that lies between the river Tanais and the Borysthenes.

413. Had ye not first my feast partook] The table was looked upon by the ancients as a sacred thing; and a violation of the laws of hospitality was esteemed the highest profanation imaginable.

562. A maiden dwells] Virgil's description of the Massylian priestess is taken from this passage:

Hæc se carminibus promittit——
Sistere aquam fluviis, et vertere sidera retro;
Nocturnosque ciet manes: mugire videbis
Sub pedibus terram, et descendere montibus ornos.
Æn. l. iv. 487.

705. Whom her friends had join'd In marriage] The chief power of disposing of their daughters in marriage, even among the heathens, was in their parents, without whose consent it was not held lawful. Thus Hermione in Euripides:

Νυμφευμάτων δὲ ἐτῶν μῶν πατὴρ ἐμὸς
Μεριμνᾷν ἕξει, κ' ὀυκ ἐμον κρινεῖν τάδε.

797. Now rising shades] Here Dr. Broome's translation begins, and continues to v. 1087; but not without considerable omissions which are supplied. Virgil has copied this exquisite description from our author. Both the poets describe minutely the profound calm and stillness of the night, in order to render the agonies of the restless heroines more affecting by such a contrast. It is impossible to give us a more lively idea of their restless situation, than by representing it in opposition to that general tranquillity which prevails through the whole creation. The silence of the night, which disposes others to rest, serves but to increase their anguish, and to swell the tumult of their passion.

'Twas night; and weary with the toils of day,
In soft repose the whole creation lay.
The murmurs of the groves and surges die,
The stars roll solemn thro' the glowing sky;
Wide o'er the fields a brooding silence reigns,
The flocks lie stretch'd along the flowery plains;
The furious savages that haunt the woods,
The painted birds, the fishes of the floods;
All, all, beneath the general darkness share
In sleep a sweet forgetfulness of care;
All but the hapless queen. Pitt.

That sudden and beautiful transition at the close of the description, At non infelix animi Phænissa, is copied with the utmost exactness from the correspondent line in our poet,

'Αλλὰ μάλ' ὀ Μήδειαν ἐπὶ γλυκερὸς λάβεν ὕπνος.

813. As from the stream-stor'd vase] Virgil has imitated this simile. Æn. viii. 22.

Sicut aquæ tremulum, &c.

So from a brazen vase the trembling stream
Reflects the lunar, or the solar beam:
Swift and elusive of the dazzled eyes,
From wall to wall the dancing glory flies:
Thence to the ceiling shoot the dancing rays,
And o'er the roof the quivering splendour plays.
Pitt.

911. This plant which rough Caucasean mountains bore] Caucasus is called by Propertius, b. i. el. 12. the Promethean mountain; because the magic herbs, for which it was famous, were said to have sprung out of the blood of Prometheus.

——————— An quæ
Lecta Prometheis dividet herba jugis.
Potter.

935. As when her limbs divine] We meet with this simile in the sixth book of Homer's Odyssey, who applies it to Nausicaa sporting with her fair attendants in the meads. Virgil applies the same simile to Dido, walking in the midst of the city,

with the Tyrian princes. See Pope's note on v. 117. Od. vi. Some of the critics have thought that no passage has been more unhappily copied by Virgil from Homer, than this comparison. But it should seem from some circumstances in his simile, that the Roman poet rather imitated this passage of Apollonius, than that of Homer.

936. The Amnesian waves] or, rather, Amnision, according to Callimachus:

——— Ἀμνισίδας εἴκοσι νύμφας.

They were so named from Amnisus, a city and river of Crete.

988. And croaking, thus Saturnia's mind express'd] Some birds were of use in divination by the manner and direction of their flight; others by the sounds they uttered; these were called oscines, of which kind were crows.

Oscinem corvum prece suscitabo
Solis ab ortu. Hor. od. xxvii. l. 3.

1005. Meanwhile the maid] No poet has succeeded better in any description than Apollonius has in the following. The anxiety with which Medea expects the arrival of Jason, expressed by her inattention and aversion to every other object, by her directing her eyes every way in search of him, and by her trembling at every breeze, are admirable strokes of nature. The appearance of Jason, flushed with all the bloom of youth, advancing hastily towards her, like the star, to which he is compared, rising from the ocean; the embarrassment which his presence occasions, the silent admiration in which they stand gazing at each other, like two tall trees in a calm, are particulars which none but the imagination of a real poet could have put together, and can never be sufficiently admired.

1099. The following night in equal shares divide] We have here a curious account of the ceremonies made use of in their sacrifices to the infernal deities. Hecate, the same with the Moon or Diana, was so called, either from her being appeased by hecatombs, or from the power she possessed of obliging those who were unburied to wander a hundred years. Virgil applies to her the epithet of ter geminam, and Horace that of triformis. She was called in Heaven Luna, or the Moon, on Earth Diana, and in Hell Proserpina, Hecate, and Brimo from her terrifying appearance.

It seems extraordinary that Diana, who is the goddess of chastity, should be represented as dispensing her favourable influence in illicit amours. But the mythologists inform us, that Diana and Venus are but one and the same divinity. The scholiast on Theocritus, Id. ii. says, that it was customary, among the ancients, for the men to implore the Sun, and women the Moon in their amours. Cicero, speaking of three Dianas, observes, that the first was thought to be the mother of winged Cupid. De Nat. Deor. l. 3.

1095. With honey, sweetest labour of the bees] Honey was a favourite ingredient with the ancients in their oblations to the gods, whether of Heaven or Hell. Homer, in his hymn to Mercury calls it

—— Θεῶν ἡδεῖαν ἐδωδήν.

Bees and honey are subjects which the Greek poets are particularly fond of introducing; and their country was plentifully supplied with these commodities.

1155. Where from Prometheus good Deucalion came] Apollonius Rhodius, according to the common opinion, supposes Deucalion to have been a native of Greece, the son of Prometheus, the son of Japetus: but in these ancient mythological accounts all genealogy must be entirely disregarded. He represents him as the first of men, through whom religious rites were renewed, cities built, and civil polity established in the world; none of which circumstances are applicable to any king of Greece. We are assured by Philo, that Deucalion was Noah. Bryant.

1245. This baneful monster was by Cadmus slain] Upon the report of the rape of Europa, her father, Agenor, sent every where in search of her, and ordered his son Cadmus not to return home till he had found her. Cadmus having traversed a part of Greece without gaining any information of her, settled in Bœotia, where he built the city of Thebes. Having sent his associates into a grove, consecrated to Mars, to fetch water, a serpent, which guarded the place, devoured them. Cadmus, to revenge their death, slew the monster; from whose teeth, which he had sown, a body of armed men sprung up. This is the fabulous account to which Apollonius alludes.

No colony, says Mr. Bryant, could settle any where, and build an orphite or serpent temple, but there was supposed to have been a contention betwixt a hero and a dragon. Cadmus was described in conflict with such an one at Thebes.

1247. An heifer to his seat] πομπαῖος relates properly to divine influence, and πομπὴ is an oracle. An ox or cow was by the Amonians esteemed very sacred and oracular. Cadmus was accordingly said to be directed πομπῇ βοός.

Bryant.

1285. Amaranthine Phasis] This river is supposed to have derived its source from a nation of that name. The poet, in describing the effects of this infernal evocation, has heaped together with great judgment, and in the true spirit of poetry, every circumstance that is capable of exciting terrour and astonishment.

1288. And now on Caucasus] Apollonius introduces his heroes on the plains of Mars with the utmost pomp and magnificence, thus artfully preparing us for the solemnities of the ensuing combat, on which the fate of Jason depends.

NOTES TO BOOK IV.

1. O GODDESS] The first and second books contain, as we have seen, the voyage of the Argonauts to Colchis. In the book we are now entering upon, the poet has given us an account of the route they took on their return. And in order to throw the utmost variety into his poem, he has conducted them to Greece by a way altogether new and unknown. He makes them sail up the Ister, and by an arm of that river, to the Eridanus, and from thence to the Rhone. Apollonius's geography is in many instances, very exceptionable. The licence which poets are allowed, quidlibet audendi, is his best excuse for inaccu-

racies of this kind. Scaliger, who seldom spares our author, does not scruple to assert, that, quod attinet ad situm orbis terrarum, sanè imperitus regionum fuit Apollonius. De Istro, dii boni! quas nugas. But let it be remembered, that not only poets have trifled in their descriptions of this river, but that historians and geographers, who have attempted to explain its course, have given very different and inconsistent accounts of it. Many curious traditions, and entertaining pieces of ancient Greek history, are interspersed throughout this book. The speeches of Medea can never be enough admired. Her sentiments are admirably suited to her condition; they are simple, unaffected, and calculated to raise our pity. Our poet has displayed a luxuriant fancy in his description of the nuptials of Jason and Medea; and he has painted the distresses of his Argonauts, on the coast of Africa, in the most glowing colours. This book appears indeed, in every view of it, equal, if not superior to any of the foregoing. We meet with some obscurities. The translator confesses his inability to ascertain the true sense of every intricate passage. Let it, however, be some alleviation of his errours, that his guides have been but few, and they not always the most intelligent; and that no part of this book, except only the story of Talus, has appeared in an English dress, before the present version was published.

32. Clung round each door] The custom of kissing beds, columns, and doors, before they were obliged to quit them, occurs frequently in the Greek tragedians.

33. A lock she tore] It was customary for young women, before the nuptial ceremony was performed, to present their hair to some deity, to whom they had particular obligations. Medea, therefore, previous to her departure and marriage with Jason, presents a lock of hair to her mother, to be deposited by her in the temple of some deity to whom it was consecrated.

64. I to the cave at Latmos] Latmos was a mountain in Caria, in whose cave the Moon was said by the poets to visit Endymion. Thus, in Valerius Flaccus, who seems to have had this passage in his eye, we read;

Latmius æstivâ residet venator in umbrâ,
Dignus amore deæ: velatis cornibus et jam
Luna venit. Lib. viii. 29.

92. Whose knees embracing] Several parts of the body were considered by the ancients as the seats of virtues and vices, of good and bad qualities. Modesty was assigned to the eyes, sagacity and derision to the nose, pride and disdain to the eye-brows, and pity to the knees; which it was customary for suppliants, when they made their requests, to touch and embrace with reverence.

123. At twilight, ere] Xenophon, de Venatione, makes the same observation, ἐξιέναι πρωΐ, exire diluculo. The same remark is made by Oppian and others.

143. Colchians, far distant] This noble hyperbole has been copied by Virgil, book vii. v. 515. where, speaking of Alecto, he says,

With her full force a mighty horn she winds;
Th' infernal strain alarms the gathering hinds.
The dreadful summons the deep forest took;
The woods all thunder'd, and the mountains shook,
The lake of Trivia heard the note profound;
The Veline fountains trembled at the sound:
The thick sulphureous floods of hoary Nar
Shook at the blast that blew the flames of war:
Pale at the piercing call, the mothers prest
With shrieks their starting infants to the breast.
Pitt.

This circumstance of the mothers clasping their infants to their breasts is a very tender and affecting one. The poets seem particularly fond of it. We meet with it in the Troades of Euripides; and Camoens, in his imitation of these striking passages in Apollonius and Virgil, was too sensible of its beauty to omit it:

Such was the tempest of the dread alarms,
The babes that prattled in their nurses' arms
Shriek'd at the sound: with sudden cold imprest,
The mothers strain'd their infants to the breast,
And shook with horrour.—
The Lusiad, b. iv. p. 124.

203. The gallant band beheld with wondering eyes] Mr. Warton is of opinion, that Virgil had this beautiful passage in his eye in the following lines:

Expleri nequit, atque oculos per singula voluit,
Miraturque, interque, manus et brachia versat.
Æn. viii. 618.

And thus Spenser, in his Fairy Queen:

But Tristram then despoiling that dead knight
Of all those goodly ornaments of praise,
Long fed his greedy eyes with the fair light
Of the bright metal, shining like sun-rays;
Handling and turning them a thousand ways.
B. vi. c. 2. st. 39.

292. And, ere bright Cynthia] By Selene, and Selenaia, is meant the ark, of which the Moon was only an emblem; and from thence the Arcades, or Arkites, had the appellation of Selenitæ. When therefore it is said, that the Arcades were prior to the Moon, it means only, that they were constituted into a nation before the worship of the ark prevailed, and before the first war upon Earth commenced. Bryant. This boast of the Arcadians, that they were a nation before the Moon gave light to the world, is also thus accounted for by some ingenious writers: the Greeks generally ordered their affairs according to the appearances of the Moon, especially those two of the new and full Moon. The Spartans held it criminal to begin any great design till after they had considered the Moon, as she appeared when new and at the full. The Arcadians, contrary to this general custom of the Greeks, transacted all their business of importance before the appearance of the new Moon, or that of the full; and were therefore called in derision, προσέληνοι, for their neglect of this religious ceremony. Which term of reproach the Arcadians applied to their commendation, and shrewdly affirmed, that they were entitled to this epithet, because their nation was more ancient than the Moon.

301. Hence rose the matchless chief] Sesostris not only overran the countries which Alexander afterward invaded; but crossed both the Indus

and the Ganges; and thence penetrated into the eastern ocean. He then turned to the north, and attacked the nations of Scythia; till he at last arrived at the Tanais, which divides Europe and Asia. Here he founded a colony; leaving behind him some of his people, as he had just before done at Colchis. He subdued Asia Minor, and all the regions of Europe; where he erected pillars with hieroglyphical inscriptions, denoting, that these parts of the world had been subdued by the great Sesostris or Sesoosis. Diodorus Sic. l. i. p. 49. Apollonius Rhodius, who is thought to have been a native of Egypt, speaks of the exploits of this prince, but mentions no name; not knowing, perhaps, by which properly to distinguish him, as he was represented under so many. He represents him as conquering all Asia and Europe; and this in times so remote, that many of the cities which he built were in ruins before the era of the Argonauts. Bryant.

311. Recording tablets keep] The Colchians, says the scholiast, still retain the laws and customs of their forefathers; and they have pillars of stone, upon which are engraved maps of the continent and of the ocean. The poet calls these pillars κύβρεις: which, we are told, were of a square figure, like obelisks. These delineations had been made of old, and transmitted to the Colchians by their forefathers; which forefathers were from Egypt. The Egyptians were very famous for geometrical knowledge. All the flat part of this country being overflowed. it is reasonable to suppose, that they made use of this science to determine their lands, and to make out their several claims, at the retreat of the waters. Bryant.

451. Rise may my furies] Thus Dido, in a fit of despondency and rage, threatens Æneas:

Et cum frigida mors anima seduxerit artus,
Omnibus umbra locis adero. Æn. iv. 385.

526. Curse of mankind] Our poet, whenever he introduces moral sentences, which is but seldom, takes care to do it with the utmost propriety; at a time when the occasion warrants the use of them, and gives additional force and lustre to the truths which they convey. Virgil has adopted this sentiment of Apollonius on a similar occasion:

Improbe amor, quid non mortalia pectora cogis!
Æn. iv. 412.

412. From the Greek word Ερως, in the original, Mr. Bryant has taken occasion to give us the following curious account of Cupid and his emblems: Iris, the rainbow, seems to have been expressed Eiras by the Egyptians. Out of Eiras the Greeks formed Eros, a god of love; whom they annexed to Venus, and made her son. And finding that the bow was his symbol, instead of the Iris, they gave him a material bow, with the addition of a quiver and arrows. Being furnished with these implements of mischief, he was supposed to be the bane of the world.

550. Turn'd from the murderous scene] The remorse and concern of Medea are very strongly expressed by this simple action, of turning aside and concealing her face from the scene of barbarity. Signs are sometimes more significant than words, however eloquent and pathetic; and silence is often the surest indication of heart-felt sorrow.

613. Where Cadmus' and Harmonia's tomb] Cadmus settling in Bœotia, married Harmonia, or Hermione, the daughter of Venus by Mars. A conspiracy being formed against him, he was obliged to quit Bœotia, and retire with his wife into Illyricum. They are said by the poets to have been transformed into serpents. Of this transformation, and of the tomb, which the people of Illyricum erected to their memory, Dionysius thus speaks:

——————ἴδοις περικυδέα τύμβον,
Τύμβον, ὃν, Ἁρμονίης Καδμοιό τε φῆμις ἐνίσπει.
Κεῖθι γὰρ εἰς ὀφίων σκολιὸν γένος ἠλλάξαντο,
Ὅππoτ' ἀπ' Ἰσμηνοῦ λιπαρὸν μετὰ γῆρας ἵκοντο.

644. Of blood yet streaming from his children slain] By Megara, the daughter of Creon king of Thebes, Hercules had several sons, whom he slew in a fit of madness. Soon after this slaughter he left Thebes, and received expiation for the murder at Athens, according to some; but according to our poet, at Macris.

689. Wak'd the brisker gales in Argo's aid] In the original,

Μηδομένη δ' ἄνυσιν τοῖο πλόου, ὦρσεν ἀέλλας
Ἀντικρύ·

Juno, anxious for the safety of her crew, and knowing they must visit Circe's isle, raised a storm for that purpose; which drove them back, up the Chronian sea, as far as the island Electris. By thus changing their direction, she shortened their voyage, and hastened their approach to the island of Circe.

727. To the far Hyperborean race] There are so many inconsistent fables among the ancients, respecting the country and situation of the Hyperboreans, that modern geographers have not been able to reconcile them. See Gesner de Navigationibus extra columnas Herculis, Præl. 2.

Callimachus, in his hymn to Delos, speaks of them as a people of high antiquity. Pindar places them near the isles of the Blest, which were supposed to have been opposite to Mauritania, and celebrates their rites. See Olymp. Od. iii. and Pyth. x.

728. Griev'd for his favourite Æsculapius] Jupiter, incensed that Æsculapius had restored Hippolitus to life, destroyed him with his thunder. Apollo, willing to revenge the death of his son, directed his darts against the Cyclops, by whose hands the thunder of Jupiter was formed. The god, for this offence, banished him from Heaven. See Virg. Æn. vii.764.

775. With chalks] In the original,

——————ἵνα ψηφῖσιν ἀπωμόρξαντο καμόντες
Ἱδρῶ ἅλις· χροιῇ δὲ κατ' αἰγιαλοῖο κέχυνται
Εἴκελοι.

The first line is obscure; for it may either mean, that they made use of the ψῆφοι as στλεγγίσματα, or strigiles, for rubbing; or that, in rubbing, the sweat dropped on the stones, ψηφῖσιν, and discoloured them. If this sense be the true one, the following lines may, perhaps, be somewhat less exceptionable than those already given:

To cleanse their sides from copious sweat they toil,
Which, trickling down, distain'd the chalky soil.

This passage will receive some illustration from Aristotle, περὶ θαυμασίων ἀκουσμάτων; who asserts, that among other monuments of the Argonautic expedition this was one, τὸ ἐπὶ τῶν ψήφων λεγόμενον. παρὰ τὸν αἰγιαλὸν ψήφους φασὶν εἶναι ποικίλας· ταύτας δὲ οἱ Ἕλληνες, οἱ τὴν νῆσον οἰκοῦντες, λέγουσι, τὴν χροιὰν λαβεῖν ἀπὸ τῶν στλεγγισμάτων ὧν ἐποιοῦντο ἀλειφόμενοι.

783. Here saw they Circe] We have the fullest description of Circe and her habitation in the 10th Odyss. of Homer: from which book succeeding poets have been supplied with ample materials, to assist them in dressing out this entertaining fiction.

It is entertaining to observe, how different poets have written on the same or similar subjects. And according as they have acquitted themselves in working them up, we may form a judgment of their taste and genius.

932. Till Themis thus] Others ascribe this discovery to Prometheus, for which Jupiter promised to release him from his chains.

946. Shall in Elysium's blissful plains] The story, here alluded to, is mentioned by several of the ancient mythologists. Medea, when in Elysium, or the Fortunate islands, gained the affections of Achilles, who then dwelt in those regions, and married her. The ancients are by no means consistent in their accounts of these Elysian fields. Some affirm them to be in the Moon, others in the milky way. But it is more generally supposed, that they are situated in some fertile and pleasant region on Earth. See Homer's Odyss. b. iv. and the note to v. 765 of Pope's Trans. and Gesner de Insulis beat. Præl. 2.

1016. Her young Achilles o'er the flame] Thus Ceres, when she undertook to bring up Triptolemus, in order to render him immortal, fed him all day with celestial food, and covered him all night with burning embers. His father Eleusinus, observing this, expressed his fears for his child. Ceres, displeased with his behaviour, struck him dead, but conferred immortality on his son.

1047. The Sirens were Cuthite and Canaanitish priests, who had founded temples, which were rendered more than ordinary famous on account of the women who officiated. With their music they enticed strangers into the purlieus of their temples, and then put them to death. The female part of their choirs were maintained for a twofold purpose; both on account of their voices and their beauty. They were said to be the children of the Muse Terpsichore; by which is meant only, that they were the daughters of harmony.

Bryant.

Orpheus, in the Argonautics ascribed to him, has not only mentioned these Sirens, but given us the song, alluded to by Apollonius, which was so efficacious as to prevent the ill effects of the Sirens' music. We have the most particular description of these enchantresses in the 12th book of Homer's Odyssey.

1054. Who lur'd, in times remote] Among others, whom Ceres sent in search of her daughter Proserpine, were the Sirens. She is said to have given them wings, to enable them to explore the country with greater ease and expedition.

1086. From whose cleft summits flames] These flaming billows must have been very alarming to the sailors, who were ignorant of the cause of them. The poet has therefore, in his description of Scylla and Charybdis, with great judgment selected these remarkable appearances, which could not fail to excite terrour and astonishment.

1091. Here o'er the sailing pine the nymphs preside] Virgil in his 1st Æn. has made use of the assistance of the sea-nymphs on a similar occasion.

> Cymothoe simul & Triton adnixus, acuto
> Detrudunt naves scopulo.

And Camoens, who seems to have been particularly pleased with this description, has, in imitation of it, summoned together a vast number of sea-nymphs to rescue the navy from destruction. See b. ii. p. 48.

1151. His father castrated] One would not expect to find in so grave a writer as Hesiod any thing like that low kind of wit, which the double sense of words gives rise to. The taste of the ancients, it has been said, was too good for these fooleries. Yet his learned annotator is of opinion, that Hesiod has availed himself of the ambiguity of the word μῆδος. He thus discusses this curious subject in a note on v. 180 in Theog.

Omninò existimo Hesiodum, et qui eum hac in re antecesserunt, aut sequuti sunt, lusisse in ambiguo. Vox μῆδος duo significabat, pudenda & consilium, cumque audissent Saturnum patri ἀποτεμεῖν μῆδος, datâ operâ ita rem acceperunt, quasi narraretur ei pudenda resecuisse, ut τερατολογίαις, quas hac de re habent, locus daretur; quamvis probè scirent consilium seu consiliarios intelligi, quorum suasu Thessaliâ excedere coactus fuerat Saturnus. Hosce consiliarios fugavit, & navibus in Asiam redire coegit.

1231. Thus Pycteus] (Note, it ought to be Nycteus.) Antiope, the daughter of Nycteus, was deflowered by Jupiter in the form of a satyr. To avoid the anger of her father, she fled to Sicyon, a city in Peloponnesus: where she was protected by Epops. Nycteus at his death requested his brother Lycus to lay siege to Sicyon, but to show no compassion to Antiope. He, willing to comply with the request of Nycteus, besieged the city, killed Epops and took Antiope prisoner.

1283. Thus Danaë] Danaë was the daughter of Acrisius. Having been informed by the oracle, that his grandson should bereave him of his life and crown, he shut her up in a tower of brass. But Jupiter, according to the fable, made his way through the roof in a shower of gold. The meaning of which fable is; Prætus, who was surnamed Jupiter, bribed the keepers, and having thus gained access to the prisoner, made her the mother of Perseus. Acrisius being apprized of this illicit commerce, and the fruits of it, ordered the mother and her son to be locked up in a chest and thrown into the sea.

1338. Snatch'd from the flames] Jupiter being in love with Semele, Juno concerted the following scheme for the destruction of her rival. She appeared to Semele in the shape of Beroë, a nurse, and insinuated to her, that if her lover were really Jupiter, he would not disguise himself like a mortal: and that the certainty of his divinity could no otherwise be ascertained, than by his appearing before her with the same majesty, which he assumed when he visited Juno. Semele followed her advice; and Jupiter having sworn by

Styx to grant her whatever she might ask, approached her in the full blaze of his glory, and Semele was consumed by his lightning. Jupiter being desirous to preserve the infant Bacchus, of whom Semele had been for some time pregnant, commissioned Mercury to deliver him from the flames, by taking him out of her womb, and conveying him to Eubœa. Here he was committed to the care of Macris. But Juno's resentment being not yet subsided, she forbade her favourite island Eubœa to give protection to the nurse of Bacchus; who now fled for refuge to Phæacia.

1505. As when] "The principal image," says Pope, Il. xiv. in a note on v. 457. "is more strongly impressed on the mind by a multitude of similes, which are the natural product of an imagination labouring to express something very vast: but finding no single idea sufficient to answer its conceptions, it endeavours by redoubling the comparisons to supply this defect." Since then the heaping together of similes, when the occasion requires, is considered as a proof of true poetical enthusiasm, it must be allowed that our poet, in this instance, as well as in many others, has shown himself capable of rising above that uniform mediocrity, which has, perhaps too hastily, been ascribed to him. For we have here an accumulation of comparisons the most elegant and apposite. The despondent heroes are likened to spectres and statues distilling drops of blood. Medea's fair attendants, lamenting their misfortunes, are compared to swallows, bereaved of their nests and screaming for their mother; and, immediately after, to the plaintive notes of dying swans.

This simile of the swallow is copied by Virgil, Æn. xii. 473.

1649. In Atlas' realm] In Africa, where, according to Virgil, Atlas reigns:

Ultimus Æthiopum locus est, ubi maximus
Atlas———

1651. The fair Hesperides] They were the daughters of Hesperus, the brother of Atlas, and shepherdesses. Hercules carried off their sheep (which, for their exquisite beauty, were called golden) and slew the shepherd, whose name was Draco. The Greek word μῆλα, which signifies apples as well as sheep, is supposed to have given rise to the fiction.

Some are of opinion, that the fable of the serpent, who guarded the golden apples, and was said to have been slain by Hercules, derives its origin from the Mosaic account of the fall.

1749. Thus sees the clown] Translated by Virgil, Æn. vi. 453.

———qualem primo qui surgere mense
Aut videt aut vidisse putat per nubila lunam.

1791. For when brave Perseus] It has been already remarked, that Danaë was enclosed in a chest by the command of her father Acrisius, and thrown into the sea. This chest was cast upon the island Seriphus, one of the Cyclades in the Ægæan sea. It was found by a fisherman, who brought it to Polydectes, king of the island. He received the mother and child with great tenderness: but falling in love with Danaë, and fearing the resentment of Perseus, now grown to manhood, he planned the following scheme for his destruction. Having invited the neighbouring princes to an entertainment, he desired each of them to bring with him some rarities for the feast. Perseus was required to bring on this occasion the head of Medusa, one of the Gorgons: an enterprize which the king imagined would prove fatal to him; but by the assistance of Minerva, he cut off the Gorgon's head; which, when he carried it to the island, turned its inhabitants into stone, and among the rest, their king, Polydectes, who had sent him out on the expedition. See Pindar's Pyth. od. xii.

1817. His corse the bright-arm'd heroes thrice surround] Virgil takes occasion to mention the same custom in the following words:

Ter circum accensos cincti fulgentibus armis
Decurrere rogos: ter mæstum funeris ignem
Lustravare in equis, ululatuque ore dederunt.
Æn. xi.

1870. Your course, that cape once doubled] It would contribute towards clearing this obscure passage, if instead of ἰθὺς, we read ὑπὲρ. This conjecture may the more readily be admitted, as we meet with the same expression, ἀγκῶνος ὑπὲρ προὔχοντος, at v. 1626.

1943. There Talus] The following is Broome's note, prefixed to his translation of the story of Talus.

The following verses from Apollonius will appear very extravagant, unless we have recourse to their allegorical meaning. Plato in his Minos writes thus:

Talus and Rhadamanthus were the assistants of Minos in the execution of his laws. It was the office of Talus to visit all parts of Crete thrice every year, to enforce them with the utmost severity. The poet alludes to this custom in these words:

Fierce guard of Crete! who thrice each year explores
The trembling isle, and strides from shores to shores.

Talus is fabled to be formed of brass, because the laws, which he carried with him in his circuit, were engraven upon brazen tables. It is not improbable, but the fable of the bursting the vein above the ankle of Talus, by which he died, arose from the manner of punishment practised by him; which was, by the opening of a vein above the ankles of criminals, by which they bled to death.

2093. Instant emerging] See on this subject Pindar's Pyth. od. iv. towards the beginning.

2096. Sintian Lemnos] The Sintians were originally Thracians; but settled afterwards at Lemnos.

2118. And added years to years exalt my verse] It was customary with the Greeks, not only to sing hymns, but to recite heroic poems in honour of the gods and heroes at their festive meetings.

THE

RAPE OF HELEN;

OR,

THE ORIGIN OF THE TROJAN WAR:

A GREEK POEM, BY COLUTHUS.

TRANSLATED BY FAWKES.

THE

RAPE OF HELEN;

OR,

THE ORIGIN OF THE TROJAN WAR.

TRANSLATED BY FAWKES.

YE nymphs of Troy, for beauty fam'd, who trace
From Xanthus' fertile streams your ancient race,
Oft on whose sandy banks your tires are laid,
And many a trinket which your hands have made,
What time to Ida's hallow'd mount ye throng,
To join the festive choir in dance and song;
No longer on your favourite banks repose,
But come, the judgment of the swain disclose.
Say from what hills, to trackless deeps unknown,
Rush'd with impetuous zeal the daring clown;
Say to what end, with future ills replete,
O'er distant oceans sail'd a mighty fleet;
What seas could this adventurous youth embroil,
Sow discord's seeds o'er what disastrous soil?
Say from what source arose the dire debate,
Which swains could end and goddesses create.
What his decision? Of the Grecian dame
Who to the shepherd's ear convey'd the name?
Speak, for ye saw, on Ida's still retreat,
Judicial Paris fill his shepherd's seat;
Venus ye saw, the Graces' darling queen,
As on her judge approv'd she smil'd serene.
What time Hæmonia's lofty mountains rung
With hymeneal songs for Peleus sung,
Officious Ganymede, at Jove's request,
Supplied with sparkling wine each welcome guest;
And all the gods to Thetis' nuptials came,
Sister of Amphitrite, honour'd dame.
Earth-shaking Neptune left his azure main,
And Jove supreme forsook his starry plain:
From Helicon, with odorous shrubs o'erspread,
The Muses' tuneful choir Apollo led.
Him Juno follow'd, wife of sovereign Jove:
With Harmony the smiling queen of love
Hasten'd to join the gods in Chiron's festive grove.
Cupid's full quiver o'er her shoulder thrown,
Persuasion follow'd with a bridal crown.
Minerva, though to nuptial rites a foe,
Came; but no helmet nodded o'er her brow.
Diana to the Centaur's grove resorts,
And for one day forgets her rural sports.
His loose locks shaking as the zephyrs play'd,
Not long behind convivial Bacchus stay'd.
War's god, as when to Vulcan's dome he sped,
No spear his hand sustain'd, no casque his head,
Such now, without his helmet or his lance,
Smiling he look'd, and led the bridal dance.
But from these blissful scenes was Discord warn'd;
Peleus rejected her, and Chiron scorn'd.
As by the gadfly stung, the heifer strays
Far from its fields, through every devious maze;
Thus, stung with envy, Discord roam'd, nor ceas'd
Her baneful arts to interrupt the feast.
Oft from her flinty bed she rush'd amain,
Then stood, then sunk into her seat again:
With desperate hand she tore her snaky head,
And with a serpent-scourge she lash'd her flinty bed.
To dart the forky lightning, and command
From Hell's abyss the Titans' impious band,
Jove from his throne with rebel arm to wrest,
Were projects form'd within the fury's breast.
But, though incens'd, she dreaded Vulcan's ire,
Who forms Jove's bolt, and checks the raging fire.

Her purpose changing, she with rattling arms
Dissension meditates and dire alarms;
If haply clattering shields can strike dismay,
And from the nuptials drive the gods away.
But Mars she dreaded, oft in arms array'd,
And this new project with complacence weigh'd.
The burnish'd apples, rich with golden rind,
Growth of Hesperian gardens struck her mind.
Resolv'd contention's baneful seeds to sow,
She tore the blushing apple from its bough,
Grasp'd the dire source whence future battles sprung,
And midst the gods the golden mischief flung.
The stately wife of Jove with wondering eyes
Beheld, and wish'd to grasp the golden prize.
Beauty's fair queen to catch the apple strove;
For 'tis the prize of beauty and of love.
Jove mark'd the contest, and, to crush debate,
Thus counsel'd Hermes, who beside him sat:
“Paris, perchance, from Priam sprung you know;
His herds he grazes on Mount Ida's brow,
And oft conducts them to the dewy meads,
Through which his streams the Phrygian Xanthus leads:
Show him yon prize, and urge him to declare
Which of these goddesses he deems most fair;
In whom, of all, his matchless skill can trace
The close-arch'd eyebrow and the roundest face,
On such a face, where bends the circling bow,
The golden apple, beauty's prize, bestow.”
Thus spoke the sire: the willing son obey'd,
And to their judge the deities convey'd.
Each anxious fair her charms to heighten tries,
And dart new lustre from her sparkling eyes.
Her veil aside insidious Venus flung;
Loose from the clasp her fragrant ringlets hung;
She then in golden cauls each curl compress'd,
Summon'd her little Loves, and thus address'd:
“Behold, my sons, the hour of trial near!
Embrace, my Loves, and bid me banish fear.
This day's decision will enhance my fame,
Crown beauty's queen, or sink in endless shame.
Doubting I stand, to whom the swain may say,
‘Bear thou, most fair, the golden prize away.’
Nurs'd was each grace by Juno's fostering hand;
And crowns and sceptres shift at her command.
Minerva dictates in th' embattled field;
And heroes tremble when she shakes her shield.
Of all the goddesses that rule above,
Far most defenceless is the queen of love.
Without or spear or shield must Venus live;
And crowns and sceptres she has none to give.
Yet why despair? though with no falchion grac'd,
Love's silken chain surrounds my slender waist.
My bow this cestus, this the dart I fling,
And with this cestus I infix my sting.
My sting infix'd renews the lover's pain,
And virgins languish, but revive again.”
Thus to her Loves the rosy-finger'd queen
Told all her fears, and vented all her spleen:
To every word they lent a willing ear,
Round their fond mother clung, and strove to cheer.
And now they reach Mount Ida's grassy steep,
Where youthful Paris feeds his father's sheep:
What time he tends them in the plains below,
Through which the waters of Anaurus flow,
Apart he counts his cattle's numerous stock,
Apart he numbers all his fleecy flock.
A wild goat's skin, around his shoulders cast,
Loose fell and flow'd below his girded waist.
A pastoral staff, which swains delight to hold,
His roving herds protected and controll'd.
Accoutred thus, and warbling o'er his song,
He to his pipe melodious pac'd along.
Unnoted oft, while he renews his lay,
His flocks desert him, and his oxen stray.
Swift to his bower retires the tuneful man,
To pipe the praise of Hermes and of Pan.
Sunk is each animal in dead repose;
No dog around him barks, no heifer lows:
Echo alone rebounds through Ida's hills,
And all the air with sounds imperfect fills.
The cattle, slunk upon their verdant bed,
Close by their piping lord repose their head.
Beneath the shades which sheltering thickets blend,
When Paris' eye approaching Hermes ken'd,
Back he retires, with sudden fear impress'd,
And shuns the presence of the heavenly guest;
To the thick shrubs his tuneful reed conveys,
And all unfinish'd leaves his warbled lays.
Thus winged Hermes to the shepherd said,
Who mark'd the god's approach with silent dread:
“Dismiss thy fears, nor with thy flocks abide;
A mighty contest Paris must decide.
Haste, judge announc'd; for whose decision wait
Three lovely females, of celestial state.
Haste, and the triumph of that face declare,
Which sweetest looks, and fairest midst the fair:
Let her, whose form thy critic eye prefers,
Claim beauty's prize, and be this apple hers.”
Thus Hermes spoke; the ready swain obey'd,
And to decide the mighty cause essay'd.
With keenest look he mark'd the heavenly dames;
Their eyes, quick flashing as the lightning's flames,
Their snowy necks, their garments fring'd with gold,
And rich embroidery wrought in every fold;
Their gait he mark'd, as gracefully they mov'd,
And round their feet his eye sagacious rov'd.
But, ere the smiling swain his thoughts express'd,
Grasping his hand him Pallas thus address'd:
“Regard not, Phrygian youth, the wife of Jove,
Nor Venus heed, the queen of wedded love:
But martial prowess if thy wisdom prize,
Know, I possess it; praise me to the skies.
Thee, fame reports, puissant states obey,
And Troy's proud city owns thy sovereign sway.
Her suffering sons thy conquering arm shall shield,
And stern Bellona shall to Paris yield.
Comply; her succour will Minerva lend,
Teach thee war's science, and in fight defend.”
Thus Pallas strove to influence the swain,
Whose favour Juno thus attempts to gain:
“Should'st thou with beauty's prize my charms reward,
All Asia's realms shall own thee for their lord.
Say, what from battles but contention springs?
Such contests shun; for what are wars to kings?
But him, whose hands the rod of empire sway,
Cowards revere, and conquerors obey.
Minerva's friends are oft Bellona's slaves,
And the fiend slaughters whom the goddess saves.”
Proffers of boundless sway thus Juno made;
And Venus thus, contemptuous smiling, said:
But first her floating veil aloft she threw,
And all her graces to the shepherd shew;
Loosen'd her little Loves' attractive chain,
And tried each art to captivate the swain.
“Accept my boon,” thus spoke the smiling dame,
“Battles forget, and dread Bellona's name.

Beauty's rich meed at Venus' hand receive,
And Asia's wide domain to tyrants leave.
The deathful fight, the din of arms I fear;
Can Venus' hand direct the martial spear?
Women with beauty stoutest hearts assail,
Beauty, their best defence, their strongest mail.
Prefer domestic ease to martial strife,
And to exploits of war a pleasing wife.
To realms extensive Helen's bed prefer,
And scoff at kingdoms, when oppos'd to her.
Thy prize with envy Sparta shall survey,
And Troy to Paris tune the bridal lay."
  The shepherd, who astonish'd stood and mute,
Consign'd to Venus the Hesperian fruit,
The claim of beauty, and the source of woes;
For dire debates from this decision rose.
Uplifting in her hand the glowing prize,
She rallied thus the vanquish'd deities:
  "To me, ye martial dames, the prize resign;
Beauty I court, and beauty's prize is mine.
Mother of mighty Mars and Vulcan too,
Fame says, the choir of Graces sprung from you:
Yet distant far, this day, your daughters stray'd,
And no one Grace appear'd to lend you aid.
Mars too declin'd t' assert his mother's right,
Though oft his brandish'd sword decides the fight.
His boasted flames why could not Vulcan cast,
And at one blaze his mother's rivals blast?
Vain are thy triumphs, Pallas, vain thy scorn;
Thou, not in wedlock, nor of woman born,
Jove's teeming head the monstrous birth contains,
And the barb'd iron ripp'd thee from his brains.
Brac'd with th' unyielding plaits of ruthless mail,
She curses Cupid and the silken veil.
Connubial bliss and concord she abhors,
In discord glories and delights in wars.
Yet know, virago, not in feats of arms
Triumph weak women, but in beauty's charms.
Nor men nor women are those mongrels base,
Like you, equivocal in form and face."
  In terms like these the laughter-loving queen
Rallied her rivals, and increas'd their spleen,
As, lifting high, she view'd with secret joy
Her beauty's triumphs and the bane of Troy.
Inspir'd with love for her, the fair unknown,
By beauty's conquering queen pronounc'd his own,
Ill-fated Paris to the forest's maze
Men vers'd in Pallas' various arts conveys.
At Pericles' command they give the blow,
And lay the glories of the forest low.
He, artist fam'd, his frantic prince obey'd,
And burden'd ocean with the ships he made.
From Ida's summits rush'd the daring swain,
And to its bowery shades preferr'd the boisterous main.
Th' extended beach with choice oblations stor'd,
And his protectress Venus oft implor'd;
The billowy deep his furrowing keel divides,
And in the Hellespont his vessel rides.
But prodigies announce approaching ill,
And with presages sad each bosom fill.
Up-heaving waves Heaven's starry concave shroud,
And round each Bear is cast a circling cloud.
Clouds and big waves discharge their watery stores;
Full on the deck the bursting torrent pours.
Their sturdy oars with unabating sweep
Far whitening agitate the angry deep.
Dardanus pass'd, and Ilion's fertile plains,
The mouth of Ismarus' lake the adventurer gains.
Now, far remote, they view Pangræa's height;
Now Phillis' rising tomb attracts their sight,
And the dull round she nine times trod in vain,
To view the faithless wanderer again.
Hæmonia's meads remote, the Trojan spies
Th' Achaian cities unexpected rise:
Phthia, with heroes far renown'd replete;
Mycenæ, fam'd for many a spacious street.
Beside the meads, where Erymanthus glides,
Sparta aspires, that boasts her beauteous brides,
Sparta with joy th' expecting swain survey'd,
Lav'd by Eurotas, by Atrides sway'd.
Nor distant far, o'ershaded by a wood,
Beneath a mountain's brow Therapnæ stood.
Short was their voyage now: the bending oar
Was heard to lash the foamy surge no more.
The sailors, safe imbosom'd in the bay,
Firm to the beach confine the corded stay.
In purifying waters plung'd the swain,
And, rising thence, pac'd slowly o'er the plain.
For much he fear'd, lest his incautious tread
O'er his wash'd feet the spatter'd mire should spread;
Or lest his hair, beneath his casque confin'd,
Should, if he ran, be ruffled with the wind.
The city's splendour Paris' eye detains,
The citizens' abodes, and glistering fanes.
Here Pallas' form, in mimic gold portray'd,
Here Hyacinthus' image he survey'd.
Him with delight the Amiclæans view'd,
Pursuing Phœbus and by him pursu'd;
But, sore displeas'd at jealous Zephyr's spite,
They urg'd the stripling to unequal fight;
For Phœbus' efforts ineffectual prov'd,
To save from Zephyr's rage the youth he lov'd.
Earth with compassion heard Apollo's cries,
And from her bosom bade a flower arise,
His favourite's name, impress'd upon whose leaf,
Still, as the god contemplates, soothes his grief.
Now Priam's son before Atrides' dome
Exulting stood in beauty's purple bloom.
Not Semele, by Jove's caresses won,
On Jove bestow'd so beautiful a son:
(Forgive me, Bacchus, seed of Jove supreme)
Such peerless graces round his person beam.
Touch'd by fair Helen's hand the bolts recede;
She to the spacious hall repair'd with speed:
Her form distinct th' unfolded portals shew;
She look'd, she ponder'd, and again withdrew.
Then on a radiant seat she bade him rest,
And, still insatiate, gaz'd upon her guest.
Awhile she likens him in graceful mien
To Love, attendant on the Cyprian queen.
But 'tis not Love, she recollects again;
Nor bow nor quiver deck this gallant swain.
"'Tis Bacchus sure, the god of wine," she said;
"For o'er his cheeks a rosy bloom is spread."
Daring at length her faltering voice to raise,
She thus express'd her wonder and her praise:
  "Whence art thou, stranger? whence thy comely race?
Thy country tell me, and thy natal place.
In thee I mark the majesty of kings:
But not from Greece thy lofty lineage springs.
Not sandy Pyle thine origin can show;
I know not thee, though Nestor's son I know.
Phthia, the nurse of heroes, train'd not thee;
For known are all th' Æacidæ to me.
Peleus, and Telamon renown'd in fight,
Patroclus' courtesy, Achilles' might."

Inspir'd by love, thus spoke the gentle dame;
And he, thus answering, fann'd the rising flame:
" If e'er recording fame, illustrious maid,
Hath to thine ear great Ilion's name convey'd,
Ilion, whose walls on Phrygian frontiers stand,
Rear'd by Apollo's and by Neptune's hand;
Him if thou know'st, most opulent of kings,
Who reigns o'er Ilion, and from Saturn springs;
I to hereditary worth aspire;
The wealthy Priam is my honour'd sire.
My high descent from Dardanus I prove;
And ancient Dardanus descends from Jove.
Th' immortals thus forsake the realms of light,
And mix with mortals in the social rite.
Neptune and Phœbus thus forsook the sphere,
Firm on its base my native Troy to rear.
But know, on three fair goddesses, of late,
Sentence I pass'd, and clos'd the long debate.
On Venus, who with charms superior shone,
I lavish'd praises and conferr'd my boon.
The Cyprian goddess, pleas'd with my decree,
Reserv'd this recompence, O queen, for me;
Some faithful fair, possess'd of heavenly charms,
Should, she protested, bless my longing arms;
Helen her name, to beauty's queen ally'd;
Helen, for thee I stemm'd the troubled tide.
Unite we now in Hymen's mystic bands;
Thus love inspires, and Venus thus commands.
Scorn not my suit, nor beauty's queen despise:
More need I add to influence the wise?
For well thou know'st, how dastardly and base
Is Menelaus's degenerate race.
And well I know, that Græcia's ample coast
No fair like thee, for beauty fam'd, can boast."
He said; on earth her sparkling eyes she cast,
Embarrass'd paus'd awhile, and spoke at last:
" To visit Ilion, and her towers survey,
Rear'd by the god of ocean and of day,
(Stupendous labours by celestials wrought)
Hath oft, illustrious guest, employ'd my thought.
Oft have I wish'd to saunter o'er the vales,
Whose flowery pasture Phœbus' flocks regales;
Where, beneath Ilion's walls, along the meads,
The shepherd-god his lowing oxen feeds.
To Ilion I'll attend thee: haste, away;
For beauty's queen forbids our long delay.
No husband's threats, no husband's search I dread,
Though he to Troy suspect his Helen fled."
The Spartan dame, of matchless charms possess'd,
Proffer'd these terms to her consenting guest.
Night, which relieves our toils, when the bright Sun,
In ocean sunk, his daily course has run,
Now gives her softest slumbers, ere the ray
Of rising morn proclaims th' approach of day.
Two gates of airy dreams she opens wide;
Of polish'd horn is this, where truths abide:
Voices divine through this mysterious gate
Proclaim th' unalterable will of fate.
But through the ivory gate incessant troop
Of vain, delusive dreams a faithless group.
Helen, seduc'd from Menelaus' bed,
Th' adventurous shepherd to his navy led;
To Troy with speed he bears the fatal freight;
For Venus' proffers confidence create.
At morning's dawn Hermione appears,
With tresses discompos'd and bath'd in tears.
She rous'd her menial train; and thus express'd
The boding sorrows of her troubled breast:
" Where, fair attendants, is my mother fled,
Who left me sleeping in her lonely bed?
For yesternight she took her trusty key,
Turn'd the strong bolt, and slept secure with me."
Her hapless fate the pensive train deplore,
And in thick circles gather round the door;
Here all contend to moderate her grief,
And by their kind condolence give relief:
" Unhappy princess, check the rising tear;
Thy mother, absent now, will soon appear.
Soon as thy sorrow's bitter source she knows,
Her speedy presence will dispel thy woes.
The virgin-cheek, with sorrow's weight o'ercome,
Sinks languid down and loses half its bloom.
Deep in the head the tearful eye retires,
There sullen sits, nor darts its wonted fires.
Eager, perchance, the band of nymphs to meet,
She saunters devious from her favourite seat,
And, of some flowery mead at length possess'd,
Sinks on the dew-bespangled lawn to rest.
Or to some kindred stream perchance she strays,
Bathes in Eurotas' streams, and round its margin plays."
" Why talk ye thus?" the pensive maid replies,
The tears of anguish trickling from her eyes:
" She knows each roseate bower, each vale and hill,
She knows the course of every winding rill.
The stars are set; on rugged rocks she lies:
The stars are up; nor does my mother rise.
What hills, what dales thy devious steps detain?
Hath some relentless beast my mother slain?
But beasts, which lawless round the forest rove,
Revere the sacred progeny of Jove.
Or art thou fallen from some steep mountain's brow,
Thy corse conceal'd in dreary dells below?
But through the groves, with thickest foliage crown'd,
Beneath each shrivel'd leaf that strews the ground,
Assiduous have I sought thy corse in vain:
Why should we then the guiltless grove arraign?
But have Eurotas' streams, which rapid flow,
O'erwhelm'd thee bathing in its deeps below?
Yet in the deeps below the Naiads live,
And they to womankind protection give."
Thus spoke she sorrowing, and reclin'd her head;
And sleeping seem'd to mingle with the dead.
For Sleep his elder brother's aspect wears;
Lies mute like him, and undisturb'd by cares.
Hence the swoln eyes of females, deep distress'd,
Oft, when the tear is trickling, sink to rest.
In this delusive dream the sleeping maid
Her mother saw, or thought she saw, portray'd.
Aloud she shriek'd, distracted and amaz'd,
And utter'd thus her anguish as she gaz'd:
" Last night, far distant from your daughter fled,
You left me slumbering in my father's bed.
What dangerous steeps have not I strove to gain?
And stroll'd o'er hills and dales for thee in vain?"
" Condemn me not," replied the wandering dame;
" Pity my sufferings, nor augment my shame.
Me yesterday a lawless guest beguil'd,
And distant tore me from my darling child.
At Cytherea's high command I rove;
And once more revel in the walks of love."
She said: her voice the sleeping maid alarms;
She springs to clasp her mother in her arms.
In vain: no mother meets her wistful eyes;
And now her tears redouble and her cries:
" Ye feathery race, inhabitants of light,
To Crete's fam'd isle direct your rapid flight.

There to my sire th' unwelcome truth proclaim,
How yesterday a desperate vagrant came,
Tore all he dotes on from his bridal bed,
And with his beauteous queen abruptly fled."
The restless fair, her mother to regain,
Thus to the winds bewail'd and wept in vain.
The Thracian town diminish'd from their view,
And fleet o'er Helle's strait the vessel flew.
The bridegroom now his natal coast descry'd,
And to the Trojan port conducts his bride.
Cassandra from her tower beheld them sail,
And tore her locks, and rent her golden veil.
But hospitable Troy unbars her gate,
Receives her citizen and seals her fate.

NOTES TO THE RAPE OF HELEN.

Coluthus Lycopolites, a Theban poet, flourished in the reign of the emperor Anastasius, about five hundred years after Christ. He is said to have been the author of several poems; none of which have come down to us except this, which in many passages is corrupt and mutilated. There is an excellent edition of this poem by Lennep. There is also an old translation of it by sir Edward Sherburne; to whom I acknowledge myself indebted for some of his useful annotations.

Did the insertion of this little poem stand in need of an apology, it might be made by observing, that the subjects of the two poems are not wholly dissimilar. In the one is celebrated the rape of Medea, in the other the rape of Helen; two events of equal celebrity in ancient story.

On the title of this poem sir Edward Sherburne makes the following not unpleasant remark: "The word rape must not be taken in the common acceptation of the expression. For Paris was more courtly than to offer, and Helen more kind-hearted than to suffer, such a violence. It must be taken rather for a transporting of her with her consent from her own country to Troy: which Virgil seems to insinuate in the first book of his Æneid, where, speaking of Helen, he says,

Pergama cum peteret, ——

The word peteret implies that the quitting of her country, and going along with Paris, was an act she desired, as well as consented to; and thus much the ensuing poem makes good."

V. 2. From Xanthus' fertile streams] The most celebrated river in Troas: it derived its source from Mount Ida.

10. Clown] The ancients esteemed the art of husbandry to be of all others the most honourable. The hands of princes sustained at the same time the crook and the sceptre. Paris, the son of Priam, king of Troy, is represented in this poem under the character of a shepherd. In our times the care of flocks and herds is committed to the lowest orders of the people. Shepherd and clown are terms with us nearly synonymous. But we must endeavour to separate from them the ideas of churlishness and ill-breeding, when applied, as the ancients applied them, to heroes and kings.

24. With hymeneal songs for Peleus sung] It was a fiction of the poets, that Peleus, the son of Æacus, and pupil of Chiron, married Thetis the daughter of Nereus, and that all the gods attended at their nuptials on Mount Pelion, except Eris or Discord, in whose presence agreement and harmony could not long subsist. See on this subject Catullus de Nupt. Pel. & Thet. and Valerius Flaccus, l. i. v. 129.

42. His loose locks] The correspondent lines in the original ought to be placed after v. 33, as Lennep rightly observes: to that place (immediately after the poet's mention of Diana) the translator has restored them.

56. With desperate hand] The conjectural reading of Vossius is here preferred; as it seems to contain more sense and more poetry than any other. He reads,

—————— χειρὶ δὲ λαιῇ
Ουδὲ τὲ κόλλοπ' ἔρυξε, καὶ ἣν ἐφυράσσατο πέτρην.

79. For 'tis the prize of beauty and of love] Apples were esteemed the symbol of love, and dedicated to Venus. They were also considered as allurements of love, and were distributed as presents among lovers. Hence the expressions μηλοβολεῖν, and malo petere, in Theocritus and Virgil.

89. The close-arch'd eyebrow] The ancients looked upon such eyebrows, which our poet calls βλεφάρων συνοχὴν, as essential to form a beautiful face. See Anacreon's description of his mistress, and Theocr. Id. viii. 72.

99. Summon'd her little Loves] They were supposed to be very numerous:

——— volucrumque exercitus omnis amorum.
Val. Flac. vi. 457.

116. My bow this cestus] The cestus of Venus, of which Homer makes particular mention, Il. xiv. 216. derives its name ἀπὸ τοῦ κεντεῖν. To which stimulating quality our poet alludes in the following line,

And with this cestus I infix my sting.

205. Beauty, their best defence, their strongest mail]

——— κάλλος,
'Αντ' ἀσπίδων ἁπασῶν
'Αντ' ἐγχέων ἁπάντων. Anacr. od. xi.

267 and 268. Ismarus—Pangræa] Mountains in Thrace. The former is also the name of a lake.

269. Now Phillis' rising tomb] Demophoon, son of Theseus, on his return from Troy passed through Thrace, where he was hospitably received by Phillis, its queen, who fell in love with and married him. He having expressed his desire to visit Athens, his native country, Phillis consented to his departure, upon condition that he would return on a certain day which she should appoint. Demophoon promised to be with her on the appointed day. When the day came, Phillis, tortured with the pangs of an impatient lover, ran nine times to the shore, which from this circumstance was called in Greek Enneados: but unable any longer to support his absence, she in a fit of despair hanged herself. See Ovid's Epist. ii. Phillis to Demoph.

274. Phthia] A province and city of Thessaly; the birth-place of Achilles. But, for a more particular account of Coluthus's geography, the reader may consult Lennep's note on v. 215, where he shows, (to make use of his own words) quam fuerit in Geographicis hospes Coluthus.

296. Him with delight] Hyacinthus was a young prince of the city Amyclæ, in Laconia. He had made so extraordinary a progress in literature, that he was considered as a favourite of Apollo. As he was playing with his fellows, he was unfortunately struck on the head by a quoit, and died of the blow. The poets have enlarged on this simple story in the following manner.

The wind which blew the quoit aside, and gave it the fatal direction, they have called Zephyrus; whom they have represented as the rival of Apollo. Zephyrus, having received for his kindnesses to Hyacinthus the most ungrateful returns, was resolved to punish him for his insolence: and having challenged him one day to a game of quoits, he struck the unfortunate youth a blow on the temples.

The inhabitants of Amyclæ, says the poet,

——————— δηϊδ' ἀήτου
Σκυζόμενος, καὶ τοῦτον ἀνήγαγεν.——

were displeased with the contest proposed by Zephyrus, and withdrew Hyacinthus from the fight; or, perhaps (still better to connect this with the following sentence) they brought him out, and spirited him on to the fight, presuming that his favourite god would enable him to come off victorious;—ἀυτὰρ 'Απόλλων, &c.

This is Lennep's conjectural reading; which, whether the true one or not, must be allowed to affix a tolerable meaning to a passage that was before very unintelligible.

302. Earth with compassion] From the blood that was spilt on the ground Apollo produced a flower, called after the name of his favourite youth. See Ovid. Metam. l. x.

331. Nestor's son] Antilochus, mentioned frequently in Hom. Il.

333. Æacidæ] The descendants of Æacus. He was the son of Jupiter and Ægina: his offspring were Phocus, Peleus, Teucer, and Telamon.

390. Two gates of airy dreams she opens wide] The fiction to which our author in this place, and Virgil in Æneid vi. allude, is borrowed from b. xix. of Hom. Odyss. It is imagined, that this story of the gates of Sleep may have had a real foundation, and have been built upon the customs of the Ægyptians. See the note on v. 656, b. xix. of Pope's Odyss. Our poet has represented these fanciful gates as opened by Night; and with great propriety.

"The ancients," says sir Edward Sherburne, "painted Sleep like a man heavy with slumber, his under garment white, his upper black, thereby expressing day and night; holding in his hand a horn, sometimes really such, sometimes of ivory in the likeness of one; through which they feigned that he conveyed dreams: true when the same was of horn, false when of ivory." Some have assigned as a reason, why true dreams pass through the gate of horn, and false ones through the gate of ivory; that horn is a fit emblem of truth, as being transparent, and ivory of falsehood, as being impenetrable.

448. For Sleep his elder brother's aspect wears] Virgil, Æn. vi. 278. calls sleep consanguineus lethi.

450. Hence the swoln eyes of females] Hence, i. e. by reason of the likeness there is betwixt these two affections.

464. At Cytherea's] The line in the original is obscure, and usually misplaced. It is given to Hermione, but without the least reason. It is here restored to its proper place; and is an observation which comes naturally enough from the mouth of Helen. See Lennep's note on the passage.

482. Cassandra from her tower] Cassandra was the daughter of Priam, and priestess of Apollo. Apollo gave her the gift of prophecy; but, on her refusing to comply with the conditions on which it was given her, he rendered it ineffectual, by ordaining that her predictions should never be believed. Hence it was, that, when Paris set sail for Greece in pursuit of Helen, her prophecy, that he should bring home a flame, which should consume his country, was not regarded. Her appearance therefore on the present occasion is quite in character; and our poet has shown his judgment by the representation he has given of her.

THE

WORKS OF ANACREON.

TRANSLATED BY FAWKES.

——Propitious Muse,
While I so late unlock thy hallow'd springs,
And breathe whate'er thy ancient airs infuse,
To polish Albion's warlike ear
This long-lost melody to hear,
Thy sweetest arts employ;
As when the winds, from shore to shore,
Through Greece thy lyre's persuasive language bore,
Till towns, and isles, and seas return'd the vocal joy.

AKENSIDE ON LYRIC POETRY.

INTRODUCTION.

It may be necessary to inform the reader that many of the following odes were translated several years ago at college for the author's amusement, without any intention of making them public. But being encouraged by the partiality of friends, and allowed to insert those odes [1] of Anacreon, which are elegantly translated by the late Dr. Broome, and a few others[2]; he determined to give an entire version of the Teian bard, as no one of this nation had hitherto done it. Mr. John Addison's Translation is incomplete, and, excepting a few odes, harsh and crude, and far from being well done. What the late ingenious and learned Mr. West says of Cowley's Pindar, may be applied to his odes of Anacreon: "That they have not the least resemblance to the manner of the author whom they pretend to imitate, or, if any, 'tis such a resemblance only as is expressed by the Italian word caricatura, a monstrous and distorted likeness."

It may be thought a bold undertaking to attempt Sappho, after the high encomiums which Mr. Addison, in the Spectator, has passed on Philips's Translation of her two odes. But, with deference to the authority of so good a judge, besides what the reader will find observed with regard to Mr. Phillips's mistaking the true sense of his author, the three first lines are amazingly rough and awkward.

Blest as th' immortal gods is *he*,
The youth who fondly sits by thee,
And hears and sees thee *all the while*, &c.

It is surprising, that such unpoetical expressions, as those here marked, should escape the censure of the accurate Mr. Addison, unless we suspect that the partiality of the friend biassed the judgment of the critic.

It is equally surprising, that the beautiful Idylliums of Bion and Moschus, which charm every reader in the original, should scarce ever have been attempted in English. The translator, therefore, may justly claim some merit in endeavouring to make these elegant Greek writers speak his native language.

He cannot conclude this short introduction, without returning his thanks to an ingenious and worthy friend (whose name would do honour to the title-page) for his revisal and correction of this little work, and for those excellent translations of the Idylliums of Moschus, marked D.

[1] Dr. Broome's odes were printed in the Gentleman's Magazine, under the name of Charles Chester, M. D.

[2] Viz. Odes 2, 11, 45, 49, and 51.

THE

LIFE OF ANACREON.

ANACREON was born at Teos, a seaport town of Ionia. Who were his parents is uncertain, though it is conjectured, from good authority, that his family was noble. The time of his birth, according to Barnes, was in the second year of the 55th Olympiad, about the beginning of the reign of Cyrus, in the year of Rome 194, and 554th before Christ. According to this account, he was about eighteen years of age, when Harpagus, the general of Cyrus, came with an army against the confederate cities of the Ionians and Æolians. The Teians, finding themselves too weak to withstand the enemy, rather chose to abandon their country than their liberty, and therefore transported themselves and their families to the city of Abdera, in Thrace; where they had not been long settled, before the Thracians, jealous of their new neighbours, endeavoured to give them disturbance. It is probable, that, in these conflicts, Anacreon lost those friends whom he laments in some of his epigrams.

We cannot expect many particulars of the life of this poet, because he seems to have been a professed despiser of business, and the cares of the world. It is certain, that wine, love, and the Muse, had the disposal of all his hours.

From Abdera he went to the court of Polycrates, tyrant of Samos, at that time one of the most gay and flourishing in Asia. A person of Anacreon's character must undoubtedly meet with a welcome reception, wherever wit and pleasure were esteemed: accordingly we find, that he was so highly honoured by Polycrates, as not only to be admitted into a share of his friendship, but even into his most secret counsels. How long he continued at Samos is uncertain; but it is probable, that the friendship of Polycrates, and the splendour of his court, had influence enough to detain him there the greatest part of his reign. This opinion also seems confirmed by Herodotus, who assures us, that Anacreon was with that prince in his chamber, when he received a message from Orætes, governor of Sardis, by whose treachery Polycrates was soon after betrayed, and inhumanly crucified[1].

A little before this remarkable incident Anacreon left Samos, and removed to Athens, having been invited thither by Hipparchus, the eldest son of Pisistratus, one of the most virtuous and learned princes of his time; who, as Plato assures us, sent the most obliging letters, with a vessel of fifty oars, to convey him over the Ægean. The same philosopher who relates this, does Anacreon the honour to style him "the wise Anacreon;" which is the foundation of Monsieur Fontenelle's ingenious dialogue, where he introduces Anacreon and Aristotle disputing the prize of wisdom, and gives the advantage to our poet.

Hipparchus being assassinated, he returned to his native country, Teos; for, after the death of Cyrus, the Teians had been suffered to reinhabit their country unmolested. Here he remained, as Suidas informs us, till another commotion in the state obliged him once more to fly to Abdera; where he died in the 85th year of his age.

[1] See Universal History, vol. viii. 8vo. page 271.

The manner of his death was very extraordinary; for we are told, that he was choked with a grape stone, as he was regaling on some new wine: which has afforded Mr. Cowley a subject for a fine elegy, the conclusion of which is very happy:

It grieves me, when I see what fate
Does on the best of mankind wait,
Poets or lovers let them be;
'Tis neither love nor poesy
Can arm against Death's smallest dart
The poet's head, or lover's heart.
But when their life in its decline
Touches th' inevitable line,
All the world's mortal to them then,
And wine is aconite to men.
Nay, in Death's hand the grape-stone proves
As strong as thunder is in Jove's.

A small part only of his works has escaped the malice of time; for, besides the odes and epigrams that still remain, he composed elegies, hymns, and iämbics. Some writers honour him with the invention of the lyre. How much he was the delight both of the ancients and moderns, appears sufficiently from those extravagant praises which they have bestowed on him. Horace mentions him with honour:

Nec, si quid olim lusit Anacreon,
Delevit ætas ——— ——— Lib. iv. ode 9.

——— blithe Anacreon's sportive lay
Still lives, in spite of time's destructive sway. Duncombe.

Anacreon had a delicate genius, and there are inexpressible charms and graces in his poetry. "His chief excellence," says Madam Dacier, "consists in imitating nature, and following reason: he presents no images to the mind but what are noble and natural." "The Odes of Anacreon," says Rapin, "are flowers, beauties, and perpetual graces: it is familiar to him to write what is natural: he has an air so delicate, easy, and graceful, that, among all the ancients, there is nothing comparable to the method he took, nor to that kind of writing he followed. He flows soft and easy, every where diffusing the joy and indolence of his mind through all his compositions, and tuning his harp to the pleasant and happy temper of his soul."

But no one has given us a juster character of his writings, than that little god who inspired them, as Mr. Cowley has made him speak:

All thy verse is softer far
Than the downy feathers are
Of my wings, or of my arrows,
Of my mother's doves, or sparrows;
Graceful, cleanly, smooth, and round,
All with Venus' girdle bound.

I cannot better conclude this account of Anacreon, than with the following epitaph, as it is translated in the Spectator, No. 551.

ON ANACREON. BY ANTIPATER.

This tomb be thine, Anacreon; all around
Let ivy wreath, let flow'rets deck the ground,
And from its earth, enrich'd by such a prize,
Let wells of milk, and streams of wine arise:
So will thine ashes yet a pleasure know,
If any pleasure reach the shades below.

To which let me add a fine stanza from Dr. Akenside's Ode on Lyric Poetry, in honour of our poet.

I see Anacreon smile and sing:
His silver tresses breathe perfume;
His cheek displays a second spring
Of roses, taught by wine to bloom.
Away, deceitful cares, away!
And let me listen to his lay,
While flowery dreams my soul employ;
While, turtle-wing'd, the laughing Hours
Lead hand in hand the festal powers,
Lead Youth, and Love, and harmless Joy.

THE

ODES OF ANACREON.

TRANSLATED BY FAWKES.

With roses crown'd, on flowers supinely laid,
Anacreon blithe the sprightly lyre essay'd,
In light fantastic measures beat the ground,
Or dealt the mirth-inspiring juice around:
No care, no thought, the tuneful Teian knew,
But mark'd with bliss each moment as it flew.

PROGRESS OF POETRY. BY A LADY.

ODE I.

ON HIS LYRE.

"WAKE, O lyre, thy silent strings,
Celebrate the brother-kings,
Sons of Atreus, fam'd afar,
Cadmus and the Theban war."—
Rapt I strike the vocal shell——
Hark—the trembling chords rebel;
All averse to arms they prove,
Warbling only strains of love.
Late I strung anew my lyre——
"Heav'nly Muse my breast inspire,

Ode I.—This ode is, with great reason and propriety, placed at the head of these beautiful little poems; for love, the argument, is in a good measure the argument of all the rest—The invention of it has been esteemed so happy and gallant, and the turn so delicate, that the best masters of antiquity have copied this excellent original. Horace had it in view, Ode 12, book 2.

Nolis longa feræ bella Numantiæ,
Nec dirum Hannibalem, nec Siculum mare,
Pœno purpureum sanguine, mollibus
Aptari citharæ modis.

Dire Hannibal, the Roman dread,
Numantian wars which rag'd so long,
And seas with Punic slaughter red,
Suit not the softer lyric song.

Lord Chief Baron Gilbert.

Ovid has imitated it in several of his elegies: In the following distich he seems to have comprehended the substance of the whole ode. Eleg. 12. book 3.

Cum Thebæ, cum Troja forent, cum Cæsaris acta;
Ingenium movit sola Corinna meum.

Tho' Thebes and Troy remain, and Cæsar's praise
Illustrious themes that might my fancy raise,
Corinna only can inspire my lays.

Bion of Smyrna has beautifully imitated this ode at the end of his fourth Idyllium.

Ην μεν γαρ βροτον αλλον η αθανατον τινα μελπω,
Καμβαινει μεν γλωσσα, καὶ ὡς πα̍ρος ουκ ετ' αειδει.
Ην δ' αυτ' ες τον Ερωτα και ες Λυκιδαν τι μελισδω,
Και τοκα μοι χαιροισα δια στοματος ρεει ωδα.

To praise a hero when I strike the lyre,
Or nobly daring to some god aspire,
In strains more ianguid flows the nerveless song,
The falt'ring accents die upon my tongue;
But when with love or Lycidas I glow,
Smooth are my lays, the numbers sweetly flow.

Ver. 3. Sons of Atreus, &c.—Cadmus and the Theban war.] Agamemnon and Menelaus, the chief commanders at the siege of Troy. By the Atridæ the poet means the Trojan, and by Cadmus the Theban war.

9. Late I strung anew my lyre—] Mr. Dacier judiciously observes, in his notes on the twenty-sixth ode of the first book of Horace, that the

While the swelling notes resound
Hercules, for toils renown'd."
Still the chords rebellious prove,
Answ'ring only strains of love!
Farewel heroes, farewel kings!
Love alone shall tune my strings.

ODE II.

BY ANOTHER HAND.

ON WOMEN.

NATURE gives all creatures arms,
Faithful guards from hostile harms;
Jaws, the lion to defend,
Horrid jaws that wide distend!
Horns, the bull, resistless force!
Solid hoofs, the vig'rous horse;
Nimble feet, the fearful hare;
Wings to fly, the birds of air.

poets, when they would celebrate any extraordinary subject, were wont to say they had new-strung their lyre.

——Hunc fidibus novis,
Hunc Lesbio sacrare plectro,
Teque tuasque decet sorores.

To sound his praise, O Muse, is thine,
In concert with the tuneful Nine,
On the fam'd Lesbian lyre new-strung,
In numbers, sweet, as old Alcæus sung.

14. Answ'ring only strains of love!] The Greek Word, αντιφωνειν, is very strong and expressive, and means, "to return a contrary sound." To understand this passage clearly, we must imagine that Anacreon is singing and playing upon the lyre, which, instead of answering to his voice in heroic numbers, returned only the sounds of love. Tibullus has a similar expression, Eleg. 4. book 3.

Tunc ego nec cithara poteram gaudere sonora,
Nec similes chordis reddere voce sonos.

No more I tun'd the loud resounding string,
Nor to the lyre's sweet melody could sing.

15. Farewel heroes, &c.]

——Heroum clara valete
Nomina, non apta est gratia vestra mihi.
Ovid, Eleg. 1. book 2.

Ye heroes of immortal fame, adieu!
Ill suits the warbling of my lyre with you.

Ode II.—Phocylides has copied a great part of this ode in his admonitory poem:

Ὁπλον ἑκαστῳ νειμε Θεος φυσιν· ηεροφοιτον
Ορνισι μεν πολλην ταχυτητ', αλκην τε λεουσι,
Ταυροις δ' αυτοχυτοις κεραεσσιν, κεντρα μελισσαις
Εμφυτον αλκαρ εδωκε· λογοι δ' ερυμ' ανθρωποισι.

Arms to all creatures God's abundant care
Affords; light pinions to the birds of air;
The lordly lion boasts his matchless might;
The bull's bright horns are terrible in fight;
The sting sharp-pointed is the bee's defence;
The shield and buckler of mankind is sense.

Fins to swim, the watery kind;
Man, the bold, undaunted mind.
Nature lavishing her store,
What for woman had she more?
Helpless woman! To be fair;
Beauty fell to woman's share.
She that's beauteous need not fear
Sword, or flame, or shield, or spear.
Beauty stronger aid affords,
Stronger far than flames or swords,
Stronger far than swords or shields;
Man himself to beauty yields.

ODE III.

CUPID BENIGHTED.

THE sable night had spread around
This nether world a gloom profound;

10. Man, the bold undaunted mind.] The Greek word φρονημα generally signifies prudence; and so Stephens has translated it: but as it would be highly absurd to suppose that Nature had forgot that useful ingredient in the composition of the ladies, we must look out for another interpretation. Φρονημα equally signifies magnanimity. It is similar to an expression of Tully, in Off. 1. 19.—Elatio & magnitudo animi: and as Mr. John Addison, in his note on this passage, observes: "By courage, when applied to man, is properly meant that superiority of mind, which is man's peculiar characteristic and charter of dominion."

14. Beauty fell to woman's share.] Coluthus, in his poem of the Rape of Helen, has the same thought, speaking of Venus:

Μουνη Κυπρις αναλκις εην θεος ου βασιληιων
Κοιρανιην, ουδ' εγχος αρηιον, ου βελος ἑλκω·
Αλλο τι δειμαινω πτεριωστιον; αντι μεν αιχμης,
Ως θοον εγχος εχουσα μελιφρονα δεσμον ερωτων.

Of all the gods, no regal sway I bear,
Nor, weak and timid, wield the martial spear;
Yet great my pow'r, for my resistless darts
Are smiles and loves that triumph over hearts.

And a little further,

Εργα μοθων ουκ οιδα· τι γαρ σακεων Αφροδιτη;
Αγλαιη πολυ μαλλον αριστευουσι γυναικες.

No fights I know, averse to war's alarms;
Idalian Venus has no need of arms:
The fair are irresistible in charms.

Nonnus introduces Venus speaking in the same manner:

Εγχος εμον πελε καλλος, εμον ξιφος επλετο μορφη.

Resistless beauty for a sword I wear, [spear.
And charms more piercing than the pointed

The Romans were so fully convinced of the power of beauty, that the word fortis, strong or valiant, signifies likewise fair or handsome; as appears by two passages in Plautus.—Bacchid. act. 2. scen. 2. 38. Sed Bacchis etiam tibi fortis visa est? Et Miles Glor. act. 4. scen. 3. 13. Ecquid fortis visa est?

Ode III.—This, as Longepierre observes, is one of the most beautiful of Anacreon's odes. Nothing

No silver moon nor stars appear,
And strong Boötes urg'd the Bear:
The race of man, with toils opprest,
Enjoy'd the balmy sweets of rest;
When from the heav'nly court of Jove
Descended swift the god of love,
(Ah me! I tremble to relate)
And loudly thunder'd at my gate.
"Who's there? I cry'd. Who breaks my door
At this unseasonable hour?"
The god, with well-dissembled sighs,
And moan insidious, thus replies:
"Pray ope the door, dear sir——'tis I,
A harmless, miserable boy;
Benumb'd with cold and rain I stray
A long uncomfortable way—
The winds with blust'ring horrour roar—
'Tis dismal dark—Pray ope the door."
Quite unsuspicious of a foe
I listen'd to the tale of woe,
Compassion touch'd my breast, and straight
I struck a light, unbarr'd the gate;
When, lo! a winged boy I spy'd
With bow and quiver at his side:
I wonder'd at his strange attire;
Then friendly plac'd him near the fire.
My heart was bounteous and benign,
I warm'd his little hands in mine,
Cheer'd him with kind assiduous care,
And wrung the water from his hair.
Soon as the fraudful youth was warm,
"Let's try," says he, "if any harm
Has chanc'd my bow this stormy night;
I fear the wet has spoil'd it quite."
With that he bent the fatal yew,
And to the head an arrow drew;
Loud twang'd the sounding string, the dart
Pierc'd thro' my liver and my heart.
Then laugh'd amain the wanton boy,
And, "Friend," he cry'd, "I wish thee joy;
Undamag'd is my bow, I see,
But what a wretch I've made of thee!"

ODE IV.

ON HIMSELF.

Reclin'd at ease on this soft bed
With fragrant leaves of myrtle spread
And flow'ry lote, I'll now resign
My cares, and quaff the rosy wine.
In decent robe, behind him bound,
Cupid shall serve the goblet round:
For fast away our moments steal,
Like the swift chariot's rolling wheel:
The rapid course is quickly done,
And soon the race of life is run;
Then, then, alas! we droop, we die,
And sunk in dissolution lie;
Our frame no symmetry retains;
Nought but a little dust remains.

can be more ingenious than the fiction, which is something similar to the fable of the Serpent and Labourer.

4. And strong Boötes urg'd the Bear:] Two constellations near the northern pole. Boötes is also called Arctophylax, or the Bear-keeper. Aratus, in his Phænomena, has three lines perfectly similar to this passage of Anacreon:

Εξοπιθεν δ' Ελικης φερεται ελαοντι εοικως,
Αρκτοφυλαξ, τον ῥ' ανδρες επικλειουσι Βοωτην,
Ουνεκ' αμαξαιης επαφωμενος ειδεται Αρκτου.

Behind, and seeming to urge on the Bear,
Arctophylax, on Earth Boötes nam'd,
Sheds o'er the arctic car his silver light.

40. Pierc'd thro' my liver] The ancients placed the seat of love in the liver, as might be proved from several passages.

Cum tibi fervens amor et libido,
Quæ solet matres furiare equorum,
Sæviet circa jecur ulcerosum.
Hor. b. 1. ode 2.

And burning love and loathsome lust,
Such as the madding fillies fires,
Still in thy canker'd liver rage.
Duncombe.

Theocrit. Idyll. 11, ver. 16.

—το οἱ ἡπατι παξε βελεμνον.

—She in his liver fix'd a dart.

And in the thirteenth Idyll. ver. 71. speaking of Hercules, he says,

——Χαλεπος γαρ εσω θεος ἡπαρ αμυσσεν.

For in his liver Love had fix'd a wound.

There is an epigram in the seventh book of the Anthologia, to the same purpose.

Ληξον, Ερως, κραδιης τε και ἡπατος. ει δ' επιθυμεις
Βαλλειν, αλλο τι μου των μελεων μεταβα.

Cease, Love, to wound my liver and my heart:
If I must suffer, choose some other part.

Ode IV.—2. With fragrant leaves of myrtle spread, &c.] Madame Dacier observes, that the ancients, by way of indulgence, used to repose themselves on large heaps of fragrant herbs, leaves, and flowers.

7.—For fast away our moments steal,
Like the swift chariot's rolling wheel.]

Seneca, in his Hercules Furens, act 1. scene 2. ver. 177. has the same sentiment.

——Properat cursu
Vita citato, volucrique die
Rota præcipitis vertitur anni.

With rapid motion, never at a stay,
Life swiftly posts along, and, day by day,
The year's great wheel incessant rolls away.

14. Nought but a little dust remains.] Anthologia, book 7.

Εν ζωοισι τα τερπνα τα Κυπριδος εν δ' Αχεροντι
Οστεα και σποδιη, παρθενε, κεισομεθα.

Phyllis, while living, let us life employ
In the soft transports of Idalian joy;
For when we die, (and die, alas! we must)
All that remains is ashes, bones, or dust.

Nos ubi decidimus
Quo pius Æneas, quo Tullus dives, et Ancus,
Pulvis et umbra sumus. Hor.

Why on the tomb are odours shed?
Why pour'd libations to the dead?
To me, far better, while I live,
Rich wines and balmy fragrance give;
Now, now, the rosy wreath prepare,
And hither call the lovely fair.
Now, while I draw my vital breath,
Ere yet I lead the dance of death,
For joy my sorrows I'll resign,
And drown my cares in rosy wine.

But to the dreary realms below
Who sink, must no return for ever know!
Inroll'd among the mighty dead,
Our body will be dust, our soul a shade.
Duncombe.

15.—Why on the tomb are odours shed?
Why pour'd libations to the dead?]

There are two epigrams in the second book of the Anthologia, very similar to this passage of Anacreon:

Και πινε, και τερπνυ, Δημοκρατες· υ γαρ ες αιει
Πιομεθ', υδ' αιει τερψιος ἑξομεθα.
Και ςεφανυς κεφαλας πυκασωμεθα, και μυρισωμεν
Αυτυς, πριν τυμβοις ταυτα φερειν ἑτερυς.
Νυν εν εμοι πιετω μεθυ το πλεον οςεα τἀμα.
Νεκρα δε Δευκαλιων αυτα κατακλυσατω.

Drink and rejoice; for let us wisely think,
My friend, we must not always laugh and drink:
Our heads we'll crown with flow'rs and rich perfumes
Before they're vainly lavish'd on our tombs.
Cares and anxieties I now resign,
Or drown them in a mighty bowl of wine.
When dead, Deucalion may, if he thinks good,
Drench my cold carcase in a watery flood.

Μη μυρα, μη ςεφανυς λιθιναις ςηλαισι χαριζυ,
Μηδε το πυρ φλεξης· εις κενον ἡ δαπανη.
Ζωντι μοι, ειτι θελεις χαρισαι.

On the cold tombs no fragrant unguents shed,
No flow'ry chaplets unavailing spread,
Nor kindle living lamps to light the dead.
Vain are these honours; rather while I live,
To me the sweet, the rich oblation give.

Of these customs of the ancients, of pouring sweet unguents on the tombs of the dead, and crowning them with flowers, &c. see Potter's Antiquities.

22. Ere yet I lead the dance of death,] The ancients believed, that happy souls in the Elysian Fields enjoyed those pleasures which they most delighted in when living. Thus Virgil,

Pars pedibus plaudunt choreas, & carmina dicunt.

Those raise the song divine, and these advance
In measur'd steps to form the solemn dance.
Pitt.

Tibullus, book 1. eleg. 3.

Sed me, quod facilis tenero sum semper amori,
Ipsa Venus campos ducet in Elysios:
Hic choreæ, cantus vigent, &c.

Then Love my ghost (for Love I still obey'd)
Will grateful usher to th' Elysian shade:
There joy and ceaseless revelry prevail,
There soothing music floats on ev'ry gale;
There painted warblers hop from spray to spray,
And, wildly pleasing, swell the gen'ral lay:
There ev'ry hedge untaught with cassia blooms,
And scents the ambient air with rich perfumes:
There ev'ry mead a various plenty yields;
There lavish Flora paints the purple fields;
With ceaseless light a brighter Phœbus glows,
No sickness tortures, and no ocean flows:
But youths associate with the gentle fair,
And stung with pleasure to the shade repair:
With them Love wanders wheresoe'er they stray,
Provokes to rapture, and inflames the play:
But chief the constant few, by death betray'd,
Reign, crown'd with myrtle, monarchs of the shade.
Grainger.

I hope the reader will not think this quotation tedious, as the passage is admirably translated, and contains a beautiful description of Elysium.

ODE V.

ON THE ROSE.

To make the beverage divine,
Mingle sweet roses with the wine;
Delicious will the liquor prove,
For roses are the flowers of love:
And while with wreaths of roses crown'd,
Let laughter and the cup go round.
Hail, lovely rose! to thee I sing,
Thou sweetest daughter of the Spring;
All mortals prize thy beauties bright;
In thee the pow'rs above delight.
Gay Cupid, with the Graces bland,
When lightly bounding hand in hand,
With nimble feet he beats the ground,
Shows his bright locks with roses crown'd.
Here then the flow'ry garland bring;
With numbers sweet I'll wake the string,
And crown'd with roses, heav'nly flow'rs!
Admitted, Bacchus, to thy bow'rs,
With snowy-bosom'd Sappho gay
I'll dance the feather'd hours away.

Ode V.—The Grecians esteemed the rose more than any other flower, and admitted it to all their entertainments; of which there needs no other proof than this ode of Anacreon, and likewise the fifty-third, where he praises this beautiful flower with the greatest address and delicacy. The Romans equally valued it. Horace says,

Huc vina et unguenta, et nimium breves
Flores amœnæ ferre jube rosæ.

Here wine, and oil, and roses bring,
Too short-liv'd daughters of the Spring.
Duncombe.

His complaint of the shortness of the rose's duration is an artful and delicate manner of praising that flower.

5. And while with wreaths of roses crown'd,] The ancients used wreaths of flowers and perfumes, at their entertainments, not only for pleasure, but because they imagined that odours prevented the wine from intoxicating them.

ODE VI.

THE PARTY OF PLEASURE.

While roses round our temples twine,
We'll gaily quaff the sparkling wine:
And, lo! the love-alluring fair
Her thyrsus brandishes in air,
With clust'ring ivy wreath'd around
Whose branches yield a rustling sound;
With graceful ease her steps she suits
To notes of soft Ionian lutes.
A youth, whose hair luxuriant flows
In curls, with breath ambrosial blows
The well-pair'd pipes, and, sweetly clear,
Pours melting music on the ear.
Here Cupid too with golden hair,
And Bacchus ever young and fair,
With Cytherea, who inspires
Delightful thoughts and warm desires,
Gay-smiling join the festive train,
And make an old man young again.

Ode VI.—This ode, in the original, bears the same title as the former, Εις ροδον, On the Rose. But, as it is universally agreed to be a mistake of the copyists, the editors of Anacreon have given it various appellations. Barnes calls it Κωμος, which he translates Festivitas amatoria, The Festival of Love. Dr. Trapp entitles it Συμποσιον, Convivium, The Banquet. Madame Dacier would have it called The Masquerade. But I agree with Longepierre, who thinks it ought to be styled The Party of Pleasure.

4. Her thyrsus brandishes in air,] The thyrsus was a spear encircled with wreaths of ivy, and sometimes vine-leaves. It was used as a weapon by those who attended the revels of Bacchus.

10. With breath ambrosial blows.] Mr. Longepierre quotes a most beautiful epigram from the seventh book of the Anthologia, near the end, similar to this passage; which, I think, cannot have justice done it in an English translation:

Κουρη τις μ' εφιλησε ποθεσπερα χειλεσιν ὑγροις·
Νεκταρ εην το φιλημα· το γαρ στομα νεκταρος επνει.
Νυν μεθυω το φιλημα, πολυν τον ερωτα πεπωκως.

Phyllis the gay, in robe of beauty drest,
Late on my lips a humid kiss imprest;
The kiss was nectar which the fair bestow'd,
For in her am'rous breath a gale of nectar flow'd.
What love, ye gods! what raptures in her kiss!
My soul was drunk with ecstacy of bliss.

12. Pours melting music on the ear.] Προχεων λιγειαν ομφην, pouring a liquid sound. The expression is very delicate. Horace has something like it, ode 24. b. 1.

Cui liquidam Pater vocem cum cithara dedit.

Who shar'st from Jove the melting voice and lyre. Duncombe.

14. Bacchus ever young and fair,] The ancient poets always represented Bacchus young and beautiful. So Ovid Metam. b. 4. v. 17.

———Tibi enim inconsumpta juventas,
Tu puer æternus, tu formosissimus alto
Conspiceris cœlo: tibi, cum sine cornibus adstas,
Virgineum caput est———

To thee eternity of youth is giv'n;
Unrival'd in thy bloom thou shin'st in Heav'n:
Conceal thy horns, and ev'ry charming grace
Of virgin beauty brightens in thy face.

ODE VII.

THE POWER OF LOVE.

Love, waving awful in his hand
His hyacinth-encircled wand,
Forc'd me, averse, with him to run;
In vain I strove the task to shun.
Swift o'er the plain our course we ply'd,
Thro' foaming floods, o'er forests wide,
O'er hills where rocks impending hung,
Till me, alas! a serpent stung:
Sore heav'd my heart with dire dismay,
My spirits sunk—I dy'd away—
Pleas'd Cupid caught my trembling hand,
My face with his soft pinions fann'd,
And cry'd, "Since now my pow'r you prove,
Dare you still boast, you will not love?"

ODE VIII.

THE DREAM.

As on a purple bed supine,
Rapt in the pleasing joys of wine,
I lull'd my weary limbs to rest,
Methought, with nymphs supremely blest,

Ode VII.—2. His hyacinth-encircled wand,] Madame Dacier and Barnes thought, ὑακινθινη might signify the colour of the wand or rod; but as the hyacinth is no where described to be of any determined colour, the interpretation will not hold good. The thought is poetical, and worthy of Anacreon, to suppose Cupid's wand adorned with little wreaths of that delicate flower tied round it. Or perhaps, by ὑακινθινη ραβδω the poet meant only a single hyacinth; for ραβδος may signify the stalk or stem of a flower: and then the moral of this charming ode will latently inculcate the irresistible force of Love, in whose hands a flower is as powerful as his bow, and arrows that are tipt with fire.

A late right reverend author, much admired for the elegance of his writings, seems to have had an eye to this ode when he composed the following lines on a fan:

Flavia the least and slightest toy
Can with resistless art employ:
This fan, in meaner hands, would prove
An engine of small force in love;
Yet she, with graceful air and mien,
Not to be told, or safely seen,
Directs its wanton motions so,
That it wounds more than Cupid's bow;
Gives coolness to the matchless dame,
To ev'ry other breast a flame.

8. Till me, alas! a serpent stung:] His being stung by a serpent, as Madame Dacier observes, was to punish his insensibility, and to show that Love, if he would submit to his dominion, would ake him under his protection.

A beauteous band, I urg'd the chase,
Contending in the rapid race;
While fairest youths, with envy stung,
Fair as Lyæus ever young,
With jealous leer, and bitter jest,
Their keen malevolence exprest.
Intent on love, I strive to greet
The gamesome girls with kisses sweet,
And, as on pleasure's brink I seem,
Wake, and, behold! 'tis all a dream.
Vex'd to be thus alone in bed,
My visionary charmers fled,
To dream once more I close my eyes;
Again, ye soft illusions, rise!

ODE IX.

THE DOVE.

"Tell me, dear, delightful dove,
Emblematic bird of love,
On your wavering wings descending,
Whence you come, and whither tending?

Ode VIII.—8. Fair as Lyæus ever young,] Lyæus was a name given to Bacchus. It is derived from the word λυειν to loose or free, because wine frees the mind from anxieties.

15. Vex'd to be thus alone in bed,
My visionary charmers fled, &c.]

Madame Dacier commends the delicacy and beauty of this ode, though in her translation all the spirit evaporates: the two last lines,

Μεμονωμενος δ' ὁ τλημων Παλιν ηθελον καθευδειν.

Thus miserably left alone, I wish'd to sleep again;

she has rendered thus: Etant donc tout triste de me voir ainsi demeure seul, je ne trouvai point de meilleure consolation, que de me remettre à dormir. There are some beautiful lines in Ovid's Epistle of Sappho to Phaon, as Mr. Pope has taught her to speak, which will elucidate this passage of Anacreon.

O night more pleasing than the brightest day,
When fancy gives what absence takes away,
And drest in all its visionary charms,
Restores my fair deserter to my arms!
But when with day the sweet delusions fly,
And all things wake to life and joy, but I,
As if once more forsaken, I complain,
And close my eyes, to dream of you again.

Ode IX.—Faber says of this ode, that it does not seem to be the work of one man only, but that the Graces joined in concert with the Muses to finish this beautiful little piece.

To understand it properly we must remember, that it was a custom among the ancients, when they undertook long journeys, and were desirous of sending back any news with uncommon expedition, to take tame pigeons along with them. When they thought proper to write to their friends, they let one of these birds loose, with letters fastened to its neck: the bird, once released, would never cease its flight till it arrived at its nest and young ones. The same custom still obtains among the Turks, and in several eastern countries.

Tell me whence your snowy plumes
Breathe such fragrance of perfumes?
And what master you obey,
Gentle bird of Venus, say!"
"Blithe Anacreon, the wise,"
Thus the feather'd page replies,
"Sends me o'er the meads and groves
To Bathyllus whom he loves,
To Bathyllus, beauteous boy,
Men's delight, and maidens' joy.
For a sonnet terse and trim,
Which the poets call a hymn,
Venus, in her sweet regard,
Sold me to the gentle bard:
Happy in his easy sway,
All his mandates I obey;
Often through the fields of air
Song or billet-doux I bear.
'If you serve me well,' says he,
'I will shortly make you free.'
He may free me, if he will,
Yet I'll stay and serve him still:

Longepierre has a quotation from Ælian, book 6. chap. 7. which proves that the crow, Κορωνη, was sometimes employed in this office. The passage may be thus translated: "In Egypt, near the lake Myris, the natives show the monument of a crow, of which they give the following account: That it was brought up by one of their kings called Marrhes, whose epistles it carried, wheresoever he pleased, with greater expedition than the swiftest of his messengers: that, when he gave his orders, it immediately understood which way to direct its flight, through what country to pass, and where to stop. To recompense these services, when it died, Marrhes honoured it with a monument and an epitaph."

6. Breathe such fragrance of perfumes?] The Greeks perfumed their birds, as we perfume our lap-dogs. Madame Dacier.

12. To Bathyllus whom he loves,] Bathyllus was a young Samian of great beauty, and admired by Anacreon. See ode 29th. Horace has taken notice of this passion:

Non aliter Samio dicunt arsisse Bathyllo
Anacreonta Teium,
Qui persæpe cavâ testudine flevit amorem,
Non elaboratum ad pedem. Epod. 14.

Such was the fate Anacreon proved,
So fondly he Bathyllus lov'd,
Accustom'd his complaints to suit
In easy measures to the lute. Duncombe.

This youth was also a favourite of Polycrates, who erected a statue to him that represented Apollo playing upon the lyre.

15, 16. For a sonnet terse and trim,
Which the poets call a hymn, &c.]

The poet could not pay himself a more delicate compliment, than by saying, that Venus, the mother of the Graces, was glad to purchase a little hymn of his composing at the price of one of her favourite doves. This passage is a proof, that Anacreon wrote hymns in honour of the gods; which are all lost, except, perhaps, part of the 50th and 52d odes to Bacchus, the 58th to Cupid, the 60th to Diana, and the 64th to Apollo. The 62d ode is also an hymeneal hymn.

For what comfort can I know
On the mountain's barren brow?
Or in deserts left alone,
There to murmur and to moan?
Or in melancholy wood,
Pecking berries, nauseous food!
Now I eat delicious bread,
By my liberal master fed;
Now I drink, of his own bowl,
Rosy wine that cheers my soul;
Sometimes dance, and sometimes play,
Ever easy, ever gay;
Or my fragrant pinions spread,
Hovering o'er my master's head:
When my limbs begin to tire,
Then I perch upon his lyre;
Soothing sounds my eyelids close,
Sweetly lulling my repose.
"Now I've told you all I know,
Friend, adieu——'tis time to go;
You my speed so long delay,
I have chatter'd like a jay."

ODE X.

CUPID IN WAX.

A RUSTIC brought, of curious mould,
A waxen Cupid to be sold:
"What price," I cry'd, "ingenuous say,
For this small image shall I pay?"
"Small is the price," reply'd the clown,
"Take it, e'en take it at your own:
To tell you all without a lie,
I make no images, not I;
But dare not in my mansion trust
This patron of unbounded lust."
"If so, then for this little coin,"
Said I, "the deity is mine."
And now, great god, my breast inspire,
There kindle all thy gentle fire:
But, if thou fail'st to favour me,
I swear I'll make a fire of thee.

35. Now I drink, of his own bowl,
Rosy wine, &c.]

The dove praises the liberality of his master for admitting him to drink of the same wine as himself; which was an indulgence the ancients never allowed to any but their favourites. Thus Homer introduces Achilles entertaining Ajax, Ulysses, and Phœnix, Iliad 9. ver. 202.

With that the chiefs beneath his roof he led,
And plac'd in seats with purple carpets spread.
Then thus—"Patroclus, crown a larger bowl,
Mix purer wine, and open every soul.
Of all the warriors yonder host can send,
Thy friend most honours these, and these thy friend." Pope.

Ode X.—The commentators observe, that Anacreon makes this young countryman speak in the Doric dialect, which was the most rustic, to ridicule the unpoliteness of a person who could be so insensible of the charms of Love, as to wish to part with his images.

11. If so, then for this little coin,] In the Greek, the price offered is a drachm, an Attic coin, value about sevenpence halfpenny English.

16. I swear I'll make a fire of thee.] Barnes observes, that it was usual for the ancient heathens to treat the images of their gods well or ill, just as they fancied they had been used by them. The modern Indians chastise their idols with scourges, whenever any calamity befalls them. There is a passage in the seventh Idyllium of Theocritus similar to this of our poet, where a person, after having made his supplication to the god Pan, pleasantly enough threatens him:

Ει δ' αλλως νευσαις, κατα μεν χροα παντ' ονυχεσσι
Δακνομενος κνασαιο, κ. τ. λ.

But may'st thou, if thou dar'st my boon deny,
Torn by fell claws on beds of netties lie;
All the cold winter freeze beneath the pole,
Where Heber's waves down Edon's mountains roll;
And in the scorching heats of summer glow,
Where under Blemyan rocks Nile's boiling waters flow.

ODE XI.

BY ANOTHER HAND.

ON HIMSELF.

OFT, with wanton smiles and jeers,
Women tell me, I'm in years;
I, the mirror when I view,
Find, alas! they tell me true;
Find my wrinkled forehead bare,
And regret my falling hair;

Ode XI.—That natural facility of thought, and that sweet simplicity of expression, which are so deservedly admired in the writings of Anacreon, abound in the original of this beautiful ode. Horace gives us his true character, when he tells us he wrote, non elaboratum ad pedem, in unlaboured verse; verse that flows with so much ease, that it seems to have cost him no care or trouble. He played upon his lyre, and the numbers came; therefore he says of him in another place:

Nec, si quid olim lusit Anacreon,
Delevit ætas——— Hor. L. 4. Od. 9.

——and blithe Anacreon's sportive lay
Still lives, in spite of time's destructive sway.
Duncombe.

We have an imitation of this ode in an epigram of Palladas in the 47th chapter of the 2d book of the Anthologia.

Γηραλεον με γυναικες αποσκωπτουσι, λεγοντες
Εις το κατοπτρον ὁραν λειψανον ἡλικιης.
Αλλ' εγω ει λευκας φορεω τριχας, ειτε μελαινας,
Ουκ αλεγω, βιοτου προς τελος ερχομενος·
Ευοδμοις δε μυροισι. και ευπεταλοις στεφανοισι,
Και βρομιῳ παυω φροντιδας αργαλεας.

To me the wanton girls insulting say,
"Here in this glass thy fading bloom survey:"
Just on the verge of life, 'tis equal quite,
Whether my locks are black, or silver-white;
Roses around my fragrant brows I'll twine,
And dissipate anxieties in wine.

6. And regret my falling hair;] The hair was always esteemed by the ancients the principal ornament of beauty. Apuleius has this remark-

White, and few, alas! I find
All that time has left behind.
But my hairs, if thus they fall,
If but few, or none at all,
Asking not, I'll never share
Fruitless knowledge, fruitless care.
This important truth I know,
If indeed in years I grow,
I must snatch what life can give;
Not to love, is not to live.

ODE XII.

ON A SWALLOW.

SAY, chattering bird, that dar'st invade
My slumbers with thy serenade,
And steal'st my visionary bliss,
How shall I punish thee for this?
Say, shall I clip thy soaring wing;
Or, like stern Tereus, Thracian king,
To swallows name of dire dismay,
Tear by the roots thy tongue away?
For, with thy execrable scream,
Thou wak'st me from a golden dream,
And from my arms hast snatch'd away
Phyllis the fair, the young, the gay.

able passage in the second book of his Milesiacs: "Even Venus herself, if she was destitute of hair, though surrounded by the Graces and Loves, would not have charms to please her own husband Vulcan." Longepierre quotes a passage from Petronius, where Eumolpus calls the hair the chief grace of beauty:

Quod summum formæ decus, cecidere capilli,
  Vernantesque comas tristis abegit hyems.
Nunc umbrâ nudata suâ jam tempora mœrent,
  Areaque attritis nidet adusta pilis.
O fallax natura deûm! quæ prima dedisti
  Ætati nostræ gaudia, prima rapis.
Infelix modo crinibus nitebas
Phœbo pulchrior, & sorore Phœbi:
At nunc lævior ære, vel rotundo
Horti tubere, quod creavit unda,
Ridentes fugis & times puellas.
Ut mortem citius venire credas,
Scito jam capitis perîsse partem.

Fall'n is thy hair, for woeful winter hoar
Has stol'n thy bloom, and beauty is no more;
Thy temples mourn their shady honours shorn,
Parch'd like the fallow, destitute of corn.
Fallacious gods! whose blessings can betray;
What first ye give us, first ye take away.
Thou, late exulting in thy golden hair,
As bright as Phœbus, or as Cynthia fair,
Now view'st, alas! thy forehead smooth and plain
As the round fungus, daughter of the rain;
Smooth as the surface of well-polish'd brass,
And fly'st with fear each laughter-loving lass.
Death hastes amain; thy wretched fate deplore;
Fall'n is thy hair, and beauty is no more.

Ode XII.—6. Or, like stern Tereus, &c.] The poet very judiciously endeavours to terrify the swallow with the mention of Tereus, whose palace, as the ancients have remarked, was carefully avoided by those birds. Pliny says, Arx regum Thraciæ, a Terei nefasto crimine invisa hirundinibus. See also Solinus. From this passage of Anacreon it should seem, that Philomela was changed into a swallow, and not Progne, as Ovid and others have asserted.

10. Thou wak'st me from a golden dream,
  And from my arms hast snatch'd away
  Phyllis the fair, the young, the gay.]

Madame Dacier says, that this passage, and another in the eighth ode——

Intent on love, I strive to greet
The gamesome girls with kisses sweet,
And, as on pleasure's brink I seem,
Wake, and, behold! 'tis all a dream.

undoubtedly furnished Horace with that beautiful sentiment in the first ode of the fourth book:

  Nocturnis te ego somniis
Jam captum teneo; jam volucrem sequor
  Te per gramina Martii
Campi, te per aquas, dure, volubiles.

Which Mr. Pope has most admirably imitated:

  Thee, dress'd in fancy's airy beam,
Absent I follow through th' extended dream;
  Now, now I seize, I clasp thy charms,
And now you burst (ah cruel!) from my arms;
  And swiftly shoot along the Mall,
Or softly glide by the Canal,
  Now shorn by Cynthia's silver ray,
And now on rolling waters snatch'd away.

Argentarius imitates this passage in an epigram, in the first book of the Anthologia, which begins,

Ορνι, τι μοι φιλον ὑπνον αφηρπασας; ἡδυ δε Πυῤῥης;
  Ειδωλον κοιτης ῳχετ' αποπταμενον.

Invidious swallow, with thy horrid scream
Why hast thou wak'd me from so sweet a dream?
Stunn'd by thy noise fair Pyrrha, like the wind,
Flew from my arms, just yielding to be kind.

Agathias has also imitated it in an epigram, in the seventh book of the Anthologia.

Πασαν εγω την νυκτα κινυρομαι· ευτε δ' επελθῃ
  Ορθρος, εληνυσαι μικρα χαριζομενος.
Αμφιπεριτρυζουσι χελιδονις· ες δε με δακρυ
  Βαλλουσι, γλυκερον κωμα παρωσαμεναι.
Ω φθονεραι παυσασθε λαλητριδες· ου γαρ εγωγε
  Την φιλομηλειαν γλωσσαν απεθρισαμην.
Αλλ' Ιτυλον κλαιοιτε κατ' ουρεα, και γοαοιτε
  Εις αιπος, κραναην αυλιν εφεζομεναι,
Βαιον ἱνα κνωσσοιμεν· ισως δε τις ἡξει ονειρος
  Ὁς με Ροδανθειοις πηχεσιν αμφιβαλοι.

All night I sigh, with cares of love opprest:
And when the morn indulges balmy rest,
These twittering birds their noisy matins keep,
Recal my sorrows, and prevent my sleep.
Cease, envious birds, your plaintive tales to tell,
I ravish'd not the tongue of Philomel.
In deserts wild, or on some mountain's brow,
Pay all the tributary grief you owe
To Itys, in an elegy of woe.
Me leave to sleep: in visionary charms
Some dream perhaps may bring Rodanthe to my arms.

ODE XIII.

ON ATYS.

As o'er the mountains, o'er the plains,
Unmanly Atys, in loud strains
Great Cybele invoking, mourn'd,
His love to sudden madness turn'd.
  Some to the Clarian fountain throng
Of laurel'd Phœbus, god of song,
And with prophetic draughts inspir'd,
Enraptur'd rave, with frenzy fir'd;
I too, inspir'd with generous wine,
While round me breathe perfumes divine,
And with fair Chloe blest, will prove
The sweetest madness—wine and love.

ODE XIV.

LOVE IRRESISTIBLE.

Yes, I yield—thy sovereign sway,
Mighty Cupid, I'll obey.
Late with soft persuasive art
Love essay'd to win my heart:
I, inflam'd with rebel pride,
His omnipotence defy'd——
With revengeful fury stung,
Straight his bow he bent, he strung,
Snatch'd an arrow wing'd for flight,
And provok'd me to the fight:
I, disdaining base retreat,
Clad in radiant arms complete,
Like Achilles, boldly wield
Glittering spear, and ample shield;
Thus equipt, resolve to prove
The terrific power of Love.
  From his bow the arrows sped;
I, alas! inglorious fled——
When the quiver at his side
Feather'd shafts no more supply'd,
Love, transform'd into a dart,
Pierc'd, like lightning, thro' my heart,

Ode XIII.—2. Umanly Atys,] A young Phrygian of great beauty, beloved by Cybele the mother of the gods, who made him her priest, on condition that he should live chaste: but he broke his vow, and, as a punishment, she afflicted him with madness; in the transports of which he deprived himself of the distinction of his sex, and would have killed himself, had not Cybele, moved with compassion, transformed him into a pinetree.

5. Some to the Clarian fountain throng] Claros was a city of Ionia near Colophon, rendered famous for a fountain consecrated to Apollo, who from thence was called Clarius. Tacitus gives an account of it in the second book of his Annals, where, speaking of Germanicus, he says, Appellitque Colophona, ut Clarii Apollinis oraculo uteretur. Non femina illic, ut apud Delphos; sed certis è familiis, & ferme Mileto accersitus sacerdos, numerum modo consultantium & nomina audit: tum in specum degressus, hausta fontis arcani aquâ, ignarus plerumque literarum & carminum, edit responsa versibus compositis super rebus quas quis mente concepit. "He landed at Colophon, to consult the oracle of Apollo at Claros. The person that delivers the oracles there is not a woman, as at Delphos, but a man selected out of certain families, and frequently from Miletus. This priest only inquires the number and names of those that consult the deity. After that, having entered his grotto, and drank of the mysterious water, he answers the question of his inquirers in verse, though he is generally illiterate, and unacquainted with the Muses."

6. Of laurel'd Phœbus,] The Greek is δαφνηφοροιο, laurel-wearing Phœbus; because when Daphne escaped his pursuit by being changed into a laurel, he consecrated that tree to himself.

Ovid. Metamorph.

Cui Deus, At quoniam conjux mea non potes esse
Arbor eris certeo, dixit, mea; semper habebunt
Te coma, te citheræ, te nostræ, Laure, pharetræ.

To whom the god—"Because thou canst not be
My mistress, I espouse thee for my tree:
Be thou the prize of honour and renown,
The deathless poet and the poem crown."

Dryden.

Ode XIV.—The subject of this ode is to show the irresistible nature of love. In this little piece Anacreon discovers a wonderful delicacy of invention: nothing can be imagined more entertaining than this combat, the preparation for it, the issue of it, and that natural and admirable reflection with which it concludes.

12. Clad in radiant arms complete, &c.] Anacreon arms himself with a spear and shield, to contend with Love. In an ancient epigram of the Anthologia, book 7, we have an account of a combatant, who put on the breast-plate of Reason, to withstand the attacks of this dangerous enemy.

Ωπλισμαι προς ερωτα περι στερνοισι λογισμον,
  Ουδε με νικησει, μουνος εων προς ένα.
Θνατος δ' αθανατω συνελευσομαι· ην δε βοηθον
  Βακχον εχη, τι μονος προς δυ' εγω δυναμαι;

With Love I war, and Reason is my shield,
Nor ever, match'd thus equally, will yield:
If Bacchus joins his aid, too great the odds;
One mortal cannot combat two such gods.

19, 20. When the quiver at his side
  Feather'd shafts no more supply'd,]

The author of an epigram, in the seventh book of the Anthologia, complains, in like manner, that Love had exhausted his quiver by shooting at him.

Μηκετι τις πτηξειε Ποθου βελος· ιοδοκην γαρ
  Εις εμε λαβρος Ερως εξεκενωσεν όλην.

No more let Cupid's shafts the world appall,
For in my bosom he has lodg'd them all.

21. Love, transform'd into a dart,
  Pierc'd, like lightning, thro' my heart.]

This thought is very beautiful and ingenious. It is taken from an ancient piece of gallantry, which ought not to be passed over in silence. The heroes of antiquity, when in any desperate engagement they found their darts spent, their strength exhausted, and saw no prospect of surviving long, would collect all their spirits and strength, and rush headlong with amazing impetuosity upon their enemies, that even in death the weight of their bodies, thus violently agitated, might bear down their adversaries. Examples of this kind of heroism are frequent in Lucan. Book 3d, speaking of a brave veteran:

——Tum vulnere multo
Effugientem animam lapsos collegit in artus
Membraque contendit toto, quicunque manebat,

Of my vitals made his prey,
And dissolv'd my soul away.
Now, alas! in vain I wield
Glittering spear and ample shield,
Victory in vain dispute,
Love, I find, is absolute;
All defence to folly turns
When within the battle burns.

ODE XV.

BY DR. BROOME.

HAPPY LIFE.

THE wealth of Gyges I despise,
Gems have no charms to tempt the wise;
Riches I leave, and such vain things,
To the low aim and pride of kings.
  Let my bright hair with unguents flow,
With rosy garlands crown my brow:
This sun shall roll in joy away;
To morrow is a distant day.

Sanguine, et hostilem, defessis robore membris,
Insiliit solo nociturus pondere puppim.
B. 3. ver. 622.

And, book 6. ver. 204, speaking of Scæva:

—— tot munera belli
Solus obit, densamque ferens in pectore sylvam
Jam gradibus fessis, in quem cadat, eligit hostem.

Encumber'd sore with many a painful wound
Tardy and stiff he treads the hostile round;
Gloomy and fierce his eyes the crowd survey,
Mark where to fix, and single out the prey.
Rowe.

Ode XV.—1. The wealth of Gyges I despise,] Gyges was the favourite of Candaules king of Lydia, whose queen was remarkably beautiful, and passionately admired by her husband. In his vanity he extolled her charms above measure to Gyges, and to convince him of her beauty, determined to show her to him naked: which he effected, but not without the queen's discovering the affront; who next morning sent privately for Gyges, and resolutely told him, he must either suffer immediate death for what he had done, or dispatch Candaules, and take her and the kingdom of Lydia for his recompense. The choice was difficult, as he greatly valued his master: however, the love of life prevailed—he stabbed Candaules, married the queen, and took possession of the kingdom.

8. To morrow is a distant day.] There is an epigram in the second book of the Anthologia, that has the same turn:

Πινε, και ευφραινου· τι γαρ αυριον, η τι το μελλον,
  Ουδεις γινωσκει· μη τρεχε, μη κοπια.
Ὡς δυνασαι χαρισαι, μεταδος, φαγε, θνητα λογιζου,
  Το ζην του μη ζην ουδεν ολως απεχει.
Πας ὁ βιος τοιοσδε, ροπην μονον αν προλαβη τις.
  Αν δε θανης, ἑτερου παντα, συ δ' ουδεν εχεις.

Cease from thy cares and toils, be sweetly gay,
And drink—To morrow is a distant day:
Improve on time; to bliss each moment give;
Not to enjoy this life, is not to live:

  Then while the hour serenely shines,
Toss the gay die, and quaff thy wines;
But ever in the genial hour,
To Bacchus the libation pour,
Lest Death in wrath approach, and cry,
"Man—taste no more the cup of joy."

ODE XVI.

BY THE SAME.

THE POWER OF BEAUTY.

SOME sing of Thebes, and some employ
Their numbers on the siege of Troy.
I mourn, alas! in plaintive strains,
My own captivity and chains.
  No navy, rang'd in proud array,
No foot, no horseman arm'd to slay,
My peace alarm: far other foes,
Far other hosts create my woes;
Strange, dangerous hosts, that ambush'd lie
In every bright, love-darting eye!

Our goods are now our own, but when we die
They come to others while in dust we lie,
And then, alas! have nothing to enjoy.

Horace expresses himself in the same manner, book 1. ode 9.

Quid sit futurum cras fuge quærere: et
Quem sors dierum cumque dabit, lucro
Appone: nec dulces amores
Sperne puer, neque tu choreas;
Dum virenti canities abest
Morosa——

To morrow and her works defy;
  Lay hold upon the present hour,
And snatch the pleasures passing by,
  To put them out of fortune's pow'r:
Nor love, nor love's delights disdain,
Whate'er thou gett'st to day is gain.
Dryden.

Ode XVI.—1. Some sing of Thebes,] Anacreon alludes to the famous war of the seven captains against Thebes, occasioned by Eteocles the son of Œdipus and Jocasta, refusing his brother Polynices his share in the government, though they had previously agreed, after their father's death, to rule alternately year by year. Æschylus wrote a tragedy on this subject.

3. I mourn, alas! in plaintive strains,
  My own captivity and chains.]

Ovid has imitated this passage—Amor. l. 2. eleg. 18.

Vincor, et ingenium sumptis revocatur ab armis,
  Resque domi gestas, et mea bella cano.

I'm conquer'd, and renounce the glorious strain
Of arms and war, to sing of love again:
My themes are acts which I myself have done,
And my Muse sings no battles but my own.

9. Dangerous hosts that ambush'd lie
  In every bright, love-darting eye!]

Nonnus calls the eyes, The archers of Love, ακοντιστηρες ερωτων; and there is something similar to this in an epigram of the Anthologia, book 7—which, speaking of love, says,

Such as destroy, when beauty arms,
To conquer, dreadful in its charms!

ODE XVII.

THE SILVER BOWL.

Mulciber, this silver take,
And a curious goblet make;
Let thy utmost skill appear
Not in radiant armour there;
Let me there no battles see;
What are arms or wars to me?
Form it with a noble sweep,
Very wide, and very deep.
Carve not there the northern Team,
Nor Orion's dreadful beam;
Pleiads, Hyads, Bears displease;
What have I to do with these?
Why should slow Boötes roll,
Why should horrid monsters prowl,
On the margin of my bowl?
Draw me, what I value more,
Vines with purple clusters store,
Bacchus ever young and fair,
Cupid with the golden hair,
Gay Bathyllus too be there,
See that, beautiful and bold,
All these figures rise in gold;
In the wine-press let them join
Hand in hand to tread the wine,

Ου με λεληθας,
Τοξοτα, Ζηνοφιλας ομμασι κρυπτομενος.

Insidious archer, not unseen you lie,
Though ambush'd close in Zenophelia's eye.

Ode XVII.—This elegant ode is quoted by Gellius, who says it was sung and played upon instruments at an entertainment where he was present.

9. Carve not there the northern Team, &c.] The poet alludes to the constellations, which Vulcan described on the shield of Achilles. See Homer's Iliad, book the 18th.

There shone the image of the master mind:
There Earth, there Heaven, there ocean he design'd;
Th' unweary'd Sun, the Moon completely round;
The starry lights that Heaven's high convex crown'd;
The Pleiads, Hyads, with the northern Team;
And great Orion's more refulgent beam,
To which, around the axle of the sky,
The Bear revolving points his golden eye,
Still shines exalted on th' etherial plain,
Nor bathes his blazing forehead in the main.
Pope.

10. Nor Orion's dreadful beam;] Anacreon calls Orion, στυγνον, odious, because he is the forerunner of tempests, and therefore dreadful to mariners. Horace calls him infestus, Epode 15.

Dum pecori lupus, et nautis infestus Orion.

As long as wolves pursue the fearful sheep,
And stern Orion rages o'er the deep.

ODE XVIII.

ON THE SAME.

Contrive me, artisan, a bowl
Of silver ample as my soul;
And in the bright compartments bring
The sweet profusion of the Spring;
Let that fair season, rich in flowers,
Shed roses in ambrosial showers;
Yet simply plain be thy design,
A festive banqueting of wine;
No hieroglyphics let it have,
No foreign mysteries engrave,
Let no blood-thirsty heroes wield
Rough armour in the silver field;
But draw me Jove's delightful boy,
Bacchus the god of wine and joy:
Let Venus with light step advance,
And with gay Hymen lead the dance.
Beneath the leaf-embellish'd vine,
Full of young grapes that promise wine,
Let Love, without his armour, meet
The meek-ey'd Graces laughing sweet.
And on the polish'd plain display
A group of beauteous boys at play;
But no Apollo, god of day.

ODE XIX.

WE OUGHT TO DRINK.

The thirsty Earth sucks up the showers
Which from his urn Aquarius pours;
The trees, which wave their boughs profuse,
Imbibe the Earth's prolific juice;
The Sea, in his prodigious cup,
Drinks all the rain and rivers up;

Ode XVIII.—19. Let Love, without his armour, meet
The meek-ey'd Graces laughing sweet.]
It is not without reason that Anacreon, after having mentioned Venus, introduces Love among the Graces; being sensible, that though beauty alone might please, yet without the aid of other charms, it could not long captivate the heart.

Καλλος ανευ χαριτων τερπει μονον· ου κατεχει δε,
Ὡς ατερ αγκιστρου νηχομενον δελεαρ.

Beauty without the graces may impart
Charms that will please, not captivate the heart;
As splendid baits without the bearded hook
Invite, not catch, the tenants of the brook.

23. But no Apollo, god of day.] The poet desires that Apollo may not be described upon his bowl, because he was so unfortunate as to kill his favourite Hyacinthus, as he was playing with him at quoits.

Ode XIX.—5. The Sea, in his prodigious cup,
Drinks all the rain and rivers up;]
The original is, Πινει θαλασσα δ' αυρας, The sea drinks up the air. All the commentators are silent here, except Dr. Trapp, who owns he did not understand the expression. Might I venture to make an easy alteration of the text, I would read, Πινει θαλασσ' αναυρους, The sea drinks up the rivers. See Ode 7th. Δια δ' ἐξιων μ' αναυρων, Through rapid rivers, or torrents. It is likewise used in the same

The Sun too thirsts, and strives to drain
The sea, the rivers, and the rain;
And nightly, when his course is run,
The merry Moon drinks up the Sun.
Then give me wine, and tell me why,
My friends, should all things drink but I?

ODE XX.

BY DR. BROOME.

TO HIS MISTRESS.

The gods o'er mortals prove their sway,
And steal them from themselves away.
Transform'd by their almighty hands,
Sad Niobe an image stands;
And Philomel up-borne on wings,
Through air her mournful story sings.
Would Heaven, indulgent to my vow,
The happy change I wish allow;
Thy envy'd mirror I would be,
That thou might'st always gaze on me;
And, could my naked heart appear,
Thou'dst see thyself—for thou art there!
Or were I made thy folding vest,
That thou might'st clasp me to thy breast!
Or, turn'd into a fount, to lave
Thy naked beauties in my wave!
Thy bosom-cincture I would grow,
To warm those little hills of snow:
Thy ointment, in rich fragrant streams
To wander o'er thy beauteous limbs;
Thy chain of shining pearl, to deck
And close embrace thy graceful neck:
A very sandal I would be,
To tread on—if trod on by thee.

sense by the best authors. Moschus, Idyllium 2, 31. See also Hoelzinus on Apollonius Rhodius, book 1, 9. This emendation makes the sense full and complete.

10. The merry Moon drinks up the Sun.] The Moon is said to drink up the Sun, because she borrows her light from that luminary.

Ode XX.—4. Sad Niobe an image stands;] Niobe was the daughter of Tantalus king of Phrygia, and wife of Amphion king of Thebes, by whom, according to Homer, having six sons and six daughters, she became so proud of her offspring and high birth that she had the vanity to prefer herself to Latona, the mother of Apollo and Diana, who, to revenge the affront offered to their parent, in one day slew all her children; upon which Niobe was struck dumb with grief, and remained stupid. For that reason, the poets have feigned her to be turned into a stone. The story is told by Ovid in the sixth book of the Metamorphoses; but perhaps better by Pope, in his translation of the twenty-fourth book of the Iliad, where Achilles is introduced thus speaking to Priam.

Nor thou, O father! thus consum'd with woe,
The common cares that nourish life forego.
Not thus did Niobe, of form divine,
A parent once whose sorrows equall'd thine:
Six youthful sons, as many blooming maids,
In one sad day beheld the Stygian shades;
These by Apollo's silver bow were slain,
Those Cynthia's arrows stretch'd upon the plain:

ODE XXI.

SUMMER.

Fill, fill, sweet girls, the foaming bowl,
And let me gratify my soul:
I faint with thirst—the heat of day
Has drank my very life away.

So was her pride chastis'd by wrath divine,
Who match'd her own with bright Latona's line:
But two the goddess, twelve the queen enjoy'd;
Those boasted twelve th' avenging two destroy'd.
Steep'd in their blood, and in the dust outspread,
Nine days neglected lay expos'd the dead;
None by to weep them, to inhume them none,
(For Jove had turn'd the nation all to stone):
The gods themselves, at length relenting, gave
Th' unhappy race the honours of a grave.
Herself a rock (for such was Heaven's high will)
Through deserts wild now pours a weeping rill;
Where, round the bed whence Achelöus springs,
The watry fairies dance in mazy rings,
There high on Sipylus's shaggy brow
She stands, her own sad monument of woe;
The rock for ever lasts, the tears for ever flow.
Pope.

There are two short epigrams in the Anthologia, which perhaps the reader will be glad to see in English.

Ὁ τυμβος ὁυτος ενδον ουκ εχει νεκρον.
Ὁ νεκρος ὁυτος εκτος ουκ εχει ταφον.
Αλλ' αυτος αυτου νεκρος εστι και ταφος.

This weeping tomb within no corse contains;
This weeping corse without a tomb remains:
For, by a strange irrevocable doom,
This image is the carcase and the tomb.

Εκ ζωης με θεοι τευξαν λιθον· εκ δε λιθοιο
Ζωην Πραξιτελης εμπαλιν ειργασατο.

I once was Niobe, and fill'd a throne,
Till Fate severe transform'd me into stone:
Behold the change which mimic art can give!
From stone Praxiteles has made me live.

I cannot conclude my notes on this ode without first observing, that this gallant original has been copied by several masters. I shall produce one example, because it is the shortest, which is an epigram of Dionysius the sophist.

Ειθ' ανεμος γενομην, συ δε γε στειχουσα παρ' αυγας,
Στηθεα γυμνωσαις, και με πνεοντα λαβοις.
Ειθε ροδον γενομην ὑποπορφυρον, οφρα με χερσιν
Αραμενη, κομισαις στηθεσι χιονεοις.
Ειθε κρινον γενομην λευκοχροον, οφρα με χερσιν
Αραμενη, μαλλον σης χροτιης κορεσῃς.

I wish myself a gentle breeze to blow,
O'er your fair bosom unconfin'd I'd flow,
And wanton on those little hills of snow.
I wish myself a rose in purple drest,
That you might place me in your snowy breast.
I wish myself a lily, lovely fair,
That I might kiss your skin, and gather whiteness there.

Ode XXI.—2. And let me gratify my soul:] The Greek is, πιειν αμυστι. Amystis, as Madame Dacier observes, was a manner of drinking among the Thracians, so called from their swallowing down a

O! lead me to yon cooling bowers,
And give me fresher wreaths of flowers;
For those that now my temples shade,
Scorch'd by my burning forehead, fade:
But O! my heart, what can remove,
What wines, what shades, this heat of love?
These are all vain, alas! I find;
Love is the fever of the mind.

ODE XXII.

BY E. G. B. ESQ.

THE BOWER.

HERE, my Chloe, charming maid,
Here, beneath the genial shade,
Shielded from each ruder wind,
Lovely Chloe, lie reclin'd!
Lo! for thee the balmy breeze
Gently fans the waving trees!
Streams, that whisper through the grove,
Whisper low the voice of Love,
Sweetly bubbling wanton sport,
Where Persuasion holds her court.
Ye who pass th' enamell'd grove,
Through the rustling shade who rove,
Sure my bliss your breast must fire!
Can you see, and not admire?

certain quantity of liquor without fetching breath, or shutting the mouth. Horace takes notice of it in book 1. ode 36.

> Neu multi Damalis meri
> Bassum Threiciâ vincat amystide.
>
> Bassus shall Damalis o'ercome,
> And drain the goblet at a draught.
>
> Duncombe.

9. But O! my heart, what can remove, &c.] The reflection the poet here makes is exceedingly natural, beautiful, and strong; " When love has once got possession of the heart, all exterior remedies will have no effect;" agreeably to the conclusion of the fourteenth ode:

> All defence to folly turns,
> When within the battle burns.

Ode XXII.—This ode is by Anacreon addressed to Bathyllus; but the translator has, with more decency and gallantry, applied it to a lady.

10. Where Persuasion holds her court.] The original is, Πηγη ρεουσα πειθους, a fountain rolling persuasion, than which nothing can be more delicate or poetical, as most of the commentators have observed.

Longepierre quotes a beautiful epigram from the Anthologia, book 1, similar to this ode; where the god Pan is supposed to speak.

> Ερχεο και κατ' εμαν ἵζευ πιτυν, ἁ το μελιχρον
> Προς μαλακους εχει κεκλιμενα ζεφυρους.
> Ηνι δε και κρουνισμα μελισταγες, ενθα μελισδων
> Ἡδυν ερημαιοις ὑπνον αγω καλαμοις.

Rest here beneath my shady pine reclin'd,
Whose tall top sweetly murmurs to the wind;
Here too a brook mellifluous flows along,
And woos me with its ever gurgling song;
Here on my solitary pipe I play,
Or sweetly sleep the tranquil hours away.

ODE XXIII.

THE VANITY OF RICHES.

IF the treasur'd gold could give
Man a longer term to live,
I'd employ my utmost care
Still to keep, and still to spare;
And, when Death approach'd, would say,
" Take thy fee, and walk away."
But since riches cannot save
Mortals from the gloomy grave,
Why should I myself deceive,
Vainly sigh, and vainly grieve?
Death will surely be my lot,
Whether I am rich or not.
Give me freely while I live
Generous wines, in plenty give
Soothing joys my life to cheer,
Beauty kind, and friends sincere;
Happy! could I ever find
Friends sincere, and beauty kind.

ODE XXIV.

ENJOYMENT.

SINCE I'm born a mortal man,
And my being's but a span;
'Tis a march that I must make;
'Tis a journey I must take:
What is past I know too well;
What is future who can tell?
Teasing Care, then set me free,
What have I to do with thee?
Ere I die, for die I must,
Ere this body turns to dust,
Every moment I'll employ
In sweet revelry and joy,

Ode XXIII. One cannot but be surprised at the wretched taste of Faber, who has rejected this ode as spurious and not Anacreon's, when perhaps it is not inferior in beauty to the best of them; as Barnes and Trapp have amply proved by explaining a Greek idiom, with which it is scarce worth while to trouble the English reader.

3, 4. I'd employ my utmost care
Still to keep, and still to spare;]

These words seem to allude to an anecdote in the history of Anacreon, which I shall explain. Stobæus tells us, that Anacreon, having received a present of five talents of gold from Polycrates, tyrant of Samos, was so embarrassed with cares and solicitudes about his treasure, that he could not sleep for two nights successively: whereupon he sent back the present, with this apology to his patron, " That, however valuable the sum might be, it was not a sufficient price for the trouble and anxiety of keeping it."

Ode XXIV.—7. Teasing Care, then set me free,] Tibullus says,

> Ite procul durum curæ genus, ite labores.
>
> Hence all ye troubles vanish into air,
> And all the wrinkled family of Care.

Laugh and sing, and dance and play,
With Lyæus young and gay.

ODE XXV.

WINE BANISHES CARES.

When gay Bacchus cheers my breast,
All my cares are lull'd to rest:
Griefs that weep, and toils that tease,
What have I to do with these?
No solicitudes can save
Mortals from the gloomy grave.
Shall I thus myself deceive?
Shall I languish? Shall I grieve?
Let us quaff the generous juice;
Bacchus gave it for our use.
For when wine transports the breast,
All our cares are lull'd to rest.

ODE XXVI.

THE TRANSPORTS OF WINE.

When gay Bacchus fills my breast,
All my cares are lull'd to rest,
Rich I seem as Lydia's king,
Merry catch or ballad sing;
Ivy-wreaths my temples shade,
Ivy that will never fade:
Thus I sit in mind elate,
Laughing at the farce of state.
Some delight in fighting fields,
Nobler transports Bacchus yields:
Fill the bowl——I ever said,
'Tis better to lie drunk than dead.

Macedonius concludes an epigram with this distich, Anthologia, book 1.

Την γαρ Ανακρεοντος ενι παραπιδεσσι φυλασσω
Παρφασιην, ότι δει φροντιδα μη κατεχειν.

I like Anacreon's counsel wond'rous well,
To let no troubles in my bosom dwell.

13, 14. Laugh and sing, and dance and play,
With Lyæus young and gay.]

Julian, in an epitaph he composed on Anacreon, makes him repeat the same lesson after he was dead.

Πολλακι μεν τοδ' αεισα, και εκ τυμβω δε βοησω·
Πινετε, πριν ταυτην αμφιβαλησθε κονιν.

What oft alive I sung, now dead I cry
Loud from the tomb, "Drink, mortals, ere you die."

Ode XXV.—1, 2. When gay Bacchus cheers my breast, [rest:]
All my cares are lull'd to

Dissipat Evius curas edaces. Hor. b. 2. 11.

Th' enlivening god will sordid care refine.
Duncombe.

—— neque aliter
Mordaces diffugiunt sollicitudines.
Book 1. 18.

'Tis wine, wine alone, that can drown every care. Duncombe.

Ode XXVI.—This ode, as Longepierre observes, is in the same style as the two preceding, and the next ensuing. There is a fragment of Bacchylides remaining, which has great affinity to these four, but chiefly to this very ode.

Γλυκει αναγκη σευομενα κυλικων
Θαλπησι θυμον Κυπριδος·
Ελπις δ' αιθυσσει φρενας
Αναμιγνυμενα Διονυσιοισι δωροις,
Ανδρασι δ' ὑψοτατω
Πεμπει μεριμνας.
Αυτος μεν πολεων
Κρηδεμνον λυει,
Πασι δ' ανθρωποις
Μοναρχησειν δοκει.
Χρυσω δ' ελεφαντι τε
Μαρμαιρουσιν οικοι.
Πυροφοροι δε κατ' αιγληεντα
Νηες αγουσιν απ' Αιγυπτου
Μεγιστον πλουτον,
Ὡς πινοντος ορμαινει κεαρ.

When the rosy bowl we drain,
Gentle Love begins to reign:
Hope, to human hearts benign,
Mingles in the friendly wine,
And with pleasing visions fair
Sweetly dissipates our care.
Warm with wine we win renown,
Conquer hosts, or storm a town,
Reign the mighty lords of all,
And in fancy rule the ball:
Then our villas charm the sight,
All with gold and ivory bright;
Ships with corn from Egypt come,
Bearing foreign treasures home:
Thus each bliss that fills the soul
Luxuriant rises from the bowl.

5, 6. Ivy-wreaths my temples shade,
Ivy that will never fade:]

Pastores hederâ crescentem ornate poetam.
Virg.

With ivy-wreaths your youthful poet crown.

On which passage Servius remarks, that poets are crowned with ivy, as being consecrated to Bacchus; either because they are enthusiasts, like the Bacchanals, or because ivy, being an evergreen, is a symbol of that eternity which they acquire by their compositions. Horace says,

Me doctarum hederæ præmia frontium
Dîs miscent superis.

An ivy crown ennobles me,
Whose darling joy is poetry. Duncombe.

ODE XXVII.

THE PRAISE OF BACCHUS.

Bacchus, Jove's delightful boy,
Generous god of wine and joy,
Still exhilarates my soul
With the raptures of the bowl;
Then with feather'd feet I bound,
Dancing in a festive round;
Then I feel, in sparkling wine,
Transports delicate, divine;

Ode XXVII.—5, 6. Then with feather'd feet I bound,
Dancing in a festive round;]

In the forty-first ode Anacreon calls Bacchus, τον

Thus the sprightly music warms,
Song delights, and beauty charms:
Debonair, and light, and gay,
Thus I dance the hours away.

ODE XXVIII.

FROM THE GUARDIAN.

HIS MISTRESS'S PICTURE.

BEST and happiest artisan,
Best of painters, if you can,
With your many-colour'd art
Paint the mistress of my heart.
Describe the charms you hear from me,
(Her charms you could not paint and see)
And make the absent nymph appear
As if her lovely self were here.
First draw her easy-flowing hair,
As soft and black as she is fair;
And, if your heart can rise so high,
Let breathing odours round her fly.
Beneath the shade of flowing jet,
The ivory forehead smoothly set,
With care the sable brows extend,
And in two arches nicely bend;
That the fair space, which lies between
The meeting shade, may scarce be seen.
The eye must be uncommon fire,
Sparkle, languish, and desire;
The flames, unseen, must yet be felt,
Like Pallas kill, like Venus melt.
The rosy cheeks must seem to glow
Amidst the white of new-fall'n snow.
Let her lips Persuasion wear,
In silence elegantly fair;
As if the blushing rivals strove,
Breathing and inviting love.
Below her chin be sure to deck
With every grace her polish'd neck;
While all that's pretty, soft, and sweet,
In the swelling bosom meet.
The rest in purple garments veil,
Her body, not her shape, conceal.
Enough!——the lovely work is done,
The breathing paint will speak anon.

THE SAME ODE IMITATED

IN THE YEAR 1755,

By another hand.

BEST of painters, show thy art,
Draw the charmer of my heart;
Draw her as she shines away
At the rout, or at the play:
Carefully each mode express,
Woman's better part is dress.
Let her cap be mighty small,
Bigger just than none at all,
Pretty, like her sense, and little,
Like her beauty, frail and brittle.
Be her shining locks confin'd
In a threefold braid behind;
Let an artificial flower
Set the fissure off before;
Here and there weave ribbon pat in,
Ribbon of the finest satin.
Circling round her ivory neck
Frizzle out the smart vandyke;
Like the ruff that heretofore
Good queen Bess's maidens wore;
Happy maidens, as we read,
Maids of honour, maids indeed.
Let her breast look rich and bold
With a stomacher of gold;
Let it keep her bosom warm,
Amply stretch'd from arm to arm;
Whimsically travers'd o'er,
Here a knot, and there a flower,
Like her little heart that dances,
Full of maggots, full of fancies.
Flowing loosely down her back
Draw with art the graceful sacque;
Ornament it well with gimping,
Flounces, furbelows, and crimping.

ἐφευρεταν χορειας, The inventor of dancing. So Tibullus,

> Ille liquor docuit voces inflectere cantu;
> Movit et ad certos nescia membra modos.
> L. 1. eleg. 7.

> This as swains quaff'd, spontaneous numbers came,
> They prais'd the festal cask, and hymn'd thy name;
> All ecstacy! to certain time they bound,
> And beat in measur'd awkwardness the ground.
> Grainger.

Ode XXVIII.—10. Soft and black as she is fair;] Neither the Greeks nor Romans seem to have esteemed one particular colour of the hair more than another; for we find both black and light colour equally admired.

19, 20. The eye must be uncommon fire,
Sparkle, languish, and desire.]

Baxter, Barnes, and Stephens, trifle ridiculously on this passage. The Greek, ὑγρον, is humid. Madame Dacier judiciously observes, "That eyes, in which there is the least degree of humidity, are uncommonly vivid and full of fire."

25. Let her lips Persuasion wear,] The ancients, to give us an idea of a mouth perfectly agreeable, generally represented it by the lips of Persuasion. Anthol. b. 7.

> Καλλος εχεις Κυπριδος, Πειθυς στομα, σωμα και ακμην
> Ειαρινων ωρων.

> Persuasion's lips, and Cyprian charms are yours,
> And the fresh beauty of the vernal Hours.

30. Her polish'd neck;] The Greek is, λυγδινω, that is, marble; from Lygdos, a place in the island of Paros, famous for the finest marble. Trapp.

33, 34. The rest in purple garments veil,
Her body, not her shape, conceal.]

Ovid has a similar passage in the first book of the Metamorphoses, v. 500.

> ——— laudat digitosque manusque,
> Brachiaque, et nudos mediâ plus parte lacertos;
> Si qua latent meliora putat.

> —— He view'd
> Her taper fingers, and her panting breast;
> He praises all he sees, and for the rest,
> Believes the beauties yet unseen are best.
> Dryden.

Let of ruffles many a row
Guard her elbows, white as snow;
Knots below, and knots above,
Emblems of the ties of love.
Let her hoop, extended wide,
Show what petticoats should hide,
Garters of the softest silk,
Stockings whiter than the milk;
Charming part of female dress,
Did it show us more or less.
Let a pair of velvet shoes
Gently press her petty-toes,
Gently press, and softly squeeze,
Tottering like the fair Chinese,
Mounted high, and buckled low,
Tott'ring every step they go.
Take these hints, and do thy duty,
Fashions are the tests of beauty;
Features vary and perplex,
Mode's the woman and the sex.

ODE XXIX.

BATHYLLUS.

Now, illustrious artisan,
Paint the well-proportion'd man;
Once again the tints prepare,
Paint Bathyllus young and fair.
Draw his tresses soft and black,
Flowing graceful down his back,
Auburn be the curl'd extremes,
Glowing like the solar beams;
Let them negligently fall,
Easy, free, and artless all.
Let his bright cerulean brow
Grace his forehead white as snow.
Let his eyes, that glow with fire,
Gentlest, mildest love inspire;
Steal from Mars the radiant mien,
Softness from th' Idalian queen;
This, with hope the heart to bless,
That, with terrour to depress.
Next, his cheeks with roses crown,
And the peach's dubious down;
And, if art can this bestow,
Let the blush ingenuous glow.
But description would be faint,
Teaching you his lips to paint:
There let fair Persuasion dwell,
Let them gently, softly swell,
Seem in sweetest sounds to break
Willing air, and silent speak.
Now you've finish'd high the face,
Draw his ivory neck with grace;
All the charms and beauty add,
Such as fair Adonis had.
Let me, next, the bosom see
And the hands of Mercury.
But I'll not presume to tell,
Artist, you who paint so well,
How the foot should be exprest,
How to finish all the rest.
I the price you ask will give,
For the picture seems to live:
Gold's too little, view this piece,
'Tis the pictur'd pride of Greece:
This divine Apollo take,
And from this Bathyllus make.
When to Samos you repair,
Ask for young Bathyllus there,
Finest figure eye e'er saw,
From Bathyllus Phœbus draw.

ODE XXX.

CUPID TAKEN PRISONER.

Late the Muses Cupid found
And with wreaths of roses bound,
Bound him fast, as soon as caught,
And to blooming Beauty brought.

Ode XXIX.—7, 8. Auburn be the curl'd extremes,
Glowing like the solar beams;]

Anacreon describes the hair of Bathyllus black towards the head, but lower down gradually inclining to a yellow. Horace calls this colour myrrheus, Myrrheum nodo cohibere crinem, b. 3, ode 14. On which an ancient critic remarks, Colorem myrrheum in crinibus hodie quoque dicunt, qui medius est inter flavum et nigrum; "Even at this day they call that hair of a myrrh colour, which is between black and yellow." Ovid describes the colour of his mistress's hair thus, Amor. l. 1. Eleg. 14.

Nec tamen ater erat, nec erat color aureus illis;
Sed quamvis neuter, mistus uterque color:
Qualem clivosæ madidis in vallibus Idæ
Ardua, direpto cortice, cedrus habet.

Nor of a black, nor of a golden hue
They were, but of a dye between the two:
Such as in rindless cedar we behold,
The black confounded with the dusky gold.

9, 10. Let them negligently fall,
Easy, free, and artless all.]

Patronius says, Crines, ingenio suo flexi, per totos se humeros effuderant: "Her hair, negligently floating where it pleased, diffused itself over her shoulders."

25. There let fair Persuasion dwell,] Meleager as Longepierre observes, calls his mistress, ἡδὺ ῥόδον πειθοῦς, The sweet rose of persuasion. Anthologia.

43, 44. This divine Apollo take,
And from this Bathyllus make.]

The poet could not give us a more perfect idea of the beauty of this young Samian: he tells the painter, "If he would draw a good likeness of Bathyllus, he must copy the portrait of Apollo, the most beautiful of the gods; and if he would make a good picture of Apollo, he must paint Bathyllus."

45. When to Samos you repair,] Bathyllus had a celebrated statue erected to his honour at Samos by Polycrates. See Apuleius.

Ode XXX.—This ode is very fine; and the fiction extremely ingenious. I believe, Anacreon would inculcate that beauty alone cannot long secure a conquest; but that when wit and beauty meet, it is impossible for a lover to disengage himself. Madame Dacier.

Venus with large ransom strove
To release the god of love.
Vain is ransom, vain is fee,
Love refuses to be free.
Happy in his rosy chain,
Love with Beauty will remain.

ODE XXXI.

THE PLEASING FRENZY.

INDULGE me, Stoics, with the bowl,
And let me gratify my soul;
Your precepts to the schools confine,
For I'll be nobly mad with wine.
Alcmæon and Orestes grew
Quite mad when they their mothers slew:
But I, no man, no mother kill'd,
No blood but that of Bacchus spill'd,
Will prove the virtues of the vine,
And be immensely mad with wine.
When Hercules was mad, we know,
He grasp'd the Iphitean bow;
The rattling of his quiver spread
Astonishment around and dread.
Mad Ajax, with his sevenfold shield,
Tremendous stalk'd along the field,
Great Hector's flaming sword he drew,
And hosts of Greeks in fancy slew.
But I with no such fury glow,
No sword I wave, nor bend the bow:
My helmet is a flowery crown;
In this bright bowl my cares I'll drown,
And rant in ecstacies divine,
Heroically mad with wine.

ODE XXXII.

THE NUMBER OF HIS MISTRESSES.

WHEN thou can'st fairly number all
The leaves on trees that fade and fall,
Or count the foaming waves that roar,
Or tell the pebbles on the shore;
Then may'st thou reckon up the names
Of all my beauties, all my flames.
At Athens, flames that still survive,
First count me only thirty-five.
At Corinth next tell o'er the fair,
Tell me a whole battalion there.
In Greece the fairest nymphs abound,
And worse than banner'd armies wound.
Count all that make their sweet abodes
At Lesbos, or delightful Rhodes.
Then Carian and Ionian dames,
Write me at least two thousand flames.
What! think'st thou this too large a sum?
Egypt and Syria are to come.
And Crete where Love his sway maintains,
And o'er a hundred cities reigns.

5, 6. Venus with large ransom strove
To release the god of love]

Moschus, in his Runaway Love, makes Venus offer a reward to any one who should only discover where he was.

—— Ὁ μανυτας γερας ἑξει
Μισθος τοι το φιλαμα το Κυπριδος.——

Whoe'er shall bring the news, his fee is this,
I Venus will reward him with a kiss.

Ode XXXI.—5. Alcmæon and Orestes] Alcmæon was the son of Amphiaraüs and Eriphyle. His father had been put to death by the contrivance of his mother, whom on that account he slew. Orestes slew his mother Clytemnestra, to revenge the death of his father Agamemnon, who, at his return from the Trojan war, had been murdered by her and her lover Ægisthus. They were both tormented by the Furies.

12. The Iphitean bow] Iphitus was the son of Eurytus king of Oechalia, and slain by Hercules, who carried off his bow.

15. Mad Ajax with his sevenfold shield] When the armour of Achilles was adjudged to Ulysses, Ajax was so enraged at the affront, that he ran mad; and falling upon a flock of sheep, which he took for so many Grecians, first slew them, and then himself. Homer celebrates his shield for its extraordinary size. Iliad, book 7.

Huge was its orb, with seven thick folds o'ercast
Of tough bull-hides; of solid brass the last.
Pope.

17. Hector's sword] Hector and Ajax made an exchange of presents (see Iliad 7.) which gave birth to a proverb, "That the presents of enemies are generally fatal:" for Ajax with this sword afterwards killed himself; and Hector was dragged, by the belt which Ajax gave him, at the chariot of Achilles.

There is an epigram to this purpose, Anthol. b. 3. c. 14.

Ἑκτωρ Αιαντι ξιφος ωπασεν' Ἑκτορι δ' Αιας
Ζωςηρ, αμφοτερων ἡ χαρις εις θανατον.

Hector bestow'd on Telamon the brave
A sword; the Greek to god-like Hector gave
A radiant belt: each gift was stamp'd with woe,
And prov'd alike destructive to the foe.

Ode XXXII.—9. At Corinth next tell o'er the fair] Corinth, the metropolis of Achaia, was so famous for rich courtezans, who would only entertain the wealthy, that it occasioned the proverb, Non cuivis homini contingit adire Corinthum, "Every man cannot go to Corinth." Lais asked Demosthenes a thousand drachms for one favour; to which he replied, "I will not buy repentance at so dear a rate." Longepierre.

19. And Crete] Anacreon says of Crete, ἁπαντ' εχυσης, abounding with all things, to express its fertility. Virgil says, it had a hundred cities:

Creta Jovis magni medio jacet insula ponto,
Centum urbes habitant magnas, uberrima regna.

Fair Crete sublimely towers amid the floods,
Proud nurse of Jove the sovereign of the gods;
A hundred cities the blest isle contains,
And boasts a vast extent of fruitful plains. Pitt.

Homer, in the Iliad, gives Crete a hundred cities, b. 2.

Crete's hundred cities pour forth all her sons.

But in the Odyssey, only ninety;

Crete awes the circling waves, a fruitful soil;
And ninety cities crown the sea-born isle. B. 19.

Therefore it is probable, that in the time of the Trojan war it had no more than ninety cities, but a hundred in the days of Homer.

Yet still unnumber'd, still remain
The nymphs of Persia and of Spain,
And Indians, scorch'd by Titan's ray,
Whose charms have burnt my heart away.

ODE XXXIII.

THE SWALLOW.

LOVELY swallow, once a year,
Pleas'd you pay your visit here;
When our clime the sun-beams gild,
Here your airy nest you build;
And, when bright days cease to smile,
Fly to Memphis or the Nile:
But, alas! within my breast
Love for ever makes his nest;
There the little Cupids lie,
Some prepare their wings to fly,
Some unhatch'd, some form'd in part,
Lie close nestling at my heart,
Chirping loud; their ceaseless noise
All my golden peace destroys:
Some, quite fledg'd and fully grown,
Nurse the younglings as their own;
These, when feather'd, others feed,
And thus propagate their breed.

Dreadful torment I sustain,
What, alas! can ease my pain:
The vast flocks of Loves that dwell
In my breast no tongue can tell.

ODE XXXIV.

TO HIS MISTRESS.

THOUGH cold winter o'er my brow
Sheds a scatter'd shower of snow,
Waving locks of silver hair;
Fly me not, capricious fair.
Though the spring's enlivening power
Blossoms in your beauty's flower,
Fly me not, nor slight my love;
In this chaplet, lo! are wove
Lucid colours blending bright
Roses red, and lilies white:
We, methinks, resemble those;
I the lily, you the rose.

ODE XXXV.

ON THE PICTURE OF EUROPA.

THIS pictur'd bull is mighty Jove,
Who meditates some prank of love;
On his broad back, with pleasing care,
He safely bears the Tyrian fair:
Lo! buoyant on the foaming tide,
He throws the circling waves aside,
Securely steering through the sea.
No other daring bull, but he,
Would leave his heifers on the plain,
To tempt the dangers of the main.

ODE XXXVI.

BY DR. BROOME.

LIFE SHOULD BE ENJOYED.

TALK not to me of pedant rules,
I leave debates to learned fools,
Who solemnly in form advise;
At best, impertinently wise.

Ode XXXIII.—5. And, when, &c.] It was an opinion generally received among the ancients, that swallows, and several other birds, crossed the sea, on the approach of winter, in search of warmer climates. Thus Virgil, Æneid 6. ver. 311.

> Quam multæ glomerantur aves, ubi frigidus annus
> Trans pontum fugat, et terris immittit apricis.

> Thick as the feather'd flocks, in close array,
> O'er the wide fields of ocean wing their way,
> When from the rage of winter they repair
> To warmer suns and more indulgent air. Pitt.

Others thought they hid themselves in the clefts of rocks. Thus Ovid, Cum glaciantur aquæ, scopulis se condit hirundo.

Pecklinius, in his book De Aëris et Elementi defectu, et vitâ sub aquis, assures us, that swallows retire to the bottom of the water during the winter; and that it is common for the fishermen on the coasts of the Baltic to take them in their nets in large knots, clinging together by their bills and claws; and that, upon their being brought into a warm room, they will separate, and begin to flutter about as in spring. Kercher, in his book De mundo subterraneo, affirms the same, and that in the northern countries they hide themselves under ground in the winter, whence they are often dug out. Longepierre.

6. Memphis, or the Nile] Memphis was a city situated on the Nile, a little below Delta, and the residence of the kings of Egypt. By the Nile, Anacreon means Ethiopia, whence that river derives its source.

8. Love for ever makes his nest] Anacreon is not singular in representing Cupid as a bird, and with propriety, because he is furnished with wings, and his flight is surprisingly rapid. Bion speaks of Love as a bird: See his second Idyllium.

Ode XXXIV.—10. Roses red, and lilies white] Virgil has very happily mixed these two colours, though upon a different occasion, Æneid. l. 12, ver. 67.

> Indum sanguineo veluti violaverit ostro
> Si quis ebur, aut mixta rubent ubi lilia multâ
> Alba rosâ——

> So looks the beauteous ivory stain'd with red;
> So roses, mix'd with lilies in the bed,
> Blend their rich hues.—— Pitt.

Ode XXXV.—This ode was composed on a picture representing the rape of Europa. See an Idyllium of Moschus upon the same subject.

Ode XXXVI.—12. With hoary locks by time o'erspread] A philosopher in Petronius makes the same reflection, Ego sic semper et ubique vixi, ut ultimam quamque lucem tanquam non redituram consumerem. "Wherever I am, I always enjoy the present day, as if I never expected to see another."

To me more pleasing precepts give,
And teach the science how to live;
To bury in the friendly draught
Sorrows that spring from too much thought;
To learn soft lessons from the fair,
How life may glide exempt from care.
Alas! I'm old—I see my head
With hoary locks by time o'erspread:
Then instant be the goblet brought,
To make me young—at least in thought.
Alas! incessant speeds the day,
When I must mix with common clay;
When I must tread the dismal shore,
And dream of love and wine no more.

ODE XXXVII.

BY DR. BROOME.

THE SPRING.

SEE! Winter's past; the seasons bring
Soft breezes with returning Spring;
At whose approach the Graces wear
Fresh honours in their flowing hair;
The raging seas forget to roar,
And smiling, gently kiss the shore;
The sportive duck, in wanton play,
Now dives, now rises into day;
The cranes from freezing skies repair,
And sailing float to warmer air;
Th' enlivening suns in glory rise,
And gaily dance along the skies;
The clouds disperse, or, if in showers
They fall, it is to wake the flowers.
See! verdure clothes the teeming earth;
The olive struggles into birth;
The swelling grapes adorn the vine,
And kindly promise future wine:
Blest juice! already I in thought
Quaff an imaginary draught.

18. And dream of love and wine no more] Horace says, in the same sense,

> Jam te premet nox, fabulæque manes,
> Et domus exilis Plutonia.——

> Too soon cut off from cheerful light,
> We must descend to sullen night,
> And, in the realms of fabled shades below,
> Thy pining ghost no joy shall know.
>
> Duncombe.

Ode XXXVII.—5. The raging seas forget to roar, &c.] The expression in Greek is extremely delicate and happy, The waves of the sea are mollified into tranquillity: Απαλυνεται γαληνη. Every letter, every syllable, is as liquid and smooth as the calm he describes. A famous old Scotch bishop, Gawin Douglas, in his description of May, seems to have had this passage in view.

> For to behald it was ane glore to se
> The stabyllit wyndys, and the calmyt se,
> The soft sessoun, the firmament serene,
> The loune illuminate are, and firth amene.

Or, as it is translated by Mr. Fawkes,

> How calm! how still! how pleasing to behold
> The sea's broad bosom where no billows roll'd!
> The season soft, the firmament serene,
> Th' illumin'd landscape, and the watry scene!

ODE XXXVIII.

ON HIMSELF.

YES, I'm old, I'm old, 'tis true;
What have I with time to do?
With the young and with the gay,
I can drink as much as they.
Let the jovial band advance,
Still I'm ready for the dance:
What's my sceptre? if you ask,
Lo! I sway a mighty flask.
Should some mettled blade delight
In the bloody scenes of fight,
Let him to this stage ascend,
Still I'm ready to contend—
Mix the grape's rich blood, my page,
We in drinking will engage.
Yes, I'm old; yet with the gay
I can be as brisk as they;
Like Silenus 'midst his train,
I can dance along the plain.

ODE XXXIX.

ON HIMSELF.

WHEN I drain the rosy bowl,
Joy exhilarates my soul;
To the Nine I raise my song.
Ever fair and ever young.

Ode XXXVIII.—7. What's my sceptre, &c.] In the Bacchanalian dances among the ancients, the leader of them bore a rod or sceptre.

17. Like Silenus, &c.] Silenus was the foster-father and tutor of Bacchus, represented by a little, flat-nosed, bald, fat, tun-bellied, old, drunken fellow, riding on an ass. Ovid draws his picture thus:

> —— Bacchæ Satyrique sequuntur,
> Quique senex ferulâ titubantes ebrius artus
> Sustinet, et pando non fortiter hæret asello.
>
> Metamorph. l. 4.

> Around the Bacchæ and the Satyrs throng;
> Behind, Silenus drunk lags slow along;
> On his dull ass he nods from side to side,
> Forbears to fall, yet half forgets to ride.
>
> Eusden.

Ode XXXIX—3. To the Nine I raise my song] Anacreon is not the only one who asserts, that Bacchus is the best friend to the Muses. If, as Horace says, you give credit to old Cratinus, the comic Greek poet, Nulla placere diu, nec vivere carmina possunt, Quæ scribuntur aquæ potoribus. "No verses long can please, or long can live, which water-drinkers write." There is an epigram in the first book of the Anthologia, which begins thus:

> Οινος τοι χαριεντι μεγας πελει ἱππος αοιδω,
> Ὑδωρ δε πινων, καλον ου τεκοις επος.

> Wine is the poet's generous horse;
> But water-drinkers works of course
> Are languid, cold, and void of force.

Aristophanes, in his comedy called Peace, humorously tells us, that, when the Lacedæmonians came to besiege Athens, Cratinus died of grief on seeing a hogshead broken, and the wine running out.

When full cups my cares expel,
Sober counsels, then farewell:
Let the winds that murmur, sweep
All my sorrows to the deep.
When I drink dull time away,
Jolly Bacchus, ever gay,
Leads me to delightful bowers,
Full of fragrance, full of flowers.
When I quaff the sparkling wine,
And my locks with roses twine,
Then I praise life's rural scene,
Sweet, sequester'd, and serene.
When I sink the bowl profound,
Richest fragrance flowing round,
And some lovely nymph detain,
Venus then inspires the strain.
When from goblets deep and wide
I exhaust the generous tide,
All my soul unbends—I play
Gamesome with the young and gay.
When the foaming bowl I drain,
Real blessings are my gain;
Blessings which my own I call:
Death is common to us all.

ODE XL.

CUPID WOUNDED.

ONCE as Cupid, tir'd with play,
On a bed of roses lay,
A rude bee, that slept unseen,
The sweet-breathing buds between,
Stung his finger, cruel chance!
With its little pointed lance.
Straight he fills the air with cries,
Weeps, and sobs, and runs, and flies;
Till the god to Venus came,
Lovely, laughter-loving dame:
Then he thus began to plain;
"Oh! undone—I die with pain—
Dear mamma, a serpent small,
Which a bee the ploughmen call,
Imp'd with wings, and arm'd with dart,
Oh!—has stung me to the heart."
Venus thus reply'd, and smil'd;
"Dry those tears, for shame! my child;
If a bee can wound so deep,
Causing Cupid thus to weep,
Think, O think! what cruel pains
He that's stung by thee sustains."

ODE XLI.

THE BANQUET OF WINE.

NOW let us gaily drink, and join
To celebrate the god of wine,
Bacchus, who taught his jovial throng
The dance, and patroniz'd the song;
In heart, in soul, with love the same,
The favourite of the Cyprian dame.
Revelry he nam'd his heir;
The Graces are his daughters fair:
Sadness in Lethe's lake he steeps;
Solicitude before him sleeps.
When in large bowls fair boys produce
The heart-exhilarating juice,
Then all our sorrows are resign'd,
They fly, and mingle with the wind.
The generous bowl then let us drain,
Dismissing care, forgetting pain:
For life, what pleasure can it give,
If with anxiety we live?
And what hereafter may betide
No living casuist can decide.

7. Let the winds that murmur, sweep] Horace has expressed himself in the same manner:

——— Tristitiam et metus
Tradam protervis in mare Creticum
Portare ventis.——

Lov'd by the Muses, to the wind
Be all my fears and griefs resign'd,
To drown them in the Cretan main. Duncombe.

Ode XL.—Theocritus has imitated this beautiful ode in his nineteenth Idyllium. See p. 217 of this volume.

13. Dear mamma, a serpent small] Madam Dacier says, that Anacreon makes Cupid speak in this manner, because, according to the Pagan theology, the language of the gods was different from that of men: but, as Longepierre ingeniously observes, "To render a passage of this nature learned, is to make it obscure; for nothing can be more natural to imagine, than that an infant, who had heard of the stinging of serpents, when he found himself stung by a little creature, he hardly knew what, should immediately think it one. The labourers might call it a bee, if they pleased: his pain and fright made him persist that it was a serpent.

Ode XLI.—3, 4. Bacchus who taught the jovial throng
The dance, and patroniz'd the song]

Tibullus says the same:

Ille liquor docuit voces inflectere cantu;
Movit et ad certos nescia membra modos.
L. 1. el. 7.

This as swains quaff'd, spontaneous numbers came,
They prais'd the festal cask, and hymn'd thy name;
All ecstacy! to certain time they bound,
And beat in measur'd awkwardness the ground.
Grainger.

8. The Graces are his daughters fair] Madam Dacier supposes this to be the passage on which the opinion, that the Graces were the daughters of Bacchus and Venus, was founded.

16. Dismissing care] Macedonius, in an epigram in the first book of the Anthologia, c. 25. says, that to banish care was a precept of Anacreon's.

Την γαρ Ανακρεοντος ενι πραπιδεσσι φυλασσω
Παρφασιην, ὅτι δει φροντιδα μη κατεχειν.

For still I hold Anacreon's rule the best,
To banish care for ever from my breast.

19, 20. And what hereafter may betide, &c.] Anacreon is not singular in enforcing the necessity of enjoying life from the brevity and uncertainty of it. Rufinus has an epigram in the seventh

The days of man are fix'd by fate,
Dark and obscure, though short the date.
Then let me, warm with wine, advance,
And revel in the tipsy dance;
Or, breathing odours, sport and play
Among the fair, among the gay.
As for those stubborn fools that will
Be wretched, be they wretched still.
But let us gaily drink, and join
To celebrate the god of wine.

ODE XLII.

ON HIMSELF.

When Bacchus, jolly god, invites,
In sprightly dance my heart delights;
When with blithe youths I drain the bowl,
The lyre can harmonize my soul:
But when indulging amorous play,
I frolic with the fair and gay,
With hyacinthine chaplet crown'd,
Then, then the sweetest joys abound;
My honest heart nor envy bears,
Nor envy's poison'd arrow fears;
By rankling malice never stung,
I shun the venom-venting tongue.
And at the jovial banquet hate
Contentions, battles, and debate:
When to the lyre's melodious sound
With Phyllis in the dance I bound,
The blooming fair, the silver lyre,
Should only dance and love inspire:
Then let us pass life's peaceful day
In mirth and innocence away.

book of the Anthologia, epigram 143, to this purpose.

Let us, my friend, in joy refine,
Bathe, crown our brows, and quaff the wine:
Short is the space for human joys;
What age prevents not, death destroys.

And Martial,

Non est, crede mihi, sapienti dicere, "vivam:"
Sera nimis vita est crastina, vive hodie.

"I'll live to morrow," 'tis not wise to say:
'Twill be too late to morrow—live to day.

Ode XLII.—13, 14. And at the jovial banquet hate
Contentions, battles, and debate]

Thus our poet in his seventh epigram says,

I ne'er can think his conversation good,
Who o'er the bottle talks of wars and blood;
But his, whose wit the pleasing talk refines,
And lovely Venus with the Graces joins.

19. Let us pass life's peaceful day] The Greek is, Βιον ησυχον φερωμεν. Anacreon esteemed tranquillity the happiest ingredient of life: Thus, Ode the 39th, he praises the γαληνην βιοτυ,

—— Life's rural scene,
Sweet, sequester'd, and serene.

ODE XLIII.

THE GRASSHOPPER.

Thee, sweet grasshopper, we call
Happiest of insects all,
Who from spray to spray canst skip,
And the dew of morning sip:
Little sips inspire to sing;
Then thou'rt happy as a king.
All, whatever thou can'st see,
Herbs and flowers belong to thee;
All the various seasons yield,
All the produce of the field.
Thou, quite innocent of harm,
Lov'st the farmer, and the farm;
Singing sweet when summer's near,
Thou to all mankind art dear;
Dear to all the tuneful Nine
Seated round the throne divine;
Dear to Phœbus, god of day,
He inspir'd thy sprightly lay,
And with voice melodious blest,
And in vivid colours drest.
Thou from spoil of time art free;
Age can never injure thee.
Wisest daughter of the earth!
Fond of song, and full of mirth;

Ode XLIII.—4, 5. And the dew of morning sip:
Little sips inspire to sing]

Dew is the nourishment of grasshoppers. Thus Virgil, ecl. 5, v. 77.

Dumque thymo pascentur apes, dum rore cicadæ.

Bees feed on thyme, and grasshoppers on dew.

The Greek poets also describe the grasshopper as a musical insect. Thus Theocritus, Idyll. 1.

—Τεττιγος επει τυγε φερτερον αδεις.

Thy song is sweeter than the grasshopper's.

Antipater, in an epigram of the Anthologia, book 1. says,

Αρκει Τεττιγας μεθυσαι δροσος, αλλα πιοντες
Αειδειν κυκνων εισι γεγωνοτεροι.

Inspir'd by dew the grasshoppers rejoice,
Nor boasts the swan so musical a voice.

15. Dear to all the tuneful Nine] Ælian, writing against those who eat grasshoppers, says: They are ignorant how much they offend the Muses, the daughters of Jupiter. Whence it appears, that these animals were esteemed sacred to the Muses, and the eating of them accounted an impiety. The following is a translation of an epigram from the first book of the Anthologia, chap. 33. containing a beautiful complaint of a grasshopper against that practice.

Τιπτε με τον, κ. τ. λ.

Why do ye, swains, a grasshopper pursue
Content with solitude, and rosy dew?
Me, whose sweet song can o'er the nymphs prevail:
I charm them in the forest, hill, or dale,
And me they call their summer-nightingale.
See, on your fruits the thrush and black-bird prey!
See, the bold starlings steal your grain away!
Destroy your foes—why should you me pursue
Content with verdant leaves, and rosy dew?

23. Wisest daughter of the earth] The Athe-

Free from flesh, exempt from pains,
No blood riots in thy veins:
To the blest I equal thee;
Thou'rt a demi-deity.

ODE XLIV.

THE DREAM.

I DREAM'D, that late I pinions wore,
And swiftly seem'd through air to soar;
Me fleeter Cupid, quick as thought,
Pursued, and in an instant caught,
Though at his feet hung weights of lead:
What can this vision mean, I said?
Its mystic sense I thus explain:
I, who ere-while have worn the chain
Of many a fair-one for a day,
Then flung the flowery band away,
Am now involv'd, and fetter'd fast
In links that will for ever last.

ODE XLV.

BY ANOTHER HAND.

CUPID'S DARTS.

As the god of manual arts
Forg'd at Lemnos missile darts,

nians called themselves Τεττιγες, grasshoppers, and some of them wore little grasshoppers of gold in their hair, as badges of honour, to distinguish them from others of later duration; and likewise as a memorial, that they were born of the earth like those insects.

25, 26. Free from flesh, exempt from pains,
No blood riots in thy veins.]

Homer represents the gods as free from blood. Speaking of Venus wounded, book 5. he says,

From the clear vein a stream immortal flow'd,
Such stream as issues from a wounded god;
Pure emanation! uncorrupted flood!
Unlike our gross, diseas'd, terrestrial blood:
(For not the bread of man their life sustains,
Nor wine's inflaming juice supplies their veins.)
Pope.

Ode XLIV.—Nothing can be more politely imagined than this ode, nor more courtly than the turn of it. "Behold," says madame Dacier, "one of the finest and most gallant odes of antiquity; and if she, for whom it was composed, was as beautiful, all Greece could produce nothing more charming."

Ode XLV.—Mons. Le Fevre was so transported with this ode, that he could not forbear crying out,

Felix, ah! nimium felix, cui carmine tali
Fluxit ab Aoniis vena beata jugis.
Quid melius dictaret amor, risusque jocique,
Et cum germanis gratia juncta suis?

Thrice happy he! to whose enraptur'd soul
Such numbers from th' Aonian mountains roll:
More finish'd what could love or laughter write,
Or what the graces dictate more polite?
John Addison.

2. Forg'd at Lemnos] Lemnos was an island of

Darts of steel for Cupid's bow,
Source of joy, and source of woe;
Venus, fast as Vulcan wrought,
Ting'd them in a honey'd draught:
But her son in bitter gall
Ting'd them, doubly-ting'd them all.
Here, releas'd from war's alarms,
Enters the fierce god of arms;
Whether led by will or chance,
Here he shakes his weighty lance.
Cupid's shafts with scornful eyes
Straight he views, and straight decries:
"This is slight, and that a toy
Fit for children to employ."
"These," said Cupid, "I admit
Toys indeed, for children fit:
But, if I divine aright,
Take it——this is not so slight."
Mars receives it; Venus smiles
At her son's well-season'd wiles.
Mars, with sudden pain possest,
Sighs from out his inmost breast:
"Cupid, you aright divine,
Not so slight this shaft of thine;
Small of size! but strong of make!
"Take it—I have try'd it—take."
"No," reply'd the wanton boy,
"Keep it, Mars, 'tis but a toy."

ODE XLVI.

THE POWER OF GOLD.

LOVE's a pain that works our woe;
Not to love, is painful too:
But, alas! the greatest pain
Waits the love that meets disdain.

the Ægean sea sacred to Vulcan, who, in the first book of the Iliad, gives an account of Jupiter's throwing him down from Heaven, and his fall upon that island:

Once in your cause I felt his matchless might,
Hurl'd headlong downward from th' etherial height;
Tost all the day in rapid circles round;
Nor, till the Sun descended, touch'd the ground:
Breathless I fell, in giddy motion lost;
The Sinthians rais'd me on the Lemnian coast.
Pope.

6. Ting'd them in a honey'd draught] Horace calls it the nectar of Venus:

——oscula quæ Venus
Quintâ parte sui nectaris imbuit.

Lips, which Venus bath'd for joy
In her celestial dew. Jeffreys.

23, 24. Mars, with sudden pain possest,
Sigh'd from out his inmost breast.]

This sentiment is extremely delicate, intimating, that one cannot even touch the darts of Cupid with safety. Moschus concludes his first Idyllium with a similar thought:

Perhaps he'll say, "Alas! no harm I know,
Here take my darts, my arrows, and my bow."
Ah! touch them not, fallacious is his aim,
His darts, his arrows all are tipt with flame.

What avails ingenuous worth,
Sprightly wit, or noble birth?
All these virtues useless prove;
Gold alone engages love.
May he be completely curst,
Who the sleeping mischief first
Wak'd to life, and, vile before,
Stamp'd with worth the sordid ore.
Gold creates in brethren strife;
Gold destroys the parent's life;
Gold produces civil jars,
Murders, massacres, and wars:
But, the worst effect of gold,
Love, alas! is bought and sold.

ODE XLVII.

YOUNG OLD-AGE.

YES, yes, I own, I love to see
Old men facetious, blithe, and free;
I love the youth that light can bound,
Or graceful swim th' harmonious round:
But when old-age jocose, though grey,
Can dance and frolic with the gay;
'Tis plain to all the jovial throng,
Though hoar the head, the heart is young.

Ode XLVI.—6. Sprightly wit, or noble birth.

Nil tibi nobilitas poterit conducere amanti.
Propertius.

Your noble birth pleads not the cause of love.

8. Gold alone engages love] Ovid says the same:

Aurea sunt verè nunc sæcula: plurimus auro
Venit honos: auro conciliatur amor.

This is the golden age; all worship gold:
Honours are purchas'd, love and beauty sold.
Our iron age is grown an age of gold,
'Tis who bids most, for all men would be sold.
Dryden.

13. Gold creates in brethren strife, &c.] Phocylides, in his Admonitory Poem, ver. 38, &c. seems to have imitated this passage.

Ἡ φιλοχρημοσυνη, κ. τ. λ.

On sordid avarice various evils wait,
And gold, false, glittering, is the tempting bait.
O cursed gold! in whom our woes combine,
Why dost thou thus with pleasing ruin shine?
Cause of the parent's curse, of brethren's strife,
Wars, murders, and all miseries of life.

Ode XLVII.—8. Though hoar the head, the heart is young] Longepierre quotes a passage from Guarini, where the same sentiment is expressed, though in a different manner; and which is translated by John Addison.

———O Corisca mia cara,
D'anima Linco e non di forze sono;
E'n questo vecchio tronco
E piu che fosse mai verde il desio.

Yes, my Corisca, Lincus is the same,
Though not in youthful force, in youthful flame;
Though age and wrinkles on my front appear,
My heart is green, and love still blossoms there.

ODE XLVIII.

BY DR. BROOME.

GAY LIFE.

GIVE me Homer's tuneful lyre,
Let the sound my breast inspire!
But with no troublesome delight
Of arms, and heroes slain in fight:
Let it play no conquests here,
Or conquests only o'er the fair!
Boy, reach that volume—book divine!
The statutes of the god of wine:
He, legislator, statutes draws,
And I, his judge, inforce his laws;
And, faithful to the weighty trust,
Compel his votaries to be just:
Thus, round the bowl impartial flies,
Till to the sprightly dance we rise;
We frisk it with a lively bound,
Charm'd with the lyre's harmonious sound;
Then pour forth, with a heat divine,
Rapturous songs that breathe of wine.

ODE XLIX.

BY ANOTHER HAND.

TO A PAINTER.

WHILE you my lyre's soft numbers hear,
Ingenious painter, lend an ear,
And, while it charms your ravish'd heart,
Display the wonders of your art.
First draw a nation blithe and gay,
Laughing and sporting life away;
Let them in sprightly dances bound,
While their shrill pipes the Bacchæ sound;

Ode XLVIII.—8. The statutes of the god of wine] It was customary with the ancients, at their entertainments, to choose a king or master of the revels, who both regulated the size of the cups, and the quantity each person was to drink: he was generally chosen by the cast of a die.

Nec regna vini sortiere talis. Hor.

No longer by the die's successful cast
Shalt thou control the gay repast.
Duncombe.

—Quem Venus arbitrum
Dicet bibendi— L. 2. ode 7.

Who, nam'd by Venus, at the jovial board
The laws of drinking shall prescribe?
Duncombe.

Ode XLIX.—5. Draw a nation blithe and gay] It is probable, that in this ode Anacreon had in view the image of peace, which Vulcan represented upon the shield of Achilles. Iliad 18.

Two cities radiant on the shield appear,
The image one of peace, and one of war;
Here sacred pomp and genial feast delight,
And solemn dance and hymeneal rite;
Along the streets the new-made brides are led,
With torches flaming, to the nuptial bed:
The youthful dancers in a circle bound
To the soft flute and cittern's silver sound;
Through the fair streets the matrons in a row
Stand in the porches, and enjoy the show.
Pope.

And, if you can perfection give,
Bid every breathing figure live:
And then, lest life insipid prove,
To make them happy, bid them love.

ODE L.

BY DR. BROOME.

THE HAPPY EFFECTS OF WINE.

SEE! see! the jolly god appears,
His hand a mighty goblet bears;
With sparkling wine full charg'd it flows,
The sovereign cure of human woes.
  Wine gives a kind release from care,
And courage to subdue the fair;
Instructs the cheerful to advance
Harmonious in the sprightly dance.
Hail! goblet, rich with generous wines!
See! round the verge a vine-branch twines.
See! how the mimic clusters roll,
As ready to refil the bowl.
  Wine keeps its happy patients free
From every painful malady;
Our best physician all the year;
Thus guarded, no disease we fear,
No troublesome disease of mind,
Until another year grows kind,
And loads again the fruitful vine,
And brings again our health—new wine.

ODE LI.

BY ANOTHER HAND.

ON A DISK, REPRESENTING VENUS.

RARE artist, whose inventive skill
Could this orb with wonders fill!
Where the mimic ocean glides
Soft with well-dissembled tides;
The waves seem floating, and above
Shines the beauteous queen of love:
The workman's fancy mounted high,
And stole th' idea from the sky.
Transporting sight!—the waves conceal
But what 'twere impious to reveal!
She, like some flower all-blossom'd gay,
Shines along the smiling way.
The amorous waters, as she swims,
Crowd to embrace her snowy limbs;
Then, proudly swelling to be prest,
Beneath her snowy fragrant breast
Ambitiously up-rise on high,
And lift the goddess to the sky;
And, while her lucid limbs they lave,
She brightens the transparent wave:
So violets enlighten'd glow,
Surrounded by the lily's snow.
  But see! a lovely, smiling train,
Conspicuous o'er the limpid main,
The queen attends! in triumph moves
Gay Cupid with his laughing Loves.
On dolphins borne, in state they ride,
And beautify the silver tide:
Dancing around in shoals they play,
And humble adoration pay.
  Rare art, that life to phantoms gives!
See! see! a second Venus lives.

ODE LII.

BY DR. BROOME.

GRAPES, OR THE VINTAGE.

Io! the vintage now is done!
And purpled with th' autumnal sun;
The grapes gay youths and virgins bear,
The sweetest product of the year!

Ode L.—4. The sovereign cure of human woes] Homer introduces Helen mixing such a bowl. Odyssy, b. 4.

Mean-time with genial joy to warm the soul,
Bright Helen mix'd a mirth-inspiring bowl;
Temper'd with drugs of sovereign use, t' asswage
The boiling bosom of tumultuous rage;
To clear the cloudy front of wrinkled care,
And dry the tearful sluices of despair.
Charm'd with that virtuous draught, th' exalted mind
All sense of woe delivers to the wind.
Though on the blazing pile his parent lay,
Or a lov'd brother groan'd his life away,
Or darling son, oppress'd by ruffian force,
Fell breathless at his feet, a mangled corse,
From morn to eve, impassive and serène,
The man entranc'd would view the deathful scene.
Fenton.

Ode LI.—6. Shines the beauteous queen of love] There are several epigrams in the fourth book of the Anthologia on Venus rising from the sea. I shall give a translation of one of them, beginning,

Ταν εκφυγυσαν, κ. τ. λ.

Apelles, rapt in sweet surprise,
Saw Venus from the ocean rise:
What art before could never give,
He made the breathing picture live.
Her radiant locks luxuriant flow'd;
Her lovely eyes serenely glow'd;
Like two round apples ripe, her breast
Rose, gently suing to be prest.

23. —a lovely smiling train, &c.]

So when bright Venus rises from the flood,
Around in throngs the wondering Nereids crowd;
The Tritons gaze, and tune the vocal shell,
And every grace unsung the waves conceal.
Garth's Disp. b. 6.

As when sweet Venus, so the fable sings,
Awak'd by Nereids, from the ocean springs;
With smiles she sees the threatening billows rise,
Spreads smooth the surge, and clears the louring skies;
Light o'er the deep with fluttering Cupids crown'd,
The pearly conch* and silver turtles bound;
Her tresses shed ambrosial odours round.
Tickell. Prosp. of Peace.

Ode LII.—3. The grapes gay youths and virgins bear] Homer, in his beautiful description of the vintage, book 18, introduces young men and maids employed in the same office.

To this one path-way gently winding leads,
Where march a train with baskets on their heads.

* In Dodsley's Miscellanies it is by mistake printed, the pearly couch. Venus, speaking of a beautiful woman, says,

Hæc & cœruleis mecum consurgere digna
Fluctibus; et nostrâ potuit considere conchâ.
Statius.

In vats the heavenly load they lay,
And swift the damsels trip away:
The youths alone the wine-press tread,
For wine's by skilful drunkards made.
Mean-time the mirthful song they raise,
Io! Bacchus, to thy praise!
And viewing the blest juice, in thought
Quaff an imaginary draught.
  Gaily through wine the old advance,
And doubly tremble in the dance;
In fancy'd youth they chant and play,
Forgetful that their locks are grey.
  Through wine the youth completes his loves;
He haunts the silence of the groves:
Where stretch'd beneath th' embowering shade
He sees some love-inspiring maid;
On beds of rosy sweets she lies,
Inviting sleep to close her eyes:
Fast by her side his limbs he throws,
Her hand he presses—breathes his vows;
And cries, "My love, my soul, comply
This instant, or, alas! I die."
In vain the youth persuasion tries!
In vain!—her tongue at least denies:
Then, scorning death through dull despair,
He storms th' unwilling willing fair;
Blessing the grapes that could dispense
The happy, happy impudence.

ODE LIII.

BY DR. BROOME.

THE ROSE.

COME, lyrist, tune thy harp, and play
Responsive to my vocal lay;
Gently touch it, while I sing
The rose, the glory of the spring.
  To Heaven the rose in fragrance flies,
The sweetest incense of the skies.
Thee, joy of Earth, when vernal hours
Pour forth a blooming waste of flowers,
The gaily-smiling graces wear
A trophy in their flowing hair:
Thee Venus, queen of beauty, loves,
And, crown'd with thee, more graceful moves.
  In fabled song, and tuneful lays,
Their favourite rose the Muses praise:
To pluck the rose the virgin-train
With blood their pretty fingers stain;
Nor dread the pointed terrours round,
That threaten, and inflict a wound:
See! how they wave the charming toy,
Now kiss, now snuff the fragrant joy.
  The rose the poets strive to praise,
And for it would exchange their bays;
O! ever to the sprightly feast
Admitted, welcome, pleasing guest!
But chiefly when the goblet flows,
And rosy wreaths adorn our brows!
  Lovely, smiling rose, how sweet
All objects where thy beauties meet!
Aurora, with a blushing ray,
And rosy fingers, spreads the day:
The Graces more enchanting show,
When rosy blushes paint their snow;
And every pleas'd beholder seeks
The rose in Cytherea's cheeks.
  When pain afflicts, or sickness grieves,
Its juice the drooping heart relieves;
And, after death, its odours shed
A pleasing fragrance o'er the dead:
And when its withering charms decay,
And sinking, fading, die away,
Triumphant o'er the rage of time,
It keeps the fragrance of its prime.

(Fair maids and blooming youths) that smiling bear
The purple product of th' autumnal year. Pope.

Ode LIII.—This ode will be understood by supposing that Anacreon celebrates a rose, and requests a lyrist to play to his voice.

13, 14. In fabled song, and tuneful lays,
  Their favourite rose the Muses praise.]

The rose was consecrated to the Muses. See Sappho.

For thy rude hand ne'er pluck'd the lovely rose
That on the mountain of Pieria blows.

21. The rose the poets strive to praise] The rose is celebrated in the fifth ode of Anacreon; in a fragment of Sappho; and in the fourteenth Idyllium of Ausonius, in which are the following beautiful lines:

Quàm longa una dies, ætas tam longa rosarum,
  Quas pubescentes longa senecta premit:
Quam modo nascentem rutilus conspexit Eoüs,
  Hanc veniens sero vespere vidit anum.

See! in the morning blooms the rose!
But soon her transient glories close:
She opens with the rising day,
And with the setting fades away.
Duncombe.

30. And rosy fingers, spreads the day] Ῥοδοδάκτυλος, rosy finger'd, is an epithet frequently used by Homer, and applied to the morning. Dryden also uses it:

The rosy-finger'd Morn appears,
And from her mantle shakes her tears.

Milton's description of the morning is also very beautiful:

——The Morn,
Wak'd by the circling Hours, with rosy hand
Unbarr'd the gates of light—— B. 6. v. 2.

35. When pain afflicts, or sickness grieves] It is well known, that the rose is used as an ingredient in the composition of several medicines.

37. And, after death, its odours shed
  A pleasing fragrance o'er the dead.]

The ancients used roses in embalming their dead. Venus anoints the body of Hector with unguent of roses, to prevent it from corruption, Iliad, book 23.

Celestial Venus hover'd o'er his head,
And roseate unguents, heavenly fragrance! shed.
Pope.

They also crowned the tombs of their friends with roses and other flowers.

41. Triumphant o'er the rage of time, &c.]

Come, lyrist, join to sing the birth
Of this sweet offspring of the Earth!
When Venus from the ocean's bed
Rais'd o'er the waves her lovely head;
When warlike Pallas sprung from Jove,
Tremendous to the powers above;
To grace the world the teeming Earth
Gave the fragrant infant birth;
And, "This," she cry'd, "I this ordain
My favourite, queen of flowers to reign."
But, first, th' assembled gods debate
The future wonder to create:
Agreed at length, from Heaven they threw
A drop of rich nectareous dew;
A bramble-stem the drop receives,
And straight the rose adorns the leaves.
The gods to Bacchus gave the flower,
To grace him in the genial hour.

ODE LIV.

BY DR. BROOME.

GROWN YOUNG.

When sprightly youths my eyes survey,
I too am young, and I am gay;
In dance my active body swims,
And sudden pinions lift my limbs.
Haste, crown, Cybeba, crown my brows
With garlands of the fragrant rose!
Hence, hoary age!—I now am young,
And dance the mirthful youths among.
Come then, my friends, the goblet drain!
Blest juice!—I feel thee in each vein!
See! how with active bounds I spring!
How strong, and yet how sweet I sing!
How blest am I, who thus excel
In pleasing arts of trifling well!

ODE LV.

BY DR. BROOME.

THE MARK.

The stately steed expressive bears
A mark imprinted on his hairs:
The turban, that adorns the brows
Of Asia's sons, the Parthian shows:
And marks betray the lover's heart,
Deeply engrav'd by Cupid's dart:
I plainly read them in his eyes,
That look too foolish, or too wise.

ODE LVI.

BY DR. BROOME.

OLD AGE.

Alas! the powers of life decay!
My hairs are fall'n, or turn'd to grey:
The smiling bloom, and youthful grace,
Is banish'd from my faded face:
Thus man beholds, with weeping eyes,
Himself half-dead before he dies.

Nothing preserves its fragrance, when dried, longer than the rose.

——και ȣ ῥοδον αυον ολειται. Theocr. Id. 27.

Blown roses hold their sweetness to the last.
Dryden.

56. A drop of rich nectareous dew, &c.] Bion tells us, that the blood of Adonis gave birth to the rose. Αἷμα ῥοδον τικτει.

Both tears and drops of blood were turn'd to flowers;
From these in crimson beauty sprung the rose,
Cerulean-bright anemonies from those.

Ode LIV.—5. Cybeba] Cybebe, or Cybele, seems to be the name of a female attendant, taken from Cybele the mother of the gods.

Ode LV.—3, 4. The turban that adorns the brows
Of Asia's sons, the Parthian [shows.]

The Greek is τιαρα, tiara, an ornament for the head like the modern turban. Addison quotes a passage from Dionysius, containing a description of the situation and manners of the Parthians; which he has thus translated:

Beyond the Caspian straits those realms extend,
Where circling bows the martial Parthians bend.
Vers'd only in the rougher arts of war,
No fields they wound, nor urge the shining share.
No ships they boast to stem the rolling tide,
Nor lowing herds o'er flowery meadows guide:
But infants wing the feather'd shaft for flight,
And rein the fiery steed with fond delight.
On every plain the whistling spear alarms,
The neighing courser, and the clang of arms;
For there no food the little heroes taste,
Till warlike sweat has earn'd the short repast.

Ode LVI.—We are indebted for this ode to Henry Stephens. It is also extant in Stobæus, who acknowledges it to be Anacreon's.

1, 2. Alas! the powers of life decay!
My hairs are fall'n, or turn'd to grey.]

Theocritus finally touches upon the progress which old-age makes on the human body.

——απο κροταφων πελομεσθα
Παντες γηραλεοι, και επισαχεω ες γενυν ερπει
Λευκαινων ὁ χρονος.——

First from our temples age begins her race,
Thence whitening time creeps softly o'er the face.
Creech.

3. The smiling bloom and youthful grace]

——fugit retro
Levis juventas, et decor, aridâ
Pellente lascivos amores
Canitie, facilemque somnum.
Hor. b. 2. od. 14.

Behold our years! how fast they fly;
Youth vanishes, and beauty fades;
Age drops her snow upon our heads,
And drives sweet slumbers from our eye!
Duncombe.

For this, and for the grave, I fear,
And pour the never-ceasing tear:
A dreadful prospect strikes the eye,
I soon must sicken, soon must die.
For this, the mournful groan I shed,
I dread—alas! the hour I dread!
What eye can stedfastly survey
Death, and its dark tremendous way?
For soon as fate has clos'd our eyes,
Man dies—for ever, ever dies!
All pale, all senseless in the urn!
Never, ah! never to return.

ODE LVII.

THAT WE SHOULD DRINK WITH MODERATION.

Bring hither, boy, a mighty bowl,
And let me quench my thirsty soul;
Fill two parts water, fill it high,
Add one of wine, for I am dry:
Thus let the limpid stream allay
The jolly god's too potent sway.
Quick, boy, dispatch—My friends, no more,
Thus let us drinking rant and roar;
Such clamorous riot better suits
Unpolish'd Scythia's barbarous brutes:
Let us, while music tunes the soul,
Mix temperance in the friendly bowl.

ODE LVIII.

THE LOVE-DRAUGHT.

As late of flow'rets fresh and fair
I wove a chaplet for my hair,
Beneath a rose, gay summer's pride,
The wanton god of love I spy'd,
I seiz'd him, resolute of soul,
And plung'd him in my flowing bowl,
Resolv'd to have a draught divine,
And fairly swallow'd him in wine:
E'er since his fluttering wings impart
Strange titillations to my heart.

ODE LIX.

TO A SCORNFUL BEAUTY.

Why thus with scornful look you fly,
Wild Thracian filly, tell me why?
Think'st thou that I no skill possess,
And want both courage and address?
Know, that whenever I think fit
To tame thee with the galling bit,
Just where I please, with tighten'd rein,
I'll urge thee round the dusty plain.
Now on the flowery turf you feed,
Or lightly bound along the mead,
So wild, so wanton, and untry'd,
You want some youth to mount and ride.

ODE LX.

EPITHALAMIUM ON THE MARRIAGE OF STRATOCLES AND MYRILLA.

Venus, fair queen of gods above,
Cupid, thou mighty power of love,
And Hymen bland, by Heaven design'd
The fruitful source of human-kind:
To you, as to the lyre I sing,
Flows honour from the sounding string;
Propitious to the numbers prove,
O Venus, Hymen, god of love.

---

14. Death, and its dark tremendous way] Catullus, speaking of Lesbia's sparrow, says,

> Qui nunc it per iter tenebricosum,
> Illuc unde negant ridire quenquam.

> Death has summon'd it to go,
> Pensive, to the shades below;
> Dismal regions! from whose bourne,
> Alas! no travellers return.

See also Moschus on the death of Bion:

> But we, the great, the brave, the learn'd, the wise,
> Soon as the hand of Death has clos'd our eyes,
> In tombs forgotten lie, no suns restore,
> We sleep, for ever sleep, to wake no more.

Ode LVII.—3. Fill two parts water] The ancients usually drank their wine mixed with water. Madam Dacier observes, that Hesiod prescribes three measures of water to one of wine in summer.

10. Unpolish'd Scythia's barbarous brutes] The Scythians were remarkable for their intemperance in drinking, and quarrelling over their cups.

Ode LVIII.—This little ode is extant in the seventh book of the Anthologia, and ascribed to Julian, *απο των ὑπαρχων Αιγυπτȣ*, a king of Egypt, who wrote several other things with elegance. As its beauty has hitherto procured it a place in most of the editions of Anacreon, it was thought worthy to be retained in this translation.

Ode LIX.—9, 10. Now on the flowery turf you feed,
Or lightly bound along the mead]

Horace has imitated this ode at the beginning of the 23d ode of the first book, the 5th of the second, but particularly in the 11th of the third.

> Quæ, velut latis equa trima campis
> Ludit exultim, metuitque tangi,
> Nuptiarum expers, et adhuc protervo
> Cruda marito.

> She sports along the verdant plain,
> Like a fleet filly, shuns the rein,
> Fears to be touch'd; nor yet will prove,
> Wild and untry'd, the pleasing pains of love.
>
> Duncombe.

Ode LX.—Theodorus Prodromus, who wrote the amours of Dosicles and Rhodanthe, has preserved this Epithalamium; which, as madam Dacier observes, is a sort of poem that used to be sung to a new-married couple on the morning after the ceremony.

4. The fruitful source of human-kind] Dionysius of Halicarnassus calls marriage, *Σωτηριαν τȣ γενȣς*, The preserver of mankind.

View, gentle youth, with rapture view
This blooming bride ordain'd for you:
Rise quick, and feast on all her charms,
Lest, like a bird, she fly your arms.
O happy youth! by Venus blest,
But happier on Myrilla's breast:
"See how the fair-one, sweetly coy,
All soft confusion, meets the joy,
Blooming as health, fresh as May-flowers,
And bright as radiant noon-tide hours."
Of all the flowers upon the plains,
The rose unmatch'd in beauty reigns;
Myrilla thus in charms excels,
She shines the rose among the belles.
O may, blest youth, the god of day
The pleasing toils of love survey:
And may a beauteous, blooming boy
Crown your soft vows with lasting joy!

ODE LXI.

ON GOLD.

When Gold, that fugitive unkind,
With pinions swifter than the wind,
Flies from my willing arms away,
(For gold with me will never stay)
With careless eyes his flight I view,
Who would perfidious foes pursue?
When from the glittering mischief free,
What mortal can compare with me!
All my inquietudes of mind
I give to murmur with the wind:
Love sweetly tunes my melting lyre
To tender notes of soft desire.
But when the vagrant finds I burn
With rage, and slight him in his turn,
He comes, my quiet to destroy,
With the mad family of Joy:
Adieu to love, and soft desire!
He steals me from my soothing lyre.
O faithless Gold! thou dear deceit!
Say, wilt thou still my fancy cheat?
This lute far sweeter transport brings,
More pleasing these love-warbled strings:
For thou with envy and with wiles
Me of my dearest love beguiles,
Dashing the cup of sweet desire,
And robb'st me of my golden lyre.
Then, for with me thou wilt not stay,
To faithless Phrygians speed'st away,
Proud and assiduous to please
Those sons of perfidy and ease.
Me from the Muse thou would'st detain,
But all thy tempting arts are vain;
Ne'er shall my voice forget to sing,
Nor this right hand to touch the string:
Away to other climes! farewell!——
Leave me to tune the vocal shell.

ODE LXII.

ON THE SPRING.

What bright joy can this exceed,
This of roving o'er the mead?
Where the hand of Flora pours,
Sweetest, voluntary flow'rs:
Where the Zephyr's balmy gale
Wantons in the lovely vale.
O! how pleasing to recline
Underneath the spreading vine,
In the close concealment laid
With a love-inspiring maid!
Fair, and sweet, and young, and gay,
Chatting all the live-long day.

ODE LXIII.

TO CUPID.

Mighty god of flames and darts,
Great controler of all hearts;
With thee Venus, lovely fair,
Venus with the golden hair,
And the bright-ey'd Dryads play,
Nymphs that on the mountains stray:
Come, propitious to my vow,
Leave the mountain's rugged brow;
Quick descend into the plain,
Where the object of my pain,
Sweet Eurypyle imparts
Anxious hopes to youthful hearts;
Melt to love the yielding fair,
Teach her not to give despair;

12. Lest, like a bird, &c.] The Greek is Μη σε φυγη περδικος αγρα, Lest the partridge should escape you; alluding to the coyness of a young bride.

15. See how, &c.] These four lines are taken from a translation of this poem, which appeared in the Student.

25. May a beauteous blooming boy, &c.] The Greek is, Κυπαριττος πεφυκοι σευ ενι κηπω, May a cypress grow in your garden! that is, "May a child, as beautiful and as long lived as a cypress, crown your happiness!" Madam Dacier observes, this was a proverbial way of speaking.

Ode LXI.—The Vatican manuscript acknow ledges this ode to be Anacreon's.

9, 10. All my inquietudes of mind
I give to murmur with the wind.]

Horace has imitated this passage, book 1. ode 26. which is an argument for the authenticity of this ode. See Ode 39.

Let the winds that murmur, sweep
All my sorrows to the deep.

28. To faithless Phrygians, &c.] The poet calls the Phrygians faithless, from their king Laomedon's deceiving Apollo and Neptune of the reward he had promised them for building the walls of Troy; and from his defrauding Hercules of his recompense, who had delivered his daughter Hesione from being devoured by a sea-monster.
Madame Dacier.

Ode LXII.—This ode has also the authority of the Vatican manuscript to claim Anacreon for its author.

7, 8. O! how pleasing to recline
Underneath the spreading vine.]

Madame Dacier remarks, that the vines in Greece were so high as to form a commodious shade.

Ode LXIII.—We owe the preservation of this fragment to Dion Chrysostom.

Thou my passion must approve,
Melt the yielding fair to love.

ODE LXIV.

TO CUPID.

IDALIAN god, with golden hair,
O Cupid, ever young and fair,
Fly to my aid, and safely shroud
Me in a purple-beaming cloud,
And on thy painted wings convey
A faithful lover on his way.
Thy blandishments disturb my rest,
And kindle tumults in my breast;
The pleasing poison was convey'd
Late from the lovely Lesbian maid;
Her sun-bright eye discharg'd a dart,
That rankling preys upon my heart:
In sparkling wit beyond compare,
She slights, alas! my silver hair,
Regardless of my heart-felt pain,
And fondly loves some happier swain.

ODE LXV.

ON HIMSELF.

I LATELY thought, delightful theme!
Anacreon saw me in a dream,

Ode LXIV.—This fragment is cited by Athenæus. Barnes supposes it to have been written on the poetess Sappho; and, to confirm his opinion, produces the testimonies of Chamæleon and Hermesianax the Colophonian; the last of which in his third elegy, says,

Και γαρ τον ὁ μελχρος κ. τ. λ.

For sweet Anacreon lov'd the Lesbian dame;
The Muse-rapt maid inspir'd the brightest flame:
And oft his native isle he would resign
For wit more brilliant, and for better wine.

10. The lovely Lesbian maid] The following lines are supposed to be part of the answer which Sappho returned to Anacreon:

Κεινον, ω χρυσοθρονε Μυσ', ενισπες
Ὑμνον, εκ της καλλιγυναικος εσθλας
Τηιος χωρας ὃν αειδε τερπνως
Πρεσβυς αγαυος.

Ye Muses, ever fair and young,
High seated on the golden throne,
Anacreon sent to me a song
In sweetest numbers, not his own;
For, by your sacred raptures fir'd,
The poet warbled what the Muse inspir'd.

Ode LXV.—This and the five following odes are not translated by Addison.

Some have imagined that this ode was not written by Anacreon, because he himself is the subject of it: but Barnes endeavours to prove it genuine from the ninth ode and the sixty-sixth, in both which Anacreon makes mention of himself; and from the frequent liberties which the best poets have taken of mentioning themselves in their own compositions.

The Teian sage, the honey'd bard,
Who call'd me with a sweet regard:
I, pleas'd to meet him, ran in haste,
And with a friendly kiss embrac'd.
'Tis true, he seem'd a little old,
But gay and comely to behold;
Still bow'd to Cytherea's shrine,
His lip was redolent of wine:
He reel'd as if he scarce could stand,
But Cupid led him by the hand.
The poet, with a gentle look,
A chaplet from his temples took,
That did of sweet Anacreon breathe,
And smiling gave to me the wreath.
I from his brow the flowery crown
Receiv'd, and plac'd it on my own:
Thence all my woes unnumber'd flow,
E'er since with raging love I glow.

ODE LXVI.

BY DR. BROOME.

ON APOLLO.

ONCE more, not uninspir'd, the string
I waken and spontaneous sing:
No Pythic laurel-wreath I claim,
That lifts ambition into fame:
My voice unbidden tunes the lay;
Some god impels and I obey.
Attend, ye groves! the Muse prepares
A sacred song in Phrygian airs;
Such as the swan expiring sings,
Melodious, by Cayster's springs,
Where listening winds in silence hear,
And to the gods the music bear.
Celestial Muse! attend and bring
Thy aid, while I thy Phœbus sing;
To Phœbus and the Muse belong
The laurel, lyre, and Delphic song.
Begin, begin the lofty strain!
How Phœbus lov'd, but lov'd in vain!
How Daphne fled his guilty flame,
And scorn'd a god that offer'd shame.
With glorious pride his vows she hears,
And Heaven, indulgent to her prayers,
To laurel chang'd the nymph, and gave
Her foliage to reward the brave.
Ah! how, on wings of love convey'd,
He flew to clasp the panting maid!
Now, now o'ertakes! but Heaven deceives
His hope—he seizes only leaves.
Why burns my raptur'd breast? ah why?
Ah! whither strives my soul to fly?
I feel the pleasing frenzy strong,
Impulsive to some nobler song:
Let, let the wanton fancy play,
But guide it, lest it devious stray.
But O! in vain—my Muse denies
Her aid, a slave to lovely eyes;
Suffice it to rehearse the pains
Of bleeding nymphs and dying swains;

Ode LXVI.—It is certain, that Anacreon wrote hymns in honour of the gods: this is undoubtedly one of them, and perhaps the most entire of any that remain. See the note on the 16th verse of the ninth ode.

Nor dare to wield the shafts of Love
That wound the gods and conquer Jove.
I yield! adieu the lofty strain;
Anacreon is himself again:
Again the melting song I play,
Attemper'd to the vocal lay.
See! see! how with attentive ears,
The youths imbibe the nectar'd airs!
And quaff, in bowery shades reclin'd,
My precepts, to regale the mind.

ODE LXVII.

ON LOVE.

To Love I wake the silver string,
And of his soft dominion sing:
A wreath of flowers adorns his brow,
The sweetest, fairest flowers that blow:
All mortals own his mighty sway,
And him the gods above obey.

ODE LXVIII.

THE SUPPLICATION.

QUEEN of the woodland chace, whose darts
Unerring pierce the mountain-harts,
Diana chaste, Jove's daughter fair,
Suppliant to thee I breathe my prayer.
Descend, propitious to my vow,
To where the streams of Lethe flow:
In pity aid a hapless race,
Bright goddess of the woodland chase;
With holy awe they own thy sway,
And meek in reverence obey.

ODE LXIX.

ARTEMON.

A FRAGMENT.

Now Artemon, a favourite name,
Inspires Eurypele with flame:

Ode LXVIII.—This is, as madame Dacier remarks, an entire hymn, or part of one, composed in honour of Diana, in favour of some town situated on the river Lethe, which she supposes to be Magnesia, near Ephesus.

It was probably made on occasion of some battle in which the Magnesians had been defeated. The poet entreats Diana to assist a people in distress, who depended only upon her protection.

Ode LXIX.—The fourth Epode of Horace has a great similitude to this ode:

Lisit superbus ambules pecuniâ, &c.

Though store of wealth you now possess,
Condition changes not with dress.
" Shall he who tir'd the lictor's hand,
Scourg'd by the magistrate's command,
With corn a thousand acres load,
With chariots wear the Appian road,
And, in contempt of Otho, sit
With the knights' order in the pit?"

Duncombe.

An upstart of ignoble blood,
Who plodded late in shoes of wood;
And round his waist, instead of vest,
Wore a cow's stinking hide undrest,
Which might, on fit occasion, yield
Rank covering for a rotten shield.
This wretch, with other wretches vile,
Liv'd hard by drudgery and toil;
Oft sentenc'd cruel pains to feel
At whipping-post, or racking wheel:
But now, conspicuous from afar,
He rides triumphant in his car;
With golden pendants in his ears,
Aloft the silken reins he bears,
Proud, and effeminately gay:
His slaves an ivory skreen display,
To guard him from the solar ray.

ODE LXX.

TO HIS BOY.

BOY, while here I sit supine,
Bring me water, bring me wine;
Bring me, to adorn my brow,
Wreaths of flowers that sweetly blow;
Love invites——O! let me prove
The joys of wine, the sweets of love.

THE EPIGRAMS OF ANACREON.

EPIGRAM I.

ON TIMOCRITUS.

THE tomb of great Timocritus behold!
Mars spares the base, but slays the brave and bold.

EPIGRAM II.

ON AGATHON.

FOR Agathon, in fighting fields renown'd
Abdera mourns his funeral pile around;
For him she mingles tears with bright applause,
Who nobly suffer'd in his country's cause:
No youth so brave, unknowing how to yield,
E'er perish'd in the thunder of the field.

Epigram I.—2. Mars spares the base, but slays the brave and bold.]

Priam, speaking of the most valiant of his sons, says

Τȣς μεν απωλεσ' Αρης—— Iliad, b. 2. ver. 260.

All those relentless Mars untimely slew,
And left me these, a soft and servile crew.

Pope.

Epig. II.—2. Abdera mourns, &c.] The Teians after their expulsion from Ionia by Harpagus the general of Cyrus, sailed into Thrace, and settled in the city of Abdera; where they had not been long, before the Thracians, jealous of their new neighbours, endeavoured to give them disturbance. It seems to be in these conflicts that Anacreon lost those friends whom he celebrates in his Epigrams. See the first, second, and thirteenth.

EPIGRAM III.

ON THE SON OF CLEENOR.

THEE, Cleënorides, the bold, the brave,
Stern Neptune sunk beneath the whelming wave:
Thy country's love so nobly fill'd thy mind,
Thou dar'dst to trust, too credulous, the wind:
The fair, though faithless, season urg'd thy doom,
And wrapp'd thy beauties in a watery tomb.

EPIGRAM IV.

ON A PICTURE REPRESENTING THREE BACCHÆ.

FIRST, Heliconias with a thyrsus past,
Xanthippe next, and Glauca is the last;
Lo! dancing down the mountains they repair,
And grateful gifts to jolly Bacchus bear;
Wreaths of the rustling ivy for his head,
With grapes delicious, and a kid well fed.

EPIGRAM V.

ON MYRON'S COW.

FEED, gentle swain, thy cattle far away,
Lest they too near the cow of Myron stray,
And thou, if chance fallacious judgment err'd,
Drive home the breathing statue with the herd.

EPIGRAM VI.

ON THE SAME.

THIS heifer is not cast, but rolling years
Harden'd the life to what it now appears:
Myron unjustly would the honour claim,
But Nature has prevented him in fame.

Epig. III.—This Cleënorides, as Barnes observes, seems to have been cast away in attempting a voyage from Abdera to his native country Teios, in the winter.

Epig. V.—Myron was the most celebrated artist of his time for casting statues in brass. Petronius, speaking of him, says, Penè hominum animas ferarumque ære comprehenderat: "He had almost found the art to enclose the souls of men and beasts in brass."

Among the many epigrams, which have been composed on Myron's cow, the following from Ausonius deserves commendation:

Bucula sum, cælo genitoris facta Myronis
  Ærea; nec factam me puto, sed genetam.
Sic me taurus init; sic proxima bucula mugit;
  Sic vitulus sitiens ubera nostra petit.
Miraris quòd fallo gregem? gregis ipse magister
  Inter pascentes me numerare solet.

By Myron's chisel I was form'd of brass;
Not Art, but Nature, my great mother was.
Bulls court my love; the heifers lowing stand;
And thirsty calves my swelling teat demand.
Nor deem this strange—the herdsman oft has err'd,
And number'd me among the grazing herd.

Epig. VI.—I found this epigram, thus excellently translated, in a paltry edition of Anacreon in English, printed by Curl.

The following epigram on an excellent modern work has expressed the same thought with the same simplicity.

ON CLARISSA.

This work is Nature's, every tittle in't
She wrote, and gave it Richardson to print.

The following epigrams were collected by Barnes, and first added to his edition of our poet: The first five on the authority of a manuscript Anthologia at Paris; the rest on the credit of a Heidleberg manuscript.

EPIGRAM VII.

ON COMPANY.

I NE'ER can think his conversation good,
Who o'er the bottle talks of wars and blood:
But his whose wit the pleasing talk refines,
And lovely Venus with the Graces joins.

EPIGRAM VIII.

A DEDICATION TO JUPITER, IN THE NAME OF PHIDOLA.

PHIDOLA, as a monument of speed,
This mare, at Corinth bred, to Jove decreed.

EPIGRAM IX.

TO APOLLO, IN THE NAME OF NAUCRATES.

GOD of the silver bow, and golden hair,
Hear Naucrates's vows, and grant his prayer!

EPIGRAM X.

ANOTHER DEDICATION.

LYCÆUS' son, Praxagoras, bestow'd
This marble statue to his guardian god:
View well the whole—what artist can surpass
The finish'd work of Anaxagoras?

EPIGRAM XI.

ANOTHER.

MINERVA's grove contains the favour'd shield,
That guarded Python in the bloody field.

Epig. VIII.—2. This mare, &c.] Pausanias, Eliac. l. 2. c. 13. mentions this mare of Phidola's, and tells us she was named Aura, or Air; and that she won the race herself, after her rider was thrown.

Epig. X.—4. Anaxagoras, a native of Ægina, was a celebrated statuary: he flourished both before and after the expedition of Xerxes. Barnes.

Epig. XI.—When the ancients escaped any imminent danger, it was usual for them to consecrate some memorial of it in the temples of their gods. Thus Horace, l. 1. ode 5.

Me tabula sacer, &c.

For me, the sacred tablet shows
That I have hung my dripping clothes
At Neptune's shrine—— Duncombe.

EPIGRAM XII.

ANOTHER, BY LEOCRATES.

WHEN Hermes' bust, Leocrates, you rais'd,
The Graces bland the beauteous image prais'd;
The joyful Academe extoll'd your name;
The speaking bust shall eternize your fame.

EPIGRAM XIII.

ON THE SON OF ARISTOCLES.

To Aristoclides, the best of friends,
This honorary verse the Muse commends:
Bold and adventurous in the martial strife,
He sav'd his country, but he lost his life.

EPIGRAM XIV.

PRAXIDICE this flowery mantle made,
Which fair Dyseris first design'd;
Mark how the lovely damsels have display'd
A pleasing unity of mind.

Epig. XII.—3. The Academe] The Athenian academy was not far distant from the Areopagus, in a grove without the city.

Epig. XIII.—Nothing among the ancient Greeks and Romans was esteemed a greater act of piety, than to fight for the good of the community; and they, who have greatly fallen in so righteous a cause, are embalmed with immortal honours. Tyrtæus wrote some noble poems on martial virtue. The following lines are translated from a fragment of his: speaking of the hero that dares to die for his country, he says,

His fair renown shall never fade away,
Nor shall the mention of his name decay.
Who glorious falls beneath the conqueror's hand,
For his dear children, and his native land,
Though to the dust his mortal part we give,
His fame in triumph o'er the grave shall live.

Anon.

Epig. XIV.—Addison quotes a passage from Shakespeare similar to this epigram:

We, Hermia, like two artificial gods,
Created with our needles both one flower,
Both on one sampler, sitting on one cushion;
Both warbling of one song, both in one key;
As if our hands, our sides, voices, and minds,
Had been incorporate. So we grew together,
Like to a double cherry, seeming parted,
But yet an union in partition,
Two lovely berries moulded on one stem;
Or with two seeming bodies, but one heart.

Midsummer Night's Dream.

EPIGRAM XV.

UNDER A STATUE.

CALLITELES first fix'd me on this base
Fair rising to the view:
His sons gave ornament and grace;
To them your thanks are due.

EPIGRAM XVI.

ANOTHER.

THIS trophy Areiphilus's son
To Bacchus consecrates, for battles won.

EPIGRAM XVII.

ANOTHER.

THESSALIA'S monarch, Echecratides,
Has fix'd me on this base,
Bacchus, the jolly god of wine, to please,
And give the city grace.

EPIGRAM XVIII.

To Mercury your orisons address,
That Timonactes meet with wish'd success,
Who fix'd these porticoes, my sweet abode,
And plac'd me sacred to the herald-god.
All who the bright-eyed Sciences revere,
Strangers and citizens are welcome here.

EPIGRAM XIX.

GREAT Sophocles, for tragic story prais'd,
These altars to the gods immortal rais'd.

EPIGRAM XX.

O MERCURY! for honours paid to thee
May Tlæas live in calm security;
Years of serenest pleasure may he gain,
And o'er th' Athenian race a long and happy reign!

Epig. XVIII.—1. To Mercury, &c.] The ancients esteemed Mercury the general protector of learning; and therefore usually placed his statue in their libraries, and in the porticoes before their public schools and academies. Addison.

Epig. XIX.—This epigram, notwithstanding what Barnes says to the contrary, is thought not to be Anacreon's; the mention of Sophocles being too repugnant to chronology, to admit it for genuine.

THE

WORKS OF SAPPHO.

TRANSLATED BY FAWKES.

Mark, Muse! the conscious shade and vocal grove,
Where Sappho tun'd her melting voice to love,
While Echo each harmonious strain return'd,
And with the soft complaining Lesbian mourn'd.

PROGRESS OF POETRY

THE

LIFE OF SAPPHO.

SAPPHO was a native of Mitylene in the island of Lesbos. Who was her father is uncertain, there being no less than eight persons who have contended for that honour; but it is universally acknowledged that Cleis was her mother. She flourished, according to Suidas, in the 42d Olympiad; according to Eusebius, in the 44th Olympiad, about 600 years before our Saviour Christ. She was contemporary with Pittachus, the famous tyrant of Mitylene, and the two celebrated poets, Stesichorus and Alcæus. Barnes has endeavoured to prove, from the testimonies of Chamæleon and Hermesianax, that Anacreon was one of her lovers; but this amour has been generally esteemed too repugnant to chronology, to be admitted for any thing but a poetical fiction.

She married one Cercolas, a man of great wealth and power in the island of Andros, by whom she had a daughter named Cleis. He leaving her a widow very young, she renounced all thoughts of a second marriage, but not the pleasures of love; not enduring to confine that passion to one person, which, as the ancients tell us, was too violent in her to be restrained even to one sex.

But no one seems to have been the object of her admiration so much as the accomplished Phaon, a young man of Lesbos; who is said to have been a kind of ferry-man, and thence fabled to have carried Venus over the stream in his boat, and to have received from her, as a reward, the favour of becoming the most beautiful man in the world. She fell desperately in love with him, and took a voyage into Sicily in pursuit of him, he having withdrawn himself thither on purpose to avoid her. It was in that island, and on this occasion, that she composed her Hymn to Venus.

Her poem was ineffectual for the procuring that happiness which she prayed for in it. Phaon was still obdurate, and Sappho was so transported with the violence of her passion, that she resolved to get rid of it at any rate.

There was a promontory in Acarnania called Leucate, on the top of which was a little temple dedicated to Apollo. In this temple it was usual for despairing lovers to make their vows in secret, and afterwards to fling themselves from the top of the precipice into the sea. For it was an established opiniou, that all those who were taken up alive, would immediately be cured of their former passion. Sappho tried the remedy; but perished in the experiment. The original of this unaccountable humour is not known. Ovid represents Sappho as advised to undertake this strange project by the vision of a sea-nymph, of which she sent the following account to the cruel Phaon:

Hic ego cum lassos, &c.

Here as I lay, and swell'd with tears the flood,
Before my sight a watery virgin stood;
She stood and cry'd, " O you that love in vain
Fly hence, and seek the fair Leucadian main:
There stands a rock, from whose impending steep
Apollo's fane surveys the rolling deep;

There injur'd lovers, leaping from above,
Their flames extinguish, and forget to love,
Haste, Sappho, haste, from high Leucadia throw
Thy wretched weight, nor dread the deeps below!"
She spoke, and vanish'd with the voice—I rise
And silent tears fall trickling from my eyes.
I go, ye nymphs, those rocks and seas to prove;
How much I fear, but, ah, how much I love!
I go, ye nymphs, where furious love inspires,
Let female fears submit to female fires.
To rocks and seas I fly from Phaon's hate,
And hope from seas and rocks a milder fate.
Ye gentle gales beneath my body blow,
And softly lay me on the waves below;
And thou, kind Love, my sinking limbs sustain,
Spread thy soft wings, and waft me o'er the main,
Nor let a lover's death the guiltless flood profane! Pope.

The Romans erected a most noble statue of porphyry to her memory; and the Mitylenians, to express their sense of her worth, and the glory they received from her being born amongst them, paid her sovereign honours after her death, and coined money with her head for the impress.

The best idea we can have of her person, is from her own description of it in Ovid:

Si mihi difficilis formam, &c.

To me what nature has in charms deny'd,
Is well by wit's more lasting charms supply'd.
Though short my stature, yet my name extends
To Heaven itself, and Earth's remotest ends.
Brown as I am, an Ethiopian dame
Inspir'd young Perseus with a generous flame;
Turtles and doves of different hues unite,
And glossy jet is pair'd with shining white.
If to no charms thou wilt thy heart resign,
But such as merit, such as equal thine,
By none, alas! by none thou canst be mov'd,
Phaon alone by Phaon must be lov'd. Pope.

To give the English reader a true notion what opinion the ancients entertained of her works, would be to collect a volume in her praise. She was honoured with the glorious title of the tenth Muse. Horace says,

Spirat adhuc amor,
Vivuntque commissi calores
Æoliæ fidibus puellæ L. 4. od. 9.

Enchanting Sappho's lyric Muse
In every breast must love infuse;
Love breathes on every tender string,
And still in melting notes we hear her sing.

Duncombe.

On the revival of learning, men of the most refined taste accounted the loss of her writings inestimable, and collected the sacred relics with the utmost assiduity: though Mr. Addison (in the Spectator, No. 223.) judiciously observes: "I do not know, by the character that is given of her works, whether it is not for the benefit of mankind that they are lost. They were filled with such bewitching tenderness and rapture, that it might have been dangerous to have given them a reading."

Vossius, in the third book of his Institutioness Poeticæ, says, that none of the Greek poets excelled Sappho in sweetness of verse; and that she made Archilochus the model of her style, but at the same time took great care to soften and temper the severity of his expression.

Hoffman, in his Lexicon, says, "Some authors are of opinion, that the elegy which Ovid made under the name of Sappho, and which is infinitely superior to his other elegies, was all, or at least the most beautiful part of it, stolen from the poems of the elegant Sappho."

She was the inventress of that kind of verse which (from her name) is called the Sapphic. She wrote nine books of odes, besides elegies, epigrams, iambics, monodies, and other pieces; of which we have nothing remaining entire, but an hymn to Venus, an ode preserved by Longinus, (which, however, the learned acknowledge to be imperfect) two epigrams, and some other little fragments. I shall conclude my account of this celebrated lady in the words of Mr. Addison, taken from the above-mentioned Spectator.

"Among the mutilated poets of antiquity, there is none whose fragments are so beautiful as those of Sappho. They give us a taste of her way of writing, which is perfectly conformable with that extraordinary character we find of her in the remarks of those great critics who were conversant with her works when they were entire. One may see, by what is left of them, that she followed nature in all her thoughts, without descending to those little points, conceits, and turns of wit with which many of our modern lyrics are so miserably infected. Her soul seems to have been made up of love and poetry: she felt the passion in all its warmth, and described it in all its symptoms. She is called by ancient authors the tenth Muse; and by Plutarch is compared to Cacus the son of Vulcan, who breathed out nothing but flame.

THE

ODES OF SAPPHO.

TRANSLATED BY FAWKES.

ODE I.

AN HYMN TO VENUS.

VENUS, bright goddess of the skies,
To whom unnumber'd temples rise,
Jove's daughter fair, whose wily arts
Delude fond lovers of their hearts;
O! listen gracious to my prayer,
And free my mind from anxious care.

If e'er you heard my ardent vow,
Propitious goddess, hear me now!
And oft my ardent vow you've heard,
By Cupid's friendly aid preferr'd,
Oft left the golden courts of Jove,
To listen to my tales of love.

The radiant car your sparrows drew;
You gave the word and swift they flew,
Through liquid air they wing'd their way,
I saw their quivering pinions play;
To my plain roof they bore their queen,
Of aspect mild, and look serene.

Soon as you came, by your command,
Back flew the wanton feather'd band,
Then, with a sweet enchanting look,
Divinely smiling, thus you spoke:
" Why didst thou call me to thy cell?
Tell me, my gentle Sappho, tell.

" What healing medicine shall I find
To cure thy love distemper'd mind?
Say, shall I lend thee all my charms,
To win young Phaon to thy arms?
Or does some other swain subdue
Thy heart? my Sappho, tell me who?

" Though now, averse, thy charms he slight,
He soon shall view thee with delight;
Though now he scorns thy gifts to take,
He soon to thee shall offerings make;
Though now thy beauties fail to move,
He soon shall melt with equal love."

Once more, O Venus, hear my prayer,
And ease my mind of anxious care;
Again vouchsafe to be my guest,
And calm this tempest in my breast!
To thee, bright queen, my vows aspire;
O grant me all my heart's desire!

ODE II.

Whatever might have been the occasion of this ode, the English reader will enter into the beauties of it, if he supposes it to have been written in the person of a lover sitting by his mistress. Addison, Spectator, No. 229.

Ode I.—We are indebted for this hymn to Dionysius of Halicarnassus, who quotes it as a pattern of perfection. Madame Dacier supposes it to be entirely historical; and that it was written after Phaon, her inconstant lover, had withdrawn himself from the island of Lesbos to Sicily, in order to avoid the importunities of an amorous mistress. It was in Sicily, therefore, and on the above-mentioned occasion, that she is supposed to have made this hymn.

13. The radiant car your sparrows drew;] Sappho says, the chariot of Venus was drawn by sparrows, because they are of all birds the most amorous.

20. Back flew the feather'd band.] There is something very pretty in this circumstance, wherein Venus is described as sending away her chariot, upon her arrival at Sappho's lodgings, to denote that it was not a short transient visit which she intended to make her. Madame Dacier.

More happy than the gods is he
Who, soft-reclining, sits by thee;
His ears thy pleasing talk beguiles,
His eyes thy sweetly-dimpled smiles.

This, this, alas! alarm'd my breast,
And robb'd me of my golden rest:
While gazing on thy charms I hung,
My voice died faltering on my tongue.

With subtle flames my bosom glows,
Quick through each vein the poison flows:
Dark, dimming mists my eyes surround;
My ears with hollow murmurs sound.

My limbs with dewy chillness freeze,
On my whole frame pale tremblings seize,
And, losing colour, sense, and breath,
I seem quite languishing in death.

Ode II.—This beautiful ode is preserved by Longinus, in his Treatise of the Sublime.

1. More happy than the gods, &c.] There is an epigram in the Anthologia, which seems to be an imitation of this stanza.

Ευδαιμων ὁ βλεπων σε, τρισσολβιος ὁς-ις ακουει,
'Ημιθεος δ' ὁ φιλων, αθανατος δ' ὁ συνων.

The youth who sees thee may rejoice,
But blest is he who hears thy voice,
A demi-god who shall thee kiss,
Who gains thee is a god in bliss.

Longinus has observed, that "this description of love in Sappho is an exact copy of nature; and that all the circumstances, which follow one another in such a hurry of sentiments, notwithstanding they appear repugnant to each other, are really such as happen in the frenzies of love." He farther says: "Sappho, having observed the anxieties and tortures inseparable to jealous love, has collected and displayed them all with the most lively exactness." And Dr. Pearce judiciously observes, that "in this ode she endeavours to express that wrath, jealousy, and anguish, which distracted her with such a variety of torture. And therefore, in the following verses of Boileau's translation the true sense is mistaken:

—— dans les doux transports, où s' egare mon ame.

"And,

—— je tombe en des douces langueurs.

As the word doux will by no means express the rage and distraction of Sappho's mind: it being always used in a contrary sense." There are two lines in Phillips's translation of this ode which are liable to the same objection:

For while I gaz'd, in transport tost.

And,

My blood with gentle horrours thrill'd.

Mr. Addison, in his Spectator on this ode, relates the following remarkable circumstance from Plutarch: "That author, in the famous story of Antiochus, who fell in love with Stratonice, his mother-in-law, and (not daring to discover his passion) pretended to be confined to his bed by sickness, tells us, that Erasistratus, the physician, found out the nature of his distemper by those symptoms of love which he had learned from Sappho's writings. Stratonice was in the room of the love-sick prince, when these symptoms discovered themselves to his physician; and it is probable, that they were not very different from those which Sappho here describes in a lover sitting by his mistress." Madame Dacier says, that this ode of Sappho is preserved entire in Longinus, whereas, whoever looks into that author's quotation of it will find, that there must at least have been another stanza, which is not transmitted to us.

FRAGMENTS.

FRAGMENT I.

The Pleiads now no more are seen,
Nor shines the silver Moon serene,
In dark and dismal clouds o'ercast;
The love appointed hour is past:
Midnight usurps her sable throne,
And yet, alas! I lie alone.

FRAGMENT II.

This seems to have been addressed to an arrogant unlettered lady, vain of her beauty and riches.

Whene'er the Fates resume thy breath,
No bright reversion shalt thou gain,
Unnotic'd thou shalt sink in death,
Nor ev'n thy memory remain:
For thy rude hand ne'er pluck'd the lovely rose,
Which on the mountain of Pieria blows.

To Pluto's mansions shalt thou go,
The stern inexorable king,
Among th' ignoble shades below
A vain, ignoble thing;
While honour'd Sappho's Muse-embellish'd name
Shall flourish in eternity of fame.

Fragment I.—6. And yet, alas! I lie alone] A shepherd in the Idyllium entitled ΟΑΡΙΣΤΥΣ (which is generally ascribed to Theocritus, but by Daniel Heinsius, is attributed to Moschus) wishes a city-girl, who had slighted him, the punishment of living and dying an old maid.

—— may you ne'er find one
Worthy your love in country or in town,
But, to a virgin-bed condemn'd, for ever lie alone!
Bowles.

Frag. II.—Sappho is not the only good writer, who, from a due sense of the excellence of their works, have promised themselves immortality.—Virgil has expressed himself in the same manner at the beginning of the third Georgic:—Horace in several places, particularly in the ode, Exegi monumentum:—but Ovid, in the strongest terms:

Jamque opus exegi, &c.

I've now compil'd a work, which nor the rage
Of Jove, nor fire, nor sword, nor eating age,
Is able to destroy ——

5. For thy rude hand ne'er pluck'd the lovely rose,
Which on the mountain of Pieria blows.]

Pieria was a mountain in Macedonia, dedicated to the Muses: by this expression Sappho seems to hint, that the lady who furnished the occasion of this satire was not conversant in the politer studies, nor acquainted with the Muses.

FRAGMENT III.

TO VENUS.

VENUS, queen of smiles and love,
Quit, O! quit the skies above;
To my lowly roof descend,
At the mirthful feast attend;
Hand the golden goblet round,
With delicious nectar crown'd:
None but joyous friends you'll see,
Friends of Venus, and of me.

FRAGMENT IV.

CEASE, gentle mother, cease your sharp reproof,
My hands no more can ply the curious woof,
While on my mind the flames of Cupid prey,
And lovely Phaon steals my soul away.

FRAGMENT V.

ON THE ROSE.

WOULD Jove appoint some flower to reign
In matchless beauty on the plain,
The rose (mankind will all agree)
The rose the queen of flowers should be;
The pride of plants, the grace of bowers,
The blush of meads, the eye of flowers:
Its beauties charm the gods above;
Its fragrance is the breath of Love;
Its foliage wantons in the air
Luxuriant, like the flowing hair;
It shines in blooming splendour gay,
While zephyrs on its bosom play.

The following is part of an Ode which Sappho is supposed to have written to Anacreon.——See the notes on the 64th Ode of Anacreon.

YE Muses, ever fair and young,
High-seated on the golden throne,
Anacreon sent to me a song
In sweetest numbers not his own;
For, by your sacred raptures fir'd,
The poet warbled what the Muse inspir'd.

TWO EPIGRAMS.

I.

MENISCUS, mourning for his hapless son,
The toil-experienc'd fisher, Pelagon,

Frag. III.—This fragment should be joined with the fourth ode of Anacreon; for as Sappho desires Venus to be her cup-bearer, so Anacreon appoints Cupid the same office:

In decent robe, behind him bound,
Cupid shall serve the goblet round.

Frag. IV.—Hephæstion produces this fragment from the seventh book of Sappho's odes. Horace seems to have had it in view, book 3. ode 12.

Tibi qualum Cythereæ puer ales
Tibi telas, operosæque Minervæ
Studium aufert, Neobule, Liparæi nitor Hebri.

The winged boy, in wanton play,
Thy work and basket steals away:
Thy web and Pallas' curious toils
Are now become fair Hebrus' spoils.
Duncombe.

Frag. V.—We are indebted to Achilles Tatius for this fragment, which is generally ascribed to Sappho. In the beginning of the second book of that romancer, Clitophon tells us, his mistress sung this eulogy on the rose at an entertainment. If the reader turns back to the fifth and fifty-third odes of Anacreon, he will find other encomiums on this beautiful flower.

Epigram I.—Longepierre observes, that it was usual among the ancients to place on the tombs of their friends the instruments peculiar to the art or mystery which they exercised when alive. Of this we have examples in Homer and Virgil. In the eleventh book of the Odyssey, ver. 75, Elpenor makes this request to Ulysses in Hell:

Σημα τε μοι χευαι, &c.

A tomb along the watery margin raise,
The tomb with manly arms and trophies grace,
To show posterity Elpenor was:
There high in air, memorial of my name,
Fix the smooth oar, and bid me live to fame.
Broome.

In the beginning of the twelfth book we find the suit was granted:

A rising tomb, the silent dead to grace,
Fast by the roarings of the main we place;
The rising tomb a lofty column bore,
And high above it rose the tapering oar.
Pope.

In the sixth book of the Æneid, ver. 232, Æneas places on the tomb of Misenus

—— suaque arma viro, remumque, tubamque.

This done; to solemnize the warrior's doom,
The pious hero rais'd a lofty tomb;
The towering top his well-known ensigns bore,
His arms, his once-lov'd trump, and tapering oar.
Pitt.

These sort of epitaphs were more general, concise, and instructive, than those which afterwards prevailed. Longepierre.

Madame Dacier also observes, that emblems of the humours of the deceased were sometimes placed on their monuments, as in this epigram on a woman named Myro:

Μη θαμβει, μαστιγα Μυρους επι σηματι λευσσων,
Γλαυκα, βιον, χαροπαν χηνα, θοαν σκυλακα.

O'er Myro see the emblems of her soul,
A whip, a bow, a goose, a dog, an owl.

The whip denoted, that she used to chastise her servants; the bow, that her mind was always bent on the care of her family; the goose, that she loved to stay at home; the dog, that she was fond of her children; and the owl, that she was assiduous in spinning and tapestry, which were the works of Pallas, to whom the owl was consecrated.
Dacier.

At the Earl of Holderness's, at Aske in Yorkshire, is an old picture, with a device which seems to be borrowed from this. It is supposed to be drawn by Hans Holbein, and represents a woman (said to be queen Elizabeth's housekeeper) standing on a tortoise, with a bunch of keys by her side, her finger on her lips, and a dove on her head. Under it is this inscription:

Has plac'd upon his tomb a net and oar,
The badges of a painful life and poor.

EPIGRAM II.

THE much-lov'd Timas lodges in this tomb,
By Death insatiate ravish'd in her bloom;
Ere yet a bride, the beauteous maid was led
To dreary coasts, and Pluto's mournful bed.
Her lov'd companions pay the rites of woe,
All, all, alas! the living can bestow;
From their fair heads the graceful curls they shear,
Place on her tomb, and drop the tender tear.

Uxor amet, sileat, servet, nec ubique vagetur:
Hoc testudo docet, claves, labra, junctaque turtur.

Which has been thus translated;

Be frugal, ye wives, live in silence and love,
Nor abroad ever gossip and roam!
This learn from the keys, the lips, and the dove,
And tortoise, still dwelling at home!

Epig. II.—From their fair heads the graceful curls, &c.]

The ceremony of cutting off the hair, among the ancients, in honour of the dead, was a token of a violent affection. Thus Achilles, in the twenty-third book of the Iliad, offers his to Patroclus. And the little Cupids tear their hair for grief at the death of Adonis: (See Bion.) Herodotus tells us that Mardonius cut off his, after his defeat. Many more instances of this extraordinary custom might be produced; but these will, probably, be thought sufficient. I shall finish my observations on this excellent poetess with an ingenious surmise in regard to the above-mentioned ceremony: It was practised, perhaps, not only in token of sorrow, but might also have a concealed meaning, that as the hair was cut from the head, and was never more to be joined to it, so was the dead for ever cut off from the living, never more to return.

THE

IDYLLIUMS

OF

BION AND MOSCHUS.

TRANSLATED BY FAWKES.

THE

LIVES OF BION AND MOSCHUS.

WE know little relating to these two celebrated pastoral poets: and therefore their history may be comprised in few words.

Bion was born at Smyrna, a famous city of Asia Minor, which also has the fairest title to the birth of Homer: for this father of poets is said to have been the son of the river Meles, which flows not far from its walls; and therefore he is called Melesigenes. To this river Moschus, in his Idyllium on the death of Bion, addresses himself; and makes that fine comparison between these two poets:

Τȣτο τοι, ω ποταμων λιγυρωτατε, κ. τ. λ.

Meles! of streams in melody the chief,
Now heaves thy bosom with another grief;
Thy Homer died, great master of the song,
Thy Homer died, the Muses sweetest tongue:
Then did thy waves in plaintive murmurs weep,
And roll'd thy swelling sorrows to the deep.
Another son demands the meed of woe,
Again thy waters weep in long-drawn murmurs slow.
Dear to the fountains was each tuneful son,
This drank of Arethuse, that Helicon.
He sung Atrides' and Achilles' ire,
And the fair dame that set the world on fire:
This form'd his numbers on a softer plan,
And chanted shepherds loves, and peaceful Pan.

We are not informed in what part of the world he lived, though it is evident that he spent much of his time in Sicily; and there it was, probably, that the wonderful sweetness of his compositions drew together great numbers of admirers and disciples; among whom was Moschus, as may be deduced from the above-mentioned poem:

I too, with tears, from Italy have brought
Such plain bucolics as my master taught;
Which, if at all with tuneful ease they flow,
To thy learn'd precepts, and thy art I owe.
To other heirs thy riches may belong;
I claim thy pastoral pipe and Doric song.

These two last verses prove, that he was not in necessitous circumstances. From the same idyllium it appears, that he died by poison, not accidentally, but by the appointment of some great man.

O hapless Bion! poison was thy fate;
The baneful potion circumscrib'd thy date.
How could fell poison cause effect so strange,
Touch thy sweet lips, and not to honey change?

Which probably was not unpunished:

But soon just vengeance will the wretch pursue.

It is likewise evident from the above-mentioned authority, that he was contemporary with Theocritus: and this famous Syracusan flourished under Ptolemy Philadelphus, who began his reign in the fourth year of the 123d Olympiad, that is, about 285 years before Christ.

Moschus was born at Syracuse, and was the disciple of Bion, as was before observed. Suidas will have him to have been a professor of grammar at Syracuse: but it is certain, that when he wrote his beautiful elegy on the death of his master, his residence was among the Italians (though perhaps in those parts that lie over against Sicily, called Great Greece); and probably he succeeded him in governing the poetic school. Some critics have formerly asserted, that Moschus and Theocritus are the same person; but they are sufficiently confuted by a passage in the elegy, where Moschus introduces Theocritus bewailing the same misfortune in another country which he was lamenting in Italy.

"The few remains of these two poets," says Kennet, "are reckoned among the sweetest pieces of the ancient delicacy. They seem, in a great measure, to have neglected that blunt rusticity and plainness, which was so admired an art of their great rival Theocritus: for they always aim at something more polite and genteel, though equally natural, in their compositions." Mr. Longepierre observes, that "the beauty of these Idylliums can never be sufficiently admired. If I dare not," says he, "affirm, that these two poets are superior to Theocritus himself; yet I may safely aver, that in general they are more correspondent to the taste of the present age; which can never be brought to relish that extreme simplicity, which abounds in Theocritus. Bion and Moschus are not less natural than he is; but though their simplicity is pure Nature, it is less rustic, and more elegant; and their poems, having a more pleasing and agreeable air, one may with justice affirm, that Bion has more grace, sweetness, and delicacy, and less rusticity (if I may be allowed the expression) than Theocritus; and that Moschus keeps the middle track between them both. However, if their works are not admitted among some for such true pastorals, they will certainly pass, among the best judges, for better poems."

There is a remarkable paper in the Guardian, No. 40, containing a parallel between the Pastorals of Mr. Pope and Mr. Phillips (by the way written by Pope himself, though the former papers on pastoral poetry were composed by Mr. Tickell). It abounds with the finest sarcastic irony, which Phillips not having penetration enough to see through, made an apology to Pope on the occasion, declaring that he had no hand in it, nor knew the author. It concludes thus: "After all that has been said, I hope none can think it any injustice to Mr. Pope that I forbore to mention him as a pastoral writer; since, upon the whole, he is of the same class with Moschus and Bion, whom we have excluded that rank; and on whose Eclogues, as well as some of Virgil's, it may be said, that they are by no means pastorals, but something better."

THE

IDYLLIUMS OF BION.

TRANSLATED BY FAWKES.

Begin, Sicilian Muse, the mournful lay—
Alas! the Muses will no longer stay,
No longer on these lovely coasts abide;
With him they warbled, and with him they died:
With Bion perish'd all the grace of song,
And all the kisses of the fair and young:
The little Loves, lamenting at his doom,
Beat their fair breasts, and weep around his tomb.

MOSCHUS ON THE DEATH OF BION.

IDYLLIUM I.

ON THE DEATH OF ADONIS.

THE death of fair Adonis I deplore;
The lovely youth Adonis is no more:
The cruel Fates have cut his vital thread,
And all the Loves lament Adonis dead.
Ah Venus! never more in purple rest,
For mournful sable change thy flow'ry vest;
Thy beauteous bosom beat, thy loss deplore
Aloud with sighs, Adonis is no more!
For the lov'd youth these copious tears I shed,
And all the Cupids mourn Adonis dead.
Methinks I see him on the mountain lie,
The boar's keen tusk has pierc'd his tender thigh;
Weltering he lies, expiring on the ground,
And near him Venus all in sorrow drown'd;
I see the crimson flood fast trickling flow
Down his white skin that vies with winter snow;
I see the lustre of his eyes decay,
And on his lips the roses fade away:
Yet who can Venus from those lips divide,
Though their sweet kisses with Adonis died?
To Venus sweet, ev'n now his breath is fled,
Yet all her kisses cannot warm the dead.
The fate of fair Adonis I deplore;
The Loves lament, Adonis is no more!
A deep wide wound is in his thigh imprest,
But Venus bears a deeper in her breast.
His beagles round a mournful howling keep;
And all the Dryads of the mountains weep:
But, Venus, quite abandon'd to despair,
Her locks dishevell'd, and her feet all bare,
Flies through the thorny brake, the briary wood,
And stains the thickets with her sacred blood:

Idyllium I.—All the beauties and graces that can possibly embellish a poem of this nature are united in this delicate Idyllium: and therefore the most polite scholars, and the best critics of every age, have deservedly esteemed it one of the finest and most perfect remains of antiquity.

20. Though their sweet kisses with Adonis died] See Moschus, ver. 97, &c.

See Venus too her beauteous bosom beat!
She lov'd her shepherd more than kisses sweet,
More than those last dear kisses which in death
She gave Adonis, and imbib'd his breath.

With piercing cries Adonis she bewails,
Her darling youth, along the winding vales;
While the blood starting from his wounded thigh,
Streams on his breast, and leaves a crimson dye.
  Ah me! what tears fair Cytherea shed,
  And how the Loves deplor'd Adonis dead!
  The queen of love, no longer now a bride,
Has lost her beauty since Adonis died;
Though bright the radiance of her charms before,
Her lover and her beauty are no more!
The mountains mourn, the waving woods bewail,
And rivers roll lamenting through the vale:
The silver springs descend in streams of woe,
Down the high hills, and murmur as they flow:
And every flower in drooping grief appears
Depress'd and languishingly drown'd in tears:
While Venus o'er the hills and valleys flies,
And, " Ah! Adonis is no more," she cries.
  Along the hills, and vales, and vocal shore,
  Echo repeats, " Adonis is no more."
  Who could unmov'd these piteous wailings hear,
Or view the love-lorn queen without a tear?
Soon as she saw him wounded on the plain,
His thigh discolour'd with the crimson stain,
Sighing she said, and clasp'd him as he lay,
" O stay, dear hapless youth! for Venus stay!
Our breasts once more let close embraces join,
And let me press my glowing lips to thine.
Raise, lov'd Adonis, raise thy drooping head,
And kiss me ere thy parting breath be fled,
The last fond token of affection give,
O! kiss thy Venus, while the kisses live;
Till in my breast I draw thy lingering breath,
And with my lips imbibe thy love in death.
This farewel kiss, which sorrowing thus I take,
I'll keep for ever for Adonis' sake.
Thee to the shades the Fates untimely bring;
Before the drear, inexorable king;
Yet still I live unhappy and forlorn;
How hard my lot to be a goddess born!
Take, cruel Proserpine, my lovely boy,
Since all that 's form'd for beauty, or for joy,
Descends to thee, while I indulge my grief,
By fruitless tears soliciting relief.
Thou dy'st, Adonis, and thy fate I weep,
Thy love now leaves me, like a dream in sleep,
Leaves me bereav'd, no more a blooming bride,
With unavailing Cupids at my side.
With thee my zone, which coldest hearts could warm,
Lost every grace, and all its power to charm.
Why didst thou urge the chase, and rashly dare
T' encounter beasts, thyself so wond'rous fair!"
  Thus Venus mourn'd, and tears incessant shed,
  And all the Loves bewail'd Adonis dead;
  Sighing they cry'd, " Ah! wretched queen, deplore
  Thy joys all fled, Adonis is no more."

43. The mountains mourn, the waving woods bewail] Virgil, Eclogue 5.

Daphni, tuum interitum, montes sylvæque loquunter.

The death of Daphnis woods and hills deplore.
Dryden.

And Eclogue 10.

Illum etiam lauri, illum etiam flevere myricæ,
Pinifer illum etiam solâ sub rupe jacentem
Mænalus, & gelidi fleverunt saxa Lycæi.

For him the lofty laurel stands in tears,
And hung with humid pearls the lowly shrub appears.
Mænalian pines the godlike swain bemoan,
When spread beneath a rock he sigh'd alone;
And cold Lycæus wept from every dropping stone.
Dryden.

44. And rivers roll lamenting] See the beginning of Moschus's Idyllium on the death of Bion.

47. And every flower in drooping grief appears.]

Ye drooping flowers, diffuse a languid breath,
And die with sorrow at sweet Bion's death.
Moschus.

55. Soon as she saw him wounded on the plain] There is a similar beautiful description in Ovid's Metamorphoses, book 4.

But when her view her bleeding love confess'd,
She shriek'd, she tore her hair, she beat her breast!
She rais'd the body, and embrac'd it round,
And bath'd with tears unfeign'd the gaping wound:
Then her warm lips to the cold face apply'd,
" And is it thus, ah! thus we meet?" she cry'd!
" My Pyramus! whence sprung thy cruel fate?
My Pyramus! ah! speak, ere 'tis too late:
I, thy own Thisbe, but one word implore,
One word thy Thisbe never ask'd before."
At Thisbe's name awak'd, he open'd wide
His dying eyes; with dying eyes he try'd
On her to dwell, but clos'd them slow, and died.
Addison.

69. Thee to the shades the Fates untimely bring, &c.]

Virgil says of Orpheus, Georg. b. 4.

—— Manesque adiit, regemque tremendum,
Nesciaque humanis precibus mansuescere corda.

Ev'n to the dark dominions of the night
He took his way, through forests void of light;
And dar'd amidst the trembling ghosts to sing,
And stood before the inexorable king.
Dryden.

72. How hard, &c.] Thus Spenser, Fairy Queen, b. 3. c. 4. st. 38.

O! what avails it of immortal seed
To been ybred, and never born to die?
For better I it deem to die with speed,
Than waste in woe, and wailful miserie.

74. Since all that's form'd for beauty, or for joy, Descends to thee]

Thus Catullus,

At vobis malè sit, malæ tenebræ
Orci, quæ omnia Bella devoratis.

Ah! death, relentless to destroy
All that's form'd for love or joy.

81. With thee my zone, &c.] The cestus of Venus is thus describ'd by Homer:

Η, και απο ϛηθεσφιν ελυσατο κεϛον, κ. τ. λ. Iliad 14, v. 214.

She from her fragrant breast the zone unbrac'd,
With various skill and high embroidery grac'd:
In this was every art, and every charm,
To win the wisest, and the coldest warm:
Fond love, the gentle vow, the gay desire,
The kind deceit, the still surviving fire,
Persuasive speech, and more persuasive sighs,
Silence that spoke, and eloquence of eyes.
Pope.

As many drops of blood, as from the wound
Of fair Adonis trickled on the ground,
So many tears she shed in copious showers:
Both tears and drops of blood were turn'd to flow'rs.
From these in crimson beauty sprung the rose,
Cerulian-bright anemonies from those.
The death of fair Adonis I deplore,
The lovely youth Adonis is no more.
No longer in lone woods lament the dead,
O queen of love! behold the stately bed,
On which Adonis, now depriv'd of breath,
Seems sunk in slumbers, beauteous ev'n in death.
Dress him, fair goddess, in the softest vest,
In which he oft with thee dissolv'd to rest;
On golden pillow be his head reclin'd,
And let past joys be imag'd in thy mind.
Though Death the beauty of his bloom devours,
Crown him with chaplets of the fairest flowers;
Alas! the flowers have lost their gaudy pride,
With him they flourish'd, and with him they died.
With odorous myrtle deck his drooping head,
And o'er his limbs the sweetest essence shed:
Ah! rather perish every rich perfume,
The sweet Adonis perish'd in his bloom.
Clad in a purple robe Adonis lies;
Surrounding Cupids heave their breasts with sighs,
Their locks they shear, excess of grief to show,
They spurn the quiver, and they break the bow.
Some loose his sandals with officious care,
Some in capacious golden vessels bear
The cleansing water from the crystal springs;
This bathes his wound, that fans him with his wings.
For Venus' sake the pitying Cupids shed
A shower of tears, and mourn Adonis dead.
Already has the nuptial god, dismay'd,
Quench'd his bright torch, for all his garlands fade.
No more are joyful hymeneals sung,
But notes of sorrow dwell on ev'ry tongue;
While all around the general grief partake
For lov'd Adonis, and for Hymen's sake.
With loud laments the Graces all deplore,
And cry, 'The fair Adonis is no more.'
The Muses, wailing the wild woods among,
Strive to recal him with harmonious song:
Alas! no sounds of harmony he hears,
For cruel Proserpine has clos'd his ears.
Cease, Venus, cease, thy soft complaints forbear,
Reserve thy sorrows for the mournful year.

93. From these in crimson beauty sprung the rose]

Some authors say, that anemonies, and not roses, sprung from the blood of Adonis. See Ovid's Metamorph. b. 10, at the end.

——— Where the blood was shed,
A flower began to rear its purple head:
Such as on punic apples is reveal'd,
Or in the filmy rind but half conceal'd.
Still here the fate of lovely forms we see,
So sudden fades the sweet anemony.
The feeble stems, to stormy blasts a prey,
Their sickly beauties droop, and pine away,
The winds forbid the flowers to flourish long,
Which owe to winds their name in Grecian song.
Eusden.

114. Surrounding Cupids heave their breasts with sighs]

Moschus imitates this in his poem on the Death of Bion:

The little Loves, lamenting at his doom,
Beat their fair breasts, and weep around his tomb.

Thus Ovid,

Ecce puer Veneris fert eversamque pharetram,
Et fractos arcus, et sine luce facem.
Aspice demissis ut eat miserabilis alis,
Pectoraque infesta tundit aperta manu.
Excipiunt lacrymas sparsi per colla capilli,
Oraque singultu concutiente sonant.
Amor. b. 3. el. 9.

See Venus' son his torch extinguish'd brings,
His quiver all revers'd, and broke his bow;
See, pensive how he droops with flagging wings,
And strikes his bared bosom many a blow.
Loose and neglected, scatter'd o'er his neck,
His golden locks drink many a falling tear:
What piteous sobs, as if his heart would break,
Shake his swoln cheek? Ah sorrow too severe!
Anon.

115. Their locks they shear, &c.] For the ceremony of cutting off the hair in honour of the dead, see the notes on the second epigram of Sappho.

118. Some in capacious golden vessels bear
The cleansing water, &c.]

The custom of washing the dead is very ancient. At the latter end of the fourth book of the Æneid, Anna says of the body of her sister Dido:

——— date vulnera lymphis
Abluam, et, extremus si quis super halitus errat,
Ore legam.———

Bring, bring me water; let me bathe in death
Her bleeding wounds, and catch her parting breath.
Pitt.

The custom of catching the parting breath may be compared with the 65th and 66th verses above, "Till in my breast," &c. See a beautiful complaint made by the mother of Euryalus, in the Æneid, b. 9, v. 486.

—— nec te tua funera mater
Produxi, pressive oculos, aut vulnera lavi, &c.

Nor did thy mother close thy eyes in death,
Compose thy limbs, nor catch thy parting breath;
Nor bathe thy gaping wounds, nor cleanse the gore,
Nor throw the rich embroider'd mantle o'er.
Pitt.

120. —— that fans him with his wings]

— Cupid caught my trembling hand,
And with his wings my face he fann'd.
Anacreon, ode 7.

136. Reserve thy sorrows for the mournful year] The time appointed for mourning for the dead, among the ancients, was ten months; which was originally the year both of the Greeks and Romans.

The anniversary of the death of Adonis was celebrated through the whole Pagan world. The ancients differ greatly in their accounts of this divinity. Plutarch maintains, that he and Bacchus are the same; and that the Jews abstained from swine's flesh, because Adonis was killed by a boar. Ausonius, in epigram 30, affirms, that Bacchus, Osiris, and Adonis, are one and the same.
Langhorne.

IDYLLIUM II.

CUPID AND THE FLOWER.

A YOUTH, once fowling in a shady grove,
On a tall box-tree spy'd the god of love,
Perch'd like a beauteous bird; with sudden joy
At sight so noble leap'd the simple boy.
With eager expedition he prepares
His choicest twigs, his bird-lime, and his snares,
And in a neighb'ring covert smil'd to see
How here and there he skipt, and hopt from tree to tree.
When long in vain he waited to betray
The god, enrag'd he flung his twigs away,
And to a ploughman near, an ancient man,
Of whom he learn'd his art, the youngster ran,
Told the strange story, while he held his plough,
And show'd the bird then perch'd upon a bough.
The grave old ploughman archly shook his head,
Smil'd at the simple boy, and thus he said:
" Cease, cease, my son, this dangerous sport give o'er,
Fly far away, and chase that bird no more:
Blest should you fail to catch him!—Hence, away!
That bird, believe me, is a bird of prey:
Though now he seems to shun you all he can,
Yet soon as time shall lead you up to man,
He'll spread his flutt'ring pinions o'er your breast,
Perch on your brow, and in your bosom nest."

IDYLLIUM III.

THE TEACHER TAUGHT.

As late I slumbering lay, before my sight
Bright Venus rose in visions of the night:
She led young Cupid; as in thought profound
His modest eyes were fix'd upon the ground;
And thus she spoke: " To thee, dear swain, I bring
My little son; instruct the boy to sing."
No more she said; but vanish'd into air,
And left the wily pupil to my care:
I, sure I was an ideot for my pains,
Began to teach him old bucolic strains;
How Pan the pipe, how Pallas form'd the flute,
Phœbus the lyre, and Mercury the lute:
Love, to my lessons quite regardless grown,
Sung lighter lays, and sonnets of his own,
Th' amours of men below, and gods above,
And all the triumphs of the queen of love.
I, sure the simplest of all shepherd swains,
Full soon forgot my old bucolic strains;
The lighter lays of Love my fancy caught,
And I remember'd all that Cupid taught.

IDYLLIUM IV.

THE POWER OF LOVE.

THE sacred Nine delight in cruel Love,
Tread in his steps, and all his ways approve:
Should some rude swain, whom Love could ne'er refine,
Woo the fair Muses, they his suit decline;
But if the love-sick shepherd sweetly sing,
The tuneful choir, attending in a ring,
Catch the soft sounds, and tune the vocal shell;
This truth by frequent precedent I tell:
For when I praise some hero on my lyre,
Or, nobly daring, to a god aspire,
In strains more languid flows the nerveless song,
Or dies in faltering accents on my tongue:
But when with Love or Lycidas I glow,
Smooth are my lays, the numbers sweetly flow.

IDYLLIUM V.

LIFE TO BE ENJOYED.

IF merit only stamps my former lays,
And those alone shall give me deathless praise:
But if ev'n those have lost their bright applause,
Why should I labour thus without a cause?
For if great Jove or Fate would stretch our span,
And give of life a double share to man,
One part to pleasures and to joy ordain,
And vex the other with hard toil and pain;
With sweet complacence we might then employ
Our hours, for labour still enhances joy.
But since of life we have but one small share,
A pittance scant which daily toils impair,
Why should we waste it in pursuit of care?

Ovid makes Venus institute this festival, Metamorph. B. 10. at the end.

—— luctus monumenta manebunt
Semper, Adoni, mei, repetitaque mortis imago
Annua plangoris peraget simulamina nostri.

For thee, lost youth, my tears, and restless pain,
Shall in immortal monuments remain:
With solemn pomp, in annual rites return'd,
Be thou for ever, my Adonis, mourn'd.

Eusden.

Idyll. II. Spenser has imitated this idyllium in his Shepherd's Calendar for the month of March, but in a language too harsh for modern ears.

8. How here and there he skipt, and hopt from tree to tree] The original Greek, Τα και τα τον Ερωτα μεταλμενον, admirably describes a bird hopping about from bough to bough, which the translator has endeavoured to imitate.

Idyl. III. This beautiful idyllium, which in a pleasing fiction describes the power of love, is preserved by Stobæus.

Idyl. IV.—12. Or dies in faltering accents on my tongue] Sappho's situation is much the same, though on a different occasion. See stanza 2.

While gazing on thy charms I hung,
My voice died faltering on my tongue.

Anacreon's first ode bears a great similitude to this idyllium.

Idyl. V.—This fragment is preserved by Stobæus.

11. But since of life we have but one small share]
Vitæ summa brevis spem nos vetat inchoare longam. Hor. l. 1. od. 4.

—— Life's short, fleeting span
Allows no long protracted plan.

Duncombe.

Why do we labour to augment our store,
The more we gain, still coveting the more?
Alas! alas! we quite forget that man
Is a mere mortal, and his life a span.

IDYLLIUM VI

CLEODAMUS AND MYRSON.

CLEODAMUS.

Say, in their courses circling as they tend,
What season is most grateful to my friend?
Summer, whose suns mature the teeming ground,
Or golden Autumn, with full harvests crown'd?
Or Winter hoar, when soft reclin'd at ease,
The fire fair-blazing, and sweet leisure please?
Or genial Spring, in blooming beauty gay?
Speak, Myrson, while around the lambkins play.

MYRSON.

It ill becomes frail mortals to define
What's best and fittest of the works divine;
The works of Nature all are grateful found,
And all the seasons in their various round.
But since my friend demands my private voice,
Then learn the season that is Myrson's choice.
Me the hot Summer's sultry heats displease;
Fell Autumn teems with pestilent disease;
Tempestuous Winter's chilling frosts I fear;
But wish for purple Spring through all the year.
Then neither cold nor heat molests the morn;
But rosy Plenty fills her copious horn:
Then bursting buds their odorous blooms display,
And Spring makes equal night, and equal day.

Non semper idem floribus est honos, &c.
—— quid æternis
Consiliis animum fatigas?
L. 2. od. 11.

Not always vernal flowers their pride retain,
And full-orb'd moons are sure to wane:
Why tire we then the narrow mind,
For cares eternal too confin'd?
Duncombe.

Thus Manilius:

Quid tam solicitis vitam consumimus annis,
Torquemurque metu, cæcaque cupidine rerum,
Æternisque senes curis, dum quærimus, ævum
Perdimus; et nullo votorum fine beati,
Victuros agimus semper, nec vivimus unquam?

Why do we thus consume our years
In blind desires, and anxious fears?
For in the search, grown grey with pain,
We lose the bliss we strive to gain:
And thus, absorb'd by distant views,
In thoughts of living, life we lose.
D.

Idyl. VI.—18. But wish for purple Spring through all the year]

Et nunc omnis ager, nunc omnis parturit arbos,
Nunc frondent sylvæ, nunc formosissimus annus.
Virg. ecl. 3.

The trees are cloth'd with leaves, the fields with grass;
The blossoms blow; the birds on bushes sing;
And Nature has accomplish'd all the Spring.
Dryden.

IDYLLIUM VII.

THE EPITHALAMIUM OF ACHILLES AND DEIDAMIA.

MYRSON AND LYCIDAS.

MYRSON.

Say, wilt thou, Lycidas, sweet shepherd-swain,
Begin some soothing, soft Sicilian strain,
Such as the Cyclops, on a rock reclin'd,
Sung to the sea-nymph, to compose his mind,
And sent it in the whispers of the wind?

LYCIDAS.

What can I sing that Myrson will commend?
With pleasure I would gratify my friend.

MYRSON.

Repeat the song which most my taste approves,
Achilles' stol'n embrace, and hidden loves;
How the bold hero laid his arms aside,
A woman's robe the manly sex belied,
And Deidamia soon became his bride.

LYCIDAS.

When with fair Helen Paris cross'd the deep,
Brought her to Troy, and made Oenone weep;
The injur'd states of Greece were all alarm'd,
Spartans, Mycenians, and Laconians arm'd;
The treachery stung their souls, and bloody vengeance warm'd:
In close disguise his life Achilles led,
Among the daughters of king Lycomed:
Instead of arms the hero learn'd to cull
The snowy fleece, and weave the twisted wool.
Like theirs, his cheeks a rosy bloom display'd,
Like them he seem'd a fair and lovely maid;
As soft his air, as delicate his tread,
Like them he cover'd with a veil his head:
But in his veins the tides of courage flow'd,
And love's soft passion in his bosom glow'd;
By Deidamia's side from morn to night
He sat, and with ineffable delight
Oft kiss'd her snow-white hand, or gently press'd
The blooming virgin to his glowing breast.
His soul was all enraptur'd with her charms,
Ardent he long'd to clasp her in his arms;
Oft in her ear these words enamour'd said,
"By pairs your sisters press the downy bed;
But we, two maids of equal age and bloom,
Still sleep divided in a separate room.
Why should the night, more cruel than the day,
Steal the sweet virgin, whom I love, away?"

* * * * * * *

IDYLLIUM VIII.

LOVE RESISLTESS.

Sweet Venus, daughter of the main,
Why are you pleas'd with mortals' pain?

Idyl. VII.—3. Such as the Cyclops, &c.] The fable of Polyphemus and Galatea has furnished matter for several poets, particularly Theocritus in his 6th and 11th Idylliums, and Ovid in the 13th book of the Metamorphoses, fable the 8th; who has borrowed freely from Theocritus. See also Bion's sixth Fragment.

9. Achilles' stol'n embrace, &c.] The story of Achilles and Deidamia is told at large by Statius in the Achilleid.

What mighty trespass have they done,
That thus you scourge them with your son?
A guileful boy, a cruel foe,
Whose chief delight is human woe.
You gave him wings, alas! and darts,
To range the world, and shoot at hearts:
For man no safety thus is found ———
His flight o'ertakes, his arrows wound.

IDYLLIUM IX.

FRIENDSHIP.

THRICE happy they! whose friendly hearts can burn
With purest flame, and meet a kind return.
With dear Pirithoüs, as poets tell,
Theseus was happy in the shades of Hell:
Orestes' soul no fears, no woes deprest;
'Midst Scythians he with Pylades was blest.
Blest was Achilles while his friend surviv'd,
Blest was Patroclus every hour he liv'd;
Blest when in battle he resign'd his breath,
For his unconquer'd friend reveng'd his death.

FRAGMENTS.

FRAGMENT I.

ON HYACINTHUS.

DESPONDING sorrow seiz'd Apollo's heart;
All cures he try'd, and practis'd every art;
With nectar and ambrosia drest the wound:
Useless, alas! all remedies are found,
When Fate with cruel shears encompasses around.

FRAGMENT II.

THUS to the smith it is not fair,
My friend, for ever to repair,
And still another's aid to ask:
Make your own pipe; 'tis no such arduous task.

FRAGMENT III.

INVITE the Muses, Love, and in your train,
Ye sacred Muses, bring me Love again!
And ever grant, my wishes to complete,
The gift of song—no remedy so sweet!

FRAGMENT IV.

INCESSANT drops, as proverbs say,
Will wear the hardest stones away.

FRAGMENT V.

ON a steep cliff, beside the sandy beach,
Sudden I stop, and, whispering soft, beseech
Relentless Galatea; even in age
Love still shall bloom, and still my hopes engage.

FRAGMENT VI.

LET me not pass without reward!
For Phœbus on each tuneful bard
Some gift bestows: the noblest lays
Are owing to the thirst of praise.

FRAGMENT VII

IN beauty boasts fair woman-kind;
Man, in a firm, undaunted mind.

Idyll. VIII.—7. You gave him wings, &c.] There is a similar thought in a Greek epigram:

Φευγειν δη τον Ερωτα κενος πονος· ȣ γαρ αλυξω
Πεζος απο πτηνȣ πυκνα διωκομενος.

Of shunning love 'tis vain to talk,
When he can fly, and I but walk.

Idyll. IX.—9. Blest when in battle, &c.] Longepierre and Laurentius Gambara have given the same interpretation of this passage; and it seems to be confirmed by what Patroclus says to Hector, in the sixteenth book of the Iliad, when he is just expiring:

Insulting man! thou shalt be soon as I;
Black Fate hangs o'er thee, and thy hour draws nigh;
Ev'n now on life's last verge I see thee stand,
I see thee fall, and by Achilles' hand. Pope.

Frag. I.—This is a small fragment of an Idyllium on the death of Hyacinthus, whom Apollo unfortunately slew as he was playing with him at quoits.

2. All cures he try'd, and practis'd every art] Apollo is said to have invented physic: he tells Daphne, Ovid Metamorph. book I.

Inventum medicina meum est, opiferque per orbem
Dicor, & herbarum subjecta potentia nobis.

Medicine is mine; what herbs and simples grow
In fields and forests, all their powers I know;
And am the great physician call'd, below.
Dryden.

Frag. II. I have always thought, that this fragment should be understood, allegorically, of those who, though they have riches (or talents) in abundance, yet make no use of them.
Longepierre.

Frag. III.—Thus Apollo, in Ovid, Metamorph. book I.

Hei mihi, quod nullis amor est medicabilis herbis!

To cure the pains of Love, no plant avails.
Dryden.

Frag. IV.—This proverb is common almost to every nation.

Thus Ovid:

Quid magis est durum saxo, quid mollius undâ?
Dura tamen molli saxa cavantur aquâ.

And,

Gutta cavat lapidem non vi, sed sæpe cadendo.

Frag. V.—This seems to have been part of a speech of Polyphemus, in an Idyllium on the subject of Acis and Galatea; which Ovid probably imitated in his Metamorph. book 13. For similar to this Fragment are the following lines:

——— gradiens ingenti littora passu
Degravat ————
——— with stalking pace he strode,
And stamp'd the margin of the briny flood.

And,—Prominet in pontum, &c.

A promontory, sharpening by degrees,
Ends in a wedge, and overlooks the seas:
On either side, below, the water flows;
This airy walk the giant lover chose. Dryden.

Frag. VII.—Similar to this is the second ode of Anacreon; for which and the notes see page 338.

THE

IDYLLIUMS OF MOSCHUS.

TRANSLATED BY FAWKES.

O Solitude, on me bestow
The heart-felt harmony of woe,
Such, such as on th' Ausonian shore
Sweet Dorian Moschus trill'd of yore!

GRAINGER'S ODE ON SOLITUDE.

IDYLLIUM I.

IN search of her son, to the listening crowd,
T'other day lovely Venus thus cry'd him aloud;
"Whoever may chance a stray Cupid to meet,
My vagabond boy, as he strolls in the street,

Idyllium I.—This beautiful Idyllium is imitated by Spenser, in his Fairy Queen, b. 3. c. 6. st. 11.

It fortuned, fair Venus having lost
Her little son, the winged god of love,
Who for some light displeasure, which him crost,
Was from her fled, as flit as airy dove,
And left her blissful bower of joy above;
(So from her often he had fled away,
When she for aught him sharply did reprove,
And wander'd in the world in strange array,
Disguis'd in thousand shapes, that none might him bewray.)
Him for to seek, she left her heavenly house,
And searched every way through which his wings
Had borne him, or his tract she mote detect:
She promis'd kisses sweet, and sweeter things,
Unto the man, that of him tidings to her brings.

And will bring me the news, his reward shall be this,
He may freely demand of fair Venus a kiss;
But, if to my arms he the boy can restore,
He's welcome to kisses, and something still more.
His marks are so plain, and so many, you'll own
That among twenty others he's easily known.
His skin is not white, but the colour of flame;
His eyes are most cruel, his heart is the same:

Meleager also has copied this fine original of Moschus, and given us a picture of Cupid much in the same manner. See Anthologia, b. 7. epig. 16.

Κηρυσσω τον Ερωτα, κ. τ. λ.

I'm in search of a Cupid that late went astray,
And stole from my bed with the dawn of the day.
His aspect is bold, his tongue never lies still,
And yet he can whine, and has tears at his will.
At human misfortunes he laughs and he sneers;
On his shoulders a quiver and pinions he wears:
'Tis unknown from what sire he deduces his birth;
'Tis not from the Air, nor the Sea, nor the Earth;
For he's hated by all—but, good people, beware;
Perhaps for a heart he's now laying a snare—
Ha, ha, cunning Cupid, I see where you lie,
With your bow ready bent:—in Zenophila's eye.

His delicate lips with persuasion are hung;
But, ah! how they differ, his mind and his tongue!
His voice sweet as honey; but nought can controul,
Whene'er he's provok'd, his implacable soul.
He never speaks truth, full of fraud is the boy;
And woe is his pastime, and sorrow his joy.
His head is embellish'd with bright curling hair;
He has confident looks, and an insolent air.
Though his hands are but little, yet darts they can fling
To the regions below, and their terrible king.
His body quite naked to view is reveal'd,
But he covers his mind, and his thoughts are conceal'd.
Like a bird light of feather, the branches among,
He skips here and there, to the old, to the young,
From the men to the maids on a sudden he strays,
And hid in their hearts on their vitals he preys.
The bow which he carries is little and light,
On the nerve is an arrow wing'd ready for flight,
A little short arrow, yet swiftly it flies
Through regions of ether, and pierces the skies.
A quiver of gold on his shoulders is bound,
Stor'd with darts, that alike friends and enemies wound:
Ev'n I, his own mother, in vain strive to shun
His arrows—so fell and so cruel my son.
His torch is but small, yet so ardent its ray,
It scorches the Sun, and extinguishes day.
O you, who perchance may the fugitive find,
Secure first his hands, and with manacles bind;
Show the rogue no compassion, though oft he appears
To weep—his are all hypocritical tears.
With caution conduct him, nor let him beguile
Your vigilant care with a treacherous smile.
Perhaps, with a laugh kisses sweet he will proffer;
His kisses are poison, ah! shun the vile offer.
Perhaps he'll say, sobbing: 'No mischief I know;
Here, take all my arrows, my darts and my bow!'
Ah! beware, touch them not—deceitful his aim;
His darts and his arrows are all tipt with flame."

13 & 14. His delicate lips with persuasion are hung;
But, ah! how they differ, his mind and his tongue!
His voice sweet as honey]

Thus the royal Psalmist, Psalm 55. v. 22. "The words of his mouth are softer than butter, having war in his heart; his words were smoother than oil, and yet be they very swords." And Solomon, Proverbs, chap. 5. v. 3. "For the lips of a strange woman drop as an honey-comb, and her mouth is smoother than oil."

41. Show the rogue no compassion, though oft he appears
To weep]

There is an epigram of Crinagoras, Anthol. b. 4. ch. 12. which may illustrate this passage: it is on an image of Cupid bound.

Και κλαι κα ςεναζε, κ. τ. λ.

Perfidious wretch, you now may cry,
And wring your hands, and sob, and sigh:
Who now your advocate will be?
Who now from chains will set you free?
You oft, by causeless doubts and fears,
From other eyes have forc'd the tears,
And, by your bitter-biting darts,
Instill'd love's poison into hearts.
O Love, who laugh'd at human bail,
Now all your arts elusive fail,
And justice will at last prevail.

46. His kisses are poison] Thus Virgil, Æneid, book 1. ver. 687.

Cum dabit amplexus, atque oscula dulcia figet,
Occultum inspires ignem, falasque veneno.

And when the queen shall strain thee in her arms,
The gentle passion by degrees inspire
Through all her breast, then fan the rising fire,
And kindle all her soul —— Pitt.

IDYLLIUM II.

EUROPA.

THE queen of love, on amorous wiles intent,
A pleasing dream to fair Europa sent.
What time still night had roll'd the hours away,
And the fresh dawn began to promise day,
When balmy slumbers, and composing rest,
Close every eye, and sooth the pensive breast,
When dreams and visions fill the busy brain,
Prophetic dreams, that never rise in vain:
'Twas then Europa, as she sleeping lay,
Chaste as Diana, sister of the Day,
Saw in her cause the adverse shore engag'd
In war with Asia; terribly they rag'd:
Each seem'd a woman; that in foreign guise,
A native this, and claim'd the lovely prize
With louder zeal: "The beauteous nymph," she said,
"Her daughter was, and in her bosom bred."
But she, who as a stranger was array'd,
Forc'd to her arms the unresisting maid;

Idyll. II.—This poem has been printed in some of the most ancient editions of Theocritus; and therefore some critics have taken it for granted that he was the author, without recollecting, that, in the time of the later Grecians, all the ancient idylliums were collected together in one volume, and the name of Theocritus prefixed to the whole: on which occasion there is an epigram in the Anthologia, ascribed to Artemidorus:

Βυκολικαι μυσαι σποραδες ποκα, νυν δ' αμα πασαι
Εντι μιας μανδρας, εντι μιας αγελας.

The past'ral Muses, scatter'd o'er the plains,
A single flock, a single fold contains.

This is one of those idylliums which has been adjudged to Moschus: besides, Ursinus tells us (as we are informed by Mr. Heskin) "that in two very ancient manuscripts which he had seen, one belonging to the Vatican, the other to the Medicean library, he observed, that the idyllium, entitled Europa, was ascribed to Moschus."

8. Prophetic dreams, that never rise in vain]

Post mediam noctem, cum somnia vera.
Hor. b. 1. sat. 10.

—— at dead of night,
When dreams are real ——
Duncombe.

Call'd her her right, by all the powers above,
Giv'n her by Fate, and Ægis-bearing Jove.
The fair Europa, struck with sudden dread,
All pale and trembling started from her bed;
Silent she sat, and thought the vision true,
Still seem'd their forms to strive before her view:
At length she utter'd thus the voice of fear;
"Ye gods, what spectres to my sight appear?
What dreams are these, in Fancy's livery drest,
That haunt my sleep, and break my golden rest?
And who that form that seem'd so wond'rous kind?
The dear idea still delights my mind.
She, like a mother, press'd me in her arms:
But, O ye gods! that send such strange alarms,
Preserve these visionary scenes from harms."
She said, and lightly from her couch she sprung,
Then sought her comrades, beautiful and young,
Her social mates; with them she lov'd to lave
Her limbs unblemish'd in the crystal wave:
With them on lawns the sprightly dance to lead,
Or pluck sweet lilies in the flowery mead.
The nymphs assembled soon, a beauteous band!
With each a curious basket in her hand;
Then reach'd those fields where oft they play'd before,
The fragrant fields along the sea-beat shore,
To gather flowers, and hear the billows roar.
Europa's basket, radiant to behold,
The work of Vulcan, was compos'd of gold;
He gave it Libya, mighty Neptune's bride,
She Telephassa, next in blood ally'd;
From her bequeath'd to fair Europa came
This splendid basket of celestial frame.
Fair in the work the milk-white Iö stood
In roughen'd gold, and lowing paw'd the flood,
(For Vulcan there had pour'd the azure main)
A heifer still, nor yet transform'd again.
Two men stood figur'd on the ocean's brim,
Who watch'd the cow, that seem'd inclin'd to swim.
Jove too appear'd enamour'd on the strand,
And strok'd the lovely heifer with his hand:
Till, on the banks of Nile again array'd,
In native beauty shone the blooming maid:
The sev'n-mouth'd Nile in silver currents roll'd,
And Jove was sculptur'd in refulgent gold.
Near piping Hermes sleepless Argus lies,
Watching the heifer with his hundred eyes:
From Argus slain a painted peacock grew,
Fluttering his feathers stain'd with various hue,
And, as a ship expands her swelling sail,
He round the basket spread his starry tail.
Such were the scenes the Lemnian god display'd,
And such the basket of the Tyrian maid.
The lovely damsels gather'd flow'rets bright,
Sweet to the smell, and beauteous to the sight;
The fragrant hyacinth of purple hue,
Narcissus, wild thyme, and the violet blue;
Some the gilt crocus or pale lily chose,
But fair Europa cropp'd the blooming rose;
And all her mates excell'd in radiant mien,
As midst the Graces shines the Cyprian queen.
Not long, alas! in these fair fields she shone,
Nor long unloos'd preserv'd her virgin zone;

51. The milk-white Iö] The fable of Iö is told at large by Ovid in the first book of the Metamorphoses, and finely translated by Mr. Dryden; to whom I refer the curious reader, the story being too long to insert here.

Saturnian Jove beheld the matchless maid,
And sudden transports the rapt god invade;
He glows with all the fervid flame of love;
For Cupid's arrows pierce the breast of Jove.
But, best his amorous intent to screen,
And shun the jealous anger of his queen,
He laid his immortality aside,
And a bull's form th' intriguing god bely'd;
But not of earthly shape, or mortal breed,
Such as at large in flowery pastures feed;

81. Saturnian Jove beheld, &c.] Ovid has told the story of the Rape of Europa in the second book of the Metamorphoses; which, to prevent the trouble of referring to the particular similar passages, I shall give altogether under this note, in the language of Mr. Addison. The English reader will see at one view, even through the medium of translation, how closely the Roman has copied the Sicilian bard.

The dignity of empire laid aside,
The ruler of the skies, the thundering god,
Who shakes the world's foundations with a nod,
Among a herd of lowing heifers ran,
Frisk'd in a bull, and bellow'd o'er the plain.
Large rolls of fat about his shoulders clung,
And from his neck the double dewlap hung.
His skin was whiter than the snow that lies
Unsully'd by the breath of southern skies;
Small shining horns on his curl'd forehead stand,
As turn'd and polish'd by the workman's hand;
His eye-balls roll'd, not formidably bright,
But gaz'd and languish'd with a gentle light.
His every look was peaceful, and exprest
The softness of the lover in the beast.
Agenor's royal daughter, as she play'd
Among the fields, the milk-white bull survey'd,
And view'd his spotless body with delight,
And at a distance kept him in her sight.
At length she pluck'd the rising flowers, and fed
The gentle beast, and fondly strok'd his head.
He stood well-pleas'd to touch the charming fair,
But hardly could confine his pleasure there.
And now he wantons on the neighb'ring strand,
Now rolls his body on the yellow sand;
And now, perceiving all her fears decay'd,
Comes tossing forward to the royal maid;
Gives her his breast to stroke, and downwards turns
His grizly brow, and gently stoops his horns.
In flowery wreaths the royal virgin drest
His bending horns, and kindly clapp'd his breast.
Till now grown wanton, and devoid of fear,
Not knowing that she press'd the Thunderer,
She plac'd herself upon his back, and rode
O'er fields and meadows, seated on the god.
He gently march'd along, and by degrees
Left the dry meadow, and approach'd the seas;
Where he now dips his hoofs, and wets his thighs,
Now plunges in, and carries off the prize.
The frighted nymph looks backward on the shore,
And hears the tumbling billows round her roar;
But still she holds him fast: one hand is borne
Upon his back, the other grasps a horn;
Her train of ruffling garments flies behind,
Swells in the air, and hovers in the wind.
Through storms and tempests he the virgin bore,
And lands her safe on the Dictæan shore;
Where now, in his divinest form array'd,
In his true shape he captivates the maid.

Whose stubborn necks beneath the yoke we bow,
Break to the wain, or harness to the plough.
His golden hue distinguish'd him afar;
Full in his forehead beam'd a silver star:
His large blue eyes, that shone serenely bright,
Languish'd with love, and sparkled with delight:
On his broad temples rose two equal horns,
Like that fair crescent which the skies adorns.
Gently he moves with peaceful look and bland,
And spreads no terrour in the virgin band:
Nearer they draw, with eager longing led
To stroke his sides, and pat his comely head:
His breath divine ambrosial odours yields,
Sweeter than fragrance of the flowery fields.
At fair Europa's feet with joy he stands,
And prints sweet kisses on her lily hands.
His foamy lips she wipes, unaw'd by dread,
And strokes his sides, and pats his comely head.
Gently he low'd, as musical and clear
As notes soft warbled on the raptur'd ear:
And, as on earth his pliant knees he bent,
Show'd his broad back, that hinted what he meant;
Then turn'd his suppliant eyes, and view'd the maid;
Who thus astonish'd, to her comrades said:
"Say, dearest mates, what can this beast intend?
Let us (for lo! he stoops) his back ascend,
And ride in sportive gambols round the mead;
This lovely bull is, sure, of gentlest breed:
So meek his manner, so benign his mind,
He wants but voice to equal human kind."
So spoke the fair, and up she rose to ride,
And call'd her lingering partners to her side:
Soon as the bull his pleasing burden bore,
Vigorous he sprung, and hasten'd to the shore.
The nymph dismay'd invok'd the virgin band
For help, and wav'd her unavailing hand.
On the soft bosom of the azure flood
With his fair prize the bull triumphant rode:
Up rose the Nereids to attend his train,
And all the mighty monsters of the main.
Cerulean Neptune was the thunderer's guide,
And for the passing pomp he smooth'd the tide:
The Tritons hail'd him as he steer'd along,
And sounded on their conchs the nuptial song.
On Jove's broad back the lovely damsel borne
Grasp'd with her fair right hand his polish'd horn,
Her left essay'd her purple robe to save,
That lightly brush'd the surface of the wave:
Around her head soft breath'd the gentle gale,
And fill'd her garment like a swelling sail.
Europa's heart throbb'd quick with chilling fear,
Far from her much-lov'd home, and comrades dear;
No sea-beat shore she saw, nor mountain's brow,
Nor aught but sky above, and waves below.
Then with a mournful look the damsel said:
"Ah! whither wilt thou bear a wretched maid?
Who, and whence art thou, wond'rous creature, say?
How canst thou fearless tread the watery way?
On the broad ocean safely sails the ship,
But bulls avoid, and dread the stormy deep.
Say, can a bull on sea-born viands feed?
Or, if descended from celestial breed,
Thy acts are inconsistent with a god:
Bulls rove the meads, and dolphins swim the flood;
But earth and ocean are alike to thee,
Thy hoofs are oars that row thee through the sea.
Perhaps, like airy birds, thou soon wilt fly,
And soar amidst the regions of the sky.
Ah! wretched maid, to leave my native home,
And simply dare with bulls in meads to roam!
And now on seas I ride—ah! wretched maid!
But, O! I trust, great Neptune, in thy aid;

93. His golden hue, &c.] Horace imitates this passage, and describes a young bullock in the same manner:

> Fronte curvatos imitatos ignes
> Tertium lunæ referentis ortum,
> Quà notam duxit, niveus videri;
> Cætera fulvus.
>
> B. 4. od. 2.

> —— on whose brows,
> Full in the front a star its lustre shows;
> A gloss of fallow hue adorns
> His skin; the crescent of his horns,
> So sharply turn'd, salutes the sight,
> Like Cynthia's fires, the third revolving night.
>
> J. Duncombe

129. Up rose the Nereids, &c.] See a simila description in Virgil's Æneid, b. 5. near the end

> A thousand forms attend the glorious god,
> Enormous whales, and monsters of the flood:
> Here the long train of hoary Glaucus rides;
> Here the swift Tritons shoot along the tides;
> There rode Palæmon o'er the watery plain,
> With aged Phorcus, and his azure train;
> And beauteous Thetis led the daughters of the main.
>
> Pitt.

See also the latter end of the fifty-first ode of Anacreon.

148. No sea-beat shore she saw, &c.] Thus Virgil, Æneid, b. 3. v. 192.

> Postquam altum tenuere rates, nec jam amplius ullæ
> Apparent terræ, cælum undique, et undique pontus.

> Now vanish'd from our eyes the lessening ground;
> And all the wide horizon stretching round,
> Above was sky, beneath was sea profound.
>
> Pitt.

Which he has borrowed from Homer, Odyss. b. 12, v. 403.

> Past sight of shore, along the surge we bound,
> And all above is sky, and ocean all around.
>
> Pope.

Horace has in a masterly manner imitated this whole idyllium, but particularly this passage, b. 3. od. 27.

> Sic et Europe niveum doloso
> Credidit tauro latus, et scatentem
> Belluis pontum, mediasque fraudes
> Palluit audax.
> Nuper in pratis studiosa florum, et
> Debitæ nymphis opifex coronæ,
> Nocte sublustri, nihil astra præter
> Vidit et undas.

> Europa thus the bull caress'd,
> And his broad back advent'rous press'd;
> But when the monsters of the main
> She saw, her heart was fill'd with throbbing pain.
> She who, along the flowery meads,
> Wove wreaths for her companions heads,
> Now in the gloom sees nought around
> But twinkling stars, and ocean's waves profound.
>
> W. Duncombe.

Soon let my eyes my great conductor hail,
For not without a deity I sail."
Thus spoke the nymph, and thus the bull reply'd:
"Courage, fair maid, nor fear the foaming tide;
Though now a bull I seem to mortal eyes,
Thou soon shalt see me ruler of the skies.
What shape I please, at will I take and keep,
And now a bull I cross the boundless deep;
For thy bright charms inspire my breast with love:
But soon shall Crete's fair isle, the nurse of Jove,
Receive Europa on its friendly strand,
To join with me in Hymen's blissful band:
From thee shall kings arise in long array,
To rule the world with delegated sway."
Thus spoke the god; and what he spoke prov'd true:
For soon Crete's lofty shore appear'd in view:
Jove straight assum'd another form and air,
And loos'd her zone; the Hours the couch prepare.
The nymph Europa thus, through powerful love,
Became the bride of cloud-compelling Jove:
From her sprung mighty kings in long array,
Who rul'd the world with delegated sway.

IDYLLIUM III.

ON THE DEATH OF BION.

Ye woods, with grief your waving summits bow,
Ye Dorian fountains, murmur as ye flow,
From weeping urns your copious sorrows shed,
And bid the rivers mourn for Bion dead:
Ye shady groves, in robe of sable hue
Bewail; ye plants, in pearly drops of dew:
Ye drooping flowers, diffuse a languid breath;
And die with sorrow at sweet Bion's death:
Ye roses change from red to sickly pale,
And all ye bright anemonies, bewail:
Now, Hyacinth, thy doleful letters show
Inscrib'd in larger characters of woe
For Bion dead, the sweetest shepherd swain.
Begin, Sicilian Muse, begin the mournful strain!
Ye nightingales, that perch among the sprays,
Tune to melodious elegy your lays,
And bid the streams of Arethuse deplore
Bion's sad fate; lov'd Bion is no more:
Nor verse nor music could his life prolong,
He died, and with him died the Doric song.
Begin, Sicilian Muse, the mournful strain!
Ye swans of Strymon, in loud notes complain,
Pensive, yet sweet, and droop the sickly wing,
As when your own sad elegy ye sing,
All the fair damsels of Oëagria tell,
And all the nymphs that in Bistonia dwell,
That Doric Orpheus charms no more the plains.
Begin, Sicilian Muse, begin the mournful strains!
No more he sooths his oxen at the yoke,
No more he chants beneath the lonely oak.
Compell'd, alas! a doleful dirge to sing,
To the grim god, the deaf Tartarean king.
And now each straggling heifer strays alone,
And to the silent mountains makes her moan;
The bulls loud bellowing o'er the forests rove,
Forsake their pasture, and forget their love.
Begin, Sicilian Muse, the mournful lay!
Thy fate, O Bion, wept the god of day;
Pan griev'd; the dancing Satyrs and the Fauns
March'd slow and sad, and sigh'd along the lawns:
Then wail'd the nymphs that o'er the streams preside,
Fast flow'd their tears, and swell'd the crystal tide.
Mute Echo now laments the rocks among,
Griev'd she no more can imitate thy song.
The flow'rets fade, and wither'd are the trees,
Those lose their beauty, and their verdure these,
The ewes no more with milky udders thrive,
No more drops honey from the fragrant hive;
The bees, alas! have lost their little store,
And what avails it now to work for more,
When from thy lips the honey's stolen away?
Begin, Sicilian Muse, begin the mournful lay!
Ne'er did the dolphin on the azure main
In such pathetic energy complain;

Idyll. III.—Some have been so absurd as to ascribe this beautiful idyllium to Theocritus, because it was originally inserted in the collection that went under his name: but that he is not the author of it, is plain from a passage in this very idyllium, which mentions Theocritus as bewailing the death of Bion.

Moschus in this idyllium so frequently alludes to Bion's, on the death of Adonis, that it will be unnecessary to point out all the resembling places.

11. Now, Hyacinth, thy doleful letters show] The story of the transformation of Hyacinthus is told by Ovid in the tenth book of the Metamorphoses:

Ipse suos gemitus foliis inscribit, et αι αι,
Flos habet inscriptum, funestaque litera ducta est.

——— the god upon its leaves
The sad expression of his sorrow weaves;
And to this hour the mournful purple wears
Ai, ai, inscrib'd in funeral characters.
Ozell.

33. And now each straggling heifer strays alone] See a similar passage in Virgil's fifth eclogue as translated by Dryden:

The swains forgot their sheep, nor near the brink
Of running waters brought their herds to drink.
The thirsty cattle, of themselves, abstain'd
From water, and their grassy fare disdain'd:
The death of Daphnis woods and hills deplore.

41. Then wail'd the nymphs that o'er the streams preside,
Fast flow'd their tears, and swell'd the crystal tide.

Thus Ovid on the death of Orpheus, Metamorph. b. 11.

—— lacrymis quoque flumina dicunt
Increvisse suis; obscuraque carbasa pullo
Naiades et Dryades, passosque habuere capillos.

Naiads and Dryads with dishevell'd hair
Promiscuous weep, and scarfs of sable wear;
Nor could the river gods conceal their moan,
But with new floods of tears augment their own.

53. Ne'er did the dolphin, &c.] Dolphins are said to utter a mournful cry, like a man in distress, and to be wonderfully fond of harmony; witness the fable of Arion. Longepierre thinks this passage alludes to the story of Hesiod; who (as Plutarch relates) being assassinated, his body was thrown into the sea, and received by a shoal of dolphins, and, on the very day when the feast of Neptune was celebrated, brought by them ashore near the city of Molicria; by which means the

Nor Philomel with such melodious woe
E'er wail'd, nor swallow on the mountain's brow:
Nor did Alcyone transform'd deplore
So loud her lover dash'd upon the shore.
Not Memnon's birds such signs of sorrow gave,
When, screaming round, they hover'd o'er his grave:
As now in melancholy mood they shed
Their plaintive tears, lamenting Bion dead.
  Begin, Sicilian Muse, the mournful lay!
The nightingales, that perch upon the spray,
The swallows shrill, and all the feather'd throng,
Whom Bion taught, and ravish'd with his song,
Now sunk in grief their pensive music ply,
And strive to sing their master's elegy;
And all the birds in all the groves around
Strain their sweet throats to emulate the sound:
Ye turtles too, the gentle bard deplore,
And with deep murmurs fill the sounding shore.
  Begin, Sicilian Muse, the mournful lay!
Who now, lov'd shepherd, on thy pipe shall play?
Still, still, methinks, the melting notes I hear,
But, ah! more faint they die upon my ear.
Echo, still listening, roves the meads along,
Or near the rocks still meditates thy song.
To Pan I'll give thy tuneful pipe, though he
Will fear, perchance, to be surpass'd by thee.
  Begin, Sicilian Muse, the mournful strain!
Thee Galatea weeps, sweet shepherd-swain;
For oft thy graceful form her bosom warm'd,
Thy song delighted, and thy music charm'd:
She shunn'd the Cyclops, and his numbers rude,
But thee with ardent love the nymph pursu'd:
She left the sea, her element, and feeds,
Forlorn, thy cattle on the flowery meads.
  Begin, Sicilian Muse, the mournful lay!
Alas! the Muses will no longer stay,
No longer on these lonely coasts abide;
With thee they warbled, and with thee they died
With Bion perish'd all the grace of song,
And all the kisses of the fair and young.
The little Loves, lamenting at his doom,
Strike their fair breasts, and weep around his tomb.
See Venus too her beauteous bosom beat!
She lov'd her shepherd more than kisses sweet,
More than those last dear kisses, which in death
She gave Adonis, and imbib'd his breath.
Meles! of streams in melody the chief,
Now heaves thy bosom with another grief;
Thy Homer died, great master of the song,
Thy Homer died, the Muses sweetest tongue:
Then did thy waves in plaintive murmurs weep,
And roll'd thy swelling sorrows to the deep:
Another son demands the meed of woe,
Again thy waters weep in long-drawn murmurs slow.
Dear to the fountains was each tuneful son,
This drank of Arethuse, that Helicon:
He sung Atrides' and Achilles' ire,
And the fair dame that set the world on fire:
This form'd his numbers on a softer plan,
And chanted shepherds loves, and peaceful Pan;
His flock he tended on the flowery meads,
And milk'd his kine, or join'd with wax the reeds;
Oft in his bosom he would Cupid take,
And Venus lov'd him for her Cupid's sake.
  Begin, Sicilian Muse, the mournful strains,
Thee all the cities of the hills and plains,
Illustrious bard, in silent grief deplore;
Ascra for Hesiod ne'er lamented more;
Not thus Bœotia mourn'd her Theban swan,
Nor thus the tears for bold Alcæus ran;
Not Ceos for Simonides, nor thus
Griev'd Paros for her bard Archilocus:
The shepherds of the Lesbian isle have long
Neglected Sappho's for thy sweeter song:
And all that breathe the past'ral reed rehearse
Thy fate, O Bion, in harmonious verse.
Sicelidas, the Samian shepherd sweet,
And Lycidas, the blithest bard of Crete,
Whose sprightly looks erst spoke their hearts elate,
Now sorrowing mourn thy sad untimely fate;
Mourns too Philetas' elegiac muse,
And sweet Theocritus of Syracuse:
I too, with tears, from Italy have brought
Such plain bucolics as my master taught;
Which, if at all with tuneful ease they flow,
To thy learn'd precepts and thy art I owe.
To other heirs thy riches may belong,
I claim thy past'ral pipe and Doric song;
In Doric song my pensive boon I pay:
  Begin, Sicilian Muse, begin the mournful lay!
Alas! the meanest flowers which gardens yield,
The vilest weeds that flourish in the field,

murderers were discovered, and suffered the punishment due to their crime.

57. Nor did Alcyone transform'd deplore, &c.] Alcyone is fabled to have been the wife of Cëyx, a king of Thrace. They were remarkable for their conjugal affection. On his being drowned, she endeavoured to cast herself into the sea; but was immediately transformed into a king's-fisher, as was likewise the body of her husband. The story is told by Ovid in the eleventh book of the Metamorphoses, and admirably translated by Dryden.

59. Not Memnon's birds, &c.] For Memnon's birds, see Ovid's Metamorphoses, b. 13.

101. Meles, &c.] The river Meles washes the walls of Smyrna, a city of Asia Minor, where Bion was born. It is also supposed to have been the birth-place of Homer, and therefore that river is said to have been his father; whence he is called Melesigenes.

123. Theban swan] Pindar.

129 to 136. These seven lines are a translation of six Greek verses which were wanting in the ancient editions of our poet. They are supposed to be supplied by Marcus Musurus of Crete; though Scaliger affirms, that they were wrote by Moschus.

131. Sicelidas, Lycidas, and Philetas are mentioned by Theocritus in his seventh Idyllium.

145. Alas! the meanest flowers which gardens yield, &c.]
This fine sentiment has been embellished by several authors. Thus Spenser;

Whence is it, that the flowret of the field doth fade,
And lieth buried long in Winter's bale?
Yet, soon as Spring his mantle hath display'd,
It flow'reth fresh, as it should never fail.
But thing on Earth that is of most avail,
    As virtue's branch, and beauty's bud,
    Reliven not for any good.

And Catullus:

Soles occidere et redire possunt:
Nobis, cum semel occidet brevis lux,
Nox est perpetua una dormienda.

Which dead in wintry sepulchres appear,
Revive in spring, and bloom another year:
But we, the great, the brave, the learn'd, the wise,
Soon as the hand of Death has clos'd our eyes,
In tombs forgotten lie, no suns restore,
We sleep, for ever sleep, to wake no more.
Thou too liest buried with the silent dead:
Fate spares the witlings, but thy vital thread
Snapp'd cruel chance! and now 'tis my hard lot
To hear the dull bards (but I envy not)
Grate their harsh sonnets, flashy, rude, and vain:
  Begin, Sicilian Muse, begin the mournful strain!
O hapless Bion! poison was thy fate;
The baneful potion circumscrib'd thy date:
How could fell poison cause effect so strange,
Touch thy sweet lips, and not to honey change?
How could the savage wretch, that mix'd the draught,
Hear heavenly music with a murderous thought?
Could not thy songs his hellish purpose sway?
  Begin, Sicilian Muse, begin the mournful lay!
But soon just vengeance will his crime pursue,
While I with pious tears thy tomb bedew.
Could I like Orpheus, as old poets tell,
Or mighty Hercules, descend to Hell;
To Pluto's dreary mansion I would go,
To hear what music Bion plays below.
List to my counsel, gentle shepherd-swain,
And softly warble some Sicilian strain,
(Such as, when living, gave divine delight)
To sooth the empress of the realms of night;
For she, ere Pluto seiz'd the trembling maid,
Sung Dorian lays, and in these meadows play'd.
Nor unrewarded shall thy numbers prove,
The dame will pity, though she cannot love;
As once she heard the Thracian's tuneful prayer,
And gave him back Eurydice the fair,
She'll pity now thy more melodious strain,
And send thee to thy hills and woods again.
Could I in powerful harmony excel,
For thee my pipe should charm the rigid king of Hell.

The Sun, that sinks into the main,
Sets, with fresh light to rise again:
But we, when once our breath is fled,
Die, and are number'd with the dead.
With endless night we close our day,
And sleep eternity away.

Admirable is that of Job, chap. 14. "Man cometh forth as a flower, and is cut down.—There is hope of a tree, if it be cut down, that it will sprout again, and that the tender branch thereof will not cease:—But man dieth, and wasteth away: yea, man giveth up the ghost, and where is he? He lieth down, and riseth not, till the Heavens be no more."

178. — and in these meadows play'd] Pluto carried away Proserpine from the fields of Enna in Sicily. Thus Milton, Paradise Lost, book 4. ver. 269.

—— not that fair field
Of Enna, where Proserpine gathering flowers,
Herself a fairer flower, by gloomy Dis
Was gather'd, which cost Ceres all that pain
To seek her through the world ———

See also Ovid's Metamorphoses, book 5.

IDYLLIUM IV.

MEGARA.

MEGARA.

"Why these complaints, and whence that dreadful sigh?
Why on thy cheek do thus the roses die?
Is it to see thy glorious son sustain,
From worthless hands, pre-eminence of pain?
A lion tortur'd by a fawn!—Great Jove!
Why such injurious treatment must I prove?
Why with such adverse omens was I born?
Wretch that I am! e'er since the nuptial morn
When to my arms my matchless lord was given,
Dear have I priz'd him as the light of Heaven;
And prize him still—— sure none has suffer'd more,
Or drank such draughts of sorrow's cup before.
With Phœbus' gift, his bow, he pierc'd the hearts
Of his own sons; or rather, arm'd with darts
Which Fates or Furies furnish'd, every child
In his own house he slew, with frenzy wild.
Than dreams more dreadful, with these streaming eyes,
(While to their mother, with incessant cries,
Their helpless mother, they exclaim'd in vain)
By their own sire I saw the children slain.
But as a bird bewails her callow brood,
While in the brake a serpent drains their blood,

Idyll. IV.—This poem contains a dialogue between Megara, the wife of Hercules, and Alcmena his mother, wherein they recapitulate their mutual misfortunes. This famous hero gave great umbrage to Eurystheus, king of Mycenæ; who fearing he would in time dispossess him of his crown, tried all methods to destroy him. Hercules, sensible of his dangerous situation, consulted the Oracle; and being answered, that it was the will of the gods that he should serve Eurestheus twelve years, was thrown into so deep a melancholy, that it turned at length into a furious frenzy; during which he put away his wife Megara, and murdered all the children he had by her, which are supposed to have been twelve, because the king imposed on him the same number of labours, as an expiation for their murder, after he had recovered his senses. Hercules is supposed to have been absent on one of these expeditions, when this dialogue commences.

21. But as a bird bewails, &c.] Virgil has happily imitated this beautiful simile in his Georgics, book 4. ver. 511.

Qualis populeâ mœrens Philomela sub umbra
Amissos queritur fœtus; quos durus arator
Observans nido implumes detraxit: at illa
Flet noctem, ramoque sedens miserabile carmen
Integrat, et mœstis late loca questibus implet.

Which is as happily translated by Dryden.

So, close in poplar shades, her children gone,
The mother-nightingale laments alone:
Whose nest some prying churl had found, and thence,
By stealth, convey'd th' unfeather'd innocence.
But she supplies the night with mournful strains,
And melancholy music fills the plains.

And, all too weak the wish'd relief to bring,
Twittering her shrill complaints, on feeble wing
At distance hovers, nor will venture near
The fell destroyer, chill'd with conscious fear;
So I, all frantic, the wide mansion o'er,
Unhappy mother! my lost sons deplore,
O blest, Diana, goddess of the chase,
Tyrant confess'd o'er woman's helpless race,
With my dear sons had thy envenom'd dart
Kindly transfix'd their mother's bleeding heart,
Then my sad parents might, with friendly care,
Have seen one pile our breathless bodies bear,
At once, with many a tear, to every shade
The decent rites of sepulture have paid,
And in one golden urn that sacred earth
Our ashes have receiv'd, which gave us birth.
But Thebes they now inhabit, fam'd for steeds,
Or toilsome till Aonia's fruitful meads:
While to my sorrows no relief is given,
At Tiryns, sacred to the queen of Heaven,
In tears unnumber'd wasting life away,
To joy a stranger, to despair a prey.
But soon my lord will bless my eyes again,
For various labours he must yet sustain
By land and sea, like iron or a rock
Unmov'd, and still superior to the shock:
While like a stream thy sorrows ever flow,
By day, by night, alike dissolv'd in woe.
Of all to me by ties of kindred join'd,
Thou only now canst cheer my anxious mind:
Far from this mansion, though in blood ally'd,
Beyond the pine-clad Isthmus they reside.
Not one remains who can console my grief,
Or to a wretched woman give relief,
Except my sister Pyrrha; all the day
She too bewails her husband snatch'd away,
Thy son Iphiclus: wretched all thy line,
Whether their sire be mortal or divine!"
Fast, while she spoke, th' o'erflowing tears distill'd
Adown her cheeks, and her fair bosom fill'd;
Her sons, her parents rising to her view:
In sad society, Alcmena too
Roll'd the big tear; and from her heaving breast,
In accents sage, her daughter thus addrest:
"Why, hapless parent, should thine eyes o'erflow?
Why should remembrance thus renew thy woe?
Why thus afflict us both? or why once more
Repeat the loss we oft have wept before?
Sure each sad day sufficient sorrows bears;
And none but wretches would recount our cares!
Be cheer'd, my daughter, and, these ills forgot,
Think that the gods a happier doom allot.
And though on grief thy thoughts are all employ'd,
I no excuse require, with pleasure cloy'd.
Much I lament, that thou so vast a weight
Of woe shouldst share in our disastrous fate.
For, O blest Proserpine and Ceres, know,
(Powers justly dreaded by the perjur'd foe)
That I not more could love thee, if my womb
With thee had teem'd, or had thy virgin-bloom
Alone remain'd a parent's hope to crown:
A truth, Megara, not to thee unknown!
Then think I view thee with no careless eye;
No, though in grief with Niobe I vie:
Grief for a son indulgence sure may gain,
To me endear'd by ten long months of pain;
And, ere I brought him to the realms of day,
My life by pangs was nearly snatch'd away.
Sent on new toils he to a distant shore
Now roams, and I may ne'er behold him more.
Besides, I lately saw, with wild affright,
A direful vision in the dead of night:
Some great impending ill, if right I deem,
Awaits my sons, from this mysterious dream.
In sleep, methought, my Hercules I spy'd,
His garments, like a labourer, thrown aside,
And, spade in hand, employ'd, with arduous toil,
To delve a ditch in some well-cultur'd soil.
But when his task the wish'd success had crown'd,
And his wide fence had girt the vineyard round,
He left his spade fix'd deeply in the plain,
And straight prepar'd to clothe his limbs again;
When, quick as thought, above the trench, behold
Destructive flames, which round the hero roll'd!
From these resistless foes alarm'd he flew,
With footsteps swift; as swiftly they pursue:

33. Then my sad parents, &c.] Megara was the daughter of Creon, king of Thebes, a city of Bœotia. It may not be improper to remark, that Moschus, contrary to the common opinion, supposes the parents of Megara to have been living when Hercules slew his children; whereas Euripides and Seneca assure us, that Lycus, a Theban exile, murdered Creon and his sons, to obtain the crown; and that Hercules did not kill his children, till he had punished Lycus.
Longepierre.

42. Tiryns] A city of Peloponnesus near Argos, where Hercules dwelt; and from thence was styled "the Tirynthian hero."

59. Thy son Iphiclus] Iphiclus was the son of Amphitryon and Alcmena, and the twin-brother of Hercules.

71. Sure each sad day sufficient sorrow bears] Thus St. Matthew, chap. 6. ver. 34. "Sufficient unto the day is the evil thereof."

86. Though in grief with Niobe I vie] For the story of Niobe, see Ovid's Metamorph. book 6. See also the notes on the twentieth ode of Anacreon.

88. Ten months] That is, ten lunar months. St. Augustine explains it thus: Quod dicunter decem menses pregnantis, novem sunt pleni; sed initium decimi pro toto accipitur.

90. My life by pangs, &c.] The birth of Hercules was attended with the most excruciating pains to Alcmena, owing to the jealousy and hatred of Juno; from which she was delivered by the address of Galanthis. See Ovid's Metamorph. book 9.

105. ——— behold
Destructive flames ——]
These were probably intended to be emblems of those flames in which this hero was afterwards consumed on Mount Oeta. See Ovid's Metamorph. book 9.

108. —— as swiftly they pursue]
This circumstance of the flames pursuing Hercules is very similar to a passage in the Iliad, book 21, where the rivers Simois and Scamander unite, pursue, and attack Achilles with all their waves:

Now here, now there, he turns on every side,
And winds his course before the following tide;
The waves flow after, wheresoe'er he wheels,
And gather fast, and murmur at his heels.
Pope.

While, like a shield, the spade now serves to guard
His half-scorch'd body, and the fire to ward.
At length Iphiclus, running to his aid,
(Such was my vision) by his feet betray'd,
Before he reach'd him, fell, with headlong force,
And there, unable to resume his course,
Lay stiff and prostrate; like a feeble sage,
Who, falling to the ground through helpless age,
There fix'd remains, till by some stranger rear'd,
Pitying his hoary hairs, and silver beard:
So on the plain was brave Iphiclus thrown.
To see my sons unaided and alone,
Fast flow'd my tears, till morn with roseate ray
Dispell'd my slumbers, and restor'd the day.
"Such were the visions of this night of dread!
Far from our house, on curs'd Eurystheus' head
These omens turn! be my presages true,
And him, O Fate, with vengeance just pursue!"

D.

IDYLLIUM V.

THE CHOICE.

When zephyrs gently curl the azure main,
On land, impatient, I can scarce sustain
At ease to dwell; a calm yields more delight:
But when old Ocean to a mountain's height
Rolls with tremendous roar, his foaming floods,
I loath the sea, and sigh for fields and woods.
Safe is the land; then piny forests please,
Though hoarse winds whistle through the bending trees:
Hapless the fisher's life! the sea his toil,
His house a bark, and faithless fish his spoil.
But O! to me how sweet are slumbers, laid
Beneath a lofty plane's embowering shade;
And thence the tinkling of a rill to hear,
Whose sound gives pleasure unallay'd by fear!

D.

IDYLLIUM VI.

CAPRICIOUS LOVE.

Pan sighs for Echo o'er the lawn;
Sweet Echo loves the dancing Faun;
The dancing Faun fair Lyda charms;
As Echo Pan's soft bosom warms,
So for the Faun sweet Echo burns;
Thus all, inconstant in their turns,
Both fondly woo, are fondly woo'd,
Pursue, and are themselves pursued.
As much as all slight those that woo,
So those that slight are slighted too:
Thus rages, by capricious Fate,
Alternate love, alternate hate.
Ye scornful nymphs and swains, I tell
This truth to you; pray, mark it well;
If to your lovers kind you prove,
You'll gain the hearts of those you love.

Idyll. V.—4. But when, &c.] Moschus perhaps in this passage had Homer in his view, Iliad, book 2.

As when the winds, ascending by degrees,
First move the whitening surface of the seas,
The billows float in order to the shore,
The wave behind rolls on the wave before;
Till, with the growing storm, the deeps arise,
Foam o'er the rocks, and thunder to the skies.

Pope.

8. —— whistle through the bending trees, &c.] In the original it is, ἁ ϖιτυς αδει, the pine-tree sings. Thus Theocritus, Idyll. 1. ver. 1. —ἁ ϖιτυς μελισδεται.

—— that pine-tree's boughs, by yonder spring,
In pleasing murmurs mix, and sweetly sing.

Creech.

Idyll. VI.—The following modern ballad is closely copied from this idyllium.

CROSS PURPOSES.

Tom loves Mary passing well,
But Mary she loves Harry;
While Harry sighs for bonny Bell,
And finds his love miscarry.
For bonny Bell for Thomas burns,
While Thomas slights her passion:
So very freakish are the turns
Of human inclination!

As much as Mary Thomas grieves,
Proud Hal despises Mary,
And all the flouts that Bell receives
From Tom, she vents on Harry.
Thus all by turns are woo'd and woo,
No turtles can be truer;
Each loves the object they pursue,
But hates the kind pursuer.

Mol gave Hal a wreath of flowers,
Which he, in amorous folly,
Consign'd to Bell, and in few hours
It came again to Molly.
If one of all the four has frown'd,
You ne'er saw people glummer;
But if one smiles, it catches round,
And all are in good humour.

Then, lovers, hence this lesson learn,
Throughout the British nation,
How much 'tis every one's concern
To smile a reformation:
And still through life this rule pursue,
Whatever objects strike you,
Be kind to them that fancy you,
That those you love may like you.

10. So those that slight are slighted too] Thus Theocritus, Idyllium 6.

—— φευγει τον φιλεοντα, και ȣ φιλεοντα διωκει.

She, driven still by an unlucky fate,
Flies those that love, and follows those that hate.

Creech.

And Horace, book 1. ode 33.

Insignem tenui fronte Lycorida
Cyri torret amor: Cyrus in asperam
Declinat Pholoen ————

For Cyrus, see! Lycoris, grac'd
With slender forehead, burns;
For Pholoe, he—— —— Duncombe.

15. If to your lovers, &c.] Thus Theocritus, Idyll. 23.

Lovers, farewell; revenge has reach'd my scorn;
Thus warn'd, be wise, and love for love return.

Dryden.

IDYLLIUM VII.

TO THE EVENING STAR.

HAIL, golden star! of ray serene,
Thou fav'rite of the Cyprian queen,
O Hesper! glory of the night,
Diffusing through the gloom delight;
Whose beams all other stars outshine,
As much as silver Cynthia thine;
O! guide me, speeding o'er the plain,
To him I love, my shepherd-swain;
He keeps the mirthful feast, and soon
Dark shades will cloud the splendid Moon.
Of lambs I never robb'd the fold,
Nor the lone traveller of gold:
Love is my crime: O lend thy ray
To guide a lover on her way!
May the bright star of Venus prove
The gentle harbinger of love!

IDYLLIUM VIII.

ALPHËUS.

FROM Pisa, where the sea his flood receives,
Alphëus, olive-crown'd, the gift of leaves,

Idyll. VII.—This idyllium has given occasion to the following ode to Cynthia, by a lady of Huntingdon; which must be allowed to have surpassed the original:

Sister of Phœbus, gentle queen,
Of aspect mild, and ray serene,
Whose friendly beams by night appear,
The lonely traveller to cheer!
Attractive power! whose mighty sway
The ocean's swelling waves obey,
And, mounting upward, seem to raise
A liquid altar to thy praise;
Thee wither'd hags, at midnight hour,
Invoke to their infernal bower:
But I to no such horrid rite,
Sweet queen, implore thy sacred light,
Nor seek, while all but lovers sleep,
To rob the miser's treasur'd heap;
Thy kindly beams alone impart,
To find the youth who stole my heart,
And guide me, from thy silver throne,
To steal his heart, or find my own!

3. Glory of the night] Thus Homer, Iliad, book 22, speaking of the same star:

Οιος δ' αςηρ, κ. τ. λ.

As radiant Hesper shines with keener light,
Far-beaming o'er the silver host of night.
Pope.

Idyll. VIII.—The story of Alphëus and Arethusa is related at large by Ovid, in his Metamorph. book 5. Virgil also mentions it in his Æneid, book 3.

Sicanio prætenta sinu jacet insula contra
Plemmyrium undosum; nomen dixere priores
Ortygiam. Alphëum fama est huc, Elidis amnem,
Occultas egisse vias subter mare; qui nunc
Ore, Arethusa, tuo Siculis confunditur undis.

An isle, once call'd Ortygia, fronts the sides
Of rough Plemmyrium, and Sicanian tides.

And flowers, and sacred dust is known to bring,
With secret course, to Arethusa's spring;
For, plunging deep beneath the briny tide,
Unmix'd, and unperceiv'd his waters glide.
Thus wonder-working Love, with mischief fraught,
The art of diving to the river taught. D.

IDYLLIUM IX.

EUNICA; OR, THE HERDSMAN.

WHEN lately I offer'd Eunica to kiss,
She fleer'd, and she flouted, and took it amiss;
"Begone, you great booby, she cry'd with a frown,
Do you think that I long for your kisses, you clown?
The sparks of the city my favours esteem—
You never shall kiss me, no, not in a dream.
How pleasing your look! and how gently you play!
How soft is your voice! and what fine things you say!
So neat is your beard, and so comely your hair!
And your lips, to be sure, are a delicate pair.
But on your dear person I never shall doat;
So pray keep your distance—you smell like a goat."
Thus spoke the proud hussey, and view'd me all round
With an eye of disdain, and thrice spit on the ground;
Then mimick'd my voice with satyrical sneer,
And sent me away with a flea in my ear.
My blood quickly boil'd, in a violent pique,
And, red as a rose, passion glow'd on my cheek;
For it vex'd me, that thus in derision she jeer'd
My looks, and my voice, and my hair, and my beard.
But, am I not handsome, ye shepherds, say true?
Or has any god alter'd my person anew?
For lately, on oaks like the ivy, with grace
My hair and my beard added charms to my face;
My brows were coal-black, and my forehead milk-white,
And my eyes, like Minerva's, were azure and bright;
My lips sweet as cream, and from them would flow
Words sweeter than honey, and softer than snow.
My songs are enchanting; nor aught can exceed
The tunes of my pipe, or the notes of my reed.
The girls of the country, if they had their wills,
Would kiss me, and press me to stay on the hills;

Hither, 'tis said, Alphëus, from his source
In Elis' realms, directs his watry course;
Beneath the main he takes his secret way,
And mounts with Arethusa's streams to day.
Pitt.

3. —— sacred dust] Moschus calls the dust sacred, because the Olympic games, which constituted no small part of the religion of the ancients, were celebrated at Elis, from whence Alphëus flowed.

Idyll. IX.—This idyllium, though commonly inserted in the works of Theocritus, has, by Daniel Heinsius and other critics, been adjudged to Moschus; and therefore is here translated. There is another idyllium, of which Moschus is supposed to have been the author, containing a dialogue between Daphnis and a shepherdess; but that is thought too loose to be here inserted. The curious reader may see it translated by Dryden.

For they say that I'm fair: but this minx of the town
Refus'd my sweet kisses, and call'd me a clown.
Alas! she forgot, or, perhaps, did not know,
That Bacchus fed herds in the valley below;
That beauty's fair queen fell in love with a swain,
And help'd him his cattle to tend on the plain;
Adonis, while living, in groves she ador'd,
And, when dead, she on groves and on mountains deplor'd.
If right my conjecture, Endymion, I ween,
Like me too once tended his steers on the green;
Yet the Moon in this herdsman took such a delight,
That she met him at Latmos, and kiss'd him all night.
Ev'n Cybele mourn'd for a herdsman; and Jove
Snatch'd a boy from his flock to be waiter above.
But Eunica disdains me, nor lists to my vow;
Is she better than Cynthia or Venus, I trow?
May she never find lovers in city or plain,
But lie always alone, yet still wishing in vain!

CUPID TURN'D PLOUGHMAN.

AN EPIGRAM.

Disguis'd like a ploughman, Love stole from the sky,
His torch, and his bow, and his quiver thrown by;
And, with pouch at his shoulder, and goad in his hand,
Began with yok'd oxen to furrow the land:
And, "O Jove, be propitious," he cry'd, "or I vow,
That I'll yoke thee, Europa's fam'd bull, to my plough." D.

This justly admired epigram makes us regret that Moschus has left us no more. Tibullus, as Broekhusius observes, probably alludes to this epigram in the beginning of his elegy 3, book 2. particularly in this verse.

Verbaque aratoris rustica discit amor.

Now Cupid joys to learn the ploughman's phrase,
And, clad a peasant, o'er the fallows strays.

Grainger.

THE

LOVES

OF

HERO AND LEANDER.

FROM THE GREEK OF MUSÆUS.

TRANSLATED BY FAWKES.

Oft, by the covert of night's shade,
Leander woo'd the Thracian maid;
Through foaming seas his passion bore,
Nor fear'd the ocean's thundering roar.
The conscious virgin, from the sea-girt tower,
Hung out the faithful torch, to guide him to her bower.

DODSLEY'S MISCELL. vol. 4. p8.

ADVERTISEMENT.

THIS celebrated poem on the loves of Hero and Leander has been admired by the politest scholars for many ages: and though Mr. Waller and several other writers of the finest taste have conjectured it to be one of the stories,

Which old Musæus so divinely sung:

yet many convincing arguments might be brought to prove it to have been the work of a later author, a grammarian of that name who lived in the fifth century.

Nor let the English reader look upon the title of grammarian as a term of reproach, though now frequently used as such. The profession, styled by the ancients Γραμματικη, was the same with the belles lettres among the moderns: and the appellation of grammarian was particularly applied to those who excelled in every kind of polite writing.

The first English translation of the following poem appeared in the year 1647, by sir Robert Stapylton. It has since that time been frequently attempted; but with what success is left to the judgment of others.

THE

LOVES

OF

HERO AND LEANDER.

TRANSLATED BY FAWKES.

SING, Muse! the conscious torch, whose nightly ray
Led the bold lover through the wat'ry way,
To share those joys which mutual faith hath seal'd,
Joys to divine Aurora unreveal'd.
Abydos, Sestos, ancient towns, proclaim
Where gentlest bosoms glow'd with purest flame.
I hear Leander dash the foaming tide!
Fix'd high in air, I see the glimmering guide!
The genial flame, the love-enkindling light,
Signal of joy that burn'd serenely bright;
Whose beams, in fair effulgency display'd,
Adorn'd the nuptials of the Sestian maid:
Which Jove, its friendly office to repay,
Should plant, all glorious, in the realms of day,
To blaze for ever 'midst the stars above,
And style it gentle harbinger of love:
For sure on Earth it shone supremely kind,
To sooth the anguish of the love-sick mind,
Till cloth'd in terrours rose the wintry blast,
Impetuous howling o'er the watry waste:
And, O! inspire me, goddess, to resound
The torch extinguish'd, and the lover drown'd.
  Against Abydos sea-beat Sestos stood,
Two neighb'ring towns, divided by the flood:
Here Cupid prov'd his bow's unerring art,
And gain'd two conquests with a single dart:
On two fond hearts the sweet infection prey'd,
A youth engaging, and a beauteous maid:
Of Sestos she, fair Hero was her name;
The youth, Leander, from Abydos came.
Their forms divine a bright resemblance bore,
Each was the radiant star of either shore.
  Thou, whom the Fates commission here to stray,
Awhile the turret's eminence survey;
Thence Hero held the blazing torch, to guide
Her lover rolling on the boisterous tide;
The roaring Hellespont, whose wave-worn strait
Still in loud murmurs mourns Leander's fate.
Say, heav'nly Muse, had Hero charms to move,
And melt the Abydinian into love?
Say, with what wiles the amorous youth inspir'd,
Obtain'd the virgin whom his soul admir'd?
  Fair Hero, priestess to th' Idalian queen,
Of birth illustrious, as of graceful mien,
Dwelt on a high sequester'd tower, that stood
Firm on the ramparts, and o'erlook'd the flood:
Chaste, and unconscious of love's pleasing pain,
She seem'd a new-born Venus of the main;
But, nice of conduct, prudently withdrew
Far from the follies of the female crew:
Blest in retreat, she shunn'd the vain delight
Of daily visits, and the dance at night,
Content in sweet tranquillity to screen
Her blooming beauty from malignant spleen;
For where superior beauty shines confest,
It kindles envy in each female breast.
To soften Venus oft with prayer she strove,
Oft pour'd libations to the god of love;
Taught by th' example of the heavenly dame,
To dread those arrows that were tipp'd with flame.
Vain all her caution, fruitless prov'd her prayer;
Love gains an easy conquest o'er the fair.

23. Against Abydos sea-beat Sestos stood] Abydos was a city of Asia, situated on the Hellespont, over-against Sestos, a city in the Thracian Chersonnesus. Geographers are of opinion, that the castles of the Dardanelles were built on the ruins of these two places: but they are manifestly mistaken; for there are no remains of antiquity to be seen near those castles, but very remarkable ones three miles farther, where the channel is considerably narrower. Le Brun assures us, that the strait at these ruins is only half a mile over, and that one of them is still called Sestos, and the other Abydos or Avido. Pliny and Herodotus say, the narrowest part of the channel is about seven stadia, or furlongs.

60. To dread, &c.] In the first idyllium of Moschus, Venus complains of Cupid, that

His darts and his arrows are all tipp'd with flame.

For now the sacred festival appear'd,
By pious Sestians annually rever'd,
At Venus' fane to pay the rites divine,
And offer incense at Adonis' shrine.
Vast crowds from all the sea-girt isles repair,
The day to rev'rence, and the feast to share.
From flowery Cyprus, circled by the main,
And high Hæmonia, hastes the youthful train;
Not one remain'd of all the female race
Thy towns, Cythera, and thy groves to grace;
Afar from spicy Libanus advance
The throngs unnumber'd, skill'd to lead the dance;
From Phrygian plains they haste in shoals away,
And all Abydos celebrates the day.
To Sestos all the mirthful youths repair,
All that admire the gay, the young, the fair;
For amorous swains, when rumour'd feasts invite,
Joy at the news, and follow with delight,
Not to the gods to pay the rites divine,
Or offer incense at some sacred shrine;
Few are their offerings, and concise their prayer,
Who give their whole devotion to the fair.
As through the temple pass'd the Sestian maid,
Her face a soften'd dignity display'd;
Thus silver Cynthia's milder glories rise,
To glad the pale dominion of the skies.
Her lovely cheeks a pure vermilion shed,
Like roses beautifully streak'd with red;
A flowery mead her well-turn'd limbs disclose,
Fraught with the blushing beauties of the rose:
But when she mov'd, in radiant mantle drest,
Flowers half unveil'd adorn'd her flowing vest,
And numerous graces wanton'd on her breast.
The ancient sages made a false decree,
Who said, the Graces were no more than three;
When Hero smiles, a thousand graces rise,
Sport on her cheek, and revel in her eyes.
Such various beauties sure conspir'd to prove
The priestess worthy of the queen of love.
Thus as she shone superior to the rest,
In the sweet bloom of youth and beauty drest,
Such softness temper'd with majestic mien,
The earthly priestess match'd the heav'nly queen.
The wondering crowds the radiant nymph admire,
And every bosom kindles with desire;
Eager each longs, transported with her charms,
To clasp the lovely virgin in his arms;
Where'er she turns, their eyes, their thoughts pursue,
They sigh, and send their souls at every view.
Then thus some ardent youth bespoke the rest,
Cast a fond look, and open'd all his breast:
"I oft at Sparta wond'ring have beheld
Young maids contending in the listed field,
Sparta, that boasts the emulated prize
Of fairest virgins, and of brightest eyes;
Yet ne'er till now beheld a nymph so fair,
Such beauty blended with such graceful air:
Perhaps (for sure immortal is her race)
Beneath the priestess Venus hides a Grace.
My dazzled eyes with constant gazing tire,
But my fond fancy ever could admire.
O! make me, Venus, partner of her bed,
Though Fate that instant strike the lover dead:
Let but my love the heavenly Hero crown,
I on the gods will look superior down.
Should you this boon deny, O queen! decree,
To bless my days, a nymph as fair as she!"

Thus spoke the general voice; the train apart
Conceal the wound deep rankling in the heart.
But when Leander saw the blooming fair,
Love seiz'd his soul instead of dumb despair;
Resolv'd the lucky moments to improve,
He sought occasion to reveal his love;
The glorious prize determin'd to obtain,
Or perish for those joys he could not gain.
Her sparkling eyes instilling fond desire
Entranc'd his soul, and kindled amorous fire.
Such radiant beauty, like the pointed dart,
With piercing anguish stings th' unguarded heart:
For on the eye the wound is first imprest,
'Till by degrees it rankles in the breast.
Now hope and confidence invade his soul;
Then fear and shame alternately control:
Fear through his bosom thrill'd; a conscious shame
Confess'd the passion which it seem'd to blame:
Her beauties fix'd him in a wild amaze;
Love made him bold, and not afraid to gaze.
With step ambiguous, and affected air,
The youth advancing fac'd the charming fair:
Each amorous glance he cast, tho' form'd by art,
Yet sometimes spoke the language of his heart;
With nods and becks he kept the nymph in play,
And tried all wiles to steal her soul away.
Soon as she saw the fraudful youth beguil'd,
Fair Hero, conscious of her beauty, smil'd;
Oft in her veil conceal'd her glowing face,
Sweetly vermilion'd with the rosy grace;
Yet all in vain to hide her passion tries,
She owns it with her love-consenting eyes.
Joy touch'd the bosom of the gentle swain,
To find his love was not indulg'd in vain.
Then, while he chid the tedious lingering day,
Down to the west declin'd the solar ray;
And dewy Hesper shone serenely bright,
In shadowy silence leading on the night.
Soon as he saw the dark involving shade,
Th' embolden'd youth approach'd the blooming maid;
Her lily hand he seiz'd, and gently prest,
And softly sigh'd the passion of his breast:
Joy touch'd the damsel, tho' she seem'd displeas'd,
And soon withdrew the lily hand he seiz'd.
The youth perceiv'd, through well-dissembled wiles,
A heart just yielding by consenting smiles;
Then to the temple's last recess convey'd
The unreluctant, unresisting maid:
Her lovely feet, that seem'd to lag behind,
But ill conceal'd her voluntary mind.
She feign'd resentment with an angry look,
And, sweetly chiding, thus indignant spoke:
"Stranger, what madness has possess'd thy brain,
To drag me thus along the sacred fane?

144. Now hope and confidence, &c.] Virgil finely describes the conflict of various passions in the breast of Turnus, Æneid, book 12, ver. 666.

——— æstuat ingens
Imo in corde pudor, mixtoque insania luctu,
Et furiis agitatus amor, et conscia virtus.

A thousand various thoughts confound the chief,
He stood, he gaz'd, his bosom swell'd with grief;
Pride, conscious valour, fury, love, and shame,
At once set all the hero in a flame. Pitt.

Go—to your native habitation, go——
'Tis quite unkind to pull my garments so.
Rich are my parents—urge not here your fate,
Lest their just vengeance you repent too late:
If not of me, of Venus stand afraid,
In her own fane soliciting a maid:
Hence speed your flight; and Venus' anger dread;
'Tis bold aspiring to a virgin's bed."
Thus chid the maid, as maids are wont to do,
And show'd her anger, and her fondness too:
The wily youth, as thus the fair complain'd,
Too well perceiv'd the victory was gain'd:
For nymphs enrag'd the more complying prove,
And chidings are the harbingers of love.
He kiss'd her snowy neck, her fragrant breast:
And thus the transport of his soul exprest:
"O lovely fair, in whom combin'd are seen
The charms of Venus, and Minerva's mien!
For sure no virgin of terrestrial race
Can vie with Hero in the bloom of face:
I deem your lineage from the gods above,
And style you daughter of Saturnian Jove.
Blest is the father from whose loins you sprung,
Blest is the mother at whose breast you hung,
Blest, doubly blest, the fruitful womb that bore
This heavenly form for mortals to adore.
"Yet, beauteous Hero, grant a lover's prayer,
And to my wishes prove as kind as fair:
As Venus' priestess, just to Venus prove,
Nor shun the gentle offices of love.
O let us, while the happy hour invites,
Propitious, celebrate the nuptial rites.
No maid can serve in Cytherea's fane;
Her eyes delight not in the virgin-train.
But would fair Hero secret rites explore,
The laws of Venus, and her pleasing lore,
Those rites are practis'd in the bridal bed,
And there must Hero, yet a maid, be led:
Then, as you fear the goddess to offend,
In me behold your husband and your friend,
Ordain'd by Cupid, greatest god above,
To teach you all the mysteries of love:
As winged Mercury, with golden wand,
Made Hercules, with distaff in his hand,
To every task of Omphale submit;
Thus Love, more powerful than the god of wit,
Sent me to you. 'Tis needless to relate
The chaste Arcadian Atalanta's fate;
Who from th' embraces of Milanion fled,
Her faithful lover, and the nuptial bed:
But vengeful Venus caus'd the nymph to burn
With equal flame, and languish in her turn.
O let example warn you to revere
The wrathful goddess, and your lover hear!"
Thus spoke the youth——his magic words control
Her wavering breast, and soften all her soul.
Silent she stood, and, rapt in thought profound,
Her modest eyes were fix'd upon the ground:
Her cheeks she hid, in rosy blushes drest,
And veil'd her lily shoulders with her vest:
On the rich floor, with Parian marble laid,
Her nimble foot involuntary play'd.
By secret signs a yielding mind is meant;
And silence speaks the willing maid's consent.
Now had the wily god's envenom'd dart
Diffus'd the pleasing poison to her heart;
Leander's form, instilling soft desire,
Woo'd her pleas'd eyes, and set her soul on fire.
While on the ground fair Hero fix'd her sight,
Leander view'd, with exquisite delight,
Her swelling breast, and neck as ivory white.
At length her face with lovely blushes spread
She rais'd, and thus in sweet confusion said:
"Stranger, thy words such magic sounds convey,
With soft compassion rocks would melt away.
Who form'd thy tongue with such persuasive art,
To pour delightful ruin on the heart?
Ah! tell me, who thus taught thee to explore
My lone retirement on the Thracian shore?
Thy speech, tho' pleasing, flow'd to me in vain:
How can a stranger Hero's love obtain?
Should I in public give to thee my hand,
My parents would forbid the nuptial band.
And should'st thou here in close concealment stay,
Our secret passion would itself betray;
For soon the voice of scandal-spreading Fame
The deed of silence would aloud proclaim.
But, gentle youth, thy name, thy country tell;
For mine, alas! by thee are known too well.
In yon high tower, which close to Sestos stands,
And all the roaring Hellespont commands,
With one attending damsel I remain;
For so my parents and the Fates ordain!
No nymphs coeval to sweet Music's sound
Lead the smooth dance, or lightly beat the ground;
But stormy winds eternal discord keep,
And blustering bellow through the boundless deep."
Thus spoke the priestess, and, with modest grace,
Conceal'd the new-born beauties of her face;
For on her cheeks the roseate blush that hung
Seem'd to condemn the language of her tongue.
Meanwhile Leander feeds the hidden fire,
Glows in each vein, and burns with fierce desire:
But anxious doubt his musing breast alarms;
How shall he gain admittance to her charms?
Nor long he paus'd, for Love in wiles abounds,
Well-pleas'd to heal the bosoms which he wounds:
'Twas he, whose arrows men and gods control,
That heal'd Leander's love-afflicted soul;
Who thus, while sighs upheav'd his anxious breast,
The nymph with artful eloquence addrest:
"For thee, dear object of my fond desire,
I'll cross the ocean, though it flame with fire:
Nor would I fear the billows' loud alarms,
While every billow bore me to thy arms;
Uncheck'd, undaunted by the boisterous main,
Tempestuous winds should round me roar in vain:
But oft as night her sable pinions spread,
I through the storm would swim to Hero's bed:
For rich Abydos is the home I boast,
Not far divided from the Thracian coast.
Let but my fair a kindly torch display,
From the high turret, to direct my way;
Then shall thy daring swain securely glide,
The bark of Cupid, o'er the yielding tide,
Thyself my haven, and thy torch my guide:
And, while I view the genial blaze afar,
I'll swim regardless of Boötes' car,
Of fell Orion, and the Northern Wain,
That never bathes his brightness in the main:
Thy star, more eminently bright than they,
Shall lead the lover to his blissful bay.
But let the torch, O nymph divinely fair!
My only safety, be thy only care;

Guard well its light, when wintry tempests roar,
And hoarse waves break tumultuous on the shore,
Lest the dire storms, that blacken all the sky,
The flame extinguish, and the lover die.
More would'st thou know? Leander is my name,
The happiest husband of the fairest dame."
Thus mutual vow'd the lovers to employ
The nights in raptures of mysterious joy;
Her task, secure th' extended torch to keep,
And his, to cross th' unfathomable deep:
On promis'd bliss their fruitful fancies fed,
Ecstatic pleasures of the nuptial bed;
Till the fond nymph, when decency requir'd,
Back to her tower unwillingly retir'd:
Leander, ere he left his lovely bride,
Mark'd well the station of the blazing guide,
Then sought Abydos cross the sounding tide.
What now but amorous scenes their thoughts employ,
Confus'd ideas of the genial joy?
Slow rose on leaden wings the morning light,
Slow noon came on—the lovers wish'd it night.
At length dark gloom a dusky mantle spread;
Sleep o'er the world his balmy influence shed.
All but Leander lay dissolv'd in rest,
Love kept a ceaseless vigil in his breast.
Silent he wander'd on the winding shore,
The deep resounded with tremendous roar:
Wide o'er the foaming waves his anxious sight
Explor'd the torch's love-proclaiming light:
He little deem'd, alas! its flame would prove
The blaze of death, tho' meant the torch of love.
Soon as fair Hero from her tower survey'd
Th' horizon darken'd in the sable shade,
The torch on high she fix'd; its flames inspire
Leander's bosom with the kindred fire:
Quick thro' his frame the bright contagion ran,
And with the glowing signal glow'd th' enamour'd man.
But when he heard the hoarse-resounding roar
Of thundering billows breaking on the shore,
Aghast he stood, he shrunk, and thus addrest
These words of courage to his trembling breast:
"Ah cruel love! whose woe the waves conspire!
The waves are water, but I burn with fire:
Be bold my heart, the foaming billows brave,
Nor fear the threatnings of the wintry wave.
Fair Venus rose propitious from the main;
She calms the ocean's rage, and sooths the lover's pain."
He spoke, and straight his lovely limbs undrest,
And folded round his head the various vest;
Then dauntless plunging in the foaming tide,
Dash'd with his arms th' intruding waves aside:
Full in his view he kept the shining mark,
Himself the pilot, passenger, and bark.
While faithful Hero, to her promise true,
Watch'd on the turret every wind that blew;
Oft with her robe she screen'd the torch's blaze
From dangerous blasts that blew a thousand ways:
Till the tir'd youth, on rolling surges tost,
Securely landed on the Sestian coast.
Soon as she saw her lover safe on shore,
Eager she ran, and led him to her tower,
Welcom'd with open arms her panting guest,
And, sweetly smiling, to her bosom prest:
Then dumb with joy the shivering youth she led,
Still wet and weary, to the genial bed;
Wip'd his fair limbs, and fragrant oils apply'd,
To cleanse his body from the oozy tide;
Then clasp'd him close, still panting, to her breast,
And thus with fond, endearing words addrest:
"My life, my lover, thou hast suffer'd more
Than fondest bridegroom e'er endur'd before;
Destin'd, alas! dread troubles to sustain,
On the rough bosom of the briny main:
Now let sweet joy succeed in sorrow's place,
And lull thy labours in my warm embrace."
She spoke: he loos'd her virgin zone, to prove
The secret rites, and mysteries of love.
No youths with measur'd dance the nuptials crown'd,
Nor tuneful hymn's congratulating sound:
No bard invok'd the heavenly queen with prayer,
To smile propitious on the wedded pair:
No nuptial torch its golden lustre shed,
Bright torch of Love, to grace the bridal bed!
No Iö Pæans musically rung;
No greeting parents hymeneals sung:
But all was gloom, and silence all around,
Instead of music's love-inspiring sound.
Beneath the covert of the night conceal'd,
They tasted pleasures mutual faith had seal'd:
In close embraces all entranc'd they lay,
In raptures never usher'd to the day:
Till the fond youth reluctant left his bride,
Still breathing love, and cross'd the foaming tide.
Thus Hero liv'd unnoted, unbetray'd,
Each night a woman, and each day a maid.
Both wish'd the hours on swiftest wings would fly,
And hail'd the evening, not the morning sky.
Thus rapt in hidden joys, each blissful night
They pass'd in ecstacies of full delight:
But soon, alas! those dear-bought pleasures fled,
And short the transports of that bridal bed!
For now relentless Winter, that deforms
With frost the forest, and the sea with storms,
Bade the wild winds o'er all the ocean reign,
And raise the rapid whirlpools of the main;
The hoarse wild winds obey, and, with harsh sound,
Roar o'er the surface of the vast profound,
Rouse from their beds the scatter'd storms that sleep
In the dark caverns of the dreary deep:
The trembling sailor hears the dreadful roar,
Nor dares the wintry turbulence explore,
But drags his vessel to the safer shore.
But thee, bold youth, no wintry storms restrain,
Nor all the deathful dangers of the main:
For when thou saw'st the torch's blaze from far,
(Of nuptial bliss the bright prophetic star)
Thee not the furious tempest could control,
Nor calm the glowing raptures of thy soul.

383. Wip'd his fair limbs, and fragrant oils apply'd.] Thus in the third book of the Odyssey, Polycaste, the daughter of Nestor, bathes and anoints Telemachus:

Sweet Polycaste took the pleasing toil
To bathe the prince, and pour the fragrant oil.

On which Dr. Broome remarks, that the practice of women bathing and anointing men frequently occurs in the Odyssey: neither is this done by women of inferior quality, but we have here a young princess bathing, anointing, and clothing the naked Telemachus.

Yet sure fair Hero, when the gloomy sky
With gathering clouds proclaim'd rough winter nigh,
Without her lover should have pass'd the night,
Nor from the tower, ill-omen'd, shown the light.
But she, ah hapless! burns with fond desire,
'Tis Love inflames her, while the Fates conspire:
The torch of death now glimmer'd from above,
No more the gentle harbinger of love.
'Twas night, and angry Æolus had hurl'd
The winds tempestuous o'er the watery world;
The bellowing winds with rage impetuous roar,
And dash the foaming billows on the shore:
Ev'n then the youth, with pleasing visions fed,
Glows with remembrance of the bridal bed;
And, while fierce tempests howl on every side,
Floats on the bosom of the briny tide.
Waves, roll'd on waves, in hideous heaps are driv'n,
Swell'd into mountains, and upheav'd to Heaven:
Bleak blasts, loud roaring, the vex'd ocean sweep,
Foam the dash'd billows, and resounds the deep.
From every part the blustering terrours fly,
Rage o'er the main, and battle in the sky:
The growling thunder of the vast profound
The rocks rebellow, and the shores rebound.
Amidst the watry war, with toils oppress'd,
O'erwhelm'd with billows, and in gulphs distress'd,
Leander oft with suppliant prayer implor'd
The sea-sprung goddess, and old ocean's lord:
Thee, Boreas, too, he summon'd to his aid,
Nor was unmindful of th' Athenian maid:
But prayers are fruitless, and petitions vain;
Love must submit to what the Fates ordain.
From wave to wave the hapless youth is tost,
Now heav'd on high, and now in whirlpools lost.
His weary'd feet no more his will obey,
His arms hang useless, and forget to play.
Borne on the surge supine, and void of breath,
He drinks the briny wave, and draws in death.
Thus while in fatal rage each wind conspires,
Extinct at once the flame, and lover's fires,
Fainting he sinks, and with the torch expires.
While on the turret Hero mourn'd his stay,
And fondly sighing, chid his long delay,
Perplexing anguish in her bosom rose,
Nor knew her eyes the blessings of repose.
Now rose the Morn, in russet vest array'd,
Still from th' impatient fair the lover stay'd:
Watchful she stood, and cast her eyes around
O'er the wide beach, and o'er the depths profound,
Haply to spy her lover, should he stray,
The light extinguish'd, 'midst the watry way:
But when she saw him breathless on the sand,
Stretch'd, ghastly-pale, by Death's relentless hand,
She shriek'd aloud; and from her throbbing breast
Rent the gay honours of her flowery vest;
Then from the tower her beauteous body cast,
And on her lover's bosom breath'd her last:
Nor could the Fates this faithful pair divide;
They liv'd united, and united died.

494. They liv'd united, and united died] "They were lovely and pleasant in their lives, and in their death they were not divided."
II Sam. chap. 1. ver. 23.

OVID'S METAMORPHOSES,

IN FIFTEEN BOOKS.

TRANSLATED BY

DRYDEN, ADDISON, GARTH, MAINWARING, CONGREVE, ROWE, POPE, GAY, EUSDEN, CROXALL, AND OTHER EMINENT HANDS.

PUBLISHED BY SIR SAMUEL GARTH, M. D.

TO HER

ROYAL HIGHNESS.

MADAM,

SINCE I am allowed the honour and privilege of so easy access to your royal highness, I dare say, I shall not be the worse received for bringing Ovid along with me. He comes from banishment to the fautress of liberty; from the barbarous to the polite; and has this to recommend him, which never fails with a clemency like yours; he is unfortunate.

Your royal highness, who feels for every one, has lately been the mournful occasion of a like sensibility in many others. Scarce an eye, that did not tell the danger you were in; even parties, though different in principles, united at that time in their grief and affectionate concern for an event of so much consequence to the interest of humanity and virtue; whilst yourself was the only person, then, unmoved.

It was remarkable, that she, who, with a manner most engaging, taught the innocent pleasures to appear more desirable than the criminal; who was every day the life of some new agreeable diversion; should behave herself, upon that cruel trial, with a magnanimity so unshaken, that those who were witnesses might have imagined she scarce ever had done any thing, but study how to die.

It is the greatest happiness can attend an age under a long depravation of morals, to be blest with examples, where virtue is set off by the advantage of birth. Such qualifications, when united, do not only persuade an imitation, but command it. Human nature is always more affected by what it sees, than what it hears of: and as those ideas, which enter by the eye, find the surest passage to the heart; so the more the object, whatever it be, seems desirable to the one, the longer it continues in the other.

There are perfections so shining, that one must be the very worst of mortals, or the very best, not to admire in all those, who possess them. To be blest with a disposition to charity, not confined by any other limits, than the modesty of those who ask it; to know, and be ready to excuse faults; yet, so strict in life, as not to want the like indulgence; to have a superiority of genius capable of judging of the highest affairs, and an application so observant, as to penetrate into the most minute; to be easy to lay down grandeur upon familiar occasions, and discerning to take it up, when dignity of station requires; to know the politer languages of the present age, as a native, and the greater occurrences, and periods of the past, as an historian, make up a character, which is so obvious, that every one will know where to apply it, except the person whose it really is: and if in this your royal highness be at a loss, I think it is the only thing within the province of your sex you are ignorant of.

I shall take up no more of your time in this dedication; because, to do every thing, that may be most acceptable to you, shall always be the endeavour of,

madam,

your royal highness's most humble

and most obedient servant,

S. GARTH.

PREFACE.

THE method I propose in writing this preface, is to take notice of some of the beauties of the Metamorphoses, and also of the faults, and particular affectations. After which I shall proceed to hint at some rules for translation in general; and shall give a short account of the following version.

I shall not pretend to impose my opinion on others with the magisterial authority of a critic; but only take the liberty of discovering my own taste. I shall endeavour to show our poet's redundance of wit, justness of comparisons, elegance of descriptions, and peculiar delicacy in touching every circumstance relating to the passions and affections; and, with the same impartiality and frankness, I shall confess the too frequent puerilities of his luxuriant fancy, and the too great negligence of his sometimes unlaboured versification.

I am not of an opinion, too common to translators, to think that one is under an obligation to extol every thing he finds in the author he undertakes: I am sure one is no more obliged to do so, than a painter is to make every face, that sits to him, handsome. It is enough if he sets the best features he finds in their full and most advantageous light. But if the poet has private deformities, though good-breeding will not allow to expose him naked, yet surely there can be no reason to recommend him, as the most finished model of harmony and proportion.

Whoever has this undistinguishing complaisance, will not fail to vitiate the taste of the readers, and misguide many of them in their judgment, where to approve, and where to censure.

It must be granted, that where there appears an infinite variety of inimitable excellencies, it would be too harsh and disingenuous to be severe on such faults as have escaped rather through want leisure and opportunity to correct, than through the erroneous turn of a depraved judgment. How sensible Ovid himself was of the uncorrectness of the Metamorphoses, appears from these lines prefixed before some of the editions by the care of his commentators.

> Orba parente suo quicunque volumina tangis,
>   His saltem vestrâ detur in urbe locus.
> Quóque magis faveas; non sunt hæc edita ab illo,
>   Sed quasi de domini funere rapta sui.
> Quicquid in his igitur vitii rude carmen habebit
>   Emendaturus, si licuisset, erat. Trist. El. vi.

Since therefore the readers are not solemnly invited to an entertainment, but come accidentally; they ought to be contented with what they find: and pray what have they to complain of? but too great variety: where, though some of the dishes be not served in the exactest order and politeness, but hashed up in haste; there are a great many accommodated to every particular palate.

To like every thing, shows too little delicacy; and to like nothing, too much difficulty. So great is the variety of this poem, that the reader, who is never pleased, will appear as monstrous as he that is always so. Here are the hurries of battles for the hero; tender emotions of soul for the lover; a search and penetration into nature for the philosopher; fluency of numbers, and most expressive figures for the poet; morals for the serious, and pleasantries for admirers of points of wit.

It is certain a poet is more to be suspected for saying too much than too little. To add is often hazardous; but to retrench, commonly judicious. If our author, instead of saying all he could, had only said all he should; Daphne had done well to fly from the god of wit, in order to crown his poet: thus Ovid had been more honoured and adored in his exile, than Augustus in his triumphs.

I shall now attempt to give some instances of the happiness and vast extent of our author's imagination. I shall not proceed according to the order of the poem, but rather transcribe some lines here and there, as my reflection shall suggest.

Nec circumfuso pendebat in aere tellus
Ponderibus librata suis——

Thus was the state of nature before the creation: and here it is obvious, that Ovid had a discerning notion of the gravitation of bodies. It is now demonstrated, that every part of matter tends to every part of matter with a force, which is always in a direct simple proportion of the quantity of the matter, and an inverse duplicate proportion of the distance; which tendency or gravitating is constant and universal. This power, whatever it be, acting always proportionably to the solid content of bodies, and never in any proportion to their superficies, cannot be explained by any material impulse. For the laws of impulse are physically necessary: there can be no *αὐτεξούσιον*, or arbitrary principle, in mere matter; its parts cannot move, unless they be moved; and cannot do otherwise when pressed on by other parts in motion; and therefore it is evident from the following lines, that Ovid strictly adhered to the opinion of the most discerning philosophers, who taught that all things were formed by a wise and intelligent mind.

Jussit et extendi campos, subsidere valles,
Fronde tegi sylvas——

The fiat of the Hebrew lawgiver is not more sublime than the jussit of the Latin poet, who goes on in the same elevated and philosophical style.

His super imposuit liquidum et gravitate carentem
Æthera——

Here the author spreads a thin veil of ether over his infant creation; and though his asserting the upper region to be void of gravitation may not, in a mathematical rigour, be true; yet it is found from the natural inquiries made since, and especially from the learned Dr. Halley's Discourse on the Barometer, that if, on the surface of the Earth, an inch of quicksilver in the tube be equal to a cylinder of air of 300 foot, it will be at a mile's height equal to a cylinder of air of 27000000: and therefore the air at so great a distance from the Earth must be rarefied to so great a degree, that the space it fills must bear a very small proportion to that which is intirely void of matter.

I think, we may be confident from what already appears, as well as from what our author has writ on the Roman feasts, that he could not be totally ignorant of astronomy. Some of the critics would insinuate from the following lines, that he mistook the annual motion of the Sun for the diurnal.

Sectus in obliquum—— Met. B. 2.

Though the Sun be always in one or other of the signs of the zodiac, and never goes by either motion more northward, or southward, than is here described; yet Phaëton being designed to drive the chariot but one day, ought to have been directed in the equator, or a circle parallel to it and not round the other oblique one of the ecliptic: a degree of which, and that by a motion contrary to the diurnal, he was obliged to go in that length of time.

I am inclined to think, that Ovid had so great an attention to poetical embellishments, that he voluntarily declined a strict observance of any astronomical system. For though that science was far from being neglected in former ages; yet the progress which was made in it, by no means equalled that of our present time.

Lucretius, though in other things most penetrating, describes the Sun scarce bigger than he appears to the eye.

Nec nimio solis major rota, nec minor ardor
Esse potest, nostris quam sensibus esse videtur.

And Homer, imagining the seats of the gods above the fixed stars, represents the falling of Vulcan from thence to the Isle of Lemnos, to continue during a whole day.

Πᾶν δ᾽ ἦμαρ φερόμην, ἅμα δ᾽ ἠελίῳ καταδύντι
Κάππεσον ἐν Λήμνῳ—— Il. lib. 1.

The Greek poet aims here to give a surprising idea of the height of the celestial mansions: but if the computation of a modern astronomer be true, they are at so much a greater distance, that Vulcan would have been more years in falling, than he was minutes.

But lest I should exceed the usual length of a preface, I shall now give some instances of the propriety of our author's similes and epithets; the perspicuity of his allegories; the instructive excellence of the morals; the peculiar happy turn of his fancy; and shall begin with the elegance of his descriptions.

——— Madidis notus evolat alis,
Terribilem piceâ tectus caligine vultum.
Barba gravis nimbis, canis fluit unda capillis,
Fronte sedent nebulæ, rorant pennæque, sinusque.
. . . .
Sternuntur segetes, et deplorata coloni
Vota jacent, longique labor perit irritus anni. Met. b. 1.

These lines introduce those of the deluge, which are also very poetical, and worthy to be compared with the next, concerning the golden age.

———Sine militis usu
Mollia securæ peragebant otia gentes.
Ipsa quoque immunis rastroque intacta, nec ullis
Saucia vomeribus, per se dabat omnia tellus.
Contentique cibis, nullo cogente, creatis,
Arbuteos fœtus, montanaque fraga legebant,
Et quæ deciderant patulâ Jovis arbore glandes.
Ver erat æternum, placidique tepentibus auris
Mulcebant Zephyri natos sine semine flores.

Virgil has also touched upon the same subject in the end of the second Georgic.

Aureus hanc vitam in terris Saturnus agebat,
Nec dum etiam audierant inflari classica, nec dum
Impositos duris crepitare incudibus enses.

And again,

Primus ab æthereo venit Saturnus Olympo
. . . .
Aurea, quæ perhibent, illo sub rege fuerunt
Sæcula: sic placidâ populos in pace regebat. Æn. b. 8. l. 319.

Some of the lines, a little foreign to the present subject, are omitted; but I shall make the most admirable author amends by transcribing at length his next description. It is of a stag, which gave the first occasion to the war betwixt the Trojans and the Rutulians: I choose this, because my design is to have these two great poets seen together, where the subject happens to be almost the same, though the nature of the poems be very different.

Cervus erat formâ præstanti, et cornibus ingens,
Tyrrheidæ pueri quem matris ab ubere raptum

Nutribant, Tyrrheusque pater, cui regia parent
Armenta, et latè custodia credita campi.
Assuetum imperiis soror omni Sylvia curâ
Mollibus intexens ornabat cornua sertis:
Pectebatque ferum, puroque in fonte lavabat.
Ille manum patiens mensæque assuetus herili
Errabat sylvis——————————— Æn. b. 7. l. 483.

The image which Ovid gives of the favourite stag slain accidentally by Cyparissus, seems not of less dignity.

Ingens cervus erat, latèque patentibus altas
Ipso suo capiti præbebat cornibus umbras:
Cornua fulgebant auro, demissaque in armos
Pendebant tereti gemmata monilia collo.
Bulla super frontem parvis argentea loris
Vincta movebatur: parilique ex ære nitebant
Auribus in geminis circum cava tempora baccæ.
Isque metu vacuus, naturalique pavore
Deposito, celebrare domos, mulcendaque colla
Quamlibet ignotis manibus præbere solebat.
Gratus erat, Cyparisse, tibi, tu pabula cervum
Ad nova, tu liquidi ducebas fontis ad undam.
. . . .
Tu modò texebas varios per cornua flores;
Nunc, eques in tergo residens, huc latus et illuc
Mollia purpureis frænabas ora capistris.

In the following lines, Ovid describes the watry court of the river Peneus, which the reader may compare with Virgil's subterranean grot of Cyrene the Naïad, mother to Aristæus.

Est nemus Hæmoniæ, prærupta quod undique claudit
Silva: vocant Tempe, per quæ Penëus ab imo
Effusus Pindo spumosis volvitur undis:
Dejectuque gravi tenues agitantia fumos
Nubila conducit, summasque aspergine sylvas
Impluit, et sonitu plus quam vicina fatigat.
Hæc domus, hæ sedes, hæc sunt penetralia magni
Amnis: in hoc residens facto de cautibus antro
Undis jura dabat, Nymphisque colentibus undas.
Conveniunt illuc popularia flumina primum;
Nescia gratentur, consolenturve parentem,
Populifer Sperchëos, et irrequietus Enipeus,
Eridanusque senex, lenisque Amphrysos, et Æas;
Moxque amnes alii, qui, quà tulit impetus illos,
In mare deducunt fessas erroribus undas. Met. b. 1.

Tristis Aristæus Penei genitoris ad undam
Stat lacrymans———————
. . . .
Jamque domum mirans genetricis, et humida regna,
Speluncisque lacus clausos, lucosque sonantes,
Ibat; et ingenti motu stupefactus aquarum,
Omnia sub magnâ labentia flumine terrâ
Spectabat diversa locis, Phasimque, Lycumque,
Et caput, unde altus primum se erumpit Enipeus,
Unde pater Tiberinus et unde Aniena fluenta,

Et gemina auratus taurino cornua vultu
Eridanus, quo non alius per pinguia culta
In mare purpureum violentior influit amnis. Georg. b. 4.

The divine poet goes on in pomp of numbers, and easy magnificence of words, until he introduces the story of Orpheus and Eurydice; in the narration of which, he is as much superior to Ovid, as the reeds of his own Mantuan shepherds are less musical than the lyre of Orpheus.

That I may not be too long on this article, I shall recommend to the reader Ovid's admirable description of sleep.

——— Est prope Cimmerios ——— Met. b. 11.

That of hunger,

——— Est locus extremis Scythiæ ——— B. 8.

That of the plague,

——— Dira lues ——— B. 7.

That of Fame,

——— Orbe locus medio est ——— B. 12.

Virgil has also touched on the two last; in the one he had Lucretius in view; in the other Homer: and I think it will not be to the disadvantage of our author to appear at the same time.

There are many other descriptions scattered in the Metamorphoses, which, for just expression of nature, and majestic modulation of words, are only inferior to those already transcribed, as they are shorter; which makes the objection, that his diction is commonly loitering into prose, a great deal too severe.

The Metamorphoses must be considered, as is observed before, very uncorrect; and Virgil's works as finished: though his own modesty would not allow the Æneids to be so. It seems it was harder for him to please himself, than his readers. His judgment was certainly great, nor was his vivacity of imagination less; for the first without the last is too heavy, and like a dress without fancy; and the last without the first is too gay, and but all trimming.

Our author's similitudes are next to be considered, which are always remarkably short, and convey some pleasing idea to the imagination. It is in this branch of the poem, that he has discovered as just a judgment as any of the classics whatever. Poets, to give a loose to a warm fancy, are generally too apt not only to expatiate in their similes, but introduce them too frequently; by doing the first, they detain the attention too long from the principal narration; and by the latter, they make too frequent breaches in the unity of the poem.

These two errours Ovid has most discerningly avoided. How short and significant are generally his comparisons! he fails not, in these, to keep a stiff rein on a high-mettled Pegasus; and takes care not to surfeit here, as he had done on other heads, by an erroneous abundance.

His similes are thicker sown by much in the fable of Salmacis and Hermaphroditus than in any other book, but always short.

The nymph clasps the youth close to her breast, and both insensibly grow one.

———Velut si quis conducto cortice ramos
Crescendo jungi, pariterque adolescere cernat. Met. b. 4.

Again, as Atalanta reddens in the race with Hippomenes,

Inque puellari corpus candore ruborem
Traxerat: haud aliter quam cum super atria velum
Candida purpureum simulatas inficit umbras. Met. b. 10.

Philomela's tongue seemed to move after it was cut out by Tereus.

Utque salire solet mutilatæ cauda colubræ,
Palpitat——————— Met. b. 6.

Cadmus sows the dragon's teeth, and the sons of the earth rise gradually.

Inde fide majus glebæ cepêre moveri;
Primaque de sulcis acies apparuit hastæ;
Tegmina mox capitum picto nutantia cono,
Mox humeri, pectusque——
Sic ubi tolluntur festis aulæa theatris
Surgere signa solent, primumque ostendere vultum,
Cætera paulatim, placidoque educta tenore
Tota patent, imoque pedes in margine ponunt. Met. b. 3.

The objection to Ovid, that he never knows when to give over, is too manifest. Though he frequently expatiates on the same thought, in different words; yet in his similes that exuberance is avoided. There is in them all a simplicity, and a confinement to the present object; always a fecundity of fancy, but rarely an intemperance: nor do I remember he has erred above once by an ill-judged superfluity. After he has described the labyrinth built by Dædalus, he compares it thus,

Non secus ac liquidus Phrygiis Mæandros in arvis
Ludit, et ambiguo lapsu refluitque, fluitque;
Et nunc ad fontes, nunc ad mare versus apertum
Incertas exercet aquas——— ——— Met. b. 8.

He should have ended at the close of the second line, as Virgil should have done at the end of the fourth in his noble simile, where Dido proceeds to the temple with her court about her.

Qualis in Eurotæ ripis, aut per juga Cynthi
Exercet Diana choros, quam mille secutæ
Hinc, atque hinc glomerantur Orëades, illa pharetram
Fert humero, gradiensque Deas supereminet omnes:
Latonæ tacitum pertentant gaudia pectus. Æn. b. 4.

I see no reason for the last line. Though the poet be justly celebrated for a most consummate judgment, yet by an endeavour to imitate Homer's similes, he is not only very long, but by introducing several circumstances, he fails of an applicable relation betwixt the principal subject, and his new ideas. He sometimes thinks fit to work into the piece some differing embroidery, which, though very rich, yet makes at best but glorious patch-work. I really believe his excellent poem had not been the less so, if, in this article, he had thought fit to have walked on in his own regular and majestic grace, rather than have been hurried forward through broken by-ways by his blind guide.

I shall transcribe one of his similes which is not culled out, but exactly of the same texture with all the rest in the four last books of the Æneids.

Turnus leaps in fury from his chariot.

Ac veluti montis saxum de vertice præceps
Cum ruit avulsum vento, seu turbidus imber
Proluit, aut annis solvit sublapsa vetustas,
Fertur in abruptum magno mons improbus actu,
Exultatque solo, sylvas, armenta, virosque
Involvens secum——— Æn. b. 12. l. 684.

It does not seem to be at all material, whether the rock was blown or washed down by wind or rain, or undermined by time.

But to return to Ovid; the reader may take notice how unforced his compliments, and how natural his transitions generally are. With how much ease does he slide into some new circumstance, without any violation of the unity of the story! The texture is so artful, that it may be compared to the work of his own Arachne, where the shade dies so gradually, and the light revives so imperceptibly, that it is hard to tell where the one ceases, and the other begins.

When he is going off from the story of Apollo and Daphne, how happily does he introduce a compliment to the Roman conquerors!

——— Et conjux quoniam mea non potes esse,
Arbor eris certè——————
Tu ducibus lætis aderis, cum læta triumphum
Vox canet, et longæ visent capitolia pompæ.
Postibus Augustis eadem fidissima custos
Ante fores stabis; mediamque tuebere quercum. Met. b. 1.

He compliments Augustus upon the assassination of Julius; and, by way of simile, takes the opportunity from the horrour that the barbarity of Lycaon gave.

——— Sic cum manus impia sævit
Sanguine Cæsareo Romanum extinguere nomen, &c.

Julius is deified, and looks down on his adopted son.

———Natique videns benefacta, fatetur.
Esse suis majora, et vinci gaudet ab illo. Met. b. 15.

And immediately follows,

Hic sua præferri quanquam vetat acta paternis,
Libera fama tamen, nullisque obnoxia jussis
Invitum præfert——————

The author in the two first lines shows the affectionate condescension of the father; in the three last, the pious gratitude of the son.

The compliments to Augustus are very frequent in the last book of the Metamorphoses: as those to the same emperor are in the Georgics of Virgil, which also strike the imagination by their agreeable flattery.

Hæc super arvorum cultu, pecorumque canebam,
Et super arboribus; Cæsar dum magnus ad altum
Fulminat Euphratem bello, victorque volentes
Per populos dat jura, viamque affectat Olympo. G. I.

Again on Julius,

Imperium Oceano, famam qui terminet astris
Julius—————— Æn. b. 1.

The compliments have a great sublimity, and are worthy of the grandeur of the heroes, and the wit of the poet.

Ovid as much deserves praise for saying a great deal in a little, as censure for saying a little in a great deal. None of the classic poets had the talent of expressing himself with more force and perspicuity.

Phaëton desires some pledge of his father's tenderness, and asks to be trusted with his chariot. He answers,

Pignora certa petis; do pignora certa timendo. Met. b. 2.

However, the latter complies with his importunity; the consequence is fatal, the world is set on fire, even the rivers feel the force of the conflagration. The Tagus boils,

——————Fluit ignibus aurum.

The Nile retreats,

Occuluitque caput, quod adhuc latet——

Xanthus is parched up.

Arsurusque iterum Xanthus———

The poet's fancy is here full of energy, as well as in the following lines. Apollo courts Daphne, and promises himself success, but is disappointed.

Quodque cupit, sperat; suaque illum oracula fallunt.

And again,

The river Achelous combats Hercules, and assumes several shapes in vain, then puts on at last that of a snake; the hero smiles in contempt.

Cunarum labor est angues superare mearum.

Ovid never excels himself so much, as when he takes occasion to touch upon the passion of love; all hearts are in a manner sensible of the same emotions; and, like instruments tuned unisons, if a string of any one of them be struck, the rest by consent vibrate.

Procris is jealous of Cephalus; she endeavours to be confirmed in her fears, but hopes the contrary,

————Speratque miserrima falli.

The next is not less natural,

————Sed cuncta timemus amantes.

Byblis is in love with Caunus. The struggle is betwixt her unlawful flame and her honour, She is all confusion at the thoughts of discovering her passion——

——miserere fatentis amorem.

She attempts to write.

Incipit et dubitat: scribit, damnatque tabellas,
Et notât, et delet: mutat, culpatque probatque.

In the end, inclination, as it does always, gets the better of discretion.

This last fable shows how touchingly the poet argues in love affairs, as well as those of Medea and Scylla. The two last are left by their heroes, and their reflections are very natural and affecting. Ovid seemed here to have had Virgil's passion of Dido in his eye, but with this difference; the one had conversed much with ladies, and knew they loved to talk a great deal: the other considered no less what was natural for them to say, than what became them to say.

Virgil has, through the whole management of this rencounter, discovered a most finished judgment. Æneas, like other men, likes for convenience, and leaves for greater. Dido, like other ladies, resents the neglect, enumerates the obligations the lover is under, upbraids him with ingratitude, threatens him with revenge, then by and by submits, begs for compassion, and has recourse to tears.

It appears from this piece, that Virgil was a discerning master in the passion of love: and they that consider the spirit and turn of that inimitable line, Qui bavium non odit, cannot doubt but he had an equal talent for satire.

Nor does the genius of Ovid more exert on the subject of love, than on all others. In the contention of Ajax, Ulysses' elocution is most nervous and persuading. Where he endeavours to dissuade mankind from indulging carnivorous appetites in his pythagorean philosophy, how emphatical is his reasoning!

Quid meruêre boves, animal sine fraude, dolisque,
Innocuum, simplex, natum tolerare laborem?
Immemor est demum, nec frugum munere dignus
Qui potuit curvi dempto modò pondere aratri
Ruricolam mactare suum—— Met. b. 15.

I think agricolam had been stronger, but the authority of manuscripts does not warrant that emendation.

Through the whole texture of this work, Ovid discovers the highest humanity, and a most exceeding good nature. The virtuous in distress are always his concern; and his wit contrives to give them an immortality with himself.

He seems to have taken the most pains in the first and second book of the Metamorphoses, though the thirteenth abounds with sentiments most moving, and with calamitous incidents, introduced with great art. The poet had here in view the tragedy of Hecuba and Euripides; and it is a wonder it has never been attempted in our own tongue. The house of Priam is destroyed, his royal daughter a sacrifice to the manes of him that occasioned it. She is forced from the arms of her unhappy friends, and hurried to the altar, where she behaves herself with a decency becoming her sex, and a magnanimity equal to her blood, and so very affecting, that even the priest wept.

——Ipse etiam flens, invitusque sacerdos, &c.

She shows no concern at approaching death, but on the account of her old, unfortunate mother,

Mors tantum vellem matrem mea fallere possit.
Mater obest, minuitque necis mea guadia; quamvis
Non mea mors illi, verum sua vita gemenda est.

Then begs her body may be delivered to her without ransom,

——Genetrici corpus inemptum
Reddite; neve auro redimat jus triste sepulchri,
Sed lacrymis: tunc, cum poterat, redimebat et auro.

The unhappy queen laments she is not able to give her daughter royal burial,

Non hæc est fortuna domûs——.

Then takes the body in her decrepit arms, and halts to the sea to wash off the blood,

——Ad littus passu processit anili
Albentes laniata comas.——

The animated thoughts, and lively images of this poem, are numerous. None ever painted more to the life than our author, though several grotesque figures are now and then seen in the same group. The most plentiful season, that gives birth to the finest flowers, produces also the rankest weeds. Ovid has shown in one line, the brightest fancy, sometimes; and in the next, the poorest affectation.

Venus makes court to Adonis,

——————Et ecce!
Opportuna suâ blanditur populus umbrâ;
Et requievit humo; pressitque et gramen et ipsum.
Met. b. 10. l. 556.

Phœbus requests Phaëton to desist from his request.

——Consiliis, non curribus utere nostris.

Cæneus in the battle of the Centaurs wounds Latreus in several places.

——Vulnusque in vulnere fecit.

These are some of our poet's boyisms. There is another affectation, called by Quintilian Ὀξύμωρον, or a witty folly, which would not have appeared quite so trifling, had it been less frequent.

Medea persuades the daughters of Pelias to kill their father, in order to have his youth renewed. She that loves him best, gives the first wound.

Et, ne sit scelerata, facit scelus—— Met. b. 7.

Althea is enraged at her son Meleager, and to do justice to the manes of his brothers, destroys him,

> Impietate pia est——

Envy enters Athens, and beholds the flourishing condition of the city,

> Vixque tenet lacrymas, quia nil lacrymabile cernit.

Ovid was much too fond of such witticisms, which are more to be wondered at, because they were not the fashion of that age, as puns and quibbles are of this. Virgil, as I remember, is not found trifling in this manner above once, or twice.

> Deucalion vacuum lapides jactavit in orbem,
> Unde homines nati, durum genus—— G. b. 1. l. 63.

Juno is in indignation at Æneas upon his arrival in Italy.

> Num capti potuere capi? num incensa cremavit
> Troja viros?—— Æn. 7. l. 295.

The poet is so far from affecting this sort of wit, that he rarely ventures on so spirited a turn of fancy, as in these following instances.

Juno upbraids Venus and Cupid, ironically, that two deities could be able to get the better of one weak woman.

> ————Memorabile nomen,
> Una dolo divûm si fœmina victa duorum est. Æn. b. 4. l. 95.

Euryalus, going upon an enterprise, expresses his concern for his surviving mother, if he should fall, and recommends her to the care of Ascanius, who answers,

> Namque erit ista mihi genitrix, nomenque Creusæ
> Solùm defuerit——

Venus is importunate in her solicitations to Vulcan, to make armour for her son: he answers,

> ————Absiste precando
> Viribus indubitare tuis—— Æn. b. 7.

At the first kindling of Dido's passion, he has this most natural thought,

> ——Illum absens absentem auditque videtque.

But to return to Ovid; though I cannot vindicate him for his points, I shall endeavour to mollify his critics, when they give him no quarter for his diction, and attack him so inflexibly for ending his lines with monosyllables, as—si quis—si non, &c. and as I think he cannot be excused more advantageously, than by affirming, that where he has done it once, Virgil has twenty times.

—— et cum	G. 1.
—— si quis	G. 2.
—— nec dum	G. 2.
—— si quam	Æn. 1.
—— si quis	Æn. 7.
—— jam bos	Æn. 12.
—— nunc nunc—&c.	

There are a great many endings of lines in this manner, and more indeed than seems consistent with the majesty of heroic verse. When lines are designed to be sermoni propriores, this liberty may be allowable, but not so when the subject requires more sonorous numbers. Virgil seems to endeavour to keep up his versification to an harmonious dignity; and therefore, when fit words do not offer with some ease, he will rather break off in an hemestich, than that the line should be lazy and languid. He well knew how essential it was in poetry to flatter the ear; and at the same time was sensible, that this organ grows tired by a constant attention to the same harmony; and therefore he endeavoured now and then to relieve it by a cadence of pauses, and a variation of measures.

Amphion Dircæus in Actæo Aracyntho. Ecl. 2.

This line seems not tuneful at the first hearing; but by repetition it reconciles itself, and has the same effect with some compositions of music, which are at the first performance tiresome, and afterward entertaining.

The commentators and critics are of opinion, that whenever Virgil is less musical, it is where he endeavours at an agreement of the sound with the sense, as,

——Procumbit humi bos.

It would show as much singularity to deny this, as it does a fanciful facility to affirm it, because it is obvious, in many places, he had no such view.

——Inventa sub ilicibus sus. Æn. 3. l. 390.
——Dentesque Sabellicus exacuit sus. G. 3. l. 255.
——Jam setis obsita, jam bos. Æn. 7. l. 791.
——Furor additus, inde lupi ceu, &c. Æn. 11. l. 355.

The places which favour most the first opinion are,

Saxa per et scopulos, et dépressas convalles. G. 3. l. 275.

——Sæpe exiguus mus.
Omnia sub magnâ labentia flumina terrâ. G. 4.

The last line is the only instance I remember (except one in Ecl. 2.) where the words terminate in the same vowel, and seem to represent the constant and uniform sound of a sliding stream.

Those that are most conversant in classic poetry must be sensible, that Virgil has been much more solicitous than Ovid to keep up his lines to an easy and a musical flow; but though the critics charge the latter with breaking through prosody and grammar, and allowing himself too often the licence of Græcisms; I take this censure to be only an arrogant pedantry in the grammarians, and groundless in itself; but though it were true, I dare be confident it is full as just upon Virgil,

——Curru subjungere tigres, Ecl. 5. l. 29,

for currui, according to the grammarians.

Often adjectives for adverbs; and the contrary.

G. 1.—Pinguia culta; an adjective for a substantive.
——Denso distinguere pingui; the same.
Æn. 11. l. 69.—Seu languentis hyacinthi; first foot of the dactyl short.
Æn. 4.—Tulerunt fastidia menses; the penultima of the verb short.
Obstupui steteruntque comæ—the same.
So Lucretius, prodiderunt, reciderunt, &c.
G. 2. l. 5.—Pampineo gravidus autumno; an iambic for a spondee.
Fluviorum rex Eridanus camposque per omnes; an anapest for a dactyl, or a spondee.
Æn. 10. l. 29.—Nec Clytio genitore minor nec fratre Mnestheo; a trochee, unless the two consonants MN of the following word be allowed.
G. 1. l. 456.—Fervere, non illâ quisquam—The penultima commonly short with Virgil, so fulgere, stridere, &c.
Æn. 12. l. 680.—Sine me furere ante furorem; a Græcism.
G. 1. l. 281.—Imponere Pelio Ossam; a Græcism, where there is no elision, but the long vowel before another made short.

The learned and reverend Dr. Clark has observed, (as he tells me) that though there be several short vowels made long in Homer, yet there is no instance on the contrary, of any long vowel (such as the first syllable of τιμή, ψυχή, νίκη, and the like) ever made short, where no vowel follows. Which shows that there is no such thing as a poetica licentia, properly so called.

Certainly no body can imagine but these two celebrated authors understood their own tongue better than the scrupulous grammarians of after-ages, who are too dogmatical, and self-sufficient, when they presume to censure either of them for not attending strictly enough to syntax, and the measure of verse. The Latin tongue is a dead language, and none can decide with confidence on the harmony or dissonance of the numbers of these times, unless they were thoroughly acquainted with their pauses and cadence. They may indeed pronounce with much more assurance on their diction; and distinguish where they have been negligent, and where more finished. There are certainly many lines in Ovid where he has been downright lazy, and where he might have avoided the appearance of being obviously so, by a very little application. In recording the succession of the Alban kings, thus,

> Epitus ex illo est, post hunc Capetusque; Capysque,
> Sed Capys ante fuit——

There are also several lines in Virgil which are not altogether tunable to a modern ear, and which appear unfinished.

> Scilicet omnibus est labor impendendus, et omnes
> Cogendæ in sulcum—— G. 2. l. 61.
> Præsertim si tempestas à vertice sylvis
> Incubuit—— G. 2. l. 310.
> Quasve referre parem? sed nunc, est omnia quando
> Iste animus supra—— Æn. 11. l. 509.
> Ista quidem quia nota mihi tua, magne, voluntas,
> Jupiter—— Æn. 12. l. 108.

But the Sun has its spots; and if amongst thousands of inimitable lines there should be some found of an unequal dignity with the rest, nothing can be said for their vindication more, than, if they be faults, they are the faults of Virgil.

As I ought to be on this occasion an advocate for Ovid, who I think is too much run down at present by the critical spirit of this nation; I dare say I cannot be more effectually so, than by comparing him in many places with his admired contemporary Virgil; and though the last certainly deserves the palm, I shall make use of Ovid's own lines, in the trial of strength betwixt Acheloüs and Hercules, to show how much he is honoured by the contention.

> ——Non tam
> Turpe fuit vinci, quam contendisse decorum. Met. b. 9.

I shall finish my remarks on our author, by taking notice of the justness and perspicuity of his allegories; which are either physical, or natural; moral, or historical. Of the first kind is the fable of Apollo and Python; in the explanation of this all the mythologists agree; exhalations and mists, being the constant effects of inundations, are here dissipated by the rays of the Sun.

Of the second kind, are Actæon torn to pieces by his own pack of dogs, and Eresicthon starved by the disease of hunger. These two allegories seem to signify, that extravagance and luxury end in want.

Of the third, is the story of the rape of Europa. History says, she was daughter to Agenor, and carried by the Candians in a galley, bearing a bull in the stern, in order to be married to one of their kings named Jupiter.

This explanation gives an occasion for a digression which is not altogether foreign to the present purpose, because it will be of use to justify Ovid on some other occasions, where he is censured for being too free with the characters of the gods. I was once representing the Metamorphoses as an excellent system of morality; but an illustrious lady, whose least advantage above her sex is that of being one of the greatest princesses in Europe, objected, that the loose and immodest sallies of Jupiter did by no means confirm my assertion.

One must consider, that what appeared an absurdity in Ovid is not so much his own fault, as that of the times before him. The characters of the gods of the old heroic age represented them unjust in their actions; mutable in their designs; partial in their favours; ignorant of events; scurrilous in their language. Some of the superior hierarchy treat one another with injurious brutalities, and are often guilty of such indecencies and misbehaviour as the lowest of mortals would blush to own. Juno calls Diana the goddess of chastity, κύον ἀδδεὲς, brazenfaced bitch; Hom. Il. b. 22. l. 481. Jupiter insults his daughter, the goddess of wisdom, for rashness and folly; bids Iris tell her, he will maul her coach horses for her like a surly bitch as she is; ἀινοτάτη κύον: Il. b. 8. from l. 400. to l. 425. then threatens in another place to beat his wife, that divine vixen, the immortal partner of the empyreal throne, καί σε πληγῆσιν ἱμάσσω. Il. b. 15. l. 17.

The commentators may endeavour to hide those absurdities under the veil of allegories: but the reader that considers the whole texture of the Iliad will find that the author's meaning, and their interpretation, are often as unlike, as the imaginary heroes of his time are to the real ones of ours.

Allegories should be obvious, and not like meteors in the air, which represent a different figure to every different eye. Now they are armies of soldiers; now flocks of sheep; and by and by nothing.

Perhaps the critics of a more exalted taste may discover such beauties in the ancient poetry, as may escape the comprehension of us pygmies of a more limited genius. They may be able to fathom the divine sense of the Pagan theology; whilst we aim at no more than to judge of a little common sense.

It is, and ever will be, a rule to a great many, to applaud and condemn with the general vogue, though never so ill grounded. The most are afraid of being particular; and rather than strive against the stream, are proud of being in the wrong with the many, rather than desirous of being in the right with the few: and though they be convinced of the reasonableness of dissenting from the common cry, yet out of a poor fear of censure, they contribute to establish it, and thus become an authority against others, who in reality are but of their own opinion.

Ovid was so far from paying a blind deference to the venerable name of his Grecian predecessor, in the character of his gods, that when Jupiter punishes Andromeda for the crimes of her mother, he calls him injustus Ammon, Met. b. 4. and takes commonly an honourable care of the decorum of the godhead, when their actions are consistent with the divinity of their character. His allegories include some religious or instructive moral, wrapped up in a peculiar perspicuity. The fable of Proserpina being sometimes in Hell, and sometimes with Ceres her mother, can scarce mean any thing else than the sowing and coming up of corn. The various dresses that Vertumnus, the god of seasons, puts on in his courtship of Pomona the garden goddess, seem plainly to express the different and most proper times for digging, planting, pruning, and gathering the increase. I shall be shorter on this head, because our countryman Mr. Sands has, by a laborious search amongst the mythologists, been very full. He has annexed his explanations to the end of each book, which deserve to be recommended to those that are curious in this figurative learning.

The reader cannot fail of observing how many excellent lessons of morality Ovid has given us in the course of his fables.

The story of Deucalion and Pyrrha teaches, that piety and innocence cannot miss of the divine protection, and that the only loss irreparable is that of our probity and justice.

That of Phaëton; how the too great tenderness of the parent proves a cruelty to the child; and that he, who would climb to the seat of Jupiter, generally meets with his bolt by the way.

The tale of Baucis and Philemon is most inimitably told. He omits not the minutest circumstance of a cottage life; and is much fuller than Virgil, where he brings in his contented old man Corycius, G. 4. Ovid represents a good old couple; happy and satisfied in a cleanly poverty; hospitable and free of the few things that Fortune had given them; moderate in desires; affectionate in their conjugal relation; so religious in life, that when they observed their homely cabin rising to a temple, all the bounty they asked of the gods they had entertained was, that they might do the office of priesthood there; and at their death, not survive one another.

The stories of Lycaon and Pentheus, not only deter from infidelity and irreverence to the gods; but the last also shows, that too great zeal produces the same effects as none at all; and that enthusiasm is often more cruel than atheism.

The story of Minos and Scylla represents the infamy of selling our country; and teaches, that even they who love the crime, abhor the criminal.

In Cippus we find a noble magnanimity, and heavenly self-denial: he preferred the good of the republic to his own private grandeur; and chose, with an exemplary generosity, rather to live a private free-man out of Rome, than to command numbers of slaves in it.

From the story of Hercules we learn, that Glory is a lady, who, like many others, loves to have her admirers suffer a great deal for her. The poet enumerates the labours of the hero; shows how he conquered every thing for others, but nothing for himself: then does him the poetical justice of an apotheosis; thinking it most fit that one, who had born the celestial orbs on his shoulders, should have a mansion amongst them.

From the assumption of Romulus; that when war is at an end, the chief business of peace should be the enacting good laws; that after a people are preserved from the enemy, the next care should be to preserve them from themselves; and therefore the best legislators deserve a place amongst heroes and deities.

From Ariadne being inhumanly deserted by Theseus; and generously received by Bacchus; we find, that as there is nothing we can be sure of, so there is nothing we ought to despair of.

From Althea burning the brand; that we should take care lest under the notion of justice, we should do a cruelty; for they that are set upon revenge, only endeavour to imitate the injury.

From Polyphemus making love to Galatea one may observe, that the most deformed can find something to like in their own person. He examines his face in the stream, combs his rueful locks with a rake, grows more exact and studious of his dress, and discovers the first sign of being in love, by endeavouring at a more than usual care to please.

The fable of Cephalus and Procris confirms, that every trifle contributes to heighten the disease of jealousy; and that the most convincing proofs can scarce cure it.

From that of Hippomenes and Atalanta we may discover, that a generous present helps to persuade, as well as an agreeable person.

From Medea's flying from Pelias's court; that the offered favours of the impious should be always suspected; and that they, who design to make every one fear them, are afraid of every one.

From Myrra; that shame is sometimes hard to be overcome, but if the sex once gets the better of it, it gives them afterwards no more trouble.

From Cenis; that effeminacy in youth may change to valour in manhood, and that as fame perishes, so does censure.

From Tereus; that one crime lays the foundation of many; and that the same person, who begins with lust, may conclude with murder.

From Midas; that no body can punish a covetous man worse than he punishes himself; that scarce any thing would sometimes prove more fatal to us, than the completion of our own wishes; and that he who has the most desires, will certainly meet with the most disappointments.

From the Pythagorean philosophy, it may be observed, that man is the only animal who kills his fellow-creature without being angry.

From Proteus we have this lesson, that a statesman can put on any shape; can be a spaniel to the lion, and a lion to the spaniel; and that he knows not to be an enemy, who knows not how to seem a friend; that if all crowns should change their ministry, as often as they please, though they may be called other ministers, they are still the same men.

The legend of Æsculapius's voyage to Rome in form of a snake, seems to express the necessary sagacity required in professors of that art, for the readier insight into distempers: this reptile being celebrated by the ancient naturalists for a quick sight.

Cur in amicorum vitium tam cernis acutum,
Quam aut aquila, aut serpens Epidaurius?——

Hor. Sat. 3. l. 26.

The venerable Epidaurian assumed the figure of an animal without hands to take fees; and therefore, grateful posterity honoured him with a temple. In this manner should wealthy physicians, upon proper occasions, practise; and thus their surviving patients reward.

If the Metamorphoses be attended to with a just application, and without prepossession; one will be the less surprised at the author's prophetic spirit, relating to the duration and success of the work.

Jamque opus exegi, &c.——

This prediction has so far proved true, that this poem has been ever since the magazine, which has furnished the greatest poets of the following ages with fancy and allusions, and the most celebrated painters with subjects and design. Nor have his poetical predecessors and contemporaries paid less regard to their own performances.

Insignemque meo capiti petere inde coronam,
Unde prius nulli velârunt tempora Musæ. Lucr. b. 1.
Nemo me lacrumeis decoret, nec funera fletu
Facsit; quur volito vivu' per ora virûm. Enn. Frag.
——Tentanda via est, quâ me quoque possim
Tollere humo, victorque virûm volitare per ora. Virg. G. 3.
Me doctarum ederæ præmia frontium
Diis miscent superis—— Hor. od. 1.

Again,

Exegi monumentum ære perennius,
Regalique situ piramidum altius,
Quod non imber edax, non aquilo impotens
Possit diruere, aut innumerabilis
Annorum series, et fuga temporum.
Non omnis moriar.—— Hor. b. 3. od. 30.

The whole ode is in a manner a continued compliment to his own writings; nor, in imitation of this celebrated author, want we poets of our present age, who have been pleased to rank themselves amongst their own admirers.

I have done with the original, and shall make no excuse for the length of the preface, because it is in the power of the reader to make it as short as he pleases. I shall now conclude with a word or two about the version.

Translation is commonly either verbal, or paraphrase, or imitation; of the first is Mr. Sands's, which I think the Metamorphoses can by no means allow of. It is agreed, that the author left it unfinished; if it had undergone his last hand, it is more than probable that many superfluities had been retrenched. Where a poem is perfectly finished, the translation, with regard to particular idioms, cannot be too exact; by doing this, the sense of the author is more entirely his own, and the cast of the periods more faithfully preserved: but where a poem is tedious through exuberance, or dark through a hasty brevity, I think the translator may be excused for doing what the author upon revising would have done himself.

If Mr. Sands had been of this opinion, perhaps other translations of the Metamorphoses had not been attempted.

A critic has observed that in his version of this book, he has scrupulously confined the number of his lines to those of the original. It is fit I should take the sum upon content, and be better bred than to count after him.

The manner that seems most suited for this present undertaking, is, neither to follow the author too close out of a critical timorousness; nor abandon him too wantonly through a poetic boldness. The original should always be kept in view, without too apparent a deviation from the sense. Where it is otherwise, it is not a version, but an imitation. The translator ought to be as intent to keep up the gracefulness of the poem, as artful to hide its imperfections; to copy its beauties, and to throw a shade over its blemishes; to be faithful to an idolatry, where the author excels; and to take the licence of a little paraphrase, where penury of fancy or dryness of expression seem to ask for it.

The ingenious gentlemen concerned in this undertaking seem to be of this opinion; and therefore they have not only consulted the reputation of the author, but their own also. There is one of them has no other share in this compliment, than by being the occasion of engaging them that have, in obliging the public. He has also been so just to the memory and reputation of Mr. Dryden, as to give his incomparable lines the advantage of appearing so near his own.

I cannot pass by that admirable English poet, without endeavouring to make his country sensible of the obligations they have to his Muse. Whether they consider the flowing grace of his versification; the vigorous sallies of his fancy; or the peculiar delicacy of his periods; they will discover excellencies never to be enough admired. If they trace him from the first productions of his youth to the last performances of his age, they will find, that as the tyranny of rhyme never imposed on the perspicuity of the sense; so a languid sense never wanted to be set off by the harmony of rhyme. And as his earlier works wanted no maturity; so this latter wanted no force, or spirit. The falling off of his hair had no other consequence, than to make his laurels be seen the more.

As a translator he was just; as an inventor he was rich. His versions of some parts of Lucretius, Horace, Homer, and Virgil throughout, gave him a just pretence to that compliment which was made to monsieur d'Ablancourt, a celebrated French translator; "It is uncertain who have the greatest obligations to him, the dead or the living."

With all these wondrous talents, he was libelled in his life-time by the very men who had no other excellencies, but as they were his imitators. Where he was allowed to have sentiments superior to all others, they charged him with theft: but how did he steal? no otherwise than like those that steal beggars' children, only to clothe them the better.

It is to be lamented, that gentlemen still continue this unfair behaviour, and treat one another every day with most injurious libels. The Muses should be ladies of a chaste and fair behaviour: when they are otherwise, they are Furies. It is certain that Parnassus is at best but a barren mountain, and its inhabitants contrive to make it more so by their unneighbourly deportment; the authors are the only corporation that endeavour at the ruin of their own society. Every day may convince them, how much a rich fool is respected above a poor wit. The only talents in esteem at present are those of Exchange-Alley; one tally is worth a grove of bays; and it is of much more consequence to be well read in the tables of interest, and the rise and fall of stocks, than in the revolutions of empires.

Mr. Dryden is still a sad and shameful instance of this truth: the man that could make kings immortal, and raise triumphant arches to heroes, now wants a poor square foot of stone, to show where the ashes of one of the greatest poets, that ever was upon Earth, are deposited.

OVID'S METAMORPHOSES.

TRANSLATED BY DRYDEN, &c. &c.

BOOK I.

Translated by Dryden.

OF bodies chang'd to various forms I sing:
Ye gods, from whom these miracles did spring,
Inspire my numbers with celestial heat;
'Till I my long laborious work complete:
And add perpetual tenour to my rhymes,
Deduc'd from nature's birth, to Cæsar's times.
Before the seas, and this terrestrial ball,
And Heav'n's high canopy, that covers all,
One was the face of nature; if a face:
Rather a rude and indigested mass:
A lifeless lump, unfashion'd, and unfram'd,
Of jarring seeds; and justly Chaos nam'd.
No Sun was lighted up, the world to view;
No Moon did yet her blunted horns renew:
Nor yet was Earth suspended in the sky;
Nor pois'd, did on her own foundations lie:
Nor seas about the shores their arms had thrown;
But earth, and air, and water, were in one.
Thus air was void of light, and earth unstable,
And water's dark abyss unnavigable,
No certain form on any was imprest;
All were confus'd, and each disturb'd the rest.
For hot and cold were in one body fixt;
And soft with hard, and light with heavy mixt.
But God, or Nature, while they thus contend,
To these intestine discords put an end; [driv'n,
Then earth from air, and seas from earth were
And grosser air sunk from ethereal Heav'n.
Thus disembroil'd, they take their proper place;
The next of kin contiguously embrace:
And foes are sunder'd, by a larger space.
The force of fire ascended first on high,
And took its dwelling in the vaulted sky:
Then air succeeds, in lightness next to fire;
Whose atoms from unactive earth retire.
Earth sinks beneath, and draws a num'rous throng
Of pondrous, thick, unwieldy seeds along.
About her coasts, unruly waters roar;
And rising, on a ridge, insult the shore.
Thus when the god, whatever god was he,
Had form'd the whole, and made the parts agree,
That no unequal portions might be found,
He moulded earth into a spacious round:
Then with a breath, he gave the winds to blow;
And bad the congregated waters flow.
He adds the running springs, and standing lakes;
And bounding banks for winding rivers makes.
Some part in earth are swallow'd up, the most
In ample oceans, disembogu'd, are lost.
He shades the woods, the valleys he restrains
With rocky mountains, and extends the plains.
And as five zones th' ethereal regions bind,
Five, correspondent, are to Earth assign'd:
The Sun with rays, directly darting down,
Fires all beneath and fries the middle zone:
The two beneath the distant poles complain
Of endless winter, and perpetual rain.
Betwixt th' extremes, two happier climates hold
The temper that partakes of hot and cold.
The fields of liquid air, enclosing all,
Surround the compass of this earthly ball:
The lighter parts lie next the fires above;
The grosser near the watry surface move: [there,
Thick clouds are spread, and storms engender
And thunder's voice, which wretched mortals fear,
And winds that on their wings cold winter bear.
Nor were those blustring brethren left at large,
On seas, and shores, their fury to discharge:
Bound as they are, and circumscrib'd in place,
They rend the world, resistless, where they pass;
And mighty marks of mischief leave behind;
Such is the rage of their tempestuous kind.
First Eurus to the rising morn is sent,
(The regions of the balmy continent;)
And eastern realms, where early Persians run,
To greet the blest appearance of the Sun.
Westward, the wanton Zephyr wings his flight;
Pleas'd with the remnants of departing light:
Fierce Boreas, with his offspring, issues forth
T' invade the frozen waggon of the north.

While frowning Auster seeks the southern sphere;
And rots, with endless rain, th' unwholesome year.
High o'er the clouds, and empty realms of wind,
The god a clearer space for Heav'n design'd;
Where fields of light, and liquid ether flow;
Purg'd from the pondrous dregs of earth below.
Scarce had the pow'r distinguish'd these, when straight
The stars, no longer overlaid with weight,
Exert their heads, from underneath the mass;
And upward shoot, and kindle as they pass,
And with diffusive light adorn their heav'nly place.
Then, every void of nature to supply,
With forms of gods he fills the vacant sky:
New herds of beasts he sends, the plains to share:
New colonies of birds, to people air;
And to their oozy beds the finny fish repair.
A creature of a more exalted kind
Was wanting yet, and then was man design'd:
Conscious of thought, of more capacious breast,
For empire form'd, and fit to rule the rest:
Whether with particles of heav'nly fire
The God of Nature did his soul inspire,
Or earth, but new divided from the sky,
And, pliant, still retain'd th' ethereal energy:
Which wise Prometheus temper'd into paste,
And, mixt with living streams, the godlike image cast.
Thus, while the mute creation downward bend
Their sight, and to their earthly mother tend,
Man looks aloft; and with erected eyes
Beholds his own hereditary skies.
From such rude principles our form began;
And earth was metamorphos'd into man.

THE GOLDEN AGE.

The golden age was first; when man, yet new,
No rule but uncorrupted reason knew:
And, with a native bent, did good pursue.
Unforc'd by punishment, unaw'd by fear,
His words were simple, and his soul sincere;
Needless was written law, where none opprest:
The law of man was written in his breast:
No suppliant crowds before the judge appear'd,
No court erected yet, nor cause was heard:
But all was safe, for conscience was their guard.
The mountain-trees in distant prospect please,
Ere yet the pine descended to the seas:
Ere sails were spread, new oceans to explore:
And happy mortals, unconcern'd for more,
Confin'd their wishes to their native shore.
No walls were yet: nor fence, nor mote, nor mound,
Nor drum was heard, nor trumpet's angry sound:
Nor swords were forg'd; but void of care and crime,
The soft creation slept away their time.
The teeming earth, yet guiltless of the plough,
And unprovok'd, did fruitful stores allow:
Content with food, which nature freely bred,
On wildings and on strawberries they fed;
Cornels and bramble-berries gave the rest,
And falling acorns furnish'd out a feast.
The flow'rs unsown, in fields and meadows reign'd:
And western winds immortal spring maintain'd.
In following years, the bearded corn ensu'd
From earth unask'd, nor was that earth renew'd.
From veins of valleys, milk and nectar broke;
And honey sweating through the pores of oak.

THE SILVER AGE.

But when good Saturn, banish'd from above,
Was driv'n to Hell, the world was under Jove.
Succeeding times a silver age behold,
Excelling brass, but more excell'd by gold.
Then Summer, Autumn, Winter did appear:
And Spring was but a season of the year.
The Sun his annual course obliquely made,
Good days contracted, and enlarg'd the bad.
Then air with sultry heats began to glow;
The wings of winds were clogg'd with ice and snow;
And shivering mortals, into houses driv'n,
Sought shelter from th' inclemency of Heav'n.
Those houses, then, were caves, or homely sheds;
With twining osiers fenc'd; and moss their beds.
Then ploughs, for seed, the fruitful furrows broke,
And oxen labour'd first beneath the yoke.

THE BRAZEN AGE.

To this came next in course, the brazen age:
A warlike offspring, prompt to bloody rage,
Not impious yet——

THE IRON AGE.

——Hard steel succeeded then:
And stubborn as the metal, were the men.
Truth, Modesty, and Shame, the world forsook:
Fraud, Avarice, and Force, their places took.
Then sails were spread, to every wind that blew,
Raw were the sailors, and the depths were new:
Trees, rudely hollow'd, did the waves sustain;
Ere ships in triumph plough'd the wat'ry plain.
Then land-marks limited to each his right:
For all before was common as the light.
Nor was the ground alone requir'd to bear
Her annual income to the crooked share,
But greedy mortals, rummaging her store,
Digg'd from her entrails first the precious ore;
Which, next to Hell, the prudent gods had laid;
And that alluring ill, to sight display'd.
Thus cursed steel, and more accursed gold,
Gave mischief birth, and made that mischief bold:
And double death did wretched man invade,
By steel assaulted, and by gold betray'd.
Now (brandish'd weapons glitt'ring in their hands)
Mankind is broken loose from moral bands;
No rights of hospitality remain:
The guest, by him who harbour'd him, is slain.
The son-in-law pursues the father's life;
The wife her husband murders, he the wife.
The step-dame poison for the son prepares;
The son inquires into his father's years.
Faith flies, and Piety in exile mourns;
And Justice, here opprest, to Heav'n returns.

THE GIANTS' WAR.

Nor were the gods themselves more safe above;
Against beleaguer'd Heav'n the giants move.
Hills pil'd on hills, on mountains mountains lie,
To make their mad approaches to the sky.
'Till Jove, no longer patient, took his time
T' avenge with thunder their audacious crime:
Red light'ning play'd along the firmament,
And their demolish'd works to pieces rent.
Sing'd with the flames, and with the bolts transfixt,
With native earth their blood the monsters mixt;
The blood, indu'd with animating heat,
Did in th' impregnant earth new sons beget:

They, like the seed from which they sprung, accurst,
Against the gods immortal hatred nurst.
An impious, arrogant, and cruel brood;
Expressing their original from blood.
Which when the king of gods beheld from high
(Withal revolving in his memory,
What he himself had found on Earth of late,
Lycaon's guilt, and his inhuman treat,)
He sigh'd; nor longer with his pity strove;
But kindled to a wrath becoming Jove:
Then call'd a general council of the gods;
Who, summon'd, issue from their blest abodes,
And fill th' assembly with a shining train.
A way there is, in Heav'n's expanded plain,
Which, when the skies are clear, is seen below,
And mortals, by the name of milky, know.
The ground-work is of stars; through which the road
Lies open to the thunderer's abode:
The gods of greater nations dwell around,
And, on the right and left, the palace bound;
The commons where they can: the nobler sort,
With winding-doors wide open, front the court.
This place, as far as Earth with Heav'n may vie,
I dare to call the Louvre of the sky.
When all were plac'd, in seats distinctly known,
And he, their father, had assum'd the throne,
Upon his iv'ry sceptre first he leant,
Then shook his head, that shook the firmament:
Air, earth, and seas, obey'd th' almighty nod;
And, with a gen'ral fear, confess'd the god.
At length, with indignation, thus he broke
His awful silence, and the powers bespoke.
"I was not more concern'd in that debate
Of empire, when our universal state
Was put to hazard, and the giant race
Our captive skies were ready to embrace:
For though the foe was fierce, the seeds of all
Rebellion sprung from one original;
Now, wheresoever ambient waters glide,
All are corrupt, and all must be destroy'd.
Let me this holy protestation make,
By Hell, and Hell's inviolable lake,
I try'd, whatever in the godhead lay:
But gangren'd members must be lopt away,
Before the nobler parts are tainted to decay.
There dwells below, a race of demi-gods,
Of nymphs in waters, and of fawns in woods:
Who, though not worthy yet in Heav'n to live,
Let them, at least, enjoy that Earth we give.
Can these be thought securely lodg'd below,
When I myself, who no superior know,
I, who have Heav'n and Earth at my command,
Have been attempted by Lycaon's hand?"
At this a murmur through the synod went,
And with one voice they vote his punishment.
Thus, when conspiring traitors dar'd to doom
The fall of Cæsar, and in him of Rome,
The nations trembled with a pious fear;
All anxious for their earthly thunderer:
Nor was their care, O Cæsar, less esteem'd
By thee, than that of Heav'n for Jove was deem'd:
Who with his hand, and voice, did first restrain
Their murmurs, then resum'd his speech again.
The gods to silence were compos'd, and sate
With reverence, due to his superior state.
"Cancel your pious cares; already he
Has paid his debt to justice, and to me.
Yet what his crimes, and what my judgments were,
Remains for me thus briefly to declare.
The clamours of this vile degenerate age,
The cries of orphans, and th' oppressor's rage,
Had reach'd the stars; 'I will descend,' said I,
'In hope to prove this loud complaint a lie.'
Disguis'd in human shape, I travell'd round
The world, and more than what I heard, I found.
O'er Mænalus I took my steepy way,
By caverns infamous for beasts of prey:
Then cross'd Cyllené, and the piny shade
More infamous by curst Lycaon made.
Dark night had cover'd Heav'n, and Earth, before
I enter'd his unhospitable door.
Just at my entrance, I display'd the sign
That somewhat was approaching of divine.
The prostrate people pray; the tyrant grins;
And, adding profanation to his sins,
'I'll try,' said he, 'and if a god appear,
To prove his deity shall cost him dear.
'Twas late; the graceless wretch my death prepares,
When I should soundly sleep, opprest with cares:
This dire experiment he chose, to prove
If I were mortal, or undoubted Jove:
But first he had resolv'd to taste my pow'r;
Not long before, but in a luckless hour,
Some legates, sent from the Molossian state,
Were on a peaceful errand come to treat:
Of these he murders one, he boils the flesh;
And lays the mangled morsels in a dish:
Some part he roasts; then serves it up, so drest,
And bids me welcome to this human feast.
Mov'd with disdain, the table I o'er-turn'd;
And with avenging flames the palace burn'd.
The tyrant in a fright, for shelter gains
The neighb'ring fields, and scours along the plains.
Howling he fled, and fain he would have spoke;
But human voice his brutal tongue forsook.
About his lips the gather'd foam he churns,
And, breathing slaughter, still with rage he burns,
But on his bleating flock his fury turns.
His mantle, now his hide, with rugged hairs
Cleaves to his back; a famish'd face he bears;
His arms descend, his shoulders sink away
To multiply his legs for chase of prey.
He grows a wolf, his hoariness remains,
And the same rage in other members reigns.
His eyes still sparkle in a narr'wer space:
His jaws retain the grin, and violence of his face.
"This was a single ruin, but not one
Deserves so just a punishment alone.
Mankind's a monster, and th' ungodly times
Confed'rate into guilt, are sworn to crimes.
All are alike involv'd in ill, and all
Must by the same relentless fury fall."
Thus ended he; the greater gods assent;
By clamours urging his severe intent;
The less fill up the cry for punishment.
Yet still with pity they remember man;
And mourn as much as heav'nly spirits can.
They ask, when those were lost of human birth,
What he would do with all this waste of earth:
If his dispeopled world he would resign
To beasts, a mute, and more ignoble line;
Neglected altars must no longer smoke,
If none were left to worship, and invoke.
To whom the father of the gods reply'd,
"Lay that unnecessary fear aside:
Mine be the care, new people to provide.
I will from wondrous principles ordain
A race unlike the first, and try my skill again."

Already had he toss'd the flaming brand;
And roll'd the thunder in his spacious hand;
Preparing to discharge on seas and land:
But stopt, for fear, thus violently driv'n,
The sparks should catch his axle-tree of Heav'n.
Rememb'ring, in the fates, a time when fire
Should to the battlements of Heav'n aspire,
And all his blazing worlds above should burn;
And all th' inferior globe to cinders turn.
His dire artill'ry thus dismist, he bent
His thoughts to some securer punishment:
Concludes to pour a watry deluge down;
And what he durst not burn, resolves to drown.
The northern breath, that freezes floods, he binds;
With all the race of cloud-dispelling winds:
The South he loos'd, who night and horrour brings;
And fogs are shaken from his flaggy wings.
From his divided beard two streams he pours,
His head, and rheumy eyes distil in show'rs.
With rain his robe and heavy mantle flow:
And lazy mists are lowring on his brow;
Still as he swept along, with his clench'd fist
He squeez'd the clouds, th' imprison'd clouds resist:
The skies, from pole to pole, with peals resound;
And show'rs enlarg'd come pouring on the ground.
Then, clad in colours of a various dye,
Junonian Iris breeds a new supply
To feed the clouds: impetuous rain descends;
The bearded corn beneath the burden bends:
Defrauded clowns deplore their perish'd grain;
And the long labours of the year are vain.
Nor from his patrimonial Heaven alone
Is Jove content to pour his vengeance down;
Aid from his brother of the seas he craves,
To help him with auxiliary waves.
The watry tyrant calls his brooks and floods,
Who roll from mossy caves (their moist abodes;)
And with perpetual urns his palace fill:
To whom in brief, he thus imparts his will.
"Small exhortation needs; your pow'rs employ:
And this bad world, so Jove requires, destroy.
Let loose the reins to all your watry store:
Bear down the dams, and open ev'ry door."
The floods, by nature enemies to land,
And proudly swelling with their new command,
Remove the living stones, that stopt their way,
And, gushing from their source, augment the sea.
Then, with his mace, their monarch struck the ground;
With inward trembling Earth receiv'd the wound;
And rising streams a ready passage found.
Th' expanded waters gather on the plain:
They float the fields, and over-top the grain;
Then rushing onwards, with a sweepy sway,
Bear flocks and folds, and lab'ring hinds away.
Nor safe their dwellings were, for, sapp'd by floods,
Their houses fell upon their household gods.
The solid piles, too strongly built to fall,
High o'er their heads behold a watry wall:
Now seas and earth were in confusion lost;
A world of waters, and without a coast.
One climbs a cliff; one in his boat is born:
And ploughs above, where late he sow'd his corn.
Others o'er chimney-tops and turrets row,
And drop their anchors on the meads below:
Or downward driv'n, they bruise the tender vine,
Or tost aloft, are knock'd against a pine.
And where of late the kids had cropt the grass,
The monsters of the deep now take their place.
Insulting Nereids on the cities ride,
And wond'ring dolphins o'er the palace glide.
On leaves, and masts of mighty oaks they browse;
And their broad fins entangle in the boughs.
The frighted wolf now swims amongst the sheep:
The yellow lion wanders in the deep:
His rapid force no longer helps the boar:
The stag swims faster than he ran before.
The fowls, long beating on their wings in vain,
Despair of land, and drop into the main.
Now hills and vales no more distinction know;
And levell'd nature lies oppress'd below.
The most of mortals perish in the flood:
The small remainder dies for want of food.
A mountain of stupendous height there stands
Betwixt th' Athenian and Bœotian lands,
The bound of fruitful fields, while fields they were,
But then a field of waters did appear:
Parnassus is its name; whose forky rise
Mounts thro' the clouds, and mates the lofty skies.
High on the summit of this dubious cliff,
Deucalion wafting, moor'd his little skiff.
He with his wife were only left behind
Of perish'd man; they two were human kind.
The mountain nymphs, and Themis they adore,
And from her oracles relief implore.
The most upright of mortal men was he;
The most sincere, and holy woman, she.
When Jupiter, surveying Earth from high,
Beheld it in a lake of water lie,
That where so many millions lately liv'd,
But two, the best of either sex, surviv'd;
He loos'd the nothern wind; fierce Boreas flies
To puff away the clouds, and purge the skies:
Serenely, while he blows, the vapours driv'n
Discover Heav'n to Earth, and Earth to Heav'n.
The billows fall, while Neptune lays his mace
On the rough sea, and smooths its furrow'd face.
Already Triton at his call appears
Above the waves; a Tyrian robe he wears;
And in his hand a crooked trumpet bears.
The sovereign bids him peaceful sounds inspire,
And give the waves the signal to retire.
His writhen shell he takes; whose narrow vent
Grows by degrees into a large extent;
Then gives it breath; the blast with doubling sound,
Runs the wide circuit of the world around:
The Sun first heard it, in his early east,
And met the rattling echos in the west.
The waters list'ning to the trumpet's roar,
Obey the summons, and forsake the shore.
A thin circumference of land appears;
And Earth, but not at once, her visage rears,
And peeps upon the seas from upper grounds;
The streams, but just contain'd within their bounds,
By slow degrees into their channels crawl;
And Earth increases, as the waters fall.
In longer time the tops of trees appear,
Which mud on their dishonour'd branches bear.
At length the world was all restor'd to view;
But desolate, and of a sickly hue:
Nature beheld herself, and stood aghast,
A dismal desert, and a silent waste.
Which when Deucalion, with a piteous look,
Beheld, he wept, and thus to Pyrrha spoke;

"Oh wife, oh sister, oh of all thy kind
The best, and only creature left behind,
By kindred, love, and now by dangers join'd;
Of multitudes, who breath'd the common air,
We two remain: a species in a pair:
The rest the seas have swallow'd; nor have we
Ev'n of this wretched life a certainty.
The clouds are still above; and while I speak,
A second deluge o'er our heads may break.
Should I be snatcht from hence, and thou remain,
Without relief, or partner of thy pain,
How couldst thou such a wretched life sustain?
Should I be left, and thou be lost, the sea,
That bury'd her I lov'd, should bury me.
Oh could our father his old arts inspire,
And make me heir of his informing fire,
That so I might abolish'd man retrieve,
And perish'd people in new souls might live!
But Heav'n is pleas'd, nor ought we to complain,
That we, th' examples of mankind, remain."
He said; the careful couple join their tears:
And then invoke the gods with pious prayers.
Thus, in devotion having eas'd their grief,
From sacred oracles they seek relief;
And to Cephisus' brook their way pursue:
The stream was troubled, but the ford they knew;
With living waters, in the fountain bred,
They sprinkle first their garments, and their head,
Then took the way, which to the temple led.
The roofs were all defil'd with moss and mire,
The desert altars void of solemn fire.
Before the gradual, prostrate they ador'd:
The pavement kiss'd; and thus the saint implor'd.
"O righteous Themis! if the pow'rs above
By pray'rs are bent to pity, and to love;
If human miseries can move their mind;
If yet they can forget, and yet be kind;
Tell how we may restore, by second birth,
Mankind, and people desolated Earth."
Then thus the gracious goddess, nodding, said;
"Depart, and with your vestments veil your head:
And stooping lowly down, with loosen'd zones,
Throw each behind your backs, your mighty mother's bones."
Amaz'd the pair, and mute with wonder, stand,
'Till Pyrrha first refus'd the dire command.
"Forbid it Heav'n," said she, "that I should tear
Those holy relics from the sepulchre."
They ponder'd the mysterious words again,
For some new sense; and long they sought in vain:
At length Deucalion clear'd his cloudy brow,
And said, "The dark enigma will allow
A meaning, which if well I understand,
From sacrilege will free the god's command:
This Earth our mighty mother is, the stones
In her capacious body are her bones:
These we must cast behind." With hope, and fear,
The woman did the new solution hear:
The man diffides in his own augury,
And doubts the gods; yet both resolve to try.
Descending from the mount, they first unbind
Their vests, and veil'd they cast the stones behind;
The stones (a miracle to mortal view,
But long tradition makes it pass for true)
Did first the rigour of their kind expel,
And suppled into softness as they fell;
Then swell'd, and swelling, by degrees grew warm,
And took the rudiments of human form;
Imperfect shapes: in marble such are seen,
When the rude chisel does the man begin;
While yet the roughness of the stone remains,
Without the rising muscles, and the veins.
The sappy parts, and next resembling juice,
Were turn'd to moisture, for the body's use:
Supplying humours, blood, and nourishment;
The rest, too solid to receive a bent,
Converts to bones; and what was once a vein,
Its former name and nature did retain.
By help of pow'r divine, in little space,
What the man threw, assum'd a manly face;
And what the wife, renew'd the female race.
Hence we derive our nature; born to bear
Laborious life; and harden'd into care.
The rest of animals, from teeming earth
Produc'd, in various forms receiv'd their birth.
The native moisture, in its close retreat,
Digested by the Sun's ethereal heat,
As in a kindly womb, began to breed:
Then swell'd, and quicken'd by the vital seed.
And some in less, and some in longer space,
Were ripen'd into form, and took a sev'ral face.
Thus when the Nile from Pharian fields is fled,
And seeks, with ebbing tides, his ancient bed,
The fat manure with heav'nly fire is warm'd;
And crusted creatures, as in wombs, are form'd;
These, when they turn the glebe, the peasants find;
Some rude, and yet unfinish'd in their kind:
Short of their limbs, a lame imperfect birth;
One half alive, and one of lifeless earth.
For heat, and moisture, when in bodies join'd,
The temper that results from either kind
Conception makes; and fighting till they mix,
Their mingled atoms in each other fix.
Thus Nature's hand the genial bed prepares
With friendly discord, and with fruitful wars.
From hence the surface of the ground with mud
And slime besmear'd (the feces of the flood)
Receiv'd the rays of Heav'n; and sucking in
The seeds of heat, new creatures did begin:
Some were of several sorts produc'd before,
But of new monsters Earth created more.
Unwillingly, but yet she brought to light
Thee, Python too, the wond'ring world to fright,
And the new nations, with so dire a sight:
So monstrous was his bulk, so large a space
Did his vast body, and long train embrace.
Whom Phœbus basking on a bank espy'd;
Ere now the god his arrows had not try'd,
But on the trembling deer, or mountain goat;
At this new quarry he prepares to shoot.
Though every shaft took place, he spent the store
Of his full quiver; and 'twas long before
Th' expiring serpent wallow'd in his gore.
Then, to preserve the fame of such a deed,
For Python slain, he Pythian games decreed,
Where noble youths for mastership should strive,
To quoit, to run, and steeds and chariots drive
The prize was fame: In witness of renown
An oaken garland did the victor crown.
The laurel was not yet for triumphs born;
But every green alike by Phœbus worn
Did, with promiscuous grace, his flowing locks adorn.

THE TRANSFORMATION OF DAPHNE INTO A LAUREL.

THE first and fairest of his loves was she,
Whom not blind Fortune, but the dire decree
Of angry Cupid forc'd him to desire:
Daphne her name, and Peneus was her sire.

Swell'd with the pride, that new success attends,
He sees the stripling, while his bow he bends,
And thus insults him; "Thou lascivious boy,
Are arms like these for children to employ?
Know, such achievements are my proper claim;
Due to my vigour, and unerring aim:
Resistless are my shafts, and Python late
In such a feather'd death, has found his fate.
Take up thy torch, (and lay my weapons by)
With that the feeble souls of lovers fry."
To whom the son of Venus thus reply'd,
"Phœbus, thy shafts are sure on all beside,
But mine on Phœbus: mine the fame shall be
Of all thy conquests, when I conquer thee."
He said, and soaring, swiftly wing'd his flight:
Nor stopt but on Parnassus' airy height.
Two diff'rent shafts he from his quiver draws;
One to repel desire, and one to cause.
One shaft is pointed with refulgent gold;
To bribe the love, and make the lover bold:
One blunt, and tipt with lead, whose base allay
Provokes disdain, and drives desire away.
The blunted bolt against the nymph he drest:
But with the sharp transfixt Apollo's breast.
Th' enamour'd deity pursues the chase;
The scornful damsel shuns his loath'd embrace:
In hunting beasts of prey her youth employs;
And Phœbe rivals in her rural joys.
With naked neck she goes, and shoulders bare;
And with a fillet binds her flowing hair.
By many suitors sought, she mocks their pains,
And still her vow'd virginity maintains.
Impatient of a yoke, the name of bride
She shuns, and hates the joys she never try'd.
On wilds, and woods, she fixes her desire:
Nor knows what youth and kindly love inspire.
Her father chides her oft; "Thou ow'st,' says he,
"A husband to thyself, a son to me."
She, like a crime, abhors the nuptial bed:
She glows with blushes, and she hangs her head.
Then casting round his neck her tender arms,
Sooths him with blanishments and filial charms;
"Give me, my lord," said she, "to live, and die,
A spotless maid, without the marriage tie.
'Tis but a small request; I beg no more
Than what Diana's father gave before."
The good old sire was soften'd to consent;
But said her wish would prove her punishment:
For so much youth, and so much beauty join'd,
Oppos'd the state, which her desires design'd.
The god of light, aspiring to her bed,
Hopes what he seeks, with flattering fancies fed;
And is, by his own oracles, misled.
And as in empty fields the stubble burns,
Or nightly travellers, when day returns,
Their useless torches on dry hedges throw,
That catch the flames, and kindle all the row;
So burns the god, consuming in desire,
And feeding in his breast a fruitless fire:
Her well-turn'd neck he view'd (her neck was bare)
And on her shoulders her dishevel'd hair;
"Oh were it comb'd," said he, "with what a grace
Would every waving curl become her face!"
He view'd her eyes, like heav'nly lamps that shone,
He view'd her lips, too sweet to view alone,
Her taper fingers, and her panting breast;
He praises all he sees, and for the rest
Believes the beauties yet unseen are best.
Swift as the wind, the damsel fled away,
Nor did for these alluring speeches stay:
"Stay nymph," he cry'd, "I follow, not a foe.
Thus from the lion trips the trembling doe;
Thus from the wolf the frighten'd lamb removes,
And, from pursuing falcons, fearful doves;
Thou shunn'st a god, and shunn'st a god, that loves.
Ah, lest some thorn should pierce thy tender foot,
Or thou shouldst fall in flying my pursuit!
To sharp uneven ways thy steps decline;
Abate thy speed, and I will bate of mine.
Yet think from whom thou dost so rashly fly;
Nor basely born, nor shepherd's swain am I.
Perhaps thou know'st not my superior state;
And from that ignorance proceeds thy hate.
Me Claros, Delphos, Tenedos obey;
These hands the Patareian scepter sway.
The king of gods begot me: what shall be,
Or is, or ever was, in fate, I see.
Mine is th' invention of the charming lyre;
Sweet notes, and heav'nly numbers, I inspire.
Sure is my bow, unerring is my dart;
But ah! more deadly his, who pierc'd my heart.
Med'cine is mine; what herbs and simples grow
In fields and forests, all their pow'rs I know;
And am the great physician call'd, below.
Alas that fields and forests can afford
No remedies to heal their love-sick lord!
To cure the pains of love, no plant avails:
And his own physic the physician fails."
She heard not half; so furiously she flies;
And on her ear th' imperfect accent dies.
Fear gave her wings: and as she fled, the wind
Increasing, spread her flowing hair behind;
And left her legs and thighs expos'd to view:
Which made the god more eager to pursue.
The god was young, and was too hotly bent
To lose his time in empty compliment:
But, led by love, and fir'd with such a sight,
Impetuously pursu'd his near delight.
As when th' impatient greyhound, slipt from far,
Bounds o'er the glebe, to course the fearful hare,
She in her speed does all her safety lay,
And he with double speed pursues the prey;
O'er-runs her at her sitting turn, and licks
His chaps in vain, and blows upon the flix:
She 'scapes, and for the neighb'ring covert strives,
And gaining shelter doubts if yet she lives:
If little things with great we may compare,
Such was the god, and such the flying fair;
She urg'd by fear, her feet did swiftly move,
But he more swiftly, who was urg'd by love.
He gathers ground upon her in the chase:
Now breathes upon her hair, with nearer pace;
And just is fast'ning on the wish'd embrace.
The nymph grew pale, and in a mortal fright,
Spent with the labour of so long a flight;
And now despairing, cast a mournful look
Upon the streams of her paternal brook;
"Oh help," she cry'd, "in this extremest need!
If water-gods are deities indeed:
Gape, Earth, and this unhappy wretch intomb;
Or change my form, whence all my sorrows come."
Scarce had she finish'd, when her feet she found
Benumb'd with cold, and fasten'd to the ground:
A filmy rind about her body grows;
Her hair to leaves, her arms extend to boughs:
The nymph is all into a laurel gone;
The smoothness of her skin remain alone.
Yet Phœbus loves her still, and casting round
Her bole his arms, some little warmth he found.

The tree still panted in th' unfinish'd part:
Not wholly vegetive, and heav'd her heart.
He fixt his lips upon the trembling rind;
It swerv'd aside, and his embrace declin'd.
To whom the god, "Because thou canst not be
My mistress, I espouse thee for my tree:
Be thou the prize of honour and renown:
The deathless poet, and the poem, crown.
Thou shalt the Roman festivals adorn,
And, after poets, be by victors worn.
Thou shalt returning Cæsar's triumph grace;
When pomps shall in a long procession pass:
Wreath'd on the post before his palace wait;
And be the sacred guardian of the gate:
Secure from thunder, and unharm'd by Jove,
Unfading as th' immortal pow'rs above:
And as the locks of Phœbus are unshorn,
So shall perpetual green thy boughs adorn."
The grateful tree was pleas'd with what he said;
And shook the shady honours of her head.

THE TRANSFORMATION OF IŌ INTO A HEIFER.

An ancient forest in Thessalia grows;
Which Tempe's pleasing valley does enclose:
Through this the rapid Peneus takes his course;
From Pindus rolling with impetuous force:
Mists from the river's mighty fall arise;
And deadly damps enclose the cloudy skies;
Perpetual fogs are hanging o'er the wood;
And sounds of waters deaf the neighbourhood.
Deep, in a rocky cave, he makes abode:
(A mansion proper for a mourning god.)
Here he gives audience; issuing out decrees
To rivers, his dependent deities.
On this occasion hither they resort;
To pay their homage, and to make their court.
All doubtful, whether to congratulate
His daughter's honour, or lament her fate.
Sperchæus, crown'd with poplar, first appears;
Then old Apidanus came crown'd with years:
Enipeus turbulent, Amphrysos tame;
And Æas last with lagging waters came.
Then, of his kindred brooks, a num'rous throng
Condole his loss; and bring their urns along.
Not one was wanting of the wat'ry train,
That fill'd his flood, or mingled with the main,
But Inachus, who in his cave, alone,
Wept not another's losses, but his own;
For his dear Iō, whether stray'd, or dead,
To him uncertain, doubtful tears he shed.
He sought her through the world; but sought in vain;
And no where finding, rather fear'd her slain.
Her, just returning from her father's brook,
Jove had beheld, with a desiring look;
And, "Oh fair daughter of the flood," he said,
"Worthy alone of Jove's imperial bed,
Happy whoever shall those charms possess!
The king of gods (nor is thy lover less)
Invites thee to yon cooler shades; to shun
The scorching rays of the meridian Sun.
Nor shalt thou tempt the dangers of the grove
Alone, without a guide; thy guide is Jove.
No puny pow'r, but he whose high command
Is unconfin'd, who rules the seas and land;
And tempers thunder in his awful hand.
Oh, fly not:" for she fled from his embrac
O'er Lerna's pastures: he pursu'd the chase
Along the shades of the Lyrcæan plain;
At length the god, who never asks in vain,
Involv'd with vapours, imitating night,
Both air and earth; and then suppress'd her flight,
And mingling force with love, enjoy'd the full delight.
Mean-time the jealous Juno, from on high,
Survey'd the fruitful fields of Arcady;
And wonder'd that the mist should over-run
The face of day-light, and obscure the Sun.
No nat'ral cause she found, from brooks, or bogs,
Or marshy lowlands, to produce the fogs:
Then round the skies she sought for Jupiter,
Her faithless husband; but no Jove was there:
Suspecting now the worst, "Or I," she said,
"Am much mistaken, or am much betray'd."
With fury she precipitates her flight:
Dispels the shadows of dissembled night;
And to the day restores his native light.
Th' almighty leacher, careful to prevent
The consequence, foreseeing her descent,
Transforms his mistress in a trice; and now
In Iō's place appears a lovely cow.
So sleek her skin, so faultless was her make,
Ev'n Juno did unwilling pleasure take
To see so fair a rival of her love;
And what she was, and whence, inquir'd of Jove:
Of what fair herd, and from what pedigree?
The god, half caught, was forc'd upon a lie:
And said she sprung from earth. She took the word,
And begg'd the beauteous heifer of her lord.
What should he do? 'twas equal shame to Jove
Or to relinquish, or betray his love:
Yet to refuse so slight a gift, would be
But more t' increase his consort's jealousy;
Thus fear, and love, by turns, his heart assail'd;
And stronger love had sure, at length, prevail'd:
But some faint hope remain'd, his jealous queen
Had not the mistress through the heifer seen.
The cautious goddess, of her gift possest,
Yet harbour'd anxious thoughts within her breast;
As she who knew the falsehood of her Jove;
And justly fear'd some new relapse of love.
Which to prevent, and to secure her care,
To trusty Argus she commits the fair.
The head of Argus (as with stars the skies)
Was compass'd round, and wore a hundred eyes.
But two by turns their lids in slumber steep;
The rest on duty still their station keep;
Nor could the total constellation sleep.
Thus, ever present to his eyes and mind,
His charge was still before him, though behind.
In fields he suffer'd her to feed by day,
But when the setting Sun to night gave way,
The captive cow he summon'd with a call;
And drove her back, and ty'd her to the stall.
On leaves of trees, and bitter herbs she fed,
Heav'n was her canopy, bare earth her bed;
So hardly lodg'd; and to digest her food,
She drank from troubled streams, defil'd with mud.
Her woeful story fain she would have told,
With hands upheld, but had no hands to hold.
Her head to her ungentle keeper bow'd,
She strove to speak, she spoke not, but she low'd:
Affrighted with the noise, she look'd around,
And seem'd t' inquire the author of the sound.
Once on the banks where often she had play'd
(Her father's banks) she came, and there survey'd
Her alter'd visage, and her branching head;
And starting, from herself she would have fled.

Her fellow nymphs, familiar to her eyes,
Beheld, but knew her not in this disguise.
Ev'n Inachus himself was ignorant;
And in his daughter did his daughter want.
She follow'd where her fellows went, as she
Were still a partner of the company:
They stroke her neck; the gentle heifer stands,
And her neck offers to their stroking hands.
Her father gave her grass; the grass she took;
And lick'd his palms, and cast a piteous look;
And in the language of her eyes she spoke.
She would have told her name, and ask'd relief,
But wanting words, in tears she tells her grief.
Which, with her foot she makes him understand:
And prints the name of Iȏ in the sand.
"Ah wretched me!" her mournful father cry'd;
She, with a sigh, to wretched me reply'd:
About her milk-white neck his arms he threw;
And wept, and then these tender words ensue.
"And art thou she, whom I have sought around
The world, and have at length so sadly found?
So found, is worse than lost: with mutual words
Thou answer'st not, no voice thy tongue affords:
But sighs are deeply drawn from out thy breast;
And speech deny'd, by lowing is express'd.
Unknowing, I prepar'd thy bridal bed;
With empty hopes of happy issue fed.
But now the husband of a herd must be
Thy mate, and bell'wing sons thy progeny.
Oh, were I mortal, death might bring relief;
But now my godhead but extends my grief;
Prolongs my woes, of which no end I see,
And makes me curse my immortality!"
More had he said, but fearful of her stay,
The starry guardian drove his charge away,
To some fresh pasture; on a hilly height
He sat himself, and kept her still in sight.

THE EYES OF ARGUS TRANSFORMED INTO A PEACOCK'S TRAIN.

Now Jove no longer could her suff'rings bear:
But call'd in haste his airy messenger,
The son of Maïa, with severe decree
To kill the keeper, and to set her free.
With all his harness soon the god was sped,
His flying hat was fasten'd on his head;
Wings on his heels were hung, and in his hand
He holds the virtue of the snaky wand.
The liquid air his moving pinions wound,
And, in the moment, shoot him on the ground.
Before he came in sight, the crafty god
His wings dismiss'd, but still retain'd his rod:
That sleep-procuring wand wise Hermes took,
But made it seem to sight a shepherd's hook.
With this, he did a herd of goats control;
Which by the way he met, and slily stole.
Clad like a country swain, he pip'd, and sung:
And playing, drove his jolly troop along.
With pleasure, Argus the musician heeds;
But wonders much at those new vocal reeds.
"And whosoe'er thou art, my friend," said he,
"Up hither drive thy goats, and play by me:
This hill has browze for them, and shade for thee."
The god, who was with ease induc'd to climb,
Began discourse to pass away the time;
And still betwixt, his tuneful pipe he plies;
And watch'd his hour, to close the keeper's eyes.
With much ado, he partly kept awake;
Not suff'ring all his eyes repose to take:
And ask'd the stranger, who did reeds invent,
And whence began so rare an instrument?

THE TRANSFORMATION OF SYRINX INTO REEDS.

Then Hermes thus; "A nymph of late there was,
Whose heav'nly form her fellows did surpass.
The pride and joy of fair Arcadia's plains,
Belov'd by deities, ador'd by swains:
Syrinx her name, by Sylvans oft pursu'd,
As oft she did the lustful gods delude:
The rural, and the woodland pow'rs disdain'd;
With Cynthia hunted, and her rites maintain'd:
Like Phœbe clad, even Phœbe's self she seems,
So tall, so straight, such well-proportion'd limbs:
The nicest eye did no distinction know,
But that the goddess bore a golden bow:
Distinguish'd thus, the sight she cheated too.
Descending from Lycæus, Pan admires
The matchless nymph, and burns with new desires.
A crown of pine upon his head he wore;
And thus began her pity to implore.
But ere he thus began, she took her flight
So swift, she was already out of sight.
Nor stay'd to hear the courtship of the god;
But bent her course to Ladon's gentle flood:
There by the river stopt, and tir'd before,
Relief from water-nymphs her pray'rs implore.
"Now while the lustful god, with speedy pace,
Just thought to strain her in a strict embrace,
He fills his arms with reeds, new-rising on the place.
And while he sighs, his ill success to find,
The tender canes were shaken by the wind;
And breath'd a mournful air, unheard before;
That much surprising Pan, yet pleas'd him more.
Admiring this new music, 'Thou,' he said,
'Who canst not be the partner of my bed,
At least shalt be the comfort of my mind:
And often, often to my lips be join'd.'
He form'd the reeds, proportion'd as they are,
Unequal in their length, and wax'd with care,
They still retain the name of his ungrateful fair."
While Hermes pip'd, and sung, and told his tale,
The keeper's winking eyes began to fail,
And drowsy slumber on the lids to creep;
'Till all the watchman was at length asleep.
Then soon the god his voice and song suppress;
And with his pow'rful rod confirm'd his rest:
Without delay his crooked falchion drew,
And at one fatal stroke the keeper slew.
Down from the rock fell the dissever'd head,
Opening its eyes in death; and falling, bled;
And mark'd the passage with a crimson trail:
Thus Argus lies in pieces, cold and pale;
And all his hundred eyes, with all their light,
Are clos'd at once, in one perpetual night.
These Juno takes, that they no more may fail,
And spreads them in her peacock's gaudy tail.
Impatient to revenge her injur'd bed,
She wreaks her anger on her rival's head;
With furies frights her from her native home;
And drives her gadding, round the world to roam:
Nor ceas'd her madness and her flight before
She touch'd the limits of the Pharian shore.
At length, arriving on the banks of Nile,
Wearied with length of ways, and worn with toil,
She laid her down; and leaning on her knees,
Invok'd the cause of all her miseries:
And cast her languishing regards above
For help from Heav'n, and her ungrateful Jove.

She sigh'd, she wept, she low'd: 'twas all she could;
And with unkindness seem'd to tax the god.
Last, with an humble pray'r, she begg'd repose,
Or death at least, to finish all her woes.
Jove heard her vows, and with a flatt'ring look,
In her behalf to jealous Juno spoke.
He cast his arms about her neck, and said,
"Dame, rest secure; no more thy nuptial bed
This nymph shall violate: by Styx I swear,
And every oath that binds the thunderer."
The goddess was appeas'd; and at the word
Was Iö to her former shape restor'd,
The rugged hair began to fall away;
The sweetness of her eyes did only stay,
Tho' not so large; her crooked horns decrease;
The wideness of her jaws and nostrils cease:
Her hoofs to hands return, in little space:
The five long taper fingers take their place,
And nothing of the heifer now is seen,
Beside the native whiteness of the skin.
Erected on her feet she walks again:
And two the duty of the four sustain.
She tries her tongue; her silence softly breaks,
And fears her former lowings when she speaks:
A goddess now, through all th' Egyptian state:
And serv'd by priests, who in white linen wait.
   Her son was Epaphus, at length believ'd
The son of Jove, and as a god receiv'd;
With sacrifice ador'd, and public pray'rs,
He common temples with his mother shares.
Equal in years, and rival in renown
With Epaphus, the youthful Phaëton,
Like honour claims; and boasts his sire the Sun.
His haughty looks, and his assuming air,
The son of Isis could no longer bear:
"Thou tak'st thy mother's word too far," said he,
"And hast usurp'd thy boasted pedigree.
Go, base pretender to a borrow'd name."
Thus tax'd, he blush'd with anger, and with shame;
But shame repress'd his rage: the daunted youth
Soon seeks his mother, and inquires the truth:
"Mother," said he, "this infamy was thrown
By Epaphus on you, and me your son.
He spoke in public, told it to my face;
Nor durst I vindicate the dire disgrace:
Even I, the bold, the sensible of wrong,
Restrain'd by shame, was forc'd to hold my tongue.
To hear an open slander, is a curse:
But not to find an answer, is a worse.
If I am Heav'n-begot, assert your son
By some sure sign; and make my father known,
To right my honour, and redeem your own."
He said, and saying cast his arms about
Her neck, and begg'd her to resolve the doubt.
   'Tis hard to judge if Clymenè were mov'd
More by his pray'r, whom she so dearly lov'd,
Or more with fury fir'd, to find her name
Traduc'd, and made the sport of common fame.
She stretch'd her arms to Heav'n, and fix'd her eyes
On that fair planet that adorns the skies;
"Now by those beams," said she, "whose holy fires
Consume my breast, and kindle my desires;
By him, who sees us both, and cheers our sight,
By him, the public minister of light,
I swear that Sun begot thee; if I lie,
Let him his cheerful influence deny:
Let him no more this perjur'd creature see;
And shine on all the world but only me.
If still you doubt your mother's innocence,
His eastern mansion is not far from hence;
With little pains you to his levee go,
And from himself your parentage may know."
With joy th' ambitious youth his mother heard,
And eager for the journey soon prepar'd.
He longs the world beneath him to survey;
To guide the chariot; and to give the day:
From Meroe's burning sands he bends his course,
Nor less in India feels his father's force;
His travel urging, till he came in sight;
And saw the palace by the purple light.

OVID'S METAMORPHOSES.

BOOK II.

Translated by Addison.

THE STORY OF PHAETON.

THE Sun's bright palace, on high columns rais'd,
With burnish'd gold and flaming jewels blaz'd;
The folding gates diffus'd a silver light,
And with a milder gleam refresh'd the sight;
Of polish'd iv'ry was the cov'ring wrought;
The matter vied not with the sculptor's thought;
For in the portal was display'd on high
(The work of Vulcan) a fictitious sky;
A waving sea th' inferior earth embrac'd,
And gods and goddesses the waters grac'd.
Ægeon here a mighty whale bestrode;
Triton, and Proteus, (the deceiving god)
With Doris here were carv'd, and all her train,
Some loosely swimming in the figur'd main,
While some on rocks their drooping hair divide,
And some on fishes through the waters glide:
Though various features did the sisters grace,
A sister's likeness was in ev'ry face.
On earth a diff'rent landscape courts the eyes,
Men, towns, and beasts in distant prospect rise,
And nymphs, and streams, and woods, and rural deities.
O'er all, the Heav'ns refulgent image shines;
On either gate were six engraven signs.
   Here Phaëton, still gaining on th' ascent
To his suspected father's palace went,
'Till pressing forward through the bright abode,
He saw at distance the illustrious god:
He saw at distance, or the dazzling light
Had flash'd too strongly on his aching sight.
   The god sits high, exalted on a throne
Of blazing gems, with purple garments on;
The Hours in order rang'd on either hand,
And Days, and Months, and Years, and Ages stand,
Here Spring appears with flowery chaplets bound;
Here Summer in her wheaten garland crown'd;
Here Autumn the rich trodden grapes besmear;
And hoary Winter shivers in the rear.
   Phœbus beheld the youth from off his throne;
That eye, which looks on all, was fix'd on one.
He saw the boy's confusion in his face,
Surpris'd at all the wonders of the place;
And cries aloud, "What wants my son? for know
My son thou art, and I must call thee so."
   "Light of the world!" the trembling youth replies;
"Illustrious parent! since you don't despise
The parent's name, some certain token give,
That I may Clymenè's proud boast believe,
Nor longer under false reproaches grieve."
   The tender sire was touch'd with what he said,
And flung the blaze of glories from his head,

And bid the youth advance: "My son," said he,
"Come to thy fathers arms! for Clymenè
Has told thee true; a parent's name I own,
And deem thee worthy to be eall'd my son.
As a sure proof, make some request, and I,
Whate'er it be, with that request comply;
By Styx I swear, whose waves are hid in night,
And roll impervious to my piercing sight."
The youth, transported, asks, without delay,
To guide the Sun's bright chariot for a day.
The god repented of the oath he took,
For anguish thrice his radiant head he shook;
"My son," says he, "some other proof require,
Rash was my promise, rash is thy desire.
I'd fain deny this wish, which thou hast made,
Or, what I can't deny, would fain dissuade.
Too vast and hazardous the task appears,
Nor suited to thy strength, nor to thy years.
Thy lot is mortal, but thy wishes fly
Beyond the province of mortality:
There is not one of all the gods that dares
(However skill'd in other great affairs)
To mount the burning axle-tree, but I;
Not Jove himself the ruler of the sky,
That hurls the three-fork'd thunder from above,
Dares try his strength: yet who so strong as Jove?
The steeds climb up the first ascent with pain,
And when the middle firmament they gain,
If downward from the Heav'ns my head I bow,
And see the earth and ocean hang below,
Ev'n I am seiz'd with horrour and affright,
And my own heart misgives me at the sight.
A mighty downfall steeps the ev'ning stage,
And steady reins must curb the horses' rage.
Tethys herself has fear'd to see me driv'n
Down headlong from the precipice of Heav'n.
Besides, consider what impetuous force
Turns stars and planets in a diff'rent course.
I steer against their motions; nor am I
Born back by all the current of the sky.
But how could you resist the orbs that roll
In adverse whirls, and stem the rapid pole?
But you perhaps may hope for pleasing woods,
And stately domes, and cities fill'd with gods;
While through a thousand snares your progress lies,
Where forms of starry monsters stock the skies:
For, should you hit the doubtful way aright,
The Bull with stooping horns stands opposite;
Next him the bright Hæmonian Bow is strung,
And next, the Lion's grinning visage hung:
The Scorpion's claws here clasp a wide extent;
And here the Crab's in lesser clasps are bent.
Nor would you find it easy to compose
The mettled steeds, when from their nostrils flows
The scorching fire, that in their entrails glows.
Ev'n I their headstrong fury scarce restrain,
When they grow warm and restiff to the rein.
Let not my son a fatal gift require,
But, O! in time, recal your rash desire;
You ask a gift that may your parent tell,
Let these my fears your parentage reveal;
And learn a father from a father's care;
Look on my face; or if my heart lay bare,
Could you but look, you'd read the father there.
Choose out a gift from seas, or earth, or skies,
For open to your wish all nature lies,
Only decline this one unequal task,
For 'tis a mischief, not a gift, you ask.
You ask a real mischief, Phaëton:
Nay hang not thus about my neck, my son:
I grant your wish, and Styx has heard my voice,
Choose what you will, but make a wiser choice."
Thus did the god th' unwary youth advise;
But he still longs to travel through the skies.
When the fond father (for in vain he pleads)
At length to the Vulcanian chariot leads.
A golden axle did the work uphold,
Gold was the beam, the wheels were orb'd with gold.
The spokes in rows of silver pleas'd the sight,
The seat with party-colour'd gems was bright;
Apollo shin'd amid the glare of light.
The youth with secret joy the work surveys,
When now the Moon disclos'd her purple rays;
The stars were fled, for Lucifer had chas'd
The stars away, and fled himself at last.
Soon as the father saw the rosy Morn,
And the Moon shining with a blunter horn,
He bid the nimble Hours, without delay,
Bring forth the steeds; the nimble Hours obey:
From their full racks the gen'rous steeds retire,
Dropping ambrosial foams, and snorting fire.
Still anxious for his son, the god of day,
To make him proof against the burning ray,
His temples with celestial ointment wet,
Of sov'reign virtue to repel the heat;
Then fix'd the beamy circle on his head,
And fetch'd a deep foreboding sigh, and said,
"Take this at least, this last advice, my son,
Keep a stiff rein, and move but gently on:
The coursers of themselves will run too fast,
Your art must be to moderate their haste.
Drive them not on directly through the skies,
But where the zodiac's winding circle lies,
Along the midmost zone; but sally forth
Nor to the distant south, nor stormy north.
The horses' hoofs a beaten track will show,
But neither mount too high nor sink too low,
That no new fires or Heaven or Earth infest;
Keep the mid way, the middle way is best.
Nor, where in radiant folds the serpent twines,
Direct your course, nor where the altar shines.
Shun both extremes; the rest let Fortune guide,
And better for thee than thyself provide!
See, while I speak, the shades disperse away,
Aurora gives the promise of a day;
I'm call'd, nor can I make a longer stay.
Snatch up the reins; or still th' attempt forsake,
And not my chariot, but my counsel, take,
While yet securely on the earth you stand;
Nor touch the horses with too rash a hand.
Let me alone to light the world, while you
Enjoy those beams which you may safely view."
He spoke in vain; the youth with active heat
And sprighty vigour vaults into the seat;
And joys to hold the reins, and fondly gives
Those thanks his father with remorse receives.
Meanwhile the restless horses neigh'd aloud,
Breathing out fire, and pawing where they stood.
Tethys, not knowing what had past, gave way,
And all the waste of Heav'n before them lay.
They spring together out, and swiftly bear
The flying youth through clouds and yielding air;
With wingy speed outstrip the eastern wind,
And leave the breezes of the Morn behind.
The youth was light, nor could he fill the seat,
Or poise the chariot with its wonted weight:

But as at sea th' unballast'd vessel rides,
Cast to and fro, the sport of winds and tides;
So in the bounding chariot toss'd on high,
The youth is hurry'd headlong through the sky.
Soon as the steeds perceive it, they forsake
Their stated course, and leave the beaten track.
The youth was in a maze, nor did he know
Which way to turn the reins, or where to go;
Nor would the horses, had he known, obey.
Then the Seven Stars first felt Apollo's ray,
And wish'd to dip in the forbidden sea.
The folded Serpent next the frozen pole,
Stiff and benumb'd before, began to roll,
And rag'd with inward heat, and threaten'd war,
And shot a redder light from every star;
Nay, and 'tis said, Boötes, too, that fain
Thou wouldst have fled, though cumber'd with thy wain.

Th' unhappy youth then, bending down his head,
Saw earth and ocean far beneath him spread.
His colour chang'd, he startled at the sight,
And his eyes darken'd by too great a light.
Now could he wish the fiery steeds untry'd,
His birth obscure, and his request deny'd:
Now would he Merops for his father own,
And quit his boasted kindred to the Sun.

So fares the pilot, when his ship is tost
In troubled seas, and all its steerage lost;
He gives her to the winds, and in despair
Seeks his last refuge in the gods and pray'r.

What could he do? his eyes, if backward cast,
Find a long path he had already past;
If forward, still a longer path they find:
Both he compares, and measures in his mind;
And sometimes casts an eye upon the east,
And sometimes looks on the forbidden west.
The horses' names he knew not in the fright,
Nor would he loose the reins, nor could he hold them right.

Now all the horrours of the Heav'ns he spies,
And monstrous shadows of prodigious size,
That, deck'd with stars, lie scatter'd o'er the skies.
There is a place above, where Scorpio bent
In tail and arms surrounds a vast extent;
In a wide circuit of the Heav'ns he shines,
And fills the space of two celestial signs.
Soon as the youth beheld him vex'd with heat
Brandish his sting, and in his poison sweat,
Half dead with sudden fear he dropt the reins;
The horses felt them loose upon their manes,
And, flying out through all the plains above,
Ran uncontrol'd where'er their fury drove;
Rush'd on the stars, and through a pathless way
Of unknown regions hurry'd on the day.
And now above, and now below they flew,
And near the Earth the burning chariot drew.

The clouds disperse in fumes, the wond'ring Moon
Beholds her brother's steeds beneath her own;
The highlands smoke, cleft by the piercing rays,
Or, clad with woods, in their own fuel blaze.
Next o'er the plains, where ripen'd harvests grow,
The running conflagration spreads below.
But these are trivial ills: whole cities burn,
And peopled kingdoms into ashes turn.

The mountains kindle as the car draws near,
Athos and Tmolus red with fires appear;
Œagrian Hæmus (then a single name)
And virgin Helicon increase the flame;
Taurus and Oetè glare amid the sky,
And Ida, spite of all her fountains, dry.
Erynx, and Othrys, and Cithæron, glow
And Rhodopè, no longer cloth'd in snow;
High Pindus, Mimas, and Parnassus sweat,
And Ætna rages with redoubled heat.
Ev'n Scythia, through her hoary regions warm'd,
In vain with all her native frost was arm'd.
Cover'd with flames the tow'ring Apennine,
And Caucasus, and proud Olympus, shine;
And, where the long-extended Alps aspire,
Now stands a huge continued range of fire.

Th' astonish'd youth, where'er his eyes could turn,
Beheld the universe around him burn:
The world was in a blaze; nor could he bear
The sultry vapours and the scorching air,
Which from below, as from a furnace, flow'd;
And now the axle-tree beneath him glow'd:
Lost in the whirling clouds that round him broke,
And white with ashes, hov'ring in the smoke,
He flew where'er the horses drove, nor knew
Whither the horses drove, or where he flew.

'Twas then, they say, the swarthy Moor begun
To change his hue, and blacken in the Sun.
Then Libya first, of all her moisture drain'd,
Became a barren waste, a wild of sand.
The water-nymphs lament their empty urns,
Bœotia, robb'd of silver Dirce, mourns,
Corinth Pyrene's wasted spring bewails,
And Argos grieves whilst Amymonè fails.

The floods are drain'd from every distant coast,
Ev'n Tanais, though fix'd in ice, was lost.
Enrag'd Caïcus and Lycormas roar,
And Xanthus, fated to be burnt once more.
The fam'd Mæander, that unweary'd strays
Through mazy windings, smokes in ev'ry maze.
From his lov'd Babylon Euphrates flies;
The big-swoln Ganges and the Danube rise
In thick'ning fumes, and darken half the skies.
In flames Ismenos and the Phasis roll'd,
And Tagus floating in his melted gold.
The swans, that on Cäyster often try'd
Their tuneful songs, now sung their last, and dy'd.
The frighted Nile ran off, and under ground
Conceal'd his head, nor can it yet be found:
His seven divided currents all are dry,
And where they row'd seven gaping trenches lie:
No more the Rhine or Rhone their course maintain,
Nor Tiber, of his promis'd empire vain.

The ground, deep-cleft, admits the dazzling ray,
And startles Pluto with the flash of day.
The seas shrink in, and to the sight disclose
Wide naked plains, where once the billows rose;
Their rocks are all discover'd, and increase
The number of the scatter'd Cyclades.
The fish in shoals about the bottom creep,
Nor longer dares the crooked dolphin leap:
Gasping for breath, th' unshapen phocæ die,
And on the boiling wave extended lie.
Nereus, and Doris with her virgin train,
Seek out the last recesses of the main;
Beneath unfathomable depths they faint,
And secret in their gloomy caverns pant.
Stern Neptune thrice above the waves upheld
His face, and thrice was by the flames repell'd.

The Earth at length, on every side embrac'd
With scalding seas that floated round her waste,
When now she felt the springs and rivers come,
And crowd within the hollow of her womb,

Up-lifted to the Heav'ns her blasted head,
And clapt her hand upon her brows, and said;
(But first, impatient of the sultry heat,
Sunk deeper down, and sought a cooler seat:)
"If you, great king of gods, my death approve,
And I deserve it, let me die by Jove;
If I must perish by the force of fire,
Let me transfix'd with thunder-bolts expire.
See, whilst I speak, my breath the vapours choke,"
(For now her face lay wrapt in clouds of smoke)
"See my sing'd hair, behold my faded eye,
And wither'd face, where heaps of cinders lie!
And does the plough for this my body tear?
This the reward for all the fruits I bear,
Tortur'd with rakes, and harass'd all the year?
That herbs for cattle daily I renew,
And food for man and frankincense for you?
But grant me guilty, what has Neptune done?
Why are his waters boiling in the Sun?
The wavy empire, which by lot was giv'n,
Why does it waste, and further shrink from Heav'n?
If I nor he your pity can provoke,
See your own Heav'ns, the Heav'ns begin to smoke!
Should once the sparkles catch those bright abodes,
Destruction seizes on the Heav'ns and gods;
Atlas becomes unequal to his freight,
And almost faints beneath the glowing weight.
If Heav'n, and earth, and sea, together burn,
All must again into their chaos turn.
Apply some speedy cure, prevent our fate,
And succour Nature, ere it be too late."
She ceas'd, for, chok'd with vapours round her spread,
Down to the deepest shades she sunk her head.
Jove call'd to witness ev'ry pow'r above,
And ev'n the god, whose son the chariot drove,
That what he acts he is compell'd to do,
Or universal ruin must ensue.
Straight he ascends the high etherial throne,
From whence he us'd to dart his thunder down,
From whence his show'rs and storms he us'd to pour,
But now could meet with neither storm nor show'r
Then, aiming at the youth, with lifted hand,
Full at his head he hurl'd the forky brand,
In dreadful thund'rings. Thus th' almighty sire
Suppress'd the raging of the fires with fire.
At once from life and from the chariot driv'n,
Th' ambitious boy fell thunder-struck from Heav'n.
The horses started with a sudden bound,
And flung the reins and chariot to the ground:
The studded harness from their necks they broke,
Here fell a wheel, and here a silver spoke,
Here were the beam and axle torn away;
And, scatter'd o'er the Earth, the shining fragments lay.
The breathless Phaëton, with flaming hair,
Shot from the chariot, like a falling star,
That in a summer's evening from the top
Of Heav'n drops down, or seems at least to drop:
Till on the Po his blasted corps was hurl'd,
Far from his country, in the western world.

PHAETON'S SISTERS TRANSFORMED INTO TREES.

The Latian nymphs came round him, and amaz'd,
On the dead youth, transfix'd with thunder, gaz'd,
And, whilst yet smoking from the bolt he lay,
His shatter'd body to a tomb convey,
And o'er the tomb an epitaph devise:
"Here he who drove the Sun's bright chariot lies;
His father's fiery steeds he could not guide,
But in the glorious enterprise he dy'd."
Apollo hid his face, and pin'd for grief,
And, if the story may deserve belief,
The space of one whole day is said to run,
From morn to wonted ev'n, without a Sun:
The burning ruins, with a fainter ray,
Supply the Sun, and counterfeit a day,
A day, that still did Nature's face disclose:
This comfort from the mighty mishief rose.
But Clymenè, enrag'd with grief, laments,
And as her grief inspires, her passion vents:
Wild for her son, and frantic in her woes,
With hair dishevel'd round the world she goes,
To seek where'er his body might be cast;
'Till, on the borders of the Po, at last
The name inscrib'd on the new tomb appears.
The dear dear name she bathes in flowing tears,
Hangs o'er the tomb, unable to depart,
And hugs the marble to her throbbing heart.
Her daughters too lament, and sigh, and mourn,
(A fruitless tribute to their brother's urn)
And beat their naked bosoms, and complain,
And call aloud for Phaëton in vain:
All the long night their mournful watch they keep,
And all the day stand round the tomb, and weep.
Four times, revolving, the full Moon return'd;
So long the mother and the daughters mourn'd:
When now the eldest, Phaëthusa, strove
To rest her weary limbs, but could not move;
Lampetia would have help'd her, but she found
Herself withheld, and rooted to the ground:
A third in wild affliction, as she grieves,
Would rend her hair, but fills her hands with leaves;
One sees her thighs transform'd, another views
Her arms shot out, and branching into boughs.
And now their legs, and breasts, and bodies stood
Crusted with bark, and hard'ning into wood;
But still above were female heads display'd,
And mouths, that call'd their mother to their aid.
What could, alas! the weeping mother do?
From this to that with eager haste she flew,
And kiss'd her sprouting daughters as they grew.
She tears the bark that to each body cleaves,
And from their verdant fingers strips the leaves:
The blood came trickling, where she tore away
The leaves and bark: the maids were heard to say,
"Forbear, mistaken parent, oh! forbear;
A wounded daughter in each tree you tear;
Farewell for ever." Here the bark increas'd,
Clos'd on their faces, and their words suppress'd.
The new-made trees in tears of amber run,
Which, harden'd into value by the Sun,
Distil for ever on the streams below:
The limpid streams their radiant treasure show,
Mix'd in the sand; whence the rich drops convey'd
Shine in the dress of the bright Latian maid.

THE TRANSFORMATION OF CYCNUS INTO A SWAN.

Cycnus beheld the nymphs transform'd, ally'd
To their dead brother on the mortal side,
In friendship and affection nearer bound;
He left the cities and the realms he own'd,
Thro' pathless fields and lonely shores to range,
And woods made thicker by the sisters' change.
Whilst here, within the dismal gloom, alone,
The melancholy monarch made his moan,
His voice was lessen'd as he try'd to speak,
And issu'd through a long-extended neck;

His hair transforms to down, his fingers meet
In skinny films, and shape his oary feet;
From both his sides the wings and feathers break;
And from his mouth proceeds a blunted beak:
All Cycnus now into a swan was turn'd,
Who, still rememb'ring how his kinsman burn'd,
To solitary pools and lakes retires,
And loves the waters as oppos'd to fires.
Mean while Apollo in the gloomy shade
(The native lustre of his brows decay'd)
Indulging sorrow, sickens at the sight
Of his own sun-shine, and abhors the light:
The hidden griefs, that in his bosom rise,
Sadden his looks, and over-cast his eyes:
As when some dusky orb obstructs his ray,
And sullies in a dim eclipse the day.
Now secretly with inward griefs he pin'd,
Now warm resentments to his griefs he join'd,
And now renounc'd his office to mankind.
"E'er since the birth of time," said he, "I've born
A long ungrateful toil, without return;
Let now some other manage, if he dare,
The fiery steeds, and mount the burning car;
Or, if none else, let Jove his fortune try,
And learn to lay his murd'ring thunder by;
Then will he own, perhaps, but own too late,
My son deserv'd not so severe a fate."
The gods stand round him, as he mourns, and [pray
He would resume the conduct of the day,
Nor let the world be lost in endless night:
Jove too himself, descending from his height,
Excuses what had happen'd, and entreats,
Majestically mixing pray'rs and threats.
Prevail'd upon at length, again he took
The harness'd steeds, that still with horrour shook,
And plies them with the lash, and whips them on,
And, as he whips, upbraids them with his son.

THE STORY OF CALISTO.

THE day was settled in its course; and Jove
Walk'd the wide circuit of the Heav'ns above,
To search if any cracks or flaws were made;
But all was safe: the Earth he then survey'd,
And cast an eye on ev'ry diff'rent coast,
And ev'ry land; but on Arcadia most.
Her fields he cloth'd, and cheer'd her blasted face
With running fountains, and with springing grass.
No tracks of Heav'n's destructive fire remain,
The fields and woods revive, and Nature smiles again.
But as the god walk'd to and fro the earth,
And rais'd the plants, and gave the Spring its birth,
By chance a fair Arcadian nymph he view'd,
And felt the lovely charmer in his blood.
The nymph nor spun, nor dress'd with artful pride,
Her vest was gather'd up, her hair was ty'd;
Now in her hand a slender spear she bore,
Now a light quiver on her shoulder wore;
To chaste Diana from her youth inclin'd,
The sprightly warriors of the wood she join'd.
Diana too the gentle huntress lov'd,
Nor was there one of all the nymphs that rov'd
O'er Mænalus, amid the maiden throng,
More favour'd once; but favour lasts not long.
The Sun now shone in all its strength, and drove
The heated virgin panting to the grove;
The grove around a grateful shadow cast:
She dropt her arrows, and her bow unbrac'd;
She flung herself on the cool grassy bed;
And on the painted quiver rais'd her head.
Jove saw the charming huntress unprepar'd,
Stretch'd on the verdant turf, without a guard.
"Here I am safe," he cries, "from Juno's eye;
Or should my jealous queen the theft descry,
Yet would I venture on a theft like this,
And stand her rage for such, for such a bliss!"
Diana's shape and habit straight he took,
Soften'd his brows, and smooth'd his awful look,
And mildly in a female accent spoke.
"How fares my girl? how went the morning chase?"
To whom the virgin, starting from the grass,
"All hail, bright deity, whom I prefer
To Jove himself, tho' Jove himself were here."
The god was nearer than she thought, and heard
Well pleas'd himself before himself preferr'd.
He then salutes her with a warm embrace:
And, ere she half had told the morning chase,
With love inflam'd, and eager on his bliss,
Smother'd her words, and stopp'd her with a kiss.
His kisses with unwonted ardour glow'd,
Nor could Diana's shape conceal the god.
The virgin did whate'er a virgin could;
(Sure Juno must have pardon'd, had she view'd)
With all her might against his force she strove;
But how can mortal maids contend with Jove?
Possest at length of what his heart desir'd,
Back to his Heav'ns th' exulting god retir'd.
The lovely huntress, rising from the grass,
With down-cast eyes, and with a blushing face,
By shame confounded, and by fear dismay'd,
Flew from the covert of the guilty shade.
And almost, in the tumult of her mind,
Left her forgotten bow and shafts behind.
But now Diana, with a sprightly train
Of quiver'd virgins, bounding o'er the plain,
Call'd to the nymph; the nymph began to fear
A second fraud, a Jove disguis'd in her;
But, when she saw the sister nymphs, suppress'd
Her rising fears, and mingled with the rest.
How in the look does conscious guilt appear!
Slowly she mov'd, and loiter'd in the rear;
Nor lightly tripp'd, nor by the goddess ran,
As once she us'd, the foremost of the train.
Her looks were flush'd, and sullen was her mien,
That sure the virgin goddess (had she been
Aught but a virgin) must the guilt have seen.
'Tis said the nymphs saw all, and guess'd aright:
And now the Moon had nine times lost her light,
When Dian, fainting in the mid-day beams,
Found a cool covert, and refreshing streams,
That in soft murmurs through the forest flow'd,
And a smooth bed of shining gravel show'd.
A covert so obscure, and streams so clear,
The goddess prais'd: "And now no spies are near
Let's strip, my gentle maids, and wash," she cries.
Pleas'd with the motion, every maid complies;
Only the blushing huntress stood confus'd,
And form'd delays, and her delays excus'd;
In vain excus'd: her fellows round her press'd,
And the reluctant nymph by force undress'd.
The naked huntress all her shame reveal'd,
In vain her hands the pregnant womb conceal'd;
"Begone!" the goddess cries with stern disdain,
"Begone! nor dare the hallow'd stream to stain:"
She fled, for ever banish'd from the train.
This Juno heard, who long had watch'd her time
To punish the detested rival's crime;
The time was come; for, to enrage her more,
A lovely boy the teeming rival bore.

The goddess cast a furious look, and cry'd,
"It is enough! I'm fully satisfy'd!
This boy shall stand a living mark, to prove
My husband's baseness, and the strumpet's love:
But vengeance shall awake: those guilty charms
That drew the thunderer from Juno's arms,
No longer shall their wonted force retain,
Nor please the god, nor make the mortal vain."
This said, her hand within her hair she wound,
Swung her to earth, and dragg'd her on the ground:
The prostrate wretch lifts up her arms in pray'r;
Her arms grow shaggy, and deform'd with hair,
Her nails are sharpen'd into pointed claws,
Her hands bear half her weight, and turn to paws;
Her lips, that once could tempt a god, begin
To grow distorted in an ugly grin.
And, lest the supplicating brute might reach
The ears of Jove, she was depriv'd of speech:
Her surly voice through a hoarse passage came
In savage sounds; her mind was still the same.
The furry monster fix'd her eyes above,
And heav'd her new unwieldy paws to Jove,
And begg'd his aid with inward groans; and tho'
She could not call him false, she thought him so.
How did she fear to lodge in woods alone,
And haunt the fields and meadows, once her own!
How often would the deep-mouth'd dogs pursue,
Whilst from her hounds the frighted huntress flew!
How did she fear her fellow-brutes, and shun
The shaggy bear, though now herself was one!
How from the sight of rugged wolves retire,
Although the grim Lycaon was her sire!
But now her son had fifteen summers told,
Fierce at the chase, and in the forest bold;
When, as he beat the woods in quest of prey,
He chanc'd to rouse his mother where she lay.
She knew her son, and kept him in her sight,
And fondly gaz'd: the boy was in a fright,
And aim'd a pointed arrow at her breast,
And would have slain his mother in the beast;
But Jove forbad, and snatch'd them through the air
In whirlwinds up to Heav'n, and fix'd them there;
Where the new constellations nightly rise,
And add a lustre to the northern skies.
When Juno saw the rival in her height,
Spangled with stars, and circled round with light,
She sought old Ocean in his deep abodes,
And Tethys, both rever'd among the gods.
They ask what brings her there: "Ne'er ask," says she,
"What brings me here; Heav'n is no place for me.
You'll see, when Night has cover'd all things o'er,
Jove's starry bastard and triumphant whore
Usurp the Heav'ns; you'll see them proudly roll
In their new orbs, and brighten all the pole.
And who shall now on Juno's altars wait,
When those she hates grow greater by her hate?
I on the nymph a brutal form impress'd,
Jove to a goddess has transform'd the beast;
This, this was all my weak revenge could do:
But let the god his chaste amours pursue,
And, as he acted after Iö's rape,
Restore th' adultress to her former shape;
Then may he cast his Juno off, and lead
The great Lycaon's offspring to his bed.
But you, ye venerable pow'rs, be kind,
And, if my wrongs a due resentment find,
Receive not in your waves their setting beams,
Nor let the glaring strumpet taint your streams."
The goddess ended, and her wish was giv'n.
Back she return'd in triumph up to Heav'n;
Her gaudy peacocks drew her through the skies;
Their tails were spotted with a thousand eyes;
The eyes of Argus on their tails were rang'd;
At the same time the raven's colour chang'd.

THE STORY OF CORONIS, AND BIRTH OF ÆSCULAPIUS.

The raven once in snowy plumes was drest,
White as the whitest dove's unsully'd breast,
Fair as the guardian of the capitol,
Soft as the swan; a large and lovely fowl;
His tongue, his prating tongue had chang'd him quite
To sooty blackness, from the purest white.
The story of his change shall here be told;
In Thessaly there liv'd a nymph of old,
Coronis nam'd; a peerless maid she shin'd,
Confest the fairest of the fairer kind.
Apollo lov'd her, 'till her guilt he knew,
While true she was, or whilst he thought her true.
But his own bird the raven chanc'd to find
The false one with a secret rival join'd.
Coronis begg'd him to suppress the tale,
But could not with repeated pray'rs prevail.
His milk-white pinions to the god he ply'd;
The busy daw flew with him, side by side,
And by a thousand teizing questions drew
Th' important secret from him as they flew.
The daw gave honest counsel, though despis'd,
And, tedious in her tattle, thus advis'd.
"Stay, silly bird, th' ill-natur'd task refuse,
Nor be the bearer of unwelcome news.
Be warn'd by my example: you discern
What now I am, and what I was shall learn.
My foolish honesty was all my crime;
Then hear my story. Once upon a time,
The two-shap'd Ericthonius had his birth
(Without a mother) from the teeming earth;
Minerva nurs'd him, and the infant laid
Within a chest of twining osiers made.
The daughters of king Cecrops undertook
To guard the chest, commanded not to look
On what was hid within. I stood to see
The charge obey'd, perch'd on a neighb'ring tree.
The sisters Pandrosos and Hersè keep
The strict command; Aglauros needs would peep,
And saw the monstrous infant, in a fright,
And call'd her sisters to the hideous sight:
A boy's soft shape did to the waist prevail,
But the boy ended in a dragon's tail.
I told the stern Minerva all that pass'd;
But, for my pains, discarded and disgrac'd,
The frowning goddess drove me from her sight,
And for her fav'rite chose the bird of night.
Be then no tell-tale; for I think my wrong
Enough to teach a bird to hold her tongue.
"But you, perhaps, may think I was remov'd,
As never by the heav'nly maid belov'd;
But I was lov'd; ask Pallas if I lie;
Though Pallas hate me now, she won't deny:
For I, whom in a feather'd shape you view,
Was once a maid (by Heav'n the story's true)
A blooming maid, and a king's daughter too.
A crowd of lovers own'd my beauty's charms;
My beauty was the cause of all my harms;
Neptune, as on his shores I wont to rove,
Observ'd me in my walks, and fell in love.

He made his courtship, he confess'd his pain,
And offer'd force, when all his arts were vain;
Swift he pursu'd: I ran along the strand,
'Till, spent and weary'd on the sinking sand,
I shriek'd aloud, with cries I fill'd the air
To gods and men; nor god nor man was there:
A virgin goddess heard a virgin's pray'r.
For, as my arms I lifted to the skies,
I saw black feathers from my fingers rise;
I strove to fling my garment on the ground;
My garment turn'd to plumes, and girt me round:
My hands to beat my naked bosom try;
Nor naked bosom now nor hands had I:
Lightly I tript, nor weary as before
Sunk in the sand, but skimm'd along the shore;
'Till, rising on my wings, I was preferr'd
To be the chaste Minerva's virgin bird:
Preferr'd in vain! I now am in disgrace:
Nyctimenè the owl enjoys my place.
"On her incestuous life I need not dwell,
(In Lesbos still the horrid tale they tell)
And of her dire amours you must have heard,
For which she now does penance in a bird,
That, conscious of her shame, avoids the light,
And loves the gloomy cov'ring of the night;
The birds, where'er she flutters, scare away
The hooting wretch, and drive her from the day."
The raven, urg'd by such impertinence,
Grew passionate, it seems, and took offence,
And curst the harmless daw; the daw withdrew;
The raven to her injur'd patron flew,
And found him out, and told the fatal truth
Of false Coronis and the favour'd youth.
The god was wroth; the colour left his look,
The wreath his head, the harp his hand forsook:
His silver bow and feather'd shafts he took,
And lodg'd an arrow in the tender breast,
That had so often to his own been prest.
Down fell the wounded nymph, and sadly groan'd,
And pull'd his arrow reeking from the wound;
And welt'ring in her blood, thus faintly cry'd,
"Ah cruel god! though I have justly dy'd,
What has, alas! my unborn infant done,
That he should fall, and two expire in one?"
This said, in agonies she fetch'd her breath.
The god dissolves in pity at her death;
He hates the bird that made her falsehood known,
And hates himself for what himself had done;
The feather'd shaft, that sent her to the fates,
And his own hand, that sent the shaft, he hates.
Fain would he heal the wound, and ease her pain,
And tries the compass of his art in vain.
Soon as he saw the lovely nymph expire,
The pile made ready, and the kindling fire,
With sighs and groans her obsequies he kept,
And, if a god could weep, the god had wept.
Her corpse he kiss'd, and heav'nly incense brought,
And solemniz'd the death himself had wrought.
But lest his offspring should her fate partake,
Spite of th' immortal mixture in his make,
He ript her womb, and set the child at large,
And gave him to the centaur Chiron's charge:
Then in his fury black'd the raven o'er,
And bid him prate in his white plumes no more.

OCYROE TRANSFORMED TO A MARE.

OLD Chiron took the babe with secret joy,
Proud of the charge of the celestial boy.
His daughter too whom on the sandy shore
The nymph Chariclo to the centaur bore,
With hair dishevel'd on her shoulders, came
To see the child, Ocyroe was her name;
She knew her father's arts, and could rehearse
The depths of prophecy in sounding verse.
Once as the sacred infant she survey'd,
The god was kindled in the raving maid,
And thus she utter'd her prophetic tale;
"Hail, great physician of the world, all hail;
Hail, mighty infant, who in years to come
Shalt heal the nations, and defraud the tomb;
Swift be thy growth! thy triumphs unconfin'd!
Make kingdoms thicker, and increase mankind.
Thy daring art shall animate the dead,
And draw the thunder on thy guilty head:
Then shalt thou die, but from the dark abode
Rise up victorious, and be twice a god.
And thou, my sire, not destin'd by thy birth
To turn to dust and mix with common earth,
How wilt thou toss, and rave, and long to die,
And quit thy claim to immortality;
When thou shalt feel, enrag'd with inward pains,
The hydra's venom rankling in thy veins!
The gods, in pity, shall contract thy date,
And give thee over to the pow'r of fate."
Thus, ent'ring into destiny, the maid
The secrets of offended Jove betray'd:
More had she still to say; but now appears
Oppress'd with sobs and sighs, and drown'd in tears.
"My voice," says she, "is gone, my language fails;
Through ev'ry limb my kindred shape prevails:
Why did the god this fatal gift impart,
And with prophetic raptures swell my heart?
What new desires are these? I long to pace
O'er flow'ry meadows, and to feed on grass;
I hasten to a brute, a maid no more;
But why, alas! am I transform'd all o'er?
My sire does half a human shape retain,
And in his upper parts preserve the man."
Her tongue no more distinct complaints affords,
But in shrill accents and misshapen words
Pours forth such hideous wailings, as declare
The human form confounded in the mare:
Till by degrees accomplish'd in the beast,
She neigh'd outright, and all the steed exprest.
Her stooping body on her hands is born,
Her hands are turn'd to hoofs, and shod in horn.
Her yellow tresses ruffle in a mane,
And in a flowing tail she frisks her train.
The mare was finish'd in her voice and look,
And a new name from the new figure took.

THE TRANSFORMATION OF BATTUS TO A TOUCH-STONE.

SORE wept the centaur, and to Phœbus pray'd;
But how could Phœbus give the centaur aid?
Degraded of his pow'r by angry Jove,
In Elis then a herd of beeves he drove;
And wielded in his hand a staff of oak,
And o'er his shoulders threw the shepherd's cloak;
On sev'n compacted reeds he us'd to play,
And on his rural pipe to waste the day.
As once attentive to his pipe he play'd,
The crafty Hermes from the god convey'd
A drove, that sep'rate from their fellows stray'd.
The theft an old insidious peasant view'd
(They call'd him Battus in the neighbourhood)
Hir'd by a wealthy Pylian prince to feed
His fav'rite mares, and watch the gen'rous breed.

The thievish god suspected him, and took
The hind aside, and thus in whispers spoke;
"Discover not the theft, whoe'er thou be,
And take that milk-white heifer for thy fee."
"Go, stranger," cries the clown, "securely on,
That stone shall sooner tell," and show'd a stone.
The god withdrew, but straight return'd again,
In speech and habit like a country swain;
And cries out, "Neighbour, hast thou seen a stray
Of bullocks and of heifers pass this way?
In the recov'ry of my cattle join,
A bullock and a heifer shall be thine." [there
The peasant quick replies, "You'll find them
In yon dark vale;" and in the vale they were.
The double bribe had his false heart beguil'd:
The god, successful in the trial, smil'd:
"And dost thou thus betray myself to me?
Me to myself dost thou betray?" says he:
Then to a touch-stone turns the faithless spy;
And in his name records his infamy.

THE STORY OF AGLAUROS TRANSFORMED INTO A STATUE.

This done, the god flew up on high, and pass'd
O'er lofty Athens, by Minerva grac'd,
And wide Munichia, whilst his eyes survey
All the vast region that beneath him lay.
'Twas now the feast, when each Athenian maid
Her yearly homage to Minerva paid;
In canisters, with garlands cover'd o'er,
High on their heads, their mystic gifts they bore:
And now, returning in a solemn train,
The troop of shining virgins fill'd the plain!
The god well pleas'd beheld the pompous show,
And saw the bright procession pass below;
Then veer'd about, and took a wheeling flight,
And hover'd o'er them: as the spreading kite,
That smells the slaughter'd victim from on high,
Flies at a distance, if the priests are nigh,
And sails around, and keeps it in her eye;
So kept the god the virgin quire in view,
And in slow winding circles round them flew.
As Lucifer excels the meanest star,
Or, as the full-orb'd Phœbe, Lucifer;
So much did Hersè all the rest outvie,
And gave a grace to the solemnity.
Hermes was fir'd, as in the clouds he hung:
So the cold bullet, that with fury flung
From Balearic engines mounts on high,
Glows in the whirl, and burns along the sky.
At length he pitch'd upon the ground, and show'd
The form divine, the features of a god.
He knew their virtue o'er a female heart,
And yet he strives to better them by art.
He hangs his mantle loose, and sets to show
The golden edging on the seam below;
Adjusts his flowing curls, and in his hand
Waves, with an air, the sleep-procuring wand;
The glitt'ring sandals to his feet applies,
And to each heel the well-trimm'd pinion ties.
His ornaments with nicest art display'd,
He seeks th' apartment of the royal maid.
The roof was all with polish'd iv'ry lin'd,
That richly mix'd, in clouds of tortoise shin'd.
The rooms, contiguous, in a range were plac'd,
The midmost by the beauteous Hersè grac'd;
Her virgin sisters lodg'd on either side.
Aglauros first th' approaching god descry'd,
And, as he cross'd her chamber, ask'd his name,
And what his business was, and whence he came.
"I come," reply'd the god, "from Heav'n, to woo
Your sister, and to make an aunt of you;
I am the son and messenger of Jove;
My name is Mercury, my bus'ness love;
Do you, kind damsel, take a lover's part,
And gain admittance to your sister's heart."
She star'd him in the face with looks amaz'd,
As when she on Minerva's secret gaz'd,
And asks a mighty treasure for her hire;
And, till he brings it, makes the god retire.
Minerva griev'd to see the nymph succeed;
And now rememb'ring the late impious deed,
When, disobedient to her strict command,
She touch'd the chest with an unhallow'd hand;
In big-swoln sighs her inward rage express'd,
That heav'd the rising ægis on her breast;
Then sought out Envy in her dark abode,
Defil'd with ropy gore and clots of blood:
Shut from the winds, and from the wholesome
In a deep vale the gloomy dungeon lies. [skies,
Dismal and cold, where not a beam of light
Invades the winter, or disturbs the night.
Directly to the cave her course she steer'd;
Against the gates her martial lance she rear'd;
The gates flew open, and the fiend appear'd.
A pois'nous morsel in her teeth she chew'd,
And gorg'd the flesh of vipers for her food.
Minerva loathing turn'd away her eye;
The hideous monster, rising heavily,
Came stalking forward with a sullen pace,
And left her mangled offals on the place.
Soon as she saw the goddess gay and bright,
She fetch'd a groan at such a cheerful sight.
Livid and meagre were her looks, her eye
In foul distorted glances turn'd awry;
A hoard of gall her inward parts possess'd,
And spread a greenness o'er her canker'd breast;
Her teeth were brown with rust, and from her
tongue,
In dangling drops, the stringy poison hung.
She never smiles but when the wretched weep,
Nor lulls her malice with a moment's sleep,
Restless in spite; while watchful to destroy,
She pines and sickens at another's joy;
Foe to herself, distressing and distrest,
She bears her own tormentor in her breast.
The goddess gave (for she abhorr'd her sight)
A short command: "To Athens speed thy flight;
On curst Aglauros try thy utmost art,
And fix thy rankest venoms in her heart."
This said, her spear she push'd against the ground,
And mounting from it with an active bound,
Flew off to Heav'n: the hag with eyes askew
Look'd up, and mutter'd curses as she flew;
For sore she fretted, and began to grieve
At the success which she herself must give.
Then takes her staff, hung round with wreaths of
thorn,
And sails along, in a black whirlwind borne,
O'er fields and flow'ry meadows: where she steers
Her baneful course, a mighty blast appears,
Mildews and blights; the meadows are defac'd,
The fields, the flow'rs, and the whole year laid
waste.
On mortals next, and peopled towns she falls,
And breathes a burning plague among their walls.
When Athens she beheld, for arts renown'd,
With peace made happy, and with plenty crown'd,
Scarce could the hideous fiend from tears forbear,
To find out nothing that deserv'd a tear.

Th' apartment now she enter'd, where at rest
Aglauros lay, with gentle sleep opprest.
To execute Minerva's dire command,
She strok'd the virgin with her canker'd hand,
Then prickly thorns into her breast convey'd,
That stung to madness the devoted maid:
Her subtle venom still improves the smart,
Frets in the blood, and festers in the heart.
To make the work more sure, a scene she drew,
And plac'd before the dreaming virgin's view
Her sister's marriage, and her glorious fate :
Th' imaginary bride appears in state;
The bridegroom with unwonted beauty glows:
For Envy magnifies whate'er she shows.
Full of the dream, Aglauros pin'd away
In tears all night, in darkness all the day;
Consum'd like ice, that just begins to run,
When feebly smitten by the distant Sun;
Or like unwholesome weeds, that set on fire
Are slowly wasted, and in smoke expire.
Giv'n up to envy (for in ev'ry thought
The thorns, the venom, and the vision wrought)
Oft did she call on death, as oft decreed,
Rather than see her sister's wish succeed,
To tell her awful father what had past:
At length before the door herself she cast;
And, sitting on the ground with sullen pride,
A passage to the love-sick god deny'd.
The god caress'd, and for admission pray'd,
And sooth'd in softest words th' envenom'd maid.
In vain he sooth'd. "Begone!" the maid replies,
"Or here I keep my seat, and never rise."
"Then keep thy seat for ever," cries the god,
And touch'd the door, wide op'ning to his rod.
Fain would she rise, and stop him, but she found
Her trunk too heavy to forsake the ground;
Her joints are all benumb'd, her hands are pale,
And marble now appears in ev'ry nail.
As when a cancer in the body feeds,
And gradual death from limb to limb proceeds;
So does the chilness to each vital part
Spread by degrees, and creeps into her heart;
'Till hard'ning ev'ry where, and speechless grown,
She sits unmov'd, and freezes to a stone.
But still her envious hue and sullen mien
Are in the sedentary figure seen.

EUROPA'S RAPE.

When now the god his fury had allay'd,
And taken vengeance of the stubborn maid,
From where the bright Athenian turrets rise
He mounts aloft, and reascends the skies.
Jove saw him enter the sublime abodes,
And, as he mix'd among the crowd of gods,
Beckon'd him out, and drew him from the rest,
And in soft whispers thus his will exprest.
"My trusty Hermes, by whose ready aid
Thy sire's commands are thro' the world convey'd,
Resume thy wings, exert their utmost force,
And to the walls of Sidon speed thy course;
There find a herd of heifers wand'ring o'er
The neighb'ring hill, and drive them to the shore."
Thus spoke the god, concealing his intent.
The trusty Hermes on his message went,
And found the herd of heifers wand'ring o'er
A neighb'ring hill, and drove them to the shore;
Where the king's daughter, with a lovely train
Of fellow-nymphs, was sporting on the plain.
The dignity of empire laid aside,
(For love but ill agrees with kingly pride)
The ruler of the skies, the thund'ring god,
Who shakes the world's foundations with a nod,
Among a herd of lowing heifers ran,
Frisk'd in a bull, and bellow'd o'er the plain.
Large rolls of fat about his shoulders clung,
And from his neck the double dewlap hung.
His skin was whiter than the snow that lies
Unsully'd by the breath of southern skies;
Small shining horns on his curl'd forehead stand,
As turn'd and polish'd by the workman's hand;
His eyeballs roll'd, not formidably bright,
But gaz'd and languish'd with a gentle light.
His ev'ry look was peaceful, and exprest
The softness of the lover in the beast.
Agenor's royal daughter, as she play'd
Among the fields, the milk-white bull survey'd,
And view'd his spotless body with delight,
And at a distance kept him in her sight.
At length she pluck'd the rising flow'rs, and fed
The gentle beast, and fondly strok'd his head.
He stood well pleas'd to touch the charming fair,
But hardly could confine his pleasure there.
And now he wantons o'er the neighb'ring strand,
Now rolls his body on the yellow sand;
And, now perceiving all her fears decay'd,
Comes tossing forward to the royal maid: [turns
Gives her his breast to stroke, and downward
His grizly brow, and gently stoops his horns.
In flow'ry wreaths the royal virgin drest
His bending horns, and kindly clapt his breast.
'Till now grown wanton and devoid of fear,
Not knowing that she prest the thunderer,
She plac'd herself upon his back, and rode
O'er fields and meadows, seated on the god.
He gently march'd along, and by degrees
Left the dry meadow, and approach'd the seas;
Where now he dips his hoofs, and wets his thighs,
Now plunges in, and carries off the prize.
The frighted nymph looks backward on the shore,
And hears the tumbling billows round her roar;
But still she holds him fast: one hand is borne
Upon his back; the other grasps a horn:
Her train of ruffling garments flies behind,
Swells in the air, and hovers in the wind.
Through storms and tempests he the virgin bore,
And lands her safe on the Dictæan shore;
Where now, in his divinest form array'd,
In his true shape he captivates the maid:
Who gazes on him, and with wondering eyes
Beholds the new majestic figure rise,
His glowing features, and celestial light,
And all the god discover'd to her sight.

OVID'S METAMORPHOSES.

BOOK III.

Translated by Addison.

THE STORY OF CADMUS.

When now Agenor had his daughter lost,
He sent his son to search on every coast;
And sternly bid him to his arms restore
The darling maid, or see his face no more;
But live an exile in a foreign clime.
Thus was the father pious to a crime.
The restless youth search'd all the world around;
But how can Jove in his amours be found?
When, tir'd at length with unsuccessful toil,
To shun his angry sire and native soil,
He goes a suppliant to the Delphic dome;
There asks the god what new-appointed home

Should end his wanderings, and his toils relieve.
The Delphic oracles this answer give:
"Behold among the fields a lonely cow,
Unworn with yokes, unbroken to the plough;
Mark well the place where first she lays her down,
There measure out thy walls, and build thy town,
And from thy guide Bœotia call the land,
In which the destin'd walls and town shall stand."
No sooner had he left the dark abode,
Big with the promise of the Delphic god,
When in the fields the fatal cow he view'd,
Nor gall'd with yokes, nor worn with servitude;
Her gently at a distance he pursued;
And, as he walk'd aloof, in silence pray'd
To the great power whose counsels he obey'd.
Her way through flowery Panopè she took,
And now, Cephisus, cross'd thy silver brook;
When to the Heav'ns her spacious front she rais'd,
And bellow'd thrice, then backward turning gaz'd
On those behind, till on the destin'd place
She stoop'd, and couch'd amid the rising grass.
Cadmus salutes the soil, and gladly hails
The new-found mountains, and the nameless vales,
And thanks the gods, and turns about his eye
To see his new dominions round him lie;
Then sends his servants to a neighbouring grove
For living streams, a sacrifice to Jove.
O'er the wide plain there rose a shady wood
Of aged trees; in its dark bosom stood
A bushy thicket, pathless and unworn,
O'er-run with brambles, and perplex'd with thorn:
Amidst the brake a hollow den was found,
With rocks and shelving arches vaulted round.
Deep in the dreary den, conceal'd from day,
Sacred to Mars, a mighty dragon lay,
Bloated with poison to a monstrous size;
Fire broke in flashes when he glanc'd his eyes:
His tow'ring crest was glorious to behold,
His shoulders and his sides were scal'd with gold;
Three tongues he brandish'd when he charg'd his foes;
His teeth stood jaggy in three dreadful rows.
The Tyrians in the den for water sought,
And with their urns explor'd the hollow vault:
From side to side their empty urns rebound,
And rouse the sleeping serpent with the sound.
Straight he bestirs him, and is seen to rise;
And now with dreadful hissings fills the skies,
And darts his forky tongues, and rolls his glaring eyes.
The Tyrians drop their vessels in the fright,
All pale and trembling at the hideous sight.
Spire above spire uprear'd in air he stood,
And gazing round him over-look'd the wood:
Then floating on the ground in circles roll'd;
Then leap'd upon them in a mighty fold.
Of such a bulk, and such a monstrous size
The serpent in the polar circle lies,
That stretches over half the northern skies.
In vain the Tyrians on their arms rely,
In vain attempt to fight, in vain to fly:
All their endeavours and their hopes are vain;
Some die entangled in the winding train;
Some are devour'd, or feel a loathsome death,
Swoln up with blasts of pestilential breath.
And now the scorching Sun was mounted high,
In all its lustre, to the noon-day sky;
When, anxious for his friends, and fill'd with cares,
To search the woods th' impatient chief prepares.
A lion's hide around his loins he wore,
The well-pois'd javelin to the field he bore,
Inur'd to blood; the far-destroying dart;
And, the best weapon, an undaunted heart.
Soon as the youth approach'd the fatal place,
He saw his servants breathless on the grass;
The scaly foe amidst their corps he view'd,
Basking at ease, and feasting in their blood.
"Such friends," he cries, "deserv'd a longer date;
But Cadmus will revenge or share their fate."
Then heav'd a stone, and rising to the throw,
He sent it in a whirlwind at the foe:
A tow'r, assaulted by so rude a stroke,
With all its lofty battlements had shook;
But nothing here th' unwieldy rock avails,
Rebounding harmless from the plaited scales,
That, firmly join'd, preserv'd him from a wound,
With native armour crusted all around.
With more success the dart unerring flew,
Which at his back the raging warrior threw;
Amid the plaited scales it took its course,
And in the spinal marrow spent its force.
The monster hiss'd aloud, and rag'd in vain,
And writh'd his body to and fro with pain;
He bit the dart, and wrench'd the wood away:
The point still buried in the marrow lay.
And now his rage, increasing with his pain,
Reddens his eyes, and beats in ev'ry vein;
Churn'd in his teeth the foamy venom rose,
Whilst from his mouth a blast of vapours flows,
Such as th' infernal Stygian waters cast;
The plants around him wither in the blast.
Now in a maze of rings he lies enroll'd,
Now all unravell'd, and without a fold;
Now, like a torrent, with a mighty force
Bears down the forest in his boist'rous course.
Cadmus gave back, and on the lion's spoil
Sustain'd the shock, then forc'd him to recoil;
The pointed jav'lin warded off his rage:
Mad with his pains, and furious to engage,
The serpent champs the steel, and bites the spear,
Till blood and venom all the point besmear.
But still the hurt he yet receiv'd was slight;
For, whilst the champion with redoubled might
Strikes home the jav'lin, his retiring foe
Shrinks from the wound, and disappoints the blow.
The dauntless hero still pursues his stroke,
And presses forward, till a knotty oak
Retards his foe, and stops him in the rear;
Full in his throat he plung'd the fatal spear,
That in th' extended neck a passage found,
And pierc'd the solid timber through the wound.
Fix'd to the reeling trunk, with many a stroke
Of his huge tail he lash'd the sturdy oak:
Till spent with toil, and lab'ring hard for breath,
He now lay twisting in the pangs of death.
Cadmus beheld him wallow in a flood
Of swimming poison, intermix'd with blood;
When suddenly a speech was heard from high,
(The speech was heard, nor was the speaker nigh)
"Why dost thou thus with secret pleasure see,
Insulting man! what thou thyself shalt be?"
Astonish'd at the voice, he stood amaz'd,
And all around with inward horrour gaz'd:
When Pallas swift descending from the skies,
Pallas, the guardian of the bold and wise,
Bids him plow up the field, and scatter round
The dragon's teeth o'er all his furrow'd ground;
Then tells the youth how to the wond'ring eyes
Embattled armies from the field should rise.
He sows the teeth at Pallas's command,
And flings the future people from his hand.

The clods grow warm, and crumble where he sows;
And now the pointed spears advance in rows:
Now nodding plumes appear, and shining crests,
Now the broad shoulders, and the rising breasts;
O'er all the field the breathing harvest swarms,
A growing host, a crop of men in arms.
So through the parting stage a figure rears
Its body up, and limb by limb appears
By just degrees; till all the man arise,
And in his full proportion strikes the eyes.
Cadmus surpris'd, and startled at the sight
Of his new foes, prepar'd himself for fight:
When one cry'd out, "Forbear, fond man, forbear
To mingle in a blind, promiscuous war."
This said, he struck his brother to the ground,
Himself expiring by another's wound;
Nor did the third his conquest long survive,
Dying ere scarce he had begun to live.
The dire example ran through all the field,
Till heaps of brothers were by brothers kill'd;
The furrows swam in blood: and only five
Of all the vast increase were left alive.
Echion one, at Pallas's command,
Let fall the guiltless weapon from his hand,
And with the rest a peaceful treaty makes,
Whom Cadmus as his friends and partners takes;
So founds a city on the promis'd earth,
And gives his new Bœotian empire birth.
Here Cadmus reign'd; and now one would have guess'd
The royal founder in his exile blest:
Long did he live within his new abodes,
Ally'd by marriage to the deathless gods;
And, in a fruitful wife's embraces old,
A long increase of children's children told;
But no frail man, however great or high,
Can be concluded blest before he die.
Actæon was the first of all his race,
Who griev'd his grandsire in his borrow'd face;
Condemn'd by stern Diana to bemoan
The branching horns, and visage not his own;
To shun his once-lov'd dogs, to bound away,
And from their huntsman to become their prey.
And yet consider why the change was wrought,
You'll find it his misfortune, not his fault;
Or, if a fault, it was the fault of chance:
For how can guilt proceed from ignorance?

THE TRANSFORMATION OF ACTÆON INTO A STAG.

In a fair chase a shady mountain stood,
Well stor'd with game, and mark'd with trails of blood.
Here did the huntsmen, till the heat of day,
Pursue the stag, and load themselves with prey;
When thus Actæon calling to the rest:
"My friends," said he, "our sport is at the best;
The Sun is high advanc'd, and downward sheds
His burning beams directly on our heads;
Then by consent abstain from further spoils,
Call off the dogs, and gather up the toils,
And ere to morrow's Sun begins his race,
Take the cool morning to renew the chase."
They all consent, and in a cheerful train
The jolly huntsmen, loaden with the slain,
Return in triumph from the sultry plain.
Down in a vale with pine and cypress clad,
Refresh'd with gentle winds, and brown with shade,
The chaste Diana's private haunt, there stood
Full in the centre of the darksome wood
A spacious grotto, all around o'er grown
With hoary moss, and arch'd with pummice stone:
From out its rocky clefts the waters flow,
And trickling swell into a lake below.
Nature had ev'ry where so play'd her part,
That ev'ry where she seem'd to vie with art.
Here the bright goddess, toil'd and chaf'd with heat,
Was wont to bathe her in the cool retreat.
Here did she now with all her train resort,
Panting with heat, and breathless from the sport;
Her armour-bearer laid her bow aside,
Some loos'd her sandals, some her veil unty'd;
Each busy nymph her proper part undress'd;
While Crocalè, more handy than the rest,
Gather'd her flowing hair, and in a noose
Bound it together, whilst her own hung loose.
Five of the more ignoble sort by turns
Fetch up the water, and unlade the urns.
Now all undrest the shining goddess stood,
When young Actæon, wilder'd in the wood,
To the cool grot by his hard fate betray'd,
The fountains fill'd with naked nymphs survey'd.
The frighted virgins shriek'd at the surprise,
(The forest echo'd with their piercing cries).
Then in a huddle round their goddess prest:
She, proudly eminent above the rest,
With blushes glow'd; such blushes as adorn
The ruddy welkin, or the purple morn;
And though the crowding nymphs her body hide,
Half backward shrunk, and view'd him from aside.
Surpris'd, at first she would have snatch'd her bow,
But sees the circling waters round her flow;
These in the hollow of her hand she took,
And dash'd them in his face, while thus she spoke;
"Tell, if thou canst, the wond'rous sight disclos'd,
A goddess naked to thy view expos'd."
This said, the man begun to disappear
By slow degrees, and ended in a deer.
A rising horn on either brow he wears,
And stretches out his neck, and pricks his ears;
Rough is his skin, with sudden hairs o'er-grown,
His bosom pants with fears before unknown:
Transform'd at length, he flies away in haste,
And wonders why he flies away so fast.
But as by chance, within a neighb'ring brook,
He saw his branching horns and alter'd look,
Wretched Actæon! in a doleful tone
He try'd to speak, but only gave a groan;
And as he wept, within the watry glass,
He saw the big round drops, with silent pace,
Run trickling down a savage hairy face.
What should he do? or seek his old abodes,
Or herd among the deer, and sculk in woods?
Here shame dissuades him, there his fear prevails,
And each by turns his aching heart assails.
As he thus ponders, he behind him spies
His op'ning hounds, and now he hears their cries:
A gen'rous pack, or to maintain the chase,
Or snuff the vapour from the scented grass.
He bounded off with fear, and swiftly ran
O'er craggy mountains, and the flow'ry plain;
Through brakes and thickets forc'd his way, and flew
Through many a ring, where once he did pursue.
In vain he oft endeavour'd to proclaim
His new misfortune, and to tell his name;
Nor voice nor words the brutal tongue supplies;
From shouting men, and horns, and dogs, he flies,
Deafen'd and stunn'd with their promiscuous cries.

When now the fleetest of the pack, that prest
Close at his heels, and sprung before the rest,
Had fasten'd on him, straight another pair
Hung on his wounded haunch, and held him there,
Till all the pack came up, and ev'ry hound
Tore the sad huntsman grov'ling on the ground,
Who now appear'd but one continu'd wound.
With dropping tears his bitter fate he moans,
And fills the mountain with his dying groans.
His servants with a piteous look he spies,
And turns about his supplicating eyes.
His servants, ignorant of what had chanc'd,
With eager haste and joyful shouts advanc'd,
And call'd their lord Actæon to the game.
He shook his head in answer to the name;
He heard, but wish'd he had indeed been gone,
Or only to have stood a looker-on.
But to his grief he finds himself too near,
And feels his rav'nous dogs with fury tear
Their wretched master panting in a deer.

THE BIRTH OF BACCHUS.

Actæon's sufferings, and Diana's rage,
Did all the thoughts of men and gods engage;
Some call'd the evils which Diana wrought
Too great, and disproportion'd to the fault:
Others again esteem'd Actæon's woes
Fit for a virgin goddess to impose.
The hearers into diff'rent parts divide,
And reasons are produc'd on either side.
Juno alone, of all that heard the news,
Nor would condemn the goddess, nor excuse:
She heeded not the justice of the deed,
But joy'd to see the race of Cadmus bleed;
For still she kept Europa in her mind,
And, for her sake, detested all her kind.
Besides, to aggravate her hate, she heard
How Semele, to Jove's embrace preferr'd,
Was now grown big with an immortal load,
And carry'd in her womb a future god.
Thus terribly incens'd, the goddess broke
To sudden fury, and abruptly spoke.
"Are my reproaches of so small a force?
'Tis time I then pursue another course:
It is decreed the guilty wretch shall die,
If I'm indeed the mistress of the sky;
If rightly styl'd among the powers above,
The wife and sister of the thund'ring Jove;
(And none can sure a sister's right deny)
It is decreed the guilty wretch shall die.
She boasts an honour I can hardly claim,
Pregnant she rises to a mother's name;
While proud and vain she triumphs in her Jove,
And shows the glorious tokens of his love:
But if I'm still the mistress of the skies,
By her own lover the fond beauty dies."
This said, descending in a yellow cloud,
Before the gates of Semele she stood.
Old Beroe's decrepit shape she wears,
Her wrinkled visage, and her hoary hairs;
Whilst in her trembling gait she totters on,
And learns to tattle in the nurse's tone.
The goddess, thus disguis'd in age, beguil'd
With pleasing stories her false foster-child.
Much did she talk of love, and when she came
To mention to the nymph her lover's name,
Fetching a sigh, and holding down her head,
"'Tis well," says she, "if all be true that's said.
But trust me, child, I'm much inclin'd to fear
Some counterfeit in this your Jupiter.
Many an honest well-designing maid
Has been by these pretended gods betray'd.
But if he be indeed the thund'ring Jove,
Bid him, when next he courts the rites of love,
Descend triumphant from th' ethereal sky,
In all the pomp of his divinity,
Encompass'd round by those celestial charms,
With which he fills th' immortal Juno's arms."
Th' unwary nymph, ensnar'd with what she said,
Desir'd of Jove, when next he sought her bed,
To grant a certain gift which she would choose;
"Fear not, reply'd the god, that I'll refuse
Whate'er you ask: may Styx confirm my voice,
Choose what you will, and you shall have your choice."
"Then," says the nymph, "when next you seek my arms,
May you descend in those celestial charms,
With which your Juno's bosom you inflame,
And fill with transport Heav'n's immortal dame."
The god surpris'd would fain have stopp'd her voice,
But he had sworn, and she had made her choice.
To keep his promise, he ascends, and shrowds
His awful brow in whirlwinds and in clouds;
Whilst all around, in terrible array,
His thunders rattle, and his lightnings play.
And yet the dazzling lustre to abate,
He set not out in all his pomp and state,
Clad in the mildest lightning of the skies,
And arm'd with thunder of the smallest size:
Not those huge bolts, by which the giants slain
Lay overthrown on the Phlegrean plain.
'Twas of a lesser mould, and lighter weight;
They call it thunder of a second-rate;
For the rough Cyclops, who by Jove's command
Temper'd the bolt, and turn'd it to his hand,
Work'd up less flame and fury in its make,
And quench'd it sooner in the standing lake.
Thus dreadfully adorn'd, with horrour bright,
Th' illustrious god, descending from his height,
Came rushing on her in a storm of light.
The mortal dame, too feeble to engage
The lightning's flashes, and the thunder's rage,
Consum'd amidst the glories she desir'd,
And in the terrible embrace expir'd.
But, to preserve his offspring from the tomb,
Jove took him smoking from the blasted womb:
And, if on ancient tales we may rely,
Enclos'd th' abortive infant in his thigh.
Here when the babe had all his time fulfill'd,
Ino first took him for her foster-child;
Then the Niseans, in their dark abode,
Nurs'd secretly with milk the thriving god.

THE TRANSFORMATION OF TIRESIAS.

'Twas now, while these transactions past on Earth,
And Bacchus thus procur'd a second birth,
When Jove, dispos'd to lay aside the weight
Of public empire and the cares of state,
As to his queen in nectar bowls he quaff'd,
"In troth," says he, and as he spoke he laugh'd,
"The sense of pleasure in the male is far
More dull and dead, than what you females share."
Juno the truth of what was said deny'd;
Tiresias therefore must the cause decide,
For he the pleasure of each sex had try'd.
It happen'd once, within a shady wood,
Two twisted snakes he in conjunction view'd,

When with his staff their slimy folds he broke,
And lost his manhood at the fatal stroke.
But, after seven revolving years, he view'd
The self-same serpents in the self-same wood:
"And if," says he, "such virtue in you lie,
That he who dares your slimy folds untie
Must change his kind, a second stroke I'll try."
Again he struck the snakes, and stood again
New-sex'd, and straight recover'd into man.
Him therefore both the deities create
The sov'reign umpire, in their grand debate;
And he declar'd for Jove: when Juno fir'd,
More than so trivial an affair requir'd,
Depriv'd him, in her fury, of his sight,
And left him groping round in sudden night.
But Jove (for so it is in Heav'n decreed,
That no one god repeal another's deed)
Irradiates all his soul with inward light,
And with the prophet's art relieves the want of [sight.

THE TRANSFORMATION OF ECHO.

FAM'D far and near for knowing things to come,
From him th'enquiring nations sought their doom;
The fair Liriope his answers try'd,
And first th' unerring prophet justified.
This nymph the god Cephisus had abus'd,
With all his winding waters circumfus'd,
And on the Nereid got a lovely boy,
Whom the soft maids ev'n then beheld with joy.
The tender dame, solicitous to know
Whether her child should reach old age or no,
Consults the sage Tiresias, who replies,
"If e'er he knows himself, he surely dies."
Long liv'd the dubious mother in suspense,
Till time unriddled all the prophet's sense.
Narcissus now his sixteenth year began,
Just turn'd of boy, and on the verge of man;
Many a friend the blooming youth caress'd,
Many a love-sick maid her flame confess'd.
Such was his pride, in vain the friend caress'd,
The love-sick maid in vain her flame confess'd.
Once, in the woods, as he pursu'd the chase,
The babbling Echo had descry'd his face;
She, who in others' words her silence breaks,
Nor speaks herself but when another speaks.
Echo was then a maid, of speech bereft,
Of wonted speech; for though her voice was left,
Juno a curse did on her tongue impose,
To sport with ev'ry sentence in the close.
Full often when the goddess might have caught
Jove and her rivals in the very fault,
This nymph with subtle stories would delay
Her coming, till the lovers slipt away.
The goddess found out the deceit in time,
And then she cry'd, "That tongue, for this thy crime,
Which could so many subtle tales produce,
Shall be hereafter but of little use."
Hence 'tis she prattles in a fainter tone,
With mimick sounds, and accents not her own.
This love-sick virgin, over-joy'd to find
The boy alone, still follow'd him behind:
When glowing warmly at her near approach,
As sulphur blazes at the taper's touch,
She long'd her hidden passion to reveal,
And tell her pains, but had not words to tell:
She can't begin, but waits for the rebound,
To catch his voice, and to return the sound.
The nymph, when nothing could Narcissus move,
Still dash'd with blushes for her slighted love,
Liv'd in the shady covert of the woods,
In solitary caves and dark abodes;
Where pining wander'd the rejected fair,
Till, harass'd out, and worn away with care,
The sounding skeleton, of blood bereft,
Besides her bones and voice had nothing left.
Her bones are petrify'd, her voice is found
In vaults, where still it doubles ev'ry sound.

THE STORY OF NARCISSUS.

THUS did the nymphs in vain caress the boy,
He still was lovely, but he still was coy;
When one fair virgin of the slighted train
Thus pray'd the gods, provok'd by his disdain,
"Oh may he love like me, and love like me in vain!"
Ramnusia pity'd the neglected fair,
And with just vengeance answer'd to her pray'r.
There stands a fountain in a darksome wood,
Nor stain'd with falling leaves nor rising mud;
Untroubled by the breath of winds it rests,
Unsully'd by the touch of men or beasts;
High bow'rs of shady trees above it grow,
And rising grass and cheerful greens below.
Pleas'd with the form and coolness of the place,
And over-heated by the morning chase,
Narcissus on the grassy verdure lies:
But whilst within the crystal fount he tries
To quench his heat, he feels new heat arise.
For, as his own bright image he survey'd,
He fell in love with the fantastic shade;
And o'er the fair resemblance hung unmov'd,
Nor knew, fond youth! it was himself he lov'd.
The well-turn'd neck and shoulders he descries,
The spacious forehead, and the sparkling eyes;
The hands that Bacchus might not scorn to show,
And hair that round Apollo's head might flow;
With all the purple youthfulness of face,
That gently blushes in the wat'ry glass.
By his own flames consum'd the lover lies,
And gives himself the wound by which he dies.
To the cold water oft he joins his lips,
Oft catching at the beauteous shade he dips
His arms, as often from himself he slips.
Nor knows he who it is his arms pursue
With eager clasps, but loves he knows not who.
What could, fond youth, this helpless passion move?
What kindled in thee this unpity'd love?
Thy own warm blush within the water glows,
With thee the colour'd shadow comes and goes,
Its empty being on thyself relies;
Step thou aside, and the frail charmer dies.
Still o'er the fountain's wat'ry gleam he stood,
Mindless of sleep, and negligent of food;
Still view'd his face, and languish'd as he view'd.
At length he rais'd his head, and thus began
To vent his griefs, and tell the woods his pain.
"You trees," says he, "and thou surrounding grove,
Who oft have been the kindly scenes of love,
Tell me, if e'er within your shades did lie
A youth so tortur'd, so perplex'd as I?
I, who before me see the charming fair,
Whilst there he stands, and yet he stands not there:
In such a maze of love my thoughts are lost:
And yet no bulwark'd town, nor distant coast,
Preserves the beauteous youth from being seen,
No mountains rise, nor oceans flow between.

A shallow water hinders my embrace;
And yet the lovely mimic wears a face
That kindly smiles, and when I bend to join
My lips to his, he fondly bends to mine.
Hear, gentle youth, and pity my complaint;
Come from thy well, thou fair inhabitant.
My charms an easy conquest have obtain'd
O'er other hearts, by thee alone disdain'd.
But why should I despair? I'm sure he burns
With equal flames, and languishes by turns.
Whene'er I stood, he offers at a kiss,
And when my arms I stretch, he stretches his.
His eyes with pleasure on my face he keeps,
He smiles my smiles, and when I weep he weeps.
Whene'er I speak, his moving lips appear
To utter something which I cannot hear.
"Ah, wretched me! I now begin too late
To find out all the long-perplex'd deceit;
It is myself I love, myself I see;
The gay delusion is a part of me.
I kindle up the fires by which I burn,
And my own beauties from the well return.
Whom should I court? how utter my complaint?
Enjoyment but produces my restraint,
And too much plenty makes me die for want.
How gladly would I from myself remove!
And at a distance set the thing I love.
My breast is warm'd with such unusual fire,
I wish him absent whom I most desire.
And now I faint with grief; my fate draws nigh;
In all the pride of blooming youth I die:
Death will the sorrows of my heart relieve.
Oh might the visionary youth survive,
I should with joy my latest breath resign!
But, oh! I see his fate involv'd in mine."
This said, the weeping youth again return'd
To the clear fountain, where again he burn'd;
His tears defac'd the surface of the well,
With circle after circle, as they fell:
And now the lovely face but half appears,
O'er-run with wrinkles, and deform'd with tears.
"Ah, whither," cries Narcissus, "dost thou fly?
Let me still feed the flame by which I die;
Let me still see, though I'm no further blest."
Then rends his garment off, and beats his breast;
His naked bosom reddens with the blow,
In such a blush as purple clusters show,
Ere yet the Sun's autumnal heats refine
Their sprightly juice, and mellow it to wine.
The glowing beauties of his breast he spies,
And with a new redoubled passion dies.
As wax dissolves, as ice begins to run,
And trickle into drops before the Sun;
So melts the youth, and languishes away,
His beauty withers, and his limbs decay;
And none of those attractive charms remain,
To which the slighted Echo su'd in vain.
She saw him in his present misery,
Whom, spite of all her wrongs, she griev'd to see.
She answer'd sadly to the lover's moan,
Sigh'd back his sighs, and groan'd to ev'ry groan:
"Ah youth! belov'd in vain," Narcissus cries;
"Ah youth! belov'd in vain," the nymph replies.
"Farewell," says he; the parting sound scarce fell
From his faint lips, but she reply'd, "Farewell."
Then on th' unwholesome earth he gasping lies,
Till death shuts up those self-admiring eyes.
To the cold shades his flitting ghost retires,
And in the Stygian waves itself admires.
For him the Naiads and the Dryads mourn,
Whom the sad Echo answers in her turn;
And now the sister nymphs prepare his urn:
When, looking for his corpse, they only found
A rising stalk, with yellow blossoms crown'd.

THE STORY OF PENTHEUS.

This sad event gave blind Tiresias fame,
Through Greece establish'd in a prophet's name.
Th' unhallow'd Pentheus only durst deride
The cheated people, and their eyeless guide.
To whom the prophet in his fury said,
Shaking the hoary honours of his head;
"'Twere well, presumptuous man, 'twere well for thee
If thou wert eyeless too, and blind, like me:
For the time comes, nay, 'tis already here,
When the young god's solemnities appear:
Which, if thou dost not with just rites adorn,
Thy impious carcase, into pieces torn,
Shall strew the woods, and hang on ev'ry thorn.
Then, then, remember what I now foretel,
And own the blind Tiresias saw too well."
Still Pentheus scorns him, and derides his skill;
But time did all the prophet's threats fulfil.
For now through prostrate Greece young Bacchus rode,
Whilst howling matrons celebrate the god:
All ranks and sexes to his orgies ran,
To mingle in the pomps, and fill the train.
When Pentheus thus his wicked rage express'd;
"What madness, Thebans, has your souls possess'd?
Can hollow timbrels, can a drunken shout,
And the lewd clamours of a beastly rout,
Thus quell your courage? can the weak alarm
Of women's yells those stubborn souls disarm,
Whom nor the sword nor trumpet e'er could fright,
Nor the loud din and horrour of a fight?
And you, our sires, who left your old abodes,
And fix'd in foreign earth your country gods;
Will you without a stroke your city yield,
And poorly quit an undisputed field?
But you, whose youth and vigour should inspire
Heroic warmth, and kindle martial fire,
Whom burnish'd arms and crested helmets grace,
Not flow'ry garlands and a painted face;
Remember him to whom you stand ally'd:
The serpent for his well of waters dy'd.
He fought the strong, do you his courage show,
And gain a conquest o'er a feeble foe.
If Thebes must fall, oh, might the Fates afford
A nobler doom from famine, fire, or sword.
Then might the Thebans perish with renown:
But now a beardless victor sacks the town;
Whom nor the prancing steed, nor pond'rous shield,
Nor the hack'd helmet, nor the dusty field,
But the soft joys of luxury and ease,
The purple vests, and flow'ry garlands please.
Stand then aside, I'll make the counterfeit
Renounce his god-head, and confess the cheat.
Acrisius from the Grecian walls repell'd
This boasted pow'r: why then should Pentheus yield?
Go quickly drag th' impostor boy to me;
I'll try the force of his divinity."

Thus did th' audacious wretch those rites profane;
His friends dissuade th' audacious wretch in vain;
In vain his grandsire urg'd him to give o'er
His impious threats; the wretch but raves the more.
So have I seen a river gently glide,
In a smooth course, and inoffensive tide;
But if with dams its current we restrain,
It bears down all, and foams along the plain.
But now his servants came besmear'd with blood,
Sent by their haughty prince to seize the god;
The god they found not in the frantic throng,
But dragg'd a zealous votary along.

THE MARINERS TRANSFORMED TO DOLPHINS.

Him Pentheus view'd with fury in his look,
And scarce withheld his hands, whilst thus he spoke:
"Vile slave! whom speedy vengeance shall pursue,
And terrify thy base seditious crew:
Thy country and thy parentage reveal,
And, why thou join'st in these mad orgies, tell."
The captive views him with undaunted eyes,
And, arm'd with inward innocence, replies.
"From high Meonia's rocky shores I came,
Of poor descent, Acœtes is my name:
My sire was meanly born: no oxen plough'd
His fruitful fields, nor in his pastures low'd.
His whole estate within the waters lay;
With lines and hooks he caught the finny prey,
His art was all his livelihood; which he
Thus with his dying lips bequeath'd to me:
'In streams, my boy, and rivers take thy chance;
There swims,' said he, 'thy whole inheritance.'
"Long did I live on this poor legacy;
Till tir'd with rocks, and my old native sky,
To arts of navigation I inclin'd;
Observ'd the turns and changes of the wind,
Learn'd the fit havens, and began to note
The stormy Hyades, the rainy Goat,
The bright Taygete, and the shining Bears,
With all the sailor's catalogue of stars.
"Once, as by chance for Delos I design'd,
My vessel, driv'n by a strong gust of wind,
Moor'd in a Chian creek; ashore I went,
And all the following night in Chios spent.
When Morning rose, I sent my mates to bring
Supplies of water from a neighb'ring spring,
Whilst I the motion of the winds explor'd;
Then summon'd in my crew, and went aboard.
Opheltes heard my summons, and with joy
Brought to the shore a soft and lovely boy,
With more than female sweetness in his look,
Whom straggling in the neighb'ring fields he took.
With fumes of wine the little captive glows,
And nods with sleep, and staggers as he goes.
"I view'd him nicely, and began to trace
Each heav'nly feature, each immortal grace,
And saw divinity in all his face.
'I know not who,' said I, 'this god should be;
But that he is a god I plainly see:
And thou, whoe'er thou art, excuse the force
These men have us'd; and oh befriend our course!'
'Pray not for us,' the nimble Dictys cry'd,
Dictys, that could the main-top mast bestride,
And down the ropes with active vigour slide.
To the same purpose old Epopeus spoke,
Who over-look'd the oars, and tim'd the stroke;
The same the pilot, and the same the rest;
Such impious avarice their souls possest.
'Nay, Heav'n forbid that I should bear away
Within my vessel so divine a prey,'
Said I; and stood to hinder their intent:
When Lycabas, a wretch for murder sent
From Tuscany, to suffer banishment,
With his clench'd fist had struck me overboard,
Had not my hands in falling grasp'd a cord.
"His base confederates the fact approve;
When Bacchus (for 'twas he) began to move,
Wak'd by the noise and clamours which they rais'd;
And shook his drowsy limbs, and round him gaz'd:
'What means this noise?' he cries; 'am I betray'd?
Ah, whither, whither must I be convey'd?'
'Fear not,' said Proreus, 'child, but tell us where
You wish to land, and trust our friendly care.'
'To Naxos then direct your course,' said he;
'Naxos a hospitable port shall be
To each of you, a joyful home to me.'
By ev'ry god, that rules the sea or sky,
The perjur'd villains promise to comply,
And bid me hasten to unmoor the ship.
With eager joy I lanch into the deep;
And, heedless of the fraud, for Naxos stand.
They whisper oft, and beckon with the hand,
And give me signs, all anxious for their prey,
To tack about, and steer another way.
'Then let some other to my post succeed,'
Said I, 'I'm guiltless of so foul a deed.'
'What,' says Ethalion, 'must the ship's whole crew
Follow your humour, and depend on you?'
And straight himself he seated at the prore,
And tack'd about, and sought another shore.
"The beauteous youth now found himself betray'd,
And from the deck the rising waves survey'd,
And seem'd to weep, and as he wept he said;
'And do you thus my easy faith beguile?
Thus do you bear me to my native isle?
Will such a multitude of men employ
Their strength against a weak defenceless boy?'
"In vain did I the godlike youth deplore;
The more I begg'd, they thwarted me the more.
And now by all the gods in Heav'n that hear
This solemn oath, by Bacchus' self, I swear,
The mighty miracle that did ensue,
Although it seems beyond belief, is true.
The vessel, fix'd and rooted in the flood,
Unmov'd by all the beating billows stood.
In vain the mariners would plough the main
With sails unfurl'd, and strike their oars in vain;
Around their oars a twining ivy cleaves,
And climbs the mast, and hides the cords in leaves:
The sails are cover'd with a cheerful green,
And berries in the fruitful canvass seen.
Amidst the waves a sudden forest rears
Its verdant head, and a new spring appears.
"The god we now behold with open'd eyes;
A herd of spotted panthers round him lies
In glaring forms; the grapy clusters spread
On his fair brows, and dangle on his head.
And whilst he frowns, and brandishes his spear,
My mates, surpris'd with madness or with fear,
Leap'd overboard; first perjur'd Madon found
Rough scales and fins his stiff'ning sides surround;
'Ah, what,' cries one, 'has thus transform'd thy look?'
Straight his own mouth grew wider as he spoke;

And now himself he views with like surprise.
Still at his oar th' industrious Libys plies;
But, as he plies, each busy arm shrinks in,
And by degrees is fashion'd to a fin.
Another, as he catches at a cord,
Misses his arms, and tumbling overboard,
With his broad fins and forky tail he laves
The rising surge, and flounces in the waves.
Thus all my crew transform'd around the ship,
Or dive below, or on the surface leap,
And spout the waves, and wanton in the deep.
Full nineteen sailors did the ship convey,
A shoal of nineteen dolphins round her play.
I only in my proper shape appear,
Speechless with wonder, and half dead with fear,
Till Bacchus kindly bid me fear no more.
With him I landed on the Chian shore,
And him shall ever gratefully adore."
"This forging slave," says Pentheus, "would prevail
O'er our just fury by a far-fetch'd tale:
Go let him feel the whips, the swords, the fire,
And in the tortures of the rack expire."
Th' officious servants hurry him away,
And the poor captive in a dungeon lay.
But, whilst the whips and tortures are prepar'd,
The gates fly open, of themselves unbarr'd;
At liberty th' unfetter'd captive stands,
And flings the loosen'd shackles from his hands.

THE DEATH OF PENTHEUS.

BUT Pentheus, grown more furious than before,
Resolv'd to send his messengers no more,
But went himself to the distracted throng,
Where high Cithæron echo'd with their song.
And as the fiery war-horse paws the ground,
And snorts and trembles at the trumpet's sound;
Transported thus he heard the frantic rout,
And rav'd and madden'd at the distant shout.
A spacious circuit on the hill there stood,
Level and wide, and skirted round with wood;
Here the rash Pentheus, with unhallow'd eyes,
The howling dames and mystic Orgies spies.
His mother sternly view'd him where he stood,
And kindled into madness as she view'd:
Her leafy jav'lin at her son she cast,
And cries, "The boar that lays our country waste!
The boar, my sisters! Aim the fatal dart,
And strike the brindled monster to the heart."
Pentheus astonish'd heard the dismal sound,
And sees the yelling matrons gath'ring round:
He sees, and weeps at his approaching fate,
And begs for mercy, and repents too late.
"Help! help! my aunt Autonoë," he cry'd;
"Remember, how your own Actæon dy'd."
Deaf to his cries, the frantic matron crops
One stretch'd-out arm, the other Ino lops.
In vain does Pentheus to his mother sue,
And the raw bleeding stumps presents to view:
His mother howl'd; and, heedless of his pray'r,
Her trembling hand she twisted in his hair,
"And this," she cry'd, "shall be Agave's share."
When from the neck his struggling head she tore,
And in her hands the ghastly visage bore.
With pleasure all the hideous trunk survey;
Then pull'd and tore the mangled limbs away,
As starting in the pangs of death it lay.
Soon as the wood its leafy honours casts,
Blown off and scatter'd by autumnal blasts,
With such a sudden death lay Pentheus slain,
And in a thousand pieces strow'd the plain.
By so distinguishing a judgment aw'd,
The Thebans tremble, and confess the god.

OVID'S METAMORPHOSES.

BOOK IV.

Translated by Mr. Eusden.

THE STORY OF ALCITHOE AND HER SISTERS.

YET still Alcithöe perverse remains,
And Bacchus still, and all his rites, disdains.
Too rash, and madly bold, she bids him prove
Himself a god, nor owns the son of Jove.
Her sisters too unanimous agree,
Faithful associates in impiety.
"Be this a solemn feast," the priest had said;
"Be, with each mistress, unemploy'd each maid.
With skins of beasts your tender limbs enclose,
And with an ivy-crown adorn your brows,
The leafy Thyrsus high in triumph bear,
And give your locks to wanton in the air."
These rites profan'd, the holy seer foreshow'd
A mourning people, and a vengeful god.
Matrons and pious wives obedience show,
Distaffs, and wool, half-spun, away they throw:
Then incense burn, and, Bacchus, thee adore,
Or lov'st thou Nysêus, or Lyæus more?
O! doubly got, O! doubly born, they sung,
Thou mighty Bromius, hail, from light'ning sprung!
Hail, Thyon, Eleêus! each name is thine:
Or, listen parent of the genial vine!
Iäcchus! Evan! loudly they repeat,
And not one Grecian attribute forget,
Which to thy praise, great deity, belong,
Styl'd justly Liber in the Roman song.
Eternity of youth is thine! enjoy
Years roll'd on years, yet still a blooming boy.
In Heav'n thou shin'st with a superior grace;
Conceal thy horns, and 'tis a virgin's face.
Thou taught'st the tawny Indian to obey,
And Ganges, smoothly flowing, own'd thy sway.
Lycurgus, Pentheus, equally profane,
By thy just vengeance equally were slain.
By thee the Tuscans, who conspir'd to keep
Thee captive, plung'd, and cut with fins the deep.
With painted reins, all-glitt'ring from afar,
The spotted lynxes proudly draw thy car.
Around, the Bacchæ, and the Satyrs throng;
Behind, Silenus, drunk, lags slow along:
On his dull ass he nods from side to side,
Forbears to fall, yet half forgets to ride.
Still at thy near approach, applauses loud
Are heard, with yellings of the female crowd.
Timbrels, and boxen pipes, with mingled cries,
Swell up in sounds confus'd, and rend the skies.
Come, Bacchus, come propitious, all implore,
And act thy sacred orgies o'er and o'er.
But Mineus' daughters, while these rites were pay'd,
At home, impertinently busy, stay'd.
Their wicked tasks they ply with various art,
And through the loom the sliding shuttle dart;
Or at the fire to comb the wool they stand,
Or twirl the spindle with a dext'rous hand.
Guilty themselves, they force the guiltless in;
Their maids who share the labour, share the sin.

At last one sister cries, who nimbly knew
To draw nice threads, and wind the finest clue,
"While others idly rove, and gods revere,
Their fancy'd gods! they know not who or where;
Let us, whom Pallas taught her better arts,
Still working, cheer with mirthful chat our hearts:
And to deceive the time, let me prevail
With each by turns to tell some antic tale."
She said: her sisters lik'd the humour well,
And smiling, bad her the first story tell.
But she awhile profoundly seem'd to muse,
Perplex'd amid variety to choose:
And knew not, whether she should first relate
The poor Dircetis, and her wond'rous fate.
The Palestines believe it to a man,
And show the lake, in which her scales began.
Or if she rather should the daughter sing,
Who in the hoary verge of life took wing;
Who soar'd from Earth, and dwelt in tow'rs on high,
And now a dove she flits along the sky.
Or how lewd Naïs, when her lust was cloy'd,
To fishes turn'd the youths she had enjoy'd,
By pow'rful verse and herbs; effects most strange!
At last the changer shar'd herself the change.
Or how the tree, which once white berries bore,
Still crimson bears, since stain'd with crimson gore.
The tree was new; she likes it, and begins
To tell the tale, and, as she tells, she spins.

THE STORY OF PYRAMUS AND THISBE.

"In Babylon, where first her queen, for state,
Rais'd walls of brick magnificently great,
Liv'd Pyramus and Thisbe, lovely pair!
He found no eastern youth his equal there,
And she beyond the fairest nymph was fair.
A closer neighbourhood was never known,
Though two the houses, yet the roof was one.
Acquaintance grew, th' acquaintance they improve
To friendship, friendship ripen'd into love:
Love had been crown'd, but impotently mad,
What parents could not hinder, they forbad.
For with fierce flames young Pyramus still burn'd,
And grateful Thisbe flames as fierce return'd.
Aloud in words their thoughts they dare not break,
But silent stand; and silent looks can speak.
The fire of love, the more it is suppress,
The more it glows, and rages in the breast.
"When the division-wall was built, a chink
Was left, the cement unobserv'd to shrink.
So slight the cranny, that it still had been
For centuries unclos'd, because unseen.
But oh! what thing so small, so secret lies,
Which scapes, if form'd for love, a lover's eyes?
Ev'n in this narrow chink they quickly found
A friendly passage for a trackless sound.
Safely they told their sorrows, and their joys,
In whisper'd murmurs, and a dying noise.
By turns to catch each other's breath they strove,
And suck'd in all the balmy breeze of love.
Oft as on diff'rent sides they stood, they cry'd,
'Malicious wall, thus lovers to divide!
Suppose, thou should'st awhile to us give place
To lock, and fasten in a close embrace:
But if too much to grant so sweet a bliss,
Indulge at least the pleasure of a kiss.
We scorn ingratitude: to thee, we know
This safe conveyance of our minds we owe.'
"Thus they their vain petition did renew
Till night, and then they softly sigh'd adieu.
But first they strove to kiss, and that was all;
Their kisses dy'd untasted on the wall.
Soon as the morn had o'er the stars prevail'd,
And, warm'd by Phœbus, flow'rs their dews exhale,
The lovers to their well-known place return,
Alike they suffer, and alike they mourn.
At last their parents they resolve to cheat,
(If to deceive in love be call'd deceit)
To steal by night from home, and thence unknown
To seek the fields, and quit th' unfaithful town.
But, to prevent their wand'ring in the dark,
They both agree to fix upon a mark;
A mark, that could not their designs expose:
The tomb of Ninus was the mark they chose.
There they might rest secure beneath the shade,
Which boughs, with snowy fruit encumber'd, made:
A wide-spread mulberry its rise had took
Just on the margin of a gurgling brook.
Impatient for the friendly dusk they stay,
And chide the slowness of departing day;
In western seas down sunk at last the light,
From western seas up-rose the shades of night.
The loving Thisbe ev'n prevents the hour,
With cautious silence she unlocks the door,
And veils her face, and marching thro' the gloom
Swiftly arrives at th' assignation-tomb.
For still the fearful sex can fearless prove;
Boldly they act, if spirited by love.
When lo! a lioness rush'd o'er the plain,
Grimly besmear'd with blood of oxen slain:
And what to the dire sight new horrours brought,
To slake her thirst the neighb'ring spring she sought.
Which, by the Moon, when trembling Thisbe spies,
Wing'd with her fear, swift as the wind, she flies;
And in a cave recovers from her fright,
But dropt her veil, confounded in her flight.
When sated with repeated draughts, again
The queen of beasts scour'd back along the plain,
She found the veil, and mouthing it all o'er,
With bloody jaws the lifeless prey she tore.
"The youth, who could not cheat his guards so soon,
Late came, and noted by the glimm'ring Moon
Some savage feet, now printed on the ground,
His cheeks turn'd pale, his limbs no vigour found:
But when, advancing on, the veil he spy'd
Distain'd with blood, and ghastly torn, he cry'd,
'One night shall death to two young lovers give,
But she deserv'd unnumber'd years to live!
'Tis I am guilty, I have thee betray'd,
Who came not early, as my charming maid.
Whatever slew thee, I the cause remain;
I nam'd, and fix'd the place where thou wast slain.
Ye lions from your neighb'ring dens repair,
Pity the wretch, this impious body tear!
But cowards thus for death can idly cry;
The brave still have it in their pow'r to die.'
Then to th' appointed tree he hastes away,
The veil first gather'd, though all rent it lay:
The veil all rent yet still itself endears,
He kiss'd, and kissing, wash'd it with his tears.
'Tho' rich,' he cry'd, 'with many a precious stain,
Still from my blood a deeper tincture gain.'
Then in his breast his shining sword he drown'd,
And fell supine, extended on the ground.
As out again the blade he dying drew,
Out spun the blood, and streaming upwards flew.

So if a conduit-pipe e'er burst you saw,
Swift spring the gushing waters thro' the flaw:
Then spouting in a bow, they rise on high,
And a new fountain plays amid the sky.
The berries, stain'd with blood, began to show
A dark complexion, and forgot their snow;
While fatten'd with the flowing gore, the root
Was doom'd for ever to a purple fruit.
"Mean time poor Thisbe fear'd, so long she stay'd,
Her lover might suspect a perjur'd maid.
Her fright scarce o'er, she strove the youth to find
With ardent eyes, which spoke an ardent mind.
Already in his arms, she hears him sigh
At her destruction, which was once so nigh.
The tomb, the tree, but not the fruit she knew;
The fruit she doubted for its alter'd hue.
Still as she doubts, her eyes a body found
Quiv'ring in death, and gasping on the ground.
She started back, the red her cheeks forsook,
And ev'ry nerve with thrilling horrours shook.
So trembles the smooth surface of the seas,
If brush'd o'er gently with a rising breeze.
But when her view her bleeding love confess'd,
She shriek'd, she tore her hair, she beat her breast.
She rais'd the body, and embrac'd it round,
And bath'd with tears unfeign'd the gaping wound.
Then her warm lips to the cold face apply'd,
'And is it thus, ah! thus we meet?' she cry'd:
'My Pyramus! whence sprung thy cruel fate?
My Pyramus!——ah! speak, ere 'tis too late.
I, thy own Thisbe, but one word implore,
One word thy Thisbe never ask'd before.'
At Thisbe's name, awak'd, he open'd wide
His dying eyes; with dying eyes he try'd
On her to dwell, but clos'd them slow, and dy'd.
"The fatal cause was now at last explor'd,
Her veil she knew, and saw his sheathless sword:
'From thy own hand thy ruin thou hast found,'
She said; 'but love first taught that hand to wound.
Ev'n I for thee as bold a hand can show,
And love, which shall as true direct the blow.
I will against the woman's weakness strive,
And never thee, lamented youth, survive.
The world may say, I caus'd, alas! thy death,
But saw thee breathless, and resign'd my breath.
Fate, tho' it conquers, shall no triumph gain,
Fate, that divides us, still divides in vain.
Now, both our cruel parents, hear my pray'r;
My pray'r to offer for us both I dare;
Oh! see our ashes in one urn confin'd,
Whom Love at first, and Fate at last has join'd.
The bliss, you envy'd, is not our request;
Lovers, when dead, may sure together rest.
Thou, tree, where now one lifeless lump is laid,
Ere long o'er two shalt cast a friendly shade.
Still let our loves from thee be understood,
Still witness in thy purple fruit our blood.'
She spoke, and in her bosom plung'd the sword
All warm and reeking from its slaughter'd lord.
"The pray'r, which dying Thisbe had preferr'd,
Both gods, and parents, with compassion heard.
The whiteness of the mulberry soon fled,
And, rip'ning, sadden'd in a dusky red:
While both their parents their lost children mourn,
And mix their ashes in one golden urn."
Thus did the melancholy tale conclude,
And a short, silent interval ensu'd.
The next in birth unloos'd her artful tongue,
And drew attentive all the sister-throng.

THE STORY OF LEUCOTHOE AND THE SUN.

"The Sun, the source of light, by beauty's pow'r
Once am'rous grew; then hear the Sun's amour.
Venus and Mars, with his far-piercing eyes,
This god first spy'd; this god first all things spies.
Stung at the sight, and swift on mischief bent,
To haughty Juno's shapeless son he went:
The goddess and her god gallant betray'd,
And told the cuckold, where their pranks were play'd.
Poor Vulcan soon desir'd to hear no more,
He dropp'd his hammer, and he shook all o'er;
Then courage takes, and full of vengeful ire
He heaves the bellows, and blows fierce the fire:
From liquid brass, tho' sure, yet subtle snares
He forms, and next a wond'rous net prepares,
Drawn with such curious art, so nicely sly,
Unseen the mashes cheat the searching eye.
Not half so thin their webs the spiders weave,
Which the most wary, buzzing prey deceive.
These chains, obedient to the touch, he spread
In secret foldings o'er the conscious bed:
The conscious bed again was quickly prest
By the fond pair, in lawless raptures blest.
Mars wonder'd at his Cytherëa's charms,
More fast than ever lock'd within her arms.
While Vulcan th' iv'ry doors unbarr'd with care,
Then call'd the gods to view the sportive pair:
The gods throng'd in, and saw in open day,
Where Mars, and beauty's queen, all naked lay.
O! shameful sight, if shameful that we name,
Which gods with envy view'd, and could not blame;
But, for the pleasure, wish'd to bear the shame.
Each deity, with laughter tir'd, departs,
Yet all still laugh'd at Vulcan in their hearts.
"Thro' Heav'n the news of this surprisal run,
But Venus did not thus forget the Sun.
He, who stol'n transports idly had betray'd,
By a betrayer was in kind repaid.
What now avails, great god, thy piercing blaze?
That youth, and beauty, and those golden rays?
Thou, who can'st warm this universe alone,
Feel'st now a warmth more pow'rful than thy own:
And those bright eyes, which all things should survey,
Know not from fair Leucothöe to stray.
The lamp of light, for human good design'd,
Is to one virgin niggardly confin'd.
Sometimes too early rise thy eastern beams,
Sometimes too late they set in western streams:
'Tis then her beauty thy swift course delays,
And gives to winter skies long summer days.
Now in thy face thy love-sick mind appears,
And spreads thro' impious nations empty fears:
For when thy beamless head is wrapt in night,
Poor mortals tremble in despair of light.
'Tis not the Moon, that o'er thee casts a veil,
'Tis love alone, which makes thy looks so pale.
Leucothöe is grown thy only care,
Not Phaëton's fair mother now is fair.
The youthful Rhodos moves no tender thought,
And beauteous Persa is at last forgot.
Fond Clytiè, scorn'd, yet lov'd, and sought thy bed,
Ev'n then thy heart for other virgins bled.
Leucothöe has all thy soul possest,
And chas'd each rival passion from thy breast.

To this bright nymph Eurynomè gave birth
In the blest confines of the spicy earth.
Excelling others, she herself beheld
By her own blooming daughter far excell'd.
The sire was Orchamus, whose vast command,
The sev'nth from Belus, rul'd the Persian land.
"Deep in cool vales, beneath th' Hesperian sky,
For the Sun's fiery steeds the pastures lie.
Ambrosia there they eat, and thence they gain
New vigour, and their daily toils sustain.
While thus on heav'nly food the coursers fed,
And night, around, her gloomy empire spread,
The god assum'd the mother's shape and air,
And pass'd, unheeded, to his darling fair.
Close by a lamp, with maids encompass'd round,
The royal spinster full employ'd he found: [rest;'
Then cry'd, 'A-while from work, my daughter,
And, like a mother, scarce her lips he prest.
'Servants retire!——nor secrets dare to hear,
Intrusted only to a daughter's ear.'
They swift obey'd: not one, suspicious, thought
The secret, which their mistress would be taught.
Then he: 'Since now no witnesses are near,
Behold! the god, who guides the various year!
The world's vast eye, of light the source serene,
Who all things sees, by whom are all things seen.
Believe me, nymph! (for I the truth have show'd)
Thy charms have pow'r to charm so great a god.'
Confus'd, she heard him his soft passion tell,
And on the floor, untwirl'd, the spindle fell:
Still from the sweet confusion some new grace
Blush'd out by stealth, and languish'd in her face.
The lover, now inflam'd, himself put on,
And out at once the god, all radiant, shone.
The virgin startled at his alter'd form,
Too weak to bear a god's impetuous storm:
No more against the dazzling youth she strove,
But silent yielded, and indulg'd his love.
"This Clytiè knew, and knew she was undone,
Whose soul was fix'd, and doted on the Sun.
She rag'd to think on her neglected charms,
And Phœbus panting in another's arms.
With envious madness fir'd, she flies in haste,
And tells the king, his daughter was unchaste.
The king, incens'd to hear his honour stain'd,
No more the father nor the man retain'd.
In vain she stretch'd her arms, and turn'd her eyes
To her lov'd god, th' enlight'ner of the skies.
In vain she own'd it was a crime, yet still
It was a crime not acted by her will.
The brutal sire stood deaf to ev'ry pray'r,
And deep in earth entomb'd alive the fair.
What Phœbus could do, was by Phœbus done:
Full on her grave with pointed beams he shone:
To pointed beams the gaping earth gave way;
Had the nymph eyes, her eyes had seen the day,
But lifeless now, yet lovely still, she lay.
Not more the god wept, when the world was fir'd,
And in the wreck his blooming boy expir'd.
The vital flame he strives to light again,
And warm the frozen blood in ev'ry vein:
But since resistless fates deny'd that pow'r,
On the cold nymph he rain'd a nectar show'r.
'Ah! undeserving thus,' he said, 'to die,
Yet still in odours thou shalt reach the sky.'
The body soon dissolv'd, and all around
Perfum'd with heav'nly fragrancies the ground.
A sacrifice for gods up-rose from thence,
A sweet delightful tree of frankincense.

THE TRANSFORMATION OF CLYTIE.

"Though guilty Clytiè thus the Sun betray'd,
By too much passion she was guilty made.
Excess of love begot excess of grief,
Grief fondly bad her hence to hope relief.
But angry Phœbus hears, unmov'd, her sighs,
And scornful from her loath'd embraces flies;
All day, all night, in trackless wilds, alone
She pin'd, and taught the list'ning rocks her moan.
On the bare earth she lies, her bosom bare,
Loose her attire, dishevel'd is her hair.
Nine times the Morn unbarr'd the gates of light,
As oft were spead th' alternate shades of night,
So long no sustenance the mourner knew,
Unless she drunk her tears, or suck'd the dew.
She turn'd about, but rose not from the ground,
Turn'd to the Sun, still as he roll'd his round:
On his bright face hung her desiring eyes,
Till fix'd to earth, she strove in vain to rise.
Her looks their paleness in a flow'r retain'd,
But here, and there, some purple streaks they gain'd.
Still the lov'd object the fond leaves pursue,
Still move their root, the moving Sun to view,
And in the heliotrope the nymph is true."
The sisters heard these wonders with surprise,
But part receiv'd them as romantic lies;
And pertly rally'd, that they could not see
In pow'rs divine so vast an energy.
Part own'd, true gods such miracles might do,
But own'd not Bacchus one among the true.
At last a common, just request they make,
And beg Alcithoë her turn to take.
"I will," she said, "and please you, if I can."
Then shot her shuttle swift, and thus began.
"The fate of Daphnis is a fate too known,
Whom an enamour'd nymph transform'd to stone,
Because she fear'd another nymph might see
The lovely youth, and love as much as she:
So strange the madness is of jealousy!
Nor shall I tell, what changes Scython made,
And how he walk'd a man, or tripp'd a maid.
You too would peevish frown, and patience want
To hear, how Celmis grew an adamant.
He once was dear to Jove, and saw of old
Jove when a child; but what he saw he told.
Crocus and Smilax may be turn'd to flow'rs,
And the Curetes spring from bounteous show'rs;
I pass a hundred legends' stale. as these,
And with sweet novelty your taste will please.

THE STORY OF SALMACIS AND HERMAPHRODITUS.

By Mr. Addison.

"How Salmacis with weak enfeebling streams
Softens the body, and unnerves the limbs,
And what the secret cause, shall here be shown;
The cause is secret, but th' effect is known.
"The Naïds nurst an infant heretofore,
That Cytherëa once to Hermes bore:
From both th' illustrious authors of his race
The child was nam'd; nor was it hard to trace
Both the bright parents thro' the infant's face.
When fifteen years in Ida's cool retreat
The boy had told, he left his native seat,
And sought fresh fountains in a foreign soil:
The pleasure lessen'd the attending toil.
With eager steps the Lycian fields he crost,
And fields that border on the Lycian coast;

A river here he view'd so lovely bright,
It show'd the bottom in a fairer light,
Nor kept a sand conceal'd from human sight.
The stream produc'd nor slimy ooze, nor weeds,
Nor miry rushes, nor the spiky reeds;
But dealt enriching moisture all around,
The fruitful banks with cheerful verdure crown'd,
And kept the spring eternal on the ground.
A nymph presides, not practis'd in the chase,
Nor skilful at the bow, nor at the race;
Of all the blue-ey'd daughters of the main,
The only stranger to Diana's train:
Her sisters often, as 'tis said, would cry,
'Fie, Salmacis: what, always idle! fie!
Or take thy quiver, or thy arrows seize,
And mix the toils of hunting with thy ease.'
Nor quiver she nor arrows e'er would seize,
Nor mix the toils of hunting with her ease.
But oft would bathe her in the crystal tide,
Oft with a comb her dewy locks divide;
Now in the limpid streams she views her face,
And drest her image in the floating glass:
On beds of leaves she now repos'd her limbs,
Now gather'd flow'rs that grew about her streams,
And then by chance was gathering, as she stood
To view the boy, and long'd for what she view'd.
"Fain would she meet the youth with hasty feet,
She fain would meet him, but refus'd to meet
Before her looks were set with nicest care,
And well deserv'd to be reputed fair.
'Bright youth,' she cries, 'whom all thy features prove
A god, and, if a god, the god of love;
But if a mortal, blest thy nurse's breast,
Blest are thy parents, and thy sisters blest:
But oh how blest! how more than blest thy bride,
Ally'd in bliss, if any yet ally'd.
If so, let mine the stolen enjoyments be;
If not, behold a willing bride in me.'
"The boy knew nought of love, and toucht with shame,
He strove, and blusht, but still the blush became:
In rising blushes still fresh beauties rose;
The sunny side of fruit such blushes shows,
And such the Moon, when all her silver white
Turns in eclipses to a ruddy light.
The nymph still begs, if not a nobler bliss,
A cold salute at least, a sister's kiss:
And now prepares to take the lovely boy
Between her arms. He, innocently coy,
Replies, 'Or leave me to myself alone,
You rude uncivil nymph, or I'll be gone.'
'Fair stranger then,' says she, 'it shall be so;'
And, for she fear'd his threats, she feign'd to go:
But hid within a covert's neighbouring green,
She kept him still in sight, herself unseen.
The boy now fancies all the danger o'er,
And innocently sports about the shore:
Playful and wanton to the stream he trips,
And dips his foot, and shivers as he dips.
The coolness pleas'd him, and with eager haste
His airy garments on the banks he cast;
His godlike features, and his heav'nly hue,
And all his beauties were expos'd to view.
His naked limbs the nymph with rapture spies,
While hotter passions in her bosom rise,
Flush in her cheeks, and sparkle in her eyes.
She longs, she burns to clasp him in her arms,
And looks, and sighs, and kindles at his charms.
"Now all undrest upon the banks he stood,
And clapt his sides, and leapt into the flood:
His lovely limbs the silver waves divide,
His limbs appear more lovely through the tide,
As lilies shut within a crystal case,
Receive a glossy lustre from the glass.
'He's mine, he's all my own,' the Naïad cries,
And flings off all, and after him she flies.
And now she fastens on him as he swims,
And holds him close, and wraps about his limbs.
The more the boy resisted, and was coy,
The more she clipt, and kist the struggling boy.
So when the wriggling snake is snatcht on high
In eagle's claws, and hisses in the sky,
Around the foe his twirling tail he flings,
And twists her legs, and writhes about her wings.
"The restless boy still obstinately strove
To free himself, and still refus'd her love.
Amidst his limbs she kept her limbs intwin'd,
'And why, coy youth,' she cries, 'why thus unkind?
Oh may the gods thus keep us ever join'd!
Oh may we never, never, never part again!'
So pray'd the nymph, nor did she pray in vain:
For now she finds him, as his limbs she prest,
Grow nearer still, and nearer to her breast;
Till, piercing each the other's flesh, they run
Together, and incorporate in one:
Last in one face are both their faces join'd,
As when the stock and grafted twig combin'd
Shoot up the same, and wear a common rind:
Both bodies in a single body mix,
A single body with a double sex.
"The boy, thus lost in woman, now survey'd
The river's guilty stream, and thus he pray'd.
(He pray'd, but wonder'd at his softer tone,
Surpris'd to hear a voice but half his own.)
'You parent-gods, whose heav'nly names I bear,
Hear your hermaphrodite, and grant my pray'r;
Oh grant, that whomsoe'er these streams contain,
If man he enter'd, he may rise again
Supple, unsinew'd, and but half a man!'
"The heav'nly parents answer'd, from on high,
Their two-shap'd son, the double votary;
Then gave a secret virtue to the flood,
And ting'd its source to make his wishes good."

Continued by Mr. Eusden.

ALCITHÖE AND HER SISTERS TRANSFORMED TO BATS.

But Mineus' daughters still their tasks pursue,
To wickedness most obstinately true:
At Bacchus still they laugh; when all around,
Unseen, the timbrels hoarse were heard to sound.
Saffron and myrrh their fragrant odours shed,
And now the present deity they dread.
Strange to relate! Here ivy first was seen,
Along the distaff crept the wond'rous green.
Then sudden springing vines began to bloom,
And the soft tendrils curl'd around the loom:
While purple clusters, dangling from on high,
Ting'd the wrought purple with a second dye.
Now from the skies was shot a doubtful light,
The day declining to the bounds of night.
The fabric's firm foundations shake all o'er,
False tigers rage, and figur'd lions roar.
Torches, aloft, seem blazing in the air,
And angry flashes of red light'nings glare.
To dark recesses, the dire sight to shun,
Swift the pale sisters in confusion run.

Their arms were lost in pinions, as they fled,
And subtle films each slender limb o'erspread.
Their alter'd forms their senses soon reveal'd;
Their forms, how alter'd, darkness still conceal'd.
Close to the roof each, wond'ring, upwards springs,
Borne on unknown, transparent, plumeless wings.
They strove for words; their little bodies found
No words, but murmur'd in a fainting sound.
In towns, not woods, the sooty bats delight,
And never, till the dusk, begin their flight;
Till Vesper rises with his ev'ning flame:
From whom the Romans have deriv'd their name.

THE TRANSFORMATION OF INO AND MELICERTA TO SEA-GODS.

THE pow'r of Bacchus now o'er Thebes had flown:
With awful rev'rence soon the god they own.
Proud Ino all around the wonder tells,
And on her nephew deity still dwells.
Of num'rous sisters, she alone yet knew
No grief, but grief which she from sisters drew.
Imperial Juno saw her with disdain
Vain in her offspring, in her consort vain,
Who rul'd the trembling Thebans with a nod,
But saw her vainest in her foster-god.
"Could then," she cry'd, "a bastard boy have pow'r
To make a mother her own son devour?
Could he the Tuscan crew to fishes change,
And now three sisters damn to forms so strange?
Yet shall the wife of Jove find no relief!
Shall she, still unreveng'd, disclose her grief!
Have I the mighty freedom to complain?
Is that my pow'r? Is that to ease my pain?
A foe has taught me vengeance, and who ought
To scorn that vengeance, which a foe has taught?
What sure destruction frantic rage can throw,
The gaping wounds of slaughter'd Pentheus show.
Why should not Ino, fir'd with madness, stray,
Like her mad sisters her own kindred slay?
Why, she not follow, where they lead the way?"
Down a steep, yawning cave, where yews display'd
In arches meet, and lend a baleful shade,
Through silent labyrinths a passage lies
To mournful regions, and infernal skies.
Here Styx exhales its noisome clouds, and here,
The fun'ral rites once paid, all souls appear.
Stiff cold, and horrour with a ghastly face
And staring eyes, infest the dreary place.
Ghosts, new-arriv'd, and strangers to these plains,
Know not the palace where grim Pluto reigns.
They journey doubtful, nor the road can tell,
Which leads to the metropolis of Hell.
A thousand avenues those tow'rs command,
A thousand gates for ever open stand.
As all the rivers, disembogu'd, find room
For all their waters in old ocean's womb:
So this vast city worlds of shades receives,
And space for millions still of worlds she leaves.
Th' unbody'd spectres freely rove, and show
Whate'er they lov'd on Earth, they love below.
The lawyers still, or right, or wrong, support,
The courtiers smoothly glide to Pluto's court,
Still airy heroes thoughts of glory fire,
Still the dead poet strings his deathless lyre,
And lovers still with fancy'd darts expire.
The queen of Heaven, to gratify her hate,
And sooth immortal wrath, forgets her state.
Down from the realms of day, to realms of night,
The goddess swift precipitates her flight.
At Hell arriv'd, the noise Hell's porter heard,
Th' enormous dog his triple head up-rear'd:
Thrice from three grizly throats he howl'd profound,
Then suppliant couch'd, and stretch'd along the ground.
The trembling threshold, which Saturnia prest,
The weight of such divinity confest.
Before a lofty, adamantine gate,
Which clos'd a tow'r of brass, the Furies sate;
Mis-shapen forms, tremendous to the sight,
Th' implacable foul daughters of the Night.
A sounding whip each bloody sister shakes,
Or from her tresses combs the curling snakes.
But now great Juno's majesty was known;
Through the thick gloom, all heav'nly bright, she shone:
The hideous monsters their obedience show'd,
And, rising from their seats, submissive bow'd.
This is the place of woe, here groan the dead;
Huge Tityus o'er nine acres here is spread.
Fruitful for pain th' immortal liver breeds,
Still grows, and still th' insatiate vulture feeds.
Poor Tantalus to taste the water tries,
But from his lips the faithless water flies:
Then thinks the bending tree he can command;
The tree starts backwards, and eludes his hand.
The labour too of Sisyphus is vain,
Up the steep mount he heaves the stone with pain,
Down from the summit rolls the stone again.
The Belides their leaky vessels still
Are ever filling, and yet never fill:
Doom'd to this punishment for blood they shed,
For bridegroom slaughter'd in the bridal bed.
Stretch'd on the rolling wheel Ixion lies;
Himself he follows, and himself he flies;
Ixion, tortur'd, Juno sternly ey'd,
Then turn'd, and toiling Sisyphus espy'd:
"And why," she said, "so wretched is the fate
Of him, whose brother proudly reigns in state?
Yet still my altars unador'd have been
By Athamas, and his presumptuous queen."
What caus'd her hate the goddess thus confest,
What caus'd her journey now was more than guest.
That hate, relentless, its revenge did want,
And that revenge the Furies soon could grant:
They could the glory of proud Thebes efface,
And hide in ruin the Cadmèan race.
For this she largely promises, entreats,
And to entreaties adds emperial threats.
Then fell Tisiphonè with rage was stung,
And from her mouth th' untwisted serpents flung.
"To gain this trifling boon, there is no need,"
She cry'd, "in formal speeches to proceed.
Whatever thou command'st to do, is done;
Believe it finish'd, though not yet begun.
But from these melancholy seats repair
To happier mansions, and to purer air."
She spoke: the goddess, darting upwards, flies,
And joyous re-ascends her native skies:
Nor enter'd there, till 'round her Iris threw
Ambrosial sweets, and pour'd celestial dew.
The faithful Fury, guiltless of delays,
With cruel haste the dire command obeys.
Girt in a bloody gown, a torch she shakes,
And round her neck twines speckled wreaths of snakes.
Fear, and Dismay, and agonizing Pain,
With frantic Rage, complete her loveless train.

To Thebes her flight she sped, and Hell forsook;
At her approach the Theban turrets shook: [cast,
The Sun shrunk back, thick clouds the day o'er-
And springing greens were wither'd as she past.
Now, dismal yellings heard, strange spectres seen,
Confound as much the monarch as the queen.
In vain to quit the palace they prepar'd,
Tisiphonè was there, and kept the ward.
She wide extended her unfriendly arms,
And all the fury lavish'd all her harms.
Part of her tresses loudly hiss, and part
Spread poison, as their forky tongues they dart.
Then from her middle locks two snakes she drew,
Whose merit from superior mischief grew:
Th' envenom'd ruin thrown with spiteful care,
Clung to the bosoms of the hapless pair. [fir'd,
The hapless pair soon with wild thoughts were
And madness by a thousand ways inspir'd.
'Tis true, th' unwounded body still was sound,
But 'twas the soul which felt the deadly wound.
Nor did th' unsated monster here give o'er,
But dealt of plagues a fresh, unnumber'd store.
Each baneful juice too well she understood,
Foam, churn'd by Cerberus, and Hydra's blood.
Hot hemlock and cold aconite she chose,
Delighted in variety of woes.
Whatever can untune th' harmonious soul,
And its mild, reas'ning faculties control,
Give false ideas, raise desires profane,
And whirl in eddies the tumultuous brain,
Mix'd with curs'd art, she direfully around
Thro' all their nerves diffus'd the sad compound.
Then toss'd her torch in circles still the same,
Improv'd their rage, and added flame to flame.
The grinning fury her own conquest spy'd,
And to her rueful shades return'd with pride,
And threw th' exhausted, useless snakes aside.
Now Athamas cries out, his reason fled,
"Here, fellow-hunters, let the toils be spread.
I saw a lioness, in quest of food,
With her two young, run roaring in this wood."
Again the fancy'd savages were seen,
As thro' his palace still he chas'd his queen;
Then tore Learchus from her breast: the child
Stretch'd little arms, and on its father smil'd:
A father now no more, who now begun
Around his head to whirl his giddy son,
And, quite insensible to nature's call,
The helpless infant flung against the wall.
The same mad poison in the mother wrought;
Young Melicerta in her arms she caught,
And with disorder'd tresses, howling, flies,
"O! Bacchus, Evôe, Bacchus!" loud she cries.
"The name of Bacchus Juno laugh'd to hear,
And said, "Thy foster-god has cost thee dear."
A rock there stood, whose side the beating waves
Had long consum'd, and hollow'd into caves.
The head shot forwards in a bending steep,
And cast a dreadful covert o'er the deep.
The wretched Ino, on destruction bent,
Climb'd up the cliff; such strength her fury lent:
Thence with her guiltless boy, who wept in vain,
At one bold spring she plung'd into the main.
Her niece's fate touch'd Cytherea's breast,
And in soft sounds she Neptune thus address'd.
"Great god of waters, whose extended sway
Is next to his, whom Heav'n and Earth obey:
Let not the suit of Venus thee displease,
Pity the floaters on th' Ionian seas.
Increase thy subject-gods, nor yet disdain
To add my kindred to that glorious train.
If from the sea I may such honours claim,
If 'tis desert, that from the sea I came,
As Grecian poets artfully have sung,
And in the name confest, from whence I sprung."
Pleas'd Neptune nodded his assent, and free
Both soon became from frail mortality.
He gave them form, and majesty divine,
And bad them glide along the foamy brine.
For Melicerta is Palæmon known,
And Ino once, Leucothöe is grown.

THE TRANSFORMATION OF THE THEBAN MATRONS.

THE Theban matrons their lov'd queen pursu'd,
And tracing to the rock, her footsteps view'd.
Too certain of her fate, they rend the skies
With piteous shrieks, and lamentable cries.
All beat their breasts, and Juno all upbraid,
Who still remember'd a deluded maid:
Who, still revengeful for one stol'n embrace,
Thus wreak'd her hate on the Cadmean race.
This Juno heard; "And shall such elfs," she cry'd,
"Dispute my justice, or my pow'r deride?
You too shall feel my wrath not idly spent;
A goddess never for insults was meant." [been,
She, who lov'd most, and who most lov'd had
Said, "Not the waves shall part me from my queen."
She strove to plunge into the roaring flood;
Fix'd to the stone, a stone herself she stood.
This, on her breast would fain her blows repeat,
Her stiffen'd hands refus'd her breast to beat.
That, stretch'd her arms unto the seas; in vain
Her arms she labour'd to unstretch again.
To tear her comely locks another try'd,
Both comely locks and fingers petrify'd.
Part thus; but Juno with a softer mind
Part doom'd to mix among the feather'd kind.
Transform'd, the name of Theban birds they keep,
And skim the surface of that fatal deep.

CADMUS AND HIS QUEEN TRANSFORMED TO SERPENTS.

MEAN time, the wretched Cadmus mourns, nor
That they who mortal fell, immortal rose. [knows
With a long series of new ills opprest,
He droops, and all the man forsakes his breast.
Strange prodigies confound his frighted eyes;
From the fair city, which he rais'd, he flies:
As if misfortune not pursu'd his race,
But only hung o'er that devoted place.
Resolv'd by sea to seek some distant land,
At last he safely gain'd th' Illyrian strand.
Cheerless himself, his consort still he cheers,
Hoary, and loaden'd both with woes and years.
Then to recount past sorrows they begin,
And trace them to the gloomy origin.
"That serpent sure was hallow'd," Cadmus cry'd,
"Which once my spear transfix'd with foolish
When the big teeth, a seed before unknown, [pride:
By me along the wond'ring glebe were sown,
And sprouting armies by themselves o'erthrown.
If thence the wrath of Heav'n on me is bent,
May Heav'n conclude it with one sad event;
To an extended serpent change the man:"
And while he spoke, the wish'd-for change began.
His skin with sea-green spots was vary'd 'round,
And on his belly prone he prest the ground.

He glitter'd soon with many a golden scale,
And his shrunk legs clos'd in a spiry tail.
Arms yet remain'd, remaining arms he spread
To his lov'd wife, and human tears yet shed.
"Come, my Harmonia, come, thy face recline
Down to my face; still touch, what still is mine.
O! let these hands, while hands, be gently prest,
While yet the serpent has not all possest."
More he had spoke, but strove to speak in vain,
The forky tongue refus'd to tell his pain,
And learn'd in hissings only to complain. [sta
Then shriek'd Harmonia, "Stay, my Cadmus,
Glide not in such a monstrous shape away!
Destruction, like impetuous waves, rolls on.
Where are thy feet, thy legs, thy shoulders gone!
Chang'd is thy visage, chang'd is all thy frame;
Cadmus is only Cadmus now in name.
Ye gods, my Cadmus to himself restore,
Or me like him transform; I ask no more."
The husband serpent show'd he still had thought,
With wonted fondness an embrace he sought;
Play'd round her neck in many a harmless twist,
And lick'd that bosom, which, a man, he kist.
The lookers-on (for lookers-on there were)
Shock'd at the sight, half-dy'd away with fear.
The transformation was again renew'd, [view'd.
And, like the husband, chang'd the wife they
Both, serpents now, with fold involv'd in fold,
To the next covert amicably roll'd.
There curl'd they lie, or wave along the green,
Fearless see men, by men are fearless seen,
Still mild, and conscious what they once have been.

THE STORY OF PERSEUS.

YET tho' this harsh, inglorious fate they found,
Each in the deathless grandson liv'd renown'd.
Thro' conquer'd India Bacchus nobly rode, [god.
And Greece with temples hail'd the conqu'ring
In Argos only proud Acrisius reign'd,
Who all the consecrated rites profan'd.
Audacious wretch! thus Bacchus to deny,
And the great thund'rer's great son defy!
Nor him alone: thy daughter vainly strove,
Brave Perseus of celestial stem to prove,
And herself pregnant by a golden Jove.
Yet this was true, and truth in time prevails;
Acrisius now his unbelief bewails.
His former thought an impious thought he found,
And both the hero and the god were own'd.
He saw, already one in Heav'n was plac'd,
And one with more than mortal triumphs grac'd.
The victor Perseus with the Gorgon-head,
O'er Libyan sands his airy journey sped.
The gory drops distill'd, as swift he flew,
And from each drop envenom'd serpents grew.
The mischiefs brooded on the barren plains,
And still th' unhappy fruitfulness remains.

ATLAS TRANSFORMED TO A MOUNTAIN.

THENCE Perseus, like a cloud, by storms was driv'n,
Thro' all th' expanse beneath the cope of Heav'n.
The jarring winds unable to control,
He saw the southern, and the northern pole:
And eastward thrice, and westward thrice was whirl'd,
And from the skies survey'd the nether world.
But when grey ev'ning show'd the verge of night,
He fear'd in darkness to pursue his flight.
He pois'd his pinions, and forgot to soar,
And, sinking, clos'd them on th' Hesperian shore:
Then begg'd to rest, till Lucifer begun
To wake the Morn, the Morn to wake the Sun.
Here Atlas reign'd, of more than human size,
And in his kingdom the world's limit lies.
Here Titan bids his weary'd coursers sleep,
And cools the burning axle in the deep.
The mighty monarch, uncontrol'd, alone,
His sceptre sways: no neighb'ring states are known.
A thousand flocks on shady mountains fed,
A thousand herds o'er grassy plains were spread.
Here wond'rous trees their shining stores unfold,
Their shining stores too wond'rous to be told,
Their leaves, their branches, and their apples, gold.
Then Perseus the gigantic prince addrest,
Humbly implor'd a hospitable rest.
"If bold exploits thy admiration fire,"
He said, "I fancy, mine thou wilt admire.
Or if the glory of a race can move,
Not mean my glory, for I spring from Jove."
At this confession Atlas ghastly star'd,
Mindful of what an oracle declar'd,
That the dark womb of time conceal'd a day,
Which should, disclos'd, the bloomy gold betray:
All should at once be ravish'd from his eyes,
And Jove's own progeny enjoy the prize.
For this, the fruit he loftily immur'd,
And a fierce dragon the strait pass secur'd.
For this, all strangers he forbad to land,
And drove them from th' inhospitable strand.
To Perseus then: "Fly quickly, fly this coast,
Nor falsely dare thy acts and race to boast."
In vain the hero for one night entreats, [threats.
Threat'ning he storms, and next adds force to
By strength not Perseus could himself defend,
For who in strength with Atlas could contend?
"But since short rest to me thou wilt not give,
A gift of endless rest from me receive."
He said, and backward turn'd, no more conceal'd
The present, and Medusa's head reveal'd.
Soon the high Atlas a high mountain stood,
His locks and beard became a leafy wood.
His hands and shoulders into ridges went,
The summit-head still crown'd the steep ascent.
His bones a solid, rocky hardness gain'd:
He, thus immensely grown, (as fate ordain'd)
The stars, the Heav'ns, and all the gods sustain'd.

ANDROMEDA RESCUED FROM THE SEA-MONSTER.

NOW Æolus had with strong chains confin'd,
And deep imprison'd ev'ry blust'ring wind,
The rising Phosphor with a purple light
Did sluggish mortals to new toils invite.
His feet again the valiant Perseus plumes,
And his keen sabre in his hand resumes:
Then nobly spurs the ground, and upwards springs,
And cuts the liquid air with sounding wings.
O'er various seas and various lands he past,
Till Æthiopia's shore appear'd at last.
Andromeda was there, doom'd to atone
By her own ruin follies not her own:
And if injustice in a god can be,
Such was the Libyan god's unjust decree.
Chain'd to a rock she stood; young Perseus stay'd
His rapid flight, to view the beauteous maid.
So sweet her frame, so exquisitely fine,
She seem'd a statue by a hand divine,

Had not the wind her waving tresses show'd,
And down her cheeks the melting sorrows flow'd.
Her faultless form the hero's bosom fires;
The more he looks, the more he still admires.
Th' admirer almost had forgot to fly,
And swift descended, flutt'ring from on high.
" O! virgin, worthy no such chains to prove,
But pleasing chains in the soft folds of love;
Thy country, and thy name," he said, " disclose,
And give a true rehearsal of thy woes."
A quick reply her bashfulness refus'd,
To the free converse of a man unus'd.
Her rising blushes had concealment found
From her spread hands, but that her hands were [bound.
She acted to her full extent of pow'r,
And bath'd her face with a fresh, silent show'r.
But by degrees in innocence grown bold,
Her name, her country, and her birth she told:
And how she suffer'd for her mother's pride,
Who with the Nereids once in beauty vy'd.
Part yet untold, the seas began to roar,
And mounting billows tumbled to the shore.
Above the waves a monster rais'd his head,
His body o'er the deep was widely spread:
Onward he flounc'd; aloud the virgin cries;
Each parent to her shrieks in shrieks replies:
But she had deepest cause to rend the skies.
Weeping, to her they cling; no sign appears
Of help, they only lend their helpless tears.
" Too long you vent your sorrows," Perseus said,
" Short is the hour, and swift the time of aid.
In me the son of thund'ring Jove behold,
Got in a kindly show'r of fruitful gold.
Medusa's snaky head is now my prey,
And through the clouds I boldly wing my way.
If such desert be worthy of esteem,
Add, if your daughter I from death redeem,
Shall she be mine? Shall it not then be thought
A bride, so lovely, was too cheaply bought?
For her my arms I willingly employ,
If I may beauties, which I save, enjoy."
The parents eagerly the terms embrace:
For who would slight such terms in such a case?
Nor her alone they promise, but beside,
The dowry of a kingdom with the bride.
As well-rigg'd galleys, which slaves, sweating, row,
With their sharp beaks the whiten'd ocean plough;
So when the monster mov'd, still at his back
The furrow'd waters left a foamy track.
Now to the rock he was advanc'd so nigh,
Whirl'd from a sling a stone the space would fly,
Then, bounding, upwards the brave Perseus sprung,
And in mid air on hovering pinions hung.
His shadow quickly floated on the main;
The monster could not his wild rage restrain,
But at the floating shadow leap'd in vain.
As when Jove's bird a speckled serpent spies,
Which in the shine of Phœbus basking lies,
Unseen, he souses down, and bears away,
Truss'd from behind, the vainly-hissing prey.
To writhe his neck the labour nought avails,
Too deep th' imperial talons pierce his scales.
Thus the wing'd hero now descends, now soars,
And at his pleasure the vast monster gores.
Full in his back, swift-stooping from above,
The crooked sabre to its hilt he drove.
The monster rag'd, impatient of the pain,
First bounded high, and then sunk low again.
Now, like a savage boar, when chaf'd with wounds,
And bay'd with opening mouths of hungry hounds,
He on the foe turns with collected might,
Who still eludes him with an airy flight;
And wheeling round, the scaly armour tries
Of his thick sides; his thinner tail now plies:
Till from repeated strokes out-gush'd a flood,
And the waves redden'd with the streaming blood.
At last the dropping wings, befoam'd all o'er,
With flaggy heaviness their master bore:
A rock he spy'd, whose humble head was low,
Bare at an ebb, but cover'd at a flow.
A ridgy hold he, thither flying, gain'd,
And with one hand his bending weight sustain'd;
With th' other, vig'rous blows he dealt around,
And the home-thrusts th' expiring monster own'd.
In deaf'ning shouts the glad applauses rise,
And peal on peal runs rattling through the skies.
The saviour-youth the royal pair confess,
And with heav'd hands their daughter's bride-groom bless.
The beauteous bride moves on, now loos'd from [chains,
The cause, and sweet reward of all the hero's pains.
Mean-time, on shore triumphant Perseus stood,
And purg'd his hands, smear'd with the monster's [blood:
Then in the windings of a sandy bed
Compos'd Medusa's execrable head.
But to prevent the roughness, leaves he threw,
And young, green twigs, which soft in waters grew,
There soft, and full of sap; but here, when lay'd,
Touch'd by the head, that softness soon decay'd.
The wonted flexibility quite gone,
The tender scyons harden'd into stone.
Fresh, juicy twigs, surpris'd, the Nereids brought,
Fresh, juicy twigs the same contagion caught.
The nymphs the petrifying seeds still keep,
And propagate the wonder through the deep.
The pliant sprays of coral yet declare
Their stiff'ning nature, when expos'd to air.
Those sprays, which did, like bending osiers, move,
Snatch'd from their element, obdurate prove,
And shrubs beneath the waves, grow stones above.
The great immortals grateful Perseus prais'd,
And to three pow'rs three turfy altars rais'd.
To Hermes this; and that he did assign
To Pallas: the mid honours, Jove, were thine.
He hastes for Pallas a white cow to cull,
A calf for Hermes, but for Jove a bull.
Then seiz'd the prize of his victorious fight,
Andromeda, and claim'd the nuptial rite.
Andromeda alone he greatly sought,
The dowry kingdom was not worth his thought.
Pleas'd Hymen now his golden torch displays;
With rich oblations fragrant altars blaze,
Sweet wreaths of choicest flow'rs are hung on high,
And cloudless pleasure smiles in ev'ry eye.
The melting music melting thoughts inspires,
And warbling songsters aid the warbling lyres.
The palace opens wide in pompous state,
And by his peers surrounded, Cepheus sate.
A feast was serv'd, fit for a king to give,
And fit for godlike heroes to receive.
The banquet ended, the gay, cheerful bowl
Mov'd round, and brighten'd, and enlarg'd each soul.
Then Perseus ask'd what customs there obtain'd,
And by what laws the people were restrain'd.

Which told; the teller a like freedom takes,
And to the warrior his petition makes,
To know, what arts had won Medusa's snakes.

THE STORY OF MEDUSA'S HEAD.

THE hero with his just request complies,
Shows, how a vale beneath cold Atlas lies,
Where with aspiring mountains fenc'd around,
He the two daughters of old Phorcus found.
Fate had one common eye to both assign'd,
Each saw by turns, and each by turns was blind.
But while one strove to lend her sister sight,
He stretch'd his hand, and stole their mutual light,
And left both eyeless, both involv'd in night.
Thro' devious wilds, and trackless woods he past,
And at the Gorgon-seats arriv'd at last:
But as he journey'd, pensive he survey'd,
What wasteful havoc dire Medusa made.
Here, stood still breathing statues, men before;
There, rampant lions seem'd in stone to roar.
Nor did he, yet affrighted, quit the field,
But in the mirror of his polish'd shield
Reflected saw Medusa slumbers take,
And not one serpent by good chance awake.
Then backward an unerring blow he sped,
And from her body lopp'd at once her head.
The gore prolific prov'd; with sudden force
Sprung Pegasus, and wing'd his airy course.
The Heav'n-born warrior faithfully went on,
And told the num'rous dangers which he run.
What subject seas, what lands he had in view,
And nigh what stars th' advent'rous hero flew.
At last he silent sat; the list'ning throng
Sigh'd at the pause of his delightful tongue.
Some begg'd to know, why this alone should wear,
Of all the sisters, such destructive hair.
Great Persus then: "With me you shall prevail,
Worth the relation, to relate a tale.
Medusa once had charms; to gain her love
A rival crowd of envious lovers strove.
They, who have seen her, own, they ne'er did trace
More moving features in a sweeter face.
Yet above all, her length of hair, they own,
In golden ringlets wav'd, and graceful shone.
Her Neptune saw, and with such beauties fir'd,
Resolv'd to compass what his soul desir'd.
In chaste Minerva's fane, he, lustful, stay'd,
And seiz'd and rifled the young, blushing maid.
The bashful goddess turn'd her eyes away,
Nor durst such bold impurity survey;
But on the ravish'd virgin vengeance takes,
Her shining hair is chang'd to hissing snakes.
These in her ægis Pallas joys to bear:
The hissing snakes her foes more sure ensnare,
Than they did lovers once, when shining hair."

OVID'S METAMORPHOSES.

BOOK V.

Translated by Arthur Maynwaring, Esq.

THE STORY OF PERSEUS CONTINUED.

WHILE Perseus entertain'd with this report
His father Cepheus, and the list'ning court,
Within the palace walls was heard aloud
The roaring noise of some unruly crowd;
Not like the songs which cheerful friends prepare
For nuptial days, but sounds that threaten'd war;
And all the pleasures of this happy feast,
To tumult turn'd, in wild disorder ceas'd:
So, when the sea is calm, we often find
A storm rais'd sudden by some furious wind.
Chief in the riot Phineus first appear'd,
The rash ringleader of this boist'rous herd,
And brandishing his brazen-pointed lance,
"Behold," he said, "an injur'd man advance,
Stung with resentment for his ravish'd wife,
Nor shall thy wings, O Perseus, save thy life;
Nor Jove himself; though we've been often told
Who got thee in the form of tempting gold."
His lance was aim'd, when Cepheus ran, and said,
"Hold, brother, hold; what brutal rage has made
Your frantic mind so black a crime conceive?
Are these the thanks that you to Perseus give?
This the reward that to his worth you pay,
Whose timely valour sav'd Andromeda?
Nor was it he, if you would reason right,
That forc'd her from you, but the jealous spite
Of envious Nereids, and Jove's high decree;
And that devouring monster of the sea,
That ready with his jaws wide-gaping stood
To eat my child, the fairest of my blood.
You lost her then, when she seem'd past relief,
And wish'd perhaps her death, to ease your grief
With my afflictions: not content to view
Andromeda in chains, unhelp'd by you,
Her spouse, and uncle; will you grieve that he
Expos'd his life the dying maid to free?
And shall you claim his merit? Had you thought
Her charms so great, you should have bravely sought
That blessing on the rocks, where fix'd she lay:
But now let Perseus bear his prize away,
By service gain'd, by promis'd faith possess'd;
To him I owe it, that my age is bless'd
Still with a child: nor think that I prefer
Perseus to thee, but to the loss of her."
Phineus on him, and Perseus, roll'd about
His eyes in silent rage, and seem'd to doubt
Which to destroy; till, resolute at length,
He threw his spear with the redoubled strength
His fury gave him, and at Perseus struck;
But missing Perseus, in his seat it stuck.
Who, springing nimbly up, return'd the dart,
And almost plung'd it in his rival's heart;
But he for safety to the altar ran,
Unfit protection for so vile a man;
Yet was the stroke not vain, as Rhætus found,
Who in his brow receiv'd a mortal wound;
Headlong he tumbled, when his skull was broke,
From which his friends the fatal weapon took,
While he lay trembling, and his gushing blood
In crimson streams around the table flow'd.
But this provok'd th' unruly rabble worse;
They flung their darts, and some in loud discourse
To death young Perseus and the monarch doom:
But Cepheus left before the guilty room,
With grief appealing to the gods above,
Who laws of hospitality approve,
Who faith protect, and succour injur'd right,
That he was guiltless of this barb'rous fight.
Pallas her brother Perseus close attends,
And with her ample shield from harm defends,
Raising a sprightly courage in his heart:
But Indian Athis took the weaker part,
Born in the crystal grottoes of the sea,
Limnatè's son, a fenny nymph, and she

Daughter of Ganges; graceful was his mien,
His person lovely, and his age sixteen.
His habit made his native beauty more;
A purple mantle fring'd with gold he wore;
His neck well turn'd with golden chains was grac'd,
His hair with myrrh perfum'd, was nicely dress'd.
Though with just aim he could the javelin throw,
Yet with more skill he drew the bending bow;
And now was drawing it with artful hand,
When Perseus, snatching up a flaming brand,
Whirl'd sudden at his face the burning wood,
Crush'd his eyes in, and quench'd the fire with
blood;
Through the soft skin the splinter'd bones appear,
And spoil'd the face that lately was so fair.
When Lycabas his Athis thus beheld,
How was his heart with friendly horrour fill'd!
A youth so noble, to his soul so dear,
To see his shapeless look, his dying groans to hear!
He snatch'd the bow the boy was us'd to bend,
And cry'd, "With me, false traitor, dare contend;
Boast not a conquest o'er a child, but try
Thy strength with me, who all thy pow'rs defy;
Nor think so mean an act a victory."
While yet he spoke he flung the whizzing dart,
Which pierc'd the plaited robe, but miss'd his heart:
Perseus, defy'd, upon him fiercely press'd
With sword unsheath'd, and plung'd it in his breast;
His eyes o'erwhelm'd with night, he stumbling
falls,
And with his latest breath on Athis calls;
Pleas'd that so near the lovely youth he lies,
He sinks his head upon his friend, and dies.
Next eager Phorbas, old Methion's son,
Came rushing forward with Amphimedon;
When the smooth pavement, slippery made with
gore,
Tripp'd up their feet, and flung them on the floor;
The sword of Perseus, who by chance was nigh,
Prevents their rise, and where they fall, they lie:
Full in his ribs Amphimedon he smote,
And then stuck fiery Phorbas in the throat.
Eurythus lifting up his ax, the blow
Was thus prevented by his nimble foe;
A golden cup he seizes, high embost,
And at his head the massy goblet tost:
It hits, and from his forehead bruis'd rebounds,
And blood and brains he vomits from his wounds;
With his slain fellows on the floor he lies,
And death for ever shuts his swimming eyes.
Then Polydæmon fell, a goddess born;
Phlegias, and Elycen with locks unshorn
Next follow'd; next, the stroke of death he gave
To Clytus, Abanis, and Lycetus brave;
While o'er unnumber'd heaps of ghastly dead,
The Argive hero's feet triumphant tread.
But Phineus stands aloof, and dreads to feel
His rival's force, and flies his pointed steel:
Yet threw a dart from far; by chance it lights
On Idas, who for neither party fights;
But wounded, sternly thus to Phineus said,
"Since of a neuter thou a foe hast made,
This I return thee," drawing from his side
The dart; which as he strove to fling, he dy'd.
Odites fell by Clymenus's sword,
The Cephon court had not a greater lord.
Hypseus his blade does in Protenor sheath,
But brave Lyncides soon reveng'd his death.
Here too was old Emathion, one that fear'd
The gods, and in the cause of Heav'n appear'd,
Who only wishing the success of right,
And, by his age, exempted from the fight,
Both sides alike condemns; "This impious war
Cease, cease," he cries; "these bloody broils for-
bear."
This scarce the sage with high concern had said,
When Chromis at a blow struck off his head,
Which, dropping, on the royal altar roll'd,
Still staring on the crowd with aspect bold;
And still it seem'd their horrid strife to blame,
In life and death, his pious zeal the same;
While clinging to the horns, the trunk expires,
The sever'd head consumes amidst the fires.
Then Phineus, who from far his javelin threw,
Broteas and Ammon, twins and brothers, slew;
For knotted gauntlets matchless in the field;
But gauntlets must to swords and javelins yield.
Ampycus next, with hallow'd fillets bound,
As Ceres' priest, and with a mitre crown'd,
His spear transfix'd, and struck him to the ground.
O Iäpetides, with pain I tell
How you, sweet lyrist, in the riot fell;
What worse than brutal rage his breast could fill,
Who did thy blood, O bard celestial! spill?
Kindly you press'd amid the princely throng,
To crown the feast, and give the nuptial song:
Discord abhorr'd the music of thy lyre,
Whose notes did gentle peace so well inspire;
Thee when fierce Pettalus far off espy'd,
Defenceless with thy harp, he scoffing cry'd,
"Go; to the ghosts thy soothing lessons play:
We loathe thy lyre, and scorn thy peaceful lay;"
And, as again he fiercely bid him go,
He pierc'd his temples with a mortal blow.
His harp he held, though sinking on the ground,
Whose strings in death his trembling fingers found
By chance, and tun'd by chance a dying sound.
With grief Lycormas saw him fall, from far,
And wresting from the door a massy bar,
Full in his pole lays on a load of knocks,
Which stun him, and he falls like a devoted ox.
Another bar Pelates would have snatch'd,
But Corythus his motions slyly watch'd;
He darts his weapon from a private stand,
And rivets to the post his veiny hand:
When straight a missive spear transfix'd his side,
By Abas thrown, and as he hung, he dy'd.
Melaneus on the prince's side was slain:
And Dorylas, who own'd a fertile plain,
Of Nasamonia's fields the wealthy lord, [hoard.
Whose crowded barns could scarce contain their
A whizzing spear obliquely gave a blow,
Stuck in his groin, and pierc'd the nerves below;
His foe beheld his eyes convulsive roll,
His ebbing veins, and his departing soul;
Then taunting said, "Of all thy spacious plains,
This spot thy only property remains."
He left him thus; but had no sooner left,
Than Perseus in revenge his nostrils cleft;
From his friend's breast the murd'ring dart he
drew,
And the same weapon at the murd'rer threw;
His head in halves the darted javelin cut,
And on each side the brain came issuing out.
Fortune his friend, his deaths around he deals,
And this his lance, and that his falchion feels:
Now Clytius dies; and by a diff'rent wound,
The twin, his brother Clanis, bites the ground.
In his rent jaw the bearded weapon sticks,
And the steel'd dart does Clytius' thigh transfix.

With these Mendesian Celadon he slew:
And Astreus next, whose mother was a Jew,
His sire uncertain: then by Perseus fell
Æthion, who cou'd things to come foretell;
But now he knows not whence the javelin flies
That wounds his breast, nor by whose arm he dies.
The squire to Phineus next his valour try'd,
And fierce Agyrtes stain'd with parricide.
As these are slain fresh numbers still appear,
And wage with Perseus an unequal war;
To rob him of his right, the maid he won,
By honour, promise, and desert his own.
With him the father of the beauteous bride,
The mother, and the frighted virgin side:
With shrieks and doleful cries they rend the air;
Their shrieks confounded with the din of war,
With clashing arms, and groanings of the slain,
They grieve unpity'd, and unheard complain.
The floor with ruddy streams Bellona stains,
And Phineus a new war with double rage maintains.
Perseus begirt, from all around they pour
Their lances on him, a tempestuous show'r,
Aim'd all at him; a cloud of darts, and spears,
Or blind his eyes, or whistle round his ears.
Their numbers to resist, against the wall
He guards his back secure, and dares them all.
Here from the left Molpeus renews the fight,
And bold Ethemon presses on the right:
As when a hungry tiger near him hears
Two lowing herds, awhile he both forbears;
Nor can his hopes of this, or that renounce,
So strong he lusts to prey on both at once;
Thus Perseus now with that or this is loth
To war distinct, but fain would fall on both.
And first Chaonian Molpeus felt his blow,
And fled, and never after fac'd his foe;
Then fierce Ethemon, as he turn'd his back,
Hurry'd with fury, aiming at his neck,
His brandish'd sword against the marble struck
With all his might; the brittle weapon broke,
And in his throat the point rebounding stuck.
Too slight the wound for life to issue thence,
And yet too great for battle, or defence;
His arms extended in this piteous state,
For mercy he would sue, but sues too late;
Perseus has in his bosom plung'd the sword,
And, ere he speaks, the wound prevents the word.
The crowds increasing, and his friends distress'd,
Himself by warring multitudes oppress'd;
"Since thus unequally you fight, 'tis time,"
He cry'd, "to punish your presumptuous crime;
Beware, my friends;" his friends were soon prepar'd,
Their sight averting, high the head he rear'd,
And Gorgon on his foes severely star'd.
"Vain shift!" says Thescelus, with aspect bold,
"Thee, and thy bugbear monster, I behold
With scorn;" he lifts his arm, but ere he threw
The dart, the hero to a statue grew.
In the same posture still the marble stands,
And holds the warrior's weapons in its hands.
Amphyx, whom yet this wonder can't alarm,
Heaves at Lyncides' breast his impious arm;
But, while thus daringly he presses on,
His weapon and his arm are turn'd to stone.
Next Nileus, he who vainly said he ow'd
His origin to Nile's prolific flood;
Who on his shield seven silver rivers bore,
His birth to witness by the arms he wore;
Full of his seven-fold father, thus express'd
His boast to Perseus, and his pride confess'd:
"See whence we sprung; let this thy comfort be
In thy sure death, that thou didst die by me."
While yet he spoke the dying accents hung
In sounds imperfect on his marble tongue;
Tho' chang'd to stone, his lips he seem'd to stretch,
And thro' th' insensate rock wou'd force a speech.
This Eryx saw, but seeing would not own;
"The mischief by yourselves," he cries, "is done.
'Tis your cold courage turns your hearts to stone.
Come follow me; fall on the stripling boy,
Kill him, and you his magic arms destroy."
Then rushing on, his arm to strike he rear'd,
And marbled o'er his vary'd frame appear'd.
These for affronting Pallas were chastis'd,
And justly met the death they had despis'd.
But brave Aconteus, Perseus' friend by chance
Look'd back, and met the Gorgon's fatal glance:
A statue now become, he ghastly stares,
And still the foe to mortal combat dares.
Astyages the living likeness knew,
On the dead stone with vengeful fury flew;
But impotent his rage, the jarring blade
No print upon the solid marble made:
Again, as with redoubled might he struck,
Himself astonish'd in the quarry stuck.
The vulgar deaths 'twere tedious to rehearse,
And fates below the dignity of verse.
Their safety in their flight two hundred found,
Two hundred by Medusa's head were ston'd.
Fierce Phineus now repents the wrongful fight,
And views his vary'd friends, a dreadful sight;
He knows their faces, for their help he sues,
And thinks, not hearing him, that they refuse:
By name he begs their succour, one by one,
Then doubts their life, and feels the friendly stone.
Struck with remorse, and conscious of his pride,
Convict of sin, he turn'd his eyes aside;
With suppliant mien to Perseus thus he prays,
"Hence with the head, as far as winds and seas
Can bear thee; hence. O quit the Cephen shore,
And never curse us with Medusa more,
That horrid head, which stiffens into stone
Those impious men who, daring death, look on.
I warr'd not with thee out of hate or strife,
My honest cause was to defend my wife,
First pledg'd to me; what crime cou'd I suppose,
To arm my friends, and vindicate my spouse?
But vain, too late I see, was our design;
Mine was the title, but the merit thine.
Contending made me guilty, I confess;
But penitence shou'd make that guilt the less:
'Twas thine to conquer by Minerva's pow'r;
Favour'd of Heav'n, thy mercy I implore;
For life I sue; the rest to thee I yield;
In pity, from my sight remove the shield."
He suing said; nor durst revert his eyes
On the grim head: and Perseus thus replies:
"Coward, what is in me to grant, I will,
Nor blood, unworthy of my valour, spill:
Fear not to perish by my vengeful sword,
From that secure; 'tis all the fates afford.
Where I now see thee, thou shalt still be seen,
A lasting monument to please our queen;
There still shall thy betroth'd behold her spouse,
And find his image in her father's house."
This said; where Phineus turn'd to shun the shield,
Full in his face the staring head he held;
As here and there he strove to turn aside,
The wonder wrought, the man was petrify'd:

All marble was his frame, his humid eyes
Dropp'd tears, which hung upon the stone like ice.
In suppliant posture, with uplifted hands,
And fearful look, the guilty statue stands.
Hence Perseus to his native city hies,
Victorious, and rewarded with his prize.
Conquest, o'er Prœtus the usurper, won,
He re-instates his grandsire in the throne.
Prœtus, his brother dispossess'd by might,
His realm enjoy'd, and still detain'd his right:
But Perseus pull'd the haughty tyrant down,
And to the rightful king restor'd the throne.
Weak was th' usurper, as his cause was wrong;
Where Gorgon's head appears, what arms are strong?
When Perseus to his host the monster held,
They soon were statues, and their king expell'd.
Thence to Seriphus with the head he sails,
Whose prince his story treats as idle tales:
Lord of a little isle, he scorns to seem
Too credulous, but laughs at that and him.
Yet did he not so much suspect the truth,
As out of pride or envy hate the youth.
The Argive prince, at his contempt enrag'd,
To force his faith by fatal proof engag'd. [takes,
" Friends, shut your eyes," he cries; his shield he
And to the king expos'd Medusa's snakes.
The monarch felt the pow'r he would not own,
And stood convict of folly in the stone.

MINERVA'S INTERVIEW WITH THE MUSES.

Thus far Minerva was content to rove
With Perseus, offspring of her father Jove:
Now hid in clouds, Seriphus she forsook,
And to the Theban tow'rs her journey took.
Cythnos and Gyaros lying to the right,
She pass'd unheeded in her eager flight;
And choosing first on Helicon to rest,
The virgin Muses in these words address'd:
" Me, the strange tidings of a new-found spring,
Ye learned sisters, to this mountain bring.
If all be true that fame's wide rumours tell,
Twas Pegasus discover'd first your well;
Whose piercing hoof gave the soft earth a blow,
Which broke the surface where these waters flow.
I saw that horse by miracle obtain
Life, from the blood of dire Medusa slain;
And now, this equal prodigy to view,
From distant isles to fam'd Bœotia flew."
The Muse Urania said, " Whatever cause
So great a goddess to this mansion draws;
Our shades are happy with so bright a guest,
You queen are welcome, and we Muses blest.
What fame has publish'd of our spring is true:
Thanks for our spring to Pegasus are due."
Then, with becoming courtesy, she led
The curious stranger to their fountain's head;
Who long survey'd, with wonder and delight,
Their sacred water, charming to the sight;
Their ancient groves, dark grottos, shady bow'rs,
And smiling plains adorn'd with various flow'rs.
" O happy Muses!" she with rapture cry'd,
" Who, safe from cares, on this fair hill reside;
Blest in your seat, and free yourselves to please
With joys of study, and with glorious ease."

THE FATE OF PYRENEUS.

Then one replies: " O goddess, fit to guide
Our humble works, and in our choir preside,
Who sure would wisely to these fields repair,
To taste our pleasures, and our labours share,
Were not your virtue and superior mind
To higher arts, and nobler deeds inclin'd;
Justly you praise our works, and pleasing seat,
Which all might envy in this soft retreat,
Were we secured from dangers and from harms;
But maids are frighten'd with the least alarms,
And none are safe in this licentious time;
Still fierce Pyreneus, and his daring crime,
With lasting horrour strikes my feeble sight,
Nor is my mind recover'd from the fright.
With Thracian arms this bold usurper gain'd
Daulis, and Phocis, where he proudly reign'd:
It happen'd once as through his lands we went,
For the bright temple of Parnassus bent,
He met us there, and, in his artful mind
Hiding the faithless action he design'd,
Conferr'd on us (whom, oh! too well he knew)
All honours that to goddesses are due.
'Stop, stop, ye Muses, 'tis your friend who calls,'
The tyrant said: ' behold the rain that falls
On every side, and that ill-boding sky,
Whose low'ring face portends more storms are nigh.
Pray make my house your own, and void of fear,
While this bad weather lasts, take shelter here.
Gods have made meaner places their resort,
And for a cottage left their shining court.'
" Oblig'd to stop, by the united force
Of pouring rains, and complaisant discourse,
His courteous invitation we obey,
And in his hall resolve awhile to stay.
Soon it clear'd up; the clouds began to fly,
The driving north refin'd the show'ry sky;
Then to pursue our journey we began;
But the false traitor to his portal ran,
Stopt our escape, the door securely barr'd,
And to our honour violence prepar'd.
But we, transform'd to birds, avoid his snare,
On pinions rising in the yielding air.
" But he, by lust and indignation fir'd,
Up to his highest tow'r with speed retir'd,
And cries, ' In vain you from my arms withdrew,
The way you go your lover will pursue.'
Then in a flying posture wildly plac'd,
And daring from that height himself to cast,
The wretch fell headlong, and the ground bestrew'd
With broken bones, and stains of guilty blood."

THE STORY OF THE PIERIDES.

The Muse yet spoke: when they began to hear
A noise of wings that flutter'd in the air;
And straight a voice, from some high-spreading bough,
Seem'd to salute the company below.
The goddess wonder'd, and inquir'd from whence
That tongue was heard, that spoke so plainly sense;
(It seem'd to her a human voice to be,
But prov'd a bird's; for in a shady tree
Nine magpies perch'd lament their alter'd state,
And, what they hear, are skilful to repeat.)
The sister to the wond'ring goddess said,
" These, foil'd by us, by us were thus repaid.
These did Evippè of Pæonia bring
With nine hard labour-pangs to Pella's king.
The foolish virgins of their number proud,
And puff'd with praises of the senseless crowd,
Through all Achaia, and th' Æmonian plains,
Defy'd us thus, to match their artless strains:
' No more, ye Thespian girls, your notes repeat,
Nor with false harmony the vulgar cheat;

In voice or skill, if you with us will vie,
As many we in voice or skill will try.
Surrender you to us, if we excel,
Fam'd Aganippè, and Medusa's well.
The conquest yours, your prize from us shall be
The Æmathian plains to snowy Pæonè;
The nymphs our judges.' To dispute the field,
We thought a shame; but greater shame to yield.
On seats of living stone the sisters sit,
And by the rivers swear to judge aright.

THE SONG OF THE PIERIDES.

"THEN rises one of the presumptuous throng,
Steps rudely forth, and first begins the song;
With vain address describes the giants' wars,
And to the gods, their fabled acts prefers.
She sings, from Earth's dark womb how Typhon rose,
And struck with mortal fear his heav'nly foes.
How the gods fled to Egypt's slimy soil,
And hid their heads beneath the banks of Nile:
How Typhon, from the conquer'd skies, pursu'd
Their routed godheads to the seven-mouth'd flood;
Forc'd ev'ry god, his fury to escape,
Some beastly form to take, or earthly shape.
Jove (so she sung) was chang'd into a ram,
From whence the horns of Libyan Ammon came.
Bacchus a goat, Apollo was a crow,
Phœbè a cat, the wife of Jove a cow,
Whose hue was whiter than the falling snow.
Mercury to a nasty ibis turn'd,
The change obscene, afraid of Typhon, mourn'd;
While Venus from a fish protection craves,
And once more plunges in her native waves.
"She sung, and to her harp her voice apply'd;
Then us again to match her they defy'd.
But our poor song, perhaps for you to hear,
Nor leisure serves, nor is it worth your ear."
"That causeless doubt remove, O Muse, rehearse,"
The goddess cry'd, "your ever-grateful verse."
Beneath a chequer'd shade she takes her seat,
And bids the sister her whole song repeat.
The sister thus: "Calliopè we chose
For the performance. The sweet virgin rose,
With ivy crown'd she tunes her golden strings,
And to her harp this composition sings.

THE SONG OF THE MUSES.

"FIRST Ceres taught the lab'ring hind to plough
The pregnant Earth, and quick'ning seed to sow.
She first for man did wholesome food provide,
And with just laws the wicked world supply'd;
All good from her deriv'd, to her belong
The grateful tributes of the Muses' song.
Her more than worthy of our verse we deem,
Oh! were our verse more worthy of the theme!
"Jove on the giant fair Trinacria hurl'd,
And with one bolt reveng'd his starry world.
Beneath her burning hills Typhœus lies,
And, struggling always, strives in vain to rise.
Down does Pelorus his right hand suppress
Tow'rd Latium, on the left Pachynè weighs.
His legs are under Lilybœum spread,
And Ætna presses hard his horrid head.
On his broad back he there extended lies,
And vomits clouds of ashes to the skies.
Oft lab'ring with his load, at last he tires,
And spews out in revenge a flood of fires,
Mountains he struggles to o'erwhelm, and towns;
Earth's inmost bowels quake, and Nature groans.
His terrours reach the direful king of Hell;
He fears his throes will to the day reveal
The realms of night, and fright his trembling ghosts.
"This to prevent, he quits the Stygian coasts:
In his black car, by sooty horses drawn,
Fair Sicily he seeks, and dreads the dawn;
Around her plains he casts his eager eyes,
And ev'ry mountain to the bottom tries.
But when, in all the careful search, he saw
No cause of fear, no ill-suspected flaw;
Secure from harm, and wond'ring on at will,
Venus beheld him from her flow'ry hill:
When straight the dame her little Cupid prest
With secret rapture to her snowy breast,
And in these words the flutt'ring boy addrest.
"'O thou, my arms, my glory, and my pow'r,
My son, whom men and deathless gods adore;
Bend thy sure bow, whose arrows never miss'd,
No longer let Hell's king thy sway resist;
Take him, while straggling from his dark abodes
He coasts the kingdoms of superior gods.
If sovereign Jove, if gods who rule the waves,
And Neptune who rules them, have been thy slaves
Shall Hell be free? The tyrant strike, my son,
Enlarge thy mother's empire, and thy own.
Let not our Heav'n be made the mock of Hell,
But Pluto to confess thy pow'r compel.
Our rule is slighted in our native skies,
See Pallas, see Diana too defies
Thy darts, which Ceres' daughter would despise.
She too our empire treats with awkward scorn;
Such insolence no longer's to be borne.
Revenge our slighted reign, and with thy dart
Transfix the virgin's to the uncle's heart.'
"She said; and from his quiver straight he drew
A dart that surely would the business do.
She guides his hand, she makes her touch the test,
And of a thousand arrows chose the best:
No feather better pois'd, a sharper head
None had, and sooner none, and surer sped.
He bends his bow, he draws it to his ear,
Through Pluto's heart it drives, and fixes there.

THE RAPE OF PROSERPINE.

"NEAR Enna's walls a spacious lake is spread,
Fam'd for the sweetly-singing swans it bred;
Pergusa is its name: and never more
Were heard, or sweeter, on Caÿster's shore.
Woods crown the lake; and Phœbus ne'er invades
The tufted fences, or offends the shades:
Fresh fragrant breezes fan the verdant bow'rs,
And the moist ground smiles with enamel'd flow'rs.
The cheerful birds their airy carols sing,
And the whole year is one eternal spring.
"Here, while young Proserpine, among the maids,
Diverts herself in these delicious shades;
While like a child with busy speed and care
She gathers lilies here, and vi'lets there;
While first to fill her little lap she strives,
Hell's grizly monarch at the shade arrives;
Sees her thus sporting on the flow'ry green,
And loves the blooming maid, as soon as seen.
His urgent flame impatient of delay,
Swift as his thought he seiz'd the beauteous prey,
And bore her in his sooty car away.
The frighted goddess to her mother cries,
But all in vain, for now far off she flies.

Far she behind her leaves her virgin train;
To them too cries, and cries to them in vain.
And while with passion she repeats her call,
The vi'lets from her lap, and lilies fall: [moan;
She misses them, poor heart! and makes new
Her lilies, ah! are lost, her vi'lets gone.
"O'er hills, the ravisher, and valleys speeds,
By name encouraging his foamy steeds;
He rattles o'er their necks the rusty reins,
And ruffles with the stroke their shaggy manes.
O'er lakes he whirls his flying wheels, and comes
To the Palici breathing sulph'rous fumes.
And thence to where the Bacchiads of renown
Between unequal havens built their town;
Where Arethusa, round th' imprison'd sea,
Extends her crooked coast to Cyanè;
The nymph who gave the neighb'ring lake a name,
Of all Sicilian nymphs the first in fame.
She from the waves advanc'd her beauteous head,
The goddess knew, and thus to Pluto said;
'Farther thou shalt not with the virgin run;
Ceres unwilling, canst thou be her son?
The maid should be by sweet persuasion won.
Force suits not with the softness of the fair;
For, if great things with small I may compare,
Me Anapis once lov'd; a milder course
He took, and won me by his words, not force.'
"Then stretching out her arms, she stopt his
But he, impatient of the shortest stay, [way;
Throws to his dreadful steeds the slacken'd rein,
And strikes his iron sceptre through the main;
The depths profound through yielding waves he cleaves,
And to Hell's centre a free passage leaves;
Down sinks his chariot, and his realms of night
The god soon reaches with a rapid flight.

CYANE DISSOLVES TO A FOUNTAIN.

"But still does Cyanè the rape bemoan,
And with the goddess' wrongs laments her own;
For the stol'n maid, and for her injur'd spring,
Time to her trouble no relief can bring.
In her sad heart a heavy load she bears,
'Till the dumb sorrow turns her all to tears.
Her mingling waters with that fountain pass,
Of which she late immortal goddess was;
Her vary'd members to a fluid melt,
A pliant softness in her bones is felt;
Her wavy locks first drop away in dew,
And liquid next her slender fingers grew.
The body's change soon seizes its extreme,
Her legs dissolve, and feet flow off in stream.
Her arms, her back, her shoulders, and her side,
Her swelling breasts in little currents glide,
A silver liquor only now remains
Within the channel of her purple veins;
Nothing to fill love's grasp; her husband chaste
Bathes in that bosom he before embrac'd.

A BOY TRANSFORMED TO AN EFT.

"Thus, while through all the earth, and all the
Her daughter mournful Ceres sought in vain; [main,
Aurora, when with dewy locks she rose,
Nor burnish'd Vesper, found her in repose.
At Ætna's flaming mouth two pitchy pines,
To light her in her search, at length she tines.
Restless, with these, through frosty night she goes,
Nor fears the cutting winds, nor heeds the snows;
And when the morning star the day renews,
From east to west her absent child pursues.
"Thirsty at last by long fatigue she grows,
But meets no spring, no riv'let near her flows.
Then looking round, a lowly cottage spies,
Smoking among the trees, and thither hies.
The goddess knocking at the little door,
'Twas open'd by a woman old and poor,
Who, when she begg'd for water, gave her ale
Brew'd long, but well preserv'd from being stale.
The goddess drank; a chuffy lad was by,
Who saw the liquor with a grudging eye,
And grinning cries, 'She's greedy more than dry.'
"Ceres, offended at his foul grimace,
Flung what she had not drunk into his face.
The sprinklings speckle where they hit the skin,
And a long tail does from his body spin;
His arms are turn'd to legs, and lest his size
Should make him mischievous, and he might rise
Against mankind, diminutive's his frame,
Less than a lizard, but in shape the same.
Amaz'd the dame the wondrous sight beheld,
And weeps, and fain would touch her quondam child.
Yet her approach th' affrighted vermin shuns,
And fast into the greatest crevice runs.
A name they gave him, which the spots exprest,
That rose like stars,[1] and vary'd all his breast.
"What lands, what seas the goddess wander'd o'er,
Were long to tell, for there remain'd no more.
Searching all round, her fruitless toil she mourns,
And with regret to Sicily returns.
At length, where Cyanè now flows she came,
Who could have told her, were she still the same
As when she saw her daughter sink to Hell;
But what she knows she wants a tongue to tell.
Yet this plain signal manifestly gave,
The virgin's girdle floating on a wave,
As late she dropt it from her slender waist,
When with her uncle thro' the deep she past.
Ceres the token by her grief confest,
And tore her golden hair, and beat her breast.
She knows not on what land her curse should fall,
But, as ingrate, alike upbraids them all,
Unworthy of her gifts; Trinacria most,
Where the last steps she found of what she lost.
The plough for this the vengeful goddess broke,
And with one death the ox and owner struck.
In vain the fallow fields the peasant tills,
The seed, corrupted ere 'tis sown, she kills.
The fruitful soil, that once such harvests bore,
Now mocks the farmer's care and teems no more.
And the rich grain which fills the furrow'd glade
Rots in the seed, or shrivels in the blade;
Or too much sun burns up, or too much rain
Drowns, or black blights destroy the blasted plain;
Or greedy birds the new-sown seed devour,
Or darnel, thistles, and a crop impure
Of knotted grass along the acres stand, [land.
And spread their thriving roots through all the
"Then from the waves soft Arethusa rears
Her head, and back she flings her dropping hairs.
'O mother of the maid, whom thou so far
Hast sought, of whom thou canst no tidings hear;
'O thou,' she cry'd, 'who art to life a friend,
Cease here thy search, and let thy labour end.
Thy faithful Sicily's a guiltless clime,
And should not suffer for another's crime;
She neither knew, nor could prevent the deed.
Nor think that for my country thus I plead;

[1] Stellio.

My country's Pisa, I'm an alien here,
Yet these abodes to Elis I prefer,
No clime to me so sweet, no place so dear.
These springs I Arethusa now possess,
And this my seat, O gracious goddess, bless:
This island why I love, and why I crost
Such spacious seas to reach Ortygia's coast,
To you I shall impart, when, void of care,
Your heart's at ease, and you're more fit to hear;
When on your brow no pressing sorrow sits,
For gay content alone such tales admits.
When through Earth's caverns I awhile have roll'd
My waves, I rise, and here again behold
The long-lost stars; and, as I late did glide
Near Styx, Proserpina there I espy'd.
Fear still with grief might in her face be seen;
She still her rape laments; yet made a queen,
Beneath those gloomy shades her sceptre sways,
And ev'n the infernal king her will obeys.'
"This heard, the goddess like a statue stood,
Stupid with grief; and in that musing mood
Continu'd long; new cares awhile supprest
The reigning pow'rs of her immortal breast.
At last to Jove her daughter's sire she flies,
And with her chariot cuts the crystal skies;
She comes in clouds, and with dishevel'd hair,
Standing before his throne, prefers her pray'r:
"'King of the gods, defend my blood and thine,
And use it not the worse for being mine.
If I no more am gracious in thy sight,
Be just, O Jove, and do thy daughter right.
In vain I sought her the wide world around,
And, when I most despair'd to find her, found:
But how can I the fatal finding boast,
By which I know she is for ever lost?
Without her father's aid, what other pow'r
Can to my arms the ravish'd maid restore!
Let him restore her, I'll the crime forgive;
My child, though ravish'd, I'd with joy receive.
Pity, your daughter with a thief should wed,
Tho' mine, you think, deserves no better bed."
"Jove thus replies: 'It equally belongs
To both, to guard our common pledge from wrongs.
But if to things we proper names apply,
This hardly can be call'd an injury.
The theft is love; nor need we blush to own
The thief, if I can judge, to be our son.
Had you of his desert no other proof,
To be Jove's brother is methinks enough.
Nor was my throne by worth superior got,
Heav'n fell to me, as Hell to him, by lot;
If you are still resolv'd her loss to mourn,
And nothing less will serve than her return;
Upon these terms she may again be yours,
(Th' irrevocable terms of fate, not ours):
Of Stygian food if she did never taste,
Hell's bounds may then, and only then, be past.'

THE TRANSFORMATION OF ASCALAPHUS INTO AN OWL.

"The goddess now, resolving to succeed,
Down to the gloomy shades descends with speed;
But adverse fate had otherwise decreed.
For long before, her giddy thoughtless child
Had broke her fast, and all her projects spoil'd.
As in the garden's shady walk she stray'd,
A fair pomegranate charm'd the simple maid
Hung in her way, and tempting her to taste,
She pluck'd the fruit, and took a short repast.
Seven times, a seed at once, she eat the food;
The fact Ascalaphus had only view'd;
Whom Acheron begot in Stygian shades
On Orphnè, fam'd among Avernal maids;
He saw what pass'd, and by discov'ring all,
Detain'd the ravish'd nymph in cruel thrall.
"But now a queen, she with resentment heard,
And chang'd the vile informer to a bird.
In Phlegeton's black stream her hand she dips,
Sprinkles his head, and wets his babbling lips.
Soon on his face, bedropt with magic dew,
A change appear'd, and gaudy feathers grew:
A crooked beak the place of nose supplies,
Rounded his head, and larger are his eyes.
His arms and body waste, but are supply'd
With yellow pinions flagging on each side.
His nails grow crooked, and are turn'd to claws,
And lazily along his heavy wings he draws.
Ill-omen'd in his form, th' unlucky fowl,
Abhorr'd by men, and call'd a screeching owl.

THE DAUGHTERS OF ACHELOUS TRANSFORMED TO SIRENS.

"Justly this punishment was due to him,
And less had been too little for his crime;
But, O ye nymphs that from the flood descend,
What fault of yours the gods could so offend,
With wings and claws your beauteous forms to spoil,
Yet save your maiden face and winning smile?
Were you not with her in Pergusa's bow'rs,
When Proserpine went forth to gather flow'rs?
Since Pluto in his car the goddess caught,
Have you not for her in each climate sought?
And when on land you long had search'd in vain,
You wish'd for wings to cross the pathless main:
The earth and sea might witness to your care:
The gods were easy, and return'd your pray'r;
With golden wing o'er foamy waves you fled,
And to the sun your plumy glory spread.
But, lest the soft enchantment of your songs,
And the sweet music of your flatt'ring tongues,
Should quite be lost, (as courteous fates ordain)
Your voice and virgin beauty still remain.
"Jove some amends for Ceres' loss to make,
Yet willing Pluto should the joy partake,
Gives them of Proserpine an equal share,
Who, claim'd by both, with both divides the year.
The goddess now in either empire sways,
Six moons in Hell, and six with Ceres stays.
Her peevish temper's chang'd; that sullen mind,
Which made ev'n Hell uneasy, now is kind.
Her voice refines, her mien more sweet appears,
Her forehead free from frowns, her eyes from tears,
As when, with golden light, the conqu'ring day
Through dusky exhalations clears a way.
Ceres her daughter's rape no longer mourn'd;
But back to Arethusa's spring return'd;
And sitting on the margin, bid her tell
From whence she came, and why a sacred well

THE STORY OF ARETHUSA.

"Still were the purling waters, and the maid
From the smooth surface rais'd her beauteous head,
Wipes off the drops that from her tresses ran,
And thus to tell Alpheus' loves began:
"'In Elis first I breath'd the living air,
The chase was all my pleasure, all my care.
None lov'd like me the forest to explore,
To pitch the toils, and drive the bristled boar.
Of fair, though masculine, I had the name,
But gladly would to that have quitted claim

It less my pride than indignation rais'd,
To hear the beauty I neglected, prais'd;
Such compliments I loath'd, such charms as these
I scorn'd, and thought it infamy to please.
"'Once, I remember, in the summer's heat,
Tir'd with the chase, I sought a cool retreat;
And, walking on, a silent current found,
Which gently glided o'er the grav'ly ground.
The crystal water was so smooth, so clear,
My eye distinguish'd ev'ry pebble there.
So soft its motion, that I scarce perceiv'd
The running stream, or what I saw believ'd.
The hoary willow, and the poplar, made
Along the shelving bank a grateful shade.
In the cool rivulet my feet I dipt,
Then waded to the knee, and then I stript;
My robe I careless on an osier threw,
That near the place commodiously grew;
Nor long upon the border naked stood,
But plung'd with speed into the silver flood.
My arms a thousand ways I mov'd, and try'd
To quicken, if I could, the lazy tide;
Where, while I play'd my swimming gambols o'er,
I heard a murm'ring voice, and frighted sprung to [shore.
Oh! whither, Arethusa, dost thou fly?
From the brook's bottom did Alpheus cry;
Again I heard him, in a hollow tone,
Oh! whither, Arethusa, dost thou run?
Naked I flew, nor could I stay to hide
My limbs, my robe was on the other side;
Alpheus follow'd fast, th' inflaming sight
Quicken'd his speed, and made his labour light:
He sees me ready for his eager arms,
And with a greedy glance devours my charms.
As trembling doves from pressing danger fly,
When the fierce hawk comes sousing from the sky;
And, as fierce hawks the trembling doves pursue,
From him I fled, and after me he flew.
First by Orchomenus I took my flight,
And soon had Psophis and Cyllene in sight;
Behind me then high Mænalus I lost,
And craggy Erimanthus scal'd with frost;
Elis was next: thus far the ground I trod
With nimble feet, before the distanc'd god.
But here I lagg'd, unable to sustain
The labour longer, and my flight maintain;
While he more strong, more patient of the toil,
And fir'd with hopes of beauty's speedy spoil,
Gain'd my lost ground, and by redoubled pace,
Now left between us but a narrow space.
Unweary'd I 'till now o'er hills, and plains,
O'er rocks, and rivers ran, and felt no pains:
The Sun behind me, and the god I kept,
But, when I fastest should have run, I stept.
Before my feet his shadow now appear'd;
As what I saw, or rather what I fear'd.
Yet there I could not be deceiv'd by fear,
Who felt his breath pant on my braided hair,
And heard his sounding tread, and knew him to be near.
Tir'd, and despairing, O celestial maid,
I'm caught, I cry'd, without thy heav'nly aid.
Help me, Diana, help a nymph forlorn,
Devoted to the woods, who long has worn
Thy livery, and long thy quiver borne.
The goddess heard; my pious pray'r prevail'd;
In muffling clouds my virgin head was veil'd.
The am'rous god, deluded of his hopes,
Searches the gloom, and through the darkness gropes;
Twice, where Diana did her servant hide
He came, and twice, O Arethusa! cry'd.
How shaken was my soul, how sunk my heart!
The terrour seiz'd on every trembling part.
Thus when the wolf about the mountain prowls
For prey, the lambkin hears his horrid howls:
The tim'rous hare, the pack approaching nigh,
Thus hearkens to the hounds, and trembles at the [cry;
Nor dares she stir, for fear her scented breath
Direct the dogs, and guide the threaten'd death.
Alpheus in the cloud no traces found
To mark my way, yet stays to guard the ground.
The god so near, a chilly sweat possest
My fainting limbs at ev'ry pore exprest;
My strength distill'd in drops, my hair in dew,
My form was chang'd, and all my substance new.
Each motion was a stream, and my whole frame
Turn'd to a fount, which still preserves my name.
Resolv'd I should not his embrace escape,
Again the god resumes his fluid shape;
To mix his streams with mine he fondly tries,
But still Diana his attempt denies.
She cleaves the ground; through caverns dark I run
A diff'rent current, while he keeps his own.
To dear Ortygia she conducts my way,
And here I first review the welcome day.'
"Here Arethusa stopt; then Ceres takes
Her golden car, and yokes her fiery snakes;
With a just rein, along mid-heaven she flies
O'er earth and seas, and cuts the yielding skies.
She halts at Athens, dropping like a star,
And to Triptolemus resigns her car.
Parent of seed, she gave him fruitful grain,
And bad him teach to till and plough the plain;
The seed to sow, as well in fallow fields,
As where the soil manur'd a richer harvest yields.

THE TRANSFORMATION OF LYNCUS.

"The youth o'er Europe and o'er Asia drives,
Till at the court of Lyncus he arrives.
The tyrant Scythia's barb'rous empire sway'd;
And, when he saw Triptolemus, he said;
'How cam'st thou, stranger, to our court, [and why?
Thy country, and thy name?' The youth did thus [reply;
'Triptolemus my name; my country's known
O'er all the world, Minerva's fav'rite town,
Athens, the first of cities in renown.
By land I neither walk'd, nor sail'd by sea,
But hither through the ether made my way.
By me, the goddess who the fields befriends,
These gifts, the greatest of all blessings, sends.
The grain she gives if in your soil you sow,
Thence wholesome food in golden crops shall grow.
"Soon as the secret to the king was known,
He grudg'd the glory of the service done,
And wickedly resolv'd to make it all his own.
To hide his purpose, he invites his guest,
The friend of Ceres, to a royal feast,
And when sweet sleep his heavy eyes had seiz'd,
The tyrant with his steel attempts his breast.
Him straight a lynx's shape the goddess gives,
And home the youth her sacred dragons drives.

THE PIERIDES TRANSFORMED TO MAGPIES.

"The chosen Muse here ends her sacred lays;
The nymphs unanimous decree the bays,
And give the Heliconian goddesses the praise.
Then, far from vain that we should thus prevail,
But much provok'd to hear the vanquish'd rail,

Calliopè resumes; ‘ Too long we've borne
Your daring taunts, and your affronting scorn;
Your challenge justly merited a curse,
And this unmanner'd railing makes it worse.
Since you refuse us calmly to enjoy
Our patience, next our passions we'll employ;
The dictates of a mind enrag'd pursue,
And, what our just resentment bids us, do.'
“The railers laugh, our threats and wrath despise,
And clap their hands, and make a scolding noise;
But in the fact there seiz'd, beneath their nails
Feathers they feel, and on their faces scales;
Their horny beaks at once each other scare,
Their arms are plum'd, and on their backs they bear
Py'd wings, and flutter in the fleeting air.
Chatt'ring, the scandal of the woods they fly,
And there continue still their clam'rous cry:
The same their eloquence, as maids or birds,
Now only noise, and nothing then but words.”

OVID'S METAMORPHOSES.
BOOK VI.

Translated by Mr. Croxall.

THE TRANSFORMATION OF ARACHNE INTO A SPIDER.

Pallas, attending to the Muses' song,
Approv'd the just resentment of their wrong;
And thus reflects; “ While tamely I commend
Those who their injur'd deities defend,
My own divinity affronted stands,
And calls aloud for justice at my hands;”
Then takes the hint, asham'd to lag behind,
And on Arachnè bends her vengeful mind;
One at the loom so excellently skill'd,
That to the goddess she refus'd to yield.
Low was her birth, and small her native town,
She from her art alone obtain'd renown.
Idmon, her father, made it his employ,
To give the spungy fleece a purple dye:
Of vulgar strain her mother, lately dead,
With her own rank had been content to wed;
Yet she their daughter, tho' her time was spent
In a small hamlet, and of mean descent,
Thro' the great towns of Lydia gain'd a name,
And fill'd the neighb'ring countries with her fame.
Oft, to admire the niceness of her skill,
The nymphs would quit their fountain, shade or hill;
Thither, from green Tymolus, they repair,
And leave the vineyards, their peculiar care;
Thither, from fam'd Pactolus' golden stream,
Drawn by her art, the curious Naiads came.
Nor would the work, when finish'd, please so much,
As, while she wrought, to view each graceful touch;
Whether the shapeless wool in balls she wound,
Or with quick motion turn'd the spindle round,
Or with her pencil drew the neat design,
Pallas her mistress shone in every line.
This the proud maid with scornful air denies;
And ev'n the goddess at her work defies;
Disowns her heav'nly mistress ev'ry hour,
Nor asks her aid, nor deprecates her pow'r.
“ Let us,” she cries, “ but to a trial come,
And, if she conquers, let her fix my doom.”
The goddess then a beldame's form put on,
With silver hairs her hoary temples shone;
Propp'd by a staff, she hobbles in her walk,
And tott'ring thus begins her old-wives' talk:
“ Young maid, attend, nor stubbornly despise
The admonitions of the old, and wise;
For age, tho' scorn'd, a ripe experience bears,
That golden fruit unknown to blooming years:
Still may remotest fame your labours crown,
And mortals your superior genius own;
But to the goddess yield, and humbly meek
A pardon for your bold presumption seek;
The goddess will forgive.” At this the maid,
With passion fir'd, her gliding shuttle stay'd;
And, darting vengeance with an angry look,
To Pallas in disguise thus fiercely spoke:
“ Thou doting thing, whose idle babbling tongue
But too well shows the plague of living long;
Hence, and reprove, with this your sage advice,
Your giddy daughter, or your awkward niece:
Know, I despise your counsel, and am still
A woman, ever wedded to my will;
And if your skilful goddess better knows,
Let her accept the trial I propose.”
“ She does,” impatient Pallas straight replies,
And, cloth'd with heavenly light, sprung from her odd disguise.
The nymphs and virgins of the plain adore
The awful goddess, and confess her pow'r;
The maid alone stood unappall'd; yet show'd
A transient blush, that for a moment glow'd,
Then disappear'd; as purple streaks adorn
The opening beauties of the rosy morn;
'Till Phœbus, rising prevalently bright,
Allays the tincture with his silver light.
Yet she persists, and obstinately great,
In hopes of conquest hurries on her fate.
The goddess now the challenge waves no more,
Nor, kindly good, advises as before.
Straight to their posts appointed both repair,
And fix their threaded looms with equal care:
Around the solid beam the web is ty'd,
While hollow canes the parting warp divide;
Thro' which with nimble flight the shuttles play,
And for the woof prepare a ready way;
The woof and warp unite, press'd by the toothy slay.
Thus both, their mantles button'd to their breast,
Their skilful fingers ply with willing haste,
And work with pleasure; while they cheer the eye
With glowing purple of the Tyrian dye:
Or, justly intermixing shades with light,
Their colourings insensibly unite.
As when a show'r transpierc'd with sunny rays
Its mighty arch along the Heav'n displays;
From whence a thousand diff'rent colours rise,
Whose fine transition cheats the clearest eyes;
So like the intermingled shading seems,
And only differs in the last extremes.
Then threads of gold both artfully dispose,
And, as each part in just proportion rose,
Some antic fable in their work disclose.
Pallas in figures wrought the heav'nly pow'rs,
And Mars's hill among th' Athenian tow'rs.
On lofty thrones twice six celestials sate,
Jove in the midst, and held their warm debate;
The subject weighty, and well known to fame,
From whom the city should receive its name.
Each god by proper features was exprest,
Jove with majestic mien excell'd the rest.
His three-fork'd mace the dewy sea-god shook,
And, looking sternly, smote the ragged rock;

When from the stone leapt forth a spritely steed,
And Neptune claims the city for the deed.
Herself she blazons, with a glitt'ring spear,
And crested helm that veil'd her braided hair,
With shield, and scaly breast-plate, implements of war.
Struck with her pointed lance, the teeming earth
Seem'd to produce a new surprising birth;
When, from the glebe, the pledge of conquest sprung,
A tree pale-green with fairest olives hung.
And then, to let her giddy rival learn
What just rewards such boldness was to earn,
Four trials at each corner had their part,
Design'd in miniature, and touch'd with art.
Hæmus in one, and Rhodopè of Thrace,
Transform'd to mountains, fill'd the foremost place;
Who claim'd the titles of the gods above,
And vainly us'd the epithets of Jove.
Another show'd, where the Pigmæan dame,
Profaning Juno's venerable name,
Turn'd to an airy crane, descends from far,
And with her pigmy subjects wages war.
In a third part, the rage of Heav'n's great queen,
Display'd on proud Antigonè, was seen;
Who with presumptuous boldness dar'd to vie,
For beauty, with the empress of the sky.
Ah! what avails her ancient princely race,
Her sire a king, and Troy her native place?
Now, to a noisy stork transform'd, she flies,
And with her whiten'd pinions cleaves the skies.
And in the last remaining part was drawn
Poor Cinyras, that seem'd to weep in stone;
Clasping the temple steps, he sadly mourn'd
His lovely daughters, now to marble turn'd.
With her own tree the finish'd piece is crown'd,
And wreaths of peaceful olive all the work surround.
Arachnè drew the fam'd intrigues of Jove,
Chang'd to a bull, to gratify his love;
How thro' the briny tide all foaming hoar,
Lovely Europa on his back he bore.
The sea seem'd waving, and the trembling maid
Shrunk up her tender feet, as if afraid;
And, looking back on the forsaken strand,
To her companions wafts her distant hand.
Next she design'd Asteria's fabled rape,
When Jove assum'd a soaring eagle's shape:
And show'd how Leda lay supinely press'd,
Whilst the soft snowy swan sat hov'ring o'er her breast.
How in a satyr's form the god beguil'd,
When fair Antiopè with twins he fill'd.
Then, like Amphitryon, but a real Jove,
In fair Alcmena's arms he cool'd his love.
In fluid gold to Danae's heart he came,
Ægina felt him in a lambent flame.
He took Mnemosynè in shepherd's make,
And for Dëois was a speckled snake.
She made thee, Neptune, like a wanton steer
Pacing the meads for love of Arnè dear;
Next like a stream, thy burning flame to slake,
And like a ram, for fair Bisaltis' sake.
Then Ceres in a steed your vigour try'd,
Nor cou'd the mare the yellow goddess hide.
Next, to a fowl transform'd, you won by force
The snake-hair'd mother of the winged horse;
And in a dolphin's fishy form, subdu'd
Melantho sweet beneath the oozy flood.
All these the maid with lively features drew,
And open'd proper landscapes to the view.
There Phœbus, roving like a country swain,
Attunes his jolly pipe along the plain;
For lovely Isse's sake, in shepherd's weeds
O'er pastures green his bleating flock he feeds.
There Bacchus, imaged like the clust'ring grape,
Melting bedrops Erigonè's fair lap;
And there old Saturn, stung with youthful heat,
Form'd like a stallion, rushes to the feat.
Fresh flow'rs, which twists of ivy intertwine,
Mingling a running foliage, close the next design.
This the bright goddess, passionately mov'd,
With envy saw, yet inwardly approv'd.
The scene of heav'nly guilt with haste she tore,
Nor longer the affront with patience bore;
A boxen shuttle in her hand she took,
And more than once Arachnè's forehead struck.
Th' unhappy maid, impatient of the wrong,
Down from a beam her injur'd person hung;
When Pallas, pitying her wretched state,
At once prevented, and pronounc'd her fate;
"Live; but depend, vile wretch," the goddess cry'd,
"Doom'd in suspense for ever to be ty'd;
That all your race, to utmost date of time,
May feel the vengeance, and detest the crime."
Then, going off, she sprinkled her with juice,
Which leaves of baneful aconite produce.
Touch'd with the pois'nous drug, her flowing hair
Fell to the ground, and left her temples bare;
Her usual features vanish'd from their place,
Her body lessen'd all, but most her face.
Her slender fingers, hanging on each side
With many joints, the use of legs supply'd,
A spider's bag the rest, from which she gives
A thread, and still by constant weaving lives.

THE STORY OF NIOBE.

SWIFT thro' the Phrygian towns the rumour flies,
And the strange news each female tongue employs:
Niobè, who before she married knew
The famous nymph, now found the story true;
Yet, unreclaim'd by poor Arachnè's fate,
Vainly above the gods assum'd a state.
Her husband's fame, their family's descent,
Their pow'r, and rich dominion's wide extent,
Might well have justify'd a decent pride;
But not on these alone the dame rely'd:
Her lovely progeny that far excell'd,
The mother's heart with vain ambition swell'd:
The happiest mother not unjustly styl'd,
Had no conceited thoughts her tow'ring fancy fill'd.
For once a prophetess, with zeal inspir'd,
Their slow neglect to warm devotion fir'd;
Thro' ev'ry street of Thebes who ran possess'd,
And thus in accents wild her charge express'd:
"Haste, haste, ye Theban matrons, and adore,
With hallow'd rites, Latona's mighty pow'r;
And to the heav'nly twins that from her spring,
With laurel crown'd, your smoking incense bring."
Straight the great summons ev'ry dame obey'd,
And due submission to the goddess paid:
Graceful, with laurel chaplets dress'd they came,
And offer'd incense in the sacred flame.
Meanwhile, surrounded with a courtly guard,
The royal Niobè in state appear'd;
Attir'd in robes embroider'd o'er with gold,
And mad with rage, yet lovely to behold:

Her comely tresses, trembling as she stood,
Down her fine neck with easy motion flow'd;
Then, darting round a proud disdainful look,
In haughty tone her hasty passion broke,
And thus began; "What madness this, to court
A goddess, founded merely on report?
Dare ye a poor pretended pow'r invoke,
While yet no altars to my godhead smoke!
Mine, whose immediate lineage stands confess'd
From Tantalus, the only mortal guest
That e'er the gods admitted to their feast.
A sister of the Pleiads gave me birth;
And Atlas, mightiest mountain upon Earth,
Who bears the globe of all the stars above,
My grandsire was, and Atlas sprung from Jove.
The Theban towns my majesty adore,
And neighb'ring Phrygia trembles at my pow'r:
Rais'd by my husband's lute, with turrets crown'd,
Our lofty city stands secur'd around.
Within my court, where'er I turn my eyes,
Unbounded treasures to my prospect rise:
With these my face I modestly may name,
As not unworthy of so high a claim;
Seven are my daughters of a form divine,
With seven fair sons, an indefective line.
Go, fools! consider this; and ask the cause
From which my pride its strong presumption draws:
Consider this; and then prefer to me
Cæus the Titan's vagrant progeny;
To whom, in travel, the whole spacious earth
No room afforded for her spurious birth.
Not the least part in earth, in Heav'n, or seas,
Would grant your out-law'd goddess any ease:
'Till pitying hers, from his own wand'ring case,
Delos, the floating island, gave a place.
There she a mother was, of two at most;
Only the seventh part of what I boast.
My joys are all beyond suspicion fix'd,
With no pollutions of misfortune mix'd;
Safe on the basis of my pow'r I stand,
Above the reach of Fortune's fickle hand.
Lessen she may my inexhausted store,
And much destroy, yet still must leave me more.
Suppose it possible that some may die
Of this my numerous lovely progeny;
Still with Latona I might safely vie:
Who, by her scanty breed, scarce fit to name,
But just escapes the childless woman's shame.
Go then, with speed your laurel'd heads uncrown,
And leave the silly farce you have begun."
The tim'rous throng their sacred rites forbore,
And from their heads the verdant laurel tore;
Their haughty queen they with regret obey'd,
And still in gentle murmurs softly pray'd.
High on the top of Cynthus' shady mount,
With grief the goddess saw the base affront;
And, the abuse revolving in her breast,
The mother her twin-offspring thus addrest:
"Lo I, my children, who with comfort knew
Your godlike birth, and thence my glory drew;
And thence have claim'd precedency of place
From all but Juno of the heav'nly race,
Must now despair, and languish in disgrace.
My godhead question'd, and all rites divine,
Unless you succour, banish'd from my shrine.
Nay more, the imp of Tantalus has flung
Reflexions with her vile paternal tongue;
Has dar'd prefer her mortal breed to mine,
And call'd me childless; which, just Fate, may she repine!"
When to urge more the goddess was prepar'd,
Phœbus in haste replies, "Too much we've heard,
And ev'ry moment's lost, while vengeance is deferr'd."
Diana spoke the same. Then both enshroud
Their heav'nly bodies in a sable cloud;
And to the Theban tow'rs descending light,
Through the soft yielding air direct their flight.
Without the wall there lies a champain ground
With even surface, far extending round,
Beaten and level'd, while it daily feels
The trampling horse, and chariot's grinding wheels.
Part of proud Niobe's young rival breed,
Practising there to ride the manag'd steed,
Their bridles boss'd with gold, were mounted high
On stately furniture of Tyrian dye.
Of these, Ismenos, who by birth had been
The first fair issue of the fruitful queen,
Just as he drew the rein to guide his horse
Around the compass of the circling course,
Sigh'd deeply, and the pangs of smart express'd,
While the shaft stuck engorg'd within his breast:
And, the reins dropping from his dying hand,
He sunk quite down, and tumbled on the sand.
Sipylus next the rattling quiver heard,
And with full speed for his escape prepar'd.
As when the pilot from the black'ning skies
A gath'ring storm of wintry rain descries,
His sails unfurl'd, and crowded all with wind,
He strives to leave the threat'ning cloud behind:
So fled the youth; but an unerring dart
O'ertook him, quick discharg'd, and sped with art;
Fix'd in his neck behind, it trembling stood,
And at his throat display'd the point besmear'd with blood.
Prone, as his posture was, he tumbled o'er,
And bath'd his courser's mane with steaming gore.
Next at young Phædimus they took their aim,
And Tantalus, who bore his grandsire's name:
These, when their other exercise was done,
To try the wrestler's oily sport begun:
And, straining ev'ry nerve, their skill express'd
In closest grapple, joining breast to breast:
When from the bending bow an arrow sent,
Join'd as they were, thro' both their bodies went:
Both groan'd, and writhing both their limbs with pain,
They fell together bleeding on the plain;
Then both their languid eyeballs faintly roll,
And thus together breathe away their soul.
With grief Alphenor saw their doleful plight,
And smote his breast, and sicken'd at the sight;
Then to their succour ran with eager haste,
And, fondly griev'd, their stiff'ning limbs embrac'd;
But in the action falls: a thrilling dart,
By Phœbus guided, pierc'd him to the heart.
This, as they drew it forth, his midriff tore,
Its barbed point the fleshy fragments bore,
And let the soul gush out in streams of purple gore.
But Damasichthon, by a double wound,
Beardless, and young, lay gasping on the ground.
Fix'd in his sinewy ham, the steely point
Stuck through his knee, and pierc'd the nervous joint:
And, as he stoop'd to tug the painful dart,
Another stuck him in a vital part;
Shot through his wezon, by the wing it hung,
The life-blood forc'd it out, and darting upward sprung.
Ilioneus, the last, with terrour stands,
Lifting in pray'r his unavailing hands;

And, ignorant from whom his griefs arise,
"Spare me, O all ye heav'nly pow'rs," he cries:
Phœbus was touch'd too late, the sounding bow
Had sent the shaft, and struck the fatal blow;
Which yet but gently gor'd his tender side,
So by a slight and easy wound he dy'd.
Swift to the mother's ears the rumour came,
And doleful sighs the heavy news proclaim;
With anger and surprise inflam'd by turns,
In furious rage her haughty stomach burns:
First she disputes th' effects of heav'nly pow'r,
Then at their daring boldness wonders more;
For poor Amphion with sore grief distrest,
Hoping to sooth his cares by endless rest,
Had sheath'd a dagger in his wretched breast.
And she, who toss'd her high disdainful head,
When through the streets in solemn pomp she led
The throng that from Latona's altar fled,
Assuming state beyond the proudest queen,
Was now the miserablest object seen.
Prostrate among the clay-cold dead she fell,
And kiss'd an undistinguish'd last farewell.
Then, her pale arms advancing to the skies,
"Cruel Latona! triumph now," she cries.
"My grieving soul in bitter anguish drench,
And with my woes your thirsty passion quench;
Feast your black malice at a price thus dear,
While the sore pangs of sev'n such deaths I bear.
Triumph, too cruel rival, and display [day.
Your conqu'ring standard; for you've won the
Yet I'll excel; for yet, though sev'n are slain,
Superior still in number I remain." [sound
Scarce had she spoke; the bow-string's twanging
Was heard, and dealt fresh terrours all around;
Which all, but Niobè alone, confound.
Stunn'd, and obdurate by her load of grief,
Insensible she sits, nor hopes relief.
Before the fun'ral biers, all weeping sad,
Her daughters stood, in vests of sable clad.
When one, surpris'd, and stung with sudden smart,
In vain attempts to draw the sticking dart:
But to grim death her blooming youth resigns,
And o'er her brothers' corpse her dying head reclines.
This to assuage her mother's anguish tries,
And, silenc'd in the pious action, dies;
Shot by a secret arrow, wing'd with death,
Her falt'ring lips but only gasp'd for breath.
One, on her dying sister, breathes her last;
Vainly in flight another's hopes are plac'd:
This hiding, from her fate a shelter seeks;
That trembling stands, and fills the air with shrieks.
And all in vain; for now all six had found
Their way to death, each by a diff'rent wound.
The last with eager care the mother veil'd,
Behind her spreading mantle close conceal'd,
And with her body guarded, as a shield.
"Only for this, this youngest, I implore,
Grant me this one request, I ask no more;
O grant me this!" she passionately cries:
But while she speaks, the destin'd virgin dies.

THE TRANSFORMATION OF NIOBE.

WIDOW'D, and childless, lamentable state!
A doleful sight, among the dead she sate;
Harden'd with woes, a statue of despair,
To ev'ry breath of wind unmov'd her hair;
Her cheek still redd'ning, but its colour dead,
Faded her eyes, and set within her head.
No more her pliant tongue its motion keeps,
But stands congeal'd within her frozen lips.
Stagnate, and dull, within her purple veins,
Its current stopp'd, the lifeless blood remains.
Her feet their usual offices refuse,
Her arms and neck their graceful gestures lose:
Action and life from ev'ry part are gone,
And ev'n her entrails turn to solid stone;
Yet still she weeps, and whirl'd by stormy winds,
Borne through the air, her native country finds;
There fix'd, she stands upon a bleaky hill,
There yet her marble cheeks eternal tears distil.

THE PEASANTS OF LYCIA TRANSFORMED TO FROGS.

THEN all, reclaim'd by this example, show'd
A due regard for each peculiar god:
Both men and women their devoirs express'd,
And great Latona's awful pow'r confess'd.
Then, tracing instances of older time,
To suit the nature of the present crime,
Thus one begins his tale: "Where Lycia yields
A golden harvest from its fertile fields,
Some churlish peasants, in the days of yore,
Provok'd the goddess to exert her pow'r.
The thing indeed the meanness of the place
Has made obscure, surprising as it was;
But I myself once happen'd to behold
The famous lake of which the story's told.
My father then, worn out by length of days,
Nor able to sustain the tedious ways,
Me with a guide had sent the plains to roam,
And drive his well-fed straggling heifers home.
Here, as we saunter'd through the verdant meads,
We spy'd a lake o'er-grown with trembling reeds,
Whose wavy tops an op'ning scene disclose,
From which an antic smoky altar rose.
I, as my superstitious guide had done,
Stopp'd short, and bless'd myself, and then went
Yet I inquir'd to whom the altar stood, [on;
Faunus, the Naiads, or some native god?
No sylvan deity, my friend replies,
Enshrin'd within this hallow'd altar lies.
For this, O youth, to that fam'd goddess stands,
Whom, at th' imperial Juno's rough commands,
Of ev'ry quarter of the earth bereav'd,
Delos, the floating isle, at length receiv'd.
Who there, in spite of enemies, brought forth,
Beneath an olive shade, her great twin-birth.
"Hence too she fled the furious stepdame's pow'r,
And in her arms a double godhead bore;
And now the borders of fair Lycia gain'd,
Just when the summer solstice parch'd the land.
With thirst the goddess languishing, no more
Her empty'd breast would yield its milky store;
When, from below, the smiling valley show'd
A silver lake that in its bottom flow'd:
A sort of clowns were reaping, near the bank,
The bending osier, and the bulrush dank;
The cress, and water-lily, fragrant weed,
Whose juicy stalk the liquid fountains feed.
The goddess came, and kneeling on the brink,
Stoop'd at the fresh repast, prepar'd to drink.
Then thus, being hinder'd by the rabble race,
In accents mild expostulates the case.
'Water I only ask, and sure 'tis hard
From Nature's common rights to be debarr'd:
This, as the genial Sun, and vital air,
Should flow alike to ev'ry creature's share.

Yet still I ask, and as a favour crave,
That which, a public bounty, Nature gave.
Nor do I seek my weary limbs to drench;
Only, with one cool draught, my thirst I'd quench.
Now from my throat the usual moisture dries,
And ev'n my voice in broken accents dies:
One draught as dear as life I should esteem,
And water, now I thirst, would nectar seem:
Oh! let my little babes your pity move,
And melt your hearts to charitable love;
They (as by chance they did) extend to you
Their little hands, and my request pursue.' [due,
"Whom would these soft persuasions not sub-
Though the most rustic and unmanner'd crew?
Yet they the goddess's request refuse,
And with rude words reproachfully abuse:
Nay more, with spiteful feet the villains trod
O'er the soft bottom of the marshy flood,
And blacken'd all the lake with clouds of rising mud.
"Her thirst by indignation was suppress'd;
Bent on revenge, the goddess stood confess'd.
Her suppliant hands uplifting to the skies,
For a redress to Heav'n she now applies.
And, 'May you live,' she passionately cry'd,
'Doom'd in that pool for ever to abide.'
"The goddess has her wish; for now they choose
To plunge, and dive among the watry ooze;
Sometimes they show their head above the brim,
And on the glassy surface spread to swim;
Often upon the bank their station take,
Then spring, and leap into the cooly lake.
Still, void of shame, they lead a clam'rous life,
And, croaking, still scold on in endless strife;
Compell'd to live beneath the liquid stream,
Where still they quarrel, and attempt to scream.
Now, from their bloated throat, their voice puts
Imperfect murmurs in a hoarser tone; [on
Their noisy jaws, with bawling now grown wide,
An ugly sight! extend on either side:
Their motley back, streak'd with a list of green,
Join'd to their head, without a neck is seen;
And, with a belly broad and white, they look
Mere frogs, and still frequent the muddy brook."

THE FATE OF MARSYAS.

SCARCE had the man this famous story told,
Of vengeance on the Lycians shown of old,
When straight another pictures to their view
The Satyr's fate, whom angry Phœbus slew;
Who, rais'd with high conceit, and puff'd with
At his own pipe the skilful god defy'd. [pride,
"Why do you tear me from myself," he cries?
"Ah cruel! must my skin be made the prize?
"This for a silly pipe?" he roaring said,
Meanwhile the skin from off his limbs was flay'd.
All bare, and raw, one large continu'd wound,
With streams of blood his body bath'd the ground.
The blueish veins their trembling pulse disclos'd,
The stringy nerves lay naked, and expos'd;
His guts appear'd, distinctly each express'd,
With ev'ry shining fibre of his breast.
The fauns, and sylvans, with the nymphs that rove
Among the satyrs in the shady grove;
Olympus, known of old, and ev'ry swain
That fed or flock or herd upon the plain,
Bewail'd the loss; and with their tears that flow'd,
A kindly moisture on the earth bestow'd;
That soon, conjoin'd, and in a body rang'd,
Sprung from the ground, to limpid water chang'd;
Which, down through Phrygia's rocks, a mighty stream, [name.
Comes tumbling to the sea, and Marsya is its

THE STORY OF PELOPS.

FROM these relations straight the people turn
To present truths, and lost Amphion mourn:
The mother most was blam'd, yet some relate
That Pelops pity'd, and bewail'd her fate,
And stript his clothes, and laid his shoulder bare,
And made the iv'ry miracle appear.
This shoulder, from the first, was form'd of flesh,
As lively as the other, and as fresh;
But, when the youth was by his father slain,
The gods restor'd his mangled limbs again;
Only that place which joins the neck and arm,
The rest untouch'd, was found to suffer harm:
The loss of which an iv'ry piece sustain'd;
And thus the youth his limbs and life regain'd.

THE STORY OF TEREUS, PROCNE, AND PHILOMELA.

To Thebes the neighb'ring princes all repair,
And with condolence the misfortune share.
Each bord'ring state in solemn form address'd,
And each betimes a friendly grief express'd.
Argos, with Sparta's and Mycenæ's towns,
And Calydon, yet free from fierce Diana's frowns:
Corinth for finest brass well fam'd of old,
Orchomenos for men of courage bold:
Cleonæ lying in the lowly dale,
And rich Messenè with its fertile vale:
Pylos, for Nestor's city after fam'd,
And Trœzen, not as yet from Pitheus nam'd:
And those fair cities, which are hemm'd around
By double seas within the Isthmian ground;
And those, which farther from the sea-coast stand,
Lodg'd in the bosom of the spacious land.
Who can believe it? Athens was the last:
Though for politeness fam'd for ages past.
For a strait siege, which then their walls en-
Such acts of kind humanity oppos'd: [clos'd,
And thick with ships, from foreign nations bound,
Seaward their city lay invested round.
These, with auxiliar forces led from far,
Tereus of Thrace, brave, and inur'd to war,
Had quite defeated, and obtain'd a name,
The warrior's due, among the sons of Fame.
This, with his wealth, and pow'r, and ancient line,
From Mars deriv'd, Pandion's thoughts incline
His daughter Procnè with the prince to join.
Nor Hymen, nor the Graces here preside,
Nor Juno to befriend the blooming bride;
But fiends with fun'ral brands the process led,
And furies waited at the genial bed:
And all night long the screeching owl aloof,
With baleful notes, sat brooding o'er the roof.
With such ill omens was the match begun,
That made them parents of a hopeful son.
Now Thrace congratulates their seeming joy,
And they, in thankful rites, their minds employ.
If the fair queen's espousals pleas'd before,
Itys, the new-born prince, now pleases more;
And each bright day, the birth and bridal feast,
Were kept with hallow'd pomp above the rest.
So far true happiness may lie conceal'd,
When by false lights we fancy 'tis reveal'd!

'Now, since their nuptials, had the golden Sun
Five courses round his ample zodiac run;
When gentle Procnè thus her lord address'd,
And spoke the secret wishes of her breast:
"If I," she said, "have ever favour found,
Let my petition with success be crown'd:
Let me at Athens my dear sister see,
Or let her come to Thrace, and visit me.
And, lest my father should her absence mourn,
Promise that she shall make a quick return.
With thanks I'd own the obligation due
Only, O Tereus, to the gods and you."
Now, ply'd with oar and sail, at his command,
The nimble gallies reach'd th' Athenian land,
And anchor'd in the fam'd Piræan bay,
While Tereus to the palace takes his way;
The king salutes, and ceremonies past,
Begins the fatal embassy at last;
Th' occasion of his voyage he declares,
And, with his own, his wife's request prefers:
Asks leave that, only for a little space,
Their lovely sister might embark for Thrace.
Thus while he spoke appear'd the royal maid,
Bright Philomela, splendidly array'd;
But most attractive in her charming face,
And comely person, turn'd with ev'ry grace:
Like those fair nymphs, that are describ'd to rove
Across the glades, and op'nings of the grove:
Only that these are dress'd for sylvan sports,
And less become the finery of courts.
Tereus beheld the virgin, and admir'd,
And with the coals of burning lust was fir'd:
Like crackling stubble, or the summer hay,
When forked lightnings o'er the meadows play.
Such charms in any breast might kindle love,
But him the heats of inbred lewdness move;
To which though Thrace is naturally prone,
Yet his is still superior, and his own.
Straight her attendants he designs to buy,
And with large bribes her governess would try:
Herself with ample gifts resolves to bend,
And his whole kingdom in th' attempt expend:
Or, snatch'd away by force of arms, to bear,
And justify the rape with open war.
The boundless passion boils within his breast,
And his projecting soul admits no rest.
And now impatient of the least delay,
By pleading Procnè's cause, he speeds his way:
The eloquence of love his tongue inspires,
And, in his wife's, he speaks his own desires;
Hence all his importunities arise,
And tears unmanly trickle from his eyes.
Ye gods! what thick involving darkness blinds
The stupid faculties of mortal minds!
Tereus the credit of good-nature gains
From these his crimes; so well the villain feigns.
And unsuspecting of his base designs,
In the request fair Philomela joins;
Her snowy arms her aged sire embrace,
And clasp his neck with an endearing grace:
Only to see her sister she entreats,
A seeming blessing, which a curse completes.
Tereus surveys her with a luscious eye,
And in his mind forestalls the blissful joy:
Her circling arms a scene of lust inspire,
And ev'ry kiss foments the raging fire.
Fondly he wishes for the father's place,
To feel, and to return the warm embrace;
Since not the nearest ties of filial blood
Would damp his flame, and force him to be good
At length for both their sakes, the king agrees;
And Philomela, on her bended knees,
Thanks him for what her fancy calls success,
When cruel fate intends her nothing less.
Now Phœbus, hast'ning to ambrosial rest,
His fiery steeds drove sloping down the west:
The sculptur'd gold with sparkling wines was fill'd,
And, with rich meats, each cheerful table smil'd.
Plenty and mirth the royal banquet close,
Then all retire to sleep, and sweet repose.
But the lewd monarch, though withdrawn apart,
Still feels love's poison rankling in his heart:
Her face divine is stamp'd within his breast,
Fancy imagines, and improves the rest:
And thus, kept waking by intense desire,
He nourishes his own prevailing fire.
Next day the good old king for Tereus sends,
And to his charge the virgin recommends;
His hand with tears th' indulgent father press'd,
Then spoke, and thus with tenderness address'd.
"Since the kind instances of pious love
Do all pretence of obstacle remove;
Since Procnè's, and her own, with your request,
O'er-rule the fears of a paternal breast;
With you, dear son, my daughter I intrust,
And by the gods adjure you to be just;
By truth, and ev'ry consanguineal tye,
To watch, and guard her with a father's eye.
And, since the least delay will tedious prove,
In keeping from my sight the child I love,
With speed return her, kindly to assuage
The tedious troubles of my ling'ring age.
And you, my Philomel, let it suffice,
To know your sister's banish'd from my eyes;
If any sense of duty sways your mind,
Let me from you the shortest absence find."
He wept; then kiss'd his child; and while he speaks,
The tears fall gently down his aged cheeks.
Next, as a pledge of fealty, he demands,
And, with a solemn charge, conjoins their hands;
Then to his daughter and his grandson sends,
And by their mouth a blessing recommends;
While, in a voice with dire forebodings broke,
Sobbing, and faint, the last farewell was spoke.
Now Philomela, scarce receiv'd on board,
And in the royal gilded bark secur'd,
Beheld the dashes of the bending oar,
The ruffled sea, and the receding shore;
When straight (his joy impatient of disguise)
"We've gain'd our point," the rough barbarian [cries;
"Now I possess the dear, the blissful hour,
And ev'ry wish subjected to my pow'r."
Transports of lust his vicious thoughts employ,
And he forbears, with pain, th' expected joy.
His gloting eyes incessantly survey'd
The virgin beauties of the lovely maid.
As when the bold rapacious bird of Jove,
With crooked talons stooping from above,
Has snatch'd, and carry'd to his lofty nest,
A captive hare, with cruel gripes opprest;
Secure, with fix'd and unrelenting eyes,
He sits, and views the helpless, trembling prize.
Their vessels now had made th' intended land,
And all with joy descend upon the strand;
When the false tyrant seiz'd the princely maid,
And to a lodge in distant woods convey'd;
Pale, sinking, and distress'd with jealous fears,
And asking for her sister all in tears.
The lecher, for enjoyment fully bent,
No longer now conceal'd his base intent;

But with rude haste the bloomy girl deflower'd,
Tender, defenceless, and with ease o'er-power'd.
Her piercing accents to her sire complain,
And to her absent sister, but in vain:
In vain she importunes, with doleful cries,
Each unattentive godhead of the skies.
She pants and trembles, like the bleating prey,
From some close-hunted wolf just snatch'd away;
That still with fearful horrour looks around,
And on its flank regards the bleeding wound.
Or, as the tim'rous dove, the danger o'er,
Beholds her shining plumes, besmear'd with gore.
And, though deliver'd from the falcon's claw,
Yet shivers, and retains a secret awe.
But when her mind a calm reflexion shar'd,
And all her scatter'd spirits were repair'd:
Torn and disorder'd while her tresses hung,
Her livid hands, like one that mourn'd, she wrung.
Then thus, with grief o'erwhelm'd her languid eyes,
"Savage, inhuman, cruel wretch!" she cries;
"Whom nor a parent's strict commands could move,
Though charg'd, and utter'd with the tears of [love,
Nor virgin innocence, nor all that's due
To the strong contract of the nuptial vow:
Virtue, by this, in wild confusion's laid,
And I compell'd to wrong my sister's bed;
Whilst you, regardless of your marriage oath,
With stains of incest have defil'd us both.
Though I deserv'd some punishment to find,
This was, ye gods! too cruel, and unkind.
Yet, villain, to complete your horrid guilt,
Stab here, and let my tainted blood be spilt.
Oh happy! had it come, before I knew
The curs'd embrace of vile perfidious you;
Then my pale ghost, pure from incestuous love,
Had wander'd spotless through th' Elysian grove.
But, if the gods above have pow'r to know,
And judge those actions that are done below;
Unless the dreaded thunders of the sky,
Like me, subdued, and violated lie;
Still my revenge shall take its proper time,
And suit the baseness of your hellish crime.
Myself, abandon'd, and devoid of shame,
Through the wide world your actions will pro- [claim;
Or though I'm prison'd in this lonely den,
Obscur'd, and bury'd from the sight of men,
My mournful voice the pitying rocks shall move,
And my complainings echo through the grove.
Hear me, O Heav'n! and, if a god be there,
Let him regard me, and accept my pray'r."
Struck with these words, the tyrant's guilty [breast
With fear, and anger, was, by turns, possest;
Now, with remorse his conscience deeply stung,
He drew the falchion that beside him hung,
And first her tender arms behind her bound,
Then dragg'd her by the hair along the ground.
The princess willingly her throat reclin'd,
And view'd the steel with a contented mind;
But soon her tongue the girding pincers strain
With anguish, soon she feels the piercing pain:
"Oh father! father!" she would fain have spoke,
But the sharp torture her intention broke;
In vain she tries, for now the blade has cut
Her tongue sheer off, close to the trembling root.
The mangled part still quiver'd on the ground,
Murmuring with a faint imperfect sound:
And, as a serpent writhes his wounded train,
Uneasy, panting, and possess'd with pain;
The piece, while life remain'd, still trembled fast,
And to its mistress pointed to the last.

Yet, after this so damn'd and black a deed,
Fame (which I scarce can credit) has agreed,
That on her rifled charms, still void of shame,
He frequently indulg'd his lustful flame.
At last he ventures to his Procnè's sight,
Loaded with guilt, and cloy'd with long delight;
There, with feign'd grief, and false, dissembled [sighs,
Begins a formal narrative of lies:
Her sister's death he artfully declares,
Then weeps, and raises credit from his tears.
Her vest, with flow'rs of gold embroider'd o'er,
With grief distress'd, the mournful matron tore,
And a beseeming suit of gloomy sable wore.
With cost, an honorary tomb she rais'd,
And thus th' imaginary ghost appeas'd.
Deluded queen! the fate of her you love,
Nor grief, nor pity, but revenge should move.
Through the twelve signs had pass'd the circling [Sun,
And round the compass of the zodiac run;
What must unhappy Philomela do,
For ever subject to her keeper's view?
Huge walls of massy stone the lodge surround,
From her own mouth no way of speaking's found.
But all our wants by wit may be supply'd,
And art makes up, what Fortune has deny'd:
With skill exact a Phrygian web she strung,
Fix'd to a loom that in her chamber hung,
Where in-wrought letters, upon white display'd,
In purple notes, her wretched case betray'd:
The piece, when finish'd, secretly she gave
Into the charge of one poor menial slave;
And then, with gestures, made him understand,
It must be safe convey'd to Procnè's hand.
The slave, with speed, the queen's apartment [sought,
And render'd up his charge, unknowing what he brought.
But when the cyphers, figur'd in each fold,
Her sister's melancholy story told,
(Strange that she could!) with silence she survey'd
The tragic piece, and without weeping read:
In such tumultuous haste her passions sprung,
They chok'd her voice, and quite disarm'd her [tongue.
No room for female tears; the furies rise,
Darting vindictive glances from her eyes;
And, stung with rage, she bounds from place to [place,
While stern revenge sits low'ring in her face.
Now the triennial celebration came,
Observ'd to Bacchus by each Thracian dame;
When in the privacies of night retir'd,
They act his rites, with sacred rapture fir'd;
By night, the tinkling cymbals ring around;
While the shrill notes from Rhodopè resound;
By night, the queen, disguis'd, forsakes the court,
To mingle in the festival resort.
Leaves of the curling vine her temples shade,
And, with a circling wreath, adorn her head:
Adown her back the stag's rough spoils appear,
Light on her shoulder leans a cornel spear.
Thus, in the fury of the god conceal'd,
Procnè her own mad headstrong passion veil'd;
Now, with her gang, to the thick wood she flies,
And with religious yellings fills the skies;
The fatal lodge, as 'twere by chance, she seeks,
And, through the bolted doors, an entrance breaks;
From thence, her sister snatching by the hand,
Mark'd like the ranting Bacchanalian band,
Within the limits of the court she drew,
Shading, with ivy green, her outward hue.
But Philomela, conscious of the place,
Felt new reviving pangs of her disgrace;

A shiv'ring cold prevail'd in ev'ry part,
And the chill'd blood ran trembling to her heart.
Soon as the queen a fit retirement found,
Stript of the garlands that her temples crown'd,
She straight unveil'd her blushing sister's face,
And fondly clasp'd her with a close embrace:
But, in confusion lost, th' unhappy maid,
With shame dejected, hung her drooping head,
As guilty of a crime that stain'd her sister's bed.
That speech, that should her injur'd virtue clear,
And make her spotless innocence appear,
Is now no more; only her hands and eyes
Appeal, in signals, to the conscious skies.
In Procnè's breast the rising passions boil,
And burst in anger with a mad recoil;
Her sister's ill-tim'd grief, with scorn, she blames,
Then, in these furious words her rage proclaims.
"Tears unavailing but defer our time,
The stabbing sword must expiate the crime;
Or worse, if wit, on bloody vengeance bent,
A weapon more tormenting can invent.
O sister! I've prepar'd my stubborn heart,
To act some hellish, and unheard-of part;
Either the palace to surround with fire,
And see the villain in the flames expire;
Or, with a knife, dig out his cursed eyes,
Or, his false tongue with racking engines seize;
Or, cut away the part that injur'd you,
And, thro' a thousand wounds, his guilty soul pur- [sue.
Tortures enough my passion has design'd,
But the variety distracts my mind."
A while, thus wav'ring, stood the furious dame,
When Itys fondling to his mother came;
From him the cruel fatal hint she took,
She view'd him with a stern remorseless look;
"Ah! but too like thy wicked sire," she said,
Forming the direful purpose in her head.
At this a sullen grief her voice supprest,
While silent passions struggle in her breast.
Now, at her lap arriv'd, the flatt'ring boy
Salutes his parent with a smiling joy:
About her neck his little arms are thrown,
And he accosts her in a prattling tone.
Then her tempestuous anger was allay'd,
And in its full career her vengeance stay'd;
While tender thoughts, in spite of passion, rise,
And melting tears disarm her threat'ning eyes.
But when she found the mother's easy heart,
Too fondly swerving from th' intended part;
Her injur'd sister's face again she view'd,
And, as by turns surveying both she stood,
"While this fond boy," she said, "can thus ex- [press
The moving accents of his fond address;
Why stands my sister of her tongue bereft,
Forlorn, and sad, in speechless silence left?
O Procnè, see the fortune of your house!
Such is your fate, when match'd to such a spouse!
Conjugal duty, if observ'd to him,
Would change from virtue, and become a crime;
For all respect to Tereus must debase
The noble blood of great Pandion's race."
Straight at these words, with big resentment fill'd,
Furious her look, she flew, and seiz'd her child;
Like a fell tigress of the savage kind,
That drags the tender suckling of the hind
Thro' India's gloomy groves, where Ganges laves
The shady scene, and rolls his streamy waves.
Now to a close apartment they were come,
Far off retir'd within the spacious dome;
When Procnè, on revengeful mischief bent,
Home to his heart a piercing poniard sent.
Itys, with rueful cries, but all too late,
Holds out his hands, and deprecates his fate;
Still at his mother's neck he fondly aims,
And strives to melt her with endearing names;
Yet still the cruel mother perseveres,
Nor with concern his bitter anguish hears.
This might suffice; but Philomela too
Across his throat a shining cutlass drew.
Then both, with knives, dissect each quiv'ring part,
And carve the butcher'd limbs with cruel art;
Which, whelm'd in boiling cauldrons o'er the fire,
Or turn'd on spits, in steamy smoke aspire:
While the long entries, with their slipp'ry floor,
Run down in purple streams of clotted gore.
Ask'd by his wife to this inhuman feast,
Tereus unknowingly is made a guest:
While she, her plot the better to disguise,
Styles it some unknown mystic sacrifice;
And such the nature of the hallow'd rite,
The wife her husband only could invite,
The slaves must all withdraw, and be debarr'd the [sight.
Tereus, upon a throne of antic state,
Loftily rais'd, before the banquet sate,
And glutton-like, luxuriously pleas'd,
With his own flesh his hungry maw appeas'd.
Nay, such a blindness o'er his senses falls,
That he for Itys to the table calls.
When Procnè, now impatient to disclose
The joy that from her full revenge arose,
Cries out, in transports of a cruel mind,
"Within yourself your Itys you may find."
Still, at this puzzling answer, with surprise,
Around the room he sends his curious eyes;
And as he still inquir'd, and call'd aloud,
Fierce Philomela, all besmear'd with blood,
Her hands with murder stain'd, her spreading hair
Hanging dishevell'd with a ghastly air,
Stept forth, and flung full in the tyrant's face
The head of Itys, goary as it was:
Nor ever long'd so much to use her tongue,
And with a just reproach to vindicate her wrong.
The Thracian monarch from the table flings,
While with his cries the vaulted parlour rings;
His imprecations echo down to Hell,
And rouse the snaky Furies from their Stygian [cell.
One while he labours to disgorge his breast,
And free his stomach from the cursed feast;
Then, weeping o'er his lamentable doom,
He styles himself his son's sepulchral tomb.
Now, with drawn sabre, and impetuous speed,
In close pursuit he drives Pandion's breed;
Whose nimble feet spring with so swift a force,
Across the fields they seem to wing their course.
And now, on real wings themselves they raise,
And steer their airy flight by diff'rent ways;
One to the woodland's shady covert hies,
Around the smoky roof the other flies;
Whose feathers yet the marks of murder stain,
Where stampt upon her breast the crimson spots remain.
Tereus, through grief, and haste to be reveng'd,
Shares the like fate, and to a bird is chang'd:
Fix'd on his head the crested plumes appear,
Long is his beak, and sharpen'd like a spear;
Thus arm'd, his looks his inward mind display,
And, to a lapwing turn'd, he fans his way.
Exceeding trouble, for his children's fate,
Shorten'd Pandion's days, and chang'd his date;

Down to the shades below, with sorrow spent,
An earlier, unexpected ghost he went.

BOREAS IN LOVE.

ERECHTHEUS next th' Athenian sceptre sway'd,
Whose rule the state with joint consent obey'd;
So mix'd his justice with his valour flow'd,
His reign one scene of princely goodness show'd.
Four hopeful youths, as many females bright,
Sprung from his loins, and sooth'd him with de- [light.
Two of these sisters, of a lovelier air,
Excell'd the rest, tho' all the rest were fair.
Procris, to Cephalus in wedlock ty'd,
Bless'd the young sylvan with a blooming bride:
For Orithyia Boreas suffer'd pain,
For the coy maid sued long, but sued in vain;
Tereus his neighbour, and his Thracian blood,
Against the match a main objection stood;
Which made his vows, and all his suppliant love,
Empty as air and ineffectual prove.
But when he found his soothing flatt'ries fail,
Nor saw his soft addresses cou'd avail;
Blust'ring with ire, he quickly has recourse
To rougher arts, and his own native force.
"'Tis well," he said; "such usage is my due,
When thus disguis'd by foreign ways I sue;
When my stern airs and fierceness I disclaim,
And sigh for love, ridiculously tame;
When soft addresses foolishly I try,
Nor my own stronger remedies apply.
By force and violence I chiefly live,
By them the louring stormy tempests drive:
In foaming billows raise the hoary deep,
Writhe knotted oaks, and sandy deserts sweep;
Congeal the falling flakes of fleecy snow,
And bruise, with rattling hail, the plains below.
I, and my brother-winds, when, join'd above,
Thro' the waste champain of the skies we rove,
With such a boist'rous full career engage,
That Heav'n's whole concave thunders at our rage.
While, struck from nitrous clouds, fierce lightnings play,
Dart thro' the storm, and gild the gloomy day.
Or when, in subterraneous caverns pent,
My breath, against the hollow earth, is bent,
The quaking world above, and ghosts below,
My mighty pow'r, by dear experience, know,
Tremble with fear, and dread the fatal blow.
This is the only cure to be apply'd,
Thus to Erechtheus I should be ally'd;
And thus the scornful virgin should be woo'd,
Not by entreaty, but by force subdu'd."
Boreas, in passion, spoke these huffing things,
And, as he spoke, he shook his dreadful wings;
At which, afar the shiv'ring sea was fann'd,
And the wide surface of the distant land:
His dusty mantle o'er the hills he drew,
And swept the lowly valleys, as he flew;
Then, with his yellow wings, embrac'd the maid,
And, wrapt in dusty clouds, far off convey'd.
The sparkling blaze of love's prevailing fire
Shone brighter as he flew, and flam'd the higher.
And now the god, possess'd of his delight,
To northern Thrace pursu'd his airy flight,
Where the young ravish'd nymph became his [bride,
And soon the luscious sweets of wedlock tried.
Two lovely twins, th' effect of this embrace,
Crown their soft labours, and their nuptials grace;
Who, like their mother, beautiful, and fair,
Their father's strength, and feather'd pinions share:
Yet these, at first, were wanting, as 'tis said,
And after, as they grew, their shoulders spread.
Zethes and Calaïs, the pretty twins,
Remain'd unfledg'd, while smooth their beardless chins:
But when, in time, the budding silver down
Shaded their face, and on their cheeks was grown,
Two sprouting wings upon their shoulders sprung,
Like those in birds, that veil the callow young.
Then as their age advanc'd, and they began
From greener youth to ripen into man,
With Jason's Argonauts they cross'd the seas,
Embark'd in quest of the fam'd golden fleece:
There, with the rest, the first frail vessel try'd,
And boldly ventur'd on the swelling tide.

OVID'S METAMORPHOSES.

BOOK VII.

Translated by Mr. Tate and Mr. Stonestreet.

THE STORY OF MEDEA AND JASON.

THE Argonauts now stemm'd the foaming tide,
And to Arcadia's shore their course apply'd;
Where sightless Phineus spent his age in grief,
But Boreas' sons engage in his relief;
And those unwelcome guests, the odious race
Of harpies, from the monarch's table chase.
With Jason then they greater toils sustain,
And Phasis' slimy banks at last they gain.
Here boldly they demand the golden prize
Of Scythia's king, who sternly thus replies:
That mighty labours they must overcome,
Or sail their Argo thence unfreighted home.
Meanwhile Medea, seiz'd with fierce desire,
By reason strives to quench the raging fire;
But strives in vain!—"Some god," she said, "withstands,
And reason's baffled counsel countermands.
What unseen pow'r does this disorder move?
'Tis love—at least 'tis like what men call love.
Else wherefore shou'd the king's commands appear
To me too hard?—But so indeed they are.
Why should I for a stranger fear, lest he
Shou'd perish, whom I did but lately see!
His death, or safety, what are they to me?
Wretch, from thy virgin-breast this flame expel,
And soon—O cou'd I, all wou'd then be well!
But love, resistless love, my soul invades;
Discretion this, affection that persuades.
I see the right, and I approve it too,
Condemn the wrong—and yet the wrong pursue.
Why, royal maid, shou'dst thou desire to wed
A wanderer, and court a foreign bed?
Thy native land, tho' barb'rous, can present
A bridegroom worth a royal bride's consent:
And whether this advent'rer lives or dies,
In fate, and fortune's fickle pleasure lies.
Yet may he live! for to the pow'rs above,
A virgin, led by no impulse of love,
So just a suit may, for the guiltless, move.
Whom wou'd not Jason's valour, youth and blood,
Invite? or cou'd these merits be withstood,
At least his charming person must incline
The hardest heart—I'm sure 'tis so with mine!
Yet, if I help him not, the flaming breath
Of bulls, and earth-born foes, must be his death.
Or, should he through these dangers force his way,
At last he must be made the dragon's prey.

If no remorse for such distress I feel,
I am a tigress, and my breast is steel.
Why do I scruple then to see him slain,
And with the tragic scene my eyes profane?
My magic's art employ, not to assuage
The savages, but to inflame their rage?
His earth-born foes to fiercer fury move,
And accessary to his murder prove?
The gods forbid—but pray'rs are idle breath,
When action only can prevent his death.
Shall I betray my father, and the state,
To intercept a rambling hero's fate;
Who may sail off next hour, and, sav'd from harms
By my assistance, bless another's arms?
Whilst I, not only of my hopes bereft,
But to unpity'd punishment am left.
If he is false, let the ingrateful bleed!
But no such symptom in his looks I read.
Nature would ne'er have lavish'd so much grace
Upon his person, if his soul were base.
Besides, he first shall plight his faith, and swear
By all the gods; what therefore canst thou fear?
Medea, haste, from danger set him free,
Jason shall thy eternal debtor be.
And thou, his queen, with sov'reign state install'd,
By Grecian dames the kind preserver call'd.
Hence idle dreams, by love-sick fancy bred!
Wilt thou, Medea, by vain wishes led,
To sister, brother, father bid adieu?
Forsake thy country's gods, and country too?
My father's harsh, my brother but a child,
My sister rivals me, my country's wild;
And for its gods, the greatest of them all
Inspires my breast, and I obey his call.
That great endearments I forsake, is true,
But greater far the hopes that I pursue:
The pride of having sav'd the youths of Greece,
(Each life more precious than our golden fleece;)
A nobler soil by me shall be possest,
I shall see towns with arts and manners blest;
And, what I prize above the world beside,
Enjoy my Jason—and when once his bride,
Be more than mortal, and to gods ally'd.
They talk of hazards I must first sustain,
Of floating islands justling in the main;
Our tender bark expos'd to dreadful shocks
Of fierce Charybdis' gulf, and Scylla's rocks,
Where breaking waves in whirling eddies roll,
And rav'nous dogs that in deep caverns howl:
Amidst these terrours, while I lie possest
Of him I love, and lean on Jason's breast,
In tempests unconcern'd I will appear,
Or only for my husband's safety fear.
Didst thou say husband?—canst thou so deceive
Thyself, fond maid, and thy own cheat believe?
In vain thou striv'st to varnish o'er thy shame,
And grace thy guilt with wedlock's sacred name.
Pull off the coz'ning mask, and oh! in time
Discover and avoid the fatal crime."
She ceas'd—the Graces now, with kind surprise,
And Virtue's lovely train, before her eyes
Present themselves, and vanquish'd Cupid flies.
She then retires to Hecate's shrine, that stood
Far in the covert of a shady wood:
She finds the fury of her flames assuag'd,
But, seeing Jason there, again they rag'd.
Blushes and paleness did by turns invade
Her tender cheeks, and secret grief betray'd.
As fire, that sleeping under ashes lies,
Fresh blown, and rous'd, does up in blazes rise,
So flam'd the virgin's breast———
New kindled by her lover's sparkling eyes.
For chance, that day, had with uncommon grace
Adorn'd the lovely youth, and through his face
Display'd an air so pleasing, as might charm
A goddess, and a vestal's bosom warm.
Her ravish'd eyes survey him o'er and o'er,
As some gay wonder never seen before;
Transported to the skies she seems to be,
And thinks she gazes on a deity.
But when he spoke, and prest her trembling hand,
And did with tender words her aid demand,
With vows, and oaths to make her soon his bride,
She wept a flood of tears, and thus reply'd;
"I see my errour, yet to ruin move,
Nor owe my fate to ignorance, but love:
Your life I'll guard, and only crave of you
To swear once more—and to your oath be true."
He swears by Hecate he would all fulfil,
And, by her grandfather's prophetic skill,
By ev'ry thing that doubting love could press,
His present danger, and desir'd success.
She credits him, and kindly does produce
Enchanted herbs, and teaches him their use:
Their mystic names and virtues he admires,
And with his booty joyfully retires.

THE DRAGON'S TEETH TRANSFORMED TO MEN.

Impatient for the wonders of the day,
Aurora drives the loit'ring stars away.
Now Mars's mount the pressing people fill,
The crowd below, the nobles crown the hill;
The king himself high-thron'd above the rest,
With iv'ry sceptre, and in purple drest.
Forthwith the brass-hoof'd bulls are set at large,
Whose furious nostrils sulph'rous flame discharge:
The blasted herbage by their breath expires;
As forges rumble with excessive fires,
And furnaces with fiercer fury glow,
When water on the panting mass ye throw;
With such a noise, from their convulsive breast,
Thro' bellowing throats, the struggling vapour prest.
Yet Jason marches up without concern,
While on th' advent'rous youth the monsters turn
Their glaring eyes, and, eager to engage,
Brandish their steel-tipt horns in threat'ning rage:
With brazen hoofs they beat the ground, and choke
The ambient air with clouds of dust and smoke:
Each gazing Grecian for his champion shakes,
While bold advances he securely makes
Thro' singeing blasts; such wonders magic art
Can work, when love conspires, and plays his part.
The passive savages like statues stand,
While he their dew-laps strokes with soothing hand;
To unknown yokes their brawny necks they yield,
And, like tame oxen, plough the wond'ring field.
The Colchians stare; the Grecians shout, and raise
Their champion's courage with inspiring praise.
Embolden'd now, on fresh attempts he goes,
With serpent's teeth the fertile furrows sows;
The glebe, fermenting with enchanted juice,
Makes the snake's teeth a human crop produce.
For as an infant, pris'ner to the womb,
Contented sleeps, 'till to perfection come,
Then does the cell's obscure confinement scorn,
He tosses, throbs, and presses to be born;

So from the lab'ring earth no single birth,
But a whole troop of lusty youths rush forth;
And, what's more strange, with martial fury warm'd,
And for encounter all completely arm'd;
In rank and file, as they were sow'd, they stand,
Impatient for the signal of command.
No foe but the Æmonian youth appears;
At him they level their steel-pointed spears;
His frighted friends, who triumph'd just before,
With peals of sighs his desp'rate case deplore:
And where such hardy warriors are afraid,
What must the tender, and enamour'd maid?
Her spirits sink, the blood her cheek forsook;
She fears, who for his safety undertook:
She knew the virtue of the spells she gave,
She knew the force, and knew her lover brave;
But what's a single champion to a host?
Yet scorning thus to see him tamely lost,
Her strong reserve of secret arts she brings,
And last, her never-failing song she sings.
Wonders ensue; among his gazing foes
The massy fragment of a rock he throws;
This charm in civil war engag'd them all;
By mutual wounds those earth-born brothers fall.
The Greeks, transported with the strange success,
Leap from their seats the conqu'ror to caress;
Commend, and kiss, and clasp him in their arms:
So would the kind contriver of the charms;
But her, who felt the tenderest concern,
Honour condemns in secret flames to burn;
Committed to a double guard of fame,
Aw'd by a virgin's, and a princess' name.
But thoughts are free, and fancy unconfin'd,
She kisses, courts, and hugs him in her mind;
To fav'ring pow'rs her silent thanks she gives,
By whose indulgence her lov'd hero lives.
One labour more remains, and, tho' the last,
In danger far surmounting all the past;
That enterprise by fates in store was kept,
To make the dragon sleep that never slept,
Whose crest shoots dreadful lustre; from his jaws
A triple tire of forked stings he draws,
With fangs, and wings of a prodigious size:
Such was the guardian of the golden prize.
Yet him, besprinkled with Lethean dew,
The fair enchantress into slumber threw;
And then, to fix him, thrice she did repeat
The rhyme, that makes the raging winds retreat;
In stormy seas can halcyon seasons make,
Turn rapid streams into a standing lake;
While the soft guest his drowzy eye-lids seels,
Th' unguarded golden fleece the stranger steals;
Proud to possess the purchase of the toil,
Proud of his royal bride, the richer spoil;
To sea both prize, and patroness he bore,
And lands triumphant on his native shore.

OLD ÆSON RESTORED TO YOUTH.

ÆMONIAN matrons, who their absence mourn'd,
Rejoice to see their prosp'rous sons return'd:
Rich curling fumes of incense feast the skies,
A hecatomb of voted victims dies,
With gilded horns, and garlands on their head,
And all the pomp of death, to th' altar led.
Congratulating bowls go briskly round,
Triumphant shouts in louder music drown'd.
Amidst these revels, why that cloud of care
On Jason's brow? (to whom the largest share
Of mirth was due)——His father was not there.
Æson was absent, once the young, and brave,
Now crush'd with years, and bending to the grave
At last withdrawn, and by the crowd unseen,
Pressing her hand (with starting sighs between)
He supplicates his kind and skilful queen.
"O patroness! preserver of my life!
(Dear when my mistress, and much dearer wife)
Your favours to so vast a sum amount,
'Tis past the pow'r of numbers to recount;
Or could they be to computation brought,
The history would a romance be thought:
And yet, unless you add one favour more,
Greater than all that you conferr'd before,
But not too hard for love and magic skill,
Your past are thrown away, and Jason's wretched still.
The morning of my life is just begun,
But my declining father's race is run;
From my large stock retrench the long arrears,
And add them to expiring Æson's years."
Thus spake the gen'rous youth, and wept the rest.
Mov'd with the piety of his request,
To his ag'd sire such filial duty shown,
So diff'rent from her treatment of her own,
But still endeav'ring her remorse to hide,
She check'd her rising sighs, and thus reply'd:
"How could the thought of such inhuman wrong
Escape," said she, "from pious Jason's tongue?
Does the whole world another Jason bear,
Whose life Medea can to yours prefer?
Or could I with so dire a change dispense,
Hecate will never join in that offence:
Unjust is the request you make, and I
In kindness your petition shall deny:
Yet she that grants not what you do implore,
Shall yet essay to give her Jason more;
Find means t'increase the stock of Æson's years,
Without retrenchment of your life's arrears;
Provided that the triple goddess join
A strong confed'rate in my bold design."
Thus was her enterprise resolv'd; but still
Three tedious nights are wanting to fulfil
The circling crescents of th' increasing Moon;
Then, in the height of her nocturnal noon,
Medea steals from court; her ancles bare,
Her garments closely girt, but loose her hair;
Thus sally'd, like a solitary sprite,
She traverses the terrours of the night.
Men, beasts, and birds in soft repose lay charm'd,
No boist'rous wind the mountain-woods alarm'd;
Nor did those walks of love, the myrtle-trees,
Of am'rous Zephyr hear the whisp'ring breeze;
All elements chain'd in unactive rest,
No sense but what the twinkling stars exprest;
To them (that only wak'd) she rears her arms,
And thus commences her mysterious charms.
She turn'd her thrice about, as oft she threw
On her pale tresses the nocturnal dew;
Then yelling thrice a most enormous sound,
Her bare knee bended on the flinty ground,
"O Night," said she, "thou confidant and guide
Of secrets, such as darkness ought to hide;
Ye stars and Moon, that, when the Sun retires,
Support his empire with succeeding fires;
And thou, great Hecate, friend to my design;
Songs, mutt'ring spells, your magic forces join;
And thou, O Earth, the magazine that yields
The midnight sorc'rer drugs; skies, mountains, fields,
Ye wat'ry pow'rs of fountain, stream, and lake;
Ye sylvan gods, and gods of night, awake,
And gen'rously your parts in my adventure take.

"Oft by your aid swift currents I have led
Through wand'ring banks, back to their fountain head;
Transform'd the prospect of the briny deep,
Made sleeping billows rave, and raving billows sleep;
Made clouds, or sunshine; tempests rise, or fall;
And stubborn lawless winds obey my call:
With mutter'd words disarm'd the viper's jaw;
Up by the roots vast oaks and rocks could draw,
Make forests dance, and trembling mountains come,
Like malefactors, to receive their doom;
Earth groan, and frighted ghosts forsake their tomb.
Thee, Cynthia, my resistless rhymes drew down,
When tinkling cymbals strove my voice to drown;
Nor stronger Titan could their force sustain,
In full career compell'd to stop his wain:
Nor could Aurora's virgin blush avail,
With pois'nous herbs I turn'd her roses pale;
The fury of the fiery bulls I broke,
Their stubborn necks submitting to my yoke;
And when the sons of Earth with fury burn'd,
Their hostile rage upon themselves I turn'd;
The brothers made with mutual wounds to bleed,
And by their fatal strife my lover freed;
And, while the dragon slept, to distant Greece,
Thro' cheated guards, convey'd the golden fleece.
But now to bolder action I proceed,
Of such prevailing juices now have need,
That wither'd years back to their bloom can bring,
And in dead winter raise a second spring,
And you'll perform't——
You will; for lo! the stars, with sparkling fires,
Presage as bright success to my desires:
And now another happy omen see!
A chariot drawn by dragons waits for me."
With these last words she leaps into the wain,
Strokes the snakes' necks, and shakes the golden rein;
That signal giv'n, they mount up to the skies,
And now beneath her fruitful Tempè lies,
Whose stores she ransacks, then to Crete she flies;
There Ossa, Pelion, Othrys, Pindus, all
To the fair ravisher a booty fall;
The tribute of their verdure she collects,
Nor proud Olympus' height his plants protects.
Some by the roots she plucks; the tender tops
Of others with her culling sickle crops.
Nor could the plunder of the hills suffice,
Down to the humble vales, and meads she flies;
Apidanus, Amphrysus, the next rape
Sustain, nor could Enipeus' bank escape;
Thro' Beebè's marsh, and thro' the border rang'd,
Whose pasture Glaucus to a Triton chang'd.
Now the ninth day, and ninth successive night,
Had wonder'd at the restless rover's flight;
Meanwhile her dragons, fed with no repast,
But her exhaling simples' od'rous blast,
Their tarnish'd scales, and wrinkled skins had cast.
At last return'd before her palace gate,
Quitting her chariot, on the ground she sate,
The sky her only canopy of state.
All conversation with her sex she fled,
Shunn'd the caresses of the nuptial bed:
Two altars next of grassy turf she rears,
This Hecate's name, that youth's inscription bears;
With forest boughs, and vervain these she crown'd;
Then delves a double trench in lower ground,
And sticks a black-fleec'd ram, that ready stood,
And drench'd the ditches with devoted blood:
New wine she pours, and milk from th' udder warm,
With mystic murmurs to complete the charm,
And subterranean deities alarm.
To the stern king of ghosts she next apply'd,
And gentle Proserpine, his ravish'd bride,
That for old Æson with the laws of fate
They would dispense, and lengthen his short date;
Thus with repeated pray'rs she long assails
Th' infernal tyrant, and at last prevails;
Then calls to have decrepit Æson brought,
And stupifies him with a sleeping-draught;
On earth his body, like a corpse, extends,
Then charges Jason and his waiting friends
To quit the place, that no unhallow'd eye
Into her art's forbidden secrets pry.
This done, th' enchantress, with her locks unbound,
About her altars trips a frantic round;
Piece-meal the consecrated wood she splits,
And dips the splinters in the bloody pits,
Then hurls them on the piles; the sleeping sire
She lustrates thrice, with sulphur, water, fire.
In a large cauldron now the med'cine boils,
Compounded of her late-collected spoils,
Blending into the mesh the various pow'rs
Of wonder-working juices, roots, and flow'rs;
With gems i'th' eastern ocean's cell refin'd,
And such as ebbing tides had left behind;
To them the midnight's pearly dew she flings,
A screech-owl's carcase, and ill-boding wings;
Nor could the wizard wolf's warm entrails scape,
(That wolf who counterfeits a human shape.)
Then, from the bottom of her conj'ring-bag,
Snakes' skins, and liver of a long-liv'd stag;
Last a crow's head, to such an age arriv'd,
That he had now nine centuries surviv'd;
These, and with these a thousand more that grew
In sundry soils, into her pot she threw;
Then with a wither'd olive bough she rakes
The bubbling broth; the bough fresh verdure takes;
Green leaves at first the perish'd plant surround,
Which the next minute with ripe fruit were crown'd.
The foaming juices now the brink o'er-swell;
The barren heath, where'er the liquor fell,
Sprang out with vernal grass, and all the pride
Of blooming May——When this Medea spy'd,
She cuts her patient's throat; the exhausted blood
Recruiting with her new-enchanted flood;
While at his mouth, and thro' his op'ning wound,
A double inlet her infusion found;
His feeble frame resumes a youthful air,
A glossy brown his hoary beard and hair.
The meagre paleness from his aspect fled,
And in its room sprang up a florid red;
Through all his limbs a youthful vigour flies,
His empty'd art'ries swell with fresh supplies:
Gazing spectators scarce believe their eyes.
But Æson is the most surpris'd to find
A happy change in body and in mind;
In sense and constitution the same man,
As when his fortieth active year began.
Bacchus, who from the clouds this wonder view'd,
Medea's method instantly pursu'd,
And his indulgent nurse's youth renew'd.

THE DEATH OF PELIAS.

THUS far obliging Love employ'd her art,
But now Revenge must act a tragic part:

Medea feigns a mortal quarrel bred
Betwixt her, and the partner of her bed;
On this pretence to Pelias' court she flies,
Who languishing with age and sickness lies:
His guiltless daughters, with inveigling wiles,
And well-dissembled friendship, she beguiles:
The strange achievements of her art she tells,
With Æson's cure, and long on that she dwells,
Till them to firm persuasion she has won,
The same for their old father may be done:
For him they court her to employ her skill,
And put upon the cure what price she will.
At first she's mute, and with a grave pretence
Of difficulty, holds them in suspense;
Then promises, and bids them, from the fold
Choose out a ram, the most infirm and old;
That so by fact their doubts may be remov'd,
And first on him the operation prov'd.
A wreath-horn'd ram is brought, so far o'ergrown
With years, his age was to that age unknown;
Of sense too dull the piercing point to feel,
And scarce sufficient blood to stain the steel.
His carcase she into a cauldron threw,
With drugs whose vital qualities she knew;
His limbs grew less, he casts his horns, and years,
And tender bleatings strike their wond'ring ears.
Then instantly leaps forth a frisking lamb,
That seeks (too young to graze) a suckling dam.
The sisters, thus confirm'd with the success,
Her promise with renew'd entreaty press;
To countenance the cheat, three nights and days
Before experiment th' enchantress stays;
Then into limpid water from the springs,
Weeds and ingredients of no force she flings;
With antic ceremonies for pretence,
And rambling rhymes without a word of sense.
Meanwhile the king with all his guards lay bound
In magic sleep, scarce that of death so sound;
The daughters now are by the sorc'ress led
Into his chamber, and surround his bed.
"Your father's health's concern'd, and can ye stay?
Unnat'ral nymphs, why this unkind delay?
Unsheath your sword, dismiss his lifeless blood,
And I'll recruit it with a vital flood:
Your father's life and health is in your hand,
And can ye thus like idle gazers stand?
Unless you are of common sense bereft,
If yet one spark of piety is left,
Dispatch a father's cure, and disengage
The monarch from his toilsome load of age:
Come—drench your weapons in his putrid gore;
'Tis charity to wound, when wounding will restore."
Thus urg'd, the poor deluded maids proceed,
Betray'd by zeal, to an inhuman deed,
And in compassion, make a father bleed.
Yes, she who had the kindest, tend'rest heart,
Is foremost to perform the bloody part.
Yet, though to act the butchery betray'd,
They could not bear to see the wounds they made;
With looks averted, backward they advance,
Then strike, and stab, and leave the blows to chance.
Waking in consternation, he essays
(Welt'ring in blood) his feeble arms to raise,
Environ'd with so many swords—"From whence
This barb'rous usage? what is my offence?
What fatal fury, what infernal charm,
'Gainst a kind father does his daughters arm?"
Hearing his voice, as thunder-struck they stopt,
Their resolution, and their weapons dropt:
Medea then the mortal blow bestows,
And that perform'd, the tragic scene to close,
His corpse into the boiling cauldron throws.
Then, dreading the revenge that must ensue,
High-mounted on her dragon-coach she flew;
And in her stately progress through the skies,
Beneath her, shady Pelion first she spies,
With Othrys, that above the clouds did rise;
With skilful Chiron's cave, and neighb'ring ground,
For old Cerambus' strange escape renown'd,
By nymphs deliver'd, when the world was drown'd;
Who him with unexpected wings supply'd,
When delug'd hills a safe retreat deny'd.
Æolian Pitanè on her left hand
She saw, and there the statu'd dragon stand;
With Ida's grove, where Bacchus, to disguise
His son's bold theft, and to secure the prize,
Made the stol'n steer a stag to represent;
Cocytus' father's sandy monument;
And fields that held the murder'd sire's remains,
Where howling Mœra frights the startled plains.
Euryphilus' high town, with tow'rs defac'd
By Hercules, and matrons more disgrac'd
With sprouting horns, in signal punishment,
From Juno, or resenting Venus sent.
Then Rhodes, which Phœbus did so dearly prize,
And Jove no less severely did chastise:
For he the vizard native's pois'ning sight,
That us'd the farmer's hopeful crops to blight,
In rage o'erwhelm'd with everlasting night.
Cartheia's ancient walls come next in view,
Where once the sire almost a statue grew
With wonder, which a strange event did move,
His daughter turn'd into a turtle-dove.
Then Hyrie's lake, and Tempè's field o'er-ran,
Fam'd for the boy who there became a swan;
For there enamour'd Phyllius, like a slave,
Perform'd what tasks his paramour would crave.
For presents he had mountain-vultures caught,
And from the desert a tame lion brought:
Then a wild bull commanded to subdue,
The conquer'd savage by the horns he drew;
But, mock'd so oft, the treatment he disdains,
And from the craving boy this prize detains.
Then thus in choler the resenting lad;
"Won't you deliver him?—You'll wish you had;"
No sooner said, but, in a peevish mood,
Leapt from the precipice on which he stood:
The standers-by were struck with fresh surprise,
Instead of falling, to behold him rise
A snowy swan, and soaring to the skies.
But dearly the rash prank his mother cost,
Who ignorantly gave her son for lost;
For his misfortune wept, till she became
A lake, and still renown'd with Hyrie's name.
Thence to Latona's isle, where once were seen,
Transform'd to birds, a monarch, and his queen.
Far off she saw how old Cephisus mourn'd
His son, into a seal by Phœbus turn'd;
And where, astonish'd at a stranger sight,
Eumelus gaz'd on his wing'd daughter's flight.
Ætolian Pleuron she did next survey,
Where sons a mother's murder did essay,
But sudden plumes the matron bore away.
On her right hand, Cyllenè, a fair soil,
Fair, till Menephron there the beauteous hill
Attempted with foul incest to defile.
Her harness'd dragons now direct she drives
For Corinth, and at Corinth she arrives;
Where, if what old tradition tells, be true,
In former ages men from mushrooms grew.

But here Medea finds her bed supply'd,
During her absence, by another bride;
And hopeless to recover her lost game,
She sets both bride and palace in a flame.
Nor could a rival's death her wrath assuage,
Nor stopt at Creon's family her rage:
She murders her own infants, in despite
To faithless Jason, and in Jason's sight;
Yet ere his sword could reach her, up she springs,
Securely mounted on her dragon's wings.

THE STORY OF ÆGEUS.

FROM hence to Athens she directs her flight
Where Phineus, so renown'd for doing right;
Where Periphas, and Polyphemon's niece,
Soaring with sudden plumes amaz'd the towns of [Greece.
Here Ægeus so engaging she addrest,
That first he treats her like a royal guest;
Then takes the sorc'ress for his wedded wife;
The only blemish of his prudent life.
Meanwhile his son, from actions of renown,
Arrives at court, but to his sire unknown.
Medea, to dispatch a dangerous heir,
(She knew him) did a pois'nous draught prepare:
Drawn from a drug, was long reserv'd in store
For desp'rate uses, from the Scythian shore;
That from the Echydnæan monster's jaws
Deriv'd its origin, and this the cause.
Through a dark cave a craggy passage lies,
To ours ascending from the nether skies;
Thro' which, by strength of hand, Alcides drew
Chain'd Cerberus, who lagg'd, and restive grew,
With his blear'd eyes our brighter day to view.
Thrice he repeated his enormous yell,
With which he scares the ghosts, and startles Hell;
At last outrageous (tho' compell'd to yield)
He sheds his foam in fury on the field;
Which, with its own, and rankness of the ground,
Produc'd a weed, by sorcerers renown'd,
The strongest constitution to confound;
Call'd aconite, because it can unlock
All bars, and force its passage through a rock.
The pious father, by her wheedles won,
Presents this deadly potion to his son;
Who with the same assurance takes the cup,
And to the monarch's health had drank it up,
But in the very instant he apply'd
The goblet to his lips, old Ægeus spy'd
The iv'ry-hilted sword that grac'd his side.
That certain signal of his son he knew,
And snatcht the bowl away; the sword he drew,
Resolv'd, for such a son's endanger'd life,
To sacrifice the most perfidious wife.
Revenge is swift, but her more active charms
A whirlwind rais'd, that snatch'd her from his arms.
While conjur'd clouds their baffled sense surprise,
She vanishes from their deluded eyes,
And thro' the hurricane triumphant flies.
The gen'rous king, altho' o'er-joy'd to find
His son was safe, yet bearing still in mind
The mischief by his treach'rous queen design'd,
The horrour of the deed, and then how near
The danger drew, he stands congeal'd with fear.
But soon that fear into devotion turns,
With grateful incense ev'ry altar burns;
Proud victims, and unconscious of their fate,
Stalk to the temple, there to die in state.
In Athens never had a day been found
For mirth, like that grand festival, renown'd.
Promiscuously the peers and people dine,
Promiscuously their thankful voices join
In songs of wit, sublim'd by sprightly wine.
To list'ning spheres their joint applause they raise,
And thus resound their matchless Theseus' praise.
"Great Theseus! thee the Marathonian plain
Admires, and wears with pride the noble stain
Of the dire monster's blood, by valiant Theseus [slain.
That now Cromyon's swains in safety sow,
And reap their fertile field, to thee they owe.
By thee th' infested Epidaurian coast
Was clear'd, and now can a free commerce boast.
The traveller his journey can pursue,
With pleasure the late dreadful valley view,
And cry, 'Here Theseus the grand robber slew.'
Cephisus' flood cries to his rescu'd shore,
'The merciless Procrustes is no more.'
In peace, Eleusis, Ceres' rites renew,
Since Theseus' sword the fierce Cercyon slew.
By him the tort'rer Sinis was destroy'd,
Of strength (but strength to barb'rous use em- [ploy'd)
That tops of tallest pines to earth could bend,
And thus in pieces wretched captives rend.
Inhuman Scyron now has breath'd his last,
And now Alcatho's roads securely past,
By Theseus slain, and thrown into the deep:
But earth nor sea his scatter'd bones would keep,
Which, after floating long, a rock became,
Still infamous with Scyron's hated name.
When Fame to count thy acts and years proceeds,
Thy years appear but ciphers to thy deeds.
For thee, brave youth, as for our commonwealth,
We pray; and drink, in yours, the public health.
Your praise the senate, and plebeians sing,
With your lov'd name the court, and cottage ring.
You make our shepherds and our sailors glad,
And not a house in this vast city's sad."
But mortal bliss will never come sincere,
Pleasure may lead, but grief brings up the rear;
While for his son's arrival, rev'ling joy
Ægeus, and all his subjects does employ;
While they for only costly feasts prepare,
His neighb'ring monarch, Minos, threatens war:
Weak in land forces, nor by sea more strong,
But pow'rful in a deep-resented wrong
For a son's murder, arm'd with pious rage;
Yet prudently before he would engage,
To raise auxiliaries resolv'd to sail,
And with the pow'rful princes to prevail.
First Anaphè, then proud Astypalæa gains,
By presents that, and this by threats obtains:
Low Myconè, Cymolus, chalky soil,
Tall Cythnos, Scyros, flat Seriphos' isle;
Paros, with marble cliffs afar display'd;
Impregnable Sithonia; yet betray'd,
To a weak foe by a gold-admiring maid,
Who, chang'd into a daw of sable hue,
Still hoards up gold, and hides it from the view.
But as these islands cheerfully combine,
Others refuse t'embark in his design.
Now leftward with an easy sail he bore,
And prosp'rous passage, to Œnopia's shore;
Œnopia once, but now Ægina call'd,
And with his royal mother's name install'd
By Æacus, under whose reign did spring
The Myrmidons, and now their reigning king.
Down to the port, amidst the rabble, run
The princes of the blood; with Telamon,
Peleus the next, and Phocus the third son:
Then Æacus, although opprest with years,
To ask the cause of their approach appears.

That question does the Gnossian's grief renew,
And sighs from his afflicted bosom drew;
Yet after a short solemn respite made,
The ruler of the hundred cities said:
"Assist our arms, rais'd for a murder'd son,
In this religious war no risk you'll run:
Revenge the dead——for who refuse to give
Rest to their urns, unworthy are to live."
"What you request," thus Æacus replies,
"Not I, but truth and common faith denies;
Athens and we have long been sworn allies:
Our leagues are fix'd, confed'rate are our pow'rs,
And who declare themselves their foes, are ours."
Minos rejoins, "Your league shall dearly cost;"
(Yet, mindful how much safer 'twas to boast,
Than there to waste his forces, and his fame,
Before in field with his grand foe he came)
Parts without blows—nor long had left the shore,
Ere into port another navy bore,
With Cephalus, and all his jolly crew;
Th' Æacides their old acquaintance knew:
The princes bid him welcome, and in state
Conduct the hero to their palace gate;
Who ent'ring, seem'd the charming mien to wear,
As when in youth he paid his visit there.
In his right hand an olive-branch he holds,
And, salutation past, the chief unfolds
His embassy from the Athenian state,
Their mutual friendship, leagues of ancient date;
Their common danger, ev'ry thing could wake
Concern, and his address successful make:
Strength'ning his plea with all the charms of sense,
And those, with all the charms of eloquence.
Then thus the king: "Like suitors do you stand
For that assistance which you may command?
Athenians, all our listed forces use,
(They're such as no bold service will refuse;)
And when y'have drawn them off, the gods be prais'd,
Fresh legions can within our isle be rais'd:
So stock'd with people, that we can prepare
Both for domestic, and for distant war,
Ours, or our friends' insulters to chastise.
"Long may ye flourish thus," the prince replies.
"Strange transport seiz'd me as I pass'd along,
To meet so many troops, and all so young,
As if your army did of twins consist;
Yet amongst them my late acquaintance miss'd:
Ev'n all that to your palace did resort,
When first you entertain'd me at your court;
And cannot guess the cause from whence could spring
So vast a change"—then thus the sighing king:
"Illustrious guests, to my strange tale attend,
Of sad beginning, but a joyful end:
The whole to a vast history would swell,
I shall but half, and that confus'dly, tell.
That race whom so deserv'dly you admir'd,
Are all into their silent tombs retir'd:
They fell; and falling, how they shook my state,
Thought may conceive, but words can ne'er relate.

THE STORY OF ANTS CHANGED TO MEN.

By Mr. Stonestreet.

"A DREADFUL plague from angry Juno came,
To scourge the land that bore her rival's name;
Before her fatal anger was reveal'd,
And teeming malice lay as yet conceal'd,
All remedies we try, all med'cines use,
Which nature could supply, or art produce;
Th' unconquer'd foe derides the vain design,
And art, and nature foil'd, declare the cause divine.
"At first we only felt th' oppressive weight
Of gloomy clouds, then teeming with our fate,
And lab'ring to discharge unactive heat:
But ere four moons alternate changes knew,
With deadly blasts the fatal south-wind blew,
Infected all the air, and poison'd as it flew.
Our fountains too a dire infection yield,
For crowds of vipers creep along the field,
And with polluted gore, and baneful steams,
Taint all the lakes, and venom all the streams.
"The young disease with milder force began,
And rag'd on birds, and beasts, excusing man.
The lab'ring oxen fall before the plough,
Th' unhappy ploughmen stare, and wonder how:
The tabid sheep, with sickly bleatings, pines;
Its wool decreasing, as its strength declines:
The warlike steed, by inward foes compell'd,
Neglects his honours, and deserts the field;
Unnerv'd, and languid, seeks a base retreat,
And at the manger groans, but wish'd a nobler fate:
The stags forget their speed, the boars their rage,
Nor can the bears the stronger herds engage:
A gen'ral faintness does invade them all,
And in the woods, and fields, promiscuously they fall.
The air receives the stench, and (strange to say)
The rav'nous birds and beasts avoid the prey:
Th' offensive bodies rot upon the ground,
And spread the dire contagion all around.
"But now the plague, grown to a larger size,
Riots on man, and scorns a meaner prize.
Intestine heats begin the civil war,
And flushings first the latent flame declare,
And breath inspir'd, which seem'd like fiery air.
Their black dry tongues are swell'd, and scarce can move,
And short thick sighs from panting lungs are drove.
They gape for air, with flatt'ring hopes t'abate
Their raging flames, but that augments their heat.
No bed, no cov'ring can the wretches bear,
But on the ground, expos'd to open air,
They lie, and hope to find a pleasing coolness there.
The suff'ring earth, with that oppression curst,
Returns the heat which they imparted first.
"In vain physicians would bestow their aid,
Vain all their art, and useless all their trade;
And they, ev'n they, who fleeting life recal,
Feel the same pow'rs, and undistinguish'd fall.
If any proves so daring to attend
His sick companion, or his darling friend,
Th' officious wretch sucks in contagious breath,
And with his friend does sympathize in death.
"And now the care and hopes of life are past,
They please their fancies, and indulge their taste;
At brooks and streams, regardless of their shame,
Each sex, promiscuous, strives to quench their flame;
Nor do they strive in vain to quench it there,
For thirst, and life, at once extinguish'd are.
Thus in the brooks the dying bodies sink
But heedless still the rash survivors drink.
"So much uneasy down the wretches hate,
They fly their beds, to struggle with their fate;
But if decaying strength forbids to rise,
The victim crawls and rolls, till on the ground he lies.

Each shuns his bed, as each would shun his tomb,
And thinks th' infection only lodg'd at home.
"Here one, with fainting steps, does slowly creep
O'er heaps of dead, and straight augments the heap;
Another, while his strength and tongue prevail'd,
Bewails his friend, and falls himself bewail'd:
This with imploring looks surveys the skies,
The last dear office of his closing eyes,
But finds the Heav'ns implacable, and dies.
"What now, ah! what employ'd my troubled mind,
But only hopes my subjects' fate to find?
What place soe'er my weeping eyes survey,
There in lamented heaps the vulgar lay;
As acorns scatter when the winds prevail,
Or mellow fruit from shaken branches fall.
"You see that dome which rears its front so high:
'Tis sacred to the monarch of the sky:
How many there, with unregarded tears,
And fruitless vows, sent up successless pray'rs!
There fathers for expiring sons implor'd,
And there the wife bewail'd her gasping lord;
With pious off'rings they appease the skies,
But they, ere yet th' atoning vapours rise,
Before the altars fall, themselves a sacrifice;
They fall, while yet their hands the gums contain,
Their gums surviving, but their off'rers slain.
"The destin'd ox, with holy garlands crown'd,
Prevents the blow, and feels an unexpected wound:
When I myself invok'd the pow'rs divine,
To drive the fatal pest from me and mine;
When now the priest with hands uplifted stood,
Prepar'd to strike, and shed the sacred blood,
The gods themselves the mortal stroke bestow,
The victim falls, but they impart the blow:
Scarce was the knife with the pale purple stain'd,
And no presages could be then obtain'd,
From putrid entrails, where th' infection reign'd.
"Death stalk'd around with such resistless sway,
The temples of the gods his force obey,
And suppliants feel his stroke, while yet they pray.
'Go now,' said he, 'your deities implore
For fruitless aid, for I defy their pow'r.'
Then with a curst malicious joy survey'd
The very altars, stain'd with trophies of the dead.
"The rest grown mad, and frantic with despair,
Urge their own fate, and so prevent the fear.
Strange madness that, when death pursu'd so fast,
T' anticipate the blow with impious haste.
"No decent honours to their urns are paid,
Nor could the graves receive the num'rous dead;
For, or they lay unbury'd on the ground,
Or unadorn'd a needy fun'ral found:
All rev'rence past, the fainting wretches fight
For fun'ral piles which were another's right.
"Unmourn'd they fall: for, who surviv'd to mourn?
And sires, and moderns unlamented burn:
Parent, and sons sustain an equal fate,
And wand'ring ghosts their kindred shadows meet.
The dead a larger space of ground require,
Nor are the trees sufficient for the fire.
"Despairing under grief's oppressive weight,
And sunk by these tempestuous blasts of fate,
'O Jove,' said I, 'if common fame says true,
If e'er Ægina gave those joys to you,
If e'er you lay enclos'd in her embrace,
Fond of her charms, and eager to possess;
O father, if you do not yet disclaim
Paternal care, nor yet disown the name;
Grant my petitions, and with speed restore
My subjects num'rous as they were before,
Or make me partner of the fate they bore.'
I spoke, and glorious lightning shone around,
And rattling thunder gave a prosp'rous sound;
'So let it be, and may these omens prove
A pledge,' said I, 'of your returning love.'
"By chance a rev'rend oak was near the place,
Sacred to Jove, and of Dodona's race,
Where frugal ants laid up their winter meat,
Whose little bodies bear a mighty weight:
We saw them march along, and hide their store,
And much admir'd their number, and their pow'r;
Admir'd at first, but after envy'd more.
Full of amazement, thus to Jove I pray'd,
'O grant, since thus my subjects are decay'd,
As many subjects to supply the dead.'
I pray'd, and strange convulsions mov'd the oak,
Which murmur'd, tho' by ambient winds unshook:
My trembling hands, and stiff-erected hair,
Exprest all tokens of uncommon fear;
Yet both the earth and sacred oak I kist,
And scarce could hope, yet still I hop'd the best;
For wretches, whatsoe'er the fates divine,
Expound all omens to their own design.
"But now 'twas night, when ev'n distraction wears
A pleasing look, and dreams beguile our cares.
Lo! the same oak appears before my eyes,
Nor alter'd in his shape, nor former size;
As many ants the num'rous branches bear,
The same their labour, and their frugal care;
The branches too alike commotion found,
And shook th' industrious creatures on the ground,
Who, by degrees (what's scarce to be believ'd)
A nobler form, and larger bulk receiv'd,
And on the earth walk'd an unusual pace,
With manly strides, and an erected face;
Their num'rous legs, and former colour lost,
The insects could a human figure boast.
"I wake, and waking find my cares again,
And to the unperforming gods complain,
And call their promise and pretences vain.
Yet in my court I heard the murm'ring voice
Of strangers, and a mixt uncommon noise;
But I suspected all was still a dream,
Till Telamon to my apartment came:
Op'ning the door with an impetuous haste,
'O come,' said he, 'and see your faith and hopes surpast:'
I follow, and, confus'd with wonder, view
Those shapes which my presaging slumbers drew:
I saw, and own'd, and call'd them subjects; they
Confest my pow'r, submissive to my sway.
To Jove, restorer of my race decay'd,
My vows were first with due oblations paid.
I then divide with an impartial hand
My empty city, and my ruin'd land,
To give the new-born youth an equal share,
And call them Myrmidons, from what they were.
You saw their persons, and they still retain
The thrift of ants, tho' now transform'd to men;
A frugal people, and inur'd to sweat,
Lab'ring to gain, and keeping what they get.
These, equal both in strength and years, shall join
Their willing aid, and follow your design,
With the first southern gale that shall present
To fill your sails, and favour your intent."

Continued by Mr. Tate.

With such discourse they entertain the day;
The ev'ning past in banquets, sport, and play:
Then, having crown'd the night with sweet repose,
Aurora (with the wind at east) arose.
Now Pallas' sons to Cephalus resort,
And Cephalus with Pallas' sons to court,
To the king's levee; him sleep's silken chain,
And pleasing dreams, beyond his hour detain;
But then the princes of the blood, in state,
Expect, and meet them at the palace gate.

THE STORY OF CEPHALUS AND PROCRIS.

To th' inmost courts the Grecian youths were
And plac'd by Phocus on a Tyrian bed; [led,
Who, soon observing Cephalus to hold
A dart of unknown wood, but arm'd with gold;
"None better loves," said he "the huntsman's
Or does more often to the woods resort; [sport,
Yet I that jav'lin's stem with wonder view,
Too brown for box, too smooth a grain for yew.
I cannot guess the tree; but never art
Did form, or eyes behold so fair a dart!" [duce
The guest then interrupts him——" 'Twou'd pro-
Still greater wonder, if you knew its use.
It never fails to strike the game, and then
Comes bloody back into your hand again."
Then Phocus each particular desires,
And th' author of the wond'rous gift inquires.
To which the owner thus, with weeping eyes,
And sorrow for his wife's sad fate, replies:
"This weapon here, O prince! can you believe
This dart the cause for which so much I grieve;
And shall continue to grieve on, till fate
Afford such wretched life no longer date?
Would I this fatal gift had ne'er enjoy'd,
This fatal gift my tender wife destroy'd:
Procris her name, ally'd in charms and blood
To fair Orythia courted by a god.
Her father seal'd my hopes with rites divine,
But firmer love before had made her mine.
Men call'd me blest, and blest I was indeed.
The second month our nuptials did succeed;
When (as upon Hymettus' dewy head,
For mountain stags my net betimes I spread)
Aurora spy'd, and ravish'd me away,
With rev'rence to the goddess, I must say,
Against my will, for Procris had my heart,
Nor would her image from my thoughts depart.
At last, in rage she cry'd, 'Ungrateful boy,
Go to your Procris, take your fatal joy;'
And so dismiss'd me: musing, as I went,
What those expressions of the goddess meant,
A thousand jealous fears possess me now,
Lest Procris had prophan'd her nuptial vow:
Her youth and charms did to my fancy paint
A lewd adultress, but her life a saint.
Yet I was absent long, the goddess too
Taught me how far a woman could be true.
Aurora's treatment much suspicion bred;
Besides, who truly love, ev'n shadows dread.
I straight impatient for the trial grew,
What courtship back'd with richest gifts could do.
Aurora's envy aided my design,
And lent me features far unlike to mine.
In this disguise to mine own house I came,
But all was chaste, no conscious sign of blame:
With thousand arts I scarce admittance found,
And then beheld her weeping on the ground
For her lost husband; hardly I retain'd
My purpose, scarce the wish'd embrace refrain'd.
How charming was her grief! Then, Phocus, guess
What killing beauties waited on her dress.
Her constant answer, when my suit I prest,
'Forbear, my lord's dear image guards this breast;
Where'er he is, whatever cause detains,
Whoe'er has his, my heart unmov'd remains.'
What greater proofs of truth than these could be?
Yet I persist, and urge my destiny.
At length, she found, when my own form return'd,
Her jealous lover there, whose loss she mourn'd.
Enrag'd with my suspicion, swift as wind,
She fled at once from me and all mankind;
And so became, her purpose to retain,
A nymph, and huntress in Diana's train:
Forsaken thus, I found my flames increase,
I own'd my folly, and I su'd for peace.
It was a fault, but not of guilt to move
Such punishment, a fault of too much love.
Thus I retriev'd her to my longing arms,
And many happy days possess'd her charms.
But with herself she kindly did confer
What gifts the goddess had bestow'd on her;
The fleetest greyhound, with this lovely dart,
And I of both have wonders to impart.
Near Thebes a savage beast, of race unknown,
Laid waste the field, and bore the vineyards down;
The swains fled from him, and with one consent
Our Grecian youth to chase the monster went;
More swift than light'ning he the toils surpast,
And in his course spears, men, and trees o'er-cast.
We slipt our dogs, and last my Lelaps too,
When none of all the mortal race would do:
He long before was struggling from my hands,
And, ere we could unloose him, broke his bands,
That minute where he was, we could not find,
And only saw the dust he left behind.
I climb'd a neighb'ring hill to view the chase,
While in the plain they held an equal race;
The savage now seems caught, and now by force
To quit himself, nor holds the same straight course;
But running counter, from the foe withdraws,
And with short turning cheats his gaping jaws:
Which he retrieves, and still so closely prest,
You'd fear at ev'ry stretch he were possess'd:
Yet for the gripe his fangs in vain prepare;
The game shoots from him, and he chops the air.
To cast my jav'lin then I took my stand;
But as the thongs were fitting to my hand,
While to the valley I o'er-look'd the wood,
Before my eyes two marble statues stood;
That, as pursu'd appearing at full stretch,
This, barking after, and at point to catch:
Some god their course did with this wonder grace,
That neither might be conquer'd in the chace."
A sudden silence here his tongue suppress,
Here he stops short, and fain would wave the rest.

The eager prince then urg'd him to impart
The fortune that attended on the dart.
"First then," said he, "past joys let me relate,
For bliss was the foundation of my fate.
No language can those happy hours express,
Did from our nuptials me and Procris bless:
The kindest pair! what more could Heav'n confer?
For she was all to me, and I to her.
Had Jove made love, great Jove had been despis'd;
And I my Procris more than Venus priz'd:

Thus while no other joy we did aspire,
We grew at last one soul, and one desire.
Forth to the woods I went at break of day,
(The constant practice of my youth) for prey:
Nor yet for servant, horse, or dog did call,
I found this single dart to serve for all.
With slaughter tir'd, I sought the cooler shade,
And winds that from the mountains pierc'd the glade:
'Come, gentle air,' so was I wont to say,
'Come, gentle air, sweet Aura, come away.'
This always was the burden of my song,
'Come 'suage my flame, sweet Aura, come along.
Thou always art most welcome to my breast;
I faint; approach, thou dearest, kindest guest!'
These blandishments, and more than these, I said,
(By fate to unsuspected ruin led):
'Thou art my joy, for thy dear sake I love
Each desert hill, and solitary grove;
When, faint with labour, I refreshment need,
For cordials on thy fragrant breath I feed.'
At last a wand'ring swain in hearing came,
And cheated with the sound of Aura's name,
He thought I had some assignation made:
And to my Procris' ear the news convey'd.
Great love is soonest with suspicion fir'd:
She swoon'd, and with the tale almost expir'd.
'Ah! wretched heart!' she cry'd, 'ah! faithless man!'
And then to curse th' imagin'd nymph began:
Yet oft she doubts, oft hopes she is deceiv'd,
And chides herself, that ever she believ'd
Her lord to such injustice could proceed,
Till she herself were witness of the deed.
Next morn I to the woods again repair,
And, weary with the chase, invoke the air;
'Approach, dear Aura, and my bosom cheer:'
At which a mournful sound did strike my ear;
Yet I proceeded, till the thicket by
With rustling noise and motion drew my eye:
I thought some beast of prey was shelter'd there,
And to the covert threw my certain spear;
From whence a tender sigh my soul did wound,
'Ah me!' it cry'd, and did like Procris sound.
Procris was there, too well the voice I knew,
And to the place with headlong horrour flew;
Where I beheld her gasping on the ground,
In vain attempting from the deadly wound
To draw the dart, her love's dear fatal gift;
My guilty arms had scarce the strength to lift
The beauteous load; my silks and hair I tore,
(If possible) to stanch the pressing gore;
For pity begg'd her keep her flitting breath,
And not to leave me guilty of her death.
While I entreat she fainted fast away,
And these few words had only strength to say;
'By all the sacred bonds of plighted love,
By all your rev'rence to the pow'rs above,
By all that made me charming once appear,
By all the truth for which you held me dear,
And last by love, the cause through which I bleed,
Let Aura never to my bed succeed.'
I then perceiv'd the errour of our fate,
And told it her, but found and told too late!
I felt her lower to my bosom fall,
And while her eyes had any sight at all,
On mine she fix'd them; in her pangs still prest
My hand, and sigh'd her soul into my breast;
Yet, being undeceiv'd, resign'd her breath
Methought more cheerfully, and smil'd in death."

With such concern the weeping hero told
This tale, that none who heard him could withhold
From melting into sympathising tears,
Till Æacus with his two sons appears;
Whom he commits, with their new-levy'd bands,
To fortune's, and so brave a gen'ral's hands.

OVID'S METAMORPHOSES.

BOOK VIII.

THE STORY OF NISUS AND SCYLLA.

By Mr. Croxall.

Now shone the morning star in bright array,
To vanquish night, and usher in the day:
The wind veers southward, and moist clouds arise,
That blot with shades the blue meridian skies.
Cephalus feels with joy the kindly gales,
His new allies unfurl the swelling sails;
Steady their course, they cleave the yielding main,
And, with a wish, th' intended harbour gain.

Meanwhile king Minos, on the Attic strand
Displays his martial skill, and wastes the land.
His army lies encampt upon the plains,
Before Alcathoe's walls, where Nisus reigns;
On whose grey head a lock of purple hue,
The strength, and fortune of his kingdom, grew.

Six moons were gone and past, when still from far
Victoria hover'd o'er the doubtful war.
So long, to both inclin'd, the impartial maid
Between them both her equal wings display'd.

High on the walls, by Phœbus vocal made,
A turret of the palace rais'd its head;
And where the god his tuneful harp resign'd,
The sound within the stones still lay enshrin'd:
Hither the daughter of the purple king
Ascended oft, to hear its music ring;
And, striking with a pebble, would release
Th' enchanted notes, in times of happy peace.
But now, from thence, the curious maid beheld
Rough feats of arms, and combats of the field:
And, since the siege was long, had learnt the name
Of ev'ry chief, his character, and fame;
Their arms, their horse, and quiver she descry'd,
Nor could the dress of war the warrior hide.

Europa's son she knew above the rest,
And more than well became a virgin breast:
In vain the crested morion veils his face,
She thinks it adds a more peculiar grace:
His ample shield, embost with burnish'd gold,
Still makes the bearer lovelier to behold:
When the tough jav'lin, with a whirl, he sends,
His strength and skill the sighing maid commends:
Or, when he strains to draw the circling bow,
And his fine limbs a manly posture show,
Compar'd with Phœbus, he performs so well,
Let her be judge, and Minos shall excel.

But when the helm put off, display'd to sight,
And set his features in an open light;
When, vaulting to his seat, his steed he prest,
Caparison'd in gold, and richly drest;
Himself in scarlet sumptuously array'd,
New passions rise, and fire the frantic maid.
"O happy spear!" she cries, "that feels his touch;"
Nay, ev'n the reins he holds are blest too much.
Oh! were it lawful, she could wing her way
Through the stern hostile troops without dismay;
Or throw her body to the distant ground,
And in the Cretans happy camp be found.

Would Minos but desire it, she'd expose
Her native country to her country's foes;
Unbar the gates, the town with flames infest,
Or any thing that Minos should request.
And as she sate, and pleas'd her longing sight,
Viewing the king's pavilion veil'd with white,
"Should joy, or grief," she said, "possess my breast,
To see my country by a war opprest?
I'm in suspense! for though 'tis grief to know
I love a man that is declar'd my foe;
Yet, in my own despite, I must approve
That lucky war, which brought the man I love.
Yet, were I tender'd as a pledge of peace,
The cruelties of war might quickly cease.
Oh! with what joy I'd wear the chains he gave!
A patient hostage, and a willing slave.
Thou lovely object! if the nymph that bare
Thy charming person, were but half so fair;
Well might a god her virgin bloom desire,
And with a rape indulge his amorous fire.
Oh! had I wings to glide along the air,
To his dear tent I'd fly, and settle there:
There tell my quality, confess my flame,
And grant him any dowry that he'd name.
All, all I'd give; only my native land,
My dearest country should excepted stand.
For, perish love, and all expected joys,
Ere with so base a thought my soul complies.
Yet, oft the vanquish'd some advantage find,
When conquer'd by a noble, gen'rous mind.
Brave Minos justly has the war begun,
Fir'd with resentment for his murder'd son:
The righteous gods a righteous cause regard,
And will, with victory, his arms reward:
We must be conquer'd; and the captive's fate
Will surely seize us, though it seize us late.
Why then should love be idle, and neglect
What Mars, by arms and perils, will effect?
Oh! prince, I die, with anxious fear opprest,
Lest some rash hand should wound my charmer's breast:
For, if they saw, no barb'rous mind could dare
Against that lovely form to raise a spear.
"But I'm resolv'd, and fix'd in this decree,
My father's country shall my dowry be.
Thus I prevent the loss of life and blood,
And, in effect, the action must be good.
Vain resolution! for, at ev'ry gate
The trusty centinels, successive, wait:
The keys my father keeps; ah! there's my grief;
'Tis he obstructs all hopes of my relief.
Gods! that this hated light I'd never seen!
Or, all my life, without a father been!
But gods we all may be; for those that dare,
Are gods, and fortune's chiefest favours share.
The ruling pow'rs a lazy pray'r detest,
The bold adventurer succeeds the best.
What other maid, inspir'd with such a flame,
But would take courage, and abandon shame?
But would, though ruin should ensue, remove
Whate'er oppos'd, and clear the way to love!
This, shall another's feeble passion dare,
While I sit tame, and languish in despair?
No; for though fire and sword before me lay,
Impatient love through both should force its way.
Yet I have no such enemies to fear,
My sole obstruction is my father's hair;
His purple lock my sanguine hope destroys,
And clouds the prospect of my rising joys."
Whilst thus she spoke, amid the thick'ning air
Night supervenes, the greatest nurse of care:
And, as the goddess spreads her sable wings,
The virgin's fears decay, and courage springs.
The hour was come, when man's o'er-labour'd breast
Surceas'd its care, by downy sleep possest:
All things now hush'd, Scylla with silent tread
Urg'd her approach to Nisus' royal bed:
There, of the fatal lock (accursed theft!)
She her unwitting father's head bereft.
In safe possession of her impious prey,
Out at a postern-gate she takes her way.
Embolden'd by the merit of the deed,
She traverses the adverse camp with speed,
Till Minos' tent she reach'd: the righteous king
She thus bespoke, who shiver'd at the thing.
"Behold th' effect of love's resistless sway!
I, Nisus' royal seed, to thee betray
My country, and my gods. For this strange task,
Minos, no other boon but thee I ask.
This purple lock, a pledge of love, receive;
No worthless present, since in it I give
My father's head."—Mov'd at a crime so new,
And with abhorrence fill'd, back Minos drew,
Nor touch'd th' unhallow'd gift; but thus exclaim'd,
(With mien indignant, and with eyes inflam'd):
"Perdition seize thee, thou, thy kind's disgrace!
May thy devoted carcase find no place
In earth, on air, or sea, by all out-cast!
Shall Minos, with so foul a monster, blast
His Cretan world, where cradled Jove was nurst?
Forbid it Heav'n!—away, thou most accurst!"
And now Alcathoë, its lord exchang'd,
Was under Minos' domination rang'd.
While the most equal king his care applies
To curb the conquer'd, and new laws devise,
The fleet, by his command, with hoisted sails,
And ready oars, invites the murm'ring gales.
At length the Cretan hero anchor weigh'd,
Repaying, with neglect, th' abandon'd maid.
Deaf to her cries, he furrows up the main;
In vain she prays, solicits him in vain.
And now she furious grows in wild despair,
She wrings her hands and throws aloft her hair.
"Where runn'st thou?" thus she vents her deep distress,
"Why shunn'st thou her that crown'd thee with success?
Her, whose fond love to thee could sacrifice
Her country, and her parent, sacred ties!
Can nor my love, nor proffer'd presents find
A passage to thy heart, and make thee kind?
Can nothing move thy pity? O ingrate,
Can'st thou behold my lost, forlorn estate,
And not be soften'd? Can'st thou throw off one
Who has no refuge left but thee alone?
Where shall I seek for comfort? whither fly?
My native country does in ashes lie:
Or were't not so, my treason bares me there,
And bids me wander. Shall I next repair
To a wrong'd father, by my guilt undone?—
Me all mankind deservedly will shun.
I, out of all the world, myself have thrown,
To purchase an access to Crete alone;
Which since refus'd, ungen'rous man, give o'er
To boast thy race; Europa never bore
A thing so savage. Thee some tigress bred,
On the bleak Syrt's inhospitable bed;

Or where Charybdis pours its rapid tide
Tempestuous. Thou art not to Jove ally'd;
Nor did the king of gods thy mother meet
Beneath a bull's forg'd shape, and bear to Crete.
That fable of thy glorious birth is feign'd;
Some wild outrageous bull thy dam sustain'd.
O father Nisus, now my death behold;
Exult, O city, by my baseness sold:
Minos, obdurate, has aveng'd ye all;
But 'twere more just by those I wrong'd to fall:
For why shouldst thou, who only didst subdue
By my offending, my offence pursue?
Well art thou match'd to one whose am'rous flame
Too fiercely rag'd, for human kind to tame;
One who, within a wooden heifer thrust,
Courted a low'ring bull's mistaken lust;
And, from whose monster-teeming womb, the Earth
Receiv'd, what much it mourn'd, a bi-form birth.
But what avail my plaints? the whistling wind,
Which bears him far away, leaves them behind.
Well weigh'd Pasiphaë, when she preferr'd
A bull to thee, more brutish than the herd.
But ah! time presses, and the labour'd oars
To distance drive the fleet, and lose the less'ning shores.
Think not, ungrateful man, the liquid way
And threat'ning billows shall enforce my stay.
I'll follow thee in spite: my arms I'll throw
Around thy oars, or grasp thy crooked prow,
And drag through drenching seas." Her eager tongue
Had hardly clos'd the speech, when forth she sprung,
And prov'd the deep. Cupid with added force
Recruits each nerve, and aids her wat'ry course.
Soon she the ship attains, unwelcome guest;
And, as with close embrace its sides she prest,
A hawk from upper air came pouring down,
('Twas Nisus cleft the sky with wings new-grown.)
At Scylla's head his horny bill he aims;
She, fearful of the blow, the ship disclaims,
Quitting her hold: and yet she fell not far,
But wond'ring, finds herself sustain'd in air.
Chang'd to a lark, she mottled pinions shook,
And, from the ravish'd lock, the name of Ciris took.

THE LABYRINTH.

Now Minos, landed on the Cretan shore,
Performs his vows to Jove's protecting pow'r;
A hundred bullocks of the largest breed,
With flowrets crown'd, before his altar bleed:
While trophies of the vanquish'd, brought from far,
Adorn the palace with the spoils of war.
Meanwhile the monster of a human beast,
His family's reproach, and stain, increas'd.
His double kind the rumour swiftly spread,
And evidenc'd the mother's beastly deed.
When Minos, willing to conceal the shame
That sprung from the reports of tattling fame,
Resolves a dark enclosure to provide,
And, far from sight, the two-form'd creature hide.
Great Dædalus of Athens was the man
That made the draught, and form'd the wond'rous plan;
Where rooms within themselves encircled lie,
With various windings, to deceive the eye.
As soft Mæander's wanton current plays,
When through the Phrygian fields he loosely strays;
Backward and forward rolls the dimpled tide,
Seeming, at once, two different ways to glide:
While circling streams their former banks survey,
And waters past succeeding waters see:
Now floating to the sea with downward course,
Now pointing upward to its ancient source:
Such was the work, so intricate the place,
That scarce the workman all its turns could trace,
And Dædalus was puzzled how to find
The secret ways of what himself design'd.
These private walls the Minotaur include,
Who twice was glutted with Athenian blood.
But the third tribute more successful prov'd,
Slew the foul monster, and the plague remov'd.
When Theseus, aided by the virgin's art,
Had trac'd the guiding thread through ev'ry part,
He took the gentle maid, that set him free,
And, bound for Dias, cut the briny sea.
There, quickly cloy'd, ungrateful, and unkind,
Left his fair consort in the isle behind;
Whom Bacchus saw, and straining in his arms
Her rifled bloom, and violated charms,
Resolves, for this, the dear engaging dame
Should shine for ever in the rolls of fame;
And bids her crown among the stars be plac'd,
With an eternal constellation grac'd.
The golden circlet mounts; and, as it flies,
Its diamonds twinkle in the distant skies;
There, in their pristine form, the gemmy rays
Between Alcides and the Dragon blaze.

THE STORY OF DÆDALUS AND ICARUS.

In tedious exile now too long detain'd,
Dædalus languish'd for his native land:
The sea foreclos'd his flight; yet thus he said;
"Though earth and water in subjection laid,
O cruel Minos, thy dominion be,
We'll go through air; for sure the air is free."
Then to new arts his cunning thought applies,
And to improve the work of nature tries.
A row of quills in gradual order plac'd,
Rise by degrees in length from first to last;
As on a cliff th' ascending thicket grows,
Or different reeds the rural pipe compose.
Along the middle runs a twine of flax,
The bottom stems are join'd by pliant wax.
Thus, well compact, a hollow bending brings
The fine composure into real wings.
His boy, young Icarus, that near him stood,
Unthinking of his fate, with smiles pursu'd
The floating feathers, which the moving air
Bore loosely from the ground, and wafted here and there.
Or with the wax impertinently play'd,
And with his childish tricks the great design delay'd.
The final master-stroke at last impos'd,
And now the neat machine completely clos'd;
Fitting his pinions on, a flight he tries,
And hung self-balanc'd in the beaten skies.
Then thus instructs his child; "My boy, take care
To wing your course along the middle air;
If low, the surges wet your flagging plumes;
If high, the Sun the melting wax consumes:
Steer between both: nor to the northern skies,
Nor south Orion, turn your giddy eyes:
But follow me: let me before you lay
Rules for the flight, and mark the pathless way."
Then teaching, with a fond concern, his son,
He took the untry'd wings, and fix'd them on;

But fix'd with trembling hands; and as he speaks,
The tears roll gently down his aged cheeks:
Then kiss'd, and in his arms embrac'd him fast,
But knew not this embrace must be the last.
And mounting upward, as he wings his flight,
Back on his charge he turns his aching sight;
As parent birds, when first their callow care
Leave the high nest to tempt the liquid air.
Then cheers him on, and oft, with fatal art,
Reminds the stripling to perform his part.
These, as the angler at the silent brook,
Or mountain-shepherd leaning on his crook,
Or gaping ploughman, from the vale descries,
They stare, and view them with religious eyes,
And straight conclude them gods; since none, but they,
Through their own azure skies could find a way.
Now Delos, Paros, on the left are seen,
And Samos, favour'd by Jove's haughty queen;
Upon the right, the isle Lebynthos nam'd,
And fair Calymnè for its honey fam'd.
When now the boy, whose childish thoughts aspire
To loftier aims, and make him ramble higher,
Grown wild, and wanton, more embolden'd flies
Far from his guide, and soars among the skies,
The soft'ning wax, that felt a nearer sun,
Dissolv'd apace, and soon began to run.
The youth in vain his melting pinions shakes;
His feathers gone, no longer air he takes.
"Oh! father, father," as he strove to cry,
Down to the sea he tumbled from on high,
And found his fate; yet still subsists by fame,
Among those waters that retain his name.
The father, now no more a father, cries,
"Ho, Icarus! where are you?" as he flies;
"Where shall I seek my boy?" he cries again,
And saw his feathers scatter'd on the main.
Then curs'd his art; and fun'ral rites conferr'd,
Naming the country from the youth interr'd.
A partridge, from a neighb'ring stump, beheld
The sire his monumental marble build;
Who, with peculiar call, and flutt'ring wing,
Chirpt joyful, and malicious seem'd to sing:
The only bird of all its kind, and late
Transform'd in pity to a feather'd state:
From whence, O Dædalus, thy guilt we date.
His sister's son, when now twelve years were past,
Was, with his uncle, as a scholar plac'd;
The unsuspecting mother saw his parts,
And genius fitted for the finest arts.
This soon appear'd; for when the spiny bone
In fishes' backs was by the stripling known,
A rare invention thence he learnt to draw,
Fil'd teeth in ir'n, and made the grating saw.
He was the first, that from a knob of brass
Made two straight arms with widening stretch to pass;
That, while one stood upon the centre's place,
The other round it drew a circling space.
Dædalus envy'd this, and from the top
Of fair Minerva's temple let him drop;
Feigning, that, as he lean'd upon the tow'r,
Careless he stoop'd too much, and tumbled o'er.
The goddess, who th' ingenious still befriends,
On this occasion her assistance lends;
His arms with feathers, as he fell, she veils,
And in the air a new-made bird he sails.
The quickness of his genius, once so fleet,
Still in his wings remains, and in his feet:
Still, though transform'd, his ancient name he keeps,
And with low flight the new-shorn stubble sweeps,
Declines the lofty trees, and thinks it best
To brood in hedge-rows o'er its humble nest;
And, in remembrance of the former ill,
Avoids the heights, and precipices still.
At length, fatigu'd with long laborious flights,
On fair Sicilia's plains the artist lights;
Where Cocalus the king, that gave him aid,
Was, for his kindness, with esteem repaid.
Athens no more her doleful tribute sent,
That hardship galant Theseus did prevent;
Their temples hung with garlands, they adore
Each friendly god, but most Minerva's pow'r:
To her, to Jove, to all, their altars smoke,
They each with victims, and perfumes invoke.
Now talking fame, through every Grecian town,
Had spread, immortal Theseus, thy renown.
From him the neighb'ring nations in distress,
In suppliant terms implore a kind redress.

THE STORY OF MELEAGER AND ATALANTA.

By Mr. Dryden.

FROM him the Caledonians sought relief;
Though valiant Meleagrus was their chief.
The cause, a boar, who ravag'd far and near:
Of Cynthia's wrath th' avenging minister.
For Oeneus with autumnal plenty bless'd,
By gifts to Heav'n his gratitude express'd:
Cull'd sheafs, to Ceres; to Lyæus, wine;
To Pan, and Pales, offer'd sheep and kine;
And fat of olives, to Minerva's shrine.
Beginning from the rural gods, his hand
Was lib'ral to the pow'rs of high command:
Each deity in ev'ry kind was bless'd,
Till at Diana's fane th' invidious honour ceas'd.
Wrath touches ev'n the gods: the queen of night,
Fir'd with disdain, and jealous of her right,
"Unhonour'd though I am, at least," said she,
"Not unreveng'd that impious act shall be."
Swift as the word, she sped the boar away,
With charge on those devoted fields to prey.
No larger bulls th' Egyptian pastures feed,
And none so large Sicilian meadows breed:
His eye-balls glare with fire suffus'd with blood;
His neck shoots up a thick-set thorny wood;
His bristled back a trench impal'd appears,
And stands erected, like a field of spears;
Froth fills his chaps, he sends a grunting sound,
And part he churns, and part befoams the ground.
For tusks with Indian elephants he strove,
And Jove's own thunder from his mouth he drove.
He burns the leaves; the scorching blast invades
The tender corn, and shrivels up the blades:
Or suff'ring not their yellow beards to rear,
He tramples down the spikes, and intercepts the year.
In vain the barns expect their promis'd load,
Nor barns at home, nor ricks are heap'd abroad:
In vain the hinds the threshing-floor prepare,
And exercise their flails in empty air.
With olives ever-green the ground is strow'd,
And grapes ungather'd shed their gen'rous blood.
Amid the fold he rages, nor the sheep
Their shepherds, nor the grooms their bulls can keep.
From fields to walls the frighted rabble run,
Nor think themselves secure within the town;
Till Meleagrus, and his chosen crew,
Contemn the danger, and the praise pursue.

Fair Leda's twins (in time to stars decreed)
One fought on foot, one curb'd the fiery steed;
Then issu'd forth fam'd Jason after these,
Who mann'd the foremost ship that sail'd the seas;
Then Theseus join'd with bold Pirithous came;
A single concord in a double name;
The Thestian sons, Idas who swiftly ran,
And Ceneus, once a woman, now a man.
Lynceus, with eagle's eyes, and lion's heart;
Leucippus, with his never-erring dart:
Acastus, Phileus, Phœnix, Telamon,
Echion, Lelix, and Eurytion,
Achilles' father, and great Phocus' son;
Dryas the fierce, and Hippasus the strong:
With twice-old Iolas, and Nestor then but young.
Laertes active, and Ancæus bold;
Mopsus the sage, who future things foretold;
And t'other seer, yet by his wife[1] unsold.
A thousand others of immortal fame;
Among the rest, fair Atalanta came,
Grace of the woods; a diamond buckle bound
Her vest behind, that else had flow'd upon the ground,
And show'd her buskin'd legs; her head was bare,
But for her native ornament of hair;
Which in a simple knot was ty'd above,
Sweet negligence! unheeded bait of love!
Her sounding quiver on her shoulder ty'd,
One hand a dart, and one a bow supply'd.
Such was her face, as in a nymph display'd
A fair fierce boy, or in a boy betray'd
The blushing beauties of a modest maid.
The Caledonian chief at once the dame
Beheld, at once his heart receiv'd the flame,
With Heav'ns averse. "O happy youth," he cry'd,
"For whom thy fates reserve so fair a bride!"
He sigh'd, and had no leisure more to say;
His honour call'd his eyes another way,
And forc'd him to pursue the now-neglected prey.
There stood a forest on a mountain's brow,
Which over-look'd the shaded plains below.
No sounding axe presum'd those trees to bite;
Coeval with the world, a venerable sight.
The heroes there arriv'd, some spread around
The toil; some search the footsteps on the ground:
Some from the chains the faithful dogs unbound.
Of action eager, and intent in thought,
The chiefs their honourable danger sought.
A valley stood below; the common drain
Of waters from above, and falling rain:
The bottom was a moist, and marshy ground,
Whose edges were with bending osiers crown'd.
The knotty bulrush next in order stood,
And all within of reeds a trembling wood.
From hence the boar was rous'd, and sprung amain,
Like lightning sudden, on the warrior train;
Beats down the trees before him, shakes the ground.
The forest echoes to the crackling sound;
Shout the fierce youth, and clamours ring around.
All stood with their protended spears prepar'd,
With broad steel heads the brandish'd weapons glar'd.
The beast impetuous with his tusks aside
Deals glancing wounds; the fearful dogs divide:
All spend their mouths aloof, but none abide.

[1] Amphiaraus.

Echion threw the first, but miss'd his mark,
And stuck his boar-spear on a maple's bark.
Then Jason; and his javelin seem'd to take,
But fail'd with over-force, and whizz'd above his back.
Mopsus was next; but ere he threw, address'd
To Phœbus thus: "O patron, help thy priest:
If I adore, and ever have ador'd
Thy pow'r divine, thy present aid afford;
That I may reach the beast." The god allow'd
His pray'r, and, smiling, gave him what he could:
He reach'd the savage, but no blood he drew:
Dian unarm'd the javelin, as it flew.
This chaf'd the boar, his nostrils flames expire,
And his red eye-balls roll with living fire.
Whirl'd from a sling, or from an engine thrown,
Amid her foes, so flies a mighty stone,
As flew the beast: the left wing put to flight,
The chiefs o'er-born, he rushes on the right.
Empalamos and Pelagon he laid
In dust, and next to death, but for their fellows' aid.
Onesimus far'd worse, prepar'd to fly,
The fatal fang drove deep within his thigh,
And cut the nerves: the nerves no more sustain
The bulk; the bulk unpropp'd, falls headlong on the plain.
Nestor had fail'd the fall of Troy to see,
But leaning on his lance, he vaulted on a tree;
Then gath'ring up his feet, look'd down with fear,
And thought his monstrous foe was still too near.
Against a stump his trunk the monster grinds,
And in the sharpen'd edge new vigour finds;
Then, trusting to his arms, young Othrys found,
And ranch'd his hips with one continu'd wound.
Now Leda's twins, the future stars, appear;
White were their habits, white their horses were:
Conspicuous both, and both in act to throw,
Their trembling lances brandish'd at the foe:
Nor had they miss'd, but he to thickets fled,
Conceal'd from aiming spears, not pervious to the steed.
But Telamon rush'd in, and happ'd to meet
A rising root, that held his fasten'd feet;
So down he fell, whom, sprawling on the ground,
His brother from the wooden gyves unbound.
Meantime the virgin-huntress was not slow
T' expel the shaft from her contracted bow:
Beneath his ear the fasten'd arrow stood,
And from the wound appear'd the trickling blood.
She blush'd for joy: but Meleagrus rais'd
His voice with loud applause, and the fair archer prais'd.
He was the first to see, and first to show
His friends the mark of the successful blow.
"Nor shall thy valour want the praises due,"
He said; a virtuous envy seiz'd the crew.
They shout; the shouting animates their hearts,
And all at once employ their thronging darts:
But out of order thrown, in air they join,
And multitude makes frustrate the design.
With both his hands the proud Ancæus takes,
And flourishes, his double-biting axe:
Then, forward to his fate, he took a stride
Before the rest, and to his fellows cry'd,
"Give place, and mark the diff'rence, if you can,
Between a woman warrior, and a man.
The boar is doom'd; nor though Diana lend
Her aid, Diana can her beast defend."
Thus boasted he; then stretch'd, on tiptoe stood,
Secure to make his empty promise good.

But the more wary beast prevents the blow,
And upward rips the groin of his audacious foe.
Ancæus falls; his bowels from the wound
Rush out, and clotted blood distains the ground.
Pirithous, no small portion of the war, [far
Press'd on, and shook his lance: to whom from
Thus Theseus cry'd; "O stay, my better part,
My more than mistress; of my heart, the heart.
The strong may fight aloof; Ancæus try'd
His force too near, and by presuming dy'd."
He said, and while he spake his javelin threw,
Hissing in air th' unerring weapon flew;
But on an arm of oak, that stood betwixt
The marksman and the mark, his lance he fixt.
Once more bold Jason threw, but fail'd to wound
The boar, but slew an undeserving hound,
And thro' the dog the dart was nail'd to ground.
Two spears from Meleager's hand were sent,
With equal force, but various in th' event:
The first was fix'd in earth, the second stood
On the boar's bristled back, and deeply drank his blood.
Now while the tortur'd savage turns around,
And flings about his foam, impatient of the wound,
The wound's great author close at hand provokes
His rage, and plies him with redoubled strokes;
Wheels, as he wheels; and with his pointed dart
Explores the nearest passage to his heart.
Quick and more quick he spins his giddy gyres,
Then falls, and in much foam his soul expires.
This act with shouts Heav'n-high the friendly band
Applaud, and strain in theirs the victor's hand.
Then all approach the slain with vast surprise,
Admire on what a breadth of earth he lies,
And scarce secure, reach out their spears afar,
And blood their points to prove their partnership of war.
But he, the conqu'ring chief, his foot impress'd
On the strong neck of that destructive beast;
And gazing on the nymph with ardent eyes,
"Accept," said he, "fair Nonacrine, my prize,
And, though inferior, suffer me to join
My labours, and my part of praise, with thine:"
At this presents her with the tusky head,
And chine, with rising bristles roughly spread.
Glad she receiv'd the gift; and seem'd to take
With double pleasure, for the giver's sake.
The rest were seiz'd with sullen discontent,
And a deaf murmur through the squadron went:
All envy'd; but the Thestyan brethren show'd
The least respect, and thus they vent their spleen aloud; [share,
"Lay down those honour'd spoils, nor think to
Weak woman as thou art, the prize of war:
Ours is the title, thine a foreign claim,
Since Meleagrus from our lineage came.
Trust not thy beauty; but restore the prize
Which he, besotted on that face, and eyes,
Would rend from us:" at this, inflam'd with spite,
From her they snatch the gift, from him the giver's right.
But soon th' impatient prince his falchion drew,
And cry'd, "Ye robbers of another's due,
Now learn the diff'rence, at your proper cost,
Betwixt true valour, and an empty boast."
At this advanc'd, and sudden as the word,
In proud Plexippus' bosom plung'd the sword:
Toxeus amaz'd, and with amazement slow
Or to revenge, or ward the coming blow,
Stood doubting; and, while doubting thus he stood,
Receiv'd the steel bath'd in his brother's blood.
Pleas'd with the first, unknown the second news,
Althæa to the temples pays their dues
For her son's conquest; when at length appear
Her grisly brethren stretch'd upon the bier:
Pale at the sudden sight, she chang'd her cheer,
And with her cheer her robes; but hearing tell
The cause, the manner, and by whom they fell,
'Twas grief no more, or grief and rage were one
Within her soul; at last 'twas rage alone;
Which burning upwards in succession, dries
The tears, that stood consid'ring in her eyes.
There lay a log unlighted on the hearth,
When she was lab'ring in the throes of birth
For th' unborn chief; the fatal sisters came,
And rais'd it up, and toss'd it on the flame:
Then on the rock a scanty measure place
Of vital flax, and turn'd the wheel apace;
And turning sung, "To this red brand and thee,
O new-born babe, we give an equal destiny;"
So vanish'd out of view. The frighted dame
Sprung hasty from her bed, and quench'd the flame.
The log, in secret lock'd, she kept with care,
And that, while thus preserv'd, preserv'd her heir.
This branch she now produc'd; and first she strows
The hearth with heaps of chips, and after blows:
Thrice heav'd her hand, and heav'd, she thrice repress'd,
The sister and the mother long contest,
Two doubtful titles, in one tender breast:
And now her eyes and cheeks with fury glow;
Now pale her cheeks, her eyes with pity flow:
Now low'ring looks presage approaching storms,
And now prevailing love her face reforms:
Resolv'd, she doubts again; the tears she dry'd
With burning rage, are by new tears supply'd.
And as a ship, which winds and waves assail,
Now with the current drives, now with the gale,
Both opposite, and neither long prevail:
She feels a double force, by turns obeys
Th' imperious tempest, and th' impetuous seas:
So fares Althæa's mind, she first relents
With pity, of that pity then repents:
Sister and mother long the scales divide,
But the beam nodded on the sister's side.
Sometimes she softly sigh'd, then roar'd aloud;
But sighs were stifled in the cries of blood.
The pious impious wretch at length decreed,
To please her brothers ghost', her son should bleed:
And when the fun'ral flames began to rise,
"Receive," she said, "a sister's sacrifice;
A mother's bowels burn:" high in her hand,
Thus while she spoke, she held the fatal brand;
Then thrice before the kindled pile she bow'd,
And the three furies thrice invok'd aloud:
"Come, come, revenging sisters, come, and view
A sister paying her dead brothers' due:
A crime I punish, and a crime commit;
But blood for blood, and death for death is fit:
Great crimes must be with greater crimes repaid,
And second fun'rals on the former laid.
Let the whole household in one ruin fall,
And may Diana's curse o'ertake us all.
Shall fate to happy Oeneus still allow
One son, while Thestius stands depriv'd of two?
Better three lost, than one unpunish'd go.
Take then, dear ghosts, (while yet admitted new
In Hell you wait my duty) take your due:

A costly off'ring on your tomb is laid,
When with my blood the price of yours is paid.
"Ah! whither am I hurry'd? Ah! forgive,
Ye shades, and let your sister's issue live;
A mother cannot give him death; though he
Deserves it, he deserves it not from me.
"Then shall th' unpunish'd wretch insult the slain,
Triumphant live, nor only live, but reign;
While you, thin shades, the sport of winds are tost
O'er dreary plains, or tread the burning coast?
I cannot, cannot bear; 'tis past, 'tis done;
Perish this impious, this detested son:
Perish his sire, and perish I withal!
And let the house's heir, and the hop'd kingdom fall!
"Where is the mother fled, her pious love,
And where the pains with which ten months I strove!
Ah! had'st thou dy'd, my son, in infant years,
Thy little hearse had been bedew'd with tears.
"Thou liv'st by me; to me thy breath resign;
Mine is the merit, the demerit thine.
Thy life by double title I require;
Once giv'n at birth, and once preserv'd from fire:
One murder pay, or add one murder more,
And me to them who fell by thee restore.
"I would, but cannot: my son's image stands
Before my sight; and now their angry hands
My brothers hold, and vengeance these exact;
This pleads compassion, and repents the fact.
"He pleads in vain, and I pronounce his doom:
My brothers, though unjustly, shall o'ercome.
But having paid their injur'd ghosts their due,
My son requires my death, and mine shall his pursue."
At this, for the last time, she lifts her hand,
Averts her eyes, and, half unwilling, drops the brand.
The brand, amid the flaming fuel thrown,
Or drew, or seem'd to draw, a dying groan;
The fires themselves but faintly lick'd their prey,
Then loath'd their impious food, and would have shrunk away.
Just then the hero cast a doleful cry,
And in those absent flames began to fry:
The blind contagion rag'd within his veins;
But he with manly patience bore his pains:
He fear'd not fate, but only griev'd to die
Without an honest wound, and by a death so dry.
"Happy Ancæus," thrice aloud he cry'd,
"With what becoming fate in arms he dy'd!"
Then call'd his brothers, sisters, sire around,
And, her to whom his nuptial vows were bound,
Perhaps his mother; a long sigh he drew,
And, his voice failing, took his last adieu.
For as the flames augment, and as they stay
At their full height, then languish to decay,
They rise and sink by fits; at last they soar
In one bright blaze, and then descend no more:
Just so his inward heats, at height, impair,
Till the last burning breath shoots out the soul in air.
Now lofty Calidon in ruins lies;
All ages, all degrees unsluice their eyes,
And Heav'n and Earth resound with murmurs, groans, and cries.
Matrons and maidens beat their breasts, and tear
Their habits, and root up their scatter'd hair:
The wretched father, father now no more,
With sorrow sunk, lies prostrate on the floor,
Deforms his hoary locks with dust obscene,
And curses age, and loaths a life prolong'd with pain.
By steel her stubborn soul his mother freed,
And punish'd on herself her impious deed.
Had I a hundred tongues, a wit so large
As could their hundred offices discharge;
Had Phœbus all his Helicon bestow'd
In all the streams, inspiring all the god;
Those tongues, that wit, those streams, that god in vain
Would offer to describe his sisters' pain:
They beat their breasts with many a bruising blow,
Till they turn livid, and corrupt the snow.
The corpse they cherish, while the corpse remains,
And exercise, and rub with fruitless pains;
And when to fun'ral flames 'tis borne away,
They kiss the bed on which the body lay:
And when those fun'ral flames no longer burn,
(The dust compos'd within a pious urn)
Ev'n in that urn their brother they confess,
And hug it in their arms, and to their bosoms press.
His tomb is rais'd; then stretch'd along the ground,
Those living monuments his tomb surround:
Ev'n to his name, inscrib'd, their tears they pay,
Till tears and kisses wear his name away.
But Cynthia now had all her fury spent,
Not with less ruin than a race content:
Excepting Gorgè, perish'd all the seed,
And her [2] whom Heav'n for Hercules decreed.
Satiate at last, no longer she pursu'd
The weeping sisters; but with wings endu'd,
And horny beaks, and sent to flit in air:
Who yearly round the tomb in feather'd flocks repair.

THE TRANSFORMATION OF THE NAIADS.

By Mr. Vernon.

THESEUS mean-while acquitting well his share
In the bold chase confed'rate like a war,
To Athens' lofty tow'rs his march ordain'd,
By Pallas lov'd, and where Erectheus reign'd.
But Achelöus stopp'd him on the way,
By rains a deluge, and constrain'd his stay.
"O fam'd for glorious deeds, and great by blood,
Rest here," says he, "nor trust the rapid flood;
It solid oaks has from its margin tore,
And rocky fragments down its current bore,
The murmur hoarse, and terrible the roar.
Oft have I seen herds with their shelt'ring fold
Forc'd from the banks, and in the torrent roll'd;
Nor strength the bulky steer from ruin freed,
Nor matchless swiftness sav'd the racing steed.
In cataracts when the dissolving snow
Falls from the hills, and floods the plains below;
Toss'd by the eddies with a giddy round,
Strong youths are in the sucking whirlpools drown'd.
'Tis best with me in safety to abide,
Till usual bounds restrain the ebbing tide,
And the low waters in their channel glide."
Theseus persuaded, in compliance bow'd;
"So kind an offer, and advice so good,
O Achelöus, cannot be refus'd;
I'll use them both," said he; and both he us'd.
The grot he enter'd, pumice-built the hall,
And tophi made the rustic of the wall;
The floor, soft moss a humid carpet spread,
And various shells the chequer'd roof inlaid.
'Twas now the hour when the declining Sun
Two-thirds had of his daily journey run;

[2] Dejanira.

At the spread table Theseus took his place,
Next his companions in the daring chase:
Pirithous here, the elder Lelex lay,
His locks betraying age with sprinkled grey.
Acharnia's river-god dispos'd the rest,
Grac'd with the equal honour of the feast,
Elate with joy, and proud of such a guest.
The nymphs were waiters, and with naked feet
In order serv'd the courses of the meat.
The banquet done, delicious wine they brought,
Of one transparent gem the cup was wrought.
Then the great hero of this gallant train,
Surveying far the prospect of the main;
"What is that land," says he, "the waves embrace?"
(And with his finger pointed at the place;)
"Is it one parted isle which stands alone?
How nam'd? and yet methinks it seems not one."
To whom the watry god made this reply;
"'Tis not one isle, but five; distinct they lie;
'Tis distance which deceives the cheated eye.
But that Diana's act may seem less strange,
These once proud Naiads were, before their change.
'Twas on a day more solemn than the rest,
Ten bullocks slain, a sacrificial feast:
The rural gods of all the region near
They bid to dance, and taste the hallow'd cheer.
Me they forgot: affronted with the slight,
My rage and stream swell'd to the greatest height;
And with the torrent of my flooding store, [tore.
Large woods from woods, and fields from fields I
The guilty nymphs, Oh! then, rememb'ring me,
I, with their country, wash'd into the sea;
And joining waters with the social main,
Rent the gross land, and split the firm champain.
Since, the Echinades, remote from shore,
Are view'd as many isles, as nymphs before.

PERIMELE TURNED INTO AN ISLAND.

"But yonder far, lo, yonder does appear
An isle, a part to me for ever dear,
From that (it sailors Perimele name)
I doting, forc'd by rape a virgin's fame.
Hippodamas's passion grew so strong,
Gall'd with th' abuse, and fretted at the wrong,
He cast his pregnant daughter from a rock;
I spread my waves beneath, and broke the shock;
And as her swimming weight my stream convey'd,
I su'd for help divine, and thus I pray'd:
'O pow'rful thou, whose trident does command
The realm of waters, which surround the land;
We sacred rivers, wheresoe'er begun,
End in thy lot, and to thy empire run.
With favour hear, and help with present aid;
Her whom I bear 'twas guilty I betray'd.
Yet if her father had been just, or mild,
He would have been less impious to his child;
In her, have pity'd force in the abuse;
In me, admitted love for my excuse.
O let relief for her hard case be found,
Her, whom paternal rage expell'd from ground,
Her whom paternal rage relentless drown'd.
Grant her some place, or change her to a place,
Which I may ever clasp with my embrace.'
"His nodding head the sea's great ruler bent,
And all his waters shook with his assent. [trest,
The nymph still swam, tho' with the fright dis-
I felt her heart leap trembling in her breast;
But hard'ning soon, whilst I her pulse explore,
A crusting earth cas'd her stiff body o'er;
And as accretions of new-cleaving soil
Inlarg'd the mass, the nymph became an isle."

THE STORY OF BAUCIS AND PHILEMON.

By Mr. Dryden.

Thus Achelous ends: his audience hear
With admiration, and admiring fear
The pow'rs of Heav'n; except Ixion's son,
Who laugh'd at all the gods, believ'd in none:
He shook his impious head, and thus replies;
"These legends are no more than pious lies:
You attribute too much to heav'nly sway,
To think they gave us forms, and take away."
The rest of better minds their sense declar'd
Against this doctrine, and with horrour heard.
Then Lelex rose, an old experienc'd man,
And thus with sober gravity began;
Heav'n's pow'r is infinite: earth, air, and sea,
The manufacture mass, the making pow'r obey:
By proof to clear your doubt; in Phrygian ground
Two neighb'ring trees, with walls encompass'd round,
Stand on a mod'rate rise, with wonder shown,
One a hard oak, a softer linden one:
I saw the place, and them, by Pittheus sent
To Phrygian realms; my grandsire's government.
Not far from thence is seen a lake, the haunt
Of coots, and of the fishing cormorant:
Here Jove with Hermes came; but in disguise
Of mortal men conceal'd their deities;
One laid aside his thunder, one his rod;
And many toilsome steps together trod:
For harbour at a thousand doors they knock'd,
Not one of all the thousand but was lock'd.
At last a hospitable house they found,
A homely shed; the roof, not far from ground,
Was thatch'd with reeds and straw, together bound.
There Baucis and Philemon liv'd, and there
Had liv'd long marry'd, and a happy pair:
Now old in love, though little was their store,
Inur'd to want, their poverty they bore,
Nor aim'd at wealth, professing to be poor.
For master, or for servant here to call,
Was all alike, where only two were all.
Command was none, where equal love was paid,
Or rather both commanded, both obey'd.
"From lofty roofs the gods repuls'd before,
Now stooping, enter'd through the little door:
The man (their hearty welcome first express'd)
A common settle drew for either guest,
Inviting each his weary limbs to rest.
But ere they sat, officious Baucis lays
Two cushions stuff'd with straw, the seat to raise;
Coarse, but the best she had: then rakes the load
Of ashes from the hearth, and spreads abroad
The living coals; and, lest they should expire,
With leaves and bark she feeds her infant fire:
It smokes; and then with trembling breath she blows,
Till in a cheerful blaze the flames arose. [these,
With brush-wood, and with chips she strengthens
And adds at last the boughs of rotten trees.
The fire thus form'd, she sets the kettle on,
(Like burnish'd gold the little seether shone)
Next took the coleworts which her husband got
From his own ground, (a small well-water'd spot;)
She stripp'd the stalks of all their leaves; the best
She cull'd, and them with handy care she drest.

High o'er the hearth a chine of bacon hung;
Good old Philemon seiz'd it with a prong,
And from the sooty rafter drew it down,
Then cut a slice, but scarce enough for one;
Yet a large portion of a little store,
Which for their sakes alone he wish'd were more.
This in the pot he plung'd without delay,
To tame the flesh, and drain the salt away.
The time between, before the fire they sat,
And shorten'd the delay by pleasing chat.
" A beam there was, on which a beechen pail
Hung by the handle, on a driven nail:
This fill'd with water, gently warm'd, they set
Before their guests; in this they bath'd their feet,
And after with clean towels dry'd their sweat.
This done, the host produc'd the genial bed,
Sallow the feet, the borders, and the stead,
Which with no costly coverlet they spread,
But coarse old garments; yet such robes as these
They laid alone at feasts, on holidays.
The good old housewife, tucking up her gown,
The table sets; th' invited gods lie down.
The trivet-table of a foot was lame,
A blot which prudent Baucis overcame,
Who thrust beneath the limping leg a sherd,
So was the mended board exactly rear'd:
Then rubb'd it o'er with newly gather'd mint,
A wholesome herb, that breath'd a grateful scent.
Pallas began the feast, where first was seen
The party-colour'd olive, black and green:
Autumnal cornels next in order serv'd,
In lees of wine well pickled, and preserv'd.
A garden-sallad was the third supply,
Of endive, radishes, and succory:
Then curds and cream, the flow'r of country fare,
And new-laid eggs, which Baucis' busy care
Turn'd by a gentle fire, and roasted rare.
All these in earthenware were serv'd to board;
And next in place an earthen pitcher, stor'd
With liquor of the best the cottage could afford.
This was the table's ornament and pride,
With figures wrought: like pages at his side
Stood beechen bowls; and these were shining clean,
Varnish'd with wax without, and lin'd within.
By this the boiling kettle had prepar'd,
And to the table sent the smoking lard;
On which with eager appetite they dine,
A sav'ry bit, that serv'd to relish wine:
The wine itself was suiting to the rest,
Still working in the must, and lately press'd.
The second course succeeds like that before,
Plumbs, apples, nuts, and of their wintry store
Dry figs, and grapes, and wrinkled dates were set
In canisters, t' enlarge the little treat:
All these a milk-white honey-comb surround,
Which in the midst the country-banquet crown'd:
But the kind hosts their entertainment grace
With hearty welcome, and an open face:
In all they did, you might discern with ease
A willing mind, and a desire to please.
" Mean-time the beechen bowls went round, and still,
Though often empty'd, were observ'd to fill;
Fill'd without hands, and of their own accord
Ran without feet, and danc'd about the board.
Devotion seiz'd the pair, to see the feast
With wine, and of no common grape, increas'd;
And up they held their hands, and fell to pray'r,
Excusing, as they could, their country fare.
" One goose they had, ('twas all they could allow)
A wakeful centry, and on duty now,
Whom to the gods for sacrifice they vow:
Her with malicious zeal the couple view'd;
She ran for life, and limping they pursu'd:
Full well the fowl perceiv'd their bad intent,
And would not make her master's compliment;
But persecuted, to the Pow'rs she flies,
And close between the legs of Jove she lies:
He with a gracious ear the suppliant heard,
And sav'd her life; then what he was declar'd,
And own'd the god. 'The neighbourhood,' said he,
'Shall justly perish for impiety;
You stand alone exempted; but obey
With speed, and follow where we lead the way:
Leave these accurs'd; and to the mountain's height
Ascend; nor once look backward in your flight.'
" They haste, and what their tardy feet deny'd,
The trusty staff (their better leg) supply'd.
An arrow's flight they wanted to the top,
And there secure, but spent with travel, stop;
Then turn their now-no-more-forbidden eyes;
Lost in a lake the floated level lies:
A watery desert covers all the plains,
Their cot alone, as in an isle remains.
Wond'ring with weeping eyes, while they deplore
Their neighbours' fate, and country now no more,
Their little shed, scarce large enough for two,
Seems from the ground, increas'd in height and bulk, to grow.
A stately temple shoots within the skies,
The crotches of their cot in columns rise:
The pavement polish'd marble they behold,
The gates with sculpture grac'd, the spires and tiles of gold.
" Then thus the sire of gods, with looks serene:
'Speak thy desire, thou only just of men;
And thou, O woman, only worthy found
To be with such a man in marriage bound.'
" Awhile they whisper; then to Jove address'd,
Philemon thus prefers their joint request:
'We crave to serve before your sacred shrine,
And offer at your altar rites divine;
And since not any action of our life
Has been polluted with domestic strife;
We beg one hour of death, that neither she
With widow's tears may live to bury me,
Nor weeping I, with wither'd arms, may bear
My breathless Baucis to the sepulchre.'
" The godheads sign their suit. They run the race
In the same tenour all th' appointed space;
Then, when their hour was come, while they relate
These past adventures at the temple gate,
Old Baucis is by old Philemon seen
Sprouting with sudden leaves of sprightly green:
Old Baucis look'd where old Philemon stood,
And saw his lengthen'd arms a sprouting wood:
New roots their fasten'd feet begin to bind,
Their bodies stiffen in a rising rind;
Then, ere the bark above their shoulders grew,
They give and take at once their last adieu.
At once, 'Farewell, O faithful spouse,' they said;
At once th' incroaching rinds their closing lips invade.
Ev'n yet, an ancient Tyanæan shows
A spreading oak, that near a linden grows;
The neighbourhood confirm the prodigy,
Grave men, not vain of tongue, or like to lie.
I saw myself the garlands on their boughs,
And tablets hung for gifts of granted vows,

And off'ring fresher up, with pious pray'r,
'The good,' said I, 'are God's peculiar care,
And such as honour Heav'n, shall heav'nly honour share."

Continued by Mr. Vernon.

THE CHANGE OF PROTEUS.

He ceas'd in his relation to proceed,
Whilst all admir'd the author, and the deed;
But Theseus most, inquisitive to know
From gods what wondrous alterations grow.
Whom thus the Calydonian stream address'd,
Rais'd high to speak, the couch his elbow press'd.
"Some, when transform'd, fix in the lasting change;
Some, with more right, through various figures range.
Proteus, thus large thy privilege was found,
Thou inmate of the seas, which earth surround.
Sometimes a blooming youth you grac'd the shore;
Oft a fierce lion, or a furious boar:
With glist'ring spires now seem'd an hissing snake,
The bold would tremble in his hands to take:
With horns assum'd a bull; sometimes you prov'd
A tree by roots, a stone by weight unmov'd:
Sometimes two wav'ring contraries became,
Flow'd down in water, or aspir'd in flame.

THE STORY OF ERISICHTHON.

"In various shapes thus to deceive the eyes
Without a settled stint of her disguise,
Rash Erisichthon's daughter had the pow'r,
And brought it to Autolycus in dow'r.
Her atheist sire the slighted gods defy'd,
And ritual honours to their shrines deny'd.
As fame reports, his hand an ax sustain'd,
Which Ceres' consecrated grove prophan'd;
Which durst the venerable gloom invade,
And violate with light the awful shade.
An ancient oak in the dark centre stood,
The covert's glory, and itself a wood;
Garlands embrac'd its shaft, and from the boughs
Hung tablets, monuments of prosp'rous vows.
In the cool dusk its unpierc'd verdure spread,
The Dryads oft their hallow'd dances led;
And oft, when round their gaging arms they cast,
Full fifteen ells it measur'd in the waist:
In height all under-standards did surpass,
As they aspir'd above the humbler grass.
"These motives, which would gentler minds restrain,
Could not make Triope's bold son abstain;
He sternly charg'd his slaves with strict decree,
To fell with gashing steel the sacred tree.
But whilst they, ling'ring, his commands delay'd,
He snatch'd an ax, and thus blaspheming said;
'Was this no oak, nor Ceres' favourite care,
But Ceres' self, this arm, unaw'd, should dare
Its leafy honours in the dust to spread,
And level with the earth its airy head.'
He spoke, and as he pois'd a slanting stroke,
Sighs heav'd, and tremblings shook the frighted oak;
Its leaves look'd sickly, pale its acorns grew,
And its long branches sweat a chilly dew.
But when his impious hand a wound bestow'd,
Blood from the mangled bark in currents flow'd.
When a devoted bull of mighty size,
A sinning nation's grand atonement, dies;
With such a plenty from the spouting veins,
A crimson stream the turfy altars stains.
"The wonder all amaz'd; yet one more bold,
The fact dissuading, strove his ax to hold.
But the Thessalian, obstinately bent,
Too proud to change, too harden'd to repent,
On his kind monitor his eyes, which burn'd
With rage, and with his eyes his weapon turn'd;
'Take the reward,' says he, 'of pious dread:'
Then with a blow lopp'd off his parted head.
No longer check'd, the wretch his crime pursu'd,
Doubled his strokes, and sacrilege renew'd;
When from the groaning trunk a voice was heard,
'A Dryad I, by Ceres' love preferr'd,
Within the circle of this clasping rind
Coëval grew, and now in ruin join'd;
But instant vengeance shall thy sin pursue,
And death is cheer'd with this prophetic view.'
"At last the oak with cords enforc'd to bow,
Strain'd from the top, and sap'd with wounds below,
The humbler wood, partaker of its fate,
Crush'd with its fall, and shiver'd with its weight.
"The grove destroy'd, the sister Dryads moan,
Griev'd at its loss, and frighted at their own:
Straight, suppliants for revenge, to Ceres go,
In sable weeds expressive of their woe.
"The beauteous goddess with a graceful air
Bow'd in consent and nodded to their pray'r.
The awful motion shook the fruitful ground,
And wav'd the fields with golden harvests crown'd.
Soon she contriv'd in her projecting mind
A plague severe, and piteous in its kind,
(If plagues for crimes of such presumptuous height
Could pity in the softest breast create.)
With pinching want, and hunger's keenest smart,
To tear his vitals, and corrode his heart.
But since her near approach by fate's deny'd
To Famine, and broad climes their pow'rs divide,
A nymph, the mountain's ranger, she address'd,
And thus resolv'd, her high commands express'd.

THE DESCRIPTION OF FAMINE.

"Where frozen Scythia's utmost bound is plac'd,
A desert lies, a melancholy waste:
In yellow crops there nature never smil'd,
No fruitful tree to shade the barren wild.
There sluggish cold its icy station makes,
There paleness, frights, and anguish trembling shakes.
Of pining famine this the fated seat,
To whom my orders in these words repeat:
Bid her this miscreant with her sharpest pains
Chastise, and sheath herself into his veins;
Be unsubdu'd by plenty's baffled store,
Reject my empire, and defeat my pow'r.
And lest the distance, and the tedious way,
Should with the toil, and long fatigue dismay,
Ascend my chariot, and convey'd on high,
Guide the rein'd dragons through the parting sky.
"The nymph, accepting of the granted car,
Sprung to the seat, and posted through the air;
Nor stopp'd till she to a bleak mountain came
Of wondrous height, and Caucasus its name.
There in a stony field the fiend she found,
Herbs gnawing, and roots scratching from the ground.
Her elfelock hair in matted tresses grew,
Sunk were her eyes, and pale her ghastly hue,
Wan were her lips, and foul with clammy dew.
Her throat was furr'd, her guts appear'd within
With snaky crawlings through her parchment skin.
Her jutting hips seem'd starting from their place,
And for a belly was a belly's space.

Her dugs hung dangling from her craggy spine,
Loose to her breast, and fasten'd to her chine.
Her joints protuberant by leanness grown,
Consumption sunk the flesh, and rais'd the bone.
Her knees, large orbits bunch'd to monstrous size,
And ankles to undue proportion rise.
"This plague the nymph not daring to draw near,
At distance hail'd, and greeted from afar.
And though she told her charge without delay,
Though her arrival late, and short her stay,
She felt keen Famine, or she seem'd to feel,
Invade her blood, and on her vitals steal.
She turn'd, from the infection to remove,
And back to Thessaly the serpents drove.
"The fiend obey'd the goddess's command,
(Though their effects in opposition stand)
She cut her way, supported by the wind,
And reach'd the mansion by the nymph assign'd.
"'Twas night when ent'ring Erisichthon's room,
Dissolv'd in sleep, and thoughtless of his doom,
She clasp'd his limbs, by impious labour tir'd,
With battish wings, but her whole self inspir'd;
Breath'd on his throat and chest a tainting blast,
And in his veins infus'd an endless fast.
"The task dispatch'd, away the fury flies
From plenteous regions, and from rip'ning skies;
To her old barren north she wings her speed,
And cottages distress'd with pinching need.
"Still slumbers Erisichthon's senses drown,
And sooth his fancy with their softest down.
He dreams of viands delicate to eat,
And revels on imaginary meat.
Chaws with his working mouth, but chaws in vain,
And tires his grinding teeth with fruitless pain;
Deludes his throat with visionary fare,
Feasts on the wind, and banquets on the air.
"The morning came, the night and slumbers past,
But still the furious pangs of hunger last;
The cank'rous rage still gnaws with griping pains,
Stings in his throat, and in his bowels reigns.
"Straight he requires, impatient in demand,
Provisions from the air, the seas, the land.
But though the land, air, seas, provisions grant,
Starves at full tables, and complains of want.
What to a people might in dole be paid,
Or victual cities for a long blockade,
Could not one wolfish appetite assuage;
For glutting nourishment increas'd its rage.
As rivers pour'd from ev'ry distant shore
The sea insatiate drinks, and thirsts for more;
Or as the fire, which all materials burns,
And wasted forests into ashes turns,
Grows more voracious, as the more it preys,
Recruits dilate the flame, and spread the blaze:
So impious Erisichthon's hunger raves,
Receives refreshments, and refreshments craves.
Food raises a desire for food, and meat
Is but a new provocative to eat.
He grows more empty, the more supply'd,
And endless cramming but extends the void.

THE TRANSFORMATIONS OF ERISICHTHON'S DAUGHTER.

"Now riches hoarded by paternal care
Were sunk, the glutton swallowing up the heir;
Yet the devouring flame no stores abate,
Nor less the hunger grew with his estate.
One daughter left, as left his keen desire,
A daughter worthy of a better sire:
Her too he sold, spent nature to sustain;
She scorn'd a lord with generous disdain,
And flying, spread her hands upon the main.
Then pray'd: 'Grant thou, I bondage may escape,
And with my liberty reward thy rape;
Repay my virgin treasure with thy aid.'
('Twas Neptune who deflower'd the beauteous maid.)
"The god was mov'd at what the fair had su'd,
When she, so lately by her master view'd
In her known figure, on a sudden took
A fisher's habit, and a manly look.
To whom her owner hasted to inquire;
'O thou,' said he, 'whose baits hide treach'rous wire;
Whose art can manage, and experienc'd skill,
The taper angle, and the bobbing quill,
So may the sea be ruffled with no storm,
But smooth with calms, as you the truth inform;
So your deceit may no shy fishes feel,
Till struck and fasten'd on the bearded steel.
Did not you standing view upon the strand
A wand'ring maid? I'm sure I saw her stand;
Her hair disorder'd, and her homely dress
Betray'd her want, and witness'd her distress.'
"'Me heedless,' she reply'd, 'whoe'er you are,
Excuse, attentive to another care.
I settled on the deep my steady eye;
Fix'd on my float, and bent on my employ.
And that you may not doubt what I impart,
So may the ocean's god assist my art,
If on the beach since I my sport pursu'd,
Or man or woman but myself I view'd.'
Back o'er the sands, deluded, he withdrew,
Whilst she for her old form put off her new.
"Her sire her shifting pow'r to change perceiv'd,
And various chapmen by her sale deceiv'd.
A fowl with spangled plumes, a brinded steer,
Sometimes a crested mare, or antler'd deer:
Sold for a price, she parted, to maintain
Her starving parent with dishonest gain.
"At last all means, as all provisions, fail'd;
For the disease by remedies prevail'd;
His muscles with a furious bite he tore,
Gorg'd his own tatter'd flesh, and gulp'd his gore.
Wounds were his feast, his life to life a prey,
Supporting nature by its own decay.
"But foreign stories why should I relate?
I too myself can to new forms translate,
Though the variety's not unconfin'd,
But fix'd in number, and restrain'd in kind:
For often I this present shape retain,
Oft curl a snake the volumes of my train.
Sometimes my strength into my horns transferr'd,
A bull I march, the captain of the herd.
But whilst I once those goring weapons wore,
Vast wresting force one from my forehead tore.
Lo my maim'd brows the injury still own;"
He ceas'd; his words concluding with a groan.

OVID'S METAMORPHOSES.

BOOK IX.

Translated by Mr. Gay and others.

THE STORY OF ACHELOUS AND HERCULES.

By Mr. Gay.

THESEUS requests the god to tell his woes,
Whence his maim'd brow, and whence his groans arose:

When thus the Calydonian stream reply'd,
With twining reeds his careless tresses ty'd:
"Ungrateful is the tale; for who can bear,
When conquer'd, to rehearse the shameful war?
Yet I'll the melancholy story trace;
So great a conqu'ror softens the disgrace:
Nor was it still so mean the prize to yield,
As great and glorious to dispute the field.
"Perhaps you've heard of Deianira's name,
For all the country spoke her beauty's fame.
Long was the nymph by num'rous suitors woo'd,
Each with address his envy'd hopes pursu'd:
I join'd the loving band; to gain the fair,
Reveal'd my passion to her father's ear:
Their vain pretensions all the rest resign,
Alcides only strove to equal mine;
He boasts his birth from Jove, recounts his spoils,
His step-dame's hate subdu'd, and finish'd toils.
"'Can mortals then,' said I, 'with gods compare?
Behold a god; mine is the watry care:
Through your wide realms I take my mazy way,
Branch into streams, and o'er the region stray:
No foreign guest your daughter's charms adores,
But one who rises in your native shores.
Let not his punishment your pity move;
Is Juno's hate an argument for love?
Though you your life from fair Alcmena drew,
Jove's a feign'd father, or by fraud a true.
Choose then; confess thy mother's honour lost,
Or thy descent from Jove no longer boast.'
"While thus I spoke, he look'd with stern disdain,
Nor could the sallies of his wrath restrain,
Which thus break forth. 'This arm decides our right;
Vanquish in words, be mine the prize in fight.'
"Bold he rush'd on. My honour to maintain,
I fling my verdant garments on the plain,
My arms stretch forth, my pliant limbs prepare,
And with bent hands expect the furious war.
O'er my sleek skin now gather'd dust he throws,
And yellow sand his mighty muscles strows.
Oft he my neck and nimble legs assails,
He seems to grasp me, but as often fails.
Each part he now invades with eager hand;
Safe in my bulk, immoveable I stand.
So when loud storms break high, and foam and roar
Against some mole that stretches from the shore;
The firm foundation lasting tempests braves,
Defies the warring winds, and driving waves.
"Awhile we breathe, then forward rush amain,
Renew the combat, and our ground maintain;
Foot strove with foot, I prone extend my breast,
Hands war with hands, and forehead forehead prest.
Thus have I seen two furious bulls engage,
Inflam'd with equal love, and equal rage;
Each claims the fairest heifer of the grove,
And conquest only can decide their love:
The trembling herds survey the fight from far,
Till victory decides th' important war.
Three times in vain he strove my joints to wrest;
To force my hold, and throw me from his breast;
The fourth he broke my gripe, that clasp'd him round,
Then with new force he stretch'd me on the ground;
Close to my back the mighty burden clung,
As if a mountain o'er my limbs were flung.
Believe my tale; nor do I, boastful, aim
By feign'd narration to extol my fame.
No sooner from his grasp I freedom get,
Unlock my arms, that flow'd with trickling sweat,
But quick he seiz'd me, and renew'd the strife.
As my exhausted bosom pants for life;
My neck he gripes, my knee to earth he strains;
I fall, and bite the sand with shame, and pains.
"O'er-match'd in strength, to wiles, and arts I take,
And slip his hold, in form of speckled snake;
Who, when I wreath'd in spires my body round,
Or show'd my forky tongue with hissing sound,
Smiles at my threats; 'Such foes my cradle knew,'
He cries, 'dire snakes my infant hand o'erthrew;
A dragon's form might other conquests gain,
To war with me you take that shape in vain.
Art thou proportion'd to the hydra's length,
Who by his wounds receiv'd augmented strength?
He rais'd a hundred hissing heads in air;
When one I lop'd, up-sprung a dreadful pair.
By his wounds fertile, and with slaughter strong,
Singly I quell'd him, and stretch'd dead along.
What canst thou do, a form precarious, prone
To rouse my rage with terrours not thy own?'
He said; and round my neck his hands he cast,
And with his straining fingers wrung me fast:
My throat he tortur'd, close as pincers clasp,
In vain I strove to loose the forceful grasp.
"Thus vanquish'd too, a third form still remains:
Chang'd to a bull, my lowing fills the plains.
Straight on the left his nervous arms were thrown
Upon my brindled neck, and tugg'd it down;
Then deep he struck my horn into the sand,
And fell'd my bulk along the dusty land.
Nor yet his fury cool'd; 'twixt rage and scorn,
From my maim'd front he tore the stubborn horn;
This, heap'd with flow'rs, and fruits, the Naiads bear,
Sacred to plenty, and the beauteous year."
He spoke; when lo, a beauteous nymph appears,
Girt like Diana's train, with flowing hairs;
The horn she brings in which all autumn's stor'd,
And ruddy apples for the second board.
Now morn begins to dawn, the Sun's bright fire
Gilds the high mountains, and the youths retire;
Nor stay'd they, till the troubled stream subsides,
And in its bounds with peaceful current glides.
But Achelous in his oozy bed
Deep hides his brow deform'd, and rustic head:
No real wound the victor's triumph show'd,
But his lost honours griev'd the watry god;
Yet ev'n that loss the willow's leaves o'erspread,
And verdant reeds, in garlands, bind his head.

THE DEATH OF NESSUS THE CENTAUR.

This virgin too, thy love, O Nessus, found,
To her alone you owe the fatal wound.
As the strong son of Jove his bride conveys,
Where his paternal lands their bulwarks raise;
Where from her slopy urn Evenus pours
Her rapid current, swell'd by wintry show'rs,
He came. The frequent eddies whirl'd the tide,
And the deep rolling waves all pass deny'd.
As for himself, he stood unmov'd by fears,
For now his bridal charge employ'd his cares.
The strong-limb'd Nessus thus officious cry'd,
(For he the shallows of the stream had try'd)
"Swim thou, Alcides, all thy strength prepare,
On yonder bank I'll lodge thy nuptial care."

Th' Aonian chief to Nessus trusts his wife,
All pale, and trembling for her hero's life:
Cloth'd as he stood in the fierce lion's hide,
The laden quiver o'er his shoulder ty'd,
(For cross the stream his bow and club were cast)
Swift he plung'd in; "These billows shall be past,"
He said, nor sought where smoother waters glide,
But stem'd the rapid dangers of the tide.
The bank he reach'd; again the bow he bears;
When, hark! his bride's known voice alarms his ears.
"Nessus, to thee I call," aloud he cries,
"Vain is thy trust in flight, be timely wise:
Thou monster double-shap'd, my right set free;
If thou no rev'rence owe my fame and me,
Yet kindred should thy lawless lust deny.
Think not, perfidious wretch, from me to fly,
Though wing'd with horse's speed; wounds shall pursue:"
Swift as his words the fatal arrow flew:
The Centaur's back admits the feather'd wood,
And through his breast the barbed weapon stood;
Which when, in anguish, through the flesh he tore,
From both the wounds gush'd forth the spumy gore
Mix'd with Lernæan venom; this he took,
Nor dire revenge his dying breast forsook.
His garment, in the reeking purple dy'd,
To rouse love's passion, he presents the bride.

THE DEATH OF HERCULES.

Now a long interval of time succeeds,
When the great son of Jove's immortal deeds,
And step-dame's hate, had fill'd Earth's utmost round;
He from Œchalia, with new laurels crown'd,
In triumph was return'd. He rites prepares,
And to the king of gods directs his pray'rs;
When Fame (who falsehood clothes in truth's disguise,
And swells her little bulk with growing lyes)
Thy tender ear, O Deianira, mov'd,
That Hercules the fair Iole lov'd.
Her love believes the tale; the truth she fears
Of his new passion, and gives way to tears.
The flowing tears diffus'd her wretched grief,
"Why seek I thus, from streaming eyes, relief?"
She cries; "indulge not thus these fruitless cares,
The harlot will but triumph in thy tears:
Let something be resolv'd, while yet there's time;
My bed not conscious of a rival's crime.
In silence shall I mourn, or loud complain?
Shall I seek Calydon, or here remain?
What though ally'd to Meleager's fame,
I boast the honours of a sister's name?
My wrongs, perhaps, now urge me to pursue
Some desp'rate deed, by which the world shall view
How far revenge, and woman's rage, can rise,
When welt'ring in her blood the harlot dies."
Thus various passions rul'd by turns her breast.
She now resolves to send the fatal vest,
Dy'd with Lernæan gore, whose pow'r might move
His soul anew, and rouse declining love.
Nor knew she what her sudden rage bestows,
When she to Lychas trusts her future woes.
With soft endearments she the boy commands
To bear the garment to her husband's hands.
Th' unwitting hero takes the gift in haste,
And o'er his shoulders Lerna's poison cast.
As first the fire with frankincense he strows,
And utters to the gods his holy vows;
And on the marble altar's polish'd frame
Pours forth the grapy stream; the rising flame
Sudden dissolves the subtle pois'nous juice,
Which taints his blood, and all his nerves bedews.
With wonted fortitude he bore the smart,
And not a groan confess'd his burning heart.
At length his patience was subdu'd by pain,
He rends the sacred altar from the plain;
Œte's wide forests echo with his cries:
Now to rip off the deathful robe he tries.
Where'er he plucks the vest, the skin he tears,
The mangled muscles and huge bones he bares,
(A ghastful sight!) or raging with his pain,
To rend the sticking plague he tugs in vain.
As the red iron hisses in the flood,
So boils the venom in his curdling blood.
Now with the greedy flame his entrails glow,
And livid sweats down all his body flow;
The cracking nerves burnt up are burst in twain,
The lurking venom melts his swimming brain.
Then, lifting both his hands aloft, he cries,
"Glut thy revenge, dread empress of the skies;
Sate with my death the rancour of thy heart,
Look down with pleasure, and enjoy my smart.
Or, if e'er pity mov'd a hostile breast,
(For here I stand thy enemy profest)
Take hence this hateful life, with tortures torn,
Inur'd to trouble, and to labours born.
Death is the gift most welcome to my woe,
And such a gift a stepdame may bestow.
Was it for this Busiris was subdu'd,
Whose barb'rous temples reek'd with strangers' blood?
Press'd in these arms his fate Antæus found,
Nor gain'd recruited vigour from the ground.
Did I not triple-form'd Geryon fell?
Or did I fear the triple dog of Hell?
Did not these hands the bull's arm'd forehead hold?
Are not our mighty toils in Elis told?
Do not Stymphalian lakes proclaim thy fame?
And fair Parthenian woods resound thy name?
Who seiz'd the golden belt of Thermodon?
And who the dragon-guarded apples won?
Could the fierce Centaur's strength my force withstand,
Or the fell boar that spoil'd th' Arcadian land?
Did not these arms the Hydra's rage subdue,
Who from his wounds to double fury grew?
What if the Thracian horses, fat with gore,
Who human bodies in their mangers tore,
I saw, and with their barb'rous lord o'erthrew?
What if these hands Nemæa's lion slew?
Did not this neck the heav'nly globe sustain?
The female partner of the thund'rer's reign
Fatigu'd, at length suspends her harsh commands,
Yet no fatigue hath slack'd these valiant hands.
But now new plagues pursue me: neither force,
Nor arms, nor darts can stop their raging course.
Devouring flame through my rack'd entrails strays,
And on my lungs and shrivel'd muscles preys;
Yet still Eurystheus breathes the vital air.
What mortal now shall seek the gods with pray'r?"

THE TRANSFORMATION OF LYCHAS INTO A ROCK.

The hero said; and with the torture stung,
Furious o'er Œte's lofty hills he sprung.
Stuck with the shaft, thus scours the tiger round,
And seeks the flying author of his wound.

Now might you see him trembling, now he vents
His anguish'd soul in groans, and loud laments;
He strives to tear the clinging vest in vain,
And with up-rooted forests strows the plain;
Now kindling into rage, his hands he rears,
And to his kindred gods directs his pray'rs.
When Lychas, lo, he spies; who trembling flew,
And in a hollow rock conceal'd from view,
Had shunn'd his wrath. Now grief renew'd his pain,
His madness chaf'd, and thus he raves again.
" Lychas, to thee alone my fate I owe,
Who bore the gift, the cause of all my woe."
The youth all pale with shiv'ring fear was stung,
And vain excuses falter'd on his tongue.
Alcides snatch'd him, as with suppliant face
He strove to clasp his knees, and beg for grace:
He toss'd him o'er his head with airy course,
And hurl'd with more than with an engine's force;
Far o'er th' Eubœan main aloof he flies,
And hardens by degrees amid the skies.
So show'ry drops, when chilly tempests blow,
Thicken at first, then whiten into snow,
In balls congeal'd the rolling fleeces bound,
In solid hail result upon the ground.
Thus, whirl'd with nervous force through distant air,
The purple tide forsook his veins, with fear;
All moisture left his limbs. Transform'd to stone,
In ancient days the craggy flint was known:
Still in th' Eubœan waves his front he rears,
Still the small rock in human form appears,
And still the name of hapless Lychas bears.

THE APOTHEOSIS OF HERCULES.

But now the hero of immortal birth
Fells Œte's forests on the groaning earth;
A pile he builds; to Philoctetes' care
He leaves his deathful instruments of war;
To him commits those arrows, which again
Shall see the bulwarks of the Trojan reign.
The son of Pæan lights the lofty pyre,
High round the structure climbs the greedy fire:
Plac'd on the top, thy nervous shoulders spread
With the Nemæan spoils, thy careless head
Rais'd on the knotty club, with look divine,
Here thou, dread hero, of celestial line,
Wert stretch'd at ease; as when a cheerful guest,
Wine crown'd thy bowls, and flow'rs thy temples drest.
Now on all sides the potent flames aspire,
And crackle round those limbs that mock the fire
A sudden terrour seiz'd th' immortal host,
Who thought the world's profess'd defender lost.
This when the thund'rer saw, with smiles he cries,
" 'Tis from your fears, ye gods, my pleasures rise;
Joy swells my breast, that my all-ruling hand
O'er such a grateful people boasts command,
That you my suff'ring progeny would aid;
Though to his deeds this just respect be paid,
Me you've oblig'd. Be all your fears forborn,
Th' Œtean fires do thou, great hero, scorn.
Who vanquish'd all things, shall subdue the flame.
That part alone of gross maternal frame
Fire shall devour; while what from me he drew
Shall live immortal, and its force subdue;
That, when he's dead, I'll raise to realms above;
May all the pow'rs the righteous act approve!
If any god dissent, and judge too great
The sacred honours of the heav'nly seat,
Ev'n he shall own his deeds deserve the sky,
Ev'n he reluctant shall at length comply."
Th' assembled pow'rs assent. No frown 'till now
Had mark'd with passion vengeful Juno's brow.
Meanwhile whate'er was in the pow'r of flame
Was all consum'd, his body's nervous frame
No more was known, of human form bereft,
Th' eternal part of Jove alone was left.
As an old serpent casts his scaly vest,
Wreathes in the sun, in youthful glory drest;
So when Alcides mortal mould resign'd,
His better part enlarg'd, and grew refin'd,
August his visage shone; almighty Jove
In his swift car his honour'd offspring drove;
High o'er the hollow clouds the coursers fly,
And lodge the hero in the starry sky.

THE TRANSFORMATION OF GALANTHIS.

Atlas perceiv'd the load of Heav'n's new guest.
Revenge still rancour'd in Eurystheus' breast
Against Alcides' race. Alcmena goes
To Iole, to vent maternal woes;
Here she pours forth her grief, recounts the spoils
Her son had bravely reap'd in glorious toils.
This Iole, by Hercules' commands,
Hyllus had lov'd, and join'd in nuptial bands.
Her swelling womb the teeming birth confess'd,
To whom Alcmena thus her speech address'd.
" O, may the gods protect thee, in that hour,
When, midst thy throes, thou call'st th' Ilithyian pow'r!
May no delays prolong thy racking pain,
As when I su'd for Juno's aid in vain!
" When now Alcides' mighty birth drew nigh,
And the tenth sign roll'd forward on the sky,
My womb extends with such a mighty load,
As Jove the parent of the burden show'd.
I could no more th' increasing smart sustain,
My horrour kindles to recount the pain;
Cold chills my limbs while I the tale pursue,
And now methinks I feel my pangs anew.
Seven days and nights amidst incessant throes,
Fatigu'd with ills I lay, nor knew repose;
When lifting high my hands, in shrieks I pray'd,
Implor'd the gods, and call'd Lucina's aid.
She came, but prejudic'd, to give my fate
A sacrifice to vengeful Juno's hate,
She hears the groaning anguish of my fits,
And on the altar at my door she sits,
O'er her left knee her crossing leg she cast,
Then knits her fingers close, and wrings them fast:
This stay'd the birth; in mutt'ring verse she pray'd,
The mutt'ring verse th' unfinish'd birth delay'd.
Now with fierce struggles, raging with my pain,
At Jove's ingratitude I rave in vain.
How did I wish for death! such groans I sent,
As might have made the flinty heart relent.
" Now the Cadmeian matrons round me press,
Offer their vows, and seek to bring redress;
Among the Theban dames Galanthis stands,
Strong-limb'd, red-hair'd, and just to my commands:
She first perceiv'd that all these racking woes
From the persisting hate of Juno rose.
As here and there she pass'd, by chance she sees
The seated goddess; on her close-press'd knees
Her fast-knit hands she leans; with cheerful voice
Galanthis cries, ' Whoe'er thou art, rejoice:

Congratulate the dame, she lies at rest,
At length the gods Alcmena's womb have blest.'
Swift from her seat the startled goddess springs,
No more conceal'd her hands abroad she flings;
The charm unloos'd, the birth my pangs reliev'd;
Galanthis' laughter vex'd the pow'r deceiv'd.
Fame says, the goddess dragg'd the laughing maid
Fast by the hair; in vain her force essay'd
Her grov'ling body from the ground to rear;
Chang'd to fore-feet her shrinking arms appear:
Her hairy back her former hue retains,
The form alone is lost; her strength remains:
Who, since the lye did from her mouth proceed,
Shall from her pregnant mouth bring forth her breed;
Nor shall she quit her long-frequented home,
But haunt those houses where she lov'd to roam."

THE FABLE OF DRYOPE.

By Mr. Pope.

SHE said, and for her lost Galanthis sighs;
When the fair consort of her son replies;
"Since you a servant's ravish'd form bemoan,
And kindly sigh for sorrows not your own,
Let me (if tears and griefs permit) relate
A nearer woe, a sister's stranger fate.
No nymph of all Œchalia could compare
For beauteous form with Dryopè the fair;
Her tender mother's only hope and pride,
(Myself the offspring of a second bride.)
This nymph, compress'd by him who rules the day,
Whom Delphi, and the Delian isle obey,
Andræmon lov'd; and blest in all those charms
That pleas'd a god, succeeded to her arms.
"A lake there was, with shelving banks around,
Whose verdant summit fragrant myrtles crown'd.
Those shades, unknowing of the fates, she sought;
And to the Naiads flow'ry garlands brought;
Her smiling babe (a pleasing charge) she prest
Between her arms, and nourish'd at her breast.
Not distant far a watry lotos grows;
The spring was new, and all the verdant boughs,
Adorn'd with blossoms, promis'd fruits that vie
In glowing colours with the Tyrian dye.
Of these she cropt, to please her infant son,
And I myself the same rash act had done,
But, lo! I saw (as near her side I stood)
The violated blossoms drop with blood;
Upon the tree I cast a frightful look,
The trembling tree with sudden horrour shook:
Lotis the nymph (if rural tales be true)
As from Priapus' lawless lust she flew,
Forsook her form; and fixing here became
A flow'ry plant, which still preserves her name.
"This change unknown, astonish'd at the sight,
My trembling sister strove to urge the flight;
Yet first the pardon of the nymphs implor'd,
And those offended sylvan pow'rs ador'd:
But when she backward would have fled, she found
Her stiff'ning feet were rooted to the ground:
In vain to free her fasten'd feet she strove,
And as she struggles only moves above;
She feels th' incroaching bark around her grow,
By slow degrees, and cover all below:
Surpris'd at this, her trembling hand she heaves
To rend her hair; her hand is fill'd with leaves;
Where late was hair, the shooting leaves are seen
To rise, and shade her with a sudden green.
The child Amphisus, to her bosom prest,
Perceiv'd a colder and a harder breast,
And found the springs, that ne'er till then deny'd
Their milky moisture, on a sudden dry'd.
I saw, unhappy, what I now relate,
And stood the helpless witness of thy fate;
Embrac'd thy boughs, the rising bark delay'd,
There wish'd to grow, and mingle shade with shade.
"Behold Andræmon, and th' unhappy sire
Appear, and for their Dryopè inquire;
A springing tree for Dryopè they find,
And print warm kisses on the panting rind;
Prostrate, with tears their kindred plant bedew,
And close embrac'd, as to the roots they grew;
The face was all that now remain'd of thee;
No more a woman, nor yet quite a tree:
Thy branches hung with humid pearls appear,
From ev'ry leaf distils a trickling tear;
And straight a voice, while yet a voice remains,
Thus through the trembling boughs in sighs complains.
"'If to the wretched any faith be giv'n,
I swear by all th' unpitying pow'rs of Heav'n,
No wilful crime this heavy vengeance bred,
In mutual innocence our lives we led.
If this be false, let these new greens decay,
Let sounding axes lop my limbs away,
And crackling flames on all my honours prey.
Now from my branching arms this infant bear,
Let some kind nurse supply a mother's care;
Yet to his mother let him oft be led,
Sport in her shades, and in her shades be fed;
Teach him, when first his infant voice shall frame
Imperfect words, and lisp his mother's name,
To hail this tree, and say with weeping eyes,
Within this plant my hapless parent lies;
And when in youth he seeks the shady woods,
Oh, let him fly the crystal lakes and floods,
Nor touch the fatal flow'rs; but warn'd by me,
Believe a goddess shrin'd in ev'ry tree.
My sire, my sister, and my spouse, farewell!
If in your breasts or love, or pity, dwell,
Protect your plant, nor let my branches feel
The browsing cattle, or the piercing steel.
Farewell! and since I cannot bend to join
My lips to yours, advance at least to mine.
My son, thy mother's parting kiss receive,
While yet thy mother has a kiss to give.
I can no more, the creeping rind invades
My closing lips, and hides my head in shades:
Remove your hands; the bark shall soon suffice,
Without their aid, to seal these dying eyes.'
She ceas'd at once to speak, and ceas'd to be;
And all the nymph was lost within the tree:
Yet latent life through her new branches reign'd,
And long the plant a human heat retain'd."

Continued by Mr. Gay.

IOLAUS RESTORED TO YOUTH.

WHILE Iolè the fatal change declares,
Alcmena's pitying hand oft wip'd her tears.
Grief too stream'd down her cheeks; soon sorrow flies,
And rising joy the trickling moisture dries:
Lo Iolaus stands before their eyes.
A youth he stood; and the soft down began
O'er his smooth chin to spread, and promise man.

Hebe submitted to her husband's pray'rs,
Instill'd new vigour, and restor'd his years.

THE PROPHECY OF THEMIS.

Now from her lips a solemn oath had past,
That Iolaus this gift alone should taste;
Had not just Themis thus maturely said, [maid.)
(Which check'd her vow, and aw'd the blooming
"Thebes is embroil'd in war. Capaneus stands
Invincible, but by the thund'rer's hands.
Ambition shall the guilty brothers [1] fire,
But rush to mutual wounds, and both expire.
The reeling Earth shall ope her gloomy womb,
Where the yet breathing bard [2] shall find his tomb.
The son [3] shall bathe his hands in parents' blood,
And in one act be both unjust and good.
Of home and sense depriv'd, where'er he flies,
The furies, and his mother's ghost, he spies.
His wife the fatal bracelet shall implore,
And Phegeus stain his sword in kindred gore.
Callirhöe shall then with suppliant pray'r
Prevail on Jupiter's relenting ear.
Jove shall with youth her infant sons inspire,
And bid their bosoms glow with manly fire."

THE DEBATE OF THE GODS.

When Themis thus with prescient voice had spoke,
Among the gods a various murmur broke;
Dissension rose in each immortal breast,
That one should grant what was deny'd the rest.
Aurora for her aged spouse complains,
And Ceres grieves for Jason's freezing veins;
Vulcan would Ericthonius' years renew;
Her future race the care of Venus drew,
She would Anchises' blooming age restore;
A diff'rent care employ'd each heav'nly pow'r:
Thus various int'rests did their jars increase,
Till Jove arose; he spoke, their tumults cease.
"Is any rev'rence to our presence giv'n,
Then why this discord 'mong the pow'rs of Heav'n?
Who can the settled will of fate subdue?
'Twas by the fates that Iolaus knew
A second youth. The fates' determin'd doom
Shall give Callirhöe's race a youthful bloom.
Arms nor ambition can this pow'r obtain;
Quell your desires; ev'n me the fates restrain.
Could I their will control, no rolling years
Had Æacus bent down with silver hairs;
Then Rhadamanthus still had youth possess'd,
And Minos with eternal bloom been bless'd."
Jove's words the synod mov'd; the pow'rs give o'er,
And urge in vain unjust complaint no more.
Since Rhadamanthus' veins now slowly flow'd,
And Æacus, and Minos bore the load;
Minos, who in the flow'r of youth, and fame,
Made mighty nations tremble at his name,
Infirm with age, the proud Miletus fears,
Vain of his birth, and in the strength of years;
And now regarding all his realms as lost,
He durst not force him from his native coast.
But you by choice, Miletus, fled his reign,
And thy swift vessel plough'd th' Ægean main;
On Asiatic shores a town you frame,
Which still is honour'd with the founder's name.
Here you Cyanëe knew, the beauteous maid,
As on her father's [4] winding banks she stray'd:
Caunus and Byblis hence their lineage trace,
The double offspring of your warm embrace.

THE PASSION OF BYBLIS.

By Stephen Harvey, Esq.

Let the sad fate of wretched Byblis prove
A dismal warning to unlawful love;
One birth gave being to the hapless pair,
But more was Caunus than a sister's care.
Unknown she lov'd, for yet the gentle fire
Rose not in flames, nor kindled to desire;
'Twas thought no sin to wonder at his charms,
Hang on his neck, and languish in his arms;
Thus wing'd with joy fled the soft hours away,
And all the fatal guilt on harmless nature lay.
But love (too soon from piety declin'd)
Insensibly deprav'd her yielding mind.
Dress'd she appears, with nicest art adorn'd,
And ev'ry youth, but her lov'd brother, scorn'd;
For him alone she labour'd to be fair,
And curs'd all charms that might with hers compare.
'Twas she, and only she, must Caunus please,
Sick at her heart, yet knew not her disease:
She call'd him lord, for brother was a name
Too cold and dull for her aspiring flame;
And when he spoke, if "sister" he reply'd,
"For Byblis change that frozen word," she cry'd.
Yet waking still she watch'd her struggling breast;
And love's approaches were in vain address'd,
Till gentle sleep an easy conquest made,
And in her soft embrace the conqueror was laid.
But oh too soon the pleasing vision fled,
And left her blushing on the conscious bed:
"Ah me!" she cry'd, "how monstrous do I seem!
Why these wild thoughts? and this incestuous dream?
Envy herself ('tis true) must own his charms,
But what is beauty in a sister's arms?
Oh were I not that despicable she,
How bless'd, how pleas'd, how happy should I be!
But unregarded now must bear my pain,
And but in dreams my wishes can obtain.
"O sea-born goddess! with thy wanton boy!
Was ever such a charming scene of joy?
Such perfect bliss! such ravishing delight!
Ne'er hid before in the kind shades of night.
How pleas'd my heart! in what sweet raptures tost!
Ev'n life itself in the soft combat lost,
While breathless he on my heav'd bosom lay,
And snatch'd the treasures of my soul away.
"If the bare fancy so affects my mind,
How should I rave if to the substance join'd?
Oh, gentle Caunus! quit thy hated line,
Or let thy parents be no longer mine!
Oh that in common all things were enjoy'd,
But those alone who have our hopes destroy'd.
Were I a princess, thou an humble swain,
The proudest kings should rival thee in vain.
It cannot be, alas! the dreadful ill
Is fix'd by fate, and he's my brother still.
Hear me, ye gods! I must have friends in Heav'n,
For Jove himself was to a sister giv'n:

[1] Eteocles and Polynices. [2] Amphiaraus. [3] Alcmæon.

[4] Mæander.

But what are their prerogatives above,
To the short liberties of human love?
Fantastic thoughts! down, down, forbidden fires,
Or instant death extinguish my desires.
Strict virtue, then, with thy malicious leave,
Without a crime I may a kiss receive:
But say should I in spite of laws comply,
Yet cruel Caunus might himself deny,
No pity take of an afflicted maid,
(For love's sweet game must be by couples play'd.)
Yet why should youth, and charms like mine despair?
Such fears ne'er startled the Æolian pair;
No ties of blood could their full hopes destroy,
They broke through all for the prevailing joy;
And who can tell but Caunus too may be
Rack'd and tormented in his breast for me?
Like me, to the extremest anguish drove,
Like me, just waking from a dream of love?
But stay! Oh whither would my fury run!
What arguments I urge to be undone!
Away, fond Byblis, quench these guilty flames;
Caunus thy love but as a brother claims;
Yet had he first been touch'd with love of me,
The charming youth could I despairing see?
Oppress'd with grief, and dying by disdain?
Ah no! too sure I should have eas'd his pain!
Since then, if Caunus ask'd me, it were done;
Asking myself, what dangers can I run?
But canst thou ask? and see that right betray'd,
From Pyrrha down to thy whole sex convey'd?
That self-denying gift we all enjoy,
Of wishing to be won, yet seeming to be coy.
Well then, for once, let a fond mistress woo;
The force of love no custom can subdue;
This frantic passion he by words shall know,
Soft as the melting heart from whence they flow."
The pencil then in her fair hand she held,
By fear discourag'd, but by love compell'd;
She writes, then blots, writes on, and blots again,
Likes it as fit, then razes it as vain:
Shame and assurance in her face appear,
And a faint hope just yielding to despair;
Sister was wrote, and blotted as a word
Which she, and Caunus too (she hop'd) abhorr'd;
But now resolv'd to be no more control'd
By scrup'lous virtue, thus her grief she told.
"Thy lover (gentle Caunus) wishes thee
That health, which thou alone canst give to me.
O charming youth! the gift I ask bestow,
Ere thou the name of the fond writer know;
To thee without a name I would be known,
Since knowing that, my frailty I must own.
Yet why should I my wretched name conceal?
When thousand instances my flames reveal:
Wan looks and weeping eyes have spoke my pain,
And sighs discharg'd from my heav'd heart in vain.
Had I not wish'd my passion might be seen,
What could such fondness and embraces mean?
Such kisses too! (Oh heedless lovely boy)
Without a crime no sister could enjoy:
Yet (though extremest rage has rack'd my soul,
And raging fires in my parch'd bosom roll)
Be witness, gods! how piously I strove
To rid my thoughts of this enchanting love.
But who could 'scape so fierce and sure a dart,
Aim'd at a tender, a defenceless heart?
Alas! what maid could suffer, I have born,
Ere the dire secret from my breast was torn.
To thee a helpless vanquish'd wretch I come,
'Tis you alone can save, or give my doom;
My life or death this moment you may choose,
Yet think, oh think, no hated stranger sues,
No foe; but one, alas! too near ally'd,
And wishing still much nearer to be ty'd.
The forms of decency let age debate,
And virtue's rules by their cold morals state;
Their ebbing joys give leisure to inquire,
And blame those noble flights our youth inspire:
Where Nature kindly summons let us go;
Our sprightly years no bounds in love should know,
Should feel no check of guilt, and fear no ill:
Lovers and gods act all things at their will.
We gain one blessing from our hated kin,
Since our paternal freedom hides the sin;
Uncensur'd in each other's arms we lie,
Think then how easy to complete our joy.
Oh, pardon and oblige a blushing maid,
Whose rage the pride of her vain sex betray'd;
Nor let my tomb thus mournfully complain,
Here Byblis lies, by her lov'd Caunus slain."
Forc'd here to end, she with a falling tear
Temper'd the pliant wax, which did the signet bear;
The curious cypher was impress'd by art,
But love had stamp'd one deeper in her heart.
Her page, a youth of confidence, and skill,
(Secret as night) stood waiting on her will;
Sighing, she cry'd, "Bear this, thou faithful boy,
To my sweet partner in eternal joy:"
Here a long pause her secret guilt confess'd,
And when at length she would have spoke the rest,
Half the dear name lay bury'd in her breast.
Thus as he listen'd to her vain command,
Down fell the letter from her trembling hand.
The omen shock'd her soul. "Yet go," she cry'd;
"Can a request from Byblis be deny'd?"
To the Mæandrian youth this message's borne,
The half-read lines by his fierce rage were torn;
"Hence, hence," he cry'd, "thou pander to her lust,
Bear hence the triumph of thy impious trust:
Thy instant death will but divulge her shame,
Or thy life's blood should quench the guilty flame."
Frighted, from threat'ning Caunus he withdrew,
And with the dreadful news to his lost mistress flew.
The sad repulse so struck the wounded fair,
Her sense was bury'd in her wild despair;
Pale was her visage, as the ghastly dead;
And her scar'd soul from the sweet mansion fled;
Yet with her life renew'd, her love returns,
And faintly thus her cruel fate she mourns:
"'Tis just, ye gods! was my false reason blind,
To write a secret of this tender kind?
With feeble craft I shou'd at first have strove,
By dubious hints to sound his distant love;
And try'd those useful, though dissembled arts,
Which women practise on disdainful hearts:
I should have watch'd whence the black storm might rise,
Ere I had trusted the unfaithful skies.
Now on the rolling billows I am tost,
And with extended sails on the blind shelves am lost.
Did not indulgent Heav'n my doom foretel,
When from my hand the fatal letter fell?

What madness seiz'd my soul? and urg'd me on
To take the only course to be undone?
I could myself have told the moving tale
With such alluring grace as must prevail;
Then had his eyes beheld my blushing fears,
My rising sighs, and my descending tears;
Round his dear neck these arms I then had spread,
And, if rejected, at his feet been dead:
If singly these had not his thoughts inclin'd,
Yet all united would have shock'd his mind.
Perhaps, my careless page might be in fault,
And in a luckless hour the fatal message brought;
Business and worldly thoughts might fill his breast,
Sometimes ev'n love itself may be an irksome guest:
He could not else have treated me with scorn,
For Caunus was not of a tigress born;
Nor steel nor adamant has fenc'd his heart;
Like mine, 'tis naked to the burning dart.
"Away false fears! he must, he shall be mine;
In death alone I will my claim resign;
'Tis vain to wish my written crime unknown,
And for my guilt much vainer to atone."
Repuls'd and baffled, fiercer still she burns,
And Caunus with disdain her impious love returns.
He saw no end of her injurious flame,
And fled his country to avoid the shame.
Forsaken Byblis, who had hopes no more,
Burst out in rage, and her loose robes she tore;
With her fair hands she smote her tender breast,
And to the wond'ring world her love confess'd;
O'er hills and dales, o'er rocks and streams she flew,
But still in vain did her wild lust pursue:
Wearied at length, on the cold earth she fell,
And now in tears alone could her sad story tell.
Relenting gods in pity fix'd her there,
And to a fountain turn'd the weeping fair.

THE FABLE OF IPHIS AND IANTHE.

By Mr. Dryden.

THE fame of this, perhaps, thro' Crete had flown:
But Crete had newer wonders of her own,
In Iphis chang'd: for near the Gnossian bounds,
(As loud report the miracle resounds)
At Phæstus dwelt a man of honest blood,
But meanly born, and not so rich as good;
Esteem'd, and lov'd by all the neighbourhood;
Who to his wife, before the time assign'd
For child-birth came, thus bluntly spoke his mind:
"If Heav'n," said Lygdus, "will vouchsafe to hear,
I have but two petitions to prefer;
Short pains for thee, for me a son and heir.
Girls cost as many throes in bringing forth;
Beside, when born, the tits are little worth;
Weak puling things, unable to sustain
Their share of labour, and their bread to gain.
If, therefore, thou a creature shalt produce,
Of so great charges, and so little use,
(Bear witness, Heav'n, with what reluctancy)
Her hapless innocence I doom to die."
He said, and tears the common grief display,
Of him who bade, and her who must obey.
Yet Telethusa still persists, to find
Fit arguments to move a father's mind;
T' extend his wishes to a larger scope,
And in one vessel not confine his hope.
Lygdus continues hard: her time drew near,
And she her heavy load could scarcely bear,
When slumb'ring, in the latter shades of night,
Before th' approaches of returning light,
She saw, or thought she saw, before her bed,
A glorious train, and Isis at their head:
Her moony horns were on her forehead plac'd,
And yellow sheaves her shining temples grac'd;
A mitre, for a crown, she wore on high;
The dog and dappled bull were waiting by;
Osiris, sought along the banks of Nile;
The silent god; the sacred crocodile;
And, last, a long procession moving on,
With timbrels, that assist the lab'ring Moon.
Her slumbers seem'd dispell'd, and, broad awake,
She heard a voice, that thus distinctly spake:
"My votary, thy babe from death defend,
Nor fear to save whate'er the gods will send.
Delude with art thy husband's dire decree:
When danger calls, repose thy trust on me:
And know thou hadst not serv'd a thankless deity."
This promise made, with night the goddess fled:
With joy the woman wakes, and leaves her bed;
Devoutly lifts her spotless hands on high,
And prays the pow'rs their gift to ratify.
Now grinding pains proceed to bearing throes,
Till its own weight the burden did disclose.
'Twas of the beauteous kind, and brought to light
With secrecy, to shun the father's sight.
Th' indulgent mother did her care employ,
And pass'd it on her husband for a boy.
The nurse was conscious of the fact alone;
The father paid his vows as for a son;
And call'd him Iphis, by a common name,
Which either sex with equal right may claim.
Iphis his grandsire was; the wife was pleas'd,
Of half the fraud by Fortune's favour eas'd:
The doubtful name was us'd without deceit,
And truth was cover'd with a pious cheat.
The habit show'd a boy, the beauteous face
With manly fierceness mingled female grace.
Now thirteen years of age were swiftly run,
When the fond father thought the time drew on
Of settling in the world his only son.
Ianthe was his choice; so wondrous fair,
Her form alone with Iphis cou'd compare;
A neighbour's daughter of his own degree,
And not more bless'd with Fortune's goods than he.
They soon espous'd; for they with ease were join'd,
Who were before contracted in the mind:
Their age the same, their inclinations too,
And bred together, in one school they grew.
Thus, fatally dispos'd to mutual fires,
They felt, before they knew, the same desires.
Equal their flame, unequal was their care;
One lov'd with hope, one languish'd in despair.
The maid accus'd the ling'ring days alone:
For whom she thought a man, she thought her own.
But Iphis bends beneath a greater grief;
As fiercely burns, but hopes for no relief.
Ev'n her despair adds fuel to her fire;
A maid with madness does a maid desire.
And, scarce refraining tears, "Alas," said she,
"What issue of my love remains for me!
How wild a passion works within my breast!
With what prodigious flames am I possest!
Could I the care of Providence deserve,
Heav'n must destroy me, if it would preserve.
And that's my fate, or sure it would have sent
Some usual evil for my punishment:

Not this unkindly curse; to rage, and burn,
Where Nature shows no prospect of return.
Nor cows for cows consume with fruitless fire;
Nor mares, when hot, their fellow-mares desire:
The father of the fold supplies his ewes;
The stag through secret woods his hind pursues:
And birds for mates the males of their own species choose,
Her females Nature guards from female flame,
And joins two sexes to preserve the game:
Wou'd I were nothing, or not what I am!
Crete, fam'd for monsters, wanted for her store,
Till my new love produc'd one monster more.
The daughter of the son a bull desir'd,
And yet ev'n then a male a female fir'd:
Her passion was extravagantly new,
But mine is much the madder of the two.
To things impossible she was not bent,
But found the means to compass her intent.
To cheat his eyes she took a different shape;
Yet still she gain'd a lover, and a leap.
Should all the wit of all the world conspire,
Should Dædalus assist my wild desire,
What art can make me able to enjoy,
Or what can change Ianthe to a boy?
Extinguish then thy passion, hopeless maid,
And recollect thy reason for thy aid.
Know what thou art, and love as maidens ought,
And drive these golden wishes from thy thought.
Thou canst not hope thy fond desire to gain;
Where hope is wanting, wishes are in vain.
"And yet no guards against our joys conspire;
No jealous husband hinders our desire;
My parents are propitious to my wish,
And she herself consenting to the bliss.
All things concur to prosper our design;
All things to prosper any love but mine.
And yet I never can enjoy the fair;
'Tis past the pow'r of Heav'n to grant my pray'r.
Heav'n has been kind, as far as Heav'n can be;
Our parents with our own desires agree;
But Nature, stronger than the gods above,
Refuses her assistance to my love:
She sets the bar that causes all my pain;
One gift refus'd makes all their bounty vain.
And now the happy day is just at hand,
To bind our hearts in Hymen's holy band:
Our hearts, but not our bodies: thus accurs'd,
In midst of water I complain of thirst.
Why com'st thou, Juno, to these barren rites,
To bless a bed defrauded of delights?
But why should Hymen lift his torch on high,
To see two brides in cold embraces lie?"
Thus love-sick Iphis her vain passion mourns;
With equal ardour fair Ianthe burns,
Invoking Hymen's name, and Juno's pow'r,
To speed the work, and haste the happy hour.
She hopes, while Telethusa fears the day,
And strives to interpose some new delay:
Now feigns a sickness, now is in a fright
For this bad omen, or that boding sight.
But having done whate'er she could devise,
And empty'd all her magazine of lies,
The time approach'd; the next ensuing day
The fatal secret must to light betray.
Then Telethusa had recourse to pray'r,
She and her daughter with dishevell'd hair;
Trembling with fear, great Isis they ador'd,
Embrac'd her altar, and her aid implor'd.
"Fair queen, who dost on fruitful Egypt smile,
Who sway'st the sceptre of the Pharian isle,
And sev'n-fold falls of disemboguing Nile,
Relieve, in this our last distress,' she said,
"A suppliant mother, and a mournful maid.
Thou, goddess, thou wert present to my sight;
Reveal'd I saw thee by thy own fair light:
I saw thee in my dream, as now I see,
With all thy marks of awful majesty:
The glorious train that compass'd thee around;
And heard the hollow timbrel's holy sound.
Thy words I noted, which I still retain;
Let not thy sacred oracles be vain.
That Iphis lives, that I myself am free
From shame and punishment, I owe to thee.
On thy protection all our hopes depend.
Thy counsel sav'd us, let thy pow'r defend."
Her tears pursu'd her words, and while she spoke
The goddess nodded, and her altar shook:
The temple doors, as with a blast of wind,
Were heard to clap; the lunar horns that bind
The brows of Isis cast a blaze around;
The trembling timbrel made a murm'ring sound.
Some hopes these happy omens did impart;
Forth went the mother with a beating heart:
Not much in fear, nor fully satisfy'd;
But Iphis follow'd with a larger stride:
The whiteness of her skin forsook her face;
Her looks embolden'd with an awful grace;
Her features and her strength together grew,
And her long hair to curling locks withdrew.
Her sparkling eyes with manly vigour shone,
Big was her voice, audacious was her tone.
The latent parts, at length reveal'd, began
To shoot, and spread, and burnish into man.
The maid becomes a youth; no more delay
Your vows, but look, and confidently pay.
Their gifts the parents to the temple bear:
The votive tables this inscription wear;
"Iphis, the man, has to the goddess paid
The vows, that Iphis offer'd when a maid."
Now when the star of day had shown his face,
Venus and Juno with their presence grace
The nuptial rites, and Hymen from above
Descending to complete their happy love;
The gods of marriage lend their mutual aid;
And the warm youth enjoys the lovely maid.

OVID'S METAMORPHOSES.

BOOK X.

Translated by Mr. Congreve, Mr. Dryden, and others.

THE STORY OF ORPHEUS AND EURYDICE.

By Mr. Congreve.

THENCE, in his saffron robe, for distant Thrace,
Hymen departs, through air's unmeasur'd space;
By Orpheus call'd, the nuptial pow'r attends,
But with ill-omen'd augury descends;
Nor cheerful look'd the god, nor prosp'rous spoke,
Nor blaz'd his torch, but wept in hissing smoke.
In vain they whirl it round, in vain they shake,
No rapid motion can its flames awake.
With dread these inauspicious signs were view'd,
And soon a more disastrous end ensu'd;
For as the bride, amid the Naïad train,
Ran joyful sporting o'er the flow'ry plain,

A venom'd viper bit her as she pass'd;
Instant she fell, and sudden breath'd her last.
When long his loss the Thracian had deplor'd,
Not by superior pow'rs to be restor'd;
Inflam'd by love, and urged by deep despair,
He leaves the realms of light, and upper air;
Daring to tread the dark Tenarian road,
And tempt the shades in their obscure abode;
Through gliding spectres of th' interr'd to go,
And phantom people of the world below:
Persephonè he seeks, and him who reigns
O'er ghosts, and Hell's uncomfortable plains.
Arriv'd, he, tuning to his voice his strings,
Thus to the king and queen of shadows sings.
"Ye pow'rs, who under Earth your realms extend,
To whom all mortals must one day descend;
If here 'tis granted sacred truth to tell,
I come not curious to explore your Hell;
Nor come to boast (by vain ambition fir'd)
How Cerberus at my approach retir'd.
My wife alone I seek; for her lov'd sake
These terrours I support, this journey take.
She, luckless wand'ring, or by fate mis-led,
Chanc'd on a lurking viper's crest to tread;
The vengeful beast, inflam'd with fury, starts,
And through her heel his deathful venom darts.
Thus was she snatch'd untimely to her tomb;
Her growing years cut short, and springing bloom.
Long I my loss endeavour'd to sustain,
And strongly strove, but strove, alas! in vain:
At length I yielded, won by mighty Love;
Well known is that omnipotence above!
But here, I doubt, his unfelt influence fails;
And yet a hope within my heart prevails,
That here, ev'n here, he has been known of old;
At least if truth be by tradition told;
If fame of former rapes belief may find,
You both by love, and love alone were join'd.
Now by the horrours which these realms surround;
By the vast chaos of these depths profound;
By the sad silence which eternal reigns
O'er all the waste of these wide-stretching plains
Let me again Eurydicè receive,
Let Fate her quick-spun thread of life re-weave.
All our possessions are but loans from you,
And soon, or late, you must be paid your due;
Hither we haste to human-kind's last seat,
Your endless empire, and our sure retreat.
She too, when ripen'd years she shall attain,
Must, of avoidless right, be yours again:
I but the transient use of that require,
Which soon, too soon, I must resign entire.
But if the destinies refuse my vow,
And no remission of her doom allow;
Know, I'm determin'd to return no more;
So both retain, or both to life restore."
Thus, while the bard melodiously complains,
And to his lyre accords his vocal strains,
The very bloodless shades attention keep,
And silent, seem compassionate to weep;
Ev'n Tantalus his flood unthirsty views,
Nor flies the stream, nor he the stream pursues;
Ixion's wond'ring wheel its whirl suspends,
And the voracious vulture, charm'd, attends;
No more the Belides their toil bemoan,
And Sisyphus reclin'd, sits list'ning on his stone.
Then first ('tis said) by sacred verse subdu'd,
The Furies felt their cheeks with tears bedew'd.
Nor could the rigid king, or queen of Hell,
Th' impulse of pity in their hearts repel.
Now, from a troop of shades that last arriv'd
Eurydicè was call'd, and stood reviv'd:
Slow she advanc'd, and halting seem'd to feel
The fatal wound, yet painful in her heel.
Thus he obtains the suit so much desir'd,
On strict observance of the terms requir'd:
For if, before he reach the realms of air,
He backward cast his eyes to view the fair,
The forfeit grant, that instant, void is made,
And she for ever left a lifeless shade.
Now through the noiseless throng their way they bend,
And both with pain the rugged road ascend;
Dark was the path, and difficult, and steep,
And thick with vapours from the smoky deep.
They well nigh now had pass'd the bounds of night,
And just approach'd the margin of the light,
When he, mistrusting lest her steps might stray,
And gladsome of the glimpse of dawning day,
His longing eyes, impatient, backward cast,
To catch a lover's look, but look'd his last;
For, instant dying, she again descends,
While he to empty air his arm extends.
Again she dy'd, nor yet her lord reprov'd;
What could she say, but that too well he lov'd?
One last farewel she spoke, which scarce he heard;
So soon he dropt, so sudden disappear'd.
All stunn'd he stood, when thus his wife he view'd
By second fate, and double death subdu'd:
Not more amazement by that wretch was shown,
Whom Cerberus beholding turn'd to stone;
Nor Olenus could more astonish'd look,
When on himself Lethea's fault he took,
His beauteous wife, who too secure had dar'd
Her face to vie with goddesses compar'd:
Once join'd by love, they stand united still,
Turn'd to contiguous rocks on Ida's hill.
Now to repass the Styx in vain he tries:
Charon averse, his pressing suit denies.
Sev'n days entire, along th' infernal shores,
Disconsolate, the bard Eurydicè deplores;
Defil'd with filth his robe, with tears his cheeks,
No sustenance but grief, and cares, he seeks:
Of rigid fate incessant he complains,
And Hell's inexorable gods arraigns.
This ended, to high Rhodopè he hastes,
And Hæmus' mountain, bleak with northern blasts.
And now his yearly race the circling Sun
Had thrice complete through wat'ry Pisces run,
Since Orpheus fled the face of womankind,
And all soft union with the sex declin'd.
Whether his ill success this change had bred,
Or binding vows made to his former bed;
Whate'er the cause, in vain the nymphs contest,
With rival eyes to warm his frozen breast:
For ev'ry nymph with love his lays inspir'd,
But ev'ry nymph repuls'd, with grief retir'd.
A hill there was, and on that hill a mead,
With verdure thick, but destitute of shade.
Where, now, the Muse's son no sooner sings,
No sooner strikes his sweet-resounding strings,
But distant groves the flying sounds receive,
And list'ning trees their rooted stations leave;
Themselves transplanting, all around they grow,
And various shades their various kinds bestow.
Here, tall Chaönian oaks their branches spread,
While weeping poplars there erect their head.
The foodful Esculus here shoots his leaves,
That turf soft lime-tree, this, fat beech receives;

Here, brittle hazels, laurels here advance,
And there tough ash to form the hero's lance;
Here silver firs with knotless trunks ascend,
There, scarlet oaks beneath their acorns bend.
That spot admits the hospitable plane,
On this the maple grows with clouded grain;
Here, wat'ry willows are with lotus seen;
There, tamarisk, and box for ever green.
With double hue here myrtles grace the ground,
And laurestines, with purple berries crown'd.
With pliant feet, now, ivies this way wind,
Vines yonder rise, and elms with vines entwin'd;
Wild ornus now, the pitch-tree next takes root,
And arbutus adorn'd with blushing fruit.
Then easy-bending palms, the victor's prize,
And pines erect with bristled tops arise.
For Rhea grateful still the pine remains,
For Atys still some favour she retains;
He once in human shape her breast had warm'd,
And now is cherish'd, to a tree transform'd.

THE FABLE OF CYPARISSUS.

AMID the throng of this promiscuous wood,
With pointed top, the taper cypress stood;
A tree, which once a youth, and heav'nly fair,
Was of that deity the darling care,
Whose hand adapts, with equal skill, the strings
To bows with which he kills, and harps to which he sings.
For heretofore, a mighty stag was bred,
Which on the fertile fields of Cæa fed;
In shape and size he all his kind excell'd,
And to Carthæan nymphs was sacred held.
His beamy head, with branches high display'd,
Afforded to itself an ample shade;
His horns were gilt, and his smooth neck was grac'd
With silver collars thick with gems enchas'd:
A silver boss upon his forehead hung,
And brazen pendants in his ear-rings rung.
Frequenting houses, he familiar grew,
And learnt by custom nature to subdue;
'Till by degrees, of fear, and wildness, broke,
Ev'n stranger hands his proffer'd neck might stroke.
Much was the beast by Cæa's youth caress'd,
But thou, sweet Cyparissus, lov'dst him best:
By thee, to pastures fresh, he oft was led,
By thee oft water'd at the fountain's head:
His horns with garlands, now, by thee were ty'd,
And, now, thou on his back wouldst wanton ride;
Now here, now there wouldst bound along the plains,
Ruling his tender mouth with purple reins.
'Twas when the summer Sun, at noon of day,
Through glowing Cancer shot his burning ray,
'Twas then, the fav'rite stag, in cool retreat,
Had sought a shelter from the scorching heat;
Along the grass his weary limbs he laid,
Inhaling freshness from the breezy shade:
When Cyparissus with his pointed dart,
Unknowing, pierc'd him to the panting heart.
But when the youth, surpris'd, his errour found,
And saw him dying of the cruel wound,
Himself he would have slain through desp'rate grief.
What said not Phœbus, that might yield relief!
To cease his mourning he the boy desir'd,
Or mourn no more than such a loss requir'd.
But he incessant griev'd: at length address'd
To the superior pow'rs a last request;
Praying, in expiation of his crime,
Thenceforth to mourn to all succeeding time.
And now, of blood exhausted he appears,
Drain'd by a torrent of continual tears;
The fleshy colour in his body fades,
And a green tincture all his limbs invades;
From his fair head, where curling locks lay hung,
A horrid bush with bristled branches sprung,
Which stiff'ning by degrees, its stem extends,
Till to the starry skies the spire ascends.
Apollo sad look'd on, and sighing, cry'd,
"Then, be for ever, what thy pray'r imply'd:
Bemoan'd by me, in others grief excite;
And still preside at ev'ry fun'ral rite."

Continued by Mr. Croxall.

Thus the sweet artist in a wond'rous shade
Of verdant trees, which harmony had made,
Encircled sat, with his own triumphs crown'd,
Of list'ning birds, and savages around.
Again the trembling strings he dext'rous tries,
Again from discord makes soft music rise.
Then tunes his voice: "O Muse, from whom I sprung,
Jove be my theme, and thou inspire my song.
To Jove my grateful voice I oft have rais'd,
Oft his almighty pow'r with pleasure prais'd.
I sung the giants in a solemn strain,
Blasted, and thunder-struck on Phlegra's plain.
Now be my lyre in softer accents mov'd,
To sing of blooming boys by gods belov'd;
And to relate what virgins, void of shame,
Have suffer'd vengeance for a lawless flame.
"The king of gods once felt the burning joy,
And sigh'd for lovely Ganymede of Troy:
Long was he puzzled to assume a shape
Most fit, and expeditious for the rape;
A bird's was proper, yet he scorns to wear
Any but that which might his thunder bear.
Down with his masquerading wings he flies,
And bears the little Trojan to the skies;
Where now, in robes of heav'nly purple drest,
He serves the nectar at th' almighty's feast,
To slighted Juno an unwelcome guest.

HYACINTHUS TRANSFORMED INTO A FLOWER.

By Mr. Ozell.

"PHŒBUS for thee too, Hyacinth, design'd
A place among the gods, had fate been kind:
Yet this he gave; as oft as wintry rains
Are past, and vernal breezes sooth the plains,
From the green turf a purple flow'r you rise,
And with your fragrant breath perfume the skies.
"You when alive were Phœbus' darling boy;
In you he plac'd his Heav'n, and fix'd his joy:
Their god the Delphic priests consult in vain;
Eurotas now he loves, and Sparta's plain:
His hands the use of bow and harp forget,
And hold the dogs, or bear the corded net;
O'er hanging cliffs swift he pursues the game;
Each hour his pleasure, each augments his flame.
"The mid-day Sun now shone with equal light
Between the past and the succeeding night;
They strip, then, smooth'd with suppling oil, essay
To pitch the rounded quoit, their wonted play:
A well-pois'd disk first hasty Phœbus threw,
It cleft the air, and whistled as it flew;
It reach'd the mark, a most surprising length;
Which spoke an equal share of art and strength.
Scarce was it fall'n, when with too eager hand
Young Hyacinth ran to snatch it from the sand;

But the curst orb, which met a stony soil,
Flew in his face with violent recoil.
Both faint, both pale, and breathless now appear,
The boy with pain, the am'rous god with fear.
He ran, and rais'd him bleeding from the ground,
Chafes his cold limbs, and wipes the fatal wound:
Then herbs of noblest juice in vain applies;
The wound is mortal, and his skill defies.
"As in a water'd garden's blooming walk,
When some rude hand has bruis'd its tender stalk,
A fading lily droops its languid head,
And bends to earth, its life and beauty fled:
So Hyacinth, with head reclin'd, decays,
And, sick'ning, now no more his charms displays.
"'O thou art gone, my boy,' Apollo cry'd,
'Defrauded of thy youth in all its pride!
Thou, once my joy, art all my sorrow now;
And to my guilty hand my grief I owe.
Yet from myself I might the fault remove,
Unless to sport, and play, a fault should prove,
Unless it too were call'd a fault to love.
Oh could I for thee, or but with thee, die!
But cruel fates to me that pow'r deny.
Yet on my tongue thou shalt for ever dwell;
Thy name my lyre shall sound, my verse shall tell;
And to a flow'r transform'd, unheard of yet,
Stamp'd on thy leaves my cries thou shalt repeat.
The time shall come, prophetic I foreknow,
When, join'd to thee, a mighty chief[1] shall grow,
And with my plaints his name my leaf shall show.'
"While Phœbus thus the laws of fate reveal'd,
Behold, the blood which stain'd the verdant field
Is blood no longer; but a flow'r full-blown,
Far brighter than the Tyrian scarlet, shone.
A lily's form it took; its purple hue
Was all that made a diff'rence to the view.
Nor stop'd he here; the god upon its leaves
The sad expression of his sorrow weaves;
And to this hour the mournful purple wears
Ai, Ai, inscrib'd in funeral characters.
Nor are the Spartans, who so much are fam'd
For virtue, of their Hyacinth asham'd;
But still with pompous woe, and solemn state,
The Hyacinthian feasts they yearly celebrate.

THE TRANSFORMATIONS OF THE CERASTÆ, AND PROPŒTIDES.

"INQUIRE of Amathus, whose wealthy ground
With veins of every metal does abound,
If she to her Propœtides would show
The honour Sparta does to him allow;
'No more,' she'd say, 'such wretches would we grace,
Than those whose crooked horns deform'd their face,
From thence Cerastæ call'd, an impious race:
Before whose gates a rev'rend altar stood,
To Jove inscrib'd, the hospitable god:
This had some stranger seen with gore besmear'd,
The blood of lambs and bulls it had appear'd:
Their slaughter'd guest it was; not flock nor herd.'
"Venus these barb'rous sacrifices view'd
With just abhorrence, and with wrath pursu'd:
At first, to punish such nefarious crimes,
Their towns she meant to leave, her once lov'd climes:
'But why,' said she, 'for their offence should I
My dear delightful plains, and cities fly?
No, let the impious people, who have sinn'd,
A punishment in death, or exile, find:
If death or exile too severe be thought,
Let them in some vile shape bemoan their fault.'
While next her mind a proper form employs,
Admonish'd by their horns, she fix'd her choice.
Their former crest remains upon their heads,
And their strong limbs an ox's shape invades.
"The blasphemous Propœtides deny'd
Worship of Venus, and her pow'r defy'd:
But soon that pow'r they felt, the first that sold
Their lewd embraces to the world for gold.
Unknowing how to blush, and shameless grown,
A small transition changes them to stone.

THE STORY OF PYGMALION AND THE STATUE.

By Mr. Dryden.

"PYGMALION loathing their lascivious life,
Abhorr'd all womankind, but most a wife:
So single chose to live, and shunn'd to wed,
Well pleas'd to want a consort of his bed.
Yet fearing idleness, the nurse of ill,
In sculpture exercis'd his happy skill;
And carv'd in iv'ry such a maid, so fair,
As Nature could not with his art compare,
Were she to work; but in her own defence
Must take her pattern here, and copy hence.
Pleas'd with his idol, he commends, admires,
Adores; and last, the thing ador'd, desires.
A very virgin in her face was seen,
And had she mov'd, a living maid had been:
One would have thought she could have stirr'd, but strove
With modesty, and was asham'd to move.
Art hid with art, so well perform'd the cheat,
It caught the carver with his own deceit:
He knows 'tis madness, yet he must adore,
And still the more he knows it, loves the more:
The flesh, or what so seems, he touches oft,
Which feels so smooth, that he believes it soft.
Fir'd with this thought, at once he strain'd the breast,
And on the lips a burning kiss impress'd.
'Tis true, the harden'd breast resists the gripe,
And the cold lips return a kiss unripe:
But when, retiring back, he look'd again,
To think it iv'ry was a thought too mean:
So would believe she kiss'd, and courting more,
Again embrac'd her naked body o'er;
And straining hard the statue, was afraid
His hands had made a dint, and hurt his maid:
Explor'd her limb by limb, and fear'd to find
So rude a gripe had left a livid mark behind.
With flatt'ry now he seeks her mind to move,
And now with gifts (the pow'rful bribes of love):
He furnishes her closet first; and fills
The crowded shelves with rarities of shells;
Adds orient pearls, which from the conchs he drew,
And all the sparkling stones of various hue:
And parrots, imitating human tongue,
And singing-birds in silver cages hung:
And ev'ry fragrant flow'r, and od'rous green,
Were sorted well, with lumps of amber laid between:
Rich fashionable robes her person deck,
Pendants her ears, and pearls adorn her neck:
Her taper'd fingers too with rings are grac'd,
And an embroider'd zone surrounds her slender waist.
Thus like a queen array'd, so richly dress'd,
Beauteous she show'd, but naked show'd the best.

[1] Ajax.

Then, from the floor, he rais'd a royal bed,
With cov'rings of Sidonian purple spread:
The solemn rites perform'd, he calls her bride,
With blandishments invites her to his side;
And as she were with vital sense possess'd,
Her head did on a plumy pillow rest.
"The feast of Venus came, a solemn day,
To which the Cypriots due devotion pay;
With gilded horns the milk-white heifers led,
Slaughter'd before the sacred altars, bled.
"Pygmalion off'ring, first approach'd the shrine,
And then with pray'rs implor'd the pow'rs divine:
'Almighty gods, if all we mortals want,
If all we can require, be yours to grant;
Make this fair statue mine,' he would have said,
But chang'd his words for shame; and only pray'd,
'Give me the likeness of my iv'ry maid.'
"The golden goddess, present at the pray'r,
Well knew he meant th' inanimated fair,
And gave the sign of granting his desire;
For thrice in cheerful flames ascends the fire.
The youth, returning, to his mistress hies,
And impudent in hope, with ardent eyes,
And beating breast, by the dear statue lies.
He kisses her white lips, renews the bliss,
And looks, and thinks they redden at the kiss;
He thought them warm before; nor longer stays,
But next his hand on her hard bosom lays:
Hard as it was, beginning to relent,
It seem'd, the breast beneath his fingers bent;
He felt again, his fingers made a print,
'Twas flesh, but flesh so firm, it rose against the dint;
The pleasing task he fails not to renew;
Soft and more soft at ev'ry touch it grew;
Like pliant wax, when chafing hands reduce
The former mass to form, and frame for use.
He would believe, but yet is still in pain,
And tries his argument of sense again,
Presses the pulse, and feels the leaping vein.
Convinc'd, o'er-joy'd, his studied thanks, and praise,
To her, who made the miracle, he pays:
Then lips to lips he join'd; now freed from fear,
He found the savour of the kiss sincere:
At this the waken'd image op'd her eyes,
And view'd at once the light, and lover with surprise.
The goddess, present at the match she made,
So bless'd the bed, such fruitfulness convey'd,
That ere ten months had sharpen'd either horn,
To crown their bliss, a lovely boy was born:
Paphos his name, who grown to manhood wall'd
The city Paphos, from the founder call'd.

THE STORY OF CINYRAS AND MYRRHA.

"Nor him alone produc'd the fruitful queen;
But Cinyras, who like his sire had been
A happy prince, had he not been a sire.
Daughters, and fathers, from my song retire;
I sing of horrour; and could I prevail,
You should not hear, or not believe my tale.
Yet if the pleasure of my song be such,
That you will hear, and credit me too much,
Attentive listen to the last event,
And, with the sin, believe the punishment:
Since nature could behold so dire a crime,
I gratulate at least my native clime,
That such a land, which such a monster bore,
So far is distant from our Thracian shore.
Let Araby extol her happy coast,
Her cinnamon, and sweet amomum boast,
Her fragrant flow'rs, her trees with precious tears,
Her second harvests, and her double years;
How can the land be call'd so bless'd, that Myrrha bears?
Nor all her od'rous tears can cleanse her crime;
Her plant alone deforms the happy clime:
Cupid denies to have inflam'd thy heart,
Disowns thy love, and vindicates his dart:
Some fury gave thee those infernal pains,
And shot her venom'd vipers in thy veins.
To hate thy sire, had merited a curse;
But such an impious love deserv'd a worse.
The neighb'ring monarchs, by thy beauty led,
Contend in crowds, ambitious of thy bed:
The world is at thy choice; except but one,
Except but him, thou canst not choose, alone.
She knew it too, the miserable maid,
Ere impious love her better thoughts betray'd,
And thus within her secret soul she said:
'Ah Myrrha! whither would thy wishes tend?
Ye gods, ye sacred laws, my soul defend
From such a crime as all mankind detest,
And never lodg'd before in human breast!
But is it sin? or makes my mind alone
Th' imagin'd sin? for nature makes it none.
What tyrant then these envious laws began,
Made not for any other beast, but man!
The father-bull his daughter may bestride,
The horse may make his mother-mare a bride;
What piety forbids the lusty ram,
Or more salacious goat, to rut their dam?
The hen is free to wed the chick she bore,
And make a husband, whom she hatch'd before.
All creatures else are of a happier kind,
Whom nor ill-natur'd laws from pleasure bind,
Nor thoughts of sin disturb their peace of mind.
But man a slave of his own making lives:
The fool denies himself what Nature gives.
Too busy senates, with an over-care
To make us better than our kind can bear,
Have dash'd a spice of envy in the laws,
And straining up too high, have spoil'd the cause.
Yet some wise nations break their cruel chains,
And own no laws, but those which love ordains;
Where happy daughters with their sires are join'd,
And piety is doubly paid in kind.
O that I had been born in such a clime,
Not here, where 'tis the country makes the crime!
But whither would my impious fancy stray?
Hence hopes, and ye forbidden thoughts, away!
His worth deserves to kindle my desires
But with the love that daughters bear to sires.
Then had not Cinyras my father been,
What hinder'd Myrrha's hopes to be his queen?
But the perverseness of my fate is such,
That he's not mine, because he's mine too much:
Our kindred-blood debars a better tie;
He might be nearer, were he not so nigh.
Eyes, and their objects, never must unite;
Some distance is requir'd to help the sight:
Fain would I travel to some foreign shore,
Never to see my native country more:
So might I to myself myself restore;
So might my mind these impious thoughts remove,
And ceasing to behold, might cease to love.
But stay I must, to feed my famish'd sight,
To talk, to kiss, and more, if more I might:
More, impious maid! what more canst thou design?
To make a monstrous mixture in thy line,
And break all statutes human and divine!

Canst thou be call'd (to save thy wretched life)
Thy mother's rival, and thy father's wife?
Confound so many sacred names in one,
Thy brother's mother! sister to thy son!
And fear'st thou not to see th' infernal bands,
Their heads with snakes, with torches arm'd their hands,
Full at thy face th' avenging brands to bear,
And shake the serpents from their hissing hair?
But thou in time th' increasing ill control,
Nor first debauch the body by the soul;
Secure the sacred quiet of thy mind,
And keep the sanctions Nature has design'd.
Suppose I should attempt, th' attempt were vain,
No thoughts like mine his sinless soul profane;
Observant of the right: and O that he
Could cure my madness, or be mad like me!'
Thus she: but Cinyras, who daily sees
A crowd of noble suitors at his knees,
Among so many, knew not whom to choose,
Irresolute to grant, or to refuse.
But having told their names, inquir'd of her
Who pleas'd her best, and whom she would prefer.
The blushing maid stood silent with surprise,
And on her father fix'd her ardent eyes;
And looking sigh'd, and as she sigh'd, began
Round tears to shed, that scalded as they ran.
The tender sire, who saw her blush, and cry,
Ascrib'd it all to maiden modesty,
And dry'd the falling drops, and yet more kind,
He strok'd her cheeks, and holy kisses join'd.
She felt a secret venom fire her blood,
And found more pleasure, than a daughter should;
And, ask'd again what lover of the crew
She lik'd the best, she answer'd, 'One like you.'
Mistaking what she meant, her pious will
He prais'd, and bid her so continue still:
The word of pious heard, she blush'd with shame
Of secret guilt, and could not bear the name.
"'Twas now the mid of night, when slumbers close
Our eyes, and sooth our cares with soft repose;
But no repose could wretched Myrrha find,
Her body rolling, as she roll'd her mind:
Mad with desire, she ruminates her sin,
And wishes all her wishes o'er again:
Now she despairs, and now resolves to try;
Would not, and would again, she knows not why;
Stops, and returns; makes and retracts the vow;
Fain would begin, but understands not how.
As when a pine is hew'd upon the plains,
And the last mortal stroke alone remains,
Lab'ring in pangs of death, and threat'ning all,
This way and that she nods, consid'ring where to fall:
So Myrrha's mind, impell'd on either side,
Takes ev'ry bent, but cannot long abide;
Irresolute on which she should relie,
At last, unfix'd in all, is only fix'd to die.
On that sad thought she rests; resolv'd on death,
She rises, and prepares to choke her breath:
Then while about the beam her zone she ties,
'Dear Cinyras, farewell,' she softly cries;
'For thee I die, and only wish to be
Not hated, when thou know'st I die for thee:
Pardon the crime, in pity to the cause:'
This said, about her neck the noose she draws.
The nurse who lay without, her faithful guard,
Though not the words, the murmurs overheard,
And sighs, and hollow sounds: surpris'd with fright,
She starts, and leaves her bed, and springs a light;
Unlocks the door, and ent'ring out of breath,
The dying saw, and instruments of death;
She shrieks, she cuts the zone with trembling haste,
And in her arms her fainting charge embrac'd:
Next, (for she now had leisure for her tears)
She weeping ask'd, in these her blooming years,
What unforeseen misfortune caus'd her care,
To loath her life, and languish in despair! [grief
The maid with down-cast eyes, and mute with
For death unfinish'd, and ill-tim'd relief,
Stood sullen to her suit: the beldam press'd
The more to know, and bar'd her wither'd breast;
Abjur'd her by the kindly food she drew
From these dry founts, her secret ill to shew.
Sad Myrrha sigh'd, and turn'd her eyes aside:
The nurse still urg'd, and would not be deny'd:
Nor only promis'd secrecy, but pray'd
She might have leave to give her offer'd aid.
'Good will,' she said, 'my want of strength supplies,
And diligence shall give what age denies:
If strong desires thy mind to fury move,
With charms and med'cines I can cure thy love:
If envious eyes their hurtful rays have cast,
More pow'rful verse shall free thee from the blast:
If Heav'n offended sends thee this disease,
Offended Heav'n with pray'rs we can appease.
What then remains, that can these cares procure?
Thy house is flourishing, thy fortune sure:
Thy careful mother yet in health survives,
And to thy comfort, thy kind father lives.'
The virgin started at her father's name,
And sigh'd profoundly, conscious of the shame
Nor yet the nurse her impious love divin'd,
But yet surmis'd that love disturb'd her mind:
Thus thinking, she pursu'd her point, and laid,
And lull'd within her lap, the mourning maid;
Then softly sooth'd her thus; 'I guess your grief:
You love, my child; your love shall find relief.
My long-experienc'd age shall be your guide;
Rely on that, and lay distrust aside:
No breath of air shall on the secret blow,
Nor shall (what most you fear) your father know.'
Struck once again, as with a thunder-clap,
The guilty virgin bounded from her lap,
And threw her body prostrate on the bed,
And to conceal her blushes, hid her head:
There silent lay, and warn'd her with her hand
To go: but she receiv'd not the command;
Remaining still importunate to know:
Then Myrrha thus; 'Or ask no more, or go;
I pr'ythee go, or staying spare my shame;
What thou would'st hear, is impious ev'n to name.'
At this, on high the beldam holds her hands,
And trembling both with age, and terrour, stands;
Adjures, and falling at her feet entreats,
Sooths her with blandishments, and frights with threats,
To tell the crime intended, or disclose
What part of it she knew, if she no farther knows.
And last, if conscious to her counsel made,
Confirms anew the promise of her aid.'
Now Myrrha rais'd her head, but soon, oppress'd
With shame, reclin'd it on her nurse's breast;
Bath'd it with tears, and strove to have confess'd:

Twice she began, and stopp'd: again she try'd;
The falt'ring tongue its office still deny'd.
At last her veil before her face she spread,
And drew a long preluding sigh, and said,
'O happy mother, in thy marriage bed!'
Then groan'd, and ceas'd. The good old woman shook,
Stiff were her eyes, and ghastly was her look:
Her hoary hair upright with horrour stood,
Made (to her grief) more knowing than she would.
Much she reproach'd, and many things she said,
To cure the madness of th' unhappy maid,
In vain: for Myrrha stood convict of ill;
Her reason vanquish'd, but unchang'd her will:
Perverse of mind, unable to reply;
She stood resolv'd, or to possess, or die.
At length the fondness of a nurse prevail'd
Against her better sense, and virtue fail'd:
'Enjoy, my child, since such is thy desire
Thy love,' she said; she durst not say, thy sire:
'Live, though unhappy, live on any terms;'
Then with a second oath her faith confirms.
"The solemn feast of Ceres now was near,
When long white linen stoles the matrons wear;
Rank'd in procession walk the pious train,
Off'ring first-fruits, and spikes of yellow grain:
For nine long nights the nuptial-bed they shun,
And sanctifying harvest, lie alone.
"Mix'd with the crowd, the queen forsook her lord,
And Ceres' pow'r with secret rites ador'd:
The royal couch now vacant for a time,
The crafty crone, officious in her crime,
The first occasion took: the king she found
Easy with wine, and deep in pleasures drown'd,
Prepar'd for love: the beldam blew the flame,
Confess'd the passion, but conceal'd the name.
Her form she prais'd; the monarch ask'd her years;
And she reply'd, 'The same thy Myrrha bears.'
Wine, and commended beauty fir'd his thought;
Impatient, he commands her to be brought.
Pleas'd with her charge perform'd, she hies her home,
And gratulates the nymph, the task was overcome'
Myrrha was joy'd the welcome news to hear;
But clog'd with guilt, the joy was unsincere:
So various, so discordant is the mind,
That in our will a diff'rent will we find.
Ill she presag'd, and yet pursu'd her lust;
For guilty pleasures give a double gust.
"'Twas depth of night: Arctophylax had driv'n
His lazy wain half-round the northern Heav'n,
When Myrrha hasten'd to the crime desir'd:
The Moon beheld her first, and first retir'd:
The stars amaz'd, ran backward from the sight,
And (shrunk within their sockets) lost their light.
Icarius first withdraws his holy flame:
The Virgin sign, in Heav'n the second name,
Slides down the Belt, and from her station flies,
And night with sable clouds involves the skies.
Bold Myrrha still pursues her black intent;
She stumbled thrice, (an omen of th' event;)
Thrice shriek'd the fun'ral owl, yet on she went,
Secure of shame, because secure of sight;
Ev'n bashful sins are impudent by night.
Link'd hand in hand, th' accomplice, and the dame,
Their way exploring, to the chamber came:
The door was ope, they blindly grope their way,
Where dark in bed th' expecting monarch lay.
Thus far her courage held, but here forsakes;
Her faint knees knock at ev'ry step she makes.
The nearer to her crime, the more within
She feels remorse, and horrour of her sin;
Repents too late her criminal desire,
And wishes, that unknown she could retire.
Her ling'ring thus, the nurse, (who fear'd delay
The fatal secret might at length betray)
Pull'd forward, to complete the work begun,
And said to Cinyras, 'Receive thy own.'
Thus saying, she deliver'd kind to kind,
Accurs'd, and their devoted bodies join'd.
The sire, unknowing of the crime, admits
His bowels, and profanes the hallow'd sheets:
He found she trembled, but believ'd she strove
With maiden modesty against her love,
And sought with flatt'ring words vain fancies to remove.
Perhaps he said, 'My daughter, cease thy fears,'
(Because the title suited with her years;)
And, 'Father,' she might whisper him again,
That names might not be wanting to the sin.
"Full of her sire, she left th' incestuous bed,
And carry'd in her womb the crime she bred.
Another, and another night she came;
For frequent sin had left no sense of shame:
Till Cinyras desir'd to see her face,
Whose body he had held in close embrace,
And brought a taper; the revealer, light,
Expos'd both crime and criminal to sight.
Grief, rage, amazement, could no speech afford,
But from the sheath he drew th' avenging sword:
The guilty fled: the benefit of night,
That favour'd first the sin, secur'd the flight.
Long-wand'ring through the spacious fields, she bent
Her voyage to th' Arabian continent;
Then pass'd the region which Panchæa join'd,
And flying, left the palmy plains behind.
Nine times the Moon had mew'd her horns; at length
With travel weary, unsupply'd with strength,
And with the burden of her womb oppress'd,
Sabæan fields afford her needful rest:
There, loathing life, and yet of death afraid,
In anguish of her spirit thus she pray'd.
'Ye pow'rs, if any so propitious are
T' accept my penitence, and hear my pray'r;
Your judgments, I confess, are justly sent;
Great sins deserve as great a punishment:
Yet since my life the living will profane,
And since my death the happy dead will stain,
A middle state your mercy may bestow,
Betwixt the realms above, and those below:
Some other form to wretched Myrrha give,
Nor let her wholly die, nor wholly live.'
"The pray'rs of penitents are never vain,
At least she did her last request obtain;
For while she spoke, the ground began to rise,
And gather'd round her feet, her legs, and thighs;
Her toes in roots descend, and spreading wide,
A firm foundation for the trunk provide:
Her solid bones convert to solid wood,
To pith her marrow, and to sap her blood:
Her arms are boughs, her fingers change their kind,
Her tender skin is harden'd into rind.
And now the rising tree her womb invests,
Now shooting upwards still, invades her breasts,
And shades the neck; when weary with delay,
She sunk her head within, and met it half the way.
And tho' with outward shape she lost her sense,
With bitter tears she wept her last offence;

And still she weeps, nor sheds her tears in vain;
For still the precious drops her name retain.
Meantime the mis-begotten infant grows,
And ripe for birth, distends with deadly throes
The swelling rind, with unavailing strife,
To leave the wooden womb, and pushes into life.
The mother-tree, as if oppress'd with pain,
Writhes here, and there, to break the bark, in vain;
And, like a lab'ring woman, would have pray'd,
But wants a voice to call Lucina's aid:
The bending bole sends out a hollow sound,
And trickling tears fall thicker on the ground.
The mild Lucina came uncall'd, and stood
Beside the struggling boughs, and heard the groaning wood;
Then reach'd her midwife hand to speed her [throes,
And spoke the pow'rful spells, that babes to birth disclose.
The bark divides, the living load to free,
And safe delivers the convulsive tree.
The ready nymphs receive the crying child,
And wash him in the tears the parent plant distill'd.
They swath'd him with their scarfs; beneath him spread
The ground with herbs; with roses rais'd his head.
The lovely babe was born with ev'ry grace,
Ev'n envy must have prais'd so fair a face;
Such was his form, as painters, when they show
Their utmost art, on naked Loves bestow:
And that their arms no diff'rence might betray,
Give him a bow, or his from Cupid take away.
Time glides along with undiscover'd haste,
The future but a length behind the past;
So swift are years. The babe, whom just before
His grandsire got, and whom his sister bore;
The drop, the thing which late the tree enclos'd,
And late the yawning bark to life expos'd;
A babe, a boy, a beauteous youth appears,
And lovelier than himself at riper years.
Now to the queen of love he gave desires,
And, with her pains, reveng'd his mother's fires.

THE STORY OF VENUS AND ADONIS.

By Mr. Eusden.

"FOR Cytherëa's lips while Cupid prest,
He with a heedless arrow raz'd her breast.
The goddess felt it, and with fury stung,
The wanton mischief from her bosom flung:
Yet thought at first the danger slight, but found
The dart too faithful, and too deep the wound.
Fir'd with a mortal beauty, she disdains
To haunt th' Idalian mount, or Phrygian plains.
She seeks not Cnidos, nor her Paphian shrines,
Nor Amathus, that teems with brazen mines:
Ev'n Heav'n itself with all its sweets unsought,
Adonis far a sweeter Heav'n is thought.
On him she hangs, and fonds with ev'ry art,
And never, never knows from him to part.
She, whose soft limbs had only been display'd
On rosy beds beneath the myrtle shade;
Whose pleasing care was to improve each grace,
And add more charms to an unrival'd face,
Now buskin'd, like the virgin huntress, goes
Through woods, and pathless wilds, and mountain-snows,
With her own tuneful voice she joys to cheer
The panting hounds, that chase the flying deer.
She runs the labyrinth of fearful hares,
But fearless beasts, and dang'rous prey forbears;
Hunts not the grinning wolf, or foamy boar,
And trembles at the lion's hungry roar.
Thee too, Adonis, with a lover's care
She warns, if warn'd thou wouldst avoid the snare:
'To furious animals advance not nigh,
Fly those that follow, follow those that fly;
'Tis chance alone must the survivors save,
Whene'er brave spirits will attempt the brave.
O! lovely youth! in harmless sports delight;
Provoke not beasts, which, arm'd by nature, fight.
For me, if not thyself, vouchsafe to fear;
Let not thy thirst of glory cost me dear.
Boars know not how to spare a blooming age;
No sparkling eyes can sooth the lion's rage.
Not all thy charms a savage beast can move,
Which have so deeply touch'd the queen of love.
When bristled boars from beaten thickets spring,
In grinded tusks a thunderbolt they bring.
The daring hunters lions rous'd devour,
Vast is their fury, and as vast their pow'r:
Curst be their tawny race! if thou would'st hear
What kindled thus my hate, then lend an ear:
The wond'rous tale I will to thee unfold,
How the fell monsters rose from crimes of old.
But by long toils I faint: see! wide display'd,
A grateful poplar courts us with a shade.
The grassy turf, beneath, so verdant shows,
We may secure delightfully repose.
With her Adonis here be Venus blest:'
And swift at once the grass and him she prest.
Then sweetly smiling, with a raptur'd mind,
On his lov'd bosom she her head reclin'd,
And thus began; but mindful still of bliss,
Seal'd the soft accents with a softer kiss.

"'Perhaps thou may'st have heard a virgin's name,
Who still in swiftness swiftest youths o'ercame.
Wond'rous! that female weakness should out-do
A manly strength; the wonder yet is true.
'Twas doubtful, if her triumphs in the field
Did to her form's triumphant glories yield;
Whether her face could with more ease decoy
A crowd of lovers, or her feet destroy.
For once Apollo she implor'd to show
If courteous fates a consort would allow:
'A consort brings thy ruin,' he reply'd;
'O! learn to want the pleasures of a bride!
Nor shalt thou want them to thy wretched cost,
And Atalanta living shall be lost.'
With such a rueful fate th' affrighted maid
Sought green recesses in the woodland glade;
Nor sighing suitors her resolves could move,
She bad them show their speed, to show their love.
He only, who could conquer in the race,
Might hope the conquer'd virgin to embrace;
While he, whose tardy feet had lagg'd behind,
Was doom'd the sad reward of death to find.
Though great the prize, yet rigid the decree,
But blind with beauty, who can rigour see?
Ev'n on these laws the fair they rashly sought,
And danger in excess of love forgot.

"'There sat Hippomenes, prepar'd to blame
In lovers such extravagance of flame.
'And must,' he said, 'the blessing of a wife
Be dearly purchas'd by a risk of life?'
But when he saw the wonders of her face,
And her limbs naked, springing to the race,
(Her limbs, as exquisitely turn'd as mine,
Or if a woman thou, might vie with thine,)

With lifted hands, he cry'd, 'Forgive the tongue
Which durst, ye youths, your well-tim'd courage wrong.
I knew not that the nymph, for whom you strove,
Deserv'd th' unbounded transports of your love.'
He saw, admir'd, and thus her spotless frame
He prais'd, and praising, kindled his own flame.
A rival now to all the youths who run,
Envious, he fears they should not be undone.
'But why,' reflects he, 'idly thus is shown
The fate of others, yet untry'd my own?
The coward must not in love's aid depend;
The god was ever to the bold a friend.'
Meantime the virgin flies, or seems to fly,
Swift as a Scythian arrow cleaves the sky:
Still more and more the youth her charms admires,
The race itself t' exalt her charms conspires.
The golden pinions, which her feet adorn,
In wanton flutt'rings by the winds are borne.
Down from her head, the long, fair tresses flow,
And sport with lovely negligence below.
The waving ribbands, which her buskins tie,
Her snowy skin with waving purple die;
As crimson veils in palaces display'd,
To the white marble lend a blushing shade.
Not long he gaz'd, yet while he gaz'd, she gain'd
The goal, and the victorious wreath obtain'd.
The vanquish'd sigh, and, as the law decreed,
Pay the dire forfeit, and prepare to bleed.
"'Then rose Hippomenes, not yet afraid,
And fix'd his eyes full on the beauteous maid.
'Where is,' he cry'd, 'the mighty conquest won,
To distance those, who want the nerves to run?
Here prove superior strength, nor shall it be
Thy loss of glory, if excell'd by me.
High my descent, near Neptune I aspire,
For Neptune was grand-parent to my sire.
From that great god the fourth myself I trace,
Nor sink my virtues yet beneath my race.
Thou, from Hippomenes o'ercome, may'st claim
An envy'd triumph, and a deathless fame.'
"'While thus the youth the virgin pow'r defies,
Silent she views him still with softer eyes.
Thoughts in her breast a doubtful strife begin,
If 'tis not happier now to lose, than win.
'What god, a foe to beauty, would destroy
The promis'd ripeness of this blooming boy?
With his life's danger does he seek my bed?
Scarce am I half so greatly worth,' she said:
'Nor has his beauty mov'd my breast to love,
And yet, I own, such beauty well might move.
'Tis not his charms, 'tis pity would engage
My soul to spare the greenness of his age:
What, that heroic courage fires his breast,
And shines through brave disdain of fate confest?
What, that his patronage by close degrees
Springs from the imperial ruler of the seas?
Then add the love, which bids him undertake
The race, and dare to perish for my sake.
Of bloody nuptials, heedless youth, beware!
Fly, timely fly from a too barb'rous fair.
At pleasure choose; thy love will be repaid
By a less foolish, and more beauteous maid.
But why this tenderness, before unknown?
Why beats and pants my breast for him alone?
His eyes have seen his num'rous rivals yield;
Let him too share the rigour of the field,
Since, by their fates untaught, his own he courts,
And thus with ruin insolently sports.
Yet for what crime shall he his death receive?
Is it a crime with me to wish to live?
Shall his kind passion his destruction prove?
Is this the fatal recompence of love?
So fair a youth, destroy'd, would conquest shame,
And nymphs eternally detest my fame.
Still why should nymphs my guiltless fame upbraid?
Did I the fond adventurer persuade?
Alas! I wish thou wouldst the course decline,
Or that my swiftness was excell'd by thine.
See! what a virgin's bloom adorns the boy!
Why wilt thou run, and why thyself destroy?
Hippomenes! Oh that I ne'er had been
By those bright eyes unfortunately seen!
Ah! tempt not thus a swift, untimely fate;
Thy life is worthy of the longest date.
Were I left wretched, did the galling chain
Of rigid gods not my free choice restrain,
By thee alone I could with joy be led
To taste the raptures of a nuptial bed.'
"'Thus she disclos'd the woman's secret heart,
Young, innocent, and new to Cupid's dart.
Her thoughts, her words, her actions wildly rove,
With love she burns, yet knows not that 'tis love.
'"Her royal sire now with the murm'ring crowd
Demands the race impatiently aloud.
Hippomenes then with true fervour pray'd,
'My bold attempt let Venus kindly aid.
By her sweet pow'r I felt this am'rous fire,
Still may she succour whom she did inspire.'
A soft, unenvious wind, with speedy care,
Wafted to Heav'n the lover's tender pray'r.
Pity, I own, soon gain'd the wish'd consent,
And all th' assistance he implor'd I lent.
The Cyprian lands, though rich, in richness yield
To that, surnam'd the Tamasenian field.
That field of old was added to my shrine,
And its choice products consecrated mine.
A tree there stands, full glorious to behold,
Gold are the leaves, the crackling branches gold.
It chanc'd, three apples in my hands I bore,
Which newly from the tree I sportive tore;
Seen by the youth alone, to him I brought
The fruit, and when, and how to use it, taught.
The signal sounding by the king's command,
Both start at once, and sweep th' imprinted sand.
So swiftly mov'd their feet, they might with ease,
Scarce moisten'd, skim along the glassy seas;
Or with a wond'rous levity be borne
O'er yellow harvests of unbending corn.
Now fav'ring peals resound from ev'ry part,
Spirit the youth, and fire his fainting heart.
'Hippomenes!' they cry'd, 'thy life preserve,
Intensely labour, and stretch ev'ry nerve.
Base fear alone can baffle thy design,
Shoot boldly onward, and the goal is thine.'
'Tis doubtful whether shouts, like these, convey'd
More pleasures to the youth, or to the maid.
When a long distance oft she could have gain'd,
She check'd her swiftness, and her feet restrain'd:
She sigh'd, and dwelt, and languish'd on his face,
Then with unwilling speed pursu'd the race.
O'er-spent with heat, his breath he faintly drew,
Parch'd was his mouth, nor yet the goal in view,
And the first apple on the plain he threw.
The nymph stop'd sudden at th' unusual sight,
Struck with the fruit so beautifully bright.
Aside she starts, the wonder to behold,
And eager stoops to catch the rolling gold.

Th' observant youth past by, and scour'd along,
While peals of joy rung from th' applauding throng.
Unkindly she corrects the short delay,
And to redeem the time fleets swift away,
Swift, as the light'ning, or the northern wind,
And far she leaves the panting youth behind.
Again he strives the flying nymph to hold
With the temptation of the second gold:
The bright temptation fruitlessly was tost,
So soon, alas! she won the distance lost.
Now but a little interval of space
Remain'd for the decision of the race.
'Fair author of the precious gift,' he said,
'Be thou, O goddess, author of my aid!'
Then of the shining fruit the last he drew,
And with his full-collected vigour threw:
The virgin still the longer to detain,
Threw not directly, but across the plain.
She seem'd awhile perplex'd in dubious thought,
If the far-distant apple should be sought:
I lur'd her backward mind to seize the bait,
And to the massy gold gave double weight.
My favour to my votary was show'd,
Her speed I lessen'd, and increas'd her load.
But lest, though long, the rapid race be run
Before my longer, tedious tale is done,
The youth the goal, and so the virgin won.
"'Might I, Adonis, now not hope to see
His grateful thanks pour'd out for victory?
His pious incense on my altars laid?
But he nor grateful thanks, nor incense paid.
Enrag'd I vow'd, that with the youth the fair,
For his contempt, should my keen vengeance share;
That future lovers might my pow'r revere,
And, from their sad examples, learn to fear.
The silent fanes, the sanctify'd abodes
Of Cybelè, great mother of the gods,
Rais'd by Echion in a lonely wood,
And full of brown, religious horrour stood.
By a long painful journey faint, they chose
Their weary limbs here secret to repose.
But soon my pow'r inflam'd the lustful boy,
Careless of rest he sought untimely joy.
A hallow'd gloomy cave, with moss o'er-grown,
The temple join'd, of native pumice stone,
Where antic images by priests were kept,
And wooden deities securely slept.
Thither the rash Hippomenes retires,
And gives a loose to all his wild desires,
And the chaste cell pollutes with wanton fires.
The sacred statues tremble with surprise,
The tow'ry goddess, blushing, veil'd her eyes;
And the lewd pair to Stygian sounds had sent,
But unrevengeful seem'd that punishment.
A heavier doom such black prophaneness draws,
Their taper fingers turn to crooked paws.
No more their necks the smoothness can retain,
Now cover'd sudden with a yellow mane.
Arms change to legs: each finds the hard'ning breast
Of rage unknown, and wond'rous strength possest.
Their alter'd looks with fury grim appear,
And on the ground their brushing tails they bear.
They haunt the woods: their voices, which before
Were musically sweet, now hoarsely roar.
Hence lions, dreadful to the lab'ring swains,
Are tam'd by Cybelè, and curb'd with reins,
And humbly draw her car along the plains.
But thou, Adonis, my delightful care,
Of these, and beasts as fierce as these, beware!
The savage, which not shuns thee, timely shun,
For by rash prowess shouldst thou be undone,
A double ruin is contain'd in one.'
"Thus cautious Venus school'd her fav'rite boy;
But youthful heat all cautions will destroy.
His sprightly soul beyond grave counsels flies,
While with yok'd swans the goddess cuts the skies.
His faithful hounds, led by the tainted wind,
Lodg'd in thick coverts chanc'd a boar to find.
The callow hero show'd a manly heart,
And pierc'd the savage with a side-long dart.
The flying savage, wounded, turn'd again,
Wrench'd out the gory dart, and foam'd with pain.
The trembling boy by flight his safety sought,
And now recall'd the lore which Venus taught;
But now too late to fly the boar he strove,
Who in the groin his tusks impetuous drove;
On the discolour'd grass Adonis lay,
The monster trampling o'er his beauteous prey.
"Fair Cytherëa, Cyprus scarce in view,
Heard from afar his groans, and own'd them true,
And turn'd her snowy swans, and backward flew.
But as she saw him gasp his latest breath,
And quiv'ring agonize in pangs of death,
Down with swift flight she plung'd, nor rage forbore,
At once her garments, and her hair she tore.
With cruel blows she beat her guiltless breast,
The fates upbraided, and her love confest.
'Nor shall they yet,' she cry'd, 'the whole devour
With uncontrol'd, inexorable pow'r:
For thee, lost youth, my tears, and restless pain,
Shall in immortal monuments remain.
With solemn pomp in annual rites return'd,
Be thou for ever, my Adonis, mourn'd.
Could Pluto's queen with jealous fury storm,
And Menthè to a fragrant herb transform?
Yet dares not Venus with a change surprise,
And in a flow'r bid her fall'n hero rise?'
Then on the blood sweet nectar she bestows,
The scented blood in little bubbles rose:
Little as rainy drops, which flutt'ring fly,
Borne by the winds, along a low'ring sky.
Short time ensu'd, till where the blood was shed,
A flow'r began to rear its purple head:
Such, as on Punic apples is reveal'd,
Or in the filmy rind but half conceal'd.
Still here the fate of lovely forms we see,
So sudden fades the sweet anemonè.
The feeble stems, to stormy blasts a prey,
Their sickly beauties droop, and pine away.
The winds forbid the flow'rs to flourish long,
Which owe to winds their names in Grecian song."

OVID'S METAMORPHOSES.

BOOK XI.

THE DEATH OF ORPHEUS.

By Mr. Croxall.

HERE, while the Thracian bard's enchanting strain
Sooths beasts, and woods, and all the list'ning plain,
The female Bacchanals, devoutly mad,
In shaggy skins, like savage creatures, clad,
Warbling in air perceiv'd his lovely lay,
And from a rising ground beheld him play.
When one, the wildest, with dishevel'd hair,
That loosely stream'd, and ruffled in the air;

Soon as her frantic eye the lyrist spy'd,
"See, see! the hater of our sex," she cry'd.
Then at his face her missive javelin sent,
Which whiz'd along, and brusht him as it went;
But the soft wreaths of ivy twisted round,
Prevent a deep impression of the wound.
Another, for a weapon, hurls a stone,
Which, by the sound subdu'd as soon as thrown,
Falls at his feet, and with a seeming sense
Implores his pardon for its late offence.
But now their frantic rage unbounded grows,
Turns all to madness, and no measure knows:
Yet this the charms of music might subdue,
But that, with all its charms, is conquer'd too;
In louder strains their hideous yellings rise,
And squeaking horn-pipes echo through the skies,
Which, in hoarse consort with the drum, confound
The moving lyre, and ev'ry gentle sound:
Then 'twas the deafen'd stones flew on with speed,
And saw, unsooth'd, their tuneful poet bleed.
The birds, the beasts, and all the savage crew
Which the sweet lyrist to attention drew,
Now, by the female mob's more furious rage,
Are driv'n, and forc'd to quit the shady stage.
Next their fierce hands the bard himself assail,
Nor can his song against their wrath prevail:
They flock, like birds, when in a clust'ring flight,
By day they chase the boding fowl of night.
So crowded amphitheatres survey
The stag, to greedy dogs a future prey.
Their steely javelins, which soft curls entwine
Of budding tendrils from the leafy vine,
For sacred rites of mild religion made,
Are flung promiscuous at the poet's head.
Those clods of earth or flints discharge, and these
Hurl prickly branches sliver'd from the trees.
And, lest their passion should be unsupply'd,
The rabble crew, by chance, at distance spy'd
Where oxen, straining at the heavy yoke,
The fallow'd field with slow advances broke;
Nigh which the brawny peasants dug the soil,
Procuring food with long laborious toil.
These, when they saw the ranting throng draw near,
Quitted their tools, and fled, possest with fear.
Long spades, and rakes of mighty size were found,
Carelessly left upon the broken ground.
With these the furious lunatics engage,
And first the lab'ring oxen feel their rage;
Then to the poet they return with speed,
Whose fate was, past prevention, now decreed:
In vain he lifts his suppliant hands, in vain
He tries, before, his never-failing strain.
And, from those sacred lips, whose thrilling sound
Fierce tigers, and insensate rocks could wound,
Ah gods! how moving was the mournful sight!
To see the fleeting soul now take its flight.
Thee the soft warblers of the feather'd kind
Bewail'd; for thee thy savage audience pin'd;
Those rocks and woods that oft thy strain had led,
Mourn for their charmer, and lament him dead;
And drooping trees their leafy glories shed.
Naïads and Dryads with dishevel'd hair
Promiscuous weep, and scarfs of sable wear;
Nor could the river-gods conceal their moan,
But with new floods of tears augment their own.
His mangled limbs lay scatter'd all around,
His head and harp a better fortune found;
In Hebrus' streams they gently roll'd along,
And sooth'd the waters with a mournful song
Soft deadly notes the lifeless tongue inspire,
A doleful tune sounds from the floating lyre;
The hollow banks in solemn concert mourn,
And the sad strain in echoing groans return.
Now with the current to the sea they glide,
Borne by the billows of the briny tide;
And driv'n where waves round rocky Lesbos roar,
They strand, and lodge upon Methymna's shore.
But here, when landed on the foreign soil,
A venom'd snake, the product of the isle,
Attempts the head, and sacred locks embru'd
With clotted gore, and still fresh-dropping blood.
Phœbus, at last, his kind protection gives,
And from the fact the greedy monster drives;
Whose marbled jaws his impious crime atone,
Still grinning ghastly, though transform'd to stone.
His ghost flies downward to the Stygian shore,
And knows the places it had seen before:
Among the shadows of the pious train
He finds Eurydicè, and loves again:
With pleasure views the beauteous phantom's charms,
And clasps her in his unsubstantial arms.
There side by side they unmolested walk,
Or pass their blissful hours in pleasing talk;
Aft or before the bard securely goes,
And, without danger, can review his spouse.

THE THRACIAN WOMEN TRANSFORMED TO TREES.

Bacchus, resolving to revenge the wrong
Of Orpheus murder'd, on the madding throng,
Decreed that each accomplice dame should stand
Fix'd by the roots along the conscious land.
Their wicked feet, that late so nimbly ran
To wreak their malice on the guiltless man,
Sudden with twisted ligatures were bound,
Like trees, deep planted in the turfy ground.
And as the fowler with his subtile gins
His feather'd captives by the feet entwines,
That flutt'ring pant, and struggle to get loose,
Yet only closer draw the fatal noose:
So these were caught; and, as they strove in vain
To quit the place, they but increas'd their pain.
They flounce and toil, yet find themselves control'd;
The root, though pliant, toughly keeps its hold.
In vain their toes and feet they look to find,
For ev'n their shapely legs are cloth'd with rind.
One smites her thighs with a lamenting stroke,
And finds the flesh transform'd to solid oak:
Another, with surprise, and grief distrest,
Lays on above, but beats a wooden breast.
A rugged bark their softer neck invades,
Their branching arms shoot up delightful shades:
At once they seem, and are a real grove,
With mossy trunks below, and verdant leaves above.

THE FABLE OF MIDAS.

Nor this suffic'd; the god's disgust remains,
And he resolves to quit their hated plains;
The vineyards of Tymole ingross his care,
And, with a better choir, he fixes there;
Where the smooth streams of clear Pactolus roll'd,
Then undistinguish'd for its sands of gold.
The Satyrs with the nymphs, his usual throng,
Come to salute their god, and jovial danc'd along.
Silenus only miss'd; for while he reel'd,
Feeble with age, and wine, about the field,

The hoary drunkard had forgot his way,
And to the Phrygian clowns became a prey;
Who to king Midas drag the captive god,
While on his totty pate the wreaths of ivy nod.
Midas from Orpheus had been taught his lore,
And knew the rites of Bacchus long before.
He, when he saw his venerable guest,
In honour of the god ordain'd a feast.
Ten days in course, with each continu'd night,
Were spent in genial mirth, and brisk delight:
Then on th' eleventh, when with brighter ray
Phosphor had chas'd the fading stars away,
The king through Lydia's fields young Bacchus sought,
And to the god his foster-father brought.
Pleas'd with the welcome sight, he bids him soon
But name his wish, and swears to grant the boon.
A glorious offer! yet but ill bestow'd
On him whose choice so little judgment show'd.
"Give me," says he, (nor thought he ask'd too much)
"That with my body whatsoe'er I touch,
Chang'd from the nature which it held of old,
May be converted into yellow gold."
He had his wish; but yet the god repin'd,
To think the fool no better wish could find.
But the brave king departed from the place,
With smiles of gladness sparkling in his face:
Nor could contain, but, as he took his way,
Impatient longs to make the first essay.
Down from a lowly branch a twig he drew,
The twig straight glitter'd with a golden hue:
He takes a stone, the stone was turn'd to gold;
A clod he touches, and the crumbling mould
Acknowledg'd soon the great transforming pow'r,
In weight and substance like a mass of ore.
He pluck'd the corn, and straight his grasp appears
Fill'd with a bending tuft of golden ears.
An apple next he takes, and seems to hold
The bright Hesperian vegetable gold.
His hand he careless on a pillar lays,
With shining gold the fluted pillars blaze:
And while he washes, as the servants pour,
His touch converts the stream to Danae's show'r.
To see these miracles so finely wrought,
Fires with transporting joy his giddy thought.
The ready slaves prepare a sumptuous board,
Spread with rich dainties for their happy lord;
Whose pow'rful hands the bread no sooner hold,
But its whole substance is transform'd to gold:
Up to his mouth he lifts the sav'ry meat,
Which turns to gold as he attempts to eat:
His patron's noble juice of purple hue,
Touch'd by his lips, a gilded cordial grew:
Unfit for drink, and wondrous to behold,
It trickles from his jaws a fluid gold.
The rich poor fool, confounded with surprise,
Starving in all his various plenty lies:
Sick of his wish, he now detests the pow'r,
For which he ask'd so earnestly before;
Amidst his gold with pinching famine curst,
And justly tortur'd with an equal thirst.
At last his shining arms to Heav'n he rears,
And in distress, for refuge, flies to pray'rs.
"O father Bacchus, I have sinn'd," he cry'd,
"And foolishly thy gracious gift apply'd;
Thy pity now, repenting, I implore;
Oh! may I feel the golden plague no more."
The hungry wretch, his folly thus confest,
Touch'd the kind deity's good-natur'd breast;
The gentle god annull'd his first decree,
And from the cruel compact set him free.
But then, to cleanse him quite from further harm,
And to dilute the relics of the charm,
He bids him seek the stream that cuts the land
Nigh where the tow'rs of Lydian Sardis stand;
Then trace the river to the fountain head,
And meet it rising from its rocky bed;
There, as the bubbling tide pours forth amain,
To plunge his body in, and wash away the stain.
The king instructed to the fount retires,
But with the golden charm the stream inspires:
For while this quality the man forsakes,
An equal pow'r the limpid water takes;
Informs with veins of gold the neighb'ring land,
And glides along a bed of golden sand.
Now loathing wealth, th' occasion of his woes,
Far in the woods he sought a calm repose;
In caves and grottos, where the nymphs resort,
And keep with mountain Pan their sylvan court.
Ah! had he left his stupid soul behind!
But his condition alter'd not his mind.
For where high Tmolus rears his shady brow,
And from his cliffs surveys the seas below,
In his descent, by Sardis bounded here,
By the small confines of Hypæpa there,
Pan to the nymphs his frolic ditties play'd,
Tuning his reeds beneath the chequer'd shade.
The nymphs are pleas'd, the boasting sylvan plays,
And speaks with slight of great Apollo's lays.
Tmolus was arbiter; the boaster still
Accepts the trial with unequal skill.
The venerable judge was seated high
On his own hill, that seem'd to touch the sky.
Above the whisp'ring trees his head he rears,
From their encumb'ring boughs to free his ears;
A wreath of oak alone his temples bound,
The pendant acorns loosely dangled round.
"In me your judge," says he, "there's no delay:"
Then bids the goatherd god begin, and play.
Pan tun'd the pipe, and with his rural song
Pleas'd the low taste of all the vulgar throng;
Such songs a vulgar judgment mostly please,
Midas was there, and Midas judg'd with these.
The mountain sire with grave deportment now
To Phœbus turns his venerable brow:
And, as he turns, with him the listening wood
In the same posture of attention stood.
The god his own Parnassian laurel crown'd,
And in a wreath his golden tresses bound,
Graceful his purple mantle swept the ground.
High on the left his iv'ry lute he rais'd,
The lute, emboss'd with glitt'ring jewels, blaz'd.
In his right hand he nicely held the quill,
His easy posture spoke a master's skill.
The strings he touch'd with more than human art,
Which pleas'd the judge's ear, and sooth'd his heart;
Who soon judiciously the palm decreed,
And to the lute postpon'd the squeaking reed.
All, with applause, the rightful sentence heard,
Midas alone dissatisfied appear'd,
To him unjustly giv'n the judgment seems,
For Pan's barbaric notes he most esteems.
The lyric god, who thought his untun'd ear
Deserv'd but ill a human form to wear,
Of that deprives him, and supplies the place
With some more fit, and of an ampler space:
Fix'd on his noddle an unseemly pair,
Flagging, and large, and full of whitish hair;

Without a total change from what he was,
Still in the man preserves the simple ass.
He, to conceal the scandal of the deed,
A purple turban folds about his head;
Veils the reproach from public view, and fears
The laughing world would spy his monstrous ears.
One trusty barber-slave, that us'd to dress
His master's hair, when lengthen'd to excess,
The mighty secret knew, but knew alone,
And, though impatient, durst not make it known.
Restless, at last, a private place he found,
Then dug a hole, and told it to the ground;
In a low whisper he reveal'd the case,
And cover'd in the earth, and silent left the place.
In time, of trembling reeds a plenteous crop
From the confided furrow sprouted up;
Which, high advancing with the ripening year,
Made known the tiller, and his fruitless care:
For then the rustling blades, and whisp'ring wind,
To tell th' important secret both combin'd.

THE BUILDING OF TROY.

PHŒBUS, with full revenge, from Tmolus flies,
Darts through the air, and cleaves the liquid skies:
Near Hellespont he lights, and treads the plains
Where great Laomedon sole monarch reigns:
Where, built between the two projecting strands,
To Panomphæan Jove an altar stands.
Here first aspiring thoughts the king employ,
To found the lofty tow'rs of future Troy.
The work, from schemes magnificent begun,
At vast expense was slowly carry'd on:
Which Phœbus seeing, with the trident god
Who rules the swelling surges with his nod,
Assuming each a mortal shape, combine
At a set price to finish his design.
The work was built; the king their price denies,
And his injustice backs with perjuries.
This Neptune could not brook, but drove the main,
A mighty deluge, o'er the Phrygian plain:
'Twas all a sea; the waters of the deep
From ev'ry vale the copious harvest sweep;
The briny billows overflow the soil,
Ravage the fields, and mock the ploughman's toil.
Nor this appeas'd the god's revengeful mind,
For still a greater plague remains behind:
A huge sea-monster lodges on the sands,
And the king's daughter for his prey demands.
To him that sav'd the damsel, was decreed
A set of horses of the Sun's fine breed:
But when Alcides from the rock unty'd
The trembling fair, the ransom was deny'd.
He, in revenge, the new-built walls attack'd,
And the twice-perjur'd city bravely sack'd,
Telamon aided, and in justice shar'd
Part of the plunder as his due reward:
The princess, rescu'd late, with all her charms,
Hesione, was yielded to his arms:
For Peleus, with a goddess bride, was more
Proud of his spouse, than of his birth before:
Grandsons to Jove there might be more than one,
But he the goddess had enjoy'd alone.

THE STORY OF THETIS AND PELEUS, &c.

FOR Proteus thus to virgin Thetis said:
"Fair goddess of the waves, consent to wed,
And take some sprightly lover to your bed.
A son you'll have, the terrour of the field,
To whom in fame and pow'r his sire shall yield."
Jove, who ador'd the nymph with boundless love,
Did from his breast the dangerous flame remove.
He knew the fates, nor car'd to raise up one,
Whose fame and greatness should eclipse his own.
On happy Peleus he bestow'd her charms,
And bless'd his grandson in the goddess' arms.
A silent creek Thessalia's coast can show;
Two arms project, and shape it like a bow;
'Twould make a bay, but the transparent tide
Does scarce the yellow-gravel'd bottom hide;
For the quick eye may through the liquid wave
A firm unweedy level beach perceive.
A grove of fragrant myrtle near it grows,
Whose boughs, though thick, a beauteous grot disclose;
The well-wrought fabric, to discerning eyes,
Rather by art than nature seems to rise.
A bridled dolphin oft fair Thetis bore
To this her lov'd retreat, her fav'rite shore.
Here Peleus seiz'd her, slumb'ring while she lay,
And urg'd his suit with all that love could say:
But when he found her obstinately coy,
Resolv'd to force her, and command the joy;
The nymph, o'erpower'd, to art for succour flies,
And various shapes the eager youth surprise:
A bird she seems, but plies her wings in vain,
His hands the fleeting substance still detain:
A branchy tree high in the air she grew;
About its bark his nimble arms he threw:
A tiger next she glares with flaming eyes;
The frighten'd lover quits his hold, and flies:
The sea-gods he with sacred rites adores,
Then a libation on the ocean pours;
While the fat entrails crackle in the fire,
And sheets of smoke in sweet perfume aspire;
Till Proteus rising from his oozy bed,
Thus to the poor desponding lover said:
"No more in anxious thoughts your mind employ,
For yet you shall possess the dear expected joy.
You must once more th' unwary nymph surprise,
As in her cooly grot she slumb'ring lies;
Then bind her fast with unrelenting hands,
And strain her tender limbs with knotted bands.
Still hold her under ev'ry different shape,
Till tir'd she tries no longer to escape."
Thus he: then sunk beneath the glassy flood,
And broken accents flutter'd where he stood.
Bright Sol had almost now his journey done,
And down the steepy western convex run;
When the fair Nereid left the briny wave,
And, as she us'd, retreated to her cave.
He scarce had bound her fast, when she arose,
And into various shapes her body throws:
She went to move her arms, and found them ty'd;
Then with a sigh, "Some god assists ye," cry'd,
And in her proper shape stood blushing by his side.
About her waist his longing arms he flung,
From which embrace the great Achilles sprung.

THE TRANSFORMATION OF DÆDALION.

PELEUS unmix'd felicity enjoy'd;
(Blest in a valiant son, and virtuous bride)
Till fortune did in blood his hands imbrue,
And his own brother by curst chance he slew:
Then driven from Thessaly, his native clime,
Trachinia first gave shelter to his crime;
Where peaceful Ceyx mildly fill'd the throne,
And like his sire, the morning planet, shone;

But now, unlike himself, bedew'd with tears,
Mourning a brother lost, his brow appears.
First to the town with travel spent, and care,
Peleus and his small company repair:
His herds and flocks the while at leisure feed
On the rich pasture of a neighbouring mead.
The prince before the royal presence brought,
Show'd by the suppliant olive what he sought;
Then tells his name, and race, and country right,
But hides th' unhappy reason of his flight.
He begs the king some little town to give,
Where they may safe his faithful vassals live.
Ceyx reply'd, " To all my bounty flows,
A hospitable realm your suit has chose.
Your glorious race, and far-resounding fame,
And grandsire Jove, peculiar favours claim.
All you can wish, I grant; entreaties spare;
My kingdom (would 'twere worth the sharing) share."
Tears stopt his speech: astonish'd Peleus pleads
To know the cause from whence his grief proceeds.
The prince reply'd: " There's none of ye but deems
This hawk was ever such as now it seems;
Know 'twas a hero once, Dædalion nam'd,
For warlike deeds and haughty valour fam'd;
Like me to that bright luminary born,
Who wakes Aurora, and brings on the morn.
His fierceness still remains and love of blood,
Now dread of birds and tyrant of the wood.
My make was softer, peace my greatest care;
But this my brother wholly bent on war;
Late nations fear'd, and routed armies fled
That force, which now the tim'rous pigeons dread.
A daughter he possest, divinely fair,
And scarcely yet had seen her fifteenth year;
Young Chionè: a thousand rivals strove
To win the maid, and teach her how to love.
Phœbus and Mercury by chance one day
From Delphi and Cyllene past this way;
Together they the virgin saw: desire [fire.
At once warm'd both their breasts with am'rous
Phœbus resolv'd to wait till close of day;
But Mercury's hot love brook'd no delay;
With his entrancing rod the maid he charms,
And unresisted revels in her arms.
'Twas night, and Phœbus in a beldam's dress,
To the late rifled beauty got access.
Her time complete nine circling moons had run;
To either god she bore a lovely son:
To Mercury Autolycus she brought,
Who turn'd to thefts and tricks his subtile thought;
Possess'd he was of all his father's sleight, [white.
At will made white, look black, and black look
Philammon born to Phœbus, like his sire,
The Muses lov'd, and finely struck the lyre,
And made his voice and touch in harmony conspire.
In vain, fond maid, you boast this double birth,
The love of gods, and royal father's worth,
And Jove among your ancestors rehearse!
Could blessings such as these e'er prove a curse?
To her they did, who with audacious pride,
Vain of her own, Diana's charms decry'd.
Her taunts the goddess with resentment fill;
' My face you like not, you shall try my skill'
She said; and straight her vengeful bow she strung,
And sent a shaft that pierc'd her guilty tongue:
The bleeding tongue in vain its accents tries;
In the red stream her soul reluctant flies.
With sorrow wild I ran to her relief,
And try'd to moderate my brother's grief.
He, deaf as rocks by stormy surges beat,
Loudly laments, and hears me not entreat.
When on the fun'ral pile he saw her laid,
Thrice he to rush into the flames essay'd,
Thrice with officious care by us was stay'd.
Now, mad with grief, away he fled amain,
Like a stung heifer that resents the pain,
And bellowing wildly bounds along the plain.
O'er the most rugged ways so fast he ran,
He seem'd a bird already, not a man.
He left us breathless all behind; and now
In quest of death had gain'd Parnassus' brow:
But when from thence headlong himself he threw,
He fell not, but with airy pinions flew.
Phœbus in pity chang'd him to a fowl,
Whose crooked beak and claws the birds control,
Little of bulk, but of a warlike soul.
A hawk become, the feather'd race's foe,
He tries to ease his own by others' woe."

A WOLF TURNED INTO MARBLE.

While they astonish'd heard the king relate
These wonders of his hapless brother's fate;
The prince's herdsman at the court arrives,
And fresh surprise to all the audience gives.
" O Peleus, Peleus! dreadful news I bear,"
He said; and trembled as he spoke for fear.
The worst affrighted Peleus bid him tell,
Whilst Ceyx too grew pale with friendly zeal.
Thus he began: " When Sol mid-heav'n had gain'd,
And half his way was past, and half remain'd,
I to the level shore my cattle drove,
And let them freely in the meadows rove.
Some stretch'd at length admire the watery plain,
Some crop'd the herb, some wanton swam the main.
A temple stands of antic make hard by,
Where no gilt domes nor marble lure the eye;
Unpolish'd rafters bear its lowly height,
Hid by a grove, as ancient, from the sight.
Here Nereus, and the Nereids they adore;
I learnt it from the man who thither bore
His net, to dry it on the sunny shore.
Adjoins a lake, enclos'd with willows round,
Where swelling waves have overflow'd the mound,
And, muddy, stagnate on the lower ground.
From thence a rushing noise increasing flies,
Strikes the still shore, and frights us with surprise.
Straight a huge wolf rush'd from the marshy wood,
His jaws besmear'd with mingled foam and blood.
Though equally by hunger urg'd, and rage,
His appetite he minds not to assuage;
Nought that he meets his rapid fury spares,
But the whole herd with mad disorder tears.
Some of our men who strove to drive him thence,
Torn by his teeth, have dy'd in their defence.
The echoing lakes, the sea, and fields and shore,
Impurpled blush with streams of reeking gore.
Delay is loss, nor have we time for thought;
While yet some few remain alive, we ought
To seize our arms, and with confederate force
Try if we so can stop his bloody course."
But Peleus car'd not for his ruin'd herd;
His crime he call'd to mind, and thence inferr'd,
That Psamathe's revenge this havoc made,
In sacrifice to murder'd Phocus' shade.
The king commands his servants to their arms,
Resolv'd to go; but the loud noise alarms

His lovely queen, who from her chamber flew,
And her half-plaited hair behind her threw:
About his neck she hung with loving fears,
And now with words, and now with pleading tears,
Entreated that he'd send his men alone,
And stay himself, to save two lives in one.
Then Peleus: "Your just fears, O queen, forget;
Too much the offer leaves me in your debt.
No arms against the monster I shall bear,
But the sea-nymphs appease with humble pray'r."
The citadel's high turrets pierce the sky,
Which home-bound vessels, glad, from far descry:
This they ascend, and thence with sorrow ken
The mangled heifers lie, and bleeding men;
Th' inexorable ravager they view,
With blood discolour'd, still the rest pursue:
There Peleus pray'd submissive towards the sea,
And deprecates the ire of injur'd Psamathè.
But deaf to all his pray'rs the nymph remain'd,
Till Thetis for her spouse the boon obtain'd.
Pleas'd with the luxury, the furious beast,
Unstopp'd, continues still his bloody feast:
While yet upon a sturdy bull he flew,
Chang'd by the nymph, a marble block he grew.
No longer dreadful now the wolf appears,
Bury'd in stone, and vanish'd like their fears.
Yet still the Fates unhappy Peleus vex'd;
To the Magnesian shore he wanders next.
Acastus there, who rul'd the peaceful clime,
Grants his request, and expiates his crime.

THE STORY OF CEYX AND ALCYONE.

By Mr. Dryden.

THESE prodigies affect the pious prince;
But more perplex'd with those that happen'd since,
He purposes to seek the Clarian god,
Avoiding Delphi, his more fam'd abode,
Since Phrygian robbers made unsafe the road.
Yet could he not from her he lov'd so well,
The fatal voyage, he resolv'd, conceal;
But when she saw her lord prepar'd to part,
A deadly cold ran shiv'ring to her heart;
Her faded cheeks are chang'd to boxen hue,
And in her eyes the tears are ever new.
She thrice essay'd to speak; her accents hung,
And falt'ring dy'd unfinish'd on her tongue,
Or vanish'd into sighs: with long delay
Her voice return'd, and found the wonted way.
"Tell me, my lord," she said, "what fault unknown
Thy once belov'd Alcyonè has done?
Whither, ah, whither, is thy kindness gone?
Can Ceyx then sustain to leave his wife,
And unconcern'd forsake the sweets of life?
What can thy mind to this long journey move?
Or need'st thou absence to renew thy love?
Yet if thou go'st by land, though grief possess
My soul ev'n then, my fears will be the less.
But ah! be warn'd to shun the watry way,
The face is frightful of the stormy sea:
For late I saw adrift disjointed planks,
And empty tombs erected on the banks.
Nor let false hopes to trust betray thy mind,
Because my sire in caves constrains the wind,
Can with a breath their clam'rous rage appease,
They fear his whistle, and forsake the seas:
Not so; for once indulg'd, they sweep the main;
Deaf to the call, or hearing, hear in vain;
But bent on mischief bear the waves before,
And not content with seas, insult the shore,
When ocean, air, and earth at once engage,
And rooted forests fly before their rage:
At once the clashing clouds to battle move,
And lightnings run across the fields above:
I know them well, and mark'd their rude comport,
While yet a child within my father's court:
In times of tempests they command alone,
And he but sits precarious on the throne:
The more I know, the more my fears augment;
And fears are oft prophetic of th' event.
But if not fears or reason will prevail,
If fate has fix'd thee obstinate to sail,
Go not without thy wife, but let me bear
My part of danger with an equal share,
And present, what I suffer only fear:
Then o'er the bounding billows shall we fly,
Secure to live together, or to die."
These reasons mov'd her starlike husband's heart,
But still he held his purpose to depart:
For as he lov'd her equal to his life,
He would not to the seas expose his wife;
Nor could be wrought his voyage to refrain,
But sought by arguments to sooth her pain:
Nor these avail'd; at length he lights on one,
With which so difficult a cause he won:
"My love, so short an absence cease to fear,
For by my father's holy flame I swear,
Before two moons their orb with light adorn,
If Heav'n allow me life, I will return."
This promise of so short a stay prevails;
He soon equips the ship, supplies the sails,
And gives the word to lanch; she trembling views
This pomp of death, and parting tears renews:
Last with a kiss, she took a long farewel,
Sigh'd, with a sad presage, and swooning fell:
While Ceyx seeks delays, the lusty crew,
Rais'd on their banks, their oars in order drew
To their broad breasts, the ship with fury flew.
The queen recover'd, rears her humid eyes,
And first her husband on the poop espies,
Shaking his hand at distance on the main;
She took the sign, and shook her hand again.
Still as the ground recedes, contracts her view
With sharpen'd sight, till she no longer knew
The much lov'd face; that comfort lost supplies
With less, and with the galley feeds her eyes:
The galley borne from view by rising gales,
She follow'd with her sight the flying sails:
When ev'n the flying sails were seen no more,
Forsaken of all sight she left the shore.
Then on her bridal bed her body throws,
And sought in sleep her wearied eyes to close:
Her husband's pillow, and the widow'd part
Which once he press'd, renew'd the former smart.
And now a breeze from shore began to blow,
The sailors ship their oars, and cease to row;
Then hoist their yards a-trip, and all their sails
Let fall, to court the wind, and catch the gales:
By this the vessel half her course had run,
And as much rested till the rising Sun;
Both shores were lost to sight, when at the close
Of day a stiffer gale at east arose;
The sea grew white, the rolling waves from far,
Like heralds, first denounce the watry war.
This seen, the master soon began to cry,
"Strike, strike the top-sail; let the main sheet fly,
And furl your sails:" the winds repel the sound,
And in the speaker's mouth the speech is drown'd.

Yet of their own accord, as danger taught
Each in his way, officiously they wrought;
Some stow their oars, or stop the leaky sides;
Another bolder yet the yard bestrides,
And folds the sails; a fourth with labour laves
Th' intruding seas, and waves ejects on waves.
In this confusion while their work they ply,
The winds augment the winter of the sky,
And wage intestine wars; the suff'ring seas
Are toss'd, and mingled as their tyrants please.
The master would command, but in despair
Of safety, stands amaz'd with stupid care,
Nor what to bid, or what forbid he knows,
Th' ungovern'd tempest to such fury grows:
Vain is his force, and vainer is his skill;
With such a concourse comes the flood of ill;
The cries of men are mix'd with rattling shrowds;
Seas dash on seas, and clouds encounter clouds:
At once from east to west, from pole to pole,
The forky lightnings flash, the roaring thunders roll.
Now waves on waves ascending scale the skies,
And in the fires above the water fries:
When yellow sands are sifted from below,
The glittering billows give a golden show;
And when the fouler bottom spews the black,
The Stygian dye the tainted waters take:
Then frothy white appear the flatted seas,
And change their colour, changing their disease.
Like various fits the Thracian vessel finds:
And now sublime she rides upon the winds;
As from a lofty summit, looks from high,
And from the clouds beholds the nether sky;
Now from the depth of Hell they lift their sight,
And at a distance see superior light;
The lashing billows make a loud report,
And beat her sides, as batt'ring rams a fort;
Or as a lion bounding in his way,
With force augmented, bears against his prey,
Sidelong to seize; or unappall'd with fear,
Springs on the toils, and rushes on the spear:
So seas impell'd by winds, with added pow'r
Assault the sides, and o'er the hatches tow'r.
The planks (their pitchy cov'rings wash'd away)
Now yield; and now a yawning breach display:
The roaring waters with a hostile tide
Rush through the ruins of her gaping side.
Mean-time in sheets of rain the sky descends,
And ocean swell'd with waters upwards tends;
One rising, falling one, the Heav'ns and sea
Meet at their confines, in the middle way:
The sails are drunk with show'rs, and drop with rain,
Sweet waters mingle with the briny main.
No star appears to lend his friendly light;
Darkness and tempest make a double night;
But flashing fires disclose the deep by turns,
And while the lightnings blaze, the water burns.
Now all the waves their scatter'd force unite;
And as a soldier, foremost in the fight,
Makes way for others, and, an host alone,
Still presses on, and urging gains the town;
So while th' invading billows come a-breast,
The hero tenth advanc'd before the rest,
Sweeps all before him with impetuous sway,
And from the walls descends upon the prey;
Part following enter, part remain without,
With envy hear their fellows' conqu'ring shout,
And mount on others' backs, in hopes to share
The city, thus become the seat of war.
An universal cry resounds aloud,
The sailors run in heaps, a helpless crowd;
Art fails, and courage falls, no succour near;
As many waves, as many deaths appear.
One weeps, and yet despairs of late relief;
One cannot weep, his fears congeal his grief,
But stupid with dry eyes expects his fate:
One with loud shrieks laments his lost estate,
And calls those happy whom their fun'rals wait.
This wretch with pray'rs and vows the gods implores,
And ev'n the skies he cannot see, adores.
That other on his friends his thoughts bestows,
His careful father, and his faithful spouse.
The covetous worldling in his anxious mind,
Thinks only on the wealth he left behind.
All Ceyx his Alcyonè employs,
For her he grieves, yet in her absence joys:
His wife he wishes, and would still be near,
Not her with him, but wishes him with her:
Now with last looks he seeks his native shore,
Which fate has destin'd him to see no more;
He sought, but in the dark tempestuous night
He knew not whither to direct his sight.
So whirl the seas, such darkness blinds the sky,
That the black night receives a deeper dye.
The giddy ship ran round; the tempest tore
Her mast, and over-board the rudder bore.
One billow mounts, and with a scornful brow,
Proud of her conquest gain'd, insults the waves below:
Nor lighter falls, than if some giant tore
Pindus and Athos with the freight they bore,
And toss'd on seas; press'd with the pond'rous blow,
Down sinks the ship within th' abyss below:
Down with the vessel sink into the main
The many, never more to rise again.
Some few on scatter'd planks, with fruitless care,
Lay hold, and swim; but while they swim, despair.
Ev'n he who late a sceptre did command,
Now grasps a floating fragment in his hand:
And while he struggles on the stormy main,
Invokes his father, and his wife, in vain.
But yet his consort is his greatest care,
Alcyonè he names amidst his pray'r;
Names as a charm against the waves and wind:
Most in his mouth, and ever in his mind.
Tir'd with his toil, all hopes of safety past,
From pray'rs to wishes he descends at last;
That his dead body, wafted to the sands,
Might have its burial from her friendly hands.
As oft as he can catch a gulp of air,
And peep above the seas, he names the fair;
And ev'n when plung'd beneath, on her he raves,
Murm'ring "Alcyonè" below the waves:
At last a falling billow stops his breath,
Breaks o'er his head, and whelms him underneath.
Bright Lucifer unlike himself appears
That night, his heav'nly form obscur'd with tears,
And since he was forbid to leave the skies,
He muffled with a cloud his mournful eyes.
Mean-time Alcyonè (his fate unknown)
Computes how many nights he had been gone;
Observes the waning Moon with hourly view,
Numbers her age, and wishes for a new;
Against the promis'd time provides with care,
And hastens in the woof the robes he was to wear:
And for herself employs another loom,
New dress'd to meet her lord returning home,
Flatt'ring her heart with joys, that never were to come:

She fum'd the temples with an od'rous flame,
And oft before the sacred altars came,
To pray for him who was an empty name.
All pow'rs implor'd, but far above the rest
To Juno she her pious vows address'd,
Her much-lov'd lord from perils to protect,
And safe o'er seas his voyage to direct:
Then pray'd, that she might still possess his heart,
And no pretending rival share a part;
This last petition heard of all her pray'r,
The rest, dispers'd by winds, were lost in air.
But she, the goddess of the nuptial bed,
Tir'd with her vain devotions for the dead,
Resolv'd the tainted hand should be repell'd,
Which incense offer'd, and her altar held:
Then Iris thus bespoke; "Thou faithful maid,
By whom thy queen's commands are well convey'd,
Haste to the house of Sleep, and bid the god
Who rules the night by visions with a nod,
Prepare a dream, in figure and in form
Resembling him, who perish'd in the storm;
This form before Alcyonè present,
To make her certain of the sad event."
Indu'd with robes of various hue she flies,
And flying draws an arch (a segment of the skies):
Then leaves her bending bow, and from the steep
Descends, to search the silent house of Sleep.

THE HOUSE OF SLEEP.

NEAR the Cimmerians, in his dark abode,
Deep in a cavern, dwells the drowsy god;
Whose gloomy mansion nor the rising Sun,
Nor setting, visits, nor the lightsome noon;
But lazy vapours round the region fly,
Perpetual twilight, and a doubtful sky:
No crowing cock does there his wings display,
Nor with his horny bill provoke the day;
Nor watchful dogs, nor the more wakeful geese,
Disturb with nightly noise the sacred peace:
Nor beast of nature, nor the tame are nigh,
Nor trees with tempests rock'd, nor human cry;
But safe repose without an air of breath
Dwells here, and a dumb quiet next to death.
An arm of Lethe, with a gentle flow
Arising upwards from the rock below,
The palace moats, and o'er the pebbles creeps,
And with soft murmurs calls the coming sleeps.
Around its entry nodding poppies grow,
And all cool simples that sweet rest bestow;
Night from the plants their sleepy virtue drains,
And passing, sheds it on the silent plains:
No door there was th' unguarded house to keep,
On creaking hinges turn'd, to break his sleep.
But in the gloomy court was rais'd a bed,
Stuff'd with black plumes, and on an ebon stead:
Black was the cov'ring too, where lay the god,
And slept supine, his limbs display'd abroad:
About his head fantastic visions fly,
Which various images of things supply, [more,
And mock their forms; the leaves on trees not
Nor bearded ears in fields, nor sands upon the shore.
The virgin, ent'ring bright, indulg'd the day
To the brown cave, and brush'd the dreams away:
The god, disturb'd with this new glare of light
Cast sudden on his face, unseal'd his sight,
And rais'd his tardy head, which sunk again,
And sinking, on his bosom knock'd his chin;
At length shook off himself, and ask'd the dame,
(And asking yawn'd) for want intent she came.

To whom the goddess thus: "O sacred Rest,
Sweet pleasing Sleep, of all the pow'rs the best!
O peace of mind, repairer of decay, [day,
Whose balms renew the limbs to labours of the
Care shuns thy soft approach, and sullen flies
Adorn a dream, expressing human form, [away!
The shape of him who suffer'd in the storm,
And send it flitting to the Trachin court,
The wreck of wretched Ceyx to report:
Before his queen bid the pale spectre stand,
Who begs a vain relief at Juno's hand."
She said, and scarce awake her eyes could keep,
Unable to support the fumes of Sleep;
But fled, returning by the way she went,
And swerv'd along her bow with swift ascent.
The god, uneasy till he slept again,
Resolv'd at once to rid himself of pain;
And, though against his custom, call'd aloud,
Exciting Morpheus from the sleepy crowd:
Morpheus, of all his numerous train, express'd
The shape of man, and imitated best;
The walk, the words, the gesture could supply,
The habit mimic, and the mien belie;
Plays well, but all his action is confin'd,
Extending not beyond our human kind.
Another, birds, and beasts, and dragons apes,
And dreadful images, and monster shapes:
This demon, Icelos, in Heav'n's high hall
The gods have nam'd; but men Phobetor call.
A third is Phantasus, whose actions roll
On meaner thoughts, and things devoid of soul;
Earth, fruits, and flow'rs he represents in dreams,
And solid rocks unmov'd, and running streams.
These three to kings and chiefs their scenes dis-
The rest before th' ignoble commons play. [play,
Of these the chosen Morpheus is dispatch'd;
Which done, the lazy monarch, over-watch'd,
Down from his propping elbow drops his head,
Dissolv'd in sleep, and shrinks within his bed.
Darkling the demon glides, for flight prepar'd,
So soft, that scarce his fanning wings are heard.
To Trachin, swift as thought, the flitting shade
Thro' air his momentary journey made:
Then lays aside the steerage of his wings,
Forsakes his proper form, assumes the king's;
And pale as death, despoil'd of his array,
Into the queen's apartment takes his way,
And stands before the bed at dawn of day:
Unmov'd his eyes, and wet his beard appears;
And shedding vain, but seeming real tears;
The briny waters dropping from his hairs.
Then staring on her with a ghastly look,
And hollow voice, he thus the queen bespoke.
"Know'st thou not me? Not yet, unhappy
Or are my features perish'd with my life? [wife?
Look once again, and for thy husband lost,
Lo all that's left of him, thy husband's ghost!
Thy vows for my return were all in vain,
The stormy south o'ertook us in the main,
And never shalt thou see thy living lord again.
Bear witness, Heav'n, I call'd on thee in death,
And while I call'd, a billow stopp'd my breath.
Think not, that flying Fame reports my fate;
I present, I appear, and my own wreck relate.
Rise, wretched widow, rise; nor undeplor'd
Permit my soul to pass the Stygian ford;
But rise, prepar'd in black, to mourn thy perish'd lord."
Thus said the player-god; and adding art
Of voice and gesture, so perform'd his part,

She thought (so like her love the shade appears)
That Ceyx spake the words, that Ceyx shed the tears.
She groan'd, her inward soul with grief opprest,
She sigh'd, she wept, and sleeping beat her breast;
Then stretch'd her arms t'embrace his body bare;
Her clasping arms enclose but empty air;
At this, not yet awake, she cry'd, "O stay;
One is our fate, and common is our way!"
So dreadful was the dream, so loud she spoke,
That starting sudden up, the slumber broke:
Then cast her eyes around, in hope to view
Her vanish'd lord, and find the vision true:
For now the maids, who waited her commands,
Ran in with lighted tapers in their hands.
Tir'd with the search, not finding what she seeks,
With cruel blows she pounds her blubber'd cheeks;
Then from her beaten breast the linen tear,
And cut the golden caul that bound her hair.
Her nurse demands the cause; with louder cries
She prosecutes her griefs, and thus replies:
"No more Alcyonè; she suffer'd death
With her lov'd lord, when Ceyx lost his breath:
No flatt'ry, no false comfort, give me none,
My shipwreck'd Ceyx is for ever gone:
I saw, I saw him manifest in view,
His voice, his figure, and his gestures knew:
His lustre lost, and ev'ry living grace,
Yet I retain'd the features of his face:
Though with pale cheeks, wet beard, and dropping hair,
None but my Ceyx could appear so fair:
I would have strain'd him with a strict embrace,
But through my arms he slipt, and vanish'd from the place:
There, ev'n just there he stood;" and as she spoke,
Where last the spectre was she cast her look:
Fain would she hope, and gaz'd upon the ground,
If any printed footsteps might be found.
Then sigh'd, and said; "This I too well foreknew,
And my prophetic fears presag'd too true:
'Twas what I begg'd, when with a bleeding heart
I took my leave, and suffer'd thee to part;
Or I to go along, or thou to stay,
Never, ah never to divide our way!
Happier for me, that all our hours assign'd
Together we had liv'd; ev'n not in death disjoin'd!
So had my Ceyx still been living here,
Or with my Ceyx I had perish'd there:
Now I die absent, in the vast profound;
And me, without myself, the seas have drown'd.
The storms were not so cruel, should I strive
To lengthen life, and such a grief survive;
But neither will I strive, nor wretched thee
In death forsake, but keep thee company.
If not one common sepulchre contains
Our bodies, or one urn our last remains,
Yet Ceyx and Alcyonè shall join,
Their names remember'd in one common line."
No farther voice her mighty grief affords,
For sighs come rushing in betwixt her words,
And stopp'd her tongue; but what her tongue deny'd,
Soft tears, and groans, and dumb complaints supply'd.
'Twas morning; to the port she takes her way,
And stands upon the margin of the sea:
That place, that very spot of ground she sought,
Or thither by her destiny was brought,
Where last he stood: and while she sadly said,
"'Twas here he left me, ling'ring here delay'd
His parting kiss, and there his anchors weigh'd;"
Thus speaking, while her thoughts past actions trace,
And call to mind, admonish'd by the place,
Sharp at her utmost ken she cast her eyes,
And somewhat floating from afar descries:
It seem'd a corpse adrift to distant sight,
But at a distance who could judge aright?
It wafted nearer yet, and then she knew,
That what before she but surmis'd, was true:
A corpse it was, but whose it was, unknown;
Yet mov'd, howe'er, she made the case her own:
Took the bad omen of a shipwreck'd man,
As for a stranger wept, and thus began:
"Poor wretch, on stormy seas to lose thy life,
Unhappy thou, but more thy widow wife."
At this she paus'd: for now the flowing tide
Had brought the body nearer to the side:
The more she looks, the more her fears increase,
At nearer sight; and she's herself the less.
Now driv'n ashore, and at her feet it lies,
She knows too much, in knowing whom she sees:
Her husband's corpse; at this she loudly shrieks,
"'Tis he, 'tis he," she cries, and tears her cheeks,
Her hair, and vest; and stooping to the sands,
About his neck she cast her trembling hands.
"And is it thus, O dearer than my life,
Thus, thus return'st thou to thy longing wife!"
She said, and to the neighbouring mole she strode,
(Rais'd there to break th' incursions of the flood.)
Headlong from hence to plunge herself she springs,
But shoots along, supported on her wings;
A bird new made, about the banks she plies,
Not far from shore, and short excursions tries;
Nor seeks in air her humble flight to raise,
Content to skim the surface of the seas:
Her bill, though slender, sends a creaking noise,
And imitates a lamentable voice.
Now lighting where the bloodless body lies,
She with a fun'ral note renews her cries:
At all her stretch, her little wings she spread,
And with her feather'd arms embrac'd the dead:
Then flick'ring to his pallid lips, she strove
To print a kiss, the last essay of love.
Whether the vital touch reviv'd the dead,
Or that the moving waters rais'd his head
To meet the kiss, the vulgar doubt alone;
For sure a present miracle was shown.
The gods their shapes to winter-birds translate,
But both obnoxious to their former fate.
Their conjugal affection still is ty'd,
And still the mournful race is multiply'd:
They bill, they tread; Alcyonè compress'd,
Sev'n days sits brooding on her floating nest:
A wintry queen: her sire at length is kind,
Calms ev'ry storm, and hushes ev'ry wind;
Prepares his empire for his daughter's ease,
And for his hatching nephews smooths the seas.

ÆSACUS TRANSFORMED INTO A CORMORANT.

THESE some old man sees wanton in the air,
And praises the unhappy constant pair.
Then to his friend the long-neck'd corm'rant shows,
The former tale reviving others' woes:
"That sable bird," he cries, "which cuts the flood
With slender legs, was once of royal blood;
His ancestors from mighty Tros proceed,
The brave Laomedon and Ganymede,
(Whose beauty tempted Jove to steal the boy)
And Priam, hapless prince! who fell with Troy:

Himself was Hector's brother, and (had Fate
But giv'n this hopeful youth a longer date)
Perhaps had rival'd warlike Hector's worth,
Though on the mother's side of meaner birth;
Fair Alyxothoè, a country maid,
Bare Æsacus by stealth in Ida's shade.
He fled the noisy town, and pompous court,
Lov'd the lone hills, and simple rural sport,
And seldom to the city would resort.
Yet he no rustic clownishness profest,
Nor was soft love a stranger to his breast:
The youth had long the nymph Hesperiè woo'd,
Oft through the thicket or the mead pursu'd:
Her haply on her father's bank he spy'd,
While fearless she her silver tresses dry'd;
Away she fled: not stags with half such speed,
Before the prowling wolf, scud o'er the mead;
Not ducks, when they the safer flood forsake,
Pursu'd by hawks, so swift regain the lake;
As fast he follow'd in the hot career;
Desire the lover wing'd, the virgin fear.
A snake unseen now pierc'd her heedless foot;
Quick thro' the veins the venom'd juices shoot:
She fell, and 'scap'd by death his fierce pursuit.
Her lifeless body, frighted, he embrac'd,
And cry'd, 'Not this I dreaded, but thy haste:
O had my love been less, or less thy fear!
The victory, thus bought, is far too dear.
Accursed snake! yet I more curs'd than he!
He gave the wound; the cause was giv'n by me.
Yet none shall say, that unreveng'd you dy'd.
He spoke; then climb'd a cliff's o'er-hanging side,
And, resolute, leap'd on the foaming tide.
Tethys receiv'd him gently on the wave;
The death he sought deny'd, and feathers gave.
Debarr'd the surest remedy of grief,
And forc'd to live, he curs'd th' unask'd relief.
Then on his airy pinions upwards flies,
And at a second fall successless tries;
The downy plume a quick descent denies.
Enrag'd, he often dives beneath the wave,
And there in vain expects to find a grave.
His ceaseless sorrow for the unhappy maid
Meager'd his look, and on his spirits prey'd.
Still near the sounding deep he lives; his name
From frequent diving and emerging came."

OVID'S METAMORPHOSES.

BOOK XII.

Translated by Mr. Dryden.

THE TROJAN WAR.

PRIAM, to whom the story was unknown,
As dead, deplor'd his metamorphos'd son:
A cenotaph his name and title kept,
And Hector round the tomb, with all his brothers wept.
This pious office Paris did not share,
Absent alone; and author of the war,
Which for the Spartan queen, the Grecians drew
T'avenge the rape, and Asia to subdue.
A thousand ships were mann'd, to sail the sea;
Nor had their just resentments found delay,
Had not the winds and waves oppos'd their way.
At Aulis, with united pow'rs they meet,
But there, cross winds or calms detain'd the fleet.
Now, while they raise an altar on the shore,
And Jove with solemn sacrifice adore;
A boding sign the priests and people see:
A snake of size immense ascends a tree,
And in the leafy summit spy'd a nest,
Which o'er her callow young a sparrow press'd.
Eight were the birds unfledg'd; their mother flew,
And hover'd round her care; but still in view:
Till the fierce reptile first devour'd the brood;
Then seiz'd the flutt'ring dam, and drunk her blood.
This dire ostent the fearful people view;
Calchas alone, by Phœbus taught, foreknew
What Heav'n decreed; and with a smiling glance,
Thus gratulates to Greece her happy chance.
"O Argives, we shall conquer: Troy is ours,
But long delays shall first afflict our pow'rs:
Nine years of labour the nine birds portend;
The tenth shall in the town's destruction end."
The serpent, who his maw obscene had fill'd,
The branches in his curl'd embraces held:
But, as in spires he stood, he turn'd to stone:
The stony snake retain'd the figure still his own.
Yet, not for this, the wind-bound navy weigh'd;
Slack were their sails; and Neptune disobey'd.
Some thought him loth the town should be destroy'd,
Whose building had his hands divine employ'd:
Not so the seer, who knew, and known foreshow'd,
The virgin Phœbe with a virgin's blood
Must first be reconcil'd: the common cause
Prevail'd; and pity yielding to the laws,
Fair Iphigenia, the devoted maid,
Was, by the weeping priests, in linen robes array'd.
All mourn her fate; but no relief appear'd;
The royal victim bound, the knife already rear'd:
When that offended pow'r, who caus'd their woe,
Relenting ceas'd her wrath, and stopp'd the coming blow.
A mist before the ministers she cast,
And, in the virgin's room, a hind she plac'd.
Th' oblation slain, and Phœbe reconcil'd,
The storm was hush'd, and dimpled ocean smil'd:
A favourable gale arose from shore,
Which to the port desir'd the Græcian gallies bore.

THE HOUSE OF FAME.

FULL in the midst of this created space,
Betwixt Heav'n, earth, and seas, there stands a place,
Confining on all three, with triple bound;
Whence all things, though remote, are view'd around,
And thither bring their undulating sound.
The palace of loud Fame, her seat of pow'r,
Plac'd on the summit of a lofty tow'r;
A thousand winding entries long and wide,
Receive of fresh reports a flowing tide.
A thousand crannies in the walls are made:
Nor gate, nor bars exclude the busy trade.
'Tis built of brass, the better to diffuse
The spreading sounds, and multiply the news:
Where echoes in repeated echoes play,
A mart for ever full, and open night and day.
Nor silence is within, nor voice express,
But a deaf noise of sounds, that never cease.
Confus'd, and chiding, like the hollow roar
Of tides receding from th' insulted shore;
Or like the broken thunder heard from far,
When Jove to distance drives the rolling war.
The courts are fill'd with a tumultuous din
Of crowds, or issuing forth, or ent'ring in:
A thoroughfare of news: where some devise
Things never heard, some mingle truth with lies;

The troubled air with empty sounds they beat,
Intent to hear, and eager to repeat.
Errour sits brooding there, with added train
Of vain credulity, and joys as vain:
Suspicion, with sedition join'd, are near,
And rumours rais'd, and murmurs mix'd, and panic fear.
Fame sits aloft, and sees the subject ground,
And seas about, and skies above; inquiring all around.
The goddess gives th' alarm; and soon is known
The Grecian fleet descending on the town.
Fix'd on defence, the Trojans are not slow
To guard their shore from an expected foe.
They meet in fight: by Hector's fatal hand
Protesilaus falls, and bites the strand
Which with expense of blood the Grecians won,
And prov'd the strength unknown of Priam's son;
And to their cost the Trojan leaders felt
The Grecian heroes; and what deaths they dealt.

THE STORY OF CYGNUS.

FROM these first onsets, the Sigæan shore
Was strew'd with carcases, and stain'd with gore:
Neptunian Cygnus troops of Greeks had slain;
Achilles in his car had scour'd the plain,
And clear'd the Trojan ranks: where'er he fought,
Cygnus, or Hector, through the fields he sought:
Cygnus he found; on him his force essay'd:
For Hector was to the tenth year delay'd.
His white-maned steeds, that bow'd beneath the yoke,
He cheer'd to courage, with a gentle stroke;
Then urg'd his fiery chariot on the foe;
And rising shook his lance, in act to throw.
But first he cry'd, "O youth, be proud to bear
Thy death, ennobled by Pelides' spear."
The lance pursu'd the voice without delay,
Nor did the whizzing weapon miss the way;
But pierc'd his cuirass, with such fury sent,
And sign'd his bosom with a purple dint.
At this the seed of Neptune, goddess-born,
"For ornament, not use, these arms are worn;
This helm, and heavy buckler, I can spare;
As only decorations of the war:
So Mars is arm'd for glory, not for need.
'Tis somewhat more from Neptune to proceed,
Than from a daughter of the sea to spring:
Thy sire is mortal; mine is ocean's king.
Secure of death, I should contemn thy dart,
Though naked; and impassible depart."
He said, and threw: the trembling weapon pass'd
Through nine bull-hides, each under other plac'd,
On his broad shield; and stuck within the last.
Achilles wrench'd it out; and sent again
The hostile gift: the hostile gift was vain.
He try'd a third, a tough well-chosen spear;
Th' inviolable body stood sincere,
Though Cygnus then did no defence provide,
But scornful offer'd his unshielded side.
Not otherwise th' impatient hero far'd,
Than as a bull, incompass'd with a guard,
Amid the circus roars, provok'd from far
By sight of scarlet, and a sanguine war:
They quit their ground, his bended horns elude;
In vain pursuing, and in vain pursu'd.
Before to farther fight he would advance,
He stood considering, and survey'd his lance.
Doubts if he wielded not a wooden spear
Without a point; he look'd, the point was there.
"This is my hand, and this my lance," he said,
"By which so many thousand foes are dead.
O whither is their usual virtue fled!
I had it once; and the Lyrnessian wall,
And Tenedos, confess'd it in their fall.
Thy streams, Caïcus, roll'd a crimson flood;
And Thebes ran red with her own natives' blood.
Twice Telephus employ'd their piercing steel,
To wound him first, and afterwards to heal.
The vigour of this arm was never vain:
And that my wonted prowess I retain,
Witness these heaps of slaughter on the plain."
He said; and doubtful of his former deeds,
To some new trial of his force proceeds.
He chose Menætes from among the rest;
At him he lanch'd his spear, and pierc'd his breast:
On the hard earth the Lycian knock'd his head,
And lay supine; and forth the spirit fled.
Then thus the hero: "Neither can I blame
The hand, or jav'lin; both are still the same.
The same I will employ against this foe,
And wish but with the same success to throw."
So spoke the chief; and while he spoke he threw;
The weapon with unerring fury flew,
At his left shoulder aim'd: nor entrance found;
But back, as from a rock, with swift rebound
Harmless return'd: a bloody mark appear'd,
Which with false joy the flatter'd hero cheer'd.
Wound there was none; the blood that was in view,
The lance before from slain Menætes drew.
Headlong he leaps from off his lofty car,
And in close fight on foot renews the war.
Raging with high disdain, repeats his blows:
Nor shield, nor armour can their force oppose;
Huge cantlets of his buckler strew the ground,
And no defence in his bor'd arms is found.
But on his flesh no wound or blood is seen;
The sword itself is blunted on the skin.
This vain attempt the chief no longer bears;
But round his hollow temples and his ears
His buckler beats: the son of Neptune, stunn'd
With these repeated buffets, quits his ground;
A sickly sweat succeeds, and shades of night;
Inverted nature swims before his sight:
Th' insulting victor presses on the more,
And treads the steps the vanquish'd trod before,
Nor rest, nor respite gives. A stone there lay
Behind his trembling foe, and stopp'd his way:
Achilles took th' advantage which he found,
O'erturn'd, and push'd him backward on the ground.
His buckler held him under, while he press'd,
With both his knees, above his panting breast;
Unlac'd his helm: about his chin the twist
He ty'd; and soon the strangled soul dismiss'd.
With eager haste he went to strip the dead:
The vanish'd body from his arm was fled.
His sea-god sire, t' immortalize his fame,
Had turn'd it to the bird that bears his name.
A truce succeeds the labours of this day,
And arms suspended with a long delay.
While Trojan walls are kept with watch and ward,
The Greeks before their trenches mount the guard.
The feast approach'd; when to the blue-ey'd maid
His vows for Cygnus slain the victor paid,
And a white heifer on her altar laid.
The reeking entrails on the fire they threw,
And to the gods the grateful odour flew.
Heav'n had its part in sacrifice: the rest
Was broil'd and roasted for the future feast.

The chief-invited guests were set around,
And hunger first assuag'd, the bowls were crown'd,
Which in deep draughts their cares and labours drown'd.
The mellow harp did not their ears employ;
And mute was all the warlike symphony:
Discourse, the food of souls, was their delight,
And pleasing chat prolong'd the summer's night.
The subjects, deeds of arms; and valour shown,
Or on the Trojan side, or on their own.
Of dangers undertaken, fame achiev'd,
They talk'd by turns; the talk by turns reliev'd.
What things but these could fierce Achilles tell,
Or what could fierce Achilles hear so well?
The last great act perform'd, of Cygnus slain,
Did most the martial audience entertain:
Wond'ring to find a body free by fate
From steel; and which could even that steel re- [bate:
Amaz'd, their admiration they renew;
And scarce Pelides could believe it true.

THE STORY OF CÆNEUS.

Then Nestor thus: "What once this age has [known,
In fated Cygnus, and in him alone,
These eyes have seen in Cæneus long before;
Whose body not a thousand swords could bore.
Cæneus, in courage, and in strength, excell'd;
And still his Othrys with his fame is fill'd:
But what did most his martial deeds adorn,
(Though since he chang'd his sex) a woman born."
A novelty so strange, and full of fate,
His list'ning audience ask'd him to relate.
Achilles thus commends their common suit:
"O father, first for prudence in repute,
Tell, with that eloquence, so much thy own,
What thou hast heard, or what of Cæneus known:
What was he, whence his change of sex begun,
What trophies, join'd in wars with thee, he won?
Who conquer'd him, and in what fatal strife
The youth, without a wound, could lose his life?"
Neleides then: "Though tardy age, and time,
Have shrunk my sinews, and decay'd my prime;
Though much I have forgotten of my store,
Yet not exhausted, I remember more.
Of all that arms achiev'd, or peace design'd,
That action still is fresher in my mind
Than aught beside. If reverend age can give
To faith a sanction, in my third I live.
"'Twas in my second cent'ry, I survey'd
Young Cænis, then a fair Thessalian maid:
Cænis the bright was born to high command;
A princess, and a native of thy land,
Divine Achilles: every tongue proclaim'd
Her beauty, and her eyes all hearts inflam'd.
Peleus, thy sire, perhaps had sought her bed,
Among the rest; but he had either led
Thy mother then, or was by promise ty'd;
But she to him, and all, alike her love deny'd.
"It was her fortune once to take her way
Along the sandy margin of the sea:
The pow'r of ocean view'd her as she pass'd,
And, lov'd as soon as seen, by force embrac'd.
So Fame reports. Her virgin-treasure seiz'd,
And his new joys, the ravisher so pleas'd,
That thus, transported, to the nymph he cry'd;
'Ask what thou wilt, no pray'r shall be deny'd.'
This also Fame relates: the haughty fair,
Who not the rape ev'n of a god could bear,
This answer, proud, return'd; 'To mighty wrongs
A mighty recompense, of right, belongs.
Give me no more to suffer such a shame;
But change the woman, for a better name;
One gift for all:' she said; and while she spoke,
A stern, majestic, manly tone she took.
A man she was: and as the godhead swore,
To Cæneus turn'd, who Cænis was before.
"To this the lover adds, without request,
No force of steel should violate his breast.
Glad of the gift, the new-made warrior goes;
And arms among the Greeks, and longs for equal foes.

THE SKIRMISH BETWEEN THE CENTAURS AND LAPITHITES.

"Now brave Pirithous, bold Ixion's son,
The love of fair Hippodamè had won.
The cloud-begotten race, half men, half beast,
Invited, came to grace the nuptial feast:
In a cool cave's recess the treat was made,
Whose entrance trees with spreading boughs o'ershade.
They sat: and summon'd by the bridegroom, came,
To mix with those, the Lapithæan name.
Nor wanted I: the roofs with joy resound:
And 'Hymen, Iö Hymen,' rung around.
Rais'd altars shone with holy fires; the bride,
Lovely herself (and lovely by her side
A bevy of bright nymphs, with sober grace)
Came glitt'ring like a star, and took her place.
Her heav'nly form beheld, all wish'd her joy;
And little wanted, but in vain, their wishes all employ.
"For one, most brutal of the brutal brood,
Or whether wine or beauty fired his blood,
Or both at once, beheld with lustful eyes
The bride; at once resolv'd to make his prize.
Down went the board; and fast'ning on her hair,
He seiz'd with sudden force the frighted fair.
'Twas Eurytus began: his bestial kind
His crime pursu'd; and each, as pleas'd his mind,
Or her, whom chance presented, took: the feast
An image of a taken town express'd.
"The cave resounds with female shrieks; we rise,
Mad with revenge to make a swift reprise:
And Theseus first, 'What phrenzy has possess'd,
O Eurytus,' he cry'd, 'thy brutal breast,
To wrong Pirithous, and not him alone,
But while I live, two friends conjoin'd in one?'
"To justify his threat, he thrusts aside
The crowd of Centaurs; and redeems the bride.
The monster nought reply'd: for words were vain,
And deeds could only deeds unjust maintain;
But answers with his hand, and forward press'd,
With blows redoubled, on his face and breast.
An ample goblet stood, of antick mold,
And rough with figures of the rising gold;
The hero snatch'd it up, and toss'd in air
Full at the front of the foul ravisher.
He falls; and falling vomits forth a flood
Of wine, and foam, and brains, and mingled blood.
Half roaring, and half neighing through the hall,
'Arms, arms,' the double-form'd with fury call;
To wreak their brother's death: a medley flight
Of bowls, and jars, at first supply the fight,
Once instruments of feasts, but now of fate;
Wine animates their rage, and arms their hate.
"Bold Amycus from the robb'd vestry brings
The chalices of Heav'n, and holy things
Of precious weight: a sconce that hung on high,
With tapers fill'd, to light the sacristy,

Torn from the cord, with his unhallow'd hand
He threw amid the Lapithæan band.
On Celadon the ruin fell; and left
His face of feature and of form bereft:
So, when some brawny sacrificer knocks,
Before an altar led, an offer'd ox,
His eye-balls rooted out, are thrown to ground;
His nose, dismantled, in his mouth is found;
His jaws, cheeks, front, one undistinguish'd wound.
"This, Belates, th' avenger, could not brook;
But, by the foot, a marble board he took,
And hurl'd at Amycus; his chin it bent
Against his chest, and down the Centaur sent:
Whom sputt'ring bloody teeth, the second blow
Of his drawn sword dispatch'd to shades below.
"Grineus was near; and cast a furious look
On the side-altar, cens'd with sacred smoke,
And bright with flaming fires; 'The gods,' he cry'd,
'Have with their holy trade our hands supply'd:
Why use we not their gifts?' Then from the floor
An altar stone he heav'd, with all the load it bore.
Altar, and altar's freight together flew,
Where thickest throng'd the Lapithæan crew:
And, at once, Broteas and Oryus slew.
Oryus' mother, Mycalè, was known
Down from her sphere to draw the lab'ring Moon
"Exadius cry'd, 'Unpunish'd shall not go
This fact, if arms are found against the foe.'
He look'd about, where on a pine were spread
The votive horns of a stag's branching head:
At Grineus these he throws; so just they fly,
That the sharp antlers stuck in either eye:
Breathless, and blind he fell; with blood besmear'd;
His eye-balls beaten out, hung dangling on his beard.
Fierce Rhætus from the hearth a burning brand
Selects, and whirling waves; till, from his hand
The fire took flame; then dash'd it from the right,
On fair Charaxus' temples, near the sight:
The whistling pest came on, and pierc'd the bone,
And caught the yellow hair, that shrivel'd while it shone:
Caught like dry stubble fir'd; or like sear wood;
Yet from the wound ensu'd no purple flood;
But look'd a bubbling mass of frying blood.
His blazing locks sent forth a crackling sound;
And hiss'd, like red-hot ir'n within the smithy drown'd.
The wounded warrior shook his flaming hair,
Then (what a team of horse could hardly rear)
He heaves the threshold-stone, but could not throw;
The weight itself forbad the threaten'd blow;
Which dropping from his lifted arms, came down
Full on Cometes' head; and crush'd his crown.
Nor Rhætus then retain'd his joy; but said,
'So by their fellows may our foes be sped;'
Then with redoubled strokes he plies his head.
The burning lever not deludes his pains,
But drives the batter'd skull within the brains.
"Thus flush'd, the conqueror, with force renew'd,
Evagrus, Dryas, Corythus, pursu'd:
First, Corythus, with downy cheeks, he slew;
Whose fall when fierce Evagrus had in view,
He cry'd, 'What palm is from a beardless prey?'
Rhætus prevents what more he had to say;
And drove within his mouth the fiery death,
Which enter'd hissing in, and chok'd his breath.
At Dryas next he flew: but weary chance
No longer wou'd the same success advance:
For while he whirl'd in fiery circles round
The brand, a sharpen'd stake strong Dryas found,
And in the shoulder's joint inflicts the wound.
The weapon stuck; which roaring out with pain,
He drew; nor longer durst the fight maintain,
But turn'd his back, for fear; and fled amain.
With him fled Orneus, with like dread possess'd;
Thaumas, and Medon wounded in the breast;
And Mermeros, in the late race renown'd,
Now limping ran, and tardy with his wound.
Pholus and Melaneus from fight withdrew,
And Abas maim'd, who boars encountering slew:
And augur Astylos, whose art in vain
From fight dissuaded the four-footed train,
Now beat the hoof with Nessus on the plain;
But to his fellow cry'd, 'Be safely slow,
Thy death deferr'd is due to great Alcides' bow.'
"Mean time strong Dryas urg'd his chance so well,
That Lycidas, Areos, Imbreus fell;
All, one by one, and fighting face to face.
Crenæus fled, to fall with more disgrace:
For, fearful, while he look'd behind, he bore,
Betwixt his nose and front, the blow before.
Amid the noise, and tumult of the fray,
Snoring, and drunk with wine, Aphidas lay.
Ev'n then the bowl within his hand he kept,
And on a bear's rough hide securely slept.
Him Phorbas with his flying dart transfix'd;
'Take thy next draught with Stygian waters mix'd,
And sleep thy fill,' th' insulting victor cry'd;
Surpris'd with death unfelt, the Centaur dy'd;
The ruddy vomit, as he breath'd his soul,
Repass'd his throat, and fill'd his empty bowl.
"I saw Petræus' arms employ'd around
A well-grown oak, to root it from the ground.
This way, and that, he wrench'd the fibrous bands;
The trunk was like a sapling, in his hands,
And still obey'd the bent: while thus he stood,
Pirithous' dart drove on, and nail'd him to the wood;
Lycus and Chromis fell, by him oppress'd;
Helops and Dictys added to the rest
A nobler palm: Helops, through either ear
Transfix'd, receiv'd the penetrating spear.
This Dictys saw; and, seiz'd with sudden fright,
Leapt headlong from the hill of steepy height;
And crush'd an ash beneath, that could not bear his weight.
The shatter'd tree receives his fall; and strikes,
Within his full-blown paunch, the sharpen'd spikes.
Strong Aphareus had heav'd a mighty stone,
The fragment of a rock; and would have thrown;
But Theseus, with a club of harden'd oak,
The cubit-bone of the bold Centaur broke,
And left him maim'd; nor seconded the stroke.
Then leapt on tall Bianor's back; (who bore
No mortal burden but his own, before)
Press'd with his knees his sides; the double man,
His speed with spurs increas'd, unwilling ran.
One hand the hero fasten'd on his locks;
His other ply'd him with repeated strokes.
The club rung round his ears, and batter'd brows;
He falls; and lashing up his heels, his rider throws.
"The same Herculean arms Nedymnus wound;
And lay by him Lycotas on the ground.
And Hippasus, whose beard his breast invades;
And Ripheus, hunter of the woodland shades:

And Tereus, us'd with mountain bears to strive,
And from their dens to draw th' indignant beasts alive.
"Demoleon could not bear this hateful sight,
Or the long fortune of th' Athenian knight:
But pull'd with all his force, to disengage
From earth a pine, the product of an age:
The root stuck fast: the broken trunk he sent
At Theseus; Theseus frustrates his intent,
And leaps aside; by Pallas warn'd, the blow
To shun: (for so he said; and we believ'd it so.)
Yet not in vain th' enormous weight was cast:
Which Crantor's body sunder'd at the waist:
Thy father's squire, Achilles, and his care;
Whom conquer'd in the Pelopeian war,
Their king, his present ruin to prevent,
A pledge of peace implor'd, to Peleus sent.
"Thy sire, with grieving eyes, beheld his fate;
And cry'd, 'Not long, lov'd Crantor, shalt thou wait
Thy vow'd revenge.' At once he said, and threw
His ashen spear; which quiver'd as it flew,
With all his force, and all his soul apply'd;
The sharp point enter'd in the Centaur's side:
Both hands, to wrench it out, the monster join'd;
And wrench'd it out; but left the steel behind;
Stuck in his lungs it stood: enrag'd he rears
His hoofs, and down to ground thy father bears.
Thus trampled under foot, his shield defends
His head; his other hand the lance protends.
Ev'n while he lay extended on the dust,
He sped the Centaur, with one single thrust.
Two more his lance before transfix'd from far;
And two, his sword had slain, in closer war.
To these was added Dorylas, who spread
A bull's two goring horns around his head.
With these he push'd, in blood already dy'd;
Him fearless I approach'd; and thus defy'd:
'Now, monster, now, by proof it shall appear,
Whether thy horns are sharper, or my spear.'
At this, I threw: for want of other ward,
He lifted up his hand, his front to guard.
His hand it pass'd; and fix'd it to his brow:
Loud shouts of ours attend the lucky blow.
Him Peleus finish'd, with a second wound,
Which through the navel pierc'd: he reel'd around;
And dragg'd his dangling bowels on the ground:
Trod what he dragg'd; and what he trod, he crush'd:
And to his mother-earth, with empty belly rush'd.

THE STORY OF CYLLARUS AND HYLONOME.

"NOR could thy form, O Cyllarus, foreslow
Thy fate; (if form to monsters men allow:)
Just bloom'd thy beard, thy beard of golden hue:
Thy locks, in golden waves, about thy shoulders flew.
Sprightly thy look; thy shapes in ev'ry part
So clean, as might instruct the sculptor's art,
As far as man extended: where began
The beast, the beast was equal to the man.
Add but a horse's head and neck; and he,
O Castor, was a courser worthy thee.
So was his back proportion'd for the seat:
So rose his brawny chest; so swiftly mov'd his feet.
Coal-black his colour, but like jet it shone:
His legs and flowing tail were white alone.
Belov'd by many maidens of his kind;
But fair Hylonomè possess'd his mind;
Hylonomè, for features, and for face,
Excelling all the nymphs of double race:
Nor less her blandishments, than beauty, move;
At once both loving, and confessing love.
For him she dress'd: for him, with female care
She comb'd, and set in curl, her auburn hair.
Of roses, violets, and lilies mix'd,
And sprigs of flowing rosemary betwixt,
She form'd the chaplet, and adorn'd her front:
In waters of the Pegasæan fount,
And in the streams that from the fountain play,
She wash'd her face; and bath'd her twice a day.
The scarf of furs, that hung below her side,
Was ermin, or the panther's spotted pride;
Spoils of no common beast: with equal flame
They lov'd: their sylvan pleasures were the same:
All day they hunted: and when day expir'd,
Together to some shady cave retir'd:
Invited to the nuptials, both repair;
And side by side, they both engage in war.
"Uncertain from what hand, a flying dart
At Cyllarus was sent; which pierc'd his heart.
The jav'lin drawn from out the mortal wound,
He faints with stagg'ring steps, and seeks the ground:
The fair within her arms receiv'd his fall,
And strove his wand'ring spirits to recall:
And while her hand the streaming blood oppos'd,
Join'd face to face, his lips with hers she clos'd.
Stifled with kisses, a sweet death he dies;
She fills the fields with undistinguish'd cries;
At least her words were in her clamour drown'd;
For my stunn'd ears receive no vocal sound.
In madness of her grief, she seiz'd the dart
New-drawn and reeking from her lover's heart;
To her bare bosom the sharp point apply'd;
And wounded fell; and falling by his side,
Embrac'd him in her arms; and thus embracing dy'd.
"Ev'n still methinks I see Phæocomes;
Strange was his habit, and as odd his dress.
Six lions' hides, with thongs together fast,
His upper part defended to his waist:
And where man ended, the continued vest
Spread on his back the houss and trappings of a beast.
A stump too heavy for a team to draw,
(It seems a fable, though the fact I saw,)
He threw at Pholon; the descending blow
Divides the scull, and cleaves his head in two.
The brains, from nose, and mouth, and either ear,
Came issuing out, as through a colander
The curdled milk; or from the press the whey,
Driv'n down by weights above, is drain'd away.
"But him, while stooping down to spoil the slain,
Pierc'd through the paunch, I tumbled on the plain.
Then Chthonius and Teleboas I slew:
A fork the former arm'd; a dart his fellow threw.
The jav'lin wounded me; (behold the scar.)
Then was my time to seek the Trojan war;
Then I was Hector's match in open field;
But he was then unborn; at least a child:
Now, I am nothing. I forbear to tell
By Periphantas how Pyretus fell;
The Centaur by the knight: nor will I stay
On Amphyx, or what deaths he dealt that day:
What honour, with a pointless lance, he won,
Stuck in the front of a four-footed man:
What fame young Macareus obtain'd in fight:
Or dwell on Nessus, now return'd from flight:

How prophet Mopsus not alone divin'd,
Whose valour equall'd his foreseeing mind.

CÆNEUS TRANSFORMED TO AN EAGLE.

"ALREADY Cæneus, with his conquering hand,
Had slaughter'd five the boldest of their band,
Pyrachmus, Helymus, Antimachus,
Bromus the brave, and stronger Stiphelus.
Their names I number'd, and remember well,
To trace remaining, by what wounds they fell.
"Latreus, the bulkiest of the double race,
Whom the spoil'd arms of slain Halesus grace;
In years retaining still his youthful might,
Though his black hairs were interspers'd with white,
Betwixt th' imbattled ranks began to prance,
Proud of his helm, and Macedonian lance;
And rode the ring around; that either host
Might hear him, while he made this empty boast.
'And from a strumpet shall we suffer shame?
For Cænis still, not Cæneus, is thy name:
And still the native softness of thy kind
Prevails, and leaves the woman in thy mind;
Remember what thou wert; what price was paid
To change thy sex; to make thee not a maid,
And but a man in show: go, card and spin;
And leave the business of the war to men.'
"While thus the boaster exercis'd his pride,
The fatal spear of Cæneus reach'd his side:
Just in the mixture of the kinds it ran;
Betwixt the nether beast, and upper man:
The monster mad with rage, and stung with smart,
His lance directed at the hero's heart:
It struck; but bounded from his harden'd breast,
Like hail from tiles, which the safe house invest.
Nor seem'd the stroke with more effect to come,
Than a small pebble falling on a drum.
He next his falchion try'd, in closer fight;
But the keen falchion had no power to bite.
He thrust; the blunted point return'd again:
'Since downright blows,' he cry'd, 'and thrusts are vain,
I'll prove his side;' in strong embraces held
He prov'd his side; his side the sword repell'd:
His hollow belly echo'd to the stroke,
Untouch'd his body, as a solid rock;
Aim'd at his neck at last, the blade in shivers broke.
"Th' impassive knight stood idle to deride
His rage, and offer'd oft his naked side;
At length, 'Now, monster, in thy turn,' he cry'd,
'Try thou the strength of Cæneus:' at the word
He thrust; and in his shoulder plung'd the sword.
Then writh'd his hand; and as he drove it down,
Deep in his breast, made many wounds in one.
"The Centaurs saw, enrag'd, th' unhop'd success;
And rushing on in crowds, together press;
At him, and him alone, their darts they threw:
Repuls'd they from his fated body flew.
Amaz'd they stood; till Monychus began,
'O shame, a nation conquer'd by a man!
A woman-man! yet more a man is he,
Than all our race; and what he was, are we.
Now, what avail our nerves? th' united force
Of two the strongest creatures, man and horse?
Nor goddess-born, nor of Ixion's seed
We seem; (a lover built for Juno's bed;)
Master'd by this half man. Whole mountains throw
With woods at once, and bury him below.
This only way remains. Nor need we doubt
To choke the soul within; though not to force it out;
Heap weights, instead of wounds.' He chanc'd to see
Where southern storms had rooted up a tree;
This, rais'd from earth, against the foe he threw;
Th' example shown, his fellow-brutes pursue.
With forest-loads the warrior they invade;
Othrys and Pelion soon were void of shade;
And spreading groves were naked mountains made.
Press'd with the burden, Cæneus pants for breath;
And on his shoulders bears the wooden death.
To heave th' intolerable weight he tries;
At length it rose above his mouth and eyes:
Yet still he heaves; and struggling with despair,
Shakes all aside, and gains a gulp of air:
A short relief, which but prolongs his pain;
He faints by fits; and then respires again:
At last, the burden only nods above,
As when an earthquake stirs th' Idæan grove.
Doubtful his death: he suffocated seem'd,
To most; but otherwise our Mopsus deem'd;
Who said he saw a yellow bird arise
From out the piles, and cleave the liquid skies:
I saw it too, with golden feathers bright;
Nor ere before beheld so strange a sight.
Whom Mopsus viewing, as it soar'd around
Our troop, and heard the pinions' rattling sound,
'All hail,' he cry'd, 'thy country's grace and love!
Once first of men below, now first of birds above.'
Its author to the story gave belief;
For us, our courage was increas'd by grief:
Asham'd to see a single man, pursu'd
With odds, to sink beneath a multitude,
We push'd the foe: and forc'd to shameful flight,
Part fell, and part escap'd by favour of the night."

THE FATE OF PERICLYMENOS.

THIS tale, by Nestor told, did much displease
Tlepolemus, the seed of Hercules:
For often he had heard his father say,
That he himself was present at the fray;
And more than shar'd the glories of the day.
"Old Chronicle," he said, "among the rest,
"You might have nam'd Alcides at the least:
Is he not worth your praise?" The Pylian prince
Sigh'd ere he spoke; then made this proud defence.
"My former woes, in long oblivion drown'd,
I would have lost; but you renew the wound:
Better to pass him o'er, than to relate
The cause I have your mighty sire to hate.
His fame has fill'd the world, and reach'd the sky;
(Which, oh, I wish, with truth I could deny!)
We praise not Hector; though his name, we know,
Is great in arms; 'tis hard to praise a foe.
"He, your great father, levell'd to the ground
Messenia's tow'rs: nor better fortune found
Elis, and Pylos; that a neighb'ring state,
And this my own: both guiltless of their fate.
"To pass the rest, twelve, wanting one, he slew;
My brethren, who their birth from Neleus drew,
All youths of early promise, had they liv'd;
By him they perish'd: I alone surviv'd.
The rest were easy conquest: but the fate
Of Periclymenos is wond'rous to relate.

To him, our common grandsire of the main
Had giv'n to change his form, and chang'd, resume again.
Vary'd at pleasure, every shape he try'd;
And in all beasts Alcides still defy'd:
Vanquish'd on Earth, at length he soar'd above;
Chang'd to the bird, that bears the bolt of Jove:
The new-dissembled eagle, now endu'd
With beak and pounces, Hercules pursu'd,
And cuff'd his manly cheeks, and tore his face;
Then, safe retir'd, and tow'r'd in empty space.
Alcides bore not long his flying foe;
But bending his inevitable bow,
Reach'd him in air, suspended as he stood:
And in his pinion fix'd the feather'd wood.
Light was the wound; but in the sinew hung
The point, and his disabled wing unstrung.
He wheel'd in air, and stretch'd his vans in vain:
His vans no longer could his flight sustain:
For while one gather'd wind, one unsupply'd
Hung drooping down, nor pois'd his other side.
He fell: the shaft that slightly was impress'd,
Now from his heavy fall with weight increas'd,
Drove thro' his neck, aslant; he spurns the ground,
And the soul issues through the weazon's wound.
"Now, brave commander of the Rhodian seas,
What praise is due from me to Hercules?
Silence is all the vengeance I decree
For my slain brothers; but 'tis peace with thee."
Thus with a flowing tongue old Nestor spoke:
Then, to full bowls each other they provoke:
At length, with weariness, and wine oppress'd,
They rise from table; and withdraw to rest.

THE DEATH OF ACHILLES.

THE sire of Cygnus, monarch of the main,
Meantime, laments his son, in battle slain,
And vows the victor's death; nor vows in vain.
For nine long years the smother'd pain he bore;
(Achilles was not ripe for fate before:)
Then when he saw the promis'd hour was near,
He thus bespoke the god, that guides the year.
"Immortal offspring of my brother Jove;
My brightest nephew, and whom best I love,
Whose hands were join'd with mine, to raise the wall
Of tott'ring Troy, now nodding to her fall,
Dost thou not mourn our pow'r employ'd in vain;
And the defenders of our city slain?
To pass the rest, could noble Hector lie
Unpity'd, dragg'd around his native Troy?
And yet the murd'rer lives: himself by far
A greater plague, than all the wasteful war:
He lives; the proud Pelides lives, to boast
Our town destroy'd, our common labour lost.
O, could I meet him! But I wish too late:
To prove my trident is not in his fate!
But let him try (for that's allow'd) thy dart,
And pierce his only penetrable part."
Apollo bows to the superior throne;
And to his uncle's anger, adds his own.
Then in a cloud involv'd, he takes his flight,
Where Greeks and Trojans mix'd in mortal fight;
And found out Paris, lurking where he stood,
And stain'd his arrows with plebeian blood:
Phœbus to him alone the god confess'd,
Then to the recreant knight he thus address'd.
"Dost thou not blush, to spend thy shafts in vain
On a degenerate, and ignoble train?
If fame, or better vengeance be thy care,
There aim: and, with one arrow, end the war."
He said; and show'd from far the blazing shield
And sword, which, but Achilles, none could wield;
And how he mov'd a god, and mow'd the standing field.
The deity himself directs aright
Th' invenom'd shaft; and wings the fatal flight.
Thus fell the foremost of the Grecian name;
And he, the base adult'rer, boasts the fame.
A spectacle to glad the Trojan train;
And please old Priam, after Hector slain.
If by a female hand he had foreseen
He was to die, his wish had rather been
The lance, and double axe of the fair warrior queen.
And now the terrour of the Trojan field,
The Grecian honour, ornament, and shield,
High on a pile th' unconquer'd chief is plac'd,
The god that arm'd him first, consum'd at last.
Of all the mighty man, the small remains
A little urn, and scarcely fill'd, contains.
Yet great in Homer, still Achilles lives;
And equal to himself, himself survives.
His buckler owns its former lord; and brings
New cause of strife, betwixt contending kings;
Who worthiest after him, his sword to wield,
Or wear his armour, or sustain his shield.
Ev'n Diomede sat mute, with down-cast eyes;
Conscious of wanted worth to win the prize:
Nor Menelaus presum'd these arms to claim,
Nor he the king of men, a greater name.
Two rivals only rose: Laertes' son,
And the vast bulk of Ajax Telamon:
The king, who cherish'd each with equal love,
And from himself all envy would remove,
Left both to be determin'd by the laws;
And to the Græcian chiefs transferr'd the cause.

OVID'S METAMORPHOSES.

BOOK XIII.

THE SPEECHES OF AJAX AND ULYSSES.

By Mr. Dryden.

THE chiefs were set; the soldiers crown'd the field:
To these the master of the seven-fold shield
Upstarted fierce: and kindled with disdain,
Eager to speak, unable to contain
His boiling rage, he roll'd his eyes around
The shore, and Græcian gallies haul'd aground.
Then stretching out his hands, "O Jove," he cry'd,
"Must then our cause before the fleet be try'd?
And dares Ulysses for the prize contend,
In sight of what he durst not once defend?
But basely fled that memorable day,
When I from Hector's hands redeem'd the flaming prey.
So much 'tis safer at the noisy bar
With words to flourish, than engage in war.
By diff'rent methods we maintain our right,
Nor am I made to talk, nor he to fight.
In bloody fields I labour to be great,
His arms are a smooth tongue, and soft deceit:
Nor need I speak my deeds, for those you see,
The Sun, and day, are witnesses for me.
Let him who fights unseen, relate his own,
And vouch the silent stars, and conscious Moon.

Great is the prize demanded, I confess,
But such an abject rival makes it less;
That gift, those honours, he but hop'd to gain,
Can leave no room for Ajax to be vain;
Losing he wins, because his name will be
Ennobled by defeat who durst contend with me.
Were my known valour question'd, yet my blood
Without that plea would make my title good:
My sire was Telamon, whose arms, employ'd
With Hercules, these Trojan walls destroy'd;
And who before with Jason sent from Greece,
In the first ship brought home the golden fleece.
Great Telamon from Æacus derives
His birth (th' inquisitor of guilty lives
In shades below; where Sisyphus, whose son
This thief is thought, rolls up the restless heavy stone.)
Just Æacus, the king of gods above
Begot: thus Ajax is the third from Jove.
Nor should I seek advantage from my line,
Unless (Achilles) it was mix'd with thine:
As next of kin, Achilles' arms I claim;
This fellow would ingraft a foreign name
Upon our stock, and the Sisyphian seed
By fraud and theft asserts his father's breed:
Then must I lose these arms, because I came
To fight uncall'd, a voluntary name,
Nor shunn'd the cause, but offer'd you my aid?
While he long lurking was to war betray'd:
Forc'd to the field he came, but in the rear;
And feign'd distraction to conceal his fear;
'Till one more cunning caught him in the snare,
(Ill for himself) and dragg'd him into war.
Now let a hero's arms a coward vest,
And he who shunn'd all honours, gain the best:
And let me stand excluded from my right,
Robb'd of my kinsman's arms, who first appear'd in fight.
Better for us, at home had he remain'd,
Had it been true the madness which he feign'd,
Or so believ'd; the less had been our shame,
The less his counsell'd crime, which brands the Græcian name:
Nor Philoctetes had been left enclos'd,
In a bare isle, to wants and pains expos'd,
Where to the rocks, with solitary groans,
His suff'rings, and our baseness he bemoans:
And wishes (so may Heav'n his wish fulfil)
The due reward to him, who caus'd his ill.
Now he, with us to Troy's destruction sworn,
Our brother of the war, by whom are borne
Alcides' arrows, pent in narrow bounds,
With cold and hunger pinch'd, and pain'd with wounds,
To find him food and clothing, must employ
Against the birds the shafts due to the fate of Troy.
Yet still he lives, and lives from treason free,
Because he left Ulysses' company;
Poor Palamede might wish, so void of aid
Rather to have been left, than so to death betray'd.
The coward bore the man immortal spite,
Who sham'd him out of madness into fight:
Nor daring otherwise to vent his hate,
Accus'd him first of treason to the state;
And then for proof produc'd the golden store,
Himself had hidden in his tent before:
Thus of two champions he depriv'd our host,
By exile one, and one by treason lost.
Thus fights Ulysses, thus his fame extends,
A formidable man but to his friends:
Great, for what greatness is in words, and sound,
Ev'n faithful Nestor less in both is found:
But that he might without a rival reign,
He left this faithful Nestor on the plain;
Forsook his friend ev'n at his utmost need,
Who tir'd, and tardy with his wounded steed,
Cry'd out for aid, and call'd him by his name;
But cowardice has neither ears nor shame;
Thus fled the good old man, bereft of aid,
And, for as much as lay in him, betray'd:
That this is not a fable forg'd by me,
Like one of his, an Ulyssean lye,
I vouch ev'n Diomede, who though his friend,
Cannot that act excuse, much less defend:
He call'd him back aloud, and tax'd his fear;
And sure enough he heard, but durst not hear.
" The gods with equal eyes on mortals look,
He justly was forsaken, who forsook:
Wanted that succour, he refus'd to lend,
Found ev'ry fellow such another friend:
No wonder, if he roar'd that all might hear;
His elocution was increas'd by fear:
I heard, I ran, I found him out of breath,
Pale, trembling, and half-dead with fear of death.
Though he had judg'd himself by his own laws,
And stood condemn'd, I help'd the common cause;
With my broad buckler hid him from the foe;
(Ev'n the shield trembled as he lay below;)
And from impending fate the coward freed:
Good Heav'n forgive me for so bad a deed!
If still he will persist, and urge the strife,
First let him give me back his forfeit life:
Let him return to that opprobrious field;
Again creep under my protecting shield:
Let him lie wounded, let the foe be near,
And let his quiv'ring heart confess his fear;
There put him in the very jaws of fate;
And let him plead his cause in that estate:
And yet when snatch'd from death, when from below
My lifted shield I loos'd, and let him go;
Good Heav'ns, how light he rose, with what a bound
He sprung from earth, forgetful of his wound;
How fresh, how eager then his feet to ply:
Who had not strength to stand, had speed to fly!
" Hector came on, and brought the gods along;
Fear seiz'd alike the feeble and the strong:
Each Greek was an Ulysses; such a dread
Th' approach, and ev'n the sound of Hector bred:
Him, flush'd with slaughter, and with conquest crown'd,
I met, and over-turn'd him to the ground.
When after, matchless as he deem'd in might,
He challeng'd all our host to single fight;
All eyes were fix'd on me: the lots were thrown;
But for your champion I was wish'd alone:
Your vows were heard; we fought, and neither yield;
Yet I return'd unvanquish'd from the field.
With Jove to friend, th' insulting Trojan came,
And menac'd us with force, our fleet with flame.
Was it the strength of this tongue-valiant lord,
In that black hour, that sav'd you from the sword?
Or was my breast expos'd alone, to brave
A thousand swords, a thousand ships to save?
The hopes of your return! And can you yield,
For a sav'd fleet, less than a single shield?

Think it no boast, O Grecians, if I deem
These arms want Ajax, more than Ajax them:
Or, I with them an equal honour share;
They honour'd to be worn, and I to wear.
Will he compare my courage with his sleight?
As well he may compare the day with night.
Night is indeed the province of his reign:
Yet all his dark exploits no more contain
Than a spy taken, and a sleeper slain;
A priest made pris'ner, Pallas made a prey:
But none of all these actions done by day:
Nor aught of these was done, and Diomede away.
If on such petty merits you confer
So vast a prize, let each his portion share:
Make a just dividend; and if not all,
The greater part to Diomede will fall.
But why for Ithacus such arms as those,
Who naked, and by night invades his foes?
The glitt'ring helm by moonlight will proclaim
The latent robber, and prevent his game:
Nor could he hold his tott'ring head upright
Beneath that motion, or sustain the weight;
Nor that right arm could toss the beamy lance;
Much less the left that ampler shield advance,
Pond'rous with precious weight, and rough with cost
Of the round world in rising gold emboss'd.
That orb would ill become his hand to wield,
And look as for the gold he stole the shield;
Which, should your errour on the wretch bestow,
It would not frighten, but allure the foe:
Why asks he, what avails him not in fight,
And would but cumber, and retard his flight,
In which his only excellence is plac'd?
You give him death, that intercept his haste.
Add, that his own is yet a maiden-shield,
Nor the least dint has suffer'd in the field;
Guiltless of fight: mine batter'd, hew'd, and bor'd,
Worn out of service, must forsake its lord.
What farther need of words our right to scan?
My arguments are deeds, let action speak the man.
Since from a champion's arms the strife arose,
Go cast the glorious prize amid the foes;
Then send us to redeem both arms, and shield,
And let him wear, who wins them in the field."
He said: a murmur from a multitude,
Or somewhat like a stifled shout, ensu'd:
Till from his seat arose Laertes' son,
Look'd down awhile, and paus'd ere he begun;
Then, to th' expecting audience, rais'd his look,
And not without prepar'd attention spoke:
Soft was his tone, and sober was his face;
Action his words, and words his action grace.
"If Heav'n, my lords, had heard our common pray'r,
These arms had caus'd no quarrel for an heir;
Still great Achilles had his own possess'd,
And we with great Achilles had been bless'd:
But since hard fate, and Heav'n's severe decree,
Have ravish'd him away from you, and me,"
(At this he sigh'd, and wip'd his eyes, and drew,
Or seem'd to draw, some drops of kindly dew)
"Who better can succeed Achilles lost,
Than he, who gave Achilles to your host?
This only I request, that neither he
May gain, by being what he seems to be,
A stupid thing; nor I may lose the prize,
By having sense, which Heav'n to him denies:
Since great or small, the talent I enjoy'd
Was ever in the common cause employ'd;
Nor let my wit, and wonted eloquence,
Which often has been us'd in your defence,
And in my own, this only time be brought
To bear against myself, and deem'd a fault.
Make not a crime, where nature made it none;
For ev'ry man may freely use his own.
The deeds of long-descended ancestors
Are but by grace of imputation ours,
Theirs in effect; but since he draws his line
From Jove, and seems to plead a right divine;
From Jove, like him, I claim my pedigree,
And am descended in the same degree.
My sire Laertes was Arcesius' heir,
Arcesius was the son of Jupiter:
No parricide, no banish'd man, is known
In all my line: let him excuse his own.
Hermes ennobles too my mother's side,
By both my parents to the gods ally'd.
But not because that on the female part
My blood is better, dare I claim desert,
Or that my sire from parricide is free;
But judge by merit betwixt him and me:
The prize be to the best; provided yet
That Ajax for a while his kin forget,
And his great sire, and greater uncle's name,
To fortify by them his feeble claim;
Be kindred and relation laid aside,
And honour's cause by laws of honour try'd:
For if he plead proximity of blood,
That empty title is with ease withstood.
Peleus, the hero's sire, more nigh than he,
And Pyrrhus, his undoubted progeny,
Inherit first these trophies of the field;
To Scyros, or to Pthia, send the shield:
And Teucer has an uncle's right; yet he
Waves his pretensions, nor contends with me.
Then since the cause on pure desert is plac'd,
Whence shall I take my rise, what reckon last?
I not presume on ev'ry act to dwell,
But take these few in order as they fell.
"Thetis, who knew the fates, apply'd her care
To keep Achilles in disguise from war;
And till the threat'ning influence was past,
A woman's habit on the hero cast:
All eyes were cozen'd by the borrow'd vest,
And Ajax (never wiser than the rest)
Found no Pelides there. At length I came
With proffer'd wares to this pretended dame;
She, not discover'd by her mien, or voice,
Betray'd her manhood by her manly choice;
And while on female toys her fellows look,
Grasp'd in her warlike hand, a javelin shook:
Whom, by this act reveal'd, I thus bespoke:
'O goddess-born! resist not Heav'n's decree,
The fall of Ilium is reserv'd for thee.'
Then seiz'd him, and produc'd in open light,
Sent blushing to the field the fatal knight.
Mine then are all his actions of the war;
Great Telephus was conquer'd by my spear,
And after cur'd: to me the Thebans owe,
Lesbos, and Tenedos, their overthrow;
Scyros and Cylla. Not on all to dwell,
By me Lyrnessus, and strong Chrysa fell:
And since I sent the man who Hector slew,
To me the noble Hector's death is due.
Those arms I put into his living hand,
Those arms, Pelides dead, I now demand.

"When Greece was injur'd in the Spartan prince,
And met at Aulis to avenge th' offence,
'Twas a dead calm, or adverse blasts, that reign'd,
And in the port the wind-bound fleet detain'd:
Bad signs were seen, and oracles severe
Were daily thunder'd in our gen'ral's ear;
That by his daughter's blood we must appease
Diana's kindled wrath, and free the seas.
Affection, int'rest, fame, his heart assail'd:
But soon the father o'er the king prevail'd:
Bold, on himself he took the pious crime,
As angry with the gods, as they with him.
No subject could sustain their sov'reign's look,
Till this hard enterprise I undertook:
I only durst th' imperial pow'r control,
And undermin'd the parent in his soul;
Forc'd him t' exert the king for common good,
And pay our ransom with his daughter's blood.
Never was cause more difficult to plead,
Than where the judge against himself decreed:
Yet this I won by dint of argument;
The wrongs his injur'd brother underwent,
And his own office, sham'd him to consent.
" 'Twas harder yet to move the mother's mind,
And to this heavy task was I design'd:
Reasons against her love I knew were vain;
I circumvented whom I could not gain:
Had Ajax been employ'd, our slacken'd sails
Had still at Aulis waited happy gales.
" Arriv'd at Troy, your choice was fix'd on me,
A fearless envoy, fit for a bold embassy:
Secure, I enter'd through the hostile court,
Glitt'ring with steel, and crowded with resort:
There, in the midst of arms, I plead our cause,
Urge the foul rape, and violated laws;
Accuse the foes, as authors of the strife,
Reproach the ravisher, demand the wife.
Priam, Antenor, and the wiser few,
I mov'd; but Paris and his lawless crew
Scarce held their hands, and lifted swords; but stood
In act to quench their impious thirst of blood:
This Menelaus knows; expos'd to share
With me the rough preludium of the war.
" Endless it were to tell what I have done,
In arms, or council, since the siege begun:
The first encounters past, the foe repell'd,
They skulk'd within the town, we kept the field.
War seem'd asleep for nine long years; at length
Both sides resolv'd to push, we try'd our strength.
Now what did Ajax, while our arms took breath,
Vers'd only in the gross mechanic trade of death?
If you require my deeds, with ambush'd arms
I trapp'd the foe, or tir'd with false alarms;
Secur'd the ships, drew lines along the plain,
The fainting cheer'd, chastis'd the rebel-train:
Provided forage, our spent arms renew'd;
Employ'd at home, or sent abroad, the common cause pursu'd.
" The king, deluded in a dream by Jove,
Despair'd to take the town, and order'd to remove.
What subject durst arraign the pow'r supreme,
Producing Jove to justify his dream?
Ajax might wish the soldiers to retain
From shameful flight, but wishes were in vain:
As wanting of effect had been his words,
Such as of course his thund'ring tongue affords.
But did this boaster threaten, did he pray,
Or by his own example urge their stay?
None, none of these: but ran himself away.
I saw him run, and was asham'd to see;
Who ply'd his feet so fast to get aboard, as he?
Then speeding through the place, I made a stand,
And loudly cry'd, 'O base degenerate band,
To leave a town already in your hand!
After so long expense of blood, for fame,
To bring home nothing, but perpetual shame!'
These words, or what I have forgotten since,
(For grief inspir'd me then with eloquence)
Reduc'd their minds; they leave the crowded port,
And to their late forsaken camp resort.
Dismay'd the council met: this man was there,
But mute, and not recover'd of his fear:
Thersites tax'd the king, and loudly rail'd,
But his wide-opening mouth with blows I seal'd.
Then, rising, I excite their souls to fame,
And kindle sleeping virtue into flame.
From thence, whatever he perform'd in fight
Is justly mine, who drew him back from flight.
" Which of the Grecian chiefs consorts with thee?
But Diomede desires my company,
And still communicates his praise with me.
As guided by a god, secure he goes,
Arm'd with my fellowship, amid the foes:
And sure no little merit I may boast,
Whom such a man selects from such an host;
Unforc'd by lots I went without affright,
To dare with him the dangers of the night:
On the same errand sent, we met the spy
Of Hector, double-tongu'd, and us'd to lye;
Him I dispatch'd, but not till undermin'd,
I drew him first to tell what treach'rous Troy design'd:
My task perform'd, with praise I had retir'd,
But not content with this, to greater praise aspir'd:
Invaded Rhesus, and his Thracian crew,
And him, and his, in their own strength I slew;
Return'd a victor, all my vows complete,
With the king's chariot, in his royal seat.
Refuse me now his arms, whose fiery steeds
Were promis'd to the spy for his nocturnal deeds:
And let dull Ajax bear away my right,
When all his days out-balance this one night.
" Nor fought I darkling still: the Sun beheld
With slaughter'd Lycians when I strew'd the field:
You saw, and counted as I pass'd along,
Alastor, Chromius, Ceranos the strong,
Alcander, Prytanis, and Halius,
Neomon, Charopes, and Ennomus;
Coon, Chersidamas; and five beside,
Men of obscure descent, but courage try'd:
All these this hand laid breathless on the ground;
Nor want I proofs of many a manly wound:
All honest, all before. Believe not me;
Words may deceive, but credit what you see."
At this he bar'd his breast, and show'd his scars,
As of a furrow'd field, well plough'd with wars.
" Nor is this part unexercis'd," said he;
" That giant-bulk of his from wounds is free:
Safe in his shield he fears no foe to try,
And better manages his blood, than I:
But this avails me not; our boaster strove
Not with our foes alone, but partial Jove,
To save the fleet: this I confess is true,
(Nor will I take from any man his due:)
But thus assuming all, he robs from you.
Some part of honour to your share will fall,
He did the best indeed, but did not all.

Patroclus in Achilles' arms, and thought
The chief he seem'd, with equal ardour fought;
Preserv'd the fleet, repell'd the raging fire,
And forc'd the fearful Trojans to retire.
"But Ajax boasts, that he was only thought
A match for Hector, who the combat sought:
Sure he forgets the king, the chiefs, and me:
All were as eager for the fight, as he:
He but the ninth, and not by public voice,
Or ours preferr'd, was only Fortune's choice:
They fought; nor can our hero boast th' event,
For Hector from the field unwounded went.
"Why am I forc'd to name that fatal day,
That snatch'd the prop and pride of Greece away?
I saw Pelides sink, with pious grief,
And ran in vain, alas! to his relief;
For the brave soul was fled: full of my friend
I rush'd amid the war, his relics to defend:
Nor ceas'd my toil, till I redeem'd the prey,
And, loaded with Achilles, march'd away:
Those arms, which on these shoulders then I bore,
'Tis just you to these shoulders should restore.
You see I want not nerves, who could sustain
The pond'rous ruins of so great a man:
Or if in others equal force you find,
None is endu'd with a more grateful mind.
"Did Thetis then, ambitious in her care,
These arms thus labour'd for her son prepare;
That Ajax after him the heav'nly gift should wear?
For that dull soul to stare, with stupid eyes,
On the learn'd unintelligible prize!
What are to him the sculptures of the shield,
Heav'n's planets, earth, and ocean's watry field?
The Pleiads, Hyads; less, and greater Bear,
Undipp'd in seas; Orion's angry star;
Two diff'ring cities, grav'd on either hand;
Would he wear arms he cannot understand?
"Beside, what wise objections he prepares
Against my late accession to the wars?
Does not the fool perceive his argument
Is with more force against Achilles bent?
For if dissembling be so great a crime,
The fault is common, and the same in him:
And if he taxes both of long delay,
My guilt is less, who sooner came away.
His pious mother, anxious for his life,
Detain'd her son; and me, my pious wife.
To them the blossoms of our youth were due,
Our riper manhood we reserv'd for you.
But grant me guilty, 'tis not much my care,
When with so great a man my guilt I share:
My wit to war the matchless hero brought,
But by this fool I never had been caught.
"Nor need I wonder, that on me he threw
Such foul aspersions, when he spares not you;
If Palamede unjustly fell by me,
Your honour suffer'd in th' unjust decree:
I but accus'd, you doom'd: and yet he dy'd
Convinc'd of treason, and was fairly try'd:
You heard not he was false; your eyes beheld
The traitor manifest; the bribe reveal'd.
"That Philoctetes is on Lemnos left,
Wounded, forlorn, of human aid bereft,
Is not my crime, or not my crime alone;
Defend your justice, for the fact's your own:
'Tis true, th' advice was mine; that staying there
He might his weary limbs with rest repair,
From a long voyage free, and from a longer war.
He took the counsel, and he lives at least;
Th' event declares I counsell'd for the best:
Though faith is all in ministers of state:
For who can promise to be fortunate?
Now since his arrows are the fate of Troy,
Do not my wit, or weak address employ;
Send Ajax there, with his persuasive sense,
To mollify the man, and draw him thence:
But Xanthus shall run backward; Ida stand
A leafless mountain; and the Grecian band
Shall fight for Troy; if, when my counsel fail,
The wit of heavy Ajax can prevail.
"Hard Philoctetes, exercise thy spleen
Against thy fellows, and the king of men;
Curse my devoted head, above the rest,
And wish in arms to meet me breast to breast:
Yet I the dang'rous task will undertake,
And either die myself, or bring thee back.
"Nor doubt the same success, as when before
The Phrygian prophet to these tents I bore,
Surpris'd by night, and forc'd him to declare
In what was plac'd the fortune of the war,
Heav'n's dark decrees and answers to display,
And how to take the town, and where the secret lay.
Yet this I compass'd, and from Troy convey'd
The fatal image of their guardian-maid:
That work was mine; for Pallas, though our friend,
Yet while she was in Troy, did Troy defend.
Now what has Ajax done, or what design'd?
A noisy nothing, and an empty wind.
If he be what he promises in show,
Why was I sent, and why fear'd he to go?
Our boasting champion thought the task not light
To pass the guards, commit himself to night;
Not only through a hostile town to pass,
But scale, with steep ascent, the sacred place;
With wand'ring steps to search the citadel,
And from the priests their patroness to steal:
Then through surrounding foes to force my way,
And bear in triumph home the heav'nly prey;
Which had I not, Ajax in vain had held,
Before that monstrous bulk, his sev'n-fold shield.
That night to conquer Troy I might be said,
When Troy was liable to conquest made.
"Why point'st thou to my partner of the war?
Tydides had indeed a worthy share
In all my toil, and praise; but when thy might
Our ships protected, didst thou singly fight?
All join'd, and thou of many wert but one;
I ask'd no friend, nor had, but him alone:
Who had he not been well assur'd, that art
And conduct were of war the better part,
And more avail'd than strength, my valiant friend
Had urg'd a better right, than Ajax can pretend;
As good at least Eurypylus may claim,
And the more mod'rate Ajax of the name:
The Cretan king, and his brave charioteer,
And Menelaus bold with sword and spear:
All these had been my rivals in the shield,
And yet all these to my pretensions yield.
Thy boist'rous hands are then of use, when I
With this directing head those hands apply.
Brawn without brain is thine: my prudent care
Foresees, provides, administers the war:
Thy province is to fight; but when shall be
The time to fight, the king consults with me.
No dram of judgment with thy force is join'd:
Thy body is of profit, and my mind.

By how much more the ship her safety owes
To him who steers, than him that only rows;
By how much more the captain merits praise,
Than he who fights, and fighting but obeys;
By so much greater is my worth than thine,
Who canst but execute, what I design.
What gain'st thou, brutal man, if I confess
Thy strength superior, when thy wit is less?
Mind is the man: I claim my whole desert
From the mind's vigour, and th' immortal part.
"But you, O Grecian chiefs, reward my care,
Be grateful to your watchman of the war:
For all my labours in so long a space,
Sure I may plead a title to your grace.
Enter the town; I then unbarr'd the gates,
When I remov'd their tutelary fates.
By all our common hopes, if hopes they be
Which I have now reduc'd to certainty;
By falling Troy, by yonder tott'ring tow'rs,
And by their taken gods, which now are ours;
Or if there yet a farther task remains,
To be perform'd by prudence, or by pains;
If yet some desp'rate action rests behind,
That asks high conduct, and a dauntless mind;
If aught be wanting to the Trojan doom,
Which none but I can manage, and o'ercome,
Award, those arms I ask, by your decree:
Or give to this, what you refuse to me."
He ceas'd: and ceasing with respect he bow'd,
And with his hand at once the fatal statue show'd.
Heav'n, air and ocean rung, with loud applause,
And by the gen'ral vote he gain'd his cause.
Thus conduct won the prize, when courage fail'd,
And eloquence o'er brutal force prevail'd.

THE DEATH OF AJAX.

HE who could often, and alone, withstand
The foe, the fire, and Jove's own partial hand,
Now cannot his unmaster'd grief sustain,
But yields to rage, to madness, and disdain;
Then snatching out his falchion, "Thou," said [he,
"Art mine; Ulysses lays no claim to thee.
O often try'd, and ever-trusty sword,
Now do thy last kind office to thy lord:
'Tis Ajax who requests thy aid, to show
None but himself, himself could overthrow:"
He said, and with so good a will to die,
Did to his breast the fatal point apply:
It found his heart, a way till then unknown,
Where never weapon enter'd, but his own.
No hands could force it thence, so fix'd it stood,
Till out it rush'd, expell'd by streams of spouting
blood.
The fruitful blood produc'd a flow'r, which grew
On a green stem; and of a purple hue:
Like his, whom unaware Apollo slew:
Inscrib'd in both, the letters are the same,
But those express the grief, and these the name.

THE STORY OF POLYXENA AND HECUBA.

By Mr. Temple Stanyan.

THE victor with full sails for Lemnos stood,
(Once stain'd by matrons with their husbands' [blood,
Thence great Alcides' fatal shafts to bear
Assign'd to Philoctetes' secret care.
These with their guardian to the Greeks convey'd,
Their ten years toil with wish'd success repaid.
With Troy old Priam falls: his queen survives;
Till all her woes complete, transform'd she grieves
In borrow'd sounds, nor with an human face,
Barking tremendous o'er the plains of Thrace.
Still Ilium's flames their pointed columns raise,
And the red Hellespont reflects the blaze.
Shed on Jove's altar are the poor remains
Of blood, which trickled from old Priam's veins.
Cassandra lifts her hands to Heav'n in vain,
Dragg'd by her sacred hair; the trembling train
Of matrons to their burning temples fly:
There to their gods for kind protection cry;
And to their statues cling till forc'd away,
The victor Greeks bear off th' invidious prey.
From those high tow'rs, Astyanax is thrown,
Whence he was wont with pleasure to look down,
When oft his mother with a fond delight
Pointed to view his father's rage in fight,
To win renown, and guard his country's right.
The winds now call to sea; brisk northern gales
Sing in the shrouds, and court the spreading sails.
"Farewell, dear Troy," the captive matrons cry;
"Yes, we must leave our long-lov'd native sky."
Then prostrate on the shore they kiss the sand,
And quit the smoking ruins of the land.
Last Hecuba on board, sad sight! appears;
Found weeping o'er her children's sepulchres:
Dragg'd by Ulysses from her slaughter'd sons,
Whilst yet she graspt their tombs, and kist their
mould'ring bones.
Yet Hector's ashes from his urn she bore,
And in her bosom the sad relic wore:
Then scatter'd on his tomb her hoary hairs,
A poor oblation mingled with her tears.
Oppos'd to Ilium lie the Thracian plains,
Where Polymnestor safe in plenty reigns.
King Priam to his care commits his son,
Young Polydore, the chance of war to shun.
A wise precaution! had not gold, consign'd
For the child's use, debauch'd the tyrant's mind.
When sinking Troy to its last period drew,
With impious hands his royal charge he slew;
Then in the sea the lifeless corse is thrown,
As with the body he the guilt could drown.
The Greeks now riding on the Thracian shore,
Till kinder gales invite, their vessels moor.
Here the wide-op'ning earth to sudden view
Disclos'd Achilles, great as when he drew
The vital air, but fierce with proud disdain,
As when he sought Briseïs to regain;
When stern debate, and rash injurious strife,
Unsheath'd his sword, to reach Atrides' life.
"And will ye go?" he said: "is then the name
Of the once great Achilles lost to fame?
Yet stay, ungrateful Greeks; nor let me sue
In vain for honours to my manes due.
For this just end, Polyxena I doom
With victim-rites to grace my slighted tomb."
The phantom spoke; the ready Greeks obey'd,
And to the tomb led the devoted maid
Snatch'd from her mother, who with pious care
Cherish'd this last relief of her despair.
Superior to her sex, the fearless maid
Approach'd the altar, and around survey'd
The cruel rites, and consecrated knife,
Which Pyrrhus pointed at her guiltless life.
Then, as with stern amaze intent he stood,
"Now strike," she said; "now spill my gen'rous
blood;
Deep in my breast, or throat, your dagger
sheath,
Whilst thus I stand prepar'd to meet my death.

For life on terms of slav'ry I despise:
Yet sure no god approves this sacrifice.
O! could I but conceal this dire event
From my sad mother, I should die content.
Yet should she not with tears my death deplore,
Since her own wretched life demands them more.
But let not the rude touch of man pollute
A virgin-victim; 'tis a modest suit.
It best will please whoe'er demands my blood,
That I untainted reach the Stygian flood.
Yet let one short, last, dying prayer be heard,
To Priam's daughter pay this last regard;
'Tis Priam's daughter, not a captive, sues;
Do not the rites of sepulture refuse.
To my afflicted mother, I implore,
Free without ransom my dead corpse restore:
Nor barter me for gain, when I am cold;
But be her tears the price, if I am sold:
Time was she could have ransom'd me with gold."
Thus as she pray'd, one common shower of tears
Burst forth, and stream'd from ev'ry eye but hers.
Ev'n the priest wept, and with a rude remorse
Plung'd in her heart the steel's resistless force.
Her slacken'd limbs sunk gently to the ground,
Dauntless her looks, unalter'd by the wound.
And as she fell, she strove with decent pride
To guard, what suits a virgin's care to hide.
The Trojan matrons the pale corpse receive,
And the whole slaughter'd race of Priam grieve.
Sad they recount the long disastrous tale;
Then with fresh tears thee, royal maid, bewail;
Thy widow'd mother too, who flourish'd late
The royal pride of Asia's happier state:
A captive lot now to Ulysses borne;
Whom yet the victor would reject with scorn,
Were she not Hector's mother: Hector's fame
Scarce can a master for his mother claim!
With strict embrace the lifeless corse she view'd;
And her fresh grief that flood of tears renew'd,
With which she lately mourn'd so many dead;
Tears for her country, sons, and husband shed.
With the thick-gushing stream she bath'd the wound;
Kiss'd her pale lips; then welt'ring on the ground,
With wonted rage her frantic bosom tore;
Sweeping her hair amidst the clotted gore;
Whilst her sad accents thus her loss deplore.
"Behold a mother's last dear pledge of woe!
Yes, 'tis the last I have to suffer now.
Thou, my Polyxena, my ills must crown:
Already in thy fate I feel my own.
'Tis thus, lest haply of my numerous seed
One should unslaughter'd fall, even thou must bleed:
And yet I hop'd thy sex had been thy guard:
But neither has thy tender sex been spar'd.
The same Achilles, by whose deadly hate
Thy brothers fell, urg'd by untimely fate!
The same Achilles, whose destructive rage
Laid waste my realms, has robb'd my childless age.
When Paris' shafts with Phœbus' certain aid
At length had pierc'd this dreaded chief, I said,
Secure of future ills, 'He can no more:'
But see, he still pursues me as before.
With rage rekindled his dead ashes burn;
And his yet murd'ring ghost my wretched house must mourn.
This tyrant's lust of slaughter I have fed
With large supplies from my too-fruitful bed.
Troy's tow'rs lie waste; and the wide ruin ends
The public woe; but me fresh woe attends.
Troy still survives to me; to none but me;
And from its ills I never must be free.
I who so late had power, and wealth and ease,
Bless'd with my husband, and a large increase,
Must now in poverty an exile mourn;
Ev'n from the tombs of my dead offspring torn:
Giv'n to Penelope, who proud of spoil,
Allots me to the loom's ungrateful toil;
Points to her dames, and cries with scorning mien:
'See Hector's mother, and great Priam's queen!'
And thou, my child, sole hope of all that's lost,
Thou now art slain, to sooth his hostile ghost.
Yes, my child falls an offering to my foe!
Then what am I, who still survive this woe?
Say, cruel gods! for what new scenes of death
Must a poor aged wretch prolong this hated breath?
Troy fall'n, to whom could Priam happy seem?
Yet was he so; and happy must I deem
His death; for O! my child, he saw not thine,
When he his life did with his Troy resign.
Yet sure due obsequies thy tomb might grace;
And thou shalt sleep amidst thy kingly race.
Alas! my child, such fortune does not wait
Our suffering house in this abandon'd state,
A foreign grave, and thy poor mother's tears,
Are all the honours that attend thy hearse.
All now is lost!—Yet no; one comfort more
Of life remains, my much-lov'd Polydore,
My youngest hope: here on this coast he lives,
Nurs'd by the guardian-king, he still survives.
Then let me hasten to the cleansing flood,
And wash away these stains of guiltless blood."
Straight to the shore her feeble steps repair
With limping pace, and torn dishevell'd hair,
Silver'd with age. "Give me an urn," she cry'd,
"To bear back water from this swelling tide:"
When on the banks her son in ghastly hue
Transfix'd with Thracian arrows strikes her view.
The matrons shriek'd; her big-swoln grief surpass'd
The pow'r of utterance; she stood aghast;
She had nor speech, nor tears to give relief:
Excess of woe suppress'd the rising grief.
Lifeless as stone, on earth she fix'd her eyes;
And then look'd up to Heav'n with wild surprise.
Now she contemplates o'er with sad delight
Her son's pale visage; then her aking sight
Dwells on his wounds: she varies thus by turns,
Till with collected rage at length she burns,
Wild as the mother-lion, when among
The haunts of prey she seeks her ravish'd young:
Swift flies the ravisher; she marks his trace,
And by the print directs her anxious chase.
So Hecuba with mingled grief and rage
Pursues the king, regardless of her age.
She greets the murd'rer with dissembled joy
Of secret treasure hoarded for her boy.
The specious tale th' unwary king betray'd.
Fir'd with the hopes of prey: "Give quick," he said
With soft enticing speech, "the promis'd store:
Whate'er you give, you give to Polydore.
Your son, by the immortal gods I swear,
Shall this with all your former bounty share."
She stands attentive to his soothing lies,
And darts avenging horrour from her eyes.

Then full resentment fires her boiling blood:
She springs upon him, 'midst the captive crowd:
(Her thirst of vengeance want of strength supplies:)
Fastens her forky fingers in his eyes;
Tears out the rooted balls; her rage pursues,
And in the hollow orbs her hand imbrues.
The Thracians, fir'd at this inhuman scene,
With darts and stones assail the frantic queen.
She snarls, and growls, nor in an human tone,
Then bites impatient at the bounding stone;
Extends her jaws, as she her voice would raise
To keen invectives in her wonted phrase;
But barks, and thence the yelping brute betrays.
Still a sad monument the place remains,
And from this monstrous change its name obtains:
Where she, in long remembrance of her ills,
With plaintive howlings the wide desert fills.
Greeks, Trojans, friends, and foes, and gods above
Her num'rous wrongs to just compassion move.
Ev'n Juno's self forgets her ancient hate,
And owns she had deserv'd a milder fate.

THE FUNERAL OF MEMNON.

By Mr. Croxall.

YET bright Aurora, partial as she was
To Troy, and those that lov'd the Trojan cause,
Nor Troy, nor Hecuba can now bemoan,
But weeps a sad misfortune, more her own.
Her offspring Memnon, by Achilles slain,
She saw extended on the Phrygian plain:
She saw, and straight the purple beams, that grace
The rosy morning, vanish'd from her face;
A deadly pale her wonted bloom invades,
And veils the low'ring skies with mournful shades.
But when his limbs upon the pile were laid,
The last kind duty that by friends is paid,
His mother to the skies directs her flight,
Nor could sustain to view the doleful sight:
But frantic, with her loose neglected hair,
Hastens to Jove, and falls a suppliant there.
"O king of Heav'n, O father of the skies,"
The weeping goddess passionately cries,
"Though I the meanest of immortals am,
And fewest temples celebrate my fame,
Yet still a goddess, I presume to come
Within the verge of your ethereal dome:
Yet still may plead some merit, if my light
With purple dawn controls the pow'rs of night;
If from a female hand that virtue springs,
Which to the gods and men such pleasure brings.
Yet I nor honours seek, nor rites divine,
Nor for more altars, or more fanes repine;
Oh! that such trifles were the only cause,
From whence Aurora's mind its anguish draws!
For Memnon lost, my dearest only child,
With weightier grief my heavy heart is fill'd;
My warrior son! that liv'd but half his time,
Nipt in the bud, and blasted in his prime;
Who for his uncle early took the field,
And by Achilles' fatal spear was kill'd.
To whom but Jove should I for succour come?
For Jove alone could fix his cruel doom.
O sov'reign of the gods, accept my pray'r,
Grant my request, and sooth a mother's care;
On the deceas'd some solemn boon bestow,
To expiate the loss, and ease my woe."
Jove, with a nod, comply'd with her desire;
Around the body flam'd the fun'ral fire;
The pile decreas'd, that lately seem'd so high,
And sheets of smoke roll'd upward to the sky;
As humid vapours from a marshy bog,
Rise by degrees, condensing into fog,
That intercept the Sun's enliv'ning ray,
And with a cloud infect the cheerful day.
The sooty ashes wafted by the air,
Whirl round, and thicken in a body there;
Then take a form, which their own heat and fire
With active life, and energy inspire.
Its likeness makes it seem to fly, and soon
It skims on real wings, that are its own;
A real bird, it beats the breezy wind,
Mix'd with a thousand sisters of the kind,
That, from the same formation newly sprung,
Up-born aloft on plumy pinions hung.
Thrice round the pile advanc'd the circling throng,
Thrice, with their wings, a whizzing concert rung.
In the fourth flight their squadron they divide,
Rank'd in two diff'rent troops, on either side:
Then two and two, inspir'd with martial rage,
From either troop in equal pairs engage.
Each combatant with beak and pounces press'd,
In wrathful ire, his adversary's breast;
Each falls a victim, to preserve the fame
Of that great hero, whence their being came.
From him their courage, and their name they take,
And, as they liv'd, they die for Memnon's sake.
Punctual to time, with each revolving year,
In fresh array the champion birds appear;
Again, prepar'd with vengeful minds, they come
To bleed, in honour of the soldier's tomb.
Therefore in others it appear'd not strange,
To grieve for Hecuba's unhappy change.
But poor Aurora had enough to do
With her own loss, to mind another's woe;
Who still in tears, her tender nature shews,
Besprinkling all the world with pearly dews.

THE VOYAGE OF ÆNEAS.

By Mr. Catcott.

TROY thus destroy'd, 'twas still deny'd by fate,
The hopes of Troy should perish with the state.
His sire, the son of Cytheréa bore,
And household-gods from burning Ilium's shore.
The pious prince (a double duty paid)
Each sacred burden through the flames convey'd.
With young Ascanius, and this only prize
Of heaps of wealth, he from Antandros flies;
But struck with horrour, left the Thracian shore,
Stain'd with the blood of murder'd Polydore.
The Delian isle receives the banish'd train,
Driv'n by kind gales, and favour'd by the main.
Here pious Anius, priest and monarch reign'd,
And either charge with equal care sustain'd,
His subjects rul'd, to Phœbus homage pay'd,
His god obeying, and by those obey'd.
The priest displays his hospitable gate,
And shows the riches of his church and state,
The sacred shrubs, which eas'd Latona's pain,
The palm, and olive, and the votive fane.
Here grateful flames with fuming incense fed,
And mingled wine, ambrosial odours shed;
Of slaughter'd steers the crackling entrails burn'd:
And then the strangers to the court return'd.
On beds of tap'stry plac'd aloft, they dine
With Ceres' gift, and flowing bowls of wine;

When thus Anchises spoke, amidst the feast:
"Say, mitred monarch, Phœbus' chosen priest,
(Or ere from Troy by cruel fate expell'd)
When first mine eyes these sacred walls beheld,
A son and twice two daughters crown'd thy bliss;
Or errs my mem'ry, and I judge amiss?"
The royal prophet shook his hoary head,
With snowy fillets bound, and sighing, said;
"Thy mem'ry errs not, prince; thou saw'st me then,
The happy father of so large a train;
Behold me now, (such turns of chance befall
The race of man!) almost bereft of all.
For (ah!) what comfort can my son bestow,
What help afford, to mitigate my woe!
While far from hence, in Andros' isle he reigns,
(From him so nam'd) and there my place sustains.
Him Delius prescience gave; the twice-born god
A boon more wond'rous on the maids bestow'd.
Whate'er they touch'd, he gave them to transmute,
(A gift past credit, and above their suit,)
To Ceres' Bacchus' and Minerva's fruit.
How great their value, and how rich their use,
Whose only touch such treasures could produce!
"The dire destroyer of the Trojan reign,
Fierce Agamemnon, such a prize to gain,
(A proof we also were design'd by fate
To feel the tempest, that o'erturn'd your state)
With force superior, and a ruffian crew,
From these weak arms the helpless virgins drew:
And sternly bade them use the grant divine,
To keep the fleet in corn, in oil, and wine.
Each, as they could, escap'd: two strove to gain
Eubœa's isle, and two their brother's reign.
The soldier follows, and demands the dames;
If held by force, immediate war proclaims.
Fear conquer'd nature in their brother's mind,
And gave them up to punishment assign'd.
Forgive the deed; nor Hector's arm was there,
Nor thine, Æneas, to maintain the war;
Whose only force upheld your Ilium's tow'rs,
For ten long years against the Grecian pow'rs.
Prepar'd to bind their captive arms in bands,
To Heav'n they rear'd their yet unfetter'd hands,
'Help, Bacchus, author of the gift,' they pray'd;
The gift's great author gave immediate aid;
If such destruction of their human frame,
By ways so wond'rous, may deserve the name.
Nor could I hear, nor can I now relate
Exact, the manner of their alter'd state;
But this in gen'ral of my loss I knew,
Transform'd to doves, on milky plumes they flew,
Such as on Ida's mount thy consort's chariot drew."
With such discourse, they entertain'd the feast;
Then rose from table, and withdrew to rest.
The following morn, ere Sol was seen to shine,
Th' inquiring Trojans sought the sacred shrine;
The mystic pow'r commands them to explore
Their ancient mother, and a kindred shore.
Attending to the sea, the gen'rous prince
Dismiss'd his guests with rich munificence:
In old Anchises' hand a sceptre plac'd,
A vest and quiver young Ascanius grac'd,
His sire, a cup; which from th' Aonian coast,
Ismenian Therses sent his royal host.
Alcon of Mylè made what Therses sent,
And carv'd thereon this ample argument:
A town with sev'n distinguish'd gates was shown,
Which spoke its name, and made the city known;
Before it, piles and tombs, and rising flames,
The rites of death, and quires of mourning dames,
Who bar'd their breasts, and gave their hair to flow,
The signs of grief, and marks of public woe.
Their fountains dry'd, the weeping Naiads mourn'd,
The trees stood bare, with searing cankers burn'd,
No herbage cloth'd the ground, a ragged flock
Of goats half-famish'd lick'd the naked rock.
Of manly courage, and with mind serene,
Orion's daughters in the town were seen;
One heav'd her chest to meet the lifted knife,
One plung'd the poniard through the seat of life,
Their country's victims; mourns the rescu'd state,
The bodies burns, and celebrates their fate.
To save the failure of th' illustrious line,
From the pale ashes rose, of form divine,
Two gen'rous youths; these fame Coronæ calls,
Who join the pomp, and mourn their mother's falls.
These burnish'd figures form'd of antic mold,
Shone on the brass, with rising sculpture bold;
A wreath of gilt acanthus round the brim was roll'd.
Nor less expense the Trojan gifts express'd;
A fuming censer for the royal priest,
A chalice, and a crown of princely cost,
With ruddy gold, and sparkling gems emboss'd.
Now hoisting sail, to Crete the Trojans stood,
Themselves rememb'ring sprung from Teucer's blood;
But Heav'n forbids, and pestilential Jove
From noxious skies the wand'ring navy drove.
Her hundred cities left, from Crete they bore,
And sought the destin'd land, Ausonia's shore;
But toss'd by storms at either Strophas lay,
Till scar'd by harpies from the faithless bay.
Then passing onward with a prosp'rous wind,
Left sly Ulysses' spacious realms behind;
Ambracia's state, in former ages known
The strife of gods, the judge transform'd to stone
They saw; for Actian Phœbus since renown'd,
Who Cæsar's arms with naval conquest crown'd;
Next pass'd Dodona, wont of old to boast
Her vocal forest; and Chaönia's coast,
Where king Molossus' sons on wings aspir'd,
And saw secure the harmless fuel fir'd.
Now to Phæacia's happy isle they came,
For fertile orchards known to early fame;
Epirus past, they next beheld with joy
A second Ilium, and fictitious Troy:
Here Trojan Helenus the sceptre sway'd,
Who show'd their fate, and mystic truths display'd.
By him confirm'd, Sicilia's isle they reach'd;
Whose sides to sea three promontories stretch'd;
Pachynos to the stormy south is plac'd,
On Lilybæum blows the gentle west;
Peloro's cliffs the northern Bear survey,
Who rolls above, and dreads to touch the sea.
By this they steer, and favour'd by the tide,
Secure by night in Zancle's harbour ride.
Here cruel Scylla guards the rocky shore,
And there the waves of loud Charybdis roar:
This sucks, and vomits ships, and bodies drown'd;
And rav'nous dogs the womb of that surround,

In face a virgin; and (if aught be true
By bards recorded once a virgin too.
A train of youths in vain desir'd her bed;
By sea-nymphs lov'd, to nymphs of seas she fled;
The maid to these, with female pride, display'd
Their baffled courtship, and their love betray'd.
When Galatea thus bespoke the fair,
(But first she sigh'd), while Scylla comb'd her hair;
"You, lovely maid, a gen'rous race pursues,
Whom safe you may (as now you do) refuse;
To me, though pow'rful in a num'rous train
Of sisters, sprung from gods, who rule the main,
My native seas could scarce a refuge prove,
To shun the fury of the Cyclops' love."
Tears chok'd her utt'rance here; the pitying maid
With marble fingers wip'd them off, and said:
"My dearest goddess, let thy Scylla know,
(For I am faithful) whence these sorrows flow."
The maid's entreaties o'er the nymph prevail,
Who thus to Scylla tells the mournful tale.

THE STORY OF ACIS, POLYPHEMUS, AND GALATEA.

By Mr. Dryden.

"Acis, the lovely youth, whose loss I mourn,
From Faunus, and the nymph Symethis born,
Was both his parents' pleasure; but, to me
Was all that love could make a lover be.
The gods our minds in mutual bands did join:
I was his only joy, and he was mine.
Now sixteen summers the sweet youth had seen;
And doubtful down began to shade his chin:
When Polyphemus first disturb'd our joy;
And lov'd me fiercely, as I lov'd the boy.
Ask not which passion in my soul was high'r,
My last aversion, or my first desire:
Nor this the greater was, nor that the less;
Both were alike, for both were in excess.
Thee, Venus, thee, both Heav'n and Earth obey;
Immense thy pow'r, and boundless is thy sway.
The Cyclops, who defy'd th' etherial throne,
And thought no thunder louder than his own,
The terrour of the woods, and wilder far
Than wolves in plains, or bears in forests are;
Th' inhuman host, who made his bloody feasts
On mangled members of his butcher'd guests,
Yet felt the force of love, and fierce desire,
And burnt for me, with unrelenting fire;
Forgot his caverns, and his woolly care,
Assum'd the softness of a lover's air;
And comb'd, with teeth of rakes, his rugged hair.
Now with a crooked scythe his beard he sleeks;
And mows the stubborn stubble of his cheeks:
Now in the crystal stream he looks, to try
His simagres, and rolls his glaring eye.
His cruelty and thirst of blood are lost;
And ships securely sail along the coast.
"The prophet Telemus (arriv'd by chance
Where Ætna's summits to the seas advance,
Who mark'd the tracks of every bird that flew,
And sure presages from their flying drew)
Foretold the Cyclops, that Ulysses' hand
In his broad eye should thrust a flaming brand.
The giant, with a scornful grin, reply'd,
'Vain augur, thou hast falsely prophesy'd;
Already Love his flaming brand has tost;
Looking on two fair eyes, my sight I lost.'
Thus, warn'd in vain, with stalking pace he strode,
And stamp'd the margin of the briny flood
With heavy steps; and weary, sought again
The cool retirement of his gloomy den.
"A promontory, sharp'ning by degrees,
Ends in a wedge, and overlooks the seas:
On either side, below, the water flows;
This airy walk the giant lover chose.
Here on the midst he sat; his flocks unled,
Their shepherd follow'd, and securely fed.
A pine so burly, and of length so vast,
That sailing ships requir'd it for a mast,
He wielded for a staff, his steps to guide:
But laid it by, his whistle while he try'd.
A hundred reeds of a prodigious growth,
Scarce made a pipe proportion'd to his mouth:
Which when he gave it wind, the rocks around,
And wat'ry plains, the dreadful hiss resound.
I heard the ruffian shepherd rudely blow,
Where, in a hollow cave, I sat below;
On Acis' bosom I my head reclin'd,
And still preserve the poem in my mind.
'"Oh lovely Galatea, whiter far
Than falling snows, and rising lilies are;
More flow'ry than the meads, as crystal bright;
Erect as alders, and of equal height:
More wanton than a kid, more sleek thy skin
Than orient shells, that on the shores are seen.
Than apples fairer, when the boughs they lade;
Pleasing, as winter suns, or summer shade;
More grateful to the sight, than goodly plains;
And softer to the touch, than down of swans,
Or curds new turn'd; and sweeter to the taste
Than swelling grapes, that to the vintage haste;
More clear than ice, or running streams, that stray
Through garden plots, but ah! more swift than [they.
'"Yet, Galatea, harder to be broke
Than bullocks, unreclaim'd, to bear the yoke,
And far more stubborn, than the knotted oak:
Like sliding streams, impossible to hold;
Like them, fallacious, like their fountains, cold;
More warping, than the willow, to decline
My warm embrace; more brittle, than the vine;
Immoveable, and fix'd in thy disdain;
Rough, as these rocks, and of a harder grain.
More violent, than is the rising flood:
And the prais'd peacock is not half so proud.
Fierce, as the fire, and sharp, as thistles are,
And more outrageous, than a mother-bear:
Deaf, as the billows, to the vows I make;
And more revengeful, than a trodden snake.
In swiftness fleeter, than the flying hind,
Or driven tempests, or the driving wind.
All other faults with patience I can bear;
But swiftness is the vice I only fear.
'"Yet if you knew me well, you would not shun
My love, but to my wish'd embraces run:
Would languish in your turn, and court my stay;
And much repent of your unwise delay.
'"My palace, in the living rock, is made
By Nature's hand, a spacious pleasing shade:
Which neither heat can pierce, nor cold invade.
My garden fill'd with fruits you may behold,
And grapes in clusters, imitating gold;
Some blushing bunches of a purple hue:
And these, and those, are all reserv'd for you.
Red strawberries, in shades, expecting stand,
Proud to be gather'd by so white a hand.

Autumnal cornels latter fruit provide,
And plums, to tempt you, turn their glossy side:
Not those of common kinds; but such alone,
As in Phæacian orchards might have grown:
Nor chesnuts shall be wanting to your food,
Nor garden-fruit, nor wildings of the wood;
The laden boughs for you alone shall bear;
And yours shall be the product of the year.
"'The flocks you see, are all my own; beside
The rest that woods and winding valleys hide;
And those that folded in the caves abide.
Ask not the numbers of my glowing store;
Who knows how many, knows he has no more.
Nor will I praise my cattle; trust not me,
But judge yourself, and pass your own decree:
Behold their swelling dugs; the sweepy weight
Of ewes, that sink beneath the milky freight;
In the warm folds their tender lambkins lie,
Apart from kids, that call with human cry.
New milk in nut-brown bowls is duly serv'd
For daily drink; the rest for cheese reserv'd.
Nor are these houshold dainties all my store:
The fields and forests will afford us more;
The deer, the hare, the goat, the savage boar.
All sorts of ven'son; and of birds the best;
A pair of turtles taken from the nest.
I walk'd the mountains, and two cubs I found,
(Whose dam had left them on the naked ground,)
So like, that no distinction could be seen:
So pretty, they were presents for a queen;
And so they shall; I took them both away;
And keep, to be companions of your play.
"'Oh raise, fair nymph, your beauteous face above
The waves; nor scorn my presents, and my love.
Come, Galatea, come, and view my face;
I late beheld it, in the wat'ry glass,
And found it lovelier, than I fear'd it was.
Survey my tow'ring stature, and my size:
Not Jove, the Jove you dream, that rules the skies,
Bears such a bulk, or is so largely spread:
My locks (the plenteous harvest of my head)
Hang o'er my manly face; and dangling down,
As with a shady grove, my shoulders crown.
Nor think, because my limbs and body bear
A thick-set underwood of bristling hair,
My shape deform'd; what fouler sight can be,
Than the bald branches of a leafless tree?
Foul is the steed without a flowing mane:
And birds, without their feathers, and their train.
Wool decks the sheep; and man receives a grace
From bushy limbs, and from a bearded face.
My forehead with a single eye is fill'd,
Round, as a ball, and ample, as a shield.
The glorious lamp of Heav'n, the radiant Sun,
Is Nature's eye; and she's content with one.
Add, that my father sways your seas, and I,
Like you, am of the wat'ry family.
I make you his, in making you my own;
You I adore; and kneel to you alone:
Jove, with his fabled thunder, I despise,
And only fear the lightning of your eyes.
Frown not, fair nymph; yet I could bear to be
Disdain'd, if others were disdain'd with me.
But to repulse the Cyclops, and prefer
The love of Acis, (Heav'ns!) I cannot bear.
But let the stripling please himself; nay more,
Please you, though that's the thing I most abhor;
The boy shall find, if e'er we cope in fight,
These giant limbs endu'd with giant might.
His living bowels from his belly torn,
And scatter'd limbs shall on the flood be borne:
Thy flood, ungrateful nymph; and fate shall find
That way for thee and Acis to be join'd.
For oh! I burn with love, and thy disdain
Augments at once my passion, and my pain.
Translated Ætna flames within my heart,
And thou, inhuman, wilt not ease my smart.'
"Lamenting thus in vain, he rose, and strode
With furious paces to the neighb'ring wood:
Restless his feet, distracted was his walk;
Mad were his motions, and confus'd his talk.
Mad, as the vanquish'd bull, when forc'd to yield
His lovely mistress, and forsake the field.
"Thus far unseen I saw: when fatal chance,
His looks directing, with a sudden glance,
Acis and I were to his sight betray'd;
Where, nought suspecting, we securely play'd.
From his wide mouth a bellowing cry he cast,
'I see, I see; but this shall be your last.'
A roar so loud made Ætna to rebound:
And all the Cyclops labour'd in the sound.
Affrighted with his monstrous voice, I fled,
And in the neighbouring ocean plung'd my head.
Poor Acis turn'd his back, and 'Help,' he cry'd,
'Help, Galatea, help, my parent gods,
And take me dying to your deep abodes.'
The Cyclops follow'd; but he sent before
A rib, which from the living rock he tore:
Though but an angle reach'd him of the stone,
The mighty fragment was enough alone,
To crush all Acis; 'twas too late to save,
But what the fates allow'd to give, I gave:
That Acis to his lineage should return;
And roll, among the river gods, his urn.
Straight issu'd from the stone a stream of blood;
Which lost the purple, mingling with the flood.
Then, like a troubled torrent, it appear'd:
The torrent too, in little space, was clear'd.
The stone was cleft, and through the yawning chink
New reeds arose, on the new river's brink.
The rock, from out its hollow womb, disclos'd
A sound like water in its course oppos'd,
When, (wond'rous to behold) full in the flood,
Up starts a youth, and navel-high he stood.
Horns from his temples rise; and either horn
Thick wreaths of reeds (his native growth) adorn.
Were not his stature taller than before,
His bulk augmented, and his beauty more,
His colour blue, for Acis he might pass:
And Acis chang'd into a stream he was.
But mine no more; he rolls along the plains
With rapid motion, and his name remains."

THE STORY OF GLAUCUS AND SCYLLA.

By Mr. Rowe.

HERE ceas'd the nymph; the fair assembly broke,
The sea-green Nereids to the waves betook:
While Scylla, fearful of the wide-spread main,
Swift to the safer shore returns again.
There o'er the sandy margin, unarray'd,
With printless footsteps flies the bounding maid;
Or in some winding creek's secure retreat
She bathes her weary limbs, and shuns the noon-day's heat.
Her Glaucus saw, as o'er the deep he rode,
New to the seas, and late receiv'd a god.

He saw, and languish'd for the virgin's love,
With many an artful blandishment he strove
Her flight to hinder, and her fears remove.
The more he sues, the more she wings her flight,
And nimbly gains a neighb'ring mountain's height.
Steep shelving to the margin of the flood,
A neighb'ring mountain bare and woodless stood;
Here, by the place secur'd, her steps she stay'd,
And, trembling still, her lover's form survey'd.
His shape, his hue, her troubled sense appall,
And dropping locks that o'er his shoulders fall;
She sees his face divine, and manly brow,
End in a fish's wreathy tail below:
She sees, and doubts within her anxious mind,
Whether he comes of god, or monster kind.
This Glaucus soon perceiv'd; and, "Oh! forbear"
(His hand supporting on a rock lay near) [fear.
"Forbear," he cry'd, "fond maid, this needless
Nor fish am I, nor monster of the main,
But equal with the wat'ry gods I reign;
Nor Proteus, nor Palæmon me excel,
Nor he whose breath inspires the sounding shell.
My birth, 'tis true, I owe to mortal race,
And I myself but late a mortal was:
Ev'n then in seas, and seas alone, I joy'd;
The seas my hours, and all my cares employ'd.
In meshes now the twinkling prey I drew;
Now skilfully the slender line I threw,
And silent sat the moving float to view.
Not far from shore, there lies a verdant mead,
With herbage half, and half with water spread:
There, nor the horned heifers browsing stray,
Nor shaggy kids, nor wanton lambkins play;
There, nor the sounding bees their nectar cull,
Nor rural swains their genial chaplets pull,
Nor flocks, nor herds, nor mowers haunt the place,
To crop the flow'rs, or cut the bushy grass:
Thither sure first of living race came I,
And sat by chance, my dropping nets to dry.
My scaly prize, in order all display'd,
By number on the greensward there I laid.
My captives, whom or in my nets I took,
Or hung unwary on my wily hook,
Strange to behold! yet what avails a lie?
I saw them bite the grass, as I sat by;
Then sudden darting o'er the verdant plain,
They spread their fins, as in their native main:
I paus'd with wonder struck, while all my prey
Left their new master, and regain'd the sea.
Amaz'd, within my secret self I sought,
What god, what herb the miracle had wrought:
'But sure no herbs have pow'r like this,' I cry'd;
And straight I pluck'd some neighb'ring herbs, and try'd.
Scarce had I bit, and prov'd the wond'rous taste,
When strong convulsions shook my troubled breast;
I felt my heart grow fond of something strange,
And my whole nature lab'ring with a change.
Restless I grew, and ev'ry place forsook,
And still upon the seas I bent my look.
'Farewell for ever! farewell, land!' I said;
And plung'd amidst the waves my sinking head.
The gentle pow'rs, who that low empire keep,
Receiv'd me as a brother of the deep;
To Tethys, and to Ocean old, they pray.
To purge my mortal earthy parts away.
The wat'ry parents to their suit agreed,
And thrice nine times a secret charm they read,
Then with lustrations purify my limbs,
And bid me bathe beneath a hundred streams:
A hundred streams from various fountains run,
And on my head at once come rushing down.
Thus far each passage I remember well,
And faithfully thus far the tale I tell;
But then oblivion dark on all my senses fell.
Again at length my thoughts reviving came,
When I no longer found myself the same;
Then first this sea-green beard I felt to grow,
And these large honours on my spreading brow;
My long-descending locks the billows sweep,
And my broad shoulders cleave the yielding deep;
My fishy tail, my arms of azure hue,
And ev'ry part divinely chang'd, I view.
But what avail these useless honours now?
What joys can immortality bestow?
What though our Nereids all my form approve?
What boots it, while fair Scylla scorns my love?"
Thus far the god; and more he would have said;
When from his presence flew the ruthless maid.
Stung with repulse, in such disdainful sort,
He seeks Titanian Circe's horrid court.

OVID'S METAMORPHOSES.

BOOK XIV.

Translated by Sir Samuel Garth, M. D.

THE TRANSFORMATION OF SCYLLA.

Now Glaucus, with a lover's haste, bounds o'er
The swelling waves, and seeks the Latian shore.
Messena, Rhegium, and the barren coast
Of flaming Ætna, to his sight are lost:
At length he gains the Tyrrhene seas, and views
The hills where baneful philtres Circe brews;
Monsters in various forms around her press;
As thus the god salutes the sorceress.
"O Circe, be indulgent to my grief,
And give a love-sick deity relief.
Too well the mighty pow'r of plants I know,
To those my figure and new fate I owe.
Against Messena, on th' Ausonian coast,
I Sylla view'd, and from that hour was lost.
In tend'rest sounds I su'd; but still the fair
Was deaf to vows, and pitiless to pray'r.
If numbers can avail, exert their pow'r;
Or energy of plants, if plants have more.
I ask no cure; let but the virgin pine
With dying pangs, or agonies, like mine."
No longer Circe could her flame disguise,
But to the suppliant god marine replies:
"When maids are coy, have manlier aims in view;
Leave those that fly, but those that like, pursue.
If love can be by kind compliance won;
See, at your feet, the daughter of the Sun."
"Sooner," said Glaucus, "shall the ash remove
From mountains, and the swelling surges love;
Or humble sea-weed to the hills repair;
Ere I think any but my Scylla fair."
Straight Circe reddens with a guilty shame,
And vows revenge for her rejected flame.
Fierce liking oft a spite as fierce creates;
For love refus'd, without aversion, hates.
To hurt her hapless rival she proceeds;
And, by the fall of Scylla, Glaucus bleeds.
Some fascinating bev'rage now she brews;
Compos'd of deadly drugs, and baneful juice.
At Rhegium she arrives; the ocean braves,
And treads with unwet feet the boiling waves.

Upon the beach a winding bay there lies,
Shelter'd from seas, and shaded from the skies:
This station Scylla chose: a soft retreat
From chilling winds, and raging Cancer's heat.
The vengeful sorc'ress visits this recess;
Her charm infuses, and infects the place.
Soon as the nymph wades in, her nether parts
Turn into dogs; then at herself she starts,
A ghastly horrour in her eyes appears;
But yet she knows not who it is she fears:
In vain she offers from herself to run;
And drags about her what she strives to shun.
Oppress'd with grief the pitying god appears;
And swells the rising surges with his tears;
From the detested sorceress he flies;
Her art reviles, and her address denies:
Whilst hapless Scylla, chang'd to rocks, decrees
Destruction to those barks, that beat the seas.

THE VOYAGE OF ÆNEAS CONTINUED.

HERE bulg'd the pride of fam'd Ulysses' fleet,
But good Æneas 'scap'd the fate he met.
As to the Latian shore the Trojan stood,
And cut with well-tim'd oars the foaming flood:
He weather'd fell Charybdis: but ere long
The skies were darken'd, and the tempest strong.
Then to the Libyan coast he stretches o'er;
And makes at length the Carthaginian shore.
Here Dido, with an hospitable care,
Into her heart receives the wanderer.
From her kind arms th' ungrateful hero flies;
The injur'd queen looks on with dying eyes,
Then to her folly falls a sacrifice.
Æneas now sets sail, and plying gains
Fair Eryx, where his friend Acestes reigns:
First to his sire does fun'ral rites decree,
Then gives the signal next, and stands to sea;
Out-runs the islands where volcanoes roar;
Gets clear of Sirens, and their faithless shore:
But loses Palinurus in the way;
Then makes Inarime, and Prochyta.

THE TRANSFORMATION OF CERCOPIANS INTO APES.

THE gallies now by Pythecusa pass;
The name is from the natives of the place.
The father of the gods, detesting lies,
Oft, with abhorrence, heard their perjuries.
Th' abandon'd race, transform'd to beasts, began
To mimic the impertinence of man.
Flat-nos'd, and furrow'd; with grimace they grin;
And look, to what they were, too near akin:
Merry in make, and busy to no end;
This moment they divert, the next offend:
So much this species of their past retains;
Though lost the language, yet the noise remains.

ÆNEAS DESCENDS TO HELL.

NOW, on his right, he leaves Parthenope:
His left, Misenus jutting in the sea:
Arrives at Cuma, and with awe survey'd
The grotto of the venerable maid:
Begs leave through black Avernus to retire;
And view the much-lov'd manes of his sire.
Straight the divining virgin rais'd her eyes;
And, foaming with a holy rage, replies:
"O thou, whose worth thy wond'rous works proclaim;
The flames, thy piety; the world, thy fame;
Though great be thy request, yet shalt thou see
Th' Elysian fields, th' infernal monarchy;
Thy parent's shade: this arm thy steps shall guide:
To suppliant virtue nothing is deny'd."
She spoke, and pointing to the golden bough,
Which in th' Avernian grove refulgent grew,
"Seize that," she bids; he listens to the maid;
Then views the mournful mansions of the dead;
The shade of great Anchises, and the place
By fates determin'd to the Trojan race.
As back to upper light the hero came,
He thus salutes the visionary dame:—
"O, whether some propitious deity,
Or lov'd by those bright rulers of the sky!
With grateful incense I shall style you one,
And doom no godhead greater than your own.
'Twas you restor'd me from the realms of night,
And gave me to behold the fields of light:
To feel the breezes of congenial air;
And Nature's blest benevolence to share."

THE STORY OF THE SIBYL.

"I AM no deity," replied the dame,
"But mortal, and religious rites disclaim.
Yet had avoided Death's tyrannic sway,
Had I consented to the god of day.
With promises he sought my love, and said,
'Have all you wish, my fair Cumæan maid.'
I paus'd; then pointing to a heap of sand,
For ev'ry grain, to live a year, demand.
But ah! unmindful of th' effect of time,
Forgot to covenant for youth, and prime.
The smiling bloom, I boasted once, is gone,
And feeble age with lagging limbs creeps on.
Sev'n cent'ries have I liv'd; three more fulfil
The period of the years to finish still.
Who'll think, that Phœbus, drest in youth divine,
Had once believ'd his lustre less than mine?
This wither'd frame (so fates have will'd) shall waste
To nothing, but prophetic words, at last."
The Sibyl mounting now from nether skies,
And the fam'd Ilian prince, at Cuma rise.
He sail'd, and near the place to anchor came,
Since call'd Cajeta from his nurse's name.
Here did the luckless Macareus, a friend
To wise Ulysses, his long labours end.
Here, wand'ring, Achæmenides he meets,
And, sudden, thus his late associate greets.
"Whence came you here, O friend, and whither bound?
All gave you lost on far Cyclopean ground;
A Greek's at last aboard a Trojan found."

THE ADVENTURES OF ACHÆMENIDES.

THUS Achæmenides: "With thanks I name
Æneas, and his piety proclaim.
I 'scap'd the Cyclops through the hero's aid,
Else in his maw my mangled limbs had laid.
When first your navy under sail he found,
He rav'd, till Ætna labour'd with the sound.
Raging he stalk'd along the mountain's side,
And vented clouds of breath at ev'ry stride.
His staff a mountain ash; and in the clouds
Oft, as he walks, his grisly front he shrowds.
Eyeless he grop'd about with vengeful haste,
And justled promontories, as he pass'd.
Then heav'd a rock's high summit to the main,
And bellow'd, like some bursting hurricane.

'Oh! could I seize Ulysses in his flight,
How unlamented were my loss of sight! [vein,
These jaws should piece-meal tear each panting
Grind ev'ry crackling bone, and pound his brain.'
As thus he rav'd, my joints with horrour shook;
The tide of blood my chilling heart forsook.
I saw him once disgorge huge morsels raw,
Of wretches undigested in his maw. [tore,
From the pale breathless trunks whole limbs he
His beard all clotted with o'erflowing gore.
My anxious hours I pass'd in caves; my food
Was forest fruits, and wildings of the wood.
At length a sail I wafted, and aboard
My fortune found an hospitable lord.
"Now, in return, your own adventures tell,
And what, since first you put to sea, befel."

THE ADVENTURES OF MACAREUS.

THEN Macareus—"There reign'd a prince of
O'er Tuscan seas, and Æolus his name. [fame
A largess to Ulysses he consign'd,
And in a steer's tough hide enclos'd a wind.
Nine days before the swelling gale we ran;
The tenth, to make the meeting land, began;
When now the merry mariners, to find
Imagin'd wealth within, the bag unbind.
Forthwith out-rush'd a gust, which backwards
Our gallies to the Læstrigonian shore, [bore
Whose crown Antiphates the tyrant wore.
Some few commission'd were with speed to treat:
We to his court repair, his guards we meet.
Two, friendly flight preserv'd; the third was doom'd
To be by those curs'd cannibals consum'd.
Inhumanly our hapless friends they treat;
Our men they murder, and destroy our fleet.
In time the wise Ulysses bore away,
And dropp'd his anchor in yon faithless bay.
The thoughts of perils past we still retain,
And fear to land, till lots appoint the men.
Polites true, Elpenor giv'n to wine,
Eurylochus, myself, the lots assign.
Design'd for dangers, and resolv'd to dare,
To Circe's fatal palace we repair.

THE ENCHANTMENTS OF CIRCE.

"BEFORE the spacious front, a herd we find
Of beasts, the fiercest of the savage kind.
Our trembling steps with blandishments they meet,
And fawn, unlike their species, at our feet.
Within upon a sumptuous throne of state,
On golden columns rais'd, th' enchantress sate.
Rich was her robe, and amiable her mien,
Her aspect awful, and she look'd a queen.
Her maids not mind the loom, nor houshold care,
Nor wage in needle-work a Scythian war.
But cull in canisters disast'rous flow'rs,
And plants from haunted heaths, and fairy bow'rs,
With brazen sickles reap'd at planetary hours.
Each dose the goddess weighs with watchful eye;
So nice her art in impious pharmacy!
Ent'ring she greets us with a gracious look,
And airs, that future amity bespoke.
Her ready nymphs serve up a rich repast;
The bowl she dashes first, then gives to taste.
Quick, to our own undoing, we comply;
Her pow'r we prove, and show the sorcery.

"Soon, in a length of face, our head extends;
Our chine stiff bristles bears, and forward bends:
A breadth of brawn new burnishes our neck;
Anon we grunt, as we begin to speak.
Alone Eurylochus refus'd to taste,
Nor to a beast obscene the man debas'd.
Hither Ulysses hastes (so fates command)
And bears the pow'rful moly in his hand;
Unsheaths his scimetar, assaults the dame,
Preserves his species, and remains the same.
The nuptial rite this outrage straight attends;
The dow'r desir'd is his transfigur'd friends.
The incantation backward she repeats,
Inverts her rod, and what she did, defeats.
"And now our skin grows smooth, our shape upright;
Our arms stretch up, our cloven feet unite.
With tears our weeping gen'ral we embrace;
Hang on his neck, and melt upon his face.
Twelve silver moons in Circe's court we stay,
Whilst there they waste th' unwilling hours away.
'Twas here I spy'd a youth in Parian stone;
His head a pecker bore; the cause unknown
To passengers. A nymph of Circe's train
The myst'ry thus attempted to explain.

THE STORY OF PICUS AND CANENS.

"PICUS, who once th' Ausonian sceptre held,
Could rein the steed, and fit him for the field;
So like he was to what you see, that still
We doubt if real, or the sculptor's skill.
The graces in the finish'd piece you find,
Are but the copy of his fairer mind.
Four lustres scarce the royal youth could name,
Till ev'ry love-sick nymph confess'd a flame.
Oft for his love the mountain Dryads su'd,
And ev'ry silver sister of the flood:
Those of Numicus, Albula, and those
Where Almo creeps, and hasty Nar o'erflows:
Where sedgy Anio glides through smiling meads,
Where shady Farfar rustles in the reeds:
And those that love the lakes, and homage owe
To the chaste goddess of the silver bow.
"In vain each nymph her brightest charms put
His heart no sov'reign would obey but one; [on,
She whom Venilia, on mount Palatine,
To Janus bore, the fairest of her line.
Nor did her face alone her charms confess,
Her voice was ravishing, and pleas'd no less.
Whene'er she sung, so melting were her strains,
The flocks unfed seem'd list'ning on the plains;
The rivers would stand still, the cedars bend,
And birds neglect their pinions to attend;
The savage kind in forest-wilds grow tame;
And Canens, from her heav'nly voice, her name.
"Hymen had now in some ill-fated hour
Their hands united, as their hearts before.
Whilst their soft moments in delights they waste,
And each new day was dearer than the past;
Picus would sometimes o'er the forests rove,
And mingle sports with intervals of love.
It chanc'd, as once the foaming boar he chas'd,
His jewels sparkling on his Tyrian vest,
Lascivious Circe well the youth survey'd,
As simpling on the flow'ry hills she stray'd.
Her wishing eyes their silent message tell,
And from her lap the verdant mischief fell.
As she attempts at words, his courser springs
O'er hills, and lawns, and ev'n a wish outwings.

'Thou shalt not 'scape me so,' pronounc'd the dame,
'If plants have pow'r, and spells be not a name.'
She said—and forthwith form'd a boar of air,
That sought the covert with dissembled fear.
Swift to the thicket Picus wings his way
On foot, to chase the visionary prey.
"Now she invokes the daughters of the night,
Does noxious juices smear, and charms recite;
Such as can veil the Moon's more feeble fire,
Or shade the golden lustre of her sire.
In filthy fogs she hides the cheerful noon;
The guard at distance, and the youth alone,
'By those fair eyes,' she cries, 'and ev'ry grace
That finish all the wonders of your face,
Oh! I conjure thee, hear a queen complain;
Nor let the Sun's soft lineage sue in vain.'
"'Whoe'er thou art,' reply'd the king, 'forbear,
None can my passion with my Canens share.
She first my ev'ry tender wish possest,
And found the soft approaches to my breast.
In nuptials blest, each loose desire we shun,
Nor time can end, what innocence begun.'
"'Think not,' she cry'd, 'to saunter out a life,
Of form, with that domestic drudge, a wife;
My just revenge, dull fool, ere long shall show
What ills we women, if refus'd, can do:
Think me a woman, and a lover too.
From dear successful spite we hope for ease,
Nor fail to punish, where we fail to please.'
"Now twice to east she turns, as oft to west;
Thrice waves her wand, as oft a charm exprest.
On the lost youth her magic pow'r she tries;
Aloft he springs, and wonders how he flies.
On painted plumes the woods he seeks, and still
The monarch oak he pierces with his bill.
Thus chang'd no more o'er Latian lands he reigns;
Of Picus nothing but the name remains.
"The winds from drisling damps now purge the air,
The mist subsides, the settling skies are fair:
The court their sovereign seek with arms in hand,
They threaten Circe, and their lord demand.
Quick she invokes the spirits of the air,
And twilight elves, that on dun wings repair
To charnels, and th' unhallow'd sepulchre.
"Now, strange to tell, the plants sweat drops of blood,
The trees are toss'd from forests where they stood;
Blue serpents o'er the tainted herbage slide,
Pale glaring spectres on the ether ride;
Dogs howl, earth yawns, rent rocks forsake their beds,
And from their quarries heave their stubborn heads.
The sad spectators stiffen'd with their fears
She sees, and sudden ev'ry limb she smears;
Then each of savage beasts the figure bears.
"The Sun did now to western waves retire,
In tides to temper his bright world of fire.
Canens laments her royal husband's stay;
Ill suits fond love with absence, or delay.
Where she commands, her ready people run;
She wills, retracts; bids, and forbids anon.
Restless in mind, and dying with despair,
Her breasts she beats, and tears her flowing hair.
Six days and nights she wanders on, as chance
Directs, without or sleep, or sustenance.
Tiber at last beholds the weeping fair;
Her feeble limbs no more the mourner bear;
Stretch'd on his banks, she to the flood complains,
And faintly tunes her voice to dying strains.
The sick'ning swan thus hangs her silver wings,
And, as she droops, her elegy she sings.
Ere long sad Canens wastes to air; whilst fame
The place still honours with her hapless name.
"Here did the tender tale of Picus cease,
Above belief the wonder I confess.
Again we sail, but more disasters meet,
Foretold by Circe, to our suff'ring fleet.
Myself unable further woes to bear,
Declin'd the voyage, and am refug'd here."

ÆNEAS ARRIVES IN ITALY.

THUS Macareus. Now with a pious aim
Had good Æneas rais'd a fun'ral flame,
In honour of his hoary nurse's name.
Her epitaph he fix'd; and setting sail,
Cajeta left, and catch'd at ev'ry gale.
He steer'd at distance from the faithless shore,
Where the false goddess reigns with fatal pow'r;
And sought those grateful groves, that shade the plain,
Where Tiber rolls majestic to the main,
And fattens, as he runs, the fair campain.
His kindred gods the hero's wishes crown
With fair Lavinia, and Latinus' throne:
But not without a war the prize he won.
Drawn up in bright array the battle stands:
Turnus with arms his promis'd wife demands.
Hetrurians, Latians, equal fortune share;
And doubtful long appears the face of war.
Both pow'rs from neighb'ring princes seek supplies,
And embassies appoint for new allies.
Æneas, for relief, Evander moves;
His quarrel he asserts, his cause approves.
The bold Rutilians, with an equal speed,
Sage Venulus dispatch to Diomede.
The king, late griefs revolving in his mind,
These reasons for neutrality assign'd.
"Shall I, of one poor dotal town possest,
My people thin, my wretched country waste?
An exil'd prince, and on a shaking throne;
Or risk my patron's subjects, or my own?
You'll grieve the harshness of our hap to hear;
Nor can I tell the tale without a tear.

THE ADVENTURES OF DIOMEDES.

"AFTER fam'd Ilium was by Argives won,
And flames had finish'd what the sword begun;
Pallas, incens'd, pursu'd us to the main,
In vengeance of her violated fane.
Alone Oïleus forc'd the Trojan maid,
Yet all were punish'd for the brutal deed.
A storm begins, the raging waves run high,
The clouds look heavy, and benight the sky;
Red sheets of lightning o'er the seas are spread,
Our tackling yields, and wrecks at last succeed.
'Tis tedious our disast'rous state to tell;
Ev'n Priam would have pity'd what befel.
Yet Pallas sav'd me from the swallowing main;
At home new wrongs to meet, as fates ordain.
Chas'd from my country, I once more repeat
All suff'rings seas could give, or war complete.
For Venus, mindful of her wound, decreed
Still new calamities should past succeed.
Agmon, impatient through successive ills,
With fury love's bright goddess thus reviles:
'These plagues in spite to Diomede are sent;
The crime is his, but ours the punishment.
Let each, my friends, her puny spleen despise,
And dare that haughty harlot of the skies.'

" The rest of Agmon's insolence complain,
And of irreverence the wretch arraign.
About to answer; his blaspheming throat
Contracts, and shrieks in some disdainful note.
To his new skin a fleece of feather clings,
Hides his late arms, and lengthens into wings.
The lower features of his face extend,
Warp into horn, and in a beak descend.
Some more experience Agmon's destiny,
And wheeling in the air, like swans they fly:
These thin remains to Daunus' realms I bring,
And here I reign, a poor precarious king."

THE TRANSFORMATION OF APPULUS.

THUS Diomedes. Venulus withdraws:
Unsped the service of the common cause.
Puteoli he passes, and survey'd
A cave long honour'd for its awful shade.
Here trembling reeds exclude the piercing ray,
Here streams in gentle falls through windings stray,
And with a passing breath cool zephyrs play.
The goatherd god frequents the silent place,
As once the wood-nymphs of the sylvan race,
Till Appulus with a dishonest air,
And gross behaviour, banish'd thence the fair.
The bold buffoon, whene'er they tread the green,
Their motion mimics, but with gest obscene.
Loose language oft he utters; but ere long
A bark in filmy net-work binds his tongue.
Thus chang'd, a base wild olive he remains;
The shrub the coarseness of the clown retains.

THE TROJAN SHIPS TRANSFORMED TO SEA-NYMPHS.

MEANWHILE the Latians all their pow'r prepare,
'Gainst fortune, and the foe to push the war.
With Phrygian blood the floating fields they stain;
But, short of succours, still contend in vain.
Turnus remarks the Trojan fleet ill-mann'd,
Unguarded, and at anchor near the strand:
He thought; and straight a lighted brand he bore,
And fire invades what 'scap'd the waves before.
The billows from the kindling prow retire;
Pitch, rosin, searwood on red wings aspire,
And Vulcan on the seas exerts his attribute of fire.
This when the mother of the gods beheld,
Her tow'ry crown she shook, and stood reveal'd;
Her brindled lions rein'd, unveil'd her head,
And hov'ring o'er her favour'd fleet, she said:
" Cease, Turnus, and the heav'nly pow'rs respect,
Nor dare to violate, what I protect.
These gallies, once fair trees on Ida stood,
And gave their shade to each descending god.
Nor shall consume; irrevocable fate
Allots their being no determin'd date."
Straight peals of thunder Heav'n's high arches rend,
The hail-stones leap, the show'rs in spouts descend.
The winds with widen'd throats the signal give;
The cables break, the smoking vessels drive.
Now, wond'rous, as they beat the foaming flood,
The timber softens into flesh and blood;
The yards, and oars new arms, and legs design;
A trunk the hull; the slender keel, a spine;
The prow a female face; and by degrees
The gallies rise green daughters of the seas.
Sometimes on coral beds they sit in state,
Or wanton on the waves they fear'd of late.
The barks that beat the seas are still their care,
Themselves rememb'ring what of late they were;
To save a Trojan sail in throngs they press,
But smile to see Alcinous in distress.
Unable were those wonders to deter
The Latians from their unsuccessful war.
Both sides for doubtful victory contend;
And on their courage, and their gods depend.
Nor bright Lavinia, nor Latinus' crown,
Warm their great soul to war, like fair renown.
Venus at last beholds her god-like son
Triumphant, and the field of battle won;
Brave Turnus slain, strong Ardea but a name,
And bury'd in fierce deluges of flame.
Her tow'rs, that boasted once a sov'reign sway,
The fate of fancy'd grandeur now betray.
A famish'd heron from the ashes springs,
And beats the ruins with disastrous wings.
Calamities of towns distrest she feigns,
And oft, with woeful shrieks, of war complains.

THE DEIFICATION OF ÆNEAS.

NOW had Æneas, as ordain'd by fate,
Surviv'd the period of Saturnia's hate:
And by a sure irrevocable doom,
Fix'd the immortal majesty of Rome.
Fit for the station of his kindred stars,
His mother goddess thus her suit prefers.
" Almighty arbiter, whose pow'rful nod
Shakes distant Earth, and bows our own abode;
To thy great progeny indulgent be,
And rank the goddess-born a deity.
Already has he view'd, with mortal eyes,
Thy brother's kingdoms of the nether skies."
Forthwith a conclave of the godhead meets,
Where Juno in the shining senate sits.
Remorse for past revenge the goddess feels:
Then thund'ring Jove th' almighty mandate seals;
Allots the prince of his celestial line
An apotheosis, and rites divine.
The crystal mansions echo with applause,
And, with her Graces, love's bright queen withdraws;
Shoots in a blaze of light along the skies,
And, borne by turtles, to Laurentum flies.
Alights, where through the reeds Numicius strays,
And to the seas his wat'ry tribute pays.
The god she supplicates to wash away
The parts more gross, and subject to decay,
And cleanse the goddess-born from seminal allay.
The horned flood with glad attention stands,
Then bids his streams obey their sire's commands.
His better parts by lustral waves refin'd,
More pure, and nearer to etherial mind,
With gums of fragrant scent the goddess strews,
And on his features breathes ambrosial dews.
Thus deify'd, new honours Rome decrees,
Shrines, festivals; and styles him Indiges.

THE LINE OF THE LATIAN KINGS.

ASCANIUS now the Latian sceptre sways;
The Alban nation Sylvius next obeys.
Then young Latinus: next an Alba came,
The grace, and guardian of the Alban name.
Then Epitus; then gentle Capys reign'd:
Then Capetis the regal pow'r sustain'd.
Next he who perish'd on the Tuscan flood,
And honour'd with his name the river god.

Now haughty Remulus begun his reign,
Who fell by thunder he aspir'd to feign.
Meek Acrota succeeded to the crown;
From peace endeavouring, more than arms, re-
To Aventinus well resign'd his throne. [nown,
The mount on which he rul'd preserves his name,
And Procas wore the regal diadem.

THE STORY OF VERTUMNUS AND POMONA.

A HAMA-DRYAD flourish'd in these days,
Her name Pomona, from her woodland race.
In garden culture none could so excel,
Or form the pliant souls of plants so well;
Or to the fruit more gen'rous flavours lend,
Or teach the trees with nobler loads to bend.
The nymph frequented not the flatt'ring stream,
Nor meads, the subject of a virgin's dream;
But to such joys her nurs'ry did prefer,
Alone to tend her vegetable care.
A pruning-hook she carry'd in her hand,
And taught the stragglers to obey command;
Lest the licentious, and unthrifty bough,
The too indulgent parent should undo.
She shows, how stocks invite to their embrace
A graft, and naturalize a foreign race
To mend the salvage teint; and in its stead
Adopt new nature, and a nobler breed.
Now hourly she observes her growing care,
And guards their nonage from the bleaker air:
Then opes her streaming sluices, to supply
With flowing draughts her thirsty family.
Long had she labour'd to continue free
From chains of love, and nuptial tyranny;
And in her orchard's small extent immur'd,
Her vow'd virginity she still secur'd.
Oft would loose Pan, and all the lustful train
Of Satyrs, tempt her innocence in vain.
Silenus, that old dotard, own'd a flame;
And he, that frights the thieves with stratagem
Of sword, and something else too gross to name.
Vertumnus too pursu'd the maid no less;
But, with his rivals, shar'd a like success.
To gain access a thousand ways he tries;
Oft, in the hind, the lover would disguise.
The heedless lout comes shambling on, and seems
Just sweating from the labour of his teams.
Then, from the harvest, oft the mimic swain
Seems bending with a load of bearded grain.
Sometimes a dresser of the vine he feigns,
And lawless tendrils to their bounds restrains.
Sometimes his sword a soldier shows; his rod,
An angler; still so various is the god.
Now, in a forehead-cloth, some crone he seems,
A staff supplying the defect of limbs;
Admittance thus he gains; admires the store
Of fairest fruit; the fair possessor more;
Then greets her with a kiss: th' unpractis'd dame
Admir'd a grandame kiss'd with such a flame.
Now, seated by her, he beholds a vine
Around an elm in am'rous foldings twine.
"If that fair elm," he cry'd, "alone should stand,
No grapes would glow with gold, and tempt the hand;
Or if that vine without her elm should grow,
'Twould creep a poor neglected shrub below.
"Be then, fair nymph, by these examples led;
Nor shun, for fancy'd fears, the nuptial bed.
Not she for whom the Lapithites took arms,
Nor Sparta's queen could boast such heavenly charms.
And if you would on woman's faith rely,
None can your choice direct so well as I.
Though old, so much Pomona I adore,
Scarce does the bright Vertumnus love her more.
'Tis your fair self alone his breast inspires
With softest wishes, and unsoil'd desires.
Then fly all vulgar followers, and prove
The god of seasons only worth your love:
On my assurance well you may repose;
Vertumnus scarce Vertumnus better knows.
True to his choice, all looser flames he flies;
Nor for new faces fashionably dies.
The charms of youth, and ev'ry smiling grace
Bloom in his features, and the god confess.
Besides, he puts on ev'ry shape at ease;
But those the most, that best Pomona please.
Still to oblige her is her lover's aim;
Their likings and aversions are the same.
Nor the fair fruit your burden'd branches bear;
Nor all the youthful product of the year,
Could bribe his choice; yourself alone can prove
A fit reward for so refin'd a love.
Relent, fair nymph, and with a kind regret,
Think 'tis Vertumnus weeping at your feet.
A tale attend, through Cyprus known, to prove
How Venus once reveng'd neglected love.

THE STORY OF IPHIS AND ANAXARETE.

"IPHIS, of vulgar birth, by chance had view'd
Fair Anaxaretè of Teucer's blood.
Not long had he beheld the royal dame,
Ere the bright sparkle kindled into flame.
Oft did he struggle with a just despair,
Unfix'd to ask, unable to forbear.
But Love, who flatters still his own disease,
Hopes all things will succeed, he knows will please.
Where'er the fair one haunts, he hovers there;
And seeks her confident with sighs, and pray'r,
Or letters he conveys, that seldom prove
Successless messengers in suits of love.
"Now shiv'ring at her gates the wretch appears,
And myrtle garlands on the columns rears,
Wet with a deluge of unbidden tears.
The nymph more hard than rocks, more deaf than
Derides his pray'rs; insults his agonies; [seas,
Arraigns of insolence th' aspiring swain;
And takes a cruel pleasure in his pain.
Resolv'd at last to finish his despair,
He thus upbraids th' inexorable fair.
"'O Anaxaretè, at last forget
The licence of a passion indiscreet.
Now triumph, since a welcome sacrifice
Your slave prepares, to offer to your eyes.
My life, without reluctance, I resign;
That present best can please a pride like thine.
But, O! forbear to blast a flame so bright,
Doom'd never to expire, but with the light.
And you, great pow'rs, do justice to my name;
The hours, you take from life, restore to fame.'
"Then o'er the posts, once hung with wreaths, he throws
The ready cord, and fits the fatal noose;
For death prepares; and bounding from above,
At once the wretch concludes his life and love.
"Ere long the people gather, and the dead
Is to his mourning mother's arms convey'd.
First like some ghastly statue she appears;
Then bathes the breathless corse in seas of tears,
And gives it to the pile; now as the throng
Proceed in sad solemnity along,

To view the passing pomp the cruel fair
Hastes, and beholds her breathless lover there.
Struck with the sight, inanimate she seems;
Set are her eyes, and motionless her limbs:
Her features without fire, her colour gone,
And, like her heart, she hardens into stone.
In Salamis the statue still is seen
In the fam'd temple of the Cyprian queen.
Warn'd by this tale, no longer then disdain,
O nymph belov'd, to ease a lover's pain.
So may the frosts in spring your blossoms spare,
And winds their rude autumnal rage forbear."
The story oft Vertumnus urg'd in vain,
But then assum'd his heav'nly form again.
Such looks and lustre the bright youth adorn,
As when with rays glad Phœbus paints the morn.
The sight so warms the fair admiring maid,
Like snow she melts: so soon can youth persuade.
Consent, on eager wings, succeeds desire;
And both the lovers glow with mutual fire.

THE LATIAN LINE CONTINUED.

Now Procas yielding to the fates, his son,
Mild Numitor succeeded to the crown:
But false Amulius, with a lawless pow'r,
At length depos'd his brother Numitor.
Then Ilia's valiant issue, with the sword,
Her parent re-inthron'd, the rightful lord.
Next Romulus to people Rome contrives;
The joyous time of Pales' feast arrives;
He gives the word to seize the Sabine wives.
The sires enrag'd take arms, by Tatius led,
Bold to revenge their violated bed.
A fort there was, not yet unknown to fame,
Call'd the Tarpeian, its commander's name.
This by the false Tarpeia was betray'd,
But death well recompens'd the treach'rous maid.
The foe on this new-bought success relies,
And silent march, the city to surprise.
Saturnia's arts with Sabine arms combine;
But Venus countermines the vain design;
Entreats the nymphs that o'er the springs preside,
Which near the fane of hoary Janus glide,
To send their succours: ev'ry urn they drain,
To stop the Sabines' progress, but in vain.
The Naiads now more stratagems essay;
And kindling sulphur to each source convey.
The floods ferment, hot exhalations rise,
Till from the scalding ford the army flies.
Soon Romulus appears in shining arms,
And to the war the Roman legions warms:
The battle rages, and the field is spread
With nothing but the dying and the dead.
Both sides consent to treat without delay,
And their two chiefs at once the sceptre sway.
But Tatius by Lavinian fury slain,
Great Romulus continu'd long to reign.

THE ASSUMPTION OF ROMULUS.

Now warrior Mars his burnish'd helm puts on,
And thus addresses Heav'n's imperial throne.
"Since the inferior world is now become
One vassal globe, and colony to Rome,
This grace, O Jove, for Romulus I claim,
Admit him to the skies, from whence he came.
Long hast thou promis'd an ethereal state
To Mars's lineage; and thy word is fate."
The sire that rules the thunder with a nod,
Declar'd the fiat, and dismiss'd the god.
Soon as the pow'r armipotent survey'd
The flashing skies, the signal he obey'd;
And leaning on his lance, he mounts his car,
His fiery coursers lashing thro' the air.
Mount Palatine he gains, and finds his son
Good laws enacting on a peaceful throne;
The scales of heav'nly justice holding high,
With steady hand, and a discerning eye.
Then vaults upon his car, and to the spheres,
Swift, as a flying shaft, Rome's founder bears.
The parts more pure, in rising are refin'd,
The gross and perishable lag behind.
His shrine in purple vestments stands in view;
He looks a god, and is Quirinus now.

THE ASSUMPTION OF HERSILIA.

Ere long the goddess of the nuptial bed,
With pity mov'd, sends Iris in her stead
To sad Hersilia. Thus the meteor maid:
"Chaste relict! in bright truth to Heav'n ally'd,
The Sabines' glory, and thy sex's pride;
Honour'd on Earth, and worthy of the love
Of such a spouse as now resides above,
Some respite to thy killing griefs afford;
And if thou wouldst once more behold thy lord,
Retire to yon steep mount, with groves o'erspread
Which with an awful gloom his temple shade."
With fear the modest matron lifts her eyes,
And to the bright ambassadress replies:
"O goddess, yet to mortal eyes unknown,
But sure thy various charms confess thee one:
O quick to Romulus thy vot'ress bear,
With looks of love he'll smile away my care:
In whate'er orb he shines, my Heav'n is there."
Then hastes with Iris to the holy grove,
And up the mount Quirinal as they move,
A lambent flame glides downward through the air,
And brightens with a blaze Hersilia's hair.
Together on the bounding ray they rise,
And shoot a gleam of light along the skies.
With op'ning arms Quirinus met his bride,
Now Ora nam'd, and press'd her to his side.

OVID'S METAMORPHOSES.

BOOK XV.

THE PYTHAGOREAN PHILOSOPHY.

By Mr. Dryden.

A king is sought to guide the growing state,
One able to support the public weight,
And fill the throne where Romulus had sat.
Renown, which oft bespeaks the public voice,
Had recommended Numa to their choice:
A peaceful, pious prince; who not content
To know the Sabine rites, his study bent
To cultivate his mind; to learn the laws
Of nature, and explore their hidden cause.
Urg'd by his care, his country he forsook,
And to Crotona thence his journey took.
Arriv'd, he first inquir'd the founder's name
Of this new colony; and whence he came.
Then thus a senior of the place replies,
(Well read, and curious of antiquities):
"'Tis said, Alcides hither took his way
From Spain, and drove along his conquer'd prey;

Then, leaving in the fields his grazing cows,
He sought himself some hospitable house:
Good Croton entertain'd his godlike guest;
While he repair'd his weary limbs with rest.
The hero, thence departing, bless'd the place;
And 'Here,' he said, 'in time's revolving race,
A rising town shall take his name from thee.'
Revolving time fulfill'd the prophecy:
For Myscelos, the justest man on Earth,
Alemon's son, at Argos had his birth:
Him Hercules, arm'd with his club of oak,
O'ershadow'd in a dream, and thus bespoke;
'Go, leave thy native soil, and make abode,
Where Æsaris rolls down his rapid flood:'
He said; and sleep forsook him, and the god.
Trembling he wak'd, and rose with anxious heart;
His country laws forbad him to depart:
What should he do? 'twas death to go away,
And the god menac'd, if he dar'd to stay.
All day he doubted, and when night came on,
Sleep, and the same forewarning dream, begun:
Once more the god stood threat'ning o'er his head;
With added curses if he disobey'd.
Twice warn'd, he study'd flight; but would convey,
At once, his person, and his wealth away:
Thus while he linger'd, his design was heard;
A speedy process form'd, and death declar'd.
Witness there needed none of his offence;
Against himself the wretch was evidence:
Condemn'd, and destitute of human aid,
To him, for whom he suffer'd, thus he pray'd.
" 'O pow'r, who hast deserv'd in Heav'n a throne,
Not giv'n, but by thy labours made thy own,
Pity thy suppliant, and protect his cause,
Whom thou hast made obnoxious to the laws.'
" A custom was of old, and still remains,
Which life or death by suffrages ordains:
White stones and black within an urn are cast;
The first absolve, but fate is in the last.
The judges to the common urn bequeath
Their votes, and drop the sable signs of death;
The box receives all black, but, pour'd from thence,
The stones came candid forth; the hue of innocence.
Thus Alemonides his safety won,
Preserv'd from death by Alcumena's son:
Then to his kinsman-god his vows he pays,
And cuts with prosp'rous gales th' Ionian seas:
He leaves Tarentum favour'd by the wind,
And Thurine bays, and Temises, behind;
Soft Sybaris, and all the capes that stand
Along the shore, he makes in sight of land;
Still doubling, and still coasting, till he found
The mouth of Æsaris, and promis'd ground;
Then saw, where on the margin of the flood,
The tomb, that held the bones of Croton, stood:
Here, by the god's command, he built, and wall'd,
The place predicted; and Crotona call'd.
Thus fame, from time to time, delivers down
The sure tradition of th' Italian town.
" Here dwelt the man divine, whom Samos bore,
But now self-banish'd from his native shore,
Because he hated tyrants, nor could bear
The chains, which none but servile souls will wear.
He, though from Heav'n remote, to Heav'n could move,
With strength of mind, and tread th' abyss above;
And penetrate, with his interior light,
Those upper depths, which nature hid from sight:
And what he had observ'd, and learnt from thence,
Lov'd in familiar language to dispense.
" The crowd with silent admiration stand,
And heard him, as they heard their god's command;
While he discours'd of Heav'n's mysterious laws,
The world's original, and nature's cause;
And what was god; and why the fleecy snows
In silence fell, and rattling winds arose:
What shook the stedfast Earth, and whence begun
The dance of planets round the radiant Sun;
If thunder was the voice of angry Jove,
Or clouds, with nitre pregnant, burst above;
Of these, and things beyond the common reach,
He spoke, and charm'd his audience with his speech.
" He first the taste of flesh from tables drove,
And argu'd well, if arguments could move:
'O mortals, from your fellows' blood abstain,
Nor taint your bodies with a food profane:
While corn and pulse by nature are bestow'd,
And planted orchards bend their willing load;
While labour'd gardens wholsome herbs produce,
And teeming vines afford their gen'rous juice;
Nor tardier fruits of cruder kind are lost,
But tam'd with fire, or mellow'd by the frost;
While kine to pails distended udders bring,
And bees their honey redolent of spring;
While earth not only can your needs supply,
But, lavish of her store, provides for luxury;
A guiltless feast administers with ease,
And without blood is prodigal to please.
Wild beasts their maws with their slain brethren fill;
And yet not all, for some refuse to kill;
Sheep, goats, and oxen, and the nobler steed,
On browse, and corn, and flow'ry meadows feed.
Bears, tigers, wolves, the lion's angry brood,
Whom Heav'n endued with principles of blood,
He wisely sundred from the rest, to yell
In forests, and in lonely caves to dwell;
Where stronger beasts oppress the weak by might,
And all in prey, and purple feasts delight.
" 'O impious use! to nature's laws oppos'd,
Where bowels are in other bowels clos'd:
Where fatten'd by their fellows' fat, they thrive;
Maintain'd by murder, and by death they live.
'Tis then for nought, that mother earth provides
The stores of all she shows, and all she hides,
If men with fleshy morsels must be fed,
And chew with bloody teeth the breathing bread:
What else is this, but to devour our guests,
And barb'rously renew Cyclopean feasts!
We, by destroying life, our life sustain;
And gorge th' ungodly maw with meats obscene.
" 'Not so the golden age, who fed on fruit,
Nor durst with bloody meals their mouths pollute.
Then birds in airy space might safely move,
And tim'rous hares on heaths securely rove:
Nor needed fish the guileful hooks to fear,
For all was peaceful; and that peace sincere.
Whoever was the wretch, (and curs'd be he)
That envy'd first our food's simplicity,
Th' essay of bloody feasts on brutes began,
And after forg'd the sword to murder man;
Had he the sharpen'd steel alone employ'd
On beasts of prey, that other beasts destroy'd,
Or man invaded with their fangs and paws,
This had been justify'd by nature's laws,
And self-defence: but who did feasts begin
Of flesh, he stretch'd necessity to sin.

To kill man-killers man has lawful pow'r,
But not th' extended licence to devour.
" 'Ill habits gather by unseen degrees,
As brooks make rivers, rivers run to seas.
The sow, with her broad snout, for rooting up
Th' intrusted seed, was judg'd to spoil the crop,
And intercept the sweating farmer's hope:
The cov'tous churl, of unforgiving kind,
Th' offender to the bloody priest resign'd:
Her hunger was no plea: for that she dy'd.
The goat came next in order to be try'd:
The goat had cropt the tendrils of the vine:
In vengeance laity and clergy join
Where one had lost his profit, one his wine.
Here was at least some shadow of offence;
The sheep was sacrific'd on no pretence,
But meek and unresisting innocence.
A patient, useful creature, born to bear
The warm, and woolly fleece, that cloth'd her
murderer;
And daily to give down the milk she bred,
A tribute for the grass on which she fed.
Living, both food and raiment she supplies,
And is of least advantage, when she dies.
" 'How did the toiling ox his death deserve,
A downright simple drudge, and born to serve?
O tyrant! with what justice canst thou hope
The promise of the year, a plenteous crop;
When thou destroy'st thy lab'ring steer, who till'd,
And plough'd with pains, thy else ungrateful field?
From his yet reeking neck, to draw the yoke,
That neck, with which the surly clods he broke;
And to the hatchet yield thy husbandman,
Who finish'd autumn, and the spring began!
" 'Nor this alone! but Heav'n itself to bribe,
We to the gods our impious acts ascribe:
First recompense with death their creatures' toil;
Then call the bless'd above to share the spoil:
The fairest victim must the pow'rs appease,
(So fatal 'tis sometimes too much to please!)
A purple fillet his broad brows adorns,
With flow'ry garlands crown'd, and gilded horns:
He hears the murd'rous pray'r the priest prefers,
But understands not 'tis his doom he hears:
Beholds the meal betwixt his temples cast,
(The fruit and products of his labours past;)
And in the water views perhaps the knife,
Uplifted to deprive him of his life;
Then broken up alive, his entrails sees
Torn out, for priests t' inspect the gods' decrees.
" 'From whence, O mortal men, this gust of
blood
Have you deriv'd, and interdicted food?
Be taught by me this dire delight to shun,
Warn'd by my precepts, by my practice won:
And when you eat the well-deserving beast,
Think, on the lab'rer of your field you feast!
' "Now since the god inspires me to proceed,
Be that, whate'er inspiring pow'r, obey'd.
For I will sing of mighty mysteries,
Of truths conceal'd, before, from human eyes,
Dark oracles unveil, and open all the skies.
Pleas'd as I am to walk along the sphere
Of shining stars, and travel with the year,
To leave the heavy Earth, and scale the height
Of Atlas, who supports the heav'nly weight;
To look from upper light, and thence survey
Mistaken mortals wand'ring from the way,
And wanting wisdom, fearful for the state
Of future things, and trembling at their fate!

" 'Those I would teach; and by right reason
To think of death, as but an idle thing. [bring
Why thus affrighted at an empty name,
A dream of darkness, and fictitious flame?
Vain themes of wit, which but in poems pass,
And fables of a world that never was!
What feels the body, when the soul expires,
By time corrupted, or consum'd by fires?
Nor dies the spirit, but new life repeats
In other forms, and only changes seats.
" 'Ev'n I, who these mysterious truths declare,
Was once Euphorbus in the Trojan war;
My name and lineage I remember well,
And how in fight by Sparta's king I fell.
In Argive Juno's fane I late beheld
My buckler hung on high, and own'd my former
shield.
" 'Then, death, so call'd, is but old matter
In some new figure, and a vary'd vest: [dress'd
Thus all things are but alter'd, nothing dies;
And here, and there th' unbody'd spirit flies,
By time, or force, or sickness dispossest,
And lodges, where it lights, in man or beast;
Or hunts without, till ready limbs it find,
And actuates those according to their kind;
From tenement to tenement is toss'd,
The soul is still the same, the figure only lost:
And, as the soften'd wax new seals receives,
This face assumes, and that impression leaves;
Now call'd by one, now by another name;
The form is only chang'd, the wax is still the same:
So death, so call'd, can but the form deface;
Th' immortal soul flies out in empty space,
To seek her fortune in some other place.
" 'Then let not piety be put to flight,
To please the taste of glutton appetite;
But suffer inmate souls secure to dwell,
Lest from their seats your parent you expel;
With rabid hunger feed upon your kind,
Or from a beast dislodge a brother's mind.
" 'And since, like Typhis parting from the shore,
In ample seas I sail, and depths untry'd before,
This let me further add. That nature knows
No stedfast station, but, or ebbs, or flows:
Ever in motion; she destroys her old,
And casts new figures in another mold.
Ev'n times are in perpetual flux, and run,
Like rivers from their fountain, rolling on:
For time, no more than streams, is at a stay;
The flying hour is ever on her way:
And as the fountain still supplies her store,
The wave behind impels the wave before;
Thus in successive course the minutes run,
And urge their predecessor minutes on,
Still moving, ever new: for former things
Are set aside, like abdicated kings:
And every moment alters what is done,
And innovates some act, till then unknown.
" 'Darkness we see emerges into light,
And shining suns descend to sable night;
Ev'n Heav'n itself receives another dye,
When weary'd animals in slumbers lie
Of midnight ease: another, when the gray
Of morn preludes the splendour of the day.
The disk of Phœbus, when he climbs on high,
Appears at first but as a bloodshot eye:
And when his chariot downward drives to bed,
His ball is with the same suffusion red;
But mounted high in his meridian race
All bright he shines, and with a better face:

For there pure particles of ether flow,
Far from the infection of the world below.
"'Nor equal light th' unequal Moon adorns,
Or in her waxing, or her waning horns;
For ev'ry day she wanes, her face is less;
But gath'ring into globe, she fattens at increase.
"'Perceiv'st thou not the process of the year,
How the four seasons in four forms appear,
Resembling human life in ev'ry shape they wear?
Spring first, like infancy, shoots out her head,
With milky juice requiring to be fed:
Helpless, though fresh, and wanting to be led.
The green stem grows in stature, and in size,
But only feeds with hope the farmer's eyes;
Then laughs the childish year with flow'rets crown'd,
And lavishly perfumes the fields around.
But no substantial nourishment receives;
Infirm the stalks, unsolid are the leaves.
"'Proceeding onward when the year began,
The Summer grows adult, and ripens into man.
This season, as in man, is most replete
With kindly moisture, and prolific heat.
"'Autumn succeeds, a sober tepid age,
Not froze with fear, nor boiling into rage;
More than mature, and tending to decay,
When our brown locks repine to mix with odious gray.
"'Last, Winter creeps along with tardy pace,
Sour is his front, and furrow'd is his face;
His scalp if not dishonour'd quite of hair,
The ragged fleece is thin; and thin is worse than bare.
"'Ev'n our own bodies daily change receive,
Some part of what was theirs before, they leave;
Nor are to day, what yesterday they were;
Nor the whole same to morrow will appear.
"'Time was, when we were sow'd, and just began,
From some few fruitful drops, the promise of a man:
Then nature's hand (fermented as it was)
Moulded to shape the soft, coagulated mass;
And when the little man was fully form'd,
The breathless embrio with a spirit warm'd;
But when the mother's throes begin to come,
The creature, pent within the narrow room,
Breaks his blind prison, pushing to repair
His stifled breath, and draw the living air;
Cast on the margin of the world he lies,
A helpless babe, but by instinct he cries.
He next essays to walk, but downward press'd
On four feet imitates his brother beast:
By slow degrees he gathers from the ground
His legs, and to the rolling chair is bound:
Then walks alone; a horseman now become,
He rides a stick, and travels round the room.
In time he vaunts among his youthful peers,
Strong-bon'd, and strung with nerves, in pride of years.
He runs with mettle his first merry stage,
Maintains the next, abated of his rage,
But manages his strength, and spares his age.
Heavy the third, and stiff, he sinks apace,
And though 'tis down-hill all, but creeps along the race.
Now sapless on the verge of death he stands,
Contemplating his former feet and hands;
And, Milo-like, his slacken'd sinews sees,
And wither'd arms, once fit to cope with Hercules,
Unable now to shake, much less to tear, the trees.
"'So Helen wept, when her too faithful glass
Reflected on her eyes the ruins of her face:
Wond'ring, what charms her ravishers could spy,
To force her twice, or ev'n but once t' enjoy!
"'Thy teeth, devouring time, thine, envious age,
On things below still exercise your rage:
With venom'd grinders you corrupt your meat,
And then, at ling'ring meals, the morsels eat.
"'Nor those, which elements we call, abide,
Nor to this figure, nor to that are ty'd;
For this eternal world is said, of old,
But four prolific principles to hold,
Four different bodies; two to Heav'n ascend,
And other two down to the centre tend:
Fire first with wings expanded mounts on high,
Pure, void of weight, and dwells in upper sky;
Then air, because unclogg'd in empty space,
Flies after fire, and claims the second place:
But weighty water, as her nature guides,
Lies on the lap of earth; and mother earth subsides.
"'All things are mix'd of these, which all contain,
And into these are all resolv'd again:
Earth rarefies to dew; expanded more,
The subtil dew in air begins to soar;
Spreads, as she flies, and weary of her name
Extenuates still, and changes into flame;
Thus having by degrees perfection won,
Restless they soon untwist the web they spun,
And fire begins to lose her radiant hue,
Mix'd with gross air, and air descends to dew;
And dew condensing, does her form forego,
And sinks, a heavy lump of earth below.
"'Thus are their figures never at a stand,
But chang'd by nature's innovating hand;
All things are alter'd, nothing is destroy'd,
The shifted scene for some new show employ'd.
"'Then, to be born, is to begin to be
Some other thing we were not formerly:
And what we call to die, is not t' appear,
Or be the thing, that formerly we were.
Those very elements, which we partake
Alive, when dead some other bodies make:
Translated grow, have sense, or can discourse;
But death on deathless substance has no force.
"'That forms are chang'd, I grant; that nothing can
Continue in the figure it began:
The golden age to silver was debas'd:
To copper that; our metal came at last.
"'The face of places, and their forms, decay;
And that is solid earth, that once was sea:
Seas in their turn retreating from the shore,
Make solid land, what ocean was before;
And far from strands are shells of fishes found,
And rusty anchors fix'd on mountain ground:
And what were fields before, now wash'd and worn
By falling floods from high, to valleys turn,
And crumbling still descend to level lands;
And lakes, and trembling bogs, are barren sands.
And the parch'd desert floats in streams unknown;
Wond'ring to drink of waters not her own.
"'Here nature living fountains opes: and there
Seals up the wombs, where living fountains were:
Or earthquakes stop their ancient course, and bring
Diverted streams to feed a distant spring.
So Lycus, swallow'd up, is seen no more,
But far from thence knocks out another door.
Thus Erasinus dives; and blind in earth
Runs on, and gropes his way to second birth,
Starts up in Argos' meads, and shakes his locks
Around the fields, and fattens all the flocks.
So Mysus by another way is led,
And, grown a river, now disdains his head:
Forgets his humble birth, his name forsakes,
And the proud title of Caïcus takes.

Large Amenane, impure with yellow sands,
Runs rapid often, and as often stands,
And here he threats the drunken fields to drown;
And there his dugs deny to give their liquor down.
"'Anigros once did wholsome draughts afford,
But now his deadly waters are abhorr'd:
Since, hurt by Hercules, as fame resounds,
The Centaurs in his current wash'd their wounds.
The streams of Hypanis are sweet no more,
But brackish lose the taste they had before.
Antissa, Pharos, Tyre, in seas were pent,
Once isles, but now increase the continent;
While the Leucadian coast, main land before,
By rushing seas is sever'd from the shore.
So Zancle to th' Italian earth was ty'd,
And men once walk'd, where ships at anchor ride;
Till Neptune overlook'd the narrow way,
And in disdain pour'd in the conqu'ring sea.
"'Two cities that adorn'd th' Achaian ground,
Buris, and Helice, no more are found,
But whelm'd beneath a lake, are sunk and drown'd;
And boatsmen through the crystal water show,
To wond'ring passengers, the walls below.
"'Near Trœzen stands a hill, expos'd in air
To winter-winds, of leafy shadows bare:
This once was level ground: but (strange to tell)
The included vapours, that in caverns dwell,
Lab'ring with colic pangs, and close confin'd,
In vain sought issue for the rumbling wind:
Yet still they heav'd for vent, and heaving still
Inlarg'd the concave, and shot up the hill;
As breath extends a bladder, or the skins
Of goats are blown t' enclose the hoarded wines:
The mountain yet retains a mountain's face,
And gather'd rubbish heals the hollow space.
Of many wonders, which I heard, or knew,
Retrenching most, I will relate but few:
What, are not springs with qualities oppos'd
Endu'd at seasons, and at seasons lost?
Thrice in a day thine, Ammon, change their form,
Cold at high noon, at morn and evening warm:
Thine, Athaman, will kindle wood, if thrown
On the pil'd earth, and in the waning Moon.
The Thracians have a stream, if any try
The taste, his harden'd bowels petrify:
Whate'er it touches, it converts to stones,
And makes a marble pavement, where it runs.
"'Crathis, and Sybaris her sister flood,
That slide through our Calabrian neighbour wood,
With gold, and amber dye the shining hair;
And thither youth resort: (for who would not be fair?)
"'But stranger virtues yet in streams we find,
Some change not only bodies, but the mind:
Who has not heard of Salmacis obscene,
Whose waters into women soften men?
Or Æthiopian lakes, which turn the brain
To madness, or in heavy sleep constrain?
Clytorian streams the love of wine expel,
(Such is the virtue of th' abstemious well,)
Whether the colder nymph that rules the flood
Extinguishes, and balks the drunken god;
Or that Melampus (so have some assur'd)
When the mad Prœtides with charms he cur'd,
And pow'rful herbs, both charms and simples cast
Into the sober spring, where still their virtues last.
"Unlike effects Lyncestis will produce;
Who drinks his waters, though with mod'rate use,
Reels as with wine, and sees with double sight;
His heels too heavy, and his head too light.
Ladon, once Pheneos, an Arcadian stream,
(Ambiguous in th' effects, as in the name)
By day is wholesome bev'rage, but is thought
By night infected, and a deadly draught.
"'Thus running rivers, and the standing lake,
Now of these virtues, now of those partake:
Time was (and all things time and fate obey)
When fast Ortygia floated on the sea;
Such were Cyanean isles, when Typhis steer'd
Betwixt their straits, and their collision fear'd;
They swam, where now they sit; and firmly join'd,
Secure of rooting up, resist the wind.
Nor Ætna vomiting sulphureous fire
Will ever belch; for sulphur will expire,
(The veins exhausted of the liquid store:)
Time was, she cast no flames, in time will cast no more.
"'For whether Earth's an animal, and air
Imbibes, her lungs with coolness to repair,
And what she sucks remits; she still requires
Inlets for air, and outlets for her fires;
When tortur'd with convulsive fits she shakes,
That motion chokes the vent, till other vent she makes:
Or when the winds in hollow caves are clos'd,
And subtle spirits find that way oppos'd,
They toss up flints in air; the flints that hide
The seeds of fire, thus toss'd in air, collide,
Kindling the sulphur, till the fuel spent,
The cave is cool'd, and the fierce winds relent.
"'Or whether sulphur, catching fire, feeds on
Its unctuous parts, till all the matter gone
The flames no more ascend; for earth supplies
The fat that feeds them; and when earth denies
That food, by length of time consum'd, the fire
Famish'd for want of fuel must expire.
"'A race of men there are, as fame has told,
Who shiv'ring suffer hyperborean cold,
Till nine times bathing in Minerva's lake,
Soft feathers, to defend their naked sides, they take.
'Tis said, the Scythian wives (believe who will)
Transform themselves to birds by magic skill;
Smear'd over with an oil of wond'rous might,
That adds new pinions to their airy flight.
"'But this by sure experiment we know,
That living creatures from corruption grow:
Hide in a hollow pit a slaughter'd steer,
Bees from his putrid bowels will appear;
Who, like their parents, haunt the fields, and bring
Their honey-harvest home, and hope another spring.
The warlike steed is multiply'd, we find,
To wasps, and hornets of the warrior kind.
Cut from a crab his crooked claws, and hide
The rest in earth, a scorpion thence will glide,
And shoot his sting, his tail in circles toss'd
Refers the limbs his backward father lost:
And worms, that stretch on leaves their filmy loom,
Crawl from their bags, and butterflies become.
Ev'n slime begets the frog's loquacious race;
Short of their feet at first, in little space
With arms and legs endu'd, long leaps they take
Rais'd on their hinder part, and swim the lake,
And waves repel: for nature gives their kind,
To that intent, a length of legs behind.
"'The cubs of bears a living lump appear,
When whelp'd, and no determin'd figure wear.
Their mother licks them into shape, and gives
As much of form, as she herself receives.

" 'The grubs from their sexangular abode
Crawl out unfinish'd, like the maggot's brood:
Trunks without limbs; till time at leisure brings
The thighs they wanted, and their tardy wings.
" 'The bird who draws the car of Juno, vain
Of her crown'd head, and of her starry train;
And he that bears th' artillery of Jove,
The strong-pounc'd eagle, and the billing dove;
And all the feather'd kind, who could suppose
(But that from sight, the surest sense, he knows)
They from th' included yolk, not ambient white, arose?
" 'There are, who think the marrow of a man,
Which in the spine, while he was living, ran;
When dead, the pith corrupted will become
A snake, and hiss within the hollow tomb.
" 'All these receive their birth from other things;
But from himself the phenix only springs:
Self-born, begotten by the parent flame
In which he burn'd, another and the same:
Who not by corn or herbs his life sustains,
But the sweet essence of amomum drains:
And watches the rich gums Arabia bears,
While yet in tender dew they drop their tears.
He, (his five centuries of life fulfill'd)
His nest on oaken boughs begins to build,
Or trembling tops of palm; and first he draws
The plan with his broad bill, and crooked claws,
Nature's artificers; on this the pile
Is form'd, and rises round, then with the spoil
Of cassia, cinnamon, and stems of nard,
(For softness strew'd beneath) his fun'ral bed is rear'd:
Fun'ral and bridal both; and all around
The borders with corruptless myrrh are crown'd;
On this incumbent, till ethereal flame
First catches, then consumes the costly frame:
Consumes him too, as on the pile he lies;
He liv'd on odours, and in odours dies.
" 'An infant phenix from the former springs,
His father's heir, and from his tender wings
Shakes off his parent dust, his method he pursues,
And the same lease of life on the same term renews.
When grown to manhood he begins his reign,
And with stiff pinions can his flight sustain.
He lightens of its load the tree, that bore
His father's royal sepulchre before,
And his own cradle; this with pious care
Plac'd on his back, he cuts the buxom air,
Seeks the Sun's city, and his sacred church,
And decently lays down his burden in the porch.
" 'A wonder more amazing would we find?
Th' hyæna shows it, of a double kind,
Varying the sexes in alternate years,
In one begets, and in another bears.
The thin cameleon fed with air, receives
The colour of the things, to which he cleaves.
" 'India when conquer'd, on the conqu'ring god
For planted vines the sharp-ey'd lynx bestow'd,
Whose urine, shed before it touches earth,
Congeals in air, and gives to gems their birth.
So coral soft, and white in ocean's bed,
Comes harden'd up in air, and glows with red.
" 'All changing species should my song recite,
Before I ceas'd, would change the day to night.
Nations and empires flourish and decay,
By turns command, and in their turns obey;
Time softens hardy people, time again
Hardens to war a soft unwarlike train.
Thus Troy for ten long years her foes withstood,
And daily bleeding bore the expense of blood:
Now for thick streets it shows an empty space,
Or only fill'd with tombs of her own perish'd race,
Herself becomes the sepulchre of what she was.
" 'Mycenè, Sparta, Thebes of mighty fame,
Are vanish'd out of substance into name.
And Dardan Rome, that just begins to rise
On Tiber's banks, in time shall mate the skies:
Widening her bounds, and working on her way;
Ev'n now she meditates imperial sway:
Yet this is change, but she by changing thrives,
Like moons new born, and in her cradle strives
To fill her infant horns; an hour shall come,
When the round world shall be contain'd in Rome.
" 'For thus old saws foretel, and Helenus
Anchises' drooping son enliven'd thus;
When Ilium now was in a sinking state,
And he was doubtful of his future fate:
'O goddess-born, with thy hard fortune strive,
Troy never can be lost, and thou alive.
Thy passage thou shalt free from fire, and sword,
And Troy in foreign lands shall be restor'd.
In happier fields a rising town I see
Greater, than what e'er was, or is, or e'er shall be:
And Heav'n yet owes the world a race deriv'd from thee.
Sages, and chiefs, of other lineage born,
The city shall extend, extended shall adorn:
But from Iülus he must draw his breath,
By whom thy Rome shall rule the conquer'd Earth:
Whom Heav'n will lend mankind on Earth to reign,
And late require the precious pledge again.'
This Helenus to great Æneas told,
Which I retain, e'er since in other mould
My soul was cloth'd; and now rejoice to view
My country walls rebuilt, and Troy reviv'd anew,
Rais'd by the fall, decreed by loss to gain;
Enslav'd but to be free, and conquer'd but to reign.
" ''Tis time my hard-mouth'd coursers to control,
Apt to run riot, and transgress the goal:
And therefore I conclude, whatever lies
In earth, or flits in air, or fills the skies,
All suffer change; and we that are of soul
And body mix'd, are members of the whole.
Then when our sires, or grandsires, shall forsake
The forms of men, and brutal figures take,
Thus hous'd, securely let their spirits rest,
Nor violate thy father in the beast,
Thy friend, thy brother, any of thy kin;
If none of these, yet there's a man within;
O spare to make a Thyestæan meal,
T' enclose his body, and his soul expel.
" 'Ill customs by degrees to habits rise,
Ill habits soon become exalted vice:
What more advance can mortals make in sin
So near perfection, who with blood begin?
Deaf to the calf, that lies beneath the knife,
Looks up, and from her butcher begs her life:
Deaf to the harmless kid, that ere he dies
All methods to procure thy mercy tries,
And imitates in vain thy children's cries.
Where will he stop, who feeds with houshold bread,
Then eats the poultry, which before he fed?
Let plough thy steers; that when they lose their breath,
To nature, not to thee, they may impute their death.
Let goats for food their loaded udders lend,
And sheep from winter-cold thy sides defend;

But neither springes, nets, nor snares, employ,
And be no more ingenious to destroy.
Free as in air, let birds on earth remain,
Nor let insidious glue their wings constrain;
Nor op'ning hounds the trembling stag affright,
Nor purple feathers intercept his flight:
Nor hooks conceal'd in baits for fish prepare,
Nor lines to heave them twinkling up in air.
"'Take not away the life you cannot give,
For all things have an equal right to live.
Kill noxious creatures, where 'tis sin to save;
This only just prerogative we have:
But nourish life with vegetable food,
And shun the sacrilegious taste of blood."'
These precepts by the Samian sage were taught,
Which god-like Numa to the Sabines brought,
And thence transferr'd to Rome, by gift his own:
A willing people, and an offer'd throne.
O happy monarch, sent by Heav'n to bless
A savage nation with soft arts of peace,
To teach religion, rapine to restrain,
Give laws to lust, and sacrifice ordain:
Himself a saint, a goddess was his bride,
And all the Muses o'er his acts preside.

THE STORY OF HIPPOLYTUS.

By Mr. Catcott.

ADVANC'D in years he dy'd; one common date
His reign concluded, and his mortal state.
Their tears plebeians and patricians shed,
And pious matrons wept their monarch dead.
His mournful wife, her sorrows to bewail,
Withdrew from Rome, and sought th' Arician vale.
Hid in thick woods, she made incessant moans,
Disturbing Cynthia's sacred rites with groans.
How oft the nymphs, who rul'd the wood and lake,
Reprov'd her tears, and words of comfort spake!
How oft in vain the son of Theseus said,
"Thy stormy sorrows be with patience laid;
Nor are thy fortunes to be wept alone,
Weigh others' woes, and learn to bear thine own.
Be mine an instance to assuage thy grief:
Would mine were none!—yet mine may bring relief.
"You've heard, perhaps, in conversation told,
What once befel Hippolytus of old;
To death by Theseus' easy faith betray'd,
And caught in snares his wicked step-dame laid.
The wond'rous tale your credit scarce may claim,
Yet (strange to say) in me behold the same,
Whom lustful Phædra oft had press'd in vain,
With impious joys my father's bed to stain;
Till seiz'd with fear, or by revenge inspir'd,
She charg'd on me the crimes herself desir'd.
Expell'd by Theseus, from his home I fled
With heaps of curses on my guiltless head.
Forlorn, I sought Pitthëan Trœzen's land,
And drove my chariot o'er Corinthus' strand;
When from the surface of the level main
A billow rising, heav'd above the plain;
Rolling, and gath'ring, till so high it swell'd,
A mountain's height th' enormous mass excell'd;
Then bellowing, burst; when from the summit cleav'd,
A horned bull his ample chest upheav'd.
His mouth, and nostrils, storms of briny rain
Expiring, blew. Dread horrour seiz'd my train.
I stood unmov'd. My father's cruel doom
Claim'd all my soul, nor fear could find a room.
Amaz'd awhile my trembling coursers stood,
With prick'd-up ears, contemplating the flood;
Then starting sudden from the dreadful view,
At once, like lightning, from the seas they flew,
And o'er the craggy rocks the rattling chariot drew.
In vain to stop the hot-mouth'd steeds I try'd,
And bending backward all my strength apply'd;
The frothy foam in driving flakes distains
The bits, and bridles, and bedews the reins.
But though, as yet untam'd they run, at length
Their heady rage had tir'd beneath my strength,
When in the spokes a stump intangling, tore
The shatter'd wheel, and from its axle bore.
The shock impetuous tost me from the seat,
Caught in the reins beneath my horses' feet.
My reeking guts dragg'd out alive, around
The jagged stump my trembling nerves were wound,
Then stretch'd the well-knit limbs, in pieces hal'd,
Part stuck behind, and part the chariot trail'd;
Till, midst my crackling joints, and breaking bones,
I breath'd away my weary'd soul in groans.
No part distinguish'd from the rest was found,
But all my parts an universal wound.
"Now say, self-tortur'd nymph, can you compare
Our griefs as equal, or in justice dare?
I saw besides the darksome realms of woe,
And bath'd my wounds in smoking streams below.
There I had stay'd, nor second life enjoy'd,
But Pæan's son his wond'rous art employ'd.
To light restor'd, by medicinal skill,
In spite of fate, and rigid Pluto's will,
Th' invidious object to preserve from view,
A misty cloud around me Cynthia threw:
And lest my sight should stir my foes to rage,
She stamp'd my visage with the marks of age.
My former hue was chang'd, and for it shown
A set of features, and a face unknown.
Awhile the goddess stood in doubt, or Crete,
Or Delos' isle, to choose for my retreat.
Delos, and Crete refus'd, this wood she chose,
Bad me my former luckless name depose,
Which kept alive the mem'ry of my woes:
Then said, 'Immortal life be thine; and thou,
Hippolytus once call'd, be Virbius now.'
Here then a god, but of th' inferior race,
I serve my goddess, and attend her chase."

EGERIA TRANSFORMED TO A FOUNTAIN.

BUT others' woes were useless to appease
Egeria's grief, or set her mind at ease.
Beneath the hill, all comfortless she laid,
The dropping tears her eyes incessant shed,
Till pitying Phœbe eas'd her pious woe,
Thaw'd to a spring, whose streams for ever flow.
The nymphs, and Virbius, like amazement fill'd
As seiz'd the swains, who Tyrrhene furrows till'd;
When heaving up, a clod was seen to roll,
Untouch'd, self-mov'd, and big with human soul.
The spreading mass in former shape depos'd,
Began to shoot, and arms and legs disclos'd,
Till form'd a perfect man, the living mould
Op'd its new mouth, and future truths foretold;
And Tages nam'd by natives of the place,
Taught arts prophetic to the Tuscan race.
Or such as once by Romulus was shown,
Who saw his lance with sprouting leaves o'ergrown,

When fix'd in earth the point began to shoot,
And growing downward turn'd a fibrous root;
While spread aloft the branching arms display'd,
O'er wond'ring crowds, an unexpected shade.

THE STORY OF CIPPUS.

By Sir Samuel Garth, M.D.

Or as when Cippus in the current view'd
The shooting horns that on his forehead stood,
His temples first he feels, and with surprise
His touch confirms th' assurance of his eyes.
Straight to the skies his horned front he rears,
And to the gods directs these pious pray'rs:
"If this portent be prosp'rous, O decree
To Rome th' event; if otherwise, to me."
An altar then of turf he hastes to raise,
Rich gums in fragrant exhalations blaze;
The panting entrails crackle as they fry,
And boding fumes pronounce a mystery.
Soon as the augur saw the holy fire,
And victims with presaging signs expire,
To Cippus then he turns his eyes with speed,
And views the horny honours of his head:
Then cry'd, "Hail conqueror! thy call obey,
Those omens I behold presage thy sway.
Rome waits thy nod, unwilling to be free,
And owns thy sov'reign pow'r as fate's decree."
He said—and Cippus, starting at th' event,
Spoke in these words his pious discontent.
"Far hence, ye gods, this execration send,
And the great race of Romulus defend.
Better that I in exile live abhorr'd,
Than e'er the capitol should style me lord."
This spoke, he hides with leaves his omen'd head,
Then prays, the senate next convenes, and said:
"If augurs can foresee, a wretch is come,
Design'd by destiny the bane of Rome.
Two horns (most strange to tell) his temples crown;
If e'er he pass the walls and gain the town,
Your laws are forfeit, that ill-fated hour;
And liberty must yield to lawless pow'r.
Your gates he might have enter'd; but this arm
Seiz'd the usurper, and withheld the harm.
Haste, find the monster out, and let him be
Condemn'd to all the senate can decree;
Or ty'd in chains, or into exile thrown;
Or by the tyrant's death prevent your own."
The crowd such murmurs utter as they stand,
As swelling surges breaking on the strand:
Or as when gath'ring gales sweep o'er the grove,
And their tall heads the bending cedars move.
Each with confusion gaz'd, and then began
To feel his fellows' brows, and find the man.
Cippus then shakes his garland off, and cries,
"The wretch you want, I offer to your eyes."
The anxious throng look'd down, and sad in thought,
All wish'd they had not found the sign they sought:
In haste with laurel wreaths his head they bind;
Such honour to such virtue was assign'd.
Then thus the senate—"Hear, O Cippus, hear;
So god-like is thy tutelary care,
That since in Rome thyself forbids thy stay,
For thy abodes those acres we convey
The plough-share can surround, the labour of a day.
In deathless records thou shalt stand inroll'd,
And Rome's rich posts shall shine with horns of gold."

THE OCCASION OF ÆSCULAPIUS BEING BROUGHT TO ROME.

By Mr. Welsted.

Melodious maids of Pindus, who inspire
The flowing strains, and tune the vocal lyre;
Tradition's secrets are unlock'd to you,
Old tales revive, and ages past renew;
You, who can hidden causes best expound,
Say, whence the isle, which Tiber flows around,
Its altars with a heav'nly stranger grac'd,
And in our shrines the god of physic plac'd.
A wasting plague infected Latium's skies;
Pale, bloodless looks were seen, with ghastly eyes;
The dire disease's marks each visage wore,
And the pure blood was chang'd to putrid gore:
In vain were human remedies apply'd;
In vain the pow'r of healing herbs was try'd:
Weary'd with death, they seek celestial aid,
And visit Phœbus in his Delphic shade.
In the world's centre sacred Delphos stands,
And gives its oracles to distant lands:
Here they implore the god, with fervent vows,
His salutary pow'r to interpose,
And end a great afflicted city's woes.
The holy temple sudden tremours prov'd;
The laurel-grove and all its quivers mov'd;
In hollow sounds the priestess thus began,
And through each bosom thrilling horrours ran.
"Th' assistance, Roman, which you here implore,
Seek from another, and a nearer shore;
Relief must be implor'd, and succour won,
Not from Apollo, but Apollo's son;
My son, to Latium born, shall bring redress:
Go with good omens, and expect success."
When these clear oracles the senate knew,
The sacred tripod's counsels they pursue,
Depute a pious and a chosen band,
Who sail to Epidaurus' neighbouring land.
Before the Grecian elders when they stood,
They pray them to bestow the healing god:
"Ordain'd was he to save Ausonia's state;
So promis'd Delphos, and unerring fate."
Opinions various their debates enlarge:
Some plead to yield to Rome the sacred charge;
Others, tenacious of their country's wealth,
Refuse to grant the pow'r who guards its health.
While dubious they remain'd, the wasting light
Withdrew before the growing shades of night;
Thick darkness now obscur'd the dusky skies:
Now, Roman, clos'd in sleep were mortal eyes,
When health's auspicious god appears to thee,
And thy glad dreams his form celestial see:
In his left hand, a rural staff preferr'd,
His right is seen to stroke his decent beard.
"Dismiss," said he, with mildness all divine,
"Dismiss your fears; I come, and leave my shrine.
This serpent view, that with ambitious play
My staff encircles, mark him ev'ry way;
His form, though larger, nobler, I'll assume,
And chang'd, as gods should be, bring aid to Rome."
Here fled the vision, and the vision's flight
Was follow'd by the cheerful dawn of light.
Now was the morn with blushing streaks o'erspread,
And all the starry fires of Heav'n were fled;
The chiefs perplex'd, and fill'd with doubtful care,
To their protector's sumptuous roofs repair,

By genuine signs implore him to express,
What seats he deigns to choose, what land to bless:
Scarce their ascending pray'rs had reach'd the sky;
Lo, the serpentine god, erected high!
Forerunning hissings his approach confest;
Bright shone his golden scales, and wav'd his lofty crest.
The trembling altar his appearance spoke;
The marble floor, and glittering ceiling shook;
The doors were rock'd: the statue seem'd to nod:
And all the fabric own'd the present god.
His radiant chest he taught aloft to rise,
And round the temple cast his flaming eyes:
Struck was th' astonish'd crowd; the holy priest,
His temples with white bands of ribbon drest,
With rev'rent awe the power divine confest!
"The god! the god!" he cries; "all tongues be still!
Each conscious breast devoutest ardour fill!
O beauteous! O divine! assist our cares,
And be propitious to thy vot'ries' prayers!"
All with consenting hearts, and pious fear,
The words repeat, the deity revere:
The Romans in their holy worship join'd,
With silent awe, and purity of mind:
Gracious to them, his crest is seen to nod,
And, as an earnest of his care, the god,
Thrice hissing, vibrates thrice his forked tongue.
And now the smooth descent he glides along:
Still on the ancient seats he bends his eyes,
In which his statue breathes, his altars rise;
His long-lov'd shrine with kind concern he leaves,
And to forsake th' accustom'd mansion grieves;
At length his sweeping bulk in state is borne
Through the throng'd streets, which scatter'd flowers adorn;
Through many a fold he winds his mazy course,
And gains the port and moles, which break the ocean's force.
'Twas here he made a stand, and having view'd
The pious train, who his last steps pursu'd,
Seem'd to dismiss their zeal with gracious eyes,
While gleams of pleasure in his aspect rise.
And now the Latian vessel he ascends;
Beneath the weighty god the vessel bends:
The Latins on the strand great Jove appease,
Their cables loose, and plough the yielding seas:
The high-rear'd serpent from the stern displays
His gorgeous form, and the blue deep surveys;
The ship is wafted on with gentle gales,
And o'er the calm Ionian smoothly sails;
On the sixth morn th' Italian coast they gain,
And touch Lacinia, grac'd with Juno's fane;
Now fair Calabria to the sight is lost,
And all the cities on her fruitful coast;
They pass at length the rough Sicilian shore,
The Brutian soil, rich with metallic ore,
The famous isles where Æolus was king,
And Pæstus blooming with eternal spring:
Minerva's cape they leave, and Capreæ's isle,
Campania, on whose hills the vineyards smile,
The city which Alcides' spoils adorn,
Naples, for soft delight and pleasure born;
Fair Stabiæ, with Cumean Sibyls' seats,
And Baia's tepid baths and green retreats;
Linternum next they reach, where balmy gums
Distil from mastic trees, and spread perfumes:
Cajeta, from the nurse so nam'd for whom
With pious care Æneas rais'd a tomb,
Vulturne, whose whirlpools suck the numerous sands,
And Trachas, and Minturnæ's marshy lands,
And Formia's coast is left, and Circe's plain,
Which yet remembers her enchanting reign;
To Antium, last, his course the pilot guides.
Here, while the anchor'd vessel safely rides,
(For now the ruffled deep portends a storm)
The spiry god unfolds his spheric form,
Through large indentings draws his lubric train,
And seeks the refuge of Apollo's fane;
The fane is situate on the yellow shore:
When the sea smil'd, and the winds rag'd no more,
He leaves his father's hospitable lands,
And furrows, with his rattling scales, the sands
Along the coast; at length the ship regains,
And sails to Tibur, and Lavinium's plains.
Here mingling crowds to meet their patron came,
Ev'n the chaste guardians of the vestal flame,
From every part tumultuous they repair,
And joyful acclamations rend the air:
Along the flow'ry banks, on either side,
Where the tall ship floats on the swelling tide,
Dispos'd in decent order altars rise,
And crackling incense, as it mounts the skies,
The air with sweets refreshes; while the knife,
Warm with the victim's blood, lets out the streaming life.
The world's great mistress, Rome, receives him now;
On the mast's top reclin'd he waves his brow,
And from that height surveys the great abodes,
And mansions, worthy of residing gods.
The land, a narrow neck, itself extends,
Round with his course the stream divided bends;
The stream's two arms, on either side, are seen,
Stretch'd out in equal length; the land between.
The isle, so call'd, from hence derives its name;
'Twas here the salutary serpent came;
Nor sooner has he left the Latian pine,
But he assumes again his form divine,
And now no more the drooping city mourns,
Joy is again restor'd, and health returns.

THE DEIFICATION OF JULIUS CÆSAR.

But Æsculapius was a foreign pow'r:
In his own city Cæsar we adore:
Him arms and arts alike renown'd beheld,
In peace conspicuous, dreadful in the field;
His rapid conquests, and swift-finish'd wars,
The hero justly fix'd among the stars.
Yet is his progeny his greatest fame:
The son immortal makes the father's name.
The sea-girt Britons, by his courage tam'd,
For their high rocky cliffs, and fierceness fam'd;
His dreadful navies, which victorious rode
O'er Nile's affrighted waves and seven-sourc'd flood;
Numidia, and the spacious realms regain'd,
Where Cinyphis or flows or Juba reign'd;
The powers of titled Mithridates broke,
And Pontus added to the Roman yoke;
Triumphal shows decreed, for conquests won,
For conquests, which the triumphs still out-shone;
These are great deeds; yet less, than to have giv'n
The world a lord, in whom, propitious Heav'n,
When you decreed the sov'reign rule to place,
You blest with lavish bounty human race.
Now lest so great a prince might seem to rise
Of mortal stem, his sire must reach the skies;

The beauteous goddess, that Æneas bore,
Foresaw it, and foreseeing did deplore;
For well she knew her hero's fate was nigh,
Devoted by conspiring arms to die.
Trembling, and pale, to every god she cry'd,
"Behold, what deep and subtile arts are try'd,
To end the last, the only branch that springs
From my Iülus, and the Dardan kings!
How bent they are! how desp'rate to destroy
All that is left me of unhappy Troy!
Am I alone by fate ordain'd to know
Uninterrupted care, and endless woe?
Now from Tydides' spear I feel the wound:
Now Ilium's tow'rs the hostile flames surround:
Troy laid in dust, my exil'd son I mourn,
Through angry seas and raging billows borne,
O'er the wide deep his wand'ring course he bends;
Now to the sullen shades of Styx descends;
With Turnus driv'n at last fierce wars to wage,
Or rather with unpitying Juno's rage.
But why record I now my ancient woes?
Sense of past ills in present fears I lose;
On me their points the impious daggers throw;
Forbid it, gods, repel the direful blow:
If by curs'd weapons Numa's priest expires,
No longer shall ye burn, ye vestal fires."
  While such complainings Cypria's grief disclose,
In each celestial breast compassion rose:
Not gods can alter fate's resistless will!
Yet they foretold by signs th' approaching ill.
Dreadful were heard, among the clouds, alarms
Of echoing trumpets, and of clashing arms;
The Sun's pale image gave so faint a light,
That the sad Earth was almost veil'd in night;
The ether's face with fiery meteors glow'd;
With storms of hail were mingled drops of blood;
A dusky hue the morning star o'erspread,
And the Moon's orb was stain'd with spots of red;
In every place portentous shrieks were heard,
The fatal warnings of th' infernal bird;
In ev'ry place the marble melts to tears;
While in the groves, rever'd through length of years,
Boding and awful sounds the ear invade,
And solemn music warbles through the shade;
No victim can atone the impious age,
No sacrifice the wrathful gods assuage;
Dire wars and civil fury threat the state;
And every omen points out Cæsar's fate;
Around each hallow'd shrine, and sacred dome,
Night-howling dogs disturb the peaceful gloom;
Their silent seats the wand'ring shades forsake,
And fearful tremblings the rock'd city shake.
  Yet could not, by these prodigies, be broke
The plotted charm, or staid the fatal stroke;
Their swords th' assassins in the temple draw;
Their murd'ring hands nor gods nor temples awe;
This sacred place their bloody weapons stain,
And virtue falls, before the altar slain.
'Twas now fair Cypria, with her woes opprest,
In raging anguish smote her heav'nly breast;
Wild with distracting fears, the goddess try'd
Her hero in th' etherial cloud to hide,
The cloud, which youthful Paris did conceal,
When Menelaus urg'd the threat'ning steel;
The cloud, which once deceiv'd Tydides' sight,
And sav'd Æneas in th' unequal fight.
  When Jove—"In vain, fair daughter, you essay
To o'er-rule destiny's unconquer'd sway:
Your doubts to banish, enter Fate's abode,
A privilege to heav'nly powers allow'd;
There shall you see the records grav'd in length,
On ir'n and solid brass, with mighty strength;
Which Heav'n's and Earth's concussion shall endure,
Maugre all shocks, eternal, and secure:
There, on perennial adamant design'd,
The various fortunes of your race you'll find:
Well I have mark'd them, and will now relate
To thee the settled laws of future fate.
He, goddess, for whose death the fates you blame,
Has finish'd his determin'd course with fame:
To thee, 'tis giv'n at length, that he shall shine
Among the gods, and grace the worshipp'd shrine:
His son to all his greatness shall be heir,
And worthily succeed to empire's care:
Ourself will lead his wars, resolv'd to aid
The brave avenger of his father's shade.
To him its freedom Mutina shall owe,
And Decias his auspicious conduct know:
His dreadful powers shall shake Pharsalia's plain,
And drench in gore Philippi's fields again:
A mighty leader, in Sicilia's flood,
Great Pompey's warlike son, shall be subdu'd:
Ægypt's soft queen, adorn'd with fatal charms,
Shall mourn her soldiers' unsuccessful arms:
Too late shall find her swelling hopes were vain,
And know, that Rome o'er Memphis still must reign:
What name I Afric, or Nile's hidden head?
For as both oceans roll, his power shall spread:
All the known earth to him shall homage pay,
And the seas own his universal sway:
When cruel war no more disturbs mankind,
To civil studies shall he bend his mind,
With equal justice guardian laws ordain,
And by his great example vice restrain.
Where will his bounty or his goodness end?
To times unborn his gen'rous views extend;
The virtues of his heir our praise engage,
And promise blessings to the coming age:
Late shall he in his kindred orbs be plac'd,
With Pylian years, and crowded honours grac'd.
Mean-time, your hero's fleeting spirit bear,
Fresh from his wounds, and change it to a star:
So shall great Julius rites divine assume,
And from the skies eternal smile on Rome."
  This spoke, the goddess to the senate flew;
Where her fair form conceal'd from mortal view,
Her Cæsar's heav'nly part she made her care,
Nor left the recent soul to waste to air;
But bore it upwards to its native skies:
Glowing with new-born fires she saw it rise;
Forth springing from her bosom up it flew,
And kindling, as it soar'd, a comet grew:
Above the lunar sphere it took its flight,
And shot behind it a long trail of light.

THE REIGN OF AUGUSTUS, IN WHICH OVID FLOURISHED.

THUS rais'd, his glorious offspring Julius view'd,
Beneficently great, and scattering good;
Deeds, that his own surpass'd, with joy beheld,
And his large heart dilates to be excell'd.
What though this prince refuses to receive
The pref'rence, which his juster subjects give;
Fame uncontroll'd, that no restraint obeys,
The homage, shunn'd by modest virtue, pays,
And proves disloyal only in his praise.

Though great his sire, him greater we proclaim:
So Atreus yields to Agamemnon's fame;
Achilles so superior honours won,
And Peleus must submit to Peleus' son;
Examples yet more noble to disclose,
So Saturn was eclips'd, when Jove to empire rose;
Jove rules the Heav'ns, the Earth Augustus sways;
Each claims a monarch's, and a father's praise.
Celestials, who for Rome your cares employ;
Ye gods, who guarded the remains of Troy;
Ye native gods, here born and fix'd by fate;
Quirinus, founder of the Roman state;
O parent Mars, from whom Quirinus sprung;
Chaste Vesta, Cæsar's houshold gods among
Most sacred held; domestic Phœbus, thou
To whom with Vesta chaste alike we bow;
Great guardian of the high Tarpeian rock;
And all ye powers whom poets may invoke;
O grant, that day may claim our sorrows late,
When lov'd Augustus shall submit to fate,
Visit those seats where gods and heroes dwell,
And leave, in tears, the world he rul'd so well!

THE POET CONCLUDES.

THE work is finish'd, which nor dreads the rage
Of tempests, fire, or war, or wasting age;
Come, soon or late, death's undetermin'd day,
This mortal being only can decay;
My nobler part, my fame, shall reach the skies,
And to late times with blooming honours rise:
Whate'er th' unbounded Roman power obeys,
All climes and nations shall record my praise:
If 'tis allow'd to poets to divine,
One half of round eternity is mine.

THE

THEBAID OF STATIUS.

TRANSLATED BY LEWIS.

Curritur ad vocem jucundam, et carmen amicæ
Thebaidos, lætam fecit cum Statius urbem,
Promisitque diem, tantâ dulcedine captos
Afficit ille animos, tantâque libidine vulgi
Auditur; sed cum fregit subsellia versu,
Esurit, intactam paridi nisi vendat agaven.

JUVENAL, Sat. 7.

All Rome is pleas'd, when Statius will rehearse,
And longing crowds expect the promis'd verse:
His lofty numbers with so great a gust
They hear, and swallow with such eager lust:
But while the common suffrage crown'd his cause,
And broke the benches with their loud applause;
His Muse had starv'd, had not a piece unread,
And by a player bought, supply'd her bread.

DRYDEN.

TO

THE MOST NOBLE PRINCE

HENRY DUKE OF BEAUFORT.

YOUR grace's condescension in permitting me to put my juvenile labours under your protection does me great honour, and claims my warmest gratitude; it was, I confess, my highest ambition to inscribe this translation to one, who had on a most public occasion distinguished himself by such classical elegance and real dignity, as justly entitled him to the universal applause of a most learned as well as splendid audience.——Nor can the translation of a poem, whose subject is the actions of heroes and princes, be inscribed with propriety to any one but a person descended like your grace from so ancient and so illustrious a line of ancestors.

I shall not presume to trouble your grace with a longer address, as I well know, that amidst all your grace's princely virtues and amiable qualities,. this is not the least conspicuous, that your heart is formed to despise every, the least, appearance of flattery. I have the honour to be,

my lord,

your grace's most obliged and

most devoted humble servant,

WILL. LILLINGTON LEWIS.

PREFACE.

IT is a general, and a true observation, that we seldom sit down with pleasure to read the author, before we have some knowledge of the man. This so natural a curiosity every editor and translator of a book should endeavour to gratify, as the life of the writer is oftentimes the best comment on the work itself. In compliance therefore with this remark, we shall collect, and lay before our readers all that has come to our knowledge of the birth, condition, character, and fortunes of our poet.

Publius Papinius Statius (for so was he called, and not Surculus, as some grammarians affirm, who confound him with the rhetorician, that flourished about the time of Nero) was born at Naples in the beginning of the emperor Claudius's reign. Those, who will have Tholouse in France, to be the place of his birth, might have been convinced of their errour, if they had attended to what he himself says in his Epithalamium of Stella and Violantilla.

> At te nascentem gremio mea prima recepit
> Parthenope, dulcisque solo tu gloria nostro
> Reptasti.

Or in his poem to Claudia.

> Nostra quoque et propriis tenuis, nec rara colonis
> Parthenope, cui mite solum trans æquora vectæ
> Ipse Dionæa monstravit Apollo Columbâ.

He was descended of a good family by his father's side, who was born at Sellæ in Epirus, not far from the celebrated Dodonæan grove, and taught rhetoric to the nobility there with singular applause, not only for his skill in that profession, but likewise for his probity and extensive learning. The honours he was distinguished with, bear testimony to this part of his character; for after having been made a citizen of Naples, he was presented with the laurel, and a crown of gold by Domitian; a proof of his favour with that prince, as the former was of his interest with the people. He married Agylline, of whom we have no farther mention, than that she died before him. See Sylvæ, l. 3. It is remarkable (says the author of Polymetis) that poetry ran more lineally in Statius's family, than perhaps in any other. He received it from his father, who had been an eminent poet in his time, and lived to see his son obtain the laurel-wreath at the Alban games, as he had formerly done himself.——Thus far Mr. Spence: and it is among the desiderata of the learned, that we have nothing extant, but what the son wrote. The Epicedion we find in his Miscellanea is at once an argument of his father's merit, and his own filial piety.

Our author discovered an early bent to poetry, which was so much cherished and improved by his father's instructions, that he soon became the public talk, and was introduced to the first wits of the age, and afterwards to the emperor himself, by his friend Paris, the player, at that time one of the chief court-favourites. His literary merit gained him so large a share of the emperor's esteem, that he was permitted to sit at table with him among his ministers and courtiers of the highest quality, and was often crowned for his verses, which were publicly recited in the theatre.

Ter me nitidis Albana ferentem
Dona comis, sanctoque indutum Cæsaris auro
Visceribus complexa tuis, sertisque dedisti
Oscula anhela meis.

Once, however, he lost the prize in the Capitol.

——Tu cum Capitolia nostræ
Inficiata lyræ; sævum, ingratumque dolebas
Mecum victa Jovem.

The frequent determination of the judges in his favour created him the envy of Martial; who piqued himself much on his extempore productions: insomuch that he has never mentioned Statius in his account of the poets, his contemporaries. The Thebaid, finished at Naples, and dedicated to Domitian, was received at Rome with the greatest applause, as Juvenal has told us in the passage, which I have chosen for my motto. This is thought by some to have been nothing more than a sneer. Mr. Dryden however, in his translation of it, and Dr. Crusius, in his life of our author, think otherwise. I shall give the reader the words of the latter. " To me the occasion of his mentioning Statius seems to be this: he observes in his satire the low state, and small encouragement given to men of letters, who were often reduced to the hard necessity of writing for bread; and that, notwithstanding the world allowed their merit, and admired their writings. Statius is brought in, as an unhappy example of this ill usage.

" Curritur ad vocem, &c.

" From this passage we learn, that Statius wrote a tragedy, which Paris purchased, who, from a player, was become the emperor's minion, the poet being reduced to sell it for his subsistence. This circumstance perhaps might have introduced our poet to that favourite, for I do not find, that after his admission to his patronage, he wanted the conveniences of life. However it does not appear from what has been quoted, that Juvenal has spoken reproachfully of him, but rather has given him great and real commendations, and has particularly taken notice of his noble style; the translator has altogether favoured this sense. This testimony deserves the more to be considered, as coming from one, whom both his friendship to Martial, and hatred to the court, might reasonably be presumed to have made our author's enemy."

But to return to our poet; he had no sooner finished his Thebaid, than he formed his plan of the Achilleid, a work, in which he intended to take in the whole life of his hero, and not one single action, as Homer has done in the Iliad. This he left imperfect, dying at Naples in the reign of Trajan, before he had well finished two books of it.

When he was young, he fell in love with, and married a widow, daughter of Claudius Apollinaris, a musician of Naples. He describes her in his poems, as a very beautiful, learned, ingenious and virtuous woman, and a great proficient in his own favourite study of poesy. Her society was a solace to him in his heavy hours, and her judgment of no small use in his poem, as he himself has confessed to us in his Sylvæ.

Longi tu sola laboris
Conscia, cumque tuis crevit mea Thebais annis.

A woman of such qualifications as these, could not fail of commanding his warmest love and respect. He inscribed several of his verses to her, and as a mark of his affection behaved with singular tenderness to a daughter, which she had by a former husband. During his absence at Naples for the space of twenty years, she behaved with the strictest fidelity, and at length followed him, and died there. He had no children by her; and therefore adopted a son, whose death he bewails in a very pathetic manner.

> Tellure cadentem
> Excepi, et vinctum genitali carmine fovi,
> Poscentemque novas tremulis ululatibus auras
> Insevui vitæ. quid plus tribuere parentes?
> Nonne gemam te, care puer, quo sospite natos
> Non cupii?

This (as Dr. Crusius observes) is a good argument, that Domitian and Paris's bounty had set him above want; one, if not the principal, end of adoption being to have one to inherit, what we leave behind us, whose grateful behaviour, and filial duty, might supply the place of a true son. Besides, the poet informs us, that he had a small country-seat in Tuscany, where Alba formerly stood.

> Parvi beatus ruris honoribus,
> Quà prisca Teucros Alba colit lares,
> Fortem atque facundum Severum
> Non solitis fidibus saluto.

With regard to his moral character, our author stands unimpeached; and from what we can collect, he appears to have been religious almost to superstition, an affectionate husband, a loyal subject, and good citizen. Some critics however have not scrupled to accuse him of gross flattery to Domitian. That he paid his court to him with a view to interest, cannot be denied: so did Virgil to Augustus, and Lucan to Nero: and it is more than probable, his patron had not yet arrived to that pitch of wickedness and impiety, at the time he wrote his poem, as he showed afterwards. Envy made no part of his composition. That he acknowledged merit, wherever he found it, his Genethliacon of Lucan, and Encomia on Virgil, bear ample testimony. Nay, he carried his reverence for the memory of the latter almost to adoration, constantly visiting his tomb, and celebrating his birth-day with great solemnity. ——His tragedy of Agave excepted, we have all his works, consisting of his Sylvæ, or miscellaneous pieces, in five books, his Thebaid in twelve, and his Achilleid in two.

Having laid before the reader the most authenticated accounts we have of our poet's life, I shall now deliver my sentiments of the work in general freely and impartially; not having the vanity to expect the world will abide by my opinion, nor invidiously detracting from the merit of other authors, to set that of Statius in a more advantageous light, as has been the practice of some literary bigots. So conscious am I of the want of critical abilities, that I should have declined saying any thing by way of dissertation, had not my more able predecessors entailed it upon me, and by their examples, rendered it the indispensable duty of each succeeding translator. Therefore if any thing is advanced contrary to the doctrine of the critics, youth must plead for me, and procure that pardon, which would be denied to persons of a more mature judgment.

As the world is no longer so bigoted to Aristotle and Bossu, as to reject a work merely because it is not written according to their particular rules, I shall not trouble myself to inquire, whether the Thebaid is an epic poem, or not. Sufficient is it to observe, that Mr. Pope thought it so; and that it has a better title to the name, than the Pharsalia of Lucan, which M. de Voltaire, in his paradoxical essay, has termed one. However, before we proceed to a critical disquisition of its merit, it is necessary to inform the reader, that the event therein spoken of, and described, happened about 1251 years before the birth of our Saviour, and 42 before the destruction of Troy. The purport of the history is this.

Laius, king of Thebes, despairing of having any children by his wife Jocasta, consulted the oracle, and received for answer, that he should have a son, who would one day murder him. To prevent this, as soon as the child was born, he bored holes through his feet, and fastening them to a tree with thongs, left him, from which misfortune he was afterwards named Oedipus. The royal infant however was preserved by the care of the servants; and in process of time, travelling near Phocis, met his father

Laius without knowing him, and upon his disputing the way, killed him in the heat of passion. He afterwards ascended the throne of Thebes, and married Jocasta his mother, at that time unknown to be so: by her he had four children, Eteocles, Polynices, Antigone, and Ismene. As soon as his sons were grown up to man's estate, they dethroned their father, and agreed between themselves to reign alternately. Eteocles was appointed by lot to rule the first year; but when that was expired, refused to resign the crown to Polynices, his younger brother. Upon this a war commenced, in which the injured prince was assisted by Adrastus, king of Argos, and five other heroes. These were all slain in battle, except Adrastus: and the two brothers falling in single fight, Creon usurped the throne, and by an inhuman act of cruelty in not suffering the dead bodies to be buried, drew upon himself the vengeance of Theseus, who marched an army against him, and took the city.

The ingenious Mr. Harte, speaking of the subject of the Thebaid, says, "It must certainly be an infinite pleasure to peruse the most ancient piece of history now extant, excepting that in holy scripture. This remark must be understood of the action of the Thebaid only, which Statius, without question, faithfully recited from the most authentic chronicles in his own age. The action of the Iliad and Odyssey happened several years after. This is evident from Homer's own words. Agamemnon in the fourth book of the Iliad recites with great transport the expedition of Tydeus, and Ulysses mentions the story of Jocasta (or Epicaste, as he calls her) in a very particular manner, in giving an account of his descent to Hell, Odyssey, book 11th. The antiquity of the Thebaid may be considered also in another view: as the poet was obliged to conform the manners of his heroes to the time of action, we in justice ought not to be so much shocked with those insults over the dead, which run through all the battles. This softens a little the barbarity of Tydeus, who expired gnawing the head of his enemy, and the impiety of Capaneus, who was thunder-struck, while he was blaspheming Jupiter. Whoever reads the books of Joshua and Judges, will find about those times the same savage spirit of insolence and fiertè."

The latter part of this observation may serve, as a defence of our author against Mr. Pope's censure of his characters (see preface to his Homer) and that of Bossu, who in his Treatise on Epic Poetry has the following extraordinary remark. "The greatest part of Statius's characters are false. The impetuosity of his genius, joined to the desire of amplifying, and making every thing he would say appear grand and marvellous, has been the occasion of this defect. He almost always carries to excess the passions he represents in his personages. He does not know what it is to preserve uniformity: he makes his heroes act extravagancies, which one would not pardon in young scholars, and often, instead of describing them as he ought, he has made chimeras of them all. These faults cannot be attributed but to want of judgment, knowledge, and a justness of thinking." Unwilling as I am to contradict a writer of such acknowledged abilities, as Mr. Bossu, I must, in justness to the poet, deny part of the charge, viz. that the greatest part of his characters are false. I know but two, which are exaggerated in the colouring: namely Tydeus and Capaneus. Eteocles and Polynices are out of the question: being such as he was obliged to describe them, in order to attain the moral end of his poem: which was to show the fatal consequences of ambition on the one hand, and of a too greedy thirst of revenge on the other. The rest, Adrastus, Amphiaraus, Parthenopæus and Hippomedon are very amiable characters. In the two former we have a lively portrait of a good king, and pious priest; and the two latter display great magnanimity, and nobleness of heart, in voluntarily taking part with the injured at the expense of their lives and fortunes. The female characters are likewise unexceptionable. Ismene and Antigone act the part of tender and loving sisters: Argia, Deiphyle, and indeed all the relicts of the seven leaders are illustrious examples of conjugal affection; and even the unhappy Jocasta herself is blameless, if considered in the light of a mother.

Let us now take a view of our author's poetical conduct and economy, an object, which should have been first attended to, had I not been insensibly drawn away to consider his characters. Here, divesting myself of all predilection and partiality, I must own, he has in many points failed. One great cause of his imperfection in this particular is his having stuck too close to history and tradition, and not sufficiently called in the assistance of fiction and invention, a lawful and necessary advantage, which all epic-writers are allowed to take. The introduction of the funeral games however, through which he has destroyed the unity of his action, and which has been oftener attacked than any one part besides, is apologized for by Mr. Harte in a very masterly manner. "The design of this book" says he, "was to give a respite to the main action, introducing a mournful, but pleasing variation from terrour to pity. It is also highly probable, that Statius had an eye to the funeral obsequies of Polydore and Anchises, mentioned in the third and fifth books of Virgil: we may also look on them as a prelude opening the mind by degrees to receive the miseries and horrours of a future war. This is intimated in some measure by the derivation of the word Archemorus. Besides the reasons above-mentioned, he would have a fine opportunity of remarking upon chief of the heroes, who must make a figure hereafter; this is represented to the eye in a lively sketch, that distributes to each person his proper lights with great advantage."

The merit of speeches and orations is determined in a great measure by the general character of the persons, who utter them; their propriety consisting in their agreement with the manners of the speaker. Adrastus must not talk like Polynices, nor Capaneus like Amphiaraus. Statius, in this particular, deserves our highest applause. His heroes always speak as they act: his orations are nervous, animated, eloquent, not so prolix as Lucan's, nor so sententious as those of Virgil. Though admirable in all, he principally excels in the mournful and pathetic. He is the same among the Romans, as Euripides among the Greeks. I forbear particularizing any speeches here, as they have been already observed in the notes.

The next point that falls under our consideration, is the sentiments; in which our author is very unequal: they are never low or vulgar, often just and noble, but sometimes ranting and unnatural. He never falls, but is often lost among the clouds by soaring too high, and too studiously avoiding every thing, that has the appearance of being flat and frigid. In this article he resembles our countryman Lee. He is less moral than Virgil, less familiar than Homer, and less philosophical than Lucan.

We now come to his descriptions, images, and comparisons, a part in which he shines with distinguished lustre. So strong is his talent this way, that whatever he describes, we seem to see in reality. In his descriptions he is full and exact, in his images bold and lively. " Your attention," says Dr. Crusius, " is always kept awake;" nay, rather the many surprising circumstances crowd in so thick upon the mind, that it finds itself almost at a loss how to take them all in, as he represents them; so far is the poet from " letting the subject grow dull and troublesome in his hands." With respect to his similies, they are for the most part proper and well drawn; but sometimes want a parity in the circumstances, which renders them obscure: this defect proceeds rather from the impetuosity of his genius, than want of judgment; for being too hasty to dwell upon particulars, he gives nothing more than the outlines of a comparison, and leaves it to the reader's imagination to fill them up.

From the descriptive part, we are naturally led to take a view of our poet's style, of which the author of the Lives of the Roman Poets has, I think, given the best account. " Strada," says he, " in his Prolusions, has placed Statius on the highest top of Parnassus; thereby intimating the strength of his genius, and the lofty spirit of his style; which indeed is generally supported by a bold and lively expression, and full flowing numbers. His manner therefore resembles rather the martial strut of a general, and the magnificence of a triumph, than the majestic port and true grandeur of a prince, which better suits the inimitable character of Virgil's style. As a soldier cannot easily lay aside the roughness of his character, neither can Statius descend from the pomp of language and loftiness of numbers, when his subject requires it."—To this remark, I must beg leave to add, that he often uses hellenisms with singular beauty and propriety. There is one fault, however, which the translator, in justice to himself, ought not to conceal, and that is his frequent obscurity.

It remains now to treat of his versification; which is scarcely inferior to that of any poet whatsoever. His numbers are correct, harmonious, sounding, expressive of the sense, and rather loftier than those of Virgil. He has nothing of Lucan's stiffness, nor of that uniform smoothness, which characterizes the verses of Claudian.

In short, if Statius has had Rapin and Bossu for his cavillers, he has had Malherbe, Rosteau, Marolles, and Scaliger for his admirers: the last of whom thinks, he comes nearest to Virgil in majesty, of all poets either ancient or modern. " He had even come nearer to him," says he, " if he had not affected it so much; for being naturally ambitious, whenever he has attempted to excel him, he has degenerated into fustian. Except the phenix Virgil, he is without dispute the prince of both Latin and Greek poets. His verses are better than Homer's: he abounds more in figures, has more poetical economy, and is more chaste and correct in his moral sentences."

I shall only trouble the reader with one quotation more on this head; and that is from the amiable Fenelon's account of the war between the ancients and moderns, in which he fancifully ascertains the rank and merits of our author, as a poet.

"Lucan being mightily incensed to see Virgil preferred before him, protested against the election, and refused to agree on any other terms, but being at least declared his colleague. Saying in sententious and haughty verse, if Virgil could not suffer an equal, he was resolved not to endure a superior; to which Virgil only made answer with a modest smile. But Lucan was hissed at by the whole assembly of ancient Latin poets, who well knew the distance betwixt him and Virgil, and therefore told him, his pretensions would only bear water amongst some moderns, that were not capable of relishing all the beauties and niceties of Latin poesy; nor could he reasonably carry his ambition higher, than to be Virgil's lieutenant. But he refused the command, and retiring with a Spanish gravity, said:

Victrix causa deis placuit, sed victa Catoni.

Giving them to understand, he would seek revenge for the wrong, he believed they had done him. Statius, in his default, was chosen by Virgil for his lieutenant-general, in preference to Silius Italicus, who pretended a title to that employment."

In another part, speaking of the arrangement of the forces, the same author says: "The army of the Latin poets was drawn up in form of battle on the left of the Grecians upon the same line. Virgil had posted his Æneids in the midst of the front, and called them the first legion: he designed to fight in person at the head of these, and named the Thebaid of Statius the second, which he disposed on the left of his own poem; and Statius was to second Virgil at the head of the epic."

To conclude, whoever will read the Thebaid in the original, will find the author to be a much better poet, than the world in general imagines. I say, imagines, because two thirds of the men of letters in this kingdom have never read him; but form their opinions from the character given him by some few prejudiced persons. Borrichius has justly observed, that he is the same among the poets, as Alexander was among heroes. He has many and great beauties, but they are blended with defects. He has more harmony than Lucan, and more spirit than Silius Italicus; and one may safely say, that if he be not equal to Virgil in some points, he approaches so near him, as to leave far behind those of his own and after times. As nothing throws a greater lustre on the fine passages in the Iliad, than Virgil's condescending to copy them; so nothing is a greater argument of Statius's merit, than the verbal imitations of Chaucer, who was perhaps a poet of the most lively imagination of any amongst the moderns. I prefer this to volumes of criticism. No one would imitate what he could exceed. Such, therefore, as he is with all his imperfections, I present him to the reader, whom I wish the same pleasure that I have found, in contemplating his many and great beauties.

Having spoken of the beauties and defects of the original, it may not be improper to acquaint the reader, what he is to expect in the following version. The great inducement to the attempting it, was its not having been wholly translated before. I had long considered it as the most illustrious work of Roman antiquity after the Æneid, and consequently was concerned, that it had never appeared in an English dress. Five books indeed have been rendered into English verse by T———rs: Mr. Pope made the first speak English, and the late ingenious Mr. Walter Harte, of St. Mary Hall, Oxon, the sixth. This is all, that to my knowledge has been translated. With more ambition, therefore, than prudence, I begun it soon after I entered at the university, at the age of eighteen, and must confess, that my chief merit consists in having had the patience to go through with it at a time of life, which is too often squandered away in a circle of follies and amusements. Those readers will be very much disappointed, who expect to find a literal version. The translator has profited too much from the fate of others, to attempt it. If he could not be just to the original in a free version, he had been much less so in a close one: such is the disparity of the two languages; and of all the Latin authors, Statius perhaps is the most difficult. It is hoped, however, the liberties which are taken will not be deemed too great, nor the deviations from the original too many. In the main parts of the poem, such as the fable, manners and sentiments, omissions and contractions are altogether unpardonable; but in others less essential, where the variation does not exceed one word, as the substituting another epithet to strengthen the idea, it is presumed, no man of candour will be offended. The abuse of triplets and Alexandrines has been very justly objected to: for which reason, the translator has scrupulously avoided them, and, unless his memory very much deceives him, has not one of either in the whole work. The incorrectness of modern rhymes has likewise given reasonable ground for censure. Great care has been taken of this point, and the translator flatters himself that very few bad rhymes will be found in the whole poem. If there is now and then a darkness, there is often a light in antiquity, which is best preserved in a literal version. Whenever the translator has found this (as indeed he has very frequently), he has always stuck close to the original. It happens sometimes again, that a whole passage is so obscure, as not to be rendered verbatim: in this case, all that can be done, is to translate in the lump, and by carefully consulting the context, give what seems to be the general sense as briefly and as poetically as one can. A translator is not accountable for the faults of the author. Now, it sometimes happens, that a thought is low and vulgar, an image not physically true, and a warrior, who has been killed, described fighting again, through a slip of the poet's memory. Whenever, therefore, the reader perceives an inaccuracy of this kind, he should turn to the passage in the original, and not throw the blame on the translator, before there is conviction that he deserves it. If there has been too great a prolixity in notes and quotations, it is but justice to ascribe it rather to the desire of gratifying his pleasure, than displaying his learning: since it is one of the most agreeable employments a rational mind can be engaged in, to compare the flowers of genius and fancy together.

After all, the translator professes himself incapable of doing Statius justice, and always keeping up that fire and spirit, which so peculiarly animates the original. His abilities are unequal to so arduous a task, and if they were greater than they are, the English language would in many points fail him. He therefore submits this version to the public, as the first-fruits of his labours; and sincerely wishes, that when his judgment is matured by time, he may be able to produce something which may show, that their present indulgence was not entirely thrown away upon him.

THE

THEBAID OF STATIUS.

TRANSLATED BY LEWIS.

BOOK I.

THE ARGUMENT.

Eteocles and Polynices having dethroned their father, Oedipus, king of Thebes, agree to reign alternately. Oedipus invokes the fury Tisiphone to punish them; she sows dissension between them. Eteocles is chosen by lot to reign the first. year. An universal discontent prevails among the Thebans. Jupiter calls a council of the Gods, and declares his intention of punishing Thebes and Argos. He sends Mercury to call up the ghost of Laius from the shades. On Eteocles's refusing to give up the sceptre at the expiration of his year, Polynices goes to Argos to solicit the aid of Adrastus against him. He is overtaken by a heavy storm, and being very much fatigued, lies down at Adrastus's gate. Tydeus arrives at the same place by chance. They quarrel and fight. Adrastus, alarmed at the noise, comes out, reconciles, and entertains them very hospitably. He relates the origin of a sacrifice which was then celebrating, and addresses a prayer to Apollo, which concludes the book.

OF guilty Thebes, to foreign arms a prey,
Fraternal rage, and impious lust of sway,
My daring Muse would sing, so Phœbus deign
To prompt the bard, and harmonize the strain.
Say, goddess, whence shall I my subject trace,
From Cadmus, author of the vicious race?

5. Say, goddess] Statius has been pretty severely handled by some ingenious critics among the moderns for this seeming doubt where to commence his narration. Tho' I cannot pretend to exculpate him entirely for running counter to the rules laid down by Horace, yet I cannot but hope, he will appear less worthy of censure than he has hitherto done, if we suppose, that the poet judged the greatest part of his Roman readers ignorant of the Theban history, (as undoubtedly they were,) and yet it was necessary they should have some previous knowledge of it, in order to understand his poem, and the allusions he frequently makes to the history and customs of that nation. But how were they to be acquainted with it? Was he to have directly collected the heads of it, and declared his intention? No: that would have been the greatest affront he could have put upon them, which our author was sufficiently aware of. Let us admire, then, the art and dexterity of the poet, who has extricated himself from the embarassments he lay under, by this polite and ingenious device. If he has offended, it is a glorious offence, or (to use the words of Mr. Pope) a grace snatch'd beyond the rules of art.

6. From Cadmus] Cadmus was the son of Agenor; this obstinate prince insisted on his travelling in quest of his sister Europa, who had been carried off by Jupiter in the form of a bull. The hero complied, but not finding his sister, settled near Thebes.

Shall I describe him on the raging sea,
Obsequious to the monarch's stern decree?
Then tell, from whence th' aspiring nation rose,
And to what source proud Thebes its grandeur owes,
How soften'd rocks (so will'd resistless fate)
Danc'd into form, to grace a future state?
What fatal causes could so far incense
The queen of Heav'n, and what the dire offence,
When Athamas, by wrath divine pursu'd,
His trembling hands in filial blood imbrued,
And his pale spouse, to shun his angry bow,
Sprung from the beach, and sought the depths below?
Wave then, whate'er to Cadmus may belong,
O Muse, and date the subject of thy song
From wretched Oedipus;—nor yet aspire
In Cæsar's praise to string thy feeble lyre,
Or tell, how twice he bade the Rhine obey,
How twice the Danube roll'd beneath his sway:
(While Dacia, daring impious war to wage,
Fell the just object of the victor's rage:)
Or how, in youthful armour clad, he strove
To vindicate the sacred rites of Jove.
Nor thou, commission'd in the rolls of fate,
To swell the glories of the Latian state,
By wild ambition led away, resign
The Roman helm to feebler hands than thine.
What tho' the stars contract their liquid space,
Well pleas'd to yield thee a serener place;
Tho' Phœbus, conscious of superior blaze,
Would intermix with thine his friendly rays;
And Jove his wide-extended empire share,
Content to rule an equal tract of air;
Yet may thy people's wishes thee detain,
And Jove enjoy an undivided reign.
The time will come, when a diviner flame
Shall prompt me to resound thy ripen'd flame,
Meanwhile permit my Muse to seek renown
In Theban wars, a prelude to thy own.
She sings of souls discordant e'en in death,
And hate, that fled not with the vital breath;
A throne, for which the vengeful fates decreed,
Two rival kings by mutual arms should bleed,
And scepter'd chiefs; who long unbury'd lay,
To birds and beasts an undistinguish'd prey;
When Dirce's source was stain'd with kindred gore,
And Thetis from the blood-impurpled shore
Beheld Ismenos roll a mingled heap
Of arms and warriors to the frighted deep.
What first, O Clio, shall adorn thy page,
Th' expiring prophet, or Ætolian's rage?
Say, wilt thou sing, how grim with hostile blood,
Hippomedon repell'd the rushing flood;
Lament th' Arcadian youth's untimely fate,
Or Jove, oppos'd by Capaneus, relate?
Now Oedipus, inur'd to deepest night,
No more in sighs bewails the loss of sight;
And tho' the rays of Phœbus ne'er invade
His dark abode, or pierce th' eternal shade,
Yet conscience haunts him with reflecting glass,
Thro' which his sins, too well distinguish'd, pass.
Their torches o'er his head the furies rear,
And threats and harsh reproaches grate his ear.
Now to th' unpitying ruler of the skies
He lifts the gloomy sockets of his eyes,
Then strikes the gaping void with impious hands,
And thus aloud infernal aid demands.
"Ye gods, who sway in Tartarus maintain,
Where guilty spirits howl with endless pain;
Thou Styx, whose gloomy banks, and shady lake
A sad impression on my senses make;
Tisiphone, on whose repeated name
I've dwelt; if Oedipus attention claim,
Oh! lend an ear, and from the realms below
Accord my wishes, and assist my vow.
If from my sire misdeem'd I took my way
To Cyrrha's fane on that important day,
When Laius bled beneath these impious hands,
Where the three paths divide the Phocian lands:
If seconded by thee, I durst chastise
Th' insidious Sphinx, and gain'd the glitt'ring prize;
Or, by thy fav'ring torch conducted, strove
To meet with equal fires Jocasta's love:
If studious of thy cause, I now prepare
Two sons, whose rising merits claim thy care;
And, too impatient of the vital light,
Forc'd from these streaming orbs the balls of sight:
Attend, and aid the vengeance I request;
If worthy thee, and what thou would'st suggest.
My sons (if sons they are) their sire disown,
Spoil'd of his eyes, and driven from his throne;

11. How soften'd] The poets feign, Amphion played so sweetly upon the lyre, that the stones and rocks danced into walls, and built the city afterwards called Thebes.

15. When Athamas] He was the father of Palæmon, and husband of Ino: but being seized with lunacy through the malice of Juno, pursued his children with his bow and arrows. Whereupon the wretched mother leaped into the sea with one of her sons.

29. Nor thou, commission'd] Virgil and Lucan gave the precedent of this fulsome and almost impious flattery, in compliment to Augustus and Nero. I hope the reader will dispense with my transcribing the passages, as they would swell the compass of these notes beyond what was intended. —See Georgics, lib. I. & Pharsalia, lib. I.

61. Now Oedipus] This is an extremely fine passage: the latter part of it alludes to the following verse in Euripides.

Ὦ Μητερ, ικετευώ σε, μὴ πίσειέ μοι
Τὰς αἱματωπὰς, και δρακοντώδεις κορας.
Αὗται γὰρ, αὗται πλησίον θρώσκουσί μου.
Orestes, v. 225.

71. Then strikes] I have rendered inane solum by gaping void, as it is spoken of the sockets of his eyes. Gronovius and Mr. Pope have taken it in the same sense, in opposition to the opinion of Bernartius and Barclay.

85. If seconded by thee] The curious reader may see the Sphynx's riddle in Greek, prefixed to the Oedipus Tyrannus of Sophocles, Johnson's edition, volume 2.

95. My sons] The Oedipus of Sophocles complains in like manner of his sons' cruelty, and wishes them a similar punishment.

'Αλλ' οἱ θεοί σφι μήτε τὴν πεπρωμένην
Ἔριν κατασβέσειαν, ἐν δ' ἐμοὶ τέλος.
Αὐτοῖν γένοιτο τῆσδε της μάχης πέρι,
Ἧς νῦν ἔχονται, κἀπαναιροῦνται δόρυ.
Ὡς οὔτ' ἂν ὃς νῦν σκῆπτρα, καὶ θρόνους εχει,
Μείνειεν, οὔτ' ἂν οὑξεληλυθὼς πολιν
Ἔλθοι πότ' αὖθις, οἵγε τὸν φύσαντ' ἐμὲ
Οὕτως ἀτίμως πατρίδος ἐξωθούμενον

And, while a guideless, helpless wretch I roam,
Deride my groans in pamp'ring ease at home.
Such is their pity, such their filial love,
And yet inactive sleep the bolts of Jove.
Then be the place of Jove by thee supply'd,
To check their insults, and reward their pride;
Let them some lasting stroke of vengeance mourn,
Which may extend to ages yet unborn:
Give them the crown, which steep'd in recent gore,
From the cleft temples of my sire I tore.
Go then, dissolve the sacred bonds of peace,
Bid discord rise, and love fraternal cease:
Urge them to dare, what may to latest times
Transmit their guilt, some yet unacted crimes.
Soon thou'lt experience (do but lead the way)
Their headstrong wills, impatient of delay;
And in the outlines of their tempers find
The truest portrait of their father's mind."
The list'ning fury now prepares to rise,
And tow'rds the suppliant wretch directs her eyes.
On sad Cocytos' banks she sate reclin'd,
And to the breeze her flowing locks resign'd.
Her snakes, unbound, along the margin glide,
Sport on the waves, or lash the sulph'ry tide.
From thence she springs; not swifter light'nings fly,
Or falling stars, that cleave the mid-way sky.
The phantoms ken her, as she soars in air,
And to the distant shades in haste repair.
Thro' dreary realms, and Pluto's wide domains
She roams, and soon th' infernal mansion gains.
The day beheld her dire approach, and shrowds
Her sick'ning glories in encircling clouds,
E'en Atlas labour'd with unwonted fears,
And shook beneath the burden of the spheres.
From Malea's humble vale she rose in flight,
And sped to Thebes, the monster's chief delight.
Not Hell itself, nor the Tartarean coast
An equal share of her esteem can boast.
A hundred serpents on her visage glare
With horrid scales, and mingle with her hair:
Her eyes, intrench'd within her bristling head,
By fits, a livid, fainty splendour shed.
Thus Cynthia blushes thro' the midnight shade,
When magic charms her lab'ring beams invade.
Her bloated skin with gather'd venom teems,
And her foul mouth exhales sulphureous steams.
Disease and death's annihilating force
From hence, as she commissions, bend their course.
Some stiffen'd rags were o'er her shoulders thrown,
And the dire monster by her dress was known.

Οὐκ ἔσκον, οὐδ' ἤμυναν, ἀλλ', ἀνάστατος
Αὐτοῖν ἐπέμφθην, κἀξεκηρυχθην φυγάς. V. 434.

There is no character in the drama more deserving of our pity, than that of Oedipus. His sins were chiefly involuntary: the gods seem to have levelled all their vengeance at him. This dreadful imprecation, however, against his own children, blackens his character, and refutes all the arguments which compassion can suggest in his favour.

124. And to] Spencer seems to have alluded to this thought in his Fairy Queen, b. 6. canto 6. stanza—

Echidna is a monster direful dread,
Whom gods do hate, and Heav'ns abhor to see;
So hideous is her shape, so huge her head,
That e'en the hellish fiends affrighted be
At sight thereof, and from her presence flee.

A crested serpent arm'd her better hand,
And in the left she toss'd a flaming brand.
When now she stood where craggy cliffs arise,
And proud Cithæron threats the neighb'ring skies,
Rang'd on her head, the scaly monsters glare,
And hiss, entwin'd in her envenom'd hair.
A signal to the Earth the shores resound,
And Greece from far returns the deaf'ning sound.
The distant summons fam'd Parnassus took,
And old Eurotas from it's summit shook:
Huge Oete nods, half sunk with all her pines,
And Isthmos scarce the parted waves disjoins;
While starting at the shock, Leucothoe press'd
The young Palæmon closer to her breast.
The fury to the palace now had come,
And shaded with her wings the splendid dome,
When here and there each furious brother flies,
And rage the place of mutual love supplies:
While jealousy and hate-ingend'ring fears
Flame in their breasts, and haunt their cred'lous ears.
Their restless minds then wild ambition fires
To break the league, and deadly wrath inspires.
Their haughty souls superior pow'r disown,
And scorn th' alternate splendours of a crown.
Such discord rises from divided sway,
When each will rule, and neither will obey.
As two young steers, when first compell'd to bow
Their stubborn necks, and trail the galling plow,
Frisk here and there, impatient of the toil,
And spread disorder o'er the furrowy soil;
Thus Discord arms the brothers in her cause,
And urges them to cancel nature's laws.
First they decreed, that each in turn should wear
The diadem in his successive year.
Unhappy youths, no longer doom'd to prove
The joys of friendship, and fraternal love!
While that in exile mourns his present state,
This dreads, alas! the same impending fate.

153. A signal] This beautiful passage is undoubtedly imitated from Virgil, Æneid, lib. 7. verse 511.

At Dea——
Pastorale canit signum, cornuque recurvo
Tartaream intendit vocem: qua protinus omne
Contremuit nemus, & silvæ intonuere profundæ.
Audiit & Triviæ longe lacus, audiit amnis
Sulfureâ Nar albus aquâ, fontesque Velini:
Et trepidæ matres pressere ad pectora natos.

Who copied it from Apollonius Rhodius, Argon. l. 4. v. 129.

——Ροιζει δέ πεχωριον, αμφι δέ μακραι
Ηιονες ποταμοιο, ϗ ασπετον ιαχεν αλσος.
Εκλυον οἱ ϗ πολλον εκας τιτηνιδος αἰης
Κολχιδα γην ενεμοντο παρα προχοησι χυκοιο,
Ος ἀποκιδναμενος ποταμου κελαδοντος Αραξεω,
Φασιδι συμφερεται ἱερον ῥοον, οἱ δέ συν αμφω
Καυκασιην ἁλαδ' εἰς ἑν ἐλαυμενοι προχεουσιν,
Δειματι δ' ἐξεγροντο λεχωίδες, αμφι δέ παισι
Νηπιαχοις, οιτεσφιν ὑπ' αγκαλιδεσσιν ιανον
Ροιζῳ παλλομενοις, χειρας βαλον ἀσχαλοωσαι.

This stroke of nature is tender and affecting to the last degree. Others would have been satisfied to have mentioned the effects of this dreadful blast upon the woods and mountains. Virgil knew, that this circumstance of the mothers' catching their infants to their breasts would more touch and interest his readers, than all the other pompous images, great as they are. Warton's Virgil.

Nor long this league withheld their impious hands,
From executing Discord's dire commands:
But ere one year was clos'd, they both gave way
To fierce contention, and desire of sway.
Yet then no gates of iv'ry did unfold
The palace, beaming with barbaric gold;
No polish'd arches, fram'd of Parian stone,
Beneath th' incumbent dome in order shone;
No guards, reclining on erected spears,
Essay'd to chase the sleepless tyrant's fears;
Nor curious gems, inlaid with art divine,
Flam'd on the brim, and sparkled in the wine.
Mere lust of pow'r the rival brothers arms,
And fills a narrow realm with war's alarms.
But while their claims yet undetermin'd stand,
And none enjoys in peace supreme command;
Law gives a sanction to injurious might,
And pow'r is hallow'd with the name of right.
Say, rivals, why ye rush to mutual death,
And why so lavish of your vital breath?
Not all th' united realms, which Sol surveys,
Adorn'd with orient, or declining rays,
When to the south he bends his rapid course,
Or the bleak north enjoys his temp'rate force;
Not all the wealth that fertile Tyre can boast,
Nor all that glitters on the Phrygian coast;
Could claim such deeds, or merit such regard,
Were all those realms the conqueror's reward.
Meanwhile the lots for the first year were thrown,
And proud Eteocles ascends the throne.
How grateful then, O tyrant, was the day,
When all around were subject to thy sway!
How pleas'd, without contention to devour
The wish'd-for sweets of undivided pow'r!
And now the disaffected Thebans vent
In whisper'd tales their growing discontent.
To th' absent prince in secret they adhere,
And curse the slow progression of the year.
Then one, by nature ready to complain,
Alike dissatisfy'd with every reign,
Well taught to feel rebellious faction's flame,
And brand with calumny the royal name,
Exclaim'd aloud: "Shall then the Theban state
Feel each vicissitude of cruel fate?
Still must our slavish necks with patience bear
Th' alternate yoke of each tyrannic heir;
Who now reverse our fates, divide the land,
And hold inferior fortune at command?
For e'er shall Thebes her sad condition mourn,
And dread each exil'd tyrant's quick return?
Is this thy fixt decree, almighty Jove,
Is this a proof of thy paternal love?
Was this a curse entail'd upon our race?
Say, from what time the omen we may trace;
When Cadmus sought his sister on the main,
Sow'd with the serpent's teeth the fertile plain,
And, forc'd on fair Bœotia's soil by fate,
Laid the foundation of the Theban state?
See, how elate with pride our king appears,
Free from competitors, and void of fears!
What threat'ning looks he wears, as if again
He scorn'd to yield his temporary reign.
Yet none before was easier of access,
More affable, or prone to give redress.
Nor wonder we: he was not then alone,
Nor without dread of a divided throne.
While we stand here, a patient servile band,
Prepar'd to act whate'er our lords command.
As when two winds contend with adverse force,
And influence by turns the vessel's course,
On this side now, obsequious to the blast,
Now there she nods, and still obeys the last:
Thus fares our state, between the doubtful sway
Of either prince, unknowing which t'obey.
Distracted, tortur'd with suspense she stands,
While this repeats his threats, and that commands."
Meanwhile the king of Heav'n, imperial Jove,
Convenes a synod of the pow'rs above;
Full in the midst, enthron'd, the thund'rer sate,
Sublime in all the pomp of regal state.
Beneath his piercing eye, in full survey,
The spacious earth, and seas contracted lay.
His brow was void of frowns, serene his look,
Yet at his nod the whole creation shook.
Their heav'nly king the rising senate greet,
And at his word resume their starry seat.
Inferior gods from ev'ry quarter come,
By rank distinguish'd in the starry dome.
None absent were of all whose force can bind,
Or on the deep discharge, the furious wind;
No rosy dryad of the shady wood,
Nor azure sister of the crystal flood.
But here, obedient to their sov'reign's will,
The winds are silent, and the waves lie still.
Thro' Heav'n's expanse a gath'ring horrour rolls,
And huge Olympus trembles to the poles.
With rays serene the wreathed pillars glare,
And a new lustre gilds the fields of air.
Its tremours now the globe began to cease,
And nature lay resign'd to downy peace;
When thus the thund'rer spoke: assenting fate
On ev'ry accent stamp'd resistless weight.
"Say, must I still of human crimes complain,
And must the thund'rer's bolts be hurl'd in vain?
Why seek they thus my tardy wrath to prove,
And scorn my proffer'd clemency and love;
While yet the Cyclops ply their arms no more,
And Ætna weeps for her exhausted store?

253. As when] It has been observed of Statius, that he shines particularly in descriptions and similies; and I will venture to say, this is not the worst of the latter in the whole work. Mediæ nutat fortuna carinæ, is a fine expression, and its spirit unattainable in English verse. However, if similies are any where unreasonable, they certainly are in speeches, and especially those delivered with any warmth. I have somewhere seen Virgil censured for putting so many similies in Æneas's mouth, during the narration of his adventures to Dido.

261. Meanwhile] This description is every way suitable to those refined ideas our author had of the Supreme Being. The images are as grand as the human mind can conceive, or fancy represent of such an assembly; and the harangue of Jove does not baulk the great expectations the preceding description has raised of him.

——— Grave & immutabile sanctis
Pondus adest verbis, & vocem fata sequuntur,

is not more sublime than concise and expressive: the sense of which an Italian or French poet would have scarce comprised in six or eight verses. I should want common justice, if I denied Mr. Pope the praise so justly deserved from the translation of this passage, which the reader may compare with the beginning of the tenth Æneid.

For this I suffer'd headstrong Phaeton
To mount the car of the reluctant Sun;
And Neptune bade th' imprison'd waters flow,
And hills and vales no more distinction know:
But all in vain; our vengeance they defy,
And triumph o'er the ruler of the sky.
To punish these, I leave the realms above,
A race descended from imperial Jove:
With Perseus Argos' sons alliance claim,
From Cadmus Thebes derives immortal fame.
Who has not heard of wretched Cadmus' fate,
And the long labours of the Theban state;
When from the silent regions of the night,
The furies sprang, and rush'd to mortal fight?
Why should I publish the fierce mother's shame,
And deeds, the pow'rs of Heav'n would blush to name?
Before I cou'd recount their num'rous crimes
From Cadmus' days unto the present times,
Phœbus wou'd seek the chambers of the main,
And rise to gild the courts of Heav'n again.
Say, without horrour can the tale be read
Of Laius slain, and his dishonour'd bed?
Dire monster! first to cause his father's death,
Then stain the womb, from whence he drew his breath.
Yet th' angry pow'rs he satisfies with groans,
And gloom eternal for his sins atones.
No more he breathes at large our upper air,
But feeds the worms of conscience with despair.
Yet say, what fury cou'd his sons inspire
Thus to torment their old, unhappy sire;
To trample on his eyes with impious feet,
And hurl him headlong from the regal seat?
Then let us pity him; nor let in vain
The wretched king of filial rage complain;
Hence shall it be my bus'ness to redress
His wrongs, and crown his wishes with success.
The day shall come, when discord from afar
Shall give whole nations to the waste of war;
When the whole guilty race in fight shall fall,
And one incircling ruin swallow all.
Adrastus shall in dire alliance join
With Heaven, and complete the Fates' design.
Nor let proud Argos triumph: 'tis decreed,
That she amid the gen'ral carnage bleed:
The craft of Tantalus, and impious feast,
Yet wake my vengeance, and inflame my breast."
  Then Juno, impotent of passion, broke
Her sullen silence, and with fury spoke.
"Why urge me thus to deeds of martial rage?
Shall Juno still in mortal strife engage?
Thou know'st, no mortals merit more my grace,
Than Argos, and the fam'd Inachian race,
By me for e'er enrich'd, and taught to wield
With sure success the weapons of the field.
Tho' there thy wiles, and providential care
O'ercame the keeper of the Pharian fair,
And the fam'd Argive was debauch'd of old,
Too fond, alas! of all-bewitching gold.
Yet these obscurer crimes I could forgive,
Did not proud Thebes my stifled ire revive;
Where Jove in all his dazzling glory shone,
And hurl'd the bolts to Juno due alone.
Let punish'd Thebes absolve th' injurious deed,
Nor both beneath divided vengeance bleed.
But if, tenacious of thy right divine,
Thou'lt thwart my will, and frustrate my design,
Descend from Heav'n, fulfil thy stern desire,
Raze Samos, wrap Mycenæ's walls in fire,
The guiltless Spartan race at once confound,
And their fair structures level with the ground.
With incense why should Juno's altars blaze,
And joyful pæans swell the note of praise?
Transfer to more deserving Isis' fane
The fatten'd victim, destin'd to be slain.
For her in Egypt bid the timbrel sound,
And Nile from ev'ry mouth her praise rebound.
But if thou wilt chastise the present age,
And sacrifice whole nations to thy rage,
If thou wilt trace obliterated crimes
From the dark annals of preceding times,
Say, from what period then it is decreed,
And to what times the guilty world shall bleed.
Begin, from whence in many a winding maze
To the Sicilian stream Alpheus strays:
There dire Arcadia's swains presum'd to found
Thy sacred temple on polluted ground;
Where stern Oenomaus' car was wont to stand,
And mould'ring skulls lie scatter'd on the sand.
Since such oblations please, since patient Jove
Yet courts the shades of Ida's guilty grove,
And favours Crete, whose impious sons presume
To show the king of Heav'n's fictitious tomb;
In Argos let thy spouse unenvy'd reign,
And share the mystic honours of the fane:
Nor waste in fight a race deriv'd from Jove,
A race, whose merits claim paternal love.
Let more detested realms in wars engage,
And feel the sad effects of filial rage."
Thus strove in vain th' indignant queen of air,
And blended in her speech reproach and prayer;
Unmov'd remains the ruler of the skies,
And thus with calmness from his throne replies.
"'Twas thus I deem'd the queen of Heav'n would plead,
Whene'er the fate of Argos was decreed:
Nor less might Bacchus thwart the will of fate,
Bacchus, the guardian of the Theban state,
But he not dares the lifted bolt to stay,
Reveres our pow'r and gives the vengeance way.

339. Then Juno] The Juno in Statius is the same with that of the Iliad and Æneid. Her summum bonum is of the negative kind, and consists chiefly in the gratification of a contradicting and perverse temper. She has always some favourites to shelter from the just vengeance of Jove, and her entreaties for pardon, or incitements to punishment, are the effects of the blindest partiality, or most inveterate prejudice. She will not permit Argos to partake of the punishment of Thebes, but hurries Jupiter on to put his threats in execution against the latter, which had been an eye-witness of his adultery.

353. Where Jove] The aspiring Semele would admit the embraces of Jupiter on no other condition, than his coming to her encircled with thunder and lightning, as he was wont to Juno. The unfortunate fair succeeded in her wishes, but perished in the completion of them.

379. Where stern Oenomaus'] Oenomaus was father of Hippodame. His daughter was promised in marriage to any one who should excel him in a chariot-race; but the loss of victory was to be attended with immediate death. The skulls here mentioned were those of the eleven suitors, who had failed in the attempt.

For by thy waves, tremendous Styx ! that flow
Thro' the drear realms of gliding ghosts below,
Not all the gods, who reign in Heav'n above,
Shall change this fixt decree, or influence Jove.
Thus have I sworn, and what I swear shall stand,
That none but Jove shall exercise command.
Haste then, my son, our orders to perform,
Mount the fleet wind, and ride the rapid storm,
To Pluto's realms with willing haste repair,
And summon Laius to the fields of air,
Whose shiv'ring ghost with lifted hands implores
A speedy passage to the farther shores.
Let his proud grandson, taught by him, disown
The mutual compact, nor resign the crown
To banish'd Polynices, who relies
On Tydeus, and his Argive sire's supplies.
From hence shall spring the seeds of mutual hate,
The rest shall follow in the course of fate."
Swift as the word, the sprightly son of May
Prepares th' Almighty's orders to obey ;
The glitt'ring sandals to his feet applies,
And to his heels the well-trim'd pinion ties.
His hat's wide-spread circumference confines
The starry radiance, that around him shines.
He grasps the wand, which draws from hollow graves,
Or drives the trembling shades to Stygian waves ;
With magic power seals up the watchful eye
In slumbers soft, or causes sleep to fly.
From the vast height with swift descent he springs;
(A slender gale supports his steady wings)
Then thro' th' etherial void conspicuous flew,
And a long trail of light behind him drew.
Meanwhile from Thebes the banish'd hero roves
Thro' barren tracts, and wide Aonian groves ;
And while the flatt'ring hopes of distant sway
Chear the bleak horrours of the tedious way,
The partial signs enlarge their heav'nly space,
And the Sun seems to run a double race :
His cares arise with each revolving ray,
And night renews the labours of the day.
In prospect he prevents his future joy,
And snatches at the visionary toy,
Surveys the glitt'ring tow'rs of Thebes his own,
Or deals out justice from a fancied throne.
Would fate permit, he'd give an age away,
And lavish all on one luxurious day :

401. For by thy waves] This was the most customary oath among the gods, and the greatest they could take ; whatever had obtained the sanction of it, was esteemed inviolable.

Stygii per flumina fratris,
Per pice torrentes atraque voragine ripas,
Annuit. Æn. 10. v. 13.

And again,

Adjuro Stygii caput implacabile fontis,
Una superstitio superis quæ reddita divis.
Lib. 12. v. 816.

411. Whose shiv'ring] The souls of the deceased wandered a hundred years, before they were admitted to pass the river Styx. Virgil introduces some departed souls in the same state as Laius.

Stabant orantes primi transmittere cursum,
Tendebantque manus ripæ ulterioris amore.
Æn. 6. v. 313.

419. Swift as the word] This description of Mercury is imitated from Virgil's in the fourth Æneid, v. 238.

—— Ille patris magni parere parabat
Imperio : et primum pedibus talaria nectit
Aurea quæ sublimem alis, sive æquora supra,
Seu terram, rapido pariter cum flamine portant.
Tum virgam capit : hac animas ille evocat orco
Pallentes, alias sub tristia Tartara mittit,
Dat somnos adimitque, & lumina morte resignat.

Who took it from Homer, Iliad, lib. 24. v. 339.

Ὣς ἔφατ', οὐδ' ἀπίθησε διάκτορος Ἀργειφόντης.
Αὐτίκ' ἔπειθ' ὑπὸ ποσσὶν ἐδήσατο καλὰ πέδιλα,
Ἀμβρόσια, χρύσεια, τά μιν φέρον ἠμὲν ἐφ' ὑγρὴν,
Ἠδ' ἐπ' ἀπείρονα γαῖαν, ἅμα πνοιῇς ἀνέμοιο.
Εἵλετο δὲ ῥάβδον τῇ τ' ἀνδρῶν ὄμματα θέλγει
Ὧν ἐθέλει, τοὺς δ' αὖτε καὶ ὑπνώοντας ἐγείρει.

Tasso has likewise improved it with many additional images in his description of the angel Gabriel, Gierus. Lib. canto 1. stanza 13.

Cosi parlògli, e Gabriel s' accinse
Veloce ad essequir l' imposte cose.
La sua forma invisibil d' aria cinse,
Ed al senso mortal la sottopose.
Umane membra, aspetto uman sinse :
Mà di celeste maestà il compose,
Trà giovane, e fanciullo età confine
Prese, & ornò di raggi il biondo crine.
Ali bianche vestì, c' han d' or le cime
Infaticabilmente agili, e preste :
Fende i venti, e le nubi, e va sublime
Sovra la terra, e sovra il mar con queste :

These are all inferior to Milton's description of the angel Raphael.

—— Six wings he wore, to shade
His lineaments divine ; the pair that clad
Each shoulder broad, came mant'ling o'er his breast
With regal ornament ; the middle pair
Girt like a starry zone his waist, and round
Skirted his loins and thighs, with downy gold,
And colours dipp'd in Heav'n : the third his feet
Shadow'd from either heel with feather'd mail,
Sky-tinctur'd grain : like Maia's son he stood
And shook his plumes, that heav'nly fragrance fill'd
The circuit wide. Par. Lost, B. 5.

433. Meanwhile] The art of characterizing is perhaps less understood than any one branch in the whole province of poetry : and indeed it may be alleged, that the qualifications requisite for it are acquired with great difficulty, and can result only from the most penetrating sagacity, joined to an intimate acquaintance with, and long study of, human nature. Young poets are apt to describe man as he ought to be, and not as he is, never considering that a completely good man is little less than a monster. Our poet has avoided this defect, and always interspersed the manly conduct of his heroes with some spices of folly and weakness ; nay, he has sometimes fallen into the other extreme, and painted men rather worse than they really are.

Despair renews, now hope dispels his gloom,
And fruitless wishes all his joys consume.
The prince at length resolves to seek for aid,
Where Danaus once th' Inachian sceptre sway'd,
From whence th' indignant Sun withdrew his light,
And hid the tyrant's crimes in sudden night:
And now, impell'd by furies, chance or fate,
He rush'd impetuous from the well-known gate,
And quits the caves, where howling matrons toil,
And slaughter'd Pentheus fertiliz'd the soil;
Then views from whence Cithæron's less'ning steep
Receives its limits from th' adjoining deep,
Or trembling hangs on Scyron's noted rock,
And from afar surveys the wat'ry shock.
To Megara the warrior next repairs,
Fam'd for the rape of Nisus' purple hairs,
From thence the straits of Corinth passes o'er,
And hears the billows break on either shore.
Now Phœbus, conscious of exhausted light,
Resigns his empire to succeeding night,
And rising Cynthia thro' the realms above
Her dew-bespangled car in silence drove.
All things were hush'd: sleep quits the fields of air,
And steals upon the watchful miser's care:
No future toils alarm his peaceful breast,
Steep'd in oblivion, and consign'd to rest.
Yet no red cloud, edg'd with a golden ray,
Foretold the glad approach of hast'ning day,
No faint reflection of the Sun invades
The night, or glimmers on the less'ning shades:
From Earth ascending, thicker vapours roll,
Form one black mist, and darken either pole.
The winds arise, and with tumultuous rage
The gath'ring horrours of the storm presage;
And whilst in Heav'n superior sway they claim,
Earth labours, and resounds the starry frame.
But Auster chiefly checks the breaking light,
In clouds encircled, and renews the night;
Then opes the sluices of the pregnant sky,
And bids the tempest from each quarter fly,
Which the fierce north, ere finish'd was its course,
Congeals to show'rs of hail with wond'rous force.
The thunder rolls, with lightning ether glows,
And bursting clouds unweary'd fires disclose.
Now Nemea, now Arcadia's cloud-capt hills
Pour on the subject vales their murm'ring rills.

456. And slaughter'd] Pentheus was the son of Echion and Agave; and torn to pieces by his mother and sisters, for despising the rites of Bacchus.

465. Now Phœbus] This is an imitation of that fine description in the fourth book of Virgil's Æneid, v. 522.

Nox erat, & placidum carpebant fessa soporem
Corpora per terras, silvæque & sæva quierant
Æquora; cum medio volvuntur sidera lapsu,
Cum tacet omnis ager; pecudes, pictæque volucres,
Quæque lacus late liquidos, quæque aspera dumis
Rura tenent, somno positæ sub nocte silenti,
Lenibant curas, & corda oblita laborum.

But the curis inserpit somnus avaris, is a circumstance which Virgil has not taken notice of, and highly worth our attention.

477. From Earth ascending] The art of the poet in working up this description deserves our greatest applause. We are led step by step from one degree of horrour to another, till all the elements are put in action, and the storm is arrived at its greatest height.

His waves in troops old Inachus sends forth,
And Erasinus, rising to the north.
Where late was dust, unnumber'd billows roar,
And Lerna spews around its liquid store:
Nor art, nor nature can the war sustain;
Mounds fail, and dams are interpos'd in vain.
Beneath its force the tallest oaks give way,
And gaping groves admit a sudden day;
Roots, leaves and boughs are hurry'd o'er the wood,
Float on the waves, and swell the loaded flood.
Meantime the Theban views with wond'ring eyes
The rocky ruin, that around him flies:
Now rural cots, and sheep-folds borne away
By the mad whirlwind's unresisted sway,
Then show'r-fed rivers from the mountain's height
Strike his quick ear, and fill his soul with fright.
Yet not more slow, unknowing where he strays,
The madding youth thro' dark and trackless ways
Pursues his course: Fear follows close behind,
And his stern brother's image haunts his mind.
As fares a mariner, when storms arise,
And clouded Phœbe quits th' unwilling skies,
Nor shines the Northern Wain: amid the strife
Of Heav'n and ocean, thoughtful for his life,
And doubtful, whether to expect his death
From storms above, or dangers underneath,
Starts at the thunder, which around him rolls,
Or dreads destruction from the neighb'ring shoals.
Not less perplex'd, the Theban warrior roves
Thro' shadowy thickets, and surrounding groves.
In vain the brambles his huge shield oppose,
His courage to his toils superior rose;
Till now he views, where from Larissa's brow
The shelving walls with light reflected glow;
Thither he posts, and from Prosymna's plain
Surveys the sacred grove, and Juno's fane;
And on the right fam'd Lerna's lake beheld,
Where fierce Alcides the fierce hydra quell'd.
At length he pass'd the gates, which open lay,
And to the royal dome pursu'd his way;
O'er the cold marble then his limbs he threw,
And sought in sleep his vigour to renew.
Adrastus o'er fair Argos sway maintain'd,
And long in peace the hoary prince had reign'd;
He drew his birth on both sides from above,
And claim'd alliance with almighty Jove.
Fate would not with a manly offspring crown
His nuptial bed. Two daughters heir'd his throne.
To him Apollo, monstrous to relate!
Disclos'd the secrets of unerring fate,
And said: "Expect thy sons on Argos' shore,
A tawny lion, and a bristling boar."
Long this revolv'd within his tender breast,
Engross'd his thoughts, and broke his nightly rest;
Long sage Amphiaraus essay'd in vain
This seeming menace of the gods t' explain,
At length perceiv'd the pow'rs' superior will,
And fate oppos'd to his predicting skill.
Here Tydeus, by resistless fortune led,
From Caledon's suspected vengeance fled,
And strove, too conscious of his brother slain,
His people's love by absence to regain.
Long sought the toiling chief a safe retreat
From the rough storm, till chance directs his feet

535. Adrastus o'er] The character and circumstances of Adrastus have a great resemblance with those of Latinus. He has no son, and receives an oracular injunction concerning the marriage of his daughters.

To the same place, where, stretch'd upon the ground,
The Theban warrior a like shelter found.
But Discord, ever fond of human blood,
Forbids the chiefs to plan each other's good;
Nor suffers them beneath one roof to share
A common shelter from th' inclement air.
Awhile harsh words, and mingled threats delay
Th' alternate labours of the bloody fray:
Then, of their garments strip'd, they both engage,
And mutual blows succeed to mutual rage.
With youth and stature flush'd, the Theban glows,
And on his lowly rival deals his blows;
But valiant Tydeus, though his dwarfish size
Could promise little to the partial eyes,
With greater confidence arose to fight,
And courage that disown'd superior might.
With swift repeated strokes their hands fly round
Their heads and cheeks; their crackling jaws re-
Thick as in war an iron tempest flies, [sound:
Or hail, that quits in rattling show'rs the skies.
Thus, when the trumpet's clanging sound proclaims
The wish'd renewal of th' Olympic games,
When clouds of dust from ev'ry part ascend,
And equal chance suspends th' impatient friend,
The diff'rent clamours of the pit engage
The list'ning rivals, and provoke their rage,
While from afar each partial mother eyes
The contest, and foredooms her son the prize.
Thus hatred, not desire of praise provokes
The sprightly chiefs, and arms their heavy strokes.
Their eyes start inward from beneath each blow,
And from their faces bloody currents flow.
Now had each vig'rous candidate for fame
With flaming sword renew'd his double claim,
And the proud Theban, stretch'd beneath the hand
Of Tydeus, dy'd with gore a foreign strand;
But old Adrastus, who with cares oppress'd,
Sigh'd for the distant joys of balmy rest,
With wonder heard th' unwonted clamours rise,
And deep-fetch'd groans, that echo'd through the
But when, Aurora bringing back the day, [skies.
Through the wide op'ning gates he took his way,
And saw their manly features rough with blood,
And their gash'd cheeks emit a crimson flood,
He thus exclaims.——"Say, what provokes your rage,
O foreign youths, and why you thus engage?
(For sure my subjects would not dare to stain
My courts with blood, and Cynthia's rule profane.)
Say, is the day too scanty, or the night
Once sacred to repose, reserv'd for fight?
But come, your country, birth, and names relate,
Say, whither bound, and whence this mutual hate?
For such high spirit, and resentment shows
A breast, that with no common ardour glows,
And in that stream of honour we may trace
A gen'rous birth, and more than vulgar race."
Scarce had he spoke, when in a mingled din
The chiefs abash'd with mutual shame, begin:
"Useless are words, O king, when wounds display
The bloody labours of this casual fray."
In vain they strive, while mutual scoffs confound
Their diff'rent accents, and perplex the sound,
Till glowing with the prospect of relief,
Intrepid Tydeus thus imparts his grief.
"From fam'd Ætolia's monster-bearing plains
I stray'd an exile, till in your domains
The night my progress check'd: and shall he dare
Deny me shelter from th' inclement air,
Because he first obtain'd a safe retreat
Beneath this roof, and hospitable seat?
Shall man alone, by boasted reason led,
Refuse to share with man the social bed,
When fiercer Cyclops live in mutual peace,
And fights between the stabled Centaurs cease?
E'en rav'ning brutes defend the common cause,
Nor deviate thus from Nature's sacred laws.
But why this flow of words? this fatal morn
Shall see my bloody spoils in triumph borne,
Or should my breast with equal vigour glow,
Nor my brisk blood forget, as erst, to flow,
This arm shall soon display my lineal fire,
And prove me worthy my celestial sire."
"Nor shall the want of martial heat disgrace,"
The Theban prince replies, "my godlike race,"
For conscious pride forbad him yet to own
His wretched sire, and claim the Theban crown.
To them the king.—"This causeless strife surceas'd,
Advance, and with us share the solemn feast.
But first resign your threats, and rage of blood
To mutual love, and cares of mutual good;
And let your hands, in sacred union join'd,
Attest the fixt intentions of the mind.
For some mysterious cause was this decreed,
Nor are the gods unconscious of the deed.
Perhaps, when length of time has seal'd the vow,
And your firm hearts with holy friendship glow,
With joy you may review the bloody fray,
Nor blush to trace this e'er-auspicious day."
Thus Jove's decree, unconscious he foreshows;
The sequel far transcends his warmest vows:

559. But Discord] We are now entering upon that part which has done Statius so much hurt in the eyes of the critics, and where we must leave him without offering a single word in his defence. He has undoubtedly erred very much in the choice of this episode: not that the piece itself, detached from the rest of the poem, is destitute of merit, but because it should not have had a place in the epopœia, and especially at this juncture. It is remarkable, that Mr. Pope has omitted the whole in his translation of this book: in my opinion, the strongest proof of its unseasonable insertion.

569. Though his dwarfish size] The dwarfish size and stature of Tydeus are taken notice of also by Homer, in Minerva's speech to Diomede.

Il. b. 5. v. 800.

῏Η ὀλιγὸν οἱ παῖδα ἐοικότα γείνατο Τυδεὺς,
Τυδεύς τοι μικρὸς μὲν ἔην δέμας, ἀλλὰ μαχητής.

605. Say, is the day] To say that this part of Adrastus's conduct is copied from that of Evander on a similar occasion, is to tell the reader what he must know already. Both princes are engaged in performing their annual vows to the gods, when the strangers arrive in their territories, and both give an account of the rise of the solemnities: but if general observations should fail of confirming what I have advanced, the passages from Virgil, which I shall quote as they occur, will sufficiently justify it.

644. Advance, and with us] Evander invites Æneas in like manner. Æneid, b. 8. v. 172.

Interea sacra hæc, quando huc venistis, amici,
Annua, quæ differre nefas, celebrate faventes
Nobiscum, et jam nunc sociorum assuescite mensis,

For Pylades was not more known to fame,
Nor Theseus, burning with an equal flame,
Tho' to redeem his bold companion lost,
He brav'd the dangers of the Stygian coast.
At length, the chiefs to reason yield the sway,
And the sage dictates of the king obey:
An air of mutual friendship they assume,
And enter, hand in hand, the spacious room.
Thus when the ruler of the stormy main
Is pleas'd the tempest's fury to restrain,
The winds, abating, smooth the vessel's course,
And on the slack'ning sails exhaust their force.
Here first the monarch, fix'd in deep amaze,
The dress and arms of either guest surveys.
A lion's tawny hide the Theban wore
(Such grac'd the godlike Hercules of yore,
Ere Nemea's boast resign'd his shaggy spoils,
To deck his shoulders, and reward his toils):
Th' Ætolian monster's pride young Tydeus bears,
Horrid with tusks, and rough with bristling hairs.
The hoary chief, astonish'd to behold
Th' events, by Phœbus' oracles foretold,
Acknowledges with joy the voice of Heav'n,
And answers, from the vocal cavern giv'n.
Then to the skies he lifts his grateful hands,
And thus the future aid of night demands,
(While thro' each vein mysterious transports roll,
And awful pleasure thrills thro' all his soul.)
" O gloomy queen of shades, whose ebon throne
The sparkling gems of Heav'n in order crown,
Beneath whose reign indulgent sleep repairs
The busy world, and buries mortal cares,
Till rising Sol warms India's fragrant soil,
And with his rays renews our daily toil;
Whose aid alone could free the doubtful way,
And the dark fates disclose to sudden day;
O speed my cause, nor let me still complain
Of lying oracles and omens vain:
So shall our sons renew these rites divine
For ages hence at this thy honour'd shrine,
And while the priests thy sacred name invoke,
Black sheep cull'd out shall fall beneath their stroke,
In curling spires the sable smoke shall rise,
And waft its grateful odours to the skies.
Hail, antient tripods, and ye dark abodes!
Exult we, fortune, for th' acknowledg'd gods,
Whose tutelary pow'r with joy I own,
And you, O long desired to heir my throne!"
He spoke, and with the princes bent his way
To th' inner court, impatient of delay,
Where yet thin fumes a fainty odour yield,
And mould'ring embers dying sparks conceal'd.

657. For Pylades] The friendship of Pylades and Orestes was so strong, that when Orestes was sent for to be put to death, Pylades said he was Orestes, to preserve his friend, and Orestes (as the truth was) avouched himself to be the man, that his friend might not for his sake lose his life, whence their names are made a proverb, to signify unfeigned friends.

659. Tho' to redeem] The companion of Theseus was Pirithous, who going to Hell in quest of Proserpine, whom he had vowed to enjoy, was slain by Cerberus. Theseus, missing his comrade, and concluding where he was gone, repaired to the infernal regions likewise, but was taken prisoner by the same monster, and detained in chains, till Hercules came and delivered him.

He then enjoins his servants to repair
The fire, and make the genial feast their care.
Swift at the word they run: the court replies
To ev'ry voice, and echoes back their cries.
With Tyrian carpets this adorns the ground,
That smooths the beds with gold and purple crown'd;
While some the tables range, count ev'ry guest,
And artfully adjust the future feast;
Others with salted entrails heap the fire,
And bid the flames from ev'ry part aspire.
From gilded roofs depending, lamps display
Nocturnal beams, and emulate the day:
The canisters are pil'd with Ceres' spoils,
And the king views with joy their rival toils.
On tapestry reclin'd, Adrastus shone
Afar conspicuous, from his iv'ry throne;
A broider'd couch supports the foreign guests,
Nor love of discord longer fires their breasts.
The monarch bids Aceste then appear,
And whispers his injunctions in her ear,
Whose bright example had to virtue train'd
His daughters, and preserv'd their fame unstain'd.
The nymphs the summons of their sire attend,
And to the hall their steps obsequious bend:
Minerva's features, and Diana's grace,
Conspir'd to stamp perfection on their face.
But as in prospect they perus'd the feast,
And met the glances of each unknown guest,
In blushes they reveal'd the first surprise,
And to their sire recall'd their wand'ring eyes,
While gath'ring shame their conscious face o'erspread,
Varying their cheeks by turns with white and red.
But when the rage of hunger was repress'd,
The meat remov'd, and satiate ev'ry guest,
A goblet in the midst Adrastus plac'd,
With sculptur'd gold, and glitt'ring figures grac'd,
In which his ancestors were wont to pour
Libations, and indulge the genial hour.
Here fraught with Gorgon's spoils, the winged horse
O'er Heav'n's expanse was seen to stretch his course,
While she her eyes in dying motions roll'd,
Her paleness imag'd in th' impassion'd gold.
There the commission'd eagle seems to bear
The Phrygian youth through tracts of yielding air;
Proud Ida's summit lessens to his sight,
And Troy rolls back beneath his rising flight;
While his sad comrades on the crowded coast
View both in clouds of ambient ether lost,
And each lov'd hound, in deeper notes of woe,
Demands his master of th' unheeding foe.
This old Adrastus fills with sacred wine,
And then in pray'r invokes the pow'rs divine:
But Phœbus, first of the celestial train,
Receives the mystic off'rings of the fane;
Him with united shouts the crowd demands,
And waves the flow'ring branches in their hands;

751. There the commission'd] Virgil relates the same story with similar circumstances, as described in a piece of embroidery.

> Intextusque puer frondosâ regius Idâ
> Veloces jaculo cervos cursuque fatigat,
> Acer, anhelanti similis; quem præpes ab Idâ
> Sublimem pedibus rapuit Jovis armiger uncis.
> Longævi palmas nequicquam ad sidera tendunt
> Custodes, sævitque canum latratus ad auras.
>
> Æneid, book 5, v. 252.

For him this annual sacrifice prepares,
While with incessant flames each altar glares.
Then thus the king.—"Perhaps these youths would know,
What claims this strict observance of our vow;
And why the pious sons of Argos pay
Such special honours to the god of day.
No superstitious zeal our sires impell'd
To constitute these rites, which you've beheld:
But when and whence these solemn customs rose,
(So ye but lend attention,) I'll disclose.
When now the Python had by Phœbus bled,
And with his bulk the Delphic plain o'erspread,
(As hanging o'er the fair Castalian flood
He fills his turgid maw with noxious food)
To th' Argive court repair'd the victor-god,
And with his presence honour'd our abode.
The king Crotopus (as the fates decreed)
Was blest with no male issue to succeed:
A nymph, unmatch'd in manners as in face,
Was the sole product of his first embrace:
Thrice happy maid! had Phœbus fail'd to move
Her tender breast, nor kindled mutual love;
For by th' enamour'd god compress'd, she bore
A godlike son on Nemea's winding shore,
Ere the tenth moon had with her borrow'd light
Supply'd the want of day, and rul'd the night.
For this constrain'd to quit her native place,
And shun approaching vengeance and disgrace,
Among the rustic swains she seeks a friend,
To whom she might her precious charge commend.
The wretched babe, beneath an homely shed,
With bleating lambkins shares a common bed;
While with the pipe his foster-father tries
To soothe his plaints, and close his infant eyes.
Hard was his lot. Yet still relentless fate
Forbad him to enjoy his poor retreat:

771. No superstitious] So Evander in the eighth book of the Æneid, verse 185.

> ——Non hæc solennia nobis
> Has ex more dapes, hanc tanti numinis aram,
> Vana superstitio, veterumque ignara Deorum
> Imposuit.

775. When now the Python] The Python was a huge serpent, so called from Πυθεῖν, to rot; because he was reported to arise from the rottenness of the earth after the deluge. Juno sent him to vex Latona, who was then with child by Jupiter: but the goddess flying to Asteria, her sister, was protected till Apollo grew up; who killed the monster; for which the Macedonians instituted the Pythian games.

775. When now] This a very fine episode, and, in my opinion, superior to that of Cacus in the eighth book of the Æneid. When I say superior, I would not be understood to mean, that this of Statius is better executed: but that it abounds with a greater variety of matter, and consequently requires less art of the poet to render it complete. The description of Psamathe and her child's unhappy fate, and the patriotic behaviour of Chorœbus are master-pieces in their kind, and cannot fail of affording the reader the highest satisfaction. Give me leave to add, that when the subject is so circumstanced as in the present case, though the poet's art should be equal, yet that episode, which contains the greatest variety of incidents, will always have the preference.

For while abandon'd to blind Fortune's care,
Beneath the shade he breathes the morning air,
The furious dogs his tender carcase tore,
And fed luxurious on the recent gore.
But when the tidings reach'd the mother's ears,
Unmindful of her former shame and fears,
She raves, the palace fills with piercing cries,
Nor shuns her father's once-avoided eyes:
Then hears, impatient of her vital breath,
The fatal sentence, and demands her death.
But Phœbus, mindful of his stol'n embrace,
Prepares t' avenge her suff'rings and disgrace,
And bids ascend, to plague the guilty Earth,
A horrid monster of infernal birth:
Her face and breast a female form disclose,
But from her head a crested serpent rose,
Whose hideous length disparts her livid brows,
And from afar with dreadful splendour glows.
When fav'ring night the busy world o'erspreads,
She roams the streets, or haunts the children's beds,
Consigns to Pluto, and a sudden night,
Those new-born babes, who scarce had seen the light,
And, unresisted by the heartless foe,
Thrives, and collects fresh strength from public woe.
With grief Chorœbus ey'd the wasteful pest,
And gen'rous rage inflam'd his patriot breast;
To some few chosen youths, who life disclaim,
And think it oversold to purchase fame,
He pleads his country's cause, and undismay'd
Extorts a promise of united aid.
These soon descry'd her, fir'd with vengeful hate,
Where the broad path, divided, fronts the gate:
Two infants, borne from some unguarded dome,
Hang at her side, unconscious what's to come,
Till her sharp claws explore their inner parts,
And seek the nearest passage to their hearts.
So sad a sight Chorœbus could not bear,
But buried in her breast his rushing spear.
The springs of life emit their crimson store,
And thro' the gap, discharg'd in issuing gore,
Her soul revisits the Tartarian coast,
And native Styx,—a lonely dreaded ghost.
Eager they press to view the monster's eyes
Livid in death, her womb's enormous size,
And breasts more filthy with the clotted blood
Of Grecian babes. The youths of Argos stood
In wonder lost; and to their recent tears
Great joys succeed, but joys appall'd with fears.
Their sole vexation now remains to find
Their rage exhausted, their revenge confin'd.
Some seem'd displeas'd, they can no longer kill,
And wish their pow'r was equal to their will:
Whilst others mangling her detested corse
With furious zeal her limbs asunder force.
To distant roosts the birds of night repair,
And shriek, impatient of the scented air:
E'en hungry dogs, and monsters of the wood,
Start from the sight, and loathe the direful food.

827. Who life disclaim] This expression is made use of by Virgil.

> Est hic, est animus lucis contemptor, et istum,
> Qui vitâ bene credat emi, quò tendis, honorem.
> Æneid, v. 206. B. 9.

And by Tasso with little variation,

> Ho core anch' io, che morte sprezza, e crede
> Che ben si cambi con l'onor la vita.
> Gierus. Lib. Canto 12. Stanza 8.

This but increas'd Apollo's former hate,
And urg'd him to revenge the monster's fate.
From cleft Parnassus' heights he bent his bow,
And hurl'd his vengeance on the realms below.
Around the god unnumber'd mischiefs wait,
And ev'ry shaft contains resistless fate.
While o'er the horizon gath'ring clouds arise,
Fraught with destruction, and infect the skies.
Death cuts the fatal sisters' threads in haste,
And the dispeopled city soon lays waste.
But Phœbus ask'd, from what mysterious source
Sirius deriv'd such unresisted force,
Demands those youths, whose hands in dust had laid
The monster's pride, to glut her vengeful shade.
Thrice happy warrior! may thy worth be crown'd
With fame, nor length of time thy glory bound;
Who, nobly lavish of thy vital breath,
Disdain'st to shun inevitable death:
And, rushing to the temple, durst provoke
The raging god, and thus demand the stroke.
'Think not desire of life, or public force
Hath to thy fane, O Phœbus, urg'd my course:
With conscious virtue arm'd, thy will I wait,
To save my country, and avert its fate.
Behold the man, who durst in fight engage
His country's pest, and bound its wasteful rage:
Whom to revenge, the Sun withheld its light,
And wrapt the skies in pestilential night.
But if such horrid scenes thy thoughts employ,
And death and slaughter are thy savage joy;
If man no more must thy protection claim,
Since the fiend's death has fann'd thy vengeful flame;
Yet why should Argos for my crimes atone,
And share the vengeance due to me alone?
Let me be deem'd the hateful cause of all,
And suffer, rather than my country fall;
Unless you view with joy our desert town,
And fun'ral flames, unrivall'd by your own.
But why do I the fatal dart arrest,
And torture with suspense each matron's breast?
Then fit the arrow to the well-strung bow,
And send me glorying to the shades below.
But, ere the fates suppress my vital breath,
Grant me to see (some solace in my death)
The plague in unoffending Argos cease,
And exil'd health restor'd again to Greece.'
Fortune consigns the coward to the grave,
But for his country's sake preserves the brave.
Relenting Phœbus quits his angry bow,
And blushing longer to remain a foe,
With rev'rence bids th' unwilling patriot live,
And health and peace in sorrowing Greece revive.
From that auspicious day with rites divine,
We worship at Apollo's honour'd shrine:
Such annual feasts his temp'rate rays require,
And thus we shun the god's returning ire.
But say, illustrious youth, from whence you came,
From whence derive your birth, and what's your claim?
Since the brave son of Oeneus stands confest,
A welcome neighbour, and more welcome guest,
And the full bowl, and silent hours invite
With various converse to contract the night."
A rising blush o'erspreads the Theban chief,
Yet glowing with the prospect of relief,
Prone to the earth he fix'd his gloomy eyes,
And with a previous sigh at length replies.
"Before these altars how shall I reveal
What conscious shame enjoins me to conceal?
Too happy! was my fortune not more known
To fame than you, or known to you alone.
But since you take such int'rest in my woe,
And the disast'rous tale desire to know,
Learn, that from Cadmus by descent I come,
Jocasta's son, and Thebes my native home."
Adrastus, touch'd with his unhappy fate,
Replies,—"Forbear the sequel to relate:
Nor think us strangers to the Theban name,
Or deaf to the divulging voice of fame.
Ev'n those who freeze beneath the northern pole,
Or view the swelling waves of Ganges roll,
Who live where ocean bounds th' Hesperian lands,
Or dread the depth of Lybia's burning sands,
All these have known the furies' vengeful ire,
And the rash actions of your wretched sire.
But if the son re-acts the father's crimes,
And shares the lineal guilt of former times,
How curst am I, on whose unhappy race
The feast of Tantalus entail'd disgrace!
Be this thy study then, with inbred worth
T' efface the stains coeval with thy birth.
But see, pale Cynthia quits th' etherial plains,
And of night's empire but a third remains;
With wine then let the sprinkled altars blaze,
And joyful Pæans swell the note of praise.
O Phœbus, author of the rising day,
Whether the Lycian mountains court thy stay,
Or fair Castalia's current claims thy care,
Where oft thou joy'st to bathe thy golden hair:
Whether proud Troy detains thee on her strands,
Rear'd by the labour of celestial hands:
Or, pleas'd to seek thy native isle no more,
Thy genial presence gilds the Cynthian shore;

859. This but increas'd] It will not perhaps be displeasing to the reader, if I subjoin the following passage from Homer, to give him an opportunity of comparing it with what he has just read.

Ὣς ἔφατ' εὐχόμενος. τοῦ δ' ἔκλυε Φοῖβος Ἀπόλλων.
Βῆ δὲ κατ' Οὐλύμποιο καρήνων χωόμενος κῆρ,
Τόξ' ὤμοισιν ἔχων, ἀμφηρεφέα τε φαρέτρην.
Ἔκλαγξαν δ' ἄρ' ὀϊστοὶ ἐπ' ὤμων χωομένοιο,
Αὐτοῦ κινηθέντος. ὁ δ' ἤϊε νυκτὶ ἐοικώς.
Ἕζετ' ἔπειτ' ἀπάνευθε νεῶν, μετὰ δ' ἰὸν ἕηκε.
Δεινὴ δὲ κλαγγὴ γένετ' ἀργυρέοιο βιοῖο.
Οὐρῆας μὲν πρῶτον ἐπῴχετο, καὶ κύνας ἀργούς.
Αὐτὰρ ἔπειτ' αὐτοῖσι βέλος ἐχεπευκὲς ἀφιεὶς,
Βάλλ'. αἰεὶ δὲ πυραὶ νεκύων καίοντο θαμειαί.

Iliad, l. 1. v. 43.

891. Yet why should Argos] Tasso has put the same noble sentiment in the mouth of Sophronia, but with an additional beauty of expression.

——E giusto, esser à mi conviene
Se fui sola al' onor, sola alle pene.

And a little lower.

A me l' onor, la morte à me si deve,
Non s' usurpi costei le pene mie.

Gierusalem Lib. Canto 2.

957. Whether proud Troy] Troy was built by the joint labour of Neptune and Apollo: hence Horace says,

Ter si resurgat murus aheneus
Auctore Phœbo, &c. Lib. 3. ode 3.

Whose graceful hand supports the fatal bow,
And darts destruction on the furious foe:
In vain old age assaults thy beardless face,
Crown'd with fresh beauty, and perennial grace.
'Tis thine to warn us with unerring skill
Of Heav'n's decrees, and Jove's resistless will;
To teach, from whence the torch of discord springs,
The change of sceptres, and the fate of kings.
Thy shafts allay'd fierce Tityos' lawless lust,
And humbled haughty Marsyas to the dust,
(Who durst aspire to match thy sacred lays)
And from the Python reap'd immortal praise:
Thy pow'r transform'd proud Niobe to stone,
And to Latona's charms adjudg'd the crown:
Megæra, fiercest fiend, at thy command
For e'er incumbent, shakes her vengeful brand
O'er the devoted head of the rash sire,
Who wrapt the Delphic fane in impious fire:
He views the proffer'd food, yet dares not taste,
And dreads the cavern'd rock above him plac'd.
Let then our fields thy constant influence share,
And Argos, sacred to the queen of air;
Whether the name of Titan please thee most,
A name rever'd on th' Achœmenian coast,
Or great Osiris, whom the Pharian swain
Decks with the first-fruits of the ripen'd grain:
Or Mitra more, to whose prolific rays
The grateful Persian adoration pays,
Who grasps the horns of the reluctant steer,
While on his head encircling lights appear."

BOOK II.

ARGUMENT.

This book opens with a description of Mercury's return from Hell, pursuant to the commands of Jove, as delivered in the first book. Laius appears to Eteocles, and to make the greater impression upon his mind, assumes the form of Tiresias. The Theban king persists in withholding the crown from his brother. The poet then transports us to Argos, and relates the marriage of the two heroes to Adrastus's daughters, by which a triple alliance is formed between Adrastus, Tydeus, and Polynices. The nuptials are interrupted by an inauspicious omen; the cause of which is attributed to Argia's wearing the necklace of Harmonia. Tydeus is deputed embassador to claim the crown of Eteocles; but meeting with a repulse, denounces war against him. The tyrant hires fifty ruffians to assassinate him in his way to Argos. These are slain all but one, whom he spares to carry the news to Thebes. The hero, flushed with his success, would have ventured himself among his enemies there, but Minerva interposes; to whom he raises a trophy of the spoils, and prefers a prayer, which concludes the book.

Now Hermes, fraught with the commands of Jove,
With wings expanded seeks the realms above.
Black mists surround him, and impervious night
Checks his bold progress, and controls his flight;
No zephyrs waft him o'er the realms below,
But still and noisome gales: on one side, flow
The branching streams of Styx in calm repose,
On t'other, fiery lakes his way oppose.
Propp'd on the wand divine, old Laius' shade
Stalks slow behind him; for the forceful blade
Thro' his pierc'd ribs an easy passage found,
Till point and hilt had clos'd the gaping wound.
Amaz'd the dreary grove and pensive glades
Survey his passage from th' infernal shades,
While flitting spectres eye the king's return
With sullen grief, and their confinement mourn:
For, like the soul, pale envy braves the tomb,
Nor with the body shares an equal doom.
But one, who sickens at another's joy,
Prone to insult, and eager to destroy,
With borrow'd smile old Laius thus address'd,
While rankling malice swell'd his envious breast.
"Thrice happy shade! (whether propitious Jove
Enjoins thy presence in the realms above,
Or madd'ning fury, or prophetic maid
Forbids thy stay in this detested shade)
Couldst thou enjoy the Sun's enliv'ning beam,
The flow'ry mead, clear skies, and crystal stream:
But soon, alas! more sorrowing thou'lt return,
And with retorted eye those pleasures mourn."
He paus'd: for Cerberus began to rear
His angry snakes, and arm'd his bristling hair;
Sternly he yawn'd: th' advancing ghosts retire,
Nor dare withstand the monster's threat'ned ire.
But Hermes with his wand Lethean clos'd
His watchful eyes, and a short truce impos'd.
A steep there is, fam'd Tænaros by name,
Whose equal summit joins the starry frame.

987. Or Mitra more] The Persians call the Sun Mitra, account him the greatest of their gods, and worship him in a cave. His statue has the head of a lion, on which a turbant, called tiara, is placed. It is clothed with Persian attire, and holds with both hands a struggling heifer.

1. Now Hermes] The beginning of this book is really valuable, as it throws considerable light on the heathen mythology, and the notions they entertained of a future state.

17. For, like the soul] This opinion of the passions inhering after death in the souls of men is confirmed by Virgil.

Quæ gratia currûm,
Armorumque fuit vivis, quæ cura nitentes
Pascere equos, eadem sequitur tellure repostos.
Æn. Lib. 6. ver. 653.

19. But one, who sickens]

Sed videt ingratos, intabescitque videndo
Successus hominum. Ovid's Metam. Lib. 2.

It appears from this passage of Statius, that the souls of the deceased were not so thoroughly weaned from the pleasures of the world, as to be averse to a return; but the most probable conjecture we can form is, that they had not undergone the purgation mentioned by Virgil.

Ergo exercentur pœnis, veterumque malorum
Supplicia expendunt. Æn. Lib. 6. v. 739.

31. He paus'd]

Cerberus hæc ingens latratu regna trifauci
Personat, adverso recubans immanis in antro:
Cui vates, horrere videns jam colla colubris,
Melle soporatam et medicatis frugibus offam
Objicit, ille fame rabidâ tria guttura pandens,
Corripit objectam, atque immania terga resolvit
Fusus humi, totoque ingens extenditur antro.
Virg. Æn. b. 5. v. 417.

Calm from its height it hears the tempest blow,
And views, secure, the breaking surge below.
Here hoarse winds, lull'd in gentle slumbers, lie,
And hurl'd from hence, the red-wing'd lightnings fly.
Collected mists its flinty sides surround,
Nor hears its head the distant thunder's sound.
But when the day declines, its length'ning steep
O'erhangs the waves, and shades the middle deep.
The crooked shore too forms an inner bay,
Where inoffensively the billows play.
The steeds of Neptune here securely feed,
Of fish and courser a promiscuous breed.
This winding path (Arcadia's sons report)
Conveys the damn'd to Pluto's gloomy court.
Here oft are heard deep groans, tumultuous cries,
And loud laments, that rend the vaulted skies;
Grim Cerb'rus howls; the furies drag their chain
And the scar'd hinds retreat to distant plains.
This way, involv'd in shades of sable night,
Great Hermes takes, and steers to Heav'n his flight.
He shakes the mists infernal from his face,
And the fresh air renews his ev'ry grace.
Then through the regions of the frozen north
He sails with steady wings.—Sleep, sallying forth
In night's dim car, extends o'er all his sway:
Both met, but Sleep resign'd the shining way.
Beneath the god the phantom flits, descries
His native country, and long-ravish'd skies,
And now surveys aspiring Cyrrha's brow,
And the stain'd fields of Phocis far below.
But as he glanc'd where his own palace stood,
And chariot still discolour'd with his blood,
He deeply groan'd: recoiling nature strove
With duty, and disputes the will of Jove.
In vain Cyllenius waves his iv'ry wand:
He halts, regardless of the god's command.
'Twas the decline of that revolving ray,
Which first gave Bacchus to the realms of day,
When joyous revels chase the drowsy night,
Nor cease, till Sol restores his absent light.
With glee the Thebans (part in open field,
And part at home) their sparkling goblets wield.
Between each draught the pipes, the cymbals sound,
And music's soft delights the banquet crown'd.
From glad Cithæron too the matrons throng,
Inspir'd by milder Bacchus, rush along.
The Thracians thus on Ossa's pine-crown'd height,
Or Rhodope, indulge the festive rite;
In luxury they snatch the lion's food,
And with new milk correct the draught of blood:
But if the strength of wine excite their rage,
Cups clash with cups, and stones with stones engage,
Nor ends the conflict, till from many a wound
Black streams of social gore distain the ground.
Such was the night, when with descending wing
Fam'd Maia's offspring reach'd the Theban king.
Stretch'd on embroider'd tapestry he lay,
And sought in sleep to doze his cares away.
Ill-fated race, whom fate forbids to know
Their destin'd woes, till she discharge the blow.
Then th' aged king with fix'd and steady mind
Prepares to execute what Jove enjoin'd;
And lest he should an airy phantom seem,
Or grisly child of some terrific dream,
Assumes the form of the Bœotian sage,
Alike in voice, in feature, and in age.
A length of hoary beard he still retains,
And the same paleness o'er his visage reigns.
But a false mitre bound his awful brow,
And in his hand he bore an olive-bough,
On which were fillets wound.—The prince's breast
With this he gently smote, and thus addrest:
"Thus sleep you, careless of the glorious strife,
As though secure of empire and of life?
Thus unambitious of the wreaths, which fame
Has woven, and thy better deeds should claim?
Less guilt attends the skilful pilot's sleep,
When gath'ring storms o'erhang the troubled deep,
The helm unmanag'd, and the ship resign'd
To sportive fortune, and th' inconstant wind.
Meanwhile the heir of old Adrastus' crown
Already deems your diadem his own,
Supports by marriage his declining cause,
And bloody Tydeus to his standard draws.
Hence springs his pride, his hopes of vengeance flow,
And a long exile to his brother-foe.
By Jove commission'd, from the skies above
I bear this proof of his paternal love.
Then keep the crown, and know, shouldst thou resign,
His soul is daring at the least as thine:
Lest through delays you mourn your empire lost,
And the fierce Argives ravaging your coast."
The phantom paus'd, (for now a bursting ray
Of light proclaim'd the glad approach of day)
Then pluck'd the borrow'd honours from his brow,
And from his hand dismiss'd the peaceful bough.

85. The Thracians thus] This account of the Thracians is confirmed by the concurring testimony of several historians, and particularly that of Herodotus.

100. What Jove enjoin'd] Jupiter's artifice to punish the Thebans will not appear unjust, if we consider, that the incestuous race of Oedipus were themselves impious, and were therefore justly doomed to destruction: and Quos Jupiter vult perdere, dementat prius.

103. Assumes the form of the Bœotian sage] Mr. Warton has been perhaps a little too severe in his strictures on this passage, in his note on verse 525 of the seventh book of Virgil's Æneid. "Statius," says he, "but with little success, upon the whole, has imitated this passage, where the shade of Laius disguised under the figure of Tiresias appears to Eteocles asleep."

111. Thus sleep you] Our author seems to have copied this speech from Homer's Iliad, book 2. verse 60.

Εὕδεις Ἀτρέος υἱὲ δαίφρονος ἱπποδάμοιο;
Οὐ χρὴ παννύχιον εὕδειν βουληφόρον ἄνδρα
Ὦ λαοί τ' ἐπιτετράφαται, καὶ τόσσα μέμηλε.
Νῦν δ' ἐμέθεν ξύνες ὦκα. Διός δέ τοι ἄγγελός εἰμι
Ὃς σεῦ ἄνευθεν ἐὼν, μέγα κήδεται.

131. The phantom paus'd] Anchises, when he is introduced appearing to his son Æneas, concludes his speech to him in the following lines.

Jamque vale: torquet medios nox humida cursu
Et me sævus equis oriens afflavit anhelis.
Virgil's Æneid, book 5. verse 738.

At length he bares his blood-impurpled breast,
And all the murder'd grandsire stands confest.
Eteocles now feels the streaming wound,
And full of horrour, rolls his eyes around
Essays to shun the spectre's hated sight,
And dares his absent brother to the fight.
Thus when a sleeping tiger from afar
Hears the shrill preludes of approaching war,
He starts, calls forth his spots, expands his jaws,
Wakes to the promis'd fight, and points his claws;
Then bounding thro' the thickets of the wood,
Bears to his bloody whelps the reeking food.
Aurora now from Tithon's saffron bed
With dawning streaks of light the skies o'erspread;
She shook the sparkling dew-drops from her hair,
And blush'd to find the peeping Sun so near:
While breaking through the clouds, the morning
star,
Advancing, tow'rds her guides his rosy car,
Nor e'er withdraws, till Sol's superior ray
Flames in the front of Heav'n, and gives the day.
Now springing from his bed, Adrastus rose,
Nor long behind the sweets of wish'd repose
Detain'd his guests: for sleep had now bedew'd
Their weary limbs, and all their strength renew'd.
But anxious cares Adrastus had opprest;
Sleep fled his eyes, and peace forsook his breast.
Musing he calls to mind the fates' decree,
And his new guests' connected destiny.
In a sequester'd room conven'd they sate,
For bus'ness calculated and debate.
Each would begin, but fears and doubts restrain:
At length the monarch rose, and eas'd their pain.
"Illustrious youths, of Heav'n the constant care,
Whom storms of thunder and inclement air
Have drove beneath my roof, by fate's decree
To fix the base of mutual amity;
Why should I dwell on what's already known
By vulgar fame through every Grecian town?
How many youths have strove (though strove in
vain)
By high desert my daughters' love to gain.
But (if a parent little credit claim)
Yourselves, the objects of their decent shame,
Saw o'er their cheeks the glowing blush arise,
When first your manly features met their eyes.
Did wealth or sway alone employ their care,
They need not of acquiring them despair:

141. Thus when a sleeping tiger] The grandeur and propriety of this simile are too obvious to be insisted upon; and were I to enlarge on it, and point out the sublimity of the expressions, the harmony of numbers, the beautiful connection of circumstances, and exact propriety of the whole, I should anticipate the reader's judgment. The greatest proof of what I advance is Mr. Cowley's imitation. He saw its beauties, and endeavoured to copy them. How well he has executed it, is left to the judicious reader to determine.

So when a Scythian tiger gazing round,
A herd of kine in some fair plain has found,
Lowing secure; he swells with angry pride,
And calls forth all his spots on ev'ry side.
Then stops, and hurls his haughty eyes on all
In choice of some strong neck, on which to fall;
Almost he scorns so weak, so cheap a prey,
And grieves to see them trembling haste away.
David.

Since many a potent king of high renown
Has wish'd them partners of th' imperial throne.
In this they might with Dejanira vie,
Or fam'd Oenomaus' boasted progeny.
But fate forbids they should the bed adorn
Of one in Elis, or in Sparta born,
To you, brave youths, decrees the beauteous pair,
And of their dotal wealth an equal share.
The god's description tallies with your own,
And Phœbus' choice agrees in you alone.
Their virgin-smiles, I ween, shall well repay
The stormy night, and labours of the fray."
The princes on each other cast an eye,
Expecting each his comrade would reply,
Till bolder Tydeus to the monarch bow'd,
And thus discharg'd the debt his duty ow'd.
"Much you enjoy of fortune and of fame,
Much more your gallant deeds and merit claim.
Of equalling your worth the best despair,
Which adds a jewel to the crown you wear.
Fierce Argos, taught by clemency t' obey,
Resigns to you the reins, and owns your sway:
And would propitious Jove consign you more,
And stretch your pow'r to Doria's double shore,
Phœbus no more should fly Mycenæ's plain,
Nor of their king Elean vales complain.
Nor do the furies only vex our state,
As thou, young warrior, better canst relate;
But I, a voluntary exile, roam,
Nor forc'd by rage fraternal fly from home."
He spoke, and thus subjoin'd the Theban chief:
"Though damp'd with sorrows, and o'ercome with
grief,
My soul, averse to Venus' mystic rites,
On other objects wastes the sleepless nights;
Yet this alliance should I now refuse,
Fancy would flag, nor furnish an excuse.
Such balmy hope allays my troubled breast,
And lulls the passions of my soul to rest,
As swells the little bark on ocean tost,
When near at hand she spies some friendly coast.
From hence alike the turns of chance we'll share,
And make each other's bliss our only care.
No fate my vow'd affection shall divide,
By marriage as by gratitude ally'd."
The princes rose, while old Adrastus strove
By strength of language to declare his love,
And vows, should fate his just emprizes crown,
His arms should soon replace them on the throne.
Meanwhile the natives, ere a vague report
Had scarce been wafted from the regal court,
With loud acclaim receive the king's decree,
And give full reins to mirth and revelry.

185. But fate forbids they should] Adrastus seems to have lain under the same restraints as Latinus.

Me natam nulli veterum sociare procorum
Fascerat, idque omnes divique hominesque canebant.

And again,

Est mihi nata, viro gentis quam jungere nostræ,
Non patrio ex adyto sortes, non plurima cœlo
Monstra sinunt.

197. Much you enjoy] I question whether, upon due consideration, there will not be found too much of the orator in Tydeus, who, according to our author's own words, was rudis fandi.

205. Phœbus no more should fly] As at the feast of Thyestes. See Ovid's Metamorphoses.

From hence Fame flies with unresisted force,
Nor hills or vales retard her airy course:
And now, a tedious length of country past,
On Cadmus' walls she fix'd herself at last.
She scares the wretched king, and brings to light
The mystic visions of the former night;
O'erwhelms his hopes, augments his growing fears,
And whispers wars and slaughter in his ears.
Soon as the wish'd-for dawn appears, to court
The sons of Argos in huge swarms resort, [stand,
Where form'd in brass their great forefathers
And art (so skilful was th' engraver's hand)
With nature vies.—Here first you might discern
Old Inachus, reclining on his urn.
Near him Iasius bends with feeble age,
And old Acrisius vents on Jove his rage.
Phoroneus, peaceful chief, was next survey'd,
And stern Chorœbus, bearing on his blade
A bloody head.—In arms great Abas shines,
And Danaus his future guilt designs.
The leaders first the slow procession wait,
While the loud rabble thunder at the gate;
The nobles next advance, a num'rous line,
And in the front, by rank distinguish'd, shine.
The inner court with fire odorous glows,
While on all sides the female tumult grows.
A throng of matrons round each bride appear,
Inspire with hope, and soothe each virgin-fear.
And now with glowing cheeks and downcast eyes
The princesses attend the sacrifice,
Known by their dignity of dress and face:
The flushing purple heightens ev'ry grace.
With pain their anxious feelings they suppress'd,
Some small regret still linger'd in their breast,
And strugglings to retain their virgin-state:
While the chaste doubts of innocence create
New blushes, that improve their nat'ral hue,
And artless tears their lovely cheeks bedew.
Decent confusion!—At the moving sight
Their tender parents melt in soft delight.
Thus should Diana, and th' Athenian maid
Descend from Heav'n in all their pomp array'd;
Each in her hands her wonted weapons bears,
And the same sternness in their looks appears.
Should Cynthia for a casque her quiver change,
And Pallas through the lawns and forests range;
The change in either would so well agree,
That safely none the pref'rence could decree:
The quiver would Minerva's shoulders grace;
And the plum'd helmet suit fair Delia's face.
Meanwhile the joyful Argives seem to vie
In public proofs of zeal and loyalty.
These waft to Jove in od'rous flames a pray'r,
And call for blessings on the royal pair;
With slaughter'd victims' entrails those appease
The gods; nor will Sabæan smoke displease,
If a pure heart direct the pious vows,
And the strong gate is deckt with flow'ring boughs.
But lo! sad omens from the gods descend,
And Jove's and Heav'n's impending rage portend;
A sadd'ning horrour ev'ry face o'erspreads,
And on their joys a solemn dulness sheds.

288. Nor will Sabæan] Our author is of Persius's opinion, whose noble lines on this subject breathe more the spirit of Christianity than heathenism.

Compositum jus, fasque animi, sanctosque recessus
Mentis, et incoctum generoso pectus honesto
Hoc cedo, ut admoveam templis, et farre litabo.
Sat. 2.

'Twas when great Hymen's sacred rites to crown,
They bent their course to fam'd Larissa's town,
Than which Munichia's hill, nor Athens' grove
Can boast superior proofs of Pallas' love.
Here (so long custom had ordain'd) are led
The nymphs, when ripen'd for the marriage-bed,
And for the frailty of the sex atone
With maiden ringlets on the altars thrown.
Ere they had scal'd the turret's gradual height,
The beam dismiss'd the buckler's sacred weight.
With horrid clangour shook the plantive ground,
The tapers crush'd, and darkness shed around.
Then, ere they durst proceed, as from the shrine
A trumpet loud proclaim'd the wrath divine.
First on the king they wildly turn their eyes;
Then, question'd, each the well-heard sound
denies.
Yet all, all feel the dreadful sign of woe,
And their first fears by various converse grow.
Nor wond'rous was it, for Argia bore
The bracelet, which Harmonia whilom wore.
O goddess! say from what mysterious source
The fatal gift deriv'd such noxious force?
Fame tells, that Vulcan wrought it, when he strove
To check the Thracian god's adult'rous love,
(For useless lay the now-neglected chain;
Threats fail'd, and punishments were schem'd in
vain:)
With many a gem 'twas fraught and preciousstone,
To deck the partner of the Theban throne.
Long did the Cyclops o'er their anvils sweat,
And their swoln sinews echoing blows repeat,
Ere th' artist had attain'd his vast design,
And stamp'd perfection on the work divine.
Of polish'd em'ralds was the curious ground,
And fatal forms of adamant surround:
Sparks of etherial temper flame above,
Fil'd remnants of the swift-wing'd bolts of Jove.
A dragon's scaly pride is here impress'd,
And there Medusa rears her snaky crest.
From golden boughs Hesperian apples sprung,
And gay to view the Colchian tree was hung.
Torn from the furies' hair a serpent shines:
To this, foul lust and various plagues he joins,
Then dips the whole in foam of lunar rays,
And hides the venom in a sprightly blaze.

314. The bracelet] Harmonia was the daughter of Mars and Venus. She married Cadmus, and was metamorphosed together with him into a serpent.

319. For useless lay the] The poet alludes to the famous chain, which Vulcan made to entrap his adulterous consort in: for a farther account of which see Homer's Odyssey; and Ovid's Metamorphoses, lib. 4. fab. 5.

This digression seems very material and necessary, since it is founded on the story, where the infectious bracelet is represented as of great importance, and it is also connected with the foregoing and following parts of it as in the case of Jocasta, mentioned by Statius, and of Eriphyle and Amphiaraus, whose fate in the following war was owing to it.

327. Of polish'd em'ralds] The antients were superstitiously exact in describing any particular suit of armour, ornaments, &c. as the shields of Achilles and Æneas, the ægis of Pallas; and here the composition of the materials and sculpture are highly consistent with the fatal virtue of this ornament.

Where'er this came, th' affrighted Graces fled;
Love pin'd, and beauty droop'd her sick'ning head:
Sorrow still haunts the mansion where it lies,
And hate-engender'd rage and fears arise.
Harmonia first its direful influence prov'd,
As o'er the furrow'd plains on spires she rov'd,
And fill'd with hissings dire th' Illyrian coast,
Till all the woman in the snake was lost;
Then Semele, for whose superior charms
The thund'rer left his jealous consort's arms.
Jocasta too, by fate's resistless will
(As fame reports) possess'd this source of ill,
And deck'd with it, in cultur'd beauty shone,
Unconscious of her crime, her guilt unknown.
Distinguish'd thus, Argia pass'd along,
And mov'd supreme amid the female throng.
Fair Eriphyle the rich gift beheld,
And her sick breast with secret envy swell'd.
Not the late omens and the well-known tale
To cure her vain ambition aught avail.
Oh! had the wretch by self-experience known
The future woes, and sorrows not her own!
But fate decrees, her wretched spouse must bleed,
And the son's phrenzy clear the mother's deed.
But when the thirteenth rising Sun had view'd
Their banquets ended, and their toils renew'd,
Revolving thoughts the banish'd prince remind
Of his lost Thebes, and empire left behind.
That day returns, when Fortune's partial hand
To his proud brother gave the whole command,
How the revolting gods against him join'd,
When to a private state reduc'd, he pin'd,
And saw his friends misdeem'd in crowds resort,
To bask beneath the sunshine of the court.
One faithful sister would have shar'd his fate,
But mourns, abandon'd at the palace-gate.
Her plaintive cries, unmov'd, the warrior hears,
For rage refus'd a passage to his tears.
Meanwhile, amid the silence of the night,
Reflecting mem'ry brings back to his sight
Those friendly few, that, ere from Thebes he stray'd,
Condol'd, and those who signs of joy display'd.
Anger and frantic grief by turns controul
His lab'ring breast, and shake his inmost soul.
While lust of pow'r, untaught to brook delay,
Flames in his breast, and chides the ling'ring day.
At length the chief prepares to steer his course
To tow'ring Thebes, and Dirce's sacred source.

355. Fair Eriphyle] Statius seems in the character of Eriphyle to have given a lesson of advice to the fair sex on their passion for dress and finery. His great master Virgil has afforded him a precedent in the episode of Camilla, whom he introduces pursuing Chloreus for the sake of his rich armour and horse-trappings.

——Unum ex omni certamine pugnæ
Cæca sequebatur, totumque incauta per agmen
Fæmineo prædæ et spoliorum ardebat amore.

Æneid, Lib. 11. 780.

361. Her wretched spouse must bleed] Her husband was Amphiaraus, a celebrated augur, whom she betrayed to Polynices for the sake of this bracelet, when he was endeavouring to avoid accompanying him in the wars, in which he knew he should certainly perish. As for her son, the distresses of his family wrought so great an impression upon his spirits, that he was at length seized with an incurable phrenzy.

Thus fares a lordly bull, when forc'd to yield
His lovely mistress, and forsake the field:
But when his wonted vigour he regains,
And a fresh tide of blood recruits his veins,
He roars, impatient for the promis'd war,
Snuffs the fresh gale, and spurns the sand afar;
Amaz'd, the swains his strength restor'd survey,
And the late victor trembles for his sway.
While thus for war the youth in secret pines,
Argia penetrates his close designs.
One morn, ere yet Aurora promis'd day,
(As in the folds of love entwin'd they lay)
"Why seeks my lord," she fondly said, "to fly?
For nought escapes an ardent lover's eye.
Say, why that bosom heaves with broken sighs,
And sleep for ever shuns those watchful eyes:
What hidden cause extorts the silent tear?
Think not a widow'd bed alone I fear,
Or the mere lust of nuptial joys should stay
The destin'd course, or prompt an hour's delay:
Though scarce twelve suns have deck'd the courts of Jove,
Since Hymen smil'd upon our mutual love.
Thy bliss alone and welfare I regard,
And only this thy parting could retard.
But oh! what rashness, helpless and alone
T' attempt th' enjoyment of the Theban crown!
Will he, whose pride and tyranny you found
Ere the first Sun had run his annual round,
Tamely resign the scepter and obey,
Till the clos'd year restore th' alternate sway?
The gods some sudden ruin sure prepare,
My boding soul presaging fibres scare.
Amid the dusky silence of the night
Imperial Juno stood confess'd to sight.
Say, what at Thebes can your attention claim,
But the fair object of a former flame?"
The smiling hero clasp'd her to his breast,
And with the stamp of love her cheeks impress'd;
Prevents with blandishments the rising tears,
And kindly thus dispels her jealous fears.
"Think not the wheel of chance will e'er remain
In this rough track. The clouds may break again,
And a far brighter sun than yet hath shone,
Survey thee partner of a double throne.
Resign thy cares to Heav'n, dismiss thy fears;
At least they suit not with thy tender years.
From Jove's strict justice and all-seeing eyes
The perjur'd villain ne'er unnotic'd flies."
From hence t' Adrastus, on whose hoary head
A length of years had their experience shed,
Speeds the young Theban; nor was Tydeus slow
T' assist, but shar'd an equal weight of woe:
For the same flame, which gen'rous souls disjoins,
With equal lustre, when united, shines.
Long they debate: at length by joint consent
Decree to sound the brother-king's intent

387. Thus fares a lordly bull] This simile is an abridgment of that beautiful description in the third book of Virgil's Georgics.

437. Nor was Tydeus slow] Amidst the tincture of barbarism and ferocity of Tydeus there is something very amiable in his character: not that I pretend to exculpate him for carrying his revenge to that savage, unprecedented height, though it was the result of friendship, and founded on an honourable basis. He quarrels and fights with Polynices; but upon the knowledge of his misfortunes strikes an alliance with him, and even sacrifices his life in his service.

By embassy, ere yet from hostile force
They seek redress, the last and worst resource.
Fraught with th' advent'rous task bold Tydeus glows,
Though long oppos'd by his dissuading spouse:
At length the compact, which in ev'ry state
Secures th' ambassador a safe retreat,
His sire's commands, and sister's tears, prevail,
O'ercome her pray'rs, and sink the doubtful scale.
Now on the woody coast the warrior strays,
And soon the fam'd Lernæan lake surveys,
Where the fell hydra was by flames subdu'd,
(For blows in vain the toiling chief renew'd)
And Nemea, where e'en now the timid swains
Rarely, as erst, chant forth their artless strains.
From thence in view of Corinth's tow'rs he came,
And left the port, which bears Palæmon's name;
Where in the midst the parting isthmus lies,
And swelling seas on either side arise.
Then Nisus' flow'ring sides the hero gains,
And on the left views Ceres' favour'd plains.
At last the glitt'ring prospect greets his eyes
Of Theban tow'rs, that shade the middle skies.
Sublime in regal pomp th' usurper sate:
A grove of spears defends th' impervious gate.
Here by his subjects fear'd, not lov'd, he reigns,
And ill-got pow'r by tyranny maintains.
He blames his brother's flight and long delay,
And wonders, he so late demands the sway:
Nor wants the tyrant e'er a specious plea
To veil his guilt, and mask his villainy.
Amid the thronging guards young Tydeus stands,
(A peaceful olive decks his waving hands)
And thus began (his name and message known)
Rough as he was in speech, and ever prone
To wrath, nor cautious to offend the ear,
Diminish'd aught the truth, howe'er severe.
" Say, tyrant, (had it been your firm design
At the due time your empire to resign)
Why heralds did not from your court appear
T' inform your brother of his ruling year?
'Twas then your duty calmly to sit down,
Till the next year replac'd you on the throne.
But he, convinc'd how well you love to reign,
Deigns thus to ask, what basely you detain.
Phœbus hath now his annual progress made,
And cloth'd the mountains with returning shade,
Since Polynices abject and alone
Hath stray'd in exile drear through realms unknown.
'Tis yours in turn th' alternate lot to share,
And bear the wintry wind and open air.
Resign it then, while guiltless shines the crown,
Nor lay too late the bright temptation down.
Your pow'r in Thebes you've long enough display'd,
In robes of Tyrian die, and gold array'd.
Now teach your subjects; those who merit sway,
Should first convince the world, they can obey."
He paus'd; and now the tyrant's looks reveal'd
The boiling wrath he had in vain conceal'd.
Thus with erected pride, the crested snake
By stones provok'd, shoots thro' the thorny brake;
His scales reflect the Sun's attracted ray:
With rolling spires he marks the furrow'd way,
And through his agitated body draws
The liquid venom to his thirsty jaws.
" Had not my brother's love of strife been known"
(He cries) " it would appear from thee alone;
In whom is stamp'd the image of his mind,
Alike of manners rude, and savage kind.
Though now thou talk'st, as if th' assailing foe
Had min'd our walls, and laid our bulwarks low;
Yet shouldst thou thus among a Scythian throng
Indulge thy lust of prate, and lawless tongue,
Thy trampled limbs and corse would scarce atone
For the bare crimes thy sland'rous mouth has done.
Avaunt; no more provoke my rage, and know,
Thy sacred office scarce can stay the blow:
But first this answer to th' Argolic lord;
That since his rashness has unsheath'd the sword,
And thus attack'd me with unkingly pride,
Bellona shall alone our rights decide,
Nor my contentious brother rule the land
Which chance and birthright gave me to command.
Meanwhile, unenvied, you may wear the crown
Which lawful Hymen has decreed your own;
The sons of Argos may thy laws obey,
And noted Lerna own thy happy sway.
Contented, we'll enjoy our Dirce's plain,
And fill the throne where Cadmus held his reign:
Nor blush the wretched Oedipus to trace
From Labdacus the founder of our race;
Though you can boast an origin divine,
And draw from Jove himself the glorious line.
Say, can the fair Argia, wont to live
In all the pomp a regal birth can give,
Forget the grandeur of her former state,
Nor cast a wish beyond our palace-gate;
Whose ornaments, the produce of our land,
We owe to our laborious sister's hand?
She'll loath perchance our mother's coarse attire,
And sordid rags, which woes like hers require.
Yet more—my father from his gloomy cell
Will grate her tender years with many a yell.
The vulgar's stubborn spirit now is broke,
Their neck inur'd to bear the royal yoke;
To this we'll add, the Thebans will not bear
The doubtful rule of each alternate heir.

462. Ceres' favour'd plains] These are the plains known to the ancients by the name of Eleusinian, from Eleusis, a neighbouring city. They were remarkably fertile, in return for which blessing the inhabitants built a temple to Ceres, their supposed benefactress.

501. Thus with erected pride] The courage and intrepidity of Tydeus are admirably well illustrated in this simile, which is taken from Homer:

Ὡς δὲ δράκων ἐπὶ χειῇ ὀρέστερος ἄνδρα μένῃσι
Βεβρωκὼς κακὰ φάρμακ', ἔδυ δέ τε μιν χόλος αἰνὸς,
Σμερδαλέον δὲ δέδορκεν ἑλισσόμενος περὶ χειῇ.
Iliad, Lib. 22. 92.

Virgil has also imitated it in his Æneid.

Qualis ubi in lucem coluber mala gramina pastus,
Frigida sub terra tumidum quem bruma tegebat,
Nunc positis novus exuviis, nitidusque juventâ,
Lubrica convolvit sublato pectore terga
Arduus ad solem, et linguis micat ore trisulcis.

Agamemnon mentions this behaviour of Tydeus as worthy to be imitated by his son Diomede. See Iliad, b. 4. 370.

525. Meanwhile unenvied] There is a vast deal of hidden sarcasm and gall in this reply. The arguments are strong and well placed, the language elegant and easy, and the whole full of spirit and fire.

531. Nor blush the wretched Oedipus] This is the very height of dissimulation: we are told by the poet, that he had despised, insulted, and drove his father from his palace; and that all the succeeding calamities were derived from his cruel usage of him.

Can I then basely sacrifice the state
To my returning brother's treasur'd hate?
Or should a resignation be my choice,
Say, can I influence the senate's voice?
Will they, to whom my gentle sway is known,
Permit me thus to give away the crown?"
More had he said, but impotent to bear,
Thus Tydeus stopt him in his full career.
" Though art and nature should conspire to form
Huge battlements against Bellona's storm,
And rocks, as erst at your Amphion's call,
Spring from their base, and form a triple wall:
Yet should those bulwarks, and those walls, beat
Compel thee to resign the guilty crown; [down,
Or should thy pride and rashness still remain
Amidst thy ruin'd town, and heaps of slain,
Torn from the head of its expiring lord
The shining spoil should deck my conqu'ring
Howe'er enrag'd, I yet must pity those, [sword.
Whom thy ambition makes my guiltless foes,
Torn from their country, wives and sons away
To sure destruction in th' unequal fray.
What breathless heaps shall raise Cithæron's height!
How shall Ismenos groan beneath the weight!
Though void of faith, and of fraternal love,
Yet dare you thus confront the gods above?
Will they in calm neutrality look down
On broken oaths, and honour's fence o'erthrown?
What wonder then? Can we expect to trace
Fair virtue's footsteps in so foul a race?
Can length of years absolve th' incestuous brood,
Or free the long confusions of their blood?
But hold—the fates revoke their first decree,
And Oedipus revives alone in thee.

557. Though art and nature] Horace has a passage equally grand and elevated.

Ter si resurgat murus aheneus
Auctore Phœbo; ter pereat meis
Excisus Argivis, ter uxor
Capta virum puerosque ploret. Lib. 3. Ode 5.

571. What breathless heaps]

Eheu quantus equis, quantus adest viris
Sudor, quanta moves funera Dardanæ
Genti! jam galeam Pallas et ægida,
Currusque et rabiem parat. B. 1. Ode 15.

581. The fates revoke their first decree] This is a stroke of the strongest satire that could possibly have been given. The thought is not one of that tinsel and flashy kind, which occurs so often in the French and Italian poets; but manly, spirited, and truly laconic.

587. Thus rag'd the boar] The passage subjoined from Ovid will exhibit to the reader's view, whence our author culled the chief circumstances which adorn this beautiful simile.

——Oeneos ultorem spreta per agros
Misit aprum.————

Riget horrida cervix:
Et setæ densis similes hastilibus horrent:
Stantque velut vallum, velut alta hastilia setæ.
Dentes æquantur dentibus Indis.
Fulmen ab ore venit.————

Licet eminus esse
Fortibus.———
Dixit, et aerata torsit grave cuspide cornum.

This prize of villainy you bear away;
Our year we claim.—But why do I delay?"
The warrior spoke, and with resistless force
Urg'd thro' the band of guards his furious course.
Thus rag'd the boar, by vengeful Cynthia sent,
To mark with ruin Caledon's extent;
His bristled back appear'd a thick-set grove,
And Jove's own thunder from his mouth he drove.
In vain the shouting sons of Greece surround,
And from hurl'd stones inflict a distant wound.
In triumph he surveys the prostrate foe,
Till at Oenides levelling a blow,
The sideling chief prevents the glancing wound,
And with his javelin nails him to the ground.
Thus anger'd, Tydeus left the guilty town,
And seem'd to make his brother's cause his own.
On earth the fruitless branch in haste he threw,
And o'er the plains with winged ardour flew;
The matrons eye from their balconies' height
The chief, and vent in curses their despight,
But not on him alone.—The tyrant bears
His share of hate convey'd in secret pray'rs.
Nor does the monarch's turn for treach'ry fail,
By nature taught too often to prevail:
With bribes and threats he gains a chosen throng
T' assault young Tydeus as he pass'd along:
Whose daring spirit and intrepid mien
Made them fit actors of so vile a scene.
Oh! fatal madness of th' ambitious soul!
What lengths can bind it, or what heights controul?
Which dares attack, what each preceding age
Had justly deem'd exempt from hostile rage.
No arts he'd leave untry'd, no means forego,
Would fortune yield him up his brother-foe.
Meanwhile th' unfolding gates disclose a train
Of chiefs ne'er destin'd to return again:
In one firm orb was rang'd the glitt'ring band,
Oppos'd, ye gods! to Tydeus' single hand,
As if prepar'd to storm some hostile town,
Or beat the walls with batt'ring engines down.
For fear had thus the scatter'd troop combin'd,
The sure attendant of a guilty mind.
Through thorny woods, a near and secret way,
They march'd, unnotic'd, wedg'd in firm array.
Far from the town two shaded hills arise,
And lose their adverse summits in the skies:

At manus Oenidæ variat: missisque duabus,
Hasta prior terrâ, medio stetit altera tergo,
Nec mora: dum sævit, dum corpora versat in orbem,
Stridentemque novo spumam sanguine fundit,
Vulneris auctor adest, hostemque irritat ad iram,
Splendidaque adversos venabula condit in armos.
Metamorph. book 8. fable 4.

603. The tyrant bears] Not all the grandeur and privileges of a crowned head, can secure it from the ill wishes of an injured people. The fear of punishment may restrain the tongue, but cannot influence the sentiments of the heart.

625. Through thorny woods, &c.] This place of ambush is not unlike that described by Virgil in the eleventh book of his Æneid.

Est curvo anfractu vallis, accommoda fraudi
Armorumque dolis: quam densis frondibus atrum
Urget utrumque latus: tenuis quo semita ducit,
Angustæque ferunt fauces, aditusque maligni.
V. 522.

One side is bounded by the grove's embrace;
A mountain's brow o'erhangs the middle space.
The nature of the place, and gloomy site
Seem'd form'd for ambuscade, and deeds of night.
A path obscure here winds the rocks between,
Beneath are spacious fields, a flow'ring scene.
Here, posted on a cliff's declining brow,
From whence she might survey the vale below,
The sphynx once dwelt.—Her cheeks were pale to view,
And her fell eyes suffus'd with gory dew.
Oft with expanded wings the monster prest
The mould'ring bones of mortals to her breast,
And hurl'd her eyes along the winding way,
Lest, unobserving, she should lose her prey.
But if his fate, or the avenging gods
Had drawn some wretch to her obscene abodes,
She clapp'd her wings distain'd with human gore,
And fill'd with yellings the retentive shore.
Then with protended nails his face she struck,
And oft her breaking teeth their hold forsook.
Thus long she reign'd: at last with headlong flight
Sprung from the rocks, and sought the realms of night,
For Oedipus, by Phœbus' aid, disclos'd
The dark enigma which she'd long propos'd.
Untouch'd the grass, neglected lies the wood,
And hungry beasts at distance seek their food.
The dryads never haunt these loathsome bow'rs,
Nor swains with incense bribe the rural pow'rs.
To other groves ill-omen'd birds repair,
And from afar abhor the tainted air.
Meanwhile the Thebans, urg'd by cruel fate,
Th' Ætolian chief in silent pomp await;
Reclining on their spears, the wood surround,
And rest their bucklers on the dewy ground.
The Sun recall'd his unavailing light,
And on the shaded ocean rush'd the night;
When Tydeus from an eminence, survey'd
Their shields and helmets glitt'ring thro' the shade,
Where thro' the scanty branches Phœbe gleams
On their bright armour with refracted beams.
Amazement seiz'd him, yet he onward hied,
And grasp'd the faithful sabre at his side:
A pointed javelin glitter'd in his hand,
While he accosts them with this stern demand.

635. Here, posted] Oedipus in Seneca speaks thus of the sphynx.

Nec sphinga cæcis verba nectentem modis
Fugi. Cruentos vatis infandæ tuli
Rictus, et albens ossibus sparsis solum.
Cumque ex superbâ rupe, jam prædæ imminens,
Aptaret alas, verbera et caudam movens,
Sævi leonis more, concuteret minas;
Carmen poposci. Sonuit horrendum; insuper
Crepuêre malæ: saxaque impatiens moræ
Revulsit unguis, viscera expectans mea.
Nodosa sortis verba, et implexos dolos,
Ac triste carmen alitis solvi feræ.

Oedipus, Act I. v. 92.

649. At last with headlong flight] Milton alludes to these verses of our author.

——The Theban monster that propos'd
Her riddle, and him that solv'd it not, devour'd;
That once found out and solv'd, for grief and spight,
Cast herself headlong from th' Ismenian steep.

665. When Tydeus from an eminence] The two adventurers in the ninth Æneid are discovered by the same accident.

Cum procul hos lævo flectentes limite cernunt;
Et galea Euryalum sublustri noctis in umbra
Prodidit immemorem, radiisque adversa refulsit.

V. 372.

673. Warriors, whence come ye?] As we are now arrived at this great action of Tydeus, it may be worth while to transcribe a passage from Crucius's Lives of the Roman Poets, relative to it.

"Nothing can equal the intrepidity of Tydeus, when he was attacked, by surprise, by fifty men that Eteocles (whom he had provoked by his haughty behaviour, during his embassy to him from Polynices) secretly dispatched after him from Thebes, to put him to death. When he comes to discover their numbers, he turns pale with anger at so base an enterprise, and, by the slaughter he makes amongst them, soon convinces them of their errour, who easily expected to overpower one man with their numbers. To secure himself from behind, he climbs up a high mountain, and from thence hurls a prodigious fragment of a rock at his pursuers, which the strongest yoke of oxen could hardly draw. This likewise is imitated from Ajax in Homer, and the poet has endeavoured to express this action in his numbers. The spondees of the first line express his contention in tearing it away from the rock: the beginning of the third breaks it off with a crack: the rest of the third and fourth heave it up, and poise it in the air.

Saxum ingens, quod vix plenâ cervice juvenci
Vertere humo, murisque valent inferre gementes,
Rupibus avellit, dein toto sanguine nixus
Sustinet, immanem quærens librare ruinam.

B. 2. Theb.

To soften the improbability of so prodigious a victory as this, which Tydeus here gained over the fifty Thebans, who were all slain but one man, whom he forced to live, and bear the fatal message of this misfortune to Thebes, the poet discovers Minerva, who is said to have secretly protected and strengthened him during the engagement, and reproves him afterwards for vainly ascribing the success to his own valour." Life of Statius, vol. 1.

"Warriors, whence come ye, and why thus profane
With war's alarms, the night's alternate reign?"
Silent they stood; and no return of sound
Convinc'd the chief he treads on hostile ground.
A javelin soon supplies the want of tongue,
By Chthonius hurl'd, the leader of the throng.
The weapon whizzes in its airy course,
Nor miss'd the mark, tho' destitute of force:
It pierc'd the Ætolian boar's erected hide,
(The chief's defence, and erst the monster's pride)
And o'er his shoulder flew, unstain'd with blood,
Where the false point deserts the feeble wood.
Then paleness cloath'd his face, but such as shows
Excess of wrath.—His stiff'ning hair arose.
And now he hurls his angry looks around,
And views, amaz'd, the num'rous foe surround.
"Whence does," he said, "this needless terrour grow,
Of meeting on the plain a single foe?
Advance, like sons of Thebes, and bravely wield
Your glittering weapons on this open field."

Scarce had he spoke, when rushing from their holds,
A num'rous band the intrepid chief infolds:
From hill and dale they pour; their bucklers yield
A silver sound, and brighten all the field.
So when the mingled cry of men and hounds
Invades the forest, or the wood surrounds,
From covert bound the stags, a fearful train,
And scour in num'rous herds the verdant plain.
The hero then ascends a mountain's height,
The best retreat from such unequal fight.
From hence, when posted on the impending brow,
He might with ease annoy the foes below..
Enrag'd, he tore the fragment of a rock,
(Earth deeply groan'd beneath the mighty shock)
Then swung it round, and poising it on high,
Sought where to let the pond'rous ruin fly.
Two steers beneath th' enormous weight would groan,
But Tydeus hurl'd it from the rock alone.
Thus, with a goblet lifted in his hand,
Brave Pholeus routed the Thessalian band.
Thus sapp'd by time, from some o'erhanging steep,
A rolling fragment thunders on the deep.
The Thebans felt it, ere they saw it fly,
And crush'd in one promiscuous ruin lie.
Four chiefs, intomb'd beneath th' oppressive weight,
Clos'd their dim eyes in one united fate;
The rest to their strong holds again repair,
Unmindful of their charge, and promis'd care.
His inward worth and virtue fail'd to save
Brave Dorylas from the relentless grave.
In vain proud Theron boasts his noble race,
And draws his lineage from the god of Thrace.
Next Halys fell, a chief whose strength could tame
The bounding steed, in arms a mighty name:
But here, alas! on foot he sought the war,
Nor join'd swift horses to the rapid car.
Last, Phædimus in death's eternal shade
Sunk, unexperiencing great Bacchus' aid.
When fiercer now, he saw them quit the fray;
He rush'd, a lion, on his helpless prey;
With swift-whirl'd javelins fed their growing fear,
Annoy'd the front, and gall'd them in the rear.
With headlong rage he issues on the plain,
(Nor cares of life or safety can detain,)
Then seiz'd a glitt'ring target, which before,
While fate permitted, valiant Theron bore:
The spacious orb he moves on ev'ry part,
And stands impervious to each hostile dart.
The flaming sabre waves their heads above,
(The shining earnest of paternal love)
Now these, now those, with fatal blows he ply'd,
And the red slaughter swells on ev'ry side.
But while the Theban troops prolong the fray,
Involv'd in night, disorder and dismay,
With heedless rage they deal their blows around,
And on their comrades oft inflict a wound:
O'er breathless heaps alternately they reel;
Darts hiss on darts, and steel descends on steel.
He presses on, o'ercoming those who try
The conflict, and o'ertaking those who fly.
Briareus thus (if Phlegra credit claim)
Oppos'd the regents of the starry frame.
The thund'rer lanch'd his flaming bolt in vain,
Nor Phœbus' shafts, nor Pallas' snakes restrain.
The spear of haughty Mars unheeded flies,
And Etna's forge in vain new bolts supplies.
Unmov'd he stalks along the fields of fight,
And with regret beholds th' exhausted fight.
Thus Tydeus in the glorious conflict glows,
And pours, like lightning, on his trembling foes;
Then, as if bent on flight, around them wheel'd,
And intercepts their anger with his shield.
Oft from its orb he pluck'd a bristling wood,
The darts, returning, drink their masters' blood.
His wounded breast stopp'd many a weapon's course;
But Heav'n disarm'd them of their fatal force.
Deiolochus beneath a whirling blow,
Not unattended, sought the shades below:
For Phlegeus, bounding with elated heart,
And axe upheav'd, rush'd on the victor's dart.
Then Lycophon, and mighty Gyan bled,
By Tydeus number'd with the vulgar dead.

700. And scour in num'rous herds] This account of the deer flying together in herds is confirmed by Virgil.

——Aliâ de parte patentes
Transmittunt cursu campos, atque agmina cervi
Pulverulenta fugâ glomerant montesque relinquunt.

705. He tore the fragment] It may not perhaps be disagreeable to the reader, to see how the heroes in Homer and Virgil handle this kind of weapon.

——Ο δέ χερμάδιον λάβε χειρὶ
Τυδείδης, μέγα ἔργον, ὃ κ' δύω γ' ἄνδρε φεροιεν
Οιοι νυν βροτοί εἴσιν, ὁ δέ μιν ῥέα πάλλε καὶ οἶος.
Lib. 5.

Turnus in the twelfth book of the Æneid, verse 896.

Saxum circumspicit ingens,
Vix illud lecti bis sex cervice subirent,
Qualia nunc hominum producit corpora terra.
Ille manu raptum trepidâ torquebat in hostem,
Altior insurgens, et cursu concitus heros.

721. His inward worth and virtue fail'd]

Α῎ξυλον δ' ἄρ ἔπεφνε βυην ἀγαθὸς Διομήδης
Τευθρανίδην, ὃς ἔναιεν ἐϋκτιμένη ἐν 'Αρίσβη,
'Αφνέιος βιὸτοιο, φίλος δ' ἦν ἀνθρώποισι.
Πάντας γὰρ φιλεεσκεν ὁδῷ ἔπι οἰκία ναίων.
'Αλλὰ οἱ ὔτις τῶν γε τότ' ἤρκεσε λυγρὸν ὄλεθρον,
Πρόσθεν ὑπαντιάσας. Iliad, b. 6. v. 12.

753. Briareus thus] Briareus was one of the bold invaders of Heaven. He is reported to have had an hundred arms and a hundred breasts. In the midst of his attempt he was struck with a thunderbolt, and buried under mount Ætna. However, at his first assault, he spread such a terrour amongst the gods, that they metamorphosed themselves into beasts and birds, and betook themselves to different countries till the storm was over.

This simile, upon the whole, is really grand and noble; and was intended to give the reader the most advantageous ideas of our hero's valour and intrepidity; and we must own, the poet has gained a double end: and does not leave us in greater admiration of Tydeus's courage, than of his own art and genius. The two last lines are elevated to the highest degree, and cannot fail of pleasing every true lover of the sublime.

In vain the braver few resist, in vain
Recall their comrades scouring o'er the plain.
The crimson horrours of the fatal night
Allay their thirst of blood, and love of fight.
When Chromis, to the Theban kings ally'd,
Proud with the capture of a lion's hide,
With knotted club in hand, amidst them ran,
And thus, a seeming Hercules, began.
Him Dryope on fair Ismenus' shore
Brought forth, when heedless of the charge she bore,
She mingled with the Bacchanalian train,
And dragg'd a bullock to her patron's fane.
Her bursting womb (an unexpected birth)
Discharg'd its burden on the clay-cold earth:
"Shall then our spoils," he cries "in triumph borne,
Ye sons of Thebes, this haughty chief adorn?
Shall he at Argos our disgrace proclaim,
(Tho' he must fail of credit and of fame?)
Fulfil ye thus the promise you have made,
And is the royal bounty thus repaid?"
More had he spoke, but whistling from above
Thro' his cleft jaws a pointed javelin drove.
Then his dull ears with hollow murmurs rung,
Th' unfinish'd accents flutter'd on his tongue,
Thro' all his limbs cold crept the shades of death,
And in thick gasps he yields his vital breath.
You too, brave Thespians, if my verse can give
Immortal honour, shall in fame revive.
Brave Periphas beneath the expiring load
Of his lov'd brother, cross'd the shining road,
(Than which nor length of time or place can prove
A brighter instance of fraternal love)
His breast beneath the cuirass heaves with sighs,
Nor the close helm restrains his streaming eyes,
When lo! a weapon flying from behind,
The subtle texture of his ribs disjoin'd;
Nor here delaying, spent its deadly force,
But fixed him to his dying brother's corse:
Who felt the stroke, though on the verge of death,
And struggling to detain the parting breath.
Thus Periphas, (whose faculties were sound,
And sense uninjur'd by the recent wound)
"O may thy sons thus press to thy embrace,
And print warm kisses on thy clay-cold face."
Thus the brave pair perform'd their mutual vow,
And sought, with hand in hand, the shades below.
Meanwhile with javelin, and protended shield
The warrior cours'd Mænetes o'er the field.
In vain he strove with safety to retreat,
The treach'rous ground betray'd his hasty feet.
In vain with blandishments he tempts the foe,
And from his throat suspends the destin'd blow.
"By Heav'n's high regents, and yon starry train,
That deck with radiant orbs th' etherial plain,

779. When Chromis] There is somewhat in the character of this warrior, like that of Numanus in the ninth book of the Æneid. They are both self-sufficient, confident bravadoes; and it may be observed, that the poets never fail of making them slain, and doing what is called poetical justice.

These little anecdotes are introduced very opportunely, and serve to recall the eyes of the reader from the scenes of blood and horrour he is almost perpetually engaged in, to objects of a more calm and tranquil nature; besides, they refresh his mind by their variety, and keep off that inattention, which will unavoidably creep on in the course of a long narration.

By sacred night, propitious to thy cause,
Oh! stay thy hand, nor scorn the just applause,
Which from my mouth thy val'rous feats shall gain,
Regardless of the tyrant's hated reign. [mourn,
So may proud Thebes her slaughter'd offspring
And joyful Argos hail thy safe return."
To whom the hero, with a gloomy frown:
"Vain are thy tears, the fatal die is thrown.
Hence to grim Pluto's realms, nor seek t' enjoy
That life thou'st sought in Tydeus to destroy.
Why lengthen thus the thread of tedious life,
Doom'd to be cut in war's approaching strife?"
This said, his spear cuts short the suppliant's pray'r,
For ever mute.—His soul dissolves in air.
Then boldly pressing on the flying crowd,
He springs, and thus in triumph vaunts aloud.
"Think not, ye dastards, this sad night renews
Great Bacchus' orgies, and triennial dues.
No howling matrons rend their floating hair,
And clad in deer-skins, wreathed javelins bear;
Or to the flute's effeminating sound,
In antic measures beat the trembling ground.
No lust-inciting timbrel here invites
To mix with eunuchs in unmanly fights.
Far other scenes of battle and of rage
Employ our arms, and all our thoughts engage.
Go, seek your comrades in the Stygian shade,
And leave to men of worth the martial trade."
While thus he raves, his sinews lose their force,
And the chill blood suspends its purple course;
Each object of his aim eludes the stroke,
And his loose knees his fleeting strength bespoke.
The boss sustains the well-known shield no more,
And dewy sweat distils from ev'ry pore.
From his warm face the bloody torrents pour,
And his discolour'd hair emits a show'r.
Thus when the king of brutes has storm'd the fold,
By famine press'd, by shepherds uncontrol'd,
He feasts luxurious on the tempting food,
And shakes his mane, erect with clotted blood:

845. Think not] Statius copied this satirical speech from that of Numanus in the ninth Æneid.

O verè Phrygiæ, neque enim Phryges! ite, per alta
Dindyma, ubi assuetis biforem dat tibia cantum.
Tympana vos buxusque vocant Berecynthia matris
Idææ. Sinite arma viris, et cedite ferro.

857. While thus he raves] Ennius has a similar passage, Ann. B. 15.

Undique conveniunt, velut imber, tela tribuno:
Configunt parmam; tinnit hastilibus umbo
Ærato sonitu galeæ: sed nec pote quisquam
Undique nitendo corpus discerpere ferro.
Semper abundantes hastas frangitque quatitque:
Totum sudor habet corpus, multumque laborat.
Nec respirandi fit copia præpete ferro.
Histri tela manu jacientes sollicitabant.

Tasso likewise imitates it, b. 9. stanza 97.

Fatto intanto hà il Soldan ciò, che è concesso
Fare a terrena forza, or piu non puote,
Tutto è sangue, e sudore, un grave, e spesso
Anhelar gli ange il petto, e i fianchi scote,
Langue sotto lo scudo il braccio oppresso,
Gira la destra il ferro in pigre rote;
Spezza, e non taglia, e divenendo ottuso,
Perduto il brando omai di brando ha l'uso.

But quickly pamper'd, bids his wrath subside,
And views the ground, with slipp'ry slaughter dy'd;
Then bites the air, and ere he hies away,
Licks the spare remnants of his mangled prey.
The warrior now to Thebes had bent his course,
And shown the marks of his superior force;
When rushing from the skies, th' Athenian maid
His rash attempt, and daring ardour stay'd.
" O thou, by whose right arm unerring fate
Decrees destruction to the Theban state,
With moderation use whate'er is giv'n,
Nor dare beyond the bounds prescrib'd by Heav'n.
All you can wish beyond these glorious spoils,
Is public credit to reward your toils.
Hæmon's prophetic offspring only lives,
Nor willing, he his slaughter'd friends survives."
He who, in wisdom and experience old,
Could fates foresee, and mystic dreams unfold,
Had warn'd the king: but by the gods' decree,
He heard and disbeliev'd the prophecy.
To him, while for delaying death he pines,
The victor chief this odious task consigns.
" Whoe'er thou art, whom mercy prompts to spare,
This message to the Theban monarch bear;
Bid him prevent each nodding turret's fall,
And with deep trenches fortify the wall:
Arm ev'ry son of Cadmus in his cause,
And subject all to military laws;
Ere soon he see me, like a ray of light,
Break thro' the cloud of hosts oppos'd in fight."
To Pallas then, assistant in his toils,
The hero dedicates the bloody spoils.

875. When rushing] This passage is borrowed from that of Homer, in the tenth Iliad, where Minerva descends from Heaven, and advises Diomede to retire, when he would have pushed his conquests farther. Her words are,

Νόστου δὴ μνῆσαι, μεγαθύμου Τυδέος υἱὲ,
Νῆας ἔπι γλαφυρὰς, μὴ καὶ πεφοβημένος ἔλθῃς,
Μήπου τις καὶ Τρῶας ἐγείρησι Θεὸς ἄλλος.

I believe every one will allow the allegory here to be just, natural, and unforced. Tydeus, flushed with success, would have returned to Thebes, loaded with the spoils of his slaughtered enemies; but while he is meditating upon it, Wisdom, expressed by Minerva, descends from Heaven, and dissuades him from so rash an attempt. Hence we may see how strongly the poetry of the ancients was connected with their religion, and of what singular importance their mythology was to set off and decorate their compositions. Had the poet observed, that his hero's rashness gave place to cooler reflections, we should have passed it over, as indifferent, and unworthy any particular notice; but when he says, that Minerva advised him against putting his projects in execution, who is not awakened, attentive, delighted?

887. But by the gods' decree] The fair Cassandra was subject to the same fatal disregard.

Tunc etiam fatis aperit Cassandra futuris
Ora, dei jussu non unquam credita Teucris.
Æn. b. 2. v. 246.

899. To Pallas then] Æneas erects a trophy of this kind to Mars, Æneid, b. 11. v. 4.

Ingentem quercum, decisis undique ramis,
Constituit tumulo, fulgentiaque induit arma,

There grew an oak which long had brav'd the rage
Of rushing tempests, and corroding age:
High on a rising eminence it stood,
The pride and glory of the subject wood.
This with the glare of crested helms he grac'd,
And shields with wounds and hostile gore defac'd;
To these a heap of shiver'd spears he joins,
And swords ne'er used before on such designs.
Then from the high-rais'd pile his hands he rears,
While echo from the hills returns his pray'rs:
" O virgin, daughter of immortal Jove,
(Nor need the sire his offspring disapprove)
Whose beamy casque a beauteous horrour crowns,
And on whose shield expressive Gorgon frowns;
To thee Bellona, great in arms, must yield,
And Mars resign the honours of the field.
O deign then (whether from Pandion's mount
You rush impetuous, or th' Aonian fount,
In whose encircling waves you bathe your hair,
Oft as the sons of Earth you make your care)
T' accept these trophies of the conquer'd foe,
Sacred by will, by gratitude and vow.
Let these awhile suffice: but should again
Kind fortune land me on my native plain,
Then to thy honour golden fanes shall rise,
And daily fumes enwrap the scented skies.
Fix'd on those hills from whose impending steep
Your eyes may range along th' Ionian deep,
Where Achelous fraught with rural spoils,
O'erflows his banks, and mocks the shepherd's toils.
Here shall be seen in brass and sculptur'd stone,
A scepter'd race, and deeds of high renown;
While the proud crest, bright lance, and captive blade,
Shall on the loaded 'scutcheon shine display'd
Which Jove and you have whilom render'd mine,
And which unwilling Thebes may yet resign.
A hundred nymphs obsequious to thy nod,
With torches shall illume the fair abode:
And in their wreaths with study'd art unite
The glowing purple and unsully'd white.
An aged matron at thy shrine shall stand,
And feed the flame with unremitting hand;
Nor rashly dare with curious eye profane
Thy mystic rites and orgies of the fane.
E'en Cynthia shall without reluctance see
The first-fruits of the year decreed to thee."
Thus Tydeus spoke, impatient of delay,
And to fam'd Argos took his weary way.

BOOK III.

THE ARGUMENT.

Eteocles, anxious for the success of the ambuscade, passes the night without sleep. In the

Mezenti ducis exuvias; tibi magne trophæum
Bellipotens: aptat rorantes sanguine cristas,
Telaque trunca viri, et bis sex thoraca petitum
Perfossumque locis; clypeumque ex ære sinistro
Subligat, atque ensem collo suspendit eburnum.

The ancients laid so great a stress upon these hostile trophies, that they despaired of conquest without having previously consecrated them to some deity, who presided over warlike affairs.

945. E'en Cynthia] Tydeus alludes here to Diana's resentment against Oeneus, his father. See Ovid, Metamorph.

morning, Mæon, the prophet, returns, and after a severe invective against the tyrant's ambition, falls upon his own sword. The king, enraged at his seeming insolence, forbids the rites of burial to be bestowed on him. In the midst of this confusion, Ide, a Theban matron, makes a pathetic lamentation over the bodies of her two sons. Alethes endeavours to mitigate the grief of his fellow-citizens, and declares his resolution of killing himself. Meanwhile, Jupiter summons Mars to take the charge of the war upon him, and deters the gods from making any opposition in favour of either nation. Mars, in his descent from Heaven, is met by Venus, who uses all her art to dissuade him from putting the commands of Jupiter in execution. Adrastus and his council are disturbed by the abrupt arrival of Tydeus, who advises them to march to Thebes that instant. The common people, exasperated at the treachery of Eteocles, are scarcely dissuaded from putting this rash counsel in execution. Adrastus sends two augurs for advice from Jupiter how to act; and is threatened with the destruction of his whole army if he makes war. Then Capaneus, a warrior of distinguished valour, puts himself at the head of the mob, and forces Amphiaraus out of his retirement, by whom he is acquainted with the fortune of the war, but to no purpose. At midnight, Argia importunes her father to give his consent to the war, whose answer concludes the book.

THE Moon had measur'd half the course of night,
And the stars shone with undiminish'd light:
But, though a tedious interval remains,
Ere fair Aurora climbs th' etherial plains,
Involv'd in cares, the Theban monarch lies:
Peace fled his breast, and sleep forsook his eyes.
While the reflection of his base designs
Preys on his mind, and fear the worst divines:
Fear, that anticipates the voice of fame,
And loves new objects of despair to frame.
Asham'd to doubt the fortune of the fray,
He seeks excuses for their long delay;
And cries: "Has fortune, or some fav'ring God
Inspir'd the foe to shun the public road?
Or fame a rumour of our ambush spread,
And rous'd all Argos to revenge the dead?
Nor have I chose a mean, inglorious train,
Averse to fight, or strangers to the plain,
But chiefs, who great in arms suffice alone
To level Argos, and secure my throne.
Fierce as great Tydeus seems and prone t' engage,
Yet may he dread my spear's resistless rage;
Though brass and adamant their strength unite,
To fence his bosom, and exclude the fight.
Whence these delays then? where the doubtful strife
And toil is ended with a single life."
Such various care his tortur'd breast inflames:
Th' advent'rers much, but more himself he blames,
Who, press'd with doubts, forbore the final blow,
And safe from Thebes dismiss'd the scornful foe.
In vain he seeks in sleep a short resource,
O'erwhelm'd with shame, distracted with remorse.
As when the pilot, tempted by the breeze
And glassy surface, seeks the middle seas,
Oft o'er the face of ether clouds arise,
And Jove in sudden show'rs forsakes the skies:
From east to west the mutt'ring thunder rolls,
And fierce Orion shakes the lab'ring poles;
Fain would he seek the shore, but from the stern
The south drives on, and hinders his return,
Till spent with useless toil, and black despair,
He quits his art, and trusts to fortune's care.
Thus, rack'd with doubts, he chides the lazy Sun,
And bids the hours with swifter motion run.
Aurora now had shot a glimm'ring ray,
And the stars vanish'd from emergent day;
When sudden tremours heav'd the guilty ground,
And Heav'n and Earth rebellow'd to the sound,
Signal of woe—while from Cithæron's brow
Rush'd a dissolving stream of ancient snow.
Upborne in air aspiring roofs engage,
And the sev'n gates thrice clash'd with martial rage.
But Mæon, rescued from th' expecting jaws
Of wish'd destruction, soon explains the cause,
Proclaims the sad reverse of partial fate,
And threats misfortunes to the Theban state.
For ere in open view he stood confest,
He deeply groan'd, and beat his manly breast.
Thus fares a shepherd, when returning light
Reveals the carnage of the former night,
(Whose flocks, retreating to some thicker wood
From the rough storm, a troop of wolves pursued)
Stretch'd on the sand, he vents his grief, yet fears
To bear the tidings to his master's ears:

5. Involv'd in cares] The pleasures of illegal acquisitions are unequal to the cares and fears arising from them. The pains of the body are curable and transient; but the stings of conscience limitable by repentance and death only. Claudian has described the torments of a guilty villain, in the person of Ruffinus, with great spirit and exact propriety.

At procul exanguis Ruffinum perculit horror:
Infectæ pallore genæ, stetit ore gelato
Incertus peteretne fugam, veniamne subactus
Posceret, an stantes sese transferret in hostes.
Quid nunc divitiæ? quid fulvi vasta metalli
Congeries? quid purpureis effulta columnis
Afria prolatæve juvant ad sidera moles?
Addit iter, numeratque dies, spatioque viarum
Metitur vitam, torquetur peste futurâ:
Nec recipit somnos, et sæpe cubilibus amens
Excutitur, pœnamque luit formidine pœnæ.

In Ruffinum, lib. 2.

47. When sudden tremours] This disaster seems to be ushered in with too much pomp and parade. A more surprising assemblage of phænomena could not have preceded the taking of Thebes. But some may say, all these prodigies were preparatory to, and presaging of it. Perhaps they were so: but they ought to have happened at a shorter distance from it; when every one must have been in suspense concerning the fate of the city, and every thing that appeared like an omen, interesting and alarming.

50. Rush'd a dissolving stream] This article of the snow's falling is mentioned by Lucan in the first book of his Pharsalia.

——vete.emque jugis nutantibus Alpes
Discussere nivem.

And, vex'd to find the vallies bleat no more,
With plaintive notes invokes the list'ning shore.
But, when the throng of matrons at the gate,
As yet unknowing their relation's fate,
Beheld him unattended, and alone,
They rush, distracted, thro' th' affrighted town.
Instead of questions, shrilling clamours rise,
And shrieks renew'd by the retentive skies.
Such is the tumult, when, its walls o'erthrown,
Bellona triumphs o'er some captive town;
Or, when a vessel, hurried down the steep
Of op'ning surges, cleaves the nether deep.
But, when the sorrowing prophet had obtain'd
Admission to the king, and audience gain'd;
"This one," he cries, "of fifty valiant lives
To bring the dismal message Tydeus gives.
Thus fortune or the vengeful fates decreed,
Or Heav'n, to punish the perfidious deed:
Or, what I speak with shame, and own with grief,
The single valour of this mighty chief
E'en I can scarcely credit, who survey'd
The bloody progress of his reeking blade.
But you, O manes of my comrades slain,
And you, bright ornaments of Cynthia's reign,
Attest, that life unask'd the victor gave,
And sav'd me from a less inglorious grave.
Thus the great arbiters of life and death
Enjoin'd: nor can we yield our vital breath,
Till the predestin'd, number'd hours are come,
And fate has seal'd th' irrevocable doom.
Else had I fall'n in war, and giv'n to fame,
What nature craves, and Pluto soon will claim;
Nor thou, for whom Bellona's torch shall burn,
The soldier bleed, and widow'd beauty mourn,
Shalt from thy banish'd brother long detain
The promis'd empire, and alternate reign:
Black fate hangs over thy devoted head,
Nor Thebes, divided from her king, shall bleed.
Full fifty ghosts shall their fresh wounds disclose,
And make thee loath the season of repose."
More had he utter'd, but the tyrant's ire
Varied his cheeks with blood, his eyes with fire.
Swift from their seats two daring villains sprung,
Prepar'd to silence his licentious tongue;
Who prone, in all the king commands, t' obey,
Shone first at court, and held the reins of sway.
Meanwhile the prophet views his naked sword,
Then smiles at the stern aspect of his lord;
And cries: "The fates forbid thee to command
A life uninjur'd by great Tydeus' hand.
My soul, discharg'd by this auspicious blade,
Shall join my comrades in th' Elysian shade."
Thus Mæon: the preventing steel suppress
Th' imperfect sounds, and quivers in his breast.
His mouth and wound emit a crimson flood,
And form a channel of united blood:
While nature shivers at approaching death,
And struggles to retain the parting breath.
Smit with the dread of these portended woes,
The nobles murmur, and the senate rose;
While faction to her side the rabble draws,
And with invented tales supports her cause.
Meanwhile the prophet's friends unite their aid,
And on their shoulders home the corse convey'd.
Frowning he seem'd as in contempt of death;
Nor fled his sternness with the vital breath.
But the fierce tyrant's rage as yet surviv'd,
Unquenchable as when its object liv'd.
Repuls'd with threats the patriot's friends retire,
Nor dare to raise him a funereal pyre.
Yet rest, illustrious shade, nor fear the rage
Of envious slander, or oblivious age.
But oh! what numbers can thy virtue paint;
(The stronger image makes description faint)
That virtue, which th' usurper durst oppose,
And warn his country of impending woes:
Which partnership in guilt did e'er disclaim,
And sought the path to freedom and to fame!
Apollo crown'd thy worth with early bays,
Nor blush'd with thee to share prophetic praise;
The nymph of Cyrrha silent shall remain,
Nor fam'd Dodona's oak an answer deign:
While round the shrine suspended nations wait,
And bribe in vain th' interpreter of fate.
Let fair Elysium hence thy presence boast,
Sequester'd from the dark Tartarean coast;
Where, nor Eteocles exerts his reign,
Nor servile Thebans brook the galling chain.
Tho' foul in dust, yet undisfigur'd lies
The carcase, guarded by the pitying skies.

65. And vex'd to find the vallies] The poets often transfer the cause of sounds from the animal authors of them, to the place in which they are represented to be. Hence Ovid says the plains low, and Hesiod, that the mountains bleat.

73. Such is the tumult] Homer has a simile something like this, upon the consternation occasioned by the death of Hector.

—— αμφι ε λαοι
Κω κυτω τ' ειχοντο και οιμωγη κατα αςυ.
Τω δε μαλις' αρ' εην εναλιγκιον, ωσει απασα
Ιλιος οφρυοεσσα πυρι μηχοιτο κατ' ακρης.
B. 22. V. 408.

103. Full fifty ghosts] Dido threatens Æneas with the same punishment.

Dido shall come with a black sulph'ry flame,
When death has once dissolv'd her mortal frame;
Shall smile to see thee, tyrant, vainly weep:
Her angry ghost, arising from the deep,
Shall haunt thee waking, and disturb thy sleep.
Dryden, Æn. 4.

129. Frowning he seem'd] Lucan has some few lines on the appearance of Pompey's countenance after death.

Nor agonies, nor livid death disgrace
The sacred features of the hero's face;
In the cold visage, mournfully serene,
The same indignant majesty was seen;
There virtue, still unchangeable, abode,
And scorn'd the spite of ev'ry partial God.
Rowe, lib. 8. v. 901.

133. Repuls'd with threats] This prohibition of the king's is the more insisted on by the poet, because the ancients had nothing in greater horrour than the want of burial. Virgil says, that the unburied on the banks of Styx

Centum errant annos, volitantque hæc littora circum,
Tum demum admissi, stagna exoptata revisunt.
Æneid, b. 6. v. 329.

153. Tho' foul in dust] The ancients held nothing, except life itself, in greater value than the burial of their bodies entire and undismembered:

Untouch'd by dogs remain his limbs and face,
While birds retire in rev'rence of the place.
Meanwhile th' Ætolian hero's feats engage
The senate's care, and fire the youth with rage.
Here age and sex no more distinction know,
But all with an impatient ardour glow,
To view the labours of a single chief,
Cheer the young bride, and soothe the parent's grief.
The weeping crowd a doleful concert yields,
While plaintive Echo from the neighb'ring fields
Sigh still with sighing answers, groan with groan,
And seems to mourn for sorrows not her own.
But when they reach'd th' unhabitable wood,
And rocks that hang incumbent o'er the flood,
A sudden tumult shakes the nether plain,
(As if the dead had yet unpitied lain:)
From one huge mouth the clamour seems to flow,
And all th' assembly wears one face of woe;
In tatter'd robes the god of sorrow stands;
Stern is his aspect, bloody are his hands:
He beckons to his vot'ries, and supplies
Their lungs with vigour, and with tears their eyes.
They lift the helmets, and rejoice to trace
The well-known features of each kindred face;
Hang o'er the clay-cold bodies, shed a flood
Of tears, and steep their hair in clotted blood:
Or seal their eyes, and, groveling on the ground,
Bathe with the stream of grief each gaping wound.
While some with fruitless care extract the darts,
Or join the sever'd limbs and kindred parts.
But wretched Ide rushes to and fro,
In all the raging impotence of woe.
Thro' thorns and clouds of dust she bends her way;
She rends her tresses venerably grey.
Horrour accompanies each streaming tear,
Nor the spectators pity her, but fear.
She seeks her sons among the num'rous dead,
And mingles with the dust her aged head.
Thus the Thessalian hag, at whose command
Reviving phantoms leave the Stygian strand,
In bloody fields explores her lifeless prey,
Lur'd with the carnage of the former day.
When night, propitious to her mystic charms,
O'er the wide globe extends her sable arms,
To various carcases, by turns she flies,
And, bending, o'er them rolls her haggard eyes:
Then, mutt'ring magic sounds with impious voice,
Demands on which to fix her doubtful choice.
The ghosts with horrour eye the world again,
And Pluto sorrows for his thinn'd domain.
Beneath a rock the happy brothers lay,
And shar'd alike the fortune of the fray.
One day, one hand suppress'd their vital breath,
And lock'd them in inseparable death.
When Ide saw, her brim-full eyes disclose
A pearly stream, and thus she speaks her woes.
"Are these your kisses? this your last embrace,
And these the smiles which death could not efface?
Has fate, propitious to the mutual vow,
Preserv'd your union in the shades below?
But say, whose languid eyes, unhappy pair,
Whose wounds shall first employ a mother's care?
Are you, late objects of my hopes and fears,
The boast and prop of my declining years!
How chang'd, alas! my offspring, since I strove
To match the daughters of Almighty Jove.
More happy she, to whom the queen of air
Denies a parent's short-liv'd joys to share;
By whom Lucina uninvok'd remains,
Who, if she tastes no pleasures, feels no pains.
Yet 'twould have been some shadow of relief,
Some small allay, and solace of my grief,
Had fame, the dying hero's only meed,
Shone on your tomb, and blaz'd the glorious deed:

hence Priam, in the 24th book of the Iliad, thus interrogates Mercury about the fate of Hector.

Η ετι παρ νηεσσιν εμος παις, ηε μιν ηδη
Ηοι κυσιν μελεις̃ι ταμων προυθηκεν Αχιλλευς. V. 409.

167. But when they reach'd] In this prelude, Statius has prepared us for all the succeeding calamities of Thebes, and has given us, as it were, all the horrours of war in miniature. The last book left us highly prepossessed in favour of Tydeus; but the poet now, like a skilful musician, changes his note, and melts us into pity and tenderness. Even the valour of Tydeus loses its lustre, when we reflect on the fatal consequences with which it was attended.

173. In tatter'd robes the god of sorrow] This personification of the passions is entirely original, and very well executed. The figure, countenance, and habit, are very consistent with the god of sorrow, and the two last lines very natural, and highly finished.

185. But wretched Ide] The character and distress of a tender mother are admirably well supported, and described in the person of Ide. But what gives the highest colouring, is the poet's remark, that her countenance rather excited horrour than compassion in the hearts of the spectators. A common poet would have described her as weeping and wringing her hands in a regular manner; but Statius represents her as frantic. She has not the face of a tender mother, but of a fury; and does not lament, but rave.

193. Thus the Thessalian hag] I must beg leave to refer my reader to the description of the sorceress Erictho, as drawn in the sixth book of Lucan's Pharsalia, in my opinion, one of the finest passages in that author. The likenesses are too strong to escape his observation, and I doubt not but the pleasure he will meet with, will abundantly compensate for the trouble of referring to it.

205. Beneath a rock] I need not acquaint the reader who these two brothers were, if he has attentively read what has gone before: but, if his memory should fail him, let him return to the 816th verse of the 2d book, where he will be fully satisfied.

211. Are these your kisses] There is no speech in the whole Thebaid more worthy our attention than this of Ide. The reader will not find in it a collection of trite sentiments, and common-place observations; but will, I doubt not, think it the most rational, pertinent, and spirited speech in the whole poem. I shall do Statius but common justice to say, that his art is here as much superior to that of Virgil in the speech of Euryalus's mother, as the Æneid is upon the whole to the Thebaid. Ide really talks like a sensible, philosophical matron; she does not wish her sons had escaped with life, but that they had fallen in a more honourable and conspicuous manner. I only wonder she so well recovered the use of her reason, as to throw out these reflections, since her appearance at first gave us little ground to expect it.

But here, alas! your lives obscure you yield,
Nor public praise survives the deathful field.
Rest then, and may no violence remove
This sacred emblem of fraternal love!
One fire shall your connected bodies burn,
And your pale ashes grace one common urn."
Others, meanwhile, in equal strains lament
Their lifeless friends, and curse the dire event.
This mourns a father, this a brother dead,
And that a partner of the nuptial bed.
High on a neighb'ring hill a thicket stood,
Whose conscious height o'erlooks the field of blood:
At this the Thebans level all their strokes,
And humble to the ground the tallest oaks.
Till thro' the trees they cleave an open way,
And the dark grove admits a sudden day.
While, clinging to the piles, they shun relief,
Averse to comfort, and o'ercharg'd with grief;
Alethes strove to calm their growing rage,
A chief advanc'd in wisdom as in age.
"Oft, on the verge of ruin, has our state
Become the sport of fortune and of fate;
Since Cadmus sow'd with serpent's teeth the soil,
And reap'd an iron harvest of his toil,
When, scar'd with the new sounds of clashing shields,
The swain forsakes his patrimonial fields.
Yet never did the sons of Cadmus show
So deep a sense, such consciousness of woe,
E'en when the palace of Agenor's son
With wasting flames, and bright destruction shone:
Or Athamas, in quest of glory, slew
His son, and home the panting carcase drew.
Not with such shrieks the Theban palace rung,
When from her throne the fierce Agave sprung,
And knew the victim of her vengeful sword,
To sense and misery at once restor'd.
If aught could match the present scene of woe,
'Twas when the patron of the silver bow
Dispatch'd, for Niobe's ambitious boast,
Her num'rous offspring to the Stygian coast.
Such dire alarms the tim'rous vulgar shook,
And thus in crowds the city they forsook.
Then ev'ry temple rung with frequent groans,
And ev'ry god was weary'd with their moans.
Sev'n ample gates imperial Thebes adorn,
Through each in pomp two funerals were borne.
Well I remember, tho' my tender years,
And youth might well excuse my want of tears,
I mourn'd the vengeance of th' immortal foe,
And from my parents catch'd th' infectious woe.
Yet less we should lament (for tears are vain)
At what the fates and equal Jove ordain.
As when, unconscious of the form impos'd,
The shouting youths and eager hounds enclos'd
Actæon, who by fatal stealth survey'd
The naked beauties of the bathing maid;
Or the chang'd virgin bath'd the Theban plains,
Whose name the grateful fountain still retains:
For this the sister-destinies decreed,
And Jove assented to the future deed.
But now the weeping sons of Thebes atone
For royal crimes, and mischiefs not their own.
Ere Fame, tho' hast'ning with the first report
Of war proclaim'd, has reach'd the Argive court,
How shall the gasping nations pant for breath,
What labours rise, what various scenes of death!
What breathless heaps, what rushing streams of blood
Shall dye the ground, and swell the neighb'ring flood!
Unhappy youths, whom Fortune only spares
For greater evils, which she now prepares:
Me Nature summons to the shades below,
And kindly snatches from approaching woe."
Thus spoke the sage; and from the tyrant's crimes
Dates all the mischief of succeeding times:
For on his mind no conscious terrours hung,
Nor check'd the honest freedom of his tongue;
Resolv'd to die, while life was in his pow'r,
Nor linger to the last predestin'd hour.
Meanwhile the scepter'd ruler of the skies
To weeping Thebes directs his awful eyes,
Surveys the carnage of the former night,
And summons Mars to plan the future fight;
Who, loaded with the spoils of conquer'd Thrace,
Impell'd his steeds along th' aerial space.
His helm with borrow'd lightning fires the pole,
Beneath his car incessant thunders roll.

259. Or Athamas] For an account of Athamas, see the note on the 15th verse of the first book.

273. Sev'n ample gates] The ancients differ concerning the number of Niobe's children. Homer and Propertius mention only twelve; but Euripides, Ovid, Sidonius, and Seneca the tragedian, affirm there were fourteen. Statius coincides with the latter, as appears from the above passage.

281. As when, unconscious] Instead of saying any thing of Actæon, whose misfortune every one is acquainted with, I shall present the reader with Ovid's description of his transformation.

—— Nec plura minata
Dat sparso capiti vivacis cornua cervi,
Dat spatium collo, summasque cacuminat aures;
Cum pedibusque manus, cum longis brachia mutat
Cruribus, et velat maculoso vellere corpus.
Additus et pavor est. Fugit Autoneius heros,
Et se tam celerem cursu miratur in ipso:
Ut vero vultus, et cornua vidit in undâ,
Me miserum! dicturus erat: vox nulla secuta est;
Ingemuit, vox illa fuit, lacrymæque per ora
Non sua fluxerunt. Mens tantum pristina mansit.
Metam. lib. 3. fab. 2.

285. Or the chang'd virgin] Dirce was the wife of Lycus after the divorcement of Antiopa, whose two sons afterwards killed Lycus, and bound Dirce to the tail of a wild horse, by which she was dragged up and down, till the gods, taking compassion of her misfortunes, changed her into a fountain of that name.

293. How shall the gasping nations] This is copied from Horace, book 1. ode 15. The words of Statius are,

Quantus equis, quantusque viris in pulvere crasso
Sudor!

Those of Horace,

Eheu quantus equis, quantus adest viris
Sudor!

313. His helm with borrow'd lightning] This description of Mars is full of that sublime imagery so peculiar to our author. The god of war is not arrayed in his own simple terrours, but calls in to his assistance those of Jupiter and Apollo. The noise of his chariot is equal to that of thunder, and the splendour of his helmet to lightning, while

His arms, enliven'd by the sculptor's art,
With golden monsters brave each hostile dart;
While his shield bears the Sun's reflected ray,
Nor shines inferior to the god of day.
When Jove beheld him in his bloody car,
Array'd in all the terrours of the war,
He cries: " Let Argos feel thy wasting force,
And death and slaughter mark thy dreadful course:
Still on thy visage may these clouds remain,
And cause a purple deluge o'er the plain.
Let Thebes no more the rage of Tydeus mourn,
But breathe revenge, and for the combat burn;
To thee devote her warriors' lives and hands,
And freely execute thy dire commands.
From hence repair to rouse the states of Greece,
Dissolve the truce, and break the bonds of peace.
'Tis thine in Heav'n to kindle fierce debate,
And fire immortal breasts with mutual hate.
Nor is this task assign'd to thee alone;
Jove has himself the seeds of discord sown:
See Tydeus, loaded with Bœotian spoils,
To Argos bears the product of his toils,
From his report shall lasting strife succeed,
And either candidate for empire bleed.
Thou but inspire the nations with belief,
And arm them to revenge their injur'd chief.
Hear then, ye pow'rs, and what you hear, approve,
Nor with entreaties tempt almighty Jove;
For thus th' impartial destinies decreed,
And have our sanction to complete the deed.
While Nature yet in wild confusion lay,
Nor Phœbe rul'd the night, nor Sol the day;
The fates had seal'd this nation's future doom,
And laid the plan of battles yet to come.
Permit me then to warn succeeding times,
(Avenging on the son his father's crimes)

the orb of his shield matches that of the Sun. The invention of his passage from Thrace (which was feigned to be the country of that god) is a very beautiful and poetical manner of celebrating the martial genius of that people, who were engaged in perpetual wars.

323. Still on thy visage] In this beautiful allegory, we may discover an amazing boldness, and exact propriety of expression. This chain or continuation of metaphors is reducible (though much superior) to a simile. Jupiter wishes, that the frowns on the brow of Mars might be as productive of an effusion of blood, as clouds are of a shower of rain. If this is not the curiosa fælicitas of Quintilian, I know not where it exists.

343. For thus th' impartial destinies] The learned differ in their opinions concerning the power of the Fates and Jupiter: some affirming the former, and others the latter to be superior. But I think the best way is to steer the middle course, and suppose them endued with an equal degree of authority, and always acting in conjunction: as here fate decrees the destruction of Thebes; but Jupiter, having the power of incidents to bring it to pass, fulfils that decree by providing means for it. Jupiter begins his speech to the gods in a similar manner in the 8th book of Homer.

Κέκλυτέ μευ πάντες τε θεοὶ, πᾶσαί τε θέαιναι,
Ὄφρ' εἴπω τά με θυμὸς ἐνὶ στήθεσσι κελεύει.
Μήτε τις οὖν θηλεια θεὸς τόγε, μητε τις ἄρσην
Πειράτω διακέρσαι ἐμὸν ἔπος· ἀλλ' ἅμα πάντες
Αἰνεῖτ', ὄφρα τάχιστα τηλευτησω τάδε ἔργα. Verse 5.

And trace from the records of distant age
Past actions which deserve my present rage.
For, by the glories of the starry sphere,
And Styx, whose awful name the gods revere,
This dreaded arm shall crush the Theban race,
And rend each structure from its solid base;
In one huge ruin heap the realms around,
And level Argive turrets with the ground:
Then bid the deep no more confinement know,
And give to Neptune all the world below.
In vain shall Juno deprecate its fall;
Or, clinging to her fane's devoted wall,
Of angry Jove, and partial fate complain:
Resent she may, but must resent in vain."
He spoke: nor durst the pow'rs of Heav'n reply:
A rev'rend horrour silenc'd all the sky.
Such stilness o'er the face of Nature reigns,
When summer smiles auspicious on the plains;
When not a breath of air disturbs the deep,
And billows on the shore reclining sleep:
The peaceful groves retain their youthful green,
And not a cloud o'ercasts the beauteous scene;
While, half-exhausted by the thirsty Sun,
Beneath their banks the peaceful rivers run.
Meanwhile the god of arms prepares for fight,
Resumes the floating reins, and shuns the right.
Prone down the steep of Heav'n the chariot flies,
Glows in the whirl, and burns along the skies;
When Venus, offspring of the briny flood,
To stay his dreaded progress adverse stood.
The steeds recoil'd, reluctant to the reins,
And smooth, in rev'rence, their erected manes:
Then champ, in honour of th' acknowledg'd fair,
The foaming bit, and snuff the trembling air.
Her snowy bosom gently press'd the yoke,
And thus, with previous tears, the goddess spoke:
" Will Mars with his own offspring then engage,
And on a guiltless nation vent his rage?
Say, shall the product of our mutual love,
And these my tears e'er unavailing prove?

379. When Venus, offspring, &c.] The ancients (to whom we owe many things) first taught us to turn the virtues and endowments of the mind into persons, to make the springs of action become visible; and because they are given by the gods, represent them as gods themselves descending from Heaven. In the same manner they described the vices, which occasion our misfortunes, as supernatural powers, inflicting them upon us, and even our natural punishments are represented as punishers themselves. Hence it is, that we find Juno and Minerva on the one side, and Venus on the other, in continual variance through the whole Iliad, Æneid, and Thebaid.

387. Will Mars then] This speech of Venus is written in the spirit of Dido's to Æneas; and in many places not only the sentiment, but even the diction is similar, as for example:

Say, shall the product] so Virgil,

Nec te noster amor, nec te data dextera quondam,
Nec moritura tenet crudeli funere Dido?

Did I for this consent, &c.]

Extinctus pudor, et, quâ solâ sidera adibam,
Fama prior.

Go then; thy flight, &c.]

Neque te teneo, neque dicta refello.
I, sequere Italiam ventis, pete regna per undas.

Did I for this consent to your embrace,
Bereft of honour, branded with disgrace?
Go then; thy flight no longer I detain;
Go; bathe in kindred blood the Theban plain.
Yet Vulcan (tho' from him I little claim)
Not thus would slight the object of his flame.
How would th' uxorious God at my demand
In toils unceasing ply his skilful hand,
And scarcely doubt (so valued are my charms)
For Mars himself to frame immortal arms!
But hold, nor let me waste my time in vain;
Or hope from Mars a trifling suit to gain:
Can hearts of adamant, or breasts of steel
The gentle impulse of compassion feel?
Yet say, for what, by whose inducements won,
You sought alliance with Agenor's son;
And forc'd the pledge of our delights to share
Woes she deserves not, and another's care?
You promis'd once a progeny divine
Of Thebans rising from the Tyrian line
Should stand renown'd in arms and martial fame,
And to succeeding times transmit their name.
But had the fates assented to my vows,
More distant climes had yielded her a spouse,
Where endless winter Thracian seas constrains,
And binds the frozen flood in chrystal chains.
Yet could my tears but bid the Thebans live,
These ancient crimes I could with ease forgive:
Though on erected spires our daughter roves,
And darts fresh poison on th' Illyrian groves."
Thus spoke the fair, with sorrow-streaming eye,
When the fierce god, half willing to comply,
Leap'd from his car, and rushing to her arms,
With eager eyes devour'd her heav'nly charms:
At length replies; while sympathetic woe
Unbends his soul, and bids the torrent flow.
"O dearer far than war, or hostile spoils,
Source of my bliss, and solace of my toils!
To whom alone of all the pow'rs of Heav'n
To meet my dreaded arms, unhurt, 'tis giv'n,
To stop my coursers in their full career,
And bid my hand dismiss the brandish'd spear.
Your former favours I can ne'er forget;
Nor words express, nor deeds discharge the debt:

407. And forc'd the pledge] This was Harmonia, who was married to Cadmus.

409. You promis'd once] The same goddess reminds Jupiter of a like promise concerning Æneas and his companions.

Certè hinc Romanos olim volventibus annis,
Hinc fore ductores revocato a sanguine Teucri,
Qui mare, qui terras omni ditione tenerent.
Virg. Æneid, lib. 1. verse 238.

423. And rushing to her arms] In the common editions, the words are,

Clyeoque receptam
Lædit in amplexu.

But Barthius very reasonably objects to this as erroneous, and corrects it thus,

Illigat amplexu,

which sense I have adopted in the translation.

429. To whom alone] Here is a latent prohibition to Venus to repeat the same indiscretion: he tells her, that she alone, being the weakest of all the gods, could have done it with impunity.

But ere oblivion shall thy name erase,
Or make me slow in Cytherea's praise,
May Pluto, and the shades of Orcus claim
This soul, bereft of its immortal frame!
Meanwhile, O queen, permit me to fulfil
The Fates' decree, and Jove's unalter'd will:
(For here thy Vulcan little would avail,
And all his boasted art and labours fail)
Hard is the task, alas! you now enjoin,
T' oppose the lord of ether's fix'd design.
I war not with the Highest: all above
Submit and tremble at the hand of Jove.
Then banish sorrow, and your fears resign,
(Secure, what Mars can do is ever thine)
And bear with patience what the Fates ordain;
To thwart is rashness, and resistance vain:
But, when Bellona waves her flaming brand,
And summons to the war each Argive band,
Myself will head in fight the Theban train,
And heap with slaughter'd foes the crimson plain.
Then, goddess, say, will Mars unjust appear,
When Argive blood shall smoke upon his spear?
This right I challenge in the field of fame,
This fate allows, nor Jove disputes my claim."
He spoke: and, eager for the promis'd war,
Urg'd o'er the vast expanse his rapid car.
Thus falls the bolt, when from the northern pole,
Jove bares his arm, and bids the thunder roll;
Pregnant with death the glaring mischief flies,
And cleaves a triple furrow in the skies:
A fatal omen to the greedy swain,
Or trembling sailors on the wat'ry main.
Meanwhile young Tydeus seeks the winding shore,
And measures back the fields he cross'd before.
His eyes, attracted with the distant glare,
Survey the temple of the queen of air.
His hair grew stiff with dust and mingled gore,
While streams of sweat distil from ev'ry pore;
His eyes, bereft of wonted sleep, display
A sanguine hue, and sicken at the day.

435. But ere oblivion] These voluntary imprecations were customary among the ancients. Thus Dido:

Sed mihi vel tellus optem prius ima dehiscat;
Vel pater omnipotens adigat me fulmine ad umbras,
Pallentes umbras Erebi, noctemque profundam,
Ante, pudor, quam te violo, aut tua jura resolvo.
Lib. 4.

441. For here thy Vulcan] Here is a sarcastical reflection on the infirmity of Vulcan, and an hint of his own superiority. His oration is delivered with the usual bluntness of a soldier, and his subsequent behaviour highly consistent. He does not stay to see what impression his excuse will make on the mind of Venus, or whether his offers in part will compensate for his non-compliance with the whole; but hurries on with a seeming indifference about the result of it.

461. Thus falls the bolt] Lucan has made use of the same comparison in the first book of his Pharsalia:

Qualiter expressum ventis per nubila fulmen
Ætheris impulsi sonitu, mundique fragore
Emicuit, rupitque diem, populosque paventes
Terruit, obliquâ præstringens lumina flammâ:
In sua templa furit: nullâque exire vetante
Materiâ, magnamque cadens, magnamque revertens
Dat stragem late, sparsosque recolligit ignes.

His toil increases, as his breath he draws,
And parching thirst inflames his clammy jaws:
Yet, unimpair'd by toils, or hostile blows,
His soul with undiminish'd ardour glows.
Thus, when the victor-bull surveys again
The subject herd, and late-abandon'd plain;
He roars, and, traversing the fields around,
Proclaims his conquest in each echoing ground;
Or eyes the swelling honours of his breast,
And blood, his adversary once possest,
While from afar, his rival with a groan,
Surveys the pleasing kingdoms once his own.
Meanwhile Oenides, as he pass'd along,
In ev'ry town convenes the rustic throng:
His words the crowd to yield him aid engage,
And fire the youth already prone to rage.
His country, name, by whom, and whither sent,
Are soon divulg'd, and what the dire event.
The sight and tale of the returning chief,
Among the trembling crowd enforce belief:
Then, sent by Mars, officious Fame appears,
Removes each doubt, and doubles all their fears.
Scarce had he reach'd the palace, when he view'd
Adrastus, studious of the public good,
Amidst his peers enthron'd; while thus they sate,
Attentive to the subject in debate,
" Arms, arms," he cries: " now, monarch, may'st thou prove
Thy blood, and martial heat deriv'd from Jove.
Justice and piety are now no more,
And slighted faith has fled the Theban shore.
More amicable treatment had I found
Where endless slaughter dyes the Scythian ground:
Or the stern guardian[1] of Bebrycia's grove
Once reign'd, in scorn of hospitable Jove.
Nor blame I those, by whom it was enjoin'd,
Nor mourn, repentant of the task assign'd.
By Jove 'twas pleasant to dispute the claim
Of boasting Thebes to military fame.
Full fifty chiefs, (forgive the seeming boast)
The flow'r, the pride, the bulwark of their host,
Came forth as if to storm some leaguer'd town,
O'erthrow its walls, or throw its ramparts down.
Tho' naked and unarm'd, I scorn'd to fly,
Resolv'd to conquer, or with honour die.
But hear the sequel: all in fight o'erthrown,
Lie wallowing in their blood before the town.
But oh! what trophies must the Thebans yield,
Would Argos lead her armies to the field
While fear prevails, while, scatter'd on the plain,
They pay the last sad office to the slain!
Myself will share the fortune of the day,
Though these few wounds require a short delay."
The senate rose: while with dejected eyes,
The warrior sprung from Cadmus, thus replies.
" How hateful to the gods, alas! I'm grown,
To view those wounds, deserv'd by me alone!
Was this, proud chief, the only way to show
Thy causeless hate, and prove thyself a foe?
Then let me not—Ah! can I wish to live,
And Tydeus, wounded in my cause, survive?
Meanwhile, may Argos flourish in repose,
Nor owe to me the cause of future woes!
No matron, angry for her children slain,
Of me, the source of mischief, shall complain.
No widow shall of me her spouse require,
Nor orphan, weeping for his absent sire.
I rush to death, nor seek ye to detain;
'Tis honour prompts me, and you urge in vain.
To Tydeus, Thebes, my country, this I owe,
Their welfare claims, nor I retard the blow."
Thus veil'd the chief the wishes of his mind,
And artfully pronounc'd the speech design'd.
At first his audience wept the injur'd chief:
Now stronger wrath supplies the place of grief.
Nor did the youth alone impatient glow,
To wrest the sceptre from th' usurping foe:
A like resentment fires the breast of age,
And rous'd the dying sparks of martial rage.
One will inclin'd to draw the glitt'ring blade,
One voice declar'd their promises of aid.
But old Adrastus, great in arts of sway,
And prudence, thus enjoins a short delay,
And cries: " Awhile, ye sons of Argos, cease
From lawless arms, nor violate the peace.
To Jove and kings alone the right belongs
Of waging battle, or avenging wrongs.
Nor thou, young warrior, of redress despair,
Thy welfare claims our seasonable care.
Let us on Tydeus now our thoughts employ,
Nor be less prone to save than to destroy.

[1] Busiris.

529. How hateful to the gods] It is an exquisite piece of art, when you seem to persuade one thing, and at the same time enforce the contrary. This kind of rhetoric is of great use in all occasions of danger, and of this Statius has afforded a most striking instance in the oration of Polynices. It is a method perfectly wonderful, and even carries in it an appearance of absurdity; for all that we generally esteem the faults of oratory, by this means become the virtues of it. Nothing is looked upon as a greater errour in a rhetorician, than to allege such arguments as either are easily answered, or may be retorted upon himself; the former is a weak part, the latter a dangerous one; and Polynices here designedly deals in both. For it is plain, that if a man must not use weak arguments, or such as may make against him, when he intends to persuade the thing he says; then on the other side, when he does not intend it, he must observe the contrary proceeding, and make what are the faults of oratory in general, the excellencies of that oration in particular, or otherwise he will contradict his own intention, and persuade the contrary to what he means. I have dwelt the longer on this remark, to render the beauty of this speech more visible and obvious; and to prevent any scrupulous objections, which might be of disadvantage to our author.

555. But old Adrastus] The reader may perhaps be at a loss to conceive how Adrastus, who had promised Polynices his aid in case of a rupture between him and his brother, should hesitate one moment about fulfilling his engagement, after such a complicated series of ill usage from Eteocles. But there were many reasons, which will justify this conduct: such as the care of his own safety (for it was uncertain what would be the event of his taking up arms). Secondly, the prevention of those calamities, which his people must necessarily undergo in the course of a long war; and, thirdly, the avoiding the anger of the gods, who ought always to be consulted upon such occasions, according to the opinion of the heathens. We may see then, that this suspension of hostilities was the result of the most consummate prudence, strict piety, and patriotic humanity.

His limbs oppress'd with toil and hostile blows,
In speedy sleep require a short repose.
Me too the same desire of vengeance warms,
But reason moderates the love of arms."
His wife and friends enclose the weary chief,
Anxious, and emulous to give relief,
While he, reclining on a pillar, stood,
Joyful amidst his toils and loss of blood.
Fam'd Idmon was at hand to prove his art,
And to the wounded warrior ease impart.
One while, the juice of lenient herbs he tries,
Then bathes the wound, or crooked knife applies,
While he relates at large, from whence arose
The wrath and ambush of his Theban foes,
How, sent by night, within the winding way,
To bar his passage, fifty warriors lay;
And, those defeated in the gloomy vale,
He spar'd but one to bear the dreadful tale.
Caught with the sound of these heroic deeds,
Each chief, in prospect, for his country bleeds:
But Polynices most the love of fame,
And thirst of empire and revenge inflame.
The Sun, descending from th' aerial steep,
Had gain'd the confines of the western deep,
And bath'd his rays in the reflecting flood;
His coursers panting on the margin stood:
Till, swift emerging from their pearly caves,
The Hours, and sea-green daughters of the waves
Releas'd them from the yoke and hated reins,
To range at will, and crop the verdant plains.
'Twas theirs his foaming horses to unbrace,
And fix the car on its immortal base.
The night succeeds, and wrapt in ambient clouds,
In one huge veil the whole creation shrouds;
While sleep consigns each anxious breast to peace,
And bids the howlings of the forest cease.
Adrastus, and the Theban prince alone
The want of sleep and inward ease bemoan.
While Tydeus charg'd with visionary spoils,
In dreams re-acts his late illustrious toils.

569. His wife and friends] This heroic behaviour of Tydeus is copied from that of Æneas on a similar occasion.

Stabat acerba fremens, ingentem nixus in hastam
Æneas, magno juvenum, et mœrentis Iüli
Concursu, lacrymisque immobilis.——
Virgil's Æneid, Lib. 12. verse 398.

591. Till, swift emerging] This circumstance of the Hours' attending on the Sun, is an imitation of a passage in the 8th book of the Iliad, where those subaltern deities are described as waiting on Minerva; but I think they are introduced with greater propriety as attendants on the Sun.

597. The night succeeds] The best description of midnight I have ever met with is the following one of Tasso.

Era la notte all' or, ch' alto riposo
Ha l' onde, e i venti, e parca muto il mondo,
Gli animai lassi, e quei, che'l mar' ondoso,
O de liquidi laghi alberga il fondo,
E chi si giace in Tana, ò in Mandra ascoso,
E i pinti Augelli nel' oblio profondo
Sotto il silentio de' secreti Orrori
Sopian gli affanni, e raddolciano i cori.
Gier. Lib. Can. 2.

Meanwhile, involv'd in shades of deepest night,
The god of war renews his airy flight.
His rattling armour thunders o'er the sky,
The subject hills and vales in turns reply.
Where e'er he moves, he kindles vengeful fires,
And love of war, and thirst of blood inspires.
Stern wrath and rage adjust his coursers' manes,
And fear array'd in armour, guides the reins.
Commission'd by the god, before the car
Fame flies, and sounds aloud the charge of war;
And, by the breathing coursers wafted, springs
Aloft in air, and shakes her clatt'ring wings.
Oft premature the watchful goddess flies,
Feigns things undone, and mingles truth with lies.
For Mars, and his impatient charioteer
With goads provoke her, and the Scythian spear.
Thus when dismiss'd from their Æolian caves,
The winds invade the calm Ægean waves,
The lord of ocean follows; while around
The tumult thickens, and the deeps resound.
Then storms and show'rs collected from afar,
Enclose the god, and rage around his car.
Scarce can the Cyclades the shock sustain,
And Delos, fearing lest she float again,
Invokes the pow'r, by whose auspicious smiles
She stands connected with her sister-isles.
Now had the seventh Aurora chas'd the night,
And deck'd the courts of Jove with new-born light,
When old Adrastus from his couch arose,
And left his chamber, satiate with repose:
Revolving much within his lab'ring breast
The future war, and wrongs of either guest:
And doubtful, whether to pollute the peace,
And summon to his aid the states of Greece;
Or for a season bid his wrath subside,
And leave the fortune of the war untry'd.

605. Meanwhile, involv'd] The characteristic of Statius, as an heroic poet, is an amazing boldness in imagery and diction. To say he always reaches the pure sublime, would be running counter to the opinion of the best critics, and consequently presumptuous and dogmatical. But to affirm he never does, would be equally unjust and unreasonable. The present passage is of the mixed kind, and, at the same time that it borders upon fustian, is not wholly destitute of sublimity. I will only add, that the most celebrated instance of this kind in Homer or Virgil, when reduced to the standard of reason, will seem a pleasing extravagance, and elaborate piece of nonsense.

617. Oft premature] So Virgil,

Tam ficti pravique tenax, quam nuncia veri.
Æn. book 4. verse 188.

628. And Delos, fearing lest she float] I know not where this passage is better illustrated than in the following lines of Virgil:

Sacra mari colitur medio gratissima tellus
Nereidum matri, et Neptuno Ægeo;
Quam pius Arcitenens oras et littora circum
Errantem, Gyaro celsâ Myconeque revinxit,
Immotamque coli dedit, et contemnere ventos.
Æn. 3. v. 73.

631. Now had the seventh Aurora] Since Tydeus had returned from his embassy to the court of Thebes.

Much he debates: at length resolves to prove
The will of Heav'n, and ask advice of Jove.
Peace was his object, peace his sole delight,
While Argos with one voice demands the fight.
To the fam'd son of Oecleus, skill'd to read
Each doubtful omen, was the charge decreed:
With him Melampus shares the task assign'd,
Endu'd from Heav'n with a prophetic mind.
Such was their skill, 'twas difficult to say
Which shone most honour'd by the god of day,
Or in whose draught a larger portion flow'd
From Cyrrha, aidful to the gift bestow'd.
The victims fall, and first the chiefs explore
The reeking fibres, and o'erflowing gore:
Their hearts, with spots o'erspread, success deny'd,
And the veins threaten'd on the hostile side.
Nor thus discourag'd, did they yet despair,
But watch'd the wing'd inhabitants of air.
There stood a mountain known to vulgar fame,
Once sacred held, and Aphesus its name;
Whose craggy top the weary clouds sustains,
And from afar o'erlooks the distant plains.
Hence, fame reports, young Perseus wing'd his way,
And sought the regions of eternal day;
While Danaë survey'd with wild affright
The bold attempt, and scarce refrain'd from flight.
Hither each anxious seer retir'd in haste,
With olive-leaves, and snow-white chaplets grac'd;
What time pale winter flies the god of day,
And earth relenting feels the genial ray.
Oeclides first preferr'd his humble pray'r:
"O thou, whose thunder rends the clouded air;
Inspir'd by whom, each vagrant of the skies,
Fraught with advice to wretched mortals, flies;
Whose wings the bold inquirer's fate disclose;
And warn him of succeeding bliss or woes!
Not Cyrrha's cave with more unerring skill,
Unfolds the king of Heav'n's eternal will;

651. Or in whose draught] The antients had a notion, that every one who had attained to any degree of skill in divination, drank of this stream, which was consecrated to Apollo. Cyrrha was a mountain near Pindus, from which this celebrated stream descended with great rapidity.

655. Their hearts] The same prognostics happened, when the Romans consulted the gods concerning the event of the civil war between Cæsar and Pompey.

——Pallida tetris
Viscera tincta notis, gelidoque infecta cruore,
Plurimus asperso variabat sanguine livor.
Cernit tabe jecur madidum: venasque minaces
Hostili de parte videt.
Lucan, Phars. b. 1, v. 763.

666. And scarce refrain'd from flight] The poet has exhibited a very beautiful image of motherly affection in the behaviour of Danaë. When she saw her son attempting to fly, her anxiety for his safety was so great, that she almost resolved to spring from the rock and follow him; and could hardly be induced to relinquish her design, even after she had considered the danger of the attempt.

677. Not Cyrrha's cave] Cyrrha was a town situated at the foot of Parnassus, from whence the oracle of Apollo was delivered.

Nor the fam'd oaks, from whence the dark decrees
Of fate are heard, low-whisper'd in the breeze.
Ammon to them must yield the prophet's bays,
And Lycian lots resign their share of praise.
No more let Apis cheat his servile train,
Nor Branchus honour'd with a Lybian fane.
No more Arcadia's trembling swains adore
The shades of Pan, or his advice implore.
More skill'd is he, to whom propitious Jove
Declares his will in omens from above.
From whence, or when this honour sprung, is known
To thee, the sole omniscient cause, alone:
Dark and obscure its origin remains,
And still deludes the vain inquirer's pains.
But, whether Nature did this task impose,
When at a word the whole creation rose;
Whether, once men, they trod some hostile plain,
And in the form of birds reviv'd again;
Or their great distance from the world below,
And purer air, this useful art bestow:
May some unerring previous signs declare
Our fate and fortune in the dubious war!
If captive Thebes, her host and walls o'erthrown,
The lawful heir, her rightful lord shall own;
Let fav'ring thunders shake the distant spheres,
And birds with voice auspicious strike our ears:

679. Nor the fam'd oaks] The oaks of this place were said to be endowed with a voice and prophetic spirit; the priests, who gave answers, concealing themselves in those trees: a practice which the pious frauds of succeeding ages have rendered not improbable.

681. Ammon to them must yield] This famous oracle was situated in Lybia, between the greater and less Catabathmus, to the west of Egypt, in what is now called the desert of Barca. For a further and more particular account, see Lucan's Pharsalia, book 9.

683. No more let Apis] Apis was an Egyptian deity, worshipped in the shape of a bull.

684. Nor Branchus] The common report is, that Branchus was a Thessalian youth beloved by Apollo; in whose honour the god commanded a temple to be erected, and sacrifices to be offered.

685. No more Arcadia's] The divine honours that were paid to Pan in Arcadia, are known to every one who is versed in the classics; nay, their partiality was so great as to prefer him before all the other deities. Hence Virgil says;

Pan etiam, Arcadiâ mecum si judice certat,
Pan etiam, Arcadiâ se victum judice dicat.
Eclogue 5. verse 58.

695. Whether, once men] The doctrine of the metempsychosis was founded upon a supposition, that the souls of the deceased passed from one body to another. Pythagoras was author of this set of philosophers, affirming that his soul entered into the bodies of five different animals; and that he was first Euphorbus, 2d Pythagoras, 3d a peacock, 4th Homer, and 5th Ennius the Roman poet.

703. Let fav'ring thunders] The heathens, among many other superstitious notions, had this in particular: that thunder coming from the left portended the favour of the gods to those who saw it. Hence Virgil:

Vix ea fatus erat senior, subitoque fragore
Intonuit lævum. Æneid, Lib. 2. verse 692.

But, if the gods averse reject our vows,
And the proud tyrant's wrongful cause espouse,
Withhold those signs: and may the plumy race
In num'rous flocks obscure th' etherial space!"
Thus spoke the sage: and on the rock reclin'd,
To the same office other gods assign'd.
From thence he views a gath'ring mist arise,
Ravish the day, and blacken all the skies.
But when they had (by old example taught)
Fresh omens from the stars and ether sought;
Melampus cries: "No fav'ring birds of prey,
Nor tuneful songsters wing their airy way,
Float on the wind, or emulously strain
Their liquid throats, and cleave th' etherial plain.
No jetty raven, from Apollo sent,
Nor owl from Pallas favours our intent;
Nor dexter eagle, stooping from above,
Proclaims our int'rest with his master Jove.
Yet see, what legions, gath'ring from afar
In quest of prey, await the future war!
Here quiv'ring hawks, and hungry vultures fly,
And cloud with spreading wings th' obstructed sky.
There horrid screech-owls with portending flight,
And screamings dire profane the hallow'd light.
What then remains?—Shall these portents prevail,
And peace or war incline the doubtful scale?
Canst thou, O source of light, unmov'd, survey
Thy rays obscur'd, and violated day?"
While thus he spake, a sudden tumult springs
From clashing talons, and obstructed wings:
They clap their pinions, and with frantic rage
Strike their own breasts, and with themselves engage.
The chief subjoins:—"Oft have these eyes beheld
Dire omens, and my skill the cause reveal'd:
Yet never felt I this excess of fear,
Or did the stars more ominous appear;
Not even when I sought the Colchian shore,
With kings and demi-gods in days of yore.
To what I urg'd they listen'd and obey'd,
And fate confirm'd whate'er Melampus said:
Nor was the son of Phœbus sooner heard
Than I, or his advice to mine preferr'd.
But see, still greater prodigies await,
And free from further doubt the will of fate.
Unnumber'd swans, collected from afar,
In one firm body wedg'd, expect the war:
Whether stern Boreas hither urg'd their course,
Or Nile o'erflows its banks from ev'ry source.
The Thebans these, who shun the deathful field,
And hold their walls before them as a shield.
But see, exulting with the hopes of prey,
A troop of eagles hither wing their way.
These are th' Inachian chiefs, who seek renown
From captive Thebes, and threat the guilty town.
With open beaks, and levell'd claws they spring,
And all the war descends upon the wing.
Beneath each blow a snowy warrior dies,
And show'rs of blood and feathers quit the skies.
Yet see, the victors triumph but to fall;
And Jove descends, alike severe to all.
This, proudly soaring through forbidden ways,
Is burnt with scorching Sol's avenging rays.
That, daring with superior strength engage,
Falls the just victim of united rage.
Here one, entangled with his foe, expires:
This, safe in flight alone, from war retires.
Another chief, o'erwhelm'd with numbers, lies,
And with his sprinkled blood pollutes the skies.
This, though he scarce retains the vital breath,
Preys on his foe, and triumphs e'en in death."—
"But whence those secret tears, that stifled groan?
Too well, alas! the fatal cause is known.

727. There horrid screech-owls] The above-quoted author says,

> Solaque culminibus ferali carmine bubo
> Sæpe queri, et longas in fletum ducere voces.
> Book 4. v. 462.

747. But see, still greater prodigies] Statius has excelled his two poetical predecessors Homer and Virgil in the choice of an omen, and in the application of it to the thing portended, in a very eminent degree. By premising this observation, I have unluckily awakened the reader's attention, and drawn myself into an indispensable necessity of giving my opinion of this part in general. To say any thing of augury, farther than it concerns the present subject of our observation, would be entirely needless, as the reader may find it described at large in Kennet and Potter. I shall only remark therefore, that out of a very dry subject, Statius has made an entertaining and agreeable narration. The different deaths of the six heroes combined against Thebes, are finely imagined in those of the six eagles. But, as the propriety of the application cannot be so well illustrated without a previous comparison, I shall defer doing it till it occurs in the course of observation. The omen described by Virgil is in the 11th book of the Æneid; and that of Homer in the 12th of the Iliad.

765. This, proudly soaring] This was Capaneus, who was thunder-struck for attempting to scale the walls of Thebes, in defiance of Jupiter.

767. That, daring with superior strength] The hero here figured was Parthenopæus, who fell in a duel with Dryas, a chief of enormous size, and distinguished strength.

769. Here one, entangled] This was Polynices, who fell encountering with his brother.

770. This, safe in flight] Adrastus is alluded to here, who returned safe home to Argos.

771. Another chief, o'erwhelm'd] Hippomedon was drowned in the river Ismenos, in the pursuit of his enemies.

773. This, tho' he scarce retains] The poet here alludes to Tydeus, who in the very pangs of death is represented as gnawing the head of his enemy.

775. But whence those secret tears] This is the most beautiful stroke in the pathetic way that I ever met with in the course of my reading. When Melampus, who had been describing the different fates of the seven heroes from those of the seven eagles, had come to that of Amphiaraus, then present, instead of pursuing the application, he burst into tears. His friend observed him, and being conscious of the cause, chides him for endeavouring to hide it. I must own I was very anxious, and unable to guess how the poet would extricate himself from this embarrassment; but was agreeably surprised to find, that he had not only cleared himself with reputation, but made it one of the most beautiful passages in the whole work. This alone might be a confutation of that false criticism which some have fallen into, who affirm, that a poet ought only to connect the great

Thus shook the trembling chiefs beneath the weight
Of imag'd mischiefs, and portended fate.
Great was their grief while yet it lay conceal'd,
But greater when their fortune was reveal'd.
From whence, ye gods! does this impatience grow
Of prying into what we fear to know?
Since prescience doubles future miseries,
Till small ills swell to a gigantic size.
We deem as certain what's a doubtful doom,
And feel th' effects before the cause is come;
To learn, perhaps, how many years remain
Of life, or what the Fates and Jove ordain.
Nor are these seeds of grief and sorrow known
From Phœbe, fibres, birds, or stars alone:
But mysteries of magic are explor'd,
And breathless carcases to life restor'd.
Yet were these arts unknown in days of old,
When Time was seen to fly on wings of gold.
The gods reserv'd them for this impious age,
When conscience threatens their impending rage.
Our virtuous sires confin'd their harmless toil
To thin the woods, or break the stubborn soil.
The depths of fate involv'd in errours lie,
Impervious, and remote from mortal eye:
Those only, who have forfeited his love,
Explore the counsels of almighty Jove.
Hence falsehood, discontent, and impious rage,
Hence ev'ry vice that stains the present age."
Meanwhile Oeclides from his temple rends
The sacred crown, and from the mount descends:
He hears the clanging trumpets from afar,
And all the tumult of approaching war.
Nor, when he reach'd the town, did he resort
Among the crowd, or mingle with the court;
But, lurking in a darksome, lonely cell,
Suppress'd in silence what he fear'd to tell.
Melampus shame and private cares detain
Where Pan and Ceres share an equal reign.
Twelve days he loiter'd on the woody coast,
Then told the imag'd fate of either host.
The god of battles, eager to perform
His sire's commands, and raise the bloody storm,
Depopulates the towns, explores the plains,
And from their toils diverts the willing swains.
Headlong they rush, impatient for the fray,
Nor pleading nature gains a short delay;
Nor weeping wives their husbands could withhold,
Such was the love of war, and Theban gold.
No more their halls, bereft of hostile spoils,
Bear witness of their sires' victorious toils.
E'en, unconsenting, Jove himself resigns
The chariots that adorn'd his awful shrines.
They scour the rusty javelin, form impart
To mutilated swords, and point the dart.
Some grace with adamant their glowing breasts,
Or fit their brighten'd helms with waving crests;
While others bend with care the Cretan bow,
And train their steeds to charge or shun the foe.
Inverted ploughs, and scythes new-temper'd wear
Another form, and with fresh lustre glare.
For spears each sacred grove its branches yields,
And oxen bleed to cloathe the burnish'd shields.
They deluge Argos, and in crowds resort
To force their monarch, and insult the court.
War is their wish, and "Arms!" the gen'ral cry;
"Arms!" in return the vaulted roofs reply;
Loud as the surge, or bellowing Ætna roars,
When the stern giant shakes the neighb'ring shores;
A burning deluge issues from above,
And hurls its anger on the courts of Jove;
The swain with horrour eyes the less'ning main,
And the cleft mountain seems to join again.
But Capaneus, the vaunted pride of Greece,
Sighs for revenge, and loaths the short-liv'd peace.

and noble particulars in his paintings. But it is in the images of things, as in the characters of persons; where a small action, or even a small circumstance of an action, lets us more into the knowledge and comprehension of them, than the material parts themselves. Plutarch has sufficiently proved this, in his apology for relating the anecdote of Agesilaus's riding upon a long pole to please his children. Nor is this found in a history only, but in a picture likewise; where sometimes a small motion or turn of a finger will express the character and action of the figure more than all the other parts of the design.

781. From whence, ye gods] It has been observed by some critics, that these philosophical inquiries and moral reflections are very un-epic, and allowable only in dramatic poetry. The authors of this observation have reason on their side, and I am glad Statius is so seldom blameable on this head. Lucan is continually splitting upon this rock; but he is more excusable than an epic poet, since the chief objection made to it is, that it breaks off the connection requisite in the epopœia, and retards the catastrophe or solution of the epic knot.

825. No more their halls] The reader may be willing, perhaps, to compare this with the following passage of Virgil.

Ardet inexcita Ausonia atque immobilis ante.
Pars, leves clypeos et spicula lucida tergunt
Arvina pingui, subiguntque in cote secures;
Tegmina tuta cavant capitum, nectuntque salignas
Umbonum crates. Alii thoracas ahenos,
Aut leves ocreas lento ducunt argento.
Vomeris huc et falcis honos, huc omnis aratri
Cessit amor: recoquunt patrios fornacibus enses:
Æn. 7. v. 632.

and with this of Lucan:

Rupta quies populi, stratisque excita juventus
Diripiunt sacris affixa penatibus arma,
Quæ pax longa dabat, nudâ jam crate fluentes
Invadunt clypeos, curvataque cuspide pila,
Et scabros nigræ morsu rubiginis enses.
Phars. lib. 1.

843. Loud as the surge] The above quoted author has made use of this comparison.

Non sic Ætneis habitans in vallibus horret
Enceladus spirante noto, cum tota cavernas
Egerit, et torrens in campos defluit Ætna.

849. But Capaneus] The character of Capaneus is poetically good, and makes a considerable figure in the Thebaid. But if we look upon it in a moral light, we shall find it an assemblage of the brightest virtues and blackest vices; and they are both so blended together, that we can neither praise or disapprove either, without an opposition from the contrary quality. He has valour in a great degree, but it is intermixed with rashness. His constancy renders him impious, and his friendship barbarous. In short, this character is built on the same plan as the Mezentius of Virgil, and Argante

Such was his stature, Jove's enormous foes,
Nor Ætna's sons in height superior rose :
And such his might, the splendours of his birth
Were darken'd by his own intrinsic worth.
Yet he contemn'd the gods, nor knew to stay,
Where vengeance or ambition led the way;
But, prodigal of life, whene'er withstood,
Oft gave his own to spill another's blood.
Before the prophet's gate, amidst a crowd
Of mingled ranks, he thus exclaims aloud.
" Say, ye bold candidates for warlike praise,
From whence these abject fears, and vain delays?
What joy to boasting Thebes! What lasting shame,
That Argos, heedless of her former fame,
Dares not thro' pious awe unsheath the sword,
Till juggling priests and prophets give the word !
Should Sol himself, whom heartless slaves adore,
And Fame reports a god, exhaust his store
Of prodigies, and scare our Argive train ;
By all deserted, would I seek the plain.
This arm and weapon aid alone afford ;
These are the gods by Capaneus ador'd.
But should this dastard seer refuse to join
In combat, nor his fraudful arts resign ;
My javelin can revenge so base a part,
And free the soul that quivers in his heart."
Shouts of acclaim the list'ning vulgar raise,
And voice to voice resounds the warrior's praise.
At length Amphiaraus his silence broke,
And, rushing from his cavern, thus he spoke.
" From whence these vaunts, this impious waste of breath?
'Tis not from mortal arms I fear my death :
Nor sought I shelter here from destin'd fight,
Nor did thy threats restore me to the light.
Another fate o'erhangs my guiltless head,
And Jove shall rank me with the num'rous dead.
Inspiring Phœbus, and a patriot's cares
Have urg'd me to reveal what fate prepares.
Hear then, nor let in vain the god disclose;
But learn, advis'd, to shun impending woes.
From thee, alone, the slighted God withholds
His oracles, nor hast'ning fate unfolds.
But say, by what malicious furies driv'n,
You take up arms, as in contempt of Heav'n ?
Is life insipid, Argos hateful grown,
And Mars of all the gods ador'd alone ?
Can home no more attractive joys afford,
And shall these omens be in vain explor'd ?
Ah ! what avails it to have read the skies,
And watch'd the course of ev'ry bird that flies?
Far better had the kindly god conceal'd
The fatal horrours of the Theban field.
Ye sacred mysteries deriv'd from Jove !
Ye wing'd inhabitants of Heav'n above !
And thou, whose guiding influence I feel,
Be witness to the truths I now reveal !
In the blue vault, as in a volume spread,
Plain might the Argive destiny be read.
The weary sisters flag, and scarcely wield
The fatal shears, such carnage hides the field.
Dismiss your arms, resign your impious rage,
Nor rashly thus, with fates averse, engage.
May fibres err, and omens threat in vain ;
Nor Argive blood enrich the Theban plain !
But let us go : our ruin is decreed,
And Thebes and Argos fatally must bleed."
Thus far the chief: a rising groan supprest,
And in eternal darkness veil'd the rest.
When Capaneus : " Fly, son of Oecleus, fly,
Thy aid we need not, and thy threats defy.
Secure thyself in flight ; nor here suggest
Fears like thy own to ev'ry soldier's breast.
May birds and fibres still thy care employ,
And ease and homely pleasures be thy joy !
Yet unreveng'd shall valiant Tydeus bleed,
And Thebes in peace applaud the guilty deed ?
Do thou assert the royal exile's cause,
And prove the force of hospitable laws.
Those ensigns of Apollo will retard
Each hostile stroke, and claim a due regard.
Does Nature, subjected to magic laws,
Disclose to light each dark, mysterious cause ?
How easy are your gods, if pray'rs can move,
And gain admission to the courts of Jove !
Fear made them first: but whence this fond delight
To scatter terrours, and retard the fight ?
Hence while thou may'st ; nor, when the morning's beam
Shall strike upon our arms at Dirce's stream,
Presume our rage, and thirst of war to stay ;
Remember this our counsel, and obey :
Lest Phœbus mourn his helpless prophet slain,
And ensigns scatter'd on the Theban plain.
There Capaneus shall act an augur's part,
And rage amidst his foes with lifted dart."
Again loud peals of acclamation rise
From ev'ry mouth, and thunder to the skies.
As when a torrent swoln with vernal rains,
And melting snows, invades the subject plains,

of Tasso : yet he has more courage than the former, and more impiety than the latter of these heroes.

857. But, prodigal of life] Tasso makes the same observation of Argante.

> E la vendetta far tanto disia.
> Che sprezza i rischi, e le difese oblia.
>
> Canto 6. st. 45.

871. This arm and weapon] This is copied from the blasphemous invocation of Mezentius.

> Dextra mihi deus et telum quod missile libro
> Nunc adsint.——
>
> Æneid. lib. 10. verse 773

919. When Capaneus] This speech of Capaneus has a great deal of spirit, humour, and sarcasm; and lets us more into the character of its author, than any hitherto has done. He is a person that cannot hearken to reason, unless agreeable to his own inclinations; and his prejudice carries him so far as to make him laugh at the noblest arts, and even the gods themselves, only because they are obstructions to his desire of waging war with Thebes. The effects of his oration are such as we may see every day in common life; where the aggressor frequently has the laugh, though his antagonist has perhaps reason on his side.

947. As when a torrent] It is doubtful whether this comparison is to be applied to the noise of the shouting Argives, or to the closing of the dispute by the interposition of night; as the poet might say with equal propriety, that the shouts of the army were as loud as the noise of a rushing torrent ; or that night closed the debate in the same manner as an eminence stops the course of an inundation. The reader, therefore, must please his

Thro' ruin'd moles the victor-wave resounds,
O'erwhelms the bridge, and bursts the lofty mounds:
Cots, herds, and trembling swains are borne away,
And hurried on with unresisted sway;
Till, bounded by some hill, it shifts its course,
And, rushing backward, seeks its distant source.
Meanwhile the Sun to western deeps retir'd,
And with his light the stern debate expir'd.
But fair Argia, steep'd in sorrow, shares
A more than half of all her husband's cares.
Impatient to divulge her grief, she rose,
And sought the royal mansions of repose.
Abandon'd to the wind her tresses fly;
Grief pal'd her cheeks, and dull'd her sparkling eye.
Thessander in her soft embraces press'd,
(Her only hope) hung smiling at her breast.
What time the Bear, of all the starry train
Alone surviving, shuns the western main,
She reach'd her sire, and, on his knees reclin'd
Thus vents the secret purpose of her mind.
" Of what avail are words to you, who know
The source and origin of all my woe?
Say, is it doubted, why I bend my course
To you, my sire, my friend, my sole resource?
Yet Heav'n attest, the silent lamp of night,
And stars alone were conscious of my flight.
Alas! nor ease, nor quiet have I known,
(But shar'd in grief and sorrows not my own,)
Since Hymen's tapers shone at your command,
And this young prince receiv'd my plighted hand.
Pangs keen as those which break my nightly rest,
Might pierce a rock, or tiger's ruthless breast.
Now on the verge of endless woe I stand,
And own no help but from thy saving hand:
Assent to war, nor let thy son bemoan
The ravish'd empire due to him alone.
But, if these tears thy pity fail to move,
Regard this infant-pledge of mutual love.
How will his foes deride his lowly birth,
And make his woes the object of their mirth!
Yet was his sire the prince, who (Phœbus said)
Should share thy scepter, and Argia's bed.
Nor was I led astray by love's delights,
Or lawless Hymen present at the rites;
But mindful e'er of what thou didst enjoin,
I taught my heart to know no choice but thine.
Say, can I freeze, when he for vengeance glows,
Or wish to smile, exempt from social woes?
The fears and cares of love, alas! are known
To those, whom fortune dooms to feel, alone.
Yet such the object of this harsh request,
I dread the grant, and what I ask, detest;
And, when the trumpet sounds the last adieu,
And the dear object lessens to my view;
I yet may wish, but then must wish in vain,
The circling moments could revolve again."
The monarch, rising, on her cheeks imprest
A tender kiss, and thus the fair addrest.
" Dismiss thy fears: e'en envy must approve
Thy just petition, and excess of love.
The threat'ning gods my lab'ring breast divide,
And bid each impulse of revenge subside.
Yet fair Argia shall not sue in vain,
Nor her brave spouse without redress complain.
Be this his solace, that this short delay
Tends to secure the fortune of the fray."
The pausing monarch from his couch arose,
And quits the silent mansions of repose;
For now Aurora, clad in eastern spoils,
Renews at once the light, and mortal toils.

BOOK IV.

THE ARGUMENT.

Adrastus having given his consent to the war, the allied army is drawn up in form of battle. They

---

own fancy, and apply it where he thinks it most applicable. I believe it will not be disagreeable to see how other poets have acquitted themselves on this subject. The reader may judge between them.

Θυνε γαρ αμπεδιον ποταμω πληθοντι εοικως
Χειμαρρω, ος τ' ωκα ρεων εκεδασσε γεφυρας·
Τονδ' ουτ' αρ τε γεφυραι εεργμεναι ισχανοωσιν,
Ουτ' αρα ερκεα ισχει αλωαων εριθηλεων,
Ελθοντ' εξαπινης οτ' επιβριση Διος ομβρος,
Πολλα δ' υπ' αυτου εργα κατηριπε καλ αιζηων.

Iliad. lib. 5.

Non sic aggeribus ruptis cum spumeus amnis
Exiit, oppositasque evicit gurgite moles,
Fertur in arva furens cumulo, camposque per omnes
Cum stabulis armenta trahit.—— Æneid. lib. 2.

Sic pleno Padus ore tumens super aggere tutas
Excurrit ripas, et totos concutit agros.
Succubuit si qua tellus, cumulumque furentem
Undarum passura ruit: tum flumine toto
Transit, et ignotos aperit sibi gurgite campos.
Illos terra fugit dominos: his rura colonis
Accedunt, donante Pado.——

Lucan Phar. book 6. ver. 276.

They are all four extremely beautiful, and have their admirers, and, unless I err very much in point of judgment, they do not appear here to the disadvantage of Statius.

965. What time the Bear, &c.] Statius is guilty of the same astronomical mistake, as his two predecessors Homer and Virgil; who both in their verses represent the Bear as the only constellation which never bathed itself in the ocean, that is to say, that did not set, and was always visible; whereas this is common to other constellations of the arctic circle; as, the Lesser Bear, the Dragon, the greatest part of Cepheus, &c. For my part, I esteem this mistake of so little consequence in a poet, that I shall not trouble the reader with a vindication, but refer him to that of Homer, by Mr. Pope. See note on verse 566 of the 18th book of the Iliad.

987. How will his foes] As being the son of an exile.

The poet in this oration does not seem to have thoroughly entered into the spirit of the cause, or kept the motives to this address sufficiently in his eye; at least I should have been inclined to have put another construction on it, and to have concluded it rather the effect of pride and ambition, than of disinterestedness and humanity, if I had not recollected that Argia was put to death by Creon, for burying her husband contrary to orders. The motives she alleges seem to be a mere feint; and indeed it is improbable that a tender wife and affectionate daughter should desire her husband and father to hazard their lives for a petty sovereignty, when the former of these relations was heir to a much larger, as Polynices was to Adrastus.

begin their march to Thebes. Eriphyle, by the acceptance of a present from Argia, lays her husband under an obligation of joining the confederates. Parthenopæus elopes during his mother's absence, and heads the Arcadian troops. She follows him, but to no effect. The priestess of Bacchus, inspired with a spirit of divination, runs up and down the city, and foretels the death of the two Theban princes, with the usurpation of the kingdom by Creon. Several prodigies happen. At length, Eteocles, alarmed at the invasion of his territories, consults with Tiresias the prophet, concerning the fate of the war. They go through a course of necromancy, and conjure up the spirit of Laius, whose ambiguous answer determines them to oppose the invaders in a hostile manner. Bacchus in his return from Thrace, meets the Argives in their route to Thebes. He leads them out of their way, and persuades the nymphs to dry up all the rivers and fountains under their care. The allies, half dead with thirst, are met by a Lemnian princess, who informs them of the river Langia, and conducts them thither. They offer up a prayer to the tutelar genius of the river, which concludes the book.

THRICE had Hyperion either tropic view'd,
The winter banish'd, and the spring renew'd;
When now the sprightly trumpet from afar
Gave the dread signal of approaching war.
When fierce Bellona, sent by Jove's command,
(The torch of discord blazing in her hand)
Bar'd her red arm from fair Larissa's height,
And whirl'd her spear, a prelude to the fight.
Whizzing it cleaves the skies: near Dirce's source
A rising hillock bounds its furious course.
Thence to the glitt'ring camp the goddess flies,
And darts from rank to rank her ardent eyes:
She strokes the steeds, and arms the warriors' hands,
The truly brave prevent her stern commands,
And e'en the coward loaths the thought of flight,
And feels a short-liv'd ardour for the fight.
The destin'd day serenely shone above,
And first a victim falls to Mars and Jove.
The trembling priest a cheerful aspect wears,
Nor to th' inquiring troops imparts his fears.
Meanwhile their friends indulge a parting view,
And press around to share the last adieu.
No bounds the gushing stream of sorrow knows;
From rank to rank the soft contagion grows:
Each pregnant eye unwonted currents pours,
Their bucklers intercept the falling show'rs.
Some through their helms a fervent kiss impart,
And nature triumphs o'er each soften'd heart.
No more the thirst of war and vengeance burns,
But exil'd tenderness in all returns.
Thus when, the storm appeas'd, a rising breeze
Invites the mariner to tempt the seas,
Their weeping friends the parting crew detain,
And for a while subsides the love of gain.
With streaming eyes, and hand fast lock'd in hand,
They put off fate, and linger on the strand.
But, when the vessel cleaves the yielding deep,
The mourners posted on some neighb'ring steep,
With eager eyes pursue the less'ning sails,
And curse the driving impulse of the gales.
Assist, O Fame! in whose immortal page
The glorious toils of ev'ry distant age
Recorded shine; to whose all-seeing eyes
Nor Heav'n, or Earth, or Hell impervious lies.
And thou, Calliope, deriv'd from Jove,
Whose music warbles in th' Aonian grove,
From whom alone heroic ardour springs,
Be present, and awake the trembling strings:
Relate, what chiefs, in quest of warlike fame,
And fir'd by Mars, to aid Adrastus came.
Surcharg'd with troubles, and a length of years,
Encircled by his host, the king appears.
A sword alone for ornament he wore,
His slaves behind the pond'rous armour bore.
Beneath the gate his fiery coursers stand;
And, while the groom divides with artful hand
His flowing mane, reluctant to the car
Arion bounds, and hopes the promis'd war.
For him Larissa arms her martial pow'rs,
And fair Prosymna grac'd with rising tow'rs.

The poet has exerted himself in a very eminent degree at the opening of this book. He awakens the reader's curiosity, and sounds an alarm to the approaching conflict. The influence of discord over the brave man and the coward is finely distinguished, and contributes to heighten the majesty of this description.

41. Assist, O Fame] It is hard to conceive any address more solemn, any opening to a subject more noble and magnificent than this invocation. The hint of it is taken from Homer, though the invocation itself is varied, as may be seen from comparing them together.

Ἔσπετε νῦν μοι Μοῦσαι ὀλύμπια δώματ᾽ ἔχουσαι·
(Ὑμεῖς γὰρ διαί εστε πάρεστέ τε, ἴστέ τε πάντα,
Ημεῖς δὲ κλέος οἶον ἀκούομεν οὐδέ τι ἴδμεν.)
Οἵτινες ἡγεμόν ες Δαναῶν, καὶ κοίρανοι ἦσαν.
Πληθὺν δ᾽ οὐκ ἂν ἐγω μυθησομαι, ᾽ουδ᾽ ὀνομηνω,
Οὐδ᾽ εἴ μοι δέκα μὲν γλῶσσαι, δέκα δὲ στόματ᾽ εἶεν.
Φωνη δ᾽ ἄρρηκτος, χάλκεον δέ μοι ἦτορ ἐνείη,
Εἰ μὴ ᾽Ολυμπιάδες μοῦσαι, Διὸς αἰγιόχοιο
Θυγατέρες, μνησαίαθ᾽ ὅσοι ὑπὸ Ἴλιον ηλθον.

Virgil has imitated it, but with little success.

Pandite nunc Helicona, deæ, cantusque movete:
Qui bello exciti reges: quæ quemque secutæ
Complerint campos acies; quibus Itala jam tum
Floruerit terra alma viris, quibus arserit armis.
Et meministis enim, divæ, et memorare potestis:
Ad nox vix tenuis famæ perlabitur aura.
Æn. 7. ver. 64.

And Tasso with some improvement.

Mente de gli anni, e del' oblio nemica,
  Delle cose custode, e dispensiera,
Vaglia mi tua ragion sì, ch'io ridica
  Di quel campo ogni duce, ed ogni schiera.
Suoni, e risplenda la lor fama antica,
  Fatta dagli anni omai tacita, e nera:
Tolto da' tuoi tefori orni mia lingua
  Cio, ch' ascolti ogni età, nulla l'estingua.
G. c. 1. st. 36.

59. For him Larissa, &c.] I think myself obliged to make a few observations on the nature of catalogues, as they have been objected to by some literati, who have delivered their critical remarks to the world with some success. To consider it then as purely poetical, (for this is all that merits our notice) we may observe first, what an air of probability is spread over the whole poem, by

To these the youth of Midea succeed,
And Phyllos, famous for her fleecy breed;
Then fair Cleone sends a valiant train,
And lowly Neris, o'er whose fertile plain
The swift Charadros rolls his rapid flood,
And Thyre, doom'd to float in Spartan blood.
From Drepanos, for snowy cliffs renown'd,
And Sicyon, with groves of olives crown'd,
A troop of grateful warriors bend their way,
Where once Adrastus held the regal sway,
Where slow Langia bathes the silent shores,
And, winding in his course, Elissos roars.
Here oft repair from Pluto's gloomy courts
The sister-furies (ancient fame reports)
While, bending o'er the brink, the serpents slake
Their thirst, and of the grateful stream partake.
But, whether these o'erturn'd the Theban state,
Or at Mycenæ kindled stern debate,
Elissos flies from the detested brood,
Such venom stains the surface of his flood.
From Ephyre a tide of warriors flows,
Who kindly bore a part in Ino's woes,
Where to the hoofs of the Gorgonean horse
A springing fountain owes its mystic source,
And the firm isthmus hears on either side
The diff'rent murmurs of the rushing tide.
From hence attend Adrastus to the fray
Three thousand warriors rang'd in bright array.
From distant lands they sought the field of fame,
Varying in manners, origin, and name.
Some knotty clubs, in fire attemper'd, bear,
While some dismiss the quiv'ring lance in air.
These ply the sounding sling with fatal art,
And rival e'en the Parthian's venom'd dart.
Amid the throng Adrastus takes his way,
Rever'd for age, but more for gentle sway.
Thus some old bull, the monarch of the meads,
His subject herd around the pasture leads.

the particularising of every nation concerned in this war. Secondly, what an entertaining scene is presented to us, of so many countries drawn in their natural colours, while we wander along with the poet amidst a beautiful variety of towns, havens, forests, groves, mountains, and rivers; and are perpetually amused with his observations on the different soils, products, situations, prospects, or with historical anecdotes, relative to the country, army, or their commanders. And lastly, there has been scarce any epic writer, but has drawn up one, which is at least a proof how beautiful it has been esteemed by the greatest geniuses in all ages. Homer gave the hint, and was followed by Virgil, Statius, Tasso, Spenser, and Milton.

83. Where to the hoofs] The fountain Hippocrene is reported to have sprung from a stroke of Pegasus's hoofs, as the etymology of the word sufficiently demonstrates; ἱππος signifying a horse, and κρηνη, a fountain.

97. Thus some old bull] This fine simile brings to my mind an equally fine one of Lucan, where he compares Pompey to an old oak: the application is obviously the same as this, though the comparison itself is not taken from the same object.

Qualis frugifero quercus sublimis in agro
Exuvias veteres populi, sacrataque gestans
Dona ducum: nec jam validis radicibus hærens,
Pondere fixa suo est: nudosque per aëra ramos

Though, spent with age, and long disus'd to fight,
His reign depends on antiquated might,
The youthful steers, without reluctance, yield
Their share of sway, nor dare dispute the field:
Such furrows on his breast, and graceful scars
Appear, the monuments of former wars.
The Theban hero, full of youthful fire,
Rode in the rank, and next his aged sire.
Beneath his standard rang'd, a valiant band
From fair Bœotia threat their native land.
Some, still impress'd with sentiments of love,
And loyalty, to fight his battles move:
While others prone to change, and to repine,
In quest of novelty, his army join.
Yet more: three wealthy cities own his sway,
And, from the father's gift, the son obey;
Whose youths embodied might increase his host,
And be some solace for his empire lost.
Such was his habit, and the same his arms,
As when he first beheld Argia's charms.
A lion's spoils across his back he wore,
And in his hand two beamy javelins bore.
The sphinx, pourtray'd, his deathful falchion grac'd,
A golden sheath the shining blade encas'd.
His mother, sisters, all that once were dear,
Rush to his thoughts, and force a tender tear.
In prospect he surveys the reign his own,
And swells on an imaginary throne.
Meanwhile, Argia from a neighb'ring tow'r,
Recalls his eyes from visionary pow'r;
The dearer object scorns an equal part
With Thebes, and claims an undivided heart.
Next joyful Tydeus joins the marching host
With troops collected on Ætolia's coast.
The trumpet sounds: he trembles with delight,
And pants, and starts, impatient for the fight.
So shines, renew'd in youthful pride, the snake,
When spring recalls him from the thorny brake,
He views with scorn the vain attacks of age,
And glows, and stiffens with collected rage.
Now rising on his spires he braves the day,
And glitters with the Sun's reflected ray:
Or, by the fatal aid of kindred green,
Amidst the grassy verdure lurks unseen.
Hapless the swain! whom near him fortune draws,
When flaming thirst dilates his venom'd jaws.
Pylene's warriors in his cause engage,
And Pleuron, conscious of Althea's rage;
They pour from Caledon's impending steep,
From Chalcis, beaten by the rolling deep,
And Olenos which boasts the birth of Jove,
Nor yields in fame to Cretan Ida's grove.

Effundens, trunco, non frondibus efficit umbram:
At quamvis primo nutet casura sub Euro,
Tot circum silvæ firmo se robore tollunt,
Sola tamen colitur.—— Pharsal. book 1.

135. So shines, renew'd] This is taken from Virgil's Æneid, book 2.

Qualis ubi in lucem coluber, mala gramina pastus,
Frigida sub terrâ tumidum quem bruma tegebat,
Nunc positis novus exuviis, nitidusque juventâ,
Lubrica convolvit sublato pectore terga
Arduus ad solem, et linguis micat ore trisulcis.

I think Statius (as every imitator should do) has improved on his original. His language is more elevated than Virgil's, and he has manifestly the advantage in inserting the two last lines, as they reflect the highest honour on Tydeus.

From Achelous some direct their course,
A stream still mindful of Herculean force.
No more, emerging from his pearly bed,
Above th' encircling waves he rears his head,
But, lurking in his azure caves, deplores
His dusty margin and exhausted shores.
A troop, selected for his guard, surrounds
The chief, distain'd with honourable wounds.
They twine young sallows to support the shield,
And in each hand a pointed javelin wield.
Mars, imag'd on their glitt'ring helms, inspires
Unwearied rage and unextinguish'd fires.
Such was the Theban's, such th' Ætolian's rage,
'Twas doubtful in whose cause the chiefs engage
Beneath a youth, as yet unknown to fame,
The Doric troops, a num'rous army, came,
With those who labour where Lyrceus leads
His copious stream along the fertile meads;
Or till with care the hoarse-resounding shores,
Where Inachus, the king of rivers, roars.
Of all, that o'er Argia bend their course,
He reigns, excell'd by none in rapid force,
When Taurus, and the wat'ry Pleiades rise,
And Jove in kindly show'rs deserts the skies.
To these succeed, whom swift Asterion laves,
And Erasine enfolds with ambient waves;
Whom Epidaure's impervious walls surround,
And Dyme, with the gifts of Bacchus crown'd.
Of Pylian youths a martial squadron came,
Tho' Pylos then could boast of little fame;
And Nestor, blooming in his second age,
Declin'd the charge, and check'd his youthful rage.
Hippomedon, their hardy chief, inspires
The love of war, and with example fires.
A triple crest his dazzling helmet grac'd,
An iron coat of mail his sides embrac'd.
A golden cuirass blazes on his breast,
With all the guilt of Danaus exprest:
The Furies light, with inauspicious hands,
The bridal torch, and tie the nuptial bands:
Their sire each instrument of wrath supplies,
And views the treach'rous swords with curious eyes.
The graceful hero rein'd a gen'rous steed,
New to the fight, and of Nemæan breed.
From earth emerging, clouds of dust arise
Beneath their rapid course, and veil the skies.
So, when Hyleus from some mountain's height,
Or hollow cliff, precipitates his flight,
The bending forests to the shock give way,
Stretch'd in long ruin, and expos'd to day.
The trembling cattle headlong seek the ground,
And Ossa shudders at the distant sound.
With horrour e'en his shaggy brethren hear
The rushing monster, nor dismiss their fear;
While Peneus' waves, suspended in their course,
Roll backward, hopeless to withstand his force.
Who to describe their numbers can aspire,
Or equal martial with Phœbean fire?
The great Alcides drains Tyrinthe's coast
Of all her youths, to form a scanty host.
Tyrinthe still the sword with glory wields,
And warriors worthy of her patron yields;
But love of glory, and a wealthy soil,
Have made them more averse to martial toil.
Few human footsteps in the fields descry'd,
The curious traveller scarce finds a guide,
To lead him where the moss-grown turret stands,
And walls, the labour of Ætnean hands.
Yet hence three hundred youths to fight repair,
Nor swords, nor sounding slings employ their care:
Each show'd, like Hercules, in savage pride,
And on his shoulders wore a lion's hide.
Their spear a trunk of pine, a quiver hung
Behind, and clatter'd as they march'd along.
They sing a Pæan in their patron's praise,
And in sonorous verse his labours raise.
With joy the god from shaded Oeta's height
Hears his immortal feats, and varied fight.
From Nemea next a social squadron came,
And where Molorchus, crown'd with endless fame,
Receiv'd the warrior, spent with recent toils,
And loaded with the monster's reeking spoils.
The straw-built mansion, and adjacent field,
With art are imag'd on each brazen shield,
The sacred oak reported to sustain
His bow unstrung, and where he press'd the plain.
But Capaneus, averse to guide the car,
On foot o'erlook'd the plain, and moving war.
A shield he bore with four thick folds o'ercast
Of tough bull-hides, of solid brass the last.
Here Vulcan frees the hydra's vital breath,
And opes each secret avenue to death;
The concave snakes, in silver carv'd, enfold,
While others seem to burn in mimic gold.
Around its iron margin Lerna leads
Her azure stream, and mingles with the meads.

151. From Achelous] Achelous contended with Hercules for the nymph Dejanira; and being overcome in a duel, was transformed into a river.

163. Such was the Theban's] It is very observable how Tydeus rises in the reader's esteem, as the poem advances. It opens with many circumstances very much to the disadvantage of his character; especially the conflict between him and Polynices: but in the second book we find him undertaking an embassy to Thebes, and endangering his life in his rival's cause: in the third book he returns covered with wounds, and yet is willing to hazard himself again, because his friend's interest required it, as he imagined; but in the fourth, he is represented at the head of his troops, breathing revenge against the Thebans, and as eager as Polynices himself, whose concern in the war was personal.

197. So, when Hyleus] Hyleus was a centaur. This is one of the noblest similes in all Statius, and the most justly corresponding in its circumstances to the thing described. The diction is lofty, the images striking, and the application obviously proper and agreeable to the subject. The version, however short it falls of the original, may be sufficient to show there was an endeavour at least to imitate it.

218. The labour of Ætnean hands] Tyrinthe is reported to have been built by the Cyclops.

237. But Capaneus] The poet ushers in Capaneus with abundance of pomp: his strength, his size, his tower-like shield, in a word, his whole figure strikes our eyes in all the strongest colours of poetry. He forces him on the observation of the reader by the grandeur of his description; and raises our expectations of him, intending to make him perform many remarkable actions in the sequel of the poem, and to become worthy of falling by the hand of Jove himself. This anecdote concerning his spear is taken from Homer, and intended to raise the idea of his hero, by giving him such as no other could wield.

His shining breast-plate was a mingled mass
Of ductile gold, and rows of mountain-brass.
Dreadful it gleam'd around : no female art
Could to the pond'rous metal form impart.
A giant on his helmet frowns imprest,
And triple were the honours of his crest.
His cypress-spear with steel encircled shone,
Not to be pois'd but by his hands alone.
Ithome's mountaineers beneath his care,
And the Messenians to the fight repair;
Where Thrion, and the craggy Æpy show
Their cliffs above, and Pteleon's walls below.
From Helos, famous for her gen'rous race
Of steeds, and Dorion, for the bard's disgrace,
They rush.—Here Thamyris in singing strove
To match the tuneful progeny of Jove:
Unskill'd to judge the future by the past,
He prov'd the Muse's matchless pow'r at last.
To silence doom'd, no more he durst aspire
To raise his voice, or string the vanquish'd lyre.
Constrain'd by threats, or with entreaties won,
The prophet seeks the fate he cannot shun.
Nor yet was prescience wanting to the deed,
Full well he saw what destiny decreed :
But Phœbus, hopeless to prolong his date,
Withholds his succour, and assents to fate.
Yet more—unmindful of the late portent,
His spouse accelerates the dire event,
And, swell'd with pride and vain ambition, sold
Her husband's life for all-bewitching gold.
Argia saw the matron's guilty views,
And that the Fates forbad her to refuse;
Then unrepining, from her snowy breast
She loos'd the gift, and thus her will exprest.
" These woeful times far other cares require
Than those of costly dress and rich attire.
No more shall art enhance Argia's charms,
While her dear consort sheaths his limbs in arms;
Awhile without reluctance I resign
Those trifles, since for him alone I shine:
Awhile the arts of Pallas shall employ
The pensive hours, and sorrow be my joy.

249. No female art] Statius alludes here to a custom among the ancient heathens, of mothers making this species of armour for their sons.

261. Here Thamyris] I am surprised, that Statius, who generally strikes out of the common track, should be such a plagiary as to relate this after Homer ; and more so, that he was so diffident of his own abilities as to copy it so closely. The words are nearly the same.

——— Δώριον, ἔνθα τε Μοῦσαι
Αντόμεναι, Θάμυριν τον Θρήϊκα παῦσαν ἀοιδῆς,
Οἰχαλίηθεν ἰόντα παρ' Εὐρύτου Οἰχαλιῆος.
Στεῦτο γὰρ εὐχόμενος νικησέμεν, εἴπερ ἂν αὐταὶ
Μοῦσαι ἀείδοιεν, κοῦραι Διὸς αἰγιόχοιο.
Αιδε χολωσαμεναι, πηρὸν θέσαν, αὐτὰρ ἀοιδὴν
Θεσπεσίην ἀφελοντο, καὶ ἐκλελαθον κίθαριστύν.
Lib. 2. v. 101. catal.

286. Since for him] This conduct of Argia, however laudable it is in itself, would be esteemed an unnecessary act of politeness by our modern belles, who are generally careless and indifferent how they appear at home, but never think themselves sufficiently decorated for the public view, as if their husbands had the least claim to their care of their persons and dress. But methinks it is highly indiscreet in them to lose the good graces of their husbands in hopes of extending their conquests :

Awhile a suppliant to the gods I'll mourn,
And weary Heav'n with vows for his return.
A greater lustre will each jewel yield,
When, crown'd with laurels from the Theban field,
My spouse shall hail me partner of his reign,
And votive choirs attend the crowded fane.
Then to my sister let it be convey'd,
If this will gain her husband's social aid."
Hence treason, murder, frenzy, all the woes
That shook the augur's guilty dome, arose.
Tisiphone with secret pleasure smiles
At her ripe project, and successful wiles.
Four rapid coursers grace the prophet's car,
Of heav'nly race, and thunder thro' the war.
From Leda's son he stole the matchless breed
By mortal mares, unequal to the steed.
Parnassian wreaths upon his forehead shone,
And by his habit was the prophet known.
Green olive-leaves his glitt'ring helm enclose,
And from between his crests a mitre rose.
A grove of spears his better hand sustains,
His other moderates the flowing reins.
Afar he shines, conspicuous in the field,
And waves the Python imag'd on his shield.
A troop of Pylian youths surround his car,
And Amyclæans, partners in the war.
From Malea's noted shore a squadron came,
And Caria, sacred to Diana's name;
From fair Eurotas, crown'd with olive-groves,
And Messe, famous for her silver doves.
Him, as their chief, a hardy race attend,
Whom Taygetus and hilly Pharis send :
Cyllenius trains them in the dusty field
To war, and breathes a soul untaught to yield.
Hence they no cares for this frail being feel,
But rush undaunted on the pointed steel.
The parents glory in their offspring's death,
And urge them to resign their vital breath :
Of all that crowd around the fun'ral pile,
The mother is observ'd alone to smile.
A pair of javelins arms their better hand,
The reins and stubborn steed the left demand.
Bare are their shoulders; floating from behind
A shaggy tunic dances in the wind.
The swan resigns the honours of his breast,
To grace their helms, and form a rising crest.
Nor did these march alone beneath his care,
But social Elis adds an equal share.
Alpheus next affords his Pisa's aid,
Who seeks thro' seas the lov'd Sicilian maid.
Their chariots hide the plain. Their horses feel,
Instead of spurs, the dart and pointed steel.
From horrid rites their present skill arose,
And to an impious source its progress owes:

as it would be deemed folly in a king to go in quest of new countries, before he had secured to himself the possession of those already acquired.

315. From Malea's] Malea was a promontory of Peloponnesus, noted for its dangerous rocks: it is situated between the bays of Argos and Laconia, and is now called Capo Malio di Santo Angelo.

337. So Lucan.

——populisque per æquora mittens
Sicaniis Alpheus aquas. Book 3. ver. 176.

341. From horrid rites] For an account of this custom, and Oenomaus, see note on the first book, verse 382.

What time Oenomaus, from his car o'erthrown,
Resigned at once his life, his fame and crown.
Their coursers champ the bit, or paw the ground,
And scatter clouds of smoke and foam around.
Parthenopæus next, by stealth repairs
To Argos, and eludes his mother's cares.
As yet a beardless youth, the troops he led,
And shone in arms, conspicuous at their head.
Chance aids his flight: for while the matron roves
Thro' distant tracts of land, and shadowy groves,
The daring youth, impell'd by adverse fates,
O'erleap'd the wall, and forc'd the palace-gates.
In form and feature ev'ry son of fame
Resigned the prize, nor durst dispute his claim.
Nor had his courage, and desert in arms
Been deem'd inferior to his outward charms,
But death o'ertook him, ere the rip'ning sun
Of manhood on his budding strength had shone.
His beauty fir'd each guardian of the grove,
The gods with envy, and the nymphs with love.
Fame tells, Diana, when she first survey'd
The little wanton sporting in the shade,
Forgave his mother's flame, and broken vow,
And grac'd him with a quiver and a bow.
He springs, impatient for the mix'd alarms
Of shrilling clarions, and resounding arms,
And burns to mingle in the dusty course
Of crimson war, and curb a captive horse.
No more he joys to range the guiltless wood
With arrows, innocent of human blood.
Above the rest he shines in flaming gold,
And Tyrian purple, glorious to behold.
His mother's combats in the Ætolian field
He bears engrav'd upon his slender shield.
A quiver, fraught with Gnossian shafts, he bore,
Of amber fram'd, with jaspers studded o'er.
A lynx's spotted hide adorns his steed,
Which match'd the stag or western wind in speed.
With pride he bounds beneath th' unwonted load
Of gleaming armour, fit to grace a God.
His master smiles: the roses on his cheek,
And youthful bloom his tender age bespeak.
To him th' Arcadian youths with joy resign
The chief command, and clad in armour shine.
Fame says, from op'ning trees they took their birth,
When human footsteps seal'd the new-born earth;
And flourish'd ere revolving Cynthia shone,
Or devious planets gleam'd around her throne.
No houses then repell'd the driving rain,
Nor Ceres glitter'd on the yellow plain;
No temples lodg'd the sculptur'd form of Jove,
Nor Hymen sanctified the flames of love.
Oft did the pregnant oak its sides unclose,
Nor ask'd Lucina's hand to ease its throes.

347. Parthenopæus] Tasso seems to have copied his account of Rinaldo's flight from this of Parthenopæus.

All'or (nè pur tre lustri avea finiti)
  Fuggì soletto, e corse strade ignote;
Varcò l'Egeo, passò di Grecia i liti,
  Giunse nel campo in region remote;
Nobilissima fuga, e che l' imiti
  Ben degna alcun magnanimo nipote.
Tre anni son, ch' è in guerra, e intempestiva
Molle piuma del mento à pena usciva. Canto 1.

As we have now seen the seven heroes armed and accoutred for battle, it will be worth while to take a critical review of them, and see how the poet has acquitted himself in the description. Though I cannot answer for the different tastes of readers, yet I flatter myself with the hopes of their approbation, with respect to the author. The chief beauty here is variety, without which all the subaltern decorations of imagery, diction, and numbers, are entirely lost, as they are common to other parts of the poem. To discover this in his characters, we need only to review them distinctly; and we shall find that of Adrastus to be no other than we can expect in a man of his years and inclinations. Exclusive of the cares for his people, old age naturally creates an aversion to war, as it is so diametrically opposite to their *summum bonum*, tranquillity. Polynices, though by no means a coward, seems to like the war no farther than as it is conducive to his interest, and the nstrument of gratifying his ambition. The love of glory, abstracted from that of empire, seems to have but little influence over him; but, when united with it, inspirits him to the highest degree of heroism. Tydeus, subject as he seems to be to the impressions of glory and fame, confides more in the justice of his cause, than any other motive. As he has no personal interest in the war, his inclination to it must arise either from the thirst of glory or desire of revenge: as to the first, we may conclude, from the whole tenour of his conduct, that it could not engage him in supporting injustice, since his attachment to Polynices was owing to his love of the opposite virtue: the desire of revenge then is the prevailing motive; but only so far as it is founded on an honourable basis, and resulting, as I have before observed, from the justice of the cause. Hippomedon and Parthenopæus are represented as two daring youths, who had no personal prejudices against the Thebans, nor lay under any obligations to the court of Argos; their sole inducements were the love of glory, and study of war, under so experienced a general as Adrastus. The warlike disposition of Capaneus arises rather from a principle of inhumanity. He is a mere homicide, and satiable by blood and carnage only. His behaviour to Amphiaraus, however palliated with the specious pretence of friendship to Tydeus, is arrogant, impious, and inhuman: his consciousness of superior valour makes him proud; his pride, impatient of reproof; and his impatience of reproof hurries him on to impiety and cruelty. The last who offers himself to our view, is Amphiaraus, a chief of a meek, dispassionate temper, who naturally prefers the sweets of peace to the hurry and fatigue of a military life. He was told that his fate was inevitable; and, in consequence of this prediction, puts a good face on it, and marches to battle with a philosophic calmness and resignation to the divine will.

387. Fame says] Evander gives a similar account of those Arcadians, who planted a colony in Italy.

Gensque virûm truncis et duro robore nata: [tauros,
Queis neque mos, neque cultus erat: nec jungere
Aut componere opes norant, aut parcere parto.
Æneid.

And Ovid mentions their antiquity.

Ante Jovem genitum terras habuisse feruntur
  Arcades, et Lunâ gens prior illa fuit.

With horrour and amaze they first survey'd
The swift vicissitudes of light and shade;
And, when the Sun withdrew its setting ray,
Fear'd an eternal absence of the day.
From Mænalos th' assembling rustics rove,
And quit, in crowds, the black Parthenian grove;
Then Rhipe, on her snowy cliffs reclin'd,
And high Enispe, obvious to the wind.
From Stratie the raging hinds descend;
Tegæan swains the exile's cause befriend.
Cyllene mourns her desert height in vain;
And Pallas weeps for her dispeopled plain.
They flock from where the gentle Ladon glides,
And rapid Cliton rolls his hoarser tides;
Where white Lampia thunders in his course,
And Peneus, whence the Styx derives his source.
From Azan then they sought the deathful field,
To which in howlings Ida's self must yield.
Like waves, they pour from the Parrhasian grove,
Sacred to Cupid, and the queen of love:
Where, to facilitate Calysto's rape,
Great Jove assum'd Diana's arms and shape:
Orchomenos, whose plains in sheep abound,
And Cynosure, for savage beasts renown'd.
Then Mars depopulates th' Æphytian plains,
And lofty Psophis of her warriors drains:
Stymphalus next, and where in days of yore
The brave Alcides slew the foaming boar.
Arcadians all: tho' various in their name,
And manners, yet their nation was the same.
For javelins some huge Paphian myrtles wield,
Whilst others arm'd with sheep-crooks take the field.
These, skilful archers, bend the stubborn bow,
And those with stakes alone provoke the foe.
One in a spreading hat his hair confines,
Another in a crested helmet shines.
Those with the spoils of some huge monster hide
Their features, glorying in terrific pride.
Mycenæ's sons alone withheld their aid,
Nor they with neutral ease the war survey'd:
The Sun's abrupt retreat, and impious rage
Of adverse brothers, all their arms engage.
Meanwhile th' ungrateful messenger in tears
The mournful tale to Atalanta bears;
How her rash son had sought the Theban fight,
With all the youths, companions in his flight.
Her fainty limbs with sudden horrour shook;
The falling bow her feeble grasp forsook:
Swift as the wind, impatient of delay,
Thro' adverse woods and streams she forc'd her way.
Her hair, dishevell'd, in confusion flies,
Her naked breasts in wild emotion rise.
The tigress thus, with dreadful anguish stung,
Pursues the spoiler, and demands her young.
At length she snatch'd his courser's foaming reins,
And the pale warrior thus awhile detains.

414. To which in howlings] There was a temple here dedicated to Cybele, whose votaries were obliged to howl in a peculiar manner, during the solemnization of the sacred rites.

418. Great Jove assum'd] There was a particular reason for his being disguised in this manner: Calysto being one of Diana's virgin attendants.

423. And where in days] This was Erymanthus.

438. Of adverse brothers] viz. Atreus and Thyestes, whose story is too well known to need any farther elucidation.

"Whence springs this impotent, this useless rage,
This heat, that ill becomes thy tender age?
Canst thou th' experienc'd soldier's hardships bear,
In toils consume the day, the night in care?
Canst thou the falchion wield, and bend the bow,
Or with the strength I wish, repel the foe?
Hast thou forgot, when on Cyllene's height
Thy slacken'd knees could scarce support thy weight,
While the fierce boar, the terrour of the wood,
Close at thy side, with threat'ning aspect stood?
How little had avail'd this useless blade,
Had my unerring shafts withheld their aid!
But here, alas! a mother's art must fail,
Nor Lycian bows, or Gnossian shafts avail.
Nor will the trusted courser aid supply,
When the loud tumult speaks the battle nigh.
In vain you mingle with the sons of Mars,
Scarce qualified to serve in Cupid's wars.
Nor were there omens wanting to disclose
Thy cruel flight, the source of future woes:
Diana's fane a sudden tremour shook;
The goddess frown'd, and angry was her look:
The falling trophies shook the sacred floor,
These arrows carry certain death no more,
But, erring from the mark, desert the bow:
Nor my faint arms their wonted vigour know.
Awhile await, and check thy youthful rage,
Till strength succeed, the gift of riper age;
Till the soft down thy tender cheeks embrace,
And stamp an air of manhood on thy face:
Nor tears, nor pray'rs shall then retard thy flight;
Myself will arm thee for the glorious fight.
Hence then—Nor let me here in vain repine;
Will you, his comrades, aid the rash design?
How well those stubborn hearts which nought can move,
Your steely race, and inbred rigour prove!"
Here paus'd the matron: the surrounding chiefs
Strive to remove her fears, and soothe her griefs.
Scarce, when the trumpet sounds the last alarms,
Can she dismiss him from her pious arms;

453. Whence springs] The abruptness of this oration admirably expresses the violence of affection in Atalanta; and the silence of Parthenopæus on the other hand, has a beautiful effect. We may suppose, it was a dreadful mortification to the young adventurer, (who assumed the man as much as possible) to be called a smock-faced boy, reminded of his weakness, and desired to return home, among a cloud of sneering warriors. Barthius, a critic of eminence, in the height of rapture on this occasion, cries out, Mirus talium artifex Papinius!

466. Nor Lycian bows] They were held in the greatest request among the ancient heathens. The arrows were called Gnossian, from Gnossus, a city of Crete.

470. Scarce qualified] Those commentators who bring an author off upon every occasion with this excuse, that he was obliged to conform to the national custom of the times, may find an apology for this raillery of Atalanta; but I am confident it would be esteemed indelicate, if not indecent and immodest, in a modern female.

475. The falling] So Lucan.

———Delapsaque templis
Dona suis. Pharsal. book 1.

491. Scarce, when the trumpet] Every one of my readers, who has undergone the like severe

Oft she commends him to the monarch's care,
And thus awhile retards the fate of war.
Meanwhile an honest shame the Thebans awes,
And cools their ardour in the royal cause;
With just aversion they awhile delay'd
The town's defence, nor march in quest of aid.
Tho' fear-inspiring fame increas'd their woes,
Doubling the strength and number of their foes;
No wonted eagerness to take the field
Impels to fix th' hereditary shield,
None fit the rein, to check or urge his speed,
And animate to fight the snorting steed:
Heartless and void of military rage,
They sought the combat, and, constrain'd, engage.
Each seeks a just pretence to shun his doom;
One pleads a num'rous progeny at home:
Another for his pregnant consort fears,
Or mourns his sire infirm and worn with years.
The god of war inspir'd no martial rage:
Their walls, decay'd with gath'ring filth and age,
And tow'rs, which at Amphion's call arose,
On ev'ry side a threat'ning gap disclose:
But now, alas! no bard with skilful hand
Repairs the breach, or bids the rampire stand.
But social love the stern Bœotian warms,
To snatch from hostile rage, and impious arms,
The liberties of Thebes, and ancient laws,
And aid the public, not the royal cause.
As when the wolf, with raging hunger bold,
Has bath'd the plain in blood, or storm'd the fold,
With paunch distended, and with lolling tongue,
He shuns the vengeance of the rustic throng;
And, conscious of the crime, at ev'ry sound
Exerts his speed, and hurls his eyes around.
Thus did each fresh report of fame suggest
The fears of vengeance to the tyrant's breast.
One spreads a rumour, that Lernæan horse
From old Asopus bent to Thebes their course;
Another, that Cithæron's tow'ring height
Was occupied, a prelude to the fight:
A third relates, that fam'd Platæa shone
With hostile fires, and splendours not her own.
Then Parian images at ev'ry pore
Were seen to sweat, and Dirce blush'd with gore.
Again on earth the speaking sphynx was heard,
And monstrous births the teeming mother scar'd.
On ev'ry breast presaging terrour sate,
Fraught with some omen of approaching fate.
But lo! a fiercer object strikes their eyes,
Forth thro' the streets the frantic priestess flies
Of Bacchus, and from his deserted fane
With hair dishevel'd rush'd along the plain.
She wildly star'd, and, urg'd with rage divine,
Shook high above her head a flaming pine.
Enthusiastic heavings swell'd her breast,
And thus her voice th' informing god addrest.
"Almighty pow'r! whose aid we boast no more,
Transferr'd from Thebes to some more favour'd shore;
Whether you shake beneath the northern pole
Your wreathed spear, and fire the Thracian's soul;
Or bid the mangled vine revive again,
While stern Lycurgus threats, but threats in vain:
Whether you rage, where down a length'ning steep
The Ganges rushes, mingling with the deep;

trial, must sympathise with the disconsolate Atalanta, and confess the poet to be a faithful interpreter of nature. It is so common in these interviews to make use of such repetitions, and summon the merest trifles to one's aid, in order to effect a short delay, and put off the anguish of the parting moment. Lucan says of Pompey:

—— Mentem jam verba paratam
Destituunt, blandæque juvat ventura trahentem
Indulgere moræ, et tempus subducere fatis.

495. Meanwhile an honest shame] The poet has made a just distinction between the disposition of the allies and the Thebans to begin hostilities. The former, conscious of their own innocence, march to battle with the greatest confidence and alacrity; the latter, sensible of the unjust cause they are engaged in, and supporting, are represented as dejected, timorous, and desponding.

521. As when the wolf] The guilty conscience of Eteocles is well illustrated in this comparison. The outlines of this speaking picture were copied from Homer on a similar subject.

'Αλλ' ὅγ' ἄρ ἔτρεσε θηρὶ κακὸν ῥέξαντι ἐοικὼς,
Ὅςε κύνα κτείνας, ἢ βȣκόλον αμφι βόεσσιν,
Φεύγει, πρίν-περ ὅμιλον ἀολλισθήμεναι ἀνδρῶν.

Virgil has copied it likewise.

Ac velut ille, prius quam tela inimica sequantur,
Continuò in montes sese avius abdidit altos
Occiso pastore lupus, magnove juvenco,
Conscius audacis facti: caudamque remulcens
Subjecit pavitantem utero, sylvasque petivit.

Virgil has undoubtedly the advantage in point of subject, though I think the simile itself is more copious, and contains a greater assemblage of images in our author.

535. Then Parian images] Some of these prognostics are mentioned by Lucan, as preceding the civil war.

Monstrosisque hominum partus, numeroque modoque
Membrorum, matremque suus conterruit infans:

And again:

Indigetes flevisse Deos, urbisque laborem
Testatos sudore lares.—— Phars. book 1.

541. But lo! a fiercer object] This is a beautiful imitation of the following passage in Lucan.

Terruerant satis hæc pavidam præsagia plebem:
Sed majora premunt. Nam qualis vertice Pindi
Edonis Ogygio decurrit plena Lyæo:
Talis et attonitam rapitur matrona per urbem,
Vocibus his prodens urgentem pectora Phœbum.

And the prophecy, annexed to it, excels the original.

553. Or bid the mangled vine] Lycurgus, king of Thrace, caused most of the vines to be rooted up, so that his subjects were obliged to mix it with water, when it was less plentiful. Hence it was feigned, that he drove Bacchus himself out of Thrace, and that Thetis received him into her bosom, according to the following lines of Homer.

Οὐδὲ γὰρ ȣδὲ Δρύαντος, ὗιος κρατερὸς Λυκόοργος·
Δὴν ἦν, ὅς ῥα θεοῖσιν ἐπȣρανίοισιν ἔριζεν.
Ος ποτε μαινομένοιο Διωνύσσοιο τιθηνάς
Σεῦε κατ' ἠγάθεον Νυσσήϊον· αἱ δ' ἅμα πᾶσαι
Θύσθλα χαμαὶ κατέχευαν, ὑπ' ἀνδροφόνοιο Λυκȣ́ργȣ
Θεινόμεναι βȣπλῆγι. Διώνυσσος δὲ φοβηθεὶς
Δύσεθ' ἁλὸς κατὰ κῦμα: Θέτις δ' ὑπεδέξατο κόλπῳ
Δειδιότα. Iliad, b. 6. v. 130.

Or from the spring of Hermus rise in gold,
Whose parting waves the sacred ore unfold:
Incline thine ear: nor let us e'er despair
Of aid, nor mourn thy alienated care.
For royal perjuries, nor crimes our own,
We weep in slaughter, and in war atone:
Yet still, O Bacchus, we thy pow'r obey,
And gifts unceasing on thy altars lay.
But, ere I speak what wretched Thebes must feel,
And truths, invidious to the great, reveal,
Transport, and waft me to the northern pole,
Where endless frosts the rays of Sol control.
Was it for this I was constrain'd to swear,
When first the sacred fillets bound my hair?
I see two stately monarchs of the mead,
Their honours equal, and the same their breed,
With clashing horns, and butting heads engage,
And fall the victims of each other's rage.
More guilty he, who scorns a share to yield,
And claims the sole possession of the field:
Meanwhile a friend to neither wears the spoils,
And reaps the harvest of their bloody toils."
Here paus'd the dame: th' exhausted fury ceas'd,
And, ebbing in her soul, the god decreas'd.
Urg'd by these omens, and superior dread,
The king for counsel to Tiresias fled;
Blind was the seer, yet boundless was his view,
The present, future, and the past he knew.
No sacrifice employs his pious cares,
Nor th' augur's art his lawful notice shares,
Nor seeks he from presaging veins to prove,
Or learn in Delphic caves the will of Jove;
No list'ning stars his potent charms invoke,
Nor fragrant altars yield prophetic smoke:
But horrid arts of magic are explor'd,
And Stygian rites, by Jove and Heav'n abhor'd.
Oft he dispeoples Pluto's airy reign,
And bids reviving phantoms breathe again.
Of blasted sheep, selected from the field,
Whose fleeces still the stench of sulphur yield,

577. Meanwhile a friend] This was Creon, who seized the kingdom of Thebes after the death of the two brothers, figured under the two bulls.

As I am not often guilty of troubling the reader with verbal criticisms and various readings, I hope he will pardon me, for barely mentioning a trifling dispute, which hath arisen about the 576th verse, between two celebrated verbal critics. One of them contends warmly that we should read mountain; alleging, the supposition to be more natural of beasts feeding there than on a field, as I have translated it. This must surely be a controversy about nothing, the meaning of the author in the words communem montem is nothing more than a pasture common to both. One of these disputants has quoted from Virgil, in support of his opinion,

Stupet inscius alto
Accipiens sonitum saxi de vertice pastor.

Forgetting that the same author had said in the 12th book,

Ac velut ingenti Sila, summove Taburno
Cum duo conversis inimica in prælia tauri
Frontibus incurrunt.

Here Taburnus and Sila are two mountains, and bulls are feeding on them; whereas in the other they are sheep, as appears from the word pastor, and the place they were feeding on, a rock.

The mangled entrails first are cull'd with care,
Then cleans'd with grass, and hallow'd with a prayer.
There grew a wood, superior to the rage
Of wintry tempests, and corroding age;
Whose boughs with interweaving union form
A shade, impervious to the sun and storm.
Invidious winds at awful distance fly,
And glancing light'nings shoot obliquely by.
No breeze in murm'ring sounds is heard to breathe,
The same eternal horrour broods beneath.
Some scatter'd images of light invade,
And but enhance the terrour of the shade.
Nor was the sacred silence of the grove
Unnotic'd by the progeny of Jove;
Latonia's form, engrav'd on ev'ry tree,
Attests the presence of the deity.
Oft have her shafts resounded thro' the glade,
And howling dogs her passing orb betray'd;
As from her uncle's dark domains she flies,
And in Diana's form deserts the skies.
But, when the mountains glitter with her light,
And the still hours to pleasing sleep invite;
Here on her quiver she reclines her head,
With heaps of glitt'ring jav'lins round her spread.
Before the entrance lies the field of Mars,
Fam'd for its iron crop and rising wars.
Bold was the wretch who durst explore again
The fatal horrours of the bloody plain;
And, heedless of the past, employ his toil
To turn, and exercise the guilty soil.
Oft (as fame tells) the earth in sounds of woe
Is heard to groan from hollow depths below,
When her indignant sons in fight engage,
And deal their blows around with airy rage.
The trembling rustic leaves his work undone,
And lowing herds the dreadful issue shun.
Here (for the place itself convenient lies
For Stygian rites, and impious aid supplies)
Are brought young steers, unknowing of the yoke,
And sable sheep to grace the fatal stroke;
Each hill and vale th' unwonted silence mourns,
And echoing Dirce groan for groan returns.
Tiresias first (as custom taught) adorns
With azure wreaths of flow'rs their tender horns,
Then fills the hollow'd entrance of the wood
With bowls of wine and milk, a mingled flood:
Honey and blood, the last with trembling hands
He pours, as oft as the parch'd earth demands.
For Hecate, first of all th' immortal train,
They heap a triple pile upon the plain;

599. There grew] The two celebrated descriptions of a wood in Lucan and Tasso are, I think, inferior to this before us. The five first verses in the original are highly finished; but the last is inexpressibly beautiful. The description of Lucan is in the 3d book of his Pharsalia, and that of Tasso in the 13th canto of his Jerusalem.

611. Latonia's form] This goddess was called Luna in Heaven, Diana upon Earth, and Proserpine in Hell. In the pagan theology it was very usual for their gods to have many names, as well as many offices. This piece of superstition is exactly copied from them by the papists, in the several employments which are assigned to their saints.

629. When her indignant sons] These were supposed to be the souls of those warriors who arose from the dragon's teeth, and fell in a conflict among themselves.

Three sylvan structures to the furies rise,
Whose less'ning summits mingle with the skies:
The last of pine to Stygian Jove they rear,
Broad was the base, the top advanc'd in air.
To Proserpine, assign'd to lasting night,
An altar rises of inferior height.
The fabric's front and ample sides they strew
With boughs of cypress, and the baleful yew.
Then with his crooked knife Tiresias trac'd
The destin'd mark, and pure libations plac'd
Between their horns: beneath the piercing wound
The victims fall, and headlong spurn the ground.
Fair Mantho, in a bowl of ample size,
Receives the blood, and to her lips applies.
The lukewarm vitals next the virgin sought
(As custom and her sire's example taught:)
Thrice round each smoking altar she convey'd
The sacred off'rings in a charger laid;
With loads of fuel heaps the kindled fire,
And bids the lambent flames to Heav'n aspire.
But, when the prophet heard the crackling wood,
And felt the heat, as near the pile he stood,
Forth from his breast these dreadful accents broke,
The flaming structure trembling as he spoke:
" Ye chearless mansions of eternal woe,
And thou, sole arbiter of all below!
Whom ruthless fate and chance ordain to sway
The Stygian realms, and empty shades obey;
Transport those phantoms that for entrance wait
And loiter yet before the gloomy gate.

653. The fabric's front] The verses in some editions of the original are

> Frondes atque omne cupressus
> Intexit plorata latus.

Which I think can scarcely be understood. Therefore, instead of frondes, read frontes, which elucidates the whole sentence, and then the sense will be clearly this: The baleful cypress covered the top and sides of the pile. This alteration seems necessary, and it is favoured by the authority of Virgil, who in the 6th book says,

> Ingentem struxere pyram, cui frondibus atris
> Intexit latera, et ferales ante cupressus
> Constituunt.

The reader will observe, that ante implies the top or front, and answers to the word frontes in our author.

667. But, when the prophet] The reader will do himself a pleasure by comparing the following account of these ceremonies with that of Lucan in the 6th book of his Pharsalia. It is evidently copied from the latter, as may be easily discerned from an attentive perusal of both. I must beg leave to observe, that the description before us is more opportune and strongly connected with the subject than in Lucan; nay, it seems more natural, that Eteocles, after such a complication of guilt and wickedness, should be anxious and solicitous concerning the event of the war, than Sextus, who was engaged in a doubly just cause. I would not be understood to speak in prejudice of Lucan, who has not only adorned his subject by this digression from it, but fully compensated for its unseasonable insertion. Give me leave to add, that Saul's application to the witch of Endor was owing to the same motives, and attended with similar circumstances.

May Charon's vessel groan beneath the weight,
And scarce restore to Styx the mighty freight.
Nor let the dead in one promiscuous train
Revive, and view the light of Heav'n again:
From fair Elysium let the just repair
Beneath thy conduct, and engage thy care;
With thee shall Hermes share the due command,
Direct their passage, and exert his wand.
But let Tisiphone the light disclose
To them whose crimes deserve eternal woes,
Without compunction and remission shake
Her flaming torch, and open ev'ry snake;
Let Cerberus his usual rage restrain,
And yield the passage to the guilty train.
Of these innumerable is the throng,
And yet the greatest part to Thebes belong."
He paus'd, unmov'd, and resolutely bent
To prove the issue, and await th' event:
Nor was the nymph deficient in her part,
For Phœbus had inur'd her tender heart.
Eteocles alone was seen to fear;
Convuls'd his limbs, and pale his cheeks appear.
One while the prophet's aged hands he press'd,
The mantle then, that grac'd his awful breast.
Would decency permit, he fain would shun
The sequel, nor conclude the rites begun.
Thus, when the bold Gætulian from afar
Hears the rous'd lion rushing to the war,
Asham'd to fly, nor daring to advance,
He stands unmov'd, and grasps the sweating lance.
His doubts to fears, his fears to anguish grow,
As nearer he perceives the wrathful foe;
So fierce he thunders through the rustling wood,
So loud he roars, and speaks his lust of food.
But old Tiresias, impotent to bear
This seeming scorn, repeats his former pray'r:
" Ye pow'rs, for whom these pure libations flow,
And Heav'n and Earth with sacred splendours glow,
Attest the fatal truth of what I say,
And learn, our charge admits of no delay.
Say, am I yet, ye sullen fiends, obey'd,
Or must I call Thessalian hags to aid?
Whose potent charms, and mystic verse shall shake
The realms of ether, and the Stygian lake:
Disclose your will, ye sisters of despair,
Say, do these just commands employ your care?
Shall Earth's weak barrier with a yawn give way,
And join the upper and the nether day?
(Since you refuse to bid the dead return,
And leave inviolate each loaded urn)
Or will ye cut and maim the bloodless head,
And cull the fibres of the recent dead?

683. With thee shall Hermes] Horace assigns this god to the same office.

> Tu pias lætis animas reponis
> Sedibus: virgâque levem coerces
> Aureâ turbam, superis Deorum
> Gratus, et imis.

701. Would decency permit] Never was the influence of conscience better proved, than in this description of Eteocles's conduct. His timidity first spurs him on to learn the fortune of the war by necromancy; but when the rites are almost finished, and the hour drawing on that must determine his future happiness or misery, the horrours of guilt increase so much upon him, that he would fain have retired, well assured in himself, that he had no reason to expect, and consequently should find nothing in his favour.

Til ye despise th' infirmities of age
Which yet retains the fatal pow'r to rage.
We know whate'er you labour to conceal,
And can, at will, those mysteries reveal.
Our vengeance lab'ring Hecate should know,
But pious awe diverts awhile the blow.
Nor does the triple king, whose name alone
You hear with terrour, as his pow'r you own,
From us lie hid;—but love of calm repose,
The joy of age, forbids me to disclose."
Here on his threat'ning speech the priestess broke,
And thus her interrupted sire bespoke.
" Forbear these useless threats, thy pray'rs have sped,
And Hell no more withholds the summon'd dead.
Elysian landscapes shine, expos'd to day,
And yawning chasms the nether shades display.
Each grove and sable stream our eyes command,
Where Acheron excites the troubled sand,
Where Phlegethon his fiery torrent rolls,
And Styx the passage of the shades controls.
I see their king, enthron'd in regal state:
Around the ministers of torment wait.
I see the consort of infernal Jove,
And conscious bed of interdicted love.
Death from an eminence surveys the throng
Of ghosts, and counts them as they pass along:
Yet still the greater part untold remains,
And o'er increasing numbers Pluto reigns.
With urn in hand the Cretan judge appears,
And lives and crimes with his assessors hears:
The conscious wretch must all his acts reveal,
Loth to confess, unable to conceal."
" Let this suffice," (replies the Theban sage)
" O guide, and prop of my declining age!
Little alas! it here avails to dwell
On these sad scenes, and paint the woes of Hell;
How the fierce centaur still his rage retains,
And giants howl in adamantine chains.
To whom is the fallacious stream unknown,
To whom the toil of the returning stone;
The pain that Tityon's mangled vitals feel,
And sad Ixion's revoluble wheel?
Once, under Hecate's auspicious care,
Myself explor'd those regions of despair,
When in each vein my blood impetuous boil'd,
Nor Heav'n these darksome orbs of light had spoil'd.
But rather strive a close access to gain
To our own Theban, and th' Argolic train.
Of milk four small libations will remove,
And force the rest to quit the dreary grove.
But mark attentive, as they pass along,
The features, aspect, mien of either throng.
Thy eyes must here supply the want of mine,
And teach me what the Fates and Heav'n design."
Swift as the word, the spotless nymph obeys,
And thrice repeats aloud her mystic lays;
Aw'd by the sound, the shades requir'd, appear,
While others fled, impell'd by sudden fear.
As Circe once, and fair Medea shone,
Now Mantho shines, surpass'd in guilt alone.
Again her list'ning sire she thus bespake:
" Agenor's son first quits the bloody lake;
With him appears the partner of his bed,
Two crested serpents hiss on either's head.
A troop of earth-born youths, in arms renown'd,
The wretched pair with hideous din surround.
The same day's Sun, that, rising, gave them birth,
Setting, restor'd them to their mother earth.
Fiercely they menace, fiercer yet engage,
And breathe revenge, and unavailing rage;
No more they seek admittance to the flood,
But wish to slake their thirst in mutual blood.
The next in order, as they pass along,
Vary in sex and age, a mingled throng.
Autonoe the first, is bath'd in tears,
And Semele the bolt, she merits, fears.
With eyes inverted, Ino shuns the foe,
And presses to her breast the source of woe.
Here sad Agave, as her sense returns,
In penitential weeds her Pentheus mourns;

735. Nor does the triple king] In the works of the ancient poets we find many confused hints and imperfect accounts concerning the existence of a great, omnipotent, and eternal being, distinguished by the name of Demogorgon. All I can collect from them amounts to show, that he was the father and creator of all the other gods; and, though bound in chains of adamant in the lowest part of Hell, was yet so terrible to all the other deities, that they could not bear the very mention of his name. Lucan has mentioned him in the following verses.

—— An ille
Compellandus erit, quo nunquam terra vocato
Non concussa tremit, qui Gorgona cernit apertam,
Verberibusque suis trepidam castigat Erinnyn,
Indespecta tenet vobis qui Tartara; cujus
Vos estis superi; Stygias qui pejerat undas.

Spenser has alluded to the notion of his preexistence to the other gods, in his apostrophe to night.

O thou, most ancient grandmother of all,
More old than Jove, whom thou at first didst breed,
Or that great house of gods celestial,
Which was begot in Demogorgon's hall,
And saw'st the secrets of the world unmade.

757. The Cretan judge] So Virgil:

Quæsitor Minos urnam movet: ille silentum
Conciliumque vocat, vitasque et crimina discit.

767. The fallacious stream] The crime of Tantalus is very well known, and for his punishment he was placed up to his chin in a pleasant stream, without being able to slake his thirst in it.

768. The toil of the returning stone] Sisyphus was a noted robber, slain by Theseus. In Hell he is represented rolling a huge stone up a hill, which rolling down again, affords him perpetual trouble and vexation.

769. The pain] Tityon made an attempt to ravish Latona, and fell by the arrows of Apollo. He is described by the poets with a vulture perpetually gnawing his liver.

770. Ixion's wheel] Ixion, boasting that he had lain with Juno, was struck down to Hell with a thunderbolt, and chained to a wheel, whose perpetual rotation was a perpetual source of anguish and torment.

799. No more they] The flood he means here, was the stream they contended about, and which, according to the poet, was the sole cause of their dispute; though the hints he has given are not sufficient to entitle me to mention it in my version.

803. Autonoe] Was the mother of Actæon.

804. And Semele] See note on the 365th verse of the first book.

She breaks her thyrsus, bares her bloody breast,
And flies to give his wand'ring spirit rest.
Through Styx and ev'ry lake above he flies,
And where th' impervious cliffs of Lethe rise;
His milder sire, Echion there he found,
To share his griefs, and ease each rankling wound.
A mournful aspect wretched Lycus wears,
And Athamas his slaughter'd infant bears.
Actæon still the form impos'd retains,
And leads the chase along the dreary plains,
Fleet are his limbs, o'er hill and dale he bounds,
And with his horns repels the rushing hounds.
Next Niobe majestic stalks along,
And shines conspicuous in the female throng.
With raptures she recounts her former woes,
Surveys th' exhausted malice of her foes;
And, pleas'd to find herself secure in death,
In loud reproaches wastes her impious breath."
While thus the priestess spoke, the list'ning sage
Uprears his hoary head, depress'd with age;
The fillets tremble on his awful brow,
And his flush'd cheeks with youthful ardour glow:
No more the staff his bending frame sustains,
Tall and erect, he stalks along the plains,
And thus replies: "O! waste thy breath no more,
The pitying gods my ravish'd sight restore:
The mists and films that lately did involve
These clouded orbs, in subtle air dissolve.
I feel the gradual entrance of the light,
And ev'ry object shines reveal'd to sight.
With eyes dejected, and dissolv'd in tears,
Each phantom of Argolic race appears.
Stern Abas here, there guilty Prætus stands,
And mild Phoroneus lifts his aged hands.
See Pelops, maim'd to glut the tyrant's lust,
And stern Oenomaus, begrim'd with dust.
In the pale aspect of each patriot shade
I see the fall of Argive pride pourtray'd.
But who are they, whose wound and gleaming arms
Bespeak them not disus'd to war's alarms?
An hostile frown and threat'ning looks they wear,
And to our view their wounded bosoms bare.
Alas! too well I know the social band
For those who fell beneath th' Ætolian's hand.
Chromis and Phegeus, skill'd to whirl the lance,
And Chthonius with impetuous strides advance:
Brave Mæon next his well-known face displays,
Mæon, distinguish'd with Phœbean bays.
From whence this rage? You tread no hostile ground,
The gods, not Tydeus, gave the fatal wound:
Thus did the cruel destinies ordain,
And human strength and art oppos'd in vain.
Mars shall again invade the Theban shore,
And, in the form of Tydeus, rage in gore."
He spoke: and, pointing to the blood above,
And sacred wreaths, the phantoms backward drove.
But pensive Laius, on the dreary steep
Of hoarse Cocytus, eyes the subject deep;
Whom late from Earth Cyllenius had convey'd,
And render'd back to rest his troubled shade.
Unmov'd by sacrifice, or hallow'd blood,
He loiter'd on the margin of the flood,
And, as askance his grandson he beheld,
High in his breast his heart indignant swell'd.
Tiresias first the mutual silence broke,
And, turning, thus th' impassive shade bespoke.
"Illustrious prince! since whose unworthy fate,
Incessant woes have vex'd the Theban state,
Here let thy rage its utmost barrier find,
Nor pass the bounds by fate and Heav'n assign'd.
Enough of vengeance to thy wrongs is paid,
And fifty bleed, to glut a single shade.
Whom dost thou fly? Thy son, depriv'd of sight,
And buried to the world, abhors the light:
What tho' he still retains his vital breath?
His pains exceed the worst degree of death.
But say, by what inducement led, you shun
A congress with his unoffending son?

815. A mournful aspect] Lycus, according to the commentator Lactantius, gave his daughter Megæra in marriage to Hercules. This so incensed Juno, that she made him a lunatic; in one of his fits he slew two of his sons, for which reason he is represented here dejected and sorrowful.

Others say he was a Theban exile, and made an attempt to ravage Megæra in the absence of her husband, who returned time enough to prevent and punish his designs with death.

834. The pitying gods] This fiction of the poet is founded upon an important truth of religion, not unknown to the Pagans, that God only can open the eyes of men, and enable them to see what they cannot discover by their own capacity. Thus Homer introduces Minerva, as enlightening the eyes of Diomede.

Α'χλὺν δ' αὖ τοι ἀπ' ὀφθαλμῶν ἕλον, ἣ πρὶν ἐπῆεν,
Ὄφρ' εὖ γινώσκῃς ἠμὲν Θεὸν, ἠδὲ καὶ ἄνδρα.
Iliad, lib. 5. v. 127.

And Milton makes Michael open Adam's eyes to see the revolutions of the world, and fortunes of his posterity.

——— He purg'd with euphrasy and rue
The visual nerve, for he had much to see,
And from the well of life three drops distill'd.
Paradise Lost, book 11.

845 In the pale aspect] This beautiful circumstance is taken from Lucan; where the shade which Erictho raises to satisfy Pompey's son about the fortune of the war, says,

—— Tristis fælicibus umbris
Vultus erat, vide Decios, natumque patremque
Lustrales bellis animas, flentemque Camillum
Et Curios, Syllam de te, Fortuna, querentem. b. 6.

864. And sacred wreaths] The verses in the original are,

Dixit, vittâque ligatis
Frondibus instantes abigit, monstratque cruorem.

Lactantius, with the usual warmth of a critic, contends, that vittaque ligatis frondibus should be referred to the fifty shades; and I wish he had given us something more to support his assertion, than his own bare word and critical authority; for I must own, I cannot easily conceive, why those fifty soldiers should wear chaplets appropriated to priests and augurs only. Besides, reason, and the context itself, seem to persuade a quite different construction, which is this, that he drove them away by showing them the blood and his wreaths, which were the ensigns of his office and authority. I would not be guilty of a positive ipse dixi, but shall refer it to the reader's own judgment to determine between us.

This description of necromancy in general, has a great resemblance with that in the 3d act of Seneca's Oedipus.

O stay your steps, and listen to his vows,
'Tis the last interview that Heav'n allows.
The lot of either warring host relate,
And be the just interpreter of fate;
If pleas'd, that we may shun the threat'ned blow,
If angry, to afford the cause of woe.
So shall the grateful vessel waft thee o'er
To the sweet banks of yon forbidden shore;
For thee the Stygian monarch shall transgress
The laws of fate, and yield the wish'd access."
The shade, relenting, steeps his paler cheeks
In the red stream, and thus the seer bespeaks.
"Ah! why am I selected to disclose
The various ills the destinies impose?
Sufficient is it to have known the past,
And prov'd, that death alone can bring the last.
But would ye learn what woes on Thebes impend,
Let him, the author, at your rites attend,
Who durst his father's blood with pleasure shed,
Ascend his mother's interdicted bed,
Thro' violated nature force his way,
And stain the sacred womb where once he lay.
E'en now the pow'rs of Hell he strives to rouse
To wrath, and wearies Heav'n with impious vows.
But, since from me alone you seek to know
Each mournful circumstance of future woe,
All I can learn, and all allow'd by fate,
With truth and accuracy I relate.
War, horrid war, the jarring world shall waste,
And thousands to their own destruction haste;
Each Grecian state her youthful warriors yields,
And ne'er before such armies hid the fields.
All these shall meet a sure, tho' various death:
Some in the glorious field shall yield their breath,
And others, blasted with etherial fire,
Or by the gaping earth o'erwhelm'd, expire.
Fair Thebes shall yet be mistress of the plain,
Nor Polynices win the promis'd reign.
But the stern sire shall triumph in success,
And Heav'n and Hell conspire to give redress."
Thus darkly he the prophecy exprest,
Part he disclos'd, the greater part supprest.
Meanwhile the scatter'd Argives bend their course
To Nemea, conscious of Herculean force;
They long to burn, to ravage, and destroy,
And war and slaughter are their only joy.
What pow'r, O Phœbus, did avert their rage,
(For scarce the fame has reach'd our distant age:)
Relate, what god obscur'd the doubtful way,
And clog'd their promis'd conquest with delay?
The god of wine, returning from the war,
From conquer'd Hæmus drove his rattling car;
The Scythian here, what time the dog-star reigns,
Nocturnal orgies to the god ordains.
The hills array'd in youthful green appear,
And scarce sustain the produce of the year.
To dearer Thebes the god pursues his way,
And plies the lash, impatient of delay:
Impetuous lynxes bear him o'er the plains
With tigers pair'd, and lick the purple reins;
Behind, a troop of bleeding wolves appear,
With wounded bears, and close the savage rear.
Stern discord, ever ready to engage,
With stagg'ring impotence, and headstrong rage,
Attend his course, and crowd around his car,
Friends of the god, and partners in the war.
But, when he saw the clouds of dust arise,
Their burnish'd armour gleaming in the skies,
And knew, that Thebes as yet was unprepar'd
To dare the combat, or their rage retard;
Astonish'd at the view, he cross'd the road,
(Tho' gorg'd and reeling with the nauseous load)
Commands the drums and shriller fifes to cease,
And thus begins, when all was hush'd in peace.
"Behold! Bellona threats the Theban tow'rs,
The queen of ether arms her Argive pow'rs,
And from the long records of distant age
Derives incitements to renew her rage.
Could not th' offender's death, nor length of time
Absolve the guilt and horrours of the crime,
When fire from Heav'n was summon'd to her doom,
And scorch'd the produce of her fertile womb?
That her exhausted anger she renews,
And the sad reliques of the name pursues.
Yet will I interpose a short delay;
Hither, ye friends of Bacchus, bend your way."
He spoke: his tigers, fleeter than the wind,
Sprung forth, and bore him to the spot design'd.
The gaudy Sun had gain'd the middle height
Of Heav'n, and flash'd intolerable light;
Each grove admits th' exhilarating ray,
And bares its dark recesses to the day;
Thick vapours issue from the steaming fields,
As the cleft earth a gradual passage yields;

891. If pleas'd] I believe this passage requires a little more illustration than was allowable in the version; the sense is, that by Laius's relating the ill fortune of the war, (for we must carry the supposition along with us of its being so) he would gain his ends, however he was disposed towards his country, viz. that if he was a foe to it, he would have the satisfaction of hearing them mourn, but if a friend, of warning them against the impending danger.

I must confess myself obliged to Lactantius for the true meaning and interpretation of this passage, and should have been at a loss for a construction, as the poet has expressed himself very obscurely.

893. So shall the grateful vessel] See note on the 414th verse of the 1st book.

933. What pow'r, O Phœbus] It was customary among the epic writers to renew their invocation to the Muses or Phœbus before the recital of any remarkable action or exploit; nor does this repetition want its uses; for it not only raises the dignity and importance of the poem in the eye of the reader, but serves likewise to awake and revive his attention to the subject and matter in hand, as it would otherwise flag and fall off in the course of a long narration. Virgil has made use of this address in his 9th book:

Quis deus, O Musæ, tam sæva incendia Teucris
Avertit? &c. v. 77.

934. For scarce the fame] This is copied from Virgil, where, in the invocation previous to his catalogue, he says,

Et meministis enim, divæ, et memorare potestis,
Ad nos vix tenuis famæ perlabitur aura.
Æn. l. 7. v. 645.

And again by Tasso:

—— Di tant' opra à noi si lunge
Debil' aura di fama pena giunga. Gier. c. 3. st. 19

965. Could not th' offender's death] This was his mother Semele, concerning whom, see note on book the 1st, verse 356.

When, rising from amidst a circling crowd
Of Naiads, thus the god exclaims aloud.
"Ye nymphs, that o'er each stream exert your reign,
Partake our honours, and adorn our train,
Assist me to repel our common foes,
Nor grudge the toil, unwilling I impose.
Withhold your sluices, dry the fertile source,
And clog with dust each stream's impetuous course:
But Nemea's most, from whence the guided foe
Pursues his wasteful path to Thebes below.
Let ev'ry torrent quit its craggy steep,
And disembogue its waters in the deep.
Propitious Phœbus seconds our designs,
As on the margin of the deep he shines;
The signs indulgent to our toils arise,
And the fierce dog-star fires th' autumnal skies.
Hence to your liquid caves awhile retire:
Your presence soon we shall again require,
When your past toils shall claim an equal share
In all the rites our votaries prepare.
No more the fauns and satyrs shall escape
Unpunish'd, or effect th' injurious rape."
He spoke: and straight a gath'ring filth o'erspreads,
And binds the streams suspended on their heads
No more the spring its wonted influence yields;
Increasing thirst inflames the wither'd fields.
Huge heaps of moisten'd dust condens'd to mud
Charge the discolour'd channel of the flood.
Pale Ceres sickens on the barren soil,
And wither'd ears elude the peasant's toil.
The flocks on the fallacious margin stood,
And mourn th' unwonted absence of the flood.
Thus, when the Nile suspends his rapid course,
And seeks with refluent waves his distant source:
In spacious caves recruits his liquid pow'rs,
And at each mouth imbibes the wintry show'rs:
The riven earth with issuing vapours smokes,
And Egypt long in vain his aid invokes;
Till, at the world's united pray'r, again
He spreads a golden harvest on the plain.
Lyrceus, and the guilty Lerna fly
To distant realms, and leave their channels dry.
No more Charadrus, with tumultuous sound,
Whirls his white foam, and floating rocks around.
With softer murmurs rough Asterion flows;
And Erasine no more confinement knows,
Who late, in sounds that match'd the noisy deep,
Or thunder, broke the shepherd's envied sleep.
Langia only, as the god ordain'd,
Preserves his stream with dust and filth unstain'd;
Langia, yet unknown to vulgar fame,
Nor glorying in the slaughter'd infant's name.
Inviolate the grove and spring remain,
And all their wonted properties retain.

983. Ye nymphs] From the beginning of this speech to the conclusion of the book, we shall find the poet exerting himself in a very eminent degree. The descriptions are particularly picturesque and lively, the sentiments noble and elevated, the speeches nervous and spirited, the diction daring and figurative, and the verses easy and harmonious.

1013. Thus, when the Nile] This comparison is drawn agreeably to truth and the general observation of travellers. The best comment upon it is in the 10th book of Lucan's Pharsalia, where the poet introduces a dialogue between Cæsar and Achoreus concerning the source and origin of the Nile.

But O! what honours the fair nymph await,
When Greece, to solemnize her infant's fate,
Shall institute triennial feasts and games,
And ages hence record their sacred names!
No more the plates their swelling chests confine,
No more the bucklers on their shoulders shine:
The fever spreads thro' each interior part,
And from the mouth invades the beating heart.
With raging pain their with'ring entrails burn,
And fiery breathings from their lungs return.
The shrinking veins contract their purple flood,
Nor feel the circling motion of the blood.
The gaping earth exhales unwholesome steams,
Resolv'd to dust by Sol's increasing beams.
The thirsty steed, impatient of the reins,
In wild disorder scours along the plains.
On the dry bit no floods of moisture flow,
In whiteness equal to the Scythian snow;
But from his mouth depends the lolling tongue,
Or to the parched roof adhesive hung.
Some, by the king commission'd, Earth explore,
And search the sources of her liquid store.
But all in vain: they view with wond'ring eyes,
Each channel dry'd, exhausted of supplies.
(Th' essential property of moisture gone)
The spring retains an empty name alone.
Nor was there greater hope of falling rain,
Than if they rang'd the desert Lybian plain,
Where Iris ever shuns the deep serene,
Nor pregnant clouds o'ershade th' unvaried scene.
At length a ray of hope dispels their grief,
And cheers them with the prospect of relief.
Hypsipile, as through the woods they stray'd,
A beauteous mourner, haply they survey'd.

1035. O! what honours] A gentleman, who has made some figure in the literary world, in perusing these lines with me, blamed our author for giving us the outlines of this piece, which he intended to fill up in the 6th book, as thinking it superfluous and disgusting. Perhaps, however, this may be so far from cloying the reader's appetite, that it may raise it, and make him desirous of seeing the picture drawn in its full length.

1049. The thirsty steed] These lines call to my mind a beautiful description in Lucan, of this noble animal in the same sickly state.

——— Non sonipes motus clangore tubarum
Saxa quatit pulsu, rigidos vexantia frænos
Ora terens, spargitque jubas, et surrigit aures,
Incertoque pedum pugnat non stare tumultu.
Fessa jacet cervix. Fumant sudoribus armi:
Oraque projectâ squallent arentia linguâ.
Pectora rauca gemunt, quæ creber anhelitus urget,
Et defecta gravis longe trahit ilia pulsus:
Siccaque sanguineis durescit spuma lupatis.
Phars. book 4. 742.

Tasso has a fine stanza on the same subject.

Langue il corsier gia sì feroce, e l' erba
Che fù suo caro cibo, à schiffo prende.
Vacilla il piede infermo, e la superba
Cervice dianzi, or giù dimessa pende:
Memoria di sue palme or più non serba,
Ne più nobil di gloria amor l' accende:
Le vincitrici spoglie, e i richi fregi
Par, che quasi vil soma, odij, e dispregi.
Canto 13. st. 62.

Opheltes, in her soft embraces prest,
(Another's hope) hung smiling at her breast.
With graceful negligence her tresses flow ;
Her humble weeds were suited to her woe :
Yet all those studied arts could not efface
Her native grandeur, and majestic grace :
With decent mixture in her stately mien
The captive and the princess might be seen.
Th' Inachian monarch first his silence broke,
And aw'd, the royal exile thus bespoke.
" O thou, whose features, and celestial air,
A more than mortal origin declare ;
Whom native Heav'n, and boundless pow'r secure
From all those wants the sons of Earth endure :
Let not an humble suppliant sue in vain,
Whether you left the chaste Diana's train,
To grace a mortal's, or immortal's arms,
(For Jove himself has pin'd for Argive charms.)
The squadrons you survey, a pious cause
To raze the guilty walls of Cadmus draws :
Yet fiery thirst our just designs controuls,
Consumes our vigour, and unmans our souls.
Whate'er you grant, with joy we shall partake,
Nor scorn the troubled stream, or standing lake :
Our pressing wants forbid us to refuse,
Nor leave as yet the liberty to choose.
No more we importune the pow'rs on high ;
Do thou the place of partial Jove supply ;
O give us strength to match our warm desires,
And nerves to second what our soul inspires.
So may this infant thrive beneath the care
Of Heav'n, and long inhale the vital air.
Yet more :—should Jove our vows with conquest
crown,
And Thebes her rightful lord and monarch own ;
For each that 'scapes the ruthless hand of death,
A slaughter'd victim shall resign his breath."

1069. Opheltes] was the son of Lycurgus, king of Nemea. His name comprehends the prediction of his death by a serpent. Ὄφις, signifying a serpent, and Ειρειν, which makes Ελον in its aorist secund. to kill.

1079. O thou] The first part of this address is a transcript of Æneas's speech to his mother Venus, in the first Æneid.

O (quam te memorem !) Virgo : namque haud
tibi vultus
Mortalis, nec vox hominem sonat : O dea, certe :
An Phœbi soror, ac nympharum sanguinis una ?
Sis felix, nostrumque leves quæcunque laborem.
Ver. 331.

1095. No more we importune] I am afraid Statius has neglected Horace's advice,

—— Servetur ad imum
Qualis ab incepto processerit, et sibi constet.

At least Adrastus seems to deviate from the pious track he first set out in. The sentiment is originally Lucan's, and I am sorry our author had the indiscretion to copy it.

Mentimur regnare Jovem, spectabit ab alto
Æthere Thessalicas, teneat cum fulmina, cædes ?
Scilicet ipse petit Pholoen ? petit ignibus Æten,
Immeritæque nemus Rhodopes, pinusque minan-
tem ?
Cassius hoc feriet potius caput ?
(Speaking of Cæsar). Phars. lib. 7.

The lines themselves are spirited and beautiful, and equally impious.

He spoke : a sudden languor seiz'd his tongue,
Inactive to the clammy jaws it hung.
His lungs no more their wonted aid supply,
And fault'ring in their course the accents die.
Pale was each face with thirst and with despair,
Faintly they heave for breath and gasp for air.
The Lemnian princess fix'd her modest eyes
Prone to the ground, and thus at length replies.
"'Tis true, O Greeks, from Heav'n I claim my birth,
And far in woe surpass the race of Earth.
Hard is my lot, a nurse's cares to prove,
And tend the produce of another's love ;
While mine, perchance, the pangs of hunger know,
And crave what on an alien I bestow.
Yet for the author of my birth I claim
A monarch great in empire as in fame.
But, why do I delay to give redress,
And aggravate with converse your distress ?
Come then, if haply yet Langia glides,
And rolls beneath the ground his silent tides.
Ne'er was he known to leave his channel dry,
Not e'en when Sirius fires the sultry sky ;
Or Cancer on his utmost limit shines,
And to the scorching Lion near inclines."
She spoke : and to procure the promis'd aid,
In haste her charge on the soft herbage laid.
Then heap'd around the choicest flow'rs, and tries
With lulling sounds to close his streaming eyes ;
Such as great Cybele, when erst she strove
To soothe the plaintive cries of new-born Jove ;
Around the babe in antic measures pass
Her jovial priests, and strike the tinkling brass,
But strike in vain : the cymbal's feeble sound,
Is in the infant's louder clamours drown'd.
Meanwhile in childish sports Opheltes past
The fatal day, of all his days the last.
One while the rising blades of grass he spurns,
Then, as his thirst, or lust of food returns,
Recalls his absent nurse with feeble cries,
Or seeks in sleep to close his heavy eyes :
To form the speech of man he now essays,
And harmless thoughts in broken sounds conveys ;
Erects his list'ning ears at ev'ry sound,
And culls the tender flow'rs that grow around :
Too credulous to the fallacious grove,
Nor conscious of the fate decreed by Jove.
Thus Mars on Thracian mountains topt with snow,
Or Hermes rang'd along Cyllene's brow.
Thus often, on his native shore reclin'd,
Apollo lay, and youthful thefts design'd,
The troops meanwhile, impatient of delay,
Thro' shades and devious thickets force their way :
One follows, where his fair conductress leads,
Another, urg'd with greater thirst precedes ;
While she repeated, as she past along,
Her promises, and cheer'd the drooping throng :

1113. From Heav'n] She was the grandaughter of Bacchus by her father Thoas's side.

1116. Of another's love] Archemorus or Opheltes.

1117. While mine] She had twins, named Thoas and Euneus, by Jason.

1133. Such as great Cybele] Cybele, or the Earth, was the mother of all the other deities. Her sacrifices were celebrated with a confused noise of timbrels, pipes, and cymbals. Hence Horace says,

——— Non acuta
Sic geminant Corybantes æra.

Soon as the rocky murmur greets their ears,
And in full view the grateful vale appears;
" A stream!" the leading chief exclaims aloud,
And waves the standard o'er the joyful crowd;
" A stream!" at once ten thousand voices cry,
" A stream!" the list'ning hills and rocks reply.
Thus, when the pilot on th' Ionian main
Discerns the summit of Apollo's fane,
The sturdy boatman quits awhile his oar,
And hails with joyful shouts the list'ning shore,
The list'ning shore returns the deaf'ning sound,
The rocks remurmur, and the deeps rebound.
Eager to drink, the rushing crowds descend,
Unmindful of their sov'reign or their friend.
Horses and charioteers, a mingled throng,
Steed press'd on steed, and man drove man along.
Here kings themselves in vain precedence claim,
In rank superior, yet their thirst the same.
Some tumble headlong from the slipp'ry rock,
Others are whelm'd beneath the wat'ry shock.
The king, to whom before a million bow'd,
Finds not a subject in the num'rous crowd.
E'en sinking friendship meets with no return
Of aid, while each becomes his own concern.
The stream, whose surface late was known to show,
Clear as a glass, the shining sands below,
Obscene with filth and gather'd mud appears,
And a discolour'd, sable aspect wears.
The flatted grass avows their heavy tread,
And bending Ceres hangs her drooping head:
Their thirst no bounds, and no distinction knows,
The more they drink, the more the fever glows.
Such is the prospect, when, o'erthrown the wall,
Bellona dooms a captive town to fall:
Vulcan and Mars with mutual aid engage,
And all is tumult, ruin, blood, and rage.
At length a chief, as in the midst he stood,
Thus gratefully bespoke the list'ning wood;
" O thou, whose verdant shades, and envied grove,
Can boast alone the patronage of Jove,
Here let thy wrath its utmost limits know,
Nor pass the bounds which Heav'n and fate allow.
Not greater was thy vengeance, when of old
Alcides slew the terrour of the fold,
When in his fatal gripe the hero prest
The throat and windpipe of the savage pest.
And thou, dispensing genius of the stream,
Impervious to the Sun's meridian beam,
Still calm, uninterrupted may'st thou range,
And from succeeding ages feel no change.
Thy channel no increase from seasons knows,
From dropping zephyrs and dissolving snows;
Nor Iris, varied by Phœbean beams,
Refunds the property of other streams:
From thy own source recruited with supplies,
Nor varied by each star that rules the skies.
Lycormas shall in vain precedence claim,
And Ladon, sacred to Apollo's name:
Sperchius shall resign his share of praise,
And Xanthus, favour'd in Mæonian lays.
But greater marks of favour shalt thou prove,
And shine in votive honours next to Jove;
Full in the shade of these encircling bow'rs,
Shall rise an altar, grac'd with native flow'rs:
So thou but open at our next return
The liquid treasures of thy sacred urn,
So thus our wasted strength again restore,
And hail us to this hospitable shore."

BOOK V.

THE ARGUMENT.

After the confederates had refreshed themselves at the river Langia, Hypsipyle, at the request

1161. Soon as the rocky murmur] This is taken from the third Æneid of Virgil.

Cum procul obscuros colles, humilemque videmus
Italiam, Italiam primus conclamat Achates,
Italiam læto socii clamore salutant. Verse 522.

And again by Tasso.

Ecco apparir Gierusalem si vede,
Ecco additar Gierusalem si scorge;
Ecco da mille voci unitamente
Gierusalemme salutar si vede. Canto 3. st. 3.

1168. The summit of Apollo's fane] Leucas was a town in the isle Leucadia in the Ionian sea, now called Santa Maura, famous for the temple of Apollo, to which those that were love-sick resorted, and were cured. Ovid describes it thus:

——Quoniam non ignibus æquis
Ureris, Ambracias terra petenda tibi.
Phœbus ab excelso, quantum patet, aspicit æquor.
Actiacum populi Leucadiumque vocant.
Heroid. Sap. to Phaon.

As for the simile, Tasso has copied it.

Così di naviganti audace stuolo,
Che mova à ricercar' estranio Lido,
E in mar dubbioso sotto ignoto polo
Provi l'onde fallaci, e'l vento infido;
S'al fin discopte il defiato suolo,
Il saluta da lungo in lieto grido,
E l'uno al' altro il mostra, e in tanto oblia
La noia, e'l mal della passata via. C. 3. st. 4.

1213. Nor Iris] The poet seems to have fancied, the rainbow drew up water from the sea or rivers, and poured it down again in showers of rain. So Lucan:

Arcus ————
Oceanum bibit, raptosque ad nubila fluctus
Pertulit, et cœlo defusum reddidit æquor.

Of all the books of the Thebaid, there is none more pleasing than the fourth. It may be divided into three parts, each of which has its particular beauties, and claims a distinct share of admiration. The first part, which comprehends an account of the warlike preparation at Argos, and a description of the troops and commanders of the confederate army, is wonderfully entertaining. The second part, which contains a description of the whole art of necromancy, the government and different compartments of the infernal regions, and a succinct account of the most celebrated personages before the Theban war, is extremely instructive. The third and last part, which is the introduction to an episode, contains a fine piece of machinery in the distress of the allies, and is a mixture of instruction and entertainment. In a word, in whatever light we contemplate it, we shall find it one of the most correct, diversified, and spirited books in the whole poem.

of Adrastus, relates her misfortunes, and in particular, describes the famous massacre of the males, the deliverance of her father, the arrival and amours of the Argonauts at Lemnos, and her abdication of the government. In the mean time, Archemorus, whom she had left behind, is slain by a serpent dedicated to Jupiter. Hypsipyle, alarmed with the screams of the dying infant, leaves the army, and is followed by Parthenopæus, whom Adrastus had sent to know the cause of her departure. As soon as the allies are acquainted with what had happened, they march with Parthenopæus to destroy the serpent. Hippomedon makes an unsuccessful attempt with a huge stone, and Capaneus kills the monster with his spear. Jupiter, enraged at this, scarcely refrains from punishing the hero with a thunderbolt, and, as a token of his displeasure, darts down a flash of lightning, which falls upon his helmet. Hypsipyle makes a lamentation over the infant's body. Lycurgus makes an attempt to slay her, but is withheld by Tydeus. This occasions a riot, which is, however, quelled by the interposition of Amphiaraus, who persuades the army to do funeral honours to Archemorus, in an oration which concludes this book.

THEIR thirst allay'd, and fervent heat of blood,
The joyful legions quit the shallower flood.
Recruited with the draught, the gen'rous steed
With louder neighings seeks the verdant mead.
As now returning health dispers'd the pain,
And lusty vigour strung their nerves again;
Th' exulting troops with fiercer ardour glow,
And threat and vow destruction to the foe;
As if some hidden virtue in the stream
Renew'd their courage and extinguish'd flame.
Again the warriors, gath'ring from afar,
Move into ranks, and wear the form of war;
Again each chief his scatter'd forces joins,
Gleams in the front, and forms the deep'ning lines.
As light'nings issue from a sable cloud,
Such from their arms the bright effulgence flow'd.
Thus, spring returning, from the sultry coast
Of Nile, the cranes, a thick embodied host,
Expand their wings, and with hoarse clangours fly
To milder climes, and a more temp'rate sky.
Their length'ning squadrons shade the plain below,
Loud and more loud the piercing clangours grow;
Till to some running stream they bend their way,
Or bask beneath the Sun's descending ray.
Amidst his circling peers Adrastus stood
Beneath an ash, the glory of the wood;
And, on the Theban hero's lance reclin'd,
Thus to the Lemnian queen reveal'd his mind.
" Whoe'er thou art, to whom these squadrons owe
Their lives, O! make us partners of thy woe.
Honours like these th' imperial lord of air,
And all th' etherial host might wish to share:
Fain would we learn, what happy spot of earth
Can boast your residence and whence your birth!
Tho' fortune frowns, impartial Heav'n exerts
Her arm of succour, and your cause asserts;
And in that air and dignity we trace
The rank and hidden glories of your race."
The princess bends awhile on earth her eyes,
And her relation ushers in with sighs.
" The odious task, O monarch, you impose,
Renews, alas! unutterable woes:
Say, conscious Lemnos, how shall I relate
Thy scenes of carnage, and thy deeds of hate?
Again the daring crime appears in sight,
And all the horrours of the fatal night.
Thrice hapless they, whose breasts the Furies fir'd,
And in whose hearts this impious rage inspir'd!
'Twas I, and I alone, who durst conceal
My sire, devoted to the ruthless steel.
Let not my simple weeds and sordid vest
Persuade you to despise your friendly guest.
But why do I divert with these delays
The cares of war, and military praise?
Know then, from Thoas, great in arms, I spring,
Tho' flying from the chains of Nemea's king."
The beauteous mourner rises in esteem,
Her talents equal to the labour seem.
All wish to know the sequel of her woes,
But chief Adrastus urg'd her to disclose.
" While these our troops unite their common aid
To force a passage thro' yon gloomy shade,

17. Thus, spring returning] This comparison seems to have been a favourite among the poets. Homer first adopted it.

Ἤΰτε περ κλαγγὴ γεράνων πέλει οὐρανόθι πρὸ,
Αἵτ' ἐπεὶ οὖν χειμῶνα φύγον, καὶ ἀθέσφατον ὄμβρον,
Κλαγγῇ ταί γε πέτονται ἐπ' Ὠκεανοῖο ῥοάων,
Ἀνδράσι Πυγμαίοισι φόνον καὶ κῆρα φέρουσαι.
Ἠέριαι δ' ἄρα ταί γε κακὴν ἔριδα προφέρονται.

Virgil borrowed it from him.

Quales sub nubibus atris
Strymoniæ dant signa grues, atque æthera tranant
Cum sonitu, fugiuntque notos clamore secundo.

Tryphiodorus has imitated it likewise.

Οἷαι δ' ἀφνειοῖο μέτηλυδες ὠκεανοῖο
Χεῖματος ἀμφὶ πολοῖ, γεράνων στίχες ἠερόφωνων,
Κυκλον ἐποχμεύουσιν ἀλήμενες ὀρχηθμοῖο,
Γειοπόνοις ἀρότησιν ἀπεχθέα κεκλήγυιαι.

Des. of Troy, v. 343.

41. The odious task] The length of this narration is abundantly compensated for by the beauties of it. The poet seems to avow his intention of imitating Virgil in his second book, by ushering it in with almost the same terms.

—— Immania vulnera, rector,
Integrare jubes——

61. While these our troops] It sometimes happens (says Longinus) that a writer, in speaking of some person, all on a sudden puts himself in that other's place, and acts his part; a figure which marks the impetuosity and hurry of the passions. The poet stops his narration, forgets his own person, and instantly, without any notice, introduces the person speaking. By this sudden transition, he prevents the reader, and the transition is made before the poet himself seems sensible he had made it. The true and proper place for this figure is when the time presses, and the occasion will not admit of any delay: it is elegant then to pass from one person to another, as in that of Hecatæus.

" The herald, extremely discontented at the orders he had received, gave command to the Heraclidæ to withdraw.—It is no way in my power to

Nor does the task require a little force,
(So thick the bushes that obstruct their course)
Each circumstance of woe relate anew,
And from the cause the dire effect pursue:
What follow'd your aversion to the crime,
And why secluded from your native clime.
'Tis pleasant to review the scenes of grief,
And to divulge our woes a short relief."
He paus'd: the captive princess thus replies:
" Encircled by the deep fair Lemnos lies;
Here weary Vulcan wastes his leisure hours,
And recollects in sleep his scatter'd pow'rs.
The cloud-capt Athos from his length'ning steep
O'erlooks our isle; his groves o'ershade the deep.
Each fronting tract of land the Thracian ploughs,
The Thracian, fatal to each Lemnian spouse.
Once great in arms and useful arts it shone,
Fertile in chiefs of valour and renown:
Not Delos, or the Samian isle could claim
A greater share of riches and of fame;
Till Heav'n to punish our offence decreed,
Nor were we wanting to promote the deed:
No temples to the queen of love were rais'd,
Nor incense on the sacred altars blaz'd.
Thus sometimes anger stings a heav'nly mind,
And vengeance sure, tho' tardy, creeps behind.
From Paphos, where a hundred altars smoke,
And love-sick votaries her aid invoke,
Careless of dress and ornament she moves,
And leaves behind her cestus and her doves.
The Moon had measur'd half the starry frame,
When the fierce goddess with the Furies came:
Far other flames than those of love she bears,
And high in air the torch of Discord rears.
Soon as the fiend-engend'red serpents roam,
Diffusing terrours o'er each wrangling dome,
The Loves, or willing, or compell'd by force,
From guilty Lemnos bend their airy course;
Lemnos, which dearer to her consort stands
Than all the cities rear'd by mortal hands.
Urg'd by no cause, the sullen bridegroom fled
From blooming beauty, and the genial bed;
No more he pays the pleasing debt of love,
When conscious Cynthia rules the realms above:
Nor sleep surprises with unnotic'd pace
The clasping pair, and strengthens their embrace:
But rage and hate in every breast arise,
And with his torch inverted Hymen flies.
The men (a plea for absence) oft complain
Of Thracian insults, and demand the plain:
And tho' from camp their eyes with ease command
Their native city, and the Lemnian strand,
Tho' nature, oft recoiling, chides their stay,
And their sad children beckon them away;
Stretch'd on the banks, they rather wish to bear
The wintry storm, th' inclemencies of air,
And listen to the hoarse-resounding roar
Of nightly surges, breaking on the shore.
Our sex in social converse seek relief,
And point to Thrace, the object of their grief:
From morn to night the stream of sorrow flows,
And Sol but sets to rise upon their woes.
How blest was I, a stranger then to love,
And all the pangs, which widow'd matrons prove.
Now thro' the zenith flaming Sol had driv'n
His panting steeds, and gain'd the middle Heav'n,
When, tho' no gath'ring clouds the day control,
Thro' skies serene portentous thunders roll;
The caverns of the smoky god display
Thick-steaming flames, and choke the face of day:
Tho' mute each blast, the rough Ægean roars,
And heavy surges lash the plaintive shores:
Then grave Polyxo thro' the city roves,
And mourns her widow'd bed and slighted loves.
Mad as the Thracian bacchanal appears,
When from afar the vocal pipe she hears,

help you; if, therefore, you would not entirely perish, and if you would not involve me too in your ruin, depart and seek a retreat among some other people."

Treatise on the Sublime, cap. 3.

92. Her cestus]. The cestus or magic girdle of Venus is thus described by Homer.

——Ἔνθα δέ οἱ θελκτήρια πάντα τέτυκτο,
Ἔνθ' ἔνι μὲν φιλότης, ἐν δ' ἵμερος, ἐν δ' ὀαριστὺς,
Πάρφασις, ἥτ' ἔκλεψε νόον πύκα περ φρονεόντων.

There is a singular propriety in making this goddess the authoress of these disturbances: the machine is allegorical, and implies, that the Lemnian matrons were excited to such a degree of lust, as to massacre their husbands for their natural impotency, or affected continence.

101. Lemnos] The reason why Vulcan is said to reside at Lemnos, was, because that island abounds with subterraneous veins of fire. He fell there from Heaven, as he himself says.

Πὰν δ' ἦμαρ φερόμην, ἅμα δ' ἠελίω καταδύντι
Κάππεσον ἐν Λήμνω.———— Hom. Iliad. b. 1.

Where philosophers say, that element has its proper place. Here it was, that he contrived the famous chain, which possibly might prejudice his consort against the Lemnians.

129. When, tho' no gath'ring clouds] This was looked upon by the ancients as very ominous: Hence Lucan enumerating the prodigies previous to the civil war between Cæsar and Pompey, says,

———Tacitum sine nubibus ullis
Fulmen.——— Phars. lib. 1.

And Horace mentions it as a warning sent from Heaven, to deter him from continuing his former irreligious course of life.

———Diespiter
Igni corusco nubila dividens,
Plerumque per purum sonantes
Egit equos, volucremque currum. Lib. 1. ode 34.

137. Mad as the Thracian bacchanal] Virgil has made choice of the same comparison to express the rage and madness of Dido, when Æneas was going to forsake her.

Sævit inops animi, totamque incensa per urbem
Bacchatur: qualis commotis excita sacris
Thyas, ubi audito stimulant trieterica Baccho
Orgia, nocturnusque vocat clamore Cithæron.
Æneid lib. 4. 300.

And Tryphiodorus likewise.

Οὐχ' οὕτω Θρήισσαν ἐνὶ δρυμοῖσι γυναῖκα
Νήδυμος αὐλὸς ἔτυψεν ὀρειμανέος Διονύσου,
Ἥτε θέω τυφθεῖσα παρήορον ὄμμα τιταίνει,
Γυμνὸν ἐπισείουσα κάρη κυανάμπυκι κισσῷ.

What he mentions of the Bacchanal's being rous-

'Evoe' she cries, and shakes the solid ground,
While echoing mountains answer to the sound.
Flush'd are her cheeks, and haggard roll her eyes,
She rends the desert town with frantic cries,
And, while the gates resound beneath her strokes,
To join in aid th' assembling dames invokes.
Four death-devoted babes, (sad scene of grief)
Hung at her side, and sought to give relief.
Swift as our leader, to Minerva's fane
We bend our course, a wild disorder'd train.
Silence enjoin'd, with confidence arose
The daring authoress of all our woes;
Her better hand a naked dagger press'd,
And thus her speech the wrathful fair address'd.
'Ye Lemnian dames, dissolv'd in barren ease,
If Venus yet retains the pow'r to please;
If empty marriage forms ye disapprove,
And hate the name without the joys of love;
Hear and attend: when Fortune points the way,
And Heav'n inspires, 'tis impious to delay:
To vengeance rise; nor let your sex be known
By want of courage, but by form alone.
Yet Hymen's privilege we may regain,
And love and genial joys revive again,
Would each the toil with just division share,
And join her private with the public care.
Three years have past, since each deserted bride
Has lost the sullen partner of her side:
No more each debt of love and duty's paid,
No more Lucina yields her timely aid.
Prompted by nature, and by love inclin'd,
The fishes, birds, and beasts increase their kind.
Stern Danaus his progeny could rouse
To vengeance for the breach of marriage vows,
And, unrestrain'd with fears, dismiss the foe,
In dreams of terrour, to the shades below:
But we, a worthless, servile, heartless train,
Had rather brook tyrannic Hymen's chain.
Yet should these old examples fail to move
Your just revenge of alienated love;
Copy the Thracian dame, who durst explore
Her spouse's heart, and drink the rushing gore.
Each doubt, and each objection to remove,
Myself will first the guilty labour prove.
Four babes, the boast and solace of their sire,
Shall first beneath the ruthless sword expire:
Nor shall their blandishments a respite gain,
But interposing Nature plead in vain:
While yet they breathe, the author of their birth
Shall crown the heap, and stain the loaded Earth.
What heroine dares thus far in guilt engage,
And second my design with equal rage?'
Meanwhile the Lemnian fleet, in all the pride
Of swelling canvas, cleaves the yielding tide.
This with pleas'd eyes the fierce Polyxo view'd,
And thus in height of joy her theme pursu'd.
'When Fortune calls, what farther can detain,
And shall the gods afford their aid in vain?
Our foes advance, impell'd by adverse fate,
To stain the sword, and glut in death our hate.
Late slighted Venus in a dream appear'd,
And o'er my head a naked falchion rear'd.
Why waste ye thus the bloom of youth? (she said)
Arise, arise, and purge the marriage bed;
On me alone for other flames rely;
Each vacant bed will I myself supply.
The goddess spoke, and on the pillow laid
This same (believe me) this same vengeful blade,
But linger on, when fair occasion calls,
And their ships ride in prospect of our walls:
At ev'ry stroke they raise the briny foam,
And bring, perhaps, their Thracian consorts home.'
Her words their hearts with manly rage inspire,
And spread from breast to breast the vengeful fire.
Not greater shouts the plains of Scythia rend,
When the fierce amazons to fight descend,
When their stern patron summons from afar
His virgin troops, and frees th' imprison'd war.
Nor discord, rising from a various choice,
Disturbs their councils with tumultuous voice;
But equal was their will, the same their haste
To desolate, and lay each mansion waste,
To strike the youth, and sire with age opprest,
To tear the wailing infant from the breast,
And subject to their unexcepting rage
Each stage of life, and each degree of age.
There grew a forest near Minerva's fane,
Whose gloomy boughs obscure the subject plain,
A steepy mount o'erhangs the nether glade,
And Sol is lost between the double shade.
Here they repair, and at the rites obscene
Attest Bellona, and the Stygian queen.
From Acheron their course the Furies bend,
And, uninvok'd, the sacrifice attend.
The Paphian goddess turns on ev'ry side
Her steps unknown, and fires each youthful bride.
Spontaneous then fell Caropeia brought
Her son (his sex, alas! his only fault);
A throng of armed priestesses surrounds,
The victim falls beneath unnumber'd wounds:
The life-blood issuing from a thousand strokes,
With horrid imprecations each invokes:
The recent shade from its dark prison springs,
And haunts the mother with encircling wings.

ed to fury by the pipe, is confirmed by Apuleius. Evantes exiliunt lucitanto tibiâ lymphaticum tripudium. Metam. lib. 8.

181. Each doubt] Cæsar has recourse to the same argument, in order to persuade his soldiers to cut down the sacred grove of Massylia, after he had given the first stroke himself.

Jam ne quis vestrûm dubitet subvertere sylvam
Credite me fecisse nefas. Lib. 3, v. 446.

199. Late slighted Venus] This fiction is palpably borrowed from the fifth book of Virgil's Æneid, where Iris, in the form of Berce, a Trojan matron, advises her supposed companions to burn the Trojan fleet, by affirming, that Cassandra had appeared to her for that purpose.

Nam mihi Cassandræ per somnum vatis imago
Ardentes dare visa faces. Lib. 5. v. 636.

213. Not greater shouts] Our author, probably, had the following simile of Virgil in his eye.

Quales Threiciæ, cum flumine Thermodontis
Pulsant, & pictis bellantur Amazones armis:
Seu circum Hippolyten, seu cum se Martia curru
Penthesilea refert; magnoque ululante tumultu,
Fæminea exultant lunatis agmina peltis.
Æneid, lib. 11. v. 659.

221. To strike the youth] Lucan has described a general massacre in a similar manner.

Non senis extremum piguit vergentibus annis
Præcipitâsse diem: nec primo in limine vitæ
Infantis miseri nascentia rumpere fata.
Crimine quo parvi cædem potuere mereri.

Struck at the sight, my limbs with horrour shook,
The blood at once my ghastly cheeks forsook.
Thus fares the hind, by rav'ning wolves pursu'd,
As first she seeks the covert of the wood;
Much she distrusts a safe retreat in flight,
But more her strength and fortune in the fight.
Now, now she seems to feel her seizing foes,
And hears with dread their jaws eluded close.
Meanwhile, their anchors dropt, the ships restore
The Lemnian warriors to their native shore:
With emulation on the deck they stand,
Contending, who should first attain the strand.
Far happier! had they press'd the Thracian plain,
Or sunk beneath the fury of the main.
The lofty fanes are hid in ambient smoke:
And votive victims grace the fatal stroke:
But the black flame and unsound entrails prove
Th' unfav'ring purpose of the gods above.
Late and unwilling to his watry bed
The Sun retir'd, and veil'd his radiant head,
Detain'd by Jove; nor ever did the day
So long before survive his setting ray.
The stars awhile withheld their gleamy light,
And sicken'd to behold the fatal night.
While other isles enjoy their usual share
Of light, and glitter with the distant glare,
O'er guilty Lemnos gath'ring clouds arise,
And low-hung vapours choke the lab'ring skies.
Lemnos, in circling darkness lost, alone
Was to the sorrowing mariner unknown.

245. Thus fares the hind] The principal images which compose this comparison, are taken from the following beautiful one of Virgil.

Inclusum veluti si quando in flumine nactus
Cervum, aut puniceæ septum formidine pennæ
Venator cursu canis & latratibus instat;
Ille autem, insidiis & ripâ territus altâ,
Mille fugit refugitque vias: at vividus Umber
'Hæret hians, jam jamque tenet, similisque tenenti
Increpuit malis, morsuque elusus inani est.'
Tum vero exoritur clamor: ripæque, lacusque
Responsant circà, & cœlum tonat omne tumultu.
Æneid, lib. 12. v. 749.

259. Unsound entrails] There is a certain mark in the entrails, which is called the god; and when this appears whole and entire, it betokens the favour of the gods. But if it is torn and maimed, it shows their displeasure. Lactantius.

261. Late and unwilling] However faulty the heathen poets have been in their descriptions of the gods, they generally take care to throw in some hints of their abhorrence of evil, and willingness to prevent or delay at least the perpetration of it, as far as is practicable, without encroaching upon the prerogative of fate. Of this we have a remarkable instance before us, where Jupiter, to testify his detestation of the matron's project, is feigned to defer the approach of night, which was appointed for the execution of it. Lucan, at the beginning of his seventh book, says,

Segnior oceano, quam lex æterna vocabat,
Luctificus Titan nunquam magis æthera contra
Egit equos, currumque polo rapiente retorsit:
Defectusque pati voluit, raptæque labores
Lucis: & attraxit nubes, non pabula flammis,
Sed ne Thessalico purus luceret in orbe.

Now from the finish'd rites they bend their way,
To drown in wine the labours of the day;
And, while the sprightly essence of the bowl
Glows in each vein, and opens ev'ry soul,
With rapture they recount their recent toils,
Their victories, and long-contested spoils.
Their wives alike indulge the genial hour,
Studious to please, and call forth beauty's pow'r;
Then love's soft queen (to crown the short repast,
And bless the night of all their nights the last)
Breath'd in each husband's breast a fierce desire
Of am'rous joys that quickly must expire.
'Twas dead of night; the matrons cease to sing,
Dumb was each voice, and mute the tuneful string;
When sleep, half-brother of approaching death,
Steep'd in soft dews exhal'd from Styx beneath,
Safe under covert of the silent hours,
With lavish hand his opiate juices pours,
But not on all: their ardour to destroy,
And watchful cares the female part employ.
At length, no longer patient of delay,
They rush impetuous on their helpless prey:
And each (a fury lodg'd within her breast),
Invades her man, with downy sleep opprest.
Thus Scythian tigresses the herd surround,
And leap amidst them with a furious bound,
When, press'd with hunger, they desert the wood,
Or their fierce whelps demand the promis'd food.
What act of guilt, or whose untimely fate
Amidst a thousand shall I first relate?
O'er Helimus, with leafy honours crown'd,
Rash Gorge stands, and meditates a wound.
Cloy'd with the banquet, he retir'd to rest,
And puff'd the fumy god from out his breast;
But sleep forsook him, ere depriv'd of breath,
And starting at the cold approach of death,
He wakes, confounded at the sudden view,
And round her neck his arms in transport threw,
But mourns the social greeting ill repaid,
As in his chest he feels the driving blade.
Nor yet resenting of his wound, he prest
Th' unworthy object closer to his breast,
And, struggling in the griping arms of death,
On Gorge dwells, and wastes his parting breath.
Dire as they were, I cannot now relate
The vulgar's countless deaths and various fate:
Suffice it private evils to disclose,
And measure by my own another's woes.
Cræneus fell, a warrior fair and bold,
And youthful Cydon, grac'd with locks of gold.
With these, the product of an alien's bed,
I pass'd my early days, together bred.
Next Gyas bled, design'd with me to prove,
Had Heav'n prolong'd his date, the joys of love.

297. Thus Scythian tigresses] I know not whether I need make an apology to the reader, for rendering the word leæ, tigresses, instead of lionesses, as the deviation is so small, and yet so necessary. At least, I should think the roughness of the verse, which a close adherence to the original in this place would infallibly occasion, more inexcusable.

301. What act of guilt] There is a beautiful interrogation of this sort in the first volume of the Musæ Anglicanæ.

Se pandit ingens area,—seu libens
Equosque currusque Arviragi sequar,
Neronianos seu furores
Ulta, vocet Boadica Musam?

Then fair Æpopeus met his mother's blade,
As at the feast the wanton stripling play'd.
Lycaste of her rage disarm'd appears,
And sheds o'er Cydimus a flood of tears;
As she beheld a face of her own mold,
And hair which she herself had trick'd with gold,
Her consort slain, her mother near her stands,
Impels with threats, and arms her trembling hands.
As when the lion, or the spotted pard,
Long from the woods and forests are debarr'd,
With equal pain and labour is renew'd
Their savage nature, as at first subdu'd.
The fair Lycaste thus resists in vain;
She rushes on him, as he press'd the plain;
Catches the welling blood, and to renew
His wounds, by the loose hair his body drew.
But as Alcimede I first survey'd,
Her sire's pale visage fix'd upon the blade,
Fear shrunk my sinews, and congeal'd my blood,
And on my head my hair erected stood.
My father's image fill'd my pious mind,
Lest equal years might equal fortune find.
From thence in haste I seek the regal seat;
Fear aids my course, and wings my tardy feet.
My sire I found perplex'd with doubts and fears,
(For now the shouts and groans awak'd his ears,
And broke his slumbers, tho' the palace stood
Sequester'd, and incompass'd with a wood)
The motives of my flight I soon disclose,
And all the series of preceding woes:
' Arise, arise, or you for ever fall;
Our female foes approach the regal hall:
Nor on our utmost speed I much rely;
The shaft may yet arrest us as we fly.'
Struck at the news, the hoary king arose,
And left the silent mansion of repose.
Thro' the least peopled parts we speed our way,
And, in a sable cloud obscur'd, survey
The passages and streets around dispread
With streams of blood and mountains of the dead.
Here blades half-buried in the recent wound,
And shiver'd lances sparkling on the ground:
There tatter'd robes discolour'd by the sword,
And heads yet bleeding on the genial board.
There bowls and tables, floating in a tide
Of slaughter, we with grief and horrour ey'd.
And warriors, vomiting a crimson flood
From their torn throats, of wine and mingled blood.
Here dy'd the lusty youth in manly bloom,
There aged sires that shar'd an equal doom;
There babes, whose infant-tongues scarce yet began
To form in broken sounds the speech of man.

343. But as Alcimede] This circumstance, with many others in this narration, is taken from the second book of Virgil's Æneid, where Æneas, after having just related the manner of Priam's death, says,

Ac me tum primùm sævus circumstetit horror:
Obstupui: subiit chari genitoris imago,
Ut regem æquævum crudeli vulnere vidi
Vitam exhalantem. Ver. 559.

351. My sire I found] Virgil has a similar passage in the second Æneid, verse 298.

Diverso interea miscentur mœnia luctu:
Et magis atque magis (quanquam secreta parentis
Anchisæ domus, arboribusque obtecta recessit)
Clarescunt sonitus, atque armorum ingruit horror.

Such scenes of carnage and debauch succeed
Thessalian feasts on Ossa's summit spread,
When Bacchus heats the cloud-born centaurs' brains,
And fires the blood that revels in their veins;
With goblets first, then weapons they engage,
And mutual deaths arise from mutual rage.
While, favour'd by the gloom, we urge our flight,
Propitious Bacchus stood reveal'd to sight;
His course from Heav'n to yield us aid he sped,
And lambent glories danc'd around his head.
Full well distinguish'd, tho' no chaplets bound
His ruddy brows, nor wreaths of vine-leaves crown'd.
A briny torrent flows adown his cheeks,
And thus the mournful god his son bespeaks.
' While Lemnos shone, defended by the fates,
In peace at home, rever'd by foreign states,
No care was wanting on my part to speed
Each enterprise, and make their toils succeed.
Our present woes the destinies ordain,
And gods implore, and men resist in vain.
With tears and blandishments I sought to move
The sire of Heav'n, and thwart the queen of love;
But at her suit the partial thund'rer nods,
Rejects our prayers, nor heeds the suppliant gods.
Haste, haste away: 'tis thine, O nymph, to share
A parent's lot, and make his life thy care;
Convey him hence thro' yon deserted gate,
And seize the fair occasion, ere too late;
In t'other, Venus, girt in armour, stands,
And animates to fight her female bands.
Whence this new thirst of blood, this vengeful flame,
That fires the bosom of so soft a dame?
Do you your father to the deep attend;
The task be mine his passage to befriend.'
This said, he soon dissolves in air again,
And while black shades conceal from us the train
Of watchful females, darts a flaming ray
That shone a guide, and pointed out the way.

379. Such scenes of carnage] For an account of the fight between the Lapithæ and Centaurs, see Ovid's Metamorphoses, book 12.

385. While, favour'd by the gloom] Barthius has observed that this introduction of Bacchus is an imitation of Virgil, who describes Venus appearing to Æneas in the following manner:

—— Mihi se non ante oculos tam clara videndam
Obtulit, & purâ per noctem in luce refulsit
Alma parens, confessa deam. B. 2. v. 589.

401. But at her suit] This nod of Jupiter was so sacred, that whatever promise obtained the sanction of it, was esteemed inviolable, as Homer informs us in the following verses;

Εἰ δ' ἄγε, τοι κεφαλῇ κατανεύσομαι, ὄφρα πεποίθῃς',
Τȣ̃το γὰρ ἐξ ἐμέθεν γε μετ' αθανάτοισι μέγιςον
Τέκμωρ· ȣ̓ γὰρ ἐμὸν παλιάγετον, ȣ̓δ' ἀπάτηλον,
Οὐδ' ἀτελεύτητόν γ' ὅ, τι κεν κεφαλῇ κατανεύσω.

415. A flaming ray] This circumstance seems borrowed from Virgil, who introduces Jupiter assisting Æneas to make his escape in the following lines;

Stella facem ducens multa cum luce cucurrit,
Iliam summa super labentem culmina tecti,
Cernimus Idæâ claram se condere sylvâ,
Signantemque vias; tum longo limite sulcus
Dat lucem, & latè circum loca sulphure fumant.
Æn. lib. 2. v. 694.

With speed the god's directions we pursue,
And soon in part the ready vessel view;
My sire embark'd, to Neptune's watchful care,
And Æolus, I oft commend with pray'r.
No bound th' alternate stream of sorrow knows,
Till beamy Phosphor, rising on our woes,
Gave warning of Aurora's hastening car,
And deep in ocean sunk each paler star.
Unwilling then the vessel I forsook,
And often backward cast a wishful look;
Till now the long-expected gales arise,
And snatch the less'ning object from my eyes.
At length the morn, the blushing morn arose,
Whose beams the horrours of the night disclose,
Black interposing clouds arise between,
And from her sight exclude the loathsome scene.
Their actions now expos'd in open day,
The trembling matrons curse the treach'rous ray;
Each would her share of guilt with joy disclaim,
And blushing meets the partner of her shame.
They burn the bodies, or inhume with speed,
And hope in vain to veil the glaring deed.
But when the Cyprian goddess, cloy'd with gore,
And her fell co-aids left the captive shore,
The wretches, stung with sharp reflection, tear
Their locks, and weep involv'd in deep despair.
An island, late enrich'd with Thracian spoils,
Fam'd for its produce, wealth, and martial toils,
Bewails the ravish'd glory of her coast,
Her infants, senate, and victorious host.
Nor does she this irreparable woe
To shipwreck, war, or wasting sickness owe;
But her own hands, the tools of envious fate,
Wrought the dire mischief, which she mourns too late.
No more her vig'rous sons exert their toil
To plough the deeps, or break the stubborn soil.
O'er the whole town unwonted silence reigns,
And clotted blood each widow'd mansion stains.
Stern phantoms, rising from the shades beneath,
The sounds of vengeance in low whispers breathe.
Within the inner court in haste I raise
A sylvan pile, to feed the fun'ral blaze;
On this the sceptre, arms and robes, that grac'd
The Lemnian monarch, are in order plac'd.

439. But when the Cyprian goddess] From the present passage, we may see to what a degree the smallest circumstance is aggrandized and heightened in the hands of a great poet. The sense of the allegory is obviously this: when their rage and passion had subsided, and gave place to cooler and more mature reflection. This personification of the affections was introduced first into Greece by the Egyptians, and translated thence to Italy. Valerius Flaccus, who has slightly touched on this subject in his Argonautics, says, they were infatuated to such a degree, as to set their own houses on fire.

—— Diras aliæ ad fastigia tædas
Injiciunt, adduntque domos.——

The latter part of this remark belongs to Barthius.

459. On this the sceptre] That this was an established custom among the ancient heathens, may be inferred from the following verses of Virgil, where Dido is introduced giving her last commands to her sister.

With looks dejected, near the pile I stand,
A bloody dagger arms my better hand.
My scatter'd hair in wild disorder flows,
My habit such as suited with my woes.
Nor tears, the token of a wounded heart,
Were wanting to complete the mourner's part.
To prove their approbation of the deed,
The Lemnian sceptre is to me decreed.
(So much my flowing tears and ready tale
Did o'er each female's easy faith prevail)
What could I do, thus press'd by their demands?
Oft I confess'd my undeserving hands
Before the gods—Constrain'd at length t'obey,
I take the crown and mutilated sway.
From hence a load of watchful cares arose,
And anxious thoughts, impatient of repose,
Polyxo's guilt in visions stands renew'd,
And Lemnian horrours in our slumbers brood;
Till altars to their angry shades we rear,
And by their ashes with devotion swear.
Thus when the savage monarch of the wood,
Impell'd with anger, or desire of food,
Has torn some lordly bull, who long had led
The subject cattle, ruler of the mead,
The headless herd in straggling parties roves,
Unmindful of their pasture or their loves;
Hush'd are the fields, the rivers cease to roar,
And the mute herds their common loss deplore.
But lo! the Argo, loaded with a train
Of heroes, cleaves th' inviolated main:

Tu secreta pyram tecto inferiore sub auras
Erige, & arma viri, thalamo quæ fixa reliquit
Dextra feras.—— Æn. lib. 4.

Philoctetes likewise, in the Hercules Oeteus of Seneca, says,

Hic nodus, inquit, nulla quem capiet manus,
Mecum per ignem flagrat, hoc telum Herculem
Tantum sequatur. Hoc quoque acciperes, ait,
Si ferre posses. Adjuvet Domini rogum.
Tum rigida secum spolia Nemæi mali
Arsura poscit.—— Act 5. v. 1660.

481. Thus when the savage] Those who always expect in Statius those minute resemblances in every branch of a comparison, which are the pride of modern similes, will frequently find themselves disappointed in the course of this work. He seems so secure of the main likeness, that he makes no scruple of neglecting the small circumstances in such a manner as to leave the reader to supply them himself, and seems more desirous of presenting the mind with a great image, than fixing it down to an exact one. The writers of the present age act in a quite different, though less judicious manner, and distract and confound the reader with a multiplicity of images, as the ingenious authors of the Monthly Review have rightly observed. Their poems are not unlike the Dutch pieces of painting, where the figures are so thick, that they are lost and confounded in each other. This simile, however, is applicable in every particular; the headless herd answers to the people of Lemnos, the silence of the fields, rivers, &c. to that of the town, and the slaughtered bull to the men massacred by the women.

490. Of heroes] They were sent by Pelias king of Thessaly, to fetch the golden fleece from Colchis. The reader may find their voyage and ad-

From Thessaly the daring warriors came,
Embolden'd by the glorious lust of fame.
On either side the hoary billows rise,
And work their foamy fury to the skies,
Like some huge mountain, white with ancient snows,
Or floating isle, the lofty vessel shows.
Soon as the lab'ring oar's enjoin'd to cease,
The hoarse-resounding deep was hush'd in peace,
From out the middle ship a voice arose,
(The middle ship the list'ning waves enclose)
Far softer than the swan expiring sings,
Or Phœbus, when he strikes the tuneful strings.
'Twas Orpheus, taught by his celestial sire,
To sing in sweet conjunction with the lyre.
The sprightly music of his varied lay
Drives ev'ry sense but hearing far away;
And all, attentive to his pleasing strains,
Forget the past, nor feel the present pains.
To farthest Scythia were th' advent'rers bound,
And where the straits of Bosphorus resound.
The crew mistaken for a Thracian band,
In straggling troops we quit the dusty strand;
Like flocks of birds, or oxen, when dismay'd,
They hear the lion in the rustling shade.
No furies were at hand to reinspire
Heroic thoughts, and wake our dormant fire.
We climb the turret, whose impending steep
Affords a prospect of the distant deep;
Here javelins, stones, and knotty clubs we bore,
And swords, polluted with their masters' gore,
Confine within the mail our jutting breasts,
And proudly strut beneath the nodding crests.
On fronting Hæmus smil'd the god of fight,
And Pallas blush'd, astonish'd at the sight.

ventures described at large in Valerius Flaccus and Apollonius, who have both written a large poem on this subject only.

503. 'Twas Orpheus] The history of Orpheus is too well known to need an explanatory note. It will be sufficient to observe, that he was a Thracian by birth, the son of Apollo and Calliope, and murdered by the Thracian Bacchanals. The extraordinary effects of his skill in music are thus summed up by Horace.

Orphea——
Arte maternâ rapidos morantem
Fluminum lapsus, celeresque ventos;
Blandum et auritas fidibus canoris
Ducere quercus. B. 1. ode 12.

510. The straits of Bosphorus] The Bosphorus is a part of the sea, which lies in two different coasts; the one by Constantinople, and the other at the entrance of the Black Sea.

523. On fronting Hæmus] The epithet adverso, which I have rendered by fronting, has afforded matter of speculation to the judicious Barthius, who informs us, that it is very doubtful whether it should be applied to the situation of the mountain, or the enmity Mars bore the Lemnians on account of their patron Vulcan. With submission to this critic's superior judgment, we must beg leave to observe, that there is a more natural reason to be given for the enmity of Hæmus, (if we suppose adversus to signify hostile in this place, which we very much doubt,) viz. the invasion of Thrace by the Lemnians a little before. Barthius had certainly forgotten this, or he never would have

Then first reflection with their fears return'd,
And their past actions with regret they mourn'd,
Lest Heav'n, to punish their presumptuous crime,
Had sent the vessel from some hostile clime.
They now had almost gain'd the sandy beach,
And stood within a Cretan arrow's reach;
When pregnant clouds o'erhang the boiling main,
And Jove descends in sluicy sheets of rain.
Horrour sits brooding o'er the liquid way,
And Sol deserts the violated day.
From ev'ry quarter rushing winds resound,
Plough up the deep, and hurl the sands around.
Surges on surges roll with hideous roar,
And clash and break, and thunder to the shore.
Obsequious to the wind the vessel plies,
And, wafted by the billows, seeks the skies,
Or, as the gaping main at once divides,
On naked sands with swift descent subsides.
The canvas flits before the driving blast,
And with a crash descends the wav'ring mast.
The pilot's art, and strength of rowers fail,
Nor demigods against the storm prevail.
While thus the tempest's growing rage demands
Their utmost care, employing all their hands,
From ev'ry eminence a mingled show'r
Of stones and jav'lins on the ship we pour;
At Telamon and mighty Peleus throw,
And threat Alcides with the Cretan bow.
At once with Mars and Neptune they engage;
Some aim the dart with unavailing rage:
Th' unsteady motion of the vessel's course,
Their efforts breaks, and lessens half their force.
The floating hold of water others clear,
And intercept with shields the rushing spear.
Nor cease we yet our missive arms to ply,
But rain a winged tempest from on high.
Vast stakes, and an enormous weight of stone,
With jav'lins recent from the flames are thrown.
Now on the leaning vessel they descend,
Or hissing in the deep their fury spend.
In ev'ry joint the groaning Argo sounds,
And gapes wide-op'ning with a thousand wounds.
As when the piercing blasts of Boreas blow,
And scatter o'er the field the driving snow,

troubled his readers with this fetched hypothesis and critical refinement.

The reader may judge from this specimen, how much patience is requisite to peruse all the notes and observations of the commentators, and learn to commiserate the translator, who must either do it, or lie under the imputation of negligence and carelessness.

551. At Telamon] Telamon was the father of Ajax; and Peleus, his brother, of Achilles. The strength of Hercules is much too well known to require a note.

554. Some aim the dart] This default was occasioned by the violent motion of the ship. Lucan says,

Incertasque manus ictu languente per undas
Exercent.

567. As when the piercing blasts] Homer has a no less beautiful comparison.

——— Ὥστε νιφάδες χιόνος πίπτουσι θαμειαὶ
Ἤματι χειμερίῳ, ὅτε τ' ὤρετο μητίετα Ζεὺς
Νιφέμεν ἀνθρώποισι, πιφαυσκόμενος τὰ ἃ κῆλα,
Κοιμήσας δ' ἀνέμους χέει ἔμπεδον, ὄφρα καλύψῃ

The beasts beneath the fleecy ruin lie,
And intercepted birds forsake the sky.
Pale Ceres droops reclining on the ground,
The mountains echo, and the deeps rebound.
But, as the light'ning, beaming thro' the shade,
The manly features of each face display'd,
The falling arms our feeble gripe forsook,
And ev'ry limb with chilling horrour shook.
Prevailing nature rose in ev'ry breast,
And tenderness, our sex's only test.
Th' Æacidæ first strike our wond'ring eyes,
And stern Ancæus of gigantic size.
Next Iphitus, who with protended spear
From threat'ning rocks preserv'd the vessel clear.
Then Hercules, impatient for the land,
We soon distinguish from th' inferior band:
The vessel leans beneath the future god,
From side to side alternate as he strode.
But nimble Jason, haply then unknown,
Amidst his comrades far conspicuous shone.
From bench to bench incessantly he flew,
And animates by turns the drooping crew.
On Ida now, Oenides then he calls,
And threatens much th' inhospitable walls;
With wrath the ling'ring Salaus he view'd,
And Tyndar's son with briny foam bedew'd,
Nor unapprov'd the son of Boreas past,
Who toil'd to fix the canvas to the mast.
With animating shouts the liquid plain,
And echoing walls they shake, but shake in vain.
The tempest grows reluctant to their toils,
And from the tow'rs each shiver'd spear recoils.
In vain the pilot plies his weary hands;
The waves and rudder hear not his commands.
Whether to right or left he turns the prow,
The labour rises, and the dangers grow;
Till Æson's offspring from the stern display'd
The olive, sacred to the martial maid;
And peace and an alliance asks aloud,
Tho' interrupted by the noisy crowd.
Scarce could the falt'ring accents reach the shore,
Lost in the louder sea's tempestuous roar.
At length the storm and war together cease,
The waves unruffle and subside in peace:
While Phœbus, issuing from a ruddy cloud,
Restor'd the day, and more serenely glow'd.
From planks compacted with a furious bound,
The warriors gain the late unfriendly ground;

Ὑψηλῶν ὀρέων κορυφὰς, καὶ πρώονας ἄκρους,
Καὶ πεδία λωτεῦντα, καὶ ἀνδρῶν πίονα ἔργα,
Καὶ τ' ἐφ' ἁλὸς πολιῆς κέχυται λιμέσιν τε καὶ ἀκταῖς,
Κῦμα δέ μιν προσπλάζον ἐρύκεται, ἄλλα τε πάντα
Εἴλυται καθύπερθ' ὅτ' ἐπιβρίσῃ Διὸς ὄμβρος.
Iliad, b. 12.

575. The falling arms] This circumstance was a favourite of the poets in their descriptions of the effects of a sudden fright.

Τῆς δ' ἐλελίχθη γυῖα, χαμαὶ δέ οἱ ἔκπεσε κερκίς.
Homer's Iliad, b. 22. v. 448.

Nuncia fama ruit, matrisque adlabitur aures
Euryali; ac ———
Excussi manibus radii, revolutaque pensa.
Virgil's Æn. b. 9. v. 474.

——— Primo qui cædis in ictu
Diriguit, ferrumque manu torpente remisit.
Lucan's Phar. b. 2. v. 77.

And by their arms and princely vestments known,
With shouts are welcom'd to the widow'd town.
Their features undisturb'd with wrath or fear,
Attract our eyes, and doubly fair appear.
Thus oft the gods (as ancient fame reports)
Resign their pomp, and quit th' etherial courts:
When to fair Æthiopia they repair,
And make awhile the genial feast their care.
To leave their passage clear, the seas divide,
And mountains, level with the vales, subside.
On Earth a sudden spring is seen to rise,
Nor Atlas groans beneath th' incumbent skies.
Here valiant Theseus, clad in shaggy spoils,
The trophies of his Marathonian toils,
The sons of Boreas, on whose temples grew
A wing, that flutter'd oft as Boreas blew,

621. Thus oft the gods] The following simile is exquisitely beautiful, and full of that sublime simplicity, which Longinus commends so much in Homer. Had that critic seen it, he had undoubtedly given it a place in his collection, and ranked it with the celebrated description of Neptune in the 13th book of the Iliad, which, if it was not for the anticlimax at the close of our poet's, would not, we believe, be thought superior. There are some stanzas in a poem on the king's coming to Oxford (where the same comparison is made use of) which, we think, are imitated from our author's with great happiness.

Ille ut superbo Jupiter agmine
Cinctus deorum, sæpius Isidis
Invisit undas, & fluenta
Jam Thamesis potiora lymphis.
Quocunque tendunt, induitur novam
Natura formam, Floraque pascuo
Miratur agresti virentes
Sponte suos properare fœtus.
Vel tecta quiddam majus & amplius
Mutata præstant, hic quasi Carolus
Palatium præsens creasset,
Artificis superans labores.
Mus. Ang. ver. 1.

The hint of this comparison was taken from Homer, who in the 1st book of the Iliad, says,

Ζεύς γὰρ ἐπ' ὠκεανὸν μετ' ἀμύμονας Αἰθιοπῆας
Χθιζὸς ἔβη μετὰ δαῖτα· θεοί δ' ἅμα πάντες ἕποντο.
Verse 423.

629. Here valiant Theseus] Theseus was the son of Ægeus, king of Athens, famous for his friendship and valorous actions, among which the slaughter of the Marathonian bull was the principal. Minos, during the preparations for a sacrifice to Jove, demanded in prayer a victim worthy of the god; upon which he sent a bull of exquisite beauty. His daughter Pasiphaë falling in love with him, persuaded her father to preserve him alive, which enraged Jupiter so much, that he caused him to go mad: at length, being tamed by Hercules, he was dedicated to Juno at Argos, from whence he escaped to Marathon, where he was slain by Theseus.

631. The sons of Boreas] Their names were Calais and Zethes. Pindar has given the following account of them.

——— καὶ γὰρ ἑκὼν
θυμῷ γελανεῖ θᾶσσον ἔν-

Great Peleus, vanquish'd by his greater son,
The daring youth, the pride of Caledon,
Admetus, by the god of day obey'd,
And Orpheus, scarce a Thracian, we survey'd.
The Spartan twins, alike in shape and size,
An errour cause in each spectator's eyes.
A shining tunic either champion wore,
Each in his hand a pointed jav'lin bore.
Bare are the cheeks of each, their shoulders bare,
And starry glories grace their sparkling hair.
Behind his lord, young Hylas tript along,
Lost and obscur'd amidst the tow'ring throng:
With pain his tender feet the stripling ply'd
To match the demigod's gigantic stride,
And sweating under the huge quiver bore
The shafts envenom'd with Lernæan gore.
The Paphian queen repeats her fraudful arts,
And tempts again with love our soften'd hearts.
Saturnia, too, divulges thro' the town
The warrior's nation, rank and high renown.
Then first our altars blaz'd, our rites began,
But Heav'n and Jove are lost in dearer man.
The gates are open to each welcome guest,
(Our late aversion to the sex suppress'd)
The dead is to the living love resign'd,
And sweet oblivion calms each anxious mind.
Then were the pleasures of the genial board,
And lost repose by pitying Heav'n restor'd,
Nor, as her crime is known, O chiefs, refuse
To hear an artless woman's just excuse.
By the late furies of our sex I vow,
And ashes of my friends inurn'd below,
Unmov'd by lust, I gave my plighted hand,
Constrain'd by fate, and adverse Heav'n's command.
But he, the treach'rous partner of my bed
(My love unheeded, and my person fled)
Adores and gazes on another's charms,
And revels in a Colchian harlot's arms.
Returning spring had now prolong'd the day,
And earth relenting felt the genial ray,
When fav'ring Heav'n, our nuptial joys to crown,
With unexpected clamours fills the town.
Myself, constrain'd a mother's throes to prove,
Disclose a double pledge of mutual love:
One still retains his wretched grandsire's name,
(The most, perhaps, that fate allows to claim.)
Full twenty suns have deck'd the courts above,
Since first they breath'd the vital air of Jove;
Lycaste then receiv'd them as her own,
From that sad day their fortune is unknown.
Calm was old ocean's face, and southern gales
In rising murmurs tempt the swelling sails.
The ship, impatient for the liquid way,
Frets in the port, and loathes the long delay.
There Jason calls the ling'ring chiefs aboard,
And the glad vessel with provision stor'd.
Oh! had he never touch'd the Lemnian shore,
But pass'd direct to Colchos, since no more
My acts of kindness his compassion move,
Nor vows, nor dearer pledges of his love.
Yet shall impartial fame to latest times
Transmit his guilt, and brand the traitor's crimes.
When now the Sun, whose next revolving beam
Must close our loves, had sought the western stream,
The groans of the late dreadful night return,
And rage again and jealous fury burn.
Scarce had Aurora chas'd the stars away,
And op'd the rosy portals of the day,
When Æson's son, conspicuous from afar,
Plies the first oar, and leads the wat'ry war.
From ev'ry rock, and hill's impending steep
We long pursue them o'er the expanded deep,
Till, the waves joining with the distant skies,
Th' excluded objects vanish from our eyes.
A rumour spread, that wafted o'er the main,
Old Thoas shares his brother's ample reign,
That all my sorrow was a feint alone,
And but for show the pyres thick flaming shone;
Stung with remorse, arose the guilty crowd,
And, for my share of slaughter, call aloud.
'Shall only she,' they cry, 'refuse to bear
A part in guilt, while joyful we appear.
No more believe we, 'twas the fates' decree,
Or will of Heav'n, if she alone is free.'
Warn'd by these words to shun their vengeful hate,
I quit the burden of imperial state,
And seek my father's well-known track of flight
Along the shore, befriended by the night;
But Bacchus then was wanting in his aid,
For, as through woods and devious wilds I stray'd,
A band of ruthless pirates forc'd aboard,
And sold me to proud Nemea's haughty lord."

τύεν βασιλευς ἀνέμων
Ζήταν Κάλαΐν τε πατὴρ Βορέας,
Ἄνδρας πλευροῖσι νωτα πε-
φρίκοντας ἄμφω πορφυρέοις. Pyth. ode Δ. epode 8.

654. But Heav'n] This line calls to my remembrance some fine ones in Mr. Pope's Eloisa and Abelard.

The dear ideas, where I fly pursue,
Rise in the grove, before the altar rise,
Stain all my soul, and wanton in my eyes.
I waste the matin lamp in sighs for thee,
Thy image steals between my God and me.
Thy voice I seem in ev'ry hymn to hear,
With ev'ry bead I drop a tender tear.
When from the censer clouds of fragrance roll,
And swelling organs lift the rising soul,
One thought of thee puts all the pomp to flight,
Priests, tapers, temples swim before my sight.

669. On another's charms] When Jason arrived at Colchos, and was informed, that the capture of the golden fleece depended on the assistance of Medea, he married, and afterwards left her for Creusa, daughter of Creon king of Corinth. Euripides and Seneca have written a tragedy on this subject.

685. The ship] The diction in this place, daring as it seems, is not too big for the sense, but just in proportion to it. A man who condemns this as extravagant, can have no relish for poetry, since it is the very soul and essence of it. 'Tis composed of what Aristotle, with great propriety, stiles living words, i. e. such as exalt and enliven the sentiment. Homer often tells us, an arrow is impatient to be discharged, and a weapon thirsts for blood, which is equally bold and flighty with this before us.

689. Oh! had he never] This is more moderate than

O! utinam tunc cum Lacedæmona classe petivit,
Obrutus insanis esset adulter aquis.

Though perhaps Hypsipile had the greatest reason to complain.

While thus the queen harangues the list'ning train,
And, by divulging it, forgets her pain;
The tender infant whom she left behind,
(So the stern gods advis'd and fates design'd)
In fatal slumbers hangs his drooping head,
The skies his canopy, the ground his bed,
And, cloy'd with sport, and weary with his toils,
Grasp'd in his hand the grass and Flora's spoils.
Meanwhile, along the fields a serpent roves,
Earth-born, the terrour of Achæan groves;
Sublime on radiant spires he glides along,
And brandishes by fits his triple tongue.
An hideous length of tail behind he draws,
And foamy venom issues from his jaws.
Three rows of teeth his mouth expanded shows,
And from his crest terrific glories rose.
The peasants consecrated him to Jove,
The tutelary patron of the grove;
Whose altars, rais'd of living turf, are stor'd
With humble off'rings, which the swains afford.
One while he rolls his curling volumes round
The sylvan fane, or ploughs the furrow'd ground;
Then round an oak his scaly length he twines,
And breaks in his embrace the toughest pines.
From bank to bank extended oft he lies,
Cut by his scales the waves high-bubbling rise.
But now, when earth is furrow'd o'er with chinks,
And ev'ry nymph within her channel sinks;
He twists, impatient of th' autumnal heats,
His spiry length, and wide destruction threats,
And thro' exhausted springs and standing lakes
In winding folds his noxious progress takes.
One while he bares his lolling tongue in air,
Thro' impotence of pain and wild despair,
Then crawls, adhesive to the groaning plain,
If haply dew or moisture yet remain.
Where'er he breathes, the blasted herbage dies,
And wasting poisons from his hissing rise.
Vast as the vengeful dragon, that around
The double summit of Parnassus wound,
Till on his back, that ouz'd at ev'ry pore
A stream of blood, a grove of spears he bore:
Or he, who round the pole meand'ring glides,
And fair Calysto from her son divides.
What god, O infant! thus adorn'd thy death,
And why so soon depriv'd of vital breath?
Was it from each succeeding age to claim
Eternal honours, and a deathless name?
Smit with his tail, the dying babe awoke,
(Nor was the serpent conscious of the stroke)
Sleep soon invades his stiff'ning limbs again,
And locks them in an adamantine chain.
His nurse, alarm'd at his half-finish'd screams,
(Such as are utter'd in terrific dreams)
Essays to fly; but, destitute of force,
Her falt'ring limbs desert her in the course.
Too certain now of the portended ill
By various omens, which her bosom fill,
She rolls her quick-discerning eyes around,
And carefully inspects the fatal ground;
Then lifts her shrill-resounding voice on high
In well-known sounds, but meets with no reply.
What could she do?—No recent marks remain
To guide her footsteps o'er the trackless plain.
Roll'd up on earth the circling monster lies,
An acre scarcely bounds his ample size.
Him as the princess unsuspecting view'd,
With sudden shrieks she rends the spacious wood.
Unmov'd, the monster keeps his former post,
Her piercing clamours reach th' Argolic host.
Sent by the king, th' Arcadian hero learn'd
The fatal cause, and with the chiefs return'd.
Soon as the glare of arms the monster spies,
And hears the growing thunder of their cries,
He rears his crest, and with a fiery glance
Expects th' assailant's terrible advance.
First stoops Hippomedon, and from the fields,
Heav'd with vast force, a rocky fragment wields.
Vast was the mass of stone, the common bound
Of neighb'ring fields, and barrier of the ground.
As when by vast machines a pond'rous stone
Descending on some hostile gate is thrown;
Thus fell the craggy rock, but fell in vain,
And made a deep impression on the plain.
The field resounds, and leaves and branches torn
Aloft in air with horrid crash are borne.
" Tho' late in vain assail'd, my keener dart
Shall thro' thy scales a fatal wound impart,

733. Meanwhile] The following description of this animal will not be thought inferior to that of Virgil in the second book.

Ecce autem gemini à Tenedo tranquilla per alta
(Horresco referens) immensis orbibus angues
Incumbunt pelago, pariterque ad littora tendunt:
Pectora quorum inter fluctus arrecta, jubæque
Sanguineæ exsuperant undas; pars cætera pontum
Pone legit, sinuatque immensa volumina tergo.
Fit sonitus spumante salo: jamque arva tenebant;
Ardentesque oculos suffecti sanguine, et igne,
Sibila lambebant linguis vibrantibus ora. V. 203.

763. Vast as the vengeful dragon] The poets feign this dragon was a favourite of Juno, and the keeper of the Hesperian garden: but was afterwards slain by Hercules, and translated to Heaven. Virgil thus describes him.

Maximus hic flexu sinuoso elabitur anguis
Circum, perque duas in morem fluminis arctos.
Georgics, b. 1. v. 244.

782. By various omens] Homer likewise calls this impotence and suspension of the animal powers, occasioned by sudden fear, an omen.

Some strange disaster, some reverse of fate
(Ye gods avert it) threats the Trojan state.
Far be the omen, which my thoughts suggest!
Pope's Iliad, b. 22. v. 583.

803. The common bound] The ancient poets, to raise our ideas of the weight and magnitude of any stone, generally call it a land-mark.

——— Campo quod forte jacebat
Limes agro positus, litem ut discerneret arvis.
Virgil's Æneid, lib. 12. ver. 897.

811. Tho' late in vain assail'd] What a beautiful transition is this from the pathetic description of the death of Archemorus!—We are alarmed with the sudden interposition of Capaneus: he breaks in upon us like a flash of lightning, and surprises the reader, who was unprepared for it. While Hippomedon and the other heroes are content with throwing stones at a distance, Capaneus, like a true descendant of Mars, advances with spear in hand, and not only threats, but puts his threats in execution. However, the chief beauty

Whether thou art the guardian of the grove,
Or, what I wish, the property of Jove,"
The vaunting Capaneus exclaims aloud,
And rushes foremost of the warrior-crowd.
Swift thro' his gaping jaws the jav'lin glides,
And the rough texture of his tongue divides;
The point was seen above his crested head,
Then stains the ground with goary filth dispread.
The furious monster, unappall'd with pain,
In rapid mazes bounds along the plain,
Then, wrench'd the jav'lin from his bleeding head,
Swift to the temple of his patron fled:
Here long he struggles in the pangs of death,
In hissing threats at length resigns his breath.
Him Lerna's lakes in gentle murmurs mourn,
And Nemea, by his frequent windings worn:
Him ev'ry nymph, that late was wont to bring
Her early tribute from the rifled spring:
For him the fauns were seen to break their reeds,
And tear the leafy honours from their heads.
E'en Jove himself the fashion'd bolt demands,
And scarce withholds his all-avenging hands,
Till the blasphemer in process of time
Should merit vengeance for a greater crime:
Yet then a flashing ray was seen to graze
His beaming helmet, and augment the blaze.
As now Hypsipyle, the serpent slain,
Seeks her lost infant on the spacious plain,
Upon a distant eminence she spy'd
The with'ring grass with drops of slaughter dy'd:
Hither in haste the beauteous mourner flies,
And soon, too soon the killing object eyes.
In vain from words she seeks a short relief,
In vain in tears to vent her swelling grief;
Short of its course the pearly current hung,
And to the roof inactive cleaves the tongue.
One while she kisses his discolour'd cheeks,
Then thro' his limbs life's luke-warm passage seeks
In vain, his face and breast misplac'd, are drown'd
In blood, and the whole body seems one wound.
As when the bird, whose nest in search of food
Some serpent climb'd, and crush'd the tender brood,
Returning, finds her clam'rous infants gone,
And blood and scatter'd feathers left alone,
She drops the meat, and spurns the nest away;
The grove responsive echoes to her lay.
Soon as the wretch had in her lap with care
Repos'd his limbs, and dry'd them with her hair,
Her voice, releas'd from sad excess of grief,
A passage found, and thus she sought relief.
"O thou, whose form and features oft have brought
My own dear offspring's image to my thought,
Whose soft caresses could alone abate
The pangs of exile and a servile state:
Say, whence these wounds? what god could thus disgrace
Thy faultless figure, and thy charms efface?
I left thee fresh in life, in beauty gay,
Engag'd in pleasure, and amus'd with play.
Where now are all those sweet attempts to speak,
The sparkling eye and rose-resembling cheek?
Where are those artful smiles, that lisping tone
To me address'd, and known to me alone?
How to procure thee slumbers did I toil,
And talk of Argo, and thy native soil!
How have I press'd thee in my folding arms,
And gaz'd and doated on thy budding charms?
Thus sooth'd, I could forget I was a slave;
To thee my breast, another's right, I gave:
Now ready to thy mouth descends again
The middle current, but descends in vain.
Nor were there omens wanting to disclose
His fate, and warn me of impending woes:
Amidst the dusky horrours of the night
The Cyprian goddess stood confest to sight.
But why should I the fatal act disclaim,
And to the guiltless gods transfer the blame?
My speedy death shall for the crime atone,
'Tis thus decreed, nor seek I death to shun.
Say, could I thus forget my precious care,
While, urg'd by vain ambition, I declare
My daring country's fortune and my own,
And court the transient blazes of renown?
Lemnos, no more against thy queen exclaim,
Our guilt is equal, our disgrace the same.

of it, which consists in the sudden and abrupt turn of the address, had been entirely lost, if the poet had followed the usual forms and said, "Then Capaneus rushes with his spear, and begins as follows."—There are more instances of this elegancy in Statius, than any author we know of, as indeed he has a greater share of vivacity.

824. To the temple] Virgil has observed the same of the serpents that slew Laocoon in his second Æneid.

At gemini lapsu delubra ad summa dracones
Effugiunt, sævæque petunt Tritonidis arces:
Sub pedibusque deæ, clypeique sub orbe teguntur.
Ver. 225.

853. As when the bird] Virgil has a beautiful simile of the same kind with this in Statius, thus excellently translated by the duke of Buckingham.

So the sad nightingale, when childless made
By some rough swain, who stole her young away,
Bewails her loss beneath a poplar shade,
Mourns all the night, in murmurs wastes the day.
Her melting songs a doleful pleasure yield,
And melancholy music fills the field.

Tasso has likewise copied it.

Come Usignuol, cui'l villan duro invole
Dal nido i figli non pennuti ancora;
Che in miserabil canto afflitte, e sole
Pinge le notti, e n' empie i boschi, e l'ora.
Al fin col novo dì rinchiude alquanto
I lumi, e'l sonno in lor serpe fra'l pianto.
Gierusal. Lib. canto 12. st. 90.

871. Where now are] This is something like that beautiful exclamation in Horace.

Quo fugit Venus heu? quove color? decens
Quo motus? quid habes illius, illius,
Quæ spirabat amores,
Quæ me surpuerat mihi? Lib. 4. Ode 13.

883. Nor were there omens] As far as we can infer from the writings of Statius, he was very superstitious. All the personages, who have a place in his poem, lay a great stress on omens, and, after any calamity has happened to them, always recollect some vision that portended it. The correction that follows has a very beautiful effect. Upon the whole, we may conclude this oration to be a master-piece in the pathetic way. That of Euryalus's mother in the 9th book of the Æneid, and of Andromache in the 22d of the Iliad, are the only ones that can stand in competition with it.

If this entreaty merits your regard,
If my past service claims this small reward,
Lead me, O quickly to the serpent lead,
Or with your swords absolve my impious deed.
Oh! never may these eyes behold again
The sire, or injur'd partner of his reign:
Tho' (what can scarcely merit your belief)
My own would equal her severest grief.
Ere from these hands she take th' ungrateful load,
Th' ungrateful load, unhappily bestow'd,
May yawning earth a sudden passage rend,
And let me thro' the dark abyss descend."
The princess spoke, and, frantic with despair,
Deforms with blood her face, with dust her hair;
Then blames the grieving warriors, in whose cause
She left the babe, too studious of applause.
And now the news had reach'd the monarch's ears,
And fill'd the royal dome with sudden tears.
Lycurgus, on that inauspicious day,
From the Persean mountain bent his way;
Where angry entrails burnt beneath the shade
To th' unregarding thunderer were paid.
All commerce with Adrastus he declin'd,
Nor in the council, or the battle join'd.
Not void of martial courage was his breast,
But piety the love of war suppress'd.
Besides the god's response, with counsel fraught,
Long lay revolving in his anxious thought.
" Lycurgus first" (the sacred voice reveal'd)
" A burial in the Theban war shall yield."
On this he dwelt, and, erring in his fate,
Preferr'd a peaceful life, and neutral state;
Yet, when he heard the clarion's loud alarms,
Wishes to sheathe his limbs in fatal arms.

910. Deforms with blood her face] This method of expressing sorrow was very customary among the orientals. We have frequent mention of it in the sacred and profane writers. Homer, in the 18th book of his Iliad, says,

Αμφοτερῃσι δε χερσιν ἑλα κονιν αιθαλοεσσαν,
Χευατο κακκεφαλης.

And again in the 22d,

Παντας δ' ελλιτανευε κυλινδομενος κατα κοπρον.

917. Entrails burnt] These pieces of meat were called prosecta by the Romans, and divided into three portions. The first was burnt; the second, consecrated and given to the priests; and the third, eaten by the person who made the sacrifice and his family. Suetonius, in the life of Augustus, says, " Cum fortè Marti rem divinam faceret, nunciatâ repente hostis incursione, semicruda exta rapta foco prosecuit, atque ita prælium ingressus victor rediit." See Arnobius, Lib. 2. Adversus Gent. et Adrian Turnebus, Adversariorum, Lib. 15. Cap. 7, Bernartius.

925. Lycurgus first] It is very remarkable in favour of Christianity, that all the oracles of the heathens were delivered in so ambiguous a manner as to admit of a double meaning. Such was the answer from the Delphic to Crœsus king of Lydia and Appius the prætor of Achaia, who thinking the oracle had warned him only to refrain from the war between Cæsar and Pompey, retired into the country called Cæla Eubœa, where, before the battle of Pharsalia, he died of a disease, and was there buried, and so possessed quietly the place which the oracle had promised him.

But soon the doubtful oracle is clear'd,
As the sad exequies in sight appear'd.
Hypsipyle the slow procession leads,
Met by the queen, array'd in sable weeds.
But pious cares no longer now withhold
The father, from his new misfortunes bold.
An angry, not a sorrowing look he wears,
And rage denies a passage to his tears.
Swift as a tiger, o'er the fields he flies,
And thus aloud to his domestics cries.
" Where is this faithless wretch, this female foe,
That spills my blood, and triumphs in my woe?
Say, lives she? breathes she yet the vital air?
Seize her, and quick, my friends, to vengeance bear;
No longer let her well-invented tale
And vain impostures o'er your faith prevail."
The monarch spoke, and from the sheath display'd
The dreadful splendours of his slaught'ring blade;
But interposing Tydeus rush'd between,
And with his shield protects the Lemnian queen;
Then shouts aloud: " Whoe'er thou art, forbear,
Nor tempt the fury of my thirsting spear."
Him stern Hippomedon, in arms renown'd,
Th' Arcadian youth, and Capaneus surround.
Their swords, impatient for the promis'd war,
With dazzling lustre glitter from afar.
To aid their king the gath'ring swains oppose,
And menace their inhospitable foes.
Then mild Adrastus, mingling with the crowd,
And good Oeclides thus exclaims aloud.
" O sheathe your swords, my friends, contend no more,
Nor stain your impious arms in kindred gore."
To this Oenides, unappeas'd, replies,
(The spark of anger beaming from his eyes)
" Dar'st thou, O tyrant, lift that guilty hand
Against the saviour of the Grecian band?
Will they, who this their present ardour owe
To her alone, resign her to the foe?
Know, that from Bacchus by descent she springs,
And claims alliance with the race of kings.
Is peace so slight a favour, whilst in arms
Thy subjects rise, impell'd with false alarms?
Yet still may'st thou enjoy it, and again
These troops behold thee weeping for the slain."
He paus'd: when, now his wrath in part suprest,
Lycurgus thus the list'ning kings addrest.
" Little I deem'd, that when you bent your course
To Thebes, we too should prove your hostile force.
But come, if social blood alone can please,
On us, our wives and harmless children seize.
From these to deeds of deeper guilt aspire,
And wrap our unavailing fanes in fire.
Still for itself will pow'r superior plead,
And sanctify the most illegal deed.

950. And with his shield] The commentators have puzzled themselves to find out a supplement to the line

Impiger objectâ——— Pectora parmâ;

one voting for proturbat, another for protentat, and a third for sustentat. Instead of weighing the respective arguments of each critic, and endeavouring to settle the true reading, we shall be content with conveying the chief idea, which is that of Hypsipyle's deliverance, in our version.

962. Nor stain your impious arms in kindred gore] The whole nation of the Greeks was descended from Perseus, the son of Danaus, from whom they were called Danai.

Will future times acknowledge your pretence,
And think you combat in a slave's defence?
Yet vengeance waits you from the pow'rs above,
And sure, tho' tardy, is the wrath of Jove."
He said, and to the city turn'd his eyes,
And there fresh scenes of blood and rage descries.
But Fame, unrivall'd in the dusty course,
In fleetness far outstrips the vig'rous horse;
From either wing she shakes the noxious seeds
Of discord, as aloft in air she speeds:
While from a thousand voices she proclaims
The monarch's vengeance, and the crowd inflames.
Too credulous, nor patient of delay,
With darts and torches they provoke the fray,
Demand Lycurgus, and advance in haste
To spoil the fanes, and lay the kingdom waste.
The screaming females rend the vaulted sphere,
And their first grief is lost in abject fear.
But old Adrastus, glitt'ring in his car,
Rode thro' the crimson ranks of noisy war:
The mournful queen of Lemnos press'd his side.
"Desist, desist from arms," aloud he cry'd;
"No more let vengeful thoughts employ your care,
Lo, our protectress breathes the vital air."
Thus, when the stormy south, and rapid north,
From their Æolian caverns issuing forth,
With sable clouds the face of Heav'n deform,
And ocean groans beneath th' incumbent storm;
If Neptune in his coral car appear,
And his hoar head above the surface rear;
The seas unruffling spread a level plain,
Exult and own the monarch of the main;
And, as the tempest and the waves subside,
The shores and mountains are again descry'd.

988. And sure, tho' tardy] This is a translation of the following lines in Tibullus, as Lactantius has remarked.

Ah! miseret, si quis primo perjuria celat,
Sera tamen tacitis pæna venit pedibus.
Eleg. p. 2. 11.

991. But Fame] This description, which affords a signal instance of our author's sublimity, is not the worse for its conciseness. It is entirely devoid of that tinsel, flashy splendour (which will pass a cursory view only, and cannot stand the test of severe criticism) and grows in our esteem from every revisal. The image of Fame shaking the seeds of discord from her wings, is very exalted, and the epithet "either" exquisitely beautiful, as it conveys to us the idea of the two different conflicts. What we value it the more for is, that it is an original, and has nothing in common with that celebrated description in the 4th book of the Æneid.

1009. Thus, when the stormy south] This simile is taken from Virgil, though the comparison of the Thebaid is the thing compared in the Æneid.

Ac veluti magno in populo cum sæpe coorta est
Seditio, sævitque animis ignobile vulgus;
Jamque faces et saxa volant; furor arma ministrat:
Tum, pietate gravem ac meritis si forte virum quem
Conspexêre, silent, arrectisque auribus astant,
Ille regit dictis animos, et pectora mulcet.
Sic cunctus pelagi cecidit fragor: æquora postquam
Prospiciens genitor, cœloque invectus aperto
Flectit equos, curruque volans dat lora secundo.
Æneid I. v. 152.

What god, propitious to her pious vows,
Recall'd the fair Hypsipyle's repose?
'Twas Bacchus, author of her noble race,
Who sent the double pledge of her embrace,
For deeds yet rip'ning in the womb of time,
Their mother brought them from their native clime.
Soon as the warders of the gates afford
Admission to their now less angry lord,
Wafted by adverse fame, the dire report
Of slain Archemorus had reach'd the court.
Therefore, t'enhance the justice of their claim
In the king's cause they seek the field of fame.
So blind are mortals to the future state,
So sudden the vicissitudes of fate!
But, as the sound of Lemnos reach'd their ears,
They pierce the thick'ning crowd, devoid of fears;
Discern their mother in the noisy ring,
And round her neck, the tears fast falling, cling.
She, like a rock, stands moveless, nor again
Dares trust the gods so oft believ'd in vain.
But, as in them she trac'd their father's charms,
And saw himself engrav'd upon their arms;
Her grief abates, and impotent to bear
The change of fortune which the gods prepare;
Prostrate she falls, and as on earth she lies,
The streams of joy swift issue from her eyes.
To cheer his issue, from a ruddy cloud
The god of wine salutes her thrice aloud:
The shouts of Bacchanals were heard on high,
And drums and cymbals shook the lab'ring sky.
At length the son of Oecleus, audience gain'd,
With words like these the list'ning host detain'd.
"Attend, ye princes, and Argolic bands,
To what Apollo by his priest commands.
The present miseries, which we deplore,
Were by the Fates predestin'd, when of yore
The future they dispos'd with certain hand,
And bade the necessary causes stand.
Hence were the springs exhausted, hence arose
The deathful serpent, author of our woes:
Hence was Archemorus depriv'd of breath,
His name deduc'd from his preluding death.
Here we must halt, and consecrate to fame
The royal infant, this his merits claim:
Let honours recompense his early doom,
And Virtue pour libations o'er his tomb.
And oh! that Sol would lengthen out the way,
And clog our progress with a fresh delay;
That accidents would intervene anew,
And Thebes retreat as fast as we pursue.
But you, who prove a more than common fate,
(Your son exalted to celestial state)

1022. The double pledge] Ovid confirms our author's assertion of Hypsipyle's twins.

Nunc etiam peperi, gratare ambobus Jason,
Dulce mihi gravidæ fecerat auctor onus.
Fælix in numero quoque sum, prolemque gemellam
Pignora Lucinâ bina favente dedi.
Jas. to Hyps. Ver. 119.

1045. To cheer his issue] This fiction seems borrowed from Virgil, who introduces Venus giving her son Æneas the same assurances of protection.

Ni signum cœlo Cytherea dedisset aperto.
Namque improviso vibratus ab æthere fulgor
Cum sonitu venit; et ruere omnia visa repente,
Tyrrhenæque tubæ mugire per æthera clangor.
Æneid viii. v. 523.

Whose honour'd name shall with oblivion strive,
And thro' each future age distinguish'd live,
While Inachus and noxious Lerna flow,
And Nemea's boughs o'ershade the fields below,
Let not your tears a deity disgrace;
A deity, tho' of terrestrial race:
Far better his untimely death appears
Than Nestor's age, and Tithon's length of years."
While thus he spoke, encircling shades arise,
And night assumes the sceptre of the skies.

BOOK VI.

ARGUMENT.

Adrastus and the Grecian princes, together with Lycurgus, Eurydice, and Hypsipyle celebrate the obsequies of Archemorus, in which is included a particular description of their felling wood, of the funeral procession, and the lamentation of Eurydice. Lycurgus and his consort are with difficulty restrained from leaping upon the funeral pyre. They throw in jewels, gold, live animals, spices, and many other things of great value. A select company of horse and foot are ordered to march round the pile. They afterwards erect a monument to the infant, on which his whole history is engraved. Adrastus institutes funeral games, and appoints prizes to those who shall conquer in them. The statues of their ancestors are carried along in procession, and exposed to public view. Then follow the chariot-race, the foot-race, the throwing the discus or quoit, the combat of the cæstus, the wrestling, and the shooting with arrows, which is attended with an omen, and concludes this book.

Now Fame from town to town, wide-wand'ring fled,
And thro' th' Argolic towns a rumour spread,
That grateful Greece prepar'd funereal games,
And various meeds, as various merit claims,
Games, in which nature might be crown'd with art,
And skill to inbred strength a grace impart,
Achaia's wonted rite. Alcmena's son
On Pisa's plain the pious strife begun,
To honour Pelops; and with conquest crown'd,
His dusty locks with wreaths of olive bound:
Next Phocis, from the serpent's windings freed,
To youths the prize of archery decreed:
Then round Palæmon's altars much bewept
The time-firm'd rites were scrupulously kept,
Oft as Leucothëa her groans renews,
And at their feasts her friendly visage shews;
Her woes with wailings either isthmus means;
Thebes echoes back her shrieks and mimick'd groans.
And now the mighty kings, whose royal birth
Exalts fair Argos o'er the foodful earth,
And whose illustrious feats the Tyrian dames,
Deep-sighing, hear, and glow with various flames;
Those mighty kings with em'lous rage contend,
And to the fight their native vigour bend.
So gallies, ere with lab'ring oars they sweep
The stormy Tyrrhene, or Ægean deep,
In some calm stream their oars and helm explore,
And learn their art, preluding near the shore;
But, well-experienc'd, tempt remoter seas,
Nor miss the land, they lose by swift degrees.
Aurora now, in early chariot drawn,
Beam'd forth her radiance on the dewy lawn,
Whilst Sleep with grief beheld his empty'd horn,
And paler Phœbe fled th' approach of morn.
With yells the streets, with groans the mournful courts
Rebellow. Echo with their sorrow sports;
From hill to hill, from grove to grove she bounds,
And catches, breaks, and multiplies the sounds.
The badge of honour from his forehead torn,
The father sits all cheerless and forlorn,
In weeds of woe array'd, and o'er his head
And length of beard a show'r of ashes spread.
Oppos'd to him, the childless mother raves,
And far out-weeps her lord. The female slaves,
Inspir'd by her example and command,
With brimful eyes around their mistress stand:
Fain would she fall upon her son's remains,
While each with friendly words her rage restrains:
Rous'd by her clamours too, the father springs
To sooth her anguish.—Soon as th' Argive kings,

1073. While Inachus] Virgil expresses himself in the same periphrastical manner.

In freta dum fluvii current, dum montibus umbræ
Lustrabunt convexa, polus dum sidera pascet,
Semper honos, nomenque tuum, laudesque manebunt. Æneid, b. 1. v. 607.

1078. Tithon's length of years] Tithon was the son of Laomedon, and ravished by Aurora for his beauty in Ethiopia, who restored his youth and beauty when he was grown old: he was at last turned into a grasshopper.

1. Now Fame] This book, which is entirely taken up in describing the games exhibited at the funeral of Archemorus, answers to the 24th of the Iliad and the 5th of the Æneid. I have given my opinion of it in the dissertation prefixed to this work, and shall therefore say nothing farther upon its general merit.

7. Achaia's wonted rite] This short sketch of the history of these institutions is a pretty opening: if the reader has a desire of being acquainted farther with their origin, he may see it at large in West's essay on the olympic games, in the first volume of his Pindar.

22. Deep-sighing] The expression in the original is suspirant, which, in all probability, was taken from Horace's ode, the 2d of the 3d book.

——— Illum ex mœnibus hosticis
Matrona bellantis tyranni
Prospiciens, et adulta virgo
Suspiret, eheu! ne rudis agminum, &c.

Upon which Mr. Francis seems to think, that the image is drawn from the 3d book of Homer's Iliad, where Helen and the Trojan dames appear upon the walls to view the camp of the Greeks.

50. Soon as th' Argive kings] The editor of Pitt's Virgil observes, that this circumstance is imitated from the 11th book of the Æneid, verse 36.

Ut vero Æneas foribus sese intulit altis,
Ingentem gemitum tunsis ad sidera tollunt
Pectoribus, mœstoque immugit regia luctu.

Catrou remarks on this passage, that it was a ceremony among the ancients, to renew their lamentations at the approach of a king or person of distinction.

Known by their awful looks and godlike port,
Had pass'd the threshold of the dreary court,
They bare afresh their bosoms, and renew
Their cries, tho' weary: tears their cheeks bedew
With drop succeeding drop. Their shrieks rebound
From ev'ry door with emulated sound,
As if the serpent had reviv'd again,
Or with a recent wound the infant slain.
The Greeks perceiv'd the odium, they design'd,
And wept the weakness, common to their kind.
Adrastus, oft as stupifying grief
Imposes silence, strives to yield relief
To the distracted sire with soft discourse:
One while he shows how vain is human force,
How hard the lot of man. He next explains
The stableness of all that Fate ordains;
And bids him not despair, since fav'ring Jove
May bless the future pledges of his love.
In vain he urg'd: unknowing check or bound,
Their plaints return'd.—In sullen silence frown'd
Th' obdurate sire, insensible of all:
So fell Ionian waves, when seamen call
For mercy, their repeated vows regard:
So slender clouds the light'ning's flight retard.
Meanwhile they crown with cypress, sign of drear,
And baleful yew, the flame-devoted bier,
And infant's bed: the nether part receives
The rustics' gift, a heap of straw and leaves:
The second row displays the various pow'rs
Of art, embroider'd o'er with short-liv'd flow'rs:
Arabian spices on the third they strew,
And Eastern sweets in lavish plenty shew;
Incense of ancient date, yet free from hoar,
And cinnamon, that grew, when Belus bore
The regal sway. A carpet wrought of gold
And richest Tyrian die, they next unfold,
And laid it on the top: from far it shone,
Instarr'd with gems, and many a precious stone.
Amidst acanthus Linus was inweav'd:
The deathful dogs their panting bosoms heav'd.
The mother held the wond'rous work in hate,
And deem'd it om'nous of her infant's fate.
Arms too, and trophies, by their grandsires won
In fight, where oft the victor is undone,
They hung around; more proper these to grace
Some honour'd hero of gigantic race:
But vain and barren fame in grief can please,
And gifts the babe's much honour'd shade appease.
Hence mournful joys and rev'rence to their tears
Arise, and presents, greater than his years,
Are brought to dignify the fun'ral pyre:
For flush'd with early hopes, the fondling sire
Devoted quivers, shafts, and shorter darts,
Untaught as yet to act their guilty parts.
Attentive to his name, she kept him steeds,
Prov'd in the course, and sprung of noted breeds;
Belts, which a greater round of waist demand,
And weapons that expect a stronger hand.
Insatiate hopes! What vests did she not frame,
Too credulous to his ambiguous name!
A purple robe, gay ensign of his reign,
And sceptre, which he might with ease sustain;
All these th' impassion'd sire to Vulcan's blaze
Consigns, and on the pile his sceptre lays,
If haply, by indulging thus his rage,
He might at length the force of grief assuage:
Meantime the augur, as the rites demand,
From out the host selects an able band,
In felling trees, their manly strength to prove,
And heap a pyre with ruins of the grove;
That Vulcan might absolve the guilty snake,
And for th' ill-omen'd war atonement make:
'Tis theirs to force thro' Tempe's gloom a way,
Hurl Nemea down, and bare the woods to day.
They level straight a venerable wood,
That long exempted from the axe had stood;
Thro' Argos and Lycæum none display'd
A greater stretch of hospitable shade.
Sacred for length of time it far extends
Its branches, nor alone in age transcends
The oldest mortal's grandsire, but has seen
The nymphs and fauns, transform'd in shape and mien:
Then swift destruction caught th' unhappy grove,
Struck by the sounding axe.—The birds above
Quit their warm nests, and savages their den,
Rous'd by the crash of trees and shouts of men.
The cypress, winter-proof Chaonian wood,
The lofty beech, the pitch-tree, Vulcan's food,

72. So fell Ionian waves, when seamen call] This seems to be copied from the sixth book of Virgil's Æneid, verse 467, where Æneas accosts Dido in the infernal regions, and meets with a rebuff from that lady.

> Talibus Æneas ardentem et torva tuentem
> Lenibat dictis animum, lacrymasque ciebat.
> Illa solo fixos oculos aversa tenebat:
> Nec magis incepto vultum sermone movetur,
> Quam si dura silex, aut stet Marpesia cautes.

75. Meanwhile they crown with cypress, sign of drear] This description, exclusive of its poetical merit, is a valuable piece of antiquity, as it lets us into the knowledge of the manner of the Grecian funerals. I hope the reader will indulge me with the use of the word drear, as I have Spenser's authority for it, and its adjective is universally adopted.

105. Attentive to his name] The oracle of Apollo, which always loved to play upon words, gave out in a response to Lycurgus, that his infant's fate was expressed in his name, which was Archemorus, and being derived from Αρχη and Μορος, might either signify, that it was his fate to reign, or that he would be the first person that should be slain in the Theban war.

> Prima, Lycurge, dabis Dircæo funera bello.

Αρχη signifying either a beginning or government, and Μορος fate or death.

137. The cypress, winter-proof] This description of felling the forests, is thought by Mr. Pope the best in our author, and copied by Spenser and Tasso.

> The sailing pine, the cedar proud and tall,
> The vine-prop elm, the poplar never dry,
> The builder oak, sole king of forests all,
> The aspin good for staves, the cypress funeral,
> The laurel, meed of mighty conquerors,
> And poets sage: the fir that weepeth still,
> The willow, worn of forlorn paramours,
> The yeugh, obedient to the bender's will,
> The birch for shafts, the sallow for the mill,
> The myrrh, sweet bleeding in the bitter wound,
> The warlike beech, the ash for nothing ill,
> The fruitful olive, and the plantane round,
> The carver holm, the maple seldom inward sound.
>
> Fairy Queen, book 1.

> Caggion recise dai pungenti ferri
> Le sacre palme, e frassini selvaggi

The holm, the yew of deadly juice, and oak,
By time uninjur'd, bow beneath their stroke;
The alder, wont to cleave the billowy flood,
And ash, that soon will drink of human blood,
The fir, th' uncultur'd ash, on mountains found,
The pine, that breathes forth fragrance from each wound,
And married elm, around whose trunks the vine
Her tendrils folds, to earth their heads decline.
Earth groans. Such vasty heaps of waste o'erspread
Mount Ismarus, when Boreas lifts his head
From his burst cave:—not with such rapid force
Red sheets of nightly flame pursue their course
O'er forests, aided by the fanning wind.
Sylvanus, Pales, and the mongrel kind
Of satyrs quit with grief their seats of ease,
Soft gurgling rills, cool grots and shady trees;
Deep groans the forest, as they take their leave:
Close to the trees th' embracing dryads cleave.
Thus, when some leader to the soldiers' rage
Resigns a captive town, they all engage
In quest of spoil, and ere the trumpets sound,
The plunder'd city's scarcely to be found.
They fell, they bear away, they load the cars;
Scarce such a din attends the work of Mars.
And now their equal toil two altars rais'd
Of equal height: one to the immortals blaz'd,
And t'other to the cheerless ghosts of Hell,
When the grave pipe proclaim'd the fun'ral knell,
Mix'd with the crooked horn.—In ancient time
This mode prevail'd o'er Phrygia's ample clime.
Pelops, as Fame reports, this rite proclaim'd
For lesser shades, and mournful dirges fram'd,
Such as were heard, when Niobe of old
To Sypilos twelve urns, disfigur'd, roll'd.

I funebri cipressi, e i pini, e i cerri,
L' elci frondose, egli alti abeti, e i faggi,
Gli olmi mariti, a cui tal' or s'appoggia
La vite, e con piè torto al ciel s'en poggia.
Altri i tassi, e le querce altri percote,
Che mille volte rinovar le chiome,
E mille volte ad ogni incontro immote
L' ire de' venti han rintuzzate, e dome:
Ed altri impose alle stridenti rote
D'orni, e di cedri e' odorate some;
Lasciano al suon dell' arme al vario grido
E le fere, e gli augei, la tana, e' l nido.
Jerus. del. c. 3. v. 76.

The editor of Pitt's Virgil, in a note on the following verses of Virgil,

Itur in antiquam sylvam, stabula alta ferarum:
Procumbunt piceæ; sonat icta securibus ilex,
Fraxineæque trabes, cuneis et fissile robur
Scinditur; advolvunt ingentes montibus ornos:

observes, that the difference between the genius of Virgil and Statius is very visible on this occasion. The latter of whom minutely, and at length, describes the different sorts of trees that were cut down to make the funeral pile for Archemorus. While Virgil observes his usual and pregnant brevity, knowing he had not leisure to dwell on this subject, merely for the sake of a florid description. It is observable, that Tasso has imitated Statius in this very particular.

172. To Sypilos] A river, into which Niobe was said to be metamorphosed, after she was slain by Phœbus and Diana.

The Grecian princes at the head appear:
The burial-gifts and sacrifice they bear,
And name aloud in titles of renown
The pious honours of their state or town.
The fun'ral bed, a length of time between,
On youthful shoulders moves (a solemn scene),
The king selected them with cautious care:
A shout uncouth succeeds and rends the air.
The peers of Lerna safe enclose their king:
The softer sex, as num'rous, form a ring
Around the mother: next the Lemnian queen,
Encircled by no slender troop, is seen:
Not mindless of the past, th' Inachian train
Intrench the mournful fair: her sons sustain
Her livid arms, and pleas'd that she is found,
Indulge her plaints, nor set her grief a bound.
There, soon as sad Eurydice, bereft
Of all her joys, the ill-omen'd dome had left,
From her bare breasts these artless accents broke,
And, with long shricks prefacing, thus she spoke.
" My son, I hop'd not to have follow'd here,
Surrounded with Argolic dames, thy bier;
Nor, frantic as I was, thy infant years
Once made a part of these my hopes and fears:
Nought cruel I fore-ween'd, for at this age
How could the Theban war my thoughts engage?
What god, however sanguine to destroy,
Would spill our blood in combat for his joy?
What drew this curse upon us? Whence arose
Such ills?—No slaughter'd babes disturb our foes.
Of tears and slaughter I've the first fruits found,
Before the sword is drawn, or trumpets sound;
While, void of thought, and fond, too fond of rest,
I trust my infant to another's breast.
What could I do? She spread a tale abroad,
Of her old sire, preserv'd by pious fraud.
Lo! the great heroine, who sole abjur'd
The mischief, vow'd by oath, and safe secur'd
Her parent from the furious Lemnian train!
Still does this daring dame your faith retain?
Was she so pious, who in desert grove
Could leave the product of another's love,
Expos'd on all sides, in a dang'rous place,
Where no huge snake of Python's monstrous race
Was needful to destroy? Th' inclement skies,
And empty terrours might alone suffice.
Nor can I blame you.—This disastrous curse
Was fated by the choice of such a nurse.
Yet wast thou kind, my son, to her alone,
The fonder parent was as yet unknown:
No mother's joys I reap'd of thee: her call
Was listen'd to, in preference of all.
How sweet thy plaints, thy laughter mixt with tears,
And murmurs must have sounded in her ears,
When first thy tongue essay'd the speech of man!
With thee a mother's office she began,
I finish it.—But shall she thus offend,
Unpunish'd, and will ye her crimes befriend,

185. Not mindless of the past] Lycurgus, in a fit of revenge, made several attempts to kill Hypsipyle, as the authoress of his son's death through her negligence. See the last book, verse 945.

209. Lo! the great heroine] Dido casts a like sneering reflection on Æneas, after she had discovered his intentions of leaving her.

——— En dextra fidesque
Quem secum patrios aiunt portare penates,
Quem subiisse humerum confectum ætate parentum!
Book 4. verse 597.

O chiefs? Why bring ye these? The fun'ral pyre,
And burial rites no useless gifts require.
Her, O ye chiefs! (his manes ask no more)
Her to a childless mother's rage restore,
By this first rage of war:—so may each dame
Of Thebes lament a son of equal fame."
Her tresses then she tore, and thus renew'd
Her pray'rs.—"Restore, nor think my soul indu'd
With savage principles, so I expire,
With vengeance cloy'd, and feed the self-same fire."
While thus she spake, at distance she beheld
Hypsipyle, whose grief no reason quell'd,
On hair and bosom vented.—This espy'd,
Ill brooking partnership in woe, she cry'd,
"This crime at least, ye peers, and thou, O king,
To whom new honours from our ruin spring,
This crime forbid, and bear the traitress hence.
Her presence gives the sacred shade offence.
Why in these sorrows does she bear a part,
And with fresh anguish rend a parent's heart?
What alien's child can she with truth bemoan,
While thus in close embrace she grasps her own?"
This said, she swoons: her plaints abruptly cease,
And the fair mourner sunk to sudden peace.
Thus when some cruel swain, or beast of prey
Has born a heifer's half-wean'd young away,
Whose strength and vital juices were sustain'd
By milky nutriment, and udders drain'd,
The childless parent to the vales complains,
And questions rivers, herds, and lonely plains:
She loaths her home, retires from field the last,
Nor ere she parts, indulges the repast.
But on the pile the sire his sceptre lays,
And casts the thund'rer's honours in the blaze;
He then curtails the locks, that scatter'd flow
Adown his back and breasts, a sign of woe,
And strewing o'er the infant, as he lies,
Weeps pious tears, and thus, impassion'd, cries.
"These ringlets, by a former contract vow'd,
On thee, perfidious Jove, I had bestow'd;
But since the priest deceiv'd me, and my pray'r
Was lost, these locks his worthier shade shall bear."
And now, a torch apply'd beneath, the fire
Cracks on the leafy summit of the pyre.
Scarce can they drive his furious friends away:
The Grecians straight the king's command obey,
And, standing with protended arms between,
Exclude the parents from the mournful scene.
Vulcan grows rich: no ashes e'er before
Were deck'd with such a mass of various ore.
The silver melts; the gems and rich attire
With gold embroider'd, crackle in the fire.
The planks of hardest oak are scented o'er
With Syrian juices: and the honey'd store
Of many a hive, and costly saffron crown'd
The heap. Full bowls of milk are hung around.
From vessels boat-wise form'd, they pour a flood
Of milk yet smoking, mix'd with sable blood.
The Grecian princes then in order led
Sev'n equal troops, to purify the dead;
Around the pile an hundred horsemen ride
With arms revers'd, and compass ev'ry side:
They fac'd the left (for so the rites require)
Bent with the dust, the flames no more aspire.
Thrice, thus dispos'd, they wheel in circles round
The hallow'd corse: their clashing weapons sound.
Four times their arms a crash tremendous yield,
And female shrieks re-echo thro' the field.
Another pile, high-heap'd with burning wood,
For slaughter'd herds and reeking victims stood.
The prophet warning them to cease their woes,
And sign of a new fun'ral, though he knows
Each omen true, all wheeling to the right,
Return: their brandish'd arms reflect the light.

265. He then curtails] Mr. Pope's note on the 166th verse of the 23d book of Homer's Iliad is well worth the reader's notice.—"The ceremony of cutting off the hair in honour of the dead, was practised not only among the Greeks, but also among other nations: thus Statius, Thebaid 6. This custom is taken notice of in holy Scripture: Ezekiel, describing a great lamentation, says, They shall make themselves utterly bald for thee, ch. 27, ver. 31. I believe it was done not only in token of sorrow, but had perhaps a concealed meaning: that as the hair was cut from the head, and was never more to be joined to it, so was the dead for ever cut from the living, never more to return. I must observe, that this ceremony of cutting off the hair was not always in token of sorrow; Lycophron in his Cassandra, ver. 976, describing a general lamentation, says

Κρατὸς δ' ἄκρον νῶτα καλλύνει φόβη.

And that the ancients sometimes had their hair cut off in token of joy is evident from Juvenal, Sat. 12. ver. 82.

——— Gaudent ibi vertice raso
Garrula securi narrare pericula nautæ.

This seeming contradiction will be solved by having respect to the different practices of different nations. If it was the general custom of any country to wear long hair, then the cutting it off was a token of sorrow; but if it was the custom to wear short hair, then the letting it grow long and neglecting it, showed, that such people were mourners."

279. Vulcan grows rich: no ashes e'er before] This part of the ceremonies is copied by Chaucer in his Palamon and Arcite, which I shall give the reader in Mr. Dryden's words.

Rich jewels in the flames the wealthy cast,
While the devouring fire was burning fast;
And some their shields, and some their lances threw,
And gave the warrior's ghost a warrior's due.
Full bowls of wine, of honey, milk, and blood,
Were pour'd upon the pile of burning wood,
And kissing flames receive, and hungry lick the food.
Then thrice the mounted squadrons ride around
The fire, and Arcite's name they thrice resound:
"Hail and farewell," they shouted thrice amain:
Thrice facing to the left, and thrice they turn'd again.
Still as they turn'd, they beat their clatt'ring shields;
The women mix their cries, and clamour fills the fields.

Virgil mentions the same circumstances in the funeral rites of Pallas, Æneas, 11.

Ter circum accensos, cincti fulgentibus armis,
Decurrêre rogos; ter mœstum funeris ignem
Lustravere in equis, ululatusque ore dedere.
Spargitur et tellus lachrymis, sparguntur et arma.
It cœlo clamorque virûm, clangorque tubarum.
Hinc alii spolia occisis direpta Latinis
Conjiciunt igni galeasque, ensesque decoros,
Frœnaque, ferventesque rotas; pars, munera nota,
Ipsorum clypeos, et non felicia tela, Ver. 188.

Each warrior there some grateful off'ring tost,
As fancy dictates: one a bit emboss'd,
Another in the blaze a helmet threw,
A belt or spear, that lighten'd, as it flew.
Each adverse field in concert hoarse replies:
The groves are fray'd with their repeated cries;
While the loud clarion and shrill-sounding horn
Pierce the quick ear with clangours scarcely borne.
Such two vast armies at the trumpet's sound,
Ere to its highest pitch their wrath is wound
By loss of blood, or slaughter dies the spear,
All beautiful with equal arms appear:
Involv'd in clouds, the pow'r of battle stands,
And doubts, on whom to turn his conqu'ring hands.
The rites were clos'd, and Vulcan's fury gone,
A heap of ashes now remain'd alone,
When, drawing near the fire, a copious show'r
Of water on the smould'ring pile they pour.
With early dawn their pious toils begun,
And scarcely ended with the setting Sun.
Nine times had Phosphor from the realms of light
Chac'd the dew-silv'ring stars and vanquish'd night,
And nine times, harbinger of Cynthia's reign,
Had chang'd his courser.—By the conscious train
Of stars, that glitter round the radiant Moon,
He's known to be the same at morn and noon:
When, sacred to the babe, a tomb arose,
Which art and speed at once united shows:
Stone was the structure. In a range display'd,
The scenes of his sad hist'ry were pourtray'd.
The princess here the thirsty Grecians guides,
To where Langia rolls his secret tides.
There creeps the luckless infant, there he lies:
The serpent writhes his spires of hideous size
Around the verge. You might expect to hear
Him hiss, so well he clasps the marble spear.
Now Fame invites the vulgar to the sight
Of sportive contests, and a bloodless fight:
Rous'd at the call, they quit the fields and town;
E'en those, to whom war's horrours are unknown,
Whom life's exhausted prime confin'd at home,
Shake off old age, and leave their peaceful dome.
Ne'er were such crowds on th' Ephyræan shore,
Or circus of Oenomaus before.
With crooked hills, and trees begirt above,
A vale subsides, the centre of a grove.
Rough, thorny ridges lie around, which yield
A length of shade, and bound it from the field;
Then hillocks, rising through a vast extent
Of grassy turf, increase the steep ascent.
There, soon as Phœbus mark'd the sylvan scene
With ruddy streaks, the martial troops convene:
'Twas pleasure there to measure with their eyes
The number, looks, and habits of th' allies
Amid the mingled crowd.—In wonder lost,
They view the strength and ardour of their host.
A hundred bulls of dusky hue they brought,
The flow'r of all the herd, and never wrought;
Then cows in number and in hue the same,
And heifers, not yet horn'd, loud-bellowing, came.

328. The ancients thought Phosphor and Vesper were not the same individual stars, as they have a different appearance at their rising; which the poet attributes to their changing horses. He says, therefore, that the stars are not deceived like mortals, who supposed that they were two distinct stars.

In order then the statues of their sires
Are borne along: the gazing crowd admires
Their life-resembling form and sculptur'd deeds.
Great Hercules the mute procession leads:
To the fell Nemean savage short of breath,
He fronts his breast, and lifts the arm of death.
The Greeks with some degree of horrour ey'd
The brazen hero, tho' their badge and pride.
Next, on the left, in order they discern
Old Inachus, who pours abroad his urn,
And, stretch'd beneath a lofty bank of reeds,
Surveys his stream slow gliding thro' the meads.
Ready for dalliance, Io stands behind;
Heart-piercing anguish touch'd the parent's mind,
As he view'd Argus, starr'd with watchful eyes:
But the more grateful ruler of the skies
Prepar'd a temple on the Pharian shore,
And bade Aurora the new pow'r adore.
Then Tantalus (not he who's feign'd to lean
O'er streams untouch'd, or starve amidst the scene
Of plenty, but the thund'rer's pious guest)
Appears above the lot of mortals blest.
At distance conqu'ring Pelops guides the reins
Of Ocean's god, and thunders o'er the plains:
False Myrtil leaves unpinn'd the chariot-wheels,
And life and vict'ry from his master steals.
Amidst the rest was sage Acrisius seen,
Choræbus, warrior of terrific mien,
Fair Danaë, who blames her guilty breast,
And Amymone, in the stream distrest:
Alcmena too the young Alcides bears;
A triple moon confines her braided hairs.
The wrangling sons of Belus join their hands
In impious leagues. More mild in aspect stands

365. In order then] Though nothing could be better contrived to excite virtue in the breasts of the Grecian princes and leaders, than this exhibition of the statues and images of their ancestors, yet I fear it will be thought too long, and had it not been in a book entirely devoted to description, it would have been absolutely unpardonable.

377. Ready for dalliance, Io stands behind] The daughter of Inachus, whom Jupiter loved, and lest his wife Juno should know it, he turned Io into an heifer: jealous Juno suspected it, and begged the heifer of her husband, and set Argus (one that had an hundred eyes) to keep her: Jupiter could not refrain, but sent Mercury to kill Argus: Juno, in revenge, sent a gad-fly that stung her and made her mad, so that she ran to Egypt, where her old form came to her again, and she was married to Osiris; after her death, the Egyptians deified and worshipped her by the name of Isis, usually sacrificing unto her a goose: when they worshipped they used to call Io, Io, whence arose that proverb. The occasion of the poet's fiction concerning Io, whom they feigned to be turned into a cow, was this; Io being with child by a Phenician mariner, and fearing her father's displeasure, went with the Phenicians into Egypt in a ship which had a painted bull.

386. Appears above the lot] Horace mentions this mark of favour conferred by Jove on Tantalus.

Occidit et Pelopis genitor conviva Deorum.

396. A triple moon confines her braided hairs] This triple moon was symbolical of Jupiter's excessive lust, who, when he lay with Alcmena, commanded he Moon to make her nightly course thrice as long as usual.

Egyptus, and with secret transport hung
On the false flatt'ry of his brother's tongue,
Unconscious of his inward hate and spite,
And all the future horrours of the night.
A thousand more were there, yet these suffice,
When virtue calls each rival to the prize.
First toil'd the coursers.—Mighty god of verse,
Theirs and their princely masters' names rehearse:
For ne'er was a more gen'rous race of steeds
Collected for the course on Grecian meads.
As if a num'rous flock of birds should try
Their active pow'rs, and wing the midway sky,
Or Æolus to the mad winds propose
The palm of swiftness, such a tumult rose.
Before them all was fleet Arion led,
Distinguish'd by his mane of fiery red:
From ocean's god (if ancient fame says true)
The gen'rous horse his honour'd lineage drew;
'Tis said, he rein'd him first with forming hand,
And curbing bit upon the dusty strand,
But spar'd the lash: for free he scours the plain,
Swift as the surge that skims along the main.
Oft in the car with other steeds, design'd
To swim the Lybian billows, was he join'd,
And train'd to carry his cerulean sire
To any coast.—The tardier clouds admire
His active strength, and each contending wind,
Notus or Eurus, follows far behind.
Amphytrion's val'rous son with equal speed
He bore, deep ruts inscrib'd upon the mead,
When for Eurystheus wars unjust he wag'd,
Yet fierce, unmanageably fierce he rag'd:
Then by the gift of Heav'n, Adrastus rein'd
The courser, and to his own service train'd;
Now, many cautions giv'n, the sire decreed
To Polynices' hands the mettled steed;
He teaches him, what arts will best assuage
His wrath, when chaf'd, and fir'd with em'lous rage.
"Give not the reins up freely, nor provoke
His headstrong fury with too frequent stroke:
With threats and spurs urge others to the course;
He'll go at will, and mock thy curbing force."
Thus Phœbus, when he lent the fiery rein,
And plac'd his offspring on the rapid wain,
With boding tears injoin'd—"Be wise, my son,
Th' untrampled zones and stars insidious shun."
With pious caution first the youth proceeds,
But fate at length sets free th' immortal steeds.
Fir'd with the prospect of the second prize,
Rapt by Oebalian steeds, the prophet flies:
Thy offspring, Cyllarus, by theft obtain'd,
When Castor on the Scythian coast remain'd,
And chang'd Amyclæ's bridle for the oar.
A robe of snowy hue the augur wore:
White were his steeds, with trappings richly drest,
The same his helm, his mitre and his crest.
Admetus too, the blissful, from the meads
Of Thessaly, scarce curbs his barren steeds:
From seed of centaurs fame reports them sprung,
Nor can I disbelieve it, since so young,
They scorn th' embraces of the male: hence force
Invests their limbs, and vigour in the course:
Their sex they thus dissemble day and night,
Black spots are seen betwixt the streaks of white.
Such was the colour of each gen'rous steed,
Nor were they far inferior to the breed,
Which, list'ning to Apollo's tuneful lays,
Forgot their pasture, lost in wild amaze.
Lo! Jason's youthful sons too, whence new fame,
And added honours crown the mother's name,
Ascend the car, which either Thoas bore,
The grandsire's proper name in days of yore,
And call'd from Euneus' omen. They display,
Like features, chariots, horses and array;
The same their vows: each wish'd the palm his own,
Or by his brother to be won alone.
Next great Hippodamus and Chromis ride:
One was by birth to Hercules ally'd,
One to Oenomaus.—'Twas hard to read,
Which drove the most untam'd and headstrong steed:
One guides the stud of Getic Diomed,
One those by his Pisæan father bred.
Dire trophies and the purple stain of war
With horrid filth begrime each hero's car.
In lieu of goals, an oak on one side stood,
Long shorn of leaves, a naked trunk of wood;
On t'other lay (a barrier of the ground)
A rocky fragment, plac'd 'twixt either bound;
Far as a dart at four times we may send,
But at three shots a shaft might reach the end.
Meanwhile Apollo charm'd the tuneful throng
Of sister-muses with celestial song:
The trembling strings responding to his hands
With silver sound, on highest Heav'n he stands,
And views Parnassian lands, his own domain.
The gods were first the subject of his strain:
To Jove and Phlegra oft his lyre he strung,
The Python, and his brother's honours sung,
And then explain'd, what pow'r the thunder drives,
Fed by what springs the boundless ocean lives;
Whence winds arise, stars glide along the sky,
And river-gods their empty urns supply:
What order guides the Sun's impetuous flight,
Contracts the day, and lengthens out the night;
Whether Earth lies the lowest, or between,
And close encompass'd by a world unseen.

405. First toil'd the coursers] We shall not be surprised to see Statius make this digression, to give us the history of his horses, when we consider to what excess the passion for fine racers is carried in our own times, and with what exactness and precision the news-papers give us their genealogy.

435. He teaches him] Nestor gives a similar caution to Antilochus in the 23d book of the Iliad, on which passage I shall refer the reader to Mr. Pope's observations, as they are equally applicable to this before us.

449. Thy offspring, Cyllarus] Frauds in the case of horses have been thought excusable in all times. Homer mentions an instance of one in the fifth book of the Iliad.

Τῆς γάρ τοι γενεῆς, ἧς Τρωΐ περ εὐρύοπα Ζεὺς
Δῶχ', υἷος ποινὴν Γανυμήδευς· οὕνεκ' ἄριστοι
Ἵππων, ὅσσοι ἔασιν ὑπ' ἠῶ τ' ἠέλιόν τε.
Τῆς γενεῆς ἔκλεψεν ἄναξ ἀνδρῶν Ἀγχίσης,
Λάθρῃ Λαομέδοντος ὑποσχὼν θήλεας ἵππους·
Τῶν οἱ ἓξ ἐγένοντο ἐνὶ μεγάροισι γενέθλης. V. 265.

And Virgil was so well pleased with it, as to introduce it in the seventh Æneid,

Absenti Æneæ currum geminosque jugales,
Semine ab æthereo, spirantes naribus ignem:
Illorum de gente, patri quos Dædala Circe
Suppositâ de matre nothos furata creavit.

503. By a world unseen] The poet alludes here

This ended, he delays to hear the Nine
Attune their lay, and whilst he tries to twine
A wreath of well-earn'd laurel for his lyre,
And to the wind resigns his loose attire,
Not distant far, brought backward by their cries,
Nemea, belov'd of Hercules, he spies,
And there a goodly sight of gen'rous steeds,
Yok'd for the race, and traversing the meads.
He knew each princely rider:—near at hand
Admetus, and the prophet took their stand.
Then to himself he said. "What pow'r above,
Enrag'd against these objects of our love,
Hath urg'd them to dispute the prize of fame?
Their pious deeds alike my favour claim,
I cannot well determine, which exceeds;
One, when I serv'd him in Thessalian meads,
(By Jove and Fate's impervious will constrain'd)
Burnt incense to his servant, nor disdain'd
The latent god; and one attends in part
My rites, a student of th' ethorial art.
What tho' Admetus in desert transcend,
Yet honour we the seer's approaching end;
Late is his death, the fatal sisters give
A length of years: to thee no joys survive;
Thou know'st, the gloomy gulf of Thebes is near,
For oft our birds have sung it in thine ear."
He said, and scarce restrain'd the rising tears:
Then straight to Nemea his course he steers,
And gleams at ev'ry bound o'er all the skies;
More swift than his great father's bolt he flies,
Or his own shafts.—Long had he trod the plain,
Yet still the traces of his flight remain
Impress'd in Heav'n, and thro' the expanse serene
And zephyrs was a track of glory seen.
Now Prothous, by the rest commission'd, took
The brazen head-piece, and impartial shook
The lots together: these to all dispose
Their port and order, as th' inscription shows.
Now men and steeds, than which no time or place
Can greater boast, the god's acknowledg'd race,
Stand to one spot confin'd. Audacious fear
And paly hope in ev'ry face appear:
Doubtful, they tremble, yet contend to start,
And fev'rish dread invades their ev'ry part.
The steeds' and horses' ardour is the same:
Their quiv'ring eye-balls dart a ceaseless flame;
They champ the sounding bit, their mouths run o'er
With frothy foam.—Bars, gates, and rails no more
Oppose their progress, while their stifled ire,
And spirit curb'd in clouds of smoke transpire.
Thus rest inglorious galls each gen'rous heart:
A thousand steps are lost before they start,
And they forerun vast tracts of distant ground,
In prospect urg'd.—The faithful grooms surround,
Confirm their courage, smooth each tortur'd mane,
And point the goal out, they must first attain.
Soon as the trumpet had the signal giv'n,
They spring forth all, with em'lous fury driv'n.
What weapons skim so thick th' embattled plain,
What clouds the Heav'ns, what sails the billowy
main?
Less swift are rivers, swoln with wintry show'rs,
Less swiftly Vulcan's wasting flame devours:
Compar'd with these, the stars, the storms are slow,
And torrents from the mountains tardier flow.
The Greeks beheld them start, and mark'd their
flight,
Now ravish'd on a sudden from their sight:
Mixt in the dust of the discolour'd field,
In one vast gloomy cloud they lie conceal'd,

to the Antipodes, a set of beings, who were supposed to live feet to feet, or diametrically opposite to us.—It is somewhat remarkable, that pope Gregory excommunicated all such as believed their existence.

520. One, when I serv'd] Apollo being exiled from Heaven by Jupiter, for killing the Cyclops, served Admetus in the capacity of cow-herd nine years, and having been treated kindly, promised him, that when the time of his death was come, another should die for him; but he found none that would take his turn, but his wife Alceste, whom for her piety Proserpine restored to life again.

539. Now Prothous] Mr. Pope in his version of the Iliad, has transcribed a note of Eustathius on the 427th line of the 23d book, which merits the attention of Statius's readers likewise. "According to these lots the charioteers took their places, but to know whether they stood all in an equal front, or one behind another, is a difficulty: Eustathius says, the ancients were of opinion, that they did not stand in one front; because it is evident, that he who had the first lot had a great advantage of the other charioteers? If he had not, why should Achilles cast lots? Madam Dacier is of opinion, that they all stood abreast to the barrier, and that the first would have a sufficient advantage, as he was nearer the bound, and stood within the rest; whereas the others must take a larger circle, and consequently were forced to run a greater compass of ground. Phœnix was placed as an inspector of the race, *i. e.* says Eustathius, he was to make report, whether they had observed the laws of the race in their several turnings. Sophocles observed the same method with Homer in relation to the inspectors in his Electra.

——— Οι τεταλμενοι βραβεις
Κληροις επιπλαι, και κατεςησαν διφρον.

The ancients say, that the charioteers started at the Sigæum, where the ships of Achilles lay, and ran towards the Phæteum, from the ships towards the shores. But Aristarchus affirmed that they ran in the compass of ground five stadia (*i. e.* about five furlongs) which lay between the wall and the tents towards the shore."

545. Audacious fear] So Virgil, speaking of the chariot-race, says,

—Spes arrectæ juvenum, exultantiaque haurit
Corda pavor pulsans. Georg. iii. v. 105.

556. A thousand steps] Mr. Hurd, in his Discourse on Poetical Imitation, might have added this instance of Pope's close copying Statius to the examples he has given us, as I think it is rather more striking than any of them. In his Windsor Forest, speaking of the courser, he says,

And ere he starts, a thousand steps are lost.

Now it is clear that

—— Pereunt vestigia mille
Ante fugam,——

are the very words of Statius: and indeed they were so very literally translated by the celebrated author above mentioned, that I could not help rendering them in his own words.

And, a thick mist fast-gath'ring o'er their eyes,
They scarcely know themselves by name or cries.
The first goal past, they kept between them clear
The utmost space allow'd in their career;
The second track blots out the former.—Now
Their bosoms touch the yoke, so prone they bow.
Then they seem double, as they pull the rein
With striving knees: the zephyrs smooth again
Their manes erect; their necks with muscles swell,
And earth imbibes the snowy show'r that fell,
From feet and wheels arise unequal sounds:
Their hands ne'er rest: the driver's lash rebounds
In echoing air.—Not thicker in the north
Pale Boreas spreads a spatt'ring tempest forth
Of noxious hail, nor from the nurse of Jove
So many show'rs oppress the nodding grove.
In prescience vers'd, Arion found with grief
The rule and guidance of an unknown chief,
And, innocent of ill, perceiv'd with dread
Th' incestuous offspring of Jocasta's bed:
E'en from the goal the burden he disdains,
And frets and flies, impetuous, o'er the plains.
The sons of Argos think his spirits rise
From praises, but the charioteer he flies;
The charioteer he threats with furious speed,
And seeks his lord o'er all the spacious mead.
Before all others, and the next by far,
Amphiaraus guides his glitt'ring car:
Thessalia's pious monarch was descry'd
With equal steps loud thund'ring at his side.
Thoas and Euneus, brother-twins succeed,
And get and lose alternately the lead;
Nor ever does immod'rate lust of fame
Impel them to forget relation's claim.
The last and greatest trials of the day
Betwixt Hippodamus, and Chromis lay;
Their heavy coursers to the labour yield,
Nor ignorant of art, they took the field:
Hippodamus, whose chariot scarce precedes,
Feels on his back his rival's breathing steeds.
The seer by Phœbus lov'd, with nice survey,
Mark'd out a narrower compass of the way,
And, drawing in the reins with all his force,
Hop'd to prevent Admetus in the course.
This the Thessalian views with careful eyes,
And glows with nearer prospect of the prize,
While fierce Arion in his lord's despight,
Runs circling round, and wanders to the right.
Oenides now was foremost in the race,
Admetus follows with redoubled pace,
When, brought at length into the path again,
The sea-born courser chases o'er the plain,
And soon o'ertakes the joyful rivals' cars:
A crash ensues, and strikes the golden stars;
The Heav'ns too tremble, and, the crowd struck down,
In open view the seats and benches shone.
But Polynices nor commands the reins,
Nor plies the whip, for pallid fear restrains:
Thus when frail reason's conquer'd by despair,
The pilot leaves his ship to fortune's care,
The stars that once deceiv'd regards no more,
And gives his art and useless labour o'er.
Again in rounds, precipitate, they wheel'd,
Then fetch'd a shorter compass o'er the field:
Again on axles axles clash, again
The wheels on spokes. No faith and peace remain:
Wars, horrid wars, by far more mild appear;
Such emulation reigns thro' the career,
They menace mutual death, unless they yield,
And oft run counter, as they cross the field.
When stripes no more avail, to mend their speed,
Admetus calls by name each weary steed,
Swift Iris, Pholoë approv'd in war,
And Thoë, wont to grace the victor's car.
The prophet too recalls to sense of shame
Cygnus, whose snowy colour suits his name,
And Aschetos.—Rous'd at their master's threat,
The champain Strymon and Æthion beat
With quicker steps. Hippodamus provokes
The Calydonian with repeated strokes,
And Thoas courts Podarces.—Gentle chief!
The Theban prince alone in silent grief
Obsequious follows, where Arion flies,
And fears to publish his mischance by cries.
Now thrice th' allotted compass had they run,
And the fourth heat with toil was scarce begun,
When the chaf'd steeds, their clammy throats on fire,
Breathe short and thick, and copiously perspire,
Till down their limbs the luke-warm current glides,
While lengthen'd gasps distend their bellying sides.
Here Fortune, doubtful long what chief to grace
With palm of conquest, hastes to close the race.
On great Æmonius Thoas' car runs foul,
While, fir'd with hope, he gathers all his soul
To pass Admetus: nor his brother brought
The wish'd-for aid, tho' earnestly he sought;
For fierce Hippodamus, of warlike mien,
Prevented his effort, and drove between:
Then Chromis, back'd with all his father's force,
And strength Herculean check'd the rapid course
Of fierce Hippodamus, just as he gain'd
The inner barrier, and his car detain'd,
Axle in axle lock'd. The steeds of Mars
Contend in vain to disengage the cars,

587. Nor from the nurse of Jove] The expression in the original is

Nec Oleniis manant tot cornibus imbres.

The fabulous history of which is as follows.—Jupiter, having been fed in Crete with the milk of a goat belonging to Amalthæa, daughter of Melissus, king of that island, after the creature was dead, inserted it among the stars, in gratitude for the nourishment received from it. This sign was supposed by the ancients to cause rain.

611. Hippodamus] Homer gives us the same image, Iliad, book 23d, verse 376.

Αἱ Φηρητιάδαο ποδώκεες ἔκφερον ἵπποι.
Τὰς δὲ μετεξέφερον Διομήδεος ἄρσενες ἵπποι
Τρώϊοι. οὐδέ τι πολλὸν ἄνευθ᾽ ἔσαν, ἀλλὰ μάλ᾽ ἐγγύς.
Αἰεὶ γὰρ δίφρου ἐπιβησομένοισιν ἐΐκτην,
Πνοιῇ δ᾽ Εὐμήλοιο μετάφρενον, εὐρέε τ᾽ ὤμω,
Θέρμετ᾽. ——

644. Admetus calls by name] I think our author commendable for not reciting speeches of his heroes to their horses, as Homer has done, who makes Antilochus speak a great deal in the very heat and hurry of the race. As Eustathius observes, he commands and soothes, counsels and threatens his horses, as if they were rational creatures.

671. Then Chromis, back'd with all his] I fear, Statius will be censured for describing his warriors so excessively brutish and inhuman in their contests: but let it be remembered, that Antilochus, in the 23d book of the Iliad, verse 423, is equally guilty of ill treatment with respect to Menelaus.

And stretch their musc'lar necks: as on the main
When sudden floods Sicilian ships restrain,
And Auster drives them with his furious gales,
In the mid ocean stand their swelling sails.
He then precipitates him from the car
All shiver'd, and had been the first by far;
But, as the Thracian tyrant's horses found
Their hapless lord, extended on the ground,
Their raging lust of wonted food returns,
And thirst for human blood redoubled burns;
Nor had he scap'd, but the Tyrinthian chief,
Careless of conquest, came to his relief,
And, turning back the reins and furious steeds,
Honour'd, tho' vanquish'd, scours along the meads.
But Phœbus, mindful of his promise, tries
On his lov'd augur to confer the prize:
At length he marks the favourable time,
And headlong shoots adown th' etherial clime;
Just as, the contest nearly at an end,
Fair vict'ry nods, and doubts whom to befriend.
A snaky-headed monster then he made
Of air impassive, and an empty shade;
Whether he form'd it in some lucky hour,
Or rais'd from Hell, the visionary pow'r
So dire a shape, such hideous features rears,
That scarce the furies (senseless deem'd of fears)
And the grim porter of th' infernal cell,
Undaunted, might behold a fiend so fell.
It would have fray'd the steeds, that whirl the car
Of Sol, or bear the god of arms to war;
For soon as her foul face Arion spies,
His stiff'ning mane of gold was seen to rise;
Upright in air his foremost feet he rears,
And with him his yoke-fellows, forceful bears.
Th' Aonian exile presses then the plains,
And, rolling on his back, resigns the reins:
Confin'd no longer by the driver's sway,
The coursers force the chariot far away.
Him, lying on the ground, the Lemnian chief,
Admetus, and the prophet ey'd with grief,
And, passing sidelong, took as large a space,
As was requir'd to shun him in the race.
At length, his trusty comrades standing round,
He lifts his weary body from the ground,
And head immers'd in gloom; then seeks again
The king, and unexpected, soothes his pain.
How much more blest, O Theban, had'st thou dy'd,
Had not th' inexorable fiend deny'd?
What wars had been prevented? Th' Argive coast,
Thebes, and thy brother then had mourn'd thee lost
In public: then had Nemea thee bemoan'd,
And Lerna's banks in hoarser concert groan'd:
Larissa had thy tomb with foliage strew'd,
And young Archemorus with envy view'd.
Oeclides then, altho' the highest meed
Of right was due to his unrivall'd speed,
(Since lighted of his lord, Arion flies)
T' o'ertake the empty car, impetuous hies.
The god recruits his strength, and cheers his soul
With hope:—as if just starting from the goal,
He throws up all the reins, and drives along
His steeds with threats, and now applies the thong;
While the loud-panting coursers, far more fleet
Than rapid Eurus, ply their sounding feet.
" Now haste at least (he cries) while none pre-
The kindling axle smokes along the meads, [cedes,'
And scatters heaps of sand thrown up afar:
Earth groans, and threats e'en then the gaudy car.
Perhaps too Cygnus then had known the course,
But Neptune favours his beloved horse:
Hence glory justly grac'd the victor-steed,
Tho' the fam'd augur gain'd the promis'd meed.
For him two youths a massy goblet bore,
Which great Alcides rear'd in days of yore
With his one hand, when brim'd with sparkling
And paid libations to the pow'rs divine. [wine,
Their eyes the figur'd centaurs sternly roll'd,
And stampt an air of terrour on the gold.
In height of anger at the hostile train
Brands, stones, and other bowls they hurl again.
On all sides faces, pale with hast'ning death,
Show wrath, that lingers with the latest breath:
Hyleus, and the chief himself engage
With far unequal strength, tho' equal rage.
To thee, Admetus, as the second meed
A robe, Mæonian produce, was decreed:
Thrice had it drank the noblest Tyrian die,
Fring'd on the borders.—Here one might descry
Leander, youth enamour'd! as he swims,
The surge sky-tinctur'd plays around his limbs:
He oars himself with shifting arms, and braves
With his opposing breast the swelling waves,
You would not think a single hair was dry.
In front of him (deep anguish in her eye)
The Sestian damsel on a turret's height
Stands, musing on the taper's dying light.
These gifts Adrastus to the victors gave,
And cheer'd the Theban with a female slave.
He then invites to urge on foot the race,
And meeds assigns the conqu'ror's speed to grace:
An useful exercise in time of peace
At sacred rites, nor when those times shall cease
In war unuseful, when mere valour fails,
And with superior arms the foe prevails.

697. A snaky-headed monster] This fiction is imitated from Virgil's Æneid, book 12, verse 845.

Dicuntur geminæ pestes, cognomine diræ;
Quas et tartaream Nox intempesta Megæram,
Uno eodemque tulit partu, paribusque revinxit
Serpentum spiris, ventosasque addidit alas.
Hæ Jovis ad solium, sævique in limine regis
Apparent, acuuntque metum mortalibus ægris,
Si quando lethum horrificum morbosque Deûm rex
Molitur, meritas aut bello territat urbes.
Harum unam celerem demisit ab æthere summo
Jupiter, inque omen Juturnæ occurrere jussit.

749. For him two youths] The chariot race is now ended; and I cannot but acknowledge, that it contains great variety of natural incidents, and still greater pomp of expression and harmony of numbers. However, the accidents and circumstances bear a striking resemblance to those of Homer; e. g. the encounter of Chromis and Hippodamus is similar to that of Antilochus and Menelaus, and Apollo's sending a phantom to frighten the horses of Polynices, to Minerva's breaking the chariot of Eumelus: nay, our author is so very unpolite to the ladies, as to undervalue a fair female, and give her to the loser as Homer has done to the great indignation of madame Dacier.

777. An useful exercise in time] Monsieur Catrou, in his note on the 377th line of the 5th book of Virgil's Æneid, remarks, that the foot race was a military exercise: the young Roman soldiers were instructed in it, according to Vegetius, agility being of great use in war.

First Idas in the lists appears: his brows
Late shaded with Olympic olive-boughs;
The Pisans and Eleans back his cause
With previous shouts, and crown him with ap-
Next Alcon (Sicyon his native place) [plause.
And Phædimus, twice victor in the race;
Then Dymas comes, once fleeter than the steed,
But length of years had lessen'd half his speed;
And many others, whom, tho' not the last
In fame, the vulgar ignorant o'erpast.
But the thick circus for th' Arcadian cries;
The shifting murmurs echo in the skies,
Mark'd with his parent's swiftness.—Who will own
Mænalian Atalanta's name unknown,
And footsteps, from her suitors well-conceal'd [1]?
The mother in her offspring shines reveal'd:
From pole to pole his glory unconfin'd
Extends.—Fame says, he caught full many a hind
In th' open plain, and stopp'd the rapid course
Of darts and arrows, sent with mighty force.
At length th' expected warrior with a bound
Springs forth, and leaps, exulting, on the ground:
Soon as his robe ungirt aside he threw,
The lovely youth unfolds to public view
His well-turn'd limbs, and falling shoulders made
More beautiful than art hath e'er pourtray'd:
Tho' all was fair, nor aught admir'd the most,
His face was in his graceful body lost.
Yet scorning beauty's praise, he drives away
Th' admiring crowd, nor patient of delay,
Makes his limbs supple for the future toil,
And stains his skin with fat Palladian oil.
The rest avail themselves of his design:
Smear'd with the juice, their glossy bodies shine.
Thus in a calm when Cynthia's starry train
Gleam on the placid surface of the main;
And the fair image of the spangled sphere
Vibrates on ocean, all things gay appear;
But brighter over all the evening star
Emits his beams, conspicuous from afar,
And radiant as in highest Heav'n he glows,
Such splendours in the world of waters shows.
Idas succeeds, the next in form and fame
Of speed, and nearly in his age the same:
Yet hasten'd on by toil, the down began
To clothe his cheeks, and mark the future man,
And some faint semblance of a beard was seen
Amidst the length of hair, that clouds his mien.
Then rightly they fore-run th' approaching race,
Explore their limbs, and try each various pace,
Instruct themselves in ev'ry needful art,
And weigh their strength and vigour, ere they start;
They bend their knees as ready for the test,
And strike with hearty claps their slipp'ry breast,
Then lift their legs, tho' heated, free and light,
And put a sudden period to their flight.
Soon as the rule had measur'd out the plain,
And smooth'd it to their feet, the naked train
Impetuous from the destin'd barrier flew,
And glitter'd in the Sun, like morning dew.
The rapid coursers, that late pass'd the mead,
Seem to have run with far inferior speed.
You'd think, so many arrows from the throng
Of Parthians or Cydonians flew along.
Thus when a herd of fleet Hircanian deer
In the lone desert hear, or seem to hear,
The hungry lion's distant roar, away
They scour in troops, collected by dismay,
And blind with terrour; as they beat the ground,
Their clashing horns incessantly resound.
Th' Arcadian leads the race, and as he flies,
Swift as the wind, eludes their dazzled eyes:
Him Idas prest, and meas'ring pace by pace,
Breath'd on his shoulders, as he urg'd the race.
Young Dymas, side by side, his rival plies,
And leaves a doubtful prospect of the prize:
Them Alcon chases.—From th' Arcadian's crown
A golden lock of hair unshorn hung down;
This for Diana, as a gift, he fed,
From his most tender age, and vainly said,
That on his country's altars it should burn,
Should he from Thebes a conqueror return;
Now loose and flowing largely down behind,
It yields at ev'ry adverse blast of wind,
And both impedes himself, and (as it flies)
Obscures his rival's view, and shades his eyes;
Soon as the youth perceiv'd th' advantage giv'n,
And time for fraud, with rival fury driv'n,
(Just as th' Arcadian prince with rapid pace
Approach'd th' extremest limit of the race)
He seiz'd, he pull'd him backward by his hair,
And touch'd the goal first, baffling all his care.
Th' Arcadians storm'd, and from the circus bent
Their steps, and vow'd the treach'ry to resent,
Should they refuse to render to his hands
The ravish'd honours which his speed demands.
There are, to whom these arts give no disgust.
Meanwhile Parthenopæus heaps with dust
And sand his weeping eyes and beauteous face:
The tears augment and heighten ev'ry grace.
One while with bloody nail his breast he tears,
And then his lovely face and guilty hairs.
On ev'ry side discordant clamours rise,
At length, the matter weigh'd, Adrastus cries,
"O youths, desist from strife.—The prize again
Shall be contended fairly on the plain;
But take a diff'rent path: that side the field
To guileful Idas, this to thee we yield.

[1] By leaving no marks of them in the sand.

808. His face was in his graceful] This observation of the poet tallies with a remark of lady M. W. Montague in one of her Letters, viz. "that if women were to go naked, their faces would be the least regarded."

815. Thus in a calm when Cynthia's] This simile, I must confess, is one of those nugæ canoræ, which according to Horace, should never take place. There is great strength of imagery and expression in it, but then it no ways illustrates the thing described, and has only a general allusion to the effects of the oil in giving a gloss to their skins, and Parthenopæus's superiority of beauty.

867. Soon as the youth] In this foot race, Statius has perhaps shown more judgment than either Homer or Virgil. The former makes Ajax lose the victory through a fall occasioned by Minerva's resentment of his disrespect in not invoking her (which is scarcely dignus vindice nodus): in the latter, Nisus is unjust to his adversary in favour of his friend, so that Euryalus wins the race by a palpable fraud (as Mr. Pope expresses it) and yet the poet gives him the greater prize. Now the action of Idas's pulling Parthenopæus back, is certainly more natural, and Adrastus acts more impartially and prudently than Æneas in making them run again.

No more be want of speed by craft supply'd."
The rivals heard, and by his words abide.
Then suppliant the Tegæan chief adores
Th' immortal pow'rs, and silently implores.
" O Phœbe, queen of forests (for to thee
This lock grew sacred from my own decree,
And from this vow arises my disgrace)
If aught of merit in the sylvan chace
My mother has display'd, or aught I claim,
Let not Arcadia prove such bitter shame,
Nor Thebes from hence a partial omen draw,
That Cynthia favours those who break her law."
The goddess heard his pray'r. Then straight he leaves
The barrier: scarce the ground his course perceives;
Scarce do his feet one grain of sand displace,
Nor in the level dust appears his trace.
He rush'd then to the goal with joyful cries,
And to the monarch back exulting flies:
The promis'd palm his raging grief appeas'd.
Now finish'd was the race, and all were pleas'd:
Parthenopæus bore a steed away
High-bred, the foremost honour of the day:
The crafty Idas a bright shield possess'd,
And Lycian shafts, much priz'd, content the rest.
He then demands, what warrior, skill'd to throw
The disk, his strength of arm and art will show?
By the good monarch Pterelas was sent
To fetch the premium; his whole body bent,
Scarce on the ground he lays the slipp'ry mass
(For the vast quoit was form'd of weighty brass).
The silent Greeks inspect with curious eyes
The disk, and weigh the labour ere they rise.
A crowd then starts.—Two of Achæan race,
At Ephyre three boast their native place;
From noted Pisa one deriv'd his birth,
The seventh had cultur'd Acarnania's earth.
More in the contest too a share had held,
But the loud clamours of the pit impell'd
Hippomedon, and fir'd his ardent soul:
Tow'ring he rose, and show'd a larger bowl.
" This rather seize, young warriors, who aspire
To break the walls of Thebes, and wrap in fire
Her loftiest bulwarks: but not ev'ry hand
Yon disk of size enormous can command:"
This said, he lifts (not all his strength apply'd)
The brazen mass, and threw with ease aside.
Astonish'd now they stand aloof, and yield,
Scarce Phlegyas and Menestheus kept the field.
(Nor had these stood the contest out, but shame
And their great friends their perseverance claim)
To these spontaneously the rest give place,
And turn inglorious, but without disgrace.
Such as the targe of Mars in Thracian fields,
A noxious light o'er all Pangæa yields,
Wide-scatt'ring splendours strike the Sun with fear,
And deeply sounds beneath the heav'nly spear.
First rose Pisæan Phlegyas with applause:
His noted skill from other objects draws
Their eyes aside: now in the golden sand
He roughens both his quoit and better hand;
The dust then shaken off upon the pit,
He turns it round, and tries which side will fit
His arm and fingers best, for well he knew
The much-lov'd game, and ponder'd, ere he threw.
Oft at a sacrifice, and ritual game
Was he renown'd, (if we may credit fame)
Where widest flows Alpheus, to throw o'er
The disk unwetted to the farthest shore.
Hence trusting to his art, nor taught to yield,
He measures the rough acres of the field,
And tracts celestial with his better hand,
And, bending either knee towards the strand,
He calls forth all his vigour, lifts on high
The massy quoit, and whirls it in the sky:
Rapid it flies, ascending in its flight,
And, whilst it seems quick-falling, grows in height.
At length, exhausted all its force, more slow
The globe return'd, and press'd the plain below.
Thus sever'd from th' astonish'd stars, the ball
Of darken'd Phœbe oft is seen to fall;
The nations, on the mighty change intent,
Their timbrels strike, and fear in vain th' event;
Whilst the victorious hag at distance smiles,
To see her charms succeed and magic wiles.
The Greeks applaud him; nor on level land
He fears Hippomedon's superior hand.
But Fortune, who her ev'ry art employs
To crush ambition, and with glee destroys
The structure of immod'rate hope, deprives
His arm of strength. In vain with her he strives.
He now prepar'd a length of space to gain,
Low-bending to the task: beneath the strain
The muscles of his vig'rous body swell:
When lo! before his feet the discus fell,
Short of his vow, and faithless to his hand:
His comrades sigh, his foes their joys command.
Menestheus then succeeds with timid art
To the bold task, and acts the cautious part:
To Maia's winged offspring much he pray'd,
And with heap'd dust the discus rougher made.
Tho' sent with far less vigour than before,
It speeds, nor stops till it had measur'd o'er
Full half the circus.—A deep, hollow sound
Ensues, and a fix'd arrow marks the ground.
Hippomedon with boding heart succeeds
The third, nor to the forceful contest speeds;
For much he ponders in his mind the woe
Of Phlegyas, and Menestheus' lucky throw.
He lifts the quoit, accustom'd to his hand,
And poising it aloft at his command,
Consults his val'rous arms, and hardy side,
And hurls it (his whole art and strength apply'd)
And follows it himself.—The discus flies
With horrid bound along the vacant skies,
And, mindful of the hand's directing force,
At distance keeps the tenour of its course;
Nor doubtfully the vanquish'd chief it pass'd,
Beside the other's limit nearly cast;
But far beyond Menestheus' mark it took
Its stand, and, as portending ruin, shook
The pillars that support the sylvan scene,
And shady roof, imbow'r'd with living green.
Such was the stone from Ætna's vap'rous height
The Cyclop threw, his hand unrul'd by sight,
When, guided by the dashing of the flood,
Ulysses' hostile vessel he pursu'd.

903. Scarce do his feet] Homer gives us a similar image in his description of the foot-race, Iliad, B. 23. v. 763.

——— Αυταρ οπισθεν
Ιχνια τυπτε ποδεσσι, παρος κονιν αμφιχυθηναι.

967. Thus sever'd] The poet in this simile alludes to a received notion of the ancients, that the eclipses of the Moon were occasioned by magic spells,; at which time they played on timbrels, cymbals, and other musical instruments, to forward her delivery, supposing her to be in labour.

1014. Ulysses'] After this verse follow three

Adrastus to the victor then assigns
As the first prize, a tiger's hide that shines
With yellow hem, refulgent to behold:
The sharpness of the claws was dull'd with gold.
With Gnossian bow and shafts Menestheus hies
Content.—To luckless Phlegyas then he cries,
" Accept this sword, Pelasgus' aid and pride,
Since adverse fortune has the palm deny'd;
Nor will th' invidious victor grieve to see
This gift allotted thee by my decree.
Decide we now, who best the cæstus wields:
Skill in this feat of vigour scarcely yields
To contests of the sword, and steely blows."
At this Argolic Capaneus uprose,
Fierce to descry, and fierce to be descry'd;
And, while upon his arm the gloves he ty'd,
Cut out of raw bull-hides, and cas'd with lead,
As hard as they, exultingly he said:
" Stands there a youth amidst yon num'rous crew,
Here let him issue forth in public view.
Yet had I rather, for my country's sake,
Some Theban rival would the challenge take,
Whom I might justly hurl to Pluto's shore,
Nor stain my stronger hand with social gore."
He said, and ceas'd.—Fear held them mute, they [gaze
In stupid wonder, and in wild amaze.
At length Alcidamas from 'midst the train
Of naked Spartans springs forth on the plain,
Unhop'd.—The Doric troops with wonder ey'd
Their king: his comrades knew that he rely'd,
More than on brutal strength, on certain rules,
Train'd up by Pollux in the sacred schools.
The god himself both fix'd his hands and form'd
His youthful arms, by holy friendship warm'd;
Oft would he place him fronting, and admire
His daring spirit, nor unequal ire,
Then catch him up, exulting, his own breast
With fervour to his naked body press'd:
Him Capaneus derides with threat'ning hands,
And, pitying, a more equal foe demands;
E'en forc'd to combat, his proud soul rebels,
And his late languid neck with fury swells.
Preparing for the combat, high in air
Their thund'ring hands th' impetuous champions [rear:
A fence their arms extended form around
Their faces, and exclude each future wound.
Such space of limbs the chief of Argos shows,
And staring bones as Tityos might disclose,
Should the fell Stygian vultures cease to feed,
And suffer him to rise, from torture freed.
The Spartan (for his strength exceeds his years)
In look a boy, in act a man appears.
Such is the prospect of his riper age,
That each spectator mourns his early rage,
And, lest he lavish too much blood away,
Wish to behold a period to the fray.
Nor all at once their wrath and blows arise;
They stay to gratify their curious eyes
In gazing on each other, and expect,
Each that his foe would the first blow direct.
Awhile alternate fears their wrath assuage,
And caution's calmer rules were join'd to rage.
Each with his hands the vacant air provokes,
And blunts the gauntlets with repeated strokes.
This husbands well his strength, (altho' he glows
With ire) and deals more sparingly his blows:
That, eager of revenge, himself neglects,
And rushes blindly on.—No skill directs
His random-strokes: his teeth in vain he grinds,
And wreaks his hasty vengeance on the winds;
For, deeply vers'd in all his country's art,
The wary Spartan parries off in part,
Or shuns his rival's blows.—One while he bows
His head, and by compliance 'scapes the blows;
Then his quick hand aside the gauntlets beat,
His head thrown back, advancing with his feet.
Oft too (so much he has at his command
The game, and such the vigour of his hand)
He boldly closes with the foe, nor fears
His giant-force, confirm'd by length of years,
But on him leaps, as on some frowning rock
A billow falls, then, broken with the shock,
Recoils.—Thus, wheeling round the furious foe,
He plies him, unrepaid, with many a blow.
He lifts his hand, and, flourishing around,
Seems on his flank and eyes to aim a wound:
This feint recals him from his proper guard;
And, whilst the threat'ned part he strives to ward,
Between his hands descends a sudden blow,
And, wounding, marks the middle of his brow.
The blood now spins forth, and a tepid rill
Stains either temple; yet the warrior still
Perceives it not, but, rolling round his eyes,
Much wonders why the sudden murmurs rise:
But, as by chance he drew back o'er his head
His weary hand, and saw the gauntlets red,
As some fierce tiger wounded with a dart,
Or gen'rous lion, glowing with the smart,

others in the earl of Arundel's manuscript copy: but as they are to be found in no other book, and Statius has so many similes drawn from this attack of the giants, I thought it needless to translate them, though they are not destitute of poetical merit, as the reader may see:

Sic et Aloidæ, cum jam celaret Olympum
Desuper Ossa rigens, ipsum glaciale terebat
Pelion, et trepido sperabant jungere cœlo.

1035. Yet had I rather] However disgusted we may be with the bullying menaces of Capaneus we cannot but be pleased with the patriotism he displays on this occasion.—He is the Epeus of Homer, and Dares of Virgil.

1079. This husbands well his strength] Upon comparison, I believe, this game of the cæstus will not be thought inferior to the foregoing in any respect. The vain-glorious fury of Capaneus, the spirit and adroitness of the young Spartan, and the different movements, attitudes, and incidents of the combat, are described in a very masterly manner.

1112. Glowing with the smart] Notwithstanding what Mr. Pope, and Mr. Hind after him have advanced, in relation to our author's studied originality, in his description of the funeral games, there are several traits in it, which bespeak it to be a copy of that in the fifth book of Virgil's Æneid, v. 53. The lines to which this note refers, are evidently imitated from the following:

At non tardatus casu, neque territus heros,
Acrior ad pugnam redit, ac vim suscitat ira.
Tum pudor incendit vires, et conscia virtus:
Præcipitemque Daren ardens agit æquore toto;

Again,

Behold again the Spartan shifts renew'd!
As the foe, &c.

Are borrowed from

Headlong he drives the youth o'er all the field,
Forc'd to give ground, yet still averse to yield;
And, gnashing horribly his teeth, he throws
His hands about, and multiplies his blows.
His rage is spent in air: his strokes in part
Fall on the cæstus: with superior art,
And active speed, the Spartan youth bewares
A thousand deaths, that rattle in his ears:
Yet, not unmindful of his art he hies,
But turns his face, and combats as he flies.
Short pantings now succeed, and toil subdues
Their harass'd limbs: more slowly he pursues,
And t'other flies: at length their falt'ring knees
Succumb, and both accept a truce of ease.
Thus when (a signal giv'n) the seamen yield
To the long labours of the wat'ry field;
Short is their rest: the watch-word soon restores
Their vig'rous toils, and they resume their oars.
Behold again the Spartan shifts renew'd!
As his foe blindly rushing on he view'd,
He falls spontaneously: with thund'ring sound
Th' assailant pitches headlong on the ground.
The wily stripling struck him ere he rose,
And smiles of joy alloy'd with terrour shows.
Th' Inachians shout: less loud the sea-beat shore,
And forests, shook by blust'ring Boreas, roar.
But when Adrastus saw the giant rise,
And lift his hands for horrid deeds, he cries;
"Haste, haste, my friends, I pray, and interpose:
With rage, unutterable rage he glows,
Resign the palm and prize to his demands,
And snatch the dying Spartan from his hands;
Lest, when his jealous wrath is at the full,
He dash within the brain his batter'd skull."
Hippomedon and Oeneus' son obey
Th' injunctions of the king without delay;
Yet scarce with all their art and force combin'd
Restrain his hands, and bend his stubborn mind.
"Away—the vict'ry's thine—'tis more than fame
To spare the vanquish'd: his connections claim
Some small regard—a partner in the fight."
Th' inexorable chief receives with slight
Their counsels, and, rejecting with his hands
The proffer'd palm and mail, his foe demands,
And cries, "Go to, and give my vengeance way,
Shall I not dig his eyes out, and repay
Those female tricks with which he hop'd to gain
The prize, and favour of a partial train;
And, mindless of his sorrowing patron, doom
His shapeless body to the silent tomb?"
He said: his comrades turn'd him far aside,
While, swoln with ire, the conquest he deny'd.

The Spartan troops deride his threats and raise
Peals of applause, and shout their champion's praise.
Now, conscious of his skill in ev'ry game,
Oenides burns to win the prize of fame.
In the foot-race the foremost name he held,
And in the quoit and cæstus both excell'd:
Yet Castor's glory, and athletic oil
Delight his heart above all other toil.
Thus was he wont his peaceful hours to spend,
And mind, fatigu'd with warlike cares, unbend.
Against the mightiest champions had he stood,
Who dwelt near Achelous' stormy flood,
And won (Heav'n-taught) the honours of the day.
Soon then as thirst of glory calls away
The youths most noted for athletic toils,
He strips his back of the terrific spoils
(The Calydonian monster's bristly hide).
Agylleus, to Cleone's race ally'd,
'Gainst him his ample limbs, high-tow'ring, rears,
Nor less than Hercules himself appears;
Such o'er the rest his brawny shoulders rise,
And his huge bulk exceeds the human size:
Yet not that hardy force, his sire could boast,
Descends to him: his strength in bulk was lost,
And a luxuriancy of blood: his skin
Was smooth without, from muscles free within.
Hence only bold Oenides hopes t'o'erthrow
Th' unwieldy might of his gigantic foe;
For tho' the smallest of the Grecian throng,
His bones were large, his arms supremely strong,
And full of sinews: nor was such a mind,
And so great strength of nature e'er confin'd
In a less body.—When with fragrant oil
Their limbs were render'd supple for the toil,
They spring impetuous from the circling train,
And occupy the middle of the plain:
Then their wet limbs with dust by turns they dry'd,
And held their arms bent in, but distant wide.
Now Tydeus brings by craft Agylleus down
(His height upon a level with his own)
And bends him forward, whilst unmov'd he stands
With stooping back and knees that sought the sands.
As on the cloud-wrapt Alps the cypress, queen
Of trees, and fairest in the sylvan scene,
To whistling winds her head, obsequious, bends,
(Tho' on the root for stay she scarce depends)
And, bowing, almost seems to kiss the plain,
Then sudden shoots up in the skies again;
Spontaneous thus Agylleus presses down
His limbs gigantic, and with many a groan
Bends himself double on his little foe:
And now their hands alternate deal a blow;

Ostendit dextram insurgens Entellus, et alte
Extulit: ille ictum venientem a vertice velox
Providit, celerique elapsus corpore cessit.
Entellus vires in ventum effudit, et ultro
Ipse gravis graviterque ad terram pondere vasto
Concidit.———

1158. Shall I not dig his eyes out] I never found myself more at a loss how to vindicate my author, than in the passage before us. If he ever deserved the censure of having made his heroes too brutal and inhuman, he has certainly done it in this place. The picture of Capaneus is drawn with too great a violence of features: and it is inconceivable, that any one could be so horridly revengeful on being foiled in a trial of skill only.

1167. Now, conscious] The poet omits no opportunity of complimenting Tydeus. The other warriors excel in one game only, whereas he is represented as equally well versed in all of them. This inclines me to think, Statius intended him as the chief character in his poems.

1207. As on the cloud-wrapt Alps, &c.] This simile does not represent the posture of the wrestlers so well as that in the 23d book of Homer's Iliad, verse 712.

Ὡς δ' ὅτ' ἀμείβοντες, τοὺς τε κλυτὸς ἤραρε τέκτων,
Δώματος ὑψηλοῖο, βίας ἀνεμῶν ἀλεείνων.

Necks, breasts, legs, foreheads, shoulders, sides, and thighs
Beneath the strokes in sudden tumours rise.
On tiptoe rais'd, their heads obliquely bent,
Each hangs on each, stretch'd out at full extent.
Scarce with such wrath two leading bulls maintain
The conflict: in the middle of the plain
Stands the fair cause, expecting which will lead
The subject herds, and rule the spacious mead.
With clashing horns the combatants engage,
Love heals their wounds, and fans their kindled rage.
As the wild boar (his eye-balls flashing fire)
Whets his dull tusks, in height of jealous ire,
Or as the shapeless bear disputes the prey
With shaggy gripes.—Thus Tydeus urg'd the fray,
And brav'd the sultry Sun, and dusty toil:
Close was his skin, inur'd with frequent toil,
And his rough limbs well-muscled.—But his foe,
Impair'd with labour, 'gan to puff and blow,
And sick to death, gapes oft with stress of pain,
And shakes the high-heap'd sand upon the plain
With copious streams of sweat, and, unsurvey'd,
By catching at the ground, his breast upstay'd.
Tydeus pursues, and while with threat'ning eyes
He mark'd his neck, runs full between his thighs:
But his hands balk the purpose of his mind,
And fall far short of what the chief design'd.
Prone fell the giant-warrior, and oppress'd
With wide extent of ruin all his breast.
Thus when th' Iberian seeks some cavern'd height
With metal fraught, and leaves the vital light,
Ere the rent Earth sends forth a sudden sound,
And trembles o'er his head the pendant ground,
His body crush'd and pent beneath the weight
Of the burst mount, and wrapt in gloomy fate,
A document of punish'd av'rice lies,
Nor the free soul regains its kindred skies.
Oenides, tho' beneath the foe he lay,
Rises in spirits, and without delay,
From the huge grasp, and heavy burden freed
Th' eluded warrior compasses with speed,
And fastens sudden on his back, then holds
His pursy sides, embrac'd in rigid folds;
Next, pressing either ham with either knee,
While the foil'd champion strove in vain to free
His limbs fast bound, and thrust beneath his side
His hand (O wonderful to be descry'd!)
He lifts the giant, rested on his breast:
Thus in his arms (fame says) Alcides prest

1221. Scarce with such wrath] This comparison is copied from Virgil's Æneid, book 12, verse 715, and is not, I think, inferior to the original.

> Ac velut ingenti Silâ, summove Taburno,
> Cum duo conversis inimica in prælia tauri
> Frontibus incurrunt, pavidi cessere magistri:
> Stat pecus omne metu mutum, mussantque juvencæ,
> Quis pecori imperitet, quem tota armenta sequantur:
> Illi inter sese multâ vi vulnera miscent,
> Cornuaque obnixi infigunt, & sanguine largo
> Colla, armosque lavant, gemitu nemus omne remugit.

1264. Thus in his arms] Every time Antæus touched the earth, he acquired fresh vigour. Lucan has described this combat with infinite spirit in the 4th book of his Pharsalia. verse 611.

His earth-born foe, and from his mother-ground
Uprais'd, when now the secret fraud he found,
Nor hope was longer left to fall, or reach
With his broad feet the surface of the beach.
A joyful shout ensues, and strikes the sky,
Rais'd by the troops.—Then poising him on high,
Sudden, and of his own accord again
He threw him down obliquely on the plain,
And following as he fell, his right hand plac'd
Upon his neck, his feet upon his waist.
Thus press'd, no more resistance had he shown,
But shame impels him on, and shame alone.
His belly wide extended on the ground,
Prostrate he lies.—At length when now he found
His sense returning, up he rose again,
And left his form imprinted on the plain.
But Tydeus, gifted with the palm and prize
Of glitt'ring arms, in height of transport, cries:
" Not half so long, I ween, had he withstood,
But Thebes has drank too freely of my blood.
These honest wounds the glorious fact atte[st."]
While thus he spake, he bar'd his manly breast,
And gave the prizes to his menial crew:
Agylleus takes the slighted mail, his due.
The Theban then, yet unconstrain'd by fate,
And Agreus, urg'd with thirst of fame, not hate,
Advance with naked swords (in armour clad)
To dare the combat: but the king forbad.
" O youths, great store of death will soon betide:
Then let your eager rage for blood subside;
Your courage, till the fight begins, restrain:
And thou, for whom we've left our own domain,
Dispeopling many cities, do not trust
Thy life to chance, nor thro' immod'rate lust
Of glory, grant the wishes of thy foes,
And thy fell brother's vows (ye pow'rs oppose)."
Then a gilt helm he gives in both their hands;
And straight, in honour of his son, commands
The crowd to wreath his brows, and by the name
Of conqueror of Thebes, proclaim his fame.
The rig'rous fates this omen render vain.
The nobles urge the monarch, to sustain
A part in the funereal games, and crown
The rites himself: and lest one chief alone
Of all the sev'n no victory should gain,
With earnest zeal they beg, that he will deign
In archery to prove his matchless art,
Or hurl with dextrous skill the flying dart.
The king assents, and, follow'd by a train
Of youths, descends with joy upon the plain:
The squire behind him bears at his command
A bow, and light-wing'd arrows in his hand.
A wild ash far beyond the circus lies,
The destin'd mark, at which his arrow flies.
Who can deny, that ev'ry omen springs
From hidden causes of terrestrial things?

1292. But the king forbad] Homer having been blamed by some of the ancients for describing this barbarous and shocking combat, Statius has very prudently waved it, and rendered Adrastus highly amiable by his prohibition of it.

1319. Who can deny] This exclamation, as well as many other passages in this work, bespeak our author to have been of a very superstitious turn of mind.

I cannot see how the poet can style this attempt a contest, and its success a victory, when there was no antagonist. It is a mere feat of archery.—Adrastus is desired by his nobles to

The book of fate lies open. We refuse
The ready prescience, offer'd to our views;
We put the pow'r to hurt in Fortune's hands:
And thus for mere chance-work each omen stands.
The fatal arrow measur'd o'er the ground,
And in the tree infix'd a slender wound;
Then (sight tremendous!) by the self-same track,
And air it cleav'd before, comes flying back,
Kept to the end the tenour of the way,
And falling, near the well-known quiver lay.
Th' erroneous chiefs mislead the list'ning crowds;
These think it driven by rencountring clouds,
And winds.—Those hold, that the re-acting wood
Impell'd it back again.——None understood
The great event, and sequel clearly shown.
Propitious was the war to him alone,
And the shaft promis'd its much favour'd lord
A safe return, and rescue from the sword.

BOOK VII.

THE ARGUMENT.

Jupiter angered at the delays of the Grecian army, sends Mercury to Mars to command him to forward the war. The temple of that deity is described. Then follows Adrastus's speech over the sepulchre of Archemorus. Mars, by means of terrour, incites the Grecians to resume their march to Thebes. Bacchus intercedes for his native city with Jupiter, who pacifies him with promises of a respite. The Theban troops and auxiliaries are drawn out to battle. Phorbas gives an account of the commanders of them to Antigone, who ascends one of the towers for that purpose. Eteocles harangues his army. The Greeks are terrified with several omens in their route to Thebes. Jocasta with her two daughters ventures into the enemies' camp, in order to bring about a reconciliation between the two brothers, which she had effected, had not the Greeks killed two tigers belonging to Bacchus. Hostilities commencing, several of note are slain on both sides. Amphiaraus, after a great slaughter of the enemy, is swallowed up by an earthquake, with an account of which prodigy the book ends.

INDIGNANT now, th' etherial king survey'd
The Theban war by fun'ral games delay'd,
And shook his head: beneath the moving god
From pole to pole the starry regions nod,
And Atlas, with unwonted weight opprest,
To the great author of the shock addrest
His just complaint.—To Maia's winged son
In awful tone th' Almighty thus begun.
"Cyllenius, mount the winds and speed thy flight
With swift descent from Heav'n's imperial height,
To where in air the Thracian domes arise,
And fair Calysto binds the northern skies,
On clouds and dews celestial feeds her beams,
And shuns old ocean's interdicted streams:
And, whether Mars, upon his spear reclin'd,
Respires from toil, or wroth with human kind,
Pursues the war near Hebrus' freezing flood,
And wantons in a sea of kindred blood,
To him our wrath in our own terms express,
Nor, cautious of offending, aught suppress:
Long since he was enjoin'd by my commands
To range in arms the Greek and Theban bands,
And kindle discord on th' Inachian shore,
And where the thund'ring waves of Malea roar.
See! fun'ral rites th' Argolic youth detain
Just on the confines of their own domain.
They act like conquerors, such shouts arise
At intervals between the sacrifice.
O Mars! is this a sample of thy rage?
See! in far other contests they engage:
Oebalian gantlets clash, and with a bound
The rising quoits aloft in air resound.
But, if the cruel horrours of the fight
Are still his joy, and give his soul delight,
Let him, averse to covenant and truce,
With fire and sword the guiltless town reduce
To ruins, slaughter in the act of pray'r,
Exhaust the world, and lay creation bare.
But now perverse, and heedless of his sire,
He quits the strife, and moderates his ire.
Yet let him speedily our will obey,
And urge the Grecian warriors to the fray;
Else (not to treat him worse) I change his kind,
And break the savage nature of his mind:
His sword and coursers else he must restore,
And claim the right of kindred blood no more.
Tritonia will suffice to the command,
And all besides shall as spectators stand."
He said: the swift-wing'd herald sallies forth,
And to the frozen climates of the north
Pursues his course. Before the polar gate
Storms, show'rs, and yawning winds his coming wait
In sable troops: then down the steepy way
The god, distracted in his flight convey.
Thick on his robe the rattling hail descends,
And ill the shading hat his ears defends.
With horrour now he casts his eyes around,
And views, where on a brazen tract of ground

give a public proof of his skill either in shooting or darting. He chooses the former, and singling out a tree which grew on the farther side of the circus, shoots, and hits the mark.—The incident of the arrow's returning back, though it borders upon the marvellous, is as natural as that of Acestes's kindling: but the application of it to the event it is intended to prognosticate is certainly more just and proper than Virgil's alluding either to the firing of the ships or the Julium Sidus, as messieurs Catrou and Warton have conjectured.

1. Indignant now] Statius has here manifested his belief of one supreme almighty being, whom he introduces with a dignity and superiority suiting his character and nature. There is a nobleness in this description that would not have disgraced Virgil himself; and the stupendous effects of the nod are finely imagined. But after all, he seems more desirous of making this deity formidable than amiable. He is just, but his justice is not tempered with mercy. We find him the author of all the blood shed between the two nations; he listens to the imprecations of Oedipus, and thinking Mars too dilatory, sends Mercury to him a second time to rouse him to battle by dint of threats.

57. With horrour now] Lewis Crusius in his life of this author, transcribes this description of Mars's temple and palace, as a very fine one: fine

Beneath the fronting height of Æmus stood
The fane of Mars, encompass'd by a wood.
The mansion, rear'd by more than mortal hands,
On columns fram'd of polish'd iron stands;
The well-compacted walls are plated o'er
With the same metal: just without the door
A thousand Furies frown. The dreadful gleam,
That issues from the sides, reflects the beam
Of adverse Phœbus, and with cheerless light
Saddens the day, and starry host of night.
Well his attendants suit the dreary place;
First frantic Passion, Wrath with redd'ning face,
And Mischief blind from forth the threshold start;
Within lurks pallid Fear with quiv'ring heart,
Discord, a two-edged falchion in her hand,
And Treach'ry striving to conceal the brand.
With endless menaces the courts resound:
Sad Valour in the midst maintains her ground,
Rage with a joyful heart, tho' short of breath,
And, arm'd with steel, the gory-visag'd Death:
Blood, spilt in war alone, his altars crowns,
And all his fire is snatch'd from burning towns.
Spoils hung around, and gaudy trophies torn
From vanquish'd states the vaulted roof adorn;
Fragments of iron gates with art engrav'd,
Vessels half burnt, or by the billows stav'd,
Sculls crush'd by wheels, or by keen falchions cleft,
And chariots of their guides and steeds bereft.
Nor were the wounds of war alone express'd,
For groans were almost seen to heave the breast.
Here grim to view was plac'd the god of fight,
So well-dispos'd, that still he was in sight
From ev'ry path, that to the centre brought:
Such was the work by skilful Vulcan wrought,
Before, by Sol betray'd, th' adult'rer rued
His treach'rous love by vengeful schemes pursued.
Scarce had Cyllenius cast his eyes around
In search of the fell demon, when the ground

however as it is, that in Dryden's Palamon and Arcite is not inferior, as the reader will perceive from a comparison.

Beneath the low'ring brow, and on a bent
The temple stood of Mars armipotent:
The frame of burnish'd steel, that cast a glare
From far, and seem'd to thaw the freezing air.
A strait long entry to the temple led,
Blind with high walls and horrour overhead:
Thence issu'd such a blast, and hollow roar,
As threatn'd from the hinge to heave the door:
In through that door a northern light there shone;
'Twas all it had, for windows there were none.
The gate was adamant, eternal frame!
Which hew'd by Mars himself, from Indian quarries came,
The labour of a god; and all along
Tough iron-plates were clench'd to make it strong.
A tun about was ev'ry pillar there:
A polish'd mirror shone not half so clear.
There saw I, how the secret felon wrought,
And treason labouring in the traitor's thought;
And midwife Time the ripen'd plot to murder brought.
There the red Anger dar'd the pallid Fear.
Next stood Hypocrisy with holy leer:
Soft smiling, and demurely looking down,
But hid the dagger underneath the gown:
Th' assassinating wife, the household fiend,
And far the blackest there, the traitor-friend.
On t'other side there stood Destruction bare;
Unpunish'd Rapine and a waste of war.
Contest with sharpen'd knives in cloisters drawn,
And all with blood bespread the holy lawn.
Loud menaces were heard, and foul disgrace,
And bawling infamy in language base;
Till sense was lost in sound, and Silence fled the place.
The slayer of himself yet saw I there,
The gore congeal'd was clotted in his hair:
With eyes half clos'd and gaping mouth he lay,
And grim, as when he breath'd his sullen soul away.
In midst of all the dome, Misfortune sate,
And gloomy Discontent and fell Debate.
And Madness laughing in his ireful mood,
And arm'd complaint on theft, and cries of blood.
There was the murder'd corpse, in covert laid,
And violent death in thousand shapes display'd:
The city to the soldiers' rage resign'd:
Successless wars, and poverty behind:
Ships burnt in fight, or forc'd on rocky shores,
And the rash hunter strangled by the boars:
The new-born babe by nurses overlaid;
And the cook caught within the raging fire he made.
All ills of Mars his nature, flame and steel,
The gasping charioteer beneath the wheel
Of his own car; the ruin'd house that falls,
And intercepts her lord betwixt the walls:
The whole division that to Mars pertains,
All trades of death that deal in steel for gains
Were there, the butcher, armourer, and smith,
Who forges sharpen'd falchions, or the scythe.
The scarlet Conquest on a tow'r was plac'd,
With shouts, and soldiers' acclamations grac'd:
A pointed sword hung threat'ning o'er his head,
Sustain'd but by a slender twine of thread.
There saw I Mars's ides, the capitol,
The seer in vain foretelling Cæsar's fall;
The last triumvirs, and the wars they move,
And Anthony, who lost the world for love.
These and a thousand more the fane adorn;
Their fates were painted ere the men were born;
All copied from the heav'ns, and ruling force
Of the red star, in his revolving course.
The form of Mars high on a chariot stood,
All sheath'd in arms, and gruffly look'd the god.
Two geomantic figures were display'd
Above his head, a warrior and a maid,
One when direct, and one when retrograde.

I hope none of my readers, but such as are insensible of the fine traits of poesy, will be displeased at this long quotation; as setting them together in this manner is the best way to show the beauties of both authors; and nothing is more agreeable to persons of taste, than comparing the flowers of genius and fancy.

96. When the ground] What a dreadful idea of Mars does the poet imprint on the imagination of the reader!—To usher him in with the greater pomp, the ground trembles, the river roars, and the gates of his palace fly open to receive him. He is represented all covered with blood; his chariot, driven by Bellona, overturns trees, hills of snow, and every thing in its way; and Mercury, a brother deity, is so daunted at his appearance, that his very blood is chilled, and he does not dare deliver Jove's message; nay, the poet tells us, that god, great as he is, would have some reverence for him, and recall the menaces he uttered.—A painter might form from this passage the portrait of Mars in all his terrours, as success-

'Gan shake, and Hebrus' horned flood to roar,
And vex with refluent waves the Thracian shore.
Then, as a sign of his approach, the steeds
Spring from their stalls, and beat the trembling
The gates of adamant, eternal frame! [meads;
Flew open. Soon as the destroyer came,
High in his car, and grac'd with hostile gore:
The wheels, swift-rolling, dash'd the meadows o'er
With crimson drops; where'er he pour'd along,
The forests and deep snows gave way.—A throng
Laden with spoils, succeeds. Bellona steers
The chariot's course, and plies her ashen spears.
All cold and stiff with terrour Hermes grew,
And turns his eyes from the terrific view.
E'en Jove himself might soften his demands,
And spare his threats.—While mute Cyllenius
The god, preventing his confusion, cries: [stands;
" What news from Jove? what orders from the
skies?
For scarce, unless some power thy will controls,
For this bleak clime beneath the northern poles
Wouldst thou resign the sweet Lycæan vales,
And Mænalos, refresh'd by summer gales."
His sire's injunctions known, without delay
Great Mars impels along the dreary way
His horses, panting yet with recent toils,
And fires the Greeks with hopes of promis'd spoils.
This seen, the cloud-compeller half resign'd
His wrath, and gentlier now his face declin'd.
Thus, when the weary blasts of Eurus cease,
And leave the deeps subdu'd, at first the peace
Is scarce discerned, as still the waves retain
Their swell, and heave the surface of the main,
Whilst, unrefresh'd, the seamen seek their oars,
And cordage, floating to the neighb'ring shores.
The fun'ral games, and harmless contests clos'd,
Adrastus silence on the crowd impos'd,
And pour'd, to glad the royal infant's soul,
A large libation from the sparkling bowl:
Then thus the discontented shade address'd:
" Grieve not, O babe, in Heav'n supremely blest,
If each third year these fun'ral rites shall see.
So may not Pelops seek with greater glee
Th' Arcadian altars, nor with iv'ry hand
Insult the temples on th' Elæan strand;
So may not Corinth, nor the Delphic coast
Superior fame, and prouder honours boast.
We deem thee more than mortal, and deny
That Styx confines a member of the sky.
Here end thy rites: but should our vows be crown'd,
And haughty Thebes lie level with the ground;
A splendid fane, and altars shall be thine,
And white-rob'd priests with holy pomp inshrine
Thy sacred ashes; nor shall Greece alone
Through all her cities make thy godhead known,
But Thebes to thy divinity appeal,
And swear by thy dread name with awful zeal."
Thus spoke the chief for all his host. The rest
In silent motions their assent express'd.
Mean time the god of battle urg'd his car
Down Ephyra's steep shores, where seen from far
The well-known mount with daring head invades
The clouds, and either sea alternate shades.
Then Terrour, dearest of his menial train,
He sends as harbinger, nor sends in vain;
Since none can on our fear so well impose,
And specious lies with more success disclose.
His aspect varies, as the fiend commands,
Unnumber'd are his tones of speech, and hands.
Whether th' existence of two suns he feigns,
Or subterraneous motions of the plains,
Whole forests shifting place, and planets hurl'd
From their own spheres, to gild the nether world,
Such is his talent, that he still deceives,
And the gull'd dotard all alike believes.
He calls forth all his art to raise a cloud
Of seeming dust, and awe the tim'rous crowd.
The chiefs, astonish'd, from the mountain's brow
Beheld it mounting o'er the fields below.
To double ev'ry fear, and spread th' alarms,
He mimics thund'ring steeds, and clashing arms;
Then with delusive shrieks he grates their ears,
And with false clamours shakes the solid spheres.
At this with sudden dread the vulgar start,
A pulse unusual flutt'ring at their heart:
"Terrour may mock us with imagin'd cries:
But can it cheat at once our ears and eyes?
See what a dust!—the Thebeans these?—tis so.
They come: such is the boldness of the foe. [vows,
But why this stand?—We'll first discharge our
And close the rites."—Thus they. The terrour grows,
A thousand different shapes the monster took,
And varied at his will his voice and look.
Now the Pisæan mode of dress he wears;
And then a suit of Pylian armour bears:
Or in the Spartan phrase, t'augment their fear,
Swears by the gods, the Theban host is near.
All passes with the crowd for genuine truth,
And gains belief from hoary age and youth.
But, when on whirlwinds borne, the direful tale
He wafts around, and brooding o'er the vale
Thrice shakes his sounding shield, thrice smites his
steeds,
And lifts the lance that flames o'er all the meads,

fully as Phidias drew that of Jupiter from Homer's description of him in the first book of the Iliad.—In short, upon the whole, this representation is so grand and full, that nothing can exceed it, but that of the same deity in the third book of this author.

99. The steeds] The seeing of a horse in a foreign country before any other object of the animal creation was reckoned by the ancients as an omen of war. Æneas, in relating his adventures to Dido, tells her that, in Italy

Quatuor hic, primum omen, equos in gramine vidi
Tondentes campum latè, candore nivali.
Et pater Anchises, bellum, terra hospita, portas.
Bello armantur equi. Book 3. verse 537.

138. So may not Pelops, &c.] The sense of this paraphrase is, " May neither the Pythian, Olympic, nor Isthmian games excel those instituted in honour of thee, O babe."

157. The well-known mount] This was a mountain in the Peloponnesian isthmus, called Acrocorinthus, i. e. the highest part of Corinth. Ephyra is an island adjoining.

159. Then Terrour] Mars is now preparing to obey Jupiter's commands by terrifying the confederates with a false account of the Theban army: but all this is told us poetically; and agreeably to the spirit of the epopæia, terrour becomes a person, and speaks and acts as an attendant of Mars. This allegorical personification is the strongest proof of a fertile imagination, and the very Ζωη και ψυχη of heroic poesy.

"Arms, arms," they shout, and, no decorum known,
Take up another's weapons for their own.
In borrow'd coats of mail, and casques they shine,
And to their comrade's car, their coursers join.
In ev'ry breast impatience to engage,
And lust of slaughter reigns. Nought checks their rage;
But on they speed, and fir'd with thirst of praise,
By present haste redeem their past delays.
Such is the tumult, when indulgent gales
Blow from the strand, and fill the spreading sails,
Before the blast the gaudy vessel flies,
The port rolls back, and lessens to their eyes.
Now on the surface of the deep their oars,
And anchors float: while the deserted shores,
And comrades left behind their eyes pursue,
Till all is lost, and vanish'd from their view.
When vine-crown'd Bacchus ey'd the Grecian throng,
As, flush'd with martial heat, they post along,
He turn'd his eyes on Thebes, and inly groan'd,
For much his native city he bemoan'd.
A look, expressive of his grief he wore;
The purple chaplets grac'd his hair no more.
Th' untasted clusters from his horns he shook,
And the wreath'd spear his better hand forsook.
Divested of his robes, before the throne
Of Jove, who press'd by chance the pole alone,
In all the negligence of woe he stands,
And, suppliant, thus bespeaks with lifted hands
His gracious sire, who well the causes knew,
Nor starts astonish'd at th' unwonted view.
" Say, father of the gods, wilt thou destroy
Thy Thebes? can none but vengeful schemes employ
Thy consort's thoughts? and does no pity move
In our behalf the tender breast of Jove?
We grant that erst it griev'd thee to the soul
To dart thy lightnings from the cloudy pole:
Yet why dost thou renew thy bitter ire,
And threat thy late-lov'd town with sword and fire?
No promises, nor oaths thy faith engage.
Alas! where wilt thou bound thy causeless rage?
Is this a proof of thy parental love?
Yet gentler far to the Parrhasian grove,
Argos and Leda's doom thou didst repair,
For then a virgin's conquest was thy care.
Is Bacchus then of all thy num'rous line
The last, who merits thy regard divine?
Bacchus, whom in far happier days of yore
(A pleasing load) the cloud-compeller bore,
And fondly prov'd a mother's keenest throes,
To usher into life, and future woes.
Yet more.—The Thebans are unskill'd in arms,
Rude and unexercis'd in war's alarms;
My martial discipline alone they know:
To weave the leafy garland for the brow,
And frame their motions to the pipe.—Can they
Who dread the wreathed lance, and female fray,
Sustain the trumpet's sound?—See furious Mars!
What feats he meditates, what wasteful wars!
How wouldst thou rage, should he to combat lead
And force the Cretans to th' embattled mead?
A tool was wanting, till entic'd by thee,
Argos must execute thy stern decree.
'Tis this reflexion that augments our woes,
We fall but to enrich our Argive foes.
I yield: but whither shall we now translate
The rites mysterious of our ruin'd state?
And what the pregnant mother left behind,
More happy had she been less fair and kind?
Shall I sue prostrate at the Thracian's feet,
Or seek in conquer'd Ind a safe retreat?
O grant thy wand'ring son a peaceful dome!
At the request of Sol no longer roam
The Delian rocks, but girt with waves, unite,
Nor envy I the happier god of light.
Minerva from her citadel belov'd
Th' invasions of the surge with ease remov'd.
Great Epaphus (as oft these eyes have view'd)
Gives laws to Egypt by his arm subdu'd.
Nor Cretan Ida, nor Cyllene care,
What hostile deeds the neighb'ring states prepare.

215. When vine-crown'd Bacchus] If Venus in Virgil pleads for the Trojans, Bacchus here intercedes for his native city, Thebes, and Statius has given Jupiter the same tender regard for him as in the Æneid he discovers for Venus. From Jupiter's answer to Bacchus on this occasion, compared to what he says elsewhere, it appears, that Jupiter himself was subject to the laws of fate: but, in reality, these are found to be no other than the fixed and immutable determinations of his own will. Here he tells that god, he does not act in compliance to Juno's caprice, but conformably to the unalterable order of destiny. But in the beginning of the Thebaid, we find him positively declaring to the gods in council, his resolution of destroying the royal families of Thebes and Argos, as a punishment for their crimes: and, perhaps, the fate of the Stoics themselves was no other than this in reality.

Lew. Crusius.

240. To the Parrhasian grove] Calysto was ravished by Jupiter in this grove. Argos was the place, where that god imposed upon Danae in the form of a shower of gold. Leda was debauched by the same god in the similitude of a swan.

243. Is Bacchus then] Lactantius informs us, that Bacchus complains of his being so often neglected by mortals, as by Lycurgus and Pentheus. To corroborate this assertion, he has cited a long passage from Ovid's Metamorphoses, where Pentheus is introduced reviling Bacchus. But this is a wrong construction; and the sense of

> Scilicet è cunctis ego neglectissima natis
> Progenies,

is, "I then am to be the most slighted of all your sons, i. e. by you."

246. (A pleasing load) the cloud-compeller] When Semele was blasted by the lightning of her lover, Bacchus, with whom she was then pregnant, was taken from her womb, and sewed up in Jupiter's thigh.

> ——genetricis ab alvo
> Eripitur, patrioque tener (si credere dignum est)
> Insuitur femori, maternaque tempora complet.

267. At the Thracian's feet] Lycurgus, king of Thrace, caused most of the vines of his country to be rooted up: hence the poets have feigned, that he fought with, and persecuted Bacchus.

270. At the request of Sol] Venus upbraids Jupiter of his partiality in like manner:

> Antenor potuit, mediis elapsus Achivis,
> Illyricos penetrare sinus, atque intima tutus

Alas! in what then can our rites offend?
Here (since in vain resistance we pretend)
Here didst thou revel in Alcmena's arms,
Here fair Antiope resign'd her charms
With eager gust, and here Europa play'd
The wanton, by thy specious form betray'd.
Desert not then the guiltless race that springs
From thee, the father of the Theban kings."
At this invidious speech th' Almighty smil'd,
And, gently raising from the ground his child,
As on his knees he sued with lifted hands,
Embrac'd, and kindly answers his demands.
" Think not, O Bacchus, that the war's design'd
To glut with slaughter Juno's vengeful mind.
We act in concert with the fates' decree:
To fall in battle was their destiny.
Peace is my sole delight: who seeks it more,
Or spills with such reluctance human gore?
Witness, thou conscious pole, and starry hall,
How oft, when mortal crimes for vengeance call,
I lay the ready bolt aside, how rare
My challeng'd thunders roar, my lightnings glare.
Scarce could I to the wrath of injur'd Mars,
And Dian, exercis'd in sylvan wars,
The Lapithæ and Calydon resign,
Tho' both had long defy'd the rage divine.
Mine is the loss and toil to re-indue
So many souls with life, and frame anew.
On Argos and her peer in guilt too late
I execute th' impartial will of fate.
To wave the sins of Greece in ancient times,
Thou know'st, how prone the Thebans are to crimes.
Thee too,— But since 'twas done in days of yore,
And we forgive, I pass the trespass o'er.
No joys incestuous hapless Pentheus knew,
No brothers he begot, no sire he slew;
Yet still dismember'd, he resign'd his breath,
And met an undeserv'd, untimely death.
With better grace thy sorrow then had flow'd,
Nor had thy eloquence been ill bestow'd.
Nor will the Thebans suffer punishment,
Tho' well deserv'd, for crimes that I resent.
Heav'n, Earth, and piety expell'd with scorn,
And nature's sacred bonds asunder torn,
And broken faith, and e'en the friends conspire
Their fall.—But thou desist to tempt our ire,
Secure, that a long interval remains
Ere we fulfil on Thebes, what fate ordains.
A new avenger in a better age
Shall rise: first Argos bleeds beneath our rage."
This heard, the god his wonted look resumes,
And with fresh youth, and new-born graces blooms.
Thus parch'd by sultry suns and southern gales,
The pale rose fades, and withers in the vales;
But if soft Zephyr fans the glowing day,
And tempers with his wings the scorching ray,
Its blush revives, the buds shines forth again,
And waft the scent thro' Flora's fair domain.
Meanwhile, their march explor'd, the scout returns,
From whom Eteocles, astonish'd, learns,
That near the confines of the Theban sway
The Grecian hosts advance, and speed their way,
And all, who view the numbers of the foe,
To vanquish'd Thebes portend approaching woe.
Of ev'ry chief he soon is taught the name,
His birth, his quality, and martial fame.
The prudent king dissembles well his fears,
And hates the message, yet attentive hears:
His host he now inspirits and demands
A faithful list of all his able bands.
By Mars excited to the deathful field,
Aonia, Phocis, and Eubœa yield
Their youth: for thus the ruler of the skies
Decreed. Thro' all the host the signal flies.
Now rang'd for war, and sheath'd in radiant arms,
Forth pour the squadrons at the first alarms,
And take the field, which next the city lay,
Thirsting for blood, and destin'd for the fray.
Before th' expected foe was yet in sight,
The matrons climb the walls to view the fight:
And teach, whilst to their sons their sires they show,
Their little hearts with early warmth to glow.
The senior princess on a turret stood,
Veil'd from the public eye. A sable hood

Regna Liburnorum, & fontem superare Timavi;
Unde per ora novem vasto cum murmure montis, &c.

287. At this invidious speech] Jupiter's behaviour to Venus after her addressing him may be compared with this to Bacchus.

> Olli subridens hominum sator atque deorum,
> Vultu, quo cœlum tempestatesque serenat,
> Oscula libavit natæ: dehinc talia fatur.
> Æneid. 1. 258.

303. The Lapithæ and Calydon] See book the first for an account of Diana's enmity to the Calydonians. The Lapithæ were a people of Thessaly, inhabiting that part of the country that lay between the mountains Pindus and Othrys. For an account of the combat betwixt them and the Centaurs, see Ovid's Metamorphoses, lib. 12.

313. No joys incestuous hapless Pentheus knew.] Pentheus was torn in pieces by the priestesses of Bacchus, for not attending the sacred rites of that deity.

331. Thus parch'd by sultry suns] Ariosto has a simile that very much resembles this of our author.

> Qual sotto il più cocente árdore estivo,
> Quando di ber piu desiosa è l' erba,
> Il fior, ch' era vicino a restar privo
> Di tutto quell' amor, ch'in vita il serba,
> Sente l'amata pioggia, e si fa vivo.
> Orlando furioso, Canto 23. Stan. 180.

361. The senior princess] Statius has also imitated Homer in many places; and he seems particularly to have had an eye to Helen's informing the old man on the walls of Troy, as she is there described in the Iliad, of the character of the several princes in the Grecian camp; for in the seventh book, Antigone, sister to Eteocles and Polynices, appears standing on a tower, attended by an old officer who had been Laius's armourbearer; who, at her desire, gives an account of the allies that came to assist the Thebans. Though some circumstances are altered, it is very easy to imagine he took his plan from the Iliad. Nor will any one condemn this conduct of his, such imitations being not only very allowable, but commendable, when made with art, and happily and fitly introduced.—— Lewis Crusius.

Lactantius observes, that in this account of the generals who took part with Thebes, and the provinces they commanded, our author has adhered

From the keen air her tender cheeks defends :
Phorbas alone of all her train attends,
The squire of Laius, whilst at Thebes he reign'd,
And in the royal service still retain'd.
Him fair Antigone with kind demand
Thus questions. " May we hope to make a stand
Against our enemies, since all the states
Of Greece descend to fight, as fame relates.
I pray thee, first inform me of the name
Of our confed'rates, and what rank they claim ?
For well I see what armour Creon wears,
What are the standards our Menæceus bears,
And how fierce Hæmon tow'rs above the rest,
A brazen sphinx well-imag'd on his crest."
Thus spake the fair unknowing. He replies :
" Yon chief, whose warlike figure strikes your eyes,
Is Dryas. From Tanagra's hill he leads
A thousand archers, train'd to warlike deeds.
The great Orion's offspring he : behold
The bolt and trident, rudely form'd in gold
Upon his shield.—Nor do his acts disgrace
Th' untainted honours of his godlike race.
From him, ye gods, avert th' invet'rate ire
Of stern Diana, fatal to his sire !
Ocaleæ, Medeon, Nisa stock'd with groves,
And Thisbe, fam'd for Cytherea's doves,
March to the fight beneath his royal care,
And to his banner, unconstrain'd, repair.
Next comes Erymedon : the weapons borne
By Faun, his rustic sire, one hand adorn,
A crest of pine-leaves trembles on his head :
The savage race his massy javelin dread,
Nor less is his desert in arms, I ween ;
With him Erythræ, rich in flocks, is seen,
Who Scolos, and the coasts of Hyle till,
Who Eteonos, rough with many a hill,
And Schœnos, Atalanta's birth-place, hold,
In manners haughty as in combat bold.
The lance of ash Pellæan, and the shield,
Impenetrable by the dart they wield.
See, with what clamours the Neptunian throng,
The natives of Onchestus, pour along !
Whom Mycalissos shades with lofty pines,
Where, as a mirror clear, Gargaphye shines,
Thy streams, O Melus, lov'd of Pallas, rise,
And Heliartos views with envying eyes
The fruit of Ceres, and, as it ascends,
With the young blades his noxious herbage blends.
Their shields are bark. Huge trunks supply the place
Of spears. A lion's hide o'erspreads their face.
These as they want a monarch of their own,
Amphion (by the damsel not unknown)
Conducts to war. The badges of the realm,
A bull and lyre are wrought upon his helm.
Proceed, brave youth, to dare the thickest foes,
And for our walls thy naked breast expose.
You too, ye warriors, favour'd of the nine !
To yield us aid forsake the mount divine.
And thou, O Olmius, and Permessus blest
With streams, whose gentle murmurs lull to rest
The weary shepherd, rouse to feats of arms
Your slothful sons, averse to war's alarms.
In strains adapted to their country's rite
They now exult, and harmonize the fight.
Thus, when in spring Sol sheds a warmer ray,
On Strymon's banks the swans renew their lay.
Pursue with cheerfulness this track to fame,
Secure, the Muses shall embalm your name
In never-dying numbers, and convey
To latest times the honours of the fray."
The princess here broke in, and thus replies.
" O father, hither turn thy aged eyes,
For sure this parity of choice declares
That those are brothers.—Mark, how either wears
The self-same armour ! equal are their crests :
But say, what motive thus cements their breasts.
Were ours as these unanimous and kind !"
She ceas'd. The sage soft smiling, thus rejoin'd.
" Nor thou, O queen, hast err'd in this alone :
Many (the real history unknown)

pretty close to Homer's catalogue, so far as regards the geography, and epithets of places.—Mr. Pope strengthens this remark. See Iliad, lib. 2.

386. Fatal to his sire] The fabulous account of this hero is as follows.—Pelasgus, a pious worshipper of the gods, hospitably entertained Jupiter, Neptune, and Mercury, for which favour they promised to grant him whatsoever he wished. Therefore, as he had no issue, he requested, that they would grant him a son. The gods promised they would ; and pissing on the hide of an ox that he had just sacrificed to them, ordered him to dig a hole for it in the earth, and take it out at the end of nine months. He did so, and found on it the child, whom he afterwards named Orion, from Ουρον, which signifies urina. When Orion grew up to man's estate, he attempted to ravish Diana, who, imploring the assistance of the earth, was delivered by a scorpion, that stung the ravisher to death. Others say, that he was slain by the shafts of that goddess, as Horace :

Virgineâ domitus sagittâ.

399. Atalanta's birth-place] There were two ladies of this name ; one an Arcadian queen, the mother of Parthenopæus, and the other (who is here meant) of Scyros. She was overcome in a foot-race by Hippomanes, who threw in her way three golden apples, which Venus had given him for that purpose.

401. The lance of ash Pellæan] Lucan mentions this sort of weapon, and particularises it, as well as our author, by the name of sarissa.

Primi Pellæas arcu fregere sarissas.

414. By the damsel not unknown] I think it not improper to take notice, that this parenthesis is not to be understood as spoken by Phorbas to Antigone, but by the author to the reader. He hints to him, that Phorbas is describing a person to Antigone, whom she very well knew ; so that we may fairly conclude, there was some love-match in the case, to which the poet alludes in this slight manner.

415. The badges of the realm, A bull and lyre] The lyre was engraved on the arms of the Thebans, because Amphion is said to have built their town by his skill in handling that instrument ; and the bull was added in honour of Cadmus, who, when he sought his sister Europa, who was ravished by Jupiter in the shape of that animal, was conducted by an heifer to the spot, where he afterwards founded the city of Thebes.

441. Nor thou, O queen] It has been observed of Statius, that in his catalogues he has happily imitated Homer and Virgil, by keeping up the

That these are brethren, have alike believ'd,
By all the signs of equal age deceiv'd.
Yet are they sire and son, tho' each appears
A brother both in stature, form, and years.
Fair Dircetis, enamour'd with the charms
Of Lapithaon, snatch'd him to her arms;
And, forcing nature, taught the boy to prove
Th' untimely joys of undigested love.
Nor was it long, before from their embrace
Alathreus sprung unmatch'd in shape and face.
He deigned not to wait the nat'ral time,
O'ertakes his father in his youthful prime,
Adopts each feature, blends their years in one:
And now they change the name of sire and son
For that of brothers, and, unknowing strife,
Tread hand in hand, the chequer'd path of life.
With each three hundred horse to fight repair,
Who breathe fam'd Coronia's temp'rate air,
And Glissas', sacred to the pow'rs divine,
One for her corn renown'd, and one for wine.
Mark Hypseus, whose enormous shield display'd
O'er four tall steeds extends its ample shade!
Huge is its orb, with sev'n bull-hides o'ercast:
The cuirass, for its strength by few surpass'd,
Three plates of iron form. His gen'rous breast
Alone it guards: he fears not for the rest.
His spear the glory of the sylvan reign,
Ne'er baulks its master's hopes, nor flies in vain:
Thro' obvious arms and hearts it takes its way,
Untaught to brook resistance and delay.
Asopus was his sire (to credit fame)
A father then, and worthy of the name,
When thro' the broken bridge and ruin'd mound
He roars, and deluges the plains around,
Or when, to brave the ruler of the skies,
In days of old he bade his waves arise.
For they report, that whilst his daughter stray'd
On the green bank he forc'd the beauteous maid.
Resenting this (for at that better time
The rape of virgins was no licens'd crime)
With Jove he durst in hardy fight engage,
And dash'd against the stars his foamy rage:
At length, unequal to the triple fire,
He slunk from combat, and resign'd his ire.
Yet some small sparks of courage still remain;
For oft in angry mood upon the plain
He pours Ætnean vapours, badge of shame,
And ashes, gather'd from the light'ning's flame.
The deeds of Hypseus we shall soon approve,
If his fair sister can but influence Jove.
Him as their chief, Ithone's troops attend;
Ithone, bless'd with Pallas for a friend.
From Arne, Græa, Mide, and the coast
Of Aulis, next he leads a banded host,
With those who exercise their rural toil
On green Plateæ, Peteon's furrowy soil,
Euripus, ebbing in his course again,
And thee, Anthedon, verge of our domain,
Where Glaucus, leaping from the grassy shore,
Plung'd headlong in the deeps, a man no more,
And view'd with sudden terrour, as he sprung,
The fishes, that around his middle clung.
With Balearic slings they cleave the wind:
Their javelins leave the swiftest shaft behind.
Nor had Narcissus shunn'd the strife of arms:
But smitten with his own reflected charms
In Thespian fields he grows. Cephissus laves
The much lov'd flow'ret with his childless waves.
Who can recount the Phocians fam'd of old,
The Phocians, in Apollo's host inroll'd?
Who Panope and Cyparissos plow,
Or Lebodea's vales, and Daulis sow?
Hyampolis on pointed rocks reclin'd,
And high Parnassus, at the top disjoin'd?
Who thro' the plains of Anemoria rove,
Thro' Cyrrha, and the dark Corycian grove;
And from Lilæa's sea-beat walls, dispread
With oozy banks, behold the fountain-head
Of hoar Cephissus, where the Pythian snake
In the fresh stream was wont his thirst to slake.
Laurels, inwoven with their crests, they wear,
And on their brazen arms insclptur'd bear
Delos, or Niobe's, or Tytion's fate,
Both sacrific'd to stern Latonia's hate.
These Iphitus, a chief well-known to fame,
Commands, whose father, Naubolus by name,
Directed once the car and warrior-steeds
Of Laius, noted for his gentle deeds,
What time (O scene heart-wounding to behold!)
His neck, convuls'd with dying motions roll'd,
And pour'd upon the ground life's purple tide.
O had I shar'd his fate, and with him dy'd!"
Whilst thus he spoke, his cheeks grew wet with tears,
And his whole visage pale and wan appears;

dignity of his style, and harmony of his numbers, and diversifying the detail with proper epithets, short descriptions, and agreeable narrations from passages of history and fable, with which he diverts and refreshes the reader at due intervals. Of his art in this last article the following anecdote is a shining instance; and though it borders upon the marvellous, does not transgress the licence of poetry.

468. He fears not for the rest] Phorbas here pays a genteel and artful compliment to the valour of Hypseus. He tells Antigone, that he had no occasion for any armour on his back, because he never turned it to his enemies.

496. Aulis] A city and haven of Bœotia where the Grecians were detained a long time by contrary winds in their expedition against Troy.

499. Euripus] A narrow sea between Bœotia and Eubœa, where, according to Gregory Nazianzen and Justin Martyr, Aristotle drowned himself, because he could not discover the cause of its ebbing and flowing, which was seven times a day.

500. Anthedon] A town situated between Eubœa and Bœotia. Glaucus was a fisherman, who laying the fish which he caught, upon the bank, observed, that by tasting a certain herb they revived, and leaped into the sea again, which he imitated, and became a god of the sea.

509. Cephissus] At present, Cepho is a river of Greece that disembogues itself into the gulph of Negropont. It rises in the mountains of Phocis, and is styled sacred by Lucan, from the nearness of its springs to the oracle of Delphos. This river was feigned to be the father of Narcissus, whose story is in every school-boy's mouth, and therefore needs not to be told here.

513. Who Panope, &c.] These lines are almost a transcript of those subjoined from Homer's catalogue. Il. B. 2.

Οἳ Κυπάρισσον ἔχον, Πυθῶνά τε πετρήεσσαν,
Κρίσσαν τε ζαθέην, καὶ Δαυλίδα καὶ Πανοπῆα,
Οἵ τ' Ἀνεμώρειαν, καὶ Ὑάμπολιν ἀμφενέμοντο.

Whilst interrupting sighs his voice represt,
And heav'd, as they would rend his swelling breast.
With lenient arts his ward removes his pain:
His voice restor'd, he faintly speaks again.
"O thou, who dost my ev'ry thought employ,
At once a pleasing care and anxious joy!
For thee I linger on life's busy stage,
And drag along the slow remains of age,
To see perchance thy princely brothers slain,
And Laius' slaughter acted o'er again.
Yet till to some brave suitor I resign
Thy virgin-charms, protract, ye pow'rs divine,
My vital thread: that charge fulfill'd I give
The loan of Nature back, and cease to live.
But whilst we thus digress the time away,
What leaders pass, unnotic'd, to the fray!
See Clonius with the seed of Abas join'd,
Whose hair depends in flowing locks behind!
Unsung Carystos, stock'd with marble veins,
Caphereus high, and Aegea's vale remains.
And now the circling troops their chief enclose,
While heralds silence on the crowd impose."
Scarce had he said, when from a rising ground,
The monarch thus bespeaks his bands around.
"Ye warrior-kings, from whose disposing hand
I take the honours of the chief command,
Or midst the vulgar herd assert my right,
Think not, I now exhort you to the fight,
Since bound by voluntary oaths, you lend
Your pow'rful aid; nor mean I to commend,
Since words can ill express my grateful sense,
Nor thanks requite your zeal in our defence,
Yet shall the gods your high desert regard,
And your own hands the victory reward.
No foe leads hither his assembled hosts,
No warlike pillager from foreign coasts
Prepares to sack the town which you defend,
But a false native, and pretended friend.
Here are his sisters, mother, aged sire,
And here his brother was.—See, flush'd with ire,
His countrymen in adverse arms he meets,
And menaces his own paternal seats.
Yet in my cause th' Aonian troops engage,
Nor leave me, monster! to thy ruthless rage;
Whose will and sentiments thou should'st have known,
Nor thus aspir'd to my forbidden crown."
This said, the king disposes all aright,
And orders, who shall take the field for fight,
Or guard the city: who shall close the rear,
Compose the flanks, or in the van appear.

555. Carystos] Now Caristo, an island bordering on the straits of Eubœa.—Caphereus was the mountain on which many of the Grecian ships were split in their return from Troy.

561. Ye warrior-kings] It will be hard to find a more artful speech than this of Eteocles to the auxiliary kings. He begins with telling them, that he is willing to resign the command of the army whenever they require it. He then pays them a genteel compliment on their readiness to assist him; and sets this expedition of his brother in the worst of lights by attributing it to the thirst of blood, disaffection to his parents, and an unnatural aversion to his native country.——In short, it is the completest piece of dissimulation I ever met with. Not the least of his malevolent disposition transpires, and no one from this harangue could form an idea of his true character.

The shepherd thus unbars at break of day
His twig-built folds, and calls the sheep away.
The fathers of the flock in order lead
The dewy way, the mother-ewes succeed.
With careful hand he tends the teeming dams,
And carries in his arms the feeble lambs.
Mean time, with wrath impell'd, the Grecian host
Pursue their march along th' Aonian coast;
From morn to night, from night to morn again
They bend beneath their armour, and disdain
The gifts of sleep, and grudge to set apart
An hour for rest, or food to cheer the heart.
They seek their enemies with equal speed,
As if pursued themselves by foes; nor heed
The prodigies, that, as they pass along,
Foretell their fate in many a boding song.
The stars, the beasts and birds of prey disclose
Destruction; o'er their banks the rivers rose:
Malignant lightnings glanc'd along the poles,
And Jove's own hand portentous thunders rolls.
Spontaneous close the holy temple-doors,
The shrine with more than mortal voices roars;
Alternate show'rs of blood and stones descend,
And kindred shades in weeping throngs attend.
Then Cyrrha's oracles respond no more,
Eleusis howls in months unknown before,
While in their op'ning fanes (a sure presage
Of future ills) the Spartan twins engage.
At depth of night (for so th' Arcadians tell)
Lycaon's frantic ghost was heard to yell.
Oenomaus renews the race again,
And guides the car o'er Pisa's cruel plain,
Whilst Achelous weeps his other horn
From his dishonour'd head unjustly torn.
Mycenæ's iv'ry Juno stands in tears,
And Perseus' statue vents in groans its fears;
Old Inachus rebellows hoarse and loud,
And with his roarings scares the rustic crowd:
While sad Palæmon o'er the double main
Was notic'd for his country to complain.
Th' Inachians heard, yet on their course they steer,
To heav'nly counsels deaf, and blind to fear.
Now on the banks of rough Asopus stood
The Grecian wings, and view'd the hostile flood,
When sudden doubts forbade them to pass o'er,
And stay'd their slack'ning steps upon the shore.

587. The shepherd thus] This simile, though taken from low life, admirably well illustrates the parental care and military vigilance of Eteocles: and with respect to the circumstances of it, Virgil himself has scarcely in all his eclogues a finer piece of rural imagery.

603. The stars, &c.] The prognostics of the civil broils between Cæsar and Pompey are many of them parallel with those preceding the Theban war. See Lucan's Pharsalia, book 1 and 7.

616. Lycaon's] Lycaon was the father of Helice, who was deflowered by Jupiter. To revenge the rape, he served up human flesh to the gods at a banquet, and was therefore turned into a wolf. See Ovid's Metamorphoses, lib. 1.

631. When sudden doubts] Cæsar's irresolution and dread at passing the Rubicon are described in a similar manner by Lucan, and the following lines in particular have a near resemblance with our author's:

——Ut ventum est parvi Rubiconis ad undas,
——————Tunc perculit horror

The river then by chance with deaf'ning sound
Descended on the trembling fields around;
Whether he ow'd his swell to mountain-snow,
Or show'rs, discharg'd from the celestial bow,
Or whether, to detain his daring foes
From sacking Thebes, spontaneous he arose.
Hippomedon first plunges in his steed,
Huge fragments of the broken bank succeed:
Then to his comrades left behind he cries,
While, bursting o'er his head, the waves arise:
" Come on, for thus to Thebes I'll show the way,
Nor walls, nor gates shall long my progress stay."
Now all rush down, dismiss their former dread,
And blush to follow, when they might have led.
Thus when the herdsman thro' some brook untry'd
Would drive his cattle to the farther side,
Just on the drink all motionless they stand,
And view the waves between, and distant strand:
But if the bolder bull pervades the ford,
And gains the wish'd-for mead, its depth explor'd,
The leap grows easy, shallower looks the stream,
And the two banks almost united seem.
Not distant far a mountain they survey,
And fields, from whence all Thebes in prospect lay:
Encamping here, they rais'd their tents and eas'd
Their limbs, so well the situation pleas'd.
Beneath, an open tract of country lies;
No hills between the town and them arise,
From whose superior height the curious foe
Might mark the motions in their camp below.
So well had Nature form'd its ev'ry part,
That nought remains improveable by art.
Here rocks in form of lofty bulwarks rose,
There hollow vales a kind of trench compose,
A battlement, self-rais'd, defends each side.
What more was wanted, their own hands supply'd,
Till Sol retir'd beneath Hesperian seas,
And sleep impos'd an interval of ease.
But O what tongue can speak the wild affright
Of Thebes, when veil'd in gloom the sleepless night
Doubles each terrour of the future fray,
And menaces the near approach of day!
They run about the walls; and in their fears
Amphion's fortress insecure appears.
Meanwhile new horrours of the foe arise,
Fame swells their number, fear augments their size.
But when they view the blazing fires, that show
The Grecian tents, from off the mountain's brow,
Their warrior-steeds and weapons, some exhort,
Others more pious to the fanes resort,
And tempt the gods with sacrifice and pray'r;
Or in the very height of their despair,
Exact a promise of the burial rite,
And fun'ral honours, if they fall in fight.
Terrific visions bring to view their foes,
And deathful dreams intrude on their repose.
To lose the life that's loathsome grown, they fear,
And call for death, but shun it when 'tis near.
In either camp the Fury takes her stand,
And brandishes a snake in either hand:
The chiefs [1] with mutual hatred she inspires;
But both against their aged parent fires:
Sequester'd in a distant cell he lies,
Implores the fiends, and re-demands his eyes.
Now fainter shone the silver lamp of night,
And the stars fled before the new-born light,
When Sol, emerging from his watry bed,
Above the waves exalts his beaming head,
And, scatt'ring from his wheels the sparks of day,
Marks his bright progress with a golden ray.
Lo! from the gate her steps Jocasta bends,
And looks the oldest of the sister fiends
In majesty of woe. Her colour flies;
Grey hairs o'erhung her cheeks and haggard eyes.
Black were her arms: an olive-branch she bore,
With wool of sable colour wreathed o'er.
Her daughters, now the better sex, sustain
The furious queen, while she exerts in vain
Her aged limbs, that, destitute of force,
Bend with her weight, and falter in the course.
She stands before the Grecians, strikes her breasts
Against the gates, and movingly requests
Accesss in terms like these.—" Ye hostile bands,
The guilty mother of the war demands
To see her son, long absent from her sight,
Nor asks it as a favour but a right."
The troops, astounded, tremble at the view,
But when she spoke, their fears increase anew.
The king's consent obtain'd, without delay
Through yielding foes, secure, she takes her way,
And, as she first th' Inachian leaders eyes,
Vents her outrageous grief in horrid cries.
" Ye chiefs of Argos, to my eyes disclose
The worst of children and the worst of foes;
O say, beneath what helm his visage lies
Conceal'd, what arms his well-known shape disguise."
While thus she spake, the summon'd prince appears;
Forth bubble from his eyes the joyful tears.
He clasps her in his arms, and, aw'd with shame,
Relieves her pains, and dwells upon her name.
His sisters now, his mother then he tends,
Who thus with pity just reproaches blends.
" O partner of Mycenæ's fair domain!
Why dost thou tears, and names respectful feign,

Membra ducis, riguere comæ, gressumque coercens
Languor in extrema tenuit vestigia ripâ.

633. The river then] Statius might have here introduced a fine piece of machinery, and taken the same advantage of the river Asopus, as Homer did of Scamander, by making it oppose the march of the Grecians.—But perhaps it was his aversion to become an imitator that made him let slip this opportunity; he rather choosing to forego an ornament than be indebted to another for the hint of it.

678. Fame swells their number] Lucan has some animated lines on the terrours that Cæsar's approach caused at Rome. Phar. B. 1.

Barbaricas sævi discurrere Cæsaris alas:
Ipsum omnes aquilas, collataque signa ferentem,
Agmine non uno, densisque incedere castris.
Nec qualem meminere vident: majorque ferusque
Mentibus occurrit, victoque immanior hoste.

[1] Eteocles and Polynices.

703. Lo! from the gate] I cannot but fancy, there is a strong resemblance between the portraits of Amata and Jocasta: though the former endeavours to sow the seeds of war, and the latter to make peace. The description of the interview between the mother and son is wrought up to the utmost height of the pathos.

735. O partner of Mycenæ's] This speech of Jocasta breathes very strongly of motherly tenderness and affection.—She opens it with declar-

And strain thy odious mother to thy breast,
Her tender bosom by thy armour press'd?
Didst thou a wretched guest and outlaw rove,
What heart's so steely that thou would'st not move?
The troops from far expect thy last commands,
And many a glitt'ring sword beside thee stands.
Alas! the cares that hapless mothers prove!
Witness, how oft I've wept, ye pow'rs above.
Yet if thou wilt the words of age revere,
And to thy friends' advice incline thy ear,
Now, while the camp is still, as in the night,
And piety suspends the dreadful fight,
I pray thee, as a king of mighty sway,
But charge thee, as my son, to speed thy way
To Thebes, and see again thy native hall,
Before to Vulcan's rage a prey it fall.
Once more address thy brother in my sight,
And I'll be judge to ascertain thy right:
Should he refuse again, he will afford
A better plea to wield again the sword.
Deem not, that by thy conscious mother's aid,
Perfidious snares are for thy ruin laid.
Some sparks of nat'ral love we still retain;
Such fears, thy sire conducting, would be vain.
Tis true, I married, and from our embrace
You sprung, the lasting badges of disgrace:
Yet vicious as you are, you share my love:
I pardon, what I yet must disapprove.
But, if thou dost persist to play the king,
A triumph ready to thy hands we bring.
Come, tie thy captive sisters' hands behind,
And to the car thy fetter'd parents bind.
Now to your shame, O Greeks, my groans I turn,
For your old sires, and babes your absence mourn.
Such then (believe me) is the secret dread,
That parents feel, such tears at home they shed.
If in so short a time so dear he's grown
To you, by whom his merits scarce were known,
What anxious thoughts must these my breasts engage,
These breasts, the solace of his tender age?

ing her doubts of her son's sincerity, then tells him, the troops are so much at his command, that they will easily dismiss their rage, if they know his inclinations are for peace. She next reminds him of her care and regard for him, and advises him to try his brother once more, adding at the same time, that if he persists in withholding the crown from him, he will then have a good pretence for commencing hostilities. She then obviates any suspicions he might entertain of her treachery, and ironically prompts him to make him and her daughters prisoners. She concludes with an apostrophe to the Grecian princes, wherein she entreats them to make peace, and use their influence with her son, to reconcile him to his friends, by telling them what anxieties their relations undergo in their absence.—It is impossible to point out the beauties of these long orations, without analysing them in this manner, and considering their several objects and motives separately.

740. What heart's so steely, that thou would'st not move] Jocasta speaks here interrogatively:—The sense is, there is no one, but what is either moved with terrour at the approaching invasion, or with compassion for your misfortunes.

From Thracian kings such usage I might bear,
But not from those who breathe the Grecian air.
Then grant my wish, and second my desire,
Or in my son's embraces I expire."
These pow'rful words the wrathful cohorts move,
And all the mother's virtuous suit approve:
Whilst on their glitt'ring shields and armour flow
The pious streams of sympathetic woe.
As when the brindled monarch of the wood
Beholds the hunter prostrate and subdu'd,
His anger past, he takes a greater joy
To spare the ready victim, than destroy:
Thus pity through their hearts unnotic'd glides,
And the fell ardour of revenge subsides.
Before them all the warrior turns his face,
To meet his loving mother's kind embrace,
And tries to yield Antigone relief,
And chase with kisses fair Ismene's grief:
While, various tempests raging in his mind,
Ambition for a time the reins resign'd.
He wills to go. Adrastus not denies;
When, mindful of past inj'ries, Tydeus cries,
"Rather let me address the gen'rous foe,
Who his experienc'd faith and honour know,
Though not a brother.—In this wounded breast
I bear his peace and covenants impress'd.
Why did'st thou not, O gentle mother-queen!
As judge and mediatress stand between,
When the fee'd guards in nightly ambush lay?
Such is the league by which thou wouldst betray
Thy son.—But lead him to yon reeking mead,
That still bears witness to the bloody deed.
Yet wilt thou follow?—Do not thus neglect
Our friendly counsels through a false respect.
Say, when the hostile weapons round thee glare,
Will she, lamenting, make thy life her care,
And turn each dagger's menac'd point away;
Or will the tyrant king forego his prey,
And send thee to our camp unhurt again?
First Inachus shall cease to seek the main,
And Achelous run back, while in my view
This lance its verdant honours shall renew.
Beneath this friendly converse lurks a sword:
Know, that our gates too will access afford:
In us, unperjur'd yet, he may confide;
Yet, should he me suspect, I step aside.
Then let him come, while privy to the scene,
His mother and his sisters stand between.
But, should he the contested crown restore,
Wilt thou resign, thy term of ruling o'er?"

801. Though not a brother] Nothing could be more aptly contrived to render Eteocles odious to his brother, and consequently to dissuade him from trusting himself in his hands, than this reflection.—He observes to Polynices, that, though he was so maltreated by Eteocles, he was not his brother; which is equivalent to saying, that he, who was his brother, would be used with a much greater degree of rigour and cruelty.

817. While in my view] The hint of this passage is taken from Valerius Flaccus, Argonautics, Book 3.

Hanc ego magnanimi spolium Didymaonis hastam,
Ut semel est avulsa jugis, a matre peremptâ.
Quæ neque jam frondes virides neque proferet umbras,
Fida ministeria, et duras obit horrida pugnas,
Testor.

This heard, their first resolves the warriors change,
And for the fight again themselves arrange.
Thus the fierce South, by sudden whirlwinds, gains
The wide-stretch'd empire of the liquid plains
From Boreas.—Peace and leagues they seek no
But give a loose to rage, and thirst for gore. [more,
Erinnys takes advantage of th' alarms,
And sows the seeds of war and future harms.
Two tigers, mild and innocent of blood,
Pursu'd their way to Dirce's sacred flood:
By Bacchus for the chariot they were broke,
And, with their country, bow'd beneath the yoke.
Now old and useless in his service grown,
They graze the fields beside the Theban town,
Gentle as lambs, and smelling as they pass,
Of Indian herbage, and Sabæan grass.
The Bacchanalian crowd, and elder priest,
At each renewal of their patron's feast,
Their sable spots with purple fillets blend,
While various clusters from their necks depend.
By flocks and herds they were alike belov'd,
Secure with them the lowing heifers rov'd,
On nought they prey, but from each friendly hand
Their daily food in placid guise demand,
And to the ground their horrid mouths incline,
To lap the purple produce of the vine.
Around the country all the day they roam,
But when at noon they seek their wonted home,
With sacred fires the domes and temples shine,
As if to grace the present god of wine.
But when her sounding lash the fury shakes,
Her sounding lash, compos'd of twisted snakes,
Their former rage returning, from the town
They break forth, by the Grecian troops unknown.
As from a diff'rent quarter of the sky,
Two thunderbolts, with ruin pregnant, fly,
And thro' the clouds a length of light extend;
Thus thro' the fields their course the tigers bend,
And, fiercely growling as they rush along,
Invade a straggler of th' Inachian throng,

835. Two tigers mild and innocent of blood] Lewis Crusius, in his account of our author, observes, that, it being more artful to let the war break out from a trivial occasion, Statius has in this passage imitated Virgil, who informs us, that the war between Æneas and Turnus was caused by the killing of a favourite stag.—I readily grant, with this ingenious gentleman, that this is an imitation of Virgil, but cannot think the death of the two tigers a trifling occasion of the war. There is certainly a wide difference between the killing a deer, the property of a country girl, and two tigers consecrated to Bacchus, the tutelary god and patron of the Thebans; and whoever considers what superstitious bigots they were at that time of day, will easily imagine, that there could not be a greater reason for the Thebans going to war, than such an insult on their gods, and such an affront to their religion.——In describing the caresses and ornaments which were bestowed on them, he has taken some of the circumstances from Virgil.

Assuetum imperiis soror omni Sylvia curâ
Mollibus intexens ornabat cornua sertis,
Pectebatque ferum, puroque in fonte lavabat.
Ille manum patiens, mensæque assuetus herili,
Errabat sylvis; rursusque ad limina nota
Ipse domum serâ quamvis se nocte ferebat.
Æn. lib. 7. ver. 486.

The prophet's charioteer, as o'er the meads
He drove to Dirce's streams his master's steeds.
Next Ida, the Tænarian, they pursue,
With him Ætolian Acamas they slew.
The coursers in disorder speed their flight,
Till brave Aconteus kindled at the sight.
Aconteus, expert in the sylvan chace,
(In fair Arcadia was his native place),
To the pursuit well-arm'd with weapons sped,
As turning to their much-lov'd Thebes, they fled,
And, eager his long-studied art to prove,
Thro' their pierc'd back, and gushing bowels drove
The levell'd javelin.——To the town again
They fly, and flying, draw upon the plain
A bloody line, while o'er their upper skin
The darts appear, the points deep-lodg'd within.
They imitate with groans the human cry,
And to the walls their wounded breasts apply.
This seen, such shrieks and mournful clamours rise,
As if (the city made a hostile prize)
The Tyrian fanes and sacred mansions shone
With Argive fires, and splendours not their own.
Less would they grieve, should Cadmus' regal hall,
Or fair Harmonia's bridal chamber fall.
But Phegeus, to revenge his injur'd god,
With haughty mien towards Aconteus strode;
And as disarm'd, he triumph'd o'er the slain,
Aim'd a destructive blow, nor aim'd in vain.
The youthful bands of Tegea fly too late,
To save the warrior, and avert his fate.
Thrown o'er the slaughter'd animals, he lies,
And to th' offended pow'r a victim dies.
The council broke and congress held in vain,
O'er all the camp loud tumults rise again.
Back thro' the hostile troops Jocasta flies,
Nor longer on her pray'rs or tears relies.
Her and her daughters thence the Greeks remove,
While Tydeus strives th' advantage to improve.
"Go, hope for peace, and the just fight delay,
Till the more prudent foe commence the fray.
Say, could ye thus the work of death adjourn,
And wait for the commission'd queen's return?"
He spoke, and to his comrades high display'd,
(A signal of the charge) his naked blade.
On either side now wrath and vengeance rise,
And one vast shout groans upward to the skies.
No martial laws observ'd, nor order known,
The soldiers with their captains mix, nor own
Superior rank: horse, foot, and rattling cars,
Form one dire chaos.—Urg'd by furious Mars,
Headlong they rush, no leisure giv'n to show
Themselves, or from the foe their comrades know.

879. To the town again] These lines are taken from the following of Virgil, who, speaking of the wounded stag, says,

Saucius at quadrupes nota intra tecta refugit,
Successitque gemens stabulis, questuque cruentus,
Atque imploranti similis, tectum omne replevit.
Æn. lib. 7. ver. 500.

905. Go, hope for peace] Our author seems in this place to have had an eye to the ironical scoff of Turnus upon the Latians in the 11th book of the Æneid, as may be seen from the præceps tempore Tydeus utitur, which is an imitation of arrepto tempore Turnus.

Imo, ait, O cives, arrepto tempore Turnus,
Cogite concilium, & pacem laudate sedentes, &c.

This mode of fight the closing armies bore;
The trumpets, horns, and clarions now no more,
As whilom, in the marching van appear,
But with the standards join'd, bring up the rear.
Such rose the conflict from few drops of blood,
And to an ocean swell'd the purple flood.
As winds at first make trial of their force
On leaves and trees, then bolder in their course,
O'erturn the forests, bear the groves away,
And lay whole mountains open to the day.
Ye Muses, now record your country's hosts,
And sing the wars that vex'd your native coasts,
For dwelling near the blood-mark'd seat of fight,
The war's whole art was obvious to your sight,
What time th' Aonian lyre's mellifluous sound
Was in the louder blast of trumpets drown'd.
The horse of Pterelas, unus'd to arms,
And new to all the battle's dire alarms,
Soon as his wearied hand had broke the reins,
Transports his master to the distant plains,
The spear of Tydeus through his shoulder flies,
Then glancing down, transpierces both his thighs,
And nails him to his seat: th' affrighted steed,
Fix'd to his rider, bounds along the mead,
And bears him on, tho' now he wields no more
His arms and bridle ting'd with reeking gore.
The centaur thus (his life in part retain'd)
Hangs from the courser which he lately rein'd.
The conflict glows. Menæceus vents his rage
On Periphas. In adverse arms engage
Hippomedon and Sybaris, while near
Rash Itys, and th' Arcadian prince appear.
A sword, O Sybaris, suppress'd thy breath;
Young Itys from a shaft receiv'd his death,
While Periphas beneath a javelin bled.
The steel of Hæmon lops away the head
Of Grecian Cœneus, whose wide-yawning eyes
Explore the sever'd trunk that bleeding lies.
This Abas saw, and rush'd to spoil the foe;
When lo! an arrow from an Argive bow
Prevents his aim,—expiring with a groan,
He quits the hostile buckler and his own.
Eunæus, thee what demon could persuade
To leave thy rosy patron's hallow'd shade,
That shade, to which thou should'st have been confin'd,
For war's tumultuous fury ill-resign'd?
Ah! hope not thou to scatter wild affright,
Whose fine-wove shield (a poor defence in fight)
With ivy-wreaths, on Nysa cull'd, is crown'd,
And whose white stole, descending on the ground,
Displays its silken fringe.—Beneath his hair
Each shoulder lies conceal'd with artful care.
The tender down his florid cheeks o'erspreads;
While his weak cuirass shines with purple threads.
A woman's bracelets on his arms he bears,
And on his feet embroider'd sandals wears.
A jasper-button, set in purest gold,
Clasp'd his robes, grac'd with many a rustling fold.
A quiver, which a lynx's hide surrounds,
And polish'd bow-case on his back resounds.
Full of the raging god, the warrior hies
Amid the press, and thus loud-vaunting cries,
"Restrain your rage.—These walls Apollo show'd
To Cadmus, for his high deserts bestow'd;
These walls to build (if we may credit fame)
The willing rocks, an happy omen came.
Our nation, sacred to the pow'rs above,
Alliance claims with Mars and greater Jove:
Nor feign we this to be the native earth
Of Hercules, and place of Bacchus' birth."
Fierce Capaneus towards the boaster steers
His course, and brandishes two beamy spears.
As when the king of beasts, at early dawn,
Springs from his thicket to the dewy lawn,
And views a deer that bounds along the green,
Or calf, whose budding horns are scarcely seen,
Tho' the stern swains a dreadful circle form,
And darted javelins rain a steely storm,
Fearless, regardless, he pursues his way,
And, unappall'd with wounds, invades the prey.
Thus Capaneus exulting o'er the foe,
With his pois'd javelin meditates a blow,
But ere the pond'rous weight of death descends,
With blasphemy reproaches thus he blends.
"Why dost thou, doom'd to bleed beneath my spear,
With shrieks unmanly strike our hosts with fear?
In wordy wars with Tyrian dames engage,
But where's the vaunted author of thy rage?
Would he were present!" Ere he scarce had said,
Unknowing of repulse, the weapon fled,
And faintly tinkled on the glitt'ring shield,
Whose folded hides a speedy passage yield.

925. As winds at first] This simile is borrowed from Virgil.

So winds, while yet unfledg'd in woods they lie,
In whispers first their tender voices try,
Then issue on the main with bellowing rage,
And storms to trembling mariners presage.
Dryden's Æn.

929. Ye Muses, now record your country's] See Note on the 41st line of the 4th Book, and 541st of the 8th.

945. The centaur thus, &c.] A poet is not confined in his comparison to things that really have an existence in nature: he may derive them as well from those that have only a place in the creation of fancy, and world of imagination. Of this latter sort is the simile before us, which admirably well illustrates the look and posture of the dying warrior, and is as strong and expressive, as it is concise.

965. Ah! hope not thou] It may be observed, that those priests and ministers of the gods, who bear a part in the Theban war, are distinguished from other leaders by the splendour and richness of their habits.——Our poet seems to have had in view the Chloreus of Virgil at the time he wrote this.

991. As when, &c.] This simile is borrowed from Homer.

Ὥστε λέων ἐχάρη μεγάλῳ ἐπὶ σώματι κύρσας,
Εὑρὼν ἢ ἔλαφον κεραὸν, ἢ ἄγριον αἶγα,
Πεινάων· μάλα γάρ τε κατεσθίει, εἴπερ ἂν αὐτὸν
Σεύωνται ταχέες τε κύνες, θαλεροί τ' αἰζηοί.
Ὣς ἐχάρη, &c.

As Virgil has copied it too, I shall give the reader an opportunity of comparing the two imitations with the original:

Impastus stabula alta leo ceu sæpe peragrans,
(Suadet enim vesana fames) si forte fugacem
Conspexit capream, aut surgentem in cornua cervum,
Gaudet hians immane, comasque arrexit et hæret
Visceribus super accumbens; lavat improba teter
Ora cruor.

Forth wells the blood, his armour knocks the ground,
And with long sobs the plates of gold resound.
He dies, he dies, the rash boy-warrior dies,
And wept and honour'd by his patron lies.
Him drunken Ismaros, (the thyrsus broke)
And Tmolus, long reluctant to the yoke,
Him Nysa, and Thesean Naxos mourn,
And Ganges, to discharge his orgies sworn.
Nor was Eteocles in combat slow;
Less oft his milder brother aims a blow.
Conspicuous in his car the prophet sate;
His steeds, as prescient of their hast'ning fate,
With dread move on, while clouds of dust arise,
Obscure the fight, and blacken half the skies.
Him Phœbus honours on his dying day,
And gives a lustre to his setting ray.
He decks his shield and helm with starry fires;
While Mars with fiercest rage his soul inspires,
And, in compliance to the god's request,
From hostile swords defends his manly breast,
That pure, nor violated here above
By wounds, he may descend to Stygian Jove.
Thus, conscious he must soon resign his breath,
Serene, he walks the dreadful path of death,
And rushes on his foes.—Despair of life
Supplies new strength and vigour in the strife.
His limbs increase in beauty, force, and size,
And ne'er before so well he read the skies.
With unextinguish'd heat of war he glows,
And pours redoubled fury on his foes.
Oft was he known to break with lenient art
The strokes of chance, and ease the human heart,
T' encroach on fate's just rights, and interpose
To save the wretched from impending woes.
Alas! how chang'd from him, who great and good
At Phœbus' shrine in holy office stood,
Who what each low'ring cloud portended knew,
And omens read from ev'ry wing that flew!
A countless herd expir'd beneath his blade
(Unhappy victims to his future shade);

1020. Less oft his milder brother] The poet here pays a great compliment to Polynices. He tells the reader, that while Eteocles is wading through blood and carnage to the crown, and making havoc among the Grecians, Polynices was checked in his conquest by the tender impulses of humanity, and regard to his countrymen.

1021. Conspicuous in his car, &c.] We find Jupiter, in the seventeenth book of the Iliad, bestowing the same honours on Hector, and dignifying his exit with a blaze of glory, as Mr. Pope expresses it.

———Δῦ δέ μιν Ἄρης
Δεινὸς ἐνυάλιος· πλῆσθεν δ᾽ ἄρα οἱ μέλε᾽ ἐντὸς
᾽Αλκῆς καὶ σθένεος.———

1038. And ne'er before] Amphiaraus is represented as being endued with a greater degree of prescience and divination just before his death, which circumstance brings to my remembrance four lines of the celebrated Waller:

——Wiser men become,
As they draw near to their eternal home,
Leaving the old, both worlds at once they view,
That stand upon the threshold of the new.

As when fell planets rule the deathful year,
And dart destruction from their baleful sphere.
Phlegyas and Phyleus fell (his javelin thrown)
His scythe-hung car mows Cremetaon down,
And Chromis; one in adverse fight was slain;
His knee cut off, the other press'd the plain.
Next Chromis, Iphinous, and Sages bled,
By missive weapons rank'd among the dead.
Unshorn Lycoreus groans his soul away,
And Gyas, sacred to the god of day;
His helm uncrested by the forceful spear,
He knew, but knew too late, the mitred seer.
Then at Alcathoüs a stone he threw,
The well-aim'd stone the hapless warrior slew.
Rear'd on the margin of Carystos' flood
His house, with infants' cries resounding, stood.
His friends at length the senseless wretch persuade
To change the sailor's for the soldier's trade;
Nor dying he prefers th' experienc'd main,
And wintry tempests to the bloody plain.
The rout and slaughter of his host survey'd,
Asopian Hypseus rushes to their aid:
Rage in his eyes, and ruin in his hand,
He galls the rear of the Tyrinthian band,
But the priest seen, the tide of wrath he turns
On him, and with redoubled fury burns.
Rang'd in a wedge, his troops beside him stood,
And form'd with spears erect an ambient wood.
He lifts, in front of all the hostile ranks,
A javelin, cull'd on his paternal banks,
And cries—"O father of th' Aonian streams,
Whose surface with etherial embers gleams,
Direct my aim: this I, thy son, demand,
And th' oaken spear, the native of thy strand.
If thou hast fought the ruler of the skies,
Give me the mighty Phœbus to despise.
From his gash'd head I'll tear the circling crown,
And with his armour in thy current drown."
Asopus heard his pray'r, but Sol deny'd
Indulgence to his son, and turn'd aside
To faithful Herses the well-darted spear,
Herses, the valiant augur's charioteer.
Apollo now directs the flowing reins,
And Aliagmon's form and visage feigns.
Their souls unmann'd, and all resistance lost,
A sudden panic seiz'd the Theban host.
Their gripe relax'd, their weapons strew the ground;
They fall thro' fear, and die without a wound.

1051. As when fell planets] Homer, Virgil, and Milton have fine similes drawn from planets, comets, &c. There is one of the last-mentioned author in particular, that is wonderfully sublime:

———He like a comet burn'd
That fires the length of Ophiuchus huge
In th' arctic sky; and from his horrid hair
Shakes pestilence and war.

1077. Rang'd in a wedge] On reading this passage, how naturally do the following verses of Milton steal in upon our memory!

While thus he spake, th' angelic squadrons bright
Turn'd fiery red, sharp'ning in mooned horns, &c.
Book 4. Line 977.

1093. Apollo now directs] This piece of machinery is beautiful to a great degree; it is imitated from the fifth book of Homer, where Pallas thrusts Sthelenus out of Diomede's chariot, and vaulting into it herself, assists that hero in his attack upon Mars.

'Twas doubtful, if th' augmented burden speeds,
Or clogs the progress of the furious steeds.
As from some cloud-capt hill a fragment worn
By dint of age, or by fierce whirlwinds torn,
Rolls down, and sweeps along in its descent
Men, trees, and cots, from their foundations rent;
Nor stops, till some deep vale confines its force,
Or river, intercepted in its course;
So rolls th' ensanguin'd car beneath the load
Of the great hero, and the greater god.
High o'er the deathful scene Apollo stands,
And wields the spears and reins with equal hands:
Unerring skill he to his priest imparts,
But mocks the Theban shooters' useless arts.
Now Antiphus, unaided by his steed,
And Mænalus lie prostrate on the mead:
Æthion then of Heliconian strain;
Polites, noted for his brother slain,
And Lampus, who, with lust transported, strove
To force fair Mantho's interdicted love:
At him the god himself directs a dart,
And drove the shining mischief to his heart.
On hills of slain the rapid coursers tread,
Destroy the living, and deform the dead.
The mangled carcases are furrow'd o'er;
And the dash'd axles blush with human gore.
O'er some the kindling car, unnotic'd, rolls,
Breaks ev'ry limb, and crushes out their souls;
Whilst others, helpless with a mortal wound,
Foresee it smoking o'er the distant ground.
Now thro' his hands the slipp'ry bridle glides,
And the besprinkled beam, unstable, slides;
The steeds, their hoofs involv'd in carnage stood,
And the spik'd wheels are clogg'd with clotted blood.
The javelins, which (their points infix'd within)
Stand extant on the surface of the skin,
The raging hero from the wounded drew,
Whose parting souls with groans the car pursue.

1101. As from] I wonder, that neither Mr. Pope nor Mr. Wharton have taken notice of this truly sublime comparison in their observation on a similar one in Homer and Virgil, especially as they have quoted one of Tasso, in my opinion, much inferior to our author's.—I shall transcribe all three.

——— Ὀλοοίτροχος ὡς ἀπὸ πέτρης,
Ὅντε κατὰ στεφάνης ποταμὸς χειμάῤῥος ὤσῃ,
Ῥήξας ἀσπέτῳ ὄμβρῳ ἀναιδέος ἔχματα πέτρης,
Ὕψι τ' ἀναθρώσκων πέτεται, κτυπέει δέ θ' ὑπ' αὐτοῦ
Ὕλη· ὃ δ' ἀσφαλέως θέει ἔμπεδον, ὄφρ' ἂν ἵκηται
Ἰσόπεδον, τότε δ' οὔτι κυλίνδεται, ἐσσύμενός περ.

Ac veluti montis saxum de vertice præceps
Cum ruit avulsum vento, ceu turbidus imber
Proluit, aut annis solvit sublapsa vetustas;
Fertur in abruptum magno mons improbus actu,
Exultatque solo, sylvas, armenta virosque
Involvens secum.

Qual gran sasso talor, ch'o la vecchiezza
Solve da un monte, o svelle ira de' venti
Ruinosa dirupa, e parta, e spezza
Le selve, e colle case anco gli armenti
Tal già trahea della, &c.

1107. So rolls] It is remarkable, that these two lines are almost a transcript of Homer's:

——— Μέγα δ' ἔβραχε φήγινος ἄξων
Βριθοσύνῃ· δεινὴν γὰρ ἄγον θεὸν ἄνδρα τ' ἄριστον.

Iliad, 5. 838.

At length (his whole divinity confess'd)
Phœbus the wond'ring augur thus address'd:
"Use well thy time, whilst in respect to me
Grim death delays the work of destiny.
We're overcome —Whate'er the fates ordain,
They execute, nor weave the woof again.
Go then, and mindful of the promise made,
Gladden Elysium with thy present shade,
Secure, no burial honours thou shalt want,
Nor sue in vain for cruel Creon's grant."
To this the chief, surcharg'd with hostile spoils,
Replies, and for a while respires from toils:
"At first I knew thee thro' thy borrow'd look;
Beneath th' unwonted weight the chariot shook:
Yet say, how long wilt thou defer my fate?
These honours ill become my wretched state.
E'en now I hear the porter's triple yell,
Hoarse-sounding Styx, and all the streams of Hell.
Take then the laurell'd honours of my head,
Too holy for the regions of the dead.
If to thy dying prophet aught is due,
With my last voice this boon I now renew,
And to thy wrath resign my trait'rous spouse;
Avenge, avenge the broken marriage-vows."
The grieving god descending on the plains,
The coursers groan, and bow'd to dust their manes.
Thus fares a vessel in a stormy night,
When the twin-stars withhold their friendly light;
Death in their thoughts, they shriek at ev'ry blast,
And deem the present moment for their last.
And now the grassy surface of the mead,
Convuls'd with frequent tremours, 'gan recede;
A thicker cloud of dust obscures the skies,
And murmurs dire from deepest Hell arise.
This sound mistaken for the crash of fight,
From field the trembling warriors urge their flight.
Another tremour now bends to the ground
Men, horses, arms, and shakes the fields around.
The leafy grove inclines its various head,
And silent from his banks Ismenos fled.
The public anger lost in private fears,
They ground their arms, and, leaning on their spears,
Start back, as on each other's face they view
Wild terrour imag'd in a pallid hue.
As when Bellona forms a naval fray,
In scorn of Neptune, on the wat'ry way:
If haply some fell tempest interpose,
Each thoughtful of himself, neglects his foes:
The common dangers cause their ire to cease,
And mutual fears impose a sudden peace:
Such was the fluctuating fight to view.
Whether from subterraneous prisons flew
Imbosom'd blasts, and gather'd from afar,
In one vast burst discharg'd the windy war:
Or latent springs had worn the rotten clay,
And open'd to themselves a gradual way:
Or on this side the swift machine of Heav'n
Inclin'd, by more than wonted impulse driv'n,
Or whether Neptune bade old Ocean roar,
And dash'd the briny foam from shore to shore:
Or Earth herself would warn by these portents
The seer, or brother-kings of both events;
Lo! she discloses wide her hollow womb:
(Night fear'd the stars, the stars the nether gloom.)
The prophet and his coursers, while they strive
To pass, the yawning cleft ingulphs alive:
Nor did he quit the reins and arms in hand,
But with them plung'd to the Tartarean strand;
And as he fell, gaz'd backward on the light;
And griev'd to see the field would soon unite,

Till now a lighter tremour clos'd again
The ground, and darken'd Pluto's wide domain.

BOOK VIII.

THE ARGUMENT.

The poet, having described the effects of Amphiaraus's coming into the infernal regions, introduces Pluto expressing his displeasure at his abrupt intrusion, and exhorting the furies to retaliate the insult by an excursion to the world above. At length, however, Amphiaraus pacifies him. The confederates, terrified by this extraordinary phenomenon, quit the field in great disorder and confusion, and express their concern for the death of the seer in a long oration. The Thebans spend the night in feasting and jollity. Adrastus calls a council in the morning, in which it is resolved, that Thiodamas should succeed Amphiaraus as augur; who, in pursuance of his election, appeases the earth by sacrifice, and delivers a funeral oration in praise of his predecessor. The battle recommencing, Tydeus on the part of the allies, and Hæmon on the part of the Thebans, signalize themselves by feats of prowess and gallantry. The Thebans, disheartened by the death of Atys, and retreat of Hæmon, are rallied by Menæceus, and renew the fight with redoubled vigour and alacrity. The poet then returns to Thebes; and while Ismene is relating a dream, which she had about her lover Atys, to her sister, he is brought into the palace just upon the point of death: this gives rise to a very affecting scene. Tydeus, in the mean time, makes a great slaughter of his enemies; and meeting with Eteocles, exchanges a dart with him; but the other flying, in the pursuit of him he is overpowered by his enemies, and receiving a mortal wound, expires gnawing the head of Menalippus, who gave it him.

SOON as the prophet reach'd the dreary coasts
Of Styx, the mansion of pale-visag'd ghosts,
Explor'd the secrets of the world below,
And pierc'd the regions of eternal woe;
His garb terrific, and loud-braying arms,
Fill Pluto's wide dominion with alarms.
The shades with horrour gaze upon his car,
His weapons, steeds distinguish'd in the war,
And his new body: for he neither came
Black from the urn, nor season'd with the flame;
But with the sweat of Mars was cover'd o'er,
And his hack'd target stain'd with dewy gore.
Nor had Erinnys yet with impious hand
O'er his cold members wav'd her flaming brand,
Or Proserpine, admitting him a ghost,
Inscrib'd his name upon the murky post.
Nor to the task the sisters' hands suffic'd;
The work as yet unfinish'd he surpris'd;
Then, nor till then, they cut the fatal thread,
And freed the seer, irregularly dead.
The manes of Elysium gaz'd around,
(Their pleasures interrupted at the sound)
And those who station'd in the gulph beneath,
An air less pure, and less enliv'ning breathe.
Then groan the lakes that parch'd with sulphur glow,
And sluggish waters, scarcely seen to flow;
While Charon, wont to plough the loaded stream,
Mourns his lost fare, a melancholy theme;
And grieves, that shades had gain'd the Stygian shore,
By chasms in Earth, and means unknown before.
In the mid part of this unhappy state
The king of Erebus in judgment sate:
The shades he question'd on their former crimes,
Displeas'd with all that fill his dreary climes;
There death in various shapes and orders stands,
The sister-fiends with vengeance in their hands,
And Punishment, distinguish'd in the throng
By chains harsh clanking, as she strides along.
With the same thumb the fates condemn and save,
Meanwhile fresh numbers issue from the grave.
There Minos with his colleague hears each cause,
Restrains the king, and mitigates the laws.
Nor was Cocytos absent, stream of woes,
And Phlegethon, that kindles as it flows,
Or Styx, whom e'en th' attesting gods revere.
Then trembling Pluto first experienc'd fear;

There is something very awful and solemn in the poet's description of the terrour and confusion which the presence of Amphiaraus occasioned in the infernal regions. But what we should principally regard it for, is the great light it throws on many parts of the heathen mythology, which would otherwise seem dark and mysterious. In short, it is altogether as fine a representation of Hell, as any we meet with in the ancient poets.

39. With the same thumb] The thumb was a token of favour and displeasure among the ancients. When a man pressed his thumb, it was a sign of his regard, as Pliny informs us, Lib. 28. cap. 11. Pollices, cum favemus, premere etiam proverbio jubemur. When the thumb was turned, his displeasure was signified, which was so great a mark of malevolence, that by this alone the people of Rome ordered the gladiators to be slain, as we learn from Juvenal, Sat. 3.

> Munera nunc edunt, et verso pollice vulgi
> Quemlibet occidunt populariter.

43. Nor was Cocytos] Milton has given us a fine picture of the rivers of Hell in the second book of Par. Lost, v. 577.

> Abhorred Styx, the flood of deadly hate,
> Sad Acheron of sorrow, black and deep;
> Cocytos, nam'd of lamentation loud
> Heard on the rueful stream; fierce Phlegethon,
> Whose waves of torrent fire inflame with rage.
> Far off from those, a slow and silent stream,
> Lethe, the river of oblivion rolls
> Her wat'ry labyrinth, whereof who drinks
> Forthwith his former state and being forgets,
> Forgets both joy and grief, pleasure and pain.

45. Or Styx] Though I have spoken of this river elsewhere, I cannot deny myself the pleasure of transcribing Hesiod's humorous account of the punishment of those gods who had swore falsely by it. "For one whole year," says he, "they must abstain from nectar and ambrosia, and lie on the ground dumb and lethargic. After a year, greater punishments await them; for they are banished for nine years, and debarred the so-

And spoke in wrath, as sick'ning he survey'd
The starry splendours, through the cleft display'd.
"What pow'r has forc'd Earth's barrier thus away,
And join'd the upper and the nether day?
Who pierc'd our gloom? Say, whence these threats
From the stern lord of ocean or the skies? [arise,
Boaster, stand forth on thy own terms of fight;
Hence let form sink to chaos, day to night.
To whom more dear!—I guard the guilty world,
Hither from Heav'n by adverse fortune hurl'd.
Nor e'en is this my own; I rule in vain,
When Jove encroaches thus upon my reign,
When on my throne the rays of Titan beat,
And light abhorr'd pervades my gloomy seat.
Wants he, the king of Heav'n, my strength to prove?
The fetter'd giants will each doubt remove,
The restless Titans (who did erst aspire
Earth to revisit) and his wretched sire.
Why wills he, that my toils should never cease?
Why must the light I lost disturb my peace?
But should it please, each kingdom I'll display,
And veil in Stygian mists the blaze of day.
Hence the twin sons of Tyndar I'll detain,
Nor render back th' Arcadian youth again.
For why does he thus journey to and fro,
And waft around the messages of woe?
Why should Ixion, with fresh labours worn,
And thirsting Tantalus my anger mourn?
How long shall living ghosts unpunish'd roam
From bank to bank, and violate my dome?
With me Pirithous durst once contend,
And Theseus sworn to his audacious friend:
Then of Alcides too (my guard remov'd)
The furious arm and strength robust I prov'd.
Now Hell, because some idle feuds arise
Between two petty princes, open lies.
I saw, when Orpheus the sad strain pursu'd,
The fiends in tears, the sisters' tasks renew'd.
The sweet musician o'er my wrath prevail'd,
Yet, heedless of the stern condition, fail'd.
Once, and but once I sought the world above,
And snatch'd in Sicily the joys of love:
The bold excursion stung th'etherial prince,
As the hard laws that quick ensu'd, evince.
At each six moons her mother at my hands
My consort for an equal term demands.
But why these plaints?—Go, minister of ill,
Revenge the insult, and our wrath fulfil.
If aught yet unconceiv'd, and unexpress'd,
Thy ready wit, and fertile brain suggest,
On which thy sisters may with envy gaze,
And I with wonder,—go, and win our praise.

ciety of the gods. At the end of the tenth year, however, they resume their pristine state and dignity."

49. What pow'r] Of all the orations in the Thebaid, there is none that can give less pleasure to the reader, and consequently less credit to the translator, than this before us. Not that Pluto speaks without spirit, but his speech has many allusions to dark circumstances in heathen mythology; so that I very much question, if, after all the pains I have taken, it is intelligible to the greatest part of my readers. It is not of a nature to shine in poetry; and all I could do to make it tolerable, was to give it as smooth numbers as possible, and curtail that length which makes it still more disgusting.

But, as an omen of our future hate,
And as a prelude to the stern debate,
Let the two brothers meet without the wall,
And, fir'd by mutual rage, in combat fall.
Let one with more than brutal fury feed
On his foe's head, expiring in the deed,
Another the last fun'ral flames deny,
And taint with carcases his native sky.
Such acts may Jupiter with pleasure view,
Nor let thy wrath our realms alone pursue.
Seek one, who may with Heav'n itself engage,
And with his shield repel the thund'rer's rage.
Why should they rather dare thro' Hell to rove,
Than with heap'd mountains scale the walls of
Jove?"
This said, he ceas'd.—His dreary palace takes
The signal dire, and to the centre shakes.
His earth, and that which overhangs him, nod
Beneath his voice, and own the speaking god.
Great was the shock, as when his brother rolls
His eyes around, and bends the starry poles.
He then rejoins.—"For thee, who durst explore
The sacred void inviolate before,
What pains can I devise?"—Half shrunk with fear,
His arms and chariot gone, proceeds the seer.
Yet still the badges of his order grace
The chief extinct, and shade his clay-cold face;
Tho' black, a fillet decks his awful brow,
And his hand grasps a wither'd olive-bough.
"If in this holy synod I may speak,
And in my own defence my silence break,
(Grand end of all things, but to me who knew
Each mystic cause, that mortal eye can view)
Source of existence, thy stern threats resign,
And to my pray'r thy willing ears incline;
Nor deign to punish one who strictly fears
To disobey, and all thy laws reveres.
No rape Herculean drew me to thy coast,
Nor was illicit venery my boast:
On these insignia for the truth rely,
Alas! my coward heart ne'er soar'd so high.
Let not our chariot pale thy consort's cheek,
Nor Cerberus with grief his cavern seek.
An augur once by Phœbus much caress'd,
The gloomy void of Chaos I attest
(For why by Sol should Pluto's subject swear?)
That for no crime this punishment I bear.
This sacred truth the Cretan's urn must know,
This sacred truth impartial Minos show.
Bought of my treach'rous wife for cursed gold,
And in the list of Argive chiefs enroll'd,
Resign'd to fate, I sought the Theban plain,
Whence flock the shades that scarce thy realms
contain.
When (how my soul yet dreads!) an earthquake
came
Big with destruction, and my trembling frame,
Rapt from the midst of gaping thousands, hurl'd
To night eternal in thy nether world.
What were my thoughts, while thro' Earth's hol-
I roll'd upheld in air, and lost in gloom? [low womb
Nought to my comrades or my country left,
Nor of my captive life by Thebes bereft;

135. No rape Herculean] The reader must observe, that Hercules himself did not design a rape upon Proserpine, but only went down to Hell with a view of rescuing Theseus and Pirithous, who had attempted it, from the punishment that Pluto had intended for them.

Doom'd never more to breathe Lernæan air,
Or to my wond'ring friends, inurn'd, repair;
No sculptur'd tomb to lengthen out my fame,
No weeping parents, nor odorous flame.
To thee the whole of fun'ral pomp I bear,
Nor shall I aught with these fleet coursers dare,
Or murmur to become a subject shade:
I wave the honours that were whilom paid:
No prescience of the future dost thou want,
Secure of all the destinies can grant.
But check thy rage, the deities regard,
And for my spouse reserve the dire reward;
If, in the process of advancing age,
She fall, a victim worthier of thy rage."
The monarch heard, nor hearing disapprov'd,
Tho' loath to spare, and scorning to be mov'd.
The lion thus, when menac'd with the sight
Of obvious weapons, calls forth all his might;
But, if his prostrate foe declines the strife,
Stalks o'er him, and disdains so cheap a life.
Meanwhile they seek the late redoubted car,
Adorn'd with fillets, and the wreaths of war,
Astonish'd, as by none it was survey'd,
Or crush'd in conflict, or a capture made.
The troops, suspicious now, recoiling yield,
Walk round the traces of the treach'rous field,
And all prefer the sweets of vital breath
To Stygian pomp, and an inglorious death.
While at a distance in the road to fame,
Adrastus guides his troops, Palæmon came,
The messenger of woe, and trembling cries,
(For scarce he trusted to his conscious eyes,
Tho' station'd near the chief ingulph'd, he saw,
All pale and sad, the discontinuous flaw:)
"O monarch, turn thy steps, and seek with speed
The Doric turrets, and our native mead;
If haply, where we left them, they remain.
No arms we need; the battle bleeds in vain.
Our unavailing swords why wield we more?
When earth (a prodigy unseen of yore)
Absorbs our warriors. From beneath our feet
The ground we press seems striving to retreat.
I view'd myself the path to night profound,
Oeclides rushing thro' the sudden wound,
Than whom of mortal race was none more dear.
To the bright lamps that gild yon azure sphere
Long did I stretch my falt'ring hands, and strain
My voice; at length convinc'd that help was vain,
I ply'd the sounding lash, and quickly left
The steaming champaign, in huge furrows cleft,
Nor common is the ill; the mother knows
Her sons, and favour to the Thebans shows."
Thus he. The monarch doubts, till Mopsus came,
And trembling Actor, who report the same.
But fame, who loves each terrour to enhance,
Relates, that more had shar'd the same mischance.
Spontaneous then the soldiers quit their ground,
Nor wait, as custom was, the trumpet's sound.
Yet was their progress slow. They scarcely trail
Their legs along, so much did fear prevail.
Their very steeds, as sensible, oppose
Their flight, regardless of repeated blows;
Nor, won by blandishments, increase their speed,
Or lift their eyes from the terrific mead.
The Thebans push'd the charge, till Vesper led
Bright Cynthia's steeds, with dusky shades o'er-spread:
Now night, that soon their terrours must increase,
Imposes a short interval of peace.
What were their aspects, when they took their fill
Of sorrow's draught? Full many a pearly rill
Stole from their helms unlac'd. Nought then could ease
Their jaded spirits that was wont to please.
They throw aside their bucklers wetted o'er,
Such as they were; nor cleans'd their darts of gore,
Nor prais'd their horses, nor for battle drest
The high-rais'd honours of the shining crest.
Such was their grief, they scarcely care to close
Their wounds, and stanch the blood that freely flows,
Or with the due resource of food and rest
Renew their strength, by toils of war opprest:
All dwell with tears on the late augur's praise,
His love of truth, and merit of the bays.
One rumour only thro' the camp is spread,
That all their fortune with the gods is fled:
"Where are his sacred arms, rever'd in war,
His crest with fillets grac'd, and laurell'd car?
Could not Castalian lakes and caves retard
His death? Was this his patron-god's reward?
Who'll teach us now, what falling stars declare,
And hallow'd light'nings inauspicious glare?
What Heav'n betokens in the victim slain,
When ye should march; what accidents detain?
What hour is most averse to dove-ey'd peace,
And when to bid the trump of discord cease?
Who now will all futurity disclose,
The just interpreter of bliss or woes?

175.] This allusion to the generosity of the lion has the sanction of all the naturalists that ever treated on this animal to confirm it. Claudian in his eulogy on Stilicon, lib. 4. says,

Obvia prosternas, prostrataque more leonum
Despicias: alacres ardent quum sternere tauros,
Transiliunt prædas humiles. Hac ipse magistrâ
Dat veniam victis, hac exhortante calores
Horrificos, et quæ nunquam nocitura timentur
Jurgia, contentus solo terrore coercet.

216. Nor wait, as custom was] Lactantius in his note on this passage furnishes us with a piece of antiquity, that, I believe, few of our readers are acquainted with: viz. that among the ancients every soldier, previously to his being enlisted, took an oath, that he would never leave the battle, before the sounding of a retreat.

225. Now night] Milton has some beautiful lines on the same subject.

Now night her course began, and over Heav'n
Inducing darkness, grateful truce impos'd,
And silence on the odious din of war.
Par. Lost, b. 6. l. 406.

239. All dwell] The reader cannot but sympathise with the Grecians on the loss of their patriot and prophet Amphiaraus, whose virtues endear him to the latest posterity. And here it may not be improper to observe, that the old proposition, "All men are alike after death," is only partially true. For the virtuous and useful member of society lives in the memory of the public, and is never thought of but with sorrow, nor mentioned but with honour; whereas the villain and pest of his country is either soon forgotten, or remembered but with infamy and detestation.

To thee the war's events were all foreknown,
And all the public evils, and thy own;
Yet, (such was virtue's influence) thou didst join
Our troops, and clad in social armour shine;
And when the fatal hour and period came,
Didst find a leisure time to purchase fame
By adverse signs o'erthrown, and heroes slain,
Till heaps of carcases deform'd the plain.
What deeds of slaughter, and what scenes of death
Might we have seen, had Heav'n prolong'd thy breath?
What lot befalls thee? Canst thou visit Earth
Again, and, as it were, renew thy birth?
Say, art thou thron'd beside thy fav'ring fates,
A counsellor in all their high debates?
Still by a grateful change dost thou obtain
The knowledge of the future, and explain?
Or did the pow'r who rules the realms below,
In pity to thy sufferings, bestow
Elysium, and her birds of hallow'd flight?
Whate'er's thy lot beneath, the god of light,
Bewailing long his loss, shall loath relief,
And Delphos mourn thy death in silent grief.
Shut on this day shall Delos e'er remain,
The sea-girt Tenedos, and Cyrrha's fane;
No bold inquirer ope the Clarian gate,
Nor Branchus from his shrine interpret fate:
For Lycia none should leave his native air,
Nor for advice to Didyma repair.
Jove's panting oaks shall on this day be mute,
Nor horned Ammon grant the pilgrim's suit:

278. Tenedos] Is an island of the Hellespont, situated over against Troy and sacred to Apollo, whence Chryses in his address to Apollo says, Τενέδοιό τε ἶφι ἀνάσσεις.

278. And Cyrrha's fane] See note on the 673d verse of the 3d book.

279. The Clarian gate] This and the other places here mentioned were noted for the most famous oracles.

280. Nor Branchus.] As a supplement to my note on the 686th verse of the 3d book, I shall transcribe the following account of Branchus from Varro. Olus quidem decimus ab Apolline, cum in peregrinatione pranderet in littore, ac deinde proficisceretur, oblitus est filium nomine Simerum, qui pervenit in saltum Patronis cujusdam, et cum esset receptus, cœpit cum suis pueris capras pascere. Aliquando prehenderunt cygnum, et illum veste cooperuerunt, dumque ipsi pugnant uter illum patri munus offerret, et essent fatigati certamine: rejecta veste mulierem invenerunt, et cum fugerent revocati ab eâ moniti sunt, ut patres unice Simerum diligerent puerum: illi quæ audierunt Patroni indicarunt. Tunc Patron Simerum pro filio suo nimio dilexit affectu, eique filiam suam ducendam locavit uxorem. Illa cum pregnans ex eo esset vidit in somniis per fauces suas introisse solem, et exisse per ventrem: ideo infans editus Branchus vocatus est, quia mater ejus per fauces sibi viderat uterum penetrasse. Hic cum in sylvis Apollinem osculatus fuisset, comprehensus est ab eo, et acceptâ corona virgaque vaticinari cœpit et subito nusquam comparuit. Templum ei factum est quod Branchiadon nominatur et Apollini Philesio pariter consecrata sunt templa, quæ ab osculo Branchi, sive certamine puerorum, Philesia nuncupantur.

The very laurels wither, rivers cease
To flow, and Trojan Thymbra rests in peace.
No certain knowledge shall the air unfold
By chirpings sage, nor destiny be told
By flapping pinions.—Soon the day shall come,
When, other oracles suprest and dumb,
Temples shall rise in honour of thy art,
And thy responses ready priests impart."
Such solemn dirges with due rev'rence paid
To the prophetic monarch's honour'd shade,
In lieu of rites funereal Greece bestows
And gives his wand'ring ghost the wish'd repose.
Then were their souls unmann'd with wild affright,
And all with equal horrour loath the fight.
Thus when some skilful pilot yields his breath,
The crew desponding at his sudden death,
Their oars seem short of half their wonted force,
And the fresh gale less aidful to their course.
But converse long indulg'd had eas'd their smart,
And dull'd each quick sensation of the heart,
When sleep unnotic'd stole to their relief,
And hush'd the voice, and clos'd the eye of grief.
Not so the joyful Thebans spent the night;
But favour'd by the stars and Phœbe's light,
In the throng'd streets and houses, madly gay,
With various sports they chas'd the hours away.
Each centinel lay dozing at his post,
And senseless riot reign'd thro' all the host.
In antic measures some obliquely bound
To the hoarse drum's and tinkling cymbal's sound,
While others pipe, and swell the mellow flute,
Or sing in concert with the shrill-ton'd lute
Their gods propitious, and in order name
The deities, whose favours worship claim.
Pæans arise to ev'ry pow'r divine,
And the crown'd goblets foam with sparkling wine.
They ridicule the Grecian augur's death,
And, as in seeming contrast, spend their breath
In praise of their Tiresias. Now they sing
The feats and prowess of each ancient king,
Thebes from its origin celestial trace,
Jove and Europa mixing in embrace,
And boast, how on his back the damsel rode,
And grasp'd his horns, unconscious of the god:
Of Cadmus, the tir'd heifer, and the field,
That erst was seen an iron crop to yield:
Of rocks that follow'd when Amphion strung
His Theban lyre, and dancing groves, they sung:
While others celebrate in equal strains
Harmonia, bound in hymeneal chains,
Or tune to pregnant Semele their lays:
None want a fable for a theme of praise.
While thus the genial banquet they prolong
In friendly guise, and urge th' unfinish'd song,

299. Thus when] Statius varies his similes with all possible art, sometimes deriving them from the animal creation, sometimes from the passions of mankind, and sometimes from the vulgar scenes and occurrences of life; but wherever we follow him, we find him a faithful copier of nature. This before us, trifling and unworthy of notice as it may appear to some for its brevity, is, notwithstanding, very just, and answers in every point to the thing described with the utmost precision and propriety. Nothing in nature could be more happily conceived, than the comparing Amphiaraus, who was the guide and oracle of his people, to the pilot of a ship.

The son of Laius, long conceal'd, forsakes
His gloomy cell, and social bliss partakes.
No wonted filth was on his visage seen,
Unruffled was his brow, his look serene.
Such wonder would arise, should Bacchus show
Barbaric trophies, and his Indian foe,
Brought from the banks of mix'd Hydaspes, grac'd
With beds of gems, and orient realms laid waste.
His friends' address with courtesy he bore,
Nor shunn'd their proffer'd solace as before;
But cleans'd his cheeks of gore, approv'd the food,
And life's long-unexperienc'd joys renew'd.
E'en Oedipus in mirth and converse gay
Assum'd a part, who late was known to pray
To Pluto, and the sister-fiends alone,
Or at his daughter's feet to pour his moan.
Yet latent was the cause. The palm of fight,
Gain'd by his country, gave him no delight;
The war was all he wish'd. To this his son
He spurr'd, nor car'd by whom the day was won.
But first with tacit vows he view'd the sword,
And all the seeds of wickedness explor'd.
Hence smil'd upon his aspect peace unknown,
And the feast pleas'd with merit not its own.
Thus Phineus, when, his limbs with hunger worn,
And the last period of his torture borne,
His palace freed from harpies he perceiv'd,
Incredulous his rescue disbeliev'd;
Then gave a loose to joy, as long unstain'd,
His vessels, beds, and costly board remain'd.
Stretch'd in their tents the Grecian cohorts lay,
And lost in sleep the labours of the day:
All but Adrastus, he, consign'd by fate
To watchful cares, the curse of regal state,
With horrour heard, unknowing the repose
His age requir'd, the revels of his foes.
He sickens at the trumpet's brazen sound,
And shouts of haughty triumph that rebound
From echoing rocks. The pipe augments his fears,
Dwells on his thoughts, and grates his loathing ears.
Then from his camp, desponding, he surveys
Their wav'ring torches, and triumphal blaze.
Thus when the fury of the tempest past,
The vessel drives with an indulgent blast,
Secure, and trusting to the settled deep,
The mariners refresh their limbs in sleep;
And all, unmindful of their office, nod,
Save the pale master, and his painted god.
Now Sol's fair sister, viewing from afar
His coursers yok'd, and ready for the car,
(While ocean roar'd beneath the rushing day,
And redden'd with Aurora's orient ray,)
Collects her beams, recalls her scatter'd light,
And with her whip compels the stars to flight.
When, ever on the public welfare bent,
Adrastus summon'd to his royal tent
The Grecian peers, the question in debate,
Who should succeed interpreter of fate,
On whom the wreaths and tripods should devolve,
And who could best their oracles resolve.
Scarce had they met, when with united voice
On fam'd Thiodamas they fix'd their choice,
To whom Amphiaraus oft reveal'd
The mysteries of Heav'n, nor blush'd to yield,
Invidious of his art, a share of fame,
But own'd his merit, and approv'd his claim.
Such unexpected honours must confound
The youth, for modesty as skill renown'd:
With awe unfeign'd he views the proffer'd leaves,
Mistrusts his art, and scarce the charge receives.
As when some youth of royal blood succeeds
To his paternal crown, and rules the Medes,
(More safe, had fate prolong'd his father's life)
With diffidence he treads the path of strife;
Much from th' aspiring temper of his peers,
And from the vulgar's headstrong will he fears,
Doubtful with whom his wide domain to share,
Whom make a partner of imperial care.
His slender grasp, he fears, will ill contain
The weighty sceptre, and his bow sustain,
And trembling takes the courser's reins in hand,
And huge tiara, badge of high command.
Soon as a chaplet for his brow he twin'd,
And in a wreath his flowing locks confin'd,
With shouts triumphant thro' the camp he went,
And as a specimen of his intent
To serve the public, piously prepares,
Earth to propitiate with due rites and prayers,
Nor useless to the Greeks the scheme appear'd.
First then two altars on the champaign rear'd,
With turf high-heap'd, and evergreens he grac'd,
And various flow'rs, in decent order plac'd,
The goddess's own gift. On these he threw,
Whate'er the vernal rays of Sol renew
On her green surface: last he pour'd a bowl
Of purest milk, and thus confirms the whole.

345. Hydaspes] A river that rises in the most northern part of India toward the mountain Imaus, and falls into the Indus, in allusion to which circumstance, I have given it the epithet mix'd.

363. Thus Phineus, when his limbs] Phineus was a king of Arcadia, who, having, at the instigation of his queen, put out the eyes of his children by a former wife, was himself struck blind by Jupiter, who sent the harpies to punish him; but directing the Argonauts in their way to Colchis, they, in return, drove away the harpies. Valerius Flaccus, who has expatiated on this fable in his Argonautics, has the following beautiful lines on Phineus's joy and astonishment on being delivered from those rapacious animals.

Ipse inter medios, ceu dulcis imagine somni
Lætus, ad oblitæ Cereris suspirat honores. B. 5.

373. With horrour heard] Homer opens the tenth book of his Iliad with a similar description of the distress Agamemnon laboured under the night after his defeat by the Trojans. The following lines seem to have given our author the hint of the six verses before us.

Τρομέοντο δέ οἱ φρένες ἐντὸς,
Ἤτοι ὅτ' ἐς πεδίον τὸ Τρωϊκὸν ἀθρήσειε,
Θαύμαζεν πυρὰ πολλὰ, τὰ καίετο Ἰλιόθι πρὸ,
Αὐλῶν, συρίγγων τ' ἐνοπὴν, ὅμαδόν τ' ἀνθρώπων.

386. And his painted god] It was a custom among the ancients to name their ships from some particular gods, whom they looked upon as tutelary patrons to them, and paint their images upon the stern.

418. And his bow sustain] The bow was borne by the Persian kings as an ensign of royalty, as we learn from Dio, book 49, who informs us, that the ambassadors sent by Mark Anthony to Phraates found him sitting on a throne of gold, and playing on his bow-string with his fingers, as I think the words, Την νευραν τȣ Τοξȣ ψαλλων, signify.

"O bland creatress of the gods above,
And men beneath, from whose omnific love
The woods are clad with verdure, rivers flow,
And animals with life's warm current glow;
Hail, fairest part of the material world,
From whom arose the stones by Pyrrha hurl'd,
Promethean arts, and food for human kind,
Improv'd by change, with various arts refin'd.
Old ocean rests sustain'd on thy embrace;
Thy wide extent contains the finny race,
The feather'd kind, and savage in his lair:
Round thee, the prop of worlds, in vacant air
Sublimely pois'd the swift machine of Heav'n,
And the bright cars by Sol and Luna driv'n,
Whose lights alternate gild the star-pav'd pole,
In motion annual and diurnal roll.
Canst thou, who, situate in the midst of things,
And undivided by the brother-kings,
So many towns and nations far and wide,
From thy vast store with nourishment supply'd,
Alone and unassisted dost sustain,
And Atlas, who without thee toils in vain
Beneath the incumbent atmosphere, his care,
Us only of thy sons refuse to bear?
Why, goddess, dost thou murmur at our weight?
O say, what crime has merited thy hate?
Is it, because a foreign birth we boast,
The wretched natives of th' Inachian coast?
Our country lies in ev'ry tract of earth: [worth,
Nor should'st thou these or those, as void of
Mark out for vengeance, or extraneous call,
Since thou'rt alike the mother of us all.
Common to all alike may'st thou remain, [plain.
Nor grudge, that aught but Thebans press thy
Still in the chance of war, and course of fate
May we expire, not whelm'd thro' sudden hate;
Snatch not our breathing bodies, ere they lie
On the known pile, but give us time to die.
Soon shall we come the path that all must tread,
When destiny has cut the fatal thread.
O stop the moving field, nor thus prevent
The sisters' hands, but to our pray'rs relent.
But thou, whom dear to Heav'n no Theban hand
Depriv'd of vital breath, nor hostile brand,
But Nature, who prepar'd a bed of rest
Between her arms, and snatch'd thee to her breast,
As if, in recompence, she would bestow
A burial-place on Cyrrha's sacred brow:
Conciliate to the gods thy wretched friend,
And let a portion of thy skill descend
To guide my breast. Whate'er thou didst prepare
To teach our grieving host, to me declare.
As thy interpreter, to thee I'll pay
My vows in absence of the god of day.
The place that snatch'd thee hence, is more divine
Than Cyrrha, Delos, or the god's own shrine."
This said, in earth he plung'd the sable herd,
And sheep, for their black fleeces much preferr'd:
Then o'er them heap'd the sand. Such rites they
For fun'ral honours to the prophet's shade. [paid
Thus toil'd the Greeks, when in the brazen sound
Of swords and martial horns their shouts are
drown'd.
The queen of furies from Theumesus' height
Her tresses shook, and rais'd the din of fight;
She mingled hissings with the clarion's tone,
And the trump breath'd a clangour yet unknown.
Cithæron starts astonish'd, and the quire
Of tow'rs that danc'd to great Amphion's lyre.
Now stern Bellona thunders at each gate,
To wake the war, and act the will of fate.
The sounding hinges ring, as they unfold:
The waves of people to the passage roll'd,
As if the Grecians press'd them from behind;
Horse mix with foot, and clashing chariots join'd.
Long in th' entangling entrance they remain,
And view the field, they strove to reach in vain.
Creon by lot from the Ogygian goes;
Neitæ then Eteocles disclose:
The Hamoloides Hæmon occupies;
Thro' Hypseus to the plain Prætides flies:
Next thro' Electræ warlike Dryas takes
His way; Eurymedon Hypsistæ shakes.
The gate of Dirce for a while retards,
Then frees the brave Menœceus with his guards.
Thus when the Nile with Heav'n's descending
show'rs,
And eastern snows retrieves his less'ning pow'rs,
Impatient of th' increase, imbib'd with force,
And foaming o'er he bursts his latent source,
Then disembogues his burden in the main, [plain,
And from sev'n mouths o'erflows the neighb'ring

435. O bland creatress] The poet has confirmed the character of Thiodomas by this beautiful hymn to the Earth. There is a genuine classical simplicity in it not without a mixture of grandeur, that none but Homer and Callimachus were truly masters of, except our Milton, whose style and manner of hymn-writing approach very near to our author's.

452. And undivided] Statius alludes here to the hemistich in the fifteenth book of the Iliad, where Neptune, speaking of the division of the world between Jupiter, Pluto and himself, says,

Γαῖα δ' ἔτι ξυνὴ πάντων.

491. In earth] The ancients always sacrificed black animals to the Earth: thus Homer in the 3d book of the Iliad.

Οἴσετε δ' ἄρν' ἕτερον λευκὸν, ἑτέρην δὲ μέλαιναν,
Γῇ τε καὶ Ἠελίῳ.

Of which (says the old scholiast) the white lamb was sacrificed to the Sun as the father of light, and the black one to the Earth, as being the mother and nurse of mankind.

511. From the Ogygian] Lactantius in his notes on our author, esteems this dull enumeration of the Theban gates as a striking elegancy: but, I confess, I fear it is folly to have translated it. Dry, however, and uninteresting as it is, I doubt not but there are many lovers of antiquity, who extol Statius to the skies for having handed down to posterity such a considerable piece of useful knowledge. All I request of the reader with respect to it, is, that he will not blame the dullness of the translator, since he could not have been faithful to the original without being so.

519. Thus when] The poet has in this comparison descended to the minutiæ of exactness; but the delicacy of the allusion, which may possibly escape the observation of the generality of our readers, is the correspondence of the seven mouths of the Nile to the seven gates of Thebes: for as each of the former discharges a torrent of water, so from each of the latter a band of warriors issues to the field of combat.

While to their caves the routed nymphs retreat,
Nor even dare their native river meet.
Meanwhile th' Inachian youths, and Spartan bands,
With those who cultivate Elæan lands,
And Pylos, seek the battle, sadly slow,
And drooping with the weight of recent woe;
Nor willing yet Thiodamas obey,
Depriv'd of their late prophet's gentle sway.
Nor, prince of augurs, does thy cohort boast
Alone of thee: the universal host
Defective seems, as thro' the wings of fight
Thy successor appears excell'd in height.
Thus should some envious cloud secrete a star
From the fair groupe that forms the Northern Car,
Short of its complement, the mangled Wain
Would scarce be known, and seamen gaze in vain.
But see! fresh labours to the poet rise,
And war unsung demands the god's supplies:
Another Phœbus then attune my lyre,
A greater Muse the growing song inspire.
The fatal hour arrives so rashly sought,
With horrour, sorrow, blood and carnage fraught;
And Death, from chains and Stygian darkness freed,
Enjoys the light, and stalking o'er the mead,
Expands his jaws, and to his arms invites
The men of worth, but vulgar triumphs slights.
He marks the chiefs who most deserve their life,
The first in arms, and foremost in the strife;
Of these, scarce number'd with the mighty dead,
The fiends rapacious snatch the vital thread.
Mars occupies the centre of the field,
His javelin dry; where'er he turns his shield,
The fatal touch erases from the mind
Wives, children, home, and leaves a blank behind.
The love of life too flies among the rest,
The last that lingers in the human breast.
Wrath sits suspended on their thirsty spears,
And half unsheath'd each angry blade appears.
Their helmets tremble, formidably gay
With nodding crests, and shed a gleamy ray.
Loud beat their daring hearts against the mails:
Nor wonder we, with men the god prevails;
The very steeds with warlike ardour glow,
And snow-white show'rs of foam the plain o'erflow.
They champ the bit, or neighing paw the ground,
And bound and prance at the shrill trumpet's sound,
As if their rider's soul transfused inspires
Their breasts with equal and congenial fires.
When now they rush, thick clouds of dust arise
From either part encount'ring in the skies.
As they advance, the middle space between
Grows less, till scarce an interval is seen.
Now front to front oppos'd in just array,
The closing hosts with groans commence the fray:
Sword is repell'd by sword, shields clash on shields,
Foot presses foot, and lance to lances yields.
Their helmets almost join, and mingling rays,
Alternately reflect each other's blaze.
Beauteous as yet the face of war appears,
No helms uncrested, and no broken spears;
Without a flaw the deep'ning lines remain,
Their belts and bucklers shine without a stain:
Fair hung the quiver at the warrior's side;
Nor did one chariot stand without a guide.
But when stern valour, prodigal of life,
And wrath arose, increasing with the strife,
Darts thrown aloft with swift succession glare,
Glow in the whirl, and hiss along the air:
A cloud of arrows intercepts the skies,
Scarce can the crowded Heav'ns for more suffice.
Not with such force the flaky sheets of snow
Descend on Rhodope's aërial brow:
Great was the crash, as when from either pole
Jove bares his arm, and bids the thunder roll:
Thus roars the storm when gloomy Boreas pours
The hail on Lybian sands in rattling show'rs.
Some fall by sent, some by returning spears,
And present death in various forms appears;

537. Thus should] This simile likewise has all the precision and justness of the former: the seven captains being represented by the seven stars in Charles's Wain.

541. But see! fresh labours] Statius is not the only author who has renewed his invocation to the deities who preside over poetry, at the middle of his book, when he is going to enter upon a different subject.

Nunc age, qui reges, Erato, &c.
Tu vatem, tu diva mone: &c.
Major rerum mihi nascitur ordo,
Majus opus moveo. Virgil, Æn. lib. 7.

And Milton likewise;

Descend from Heav'n, Urania, &c.
Half yet remains unsung, &c. Par. Lost, b. 7.

547. And Death] We are here dazzled and confounded with a variety of scenes, and complication of imagery. What can be more grand and magnificent than the prelude to this battle? We see Death let loose from Hell, and striding with open mouth over the field, Mars spiriting the soldiers, and with the touch of his shield infusing a forgetfulness of all domestic connections, and the very horses seemingly voluntary in their masters' service.

575. As they advance, the middle] These are good lines, though I cannot think them equal to the following.

————For now
'Twixt host and host a narrow space was left,
A dreadful interval, and front to front
Presented stood in terrible array
Of hideous length. Par. Lost, b. 6. 103.

579. Sword is] The lines in the original, viz.

Jam clypeus clypeis, umbone repellitur umbo,
Ense minax ensis, pede pes & cuspide cuspis,

are imitated (says Mr. Pope) very happily from the following lines in the fourth book of the Iliad, verse 446.

Οἱ δ᾽ ὅτε δήρ᾽ ἐς χῶρον ἕνα ξυνιόντες ἵκοντο,
Σύν ῥ᾽ ἔβαλον ῥινὺς, σὺν δ᾽ ἔγχεα, καὶ μένε᾽ ἀνδρῶν
Χαλκεοθωρήκων, ἀτὰρ ἀσπίδες ὀμφαλόεσσαι
Ἔπλην τ᾽ ἀλλήλησι ———— ———

595. Not with such force] The reader may compare this with the following, quoted from Virgil's Æneid, book 9. verse 668.

Quantus ab occasu veniens pluvialibus hœdis
Verberat imber humum: quam multâ grandine nimbi
In vada precipitant, cum Jupiter horridus austris
Torquet aquosam hyemem, & cœlo cava nubila rumpit.

With stakes, in lieu of javelins, they engage,
And mutual blows are dealt with mutual rage.
Their whizzing slings a stony tempest rain;
The bullets flash, like lightning, o'er the plain.
A double fate is lodg'd in ev'ry dart,
And, the steel failing, poison saps the heart.
No random weapons fly without a wound;
The press so thick, they cannot reach the ground.
Oft ignorant they kill, and fall in fight,
And fortune does the work of val'rous might.
They gain and lose with swift vicissitude
The well-fought ground, pursuing and pursu'd.
As when great Jove of adverse winds and storms,
To vex the world, a double tempest forms;
The skies and surges waver with the blast
Which then prevails, and still obey the last;
Till the light clouds with driving Auster sweep,
Or stronger Boreas rules the wat'ry deep.
Asopian Hypseus first the slaughter led,
And slew Menalcas at his people's head.
Th' Oebalians proud, who, wedg'd in firm array
With close-compacted shields, had forc'd their
way
Thro' the Eubœan ranks, their mightiest slain,
They swerv'd aside and sorrowing quit the plain.
He, a rough native of the rapid flood,
A Spartan both in nature and by blood,
Back thro' his bowels drew the thrilling dart,
That quiver'd in his bosom near his heart,
(Lest in his back by sinking deeper found,
His troops should deem it a dishonest wound.)
Then at his foe the weapon faintly threw,
The bloody weapon unavailing flew.
Here end the rural sports of the deceas'd,
His wars, and stripes that erst his mother pleas'd.
At Phædimus Amyntas lifts his bow;
When (ah! how swift the sisters wing the blow)
Supine the chief lies panting on the ground,
Ere the recoiling string had ceas'd to sound.
On Phegeus next a forceful stroke descends,
And his right arm from off the shoulder rends.
Long trembling on the pain the member stay'd,
Nor from its faithful grasp dismiss'd the blade;
Acetes view'd with horrour, as it lay
'Midst other arms, and lopp'd the hand away.
Stern Athamas his furious lance impell'd
At Iphis, angry Pheres Abas fell'd;
The sword of savage Hypseus Argus found:
They lay, lamenting each a diff'rent wound.
Rapt in a chariot, Abas sought the mead;
Argus on foot: but Iphis rein'd the steed.
Two Theban twins together rang'd the field,
In casques, the fatal mask of war, conceal'd;
These, as along the paths of fight they sped,
Two twins of Argos mingled with the dead:
But when each kindred feature they descry'd,
As to despoil them of their arms they try'd;
They gaze upon each other, and bemoan
The cruel lot, that soon may be their own.
Unhappy Daphnis by fierce Ion bleeds,
Who took advantage of his headstrong steeds:
Jove smiles in triumph, Phœbus mourns in vain;
This dwelt at Pisa, that on Cyrrha's plain.
Two chiefs above the rest were mark'd with fame;
By fortune, heroes of distinguish'd name;
Fierce Hæmon chas'd the Grecians o'er the field,
The Theban troops to raging Tydeus yield:
In him Alcides gen'rous heat instills,
Him Pallas fires.—Thus from their echoing hills
Two torrents rush, increas'd with wintry rains,
And pour a double ruin on the plains,

615. As when great Jove] So Silius Italicus, l. 4.

Hac pontum vice (ubi exercet discordia ventos)
Fert Boreas, Eurusque refert, molemque profundi,
Nunc huc alterno, nunc illuc flamine gestant.

636. And stripes that erst his mother pleas'd] Orestes having transported the image of Diana from Scythia into Sparta, and that goddess being only placable with human blood, lest the divine vengeance should be incurred by an intermission of sacrifice, and that their cruelty might not excite the Greeks to a rebellion, they inured their children to undergo a severe scourging with a kind of emulous patience and fortitude, till the blood gushed out in such a quantity as might appease the cruel goddess. Tertullian in his proem to his lives of the martyrs gives much the same account: Nam quod hodie apud Lacedæmonios solemnitas maxima est Διαμαστιγωσις [i. e. Flagellatio] non latet. In quo sacro ante aram nobiles quique adolescentes flagellis affliguntur astantibus parentibus & propinquis & uti perseverent adhortantibus.

637. At Phædimus] As the perpetual horrour of combats and a succession of images of slaughter could not but tire the reader in the course of a long work, Statius has endeavoured to remedy this defect by a constant variety in the deaths of his heroes. These he distinguishes several ways: sometimes by the characters of the men, their age, office, profession, nation, and family, sometimes by the difference of their wounds, and at others by the several postures and attitudes in which his warriors are described, either falling or fighting.

670. Thus from their echoing hills] I shall take this opportunity of presenting my readers with three very fine similes from three different authors; the last of which is perhaps as pompous, copious, picturesque, not to say every way poetical, as ever was drawn from this part of the creation.

Ut torrens celsi præceps e vertice Pindi
Cum sonitu ruit ad campum, magnoque furore
Convulsum montis volvit latus, obvia passim
Armenta, immanesque feræ, sylvæque trahuntur.
Spumea saxosis clamat convallibus unda.
Silius Italicus de Bello Punico, lib. 4.

Con quel furor, che'l re de fiumi altiero,
Quando rompe tal volta argini e sponde,
E che nei campi Ocnei s' apre il sentiero,
Ei grassi solchi, e le biade feconde,
E con le sue Capanne il gregge intiero,
E coi cani i pastor porta nell' onde.
Ariosto's Orlan. Furioso, canto 40.

Comme un voit un torrent du haut des Pirennées,
Menacer des vallons les nymphes consternées;
Cent digues qu'on oppose a ses flots orageux,
Soutiennent quelque temps son choc impetueux:
Mais bientot renversant sa barriere impuissante,
Il porte au loin le bruit, la mort, & l'epouvante;
Deracine en passant ces chenes orgueilleux,
Qui bravoient les hivers, & qui touchoient les
cieux,
Detache les rochers du pendant des montagnes,
Et poursuit les troupeaux fuiant dans les campagnes.
Voltaire's Henr. Chant. 6.

Contending, who should highest overflow
The bridge, or soonest lay the forest low;
Till some strait vale unites their watry force,
And joins their streams in one continu'd course;
Then, ocean near, they labour to disjoin
Their currents, ere they mingle with the brine.
Bold Idas issued thro' the middle fight,
And wav'd a torch that shed a smoky light:
The warrior's frolic struck his foes with fear;
They shunn'd his sight, and left the passage clear:
But Tydeus's lance pursu'd him, as he sped,
Tore off his helm, and pierc'd his naked head.
Supine the giant lay, the barbed spear
Stands fixed upon his forehead. Round his ear,
And temple swift the curling flames arise,
When Tydeus thus in triumph boasting cries;
" O call not Argos cruel in return
For this thy fun'ral pile; in quiet burn."
As the gaunt wolf, pleas'd with the first essay
Of slaughter, flies, uncloy'd to make a prey
Of the whole flock. Thus rush'd the vengeful son
Of Oeneus to complete the task begun.
Brave Aon perish'd by a well-aim'd stone;
His sword hew'd Pholus and bold Chromis down.
The sons of Mæra sunk to nether night
Beneath his piercing dart, whom in despite
Of Venus, once her patroness, she bare:
Mean time the matron wearies Heav'n with pray'r.
Nor with less wrath insatiate Hæmon glows,
But dies the ground with purple as he goes;
In ev'ry quarter of the field engag'd,
But mostly where the thickest combat rag'd.
At length as on he sped, tho' short of breath,
Yet still unwearied with the work of death;
He falls on Butes, who address'd his host
To dare the threatened shock, nor quit their post:
On the fair youth, unknowing whence it came,
Descends the pole-ax with unerring aim,
And cleaves his temples, grac'd with youthful charms;
His locks divided fall upon his arms.
The crimson life gush'd upward from the wound;
Prone falls the chief, and falling spurns the ground.
Polites then beneath his falchion bow'd,
And Hypanis, who long unshorn had vow'd
Their hair to Bacchus, and the god of day:
Yet neither came to drive the pest away.
To these the warrior Hyperenor join'd,
And Damasus, who fain would have declin'd
Th' unequal conflict; but the spear he threw,
Athwart his breast, and thro' his shoulders flew;
From his tenacious grasp the buckler tore,
And on its point in seeming triumph bore.
Much more had Hæmon too that day achiev'd,
The pow'r assisting: but Minerva griev'd
For her slain Greeks, and to his wrath oppos'd
Oenides.—Now the god and goddess clos'd
In converse mutual, when Alcmene's son,
Peace at his heart, serenely thus begun.
" Say, faithful sister, by what fortune driv'n,
We meet in battle? Has the queen of Heav'n,
For ever studious in promoting ill,
Devis'd this scheme?—Whatever is thy will,
Let that be done: much sooner I'd withstand
The wrath of Heav'n, and brave the thund'rer's hand.
Dear as my Hæmon is, him I disown,
If Pallas favours heroes of her own.
No more with thee in any mortal's cause
I combat, tho' thy favour'd Tydeus draws
On Hyllus, or should menace with his spear
Amphitryon, recent from the nether sphere.
Fresh in my mind thy favours I retain;
How oft (when o'er the spacious earth and main
I roam'd) that hand upheld me in the fray,
And Jove's own ægis gave my arm the day!
With me the realms of Styx thou hadst explor'd,
Could Acheron to gods access afford.
To thee my rank and place in Heav'n I owe,
My sire, and more than I can utter now.
Then act thy will on Thebes,—to thee I yield
The sole command, and guidance of the field."
This said, he strode away.—His words assuage
The wrath of Pallas, and appease her rage.
Her anger past, the wonted smiles return;
The snakes subside, her eyes desist to burn.
The warrior, conscious that the god retir'd,
No more with strength endued, with ardour fir'd,
With faint effort whirls round his useless brand,
Nor in one stroke descries his patron's hand.
Would pride and shame permit, he fain would fly:
He blushes to retreat, yet fears to die.
Oenides urges his retreating foe;
And brandishing what no one else could throw,
Directs his arm, where 'twixt his helm and shield,
The joining throat and neck a passage yield.
Nor err'd his hand, but Pallas chose to spare
The hapless youth, and made his life her care.

691. As the gaunt wolf] Tasso has paraphrased this.

> Come dal chiuso ovil cacciato viene
> Lupo tal'or, che fugge, e si nasconde;
> Che se ben del gran ventre omai ripiene
> Ha l' ingorde voragine profonde.
> Avido pur di sanguo anco fuor tiene
> La lingua, e'el sugge dalla labra immonde;
> Tal'ei sen gia dopo il sanguigno Stratio
> Della sua cupa fame anco non satio.
>
> Gier. Lib. canto 10. stanza 2.

716. Who long unshorn had vow'd] Their letting their hair grow to a great length, and dedicating it to the gods, was esteemed a principal act of religion by the ancients. Thus we find Achilles consecrated his hair to the river Sperchius in order to procure himself and friend a safe return from Troy.

> Ἔνθ' αὖτ' ἄλλ' ἐνόησε ποδάρκης δῖος Ἀχιλλεύς,
> Στὰς ἀπάνευθε πυρῆς ξανθὴν ἀπεκείρατο χαίτην,
> Ἣν ῥα Σπερχειῷ ποταμῷ τρέφε τηλεθόωσαν.

741. On Hyllus] Hyllus and Amphitryon were his sons by Omphale.

743. Fresh in my mind thy favours] In the eighth book of the Iliad, Pallas mentions Jove's ingratitude in not rewarding her for the services she had done his son Hercules at his request, when distressed by the artifice of Juno.

756. The snakes subside] The poet must here allude to the snakes on Medusa's head, depictured on Jupiter's ægis, which Pallas generally carried about her.

> Ἀμφὶ δ' ἄρ' ὤμοισιν βάλετ' Αἰγίδα θυσσανόεσσαν
> Δεινὴν, ἣν περὶ μὲν πάντῃ φόβος ἐστεφάνωτο.
> Ἐν δ' ἔρις, ἐν δ' ἀλκὴ, ἐν δὴ κρυόεσσα ἰωκή·
> Ἐν δέ τε Γοργείη κεφαλὴ δεινοῖο πελώρου.
>
> Iliad 5. Ver. 738.

The dart, diverted from its destin'd course,
His shoulder graz'd, and spent in air its force.
A fate so near him chills his soul with dread;
At once his fortitude and vigour fled:
No more he dares prolong th' unequal fight,
But even sickens at the hero's sight.
Thus, when some hunter's spear has drawn the gore
From the tough forehead of a bristled boar,
But lightly raz'd the skin, nor reach'd the brain;
The daunted savage wheels around with pain,
Grinding his tusks, or stands aloof thro' fear,
Nor tempts again the fury of his spear.
Long had brave Prothous with unerring hand
Dealt out his shafts, and gall'd the Grecian band:
This Tydeus saw, and rushing at the foe
And his gay courser, aim'd a double blow.
On him, as prone he tumbles on the plains,
Falls the pierc'd steed, and, while he seeks the reins,
Stamps on the helm, till by his feet comprest
On his lord's face, it crush'd his shielded breast;
Then spouting out amidst a purple tide
The bit, expir'd recumbent at his side.
Thus often on the cloud-supporting crown
Of Gaurus, vine and elm are both o'erthrown,
A double damage to the swain: but most
Th' uxorious elm bewails his consort lost;
Nor groans so much for his own hapless fate,
As for the grapes he presses with his weight.
Chorœbus, comrade of the nine, forsook
His native mount, and the Castalian brook;
Though oft Urania from th' inspected stars
Forewarn'd his death, and bade him shun the wars:
Heedless he mixes with the daring throng,
And, while he meditates the future song,
Becomes himself a theme of public praise;
The sisters weep, forgetful of their lays.
Swoll'n with ambitious hopes, young Atys came
From Phocian Cyrrha to the field of fame,
To fair Ismena from his tender age
Espous'd; nor did her father's impious rage,
Or the neglected beauties of her face,
The idol fair one in his eyes disgrace.
Nor in her turn the damsel disapproves
His faultless person; mutual were their loves.
But war forbids their nuptials; hence arose
The champion's hatred to his Argive foes.
He shines the foremost in the deathful scene,
And, lab'ring to be notic'd by his queen,
Now wars on foot, and now with loosen'd reins,
And foaming horses pours along the plains.
His doating mother deck'd his am'rous breast
And graceful shoulders with a purple vest.
His arms and trappings were emboss'd with gold,
Lest he should seem less glorious to behold
Than his fair spouse.—On these the chief rely'd,
And the stern Greeks to single fight defy'd;
The weakest of his enemies subdu'd,
And none attack'd, who were not first pursu'd.
Trembling he bears their trophies to his train,
And with his troops, inglorious, herds again.
Thus the young lion in the Caspian shade,
(No length of mane terrific yet display'd)
Yet innocent of slaughter'd bull or ram,
If chance he lights upon a straggling lamb
Without the fold, in absence of the swain,
Riots in blood, and glories in the slain.
On Tydeus then unknown he casts his eyes,
And measuring his valour by his size,
Proudly presumes to make an easy prey
Of the slain chief, and bear his arms away.
He now had levell'd many a distant blow,
Ere the brave prince perceiv'd his puny foe:
At length contemptuously he view'd the man,
And formidably smiling, thus began:
"I see, vain fop, too prodigal of breath,
Thou seekest honour from a glorious death."
He paus'd; nor deigning to discharge a blow
With sword or spear on such a worthless foe,
His arm scarce rais'd, a slender javelin threw,
With fatal certainty the weapon flew;
And, as if driven with his utmost force,
Deep in his groin infix'd, there stopp'd its course.
The chief of life thus seemingly bereft,
The gen'rous victor passes on, and left
His arms untouch'd, and thus jocosely said,
"These suit not Mars, nor thee, O fav'ring maid:
What man of courage would not blush to wear
Such gaudy trifles?—Nay, I scarce would dare
Present them, by my consort to be borne,
Lest she reject them with indignant scorn."
Thus spake Oenides, fir'd with lust of fame,
And sallies forth in quest of nobler game.
Thus, when the lion roams, where heifers feed,
And lowing beeves expatiate o'er the mead,
The royal savage traversing the plain
In sullen majesty, and sour disdain,

827. He bears their trophies] This passage gives us an insight into the ancient method of fighting. We see the leaders advancing before their troops, and making an excursion, and as soon as they had obtained the spoils of the vanquished, returning to them again. If this passage is attended to, it will clear up many things in Homer, and his imitators, which would otherwise seem very absurd.—Atys would have made a good hero in a romance. He was one of those gentlemen who go to war only to please the ladies, and mix the beau with the hero, two characters the most inconsistent in nature, though often united in practice. Whilst, however, we are pitying the rash and ill-timed gallantry of this young man, we cannot but applaud the rough soldier-like behaviour of Tydeus, and the blunt wit he shows on this occasion. I shall only observe farther, that this character is admirably well supported, and is a sufficient proof of our author's vein for satire.—The former part of this note belongs to Barthius.

861. Thus, when the lion] In order to obviate any objection that may arise to the frequent repetition of similes drawn from the same object, I shall transcribe Mr. Pope's defence of Homer on that point. ——"Is it not more reasonable to compare the same man always to the same animal, than to see him sometimes a sun, sometimes a tree, and sometimes a river? Though Homer speaks of the same creature, he so diversifies the circumstances and accidents of the comparison, that they always appear quite different. And to say truth, it is not so much the animal or the thing, as the action or posture of them that employs our imagination: two different animals in the same action are more like each other than one and the same animal is to himself in two different actions. And those who, in reading Homer, are shocked that 'tis always a lion, may as well be angry that it is always a man." See Essay on Homer's Battles.

Spares the weak herd, and culling out their head,
Some lordly bull, arrests and lays him dead.
Menæceus, list'ning to the dying cries
Of Atys, swiftly to his rescue flies;
And lest his steeds should flag, deserts his car,
And bounds impetuous thro' the ranks of war.
Th' Arcadian youths advanc'd to strip the slain;
Nor did the Thebans labour to restrain,
Till brave Menæceus thus:—"O foul disgrace
To boasted Cadmus! O degen'rate race!
Shall foreign Atys gain deserv'd applause
By nobly bleeding in another's cause,
While we decline the danger of the day,
And children, wives, and all that's dear betray?"
Each tender care reviv'd, the troops arise,
Shame in their breasts, and anger in their eyes.
Meanwhile the Theban princesses, a pair
Alike in manners, and supremely fair,
Retiring to their chambers, give a vent
To mutual grief, and mutual discontent:
Nor do they weep the present ills of fate,
But from the earliest æra of their state
Seek matter of complaint; one mourns her sire,
And one the mother-queen's incestuous fire;
This weeps her absent brother's baneful stars,
The monarch that, but both detest the wars.
Their vows suspended by an equal love,
They fondly pity whom they can't approve,
And doubt, whom they had rather have prevail:
At length the favour'd exile sinks the scale.
Thus Pandionian birds, when they regain
Their native clime in winter's dreary reign,
Perch'd on their nests, in plaintive accents tell,
And hear what various accidents befel

873. O foul disgrace] This little exhortation of Menæceus to his soldiers is at once concise and pithy. A longer speech at this juncture would have been very absurd. He has said all that was wanted, and nothing but what he ought. It is something like that comprehensive harangue of the great Gustavus, "Look ye at those fellows; either fell them, or they'll fell you."—It is remarked of Homer, that his longest orations are such as were delivered in the heat of battle, a fault which none can accuse our author of without manifest injustice.

891. Their vows suspended] This recals to my remembrance four beautiful lines from Seneca the tragedian, who, in his Thebais, introduces Jocasta speaking as follows:

Utramque quamvis diligam affectu pari,
Quo causa melior sorsque deterior tradit,
Inclinat animus, semper infirmo favens
Miseros magis fortuna conciliat suis.

Though, by the by, the poet seems to contradict what he said before, viz. that Antigone preferred Polynices in her esteem.

895. Thus Pandionian birds, when] Statius is not the first poet who has likened the chattering of women to the chirping of birds. Virgil in his Æneid compares the loquacious Juturna to one of them.

Nigra velut magnas domini cum divitis ædes
Pervolat, et pennis alta atria lustrat hirundo,
Pabula parva legens, nidisque loquacibus escas:
Et nunc porticibus vacuis, nunc humida circum
Stagna sonat. Lib. 12. ver. 473.

Each other absent, and by turns rejoice
In notes that emulate the human voice.
Tears making way, the chaste Ismene broke
Her silence first, and thus, exclaiming, spoke:
"O sister! what deluding errours blind
And mock the easy faith of human kind!
When images, in dreams returning, play
Before our eyes, distinct as in the day;
And sleep is mark'd by care: for yesternight
My fancy labour'd with the sudden sight
Of nuptials, which in peace were never sought,
Nor enter'd in my most unguarded thought.
The bridegroom too among the rest was shown,
Scarce known in person: once indeed I own
I saw him, when my marriage was propos'd,
At court.—But soon the glitt'ring scene was clos'd.
The fires extinguish'd suddenly I view'd,
And omens and prognostics dire ensu'd.
My mother follow'd then, with fury fir'd,
And Atys at my hands with shouts requir'd.
What mean these dark portents of death obscure?
I fear not, while our house is thus secure,
While the foe stands aloof, and hope remains,
Fraternal concord may reward our pains."
While thus each other's sorrows they report,
A sudden tumult fills the spacious court;
And Atys enters (moving scene of woe)
By toil and sweat recover'd from the foe.
Life's ebbing stream ran trickling on the ground,
One feeble hand reclin'd upon the wound,
And his loose hairs his bloodless face conceal'd,
His languid neck dependent on the shield.
Jocasta first the killing object ey'd,
And trembling call'd his fair intended bride.
This he requests, that with his dying voice
And last farewell he may confirm his choice.
Her name alone, a pleasing sound, long hung
On his pale lips, and trembling on his tongue.
The servants shriek, the virgin with her hands
Conceals her blushes: modesty commands.
The queen, indulgent to th' entreating chief,
Constrains her to impart this last relief.
Thrice at her name he lifts his drooping head,
And thrice sinks back, his vital spirits fled.
On her, the light of Heav'n no more enjoy'd,
He feasts his eyes, admiring and uncloy'd.
No parents near to rear the sacred pyre,
Nor frantic mother, or desponding sire;
To her th' ungrateful office they assign,
To tend his obsequies and rites divine.
There, no one present, o'er the corse she sighs,
Closes each wound, and seals her lover's eyes.
Meanwhile Bellona wak'd anew the fray,
And turn'd the doubtful fortune of the day:
She chang'd her torch, and other serpents wore,
Heap'd slain on slain, and swell'd the stream of gore,
As if the toil of fight was scarce begun,
Much work of death remaining to be done.

923. While thus] This description of the distress of the two lovers is beyond all the encomiums that can be given it; though the grief of Ismene on this occasion is not so outrageous, as if she had not been prepared for it by a previous dream. The dying warrior is very artfully introduced, his condition and appearances are very picturesque, and the effects of his violent passion finely imagined, though at the same time very natural.

But Tydeus shines the most; tho', sure to wound,
Parthenopæus deals his shafts around,
Tho' fierce Hippomedon impels his horse
Thro' the gor'd war, and crushes many a corse,
And Capaneus' javelin wings its flight,
Afar distinguish'd in the ranks of fight,
His was the day: before him trembling flies
The Theban herd, as thus aloud he cries:
"Why this retreat, when unreveng'd remain
Your valiant comrades, late in ambush slain?
Behold the man, by whom alone they bled:
Behold, and wreak on his devoted head
Your wrath collected.—Can ye thus forego
The chance of war, and spare the present foe?
Is there a man whom this wide-wasting steel
Has wrong'd, for vengeance let him here appeal.
Now by my soul it grieves me, that content
With fifty deaths, my course I backward bent
To fair Mycenæ.—Fly then, but this day
The proud usurper for your flight shall pay."
Scarce had he spoke, when on the left he spy'd
The king conspicuous for his plumy pride,
Rallying his routed forces.—At the view
The kindling hero to th' encounter flew,
As on a swan the royal eagle springs
With swift descent, and shades him with his wings.
Then thus.—"O monarch, studious of the right,
Meet we thus fairly by Apollo's light?
Or hadst thou rather trust thy worthless life
To night and ambuscades, than open strife?"
To this the sullen tyrant nought replies,
But at the foe a spear loud whizzing flies,
Charg'd with an answer. Rapid was its force;
But towards the period of its furious course
Oenides beat it off, and whirls his own
With strength and vigour until then unknown.
Swift rush'd the lance, and promis'd in its flight
To put an end to the destructive fight.
The fav'ring gods of either party bent
Their eyes towards it, anxious for th' event;
But for his brother the fell fiend preserv'd
Eteocles. Aside the jav'lin swerv'd
To Phlegyas, his squire, where 'midst the press
He toil'd with equal honour and success.
Now fiercer grown, th' Ætolian draws his sword,
And rushes, but the Theban arms afford
A grateful shelter to the coward king.
As when the shepherds, gath'ring in a ring,
Attempt to drive the nightly wolf away;
The prowling savage, heedful of his prey,
Pursues that only, nor attacks his foes,
Whose clubs and stones annoy him as he goes.
Thus Tydeus disregards th' inferior crowd,
And vengeance on their guilty monarch vow'd.
Yet, scorning opposition in the chace,
He struck the daring Thoas in his face;
A well-aim'd dart Deilochus arrests,
And left its point deep-buried in his breasts:
Pierc'd in the side, then Clonius bit the ground,
And stern Hippotades, from whose wide wound
The bowels gush'd.—Full helmets oft he skims
In air, and to the trunk restores his limbs.
And now the prince, unweary'd yet with toils,
Block'd himself up with carcases and spoils:
With him alone the circling hosts engage,
The single object of their missile rage.
Part glitter on the surface of his skin,
Part frustrate fall, and part are lodg'd within:
Some Pallas plucks away. His targe appears
An iron grove, thick set with gleamy spears.
No crest is extant; thro' the bristling hide
His naked back and shoulders are descry'd:
And Mars, which on his casque depictur'd sate,
Fell off, a joyless omen of his fate.
The shiver'd brass into his body pent,
Wrought him such pain as might have made relent
The bravest heart, when lo! a stroke descends,
And from the gums his gnashing grinders rends.
His breast is delug'd with a tide of gore,
With dust embrown'd, while each dilated pore
In copious drops perspires.—Pleas'd he survey'd
His bands applauding, and the martial maid,
Who o'er her eyes the spreading ægis threw,
As to her sire in his behalf she flew.
But see, an ashen jav'lin cuts the wind,
And leaves, with anger charg'd, the clouds behind.
Long was the author of the deed unknown,
Great Menalippus, for he durst not own:
At length the foe's untimely joy display'd
The warrior, herding in his troop, betray'd.

957. But Tydeus shines the most] The picture of Tydeus in the following lines is very elaborately drawn. As his fate is near at hand, the poet endeavours to make him quit the stage with honour, and immortalize him in his verses. Accordingly, this being the last scene he is to appear in, he is ushered in with the greatest pomp; and lest there should be any doubt of his superiority, after having been compared to the king of beasts, he is represented by the eagle, king of birds. The poet, by this accumulation of similes, raises our ideas of his hero much higher than any simple description can reach.

981. As on a swan] This comparison is very minutely copied from Homer, as may be seen from the circumstance of the shadowing of the eagle's wings.

So the strong eagle from his airy height,
Who marks the swans' or cranes' embodied flight,
Stoops down impetuous, as they light for food,
And stooping, darkens with his wings the flood.
Pope's Iliad.

1019. And now the prince] The magnanimous Scæva is in much the same plight in the sixth book of Lucan's Pharsalia.

Illum tota premit moles, illum omnia tela.
———Fortis crebris sonat ictibus umbo,
Et galeæ fragmenta cavæ compressa perurunt
Tempora: nec quicquam nudis vitalibus obstat
Jam pater stantes in summis ossibus hastas.
———Stat non fragilis pro Cæsare murus,
Pompeiumque tenet: jam pectora non tegit armis:
Ac veritus credi clypeo, lævaque vacasse,
Aut culpa vixisse sua non vulnera belli
Solus obit, densamque ferens in pectore sylvam,
Tum gradibus fessis, in quem cadet, eligit hostem.

1041. But see, an ashen jav'lin] These verses are imitated from Virgil.

Has inter voces, media inter talia verba,
Ecce viro stridens alis allapsa sagitta est:
Incertum quâ pulsa manu, quo turbine adacta;
Quis tantam Rutulis laudem, casusne, Deusne,
Attulerit: pressa est insignis gloria facti,
Nec sese Æneæ jactavit vulnere quisquam.
Æneid, Lib. 12, ver. 323.

For the pierc'd hero, now no longer steel'd
Against the growing anguish, loos'd his shield,
And bent beneath the wound. This seen, the Greeks
Rush to his aid with groans, nor manly shrieks:
The sons of Cadmus, smiling at their grief,
With shouts triumphant intercept relief.
The chief, inspecting close the adverse side,
The marksman, lurking in the crowd, espy'd,
Collects his whole remains of life and strength,
And throws a weapon of enormous length,
Which neighb'ring Hopleus gave, nor gave in vain:
Forth spouts the blood, extorted by the strain.
By force his sad companions drag him thence,
(While yet unconscious of his impotence)
Then bear him to the margin of the field,
His sides supported in a double shield;
And promise, he shall quickly re-engage,
When strength shall second his undaunted rage.
But he himself perceives his failing breath,
And shudd'ring at the chilling hand of death,
Reclines on earth, and cries,—" I die in peace;
But pity me, O sons of fertile Greece!
I ask you not these relics to convey
To Argos, or the seat of regal sway,
Regardless of my body's future doom,
Nor anxious for the honours of the tomb.
Curst are the brittle limbs, which thus desert
The soul, when most their strength they should exert.
All I solicit farther is the head
Of Menalippus; for my jav'lin sped,
And stretch'd, I trust, the dastard on the plains:
Then haste, Hippomedon, if aught remains
Of Argive blood; and thou, Arcadian youth,
In praise of whom fame e'en detracts from truth:
Go, valiant Capaneus, thy country's boast,
And now the greatest of th' Argolic host."
All mov'd; but Capaneus arrives the first,
Where breathing yet he lay, deform'd with dust,
And took him on his shoulders. Down his back
Flows the warm blood, and leaves a crimson track.
Such look'd Alcides, when in times of yore
He enter'd Argos with the captive boar.
O'ercome with joy and anger, Tydeus tries
To raise himself, and meets with eager eye
The deathful object, pleas'd as he survey'd
His own condition in his foe's pourtray'd.
The sever'd head impatient he demands,
And grasps with fervour in his trembling hands,
While he remarks the restless balls of sight,
That sought and shunn'd alternately the light.
Contented now, his wrath began to cease,
And the fierce warrior had expir'd in peace;
But the fell fiend a thought of vengeance bred,
Unworthy of himself, and of the dead.
Mean while, her sire unmov'd, Tritonia came,
To crown her hero with immortal fame;
But, when she saw his jaws besprinkled o'er
With spatter'd brains, and ting'd with living gore;
Whilst his imploring friends attempt in vain
To calm his fury, and his rage restrain:
Again, recoiling from the loathsome view,
The sculptur'd target o'er her face she threw;
And, her affection chang'd to sudden hate,
Resign'd Oenides to the will of fate:
But, ere she join'd the senate of the skies,
Purg'd in Ilyssos her unhallow'd eyes.

BOOK IX.

THE ARGUMENT.

The Thebans, spirited up by Eteocles to revenge the insult offered to Menalippus's body, renew the fight with great ardour. Polynices, almost

1062. His sides] The ancients were wont to carry their generals who fell in battle on a shield; as we learn from Virgil, book 10.

———At socii multo gemitu, lacrymisque,
Impositum scuto referunt Pallanta frequentes.

Again, book 10.

At Lausum socii exanimum super arma ferebant.

The losing a shield in combat was looked upon as the greatest disgrace that could befall a man:

Tecum Philippos et celerem fugam
Sensi, relictâ non bene parmulâ,

says Horace: hence the famous saying of the Spartan lady, when she gave her son a shield; Aut cum illo, aut in illo; *i.e.* " Either return with it, or upon it."——Part of this note belongs to Bernartius.

1093. The sever'd head] We are now come to that remarkable action of Tydeus which so much offended Mr. Pope, that, in vindicating a passage of Homer, where Achilles wishes he could eat the flesh of Hector, he says, " However, this is much more tolerable than a passage in the Thebaid of Statius, where Tydeus, in the very pangs of death, is represented as gnawing the head of his enemy."—But, with deference to the memory of that great man, I must beg leave to offer something in my author's defence, which I shall leave the reader to consider.

First, With respect to the fact taken absolutely, and in itself, the poet does not recite it as worthy of imitation, or praise his hero for the perpetration of it; but expresses his abhorrence of it, and informs us, that Tisiphone suggested it to Tydeus, and that Pallas herself, his stanch patroness, was so disgusted as utterly to desert him: these are circumstances that sufficiently absolve the poet from the censure of making his favourite character so monstrously brutish and inhuman.

Secondly, If we consider it comparatively, we must observe, that the will and intention, which only render moral actions culpable, were the same both in Achilles and Tydeus. The former wishes he could eat his enemy's flesh, the latter does it; so that the only difference is, that Tydeus had a better appetite, and less aversion to human flesh than Achilles.

Lastly, If it is really a fault, the commission of it was owing to the extravagant veneration that Statius had for Homer, as it is evidently imitated from the above-mentioned passage in the Iliad: so that the original thought will still be chargeable on that great author.

1112. Ilyssos] Is a river of Elysium, which the poet terms guiltless, because it makes guiltless, *i. e.* purifies. It is opposed to Styx, a stream of Hell; and called in Greek Ηλυσσος, from Λυσις,'that is to say, solution, because souls, after the solution of their corporeal bonds, descend to those fields.

overcome with grief for the death of Tydeus, laments very pathetically over him. Hippomedon opposes the enemy's onset with unparalleled fortitude. Lycus wounds him. He is assisted by Alcon, and kills Mopsus, Polites, and many others of note. The fury Tisiphone draws him off from attacking the Thebans by a false insinuation of Adrastus's being taken prisoner. In the mean time the Grecians are worsted, and the body of Tydeus is wrested from them: Hippomedon returns to the combat, pursues them into the river, and after a great slaughter of them, is opposed by the god of the stream himself, and being cast on shore, is overpowered by their numbers, and slain, notwithstanding Juno's interposition with Jupiter in his behalf. Parthenopæus then signalizes himself by his feats of archery, and is presented by Diana with a set of poisoned arrows. She solicits Apollo in his favour, but to no purpose. He is near being slain by Amphion, but the goddess and Dorceus rescue him. At length Dryas, at the instigation of Mars, slays him, and is killed himself by an invisible agent, supposed to be Diana herself. The young Arcadian, just at the point of death, gives his last commands to Dorceus, with which the book concludes.

THE brutal rage of bloody Tydeus fires
His foes, and th' ardour of revenge inspires.
E'en his own Grecians less deplore his fate,
And blame his fury and excess of hate.
Mars too, severest on th' embattled mead,
Fame represents disgusted at the deed,
What time, a vig'rous agent in the war,
O'er hills of slain he drove his rattling car.
So dire a scene the god could not survey,
But turn'd his steeds, and measur'd back the way.
To punish, then, the injury sustain'd
By Menalippus, on his corse prophan'd
The Theban youth with wrath rekindled rise.
From man to man th' infectious vengeance flies,
As if some foe their sires should disintomb,
And their remains a prey to monsters doom.
The monarch fans the fire, and thus bespeaks:
" Who now will favour, and account the Greeks
As men?—Behold, with arms supply'd no more
They ply their teeth, and lap the Theban gore.
Say, do we not with Lybian lions fight,
With human art opposing savage might?
See Tydeus, as a lenitive in death,
Feeding on hostile flesh resigns his breath.
With fire and sword contented we engage;
Their want of weapons is supply'd by rage.
Refining cruelty, full in the view
Of Jove, this impious track may they pursue.
Yet truly they the prophet's end bemoan,
And curse the land for mischiefs not its own."
In words like these the king harangu'd aloud,
And vainly stalk'd before th' obsequious crowd.
In all an equal fury burns, to gain
The spoils and hated corse of Tydeus slain.
Thus fowls obscene hang o'er the liquid way,
When from afar the wafting gales convey
The scent of bodies that unburied lie,
And taint the thick'ning ether.—As they fly,
With flapping pinions all the skies resound:
The lesser birds retire, and quit their ground.
Fame flies from man to man, from band to band,
And spreads vague murmurs o'er the Theban land;
More swift than wont she plies her sable wings,
When woeful tidings to some wretch she brings.
To trembling Polynices now she bears
The dismal news, and thunders in his ears.
His tears congeal'd, all petrified with grief
He stands, and for a time withholds belief.
For his superior valour, so well known,
Forbids him to believe the chief o'erthrown:
But when a fresh report pronounc'd him dead,
A cloud of grief his eyes and mind o'erspread;
All circulation ceasing in his veins,
He faints, he falls; his arms bestrew the plains.
His tears now gush forth at the last effort,
And the bright greaves his falling shield support.
Lonely he walks amidst a circling throng,
And scarcely drags his falt'ring knees along,
And cumbrous spear, as though he was deprest
With countless wounds, and pain'd above the rest.
The breathless hero by his comrades shown,
Who the sad prince attend with many a groan,
He grovels o'er the corse, (while from his eyes
The tears run copious) and desponding cries:
" O Tydeus, hope of all my warlike toils,
Prop of my cause, and partner of my spoils!
Is this the recompense I should bestow,
Are these the thanks which to my friend I owe,
That in my sight I suffer thee to lie
Unwept and bare beneath a foreign sky?
In exile now far worse than death I rove,
Depriv'd in thee of more than brother's love.
Nor seek I now the crown by lot decreed,
And sullied throne to which I should succeed:
Little I prize the badges of command,
And sceptre, which I take not from thy hand.

1. The brutal rage] The poet, foreseeing as it were, that he should offend the delicacy of the critics by this narrative, seems in this passage to have endeavoured to obviate the censure, and assure the reader, that he did not propose this action of his hero as worthy of imitation, but quite the reverse:—with a view to this, he represents Mars expressing his abhorrence of it in the strongest manner, and introduces Eteocles taking advantage of this act of brutality, to rally the Thebans to the charge.

35. Thus fowls obscene] Milton has a noble simile conceived in the genuine spirit of this author:

As when a flock
Of rav'nous fowl, though many a league remote,
Against the day of battle, to a field
Where armies lie incamp'd, come flying, lur'd
With scent of living carcases, design'd
For death the following day, in bloody fight.
Par. Lost, book 10. v. 273.

65. O Tydeus] These reflections of Polynices on the death of Tydeus are very manly and pathetic; they display a dignity of soul, a disinterestedness of friendship, and an overflowing of gratitude, that is rarely to be found in the breast of the ambitious; and I doubt not, but readers of the same delicate mould as the speaker here seems to be, will meet with a great deal of entertainment in the perusal of this masterly oration.

Stand off, ye warriors, and to me alone
Resign the fight:—the fortune is my own.
No longer now your useless arms employ,
Nor in pursuit of vengeance still destroy.
What greater proof of malice can you give,
Or how can I atone, while I survive,
For my friend's death?—O king, O conscious night,
Begun with strife, but closing with delight!
O Argos, dearest to the gods above,
And short-liv'd wrath, the pledge of lasting love!
Oh! hadst thou (while my life was in thy hand)
Stretch'd me unpity'd on a foreign strand!
Yet more—great chief, thou didst adopt my cause,
And, trusting Jove and hospitable laws,
Repair to Thebes, whence none would have return'd
Less brave.—So strong the flame of friendship burn'd.
Fame hath e'en now of Theseus ceas'd to boast,
And Telamon's renown in thine is lost.
How chang'd thy form! ah! what a diff'rent air!
But say, what wounds shall first employ my care?
How shall I know the Theban blood from thine?
And in thy death what numbers did combine?
Full well I ween, this envious Jove decreed;
And Mars with all his javelin help'd the deed."
He spake, and washes with his tears away
The clots of blood that on the visage lay;
And ev'ry limb compos'd, thus cries anew:
"Could'st thou thus far my just revenge pursue,
And I still breathe?"—This said, with woe distress'd,
He points the naked sceptre to his breast.
His pitying friends restrain'd his daring hands,
While the good king his rashness reprimands,
And soothes his rage, revolving in his mind
The turns of war, and what the fates design'd;
Then from the much-lov'd corse, from which arose
His love of death, and bitterness of woes,
He steals the youth, and, whilst his words afford
A sweet delusion, sheathes unseen the sword.
Such o'er th' unfinish'd field (his comrade dead)
The bull inactive with despair, is led:
Part of the yoke on his bent neck he wears,
And part the swain, the tears fast streaming, bears.
But see! the flow'r of all the Theban band,
Fir'd with their chief's example and command,
Appears, whose prowess Mars might not despise,
Nor Pallas view their skill but with surprise.
Unmov'd Hippomedon the shock withstands,
A shield and spear protended in his hands;
As some high cliff, whose bleak and rugged brow
O'erhangs the deeps, nor fears the surge below,
Nor storms above, but stands by both unmov'd,
Their threats defy'd, their utmost fury prov'd.
E'en worsted Neptune shuns th' unequal war,
And shatter'd ships decline it from afar.
Etcocles first ey'd the godlike man,
And, ere he whirl'd his javelin, thus began:
"Say, are ye not asham'd to war in sight
Of Heav'n, for one whose deeds disgrace the fight?
Is it such merit, such renown to save
A savage monster's relics for the grave;
Lest unlamented, uninterr'd he lie,
And his corse rot beneath a foreign sky?
Dismiss your cares; nor beasts nor birds of prey
Will drink his gore, and bear his flesh away;
Nay, should his corse to Vulcan's rage be doom'd,
The pious flames would leave it unconsum'd."
He ceas'd, and flung a javelin, which the brass
Forbade beyond the second orb to pass.
Then Pheres, and the vig'rous Lycus threw,
Short of its aim the dart of Pheres flew;
While that of vig'rous Lycus lightly graz'd
The nodding helm with sculptur'd forms imblaz'd.
Cleft by the point, the crests asunder fled,
And thro' the casque appear'd his naked head.
Astounded with the stroke, he dares not fly,
Nor on his own defence alone rely;
But wheresoe'er he turns the corse he views,
And standing or advancing, still pursues
That for his object, nor to aim a blow,
Desists to watch the motions of the foe.
Not thus, with all a mother's fury stung,
The lowing heifer guards her first-born young,

77. Stand off, ye warriors] This action, which proves the great courage of Polynices, has been censured in Achilles, as a mark of the utmost rashness and fool-hardiness; yet it is remarkable, that Virgil and Milton, as well as our author, have imitated it from Homer.

At pius Æneas dextram tendebat inermem
Nudato capite, atque suos clamore vocabat.
Quo ruitis? quæve ista repens discordia surgit!
O cohibete iras: ictum jam fœdus, et omnes
Compositæ leges, mihi jus concurrere soli;
Me sinite atque auferte metus.——
Æneid, L. 12.

115. Such o'er th' unfinish'd] The hint of this beautiful simile was taken from one in the 13th book of Homer's Iliad:

Ἀλλ' ὥς τ' ἐν νειῷ βόε οἴνοπε πηκτὸν ἄροτρον
Ἶσον θυμὸν ἔχοντε τιταίνετον, ἀμφὶ δ' ἄρα σφιν
Πρυμνοῖσιν κεράεσσι πολὺς ἀνακηκίει ἱδρώς,
Τὼ μὲν τε ζυγὸν οἶον ἐΰξοον ἀμφὶς ἐέργει
Ἱεμένω κατὰ ὦλκα, τέμνει δέ τε τέλσον ἀρούρης. V. 706.

121. Whose prowess Mars might not despise] This distinction of skill and prowess cannot appear superfluous to any one who considers, that valour tempered with prudence was the characteristical property of Pallas, and that mere brutal courage only was attributed to Mars.

125. As some high cliff] Virgil and Tasso have two comparisons upon this subject.

Ille, velut pelagi rupes immota, resistit:
Ut pelagi rupes, magno veniente fragore,
Quæ sese multis circum latrantibus undis,
Mole tenet: scopuli nequicquam et spumea circum
Saxa fremunt, laterique illisa refunditur alga.
Æn. 7. v. 586.

Ma come alle procelle esposto monte,
Che percosso dai flutti al mar sovraste,
Sostien firme in se stesso i tuoni, e l'onte
Del ciel irato, e i venti, e l'onde vaste:

The repetition of Pelagi rupes adds greatly to the merit of Virgil's: Tasso's is too confined to admit of any heightening circumstances, and our author's is spoiled by that unlucky pathos at the close.

157. Not thus, with all a mother's] This description of the contest for the body of Tydeus is imitated from that over the body of Patroclus in the 17th book of the Iliad, though diversified with many additional circumstances: and this

When the gaunt wolf her straw-built fortress storms;
A circle, wheeling, with her horns she forms,
And dauntless foams, not mindful of her sex,
With more than female rage the war expects.
At length the cloud of flying javelins o'er,
The weapons to their owners they restore.
First Sicyonian Alcon lent his aid,
And with him brought from Pisan Ida's shade
A troop of youths.—On these the chief relies,
And hurls a beam against his enemies.
Swift as a shaft the ruin wings its way
Across the field, nor knowing of delay,
A passage through the shield of Mopsus broke,
And fell'd Polites with a sudden stroke.
At Cydon and Phalanthus then he threw,
And Eryx, wounded through his helmet, slew,
Whilst in the search of weapons back he turn'd,
Nor fearing death, with hopes of conquest burn'd:
As quiv'ring in his jaws the lance he views,
In death's last anguish the tough wood he chews,
While mix'd with murmurs, gush'd the purple spring,
And on the point his teeth all loosen'd ring.
Leonteus, hid behind his social band,
Forth from the rank advanc'd his trembling hand,
And seizing by the hair, in quest of prey,
Essay'd to draw the warrior's corse away.
Hippomedon the dastard's aim descries,
And though from ev'ry quarter dangers rise,
Sheer from his arm the guilty hand divides
With his keen blade, and thus insulting chides.
" Be this thy punishmeut, vile wretch, and know,
'Tis Tydeus, Tydeus gives the wrathful blow:
Henceforth the relics of the dead revere,
And the revenge of breathless heroes fear."
Thrice did the Thebans bear away the slain,
And thrice the Grecian phalanx bid regain.
As in a storm on the Sicilian main,
An anxious vessel wanders (whilst in vain
The pilot struggles with the driving wind)
And measures back the space she left behind.
Nor then, repuls'd by countless enemies,
Hippomedon had quitted his emprize,
Tho' their loud-thund'ring engines interpos'd,
The total force of Thebes had with him clos'd,
And cover'd with join'd shields their banded pow'rs,
(A mode of fight the bane of lofty tow'rs)
But the fell fury, mindful of her lord,
And Tydeus' rage detested and abhorr'd,
Invades by stealth the centre of the field,
Transform'd her person, and her garb conceal'd.
Both hosts perceiv'd her, and thro' horse and man
The dewy sweat of sudden horrour ran:
Though her stern face relax'd into a smile,
Halys she shows, to carry on the guile.
The snakes desist to hiss at her command;
Nor scourge, nor torch obscene was in her hand.
Array'd in arms, and bland in voice and look,
Besides Hippomedon her stand she took;
Yet, while her artful tale the warrior heard,
He fear'd her looks, and wonder'd why he fear'd.
To whom, dissolv'd in tears, the fury said:
" Illustrious hero, vain is all thine aid
To guard the bodies scatter'd on the plain,
(But, are we anxious for th' unburied slain?)
Behold, encompass'd by a barb'rous throng,
The great, the good Adrastus dragg'd along!
In preference to all the Grecian band
On thee he calls, and beckons with his hand.
I saw him fall (a scene scarce to be borne)
The crown from off his hoary temples torn.
Not far from hence he toils.—Direct thine eyes,
Where thick in air the clouds of dust arise."
Pond'ring at this a while the warrior stands,
And weighs his fears, the fury reprimands.
" Why dost thou hesitate? Say, do we go,
Or yield the dead and living to the foe?"
He leaves the wretched office to his friends,
And, to relieve the king, his progress bends;
Yet oft reverts his eyes towards the slain,
Prepar'd, whene'er recall'd, to turn again.
He blindly follow'd where the fury led,
And here and there his course erroneous sped,
Till, casting back her shield, she wing'd her flight,
Burst by the snakes, her casque admits the light.
The clouds dispersing, he beholds from far
Adrastus safe and fearless in his car.
The Thebans the contested corse possess,
And notify with clamours their success:
Their shouts victorious dwell upon their ears,
And strike the Grecians' souls with grief and fears.
See Tydeus, (thus all-potent fate decreed)
Dragg'd to and fro across the hostile mead!
Tydeus, whom not the mightiest chief withstood;
But often as the Thebans he pursu'd,
A passage open to his progress lay,
Whether on foot or horse he took his way.
No rest their arms or wearied hands obtain,
Employ'd to wreak their vengeance on the slain.
Securely now they pierce his clay-cold face,
And the great dead with wounds unfelt disgrace.

elegant comparison is paraphrased from one in the beginning of the above-mentioned book:

Οὐδ' ἔλαθ' Ἀτρέος υἱὸν ἀρηΐφιλον Μενέλαον
Πάτροκλος Τρώεσσι δαμεὶς ἐν δηϊοτῆτι·
Βῆ δὲ διὰ προμάχων κεκορυθμένος αἴθοπι χαλκῷ·
Ἀμφὶ δ' ἄρ' αὐτῷ βαῖν', ὥς τις περὶ πόρτακι μήτηρ
Πρωτοτόκος κινυρὴ, οὐ πρὶν εἰδυῖα τόκοιο·
Ὣς περὶ Πατρόκλῳ βαῖνε ξανθὸς Μενέλαος.

190. 'Tis Tydeus, Tydeus gives the wrathful]

———Pallas te hoc vulnere, Pallas
Immolat, et pœnam scelerato ex sanguine sumit.

193. Thrice did the Thebans] Statius in this passage had an eye to the following lines in the Iliad:

Τρὶς μὲν μιν μετόπισθε ποδῶν λάβε φαίδιμος Ἕκτωρ,
Ἑλκέμεναι μεμαὼς, μέγα δὲ Τρώεσσιν ὁμόκλα.
Τρὶς δὲ δύ' Αἴαντες θοῦριν ἐπιειμένοι ἀλκὴν,
Νεκροῦ ἀπεστυφέλιξαν·

205. But the fell fury] This piece of machinery is very well conducted, and the description of Tisiphone full of that sublime imagery, which constitutes the chief beauty of heroic poesy: the gods, goddesses, and other supernatural deities, very often are introduced in this manner, and in particular there is one instance of it in the 13th book of the Iliad, where Neptune, in the form of Chalchas, inspirits the two Ajaxes to continue the battle; from whence, I presume, this was taken.

257. Securely now] The unfortunate Hector meets with the same ungenerous treatment from the Grecians. Homer's Iliad, lib. 22. ver. 369.

———Ἄλλοι δὲ περίδραμον υἷες Ἀχαιῶν,
Οἳ καὶ θηήσαντο φυὴν, καὶ εἶδος ἀγητὸν
Ἕκτορος· οὐδ' ἄρα οἵ τις ἀνουτητί γε παρέστη·

Promiscuous here the brave and tim'rous stood,
Deeming their hands ennobled with his blood,
And to their wives and tender infants show
The weapons, stain'd with carnage of the foe.
Thus when, with force combin'd, the Lybian swains
Have quash'd the stern dispeopler of the plains,
Thro' dread of whom each night the folds were barr'd,
And the sad shepherds form'd a watchful guard,
The fields exult, with shouts the hinds arise,
They pluck his mane, and gaze with wond'ring eyes;
And, while his hideous yawn and bulk engage
Their notice, call to mind his living rage,
Whether upon some rustic's wall he's view'd,
Or decks an ancient daughter of the wood.
But fierce Hippomedon returns again,
And, though he clearly sees, he fights in vain,
For the rap'd body lends his useless aid,
And brandishes aloft his fatal blade.
Scarce he selects his comrades from his foes,
Whilst, unresisted, through the war he goes.
But now the ground, with slipp'ry slaughter dy'd,
Arms, dying warriors, cars without a guide,
And his left thigh, whose wound he would not own,
Or which in time of conflict was unknown,
Retard the chace, and oft his trembling knees
Refuse their aid.—Hopleus at length he sees,
The squire and comrade of th' Ætolian chief:
Who, bath'd in sorrow, and entranc'd with grief,
On his great master's gen'rous courser sate.
The steed unknowing this last act of fate,
Neighs and curvets (his graceful neck depress'd)
And only grieves at th' interval of rest.
Embolden'd now against th' inferior band
Of infantry, sad Hopleus takes in hand
The reins, and strokes the steed that will not own
Another lord, and bear a load unknown.
Then thus accosts him :—"Why, unhappy steed,
Dost thou desert me at my greatest need,
And, mindless of command, refuse to bear?
No longer regal trappings shalt thou wear,
Nor, pamper'd on Ætolia's verdant plain,
In the clear current bathe thy flowing mane.
For what remains, avenge thy master's shade,
At least pursue them; nor, a captive made,
Endure the burden of a foe abhorr'd,
Nor after Tydeus take a foreign lord."
The horse, as sensible of his discourse,
Springs forth resistless as the lightning's force,
Transports him like a torrent o'er the plains,
Nor scorns his equal guidance of the reins.
The centaur thus from Ossa's piny brow
Descends impetuous to the vales below,
Half man, half beast; where'er his course he takes,
The hill, the dale, the grove, the forest shakes.
Collected in one herd, the Theban race
Retires, while headlong he pursues the chase,
And mows them down, ere scarce they feel the wound;
The headless trunks fall backward on the ground.
The vanquish'd warriors now in prospect reach
Their native stream, and press to gain the beach;
Above his wonted swell Ismenos rose,
A certain signal of impending woes.
Here from the labours of the longsome way
Respiring they indulge a short delay.
The waves, astonish'd at th' uncouth alarms,
Roll back, and glitter with the blaze of arms,
They plung'd with half the bank into the tide,
While clouds of dust conceal'd the farther side.
He too leaps fearless from the broken steep,
Accoutred as he was, and tempts the deep,
Tenacious of the reins, while heap'd on high,
The hostile billows thick before him fly.
Beside a poplar, that o'erhangs the flood,
On the green turf his darts conspicuous stood.

263. Thus when, &c.] This comparison is a fine illustration of what the poet has heretofore said of this hero; and here it may not be mal-a-propos to remark, that our author, with a truly becoming spirit, deigns very rarely to tread in the path of his predecessors, and adopt in his works the allusions of others. This the reader must have observed, as I have always confronted him with the original, whenever he does it. Nor are his imitations, like those of Virgil from Homer, a servile copy: a hint is sufficient to him; he only takes the outlines of a picture, and fills them up with masterly traits of his own fancy, which give it an air of originality, and do not less honour to his genius than judgment.

295. Why, unhappy steed] There is something extremely pathetic in this address, and Statius is not singular in making his heroes accost their horses. Hector, in the 8th book of the Iliad, and Achilles in the 19th, makes a formal speech to these animals. The harangue of Mezentius to his courser in the 10th book of the Æneid is in some respects like this before us.

——— Aut hodie victor spolia illa cruenta
Et caput Æneæ referes, Lausique dolorum
Ultor eris mecum; aut, aperit si nulla viam vis,
Occumbes pariter, neque enim, fortissime, credo
Jussa aliena pati, et dominos dignabere Teucros.
V. 862.

309. The centaur] This comparison is imitated from Virgil, Æneid 7.

Ceu duo nubigenæ cùm vertice montis ab alto
Descendunt centauri, Omolen, Othrynque nivalem
Linquentes cursu rapido: dat euntibus ingens
Sylva locum, et magno cedunt virgulta fragore.

Those who think Virgil had not a strong and sublime imagination (says the editor of Pitt's version) are desired to consider this simile: all the circumstances of it are painted with Homeric spirit and magnificence, particularly,

Dat euntibus ingens
Sylva locum, et magno cedunt virgulta fragore.

To have a just idea of the thing described, says Burmannus, we are to suppose these centaurs half horse and half man, but resembling the horse in the fore-part, and so bearing down with their breast all that stood in their way. Statius Theb. 9. 220. imitates our author in a manner rather bold than just.—Thus far Mr. Warton, from whose sentence in matters of taste there lies no appeal. However, I wish he had specified in what our author has not imitated this comparison justly.

325. They plung'd with half the bank into] This battle in the river Ismenos is copied from that of Homer in the 21st Iliad; and I doubt not, but, after an attentive comparison, the reader will find it diversified with equally striking circumstances, and adorned with all that variety of imagery, which has been so much admired in the original.

Dispirited with fear, and scarce alive,
They cast away their arms and basely dive,
Their helms unlac'd, beneath the whelming surge,
Nor while their breath permits, again emerge:
While some by swimming hope the shore to gain,
But, cumber'd by their armour, hope in vain;
The radiant belts around their middles thrown,
And wetted breastplates help to weigh them down.
As when in ocean the sky-tinctur'd race
Of fishes spy some dolphin on the chase,
Whose spouting gills, and storm-exciting tail
Upturns the sands, so much their fears prevail
That in huge shoals they seek their watry caves,
Mix with the weeds, or lurk beneath the waves;
Nor from the deeps emerge, till far away
He swims, to make some well mann'd ship his prey:
Thus the fierce hero drives the scatter'd trains,
And in mid-water moderates the reins,
And grasps his arms: he still maintains his seat,
And buoys his steed up, rowing with his feet,
Whose hoof accustom'd only to the land,
Slides to and fro, and seeks the firmer sand.
Chromis slew Ion, Antiphus lays dead
Chromis, and Antiphus by Hypseus bled.
Then o'er Astiages black death impends,
And Linus, who, the river pass'd, ascends
The bank; but fate forbidding him to land,
He tumbles back beneath great Hypseus' hand.
With equal rage the Greek and Theban burn,
From that same stream ne'er destin'd to return.
At both the river casts a fearful view,
While both to crimson change its sable hue.
Now mangled skulls and members of the slain,
Light helmets which the floating crests sustain,
Darts, bows unbent, and shields of ductile gold
Adown the bellowing current glitt'ring roll'd.
With wand'ring arms the surface is o'erspread,
The bottom with the corses of the dead:
There warriors struggling in the pangs of death,
The stream oppos'd drives back their issuing breath.
Whilst, borne away by the resistless flood,
Young Agrius seiz'd a lowly elm that stood
On the green bank (his slidd'ring steps to stay)
The stern Menœceus lops his arms away.
Supine he tumbles: the shock'd tree surveys
His hands, still clenching its expanded sprays.
The spear of Hypseus hapless Sages found:
The hero sinks, deform'd with many a wound,
Whilst for his body blood alone returns.
His brother to regain, Agenor burns,
Ill-fated chief! and from the steepy strand
Leap'd headlong down, and grasp'd him in his hand;
But with the stream imbib'd more heavy grown,
The wounded Sages sinks Agenor down,
Who from the deeps might have emerg'd again,
But love detain'd him there, his brother slain.
Whilst rising Chaletus attempts a wound,
By circling eddies in the gulph profound
He sinks absorb'd: the gath'ring billows rise
Above his head, till all conceal'd he lies.
No more his hand is seen, his sword beneath
The depth descends, divided from the sheath.
In various shapes, and countless forms appear
Ruin and death.—A Mycalesian spear
Agyrtes strikes: in vain he looks behind,
The latent owner of the dart to find;
But hurried onward by the rapid flood,
The flying lance drank deeply of his blood.
The courser next of Caledonian strain
(His shoulders pierc'd) stung with the deathful [pain,
Rears up, and, resting on his feet behind,
With hoofs uplifted paws the yielding wind.
Firm'd as he was against the watry force,
The hero pities his expiring horse,
And, whilst deep groans burst from his heaving [heart,
Resigns the reins and then extracts the dart.
Safer in gait and aim, the chief renews
On foot the conflict, and the foe pursues.
To Nomius first, his conquest he extends,
On Mimas and Licetas next descends
His blade: then Lichas of Thisbæan strain,
And young Thespiades, a twin, was slain.
To rash Penemus then he cries:—"Yet live,
And thy sad brother's helpless fate survive:

341. As when in ocean] The poet, judiciously varying the subject of his similes with the element, compares Hippomedon pursuing the Thebans in the river Ismenos, to a dolphin in chase of the lesser fry. The reader may see the materials, on which our author worked, by perusing the following lines of Homer; but what he has drawn up in a simple unadorned manner, his copier has enriched with all the flowers of language and luxuriancy of description.

Ὡς δ' ὑπὸ δελφῖνος μεγακήτεος ἰχθύες ἄλλοι
Φεύγοντες, πιμπλᾶσι μυχοὺς λιμένος εὐόρμου
Δειδιότες· μάλα γάρ τε κατεσθίει ὅν κε λάβῃσιν.

Il. b. 21.

382. His brother to regain] Of all the instances of brotherly love and friendship, I think this is at once the most strong and delicate. It is one of that kind of incidents, which, whilst they take off from and lessen the horrours of war, plunge us into the depth of distress, and call forth that exquisite sensibility, which is an ornament to our nature, and the greatest proof of a good and generous heart. Neither will those think this action merely poetical, who have read the epitaph on the two Lytteltons in Magdalen College chapel, Oxon; one of whom slipping into the water, his brother jumped in, and was drowned with him. Neither Homer, Virgil, nor any other author presents us with an anecdote of their warriors equally beautiful.

413. Of Thisbæan strain] Though I have not translated the epithets annexed to Nomius, Mimas, Lycetus, and other doughty heroes, as they convey no particular idea, yet I could not pass over that of Thisbæan, which belongs to Lichas, after the strenuous endeavours of the learned commentator Gronovius to settle it thus. I shall transcribe his conjectures as well for the entertainment of my readers, as a sanction to my adopting this particular epithet in my version.

"In most of the MSS. it is Thæbeumque Lichan. Some will have it to be Phœbeumque or Phœleumque: but the adjective Thebæus for Thebanus is new and too much a Grecism. I have found at length in one book, Thisbæumque, and that is the true reading. In this very book one is killed by Parthænopeus, quem candida Thisbe miserat. You have in the 2d Iliad, in the catalogue of the Bœotians, πολυτρήρωνα τε Θίσβην. Ovid 2 Met. Quæ nunc Thisbæas agitat mutata columbas."

To the dire walls of Thebes depart alone,
To thy sad parents henceforth better known.
'Tis well, ye gods, that with her bloody hand
Bellona chang'd the combat from the land
To this same river, since the timid throng
Is by their own Ismenos dragg'd along.
Nor Tydeus' shade shall wail around your fire,
Debarr'd of what his country's rites require,
But earth resolve him to his pristine state;
While you shall prove a far more rig'rous fate,
The fishes' prey."—Such taunts he deals around,
And with harsh words embitters ev'ry wound.
Now at the foe the floating darts he throws,
Then with his falchion aims wide slaught'ring blows.
Theron, a comrade of the sylvan maid,
And rustic Gyas felt his thrilling blade:
Erginus, skill'd in naval arts he slew,
Herses, who ne'er the rites of tonsure knew,
And Cretheus, bold advent'rer on the main,
Who in the depth of winter's dreary reign,
Had often past Eubœa's highest cliff,
The dread Caphareus, in a slender skiff.
What cannot fate achieve?—transfix'd his breast,
On waves he floats, a terrour to the rest.
While gay Pharsalus o'er the liquid plain
Guides his high car, to seek his social train,
A Doric javelin, hissing from afar,
Precipitates the vaunter from his car.
Th' encumb'ring juncture of the chariot-beam
Immers'd the steeds beneath the rapid stream.
Ye learned Nine! who make such themes your care,
Indulge my thirst of knowledge, and declare,
What watry toils the Grecian prince engag'd,
And why in obvious arms Ismenos rag'd?
'Tis yours to vindicate the voice of fame,
And trace it to the source from whence it came.
Crenæus (as preceding bards have sung)
From fair Ismenis, and a satyr sprung,
With youthful spirits flush'd, and vig'rous blood,
Rejoic'd to war in his maternal flood.
The bank his cradle, there he first drew breath,
And there, the bank his grave, he found his death.
Presuming, that the furies here employ
Their arts in vain, with more than wonted joy,
He passes now the flatt'ring river o'er,
And fords alternately from shore to shore.
If down, or cross the stream he takes his way,
The waves assist him; nor his progress stay,
When obvious to the driving tide he goes;
But back with him th' obsequious current flows.
Not with more care the circling deeps defend
The body of their Anthedonian friend:
Thus Triton labours to compose the main,
When to his mother's kind embrace again
Palæmon hastes, and as he moves along,
Strikes the slow dolphin with his sounding thong.
Array'd in golden panoply, he fought,
The Theban story on his target wrought.
Here (while no fears disturb her tender breast)
Fair to the view the Tyrian damsel press'd
The bull's white back: no more her fingers hold
His beauteous horns; in curling billows roll'd,
The sportive sea her feet, exulting, laves,
You'd think the lover swims and cuts the waves.
The water firms our faith, nor does the stream
Of colour diff'rent from main ocean seem.
Now at Hippomedon he boldly aims
His darts, and with exulting voice exclaims:
"No poisons of Lernæan rankness stain
Our riv'lets, nor Herculean serpents drain.
This violated stream (as thou shalt prove)
Is doubly sacred to the pow'rs above."
Without reply the chief against him goes,
Whilst in his offspring's aid the river rose,
And check'd his hand, which yet discharg'd a wound;
The piercing lance life's warm recesses found.
The daring mischief terrified the flood,
And streams of grief distill'd from either wood;
Each hollow bank with deeper murmurs rung,
While the last sound, that linger'd on his tongue,
Was "Mother, mother."—Here he ceas'd: the rest
The whelming surge with hideous roar suppress.
Ismenis, compass'd with her nymphs around,
Springs from her cavern with a furious bound,
Her hair dishevell'd, rends her sea-green vest,
And mars with frequent stripes her face and breast.

418. To thy sad parents henceforth better known] The poet here, though somewhat obscurely, hints at the following verses of Virgil and Lucan, who imitated him.

Daucia Laride, Thymberque simillima proles,
Indiscreta suis gratusque parentibus error,
At nunc dura dedit vobis discrimina Pallas.
Æneid 10.

Stant gemini fratres, fecundæ gloria matris,
Quos eadem variis genuerunt viscera fatis:
Discrevit mors sæva viros: unumque relictum
Agnorunt miseri, sublato errore, parentes.
Pharsalia lib. 3.

447. Ye learned nine] The poet's stopping abruptly in his relation, and breaking out in this solemn address to the Muses, alarms the reader, and greatly raises his attention: but as I have spoken so openly and so copiously of the nature and reason of these extraordinary invocations, I shall take no farther notice of them. See the note on the 41st and 935th verses of the 4th book.

453. Crenæus] The motive of Ismenos's rage against Hippomedon was the same as that of Xanthus's against Achilles: the former slew Crenæus, and the latter Asteropœus, who were both favourites of the two river gods abovementioned.

475. Here (while no fears] I cannot help thinking with the editor of Pitt's Virgil, that Statius has indulged his fancy too much in describing shields of this sort; and here by the way, that gentleman observes, that our author's genius seems to be particularly suited to such kinds of description.

489. Without reply] This silence is more expressive of true valour, and more consistent with the real character of a hero than the most bitter and satyrical retort could have been. A brave man is always more ready to justify himself by deeds than words. Thus the great Hector, when accused of cowardice by Sarpedon, does not stay to make any answer, but rushes among his enemies to give the accuser ocular demonstration of his courage, and make him ashamed of his unjust imputation.

Soon as above the waves she lifts her eyes,
Her son she calls with unavailing cries:
One token of his death is seen alone,
The shield, too well by his sad parent known.
Far off he lies, where, bellowing down the steep,
Ismenos disembogues into the deep
His streams.—Thus the deserted halcyon groans,
And her wet dome, and floating nest bemoans,
When the relentless south, and envious flood
Have borne away to sea her feather'd brood.
Again the childless matron dives, and hides
Her well-turn'd limbs beneath the circling tides;
Thro' many a liquid path she takes her way,
Which far beneath the glassy surface lay.
In vain the wretched warrior's corse she seeks,
And in loud plaints her agony bespeaks:
The dreadful river oft obstructs her view,
Its colour darken'd to a sanguine hue.
Headlong on missive weapons now she lights,
And falchions, blunted in repeated fights,
Then handles helms, disguis'd with clefts and gore,
And turns the mangled bodies o'er and o'er.
Nor from the briny deeps did she retire
To bitter Doris, till the pitying choir
Of Nereids saw him floating on the main,
And shov'd him to her longing arms again.
She clasps as still alive, and with her hand
Extends his body on the grassy strand;
With her soft hair his humid visage dries,
And adds these words, a sequel to her cries.
"Say, did Ismenos of immortal line,
And thy great parents this sad lot assign?
Thus dost thou exercise supreme command,
And rule our river?—In a foreign land
More safe thou'dst been, more safe on hostile shores,
And the salt wave of Neptune; that restores
Thy body, all deform'd in cruel fight,
And with thy presence glads and shocks my sight.
Are these thy father's eyes, is this my face,
And did such locks thy grandsire's shoulders grace?
Art thou that youth, who late conspicuous stood,
Pride of the stream, and glory of the wood?
No more attended by my nymphs I move
Queen of the flood, and goddess of the grove.
Where are those frequent suitors, that of late
Were seen to press around thy mother's gate;
And nymphs contending who should serve thee most?
Why should I now inter thee on the coast,
And not in my embrace?—O had I dy'd
O'erwhelm'd amidst the roarings of the tide!
Does not such slaughter, O thrice rigid sire!
With pity and with shame thy breast inspire?
What lake, in this thy daughter's dire distress,
Conceals thee thus, whose deep and dark recess
Nor thy now breathless grandson's early fate,
Nor our complaints and groans can penetrate?
See still Hippomedon thy godhead braves,
And rages, uncontroll'd, amidst thy waves!
Unwonted tremours seize the banks and flood,
And the ting'd billows drink Aonian blood.
Tho' slow in our defence, thy ready aid
Attends the Greeks.—Yet see due honours paid
To my son's last remains; and be it known,
That soon another's death thou shalt bemoan."
These words, accompanied with tears, she spoke,
And stains her gen'rous breast with many a stroke.
The sea-green sisters make her loss their own,
Sigh back her sighs, and echo groan with groan.
Ismenos then lay buried in a cave,
Whence thirsty clouds and gales imbibe the wave,
Whence with fresh juice the show'ry bow is fed,
And golden crops the Tyrian fields o'erspread:
But when he heard from far the doleful sound,
In which the murmurs of the surge were drown'd,
He lifts his neck with shaggy moss o'ergrown,
And temples circled with an icy crown;

509. Thus the deserted halcyon groans] Statius with a propriety rarely to be found (as I have already remarked in the simile of the dolphin) frequently shifts the subject of his comparisons with the element, and descends to the very minutiæ of similitude. A poet of less taste and fancy would have been content to have illustrated the sorrow of Ismenis by that of a swallow, a nightingale, or any other bird for the loss of her young; but our author very judiciously takes in the circumstance of her being a water-nymph, and compares her to the halcyon, which always builds her nest on the banks of the sea, or large rivers.

544. Pride of the stream] Crenæus was prince of the stream by right of his grandfather Ismenos, and of the grove by virtue of being the son of the faun or satyr.

545. No more attended] There is a wide difference between the lamentations of Ismenis and other mothers for the loss of their children. She chiefly laments, that all her honours must cease with his death. The prospect of this supersedes all other considerations, and seems to affect her in a more particular manner. In short, she mourns in as womanish a manner as Eve, when Michael denounces her departure from Eden.

Must I thus leave thee, Paradise? thus leave
Thee, native soil, those happy walks and shades,
Fit haunt of Gods? where I had hope to spend,
Quiet, though sad, &c. Par. Lost, b. 11. v. 269.

566. Soon another's death thou shalt bemoan] Barthius treats our author's want of thought in this place with great humour. Ismenis (says he) reproaches her father as quite ignorant of the death of his son and others. But when his grandson's fate approached, he opposes his waves to Hippomedon.

——In his offspring's aid the river rose,
And check'd his hand.———

Did Ismenis do this in a dream, or did our truly good author nod over this passage?—The latter I take to have been the case.

570. Sigh back her sighs] After this verse follows a simile which is so very obscure, and consists of such filthy images, that I have ventured to omit it by my friends' advice.

571. Ismenos then] From this line to the speech of Ismenos to Jupiter there runs one continued chain of sublimity and imagery scarce inferior to any thing I have ever read.—The picture of the abode and habit of this water-god is superior to Virgil's description of the Tiber; and that of the river's resistance to Hippomedon is equal at least in point of circumstances and variety to that of Xanthus, in the 21st book of Homer's Iliad, against Achilles.

And rushing on, a full-grown pine o'erturns,
As down the stream he rolls his copious urns.
The woods and lesser brooks his progress eye
With wonder, as he leaves his channel dry,
His stony channel, and with dashing waves
From either bank the slime invet'rate laves.
Sonorous in his course, the river roars,
And foaming, far o'ertops the subject shores;
While from his sea-green beard in many a rill
The lucid drops upon his breast distil.
One nymph alone he meets, who soon makes known
His grandson's fate, and evils soon his own,
Presses his hand, and the fell Grecian shows,
Hippomedon, sole author of his woes.
Suspended in mid-air the wrathful flood
Awhile, with all his waves encircled, stood,
Then shook his horns, with verdant sedge entwin'd;
And thus he vents his turbulence of mind.
" Is this, O ruler of the gods above,
The best reward my services must prove?
Wink'd I for this (thyself our honour'd guest,
At deeds, which friendship, and not fear suppress'd)
As when a borrow'd pair of horns adorn'd
Thy guilty brows, or Phœbe was suborn'd
To lengthen out the night, and (oh! disgrace
To the whole sex, and all the Theban race)
Proud Semele to Juno's rank aspir'd,
And for a dow'r etherial flames requir'd?
Was it so slight a favour to defend
Thy foster'd offspring, and their youth befriend?
For refuge to this stream Tyrintheus came,
And here, O Bacchus, temper'd we thy flame.
Behold! what heaps of carnage choke my stream,
What shiver'd weapons on my surface gleam!
War rages thro' our ford, the billows breathe
Confusion, rout, and death; above, beneath,
Souls wander, recent from their bloody doom,
And hov'ring, spread o'er either bank a gloom.
All votaries invoke my chrystal wave
With holy yellings: 'tis my praise to lave
In the clear stream great Bacchus' sacred horns,
And the soft thyrsus that his head adorns.
In vain I seek the straits.—Not Strymon's flood,
Dire as it seems, is thus deform'd with blood;
Nor foaming Hebrus bears the stain of gore
So deep, when warring Mars invades the shore.
Remember, that the stream which now demands
Jove's timely aid, deserves it at his hands.
Does Bacchus blot his parents from his mind,
Or is Hydaspes more to peace inclin'd?
Nor thou, whom the gay spoils and trophies, torn
From brave Crenæus, hapless boy, adorn,
Shalt pay to Inachus the votive crown,
Or hail with conqu'ring shouts thy native town,
Unless the mortal progeny of earth
I prove, and more than human is thy birth."
Raging he spake, and to the ready wave
A token of his vengeful purpose gave.
First bleak Cithæron from his hoary brows
Pours many a rill of long collected snows;
Asopus then by stealth his wants supplies
With streams, that from his op'ning springs arise.
The scrutinizing god himself explores
Earth's hollow entrails, and recruits his stores
From marshes, pools, and lakes with filth o'erspread;
And lifting to the skies his dropping head,
Exhausts the clouds of moisture, and inhales
The humid vapours lodg'd in show'ry gales.
And now o'er both his banks Ismenos rose,
And all around a foamy deluge throws.
Hippomedon, who fording half the tide,
Its greatest depth and utmost rage had try'd,
Unbath'd his shoulders, wonders as he sees
The flood invading them by quick degrees.
Swelling on either side, the billows form
A watry bulwark: as when some huge storm
Drains the Plëiades, in winter's reign,
And dashes black Orion on the main.
Thus the Theumesian stream the warrior toss'd
On its salt surface: on his shield imboss'd
He breaks his fury: o'er its orb he boils
With black'ning foam, and all resistance foils.
Though oft repuls'd, in greater troops again
The surges mount. The hero toils in vain;
For not content with his own liquid force,
The rapid current gathers in its course
Beams, stones torn from the bottom, shrubs that grow
On the green verge, and whirls them at the foe.
Unequal hangs the fight: more fierce he raves,
As undismay'd the chief his anger braves:
For neither does he turn his back, or yield
To any threats; but bending to the field
His steps, still boldly meets the rushing tides,
And, with his shield oppos'd, the flood divides.
His feet upheld, still with the moving ground
He moves, the slipp'ry pebbles floating round,
And struggles, while, his knees relax'd with toil,
Far from beneath him slides the slimy soil.
" Ismenos, say," th' upbraiding warrior cries,
" From whence these sudden gusts of passion rise?
Whence hast thou drawn this strength? Some mightier friend
Than Bacchus must thy desp'rate cause defend:
For, till the present war, thy peaceful flood
Was never crimson'd but with female blood,
When pipes unequal at your orgies roar,
And madd'ning matrons stain your rites with gore."
He said: and now the pow'r himself appears,
And o'er the waves his head spontaneous rears.
A load of filth to his marr'd visage clung,
Mute was his rage, and silent was his tongue.
Now face to face the god and hero stood,
When, rising to the stroke, the furious flood
Impell'd a leafless oak: four times unmov'd
The dire assault and thund'ring shock he prov'd:
At length, his shield struck down, the chief withdrew
By tardy steps, the billows thick pursue,
Back'd by their leader: while with hissing sound,
A show'r of darts and stones is rain'd around,
And, rang'd along the beach, his Theban foes
His landing with protended arms oppose.
What can he do, besieg'd with waves and spears?
Nor hope of flight, nor glorious death appears.
Just on the brink ('twas doubtful if it stood
Fix'd on the land, or rooted in the flood)

621. Not Strymon's flood] Strymon and Hebrus are two rivers of Thrace: the one famous for the battles between the pygmies and cranes, and the other for those of Mars.

701. Just on the brink] This beautiful incident is borrowed from the 21st book of the Iliad, but diversified and enlarged with many additional circumstances.

An ash with far-projecting branches grew,
And o'er the stream a shade wide-spreading threw.
Hither he sped his course in quest of aid,
(For how could he the guarded beach invade?)
And snatch'd a branch, his slidd'ring steps to stay,
But, faithless to his grasp, the tree gives way,
Beneath his dragging weight uprooted falls,
An earthy fragment in the water hales,
Torn from the border, and from side to side
In length extended, bridges the rough tide.
Here meet the rushing waves; the settling mud
Sinks to the bottom.—Now the circling flood
Invades the neck and shoulders of the chief:
At length, oppress'd with more than vulgar grief,
He cries:—"O Mars, shall I resign my breath
In this vile river? Such inglorious death
Attends the swain, whom to the neighb'ring deeps,
Increas'd by sudden show'rs a torrent sweeps.
Why fell I not beneath the hostile sword?
Argos had then wept o'er my corse restor'd."
Mov'd by these pray'rs at length Saturnia seeks
The courts of Jove, and thus her spouse bespeaks.
"How long, illustrious sire of gods above,
Shall wretched Greece thy studied vengeance prove?
By Pallas hated, Tydeus press'd the plain,
And silent Delphos wails her augur slain.
Say, shall Hippomedon, whose native place
Is Argos, sprung of fam'd Mycenæ's race,
Deserted by the pow'r, whose grace he woo'd,
Glut the fell monsters of the sea with food?
The vanquish'd sure have shar'd the fun'ral rite.
Where are the flames that must succeed the fight
By Theseus kindled?"—He receives her pray'r,
And makes the object of her suit his care, [again
His eyes turn'd back on Thebes.—The stream
Sinks at his nod, and spreads a level plain.
Above the surface now his shoulders rise,
And hope returning sparkles in his eyes.
So, when a tempest rais'd by winds, subsides,
And Neptune's trident calms the ruffled tides,
The rocks lift up their heads to sight long-lost,
And the glad seamen eye the wish'd-for coast.
Ah! what avails it to have gain'd the beach,
Since still he stands within the javelin's reach?
The Tyrian cohorts press on ev'ry side,
No more the mail and shield his body hide;
But the whole man's expos'd to death.—The blood
That long had lain congeal'd beneath the flood,
Now issues copious, thaw'd in open air,
And all his honest wounds again lie bare.
Drain'd of life's juice, relax'd appears each vein,
Nor his chill'd feet his trembling frame sustain.
He drops; as from some mountain's airy crown,
Torn by the winds, a tall oak tumbles down,
Which late was seen with shading boughs to rise,
Its root in earth, its summit in the skies.
Whilst, as a prelude to its fate, its head
Threat'ning it nods, the grove and mountain dread,
Lest falling, it deform the sylvan reign,
And spread a length of ruin on the plain.

——Ὁ δὲ πτελέην ἕλε χερσὶν
Εὐφυέα, μεγάλην, ἡ δ' ἐκ ῥιζων ἐριπῦσα
Κρημνὸν ἅπαντα διῶσεν, ἐπέσχε δὲ καλα ῥέεθρα
Ὄζοισιν πυκινοῖσι, γεφύρωσεν δέ μιν αὐτὸν,
Εἴσω πᾶσ' ἐριπῦς.——

Some of the verses (as Mr. Pope has observed of Homer's) run hoarse, full and sonorous, like the torrent they describe; others, by their broken cadences and sudden stops, image the difficulty, labour and interruption of the hero's march against it. The fall of the tree, the tearing up of the bank, the rushing of the branches in the water, are all put into such words, that almost every letter corresponds in its sound, and echoes to the sense in this particular.

717. O Mars, shall I resign my breath] The behaviour and speech of Hippomedon have so many precedents, that I should not know from what original it is copied, had not the poet himself left a mark of distinction, which is the allusion to the shepherd.

Ὥς μ' ὄφελ' Ἕκτωρ κτεῖναι, ὃς ἐνθάδε τέτραφ' ἄριστος,
Τωκ' ἀγαθὸν μὲν ἔπεφν', ἀγαθὸς δέ κεν ἐξενάριζε·
Νῦν δε με λευγαλέω θανάτω ἑιμαρτο ἁλωναι
Ἐρχθέντ' ἐν μεγαλω ποταμω, ὡς παῖδα συφορβὸν,
Ὅν ῥά τ' ἔναυλος ἀποέρσει χειμῶνι περωντα.

Homer again in his Odyssey, Virgil, and Lucan have all similar passages in their respective works; which circumstance, I think, sufficiently clears up the two former from the imputation of having represented their heroes as cowards. They do not lament, that they must die, but only dislike the mode of death. Drowning, it was thought by the ancients, hindered their bodies from being buried: we must not wonder, therefore, that they abominated it, as they could not be admitted into the number of the blessed, until they had received the funeral rites.—See Palinurus's speech to Æneas in the sixth book of Virgil's Æneid.

741. So, when a tempest] This is a very elegant similitude, and well adapted to the circumstances of the person. Our poet would not, as he had before compared him to a rock for his fortitude, degrade him in his distress by illustrating his situation in a meaner comparison, and therefore compares him to a rock again.

Servatur ad imum
Qualis ab incepto processerit, & sibi constet.

755. As from some mountain's airy crown] Homer, Virgil, and Silius Italicus have all comparisons derived from this subject, which I shall lay before the reader, without anticipating his judgment by any remarks of my own.

——Ὁ δ' ἐν κονίησι χαμαὶ πέσεν αἴγειρος ὣς,
Ἥ ῥά τ' ἐν ἑιαμενῇ ἕλεος μεγάλοιο πεφύκει
Λείη, ἀτὰρ τέ οἱ ὄζοι ἐπ' ἀκροτάτη πεφύασι·
Τὴν μέν θ' ἁρματοπηγὸς ἀνὴρ αἴθωνι σιδήρω,
Ἐξέταμ' ὄφρα ἴτον κάμψη περικαλλεϊ δίφρω,
Ἣ μέν' ἀζομένη κεῖται ποταμοῖο παρ' ὄχθας.
Iliad. lib. 4. v. 482.

Ac veluti in summis antiquam montibus ornum,
Cum ferro accisam crebrisque bipennibus instant
Eruere agricolæ certatim; illa usque minatur,
Et tremefacta comam concusso vertice nutat;
Vulneribus donec paulatim evicta supremum
Ingemuit, traxitque jugis avulsa ruinam.
Æneid, lib. 2. ver. 626.

Ceu Zephyrus quatit antiquos ubi flamine lucos,
Fronte super tremuli vix tota cacuminis hærens
Jactatur, pariter nido luctante volucris.
Procubuit tandem multa devicta securi
Suffugium infelix miseris, & inhospita quercus,
Elisitque virum spatiosa membra ruina.
Bellum Pun. l. 5.

Yet no one durst despoil the chief bereft
Of life: untouch'd his sword and helm were left.
Scarce trusting to their eyes, aloof they stand,
And fear the blade he clenches in his hand.
Hypseus at length their doubts remov'd, withdrew
The casque and his stern face disclos'd to view:
Then boastful thro' the Theban ranks he goes,
And on his sabre's point high-glitt'ring shows
The spoil suspended, and exulting cry'd:
"Behold the conqu'ror of the bloody tide,
And vow'd avenger of great Tydeus dead,
Hippomedon!—how well his schemes have sped!"
Brave Capaneus beheld the glorying chief
From far, but from the foe conceal'd his grief,
And as the brandish'd weapon he survey'd,
Accosts it thus:—"Be present with your aid,
My arm and sword; so ye assist my stroke,
No other deities I will invoke."
This said, elate in thought the warrior glows,
And rushes, self-secure of all his vows.
Now thro' the shield, which strong bull-hides in-fold,
And brazen mail, all rough with scales of gold,
The trembling javelin passes, and arrests
The prince, deep-buried in his gen'rous breasts.
He sinks, as some high tow'r that long hath stood
Bellona's fiercest shocks, at length subdu'd
With oft repeated strokes it thunders down,
And opens to the foe the fenceless town.
Then striding o'er th' expiring chief, he cries:
"The fame of death we grant thee: lift thine eyes,
And mark th' illustrious author of the wound:
Go—vaunt of this in the drear Stygian sound."
The sword and head-piece seiz'd, he takes again
The target, wrested from the Grecian slain,
And placing o'er the corse, says with a groan:
"Receive these hostile trophies with thy own,
And sleep secure, that rescu'd from the foe,
Thy manes shall the rites of burial know.
But while thy solemn fun'rals we prepare,
Accept this earnest of my future care."
Thus long the combat hung in even scales,
And either host alternately prevails:
Mars aids them both, like an impartial lord,
And with commutual wounds the battle gor'd.
In turn they mourn the Greek and Theban chief,
And from each other's sorrows find relief.
Meanwhile, disturbed by visions of the night,
And dreams, * th' Arcadian princess bends her flight
To Ladon's gelid spring, to wash away
Her noxious sleep, before the destin'd day.

* Atalanta, mother of Parthenopæus.

787. As some high tow'r] Our author in this comparison has set the Theban hero in a stronger light than the Grecian.—He illustrates the falling of Hippomedon by that of an oak, but compares Hypseus to a tower, which is more expressive of the character of a valiant leader: a tower being the defence of a city, as a valiant commander is of his army.—This simile though not very long, is paraphrased from the verse of Homer subjoined.

Ἤριπε δ' ὡς ὅτε πύργος ἐνὶ κρατερῇ ὑσμίνῃ.

793. And mark th' illustrious] Æneas closes his address of commiseration to Lausus in much the same boastful manner.

Hoc tamen infelix miseram solabere mortem:
Æneæ magni dextrâ cadis. Æn. 10. line 829.

Loose was her dress, dishevelled was her hair,
And, as the rites required, her feet were bare.
For anxious thoughts and weighty cares opprest
Her mind in sleep, and broke her nightly rest.
Ofttimes the spoils, which, she had sacred made,
Torn from the shrine, or fallen she survey'd:
Ofttimes she fancied, that, expelled the groves,
In tombs and sepulchres unknown she roves,
And that her victor son's return'd again,
Yet only sees his courser, arms and train.
Untouch'd the quivers from her shoulders fall,
And her own effigies, that grac'd the hall,
Was heard to hiss and crackle in the flames:
But the past night the greatest woes proclaims.
'Twas this that fill'd her soul with anxious fears,
And call'd forth all a mother's tender cares.
In fair Arcadia's blissful bow'rs there stood
A noted oak: the nymphs that haunt the wood,
Had vow'd it sacred to their guardian-maid,
And at the rites divine due off'rings paid.
Here she was wont her bow and shafts to place,
And high display the trophies of the chase,
The lion's brindled hide its boughs adorns,
The boar's sharp tusks, and stag's wide-branching horns.
Such honours heap this monarch of the grove,
That scarce the crowded limbs have room to move;
While the refulgent steel destroys the shade,
Dispels the gloom, and lightens all the glade.
As haply from the hills she took her way,
Tir'd with the longsome labours of the day,
And in her hand a bear's grim visage bore,
Yet warm with life, and reeking still with gore,
She spies the foliage strew'd upon the ground,
And the hack'd branches, red with many a wound.
At length a nymph informs her, Bacchus rag'd,
Against the Greeks with all his priests engag'd.
While, dreaming, thus she groans, and beats her breast,
Sleep quits her eyes, and from the couch of rest,
Starting as from a trance, in vain she seeks
The pearly current that bedew'd her cheeks.
Thrice then she bathes her tresses in the stream,
T'avert the mischiefs imag'd in the dream,
Adds magic sounds, impower'd to control
The mother's grief, and cheer her anxious soul,
And hast'ning to the weapon'd virgin's fane,
What time the dew-drops glitter on the plain,
Beholds again with joy the verdant wood,
And the known oak unchang'd, and free from blood.
Now in the hallow'd vestible she stands,
And thus invokes the Pow'r with lifted hands;
"O sylvan queen, whose more than female arms
I bear, not mindful to improve my charms
Like others of my sex, pursue afar
Thy hardy steps, and dare the savage war.
With Amazons I boast an equal name,
Nor do the Colchian dames outshine my fame.
If to no rites of Bacchus I resort,
Nor mix in nightly choirs and wanton sport;
If true to thee, I wield no wreathed dart,
Nor in unseemly actions bear a part,
But though defil'd in Hymen's hateful bed,
Pursue the toils, to which I first was bred,
And to the chase and rural shades inclin'd,
For thee reserve a pure, unwedded mind.
Nor in the dark recesses of the grove
Hid I the token of my vicious love,

878. Hid I the token of my vicious love] The

But op'ning all my guilt, without deceit
Produc'd the boy, and plac'd him at thy feet.
Nor blood degen'rate sallies in his veins;
His early virtue justified my pains:
For, when an infant, he could scarcely go,
He stretch'd his little hands, and lisp'd, 'A bow:'
Him (ah! what om'nous dreams my soul dismay,
And damp my ruffled spirits?) him, I pray,
Who trusting to thy aid (his mother's right)
In youthful folly rushes to the fight,
Restore victorious, or (if I demand
Too much) uninjur'd to his native land.
Here may he toil, and bear thy arms alone:
But O! remove these signs of ills unknown.
In bow'rs Arcadian, why should Bacchus reign,
And Theban gods encroach on thy domain?
Why to myself (but may the watchful throng
Of demons render this construction wrong)
Take I the mischiefs, shadow'd in the oak?
But, if the gods intend this dreaded stroke,
O mild Dictynna, by the mother's throes,
And yon fraternal orb that récent glows,
Transfix me with thy darts, and set me free;
'Tis ease, 'tis mercy to a wretch like me:
And, if a martial death must end his date,
Let him, O let him first bemoan my fate."
Here paus'd the queen, and wept; nor wept alone:
For tears descended from the sculptur'd stone.
While thus she press'd the sacred threshold, bare,
And brush'd the clay-cold altars with her hair;
Abruptly the rough goddess leaves her, flies
O'er Mænalos, high-branching in the skies,
Directs her progress to the Theban town
By a bright, inner path, to all unknown
But deities, and from a point on high
O'er Earth's vast globe extends her boundless eye.
And now near Helicon's inspiring source
She halts awhile (completed half her course)
When through a cloud far-beaming she discern'd
Her brother from th' Aonian war return'd.
Uncouth his visage show'd, disguis'd with grief,
For much he mourn'd the prophet, luckless chief.
More fiercely glow the planets in embrace,
And paint with crimson streaks th' aerial space;
Loud clash the bows, and through the skies around
The quivers echo back the solemn sound.
Apollo took the word, and thus bespeaks:
"Full well I know, my dearest sister seeks
Th' Arcadian youth, who dares beyond his might,
And mixes, fearless, in th' unequal fight.
His mother sues, and would th' immortals give
Assent to save, the warrior long should live.
Myself (it shames me, that I could not aid)
The prophet with his arms and wreaths survey'd,
When, urged by fate, he sunk to deepest Hell,
And look'd at me for succour, as he fell.
Nor could I keep my car, and earth re-join,
Tho' stern, nor worthy more of rites divine.
Thou seest my silent dome, and wailing cave:
This sole reward my pious comrades have.
No more my unavailing help implore;
Heav'n wills, we give the fruitless labour o'er:
His hour draws on, the destinies ordain,
Nor are our oracles believ'd in vain."
Thus, all confus'd, the heav'nly maid reply'd,
In turn: "His want of days then be supply'd
With lasting fame, some recompense bestow,
And add in glory what in life you owe.
Nor shall he 'scape unpunish'd for the deed,
By whom fate dooms the guiltless chief to bleed:
Our raging arrows shall avenge the slain,
And fix the quiv'ring dastard to the plain."
She ceas'd; nor willing to his lips applies
Her vermil cheeks, but to the conflict flies.
Now fiercer burns the fight on either side,
And mutual vengeance swells the purple tide

reader must take notice, that the poet only calls this love vicious, inasmuch as it was a breach of vow; all virgins, who entered into Diana's service, being obliged at their initiation, to make a vow of perpetual virginity.

896. Of demons] I think the word demons in this place a more proper term than gods, as the former, being a subordinate class of deities, were supposed by the ancients to superintend the affairs of mankind in a more particular manner.—In the least deviation from the original I shall always hold it incumbent on me to give my reasons for it.

899. O mild Dictynna] If the reader has any curiosity to know the origin of this name, let him attend to what Lactantius says on this subject.—Briton, a Cretan virgin and daughter of Mars, was consecrated to Diana; and to avoid an attempt made by Minos on her chastity, threw herself into the sea, and was taken up in fishing-nets, which in Greek are called dictua. Soon after this the Cretans were punished by a heavy pestilence, that raged amongst them, and were informed, that they could not remove it but by building a temple to the offended goddess, which they did, and called it Dictynnæ from the fishing-nets.

906. For tears descended from the sculptur'd stone] The poet means the marble statue of Diana: Lucan, speaking of the prognostics, which preceded the civil wars, says:

> The face of grief each marble statue wears,
> And Parian gods and heroes stand in tears.

908. And brush'd] The words in the original are

> ——Gelidas verrentem crinibus aras.

In the former editions it was verentem, which Bernartius has judiciously altered to verrentem, and supported it by the following quotations: Stratæ passim matres, crinibus templa verrentes, veniam irarum cœlestium exposcunt.—Livy, book 3.

Matronæ circa deûm delubra discurrunt, crinibus passis aras verrentes.—Livy, book 26.

Tunc Psyche uberi fletu rigans deæ vestigia, humumque verrens crinibus suis.——Apuleius, book 5.

Matres Italæ pensa manibus abjecerunt, parvos liberos abreptos ad templa traxerunt, ibi ædes sacras passo capillo suo quæque verrebat.—Mamertinus, Panegyrick on Maximian.

953. Now fiercer burns the fight] There is great strength of imagery and expression in these, and the following lines; but as I am conscious my translation will not make my assertion good, I shall transcribe the author's own words: and in this, as well as in all other places, where I pass encomiums, I hope the reader will always understand them as spoken of the original.

For their lost leaders.—Here the pensive band
Of Hypseus mourns, depriv'd of his command;
There brave Hippomedon's stout warriors glow,
Nor screen their bosoms from the menac'd blow.
Fiercely they give, serenely take a wound,
Strive hard to gain but never quit their ground.
In close array they move, and to their foes
The seat of honour, not of shame expose,
When swift Latonia, gliding thro' the skies,
On Dirce's summit stands with watchful eyes.
Beneath her step the waving forests nod,
And quaking mountains own the present god;
As when at fruitful Niobe she bent
Her shafts, and all her well-stor'd quiver spent.
The youthful warrior in the centre stood,
And gaz'd, exulting, o'er the scene of blood.
A hunting steed transports him o'er the plains,
New to the fight, and guidance of the reins;
A tiger's motley hide his back o'erspread,
And beat with gilded claws, as on he sped.
His neck was musculous, his mane, confin'd
In twisted ringlets, mocks the fanning wind.
The poitrel with his snow-white teeth he champ'd,
And with black spots his dappled chest was stamp'd.
The rider too in vests embroider'd shone,
(These Atalanta wrought, and these alone)
A costly robe o'er the gay tunic lies,
That twice had drank the noblest Tyrian dyes,
Bound in a chain, with radiant jaspers strung:
The target from his steed's left shoulder hung.
His weighty sword, girt to his tender side,
Blaz'd at each motion with a martial pride.
A golden clasp the circling belt confin'd.
The youth exults, as in the passing wind
He hears the sheath, the quiver that depends,
And the chain's clank, that from the helm descends.

At pugna ereptis major crudescit utrimque
Regibus, alternosque ciet vindicta Furores.
Hypseos hinc turmæ, desolatumque magistro
Agmen, at hinc gravius fremit Hippomedontis adempti
Orba cohors. Præbent obnixi pectora ferro:
Idem ardor rabidis externum haurire cruorem,
Ac fudisse suum: nec se vestigia mutant.
Stat cuneo defixa acies, hostique cruento
Dant animas, et terga negant.——

966. The present god] Availing myself of the precedent, which Mr. Pope has given me, I have not scrupled to use the word god for goddess in my version. The Greeks apply Θεὸς indiscriminately for both genders. Our poet himself in his fourth book, speaking of Diana, says,

Nec caret umbra Deo.

And the chaste and correct Virgil in the second book of his Æneid says;

Descendo, ac ducente Deo, flammam inter et hostes
Expedior.————

969. The youthful warrior] Statius, more in the Ovidian than in the Virgilian taste, has given full reins to his fancy in describing the horse, habit, and person of this juvenile adventurer, like the ancient priests, who before a sacrifice, tricked out their victims with flowers, garlands, and such like ornaments.

One while he shakes his casque with gems inchas'd,
And nodding crest with various plumage grac'd;
But, when his head is heated, throws for air
His helm aside, and leaves his visage bare.
More charming then his glossy ringlets shine,
His vivid eyes, that scatter'd rays divine,
And rosy cheeks, o'er which the down began
But faintly to appear, and promise man.
Nor does he plume himself with beauty's praise;
But strives to lessen it by various ways,
And knits his brows, yet anger clothes his face
With majesty, and heightens ev'ry grace.
The Thebans, mindful of their children, yield
Their ground thro' pity, nor dispute the field
With the boy-warrior: he their flight pursues
With darts, and tempts the fray, which they refuse.
The Tyrian damsels, who behold the fight
From high Teumesus, feast their greedy sight
On his fair features, seen thro' the disguise
Of war, and vent their flame in secret sighs.
Grief touch'd Diana's bosom, as she ey'd
The too rash youth. "Ah! how can I" (she cry'd,
While copious ran the pearly stream of woe)
"Ward off, or e'en delay th' impending blow?
Spontaneous hast thou sought then, cruel boy,
And are the perils of the fight thy joy?
Alas! thy early courage is thy bane,
And glory spurs thee to the deathful plain.
Scarce till of late thro' the Mænalian grove,
Without a guide, securely could'st thou rove;
Nor was it safe to pierce the woodland shade
And haunts of beasts, without thy mother's aid,
Whose sylvan arms, the quiver, shafts, and bow,
Thy shoulders scarce suffic'd to bear till now.
To our deaf altars, weeping, she repairs,
And wearies Heav'n with unavailing pray'rs;
Whilst in the toils of fight thou dost rejoice,
And listen, pleas'd, to the shrill clarion's voice.
Go then, secure of an immortal crown,
And to thy mother doom'd to die alone."
She ceas'd, and, his victorious fame to raise
And crown his exit with distinguish'd praise,
Rush'd thro' the lines (a dusky veil of clouds
From mortal eyes the bashful goddess shrowds)
And stole the faithless arrows that he bore,
Recruiting th' emptied quiver with a store
Of ointed shafts: of these none flies in vain,
Nor touches, innocent of blood, the plain.
She sprinkles then the warrior and his horse
With dews ambrosial, lest his wounded corse

1039. She sprinkles then the warrior] This fiction is imitated from Homer's Iliad, book the 6th, where Apollo discharges the same kind office to Sarpedon:

——Οὐδ' ἄρα πατρὸς ἀνηκούστησεν Απόλλων.
Βῆ δὲ κατ' 'Ιδαίων ὀρέων ἐς φύλοπιν αἰνην,
Αὐτίκα δ' ἐκ βελέων Σαρπηδόνα δῖον ἀείρας
Πολλὸν ἄπο προφέρων λοῦσεν ποταμοῖο ῥοῆσι,
Χρῖσεν τ' ἀμβροσίη.————

And again in the 19th:

Πατρόκλω δ' αὖτ' ἀμβροσίην καὶ νέκταρ ἐρυθρὸν
Στάξε κατὰ ῥινῶν, ἵνα οἱ χρὼς ἔμπεδος εἴη.

Virgil has also imitated it:

——Spargitque salubres
Ambrosiæ succos, et odoriferam panaceam.

Should be abus'd before he yields his breath;
And, as a charm to break the pangs of death,
Adds holy murmurs, and mysterious songs,
Such as in secret caves the Colchian throngs
She teaches, at the season of repose,
And shows each noxious plant and herb that grows.
More furious now he deals his shafts around,
To reason deaf; his wrath no limits bound;
But, mindless of his country, self, and friends,
The fated darts without reserve he sends.
The youthful lion thus, whose tender age
Was nurs'd with blood, the source of savage rage,
By his Gætulian dam, when he surveys
The mane, that o'er his neck redundant plays,
And his sharp claws, protended for the fight,
He springs forth, conscious of his nat'ral right
From his loath'd den, and with a sour disdain
Of proffer'd food, explores his new domain.
Say, valiant youth, who press'd their native mead,
By thy Parrhasian bow to death decreed?
Choræbus of Tanagra spurn'd the field
The first. Between the margin of the shield
And helm, the dart a narrow passage found:
His jaws are crimson'd with the gushing wound,
And o'er his face the sacred venom glows,
Wide-spreading.—At Eurytion then he throws
A triple-pointed shaft: the weapon flies,
And deep in his left eye-ball buried lies.
The dart extracted from the wound by force,
Against the foe Eurytion bends his course;
But ah! what cannot heav'nly shafts?—again
An arrow speeds, unerring, o'er the plain,
And doubles his distress: yet still the foe
He chas'd, as far as memory could go;
Then fell, and Ida crush'd, who near him stood:
Here, midst the rage of war and scene of blood,
In thick short sobs he gasps away his breath,
Devoting friends and foes alike to death.
The sons of Abas next his fury prove;
Cydon, subservient to th' incestuous love

1051. The youthful lion] This simile is a strong proof of the fruitfulness of the poet's imagination, and judicious taste. It is bold with correctness, natural without being vulgar, and copious without prolixity: and what is still adding to its merit is, that it is an original.

1059. Say, valiant youth] This beautiful interrogation is imitated from the 16th book of the Iliad.

> Ἔνθα τίνα πρωτον, τίνα δ' ὕςατον ἐξενάριξας
> Πατρόκλεις, ὅτε δή σε θεοὶ θάνατόν δε καλεσσαν.

Virgil has also copied it.

> Quem telo primum, quem postremum, aspera virgo,
> Dejicis? aut quot humi morientia corpora fundis?

I shall transcribe Mr. Pope's judicious observations on the above-cited passage in Homer, as they are equally applicable to our author's.—The poet in a very moving and solemn way turns his discourse to Patroclus. He does not accost his Muse, as it is usual with him to do, but inquires of the hero himself who was the first, and who the last, who fell by his hand? This address distinguishes and signalizes Patroclus, (to whom Homer uses it more frequently, than I remember on any other occasion) as if he was some genius or divine being, and at the same time it is very pathetical, and apt to move our compassion.

Of his sad sister, and fair Argus fam'd
For his sleek hair.—Pierc'd by a lance well-aim'd,
Young Cydon's parts obscene lie bare to view;
A dart oblique thro' t'other's temples flew.
In one the steel, in one the feather's seen, [green.
The blood flows down from both, and stains the
On all alike th' impartial darts descend.
His peerless charms gay Lamus ill defend;
Young Æolus fills an untimely grave:
Nor could his mitred honours Lygdus save.
Fair Lamus mourns his face: a lance impales
The groin of Lygdus: Æolus bewails
His snowy brows.—The first unhappy swain
Eubœa own'd: on Thisbe's rocky plain
The second dwelt: the third Amyclæ bore,
Yet never, never shall behold him more.
Such is his art, no missile flies in vain,
And such their force, that all they wound, are slain.
His hand ne'er rests, but shaft to shaft succeeds,
And the long hiss runs echoing o'er the meads.
'Twas almost past belief, a single bow,
And one weak hand could work such mighty woe.
Where least the foe suspects, his darts he sends;
And oft, in act to shoot, his arms extends,
Then sudden quits the mark: when they draw
He flies, and turning lets his arrows fly. [nigh,
To vengeance now the sons of Cadmus rise,
Wrath in their breasts, amazement in their eyes,
And first Amphion, sprung of race divine,
(From Jove himself he drew his natal line)
Unknowing yet, what carnage had o'erspread
The fatal champaign, thus insulting, said.
"How long wilt thou protract thy vital date,
O luckless boy, and gain delays from fate?
Do insolence and high presumption reign
In that vile breast, because thy foes disdain
To take th' advantage, and in fight engage
With one so far beneath a soldier's rage?
Hence to thy equals, and, secure from harms,
At home act o'er the fray with mimic arms;
There long enjoy, if war be thy delight,
The pomp without the dangers of the fight,
Or, if surviving glory be thy aim,
We grant, at thy request, a death of fame."
Here on his speech th' impatient hero broke,
And thus in terms of equal wrath bespoke.
"Small as my strength is, it avails to gain
The palm, and drive the Thebans from the plain.
Lives there so much a boy, as to decline
The strife with you, a soft enervate line?
In me, bold, rough, and hardy, thou shalt find
A sample of the whole Arcadian kind:

1083. Young Cydon's parts obscene lie bare to view] Our author makes the incestuous Cydon punished in that part, with which he had offended. This is poetical justice in the strictest sense of the word.

1097. Such is his art] I should be thought too mistrustful of the reader's taste, should I point out to him the beauties of these lines. My version, I confess, falls infinitely short of the original, and indeed the

> Solo respicit arcu

cannot be rendered in our language with a suitable dignity.

1131. In me, bold, rough, and hardy] The latter part of this speech is very much like that of Numanus in the ninth book of the Æneid

Me no fair priestess, by her god compress'd,
Brought forth to woe, in the still hours of rest.
No spears inverted in our hands we bear,
Nor on our heads unmanly turbans wear,
Train'd from our birth, to dare the frozen flood,
Explore the savage haunts, and range the wood.
To close the whole—(for why should I delay
With needless words the business of the fray?)
Our mothers wield the bow—your slothful sires
Strike hollow timbrels, and attend the quires."
These taunts, tho' just, Amphion could not hear,
But at the speaker's mouth directs a spear
Of dreadful size.—Astonish'd at the glare,
The courser rears aloft his feet in air,
And flound'ring on one side his master cast,
Then fell himself: the devious javelin past.
More fierce at this, the foe unsheath'd his blade,
And rush'd tumultuous: Cynthia this survey'd,
And anxious for his safety, interpos'd,
Her look disguis'd, and features undisclos'd.
Fir'd with chaste love, and friendship's holy flame,
Beside him Dorceus stood, and shar'd his fame:
To him the queen consign'd his tender years,
And youthful wars, the source of all his fears.
In his resembled form, and borrow'd vest
The goddess thus her favour'd youth address'd.
"No more, O prince! Here let thy fury cease,
Enough is given to vengeance, fame, and Greece.
Now spare the wretched Atalanta, spare
Those guardian-gods, who make thy life their care."
The youth replies:—"Indulge this once thy friend,
And wait till on the ground my spear extend
This daring wretch, who equal weapons bears,
Boasts equal reins, and equal vestments wears.
His reins shall grace my steed, his vests the door
Of Dian's temple, and his feather'd store
My mother's quiver."—Weeping Cynthia hears
Th' insulting vaunt, and smiles amidst her tears.
This from a distant quarter of the skies,
Couch'd in th' embrace of Mars, fair Venus eyes;
And while she sues, recalling to his mind
Harmonia and her offspring left behind,
By timely arts awakes the grief, suppress
In the recesses of his gloomy breast.
"Behold, O god of arms, yon wanton dame
With mortals mixing in the field of fame!
How boldly she confines the war's alarms,
And fixes, where she lists, the stress of arms.
Yet more—she rages not alike on all;
Gall'd by her darts, the Thebans only fall.
The charge and sway of fight to her transferr'd,
'Tis thine with darts to pierce the tim'rous herd."
Fir'd by these just complaints, the warrior-god
Sprung from her arms, and to the combat strode:
His other furies toiling at the fray,
Anger alone attends him in the way.
He checks the goddess in her rapid course,
And from the fight deters with menac'd force.
"The fates to Cynthia diff'rent wars decree;
The field of battle is no sphere for thee:
Then quit it, or by Styx thou soon shalt know,
Not Pallas' self is a more dreadful foe."
What can she do?—Here threat'ning Mars withstands,
There Fate, a loaded distaff in her hands;
While Jove leans from the stars, all stern to view.
Through rev'rence then the bashful pow'r withdrew.
Now thro' the Theban lines Mars darts his eyes,
And Dryas, sprung from great Orion, spies;
Him, for his hatred to the sylvan dame,
He singles out, and sets his soul on flame.
More furious now against the race abhorr'd,
He slays th' Arcadians, and disarms their lord.
Cyllene's bands, and Tegea's hardy swains
In long rows slaughter'd, press the sanguine plains.
Th' Ægytian chiefs, and troops of Pheneum fly:
Man falls on man, and all or yield or die.
Th' Arcadian prince himself he next pursues
With hopes of vengeance, though his hands refuse
To toss the lance.—He, wheeling, shifts his course,
And dreads the giant-chief's superior force.
Presages dire the lab'ring chief oppress,
Unman his soul, and heighten his distress.
And now the real Dorceus he descry'd
Sorrowing! a faithful few remain'd beside.
His strength recedes, and, as the quiver grew
More light, his want of shafts he quickly knew.
Less easy now the weight of arms he bears,
And to himself a boy at length appears:
But when he view'd the hostile buckler's flame,
A sudden tremour shot through all his frame.
As when a swan surveys the bird of Jove,
For prey descending from his walks above,

———Natos ad flumina primum
Deferimus, sævoque gelu duramus & undis.
Venatu invigilant pueri, sylvasque fatigant:

And again;

Vobis picta croco, & fulgenti murice vestis:
Desidiæ cordi; juvat indulgere choreis:
Et tunicæ manicas, & habent redimicula mitræ.

1153. Fir'd with chaste love] Statius seems to have endeavoured by this distinction to prevent any suspicions of his immorality, which Virgil lay under from having mentioned in different parts of his works the love of boys and young men with some degree of warmth.

1171. This from a distant quarter of the skies] Venus here, as well as in the Æneid, takes advantage of the amorous fits of her gallants, to win them over to her purpose. And exclusive of her charms, this speech is very well calculated to procure her what she wanted. Nothing could prevail more with Mars than the apprehension of an encroachment upon his prerogative: and these two lines in particular are very humorous and witty:

The charge and sway of fight to her transferr'd,
'Tis thine with darts to pierce the tim'rous herd.

1200. Sprung from great Orion] Orion was stung to death by a scorpion on Diana's account. It was therefore very judicious in the poet to make Dryas his son.

1223. As when a swan surveys the bird of Jove] This similitude is very expressive of the terrour and consternation of Parthenopæus. Homer in the 21st of his Iliad has one something like it, where he compares Diana, afraid of Juno, to a dove afraid of a falcon.

Δακρυόεσσα δ' ἔπειτα θεὰ φύγεν ὥστε πέλεια,
Ἥ ῥά θ' ὑπ' ἴρηκος κοίλην εἰσέπτατο πέτρην
Χηραμόν, οὐδ' ἄρα τῇγε ἁλώμεναι αἴσιμον ἦεν.
v. 493.

She seeks some cavern, and with fear deprest,
Claps close her quiv'ring pinions to her breast;
Thus when Parthenopæus near discerns
His foe's gigantic size, his anger turns
To deathful horrour: yet he still relies
On arms, and fixing on the heav'ns his eyes,
Invokes his patroness, and aims a blow,
The forky weapon fitted to the bow.
Now with full force he bends the stubborn yew,
The string approach'd his breast, so close he drew,
And the far distant horns already join'd,
Drawn to an arch: when, swifter than the wind,
Th' Aonian javelin obvious flies, and broke
The sounding string; his arm beneath the stroke
Is numb'd, and guiltless of th' intended wound,
The bow unbent, the shaft drops on the ground.
At length, in height of agonizing pain,
He quits the reins, and weapons, grasp'd in vain,
(For through his mail the spear had wing'd its flight,
Just where the shoulder and the arm unite)
When lo! a second lance, impell'd with force,
Transpierc'd the courser's knee, and stops his course.
Then haughty Dryas (wonderful to tell!)
Unconscious of the hand by which he fell,
Himself was slain: nor was the weapon found,
And daring author of so great a wound.
But his sad comrades on an ample shield
Remove the youthful hero from the field,
Who grieves not for himself, but for his steed:
O early age for such a glorious deed!
His beauteous face grows wan, his helm unty'd,
And on his trembling cheeks the graces died.
Thrice did they raise his head, and thrice depress'd,
His neck reclines upon his snowy breast;
Down which (Oh! ruthless vengeance of his foes!)
The gushing blood in purple currents flows.
To Dorceus now he gave his dying hand,
And, sighing, thus address'd his last command
"Life ebbs apace: but thou with lenient art
Some solace to my mother's grief impart:
She in terrific visions of the night,
In dreams, or in some bird's ill-omen'd flight,
Has seen my doom.—Yet study some pretence,
Some pious frauds to keep her in suspense.
Nor break it suddenly, nor when she stands,
The chace just o'er, with weapons in her hands.
But these my words repeat, when forc'd to tell:
'O mother, through my own deserts I fell,
As in contempt of thee, I sought the plain,
Thy pray'rs rejected, thy dissuasions vain:
And, heedless of thy counsels, still engag'd,
Where glory call'd, and where the combat rag'd.
Live therefore, and thy fruitless grief resign'd,
Resent, not pity, my too froward mind.
In vain from fam'd Lycæus' snow-capt brow,
Thou lookest, anxious, on the plain below,
If chance some shout re-echoes in the skies,
And clouds of dust beneath our feet arise.
I press a foreign strand, nor art thou nigh
To catch my parting breath, and close my eye.
Yet, honour'd parent, for the giver's sake,
This lock, in lieu of the whole body, take:
This thou wast wont to deck, in my despite,
And make the tender office thy delight.
To this funereal rites thou shalt assign;
And oh! remember, what I now enjoin:
My sylvan weapons grant to no demands,
Lest they grow blunt in unexperienced hands:
Let my lov'd hounds enjoy repose, nor own
Another lord, and feed from hands unknown:
But burn these useless arms on yonder plain,
Or hang them up in cruel Cynthia's fane.'"

1253. Now with full force] The posture and attitude of the shooter are painted in a very lively and beautiful manner. Dryas pierces his enemy near the articulation of the arm and shoulder, so that the former loses all its strength.—This is a just representation of the consequence of such a wound, and I believe every one will readily allow this passage to be a speaking picture.

1263. Life ebbs apace] The beginning of this speech cannot be too much commended for the filial piety and affection it displays, and the simplicity of the latter part is not disgusting as it comes from the mouth of so young a person as Parthenopæus, and here I cannot help observing, that the combat of Hippomedon with Ismenos is a sublime piece of machinery, and the description of the exploits and death of Parthenopæus equally tender and affecting. In short there is no part of the Thebaid that has more force of imagination, and a greater exertion of the inventive faculties of our author.

BOOK X.

THE ARGUMENT.

This book opens with an harangue of Eteocles to his soldiers, in which he advises them to attack the Grecians' camp by night. The ladies of Argos go in procession to Juno's temple, and implore the blessing of that goddess upon the arms of the allies. She sends Iris to Somnus, to persuade him to set the Thebans in a deep sleep. This being done, Thiodamas influences the troops to sally forth, and massacre the Thebans in their intrenchments. A select party is ordered to accompany him by Adrastus. They make a great slaughter, and morning drawing near, devote the trophies to Apollo, and then retire. Hopleus and Dymas go in quest of the bodies of Tydeus and Parthenopæus, but are intercepted by Amphion and slain. A party of the enemy rush into Thebes, and fall victims to their own rashness. The citizens, in great consternation at this irruption, apply to Tiresias, who informs them, that they can only be saved by the voluntary death of Menœceus. That hero, touched with compassion for his country, first stabs himself, and then leaps off the tower upon his enemies. In the mean time Capaneus exerts himself in a very extraordinary manner, and having scaled the walls of Thebes, is struck down and killed by Jupiter with lightning for his impiety.

Sol's evening wheels o'erhung th' Hesperian strand,
And dewy night advanc'd at Jove's command,
Who from Olympus with unpitying eyes
The rage and slaughter of the fight descries;

1. Sol's ev'ning wheels o'erhung] As in every just history-picture (to use the allusion of Mr. Pope) there is one principal figure, to which all

Yet grieves, so many alien troops should fall
By fates unjust before the Theban wall.
The plain unfolds a scene of horrour.—Here
Confus'dly heap'd, cars, horses, arms appear,
Dismember'd heroes, hearts that beat no more
To glory's call, and trunks disguis'd with gore.
Then the dishonour'd host, their ensigns torn,
Withdraw their bands, with length of combat worn:
The gates, unclos'd, admit the lessen'd train
With half the ease, they sent them to the plain.
They grieve, yet find some solace to their griefs,
As four, the bravest of the Grecian chiefs
Were slain.—Their legions roam without a guide,
Like vessels tost on ocean's billowy tide,
Whose course unsteer'd the winds and tempests sway,
And chance conducts them o'er the watry way.
From this alone the Tyrians bolder grown,
No longer fear the capture of the town,
But hoping conquest, study to prevent
The foe's escape, should that be their intent.
The watch-word flies through all th' assembled host;
The guards, by turns dispos'd, maintain their post.
By lot to Meges, and to Lycus falls
The post of honour.—Now beneath the walls
At their command arms, food, and fire they bring,
Harangu'd, as follows, by the joyful king.
" Assume, ye vanquishers of Greece, ye rods
To scourge the foes of Thebes and of the gods,
Fresh courage, and your ravish'd fame retrieve;
Nor at this interval of darkness grieve,
Which bounds our ire: we'll finish what's begun
Before the setting of to morrow's Sun.
See Lerna's glory humbled in the dust,
The chiefs, in whom she most repos'd her trust!
By vengeful Heav'n her boasted Tydeus fell;
The seer's black shade surpris'd the pow'rs of Hell.
With stern Hippomedon's triumphal spoils
Ismenos swells, nor midst our warlike toils
Rank we th' Arcadian's death.—The premium lies
In our own breasts, and plunder is our prize.
No more, each at his cohort's van, appear
The sev'n fam'd crests, or glitter in the rear.
Then fear ye Capaneus, whose valour's rage,
My brother's youth, and th' Argive monarch's age?
Haste, warriors, haste, and while intrench'd they lie,
Surround with flames, nor give them time to fly.
Within our reach the glorious conquest stands,
And the rich prey lies ready to our hands."
The Thebans thus he fires with promis'd spoils,
And urges to renew their prosp'rous toils.
They turn'd just as they were, nor wash'd away
The sweat and blood of the preceding day:
Their dearest friends from their embrace they shook,
No pause they make, and no inquiries brook.
The troops in sev'ral parties then divide,
And gird the front, the back, and either side
Of the Greek trench with flames.—At depth of night
Thus rav'ning wolves in hideous throngs unite,
And, urg'd with lust of long-untasted food,
Desert their haunts, and seek the fleecy brood.
Vain hope torments their maws, as in the gale
They snuff their breath, and list'ning at the pale,
Catch their hoarse bleatings. Stiff at length with cold,
In impotence of anger, at the fold
They dart their claws, and while the foam runs o'er,
Gnash their sharp teeth, and threat th' obstructing door.
Meanwhile at Argos an assembled train
Of suppliant dames proceed to Juno's fane:
There, prostrate at her altars, they implore
Her aid divine, and urge her to restore

the rest refer and are subservient; so in each battle of the Thebaid there is one principal person, that may properly be called the hero of that day and action. This conduct preserves the unity of the piece, and keeps the imagination from being distracted and confused with a wild number of independent figures, which have no subordination to each other. In this particular Statius has followed the example of Homer, as the reader must have observed. In the seventh book Amphiaraus is the leading character, in the eighth Tydeus, in the ninth Hippomedon, in the eleventh Polynices; and in this, Capaneus, whose death and exploits, with the description of the palace of Sleep, render this book equal, if not superior to any of the preceding.

61. At depth of night] Virgil has an equally fine simile in his ninth book, derived from the same animal.

Ac veluti pleno lupus insidiatus ovili,
Cum fremit ad caulas, ventos perpessus, et imbres,
Nocte super mediâ: tuti sub matribus agni
Balatum exercent: ille asper, et improbus irâ,
Sævit in absentes: collecta fatigat edendi
Ex longo rabies, et siccæ sanguine fauces.

Tasso has transcribed the first part of this comparison in the nineteenth canto of his Jerusalem;

Qual lupo predatore al' aer bruno
Le chiuse mandre, insidiando, aggira,
Secco l' avide fauci, e nel digiuno
Da nativo odio stimolato, e d' ira.

71. Meanwhile at Argos an assembled train] This procession of the Grecian matrons to the temple of Juno, with their offerings, and the ceremonies, is copied from the sixth book of the Iliad, where the Trojan women make the same procession to Minerva's temple.

Αἱ δ' ὅτε νηὸν ἵκανον Ἀθήνης ἐν πόλει ἄκρῃ,
Τῇσι θύρας ὤϊξε Θεανὼ καλλιπάρῃος,
Αἱ δ' ὀλολυγῇ πᾶσαι Ἀθήνῃ χεῖρας ἀνέσχον.
Ἡ δ' ἄρα πέπλον ἑλοῦσα Θεανὼ καλλιπάρῃος
Θῆκεν Ἀθηναίης ἐπὶ γούνασιν ἠϋκόμοιο.

Virgil has also introduced it among the figures in the picture at Carthage. Æneid, l. v. 483.

Interea ad templum non æquæ Palladis ibant
Crinibus Iliades passis, peplumque ferebant
Suppliciter tristes, et tunsæ pectora palmis.

He has copied it again in the eleventh book:

Necnon ad templum summasque ad Palladis arces
Subvenitur magnâ matrum regina catervâ,
Dona ferens:
Succedunt matres, et templum thure vaporant,
Et mœstas alto fundunt de limine voces.

But I think, our author's is more conformable to the christian system; the worship whereof is grounded more on love than fear, and seems directed rather to implore the assistance and protection of a benevolent being, than avert the malice and anger of a wrathful and mischievous demon.

Their absent friends. On the cold stones they fall,
They press their faces to the doors and wall,
And teach their little sons religion's care.
Now sets the day, consum'd in vows and pray'r,
And night succeeds, when, heap'd with watchful fires,
Their altars blaze: the smoke ascends in spires.
A costly veil too, as a gift, they brought,
No barren hand the shining vest had wrought;
Rich was its texture, and its every part
Was labour'd o'er with more than vulgar art.
The ground was purple, glorious to behold,
With foliage interwove, and flow'rs of gold.
There Juno's self with eyes cast downward stands,
Betroth'd, not fetter'd yet in nuptial bands;
Asham'd to sink the sister in the spouse,
Her rosy cheek with graceful blushes glows,
And, yet a stranger to his furtive love,
She prints sweet kisses on her youthful Jove.
With this the sacred iv'ry they invest,
And, weeping, thus their humble suit addrest:
"O queen of Heav'n, and all th' ethereal pow'rs!
Behold the Tyrian harlot's impious tow'rs!
Burst all her gates, hurl all her rampires down,
And with new light'nings blast the guilty town."
How can she act!—She knows the will of fate,
And fears with Jove to enter in debate;
Yet sorrows, lest the gifts of mighty cost,
Their ardent pray'rs, and sacrifice be lost.
While thus she mus'd, auspicious chance bestows
A time to aid, and grant their pious vows.
From her bright throne she sees the portals clos'd,
And wakeful guards around the trench dispos'd.
Wrath and revenge her spleenful bosom strook,
And as she mov'd, her crown terrific shook.
Such was her rage, when from her starry plain
She view'd Alcmene's son with stern disdain,
And griev'd, that Thebes should bring two bastard-boys *
To light, the fruits of Jove's adult'rous joys.
She dooms the Thebans then to death, who keep
The mighty watch, when lock'd in sudden sleep:
In Iris now she vests the whole command,
And lodges all the weighty charge in hand,
Who bends her progress to the world below,
Suspending high in air her various bow.
Far on the confines of the western main,
Where Æthiopia bounds her wide domain,
There stands a grove, that casts a shade afar,
Impenetrable to the brightest star,
Beneath whose hollow rocks a cave descends
Of depth immense, and in the mountain ends.
Here all-disposing Nature fix'd th' abode
Of Somnus, and secur'd the drowsy god.
Sloth, who scarce knows an interval from sleep,
Rest motionless, and dark Oblivion keep
Eternal sentry at the gloomy gate:
There listless Ease, and awful Silence sate
With close-contracted wings, and, still as Death,
Repel the winds, and hush each murmur's breath:
No rustling foliage here is heard to move,
No feather'd songsters warble through the grove;
No lightnings glare, no crashing thunders roar,
No foamy waves, rebounding from the shore.
The neighb'ring stream along the valley glides,
And rolls between the rocks his noiseless tides.
The sable herds and flocks from food abstain,
Or only graze, recumbent on the plain:
Nor stops th' infection here, but spreads around,
And withers herbs just springing from the ground.
"Within, a thousand statues of the god
Were grav'd by Vulcan.—Here was seen to nod
Pleasure, with overacted joys oppress'd,
And healthful toil, ne'er physick'd into rest.
There Love from am'rous cares a respite stole,
And Bacchus snor'd o'er a half-finish'd bowl.
Deep, deep within, Death, his half-brother, lies,
His face was void of terrour, clos'd his eyes."
Beneath the dew-bespangled cavern lay
The god himself, and dos'd his cares away.
The roof was verdant; his own poppies spread
A carpet soft, and swell'd the rising bed.
His mouth, half-shut, breathes soporific steams,
And his warm vests exhale the vap'ry streams.
One hand sustains his head; the horn drops down,
Unheeded, from his other torpid grown.
A thousand various dreams attend their chief,
Truths mix'd with falsehood, joys alloy'd with grief:
The sons of darkness these, and night's black hosts,
On earth they lie, or cleave to beams and posts.
Some slender glimm'rings faintly shine between,
And serve to make the gloom more clearly seen.
Here, pois'd on equal pinions, Iris flies,
And draws a thousand colours from the skies.

* Hercules and Bacchus, the former being the son of Alcmene, and the latter of Semele.

119. Far on the confines] The poets have differed in their accounts of the situation of this court of Morpheus: Homer places it at Lemnos, Ovid with the Cimmerians, a people of Scythia, and ours above Ethiopia. The verses marked are some that are not in all the editions, but which I have rendered on the authority of Gronovius. This description is preferable to that of the temple of Mars in the seventh book, but rivalled by that of the palace of this deity in the eleventh book of the Metamorphoses.

Est prope Cimmerios longo spelunca recessu,
Mons cavus, ignavi domus et penetralia Somni;
Quo nunquam radiis oriens, mediusve, cadensve
Phœbus adire potest. Nebulæ caligine mistæ
Exhalantur humo: dubiæque crepuscula lucis.
Non vigil ales ibi cristati cantibus oris
Evocat Auroram: nec voce silentia rumpunt
Sollicitive canes, canibusve sagacior anser.
Non fera, non pecudes, non moti flumine rami,
Humanæve sonum reddunt convicia linguæ.
Muta quies habitat. Saxo tamen exit ab imo
Rivus aquæ Lethes: per quem olim murmure labens
Invitat somnos crepitantibus unda lapillis.
Ante fores antri fœcunda papavera florent,
Innumeræque herbæ, quarum de lacte soporem
Nox legit, et spargit per opacas humida terras.
Janua, quæ verso stridorem cardine reddat,
Nulla domo totâ est; custos in limine nullus.
At medio torus est, ebeno sublimis in atra,
Plumeus, atricolor, pullo velamine tectus:
Quo cubat ipse deus, membris languore solutis.
Hunc circa passim varias imitantia formas
Somnia vana jacent totidem, quot messis aristas,
Silva gerit frondes, ejectas littus arenas.

I think the Ovidian circumstance of its having no gates, which might make a noise by the turning of their hinges, is proper enough: but our author's account of the greatest provocatives to sleep is very just, and a great improvement on the preceding description.

At her approach the woods, the vales below
Smile, and reflect the radiance of her bow:
While the dark dome, struck by her glitt'ring zone,
Bursts into light, and splendours not its own.
Still proof against th' irradiating gleams,
And heav'nly voice, the sluggish godhead dreams,
Till with fresh light she strengthen'd every ray,
And in his eyes infus'd the golden day:
Then scarce awake, and half unclos'd his eyes,
He lifts his head.—The show'ry goddess cries:
" O Somnus, gentlest of the pow'rs above,
At Juno's suit, the sister-queen of Jove,
On Thebes thy soporific arts employ,
Who, flush'd with conquest and unruly joy,
The Grecian trench beleaguer; disobey
Thy just commands, and Night's alternate sway.
Grant her request then, snatch the time to please
That rarely comes, and wrathful Jove appease
By means of Juno's interceding aid."——
This mandate giv'n, the many-colour'd maid
Ceas'd not, but lest she give her charge in vain,
Thrice shook him, and repeats it o'er again.
Thus importun'd the pow'r of slumbers nods
Assent. The fair attendant of the gods,
Clogg'd with thick vapours, quits the dark domain,
And points her rays, grown blunt with frequent rain.
He too call'd forth his speed and active pow'rs,
With blust'ring winds disturb'd the peaceful hours,
And spreads his mantle out, contracted, bent,
And stiffen'd with the freezing element;
Then, bending through the skies his silent flight,
O'erhangs the Tyrian plains from Heav'n's mid-height.
His breath alone extends upon the ground,
Herds, flocks, and birds, and stills the world around.
Where'er he takes his way, the billows slide
From off the rocks, and howling storms subside:
The clouds condense, the forests nod on high,
And falling stars desert the drowsy sky.
First sudden mists, wide-spreading o'er the field,
The presence of the deity reveal'd,
Then straight the senseless dins and riot cease,
And the late noisy camp is hush'd in peace:
But, when he stretches out his humid wings,
And, circumfus'd in pitchy darkness, flings
His poppies far and wide, they roll their eyes,
And on the tongue th' imperfect accent dies,
Then from their op'ning hands, disarm'd by rest,
They drop their shields and spears: their heads deprest
With weight unwonted on their bosoms fall.
And now the god of silence reigns o'er all:
The coursers sink to sleep at his command,
And sudden ashes quench'd each flaming brand.
But the bland pow'r of night (as was injoin'd)
To Thebes alone his opiate gifts confin'd;
From the confed'rate camps he drives away
His mists:—awake, as in the blaze of day,
They stand in arms, and, fir'd with just disdain,
Expect the menac'd fray, and hostile train.
Lo! chilling horrour creeps through all the breast
Of their sage prophet, by the god possest,
And urges him tumultuous to disclose
The fates' designs upon his country's foes.
Whether this insight Phœbus had inspir'd,
Or Juno with prophetic fury fir'd,
Dreadful in voice and look, he springs abroad,
By Heav'n's informing spirit over-aw'd,
And foams and quakes, unable to control
The lab'ring impulse of his master'd soul.
His haggard face with heat unwonted glows,
And by quick turns his colour comes and goes:
He rolls his eyes around; his locks, that flow
Disorder'd, shake the chaplet on his brow.
At periods thus the Phrygian zealot raves,
Whom Cybele from his terrific caves,
Or shrines allures; nor though he bleeds, he knows
His arms are hack'd and seam'd with frequent blows.
He plies the holy pine, and whirls around
His hair: the motion deadens ev'ry wound.
The field and gory tree are seiz'd with fear,
And the scar'd lions high her chariot rear.
Now to the council-hall, and awful dome
With standards hung, the madding seer had come:
Adrastus here presides o'er the debate,
And plans the welfare of th' endanger'd state:
The peers of Argos stand, and form a ring
About the throne of their consulting king,
Advanc'd by the late deaths, nor do they thank
The cruel stroke, that elevates their rank.

184. And wrathful Jove appease] We know not in what Somnus offended Jupiter, unless it was in setting him to sleep, in order that Juno might shipwreck Hercules in his voyage home from Troy, as he himself tells that goddess in the fourteenth book of the Iliad.

Ἤτοι ἐγὼ μὲν ἔθελξα Διὸς νόον αἰγιόχοιο
Νήδυμος ἀμφιχυθείς. Σὺ δέ οἱ κακὰ μήσαο θυμῷ,
Ὄρσασ' ἀργαλέων ἐπὶ πόντον ἀήτας.
Καί μιν ἔπειτα Κόων δεῦ ναιομένην ἀπένεικας
Νόσφι φίλων πάντων. ὁ δ' επεγρόμενος χαλέπαινε.

225. Lo! chilling horrour] Compare this with the following passages of Virgil and Tryphiodorus.

Ventum erat ad limen, cum virgo: " Poscere fata
" Tempus, ait: Deus, ecce Deus." Cui talia fanti
Ante fores, subito non vultus, non color unus,
Non comptæ mansere comæ: sed pectus anhelum,
Et rabie fera corda tument, majorque videri,
Nec mortale sonans: afflata est numine quando
Tam propiore Dei. Æn. 6.

Κουρη δ' ἐκ θαλαμοιο θεηλατος ουκετι μιμνειν
Ηθελεν ἐν θαλαμοισι. διαῤῥηξασα δ' ὀχηας,
Εδραμεν——
Τοιη μαντιπολοιο βολης ὑπὸ νυγματικουρη
Πλαζομενη κραδιην ἱερην ἀνεσειετο δαφνην.
Παντη δε βρυχατο κατὰ πτολιν.——
Οὐκ ουτω Θρηισσαν ἐνὶ δρυμοισι γυναικα.
Νηδυμος αὐλὸς ετυψεν ορειμανεος Διονυσου,
Ητε θεω τυφθεισα παρηορον ομμα τιταινει,
Γυμνον ἐπὶ σειουσα καρη κυαναμπυκι κισσα.
Ἧς ηγε πτολεοφοντος ἀναΐξασα νοοιο.
Κασσανδρη νεοφοντος ἐμαινετο· πυκνα δε καιτην
Κοπτομενη καὶ στερνον, ἀνιαχος μαιναδι φανη.
Destruction of Troy.

There is one circumstance of similitude between the descriptions of Tryphiodorus and Statius, that makes me think one of them borrowed from the other; and that is the likeness of the comparison: for as the phrenzy of Thiodamas is compared to that of one of Cybele's priests, so the fury of Cassandra is illustrated by that of a Thracian bacchanal. But who is the original in this case cannot be known, till the time in which Tryphiodorus flourished is ascertained, which Mr. Merrick, his translator, assures us is not yet done.

As when a vessel has her pilot lost
In a mid-voyage, half the ocean cross'd,
One, who with skill the prow or side-decks guides,
Succeeds, and at the widow'd helm presides;
Th' astonish'd ship then wonders as she goes,
With equal speed, and equal steerage knows.
Thus to the Greeks the sprightly seer imparts
Fresh spirits, and re-fortifies their hearts:
" Heav'n's mandates, and advice of high import
To you, renowned chieftains, we report.
Think not, these weighty accents are my own;
A god inspires them, whose prophetic crown
Approv'd by your consenting voice, I wear,
Nor in despite of him, these ensigns bear.
This night, now big with many a daring deed,
By fate for glorious treachery's decreed;
Lo! honour calls, and fortune asks your hands
To act, and hearts to dare, what she commands.
The Thebans sleep—Then let this night repay
The deathful feats, and carnage of the day.
To arms, to arms—this hour shall make amends
For all, and serve as fun'rals to our friends;
Burst we the gates, should they our wrath oppose,
And turn the tide of vengeance on our foes.
For by these tripods, and th' untimely fate
Of our late augur, in the last debate,
This, warn'd by fav'ring omens, I beheld,
What time our host, by hostile force repell'd,
Forsook the fight; but now the pow'rs divine
Confirm, repeat, and clear the former sign.
Beneath the covert of the silent night,
The seer himself stood manifest to sight,
From earth emerg'd; such as alive he shone,
The colour of his steeds was chang'd alone.
I speak no visions of the night profound,
Nor prodigies in slumber only found.
' Dost thou' he cry'd, ' permit the Greeks to lose
This fair occasion, sure they can't refuse?
Restore, degen'rate chief, these wreaths restore,
So ill deserv'd, nor so disgrac'd before.
I taught thee not for this the mysteries
Of Heav'n, or how to read each wing that flies.
But come at least—on Thebes revenge my death,
And with thy sword suppress their forfeit breath.'
He said, and urg'd me to the nightly war,
With his uplifted spear, and all his car.
Snatch then the vengeance which the gods bestow;
No more, man clos'd with man, we seek the foe;
Fenceless they lie, and we' ve full pow'r to rage:
But who with me will in th'emprize engage,
And, while the fates permit, his glory raise
On this firm base, and win eternal praise?
Mark yon repeated omens of the night,
Auspicious birds! I'll follow them to fight,
Tho' none should second me; for lo! again
He drives his rattling chariot o'er the plain."
Thus with exalted voice the chief exclaims,
Piercing the night's dull ear, and all inflames;
As by one pow'r inspir'd, with him they join,
Resolv'd to share whate'er the fates design.
Full thirty warriors, at the king's command,
He singles out, the flow'r of all the band;
But envy swell'd each other Argive's breast,
Eager of action, enemy to rest;
Some deem their race a merit, and make known
Their grandsires' actions, others boast their own,
Or will, that lots be cast.—This seen, the king
Exults, buoy'd up on hope's aspiring wing.
On Pholoë thus the rearer of the steed,
When the kind spring renews his gen'rous breed,
With joy views these strain up the mountain-steep,
Those with their dams contend, or dare the deep;
Then much he muses, which are fit to train
For rural labours, or th' embattled plain,
Which best would serve the chase, or soonest rise
To palms Elean, and th' Olympic prize?
Such honest glee the hoary monarch shows,
Nor checks their ardours, nor less eager glows.
" What gods," he cries, " so sudden, yet so late
Thus interpose to save th' afflicted state?
Are these the seeds of courage, that withstood
Distress so long, the ebb of gen'rous blood?
Illustrious youths, I praise you, and enjoy
Sedition, rais'd thro' ardour to destroy;
But, as we meditate a fraudful blow,
Our motions must be private, lest they know.
A noisy crowd ill suits with dark designs,
Restrain your rage, till Sol returning shines,
Then we'll all sally out, to war releas'd."
Sooth'd by these words, their youthful fury ceas'd:
As when stern Æolus rolls the huge stone
Before his cave, and from his airy throne
Confines the winds, all eager to engage,
And pour upon the deeps their blust'ring rage.

269. This night, now big with many a] This machine is very beautiful; and indeed a contrivance to repair the acts of the last day by this night-adventure was very necessary, as the Greeks were very much dispirited by the death of the four leaders. The hint of it is taken from the 10th book of the Iliad, where Diomede and Ulysses sally out upon the like errand; or from the 9th of the Æneid, where Nisus and Euryalus make an expedition of this kind, and give rise to a noble episode. And here I cannot but take notice how amiable Adrastus appears to us, who, ever anxious for the good of his people, keeps awake and calls a council to settle the means of their preservation. In this behaviour we may discover the marks of an affectionate father, a sincere friend, a patriotic king, and a prudent general.

308. I'll follow them to fight] This recalls to my remembrance a similar rant, which Homer puts into the mouth of Diomede, though perhaps with less propriety; as in him it was the result of downright rashness, but in our augur of an honest confidence in the Deity.

'Αλλ' ἄλλοι μενέυσι καρηκομόωντες Ἀχαιοὶ
Εἰσόκε περ Τροίην διαπέρσομεν, εἰ δὲ καὶ αὐτοὶ
Φευγόντων συν νηυσὶ φίλην ἐς πατρίδα γαῖαν.
Νῶϊ δ' ἐγὼ, Σθένελός τε μαχησόμεθ', εἰσόκε τέκμωρ
Ἰλίου εὕρωμεν. σὺν γὰρ θεῳ εἰλήλουθμεν.
Iliad, b. 9. v. 45.

323. On Pholoë thus] Homer illustrates the joy which Æneas displays on viewing the discipline and valour of his troops by that of a shepherd, on seeing his flocks in good plight, as he leads them to water.

————Αὐτὰρ επειτα
Λαοι εποιθ', ωσει τε μετα κτιλον ἕσπετο μηλα
Πιομεν' ἐκ βοτανης, γανυται δ' αρα τε φρενα ποιμην.
Ως Αινεια θυμος ἐνὶ στηθεσσι γεγηθει,
Ως ιδε λαων εθνος ἐπισπομενον εοι αὐτω.

The seer Agylleus to the task assign'd,
And Actor.—This was skill'd to sway the mind
With bland persuasion; that, Alcides' son,
Boasts equal strength, and equal trophies won.
Beneath each chief ten warriors take their way;
Which might alone the Theban host affray
In open fight.—The seer himself lays down
The ensigns of his God, the laurel-crown,
And fillet, that confines his flowing hair,
Commended to the aged monarch's care:
In Polynices' mail his breast he cas'd,
And on his head the proffer'd helmet lac'd,
Stern Capaneus a sword to Actor gave,
For he himself, immoderately brave,
Disdains Heav'n's guidance, and the night's alarms.
With Nomius then Agylleus changes arms;
For little would avail the archer now,
The shafts Herculean, and unerring bow.
Thus, sheath'd in radiant arms, they quit their tents,
And, headlong, from the steepy battlements
Leap down, lest, should they thro' the portals take
Their way, the brazen hinge the Thebans wake.
Stretch'd on the ground, they view the ready prey;
As slain already, motionless they lay.
" Where'er you list, my brave companions, go,
And hew a passage thro' the sleeping foe,"
(With voice distinct, the priest exhorting cry'd)
" Nor spare the blessing which the gods provide.
You see the foe expos'd upon the plain;
Did these (I speak with anger and disdain)
Did these coop up our warriors in their wall,
Blind to their int'rest, deaf to glory's call?"
This said, in wrath he drew his glitt'ring brand,
And pass'd the dying troops with rapid hand.
Who can recount the slaughter? who can name
The group of vulgar deaths, unknown to fame?
His rage no rule, his sword no limits knows,
But bathes his steps in purple, as he goes;
Limbs, trunks, and sever'd heads he leaves behind,
And hears their groans remurmur'd in the wind.

361. Stern Capaneus a sword to Actor] That it was a custom among the ancients to make presents of this kind to adventurers, before they set out on an expedition, is evident from Homer's Iliad, book the 10th, v. 255.

Τυδέιδη μὲν δῶκε μενεπτόλεμος Θρασυμήδης
Φασγανον ἄμφηκες [τὸ τ' ἐὸν παρὰ νηυσὶ λέλειπτο]
Καὶ σάκος· ἀμφὶ δε οἱ κυνέην κεφαλῆφιν ἔθηκε
Ταυρέιην, ἀφαλόντε, καὶ ἄλοφον, ἥτε καταῖτυξ
Κέκληται. Ῥύεται δὲ καρη θαλερῶν αἰζηῶν.
Μηριόνης δ' Ὀδυσῆϊ δίδȣ βιὸν, ἠδὲ φαρέτρην,
Καὶ ζίφος. ἀμφὶ δὲ οἱ κυνέην κεφαλήφιν ἔθηκε
Ῥινȣ ποιητήν.——

And from Virgil's Æneid, book the 9th, line 303.

Sic ait illacrymans: humero simul exuit ensem
Auratum, mirâ quem fecerat arte Lycaon
Gnossius, atque habilem vaginâ aptarat eburnâ.
Dat Niso Mnestheus pellem, horrentisque leonis
Exuvias: galeam fidus permutat Alethes.

The holy scriptures likewise make mention of a similar gift; Samuel, book 1st, chap. 18. ver. 4. " And Jonathan stript himself of the robe that was upon him, and gave it to David, and his garments even to his sword, and to his bow, and to his girdle."

Stretch'd on a couch one doz'd, one press'd the field,
Another, stumbling, overlaid his shield:
Here goblets lie, there weapons strew'd between,
Of war, and foul debauch, a motley scene.
Some on their massy bucklers stood reclin'd,
Like lifeless statues; just as they're confin'd
By Morpheus in the bands of soft repose,
So various were the postures of the foes.
Here clad in arms, Saturnia takes her stand,
A torch held forth to guide her favour'd band;
She points the bodies out, with fury warms
Their gen'rous breasts, and strings their nervous arms.
Thiodamas perceiv'd her, but suppress'd
The silent joy beneath his conscious breast.
Dull'd with success, his wrath is at a stand;
Blunt grows the falchion, weary is his hand.
As when the native of the Caspian wood
(Some tiger fierce) has gorg'd his maw with food,
His beauteous spots confus'd with clotted gore,
He views the prey, and grieves his hunger's o'er,
The weary prophet thus surveys the slain,
And mourns his vanquish'd arm, but mourns in vain;
He wishes now a fresh increase of might,
A hundred arms, and hundred hands to fight,
Then tir'd of menaces, and wordy rage,
He hopes the rising Thebans may engage.
At distance Actor, and the chief who trac'd
His lineage from Alcmena's son, lay waste
The Tyrian forces.—Each a crowd succeeds,
And trails a bloody path along the meads.
The matted grass stands high in sable blood,
And from the tents descends a reeking flood.
The breath of sleep and death thick steams around,
And with the recent slaughter smokes the ground.
Supinely as at first, each Theban lies,
Nor lifts his head, nor opes his heavy eyes.
With such wide-hov'ring wings the god invades
The wretched crew, and spreads o'er all his shades.
Ialmenus, unknowing rest, had strung
His harp to Phœbus, and in concert sung
A lofty pæan in the Tyrian strain,
Doom'd never to behold him rise again:
His neck, with sleep's incumbent weight depress'd,
Swerv'd to the left, and sunk upon his breast;
This seen, Agylleus drove his piercing brand
Sheer thro' his breast, and struck his better hand;
Whose taper fingers trembled on the strings.
Forc'd by the stroke the vital spirit wings
Its way to Hell.—The tables down he spurns,
And backward in the bowls the wine returns:
The wid'ning wound emits a copious flood
Of Bacchus' heady juice, and mingled blood.
At Thamyrus the furious Actor flies,
As in his brother's arms entwin'd he lies;
Pierc'd in the back Etheclus Tagus slew;
From off his neck the head of Hebrus flew
By Danaus' stroke; unconscious of his death,
Without one pang or groan he yields his breath.
Young Palpetus beneath the chariot press'd
The clay-cold earth, and puffing from his breast
The nauseous fumes, his coursers terrified,
That cropp'd the flow'ry herbage at his side.
From his gorg'd mouth the filthy liquor flows,
And in his veins, intoxicating, glows;
When lo! th' Inachian prophet, as he snor'd,
Deep in his throat infix'd the shining sword:
Wine from his wound came issuing as he died,
And drown'd th' imperfect murmur in the tide.

A deathful vision haply then was sent
In which he saw pourtray'd the dire event;
Thiodamas his breast unguarded tore;
So dream'd the luckless chief, and wak'd no more.
The clouds dissolve in dew upon the plains,
And of night's reign a fourth alone remains:
Bootes flies before the greater car
Of Sol, and dim grows each inferior star;
And, matter failing, slaughter found an end,
When prudent Actor thus accosts his friend.
" Thiodamas, let this unhop'd-for joy
Find its due bounds; here cease we to destroy.
Scarce one, I ween, of all this num'rous train
Survives to war, and visit Thebes again;
Unless the deep'ning streams of blood conceal
Th' inglorious coward from the vengeful steel.
Then moderate thy yet successful rage:
There want not gods, who will for Thebes engage,
And even those who aided us before,
May fly, and give the longsome labour o'er."
The seer obeys, and lifting to the skies
His hands, embru'd in recent slaughter, cries:
" Phœbus, the well-earn'd trophies of the night,
And first fruits of the war, thy lawful right,
Accept from me, thy soldier and thy priest,
Though foul and reeking from the bloody feast.
If patient of thee, right thy gifts I use,
Thy spirit often in my breast infuse.
These arms, and bloody honours now suffice:
But, when our country glads again our eyes,
So many gifts shall answer thy demand,
And oxen bleed beneath the pontiff's hand."
This said, his pious pray'r the chieftain ends,
And from the fray recals his pious friends.
From Calydon and Mænalus there came
Two mighty warriors not unknown to fame,
Hopleus and Dymas, by their kings approv'd,
Their faith rewarded, and their presence lov'd:
Their leaders lost, they loath the light of life,
Th' Ætolian first promotes the glorious strife.
" Say, dearest Dymas, does no care remain,
No small compassion for thy sov'reign slain,
Whose corse perhaps the famish'd fowls of air,
Or Theban dogs with rage relentless tear?
What then is left to grace his country's urn?
See, his fierce mother waits for your return!
But still the ghost of Tydeus, void of rest,
Stalks in my view, and rages in my breast.
Though less expos'd to Phœbus he appears,
His limbs well-harden'd, and confirm'd with years;
Yet in the search I'll range the champain o'er,
And force my way to Thebes."—He said no more,
For Dymas cut him short and thus reply'd:
" By the chief's wand'ring shade, my greatest guide,
And yon bright stars, that gild the skies, I swear,
That this same heat and energy I share.
Long have I sought a partner in the deed;
Now, back'd by thy assistance, I'll precede."
This said, he leads the way, and to the skies
Lifting his hands, in height of anguish cries,
" O Cynthia, queen of the mysterious night,
If truly Fame reports it thy delight
To wear a triple form, and often change
Thy virgin-aspect in the sylvan range,
Look down from Heav'n, and to these eyes restore
Thy comrade's corse (thy comrade now no more):
He, fairest far of all th' Arcadian boys,
Excites our vengeance, and our search employs."
The goddess heard, and bright'ning ev'ry ray,
Points her sharp horn to where the body lay:
Then Thebes shines forth, Cithæron's hills arise
In prospect fair, and steal into the skies.
Thus when at depth of night avenging Jove
Rolls his hoarse thunders through the realms above,
The clouds divide, the stars serenely glow,
And sudden splendours gild the world below.
Brave Hopleus catch'd the rays, whose piercing light
Presents the corse of Tydeus to his sight.
Both bodies found, they raise a gladsome cry,
(The sign agreed) and to the weight apply
Their shoulders; pleas'd, as if preserv'd from death,
Each corse was re-inspir'd with vital breath.
Nor durst they give full vent to tears or words;
Th' unfriendly dawn no leisure-time affords.
With grief the paler darkness they survey,
As through the silent shades they bend their way.
To pious heroes Fate success denies,
And Fortune rarely crowns the bold emprize.
The burden now grows lighter in their hand,
As the whole camp in prospect they command,
When from behind black clouds of dust arise,
And sudden sounds run echoing through the skies.
Amphion, eager at the king's command,
Conducts a troop of horse, to scour the land,
And watch the foe.——While far before his train,
He spurs his courser through the trackless plain,
He catch'd a transient glance (for yet the light
Had but in part dispell'd the shades of night)
Of some faint object, that at distance strays,
He looks again, and doubts if he surveys.
The fraud detected,—" Stand, whoe'er you are,"
(Amphion cries) "and whence you come, declare."
Confess'd at length, the wretched pair appear,
The wretched pair rush on with speed, and fear

457. A deathful vision] This image is very natural, and imitated from the tenth book of the Iliad, ver. 496.

——Κακὸν γὰρ ὄναρ κεφαλῆφιν ἐπέστη
Τὴν νυκτ', Οἰνέιδαο ϖαϊ, διὰ μῆτιν 'Αθήνης.

Shakspeare's tragedy of Macbeth presents us with as fine a picture, where two of Duncan's soldiers, just as their king was assassinated, are described starting out of their sleep in the greatest perturbation.

There's one did laugh in his sleep, and one cry'd,
Murder;
They wak'd each other, and I stood and heard them;
One cry'd, God bless us, and Amen the other,
As they had seen me with these hangman's hands.

549. Amphion, eager at the king's command] The manner of the discovery is similar to that of the adventurers in the ninth book of the Æneid, and the question put to them by the enemy much the same.

Interea præmissi equites ex urbe Latina,
Cætera dum legio campis instructa moratur,
Ibant et Turno regi responsa ferebant,
Tercentum, scutati omnes, Volscente magistro.
Jamque propinquabant castris, murosque subibant,
Cum procul hos lævo flectentes limite cernunt:
Et galea Euryalum sublustri noctis in umbra
Prodidit immemorem, radiisque adversa refulsit.

Not for themselves.——He shakes his javelin now,
And seems to meditate a deathful blow;
Yet high in air the missile weapon cast,
Which wilful err'd, the object far o'erpast:
Before the face of Dymas fix'd it lay,
(Who started first) and check'd him in the way.
But valiant Æpytus his javelin toss'd
With care, nor will'd the fair occasion lost.
Through Hopleus' back the well-aim'd dart he flung,
And graz'd the corse, that on his shoulders hung.
He falls, not mindless of his lord in death,
But in the painful grasp expires his breath:
Too happy, had he reach'd the Stygian coast
Just then, unknowing that the corse was lost.
This scap'd not Dymas: as he turn'd behind,
He sees the troops, in his destruction join'd,
Uncertain or to tempt th' approaching foes
With soothing blandishments, or ply with blows.
Wrath spurs to combat, fortune bids him try
The force of pray'r: on none he can rely.
Too wroth to sue, before his feet he plac'd
The wretched corse, with wounds unfelt disgrac'd;
And tossing to the left a weighty hide,
(Which grac'd his back, and hung with martial pride,
A tiger's spoils) protends his naked blade,
And guards the hero's body, undismay'd:
Prepar'd for ev'ry dart that comes, he turns:
And with the thirst of death or conquest burns.
As the gaunt lioness, whose cruel den
Is thick beset with clam'rous hounds and men,
Stands o'er her whelps, erect, and sends around,
Perplex'd with doubts, a mournful, angry sound.
With ease she might disperse the sable train,
And knap the weapons with her teeth in twain,
But nat'ral love o'ercomes the lust of fight:
She foams with rage, yet keeps her whelps in sight.
The falchion now lops off his weaker hand,
Though great Amphion check'd the furious band,
And by his hair the youth is dragg'd along,
By fate resign'd to an insulting throng.
Then, nor till then, in suppliant guise he bow'd
His sword, and thus address'd the ruthless crowd,
" More gently treat the tender boy, I pray,
By that blest cradle, where young Bacchus lay,
By luckless Ino's flight, and female fears,
And your Palæmon's almost equal years.
If one among you tastes domestic joys,
If any here paternal care employs,
Heap o'er his poor remains a little sand,
And to his pyre apply one kindled brand.
His looks, behold! his looks this boon implore.
First let the monsters lap my spatter'd gore:
Me, me resign to the fell birds of prey;
'Twas I, who train'd, and forc'd him to the fray."
" If such is thy desire" (Amphion cries)
" To deck his corse with fun'ral obsequies,
What, to redeem their loss, the Greeks prepare,
Their schemes, their counsels, and resolves declare.
As a reward, the light of life enjoy,
And, as thou wilt, intomb th' unhappy boy."
Th' Arcadian, full of horrour, scorn'd a part
So base, plung'd all the poniard in his heart,
And cry'd, " Did nought, save this, remain to close
My country's fate, that I should tell her foes
Her fix'd intents?—We buy no fun'ral pyre
On terms like these, nor would the prince require."
He spake, and on his youthful leader laid
His breast, wide-open'd by the trenchant blade,
And said in dying accents, " Thou shalt have
My lifeless corse, a temporary grave."
Thus did the warriour of Ætolian race,
And brave Arcadian, in the wish'd embrace

Haud temere est visum. Conclamat ab agmine
 Volscens,
State, viri: quæ causa viæ? quive estis in armis?
Quove tenetis iter?——Verse 367.

561. He shakes his javelin now] This circumstance is borrowed from the tenth book of Homer's Iliad, v. 372.

Ἦρα, καὶ ἔγχος ἀφῆκεν, ἑκὼν δ' ἡμάρτανε φωτός.
Δεξιτερὸν δ' ὑπὲρ ὦμον ἐΰξόυ δυρὸς ἀκωκὴ
Ἐν γαίῃ ἐπάγη. ὁ δ' ἄρ' ἔςη, τάρβησέν τε.

581. Too wroth to sue, before his feet he plac'd] Nothing can exceed the valour and magnanimity of this hero.——He would not surrender up the body of his friend, and knew that it was impossible to preserve it by carrying it on his back, as it must necessarily tie up his hands from making any defence: he therefore places it on the ground before his enemies, as the prize for which they were to fight.—His various movements and situation on this occasion are well illustrated by the subsequent comparison, which is imitated from Homer.

——————Ὥς τις τε λέων περὶ οἷσι τέκεσσιν·
Ὧι ῥά τε νήπι' ἄγοντι συναντήσονται ἐν ὕλῃ
Ἄνδρες ἐπακτῆρες, ὁ δέ τε σθένεϊ βλεμεαίνει,
Πᾶν δὲ τ' ἐπισκυνίον κάτω ἕλκεται, ὄσσε καλύπτων.
Iliad, b. 17. v. 133.

Ariosto in his Orlando Furioso has translated our author's comparison almost literally, with the single difference of substituting a she-bear instead of a lioness.

Com' orsa, che l' alpestre cacciatore
Nella pietrosa tana assalito abbia:
Sta sopra i figli con incerto core,
E freme in suoni di pieta, e di rabbia,
Ira la invita, e natural furore
A spiegar l' ugna, e insanguinar la sabbia;
Amor la intenerisce, e la ritira
A riguardar i figli in mezo all' ira.

609. Heap o'er his poor remains] So Horace, lib. 1. ode 28.

At tu, nauta, vagæ ne parce malignus arenæ
 Ossibus et capiti inhumato
Particulam dare.

It was sufficient for all the rites of burial, that dust should be thrice thrown on an unburied body. This kind of sepulture is by Quintilian called Collatitia sepultura. It was an act of religion so indispensable, that no person could be excused, and even the pontifices, who were forbidden to approach or look on a dead body, were obliged to perform this duty, as Servius tells us in his notes on the sixth book of Virgil's Æneid. Thus, among the Jews, the high priest was forbidden to approach his father's or mother's, and yet he was enjoined to inter any dead body, which he found in the road.—Francis's Horace,

Of their lov'd kings, expire their vital breath,
Rush on destruction, and enjoy their death.
Embalm'd in verse, illustrious shades, you live,
And share alike the praise my Muse can give,
Though rank'd at distance in th' Aonian quire,
She boasts not loftier Maro's tuneful lyre:
Perchance too Nisus and his friend may deign
To style you comrades in th' Elysian plain.
But fierce Amphion to the regal court
A herald sends, commission'd to report
His feats of triumph, the device explain,
And render back each captive corse again.
He flies himself to brave the leaguer'd foes,
And each associate's sever'd visage shows.
Meantime the Grecians from the walls discern
Thiodamas, and hail his safe return;
Nor could they check the gush of joy, and hide
The smiles of secret transport, when they spy'd
The naked swords, distain'd with blood.—Again
A louder clamour runs through all the train,
Whilst, leaning o'er the ramparts, they look down
For the returning troops, each for his own.
Thus when a callow brood of birds descry
Their dam long-absent, as she cleaves the sky,
They long to meet her, and put forth their heads
Far from the nest, whilst anxiously she dreads
Lest, ere she reach the tree, they fall,—then clings
To the warm nest, and flaps her loving wings.
But, whilst they clasp their friends in their embrace,
And count the slaughter of the Theban race,
For absent Hopleus some concern they show,
And oft complain, that Dymas is too slow.
Behold! the leader of the Tyrian band,
Amphion comes, a falchion in his hand.
Damp'd was his joy for the two warriors slain,
When he beheld, what carnage heap'd the plain,
The strength, and bulwark of the Thebans lost,
And in one ruin stretch'd a mighty host.
His vital frame a sudden tremour shook,
Such as attends the wretch, by thunder struck:
Fix'd as a stone, and motionless he stood,
And lost at once his voice, his sight, and blood.
The courser turns him, ere he bursts in sighs:
The dust rolls backward, as the cohort flies.
With lengthen'd strides the Tyrians sought the gate,
When the brave Grecians, hearten'd and elate
With their nocturnal triumph, to the meads
Spring, full of hopes, and urge their foaming steeds
O'er arms, and blood and bodies of the slain,
Excite the dust, and thunder through the plain,
Their heavy hoofs the limbs of heroes tore,
And the stain'd axle-trees are clogg'd with gore.
Sweet is the vengeance, pleasant is the way,
As if all Thebes in dust low-humbled lay,
And trampled with their feet.—To these began
Great Capaneus.—"No longer on the plan
Of timid caution, urge we the dark fight,
But let our deeds be witness'd by the light.
By me no other omens are explor'd,
Than my victorious hand, and naked sword."
He said. Adrastus and his son inspire
The troops with courage, and add fire to fire:
The augur then more sad and slow succeeds.
And now that day had clos'd their martial deeds,
The city enter'd; (while the wordy chief
Recounts their loss, and tells the tale of grief)
But Megareus the black battalion ey'd
Rising on sight, and from the watch-tow'r cry'd,
"Shut, sentry, shut the gates, the foe is near."
There is a season, when excess of fear
Augments our vigour. At the word they rose,
And all the gates, save one, were seen to close:
For whilst slow Echion at th' Ogygian toils,
The Spartan youth, inflam'd with lust of spoils,
Rush boldly in, and in the threshold fall,
Their blood thick dash'd against the hostile wall:
Brave Panopeus from high Taygetus came,
To rough Eurotas Œbalus laid claim:
And thou, Alcidamas, whom fame reports
A recent victor in Nemean sports,
Whose wrists first Tyndar's son with gantlets bound,
And with the season'd cincture girt thee round,
With dying eyes behold'st thy patron's star,
That sets, and gives thee to the rage of war.
Th' Œbalian grove, the margin of the stream,
From fair Lacæna styl'd, the poet's theme,
And haunt of the false swan, thy death shall mourn,
And Dian's nymphs the doleful notes return.

639. Perchance too Nisus and his friend] This is a very modest character of one of the most beautiful episodes I know. Neither can I think it so much inferior to that of Nisus and Euryalus, as the author seems to do himself. In Virgil we admire friendship for the living, but in Statius a generous gratitude to the dead; which, however, is given up to the service of the public. The reply, which Dymas makes to Amphion, who tempted him to betray his countrymen, with the promise of life and the body of his friend, is equal to any thing I have ever read in the sentimental way.

655. Thus when a callow brood] There is an agreeable simplicity in this comparison, which may disgust many, who do not observe, that the poet, accommodating himself to the occasion, means only to describe the impatience of the Thebans to see their friends, who had accompanied the expedition, and the manner and attitude, in which they posted themselves for observation. He must have a very depraved taste for poetry, who would have this image suppressed.

677. With lengthen'd strides] Homer paints Hector's progress in the eleventh book of the Iliad, with the same heat of imagination.

Ὣς ἄρα φωνήσας, ἵμασεν καλλίτριχας ἵππους
Μάστιγι λιγυρῇ· τοὶ δὲ, πληγῆς ἀίοντες,
Ῥίμφ' ἔφερον θοὸν ἅρμα μετὰ Τρῶας ϗ Ἀχαιοὺς,
Στείβοντες νέκυάς τε ϗ ἀσπίδας· αἵματι δ' ἄξων
Νέρθεν ἅπας πεπάλακτο, ϗ ἄντυγες αἳ περὶ δίφρον,
Ἃς ἄρ' ἀφ' ἱππείων ὁπλέων ῥαθάμιγκες ἔβαλλον,
Ἅς τ' ἀπ' ἐπισσώτρων.——

688. No longer on the plan] With what a beautiful abruptness does Capaneus break in upon us, and what a pleasingly terrible effect has his speech upon our minds! Some may admire the deliberate valour of Æneas; but give me the impetuosity of Achilles and Capaneus: the former indeed is of the greatest service to the state, but the latter makes the finest figure in poesy. There is an eclat of sentiment in this blunt and soldier-like speech, that forces and commands our attention: every word is animated with an enthusiastic courage, and worthy to be delivered by a gallant officer.

Thy mother too, who martial precepts gave,
And whose sage lessons form'd thee wise and brave,
Shall think, thou learn'dst too much.—Thus in
Mars rages on, and acts the will of fate. [the gate
At length, their shoulders to the mass oppos'd,
Great Alimenides, and Acron clos'd
The valves of iron—kept the foes at bay,
Barr'd the strong portals, and exclude the fray.
Thus two stout bullocks, groaning as they bow
Their necks, through fields long-fallow from the plough.
Their loss, alas! was equal to their gain:
For they exclude their friends, while they retain
Their enemies, coop'd up within the walls.
First Ormenus of Grecian lineage falls.
In suppliant posture whilst Amynthor stood,
And with extended hands for mercy su'd,
His parted visage fell upon the ground,
Th' unfinish'd accents ceas'd beneath the wound,
And his gay chain, the work of artful hands,
Clinks, dust-dishonour'd on the hostile sands.
Meantime the trench is broke, the outworks fall,
And leave a passage open to the wall,
Near which in lines was rang'd the num'rous band
Of infantry.—The coursers trembling stand,
Nor, though impatient, dare the trench o'erleap,
The prospect was so dark, the gulph so deep.
Just on the margin eagerly they neigh,
Then suddenly start back with wild affray.
These strive to force the gates, those pluck away
The pales, that in the ground deep-fasten'd lay;
The iron bars some labour to remove,
Whilst others from their sounding places shove
Huge stones.—Part see with joy the brands, they flung,
Stuck to the spires, or on the turrets hung:
Part search the basis, and apply the pow'r
Of the dark shell, to sap each hollow tow'r.
But the besieg'd (for this resource alone
Remain'd) the summit of the bulwarks crown;
And stakes, well-season'd in the flames, vast beams,
Well-polish'd darts, that shed incessant gleams,
And heated bullets from the ramparts throw,
And rob the walls of stones, to gall the foe.
The weapon'd windows hissing javelins pour,
And thick around descends the steely show'r.

As when on Malea, or Ceraunia's hill
The cloud-wrapt tempests, motionless and still,
Collect new forces, and augment their rage,
Then sudden combat with old Ocean wage,
Thus the beleag'ring Greeks without the wall
Of Thebes, o'erpow'r'd with hostile numbers fall.
Their breasts and faces obvious to the fray,
The thick'ning tempest drives them not away:
Mindless of death, straight to the walls they turn
Their looks, and their own darts alone discern.
His scythe-hung car round Thebes while Antheus
A Tyrian lance arrests him from above: [drove,
Numb'd with the stroke, his hand dismiss'd the rein:
He tumbles backward, fasten'd to the wain
By his bright greaves.—O wondrous fate of war!
His arms are trail'd by the swift-rolling car.
Beneath the smoking wheels two ruts appear,
The third imprinted by the hanging spear:
His graceful head depending on the strand,
His bloody tresses purple all the sand.
Meantime the trumpet kindles fierce alarms
Through the sad city, and excites to arms,
Thund'ring at ev'ry door its baleful call.
Their posts assign'd by lot, before them all
The standard-bearer carries in his hand
Th' imperial ensign of the Tyrian band.
Dire was the face of things, with such a scene
Not Mars himself would have delighted been.
Flight, circumfus'd in gloom, nor rul'd by thought,
Fear, sorrow, and despair, to fury wrought,
The madding town with doubtful horrours rend,
And in one subject various passions blend. [sound
You'd swear, the war was there.—The tow'rs re-
With frequent steps; the streets are fill'd around:
With fancy's eye they view the fire and sword,
And wear the fetters of an Argive lord.
Preventing fear absorb'd the time to come:
They fill with shrieks each house and holy dome;
Th' ungrateful altars are besieg'd with tears,
And the same terrour rules all ranks and years.
The old men pray for death: the youth by turns
Grows pale with fright, or with resentment burns:
The trembling courts the female shrieks rebound,
Their infant-sons, astonish'd at the sound,
Nor knowing whence the streams of sorrow flow,
Condole, and melt in sympathetic woe.
Love calls the dames together.—At this hour
The sense of shame gives place to fortune's pow'r.
They arm the men, with courage fire each breast,
Schemes of revenge with ready wit suggest,
And, rushing with them, lay before their eyes
Their homes, and babes, the pledge of nuptial ties.

729. Thus two stout bullocks] The image here given of the two warriors is as lively as it is exact. Their toil, vigour, nearness to each other, and the difficulties they encounter with, perfectly answer to each circumstance in the comparison, which is abridged from Homer's Iliad.

Ἀλλ' ὥς τ' ἐν νειῷ βόε οἴνοπε πηκτὸν ἄροτρον,
Ἶσον θυμὸν ἔχοντε, τιταίνετον, ἀμφὶ δ' ἄρα σφιν
Πρυμνοῖσιν κεράεσσι πολὺς ἀνακηκίει ἱδρώς.
Τὼ μέν τε ζυγὸν οἶον ἐΰξοον ἀμφὶς ἐέργει,
Ιεμένω κατὰ ὦλκα· τέμνει δέ τε τέλσον ἀρούρης.
Book 13. line 703.

744. The coursers trembling stand] These lines are imitated from the twelfth book of the Iliad, line 50.

——Τάφρον ἐποτρύνων διαβαινέμεν, οὐδὲ οἱ ἵπποι
Τόλμων ὠκύποδες. μάλα δὲ χρεμέτιζον ἐπ' ἄκρῳ
Χείλει ἐφεσταότες. ἀπὸ γὰρ δειδίσσετο τάφρος
Εὐρεῖ' οὔτ' ἂρ ὑπερθορέειν σχεδὸν, οὔτε περῆσαν
Ῥηϊδίη.——

785. Meantime the trumpet] After this melancholy description of the fate of Antheus, how are we startled at the sudden sound of the clarion! There is an equally abrupt transition from the pathetic to the terrible, in the ninth book of Virgil's Æneid, where our concern for the distressed mother of Euryalus is interrupted by

At tuba terribilem sonitum procul ære canoro
Increpuit.

805. The old men] The description of the different effects this consternation had upon the different stages of life, is executed with an amazing spirit and propriety; every circumstance is nature, and nature without disguise.

Thus when some shepherd-swain essays to drive
The bees thick cluster'd from their cavern'd hive,
In sable clouds they rise, assert their right,
And, buzzing, urge each other to the fight:
At length, deserted by their blunted stings,
They clasp the honey'd sweets with weary wings,
And, pressing to them, take a last farewell
Of their long-labour'd combs, and captive cell.
The vulgar too each other's schemes oppose;
Kindled by them, the flame of discord glows.
With open voice these wish the crown restor'd,
And claim great Polynices for their lord.
All rev'rence lost,—"No longer let him roam"
(One cries) "remote from his paternal home,
But hail his household-gods, his sire again,
And take possession of his annual reign.
Say, why should I with frequent blood atone
For the king's crimes, and perj'ry not my own?
"Late, much too late" (another chief replies)
"Comes that advice, when the wrong'd foe relies
On speedy conquest."—A more abject crew
With pray'rs and tears to sage Tiresias sue,
And, as some solace, urge him to disclose
The future times, or fraught with bliss or woes.
But he the mighty secret still suppress'd
Within the dark recesses of his breast,
And thus.—"Why did your king my counsel slight,
When I forbade him the perfidious fight?
Yet thee, ill-fated Thebes! should I pass o'er,
And lose th' occasion, which returns no more?
I cannot hear thy fall, nor view the light
Of Grecian fires with these dim orbs of sight.
Then yield we, Piety.—O damsel, place
A pile of altars to th' immortal race."
This done, the nymph inspects with curious eyes,
And tells her sire, that ruddy tops arise
From the divided flames, but at the height
The middle fire emits a clearer light;
Then she informs him doubtful, that the blaze
Describ'd a snake, roll'd up in circling maze,
And varying, almost lost its bloody hue,
And paints all to his intellectual view.
By her instructions taught, the pious sire
With joy embrac'd the wreath-encircled fire,
And catches on his glowing face, and brows,
The vapours, that the will of Fate disclose.
His sordid locks, now stiff with horrour, stand,
And lift above his head the trembling band:
You'd think, his eyes unclos'd, his cheeks resume
Their long-lost colour, and exhausted bloom.
At length he gave a loose to rage, and cried,
"Ye guilty Thebans, hear what fates betide
Your city, the result of sacrifice:
Its safety may be bought, though high the price.
The snake * of Mars, as his due rite, demands
A human victim from the Theban bands;
Fall he, whoe'er amidst our num'rous trains
The last of the fell dragon's race remains:
Thrice happy, who can thus adorn his death,
And for so great a meed resign his breath!
Near the fell altars of the boding chief
Sad Creon stood, and fed his soul on grief:
Yet then he only wept his common fate,
And the near ruin of th' Aonian state,
When sudden as the vengeful shaft arrests
Some hapless wretch, deep sinking in his breasts,
Pale horrour fix'd him, when he heard the call,
Which summons brave Menœceus to his fall.
A clammy sweat crept cold o'er ev'ry part,
Fear froze his veins, and thrill'd thro' all his heart.
Thus the Trinacrian coast sustains the tide
Afar rebounding from the Lybian side.
Whilst for the victim the stern prophet cries,
Full of th' inspiring god, in suppliant guise
Around his knees the tender father clung,
And strove in vain to curb his boding tongue.
Swift Fame then makes the sacred answer known,
And the dead oracle flies round the town.
Now, Clio, say, who this young warrior fir'd,
And in his breast contempt of death inspir'd!
(For ne'er, in absence of the pow'rs divine,
Could mortal harbour such a brave design)
Pursue the mighty theme: to thee alone
The storied deeds of early times are known.
Jove's fav'rite goddess press'd the throne, from whence
The gods rare virtue's costly gifts dispense
'Midst Earth's best sons:—whether almighty Jove
Consign'd it to them from well-founded love,
Or, mindful of their merits, she might choose
In ample breasts the glorious sparks t' infuse;
She sprung, all gladsome, from the realms of day:
With def'rence meet the brightest stars give way,
And signs, which for their feats and genuine worth
Herself had fix'd in Heav'n.—She lights on Earth,
Her face not far remote from air, appears
In Mantho's form, and looks of equal years.
That her responses might due credit gain,
She quits awhile the badges of her reign:
No more of terrour in her eyes is seen;
Smooth is her brow, and less severe her mien:
The sword and arms of death are thrown aside,
And by the augur's staff their place supply'd.
Her loosely-flowing garments sweep the ground,
And her rough laurell'd hair with fillets bound.
Yet her stern visage, and the steps she trod
With longsome strides reveal the latent god.
Thus smil'd the Lydian queen when she descry'd
Alcides, stript of his terrific hide,

817. Thus when] This simile seems to have been taken from one in the twelfth book of the Æneid, which, according to Mons. Catrou, is imitated from Apollonius Rhodius's Argonautics, lib. 1. verse 130.

῞Ως δὲ μέλισσαων σμῆνος μέγα μηλοβοτῆρες
Ἠὲ μελισσόκομοι πέτρῃ ἔνι καπνιόωσιν,
Αι δέ τοι τείως μὲν πολλεες ω ενι σίμβλω
Βομβηδὸν κλονέονται, ἐπὶ πρὸ δὲ λιγνυόεντι
Καπνω τύφομεναι πέτρης ἑκὰς ἀΐσσουσιν.

Virgil's is

Inclusas ut cùm latebroso in pumice pastor
Vestigavit apes, fumoque implevit amaro;
Illæ intus trepidæ rerum per cerea castra
Discurrunt, magnisque acuunt stridoribus iras.
Volvitur ater odor tectis; tum murmure cœco
Intus saxa sonant: vacuas it fumus ad auras.

* The dragon whose teeth were sown by Cadmus.

895. Now, Clio, say] The grandeur of this machinery must delight every one who has the least tincture of taste; and indeed this whole story is very affecting. The patriotic heroism of Menœceus in particular, is finely contrasted by the tender affection and fatherly love of Creon.

923. Thus smil'd the Lydian queen] The for-

Shine in embroider'd vests, and robes of cost,
On his broad back, and brawny shoulders lost,
When Pallas' arts with ill success he try'd,
And broke the timbrel, which in vain he ply'd.
Nor thee, Menœceus, does the goddess find
Unworthy of the honours she design'd:
Before the Theban tow'rs she sees thee stand,
With early worth preventing her command.
Soon as th' enormous portals wide unclose,
How didst thou quash the pride of Argive foes!
Thus Hæmon rages too; but tho' you shine
Brothers in all, the greater praise is thine.
The breathless carcases are heap'd around;
Sure flies each dart, each weapon bears a wound.
Nor yet was virtue present.—Ne'er he stands,
Unbent his mind, unexercis'd his hands:
His arms no leisure know, the sphinx pourtray'd
Upon his helm seems mad; the blood survey'd,
Th' enliven'd effigy springs forth to view,
And the dull copper wears a brighter hue:
When now the goddess check'd his furious hand,
And thus accosts him, as he lifts the brand.
" O noble youth, whose claim of lineage Mars
With joy accepts, resign these humble wars;
This palm is not thy due.—The stars invite
Thy soul away, and promise more delight.
My sire now rages in the joyful fane;
This sense the flames and fibres ascertain,
This Phœbus urges; thee all Thebes demands,
To save the rest of her devoted bands.
Fame sings the sacred answer, and our youth
With shouts of triumph hail the voice of truth.
Embrace the glorious offer then, nor waste
The time away, but to fruition haste,
Lest Hæmon start before thee."—Thus she spake,
And fann'd the sparks of virtue still awake;
Then, clearing all his doubts with lenient art,
She winds herself, unseen, into his heart.
Swift as assail'd by Jove's unerring aim,
The blasted cypress takes th' ethereal flame,
From top to stern with bright contagion spread;
The youth (so well her forceful influence sped)
Feeds the new ardours kindled in his breast,
And longs for death, each meaner thought supprest.
But when he 'gan at leisure to survey
Her gait and habit, as she turns away,
And mingling with the clouds, eludes his eyes,
In height of admiration, thus he cries.
" Willing, O goddess, we obey thy call,
Nor meet with passive sloth the destin'd fall:"
—And while from fight, obsequious, he withdrew,
Agreus of Pylos near the trenches slew.
At length, supported by his menial train,
He goes; the vulgar hail him o'er the plain
With names of patriot, champion, god, inspire
An honest pride, and set his soul on fire.
And now to Thebes his hasty course he bends,
Well-pleas'd to have escap'd his wretched friends,
When Creon met him, and would fain accost,
But his breath fail'd, his utterance was lost.
Awhile both silent and dejected stand,
At length his sire began with kind demand.
" Say, prythee, what new stroke of fortune calls
My son from fight, when Greece surrounds our walls?
What worse than cruel war dost thou prepare,
Why do thy eyes with rage unwonted glare,
Why o'er thy cheeks such savage paleness reigns,
And ill thy face a father's look sustains?
Heard'st thou the forg'd responses?—It appears
Too well.—My son, by our unequal years,
I pray thee, and thy wretched mother's breasts,
Trust not, O trust not, what the seer suggests.
Think'st thou, the pow'rs that haunt yon starry
Vouchsafe to shed down intellectual light [height,
On such a dotard, whose perpetual gloom
And age approach th' incestuous monarch's doom?
Yet more—the king may deal with secret fraud,
And for some end spread these reports abroad,
For well I ween, he views with jealous eye
Thy first-rate valour and nobility.
Perchance these pompous words, which we suppose
Divine, from his too fertile brain arose.
Give not thy heated mind the reins of sway,
Allow some interval, some short delay:
Impetuous haste misguides us oft.—O grant
This last, this modest boon; 'tis all I want.
So be thy temples silver'd o'er with age;
So may a father's cares thy thoughts engage,
And cause the fears thy rash designs inspire;
Ne'er then, O ne'er forsake thy wretched sire.
Why should the pledges of another's love,
And alien parents thy compassion move?
If aught of shame remains, first tend thy own:
This is true piety, and true renown.
The other's a mere shade, a transient breath
Of fame, and titles lost in gloomy death.
Nor think I check thee thro' excess of fear:
Go, mix in combat—toss the pointed spear,

titude of Hercules was not equal to his amorousness. He fell in love with Omphale, queen of Lydia, and in order to win her affections by his obsequiousness, condescended to change the lion's hide for a suit of purple, and the club for a distaff.

941. The sphinx pourtray'd] Though some readers may think this image too bold, it is evident Tasso did not, from his imitation of it. Gierus. lib. can. 9. st. 25.

> Porta il Soldan su'l elmo orrido e grande
> Serpe, che si dilunga, e'l collo snoda
> Su le zampe s' inalza, e l' ali spande,
> E piega in arco la forcuta coda,
> Par che tre lingue vibri, e che fuor mande
> Livida spuma, e che l' suo fischio s' oda.
> Ed or, ch' arde la pugna anch' ei s' infiamma
> Nel moto, e fumo versa insieme, e fiamma.

949. The stars invite] These verses are imitated by the last-quoted author, in the second book of his Jerusalem, where Sophronia says to Olindo,

> ——Lieto aspira alta superna fede:
> Mira il ciel, com' e bello, e mira il sole,
> Ch' a se par, che n' inviti, e ne console. Stan. 36.

987. Say, prythee] One seldom meets with a finer piece of dissuasive and pathetic eloquence, than this oration of Creon. The circumstances of distress show a judicious choice in the poet, and are expressed in a very happy manner. The question Creon puts to his son, in "Heard'st thou, &c." and the preventing his confusion by answering it himself, is a striking instance of the poet's taste in the use of figures. The odium he afterwards throws on Eteocles, and the ridiculous light he sets Tiresias in, to give weight to his dehortation, is very artful.

And dare the thickest horrours of the plain:
Where chance is equal, I will ne'er restrain.
O let me cleanse with tears the stain of blood,
And with my hairs dry up the surging flood;
Thus thou may'st fight, o'ercome, and triumph still;
This is thy country's choice, thy father's will."
Thus in embrace his troubled son he holds,
And round his neck his arms encircling folds;
But neither could the copious stream of grief,
Nor words unbend the Heav'n-devoted chief.
Yet more, the gods suggesting, he relieves
His father's fears, and with this tale deceives.
"O best of parents! let not idle fear
Disturb thy bliss; no phrenzy of the seer,
No phantoms of the dead, nor signs from Jove
Solicit me to quit this light above.
Still may Tiresias to his friends impart
The god's response, and try each priestly art;
Nor should I lay aside my fix'd design,
Tho' Phœbus warn me from his open shrine.
But my dear brother's sad mischance recalls
My willing steps to these ill-omen'd walls;
Pierc'd by an Argive spear, my Hæmon lies
Between both hosts, and soon the Grecians' prize;
So thick the foesurrounds, that scarce, I trust,
This arm can reach him 'midst th' insanguin'd dust.
But why do I delay?—Go, raise again
His drooping spirits, and command the train
To bear him off with care.—I haste to find
Eetion, skill'd, o'er all the healing kind,
To close up wounds, to stanch the flux of blood,
And stop the flight of life's low-ebbing flood."
His speech broke off, away the hero sped;
A sudden gloom his father's mind o'erspread;
His love's divided, ill his tears agree,
Yet he believes, impell'd by destiny.
Meantime fierce Capaneus pursues the train,
Whom Tyrian portals vomit on the plain,
And swells with frequent deaths the guilty field;
Horse, foot, and charioteers before him yield;
And, their pierc'd drivers thrown, th' unbridled steeds
Crush out their souls, and thunder o'er the meads.
He reeks in blood, the lofty tow'rs assails
With stones, and wheresoe'er he turns, prevails.
One while he plied his sling, and dealt around
From swift-hurl'd bullets a new kind of wound,
Then, lanching forth a dart, his arm he swung
Aloft. No weapon idle fell, he flung,
Nor, innocent of blood, return'd again,
But levell'd some proud warrior on the plain.
Their place by him supplied, the Grecian host
No longer deem their mightiest leaders lost,
Oenides, Atalanta's youthful son,
Amphiaraus, and stern Hippomedon:
In him they meet, inspire an equal flame,
And animate by turns his vital frame.
Nor age, nor rank, nor form, his pity moves,
The proud and meek alike his fury proves.
Not one durst with him try the chance of war,
Or stand in arms oppos'd.—They dread from far
His temper'd armour, his tremendous crest,
And glitt'ring helm, with various forms imprest.
Meanwhile Menœceus on the walls was seen,
Divine his aspect, more august his mien;
His casque aside the pious hero threw,
And stood a while, confess'd to public view;
From thence he cast an eye of pity down,
On either host, that fought before the town,
And silence, and a truce from war enjoin'd,
Thus spoke the purpose of his gen'rous mind.
"Ye pow'rs of war, and thou, whose partial love
Grants me this honour, Phœbus, son of Jove,
O give to Thebes the joys so dearly sought,
Those mighty joys, by my own life-blood bought:
Return the war, on Lerna's captive coast
Dash the foul remnants of her vanquish'd host;
And let old Inachus with adverse waves
Shun his fam'd offspring, now dishonour'd slaves.
But let the Thebans by my death obtain
Their fanes, lands, houses, children, wives again.
If aught of merit my submission claim,
If, undismay'd, I heard the prophet name
Myself the victim, nor with fear withdrew,
Assenting, ere my country deem'd it true,
To Thebes, I pray, in lieu of me be kind;
And teach my cred'lous sire to be resign'd."
He said, and pointing to his virtuous breast
The glitt'ring blade, attempts to set at rest
Th' indignant soul, that frets and loaths to stay,
Imprison'd in its tenement of clay:
He lustrates with his blood the walls and tow'rs,
And throws himself amidst the banded pow'rs,
And, grasping still the sabre in his hands,
Essays to fall on the stern Grecian bands.
But piety and virtue bear away,
And gently on the ground his body lay;
While the free spirit stands before the throne
Of Jove, and challenges the well-earn'd crown.
Now to the walls of Thebes with joyful care
The hero's corse, with ease obtain'd, they bear.
The Greeks with decent reverence survey
The solemn pomp, and willingly give way:
On youthful shoulders borne, amidst a train
Of either sex, who break into a lane,
He passes on, to rank celestial rais'd,
And more than Cadmus or Amphion prais'd.

1059. Meantime fierce Capaneus] With what dreadful pomp is Capaneus ushered in here! in what bold colours has the poet drawn his impetuosity and irresistibility, and what a grand idea does he give us of his hero, when he tells us, that by his valorous feats he kept the Greeks in such a perpetual round of attention, that they had not time to reflect upon the loss of their four commanders, or if they did, that they thought Capaneus was equal to all of them together, and that his body was animated by their souls.

1119. While the free spirit] This passage recalls to my mind some fine lines of Lucan, in which he describes the residence of Pompey's soul, after it was separated from the body:

At non in Pharia manes jacuêre favillâ:
Nec cinis exiguus tantam compescuit umbram.
Prosiluit busto, semiustaque membra relinquens,
Degeneremque rogum, sequitur convexa Tonantis,
Quâ niger astriferis connectitur axibus aer,
Quodque patet terras inter lunæque meatus
Semidei manes habitant: quos ignea virtus
Innocuos vitâ patientes ætheris imi
Fecit, et æternos animam collegit in orbes:
Non illuc auro positi, nec thure sepulti
Perveniunt; illic postquam se lumine vero
Implevit stellasque vagas miratur, et astra
Fixa polis, vidit quanta sub nocte jaceret
Nostra dies, risitque sui ludibria trunci.

Phars. lib. 9.

These o'er his lifeless limbs gay garlands fling;
Those single flow'rs, the produce of the spring,
And in his ancestors' time-honour'd tomb
Depose the body, od'rous with perfume.
The rites of praise perform'd, they straight renew'd
The combat.—Here, his wrath at length subdu'd,
In groans the mournful Creon seeks relief,
And the sad mother weeps away her grief.
" For cruel Thebes by me then wast thou bred,
And have I nourish'd thy devoted head, [done,
Like some vile dame?—What mischiefs have I
And to what gods thus odious am I grown?
No interdicted pleasures did I prove,
Nor wast thou offspring of incestuous love.
Jocasta's sons command the deathful plain,
Fate gives the sceptre, and she sees them reign.
Let us for this ill-omen'd war atone,
That they may mount by turns the sully'd throne.
(This pleases thee, O cloud-compelling Jove!)
Why censure I or men or gods above?
'Tis thou, Menœceus, who has caus'd my fall;
On thee it rests, the guilty source of all.
From whence this love of death that seiz'd my
And holy rage? How diff'rent in their kind [mind,
From their sad mother these my children prove,
Fruit of my throes, and pledges of my love!
Full well, alas! the fatal cause I read
In the fell snake, and war-producing mead:
Hence headstrong valour, impotent of rest,
Usurp'd my share in guidance of thy breast,
And, unconstrain'd, nay 'gainst the will of fate,
Thou wing'st thy way to Pluto's gloomy state.
Much of the Greeks and Capaneus I heard;
Yet this, this hand alone was to be fear'd,
And weapon, which imprudently I gave:
Yet why?—It was fit present for the brave.
See, the wide wound absorbs the length of sword,
Deep as the fiercest Argive could have gor'd."
More had she said, unknowing check or bound,
And sadden'd with her wailings all around;
But her consoling comrades homeward led
Th' unwilling dame, and plac'd her on the bed:
There, her torn cheeks suffus'd with blood, she lay
Deaf to advice, and sick'ning at the day;
And, her voice gone, and all confus'd her mind,
Still kept her languid eyes on earth declin'd.
The Scythian tigress thus beneath some cave
For her stol'n whelps is often seen to rave,
And, couching at the vasty mouth alone,
Scents the fresh trace, and licks the tepid stone.
Her hunger, wrath, and native rage subside,
In grief consum'd. Securely by her side,
With passive impotency she surveys
The flocks and herds on verdant pasture graze:
For where are those, for whom she now should feed
Her dugs, and range, in quest of prey, the mead?
Thus far have arms and death adorn'd our lays,
And war's grim horrours been a theme of praise:
Now be the song to Capaneus transferr'd.
No more I grovel with the vulgar herd,
But, catching fury from th' Aonian grove,
Uncircumscrib'd, thro' realms of ether rove.
With me, ye Muses, prove the high event—
Whether from deepest night this rage was sent,
Or the dire furies, rang'd beneath his sign,
Impell'd him to confront the pow'rs divine,
Or rashness urg'd him on, or lust of fame,
Which woos by per'lous feats a deathless name;
Or preludes of success Heav'n sent to draw
The guilty wretch, to break calm caution's law;
He loaths all earthly joys; the rage of fight
Palls on his soul, and slaughter shocks his sight:
And, all his quiver spent, he lifts on high
His weary arm, and points it to the sky.
He rolls his wrathful eyes round, metes the height
Of the tall rampires, and th' unnumber'd flight
Of steps, and straight of two compacted trees
A ladder forms, to scale the walls with ease.
Now, dreadful from afar, he bares to view
A clefted oak, that lighten'd as he flew:
His burnish'd arms too ruddy splendours yield,
And the flame kindles on his blazing shield.
" Virtue directs me by this path" (he cry'd)
" To Thebes, by which the slipp'ry tow'r is dy'd
With brave Menœceus' blood.—Then let me try
If sacred rites avail, or Phœbus lie."
He said, and, mounting up the captive wall
By steps alternate, menaces its fall.
Such in mid air the fierce Alcidæ show'd,
When Earth's bold sons with vain ambition glow'd,
Ere Pelion (hideous height!) was hurl'd above,
Or Ossa cast a shade on trembling Jove.
Th' astonish'd Thebans then, on th' utmost verge
Of fated ruin, the sharp contest urge,
Nor less than if Bellona, torch in hand,
Was bent to fire their town, and waste their land,
Huge beams and stones from ev'ry quarter fling,
And ply with haste the Balearic sling:
(For now no hope, no dawn of safety lies
In darts, and random shafts, that wing the skies)
Vast engines too, in passion's giddy whirl,
And massy fragments at the foe they hurl.

1132. Od'rous] I cannot but think *adoratum* a typographical errour, and would therefore substitute *odoratum* in its stead, which those who are acquainted with the funeral rites of the ancients will, I doubt not, approve of, it being the custom to perfume the bodies of the dead before burial. I hope the reader will pardon this conjecture, if he does not coincide with me.

1175. The Scythian tigress thus] The grief of Menœceus's mother for the loss of her son, is aptly enough pourtrayed by this simile of the tigress; the hint of it may have possibly been taken from the following comparison in the eighteenth book of Homer's Iliad.

——Ὥσπερ λῖς ἠϋγένειος
Ὧι ῥά θ' ὑπὸ σκυμνους ἐλαφηβόλος ἁρπάσῃ ἀνὴρ
Ὕλης ἐκ πυκινῆς· ὁ δέ τ' ἄχνυται ὕστερος ἐλθών.
Πολλὰ δέ τ' ἄγχι ἐπῆλθε μετ' ἀνέρος ἴχνι' ἐρευνῶν,
Εἴποθεν ἐξεύροι. μαλα γὰρ δριμὺς χόλος αἱρεῖ.
Verse 318.

This is natural enough, but the images contained in

—— Tepidi lambit vestigia saxi.
———— Eunt præter secura armenta, gregesque
Aut quos ingenti premat expectata rapina:

are perhaps equal to any thing in the Homeric allusion.

1185. Thus far have arms] The poet raises the character of his hero very much by this invocation. One muse sufficed before, but he now summons all the nine, by which the grandeur of the subject is very much enhanced, and the difficulty of singing his great exploits very strongly imaged.

The weapons that from ev'ry part are thrown
Deter him not, nor fetch the warrior down:
Hanging in empty air, his steps he guides,
Secure of danger, and with longsome strides,
As on plain ground, maintains an equal pace,
Tho' death on all sides stares him in the face.
Thus some deep river, thund'ring in its course,
Turns on an aged bridge its wat'ry force;
And, as the loosen'd stones and beams give way,
Doubles its rage, and strives to wash away
The mass inert, nor ceases, till it sees
Th' obstructing pile dispers'd, and flows with ease.
Soon as he reach'd the turret's long-sought height,
(Tho' lessen'd, yet conspicuous to the sight)
And scar'd the Thebans with his bulky shade,
He cast a downward look, and vaunting said:
" Are these the bulwarks then, is this the wall,
That erst obey'd Amphion's tuneful call?
Are these the fabled theme, and storied boast
Of Thebes? Shall these oppose our conqu'ring host?
What honour, tho' beneath our frequent stroke
These lyre-constructed tow'rs should yield?"—He spoke,
And with his hands and feet fast hurling down
The coins and beams compacted, lays the town
Part open.—Then the bridge-form'd works divide,
And the stone joists from off the ridges slide.
The fortress broken down, again he takes
Advantage of the ruin which he makes,
And, gath'ring rocky fragments as they fall,
Destroys the town with its own shiver'd wall.
Mean time round Jove's bright throne the pow'rs divine
For Thebes and Greece in fierce contention join:
To both alike impartial, he descries
Their animated wrath with careless eyes.
Restrain'd by Juno, Bacchus inly groans;
Then, glancing at his sire, he thus bemoans:
" O Jove, where is that cruel hand, which aims
The forked bolt, and lanches livid flames,
My cradle once?"—Sol for those mansions sighs,
Which erst he gave to Cadmus as a prize.
His equal love sad Hercules extends
To both, and doubts, whilst yet his bow he bends;
His mother's birth-place* Perseus much laments,
And Venus for Harmonia's people vents
Her grief in tears: suspicious of her spouse,
She stands aloof, and, wroth for broken vows,
In secret Mars regards.—The martial dame
On Tyrian gods, audacious, casts the blame:
A furious silence tortures Juno's breast,
Yet nought avails to break th' Almighty's rest;
Nay e'en the strife had ceas'd, when in the skies
The voice of Capaneus was heard.—He cries:
" On part of Thebes then no immortals stand;
Where are the natives of the guilty land,
Bacchus and Hercules?—It gives me shame
To challenge any of inferior name.
Come, Jove, (for who's more worthy to engage?)
Thy harlot's threat'ned ashes claim thy rage;
Come, gather all thy lightning to the blow,
And plunge me flaming to the shades below:
Abler perchance the timid sea to scare
With empty sound, and unavailing glare,
Or wreak thy spite on Cadmus' bridal bed."
The gods deep groan'd, yet nought in rev'rence said.
Th' Eternal, smiling at his rashness, shakes
The honours of his head, and thus bespeaks.
" Survives then mortal pride dire Phlegra's fight,
And wilt thou too my slumb'ring wrath excite?"
This heard, the pow'rs eternal prompt his hand
Long-ling'ring, and his vengeful darts demand;
Nor now the partner of imperial state,
Saturnia, durst resist the will of fate.
His regal dome in empyreal Heav'n
Spontaneous thunders, ere a sign was giv'n.
The show'rs collect, the clashing clouds are join'd
In conflict fierce, without one blast of wind;
You'd think Iapetus had broke his chain,
Or fell Typhœus was releas'd again,
Inarime, and Ætna rear'd on high.
Th' immortals blush to fear, but when they spy
In mid-way air an earth-born warrior stand
Oppos'd to Jove, and the mad fight demand;
Th' unwonted scene in silence they admire,
And doubt, if he'll employ th' etherial fire.
Now 'gan the pole just o'er th' Ogygian tow'r
To thunder, prelude of almighty pow'r,
And Heav'n was ravish'd from each mortal eye:
Yet still he grasps the spires, he can't descry;
And oft, as gleams shone thro' the breaking cloud,
" This flash comes opportune" (he cries aloud)
" To wrap proud Thebes in fire; at my demand
'Twas sent to wake anew my smould'ring brand."
While thus he spake, the lord of all above
Bar'd his right arm, and all his thunder drove;
Dispers'd in ambient air, his plumes upflew,
And his shield falls, discolour'd to the view;
And now his manly members all lie bare:
Both hosts, astounded at the dazzling glare,
Recede, lest, rushing with his whelming weight,
And flaming limbs, he hasten on their fate.
His helmet, hair, and torch now hiss within,
And from the touch quick shrinks his shudd'ring [skin;
He shoves his mail away, amaz'd to feel
Beneath his breast the cinders of the steel,
And places full against the hated wall
His smoking bosom, lest, half-burnt, he fall.
At length, his earthly part resolv'd away,
The spirit quits its prison-house of clay;
And, had his hardy corse consum'd more slow,
He might have well deserv'd a second blow.

* Argos.

1237. Thus some deep river] I know nothing that can give us a more terrible idea of Capaneus assaulting the Theban fortifications, than this comparison of a river's beating with violence against a bridge: there is great majesty of style, and variety of images in it, and the simile itself contains such an exact point of likeness, as cannot fail of pleasing every reader of taste.

1261. Mean time round Jove's bright throne] Statius gives the Greeks the same auxiliary deities as Homer does. In this particular he has shown great judgment, but still greater, in not imitating the ridiculous battle of the gods, which characterises the 21st book of the Iliad.

1269. My cradle once] The poet alludes to the supposed notion, that Bacchus was taken out of Jupiter's thigh.

1288. Thy harlot's threat'ned ashes] Semele, who was burnt by lightning. Her ashes were preserved in an urn, and held in great veneration by the Thebans.

1340. He might have well deserv'd] I cannot conclude my notes on this book, without taking

BOOK XI.

THE ARGUMENT.

The Greeks being disheartened by the death of Capaneus, the Thebans make a great slaughter of them. Tisiphone persuades her sister Megæra to assist her in forwarding the duel between the two brothers. Jupiter calls a council of the gods, and advises them to retire from the sight of the combat. Tisiphone goes in quest of Polynices, and by her machinations prevails on him to challenge his rival. He informs Adrastus of his intention, whose attempts to deter him from it are frustrated by the fury. Eteocles returns thanks to Jupiter for his victory by a sacrifice, which is attended with several inauspicious omens. Æpytus bears the challenge to the king. His courtiers dissuade him from accepting it, but Creon insolently insists on it. Jocasta uses her interest with him to hinder the congress. Antigone addresses Polynices to the same purpose, and would have gained her point, had not the fury interposed. They engage. Adrastus endeavouring in vain to part them, retreats to Argos. Piety descends from Heaven to the same effect, but is repulsed by Tisiphone. Polynices overcomes Eteocles; but attempting to strip him of his arms, receives a mortal wound. They both expire. Œdipus laments over their bodies, and endeavours to kill himself, as does Jocasta, who is prevented by Ismene. Creon usurps the crown, and prohibits the burial of the dead bodies. He then threatens to banish Œdipus, who loads him with a volley of imprecations: Antigone intercedes, and procures his pardon. The remains of the confederate army decamp by night, and fly to Adrastus's dominions.

When dying Capaneus had now supprest
The daring fury of his impious breast,
And the vindictive bolt, well pleas'd to prove
Its pow'r obsequious to the will of Jove,
Spent on the walls the remnant of its force,
And to the blasted earth pursu'd its course;
The Thunderer withholds his vengeful hand,
Recalls the day, and spares the guilty land;
While from their thrones sublime the gods arise,
And hail with shouts the monarch of the skies,

some notice of the exploits of Capaneus, which make, in my opinion, the finest part, not only of this book, but of the whole work. There is great strength of imagination and an animated turn of expression in it, which must engage every one, who admires the flights of an irregular and eccentric genius. The violence and impetuosity of Capaneus is finely contrasted by the calm consciousness of superiority in Jupiter; but it may be observed, that as our poet has elevated the character of his hero up to the gods, so he has put that of the gods upon a level with men. Witness that hemistich,

Th' immortals blush to fear.

This, however, is not the fault of Statius in particular, but of all the authors who have introduced machinery in their poems.

As when from Phlegra conqu'ring he return'd,
And crush'd Enceladus his anger mourn'd.
But Capaneus, consign'd to deathless fame
For acts which Jove chastis'd, but durst not blame,
Retains the frowns which death could not efface,
Whilst his huge arms a shatter'd tow'r embrace.
As Tityus, monster of enormous size,
Stretch'd o'er nine acres near Avernus lies;
Whose giant-limbs if chance the birds survey,
They start, and trembling quit th' immortal prey;
While still his fruitful fibres spring again,
Swell, and renew the bold offender's pain.
Thus groan'd the plain beneath th' oppressive load,
And with bright flames of livid sulphur glow'd.
Now paus'd the battle; and the chosen train
Of weeping suppliants quit each hallow'd fane.
Here all their vows, here all their sorrows cease,
And each fond mother's pray'r is hush'd in peace.
Mean while the Greeks in broken squadrons yield,
And to their victor-foes resign the field.
They fear not human threats, or hostile darts,
But angry Jove unmans their drooping hearts.
His thunder-storms still dwell upon their ears,
And fancy'd lightnings cleave the starry spheres.

Among all the books of the Thebaid, there is none in which the poet has conducted that part which concerns the marvellous with greater art and address. The intrigue of the furies to procure a duel between the two rivals has something in it pleasingly terrible. Add to this the spirit and propriety of the several speeches, among which those of Eteocles, Polynices, Antigone, and Œdipus are master-pieces in their kind, and inimitably beautiful. But, bating these perfections, which characterize it in particular, the subject and matter of it in general is too interesting not to require a double degree of attention in perusing it. We see in the conclusion of it poetical justice administered with great impartiality and propriety; and the grand end of the poem answered, which was, the showing the ill effects of ambition, exemplified in the death of the two brothers. We are only therefore to look upon the twelfth book as an ornamental supplement, as the poem might have ended here without violating the laws of the epopœia.

11. Phlegra] Phlegra was a city of Macedonia, where the giants fought the gods. It is situated under mount Pindus.

17. As Tityus] Lucretius has beautifully explained the fable of Tityus according to its allegorical sense.

Nec Tityon volucres ineunt Acheronte jacentem;
Nec, quod sub magno scrutetur pectore, quidquam
Perpetuam ætatem poterunt reperire profecto,
Quamlibet immani projectu corporis exstet,
Qui non sola novem dispersis jugera membris,
Obtineat, sed qui terrai totius orbem:
Non tamen æternum poterit perferre dolorem,
Nec præbere cibum proprio de corpore semper,
Sed Tityos hic est nobis, in amore jacentem
Quem volucres lacerant, atque exest anxius angor;
Aut aliâ quâvis scindunt cupedine curæ.

33. His thunder-storms] Any noise or sight that makes a deep impression on us, affects our organs of sensation, as it were by a kind of echo, long after the object is removed. It is thus we see Adam affected after the angel's relation:

He seems himself to press the flying band,
And lanch his bolts with unremitting hand.
The Theban monarch, eager to improve
The fair occasion proffer'd him by Jove,
Pricks onward to the rout, and o'er the mead
With goring spurs impels his foaming steed.
Thus when the royal savage, gorg'd with food,
Retires, th' inferior natives of the wood,
Bears, wolves, and spotted lynxes haste away,
To seize the scanty relics of his prey.
Eurymedon succeeds, who weapons bore
Of form uncouth, and rustic armour wore;
Pan was his boasted sire; like him he courts
A modest fame, and shines in rural sports.
Next came Alatreus, flush'd with early fire,
And matching, while a boy, his youthful sire.
Thrice happy both, but far more envy'd he,
Whom fate adorn'd with such a progeny.
Their years unequal, equal their renown,
By both with equal strength the dart was thrown.
Where the deep trench in length extended lay,
Compacted troops stand wedg'd in firm array.
Alas! how fickle is the god of fight!
How vain, oppos'd to Heav'n, is human might!
The Greeks, who late the walls of Cadmus scal'd,
In turn behold with grief their tents assail'd.
As driving clouds before a whirlwind fly,
And break and scatter thro' the ruffled sky;

> The angel ended, and in Adam's ear
> So charming left his voice, that he awhile
> Thought him still speaking.
>
> Par. Lost, B. 8. L. 1.

It is thus we must account for the seeming inconsistency in the following verses of Homer.

> Ἤτοι ὅτ' ἐς πεδίον τὸ Τρωϊκὸν ἀθρήσειε,
> Θαύμαζεν πυρὰ πολλὰ, τὰ καίετο Ἰλιόθι πρὸ,
> Αὐλῶν, συρίγγων τ' ἐνοπὴν, ὅμαδόν τ' ἀνθρώπων. B. 10.

or as Aristotle answers a criticism of some censurers of Homer on this place, who asked, how it was that Agamemnon, shut up in his tent in the night, could see the Trojan camp at one view, and the fleet at another, as the poet represents it? Το δε κατα μεταφοραν ειρηται (says he), that is, 'tis only a metaphorical manner of speech; to cast one's eye, means but to reflect upon, or to revolve in one's mind; and that employed Agamemnon's thoughts in his tent, which had been the chief object of his sight the day before.

61. As driving clouds] As some critics have objected against heaping comparisons one upon another, to prevent any prejudices which the unwary reader may form, we shall lay before him Mr. Pope's defence of the following verses of Homer:

> Ουτε θαλασσης κυμα τοσον βοαα ποτι χερσον,
> Ποντόθεν ορνυμενον πνοιῃ Βορεω αλεγεινη.
> Ουτε πυρος τοσσος γε ποτι βρομος αιθομενοιο,
> Ουρεος εν βησσης, οτε τ' ωρετο καιεμεν υλην·
> Ουτ' ανεμος τοσσονγε ποτι δρυσιν υψικομοισιν
> Ηπυει, ος τε μαλιστα μεγα βρεμεται χαλεπαινων.

"In this case," says he, "the principal image is more strongly impressed on the mind by a multiplication of similes, the natural product of an imagination labouring to express something vast: but finding no single idea sufficient to answer its conceptions, it endeavours, by redoubling the comparisons, to supply this defect; the different sounds of waters, winds, and flames, being as it were united in one. We have several instances of this sort even in so castigated and reserved a writer as Virgil, who has joined together the images of this passage in the fourth Georgic, and applied them, beautifully softened by a kind of parody, to the buzzing of a bee-hivé.

> Frigidus ut quondam sylvis immurmurat Auster,
> Ut mare sollicitum stridet refluentibus undis,
> Æstuat ut clausis rapidus fornacibus ignis.

Tasso has not only imitated this particular passage of Homer, but likewise added to it. Canto 9. stanza 22.

> Rapido si che torbida procella
> Da' cavernosi monti esce piu tarda:
> Fiume, ch' arbori insieme, e case svella:
> Folgore, che le torri abbatta, et arda:
> Terremoto, che'l mondo empia d'orrore,
> Son picciole sembianze al suo furore.

As angry billows lave the rocky strand,
And now disclose, and now o'erwhelm the sand;
Or when on Ceres southern gusts descend,
Before the blast the nodding harvests bend:
Thus fall the rough Tyrinthian youths beneath
The scythe of death, who, like Alcides, sheath
Their limbs in savage trophies. From on high
Their patron views their hapless destiny,
And pities, as he marks their shaggy spoils,
Memorials of his own illustrious toils.
Enipeus, urg'd by some unfriendly pow'r,
O'erlook'd the conflict from a Grecian tow'r;
Of either army none was more renown'd
The warrior-trumpet in the field to sound:
But while, an advocate for speedy flight,
He sounded a retreat from adverse fight,
Hurl'd by some envious foe, a whizzing spear
Transfix'd his hand, and nail'd it to his ear:
Nor ceas'd the clarion, when the hand of Death
Impos'd a truce, and Fate suppress'd his breath,

76. The warrior-trumpet] Statius has been blamed by some ingenious philologists for confounding the manners of the times he wrote of, with those of the times he lived in, by introducing a trumpeter upon the stage. They quote Eustathius and Didymus, to prove that the use of that instrument was not known during the Theban war. But with deference to their superior abilities, we must beg leave to observe, that the testimony of the poet is much more valid than that of the above-mentioned authors, as he lived nearer those times, and consequently had a better opportunity of making researches and inquiries. Virgil has likewise introduced it as used in the Trojan war, which was not long after that of Thebes, and the sacred writers make mention of them very frequently in their history of ages at least as early as this.

81. Nor ceas'd the clarion] The hint of this beautiful circumstance seems taken from the description of Orpheus's death in the fourth book of the Georgics.

> Tum quoque marmoreâ caput a cervice revulsum,
> Gurgite cum medio portans Œagrius Hebrus
> Volveret, Eurydicen vox ipsa et frigida lingua,
> Ah miseram Eurydicen, animâ fugiente, vocabat.

But, to th' amazement of the list'ning throngs,
Th' unvary'd soothing strain awhile prolongs.
Meantime the fiend, embolden'd by success,
And pleas'd to view the Grecian host's distress,
Thinks nothing done, till, fir'd with mutual rage,
The rival kings in impious fight engage;
And lest, unaided, her attempts should fail,
When force combin'd might easily prevail,
Megæra partner of her toils she makes,
And summons to the charge her kindred snakes.
For this a passage with her Stygian blade
In a lone valley for her voice she made;
And mutters words, that shook the depth of Hell,
And rous'd the fury from her gloomy cell:
Then a loud-hissing horned snake she rears,
Conspicuous midst the matted tuft of hairs:
Earth groans disparting at the dreadful sound,
Olympus trembles, and the deeps rebound;
While, wak'd to sudden wrath, th' ethereal sire
Demands his bolts, and threats the world with fire.
Her comrade at the distant summons shook,
As near her parent's side her stand she took;
While Capaneus harangues th' assembled ghosts,
And loud applauses rend the Stygian coasts.
Swift from the baleful regions of the dead
Th' ascending monster bar'd her horrid head.
The shades rejoice: the circling clouds give way,
And Hell exults with unexpected day.
Her sister flew to meet her, swift as wind;
And thus unfolds the purpose of her mind.
"Thus far our father's harsh commands I've borne,
Alone on Earth, expos'd to mortals' scorn,
While you, exempt from war and hostile rage,
The pliant ghosts with gentle sway assuage.
Nor are my hopes deceiv'd, or labours vain:
Witness this crimson stream, and reeking plain;
To me dread Pluto owes the num'rous shades,
That swarm in Styx, and the Lethæan glades.
These are my triumphs, this the dire success
Acquir'd by toils, and purchas'd with distress.
Let Mars command the fates of either host;
'Tis not of vulgar deaths alone I boast:
Ye saw (for sure his figure must command
Your notice, as he stalk'd along the strand)
A martial chief, whose terrour-breathing face
And hands black streams of lukewarm gore disgrace.
Inspir'd by me, on human flesh he fed,
And with his teeth defac'd the victor's head.
Ye heard (for Nature felt the thunder-shock,
That might have riv'd an adamantine rock)
When Jove in all his terrours sate array'd,
And summon'd all the godhead to his aid,
To wreak his vengeance on a son of Earth:
I smil'd, for such a scene provok'd my mirth.
But now (for ever unreserv'd and free
I trust the secrets of my soul to thee)
My hands refuse the blunted torch to rear,
And the tir'd serpents loath this upper air.

97. Then a] The cerastes has horns like a ram's, and a very small body. It was probably from this description Milton took the hint of the following verses.

But on they roll'd in heaps, and up the trees
Climbing, sat thicker than the snaky locks
That curl'd Megæra. Par. Lost, b. 10. v. 558.

113. Thus] One cannot sufficiently admire the fire, spirit, and propriety of this oration, and with what art the character of the fury Tisiphone is supported.

But thou, whose rage as yet entire remains,
Whose snaky tire its wonted health retains;
Thy forces join, and all my labours share,
For schemes like these demand our utmost care.
Faint as I seem, from toil I shall not breathe,
Till the two brother-kings their swords unsheath.
On this I stand resolv'd, though Nature plead,
And start recoiling at th' accursed deed.
Great is the task, then let us steel our hearts
With rage, and act with vigour each our parts.
Whence these delays? For once forget to spare,
And choose the standards you prefer to bear.
They both are tutor'd ready to our hands,
And fir'd by Discord, wait but our commands.
Yet will, I fear, Antigone prevail,
And with her artful conduct turn the scale,
Or Œdipus, whose importuning pray'r
Experience tells us oft has urg'd to spare.
Oft is he seen from converse to retire,
In secret weep, and act again the sire.
For this my bold excursion I postpone
To Thebes, despairing to succeed alone.
Then let the banish'd prince your cares engage,
Lest length of time o'ercome his less'ning rage.
But most beware, lest mild Adrastus sway
His youthful mind, and interrupt the fray."
Their parts assign'd, the sister-furies sped
Each diff'rent ways, as their engagements led.
As when two winds from adverse quarters try
With equal lungs their titles to the sky,
Beneath the blast the waves and woods resound,
And one mis-shapen waste deforms the ground;
The mourning hinds their various loss deplore,
Yet thank that lot which kept them safe on shore.
When Jove, enthron'd in open air, survey'd
The day polluted with a double shade,
While murky spots obscur'd the louring skies
And Phœbus, sternly to the gods he cries:
"We saw the furies impious combat wage,
And brook'd, while moderation check'd their rage:
Though one to fight unequal durst aspire,
And fell the victim of celestial ire.
But deeds approach, as yet on Earth unknown,
For which the tears of ages can't atone.
O turn your eyes, nor let the gods survey
The fatal horrours of this guilty day.
Sufficient was the specimen, I ween,
When Sol, disgusted at the rites obscene
Of impious Tantalus, recall'd his light;
And now again ye mourn a sudden night.
Great as the crime appears, at Mercy's pray'r
The tenants both of Heav'n and Earth I spare.
But Heav'n forbid, Astræa's chaster eye,
Or the fair Twins, such hellish acts descry."

152. And choose the standards] The meaning of this is, choose whether you will inspirit Eteocles or Polynices to the combat.

169. As when] The winds perhaps have been the subject of more comparisons than any one thing in nature. Homer, Virgil, and the greatest geniuses of ancient and modern times abound in them, out of which the following comes nearest our author's.

Adversi rupto ceu quondam turbine venti
Confligunt, Zephyrusque Notusque et lætus cois
Eurus equis: stridunt sylvæ: sævitque tridenti
Spumeus, atque imo Nereus ciet æquora fundo.
Æn. b. 2.

The Thund'rer spoke, and as he turn'd away,
A sudden gloom o'erwhelm'd th' inverted day.
Meanwhile the virgin daughter of the night
Seeks Polynices through the ranks of fight.
Beneath the gate the musing chief she found,
For various omens did his soul confound;
Yet unresolv'd to tempt his doubtful fate,
And in a duel end the stern debate.
He saw, as roaming in the gloom of night
Along the trench he ponder'd on the fight,
Argia's image pensive and forlorn,
Her torches broken, and her tresses torn
(For Jove's all-gracious will had thus decreed
To warn him of the near-approaching deed).
In vain the warrior importun'd to tell
The motive of her flight, and what befel:
Nought to the tender question she replies,
But from his sight, the tears fast-falling, flies.
Yet well, too well he guess'd the fatal cause,
That his fair consort from Mycenæ draws,
Discerns the dire prediction of his death,
And trembles, to resign his vital breath.
But when the goddess thrice her scourge had ply'd,
And smote the mail that glitter'd on his side;
He raves, he burns with fury not his own,
Nor seeks so much to mount the Theban throne,
As o'er his slaughter'd brother to expire,
At length he thus accosts his aged sire.
"Too late, O best of fathers, I've decreed
In single fight to conquer or to bleed,
When only I of all my peers survive,
For nought but misery condemn'd to live.
O had I thus determin'd, ere the plain
Yet whiten'd with the bones of thousands slain,
Rather than see the flow'r of Argos fall,
And royal blood begrime the guilty wall!
Say, was it just, I should ascend the throne,
Through which so many widow'd cities moan?
Yet since too late the wreaths of praise I claim,
Revenge shall prompt, and act the part of fame.
Say, can one spark of pity warm thy breast
For him who robb'd thy ancient limbs of rest,
For him, by whose unhappy conduct led,
And in whose cause so many chiefs have bled?
This well thou know'st, though willing to conceal
My shameless actions through paternal zeal.

195. And as he turn'd, &c.] This fiction of Jupiter's turning away his eyes is borrowed from the following lines in the 16th book of Homer.

> The god, his eyes averting from the plain,
> Laments his son, predestin'd to be slain
> Far from the Lycian shores, his native reign.
>
> Pope's Iliad.

223. Too late] This speech of Polynices is not without its particular graces. There is an air of majesty and greatness that dignifies the whole; and the beautiful confusion and irregularity that it displays is excellently adapted to the circumstances of the speaker. In the beginning of it he blames himself for not preventing the vast effusion of blood by a single combat with his brother Eteocles. He then artfully sounds Adrastus concerning his affection, with a view to the request he afterwards makes. In short, our author has approved himself no less skilful in moving the passions, than in describing the more tumultuous scenes of war and devastation.

O had I dy'd, ere to these walls I fled;
But wreak thy vengeance on my guilty head.
To single combat I my brother dare.
'Tis thus resolv'd. For fight I now prepare.
Nor thou dissuade: for by almighty Jove
Thy pray'rs and tears must ineffectual prove.
Should e'en my parents, half-dissolv'd in tears,
Or sisters rush between our clashing spears,
And fondly strive to check my furious course,
They strive in vain: for vain are art and force.
Say, shall I drink the little that remains
Of Grecian blood, and waste it on the plains?
I saw, unmov'd, th' unclosing earth give way,
And snatch the prophet from the realms of day.
I saw the blood of gen'rous Tydeus spilt,
A more than equal partner of his guilt.
In vain th' Arcadian queen and Tegea raves,
While this her son, and that her monarch craves.
Why fell I not, like bold Hippomedon,
Surcharg'd with martial wreaths and trophies won?
Why durst I not, like Capaneus, engage,
And mingle mortal with immortal rage?
What coward terrours check my trembling hand?
Avaunt—I give the justice ye demand.
Here let the childless matron, hoary sire,
And youthful widow, flush'd with am'rous fire,
With all, whose joys I cropp'd before the time,
Convene, and curse me for the fatal crime.
Here let them stand spectators of the fray,
And for my foe with hands uplifted pray.
And now, my spouse, and all that's dear, adieu;
Nor thou, O king, beyond the grave pursue
Thy vengeance; nor to us alone impute [suit,
The guilt, which Heav'n partakes; but grant my
And rescue from my conqu'ring brother's ire
My last remains.—This only I require.
O may thy daughter happier nuptials prove,
And bless a chief more worthy of her love."
He paus'd; and manly tears their cheeks o'erflow:
Thus, when returning spring dissolves the snow,
Of Hæmus nothing save the name remains,
And Rhodope sinks level with the plains.
To calm his passion with the words of age,
And moderate his now-redoubled rage,
Essay'd Adrastus; but the Stygian queen
Broke off his speech with a terrific scene.
A winged steed, and fatal arms she brought;
And lest he flag, to sudden pity wrought,
A polish'd helm she fix'd upon his head,
And thus, in aspect like Perinthus, said.
"No more delays.—The object of thy hate,
(As fame informs us) issues from the gate."

279. He paus'd] Ariosto has imitated this simile in the 36th canto of his Orlando Furioso, stanza 40.

> Come a meridional tiepidi venti,
> Che spirano dal mare il fiato caldo:
> Le nevi si dissolvono e i torrenti,
> E'l ghiaccio, che pur dianzi era se saldo.

285. But the Stygian queen] The introduction of the fury Tisiphone as the authoress of the duel is imitated from the seventh book of the Æneid, where Alecto is engaged in almost the same illaudable office. And perhaps after the reader has well weighed the two passages together, and observed with what art the machinery is conducted by our poet, he will not think the copy much inferior to the original.

The fiend prevails, and mounting him by force,
With joy beholds him take the wish'd-for course:
Pale as a spectre, o'er the plain he flies,
And her dire shadow, looking round, descries.
In vain the Theban leader sought to prove
His gratitude to cloud-compelling Jove
By sacred honours.—The celestial sire
Unheeding sees the curling fumes aspire,
Nor to the fane one deity descends;
Tisiphone alone the rites attends.
Amid the crowd she stands, and wafts his vows
From Jove to Proserpine's tremendous spouse.
" O thou, from whom (though envying Argos boast
Saturnia's presence on her favour'd coast)
We sprung, a race of origin divine,
What time, a votary to Cupid's shrine,
Great Jove was seen in less than human shape,
Our orgies interrupted by the rape,
Whilst on thy back the cheated fair one rode,
Unconscious of th' embraces of a god;
Nor only then (if we may credit fame)
Wert thou enamour'd of a Theban dame!
At length our walls have prov'd thy grateful sense
Of ancient services: as in defence
Of thy own Heav'n the vengeful thunders roll'd,
Such as our sires with horrour heard of old.
Accept these off'rings then, thy mercies claim,
Nor let in vain the votive altars flame.
Let these suffice.—Our best endeavours prove
A trivial recompense for heav'nly love.
To Bacchus and Alcides we resign
This office, where 'tis theirs alone to shine."
He paus'd; when bursting forth with sable glare,
The flames invade his diadem and hair.
The victim then, uninjur'd by the wound,
With bloody foam distain'd the sacred ground,
At the bright altar aim'd a furious stroke,
And thro' th' opposing crowd impetuous broke.
Forth from the fane the pale attendants spring,
And the sage augur scarce consoles the king.
At length he issues orders to renew
The rites, and screens his fears from public view.
Thus Hercules, when first he felt the pains
Of the slow poison raging in his veins,
Patient awhile his part at th' altar bore:
Then, as his anguish grew at ev'ry pore,

313. Nor only then] The lady here hinted at is Semele, to whom he alludes in the following verse:

Such as our sires with horrour heard of old.

325. When bursting] This ominous incident seems taken from Virgil, who says in his seventh Æneid,

Præterea castis adolet dum altaria tædis,
Et juxta genitorem astat Lavinia virgo:
Visa, nefas, longis comprendere crinibus ignem,
Atque omnem ornatum flammâ crepitante cremari,
Regalesque accensa comas, accensa coronam
Insignem gemmis: tum fumida lumine fulvo
Involvi, ac totis Vulcanum spargere tectis. V. 71.

335. Thus Hercules] I believe most of my readers are acquainted with the history of this affair: and therefore shall make no apology for referring those who are not to Seneca, who has written a play on this subject, entitled Hercules Œtæus.

Gave vent to groans that pierc'd the pitying skies,
And wildly left th' unfinish'd sacrifice.
Whilst anxious cares perplex his tortur'd mind,
Young Æpytus (his porter's charge assign'd
To substitutes less swift of foot) drew near,
And, panting, thus salutes the royal ear.
" O wave these rites, ye solemnize in vain;
Nor let such cares withhold you from the plain.
When groves of hostile spears beset our gates,
Our fate depends on action, not debates.
Thy foe, O monarch, thunders at the walls;
And thee to combat, thee alone he calls."
His comrades turn away, and while he speaks,
Sighs heave each breast, and tears bedew their
His army vent their murmurs to the skies; [cheeks.
At length in agony of grief he cries,
" Say, why was guiltless Capaneus destroy'd?
Here rather be thy bolts, O Jove, employ'd."
In the king's breast now fear and anger wage
A short-liv'd war, but soon are lost in rage.
Thus when the victor-bull hears from afar
His exil'd rival hast'ning to the war,
He stalks, exulting in collected might,
Foams with excess of rage, and hopes the fight:
His heels the sand, his goring horns provoke
The passive air with many a well-aim'd stroke;
While the fair herd, with anxious horrour mute,
Expect the issue of the stern dispute.
Nor were they wanting, who the king befriend;
" Let him his empty wrath, unheeded, spend
On these our walls: nor wonder, should he dare
E'en greater things, when prompted by despair.
In rash exploits, and fruitless schemes t' engage,
Is the last effort of declining rage.
Rest thou secure, and trust to us alone, [throne.
Whose arms shall guard thee on the well-earn'd
At thy command all Thebes shall arm again."
Thus spake of sycophants th' encircling train.
But Creon took advantage of the times,
To tell the monarch of his num'rous crimes;

345. O wave these rites] From the beginning of this speech to the close of the book there is a constant succession of all the graces of poetry. The pleasing and terrible, the sublime and the pathetic, are here worked up to perfection, and shown in their proper colours. They not only force the reader's attention, but admiration. The distress is here wound up to its highest pitch, and the characters of Eteocles, Polynices, Antigone, and Œdipus, admirably supported. The reader will, I hope, excuse this and other sallies of enthusiasm, as it is but natural for a translator to have some predilection for his author, which may sometimes transport a young critic too far. It is hoped however that men of taste will acknowledge that Statius in this book deserves a high degree of praise and admiration.

359. Thus when, &c.] The reader may compare this with the following simile from Tasso.

Non altramente il tauro, ove l' irriti
Geloso amor con stimuli pungenti,
Horribilmente mugge, e co' muggiti
Gli spirti in se risveglia, e l' ire ardenti,
E'l corno aguzza ai tronchi, e par, ch' inviti
Con vani colpi alla battaglia i venti,
Sparge co'l piè l' arena, e'l suo rivale
Da lunge sfida à guerra aspra, e mortale.
Gierus. c. 7. st. 55.

A spirit yet untam'd and uncontrol'd,
With grief for brave Menæceus made him bold.
No rest he knows: alike are day and night,
His son is ever present to his sight.
Still he beholds him falling from the tow'r,
While his torn breast emits a bloody show'r.
As still the monarch on the challenge mus'd,
Dar'd not accept it, nor had yet refus'd,
He cries.—" O tyrant insolent and base,
Employ'd by Heav'n to plague a guilty race,
No longer hope the Thebans to command,
And meanly conquer by another's hand.
No longer shalt thou here in soft repose
Insult our fears, and triumph in our woes.
Too long beneath the wrath of Jove we've groan'd,
And for another's perjuries aton'd.
No longer Thebes her treasur'd wealth can boast,
Her youthful warriours, and well-peopled coast:
So few are left, that shouldst thou longer sway,
Slaves would be even wanted to obey.
Some hath Ismenos wafted to the deep,
And some, depriv'd of fun'ral honours, sleep,
While others seek their limbs dispers'd around,
Or prove their art on many a mortal wound.
Restore our brothers, sires, and sons their own,
Nor let our desert fields and houses moan.
Say, why is Dryas absent now so long,
Eubœa's leaders, and the Phocian throng?
Yet them th' impartial arbiter of fight
Consign'd to mansions of eternal night.
But thou, my son, as worthy that alone,
Hast fallen to secure the tyrant's throne,
Devoted as the first-fruits of the war,
To Mars, a sacrifice the gods abhor.
And shall our king (O scandal to the name)
Delay when challeng'd to assert his claim?
Or does Tiresias bid another go,
And basely frame new oracles of woe?
For why should Hæmon any longer live,
And his more gen'rous brother still survive?
Let him defend thy right to kingly pow'r
While thou may'st sit spectator from the tow'r.
Why dost thou murm'ring vent thy threats in vain,
And look for vengeance from this menial train?
Not these alone, but they who gave thee breath,
And e'en thy sisters wish thy speedy death.
Thy threat'ning brother labours at the gate;
Nor canst thou here much longer shun thy fate
So long deserv'd."—Thus spoke th' impassion'd sire;
The king replies, inflam'd with equal ire:
" Think not, O traitor, by this weak pretence
To veil thy hopes, and triumph o'er our sense:
No grief could move thee for Menæceus' death,
But rather joy he thus resign'd his breath.
Fearing, thy impious thoughts should be descry'd,
Thou seek'st in tears the swelling joy to hide,
Through vain presumption, that if I should fall,
Thou, as next heir, must sway the regal hall.
Yet hope not Fortune, adverse as she seems,
Will second thee in these ambitious schemes;
E'en now thy wretched life is in my hands,
But first my arms, my arms, ye faithful bands.
While we're in fight, thou, Creon, may'st assuage
Thy groans, and take advantage of our rage.
Yet should the fortune of the day be mine,
Immediate death, vile miscreant, shall be thine."
Thus spoke the monarch, and his shining sword,
Drawn forth in anger, to the sheath restor'd.
Thus, when excited by a random wound,
The snake, on spires erected, cleaves the ground,
And, fraught with ire, from his whole body draws
A length of poison to his thirsty jaws,
If chance his foe, unheeded, turns aside,
His high-wound wrath is quickly pacified;
He drinks the venom, which he wrought in vain,
And his distended neck subsides again.
But when the sad Jocasta had receiv'd
The dire account, too hastily believ'd,
Unmindful of her sex, and ev'ry care,
She bar'd her bloody breast, and rent her hair.
As when Agave climb'd the mountain's brow,
To bring the promis'd head (her impious vow),
Such rush'd the queen, distracted in her mind,
And left her daughters, and her slaves behind.
Despair her nerves with unknown vigour strung,
And violence of sorrow made her young.
Meanwhile the chief his graceful helmet took,
And in his hand two pointed javelins shook,
When in his mother rushes. At the sight
He and his train grew pale with wild affright,
He renders back in haste a proffer'd dart,
While thus she strives to work upon his heart.

387. O tyrant] Notwithstanding the great character of Drances's invective in the eleventh book of the Æneid, this of Creon may at least bear to be compared with it. If the former is full of spirited satire and humorous sarcasms, the latter is no less so, to which are superadded some fine strokes of the pathos, which the subject of Drances's speech would not admit of. But as general remarks are less convincing than particulars, we shall confront some parallel passages.

393. Too long] So Virgil.

O Latio caput horum et causa malorum!
Pone animos, et pulsus abi: sat funera fusi
Vidimus, ingentes et desolavimus agros.

399. Some hath Ismenos]

Nos, animæ viles, inhumata, infletaque turba,
Sternamur campis.

407. Yet them] The transition from the death of the other heroes to that of his son is very artfully conducted, and merits the highest applause from all lovers of the pathetic.

413. And shall our king]

Et jam tu, si qua tibi vis,
Si patrii quid Martis habes, illum aspice contra
Qui vocat.————

458. She bar'd her bloody breast] The speech of Jocasta opens with great tenderness, and is preluded by actions expressive of the highest misery. The circumstance, in particular, of showing that breast to her son, which had supported him in his infancy, is (to use the words of Mr. Pope) extremely moving. It is a silent kind of oratory, and prepares the heart to listen by prepossessing the eye in favour of the speaker. Priam and Hecuba are represented in much the same condition, when endeavouring to dissuade their son Hector from a single combat with Achilles, though I must observe, in praise of our author, that there is more passion in Jocasta's speech, and the contrast of terrour and pity considerably more heightened.

"Say, whence this rage, and why so soon again
The warring furies quit their nether reign?
Was it so slight two adverse hosts to lead,
And fight by proxy on th' ensanguin'd mead,
That nothing but a duel can appease
Your mutual wrath, nor less than murder please?
Where will the victor have recourse for rest?
Say, will he court it on this slighted breast?
Thrice happy spouse in this thy gloomy state!
O had these eyes but shar'd an equal fate!
And must I see?—Ah! whither dost thou turn
Those eyes that with revengeful fury burn?
What mean these symptoms of a tortur'd breast,
Harsh-grinding teeth, and murmurs half-supprest?
Hop'st thou to see thy mother overcome?
First thou must try these odious arms at home.
I'll stop thee in the threshold of the gate,
And, while I can, oppose the fell debate.
First thou shalt pierce, in fulness of thy rage,
These breasts, that fed thee in thy tender age;
While hurried on by thee, the furious horse
Spurns my hoar head, and tramples on my corse.
Why dost thou thus repel me with thy shield?
Forbear, and to my just entreaties yield.
No honours to the furies have I paid,
Nor against thee invok'd infernal aid.
'Tis not stern Œdipus, thy vengeful sire,
Thy bliss, thy welfare only I desire.
I ask thee but to halt awhile, and weigh
The guilt and dangers of th' intended fray.
What tho' thy brother summons thee to fight,
Presuming on imaginary might?
No friend is near his fury to restrain:
Thee all entreat, thee all entreat in vain.
Him to the fight Adrastus may persuade,
Or should he check, scarce hopes to be obey'd.
Wilt thou then leave us here absorb'd in woe,
To vent thy anger on a brother foe?"
Nor did a virgin's tender fears withhold
The fair Antigone, but nobly bold
She rush'd amidst the crowd, resolv'd to gain
The wall, whose height commands the subject plain.
Old Actor follows with unequal pace,
Enfeebled ere he reach'd the destin'd place.
Her brother she discern'd not, as afar
She saw him glitter in the pomp of war:
But when she heard him insolently loud
Discharge his darts, and thunder in the crowd,
She screams, and as about to quit the walls,
On Polynices thus aloud she calls.
"Awhile thy arms, and horrid crest resign,
And to yon tow'r thy roving eyes confine.
Know'st thou thy foes, and dost thou thus demand
Our lawful share of the supreme command?
Whate'er may be the merits of the cause,
Such conduct cannot meet with our applause.
By all the gods of Argos, (for our own
Dishonour'd and of no repute are grown)
By thy fair spouse, and all thy soul holds dear,
O calm thy passion, and a sister hear.
Of either host behold a num'rous train,
Permit not these to sue, and sue in vain.
This, only this I claim as the reward
Of my suspected love, and firm regard.
Unbind the martial terrours of thy brow,
Dismiss each frown, and give me yet to know,
That what with honest freedom I impart
Has wrought a just impression on thy heart.
Fame says, thy mother's suppliant groans have won
Eteocles, her more obsequious son:
But I return repulsed, who day and night
Have wept thy exile, and bemoan'd thy flight.
By me thy haughty father was appeas'd,
E'en the stern Œdipus, so rarely pleas'd.
Thy brother stands acquitted of the crime:
What tho' he reign'd beyond th' allotted time,
And broke his faith? yet he repents at last,
And wisely shuns the censure of the past."
Still'd by these words, his rage began to cease,
And his tumultuous soul was hush'd to peace;
His grasp relax'd, he gently turns the reins,
And sadly silent for a while remains.
Thick-issuing groans his blunted anger show,
And tears, by nature only taught to flow.
But while he hesitates as in a trance,
Asham'd alike to linger or advance,
The gates broke down, his mother thrust aside,
Freed by the fury, thus his rival cried.
"Brother, at length I come, yet much repine
The glory of the challenge must be thine.
Yet trust me, 'twas my mother who delay'd
The wish'd for combat, and withheld my blade.
Soon shall this headless state, our native land,
Be subject to the conqueror's command."
Nor was the prince more mild in his replies:
"Now, tyrant, dost thou know thy faith?" he cries:
"Thou actest now at length a brother's part;
But come, and prove the fury of my dart.
Such covenants alone to choose remain,
These are the laws that must secure our reign."
This answer, stern to view, the chief return'd;
For his proud heart with secret envy burn'd,
As he descry'd his brother's num'rous train,
That swarm'd around him, and half hid the plain,
The purple trappings that his steed adorn,
And studded helm, by monarchs only borne,
Though he himself no common armour bore,
Nor on his back a vulgar tunic wore;
Th' embroidery his skilful consort (taught
Each art that Lydian damsels practise) wrought.
And now they sally to the dusty plain,
The furies follow, mingling in the train.
Like trusty squires, beside the steeds they stand,
Adjust their trappings with officious hand,

527. For our own] This is a very bitter remonstrance of his disregard to his native town, by bringing a foreign army to besiege it.

534. Of my suspected love] Antigone is reported to have confined her affection to her younger brother Polynices, and even to have admitted him to her embraces. Lactantius.

581. And now they sally to the] It is impossible but the whole attention of the reader must be awakened at this crisis. Nothing could be better contrived to prepossess him with a just detestation of this impious and unnatural combat than the fiction that preludes it. The images have something in them wonderfully grand and magnificent. We hear Pluto thundering, feel the earth shaking under us, and see Mars, Pallas, and the subaltern deities of war, retiring with the utmost precipitation from so horrid a spectacle. Even the furies themselves, who were accessory to the duel, when it is upon the point of being fought, are represented as shocked, abashed, and astonished. The circumstance of the mothers driving away their children has not more of art than nature in its invention.

And, while they seem attentive to the reins,
With intermingled snakes augment their manes.
Two brothers meet in fight, alike in face,
Sprung from one womb, tho' not from one embrace.
Now cease the signals of the war around,
Nor the hoarse horns, nor shriller trumpets sound,
When Pluto thunder'd from his gloomy seat,
The conscious earth thrice shook beneath their feet.
Mars lash'd his steeds, and all the pow'rs of war
Retire from scenes they cannot but abhor.
Bellona quench'd in haste her flaming brand,
And laurell'd valour quits the guilty land.
The sister furies blush at their own deeds;
While to the walls the wretched vulgar speeds,
A just aversion mix'd with pity show,
And rain their sorrows on the crowd below.
Here hoary sires, a venerable throng,
Complain to Heav'n, and cry, "We've liv'd too long;"
There sadder matrons their bare breasts display,
And kindly drive their eager sons away.
Astonish'd at the deed, infernal Jove
Opens each passage to the realms above.
The phantoms, freed, on ev'ry mountain's brow
Recline, spectators of their country's woe;
Around a mist of Stygian gloom they cast,
Glad that their greatest crimes are now surpast.
Soon as Adrastus was inform'd by fame,
The wrathful combatants, unaw'd by shame,
Had issued forth to close the bloody scene,
He urg'd his steeds, and kindly rush'd between.
Much was he reverenc'd for rank and age,
But what could these avail to calm their rage,
When nature's ties experienc'd no regard?
Yet thus he strives their conflict to retard.
"Shall then the Greek and Tyrian armies too
Your crime, as yet unmatch'd, unacted, view?
Can there be pow'rs above, and laws divine?
But come, your wrath at my request resign.
I ask thee, monarch! tho' we act as foes,
Yet know, our strife from our relation rose.
Of thee a son's obedience I demand;
Yet if he thus desire supreme command,
I lay aside the garb of sov'reign sway,
Argos and Lerna shall your laws obey."
He spake: their stubborn purpose they retain,
Nor his sage counsels more their will restrain,
Than the sea listens to the sailor's cry,
When the surge bellows, and the storm runs high.
When he perceiv'd his mild entreaties vain,
And the two knights encount'ring on the plain,
While each, impatient, anxious first to wound,
Inserts his dart, and whirls the sling around,
He lash'd Arion (who, his silence broke,
The stern decrees of fate, portentous, spoke)
Yields all the reins, and flying swift as wind,
His camp, his son, and army leaves behind.
Not paler look'd the ruler of the ghosts,
When he compar'd his own Tartarian coasts
With the more blissful scenes of Heav'n above,
By fav'ring lot assign'd to happier Jove.
Nor Fortune was indulgent to the fray,
But by a blameless errour of the way
She kept their rushing coursers long apart,
And kindly turn'd aside each guiltless dart.
At length the chiefs, impatient for the fight,
With spurs and loosen'd reins their steeds excite,
While direful omens from the gods above
Both armies to renew the battle move.
Through either camp a busy murmur rolls,
And glorious discord fires their inmost souls.
Oft passion urges them to rush between,
And intercept with arms the bloody scene;
But Piety, who view'd with equal scorn
The gods, and those of mortal mothers born,
Sat in a distant part of Heav'n, alone,
Nor habited as she was whilom known.
A gloomy discontented look she wore,
The snow-white fillet from her tresses tore,
And like a mother or a sister show'd
Her tender heart in tears, that freely flow'd.
The guilty fates and Saturn's son she blam'd,
And with a voice that pierc'd the skies, exclaim'd,

638. The stern decrees] The impropriety of this fiction is not so flagrant as some may apprehend it, and our author has the sanction of fable and history to justify his using it. Livy tells us of two oxen, who forewarned the city of Rome in these words, Roma cave tibi: and Pliny observes, that these animals were remarkable for vaticination. Est frequens in prodigiis priscorum, bovem esse locutum. Homer introduces the horses of Achilles prophesying their master's death: and if he has done it without censure from the critics, why may not Statius be allowed the same liberty after him?

641. Not paler look'd] The following verses of Homer, with Mr. Pope's note on them, will clear up the mystery of this simile, if there be any.

Τρεῖς γάρ τ' ἐκ Κρόνου ἐσμὲν ἀδελφεοὶ, οὓς τέκε Ῥέιη,
Ζεὺς καὶ ἐγὼ, τρίτατος δ' Ἀΐδης ἐνέροισιν ἀνάσσων,
Τριχθὰ δὲ πάντα δέδασται, ἕκαστος δ' ἔμμορε τιμῆς·
Ἤτοι ἐγὼν ἔλαχον πολιὴν ἅλα ναιέμεν αἰεὶ
Παλλομένων, Ἀΐδης δ' ἐλάχεν ζόφον ἠερόεντα·
Ζεὺς δ' ἔλαχ' οὐρανὸν εὐρὺν ἐν αἰθέρι καὶ νεφέλησι·
Γαῖα δ' ἔτι ξυνὴ πάντων καὶ μακρὸς ὄλυμπος.

Homer's Iliad, b. 15.

Some have thought the Platonic philosophers drew from hence the notion of their triad, (which the christian Platonists since imagined to be an obscure hint of the sacred Trinity.) The trias of Plato is well known, τὸ αὐτό ον νοῦς ὁ δημιουργὸς, ἡ του κοσμου ψυχη. In his Gorgias he tells us, τὸν Ὅμηρον (autorem sc. fuisse) τῆς τῶν δημιουργικῶν Τριαδικῆς ὑποστασεως. See Proclus in Plat. Theol. lib. 1. c. 5. Lucian, Philopatr. Aristoteles de cœlo, lib. 1. c. 1. speaking of the ternarian number from Pythagoras, has these words: Τα τρια πάντα, καὶ τὸ τρὶς παντη. καὶ πρὸς τας αριστέιας τῶν θεῶν χρώμεθα τῷ ἀριθμῷ τούτῳ. καθάπερ γαρ φασιν καὶ οἱ Πυθαγόρειοι τὸ πᾶν καὶ τὰ πάντα τοῖς τρισὶν ὥρισται· Τελευτὴ γὰρ καὶ μέσον καὶ ἀρχὴ τὸν ἀριθμὸν ἔχει τὸν τοῦ παντος ταῦτα δὲ τὸν τῆς Τριάδος. From which passage Trapezuntius endeavoured very seriously to prove that Aristotle had a perfect knowledge of the Trinity. Duport, (who furnished me with this note, and who seems to be sensible of the folly of Trapezuntius) nevertheless, in his Gnomologia Homerica, has placed opposite to this verse that of St. John: "There are three who give testimony in Heaven, the Father, the Son, and the Holy Ghost." I think this the strongest instance I ever met with of the manner of thinking of such men, whose too much learning has made them mad.

She soon would quit the starry realms of Jove,
And seek a mansion in the Stygian grove.
" Why was I form'd, O author of my birth,
To sway the sons of Heav'n, and sons of Earth?
Suspended are my honours, lost my fame,
And Piety is nothing but a name.
O madness, fatal madness of mankind,
And arts, by rash Prometheus ill design'd.
Far better had the world continued void,
And the whole species been at once destroy'd.
Try we howe'er their fury to restrain,
Some praise is due should we but try in vain."
She spoke, and watching for a fav'ring time,
With swift descent forsook th' aërial clime.
Sad as she seem'd, a snowy trail of light
Pursu'd her steps, and mark'd her rapid flight.
Scarce had she landed, when, their wrath supprest,
The love of peace prevails in ev'ry breast.
Adown their cheeks the tears in silence steal,
And the two foes a transient horrour feel.
Fictitious arms, and male attire she wears,
And thus aloud her high behests declares.
" Hither, whoe'er fraternal friendship knows,
If yet we may restrain these brother-foes."
Then (for I ween Heav'n pitied) from each hand
The weapons fell, and fix'd the coursers stand.
E'en Fortune seem'd to spin a short delay,
And rush between to close the dreadful fray;
But stern Erinnys pierc'd the thin disguise,
And swift as lightning to the goddess flies.
" What urg'd thee, who to peace art more inclin'd,
To mingle in the wars of human kind?
Retire, advis'd, and give the vengeance way;
Ours is the field, and fortune of the day.
Why wert thou wanting, when a just pretence
Was offered thee to war in their defence?
When Bacchus bath'd his arms in kindred blood,
And Mars's serpent drank the guilty flood;
When the Sphinx fell, and Cadmus sow'd the plain;
When Laius by his son was rashly slain,
Or, guided by our torch, Jocasta press'd
The bed of incest?"—Thus the fiend address'd
The bashful pow'r, pursu'd her as she fled
With snakes, and wav'd her torch around her head.
The goddess draws the veil before her eyes,
And for redress to Jove all-potent flies.
Soon as she left the heroes, by degrees
Their ire returns, and nought but arms can please.
The perjur'd monarch first his jav'lin flings;
Full on the middle orb the weapon rings,
Nor pierc'd the gold, but bounding from the shield
Exhausts its blunted fury on the field.
The prince advances next, in act to throw,
But first bespeaks the pow'rs that rule below:
" Ye gods, of whom with more than hop'd success
The son of Laius whilom ask'd redress,
To this less impious pray'r your ears incline,
And realise the mischief I design.
Nor think, my rival slain, I wish to live,
This guilty spear shall absolution give.
Give me but breath to tell him that I reign,
And by surviving, double all his pain."
The rapid spear, with forceful vigour cast,
Between the rider's thigh and courser past.
A double death the vengeful marksman meant,
But the wise chief his knee alertly bent;
Nor innocent of blood the lance descends,
But the short ribs with glancing fury rends.
The steed wheels round, impatient of the reins,
And draws a bloody circle on the plains.
The prince, presuming it his rival's wound,
(He too believes it) with a furious bound
Springs forward, and advancing o'er the mead,
Pours all his fury on the wounded steed.
Reins mix'd with reins, and hand inlock'd in hand,
At once the falling coursers press the strand.
As ships, entangled by the wind, contend,
Their oars exchange, their mingled rudders rend,
And, while they struggle in the gloomy storm
To break the knot, a stricter union form;
Then, all the pilot's art in vain applied,
Together in a depth of sea subside;
Such was the scene of conflict. Art they scorn,
By mutual anger on each other borne.
The sparks, that issue from each other's eyes,
Kindle their ire, and bid their fury rise:
Entwin'd in one their hands and swords were seen,
So close, no interval was left between;
But mutual murmurs, as in stern embrace
They mix, supply the horn, and trumpet's place.
As when, with anger stung and jealous rage,
Two boars, the terrour of the wood, engage,
They gnash their iv'ry tusks, their bristles rise,
And lightning flashes from their glaring eyes;
While the pale hunter, from some mountain's height,
Stills the shrill-baying hounds, and views the fight;
Thus fought the chiefs; nor tho' they yet had found
Their strength exhausted by a mortal wound,

712. And for redress] Barthius with more than usual propriety observes, that our author, like the great Homer, has nodded over this passage. " How," says he, " is it probable, that Piety should have recourse to Jupiter for redress, on whom, with all the other deities, she had thrown out the most bitter invectives, and threatened, as he informs us,

> She soon would quit the starry realms of Jove,
> And seek a mansion in the Stygian grove.

727. Give me but breath] I am inclined to believe this was one of those passages that induced Mr. Pope to remark on our author's heroes, that an air of impetuosity runs through them all: the same horrid and savage courage appears in Capaneus, Tydeus, Hippomedon, &c. They have a parity of character which makes them seem brothers of one family.——Lucan puts a wish in Cæsar's mouth, which is not very dissimilar.

————————Mihi funere nullo
Est opus, O Superis lacerum retinete cadaver
Fluctibus in mediis; desint mihi busta, rogusque,
Dum metuar semper, terrâque expecter ab omni.
Ph. l. 5.

757. As when] The poet has here given us an image of the two combatants with great precision and exactness. If he had compared them to a boar and a lion fighting, he had not taken in the circumstance of relation between the two heroes, which constitutes the essence of the comparison. The hunter and his dogs very properly correspond with the soldiery, who were spectators of the duel. In short (as Mr. Pope observes of a simile in Homer) there is no circumstance of their present condition that is not to be found in the comparison, and no particular in the comparison that does not resemble the action of the heroes.

Yet flow'd the blood, the mischief was begun,
Nor aught the fiends could wish remain'd undone.
They grieve, the wrath of man can yet do more,
And praise the strict observance of their lore.
Each aims a deadly blow, and thirsts for blood,
Nor sees his own, that forms a purple flood.
Full on his foe th' impetuous exile flies,
Exhorts his hand, and ev'ry nerve applies:
Much he presumes upon his righteous cause,
And juster anger, then his falchion draws,
And in his brother's groin the steel inserts,
Where his ill-guarding mail the cincture girts.
The king, alarm'd as he began to feel
The cold invasion of the griding steel,
Retires beneath his target. He pursues,
As the wide wound and issuing gore he views,
And with a voice that shook the fields around,
Insults him thus, as still he quits his ground:
" Brother, why this retreat?—O transient sleep
And vigils, which th' ambitious ever keep!
Behold these limbs, by want and exile steel'd,
And learn to bear the hardships of the field;
Nor trust the fortune, that bestows a throne,
And rashly call, what she but lends, thy own."
The king as yet his vital breath retain'd,
And ebbing still the stream of life remain'd.
Spontaneously supine he press'd the ground,
And meditates in death a fraudful wound.
His brother, hoping now the day his own,
Extends his hands to Heav'n, and in a tone
That shook Cithæron, echoing thro' the skies,
Thus o'er his prostrate foe, insulting, cries: [breath,
" 'Tis well.—The gods have heard.—He pants for
And his eyes darken with the shades of death.
Let some one bring the crown, and robe of state,
While yet he sees, and struggles with his fate."
He paus'd, inspir'd by some unfriendly pow'r,
To strip his rival in his dying hour,
As if his ill-earn'd spoils, in triumph borne,
Would raise his glory, and the fanes adorn.
The monarch, who, tho' feigning to expire,
Surviv'd to execute his vengeful ire,
When he perceiv'd the posture of his foe,
(His bosom obvious to a mortal blow)
Unseen his falchion raises, and supplies
With rage the strength that ebbing life denies,
Then in his unsuspecting brother's heart
With joyful anger sheathes the steely part.
The prince rejoins.—" Then art thou yet alive,
And does thy thirst of vengeance still survive?
Base wretch! thy perfidy can never gain
A blissful mansion in th' Elysian plain.
Hence to the shades, there I'll renew my claim
Before the Cretan, who is said by fame
To shake the Gnossian urn, and woes prepare
For perjur'd kings, and all who falsely swear."
This said, he sunk beneath the deathful blow,
And with the weight of arms o'erwhelm'd his foe.
Go, cruel shades, the pains of Hell exhaust,
Mourn all ye fiends, the palm of guilt is lost.
Henceforward learn the sons of Earth to spare,
Nor punish deeds, which ill with these compare;
Deeds, that are yet unmatch'd in any clime,
Nor known in all the spacious walks of Time.
Let dark oblivion veil the guilty fight,
And kings alone th' enormous crime recite.
When Œdipus had heard, the brothers fell
By mutual wounds, his subterraneous cell
He quits in haste, and drags to scenes of strife
His wretched load of unillumin'd life.
Invet'rate filth and clotted gore dispread
The silver honours of his aged head.
Dire to the view his hollow cheeks arise,
And frightful yawn the ruins of his eyes.
His right hand on the staff was seen to rest,
His left the shoulder of his daughter prest.
Such here on Earth would hoary Charon seem,
Should he forsake awhile the Stygian stream;
The stars would blush to view his hideous mien,
And Phœbus sicken at his form obscene.
Nor he himself would long avail to bear
The change of climate, and a foreign air,
While in his absence swells the living freight,
And ages on the banks his coming wait.
Soon as they reach'd the field, aloud he cries,
" O thou, on whom alone my age relies,
Direct me to my sons, and let me share
The fun'ral honours which their friends prepare."
The virgin, ignorant of his command,
Replies in groans, and lingers on the strand;
While chariots, arms, and warriors heap the way,
Their feet entangle, and their progress stay.
Scarce can his aged legs the sire sustain,
And his conductress labours oft in vain.
Soon as her shrieks proclaim'd the fatal place,
He mix'd his limbs with theirs in cold embrace.
Speechless he lies, and murmurs o'er each wound,
Nor for a while his words a passage found.
But while their mouths beneath their helms he seeks,
His sighs give way, and all the father speaks.
" Does then affection bear again its part
In decent grief, and can this stubborn heart,
By wrongs inur'd, and by distresses steel'd,
To conqu'ring nature's late impressions yield?
Else why these tears, that long had ceas'd to flow,
And groans, that more than vulgar sorrow show?
Accept then, what, as sons, you rightly claim,
(For well your actions justify the name.)
Fain would I speak, but know not which demands
The preference by birth:—then say whose hands
I grasp.—How shall I give your shades their due,
And with what pomp your obsequies pursue?
O that my eyes could be restor'd again,
And the lost power of renewing pain!
To Heav'n, alas! too just my cause appear'd,
And too successfully my pray'rs were heard.
What god was near me when, by passion sway'd,
My vows to Pluto, and the fiends I paid,
And faithfully convey'd the curse to fate?
Charge not on me, my sons, the dire debate,
But on my parents, throne, infernal foes,
And injur'd eyes, sole authors of your woes.
My guiltless guide, and Pluto loth to spare,
I call to vouch the sacred truth I swear.

831. When Œdipus] Of all the pictures which the pencil of poetry ever presented to the eye of the mind, none abounds in more masterly strokes and touches than this before us. Œdipus appears here in all the pomp of wretchedness, (if I may use that expression,) and can only be equalled by Shakspeare's King Lear.

845. Nor he] Our author has taken the hint of this hypothesis from Ovid's Metamorphoses.

Est via declivis, per quam Tyrinthius heros
Restantem, contraque diem, radiosque micantes
Obliquantem oculos, nexis adamante catenis
Cerberon attraxit.————Lib. 8.

Thus worthily may I resign my breath,
Nor Laius shun me in the realms of death.
Alas! what bonds, what wounds are these I feel?
O loose your hands, no longer grasp the steel.
No longer let these hostile folds be seen,
And now at least admit your sire between."
Thus wail'd the wretched king, and sick of life
In secret sought the instrument of strife;
But she, suspicious of his rash designs,
Conceal'd it, whilst in rage he thus rejoins.
"Ye vengeful furies! can no sword be found?
Was all the weapon buried in the wound?"
His comrade, raising him, her grief suppress,
And much rejoic'd, that pity touch'd his breast.
Meanwhile, impatient of the vital light,
And dreading to survive the threaten'd fight,
The queen the sword of hapless Laius sought,
(A fatal spoil, with future mischiefs fraught,)
And, much complaining of the pow'rs above,
Her furious son, and her incestuous love,
Attempts to pierce her breast. Her falt'ring hand
Long struggled to infix the weighty brand,
At length with toil her aged veins she tore,
And purg'd the bed of guilt with issuing gore.
The fair Ismene to her rescue flew,
Her snowy arms around her mother threw,
To dry the wound her ev'ry care applied,
And rent her tresses, sorrowing at her side.
Such erst in Marathon's impervious wood
Erigone beside her father stood,
When, hast'ning to discharge her pious vows,
She loos'd the knot, and cull'd the strongest boughs:
But Fortune, who with joy malign survey'd
The hopes of either rival frustrate made,
Transfers the sceptre thence with envious hand,
And gives to Creon the supreme command.
Alas! how wretched was the term of fight!
Another rules, while they dispute their right.
Him all invite with one approving voice,
And slain Menœceus justifies their choice.
At length he mounts the long-contested throne
Of Thebes, to kings of late so fatal grown.
O flatt'ring empire, and deluding love
Of pow'r! shall such examples fruitless prove?
See, how he frowns upon his menial train,
And waves the bloody ensign of his reign!
What more, should Fortune all her store exhaust?
Behold the father in the monarch lost!
He whilom mourn'd his son's untimely death;
Now glories that he thus resign'd his breath.
Scarce had he reign'd, the tyrant of a day,
When, as a sample of his future sway,
The last funereal honours he denies
To the slain Greeks, expos'd to foreign skies;
And, ever mindful of an insult past,
Forbids their wand'ring shades to rest at last.
Then meeting, as he pass'd th' Ogygian gate,
The son of Laius, object of his hate,
At first his age and title he rever'd,
And for a while his eyeless rival fear'd:
But soon the king returns; and inly stung,
He cries with all the virulence of tongue:
"Avaunt, fell omen to the victors, hence,
Nor longer by delays my wrath incense;
Hence with thy furies, while thy safety calls;
And let thy absence purify our walls.
Thy wishes granted, and thy children slain,
What hopes, or impious vows can now remain?"
At this reproach, as some terrific sight,
His meagre cheeks stood trembling with affright.
Old age awhile recedes; his hand resigns
The staff, nor on his guide he now reclines:
But, trusting to his rage, with equal pride,
And bitterness of words, he thus reply'd.
"What tho' the slain no more thy thoughts engage,
And thou hast leisure here to vent thy rage,
Yet know, the crown, which late adorn'd my head,
Affords thee no pretence to wrong the dead,
And trample on the ruins of those kings,
From whose misfortunes thy short glory springs.
Go on, and merit thus the regal sway.
But why this caution, and this long delay?
Give tyranny at once the length of reins,
And boldly act whate'er thy will ordains.
Would'st thou with exile punish an offence,
Know, exile argues too much diffidence
Of thy own pow'r: then check thy rage no more,
But auspicate thy reign with human gore.
Expect not I shall deprecate the stroke,
And on my knees thy clemency invoke:
Long since in me the source of fear is dry;
And death with all its horrours I defy.
Is banishment decreed?—The world I left,
Of all its joys spontaneously bereft;
And, long impatient of the scenes of light,
Forc'd from their orbs the bleeding balls of sight.
What equal punishment canst thou prepare?
I fly my country, and its tainted air.
It moves me not, in what so distant clime
I pass the wretched remnant of my time.
No land, I ween, will to my pray'rs deny
The little spot that I shall occupy.
Yet Thebes most pleases, as it gave me birth,
And lodges all my soul holds dear on Earth.
Th' Aonian sceptre long may'st thou possess,
And rule the Thebans with the same success
As Cadmus, I, and Laius rul'd before;
Nor fortune's sunshine beam upon thee more.
May sons and loves like mine thy woes enhance,
Nor virtue guard thee from the strokes of chance.

917. Such erst in Marathon's] Erigone was the daughter of Icarus; and being directed by her dog to the place where her father was slain, through excess of grief hung herself upon a neighbouring tree; but the branch breaking down with her weight, she was said to seek stronger boughs. At length she accomplished her purpose, and for her piety was translated into Heaven, and became the constellation we call Virgo.

939. Scarce had he reign'd] Seneca, in his Thyestes, says: Ut nemo doceat fraudis, scelerumque viam, regnum docebit: a truth which the history of every age and country will evince to us. Μέγαν ὄλβον καταπέψαι ὀ δύνανται, (says Pindar) or in other words, Good fortune is less tolerable than bad. That we are the more liable to fall into vices, when we have the means of gratifying them, is indisputably true; how little, then, ought those to repine, whom Providence has placed in a lowly situation of life, secure from many temptations to which the great and the rich are exposed; or ought we not rather to look upon it as the most distinguishing mark of favour which could possibly be conferred upon us?

997. May sons] Perverse children are not reckoned the greatest evil of life by our poet only; king Lear, inflaming nature against his daughter Gonerill, says,

Much may'st thou love the life thou'rt doom'd to lose,
And sue for pardon, which thy foes refuse.
Suffice these curses to deform thy reign.——
Then lead me, daughter, from his curs'd domain.
But why shouldst thou partake paternal woe?
Our potent monarch will a guide bestow."
The princess, fearing to be left behind,
Rever'd his pray'rs, and cries, on earth reclin'd,
"By this thy kingdom, and the sacred ghost
Of brave Menœceus, our support and boast,
Forgive, if, heated in his own defence,
His answer sounds like pride and insolence.
From long complaints arose this haughty style;
Nor thee alone he glories to revile;
But e'en the gods, and I, who ne'er offend,
Oft prove the rancour which he cannot mend.
To quit this hated life is all his aim,
And fatal liberty his only claim;
For this he spends in obloquies his breath,
And hopes by scandal to procure his death.
But may the pow'rs of Heav'n direct thy sway,
And with fresh gifts distinguish ev'ry day.
Such impotence resent not, but despise;
And keep my father's fate before thine eyes.
In gold and regal purple once he shone,
And, girt with arms, sublimely fill'd the throne,
From whence he gave to all impartial laws,
With patience heard, with justice clos'd the cause.

——————If she must teem,
Create her child of spleen, that it may live,
And be a thwart, disnatur'd torment to her;
Let it stamp wrinkles on her brow of youth,
With cadent tears fret channels in her cheeks,
Turn all her mother's pains and benefits
To laughter and contempt; that she may feel
How sharper than a serpent's tooth it is,
To have a thankless child. Act 1. Scene 15

1007. By this thy kingdom] Œdipus having exasperated Creon by his spirited, though insolent reply, the princess Antigone takes upon her to calm his anger; her oration is therefore framed with an opposite air to all which has been hitherto said, sedate and inoffensive. She begins with an apology for her father's disrespect; tells him, that the greatest favour he could confer would be to sentence him to death, sets her good wishes in opposition to his imprecations, reminds him of his enemy's former rank and dignity, but present inability to injure him, and concludes with evincing the ill policy of banishing him. In short, this specimen suffices to show Antigone's good sense, and the power of female oratory in mollifying the almost implacable hatred of Creon to her father.

1023. In gold, &c.] Barthius observes, that this passage is a contradiction of what the poet says in the first book, verse 191.

Yet then no gates of iv'ry did unfold
The palace, &c.

Notwithstanding this, I could have defended this oversight with some seemingly ingenious conjectures, after the example of those commentators who never fail their author at a pinch; but as I have no intention of introducing the Thebaid upon the public as a perfect poem, I shall most willingly subscribe to Barthius's opinion, that the passage before us is highly exceptionable.

Alas! of all his once-unnumber'd trains,
A single guide and comrade now remains.
Can he thy weal oppose? and wilt thou rage
Against an enemy, disarm'd by age?
Must he retire, because he loudly groans,
And grates thy ears with inauspicious moans?
Resign thy fears; at distance from the court
Hence shall he mourn, nor interrupt thy sport.
I'll break his spirit, urge him to retreat,
And close confine him to his gloomy seat.
But should he wander, exil'd and distrest,
What city would admit him as a guest?
Wouldst thou to polish'd Argos he should go,
Crawl to Mycenæ in the garb of woe,
And, crouching at their vanquish'd monarch's gate,
The rout and slaughter of our host relate?
Why should he thus expose the nation's crimes,
And open all the sorrows of the times?
Conceal whate'er we suffer; at thy hand
No mighty favours, Creon, we demand.
Pity his sorrows, and revere his age,
Nor wrong the dead in fulness of thy rage;
The slaughter'd Thebans may enjoy at least
Funereal rites."—The prostrate princess ceas'd:
Her sire withdraws her, and with threats disdains
The grant of life, which scarcely she obtains.
The lion thus, who green in years had sway'd
The forests round, by ev'ry beast obey'd,
Beneath some arching rock in peace extends
His listless bulk; and tho' no strength defends
His age from insults, yet secure he lies;
His venerable form access denies:
But if a kindred voice pervade his ears,
Reflecting on himself, his limbs he rears,
And wishing much his youth restor'd again,
With envy hears the monarchs of the plain.
At length compassion touch'd the tyrant's breast;
Yet he but grants a part of her request,
And cries,—"Not distant from his native coasts,
Of whose delights so much he vainly boasts,
Shall he be banish'd, so he cease to roam,
And leave inviolate each holy dome.
Let him possess his own Cithæron's brow,
The wood contiguous, and the fields below,
O'er which the shades of heroes, slain in fight,
Are seen to flit, and shun the loathsome light."
This said, his course th' usurper homeward bent,
Nor durst the crowd withhold their feign'd assent.
Meanwhile the routed Greeks by stealth retire,
And leave their camp expos'd to hostile fire.
To none their ensigns and their chiefs remain,
But, silent and dispers'd, they quit the plain;
And to a glorious death and martial fame,
Prefer a safe return, and living shame.
Night favours their design, assistance yields,
And in a cloud the flying warriors shields.

BOOK XII.

THE ARGUMENT.

The Thebans, after some doubts concerning the reality of the enemy's flight, repair to the field

1053. The lion thus] This comparison is as just as language can make it. I cannot find, that Statius is indebted for it to any of his poetical predecessors. The non adeunda senectus is a beauty of diction I could not preserve in my translation, nor indeed will the English idiom admit of it.

of battle, and bury their dead. Creon discharges his son's obsequies with great solemnity, and laments over him in a very pathetic manner; he then forbids his subjects to burn the Greeks. In the mean time, the wives of the six captains slain in the siege march in procession to Theseus, king of Athens, to solicit his assistance in procuring the dead bodies. Argia leaves them, goes to Thebes, accompanied only by Menætes, and burns the body of Polynices on Eteocles's pile. She there meets with Antigone, who assists her. They are taken, and brought before Creon, who sentences them both to death. By the interposition of Pallas, the Argive ladies meet with a favourable reception from Theseus, who sends a herald to Creon, and orders him to procure funeral rites for the Greeks, or declare war against him. Upon the tyrant's obstinate refusal, the Athenians march to Thebes, which upon the death of Creon surrenders to Theseus, and entertains him in an hospitable manner. The princesses having obtained the bodies, discharge their funeral rites in a very sumptuous manner, a particular description of which the poet waves, and concludes the work with an address to his poem.

'Twas now the time, that on the vault serene
Of Heav'n a smaller group of stars was seen,
And Phœbe glimmer'd with diminish'd horn;
When fair Aurora, harbinger of morn,
Dispels afar the trembling shades of night,
And re-salutes the world with orient light.
Now thro' the desert town the Thebans stray,
And mourn the tardy progress of the day.
Tho', since the conflict with their Argive foes,
Now first they taste the sweets of soft repose,
Nor yet the fears of hostile vengeance cease;
Sleep hovers round the bed of sickly peace,
Nor rests.—They scarcely dare to quit the gate,
And pass the trench; the mem'ry of their fate,
And horrours of the late embattled plain,
Deep in their timid breasts infix'd remain.
As mariners long absent, when they land,
Perceive a seeming motion in the strand;
Thus, at each noise, the troops, recoiling, halt,
And listen, fearful of a new assault:
As when the serpent scales some tow'r, possest
By doves Idalian; as their fears suggest,
The white-plum'd parents drive their offspring home;
Then with their claws defend th' aerial dome,
And call their little rage forth to the fray;
Straight tho' the scaly monster hies away,
The danger past, they dread to leave their brood,
And sally forth in quest of wonted food;
At length with cautious fear they wing their flight,
And oft look back from Heav'n's impervious height.
They seek their slaughter'd comrades on the coast,
(The bloodless relics of the mangled host)
And wander o'er the blood-impurpled mead,
Where grief and sorrow (guides unpleasing) lead.
Some but the bodies of their friends descry,
While near another's limbs and visage lie;
Others bemoan the chariots, or accost
(All that remains) the steeds whose lords are lost:
Part kiss the gaping wounds of heroes slain,
And of their too great fortitude complain.
Digested now the scene of slaughter lies;
Part bear huge spears erected in their eyes;
Here sever'd from their arms are hands display'd,
Tenacious still of the discolour'd blade;
In some no traces of their death appear;
Their comrades rush, and shed the ready tear.
Around the shapeless trunks debates arise,
The question, who should solve their obsequies.
Oft (fortune sporting with their woe) they pour
O'er hostile chiefs a tributary show'r;
Nor can the friend his slaughter'd friend implore,
Or know the Theban from the Grecian gore.
But those, whose family entire remains,
From sorrow free, expatiate o'er the plains,
Inspect the tents once fill'd with Argive bands,
And fire them in revenge with flaming brands;
While others seek the place where Tydeus lies,
And the fam'd seer was ravish'd from their eyes:
Or search, if still on Jove's blaspheming foe
Th' ethereal lightnings unextinguish'd glow.
Now Phœbus set on their unfinish'd grief,
And Vesper rose; yet heedless of relief,
The lengthen'd strain, unwearied, they pursue,
And feasting on the scene, their fears renew:
There, disregarding the departed light,
In crowds they lie, and sorrowing out the night,
Alternate groan; (while far away retire
The savage monsters, scar'd with noise and fire.)
Nor did their eyes with constant weeping close,
The stars in vain persuading to repose.

The propriety of adding this last book depends entirely on the kind of poem, which the critics determine this to be. If they settle it to be an heroic or historical poem only, they grant of consequence the necessity of adding it, in order to render the poem complete; but if it is an epic poem, it should have ended at the death of the two brothers, according to the Aristotelian and Bossuvian system. But after all, I cannot see any great impropriety in superadding to the grand catastrophe, if the excrescence grows naturally out of the subject, and is equally well executed with the former, as I think no one will deny of this before us. I shall conclude this note with observing, that Virgil is the only writer who has strictly adhered to this form.

22. By doves Idalian] The expression in the original is, Idaliæ volucres; which, as Idalus was a mount consecrated to Venus, and the dove was the favourite of that goddess, cannot be supposed to mean any other species of birds; but it is very extraordinary, Statius should represent them so very bold.

53. But those] We find the Trojans diverting themselves in a similar manner after the supposed retreat of the Grecian army.

Ergo omnis longo solvit se Teucria luctu;
Panduntur portæ, juvat ire, et Dorica castra,
Desertosque videre locos, littusque relictum.
Hic Dolopum manus, hic sævus tendebat Achilles:
Classibus hic locus; hic acies certare solebant.
Virg. Æn. L. 2.

70. The stars] The original is, nec dulcibus astris victa, coierunt lumina, which I have translated thus from the authority of Virgil.

————Suadentque cadentia sidera somnos.

Now Phosphor thrice an orient lustre shed
O'er Heav'n, and gleam'd on the pale-visag'd dead;
When the thinn'd groves and widow'd mountains mourn
Their leafy pride on rolling waggons borne.
Cithæron, wont to grace funereal piles,
And fair Theumesus, yield their verdant spoils:
Prostrate on earth the forest's glory lies,
While thick around the flaming pyres arise.
The Theban shades with joyful eyes survey'd
This last kind office to their relics paid:
But the sad Argives, hov'ring round, bemoan
The hostile fires, and honours not their own.
No regal exequies and pomp adorn
The tyrant-king, neglected and forlorn;
Nor his fierce brother for a Grecian held,
And from his country exil'd and expell'd;
But Thebes and Creon for his son prepare
More than plebeian rites, their common care.
A costly pile of choicest wood they raise,
High as his worth, and spreading as his praise:
On this they heap the trophied spoils of Mars,
Arms, batter'd bucklers, and unwieldy cars.
The chief, as conqueror, on these is laid,
With fillets grac'd, and wreaths that never fade.
Alcides thus mount Œta press'd of yore,
By Heav'n forbad on Earth to linger more.
To crown the whole, the captive Greeks were slain,
And hurried in their youth to Pluto's reign.

95. Alcides thus] As this funeral is very elegantly described by Seneca, I shall make no apology for transcribing it here.

Ut omnis Oeten mœsta corripuit manus,
Hinc fagus umbras perdit, et toto jacet
Succisa trunco; flexit hinc pinum ferox
Astris minantem, et nube de media vocat;
Ruitura cautes movit, et sylvam trahit
Secum minorem. Chaonis quondam loquax
Stat vasta late quercus, et Phœbum vetat,
Ultraque totos porrigit ramos nemus.
Gemit illa multo vulnere impresso minax,
Frangitque cuneos, resilit excussus chalybs,
Vulnusque ferrum patitur, et truncum fugit.
Commota tantum est; tunc cadens lenta morâ
Duxit ruinam, protinus radios locus
Admisit omnes ————
Aggeritur omnis sylva, et alternæ trabes
In astra tollunt Herculi angustum rogum.
Ut pressit Œten, ac suis oculis rogum,
Lustravit, omnes fregit impositus trabes,
Arcumque poscit:————
Tum rigida secum spolia Nemæi mali
Arsura poscit, latuit in spolia rogus.

Herc. Œt. Act. 5. sc. I.

97. The captive Greeks] Shocking as this act of cruelty may appear to some christian readers, it was authorised by the military customs and religious laws of those times, as may be seen from Homer and Virgil, who have both made their heroes guilty of it in discharging the burial-rites of Patroclus and Pallas.

———— πίσυρας δ' ἐριαύχενας ἵππους
Ἐσσυμένως ἐνέβαλλε πυρῇ, μεγάλα στοναχίζων.
Ἐννέα τῷ γε ἄνακτι τραπεζῆες κύνες ἦσαν,
Καὶ μὲν τῶν ἐνέβαλλε πυρῇ δύο δειροτομήσας·
Δώδεκα δὲ Τρώων μεγαθύμων υἱέας ἐσθλοὺς
Χαλκῷ δηϊόων· ————

Iliad. lib. 23. 173.

Then well-rein'd steeds, the strength of war, are thrown
Beside their lord: the sire heaves many a groan,
When Vulcan on the high-heap'd victims preys;
Then thus he cries, deep-musing on the blaze:
"O thou design'd to share with me the throne,
And after me to govern Thebes alone,
Hadst thou not, prodigal of vital breath,
To save the realm, preferr'd a glorious death:
The sweets of empire, and imperial state
Are all embitter'd by thy early fate.
What tho' thy presence grace the courts of Jove,
And mortal virtue shine in Heav'n above:
To thee, my deity, shall vows be paid,
And tears, a constant tribute to thy shade.
Let Thebes high temples raise, and altars heap:
Give me alone the privilege to weep.
And now, alas! what rites shall I decree,
What honours worthy of myself and thee?
O that the gods, to deck thy sculptur'd bust,
Would lay the pride of Argos in the dust!
I'd crown the pile, and yield my forfeit breath
With all the honours, gain'd me by thy death.
Has the same day, and the same impious fight
Consign'd with thee to shades of endless night
The brother-kings?—then, Œdipus, we bear
An equal part in sorrow and despair:
Yet how resembling are the shades we moan,
Witness, O Jove; to thee their worth is known.
Accept, sweet youth, the first-fruits of my reign,
Nor these bright ensigns of command disdain,
Which e'en Ambition's self might blush to wear,
When purchas'd with the price of blood so dear.
May proud Eteocles thy pomp survey,
And sicken at his alienated sway."
This said, his crown and sceptre he resigns,
And with redoubled fury thus rejoins:
"Censure who will, 'tis my command that none
Shall mix their burial-rites with thine, my son.
O could I lengthen out their sense of pain,
And drive from Erebus the Grecians slain!
Yet birds and beasts shall on their leader prey,
And to the public eye his heart display.
But Sol resolves them to their pristine state,
And Earth conceals from my revengeful hate:
This edict I repeat, that none offend
Through ignorance, or ignorance pretend.
What wretch but rears a tomb, or wills to rear,
And makes the relics of a foe his care,
His carcase shall the Grecian's place supply:
Attest, my son, and ye that rule the sky."

Addit equos et tela, quibus spoliaverat hostem.
Vinxerat et post terga manus, quos mitteret umbris
Inferias, cæso sparsuros sanguine flammam;
Indutosque jubet truncos hostilibus armis
Ipsos ferre duces, inimicaque nomina figi.

Æneid, b. 11. v. 80.

137. O could] In this address of Creon to his son we may observe a mixture of tenderness and ferocity, which is very consistent with and agreeable to his character: and while we are displeased with the implacable enemy, we should not withhold the praise due to the loving and affectionate parent. I think, this behaviour is a sufficient confutation of Eteocles's calumny in the preceding book.

No grief could move thee for Menœceus' death,
But rather joy he thus resign'd his breath.

He spoke; nor willing sought the regal court.
Meanwhile, assembled at the first report
Of Creon's rage, the dames of Argive strain,
Who wept their fathers and their husbands slain,
Attir'd as mourners, or a captive band,
In sad procession move along the strand,
All gash'd with wounds: dishevell'd was their hair,
The same their habit, and their breasts were bare:
From their torn cheeks a crimson current flows,
And their soft arms were swoln with cruel blows.
Argia, senior of the sable train,
Whose falt'ring steps two grieving maids sustain,
Majestically sad and slow precedes,
And asks the way, unknowing where she leads.
The palace loath'd, her sire no more at heart,
And all neglected, but her better part;
She dwells upon the valour of her spouse,
And love, tenacious of the marriage-vows:
And Thebes, the ruin of her country's host,
Prefers to Argos, and th' Inachian coast.
To her the consort of th' Ætolian chief
Succeeds, and equals in the pomp of grief
Her sister-queen: with her a mingled throng
From Calydon and Lerna march along;
More wretched, as she heard th' unworthy fate
Of Menalippus, and her spouse's hate.
Yet she forgives, and, while she disapproves
The flagrant sin, the pleasing sinner loves.
Next came Hippomedon's dejected queen,
Of manners soft, though savage was her mien.
Then Eriphyle, who presumes in vain
By pompous rites to wash away her stain.
Diana's childless comrade clos'd the rear,
The fair Mænalian nymphs beneath her care;
With her Evadne pregnant: one exclaims
Against her daring son's ambitious aims;
But, mindful of her spouse, and parent Mars,
The other, stern in tears, upbraids the stars.
Chaste Hecate from the Lycean grove
Beheld, and heav'd a sigh; while as they rove
Along the double shore, Leucothea spies,
And from her Isthmian tomb loud-wailing cries.
Ceres, her private woes in theirs forgot,
Held forth the mystic torch, and wept their lot.
E'en Juno, partner of aerial sway,
Conducts them through a safe, though secret way,
Lest, should their people meet, th' emprize be [cross'd,
And all its promis'd fame and glory lost.
Nor various Iris less employ'd her care
To guard the dead from putrefying air:
O'er ev'ry tainted limb with skill she pours
Ambrosial dews, and mystic juices show'rs;
Lest they decay before the flames consume,
And their sad friends consign them to the tomb.
But Ornithus, disabled in the fray,
And by his troops deserted, takes his way
Through thick recesses, that exclude the light
Of Sol, a recent wound impedes his flight:
Pale were his cheeks with loss of blood and fear,
His steps supported by a broken spear.

197. Nor various Iris] This fiction is borrowed from Homer, who introduces Thetis performing the same kind office to the body of Patroclus; though I think the allegory is not so just and natural in the imitation.

Πατρόκλῳ δ' αὖτ' ἀμβροσίην ϗ νέκταρ ἐρυθρὸν
Στάξε κατὰ ῥινῶν, ἵνα οἱ χρὼς ἔμπεδος εἴη·
Iliad. l. 19. v. 38.

Soon as he hears th' unwonted tumult rise,
And views the female cohorts with surprise;
Inquiries none he makes about their woes,
Nor asks the reasons, which themselves disclose,
But took the word, and first his silence broke,
The stream of grief descending, as he spoke:
" Say, wretches, whither haste ye, what you are,
And why this fun'ral pageant you prepare;
When day and night commission'd soldiers stand
To guard the shades by Creon's harsh command;
When inaccessible to all remain,
But birds and beasts, the bodies of the slain,
Unwept and uninterr'd?—Will he relent,
His stubborn soul by your entreaties bent?
Believe me, sooner might your pray'rs assuage
Th' Egyptian tyrant's altars, and the rage
Of Diomede's half-famish'd steeds: or move
Sicilian gods, the progeny of Jove.
If well I know the man, perchance he'll dare
To seize your persons in the act of pray'r,
And slaughter each, not o'er her husband's corse,
But distant far, unknowing of remorse.
Retreat ye then, while yet secure you may;
And when you reach again Mycenæ, pay
A cenotaph, the utmost that remains
While thus the breathless heroes press the plains.
Or will ye stay t' implore the passing aid
Of Theseus, who, with ensigns high-display'd,
Returns in triumph from Thermodon's shore,
Clogg'd with the dead, and red with female gore?
Arms must compel him to commence the man,
And form his morals on a juster plan."
He said: their tears with horrour stand congeal'd,
And grief and passion to amazement yield;
From ev'ry face at once the colour flies,
And all their ardour for th' adventure dies.
Thus, when the tiger's howl (terrific sound)
Has reach'd the herd in some capacious ground,
Through the whole field a sudden terrour reigns:
And all, forgetful of the grassy plains,

224. Th' Egyptian tyrant's] Busiris king of Egypt was wont to sacrifice strangers to his gods; but being overcome by Hercules underwent the same fate.

Diomede king of Thrace fed his horses with human flesh, and was slain by the above-mentioned hero.

226. Sicilian gods] Lactantius gives us the following account of these deities.

The nymph Ætna having consented to the embraces of Jupiter was pursued by Juno, and imploring the assistance of the Earth was received into her bosom, and bore two twins, who for their virtues were admitted into the society of the gods, and had divine honours paid them, but they were only appeased with human blood.

233. A cenotaph] This was a kind of mock funeral, and is thus described by Virgil in the third book of his Æneid.

Ante urbem in luco falsi Simoentis ad undam
Libabat cineri Andromache, manesque vocabat
Hectoreum ad tumulum, viridi quem cespite inanem;
Et geminas, causam lacrymis, sacraverat aras.

For a farther account of this ceremony see Xenophon's Κυρου Αναβασις, lib. 6. and Tacitus's Annals, lib. 1. and 11. and Suetonius in the Life of Claudius.

Stand mute with expectation, who shall please,
And first the foe's rapacious maw appease.
Forthwith a series of debates arose,
And various schemes in order they propose:
Some will, to Thebes that instant they repair,
And tempt the king by blandishment and pray'r;
For aid on Theseus others would rely:
But all disdain, nought enterpris'd, to fly.
Not thus Argia with the rest despairs;
With more than female fortitude she bears
The news dissuasive, and, her sex resign'd,
Attempts a deed of the most daring kind.
She glows with hope of dangerous applause,
Won by the breach of Creon's impious laws,
And courts, what the most hardy Thracian dame,
Though fenc'd with virgin-cohorts, would disclaim.
She meditates, by what fallacious cheat,
Unnotic'd by the rest, she may retreat,
Rash and regardless of her life through grief,
And urg'd by love of her much injur'd chief,
Or gain his dear remains, or else provoke
The tyrant to inflict a deadly stroke.
In ev'ry act and character appear'd
Her spouse confest; one while a guest rever'd,
Now at the altars of the pow'rs above,
And now the sweet artificer of love;
Then sheath'd in arms, and quitting her embrace,
With ling'ring eyes, and anguish in his face.
Yet most that imag'd form recurs to sight,
Which, bare and naked from the scene of fight,
Demands the pile: disturb'd with cares like these,
She sickens, and since nought her griefs can ease,
Flies to grim death for yet-untasted rest,
(The chastest ardour in a female breast)
Then, turning to her Argive comrades, cries:
" Do you, in favour of our just emprise,
Solicit Theseus, crown'd with hostile spoils,
And may success attend your pious toils.
But suffer me, from whom alone arose
These grievous ills and yet unequall'd woes,
To penetrate the Theban court, and prove
The menac'd thunder of this earthly Jove.
Nor at our entrance shall we find the town
Inhospitable, or ourselves unknown;
My husband's sire and sisters will defend
His wretched widow, and her cause befriend.
Only retreat not; to these hostile walls
My own desire, an happy omen, calls."
She ceas'd: and as a partner of the way,
Menœtes took (beneath whose gentle sway
Her youthful age receiv'd an early store
Of mental charms, resign'd to virtue's lore)
And, though a stranger to the road, pursu'd
The steps of Ornitus, distinctly view'd.
But when, impetuous as the driving wind,
She'd left the partners of her woe behind,
" Shall I, O much lov'd source of grief," she cries,
" While foul in dust thy slighted carcase lies,
Expect an answer from th' Athenian king,
And wait for aid, which he may never bring;
Or hesitate for sanction from above,
To execute the dictates of my love?
While thy remains decrease by this delay,
Why do I yield not to the birds of prey
These viler limbs? And now, alas! if aught
Of sense survives, or soul-engend'red thought,
To Stygian gods perchance thou dost complain,
And wonder what can thus thy wife detain;
Whether intomb'd, or bare beneath the skies
Thy corse remains, on me th' omission lies.
No more then death and Creon shall withstand,
Nor love and Ornitus in vain command."
This said, she scours the Megareian plain
With rapid pace, and seeks the small domain
Of Creon; each she meets, in haste replies
To her demands, and turns aside his eyes,
Affrighted at her garb.—Thus on she goes,
Of aspect stern, confiding in her woes:
Alike intrepid in her heart and ear;
And, far from fearing, she inspires with fear.
In Phrygia thus when Dindymus rebounds
With shrieks nocturnal, and with doleful sounds,
The frantic leader of the matrons flies
To where the waves of Simoïs arise;
Whose sacred blade the goddess did bestow,
What time with wreaths she grac'd her awful brow.
Hyperion now in western deeps had hurl'd
His flaming car, and sought the nether world;
When imperceptibly the tedious day,
Beguil'd by toils of sorrow, steals away.
Secure o'er darksome meads, and rocks, 'twixt beams
That totter to their fall, through swelling streams,
And groves that ne'er admit the piercing rays
Of Phœbus, baffling his meridian blaze,
And dykes, and furrows of th' indented field,
From her incurious eyes by night conceal'd,
Through the green couch of monsters, and the den
Possess'd by beasts, and unexplor'd by men,
Direct and unoppos'd she speeds her flight:
No toils fatigue her, and no perils fright.
Menœtes follows slow: shame stings his mind,
And wild amazement to be left behind.
Where for instruction did she not apply,
Whilst her chaste bosom heav'd with many a sigh?
Oft the path lost, a devious way she took,
When, her chief solace, the bright flames forsook
Her erring feet, or the cold shades of night,
Back'd by the wind, expell'd the guiding light.
But when the mount of Pentheus they descend,
And, weary, to the vale their footsteps bend;
Menœtes, nearly spent, the nymph addrest,
While frequent pantings heav'd his aged breast.
" Not far (if hope of the near-finish'd way
Flatters me not) the champaign I survey,
Where the fell scene of blood and carnage lies,
And, intermix'd with clouds, the domes arise.
A noisome stench pervades the steaming air,
And rav'nous birds in flocks obscene repair.
This is the fatal plain, the seat of war;
Nor is the town of Cadmus distant far.
See, how the field projects the length'ning shade
Of walls, upon its surface wide display'd,

329. In Phrygia thus when Dindymus] Dindymus or Dindyma were two mountains near Ida in Phrygia, consecrated to Cybele, and famous for the solemnization of her sacred rites, as we learn from Virgil.

O vere Phrygiæ, neque enim Phryges! ite per alta
Dindyma, ubi assuetis biforem dat tibia cantum.
Tympana vos buxusque vocant Berecynthia matris
Ideæ.———— Æneid, b. 9. v. 617.

369. See, how the field] This description is scarce inferior to any in the whole work. It is as beautiful a night-piece as can be found in poetry. The shade of the walls projecting into the field before the city, the light on the watch-towers

While dying Vulcan faintly shines between
From the watch-tow'r, and swells the solemn scene!
The night was late more still, the stars alone
Cast a faint lustre round her ebon throne."
So spake Menœtes; and the trembling fair
With hands extended thus addrest her pray'r:
" O Thebes, once sought with more than vulgar toil,
Though hostile now, again a friendly soil
Should Creon deign to render back entire
My lord's remains, to feed the fun'ral fire!
View, with what pomp, what followers at her call,
The wife of Polynices seeks thy wall!
Full modest is my suit, nor hard the task
To gratify: my spouse is all I ask;
My spouse long outlaw'd, and expos'd to want,
(His throne usurp'd) to my entreaties grant.
Nor linger thou in Pluto's griesly dome,
If aught of form subsist, and phantoms roam;
But if thy favours I deserve, precede,
And to thy earthly part thy consort lead."
She said: and hast'ning to a neighb'ring cot,
Some simple swain's secure, though slender lot,
Repairs her torch extinguish'd by the wind,
And rushes forwards, turbulent of mind.
Such was the search that pensive Ceres made,
(Her child convey'd to the Tartarean shade)
With lamp in hand, whose well-reflected light
Varied each side, with rays alternate bright,
She trac'd the chariot-ruts, distinctly view'd,
And step by step the ravisher pursu'd.
Th' imprison'd giant echoes back again
Her frantic shrieks, and lightens all the plain
With bursting fire from the Vulcanian hall;
And rivers, forests, hills, and valleys, call
Persephone: the court of Dis alone
Is silent midst the universal groan.
Her friend reminds her oft of Creon's ire,
And warns to hide the interdicted fire.
Thus she, who reign'd o'er many a Grecian town,
With ev'ry virtue that adorns a crown,
In war redoubted, and in peace belov'd,
Admir'd for beauty, and for worth approv'd,
Amidst the dreary horrours of the night,
Without a social guide, her foes in sight,
Undaunted strays through meadows cover'd o'er
With deathful arms, and slippery with gore,
While injur'd ghosts flit round her, and demand
Their limbs disjoin'd, and scatter'd on the strand.
Oft as the lifeless bodies are explor'd
With curious inquest, on the spear or sword
She treads unheeding, all her thoughts employ'd
Her lord's mistaken relics to avoid.
Now leaning o'er the carcases, she strains
Her eyes, and of the want of light complains;
When Juno, who, to save her chosen race,
Had stolen from the Thunderer's embrace,
And, taking all advantage of the time,
Shot down to Athens from th' aerial clime,
To move the mind of Pallas, and prepare
The city to receive each suppliant fair;
Beheld th' Inachian princess, as in vain
She toil'd erroneous on the spacious plain,
And grieving at the sight, awhile resign'd
To pity's gentle lore her tender mind:
And, stopping near the sister of the Sun
Her chariot, thus in accents mild begun:
" At Cynthia's hands if Juno claim regard,
Her merit with a due return reward.

breaking out by fits here and there, and the stillness of the night, present a fine picture to the imagination. The colouring is so strong, that one may almost fancy seeing the disconsolate princess walking under the walls, and deliberating how to act.

388. If aught of form subsist] Mr. Pope's note on the following verses of Homer,

> Ω ποποι, ἠρά τις ἐςὶ ϗ εἰν Αιδαο δομοισιν
> Ψυχη ϗ εἴδωλον, ἀταρ φρενες ὀυκ ἐνι παμπαν.

will throw a good deal of light on this matter.

" This passage will be clearly understood, by explaining the notion which the ancients entertained of the souls of the departed, according to the forecited triple division, or mind, image, and body. They imagined, that the soul was not only separated from the body at the hour of death, but that there was a farther separation of the φρην, or understanding, from its Ειδωλον, or vehicle; so that the Ειδωλον, or image of the body, being in Hell, the φρην, or understanding, might be in Heaven: and that this is a true explanation is evident from a passage in the Odyssey. B. 11. v. 600.

> Τὸν δὲ μετ' εισενοησα βιην Ηρακληειην
> Ειδωλον· αὐτὸς δὲ μετ' αθανατοισι θεοισι
> Τερπεται εν θαλιης, ϗ ἔχει καλλισφυρον Ηβην·

By this it appears that Homer was of opinion that Hercules was in Heaven, while his Ειδωλον, or image, was in Hell: so that when this second separation is made, the image or vehicle becomes a mere thoughtless form.

" We have this whole doctrine very distinctly delivered by Plutarch in these words: ' Man is a compound subject; but not of two parts, as is commonly believed, because the understanding is generally accounted a part of the soul; whereas indeed it as far exceeds the soul, as the soul is diviner than the body. Now the soul, when compounded with the understanding, makes reason, and when compounded with the body, passion: whereof the one is the source or principle of pleasure or pain, the other of vice or virtue. Man therefore properly dies two deaths; the first death makes him two of three, and the second makes him one of two.'—Plutarch of the Face in the Moon." See Homer's Iliad, vol. 2. lib. 22.

424. And of the want of light complains] Lactantius, contrary to the general practice of commentators, convicts Statius of a slip of his memory in representing Argia without a torch, and presently after hinting that she had one; condemning him from his own words,

> ———Aliamque ad busta ferebat
> Antigone miseranda facem——— Verse 349.

How (says he) could Antigone be said to bear another torch, unless Argia had one before? But this is a mere critical cavil. Argia might have a torch at the time the poet mentions, though not before. It may then be asked, why the poet did not tell us of it?—To this I answer, that it was needless he should inform us of it, unless he could do it without seeming desirous of it, and going out of his subject on purpose.

For night prolong'd, to crown a vicious flame,
And other insults, I forbear to name,
Grant my request, and by compliance shun
The wrath incurr'd for crimes already done.
See, circumfus'd in night Argia strays,
A dame as worthy of our aid as praise!
In vain she toils around th' ensanguin'd field,
Until thy stronger rays assistance yield.
Exert thy horns, and, nearer in thy course,
Shine down on Earth with more than wonted force;
While Sleep, who guides thy chariot thro' the skies,
Descends to close each watchful Theban's eyes."
Scarce had she spoke, when from a bursting cloud
The goddess held her orb forth midst a crowd
Of lesser stars, and gilds the dewy plains:
The dazzling lustre Juno scarce sustains.
The princess viewing now, recals to thought
The purple robe, her skilful hands had wrought,
Although the texture was effac'd with gore,
Nor the bright hue so vivid as before;
And while she calls on Heav'n in plaintive strains,
And fears, that this small gift alone remains
To grace his obsequies, and future bust,
She sees his body trampled in the dust.
Forthwith her speech, her sight, her motion flies,
And grief suspends the torrent in her eyes.
Then grov'ling o'er the slain, with warm embrace
She clasp'd his limbs, and kiss'd his clay-cold face;
And from his stiff'ning hair, and costly vest,
The clotted gore with care assiduous press'd.
Her voice returning, on her spouse she roll'd
Her eyes, and cry'd,—"Art thou, whom I behold,
Adrastus' heir, and leader of the fight,
In bold assertion of a monarch's right?
And do I thus array'd thy triumphs meet?
See, see Argia seeks a safe retreat
At Thebes.—O lead her then within the walls
To thy paternal roof and regal halls;
And seize th' occasion which she gives, to prove
Thy grateful sense of her experienc'd love.
Alas! what do I ask?—a slender spot
Of native earth is all my consort's lot.
For what this quarrel then, and impious fray?
Forbid it Heav'ns, his brother e'er should sway

439. For night prolong'd] Jupiter, having lain with Alcmena in the form of her husband Amphitryon, thinking the space of one night insufficient for his pleasures, ordered the Moon to make it as long as three, which (we find from this speech of Juno) she complied with.—Lactantius.

Ovid also takes notice of it in Dejanira's epistle to Hercules.

At non ille velit, cui Nox si creditur una
Non tanti, ut tantus concipere, fuit.

463. Forthwith her speech] Mr. Dryden in his poem on the death of Charles the Second has some fine lines, that very nearly resemble our author's.

Thus long my grief has kept me dumb:
  Sure there's a lethargy in mighty woe,
  Tears stand congeal'd, and cannot flow;
And the sad soul retires into her inmost room:
  Tears, for a stroke foreseen, afford relief;
  But unprovided for a sudden blow,
    Like Niobe, we marble grow;
    And petrify with grief.

Weeps not Jocasta, tender-hearted dame?
Where is Antigone, so known to fame?
Fate wills then, thou should'st lie for me alone,
To torture me, in cruel fight o'erthrown.
In vain I said, 'Ah! whither dost thou fly
For crowns and sceptres, which the gods deny?
Let Argive honours bound thy rash desire,
Nor thus beyond what fortune grants aspire.'
Yet why do I complain?—I gave the sword,
And my sad sire in thy behalf implor'd,
To find thee thus.—Yet will I not repine;
Resign to your decrees, O pow'rs divine!
His relics by your aid obtain'd repay
The toils and anxious sorrows of the way.
Alas! with what a gape descends the wound!
Was this his brother? On what spot of ground
Lies the fell murd'rer?—Could I know the way,
I'd rob the beasts, and vultures of their prey.
But he perhaps enjoys a decent pyre;
And shalt thou mourn the want of ritual fire?
Ah! no.—With equal honours shalt thou burn,
And tears rain copious o'er the golden urn,
To kings deny'd: thy tomb for e'er shall prove
The pleasing duty of my widow'd love;
And young Thessander to thy bed succeed,
A witness to the woes on which I feed."
Behold Antigone with trembling hand
Bear for the furtive rites another brand,
Shares all the woe, and heaves the distant groan;
Scarce could she gain an egress from the town;
For Creon, ever wary to retard
The breach of his command, increas'd the guard;
So that more oft revolves the watching-hour,
And thicker burns the fire on ev'ry tow'r.
Her brother therefore, and the gods she prays,
To speed her flight, and pardon her delays;
And, frantic, rushes from the silent walls,
While drowsy Morpheus on the sentry falls.
With such a bound along the meadow springs
The virgin-lioness, when anger wings
Her rapid progress, or when hopes of prey
Allure her from her shady den away.
Nor a long time elaps'd, before she gain'd
The place by Polynices' blood distain'd.
Menœtes meets her traversing the plains,
And his dear pupil's deep-fetch'd groans restrains.
But, when the growing noise had reach'd the ear
Of the sad virgin all erect thro' fear;
And by the torches' light, and friendly rays
Of Cynthia, more distinctly she surveys
Argia's bloody face, dishevell'd hair,
And sable vest, she thus bespeaks the fair:
"Say, daring wretch, what chief o'erthrown in fight
Thou seek'st, encroaching on my proper right?"
To this she nought replies, but o'er her spouse,
And her own face, a sable veil she throws,
For fear at first her ev'ry thought possest,
And grief awhile forsook her tender breast.
This length of silence but the more increas'd
The dame's surmise, nor her inquiries ceas'd:
Her comrade then she presses, while they gaze
With horrour fix'd, and silent with amaze:

507. And young Thessander] This is an allusion to the famous speech of Dido in the fourth book of Virgil's Æneid.

Saltem si qua mihi de te suscepta fuisset
Ante fugam soboles; si quis mihi parvulus aulâ
Luderet Æneas, qui te tantum ore referret.
Barthius.

At length the princess thus her silence broke,
And, clasping in her arms the body, spoke.
" If, in the search of some relation slain,
Thou roamest, darkling, thro' the bloody plain,
And fearest angry Creon's stern decree,
My secret purpose I reveal to thee.
If thou art wretched (as thy tears avow)
Why join we not our hands, and make a vow
Of amity ?—Adrastus' daughter I,
Hopeful by stealth, and mutual secrecy,
My Polynices' poor remains to burn,
And close his ashes in a precious urn :
But who art thou ?"—Astonish'd with surprise,
The Theban damsel, trembling, thus replies.
" Me then (O ignorance of human race !)
Me dost thou fear, and hold in thy embrace
My brother's limbs, unwilling to disclose ?
To thee, the tender partner of my woes,
The friendly task with blushes I resign,
And own my lukewarm love excell'd by thine."
Thus she.--When, grov'ling with disorder'd charms
Around the prince, they fold him in their arms ;
Their falling tears, and hair together blend,
(While eagerly to kiss him they contend)
And with mix'd groans their lips by turns employ
On his dear face and neck, and share the joy.
A brother one, and one a husband plains ;
And Thebes and Argos in alternate strains
They sing ; but most Argia calls to mind
Their num'rous griefs, hard lot and fates unkind.
" By this our common rite of secret woe,
Yon social manes, and the stars that glow
In Heaven, conscious of the truth, I swear,
That never, when he breath'd our Argive air,
His dear, though absent, sister 'scap'd his thought ;
Her only he desir'd, her only sought.
Whilst his lov'd mother, and his native clime,
His crown detain'd beyond th' allotted time,
Without one tear or sigh were left behind,
And I, a lesser care, with ease resign'd.
But thou perhaps from some huge turret's height,
Hast seen him toiling thro' the ranks of fight,
While, as with martial air he strode along,
With eyes reverted from amidst the throng,
He wav'd his sword, and bow'd his triple crest,
An honour paid to those he lov'd the best,
While we at distance pin'd.—What god could fire
The furious pair to such excess of ire ?
Could not your prayers move his stubborn breast?
And was a sister's suit in vain address'd ?"
Now had the dame the woeful fact disclos'd,
But thus their faithful comrade interpos'd :
" Come on, and first your enterprize pursue ;
The stars, retiring, wear a paler hue,
And morn advances.—When the work is sped,
Then pour your boundless sorrows o'er the dead."
Not far remote, Ismenos roll'd his flood,
Still foul with slaughter, and distain'd with blood.
Hither the feeble pair by mutual aid
The warrior's lacerated corpse convey'd,
The little strength he has Menœtes lends,
And to support the load his arm extends.
Thus Phaeton, from Vulcan's fury sav'd,
In Po's warm stream his pious sisters lav'd,
To trees transform'd, and sorrowing for his doom,
Ere scarce his smoking body fill'd the tomb.
Soon as they cleans'd their brother in the ford,
And to their proper form his limbs restor'd,
They print the parting kiss on either cheek,
And fire, to close the rites, assiduous seek :
But ev'ry spark extinct, and flame o'ercome
By vap'ry damps, desponding long they roam.
Preserv'd by chance, or Providence, there stood,
Not distant far, a high-heap'd pile of wood :
Whether some fiend the fires discordant spar'd,
Or nature for new prodigies prepar'd,
Is yet unsaid, the cause remains unknown ;
Eteocles upon the top was thrown.
Here they perceive a slender gleam of light
From sable oaks, and, joyful at the sight,
In haste implore the unknown shade, who claims
The structure, to divide the grateful flames
With Polynices, nor disdain to burn
On the same pyre, and share one common urn.
Again behold the brothers !—When the fire
Pervades their limbs in many a curling spire,
The vast pile trembles, and th' intruder's corse
Is driven from the pile with sudden force ;
The flames, dividing at the points, ascend,
And at each other adverse rays extend.
Thus, when the ruler of th' infernal state
(Pale-visag'd Dis) commits to stern debate
The sister-fiends, their brands, held forth to fight,
Now clash, then part, and shed a transient light.
The very beams disjoin before their eyes:
With hell-bred terrours smit, each virgin cries:
" Through our default then do the flames engage,
And have our hands renew'd fraternal rage ?
For who, however cruel in the fray,
Would drive an injur'd Theban's shade away ?

575. By this our common rite] Our author, to put a finishing stroke to the characters of Argia and Antigone, presents us with an interview between them, in which their dispositions and manners are conveyed to us through the channel of discourse. From a comparison of the conduct of these ladies we may infer, that love transcends natural affection in a very eminent degree. Argia, fearing lest her sister should not persevere in assisting at the funeral rites of her husband through dread of Creon's displeasure, tells her of his sincere regard and esteem, and prompts her to exer herself, without seeming to do it.—The art of the poet is very visible on this occasion.

595. Now had the dame] This seems an indirect stroke on female loquacity. The two princesses, forgetful of the object of their enterprize, fall into a long conversation, which in all probability might have lasted till day-light, had not their good friend Menœtes admonished them of their duty.

607. Thus Phaeton] The story of Phaeton's fall from Heaven is too well known to be enlarged upon in a note. See Ovid's Metamorphoses, lib. 2. fable 1.

629. Again behold the brothers] This fiction is very properly inserted, and if it is not the poet's invention, does great honour to his judgment. Such traits of the marvellous have a fine effect in poetry. Lucan has imitated it in his account of the prodigies that ushered in the civil war between Cæsar and Pompey. Pharsalia, lib. 1.

——— ——— ———Vestali raptus ab arâ
Ignis, et ostendens confectas flamma Latinas
Scinditur in partes, geminoque cacumine surgit.
Thebanos imitata rogos.———

But our Eteocles?—The shield I know,
And half-burnt girdle of the brother foe.
Mark, how the fire recedes, then joins again!
Deep fix'd as erst their enmities remain.
Fruitless the war! In vain afresh they join
In fight, O tyrant, for the palm is thine;
Whence then this useless rage, this martial heat,
When he usurps the crown, and regal seat?
Resign your threats; and thou, the younger, bend,
Nor more for alienated sway contend.
At our joint suit, O close the direful scene:
Or, to prevent your rage, we rush between."
Scarce had she spoke, when with a rumbling sound
The field and lofty houses shook around;
The pile yawn'd wider, and his slumbers broke,
From dreams of woe the starting soldier woke,
And, running o'er the plain with naked sword,
Each secret pass and avenue explor'd.
Menœtes only dreads th' advancing band;
While they before the pyre, undaunted, stand,
Avow the breach of Creon's harsh decree,
And lift the shout of triumph, as they see
Their brother's body to the flames a prey,
And ev'ry mould'ring limb consum'd away.
If aught disturbs the tenour of their mind,
'Tis but the fear that Creon should be kind.
They both dispute whose labours merit most
Of glory, and the crime alternate boast.
"I brought the corse, and I the structure fir'd,
Me love," they cry, "me piety inspir'd."
The cruel punishment thus each demands,
And thro' the chains, delighted, thrusts her hands.
No more that caution to offend remains,
Nor mutual reverence their stile restrains:
Both angry seem, such jarring clamours rise
On either side, and rend the vaulted skies.
The guards who seiz'd them are dispatch'd to court,
Before the king the matter to report.
But Pallas ushers in the female band
To the Cecropian town, at the command
Of Juno, crowns their sorrows with applause,
And interests the people in their cause. [plies
Their hands with boughs, their foreheads she sup-
With wreaths, and teaches them in humble guise
To veil their face, the suppliant knee to bend,
And empty urns to public view extend.
Of ev'ry age a crowd of gazers roams,
Some seek the streets, and others mount their domes.
"From whence this swarm of wretched dames?"
they cry:
"Why flows the tear, and heaves the broken sigh?"
In concert, ere they learn the cause, they groan.
The goddess, mixt with either train, makes known
The object of their suit, their native land,
And whom they mourn, and answers each demand.
On all occasions they themselves disclose
The source and origin of all their woes,
And, murm'ring out th' inhuman tyrant's law,
In throngs around a vulgar audience draw.

669. If aught] The magnanimity of these two heroines is equal to any thing recorded of the fair sex both in fable and history. One cannot but cry out with Tasso,

> O spettacolo grande, ove à tenzone
> Sono amore, e magnanima virtute!
> Ove la morte al vincitor si pone
> In premio, e'l mal del vinto è la salute!

Thus from their nests the Thracian birds complain
In broken notes, and many a twitt'ring strain,
To strangers when th' incestuous rape they sing,
And wail th' injustice of the lustful king.
There stood as in the centre of the town
An altar, sacred to the poor alone;
Here gentle Clemency has fix'd her seat,
And none but wretches hallow the retreat.
A train of votaries she never wants.
And all requests and suits, impartial, grants.
Whoe'er implore, a speedy audience gain;
And open night and day her gates remain:
That misery might ever find access,
And by complaints alone obtain redress.
Nor costly are her rites: no blood she claims
From slaughter'd victims, nor odorous flames;
Her altars sweat with tears; and wreaths of woe,
Her suitors, tearing from their hair, bestow;
Or garments in her fane are left behind,
When Fortune shifts the scene, to her resign'd.
A grove surrounds it, where in shadowy rows
The laurel tree and suppliant olive grows.
No well wrought effigy her likeness bears,
Her imag'd form no sculptur'd metal wears:
In human breasts resides the pow'r divine,
A constant levee trembling at her shrine.
The place, deform'd with horrours not its own,
To none but objects of distress is known.
Fame says, the sons of great Alcides rear'd
The fane, in honour of the pow'r rever'd,
(A temple to their father first decreed)
But Fame diminishes the glorious deed.
'Tis juster to believe, the pow'rs above,
Of whose protection and parental love
Fair Athens shar'd a more than equal part,
The pile erected, not a mortal's art;
That mercy might, by rushing in between
Offended justice and th' offender, screen
The guilty wretch. For this the structure rose,
A common refuge in the greatest woes.

703. Thus from their nests] Tereus, king of Thrace, having married Progne, the daughter of Pandion king of Athens, and ravished her sister Philomela, cut out her tongue, and shut her up in a prison, where she wrote the story in needle-work, and sent it to her sister. Progne was transformed to a swallow, and Philomela to a nightingale.—We had a simile drawn from this bird in the eighth book. I do not like the repetition; but think it much more tolerable than one in the fifteenth book of the Iliad, which is copied verbatim from one in the sixth: I mean that of a horse set at liberty and ranging the pastures: whereas our author has varied his language and the circumstances of the comparison.

709. Here gentle Clemency] Chaucer, who in his Palamon and Arcite has taken great liberties with our author, and almost transcribed some passages (as will be seen in the sequel) mentions the Argive ladies entering this temple.

> Here in this temple of the goddesse Clemence,
> We have been waiting all this fourtenight: &c.

There is a vast luxuriance of fancy, as well as propriety displayed in this description. The building, sacrifices, and votaries are such as are highly consistent with the nature of the thing, and character of this goddess.

No human blood th' unspotted pavements stains;
But threat'ning Vengeance with her clanking chains,
And instruments of anger, howls aloof,
Nor Fortune frowns beneath this hallow'd roof.
Through all the globe is this asylum known.
Here kings depos'd, and chiefs in war o'erthrown,
And those, whose errour was their only crime,
Convene, repairing from each distant clime.
This hospitable goddess soon o'ercame
The rage of Œdipus, whose vengeful flame
The Furies kindled; and Orestes freed
From the fell horrours of the murd'rous deed.
Hither the pensive dames of Lerna come,
Conducted by a crowd: before the dome
A train of pilgrims stood, but all give way.
Soon as more pleasing thoughts their cares allay,
They shout aloud.—Thus when a well-rang'd host
Of feather'd cranes survey the Pharian coast,
They stretch their necks, and clapping as they fly,
Their wings expanded, shade a length of sky:
Such is their joy to scape the winter's reign,
And share in Nile the summer heats again.
Now Theseus, grac'd with conquest and renown
From Scythian battles, seeks th' Athenian town.
A pair of snow-white steeds his chariot draws,
His chariot wreath'd with laurels, while th' applause
Of shouting thousands, and pacific sound
Of breathing clarions wafts his praise around.
To swell the pomp, before the chief are borne
The spoils and trophies from the vanquish'd torn;
The car, the pageant charg'd with many a crest,
The sorrowing steed, with trappings gaily drest,
The pole-axe, wont to lay the forest low,
And thin Mæotis, the well-polish'd bow,
The quiver light, the girdle studded o'er
With gems, and shield deform'd with female gore.
But they, intrepid still, their sex disclose,
And in no vulgar groans express their woes;
To sue for life unworthily disdain,
And seek the martial virgin's holy fane.
The reigning passion now is to behold
The victors, glitt'ring with Barbaric gold:
But most Hippolyte their notice drew,
No longer frowning, but serene to view,
And reconciled to nuptial rites.—They gaze
Askance, with looks expressive of amaze,
And mutter out their wonder, that she broke
Her country's laws, and, patient of the yoke,

752. The rage of Œdipus] Œdipus, being expelled Thebes, by the command of Creon, fled to Colonos, where there was a temple consecrated to the Furies, but was taken thence by the Athenians, and very hospitably entertained. Aristophanes wrote a tragedy on this subject.—Lactantius.

759. A well-rang'd host] The cranes in their flight (as here from a colder to a warmer climate) usually kept in the form of one of these three Greek letters, Δ, Λ, or Υ, unless the violence of the wind or any other accident broke their order.

785. Hippolyte] Bernartius gives himself much trouble about the name of this lady of Theseus, and endeavours to prove, from a passage in Pausanias, that it was not Hippolyte, but Antiope. But as what he advances is very dry and tedious, and as the subject itself is not interesting (a poet not being tied down to historical precision) I shall take no farther notice of it, as the reader may see it at large in the Variorum edition by Veenhusen.

With artful braidings trick'd her auburn hair,
And veil'd her sun-burnt bosom, whilom bare;
That, pleas'd, she mixes in the gaudy show,
And brooks th' embraces of an Attic foe.
By slow degrees the suppliants quit the fane,
And, standing full in prospect of the train,
Admire the triumph, and recal to mind
Their husbands, to the fowls of air resign'd.
The coursers halting, from his chariot's height
The monarch lean'd, and, musing at the sight,
Inquires the cause.—To his demand replied
The wife of Capaneus, and boldly cried:
" O valiant Theseus, of whose future praise,
And glory, Fortune on our ruins lays

795. By slow degrees] So Chaucer:

This duke, of whom I make mencioune,
When he was come almost to the town
In all his well and his most pride,
He was ware, as he cast his eye aside,
Where that there kneeled in the high wey
A companie of ladies, twey and twey:
Each after other clad in clothes blacke,
But such a crie and such a woe they make,
That in this world nys creature living
That ever heard such a waimenting:
And of this crie they would never stenten,
Till they the reines of his bridell henten.

803. O valiant Theseus] It will not, I apprehend, be an unpleasing task to the reader to compare this speech with the last-quoted author's on the same subject.

The oldest ladie of them all spake,
Whan she had souned with a deadlie chere,
That it was ruth for to see and here:
She said, " Lord to whom Fortune hath yene
Victory, and a conqueror to live;
Nought greveth us your glory and honour,
But we bespeke you of mercy and socour.
And have mercy on our wo and distresse,
Some drop of pity through the gentilnesse
Upon us wretched wymen let thou fall.
For certes, lord, there nys none of us all
That shene hath been a dutchesse or a quene,
Nor be we caytifs, as it is well isene:
Thanked be Fortune, and her false whele
That none estate assureth for to be well.
Now certes, lord, to abyde your presence,
Here in this temple of the goddesse Clemence,
We have be waiting all this fourtenight:
Helpe us, lord, sith it lieth in thy might.
I wretch, that wepe and waile thus,
Whilom wife to king Capaneus,
That starfe at Thebes, cursed be the day,
And all we that ben in this array,
And maken all this lamentation,
We losten all our husbondes at that town,
While that the siege thereabout laie;
And yet the old Creon (wel awaie)
That lord is nowe of Thebes cite,
Fulfilled of yre, and of iniquite,
He for dispute, and for his tiranny
To done the deed bodies villanie,
Of all our lords, which that benslawe
Hath all the bodies on an heape idrawe;
And will not suffer them by none assent
Neither to be buried, ne to be brent,
But maketh hounds to eat hem in dispite."
And with that word without more respite

The basis, deem us not a guilty train
For crimes far exil'd, or of foreign strain:
Since all of us attain'd the rank before
Of royalty, and rul'd th' Inachian shore,
The wives of kings who met an early grave
In Theban wars, unfortunately brave.
Though griev'd, we cannot of their deaths complain,
For this the laws and chance of arms ordain.
Nor were they centaurs, or of monstrous birth,
The sport of Nature, and the dregs of Earth.
To wave their race, and glorious ancestry,
Suffice it, noble Theseus, that with thee
They bore a manly form, a thinking mind,
And all the properties of human kind:
Yet Creon, ruthless as the king of Hell,
And, as th' infernal boatsman, stern and fell,
To breathless carcases extends his ire,
Nor grants the last sad honours of the pyre:
Beneath the doubtful axle of the sky,
And Erebus, unburied still they lie.
Alas! O Nature, how art thou debas'd!
Through our defaults insulted and disgrac'd.
Where now is Athens? where the gods above?
Why sleeps the thunderbolt of partial Jove?
Meanwhile the sev'nth bright harbinger of day
Turns far from Thebes her orient steeds away.
The stars, that gild yon spangled sphere with light,
Avert their rays, and sicken at the sight.
The very birds and monsters of the wood
Abhor th' ill-scented field and noisome food,
From the corrupted blood such steams arise,
Taint the fresh gale, and poison half the skies.
Nought save the putrid gore to burn remains,
And naked bones, that whiten all the plains.
Haste, venerable sons of Cecrops, haste
To lay the realms of haughty Creon waste:
Such vengeance well becomes you—haste before
He pours his fury on the Thracian shore,
Before each nation shares an equal fate,
And millions rot beneath his impious hate.
For say, what lengths will bound his lawless rage,
If thoughts of vengeance yet his breast engage?
'Tis true, they fought, and vanquish'd press'd the plains:
Yet why should he pursue their cold remains?
Not thus thy wrath, as fame reports the deed,
Base Sinis to his brother brutes decreed;
But, as thy valour great, thy pity gave
Him and his ill-deserving peers a grave.
Thy piety, I ween, the foe admires,
And Tanais shines bright with frequent fires.
No wonder then, the pow'rs of battle bless
Thy dreaded arms with more than hop'd success.
Yet oh what wreaths thy forehead should adorn,
More glorious than the palm of conquest borne,
Wouldst thou but grace the dead with obsequies,
And ease the realms of Dis, the earth, and skies;
If Crete, and thy own Marathonian plain
Thou freed'st, nor the sage matron wept in vain!
O grant our suit: so through th' ensanguin'd field
May Pallas guide thee, and from danger shield:
Nor Hercules with envious hate pursue
Thy equal feats: but may thy mother view
An endless round of triumphs, nor the state
Of Athens prove at any time our fate."
She said and ceas'd: with hands upheld the rest
Echo her shrieks, and second her request.
At this the stream of grief begins to flow,
And his wet cheeks with rising blushes glow.
But soon his tears are dried in vengeful flames;
And, fir'd with just resentment, he exclaims:
" What fury thus deforms the moral plan
Of kings, and in the monster sinks the man?
Thank Heav'n, my virtue is not left behind,
Nor with my climate have I chang'd my mind.
Whence this new phrenzy, Creon? Hast thou thought
My spirits broken with the toils I wrought?
I come, I come, unwearied as before,
And my spear thirsts for thy devoted gore.
Then quick, my faithful Phegeus, turn thy steed,
And bear to Creon this my will decreed,
' Thebes or the Grecian carcases shall burn:'
Go, and prevent our hopes with thy return."
This said, forgetful of his recent toils,
He cheers his troops to fight with promis'd spoils,
And heals their strength impair'd—Thus when again
The victor-bull recovers his domain
And herd, if haply the rebellowing grove
Betrays a second rival to his love,

They fallen grossly, and crien piteously,
" Have on us wretched wymen some mercie
And let our sorowe sinke in thine hert."

850. Base Sinis] Sinis, Cercyon, and Scyron, were notorious robbers, whom this hero killed. Of the former Pausanias in his Corinthiacs gives the following account: "In the Isthmus there is a place, where Sinis, the robber, bending the branches of several pines to the ground, bound the wretches that he overcame to them in such a manner, that when the trees unbent themselves, they tore their bodies to pieces. He was punished in the same way by Theseus."

Propertius alludes to this fact. Book third.

Arboreasque cruces Sinis et non hospita Graiis
Saxa, et curvatas in sua fata trabes.

See Plutarch likewise in the Life of Theseus.
Bernartius.

854. And Tanais] Tanais was a famous river in the country of the Amazons.

861. If Crete, and, &c.] He killed the Marathonian bull, and minotaur of Crete.

869. She said and ceas'd] Let us see what Chaucer says:

This gentil duke downe from his horse stert,
With hert piteous, when he herd hem speke.
Him thought that his hert woulde breke,
Whan he saw hem so piteous and so mate,
That whilom were of so grete estate:
And in his armes he hem all up hent,
And hem conforted in full good entent:
And swore his othe, as he was true knight
He wolde don so ferforthly his might
Upon the tyrant Creon hem to wreake,
That all the people of Grece shulde speake
How Creon was of Theseus yserved;
As he that hath his deth full well deserved.

889. Thus when again] There is a great deal of what the French call *naiveté vivace* in this comparison, and it may be observed, to the honour of our author, that he never fails in this article through the whole work.

———— Servatur ad imum,
Qualis ab incœpto processerat, et sibi constat.

Though from his head and neck the bloody show'rs
Distil, he recollects his scatter'd pow'rs,
And, ev'ry groan suppress'd, and wound conceal'd,
Expatiates o'er the mead, untaught to yield.
Tritonia shakes the terrours of her breast:
And straight the snakes, that form Medusa's crest,
With hostile hissings all at once arise,
And at the walls of Cadmus dart their eyes.
Nor had th' Athenian host prepar'd to go,
When Dirce trembled at the trump of woe.
Now to the war not only those, who shar'd
The laurels reap'd on Caucasus, repair'd
With unextinguish'd heat, but ev'ry plain
To combat sends a rude, unmarshall'd train:
Beneath the standards of their chief convene
The hinds, who cultivate the pastures green
Of Brauron, and the Pyreæan strand,
Dreadful tho' firm to seamen, when they land.
From Marathon, inur'd to martial toils,
Though yet unnotic'd for its Persian spoils,
A band arrives; with these a cohort speeds
From fair Melænæ's ever-verdant meads.
Then from Icarius' hospitable dome,
To gods a feasting-house, the warriors roam,
From Parnes, with a purple harvest crown'd,
Egaleos, for its fertile groves renown'd,
And Lycabessos, not unknown to fame
For olives.—Next the stern Ileus came,
The rough Hymettian, and the swains who wreathe
The thyrsus in Acharne's vales beneath.
Sunium, by eastern prows afar perceiv'd,
Is left, from whence the Cretan ship deceiv'd
The sire with sable sails, as o'er the steep
He bent, in act to fall, and name the deep.
These Salamis, and those Eleusis sends,
O'er whose rich furrows Ceres wide extends
The scene of plenty: on they bend their way,
Their ploughs suspended for the dreadful fray.
Now march the troops whom, hardy, fierce, and bold,
Callirhoe's nine meand'ring streams infold,
And fair Ilyssos, who conceal'd with care
The Thracian ravisher, and Attic fair.
The citadel resigns its guards for fight,
Where Neptune and Minerva vy'd in might,
Till from the doubtful cliff an olive sprung,
And th' ebbing seas with length'ning shade o'erhung.
Nor had the Scythian queen withheld her aid;
She join'd the host with ensigns high-display'd;
But Theseus, mindful of her growing pains,
And swelling womb, her youthful heat restrains,
And warns her, safe at home from war's alarms,
To deck the nuptial bed with votive arms.
Soon as the chief surveys their martial rage,
While prone to fight, and ardent to engage,
They greet their offspring with a short embrace,
Thus from his car he speaks: "O gen'rous race!
With me selected to defend the laws
Of nations, and assert the common cause,
Exert your pow'rs, and to the combat rise
With courage equal to the vast emprize.
With us is Nature, ever faithful guide,
The gods, inclining to the juster side,
And, to our view disclos'd, th' Elysian band
In approbation of our conduct stand:
The snake-hair'd fiends the sons of Cadmus head,
And to the wind their floating banners spread.
On then, my friends, to conquer or to die,
And on the justice of your cause rely."
The monarch spoke, and hurl'd a sounding lance,
Prelude to fight, and signal to advance.
As when the cloudy son of Saturn forms
The winter's reign, and vexes with his storms
The northern pole, the face of Heav'n's o'ercast,
And all Æolia shakes beneath the blast,
While Boreas, scorning his inactive ease,
Acquires fresh strength, and whistles o'er the seas:
Then groan the waves and hills, the lightnings shine,
The thunders roar, the clouds in conflict join:
Thus with repeated strokes the plains resound,
And wheels and hoofs indent the smoking ground.
Troop follows troop: beneath their feet arise
Black clouds of dust, and intercept the skies,
Yet through the thick'ning gloom by fits is seen
The transient light of arms, that gleams between,
Their javelins glare with intermingled rays,
And strike each other with reflected blaze.

912. Though yet unnotic'd] The Athenians gained a great victory here over the Persian army commanded by Dates and Ataphernes, whose history every one is well acquainted with.

925. With sable sails] The lot falling upon Theseus to go to Crete according to the compact with Minos, he went on board a ship, whose sails and tackle were black, and received this command from his father Ægeus, that if he escaped the dangers, he should change his black sails into white ones: but the hero forgetting this injunction, his father seeing the black sails imagined that his son was dead, and cast himself headlong from the promontory of Sunium into the sea, which was afterwards called the Ægean from his name and destiny.

933. Who conceal'd with care] Boreas ravished Orythia, the daughter of king Erectheus, by whom he had the two twins, Zetus and Calais. Lactantius.

936. Where Neptune and Minerva] The poet means the Acropolis, where the above-mentioned deities made a trial of their power. The former, by striking the earth, caused a horse to spring from it, which is the token of war: but the latter produced an olive-tree, the ensign of peace.

944. To deck] It was a custom of the ancients after a victory, or when they had resigned their military employments, to hang up their arms, and consecrate them.—Horace alludes to this ceremony, lib. 3. ode 26.

> Vixi puellis nuper idoneus,
> Et militavi non sine gloria:
> Nunc arma, defunctumque bello
> Barbiton hic paries habebit:
> Lævum marinæ qui Veneris latus
> Custodit: hic, hic ponite lucida
> Funalia, et vectes, et arcus
> Oppositis foribus minaces.

961. And hurl'd a sounding lance] The poet has here (as it sometimes happens with the most accurate writers) confounded the customs of other countries with those of his own, in representing Theseus giving the signal of war by darting a javelin into the frontiers of his enemy's country, which ceremony was peculiar to the Romans only, and performed by their feciales or heralds at arms, as we learn from Livy, book 1.

Now thro' the shades of night they seek their foes :
Meanwhile a contest emulous arose,
Who first could reach the town, and in the wall
Infix his dart. Conspicuous o'er them all,
Neptune's great offspring stalks along the field
With haughty strides, and waves his ample shield,
The sculptur'd surface of whose boss displays
Crete's hundred towns, the first essay of praise.
Himself is there pourtray'd, as rashly brave
Within the horrid windings of the cave,
He twists the monster's neck, and to his hands
And brawny arms applies the strait'ning bands,
Or from his threat'ning horns withdraws away
His face, and shuns with art th'unequal fray.
Fear seiz'd the Theban host, as they survey'd
The warrior's image on the targe pourtray'd;
Such was th' engraver's skill, they seem'd to view
A double Theseus, wet with gory dew.
The hero at the sight recals to mind
His ancient deeds, his friends of noble kind,
The late-fear'd threshold, and the Gnossian fair
Pursuing the lost clue with busy care.
Meantime the dames, for speedy death design'd
By Creon's law, their hands fast-bound behind,
Are from the loathsome prison-house convey'd
Beneath a double guard. Both undismay'd,
Triumphant would resign their vital breath,
Smile at the dagger drawn, and rush on death,
And dying disappoint the tyrant's aim ;
When to the court th' Athenian legate came.
An olive's peaceful branch indeed he bears,
But war in high insulting tone declares ;
And mindful of his lord's supreme command,
Informs the Theban king, that near at hand
His master's troops are station'd, and but wait
His answer to commence the stern debate.
The tyrant, floating in a sea of care,
Now doubts to persevere in wrath, or spare:
At length with an assum'd, embitter'd smile
Confirm'd, he thus replies in haughty style :
" Since then no samples of our ire suffice
To make a rash and doating people wise,
Let self-experience.—See the foe again
Insults our walls. We'll meet them on the plain.
Let them prepare to share their neighbour's fate ;
Repent they may, but they repent too late.
This is our law, and on these terms we take
The field."—While thus in angry mood he spake,
A cloud of dust, ascending in his sight,
Obscures the day, and hides the mountain's height.
Impassion'd as he was, he warns his bands
To arm, and armour for himself demands.
Sudden he sees (an omen of his fall)
The furies seated in the middle hall,
Menœceus weeping his devoted sire,
And the glad Argives flaming on the pyre.
How fatal to the Thebans was the day,
When peace, by blood obtain'd, was chas'd away !
Their weapons, scarce hung up, they now resume,
Hack'd shields, unable to prevent their doom,
Helms, of their crests bereft in days of yore,
And javelins yet distain'd with clotted gore :
None is distinguish'd on th' embattled mead
For his neat quiver, sword, and well-reined steed.
No longer in the trenches they confide :
The city walls gape wide on every side,
No gates nor bulwarks guard the guilty town,
By Capaneus dismantled, and o'erthrown.
Nor now the heartless youth, before they quit
Their wives and children, in embraces knit
Their spreading arms, nor the last kiss bestow ;
E'en the crazed parents part without a vow.
But when th' Athenian saw the solar beam
From bursting clouds upon his armour gleam,
With headlong fury on the field he leaps,
Where many an Argive chief unburied sleeps :
And, as he views the blood-polluted streams,
And breathes an air condens'd by vap'ry steams,
Beneath his dusty helmet, at the sight
Inflam'd, he groans, and rushes to the fight.
Some reverence at least the Theban shows,
Some honour on the Grecians he bestows,
As for the fight another plain he chose,
Nor mingled with the dead his living foes.
But, to fill up the measure of his guilt,
And save the blood, devoted to be spilt,
A field untill'd, and never furrow'd o'er
He singles out, to drink the hostile gore.
And now Bellona sets in adverse arms
Both hosts, and shakes the plain with war's alarms.

989. The monster's neck] The minotaur was half man, half beast, and kept in the labyrinth made by Dædalus, where he devoured yearly seven of the noblest Athenian youths, till the third year Theseus slew him, and escaped by the help of Ariadne.

995. They seem'd to view] Tasso seems to have imitated this fiction in the last canto of his Jerusalem Delivered, where he tells us, that Rinaldo's motions were so sudden and rapid, that every time he brandished his sword, his enemies thought he brandished three.

Qual tre lingue vibrar sembra il serpente,
Che la prestezza d' una il persuade ;
Tal credea lui la sbigottita gente
Con la rapida man girar tre spade
L' occhio al moto deluso il falso crede.
E' l terrore a que' monstri accresce fede.

1001. Meantime the dames] There is a great similitude between this book and the second of Tasso's Jerusalem. The magnanimity of Olindo and Sophronia resembles that of Antigone and Argia. The former are delivered from punishment by the mediation of Clorinda, and the latter by the interposition of the Athenian ambassador. Nor is the haughty deportment of Phegeus unlike that of Argante.

1027. A cloud of dust, ascending in the sight] Occasioned by the march of the Athenian army.

1031. Sudden he sees] To make this fiction tolerable, we must not take the words of the original in a literal sense, but suppose, that Creon, oppressed with cares and anxiety, fell asleep, and saw these images in a dream ; as Richard the Third in Shakspeare, the night before the battle of Bosworth, saw the ghosts of those he had murdered, and was by them threatened with his approaching death.

1047. Before they quit] The farewell kiss was so much insisted on by the ancients at parting from, or seeing one another again after a long absence, that Suetonius informs us, Nero was censured, and looked upon as an uncourteous brute for the omission of it. " Quod neque adveniens, neque proficiscens, quenquam osculo impertivit," Life of Nero, cap. 37.

With shouts the Theban bands the strife commence:
But martial trumps th' Athenian troops incense.
With downcast looks the sons of Cadmus stand,
And feebly grasp the weapons in their hand;
Their arms yet unemploy'd, they yield their ground,
And show old scars, and many a streaming wound.
Nor in th' Athenian chieftains as before
The thirst of vengeance glows; their threats are [o'er,
And, unoppos'd, their courage dies away.
Thus, when the yielding woods decline the fray,
The winds grow placid; and the waves subside,
If no firm shore repels the briny tide.
But as the son of Ægeus high display'd
The spear of Marathonian oak, whose shade
O'erhangs the foe, whilst dreadful to the sight,
Its steely point emits a beamy light,
His foes pale horrour urges from behind,
And wings them with the fleetness of the wind:
As when from Hæmus Mars impels his car,
And scatters havoc from the wheels of war,
Before him carnage, rout, disorder fly,
His harbingers, and all or kill or die.
But Theseus scorns to stain with vulgar gore
His sword. The flying herd he passes o'er,
To weaker hands such easy conquests yields,
And scours, in quest of nobler game, the fields.
Thus dogs and wolves invade the ready prey,
While the more gen'rous lion stalks away.
Yet Thamirus and bold Olenius too,
Presuming to contend in arms, he slew;
This, as he lifts a stone, in act to throw,
That, as he fits his arrow to his bow.

1070. But martial trumps] Euripides tells us, that Theseus before the battle declared to either army by an herald, that he had no other view in this expedition, but to have justice done to the Argives, by having them buried in a decent proper manner; and that Creon made no answer to this declaration. Barthius.

1087. As when from Hæmus] Statius by this comparison sets the valour of Theseus in a very exalted light. He is no less formidable than Mars himself. We look upon him as more than human, and are not astonished so much at the effects of his prowess. The first hint of comparing heroes to the gods was Homer's, who in his Iliad likens Idomeneus to this same deity.

Lib. 13. verse 298.

Οἷος δὲ βροτολοιγὸς Ἄρης πόλεμονδε μέτεισι,
Τῷ δὲ φόβος φίλος υἱὸς ἅμα κρατερὸς καὶ ἀταρβὴς
Εσπετο, ὅς ἐφόβησε ταλάφρονά περ πολεμιστήν.

Virgil has enlarged on this simile, and thrown in several beautiful images. Æneid, book 12. v. 331.

Qualis apud gelidi cum flumina concitus Hebri
Sanguineus Mavors clypeo increpat, atque furentes
Bella movens immittit equos: illi æquore aperto
Ante Notos Zephyrumque volant: gemit ultima pulsu
Thraca pedum: circumque atræ Formidinis ora,
Iræque, Insidiæque, dei comitatus, aguntur.

Silius Italicus has likewise imitated it in his Punic War, book 1.

Quantus Bistoniis latè gradivus in oris
Belligero rapitur curru, telumque coruscans
Titanum quo pulsa cohors, flagrantia bella
Cornipedum afflatu domat, et stridoribus axis.

Then fell three sons of Alceus side by side,
Whilst in their strength united they confide,
Pierc'd by three spears: first, wounded in his breast,
Rash Phileus sought the shades of endless rest;
Next, the lance piercing thro' the shoulder-joint,
Iapix dies; last Helops bit the point.
Now Hæmon in his car he sought: his blade,
Wav'd round, in air a dazzling circle made:
But he retires.—The spear with whizzing sound
Two chiefs transfix'd with one continued wound,
And aim'd a third, but th' axle-tree withstood,
And lodg'd the dart, deep-buried in the wood.
But Creon only through the ranks of fight
He seeks, and challenges to prove his might:
The tyrant in the van, though far apart,
He soon espies, whilst using ev'ry art,
To dare th' attack he reincites his band,
And makes the last effort: him, by command
Of Theseus, his retiring troops resign
To his own valour, and the pow'rs divine.
The king recals them, but, when he descry'd
Himself alike abhorr'd by either side,
Bold with despair, his utmost rage collects,
And thus to Theseus his discourse directs:
" Think not, thou comest here a war to wage
With Amazons, or wreak thy female rage
On female foes.—Thou meet'st with manly arms,
Chiefs old in war, and nurs'd amidst alarms;
Beneath whose might Hippomedon was slain,
And Capaneus and Tydeus press'd the plain.
What phrenzy prompts thee thus to tempt thy fate?
See, in whose cause thou kindlest the debate!"
He spoke, and at the foe a javelin flings,
Faint on the surface of the shield it rings.
But Theseus, smiling at the feeble blow,
Shakes his enormous lance, in act to throw,
But, ere he lets th' impatient weapon fly,
In thund'ring accents makes this stern reply:
" Ye Grecian shades, to whom Ægides sends
This sacrifice, prepare the vengeful fiends
For his reception, and unbar the domes
Of Tartarus: he comes, the tyrant comes."
He said, with force dismiss'd, the quiv'ring dart
Pervades the skies, and lights, where near his heart
The slender chains, well wrought of ductile gold,
The cuirass, arm'd with many a plate, infold.
The blood spins upward from a thousand holes:
He sinks, and, doubting where to fix them, rolls
His eyes around.—The victor stands beside
To spoil his arms, and thus insulting cry'd:

1118. Him, by command] Our author seems to have taken this circumstance from Virgil's Æneid, lib. 12. verse 758.

Ille simul fugiens, Rutulos simul increpat omnes,
Nomine quemque vocans; notumque efflagitat [ensem.
Æneas mortem contra præsensque minatur
Exitium, si quisquam adeat; terretque trementes
Excisurum urbem minitans.——

1125. Think not] Numanus in the ninth book of the Æneid insults the Trojans in almost the same strain.

Quis deus Italiam, quæ vos dementia adegit?
Non hic Atridæ, nec fandi fictor Ulysses.

Creon however, in the heat of his passion, transgresses the bounds of truth, and very ungratefully forgets his deliverer, in attributing the death of Capaneus to a mortal hand.

"Now wilt thou rev'rence justice, nor disdain
To grant interment to the Grecians slain?
Go, meet the vengeance thy demerits claim,
Secure howe'er of the last fun'ral flame."
With pious tumult now both hosts embrace,
Join hand in hand, and mingle face with face.
Peace and a league the sons of Thebes request;
And, hailing Theseus by the name of guest,
Court him to march his army to the town,
And use the royal mansion as his own.
The chief assents. The Theban dames rejoice,
And greet his entrance with applauding voice.
Thus did the banks of Ganges once resound
The victor's praise, with wreaths of vine-leaves crown'd.
Now from the summit of the fronting hill,
Whose shady groves o'erhang the sacred rill
Of Dirce, the Pelasgian dames descend,
And with shrill shouts the vaulted ether rend.
Thus, when the frantic choir of matrons join
With hideous yell the jolly god of wine,
They rage and foam, as if they had decreed
To do, or late had done some flagrant deed.
Far other tears gush forth, the tears of joy,
And various objects their pursuit employ.
To Theseus these, to Creon those repair,
Whilst others make the dead their earliest care.
Scarce could I dignify their woes in verse,
And all the pomp in equal strains rehearse,
Should gentle Phœbus fortify my lungs,
And give locution from a hundred tongues:
To sing, with what a bound and placid smile
Evadne leap'd upon the fun'ral pile,
And, folding in her arms her husband's corse,
Explor'd the traces of the lightning's force;
How his fair spouse with kisses stamps the face
Of cruel Tydeus, clasp'd in her embrace;
Or to her sister with fast-streaming eyes
Argia tells the former night's emprize; [mands
With what loud shrieks th' Arcadian queen de-
Her son, bewail'd by all his subject bands,
Her son, whose beauty fled not with his breath,
Her son, esteem'd in life, and wept in death.
For such a mighty task the new supplies
Of some inspiring god would scarce suffice.
Yet more.—My ship, long tost upon the seas,
Requires a port, and interval of ease.
O Thebaid, dear object of my toil,
For twelve long years pursu'd by midnight oil!
Wilt thou survive thy author, and be read,
His lamp of life extinct, his spirit fled?
For thee already Fame has pav'd the way
To future praise, and cherishes thy lay.
Taste stamps thee current, marks thee for her own,
And makes thy few deserts, and beauties known
To gen'rous Cæsar, whilst the studious youth
From thy chaste page imbibes the moral truth
With fiction temper'd.—Claim thy proper bays,
Nor emulate the greater Æneid's praise;
At awful distance follow, and adore
Its sacred footsteps: thus, the tempest o'er,
Through envy's cloud distinguish'd, thou shalt shine,
And after me enjoy a name divine.

1151. Now wilt thou rev'rence justice] It may be worth while to compare the conduct of Theseus with that of Achilles on a similar occasion. The former, we see, when Creon was just dying, only upbraids him of his cruelty in a gentle manner, and with great humanity promises him, he shall not want the funeral rites which he denied to others; whilst the latter, as it were to sharpen and embitter the agonies of death, with the utmost ferocity threatens Hector, that no motives shall ever prevail with him to suffer his body to be buried.—Here Homer has outraged nature, and not represented his hero as a man, but a monster; and yet Mr. Pope, in the preface to his version, after having praised his author's talent for drawing characters, and his lessons of morality, remarks of Statius's heroes, that an air of impetuosity runs through them all; the same horrid and savage courage appears in his Capaneus, Tydeus, and Hippomedon. They have a parity of character (says he) which makes them seem brothers of one family.—This observation may suffice to show the reader, to what lengths a predilection for his author will carry a translator.

1179. Should gentle Phœbus] Our author has imitated this from Homer, book 2d, verse 488.

Πληθὺν δ' οὐκ ἂν ἐγὼ μυθήσομαι, οὐδ' ὀνομήνω,
Οὐδ' εἴ μοι δέκα μὲν γλῶσσαι, δέκα δὲ στόματ' εἶεν,
Φωνὴ δ' ἄῤῥηκτος, χάλκεον δέ μοι ἦτορ ἐνείη.

Nor is he singular in his imitation.

Non, mihi si linguæ centum sint, oraque centum,
Ferrea vox, omnes scelerum comprendere formas,
Omnia pœnarum percurrere nomina possum.
Virg. Æn. l. 6.

Tasso has also borrowed the thought. Jerusalem Delivered, Canto 9. Stan. 92.

Non io, se cento bocche, e lingue cento
Avessi, e ferrea lena, e ferrea voce,
Narrar potrei quel numero, che spento
Ne' primi assalti hâ quel drappel feroce.

1182. Evadne leap'd upon the fun'ral pile] This heroine threw herself upon the pile of her husband Capaneus, and was burnt with him. There are equal instances of affection amongst the eastern nations of our time, and Montaigne acquaints us, that it is a custom in some parts of India, whenever their prince dies, to burn his most beloved concubine on the same pile with him.

1191. Her son] This repetition of the hero's name three times leaves a great impression of him on the mind of the reader, and is so very beautiful, that I thought myself obliged to preserve it in the translation. Homer has one equally delicate.

Νιρεὺς δ' αὖ Σύμηθεν ἄγεν τρεῖς νῆας ἐΐσας,
Νιρεὺς Ἀγλαΐης υἱὸς, Χαρόποιό τ' ἄνακτος,
Νιρεὺς, ὃς κάλλιστος ἀνὴρ ὑπὸ Ἴλιον ἦλθε.

1197. O Thebaid] The poet in this address very artfully takes his leave of the reader, and at the same time sings his own panegyric, which he has done in a decent modest manner, and paid a genteel compliment to the author of the Æneid. In this self-notice he has the authority of Pindar, Lucretius, Ovid, and Lucan, who have all given him precedents.

THE

WORKS

OF

H E S I O D.

TRANSLATED BY COOKE.

TO HIS GRACE

JOHN DUKE OF ARGYLL AND GREENWICH, &c.

MY LORD,

As this is the only method by which men of genius and learning, though small perhaps my claim to either, can show their esteem for persons of extraordinary merit, in a superior manner to the rest of mankind, I could never embrace a more favourable opportunity to express my veneration for your grace than before a translation of so ancient and valuable an author as Hesiod. Your high descent, and the glory of your illustrious ancestors, are the weakest foundations of your praise; your own exalted worth attracts the admiration, and I may say the love, of all virtuous and distinguishing souls; and to that only I dedicate the following work. The many circumstances which contributed to the raising you to the dignities which you now enjoy, and which render you deserving the greatest favours a prince can bestow, and, what is above all, which fix you ever dear in the affection of your country, will be no small part of the English history, and shall make the name of Argyll sacred to every generation; nor is it the least part of your character, that the nation entertains the highest opinion of your taste and judgment in the polite arts.

You, my lord, know how the works of genius lift up the head of a nation above her neighbours, and give it as much honour as success in arms; among these we must reckon our translations of the classics; by which, when we have naturalized all Greece and Rome, we shall be so much richer than they were, by so many original productions as we shall have of our own. By translations, when performed by able hands, our countrymen have an opportunity of discovering the beauties of the ancients, without the trouble and expense of learning their languages; which are of no other advantage to us than for the authors who have writ in them; among which the poets are in the first rank of honour, whose verses are the delightful channels through which the best precepts of morality are conveyed to the mind; they have generally something in them so much above the common sense of mankind, and that delivered with such dignity of expression, and in such harmony of numbers, all which put together constitute the *os divinum,* that the reader is inspired with sentiments of honour and virtue, he thinks with abhorrence of all that is base and trifling; I may say, while he is reading, he is exalted above himself.

You, my lord, I say, have a just sense of the benefits arising from works of genius, and will therefore pardon the zeal with which I express myself concerning them: and great is the blessing, that we want not persons who have hearts equal to their power to cherish them: and here I must beg leave to pay a debt of gratitude to one, who, I dare say, is as highly thought of by all lovers of polite learning as by myself, I mean the earl of Pembroke; whose notes I have used in the words in which he gave them to me, and distinguished them by a particular mark from the rest. Much would I say in commendation of that great man; but I am checked by the fear of offending that virtue which every one admires. The same reason makes me dwell less on the praise of your grace than my heart inclines me to.

The many obligations which I have received from a lady, of whose virtues I can never say too much, make it a duty in me to mention her in the most grateful manner; and particularly before a translation, to the perfecting which I may with propriety say she greatly conduced by her kind solicitations in my behalf, and her earnest recommendation of me to several persons of distinction. I believe your grace will not charge me with vanity, if I confess myself ambitious of being in the least degree of favour with so excellent a lady as the marchioness of Annandale.

I shall conclude, without troubling your grace with any more circumstances relating to myself, sincerely wishing what I offer was more worthy your patronage; and at the same time I beg it may be received as proceeding from a just sense of your eminence in all that is great and laudable. I am,

my Lord,

with the most profound respect,

your grace's

most obedient and most humble servant,

THOMAS COOKE.

January, 1728.

A DISCOURSE ON THE LIFE OF HESIOD.

THE lives of few persons are confounded with so many incertainties, and fabulous relations, as those of Hesiod and Homer; for which reason, what may possibly be true is sometimes as much disputed as the romantic part of their stories. The first has been more fortunate than the other, in furnishing us, from his writings, with some circumstances of himself and family, as the condition of his father, the place of his birth, and the extent of his travels; and he has put it out of dispute, though he has not fixed the period, that he was one of the earliest writers of whom we have any account.

He tells us, in the second book of his Works and Days, that his father was an inhabitant of Cuma, in one of the Æolian isles; from whence he removed to Ascra, a village in Bœotia, at the foot of mount Helicon; which was doubtless the place of our poet's birth, though Suidas, Lilius Gyraldus, Fabricius, and others, say he was of Cuma. Hesiod himself seems, and not undesignedly, to have prevented any mistake about his country; he tells us positively, in the same book, he never was but once at sea, and that in a voyage from Aulis, a seaport in Bœotia, to the island Eubœa. This, connected with the former passage of his father sailing from Cuma to Bœotia, will leave us in no doubt concerning his country.

Of what quality his father was we are not very certain; that he was drove from Cuma to Ascra, by misfortunes, we have the testimony of Hesiod. Some tell us he fled to avoid paying a fine; but what reason they have to imagine that I know not. It is remarkable that our poet, in the first book of his Works and Days, calls his brother διον γενος; we are told indeed that the name of his father was Dïos, of which we are not assured from any of his writings now extant; but if it was, I rather believe, had he designed to call his brother of the race of Dios, he would have used Διογενης or Διυ γενος; he must therefore by διον γενος intend to call him of race divine. Le Clerc observes, on this passage, that the old poets were always proud of the epithet divine, and brings an instance from Homer, who styled the swineherd of Ulysses so; in the same remark he says, he thinks Hesiod debases the word in his application of it, having spoke of the necessitous circumstances of his father in the following book. I have no doubt but Le Clerc is right in the meaning of the word διον, but at the same time I think his observation on it trifling; because, if his father was reduced to poverty, we are not to infer from thence he was never rich, or, if he was always poor, that is no argument against his being of a good family; nor is the word divine in the least debased by being an epithet to the swineherd, but a proof of the dignity of that office in those times. We are supported in this reading by Tzetzes: and Valla, and Frisius, have took the word in the same sense, in their Latin translations of the Works and Days:

——Frater ades (says Valla) generoso e sanguine Perse.

And Frisius calls him, Perse divine.

The genealogy likewise which the author of the contention betwixt Homer and Hesiod gives us very much countenances this interpretation: we are told in that work, that Linus was the son of Apollo and of Thoose the daughter of Neptune; king Pierus was the son of Linus, Oeagrus of Pierus and the nymph Methone, and Orpheus of Oeagrus and the muse Calliope; Orpheus was the father of Othrys, Othrys of Harmonides, and Harmonides of Philoterpus; from him sprung Euphemus, the father of Epiphrades, who begot Menalops, the father of Dios; Hesiod and Perses were the sons of Dios by Pucamede, the daughter of Apollo; Perses was the father of Mæon, whose daughter, Crytheis, bore Homer to the river Meles. Homer is here made the great grandson of Perses the brother of Hesiod. I do not give this account with a view it should be much depended on; for it is plain, from the poetical etymologies of the names, it is a fictitious generation; yet two useful inferences may be made from it; first, it is natural to suppose, the author of this genealogy would not have forged such an honourable descent unless it was generally believed he was of a great family; nor would he have placed him so long before Homer, had it not been the prevailing opinion he was first.

Mr. Kennet quotes the Danish astronomer, Longomontanus, who undertook to settle the age of Hesiod from some lines in his Works and Days; and he made it agree with the Arundelian marble, which makes him about thirty years before Homer.

Herodotus assures us that Hesiod, whom he places first in his account, and Homer, lived four hundred years, and no more, before himself; this must carry no small weight with it, when we consider it as delivered down to us by the oldest Greek historian we have.

The pious exclamation against the vices of his own times, in the beginning of the iron age, and the manner in which the description of that age is wrote, most of the verbs being in the future tense, give us room to imagine he lived when the world had but just departed from their primitive virtue, just as the race of heroes was at an end, and men were sunk into all that is base and wicked.

Justus Lipsius, in his notes to the first book of Velleïus Paterculus, says, "there is more simplicity, and a greater air of antiquity, in the works of Hesiod than of Homer," from which he would infer he is the older writer: and Fabricius gives us these words of Ludolphus Neocorus, who writ a critical history of Homer; "if a judgment of the two poets is to be made from their works, Homer has the advantage, in the greater simplicity, and air of antiquity, in his style. Hesiod is more finished and elegant." One of these is a flagrant instance of the random judgment which the critics, and commentators, often pass on authors, and how little dependance is to be laid on some of them. In short they are both in an errour; for had they considered through how many hands the Iliad and Odysses have been, since they came from the first author, they would not have pretended to determine the question, who was first, by their style.

Dr. Samuel Clarke (who was indeed a person of much more extensive learning and nicer discernment than either Neocorus or Lipsius) has founded an argument for the antiquity of Homer on a quantity of the word καλος: in his note on the 43d verse of the 2d book of the Iliad he observes that Homer has used the word καλος in the Iliad and Odyssey above two hundred and seventy times, and has in every place made the first syllable long; whereas Hesiod frequently makes it long, and often short: and Theocritus uses it both long and short in the same verse: from which our learned critic infers that Hesiod could not be cotemporary with Homer (unless, says he, they spoke different languages in different parts of the country) but much later; because he takes it for granted that the liberty of making the first syllable of καλος short was long after Homer; who uses the word above two hundred and seventy times, and never has the first syallable short. This is a curious piece of criticism, but productive of no certainty of the age of Homer or Hesiod. The Ionic poets, Dr. Clarke observes, had one fixed rule of making the first syllable in καλος long: the Attic poets, Sophocles, Euripides, and Aristophanes, in innumerable places, he says, make it short; the Doric poets do the same: all therefore that can be inferred from this is, that Homer always used it in the Ionic manner, and Hesiod often in the Ionic, and often in the Doric. This argument of Dr. Clarke's, founded on a single quantity of a word, is entirely destructive of sir Isaac Newton's system of chronology; who fixes the time of Troy being taken but thirty-four years before Hesiod flourished. Troy, he says*, was taken nine hundred and four years before Christ, and Hesiod, he says, flourished eight hundred and seventy. This shows sir Isaac Newton's opinion of the age of Hesiod in regard to his vicinity to Homer: his bringing the chronology of both so low as he does is to support his favourite scheme of reducing all to Scripture chronology.

After all, it is universally agreed he was before, or at least cotemporary with, Homer; but I think we have more reason to believe him the older; and Mr. Pope, after all the authorities he could find in behalf of Homer, fixes his decision on the Arundelian marble. To enter into all the disputes which have been on this head would be endless, and unnecessary; but we may venture to place him a thousand years before Christ, without exceeding an hundred, perhaps, on either side.

Having thus far agreed to his parents, his country, and the time in which he rose, our next business is to trace him in such of his actions as are discoverable; and here we have nothing certain but what occurs to us in his works. That he tended his own flocks on mount Helicon, and there first received his notions of poetry, is very probable from the beginning of his Theogony; but what he there says of the Muses appearing to him, and giving him a sceptre of laurel, I pass over as a poetical flight. It

* In his Chronology of Ancient Kingdoms amended.

likewise appears, from the first book of his Works and Days, that his father left some effects, when he died, on the division of which his brother Perses defrauded him, by bribing the judges. He was so far from being provoked to any act of resentment by this injustice, that he expressed a concern for those poor mistaken mortals, who placed their happiness in riches only, even at the expense of their virtue. He lets us know, in the same poem, that he was not only above want, but capable of assisting his brother in time of need; which he often did after the ill usage he had met with from him. The last passage, relating to himself, is his conquest in a poetical contention. Amphidamas, king of Eubœa, had instituted funeral games in honour of his own memory, which his sons afterwards saw performed: Hesiod here was competitor for the prize in poetry, a tripod, which he won, and, as he tells us himself, consecrated to the Muses.

Plutarch, in his Banquet of the Seven Wise Men, makes Periander give an account of the poetical contention at Chalcis; in which Hesiod and Homer are made antagonists; the first was conqueror, who received a tripod for his victory, which he dedicated to the Muses, with this inscription;

Ησιοδος Μουσαις Ελικωνισι τονδ' ανεθηκεν,
Υμνω νικησας εν χαλκιδι θειον Ομηρον.

This Hesiod vows to th' Heliconian Nine,
In Chalcis won from Homer the divine.

This story, as related by Plutarch, was doubtless occasioned by what Hesiod says of himself, in the second book of his Works and Days; which passage might possibly give birth to that famous treatise, Αγων Ομηρου και Ησιοδου, mentioned in the fourth section of this discourse. Barnes, in his Præloquium to the same treatise, quotes three verses, two from Eustathius, and the third added by Lilius Gyraldus, in his life of our poet, which inform us, that Hesiod and Homer sung in Delos to the honour of Apollo.

Εν Δηλῳ τοτε πρωτον εγω και Ομηρος, αοιδοι,
Μελπομεν, εν νεαροις υμνοις ραψαντες αοιδην,
Φοιβον Απολλωνα χρυσαορον ον τεκε Λητω.

Homer, and I, in Delos sung our lays,
There first we sung, and to Apollo's praise;
New was the verse in which we then begun
In honour to the god, Latona's son.

But these, together with the contention betwixt these two great poets, are regarded as no other than fables: and Barnes, who had certainly read as much on this head as any man, and who seems, by some expressions, willing to believe it if he could, is forced to decline the dispute, and leave it in the same uncertainty in which he found it. The story of the two poets meeting in Delos is a manifest forgery; because, as I observed before, Hesiod positively says he never took any voyage but that to Chalcis; and these verses make his meeting in Delos, which is contrary to his own assertion, precede his contention at Chalcis. Thus have I collected, and compared together, all that is material of his life; in the latter part of which, we are told, he removed to Locris, a town near the same distance from mount Parnassus as Ascra from Helicon. Lilius Gyraldus, and others, tell us he left a son, and a daughter; and that his son was Stesichorus the poet; but this wants better confirmation than we have of it. It is agreed by all that he lived to a very advanced age.

The story of his death, as told by Solon, in Plutarch's Banquet of the Seven Wise Men, is very remarkable. The man, with whom Hesiod lived at Locris, ravished a maid in the same house. Hesiod, though entirely ignorant of the fact, was maliciously accused, as an accomplice, to her brothers, who barbarously murdered him with his companion, whose name was Troilus, and throwed their bodies into the sea. The body of Troilus was cast on a rock, which retains the name of Troilus from that accident. The body of Hesiod was received by a shoal of dolphins as soon as it was hurled into the water, and carried to the city Molicria, near the promontory Rhion; near which place the Locrians then held a solemn feast, the same which is at this time celebrated with so much pomp. When they saw a floating carcase they ran with astonishment to the shore, and finding it to be the body of Hesiod, newly slain, they resolved, as they thought themselves obliged, to detect the murderers of a person they so much esteemed and honoured. When they had found out the wretches who committed the murder, they plunged them alive into the sea, and afterwards destroyed their houses. The remains of Hesiod were deposited in Nemea; and his tomb is unknown to most strangers: the reason of it being concealed was because of the Orchomenians, who had a design, founded on the advice of an oracle, to steal his remains from thence, and to bury them in their own country. This account of the oracle, here mentioned by Plutarch, is related by Pausanias, in his Bœotics. He tells us the Orchomenians were advised by the oracle to bring the bones of Hesiod into their country, as the only means to drive away a pestilence which raged among them. They obeyed the oracle, found the bones, and brought them home. Pausanias says they erected a tomb over him, with an inscription to this purpose on it;

Hesiod, thy birth is barren Ascra's boast,
Thy dead remains now grace the Minyan coast;
Thy honours to meridian glory rise,
Grateful thy name to all the good and wise.

We have the knowledge of some few monuments which were raised in honour of this great and ancient poet: Pausanias, in his Bœotics, informs us, that his countrymen the Bœotians erected to his memory an image with a harp in his hand: the same author tells us, in another place, there was likewise a statue of Hesiod in the temple of Jupiter Olympicus. Fulvius Ursinus, and Boissard, in his antiquities, have exhibited a breast with a head, a trunk without a head, and a gem, of him: and Ursinus says there is a statue of him, of brass, in the public college at Constantinople: the only original monument of him besides, now remaining, or at least known, is a marble busto in the Pembroke collection at Wilton: what Fulvius Ursinus has published resembles that, but is only a basso relievo. From the manner of the head being cracked off from the lower part, which has some of the hair behind, it appears that both the parts are of the same work and date.

For his character we need go no farther than his Works and Days: with what a dutiful affection he speaks of his father, when he proposes him as a pattern to his brother! His behaviour, after the unjust treatment from Perses and the judges, proves him both a philosopher and a good man. His moral precepts, in the first book, seem to be as much the dictates of his heart as the fruits of his genius; there we behold a man of the chastest manners, and the best disposition.

He was undoubtedly a great lover of retirement and contemplation, and seems to have had no ambition but that of acting well. I shall conclude my character of him with that part of it which Paterculus so justly thought his due: perelegantis ingenii, et mollissimâ dulcedine carminum memorabilis; otii quietisque cupidissimus: "of a truly elegant genius, and memorable for his most easy sweetness of verse; most fond of leisure and quietude."

A DISCOURSE ON THE WRITINGS OF HESIOD.

OF all the authors who have given any account of the writings of our poet, I find none so perfect as the learned Fabricius, in his Bibliotheca Græca; he there seems to have left unread no work that might in the least contribute to the completing his design: him I shall follow in the succeeding discourse, so far as relates to the titles of the poems, and the authorities for them.

I shall begin with the Theogony, or Generation of the Gods, which Fabricius puts out of dispute to be of Hesiod: nor is it doubted, says he, that Pythagoras took it for his, who feigned he saw the soul of our poet in Hell chained to a brazen pillar; a punishment inflicted on him for the stories which he invented of the gods. This doubtless is the poem that gave Herodotus occasion to say that Hesiod, with Homer, was the first who introduced a Theogony among the Grecians; the first who gave names to the gods, ascribed to them honours and arts, giving particular descriptions of their persons. The first hundred and fifteen lines of this poem have been disputed; but I am inclined to believe them genuine, because Pausanias takes notice of the sceptre of laurel, which the poet says, in those verses, was a present to him from the Muses: and Ovid, in the beginning of his Art of Love, alludes to that passage of the Muses appearing to him; and Hesiod himself, in the second book of his Works and Days, has an allusion to these verses.

The Works and Days is the first poem of its kind, if we may rely on the testimony of Pliny; it being very incertain, says Fabricius, whether the poems attributed to Orpheus were older than Hesiod; among which the critics and commentators mention one of the same title with this of our poet. Pausanias, in his Bœotics, tells us he saw a copy of this wrote in plates of lead, but without the first ten verses with which it now begins. The only dispute about this piece has been concerning the title, and the division into books. Some make it two poems; the first they call Εργα Works, and the second Ημεραι Days: others call the first Εργα και Ημεραι Works and Days, and the second Ημεραι only, which part consists of but sixty-four lines: where I mention the number of verses, in this discourse, I speak of them as they stand in the original. We find, in some editions, the division beginning at the end of the moral and religious precepts; but Grævius denies such distinctions being in any of the old manuscripts. Whether these divisions were in the first copies signifies little; for as we find them in several late editions, they are very natural, and contribute something to the ease of the reader, without the least detriment to the original text. I am ready to imagine we have not this work delivered down to us so perfect as it came from the hands of the poet; which I shall endeavour to show in the next section. This poem, as Plutarch, in his Symposiacs, assures us, was sung to the harp.

The Theogony, and Works and Days, are the only undoubted pieces of our poet now extant; the Ασπις Ηρακλεους, the Shield of Hercules, is always printed with those two, but has not one convincing argument in its favour, by which we may positively declare it a genuine work of Hesiod. We have great reason to believe those two poems only were remaining in the reign of Augustus: Manilius, who was an author of the Augustan age, in the second book of his astronomy, takes notice, in his commendation of our poet and his writings, of no other than the Theogony, and Works and Days. The verses of Manilius are these:

> Hesiodus memorat divos, divûmque parentes,
> Et chaos enixum terras, orbemque sub illo
> Infantem, primum[1], titubantia sidera, corpus,

[1] Dr. Bentley, whose Manilius was published ten years after the first edition of this discourse, gives primos titubantia sidera partus: the old copies, he says, have primos; and partus is supplied by

Titanasque senes, Jovis et cunabula magni,
Et sub fratre viri nomen, sine fratre parentis,
Atque iterùm patrio nascentem corpore Bacchum,
Omniaque immenso volitantia numina mundo:
Quinetiam ruris cultus, legesque rogavit[2],
Militiamque Soli, quos colles Bacchus amaret,
Quos fœcunda Ceres campos, quod Bacchus utrumque[3],
Atque arbusta vagis essent quod adultera pomis,
Sylvarumque deos, sacrataque numina Nymphas;
Pacis opus, magnos naturæ condit in usus.

Thus translated by Mr. Creech,

——Hesiod sings the gods' immortal race,
He sings how chaos bore the earthy mass,
How light from darkness struck did beams display,
And infant-stars first stagger'd in their way,
How name of brother veil'd an husband's love,
And Juno bore unaided by her Jove,
How twice-born Bacchus burst the Thund'rer's thigh,
And all the gods that wander through the sky:
Hence he to fields descends, manures the soil,
Instructs the ploughman, and rewards his toil;
He sings how corn in plains, how vine in hills,
Delight, how both with vast increase the olive fills,
How foreign grafts th' adulterous stock receives,
Bears stranger fruit, and wonders at her leaves;
An useful work when peace and plenty reign,
And art joins nature to improve the plain.

The observation which Mr. Kennet makes on these lines is, that "those fine things which the Latin poet recounts about the birth of the gods, and the making the world, are not so nearly allied to any passages in the present Theogony as to justify the allusion." An author, who was giving an account of an ancient poet, ought to have been more careful than this biographer was in his judgment of these verses; because such as read him, and are at the same time unlearned in the language of the poet, are to form their notions from his sentiments. Mr. Kennet is so very wrong in his remark here, that in all the seven lines, which contain the encomium on the Theogony, I cannot see one expression that has not an allusion, and a strong one, to some particular passage in that poem. I am afraid this gentleman's modesty made him distrust himself, and too servilely follow this translation, which he quotes in his life of Hesiod, where he seems to lay great stress on the judgment of the translator. Mr. Creech has in these few lines so unhappily mistook his author, that in some places he adds what the poet never thought of, leaves whole verses untranslated, and in other places gives a

his own judgment: but primos partus for titubantia sidera is not consistent with the genealogy of these natural bodies in the Theogony of Hesiod: an exact genealogical table to which, I have given at the end of my notes to that poem. I must, with great deference to the superior knowledge of that learned critic, prefer the common reading primum corpus: Dr. Bentley's chief objection to this reading is founded on making primum to be understood first in point of time; therefore, says he, quomodo vero sidera primum erant corpus, cum ante illa extiterint Chaos, Terræ, Orbis? Very true; but primum must be taken as I have used it in my explanation of it.

[2] For legesque rogavit Dr. Bentley gives legesque novandi, on the authority of no copy, but from a dislike to the expression of rogavit cultus and rogavit militiam; but, as the old reading rogavit is agreeable to my construction of it, I am for keeping it in.

[3] For Bacchus utrumque Dr. Bentley gives Pallas utrumque; and in that sense Mr. Creech has translated it; which would be the more eligible reading, if Hesiod had treated of olives. Bacchus utrumque is a foolish repetition, as Dr. Bentley observes.

sense quite different to what the poet designed. I shall now proceed to point out those passages to which Manilius particularly alludes: his first line relates to the poem in general, the generation of the gods; though we must take notice that he had that part of Hesiod's system in view where he makes matter precede all things, and even the gods themselves; for by divûm parentes the Latin poet means Chaos, Heaven, Earth, &c. which the Greek poet makes the parents of the gods. Hesiod tells us, verse the hundred and sixteenth, Chaos brought forth the earth her first offspring; to which the second line here quoted has a plain reference; and orbemque sub illo infantem, which Mr. Creech has omitted, may either mean the world in general, or, by sub illo being annexed, Hell, which, according to our poet, was made a subterranean world. Primum, titubantia sidera, corpus, which is here rendered, And infant stars first stagger'd in their way, are the Sun and Moon; our poet calls them Ηελιον τε μεγαν, λαμπραν τε σεληνην, the great sun, and the bright moon; the Roman calls them the wandering planets, the chief bodies in the firmament, not the first works of Heaven, as is interpreted in the Dauphin's edition of Manilius: the fourth verse, which refers to the birth of Jove, and the wars of the giants and the gods, one of the greatest subjects of the Theogony, the English translator has left untouched. I am not ignorant of a various reading of this passage; viz.

Titanasque juvisse senis cunabula magni,

which has a stronger allusion to the battle of the gods than the other reading, senis cunabula magni meaning the second childhood, or old age, of Saturn. The next verse, which is beautifully expressed in these two lines,

How name of brother veil'd an husband's love,
And Juno bore unaided by her Jove,

plainly directs to Jupiter taking his sister Juno to wife, and Juno bearing Vulcan, ου φιλοτητι μιγεισα, by which Hesiod means without the mutual joys of love. The succeeding line has a reference to the birth of Bacchus, and the seventh to the whole poem; so that he may be said to begin and end his panegyric on the Theogony with a general allusion to the whole. The Latin poet, in his six verses on the Works and Days, begins, as on the Theogony, with a general observation on the whole poem: Hesiod, says he, inquired into the tillage and management of the country, and into the laws, or rules, of agriculture; I do not question but Manilius, in legesque rogavit, had his eye on these words of our poet, Ουτος τοι πεδιων πελεται νομος, this is the law of the fields. What the Roman there says of Bacchus loving hills, and of grafting, has no allusion to any part of the present Works and Days; but we are not to infer from thence that this is not the poem alluded to, but that those passages are lost; of which I have not the least doubt, when I consider of some parts of the Works and Days, which are not so well connected as I wish they were. I think it is indisputable that Hesiod writ more of the vintage than we have now extant, and that he likewise laid down rules for the care of trees: this will appear more clearly, if we observe in what manner Virgil introduces this line,

Ascræumque cano, Romana per oppida, carmen.

This is in the second book of the Georgics, the chief subjects of which book are the different methods of producing trees, of transplanting, grafting, of the various kinds of trees, the proper soil for each kind, and of the care of vines, and olives; and he has in that book the very expression Manilius applies to Hesiod. Bacchus amat colles, says Virgil; rogavit quos colles Bacchus amaret, says the other of our poet, he inquired after what hills Bacchus loved.

I should not have used Mr. Creech, and Mr. Kennet, with so much freedom as I have, had not the translation of one, and the remark of the other, so nearly concerned our poet; but I hope the clearing a difficult and remarkable passage in a classic will, in some measure, atone for the liberties I have took with those gentlemen.

We have now, ascribed to Hesiod, a poem under the title of Ασπις Ηρακλεους, the Shield of Hercules; which Aristophanes the grammarian supposes to be spurious, and that it is an imitation of the Shield of Achilles in Homer. Lilius Gyraldus, and Fabricius, bring all the testimonies they can for it being writ by Hesiod; but none of them amount to a proof. Fabricius gives us the opinion of Tanaquil Faber, in these words; "I am much surprised that this should formerly have been, and is now, a matter of dispute; those who suppose the Shield not to be of Hesiod, have a very slender knowledge of the Greek poetry." This is only the judgment of one man against a number, and that founded on no authority. I know not what could induce Tanaquil Faber so confidently to assert this, which looks, if I may use the expression, like a sort of bullying a person into his opinion, by forcing him into the dreadful apprehension of being thought no judge of Greek poetry if he will not come in: I say, I know not what could induce him to assert this, for there is no manner of similitude to the other works of our poet: and here I must call in question the judgment of Aristophanes, and of such as have followed him, for supposing it to be an imitation of the Shield of Achilles. The whole poem consists of four hundred and fourscore verses; of which the description of the shield is but one hundred and fourscore; in this description are some similar passages to that of Achilles, but not sufficient to justify that opinion: there are likewise a few lines the same in both; but after a strict examination they may possibly appear as much to the disadvantage of Homer as to the author of this poem. The other parts have no affinity to any book in the two poems of Homer. The poet begins with a beautiful description of the person of Alcmena, her love to Amphitryon, and her amour with Jupiter; from thence he proceeds to the characters of Hercules, and Iphiclus, and goes on regularly to the death of Cygnus, which concludes the poem, with many other particulars, which, as I said before, have no relation to any part of Homer. Among the writings of our poet which are lost we have the titles of Γυναικων, or Ηρωιδων, Καταλογος, and of Γυναικων Καταλογος, or Ηοιαι Μεγαλαι: both these titles are likely to belong but to one poem, and to that which Suidas mentions, the Catalogue of Heroic Women, in five books: that he composed such a work is probable from the two last verses of the Theogony, and it being often mentioned by ancient writers: we have an account of another poem under the title of Ηρωγονια, the Generation of Heroes: the favourers of the Shield of Hercules would have that poem received as a fragment of one of these; and all that Le Clerc says in defence of it is, "since Hercules was the most famous of heroes, it is not absurd to imagine the Shield to be a part of the Ηρωγονια, though it is handed down to us as a distinct work, and yet is but a fragment of it." Thus we see all their arguments, both for it being genuine, and a fragment of another poem, are but conjectures. I think they ought not to suspect it a part of another work, unless they could tell when, where, or by whom, the title was changed. It is certainly a very ancient piece, and well worth the notice of men of genius.

Besides the pieces just mentioned, we find the following catalogue in Fabricius attributed to Hesiod, but now lost.

Παραινεσις or Υποθηκαι χειρωνος: this was concerning the education of Achilles under Chiron; which Aristophanes, in one of his comedies, banters as the work of Hesiod.

Μελαμποδια or εις τον Μαντιν Μελαμποδα: a poem on divination: the title is supposed to be took from Melampus an ancient physician, said to be skilled in divination by birds. Part of this work is commended by Athenæus, book 13.

Αστρονομια μεγαλη or Αστρικη βιβλος: a treatise of astronomy. Pliny says, "according to Hesiod, in whose name we have a book of astrology extant, the early setting of the Pleïades is about the end of the autumn equinox." Notwithstanding this quotation, Fabricius tell us, that Athenæus and Pliny, in some other place, have given us reason to believe they thought the poem of astronomy supposititious.

Επικηδειος εις Βατραχυν: this is mentioned by Suidas, with the addition of τινα ερωμενον αυτȣ, a funeral song on Batrachus, whom he loved.

Περι Ιδαιων Δακτυλων: this was of the Idæi Dactyli, "who," says Pliny, in his seventh book, "are recorded by Hesiod, as discoverers of iron in Crete:" this is likewise in the catalogue of Suidas.

Επιθαλαμιος Πελεως και Θετιδος: an epithalamium on the marriage of Peleus and Thetis; two verses of which are in the Prolegomena of Isaac Tzetzes to Lycophron.

Γης περιοδος: this book of geography is mentioned by Strabo.

Αιγιμιος: a poem on one Ægimius; this, Athenæus tells us, was writ by Hesiod, or Cercops; a wretch whose name is now remembered only for being to Hesiod what Zoilus was to Homer.

Θησεως εις τον αιδην καταβασις: the descent of Theseus into Hell: this is attributed to Hesiod by Pausanias, in his Bœotics.

Επη μαντικα και εξηγησεις επι τερασιν: on prophecies or divination, with an exposition of prodigies or portents: this is likewise mentioned by Pausanias.

Θειοι λογοι: divine speeches; which Maximus Tyrius takes notice of in his sixteenth dissertation.

Μεγαλα εργα: great or remarkable actions: we find the title of this work in the eighth book of Athenæus.

Κηυκος γαμος: the marriage of Ceyx; we have an account of this poem both by Athenæus, and Plutarch in his Symposiacs.

Of all these labours of this great poet we see nothing but the titles remaining, excepting some fragments preserved by Pausanias, Plutarch, Polybius, &c. We are told that our poet composed some other works, of which we have not even the titles. We are assured, from divers passages in Pliny, that he wrote of the virtues of herbs; but here Fabricius judiciously observes, that he might, in other poems, occasionally treat of various herbs; as in the beginning of his Works and Days he speaks of the wholesomeness of mallows, and the daffodil, or asphodelos. Quintilian, in his fifth book, denies the fables of Æsop to have been written originally by him, but says the first author of them was Hesiod; and Plutarch informs us that Æsop was his disciple: but this opinion, though countenanced by some, is exploded by others.

When we reflect on the number of titles, the poems to which are irreparably lost, we should consider them as so many monuments to raise our concern for the loss of so much treasure never to be retrieved. Let us turn our thoughts from that melancholy theme, and view the poet in his living writings; let us read him ourselves, and incite our countrymen to a taste of the politeness of Greece. Scaliger, in an epistle of Salmasius, divides the state of poetry in Greece into four periods of time: in the first arose Homer and Hesiod; on which he has the just observation that concludes my discourse: "this," says he, "you may not improperly call the spring of poesy, but it is rather the bloom than infancy."

THE GENERAL ARGUMENT TO THE

WORKS AND DAYS,

FROM THE GREEK OF DANIEL HEINSIUS.

THE poet begins with the difference of the two contentions, and, rejecting that which is attended with disgrace, he advises his brother Perses to prefer the other. One is the lover of strife, and the occasion of troubles. The other prompts us on to procure the necessaries of life in a fair and honest way. After Prometheus had, by subtlety, stole the fire clandestinely from Jove (the fire is by the divine Plato, in his allusion to this passage, called the necessaries or abundance of life; and those are called subtle who were solicitous after the abundance of life) the god created a great evil, which was Pandora, that is Fortune, who was endowed with all the gifts of the gods, meaning all the benefits of nature: so Fortune may from thence be said to have the disposal of the comforts of life; and, from that time, care and prudence are required in the management of human affairs. Before Prometheus had purloined the fire, all the common necessaries of life were near at hand, and easily attained; for Saturn had first made a golden age of men, to which the earth yielded all her fruits spontaneously: the mortals of the golden age submitted to a soft and pleasant death, and were afterwards made demons, and honour attended their names. To this succeeded the second, the silver age, worse in all things than the first, and better than the following; which Jupiter, or Fate, took from the Earth, and made happy in their death. Hence the poet passes to the third, the brazen age, the men of which, he says, were fierce and terrible, who ignobly fell by their own folly and civil discord; nor was their future fate like to the other, for they descended to Hell. This generation is followed by a race of heroes, Eteocles and Polynices, and the rest who were in the first and oldest Theban war, and Agamemnon and Menelaus, and such as are recorded by the poet[1] to be in the Trojan war, of whom some perished entirely by death, and some now inhabit the isles of the blessed. Next he describes the iron age, and the injustice which prevailed in it. He greatly reproves the judges, and taxes them with corruption, in a short and beautiful fable. In the other part of the book, he sets before our eyes the consequences of justice and injustice; and then, in the most sagacious manner, lays down some of the wisest precepts to Perses. The part which contains the precepts is chiefly writ in an irregular, free, and easy way; and his frequent repetitions, which custom modern writers have quite avoided, bear no small marks of his antiquity. He often digresses, that his brother might not be tired with his precepts, because of a too much sameness. Hence he passes to rules of economy, beginning with agriculture. He points out the proper season for the plough, the harvest, the vintage, and for felling wood; he shows the fruits of industry, and the ill consequences of negligence. He describes the different seasons, and tells us what works are proper to each. These are the subjects of the first part of his economy. In process of time, and the thirst of gain increasing in men, every method was tried to the procuring riches; men began to extend their commerce over the seas; for which reason the poet laid down precepts for navigation. He next proceeds to a recommendation of divine worship, the adoration due to the immortal gods, and the various ways of paying our homage to them. He concludes with a short observation on days, dividing them into the good, bad, and indifferent.

[1] I suppose Heinsius means Homer.

THE

WORKS OF HESIOD.

TRANSLATED BY COOKE.

WORKS AND DAYS.

BOOK I.

THE ARGUMENT.

This book contains the invocation to the whole, the general proposition, the story of Prometheus, Epimetheus, and Pandora, a description of the golden age, silver age, brazen age, the age of heroes, and the iron age, a recommendation of virtue, from the temporal blessings with which good men are attended, and the condition of the wicked, and several moral precepts proper to be observed through the course of our lives.

SING, Muses, sing, from the Pierian grove;
Begin the song, and let the theme be Jove;
From him ye sprung, and him ye first should praise;
From your immortal sire deduce your lays;
To him alone, to his great will, we owe,
That we exist, and what we are, below.
Whether we blaze among the sons of fame,
Or live obscurely, and without a name,
Or noble, or ignoble, still we prove
Our lot determin'd by the will of Jove.
With ease he lifts the peasant to a crown,
With the same ease he casts the monarch down;
With ease he clouds the brightest name in night,
And calls the meanest to the fairest light;
At will he varies life through ev'ry state,
Unnerves the strong, and makes the crooked strait.
Such Jove, who thunders terrible from high,
Who dwells in mansions far above the sky.
Look down, thou pow'r supreme, vouchsafe thine [aid,
And let my judgment be by justice sway'd;
O! hear my vows, and thine assistance bring,
While truths undoubted I to Perses sing.
As here on Earth we tread the maze of life,
The mind's divided in a double strife;
One, by the wise, is thought deserving fame,
And this attended by the greatest shame,
The dismal source whence spring pernicious jars,
The baneful fountain of destructive wars,
Which, by the laws of arbitrary fate,
We follow, though by nature taught to hate;
From night's black realms this took its odious birth:
And one Jove planted in the womb of earth,
The better strife; by this the soul is fir'd
To arduous toils, nor with those toils is tir'd;
One sees his neighbour, with laborious hand,
Planting his orchard, or manuring land;
He sees another, with industrious care,
Materials for the building art prepare;
Idle himself he sees them haste to rise,
Observes their growing wealth with envious eyes,
With emulation fir'd, beholds their store,
And toils with joy, who never toil'd before:
The artist envies what the artist gains,
The bard the rival bard's successful strains.
Perses, attend, my just decrees observe,
Nor from thy honest labour idly swerve;
The love of strife, that joys in evils, shun,
Nor to the forum, from thy duty, run.
How vain the wranglings of the bar to mind,
While Ceres, yellow goddess, is unkind!
But when propitious she has heap'd your store,
For others you may plead, and not before;
But let with justice your contentions prove,
And be your counsels such as come from Jove;
Not as of late, when we divided lands,
You grasp'd at all with avaricious hands;
When the corrupted bench, for bribes well known,
Unjustly granted more than was your own.
Fools, blind to truth! nor knows their erring soul
How much the half is better than the whole,
How great the pleasure wholesome herbs afford,
How bless'd the frugal, and an honest, board!
Would the immortal gods on men bestow
A mind, how few the wants of life to know,
They all the year, from labour free, might live
On what the bounty of a day would give,
They soon the rudder o'er the smoke would lay,
And let the mule, and ox, at leisure stray:
This sense to man the king of gods denies,
In wrath to him who daring robb'd the skies;
Dread ills the god prepar'd, unknown before,
And the stol'n fire back to his Heav'n he bore;
But from Prometheus 'twas conceal'd in vain,
Which for the use of man he stole again,
And, artful in his fraud, brought from above,
Clos'd in a hollow cane, deceiving Jove:
Again defrauded of celestial fire,
Thus spoke the cloud compelling god in ire:
" Son of Iäpetus, o'er-subtle, go,
And glory in thy artful theft below;
Now of the fire you boast by stealth retriev'd,
And triumph in almighty Jove deceiv'd;
But thou too late shall find the triumph vain,
And read thy folly in succeeding pain;
Posterity the sad effect shall know,
When, in pursuit of joy, they grasp their woe."
He spoke, and told to Mulciber his will,
And, smiling, bade him his commands fulfil,
To use his greatest art, his nicest care,
To frame a creature exquisitely fair,
To temper well the clay with water, then
To add the vigour, and the voice, of men,

To let her first in virgin lustre shine,
In form a goddess, with a bloom divine:
And next the sire demands Minerva's aid,
In all her various skill to train the maid,
Bids her the secrets of the loom impart,
To cast a curious thread with happy art:
And golden Venus was to teach the fair
The wiles of love, and to improve her air,
And then, in awful majesty, to shed
A thousand graceful charms around her head:
Next Hermes, artful god, must form her mind,
One day to torture, and the next be kind,
With manners all deceitful, and her tongue
Fraught with abuse, and with detraction hung.
Jove gave the mandate; and the gods obey'd.
First Vulcan form'd of earth the blushing maid;
Minerva next perform'd the task assign'd,
With ev'ry female art adorn'd her mind.
To dress her Suada, and the Graces, join;
Around her person, lo! the di'monds shine.
To deck her brows the fair-tress'd Seasons bring
A garland breathing all the sweets of Spring.
Each present Pallas gives its proper place,
And adds to ev'ry ornament a grace.
Next Hermes taught the fair the heart to move,
With all the false alluring arts of love,
Her manners all deceitful, and her tongue
With falsehoods fruitful, and detraction hung.
The finish'd maid the gods Pandora call,
Because a tribute she receiv'd from all:
And thus, 'twas Jove's command, the sex began,
A lovely mischief to the soul of man.
When the great sire of gods beheld the fair,
The fatal guile, th' inevitable snare,
Hermes he bids to Epimetheus bear.
Prometheus, mindful of his theft above,
Had warn'd his brother to beware of Jove,
To take no present that the god should send,
Lest the fair bride should ill to man portend;
But he, forgetful, takes his evil fate,
Accepts the mischief, and repents too late.
Mortals at first a blissful Earth enjoy'd,
With ills untainted, nor with cares annoy'd;
To them the world was no laborious stage,
Nor fear'd they then the miseries of age;
But soon the sad reversion they behold,
Alas! they grow in their afflictions old;
For in her hand the nymph a casket bears,
Full of diseases, and corroding cares,
Which open'd, they to taint the world begin,
And Hope alone remains entire within.
Such was the fatal present from above,
And such the will of cloud-compelling Jove.
And now unnumber'd woes o'er mortals reign,
Alike infected is the land, and main,
O'er human race distempers silent stray,
And multiply their strength by night and day;
'Twas Jove's decree they should in silence rove;
For who is able to contend with Jove?
And now the subject of my verse I change;
To tales of profit and delight I range;
Whence you may pleasure and advantage gain,
If in your mind you lay the useful strain.
Soon as the deathless gods were born, and man,
A mortal race, with voice endow'd, began,
The heav'nly pow'rs from high their work
behold,
And the first age they style an age of gold.
Men spent a life like gods in Saturn's reign,
Nor felt their mind a care, nor body pain;
From labour free they ev'ry sense enjoy;
Nor could the ills of time their peace destroy;
In banquets they delight, remov'd from care;
Nor troublesome old age intruded there:
They die, or rather seem to die, they seem
From hence transported in a pleasing dream.
The fields, as yet untill'd, their fruits afford,
And fill a sumptuous, and unenvied board:
Thus, crown'd with happiness their ev'ry day,
Serene, and joyful, pass'd their lives away.
When in the grave this race of men was laid,
Soon was a world of holy demons made,
Aërial spirits, by great Jove design'd
To be on Earth the guardians of mankind;
Invisible to mortal eyes they go,
And mark our actions, good or bad, below;
Th' immortal spies with watchful care preside,
And thrice ten thousand round their charges glide:
They can reward with glory, or with gold;
A pow'r they by divine permission hold.
Worse than the first, a second age appears,
Which the celestials call the silver years.
The golden age's virtues are no more;
Nature grows weaker than she was before;
In strength of body mortals much decay;
And human wisdom seems to fade away.
An hundred years the careful dames employ,
Before they form'd to man th' unpolish'd boy;
Who when he reach'd his bloom, his age's prime,
Found, measur'd by his joys, but short his time.
Men, prone to ill, denied the gods their due,
And, by their follies, made their days but few.
The altars of the bless'd neglected stand,
Without the off'rings which the laws demand;
But angry Jove in dust this people laid,
Because no honours to the gods they paid. [span,
This second race, when clos'd their life's short
Was happy deem'd beyond the state of man;
Their names were grateful to their children made;
Each paid a rev'rence to his father's shade.
And now a third, a brazen, people rise,
Unlike the former, men of monstrous size:
Strong arms extensive from their shoulders grow,
Their limbs of equal magnitude below;
Potent in arms, and dreadful at the spear,
They live injurious, and devoid of fear:
On the crude flesh of beasts, they feed, alone,
Savage their nature, and their hearts of stone;
Their houses brass, of brass the warlike blade,
Iron was yet unknown, in brass they trade:
Furious, robust, impatient for the fight,
War is their only care, and sole delight.
To the dark shades of death this race descend,
By civil discords, an ignoble end! [might,
Strong tho' they were, death quell'd their boasted
And forc'd their stubborn souls to leave the light.
To these a fourth, a better, race succeeds,
Of godlike heroes, fam'd for martial deeds;
Them demigods, at first, their matchless worth
Proclaims aloud, all through the boundless Earth.
These, horrid wars, their love of arms, destroy,
Some at the gates of Thebes, and some at Troy.
These for the brothers fell, detested strife!
For beauty those, the lovely Grecian wife!
To these does Jove a second life ordain,
Some happy soil far in the distant main,
Where live the hero-shades in rich repast,
Remote from mortals of a vulgar cast:
There in the islands of the bless'd they find,
Where Saturn reigns, an endless calm of mind;

And there the choicest fruits adorn the fields,
And thrice the fertile year a harvest yields.
O! would I had my hours of life began
Before this fifth, this sinful, race of man;
Or had I not been call'd to breathe the day,
Till the rough iron age had pass'd away!
For now, the times are such, the gods ordain,
That ev'ry moment shall be wing'd with pain;
Condemn'd to sorrows, and to toil, we live;
Rest to our labour death alone can give;
And yet, amidst the cares our lives annoy,
The gods will grant some intervals of joy:
But how degen'rate is the human state!
Virtue no more distinguishes the great;
No safe reception shall the stranger find;
Nor shall the ties of blood, or friendship, bind;
Nor shall the parent, when his sons are nigh,
Look with the fondness of a parent's eye,
Nor to the sire the son obedience pay,
Nor look with rev'rence on the locks of grey,
But, O! regardless of the pow'rs divine,
With bitter taunts shall load his life's decline.
Revenge and rapine shall respect command,
The pious, just, and good, neglected stand.
The wicked shall the better man distress,
The righteous suffer, and without redress;
Strict honesty, and naked truth, shall fail,
The perjur'd villain, in his arts, prevail.
Hoarse Envy shall, unseen, exert her voice,
Attend the wretched, and in ill rejoice.
At last fair Modesty and Justice fly,
Rob'd their pure limbs in white, and gain the sky;
From the wide Earth they reach the bless'd abodes,
And join the grand assembly of the gods,
While mortal men, abandon'd to their grief,
Sink in their sorrows, hopeless of relief.
While now my fable from the birds I bring,
To the great rulers of the Earth I sing.
High in the clouds a mighty bird of prey
Bore a melodious nightingale away;
And to the captive, shiv'ring in despair,
Thus cruel spoke the tyrant of the air.
"Why mourns the wretch in my superior pow'r?
Thy voice avails not in the ravish'd hour;
Vain are thy cries; at my despotic will,
Or I can set thee free, or I can kill.
Unwisely who provokes his abler foe,
Conquest still flies him, and he strives for woe."
Thus spoke th' enslaver with insulting pride.
O! Perses, justice ever be thy guide;
May malice never gain upon thy will,
Malice that makes the wretch more wretched still.
The good man injur'd, to revenge is slow,
To him the vengeance is the greater woe.
Ever will all injurious courses fail,
And justice ever over wrongs prevail;
Right will take place at last, by fit degrees;
This truth the fool by sad experience sees.
When suits commence, dishonest strife the cause,
Faith violated, and the breach of laws,
Ensue; the cries of justice haunt the judge,
Of bribes the glutton, and of sin the drudge.
Through cities then the holy demon runs,
Unseen, and mourns the manners of their sons,
Dispersing evils, to reward the crimes
Of those who banish justice from the times.
Is there a man whom incorrupt we call,
Who sits alike unprejudic'd to all,
By him the city flourishes in peace,
Her borders lengthen, and her sons increase;
From him far-seeing Jove will drive afar
All civil discord, and the rage of war.
No days of famine to the righteous fall,
But all is plenty, and delightful all;
Nature indulgent o'er their land is seen,
With oaks high tow'ring are their mountains green,
With heavy mast their arms diffusive bow,
While from their trunks rich streams of honey [flow;
Of flocks untainted are their pastures full,
Which slowly strut beneath their weight of wool;
And sons are born the likeness of their sire,
The fruits of virtue, and a chaste desire:
O'er the wide seas for wealth they need not roam,
Many and lasting are their joys at home.
Not thus the wicked, who in ill delight,
Whose daily acts pervert the rules of right;
To those the wise disposer, Jove, ordains
Repeated losses, and a world of pains:
Famines and plagues are unexpected nigh;
Their wives are barren, and their kindred die;
Numbers of these at once are swept away;
And ships of wealth become the ocean's prey.
One sinner oft provokes th' Avenger's hand;
And often one man's crimes destroy a land.
Exactly mark, ye rulers of mankind,
The ways of truth, nor be to justice blind;
Consider, all ye do, and all ye say,
The holy demons to their god convey,
Aërial spirits, by great Jove design'd,
To be on Earth the guardians of mankind;
Invisible to mortal eyes they go,
And mark our actions, good or bad, below;
Th' immortal spies with watchful care preside,
And thrice ten thousand round their charges glide.
Justice, unspotted maid, deriv'd from Jove,
Renown'd, and reverenc'd by the gods above,
When mortals violate her sacred laws,
When judges hear the bribe, and not the cause,
Close by her parent god behold her stand,
And urge the punishment their sins demand.
Look in your breasts, and there survey your crimes,
Think, O! ye judges, and reform betimes,
Forget the past, nor more false judgments give,
Turn from your ways betimes, O! turn and live.
Who, full of wiles, his neighbour's harm contrives,
False to himself, against himself he strives;
For he that harbours evil in his mind
Will from his evil thoughts but evil find;
And lo! the eye of Jove, that all things knows,
Can, when he will, the heart of man disclose;
Open the guilty bosom all within,
And trace the infant thoughts of future sin.
O! when I hear the upright man complain,
And, by his injuries, the judge arraign,
"If to be wicked is to find success,"
I cry, "and to be just to meet distress,
May I nor mine the righteous path pursue,
But int'rest only ever keep in view:"
But, by reflection better taught, I find
We see the present, to the future blind.
Trust to the will of Jove, and wait the end,
And good shall always your good acts attend.
These doctrines, Perses, treasure in thy heart,
And never from the paths of justice part:
Never by brutal violence be sway'd;
But be the will of Jove in these obey'd.
In these the brute creation men exceed,
They, void of reason, by each other bleed,
While man by justice should be kept in awe,
Justice, of nature well ordain'd the law.

Who right espouses through a righteous love,
Shall meet the bounty of the hands of Jove:
But he that will not be by laws confin'd,
Whom not the sacrament of oaths can bind,
Who, with a willing soul, can justice leave,
A wound immortal shall that man receive;
His house's honour daily shall decline:
Fair flourish shall the just from line to line.

O! Perses, foolish Perses, bow thine ear
To the good counsels of a soul sincere.
To wickedness the road is quickly found,
Short is the way, and on an easy ground.
The paths of virtue must be reach'd by toil,
Arduous and long, and on a rugged soil,
Thorny the gate, but when the top you gain,
Fair is the future, and the prospect plain.
Far does the man all other men excel,
Who, from his wisdom, thinks in all things well,
Wisely consid'ring, to himself a friend,
All for the present best, and for the end;
Nor is the man without his share of praise,
Who well the dictates of the wise obeys;
But he that is not wise himself, nor can
Hearken to wisdom, is a useless man.

Ever observe, Perses, of birth divine,
My precepts, and the profit shall be thine;
Then famine always shall avoid thy door,
And Ceres, fair-wreath'd goddess, bless thy store.
The slothful wretch, who lives from labour free,
Like drones, the robbers of the painful bee,
Has always men, and gods, alike his foes;
Him famine follows with her train of woes.
With cheerful zeal your mod'rate toils pursue,
That your full barns you may in season view.
The man industrious, stranger is to need,
A thousand flocks his fertile pastures feed;
As with the drone, with him it will not prove,
Him men and gods behold with eyes of love.
To care and labour think it no disgrace,
False pride! the portion of the sluggard race:
The slothful man, who never work'd before,
Shall gaze with envy on thy growing store:
Like thee to flourish, he will spare no pains;
For lo! the rich virtue and glory gains.

Strictly observe the wholesome rules I give,
And, bless'd in all, thou like a god shalt live.
Ne'er to thy neighbour's goods extend thy cares,
Nor be neglectful of thine own affairs.
Let no degen'rate shame debase thy mind,
Shame that is never to the needy kind;
The man that has it will continue poor;
He must be bold that would enlarge his store:
But ravish not, depending on thy might,
Injurious to thyself, another's right.
Who, or by open force, or secret stealth,
Or perjur'd wiles, amasses heaps of wealth,
Such many are, whom thirst of gain betrays,
The gods, all-seeing, shall o'ercloud his days;
His wife, his children, and his friends, shall die,
And like a dream, his ill-got riches fly:
Nor less, or to insult the suppliant's cries,
The guilt, or break through hospitable ties.
Is there who, by incestuous passion led,
Pollutes with joys unclean his brother's bed,
Or who, regardless of his tender trust,
To the poor helpless orphan proves unjust,
Or, when the father's fatal day appears,
His body bending through the weight of years,
A son who views him with unduteous eyes,
And words of comfort to his age denies,
Great Jove vindictive sees the impious train,
And, equal to their crimes, inflicts a pain.

These precepts be thy guide thro' life to steer:
Next learn the gods immortal to revere:
With unpolluted hands, and heart sincere,
Let from your herd or flock an off'ring rise:
Of the pure victim burn the white fat thighs;
And to your wealth confine the sacrifice.
Let the rich fumes of od'rous incense fly,
A grateful savour, to the pow'rs on high;
The due libation nor neglect to pay,
When ev'ning closes, or when dawns the day:
Then shall thy work, the gods thy friends, succeed;
Then may you purchase farms, nor sell through
[need.

Enjoy thy riches with a lib'ral soul,
Plenteous the feast, and smiling be the bowl;
No friend forget, nor entertain thy foe,
Nor let thy neighbour uninvited go.
Happy the man, with peace his days are crown'd,
Whose house an honest neighbourhood surround;
Of foreign harms he never sleeps afraid,
They, always ready, bring their willing aid;
Cheerful, should he some busy pressure feel,
They lend an aid beyond a kindred's zeal;
They never will conspire to blast his fame;
Secure he walks, unsully'd his good name:
Unhappy man, whom neighbours ill surround,
His oxen die oft by a treach'rous wound.
Whate'er you borrow of your neighbour's store,
Return the same in weight, if able, more;
So to yourself will you secure a friend,
He never after will refuse to lend.
Whatever by dishonest means you gain,
You purchase an equivalent of pain.

To all a love for love return: contend
In virtuous acts to emulate your friend.
Be to the good thy favours unconfin'd;
Neglect a sordid, and ungrateful, mind.
From all the gen'rous a respect command,
While none regard the base ungiving hand:
The man who gives from an unbounded breast,
Though large the bounty, in himself is bless'd:
Who ravishes another's right shall find,
Though small the prey, a deadly sting behind.
Content, and honestly, enjoy your lot,
And often add to that already got;
From little oft repeated much will rise,
And, of thy toil the fruits, salute thine eyes.
How sweet at home to have what life demands,
The just reward of our industrious hands,
To view our neighbour's bliss without desire,
To dread not famine, with her aspect dire!
Be these thy thoughts, to these thy heart incline,
And lo! these blessings shall be surely thine.

When at your board your faithful friend you
Without reserve, and lib'ral, be the treat: [greet,
To stint the wine a frugal husband shows,
When from the middle of the cask it flows.
Do not, by mirth betray'd, your brother trust,
Without a witness, he may prove unjust:
Alike it is unsafe for men to be,
With some too diffident, with some too free.

Let not a woman steal your heart away,
By tender looks, and her apparel gay;
When your abode she languishing inquires,
Command your heart, and quench the kindling
If love she vows, 'tis madness to believe, [fires;
Turn from the thief, she charms but to deceive:
Who does too rashly in a woman trust,
Too late will find the wanton prove unjust.

Take a chaste matron, partner of your breast,
Contented live, of her alone possess'd;
Then shall you number many days in peace,
And with your children see your wealth increase;
Then shall a duteous careful heir survive,
To keep the honour of the house alive.
If large possessions are, in life, thy view,
These precepts, with assiduous care, pursue.

BOOK II.

THE ARGUMENT.

In this book the poet instructs his countrymen in the arts of agriculture and navigation, and in the management of the vintage: he illustrates the work with rural descriptions, and concludes with several religious precepts, founded on the custom and manners of his age.

WHEN the Pleïades, of Atlas born,
Before the Sun's arise illume the morn,
Apply the sickle to the ripen'd corn;
And when, attendant on the Sun's decline,
They in the ev'ning ether only shine,
Then is the season to begin to plough,
To yoke the oxen, and prepare to sow:
There is a time when forty days they lie,
And forty nights, conceal'd from human eye,
But in the course of the revolving year,
When the swain sharps the scythe, again appear.
This is the rule to the laborious swain,
Who dwells or near, or distant from, the main,
Whether the shady vale receives his toil,
And he manures the fat, the inland soil.
Would you the fruits of all your labours see,
Or plough, or sow, or reap, still naked be;
Then shall thy barns, by Ceres bless'd, appear
Full of the various produce of the year;
Nor shall the seasons then behold thee poor,
A mean dependant on another's store.
Though, foolish Perses, bending to thy pray'rs,
I lately heard thy plaints, and eas'd thy cares,
On me no longer for supplies depend,
For I no more shall give, no more shall lend.
Labour industrious, if you would succeed;
That men should labour have the gods decreed,
That with our wives and children we may live
Without th' assistance that our neighbours give,
That we may never know the pain of mind,
To ask for succour, and no succour find:
Twice, thrice, perhaps, they may your wants supply;
But constant beggars teach them to deny;
Then wretched may you beg, and beg again,
And use the moving force of words in vain.
Such ills to shun, my counsels lay to heart;
Nor dread the debtor's chain, nor hunger's smart.
A house, and yoke of oxen, first provide,
A maid to guard your herds, and then a bride;
The house be furnish'd as thy need demands,
Nor want to borrow from a neighbour's hands.
While to support your wants abroad you roam,
Time glides away, and work stands still at home.
Your business ne'er defer from day to day,
Sorrows and poverty attend delay;
But lo! the careful man shall always find
Increase of wealth according to his mind.
When the hot season of the year is o'er
That draws the toilsome sweat from ev'ry pore,
When o'er our heads th' abated planet rolls
A shorter course, and visits distant poles,
When Jove descends in show'rs upon the plains,
And the parch'd earth is cheer'd with plenteous rains,
When human bodies feel the grateful change,
And less a burden to themselves they range,
When the tall forest sheds her foliage round,
And with autumnal verdure strews the ground,
The bole is incorrupt, the timber good;
Then whet the sounding axe to fell the wood.
Provide a mortar three feet deep, and strong;
And let the pestle be three cubits long.
One foot in length next let the mallet be,
Ten spans the wain, seven feet her axletree;
Of wood four crooked bits the wheel compose,
And give the length three spans to each of those.
From hill or field the hardest holm prepare,
To cut the part in which you place the share;
Thence your advantage will be largely found,
With that your oxen long may tear the ground;
And next, the skilful husbandman to show,
Fast pin the handle to the beam below:
Let the draught-beam of sturdy oak be made,
And for the handle rob the laurel shade;
Or, if the laurel you refuse to fell,
Seek out the elm, the elm will serve as well.
Two ploughs are needful; one let art bestow,
And one let nature to the service bow;
If use, or accident, the first destroy,
Its fellow in the furrow'd field employ.
Yoke from the herd two sturdy males, whose age
Mature secures them from each other's rage;
For if too young they will unruly grow,
Unfinish'd leave the work, and break the plough:
These, and your labour shall the better thrive,
Let a good ploughman, year'd to forty, drive;
And see the careful husbandman be fed
With plenteous morsels, and of wholesome bread:
The slave who numbers fewer days, you'll find
Careless of work, and of a rambling mind;
Perhaps, neglectful to direct the plough,
He in one furrow twice the seed will sow.
Observe the crane's departing flight in time,
Who yearly soars to seek a southern clime,
Conscious of cold; when the shrill voice you hear,
Know the fit season for the plough is near;
Then he for whom no oxen graze the plains,
With aking heart, beholds the winter rains;
Be mindful then the sturdy ox to feed,
And careful keep within the useful breed.
You say, perhaps, you will entreat a friend
A yoke of oxen, and a plough, to lend:
He your request, if wise, will thus refuse,
" I have but two, and those I want to use;
To make a plough great is th' expense and care;
All these you should, in proper time, prepare."
Reproofs like these avoid; and, to behold
Your fields bright waving with their ears of gold,
Let unimprov'd no hour, in season, fly,
But with your servants plough, or wet, or dry;
And in the spring again to turn the soil
Observe; the summer shall reward your toil.
While light and fresh the glebe, insert the grain;
Then shall your children smile, nor you complain.
Prefer with zeal, when you begin to plough,
To Jove terrene, and Ceres chaste, the vow;
Then will the rural deities regard
Your welfare, and your piety reward,

Forget not, when you sow the grain, to mind
That a boy follows with a rake behind;
And strictly charge him, as you drive, with care
The seed to cover, and the birds to scare.
Through ev'ry task, with diligence, employ
Your strength; and in that duty be your joy;
And, to avoid of life the greatest ill,
Never may sloth prevail upon thy will:
(Bless'd who with order their affairs dispose!
But rude confusion is the source of woes.)
Then shall you see, Olympian Jove your friend,
With pond'rous grain the yellow harvest bend:
Then of Arachne's web the vessels clear,
To hoard the produce of the fertile year.
Think then, O! think, how pleasant will it be,
At home an annual support to see,
To view with friendly eyes your neighbour's store,
And to be able to relieve the poor.
  Learn now what seasons for the plough to shun:
Beneath the tropic of the winter's sun
Be well observant not to turn the ground,
For small advantage will from thence be found:
How will you sigh when thin your crop appears,
And the short stalks support the dusty ears!
Your scanty harvest then, in baskets press'd,
Will, by your folly, be your neighbour's jest:
Sometimes indeed it otherwise may be;
But who th' effect of a bad cause can see?
If late you to the ploughman's task accede,
The symptoms these, the later plough must speed.
When first the cuckoo from the oak you hear,
In welcome sounds, foretel the spring-time near,
If Jove, the ploughman's friend, upon the plains,
Three days and nights, descends in constant rains,
Till on the surface of the glebe the tide
Rise to that height the ox's hoof may hide,
Then may you hope your store of golden grain
Shall equal his who earlier turn'd the plain.
Observe, with care, the precepts I impart,
And may they never wander from thy heart;
Then shall you know the show'rs what seasons bring,
And what the bus'ness of the painted spring.
  In that bleak, and dead, season of the year,
When naked all the woods, and fields, appear,
When nature lazy for a while remains,
And the blood almost freezes in the veins,
Avoid the public forge where wretches fly
Th' inclement rigour of the winter sky:
Thither behold the slothful vermin stray,
And there in idle talk consume the day;
Half-starv'd they sit, in evil consult join'd,
And, indolent, with hope buoy up their mind;
Hope that is never to the hungry kind!
Labour in season to increase thy store,
And never let the winter find thee poor:
Thy servants all employ till summer's pass'd,
For tell them summer will not always last.
  The month all hurtful to the lab'ring kine,
In part devoted to the god of wine,
Demands your utmost care; when raging forth,
O'er the wide seas, the tyrant of the north,
Bellowing thro' Thrace, tears up the lofty woods,
Hardens the earth, and binds the rapid floods.
The mountain oak, high tow'ring to the skies,
Torn from his root across the valley lies;
Wide-spreading ruin threatens all the shore,
Loud groans the earth, and all the forests roar:
And now the beast amaz'd, from him that reigns
Lord of the woods to those which graze the plains,
Shiv'ring, the piercing blast, affrighted, flies,
And guards his tender tail betwixt his thighs.
Now nought avails the roughness of the bear,
The ox's hide, nor the goat's length of hair:
Rich in their fleece, alone the well cloth'd fold
Dread not the blust'ring wind, nor fear the cold.
The man who could erect support his age,
Now bends reluctant to the north-wind's rage:
From accidents like these the tender maid,
Free and secure, of storms nor winds afraid,
Lives, nurtur'd chaste beneath her mother's eye,
Unhurt, unsully'd, by the winter's sky;
Or now to bathe her lovely limbs she goes,
Now round the fair the fragrant ointment flows;
Beneath the virtuous roof she spends the nights,
Stranger to golden Venus, and her rites.
Now does the boneless polypus, in rage,
Feed on his feet, his hunger to asswage;
The Sun no more, bright shining in the day,
Directs him in the flood to find his prey;
O'er swarthy nations while he fiercely gleams,
Greece feels the pow'r but of his fainter beams.
Now all things have a diff'rent face below;
The beasts now shiver at the falling snow;
Thro' woods, and thro' the shady vale, they run
To various haunts, the pinching cold to shun;
Some to the thicket of the forest flock,
And some, for shelter, seek the hollow rock.
  A winter garment now demands your care,
To guard the body from th' inclement air;
Soft be the inward vest, the outward strong,
And large to wrap you warm, down reaching long:
Thin lay your warp, when you the loom prepare,
And close to weave the woof no labour spare.
The rigour of the day a man defies,
Thus cloth'd; nor sees his hairs like bristles rise.
Next for your feet the well hair'd shoes provide,
Hairy within, of a sound ox's hide.
A kid's soft skin over your shoulders throw,
Unhurt to keep you from the rain or snow;
And for your head a well made cov'ring get,
To keep your ears safe from the cold and wet.
  When o'er the plains the north exerts his sway,
From his sharp blasts piercing begins the day;
Then from the sky the morning dews descend,
And fruitful o'er the happy lands extend.
The waters by the winds convey'd on high,
From living streams, in early dew-drops lie
Bright on the grass; but if the north-wind swells
With rage, and thick and sable clouds compels,
They fall in ev'ning storms upon the plain:
And now from ev'ry part, the lab'ring swain
Foresees the danger of the coming rain;
Leaving his work, panting behold him scour
Homeward, incessant to outrun the show'r.
This month commands your care, of all the year,
Alike to man and beast, the most severe:
The ox's provender be stinted now;
But plenteous meals the husbandman allow;
For the long nights but tedious pass away.
These rules observe while night succeeds the day,
Long as our common parent earth shall bring
Her various offsprings forth to grace the spring.
  When from the tropic of the winter's sun,
Thrice twenty days and nights their course have run,
And when Arcturus leaves the main, to rise
A star, bright shining in the ev'ning skies,
Then prune the vine: 'tis dang'rous to delay
Till with complaints the swallow breaks the day.

When with their domes the slow-pac'd snails retreat,
Beneath some foliage, from the burning heat
Of the Pleïades, your tools prepare;
The ripen'd harvest then demands your care.
Now fly the jocund shades your morning sleep,
And constant to their work your servants keep;
All other pleasures to your duty yield;
The harvest calls, haste early to the field.
The morning workman always best succeeds;
The morn the reaper, and the trav'ler, speeds:
But when the thistle wide begins to spread,
And rears in triumph his offensive head,
When in the shady boughs, with quiv'ring wings,
The grasshopper all day continual sings,
The season when the Dog rèsumes his reign,
Weakens the nerves of man and burns the brain,
Then the fat flesh of goats is wholesome food,
And to the heart the gen'rous wine is good;
Then nature through the softer sex does move,
And stimulates the fair to acts of love:
Then in the shade avoid the mid-day sun,
Where zephyrs breathe, and living fountains run;
There pass the sultry hours, with friends, away,
And frolic out, in harmless mirth, the day;
With country cates your homely table spread,
The goat's new milk, and cakes of milk your bread;
The flesh of beeves, which brouse the trees, your meat;
Nor spare the tender flesh of kids to eat;
With Byblian wine the rural feast be crown'd;
Three parts of water, let the bowl go round.
Forget not, when Orion first appears,
To make your servants thresh the sacred ears;
Upon the level floor the harvest lay,
Where a soft gale may blow the chaff away;
Then, of your labour to compute the gain,
Before you fill the vessels, mete the grain.
Sweep up the chaff, to make your work complete;
The chaff, and straw, the ox and mule will eat.
When in the year's provision you have laid,
Take home a single man, and servant-maid;
Among your workmen let this care be shown
To one who has no mansion of his own.
Be sure a sharp-tooth'd cur well fed to keep,
Your house's guard, while you in safety sleep.
The harvest pass'd, and thus by Ceres bless'd,
Unyoke the beast, and give your servants rest.
Orion and the Dog, each other nigh,
Together mounted to the midmost sky,
When in the rosy morn Arcturus shines,
Then pluck the clusters from the parent vines;
Forget not next the ripen'd grapes to lay
Ten nights in air, nor take them in by day;
Five more remember, ere the wine is made,
To let them lie, to mellow in the shade;
And in the sixth briskly yourself employ,
To cask the gift of Bacchus, sire of joy.
Next, in the round, do not to plough forget,
When the Seven Virgins, and Orion, set:
Thus an advantage always shall appear,
In ev'ry labour of the various year.
If o'er your mind prevails the love of gain,
And tempts you to the dangers of the main,
Yet in her harbour safe the vessel keep,
When strong Orion chases to the deep
The Virgin Stars; then the winds war aloud,
And veil the ocean with a sable cloud:
Then round the bark, already haul'd on shore,
Lay stones, to fix her when the tempests roar;
But first forget not well the kell to drain;
And draw the pin to save her from the rain.
Furl the ship's wings, her tackling home convey,
And o'er the smoke the well made rudder lay.
With patience wait for a propitious gale,
And a calm season to unfurl the sail;
Then lanch the swift-wing'd vessel on the main,
With a fit burden to return with gain.
So our poor father toil'd his hours away,
Careful to live in the unhappy day;
He, foolish Perses, spent no time in vain,
But fled misfortunes, through the wat'ry plain;
He, from Æolian Cuma, th' ocean pass'd,
Here, in his sable bark, arriv'd at last.
Not far from Helicon he fix'd his race,
In Ascra's village, miserable place!
How comfortless the winter season there!
And cheerless, Ascra, is thy summer air.
O! Perses, may'st thou ne'er forget thy sire,
But let thy breast his good example fire:
The proper business of each season mind;
And O! be cautious when you trust the wind.
If large the vessel, and her lading large,
And if the seas prove faithful to their charge,
Great are your gains; but, by one evil blast,
Away your hopes are with your venture cast.
If diligent to live, from debtors free,
You rashly are resolv'd to trade by sea,
To my instructions an attention pay,
And learn the courses of the liquid way;
Though nor to build, nor guide a ship, I know,
I'll teach you when the sounding main to plow.
Once I have cross'd the deep, and not before,
Nor since, from Aulis to Eubœa's shore,
From Aulis, where th' assembled Greeks lay bound,
All arm'd, for Troy, for beauteous dames renown'd:
At Chalcis, there, the youth of noble mind,
For so their great forefather had enjoin'd,
The games decreed, all sacred to the grave
Of king Amphidamas, the wise and brave;
A victor there in song the prize I bore,
A well-ear'd tripod, to my native shore;
Which to the sacred Heliconian nine
I offer'd grateful for their gift divine,
Where with the love of verse I first was fir'd,
Where by the heav'nly maids I was inspir'd;
To them I owe, to them alone I owe,
What of the seas, or of the stars, I know;
Mine is the pow'r to tell, by them reveal'd,
The will of Jove, tremendous with his shield;
To them, who taught me first, to them belong
The blooming honours of th' immortal song.
When, from the tropic of the summer's sun,
Full fifty days and nights their course have run,
Fearless of danger, for the voy'ge prepare,
Smooth is the ocean, and serene the air:
Then you the bark, safe with her freight, may view,
And gladsome as the day the joyful crew,
Unless great Jove, the king of gods, or he,
Neptune, that shakes the earth, and rules the sea,
The two immortal pow'rs on whom the end
Of mortals, good and bad, alike depend,
Should jointly, or alone, their force employ,
And, in a luckless hour, the ship destroy:
If, free from such mischance, the vessel flies,
O'er a calm sea, beneath indulgent skies,
Let nothing long thee from thy home detain,
But measure, quickly, measure back the main.

Haste your return before the vintage pass'd,
Prevent th' autumnal show'rs, and southern blast,
Or you, too late a penitent, will find
A ruffled ocean, and unfriendly wind.
Others there are who choose to hoist the sail,
And plough the sea, before a spring-tide gale,
When first the footsteps of the crow are seen,
Clearly as on the trees the budding green:
But then, may my advice prevail, you'll keep
Your vessel safe at land, nor trust the deep;
Many, surprising weakness of the mind,
Tempt all the perils of the sea and wind,
Face death in all the terrours of the main,
Seeking, the soul of wretched mortals, gain.
Would'st thou be safe, my cautions be thy guide;
'Tis sad to perish in the boist'rous tide.
When for the voy'ge your vessel leaves the shore,
Trust in her hollow sides not half your store;
The less your loss should she return no more:
With all your stock how dismal would it be
To have the cargo perish in the sea!
A load, you know, too pond'rous for the wain,
Will crush the axletree, and spoil the grain.
Let ev'ry action prove a mean confess'd;
A moderation is, in all, the best.
Next to my counsels an attention pay,
To form your judgment for the nuptial day.
When you have number'd thrice ten years in time,
The age mature when manhood dates his prime,
With caution choose the partner of your bed:
Whom fifteen springs have crown'd, a virgin wed.
Let prudence now direct your choice; a wife
Is or a blessing, or a curse, in life;
Her father, mother, know, relations, friends,
For on her education much depends:
If all are good, accept the maiden bride;
Then form her manners, and her actions guide:
A life of bliss succeeds the happy choice;
Nor shall your friends lament, nor foes rejoice.
Wretched the man condemn'd to drag the chain,
What restless ev'nings his, what days of pain!
Of a luxurious mate, a wanton dame,
That ever burns with an insatiate flame,
A wife who seeks to revel out the nights
In sumptuous banquets, and in stol'n delights:
Ah! wretched mortal! though in body strong,
Thy constitution cannot serve thee long;
Old age, vexatious, shall o'ertake thee soon;
Thine is the ev'n of life before the noon.
Observe in all you do, and all you say,
Regard to the immortal gods to pay.
First in your friendship let your brother stand,
So nearly join'd in blood, the strictest band;
Or should another be your heart's ally,
Let not a fault of thine dissolve the tie;
Nor e'er debase the friendship with a lie.
Should he, offensive, or in deed, or speech,
First in the sacred union make the breach,
To punish him may your resentments tend;
For who more guilty than a faithless friend?
But if, repentant of his breach of trust,
The self-accuser thinks your vengeance just,
And humbly begs you would no more complain,
Sink your resentments, and be friends again;
Or the poor wretch, all sorrowful to part,
Sighs for another friend to ease his heart.
Whatever rage your boiling heart sustains,
Let not the face disclose your inward pains.
Be your companions o'er the social bowl
The few selected, each a virtuous soul.
Never a friend among the wicked go,
Nor ever join to be the good man's foe.
When you behold a man by fortune poor,
Let him not leave with sharp rebukes the door:
The treasure of the tongue, in ev'ry cause,
With moderation us'd, obtains applause:
What of another you severely say
May amply be return'd another day.
When you are summon'd to the public feast,
Go with a willing mind a ready guest;
Grudge not the charge, the burden is but small;
Good is the custom, and it pleases all.
When the libation of black wine you bring,
A morning off'ring to the heav'nly king,
With hands unclean if you prefer the pray'r,
Jove is incens'd, your vows are lost in air;
So all th' immortal pow'rs on whom we call,
If with polluted hands, are deaf to all.
When you would have your urine pass away,
Stand not upright before the eye of day;
And scatter not your water as you go,
Nor let it, when you're naked, from you flow:
In either case 'tis an unseemly sight:
The gods observe alike by day and night:
The man that we devout and wise may call
Sits in that act, or streams against a wall.
Whate'er you do in amorous delight,
Be all transacted in the veil of night;
And when, transported, to your wife's embrace
You haste, pollute no consecrated place;
Nor seek to taste her beauties when you part
From a sad fun'ral with a heavy heart:
When from the joyous feast you come all gay,
In her fair arms revel the night away.
When to the rivulet to bathe you go,
Whose lucid currents, never ceasing, flow,
E're to deface the stream, you leave the land,
With the pure limpid waters cleanse each hand;
Then on the lovely surface fix your look,
And supplicate the guardians of the brook:
Who in the river thinks himself secure,
With malice at his heart, and hands impure,
Too late a penitent, shall find, ere long,
By what the gods inflict, his rashness wrong.
When to the gods your solemn vows you pay,
Strictly attend while at the feast you stay;
Nor the black iron to your hands apply,
From the fresh parts to pare the useless dry.
The bowl, from which you the libation pour
To Heav'n, profane not in the social hour:
Who things devote to vulgar use employ,
Those men some dreadful vengance shall destroy.
Never begin to build a mansion seat,
Unless you're sure to make the work complete;
Lest, on th' unfinish'd roof high perch'd, the crow
Croak horrid, and foretel approaching woe.
'Tis hurtful in the footed jar to eat,
Till purify'd: nor in it bathe your feet.
Who in a slothful way his children rears,
Will see them feeble in their riper years.
Never by acts effeminate disgrace
Yourself, nor bathe your body in the place
Where women bathe; for time and custom can
Soften your heart to acts beneath a man.
When on the sacred rites you fix your eyes,
Deride not, in your breast, the sacrifice;
For know, the god, to whom the flames aspire,
May punish you severely in his ire.

Sacred the fountains, and the seas, esteem,
Nor by indecent acts pollute their stream.
These precepts keep, fond of a virtuous name,
And shun the loud reports of evil fame:
Fame is an ill you may with ease obtain,
A sad oppression to be borne with pain;
And when you would the noisy clamours drown,
You'll find it hard to lay your burden down:
Fame, of whatever kind, not wholly dies,
A goddess she, and strengthens as she flies.

BOOK III.

THE ARGUMENT.

The poet here distinguishes holy days from other, and what are propitious, and what not, for different works, and concludes with a short recommendation of religion and morality.

Your servants to a just observance train
Of days, as Heav'n and human rites ordain;
Great Jove, with wisdom, o'er the year presides,
Directs the seasons, and the moments guides.
Of ev'ry month, the most propitious day,
The thirtieth choose, your labours to survey;
And the due wages to your servants pay.
The first of ev'ry moon we sacred deem,
Alike the fourth throughout the year esteem;
And in the seventh Apollo we adore,
In which the golden god Latona bore;
Two days succeeding these extend your cares,
Uninterrupted, in your own affairs;
Nor in the next two days, but one, delay
The work in hand, the bus'ness of the day,
Of which th' eleventh we propitious hold
To reap the corn, the twelfth to shear the fold;
And then behold, with her industrious train,
The ant, wise reptile, gather in the grain;
Then you may see, suspended in the air,
The careful spider his domain prepare,
And while the artist spins the cobweb dome
The matron cheerful plies the loom at home.
Forget not in the thirteenth to refrain
From sowing, lest your work should prove in vain;
Though then the grain may find a barren soil,
The day is grateful to the planter's toil:
Not so the sixteenth to the planter's care;
A day unlucky to the new-born fair,
Alike unhappy to the married then;
A day propitious to the birth of men:
The sixth the same both to the man and maid;
Then secret vows are made and nymphs betray'd;
The fair by soothing words are captives led;
The gossip's tale is told, detraction spread;
The kid to castrate, and the ram, we hold
Propitious now; alike to pen the fold.
Geld in the eighth the goat, and lowing steer;
Nor in the twelfth to geld the mule-colt fear.
The offspring male born in the twentieth prize,
'Tis a great day, he shall be early wise.
Happy the man-child in the tenth day born;
Happy the virgin in the fourteenth morn;
Then train the mule obedient to your hand,
And teach the snarling cur his lord's command;
Then make the bleating flocks their master know,
And bend the horned oxen to the plough.
What in the twenty-fourth you do, beware;
And the fourth day requires an equal care;
Then, then, be circumspect in all your ways,
Woes, complicated woes, attend the days.
When, resolute to change a single life,
You wed, on the fourth day lead home your wife;
But first observe the feather'd race that fly,
Remarking well the happy augury.
The fifths of ev'ry month your care require,
Days full of trouble, and afflictions dire;
For then the Furies take their round, 'tis said,
And heap their vengeance on the perjur'd head.
In the seventeenth prepare the level floor;
And then of Ceres thresh the sacred store;
In the same day, and when the timber's good,
Fell, for the bedpost, and the ship, the wood.
The vessel, suff'ring by the sea and air,
Survey all o'er, and in the fourth repair.
In the nineteenth 'tis better to delay,
Till afternoon, the business of the day.
Uninterrupted in the ninth pursue
The work in hand, a day propitious through;
Themselves the planters prosp'rous then employ;
To either sex in birth, a day of joy.
The twenty-ninth is best, observe the rule,
Known but to few, to yoke the ox and mule;
'Tis proper then to yoke the flying steed;
But few, alas! these wholesome truths can read;
Then you may fill the cask, nor fill in vain;
Then draw the swift ship to the sable main.
To pierce the cask till the fourteenth delay,
Of all most sacred next the twentieth day;
After the twentieth day few of the rest
We sacred deem, of that the morn is best.
These are the days of which the observance can
Bring great advantage to the race of man;
The rest unnam'd indiff'rent pass away,
And nought important marks the vulgar day:
Some one commend, and some another praise,
But most by guess, for few are wise in days:
One cruel as a stepmother we find,
And one as an indulgent mother kind.
O! happy mortal, happy he, and bless'd,
Whose wisdom here is by his acts confess'd;
Who lives all blameless to immortal eyes,
Who prudently consults the auguries,
Nor, by transgression, works his neighbour pain,
Nor ever gives him reason to complain.

OBSERVATIONS ON THE ANCIENT GREEK MONTH.

I believe it will be necessary, for the better understanding the following table, to set in a clear light the ancient Greek month, as we may reasonably conclude it stood in the days of Hesiod, confining ourselves to the last book of his Works and Days.

The poet makes the month contain thirty days, which thirty days he divides into three parts: the first he calls ιϛαμενȣ, or ιϛαμενȣ μηνος, in the genitive case, because of some other word which is commonly joined requiring it to be of that case; the root of which, ιϛημι or ιϛαω, signifies, I erect, I set up, I settle, &c. and Henry Stephens interprets the words ιϛαμενȣ μηνος, ineunte mense, the entrance of the month, in which sense the poet uses them; which entrance is the first decade, or first ten days. The second he calls μεσȣντος, which is from μησοω, I am in the midst, meaning the middle decade of the month. The third part he calls φθινοντος, from φθινω, which is from φθιω, or φθεω, I waste away, meaning the decline, or last decade, of the month. Sometimes these words are used in the nominative case.

Before I leave these remarks I shall show the manner of expression, of one day, in each decade, from the last book of our poet, which will give a clear idea of all.

Εκτη δ' η μεσση μαλ' ασυμφορος εστι φυτοισιν. Ver. 8.

The middle sixth is unprofitable to plants.

That is, the sixth day of the middle decade.

πεφυλαξο δε θυμω

Τετραδ' αλευασθαι φθινοντος θ' ισταμενης τε. Ver. 33.

Keep in your mind to shun the fourth of the entrance, and end, of the month. That is, the fourth of the entrance, or first decade, and the fourth of the end, or last decade.

It is proper to observe that those days which are blanks are, by our poet, called indifferent days, days of no importance, either good or bad. It is likewise remarkable, that he makes some days both holy days and working days, as the fourth, fourteenth, and twentieth: but, to clear this, Le Clerc tells us, from our learned countryman Selden, that ιερον ημαρ, though litterally a holy day, does not always signify a festival, but often a day propitious to us in our undertakings.

A TABLE OF THE ANCIENT GREEK MONTH, AS IN THE LAST BOOK OF THE WORKS AND DAYS OF HESIOD.

DECADE I.

1. Day of decade I. Holy day.
2.
3.
4. Holy day. Propitious for marriage, and for repairing ships. A day of troubles.
5. In which the Furies take their round.
6. Unhappy for the birth of women. Propitious for the birth of men, for gelding the kid and the ram, and for penning the sheep.
7. The birthday of Apollo. A holy day.
8. Geld the goat, and the steer.
9. Propitious quite through. Happy for the birth of both sexes. A day to plant in.
10. Propitious to the birth of men.

DECADE II.

1. Day of decade II, or 11th of the month. To reap.
2. For women to ply the loom, for the men to shear the sheep, and geld the mule.
3. A day to plant in, and not to sow.
4. Propitious for the birth of women. Break the mule and the ox. Teach your dog, and your sheep, to know you. Pierce the cask. A holy day.
5.
6. A day unlucky for the marriage and birth of women. Propitious for the birth of men, and to plant.
7. Thresh the corn, and fell the wood.
8.
9. Luckiest in the afternoon.
10. Happy for the birth of men. Most propitious in the morning. A holy day.

DECADE III.

1. Day of decade III, or 21st of the month.
2.
3.
4.
5.
6.
7.
8.
9. Yoke the ox, the mule, and the horse. Fill the vessels. Lanch the ship.
10. Look over the business of the whole month; and pay the servants their wages.

Those days which are called holy days in the Table are, in the original, ιερον ημαρ.

A VIEW OF THE WORKS AND DAYS.

Now we have gone through the Works and Days, it may possibly contribute, in some degree, to the profit and delight of the reader to take a view of the poem as we have it delivered down to us. I shall first consider it as an ancient piece, and, in that light, enter into the merit and esteem that it reasonably obtained among the ancients: the authors who have been lavish in their commendations of it are many; the greatest of the Roman writers in prose, Cicero, has more than once expressed his admiration for the system of morality contained in it; and the deference the greatest Latin poet has paid to it I shall show in my comparison of the Works and Days with the Latin Georgic: nor is the encomium paid by Ovid, to our poet, to be passed over.

Vivet et Ascræus, dum mustis uva tumebit,
Dum cadet incurvâ falce resecta Ceres.

While swelling clusters shall the vintage stain,
And Ceres with rich crops shall bless the plain,
Th' Ascræan bard shall in his verse remain.
Eleg. 15. Book I.

And Justin Martyr[1], one of the most learned fathers in the Christian church, extols the Works and Days of our poet, while he expresses his dislike to the Theogony.

While our poet addresses to Perses his brother, he instructs his countrymen in all that is useful to know for the regulating their conduct, both in the business of agriculture, and in their behaviour to each other. He gives us an account of the first ages, according to the common received notion among the Gentiles. The story of Pandora has all the embellishments of poetry which we can find in Ovid, with a clearer moral than is generally in the fables of that poet. His system of morality is calculated so perfectly for the good of society, that there is scarcely any precept omitted that could be properly

[1] In his second discourse or cohortation to the Greeks.

thought of on that occasion. There is not one of the ten commandments of Moses, which relates to our moral duty to each other, that is not strongly recommended by our poet; nor is it enough, he thinks, to be observant of what the civil government would oblige you to, but, to prove yourself a good man, you must have such virtues as no human laws require of you, as those of temperance, generosity, &c. these rules are laid down in a most proper manner to captivate the reader; here the beauties of poetry and the force of reason combine to make him in love with morality. The poet tells us what effect we are reasonably to expect from such virtues and vices as he mentions; which doctrines are not always to be took in a positive sense: if we should say a continuance of intemperance in drinking, and in our commerce with women, would carry us early to the grave, it is morally true, according to the natural course of things; but a man of a strong and uncommon constitution may wanton through an age of pleasure, and so be an exception to this rule, yet not contradict the moral truth of it. Archbishop Tillotson has judiciously told us in what sense we are to take all doctrines of morality; "Aristotle," says that great divine, "observed, long since, that moral and proverbial sayings are understood to be true generally, and for the most part; and that is all the truth is to be expected in them; as when Solomon says, 'train up a child in the way wherein he shall go, and when he is old he will not depart from it:' this is not to be taken, as if no child that is piously educated did ever miscarry afterwards, but that the good education of children is the best way to make good men."

The second book, which comes next under our view, will appear with more dignity when we consider in what esteem the art of agriculture was held in those days in which it was writ: the Georgic did not then concern the ordinary and middling sort of people only, but our poet writ for the instruction of princes likewise, who thought it no disgrace to till the ground which they perhaps had conquered. Homer makes Laertes not only plant but dung his own lands; the best employment he could find for his health, and consolation, in the absence of his son. The latter part of this book, together with all the third, though too mean for poetry, are not unjustifiable in our author. Had he made those religious and superstitious precepts one entire subject of verse, it would have been a ridiculous fancy, but, as they are only a part, and the smallest part, of a regular poem, they are introduced with a laudable intent. After the poet had laid down proper rules for morality, husbandry, navigation, and the vintage, he knew that religion towards the gods, and a due observance of what was held sacred in his age, were yet wanted to complete the work. These were subjects, he was sensible, incapable of the embellishments of poetry; but as they were necessary to his purpose he would not omit them. Poetry was not then designed as the empty amusement only of an idle hour, consisting of wanton thoughts, or long and tedious descriptions of nothing, but, by the force of harmony and good sense, to purge the mind of its dregs, to give it a great and virtuous turn of thinking: in short, verse was then but the lure to what was useful; which indeed has been, and ever will be, the end pursued by all good poets: with this view Hesiod seems to have writ, and must be allowed by all true judges to have wonderfully succeeded in the age in which he rose.

This advantage more arises to us from the writings of so old an author; we are pleased with those monuments of antiquity, such parts of the ancient Grecian history, as we find in them.

I shall now endeavour to show how far Virgil may properly be said to imitate our poet in his Georgic, and to point out some of those passages in which he has either paraphrased, or literally translated from the Works and Days. It is plain he was a sincere admirer of our poet, and of this poem in particular, of which he twice makes honourable mention, and where it could be only to express the veneration that he bore to the author. The first is in his third pastoral.

In medio duo signa, Conon, et quis fuit alter,
Descripsit, radio, totum qui gentibus orbem,
Tempora quæ messor, quæ curvus arator, haberet?

Two figures on the sides emboss'd appear,
Conon, and what's his name who made the sphere,
And show'd the seasons of the sliding year?
Dryden.

Notwithstanding the commentators have all disputed whom this interrogation should mean, I am convinced that Virgil had none but Hesiod in his eye. In the next passage I propose to quote, the greatest honour that was ever paid by one poet to another is paid to ours. Virgil, in his sixth pastoral, makes Silenus, among other things, relate how Gallus was conducted by a Muse to Helicon, where Apollo, and all the Muses, arose to welcome him; and Linus, approaching him, addressed him in this manner:

——hos tibi dant calamos, en, accipe, Musæ,
Ascræo quos antè Seni; quibus ille solebat
Cantando rigidas deducere montibus ornos.

Receive this present by the Muses made,
The pipe on which th' Ascræan pastor play'd;
With which, of old, he charm'd the savage train,
And call'd the mountain ashes to the plain.
Dryden.

The greatest compliment which Virgil thought he could pay his friend and patron, Gallus, was, after all that pompous introduction to the choir of Apollo, to make the Muses present him, from the hands of Linus, with the pipe, or calamos, Ascræo quos antè seni, which they had formerly presented to Hesiod; which part of the compliment to our poet Dryden has omitted in his translation.

To return to the Georgic. Virgil can be said to imitate Hesiod in his first and second books only; in the first is scarcely any thing relative to the Georgic itself, the hint of which is not took from the Works and Days; nay more, in some places whole lines are paraphrased, and some literally translated. It must indeed be acknowledged, that the Latin poet has sometimes explained, in his translation, what was difficult in the Greek, as where our poet gives directions for two ploughs:

Δοια δε θεσθαι αροτρα πονησαμενος κατα οικον
Αυτογυον και πηκτον.

by αυτογυον he means that which grows naturally into the shape of a plough, and by πηκτον that made by art. Virgil, in his advice to have two ploughs always at hand, has this explanation of αυτογυον;

Continuò in sylvis magnâ vi flexa domatur
In burim, et curvi formam accipit ùlmus aratri.
Georg. 1.

Young elms, with early force, in copses bow,
Fit for the figure of the crooked plough.
Dryden.

Thus we find him imitating the Greek poet in the most minute precepts. Hesiod gives directions for the making a plough; Virgil does the same. Even that which has been the subject of ridicule to many of the critics, viz. plough and sow naked, is translated in the Georgic; nudus ara, sere nudus. Before I proceed any farther, I shall endeavour to obviate the objection which has been frequently made against this precept. Hesiod means to insinuate, that ploughing and sowing are labours which require much industry, and application; and he had doubtless this physical reason for his advice, that where such toil is required it is unhealthful, as well as impossible, to go through with the same quantity of clothes as in works of less fatigue. Virgil doubtless saw this reason, or one of equal force, in this rule, or he would not have translated it. In short, we may find him a strict follower of our poet in most of the precepts of husbandry in the Works and Days. I shall give but one instance more, and that in his superstitious observance of days:

———quintum fuge; pallidus Orcus,
Eumenidesque satæ: &c.

————the fifths be sure to shun,
That gave the Furies, and pale Pluto, birth.
Dryden.

If the judgment I have passed from the verses of Manilius, and the second book of the Georgic, in my Discourse on the Writings of Hesiod, be allowed to have any force, Virgil has doubtless been as much obliged to our poet in the second book of his Georgic, as in the first; nor has he imitated him in his precepts only, but in some of his finest descriptions, as in the first book describing the effects of a storm:

————quo, maxima, motû,
Terra tremit, fugere feræ; &c.

and a little lower in the same description:

Nunc nemora, ingenti vento, nunc litora plangunt:

which is almost literal from Hesiod, on the power of the north wind:

————μεμυκε δε γαια και υλη, &c.

Loud groans the earth, and all the forests roar.

I cannot leave this head, without injustice to the Roman poet, before I take notice of the manner in which he uses that superstitious precept πεμπλας δ' εξαλεασθαι, &c. what in the Greek is languid, is by him made brilliant:

———quintum fuge; pallidus Orcus,
Eumenidesque satæ: tum partu, terra, nefando,
Cœumque Japetumque creat, sævumque Typhœum,
Et conjuratos cœlum rescindere fratres:
Ter sunt conati, &c.

————the fifths be sure to shun,
That gave the Furies, and pale Pluto, birth,
And arm'd against the skies the sons of earth;
With mountains pil'd on mountains thrice they strove
To scale the steepy battlements of Jove;
And thrice his light'ning and red thunder play'd,
And their demolish'd works in ruin laid.
Dryden.

As I have showed where the Roman has followed the Greek, I may be thought partial to my author, if I do not show in what he has excelled him: and first, he has contributed to the Georgic most of the subjects in his two last books; as, in the third, the management of horses, dogs, &c. and, in the fourth, the management of the bees. His style, through the whole, is more poetical, more abounding with epithets, which are often of themselves most beautiful metaphors. His invocation on the deities concerned in rural affairs, his address to Augustus, his account of the prodigies before the death of Julius Cæsar, in the first book, his praise of a country life, at the end of the second, and the force of love in beasts, in the third, are what were never excelled, and some parts of them never equalled, in any language.

Allowing all the beauties in the Georgic, these two poems interfere in the merit of each other so little that the Works and Days may be read with as much pleasure as if the Georgic had never been written. This leads me into an examination of part of Mr. Addison's Essay on the Georgic: in which that great writer, in some places, seems to speak so much at venture, that I am afraid he did not remember enough of the two poems to enter on such a task. "Precepts," says he, "of morality, besides the natural corruption of our tempers, which makes us averse to them, are so abstracted from ideas of sense, that they seldom give an opportunity for those beautiful descriptions and images which are the spirit and life of poetry." Had he that part of Hesiod in his eye, where he mentions the temporal blessings of the righteous, and the punishment of the wicked, he would have seen that our poet took an opportunity, from his precepts of morality, to give us "those beautiful descriptions and images which are the spirit and life of poetry." How lovely is the flourishing state of the land of the just there described, the increase of his flocks, and his own progeny! The reason which Mr. Addison gives against rules of morality in verse is to me a reason for them; for if our tempers are naturally so corrupt as to make us averse to them, we ought to try all the ways which we can to reconcile them, and verse among the rest; in which, as I have observed before, our poet has wonderfully succeeded.

The same author, speaking of Hesiod, says, "the precepts he has given us are sown so very thick, that they clog the poem too much." The poet, to prevent this, quite through his Works and Days, has staid so short a while on every head, that it is impossible to grow tiresome in either; the division of the work I have given at the beginning of this View, therefore shall not repeat it. Agriculture is but one subject, in many, of the work, and the reader is there relieved with several rural descriptions, as of the north wind, autumn, the country repast in the shades, &c. The rules for navigation are dispatched with the utmost brevity, in which the digression concerning his victory at the funeral games of Amphidamas is natural, and gives a grace to the poem.

I shall mention but one oversight more which Mr. Addison has made, in his essay, and conclude this head: when he condemned that circumstance of the virgin being at home in the winter season free from the inclemency of the weather, I believe he had forgot that his own author had used almost the same image, and on almost the same occasion, though in other words:

Nec nocturna quidem carpentes pensa puellæ
Nescivere hyemem; &c. Georg. 1.

The difference of the manner in which the two poets use the image is this. Hesiod makes her with her mother at home, either bathing, or doing what most pleases her; and Virgil says, " as the young women are plying their evening tasks, they are sensible of the winter season, from the oil sparkling in the lamp, and the snuff hardening."

The only apology I can make for the liberty I have taken with the writings of so fine an author as Mr. Addison, is that I thought it a part of my duty to our poet, to endeavour to free the reader from such errours as he might possibly imbibe, when delivered under the sanction of so great a name.

I must not end this View without some observations on the fourth eclogue of Virgil, since Probus, Grævius, Fabricius, and other men of great learning, have thought fit to apply what has there been generally said to allude to the Cumæan sybil to our poet:

Ultima Cumæi venit jam carminis ætas.

This line, say they, has an allusion to the golden age of Hesiod; Virgil therefore is supposed to say, " the last age of the Cumæan poet now approaches." By last he means the most remote from his time; which Fabricius explains by antiquissima, and quotes an expression from Cornelius Severus, in which he uses the word in the same sense, ultima certamina for antiquissima certamina. The only method by which we can add any weight to this reading is by comparing the eclogue of Virgil with some similar passages in Hesiod. To begin, let us therefore read the line before quoted with the two following:

Ultima Cumæi venit jam carminis ætas;
Magnus ab integro sæclorum nascitur ordo;
Jam redit et Virgo, redeunt Saturnia regna.

which will bear this paraphrase: " The remotest age mentioned in the verse of the Cumæan poet now approaches; the great order, or round, of ages, as described in the said poet, revolves; now returns the virgin Justice, which, in his iron age, he tells us, left the Earth; and now the reign of Saturn, which is described in his golden age, is come again." If we turn to the golden and iron ages, in the Works and Days, we shall find this allusion very natural.

Let us proceed in our connection and comparison of the verses. Virgil goes on in his compliment to Pollio on his new-born son:

Ille deûm vitam accipiet.

" He shall receive, or lead, the life of gods," as the same poet tells us they did in the reign of Saturn.

Ως τε θεοι δ' εζωον.——————
Νοσφιν ατερ τε πονων.——————

" They lived like gods, and entirely without labour."

——————feret omnia tellus;
Non rastros patietur humus, non vinea falcem:
Robustus quoque jam tauris juga solvet arator.

" The earth shall bear all things; there shall be no occasion for instruments of husbandry, to rake the ground, or prune the vine; the sturdy ploughman shall unyoke his oxen, and live in ease;" as they did in the reign of Saturn, as we are told by the same Cumæan poet.

———καρπον δ' εφερε ζειδωρος αρουρα
———Αυτοματη, πολλον τε και αφθονον.

" The fertile earth bore its fruit spontaneously, and in abundance."

Here we see several natural allusions to our poet, whence it is not unreasonable, for such as mistake the country of Hesiod, to imagine, that all Virgil would say to compliment Pollio, on the birth of his son, is, that now such a son is born, the golden age, as described by Hesiod, shall return; and granting the word Cumæi to carry this sense with it, there is nothing of a prophecy mentioned, or hinted at, in the whole eclogue, any more than Virgil's own, by poetical licence.

A learned prelate of our own church asserts something so very extraordinary on this head, that I cannot avoid quoting it, and making some few remarks upon it: his words are these, " Virgil could not have Hesiod in his eye in speaking of the four ages of the world, because Hesiod makes five ages before the commencement of the golden." And soon after, continues he, " the predictions in the prophet (meaning Daniel) of four successive empires, that should arise in different ages of the world, gave occasion to the poets, who had the knowledge of these things only by report, to apply them to the state of the world in so many ages, and to describe the renovation of the golden age in the expressions of the prophet concerning the future age of the Messias, which in Daniel is the fifth kingdom." Bishop Chandler towards the conclusion of his Vindication of his Defence of Christianity. What this learned parade was introduced for, I am at loss to conceive! First, in that beautiful eclogue, Virgil speaks not of the four ages of the world: secondly,

Hesiod, so far from making five ages before the commencement of the golden, makes the golden age the first: thirdly, Hesiod could not be one of the poets who applied the predictions in the prophet Daniel to the state of the world in so many ages, because he happened to live some hundred years before the time of Daniel.

This great objection to their interpretation of Cumæi still remains, which cannot very easily be conquered, that Cuma was not the country of Hesiod, as I have proved in my Discourse on the Life of our poet, but of his father; and, what will be a strong argument against it, all the ancient poets, who have used an epithet taken from his country, have chose that of Ascræus. Ovid, who mentions him as often as any poet, never uses any other; and, what is the most remarkable, Virgil himself makes use of it in every passage in which he names him; and those monuments of him, exhibited by Ursinus and Boissard, have this inscription;

Ι Σ Ι Ο Δ Ο Σ
Δ Ι Ο Υ
Α Σ Κ Ρ Α Ι Ο Σ.

Ascræan Hesiod, the son of Dios.

THE

THEOGONY OF HESIOD.

TRANSLATED BY COOKE.

TO THE MOST HONOURABLE

GEORGE [1] MARQUIS OF ANNANDALE.

MY LORD,

THE reverence I bear to the memory of your late grandfather, with whom I had the honour to be particularly acquainted, and the obligations I have received from the incomparable lady your mother, would make it a duty in me to continue my regard to their heir; but stronger than those are the motives of this address: since I have had the happiness to know you, which has been as long as you have been capable of distinguishing persons, I have often discovered something in you that surpasses your years, and which gives fair promises of an early great man; this has converted what would otherwise be but gratitude to them to a real esteem for yourself. Proceed, my lord, to make glad the heart of an indulgent mother with your daily progress in learning, wisdom, and virtue. Your friends, in their different spheres, are all solicitous to form you; and among them permit me to offer my tribute, which may be no small means to the bringing you more readily to an understanding of the classics; for on the theology of the most ancient Greeks, which is the subject of the following poem, much of succeeding authors depends. Few are the writers, either Greek or Roman, who have not made use of the fables of antiquity; historians have frequent allusions to them; and they are sometimes the very soul of poetry; for these reasons let me admonish you to become soon familiar with Homer and Hesiod, by translations of them: you will perceive the advantage in your future studies, nor will you repent of it when you read the great originals. I have, in my notes[2], spared no pains to let you into the nature of the Theogony, and to explain the allegories to you; and indeed I have been more elaborate for your sake than I should otherwise have been. While I am paying my respect to your lordship, I would not be thought forgetful of your brother, directing what I have here said at the same time to him. Go on, my lord, to answer the great expectations which your friends have from you; and be your chief ambition to deserve the praise of all wise and good men. I am,

my lord,

with the greatest respect and most sincere affection,

your most obedient and most humble servant,

THOMAS COOKE.

[1] Lord George Johnston when this was first published in the year 1728.

[2] These notes are omitted in the present edition. C.

THE

THEOGONY,

OR

THE GENERATION OF THE GODS.

THE ARGUMENT.

After the proposition, and invocation, the poet begins the generation of the gods. This poem, besides the genealogy of the deities and heroes, contains the story of Heaven and the conspiracy of his wife and sons against him, the story of Styx and her offsprings, of Saturn and his sons, and of Prometheus and Pandora: hence the poet proceeds to relate the war of the gods, which is the subject of above three hundred verses. The reader is often relieved, from the narrative part of the theogony, with several beautiful descriptions, and other poetical embellishments.

BEGIN, my song, with the melodious nine
Of Helicon the spacious and divine;
The Muses there, a lovely choir, advance,
With tender feet to form the skilful dance,
Now round the sable font in order move,
Now round the altar of Saturnian Jove;
Or, if the cooling streams to bathe invite,
In thee, Permessus, they awhile delight;
Or now to Hippocrene resort the fair,
Or, Olmius, to thy sacred spring repair.
Veil'd in thick air, they all the night prolong,
In praise of ægis-bearing Jove, the song;
And thou, O Argive Juno, golden shod,
Art join'd in praises with thy consort god;
Thee, goddess, with the azure eyes, they sing,
Minerva, daughter of the heav'nly king;
The sisters to Apollo tune their voice,
And, Artemis, to thee whom darts rejoice;
And Neptune in the pious hymn they sound,
Who girts the Earth, and shakes the solid ground
A tribute they to Themis chaste allow,
And Venus charming with the bending brow,
Nor Hebe, crown'd with gold, forget to praise,
Nor fair Dione in their holy lays;
Nor thou, Aurora, nor the day's great light,
Remain unsung, nor the fair lamp of night;
To thee, Latona, next the numbers range;
Iăpetus, and Saturn, wont to change,
They chant; thee, Ocean, with an ample breast,
They sing, and Earth, and Night in sable dress'd;
Nor cease the virgins here the strain divine;
They celebrate the whole immortal line.
Erewhile as they the shepherd swain behold
Feeding, beneath the sacred mount, his fold,
With love of charming song his breast they fir'd;
There me the heav'nly Muses first inspir'd;
There, when the maids of Jove the silence broke,
To Hesiod thus, the shepherd swain, they spoke.
"Shepherds, attend, your happiness who place
In gluttony alone, the swain's disgrace;
Strict to your duty in the field you keep,
There vigilant by night to watch your sheep:
Attend, ye swains on whom the Muses call,
Regard the honour not bestow'd on all;
'Tis ours to speak the truth in language plain,
Or give the face of truth to what we feign."
So spoke the maids of Jove, the sacred nine,
And pluck'd a sceptre from the tree divine,
To me the branch they gave, with look serene,
The laurel ensign, never-fading green:
I took the gift with holy raptures fir'd,
My words flow sweeter, and my soul's inspir'd;
Before my eyes appears the various scene
Of all that is to come, and what has been.
Me have the Muses chose, their bard to grace,
To celebrate the bless'd immortal race;
To them the honours of my verse belong,
To them I first and last devote the song:
But where, O where, enchanted do I rove,
Or o'er the rocks, or through the vocal grove?
Now with th' harmonious nine begin, whose voice
Makes their great sire, Olympian Jove, rejoice;

The present, future, and the past, they sing,
Join'd in sweet concert to delight their king;
Melodious and untir'd their voices flow;
Olympus echoes, ever crown'd with snow.
The heav'nly songsters fill th' ethereal round;
Jove's palace laughs, and all the courts resound:
Soft warbling endless with their voice divine,
They celebrate the whole immortal line:
From Earth, and Heav'n, great parents, first they trace
The progeny of gods, a bounteous race;
And then to Jove again returns the song,
Of all in empire, and command, most strong;
Whose praises first and last their bosom fire,
Of mortals, and immortal gods, the sire:
Nor to the sons of men deny they praise,
To such as merit of their heav'nly lays;
They sing the giants of puissant arm,
And with the wond'rous tale their father charm.
Mnemosyne, in the Pierian grove,
The scene of her intrigue with mighty Jove,
The empress of Eleuther, fertile Earth,
Brought to Olympian Jove the Muses forth;
Bless'd offsprings, happy maids, whose pow'rful art
Can banish cares, and ease the painful heart.
Absent from Heav'n, to quench his am'rous flame,
Nine nights the god of gods compress'd the dame.
Now thrice three times the Moon concludes her race,
And shows the produce of the god's embrace,
Fair daughters, pledges of immortal Jove,
In number equal to the nights of love;
Bless'd maids, by harmony of temper join'd;
And verse, their only care, employs their mind.
The virgin songsters first beheld the light
Near where Olympus rears his snowy height;
Where to the maids fair stately domes ascend,
Whose steps a constant beauteous choir attend.
Not far from hence the Graces keep their court,
And with the god of love in banquets sport;
Meanwhile the nine their heav'nly voices raise,
To the immortal pow'rs, the song of praise;
They tune their voices in a sacred cause,
Their theme the manners of the gods, and laws:
When to Olympus they pursue their way,
Sweet warbling, as they go, the deathless lay,
Measuring to Jove, with gentle steps, the ground,
The sable earth returns the joyful sound.
Great Jove, their sire, who rules th' ethereal plains,
Confirm'd in pow'r, of gods the monarch reigns;
His father Saturn hurl'd from his command,
He grasps the thunder with his conqu'ring hand;
He gives the bolts their vigour as they fly,
And bids the red-hot light'ning pierce the sky;
His subject deities obey his nod,
All honours flow from him, of gods the god;
From him the Muses sprung, no less their sire,
Whose attributes the heav'nly maids inspire:
Clio begins the lovely tuneful race,
Melpomene which, and Euterpe, grace,
Terpsichore all joyful in the choir,
And Erato, to love whose lays inspire;
To these Thalia and Polymnia join,
Urania, and Calliope divine,
The first, in honour, of the tuneful nine;
She the great acts of virtuous monarchs sings,
Companion only for the best of kings.
Happy of princes, foster sons of Jove,
Whom at his birth the nine with eyes of love
Behold, to honours they his days design;
He first among the sceptred hands shall shine;
Him they adorn with every grace of song,
And soft persuasion dwells upon his tongue;
To him, their judge, the people turn their eye,
On him for justice in their cause rely,
Reason alone his upright judgment guides,
He hears impartial, and for truth decides;
Thus he determines from a sense profound,
And of contention heals the pois'nous wound.
Wise kings, when subjects grow in faction strong,
First calm their minds, and then redress their wrong,
By their good counsels bid the tumult cease,
And sooth contending parties into peace;
His aid with duteous rev'rence they implore,
And as a god their virtuous prince adore:
From whom the Muses love such blessings flow,
To them a righteous prince the people owe.
From Jove, great origin, all monarchs spring,
From mighty Jove, of kings himself the king;
From the Pierian maids, the heav'nly nine,
And from Apollo, sire of verse divine,
Far-shooting deity, whose beams inspire,
The poets spring, and all who strike the lyre.
Bless'd whom with eyes of love the Muses view,
Sweet flow his words, gentle as falling dew.
Is there a man by rising woes oppress'd,
Who feels the pangs of a distracted breast,
Let but the bard, who serves the nine, rehearse
The acts of heroes pass'd, the theme for verse,
Or if the praise of gods, who pass their days
In endless ease above, adorns the lays,
The pow'rful words administer relief,
And from the wounded mind expel the grief;
Such are the charms which to the bard belong,
A gift from gods deriv'd, the pow'r of song.
Hail, maids celestial, seed of Heav'n's great king,
Hear, nor unaided let the poet sing,
Inspire a lovely lay, harmonious nine,
My theme th' immortal gods, a race divine,
Of Earth, of Heav'n, which lamps of light adorn,
And of old sable Night, great parents, born,
And, after, nourish'd by the briny Main:
Hear, goddesses, and aid the vent'rous strain;
Say whence the deathless gods receiv'd their birth,
And next relate the origin of Earth,
Whence the wide sea that spreads from shore to shore,
Whose surges foam with rage, and billows roar,
Whence rivers which in various channels flow,
And whence the stars which light the world below,
And whence the wide expanse of Heav'n, and whence
The gods, to mortals who their good dispense;
Say how from them our honours we receive,
And whence the pow'r that they our wants relieve;
How they arriv'd to the ethereal plains,
And took possession of the fair domains:
With these, Olympian maids, my breast inspire,
And to the end support the sacred fire,
In order all from the beginning trace,
From the first parents of the num'rous race.
Chaos, of all the origin, gave birth
First to her offspring the wide-bosom'd Earth,
The seat secure of all the gods, who now
Possess Olympus ever cloth'd with snow;
Th' abodes of Hell from the same fountain rise,
A gloomy land that subterranean lies;
And hence does Love his ancient lineage trace,
Excelling fair of all th' immortal race;
At his approach all care is chas'd away,
Nor can the wisest pow'r resist his sway;
Nor man, nor god, his mighty force restrains,
Alike in ev'ry breast the godhead reigns:

And Erebus, black son, from Chaos came,
Born with his sister Night, a sable dame.
Night bore, the produce of her am'rous play
With Erebus, the sky, and cheerful day.
Earth first an equal to herself in fame
Brought forth, that covers all, the starry frame,
The spacious Heav'n, of gods the safe domain,
Who live in endless bliss, exempt from pain;
From her the lofty hills, and ev'ry grove,
Where nymphs inhabit, goddesses, and rove:
Without the mutual joys of love she bore
The barren sea, whose whit'ning billows roar.
At length the Ocean, with his pools profound,
Whose whirling streams pursue their rapid round,
Of Heav'n and Earth is born; Cœus his birth
From them derives, and Creus, sons of Earth;
Hyperion and Japhet, brothers, join:
Thea, and Rhea, of this ancient line
Descend; and Themis boasts the source divine,
And thou Mnemosyne, and Phœbe, crown'd
With gold, and Tethys, for her charms renown'd:
To these successive wily Saturn came,
As sire and son in each a barb'rous name.
Three sons are sprung from Heav'n and Earth's embrace,
The Cyclops bold, in heart a haughty race,
Brontes, and Steropes, and Arges brave,
Who to the hands of Jove the thunder gave;
They for almighty pow'r did light'ning frame,
All equal to the gods themselves in fame;
One eye was plac'd, a large round orb, and bright,
Amidst their forehead to receive the light;
Hence were they Cyclops call'd; great was their skill,
Their strength, and vigour, to perform their will.
The fruitful Earth by Heav'n conceiv'd again,
And for three mighty sons the rending pain
She suffer'd; Cottus, terrible to name,
Gyges, and Briareus, of equal fame;
Conspicuous above the rest they shin'd,
Of body strong, magnanimous of mind;
Fifty large heads their lusty shoulders bore,
And dang'rous to approach, hands fifty more:
Of all from Heav'n, their sire, who took their birth,
These were most dreadful of the sons of Earth;
Their cruel father, from their natal hour,
With hate pursued them, to his utmost pow'r;
He from the parent womb did all convey
Into some secret cave remote from day:
The tyrant father thus his sons oppress'd,
And evil meditations fill'd his breast.
Earth deeply groan'd for these her sons confin'd,
And vengeance for their wrongs employ'd her mind;
She yields black iron from her fruitful vein,
And of it forms an instrument of pain;
Then to her children thus, the silence broke,
Without reserve she, deeply sighing, spoke.
"My sons, descended from a barb'rous sire,
Whose evil acts our breasts to vengeance fire,
Attentive to my friendly voice incline;
Th' aggressor he, and to revenge be thine."
The bold proposal they astonish'd hear;
Her words possess'd them with a silent fear;
Saturn, at last, whom no deceit can blind,
To her responsive thus declar'd his mind.
"Matron, for us the throeing pangs who bore,
Much we have suffer'd, but will bear no more;
If such as fathers ought ours will not be,
The name of father is no tie to me;
Patient of wrongs, if they th' attempt decline,
Th' aggressor he, all to revenge be mine."
Earth greatly joy'd at what his words reveal'd,
And in close ambush him from all conceal'd;
Arm'd with the crooked instrument she made,
She taught him to direct the sharp-tooth'd blade.
Great Heav'n approach'd beneath the veil of Night,
Proposing from his consort, Earth, delight;
As in full length the god extended lay,
No fraud suspecting in his am'rous play,
Out rush'd his son, complotter with his wife,
His right hand grasp'd the long, the fatal, knife,
His left the channel of the seed of life,
Which from the roots the rough-tooth'd metal tore,
And bath'd his fingers with his father's gore;
He throw'd behind the source of Heaven's pain,
Nor fell the ruins of the god in vain;
The sanguine drops which from the members fall
The fertile earth receives, and drinks them all:
Hence, at the end of the revolving year,
Sprung mighty Giants, pow'rful with the spear,
Shining in arms; the Furies took their birth
Hence, and the Wood-Nymphs of the spacious earth.
Saturn the parts divided from the wound,
Spoils of his parent god, cast from the ground
Into the sea; long through the watry plain
They journey'd on the surface of the main:
Fruitful at length th' immortal substance grows,
Whit'ning it foams, and in a circle flows:
Behold a nymph arise divinely fair,
Whom to Cythera first the surges bear:
Hence is she borne safe o'er the deeps profound
To Cyprus, water'd by the waves around:
And here she walks endow'd with every grace
To charm, the goddess blooming in her face;
Her looks demand respect; and where she goes,
Beneath her tender feet the herbage blows;
And Aphrodite, from the foam, her name,
Among the race of gods and men the same;
And Cytherea from Cythera came;
Whence, beauteous crown'd, she safely cross'd the sea,
And call'd, O Cyprus, Cypria from thee;
Nor less by Philomedea known on earth,
A name deriv'd immediate from her birth:
Her first attendants to th' immortal choir
Were Love, the oldest god, and fair Desire:
The virgin whisper, and the tempting smile,
The sweet allurement that can hearts beguile,
Soft blandishments which never fail to move,
Friendship, and all the fond deceits in love,
Constant her steps pursue, or will she go
Among the gods above, or men below.
Great Heav'n was wroth thus by his sons to bleed,
And call'd them Titans from the barb'rous deed;
He told them all, from a prophetic mind,
The hours of his revenge were sure behind.
Now darksome Night fruitful began to prove,
Without the knowledge of connubial love;
From her black womb sad Destiny and Fate,
Death, Sleep, and num'rous dreams, derive their date:
With Momus the dark goddess teems again,
And Care, the mother of a doleful train;
Th' Hesperides she bore, far in the seas
Guards of the golden fruit, and fertile trees:
From the same parent sprung the rig'rous three,
The goddesses of fate and destiny,
Clotho and Lachesis, whose boundless sway,
With Atropos, both men and gods obey;
To human race they, from their birth, ordain
A life of pleasure or a life of pain;
To slav'ry, or to empire, such their pow'r,
They fix a mortal at his natal hour;

The crimes of men, and gods, the Fates pursue,
And give to each alike the vengeance due;
Nor can the greatest their resentment fly,
They punish ere they lay their anger by:
And Nemesis from the same fountain rose,
From hurtful Night, herself the source of woes:
Hence fraud, and loose desire, the bane of life,
Old age vexatious, and corroding strife.
From strife pernicious, painful labour rose,
Oblivion, famine, and tormenting woes;
Hence combats, murders, wars, and slaughters, rise,
Deceits, and quarrels, and injurious lies;
Unruly licence hence that knows no bounds,
And losses spring, and sad domestic wounds;
Hence perjury, black perjury, began,
A crime destructive to the race of man.
Old Nereus to the Sea was born of Earth,
Nereus who claims the precedence in birth
To their descendants; him old god they call,
Because sincere, and affable, to all;
In judgment moderation he preserves,
And never from the paths of justice swerves.
Thaumas the great from the same parents came,
Phorcys the strong, and Ceto beauteous dame:
To the same sire did Earth Euribia bear,
As iron hard her heart, a cruel fair.
Doris to Nereus bore a lovely train,
Fifty fair daughters, wand'rers of the main;
A beauteous mother she, of Ocean born,
Whose graceful head the comeliest locks adorn:
Proto, Eucrate, nymphs, begin the line,
Sao to whom, and Amphitrite join;
Eudore, Thetis, and Galene, grace,
With Glauce, and Cymothoe, the race;
Swift-footed Spio hence derives her birth,
With thee, Thalia, ever prone to mirth;
And Melite, charming in mien to see,
Did the same mother bear, Eulimene,
Agave too, Pasithea and thee;
From whom sprung Erato, Eunice, you,
With arms appearing of a rosy hue;
Doto and Proto join the progeny,
With them Pherusa and Dunamene;
Nisæa and Actæa boast the same,
Protomedia from the fruitful dame,
And Doris, honour'd with maternal name;
And hence does Panope her lineage trace,
And Galatea, with a lovely face;
And hence Hippothoe, who sweetly charms,
And thou, Hipponoe, with thy rosy arms;
And hence Cymodoce, the floods who binds,
And with Cymatolege stills the winds;
With them the pow'r does Amphitrite share,
Of all the main the loveliest-footed fair;
Cumo, Heïone, and Halimed,
With a sweet garland that adorns her head,
Boast the same rise, joyful Glauconome,
Pontoporea, and Liagore;
Evagore, Laomedia, join,
And thou, Polynome, the num'rous line;
Autonoe, Lysianassa, name,
Sisters descended from the fertile dame;
In the bright list Evarne fair we find,
Spotless the nymph both in her form and mind,
And Psamathe, of a majestic mien;
And thou, divine Menippe, there art seen;
To these we Neso add, Eupompe, thee,
And thee, Themisto, next, and Pronoe;
Nemertes, virgin chaste, completes the race,
Not last in honour, though the last in place;
Her breast the virtues of her parent fire,
Her mind the copy of her deathless sire.
From blameless Nereus these, the fruits of joy,
And goodly offices the nymphs employ.
Of Ocean born, Electre plights her word
To Thaumas, and obeys her rightful lord;
Iris to whom, a goddess swift, she bears;
From them the Harpies with their comely hairs
Descend, Aëllo, who pursues the wind,
And with her sister leaves the birds behind;
Ocypete the other; when they fly,
They seem with rapid wings to reach the sky.
Ceto to Phorcys bore the Graiæ, grey
From the first moment they beheld the day;
Hence gods and men these daughters Graiæ name;
Pephredo lovely veil'd from Ceto came,
And Enyo with her saffron veil: the same
To Phorcys bore the Gorgons, who remain
Far in the seat of Night, the distant main,
Where, murm'ring at their task, th' Hesperides
Watch o'er the golden fruit, and fertile trees:
The number of the Gorgons once were three,
Stheno, Medusa, and Euryale;
Of which two sisters draw immortal breath,
Free from the fears of age as free from death;
But thou, Medusa, felt a pow'rful foe,
A mortal thou, and born to mortal woe;
Nothing avail'd of love thy blissful hours,
In a soft meadow, on a bed of flow'rs,
Thy tender dalliance with the ocean's king,
And in the beauty of the year, the spring;
You by the conqu'ring hand of Perseus bled,
Perseus whose sword laid low in dust thy head;
Then started out, when you began to bleed,
The great Chrysaor, and the gallant steed
Call'd Pegasus, a name not given in vain,
Born near the fountains of the spacious main.
His birth will great Chrysaor's name unfold,
When in his hand glitter'd the sword of gold;
Mounted on Pegasus he soar'd above,
And sought the palace of almighty Jove;
Loaded with light'ning through the skies he rode,
And bore it with the thunder to the god.
Chrysaor, love the guide, Calliroe led,
Daughter of Ocean, to the genial bed;
Whence Geryon sprung, fierce with his triple head;
Whom Hercules laid breathless on the ground,
In Erythea, which the waves surround;
His oxen lowing round their master stand,
While he falls gasping from the conqu'ror's hand:
That fatal day beheld Eurytion fall,
And with him Orthus in a gloomy stall;
By his strong arm the dog and herdsman slain,
The hero drove the oxen cross the main;
The wide-brow'd herds he to Tirynthus bore,
And safely landed on the sacred shore.
Calliroe in a cave conceiv'd again,
And for Echidna bore maternal pain;
A monster she of an undaunted mind,
Unlike the gods, nor like the human kind;
One half a nymph of a prodigious size,
Fair her complexion, and asquint her eyes;
The other half a serpent dire to view,
Large and voracious, and of various hue;
Deep in a Syrian rock her horrid den,
From the immortal gods remote, and men;
There, so the council of the gods ordains,
Forlorn, and ever young, the nymph remains.
In love Echidna with Typhaon join'd,
Outrageous he, and blust'ring, as the wind;

Of these the offsprings prov'd a furious race;
Orthus, the produce of the first embrace,
Was vigilant to watch his master's herd,
The dog of Geryon, and a trusty guard:
Next Cerberus, the dog of Pluto, came,
Devouring, direful, of a monstrous frame;
From fifty heads he barks with fifty tongues,
Fierce, and undaunted, with his brasen lungs:
The dreadful Hydra rose from the same bed,
In Lerna by the fair arm'd Juno bred,
Juno, with hate implacable who strove,
Against the virtues of the son of Jove;
But Hercules, with Iolaus join'd,
Amphitryon's race, and of a martial mind,
Bless'd with the counsel of the warlike maid,
Dead at his feet the horrid monster lay'd:
From the same parents sprung Chimæra dire,
From whose black nostrils issued flames of fire;
Strong, and of size immense; a monster she
Rapid in flight, astonishing to see;
A lion's head on her large shoulders grew,
The goat's and dragon's, terrible to view;
A lion she before in mane and throat,
Behind a dragon, in the midst a goat;
Her Pegasus the swift subdued in flight,
Back'd by Bellerophon, a gallant knight.
From Orthus and Chimæra, foul embrace,
Is Sphinx deriv'd, a monster to the race
Of Cadmus fatal: from the same dire veins
Sprung the stern ranger of Nemean plains,
The lion nourish'd by the wife of Jove,
Permited lord of Tretum's mount to rove;
Nemea he, and Apesas, commands,
Alarms the people, and destroys their lands;
In Hercules at last a foe he found,
And from his arm receiv'd a mortal wound.
Ceto and Porcys both renew'd their flame;
From which amour a horrid serpent came;
Who keeps, while in a spacious cave he lies,
Watchful o'er all the golden fruit his eyes.
Tethys and Ocean, born of Heav'n, embrace,
Whence springs the Nile, and a long wat'ry race,
Alpheus, and Eridanus the strong,
That rises deep, and stately rolls along,
Strymon, Mæander, and the Ister clear;
Nor, Phasis, are thy streams omitted here;
To the same rise Rhesus his current owes,
And Achelous, that like silver flows;
Hence Nessus takes his course, and Rhodius,
With Haliacmon, and Heptaporus;
To these the Granic and Æsapus join,
Hermus to these, and Simoïs divine,
Penëus, and the Caic flood, that laves
The verdant margins with his beauteous waves;
The great Sangarius, and the Ladon, name,
Parthenius, and Evenus, streams of fame,
And you, Ardescus, boast the fruitful line,
And lastly you, Scamender the divine.
From the same parents, fertile pair, we trace
A progeny of nymphs, a sacred race;
Who, from their birth, o'er all mankind the care
With the great king Apollo jointly share;
In this is Jove, the god of gods, obey'd,
Who grants the rivers all to lend their aid.
The nymphs from Tethys, and old Ocean these,
Pitho, Admete, daughters of the seas,
Ianthe, and Electra, nymphs of fame,
Doris, and Prymno, and the beauteous dame
Urania, as a goddess fair in face;
Hence Hippo, and hence Clymene, we trace,
And thou, Rodia, of the num'rous race;
Zeuxo to these succeeds, Calliroe,
Clytie, Idya, and Pasithoe;
Plexaure here, and Galaxaure, join,
And lovely Dion, of a lovely line;
Molobosis, and Thoe, add to these,
And charming Polydora, form'd to please,
Cerces, whose beauties all from nature rise,
And Pluto, with her large majestic eyes;
Perseïs, Xanthe, in the list we see,
And Ianira, and, Acaste, thee;
Menestho, nor Europa, hence remove,
Nor Metis, nor Petræa, raising love;
Crisie and Asia boast one ancient sire,
With fair Calypso, object of desire,
Telestho, saffron-veil'd, Eurynome,
Eudore, Tyche, and Ocyroe,
And thou, Amphiro, of the source divine,
And Styx, exceeding all the lovely line;
These are the sons first in the list of fame,
And daughters, which from ancient Ocean came,
And fruitful Tethys, venerable dame:
Thousands of streams which flow the spacious earth
From Tethys, and her sons, deduce their birth;
Numbers of tides she yielded to her lord,
Too many for a mortal to record;
But they who on, or near, their borders dwell,
Their virtues know, and can describe them well.
The fruits of Thia and Hyperion rise,
And with refulgent lustre light the skies,
The great, the glorious Sun, transcending bright,
And the fair splendid Moon, the lamp of night;
With them Aurora, when whose dawn appears,
Who mortal men, and gods immortal, cheers.
To Creus, her espous'd, a son of Earth,
Eurybia gave the great Astræus birth;
Perses from them, of all most skilful, came,
And Pallas, first of goddesses in fame.
Aurora brought to great Astræus forth
The West, the South-wind, and the rapid North;
The morning-star, fair Lucifer, she bore,
And ornaments of Heav'n, ten thousand more.
From Styx, the fairest of old Ocean's line,
And Pallas, sprung a progeny divine,
Zeal to perform, and Vict'ry in her pace
Fair-footed, Valour, Might, a glorious race!
They hold a mansion in the realms above,
Their seat is always near the throne of Jove;
Where the dread thund'ring god pursues his way,
They march, and close behind his steps obey.
This honour they by Styx, their mother, gain'd;
Which by her prudence she from Jove obtain'd:
When the great pow'r that e'en the gods commands,
Who sends the bolts from his almighty hands,
Summon'd th' immortals, who obey'd his call,
He thus address'd them in th' olympian hall.
"Ye gods, like gods, with me who dauntless dare
To face the Titans in a dreadful war,
Above the rest in honour shall ye stand,
An ample recompense shall load your hand:
To Saturn's reign who bow'd, and unprefer'd,
Void of distinction, and without reward,
Great, and magnificently rich, shall shine,
As right requires, and suits a pow'r divine."
First as her father counsell'd, Styx ascends,
And her brave offsprings to the god commends;
Great Jove receiv'd her with peculiar grace,
Nor honour'd less the mother than her race;

Enrich'd with gifts she left the bright abodes,
By Jove ordain'd the solemn oath of gods;
Her children, as she wish'd, behind remain,
Constant attendants on the thund'rer's train:
Alike the god with all maintain'd his word,
And rules, in empire strong, of lords the lord.
  Phœbe with fondness to her Cœus cleav'd,
And she, a goddess, by a god conceiv'd;
Latona, sable-veil'd, the produce proves,
Pleasing to all, of their connubial loves,
Sweetly engaging from her natal hour,
The most delightful in th' olympian bow'r:
From them Asteria sprung, a nymph renown'd,
And with the spousal love of Perses crown'd;
To whom she bore Hecate, lov'd by Jove,
And honour'd by th' inhabitants above,
Profusely gifted from th' almighty hand,
With pow'r extensive o'er the sea and land,
And great the honour she, by Jove's high leave,
Does from the starry vault of Heav'n receive.
When to the gods the sacred flame aspire,
From human off'rings, as the law require,
To Hecate the vows are first prefer'd;
Happy of men whose pray'rs are kindly heard,
Success attends his ev'ry act below,
Honour, wealth, pow'r, to him abundant flow.
The gods, who all from Earth and Heav'n descend,
On her decision for their lots depend;
Nor what the earliest gods, the Titans, claim,
By her ordain'd, of honour or of fame,
Has Jove revok'd by his supreme command,
For her decrees irrevocable stand:
Nor is her honour less, nor less her pow'r,
Because she only bless'd the nuptial hour;
Great is her pow'r on Earth, and great her fame,
Nor less in Heav'n, and o'er the main the same,
Because Saturnian Jove reveres the dame:
The man she loves she can to greatness raise,
And grant to whom she favours public praise;
This shines for words distinguish'd at the bar;
One proudly triumphs in the spoils of war;
And she alone can speedy vict'ry give,
And rich in glory bid the conqu'rer live:
And where the venerable rulers meet
She sits supreme upon the judgment-seat:
In single trials or of strength, or skill,
Propitious she presides o'er whom she will;
To honour she extends the beauteous crown,
And glads the parent with the son's renown,
With rapid swiftness wings the gallant steeds,
And in the race the flying courser speeds.
Who, urg'd by want, and led by hopes of gain,
Pursue their journey cross the dang'rous main,
To Hecate they all for safety bow,
And to their god and her prefer the vow.
With ease the goddess, venerable dame,
Gives to the sportsman's hand his wish'd-for game;
Or now the weary'd creature faintly flies,
And, for a while, eludes the huntsman's eyes,
Who stretches, sure to seize the panting prey,
And bear the glory of the chase away,
Till, by the kind protect'ress of the plains,
Her strength recovers, and new life she gains,
She starts, surprising, and outstrips the wind,
And leaves the masters of the chase behind.
With Mercury the watchful goddess guards
Of goats the straggling flocks, the lowing herds,
And bleating folds, rich with the pond'rous fleece;
By her they lessen, and by her increase.
The only daughter of her mother born,
And her the gods with various gifts adorn:
O'er infants she, so Jove ordain'd, presides,
And the upgrowing youth to merit guides;
Great is the trust the future man to breed,
A trust to her by Saturn's son decreed.
  Rhea to Saturn bore, her brother god,
Vesta and Ceres; Juno, golden shod,
And Pluto, hard of heart, whose wide command
Is o'er a dark and subterranean land,
A pow'rful monarch, hence derive their birth,
With Neptune, deity who shakes the Earth;
Of these great Jove, the ruler of the skies,
Of gods and men the sire, in council wise,
Is born; and him the universe adores,
And the Earth trembles when his thunder roars.
Saturn from Earth, and Heav'n adorn'd with stars,
Had learn'd the rumour of approaching wars,
Great as he was a greater should arise
To rob him of the empire of the skies,
The mighty Jove, his son, in council wise:
With dread the fatal prophecy he hear'd,
And for his regal honours greatly fear'd,
And that the dire decree might fruitless prove,
Devour'd his pledges, at their birth, of love:
Now Rhea, who her slaughter'd children griev'd,
With Jove, the sire of gods and men, conceiv'd,
To Earth and Heav'n she for assistance runs,
And begs their counsel to revenge her sons,
To guard her Jove from wily Saturn's ire,
Secret to keep him from a barb'rous sire:
They to their daughter lend a willing ear,
And to her speak the hour of vengeance near,
Nor hide they from her what the Fates ordain
Of her great-minded son, and Saturn's reign:
Her safe to Crete the parent gods convey,
In Lyctus there, a fertile soil, she lay;
At length the tedious months their course had run,
When mighty Jove she bore, her youngest son;
Wide-spreading Earth receiv'd the child with joy,
And train'd the god up from a newborn boy.
Rhea to Lyctus safely took her flight,
Protected by the sable veil of night;
Far in the sacred earth her son she lay'd,
On mount Ægæus ever crown'd with shade.
When the old king, who once could boast his reign
O'er all the gods, and the etherial plain,
Came jealous of the infant's future pow'r,
A stone the mother gave him to devour;
Greedy he seiz'd th' imaginary child,
And swallow'd heedless, by the dress beguil'd;
Nor thought the wretched god of ought to fear,
Nor knew the day of his disgrace was near;
Invincible remains his Jove alive,
His throne to shake, and from his kingdom drive
The cruel parent, for to him 'tis giv'n
To rule the gods, and mount the throne of Heav'n.
Well thriv'd the deity, nor was it long
Before his strength increas'd, and limbs grow'd strong.
When the revolving year his course had run,
By, Earth, thy art, and Jove his pow'rful son,
The crafty Saturn, once by gods ador'd,
His injur'd offsprings to the light restor'd:
First from within he yielded to the day
The stone deceitful, and his latest prey;
This Jove, in mem'ry of the wond'rous tale,
Fix'd on Parnassus in a sacred vale,
In Pytho the divine, a mark to be,
That future ages may astonish'd see:

And now a greater task behind remains,
To free his kindred heav'n-born race from chains,
In an ill hour by Saturn rashly bound,
Who from the hands of Jove their freedom found;
With zeal the gods perform'd a thankful part,
The debt of gratitude lay next their heart;
Jove owes to them the bolts which dreadful fly,
And the bright lightning which illumes the sky;
To him th' exchange for liberty they bore,
Gifts deep in earth conceal'd, unknown before;
Now arm'd with them, he reigns almighty Jove,
The lord of men below and gods above.
Clymene, ocean-born, with beauteous feet,
And Japhet, in the bands of wedlock meet;
From whose embrace a glorious offspring came,
Atlas magnanimous, and great in fame,
Menœtius, thou with lasting honours crown'd,
Prometheus for his artifice renown'd,
And Epimetheus of instedfast mind,
Lur'd to false joys, and to the future blind,
Who, rashly weak by soft temptations mov'd,
The bane of arts and their inventors prov'd,
Who took the work of Jove, the virgin fair,
Nor saw beneath her charms the latent snare.
Blasted by light'ning from the hands of Jove,
Menœtius fell in Erebus to rove;
His dauntless mind that could not brook command,
And prone to ill, provok'd th' almighty hand.
Atlas, so hard necessity ordains,
Erect the pond'rous vault of stars sustains;
Not far from the Hesperides he stands,
Nor from the load retracts his head or hands:
Here was he fix'd by Jove in council wise,
Who all disposes, and who rules the skies:
To the same god Prometheus ow'd his pains,
Fast bound with hard inextricable chains
To a large column in the midmost part,
Who bore his suff'rings with a dauntless heart;
From Jove an eagle flew with wings wide spread,
And on his never-dying liver fed;
What with his rav'nous beak by day he tore
The night supply'd, and furnish'd him with more:
Great Hercules to his assistance came,
Born of Alcmena, lovely-footed dame;
And first he made the bird voracious bleed,
And from his chains the son of Japhet freed;
To this the god consents, th' olympian sire,
Who, for his son's renown, suppress'd his ire,
The wrath he bore against the wretch who strove
In counsel with himself, the pow'rful Jove;
Such was the mighty thund'rer's will, to raise
To greatest height the Theban hero's praise.
When at Mecona a contention rose,
Men and immortals to each other foes,
The strife Prometheus offer'd to compose;
In the division of the sacrifice,
Intending to deceive great Jove the wise,
He stuff'd the flesh in the large ox's skin,
And bound the entrails, with the fat, within,
Next the white bones, with artful care, dispos'd,
And in the candid fat from sight enclos'd:
The sire of gods and men, who saw the cheat,
Thus spoke expressive of the dark deceit.
"In this division how unjust the parts,
O Japhet's son, of kings the first in arts!"
Reproachful spoke the god in council wise;
To whom Prometheus full of guile replies,
"O Jove, the greatest of the pow'rs divine,
View the division, and the choice be thine."
Wily he spoke from a deceitful mind;
Jove saw his thoughts, nor to his heart was blind;
And then the god, in wrath of soul, began
To plot misfortunes to his subject man:
The lots survey'd, he with his hands embrac'd
The parts which were in the white fat incas'd;
He saw the bones, and anger sat confess'd
Upon his brow, for anger seiz'd his breast:
Hence to the gods the od'rous flames aspire
From the white bones which fed the sacred fire.
The cloud-compelling Jove, by Japhet's son
Enrag'd, to him in words like these begun.
"O! who in male contrivance all transcend,
Thine arts thou wilt not yet, obdurate, end."
So spoke th' eternal wisdom, full of ire,
And from that hour deny'd the use of fire
To wretched men, who pass on Earth their time,
Mindful, Prometheus, of thy artful crime:
But Jove in vain conceal'd the splendid flame;
The son of Japhet of immortal fame,
Brought the bright sparks clandestine from above
Clos'd in a hollow cane; the thund'ring Jove
Soon, from the bitterness of soul, began
To plot destruction to the peace of man.
Vulcan, a god renown'd, by Jove's command,
Form'd a fair virgin with a master hand,
Earth her first principle, her native air
As modest seeming as her face was fair.
The nymph, by Pallas, blue-ey'd goddess, dress'd,
Bright shin'd improv'd beneath the candid vest;
The rich wrought veil behind, wond'rous to see,
Fruitful with art, bespoke the deity;
Her brows to compass did Minerva bring
A garland breathing all the sweets of spring:
And next the goddess, glorious to behold,
Plac'd on her head a glitt'ring crown of gold,
The work of Vulcan by his master hand,
The labour of the god by Jove's command;
There seem'd to scud along the finny breed;
And there the beasts of land appear'd to feed;
Nature and art were there so much at strife,
The miracle might well be took for life.
Vulcan the lovely bane, the finish'd maid,
To the immortal gods and men convey'd;
Graceful by Pallas dress'd the virgin trod,
And seem'd a blessing or for man or god:
Soon as they see th' inevitable snare,
They praise the artist, and admire the fair;
From her, the fatal guile, a sex derives
To men pernicious, and contracts their lives,
The softer kind, a false alluring train,
Tempting to joys which ever end with pain,
Never beheld with the penurious race,
But ever seen where lux'ry shews her face.
As drones oppressive habitants of hives,
Owe to the labour of the bees their lives,
Whose work is always with the day begun,
And never ends but with the setting Sun,
From flow'r to flow'r they rove, and loaded home
Return, to build the white, the waxen comb,
While lazy the luxurious race remain
Within, and of their toils enjoy the gain,
So woman, by the thund'rer's hard decree,
And wretched man, are like the drone and bee:
If man the galling chain of wedlock shuns,
He from one evil to another runs;
He, when his hairs are winter'd o'er with gray,
Will want a helpmate in th' afflicting day;
And if possessions large have bless'd his life,
He dies, and proves perhaps the source of strife;

A distant kindred, far ally'd in blood,
Contend to make their doubtful titles good:
Or should he, these calamities to fly,
His honour plight, and join the mutual tie,
And should the partner of his bosom prove
A chaste and prudent matron, worthy love;
Yet he would find this chaste, this prudent wife
The hapless author of a checquer'd life:
But should he, wretched man, a nymph embrace,
A stubborn consort, of a stubborn race,
Poor hamper'd slave, how must he drag the chain!
His mind, his breast, his heart, o'ercharg'd with
What congregated woes must he endure! [pain!
What ills on ills which will admit no cure!
Th' omnipotence of Jove in all we see,
Whom none eludes, and what he wills must be;
Not thou, to none injurious, Japhet's son,
With all thy wisdom, could his anger shun;
His rage you suffer'd, and confess'd his pow'r
Chain'd in hard durance in the penal hour.
  The brothers Briareus and Cottus lay,
With Gyges, bound in chains, remov'd from day,
By their hard-hearted sire, who with surprise
View'd their vast strength, their form, and monstrous size:
In the remotest parts of Earth confin'd
They sat, and silent sorrows wreck'd their mind,
Till by th' advice of Earth and aid of Jove,
With other gods, the fruits of Saturn's love
With Rhea beauteous dress'd, they broke the chain,
And from their dungeons burst to light again.
Earth told them all, from a prophetic light,
How gods encount'ring gods should meet in fight,
To them foretold, who stood devoid of fear,
Their hour of vict'ry and renown was near;
The Titans, and the bold Saturnian race,
Should wage a dreadful war, ten years the space.
The Titans brave on lofty Othrys stand,
And gloriously dare the thund'rer's hand;
The gods from Saturn sprung ally their pow'r;
(Gods Rhea bore him in a fatal hour:)
From high Olympus they like gods engage,
And dauntless face, like gods, Titanian rage.
In the dire conflict neither party gains,
In equal balance long the war remains;
At last by truce each soul immortal rests,
Each god on nectar and ambrosia feasts;
Their spirits nectar and ambrosia raise,
And fire their gen'rous breasts to acts of praise;
To whom, the banquet o'er, in council join'd,
The sire of gods and men express'd his mind:
  "Gods, who from Earth and Heav'n, great rise, descend,
To what my heart commands to speak attend:
For vict'ry long, and empire, have we strove,
Long have ye battel'd in defence of Jove;
To war again, invincible your might,
And dare the Titans to the dreadful fight;
Of friendship strict observe the sacred charms,
Be that the cement of the gods in arms;
Grateful remember, when in chains ye lay,
From darkness Jove redeem'd ye to the day."
  He spoke, and Cottus to the god replies;
"O venerable sire, in council wise,
Who freed immortals from a state of woe,
Of what you utter well the truth we know:
Rescu'd from chains and darkness here we stand,
O son of Saturn, by thy pow'rful hand;
Nor will we, king, the rage of war decline,
Till pow'r, indisputable pow'r, is thine;
The right of conquest shall confirm thy sway,
And teach the Titans whom they must obey."
  He ends, the rest assent to what he says;
And the gods thank him with the voice of praise:
He more than ever feels himself inspir'd,
And his mind burns with love of glory fir'd.
All rush to battle with impetuous might,
And gods and goddesses provoke the fight.
The race that Rhea to her lord conceiv'd,
And the Titanic gods by Jove reliev'd
From Erebus, who there in bondage lay,
Ally their arms in this immortal day.
Each brother fearless the dire conflict stands,
Each rears his fifty heads, and hundred hands;
They mighty rocks from their foundations tore,
And fiercely brave against the Titans bore.
Furious and swift the Titan phalanx drove,
And both with mighty force for empire strove:
The ocean roar'd from ev'ry part profound,
And the earth bellow'd from her inmost ground:
Heav'n groans, and to the gods conflicting bends,
And the loud tumult high Olympus rends.
So strong the darts from god to god were hurl'd,
The clamour reach'd the subterranean world;
And where with haughty strides each warrior trod,
Hell felt the weight, and sunk beneath the god;
All Tartarus could hear the blows from far:
Such was the big, the horrid, voice of war!
And now the murmur of incitement flies,
All rang'd in martial order, through the skies;
Here Jove above the rest conspicuous shin'd,
In valour equal to his strength his mind;
Erect and dauntless see the thund'rer stand,
The bolts red hissing from his vengeful hand;
He walks majestic round the starry frame;
And now the light'nings from Olympus flame;
The earth wide blazes with the fires of Jove,
Nor the flash spares the verdure of the grove.
Fierce glows the air, the boiling ocean roars,
And the seas wash with burning waves their shores;
The dazzling vapours round the Titans glare,
A light too pow'rful for their eyes to bear!
One conflagration seems to seize on all,
And threatens Chaos with the gen'ral fall.
From what their eyes behold, and what they hear,
The universal wreck of worlds is near: [scend,
Should the large vault of stars, the Heav'ns, de-
And with the Earth in loud confusion blend,
Like this would seem the great tumultuous jar:
The gods engag'd, such the big voice of war!
And now the batt'ling winds their havock make,
Thick whirls the dust, Earth, thy foundations
The arms of Jove thick and terrific fly, [shake;
And blaze and bellow through the trembling sky;
Winds, thunder, lightning, thro' both armies drove,
Their course impetuous from the hands of Jove;
Loud and stupendous is the raging fight,
And now each warrior god exerts his might.
Cottus, and Briareus, who scorn to yield,
And Gyges panting for the martial field,
Foremost the labours of the day increase,
Nor let the horrours of the battle cease:
From their strong hands three hundred rocks they
And, oft repeated, overwhelm the foe; [throw,
They forc'd the Titans deep beneath the ground,
Cast from their pride, and in sad durance bound,
Far from the surface of the Earth they lie,
In chains, as Earth is distant from the sky;
From Earth the distance to the starry frame,
From Earth to gloomy Tartarus, the same.

From the high Heav'n a brazen anvil cast,
Nine nights and days in rapid whirls would last,
And reach the Earth the tenth, whence strongly hurl'd,
The same the passage to th' infernal world,
To Tart'rus; which a brazen closure bounds,
And whose black entrance threefold night surrounds,
With earth thy vast foundations cover'd o'er;
And there the ocean's endless fountains roar:
By cloud-compelling Jove the Titans fell,
And there in thick, in horrid darkness dwell:
They lie confin'd, unable thence to pass,
The wall and gates by Neptune made of brass;
Jove's trusty guards, Gyges and Cottus, stand
There, and with Briareus the pass command.
The entrance there, and the last limits, lie
Of earth, the barren main, the starry sky,
And Tart'rus; there of all the fountains rise,
A sight detested by immortal eyes:
A mighty chasm, horror and darkness here;
And from the gates the journey of a year:
Here storms in hoarse, in frightful murmurs play,
The seat of Night, where mists exclude the day.
Before the gates the son of Japhet stands,
Nor from the skies retracts his head or hands;
Where Night and Day their course alternate lead;
Where both their entrance make, and both recede,
Both wait the season to direct their way,
And spread successive o'er the Earth their sway:
This cheers the eyes of mortals with her light;
The harbinger of Sleep, pernicious Night:
And here the sons of Night their mansion keep,
Sad deities, Death and his brother Sleep;
Whom, from the dawn to the decline of day,
The Sun beholds not with his piercing ray:
One o'er the land extends, and o'er the seas,
And lulls the weary'd mind of man to ease;
That iron-hearted, and of cruel soul,
Brazen his breast, nor can he brook controul,
To whom, and ne'er return, all mortals go,
And even to immortal gods a foe.
Foremost th' infernal palaces are seen
Of Pluto, and Persephone his queen;
A horrid dog, and grim, couch'd on the floor,
Guards, with malicious art, the sounding door;
On each who in the entrance first appears,
He fawning wags his tail, and cocks his ears;
If any strive to measure back the way,
Their steps he watches, and devours his prey.
Here Styx, a goddess, whom immortals hate,
The first-born fair of Ocean, keeps her state;
From gods remote her silver columns rise,
Roof'd with large rocks her dome that fronts the skies:
Here, cross the main, swift footed Iris brings
A message seldom from the king of kings;
But when among the gods contention spreads,
And in debate divides immortal heads,
From Jove the goddess wings her rapid flight
To the fam'd river, and the seat of Night,
Thence in a golden vase the water bears,
By whose cool streams each pow'r immortal swears.
Styx from a sacred font her course derives,
And far beneath the earth her passage drives;
From a stupendous rock descend her waves,
And the black realms of Night her current laves:
Could any her capacious channels drain,
They'd prove a tenth of all the spacious main;
Nine parts in mazes clear as silver glide
Along the earth, or join the ocean's tide;
The other from the rock in billows rolls,
Source of misfortune to immortal souls.
Who with false oaths disgrace th' olympian bow'rs,
Incur the punishment of heav'nly pow'rs:
The perjur'd god, as in the arms of death,
Lethargic lies, nor seems to draw his breath;
Nor him the nectar and ambrosia cheer,
While the Sun goes his journey of a year;
Nor with the lethargy concludes his pain,
But complicated woes behind remain:
Nine tedious years he must an exile rove,
Nor join the council, nor the feasts, of Jove;
The banish'd god back in the tenth they call
To heav'nly banquets and th' olympian hall:
The honours such the gods on Styx bestow,
Whose living streams thro' rugged channels flow,
Where the beginning, and last limits, lie
Of earth, the barren main, the starry sky,
And Tart'rus; where of all the fountains rise;
A sight detested by immortal eyes.
Th' inhabitants through brazen portals pass,
Over a threshold of e'erlasting brass,
The growth spontaneous, and foundations deep;
And here th' allies of Jove their captives keep,
The Titans, who to utter darkness fell,
And in the farthest parts of Chaos dwell.
Jove grateful gave to his auxiliar train,
Cottus and Gyges, mansions in the main;
To Briareus, for his superior might
Exerted fiercely in the dreadful fight,
Neptune who shakes the earth, his daughter gave,
Cymopolia, to reward the brave.
When the great victor god, almighty Jove,
The Titans from celestial regions drove,
Wide Earth Typhœus bore, with Tart'rus join'd,
Her youngest born, and blust'ring as the wind;
Fit for most arduous works his brawny hands,
On feet as durable as gods he stands;
From heads of serpents hiss an hundred tongues,
And lick his horrid jaws, untir'd his lungs;
From his dire hundred heads his eye-balls stare,
And, fire-like, dreadful to beholders, glare;
Terrific from his hundred mouths to hear,
Voices of ev'ry kind torment the ear;
His utt'rance sounds like gods in council full;
And now he bellows like the lordly bull:
And now he roars like the stern beast that reigns
King of the woods, and terrour of the plains;
And now, surprising to be hear'd, he yelps,
Like, from his ev'ry voice, the lion's welps;
And now, so loud a noise the monster makes,
The loftiest mountain from its basis shakes:
And now Typhœus had perplex'd the day,
And over men and gods usurp'd the sway,
Had not the pow'rful monarch of the skies,
Of men and gods the sire, great Jove the wise,
Against the foe his hottest vengeance hurl'd,
Which blaz'd and thunder'd thro' th' etherial world;
Thro' land and main the bolts red hissing fell,
And thro' old Ocean reach'd the gates of Hell.
Th' almighty rising made Olympus nod,
And the earth groan'd beneath the vengeful god.
Hoarse thro' the cœrule main the thunder roll'd
Thro' which the lightning flew, both uncontroul'd;
Fire caught the winds which on their wings they bore,
Fierce flame the earth and Heav'n, the seas loud roar,
And beat with burning waves the burning shore;
The tumult of the gods was hear'd afar:
How hard to lay this hurricane of war!
The god who o'er the dead infernal reigns,
E'en Pluto, trembled in his dark domains;

Dire horrour seiz'd the rebel Titan band,
In Tartarus who round their Saturn stand:
But Jove at last collected all his might,
With lightning arm'd, and thunder, for the fight,
With strides majestic from Olympus strode;
What pow'r is able now to face the god!
The flash obedient executes his ire;
The giant blazes with vindictive fire;
From ev'ry head a diff'rent flame ascends;
The monster bellows, and Olympus bends:
The god repeats his blows, beneath each wound
All maim'd the giant falls, and groans the ground.
Fierce flash the lightnings from the hands of Jove,
The mountains burn, and crackles ev'ry grove.
The melted earth floats from her inmost caves,
As from the furnace run metallic waves:
Under the caverns of the sacred ground,
Where Vulcan works, and restless anvils sound,
Beneath the hand divine the iron grows
Ductile, and liquid from the furnace flows;
So the earth melted: and the giant fell,
Plung'd by the arms of mighty Jove to Hell.
Typhœus bore the rapid winds which fly
With tempests wing'd, and darken all the sky;
But from the bounteous gods derive their birth
The gales which breathe frugiferous to earth,
The south, the north, and the swift western wind,
Which ever blow to profit human kind:
Those from Typhœus sprung, an useless train,
To men pernicious, bluster o'er the main;
With thick and sable clouds they veil the deep,
And now destructive cross the ocean sweep:
The mariner with dread beholds from far
The gath'ring storms, and elemental war;
His bark the furious blast and billows rend;
The surges rise, and cataracts descend;
Above, beneath, he hears the tempest roar;
Now sinks the vessel, and he fears no more:
And remedy to this they none can find,
Who are resolv'd to trade by sea and wind.
On land in whirlwinds, or unkindly show'rs,
They blast the lovely fruits and blooming flow'rs;
O'er sea and land the blust'ring tyrants reign,
And make of earth-born men the labours vain.
And now the gods, who fought for endless fame,
The god of gods almighty Jove proclaim,
As Earth advis'd: nor reigns olympian Jove
Ingrate to them who with the Titans strove;
On those who warr'd beneath his wide command
He honours heaps with an impartial hand.
And now the king of gods, Jove, Metis led,
The wisest fair one, to the genial bed;
Who with the blue-ey'd virgin fruitful proves,
Minerva, pledge of their celestial loves;
The sire, from what kind Earth and Heav'n reveal'd,
Artful the matron in himself conceal'd;
From her it was decreed a race should rise
That would usurp the kingdom of the skies;
And first the virgin with her azure eyes,
Equal in strength, and as her father wise,
Is born, th' offspring of th' almighty's brain:
And Metis by the god conceiv'd again,
A son decreed to reign o'er Heav'n and Earth,
Had not the sire destroy'd the mighty birth:
He made the goddess in himself reside,
To be in ev'ry act th' eternal guide.
The Hours to Jove did lovely Themis bear,
Eunomie, Dice, and Irene fair;
O'er human labours they the pow'r possess,
With seasons kind the fruits of earth to bless:
She by the thund'ring god conceiv'd again,
And suffer'd for the Fates the rending pain,
Clotho and Lachesis, to whom we owe,
With Atropos, our shares of joy or woe;
This honour they receiv'd from Jove the wise,
The mighty sire, the ruler of the skies.
Eurynome, from Ocean sprung, to Jove
The beauteous Graces bore inspiring love,
Aglaia, and Euphrosyne the fair,
And thou Thalia of a graceful air;
From the bright eyes of these such charms proceed
As make the hearts of all beholders bleed.
He Ceres next, a bounteous goddess, led
To taste the pleasures of the genial bed;
To him fair-arm'd Persephone she bore,
Whom Pluto ravish'd from her native shore:
The mournful dame he of her child bereft,
But the wise sire assented to the theft.
Mnemosyne his breast with love inspires,
The fair-tress'd object of the god's desires;
Of whom the Muses, tuneful nine, are born,
Whose brows rich diadems of gold adorn;
To them uninterrupted joys belong,
Them the gay feast delights, and sacred song.
Latona bore, the fruits of Jove's embrace,
The loveliest offsprings of th' ethereal race;
She for Apollo felt the child-bed throw;
And, Artemis, for thee who twang the bow.
Last Juno fills th' almighty monarch's arms,
A blooming consort, and replete with charms;
From her Lucina, Mars, and Hebe, spring;
Their sire of gods the god, of kings the king.
Minerva, goddess of the martial train,
Whom wars delight, sprung from th' almighty's brain;
The rev'rend dame, unconquerable maid,
The battle rouses, of no pow'r afraid.
Juno, proud goddess, with her consort strove,
And soon conceiv'd without the joys of love;
Thee she produc'd without the aid of Jove,
Vulcan, who far in ev'ry art excel
The gods who in celestial mansions dwell.
To Neptune beauteous Amphitrite bore
Triton, dread god, who makes the surges roar;
Who dwells in seats of gold beneath the main,
Where Neptune and fair Amphitrite reign.
To Mars, who pierces with his spear the shield,
Terrour and Fear did Cytherea yield;
Dire brothers who in war disorder spread,
Break the thick phalanx, and increase the dead;
They wait in ev'ry act their father's call,
By whose strong hand the proudest cities fall:
Harmonia, sprung from that immortal bed,
Was to the scene of love by Cadmus led.
Maia, of Atlas born, and mighty Jove,
Join in the sacred bands of mutual love;
From whom behold the glorious Hermes rise,
A god renown'd, the herald of the skies.
Cadmean Simele, a mortal dame,
Gave to th' almighty's love a child of fame,
Bacchus, from whom our cheerful spirits flow,
Mother and son alike immortal now.
The mighty Hercules Alcmena bore
To the great god who makes the thunder roar.
Lame Vulcan made Aglaia fair his bride,
The youngest Grace, and in her blooming pride.
Bacchus, conspicuous with his golden hair,
Thee Ariadne weds, a beauteous fair,
From Minos sprung, whom mighty Jove the sage
Allows to charm her lord exempt from age.

Great Hercules, who with misfortune strove
Long, is rewarded with a virtuous love,
Hebe, the daughter of the thund'ring god,
By his fair consort Juno golden shod;
Thrice happy he safe from his toils to rise,
And ever young a god to grace the skies.
From the bright Sun, and thee, Perseïs, spring,
Fam'd offsprings, Circe, and Æetes king.
Æetes thee, beauteous Idya, led,
Daughter of Ocean, to the genial bed;
And with th' applause of Heav'n your loves were crown'd;
From whom Medea sprung, a fair renown'd.
All hail, olympian maids, harmonious Nine,
Daughters, of Ægis-bearing Jove, divine,
Forsake the land, forsake the briny main,
The gods and goddesses, celestial train;
Ye Muses, each immortal fair record
Who deign'd to revel with a mortal lord,
In whose illustrious offsprings all might trace
The glorious likeness of a godlike race.
Jason, an hero thro' the world renown'd,
Was with the joyous love of Ceres crown'd;
Their joys they acted in a fertile soil
Of Crete, which thrice had bore the plowman's toil;
Of them was Plutus born, who spreads his hand,
Dispersing wealth, o'er all the sea and land;
Happy the man who in his favour lives,
Riches to him, and all their joys he gives.
Cadmus Harmonia lov'd, the fair and young,
A fruitful dame, from golden Venus sprung;
Ino, and Simele, Agave fair,
And thee, Autonoë, thy lover's care,
(Young Aristæus with his comely hair,)
She bore; and Polydore completes the race,
Born in the walls of Thebes, a stately place.
The brave Chrysaor thee, Calliroe, led,
Daughter of Ocean, to the genial bed;
Whence Geryon sprung fierce with his triple head;
Whom Hercules laid breathless on the ground,
In Erythia which the waves surround;
By his strong arm the mighty giant slain,
The hero drove his oxen cross the main.
Two royal sons were to Tithonus born,
Of thee, Aurora, goddess of the morn;
Hemathion from whom and Memnon spring,
Known by his brazen helm was Æthiop's king.
Pregnant by Cephalus the goddess proves,
A son of high renown rewards their loves;
In form like the possessors of the skies,
Great Phaëton; whom with desiring eyes
Fair Aphrodite views: in blooming days
She to her sacred fane the youth conveys;
Inhabitant divine he there remain'd,
His task nocturnal by the fair ordain'd.
When Pelies, haughty prince of wide command,
Of much th' achiever with an impious hand,
Success attending his injurious mind,
Gave the swell'd sails to fly before the wind,
Æsonides, such gods were thy decrees,
The daughter of Æetes cross the seas
Rap'd from her sire; the hero much endur'd
Ere in his vessel he the fair secur'd;
Her to Iolcus, in her youthful pride,
He bore, and there possess'd the charming bride:
To Jason, her espous'd, the lovely dame
Medeus yields, pledge of the monarch's flame;
Whom Chiron artful by his precepts sway'd:
Thus was the will of mighty Jove obey'd.
The Nereid Psamathe did Phocus bear
To Æacus, herself excelling fair.
To Peleus Thetis, silver-footed dame,
Achilles bore, in war a mighty name.
Fair Cytherea, ever flush'd with charms,
Resign'd them to a mortal hero's arms:
To thee, Anchises, the celestial bride
Æneas bore high in the shades of Ide.
Circe, the daughter of the Sun, inclin'd
To thee, Ulysses, of a patient mind;
Hence Agrius sprung, and hence Latinus came,
A valiant hero, and a spotless name:
The sacred isles were by the brothers sway'd;
And then the Tyrrhenes, men renown'd obey'd.
Calypso with the sage indulg'd her flame;
From them Nausithous and Nausinous came.
Thus each immortal fair the Nine record
Who deign'd to revel with a mortal lord;
In whose illustrious offsprings all might trace
The glorious likeness of a god-like race:
And now, olympian maids, harmonious Nine,
Daughters, of Ægis bearing Jove, divine,
In lasting song the mortal dames rehearse;
Let the bright belles of Earth adorn the verse.

A DISCOURSE ON THE THEOLOGY AND MYTHOLOGY OF THE ANCIENTS.

In the following discourse I shall confine myself to the theology and mythology of the ancient Greeks, shewing their rise and progress, with a view only to the theogony of Hesiod, intending it but as an appendix to the notes.

The Greeks doubtless derived great part of their religion from the Egyptians; and though Herodotus tells us, in one place, that Hesiod, with Homer, was the first who introduced a theogony among the Grecians, and the first who gave names to the gods, yet he contradicts that opinion in his second book, where he says Melampus seems to have learned the stories of Bacchus from Cadmus and other Tyrians which came with him from Phœnicia to the country now called Bœotia; he must therefore mean that Hesiod and Homer were the first who gave the gods a poetical dress, and who used them with more freedom in their writings than preceding authors.

Herodotus, Diodorus Siculus, and Pausanias, all mention Cadmus settling in Bœotia, and Egyptian colonies in other parts of Greece; and Herodotus says almost all the names of the gods in Greece were from Egypt; to enforce which I have translated the following account from Diodorus Siculus.

We learn from the Egyptians that many by nature mortal were honoured with immortality for their wisdom and inventions which proved useful to mankind, some of which were kings of Egypt; and to such they gave the names of the celestial deities. Their first prince was called Ηλιος from the planet of that name the Sun. We are told that Ηφαιστος, or Vulcan, was the inventor of fire, that is the use of it; for seeing a tree on the mountains blasted from Heaven, and the wood burning, he received much comfort from the heat, being then winter; from this he fired some combustible matter, and preserved the use of it afterwards to men; for which reason he was made ruler of the people. After this Chronos, or Saturn, reigned, who married his sister Rhea, of whom five deities were born, whose names were Osiris, Isis, Typhon, Apollo, Aphrodite. Osiris is Bacchus, and Isis

Ceres or Demeter. Isis was married to Osiris, and, after she shared the dominion, made many discoveries for the benefit of life; she found the use of corn, which grew before neglected in the fields like other herbs; and Osiris begun to cultivate the fruit-trees. In remembrance of these persons annual rites were decreed, which are now preserved; in the time of harvest they offer the first-fruits of the corn to Isis, and invoke her. Hermes invented letters, and the lyre of three chords; he first instituted divine worship, and ordained sacrifices to the gods.

The same historian proceeds to relate the expedition of Osiris, who was accompanied by his brother Apollo, who is said to be the first that pointed out the laurel. Osiris took great delight in music, for which reason he carried with him a company of musicians, among which were nine virgins eminent for their skill in singing, and in other sciences, whom the Greeks call the Muses, and Apollo they style their president. Osiris at his return was deified, and afterwards murdered by his brother Typhon, a turbulent and impious man. Isis and her son revenged themselves on Typhon and his accomplices.

Thus far Diodorus in his first book; and Plutarch, in his treatise of Isis and Osiris, seems to think the Grecian poets, in their stories of Jupiter and the Titans, and of Bacchus and Ceres, indebted to the Egyptians.

Diodorus, in his third book, tells us Cadmus, who was derived from Egypt, brought letters from Phœnicia, and Linus was the first among the Greeks who invented poetic numbers and melody, and who writ an account of the actions of the first Bacchus; he had many disciples, the most renowned of which were Hercules, Thamyris, and Orpheus. We are told by the same author that Orpheus, who was let into the theology of the Egyptians, applied the generation of the Osiris of old to the then modern times, and, being gratified by the Cadmeans, instituted new rites. Simele, the daughter of Cadmus, being defloured, bore a child of the same likeness, which they attributed to Osiris of Egypt; Orpheus, who was admitted into the mysteries of the religion, endeavoured to veil her shame by giving out that Simele conceived by Jove, and brought forth Bacchus. Hence men, partly through ignorance, and partly through the honour which they had for Orpheus, and confidence in him, were deceived.

From these passages we learn that the religion and gods of Egypt were, in part, translated with the colonies into Greece; but they continued not long without innovations and alterations. Linus first sung the exploits of the first Bacchus or Osiris; he doubtless took all the poetical liberty that he could with his subject: Orpheus after him banished the first Bacchus from the theology, and introduced the second with a lie to conceal the shame of a polluted woman. In short, all the stories which were told in honour of those Egyptians who had deserved well of their country were, with their names, applied to other persons. Thus, according to the historian, the divine Orpheus set out with bribery, flattery, and delusion.

Hesiod begins his Theogony with the first principle of the heathen system, that Chaos was the parent of all, and Heaven and Earth the parents of all visible things. That Heaven is the father, says Plutarch, in his Inquiry after God, appears from his pouring down the waters which have the spermatic faculty, and Earth, the mother because she brings forth. This, according to the opinion of Plutarch and many more, was the origin of the multiplicity of gods, men esteeming those bodies in the heavens and on the earth, from which they received benefit, the immediate objects of their gratitude and adoration: the same were the motives afterwards which induced them to pay divine honours to mortal men, as we see in the account we have from Diodorus. The design of the poet was to give a catalogue of those deities who were, in any sense, esteemed as such in the times in which he lived, whether fabulous, historical, or physical; but we must take notice that even where a story had rise from fable, or history, he seems to labour at reducing it to nature, as in that of the Muses: what was before of mean original from nine minstrels, slaves to a prince, is rendered great by the genius of the poet.

I shall conclude, thinking it all that is farther necessary to be said, and particularly on the mythology, with the following translation from the preface of lord Bacon to his treatise on the Wisdom of the Ancients.

"I am not ignorant how incertain fiction is, and how liable to be wrested to this or that sense, nor how prevalent wit and discourse are, so as ingeniously to apply such meanings as were not thought of originally: but let not the follies and license of few lessen the esteem due to parables; for that would be prophane and bold, since religion delights in such veils and shadows: but, reflecting on human wisdom, I ingeniously confess my real opinion is, that mystery and allegory were from the original intended in many fables of the ancient poets: this appears apt and conspicuous to me, whether ravished with a veneration for antiquity, or because I find such coherence in the similitude with the things signified, in the very texture of the fable, and in the propriety of the names which are given to the persons or actors in the fable: and no man can positively deny that this was the sense proposed from the beginning, and industriously veiled in this manner. How can the conformity and judgment of the names be obscure to any? Metis being made the wife of Jove plainly signifies counsel. No one should be moved if he sometimes finds any addition for the sake of history, or by way of embellishment, or if chronology should happen to be confounded, or if part of one fable should be transferred to another, and a new allegory introduced; for these were all necessary and to be expected, seeing they are the inventions of men of different ages, and who writ to different ends, some with a view to the nature of things, and other to civil affairs.

"We have another sign, and that no small one, of this hidden sense which we have been speaking of; which is, that some of these fables are in the narration, that is, in themselves literally understood, so foolish and absurd, that they seem to proclaim a parable at a distance. Such as are probable may be feigned for amusement, and in imitation of history; but where no such designs appear, but they seem to be what none would imagine or relate, they must be calculated for other uses. What a fiction is this! Jove took Metis for his wife, and as soon as he perceived her pregnant eat her, whence he himself conceived, and brought forth Pallas armed from his head. Nothing can appear more monstrous, more like a dream, and more out of the course of thinking, than this story in itself. What has a great weight with me is, that many of these fables seem not to be invented by those who have related them, Homer, Hesiod, and other writers; for were they the fictions of that age, and of those who delivered them down to us, nothing great and exalted, according to my opinion, could be expected from such an origin: but if any one will deliberate on this subject attentively, these will appear to be delivered and related as what were before believed and received, and not as tales then first invented and communicated; besides, as they are told in different manners by authors of almost the same times, they are easily perceived to be common, and derived from old memorial tradition, and are various only from the additional embellishments which diverse writers have bestowed on them.

"In old times, when the inventions of men, and the conclusions deduced from them, were new and uncommon, fables, parables, and similes, of all kinds abounded. As hieroglyphics were more ancient than parables, parables were more ancient than arguments. We shall close what we have here said with this observation; the wisdom of the ancients was either great or happy, great if these figures were the fruits of their industry, and happy if they looked no farther, that they have afforded matter and occasion so worthy contemplation."

POSTSCRIPT.

I CANNOT take my leave of this work without expressing my gratitude to Mr. Theobald for his kind assistance in it. Much may with justice be said to the advantage of that gentleman, but his own writings will be testimonies of his abilities, when, perhaps, this profession of my friendship for him, and of my zeal for his merit, shall be forgot.

Such remarks as I have received from my friends I have distinguished from my own, in justice to those by whom I have been so obliged, lest, by a general acknowledgment only, such errours as I may have possibly committed, should, by the wrong guess of some, be unjustly imputed to them. The few notes which were writ by the earl of Pembroke are placed betwixt two asterisms[1].

THOMAS COOK.

Feb. 15, 1728.

[1] As before observed, the whole of the notes are omitted in this collection. *C.*